Routledge Encyclopedia of
PHILOSOPHY

General Editor
EDWARD CRAIG

London and New York

First published 1998
by Routledge
11 New Fetter Lane, London EC4P 4EE
Simultaneously published in the USA and Canada
by Routledge
29 West 35th Street, New York, NY 10001

©1998 Routledge

Typeset in Monotype Times New Roman by
Routledge

Printed in England by
T J International Ltd, Padstow, Cornwall, England

Printed on acid-free paper which conforms to ANS1.Z39, 48-1992 and ISO 9706 standards

British Library Cataloguing-in-Publication Data
A catalogue record for this book is available from the British Library

The Library of Congress Cataloguing-in-Publication data is given in volume 10.

ISBN: 0415-07310-3 (10-volume set)
ISBN: 0415-18706-0 (volume 1)
ISBN: 0415-18707-9 (volume 2)
ISBN: 0415-18708-7 (volume 3)
ISBN: 0415-18709-5 (volume 4)
ISBN: 0415-18710-9 (volume 5)
ISBN: 0415-18711-7 (volume 6)
ISBN: 0415-18712-5 (volume 7)
ISBN: 0415-18713-3 (volume 8)
ISBN: 0415-18714-1 (volume 9)
ISBN: 0415-18715-X (volume 10)

ISBN: 0415-16916-X (CD-ROM)
ISBN: 0415-16917-8 (10-volume set and CD-ROM)

Contents

Using the *Encyclopedia*

List of entries

Using the *Encyclopedia*

The *Routledge Encyclopedia of Philosophy* is designed for ease of use. The following notes outline its organization and editorial approach and explain the ways of locating material. This will help readers make the most of the *Encyclopedia*.

SEQUENCE OF ENTRIES

The *Encyclopedia* contains 2,054 entries (from 500 to 19,000 words in length) arranged in nine volumes with a tenth volume for the index. Volumes 1–9 are arranged in a single alphabetical sequence, as follows:

Volume 1: A posteriori *to* Bradwardine, Thomas

Volume 2: Brahman *to* Derrida, Jacques

Volume 3: Descartes, René *to* Gender and science

Volume 4: Genealogy *to* Iqbal, Muhammad

Volume 5: Irigaray, Luce *to* Lushi chunqiu

Volume 6: Luther, Martin *to* Nifo, Agostino

Volume 7: Nihilism *to* Quantum mechanics, interpretation of

Volume 8: Questions *to* Sociobiology

Volume 9: Sociology of knowledge *to* Zoroastrianism

Alphabetical order

Entries are listed in alphabetical order by word rather than by letter with all words including *and*, *in*, *of* and *the* being given equal status. The exceptions to this rule are as follows:

- biographies: where the forenames and surname of a philosopher are inverted, the entry takes priority in the sequence, for example:

Alexander, Samuel (1859–1938)
Alexander of Aphrodisias (*c.* AD 200)
Alexander of Hales (*c.* 1185–1245)

- names with prefixes, which follow conventional alphabetical placing (see Transliteration and naming conventions below).

A complete alphabetical list of entries is given in each of the Volumes 1 to 9.

Inverted titles

Titles of entries consisting of more than one word are often inverted so that the key term (in a thematic or signpost entry) or the surname (in a biographical entry) determines the place of the entry in the alphabetical sequence, for example:

Law, philosophy of *or*
Market, ethics of the *or*
Hart, Herbert Lionel Adolphus (1907–93)

Conceptual organization

Several concerns have had a bearing on the sequence of entries where there is more than one key term.

In deciding on the sequence of entries we have tried, wherever possible, to integrate philosophy as it is known and studied in the USA and Europe with philosophy from around the world. This means that the reader will frequently find entries from different philosophical traditions or approaches to the same topic close to each other, for example, in the sequence:

Political philosophy [signpost entry]
Political philosophy, history of
Political philosophy in classical Islam
Political philosophy, Indian

Similarly, in entries where a philosophical tradition or approach is surveyed we have tried, whenever appropriate, to keep philosophical traditions from different countries together. An example is the sequence:

Confucian philosophy, Chinese
Confucian philosophy, Japanese
Confucian philosophy, Korean
Confucius (551–479 BC)

Finally, historical entries are usually placed with contemporary entries under the topic rather than the historical period. For example, in the sequence:

Language, ancient philosophy of
Language and gender
Language, conventionality of
Language, early modern philosophy of
Language, Indian theories of
Language, innateness of

DUMMY TITLES

The *Encyclopedia* has been extensively cross-referenced in order to help the reader locate their topic of interest. Dummy titles are placed throughout the alphabetical sequence of entries to direct the reader to the actual title of the entry where a topic is discussed. This may be under a different entry title, a synonym or as part of a larger entry. Wherever useful we have included the numbers of the sections (§§) in which a particular topic or subject is discussed. Examples of this type of cross-reference are:

AFRICAN AESTHETICS *see*
AESTHETICS, AFRICAN

CANGUILHEM, GEORGES *see*
FRENCH PHILOSOPHY OF SCIENCE §§3–4

TAO *see* DAO

GLOSSARY OF LOGICAL AND MATHEMATICAL TERMS

A glossary of logical and mathematical terms is provided to help users with terms from formal logic and mathematics. 'See also' cross-references to the glossary are provided at the end of entries where the user might benefit from help with unfamiliar terms. The glossary can be found in Volume 5 under L (LOGICAL AND MATHEMATICAL TERMS, GLOSSARY OF).

THE INDEX VOLUME

Volume 10 is devoted to a comprehensive index of key terms, concepts and names covered in Volumes 1–9, allowing readers to reap maximum benefit from the *Encyclopedia*. A guide to the index can be found at the beginning of the index. The index volume includes a full listing of contributors, their affiliations and the entries they have written. It also includes permission acknowledgements, listed in publisher order.

STRUCTURE OF ENTRIES

The *Routledge Encyclopedia of Philosophy* contains three types of entry:

- 'signpost' entries, for example, METAPHYSICS; SCIENCE, PHILOSOPHY OF; EAST ASIAN PHILOSOPHY. These entries provide an accessible overview of the sub-disciplines or regional coverage within the *Encyclopedia*; they provide a 'map' which directs the reader towards and around the many entries relating to each topic;
- thematic entries, ranging from general entries such as KNOWLEDGE, CONCEPT OF, to specialized topics such as VIRTUE EPISTEMOLOGY;
- biographical entries, devoted to individual philosophers, emphasizing the work rather than the life of the subject and with a list of the subject's major works.

Overview

All thematic and biographical entries begin with an overview which provides a concise and accessible summary of the topic or subject. This can be referred to on its own if the reader does not require the depth and detail of the main part of the entry.

Table of contents

All thematic and biographical entries over 1000 words in length are divided into sections and have a numbered table of contents following the overview. This gives the headings of each of the sections of the entry, enabling the reader to see the scope and structure of the entry at a glance. For example, the table of contents in the entry on HERACLITUS:

1 Life and work
2 Methodology
3 Unity of opposites and perspectivism
4 Cosmology
5 Psychology, ethics and religion
6 Influence

Cross-references within an entry

Entries in the *Encyclopedia* have been extensively cross-referenced in order to indicate other entries that may be of interest to the reader. There are two types of cross-reference in the *Encyclopedia*:

1. 'See' cross-references

Cross-references within the text of an entry direct the reader to other entries on or closely related to the topic under discussion. For example, a reader may be directed from a conceptual entry to a biography of the philosopher whose work is under discussion or vice versa. These internal cross-references appear in small capital letters, either in parentheses, for example:

Opponents of naturalism before and since Wittgenstein have been animated by the notion that the aims of social science are not causal explanation and improving prediction, but uncovering rules that make social life intelligible to its participants (see EXPLANATION IN HISTORY AND SOCIAL SCIENCE).

or sometimes, when the reference is to a person who

has a biographical entry, as small capitals in the text itself, for example:

> Thomas NAGEL emphasizes the discrepancy between the objective insignificance of our lives and projects and the seriousness and energy we devote to them.

For entries over 1,000 words in length we have included the numbers of the sections (§) in which a topic is discussed, wherever useful, for example:

> In *Nicomachean Ethics*, Aristotle criticizes Plato's account for not telling us anything about particular kinds of goodness (see ARISTOTLE §§ 21–6).

2. 'See also' cross-references

At the end of the text of each entry, 'See also' cross-references guide the reader to other entries of related interest, such as more specialized entries, biographical entries, historical entries, geographical entries and so on. These cross-references appear in small capitals in alphabetical order.

References

References in the text are given in the Harvard style, for example, Kant (1788), Rawls (1971). Exceptions to this rule are made when presenting works with established conventions, for example, with some major works in ancient philosophy. Full bibliographical details are given in the 'List of works' and 'References and further reading'.

Bibliography

List of works

Biographical entries are followed by a list of works which gives full bibliographical details of the major works of the philosopher. This is in chronological order and includes items cited in the text, significant editions, dates of composition for pre-modern works (where known), preferred English-language translations and English translations for the titles of untranslated foreign-language works.

References and further reading

Both biographical and thematic entries have a list of references and further reading. Items are listed alphabetically by author's name. (Publications with joint authors are listed under the name of the first author and after any individual publications by that author). References cited in the text are preceded by an asterisk (*). Further reading which the reader may find particularly useful is also included.

The authors and editors have attempted to provide the fullest possible bibliographical information for every item.

Annotations

Publications in the 'List of works' and the 'References and further reading' have been annotated with a brief description of the content so that their relevance to readers' interests can be quickly assessed.

EDITORIAL STYLE

Spelling and punctuation in the *Encyclopedia* have been standardized to follow British English usage.

Transliteration and naming conventions

All names and terms from non-roman alphabets have been romanized in the *Encyclopedia*. Foreign names have been given according to the conventions within the particular language.

Arabic

Arabic has been transliterated in a simplified form, that is, without macrons or subscripts. Names of philosophers are given in their Arabic form rather than their Latinate form, for example, IBN RUSHD rather than AVERROES. Arabic names beginning with the prefix 'al-' are alphabetized under the substantive part of the name and not the prefix, for example:

> KILWARDBY, ROBERT (d. 1279)
> AL-KINDI, ABU YUSUF YAQUB IBN ISHAQ (d. *c*.866–73)
> KNOWLEDGE AND JUSTIFICATION, COHERENCE THEORY OF

Arabic names beginning with the prefix 'Ibn' are alphabetized under 'I'.

Chinese, Korean and Japanese

Chinese has been transliterated using the Pinyin system. Dummy titles in the older Wade–Giles system are given for names and key terms; these direct the reader to the Pinyin titles.

Japanese has been transliterated using a modified version of the Hepburn system.

Chinese, Japanese and Korean names are given in Asian form, that is, surname preceding forenames, for example:

> WANG FUZHI
> NISHITANI KEIJI

The exception is where an author has chosen to present their own name in conventional Western form.

Hebrew

Hebrew has been transliterated in a simplified form, that is, without macrons or subscripts.

Russian

Cyrillic characters have been transliterated using the Library of Congress system. Russian names are usually given with their patronymic, for example, BAKUNIN, MIKHAIL ALEKSANDROVICH.

Sanskrit

A guide to the pronunciation of Sanskrit can be found in the INDIAN AND TIBETAN PHILOSOPHY signpost entry.

Tibetan

Tibetan has been transliterated using the Wylie system. Dummy titles in the Virginia system are given for names and key terms. A guide to Tibetan pronunciation can be found in the INDIAN AND TIBETAN PHILOSOPHY signpost entry.

European names

Names beginning with the prefixes 'de', 'von' or 'van' are usually alphabetized under the substantive part of the name. For example:

> BEAUVOIR, SIMONE DE
> HUMBOLDT, WILHELM VON

The exception to this rule is when the person is either a national of or has spent some time living or working in an English-speaking country. For example:

> DE MORGAN, AUGUSTUS
> VON WRIGHT, GEORG HENRIK

Names beginning with the prefix 'de la' or 'le' are alphabetized under the prefix 'la' or 'le'. For example:

> LA FORGE, LOUIS DE
> LE DOEUFF, MICHÈLE

Names beginning with 'Mc' or 'Mac' are treated as 'Mac' and appear before Ma.

Historical names

Medieval and Renaissance names where a person is not usually known by a surname are alphabetized under the forename, for example:

> GILES OF ROME
> JOHN OF SALISBURY

List of entries

Below is a complete list of entries in the order in which they appear in the *Routledge Encyclopedia of Philosophy*.

An alphabetical list of contributors, their affiliations and the entries they have written can be found in the index volume (Volume 10).

GENEALOGY

'Genealogy' is an expression that has come into currency since the 1970s, a result of Michel Foucault's works Surveiller et punir *(1975) (*Discipline and Punish, *1977) and* The History of Sexuality *(1976, 1984a, 1984b). Foucault's use of the term continues Nietzsche's in his* On the Genealogy of Morals *([1887] 1967). For both philosophers, genealogy is a form of historical critique, designed to overturn our norms by revealing their origins. Whereas Nietzsche's method relies on psychological explanations, and attacks modern conceptions of equality in favour of a perfectionist ethic, Foucault's relies on micro-socio-logical explanations, and attacks modern forms of domination in favour of radical politics.*

1   **Genealogy as philosophical method**
2   **Nietzsche**
3   **Foucault**

1   Genealogy as philosophical method

While some claim that genealogy is a new method for investigating history, others have maintained that genealogy is simply historical investigation itself, and nothing new. Neither of these claims captures what is distinctive about Nietzsche's and Foucault's enter-prises. Rather, genealogy is a new method of applying historical investigation to philosophical concerns.

In Book I of the *Republic*, Plato portrays Socrates as seeking substantive philosophical knowledge of justice by discussing proposed definitions of 'justice'. The *elenchus* is the method for testing proposed definitions. In the second essay of *On the Genealogy of Morals* ([1887] 1967, II: 13) Nietzsche claims that 'only that which has no history is definable'. If the expressions which concern us have a history, then Socrates' project fails. We can better clarify the sense behind such expressions as 'justice' by examining the history of the practices that have shaped our disposition to classify some acts as just. According to Plato, we apprehend an unchanging, independently real *eidos* of justice, and it is our capacity to intuit the presence of justice in an act that accounts for our linguistic dispositions. Consequently, the history of our linguistic dispositions can only be the history of our clear vision of what is always already there; such a history cannot possess much philosophical interest. On the genealogist's view, however, there is no such *eidos*. Therefore, it cannot be responsible for our semantic intuitions or our consensus about them. For the genealogist, history itself moulds and shapes our practices and intuitions over time; in an account of what moulds the history, we will find nothing but

competing and cooperating forces, interpretations, interests. The genealogist's interest is thus directed at normative practices whose dominance requires that their participants not understand how the practice came to be.

As Nietzsche and Foucault view it, genealogy supersedes earlier forms of philosophy. The sweeping character of this methodological claim rests on the genealogist's confidence that traditional philosophical strategies fail on their own terms. (This point is crucial for escaping the common complaint that the genealogist commits the genetic fallacy.) Traditional strategies falsely presuppose that our intuitions are reliable. If, for example, our moral intuitions were broadly unreliable, traditional moral theory would collapse, given the moral theorist's reliance on these intuitions for data by which to judge the moral theories under discussion. If our conceptual or semantic intuitions are unreliable, similar considera-tions will apply to conceptual or linguistic analysis.

History, according to genealogists, is not teleologi-cal (as it is for Hegel). They cannot identify a *goal* of a historical process, and then go on to show how it gradually emerged from its embryonic beginnings. Rather, they chart the processes that, by contingent confluence, produce a contemporary result. Hence the metaphor: no individual is the goal of a family history. Rather, a family is a vast fabric of relation-ships, and any one individual represents only one among many confluences of past lines of descent.

To avoid the temptation of projecting current norms into the past, which would promote a teleological picture, genealogy adopts the German historicist view that each cross-section of history has its own autonomous structures, meanings, values, etc. which the historian must work to recover hermeneu-tically (see HISTORICISM; HERMENEUTICS). However, unlike the hermeneutic historian, the genealogist allows that the alien culture's self-understanding is not the end, but the beginning of investigation. Since the function of genealogy is to undermine our own hermeneutical self-understanding, we cannot grant self-understanding final authority elsewhere either.

What determines the content of such a self-under-standing is, ultimately, multiple conflicting interests and interested interpretations. Genealogy charac-terizes the underlying historical processes as a 'power struggle'. Just as an account of a war will differ depending upon which combatant pens it, aspects of these historical processes will appear differently to different viewers. Attention to this plurality of 'perspectives' leads the genealogist to claim that there is no absolute fact as to the significance or value of a particular historical event or process. If we add the claim that experienced fact is largely constituted by the interpretations of those experiencing it, a question arises: does it make sense to speak of historical fact at all? This feature of genealogy raises familiar epistemological problems, and sits uncomfortably with its intended critical function. However that may be, the genealogist does *not* claim that one perspective is as good as another, either normatively or cognitively. Genealogy serves a critical function, undermining the myths and mystifications a particular contemporary perspective may have about itself. To the extent that the perspective depends upon mystification, participants' understanding of the processes that constructed the perspective will lead to its disintegration.

The critical nature of genealogy can be understood as follows. The genealogist is concerned to undermine ahistorical and inflationary interpretations of mundane facts about human life. These interpretations typically appeal to structures, norms, entities, etc. which stand above both nature and history. The genealogist is also apt to undermine the propensity to regard what is artificial (and therefore mutable) as naturally, rationally or metaphysically necessary (and therefore immutable). Norms may appear to possess a greater degree of legitimacy if they are associated with such necessities as opposed to artifice. If norms are artificial, produced by struggle and veiled by mystification, they will be an expression of someone's pragmatic interests. Inflationary interpretations conceal these interests and the ways that the practice in question promotes them.

Finally, genealogists must accept that they too are engaged in a practice (doing genealogy) which has a history, which expresses various pragmatic interests, which is perspectival, etc. Whether genealogy's reflexivity hoists the genealogists by their own petard has been much discussed since the 1970s.

Many broad themes of contemporary genealogical inquiry have resonances in earlier European intellectual history. The notion of the artificiality of norms, and their emergence from conflict is central to social contract theory since Hobbes (see CONTRACTARIANISM). However, modern dissenters from social contract theory laid the groundwork for Nietzsche's novel interpretation of morality. Though himself a social contract theorist, in the *Discourse on Inequality* ([1755] 1988) ROUSSEAU transforms the model *state of nature–contract–civil society* into an anthropological and historical, if speculative, narrative. Rousseau outlines how we might have first become social. Later, through mystified economic processes, we come to consent to political institutions which benefit the wealthy at the expense of the poor. By emphasizing the historical and artificial character of this process, Rousseau rejects the social contract arguments

defending the economic and political institutions of his day.

2 Nietzsche

The image of Rousseau haunted NIETZSCHE throughout his career. Both the similar styles of argumentation, and the aristocratic values Nietzsche champions make 'A Discourse on Equality' an apt alternate title for his *Genealogy*. Nietzsche's thoughts on the development of morality can be seen in several texts prior to the *Genealogy*. In 'On the Utility and Liability of History for Life '([1873b] 1995), Nietzsche deplores the rise of 'disinterested' historical research, which has replaced more edifying and useful portrayals of the past with pointless accumulations of fact. Creative living requires that we often forget the past. If we are to benefit from the study of the past, we must practise history with one or more of three aims in mind. 'Antiquarian history' seeks to revive the lost cultural treasure house of the past. 'Monumental history' seeks to memorialize ethically exceptional individuals and deeds, which we might wish to emulate. 'Critical history' uncovers the evils of the past that we might better renounce them in the present. All three forms appear woven together in several later works: 'On Truth and Lie in an Extra-moral Sense' ([1873a] 1990), 'On the History of the Moral Sensations' in the first volume of *Human, All Too Human* ([1878] 1986), 'Natural History of Morality' in *Beyond Good and Evil* ([1886] 1966) and the *Genealogy* itself.

In the first essay of the *Genealogy*, Nietzsche argues that 'English psychologists' err in regarding the original sense of 'good' as 'useful'. The sense of 'good' varied, depending upon which class perceived it. For the dominant class, or 'masters', the primary sense of what is good is the self and that which resembles the self. By contrast, the socially subordinated, the 'slaves' behave in very different ways, which the master designates as 'bad', ignoble or base. However, from the slave perspective, what the master calls 'good' causes the slave's suffering and subordination. Thus, he designates the master as 'evil' or wicked. The slave then invents the fiction of free will. The master is free to not behave in a wicked way, and the slave is equally free to begin to do so. The slave then constructs a moral scheme according to which his own passivity makes him morally superior to the master and therefore 'good'. Here we see many characteristic themes of genealogy sounded: pragmatic interests, perspectivality, demystification. The relevance of Nietzsche's critique of Christianity is clear. Beyond that, he broadens his analysis by claiming that modern liberal institutions, norms and intuitions are so much secularized Christianity. Thus liberalism inherits much of Christianity's unappetizing 'slavishness' without the religious rationale which legitimated it.

In the second essay of the *Genealogy*, Nietzsche traces the psychological origin of guilt to the primitive experience of debt (at a time when enforcement of debt was more cruel than now). Anticipating Freud, he speculates that the inner mechanism mediating this experience is the product of introjected aggression. While we cannot dismantle the conscience, we can 'reprogramme' it with values and standards other than those derived from slave morality. In the third essay, Nietzsche asks why we regard asceticism so highly. He reveals its psychological roots in the sour grapes of the ascetic. Its persistence is due to the socially stabilizing function of the ascetic's ideology of sin and contrition. Furthermore, modern science is an outgrowth of the ascetic ideal, its self-hating contempt for pleasurable illusion expressing itself as a commitment to truth. These essays stand as early paradigms of genealogical critique.

3 Foucault

FOUCAULT turned towards Nietzsche and genealogy late in his career. In his earlier, 'archaeological' works, Foucault analysed medicine, the human sciences (for example, economics, linguistics, biology) and philosophy. According to Foucault, structured codes organize scientists' perception, discourse and social practices at a level unknown to them. Such codes, or 'epistemes', play a quasi-Kantian role, as 'conditions of the possibility' of knowledge. Foucault's conception of episteme thus makes the work of scientists subject to a cultural force beyond anyone's conscious control. His conception of these epistemes and their historical succession is indebted to the later Heidegger's conception of a 'history of being' as well as to the work of the structuralists (for example, Althusser, Lacan, Lévi-Strauss) (see HEIDEGGER, M.; STRUCTURALISM). His later turn to genealogy would inherit both the culturalism, and the epistemological interests, of his earlier work.

Foucault came to believe that he was reifying unduly in claiming that epistemes, which are abstract, governed (at least some domains of) social life. Instead, he substituted the notion of regimes of power, which coerce people into following specific norms. The mechanisms which maintain this coercion are micro-practices demanding specific kinds of behaviour in specific contexts (for example, the use of time-cards and clocks in factories). Although these micro-practices in effect subordinate some people to the benefit of others, they need not be the products of any deliberate design.

Foucault's analysis of society often seems to jump from detailed concrete descriptions of micro-practices, to more impressionistic claims about the common style of the micro-practices. This common style betrays a pervasive, invisible, impersonal force: power. Power structures behaviour; at the same time, it structures the perception, discourse and practices of scientists who are concerned to understand human behaviour scientifically. Foucault's account of the relationship between power and knowledge echoes Nietzsche's in *Genealogy* Essay III. However, where Nietzsche's analysis of the will to truth depends on *psychological* explanations, in Foucault's, micro-sociology and a broad cultural thematics replace psychology.

Foucault's genealogical method, which he sketches in 'Nietzsche, genealogie, histoire' (1971), does not merely echo Nietzsche's concern with power. Both philosophers' historical inquiries are directed at practices whose character bears on philosophical concerns (for example, the nature of personal and political freedom, the value of self-knowledge). Furthermore, Foucault's analyses, like Nietzsche's, portray historical processes with an emphasis on their contingent, non-teleological character. He is sensitive to how alien even something as recent as the Enlightenment can appear, if viewed through historicist lenses. However, what links him most decisively with Nietzsche is his commitment to demystifying accounts of the historical processes that most concern him. We easily ignore our 'disciplinary' practices in their institutional home, the prison, because our ideological commitments interpret such practices as just. Once we see the practices described in coolly non-ideological terms and in concrete detail, we clearly perceive their outrageousness. What is more, the presence of similar 'carceral' practices in other social domains can then be more clearly perceived. Foucault intends his readers to transpose their outrage from the one setting to the other. His work thus shares Nietzsche's critical intent: Nietzsche wishes to use his critique as a tool to re-animate 'noble' values, whereas Foucault places his critique in the service of radical politics.

Foucault had intended to continue his genealogy of modernity. He meant to supplement his account in *Discipline and Punish* (1975) of the growing 'carceralization' of modernity with a parallel account of its growing 'sexualization' in the projected multi-volume *History of Sexuality*. However, after one promising introductory volume, Foucault turned his attention away from the historical processes that culminated in contemporary society. Instead, he turned toward the genealogy of Western ethical ideals, and their relationship to sexual self-mastery. This project begins with an analysis of Greek ethics in *The Use of Pleasure* (1984a), and continues with an account of Roman ethics in *The Care of the Self* (1984b). A final volume, which was to deal with medieval ethics and the 'hermeneutics of the self' has not yet appeared. In these final works, Foucault relegates his political passion, so reminiscent of Rousseau, to the background. Instead, we see the beginnings of work much closer in subject and spirit to Nietzsche's original concerns.

See also: POST-STRUCTURALISM IN THE SOCIAL SCIENCES §3

References and further reading

Dreyfus, H.L. and Rabinow, P. (1982) *Michel Foucault: Beyond Structuralism and Hermeneutics*, Chicago, IL: University of Chicago Press. (An accessible introduction to Foucault's thought, with extensive discussion of the methodological issues raised by genealogy.)

* Foucault, M. (1971) 'Nietzsche, généalogie, histoire', in *Hommage à Jean Hyppolite*, Paris: Presses Universitaires de France; trans. D. Bouchard and S. Simon, 'Nietzsche, Genealogy, History', in *Language, Counter-memory, Practice*, ed. D. Bouchard, Ithaca, NY: Cornell University Press, 1977; reprinted in P. Rabinow (ed.) *The Foucault Reader*, New York: Pantheon Books, 1984. (This latter volume also includes extensive selections from *Discipline and Punish* and *History of Sexuality*, vols 1 and 2, and makes a good starting point for reading Foucault.)

* —— (1975) *Surveiller et punir: naissance de la prison*, Paris: Gallimard; trans. A. Sheridan, *Discipline and Punish: The Birth of the Prison*, New York: Pantheon Books, 1977. (Foucault's first genealogical exercise, focusing on the relationships between the history of punitive practices, criminology and the formation of the modern subject.)

* —— (1976) *La Volonté de savoir* (The Will to Knowledge), trans. R. Hurley, *The History of Sexuality*, vol. 1, *An Introduction*, New York: Pantheon Books, 1978. (Foucault's second genealogical exercise, never completed, was to trace connections between sexology, psychiatry, the 'sexualization' of modern culture and the emergence of the hermeneutical, self-interpreting subject.)

* —— (1984a) *L'Usage des plaisirs*, Paris: Gallimard; trans. R. Hurley, *The History of Sexuality*, vol. 2, *The Use of Pleasure*, New York: Pantheon Books, 1985. (The first of two studies in Foucault's self-described 'genealogy of ethics' proposes that ancient Greek ethics was inseparable from personal projects of sexual self-mastery.)

* —— (1984b) *Le Souci de soi*, Paris: Gallimard; trans. R. Hurley, *The History of Sexuality*, vol. 3, *The Care of the Self*, New York: Pantheon Books, 1986. (In the second of two studies in ancient ethics. Foucault turns his attention to Rome.)

* Nietzsche, F. (1873a) 'On Truth and Lie in an Extra-moral Sense', trans. D. Breazeale, in *Philosophy and Truth*, Atlantic Highlands, NJ and London: Humanities Press International, 1990. (This early text of Nietzsche's critically discusses the development of the 'drive for truth' in a manner that anticipates his later genealogies. It has been very influential in both philosophical and literary theory circles.)

* —— (1873b) 'Vom Nutzen und Nachtheil der Historie für das Leben', Leipzig: Fritzsch; trans. R.T. Gray, 'On the Utility and Liability of History for Life', in *The Complete Works of Friedrich Nietzsche*, vol. 2, ed. E. Behler, Stanford, CA: 1995. (Vol. 2 is the only volume of this twenty-volume 'Stanford Edition' to have appeared at the time of writing. This edition is based on the Colli-Montinari *Kritische Studienausgabe*, a large subset of the *Kritische Gesamtausgabe Werke*, which is regarded as the definitive German edition. 'On Truth and Lie in an Extra-moral Sense' will appear in vol. 1; *Human, All Too Human* will appear in vols 3 and 4; *Beyond Good and Evil* and *On the Genealogy of Morals* will appear in vol. 8.)

* —— (1878) 'Zur Geschichte der moralischen Empfindungen', in *Menschliches, Allzumenschliches*, Chemnitz: E Schmeitzner; trans. R.J. Hollingdale, 'On the History of the Moral Sensations', in *Human, All Too Human*, Cambridge: Cambridge University Press, 1986. (These aphorisms represent Nietzsche's first attempt at a genealogy of morals.)

* —— (1886) 'Zur Naturgeschichte der Moral', in *Jenseits von Gut und Böse*, Chemnitz: E. Schmeitzner; trans. W. Kaufmann, 'Natural History of Morals', in *Beyond Good and Evil*, New York: Random House, 1966. (A precis of the late Nietzsche's genealogy of morals.)

* —— (1887) *Zur Genealogie der Moral*, Chemnitz: E. Schmeitzner; trans. W. Kaufmann and R.J. Hollingdale, *On the Genealogy of Morals*, New York: Random House, 1967. (The classic text which introduced the concept of 'genealogy' into philosophical discussion.)

* Plato (*c.*380s–370s BC) *Republic*, trans. G.M.A. Grube, revised C.D.C. Reeve, Indianapolis, IN: Hackett Publishing Company, 1992. (Reeve's introduction is especially relevant.)

* Rousseau, J.-J. (1755) *Discours sur l'origine de*

l'inégalité, in *Oeuvres complètes*, vol. 3, Paris: Gallimard, 1975; trans. J. Conaway Bondanella, *Discourse on Inequality*, in *Rousseau's Political Writings*, ed. A. Ritter and J. Conaway Bondanella, New York and London: W.W. Norton, 1988. (Rousseau's critique of inegalitarian attitudes, practices and institutions rests on demystifying historical narrative in a fashion which anticipates Nietzsche, despite the latter's opposing normative commitments.)

* —— (1762) *Contrat social*, in *Oeuvres complètes*, vol. 3, Paris: Gallimard, 1975; trans. J. Conaway Bondanella, *On the Social Contract*, in *Rousseau's Political Writings*, ed. A. Ritter and J. Conaway Bondanella, New York and London: W.W. Norton, 1988. (Rousseau's contribution to liberal political theory also emphasized the artificiality of the social.)

Schacht, R. (1983) *Nietzsche*, London and New York: Routledge, 2nd edn, 1992. (Systematic, thorough, moderately difficult. Issues associated with genealogy can be found throughout, but see especially chapters 2, 5, 6 and 7.)

—— (ed.) (1994) *Nietzsche, Genealogy, Morality: Essays on Nietzsche's Genealogy of Morals*, Berkeley, CA: University of California Press. (This collection is an ideal starting point for further reading about Nietzsche's *Genealogy*.)

R. KEVIN HILL

GENERAL RELATIVITY, PHILOSOPHICAL RESPONSES TO

Much of the early philosophical attention given Einstein's theory of gravitation was not uncontaminated by a grim post-war atmosphere conducive to public diversions, hysteria and national chauvinism. Most was ill-informed regarding the mathematical and physical content of the theory. Even amongst the scientifically literate, there was disagreement as to the theory's philosophical implications. In part, this lack of clarity is due to Einstein. In an endeavour to eliminate references to 'absolute space' as the earlier special (or, as it was then known, restricted) theory of relativity (STR) had eliminated reference to 'absolute time', Einstein had motivated his theory of gravitation as arising from an epistemologically mandated generalization of the relativity principle of STR, which governed only inertial motions, and he misleadingly baptized it a theory of 'general relativity', wherein all motions are regarded as relative to other bodies. This the theory does not show. Also, some incautiously expressed remarks on the formal requirement of general covariance were seized upon as evidence for antithetical epistemological and ontological attitudes. Amidst such confusions, it is not at all surprising that inherently antagonistic philosophical outlooks claimed vindication or confirmation by the general theory of relativity (GTR). In turn, the perceived failure of both Machian positivism and Neo-Kantianism to accommodate the revolutionary theory spurred the development of a new 'scientific philosophy', logical positivism. The subsequent course of philosophy of science in the twentieth century was indelibly marked by this development. Yet it would turn out that Einstein himself refused to be a cooperative exemplar for any of the major philosophical schools, positivism, Kantianism, or, to its embarrassment, logical positivism.

1 Positivism
2 Neo-Kantianism
3 Logical positivism
4 Einstein's response

1 Positivism

Positivists generally welcomed the special theory of relativity (STR), viewing Einstein's operational analysis of the 'simultaneity' of separated events as a vindication of Mach's account of concepts as mere tools, economical shorthand for operations exhibiting the dependence of phenomena on one another (see LOGICAL POSITIVISM §§2, 4; MACH, E.; OPERATIONALISM). Some of Einstein's epistemological remarks in the context of STR appear to underscore this alignment: for example, 'The concept does not exist for the physicist until he has the possibility of discovering whether or not it is fulfilled in an actual case' (Einstein 1917: 22). Such pronouncements served to cast Einstein's philosophical orientation in a positivist light and, naturally enough, promoted tendencies both to fashion similar interpretations of the general theory of relativity (GTR) and, in view of ensuing difficulties, to criticize GTR as a violation of Einstein's own methodological precepts (Bridgman 1949).

A single passage from section three of Einstein's 1916 exposition of GTR provided further grist for the mill of Machian positivism. There, in the course of a heuristic 'reflection' on the reason for the necessity of general covariance of the field equations of gravitation (that they remain unchanged under arbitrary transformation of the coordinates), Einstein proclaimed that this requirement, 'takes away from space and time the last remnant of physical objectivity' since 'all our space-time verifications invariably amount to a determination of space-time coincidences' and that consequently, 'all our physical experience can ultimately be reduced to [point-event] coincidences'. Following the interpretation given these remarks by the Machian physicist Philipp Frank, the philosopher Joseph Petzoldt stated that 'the theory of relativity rests, in the end, on the perception of the coincidence of sensations' and, in particular, that GTR 'is fully in accord with Mach's world-view, which is best characterized as relativistic positivism', his designation for Mach's philosophical direction (see Petzodt 1921: 516). Despite the obvious embarrassment of Mach's apparent disavowal of the theory of relativity in the 'Preface', dated 1913, to his posthumously published (1921) book on physical optics (Mach died in 1916), Einstein's illustrative reflection seemed an incontrovertible avowal of the centrepiece of Mach's phenomenalist epistemology with its attendant ontological parsimony.

Contemporary scholarship has shown that these remarks of Einstein were but elliptical references to an argument for a different and considerably more intricate conclusion, that the points of the spacetime manifold have no inherent individuality (inherited say, from the underlying topology) (see SPACETIME), hence they have no reality independently of the presence of physical fields defined on the manifold (Stachel 1989). And while Einstein made no secret of his ambition in the context of GTR (in recognition of a 'general principle of relativity') to fully implement what he termed 'Mach's programme' against Newtonian 'absolute motions', he had already distanced himself from Mach's phenomenalist epistemology. As for the infamous 'Preface', a strong case has recently been made that it was forged after Mach's death by his son Ludwig, under the influence of a rival guardian of Mach's legacy, Hugo Dingler.

2 Neo-Kantianism

Among the scientifically minded philosophical community of Wilhelmian and early Weimar Germany, the philosophy of Kant held pride of place, with that of Mach a distant second. Only a few Kantians adopted strategies to preserve Kantian orthodoxy intact in the face of empirical success of GTR, for example, claiming that Kant's views on space and time pertained solely to a psychological 'intuitive space' and were not touched by Einstein's empirical theory of spacetime (Sellien 1919). Others sought vindication on grounds which downplayed the doctrine of space and time, for example, holding that Einstein's finite but unbounded universe supported the dialectical argument of the first antinomy of pure

reason (Schneider 1921). But since, according to GTR, the behaviour of light rays and measuring rods in gravitational fields no longer corresponded to the relations of Euclidean geometry, knowledgeable Kantians concluded that the necessarily Euclidean character of space claimed in the transcendental aesthetic (TA) was untenable (see KANT, I. §5). At least, that is, in finite regions, for it could be maintained that those (essentially gravitation-free) infinitesimal regions where the rigorous validity of STR was upheld within GTR did conform to Kantian a priori conditions of experience (Cassirer 1921: 436–7; Bollert 1921: 61). As a matter of mathematical fact, the metric in the immediate neighbourhood of any point in a Riemannian manifold (such as is employed in Einstein's theory of gravitation) is 'locally Euclidean' (in spacetime, pseudo-Euclidean, for example a Minkowski metric); in such regions the spacetime manifold is homogeneous, isotropic and flat. But it is not generally possible to extend this metrical characterization to cover the entire spacetime manifold since the generic spacetimes allowed in GTR are inhomogeneous and variably curved (see SPACETIME §3). And these latter do fall outside the supposed necessity of conditions of possible experience.

Characteristically, the deliverances of the new physics were accepted as fact while resources broadly within Kantian orthodoxy were sought for updating 'critical idealism'. Bollert (1921, cited by Gödel 1946/9) 'clarifies' the latter as concerned with the identification of progressively deeper 'levels of objectivation' underlying physics; in this regard, GTR, with its variably curved spacetimes, is a further step below the space and time of both Newton and STR. More influential was Ernst Cassirer's interpretation of Einstein's comment that space and time have lost 'the last remnants of physical objectivity'. According to Cassirer, GTR confirms the pivotal Kantian lesson of the ideality of space and time, that space and time are not 'things' but only 'forms of appearance' or, better, 'ideal principles of order'; each is a schema applying to the phenomena of the external world as a necessary condition of their possible experience (see SPACE §3). GTR has thus given explicit formulation to what Kant tried, with partial success, to articulate in the doctrine of 'pure intuition', namely, space and time are methodological presuppositions of empirical knowledge in physics. What remains of 'pure intuition' are 'the serial form of the relations of coexistence and succession', a structure consisting of (broadly speaking) topological relations which is far more impoverished than a globally Euclidean metric. In the light of GTR, Cassirer recast Kant's doctrine of space and time as essentially a version of Leibnizian relationism (see LEIBNIZ, G.W. §11).

A more radical revision of Kant is given in Winternitz (1924) for whom the essential Kantian conception is just the recognition that the world is *nicht gegeben, sondern aufgegeben* (not given but posed) to us as a task (see Kant, I., *Critique of Pure Reason*, A498/B526). Regarding the TA as undeniably asserting the necessarily Euclidean character of geometry, hence in direct contradiction with GTR, Winternitz accordingly jettisoned it as a confusing and unnecessary appendage to what is taken as the fundamental Kantian endeavour: to establish the a priori presuppositions of physical knowledge. These are spatiality and temporality as 'unintuitive schemata of order' in general (as distinct from any particular chronometrical relations), the law of causality and assumption of continuity of physical processes, the principle of sufficient reason, and the conservation laws. Remarkably, the *necessity* of each of these putative a priori elements was soon to be challenged by the new quantum mechanics (see QUANTUM MECHANICS, INTERPRETATIONS OF).

3 Logical positivism

The last redoubt still held by Kantians concerned the existence of synthetic a priori elements of physical knowledge; their defence was also attempted in the earliest works of Rudolf Carnap and Hans Reichenbach. Carnap's first philosophical publication, his dissertation on space (1922), essentially seeks a reconciliation between GTR and the Kantian notion of a form of intuition. Carefully distinguishing between intuitive, physical and mathematical conceptions of space, Carnap also draws upon the infinitesimal validity of Euclidean geometry in a Riemannian manifold to argue that this geometry is presented in the intuition of a limited region. But since the global extension of this structure depends upon conventions, Euclidean geometry is not constitutive of experience in Kant's sense. Instead, inspired by Einstein's remarks on point coincidences, Carnap conceives the empirical content of physics ('matters of fact') as entirely given by spacetime coincidences while, as a synthetic a priori condition of the possibility of experience, intutive space is assigned a structure of topological relations since these alone preserve empirical content for all possible metric stipulations. By the late 1920s, Carnap had come to view form solely in logical or analytic, not synthetic, terms, concluding that 'there is no synthetic a priori'. This declaration became an article of faith among logical empiricists (see CARNAP, R.).

Of all the logical empiricists, Reichenbach wrote the most extensively about problems of space and time and the philosophical interpretation of GTR.

His early work (1920) also attempts to reconcile GTR with the Kantian emphasis on the a priori, although a modification in the conception of the a priori must be made in view of inconsistencies resulting from a straightforward combination of Kantian precepts and empirically confirmed principles of GTR (for example, the equivalence of inertial and gravitational mass). Reichenbach suggested that of the two primary senses of the Kantian a priori, as valid for all time and as constitutive of the object of knowledge, only the latter was compatible with the new physics of GTR. The remnant of the a priori is placed in 'principles and axioms of coordination', linking the (analytic) mathematics of physical theory with objects in the physical world, in effect, 'constituting' the latter. The systematic task of the philosopher of science now becomes the provision of an 'axiomatic' analysis of domains of physical knowledge. The aim here is to locate a theory's empirical core and then sharply to separate this 'objective content' from 'the subjective contribution of reason', systems of equations and the respective principles of coordination (see THEORIES, SCIENTIFIC). Reichenbach came to view the important role of coordinative principles in less and less Kantian terms, stressing instead their character as freely chosen conventions or definitions, not derived from experience but essential to the applicability of mathematical theory to physical reality. From this viewpoint, 'the philosophical significance' of GTR is that it shows how empiricist analyses of scientific knowledge must be tempered with a recognition of the fundamental role of conventional elements in the basic propositions of physical theory. Thus, in order to obtain empirical spacetime measurements, certain stipulations must first be made governing the behaviour of measuring rods and clocks. Reichenbach's analysis of the relation of mathematical theory to empirical objects in terms of 'coordinative definitions' became a central tenet of the standard 'received view' of scientific theories dominant in philosophy of science till the 1960s (see REICHENBACH, H.).

The founder of the Vienna Circle, Moritz Schlick, was already an opponent of the Kantian conception of physical knowledge; he had not yet embraced neopositivism (see SCHLICK, F.A.M. §1). In one of the earliest lay monographs on GTR, Schlick argued (1917), in a concluding philosophical section applauded by Einstein, for a tempered realism about physical theories which nonetheless recognized that no physical theory fails to have at least some arbitrary elements. Subsequently (1921), he subjected Cassirer's very general defence of a priori elements as methodological presuppositions in physical knowledge to a withering critique, arguing that such vague formulations could have no physical significance and hence were best abandoned. Together with H. WEYL, who was fundamentally opposed to positivism, Schlick emphasized that the union of space, time, *and* matter wrought by the geometrization of gravity in GTR is a mind-independent reality. Of course, Kant does not allow, on pain of surrendering transcendental idealism, that there is a coherent conception of space except as a form of sensibility.

4 Einstein's response

Einstein's reaction to the various philosophical appropriations of his theory are perhaps most widely known through casual remarks made in other contexts, but they may be tracked more closely in several explicit encounters: a meeting at the Sorbonne in Paris on 6 April 1922, with French philosophers, physicists and mathematicians, and in several rare book reviews of philosophical works dealing with his theory. The significance of these encounters lies in how Einstein distinguishes his views from others, not in the presentation of a comprehensive alternative. At the Paris meeting, Einstein made short shrift of Machian philosophy, praising Mach as a 'good mechanician' (no doubt in reference to Mach's views of the relativity of motion) but as a 'deplorable philosopher'. In this venue Einstein also suggestively remarked that 'each philosopher has his own Kant', probably alluding to the plethora of Kantian attempts to assimilate GTR, but perhaps as well intentionally including himself. In this regard, it is instructive to consider that his most fully articulated objection to claims of the necessity of a priori elements in physical knowledge, voiced in a review of an otherwise forgettable book by a student of Cassirer (Elsbach 1924), is considerably different from the verificationist objections of Schlick. It is not that such elements are so general as to be beyond empirical confirmation or disconfirmation but rather that it is entirely arbitrary *which* components of a theoretical system are to be considered a priori. Here also Einstein concedes the justice of the criticism, already implicitly made by Cassirer, of his remark (cited in §1 above) that concepts in physics have validity only if they are individually connected with experience; now an explicitly holist line is affirmed: 'in general, it is not to single concepts but only to the system as a whole that possible experiences must correspond' (1924b: 1,692). Reviewing Winternitz's book, Einstein expressly agrees with the Kantian point that the fundamental principles of a theoretical structure 'do not themselves originate in experience'; the difference with Kantians arises only in Einstein's view that such principles are '*insgesamt* [collectively] mere conven-

tions like the ordering principle of words in a dictionary' (1924a: 22). Interestingly, late in life Einstein returns to the language of Winternitz's formulation of the essential Kantian postulate, that the world is 'not given but posed' as comprising 'the truly valuable' in Kantian doctrine. As before, however, Einstein takes the so-called categories not as 'unalterable' but as '(in the logical sense) free conventions' (1949: 680, 674). Finally, in a review of a work which emphasized the on-going development (then underway by Einstein and others) of GTR into a 'unified field theory' which would contain all laws of nature as logical consequences, Einstein appears to endorse Meyerson's explicitly realist orientation, noting that 'at the basis of all physical science lies a philosophical realism' (1928: 253) (see MEYERSON, É.). Expressions of such 'metaphysical' articles of faith, made with increasing frequency in his later years, were anathema to logical positivism.

See also: BRIDGMAN, P.W.; EINSTEIN, A.; GEOMETRY, PHILOSOPHICAL ISSUES IN §3; RELATIVITY THEORY, PHILOSOPHICAL SIGNIFICANCE OF

References and further reading

* Bollert, K. (1921) *Einstein's Relativitätstheorie und ihre Stellung im System der Gesamterfahrung* (Einstein's Theory of Relativity and its Position in the System of Experience as a Whole), Leipzig: Steinkopff. (Technically proficient Neo-Kantian interpretation.)
* Bridgman, P.W. (1949) 'Einstein's Theories and the Operational Point of View', in P.A. Schilpp (ed.) *Albert Einstein: Philosopher–Scientist*, Evanston, IL: Northwestern University Press, 335–54. (Indicts GTR as not following methodology of STR.)
* Carnap, R. (1922) *Der Raum. Ein Beitrag zur Wissenschaftslehre* (Space. A Contribution to the Theory of Science), Berlin: Reuther & Reichard. (Sophisticated discussion of different conceptions of space and their interrelations.)
* Cassirer, E. (1921) *Zur Einstein'schen Relativitätstheorie*, Berlin: Bruno Cassirer; trans. W.C. Swabey and M.C. Swabey, *Substance and Function and Einstein's Theory of Relativity*, Chicago, IL: Open Court, 1923. (Richly textured, historically-oriented Neo-Kantian interpretation.)
* Einstein, A. (1917) *Ueber die spezielle und die allgemeine Relativitätstheorie*, Braunschweig: Vieweg; trans. R.W. Lawson, *Relativity: The Special and the General Theory*, New York: Crown, 1961. (His lay exposition of special and general relativity.)
* —— (1924a) 'Review of *Relativitätstheorie und*

Erkenntnislehre by J. Winternitz', *Deutsche Literaturzeitung*, 20–2. (Conventionalism of a priori elements in physical knowledge.)

* —— (1924b) 'Review of *Kant und Einstein* by A. Elsbach', *Deutsche Literaturzeitung* 45: 1,685–92. (Early statement of holist views on the relation of theory to experience.)

* —— (1928) 'À Propos de *La Déduction Relativiste* by É. Meyerson', *Revue philosophique de la France et de l'étranger*, 105: 161–6; trans. in É. Meyerson, *The Relativistic Deduction*, Dordrecht: Reidel, 1985, 252–6. (Endorses author's realist orientation.)

* —— (1949) 'Replies to Crticicisms', in P.A. Schilpp (ed.) *Albert Einstein: Philosopher–Scientist*, Evanston, IL: Northwestern University Press, 665–88. (Einstein's later philosophical views.)

* Elsbach, A. (1924) *Kant und Einstein*, Berlin and Leipzig: de Gruyter. (Neo-Kantian work drawing heavily upon Cassirer.)

* Gödel, K. (1946/9) 'Some Observations about the Relationship between Theory of Relativity and Kantian Philosophy', in S. Feferman *et al.* (eds) *Kurt Goedel Collected Works*, New York: Oxford University Press, 1995, vol. III, 230–59. (Two versions of an unpublished essay attempting to minimize Kantian difficulties with general relativity.)

Hentschel, K. (1990) *Interpretationen und Fehlinterpretationen der speziellen und der allgemeinen Relativitätstheorie durch Zeitgenossen Albert Einstein* (Interpretations and Misinterpretations of the Special and the General Theory of Relativity by Einstein's Contempories), Basel-Boston-Berlin: Birkhäuser. (Encyclopedic reference of all the various 'schools' of interpretation.)

* Mach, E. (1921) *Die Prinzipien der physikalischen Optik. Historisch and erkenntnispsychologisch entwickelt*, Leipzig: J.A. Barth; trans. J. Anderson and A. Young, *The Principles of Physical Optics: An Historical and Philosophical Treatment*, London: Methuen, 1926; repr. New York: Dover, 1953. (Published posthumously, contains the preface of July 1913 refered to in §1.)

Meyerson, É. (1925) *La Déduction Relativiste*, Paris: Payot; trans. with supplementary material D.A. Sipfle and M.A. Sipfle, *The Relativistic Deduction*, Dordrecht: Reidel, 1985. (GTR carries out Descartes' 'geometrization of Nature'.)

* Petzoldt, J. (1921) 'Das Verhältnis der Machschen Gedankenwelt zur Relativitätstheorie' (The Relation of Mach's Philosophy to the Theory of Relativity), an appendix to E. Mach, *Die Mechanik in ihrer Entwicklung: Historisch-Kritisch Dargestellt*, 8th edn, Leipzig: Brockhaus, 490–517. (Machian assimilation of GTR.)

* Reichenbach, H. (1920) *Relativitätstheorie und Erkenntnis A priori*, Berlin: Springer; trans. M. Reichenbach, *The Theory of Relativity and A Priori Knowledge*, Berkeley, CA: University of California Press, 1965. (Early attempt to modify Kant to accommodate GTR.)

—— (1928) *Philosophie der Raum-Zeit-Lehre*, Berlin and Leipzig: de Gruyter; trans. M. Reichenbach and J. Freund, *The Philosophy of Space and Time*, New York: Dover, 1957. (GTR shows role of stipulations in knowledge of nature.)

* Schlick, M. (1917) *Raum und Zeit in der gegenwärtigen Physik*, Berlin: Springer; trans. of 4th edn of 1922 by H.L. Brose and P. Heath, 'Space and Time in Contemporary Physics', *Moritz Schlick: Philosophical Papers*, Dordrecht: Reidel, 1979, vol. 1, 207–69. (Concluding philosophical chapter praised by Einstein.)

* —— (1921) 'Kritizistische oder empiristische Deutung der neuen Physik?', *Kant-Studien* 26, 96–111; trans. P. Heath, 'Critical or Empiricist Interpretation of Modern Physics', in *Moritz Schlick: Philosophical Papers*, Dordrecht: Reidel, 1979, vol. 1, 322–34. (Attack upon a priori principles as unverifiable.)

* Schneider, I. (1921) *Das Raum-Zeit Problem bei Kant und Einstein* (The Space-Time Problem in Kant and Einstein), Berlin: Springer. (Novel Neo-Kantian assimilation of Einstein's cosmology.)

* Sellien, E. (1919) *Die erkenntnistheoretische Bedeutung der Relativitätstheorie*, Berlin: Reuther & Reichard. (Argues Kant's doctrine of space and time is unscathed by GTR.)

* Stachel, J. (1989) 'Einstein's Search for General Covariance, 1912–1915', in D. Howard and J. Stachel (eds) *Einstein and the History of General Relativity*, Boston-Basel: Birkhäuser, 48–100. (Uncovers elliptically expressed significance of talk of 'point coincidences'.)

* Winternitz, J. (1924) *Relativitätstheorie und Erkenntnislehre* (Theory of Relativity and the Theory of Knowledge), Leipzig and Berlin: B.G. Teubner. (Neo-Kantian interpretation abandoning Transcendental Aesthetic.)

T.A. RYCKMAN

GENERAL WILL

The fundamental claim for general will is that the members of a political community, as members, share a public or general interest or good which is for the benefit of them all and which should be put before private interests. When the members put the general good first, they are willing the general will of their community. The claim was given special and influential shape by Rousseau. He produced a comprehensive theory of the legitimacy of the state and of government, revolving around the general will. Some contend this solves the central problem of political philosophy – how the individual can both be obliged to obey the state's laws, and be free. If laws are made by the general will, aimed at the common good and expressed by all the citizens, the laws must be in accordance with the public interest and therefore in the interest of each, and each is obliged by the law yet free because they are its author. Rousseau's formulation has been much criticized. But others have found it essentially true and have variously adapted it.

1 **Rousseau and the general will**
2 **Criticisms**
3 **Later versions**

1 Rousseau and the general will

Rousseau's general will is the will of a people or state (see ROUSSEAU, J.-J. §§2–3). A people is not a natural society as is the family, but conventional. Rousseau uses the framework of social contract theory: independent individuals (men only) freely, equally and unanimously bind themselves into a single association (see CONTRACTARIANISM §6). Thereby private persons become a public person, the people, and a collective body, the state, with a single will. That will is necessarily general in its object, its source and its application. (1) It aims exclusively at the common good of the whole body, which is the good of every member, good being moral person-hood, freedom, and security under the law, possible only in a state. (2) The will of the whole body can be expressed only through the wills of its parts, that is, by all the members voting together. It is impossible to transfer one's will, so no member can give his right to express the general will to a representative or government or leader. Rousseau thus ties the general will to direct popular sovereignty. (3) The general will, in the form of laws, applies equally to all members.

The laws of a society ought to conform to the general will, and its government ought to conform to the laws. Rousseau realizes this would happen only if certain conditions are met, and the individual associates together consider themselves a single body so that they have a single will. The members of the state, the citizens, must be socialized to be patriotic and public spirited. There must be no extremes of wealth and poverty to heighten conflicting private interests. Private associations, factionalizing society and encouraging citizens to substitute a partial interest for the general interest, must be prevented or controlled. The government, appointed by the people as its servant, and potentially the most dangerous partial interest, must be kept in its place.

These conditions met, the general will is obvious to every citizen and guides the state according to the common end for which it was instituted. The citizens remain equal; none can impose a burden on others without undertaking it himself. The laws are just, being in the common interest. Everyone is free, because each individual obeys laws which he has made himself and which require what everyone wants for himself.

2 Criticisms

Some common criticisms rest on misunderstanding. Rousseau is attacked for stating that the general will is 'always right', that if one is outvoted that shows one made a mistake, and that one can be 'forced to be free'. These claims startle, but can be understood as true by definition provided the conditions for the expression of the general will are met.

Other criticisms, of both the general will having a general object and of its being willed generally, are more serious. It can be denied that individuals in a society constitute, or can constitute themselves, by a contract, a kind of person with a single will. This objection raises controversial and unsettled issues about the nature of social wholes. Even if such a 'person' is possible, it can still be denied that there can be a general interest which is in the interest of all members of a society. It can be argued that on specific matters, there is no policy or action which is in everyone's interest because individuals tend to have different aims and desires. People may agree, but that agreement is contingent, temporary, subjective and possibly arbitrary. Rousseau's belief that all men have the same basic moral and material interests (see his *Discourse on the Origins of Inequality* (1755)), so that they share a permanent and objective interest, requires assumptions about human nature and men's true interests which are disputable (see PUBLIC INTEREST §2).

If the idea of a public interest and a general will aiming at it is accepted, it is still vulnerable to powerful criticism. It can only be expressed through the votes of all the citizens, unanimously or by a majority. Rousseau admits the people's deliberations are not always right: a people is often fooled. But he offers no clear way of determining which majority decisions express the general will and which do not.

Even when the public interest is known, Rousseau

recognizes that men are inclined to give preference to their own personal interests (which may be opposed to each other and to the public interest), following their private, particular will rather than the general will. This could be prevented, but only under improbable conditions and at great cost. In a suitably small and socially homogeneous society, if it could be established, all the citizens might well be sufficiently close in their values and aims to agree on common interests and put them first, as Rousseau found so admirable in ancient Sparta. However this would involve a high degree of deliberate socialization. The society's institutions would be designed to make citizens uniform. Under such conditions, the emergence of a general will is more plausible; but the price would be a society in which individuality was not developed but discouraged. There is always a balance to be struck between the freedom of individual members of society and the restrictions necessary for its existence. Rousseau's general will seems to require minimizing the individual's freedom, in the public sphere at least.

3 Later versions

Attempts, not altogether successful, have been made to retain the essence of Rousseau's idea while abandoning elements which are subject to criticism. KANT (§10) holds that it is not necessary that the people actually express the general will: it is enough if the law is what the people ought to have willed if they had been asked. The general will becomes hypothetical, what rational men would will, and operates as a 'regulative ideal', a standard to guide conduct. This avoids the practical problems in Rousseau. However, an acceptable test of what laws it is rational to will is needed, and what Kant provides – a political version of his categorical imperative – is disputable.

HEGEL (§8) dispenses with social contract theory, and its individualism, instead situating the general will in actual historical societies. The moral and cultural beliefs and ideals of a society, and the legal, moral, economic, social and political institutions and practices which embody them, are its general will as it has developed; each society has established its own view of the public good. Its individual members learn this as they grow up, and express it and contribute to its further development as they live their lives in and through the society and its beliefs, rules and institutions. The general will ceases to be an ideal, hard to realize practically, and is given specific concrete content. Responsibility for expressing it is given to the civil service and the government. The people does not legislate directly, but elects representatives. Private associations are no longer seen as factional but as

important media for the education of citizens. This is the general will brought down to earth – perhaps too much. Hegel realizes the ideas and institutions of one's society are inadequate in various ways; however, the direction of reform is indicated only very generally.

Recently the general will has been considered in terms of social choice theory (see SOCIAL CHOICE). This has led to some clarification, especially of how the general will might emerge through voting. However, to the extent that this approach aggregates individual preferences (taking individuals as isolable from their society), and sets no moral limit to the content of decisions, it departs significantly from Rousseau's and gives the term a different meaning. Rousseau's general will requires the existence of a social unity between individuals, who thereby have a collective interest as members of that union in addition to their private interests as individuals; their general interest is to have a certain kind of society, bringing everyone specific moral benefits; and the verdict on what the general will is in any particular case must be delivered by the citizens themselves. Hence Rousseau's ideas, although complex and problematic, remain relevant, for instance to debates about freedom, democracy, republicanism and communitarianism.

References and further reading

Bosanquet, B. (1899) *The Philosophical Theory of the State*, London: Macmillan, chaps 4–7. (Reworks Rousseau on Hegelian lines.)

Emmet, D. (1994) *The Role of the Unrealisable: A Study of Regulative Ideals*, London: Macmillan, chaps 1–4. (Regulative ideals, and the general will as one.)

Grofman, B. and Feld, S.L. (1988) 'Rousseau's General Will: A Condorcetian Perspective', *American Political Science Review* 82 (2): 567–76. (How the general will could emerge through voting.)

Hiley, D.R. (1990) 'The Individual and the General Will: Rousseau Reconsidered', *History of Philosophy Quarterly* 7 (2): 159–78. (Connects Rousseau with contemporary debates between liberals and communitarians.)

Levine, A. (1993) *The General Will: Rousseau, Marx, Communism*, Cambridge: Cambridge University Press. (The use of the idea of the general will in current political philosophy.)

Nicholson, P.P. (1990) *The Political Philosophy of the British Idealists: Selected Studies*, Cambridge: Cambridge University Press, study VI. (Rousseau, Kant and Hegel discussed briefly, Bosanquet fully.)

Riley, P. (1986) *The General Will Before Rousseau:*

The Transformation of the Divine into the Civic, Princeton, NJ: Princeton University Press. (Traces the theological origins of the idea of the general will in writers such as Pascal and Malebranche.)

Rousseau, J.-J. (1762) *Social Contract, Discourse on the Virtue Most Necessary For a Hero, Political Fragments, and Geneva Manuscript*, trans. J.R. Bush, R.D. Masters, C. Kelly and T. Marshall in R.D. Masters and C. Kelly (eds) *The Collected Writings of Rousseau*, Hanover, NH, and London: University Press of New England, 1994, vol. 4. (Rousseau's fullest account of the general will.)

* —— (1755) *Discourse on the Origins of Inequality Among Men (Second Discourse) Polemics and Political Economy*, trans. J.R. Bush, R.D. Masters, C. Kelly and T. Marshall in R.D. Masters and C. Kelly (eds) *The Collected Writings of Rousseau*, Hanover, NH, and London: University Press of New England, 1992, vol. 3. (Rousseau's view of human nature.)

Runciman, W.G. and Sen, A.K. (1965) 'Games, Justice and the General Will', *Mind* 74: 554–62; repr. in W.G. Runciman, *Sociology in its Place and Other Essays*, Cambridge: Cambridge University Press, 1970, 224–32. (Claims a useful sense may be given to the general will by reference to the Prisoner's Dilemma.)

PETER P. NICHOLSON

GENETICS

Genetics studies the problem of heredity, namely why offspring resemble their parents. The field emerged in 1900 with the rediscovery of the 1865 work of Gregor Mendel. William Bateson called the new field 'genetics' in 1905, and W. Johannsen used the term 'gene' in 1909. By analysing data about patterns of inheritance of characters, such as yellow and green peas, Mendelian geneticists infer the number and type of hypothetical genes. The major components of the theory of the gene, which proposed the model of genes as beads on a string, were in place by the 1920s. In the 1930s, the field of population genetics emerged from the synthesis of results from Mendelian genetics with Darwinian natural selection. Population geneticists study the distribution of genes in the gene pool of a population and changes caused by selection and other factors. The 1940s and 1950s saw the development of molecular genetics, which investigates problems about gene reproduction, mutation and function at the molecular level.

Philosophical issues arise: the question about the evidence for the reality of hypothetical genes, and the status of Mendel's laws, given that they are not universal generalizations. Debates have occurred about the nature of the relation between Mendelian and molecular genetics. Population genetics provides the perspective of the gene as the unit of selection in evolutionary theory. Molecular genetics and its accompanying technologies raise ethical issues about humans' genetic information, such as the issue of privacy of information about one's genome and the morality of changing a person's genes. The nature–nurture debate involves the issue of genetic determinism, the extent to which genes control human traits and behaviour.

1   Historical development of Mendelian genetics
2   Reality of the genes
3   Universality of genetic laws
4   Reduction and theory change in genetics
5   The gene as the unit of selection
6   Genetic determinism and sociobiology

1   Historical development of Mendelian genetics

Mendelian genetics arose from three traditions in the nineteenth century: one, the hybridist tradition of Mendel; two, speculative theories of heredity, variation and development; and, three, studies of the hereditary variation important in evolutionary change. Genetics emerged when the problems of heredity and embryological development were separated: the transmission of hereditary characters through generations can be studied independently of the development of the characters in embryos. Thus, bifurcation rather than unification marked early progress in genetics. Only recently have efforts to reunite genetics and embryology begun to be fruitful.

Mendel and Darwin viewed organisms as being composed of separable unit-characters that could vary independently of one another. The focus on contrasting variations among individual organisms, rather than on the similarities on which taxonomists had focused, was a key conceptual shift that enabled the development of both Darwinian natural selection and Mendelian genetics (see EVOLUTION, THEORY OF §1).

Mendelian genetics is usually presented by following the details of an exemplary cross-breeding experiment. The technique used by the Mendelian geneticist is artificial breeding. For example, pure breeding plants that produce yellow peas are bred with others that produce only green peas. The resulting hybrid peas are all yellow. After the hybrids self-fertilize, the resulting peas occur in a ratio of three yellow to one green. The empirical generalization of 3:1 ratios is explained by assuming the existence of paired genes. It is a matter of dispute how much of this explanation is found in Mendel's paper. The post-1900 account assumes that paired genes occur in the pure breeding parents: designate yellow, AA; green, aa. The hybrid has the 'phenotype' of the dominant parent, yellow, but its 'genotype' is Aa. During the formation of germ cells in the hybrid, the two genes segregate (separate) to form germ cells (pollen and eggs) that are either A or a. Segregation is the key theoretical assumption of Mendelian genetics. The two types of germ cell form in equal numbers and combine randomly during fertilization; symbolically: $(A + a)(A + a) = 1AA + 2Aa + 1aa$. The AA and Aa plants have yellow peas; the aa, green. These theoretical assumptions thus explain the empirical generalization of $3:1$ ratios. Numerous characters in plants and animals exhibit such ratios. The law of segregation is also called 'Mendel's first law'.

Although Mendel himself did not distinguish them, Mendelian genetics came to contain what are called 'Mendel's two laws'. Mendel's second law was formulated separately only after exceptions were found, and is called the 'law of independent assortment'. The law states that genes for different traits, such as pea colour and pea shape, are inherited independently. In 1910, Morgan explained anomalies for independent assortment by postulating that some genes are linked in inheritance. Thus, the overgeneralization that all genes assort independently was specialized to the claim that all genes in different linkage groups assort independently. Linkage is explained by the chromosome theory, which is discussed in §2. Because of the significant changes that linkage introduced, the field is sometimes called 'Mendelian–Morganist genetics'.

In 1926, Morgan stated what he called 'the theory of the gene':

> The theory [of the gene] states that the characters of the individual are referable to paired elements (genes) in the germinal material that are held together in a definite number of linkage groups; it states that the members of each pair of genes separate when their germ-cells mature in accordance with Mendel's first law, and in consequence, each germ-cell comes to contain one set only; it states that the members belonging to different linkage groups assort independently in accordance with Mendel's second law; it states that an orderly interchange – crossing over – also takes place, at times between the elements in corresponding linkage groups; and it states that the frequency of crossing-over furnishes evidence of the linear order of the elements in each linkage group and of the relative position of the elements with respect to each other.

(Morgan 1926: 25)

The occasional crossing over between genes in corresponding linkage groups enables the construction of genetic maps, which show the relative positions of genes to each other. Numerous questions were left unanswered by the theory of the gene of the 1920s. What is the chemical nature of the gene? What is the size of the gene? How do genes mutate and then stably reproduce those mutations? How do genes function to produce characters? These questions were not answerable by the technique of artificial breeding of Mendelian genetics.

2 Reality of the genes

The genes were hypothetical, theoretical entities, whose numbers and types were inferred in order to explain the distribution of characters in breeding experiments. The first step in providing the physical basis of heredity was the proposal in 1903–4 of the chromosome theory, the claim that Mendelian genes are arranged linearly along the chromosomes, which are thread-like bodies in the nuclei of cells. The chromosome theory was an interfield theory which integrated findings from the fields of cytology and genetics. Information about chromosomes, obtained by fixing and staining parts of cells and viewing them in a microscope, was related to information about genes, inferred from patterns of inheritance of characters. Predictions were made about the behaviour of chromosomes, based on genetic information, and vice versa. Chromosomes are chemically composed of proteins and deoxyribonucleic acid (DNA). Early speculations were that the genes were proteins. That view was challenged in the 1940s and 1950s as evidence mounted that DNA is the genetic material (or occasionally ribonucleic acid – RNA). The field of molecular biology (also called 'molecular genetics') emerged with the discovery of the double helix structure of DNA by Watson and Crick in 1953. By 1970, numerous problems had been solved: gene reproduction (opening and copying of the double helix of DNA), the genetic code and the sequence hypothesis (three bases along the linear length of the DNA code for one amino acid in a linear protein), and genetic function (DNA is transcribed to messenger RNA which is translated to protein). From a molecular genetics perspective, genes are segments of DNA or RNA which code for a molecular product or regulate or otherwise influence other genes. After 1970, a new era of molecular genetics began. With the discovery of enzymes that precisely cut and ligate

13

DNA, DNA from widely divergent species can be recombined. Techniques for sequencing DNA have made possible the human genome project in which all the DNA in a human will be sequenced (see MOLECULAR BIOLOGY; SCIENTIFIC REALISM AND ANTIREALISM).

3 Universality of genetic laws

Philosophers trained in logic are fond of universal generalizations. At least some laws in physics appear to be universal generalizations, admitting of no exceptions, applying to all objects in the universe and throughout all time (at least after the first three minutes following the Big Bang). Biology seems to lack such strong universal generalizations. Although all living things on earth share enough of their metabolic and genetic machinery to indicate a common origin for all life, exceptions to generalizations abound. Certainly Mendel's two laws are not without exceptions. The 1:1 segregation of genes is violated when one gene knocks out its competitor. Such segregation distortion is uncommon, but does constitute an exception to the law of segregation. The oversimplification that one gene is associated with one character was complicated when it was found that one gene can influence many characters and one character may be influenced by many genes. One character is not always dominant over another; the hybrid can show a blend of the two parental characters or even a character different from those of its parents. Special-case exceptions also exist for the general claims of molecular genetics, such as the universality of the genetic code and the claim that DNA is the genetic material.

Given the perspective of evolutionary theory, namely that adapted variants survive in natural selection, such variation and lack of universality are not surprising. Furthermore, the genetic apparatus in sexually breeding organisms, which is the object of study in Mendelian genetics, is itself a product of evolution. Future evolutionary changes may result in segregation being the special case or even disappearing, if other mechanisms prove more advantageous.

Defenders of the claim that there are laws in biology take a more local or conditional perspective on the nature of laws. Within the time span of genetic experiments, Mendel's laws support predictions about the ratios of characters expected in hybrid crosses (see LAWS, NATURAL §1).

4 Reduction and theory change in genetics

Philosophers have debated whether the relation between Mendelian and molecular genetics is one of theory reduction. Theory reduction, in the sense proposed by the logical empiricists, requires that theories be in axiomatic form, such that the reduced theory can be deductively derived from the reducing theory. Furthermore, any term in the reduced theory not also in the reducing theory must be connected to a term in the reducing theory by a 'reduction function'. Severe complications arise when trying to connect the Mendelian gene, characterized in terms of effects upon one or many phenotypic characters, and the molecular gene, which may code for a single protein that has myriad effects upon numerous biosynthetic pathways. Furthermore, although some possibility exists for putting Mendel's laws of segregation and independent assortment into an axiomatic form, no 'laws of molecular biology' seem identifiable. No deduction seems possible.

The debate about derivational theory reduction arose within the context of the logical empiricist approach to philosophy of science (see LOGICAL POSITIVISM §4; UNITY OF SCIENCE). Alternatives to reduction have arisen within the context of the study of theory change, rather than the analysis of logical relations between static, axiomatically characterized, atemporal theories. From this historical perspective, one view is that Mendelian genetics was replaced by molecular genetics. Another view is that molecular genetics is the later development of the research programme begun by Mendelian genetics. In this latter alternative, Mendelian segregation, for example, is viewed as being explained at the level of the chromosome. Pairs of chromosomes separate in the formation of germ cells and this explains why genes, carried by the chromosomes, segregate. However, the problems of gene reproduction and gene function were not solved at the chromosomal level. Their solution required the level of the macromolecule. Molecular genetics thus solved problems posed by, but not solvable by, Mendelian genetics and the chromosome theory (see REDUCTION, PROBLEMS OF).

5 The gene as the unit of selection

Philosophers of biology, as well as evolutionary biologists, have debated the appropriate unit for evolutionary theory. Dawkins (1982) proposed that 'selfish' genes construct extended phenotypes to increase their chances of survival in future generations. Extended phenotypes include not only the hereditary characters of typical Mendelian phenotypes, but also any behaviour under genetic control, such as the building of dams by beavers. The genes are the replicators and the important units of selection; the extended phenotypes are vehicles for carrying the genes. Others have objected that the phenotype is the unit that interacts with the environment and hence the phenotype (the interactor) is the more important unit in selection. Other critics of genic selection argue that attempting to reduce the theory of evolution to an account of changes in individual genes produces artifacts, because the individual genes are usually parts of gene complexes that produce phenotype characters in complex ways. Also, the selective advantage of a gene may be dependent on its relative frequency in a gene pool; thus, say critics of genic selection, the genetic context is relevant to the selective advantage of a given gene. Reducing evolutionary theory to the level of the single gene may be too low a level for an adequate theory. Defenders of genic selectionism disagree.

There is another problem with characterizing the units of selection theory as the replicator and the interactor – it neglects the essential role of genetic variation in producing the raw material on which selection acts. Selection type theories are characterized by genetic variation, then interaction, which causes a benefit to accrue to some of the variants, a benefit which may include genetic replication (see EVOLUTION, THEORY OF §3).

6   Genetic determinism and sociobiology

The issue of the role of genes in determining human traits has occasioned much debate. Human sociobiology raises new questions for the old nature–nurture debate about the role of genes in determining human social behaviour and the past evolutionary advantage of such hypothetical genes (see SOCIOBIOLOGY). The fallacy of genetic fatalism is the erroneous assumption that possession of a gene infallibly leads to a single phenotypic expression of the genetic trait. Different phenotypic responses are possible, given the genetic context and environmental variables that play a role in the expression of a trait.

See also: GENETICS AND ETHICS; SPECIES

References and further reading

Beatty, J. (1995) 'The Evolutionary Contingency Thesis', in J.G. Lennox and G. Wolters (eds) *Philosophy of Biology*, Konstanz: University of Konstanz Press and Pittsburgh, PA: University of Pittsburgh Press, 45–81. (Argues against the claim that there are biological laws. See §3.)

Brandon, R.N. (1990) *Adaptation and Environment*, Princeton, NJ: Princeton University Press. (Argues for a phenotypic perspective in evolutionary theory.)

Brandon, R.N. and Burian, R. (eds) (1984) *Genes, Organisms and Populations*, Cambridge, MA: MIT Press. (Collection of articles by both biologists and philosophers about units of selection.)

Carlson, E.A. (1966) *The Gene: A Critical History*, Philadelphia, PA: Saunders. (History of the gene concept.)

Darden, L. (1991) *Theory Change in Science: Strategies from Mendelian Genetics*, New York: Oxford University Press. (Discusses reasoning strategies in theory change by tracing the development of Morgan's theory of the gene.)

Darden, L. and Cain, J.A. (1989) 'Selection Type Theories', *Philosophy of Science* 56: 106–29. (Argues for the role of genetic variation, in addition to interaction and replication, in natural selection.)

Darden, L. and Maull, N. (1977) 'Interfield Theories', *Philosophy of Science* 44: 43– 64. (Discusses the chromosome theory mentioned in §2, as well as theories from molecular biology that bridge two fields.)

* Dawkins, R. (1982) *The Extended Phenotype*, New York: Oxford University Press. (An extended argument for the selfish gene perspective.)

Dunn, L.C. (1965) *A Short History of Genetics*, New York: McGraw-Hill. (History of genetics from Mendel to 1939.)

Judson, H.F. (1979) *The Eighth Day of Creation*, New York: Simon & Schuster. (Account of the development of molecular biology, with extensive quotations from interviews with participants.)

Kevles, D.J. and Hood, L. (eds) (1992) *The Code of Codes: Scientific and Social Issues in the Human Genome Project*, Cambridge, MA: Harvard University Press. (Useful collection of articles from diverse perspectives.)

Kitcher, P. (1984) '1953 and All That: A Tale of Two Sciences', *The Philosophical Review* 93: 335–73; repr. in Sober, E. (ed.) *Conceptual Issues in Evolutionary Biology*, Cambridge, MA: MIT Press, 1994, 2nd edn, 379–99. (Argues against derivational reduction; in favour of molecular genetics as an 'explanatory extension' of classical genetics and in favour of autonomous levels of biological explanation.)

Morgan, T.H., Sturtevant, A.H., Muller, H.J. and Bridges, C.B. (1915) *The Mechanism of Mendelian Heredity*, New York: Holt. (Seminal monograph on the chromosome theory of Mendelian heredity.)

* Morgan, T.H. (1926) *The Theory of the Gene*, New Haven, CT: Yale University Press. (The classic statement of the theory by its principal architect.)

Olby, R. (1985) *Origins of Mendelism*, Chicago, IL: University of Chicago Press, 2nd edn. (Places Mendel in the older hybridist tradition rather than as the first Mendelian geneticist.)

—— (1974) *The Path to the Double Helix*, Seattle, WA:

University of Washington Press. (History of developments from 1930s to the 1953 Watson–Crick discovery of the structure of DNA.)

Sober, E. and Lewontin, R. (1982) 'Artifact, Cause, and Genic Selection', *Philosophy of Science* 47: 157–80. (Argues against genic selectionism. See §5)

Sterelny, K. and Kitcher, P. (1988) 'The Return of the Gene', *Journal of Philosophy* 85: 339–61. (A defence of genic selectionism. See §5.)

Stern, C. and Sherwood, E. (eds) (1966) *The Origin of Genetics, A Mendel Source Book*, San Francisco, CA: W.H. Freeman. (Contains translations of Mendel's original papers, letters and the papers of his rediscovers, Hugo de Vries and Carl Correns.)

Strickberger, M. (1985) *Genetics*, New York: Macmillan, 3rd edn. (A standard genetics textbook with more detail on Mendelian genetics, which was presented briefly in §1.)

Waters, C.K. (1990) 'Why the Anti-reductionist Consensus Won't Survive the Case of Classical Mendelian Genetics', in A. Fine, M. Forbes and L. Wessels (eds) *PSA 1990*, East Lansing, MI: Philosophy of Science Association, vol. 1, 125–39; repr. in E. Sober (ed.) *Conceptual Issues in Evolutionary Biology*, Cambridge, MA: MIT Press, 1994, 2nd edn, 401–17. (A defence of reduction and a source for references to the reduction debate discussed in §4.)

Watson, J. (1980) *The Double Helix, A Norton Critical Edition*, New York: W.W. Norton. (Watson's autobiographical account of the discovery of the DNA double helix, reprints of original articles, and other related material.)

Watson, J., Hopkins, N.H., Roberts, J.W., Steitz, J.A. and Weiner A.M. (1988) *Molecular Biology of the Gene*, Menlo Park, CA: Benjamin Cummings, 4th edn. (Developments in molecular biology can be traced by examining the changes through the four editions of Watson's textbook.)

Wimsatt, W. (1980) 'Reductionist Research Strategies and their Biases in the Units of Selection Controversy', in T. Nickles (ed.) *Scientific Discovery: Case Studies*, Dordrecht: Reidel, 213–59. (Relates the issues of reduction and the controversy about units of selection, discussed in §4 and §5.)

LINDLEY DARDEN

GENETICS AND ETHICS

The identification of human genes poses problems about the use of resources, and about ownership and use of genetic information, and could lead to over-emphasis of the importance of genetic make-up. Genetic screening raises problems of consent, stigmatization, discrimination and public anxiety. Counselling will be required, but whether this can facilitate individual choice is unclear. It will also involve problems of confidentiality. On the other hand genetic knowledge will pave the way for genetic therapies for hereditary disease. This raises the question whether a therapy which alters an individual at the genetic level is different in kind from conventional medical treatment. Genetic alterations passed on to future generations raise problems regarding consent. Genetic intervention could also be used to make 'improvements' in human genetic potential, leading to anxieties about eugenic attempts to design the species. Transgenics, the introduction of foreign genes into a genome, raises questions about the integrity of species boundaries and the assessment of risk.

1 **Genetic screening, determinism and discrimination**
2 **Genetic counselling**
3 **Gene therapy**
4 **Eugenics and transgenics**
5 **The human genome project**

1 Genetic screening, determinism and discrimination

It is with regard to the medical implications of genetic research that most ethical issues arise. The first concerns genetic screening. There is a distinction between screening and testing, although similar ethical issues arise in both cases: whereas testing applies to the analysis of the genetic make-up of individuals, to establish whether they carry a certain gene, screening determines the prevalence of a gene in a particular population. Different kinds of screening can be distinguished. (1) Neonatal screening, such as that used for phenylketonuria, which is primarily for identifying those suffering from diseases that can be ameliorated by early treatment. (2) Screening or testing in childhood, which will facilitate both the detection of those predisposed to develop late-onset diseases, and the identification of carrier status prior to reproductive age. There are particular problems here with consent, possible stigmatization, and the disclosure of information to the child. (3) Preconception screening of adults, which may increase the possibilities of informed reproductive choice. (4) Prenatal screening, which will have particular relevance for assessing the status of the foetus, with the associated ethical dilemmas concerning abortion (see REPRODUCTION AND ETHICS).

Screening of adults will increasingly have implications beyond reproductive choice. Whereas in the past, screening tended to be targeted at

16

individuals known to be at risk, greater genetic knowledge will facilitate the screening of whole populations, given available resources. It may become possible to do 'broad spectrum' screening of individuals for a wide range of conditions, with the associated likelihood of increased public anxiety arising from changes in self-image following testing, and the danger of stigmatization.

Three categories of ethical issue arise. What criteria should be satisfied before the introduction of a particular screening programme? In accordance with what principles should a screening programme be carried out? What are the criteria for success – how should it be evaluated afterwards? This may involve follow-up of individuals screened, for example, with problems of privacy and confidentiality.

Genetic screening could lead to new forms of discrimination on the basis of a person's genetic make-up, irrespective of symptoms. The implementation of sickle-cell screening in the USA led to stigmatization of carriers, despite the fact that they did not have sickle-cell disease. Further worry surrounds the use of screening and testing to identify people who have a genetic predisposition to develop a disease in later life which has a genetic component, but which may require some environmental component to trigger it. If it were possible to identify which individuals were at increased risk, because of their genetic make-up, of succumbing to cancer caused by a particular toxin in the workplace, such individuals might find themselves unemployable or uninsurable. There is a question concerning what information about genetic predispositions ought to be made available to employers and insurers, and a conceptual question about what counts as a predisposition: there is a danger that the distinction between 'predisposed' and 'predetermined' might become blurred.

Arguments against genetic discrimination, or 'geneticism', are analogous to those opposing racism and sexism. There are worries, however, that greater genetic knowledge may lead to less tolerance of genetic disease, which may come to be seen as avoidable. A distinction has to be drawn, however, between the evaluation of a particular genetic condition and the value of the individual who suffers from it. Hence there are issues about choice of terminology. The choice between 'handicap', 'defect', 'disorder' and 'variant' is not ethically neutral.

2 Genetic counselling

Genetic screening programmes will increase the need for counselling. Genetic counselling is commonly understood to include the following elements: esti-mating the risk of having or propagating a genetic

disorder; advising the counsellee at risk about the medical facts underlying the disorder; and facilitating and supporting a decision by the counsellee.

The first ethical dilemma concerns autonomy (see AUTONOMY, ETHICAL). There is a question whether the very existence of genetic screening and counselling encourages pressure on individuals to make particular reproductive decisions. In line with the importance commonly given to autonomy, the prevailing model in genetic counselling has been 'nondirective'. Counsel-ling, in facilitating counsellee decision-making, is thus distinguished from advice. It has been suggested, however, that the very structure of the counselling interview undermines the possibility of nondirective-ness, and the fact that, for example, termination is an option may somehow suggest to clients that this is a choice they ought to make.

Informed consent is particularly problematic in genetic counselling, when variation in perceptions of risk is taken into account. To a couple being counselled about a one in four chance of giving birth to a child suffering from a recessive genetic condition, the numerical probability may be less meaningful than the nature of the condition itself. Furthermore, individuals' perception of risk can be affected by the way in which information is presented. The introduc-tion of population broad-spectrum screening will further complicate the issues. Informed consent will be yet more difficult when a number of diseases are at issue at the same time (see CONSENT).

The applicability of principles of medical ethics to genetic counselling is also complicated by the fact that the 'client' in this context is normally a couple or family rather than an individual. This raises the issue of confidentiality, relevant to both screening and counselling. The discovery of nonpaternity is an example of a dilemma that might arise. For example, genetic testing of a child and its parents may reveal that the male partner is not the genetic father of the child. Does he have a right to this information, or does the mother have a right to confidentiality?

The issue of confidentiality is linked with that of ownership, and the sense in which an individual can be said to own their genes. The fact that genetic relatives share genes has been advanced as a reason for questioning the individual's right to confidenti-ality in some cases, where there is information that might affect the reproductive decisions of others.

3 Gene therapy

Genetic knowledge will facilitate gene therapy, which is controversial because it involves alteration of an individual at the genetic level. An analogy is frequently drawn, however, between gene therapy and organ transplants. Fears that genetic alteration would somehow interfere with the identity of the person are unrealistic in the light of proper understanding of what the techniques involve, and appreciation of the extent to which individuals can be affected by environmental techniques. Regarding the view that gene therapy should be seen in the same way as other forms of therapy, and similarly subject to requirements of informed consent, there are two complicating factors, however. One is the difference between somatic and germline gene therapy; the other is the potential use of gene therapy techniques for enhancement purposes.

Somatic gene therapy is the treatment of the body cells of an individual; the genetic alteration will not be passed on to descendants. Germline therapy, however, will involve changes that will affect subsequent generations. Many commentators see a moral difference between these two, suggesting that somatic, but not germline, therapy is acceptable. The arguments for this position are, first, that there is at present insufficient knowledge to justify taking risks that may be irrevocable (see RISK). If, for example, action were taken to eliminate a particular gene from the gene pool, we may discover too late that it had some hidden advantage and lose valuable genetic diversity. Second, whereas the individual undergoing somatic therapy has the opportunity to consent to or refuse therapy, those affected by germline therapy will be as yet unborn generations, who cannot express a choice in the matter. This raises the general ethical question whether we have obligations to future generations (see FUTURE GENERATIONS, OBLIGATIONS TO). Third, there is an argument that individuals have a right to an unmodified genetic inheritance. In a more plausible form the argument claims a right to a genetic inheritance that has not been tampered with except to remove pathology. Here it slides into the therapy/ enhancement distinction.

A further problem associated with germline therapy concerns the means of carrying it out. It must either target the germ cells of an adult or be carried out at the embryonic stage. Its development will therefore involve research on human embryos and the associated ethical dilemmas.

On the other hand, there are arguments in favour of a positive obligation to develop germline therapy. First, there is said to be a general obligation to relieve suffering where we can, in this case by seeking treatments for genetic disease. Second, there is an argument from scientific freedom, though this is largely connected with a view that classifies gene therapy as research. Third, there is an argument from reproductive autonomy. Germline therapy might be, for some couples, the only way they can achieve a 'winning combination' of genes. Even if this is not the case, if a woman can consent to somatic therapy on her child, why cannot she ensure that all her descendants should be free of a condition such as Huntington's chorea?

The debate over the distinction between gene therapy and genetic enhancement raises the question of what the goals of medicine should be. If medical technology is not limited to therapeutic interventions elsewhere, it is difficult to see the argument for limiting it in the genetic sphere alone: particular uses would have to be considered on their individual merits. An example to illustrate the distinction is the use of growth hormone to treat dwarfism, on the one hand, and to produce talented basketball players, on the other.

4 Eugenics and transgenics

Underlying many of the objections to genetic screening, genetic counselling with the option of termination of affected foetuses, and gene therapy, is an anxiety about eugenics, the attempt to improve the human gene pool. This arises because of historical precedents which show the potential for abuse. It is also one factor in the drive towards the upholding of nondirectiveness in counselling. The question arises as to the extent to which it is possible to advocate steps to improve genetic public health without the associations of discredited genetic eugenic policies. If public health is a good that should be pursued, then, *a fortiori*, genetic public health is a good that should be pursued. A distinction has commonly been drawn between negative and positive eugenics, negative being the attempt to reduce the frequency of genetic disease and positive the attempt to improve such qualities as intelligence or moral sensitivity. Some take the view that all eugenics is unacceptable; some that negative eugenics is morally acceptable, but not positive; others that both, under certain conditions, are acceptable. There are conceptual problems about how the negative–positive distinction is to be drawn, and also problems about the arguments for a moral distinction. There are arguments about the greater moral urgency of relieving suffering, but also intuitive objections to 'designer babies', the basis of which is not always clear, but which rely partly on an appeal to human dignity, partly on an objection to 'playing God', and partly on an appeal to lack of sufficient knowledge.

Transgenics, the incorporation of foreign genes into the genome of an organism, is commonly discussed in connection with animals and plants. One issue concerns the rights of the host organism, particularly in cases where suffering is likely to ensue. A more fundamental question is whether there is anything wrong in principle in crossing species barriers. Supporters point out that cross-breeding is nothing new, and that the definition of species is itself problematic (see SPECIES). Opponents may fall back on arguments about what is natural to a certain form of life, or point to the risks of releasing genetically engineered organisms into the environment. In addition to the interests of the modified organisms themselves, there are consequences for human health, for other species, and for the biosphere to be considered. There is a question, first, as to what constitutes 'release', and, second, as to whether risk-assessment exhausts the moral issues.

5 The human genome project

The attempt to map and sequence the entire human genome raises ethical questions about whether that attempt is worthwhile. Large parts of the genome, for example, are referred to as 'junk DNA' – are they worth sequencing? The project is defended on the grounds that knowledge is worthwhile in itself: junk DNA may have functions we are as yet unaware of, and the mapping of the human genome will give us insight into the nature of humanity. The latter point is attacked as an overly reductionist view of human beings which ignores spiritual and environmental factors (see HUMAN NATURE §2).

A second problem concerns ownership and exploitation of results of human genome analysis: whether, for example, it is permissible to patent human genetic sequences, and how the benefits of the knowledge gained will be distributed, given that there is a sense in which the genome belongs to the whole of humanity (see RESPONSIBILITIES OF SCIENTISTS AND INTELLECTUALS §3). These issues have been given added urgency by the result of a recent genetic experiment: the succesful cloning of a sheep. Nicknamed 'Dolly', the cloned sheep was produced by isolating a segment of DNA from another sheep and replicating it in a laboratory. It has been admitted by the scientists who performed the experiment that the same process could be applied to humans.

Because of their revolutionary and far-reaching potential, and because the fact of genetic relatedness poses particular problems for an individualistic ethic, advances in genetics have provoked discussion about the appropriate ethical framework to apply: whether there is any categorical objection to genetic interventions or whether some form of consequentialist analysis is adequate (see CONSEQUENTIALISM; DEONTOLOGICAL ETHICS); whether established principles of medical ethics are applicable or whether an ethics of

care based on feminist thought is preferable (see MEDICAL ETHICS; FEMINIST ETHICS).

See also: APPLIED ETHICS; BIOETHICS; GENETICS; TECHNOLOGY AND ETHICS

References and further reading

Annas, G.J. and Elias, S. (eds) (1992) *Gene Mapping: Using Law and Ethics as Guides*, New York: Oxford University Press. (Focuses on the medical implications of genetic research.)

Chadwick, D. *et al.* (1990) *Human Genetic Information: Science, Law and Ethics*, Chichester: John Wiley. (Deals with issues raised by the attempt to map and sequence the human genome.)

Chadwick, R. (1988) 'Genetic improvement', in D. Braine and H. Lesser (eds) *Ethics, Technology and Medicine*, Aldershot: Avebury. (On the distinction which has been drawn between negative and positive eugenics, negative being the attempt to reduce the frequency of genetic disease and positive the attempt to improve such qualities as intelligence or moral sensitivity.)

—— (1992) *Ethics, Reproduction and Genetic Control*, London: Routledge. (Examines issues relating to eugenics.)

Clarke, A. (1991) 'Is non-directive counselling possible?', *Lancet* 338: 998–1001. (Considers issues in genetic counselling.)

Clothier, C.M. *et al.* (1992) *Report of the Committee on the Ethics of Gene Therapy*, London: HMSO. (Multi-authored report on the ethical issues raised by gene therapy.)

Macer, D.R.J. (1990) *Shaping Genes*, Christchurch, New Zealand: Eubios Ethics Institute. (Contains material on transgenics; has a good bibliography and survey of relevant literature.)

Pembrey, M.E. (1991) 'Embryo therapy: is there a clinical need?', in D.R. Bromham *et al.* (eds) *Ethics in Reproductive Medicine*, London: Springer-Verlag. (On germline therapy and the possibility of a winning combination of genes.)

Wertz, D.C. and Fletcher, J.C. (1991) 'Privacy and disclosure in medical genetics examined in an ethics of care', *Bioethics* 5: 212–32. (Considers privacy and disclosure as they arise in relation to issues in genetics.)

RUTH CHADWICK

GENTILE, GIOVANNI (1875–1944)

Best known as the self-styled philosopher of Fascism, Gentile, along with Benedetto Croce, was responsible for the ascendance of Hegelian idealism in Italy during the first half of the twentieth century. His 'actual' idealism or 'actualism' was a radical attempt to integrate our consciousness of experience with its creation in the 'pure act of thought', thereby abolishing the distinction between theory and practice. He held an extreme subjectivist version of idealism, and rejected both empirical and transcendental arguments as forms of 'realism' that posited the existence of a reality outside thought.

His thesis developed through a radicalization of Hegel's critique of Kant that drew on the work of the nineteenth-century Neapolitan Hegelian Bertrando Spaventa. He argued that it represented both the natural conclusion of the whole tradition of Western philosophy, and had a basis in the concrete experience of each individual. He illustrated these arguments in detailed writings on the history of Italian philosophy and the philosophy of education respectively. He joined the Fascist Party in 1923 and thereafter placed his philosophy at the service of the regime. He contended that Fascism was best understood in terms of his reworking of the Hegelian idea of the ethical state, a view that occasionally proved useful for ideological purposes but which had little practical influence.

1 Life and works
2 Actualism
3 Social and political philosophy

1 Life and works

Giovanni Gentile was born on 30 May 1875 at Castelvetrano in Sicily. He studied philosophy at the University of Pisa under Donato Jaja, a pupil of Bertrando Spaventa. Spaventa's ideas were also to have a profound impact on Gentile's thought. He graduated in 1897 with a thesis on the nineteenth-century Italian philosophers Rosmini and Gioberti, through whom he explored Kant and Hegel respectively. He later claimed that the germs of his mature philosophy were already present in this early attempt to pursue the Hegelian critique of Kant. This study was published in 1898 and was followed the next year by a critical examination of the writings of Karl Marx, *La filosofia di Marx: Studi critici* (The Philosophy of Marx: Critical Studies), which took this project further. In this work he offered one of the earliest Hegelian readings of Marxism. Although he

maintained that Marx's materialism involved an unsuperseded dualism between mind and matter, he shared his belief in the unity of thought and practice. He translated Marx's *Theses on Feuerbach* into Italian for the first time, using them to assimilate the Marxian doctrine of praxis to Vico's notion that we can only know what we have made. His own doctrine largely grew out of a radicalization of this thesis: namely, that we make the world through thought.

Gentile's friendship with Croce began during this period (see CROCE, B. §§1, 4). Their collaboration on the latter's journal *La critica* was to have a profound impact on Italian cultural life. Together they attacked the dominant positivist tradition and worked for a revival of the idealist tradition of the Neapolitan Hegelians. In pursuance of this goal, Gentile contributed a series of detailed historical studies of Italian philosophy in the eighteenth and nineteenth centuries to *La critica*, and republished the works of Spaventa.

Gentile first developed his own theory through writings on the philosophy of education, beginning with his essay 'Il concetto scientifico della pedagogia' (The Scientific Concept of Education) (1901) and culminating in his two-volume *Sommario di pedagogia come scienza filosofica* (Summary of the Philosophy of Education) (1913–14). He became a *Privatdozent* at Naples in 1903, but only secured a permanent post in 1906, when he became professor of philosophy at the university of Palermo. He began to work out his theory in earnest, publishing an important article in 1912, 'L'atto di pensare come atto puro' (The Act of Thought as Pure Act), and a series of essays in 1913, *La riforma della dialettica hegeliana* (The Reform of the Hegelian Dialectic). Up until this time, his relationship with Croce had been one of friendly and creative disagreement. Indeed, he could claim to have had an important influence on Croce, moving him in a more markedly historicist direction. Croce, however, now accused him of advocating either emotivism or a mystical spiritualism, while Gentile countered that his friend remained at heart a naturalist. Their disagreements, hitherto confined to private correspondence, went public in 1913 in a famous debate in the journal *La voce*. It marked the first step to their eventual dramatic split.

In 1914, Gentile succeeded to Jaja's chair at Pisa, where he wrote his major work, the *Teoria generale della spirito come atto puro* (The Theory of Mind as Pure Act) (1916). In 1917 he moved to Rome, where he completed the systematic exposition of his thesis with his two-volume *Sistema di logica come teoria del conoscere* (System of Logic as Theory of Knowing) (1917, 1923). In 1920 he started up the *Giornale di filosofia italiana* (Journal of Italian Philosophy) as an organ for his students, although he continued to write for *La critica*.

In 1922 Gentile entered Mussolini's first cabinet as Minister of Education, instituting *La riforma Gentile*, a comprehensive overhaul of the secondary education system. In 1923 he joined the Fascist Party and thereafter became the self-styled philosopher of Fascism – a move that precipitated the final break with Croce, who remained a confirmed liberal. From 1924 he was director of the National Fascist Institute of Culture. He also acted as editorial director of the *Enciclopedia italiana* from its inception in 1925 to its completion in 1937. The only books of philosophical note from this period were his *Filosofia dell'arte* (The Philosophy of Art) (1931), which criticizes Croce's aesthetics, and *Genesi e struttura della società* (Genesis and Structure of Society) (1946), which offers the fullest account of his social and political philosophy. This last was written following the outbreak of civil war in Italy and was published posthumously. Gentile had joined the last ditchers in the German puppet Fascist Social Republic of Salò, and was assassinated by communist partisans in Florence on 15 April 1944.

2   Actualism

Gentile sought to elaborate a theory of knowledge that rejected all presuppositions of either a transcendent or an empirical reality lying outside human consciousness. Following Hegel, Gentile believed that by positing a fixed noumenal world as the transcendental ground of phenomenal experience Kant denied the truly creative faculty of the Understanding (see KANT, I. §5). Hegel's criticism did not go far enough for Gentile, however. Hegel did not wish to replace transcendental with subjectivist idealism. The contribution of the thinking subject was vital, but this did not mean that all knowledge was relative to the knower. Hegel's epistemology was underwritten by an ontological argument, which regarded being and consciousness as logically related as part of the development of a metaphysical entity – Spirit or Mind – immanent to them both (see HEGEL, G.W.F. §3). Gentile argued that this solution remained unsatisfactory because the Hegelian Spirit was as transcendent from the human viewpoint as the Kantian categories. He believed the Hegelian distinction between *Phenomenology*, or the development of individual consciousness, and *Logic*, which regarded reality as the product of Spirit, created an apparent dualism between Spirit as the essence of everything and human thought. Drawing on Spaventa, Gentile sought to overcome this alleged Hegelian dualism by identifying the individual mind of the *Phenomenology* with the Spirit of the *Logic*. Transcendence was finally overcome in a philosophy of absolute immanence, in which the activity of the thinking subject was the sole basis for human knowledge and hence of the objects that constituted human experience.

Gentile, via Hegel and Spaventa, concluded by transferring to thought *tout court* the faculties originally ascribed by Kant to the transcendental subject and by Hegel to Spirit. The method of immanence, he contended, rendered thought a 'pure act' that is presuppositionless, the absolute foundation of the human world of experience. Sensation, on this theory, is misconstrued as a response to an object external to the subject. Rather, it represents an act of self-awareness on the part of the thinking subject through which the external world is internally comprehended as part of a process of self-constitution (*autoctisi*).

There is a clear danger that Gentile's theory risks degenerating into solipsism. He attempted to avoid this pitfall through a theory of language that in a number of respects anticipates the arguments of Wittgenstein. Language, Gentile argued, is the embodiment of thought through which we organize experience. It is the form and not simply the vehicle of consciousness. However, there can be no purely personal or private language (see PRIVATE LANGUAGE ARGUMENT §§1–2; WITTGENSTEIN, L.J.J. §13). The very concept of language entails a spiritual universe comprised of a system of meanings that are essentially public and communicable. Consequently, all thought implied the existence of an 'other' with whom we entered into dialogue within our own consciousness. The search for self-knowledge, and in the process truth, involved the aspiration to membership of an ideal community speaking a shared universal language.

Gentile provided two proofs of his 'theory of spirit as pure act'. First, he claimed it was the logical outcome of the rationalist enterprise of modern philosophy since Descartes and, borrowing from Hegel, the essence of Christianity. He adopted Spaventa's theory of the 'circulation of European thought' to illustrate this thesis in order to show how the ideas of the German philosophers he admired were adopted, or independently conceived, by Italian thinkers as part of a single philosophical tradition. Second, he maintained that the theory reflected the phenomenological development of human consciousness within the individual. This argument provided the main theme of his writings on education and influenced his practical proposals for changes in the school curriculum, which gave pride of place to languages and philosophy and treated history and the natural sciences as preliminary stages of human understanding.

3 Social and political philosophy

Gentile's 'actual idealism' entailed the unity of theory and practice. Thinking and acting formed part of the same activity of self-constitution, whereby experience involved thought simultaneously comprehending and transforming the world. Drawing on Marx and Vico, Gentile elaborated an idealist theory of praxis whereby thought creates the world of fact through the transformation of nature – a process he termed the 'humanization of labour'. Actualism was the only philosophy compatible with human autonomy. It brought moral freedom back to earth from the noumenal world where Kant placed it, to become part of our everyday economic and political activity for which we were totally responsible. As he put it in a famous speech in support of the Fascist *squadristi*, it is impossible 'to distinguish moral force from material force .... Every force is a moral force, for it is always an expression of will, and whatever method of argument it uses – from sermon to cudgel – its efficacy cannot be other than that of entreating the inner man and persuading him to agree' (1925: 50–1).

Just as his subjectivist idealism risks solipsism at the level of theory, so it appears to endorse a Hobbes-like 'war of all against all', in which might is right, at the level of practice. Once again, Gentile's solution to this dilemma was to argue that action, like consciousness, presupposed interaction with a community of values. Drawing on both the Hegelian conception of the state as the rational expression of the ethical life of the nation and Giuseppe Mazzini's theory of nationalism as the spiritual expression of 'God and People', he argued that each individual came to appreciate how their self-realization was intimately bound up with those of their fellows through social institutions that embodied shared cultural traditions and were oriented towards the common good. His defence of Fascism was largely in these terms, although this involved a considerable blindness to the difference between official doctrine and the practical reality. He coined the term totalitarianism to signify his ideal of the ethical state as the unity of the whole nation's thought and action. However, the Fascist corporatist state he idealized as the mechanism for bringing this unification about never had more than a merely formal existence.

The central difficulty of Gentile's thought lies in his attempt to reconcile an extreme subjectivism with a universalist theory of meaning and a collectivist conception of the state. Arguably the clearest account of his position comes in Chapter 4 of the posthumously published *Genesis and Structure of Society* on 'Transcendental Society or Society *in interiore homine*'. Gentile insisted that our consciousness of society and the community of meaning comes not from our actual interaction with other people but is generated within ourselves and the reflection of individuals upon themselves. Society and even language originates from within the individual (*in interiore homine*), not between individuals (*inter homines*), a view Gentile condemned as atomistic. The temptation to slip from this position into the assumption of an undifferentiated identity among individuals is all too easy, however, as Gentile's connivance with a highly repressive and authoritarian regime amply testifies.

See also: ITALY, PHILOSOPHY IN §3

List of works

Gentile, G. (1950–) *Opere complete*, Florence: Sansoni, 55 vols. (The definitive edition of Gentile's works.)

—— (1991) *Opere filosofiche*, ed. E. Garin, Milan: Garzanti. (A collection of the principal philosophical works leading up to and including the *Teoria generale dello spirito come atto puro*, together with a useful editorial introduction.)

—— (1899) *La filosofia di Marx: Studi critici* (The Philosophy of Marx), Pisa: Spoerri. (This book contains Gentile's *abilitazione* thesis in the history of philosophy of 1897 on historical materialism and studies on the philosophy of praxis emerging out of his discussions with Sorel, Labriola and Croce, to whom it was dedicated.)

—— (1901) 'Il concetto scientifico della pedagogia' (The Scientific Concept of Education), *Rendiconti Accademia Lincei* 9; repr. *Scritti pedagogia I: Educazione e scuola laica*, 4th edn, Milan: Treves, 1932, 1–47. (Gentile's early work on the philosophy of education.)

—— (1912) 'L'atto di pensare come atto puro' (The Act of Thought as Pure Act), *Annuario della Biblioteca filosofica di Palermo* 1; repr. in Gentile 1991, vol. 27, 138–95. (The first statement of Gentile's 'actualism'.)

—— (1913) *La riforma della dialettica hegeliana* (The Reform of the Hegelian Dialectic), Messina: Principato. (Collects Gentile's early essays outlining his Spaventian reinterpretation of Hegel and the 'actualism' he derived from it.)

—— (1913–14) *Sommario di pedagogia come scienza filosofica* (Summary of the Philosophy of Education), Bari: Laterza, 2 vols. (Gentile's main treatise on the philosophy of education.)

—— (1916) *Teoria generale della spirito come atto puro*, Pisa: Mariotti; trans. H. Wildon Carr, *The Theory of Mind as Pure Act*, London: Macmillan,

1922. (Presents the first full account of Gentile's actualist doctrine.)

—— (1917, 1923) *Sistema di logica come teoria del conoscere* (System of Logic as Theory of Knowing), Pisa: Spoerri. (The final extended statement of Gentile's theory.)

—— (1920) *La riforma dell'educazione. Discorsi ai maestri di Triestre*, Bari: Laterza; trans. D. Bigongiari, *The Reform of Education*, New York: Harcourt Brace, 1922. (A collection of lectures delivered to Italian school teachers which offers the most accessible introduction to Gentile's ideas. It includes an interesting preface by Croce.)

—— (1925) *Che cosa è il fascismo? Discorsi e polemiche* (What is Fascism?), Florence: Vallecchi. (A collection of Gentile's early articles and speeches supporting fascism.)

—— (1931) *Filosofia dell'arte*, Milan: Treves; trans. G. Gullace, *The Philosophy of Art*, Ithaca, NY: Cornell University Press, 1972. (The fullest account of Gentile's aesthetic theory, which had a major influence on that of the British philosopher R.G. Collingwood.)

—— (1946) *Genesi e struttura della società*, Florence: Sansoni; trans. H.S. Harris, *Genesis and Structure of Society*, Urbana, IL: University of Illinois Press, 1960. (The fullest exposition of Gentile's social and political thought. The introduction to the translation traces the influence of Gentile outside Italy, particularly on Collingwood.)

References and further reading

Bellamy, R.P. (1987) *Modern Italian Social Theory: Ideology and Politics from Pareto to the Present*, Cambridge: Polity Press, ch. 6. (Locates Gentile's ideas within the context of the Italian idealist tradition and the political concerns of the times.)

Del Noce, A. (1990) *Giovanni Gentile. Per una interpretazione filosofica della storia contemporania*, Bologna: Il Mulino. (A sympathetic and at times contentious defence of Gentile's ideas.)

Harris, H.S. (1960) *The Social Philosophy of Giovanni Gentile*, Urbana, IL: University of Illinois Press. (The best account of Gentile's philosophy, with particular reference to his social and political thought.)

Holmes, R.W. (1937) *The Idealism of Giovanni Gentile*, New York: Macmillan. (A useful, if somewhat dated overview.)

Jacobelli, J. (1989) *Croce e Gentile: Da sodalizio al dramma*, Milan: Rizzoli. (An account of the intellectual relationship between Croce and Gentile.)

Turi, G. (1995) *Giovanni Gentile. Una biografia*, Florence: Giunti. (The most recent intellectual and political biography.)

RICHARD BELLAMY

GENTZEN, GERHARD KARL ERICH (1909–45)

The German mathematician and logician Gerhard Gentzen devoted his life to proving the consistency of arithmetic and analysis. His work should be seen as contributing to the post-Gödelian development of Hilbert's programme. In this connection he developed several logical calculi. The main device used in his proofs was a theorem in which he proved the eliminability of the inference known as 'cut' from a variety of different kinds of proofs. This 'cut-elimination theorem' yields the consistency of both classical and intuitionistic logic, and the consistency of arithmetic without complete induction. His later work was aimed at providing consistency proofs for less restricted systems of arithmetic and analysis.

Gerhard Gentzen studied mathematics at Greifswald, where he was born, Göttingen, Munich and Berlin. In 1933 he obtained his doctoral degree at Göttingen under the supervision of Hermann Weyl and then from 1935 to 1943 he carried out research as an assistant to David Hilbert. Gentzen was conscripted in 1939 and then released from military service in 1942 after having become seriously ill. On his release, he took up a post at the University of Göttingen, where he had completed his post-doctoral thesis in 1940, moving to the German university in Prague in 1943. Gentzen was imprisoned by the Czech authorities in May 1945 because of his membership of National Socialist organizations. Three months later he died of malnutrition.

Gentzen was one of the most important contributors to Hilbert's programme of founding classical mathematics via finitary consistency proofs (see HILBERT'S PROGRAMME AND FORMALISM). For this purpose he developed several logical calculi building on earlier work on logical deduction by the Göttingen physicist Paul Hertz (see Gentzen 1933). Gentzen's main idea, already present in his doctoral dissertation, 'Untersuchungen über das logische Schließen' (Investigations into Logical Deduction), was to replace Hilbert-style calculi, in which theorems are deduced from axioms, by 'calculi of natural deduction' which start not with axioms but with sets of formulas considered as assumptions (see NATURAL DEDUCTION, TABLEAU AND SEQUENT SYSTEMS). The general form of an inference figure in such calculi is

$$\frac{A_1 \dots A_v}{B} \quad (v \geqslant 1),$$

where $A_1, \dots, A_v, B$ are formulas, and where the 'lower formula' B is deduced from the 'upper formulas' $A_1, \dots, A_v$. Propositional connectives and quantifiers are defined by rules governing their introduction and elimination in proofs, and theorems are derived tree-style beginning with certain initial formulas treated as (possibly hypothetical) 'assumptions'. The idea was that such a procedure would be more like our 'natural' way of reasoning in mathematics than are the procedures of a Hilbert-style system. The resulting intuitionist calculus (NJ) can be extended into a complete classical calculus (NK) by simply admitting additional assumption formulas, for example, in the case of propositional logic, sentences of the form $A \vee \neg A$.

In order to avoid assumption formulas, Gentzen suggested intuitionist and classical 'sequent calculi' (LJ and LK, respectively). A metalogical sequent of the type $A_1, \dots, A_v \vdash B_1, \dots, B_\mu$ can be read as an abbreviation of the logical formula $A_1 \wedge \dots \wedge A_v \supset B_1 \vee \dots \vee B_\mu$. Sequents can be arranged in derivations with initial sequents of the unconditional form $D \vdash D$. Besides the operational rules for introduction and elimination of particular operators, Gentzen introduced structural rules (so-called 'inference figure schemes'). They include 'thinning', which allows the introduction of extra formulas in antecedents, 'contraction' of formulas stated more than once, 'interchange' of formulas in antecedents and consequents, and the important 'cut' rule

$$\frac{\Sigma \vdash A \quad \Sigma, A \vdash B}{\Sigma \vdash B},$$

with Σ an arbitrary set of formulas. Gentzen's cut-elimination theorem ('*Hauptsatz*') says that every derivation in LJ or LK can be transformed into a derivation with the same end sequent in which the cut rule is not used. The *Hauptsatz* can be used to prove the consistency of classical and intuitionist predicate logic. Gentzen also used it to solve the decision problem for intuitionistic propositional logic and to give a new proof that the law of excluded middle cannot be derived in formalized intuitionistic logic.

Using a sharpened form of the cut-elimination theorem (commonly referred to as the Gentzen–Herbrand theorem) and the subformula property (stating that all formulas occurring in the course of a derivation in the sequent calculus without cuts are subformulas of the formulas in the end sequent), Gentzen succeeded in proving the consistency of arithmetic without complete induction. However, he saw this as only a first step, since, as he noted, arithmetic without induction is of only little practical significance in number theory (1969: 115). In approaching the project of finding consistency proofs for less restricted systems of arithmetic and analysis Gentzen had to face Gödel's result that the consistency of a formalized theory embracing arithmetic cannot be proved using only means formalizable in this theory. For Gentzen, this did not yield the impossibility of consistency proofs for such theories. He admitted a 'restricted transfinite induction' up to Cantor's first epsilon number ε_0 (the limit of $\omega, \omega^\omega, \omega^{\omega^\omega}, \dots$), which cannot be formalized in classical arithmetic, which he nevertheless claimed could be interpreted constructively (1969: 231). Hence he regarded a consistency proof using ε_0-induction as a contribution to the realization of a liberalized Hilbert's programme although the form of induction used goes beyond the finitary methods of proof as described by Hilbert.

In 'Die Widerspruchsfreiheit der reinen Zahlentheorie' (1936a), Gentzen offered a first proof of the consistency of classical arithmetic by arranging the proofs of classical number theory into an ordering of type ε_0 such that the consistency of a given proof in the sequence follows from that of its predecessors. This done, an application of ε_0-induction secures the proof of the consistency of the full family of proofs of classical arithmetic.

Gentzen provided new insights into the interrelationship between the intuitionist and formalist approaches to the philosophy of mathematics. He aimed at reconciling both positions with the help of a consistency proof which saved all of classical analysis by constructive techniques. The techniques he developed are now standard in proof theory.

See also: GÖDEL'S THEOREMS; LOGICAL AND MATHEMATICAL TERMS, GLOSSARY OF; PROOF THEORY

List of works

Gentzen, G. (1969) *The Collected Papers of Gerhard Gentzen*, ed. M.E. Szabo, Amsterdam and London: North Holland. (English translations of most of Gentzen's papers, including the first publication of some. See also Szabo's 'Biographical Sketch' and 'Introduction'.)

—— (1933) 'Über die Existenz unabhängiger Axiomensysteme zu unendlichen Satzsystemen', *Mathematische Annalen* 107: 329–50; trans. 'On the Existence of Independent Axiom Systems for Infinite Sentence Systems', in *The Collected*

Papers, 1969, 29–52. (A discussion of Paul Hertz's theory of logical deduction.)

—— (1935) 'Untersuchungen über das logische Schließen', *Mathematische Zeitschrift* 39: 176–210, 405–565; repr. Darmstadt: Wissenschaftliche Buchgesellschaft, 1969; trans. 'Investigations into Logical Deduction', in *The Collected Papers*, 1969, 68–131. (Gentzen's doctoral dissertation, including the calculi of natural deduction and sequents, and the consistency proof for arithmetic without complete induction.)

—— (1936a) 'Die Widerspruchsfreiheit der reinen Zahlentheorie', *Mathematische Annalen* 112: 493–565; repr. Darmstadt: Wissenschaftliche Buchgesellschaft, 1967; trans. 'The Consistency of Elementary Number Theory', in *The Collected Papers*, 1969, 132–213. (Includes a discussion of finitism and the introduction of transfinite induction.)

—— (1936b) 'Die Widerspruchsfreiheit der Stufenlogik', *Mathematische Zeitschrift* 41 (3): 357–66; trans. 'The Consistency of the Simple Theory of Types', in *The Collected Papers*, 1969, 214–22. (Discusses the consistency of the simple theory of types.)

—— (1938) *Die gegenwärtige Lage in der mathematischen Grundlagenforschung: neue Fassung des Widerspruchsfreiheitsbeweises für die reine Zahlentheorie*, Leipzig: Hirzel; part 1 repr. in *Deutsche Mathematik* 3: 255–68, 1939; repr. Darmstadt: Wissenschaftliche Buchgesellschaft, 1969; trans. 'The Present State of Research into the Foundations of Mathematics', in *The Collected Papers*, 1969, 234–51. (The first part gives an excellent account of the state of proof theory in the 1930s.)

—— (1943) 'Beweisbarkeit und Unbeweisbarkeit von Anfangsfällen der transfiniten Induktion in der reinen Zahlentheorie', *Mathematische Annalen* 119 (1): 140–61; trans. 'Provability and Nonprovability of Restricted Transfinite Induction in Elementary Number Theory', in *The Collected Papers*, 1969, 287–308. (Gentzen's post-doctoral thesis.)

References and further reading

Prawitz, D. (1965) *Natural Deduction: A Proof-Theoretical Study*, Stockholm Studies in Philosophy 3, Stockholm, Göteborg and Uppsala: Almqvist & Wiksell. (A classic study of Gentzen's logic and its development up to 1965.)

Vihan, P. (1995) 'The Last Months of Gerhard Gentzen in Prague', *Collegium Logicum* 1: 1–7. (An account of Gentzen's imprisonment.)

VOLKER PECKHAUS

GEOLOGY, PHILOSOPHY OF

In the mid-1960s, geology underwent a conceptual revolution. Prior to that time, most geologists believed that the continents and oceans were fixed and permanent, the basic features of the earth's crust. Subsequently they came to agree that the earth was covered by rigid plates, thin in relation to the earth's diameter, in which the continents were embedded like logs in icebergs. It was the creation, movement and destruction of these plates that were responsible for the mid-ocean ridges, the areas of mountain building and earthquake activity, and the deep ocean trenches.

This conceptual revolution also marks a shift in the philosophy of geology. From the early nineteenth century, the chief philosophical question posed by geology was whether a historical science encountered special epistemic problems, a question that was usually answered by invoking the principle of uniformitarianism. In its strict form this stated that the only kind and intensities of causes that could be used to explain past geological phenomena were those that could be directly observed. Many sloppier formulations were invoked under the same name. Since the revolution, philosophers have turned to geology chiefly to use the revolution to exemplify or challenge one or another theory of scientific change.

1 Geology as a historical science: uniformitarianism
2 Scientific change and the plate tectonic revolution

1 Geology as a historical science: uniformitarianism

Early in the nineteenth century, geologists, who had previously concerned themselves primarily with the location and chemistry of economically valuable ores, began instead to concentrate on unravelling the earth's history. For the next century-and-a-half, the major issue in philosophy of geology was what it was to be a historical science. Most of the hard thinking about this was done by geologists, not philosophers.

Often cited in this regard is James Hutton, the late-eighteenth-century Scottish geologist and natural philosopher, who coined the phrase that the processes of geology showed 'no vestige of a beginning, no prospect of an end'. But in fact the major analysis of geology as a historical science was advanced by Charles Lyell, the British geologist, in his three-volume *Principles of Geology* (1830–3). Although Lyell himself did not call this analysis uniformitarianism, the Victorian philosopher-scientist William Whewell dubbed it so in the *Quarterly Review* in 1832. What Lyell had suggested was: one, that the laws of nature have not changed over time (law uniformitarianism); two, that the kinds of cause operating have not changed over time (kind uniformitarianism); and three, that the intensity of those causes has not changed over time either (degree uniformitarianism).

Law uniformitarianism was an uncontroversial position in the early nineteenth century. Geologists agreed that the laws of nature had neither changed nor been suspended. With the possible exception of the introduction of new animal and plant species, miracles were no longer part of the geological repertoire. Even in the case of new species, their possibly miraculous creation did not signify a change of natural law but an exception to it. Lyell himself dealt with this by having new species created in a law-like manner.

Kind and degree uniformitarianism, by contrast, were controversial. It seems plausible to believe that Lyell had taken these positions as a result of adapting a well-known methodological principle to geology, the principle of true causes (or vera causa principle) laid down by Newton in the Rules of Reasoning in the *Principia mathematica* (1687). This stated that the scientist should 'admit no more causes of natural things than such as are both true and sufficient to explain their appearances'. Newton's prestige was such that, during the eighteenth century, many different glosses were placed on the method of true causes (see SCIENTIFIC METHOD §2). It seems likely that Lyell took his particular interpretation from the Scottish philosopher Thomas REID (1710–96), who argued in his *Essays on the Intellectual Powers of Man* (1785) that the vera causa principle meant that: one, there must be direct observational evidence that causes of the kind assumed do exist, and two, there must be evidence that the causes were sufficient to produce the purported effects.

As Lyell saw it, the problem for the geologist who attempted to interpret the past was the lack of direct observational access to past causes. The only causes that could be readily observed were those acting at present. Therefore the geologist who attempted to follow the method of true causes was in general limited to causes of a kind that operate at present. Equally, in conjecturing about the unknown effects of some observed cause, geologists must confine themselves in a similar way. In short, kind and degree uniformitarianism can be seen as a straightforward extension of the principle of true causes to situations in which cause and effect are widely separated in time.

Geologists' attempts to reconstruct the past, therefore, posed a special case of an epistemic problem central to the other sciences: how to go from the known to the unknown, from the observable to the unobservable. But whereas for physicists this jump was generally from the macro-world to the micro, for geologists it was from the present to the past. Even if geology were an historical science, its epistemic problems could be tackled by a suitable modification of methodological principles already established in the other sciences.

Lyell put his principle of uniformitarianism to good effect in constructing his system of geology. He was unhappy with the common belief that the earth had once been molten and that its temperature was declining. Such a theory did not meet his vera causa criterion for there was no direct observational access to the original state of the globe. There was, however, evidence (fossilized tropical plants, for example) that the temperature of the northern hemisphere had been lower in the past. To explain this, Lyell proposed an alternative. At present, the earth's temperature at a given spot depends not solely on latitude but also on the distribution of land and sea, continental climates being very different from oceanic ones. Distribution of land and sea is thus a vera causa of climate. If the distribution of continents and islands had been different in the past, then the temperature in the northern hemisphere could have been warmer even though the average temperature of the globe remained the same.

Lyellian uniformitarianism won certain influential adherents in the nineteenth century, among them the astronomer and philosopher of science John Herschel, the mathematician Charles Babbage, and the natural historian Charles DARWIN. Indeed, all three, realizing that the success of Lyell's vera causa theory of climate depended on a prior vera causa theory of the elevation and depression of land masses, attempted to identify a 'true cause' for land elevation, something that Lyell had not succeeded in doing in the *Principles*.

Most geologists, though, were sceptical. To them, it appeared quite possible that certain causes now in operation (ice, for example) might not have existed in the past (if the globe had been warmer, for example). To almost all geologists, the suggestion that causes had never varied in intensity was little short of perverse. Consequently most subscribed to the rival position, termed catastrophism by Whewell, which admitted the possibility of past causes different in kind and in intensity from those currently operating. Catastrophism in this strict sense was not tantamount to asserting that all geological effects were to be explained by sudden and dramatic changes and certainly not to the assertion that the laws of nature had changed over time.

In the twentieth century, for reasons that are not entirely clear, it became geological orthodoxy to invoke uniformitarianism, though by now much of the force of Lyell's original thesis had been lost. The term was frequently used to mean 'actualism' – that the past should be interpreted in terms of present causes. Lyell himself had never simplistically equated the 'present' and the 'known'. For him, the core dichotomy was between the observable and the unobservable, not between the present and the past. While most observable causes were present causes, sometimes we had access to past causes from the written records of antiquity. For example, on the basis of historical records of volcanic activity, Lyell was quite prepared to argue that the places where volcanoes would erupt in the future would vary just as they had varied in the past.

Uniformitarianism was also confused with 'gradualism', the belief that all geological processes had acted slowly and gradually, again something that Lyell never claimed. For him, the question of the pace of geological processes was simply a matter of what was observed. If there was observational evidence of meteor impact or of large-scale floods, then such agencies could be invoked in the past.

In the 1980s and 1990s, catastrophism (understood as anti-gradualism) became newly fashionable as geologists came to understand the effect of sudden and dramatic changes on the earth's surface. The detailed investigation of mass extinctions and the debate about whether these could be explained by meteor impact contributed to this (see EVOLUTION, THEORY OF §3). (Lyell would have been quite happy to accept our current evidence of meteor impact as adequate to establish meteors as a vera causa of geological change.)

Meanwhile, throughout the first half of the twentieth century, professional philosophers remained silent about the problems of geology. When they did speak, it was to say that, since geology dealt with the past, its laws must perforce be supplied by physics and chemistry. Hence, once the philosophical problems of physics and chemistry had been solved, solutions to the problems of geology would follow without further ado.

2 Scientific change and the plate tectonic revolution

During the 1960s, geology underwent a sudden and dramatic theoretical revolution. According to the new plate tectonic theory, the earth is covered by a limited number of rigid plates, thin in relation to the diameter of the earth, created at mid-ocean ridges (actually large mountain chains), spreading out from those ridges to be consumed again in subduction zones. Other phenomena – mountain building, earthquake activity, gravity anomalies, and so on – are explained in relation to the movement and intersection of these plates.

The revolution changed the emphasis of geology once more; reconstructing the earth's past declined in importance and understanding the causal processes going on at present became the major focus of attention. These causes, while in principle compatible with those invoked by physicists and chemists, were in practice of a different order, including creation of new land at mid-ocean ridges, mountain building where one plate overrode another, destruction of land in subduction zones, and possible convection currents in the earth's interior. Nonetheless, neither geologists nor philosophers have worried overtly about the philosophical foundations of the entities and processes asserted in plate tectonic theory. Instead the attention has gone to the plate tectonic revolution as a case of scientific change.

The plate tectonic revolution disturbed geologists deeply: within a matter of a few years, their most basic ideas about the structure of the earth were overturned. Equally important, their implicit philosophy of science simply gave no warrant for such a change. Ultimately derived from positivism, geologists' image of science suggested that it progressed by a simple confrontation of hypothesis and evidence so that gradually and cumulatively a body of well-founded conclusions was established (see LOGICAL POSITIVISM §4).

Casting around for some interpretation of science that would make sense of this event, geologists involved in the revolution quickly lit upon Thomas Kuhn's *Structure of Scientific Revolutions*, serendipitously published just a few years previously in 1962. This gave licence for the possibility of revolutionary change in the most basic postulates of a science (see KUHN, T.S.).

Philosophers of science, while agreeing that the changes were indeed dramatic, have been less inclined to treat the revolution as specifically Kuhnian. They have denied both that pre-plate tectonic geology was immature and that it fitted Kuhn's description of normal science. They have questioned whether geological methods and aims changed concurrently with theory. They have dismissed the idea that pre-plate tectonic geology and plate tectonics were incommensurable (see INCOMMENSURABILITY).

But while being unconvinced that the geological revolution could be characterized as Kuhnian, they have agreed with geologists that this dramatic theoretical change does pose a challenge to the methodologies of science proposed by positivists. There is now a substantial and growing literature that seeks to interpret these changes in light of different methodologies.

See also: CAUSATION; LAWS, NATURAL; OBSERVATION; SCIENCE, 19TH CENTURY

PHILOSOPHY OF; SCIENTIFIC REALISM AND
ANTIREALISM

References and further reading

Frankel, H. (1987) 'The Continental Drift Debate', in H. Tristram Engelhardt Jr. and A.L. Caplan (eds) *Scientific Controversies: Case Studies in the Resolution and Closure of Disputes in Science and Technology*, Cambridge: Cambridge University Press. (A good short account of the history of plate tectonics, both historically and philosophically sophisticated.)

Kitts, D. (1977) *The Structure of Geology*, Dallas, TX: Southern Methodist University Press. (The sole significant attempt to apply positivist philosophy of science to geology.)

Laudan, R. (1987) *From Mineralogy to Geology: The Foundations of a Science, 1650–1830*, Chicago, IL: University of Chicago Press. (Uses history to explore the conceptual foundations of geology.)

LeGrand, H. (1988) *Drifting Continents and Shifting Theories*, Cambridge: Cambridge University Press. (Contrasts philosophical and sociological accounts of scientific change.)

* Lyell, C. (1830–3) *Principles of Geology*, London: John Murray, 3 vols; repr. Chicago, IL: Chicago University Press, 1989. (The classic formulation of uniformitarianism aptly introduced by Martin Rudwick, a leading historian of geology.)

RACHEL LAUDAN

GEOMETRY, PHILOSOPHICAL ISSUES IN

The least abstract form of mathematics, geometry has, from the earliest Hellenic times, been accorded a curious position straddling empirical and exact science. Its standing as an empirical and approximate science stems from the practical pursuits of land surveying and measuring, from the prominence of visual aids (figures and constructions) in geometric proofs and, in the twentieth century, from Einstein's General Theory of Relativity, which holds that the geometry of spacetime is dependent upon physical quantities. On the other hand, very early on, the symmetry and perfect regularity of certain geometric figures were taken as representative of a higher knowledge than that afforded by sense experience. And its concern with figures and constructions, rather than with number and calculation, rendered geometry amenable to axiomatic formulation and syllogistic deduction, establishing a paradigm of

demonstrative knowledge which endured for two millennia. While the progress of mathematics has surmounted traditional distinctions between geometry and the mathematics of number, leaving only a heuristic role for geometric intuition, geometric thinking remains a vital component of mathematical cognition.

1 **The idea of a demonstrative science**
2 **Towards formal rigour**
3 **The nature of geometry**
4 **Geometry of physical space**
5 **But what is geometry?**

1 The idea of a demonstrative science

The earliest records of activity in geometry come from Babylon. What we know as Pythagoras' theorem appears in cuneiform texts of around 2600 BC, where it is given an empirical and approximate verification. As the name indicates, the subject of geometry originated in the practical pursuits of land measurement and surveying (though probably not first among the Egyptians, as Herodotus famously reports). Although the Greeks did not originate geometry, it is to them that we owe the conception of geometry as an exact demonstrative science as against an empirical and practical discipline. While anecdotal evidence identifies Thales of Miletus as the originator of the idea that geometric statements are to be proved, it is generally accepted that the Pythagoreans had transformed mathematics into a deductive science by around 500 BC. Pythagoras himself is said to have conferred upon geometry the standing of *theōria*, the manner of contemplative knowledge alone worthy of a free and not a slave people; and to have propounded the belief that its true subject matter pertained to intelligible objects rather than to sense experience. Later, in Plato, geometric figures – circles, triangles, the regular solids – became archetypal ideal forms: perfect, universal, absolute, eternal and harmonious; whereas their sensible instantiations in matter were seen as inexact, particular, relative, temporal and discordant (see PYTHAGOREANISM §2).

Early Pythagorean methods of proof had probably not advanced much beyond primitive diagrammatic methods. By arranging pebbles in simple geometric arrays, a number of elementary theorems had been discovered by direct observation. Other visual methods included superposition, whereby the identity or congruence of two geometric figures was established by moving one figure into point-for-point coincidence with another. Some have conjectured that the first Greek proofs of the Pythagorean theorem were discovered in this manner. While such methods were suitable to the discovery of simple arithmetic and geometric facts, they were not as conclusive as the deductive methods canonically compiled in Euclid's *Elements of Geometry* (*c.*300 BC). Through its influence, the idea of a demonstrative science was established and geometry became the paradigm of systematic presentation of a body of knowledge in terms of logical deductions from axioms, whose truth was antecedently recognized.

At the basis of geometry, Euclid distinguished axioms, postulates and definitions. Euclid calls axioms 'common notions' which, as the starting points of demonstration, are held to be immediately evident, non-demonstrable truths or 'intelligible principles' deniable only on pain of absurdity. In this, he followed Aristotle rather than Plato, for whom a dialectical demonstration of the starting point of any particular systematic inquiry into the nature of things was required (*Republic* VII.533c). The five axioms all concern the concept of equality and might be considered as stipulating properties of identity applicable to magnitudes generally, for example, the third: 'Two things equal to a third thing are equal to each other.'

In addition to his axioms or 'common notions', Euclid also stated five postulates which are not asserted as true but rather as hypotheses to be tested through the conformity with experience of results deduced from them. The first three outline the permissible means by which geometric figures may be constructed: (1) by drawing a straight line from any point to any other point; (2) by producing a finite straight line continuously in a straight line; (3) by describing a circle with any given point as centre and any given distance as radius. These postulates essentially delimit geometric construction as a procedure involving only straight edge and compass. This bounds what has been traditionally termed 'elementary geometry' and one may ask why such constructions were singled out, for at an early date Greek geometers had already recognized that there were many interesting problems in construction which did not appear to be solvable by these means alone. Three famous examples known in ancient times are: to construct a square having the area of a given circle ('squaring the circle'); to trisect a given angle; and to construct a cube having double the volume of a given cube. Plutarch (*c.*46–120) reports that Plato was incensed by the attempts by Eudoxus and Archytas to solve the problem of doubling the cube by employing mechanical instruments in trial and error fashion; for Plato, such methods accorded sense experience an unwarranted legitimacy and hence were a corruption of the 'pure excellence of geometry'. In fact, not until the nineteenth century were rigorous proofs given that these are impossible ruler and

compass constructions, each additionally requiring some version of a principle of continuity.

Of the remaining two postulates, (4) All right angles are equal to each other, and (5) Given a line *l* and a point P not on it, there is a unique line parallel to *l* through P, (5) was often singled out as lacking the evidential force of the others. As a result, from Euclid's time up to the early part of the nineteenth century, many attempts were made in vain to derive it from Euclid's other assumptions. (Mathematical practice over the centuries had largely submerged Euclid's evidential distinction between axioms and postulates.) Reflecting on this dismal record in 1819, C.F. Gauss had to admit that 'In the theory of parallels, we are still no further than Euclid', a situation he called 'the shame of mathematics'. Resolution took quite an unexpected form. After unsuccessfully attempting to demonstrate the postulate, both J. Bolyai (in 1823) and N. Lobachevskii (in 1826) independently formulated a consistent non-Euclidean (hyperbolic) geometry in which the fifth postulate did not hold, the other Euclidean axioms and postulates remaining intact. Gauss himself had privately entertained such thoughts as early as 1799. Significantly, Gauss and Lobachevskii (but not Bolyai, who conceived of geometry as a purely logical system based upon axioms) seem to have thought that the truth as to the Euclidean or non-Euclidean character of geometry was an empirical matter to be resolved by certain observations in geodesy or astronomy (for example, stellar parallax). The mathematical and philosophical ramifications of these discoveries were slow to emerge; Bolyai and Lobachevskii had published obscurely and Gauss not at all. But by mid-century, a transformation was underway in the Euclidean conception of geometric knowledge as a unique body of truths concerning space whose certainty was secured by intuition.

2 Towards formal rigour

For nearly two millennia, Euclid's *Elements* was the exemplar of exact reasoning. It is instructive to consider the developments which resulted in overturning this perspective. The first took place between the end of the seventeenth and the end of the eighteenth centuries. For Hobbes, Spinoza and Descartes, reasoning *more geometrico* ('in the geometric manner') attained the deductive ideal, whereby the truth of single propositions inexorably followed from propositions either antecedently established or accepted as fundamental truths. According to Pascal (*c.*1657), the 'art of persuasion' is identified with the method whereby evident axioms are laid down, clear definitions of non-primitive terms are given, and demonstration proceeds in step-by-step fashion. Even Newton, the co-discoverer of the differential and integral calculus, wrote his *Mathematical Principles of Natural Philosophy* (1687) in the axiomatic style of a classical geometric treatise, employing geometric methods of proof where the new methods of the calculus would have been more appropriate.

However, the enormous progress of mathematics in the eighteenth century was almost entirely due to developments in algebra and the new science of analysis, the study of functions and variables pioneered, above all, by Euler. Correspondingly, the guiding ideal of rigour in mathematical proof shifted from the figures and constructions of geometry to the permitted manipulations and transpositions of symbols characteristic of algebra and analysis. Thus Lagrange would famously boast in the beginning of his *Mécanique analytique* (1788) that 'One will not find any figures in this work. The methods that I present require neither constructions, nor geometrical or mechanical reasoning, but only algebraic operations subjected to a regular and uniform development'. Another shift took place at the end of the nineteenth century in tandem with the programme of seeking greater rigour in the calculus, the so-called 'arithmetization' of analysis. Here, the analytic idea of rigour was carried into geometry itself in the demand that deduction not only be independent of diagrams and figures but also of the meaning of geometric concepts. In 1882, Pasch provided an initial account of Euclidean geometry as a hypothetico-deductive system in which the Euclidean definitions of 'point', 'line' and 'plane' were replaced by stipulated unanalysed relations between these concepts. However, the classic exposition of this point of view is Hilbert's *Grundlagen der Geometrie* (1899) which famously posits 'three different systems of things:... points... straight lines... and planes', entities defined only implicitly through relations designated by terms such as 'lie upon', 'between', 'parallel', 'congruent' and 'continuous' whose complete characterization, in turn, lies in those propositions derivable from the chosen axioms. In this abstract conception, there is no longer any trace of the traditional conception of geometry as a theory of *actual* space and its properties. By the early twentieth century, this trend towards axiomatic formalism had completely supplanted the Euclidean paradigm of an exact science.

3 The nature of geometry

According to a once-customary view of mathematics, the two primordial mathematical conceptions are the notions of whole number (as exhibited in counting or ordering) and continuous magnitude or mere extension (as determined in measurement); hence mathematics is ultimately rooted in the sciences of number (arithmetic, algebra, analysis) and the science of space (geometry). However, the conception of geometry as the science of space seems only to have emerged in the late Renaissance, as the modern notion of 'space' arose around 1600 AD (see SPACE), whereas the science of number has a pedigree reaching back to the speculations of the Pythagoreans. Indeed, the Pythagoreans initially did not clearly distinguish geometry from number. Number was the essential reality, though numbers appear to have been conceived as dots in particular geometric arrangements (thus, for example, the terms 'square number' and 'triangular number', which still survive). The Pythagorean discovery of incommensurable lines (for example, $\sqrt{2}$ which is the diagonal of a unit square) perhaps first effected a separation, for a 'horror of the irrational' prevented a generalization of the concept of number suitable for measurement as well as counting. Hence, irrational magnitudes could only be represented geometrically. As a result, the science of number remained paramount and, in the *Republic*, Plato places the study of geometry after the study of number on the grounds that, unlike the figures of geometry, numbers have no sensible and tangible bodies but are purely objects of thought accessible only to the soul (VII.526). A more compelling reason for the subordination is simply that geometry, in speaking of triangles, quadrilaterals and so on, presupposes number.

The ancient distinction of geometry and the science of number was blurred by the invention of analytic geometry by Fermat (1629) and Descartes (1637). The essential idea here – the introduction of numerical coordinates into the plane – establishes a one-to-one correspondence between plane curves and equations in two variables: to each distinct curve corresponds a definite equation $f(x, y) = 0$. This permits the study of the geometric properties of curves through algebraic or analytic relations connecting their equations, an innovation greatly expanding the variety of curves and figures which can be submitted to precise mathematical treatment. Moreover, coordinates provide a ready means of generalizing from two to three dimensions, and then, as Grassmann (1844) showed, to *n*-dimensional spaces. Thus it is only with the introduction of coordinates that geometry acquires the requisite generality of a 'science of space' (and indeed, more than the requisite generality); ironically, geometry obtains the status of 'science of space' through methods which enable a reduction of geometry to number.

However, the triumph of analytic methods in

geometry was carefully circumscribed. Newton, for example, held that equations as 'Expressions of Arithmetical Computation . . . properly have no place in Geometry', and he celebrated 'the Ancients' over 'the Moderns', in that the former 'never introduced Arithmetical Terms into Geometry' whereas the latter 'by confounding both, have lost the simplicity in which all the Elegancy of Geometry consists' ([1707] 1728: 228; 1967: 120). Newton's intent, it seems, was to insulate only elementary geometry from algebraic methods but not higher geometry, where coordinate methods were actively employed and extended. Other dissenters from the 'triumph of analysis' soon emerged. Most influential were the early nineteenth century French school of projective geometers (L. Carnot, Chasles, Poncelet, among others). Expressing empiricist disdain for the use in calculus and algebra of such 'metaphysical' entities as infinitesimals and negative numbers, they championed instead coordinate-free 'synthetic' methods of proof whereby mathematical certainty was safeguarded by exclusive focus upon a constructed figure (see Poncelet 1822).

At issue here is the status of the diagrams employed in geometric proofs. Were constructed figures merely superfluous, *in concreto* visual aids to clarify bits of abstract reasoning in the text? Or were geometric truths somehow necessarily connected with the quasi-visual evidence provided by representation in 'the mind's eye' of intuition? For Kant, it was clearly the latter. Euclidean geometry characterizes that 'pure form of our sensible intuition' which is space, a condition imposed by the mind upon the experience of the outer sensible world and thus a condition of the possibility of experience of this world. Furthermore, the ruler and compass constructions of Euclidean geometry are examples *par excellence* of how, for Kant, mathematical knowledge is attained solely through construction of concepts, that is, exhibition a priori of an intuition (for example, a figure such as a triangle) corresponding to its concept which, though particular, is none the less representative of all the universality contained in the concept. A geometric proof is thus 'a chain of inference guided throughout by intuition' (1781/1787: a717; b745).

Mathematical developments in the nineteenth century undermined Kant's conception. First, as noted above, the discovery of consistent (that is, relative to Euclidean geometry) non-Euclidean geometries undercut the prevalent belief in the necessary truth of Euclidean geometry as a characterization of space. Second, the development of projective geometry led to a vastly generalized conception of a geometry as the study of properties of figures invariant under a given group of transformations. Thus, there are as many geometries as there are

groups of transformations acting on a space. Third, under the influence of Riemann (see below), physical space came to be seen as a special three-dimensional case of a more general geometric structure. From each of these developments, it followed that the structure of physical space was no longer geometry's sole subject matter. Thus different 'mathematical spaces' came to be distinguished from physical space, and both from a quasi-perceptual and psychological 'space of intuition'. Finally, the trend towards greater rigour in mathematical proof in the latter part of the century denied intuition any intrinsic evidential standing. This in turn promoted axiomatic formalism in geometry, where an explicit recognition that geometric primitives have no pre-axiomatic meaning replaced the traditional view of its primitive terms as indefinable but intuitively secure concepts.

4 Geometry of physical space

Once the conceptual possibility opened that the geometry of physical space is not necessarily Euclidean, the question concerning the structure of this space appeared to be empirically resolvable through measurement. Poincaré (1902) argued, however, that any empirical determination of the geometry of physical space must rest on certain prior conventions concerning metric concepts, such as whether the path of a light ray is considered 'straight'. Others saw a still more fundamental problem concerning what is presupposed by measurement at all. To this, Riemann (1854) and Helmholtz (1868) provided superficially similar but in fact quite different solutions. For both, measurement rests upon the possibility of free mobility of the standard of measurement. However, Riemann interpreted this to mean that magnitudes are independent of their position in what he termed an n-fold extended quantity, of which physical space is merely a particular three-dimensional instance (see SPACE §4). Riemann postulated an analytical expression, a generalization of the Pythagorean theorem to n dimensions, which is an invariant measure of the infinitesimal lengths between neighbouring points in such a structure, roughly the modern idea of a real n-dimensional differentiable manifold. Given this measure, one can define the arc length of a curve, the angle between intersecting curves, the volume of a region and other geometric concepts. This geometry is locally Euclidean in that it gives a Euclidean metric structure to the tangent space at each point P, hence the measure applies generally to flat and to curved manifolds and also to manifolds with variable (non-constant) curvature. However, in this latter type of manifold, Riemann went on to observe, the magnitude of a solid body is not independent of the position of the body.

Helmholtz, on the other hand, saw the postulate of free mobility as resting upon presumed facts about the behaviour of such bodies *in physical space*, in particular, that there are rigid motions. While acknowledging that the notion of a perfectly rigid body is an idealization to which nothing in the physical world corresponds, Helmholtz none the less saw this concept as a presupposition of measurement in general and hence of the geometry of physical space. As subsequently refined by Reichenbach (1928), who emphasized the impossibility of actually ascertaining whether a physical measuring rod undergoes alterations of length in transport, this view introduces an arbitrary element into measurement in that it makes determinations of the geometry of physical space rest on the adoption of conventions regarding the behaviour of rigid bodies. However, in the generic case of variably curved space-times permitted by Einstein's Theory of General Relativity (1915), the notion of a rigid body is suspect for just the reason suggested 61 years earlier by Riemann: there are no congruences corresponding to the supposed invariant length of a rigid body. In this situation the most consistent procedure, as Weyl pointed out, is to renounce the concept of a transportable standard length. Weyl then showed (1921) how metric properties of the space-time manifold could be mathematically derived from weaker conformal and affine properties having, as their respective empirical correlates, two metric-independent physical processes, the paths of light rays (so-called null geodesics) and the inertial trajectories of point masses (particles 'too small' to be affected by forces of surrounding physical fields). The essentials of this procedure remain a matter of live interest among general relativists (see Ehlers 1988).

5 But what is geometry?

With the triumph of formal axiomatics, geometry had lost its two most distinctive characteristics: its standing as the theory of physical space and the intuitional trappings attending its traditional reliance on figures and constructions. What then distinguishes geometry from any other formally axiomatized mathematical theory? Surveying the subject in 1932, two eminent geometers wrote:

The question then arises why the name geometry is given to some mathematical sciences and not to others. It is likely that there is no definite answer to this question, but that a branch of mathematics is called a geometry because the name seems good,

on emotional and traditional grounds, to a sufficient number of competent people.

(Veblen and Whitehead 1932: 17)

Yet, as Cartan (1936) quickly pointed out, even in mathematics such a consensus may be difficult to achieve. This is not to say that boundaries are not still drawn. A leading contemporary geometer recently suggested that 'a property is geometrical, if it does not deal directly with numbers or if it happens on a manifold, where the coordinates themselves have no meaning' (Chern 1990: 685). In any case, it must be admitted that geometry has not been completely assimilated into the rest of mathematics, in part, perhaps, because the physical world continues to suggest geometric analogies. Moreover, mathematicians continue to speak of 'geometric intuition' as a fertile source of mathematical invention, even while recognizing that distinctions between geometry and other areas of mathematics remain a matter of taste. And although some mathematicians doubt that 'the psychological aspects of true geometric intuition' will ever be 'cleared up' (Weil 1978), others speculate that the visual-intuitive mode of cognition so characteristic of geometry stems from a lateral specialization of the brain localized in the right hemisphere of the cerebral cortex (Yaglom 1988: 26).

See also: CONVENTIONALISM; EINSTEIN, A.; HELMHOLTZ, H. VON; HILBERT'S PROGRAMME AND FORMALISM; KANT, I.; LOGICAL AND MATHEMATICAL TERMS, GLOSSARY OF; MATHEMATICS, FOUNDATIONS OF; POINCARÉ, J.H.; RELATIVITY THEORY, PHILOSOPHICAL SIGNIFICANCE OF; SPACETIME; WEYL, H.

References and further reading

Atiyah, M. (1982) 'What is Geometry?', *The Mathematical Gazette* 66: 179–84. (The suggestion, by an eminent geometer, that geometry is that part of mathematics where visual thought is dominant.)

Boyer, C. (1956) *History of Analytic Geometry*, New York: Scripta mathematica. (A comprehensive account of the innovations of Fermat and Descartes.)

* Cartan, E. (1936) 'Le rôle de la théorie des groupes de lie dans l'évolution de la géométrie moderne', *Comptes rendus du congrès international des mathématiciens* 1: 92–103. (The case for continuous groups as the unifying concept in geometry.)

* Chern, S.-S. (1990) 'What is Geometry?', *American Mathematical Monthly* 97: 679–86. (A survey from Euclid to fibre bundles.)

Coolidge, J. (1940) *A History of Geometrical Methods*,

Oxford: Clarendon Press. (Compendium covering Babylonia to Weyl's generalization of Riemannian geometry.)

Daston, L.J. (1986) 'The Physicalist Tradition in Early Nineteenth Century French Geometry', *Studies in the History and Philosophy of Science* 17: 269–95. (An informative essay on the geometric empiricism of an influential school of projective geometers.)

* Descartes, R. (1637) *La Géométrie*, Leiden: Maire; trans. D.E. Smith and M.L. Latham, *The Geometry of René Descartes*, with a facsimile of the 1st edn, New York: Dover, 1954. (The first published account of analytic geometry.)

* Ehlers, J. (1988) 'Einführung der Raum-Zeit-Struktur mittels Lichtstrahlen und Teilchen' (The Introduction of Space-Time Structure through Light Rays and Particles), in J. Audretsch and K. Mainzer (eds) *Philosophie und Physik der Raum-Zeit*, Mannheim: Wissenschaftsverlag, 145–62. (A discussion of the problem of measurement in General Relativity.)

* Euclid (c.300 BC) *The Thirteen Books of Euclid's Elements*, trans. T. Heath, Cambridge: Cambridge University Press, 2nd edn, 1956, 3 vols. (First articulated conception of geometry as a deductive science, based upon axioms, postulates and definitions.)

* Fermat, P. de (1629) 'Ad Locos Planos et Solidos Isagoge', in *Oeuvres*, ed. P. Tannery and C. Henry, Paris: Gauthiers-Villars, 1891–1922, vol. 1, 91–110 (Latin); vol. 3, 85–101 (French); partial English translation in D.E. Smith (ed.) *A Source Book in Mathematics*, New York: Dover, 1984, vol. 2, 389–96. (Fermat's discovery of analytic geometry, published posthumously.)

* Grassmann, H. (1844) *Die lineale Ausdehnungslehre, ein neuer Zweig der Mathematik*, Leipzig: Otto Wigand, 2nd edn, 1862; trans. L.C. Kannenberg, 'The Linear Theory of Extension: A New Branch of Mathematics', in *A New Branch of Mathematics: The 'Ausdehnungslehre' of 1844, and Other Works*, La Salle, IL: Open Court, 1995. (Incipient general formulation of vector analysis in *n*-dimensional space.)

* Helmholtz, H. von (1868) 'Über die Tatsachen, die der Geometrie zugrunde liegen', *Nachrichten der Königlichen Gesellschaft der Wissenschaften zu Göttingen* 9: 193–221; trans. M. Lowe, 'On the Facts Underlying Geometry', in *Epistemological Writings*, ed. P. Hertz and M. Schlick, Dordrecht: Reidel, 1977, 39–71. (The view that measurement presupposes the notion of a rigid body.)

* Hilbert, D. (1899) *Grundlagen der Geometrie*, Leipzig: Teubner, 7th edn, 1930; 2nd edn trans. L. Unger and P. Bernays, *Foundations of Geometry*, La Salle,

IL: Open Court, 1971. (Influential abstract axiomatization of Euclidean geometry.)

* Kant, I. (1781/1787) *Critique of Pure Reason*, trans. N. Kemp Smith, London: Macmillan, 1929. (The 'Transcendental Aesthetic' and 'Transcendental Doctrine of Method' sections give Kant's views on geometry.)

Klein, F. (1895) *Vorträge über ausgewahlte Fragen der Elementargeometrie*, Leipzig: Barth; trans. *Famous Problems of Elementary Geometry*, New York: Dover, 1956. (Classic examination of ruler and compass constructions involving no higher mathematics.)

Müller, I. (1981) *Philosophy of Mathematics and Deductive Structure in Euclid's Elements*, Cambridge, MA: MIT Press. (A modern perspective on axiomatic method in Euclid.)

Nagel, E. (1939) 'The Formation of Modern Conceptions of Formal Logic in the Development of Geometry', *Osiris* 7: 142–224; repr. in *Teleology Revisited and Other Essays in the Philosophy and History of Science*, New York: Columbia University Press, 1982, 195–259. (Classic study of the rise of the 'formalistic' conception of geometry.)

* Newton, I. (1687) *The Mathematical Principles of Natural Philosophy*, trans. A. Motte (1729) and ed. F. Cajori, Berkeley, CA: University of California Press, 1962, 2 vols. (Its propositions are demonstrated synthetically, 'that the system of the heavens might be founded on good geometry'.)

* —— (1707) *Arithmetica Universalis*, Cambridge: Whiston; trans. Ralphson and Cunn (1722), *Universal Arithmetik: Or, A Treatise of Arithmetical Composition and Resolution*, London: Sener, 2nd and very much revised edn, 1728; repr. in *The Mathematical Works of Isaac Newton*, ed. D.T. Whiteside, London and New York: Johnson Reprint, 1967, vol. 2, 1–257. (Criticism of the Cartesian association of algebra and geometry.)

* Pascal, B. (c.1657) *De l'esprit géométrique*, fragments published posthumously in *Oeuvres complètes*, Paris: Desclée de Brouwer, 1991, vol. 3, 390–428; trans. R. Schofield in *Scientific Treatises*, Chicago, IL, and London: Encyclopaedia Britannica, 1952, 430–46. (The view that 'geometry has all the perfection men are capable of'.)

* Plato (c.380–367 BC) *Republic*, trans. P. Shorey (1930), London and Cambridge, MA: Loeb Classical Library, Heinemann and Harvard University Press, 1969, 2 vols. (Book VII locates the study of geometry as knowledge of 'the eternally existent' in the curriculum for future guardians of the ideal state.)

* Plutarch (c.46–120) *Lives*, vol. 5, Cambridge, MA: Harvard University Press (Loeb Classical Library),

1961, 472–3. (Report of Plato's wrath at empirical methods in geometry.)

* Poincaré, H. (1902) *La Science et l'hypothèse*, Paris: Flammarion; trans. W. Greenstreet, *Science and Hypothesis*, New York: Dover, 1952, ch. 5. (Classic statement of geometric conventionalism.)

* Poncelet, J.V. (1822) *Traité des propriétés projectives des figures (Treatise on the Projective Properties of Figures)*, Paris: Bachelier; trans. selections entitled 'On Projective Geometry', in D.E. Smith (ed.) *A Source Book in Mathematics*, New York: Dover, 1984, vol. 2, 315–23. (Sketch of the significance of coordinate-free projective methods.)

* Reichenbach, H. (1928) *Philosophie der Raum-Zeit Lehre*, Berlin: de Gruyter; trans. M. Reichenbach and J. Freund, *The Philosophy of Space and Time*, New York: Dover, 1982. (The case for conventionalism in the context of the General Theory of Relativity.)

* Riemann, B. (1854) 'Über die Hypothesen, welche der Geometrie zu Grunde liegen', *Abhandlungen der Königlichen Gesellschaft der Wissenschaften zu Göttingen* 13: 133–52; trans. with mathematical commentary, 'On the Hypotheses which lie at the Foundations of Geometry', in M. Spivak, *A Comprehensive Introduction to Differential Geometry*, Houston: Publish or Perish, 2nd edn, 1990, vol. 2, 135–53. (Densely compressed, the deep mathematical and philosophical content of this article repays study.)

Szabó, A. (1964) 'The Transformation of Mathematics into Deductive Science and the Beginnings of its Foundation on Definitions and Axioms', *Scripta Mathematica* 28: 27–48A, 113–39. (A scholarly yet speculative account of the Pythagorean origins of mathematics as a demonstrative science.)

Tarski, A. (1959) 'What is Elementary Geometry?', in L. Henkin, P. Suppes and A. Tarski (eds) *The Axiomatic Method*, Amsterdam: North Holland, 16–29. (A logical formulation of elementary geometry without a set-theoretic basis.)

Torretti, R. (1978) *Philosophy of Geometry from Riemann to Poincaré*, Dordrecht: Reidel. (A work of high mathematical and philosophical distinction.)

* Veblen, O. and Whitehead, J.H.C. (1932) *The Foundations of Differential Geometry*, London: Cambridge University Press. (A concise account reflecting stimulus provided by the theory of General Relativity.)

* Weil, A. (1978) 'S.S. Chern as Geometer and Friend', in S.-S. Chern, *Selected Papers*, New York and Berlin: Springer, 1989, ix–xii. (Assessment of the place of geometry within mathematics by a leading number theorist.)

* Weyl, H. (1921) 'Zur Infinitesimal Geometrie: Einordnung der projektiven und konformen Auffassung', *Nachrichten der Königlichen Gesellschaft der Wissenschaften zu Göttingen, mathematisch-physikalische Klasse*, 99–112; repr. in *Gesammelte Abhandlungen*, Berlin and New York: Springer, 1968, vol. 2, 195–207. (The theorem that conformal and affine properties of a Riemannian manifold determine the metric.)

* Yaglom, I.M. (1988) *Felix Klein and Sophus Lie; Evolution of the Idea of Symmetry in the Nineteenth Century*, trans. S. Sossinsky, Boston, MA, and Basle: Birkhäuser. (A readable account of the development of the group concept in geometry.)

T.A. RYCKMAN

GEORGE OF TREBIZOND (c.1396–c.1472)

George was a fifteenth-century humanist important for his work in rhetoric, his translations from the Greek, and his role in the Renaissance Plato–Aristotle controversy. In 1458, as a fierce opponent of Plato and supporter of Aristotle, he transformed what had previously been a quarrel among Byzantines into a major European controversy. He also wrote the first and, for a time, the most popular humanist manual of logic.

Born and brought up in Crete (his Greek name 'Trapezountios' is a patronymic, not a toponymic), George emigrated to Italy around 1416 when twenty years old. Mastering Latin with startling speed, he became a teacher of Latin eloquence in northern Italy. He confirmed his reputation with the publication at Venice in 1433–4 of his book on rhetoric, which was the first full-fledged work on the subject in the classical mode since antiquity. In the late 1430s, at Florence, he published an *Isagoge Dialectica* (Introduction to Logic), which became a best-seller in the first half of the sixteenth century as humanists attempted to wrest the teaching of logic from the philosophers (see LOGIC, RENAISSANCE). George himself had no polemical purpose. He merely wished to extract from ARISTOTLE and the manuals of contemporary Aristotelians that small and simplified amount of logic needed by someone primarily interested in rhetoric and literature. Around this time he also joined the papal bureaucracy, becoming eventually a papal secretary. In Florence and (after 1442) in Rome, he continued to teach rhetoric, but he also began to translate from the Greek. His work as a translator peaked under Pope Nicholas V (1447–55), who commissioned him to translate into Latin all of Aristotle's zoological works, the pseudo-Aristotelian *Problemata*, Plato's *Laws*, Ptolemy's *Almagest* and patristic texts (including Eusebius of Caesaria's *Preparation of the Gospels*, which preserves a great many classical philosophical fragments). A quarrel with the pope over his commentary on Ptolemy's *Almagest* drove George to the Neapolitan court of King Alfonso of Aragon in 1452, but he returned to Rome in 1455. Thereafter, he lived in Rome until he died about 1472 (apart from a foray to Venice in 1460–1, where he propounded the theory that the Venetians had realized the ideal mixed constitution of monarchy, aristocracy and democracy).

In the mid-1450s George turned on the Greek Cardinal Bessarion. Though himself a pious Christian, Bessarion had studied with the neo-pagan Byzantine Platonist Pletho. George became convinced that Bessarion and his circle of Greek and Latin humanists were engaged in a Platonic conspiracy to paganize the Latin West. The first result was George's treatise of 1456, the *Protectio Aristotelis Problematum* (Protection of Aristotle's *Problemata*), which warned of the attempt of the Bessarion circle (and especially Bessarion's client, the Greek scholar Theodore Gaza) to undermine Latin Aristotelianism and theology by disseminating perverse translations of Aristotle. In 1458 George published (in manuscript form) the first major Latin work in the Plato–Aristotle controversy, the *Comparatio Philosophorum Aristotelis et Platonis* (Comparison of the Philosophers Aristotle and Plato) (printed in 1523 as *Comparationes philosophorum Aristotelis et Platonis*).

The *Comparatio* is divided into three books. In the first, George compares the two philosophers as scholars, and seeks to demonstrate that while Aristotle is the foundation of scientific knowledge, Plato was a mere literary dabbler. In the second, he measures the doctrines of both Aristotle and Plato against the standard of Christian truth. Plato fails miserably because he believed in the transmigration of souls, creation from pre-existent matter, and a hierarchy of gods. Aristotle, on the other hand, taught the immortality of the soul, creation of the world from nothing, and monotheism. George even argues that Aristotle had an inkling of the Christian Trinity. To prove the latter contention, George resorted to the exemplarist doctrine of the medieval Platonic tradition, which found Trinitarian vestiges in all creation. George attributed to Aristotle a hylomorphic conception of the soul and argued that creation *ex nihilo* was a philosophically necessary doctrine. Ironically, both positions reflected the medieval Platonic tradition of the Franciscan-

Augustinian school rather than the Christian Aristotelianism of Thomas AQUINAS, whom George cited. In Book 3, George revealed his true purpose: to warn the West of the Platonic conspiracy. He showed that Platonists propounded and practised homosexuality. He warned that their doctrines had been the cause of Christian heresies, that Muhammad himself had been trained by a Platonist, and that more recently Pletho had tried to revive heathenism. Now, the Platonists (meaning Bessarion and his circle) stood poised to capture the church. Bessarion answered George in 1469 with his monumental *In calumniatorem Platonis* (Against Plato's Calumniator), which rehabilitated Plato by making him a semi-Christian Neoplatonist, by arguing that Aristotle was a pagan, and by ignoring George's attack on Pletho's pagan agenda. This phase of the Plato–Aristotle controversy ended with the deaths of Bessarion and George about 1472.

See also: ARISTOTELIANISM, RENAISSANCE; HUMANISM, RENAISSANCE; PLATONISM, RENAISSANCE

List of works

George of Trebizond [Georgius Trapezuntius] (c. 1438) *Isagoge Dialectica* (Introduction to Logic), Cologne: Eucharius, 1539; repr. Frankfurt am Main: Minerva, 1966. (A simplified Aristotelian logic, useful in rhetorical education. George's *Isagoge* went through many early modern editions; the Minerva edition is a photographic reprint of Eucharius.)

—— (1456) *Protectio Aristotelis Problematum* (Protection of Aristotle's *Problemata*), in L. Mohler (ed.) *Kardinal Bessarion*, Paderborn: Schöningh, 1923–42; repr. Aalen: Scientia and Paderborn: Schöningh, 1967, vol. 3, 274–342. (A critique of Theodore Gaza's translation of pseudo-Aristotle's *Problemata* and an attack on those who would subvert Aristotelianism.)

—— (1458) *Comparationes Philosophorum Aristotelis et Platonis* (Comparisons of the Philosophers Aristotle and Plato), Venice: Iacobus Pentius, 1523; repr. Frankfurt am Main: Minerva, 1965. (Condemns Plato as an incompetent philosopher whose latter-day followers subvert Christianity, but praises Aristotle for giving philosophical support to Christian truths and for having intimations of some Christian mysteries. The manuscript (published in 1458) gives the title of this work as *Comparatio philosophorum Aristotelis et Platonis*.)

References and further reading

Monfasani, J. (1976) *George of Trebizond: A Biography and a Study of His Rhetoric and Logic*, Leiden: Brill. (The Plato–Aristotle controversy is treated at length.)

—— (ed.) (1984) *Collectanea Trapezuntiana: Texts, Documents, and Bibliographies of George of Trebizond*, Binghamton, NY: Medieval & Renaissance Texts & Studies. (The Greek texts are accompanied by an English translation.)

JOHN MONFASANI

GERARD, ALEXANDER (1728–95)

Alexander Gerard was Professor of Moral Philosophy and Logic (1752) and Professor of Divinity (1759) at Marischal College, and Professor of Divinity (1773) at King's College, Aberdeen. A leading member of the Aberdeen Philosophical Society, he wrote a new plan of education for Marischal College as well as works on divinity. He is best known, however, for his Essay on Taste *(1759). In 1774, he returned to the subject with* An Essay on Genius. *Gerard was associated with Thomas Reid (1710–96) in the Philosophical Society until Reid's transfer to Glasgow in 1764. The work of David Hume (1711–76) was a principal influence.*

Alexander Gerard's aesthetic philosophy is a response to the theories of Francis HUTCHESON (1694–1746) and David Hume (see HUME, D. §3). Like Hutcheson, Gerard made use of the concepts of an internal sense and of association to explain the subjectivity of taste. However, Gerard's use of an internal sense, which he called a reflex act, must be severely qualified. He distinguished two ways of considering taste:

> It may be considered either as a species of *sensation*, or as a species of *discernment*.... Taste considered in the former of these lights, in respect of what we may call its *direct exercise*, cannot properly admit any standard...But notwithstanding this, there may be a standard of taste in respect of its *reflex acts*: and it is only in respect of these, that a standard should be sought for.
>
> (1759: 214–6)

This distinction distances Gerard from Hume's more radical reliance on sentiment and Hutcheson's elaborate theory of an internal sense. Gerard depended on a species of induction (perhaps derived from another

Aberdeen philosopher, George TURNBULL) to correct immediate sensation.

Gerard's own theory rests on a view of the imagination as exercising the mind. Freed of the need for the actual presence of objective sources, which limit the external senses, the imagination combines reflective ideas supplied by fancy. The operation of the imagination exercises the mind, and when that exercise falls within a moderate range, it is experienced as pleasurable. If it is either too languid and easy or too excited and difficult, discomfort (or indifference) results. From the beginning, these were the controlling principles of Gerard's discussion. But the terms of the problem set for him (and in some sense his essay was a set piece for the Edinburgh Society for the Encouragement of Arts, Sciences, Manufactures and Agriculture) come from Hutcheson's internal sense theory and Hume's search for a standard of taste. So Gerard used 'taste' as a vehicle to explain the faculty of the imagination. He was not always consistent, and sometimes it seems that he forgot that the problem of taste arose because an internal sense would lack the checks and confirmations of an external sense.

Gerard tended to multiply senses because they were little more to him than aesthetic predicates. Association establishes the reference for such predicates. Thus, while continuing to use the language of taste and internal sense, he was moving decisively in the direction of Archibald Alison's more elaborate scheme of imaginative and associative aesthetics (see ALISON, A.). At the same time, Gerard remains within the scope set by REID and his school.

See also: ABERDEEN PHILOSOPHICAL SOCIETY; EMOTION IN RESPONSE TO ART; ENLIGHTENMENT, SCOTTISH; ARTISTIC TASTE

List of works

Gerard, A. (1759) *An Essay on Taste*, London: Miller; 3rd edn repr. Gainsville, FL: Scholars' Facsimiles and Reprints, 1963. (Gerard's prize essay for The Edinburgh Society for the Encouragement of the Arts, Sciences, Manufactures and Agriculture. The Essay on Taste sifts internal sense toward a theory of imagination and association. Includes a useful introduction by W.J. Hipple, Jr.)

—— (1774) *An Essay on Genius*, London: Strahan; repr. ed. B. Fabian, Munich: Fink. (Less widely read because it fails to break new ground. Continues Gerard's emphasis on imagination and association as the leading concepts of an aesthetic psychology.)

References and further reading

Dickie, G. (1996) *The Century of Taste*, Oxford: Oxford University Press. (A defence of Hume against the forms of association advocated by Alison and Gerard.)

Kivy, P. (1976) *The Seventh Sense*, New York: Burt Franklin. (Traces the concept of internal sense through eighteenth-century aesthetics.)

McCosh, J. (1875) *The Scottish Philosophy*, New York: Carter, 1911–2; repr. Bristol: Thoemmes, 1990. (Brief biographical sketch and commentary.)

Stulmitz, J. (1961) 'Beauty: Some Stages in the History of Ideas', *Journal of the History of Ideas* 22: 185–204. (Locates Gerard as the mediator between the internal sense theory of Hutcheson and the associationism of A. Alison.)

Townsend, D. (1987) 'From Shaftesbury to Kant', *Journal of the History of Ideas* 48: 287–305. (Traces the development of the empiricist tradition, including Gerard. Argues that activity of the mind is more important than association or sense to Gerard.)

DABNEY TOWNSEND

GERARD OF CREMONA (1114–87)

Gerard of Cremona was the most important translator of philosophical works from Arabic to Latin in the twelfth century. During a career of about forty years, he translated at least seventy books. The most famous translations are those of works of Aristotle, including Posterior Analytics, Physics, On the Heavens, On Generation and Corruption *and* Meteorology 1–3. *Gerard also translated a number of works as part of the Aristotelian corpus that were not at all Aristotelian; the most important of these is the so-called* Liber de causis (Book of Causes). *However, the Aristotelian translations were only a small part of his labour. He translated many more works that were medical, astronomical or mathematical, bringing into Latin several small libraries of fundamental natural science.*

What is known of Gerard's life comes principally from three related documents: a list of his translations prepared by his assistants, a later biographical note and a verse eulogy. According to the biographical note, Gerard came to Toledo from Italy in search of Ptolemy's *Almagest*. He stayed to learn Arabic when he discovered just how much in that language was inaccessible to the Latins. So far as modern scholarship can determine, this would have been about 1140.

His first translation seems indeed to have been of Ptolemy, since it is only for this work that the list of translations assigns a native collaborator. After the *Almagest*, Gerard is known to have translated at least seventy more works.

Gerard's assistants divided the translated works by subject. The richest subjects are medicine (24 works), mathematics, including optics, weight and dynamics (17 works), and logic or philosophy (14 works). The last group contains some of Gerard's most famous translations, including Aristotle's *Posterior Analytics* (revised from the version of James of Venice, with the commentary of THEMISTIUS), *Physics* (with the commentary of AL-FARABI), *On the Heavens, On Generation and Corruption* and *Meteorology* 1–3. It should be noted that Gerard was concerned to provide commentaries alongside the Aristotelian texts. Some of these commentaries were originally Greek (as in the case of Themistius on the *Posterior Analytics*), though Gerard brought them in from Arabic. Other commentaries and expository treatises had been written in Arabic as part of the Arab peoples' own appropriation of Greek learning (as in the case of al-Farabi's commentary on the *Physics*).

Gerard also translated a number of works as part of the Aristotelian corpus that were not at all Aristotelian. The most important of these is the so-called *Liber de causis* (Book of Causes), a compilation of material mostly from PROCLUS (see LIBER DE CAUSIS). This treatise on the cosmic participation of such transcendental features as goodness or unity was read for about a century after Gerard's translation as if it had been written by Aristotle, and guided interpretations of the whole Aristotelian corpus.

Gerard's translations are notable for their fidelity to the Arabic. They preserve its syntax and its lexicon as much possible. Even when Gerard had access to an earlier Latin translation based on the Greek, he would weigh its meaning against what he had gathered from the Arabic, often standardizing the technical terminology to reflect Arabic usage. When the original was in Arabic, Gerard would revise earlier Latin versions and restore passages that had been abridged or omitted. The resulting version does not always make for easy reading, but Gerard seems to have imagined that the texts would not function as isolated discourses so much as parts or stages of a complete curriculum. The influx of Arabic learning into the Latin West was an influx of new texts that mediated organized bodies of knowledge. It was not enough that the texts be put into a passable Latin; they had to be glossed, interpreted, reconciled and corrected in circumstances very different from the circumstances of their Arabic transmission. Gerard meant to help this labour by providing not just single texts, but groups of texts that would serve to introduce bodies of knowledge in a coherent and ordered way. Gerard was not just translating Arabic texts, he was importing Arabic curricula. It would be at least a century before these curricula would be appropriated in any active way by his Latin readers.

See also: ARISTOTELIANISM, MEDIEVAL; TRANSLATORS; ISLAMIC PHILOSOPHY: TRANSMISSION INTO WESTERN EUROPE

List of works

Gerard of Cremona (before 1187) Revision of James of Venice's translation of Aristotle's *Posterior Analytics*, ed. L. Minio-Paluello and B. Dod, Aristoteles Latinus 4.3, 2nd edn, Leiden: Brill, 1968. (This Aristotelian work was fundamental for the medieval reconceiving of the nature of knowledge.)

—— (before 1187) Translation of Aristotle's *Meterology* 1–3, ed. A. Pattin and É. van de Vyver, *Études d'histoire littéraire sur la scolastique médiévale*, Philosophes Médiévaux 8, Louvain and Paris: Publications universitaires, 1964, 241–71. (This Aristotelian work provided medieval Latin readers with the bases for an account of elemental interactions.)

—— (before 1187) Translation of Themistius' commentary on Aristotle's *Posterior Analytics*, ed. J.R. O'Donnell, *Mediaeval Studies* 20, 1958, 239–315. (Themistius' commentary provided medieval Latin readers with some access to late classical readings of Aristotle.)

—— (before 1187) Translation of al-Kindi's *De quinque essentiis* (On the Five Essences), ed. A. Nagy, *Die philosophischen Abhandlungen des Ja'qub ben Ishaq al-Kindi*, Beiträge zur Geschichte der Philosophie des Mittelalters 2.5, Münster: Aschendorff, 1897, 28–40. (This text provided medieval Latin readers with an introduction to Neoplatonic cosmology.)

—— (before 1187) Revision of Gundissalinus' abridgement of al-Farabi's *Catalogue of Sciences*, ed. A. González Paléncia, Madrid and Granada: Instituto Miguel Asin, 1953. (The *Catalogue* describes a hierarchy of liberal arts and philosophical sciences.)

—— (before 1187) Revision of an earlier translation of the *Liber de causis* (Book of Causes), ed. A. Pattin, *Tijdschrift voor Filosofie* 28, 1966, 90–203. (The *Liber de causis*, believed still to be a work of Aristotle, provided a deeply Neoplatonic ontology.)

Anon. (*c.*1187) List of Gerard's Translations, ed. F. Wüstenfeld, 'Die Übersetzungen arabischer Werke in das lateinische seit dem XI. Jahrhunderts,' *Sitzungsberichte der K. Akademie der Wissenschaften in Wien*, Phil.-hist. Kl. 149 (4), 1904, and 151 (1), 1906; trans. M. McVaugh in *A Source Book in Medieval Science*, ed. E. Grant, Cambridge, MA: Harvard University Press, 1974, 35–8. (List of Gerard's translations compiled by his assistants.)

References and further reading

Lemay, R. (1978) 'Gerard of Cremona,' *Dictionary of Scientific Biography* 15 (Supplement 1): 173–92. (The most useful introduction in English; contains an exhaustive list of the translations, with bibliography.)

MARK D. JORDAN

GERARD OF ODO
(*c.*1290–*c.*1349)

Gerard of Odo, a scholastic philosopher and theologian who wrote a long commentary on Aristotle's Nicomachean Ethics, *is one of many scholastics who attempted to reconcile Aristotle's teachings with the views of Christian authorities. Gerard's work declares the subject of ethics to be the human being as free, makes the will's power of self-determination a necessary condition for moral responsibility, and in other respects reflects the voluntarism commonly found in Franciscan writings of the period.*

Gerard of Odo has long been remembered by Church historians as the papal associate who became minister general of the Franciscan order in 1329. At the time, the Franciscans were badly divided about the kind of life required by their vow of poverty. Pope John XXII deposed the head of the order and nominated Gerard, his own candidate, as the new minister general. Gerard continued in that position until 1342, when he was named patriarch of Antioch and bishop of Catania.

Gerard's accomplishments as a bachelor and master of theology at Paris were better received than his performance as an administrator. His writings include a commentary on the *Sentences* of Peter LOMBARD, two treatises on logic – one on syllogisms, the other on supposition (*De suppositionibus*) – as well as a treatise on economics (*De contractibus*) and a long commentary on the *Nicomachean Ethics*. His discussion of continua, once thought to be a fragment of some lost work on Aristotle's *Physics*, comes from his *Sentences* commentary.

Gerard's most important contribution by far was his commentary on Aristotle's *Ethics*, which might explain how he came to be called 'the Moral Doctor.' The better-known *Ethics* commentary by the nominalist John BURIDAN borrows extensively from Gerard's work, which favours a more realist, Neoplatonist metaphysics. Despite the seemingly prohibitive metaphysical differences, Buridan plainly found the work of the Moral Doctor well worth his attention (Walsh 1975).

Gerard's commentary on the *Ethics*, probably the first such work by a Franciscan, signals its emphasis on freedom from the outset. The prologue declares the subject of ethics to be the human being as *free*. Though this opens the possibility that ethics extends to angels, Gerard argues that angelic freedom differs significantly from human freedom, and since we know little about angels in any case, we apply ethics only to mankind. Nevertheless, he adds, ethics could apply to other creatures if any possessed a freedom similar to our own.

Gerard sees the will's power of self-determination as the source of freedom and a necessary condition for moral responsibility. Among the powers of the soul, the will holds the position of king, the intellect only of king's counsellor. Because the will can act against the advice of the intellect, and the intellect cannot influence the emotions without the concurrence of the will, moral weakness arises from weakness of will. In a similar vein, Gerard opposes AQUINAS in insisting that all moral virtues must belong to the will. Aquinas' commentary on the *Ethics* claims that temperance and courage have to do mainly with how someone is internally affected by the passions, whereas justice has mainly to do with how one acts externally; thus the former are virtues of the emotional part of the soul, while the latter is a virtue of the will. Quoting Aquinas with strong disapproval, Gerard argues that *all* moral virtues moderate passion but nonetheless are principally concerned with action. For him, all moral virtues are habits of choice: hence habits of the will, since choice is an act of the will (see FREE WILL).

On these and many other points, Gerard's commentary reflects the voluntarism so often found in Franciscan writings of the late thirteenth and early fourteenth centuries. His work attempts to interpret Aristotle's *Ethics* in such a way that it supports, or at least does not contradict, teachings prevalent in his own order (Kent 1984).

Gerard's *Sentences* commentary placed him among the 'indivisibilists' in the scholastic debate about continuous magnitudes. He argues that a continuum is composed of extensionless points, distinct from mathematical points in admitting relative differences in time and space (Zoubov 1959). Here, as in the metaphysics of his *Ethics* commentary, Gerard diverges sharply from Aristotle's teachings. The arguments against indivisibles in Book VI of the *Physics* allow for no genuine doubt about Aristotle's views.

See also: ARISTOTELIANISM, MEDIEVAL

List of works

Gerard of Odo (c.1320–9) *Expositio in Aristotelis Ethicam* (Commentary on Aristotle's *Nicomachean Ethics*), Venice: De Lovere, 1500. (Gerard's best known work, which influenced John Buridan.)

—— (c.1320–9) *De suppositionibus* (On Supposition), ed. S. Brown, 'Gerard Odon's 'De Suppositionibus'', *Franciscan Studies* 35, 1975, 5–44. (Logical treatise, on suppositions.)

—— (c.1326–8) *In quattuor libros Sententiarum*, MS Sarnano E. 98; MS Paris, BN lat. 3068. (No edition of this work exists. Other useful manuscripts can be found in the national library in Naples and the cathedral library in Valencia.)

—— (??) *De contractibus*, MS Siena Bcom. U.V.8. (Discussed in Langholm (1979), chapter 6, this work is quoted extensively and with approval by St Bernardino of Siena.)

References and further reading

* Kent, B. (1984) 'Aristotle and the Franciscans: Gerald Odonis' Commentary on the "Nicomachean Ethics"', Ph.D dissertation, Columbia University. (Places Gerard's *Ethics* commentary in the context of late thirteenth- and early fourteenth-century Franciscan psychology and ethics.)

Langholm, O. (1979) *Price and Value in the Aristotelian Tradition*, Bergen: Universitetsforlaget. (Discusses Gerard's *De contractibus* and other scholastic works on economics.)

Murdoch, J.E. (1982) 'Infinity and continuity,' in N. Kretzmann, A. Kenny and J. Pinborg (eds) *The Cambridge History of Later Medieval Philosophy*, Cambridge: Cambridge University Press. (Explains fourteenth-century debate regarding indivisibles.)

Saarinen, R. (1994) *Weakness of the Will in Medieval Thought: From Augustine to Buridan*, Leiden: Brill. (Exegesis of teachings by Gerard and other medieval thinkers on the problem of *akrasia*.)

* Walsh, J.J. (1975) 'Some Relationships Between Gerald Odo's and John Buridan's Commentaries on Aristotle's 'Ethics',' *Franciscan Studies* 35: 237–75. (Analysis of Buridan's borrowings from Gerard's commentary.)

* Zoubov, V. (1959) 'Walter Catton, Gérard d'Odon et Nicolas Bonet,' *Physis* 1: 261–78. (Gerard's arguments regarding the composition of continua and his influence on other thinkers.)

BONNIE KENT

GERBERT OF AURILLAC (938–1003)

Gerbert is chiefly remembered as an educational reformer. He established a syllabus for the university course in logic, the logica vetus, *that remained in use until the mid-twelfth century. Most of his academic writings are instructional works on mathematics. In his single philosophical work,* De rationali et ratione uti *(On That Which is Rational and Using Reason), he uses Boethius' logical commentaries to develop a distinctly Platonic solution to a problem he derives from Porphyry's* Isagōgē.

Gerbert began his studies as a Cluniac monk at Aurillac. It is generally supposed, although documentation for this period is not good, that he was exposed to Islamic science and mathematics during a subsequent stay in Catalonia. He moved to Rheims around 972 to continue his studies, and later became director of schools there. After a brief and stormy tenure as Abbot of Bobbio, *circa* 980–3, he returned to Rheims, where he continued to engage in political controversy. In 991 he was made archbishop, and in 998 was transferred to Ravenna. He was elected as Pope Sylvester II in 999, and died in Rome in 1003.

During Gerbert's first stay at Rheims, he instigated educational reforms which were to influence the curriculum of cathedral schools and universities for at least the following two centuries. Gerbert is the first person documented to have taught the syllabus of the *logica vetus*, the basis for logic teaching until the mid-twelfth century. He used Porphyry's *Isagōgē* in the translations of MARIUS VICTORINUS and BOETHIUS, Aristotle's *Categories* and *De interpretatione* in Boethius' versions, Cicero's *Topics*, Boethius' commentaries on these works and Boethius' own logical works (see ARISTOTLE; CICERO; PORPHYRY). In addition to studying these works, his students were required to engage in 'controversies' on set questions (see also LANGUAGE, MEDIEVAL THEORIES OF; LOGIC, MEDIEVAL).

In teaching astronomy, Gerbert used a spherical model to illustrate the movement of the planets and had his students make astronomical observations. Mathematics was an area of particular interest for Gerbert; several of his letters include mathematical discussions in response to questions from his students, and he also wrote longer mathematical treatises. He taught arithmetic using the arabic numerals from one to nine rather than Roman numerals (though he did not adopt the arabic zero), and instructed his students in the use of the abacus. His treatise on the use of the abacus later became a standard work. For geometry, he supplemented a fragmentary version of Euclid with his own treatise. Gerbert is also known to have reintroduced the study of classical authors including Virgil, Terence, Horace, Persius, Lucan, Seneca and Quintilian. Fulbert of Rheims, founder of the school of Chartres, was one of his students (see CHARTRES, SCHOOL OF).

Gerbert's one extant philosophical work, *De rationali et ratione uti* (On That Which is Rational and Using Reason) has been examined by Marenbon (1983). It shows Gerbert using Porphyry's *Isagōgē*, Aristotle's *De interpretatione* and Boethius' commentaries on the same works to explain a problem arising from Porphyry's discussion of differentia: why *ratione uti* can be predicated of *rationale*. As Marenbon explains, Gerbert uses the opposition between act and potency (discussed in both the *Isagōgē* and the *De interpretatione*), Aristotle's remarks on psychology at the beginning of the *De interpretatione* and a metaphysical hierarchy from the beginning of Boethius's first *Isagōgē* commentary in developing his solution. Gerbert claims that when *rationale* is considered just as a concept, apart from any instance in a human being, then its scope is no narrower than that of *ratione uti*. It is only when the concept *rationale* is attached to a corporeal human being that it is no longer always in act, but becomes a potentiality realized in act only when the person who is rational is indeed using reason. When *rationale* is attached to a corporeal being, then, it is acceptable to predicate *ratione uti* of it. When we say 'that which is rational uses reason', it is understood that we are referring to some particular rational being which is currently using its reason, not to 'that which is rational' taken in a general sense.

A philosophical debate between Gerbert and Otric held before Emperor Otto II is recounted by Gerbert's student Richer. While the word-for-word dialogue Richer includes is most likely of his own composition, the event may well have occurred. According to Richer, the debate ranged over the proper division of philosophy, the cause of the creation of the world, whether all causes can be expressed by the single word 'good', the cause of a shadow and whether 'mortal' or 'rational' is the wider concept. Whether or not Richer's account faithfully reports Gerbert's replies, it remains a testimony to his effective teaching.

See also: CHARTRES, SCHOOL OF; LOGIC, MEDIEVAL; NATURAL PHILOSOPHY, MEDIEVAL (§1)

List of works

Gerbert of Aurillac (*c.*972–99) *Opera* (Works), ed. A. Duchesne in J.-P. Migne, *Patrologia Latina* 139: 201–64; revised edn, ed. A. Olleris, *Oeuvres de Gerbert, pape sous le nom de Sylvestre ii*, Clermont-Ferrand: Thibaud and Paris: Dumoulon, 1867. (Collected works of Gerbert.)

—— (*c.*972–99) *Gerberti opera mathematica* (Mathematical Works of Gerbert), ed. N. Bubnov, Berlin: Berloni (R. Friedlander & Sohn), 1889. (Includes the mathematical letters as well as the treatises.)

—— (983–97) Letters, ed. J.V. Havet, *Lettres de Gerbert, 983–97*, Paris: A. Picard, 1889; re-edited and trans. H.P. Lattin, *The Letters of Gerbert with his Papal Privileges as Sylvester II*, Records of Civilization, Sources and Studies 60, New York: Columbia University Press, 1961. (Mathematical discussions and requests for books are included.)

—— (*c.*972–99) *De rationale et ratione uti* (On That Which is Rational and Using Reason), ed. A. Olleris, *Oeuvres de Gerbert, pape sous le nom de Sylvestre ii*, Clermont-Ferrand: Thibaud and Paris: Dumoulon, 1867, 297–310. (A short treatise on why 'using reason' can be predicated of 'that which is rational'.)

References and further reading

Amann, E. (1941) 'Silvestre II', in *Dictionnaire de théologie catholique*, Paris: Letouzey et Ane, vol. 14 (2), cols 2075–83. (Still provides the most extensive bibliography of work on Gerbert.)

* Marenbon, J. (1983) *Early Medieval Philosophy (480–1150)*, London: Routledge & Kegan Paul, 82–3. (A clear, accessible exposition of *De rationali et ratione uti*.)

Lindgren, U. (1976) *Gerbert von Aurillac und das Quadrivium* (Gerbert of Aurillac and the Quadrivium), Wiesbaden: Steiner. (Discusses Gerbert's mathematical and scientific interests and teaching.)

* Richer (*c.*980–1000) *Histoire de France 888–995*, ed. R Latouche, Paris: H. Champion, 1937, vol. 2, 54–64. (This historian, a student of Gerbert's, recounts Gerbert's career and gives details of his teaching and of his debate with Otric before emperor Otto II.)

FIONA SOMERSET

GERDIL, GIANCINTO SIGISMONDO (1718–1802)

A lifelong member of the Barnabite religious order, Gerdil became well-known as the most eminent Italian disciple of Malebranche (and critic of Locke); in 1764 he published a critique of Émile *(1762) which Rousseau himself called the only attack worth reading in its entirety. Only extreme old age kept Cardinal Gerdil from being elected Pope at Venice in 1798.*

Born in Savoy, Gerdil became a lifelong member of the Barnabite religious order and, as a Cardinal in 1798, was kept from being elected Pope at Venice only by extreme old age. He is best-known, however, as the most eminent Italian disciple of MALEBRANCHE (1638–1715) and a critic of LOCKE and ROUSSEAU.

As a follower of Malebranche, Gerdil defended the principal doctrines of the celebrated Oratorian Father: that God governs the universe through consent, uniform *volontés générales* (general wills), not through *ad hoc* miraculous *volontés particulières* (particular wills); that human beings are only the 'occasional' causes of their own acts (while God is the true cause); that 'we see all things in God', not in Lockean sense-perception. Gerdil was also distressed by the Lockean notion that the natural immortality of the soul is only highly 'probable', that only revelation (but not reason) can offer certainty on this point. Here Gerdil's key works are *The Immateriality of the Soul, Demonstrated against Locke* and *Defence of the Sentiment of Father Malebranche against this Philosopher* (both published 1747–8).

But it was as a critic of Rousseau that Gerdil gained a European reputation. In his *Réflexions* on Rousseau's political, religious and pedagogical theory (1764), Gerdil urged that 'the purpose of *The Social Contract* is the universal overturning of the civil order; the purpose of *Émile* (1762) is to prepare minds for this through a total revolution in ways of thinking'. Granting Rousseau's eloquence and 'brilliance of colouring' as a writer, Gerdil insisted that Jean-Jacques' clinging to (supposedly uncorrupted) 'nature' would produce 'bad Christians and bad citizens'. Rousseau's supposed 'natural man', for Gerdil, is 'the most factitious [being] that has ever existed in the mind of any philosopher': 'no one today has seen a man detached from every social institution, no one can say what he is'. Despite the 'persuasiveness' of Rousseau's 'blinding' eloquence, in Gerdil's view, the citizen of Geneva's thought amounts to:

> contempt for all revealed religion, and for Christianity in particular...; a revolt against all legitimate authority: ...a false indulgence in not

reprimanding the faults arising from children's natural liberty; a false determination not to reason with them, and not to cultivate their minds by any of the studies suitable to their age – such are the fruits of this new plan for education.

Réflexions

If Rousseau alone is right, Gerdil adds tartly, then Socrates, Plato, Cicero, Seneca, Plutarch, Bacon, Bossuet and Fénelon knew nothing about human nature or suitable education. And he ends the *Réflexions* with a paragraph whose literary effectiveness Rousseau himself acknowledged: 'M. Rousseau is opening a new career. Men will no longer be depraved by arbitrary institutions, they will no longer be terrified by the importunate threats of religion; they will no longer be fatigued by studies which are so remote from their nature. What chimeras! What visions!'

List of works

Gerdil, G.S. (1806–21) *Opere* (Works), Rome, 20 vols.
——(1747–8) *L'immatérialité de l'âme, démontrée contre Locke* (The Immateriality of the Soul, Demonstrated against Locke), together with *Défense du sentiment du P. Malebranche, contre ce philosophe* (Defence of the Sentiment of Father Malebranche against this Philosopher), Turin.
—— (1764) *Réflexions sur la théorie et la pratique de l'éducation, contre les principes de J.J. Rousseau* (Reflections on the theory and practice of education, against the principles of J.-J. Rousseau), Paris.

References and further reading

Biographie universelle (1816) 'Gerdil', Paris, vol. 17.
Geymonat, L. (ed.) (1971) *Storia del pensiero filosofico e scientifico* (History of Philosophical and Scientific Thought), vol. 3: 486–8, Milan.

PATRICK RILEY

GERMAN IDEALISM

From the late eighteenth century until the middle of the nineteenth, German philosophy was dominated by the movement known as German idealism, which began as an attempt to complete Kant's revolutionary project: the derivation of the principles of knowledge and ethics from the spontaneity and autonomy of mind or spirit. However, German idealists produced systems whose relation to Kant is controversial, due to their emphasis on the absolute unity and historical development of reason.

As a movement to complete Kant's project, German idealism was punctuated by controversies about whether certain Kantian distinctions constitute *dualisms* – unbridgeable gaps between elements whose underlying unity must be demonstrated – and about how such dualisms can be overcome (see KANT, I. §3). One controversy concerned the distinction between the form of knowable objects – contributed by the mind, according to Kant – and the *matter* of sensation – contributed by mind-independent things-in-themselves. JACOBI objected that things-in-themselves lay beyond the boundaries of human knowledge, so Kant should profess 'transcendental ignorance' about the origin of sensible matter, leaving open the possibility that reality is mind-dependent. Another controversy concerned Kant's distinction between the spatio-temporal forms of sensibility and the categorial forms of understanding. Maimon (1790) argued that unless the underlying unity of this distinction were demonstrated, the applicability of categories to sensible objects could not be demonstrated against sceptics like HUME. Instead of defeating scepticism as he intended, some thought Kant had ensured its triumph by establishing unbridgeable dualisms between mind and reality, and between understanding and sensibility.

In the 1790s, some Kantians – notably REINHOLD, Fichte and Schelling – sought to complete Kant's project through systematization. Troublesome dualisms would be overcome by positing distinct mental forms, as well as the distinction between mind and reality, as necessary conditions of the mind's free and unitary activity, and thus as necessary elements of a unified system (see FICHTE, J.G. §3; SCHELLING, F.W.J. VON §1). However, other Kantians – notably Buhle – accused the systematizers of undermining the distinctness of form and matter, and of attempting to generate matter from pure form. Meanwhile the systematizers, seeking to defeat scepticism, claimed metaphysical knowledge grounded in intellectual intuition of the mind's spontaneity (see FICHTE, J.G. §5). But Kant had explicitly denied that humans could attain such knowledge.

Professing continued allegiance to Kant despite these apparent departures, some systematizers – notably Fichte – claimed that Kant's teaching was only intelligible from a special standpoint and that, having attained that standpoint, they were expressing Kant's spirit, if not his letter. However, in his 1799 *Open Letter on Fichte's Wissenschaftslehre*, Kant publicly repudiated all attempts to discern his philosophy's spirit from a special standpoint and rejected any endeavour to bridge the gap between form and matter. But those who were repudiated did not change their ways. Finding Kant unable to complete the revolution he had started, they henceforth constructed their systems more independently of Kant's writings. The influence of pre-Kantian philosophers, notably SPINOZA, was explicitly acknowledged.

In order to overcome Kantian dualisms without ignoring his distinctions, Idealists produced a variety of developmental monisms (see FICHTE, J.G. §3; SCHELLING, F.W.J. VON §2; HEGEL, G.W.F. §4). Such systems portray a single, developing principle expressing itself in dualisms whose unstable, conflictual nature necessitates further developments. Thus reality is a developing, organic whole whose principle can be grasped and whose unity can be articulated in a philosophical system. But the dualisms encountered in everyday experience are not illusory. Rather, they are necessary stages in reality's development towards its full realization. This conception of development is often called dialectic.

Developmental monism emphasized the sociality and historicity of reason. Fichte was the first to emphasize sociality, arguing that the development of individual self-consciousness required consciousness of another mind, and deriving a theory of justice from the idea of one individual *recognizing* another as such (see FICHTE, J.G. §7). Hegel placed particular emphasis on historicity, portraying human history as a series of conflicts and resolutions culminating in a just society that would enable the reciprocal recognition of individuals, as well as the perfect self-recognition of reason at which philosophy had always aimed (see HEGEL, G.W.F. §8). Thus history – especially the history of philosophy – acquired unprecedented significance as the narrative of the mind's ascent to self-knowledge. And it was hoped that a philosophical account of society's historical development would correct the deficiencies of the French revolution, which was often called the political equivalent of Kant's revolution.

Idealists disagreed about whether Kant's distinction between mind and nature was another problematic dualism. Schelling and Hegel argued that a systematic philosophy must portray nature as the mind's preconscious development. But Fichte regarded their philosophy of nature as a betrayal of Idealism that explained the mind in nonmental terms and deprived the mind of its autonomy. By 1801 the disagreement was explicit (see FICHTE, J.G. §6; SCHELLING, F.W.J. VON §§1, 2; HEGEL, G.W.F. §§3, 7).

Controversy about another putative dualism – between concept and intuition – ended the alliance between Schelling and Hegel. Without naming him,

Hegel's *Phenomenology of Spirit* (1807) appeared to criticize Schelling's view that philosophy can only be understood by those innately able to intuit – to grasp non-discursively – the identity implicit in apparent dualisms. Hegel argued that the completed philosophical system must be conceptualized and rendered discursively intelligible to everyone. However, only those who transformed their accustomed ways of thinking could understand the system (see HEGEL, G.W.F. §§5, 6). So Hegel undertook to guide his readers through a series of transformations of consciousness representing the history of human thought, as well as the education of the individual. The Napoleonic wars forced Hegel from university life, but after his return in 1814, and especially after his move to Berlin in 1818, his version of idealism – with its portrayal of reason developing in both nature and culture towards conceptual articulation – became dominant.

However, Hegel died in 1831 and Schelling raised influential criticisms of Hegel when he began teaching in Berlin in 1841. In an inaugural lecture before an audience including Engels and Kierkegaard, Schelling argued that Hegel's system was an inevitably failed attempt to overcome the dualism between conceptual thought and intuited existence. Schelling's criticism was seminal for Marxism and existentialism and was more influential than his alternative proposals, which he had been developing under the influence of theosophy since 1809 (see EXISTENTIALISM; MARXISM, WESTERN; SCHELLING, F.W.J. VON §§3, 4; HEGELIANISM §3). The relationship between thought and existence remains problematic for post-idealist philosophy, and German idealism remains both an object of criticism and a source of insight.

See also: ABSOLUTE, THE; IDEALISM; ROMANTICISM, GERMAN; ROSENZWEIG, F.; BUDDHISM, YOGĀCĀRA SCHOOL OF §2

List of works

Collected works, critical editions and English translations can be found in the entries on individual philosopher throughout the *Encylopedia*. Below are listed some texts of particular importance for the historical development of German idealism.

Behler, E. (ed.) (1985) *Fichte, Jacobi and Schelling: Philosophy of German Idealism*, New York: Continuum. (Contains translations of Fichte's Sun-Clear Report and Jacobi's Letter to Fichte, both relevant to the controversy about whether Idealism has atheistic and nihilistic implications, as well as important writings by Schelling on aesthetics, the philosophy of nature and the difficulties facing any philosophical account of the freedom to do evil.)

Giovanni, G. di and Harris, H. (eds) (1985) *Between Kant and Hegel: Texts in the Development of Post-Kantian Idealism*, Albany, NY: State University of New York Press. (Contains translated and annotated extracts from important texts by Reinhold, Aenesidemus, Maimon and Beck that were pivotal in the debate between sceptical and systematic interpretations of Kant, as well as articles from the *Critical Journal* of Hegel and Schelling, dating from their early alliance.)

Hegel, G.W.F. (1807) *Phänomenologie des Geistes* (Phenomenology of Spirit), trans. A.V. Miller, Oxford: Clarendon Press, 1977. (Hegel's early attempt to complete Kant's revolution by leading the reader through a series of dualistic forms of consciousness, representing the history of human thought, until the reader reaches the standpoint of absolute knowledge by seeing the dialectical development of each form into the next, and the dialectical development of the entire series into knowledge free of dualism.)

Hegel, G.W.F., Schelling, F.W.J., Hölderlin, J.C.F. (1796) *Das älteste Systemprogram; Studien zur Frühgeschichte des deutschen Idealismus*, ed. R. Bubner, Bonn: Bouvier, 1973; trans. as *The Oldest System Programme of German Idealism*, in E. Behler (ed.) *Fichte, Jacobi and Schelling: Philosophy of German Idealism*, New York: Continuum, 1985. (Written in Hegel's hand but of disputed authorship, this provides a remarkable glimpse of the origins of German idealism; for interpretation and reception-history see F.-P. Hansen's *'Das älteste Systemprogram': Rezeptionsgeschichte und Interpretation*, Berlin and New York: de Gruyter, 1989. The Bubner volume contains useful German articles on the content and authorship of the manuscript.)

Jacobi, F. (1785–1815) *The Main Philosophical Writings and the Novel Allwill*, trans. G. di Giovanni, Montreal and Kingston, London, Buffalo, NY: McGill-Queen's University Press, 1994. (Collection of important texts, with an introduction, notes and bibliography. Although Jacobi was not, strictly speaking, a German idealist, many of his ideas greatly influenced Idealism. For example, the Idealists should be understood as accepting his criticism of Kant's conception of the thing-in-itself, and as inspired by the Spinozism he brought to their attention, although Jacobi himself publicized Spinozism only in order to reject it.)

Kant, I. (1799) 'Erklärung in Beziehung auf Fichtes Wissenschaftslehre' (Open Letter on Fichte's Wissenschaftslehre), in *Kant: Philosophical Correspon-*

dence, 1759–99, ed. and trans. A. Zweig, Chicago, IL: University of Chicago Press, 1967, 253–4. (Kant publicly repudiates Fichte and Beck for claiming that the correct interpretation of his writings would be understood only from a special standpoint, according to the spirit and not the letter. Implicitly repudiated are Schelling, Hegel and all others who distinguish, in their own ways, between the letter and the spirit of Kant's philosophy.)

Maimon, S. (1790) 'Versuch über die Transcendentalphilosophie mit einem Anhang über die symbolische Erkenntnis und Anmerkungen' (Essay on Transcendental Philosophy with an Appendix on Symbolic Cognition and Annotations), in S. Maimon, *Gesammelte Werke*, ed. V. Verra, Heidelberg: G. Olms, 1965–75, vol. 2. (An influential work that presses the case against various Kantian dualisms with great clarity, and proposes a monistic solution whereby the dualisms afflicting the finite, human mind represent an imperfect yet necessary stage on the way towards the realization of the infinite, divine mind.)

Simpson, D. (ed.) (1984) *German Aesthetic and Literary Criticism: Kant, Fichte, Schelling, Schopenhauer, Hegel*, Cambridge: Cambridge University Press. (Contains texts relevant to the philosophy of art and literature.)

References and further reading

Beiser, F. (1987) *The Fate of Reason: German Philosophy from Kant to Fichte*, Cambridge, MA: Harvard University Press. (Indispensable account of the immediate reaction to Kant's revolution.)

—— (1992) *Enlightenment, Revolution and Romanticism: The Formation of Modern German Political Thought, 1792–1800*, Cambridge, MA: Harvard University Press. (Important account of the political dimension of early Idealism.)

Breazeale, D. (1981) 'Fichte's *Aenesidemus* Review and the Transformation of German Idealism', *Review of Metaphysics* 34: 545–68. (Clear, accessible account of the important role of sceptical challenges to Kant and Reinhold in the development of Fichte's thought.)

—— (1982) 'Between Kant and Fichte: Karl Leonhard Reinhold's "Elementary Philosophy"', *Review of Metaphysics* 35: 785–822. (Clear, accessible account of this neglected philosopher's important contribution to early German idealism: the idea of completing Kant's revolution through systematization.)

Cassirer, E. (1917) *Das Erkenntnisproblem in der Philosophie und Wissenschaft der neueren Zeit* (The Problem of Knowledge in the Philosophy and Science of the Modern Age), vol. 2, Darmstadt: Wissenschaftliche Buchgesellschaft. (Classic study of the development from Kant to Hegel, challenging the traditional view of that development as leading inexorably to Hegel; a useful corrective to Kroner.)

Henrich, D. (1997) *The Course of Remembrance and Other Essays on Hölderlin*, ed. E. Förster, Stanford, CA: Stanford University Press. (Important collection of essays by a leading German researcher, reporting groundbreaking work on the origins of German idealism at the University of Jena, and focusing on some neglected but influential figures.)

Kroner, R. (1921) *Von Kant bis Hegel* (From Kant to Hegel), Tübingen: JCB Mohr, 3rd edn. (The classic account of German idealism as a dialectic culminating in Hegel.)

Nauern, F.-G. (1971) *Revolution, Idealism and Human Freedom: Schelling, Hölderlin and Hegel and the Crisis of Early German Idealism*, The Hague: Martinus Nijhoff. (Accessible account of the early thought of three important figures who studied together at the Tübingen theological seminary at the time of the French revolution.)

Royce, J. (1919) *Lectures on modern idealism*, foreword by J.E. Smith, New Haven, CT: Yale University Press, 1964. (A classic, if rather outdated, account of German idealism by a major US philosopher of the nineteenth and early twentieth centuries.)

Solomon, R. (1981) *Introducing the German idealists: mock interviews with Kant, Hegel, Fichte, Schelling, Reinhold, Jacobi, Schlegel, and a letter from Schopenhauer*, Indianapolis, IN: Hackett Publishing Company. (Accessible introduction to some important figures in German idealism.)

Solomon, R. and Higgins, K. (1993) *The Age of German Idealism*, London and New York: Routledge. (Accessible and useful collection of articles on individual thinkers, well suited to beginners.)

Taylor, C. (1979) *Hegel and Modern Society*, Cambridge: Cambridge University Press. (Illuminating and accessible account of the cultural and social background against which German idealism developed.)

PAUL FRANKS

GERSON, JEAN (1363–1429)

Gerson was one of the leading theologians of the via moderna, *the 'modern way' of nominalism. A fervent critic of the 'formalists' of the* via antiqua, *Gerson stood in the Ockhamist tradition as a pastoral theologian opposed to strictly speculative questions. His overarching interests lay in the pastoral foundations of theology and opposed abstract and hence 'unedifying' metaphysical questions, as these dominated scholastic discourse in the theological faculty at Paris. He sought to mediate between increasingly polemical school disputes, arguing for the recovery of a 'biblical' theology that led away from speculative questions toward mystical encounter with God. Later known as* doctor christianissimus *(the most Christian doctor), Gerson exerted such a profound influence upon the subsequent theological horizon that one historian has aptly called the fifteenth century 'le siècle de Gerson'.*

Educated at the College of Navarre in Paris, Gerson attained his *licentia* (1381) and *magister* (1382) in arts before completing his *baccalaureus formatus* in 1390–2 and attaining the licentiate in theology in 1392. In 1395 he was appointed chancellor of Notre Dame and assumed administrative oversight for the University of Paris. Gerson's tenure of this office shaped in practical ways his approach to philosophical questions. His opposition to 'speculative' metaphysical questions that exceeded the 'revealed' truths of scripture must be set alongside his lifelong interest in 'mystical' theology (see for example his *De mystica theologia* (On Mystical Theology)), but he conceived of the latter not as an abstract or speculative form of cognition but in terms of its transformative power that led toward an experiential and affective understanding (*cognitio experimentalis et affectualis*). At the conclusion of the Council of Constance (1414–8), which Gerson attended as representative of the university and the province of Sens, he completed his important treatise *De consolatione theologiae* (On the Consolation of Theology), a dialogue about ecclesial and theological questions which sought to extend rather than simply imitate the philosophical precedent of BOETHIUS.

Gerson eventually returned to Lyons, where he took up residence at the Coelestine Priory and completed works of a wide topical range. Among these are several works devoted to epistemological questions, including a treatise exploring the relation of scholastic and mystical theology, *De elucidatione scholastica mysticae theologiae* (On the Scholastic Elucidation of Mystical Theology), and two works of fifty propositions each, devoted to the epistemological debate between realists of the *via antiqua* and nominalists of the *via moderna*, *De modis significandi* (On Modes of Signifying) and *De concordia metaphysicae cum logica* (On the Harmony of Metaphysics and Logic). Although he retained his appointment as university chancellor until his death, Gerson never returned to Paris after the council. He died on 12 July 1429, and was buried in the church of St Lawrence at Lyons.

The question of Gerson's philosophical commitments has been much disputed in recent studies. This derives in part from the moderating character of his thought, and in part from developments in his own thinking. The most convincing portrait of Gerson's mature philosophical position remains that offered by Gerhard Ritter (1922), who situates him as a philosophical theologian interested in finding a mediating position that would secure the foundation for a philosophical metaphysics on the basis of a nominalist epistemology. Gerson sought to maintain, according to Ritter, the nominalist distinction of signs and things signified, and identified 'natural reason' as limited to the former. At the same time, Gerson insisted that such signs were not devoid of true signification, and thus metaphysical arguments could hold real epistemological certitude. On the basis of Gerson's strong syncretistic tendencies, Ritter represents him as a conciliatory figure attempting to follow a middle way between the 'modern' heirs of WILLIAM OF OCKHAM and advocates of an earlier realist tradition.

Such later tendencies are already evident in his earlier program for curricular reform (see for example his letter to Pierre d'Ailly in 1401, in *Oeuvres Complètes* 2: 26–), as in his larger treatise *Contra curiositatem studentium* (Against the Curiosity of Scholars). In these writings, Gerson avoided theoretical questions by evaluating the legitimate place of *philosophia* in terms of pastoral questions and concerns. Thus he insisted that the *articuli fidei* (articles of faith) were in no way contrary to 'natural reason'; the human pursuit of knowledge should respect certain limited boundaries within which philosophical speculation might legitimately proceed. Such 'natural reasoning' should not, he argued, apply itself through 'vain curiosity' to unedifying questions removed from the actual practice of Christian life, since this often transgressed the boundaries both of reason and of faith and penetrated the hidden realm of the divine will (*secretum divinae voluntatis*). Rather, one should be guided by humility to accept as sufficient the knowledge gained by scaling the ladder of scripture (*scala scripturarum*), even though one should 'elucidate humbly [through the use of natural reason] the truth of holy scripture within the limits where this is possible' (*Contra curiositatem studentium*, in *Oeuvres Complètes* 3: 233). At stake for Gerson was how to apply reason properly to unfold the revealed truths of faith, in order to strive beyond such knowledge by mounting the 'other ladder'

leading toward the 'higher [mystical] knowledge of God' (*Contra curiositatem studentium*: 233).

Later writings, particularly his *De consolatione theologiae*, further develop this argument. Here Gerson insists that the revealed truths of scripture (*articuli fidei*), while not immediately accessible to 'natural reason,' are not on this account irrational. Applying Thomist logic to this question, he suggests that 'just as grace exceeds [but does not destroy or oppose] nature ... so does theology surpass philosophy – not by rejecting it but by taking it into servitude' (*De consolatione theologiae*, in *Oeuvres Complètes* 9: 188). Philosophy brings us to the 'summit' of natural reason and its consolations, only to yield to the higher reaches accessible only by theology. Thus *philosophia* for Gerson established a useful but limited prolegomenon for theology, finally directing us toward the 'higher' knowledge of faith revealed in and through the church. On the basis of such a mediating position, it is not surprising to note that the official controversy over nominalism that took place in the later fifteenth century found Parisian nominalists seeking to claim Gerson as an authority endorsing their position, while the official edict condemning this movement did not include him among the 'new doctors' condemned.

See also: NOMINALISM; WILLIAM OF OCKHAM

List of works

Gerson, J. (1401–26) *Opera omnia*, ed. P. Glorieux, *Oeuvres Complètes*, 10 vols, Paris: Desclée, 1960–73. (This is the standard critical edition of Gerson's works. Gerson's extensive writings were already compiled and published in several editions during the later fifteenth century, the first by Johannes Koelhoff, Cologne, 1483/4, and the second by Geiler von Kaysersberg and Petrus Schott, Strassburg, 1488 (repr. 1489, 1494). An early modern edition was prepared by E. du Pin, *Opera omnia*, 4 vols, Antwerp, 1706.)

—— (1402) *Contra curiositatem studentium* (Against the Curiosity of Scholars), in P. Glorieux (ed.) *Oeuvres Complètes*, Paris: Desclée, 1960–73. (Treatise on educational reform.)

—— (1402–3) *De mystica theologia* (On Mystical Theology), in P. Glorieux (ed.) *Oeuvres Complètes*, Paris: Desclée, 1960–73. (Reflects Gerson's lifelong interest in mystical theology.)

—— (1418) *De consolatione theologiae* (On the Consolation of Theology), in P. Glorieux (ed.) *Oeuvres Complètes*, Paris: Desclée, 1960–73. (Influenced by Boethius, Gerson here argues that the revealed truths of scripture are not irrational simply because they are not immediately accessible to natural reason.)

—— (1424) *De elucidatione scholastica mysticae theologiae* (On the Scholastic Elucidation of Mystical Theology), in P. Glorieux (ed.) *Oeuvres Complètes*, Paris: Desclée, 1960–73. (Treatise exploring the relationship between scholasticism and mystical theology.)

—— (1426) *De modis significandi* (On the Mode of Signifying), in P. Glorieux (ed.) *Oeuvres Complètes*, Paris: Desclée, 1960–73. (Propositions exploring the debate between realism and nominalism.)

—— (1426) *De concordia metaphysicae cum logica* (On the Harmony of Metaphysics and Logic), in P. Glorieux (ed.) *Oeuvres Complètes*, Paris: Desclée, 1960–73. (Propositions exploring the debate between realism and nominalism.)

References and further reading

Burger, C. (1986) *Aedificatio, Fructus, Utilitas. Johannes Gerson als Professor der Theologie und Kanzler der Universität Paris* (Edification, Fruition, Usefulness: Jean Gerson as Professor of Theology and Chancellor of the University of Paris), Tübingen: J.C.B. Mohr (Paul Siebeck). (Critical overview of Gerson's university writings to 1415, emphasizing the pastoral tone and ecclesial context of his thought.)

Burrows, M. (1991) *Jean Gerson and 'De Consolatione Theologiae' (1418): The Consolation of a Biblical and Reforming Theology for a Disordered Age*, Tübingen: J.C.B. Mohr (Paul Siebeck). (Oriented toward Gerson's writings from 1415, with opening discussion of current Gerson historiography, full bibliography and detailed consideration of how pastoral and ecclesiological concerns shaped philosophical and theological arguments.)

Combes, A. (1945–72) *Essai sur la critique de Ruysbroeck par Gerson* (A Study of Gerson's Criticism of Ruysbroeck), Paris: Vrin, 3 vols. (Detailed analysis of Gerson's theological criticism of Ruysbroeck's union mysticism, with careful attention to theological and soteriological questions.)

—— (1963–4) *La théologie mystique de Gerson. Profil de son évolution* (Gerson's Mystical Theology: Profile of its Develpment), Paris: Vrin, 2 vols. (Masterly survey of Gerson's mystical theology, early and late, with detailed discussion of how his thought related to that of his contemporaries.)

Delaruelle, E. (1964) *L'Eglise au temps du Grand Schisme et de la crise conciliaire* (The Church from the Time of the Great Schism to the Conciliar Crisis), Brussels: Bloud & Gay, 1964. (Standard French study of the period, emphasizing the relationship of institutional and intellectual developments.)

* Ritter, G. (1922) *Studien zur Spätscholastik* (Studies of Late Scholasticism), vol. 2, *Via antiqua und via moderna auf den deutschen Universitäten des XV. Jahrhunderts* (The *Via Antiqua* and *Via Moderna* in German Universities in the Fifteenth Century), Heidelberg: Carl Winter. (Careful, technically demanding study of late-scholastic philosophical debates between advocates of 'old' and 'new' schools; unsurpassed by subsequent studies.)

Vignaux, P. (1948) *Nominalisme au XIVe siècle* (Nominalism to the Fourteenth Century), Paris: Vrin. (Broad and masterful orientation to late medieval nominalism, with subtle interpretation of both philosophical issues and their theological consequences.)

MARK S. BURROWS

GERSONIDES (1288–1344)

Living all his life in southern France, Levi ben Gershom, known as Gersonides in Latin texts, was an accomplished astronomer and mathematician as well as a philosopher. A prolific and engaged exegete, Gersonides wrote biblical commentaries that are still studied today. His philosophical magnum opus, Milhamot ha-Shem (The Wars of the Lord), reached original and often unorthodox conclusions regarding many of the great issues of medieval philosophical theology. It denied creation ex nihilo, preferring a modified version of the doctrine of formatio mundi traditionally ascribed to Plato (formation of the world from pre-existing matter). It qualified traditional doctrines of divine omniscience by denying God's determinate knowledge of future contingent events. And it confined personal immortality to the rational portion of the soul, that is, the intellect.

1 **Life and works**
2 **Creation**
3 **Divine knowledge**
4 **Immortality**
5 **Conclusion**

1 Life and works

Known in traditional Hebrew sources by the acronym Ralbag (Rabbi Levi ben Gershom), Gersonides was born in Provence and lived there all his life. Besides his philosophical work, he made important contributions to astronomy, mathematics, and biblical exegesis. Both a theorist and an observer in astronomy, he held to the Ptolemic system but rejected the epicycles and other aspects of the medieval Ptolemaic worldview. His commentaries on the Pentateuch, Proverbs, Job, the Former Prophets and several of the smaller Hagiographia are full of philosophy, which he saw as the key to the true understanding of Scripture. He continued the Jewish tradition of writing supercommentaries on Averroes' commentaries on Aristotle, but his original philosophical work, *Milhamot ha-Shem*, written in Hebrew in six books, covers the full range of medieval psychology, metaphysics, philosophy of nature and cosmology. Gersonides was less interested in moral and political philosophy, but his biblical commentaries do reflect on these topics. This essay will consider three of the central issues treated in *Milhamot ha-Shem*: creation, divine knowledge, and immortality.

2 Creation

Creation was a persistent problem in medieval philosophy (see CREATION AND CONSERVATION, RELIGIOUS DOCTRINE OF). Both Aristotelians and the Neoplatonists regarded the universe as eternal; yet the Bible and the Qur'an teach creation. Since Gersonides believed that philosophy and the Torah teach the same truth, the apparent disagreement needed to be resolved. His admired philosophical predecessors Averroes (see IBN RUSHD) and Moses MAIMONIDES had taught two contrary theses: Averroes, that the universe is eternal, Maimonides, that it was created *ex nihilo* but that neither the world's creation nor its eternity is demonstrable. Gersonides rejected both views in favour of *formatio mundi*: creation was not bringing something into existence from nothing but the organizing of an eternal, hitherto formless matter. This theory, Gersonides urged, is demonstrable. He devoted the longest part of *Milhamot ha-Shem* to formulating numerous arguments in support of some form of creation. These fall into three distinct groups.

(1) Clearly favouring teleology in metaphysics and cosmology, Gersonides makes the classic argument from design a key proof not just of the existence of God but of creation as he understands it. Anything with teleological properties, he argues, must be the work of a purposive agent – unless it is a chance phenomenon. Focusing on the heavenly bodies, eternal beings for ARISTOTLE (§16), and certainly not chance phenomena in Aristotelian philosophy, Gersonides urges that these do exhibit teleological properties, most plainly in the case of the sun, whose beneficent functioning is obvious. The system and arrangement of the heavenly bodies in general similarly manifest order and design and so show them to be products of purpose and intent, thus, created (Milhamot ha-Shem: 6.1, 7 and 9).

(2) Gersonides reinforces this argument with the 'particularization argument' often favoured by Muslim theologians of the *kalam* (see ISLAMIC THEOLOGY). Aristotle's heavenly bodies all consist of a fifth element (the 'quintessence' of the scholastics). Yet they exhibit diverse properties. Mars, for example, emits a reddish light, whereas Venus has a bluish cast. Aristotle's attempt to explain such properties in terms of distances from the earth fails, since Saturn and Jupiter both emit a whitish light, although Saturn is much further from the earth than Jupiter. Since chance was excluded by Aristotle himself, the observed differences can be explained only by reference to a 'producing agent' (Milhamot ha-Shem: 6.1, 8).

(3) Relying on Aristotle's doctrine (*Physics* III 4–8) that an actual infinity is impossible, Gersonides argues, in the style of *kalam*, that the world's eternity would entail an actual infinity. Among his several variations on this long familiar line of argument one is especially interesting, since it is not invalidated by modern astronomy or mathematics: Gersonides argues from our intuition that the past is closed and the future open. Unlike the future, where it is often not determined whether p or ¬p, for all states of affairs in the past it is already the case that p or ¬p; that is, the past is completely determinate. Each fact about the past is real: it is a definite outcome of a preceding state of affairs and has causal consequences, many of which have lasting effects. In this sense the past is always with us. To Gersonides this means that unlike the future, which to a considerable extent is empty, the past is actual. If it were infinite, we would have an actual infinity (Milhamot ha-Shem: 6.1, 10–11) (ETERNITY OF THE WORLD, MEDIEVAL VIEWS ON).

Concluding that the world must be created, Gersonides goes on to argue that its creation cannot be *ex nihilo*. Here he relies on Aristotle's physics and on the fact that familiar cases of generation are always from, or out of, something. He also appeals to the idea that in nature 'like produces like'. Anticipating the critics of Cartesian mind-body interaction, he finds it implausible to say that pure form could bring bodies into being from no pre-existing matter. God, an incorporeal being, could no more create something physical *ex nihilo* than a stallion and a mare could produce a bear.

Defenders of *ex nihilo* creation might not feel troubled by these objections, since creation for them is no ordinary natural event but the 'mother of miracles'. Why should we expect it to conform to the familiar natural laws? But Gersonides goes further. Creation *ex nihilo*, he argues, would entail a vacuum, both before and after the event. And a vacuum, it was widely assumed, was not just a natural but a logical impossibility. In the beginning, according to the adherents of absolute creation, there was only God; then a world was made. If this world was preceded by and subsequently located in empty space – since it is a finite body – then there would inevitably be a vacuum not only prior to the world's creation, but even afterwards, unless the world were infinite in size, a possibility that Aristotle was generally thought to have ruled out (*Physics* IV 7; *On the Heavens* III 2; see Milhamot ha-Shem 6.1, 17–8).

In response to these difficulties, Gersonides adopted the account that medieval thinkers usually thought of as Plato's: the Creator fashioned the universe out of a pre-existing matter (see PLATO §16). Although eternal, this matter was not divine. For it was unstable and utterly imperfect, having no intrinsic form or shape. 'Not preserving its shape', it is no competition to God, who is immutable and utterly perfect. Matter is not worthy of worship. It is simply the raw material from which our world was manufactured. It is also the source of all disorder and defect – including moral imperfection (Perush 'al Sefer Iyyov (Commentary on Job – introduction).

Gersonides caps his cosmology by arguing that the universe is indestructible, although generated, contrary to Aristotle, who held that whatever is generated is destroyed (*On the Heavens* I 12). Both Plato and MAIMONIDES had believed the world indestructible, but they ascribed its endurance to God's will (see Plato, *Timaeus* 41a–b; Maimonides, *Guide to the Perplexed* II 27). Gersonides went further, arguing that the cosmos is intrinsically indestructible, since it contains no inherent cause of corruption. God not only would not but could not destroy it; for God would have no reason to destroy what is as perfect as it can be. Once created, then, the world endures forever (Milhamot ha-Shem: 6.1, 16).

3 Divine knowledge

Gersonides deviates from familiar views on divine omniscience as well. Ever since AUGUSTINE, most medieval thinkers had opted for some kind of compatibilist solution to the venerable difficulties of reconciling divine foreknowledge with human freedom. Not so Gersonides. Embracing the position of the 'philosophers' (that is, Neoplatonic Aristotelians), he concludes that an eternal and incorporeal God cannot know spatio-temporal particulars as such, least of all, future contingent events. If God knew these as particulars, they would lose their contingency. In an argument that anticipates the thinking of recent philosophers, Gersonides preserves

human freedom even at the cost of limiting God's knowledge: God knows the general laws governing human behaviour – how humans in general would react to a divine command to kill their only child, and that it is possible for someone to be willing to do so. But God does not know whether Abraham or Jephtha is that person. For humans have the power to act contrary to the biological-psychological generalities of human behaviour, and God knows that these patterns can be broken by human freedom (see FREE WILL; OMNISCIENCE).

Gersonides did not regard his solution as a weakening of God's omniscience, since an omniscient being knows only what is knowable. Future contingent events are not knowable in principle. If they were, they would forfeit their contingency (see Aristotle, *On Interpretation* IX). If it is objected that this means that God lacks knowledge of particulars that even a child might know, Gersonides is ready with an answer: ignorance of spatio-temporal events is not a genuine deficiency in a being who transcends the spatio-temporal order.

Thomas AQUINAS admitted that God would not know future events as future but as 'eternally present' (*Summa theologiae* Ia.14.13). Gersonides goes further, holding that an eternal being does not know temporal particulars at all. For, as Aristotle claims, genuine knowledge is of the universal (*On the Soul* II 5).

How then can we make sense of the biblical stories in which God speaks to individuals such as Abraham and Moses at specific times? Here Gersonides calls on the aid of the highly regarded twelfth-century biblical exegete, Abraham IBN EZRA, who had reached the same conclusion about divine knowledge. Relying heavily on the traditional hermeneutical liberty to interpret biblical texts so as to reconcile them with philosophical knowledge (Milhamot ha-Shem 3.6), he adapts his reading of Scripture to fit his philosophical conclusions; for example, Bilaam's donkey didn't really speak: that incident was just one episode in Bilaam's prophetic dream. More literal readers of the Bible might find the outcome strained. But Gersonides' boldness is noteworthy and admirable: he does not allow even the authority of text or tradition to subvert his philosophical conclusions but bends both to accommodate the truth as he believes argument to have shown it.

4 Immortality

Gersonides shows similar independence regarding immortality. By his time the question had become quite focused: what exactly in humans is immortal and how does it become immortal? Within Gersonides' philosophical orbit the standard reply was that the human intellect becomes immortal through 'conjunction', or linkage with the 'active intellect'. This active intellect was a transcendent, incorporeal cosmic intelligence responsible not only for human intellectual knowledge (including prophecy) but also for informing all things with their objective natures and thus for the governance of biological reproduction and development. The idea of the active intellect stems from a somewhat elusive paragraph in Aristotle's *On the Soul* (III 5), which speaks of an active intellect that is a precondition of human understanding. In interpreting this passage, Gersonides follows the tradition laid down by ALEXANDER OF APHRODISIAS (*fl. c.*AD 200), who regarded the active intellect as a transcendent and eternal power but the human intellect as a material disposition or capacity of the body, specifically, of the imagination. Other interpreters such as THEMISTIUS and Avicenna (see IBN SINA) believed the human intellect to be an incorporeal substance, inherently capable of immortality. How could Gersonides, as a follower of Alexander's tradition, account for immortality, if the human intellect was just a biological function and thus susceptible to corruption?

Unlike Alexander or Averroes (whose position is closer to that of Themistius), Gersonides rejected 'linkage' with the active intellect. He did not think that we ever reach an intellectual level that would allow so intimate a bond with the transcendent. Besides, the Averroist version of 'conjunction' implied the obliteration of individuality: all minds become one in the active intellect. Such loss of identity was objectionable both philosophically and religiously. What Gersonides was seeking was personal immortality.

If the human intellect is only a capacity of the imagination to acquire knowledge, by abstraction from and generalization about sense-data, albeit with the aid of the active intellect, what persists after physical death? Gersonides turns for help to Plato: although the senses are needed initially to acquire the data from which we derive our general concepts, these concepts are grounded not only in the natural world, in the types, or natural kinds, of things, but also in the active intellect itself, which exhibits the 'rational order' (a favourite phrase of Gersonides') of the terrestrial world. Like Plato's eternal paradigm (*Timaeus* 28–9) the rational order in the active intellect is an everlasting blueprint for the natural world (see PLATO §16). In so far as the human mind apprehends, or 'participates', in this plan it becomes incorruptible and everlasting. This is the meaning of the expression 'acquired intellect' as used in Alexander's psychology. That intellect in us is the repository of the intellectual capital our minds have accrued. Immortality is achieved not through conjunction with the active intellect but by our individual intellectual efforts and successes. Since what is immortal is our own knowledge, unique to each individual, the immortality we are assured is personal.

5 Conclusion

Although working within a well-defined philosophical tradition that continually tried to show its religious fidelity, Gersonides departed from some of the central doctrines of traditional medieval faith. His loyalty to biblical creation led him to reject Aristotle's notion of the eternity of the universe; but his commitment to Aristotle's physics and metaphysics forced him to reject *creatio ex nihilo* as well. In his theories of divine omniscience and human immortality, he sided with the 'philosophers' more than with the 'theologians'. Yet he did not reject divine omniscience and he worked creatively to sustain individual immortality. His views provoked much controversy, and the *Milhamot ha-Shem* received hostile criticism (notably from CRESCAS). But Gersonides' biblical commentaries, which often voice his philosophical conclusions, are still studied by traditional Jews. Like Maimonides, Gersonides could think radically and originally, even to the point of heterodoxy, but could win the acceptance of the religious community through a combination of philosophical acumen, biblical and rabbinic erudition, and a life conducted within the norms and traditions of practice of the community.

See also: ARISTOTELIANISM IN ISLAMIC PHILOSOPHY; ARISTOTELIANISM, MEDIEVAL; ETERNITY OF THE WORLD, MEDIEVAL VIEWS OF; GOD, CONCEPTS OF; MAIMONIDES, M.; NATURAL PHILOSOPHY, MEDIEVAL; PLATONISM, MEDIEVAL; SOUL, NATURE AND IMMORTALITY OF THE

List of works

Levi ben Gershom (Gersonides) (1317–29) *Milhamot ha-Shem* (The Wars of the Lord), Leipzig: Lorck, 1866; Books 1–4 trans. S. Feldman, *The Wars of the Lord*, Philadelphia, PA: Jewish Publication Society, 1984, 1987, 2 vols. (Covers the full range of medieval psychology, metaphysics, philosophy of nature and cosmology. The longest part of the work is devoted to formulating numerous arguments in support of some form of creation. Volume 3 of the Jewish Publication Society edition is due to be published, containing Books 5 and 6, a bibliography and indices.)
—— (1325) *Perush 'al Sefer Iyyov* (Commentary on the Book of Job), trans. A. Lassen, *Commentary of*

Levi ben Gershom on the Book of Job, New York: Bloch Publishing House, 1946. (In the introduction to his commentary, Gersonides makes the argument that matter is not worthy of worship. This argument suggests that matter is simply the raw material from which our world was manufactured, and that it is the source of all disorder and defect – including moral imperfection.)

—— (1319) *Sefer ha-Heqqesh ha-Yashar* (Book of the Correct Syllogism), trans. C. Manekin, *The Logic of Gersonides: A Translation of the Sefer ha-Heqqesh ha-Yashar*, Dordrecht: Kluwer Academic Publishers, 1992. (Influenced by the works of Aristotle and Averroes, Gersonides wrote this work, criticizing several arguments of Aristotle.)

—— (1329–38) *Perush 'al ha-Torah* (Commentary on the Torah), ed. J. Levy, *Perushei Ralbag 'al ha-Torah*, Jerusalem: Mossad Ha-Rav Kook, 1992, 1994, 2 vols. (The two volumes which comprise the Levy edition are the parts of the commentary on Genesis (1992) and Exodus (1994).)

—— (1328–40) *The Astronomy of Levi ben Gershom (1288–1344)*, trans. with commentary by B. Goldstein, New York: Springer, 1985. (This translation is of the first 20 chapters of the astronomical-mathematical portion of Book 5, part 1 of the *Milhamot ha-Shem*.)

References and further reading

Dahan, G. (ed.) (1991) *Gersonides en son temps*, Louvain and Paris: E. Peeters. (A collection of recent essays on Gersonides' life and thought, with a good bibliography.)

Feldman, S. (1967) 'Gersonides' Proofs for the Creation of the Universe', *Proceedings of the American Academy of Jewish Research* 35: 113–37. (Detailed analysis of Gersonides' various proofs for the creation of the universe.)

—— (1975) 'Platonic Themes in Gersonides' Cosmology', *Salo W. Baron Jubilee Volume*, ed. S. Lieberman and A. Hyman (Jerusalem: American Academy for Jewish Research) 1: 383–405. (Intensive discussion of Gersonides' critique of *ex nihilo* creation and defence of creation out of eternal formless matter; arguments for the indestructibility of a created universe.)

—— (1978) 'Gersonides on the Possibility of Conjunction with the Agent Intellect', *Association for Jewish Studies Review* 3: 99–120. (Philosophical and historical analysis of Gersonides' critique of Averroes' theory of intellect and immortality.)

Goldstein, B. (1969) 'Preliminary Remarks on Levi ben Gerson's Contribution to Astronomy', *Proceedings of the Israel Academy of Sciences and Humanities* 3 (9): 239–254. (A good introduction to Gersonides' astronomy.)

Kellner, M. (1980) 'Gersonides on the Problem of Volitional Creation', *Hebrew Union College Annual* 51: 111–28. (A critical analysis of Gersonides' doctrine of creation, especially his rejection of *ex nihilo* creation.)

Manekin, C. (1985) 'Preliminary Observations on Gersonides' Logical Writings', *Proceedings of the American Academy for Jewish Research* 52: 85–113. (A good but technical treatment of some of the more significant issues in Gersonides' logic.)

Rudavsky, T. (1983) 'Divine Omniscience and Future Contingents in Gersonides', *Journal of the History of Philosophy* 21: 513–36. (Good but difficult discussion of Gersonides' doctrine of divine omniscience, focusing upon its philosophical adequacy and fidelity to Scripture.)

Samuelson, N. (1972) 'Gersonides' Account of God's Knowledge', *Journal of the History of Philosophy* 10: 399–416. (Comprehensive philosophical analysis of Gersonides' doctrine of divine foreknowledge.)

Touati, C. (1973) *La Pensée philosophique et théologique de Gersonide*, Paris: Les Editions de Minuit. (The most comprehensive study of Gersonides' philosophy.)

Wolfson, H. (1953) 'Maimonides and Gersonides on Divine Attributes as Ambiguous Terms', *Mordecai M. Kaplan Jubilee Volume* (ed. M. Davis, New York: Jewish Theological Seminary of America), 515–30. (Classic treatment of the philological-textual background of this problem.)

SEYMOUR FELDMAN

GESTALT PSYCHOLOGY

The term 'Gestalt' was introduced into psychology by the Austrian philosopher Christian von Ehrenfels. 'Gestalt', in colloquial German, means 'shape' or 'structure'. Ehrenfels demonstrates in his essay of 1890 that there are certain inherently structural features of experience that must be acknowledged in addition to simple tones, colours and other mental 'atoms' or 'elements' if we are to do justice to the objects towards which perception, memory and abstract thinking are directed. His essay initiated a reaction against the then still dominant atomism in psychology, a reaction that led in turn to the ideas on 'cerebral integration' of the so-called Berlin school of Gestalt psychology and thence to contemporary investigations of 'neural networks' in cognitive science. Many of the specific empirical facts discovered by the Gestaltists about the perception of movement and contour, about perceptual constancy and perceptual illusions, and about the role of 'good form' in perception and memory have been absorbed into psychology as a whole.

1 **Ehrenfels v. Mach**
2 **The Austro-Italian production theory**
3 **The Berlin school and contemporary influence**

1 Ehrenfels v. Mach

Christian von Ehrenfels belonged to an impressive list of thinkers – including also Edmund Husserl, Alexius Meinong and Carl Stumpf – who were students of Franz Brentano. One of Ehrenfels' central concerns was a criticism of the treatment of complex presentation put forward by Ernst Mach. For Mach (1886), the only satisfactory story of the universe is one told exclusively in terms of sensory atoms. All other putative entities – including not only melodies and shapes but also bodies and selves – are, he says, merely 'auxiliary aids' introduced 'for purposes of thought economy'. Only the 'elements', sensations, are real (see MACH, E.; PHENOMENALISM; SENSE-DATA).

How, then, do we account for the fact that we recognize different spatial figures as the same? By means of an appeal, Mach says, to additional elementary sensations *outside* the sphere of visual perception (1865). When I see a square, for example, then in addition to the perceived elements (the points, lines or segments) there is also a peculiar nervous or 'muscular' sensation that I have as a result of the innervations of the muscles of my eyes, a sensation that is repeated, spontaneously and without any effort on my part, whenever I see a similar figure.

But how can this account do justice to the unity of complex experiences: why is the muscular sensation not just a further item super-added to the sum of elementary visual sensations? How can Mach's account be generalized to other sensory modalities? As Ehrenfels saw, such additional sensations can at best explain our perception of what is complex only in relation to what is presented simultaneously, that is, simple spatial figures, simple smells, simple musical chords. A melody, however, is a unitary complex that is extended in time, and there is no point at which some putative associated elementary feeling-sensation could be associated with *all* the separate auditory sensations. Through these and other arguments, atomistic psychology of the sort that Mach defended was replaced in its position of dominance by the tradition of Gestalt psychology.

Ehrenfels (1890) pointed out that our perceptual experience of complex objects is something distinct from the experience of a mere sum of sensory elements. This is shown also by the fact that we can apprehend the same shape in association with sensory elements that, taken individually, have nothing in common: we can recognize the shape of a head, for example, by looking at a drawing or shadow, just as we can recognize a melody that has been transposed into a different key.

Consider the relation between the successive notes in a melody and the melody itself. Ehrenfels' proposal is that wherever we have a relation of this sort, between a complex of sensory elements and a single invariant structure, we are to conceive the latter as a new sort of abstract entity that he calls a 'Gestalt quality'. A surprisingly wide variety of Gestalt qualities can be distinguished on this basis, including mixed Gestalt qualities, such as dances, marches, operas, that arise when data from different sensory modalities are combined. Ehrenfels allows also higher levels of Gestalt complexity, where Gestalt qualities themselves would be combined together in cumulative fashion.

2 The Austro-Italian production theory

For Ehrenfels, the Gestalt quality exists as an object of experience if an appropriate constellation of elements is present in sensation. For MEINONG and his followers in Graz, however, the Gestalt quality is an abstract 'object of higher order' that is the product of a specific sort of cognitive processing. As Benussi (1914) saw, if Gestalt presentations are brought about on the basis of stimulus-presentations via additional cognitive processing, such presentations can display a certain 'Gestalt-ambiguity' in relation to the stimulus. Standard examples of such ambiguities are afforded by the Necker cube and the 'duck–rabbit' figure:

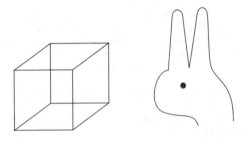

Benussi and his colleagues in Graz were the first to subject this 'Gestalt-switch' phenomenon (the phenomenon of 'seeing as') to detailed theoretical and experimental treatment (see also WITTGENSTEIN,

L. J. J.). Benussi went on to establish a tradition of experimental Gestalt psychology in Italy that, through the work of Kanizsa, Bozzi and others, is still alive today, producing valuable results, for example in the investigation of transparency, and of subjective contours or 'amodal' completion, as in such figures as the so-called Kanizsa triangle:

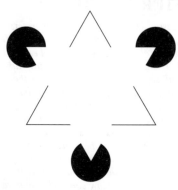

Associated investigations were carried out also by Albert Michotte and his school in Louvain, who showed on the basis of work with simple cartoon figures of moving discs and squares how, even in the absence of any specific sensory stimulus, we can enjoy a perceptual awareness of causality and of other 'functional connections'.

3 The Berlin school and contemporary influence

The Berlin school initiated in Stumpf's laboratory by Max Wertheimer, Wolfgang Köhler and Kurt Koffka also studied phenomenal motion. Wertheimer discovered that, when subjects are exposed under certain conditions to two alternately flashing lights a short distance apart, they have an experience of movement back and forth from the one to the other, what he called the 'phi-phenomenon' (the basis of cinematography). The phi-phenomenon is clearly not a matter of any discrete and independent 'elementary' sensory data: what one perceives is, as Wertheimer says, a certain *sui generis* dynamic character of 'across' (see SENSE-DATA).

From the perspective of the Berlin school, moreover, we should speak not of 'sensory presentations' or 'sensory data' but always rather of activity at the cortical and peripheral ends of sensory nerves. The perceived Gestalt, too, is not abstract on the Berlin theory but a part of nature. It is an integral whole that includes among its parts the putative sensory data experienced 'integrally' together by the perceiving subject. Later, J.J. Gibson sought to use this Gestaltist naturalism as the basis of a 'direct realist' theory

according to which acts of perception would be directed towards parts of the environment of the perceiving subject, including edges, surfaces and other 'affordances' (Katz 1987; VISION §§2–3).

Most characteristic of the Berlin school is its account of the relation between conscious phenomena and the brain events that underlie them. Köhler (1920) advanced the postulate of 'psychophysical isomorphism' according to which conscious events and brain events would be related by 'real structural properties' that they shared in common. This view has been described as the first conception of psychic activity that made possible a serviceable physiological approach to the workings of the mind in the modern sense. Yet Köhler's own variant of the isomorphism hypothesis fared badly in a number of crucial experiments in mid-century, experiments which coincided with the geographic dispersal of the Berlin school and also with the deprivation of its prior position of dominance.

While many results and concerns of the Gestaltists came to be absorbed into standard textbook psychology in mid-century, the Gestaltist label was normally dropped. Gestalt ideas have been revivified of late also by cognitive scientists, for example in work on imagery, on prototypes in categorization and learning, on naïve or qualitative physics, and in the work of the so-called 'cognitive linguists' who, like the Gestaltists, see human cognition as a part of nature, and who seek an integrated account of its various facets.

See also: CONNECTIONISM; PERCEPTION

References and further reading

Ash, M.G. (1995) *Gestalt Psychology in German Culture 1890–1967: Holism and the Quest for Objectivity*, Cambridge and New York: Cambridge University Press. (Definitive history of the Berlin school.)

* Benussi, V. (1914) 'Gesetze der inadäquaten Gestaltauffassung' (Laws of Inadequate Comprehension of Gestalt), *Archiv für die gesamte Psychologie* 32: 396–419. (On Gestalt ambiguity and other forms of inadequacy of Gestalt perception especially as exemplified in the experience of optical illusions.)

* Ehrenfels, C.V. (1890) 'Über "Gestaltqualitäten"', *Vierteljahrsschrift für wissenschaftliche Philosophie* 14: 242–92; repr. in *Philosophische Schriften* (Philosophical Writings), vol. 3, *Psychologie, Ethik, Erkenntnistheorie* (Psychology, Ethics, Theory of Knowledge), ed. R. Fabian, Munich and Vienna: Philosophia, 1993; trans. 'On "Gestalt Qualities"',

in Smith (1998), 82–117. (Introduction of 'Gestalt' as a technical term of psychology.)

Kanizsa, G. (1979) *Organization in Vision: Essays on Gestalt Perception*, New York: Praeger. (Classic papers by a leading contemporary representative of the Austro-Italian Gestalt school.)

* Katz, S. (1987) 'Is Gibson a Relativist?', in A. Costall and A. Still (eds) *Cognitive Psychology in Question*, Brighton: Harvester, 115–27. (On problems with Gibson's 'direct realism'.)

Koffka, K. (1915) 'Beiträge zur Psychologie der Gestalt. III Zur Grundlegung der Wahrnehmungspsychologie. Eine Auseinandersetzung mit V. Benussi' (Contributions to Gestalt Psychology. III On the Foundations of the Psychology of Perception. A debate with V. Benussi), *Zeitschrift für Psychologie* 73: 11–90. (Early statement of Gestaltist critique of the doctrine of elementary sense-data.)

* Köhler, W. (1920) *Die physischen Gestalten in Ruhe und im stationären Zustand. Eine naturphilosophische Untersuchung* (Physical Gestalts at Rest and in the Stationary State. An Investigation in Natural Philosophy), Braunschweig: Vieweg. (Classic work on Gestalts in the physical, biological and psychological domains.)

* Mach, E. (1865) 'Bemerkungen zur Lehre vom räumlichen Sehen' (Observations on the Theory of Spatial Vision), *Zeitschrift für Philosophie und philosophische Kritik* 46: 1–5; trans. in *Popular-Scientific Lectures*, La Salle, IL: Open Court, 1943. (Introduces the view of complex perception as a function of 'muscular sensations'.)

* —— (1886) *Beiträge zur Analyse der Empfindungen*, Jena: Fischer; trans. C.M. Williams, *Contributions to the Analysis of Sensations*, Chicago, IL: Open Court, 1897. (Classic statement of Mach's phenomenalism, and of the view that entities are categorized as 'mind' and 'matter' not because of intrinsic qualities but because of the relational contexts in which they occur.)

Michotte, A. (1963) *The Perception of Causality*, London: Methuen. (Classic treatment of causality; demonstrates the baselessness of Hume's assertion that causality is not perceived, by revealing the precise conditions under which there occur perceptions of a range of different types of causality.)

Smith, B. (ed.) (1988) *Foundations of Gestalt Theory*, Munich and Vienna: Philosophia. (Survey of Gestalt tradition with extensive annotated bibliography; includes translations also of writings on the logic of Gestalt by Kurt Grelling and Paul Oppenheimer.)

Smith, B. and Casati, R. (1994) 'Naïve Physics', *Philosophical Psychology* 7 (2): 225–44. (Study of Gestaltist and other early studies of naïve and qualitative physics.)

BARRY SMITH

GETTIER PROBLEMS

The expression 'the Gettier problem' refers to one or another problem exposed by Edmund Gettier when discussing the relation between several examples that he constructed and analyses of knowing advanced by various philosophers, including Plato in the Theatetus. *Gettier's examples appear to run counter to these 'standard' or 'traditional' analyses. A few philosophers take this appearance to be deceptive and regard the genuine problem revealed by Gettier to be: 'How can one show that Gettier's examples are not really counterexamples to the standard analyses?' But most philosophers take seriously the problem which is the central concern of this entry: 'How can such standard analyses be altered so that Gettier's cases do not constitute counterexamples to the modified analyses (and without opening the analyses to further objections?)'.*

Gettier's short paper spawned many important, ongoing projects in contemporary epistemology – for instance, attempts to add a fourth condition of knowing to the traditional analyses, attempts to replace some conditions of those analyses, such as externalist accounts of knowing or justification (causal theories and reliability theories), and revived interest . in scepticism, including an investigation of the deductive closure principle. Difficulties uncovered at each stage of this research have generated an ever more sophisticated set of accounts of knowing and justification, as well as a wealth of examples useful for testing proposed analyses. In spite of the vast literature that Gettier's brief paper elicited, there is still no widespread agreement as to whether the Gettier problem has been solved, nor as to what constitutes the most promising line of research.

1 **Gettier-type cases**
2 **Defeasibility analyses**
3 **Causal analyses and proper functioning**
4 **The role of false propositions**

1 Gettier-type cases

Clarifying the Gettier problem as most philosophers have seen it ('How can the standard analyses be altered so that Gettier-type cases do not constitute counterexamples to the modified analyses, and without opening the analyses to further objections?') involves clarifying the terms 'a standard analysis' and

'Gettier-type cases'. We may here sidestep concern with the former (but see Shope 1981) by rephrasing the problem as: 'What aspect of a correct analysis of one's knowing that *p* prevents Gettier-type cases from constituting counterexamples to it?' Philosophers who adopt the broadest perspective regard a Gettier-type case as any situation where justified, true believing falls short of knowing. Others are influenced by the manner in which they expect the central problem to be resolved. For example, those who think that the counterexamples in question can be avoided by clauses in a correct analysis ruling out the falsity of specific types of propositions to which the knower is related will characterize Gettier-type cases as situations where knowledge is absent because various propositions are false. Those who hope to avoid the counterexamples by strictures on the durability or degree of justification of one's believing that *p* may prefer to define 'Gettier-type case' by mentioning aspects of such justification. Alternatively, Alvin Plantinga (1993b) suggests that Gettier-type cases involve a slight mismatch between the proper functioning of one's cognitive equipment and one's circumstances.

Approaches to resolving the central problem have been too multifarious for a brief summary. So, setting aside differences over what constitutes an analysis (Shope 1981, and forthcoming), consider how variations on the following important Gettier-type case (Lehrer 1965) impact on a number of prominent attempts to analyse knowing:

Mr Nogot: Somebody in one's office, Mr Nogot, has given evidence, *e*, that completely justifies one in believing that *f*: 'Mr Nogot, who is in the office, owns a Ford'. Evidence *e* consists in such things as Nogot's having been reliable in dealings with one in the past, having just said to one that he owns a Ford, and having just shown legal documents confirming it. From the proposition that *f*, one deduces and thereby comes to believe that *p*: 'Somebody in the office owns a Ford'. Unsuspectedly, Nogot has been lying and it is someone else in the office who happens to own a Ford. One has true, justified belief that *p* but not knowledge that *p*.

This case differs slightly from one of Gettier's original (1963) examples, in which one notices that by picking at random a city name such as 'Barcelona', one can deduce from the unsuspectedly false proposition that *f'*, 'Jones owns a Ford', the conclusion that *p'*, 'Either Jones owns a Ford or Brown is in Barcelona', which one proceeds to believe on the grounds of the proposition that *f'*.

In Gettier's other original example, one justifiably believes the unsuspectedly false proposition that *f''*:

'Jones, who is not myself, is the man who will get the job, and Jones has ten coins in his pocket', and one sees that it entails that *p''*: 'The man who will get the job has ten coins in his pocket', which one then believes on the grounds of the proposition that *f''*. Unsuspectedly, not only does one have ten coins in one's own pocket, but it is oneself who is going to get the job.

Some variants of the Nogot case do not involve one's having relevant false beliefs. (Indeed, Gettier only spoke of a *proposition* as the basis for one's inferring that *p'* [that *p''*].) For instance, one may happen to be a clever and cautious reasoner not interested in who owns a Ford but only in whether it is true that *p*, and realizing that someone in the office other than Nogot might happen to own a Ford, one decides that it is safer merely to accept that *p* than to believe that *f* (see Lehrer 1974). Alternatively, Richard Feldman (1974) has noted that one may not arrive at a belief that *p* by relying upon considerations about the proposition that *f*, but instead by utilizing as a basis for believing that *p* the following true existential generalization of one's evidence: 'There is someone in the office who has provided me with evidence *e*'.

2 Defeasibility analyses

Defeasibility analyses of knowing attempt to exploit the insight that specific propositions are true (for example, 'Nogot owns no Ford'), whose hypothetical inclusion in the set of propositions that one believes would have a negative impact either upon the justified status of the belief or upon the justified status of the proposition that *p* (see KNOWLEDGE, DEFEASIBILITY THEORY OF). For instance, Peter Klein (1971) advanced the requirement: 'No proposition is true such that if one were to believe it, then the justification condition would not hold'. We might call such a truth a 'defeater' of *p*. The requirement shows that one fails to know that *p* in the following case:

Tom Grabit's Twin: One is well-acquainted with Tom Grabit, and clearly sees him steal a book from the library. But in consequently coming to believe that *p*, 'Tom stole the book', one does not realize that *t*, 'Tom has an identical twin and that the twin was in the library around the time of the theft'.

Similarly, if in the two variants of the Nogot case mentioned above one were also to have the true belief that not-*f*, then one would not be justified in believing that *p*.

But here we encounter the difficulty of avoiding Gettier-type cases without creating further problems, one such problem being the generation of non-

Gettier-type counterexamples. Klein's defeasibility analysis faces this difficulty concerning a variant of the Tom Grabit case as it was originally described by Keith Lehrer and Thomas Paxson (1969) – one indeed knows that p but does not realize that t: 'Tom's mother has testified to police that f: "Tom has an identical twin and was miles away from the library at the time of the theft"', and that t': 'The twin is not real and Mrs Grabit is lying'. If one were merely to come to believe the misleading evidence that t without also coming to believe the truth that t', one would not be justified in believing that p.

In response, Klein (1981) deepened the defeasibility approach by requiring, roughly, that the combination of a defeater (such as t) with S's evidence should not remove S's justification for believing p, essentially through justifying S in believing a false proposition (such as f). But the resulting analysis of knowing is too weak to deal with a variant of the Nogot case in which (1) after coming to believe that n: 'Nogot owns a Ford', S sees, as luck would have it, a true sentence expressing a disjunction, d, which, unsuspected by S, is such that any defeater of n entails one or another disjunct of d that S is not presently justified in believing; (2) on the basis of believing that n, S comes to believe that p: 'n or d'; (3) it is true that n because Nogot is lucky enough to win a Ford in a raffle while in the company of S. Defeaters of n fail to be defeaters of p, since they support its second disjunct. Yet there need be no other truths that defeat p. So Klein does not show why S fails to know that p.

Perhaps this case of Lucky S and Lucky Nogot could be handled by a sufficiently clarified defeasibility condition inspired by John Barker's (1976) concern with the fact that there may be other truths, which, when combined with a defeater of p and with S's evidence for p, restore S's original justification for believing p. (Yet Klein's 1981 work pointed out that restoring evidence may be too easy to come by, for example, exact specifications of nearby lookalikes whose nearness should deny knowledge – such as a real twin in a variant of the Grabit case; see also the case of the Back-Up Volcano in Shope (1981).)

In a sophisticated defeasibility account, Barker's perspective is extended by John Pollock (but in a fashion that may fail to handle the case of Lucky S and Lucky Nogot). Pollock (1986) focuses on the justification for the statement that p which is provided by an argument whose premises are drawn from the reasons forming one's basis for believing that p. He defines the defeat of such an argument by a set, S, of propositions as a situation where: (1) one has the reasons in question and it is logically possible for one to become justified in believing that p on the basis of those reasons; and (2) one believes the members of set

S, where S is consistent with the proposition that p and is such that it is not logically possible for one to become justified in believing that p on the basis of the combination of one's present reasons and the members of S. As a condition of one's knowing that p, Pollock proposes that the rational presumption in favour of believing that p created by reasons drawn from one's present reasons for believing that p is undefeated by the set of all truths. Pollock appears to be requiring that the following conditional proposition, R, must be true: 'If one were to retain one's present reasons for believing that p and were to believe the members of the set of all truths, then one would be justified in believing that p on that basis'. Thus, one lacks knowledge in the original Nogot case because of the inclusion of the proposition that Nogot owns no Ford in the set of all truths. In contrast, one succeeds in knowing in the case of the lying Mrs Grabit thanks to the inclusion in the set of all truths of the proposition that t' (Plantinga 1993a gives fuller exposition).

Some examples of introspective knowledge are a challenge for defeasibility theories and Pollock (1992) seeks to handle them by treating conditionals as true when they have logically or metaphysically impossible antecedents. For instance, when one knows that p: 'I believe that f', one's reasons for believing may include the presence of the introspected state, one's believing that f. Suppose that one does not realize that it is false that f. At least for some instantiations for 'f', the antecedent of Pollock's conditional involves the impossible situation of retaining one's reason, that is continuing to believe that f, while also believing that not-f – since the proposition that not-f belongs to the set of all truths. (In contrast, Klein needs here to maintain the less-than-obvious claim that S's believing the conjunction 'Not-f and S believes that f' justifies S's believing that S believes that f.)

But Pollock's treatment of conditionals as being true when they have impossible antecedents opens his analysis to non-Gettier-type counterexamples concerning one's coming to believe that one is in a particular mental state through inference from false beliefs rather than through introspection. On the basis of a justified but imperfect psychological theory, I may justifiably believe the following two propositions that I do not realize are false – f_1: 'Everyone has memories of early childhood', and f_2: 'Everyone who has memories of early childhood believes everyone to have memories of early childhood'. On this basis I come justifiably to believe the true proposition that b: 'I believe that f_1'. Pollock's account incorrectly entails my knowing that b, since it will be impossible for me to retain my reasons for believing that b while adding the true beliefs that not-f_1 and that not-f_2.

3 Causal analyses and proper functioning

The preceding Gettier-type cases involve no causal relationship between one's believing that *p* and the state of affairs that one believes to obtain. So various analyses requiring such specified causal connections have been proposed (see KNOWLEDGE, CAUSAL THEORY OF). Alternatively, sometimes conditionals have been included in a fourth condition of knowing, relating believing that *p* to what one believes to obtain. For instance, Robert Nozick (1981) initiated a new line of research by requiring that if it were the case that *p* then one would believe that *p*. As it stands, this suggestion faces a difficulty that also affects simple versions of causal theories: these views fail to rule out knowledge in a refinement of another variant of the Nogot case that was devised by Keith Lehrer (1979). Here he imagines that Nogot is manifesting a compulsion to trick people into justifiedly believing truths by concocting Gettierized evidence of type *e* for those truths. Nozick's conditional is satisfied if we add the details that: (1) Mr Nogot's neurosis is highly specific to the type of information contained in the proposition that *p*; (2) his compulsion is not easily changed; (3) while in the office he has no other easy trick of the relevant type to play on one; and (4) one arrives at one's belief that *p* not by reasoning through false beliefs but by basing the belief that *p* on a true existential generalization of one's evidence (Shope 1992).

Further variations on the case of tricky Mr Nogot challenge Alvin Plantinga's (1993b) proposal that one's knowing that *p* requires not only that one have a true, justified, sufficiently strong belief that *p*, but that one also meets the following requirements: (*1*) the cognitive faculties involved in the production of one's belief are functioning properly in an environment sufficiently similar to the one for which they were designed; (*2*) the portion of one's design plan covering formation of beliefs when in the latter circumstances specifies that such formation directly serves the function of forming true beliefs; (*3*) if those circumstances include additional beliefs or testimony, then the latter are or express beliefs also satisfying (*2*) – and so on, backwards through any chain of input beliefs or testimony from one person to another; (*4*) there is a high statistical or objective probability that a belief produced in accordance with that portion of one's design plan in one's type of circumstances is true.

Plantinga notes that the original Nogot case involves credulity, that is believing for the most part what one's fellows tell one. When Nogot says that he owns a Ford, credulity helps to produce one's false belief that *f*, which serves as further input to one's belief-forming faculties so as to generate the true belief that *p*. Plantinga suggests that credulity was designed to function in circumstances where testimony from our fellows does not deceive us and is intended to produce true beliefs in us. Both of the latter circumstances are absent when Nogot brags about his Ford and one comes to believe that *f*.

But in the case of tricky Mr Nogot the informant does intend to produce a true belief in one. Of course, the case does not satisfy (*4*), since it is likely that one will not only believe that *p*, but also believe that *f*. So consider instead a variant of the case where one is in addition a clever and cautious reasoner of the type described earlier, highly likely to avoid believing that *f*, and suppose that Nogot realizes this. He then takes no significant risk of one's forming a false belief.

The example may violate (*3*) if the purpose specified in the design plan for the use of testimony is to induce or sustain belief on the part of another *in what the testifier says*. But Plantinga admits that Nogot provides a wide variety of evidence that supports both the proposition that *f* and the proposition that *p*. So the Nogot case can be altered by imagining that he provides a large quantity of evidence involving no false testimony. Then it is obscure how Plantinga can show that tricky Mr Nogot is providing evidence for a non-designed purpose, since evidence never supports only one proposition, and we rarely, if ever, come to believe everything for which we have evidence.

Suppose that Plantinga is defended by the suggestion that the circumstances in which one's relevant cognitive faculties were designed to operate exclude the type found when tricky Mr Nogot meets the clever reasoner. This response exposes a 'generality problem' in Plantinga's account: what level of generality is relevant to specifying the circumstances pertinent to conditions (*2*), (*3*) and (*4*)? Plantinga rejects the possibility of a naturalistic account of proper function, and focuses attention on what a theistic God would have in mind when designing us in his image, part of which would involve our powers as knowers being analogous to God's in so far as he has beliefs that are true and he, although not designed, fulfils a specification that is an ideal for cognitive design plans, namely, to believe that *p* if and only if it is true that *p*. So what does it matter that a neurosis is what motivates the way in which evidence is provided by tricky Mr Nogot, since true beliefs are ensured?

In any event, Plantinga's requirements are too weak to deal with the following variant of the original Nogot case: Nogot is entirely sincere but his Ford has, unknown to everyone in the office, been repossessed or destroyed by a meteorite since he parked it. Requirement (*3*) implies that when one's belief depends upon a chain of testimony, then at each stage the input propositions must have the right kind of credentials, namely, being a belief that has warrant for the testifier. But the sincere Nogot would have warrant for believing the truth that f in a variant of the above case where nothing untoward happens to his Ford. So it is difficult to see how the repossession or meteorite strike removes such warrant in the former case. (Moreover, the case of unlucky, sincere Mr Nogot could also be varied so as not to include any false testimonial evidence.)

4 The role of false propositions

Solutions concerning the role of false propositions continue to intrigue researchers. Roderick Chisholm (1966) requires that when one knows that p, something makes p evident for one without making any falsehood evident for one – unless the proposition that p is a conjunction (for example, 'Nogot is in the office and has presented e'), in which case Chisholm also requires that there is something that makes any given conjunct evident for one without making any falsehood evident for one. But the physicist Millikan, who mistakenly accepted the false statement that the charge of the electron was a certain value, did at least know that the value was very, very close to the one that he picked. Anything that made the latter proposition evident for Millikan also made the former falsehood evident for him (Plantinga 1993a provides other counterexamples).

Another solution of the Gettier problem that concerns the exclusion of falsehoods requires that one's believing that p be justified through one's grasping enough of a 'justification-explaining chain' – a specific type of structure of justified propositions concerning what explains the justification of other members without including falsehoods at certain locations (see Shope 1981). The rationale for such a requirement is that fully satisfactory explanations avoid crucial reliance on falsehoods. We must acknowledge and analyse a broader category of knowing that p than the narrower, debate-oriented species of concern in a standard analysis, a genus that grants some knowledge to infants and perhaps even to some brutes. Then we may say that: (1) grasping a proposition within a justification-explaining chain, for example, the proposition that h, is having knowledge that h belonging to the broad category; and (2) the amount of the chain that one must grasp in this way in order to have knowledge that p belonging to the narrow category is an amount that suffices for having knowledge that p belonging to the broad category (see Shope forthcoming).

See also: INTERNALISM AND EXTERNALISM IN EPISTEMOLOGY; INTROSPECTION, EPISTEMOLOGY OF; RELIABILISM

References and further reading

* Barker, J. (1976) 'What You Don't Know Won't Hurt You?', *The American Philosophical Quarterly* 13 (4): 303–8. (Defeasibility approach mentioned in §2 above, which was the first to deal with misleading defeaters, such as t.)
* Chisholm R. (1966) *Theory of Knowledge*, Englewood Cliffs, NJ: Prentice Hall, 3rd edn, 1989. (The third edition of this textbook refines earlier research by its author and presents a solution mentioned in §4 above concerning falsehoods.)
* Feldman, R. (1974) 'An Alleged Defect in Gettier Counter-Examples', *The Australasian Journal of Philosophy* 52 (1): 68–9. (Describes an example mentioned above in §1 not involving falsely believing.)
* Gettier, E. (1963) 'Is Justified True Belief Knowledge?', *Analysis* 23 (6): 121–3; repr. in M. Roth and L. Galis (eds) *Knowing: Essays in the Analysis of Knowledge*, New York: Random House, 1970, 35–8. (Gettier's presentation of his own two examples.)
* Klein, P. (1971) 'A Proposed Definition of Propositional Knowledge', *The Journal of Philosophy* 68 (16): 471–82. (A defeasibility analysis presenting the Tom Grabit example mentioned above in §2 that has inspired important variants.)
* —— (1981) *Certainty: A Refutation of Scepticism*, Minneapolis, MN: University of Minnesota Press. (Defends an improvement upon Klein (1971) mentioned in §2 above; relates defeasibility to issues about certainty and scepticism.)
* Lehrer, K. (1965) 'Knowledge, Truth, and Evidence', *Analysis* 25 (5): 168–75; repr. in M. Roth and L. Galis (eds) *Knowing: Essays in the Analysis of Knowledge*, New York: Random House, 1970, 55–66. (A defeasibility analysis presenting the Mr Nogot example mentioned in §2 above that has inspired important variants.)
* —— (1974) *Knowledge*, London: Oxford University Press. (Presents the clever reasoner example mentioned in §1 above, and analyses knowing so as to accommodate it.)
* —— (1979) 'The Gettier Problem and the Analysis of Knowledge', in G. Pappas (ed.) *Justification and Knowledge*, Dordrecht, Boston, MA, and London: Reidel, 65–78. (Presents the tricky Mr Nogot example mentioned in §3 above.)
—— (1990) *Theory of Knowledge*, Boulder, CO and

San Francisco, CA: Westview Press. (A textbook refining earlier research by its author.)

* Lehrer, K. and Paxson, T., Jr. (1969) 'Knowledge: Undefeated Justified True Belief', *The Journal of Philosophy* 66 (8): 225–37; repr. in M. Roth and L. Galis (eds) *Knowing: Essays in the Analysis of Knowledge*, New York: Random House, 1970, 55–66. (Presents a defeasibility analysis and describes a variant of the Tom Grabit example mentioned above in §2.)

Moser, P. (1989) *Knowledge and Evidence*, Cambridge: Cambridge University Press. (Presents a defeasibility analysis related to Barker's; contains a critique of the solution to the Gettier problem proposed in Shope (1981).)

* Nozick, R. (1981) *Philosophical Explanation*, Cambridge, MA: Harvard University Press. (Contains a section on epistemology analysing knowing in terms of 'tracking the truth,' which involves conditionals including the one mentioned in §3 above.)

* Plantinga, A. (1993a) *Warrant: the Current Debate*, New York and Oxford: Oxford University Press. (A thorough survey and critique of contemporary attempts to develop a fourth condition of knowing, which includes counterexamples to Chisholm's account.)

* —— (1993b) *Warrant and Proper Function*, New York and Oxford: Oxford University Press. (Presents the analysis of knowing discussed in §3 above.)

* Pollock, J.L. (1986) *Contemporary Theories of Knowledge*, Totowa, NJ: Rowman & Littlefield. (A textbook including one of the most sophisticated defeasibility analyses, discussed above in §2.)

* —— (1992) 'Reply to Shope', *Philosophy and Phenomenological Research* 52 (2): 411–3. (Explains how his defeasibility theory relates to introspective knowledge; discussed in §2 above.)

* Shope, R.K. (1981) *The Analysis of Knowing: a Decade of Research*, Princeton. NJ: Princeton University Press. (Surveys and assesses analyses of knowing presented after the period covered by Slaught (1977), especially in regard to the Gettier problem; offers a characterization of the problem and sketches a solution mentioned above in §4.)

* —— (1992) 'Propositional Knowledge', in J. Dancy and E. Sosa (eds) *A Companion to Epistemology*, Oxford: Blackwell, 396–401. (A brief handbook survey of main types of analyses of knowing prior to that offered in Plantinga (1993b), with some consideration of their relation to the Gettier problem.)

* —— (forthcoming) *Knowledge as Power*. (Completes the sketch in Shope (1981) of a solution to the Gettier problem in the fashion mentioned above in §4 and defends it against critics, including Moser (1989).)

Slaught, R.L. (1977) 'Is Justified True Belief Knowledge?: A Selective Critical Survey of Recent Work', *Philosophy Research Archives* 3: 1–135. (A thorough survey of early literature concerning the Gettier problem.)

ROBERT K. SHOPE

GEULINCX, ARNOLD (1624–69)

Rediscovered in the middle of the nineteenth century, for a long time it was only because of his relation with other more conspicuous philosophers, such as Spinoza, Leibniz and Kant, that interest in Geulincx arose. It has since become clear that he was an original thinker in his own right, who proposed an intriguing metaphysics and made interesting contributions to logic.

1 **Life and works**
2 **Logic**
3 **Metaphysics and moral philosophy**
4 **Relation to other thinkers**

1 Life and works

Arnold Geulincx was born in Belgium at Antwerp. In 1641 he matriculated at Louvain, where he became a professor of philosophy in 1646. For reasons that are not clear but were probably of a religious nature (at Catholic Louvain there was much sensitivity over Jansenism), he was suspended from his duties and subsequently dismissed in 1657/8. He moved to Leiden and converted to Calvinism. After taking a degree in medicine he obtained permission to lecture on philosophy, but his position was regularized only in 1662 when he was appointed reader in logic. He became professor 'extra ordinem' in 1665, but died in 1669 from the plague. Most of his works, dealing with logic, moral philosophy, physics and metaphysics, were published posthumously.

2 Logic

Although the main merits of Geulincx's works on logic seem to be their elegance and precision, Dürr and Nuchelmans have shown that he made some important steps towards a logic of propositions. According to him, words like *est* and *non* are signs (*notae*) by which to indicate the mental act performed with respect to a particular content. Every denial is the negation of an affirmative claim, and that means that an affirmation has been present to the mind (*affirmatio inclusa*). Accordingly, 'Peter is not learned' must be interpreted as 'It is not the case that Peter is learned', or also as 'The sentence "Peter is learned" is false'. Speaking of compound conditional sentences, Geulincx defines an antecedent as a statement which says that the whole of that which some other statement (the consequent) says to be the case is indeed the case. Consequence is a form of containment (*continentia*): between two statements *A* and *B* there obtains a relation of consequence if *A* says the dictum of *B*. Both the theory of containment and the theorem that every *A* implies the statement '*A* is true' are corollaries of the idea put forward by Geulincx that by making a statement one commits oneself to the truth of that statement and of everything entailed by that statement. For example, if one says 'I am standing', this must be taken as an affirmation of whatever is entailed by that statement, such as, for example, 'I am capable of standing'. Accordingly 'I am standing' serves as the antecedent of any number of other statements to the truth of which we commit ourselves (see CONDITIONALS; PROPOSITIONAL LOGIC).

3 Metaphysics and moral philosophy

According to Geulincx, metaphysics is first philosophy or first science. It deals with the human subject, body and God, each of which are the object of a separate science: autologia, somatologia and theologia. The autologia consists in an exploration of the Cartesian *Cogito*, which, however, Geulincx does not see as the basic principle of his philosophy but, rather, as a way to gain access to the realm of necessary truths (see DESCARTES, R. §5). In fact, the more fundamental principle is the axiom that we can truly be said to make or do something only if we know how it is made or done (*quod nescis quomodo fiat id non facis*). This axiom allows Geulincx to claim that we are passive spectators of the world, our only activities being to will and think, albeit in a purely immanent way. Indeed, the world cannot be the cause of our seeing and perceiving: since it can neither think nor know anything, it cannot be active. The only true cause is God and the only truly causal relation is that between God and the world. In fact, all philosophy should begin with the concept of God; we have to start with the *Cogito* only because the Fall has obscured our faculties. The result of Geulincx's analysis is that God is Being simpliciter as well as Mind simpliciter. This implies not only that all reality is ultimately mental but also that whatever is neither God nor part of God is nothing but an appearance. In fact, there are only two things that really exist: Mind,

which is the creator, and Body, which is the created. Our minds are parts of the Divine mind. Our bodies are part of a phenomenal world. Particular three-dimensional bodies can be understood as limitations of the archetypal Extension that was produced in the act of creation. However, that there is a world extended in three dimensions can be known through the sensations God causes us to have. Finally, since contingent facts cannot be accounted for by principles of metaphysics (which explain only what is necessary), physics makes use of 'hypotheses'. These must consist of clear and distinct ideas which together with the principles of metaphysics must be sufficient to explain all phenomena (see PERSONS; GOD, CONCEPTS OF).

Like his metaphysics, Geulincx's moral philosophy is based on a corollary of his fundamental axiom, namely, that where there is no possibility to act there can be no will either (*ubi nihil vales, ibi etiam nihil velis*). In whatever way we act, it is God that makes us act in that particular way. Accordingly, virtue is not to act in a particular way but to yield internally to God's will. Morality lies in the intention, not in the act. As a result, the cardinal virtues are dispositions: diligence, obedience, justice and, above all, humility. Passions on the other hand are like sense impressions. Although they belong to human nature, they are relevant only in so far as they prevent us from developing the right attitude towards God's will. The most dangerous passion in this respect is self-love. In any case, the reward of virtue is that, freed from self-love, we enjoy peace and tranquillity in this life.

4 Relation to other thinkers

Although much in Geulincx's philosophy goes back to Descartes, it would probably be wrong to call him a Cartesian. For not only are the various parts of his philosophy differently connected, his metaphysics is crowned by his moral philosophy, not by his physics, which is basically an attempt to provide a metaphysical account of Divine Creation. Accordingly, his philosophy has more affinity with Malebranche, with whom Geulincx shares a basically occasionalist interpretation of causality (see MALEBRANCHE, N. §4). There is also some similarity with Spinoza's philosophy – except, of course, that Spinoza rejects the idea of creation (see SPINOZA, B. DE §4). In fact, Geulincx's starting point is fundamentally different. Whereas Spinoza argues that on the basis of Cartesian metaphysics it is impossible to account for creation, Geulincx takes creation to be a fact and attempts to make sense of it in terms of Cartesian metaphysics. However, the only way to do this is, he believes, to assume that creation consists in producing a world of appearance. Geulincx's physics is also different from that of Descartes, not because it would involve different concepts but because they understand the status of concepts differently: concepts are 'hypotheses' which, even if clear and distinct, are not automatically and necessarily true. This doctrine, which involves an interplay of empirical and metaphysical principles, has often been associated with Kant's theory of judgment (Cassirer 1911, De Vleeschauwer), but this is somewhat far fetched (see KANT, I. §7). The best characterization seems to be that he is a Christian philosopher trying to find his way in the world of post-Aristotelian philosophy and availing himself of the language and concepts of his contemporaries to provide an intelligible account of the mysteries of faith.

List of works

Geulincx, A. (1891–3) *Opera philosophica*, ed. J.P.N. Land, The Hague: Martinus Nijhoff, 3 vols; repr. with some additions, *Sämtliche Schriften*, ed. H.J. De Vleeschauwer, Stuttgart Bad Canstatt: Frommann, 1965–8, 3 vols.

—— (1653) *Quaestiones quodlibeticae*, Antwerp; repr. Leiden, 1665; repr. *Opera philosophica/Sämtliche Schriften*, vol. 1, 67–147.

—— (1662) *Logica suis fundamentis restituta*, Leiden; repr. Amsterdam 1689; repr. *Opera philosophica/ Sämtliche Schriften*, vol. 1, 165–454.

—— (1663) *Methodus inveniendi argumenta*, Leiden; repr. *Opera philosophica/Sämtliche Schriften*, vol. 2, 1–111.

—— (1667) *Van de Hooft-deuchden*, Leiden; repr. ed. J.P.N. Land, Antwerp, 1895; repr. ed. C. Verhoevan, Baarn: Ambo, 1986. (Dutch translation of Book 1 of the *Ethica*.)

—— (1675) *'Gnoti seauton' sive Ethica integra*, ed. 'Philaretus' (Cornelis Bontekoe), Leiden; 5th edn, 1709; repr. *Opera philosophica/Sämtliche Schriften*, vol. 3, 1–271.

—— (1688) 'Physica vera', in C. Bontekow, *Metaphysica*, Leiden; repr. *Opera philosophica/ Sämtliche Schriften*, vol. 2, 368–446.

—— (1690) *Annotata praecurrentia ad R. Cartesii Principia*, Dordrecht.

—— (1691a) *Annotata majora in Principia philosophiae Renati Des Cartes*, Dordrecht; repr. *Opera philosophica/Sämtliche Schriften*, vol. 3, 361–521.

—— (1691b) *Metaphysica vera et ad mentem peripateticam*, Amsterdam; repr. *Opera philosophica/Sämtliche Schriften*, vol. 2, 137–265.

References and further reading

* Cassirer, E. (1911) *Das Erkenntnisproblem in der Philosophie und Wissenschaft der neueren Zeit*, Darmstadt: Wissenschaftliche Buchgesellschaft, 1971–3, vol. 1, 532– 43.

Cooney, B. (1972) *The Development of Cartesian metaphysics: Descartes, Malebranche, Geulincx*, Ph.D. dissertation, McGill University, Montreal.

—— (1978) 'Arnold Geulincx: A Cartesian idealist', *Journal of the History of Philosophy* 16: 167–80.

de Lattre, A. (1966) *L'occasionalisme d'Arnold Geulincx*, Paris: éditions de Minuit.

De Vleeschauwer, H.J. (1957) *Three centuries of Geulincx research*, Communications of the University of South Africa, vol. 1, Pretoria.

—— (1961) *More seu ordine geometrico demonstratum*, Communications of the University of South Africa, vol. 48, Pretoria.

—— (1965) *Le problème du suicide dans la philosophie morale d'Arnold Geulincx*, Communications of the University of South Africa, vol. 54, Pretoria.

Dürr, K. (1939–40) 'Die mathematische Logik des Arnold Geulincx', *Erkenntnis* 8: 361–68.

—— (1965) 'Arnold Geulincx und die klassische Logik des 17, Jahrhunderts', *Studium generale* 18: 520–41.

Land, J.P.N. (1895) *Arnold Geulincx und seine Philosophie*, The Hague: Martinus Nijoff.

Malbreil, G. (1974) 'L'occasionalisme d'Arnold Geulincx', *Archives de Philosophie* 37: 77–105. (Based on Alain de Lattre).

Monchamp, G. (1886) *Histoire du cartésianism en Belgique*, Brussels, 219–46.

Nuchelmans, G. (1983) *Judgment and proposition from Descartes to Kant*, Amsterdam, Oxford and New York: North Holland, 99–120.

—— (1984) *'Geulincx' karakterisering van relationele predikaten en van voegwoorden. Mededelingen van de Koninklijke Akademie voor Wetenschappen, Letteren en Schone Kunsten van Belgie. Klasse der Letteren*, Brussels, 73–89.

—— (1986) *Geulincx' containment theory of logic*, Amsterdam, Oxford and New York: North Holland.

Vander Haeghen, V. (1886) *Geulincx: étude sur sa vie, sa philosophie et ses ouvrages*, Gent.

THEO VERBEEK

AL-GHAZALI, ABU HAMID (1058–1111)

Al-Ghazali is one of the greatest Islamic jurists, theologians and mystical thinkers. He learned various branches of the traditional Islamic religious sciences in his home town of Tus, Gurgan and Nishapur in the northern part of Iran. He was also involved in Sufi practices from an early age. Being recognized by Nizam al-Mulk, the vizir of the Seljuq sultans, he was appointed head of the Nizamiyyah College at Baghdad in AH 484/AD 1091. As the intellectual head of the Islamic community, he was busy lecturing on Islamic jurisprudence at the College, and also refuting heresies and responding to questions from all segments of the community. Four years later, however, al-Ghazali fell into a serious spiritual crisis and finally left Baghdad, renouncing his career and the world. After wandering in Syria and Palestine for about two years and finishing the pilgrimage to Mecca, he returned to Tus, where he was engaged in writing, Sufi practices and teaching his disciples until his death. In the meantime he resumed teaching for a few years at the Nizamiyyah College in Nishapur.

Al-Ghazali explained in his autobiography why he renounced his brilliant career and turned to Sufism. It was, he says, due to his realization that there was no way to certain knowledge or the conviction of revelatory truth except through Sufism. (This means that the traditional form of Islamic faith was in a very critical condition at the time.) This realization is possibly related to his criticism of Islamic philosophy. In fact, his refutation of philosophy is not a mere criticism from a certain (orthodox) theological viewpoint. First of all, his attitude towards philosophy was ambivalent; it was both an object and criticism and an object of learning (for example, logic and the natural sciences). He mastered philosophy and then criticized it in order to Islamicize it. The importance of his criticism lies in his philosophical demonstration that the philosophers' metaphysical arguments cannot stand the test of reason. However, he was also forced to admit that the certainty of revelatory truth, for which he was so desperately searching, cannot be obtained by reason. It was only later that he finally attained to that truth in the ecstatic state (fana') of the Sufi. Through his own religious experience, he worked to revive the faith of Islam by reconstructing the religious sciences upon the basis of Sufism, and to give a theoretical foundation to the latter under the influence of philosophy. Thus Sufism came to be generally recognized in the Islamic community. Though Islamic philosophy did not long survive al-Ghazali's criticism, he contributed greatly to the subsequent philosophization of Islamic theology and Sufism.

1   Life
2   Theological conceptions
3   Refutation of philosophy
4   Relation to philosophy

1   Life

The eventful life of Abu Hamid Muhammad ibn Muhammad al-Ghazali (or al-Ghazzali) can be divided into three major periods. The first is the period of learning, first in his home town of Tus in Persia, then in Gurgan and finally in Nishapur. After the death of his teacher, Imam al-Haramayn AL-JUWAYNI, Ghazali moved to the court of Nizam al-Mulk, the powerful vizir of the Seljuq Sultans, who eventually appointed him head of the Nizamiyyah College at Baghdad in AH 484/AD 1091.

The second period of al-Ghazali's life was his brilliant career as the highest-ranking orthodox 'doctor' of the Islamic community in Baghdad (AH 484-8/AD 1091-5). This period was short but significant. During this time, as well as lecturing on Islamic jurisprudence at the College, he was also busy refuting heresies and responding to questions from all segments of the community. In the political confusion following the assassination of Nizam al-Mulk and the subsequent violent death of Sultan Malikshah, al-Ghazali himself fell into a serious spiritual crisis and finally left Baghdad, renouncing his career and the world.

This event marks the beginning of the third period of his life, that of retirement (AH 488-505/AD 1095-1111), but which also included a short period of teaching at the Nizamiyyah College in Nishapur. After leaving Baghdad, he wandered as a Sufi in Syria and Palestine before returning to Tus, where he was engaged in writing, Sufi practices and teaching his disciples until his death.

The inner development leading to his conversion is explained in his autobiography, *al-Munqidh min al-dalal* (The Deliverer from Error), written late in his life. It was his habit from an early age, he says, to search for the true reality of things. In the process he came to doubt the senses and even reason itself as the means to 'certain knowledge', and fell into a deep scepticism. However, he was eventually delivered from this with the aid of the divine light, and thus recovered his trust in reason. Using reason, he then set out to examine the teachings of 'the seekers after truth': the theologians, philosophers, Isma'ilis and Sufis. As a result of these studies, he came to the realization that there was no way to certain knowledge except through Sufism. In order to reach this ultimate truth of the Sufis, however, it is first necessary to renounce the world and to devote oneself to mystical practice. Al-Ghazali came to this realization through an agonising process of decision, which led to a nervous breakdown and finally to his departure from Baghdad.

The schematic presentation of *al-Munqidh* has

allowed various interpretations, but it is irrelevant to question the main line of the story. Though certain knowledge is explained in *al-Munqidh* as something logically necessary, it is also religious conviction (*yaqin*) as mentioned in the *Ihya' 'ulum al-din* (The Revival of the Religious Sciences). Thus when he says that the traditional teachings did not grip him in his adolescence, he means to say that he lost his conviction of their truth, which he only later regained through his Sufi mystical experiences. He worked to generalize this experience to cure 'the disease' of his time.

The life of al-Ghazali has been thus far examined mostly as the development of his individual personality. However, since the 1950s there have appeared some new attempts to understand his life in its wider political and historical context (Watt 1963). If we accept his religious confession as sincere, then we should be careful not to reduce his thought and work entirely to non-religious factors. It may well be that al-Ghazali's conversion from the life of an orthodox doctor to Sufism was not merely the outcome of his personal development but also a manifestation of a new stage in the understanding of faith in the historical development of Islam, from the traditional form of faith expressed in the effort to establish the kingdom of God on Earth through the *shari'a* to a faith expressed as direct communion with God in Sufi mystical experience. This may be a reflection of a development in which the former type of faith had lost its relevance and become a mere formality due to the political and social confusion of the community. Al-Ghazali experienced this change during his life, and tried to revive the entire structure of the religious sciences on the basis of Sufism, while at the same time arguing for the official recognition of the latter and providing it with solid philosophical foundations.

2 Theological conceptions

Al-Ghazali wrote at least two works on theology, *al-Iqtisad fi'l-i'tiqad* (The Middle Path in Theology) and *al-Risala al-Qudsiyya* (The Jerusalem Epistle). The former was composed towards the end of his stay in Baghdad and after his critique of philosophy, the latter soon afterwards in Jerusalem. The theological position expressed in both works is Ash'arite, and there is no fundamental difference between al-Ghazali and the Ash'arite school (see ASH'ARIYYA AND MU'TAZILA). However, some changes can be seen in the theological thought of his later works, written under the influence of philosophy and Sufism (see §4).

As Ash'arite theology came into being out of criticism of Mu'tazilite rationalistic theology, the two schools have much in common but they are also not without their differences. There is no essential difference between them as to God's essence (*dhat Allah*); al-Ghazali proves the existence of God (the Creator) from the createdness (*hadath*) of the world according to the traditional Ash'arite proof. An atomistic ontology is presupposed here, and yet there are also philosophical arguments to refute the criticism of the philosophers. As for God's attributes (*sifat Allah*), however, al-Ghazali regards them as 'something different from, yet added to, God's essence' (*al-Iqtisad*: 65), while the Mu'tazilites deny the existence of the attributes and reduce them to God's essence and acts. According to al-Ghazali, God has attributes such as knowledge, life, will, hearing, seeing and speech, which are included in God's essence and coeternal with it. Concerning the relationship between God's essence and his attributes, both are said to be 'not identical, but not different' (*al-Iqtisad*: 65). The creation of the world and its subsequent changes are produced by God's eternal knowledge, will and power, but this does not necessarily mean any change in God's attributes in accordance with these changes in the empirical world.

One of the main issues of theological debate was the relationship between God's power and human acts. The Mu'tazilites, admitting the continuation of an accident (*arad*) of human power, asserted that human acts were decided and produced (or even created) by people themselves; thus they justified human responsibility for acts and maintained divine justice. In contrast, assuming that all the events in the world and human acts are caused by God's knowledge, will and power, al-Ghazali admits two powers in human acts, God's power and human power. Human power and act are both created by God, and so human action is God's creation (*khalq*), but it is also human acquisition (*kasb*) of God's action, which is reflected in human volition. Thus al-Ghazali tries to harmonize God's omnipotence and our own responsibility for our actions (see OMNIPOTENCE).

As for God's acts, the Mu'tazilites, emphasizing divine justice, assert that God cannot place any obligation on people that is beyond their ability; God must do what is best for humans and must give rewards and punishments according to their obedience and disobedience. They also assert that it is obligatory for people to know God through reason even before revelation. Al-Ghazali denies these views. God, he says, can place any obligations he wishes upon us; it is not incumbent on him to do what is best for us, nor to give rewards and punishments according to our obedience and disobedience. All this is unimaginable for God, since he is absolutely free and is under no obligation at all. Obligation (*wujub*), says al-Ghazali, means something that produces serious harm unless performed, but nothing does harm to God. Furthermore, good (*hasan*) and evil (*qabih*) mean respectively congruity and incongruity with a purpose, but God has no purpose at all. Therefore, God's acts are beyond human ethical judgment. Besides, says al-Ghazali, injustice (*zulm*) means an encroachment on others' rights, but all creatures belong to God; therefore, whatever he may do to his creatures, he cannot be considered unjust.

The Mu'tazilites, inferring the hereafter from the nature of this world, deny the punishment of unbelievers in the grave from their death until the resurrection, and also the reality of the various eschatological events such as the passing of the narrow bridge and the weighing on the balance of human deeds (see ESCHATOLOGY). Al-Ghazali, on the other hand, rejecting the principle of analogy between the two worlds, approves the reality of all these events as transmitted traditionally, since it cannot be proven that they are rationally or logically impossible. Another important eschatological event is the seeing of God (*ru'ya Allah*). While the Mu'tazilites deny its reality, asserting that God cannot be the object of human vision, al-Ghazali approves it as a kind of knowledge which is beyond corporeality; in fact, he later gives the vision of God deep mystical and philosophical meaning. In short, the Mu'tazilites discuss the unity of God and his acts from the viewpoint of human reason, but al-Ghazali does so on the presupposition that God is personal and an absolute reality beyond human reason.

3 Refutation of philosophy

Al-Ghazali's relationship with philosophy is subtle and complicated. The philosophy represented by AL-FARABI and IBN SINA (Avicenna) is, for al-Ghazali, not simply an object of criticism but also an important component of his own learning. He studied philosophy intensively while in Baghdad, composing *Maqasid al-falasifa* (The Intentions of the Philosophers), and then criticizing it in his *Tahafut al-falasifa* (The Incoherence of the Philosophers). The *Maqasid* is a precise summary of philosophy (it is said to be an Arabic version of Ibn Sina's Persian *Danashnamah-yi ala'i* (Book of Scientific Knowledge) though a close comparative study of the two works has yet to be made). In the medieval Latin world, however, the content of the *Maqasid* was believed to be al-Ghazali's own thought, due to textual defects in the Latin manuscripts. As a result, the image of the 'Philosopher Algazel' was created. It was only in the middle of the nineteenth century that Munk corrected this mistake by making use of the complete manuscripts of the Hebrew translation. More works by al-Ghazali

began to be published thereafter, but some contained philosophical ideas he himself had once rejected. This made al-Ghazali's relation to philosophy once again obscure. Did he turn back to philosophy late in life? Was he a secret philosopher? From the middle of the twentieth century there were several attempts to verify al-Ghazali's authentic works through textual criticism, and as a result of these works the image of al-Ghazali as an orthodox Ash'arite theologian began to prevail. The new trend in the study of al-Ghazali is to re-examine his relation to philosophy and to traditional Ash'arism while at the same time recognizing his basic distance from philosophy.

Al-Ghazali composed three works on Aristotelian logic, *Mi'yar al-'ilm* (The Standard Measure of Knowledge), *Mihakk al-nazar fi'l-mantiq* (The Touchstone of Proof in Logic) and *al-Qistas al-mustaqim* (The Just Balance). The first two were written immediately after the *Tahafut* 'in order to help understanding of the latter', and the third was composed after his retirement. He also gave a detailed account of logic in the long introduction of his writing on legal theory, *al-Mustasfa min 'ilm al-usul* (The Essentials of Islamic Legal Theory). Al-Ghazali's great interest in logic is unusual, particularly when most Muslim theologians were antagonistic to it, and can be attributed not only to the usefulness of logic in refuting heretical views (*al-Qistas* is also a work of refutation of the Isma'ilis), but also to his being fascinated by the exactness of logic and its effectiveness for reconstructing the religious sciences on a solid basis.

There is a fundamental disparity between al-Ghazali's theological view and the Neoplatonic–Aristotelian philosophy of emanationism. Al-Ghazali epitomizes this view in twenty points, three of which are especially prominent: (1) the philosophers' belief in the eternity of the world, (2) their doctrine that God does not know particulars, and (3) their denial of the resurrection of bodies. These theses are ultimately reducible to differing conceptions of God and ontology. Interestingly, al-Ghazali's criticism of philosophy is philosophical rather than theological, and is undertaken from the viewpoint of reason.

First, as for the eternity of the world, the philosophers claim that the emanation of the First Intellect and other beings is the result of the necessary causality of God's essence, and therefore the world as a whole is concomitant and coeternal with his existence (see CREATION AND CONSERVATION, RELIGIOUS DOCTRINE OF). Suppose, say the philosophers, that God created the world at a certain moment in time; that would presuppose a change in God, which is impossible. Further, since each moment of time is perfectly similar, it is impossible, even for God, to choose a particular moment in time for creation. Al-Ghazali retorts that God's creation of the world was decided in the eternal past, and therefore it does not mean any change in God; indeed, time itself is God's creation (this is also an argument based on the Aristotelian concept of time as a function of change). Even though the current of time is similar in every part, it is the nature of God's will to choose a particular out of similar ones.

Second, the philosophers deny God's knowledge of particulars or confine it to his self-knowledge, since they suppose that to connect God's knowledge with particulars means a change and plurality in God's essence. Al-Ghazali denies this. If God has complete knowledge of a person from birth to death, there will be no change in God's eternal knowledge, even though the person's life changes from moment to moment.

Third, the philosophers deny bodily resurrection, asserting that 'the resurrection' means in reality the separation of the soul from the body after death. Al-Ghazali criticizes this argument, and also attacks the theory of causality presupposed in the philosophers' arguments (see CAUSALITY AND NECESSITY IN ISLAMIC THOUGHT). The so-called necessity of causality is, says al-Ghazali, simply based on the mere fact that an event A has so far occurred concomitantly with an event B. There is no guarantee of the continuation of that relationship in the future, since the connection of A and B lacks logical necessity. In fact, according to Ash'arite atomistic occasionalism, the direct cause of both A and B is God; God simply creates A when he creates B. Thus theoretically he can change his custom (sunna, 'ada) at any moment, and resurrect the dead: in fact, this is 'a second creation'.

Al-Ghazali thus claims that the philosophers' arguments cannot survive philosophical criticism, and Aristotelian logic served as a powerful weapon for this purpose. However, if the conclusions of philosophy cannot be proved by reason, is not the same true of theological principles or the teachings of revelation? How then can the truth of the latter be demonstrated? Herein lies the force of al-Ghazali's critique of reason.

4 Relation to philosophy

Philosophy declined in the Sunni world after al-Ghazali, and his criticism of philosophy certainly accelerated this decline. Nearly a century later, IBN RUSHD (Averroes) made desperate efforts to resist the trend by refuting al-Ghazali's *Tahafut* in his *Tahafut al-tahafut* (The Incoherence of the Incoherence) and *Fasl al-maqal* (The Decisive Treatise), but he could not stop it. Philosophy was gradually absorbed into

Sufism and was further developed in the form of mystical philosophy, particularly in the Shi'ite world (see MYSTICAL PHILOSOPHY IN ISLAM). In the Sunni world also, Aristotelian logic was incorporated into theology and Sufism was partially represented philosophically. In all this, al-Ghazali's influence was significant.

Ghazali committed himself seriously to Sufism in his later life, during which time he produced a series of unique works on Sufism and ethics including *Mizan al-'amal* (The Balance of Action), composed just before retirement, *Ihya' 'ulum al-din*, his *magnum opus* written after retirement, *Kitab al-arba'in fi usul al-din* (The Forty Chapters on the Principles of Religion), *Kimiya'-yi sa'adat* (The Alchemy of Happiness), *Mishkat al-anwar (The Niche of the Lights)* and others. The ultimate goal of humankind according to Islam is salvation in paradise, which is depicted in the Qur'an and Traditions as various sensuous pleasures and joy at the vision of God. The greatest joy for al-Ghazali, however, is the seeing of God in the intellectual or spiritual sense of the beatific vision. In comparison with this, sensuous pleasures are nothing. However, they remain necessary for the masses who cannot reach such a vision.

Resurrection for IBN SINA means each person's death – the separation of the soul from the body – and the rewards and punishments after the 'resurrection' mean the pleasures and pains which the soul tastes after death. The soul, which is in contact with the active intellect through intellectual and ethical training during life, is liberated from the body by death and comes to enjoy the bliss of complete unity with the active intellect. On the other hand, the soul that has become accustomed to sensual pleasures while alive suffers from the pains of unfulfilled desires, since the instrumental organs for that purpose are now lost. Al-Ghazali calls death 'the small resurrection' and accepts the state of the soul after death as Ibn Sina describes. On the other hand, the beatific vision of God by the elite after the quickening of the bodies, or 'the great resurrection', is intellectual as in the view of the philosophers. The mystical experience (*fana'*) of the Sufi is a foretaste of the real vision of God in the hereafter.

A similar influence of philosophy is also apparent in al-Ghazali's view of human beings. Human beings consist of soul and body, but their essence is the soul. The human soul is a spiritual substance totally different from the body. It is something divine (*amr ilahi*), which makes possible human knowledge of God. If the soul according to al-Ghazali is an incorporeal substance occupying no space (as Ibn Sina implies, though he carefully avoids making a direct statement to that effect), then al-Ghazali's concept of the soul is quite different from the soul as 'a subtle body' as conceived by theologians at large. According to al-Ghazali, the body is a vehicle or an instrument of the soul on the way to the hereafter and has various faculties to maintain the bodily activities. When the main faculties of appetite, anger and intellect are moderate, harmonious and well-balanced, then we find the virtues of temperance, courage, wisdom and justice. In reality, however, there is excess or deficiency in each faculty, and so we find various vicious characteristics. The fundamental cause for all this is love of the world (see SOUL IN ISLAMIC PHILOSOPHY).

The purpose of religious exercises is to rectify these evil dispositions, and to come near to God by 'transforming them in imitation of God's characteristics' (takhalluq bi-akhlaq Allah). This means transforming the evil traits of the soul through bodily exercises by utilizing the inner relationship between the soul and the body. Al-Ghazali here makes full use of the Aristotelian theory of the golden mean, which he took mainly from IBN MISKAWAYH. In order to maintain the earthly existence of the body as a vehicle or an instrument of the soul, the mundane order and society are necessary. In this framework, the traditional system of Islamic law, community and society are reconsidered and reconstructed.

The same is also true of al-Ghazali's cosmology. He divides the cosmos into three realms: the world of mulk (the phenomenal world), the world of malakut (the invisible world) and the world of jabarut (the intermediate world). He takes this division from the Sufi theorist Abu Talib al-Makki, although he reverses the meanings of malakut and jabarut. The world of malakut is that of God's determination, a world of angels free from change, increase and decrease, as created once spontaneously by God. This is the world of the Preserved Tablet in heaven where God's decree is inscribed. The phenomenal world is the incomplete replica of the world of malakut, which is the world of reality, of the essence of things. The latter is in some respects similar to the Platonic world of Ideas, or Ibn Sina's world of intelligibles. The only difference is that the world of malakut is created once and for all by God, who thereafter continues to create moment by moment the phenomenal world according to his determination. This is a major difference from the emanationist deterministic world of philosophy. Once the divine determination is freely made, however, the phenomenal world changes and evolves according to a determined sequence of causes and effects. The difference between this relationship and the philosophers' causality lies in whether or not the relation of cause and effect is necessary. This emphasis on causal

relationship by al-Ghazali differs from the traditional Ash'arite occasionalism.

The Sufis in their mystical experience, and ordinary people in their dreams, are allowed to glimpse the world of the Preserved Tablet in heaven, when the veil between that world and the soul is lifted momentarily. Thus they are given foreknowledge and other forms of supernatural knowledge. The revelation transmitted by the angel to the prophets is essentially the same; the only difference is that the prophets do not need any special preparation. From the viewpoint of those given such special knowledge of the invisible world, says al-Ghazali, the world is the most perfect and best possible world. This optimism gave rise to arguments and criticism even in his lifetime, alleging that he was proposing a Mu'tazilite or philosophical teaching against orthodox Ash'arism. He certainly says in his theological works that it is not incumbent upon God to do the best for humans; however, this does not mean that God will not in fact do the best of his own free will. Even so, behind al-Ghazali's saying that God does so in actuality, we can see the influence of philosophy and Sufism.

Al-Ghazali's criticism of philosophy and his mystical thought are often compared to the philosophical and theological thought of Thomas AQUINAS, NICHOLAS OF AUTRECOURT, and even DESCARTES and PASCAL. In the medieval world, where he was widely believed to be a philosopher, he had an influence through the Latin and Hebrew translations of his writings and through such thinkers as Yehuda HALEVI, Moses MAIMONIDES and Raymond Martin of Spain.

See also: ASH'ARIYYA AND MU'TAZILA; CAUSALITY AND NECESSITY IN ISLAMIC THOUGHT; IBN SINA; IBN RUSHD; ISLAM, CONCEPT OF PHILOSOPHY IN; MYSTICAL PHILOSOPHY IN ISLAM; NEOPLATONISM IN ISLAMIC PHILOSOPHY

List of works

Al-Ghazali (1094) *Maqasid al-falasifa* (The Intentions of the Philosophers), ed. S. Dunya, Cairo: Dar al-Ma'arif, 1961. (A precise summary of Islamic philosophy as represented by Ibn Sina.)

—— (1095) *Tahafut al-falasifa* (The Incoherence of the Philosophers), ed. M. Bouyges, Beirut: Imprimerie Catholique, 1927; trans. S.A. Kamali, *Al-Ghazali's Tahafut al-Falasifah*, Lahore: Pakistan Philosophical Congress, 1963. (Al-Ghazali's refutation of Islamic philosophy.)

—— (1095) *Mi'yar al-'ilm* (The Standard Measure of Knowledge), ed. S. Dunya, Cairo: Dar al-Ma'arif, 1961. (A summary account of Aristotelian logic.)

—— (1095) *Mihakk al-nazar fi'l-mantiq* (The Touchstone of Proof in Logic), ed. M. al-Nu'mani, Beirut: Dar al-Nahdah al-Hadithah, 1966. (A summary of Aristotelian logic.)

—— (1095) *al-Iqtisad fi'l-i'tiqad* (The Middle Path in Theology), ed. I.A. Çubukçu and H. Atay, Ankara: Nur Matbaasi, 1962; partial trans. A.-R. Abu Zayd, *Al-Ghazali on Divine Predicates and Their Properties*, Lahore: Shaykh Muhammad Ashraf, 1970; trans. M. Asín Palacios, *El justo medio en la creencia*, Madrid, 1929. (An exposition of al-Ghazali's Ash'arite theological system.)

—— (1095) *Mizan al-'amal* (The Balance of Action), ed. S. Dunya, Cairo: Dar al-Ma'arif, 1964; trans. H. Hachem, *Ghazali: Critère de l'action*, Paris: Maisonneuve, 1945. (An exposition of al-Ghazali's ethical theory.)

—— (1095–6) *al-Qistas al-mustaqim* (The Just Balance), ed. V. Chelhot, Beirut: Imprimerie Catholique, 1959; trans. V. Chelhot, 'Al-Qistas al-Mustaqim et la connaissance rationnelle chez Ghazali', *Bulletin d'Études Orientales* 15, 1955–7: 7–98; trans. D.P. Brewster, *Al-Ghazali: The Just Balance*, Lahore: Shaykh Muhammad Ashraf, 1978. (An attempt to deduce logical rules from the Qur'an and to refute the Isma'ilis.)

—— (1096–7) *Ihya' 'ulum al-din* (The Revival of the Religious Sciences), Cairo: Matba'ah Lajnah Nashr al-Thaqafah al-Islamiyyah, 1937–8, 5 vols; partial translations can be found in E.E. Calverley, *Worship in Islam: al-Ghazali's Book of the Ihya' on the Worship*, London: Luzac, 1957; N.A. Faris, The *Book of Knowledge, Being a Translation with Notes of the Kitab al-'Ilm of al-Ghazzali's Ihya' 'Ulum al-Din*, Lahore: Shaykh Muhammad Ashraf, 1962; N.A. Faris, *The Foundation of the Articles of Faith: Being a Translation with Notes of the Kitab Qawa'id al-'Aqa'id of al-Ghazzali's Ihya' 'Ulum al-Din*, Lahore: Shaykh Muhammad Ashraf, 1963; L. Zolondek, *Book XX of al-Ghazali's Ihya' 'Ulum al-Din*, Leiden: Brill, 1963; T.J. Winter, *The Remembrance of Death and the Afterlife: Book XL of the Revival of Religious Sciences*, Cambridge: The Islamic Text Society, 1989; K. Nakamura, *Invocations and Supplications: Book IX of the Revival of the Religious Sciences*, Cambridge: The Islamic Text Society, 1990; M. Bousquet, *Ih'ya 'ouloûm ed-din ou vivification de la foi, analyse et index*, Paris: Max Besson, 1951. (Al-Ghazali's summa of the religious sciences of Islam.)

—— (1097) *al-Risala al-Qudsiyya* (The Jerusalem Epistle), ed. and trans. A.L. Tibawi, 'Al-Ghazali's Tract on Dogmatic Theology', *The Islamic Quarterly* 9 (3/4), 1965: 62–122. (A summary of al-Ghazali's theological system, later incorporated into the *Ihya'*.)

—— (1106–7) *Mishkat al-anwar* (The Niche of the Lights), ed. A. Afifi, Cairo, 1964; trans. W.H.T. Gairdner, *Al-Ghazzali's Mishkat al-Anwar*, London: The Royal Asiatic Society, 1924; repr. Lahore: Shaykh Muhammad Ashraf, 1952; R. Deladrière, *Le Tabernacle des lumières*, Paris: Éditions du Seuil, 1981; A.-E. Elschazli, *Die Nische der Lichter*, Hamburg: Felix Meiner, 1987. (An exposition of al-Ghazali's mystical philosophy in its last phase.)

—— (1109) *al-Mustafa min 'ilm al-usul* (The Essentials of the Islamic Legal Theory), Cairo: al-Matba'ah al-Amiriyyah, 1322–4 AH. (An exposition and standard work of the Islamic legal theory of the Shafi'ite school.)

—— (c. 1108) *al-Munqidh min al-dalal* (The Deliverer from Error), ed. J. Saliba and K. Ayyad, Damascus: Maktab al-Nashr al-'Arabi, 1934; trans. W.M. Watt, *The Faith and Practice of al-Ghazali*, London: Allen & Unwin, 1953; trans. R.J. McCarthy, *Freedom and Fulfillment: An Annotated Translation of al-Ghazali's al-Munqidh min al-Dalal and Other Relevant Works of al-Ghazali*, Boston, MA: Twayne, 1980. (Al-Ghazali's spiritual autobiography.)

References and further reading

Abu Ridah, M. (1952) *Al-Ghazali und seine Widerlegung der griechischen Philosophie* (Al-Ghazali and His Refutation of Greek Philosophy), Madrid: S.A. Blass. (An analysis of al-Ghazali's refutation of philosophy in the framework of his religious thought.)

Campanini, M. (1996) 'Al-Ghazzali', in S.H. Nasr and O. Leaman (eds) *History of Islamic Philosophy*, London: Routledge, ch. 19, 258–74. (The life and thought of al-Ghazali is discussed in detail, with a conspectus of his thought through his very varied career.)

Frank, R. (1992) *Creation and the Cosmic System: al-Ghazali and Avicenna*, Heidelberg: Carl Winter Universitätsverlag. (One of the recent works clarifying the philosophical influence upon al-Ghazali, representing a new trend in the study of al-Ghazali.)

—— (1994) *Al-Ghazali and the Ash'arite School*, Durham, NC: Duke University Press. (A new attempt to prove al-Ghazali's commitment to philosophy and his alienation from traditional Ash'arism.)

Ibn Rushd (c. 1180) *Tahafut al-tahafut* (The Incoherence of Incoherence), trans. S. Van den Bergh, *Averroes' Tahafut al-Tahafut*, 2 vols, London: Luzac, 1969. (A translation with detailed annotations of Ibn Rushd's refutation of al-Ghazali's criticism of philosophy.)

Jabre, F. (1958a) *La notion de certitude selon Ghazali*

dans ses origines psychologiques et historiques (The Notion of Certitude According to al-Ghazali and Its Psychological and Historical Origins), Paris: Vrin. (A comprehensive analysis of al-Ghazali's important concept of certitude.)

—— (1958b), *La notion de la ma'rifa chez Ghazali* (The Notion of Gnosis in al-Ghazali), Beirut: Librairie Orientale. (An analysis of the various aspects of the notion of mystical knowledge.)

Laoust, H. (1970) *La politique de Gazali* (The Political Thought of al-Ghazali), Paris: Paul Geuthner. (An exposition of al-Ghazali's political thought, showing him as an orthodox jurist.)

Lazarus-Yafeh, H. (1975) *Studies in al-Ghazali*, Jerusalem: The Magnes Press. (Literary stylistic analyses applied to al-Ghazali's works.)

Leaman, O. (1985) *An Introduction to Medieval Islamic Philosophy*, Cambridge: Cambridge University Press. (A good introduction to al-Ghazali's philosophical arguments against the historical background of medieval Islamic philosophy.)

—— (1996) 'Ghazali and the Ash'arites', *Asian Philosophy* 6 (1): 17–27. (Argues that the thesis of al-Ghazali's distance from Ash'arism has been overdone.)

Macdonald, D.B. (1899) 'The Life of al-Ghazzali, with Especial Reference to His Religious Experiences and Opinions', *Journal of the American Oriental Society* 20: 71–132. (A classic biography, still useful.)

Marmura, M.E. (1995) 'Ghazalian Causes and Intermediaries', *Journal of the American Oriental Society* 115: 89–100. (Admitting the great influence of philosophy on al-Ghazali, the author tries to demonstrate al-Ghazali's commitment to Sufism.)

Nakamura Kojiro (1985) 'An Approach to Ghazali's Conversion', *Orient* 21: 46–59. (An attempt to clarify what Watt (1963) calls 'a crisis of civilization' as the background of al-Ghazali's conversion.)

—— (1993) 'Was Ghazali an Ash'arite?', *Memoirs of Research Department of the Toyo Bunko* 51: 1–24. (Al-Ghazali was still an Ash'arite, but his Ash'arism was quite different from the traditional form.)

Ormsby, E.L. (1984) *Theodicy in Islamic Thought: The Dispute over al-Ghazali's 'Best of All Possible Worlds'*, Princeton, NJ: Princeton University Press. (A study of the controversies over al-Ghazali's 'optimistic' remarks in his later works.)

Shehadi, F. (1964) *Ghazali's Unique Unknowable God: A Philosophical Critical Analysis of Some of the Problems Raised by Ghazali's View of God as Utterly Unique and Unknowable*, Leiden: Brill. (A careful philosophical analysis of al-Ghazali's religious thought.)

Sherif, M. (1975) *Ghazali's Theory of Virtue*, Albany, NY: State University of New York Press. (A careful analysis of al-Ghazali's ethical theory in his Mizan and the philosophical influence on it.)

Smith, M. (1944) *Al-Ghazali the Mystic*, London: Luzac. (A little dated, but still a useful comprehensive study of al-Ghazali as a mystic and his influence in both the Islamic and Christian worlds.)

* Watt, W.M. (1963) *Muslim Intellectual: A Study of al-Ghazali*, Edinburgh: Edinburgh University Press. (An analysis of al-Ghazali's life and thought in the historical and social context from the viewpoint of sociology of knowledge.)

Zakzouk, M. (1992) *Al-Ghazali's Philosophie im Vergleich mit Descartes* (Al-Ghazali's Philosophy Compared with Descartes), Frankfurt: Peter Lang. (A philosophical analysis of al-Ghazali's thought in comparison with Descartes with reference to philosophical doubt.)

KOJIRO NAKAMURA

GILBERT OF POITIERS (c.1085–1154)

Gilbert's most important work is his commentary on the theological treatises of Boethius. His contemporaries valued him not only as a theologian but also as a philosopher, especially as a logician. Their estimation was well-founded. Although today we possess only theological writings from his own hand, these allow us to reconstruct a body of rich and independent philosophical thought.

The most salient characteristic of Gilbert's thought is the precise, analytical reflection that he brought to bear on the linguistic and conceptual means by which we think about whatever exists. In Gilbert's thought, two things go hand in hand: a philosophy of the concrete and the particular and an intellectual viewpoint whose conceptual resources are manifestly Platonist. In the history of philosophy, these two things are not usually found together.

1   Life
2   The multiformity of being
3   The individual
4   Theory of knowledge
5   The nature of theological discourse

1   Life

Gilbert of Poitiers, named after the city of his birth, studied in Chartres and Laon and then taught theology in Chartres and in Paris. In 1142 he was made Bishop of Poitiers. At two Councils he had to defend his doctrine of the Trinity against charges of heresy. In both cases his learning, power of argumentation and self-assured presence were convincing, and his defence succeeded. He died, highly respected, in 1154 (see CHARTRES, SCHOOL OF).

Gilbert's influence survived for some time after his death, thanks to the efforts of his students. The school he founded (named apparently after the Porretain quarter in Paris, in which it was located, rather than after Gilbert himself) survived well into the second half of the twelfth century, teaching grammar, logic and theology according to the philosophical methods and concepts that Gilbert had introduced.

2 The multiformity of being

At the foundation of Gilbert's whole ontology lies the distinction between 'that which is' (*quod est*) and 'that through which a particular thing is' (*quo est*). Corresponding to this distinction, there are different kinds of linguistic expression. 'That which is' is referred to and described by concrete terms (such as 'human being', 'bodily, body', 'colourful, the coloured'). Every concrete term in turn has a correlated abstract term (such as 'humanity', 'corporeity', 'colour'). The abstract term designates 'forms', or determinations of that which is. Thus every being can be referred to and described in many different ways. Gilbert construes this fact as meaning that one can see each being as a concretion of many formal determinations; any being is multiform, in that it is constituted by a plurality of formal determinations. Conversely, forms are real only through their concretion; they have no independent existence.

Among the forms that determine any being, there are some that determine a given being with respect to its essence. These make up 'the being of something with respect to what it is' (*esse aliquid in eo quod quid est*) (Commentary on Boethius' *De hebdomadibus* 1, nn. 46–7, 11.255–62). Other forms also make a being be something particular, but they determine the being only with respect to some non-essential property (*esse aliquid tantum*), not with respect to what it is. Gilbert calls a being, considered with regard to its essential determinations, 'a subsistent something' (*subsistens*), and he calls these formal determinations 'subsistences' (*subsistentiae*), belonging to the subsistent something. Every subsistent something has several subsistences, for everything determines a being essentially that belongs to its definition or to the further explanation of a determination referred to in the definition. For each being, it is the task of the natural sciences to discern correctly the boundaries

between the determinations belonging to the being's definition and those having to do with its merely accidental properties. The criterion for making this decision between the ways that a form determines a being is the regularity with which a given being has certain properties (*consuetudo rerum*). It is generally possible that some formal determination that is a subsistence in relation to one being is accidental in relation to another.

Gilbert distinguishes sharply between designations or descriptions that apply to something in and of itself, and those that characterize it in comparison with something else. Aside from the subsistences of a thing, only its qualitative and quantitative determinations pertain to the thing's own being. Determinations of space, time and position, as well as determinations of how a thing acts or is affected and of what a thing possesses, always characterize a thing in relation to other things. Such determinations are relational, pertaining to the circumstances in which a thing exists.

3 The individual

Anything that subsists is a singular thing (*singulare*); and every subsistence, and every quality and quantity, is also single. Any single entity is different from every other. Gilbert adheres to this proposition closely. When one and the same subsistence, or one and the same property, belongs to different things, then these things are 'the same in form' (*conformes*) with regard to each subsistence or property: but the form, considered as the form of some one thing, is different from the form of some other thing even though it is the same in content. Every human being is a human being through its own humanity; every white thing is white through its own whiteness.

In Gilbert's view, the singularity of form is the basis of the singularity of that which is formed by it (Commentary on Boethius' *De trinitate* I, 5, n. 23, 1.162). Consequently, when Gilbert considers what individuality consists in, he takes forms, not what is formed, as his starting point. Formal determinations are either simple or complex (for example, humanity is complex compared with being rational since rationality is a conceptual element of humanity.) All simple formal determinations are suited to determine equally a number of subsistent things. Gilbert calls such forms 'divisible among many' (*dividua*). If two things *a* and *b* are the same in form with respect to the form *F*, then *F* is 'divisible' with respect to *a* and *b* (and probably with respect to other things as well). A complex formal determination could be represented by a conjunction of expressions standing for single forms (*F* and *G* and ...) or, considered as the form of *a*, by the conjunction (*F(a)* and *G(a)* and . . .). Such a formal complex remains divisible as long as it can be completed by further formal elements and, while it is not complete, the complex taken as a whole could apply to other things. However, the complete formal determination, to which nothing further can be added, is not divisible. With respect to it, no two things are the same in form. Formal determination is thus the basis of individuality: an individual, determined in every respect by its complete form, may be similar to other individuals in many ways, but as a whole it is dissimilar from every other individual.

Finite reason can never grasp the individuality of an individual with regard to its content, because finite reason is discursive (that is, it proceeds by joining together partial determinations of things). Any content attainable by finite reason is always partial and therefore 'divisible'. When we want to refer unmistakably to precisely one individual, we have surrogates of complete understanding, such as dating and locating. But individuals are not individuated by their place in space and time; rather, they are individuated by their complete form. The complete form is inherently unrepeatable, and thus individual things are unrepeatable. This proposition is indemonstrable; it is a first principle of Gilbert's ontology.

4 Theory of knowledge

Gilbert distinguishes three branches of theoretical knowledge: physics, mathematics, and theology. This distinction is common in medieval philosophy. Its ultimate derivation is from Aristotle's *Metaphysics*, Book E, recalled by Boethius in the first of his treatises on the Trinity. However, in the twelfth century, at the time that Gilbert was commenting on Boethius, Aristotle's *Metaphysics* itself was not yet known in the West.

In his interpretation of the distinction, Gilbert arrives at a special understanding of the three sorts of theoretical knowledge. His first step is to take up objects of knowledge. We consider objects that are either concrete or abstract, and we consider what is abstract when we consider the first principles of all being in their simple being in themselves. Gilbert often speaks of unformed matter and of form which is not the form of some matter as principles. For Gilbert, however, there is ultimately just a single 'separated' first principle of being, God. Theology is the science whose object is the non-concrete.

Gilbert's second step is to take up different ways of knowing. That which is concrete can be considered either as it is, or in an abstract way (*abstractim*) when we attend only to forms, disregarding matter. The first way Gilbert calls 'natural consideration', the second

he calls 'mathematical consideration' (or sometimes also *mathesis* or *disciplina*). It should be noted that *mathesis* concerns not quantities but abstracted forms.

The first way of knowing considers natural things in a 'natural' way and describes things as they present themselves in experience. What is concrete is complex and multiform; its formal aspects are understood as they are found in their concretion. This is reflected in the language of natural science. In its statements, which are descriptive, there are concrete terms in both subject position and predicate position, though a predicate term can be filled out by an abstract term in the ablative case (for example, 'Socrates is a human being *on account of humanity*', or 'something is white *on account of whiteness*').

Mathesis does not have its own sphere of objects, separable with regard to content from the objects of natural science. *Mathesis* is special because it is a certain way of knowing, consisting in conceptual analysis. Its inquiry concerns the meaning of concepts such as corporeity or life. Thus concepts of forms are freed from the concrete state of affairs with which they are connected. *Mathesis* concerns itself with the question of what other concepts are implied by the range of meaning of a certain concept: with what other concepts is a given concept compatible or incompatible? It is mathematical rather than natural consideration of objects that leads to general concepts under which other concepts are ordered. Ultimately, such consideration leads to the Aristotelian categories. Gilbert emphasizes explicitly that the categories are referred to more adequately by abstract than by concrete terms (Commentary on Boethius' *De trinitate* I, 4, nn. 7-21).

Natural and mathematical consideration must not be mixed together. Nor must concrete and abstract terms be mixed together in statements, for instance, by putting a concrete term in subject position and an abstract term in predicate position or vice versa. The descriptive consideration *of things* and the consideration that develops theories *about the concepts of forms* are different and complementary.

5 The nature of theological discourse

Theological discourse is reflective and has no special language appropriate to it. We put together statements using concrete or abstract terms, but none of these statements conveys God's simplicity (see SIMPLICITY, DIVINE). This inappropriateness is something about which the theologian or metaphysician thinks, but he cannot make statements that are in fact appropriate to the object under consideration.

From Gilbert's writings, we can infer a methodology of speculative theology. This methodology consists in precisely regulated transpositions (*transsumptio*) of ways of using expressions and making statements. The ways of using expressions and making statements cannot themselves be altered, for we cannot speak in any other ways than those resulting from natural or mathematical consideration, using concrete and abstract terms. Gilbert's theory of transpositions is a theory about the sort of altered sense that statements of an ordinary form must be understood as having when they are used in theological discourse. One of the first transpositions is that of word meaning. The predicate 'is powerful' has a different meaning when applied to God than when applied to a king. When God is said to be just, this is not to be understood as a determination of a quality; nor, when God is said to be greatest, is this to be understood as the determination of a quantity (Commentary on Boethius' *De trinitate* I, 4, n. 28, ll.161–9).

More important is the transposition of the meaning of predication. Ordinarily, when we say of something that it is, or that it is powerful, or that it is wise, we are making very different statements. Recourse to the abstract concepts of existence, reality, power or wisdom serves to make clear the differences between these formal determinations. However, God must not be thought of as multiform. When it is said of God that he exists, or is powerful, or is wise, these statements are just various approximations – from the human standpoint – regarding the being who is simple. Every statement about God must be understood as expressing its object as a whole. Whereas ordinarily we must understand and evaluate the statements that we made about something separately (*divisive*), in theology we must understand all statements as conjoined and interrelated (*coniuncte et copulate*), in other words, in such a way that each statement is thought of as including all other statements (Commentary on Boethius' *De trinitate* I, 4, nn. 37–48).

When reflecting on the inappropriateness of our talk about God, Gilbert occasionally makes statements of the following form, which he otherwise rejects: 'God is not powerful but rather power itself'. It is a mistake to think that in statements of this form, one has discovered the special language appropriate to theological discourse. Such statements are only admissible in the development of theological inquiry, arising as our thought about God corrects itself, and should not be taken as fixed results of theological consideration. Abstract terms ordinarily are indications of a possible conformity among beings; but there is no conformity between God and anything else.

Gilbert sees theology as a reflection on that which is primordial, that is, as providing a theory of first principles. However, such a theory must also teach us to see that which has come into being (that which derives from first principles) in a new light. The path of human thought leads from what has come into being to what is primordial, and it also leads back again, connecting our consideration of the primordial to our concepts of what has come into being. Although the primordial is incomprehensible, our thinking about it changes our understanding of what has come into being.

In Gilbert's view, there is not just one transposition; there is also another, complementary transposition leading from thought about God to a new understanding of the natural world. Gilbert demonstrates this reversal of the direction of transposition in the case of the predicate 'good'. He explains that the proposition that every being is good insofar as it is a being lies beyond any natural consideration, springing instead from theology. Because God is good insofar as he is, everything created by him is good. In its primary sense, therefore, 'is good' is predicated of God, and when we say of a creature that it is good, we are using a derivative designation (*denominatio*) (Commentary on Boethius' *De hebdomadibus* 2, nn. 150–6).

It is clear that construing the predicate 'is good' along these lines is not just an *ad hoc* idea, for Gilbert interprets each of the axioms that Boethius presents in his treatise *De hebdomadibus* in two ways (with the exception of the axiom concerning simplicity, which can only be understood theologically). Thus being (*id quod est*) should be treated in the following two ways: theologically speaking, God is the being of everything; ontologically speaking, the totality of its subsistences is the being of each existent thing. Theologically speaking, then, God alone is, in the full sense of the word 'is'. Each particular thing is just that particular thing, and is not something else that also is. Given the historical context, it is surprising that in his theological works Gilbert construes the Boethian axioms ontologically as well as theologically. Indeed, Gilbert apparently takes special interest in the ontological interpretation, one which is clearly not demanded by Boethius' text. From a philosophical perspective, the converse is equally noteworthy: in Gilbert's view, to speak of the being of natural beings is to speak of 'being' and 'beings' in respect of a certain derivative designation (*denominatio*).

See also: ARISTOTELIANISM, MEDIEVAL; BEING; BOETHIUS, A.M.S.; CHARTRES, SCHOOL OF; LANGUAGE, MEDIEVAL THEORIES OF (§8); NATURAL THEOLOGY

List of works

Gilbert of Poitiers (*c*.1085–1154) Commentaries on Boethius, ed. N.M. Häring, *The Commentaries on Boethius by Gilbert of Poitiers*, Toronto, Ont.: Pontifical Institute of Mediaeval Studies, 1966. (Includes Gilbert's commentaries on *De hebdomadibus* and *De trinitate*.)

—— (*c*.1085–1154) *Compendium logicae* (Compendium of Logic), ed. S. Ebbesen, K.M. Fredborg and L.O. Nielsen, *Compendium Logicae Porrentanum ex codice Oxoniensi collegii Corporis Christi 250: A Manual of Porretan Doctrine by a Pupil of Gilbert's*, Cahiers de l'Institut du Moyen-Âge Grec et Latin 57, 11–67, Copenhagen: Paludan, 1983. (Gilbert's work on logic.)

References and further reading

Elswijk, H.C. van (1966) *Gilbert Porreta, Sa Vie, son oeuvre, sa pensée* (Gilbert of Poiters: His Life, Work and Thought), Louvain: Spicilegium sacrum Lovaniense. (Reliably informative about Gilbert's life and work.)

Gracia, J.J.E. (1984) *Introduction to the Problem of Individuation in the Early Middle Ages*, Munich: Philosophia Verlag, 155–78, 187–93. (Systematic investigation of the history of the problem, carried out on a high analytical level.)

Jacobi, K. (1995) 'Einzelnes-Individuum-Person. Gilbert von Poitier's Philosophie des Individuellen' (Particular-Individual-Person: Gilbert of Poitier's Philosophy of Individuals), in J. Aertsen and A. Speer (eds) *Individuum und Individualität im Mittelalter*, Miscellanea Mediaevalia 23, Berlin: de Gruyter. (An elaboration of the material in §2 above.)

Maioli, B. (1979) *Gilberto Porretano. Della grammatica speculativa alla metafisica del concreto* (Gilbert of Poitiers: From Speculative Grammar to the Metaphysics of the Concrete), Biblioteca di cultura 173, Roma: Bulzoni Editore. (A good presentation of Gilbert's philosophy, taking into account the historical context of this thought.)

Nielsen, L.O. (1982) *Theology and Philosophy in the Twelfth Century: A Study of Gilbert Porreta's Thinking and the Theological Exposition of the Doctrine of the Incarnation during the Period 1130–1180*, Leiden: Brill. (Part I, *Gilbert Porreta's Life, Works and Thought* begins with an informative biography at the cutting edge of Gilbert scholarship. It is followed by a well thought-out presentation of Gilbert's metaphysics, theory of science, philosophy of language and theology.)

Rijk, L.M. de (1988–9) 'Semantics and Metaphysics in Gilbert of Poitiers: A Chapter of Twelfth-Century Platonism', *Vivarium* 26 (2): 73–112; 27 (1): 11–35. (Important excerpts from Gilbert's commentaries are carefully selected, translated and commented on, in accordance with the central concepts and themes of Gilbert's philosophy.)

Schmidt, M.A. (1956) *Gottheit und Trinität, nach dem Kommentar des Gilbert Porreta zu Boethius, De Trinitate* (Godhead and Trinity in Gilbert of Poitiers' Commentary on Boethius' *De trinitate*), Studia Philosophica, Jahrbuch der Schweizer Philosophischen Gesellschaft, Suppl. 7, Basel: Verlag für Recht und Gesellschaft. (A study of Gilbert's theology, full of sound philosophical observations.)

Translated by Hannes Jarka-Sellers

KLAUS JACOBI

GILES OF ROME (*c*.1243/7–1316)

Giles of Rome was one of the most eminent theologians and commentators on the works of Aristotle at the University of Paris in the second half of the thirteenth century. He was probably a pupil of Thomas Aquinas, who exerted a deep influence on Giles' metaphysical and theological thought. Giles' reception of Aquinas' positions, however, was often critical and original.

*For historians of medieval philosophy, Giles' name is mainly associated with the doctrine of 'the real distinction' between essence (*essentia*) and existence (*esse*). According to this doctrine, essence and existence are two completely distinct things (*res*) of which the ontological structure of every created being is composed. On the issue of the relationship between essence and existence Giles took a firm position against his contemporary Henry of Ghent, who maintained that existence is a mere relation of the essence of a created being to its creator. Giles was also involved in the debate over the unity of the substantial form in composite substances, another burning issue in the thirteenth century. As a commentator on Aristotle's works, Giles made original contributions to the tradition of Aristotelian natural philosophy, especially in his treatment of extension, place, time and motion in a vacuum.*

1 Life
2 Metaphysics
3 Theory of soul and of knowledge
4 Natural philosophy
5 Theology
6 Politics

1 Life

Giles of Rome was born, probably in Rome, in the fifth decade of the thirteenth century. It seems that he entered the Augustinian Order at Rome. In order to study philosophy and theology he was sent to Paris, where he probably attended Thomas Aquinas' lectures during the years 1269–72. Giles started his academic carrier as a bachelor of theology at the university of Paris around 1270, and in the period between 1270 and 1277 he lectured on the four books of the *Sentences* by Peter LOMBARD and wrote most of his commentaries on Aristotle's works.

In 1277 he was one of those whose views were attacked in the condemnation of heterodox Aristotelianism initiated by the bishop of Paris, Etienne Tempier (see ARISTOTELIANISM, MEDIEVAL). Three main reasons for Giles' condemnation have been detected: first, the similarities between some of his doctrinal positions and those of the masters of arts who were the principal targets of the condemnation (for example, SIGER OF BRABANT); second, his critical attitude towards some masters of theology, especially HENRY OF GHENT; and third, his defence of some Thomist positions, such as those about the unity of the substantial form and the possibility of an eternal world (see AQUINAS, T.; ETERNITY OF THE WORLD, MEDIEVAL VIEWS OF). As a reaction against the condemnation, he wrote the sharply polemic treatise *Contra gradus et pluralitatem formarum* (Against the Degrees and Plurality of Forms), in which he argued that the doctrine of the unity of substantial form is not only sound but also the only one in agreement with faith.

Little is known about Giles' activity in the years immediately after 1277. He probably left Paris and returned to Italy. During this period he wrote the *De regimine principum* (On the Governance of Princes), dedicated to the future French king Philip the Fair, whose tutor he is said to have been, possibly in the period between 1277/8 and 1281.

In 1285 Giles returned to Paris, where he was appointed master of theology. His activity in this position is mainly represented by six *Quodlibeta* discussed between 1286 and 1291 and by several collections of *Quaestiones disputatae* (Disputed Questions). The most heated phase of Giles' polemic against Henry of Ghent on the issue of the distinction between essence and existence also dates to this period. In 1287 his teachings became the official doctrine of the Augustinian Order, of which he was elected prior general in 1292.

In 1295, Pope Boniface VIII appointed Giles archbishop of Bourges. He took an active part in the ecclesiastical life of that period. On the occasion of the controversy over the legitimacy of Boniface VIII's election, Giles wrote the *De renuntiatione papae* (On the Abdication of the Pope), in which he took the pope's side. In connection with the conflict between Boniface VIII and Philip the Fair, he wrote the *De ecclesiastica potestate* (On the Ecclesiastical Power), a work which exerted a strong influence on the pope. Giles died in Avignon on 22 December 1316.

2 Metaphysics

Giles' philosophical and theological thought is much influenced by the writings of AQUINAS, but his views do not faithfully express those of Aquinas. On the contrary, Giles often criticizes Aquinas' positions, although in most cases his criticisms aim at correcting and integrating Aquinas' doctrines rather than rejecting them completely. Furthermore, Giles' methodological approach to philosophical problems is not the same as that of Aquinas. Giles pays more attention to the logical structure of argumentation and linguistic analysis, and also tries to formulate more general solutions.

Giles' metaphysics is mainly characterized by two doctrines: the real distinction between essence and existence and the unity of the substantial form. As to the first doctrine, although Giles finds a distinction between essence and existence in Aquinas' writings, he is particularly original in his interpretation of this distinction. Indeed, Giles' view on this topic is much more clear-cut and radical than that of Aquinas, for he maintains that essence and existence are two completely distinct things (*res*), of which the ontological structure of any created being is composed. According to Giles, in order to account for the passage of an entity from potentially existing to actually existing, it is necessary to regard existence as a *res* which is added to the essence of this entity. On the basis of this account of coming into being, Giles strongly criticizes and rejects Henry of Ghent's notion of existence as a mere relation of the created essence to the creator. Despite Giles' refusal to identify existence with an accidental form, the essence–existence relationship in his treatment of it turns out to be very similar to the Aristotelian substance–accident relationship (see ARISTOTLE). This implies in particular that essence is ontologically prior to existence. In this respect, Giles' position is closer to an Avicennian than to a Thomist position (see EXISTENCE; IBN SINA).

Giles' position on the issue of the unity of the substantial form is not perfectly uniform. In the *Errores philosophorum* (Errors of the Philosophers) he criticizes Aristotle's theory of the unity of the substantial form in every composite substance (however, Giles' authorship is not certain). On the contrary, in the *Contra gradus et pluralitatem formarum* he denies the plurality of forms in any composite. In his later writings, however, he seems to be more concerned with the theological implications of the doctrine as applied to the human being, and adopts a more prudent view, holding that there is only one substantial form in any composite with the exception of the human being, and leaving the question open in this latter case.

The nature of individuation is another important topic in Giles' metaphysics. Following Aquinas, he maintains that prime matter is pure potentiality and that therefore a quantitative principle must be added to matter in order to account for the multiplication of the substantial form. This quantitative principle is described by Giles in terms of Averroes' notion of indefinite dimension (*dimensio indeterminata*), where the adjective 'indefinite' reflects the fact that this dimension exists in matter prior to the substantial form (see IBN RUSHD). In replying to some objections against the priority of extension over substance resulting from his account of individuation, Giles specifies that the principle of individuation is not quantity conceived of as a thing distinct from matter, but a quantitative mode (*modus quantitativus*) of being which indefinite dimensions confer upon matter (see MATTER).

3 Theory of soul and of knowledge

Giles' psychology and epistemology reflect mainly Aristotelian and Thomistic principles, with no special inclinations towards Augustinian or Averroistic positions. As to the theory of soul, for instance, Giles follows Aquinas' view on the real distinction between the soul and its faculties. In theory of knowledge, Giles emphasizes the Aristotelian principle that any knowledge starts from sense experience. Accordingly, he rejects the Platonic theory of innate ideas as well as the Augustinian theory of illumination (see AUGUSTINIANISM; PLATONISM, MEDIEVAL). While the starting point of intellectual knowledge is the sensory cognition of sensible substances, its proper object is the immaterial quiddity of these substances. Therefore, intellectual knowledge also requires a process of abstraction from material conditions, in which, according to Giles, both the agent intellect (*intellectus agens*) and an intelligible species (*species intelligibilis*) play an essential role (see KNOWLEDGE, CONCEPT OF).

As to the theory of truth, while in Aquinas both the Augustinian–Anselmian and the Aristotelian traditions are combined, Giles firmly adopts the latter. That is, he maintains that truth is not a property

inhering in extra-mental things independently of any cognitive act, but a correspondence between these things and the propositions formed by the intellect (*adaequatio intellectus et rei*).

Regarding the issue of the unicity of the intellect, Giles strongly rejects both the doctrine of the unicity of the agent intellect, which he ascribes to Avicenna (see IBN SINA §3) and the Averroistic doctrine of the unity of the possible intellect (see AVERROISM) In Giles' view, individual knowledge and the ontological status of the intellect as an intermediate entity between material and immaterial forms can be accounted for only if rational soul is the form of the body and is multiplied by inhering in different bodies.

4 Natural philosophy

Giles' natural philosophy is still basically Aristotelian. His most systematic and extensive treatment of physical concepts is contained in his commentary on Aristotle's *Physics*, which was widely used by later commentators. In addition to a careful exegesis of Aristotle's text, Giles also presents original positions on some of the fundamental issues of Aristotelian natural philosophy, as for instance extension, place, time and the eternity of the world.

In order to account for the processes of condensation and rarefaction, Giles postulates the existence of two independent quantities inhering in a physical body: the corporeal dimensions, which vary when the body is condensed or rarefied, and the quantity of matter (*quantitas materiae*), which does not vary. This distinction has strong similarities to the modern distinction between volume and mass.

Giles also distinguishes between material place (*locus materialiter*) and formal place (*locus formaliter*). Material place is place in the Aristotelian sense, that is, the inner surface of the containing body. Formal place is an order (*ordo*) or a distance (*distantia*) between the located body and the fixed points of the universe. Following Aquinas, Giles introduces the notion of formal place in order to account for the immobility of place, but he departs from Aquinas regarding the relationship between material place and formal place. In Giles' view, formal place is not a property of material place, but something independent of it. His motivation for separating formal from material place is to be found in the distinction between two roles that the notion of place must play: first, a principle of delimitation of the extension of the located body; and second, a frame of reference for describing the body's motion and rest. The first requirement is adequately met by material place, the second by formal place.

Although Giles agrees with most of Aristotle's

presuppositions about time, he also admits the simultaneous existence of many temporal durations and the existence of a discrete time, that is, of a succession of instants conceived of as temporal atoms rather than as mere cuts in a temporal continuum, whereas Aristotle holds that there is just one time and that it is a continuum. In particular, the notion of a discrete time plays an important role in Giles' treatment of motion in the void, since he argues that such a motion would not take place instantaneously, as Aristotle and Averroes claim, but in a succession of instants, that is, in a discrete time.

On the issue of the eternity of the world, in his early writings Giles follows a Thomistic position. On the one hand, he claims that Aristotle's and Averroes' arguments for an eternal world are not conclusive, since they falsely assume that any production involves motion; on the other hand, however, he admits that an eternal world is at least theoretically possible. After the condemnation of 1277, Giles takes a more moderate position, according to which it is theoretically possible to prove that the world had a temporal beginning, although adequate arguments for this conclusion have not yet been proposed (see ETERNITY OF THE WORLD, MEDIEVAL VIEWS OF; NATURAL PHILOSOPHY, MEDIEVAL).

5 Theology

Giles' conception of God centres on the notion of divine unity, which he regards as the primary divine attribute. The priority of divine unity is particularly evident in his approach to trinitarian problems, in which he stresses the supremacy of the unity of the divine essence over the multiplicity of the divine relations. Giles' emphasis on the unity of God, however, does not imply that divine relations are weakened. On the contrary, his doctrine of divine relations is much more complex and articulated than that of Aquinas. Giles' doctrine is based on a distinction between three kinds of relations (opposite, disparate and similar), which turns out to be a very powerful conceptual tool for dealing with some traditional problems of trinitarian theology, such as those concerning the priority–posteriority relationship among divine relations, their real distinction and their multiplication.

Among divine attributes, infinity ranks second only to unity. The importance of the infinity of God appears especially in Giles' discussion of the problem of the object of theology. Contrary to Aquinas, he constantly remarks that the object of theology cannot be God as God, since our finite intellect cannot grasp the infinity of God. Instead, the object of theology is to be identified with God regarded as the 'principle of

our restoration and the completion of our glorification' (*principium nostrae restaurationis et consummatio nostrae glorificationis*), according to the formula which characterized Giles' position in a long lasting debate in which Henry of Ghent and GODFREY OF FONTAINES were also involved. Giles' emphasis on the wide gap between finite creatures and infinite God does not lead him to a sceptical conclusion about the possibility of rational knowledge of the divine nature. He shows, for instance, an optimistic attitude towards our knowledge of the Trinity, since he maintains that natural reason can prove that the arguments against the Trinity of the divine persons are not conclusive (see GOD, CONCEPTS OF; TRINITY).

Finally, Giles was also a preacher. His preaching activity, as attested to by a collection of seventy-six sermons written by Giles himself, is one of the most original in the thirteenth century, since it is characterized by strong doctrinal commitments and is closely related to his theological works. Indeed most of Giles' sermons can be considered as short theological treatises and represent an important source for a final assessment of his theological thought.

6 Politics

Giles' political thought centres on the theory of the supremacy of spiritual power over temporal power. In the *De regimine principum* he holds that the state originates from the natural tendency of human beings to live in a civil society, but in the *De ecclesiastica potestate* he also stresses that the state must be subordinated to spiritual power. In Giles' view, the distinction between temporal and spiritual power is based on the distinction in the human being between body and soul, but the subordination of temporal to spiritual power is based on the order in the universe, according to which only spiritual power derives directly from God, whereas temporal power is dependent upon the spiritual.

See also: AQUINAS, T.; ARISTOTELIANISM, MEDIEVAL; AUGUSTINIANISM; GODFREY OF FONTAINES; HENRY OF GHENT §2; NATURAL PHILOSOPHY, MEDIEVAL

List of works

Giles' works can be chronologically divided into four chronological periods: before 1277/8, 1278–85, 1286–95 and 1296–1316. The main works belonging to each of these groups are listed below, after the complete works.

Giles of Rome [Aegidius Romanus] (before 1271–after 1309) *Aegidii Romani Opera Omnia* (Complete

Works of Giles of Rome). In addition to the volume containing the edition of Giles' *Apologia* and the one containing the *Repertorio dei sermoni*, noted above, the following volumes of *census* and description of the manuscripts have been published: *Aegidii Romani Opera Omnia*, Catalogo dei manoscritti: I, 1, 1 (Vatican), a cura di B. Faes de Mottoni and C. Luna, Florence: Olschki, 1987; I, 1, 2* (Florence, Padua, Venice), a cura di F. Del Punta and C. Luna, Florence: Olschki, 1989; I, 1, 3* (Dipartimenti), a cura di F. Del Punta and C. Luna, Florence: Olschki, 1987; I, 1, 3** (Paris), a cura di C. Luna, Florence: Olschki, 1988; I, 1, 5* (Munich), a cura di B. Faes de Mottoni, Florence: Olschki, 1990; I, 1, 11 (*De Regimine Principum*) (Vatican), a cura di F. Del Punta and C. Luna, Florence: Olschki, 1993.

Before 1277/8

—— (before 1271) *Super librum I Sententiarum, reportatio* (On the First Book of the Sentences), ed. C. Luna (1990), 'Fragments d'une reportation du commentaire de Gilles de Rome sur le premier livre des *Sentences*. Les extraits des mss. Clm. 8005 et Paris, B. N., Lat. 15819', *Revue des sciences philosophiques et théologiques* 74: 234–54, 446–56. (Giles' commentary on the first book of the *Sentences* of Peter Lombard.)

—— (before 1271) *Super librum II Sententiarum, reportatio* (On the Second Book of the Sentences). (An edition of this recently discovered work is in preparation.)

—— (before 1271) *Super librum III Sententiarum, reportatio* (On the Third Book of the Sentences), ed. C. Luna (1990), 'La *Reportatio* della lettura di Egidio Romano sul libro III delle *Sentenze* e il problema dell'autenticità dell'*Ordinatio*', *Documenti e studi sulla tradizione filosofica medievale* 1 (1): 179–225. (Giles' commentary on the third book of the *Sentences* of Peter Lombard.)

—— (before 1271) *Super librum IV Sententiarum, reportatio* (On the Fourth Book of the Sentences), ed. C. Luna (1990), 'La lecture de Gilles de Rome sur le quatrième livre des *Sentences*. Les extraits du Clm. 8005', *Recherches de théologie ancienne et médiévale* 57: 216–54. (Giles' commentary on the fourth book of the *Sentences* of Peter Lombard.)

—— (c.1269–72/3) *Quaestiones metaphysicales, reportatio* (Metaphysical Questions), Venice, 1501. (Edition of questions on metaphysics.)

—— (c.1271–3) *Super librum I Sententiarum, ordinatio* (On the First Book of Sentences), Venice, 1521. (Further commenary on the *Sentences* of Peter Lombard.)

—— (c.1271–4) *Super libros Rhetoricorum* (On Aristotle's *Rhetoric*), Venice, 1515. (Commentary on Aristotle.)

—— (c.1274) *Super De generatione et corruptione* (On Aristotle's *On Generation and Corruption*), Venice, 1505. (Commentary on Aristotle.)

—— (c.1274) *Quaestiones super librum I De generatione et corruptione* (Questions on the first book of Aristotle's *On Generation and Corruption*), Venice, 1505. (Questions on Aristotle.)

—— (c.1274) *Theoremata de Corpore Christi* (Theorems about Christ's Body), Rome, 1554. (Metaphysical work.)

—— (c.1274–5) *Super libros Elenchorum* (On Aristotle's *Sophistical Refutations*), Venice, 1496. (Commentary on Aristotle.)

—— (c.1274–5) *Super Physicam* (On Aristotle's *Physics*), Venice, 1502. (Commentary on Aristotle.)

—— (after 1274) *De plurificatione intellectus possibilis* (On the Multiplication of the Possible Intellect), Venice, 1500; ed. H. Bullotta, Rome: Barracco, 1957. (Giles on the intellect.)

—— (before 1275) *Errores philosophorum* (Errors of the Philosophers), ed. J. Koch, Milwaukee, WI, 1944. (Criticizes Aristotle on the unity of the substantial form.)

—— (c.1276) *Super De anima* (On Aristotle's *On the Soul*), Venice, 1500. (Commentary on Aristotle.)

—— (1277–8) *Contra gradus et pluralitatem formarum* (Against the Degrees and Plurality of the forms), Venice, 1500. (Argues that the doctrine of the unity of substantial form is in agreement with faith.)

1278–85

—— (c.1280) *De regimine principum* (On the Governance of Princes), Rome, 1607. (Gives the view that the state originates from the natural tendency of human beings to live in a civil society.)

—— (1281) *Quaestiones disputatae in capitulo generali Paduae* (Questions Disputed at the General chapter of Padua), ed. G. Bruni (1939), *Analecta Augustiniana* 17: 125–50. (Edition of disputed questions.)

—— *Theoremata de esse et essentia* (Theorems on Being and Essence), ed. E. Hocedez, Louvain: Musuem Lessianum, 1930. (Metaphysical theorems.)

1286–95

—— (c.1286–7) *Quaestiones de esse et essentia* (Questions on Being and Essence), Venice, 1503. (Metaphysical questions.)

—— (before 1288) *De materia caeli contra Averroistas*

(On the Matter of the Heavens, Against Averroists), Venice, 1500. (Treatise against the Averroists.)

—— (c.1287–8) *Quaestiones de cognitione angelorum* (Questions on the Angels' Knowledge), Venice, 1503. (Early edition; no modern edition exists at present.)

—— (c.1288–9) *Quaestiones de mensura angelorum* (Questions on the Measure of the Angels), Venice, 1503. (Early edition; no modern edition exists at present.)

—— (c.1287–90) *Quaestiones de compositione angelorum* (Questions on the Composition of the Angels). (No published edition exists. The work can be found in manuscript at Toulouse, Bibl. Mun., ms. 739, fols. 96ra–103vb.)

—— (1286–91) *Quodlibeta*, Louvain, 1646. (Edition of Giles' quodlibetal questions.)

—— (c.1289–91) *Super De causis* (On the Book of the Causes), Venice, 1550. (Commentary on Aristotle.)

—— (after 1288) *Tractatus de subiecto theologiae* (Treatise on the Object of Theology), Venice, 1504; ed. C. Luna (1991) 'Una nuova questione di Egidio Romano *De subiecto theologiae*', *Freiburger Zeitschrift für Philosophie und Theologie* 38: 129–58. (Theological treatise.)

—— (after 1288–9) *Quaestiones de motu angelorum* (Questions on the Movement of the Angels), ed. G. Bruni (1939) *Analecta Augustiniana* 17: 22–66. (Metaphysical work.)

—— (after 1288–9) *Super Posteriora Analytica* (On Aristotle's *Posterior Analytics*), Venice, 1488. (Commentary on Aristotle.)

—— (after 1288–9) *De formatione corporis humani in utero* (On the Formation of the Human Body in the Uterus), Arimini, 1626. (Scientific work.)

—— (after 1288–9) *Quaestio de subiecto theologiae* (Question on the Subject of Theology), ed. C. Luna (1990) 'Una nuova questione di Egidio Romano *De subiecto theologiae*', *Freiburger Zeitschrift für Philosophie und Theologie* 37: 429–39. (Edition of a theological question.)

1296–1316

—— (after May–June 1297) *De renuntiatione papae* (On the Abdication of the Pope), Rome, 1554. (Sides with Pope Boniface VIII in the dispute over the latter's election.)

—— (finished before 1303) *Hexaemeron*, Rome, 1555. (No modern edition of this work exists at present.)

—— (1301–2) *De ecclesiastica potestate* (On the Ecclesiastical Power), ed. R. Scholz, Weimar: Hermann Böhlaus Nachfolger, 1929. (On the

conflict between Pope Boniface VIII and King Philip IV of France.)

—— (finished not before 1309) *Super librum II Sententiarum, ordinatio* (On the Second Book of the Sentences), Venice, 1581. (Further work on the second book of Peter Lombard's *Sentences*.)

—— *Super librum III Sententiarum, ordinatio* (On the Third Book of the Sentences), Rome, 1623. (Spurious. See C. Luna (1990–1) 'La *Reportatio* della lettura di Egidio Romano sul libro III delle *Sentenze* e il problema dell'autenticità dell'*Ordinatio*', *Documenti e studi sulla tradizione filosofica medievale* 1 (1): 113–78; 2 (1): 75–146.)

Undated and complete works

—— (n.d.) *Sermones* (Sermons), partially published in C. Luna, *Aegidii Romani Opera Omnia*, I, 6, *Repertorio dei sermoni*, Florence: Olschki, 1990. (Edition of Giles' collected sermons.)

References and further reading

Bruni, G. (1933) 'Egidio Romano antiaverroista', *Sophia* 1: 208–19. (An assessment of Giles' anti-Averroistic position on the issue of the unity of the intellect.)

Conti, A.D. (1992) 'Conoscenza e verità in Egidio Romano', *Documenti e studi sulla tradizione filosofica medievale* 3 (1): 305–61. (A detailed account of Giles' theory of truth and of knowledge and of its relation to Aquinas' positions.)

Del Punta, F., Donati, S. and Luna, C. (1993) 'Egidio Romano', in *Dizionario biografico degli italiani* 42: 319–41. (The most up-to-date biography, with a full and comprehensive bibliography.)

Donati, S. (1988) 'La dottrina delle dimensioni indeterminate in Egidio Romano', *Medioevo* 14: 149–233. (An expansion of the material in §2 of this entry on individuation and in §4 on extension.)

—— (1990–1) 'Studi per una cronologia delle opere di Egidio Romano. I: Le opere prima del 1285. I commenti aristotelici', *Documenti e studi sulla tradizione filosofica medievale* 1 (1): 1–112; 2 (1): 1–74. (A systematic study of the relative and absolute chronology of Giles' commentaries on Aristotle's works before 1285.)

Lambertini, R. (1992) 'Tra etica e politica: la *prudentia* del principe nel *De regimine* di Egidio Romano', *Documenti e studi sulla tradizione filosofica medievale* 3 (1): 77–144. (An account of Giles' theory of practical wisdom in the *De regimine principum*.)

Luna, C. (1988) 'Essenza divina e relazioni trinitarie

nella critica di Egidio Romano a Tommaso d'Aquino', *Medioevo* 14: 3–69. (An expansion of the material in §5 above on Giles' conception of God and of the trinitarian relations.)

—— (1991) 'Théologie trinitaire et prédication dans les sermons de Gilles de Rome', *Archives d'histoire doctrinale et littéraire du Moyen Age* 58: 99–135. (An analysis of the relationship between Giles' theological treatment of trinitarian problems and his preaching activity.)

Nash, P.W. (1950) 'Giles of Rome on Boethius' *Diversum est esse et id quod est*', *Mediaeval Studies* 12: 57–91. (A study on Giles' doctrine of the real distinction between essence and existence. An expansion of the material in §2 above on this topic.)

Trifogli, C. (1988) 'La dottrina del luogo in Egidio Romano', *Medioevo* 14: 235–90. (An expansion of the material in §4 above on place.)

—— (1990) 'La dottrina del tempo in Egidio Romano', *Documenti e studi sulla tradizione filosofica medievale* 1 (1): 247–76. (An expansion of the material in §4 above on time.)

—— (1992) 'Giles of Rome on Natural Motion in the Void', *Mediaeval studies* 54: 136–61. (An account of Giles' position in the debate on natural motion in the void.)

—— (1993) 'Giles of Rome on the Instant of Change', *Synthese* 96 (1): 93–114. (An account of Giles' doctrine of the change between contradictory states.)

FRANCESCO DEL PUNTA
CECILIA TRIFOGLI

GILSON, ETIENNE

see THOMISM (§3)

GINZBERG, ASHER *see* HA'AM, AHAD

GIOBERTI, VINCENZO (1801–52)

The work of Vincenzo Gioberti was a life-long attempt to reconnect philosophy and Christianity, and tradition and progress, within the political turmoil of early nineteenth-century Italy and the rise of new philosophies of history. His critique of subjectivism led him to propose a Neoplatonic scheme (epitomized in what he called the 'ideal formula'), which finds its root in an original intuition of being. From this intuition he deduced that the Being as the creator is God. But reflective judgment is not mere contemplation: as thinking and creating are the same in God (God is 'the first philosopher'), so thinking and acting are the same in man, as an image of God. History and civilization are the continuation of the creative process in which the return of existence to being leads duality to unity again, although it keeps the ontological gap of creatural relationship.

Gioberti was an outstanding intellectual of the Italian Risorgimento and the leader of the Neo-guelphic movement, whose aim was national unification under the Pope's leadership and national identity based on Catholicism. However, despite his involvement in active politics (he was both exiled and later became Prime Minister of Piedmont), his philosophical vocation was constantly pre-eminent.

Gioberti's philosophy took systematic shape in *Introduzione allo studio della filosofia* (Introduction to the Study of Philosophy) (1840). For him the main object of philosophy is the Idea, which cannot be considered as a mere mental representation or as a psychological construction. Gioberti's argument starts from a critique of Descartes' philosophy of the subject, which he calls 'psychologism'. This is 'the modern heterodoxy of philosophical sciences' which alters the legitimate notion of Idea, whose meaning expresses 'neither our concept, nor any other created thing or property, but the absolute and eternal truth, as it reveals itself to man's intuition' (1840 (2): 1). According to Gioberti, Descartes did in philosophy what Luther had done in theology. In both cases truth is derived from the state of the subject, from its intimate sense. The priority of the Idea is denied and what takes its place is a conceptual simulacrum, in which sensibilia and intelligibilia are mixed into a contradictory synthesis. Gioberti describes five possible developments of Descartes' position which correspond to five moments of modern philosophy: (1) Cartesianism itself; (2) Lockean empiricism; (3) Spinozism and German idealism; (4) Kantianism and French sensism; and (5) Humean scepticism. The order of classification finds its own consistency in the progressive shift of Descartes' subjective foundation towards the giving up of every ontological perspective until the Humean elision of the foundation itself. In this sequence, the third moment takes a central and recursive place. Between the permanence of an ontology which contradicts its own foundation, as in Cartesianism, and the negation of any ontology, as in Hume, this moment presents an attempt to construct a new ontology fully consistent with the new method and therefore totally different from traditional ontology.

Gioberti's argument is that the new method perverts the ontological outlook implied in all men by original intuition, and leads it to pantheism, that is, an ontology which confuses being and existence, through a reflection misled by subjectivism. As Spinozism was a necessary result of Cartesianism, so the necessary outcome of Kantian criticism was German idealism. Gioberti's notion of pantheism is very wide-ranging and covers several philosophical positions, for it summarizes the consequences of a deceptive approach to the relationship between intuition and reflection. Its real meaning is clarified by the polemic Gioberti elaborated in *Degli errori filosofici di Antonio Rosmini* (On the Philosophical Mistakes of Antonio Rosmini) (1841–43). Although Gioberti was close to Rosmini in his judgment of post-Cartesian philosophy, he could not accept his claim that being, which is the object of our intuition, is, first of all, ideal being. Rosmini's being is a psychological *primum* – a mental object and, therefore, a form of the human mind – and not an ontological *primum*: the latter should be founded on the former and their coincidence should be the aim of the reflection (see ROSMINI-SERBATI, A.). Against Rosmini, Gioberti asserts that the Idea itself is present as a true reality to intuition, whose passivity we have to acknowledge. Truth does not belong to a performance of mind, but to the Idea which becomes evident by penetrating the mind and making it partake of itself. In this way it is possible to escape psychologistic anthropocentrism: philosophy performs a reflective judgment which is really 'voluntary, subjective, human', although it finds legitimacy and objectivity because it is a repetition of intuitive judgment, which precedes, establishes and authorizes it.

This is the birth of the 'ideal formula' by which Gioberti expresses his own philosophical position called 'ontologism'. The formula consists of three statements connected to each other: (1) being is by necessity, (2) being creates the existent and (3) the existent comes back to being. These statements identify two cycles. The first clarifies the relation between Creator and creatures; for existing-beings are literally so (as *ex-sistentes*) and their reason is outside themselves, in being as a creator. In the second cycle, man, as an image of being, finds his own creative dimension in thinking. The return to being takes the features of the human *methexis* of being's activity: it is man who makes himself the creator of history, institutions and culture, and it is man's creative progress which makes intelligible the sensible of nature by realizing its potential to be word.

The ideal formula formed a theoretical structure for a philosophical encyclopedia, whose first devel-opments were the writings *Del bello* (On Beauty) (1841) and *Del buono* (On Good) (1843a), and to which are correlated *Primato morale e civile degli Italiani* (Moral and Civil Primacy of Italians) (1843b) and *Del rinnovamento civile in Italia* (Of Italy's Civil Renewal) (1851). These mark the birth of the Neo-guelphic project and its fall as a result of the First War of National Liberation (1848–9). In *Primato* Gioberti attributed to Italian national events a crucial role in the fate of Europe and at the same time wished to force the Catholic Church to become the guarantor of progress and of liberties. This explains his polemic against the Jesuits in *Il Gesuita moderno* (The Modern Jesuit) (1846–7). In *Del rinnovamento* a secular Papacy is no longer given a central role, and the defence of the internal *status quo* of states gives way to the acceptance of the ineluctable republican destiny of post-1848 Europe. Sovereignty is of the Idea, the choice between monarchy or republic only a matter of political opportunity: the Piedmontese way to Italian unity is supported, but only on this basis. What remains is the emphasis on the religious determination of progress: its catholicity.

Gioberti's legacy in Italian philosophy is linked to the participative moment of the second cycle of the ideal formula and especially to its version as it appears in the posthumously published *Protologia* (First Science) (1857). This work uses a great deal of Hegelian vocabulary and puts more stress on the dialectical determination of the formula. Man's thought in his return to being takes on the character of a con-creation, and Gioberti goes so far as to speak of a real 'palingenesis'. Some scholars see here a new phase in Gioberti's philosophy, where the opposition between transcendence and immanence loses its traditional sharpness. Supporting this interpretation, Bertrando Spaventa in his book *La filosofia di Gioberti* (Gioberti's Philosophy) (1863) recognized in Gioberti's work the inquiry of a principle of all things not in the absolute objectivity, material or ideal, but in the absolute mind. For him it represented a moment of the homecoming of Italian thought which had its origins in Bruno and Vico, and thence emigrated into German philosophy. In the late nineteenth century these aspects of Gioberti's work contributed to the theoretical roots of the actualism of Giovanni GENTILE (§2).

See also: GERMAN IDEALISM; ITALY, PHILOSOPHY IN §2

List of works

Gioberti, V. (1838) *Teorica del sovrannaturale* (Theory

of the Supernatural), Padua: Cedam, 1972. (An early statement of Gioberti's philosophy.)

—— (1840) *Introduzione allo studio della filosofia* (Introduction to the Study of Philosophy), Milan: Bocca, 2 vols, 1939–41. (The most organized exposition of Gioberti's philosophical system.)

—— (1841) *Del bello*, Milan: Bocca, 1939; trans. E. Thomas, *On Beauty*, London, Taylor, 1871. ('Ideal formula' and aesthetics in Gioberti.)

—— (1841–4) *Degli errori filosofici di A. Rosmini* (On the Philosophical Mistakes of Antonio Rosmini), Milan: Bocca, 1939. (Gioberti's critique of Rosmini's view of the Idea.)

—— (1843a) *Del buono* (On Good), Milan: Bocca, 1940. (A reflection on ethics and politics strongly connected with the *Primato*.)

—— (1843b) *Primato morale e civile degli italiani* (Moral and Civil Primacy of Italians), Milan: Bocca, 1939. (The most famous work by Gioberti and a major text of the Italian Risorgimento.)

—— (1847) *Il Gesuita Moderno* (The Modern Jesuit), Milan: Bocca, 1940. (The polemic against Jesuits and their reading of the *Primato*.)

—— (1851) *Del Rinnovamento Civile d'Italia* (Of Italy's Civil Renewal), Rome: ABETE, 1969. (Gioberti's view of the political condition of Europe and Italy after 1848.)

—— (1857) *Protologia* (First Science), ed. G. Massari, Padua: Cedam, 1983–6. (A posthumous collection of fragments documenting the so-called second phase of Gioberti's thought.)

Listed twentieth-century editions belong to the National Edition of *Opere edite e inedite Vincenzo Gioberti*, (originally edited by Enrico Castelli) which began in 1939 and is still being printed by several publishers.

References and further reading

Gentile, G. (1898) *Rosmini e Gioberti. Saggio storico sulla filosofia italiana del Risorgimento* (Rosmini and Gioberti. Historical Essay on Italian Philosophy of Risorgimento), Florence: Sansoni; 3rd edn, 1958. (The actualistic version of the idealistic interpretation of Gioberti.)

Derossi, G. (1970) *La teoria giobertiana del linguaggio come dono divino e il suo significato storico e speculativo* (Gioberti's Theory of Language as a Divine Gift and Its Historical and Theoretical Meaning), Milan: Marzorati. (The linguistic side of Gioberti's philosophy.)

Padovani, U. (1927) *Gioberti e il cattolicesimo* (Gioberti and Catholicism), Milan: Vita &

Pensiero. (Represents the criticism of Gioberti by the Catholic orthodoxy.)

Portale, V. (1968) *Vincenzo Gioberti e l'ontologismo* (Vincenzo Gioberti and Ontologism), Cosenza: Pellegrini. (A useful tool for a first approach.)

* Spaventa, B. (1863) *La filosofia di Gioberti* (Gioberti's Philosophy), Naples: Vitale. (The main text in the Italian idealistic reception of Gioberti.)

Stefanini, L. (1947) *Gioberti*, Milan: Bocca. (A wide study which stresses the elements of continuity in Gioberti's thought against the neo-idealistic interpretation.)

MARIO PICCININI

GIVEN, PROBLEM OF

see PERCEPTION, EPISTEMIC ISSUES IN; PHENOMENOLOGY, EPISTEMIC ISSUES IN

GLANVILL, JOSEPH (1636–80)

Joseph Glanvill was an opponent of the scholastic philosophy which he had been taught in England, supporting instead the new learning associated with Francis Bacon and the Royal Society of which he became a Fellow in 1664. Although he called himself a sceptic and is often so classified, this may easily give a misleading picture of his philosophy. He was a sceptic in so far as he believed that human knowledge is very limited, opposing both the extravagant religious 'enthusiasm' for doctrines to the contrary which still retained adherents throughout his life, and the more general dogmatism which holds firmly to an opinion even though the evidence does not warrant it. Although he was not untouched by the revival of Platonic philosophies in Cambridge and was a great admirer of Henry More, in general he advocated an anti-dogmatic and generally empirical philosophy which in some ways anticipates the thought of Locke. In one area he might be accused of succumbing to the enthusiasm of his opponents, and that was in his espousal of a belief in witchcraft, though he claimed that in his explorations of the spirit world he was merely concerned to gather empirical evidence for a religious view. His analysis of causation has been held to anticipate that of Hume. Although it is true that he does have some of Hume's insights, the extent of that anticipation has sometimes been exaggerated.

1   The way to science

The tone of the English philosopher Glanvill's thought is almost always aimed at reconciling the new philosophy, associated with Francis BACON, DESCARTES and the early members of the Royal Society, with traditional Christian doctrine as espoused by the Anglican Church. In doing so he laid great stress on the merits of the new philosophy and the limitations of human knowledge, itself substantially, but not wholly, the product of experience.

Glanvill's first and most important work, *The Vanity of Dogmatizing* (1661), was somewhat modified and improved as *Scepsis Scientifica* (1665). In them he sees 'confest ignorance as the way to science'. He argues that a proper recognition of our limited understanding of the world will provide an antidote to the dogmatic but unwarranted claims to knowledge all too often made, especially by the Aristotelians whom he regarded as the major opponents. Conceits and fancies too often stand in the way to true knowledge and we must recognize that, since the fall of man, ignorance has been the dominant human condition. The book develops examples of that ignorance: as the 'divine Plato' said, we have both mind and body. But how they are connected is a mystery. We can give no account of the nature of spirit. Even the 'ingenious Descartes' cannot help us. We are entirely dependent on our senses for our knowledge but, as we can see only the surface of things, our knowledge is scant and limited.

Despite these limitations, Glanvill regards Descartes' philosophy as providing the best alternative to Aristotelianism, although his understanding of Descartes' philosophy as providing merely hypothetical explanations of phenomena is undoubtedly one that Descartes would not have recognized. And although his empiricism was tempered with a commitment to some innate knowledge of the Platonic kind, he was not a rationalist in any serious sense. He follows Descartes in accepting a distinction between primary and secondary qualities and a generally mechanical philosophy.

Several chapters are a direct attack on Aristotelian philosophy, regarded as entirely devoid of merit. It is merely verbal, litigious, gives no account of the phenomena, makes no discoveries and is inconsistent with both divinity and itself.

2   Causation and contingency

Among the many other examples of our sources of error and ignorance given by Glanvill, the one that has drawn most attention to his writings over the years has been his account of causation, which in important ways anticipates the much more famous analysis of David HUME in the following century. The crucial section in Glanvill is very short:

> All knowledge of causes is *deductive*: for we know none by simple intuition; but through the mediation of their effects. So that we cannot conclude, anything to be the cause of another; but from its continual accompanying it: for the *causality* it self is *insensible*. But now to argue from a concomitancy to a causality, is not infallibly conclusive: yea in this way lies notorious delusion.
>
> (Glanvill 1665: 142)

Glanvill, like Hume, recognizes the contingency of causal inference, its empirical basis in constant conjunction, and its fallibility. To claim knowledge of causes from our simple observations of constancies is merely a conceit, we never have more than conjectures.

In recognizing that we cannot observe the causal relationship but only the constant conjunction, Glanvill clearly went a long way towards Hume's position. Nor is this so surprising, given that both of them begin from the empiricist position that the source of knowledge is experience. And, whatever Hume's position might be, it is also clear that Glanvill does not deny the reality of causal relations in the world, only the certainty of our knowledge of them. His argument is entirely epistemic: we have no knowledge of necessary connection, but that does not entail that necessary connections do not exist. He does not explore the further question as to whether we have any reason at all to believe that there are any such connections. But this was in a sense already excluded by his realist commitment to the physical world, which remains an unexamined assumption in his philosophy. This emerges clearly in his account of our ignorance of the natural causes of phenomena in a later chapter. We cannot, he says, infer to the hidden causes of phenomena except by analogy, but this is notoriously unreliable because there is so often little resemblance between an effect and its cause. To claim that the causes must be as we conceive them is to set unwarranted bounds to omnipotency. We have to settle for the limited knowledge we have through our senses and refrain from the all-too-human tendency to make dogmatic claims which extend beyond our ability to know.

3 Glanvill and More

Glanvill can sound extremely modern and he does anticipate the later British empiricists, particularly Locke and Hume, in important ways. But we should also appreciate that he combined his empiricism with an early admiration for the philosophy of Henry MORE and Plato which fits less easily with that empirical tradition. In his early *Lux Orientalis* (1662) he followed More, Origen, Plato and the Cambridge Platonist George Rust in a commitment to pre-existence (see CAMBRIDGE PLATONISM). Yet, consistent with his position in *The Vanity of Dogmatizing*, he recognized that he had shown only that it is probably true and not that it must be.

Glanvill, once again following More, argues that, although spirit is primary, it is totally insensate without body and never acts 'but in some body or other', even though that body does not have to be the one we have now. He also sees the arguments for pre-existence as providing evidence for the independent existence of the soul and thus for the possibility of immortality. In subscribing to the Platonist theory he also commits himself to a theory of plastic nature which seems somewhat at odds with his cautious scepticism in other areas.

4 Witches and spirits as natural phenomena

Glanvill maintained a strong commitment to the existence of witches, which appeared in several of his publications. He claimed there was strong empirical evidence for their existence, and that they did exist itself argued for the spiritual world and our immortality. To deny their existence, as did HOBBES, was a short step away from atheism. Witchcraft and the world of spirits Glanvill regarded as further natural phenomena that deserved investigation entirely within the spirit of the Royal Society.

It is this last point that is perhaps the central feature of Glanvill's thought and which gives him a modest but real place in the history of philosophy. For in the early decades of the Royal Society he provided a philosophical defence of its methods and procedures against its assailants, in particular Henry Stubbe and Meric Casaubon. Central to much of Glanvill's argument was the belief that the study of nature in the way advocated by the Royal Society provided strong support for religion, rather than the opposite, particularly in exhibiting, as he expressed it in *Philosophia Pia* (1671: 17), 'the wonderful art, and contrivance that is in the context of the effects of nature'. In mounting this defence of a rational, cautious empiricism as a road to a deeper religious knowledge, Glanvill contributed substantially to the intellectual respectability of the new natural sciences without ever reaching a philosophical depth comparable to that achieved later in the century by John Locke.

See also: ARISTOTELIANISM IN THE 17TH CENTURY

List of works

Glanvill, J. (1661) *The Vanity of Dogmatizing: or Confidence in Opinions. Manifested in a Discourse of the Shortness and Incertainy of our Knowledge, and its Causes, with some reflections on Peripateticism; and an Apology for Philosophy*, London. (With *Scepsis Scientifica*, Glanvill's most important work. It argues a cautious empiricist philosophy in keeping with the programme of the Royal Society.)

—— (1662) *Lux Orientalis, or An Enquiry into the Opinion of the Eastern Sages, Concerning the Præexistence of Souls. Being a key to unlock the Grand Mysteries of Providence, In relation to mans sin and misery*, London. (Argues for the Platonic doctrine of the plausibility of the pre-existence of souls. The argument is much indebted to Henry More.)

—— (1665) *Scepsis Scientifica: or Confest Ignorance, the way to Science; In an Essay of the Vanity of Dogmatizing, and Confident Opinion. With a Reply to the Learned Thomas Albius*, London. (Essentially a second edition of *The Vanity of Dogmatizing*.)

—— (1667) *Some Philosophical Considerations Touching the Being of Witches and Witchcraft*, London. (Argues that there is substantial empirical evidence for the existence of witches, which itself is evidence of a spiritual world.)

—— (1668a) *A Blow at Modern Sadducism in some Philosophical Considerations about Witchcraft*, London. (Further evidence for witches and therefore for spirits.)

—— (1668b) *Plus Ultra: or The Progress and Advancement of Knowledge since the Days of Aristotle*, London. (A championing of modern learning and a defence of the Royal Society against those who asserted the superiority of the ancients.)

—— (1671) *Philosophia Pia; or, A discourse of the Religious Temper, and Tendencies of the Experimental Philosophy, which is profest by the Royal Society*, London. (A further defence of the Royal Society and its goals, especially with regard to the religious implications of its method and findings which Glanvill claims strongly supported the religious position.)

—— (1676) *Essays on Several Important Subjects in Philosophy and Religion*, London. (Essays defending positions he had already advocated on reason, spirits, religion, scepticism and knowledge.)

—— (1681) *Sadducismus Triuphatus: or, Full and Plain Evidence concerning Witches and Apparitions. In two Parts. the First treating of their Possibility, the Second of their Real Existence*, London. (Yet more argument and evidence for the existence of witches.)

References and further reading

Cope, J.I. (1956) *Joseph Glanvill. Anglican Apologist*, St Louis, MO: Washington University Studies. (A scholarly and comprehensive intellectual biography.)

Leeuwan, H.G. van (1970) *The Problem of Certainty in English Thought 1630–1690*, The Hague: Martin Nijhoff. (Pages 71–89 are useful on Glanvill, and the remainder of the book provides the context of Glanvill's thought.)

Popkin, R.H. (1953) 'Joseph Glanvill: A Precursor of David Hume', *Journal of the History of Ideas* 14: 293–303; repr. in R.H. Popkin *The High Road to Pyrrhonism*, Indianapolis, IN: Hackett Publishing Company, 1993. (Argues that Glanvill anticipated Hume on the fallacy of induction.)

G.A.J. ROGERS

GLOSSARY OF LOGICAL TERMS *see* LOGICAL AND MATHEMATICAL TERMS, GLOSSARY OF

GNOSTICISM

Gnosticism comprises a loosely associated group of teachers, teachings and sects which professed to offer 'gnosis', saving knowledge or enlightenment, conveyed in various myths which sought to explain the origin of the world and of the human soul and the destiny of the latter. Everything originated from a transcendent spiritual power; but corruption set in and inferior powers emerged, resulting in the creation of the material world in which the human spirit is now imprisoned. Salvation is sought by cultivating the inner life while neglecting the body and social duties unconnected with the cult. The Gnostic movement emerged in the first and second centuries AD and was seen as a rival to orthodox Christianity, though in fact some Gnostic sects were more closely linked with Judaism or with Iranian religion. By the fourth century its influence was waning, but it persisted with sporadic revivals into the Middle Ages.

1 **Basic doctrines**
2 **Definitions, origins and dating**
3 **Sources**
4 **Philosophical content and value**

1 Basic doctrines

Gnosticism can best be understood in terms of family likeness. One can identify characteristic features, most of which are found in most Gnostic sects; but the attempts often made to define Gnosticism in terms of universally present common features can only approximate to the truth.

Characteristic tenets include:

1 A radical dualism, contrasting a transcendent realm of pure spirit with the world of gross matter. The human makeup likewise presents a sharp contrast of spirit and sensuality, with a corresponding distinction between the 'elect' or spiritual people and the rest of society, though some systems introduce an intermediate grade.
2 A creator presented as imperfect or evil, though commonly identified with the God of Judaism, and sharply contrasted with the supreme divinity, who is his ultimate source. His existence is explained by various myths depicting events prior to the creation and claiming to show how evil dispositions arose by accumulated lapses among the heavenly powers.
3 The human spirit originated in the higher realm, but is now imprisoned in the form of a soul within the material body. Many Gnostic sects taught that the same spirit can live many lives. But it is often seen as predestined to salvation or the reverse.
4 The Gnostics' aim was to liberate their spirits from all attachment to material things, and thereby return with the elect minority to ultimate happiness. Most Gnostic sects therefore adopted a puritan ethic, though some held that all physical actions are contemptible and approved licentious conduct as a sign of liberation.

2 Definitions, origins and dating

'Gnosticism' is a term coined by modern scholars. Ancient writers allude to 'gnosis', that is, knowledge, especially spiritual knowledge or enlightenment, St Paul speaks disparagingly of Christians who laid claim to it (1 Corinthians 8: 1), but it was nevertheless commended by CLEMENT OF ALEXANDRIA and others. Clement also uses 'Gnostic' to mean a devout and instructed Christian. The Gnostic sects themselves had no common self-designation parallel to 'Jew' or 'Christian', and were commonly named after their founders. Irenaeus (c. 130–c. 200), however, implies that the term was appropriated by several sects, and its use was soon extended to include all similar schools.

There has been much debate about the origins of Gnosticism, whether Greek, Jewish or Iranian. It now appears that the movement was too diversified for any single-source theory to be acceptable, and many forms of it clearly presuppose an amalgamation of different cultures. Its ablest exponents, including Valentinus and Marcion (fl. c. 140–60), inherit the traditions of Hellenistic Judaism, incorporating Christian elements; the rest are unlikely to interest students of philosophy.

The problem of dating has been complicated by ill-defined terminology. It has been claimed that Gnosticism originated in Iran before the Christian movement emerged. But it now appears that the emergence of *systematic* Gnostic teaching is roughly contemporaneous with a parallel Christian development, though many of the ideas found in Gnosticism were current earlier. Scholars, especially in Germany, now tend to reserve the term 'Gnosticism' for the elaborate systems described by Irenaeus around 180 AD, for example, using 'Gnosis' as an inclusive term for its constituent ideas.

Mandaeism, a small Gnostic sect unnoticed by Christian writers, has attracted some attention from scholars, as the sect still survives and has preserved sacred writings of great antiquity. Its claim to derive from John the Baptist is probably unfounded.

3 Sources

For many centuries Gnosticism was known only through the writings of its Christian opponents, notably Irenaeus, TERTULLIAN and Clement, who did however embody quotations from the works they criticized. Some later Gnostic texts of dubious value emerged in the eighteenth century, supplemented by the important Berlin Codex 8502 (discovered 1901, fully edited 1955). But the situation was transformed by the discovery of forty-four books in codex form at Nag-Hammadi in Upper Egypt in 1944 (though once again publication was delayed). Most are Coptic translations of Greek originals, some of which probably date from the first century AD. Many of them introduce biblical characters, though strongly influenced by Gnostic assumptions. Three may be mentioned in particular: the Apocryphon of John, which abounds in fanciful mythology, but was apparently authoritative and survives in several copies; the Gospel of Thomas, a collection of sayings ascribed to Jesus, isolated from their settings and

accompanying actions, but sometimes presenting variant forms of canonical Gospel texts; and the so-called Gospel of Truth (*Evangelium veritatis*), the one item in the collection which could without absurdity be annexed to the Christian scriptures; it has no marked heretical features and offers an original meditation on the passion of Christ.

The list of sources should be extended by a brief note on Manicheism, a Gnostic sect founded by Mani (Manes, Manichaeus) around 216–76 AD in Iran, and influential especially in the fourth century, when it briefly captured St Augustine (see MANICHEISM). Earlier patristic and Muslim sources can now be compared with Manichean documents found at Turfan from 1898 and in Egypt from 1930 onwards, including a biography of the founder.

4 Philosophical content and value

Early Christian writers, especially Hippolytus (c. 170–c. 236), argued that the Gnostics were influenced by Greek philosophy. In most cases this is unlikely, and where such influence existed it has been overlaid by mythology. Some philosophical schools, for example, Sceptics and Epicureans, can be discounted; Stoic influence was slight and indirect. One must also exclude the dominant Platonism, which taught the eternity of the world, taking the *Timaeus* to symbolize its eternal dependence on creative goodness. But some Gnostic sects echo the Jewish and Christian Platonism that assimilated the early chapters of Genesis with the *Timaeus* interpreted historically, as it was by PLUTARCH and Atticus. The Nag-Hammadi texts include an extract from Plato's *Republic* (588a–589b) inaccurately reproduced in Coptic. Pythagorean influence appears in the significance assigned to numbers, already present in the Jewish practice of Gematria, where numbers, commonly expressed by letters, are regrouped to yield significant words; thus 666, 'the number of the beast' (Revelation 13: 18), can be split up, it is alleged, to yield the letters NERO CAESAR.

Platonic traits appear clearly in the Valentinian system, which was widely influential and is commonly taken as typical. Valentinus was a gifted man who hoped to be made Bishop of Rome, and so presumably restrained his speculative powers, as his scanty surviving fragments suggest. Yet the Valentinian system, as known only one generation later, presents a bewilderingly complex mythology, clearly unacceptable to mainstream Christians.

Note however the following features:

1 Dualism is modified to include an intermediate grade: three levels of being – spirit, soul and

matter; and three classes of people – the Gnostic elect, the conventional church member, the unregenerate outsider – which recalls the three classes of citizens in Plato's *Republic*.

2 Evil is traced to defective cognition.

3 The ultimate divinity expands to form a series of powers or 'Aeons'. The first derivative is God's self-knowledge (his 'Ennoia'). But the process goes wrong: in the developed Valentinian myth, the primal fault is ascribed to the last in a series of thirty Aeons, who nevertheless bears the prestigious name of Sophia. This may point to an earlier conception in which it is the *first* derivative, Ennoia-Sophia, who fails. Conversely, Irenaeus describes a further development in which the erring Sophia herself is duplicated.

The myth serves to express a fundamental problem of theology. The ancients commonly thought of knowledge as a process of copying; thus we may be said to know someone when we can recall that person's features. Thus any knowledge of God must be a kind of replica. But it cannot be perfect, or it would amount to a second divinity. So any attempt to elucidate God must be presumptuous. The most thoughtful treatment of the problem appears in the Tripartite Tractate from Nag-Hammadi. Here God's nature is expressed in a series of powers which at first appear as impersonal attributes; but to replicate God's being each one must become a sovereign will; they thus incur a common failure, as each one fails to consider its own incompleteness and its need of the others. This account of the primary fault is clearly more persuasive than the official Valentinian theory, which fixes the blame exclusively on Sophia. But the majority of Gnostic teachers were catering for untrained minds, and sought to impress them with increasingly complex and pretentious mythology, a feature which today baffles and repels many philosophers.

References and further reading

Foerster, W. (ed. and trans.) (1972, 1974) *Gnosis*, Oxford: Clarendon Press. (An English translation of Gnostic texts in two volumes: 1, Patristic Evidence: 2, Coptic and Mandaean Sources.)

Grant, R.M. (ed. and trans.) (1961) *Gnosticism, An Anthology*, London: Collins. (Good introductory collection.)

Jonas, H. (1958) *The Gnostic Religion*, Boston, MA: Beacon Press. (Authoritative brief survey.)

Koester, H. (1990) *Ancient Christian Gospels, their History and Development*, London: SCM Press. (Compares the canonical Gospels with Gnostic parallels.)

Layton, B. (ed. and trans.) (1987) *The Gnostic Scriptures: A New Translation*, London: SCM. (Complete English version of the Nag-Hammadi texts.)

Pagels, E.H. (1975) *The Gnostic Paul*, Philadelphia, PA: Fortress Press. (Introduces Gnostic biblical scholarship.)

—— (1979) *The Gnostic Gospels*, New York: Random House; repr. Harmondsworth: Penguin, 1982. (Introduces Gnostic biblical scholarship.)

Robinson, J.M. (ed. and trans.) (1988) *The Nag-Hammadi Library*, Leiden: Brill. (Complete translation of the collection.)

Rudolph, K. (1983) *Gnosis*, Edinburgh: T. & T. Clark. (Authoritative, comprehensive study.)

Stead, G.C. (1969) 'The Valentinian Myth of Sophia', *Journal of Theological Studies* 20: 75–104. (Examines the growth of a Gnostic myth).

Wilson, R.M. (1968) *Gnosis and the New Testament*, Oxford: Blackwell. (Fairly simple in treatment, but totally reliable.)

Yamauchi, E. (1973) *Pre-Christian Gnosticism*, London: Tyndale Press. (Discusses the question whether Gnosticism antedates Christianity.)

CHRISTOPHER STEAD

GOD, ARGUMENTS FOR THE EXISTENCE OF

Arguments for the existence of God go back at least to Aristotle, who argued that there must be a first mover, itself unmoved. All the great medieval philosophers (Arabic and Jewish as well as Christian) proposed and developed theistic arguments – for example, Augustine, al-Ghazali, Anselm, Moses Maimonides, Thomas Aquinas and Duns Scotus. Most of the great modern philosophers – in particular René Descartes, Gottfried Leibniz and Immanuel Kant – have also offered theistic arguments. They remain a subject of considerable contemporary concern; the twentieth century has seen important work on all the main varieties of these arguments.

These arguments come in several varieties. Since Kant, the traditional Big Three have been the cosmological, ontological and teleological arguments. The cosmological argument goes back to Aristotle, but gets its classic statement (at least for European philosophy) in the famous 'five ways' of Aquinas, in particular his arguments for a first uncaused cause, a first unmoved mover, and a necessary being. According to the first-mover argument (which is a special case of the first-cause argument), whatever is moved (that is, caused to move) is moved by something else. It is impossible, however, that there should be an infinite series of moved and moving beings; hence there must be a first unmoved mover. Aquinas goes on to argue that a first mover would have to be both a first cause and a necessary being; he then goes on in the next parts (Ia, qq.3–11) of the Summa theologiae *to argue that such a being must have the attributes of God.*

The perennially fascinating ontological argument, in Anselm's version, goes as follows: God is by definition the being than which none greater can be conceived. Now suppose God did not exist. It is greater to exist than not to exist; so if God did not exist, a being greater than God could be conceived. Since God is by definition the being than which none greater can be conceived, that is absurd. Therefore the supposition that God does not exist implies an absurdity and must be false. This argument has had many illustrious defenders and equally illustrious attackers from Anselm's time to ours; the twentieth century has seen the development of a new (modal) version of the argument.

Aquinas' fifth way is a version of the third kind of theistic argument, the teleological argument; but it was left to modern and contemporary philosophy to propose fuller and better-developed versions of it. Its basic idea is simple: the universe and many of its parts look as if they have been designed, and the only real candidate for the post of designer of the universe is God. Many take evolutionary theory to undercut this sort of argument by showing how all of this apparent design could have been the result of blind, mechanical forces. Supporters of the argument dispute this claim and retort that the enormously delicate 'fine tuning' of the cosmological constants required for the existence of life strongly suggests design.

In addition to the traditional Big Three, there are in fact many more theistic arguments. There are arguments from the nature of morality, from the nature of propositions, numbers and sets, from intentionality, from reference, simplicity, intuition and love, from colours and flavours, miracles, play and enjoyment, from beauty, and from the meaning of life; and there is even an argument from the existence of evil.

1   **Cosmological arguments**
2–3 **Ontological arguments**
4–5 **Teleological arguments**
6   **Other theistic arguments**

1   Cosmological arguments

Cosmological arguments start from some obvious and general but a posteriori fact about the universe: that there are contingent beings, for example, or that things move or change. We find first steps towards

such an argument in Plato (*Laws* 10); ARISTOTLE (§16) (*Metaphysics* 12; *Physics* 7, 8) gives it a fuller statement; the medieval Arabic (especially al-Ghazali) and Jewish philosophers (especially Maimonides) gave elaborate statements of the argument; but its *locus classicus* (for Westerners, anyway) is the first three of the famous 'five ways' of Aquinas' *Summa theologiae*. Following Aquinas, DUNS SCOTUS (§§7–11) presented a subtle and powerful version of the argument, and in modern times the most influential versions of the argument are to be found in the works of LEIBNIZ (§3) and Samuel CLARKE (§1). (The most influential criticisms of the argument are given by HUME (§6) and KANT (§8).)

Following William Craig (1980), we may distinguish substantially three versions of the cosmological argument. First, the so-called *kalam* (Arabic, 'speculative theology') argument, developed by Arabic thinkers (for example, AL-KINDI (§2) and al-Ghazali). Put most schematically, this argument goes as follows:

(1) Whatever begins to exist is caused to exist by something else.
(2) The universe began to exist.
(3) Therefore the universe was caused to exist; and the cause of its existence is God.

The second premise was supported by arguments for the conclusion that an 'actual infinite' is not possible: it is not possible, for example, that there have been infinitely many temporally non-overlapping beings each existing for at least a second; alternatively, it is not possible that an infinite number of seconds have elapsed. These arguments proceed by pointing out some of the paradoxes or peculiarities that an actual infinite involves (see INFINITY). For example, suppose there were a hotel with infinitely many rooms ('Hilbert's Hotel'). The hotel is full; a new guest arrives; despite the fact that each room is already occupied, the proprietor accommodates the guest by putting them in room 1, moving the occupant of room 1 to room 2, of room 2 to room 3, and in general the occupant of n to $n+1$. No problem! Indeed, when a large bus containing infinitely many new guests pulls up, they too can all be accommodated: for any odd-numbered room n, move its occupant into room $2n$ (moving the occupant of *that* room n^* into $2n^*$, and so on), thus freeing up the infinitely many odd-numbered rooms. In fact, if it is a busy weekend and an infinite fleet of buses pulls up, each with infinitely many new guests, they too can all be easily accommodated. And the question is: is it really possible, in the broadly logical sense, that such a hotel could actually exist? The friend of the *kalam* argument thinks not, and adds that no other actual infinite is possible either. If so, then the universe has not existed for an infinite stretch of time, but had a beginning. Contemporary cosmological theory in physics has seemed to some to provide scientific, empirical support for the claim that the universe had a beginning; according to 'Big Bang' cosmology, the universe came into being something like 15 billion years ago, give or take a few billion (see COSMOLOGY §3).

Given that the universe has a beginning, the next step is to argue (by way of the first premise) that it must therefore have had a cause; it could not have popped into existence uncaused. And the final step is to argue that the cause of the universe would have to have certain important properties – properties of God.

The second kind of cosmological argument is the kind to be found in the first three of Aquinas' five ways. His second way, for example, goes like this:

(1) Many things in nature are caused.
(2) Nothing is a cause of itself.
(3) An infinite regress of essentially ordered efficient causes is impossible.
(4) Therefore, there is a first uncaused cause – 'to which', says Aquinas, 'everyone gives the name of God.'

There are two points of particular interest about this argument. First, Aquinas disagrees with a premise of the *kalam* argument, according to which it is impossible that there be an actual infinite. He argues that it cannot be proved that the universe had a beginning; he thinks it possible (though false) that the universe has existed for an infinite stretch of time. How then are we to understand premise (3)? Aquinas is here speaking of a certain kind of series, an 'essentially ordered' series, a series of causes in which any cause of an effect must be operating throughout the whole duration of the effect's operation. It is only such series, he says, that cannot proceed to infinity. (Aquinas gives the example of a stick moving a stone, a hand moving the stick, and so on.) So the upshot of the argument, if it is successful, is that there exists at least one thing which causes other things to exist, but is not itself caused to exist by anything else.

But could there not be many such things? And would each of them be God? This brings us to the second point of interest. Aquinas argues that there must be a first unmoved mover, a first uncaused cause, a necessary being, and the like; but his theistic argument is not finished there. In the next eight questions he argues that anything that was a first efficient cause would have to be immaterial, unchanging, eternal, simple and the possessor of all the perfections to be found in those things dependent upon it – in a word, God. It is therefore incorrect to follow the usual custom of criticizing Aquinas for

hastily concluding that a first cause or unmoved mover or necessary being would have to be God.

The third sort of cosmological argument is associated especially with Leibniz and Samuel Clarke; according to this version of the argument, there must be a sufficient reason for the actuality of any contingent state of affairs. Therefore there must be a sufficient reason for the existence of any contingent being – but also, says Leibniz, for the whole series of contingent beings. This sufficient reason must be the activity of God.

2 Ontological arguments

Anselm's ontological argument has excited enormous controversy (see ANSELM OF CANTERBURY §§3–4). Aquinas rejected it, Duns Scotus 'coloured' it a bit and then accepted it; DESCARTES (§6) and Malebranche endorsed it; like Duns Scotus, Leibniz thought it needed just a bit of work to be successful; Kant rejected it and delivered what many thought to be the final quietus (though others have found Kant's criticisms both intrinsically obscure and of doubtful relevance to the argument); and Schopenhauer thought it a 'charming joke'. Although in the twentieth century it was defended by (among others) Charles Hartshorne, Norman Malcolm and Alvin Plantinga, probably most contemporary philosophers reject the argument, thinking it a joke, but not particularly charming.

Anselm's version goes as follows:

Hence, even the fool is convinced that something exists in the understanding, at least, than which nothing greater can be conceived.... And assuredly that, than which nothing greater can be conceived, cannot exist in the understanding alone; for suppose it exists in the understanding alone; then it can be conceived to exist in reality; which is greater.

Therefore, if that, than which nothing greater can be conceived, exists in the understanding alone, the very being, than which nothing greater can be conceived is one, than which a greater can be conceived. But obviously this is impossible. Hence, there is no doubt that there exists a being, than which nothing greater can be conceived, and it exists both in the understanding and in reality.

(*Proslogion*, ch. 2)

This argument is a *reductio ad absurdum*: postulate the nonexistence of God, and show that this leads to an absurdity. Perhaps we can outline the argument as follows:

(1) A maximally great being (one than which nothing

greater can be conceived) exists in the understanding (that is, is such that we can conceive of it).

(2) It is greater to exist in reality than to exist merely in the understanding.

(3) Therefore, if the maximally great being existed *only* in the understanding, it would be less than maximally great.

But it is impossible that the maximally great being be less than maximally great; hence this being exists in reality as well as in the understanding – that is, it exists. And clearly this maximally great being is God.

The earliest objection to this argument was proposed by Anselm's contemporary and fellow monk Gaunilo in his *On Behalf of the Fool* (Psalm 14: 'The fool has said in his heart "There is no God"'). According to Gaunilo, the argument must be defective, because we can use an argument of the very same form to demonstrate the existence of such absurdities as an island (or chocolate sundae, or hamster, for that matter) than which none greater can be conceived. (Says Gaunilo: 'I know not which I ought to regard as the greater fool: myself, supposing that I should allow this proof; or him, if he should suppose that he had established with any certainty the existence of this island.') But Anselm has a reply: the notion of a maximally great island, like that of a largest integer, does not make sense, cannot be exemplified. The reason is that the properties that make for greatness in an island – size, number of palm trees, quality of coconuts – do not have intrinsic maxima; for any island, no matter how large and no matter how many palm trees, it is possible that there be one even larger and with more palm trees. But the properties that make for greatness in a being – knowledge, power and goodness, for example – do have intrinsic maxima: omniscience, omnipotence and being perfectly good.

3   Ontological arguments (cont.)

The most celebrated criticism of the ontological argument comes from Immanuel Kant, who apparently argues in his *Critique of Pure Reason* (Transcendental Dialectic, bk II, ch. III, section 4) that if this argument were sound, the proposition 'there is a being than which none greater can be conceived' would have to be logically necessary; but there cannot be an existential proposition that is logically necessary. Sadly, his reason for making this declaration is itself maximally obscure. He adds that 'existence is not a real predicate', which is widely quoted as the principal objection to the argument. Unfortunately this dictum is of dubious relevance to Anselm's

argument and a dark saying in its own right. What might it mean to say that existence is not a real property or predicate? And if it is not, how is that relevant to the argument? Why should Anselm care whether it is or not?

Perhaps we can understand Kant as follows. The argument as stated begins with the assertion that a maximally great being exists in the understanding; the idea is that this much is obvious, whether or not this being also exists in reality (that is, actually exists). Anselm then goes on to reason about this being, arguing that a being with the properties this one has – of being maximally great – cannot exist only in the understanding, but must exist in reality as well. So the argument depends upon the assumption that there *is* a maximally great being, and now the question is: does this being actually exist? Use the term 'actualism' for the view that there are not (and could not be) things that do not exist; the things that exist are all the things there are. Note that if this is true, then existence is a very special property: it is redundant, in that it is implied by every other property; anything that has *any* property (including the property of being maximally great) also has existence. But if actualism is true, the ontological argument as formulated above cannot work. For if it is not possible that there be things that do not exist, then in saying initially that there is a maximally great being, one that at any rate exists in the understanding, we are already saying that there exists a maximally great being, thus begging the question. If no maximally great being exists, then there simply is no such thing as a maximally great being, in which case we cannot (following Anselm) suppose initially that the maximally great being does not exist in reality and then argue that this being would be greater if it did exist in reality. If actualism is true, existence is a redundant property; but then to say that there is a maximally great being that exists in the understanding is already to say that there really exists a maximally great being. So perhaps Kant's puzzling dictum should be seen as an early endorsement of actualism.

Of course Anselm might reply that the fault lies not with his argument, but with actualism; in any event, there are other versions that do not conflict with actualism. Charles Hartshorne (1941) claimed to detect two quite different versions of the argument in Anselm's work; the second version is consistent with actualism and thus sidesteps Kant's criticism. This version proceeds from the thought that a really great being would be one that would have been great even if things had been different; its greatness is stable across possible worlds, to put it in a misleading if picturesque way. So say that a being has *maximal excellence* in a given possible world W if and only if it is omnipotent, omniscient and wholly good in W; and say that a being has *maximal greatness* if it has maximal excellence in every possible world. Then the premise of the argument (thus restated) is simply:

Maximal greatness is possibly exemplified.

That is, it is possible that there be a being that has maximal greatness. But (given the widely accepted view that if a proposition is possibly necessary in the broadly logical sense, then it is necessary), it follows by ordinary modal logic that maximal greatness is not just possibly exemplified, but exemplified in fact. For maximal greatness is exemplified if and only if there is a being B such that the proposition

B is omnipotent and omniscient and wholly good (has maximal excellence)

is necessary. If maximal greatness is possibly exemplified, therefore, then some proposition of that sort is possibly necessary. By the above principle, whatever is possibly necessary is necessary; accordingly, that proposition is necessarily true and hence true.

So stated, the ontological argument breaches no laws of logic, commits no confusions and is entirely immune to Kant's criticism. The only remaining question of interest is whether its premise, that maximal greatness is possibly exemplified, is indeed true. That certainly seems to be a rational claim; but it is not one that cannot rationally be denied. A remaining problem with the argument, perhaps, is that it might be thought that the epistemic distance between premise and conclusion is insufficiently great. Once you see how the argument works, you may think that asserting or believing the premise is tantamount to asserting or believing the conclusion; the canny atheist will say that he does not believe it is possible that there be a maximally great being. But would not a similar criticism hold of any valid argument? Take any valid argument: once you see how it works, you may think that asserting or believing the premise is tantamount to asserting or believing the conclusion. The ontological argument remains as intriguing as ever.

4 Teleological arguments

Teleological arguments start from contingent premises that involve more specific features of the universe, features which in one way or another suggest that the universe has been designed by a conscious and intelligent being. These arguments have often been developed in close connection with modern science; they have been endorsed by many of the giants of modern science, including Isaac Newton.

Here is a classic statement of the argument by William PALEY (§2):

> In crossing a heath, suppose I pitched my foot against a *stone*, and were asked how the stone came to be there, I might possibly answer that for any thing I know to the contrary, it had lain there for ever: nor would it perhaps be very easy to show the absurdity of this answer. But suppose I had found a *watch* upon the ground and it should be inquired how the watch happened to be in that place, I should hardly think of the answer which I had before given, that, for any thing I know the watch might have always been there. Yet why should not this answer serve for the watch, as well as for the stone? For this reason and for no other: viz., that, when we come to inspect the watch, we perceive (what we could not discover in the stone) that its several parts are framed and put together for a purpose...
>
> ([1802] 1804: 1–2)

Paley then points out that the universe and some of its parts – for example, living things and their organs – resemble a watch, in that they give the appearance of having been designed in order to accomplish certain purposes. An eye, for example, looks like an extremely subtle and sophisticated mechanism designed to enable its owner to see. But the only serious candidate for the post of designer of the universe is God.

Kant, who had little but contempt for the cosmological and ontological arguments, was much less dismissive of this one. He still rejected the argument, however, pointing out that at most it shows that it is likely that there is a designer or architect of the universe; and it is a long way from a designer to the God of the theistic religions, an almighty, omniscient, wholly good creator of the world, by whose power the universe sprang into being. Of course, a cosmic architect – a being who has designed our entire universe, with its elements ranging across many orders of magnitude from gigantic galaxies to the minutest things we know – is no mean conclusion, and it seems churlish to dismiss it with an airy wave in order to point out that there is something even stronger that the teleological argument does not show.

5 Teleological arguments (cont.)

Many people, however, have rejected the teleological argument even taken as an argument for a designer. The eighteenth-century proponents of the argument invariably mentioned the apparent teleology in the biological world; but (so say the critics) Darwin changed all that. We now know that the apparent design in the world of living things is *merely* apparent.

The enormous variety of flora and fauna, those enormously elaborate and articulate mechanisms, and finely detailed systems and organs such as the mammalian eye and the human brain give a powerful impression of design; but in fact they are the product of such blind mechanisms as random genetic mutation and natural selection. The idea is that there is a source of genetic variation which produces mutation in the structure and function of existing organisms. Most of these mutations are deleterious; a few are adaptive and their lucky owners will have an adaptive edge, eventually coming to predominate in a population. Given enough time, so the story goes, this process can produce all the splendid complexity and detail that characterize the contemporary living world (see EVOLUTION, THEORY OF).

Of course there is little real evidence that these processes can in fact achieve this much: naturally enough, we have not been able to follow their operation in such a way as to observe them produce, say, birds or mammals from reptiles, or even human beings from simian precursors. And even if we did observe the course of animate history (even if we had a detailed record on film), this would by no means show that blind mechanisms are in fact sufficient for this effect; for of course there would be nothing in the film record to show that those random genetic mutations were not in fact guided and orchestrated by God.

Still, the critic of the teleological argument claims not that in fact evolution has been accomplished just by these blind mechanisms, but that it could have been; if so, there is a real alternative to design. That these mechanisms really could have produced effects of this magnitude is far from clear; we have little real reason to suppose that there is a path through the space of possible animal design plans, a path leading from bacteria to human beings, and such that each new step is both adaptive and reachable from the previous step by mechanisms we understand. Still, the suggestion does perhaps damage the teleological argument by suggesting a naturalistic candidate for the post of producer of apparent design.

But organic evolution addresses only one of the areas of apparent design. There is also the origin of life; even the simplest unicellular creatures (prokaryotes such as bacteria and certain algae, for example) are enormously complex and upon close inspection look for all the world as if they have been designed; it is fair to say that no one, so far, has a decent idea as to how these creatures might have come into being just by way of the operation of the regularities of physics and chemistry. There are also the various considerations connected with the so-called 'fine tuning' of the universe. First, there is the 'flatness' problem. The

mass density of the universe is at present very close to the density corresponding to the borderline between an open universe (one that goes on expanding for ever) and a closed universe (one that expands to a certain size and then collapses). The ratio between the forces making for expansion and those making for contraction is close to one. But then shortly after the Big Bang this value would have to have been inside a very narrow band indeed. Thus Stephen Hawking (1974): 'reduction of the rate of expansion by one part in 10^{12} at the time when the temperature of the Universe was 10^{10} K would have resulted in the Universe's starting to recollapse when its radius was only 1/3000 of the present value and the temperature was still 10,000 K' – much too warm for the development of life. On the other hand, if the rate of expansion had been even minutely greater, the universe would have expanded much too fast for the formation of stars and galaxies, required for the formation of the heavy elements necessary for the development of life.

Another kind of fine tuning was also necessary: of the fundamental physical constants. If any of the four fundamental forces (weak and strong nuclear forces, electromagnetic force, electron charge) had been even minutely different, the universe would not have supported life; they too must have been fine-tuned to an almost unbelievable accuracy. And the suggestion, again, is that given the infinite range of possible values for the fundamental constants, design is suggested by the fact that the actual values fall in that extremely narrow range of values that permits the development of intelligent life.

But there is a naturalistic riposte. Since the 1970s, several different sorts of 'inflationary' scenario have shown up. These postulate the formation (at very early times) of many different universes or subuniverses, with different rates of expansion, and different values for the fundamental constants. These inflationary models are motivated, in part, by a desire to avoid singularities and the accompanying appearance of design. If all possible values for the fundamental constants and the rate of expansion are actually exemplified in different subuniverses, then the fact that there is a subuniverse with the values ours displays no longer requires explanation or suggests a Designer. Many of these scenarios are wildly speculative and unencumbered by empirical evidence, but (if physically acceptable) they do tend to blunt the force of a design argument from fine tuning. (Of course, someone who already believed in God and saw no need to eliminate suggestions of design might be inclined to reject these suggestions as metaphysically extravagant.) But there are also counterarguments here; the discussion goes on. It is hard to see a verdict, at present, on the prospects of this form of the argument. The teleological argument seems to have enormous vitality; its epitaph is often read, but the argument regularly reappears in new forms. As for a final evaluation, the best perhaps comes from Kant, who said that this argument 'always deserves to be mentioned with respect. It is the oldest, the clearest and the most accordant with the common reason of mankind' (1787: 520).

6   Other theistic arguments

We have examined the Big Three among theistic arguments, but there are many more. First, there are moral arguments of at least two sorts. These are arguments that the very nature of morality – the unconditioned character of the moral law – requires a divine lawgiver. You might find yourself utterly convinced that:

Morality is objective, not dependent upon what human beings know or think or do.

You may also be convinced that:

The objective character of morality cannot be explained in terms of any 'natural' facts about human beings (or other things), so there could not be such a thing as objective moral law unless there were a being like God who legislates it.

Then you will have a theistic argument from the nature of morality. This argument can go in either of two directions: some people think we can simply *see* that moral obligation is impossible apart from a divine will and lawgiver, while others think that the dependence of moral obligation upon the will of God is the best explanation for its objectivity and special deontological force.

A second main type of moral argument is due to Kant (1788), who argues first that virtue deserves to be proportionally rewarded with happiness: the more virtuous you are, the more happiness you deserve. But nature by itself does not seem able to guarantee anything like this sort of coincidence. If morality is to make sense, however, it must be supposed that there is such a coincidence; practical reason, therefore, is entitled to postulate a supernatural being with enough knowledge, power and goodness to ensure that we receive the happiness we deserve as a reward for our virtue. So taken, the argument is for the rationality of making the assumption that there is a being of this sort; it is not really an argument for the actual existence of such a being. This argument receives criticism from several sides: some hold that we do not have to assume that there is proportionality between virtue and happiness in order to carry out the moral

life; others (for example, many Christians) argue that both happiness and the ability to live a moral life are gifts of grace and that if we really got what we deserve, we should all be thoroughly miserable.

There are many other theistic arguments – arguments from the nature of proper function, from the nature of propositions, numbers and sets, from intentionality, from counterfactuals, from the confluence of epistemic reliability with epistemic justification, from reference, simplicity, intuition, love, colours and flavours, miracles, play and enjoyment, morality, beauty, the meaning of life, and even from the existence of evil. There is no space even to outline all these arguments, so we will look at just three.

First, the argument from intentionality (or about-ness). Consider propositions – the things that are true or false, that are capable of being believed, and that stand in logical relations to one another. Propositions have another property: *aboutness* or *intentionality*. They represent reality or some part of it as being thus and so, and it is by virtue of this property that propositions (as opposed, for example, to sets) are true or false. Most who have thought about the matter have found it incredible that propositions should exist apart from the activity of minds. How could they just *be* there, if never thought of? Further, representing things as being thus and so – being about something or other – seems to be a property or activity of minds or perhaps thoughts. It is therefore extremely plausible to think of propositions as ontologically dependent upon mental or intellectual activity in such a way that either they just *are* thoughts, or else at any rate could not exist if not thought of. But propositions cannot be human thoughts; there are far too many of them for that. (For each real number r, for example, there is the proposition that r is distinct from the Taj Mahal.) Hence the only viable possibility is that they are divine thoughts, God's thoughts (so that when we think, we literally think God's thoughts after him).

Second, there is the argument from sets or collections. Many think of sets as displaying the following characteristics: (1) no set is a member of itself; (2) sets (unlike properties) have their extensions essentially – hence many sets are contingent beings and no set could have existed if one of its members had not; (3) sets form an iterated structure – at the first level, there are sets whose members are nonsets, at the second, sets whose members are nonsets or first level sets, . . . , at the nth level, sets whose members are nonsets or sets of index less than n, . . . , and so on.

It is also natural to follow Georg Cantor, the father of modern set theory, in thinking of sets as collections – that is, as things whose existence depends upon a certain sort of intellectual activity, a collecting or 'thinking together' as Cantor put it. If sets were collections, that would explain their having the first three features. But of course there are far too many sets for them to be a product of human thinking together; there are many sets such that no human being has ever thought their members together and many such that no human being *could* think them together. That requires an infinite mind – one such as God's.

For a third example, consider the argument from appalling evil. Many philosophers offer antitheistic arguments from evil, and perhaps they have some force. But there is also a *theistic* argument from evil. The premise is that there is real and objectively horrifying evil in the world. Examples would be certain sorts of appalling evil characteristic of Nazi concentration camps: guards found pleasure in devising tortures, making mothers decide which of their children would go to the gas chamber and which be spared; small children were hanged, dying (because of their light weight) a slow and agonizing death; victims were taunted with the claim that no one would ever know of their fate and how they were treated. Of course, Nazi concentration camps have no monopoly on this sort of evil: there are also Stalin, Pol Pot and a thousand lesser villains. These states of affairs, one thinks, are objectively horrifying, in the sense that they would constitute enormous evil even if we and everyone else came perversely to approve of them.

Naturalism does not have the resources to accommodate or explain this fact about these states of affairs. From a naturalistic point of view, about all one can say is that we do indeed hate them; but this is far short of seeing them as intrinsically horrifying. How can we understand this intrinsically horrifying character? After all, as much misery and suffering can occur in a death from cancer as in a death caused by someone else's wickedness. What is the difference? The difference lies in the perpetrators and their intentions. Those who engage in this sort of evil are purposely and intentionally setting themselves to do these wicked things. But why is that objectively horrifying? A good answer (and one for which it is hard to think of an alternative) is that this evil consists in defying God, the source of all that is good and just, and the first being of the universe. What is horrifying here is not merely going contrary to God's will, but consciously choosing to invert the true scale of values, explicitly aiming at what is abhorrent to God. This is an offence and affront to God; it is defiance of God himself, and so is objectively horrifying. Appalling evil thus has a sort of cosmic significance. But of course there could be no evil of this sort if there were no such being as God.

See also: AGNOSTICISM; ATHEISM; DEISM; GOD, CONCEPTS OF; NATURAL THEOLOGY; RELIGION AND EPISTEMOLOGY; RELIGIOUS EXPERIENCE

References and further reading

* Aquinas, T. (1266–73) *Summa theologiae*, London: Eyre & Spottiswoode, and New York: McGraw-Hill, for Blackfriars, 1964, 60 vols, Ia, qq.2–11. (The *locus classicus* of the cosmological argument; there is also a fuller statement of the first of the five ways in Aquinas' *Summa contra gentiles* I, 12–22.)
* Anselm (1077–8) *Proslogion*, in *Opera omnia*, ed. F.S. Schmitt, Stuttgart: F. Frommann, 1984. (Contains the original statement of the ontological argument(s).)
* Aristotle (*c.*350 BC) *Metaphysics* 12, in *The Complete Works of Aristotle*, ed. J. Barnes, Princeton, NJ: Princeton University Press, 1984. (An early source for the cosmological argument.)
* —— (*c.*350 BC) *Physics* 7, 8, in *The Complete Works of Aristotle*, ed. J. Barnes, Princeton, NJ: Princeton University Press, 1984. (A version of the cosmological argument can also be found here.)
  Clarke, S. (1705, 1706) *A Demonstration of the Being and Attributes of God* and *A Discourse Concerning the Unchangeable Obligations of Natural Religion*, London: Faksimile-Neudruck der Londoner Ausgaben. (Clarke's Boyle Lectures, containing an elaborate statement of the 'sufficient reasons' version of the cosmological argument, the one criticized by Hume.)
  Clifford, W.K. (1879) 'The Ethics of Belief', in *Lectures and Essays*, London: Macmillan. (Classic statement of the view that one needs evidence in order to be justified (within one's intellectual rights) in believing that there is such a person as God.)
* Craig, W. (1980) *The Cosmological Argument from Plato to Leibniz*, London: Macmillan. (An excellent history of the cosmological argument, especially good on the versions given by the medieval Arabic and Jewish philosophers.)
  Descartes, R. (1641) *Meditations*, New York: Dover, 1955. (Contains a classic statement of the ontological argument, the statement that (apparently) Kant had in mind in arguing that no version of the argument could be successful; contains also Descartes' own idiosyncratic version of the cosmological argument.)
* Gaunilo (*c.*1078) *On Behalf of the Fool*, in Anselm, *Monologion and Proslogion: with the replies of Gaunilo and Anselm*, Indianapolis, IN, 1966. (A criticism of Anselm's ontological argument.)
* Hartshorne, C. (1941) *Man's Vision of God*, New

York: Harper & Row. (The first modal version of the ontological argument.)

* Hawking, S. (1974) 'The Anisotropy of the Universe at Large Times', in M.S. Longair (ed.) *Confrontation of Cosmological Theories with Observational Data*, Dordrecht: Reidel, 72. (An early statement of and response to fine-tuning issues by one of the most eminent contemporary physicists.)

* Kant, I. (1781/1787) *Critique of Pure Reason*, trans. and ed. N. Kemp Smith, London: Macmillan, 1929. (Contains influential criticisms of the cosmological, teleological and ontological arguments; Kant holds that the first two are unsuccessful without the third, but the third is vitiated by the fact (as Kant sees it) that 'existence is not a predicate'.)

* —— (1788) *Critique of Practical Reason*, trans. and ed. L. White Beck, New York: Macmillan, 1993. (Presents a moral argument: postulation of the existence of God is a necessary condition for morality.)

Leibniz, G.W. (1714) *Monadology*, in *The Monadology and other Philosophical Writings*, trans. R. Latta, Oxford: Oxford University Press, 1898. (Contains Leibniz's statement of the 'sufficient reasons' version of the cosmological argument, as well as one of his statements of the ontological argument; Leibniz accepted the ontological argument, but thought it was necessary to prove and add as a preliminary premise the proposition that it is possible that there is such a person as God.)

Mavrodes, G. (1986) 'Religion and the Queerness of Morality', in R. Audi and W. Wainwright (eds) *Rationality, Religious Belief and Moral Commitment*, Ithaca, NY: Cornell University Press. (Mavrodes argues that if naturalism were true, there would be no such thing as morality; this is therefore a moral argument for the existence of God.)

* Paley, W. (1802) *Natural Theology, or Evidences of the Existence and Attributes of the Deity collected from the Appearances of Nature*, London: R. Faulder & Son; Weybridge: S. Hamilton, 1804. (Classic modern statement of the teleological argument.)

Plantinga, A. (1974) *The Nature of Necessity*, Oxford: Clarendon Press. (Contains a version of the ontological argument developed in terms of the metaphysics of modality (possible worlds) that is immune to Kant's criticism (whatever precisely it was).)

—— (1983) 'Reason and Belief in God', in A. Plantinga and N. Wolterstorff (eds) *Faith and Rationality*, Notre Dame, IN: University of Notre Dame Press. (Argues against the claim that propositional evidence (as in the theistic arguments) is needed for rational justification in believing in God; see also the other essays in the collection.)

* Plato (c.360 BC) *Laws*, Chicago, IL: University of Chicago Press. (One of the earliest adumbrations of the cosmological argument.)

Rowe, W. (1975) *The Cosmological Argument*, Princeton, NJ: Princeton University Press. (A penetrating and thorough examination of the several forms of the cosmological argument.)

Swinburne, R. (1979) *The Existence of God*, Oxford: Oxford University Press. (Contains a very full and sophisticated version of the teleological argument, developed in terms of probability.)

ALVIN PLANTINGA

GOD, CONCEPTS OF

We think of God as an ultimate reality, the source or ground of all else, perfect and deserving of worship. Such a conception is common to both Eastern and Western religions. Some trace this to human psychology or sociology: Freud regarded God as a wish-fulfilling projection of a perfect, comforting father-figure; Marxists see belief in God as arising from the capitalist structure of society. Believers, however, trace their belief to religious experience, revealed or authoritative texts, and rational reflection.

Philosophers flesh out the concept of God by drawing inferences from God's relation to the universe ('first-cause theology') and from the claim that God is a perfect being. 'Perfect-being' theology is the more fundamental method. Its history stretches from Plato and Aristotle, through the Stoics, and into the Christian tradition as early as Augustine and Boethius; it plays an important role in underwriting such ontological arguments for God's existence as those of Anselm and Descartes. It draws on four root intuitions: that to be perfect is perfectly to be, that it includes being complete, that it includes being all-inclusive, and that it includes being personal. Variously balanced, these intuitions yield our varied concepts of God.

Criticisms of perfect-being theology have focused both on the possibility that the set of candidate divine perfections may not be consistent or unique, and doubts as to whether human judgment can be adequate for forming concepts of God. Another problem with the method is that different accounts of perfection will yield different accounts of God: Ibn Sina and Ibn Rushd, for instance, appear to have held that God would be the more perfect for lacking some knowledge, while most Christian writers hold that perfection requires omniscience.

93

Views of God's relation to the universe vary greatly. Pantheists say that God is the universe. Panentheists assert that God includes the universe, or is related to it as soul to body. They ascribe to God the limitations associated with being a person – such as limited power and knowledge – but argue that being a person is nevertheless a state of perfection. Other philosophers, however, assert that God is wholly different from the universe.

Some of these think that God created the universe ex nihilo, that is, from no pre-existing material. Some add that God conserves the universe in being moment by moment, and is thus provident for his creatures. Still others think that God 'found' some pre-existing material and 'creates' by gradually improving this material – this view goes back to the myth of the Demiurge in Plato's Timaeus, and also entails that God is provident. By contrast, deists deny providence and think that once God made it, the universe ran on its own. Still others argue that God neither is nor has been involved in the world. The common thread lies in the concept of perfection: thinkers relate God to the universe in the way that their thoughts about God's perfection make most appropriate.

1 **The logic of 'God'**
2 **Data and methods**
3 **Perfect-being theology**
4 **Limits of perfect-being theology**
5 **Intuitions about perfection**
6 **Classical theism**
7 **Pantheism**
8 **Panentheism**

1 The logic of 'God'

We use the term 'God' in two main ways. We use 'God' to address God, as in prayer. So used, 'God' seems like a proper name. We also use 'God' like a general predicate. For we can and do ask whether there is more than one God: the concept of God allows this question a 'yes' answer. The concept of Moses does not allow a 'yes' answer to 'was there more than one Moses?' One cannot use proper names this way, for there cannot have been two Moseses. If 'two' people are identical with Moses, they are one person, not two. 'Was there more than one Moses?' makes sense only taken as 'was there more than one man called Moses?' or 'did one person do the deeds in the Moses story, or does the story conflate the deeds of many men?'

The ambiguity between name and predicate suggests that 'God' is a title-term, like 'Pastor' or 'Bishop'. Many people can be bishops; in this way title-terms are like general predicates. But one can also address the office-holder by the title ('Dear Bishop...'); one can use the title as a name for the person who holds the office. Thus, the concept of God is a concept of an individual holding a special office.

Thinkers have disagreed about what this office is. AQUINAS (§9) suggests that to be God is to have providence over all (*Summa theologiae* Ia, q.13, a.8). But without obviously contradicting themselves, some philosophers (such as ARISTOTLE (§16) and PLOTINUS (§§3–5)) deny that God provides for creatures. Some say that to be God is to deserve worship. But arguably one's act cannot be an act of worship if one does not take its object to be truly divine, and something cannot deserve worship if it is not divine. If either of these claims is true, 'to be God is to deserve worship' amounts to something like 'to be God is to deserve to be treated as God' – which is true but not helpful.

The suggestion that this entry will explore is that the role or office of God is that of ultimate reality, than which no reality is more basic. Consider some claims on which Eastern and Western religions agree:

(1) Nothing made God; anything that was made is not God.
(2) God is the source or ground of all that is not God.

Eastern and Western religions also agree that God is the Supreme Being. They use 'supreme' to speak of God's perfection and authority and so agree that:

(3) God rules all that is not God.
(4) God is the most perfect being.

(1)–(4) are necessary truths *de dicto*; they state requirements for counting as God. All express facets of God's ultimacy. (1) states that nothing is causally more basic than God. On (1), no account of why things exist can go beyond God; if God explains anything, God is an ultimate explainer. On (2), all explanations of existence do in fact terminate in God. On (3), God has ultimate control over all things; on (4), God is ultimate in perfection. If (1)–(4) are near the core of the concept of God, so is ultimacy.

Quite diverse religious contexts tie ultimacy and deity. Revelation 21: 12 calls God 'the Alpha and the Omega, the beginning and the end'. To be last is to be ultimate. That is first to which nothing is prior. So being first is also a way to be ultimate, and being first is a prerequisite of being taken as God. John Chrysostom comments that 'men most honour the eldest of beings which was before all, and account this to be God' (*Homilies on St John* [1994: 7]). Pantheists claim not to twist the meaning of 'God' in calling the universe 'God' because, as they see it, the universe is the ultimate reality; there is nothing beyond it. Even believers in many gods sometimes distinguish mere gods from God on grounds of ultimacy. Thus, Hindus see their many *devas* (gods) as finally just creations and manifestations of the one ultimate being, Brahman (see GOD, INDIAN CONCEPTIONS OF); and PROCLUS (§4), a Neoplatonic polytheist, writes that:

> God and the One are the same because there is nothing greater than God and nothing greater than the One...[Plato's] Demiurge is a god, not God. The god that is the One is not a god, but God simply.
>
> (*Commentary on Plato's Parmenides* 641–3)

Proclus' One counts as God precisely because it is, in Proclus' view, the ultimate reality. TILLICH (§§2–3) sums it up: 'Only [an] ultimate reality can...be our unconditional concern [that is, a genuine God]. Faith in anything which has only preliminary reality is idolatrous' (1955: 59). Thus, concepts of God are concepts of what the ultimate reality is and how it is related to the rest of reality.

2   Data and methods

Human beings draw their views of God from religious experience, revealed or authoritative texts, and rational reflection. The third is, in a way, basic. Not all seeming experience of God is genuine. Texts and philosophical thought help sort the true from the illusory. Then, too, the genuine experiences of God, once found, do not wear their meanings on their sleeves. They need interpretation, which texts and reason provide. Finally, authoritative texts themselves need interpretation, and reason provides this. So religious experience and authoritative texts are data, which philosophical and theological reasoning work into fully articulate theories of the nature of God.

Some trace views of God to still other sources. For example, Freud argued that belief in God is a form of wish-fulfilment, in which human beings give themselves the protected, loved feeling of an idealized childhood by projecting into reality a vision of a perfect, benevolent father-figure who will make everything right in the end. Other psychologists take a still dimmer view of God, seeing him as not a comforting dream but the projection into reality of neurotic self-loathing; they see belief in divine judgment (for example) as a form of self-persecution. DURKHEIM (§4) (1915) regarded the concept of God as a symbol expressing society's role in our lives. Marxists see this role as oppressive, at least under capitalism, and so see concepts of God as reflecting and reacting to social evils. On their view, belief in God is doomed to wither away when society progresses.

These are all speculations, and beliefs may be true even if one can explain our holding them in purely psychological or sociological terms. But still, theists claim that reason, experience and authority yield *warranted* belief. On some views, beliefs are warranted only if their sources are reliably truth-producing ways of forming beliefs. Wish-fulfilment and neurosis-expression are not reliably truth-producing ways of forming beliefs. So, on these views of warrant, a persuasive psychological or sociological explanation of apparent religious experience or the intuitions that guide theistic reasoning could undermine theists' claims to warranted belief. Again, some think a belief warranted only if one holds it for the right kind of reason. 'To feel good' is not the right kind of reason.

Still, the concept of God gives as much grist to wish-fulfilment as to self-persecution or Marxist theories. Consequently, the two sorts may cancel out: the facets of God which count *for* the one count *against* the other. Belief in God cannot both comfort and torment us. It can at most comfort one part of us and torment another part. But the more elaborate the genetic account of theism's attractions, the less plausible the account becomes. Furthermore, one can give equally unflattering accounts of the appeal of atheism, Freudianism and Marxism. If so, the genetic argument again cancels out.

Western philosophy works up theories about God in two main ways. *First-cause theology* draws out implications of God's relation to the universe. *Perfect-being theology* reasons out consequences of the claim that God is a perfect being. Each method gets at part of God's ultimacy. First-cause theology explores God's causal ultimacy. Perfect-being theology explores God's ultimacy in value. Most religious thinkers use both methods. Aquinas, for instance, sets up his basic descriptions of God by giving five ways to argue for God's existence (*Summa theologiae* Ia, q.2, a.3). The first three ways argue the existence of a first cause, the fourth that of a perfect being, and the fifth that of an intelligent designer of nature. Aquinas then argues that a first cause must be purely actual and so perfect and uses both perfect-being and first-cause theology to work out his concept of God.

Perfect-being theology is the more basic theological method. In the West, for instance, first-cause theology often explicates and/or argues the claim that God created the universe *ex nihilo* (see CREATION AND CONSERVATION, RELIGIOUS DOCTRINE OF §§1–2). But while Western Scriptures say that God created the universe, they do not so clearly state that God made it *ex nihilo*. The most famous biblical passage on creation is Genesis 1: 1–2: '[1]In the beginning God created the heavens and the earth. [2]Now the earth was formless and empty, darkness was over the surface of the deep, and the Spirit of God was hovering over the waters.' Verse 1 could assert a creation *ex nihilo*, with verse 2 describing that act's initial result. But verse 1 could just be a topic statement for the overall creation story, which might begin in verse 2. In that case, in the story, God finds some initial chaotic state of things, and creates a universe by forming or moulding that chaos into the structured world we now inhabit. This second reading does not involve creation *ex nihilo*. It is perfect-being theology that leads Western thinkers to take creation as *ex nihilo*; by doing so, they magnify things' dependence on God and God's importance for and superiority to the universe. We ought, then, to focus on perfect-being theology.

3 Perfect-being theology

Perfect-being theology has a long history. PLATO (§14) assumes that gods are 'the...best possible' to argue that they are immutable (*Republic* II, 381c). To work out the nature of God, Aristotle takes as a premise that God is 'the best substance' (*Metaphysics* XII, 9, 1074b). CICERO (§3) records the perfect-being arguments of the early Stoic ZENO OF CITIUM:

> That which is rational is better than that which is not rational. But nothing is better than the cosmos. Therefore the cosmos is rational. One can prove in a similar manner that the cosmos is wise, happy and eternal, since all of these are better than things which lack them, and nothing is better than the cosmos.
>
> (*On the Nature of the Gods* II, 21)

Zeno plainly envisages many applications of this basic argument form:

(5) Whatever is *F* is more perfect than whatever is not *F*.

(6) Whatever is most perfect is more perfect than everything else.

(7) So whatever is most perfect is *F*.

(8) *X* is most perfect.

(9) So *X* is *F*.

The project of filling out a concept of God by successive applications of (5)–(9) is a version of perfect-being theology. To many, Zeno's taking 'the cosmos' as a value of *X* in (8) will look odd. Cicero's case for Zeno is that 'since the cosmos includes everything and since there is nothing which is not in it, it is perfect in all respects' (*On the Nature of the Gods*). Cicero's thought is perhaps this: the cosmos is composed of other objects, its parts. So the cosmos' perfection is the sum of its parts' perfections, and thus it is greater than the perfection of every object it contains. But the cosmos contains every object other

than itself. So the cosmos is the most perfect actual being.

Cicero seems even to think that the cosmos is the most perfect *possible* being:

> Nothing at all is better...than the cosmos. Not only *is* nothing better, but nothing can even be conceived of which is better. And if nothing is better than reason and wisdom, it is necessary that these be present in that which we have granted to be the best.
>
> (*On the Nature of the Gods* II, 18)

Reasoning out the nature of a greatest *possible* being is another form of perfect-being theology. Taking the cosmos as the greatest *possible* being, Cicero applies to 'reason' and 'wisdom' a form of argument which, like (5)–(9), yields a general theological programme. Why might Stoics call the cosmos the most perfect possible being? Suppose that to be a cosmos is to be all-inclusive, a sum of all other things. If so, then no matter what, if anything exists, a cosmos also exists: there is a sum of all things, and this sum is the most perfect actual thing. Suppose we now add that no matter what objects made it up, the cosmos which existed would be the same individual cosmos as the one which now exists. It then follows that the cosmos is the greatest possible being, in the sense that no matter what possible things existed, our cosmos would be greater than any of them. Stoics may have thought this way (see STOICISM §§3–5).

The Christian tradition invokes perfect-being theology at least as early as AUGUSTINE (§7), who wrote: 'When we think of...God...thought takes the form of an attempt to conceive something than which nothing more excellent or sublime exists' (*Christian Doctrine* I, 7, 7). Augustine tells us to construct a concept of God by seeking a concept of the most perfect being there is. He adds two concrete rules. One is to deny God whatever attributes we think to be imperfections, the other is to affirm of God in the highest degree any attributes we find to be perfections (*On the Trinity* V, 1, 2; XV, 4, 6).

BOETHIUS (§5) stated an axiom stronger than Augustine's, that God is such that nothing greater than him is even conceivable (*The Consolation of Philosophy* III, 10). ANSELM OF CANTERBURY (§§3–4) at first based his perfect-being theology on Augustine's axiom, that God is the greatest actual being (*Monologion*, chaps 1–3). To fill out the concept of God, Anselm directed, ascribe to God all attributes *F* such that whatever is *F* is better than whatever is not *F* (*Monologion*, ch. 15). Thus Anselm's *Monologion* recaps Zeno's theological programme. In his *Proslogion*, Anselm switches to Boethius' axiom, and suggests filling out the concept of God by many arguments of this form:

(10) Nothing greater than God is conceivable.
(11) If God is not F, something greater than God is conceivable.
(12) So God is F.

Replacing 'is conceivable' with 'is possible' yields a form of argument theistic philosophers still respect. Replacing 'F' with 'existent' yields Anselm's ontological argument for God's existence (see GOD, ARGUMENTS FOR THE EXISTENCE OF §2).

4 Limits of perfect-being theology

Duns Scotus' gloss on Boethius' axiom calls God the greatest being conceivable without contradiction (*On the First Principle*, 4.65) (see DUNS SCOTUS, J. §§7–11). So perhaps Duns Scotus saw a question LEIBNIZ (§3) was to raise explicitly: what if some values of F are incompatible? What if nothing can have all values of F? Perfect-being theology replies: if so, God has a set of compatible attributes S which does not include all values of F, such that nothing can be greater than a thing with all members of S. This raises another question. Suppose that there is such a set. There may also be a second set T such that nothing can be greater than a thing with all members of T, but either an S-God would be just as great as a T-God or an S-God would be neither greater than, less great than nor as great as a T-God. What then? Perfect-being theology can say that God has any attributes common to S and T and can try to decide between S and T on further grounds, but may have to settle for saying that God has either S or T. There is no guarantee that perfect-being theology alone can fill out the concept of God.

The metaphysics one brings to perfect-being theology affects one's conclusions. The Stoics agreed with Christians that being an agent is a perfection. But the Stoics thought that only material things can act. They inferred that God must be material and so must be the most perfect material thing, the cosmos. Being perfect is being maximally good, and so thinkers' intuitions about what is perfect can differ and be as hard to reconcile as their intuitions about what is good. But perfect-being theology yields divergent results when those who do it do not share intuitions about what it is to be perfect. Anselm, a Christian, thought that a perfect being must be all-knowing (*Proslogion*, ch. 6). But ALCINOUS, a second-century Platonist, held that all God's ideas are 'eternal and perfect' and therefore denied that God has ideas – or therefore knowledge – of disease, artefacts, dirt or individuals as such (*The Handbook of Platonism*, 9.2,

7; 11.27–31). Ibn Sina and Ibn Rushd too seem to have thought that a perfect being has some but not all knowledge – that there is knowledge that is not good, so that God is more perfect without it (see IBN RUSHD §2). It is not clear that perfect-being theology can adjudicate such differences. So while it may help one work out one's own concept of God, perfect-being theology may have less promise as an avenue of theological agreement. This might in turn cast doubt on perfect-being theology's ability to give theological beliefs *warrant*.

Some theists reject perfect-being theology. Plotinus held with Plato that goodness is 'superior to being' (*Republic* VI, 509b). He thus refused to use perfect-being theology to explicate his view of the truly ultimate God, the One or Good; Plotinus' 'perfect being' is his second, subordinate god, *Nous*, the divine mind. For Plotinus, then, being truly ultimate is incompatible with being the subject of perfect-being theology. Theists who hold that God is utterly ineffable or entirely beyond our conceptual grasp doubt that perfect-being theology's development of human concepts of perfection can really explicate God's nature. As one's concept of perfection reflects one's concept of goodness, theists in the tradition of Augustine and CALVIN (§§2–3), who emphasize the corrupting effects of sin on the human power to judge what is good, find perfect-being theology radically unreliable. Freudian views of religious belief can also question perfect-being theology, for it can look like explicit, conscious wish-fulfilment: is it not a way of ascribing to God a 'wish list' of perfections? Finally, those who criticize the ontological argument for God's existence may also criticize perfect-being theology. For perfect-being theology underwrote the ontological argument in Anselm and DESCARTES (§6), and its connection with that argument is not accidental. Perfect-being theology claims in effect that in God's case, 'ought' implies 'is', and one thing God ought to be is existent.

5 Intuitions about perfection

Four intuitions about what it is to be perfect are found in the history of philosophical theology. One is that to be perfect is perfectly to be, and so draws on an account of what it is to *be*. We find this account and its consequences in PARMENIDES (§6) and in Plato's account of his Forms. Augustine puts it this way:

> Something which changes does not retain its own being. A thing which can change, even if it does not change, cannot be what it had been. So only what does not only not change but also cannot at all

change falls most truly...under the category of being.

(*On the Trinity* V, 2–3)

A God perfect in this way must be wholly discrete from the universe: the universe changes, God does not.

The Latin root of 'perfect', *perficio*, has the sense of 'complete'. Thus, a second perfection-intuition has been that what is perfect lacks nothing, is fully self-sufficient, and so is independent of all else. If persons by nature change, are finite or incomplete in various ways, or require others for their full flourishing, a God whose perfection reflects these first two intuitions may be personlike, but is not in the ordinary sense a person. A third intuition is that what is perfect, being complete, is all-inclusive. Classical theism takes God to be all-inclusive in perfection. Thus, Aquinas argues that if a being lacks some perfection, it is not a God (*Summa theologiae* Ia, q.11, a.3). The Stoics and Parmenides took being perfect as being all-inclusive and reasoned that as all-inclusive, a perfect being must include the universe. One way to develop this thought holds that God is the universe, and so sees God as impersonal. A second way to develop this view sees God as including, but also as being 'more than', the universe, just as persons include but are more than their bodies. The last intuition takes persons as the standard of perfection, and so insists that any perfect being must know, will and (according to some philosophers) feel.

Below is a survey of some of the main concepts of God that these intuitions have yielded.

6 Classical theism

Classical theism's ancestry includes Plato, Aristotle, Middle Platonism and Neoplatonism. It entered Judaism through PHILO OF ALEXANDRIA (§4), reaching its apogee there in MAIMONIDES (§3). It entered Christianity as early as Irenaeus and CLEMENT OF ALEXANDRIA and became Christian orthodoxy as the Roman Empire wound down. Though more and more challenged after 1300, it remains orthodox. Classical theism filtered into Islam as early as AL-KINDI (§§1–2). AL-GHAZALI attacked it as the view of Islamic Aristotelians, and it suffered in Islamic orthodoxy's successful reaction against Aristotle.

Much of classical theism's concept of God unfolds from the claim that God is the ultimate reality. According to classical theism, God is:

A se – wholly independent of all else. God is absolutely the first being. He exists before there is anything else for him to depend on. So he must need or depend on nothing in any way other than himself.

(Classical theism sits well with intuitions that, as perfect, God is self-sufficient.)

Simple – completely without parts. Whatever has parts depends on them for its existence and nature; bricks make a wall and make it what it is. So a God wholly *a se* has no parts (see SIMPLICITY, DIVINE).

Having no parts, God is:

Immaterial – whatever is made of matter has parts, for the matter of which it is made has parts. So a partless God cannot be made of matter, or include matter in any way which makes its parts his.

Not spatially extended – whatever extends through space has parts covering the parts of the space through which it extends (or so most think).

Without accidents – lacking non-relational contingent attributes. If God has attributes distinct from himself, he depends on them for his nature and existence. So if he is entirely *a se*, he has no such attributes: God's attributes = God. Nothing can be identical with a contingent attribute. For if one has an attribute contingently, one can only be contingently identical with it. But all genuine identities are necessary. So God has no accidents.

If so, God is:

Immutable – or unable to undergo real, intrinsic change. For real, intrinsic change is change in accident (see IMMUTABILITY).

If *a se*, God is also:

Impassible – unable to be affected by beings other than himself. For if we affected God – if, say, our suffering made him sorrowful – his emotional state would depend on us, and so God would not be wholly *a se*.

According to classical theism, God is also:

Eternal – in the sense of timeless, that is, alive without past or future, living a life neither containing nor located in any series of earlier and later events. Much traditional perfect-being theology converges on this claim. Boethius, for instance, argued that a perfect being must be timeless because timeless existence is superior to temporal existence. Temporal beings lose their pasts and lack their futures, and so enjoy only an instant-thin slice of their existences at any one time. Timeless life has no past or future. A timeless being enjoys its entire life in one timeless present. Thus Boethius saw timeless life as 'the all-at-once and perfect possession of interminable life' (*The Consolation of Philosophy* V, 6), and so most appropriate to a perfect being (see ETERNITY).

Necessarily existent – perfect-being theology yields divine necessity. To exist contingently is to be able not to exist. A being is more perfect if wholly immune to nonexistence (see NECESSARY BEING).

Omnipresent – present in all space and time, though not contained by either (see OMNIPRESENCE). This follows via perfect-being theology: a God not in some way everywhere and everywhen would be more limited and less perfect than a God with these attributes. As creator and sustainer, God is present everywhere and everywhen in the sense that he sustains in being and knows immediately every place and time and their contents.

Classical theism thinks God personal enough to have intellect and will. Perfect-being theology backs this if nothing incompatible with intellect and will adds more value to the concept of God. If God has intellect and will, perfect-being theology ascribes to him also the perfect versions of these.

Perfect intellect includes *perfect wisdom and rationality* and *perfect knowledge*. It thus includes omniscience, variously defined as knowing all truths and/or all facts, or all that is knowable, or having the greatest amount of knowledge possible for a single individual (see OMNISCIENCE). Classical theism typically holds that God's knowledge includes knowledge of free creaturely actions that, with respect to us, are future; this raises the question of how such knowledge is compatible with creaturely freedom. Perfection in knowledge also includes having knowledge in the best possible way (perhaps immediately rather than inferentially, or by direct intuition of fact rather than through grasping some representation such as a proposition) and on the best possible grounds. As perfectly wise or rational, God makes optimal use of his knowledge.

Perfect will includes *perfect power* and *perfect goodness*. Perfect power includes omnipotence, defined roughly and with some qualifications as the power to actualize any broadly logically possible state of affairs (see OMNIPOTENCE). Perfect goodness includes always acting as moral norms dictate, doing great supererogatory good and having perfect versions of at least some moral virtues (justice, mercy, altruistic love). The claim that God is perfect in knowledge, power and goodness sets up the various versions of the problem of evil (see EVIL, PROBLEM OF). The simplest version is this: if God knows that and when each evil will occur if he does not intervene, and God has the power to prevent each evil, and God is perfectly good and so does not approve of evil, how then can evil occur?

Classical theism constrains what we make of God's personal attributes. For instance, if wholly *a se*, God cannot know creatures by observing them, since states of observational knowledge causally depend on the objects observed. If I know that Fido is here by seeing Fido, then as Fido helps cause my seeing, Fido helps cause my knowing. Perfect-being theism also affects our view of God's personal attributes. It would be better to be necessarily omniscient, omnipotent and

so on than merely contingently so. So perfect-being theism pushes us to say that God has necessarily his personal perfections. This can raise questions about, for example, God's goodness: some argue that if God necessarily does no wrong, he does not qualify as a morally responsible agent (see FREEDOM, DIVINE).

Classical theism holds God wholly discrete from the world in substance. Classical theists differ over God's relation to the world. Aristotle held that God is merely a final cause, a lure who draws the universe's efficient causes into action (*Metaphysics* XII, 6–7). But most classical theists hold that God efficiently causes the world to exist by creating it from no pre-existing material; classical theists often compare this with our thinking up imaginary worlds just as we choose (without implying that the universe is a figment of God's imagination).

Most classical theists hold that God created freely and directly rather than via an intermediary. Other classical theists demur. Plotinus, for instance, argued that his ultimate reality, the One, creates necessarily (*Enneads* II, 9, 3), and has as its direct effect only a second deity, the divine mind, which creates all 'lower' beings. Both claims have had later partisans in classical theism – for example, such Arabic Aristotelians as Ibn Sina and Ibn Rushd.

Most classical theists who hold that God creates also hold that God conserves the world – that is, they hold that the universe depends on God for its being not merely in its first instant of existence (if any), but equally throughout its duration. For classical theists, God would not have to do anything positive to annihilate the universe. He would merely have to stop doing what he is always doing to keep it in existence. As a book falls to the floor once a supporting hand is withdrawn, so the world would fall back into nothingness were God's supporting power withdrawn (see CREATION AND CONSERVATION, RELIGIOUS DOCTRINE OF §5). If God conserves the world, God also is provident for his creatures, at least in keeping in being the things they need. Creation and conservation raise again the problem of evil: if all things stem from God and God actively preserves them, how can God avoid responsibility for the evils things bring?

Classical theism's God is infinite or unlimited in not depending on other things, and in perfection, power, knowledge, goodness and creative responsibility. Thus, to some, the God of classical theism is personlike but not a person (as some say of Brahman, conceived as being, consciousness and bliss). Some have denied classical theism because they see God as limited in some of these ways and more like the persons we know. Some deists denied divine providence, and perhaps conservation (see DEISM §§1–2). Plato held that the Demiurge 'found' a disordered cosmos, and 'created' only by bringing it into better order (*Timaeus*, 30a), thus freeing him from responsibility for evil (*Republic* II, 379c). Theists such as John Stuart Mill and William JAMES (§4) tried to free God of this responsibility by supposing that God has only limited power and/or knowledge.

7 Pantheism

Pantheism consists of two theses: that (a) all things are parts of, appearances of or really identical with some one being, and (b) this being is divine. Claim (a) is compatible with the view that all items not identical with this one being are unreal, or ultimately unreal, but does not entail it. Nor does (a) entail (b), for one who holds that there is just one really real or all-inclusive thing need not treat it as divine. Still, if there is just one thing, or an all-inclusive thing, that thing is the ultimate thing, and has a claim to be the most perfect thing. So given the tie between ultimacy and deity and the tradition of perfect-being theism, those who hold (a) naturally tend towards (b).

Reverence for nature and mystical experiences of the unity of all things are a perennial source of pantheism, the former persuasive to nineteenth-century Romantics, the latter to Eastern thinkers. Once tilted towards this view of God, pantheists sometimes argue that their Unity has some attributes classical theism calls distinctively divine. Stoics argue that the universe is conscious and wise, SPINOZA (§§2–4) that the one universal substance is simple, Hegel that the world-spirit exercises a kind of providence, and some contemporary philosophers that the universe viewed tenselessly exists independently and is eternal. The universe is certainly omnipresent in the sense that every place is part of it, though not as in classical theism (in which God is present *as a whole* in every place and time). In pantheism, God = universe, and so the claim that God and universe are causally related is problematic. Spinoza tries to preserve an efficient-causal relation by distinguishing an active aspect of the universe (*natura naturans*) from a passive (*natura naturata*). Hegel sees God as the universe's final cause, claiming that full realization of its divine nature is the goal towards which the universe's development moves.

The line between pantheism and panentheism is narrow. Pantheism holds that God is the sum of, the reality behind or the true identity of all things, and nothing beyond this. If a being with awareness and/or will is in some way more than its body, then a view can remain pure pantheism only by denying that God is a person or personlike, and many thinkers usually called pantheists (for example, Spinoza, the Stoics, some Hindus) may actually have been panentheists.

Many find pantheism's implications distasteful. If everything is part of God, or an aspect of him, and so forth, then God includes or really is the most unsavoury items, and (for example) whoever eats, chews on God. Thus 'pantheist' often serves as a term of theological abuse, and not everyone given the label deserves it.

8 Panentheism

Panentheism can be traced back at least to the Hindu thinker RĀMĀNUJA (§3); its chief twentieth-century friends have been 'process philosophers' (see PROCESS THEISM). Panentheism seeks a middle ground between classical theism and pantheism, preserving the former's claim that God has intellect and will and the latter's sense of intimate connection between God and universe. In panentheism, God is a person who includes the universe, or a soul whose body is the universe. Thus, God is larger than but also like the persons we know: physically embodied in a finite material object, growing older through time and changing as his material parts change. Panentheists claim that even so, God is perfect, because persons are the acme of perfection. Panentheists deny that God is immaterial; most also affirm that he has spatial extension, and offer their own distinctive slants on other traditional divine attributes.

The panentheist's God includes other things, and so depends on them. Such a God is thus not *a se* in the classical sense. But such a God may still be more independent than anything else. He depends only on things he includes, in contrast to depending on things that include him or that lie beyond him. Some panentheists (such as Charles Hartshorne) see some sorts of dependence as perfections. Compassion and sympathy are (they argue) moral perfections that involve having feelings that depend on others' fortunes, and all knowledge depends on the objects known. The panentheist's God has the complexity of the universe and changes as it does. But some panentheists (such as Hartshorne) maintain that God's abstract nature is simple, while Rāmānuja sites all complexity in God's body, the universe, holding that God's inner self, the pure Brahman, is partless. Hartshorne and Rāmānuja claim that God is immutable in certain respects, Hartshorne that his basic character (perfect benevolence, and so forth) cannot change, Rāmānuja that all change occurs in God's body, the universe, not in Brahman proper. Panentheists hold that God is eternal in the sense of everlasting in time; Hartshorne defends a version of the ontological argument, contending that God exists necessarily. Process panentheists usually claim that God cannot know the future, as it is indeterminate and so unknowable, and that God's power, while greater than any other being's, is not literally omnipotence. In this they follow Plato, whose Demiurge seeks to mould the world into a better place, but is limited by the recalcitrant material with which he works.

See also: BIBLE, HEBREW; FEMINIST THEOLOGY; GOD, ARGUMENTS FOR THE EXISTENCE OF; GOODNESS, PERFECT; INCARNATION AND CHRISTOLOGY §1; KABBALAH §3; MONOTHEISM; PANTHEISM; POSTMODERN THEOLOGY; THEOLOGY, RABBINIC; TIAN; TRINITY

References and further reading

* Alcinous (2nd century AD) *The Handbook of Platonism*, trans. J. Dillon, New York: Oxford University Press, 1993. (Synopsis of Middle Platonism.)

Alston, W. (1989) *Divine Nature and Human Language*, Ithaca, NY: Cornell University Press. (Important essays on divine action, knowledge and timelessness.)

* Anselm (1076) *Monologion*, trans. J. Hopkins and H. Richardson, in J. Hopkins and H. Richardson (eds and trans), *Anselm of Canterbury*, Toronto, Ont.: Edwin Mellen Press, 1974, vol. 1. ('Perfect-being' account of God's existence and nature.)

* —— (1077–8) *Proslogion*, trans. J. Hopkins and H. Richardson, in J. Hopkins and H. Richardson (eds and trans), *Anselm of Canterbury*, Toronto, Ont.: Edwin Mellen Press, 1974, vol. 1. (*Locus classicus* of perfect-being theology.)

* Aquinas, T. (1266–73) *Summa theologiae*, New York: Benziger Brothers, 1948. (*Locus classicus* of classical theism.)

* Aristotle (mid 4th century BC) *Metaphysics*, trans. W.D. Ross, in R. McKeon (ed.) *The Basic Works of Aristotle*, New York: Random House, 1941. (Primary source for his philosophical theology.)

* Augustine (397–426) *Christian Doctrine*, trans. F. Shaw, in P. Schaff (ed.) *Nicene and Post-Nicene Fathers*, series 1, Peabody, MA: Hendrickson Publishers, 1994, vol. 2. (On how to interpret Scripture.)

* —— (398–425) *On the Trinity*, trans. A. Haddan and W. Shedd, in P. Schaff (ed.) *Nicene and Post-Nicene Fathers*, series 1, Peabody, MA: Hendrickson Publishers, 1994, vol. 3. (His central treatment of the nature of God.)

—— (388) *On the Morals of the Manichaeans*, trans. R. Stothert, in P. Schaff (ed.) *Nicene and Post-Nicene Fathers*, series 1, Peabody, MA: Hendrick-

son Publishers, 1994, vol. 4. (Polemical work, on ethics and metaphysics.)

* Boethius, A.M.S. (*c.*522–4) *The Consolation of Philosophy*, trans. V.E. Watt, New York: Penguin Books, 1969. (On the nature of happiness, luck, freedom and divine foreknowledge.)

* Chrysostom, J. (390–8) *Homilies on St. John*, trans. P. Schaff, in P. Schaff (ed.) *Nicene and Post-Nicene Fathers*, series 1, Peabody, MA: Hendrickson Publishers, 1994, vol. 14. (Series of occasionally philosophical sermons.)

* Cicero (45 BC) *De natura deorum*, trans. H. Rackham, *On the Nature of the Gods*, London: Heinemann, 1933. (Rich source of Graeco-Roman philosophical theology.)

Davis, S.T. (1983) *Logic and the Nature of God*, Grand Rapids, MI: Eerdmans. (Readable account of central divine attributes; slightly harder than Morris (1991).)

* Duns Scotus, J. (*c.*1306) *On the First Principle*, trans. A. Wolter, Chicago, IL: Franciscan Herald Press, 1966. (Fullest version of his argument for God's existence, compact outline of his view of God.)

* Durkheim, É. (1915) *The Elementary Forms of the Religious Life*, London: Allen & Unwin. (Sociological account of religion.)

Freud, S. (1927) *The Future of an Illusion*, trans. J. Strachey, New York: W.W. Norton & Co., 1961. (Psychological critique of religious belief.)

Hartshorne, C. (1948) *The Divine Relativity*, New Haven, CT: Yale University Press. (Exposition of 'process' panentheism.)

Hartshorne, C. and Reese, W. (1953) *Philosophers Speak of God*, Chicago, IL: University of Chicago Press. (Selective, idiosyncratic history, coloured by the authors' panentheist views.)

Levine, M. (1994) *Pantheism*, New York: Routledge. (Fullest presentation of this view to date.)

Morris, T.V. (ed.) (1987) *The Concept of God*, New York: Oxford University Press. (Collection of important recent articles. Rigorous but not technical.)

—— (1991) *Our Idea of God*, Notre Dame, IN: University of Notre Dame Press. (Good introduction to issues in philosophical theology.)

* Plato (*c.*380–367 BC) *Republic*, trans. G.M.A. Grube and C.D.C. Reeve, Indianapolis, IN: Hackett Publishing Company, 1992. (The nature of justice, in individuals and society.)

* —— (*c.*366–360 BC) *Timaeus*, trans. B. Jowett, in E. Hamilton and H. Cairns (eds) *Collected Dialogues of Plato*, Princeton, NJ: Princeton University Press, 1961. (His cosmology, with some attention to philosophical theology.)

* Plotinus (*c.*250–66) *Enneads* II, trans. A.H. Arm-

strong, Cambridge, MA: Harvard University Press, 1979. (First Neoplatonist metaphysical system.)

* Proclus (c.460–70) *Commentary on Plato's Parmenides*, trans. G. Morrow and J. Dillon, Princeton, NJ: Princeton University Press, 1987. (Really an exposition of Neoplatonist metaphysics and theology.)

Sontag, F. (1962) *Divine Perfection*, New York: Harper. (Impressionistic account of relevant intuitions.)

Swinburne, R. (1993) *The Coherence of Theism*, New York: Oxford University Press, revised edn. (Clear, careful treatment of central divine attributes.)

* Tillich, P. (1955) *Biblical Religion and the Search for Ultimate Reality*, Chicago, IL: University of Chicago Press. (On religion's relation to philosophy.)

BRIAN LEFTOW

GOD, INDIAN CONCEPTIONS OF

In the Ṛg Veda, the oldest text in India, many gods and goddesses are mentioned by name; most of them appear to be deifications of natural powers, such as fire, water, rivers, wind, the sun, dusk and dawn. The Mīmāṃsā school started by Jaimini (c. AD 50) adopts a nominalistic interpretation of the Vedas. There are words like 'Indra', 'Varuṇa', and so on, which are names of gods, but there is no god over and above the names. God is the sacred word (mantra) which has the potency to produce magical results. The Yoga system of Patañjali (c. AD 300) postulates God as a soul different from individual souls in that God does not have any blemishes and is eternally free. The ultimate aim of life is not to realize God, but to realize the nature of one's own soul. God-realization may help some individuals to attain self-realization, but it is not compulsory to believe in God to attain the summum bonum *of human life. Śaṅkara (c. AD 780), who propounded the Advaita Vedānta school of Indian philosophy, agrees that God-realization is not the ultimate aim of human life. Plurality, and therefore this world, are mere appearances, and God, as the creator of the world, is himself relative to the concept of the world. Rāmānuja (traditionally 1016–1137), the propounder of the Viśiṣṭādvaita school, holds God to be ultimate reality, and God-realization to be the ultimate goal of human life. The way to realize God is through total self-surrender to God. Nyāya theory also postulates one God who is an infinite soul, a Person with omniscience and omnipresence as his attributes. God is the creator of language, the author of the sacred Vedas, and the first teacher of all the arts and crafts.*

1 Mysticism in the Ṛg Veda
2 The Pūrva-Mīmāṃsā conception
3 The Vedānta conception
4 The Yoga conception
5 The Nyāya conception

1 Mysticism in the Ṛg Veda

The Vedic texts (c.2000–1500 BC) suggest that divinity permeates the whole universe, the fields, the crops, animals, human speech, and so on. This conception involves many gods and goddesses, but it is not polytheism, for each god or goddess is praised as the supreme deity in the verses addressed to them. Max Müller has coined the term 'henotheism' to denote systems where the position of supreme deity is occupied now by one god or goddess, then by another, and so on (see Chatterjee and Datta 1984). No more than one god is ever worshipped at a time. There is also an emphasis on monotheism, pantheism and mysticism; the different gods and goddesses are said to be different only in name.

It is often claimed that the Ṛg Veda (c.200 BC) represents nature worship, polytheism and a rather crude imagery of gods and goddesses. This claim is certainly unjustified, for all through the Ṛg Veda there is a sense of all-pervasive divine presence, immanent in humanity and nature, unifying the universe and illuminating it. To the seers (ṛṣis) of the Ṛg Veda, nature is a living divine presence with which they can have communion and be existentially united. They worship the sun, the moon, the dawn, the night, the firmament, fire, water, rivers, seasons, herbs, trees, forests, the grass, the furrows, agriculture, mountains, stones, wind and so forth not as mere natural forces, not as anthropomorphic gods and goddesses, but as the various expressions of one divine foundational reality. 'The real is one, the learned call it by various names: Agni, Yama, Mātariśvan' (Ṛg Veda 1.164.46). The only mode of worship is performing sacrifices to gods and goddesses. It is not merely that the gods are one, but that the whole of the universe in its physical, material and natural aspects is permeated by one divine presence. Even in the description of the horse sacrifice (1.162), the entire sacrifice, the apparent victim, all the implements used and actions performed are united in the all-comprehending divine presence. The result of this sacrifice, too, is all-pervasive, mundane as well as spiritual.

The whole of Ṛg Veda 1.164 is permeated with a sense of divine unity in all creation. The human being has a body and a soul, which is the principle of consciousness. This consciousness has two levels. At the surface level, the human subject knows objects, performs actions and experiences pleasure and pain. Then there is the deeper level of consciousness, where the subject is simply the witness of the empirical self, unaffected by its pleasures and sufferings, by wants and needs, by motives and intentions. This deeper consciousness is the same as the divinity of the whole universe. This the predominant tradition in the *Ṛg Veda*, but there is a second tradition, which is found in one hymn of the tenth chapter (10.136). This is the tradition of the Munis, who are completely different from the members of mainstream society. Physically, the Munis have long hair, are dirty and wear yellow clothes. They are wanderers, not living in societies or performing any social function and not performing any sacrifices. The Munis claim that spiritual realization brings magical powers – a doctrine that is otherwise absent in the *Ṛg Veda*. According to Sāyana (after *c.*AD 780) the Munis 'become gods by the might of their penance'. This is also the first time we find a reference to penance in the *Ṛg Veda*. The Munis have the power to transmit spiritual excellence and power to others: 'Exhilarated by the sanctity of the Munis, we have mounted upon the winds' (10.136.3). The plurality of gods and goddesses does not make any difference to the spiritual realization of the Muni, who is equally attached to all of them, 'the friend of each deity' (10.136.4). All persons also regard the Munis as their true friends, 'sweet and most delightful friends' (10.136.6).

2   The Pūrva-Mīmāṃsā conception

God is supposed to be known from the revealed scriptures (Vedas). Pūrva-Mīmāṃsā philosophers reject this theory. The revealed texts are only the source of knowing our duty, which is to perform sacrifices. There are names of gods and goddesses, but they do not have any reference beyond these names; there is no divinity beyond the names. There is nothing real beyond the texts. The revealed texts are eternal; they do not have any author. So God is not their author. The universe, too, is eternal and self-sustaining; God cannot, therefore, be postulated as the creator, sustainer and destroyer of the world. So gods and goddesses are just names that have magical powers to produce merit. When performing sacrifices one has to utter the sentences very carefully; as a result, one goes to heaven after death. Neither God-realization nor self-realization is the ultimate aim. In heaven, there are no gods or goddesses, for they are only names. To be in heaven is to enjoy bliss eternally; there can be no fall from heaven (see MĪMĀṂSĀ).

3   The Vedānta conception

According to ŚAṄKARA (*c.* AD 780), who propounded the Advaita Vedānta school of Indian philosophy, God-realization is not the ultimate aim of human life. God is one; he is the creator, sustainer and destroyer of the world, and is therefore omnipotent and omniscient, and the object of worship. But God is not the ultimate reality. For plurality, and therefore this world, are mere appearances (*māyā*), and God, as the creator of the world, is himself related to appearance. Ultimate reality (Brahman), on the other hand, is beyond all relations to objects, to humanity, to thought and to language. Ultimate reality is pure, impersonal, universal consciousness, devoid of any internal or external difference. This consciousness is identical with the self of the individual, which is different from other selves and material objects only at the surface level. At the deepest level, every person, as also every material object, is identical with Brahman. All reality is Brahman. One cannot worship Brahman, for worshipping presupposes a distinction between the subject and object of worship. Brahman is pure subject and can never become an object of worship or even of knowledge. One can only *be* Brahman, that is, realize that one is pure, impersonal, universal consciousness (see BRAHMAN; VEDĀNTA).

In the Vedānta system, God is conceived under two aspects: God pervades the world, and is also beyond it. God is both immanent and transcendent. The world of material objects and living beings contains a plurality of innumerable objects. The question which arises here is: how can the immanent unity be reconciled with the phenomenal plurality? The two major schools of Vedānta, the Advaita Vedānta of Śaṅkara and the Viśiṣṭādvaita of RĀMĀNUJA, answer this question differently. According to Śaṅkara, manyness or plurality is inconsistent with unity, and as the inner reality is one, the surface reality, that is, the phenomenal world, is only apparent. This apparent world, the world-show, cannot be really related to the inner unity which is God. The relation between God and the world is like the relation between a piece of rope and the illusory snake for which it is mistaken. The piece of rope is, of course, necessary as the foundation of the illusory snake. So also God is the foundation of the illusory world. The cause of this illusory appearance is *māyā*, which has the dual function of covering reality and projecting illusory objects. The world projected by *māyā* is not real, but it is not wholly unreal. Thus the illusory object, the appearance, is neither real nor unreal. It is not real, for when one has spiritual illumination the world-show vanishes, just as, in good light, the illusory snake vanishes and the piece of rope is seen (see ERROR AND ILLUSION, INDIAN CONCEPTIONS OF §1). Nor is it wholly unreal, for a wholly unreal thing (such as a barren woman's son) cannot be perceived. The world is not unreal, for it is perceived to be real; the world is not real, for it is contradicted by spiritual realization of the universal unity. The bare identity of consciousness is the only reality; this consciousness is universal, impersonal, eternal. If the conception of God is necessarily that of a Person, then this universal consciousness cannot be called God; it is Brahman. So, according to Śaṅkara, Brahman is not the creator of the world, for the world is not eternal, and whatever follows from Brahman must partake of its eternal reality. Brahman is the foundation of the world in the sense in which a real object is the foundation of an illusory object. There cannot be any illusion unless there is a real object which is mistaken for an illusory object. Thus illusion differs from hallucination. Identity cannot tolerate any difference; so Brahman is pure identity devoid of all internal and external difference. Being aware of identity with Brahman, the illumination of the real self, is the ultimate aim of life.

Rāmānuja, on the other hand, argues that the empirical world of plurality cannot be illusory, for it is reality related to God, who is infinite. The world is, of course, not created by an antecedently existing God; God and the world are necessary for each other. Rāmānuja, in his Viśiṣṭādvaita philosophy, conceives the relation between God and the world on the analogy of the self and body of a human being. Just as a human being is an embodied consciousness, so also God is the self and the world is his body. The entire empirical universe is the body of God, who, as the indwelling spirit, is immanent in the universe. But even though both God and the world are real, still God as the soul of the world has supremacy over the world. Thus unity and plurality are both real; the ultimate reality – God – is unity in difference. To see God through self-surrender, not to be identical with him, is the ultimate aim of human life. Going to heaven cannot be the *summum bonum*, for one can stay in heaven only so long as one's merit is not exhausted. So there is necessarily a fall from heaven.

4 The Yoga conception

Patañjali, founder of the Yoga system, postulates God as a soul different from individual souls in that he does not have any blemishes and is eternally free. God is omniscient and omnipresent and is the creator of the world, which arises from ultimate matter (*prakṛti*) because of its association with individual souls due to nescience. All souls, individual as well as divine, are of the nature of consciousness not really affected by pain and suffering. The ultimate aim of life is not to realize God, but to realize the nature of one's own soul, which is wrongly believed to be associated with the body. But God-realization may help some individuals to attain self-realization. It is not compulsory to believe in God to attain the *summum bonum* of human life.

Patañjali did not feel the necessity of God for solving any theoretical problem of philosophy. For him, God has more a practical than a theoretical value. Devotion to God is considered to be of great practical value, inasmuch as it forms part of the practice of yoga and is one of the many means for the final attainment of concentration leading to yoga, defined as 'restraint of the mind'. The ultimate aim of human life is self-realization; God-realization is an optional means.

According to the Yoga system, God is the Supreme Person who is above all individual selves and free from all defects. He is the Perfect Being, eternal, all-pervading and omniscient. All individual selves are more or less subject to the afflictions (*kleśa*) of ignorance, egoism, desire, aversion and dread of death. They have to do various kinds of works (*karma*) – good, bad and indifferent – and reap the consequences (*vipāka*) thereof. They are also infected and influenced by the latent impressions of their past experiences (*āśaya*). Even if the liberated self is released from all these troubles, it cannot be said that it was always free from them. It is God and God alone who is eternally free from all defects. God is a perfect immortal spirit who remains ever untouched by afflictions and actions, and their effects and impressions. He possesses a perfect nature and also the fullest possible knowledge of all acts; he is, therefore, capable of maintaining the whole world by his mere wish or thought. He is the Supreme Ruler of the world and has infinite knowledge, unlimited power and the wisest desires, which distinguish him from all other selves.

5 The Nyāya conception

According to Nyāya, both old and new, God is a self-substance which has special qualities that distinguish God from individual selves. God as Supreme Self (*paramātman*) has eight qualities: number, magnitude, separateness, conjunction, disjunction, consciousness or knowledge, desire or will, and inner effort. God does not have pleasure, pain, aversion, memory traces, merit or demerit. This conception of God is fundamentally different from the Advaita Vedānta theory of Brahman, which identifies Brahman with existence, consciousness and bliss. The Nyāya conception of God, on the other hand, is of a substance which has existence, consciousness, will and inner effort, but not bliss, as special qualities. Moreover, God is one real object among many. There are several qualities that make God the Supreme Self. So far as omnipresence is concerned, God and individual selves have this quality in the same sense; both God and individual selves (or souls) are ubiquitous substances. It does not make sense to say that God is in the world or in humanity, or immanent in any sense. This is because ubiquitous substance cannot be in anything. On the other hand, all substances of finite magnitude are in contact with ubiquitous substances; they are in these substances, but these substances are not in anything.

The difference between individual selves and God consists primarily in his not having any body. God is the Supreme Self without any body. The supremacy of the Supreme Self consists in his omniscience and omnipotence. But these qualities are conceived very differently in new Nyāya (Navya-Nyāya) than in other Indian philosophical systems. God's knowledge of all things and events, past, present and future, is one cognition and is eternal. Although God knows all objects, he does not know them in different cognitive states. He has only one cognition, which is eternally there. Moreover, this eternal knowledge can only be perceptual; it cannot be inferential, for any mediate cognition has to be produced by another cognition. But as God does not have a plurality of cognitions, and as his knowledge is eternal, his knowledge cannot be produced at all; for whatever is produced cannot be eternal.

The omnipotence of God is also conceived very differently in Navya-Nyāya than in other Indian philosophical systems. God creates everything through his will guided by his knowledge. Again, the will of God is one act of will and is eternal: God does not have to perform more than one act of will to create the world. Furthermore, God does not create everything that there is. According to Navya-Nyāya, there are eternal objects of various categories, such as the self, atoms, space, time, the mind (manas) and ether (ākāsa), all of which are substances. Also eternal are universals, the relation of inherence (samavāya) and the individuality (viśeṣa) that belongs to each eternal substance (see NYĀYA-VAIŚEṢIKA §§4–5). These objects are all coeternal with God and cannot be created by him. Thus God's omnipresence and omnipotence are very much restricted in that he cannot be present in any ubiquitous substance such as space or time, nor in our souls. However, he does have unrestricted, eternal perception of all things past, present and future, as also of all eternal substances and objects.

See also: GAUḌĪYA VAIṢṆAVISM; GOD, CONCEPTS OF; HEAVEN, INDIAN CONCEPTIONS OF

References and further reading

Bhattacharyya, S. and Potter, K.H. (eds) (1993) *Encyclopedia of Indian Philosophies*, vol. 6, *Indian Philosophical Analysis: Nyāya-Vaiśeṣika from Gaṅgeśa to Raghunātha Śiromaṇi*, Princeton, NJ: Princeton University Press. (See especially page 211 of Part Two, chapter one (on Gaṅgeśa) for proofs of the existence of God in Nyāya.)

Chatterjee, S.C. and Datta, D.M. (1984) *An Introduction to Indian Philosophy*, Calcutta: University of Calcutta. (Includes an explanation of Müller's conception of henotheism.)

Frauwallner, E. (1973) *History of Indian Philosophy*, trans. V.M. Bedekar, Delhi: Motilal Banarsidass, 2 vols. (Contains original researches into many Indian systems.)

Radhakrishan, S. (1923) *Indian Philosophy*, Delhi: Oxford University Press, 1989, 2 vols. (Contains detailed information about all the Indian systems.)

* *Ṛg Veda* (c.1200 BC), trans. H.H. Wilson, *Ṛg-Veda Samhita*, Delhi: Nag Publishers, 1990, 7 vols. (An English translation of the entire Ṛg Veda. The Indian tradition is that the Vedas are beginningless; Wilson is of the opinion that they are of human composition.)

SIBAJIBAN BHATTACHARYYA

GÖDEL, KURT (1906–78)

The greatest logician of the twentieth century, Gödel is renowned for his advocacy of mathematical Platonism and for three fundamental theorems in logic: the completeness of first-order logic; the incompleteness of formalized arithmetic; and the consistency of the axiom of choice and the continuum hypothesis with the axioms of Zermelo–Fraenkel set theory.

A Sudeten German born in Brno, Moravia, Gödel received his doctorate in 1930 at the University of Vienna. His dissertation, extending earlier work by Skolem, demonstrated that first-order predicate calculus is semantically complete, that is, that every logical truth is provable. His incompleteness paper (1931, subsequently his *Habilitationsschrift*) showed that every ω-consistent recursively axiomatizable formalization of Peano arithmetic yields statements that are formally undecidable (neither provable nor refutable) within the theory. Rosser later showed that 'ω-consistent' could be weakened to 'consistent'. One of the undecidable sentences expresses the theory's own consistency. Hilbert's goal of reducing the consistency of arithmetic to that of weaker systems (see HILBERT'S PROGRAMME AND FORMALISM) thus cannot be realized.

While *Privatdozent* at the University of Vienna (1933–9) Gödel published several papers bearing on the decision problem (see PROOF THEORY) and the relation between classical and intuitionistic logic (see INTUITIONISM). He also attended some meetings of the Vienna Circle, but disagreed with its philosophy (see LOGICAL POSITIVISM).

Gödel spent the academic year 1933–4 at the Institute for Advanced Study in Princeton. Then, after recovering from an incapacitating bout of depression, he turned to set theory. In his address to the International Congress of Mathematicians in 1900, Hilbert had asked for a proof that every infinite set of real numbers is equinumerous either with the integers or the set of all reals (Cantor's continuum hypothesis). Gödel showed in 1938 that that assumption cannot be disproved within Zermelo–Fraenkel set theory, since it and the axiom of choice hold within a particular model thereof (see SET THEORY).

In 1940 Gödel emigrated to the United States. He returned to the Princeton Institute and remained there until his death from malnutrition – the result of further psychiatric disturbance – in 1978.

After 1942, frustrated by his failure to prove that the negation of the continuum hypothesis is also consistent with the axioms of set theory (a result finally established by Paul Cohen in 1963 – see Cohen 1966), Gödel worked primarily in philosophy and cosmology. Among the philosophical works published during his lifetime his commentary on 'Russell's Mathematical Logic' (1944) and his essay 'What is Cantor's Continuum Problem?' (1947, revised 1964) are notable for their mathematical Platonism. In the former, Gödel maintained that 'classes and concepts may... be conceived as real objects' whose existence is as tenable as that of physical bodies; in the latter that 'despite their remoteness from sense experience, we... have something like a perception also of the objects of set theory', whose 'axioms force themselves upon us as being true'. Posthumous philosophical works include a modal formalization of Leibniz's ontological proof.

See also: CANTOR'S THEOREM; CHURCH'S THEOREM AND THE DECISION PROBLEM; COMPUTABILITY THEORY; CONTINUUM HYPOTHESIS; GÖDEL'S THEOREMS; LOGICAL AND MATHEMATICAL TERMS, GLOSSARY OF; PROVABILITY LOGIC; REALISM IN THE PHILOSOPHY OF MATHEMATICS; TIME TRAVEL; TURING MACHINES

List of works

Gödel, K. (1986–95) *Kurt Gödel: Collected Works*, vol. 1, *Publications 1929–1936*, 1986; vol. 2, *Publications 1938–1974*, 1990; vol. 3, *Unpublished Essays and Lectures*, 1995, ed. S. Feferman *et al.*, New York and Oxford: Oxford University Press. (Contains full texts of all Gödel's published works as well as some previously unpublished work, with commentaries and an extensive bibliography. Includes parallel English translations of all German items.)

—— (1930) 'Die Vollständigkeit der Axiome des logischen Funktionenkalküls', *Monatshefte für Mathematik und Physik* 37: 349–60; trans. 'The Completeness of the Axioms of the Functional Calculus of Logic', in J. van Heijenoort (ed.) *From Frege to Gödel: A Source Book in Mathematical Logic, 1879–1931*, Cambridge, MA: Harvard University Press, 1967, 582–91. (Revised version of Gödel's doctoral dissertation.)

—— (1931) 'Über formal unentscheidbare Sätze der *Principia Mathematica* und verwandter Systeme I', *Monatshefte für Mathematik und Physik* 38: 173–98; trans. 'On Formally Undecidable Propositions of *Principia Mathematica* and Related Systems', in J. van Heijenoort (ed.) *From Frege to Gödel: A Source Book in Mathematical Logic, 1879–1931*, Cambridge, MA: Harvard University Press, 1967, 592–617. (The incompleteness paper.)

—— (1940) *The Consistency of the Axiom of Choice and of the Generalized Continuum Hypothesis with the Axioms of Set Theory*, Annals of Mathematics Studies, vol. 3, Princeton, NJ: Princeton University Press. (A monograph including full details of Gödel's consistency proofs.)

—— (1941) 'In What Sense is Intuitionistic Logic Constructive?', in *Collected Works*, vol. 3, 189–201. (A particularly lucid discussion of the ideas underlying Gödel's consistency proof for arithmetic via functionals of finite type.)

—— (1944) 'Russell's Mathematical Logic', in P.A. Schilpp (ed.) *The Philosophy of Bertrand Russell*, Library of Living Philosophers, vol. 5, Evanston, IL: Northwestern University Press. (An intricate critique of Russell's contributions to logic.)

—— (1946–9) 'Some Observations About the Relationship Between Theory of Relativity and Kantian Philosophy' (two versions), in *Collected Works*, vol. 3, 230–60. (The accompanying introductory note, by Howard Stein, provides penetrating historical and technical commentary.)

—— (1947) 'What is Cantor's Continuum Problem?', *American Mathematical Monthly* 54: 515–25; errata, 55: 151. (A discussion of the problem of determining the cardinality of the continuum, written for a general mathematical audience.)

—— (1953–9) 'Is Mathematics Syntax of Language?' (two versions), in *Collected Works*, vol. 3, 334–63. (An essay opposing views of Rudolf Carnap.)

—— (1970) 'Ontological Proof', in *Collected Works*, vol. 3, 403–4. (Preceded by an illuminating note by Robert M. Adams.)

References and further reading

Boolos, G. (1979) *The Unprovability of Consistency: An Essay in Modal Logic*, Cambridge: Cambridge University Press. (The work of Gödel and Löb, viewed from a modal perspective.)

—— (1993) *The Logic of Provability*, Cambridge: Cambridge University Press. (Revised and expanded sequel to Boolos (1979).)

* Cohen, P. (1966) *Set Theory and the Continuum Hypothesis*, New York: Benjamin. (A self-contained exposition of Cohen's independence proofs.)

Dawson, J. (1997) *Logical Dilemmas: The Life and Work of Kurt Gödel*, Wellesley, MA: Peters. (A full-length scientific biography.)

Nagel, E. and Newman, J.R. (1958) *Gödel's Proof*, New York: New York University Press; repr. London: Routledge, 1971. (Still a classic exposition of Gödel's incompleteness results for the lay reader.)

Shanker, S. (ed.) (1988) *Gödel's Theorem in Focus*, London: Croom Helm. (An anthology of essays about Gödel's life and work, together with a translation of his incompleteness paper.)

Yourgrau, P. (1991) *The Disappearance of Time: Kurt Gödel and the Idealistic Tradition in Philosophy*, Cambridge: Cambridge University Press. (A study of the implications of Gödel's cosmological work for the philosophy of time.)

JOHN W. DAWSON, JR

GÖDEL'S THEOREMS

Utilizing the formalization of mathematics and logic found in Whitehead and Russell's Principia Mathematica *(1910), Hilbert and Ackermann (1928) gave precise formulations of a variety of foundational and methodological problems, among them the so-called 'completeness problem' for formal axiomatic theories – the problem of whether all truths or laws pertaining to their subjects are provable within them. Applied to a proposed system for first-order quantificational logic, the completeness problem is the problem of whether all logically valid formulas are provable in it.*

In his doctoral dissertation (1929), Gödel gave a positive solution to the completeness problem for a system of quantificational logic based on the work of Whitehead and Russell. This is the first of the three theorems that we here refer to as 'Gödel's theorems'.

The other two theorems arose from Gödel's continued investigation of the completeness problem for more comprehensive formal systems – including, especially, systems comprehensive enough to encompass all known methods of mathematical proof. Here, however, the question was not whether all logically valid formulas are provable (they are), but whether all formulas true in the intended interpretations of the systems are.

For this to be the case, the systems would have to prove either S or the denial of S for each sentence S of their languages. In his first incompleteness theorem, Gödel showed that the systems investigated were not complete in this sense. Indeed, there are even sentences of a simple arithmetic type that the systems can neither prove nor refute, provided they are consistent. So even the class of simple arithmetic truths is not formally axiomatizable.

The idea behind Gödel's proof is basically as follows. Let a given system T satisfy the following conditions: (1) it is powerful enough to prove of each sentence in its language that if it proves it, then it proves that it proves it, and (2) it is capable of proving of a certain sentence G (Gödel's self-referential sentence) that it is equivalent to 'G is not provable in T'. Under these conditions, T cannot prove G, so long as T is consistent. For suppose T proved G. By (1) it would also prove 'G is provable in T', and by (2) it would prove 'G is not provable in T'. Hence, T would be inconsistent.

Under slightly stronger conditions – specifically, (2) and (1') every sentence of the form 'X is provable in T' that T proves is true – it can be shown that a consistent T cannot prove 'not G' either. For if 'not G' were provable in T it would follow by (2) that 'G is provable in T' would also be provable in T. But then by (1') G would be provable. Hence, T would be inconsistent.

The proof of Gödel's second incompleteness theorem essentially involves formalizing in T a proof of a formula expressing the proposition that if T is consistent, then G. The second incompleteness theorem (that is, the claim that if T is consistent it cannot prove its own consistency) then follows from this and the first part of the proof of the first incompleteness theorem.

The two incompleteness theorems have been applied to a wide variety of concerns in philosophy. The best known of these are critical applications to Hilbert's programme and logicism in the philosophy of mathematics and to mechanism in the philosophy of mind.

1 Background

Interest in questions of completeness dates from quite early on in the history of logic and the foundations of mathematics. Aristotle (*Posterior Analytics* 87b) described the goal of science as the complete identification of the laws pertaining to its various areas. Much later, Kant expressed concern with completeness when he described human reason as inevitably disposed to pose questions to itself that it cannot answer. Clearer still, perhaps, are various statements in letters by Gauss (1817, 1829), in which he asserted that it may in principle be impossible for us to give a complete specification of the laws of geometry a priori owing to the fact that its object, space, is at least partially 'external' to our minds. (See Kronecker ([1887] 1932: 265) for an expression of the same view.) Finally, we find something approaching modern formulations of the notion in Hilbert ([1900] 1930: 242), where it is said to be a duty to show that a set of axioms for geometry capture every geometric law, and in Huntington (1905: 17), where a set of postulates for real algebra is said to form a 'complete' axiomatic basis for the subject.

However, it was not until the appearance of Hilbert and Ackermann's *Grundzüge der theoretischen Logik* (1928: 42–3) that the completeness problem received its first fully explicit, precise and general formulation. Hilbert and Ackermann believed that the formal–symbolic approach of modern mathematics had contributed greatly to its remarkable development, and they therefore advocated taking the same approach to logic. Such an approach would, they believed, pave the way for a mathematically precise study of both logical and mathematical thinking, and would make it possible to settle in a mathematical way various of the methodological and foundational questions pertaining to them. Among these was the question of 'completeness' – that is, whether the full class of truths or laws properly pertaining to a given domain of thought can be proved in a given system purporting to formalize it. Whitehead and Russell (1910) presented a formalism (PM) for logic and mathematics, and this became the focus of the early investigations of the completeness problem.

The first results were obtained (independently) by Bernays, in his unpublished *Habilitationsschrift* of 1918 (see Bernays 1926), and Post, in his doctoral

dissertation of 1920 (see Post 1921). They isolated the propositional part of Whitehead and Russell's PM and showed that it proved all valid sentences of the propositional variety. Post indeed proved the stronger result (known as 'Post-completeness') that no sentence of the propositional variety can be added to PM without creating an inconsistency.

Hilbert and Ackermann observed that the broader logical system known as the 'restricted', or 'first-order' predicate calculus is not Post-complete (1928: 92). With this as his point of departure, Gödel, in his doctoral dissertation (1929), then took up the ordinary completeness problem for this system. Using ideas introduced by Löwenheim (1915) and Skolem (1923), he obtained the basic positive result that every valid formula of the first-order quantificational variety is provable in PM. Indeed, he proved the somewhat stronger result that every first-order quantificational formula is either refutable in PM or is satisfiable in a denumerable domain. He then extended the basic result to first-order logic with identity and the stronger result from single formulas to denumerable systems of formulas. In this latter extension, he made use of a 'compactness' result (namely, that a denumerably infinite set of formulas is satisfiable if and only if each of its finite subsets is) that he proved by semantic means.

In the introduction to his dissertation (deleted from the version published in 1930), Gödel expressed awareness of the possibility that the completeness problem for other areas of mathematical thought might not result in the same positive type of result as the completeness problem for PM. It was therefore not surprising that in 1930 he turned his attention to the completeness problem for the architectonic systems of Whitehead and Russell and Zermelo and Fraenkel (see Gödel 1930, 1931). These systems interested Gödel precisely because of their comprehensiveness. Such comprehensiveness might, he noted, lead some to conjecture that they can decide all mathematical questions formulable in their languages. What Gödel showed was that this is mistaken. There are problems – indeed, relatively elementary problems of the arithmetic of the integers – that even the most comprehensive systems cannot decide. Gödel's investigation of the completeness problem thus ended with a negative result.

There is a relationship between Gödel's 1929/1930 and 1931 studies that seems worth noting, even though he himself did not note it. It stems from the fact that every formal system is composed of both a logical and a non-logical part, deficiencies in either of which can lead to incompleteness. A defect of the first sort would mean that though the non-logical part might itself be perfect in content, the logical part would not be able fully to extract that content.

Gödel ([1929] 1930) can be seen as showing that incompleteness in systems whose logic is rightly taken to be first-order is due to deficiencies in the non-logical part, and his 1931 paper can then be seen as showing that such deficiencies extend to a wide range of systems. The latter also points to *logical* deficiencies in another class of systems, however – namely, systems whose non-logical parts are composed of the second-order Peano postulates and whose logical part is some formalizable scheme of second-order logical principles. This is a result of the categoricity of the second-order Peano postulates (first established in Dedekind 1888). Being categorical, they are in a certain sense perfect in their content. Still, Gödel (1931) establishes that any formal system based on them must be incomplete. Hence, any formalizable scheme of second-order logical consequence must fail to capture some of the content latent in them. In other words, any formal system of second-order logic must fail to capture some valid second-order logical principle. The 1931 paper can thus be seen as rounding out the logical investigations of the 1930 paper by providing a negative solution to the completeness problem for second-order logic.

2 The completeness theorem

Gödel's original completeness proof was based on a normalization of quantificational formulas developed by Löwenheim (1915) and Skolem (1923). According to this normalization, there is an effective way of finding, for each formula ϕ of a first-order quantificational language L, a formula $\sigma(\phi)$ such that ϕ is satisfiable iff $\sigma(\phi)$ is, and $\sigma(\phi)$ is of the form U–E–QF, where U is a (non-empty) string of universal quantifiers, E a (possibly empty) string of existential quantifiers and QF a quantifier-free formula. Gödel showed how to construct conjunctions $K_n = QF_1 \& \ldots \& QF_n$ of instances QF_i of QF such that either for every n, K_n is truth-functionally satisfiable, or, for some n, K_n is not. Like Skolem, he then showed that if the first alternative holds, $\sigma(\phi)$ is satisfiable in the domain of the natural numbers. Finally, he was able to show – and this was his distinctive contribution – that if the second alternative holds, $\sigma(\phi)$ is refutable (that is, $\vdash_{PM} \neg\sigma(\phi)$). With this came the crucial link between satisfiability and derivability in PM needed to prove PM's completeness.

It follows that $\sigma(\phi)$ is either denumerably satisfiable or refutable, and from this and the fact (also used by Gödel) that $\sigma(\phi)$ is refutable only if ϕ is, it then follows that for any formula ϕ of the language of the pure predicate calculus either ϕ is (denumerably) satisfiable or ϕ is refutable.

Gödel's proof was given for a specific logical calculus having a countable language (that is, a language containing countably many individual constants). Since then, completeness proofs have been devised both for a wider variety of calculi having countable languages (see, for example, Henkin 1949; Hasenjäger 1953; Hintikka 1955) as well as for calculi with uncountable languages (see Maltsev 1936). From this work, the following general method for constructing models for consistent sets of sentences of infinite cardinality has emerged.

To construct a model of infinite cardinality α for a consistent set S of sentences of language L of cardinality not exceeding α, one begins by adding α-many constants to L to form the language L^*. One then extends S to a maximal consistent and term-complete set S^*. (A consistent set is 'maximal consistent' iff no set properly containing it is consistent. A set is 'term-complete' just in case for every formula ϕ and all terms $t_1, \ldots, t_i, \ldots, t_\alpha$ of L^*, if $\phi(t_1), \ldots, \phi(t_i), \ldots, \phi(t_\alpha)$ are all elements of the set, then so is $\forall x \phi(x)$.) Next one constructs a model for S^* whose domain is the class of constants of L^*. And finally, one restricts this model to L and automatically obtains a model for S.

The proof that this construction yields a model M proceeds roughly as follows. (1) For every closed term c that appears in S^*, let M assign c itself as value. In this way, every element of the domain of M becomes the referent of a term of L^*. (2) For each basic n-ary predicate P^n of L^*, let M assign the n-tuple $\langle t_1, \ldots, t_n \rangle$ to the extension of P^n iff $P^n(t_1, \ldots, t_n)$ is an element of S^*. In this way, all atomic sentences and all denials of atomic sentences that are elements of S^* become true in M. This is so because S^*, being consistent, does not contain any atomic sentence that is denied by another element of S^*.

This completes the basis clause. In the induction step one calls upon the fact that, owing to its maximal consistency (and, in the case of quantified sentences, its term-completeness), S^* contains, for each of its compound elements σ_c (of complexity greater than that of the denial of an atomic sentence), a set of less complex elements whose joint truth suffices for the truth of σ_c. These less complex sentences fall under the hypothesis of the induction. The truth of the sentences of the basis clause thus 'induces' the truth of all elements of S^* of the next higher degree of complexity, and this process continues through all degrees of complexity. The truth-in-M of the sentences covered in the basis step thus eventually 'oozes up' to each element of S^*.

Every consistent set of sentences thus has a model.

From this, both 'weak' completeness (every valid sentence is derivable) and 'strong' completeness (every sentence validly implied by a set of sentences is derivable from it) follow for systems admitting the usual types of derivations.

3 The first incompleteness theorem

Gödel made use of a formalization of mathematics in his 1931 paper that was related to that given in Whitehead and Russell (1910). But he added a new device – the 'arithmetization' of formal systems. This was based upon a division of the objects of a formal language into three basic categories: (1) the basic symbols of the language; (2) finite sequences of these symbols; and (3) finite sequences of finite sequences of them. In order to express properties and propositions concerning these objects as predicates and sentences of arithmetic, Gödel defined a correlation (now called a 'Gödel-numbering') between the objects of these three types and the natural numbers. He coded the individual symbols of the systems by distinct odd numbers. To each finite sequence $\sigma_1, \ldots, \sigma_n$ of symbols he then assigned the number

$$2^{g(\sigma_1)} \cdot 3^{g(\sigma_2)} \cdot \ldots \cdot p_n^{g(\sigma_n)},$$

where p_n is the nth prime number and $g(\sigma_i)$ $(1 \leqslant i \leqslant n)$ the Gödel number of σ_i. Finally, to each finite sequence of finite sequences of symbols $\Sigma_1, \ldots, \Sigma_k$, he assigned the number

$$2^{g(\Sigma_1)} \cdot 3^{g(\Sigma_2)} \cdot \ldots \cdot p_k^{g(\Sigma_k)},$$

where p_k is the kth prime number and $g(\Sigma_i)$ $(1 \leqslant i \leqslant k)$ the Gödel number of Σ_i.

Infinitely many others schemes would be possible. The essential features are that distinct expressions are assigned distinct numbers and that there are effective procedures for encoding expressions and for decoding numbers to find which expression (if any) they represent.

Under such an encoding, certain formulas express not only arithmetic statements about numbers but also metamathematical statements about such objects as formulas, axioms and proofs. Using this observation, Gödel exploited an analogy with the Richard and liar paradoxes (see PARADOXES OF SET AND PROPERTY §6). (In passing he also observed that any other 'epistemological antinomy' could be put to similar use. See Gödel (1931: 598).) The analogy runs as follows.

Suppose that a theory T proves only true sentences and that a sentence G 'says' of itself that it is not provable in T. Neither G nor $\neg G$ is then provable in T. For if G is true then it is not provable in T, and if G is

false then it cannot be provable because T proves only true sentences. So G is not provable in T and hence true. Its denial, $\neg G$, is thus false and hence unprovable in T since T proves only true sentences.

Gödel's proof follows this reasoning with one exception that he himself emphasized (1931: 599): it replaces the assumption that T proves only true sentences with the weaker assumption of ω-consistency (see below). The core of the proof is the construction of the 'self-referential' sentence G in the so-called 'diagonal lemma'. In its general form, this lemma states that for every formula F of L_T (that is, the language of T) of one free variable, there is a sentence D of L_T such that $\vdash_T D \leftrightarrow F(\ulcorner D \urcorner)$ (the term '$\ulcorner D \urcorner$' stands for the numeral of L_T whose referent under the standard interpretation of L_T is the Gödel number of D). We need only the following specialization of the diagonal lemma to G:

(DL) For every theory T that contains a certain fragment of arithmetic, there is a sentence G of L_T such that $\vdash_T G \leftrightarrow \neg \mathrm{Prov}_T(\ulcorner G \urcorner)$.

This lemma is also referred to as Gödel's 'fixed point theorem', A being a 'fixed point' in T of a formula $\phi(x)$ just in case $\vdash_T A \leftrightarrow \phi(\ulcorner A \urcorner)$. The formula $\mathrm{Prov}_T(x)$ 'expresses' the notion of a formula's being provable in T in the limited sense that the set of A such that $\vdash_T \mathrm{Prov}_T(\ulcorner A \urcorner)$ is the set of theorems of T. In the standard terminology, $\mathrm{Prov}_T(x)$ 'weakly represents' the set of Gödel numbers of theorems of T in T; that is

(WR) For every sentence A of L_T, $\vdash_T A$ iff $\vdash_T \mathrm{Prov}_T(\ulcorner A \urcorner)$.

From DL and WR, the proof of Gödel's first incompleteness theorem (G1) proceeds in two parts.

Part 1. If T is a consistent theory and $\mathrm{Prov}_T(x)$ satisfies both WR in the 'only if' direction and DL, then $\nvdash_T G$.

Proof. Suppose that

(1) $\vdash_T G$.

From this and WR in the 'only if' direction, we get

(2) $\vdash_T \mathrm{Prov}_T(\ulcorner G \urcorner)$.

But by (1), DL and the assumption that the logic of T allows *modus ponens* inference, we get

$\vdash_T \neg \mathrm{Prov}_T(\ulcorner G \urcorner)$,

which together with (2) implies the inconsistency of T.

Part 2. If T is consistent and $\mathrm{Prov}_T(x)$ satisfies both WR in the 'if' direction and DL, then $\nvdash_T \neg G$.

Proof. Suppose that

(3) $\vdash_T \neg G$.

From (3), DL and the fact that the logic of T allows both *modus tollens* inference and inference from $\neg\neg A$ to A, it follows that

$\vdash_T \text{Prov}_T(\ulcorner G \urcorner)$.

But this and WR in the 'if' direction imply that

$\vdash_T G$,

which together with (3) implies the inconsistency of T. Together, parts 1 and 2 establish

(G1) If T is consistent and $\text{Prov}_T(x)$ satisfies DL and WR, then $\nvdash_T G$ and $\nvdash_T \neg G$.

It should be noted that WR in the 'if' direction is a different condition from that of the consistency of T. It forces all theorems of T of the form $\text{Prov}_T(\ulcorner A \urcorner)$ to be true. Equivalently, given the decidability in T of the arithmetized proof relation of T, it forces T to be ω-consistent (that is, it forces T not to prove, for any formula ϕ, both all instances of $\phi(n)$ and also $\exists x \neg \phi(x)$). ω-consistency, which was explicitly used as a condition in Gödel's original proof, thus figures in our proof as well. Using a more complicated fixed point formula than G and a more complicated proof than the one just given, Rosser (1936) proved a version of G1 that does not require ω-consistency.

Parts 1 and 2 reveal the basic structure of the proof for G1. The details that remain are proofs of DL and WR. These can be found in many standard logic texts (for example, Enderton 1972; Boolos and Jeffrey 1974). Since Gödel's proof in 1931, a mathematically more interesting case of a purely combinatorial sentence undecidable in first-order Peano arithmetic (PA) has been given, in Paris and Harrington (1977). In the early 1980s, Friedman gave a still more striking case (involving Kruskal's theorem) of an arithmetical sentence undecidable in fragments of second-order Peano arithmetic considerably stronger than PA.

4 The second incompleteness theorem

Gödel arrived at the idea for his second incompleteness theorem (G2) by noting that, using the provability expression $\text{Prov}_T(x)$ of part 1 of the proof of G1, one can define a consistency formula Con_T for T and that the proof of part 1 can then be carried out in T. In other words, one can prove '$\text{Con}_T \to G$' in T. Together with part 1, this then implies the unprovability in T of Con_T.

The proof of '$\text{Con}_T \to G$', however, requires conditions on $\text{Prov}_T(x)$ that are different from those (namely DL and WR) required for the proof of G1.

What exactly these conditions are becomes clear from the proof of '$\text{Con}_T \to G$' given below.

The details of this proof require that we choose a specific definition of the consistency expression, Con_T. The definition we choose is the basic one, the formula '$\forall x(\text{Prov}_T(x) \to \neg\text{Prov}_T(\text{neg}(x)))$' (where $\text{neg}(x)$ stands for the function that sends the Gödel number of a formula to the Gödel number of its negation). We could define Con_T differently without altering the conditions on $\text{Prov}_T(x)$ that are required for the proof of '$\text{Con}_T \to G$' in T. The present definition, however, has the virtues of being both familiar and basic. We therefore proceed with the proof of

(G2 lemma) $\qquad\qquad \vdash_T \text{Con}_T \to G$.

Its core element is the construction of a derivation in T of $\neg\text{Con}_T$ from $\neg G$. We begin by stating five schemata whose provability in T will be assumed in the proof:

(a) $\text{Prov}_T(\ulcorner A \urcorner) \to \text{Prov}_T(\ulcorner \text{Prov}_T(\ulcorner A \urcorner) \urcorner)$

(b) $\text{Prov}_T(\ulcorner A \leftrightarrow B \urcorner) \to \text{Prov}_T(\ulcorner \neg B \leftrightarrow \neg A \urcorner)$

(c) $\text{Prov}_T(\ulcorner A \leftrightarrow B \urcorner) \to \text{Prov}_T(\ulcorner A \to B \urcorner)$

(d) $\text{Prov}_T(\ulcorner A \to B \urcorner) \to (\text{Prov}_T(\ulcorner A \urcorner) \to \text{Prov}_T(\ulcorner B \urcorner))$

(e) $\text{Prov}_T(\ulcorner A \urcorner) \to \text{Prov}_T(\ulcorner \neg\neg A \urcorner)$.

The proof proper begins by taking $\neg G$ as a hypothesis in T. We then reason in T as follows. Applying DL (whose content '$G \leftrightarrow \neg\text{Prov}_T(\ulcorner G \urcorner)$' is available in T), we get

(4) $\text{Prov}_T(\ulcorner G \urcorner)$.

From (4) and an instance of (a), we get

(5) $\text{Prov}_T(\ulcorner \text{Prov}_T(\ulcorner G \urcorner) \urcorner)$.

We now add a T-theoretic 'formalization' of DL; that is,

$\text{Prov}_T(\ulcorner G \leftrightarrow \neg\text{Prov}_T(\ulcorner G \urcorner) \urcorner)$.

This together with an instance of schema (b) gives

$\text{Prov}_T(\ulcorner \neg\neg\text{Prov}_T(\ulcorner G \urcorner) \leftrightarrow \neg G \urcorner)$,

which together with an instance of (c) then yields

$\text{Prov}_T(\ulcorner \neg\neg\text{Prov}_T(\ulcorner G \urcorner) \to \neg G \urcorner)$.

From this and an instance of (d) we get

$\text{Prov}_T(\ulcorner \neg\neg\text{Prov}_T(\ulcorner G \urcorner) \urcorner) \to \text{Prov}_T(\ulcorner \neg G \urcorner)$,

which with an instance of (e) gives us

$\text{Prov}_T(\ulcorner \text{Prov}_T(\ulcorner G \urcorner) \urcorner) \to \text{Prov}_T(\ulcorner \neg G \urcorner)$.

This and (5) via *modus ponens* in T imply

(6) $\text{Prov}_T(\ulcorner \neg G \urcorner)$.

111

(6) together with (4) then gives us

$$\neg(\text{Prov}_T(\ulcorner G\urcorner) \to \neg\text{Prov}_T(\ulcorner \neg G\urcorner)).$$

This and the definition of Con_T imply $\neg\text{Con}_T$. This is what was to be proved in T from our hypothesis $\neg G$. Discharging this hypothesis, we then get

$$\neg G \to \neg\text{Con}_T,$$

and from this, by contraposition in T, we conclude

$$\text{Con}_T \to G.$$

Inspecting this proof we see that it makes various common assumptions concerning the logic of T; for example, that it allows *modus ponens* inference, classical contraposition and universal instantiation. It also utilizes various conditions on $\text{Prov}_T(x)$ – specifically, schemata (a)–(e) and the 'formalized' version of DL. All of these, we will now show, can be obtained from the following 'derivability conditions'.

(DC1) For every sentence A of L_T, $\vdash_T A$ only if $\vdash_T \text{Prov}_T(\ulcorner A\urcorner)$.

(DC2) For all formulas A and B of L_T,
$$\vdash_T \text{Prov}_T(\ulcorner A \to B\urcorner)$$
$$\to (\text{Prov}_T(\ulcorner A\urcorner) \to \text{Prov}_T(\ulcorner B\urcorner)).$$

(DC3) For every sentence A of L_T,
$$\vdash_T \text{Prov}_T(\ulcorner A\urcorner) \to \text{Prov}_T(\ulcorner \text{Prov}_T(\ulcorner A\urcorner)\urcorner).$$

The sufficiency of DC1–3 can be seen as follows. Schema (a) is simply DC3 and schema (d) is DC2. The 'formalized' version of DL used above is obtained immediately by applying DC1 to DL. Schema (b) is obtained by applying DC1 to the logical truths of the form $(A \leftrightarrow B) \to (\neg B \leftrightarrow \neg A)$ to get the several instances of $\text{Prov}_T(\ulcorner (A \leftrightarrow B) \to (\neg B \leftrightarrow \neg A)\urcorner)$, and then applying DC2. The remaining schemata are similarly obtained. Schema (c) is obtained by applying DC1 to the logical principle $(A \leftrightarrow B) \to (A \to B)$ to get $\text{Prov}_T(\ulcorner (A \leftrightarrow B) \to (A \to B)\urcorner)$, which then, by DC2, yields (c). Schema (e) is obtained by application of DC1 to $A \to \neg\neg A$ to get $\text{Prov}_T(\ulcorner A \to \neg\neg A\urcorner)$, and then application of DC2.

We thus arrive at the following generalized version of Gödel's second incompleteness theorem.

(G2) If T is consistent, Con_T is defined as $\forall x(\text{Prov}_T(x) \to \neg\text{Prov}_T(\text{neg}(x)))$ and $\text{Prov}_T(x)$ satisfies DC1–3, then $\nvdash_T \text{Con}_T$.

5 The derivability conditions

DC1–3 represent a streamlining of the original 'Ableitbarkeitsforderungen' used in Hilbert and Bernays (1939: 285–6) to give the first full proof of G2. The improvements are due mainly to Löb (1955),

though his aim was to identify a set of conditions on $\text{Prov}_T(x)$ sufficient to solve a problem of Leon Henkin's and not to provide a general set of conditions under which G2 holds.

Jeroslow (1973) produced a further streamlining of the derivability conditions by showing how to eliminate DC2. The key idea was a new fixed-point or diagonalization construction – referred to as a 'literal' fixed point. It states that

> For every formula $\psi(x)$ of L_T of one free variable, one can effectively find a formula ϕ and a closed term τ of L_T such that ϕ is $\psi(\tau)$, and $\vdash_T \tau = \ulcorner\phi\urcorner$.

What Jeroslow proved was a version of G2 lemma with a literal Gödel sentence G_{Lit} – that is, a sentence of the form $\neg\text{Prov}_T(\tau)$, where $\vdash_T \tau = \ulcorner G_{\text{Lit}}\urcorner$, and not merely a sentence provably equivalent in T to the sentence $\neg\text{Prov}_T(\ulcorner G_{\text{Lit}}\urcorner)$ – in place of the usual Gödel sentence G. His proof relies only upon the literal diagonal lemma, DC1 and DC3. Likewise, the relevant part of Jeroslow's version of G1 – namely, that if T is consistent, then $\nvdash_T G_{\text{Lit}}$ – relies only upon the literal diagonal lemma and DC1. Together these two results yield a version of G2 that requires only the literal diagonal lemma, DC1 and DC3. We thus see that G2 can hold even when the formula expressing provability does not satisfy DC2. Among other things, this appears to distinguish G2 from Löb's theorem (that is, the theorem that for any sentence A of L_T and any formula $\text{Prov}_T(x)$ satisfying DC1–3, if $\vdash_T \text{Prov}_T(\ulcorner A\urcorner) \to A$, then $\vdash_T A$), since the known proofs of the latter demand satisfaction of DC2 (see Kreisel and Takeuti 1974: 7–8).

The approaches of Hilbert and Bernays (1939), Löb (1955) and Jeroslow (1973) are what might be called 'derivability conditions' approaches since they all rely for their application upon the satisfaction of some set of abstract conditions on $\text{Prov}_T(x)$. Feferman (1957, 1960) has criticized such approaches on the ground that, for a given theory T and a given formula $\text{Prov}_T(x)$ weakly representing the theorems of T, it is often difficult to determine whether or not such a set of conditions holds. He therefore sought a condition on provability expressions whose satisfaction or non-satisfaction is easier to determine, but which is still sufficient for G2.

By requiring that provability expressions preserve the logical and inductive structures of the usual definitions of formal provability, Feferman was able to reduce his condition to one governing the choice of expressions for the axioms of a system. That requirement is that the axiomhood formula be RE, where, roughly, this means that it preserves the way in which the axioms are 'presented'. An RE ('recursively enumerable') formula is one which transparently defines a recursively enumerable set of axioms. An RE formula representing an infinite set of axioms (which is the difficult case) imitates the inductive character of the metamathematical definition of that set (see Smullyan 1961; Kreisel 1965; Feferman 1982, 1989). The advantage of using the RE criterion for G2 is that the RE representations form a primitive recursive set. Because of this, the question of whether a given expression of provability is RE is generally easier to answer than the question of whether it satisfies a given set of derivability conditions.

Using his new condition, Feferman proved the following version of G2 (1960: theorem 5.6).

> If T is a system containing a minimal amount of arithmetic, $Ax_T(x)$ is an RE formula representing the axioms of T in T, and Con_T is built up from $Ax_T(x)$ in a way that corresponds to any of the usual ways in which the definition of consistency is related to the definition of axiomhood for T, then $\nvdash_T Con_T$.

He also showed (theorem 5.9) that the restriction to RE cases of $Ax_T(x)$ is important since there are theories S and non-RE representations of their axioms $Ax_S^*(x)$ such that consistency formulas Con^*S – built up from $Ax_S^*(x)$ in exactly the same way that Con_T is built up from $Ax_T(x)$ – are provable in S. See Feferman (1982, 1989) for further development of his search for a general, readily applicable characterization of the representations of metamathematical notions with respect to which G2 holds.

Derivability conditions approaches have generally been enhanced by the recent development of provability logics (see PROVABILITY LOGIC). The choice between the two types of approaches is complicated by the fact that Jeroslow's criterion for G2 appears to apply to theories to which Feferman's does not (namely, various cut-free systems of analysis – see Kreisel and Takeuti 1974). Thus, though Feferman's G2 criterion may generally be easier to apply than those of the derivability conditions approaches, it does not appear to be as broad in scope (see Feferman's remark 1 in Gödel (1990: 282–7) for a related discussion).

6 Philosophical applications

There have been many attempts to apply Gödel's incompleteness theorems to philosophical concerns. For the most part, these have to do with issues in the philosophy of mathematics and the philosophy of mind, though there have also been attempts in other areas of philosophy, and also in areas of intellectual life not lying wholly within philosophy (see Thomas

1995). Here we consider some of the better-known and/or better-developed applications.

In the philosophy of mathematics the chief application is to Hilbert's programme which is widely believed to have been refuted by G2. This is so because G2 is seen as prohibiting the finitary consistency proof that Hilbert demanded for classical mathematics (see, for example, Gödel 1958; Kitcher 1976; Kreisel 1958; Prawitz 1981; Resnik 1974; Smorynski 1977, 1985; Simpson 1988; for a dissenting view see Detlefsen 1986, 1990). G1 has been presented as having a similar effect through its exhibition of a recognizedly true real sentence of classical mathematics (namely, G) that is not finitarily provable (see Smorynski 1977, 1985; HILBERT'S PROGRAMME AND FORMALISM §4).

Gödel's theorems have also been used to argue against logicism. One example of this is in Hellman (1981), which maintains that G2 implies that no finitely axiomatizable logicist system exists. For non-finitely axiomatizable systems, the claim is weaker: such systems may exist, but G2 prohibits our being able to know of any particular system that it is one of them. A major attraction of Hellman's argument is that, unlike other arguments against logicism, it does not require that one know where to draw the line between logic and non-logic.

Gödel's theorems have also figured in philosophical discussions concerning the nature of proof. Among the more interesting of these are Myhill (1960) and Reinhardt (1985, 1986). Myhill argues that G1 and G2 establish that for any correct system containing arithmetic there are 'correct' inferences – inferences to whose acceptability the user of the system is rationally committed – that cannot be captured in it. There is thus, he says, an absolute epistemic notion of provability (neither syntactic, nor semantic nor psychological in character), according to which Gödel's undecidable sentences are provable. Hence, this notion of absolute provability is not formalizable. Reinhardt (1985, 1986) refines aspects of this argument and also argues that if 'humanly provable' means 'formally provable' there must be absolutely undecidable sentences of arithmetic. He urges the view that G2 is an epistemic phenomenon – one that arises from the epistemic properties of that type of belief that mathematical proof is supposed to sponsor. These properties, it turns out, lead to something tantamount to the derivability conditions.

In a related vein, Dummett (1963) has used G1 to argue that mathematical proof (including that which lies within a well-circumscribed subject area) is an 'indefinitely extensible concept' and cannot therefore be identified with derivation in any formal system. Since, he believes, the meanings of mathematical statements are to be given in terms of a concept of proof, this means that the notion of proof that determines the meanings of mathematical statements must be an essentially vague and unformalizable one. In this he sounds a theme similar in certain respects to one associated with the intuitionist, Brouwer.

Chaitin (1974, 1975, 1982) offers an analysis of Gödel's theorems that links them to limits on the extent to which information in a given mathematical field can be 'compressed' into a formal system. They thus, according to Chaitin, point up the need for a continuing search for new axioms (see COMPUTABILITY AND INFORMATION). This view of the relationship between Gödel's theorems and algorithmic information theory is challenged in van Lambalgem (1989).

In the philosophy of mind and metaphysics, the main application of the theorems is to the question of mechanism ('Do human-like minds have only such capabilities as are simulable by computational devices?' – see MIND, COMPUTATIONAL THEORIES OF §5) and, more generally, to the question of materialism ('Are all objects, events and/or forces in the world reducible to physical matter and its physical properties?' – see MATERIALISM; MATERIALISM IN THE PHILOSOPHY OF MIND). Gödel himself (1951) presented such an application, arguing that either the mind of the human mathematician cannot be codified by any formal system or that there exist absolutely unsolvable arithmetical problems of an elementary sort. On the former alternative, supposing Church's thesis, mechanism clearly fails. On the latter, Gödel argued, materialism fails. For if there are mathematical problems that are absolutely unsolvable, then mathematics is not our own creation; and if this is so, its objects must exist independently of us, in which case a materialist view of reality fails. See Wang (1993) for a useful discussion of Gödel's argument.

The most well-known anti-mechanist argument is that of Lucas (1961), modified by Benacerraf (1967) and repeated in Penrose (1989, 1994). In outline, the argument is as follows. (1) If human minds were mechanizable (or, in some versions, if they could be known to be identical to some particular machine), then, by G2, they could not know that their beliefs are consistent. But (2) human minds can know that their beliefs are consistent; therefore, (3) they are not mechanizable (or, as in Benacerraf's variant, they cannot be known to be identical to any particular machine).

Lucas' argument has been widely criticized (see, for example, Boolos 1968; Chihara 1972; Dennett 1978; Putnam 1960 (before the fact); Smart 1961; Wang 1974; Webb 1968, 1980). Its chief difficulty is perhaps one that is partially concealed by the unclarity of premise (2). It is true that humans are capable of

examining various of their sets of beliefs and arriving at credible judgments regarding their consistency. It does not follow from this, however, that among the sets of beliefs they can judge to be consistent are some that contain that very consistency judgment itself. Indeed, if fixing a set of beliefs is a typical precondition for its evaluation, it would seem that consistency judgments do not typically belong to the sets to which they are applied; for at the time the beliefs are fixed such judgments would not yet have been made and so would not exist as elements of the set being evaluated. For consistency evaluations not requiring such prior fixing of beliefs, on the other hand, it is not clear that G2 applies. Either way, Lucas-type arguments face serious difficulties (see Detlefsen 1995).

See also: CHURCH'S THEOREM AND THE DECISION PROBLEM; CHURCH'S THESIS; COMPUTABILITY THEORY; LOGICAL AND MATHEMATICAL TERMS, GLOSSARY OF; ORDINAL LOGICS; PROOF THEORY

References and further reading

* Benacerraf, P. (1967) 'God, the Devil, and Gödel', *The Monist* 51: 9–32. (A revised and chastened version of Lucas' anti-mechanist argument from the incompleteness theorems.)
* Bernays, P. (1926) 'Axiomatische Untersuchung des Aussagen-Kalküls der *Principia Mathematica*' (Axiomatic Investigation of the Propositional Calculus of *Principia Mathematica*), *Mathematische Zeitschrift* 25: 305–20. (Condensed version of the author's 1918 *Habilitationsschrift* in which the first proof of the completeness of the propositional calculus of Whitehead and Russell was given.)
* Boolos, G. (1968) 'Review of "Minds, Machines and Gödel", by J.R. Lucas, and "God, the Devil, and Gödel", by P. Benacerraf', *Journal of Symbolic Logic* 33: 613–15. (Critical review of Lucas (1961) and Benacerraf (1967).)
* Boolos, G. and Jeffrey, R. (1974) *Computability and Logic*, Cambridge: Cambridge University Press, 3rd edn, 1989. (Thorough and well-written textbook of mathematical logic that provides much of the technical material required for the proofs given here.)
* Chaitin, G.J. (1974) 'Information-Theoretic Limitations of Formal Systems', *Journal of the Association for Computing Machinery* 21: 403–24. (Introduction to Chaitin's analysis of Gödel's incompleteness theorems; argues that they show a limit on the information that can be 'compressed' into a formal axiomatic system, and infers that the search for new axioms must be an enduring part of mathematical research.)

* —— (1975) 'Randomness and Mathematical Proof', *Scientific American* 232: 47–52. (Less technical version of various of the ideas in Chaitin (1974).)

* —— (1982) 'Gödel's Theorem and Information', *International Journal of Theoretical Physics* 21: 941–54. (Attempt to explain Gödelian incompleteness as a phenomenon in algorithmic information theory.)

* Chihara, C. (1972) 'On Alleged Refutations of Mechanism Using Gödel's Incompleteness Results', *Journal of Philosophy* 69: 507–26. (Critical discussion of attempted anti-mechanist applications of Gödel's incompleteness theorems.)

* Dedekind, R. (1888) *Was sind und was sollen die Zahlen?*, Braunschweig: Vieweg; trans. W.W. Beman (1901), 'The Nature and Meaning of Numbers', in *Essays on the Theory of Numbers*, New York: Dover, 1963. (Includes Dedekind's proof of the categoricity of the second-order Peano postulates, chapter 10, theorem 132.)

* Dennett, D.C. (1978) 'The Abilities of Men and Machines', in *Brainstorms: Philosophical Essays on Mind and Psychology*, Cambridge, MA: MIT Press, 1981. (Criticism of Lucas (1961) and similar arguments.)

* Detlefsen, M. (1986) *Hilbert's Program: An Essay on Mathematical Instrumentalism*, Boston, MA, and Dordrecht: Reidel. (Detailed critical examination of the arguments from Gödel's incompleteness theorems against Hilbert's programme; focuses primarily on the arguments from G2 and the question of what is required of formulas that are to express consistency.)

* —— (1990) 'On an Alleged Refutation of Hilbert's Program using Gödel's First Incompleteness Theorem', *Journal of Philosophical Logic* 19: 343–77. (Critical examination of the arguments against Hilbert's programme from G1.)

* —— (1995) 'Wright on the Non-Mechanizability of Intuitionist Reasoning', *Philosophia Mathematica*, series 3, 3: 103–19. (Critical examination of an argument by Crispin Wright that Gödel's theorems imply the non-mechanizability of intuitionist mathematics. Includes brief statement of what the author regards as the central mistake of all Lucas-type arguments.)

* Dummett, M.A.E. (1963) 'The Philosophical Significance of Gödel's Theorem', in *Truth and Other Enigmas*, Cambridge, MA: Harvard University Press, 1978. (Includes Dummett's argument that Gödel's incompleteness theorems show that the notion of mathematical proof is essentially unformalizable.)

* Enderton, H.B. (1972) *A Mathematical Introduction to Logic*, New York: Academic Press, 1972. (Well-conceived and -executed basic textbook of mathematical logic; supplies definitions and proofs of the basic notions and results needed to prove G1. Treatment of G2 is sketchy.)

* Feferman, S. (1957) 'Formal Consistency Proofs and Interpretability of Theories', in *Summaries of Talks Presented at the Summer Institute of Symbolic Logic in 1957 at Cornell University*, vol. 1, 71–7. Mimeographed. (A succinct and readable summary of the author's Berkeley doctoral dissertation.)

* —— (1960) 'Arithmetization of Metamathematics in a General Setting', *Fundamenta Mathematicae* 49: 3–92. (Thorough treatment of the differences between G1 and G2 as regards the conditions they require of arithmetical expressions of metamathematical notions. Develops a novel and interesting alternative to the traditional derivability conditions approach to the proof of G2.)

* —— (1982) 'Inductively Presented Systems and the Formalization of Metamathematics', in D. van Dalen, D. Lascar and T. Smiley (eds) *Logic Colloquium '80*, Studies in Logic and the Foundations of Mathematics, 108, Amsterdam: North Holland, 1982. (Outline of investigation designed to extend and refine the study begun in the author's dissertation and 1960 paper. The aim is a fully explicit and precise account of canonical representations of the various metamathematical notions pertaining to formal axiomatic systems.)

* —— (1989) 'Finitary Inductively Presented Logics', in R. Ferro, Bonotto, S. Valentini and A. Zanardo (eds) *Logic Colloquium '88*, Studies in Logic and the Foundations of Mathematics, 127, Amsterdam: North Holland, 1989. (Continuation of the author's long-standing study of what is required for the canonical representation of formal systems.)

* Gauss, K. (1817, 1829) letter to Olbers (1817), in *Briefwechsel mit H.W.M. Olbers*, Hildesheim: Olms, 1976; letter to Bessel (1829), in *Werke*, Leipzig: Teubner, 1863–1903, vol. 8, 200. (Statement of Gauss' belief that though a human knower might be able to attain complete knowledge of the laws of arithmetic a priori, the same would not be true of the laws of geometry.)

* Gödel, K. (1929) 'Über die Vollständigkeit des Logikkalküls', doctoral dissertation, University of Vienna; trans. 'On the Completeness of the Logical Calculus', in Gödel (1986), 44–101; slightly modified version, 'Die Vollständigkeit der Axiome des logischen Funktionenkalküls', *Monatshefte für Mathematik und Physik* 37: 349–60, 1930; trans. 'The Completeness of the Axioms of the Functional Calculus of Logic', in van Heijenoort (1967), 582–91; and in Gödel (1986), 102–23. (Gödel's doctoral dissertation in which he first proved the

completeness of the quantificational portion of the logic of Whitehead and Russell.)

—— (1930) 'Einige metamathematische Resultate über Entscheidungsdefinitheit und Widerspruchsfreiheit', repr. and trans. 'Some Metamathematical Results on Decidability and Consistency', in Gödel (1986); trans. in van Heijenoort (1967). (Brief announcement of Gödel's incompleteness theorems.)

* —— (1931) 'Über formal unentscheidbare Sätze der *Principia Mathematica* und verwandter Systeme I', *Monatshefte für Mathematik und Physik* 38: 173–98; trans. 'On Formally Undecidable Propositions of *Principia Mathematica* and Related Systems', in van Heijenoort (1967), 592–617; and in Gödel (1986), 144–95. (Paper in which were originally published Gödel's proofs of his incompleteness theorems.)

* —— (1951) 'Some Basic Theorems on the Foundations of Mathematics and Their Implications', in Gödel (1995). (Edited text of Gödel's 1951 Josiah Gibbs Lecture delivered at Brown University at a meeting of the American Mathematical Society. Gödel here formulated his argument concerning the anti-materialist implications of his incompleteness theorems; also includes an argument for a Platonist conception and an argument against a conventionalist conception of mathematics. Useful introductory essay by George Boolos.)

* —— (1958) 'Über eine bisher noch nicht benützte Erweiterung des finiten Standpunktes', repr. and trans. 'On a Hitherto Unexploited Extension of the Finitary Standpoint', in Gödel (1990). (Gödel's attempt to find a legitimate epistemological extension of Hilbert's finitary standpoint that is capable of providing the kinds of soundness proofs for classical mathematics that Hilbert called for. Includes Gödel's statement that, unlike in his 1931 paper, he now accepted the idea that G2 essentially refutes Hilbert's programme.)

—— (1986–95) *Collected Works*, ed. S. Feferman *et al.*, vol. 1, *Publications 1929–1936*, 1986; vol. 2, *Publications 1938–1974*, 1990; vol. 3, *Unpublished Essays and Lectures*, 1995, New York and Oxford: Oxford University Press. German originals and English translations. (Accurate yet readable translations, useful introductory essays and bibliography.)

* Hasenjäger, G. (1953) 'Eine Bemerkung zu Henkins Beweis für die Vollständigkeit des Prädikatenkalküls der ersten Stufe' (A Remark on Henkin's Proof of the Completeness of the First-Order Predicate Calculus), *Journal of Symbolic Logic* 18: 42–8. (A simplification of Henkin's completeness proof.)

Heijenoort, J. van (ed.) (1967) *From Frege to Gödel: A Source Book in Mathematical Logic,* *1879–1931*, Cambridge, MA: Harvard University Press. (Basic papers in mathematical logic and the foundations of mathematics, with useful forewords and bibliography.)

* Hellman, G. (1981) 'How to Gödel a Frege–Russell: Gödel's Incompleteness Theorems and Logicism', *Noûs* 25: 451–68. (Argues that G2 counts against logicism.)

* Henkin, L. (1949) 'The Completeness of the First-Order Functional Calculus', *Journal of Symbolic Logic* 14: 159–66. (First presentation of the currently prevailing method for completeness proofs; introduced devices making the proof less dependent upon the details of the particular calculus involved and, hence, more general in scope.)

—— (1952) 'A Problem concerning Provability', *Journal of Symbolic Logic* 17: 160. (Posed the question 'Is a sentence expressing the statement that it is itself provable in *T*, a first-order formal system containing enough arithmetic to enable it to represent all recursive relations of natural numbers, provable in *T* or not?' Solved in the affirmative by Löb (1955).)

* Hilbert, D. (1900) 'Über den Zahlbegriff' (On the Number-Concept), *Jahresbericht der Deutschen Mathematiker-Vereinigung* 8; revised as appendix 6 of *Grundlagen der Geometrie*, Leipzig and Berlin: Teubner, 7th edn, 1930. (Early statement by Hilbert of the chief aims of foundational studies. Explicitly identified are a completeness problem, and the consistency problem, which is described as necessary for the demonstration of the existence of a concept.)

* Hilbert, D. and Ackermann, W. (1928) *Grundzüge der theoretischen Logik*, Berlin: Springer, 2nd edn, 1938; 2nd edn trans. L.M. Hammond, G.G. Leckie and F. Steinhardt, *Principles of Mathematical Logic*, ed. R.E. Luce, New York: Chelsea, 1950. (Text in which the standard problems of metamathematics – consistency, completeness, independence and decidability – received their first precise formulations; readable and illuminating source for students today. These formulations guided Gödel and Church in their subsequent research.)

* Hilbert, D. and Bernays, P. (1939) *Grundlagen der Mathematik* (Foundations of Mathematics), vol. 2, Berlin: Springer; 2nd edn, 1970. (Classic work of mathematical logic; gives the first full proof of G2.)

* Hintikka, J. (1955) 'Form and Content in Quantification Theory', *Acta Philosophica Fennica* 8: 7–55. (Description of a tableau method that supports a simple proof of completeness.)

* Huntington, E.V. (1905) 'A Set of Postulates for Real

Algebra, Comprising Postulates for a One-Dimensional Continuum and for the Theory of Groups', *Transactions of the American Mathematical Society* 6: 17–41. (Includes early explicit mention of completeness as a property of an axiom system (see page 17).)

* Jeroslow, R. (1973) 'Redundancies in the Hilbert–Bernays Derivability Conditions for Gödel's Second Incompleteness Theorem', *Journal of Symbolic Logic* 38: 359–67. (Shows how to eliminate DC2 as a condition on provability expressions whose associated consistency expressions support a version of G2.)

* Kitcher, P. (1976) 'Hilbert's Epistemology', *Philosophy of Science* 43: 99–115. (Useful discussion of the epistemic character of Hilbert's so-called 'finitary' judgments and of the bearing of Gödel's theorems on Hilbert's programme.)

* Kreisel, G. (1958) 'Hilbert's Programme', *Dialectica* 12: 346–72; revised version in P. Benacerraf and H. Putnam (eds) *Philosophy of Mathematics: Selected Readings*, Cambridge: Cambridge University Press, 2nd edn, 1983. (Essay on the plausibility of Hilbert's programme in light of Gödel's theorems and other developments; discusses the differences between G1 and G2 and between what Kreisel calls the broader and narrower versions of Hilbert's programme; claims that G1 counts against the broader version.)

* —— (1965) 'Mathematical Logic', in T.L. Saaty (ed.) *Lectures in Modern Mathematics*, vol. 3, New York: Wiley. (Survey of modern mathematical logic. Considers the conditions that must be satisfied by formulas expressing metamathematical notions, and introduces the notion of a 'canonical' representation.)

* Kreisel, G. and Takeuti, G. (1974) 'Formally Self-Referential Propositions for Cut-Free Classical Analysis and Related Systems', *Dissertationes Mathematicae* 118: 4–50. (Useful study of the conditions on formulas expressing provability that are required for G2 and such related results as Löb's theorem. Shows how the streamlining of the derivability conditions discovered by Jeroslow allows a proof of G2 for certain cut-free systems of analysis.)

* Kronecker, L. (1887) 'Über den Zahlbegriff' (On the Concept of Number), *Journal für die reine und angewandte Mathematik* 101: 337–55; repr. in *Werke*, ed. K. Hensel, Leipzig: Teubner, 1932, vol. 3, part 1, 249–74. (Kronecker's only philosophical essay, in which he expresses the view, also expressed earlier by Gauss, that although humans might be able to attain a complete knowledge of the laws of arithmetic a priori, the same cannot be expected of the laws of geometry.)

* Lambalgem, M. van (1989) 'Algorithmic Information Theory', *Journal of Symbolic Logic* 54: 1,389–400. (Argues that Chaitin's analysis of Gödel's theorem in terms of algorithmic information theory does not in fact explain it.)

* Löb, M.H. (1955) 'Solution of a Problem of Leon Henkin', *Journal of Symbolic Logic* 20: 115–18. (Positive solution of the problem posed by Henkin (1952). Streamlined the original conditions on provability expressions used in the first full proof of G2 in Hilbert and Bernays (1939).)

* Löwenheim, L. (1915) 'Über Möglichkeiten im Relativkalkül', *Mathematische Annalen* 76: 447–70; trans. S. Bauer-Mengelberg, 'On Possibilities in the Calculus of Relatives', in van Heijenoort (1967), 232–51. (Includes a proof of Löwenheim's theorem that a formula true in all finite and denumerably infinite domains is true in all domains. Makes use of a normal form for first-order formulas that Gödel also made use of in his completeness proof.)

* Lucas, J.R. (1961) 'Minds, Machines, and Gödel', *Philosophy* 36: 112–27; revised version appears in *Freedom of the Will*, Oxford: Clarendon Press, 1970. (First statement of a well-known and widely discussed argument that Gödel's incompleteness theorems refute mechanism.)

—— (1970) *Freedom of the Will*, Oxford: Clarendon Press. (Includes responses to some of the criticisms of the earlier version of the argument (1961) and gives a select bibliography of the anti-mechanist argument from Gödel's theorems.)

* Maltsev, A.I. (1936) 'Untersuchungen aus dem Gebiete der mathematischen Logik', *Matematicheskii Sbornik* 1: 323–6; trans. 'Investigations in the Area of Mathematical Logic', in B. Wells (ed.) *The Metamathematics of Algebraic Systems: Collected Papers, 1936–1967*, Amsterdam: North Holland, 1971. (Extends to uncountable sets of formulas the proof of compactness given in Gödel (1930) for countable sets of formulas.)

* Myhill, J. (1960) 'Some Remarks on the Notion of Proof', *Journal of Philosophy* 62: 461–70. (Argues that Gödel's incompleteness theorems show that for any correct formal system containing arithmetic there are inferences to whose acceptability the user of the system is rationally committed that cannot be captured in it.)

* Paris, J. and Harrington, L. (1977) 'A Mathematical Incompleteness in Peano Arithmetic', in J. Barwise (ed.) *Handbook of Mathematical Logic*, Amsterdam: North Holland. (First proof of a reasonably natural and true statement of pure combinatorics

that is not provable in first-order Peano arithmetic. Followed a few years later by an even more striking discovery of Harvey Friedman's (see Simpson 1985).)

* Penrose, R. (1989) *The Emperor's New Mind: Concerning Computers, Minds, and the Laws of Physics*, New York: Oxford University Press. (Argues against mechanism in a manner essentially that of Lucas (1961).)

* —— (1994) *Shadows of the Mind: A Search for the Missing Science of Consciousness*, New York: Oxford University Press. (Includes replies to critics of the anti-mechanist argument of Penrose (1989). Essential elements of the argument remain unchanged.)

* Post, E. (1921) 'Introduction to a General Theory of Elementary Propositions', *American Journal of Mathematics* 43: 163–85; repr. in van Heijenoort (1967), 264–83. (First published proof of the completeness of the propositional calculus of Whitehead and Russell; also proved its Post-completeness.)

* Prawitz, D. (1981) 'Philosophical Aspects of Proof Theory', in G. Fløistad (ed.) *Contemporary Philosophy: A New Survey*, vol. 1, The Hague: Martinus Nijhoff, 1981. (Useful presentation of the case against Hilbert's programme via Gödel's theorems, especially G1.)

* Putnam, H. (1960) 'Minds and Machines', in S. Hook (ed.) *Dimensions of Mind: A Symposium*, New York: Macmillan. (Predates Lucas (1961), but none the less has the makings of an effective argument against it.)

* Reinhardt, W. (1985) 'Absolute Versions of Incompleteness Theorems', *Noûs* 19: 317–46. (Argues that epistemic properties of an intuitive notion of provability give rise to G1 and G2 phenomena.)

* —— (1986) 'Epistemic Theories and the Interpretation of Gödel's Incompleteness Theorems', *Journal of Philosophical Logic* 15: 427–74. (Extends and refines the discussion of Reinhardt (1985).)

* Resnik, M. (1974) 'The Philosophical Significance of Consistency Proofs', *Journal of Philosophical Logic* 3: 133–47. (Discussion of certain elements of Feferman (1960) and the question of the difference between normal and 'pathological' expressions of metamathematical notions.)

* Rosser, J.B. (1936) 'Extensions of Some Theorems of Gödel and Church', *Journal of Symbolic Logic* 1: 87–91. (Proof of a version of G1 that does not rely upon a theory's being ω-consistent.)

Simpson, S. (1985) 'Nonprovability of certain combinatorial properties of finite trees', in L. Harrington et al. (eds) *Harvey Friedman's Research in the Foundations of Mathematics*, Amsterdam: North Holland, 1985. (First published presentation of Friedman's proof in the early 1980s that a certain proposition of finite combinatorics (a form of Kruskal's theorem on finite trees) is independent not only of first-order Peano arithmetic but also of two subsystems of second-order Peano arithmetic that go well beyond it.)

* —— (1988) 'Partial Realization of Hilbert's Program', *Journal of Symbolic Logic* 53: 349–63. (Useful survey and basic exposition of the work of the so-called 'reverse mathematics' programme begun by Harvey Friedman. Argues that though Hilbert's programme in its original form is refuted by G2, a significant portion of that programme can still be carried out.)

* Skolem, T. (1923) 'Einige Bemerkungen zur axiomatischen Begründung der Mengenlehre', in *Matematikerkongressen i Helsingfors den 4–7 Juli 1922, Den femte skandinaviska matematikerkongressen, Redogörelse*, Helsinki: Akademiska Bokhandeln, 217–32; trans. S. Bauer-Mengelberg, 'Some Remarks on Axiomatized Set Theory', in van Heijenoort (1967), 291–301. (Anticipated the chief result of Gödel (1930). Gödel was apparently unaware of it at the time he wrote his paper.)

* Smart, J.J.C. (1961) 'Gödel's Theorem, Church's Theorem and Mechanism', *Synthese* 13: 105–10. (Critical discussion of Lucas-type arguments.)

* Smorynski, C. (1977) 'The Incompleteness Theorems', in J. Barwise (ed.) *Handbook of Mathematical Logic*, Amsterdam, North Holland. (Exposition of Gödel's incompleteness theorems, their proofs and some of their applications.)

* —— (1985) *Self-Reference and Modal Logic*, New York: Springer. (Good exposition of provability logic. Chapter 0 presents argument against Hilbert's programme via G1.)

* Smullyan, R. (1961) *Theory of Formal Systems*, Princeton, NJ: Princeton University Press. (Important study of the nature of formal systems and what is required for the adequate representation of metamathematical notions via arithmetization.)

* Thomas, D. (1995) 'Gödel's Theorem and Postmodern Theory', *Publications of the Modern Language Association* 110: 248–61. (Discussion of the significance of Gödel's incompleteness theorems for literary criticism.)

* Wang, H. (1974) *From Mathematics to Philosophy*, New York: Humanities Press. (Includes worthwhile discussion of a variety of aspects of Gödel's theorems and of his philosophical ideas; also a critical discussion of Lucas-type arguments against mechanism.)

* —— (1993) 'Can Machines Think?', *Philosophia Mathematica*, series 3, 1: 97–138. (Discussion of

Gödel's ideas on mechanism. Reconstructs the many conversations between the author and Gödel on the subject.)

* Webb, J. (1968) 'Metamathematics and the Philosophy of Mind', *Philosophy of Science* 35: 156–78. (Interesting discussion of some of the difficulties involved in trying to link Gödel's incompleteness theorems to anti-mechanist views of mind.)

* —— (1980) *Mechanism, Mentalism, and Metamathematics: An Essay on Finitism*, Boston, MA: Reidel. (Thorough study of various themes in philosophy with which Gödel's incompleteness theorems have sometimes been associated. Argues that, contrary to the opinion of some, these theorems actually confirm a type of formalism in the philosophy of mathematics.)

* Whitehead, A.N. and Russell, B.A.W. (1910) *Principia Mathematica*, vol. 1, Cambridge: Cambridge University Press; 2nd edn, 1925; repr. 1994. (The classical symbolic formalization of logic and mathematics; basis of much of the greatest work in mathematical logic and the foundations of mathematics in the twentieth century.)

MICHAEL DETLEFSEN

GODFREY OF FONTAINES (*c*.1250–*c*.1306/9)

Godfrey of Fontaines studied philosophy and theology at the University of Paris and subsequently taught theology there. A theologian by profession, he developed a highly interesting philosophy, especially a metaphysics. For Godfrey, metaphysics studies being as being. Being itself is divided into cognitive being and real being, and real being is divided into being in act and being in potency. In finite beings, essence and existence are neither really distinct nor intentionally distinct; they are identical. Human reason can prove that God exists, and reach some imperfect knowledge concerning what God is, but cannot prove that the world began to be. For Godfrey, corporeal entities in this world are composed of matter and form, but heavenly bodies probably lack prime matter. On philosophical grounds, he favours the theory that there is only one substantial form in human beings – the intellective soul – but for theological reasons leaves this question open. His philosophy is somewhat more Aristotelian and less Neoplatonic than that of most of his contemporaries.

1   Life and works
2   Theory of being
3   Theory of essence and existence
4   Philosophical knowledge of God
5   Eternal creation
6   Substance and accidents
7   Matter and form

1   Life and works

Born in the principality of Liège in modern Belgium, probably shortly before 1250, Godfrey of Fontaines studied philosophy at the Faculty of Arts of the University of Paris, presumably before 1274, and then completed the lengthy programme in the theology faculty, eventually becoming regent master in theology in 1285. He continued to teach theology at Paris until about 1298–9, and then returned to the same position around 1303–4. He died around 1306, or perhaps in 1309.

His major contributions to philosophical and theological literature were his fifteen *Quodlibeta* (Quodlibetal Questions). These originated from public disputations which were open to anyone who might wish to pose questions about any reasonable topic, and which were again disputed and 'determined' (resolved) by the presiding master on some following day. Godfrey also conducted other 'ordinary' disputations, and some of these have been preserved. His philosophy, especially his metaphysics, is highly interesting, and he often turned to it in deciding theological issues.

2   Theory of being

With ARISTOTLE, Godfrey holds that metaphysics has being as being as its subject. Being is the most general notion the human mind can discover, and is affirmed primarily of substance and of everything else as in some way ordered to substance. Godfrey divides being into cognitive being (being in the mind of a knower, whether human or divine), and real being (being outside the mind). Real being is divided into being in potency and being in act. For a thing to have being in potency is for it to exist in one or more causes which have the capacity to bring it into actual being. A thing may have potential being by reason of an intrinsic cause, for example, pre-existing matter which would enter into that thing's structure when it receives actual being, or by reason of an extrinsic cause (or causes) which can bring it into actual being. For a thing to have actual being is for it to exist in its own right with its own complete form or nature (see BEING).

3   Theory of essence and existence

Much debated during Godfrey's time was how essence is related to existence in created entities. It was generally conceded that they are identical in God. Godfrey strongly rejects the view that essence and existence are really distinct in creatures. He directs special attention to the way this theory was defended by GILES OF ROME, who had referred on some occasions to this as a distinction between two 'things'. However, Godfrey also rejects, at least by implication, the more nuanced distinction of essence and act of being (esse) defended by Thomas AQUINAS. He also rejects Henry of Ghent's claim that they are intentionally distinct, that is, by a distinction that is less than real but more than purely mental (see HENRY OF GHENT). For Godfrey, essence and existence are really identical, so strictly so that whatever is true of one is true of the other, and whatever is known of one is known of the other. He denies (against Thomas and Giles, but also against Henry) that one can know what something is (its essence) without knowing that it is (its existence). He tries to account for our awareness of nonexistent possible entities simply by appealing to the distinction between our knowing something as only potentially existing and our knowing it as actually existing. Neither real nor intentional distinction of essence and existence is needed to account for this (see EXISTENCE).

To account for the non-simple character of created entities, especially purely spiritual entities such as angels, Godfrey maintains that such beings fall short of God, the supreme or first 'One', by possessing an intermediary nature. In comparison with God they may be regarded as potential, but in comparison with less perfect created beings they may be regarded as actual. This is enough for him to defend their act-potency 'composition' and thereby distinguish them from God. This solution blends Aristotelianism (act-potency composition) and Neoplatonism (Proclus' notion that what participates in the 'One' or God, is both one and not one) (see ARISTOTELIANISM, MEDIEVAL; PLATONISM, MEDIEVAL).

4 Philosophical knowledge of God

Godfrey accepts the prevailing view of his time that in this life human beings do not enjoy direct or intuitive knowledge of God. In addition to the knowledge of God afforded believers by divine revelation, Godfrey defends the human mind's ability to reason from knowledge of effects to knowledge of God as their first cause. He assigns some role in this process to argumentation based on motion which concludes to a First Mover in accord with Aristotle's procedure in the *Physics*, but reserves more precise knowledge of God to metaphysics.

Godfrey does not fully accept Aquinas's view that by reasoning philosophically we can know that God is

and what God is not (with which Godfrey agrees) but not what God is. Godfrey maintains that through appropriate metaphysical reasoning we can also know something about what God is, though such knowledge will always be incomplete and imperfect. In discussing God's knowledge and production of created entities, Godfrey appeals to a theory of divine ideas. For him these are simply different ways in which God understands his essence as capable of being imitated by creatures. The divine ideas are not really distinct either from one another or from the divine essence. Even so, Godfrey does postulate a plurality of divine ideas to correspond to different specific classes of creatures but, against the prevailing view of his time and in agreement with Henry of Ghent, he denies that divine ideas are multiplied to correspond to different individuals within species (see GOD, CONCEPTS OF).

5 Eternal creation

Sharply contested during Godfrey's time was the issue concerning whether or not philosophical argumentation can demonstrate that the world began to be. All participants in this discussion acknowledged that, on the strength of Scripture, we can be certain that the world began to be, but some, such as Henry of Ghent, maintained that human argumentation can demonstrate this conclusion. Others, including Thomas Aquinas, SIGER OF BRABANT and BOETHIUS OF DACIA denied that human reason can prove this. In addition some, including Aquinas near the end of his career in his *De aeternitate mundi* (On the Eternity of the World), went so far as to maintain that human reason can establish the possibility of an eternally created world. Godfrey holds that human reason cannot prove that the world began to be, but, while he is heavily dependent on Aquinas' *De aeternitate mundi*, he refuses to go so far as to claim that human reason can prove that an eternally created world is possible (see ETERNITY OF THE WORLD, MEDIEVAL VIEWS OF).

6 Substance and accidents

Godfrey accepts the usual Aristotelian distinction between substance and accidents, but rigidly applies the equally Aristotelian theory of act and potency to their relationship. If accidents inhere in their appropriate substances as secondary actualities in an underlying potential subject, can a substance efficiently cause any of the accidents that inhere in it? For Godfrey this is impossible, for it would mean that a substance would be active (as efficiently causing its accidents) and passive (as receiving them) at one and the same time with respect to the same thing. He is especially critical of Henry of Ghent's claim that a substance may be regarded as the proximate efficient cause of its proper accidents and operations. One particular point of disagreement had to do with the causal explanation of human activities, especially volition. In such cases Henry maintains that a human agent, because of the spiritual nature of the will, can reduce itself from what he calls virtual act to formal act, and that this happens in acts of choice (see HENRY OF GHENT). For Godfrey this would violate the Aristotelian view that whatever is moved is moved by something else and that nothing can reduce itself from potency to act. The human will is not the efficient cause of its acts of choice since they inhere in the will itself: their efficient cause is rather the object of choice insofar as this is presented to the will by the intellect. Not surprisingly, Godfrey's highly intellectualist account of human choice was criticized by some as leading to determinism. Closely connected with Godfrey's position concerning this is his defence of a real distinction between the soul and its powers, including the intellect and the will.

7 Matter and form

Godfrey accepts the Aristotelian view that corporeal entities are composed of prime matter and substantial form, and that they unite as potency and act to constitute the essence of such entities. He strongly insists that prime matter is pure potency, and denies, especially against Henry of Ghent, that it enjoys some minimum degree of actuality in itself that would be sufficient for God to keep it in existence without any form. In arguing for the matter–form composition of material entities to account for the change of one material substance into another, Godfrey is ultimately inspired by Aristotle's procedure in *Physics* I. Against the view defended by some thirteenth-century thinkers, Godfrey rejects any kind of matter–form composition of purely spiritual entities such as human souls and angels. He also rejects the view proposed by some, such as Aquinas, that because of their incorruptible character, heavenly bodies are composed of a special kind of prime matter and their appropriate substantial forms. Because he also accepts the prevailing view that heavenly bodies are not subject to corruption, Godfrey is forced into a difficult position. Drawing upon Averroes, he proposes that it is better to say that there is no matter in the proper sense in the heavenly bodies; for if there were, they would be subject to corruption (see IBN RUSHD). Godfrey refers to this position as being 'more probable'.

Closely related to Godfrey's views on matter and

form is his consideration of another contested issue: unity versus plurality of substantial forms in corporeal substances, especially in human beings. Aquinas had argued that in human beings the intellective soul is their single substantial form, but his position had been condemned after his death by two Archbishops of Canterbury, Robert KILWARDBY in 1277 and John PECHAM in 1284 and 1286. Godfrey's philosophical argumentation leads him to favour unicity of substantial form in all corporeal entities, including human beings. However, theological concerns, especially the need to explain how the body of Christ could continue to retain its identity as his body during the three days in the tomb, perplex him. Hence, while he insists upon the theologian's right to defend unicity of substantial form, Godfrey styles this theory as more probable but does not adopt it definitively.

Godfrey devotes considerable effort to determining the respective roles of form, prime matter, and quantity in the individuation of material entities. He concludes that a thing's substantial form is its formal principle of individuation, and that quantity plays the role of material dispositive cause by rendering matter divisible into numerically distinct parts which can therefore receive different substantial forms of the same kind. His philosophy is somewhat more Aristotelian and somewhat less Neoplatonic than that of most of his contemporaries.

See also: ARISTOTELIANISM, MEDIEVAL; HENRY OF GHENT §2

List of works

Godfrey of Fontaines (1285–1304) *Quodlibeta* (Quodlibetal Questions), ed. M. De Wulf, J. Hoffmans and O. Lottin in Les Philosophes Belges II–V, XIV, Louvain: Institut supérieur de Philosophie de l'Université, 1904–37. (Quodlibets 1–4 are in vol. II, ed. M. De Wulf and J. Hoffmans, 1904; Quodlibets 5–7 are in vol. III, ed. M. De Wulf and J. Hoffmans, 1914; Quodlibets 8–10 are in vol, IV, ed. J. Hoffmans, 1924–31; Quodlibets 11–14 are in vol. V, ed. J. Hoffmans, 1932–35; Quodlibets 15 plus three ordinary questions are in vol. XIV, ed. O. Lottin, 1937. Wippel (1981) has proposed dates of composition for individual quodlibets.)

—— (c.1285) Disputed Questions. (Edited questions can be found in B. Neumann, *Der Mensch und die himmlische Seligkeit nach der Lehre Gottfrieds von Fontaines*, Limburg: Lahn-Verlag, 1958; O. Lottin, *Psychologie et morale aux XIIᵉ et XIIIᵉ siècle*, Louvain: Abbaye du Mont César, and Gembloux, J. Duculot, 1954; and J.F. Wippel, 'Godfrey of Fontaines: Disputed Questions 9, 10 and 12',

Franciscan Studies 33: 356–72. For a listing of those questions which have been edited either in whole or in part see Wippel 1981: xxxi-xxxii.)

References and further reading

De Wulf, M. (1904) *Un théologien-philosophe du XIIIe siècle. Etude sur la vie, les oeuvres et l'influence de Godefroid de Fontaines* (A Theologian-Philosopher of the Thirteenth Century: Study on the Life, Works and Influence of Godfrey of Fontaines), Brussels: Hayez. (Still the most thorough account of Godfrey's life.)

Putallaz, F.-X. (1995) *Insolente liberté – controverses et condamnations au XIIIᵉ siècle*, Fribourg: Éditions Universitaires de Fribourg Suisse. (Chapters (here called 'situations') VI and VII are especially helpful on Godfrey's place in late thirteenth-century discussions concerning the respective roles of the intellect and the will in accounting for human choice.)

Wippel, J.F. (1981) *The Metaphysical Thought of Godfrey of Fontaines: A Study in Late Thirteenth-Century Philosophy*, Washington, DC: Catholic University of America Press. (A general account of Godfrey's metaphysical thought and his contributions to philosophy, with bibliography.)

—— (1982) 'Godfrey of Fontaines' Disputed Questions 9 and 10 (Bruges 491): by Godfrey or by Giles of Rome?', *Franciscan Studies* 42: 216–47. (On the authenticity of two Disputed Questions attributed to Godfrey and edited by Wippel in 1973.)

—— (1984) 'Possible Sources for Godfrey of Fontaines' Views on the Act-Potency 'Composition' of Simple Creatures', *Mediaeval Studies* 46: 222–44. (Proposes an anonymous set of questions on Aristotle's *Posterior Analytics* as another source for Godfrey's theory in addition to Siger and Proclus.)

JOHN F. WIPPEL

GODWIN, WILLIAM (1756–1836)

William Godwin is considered the founder of philosophical anarchism. His An Enquiry Concerning Political Justice *(1793) contends that although government is a corrupt force in society, perpetuating dependence and ignorance, it will increasingly be rendered impotent by the gradual spread of knowledge. Politics will be displaced by an enlarged morality as truth conquers error and mind subordinates matter. He predicts the end to cooperative activities (which restrain individual freedom), the abandonment of marriage and private property, and increasing longevity and ultimate immortality.*

Godwin's moral theory is often described as utilitarian, but he understands pleasure to be inseparable from the development of truth and wisdom through the full and free exercise of private judgment and public discussion. As such, his position is better understood as perfectionist.

1 Life
2 Ethics
3 Anarchism and liberalism

1 Life

William Godwin was born 3 March 1756, the son of a Dissenting minister, and was educated for the ministry at the Hoxton Dissenting Academy. When his vocation failed he turned to political journalism. Caught up in the wave of enthusiasm which greeted the French Revolution in 1789, he took an active interest in the controversy which followed Edmund Burke's attack (see BURKE, E.) on the revolutionaries and their English supporters (notably Richard PRICE and the Dissent-dominated London Revolution Society). Godwin's *Enquiry Concerning Political Justice*, written between September 1791 and January 1793, was intended as a summary of recent developments in moral and political philosophy. It begins with evident debts to the *philosophes* (especially Baron d'Holbach, Claude-Adrien HELVETIUS and Jean-Jacques Rousseau), to Thomas Paine's *Common Sense* (1775) and *Rights of Man* (1791–2; see PAINE, T.) and to Price's Platonism. But as the work develops, Godwin's own position emerges, the *philosophe* influence is displaced by a secular interpretation of several central themes of rational dissent: notably the importance of candour, the doctrine of philosophical necessity, the irresistible power of truth, and the sanctity of private judgment. From these materials Godwin forges a resounding attack on contemporary political institutions and a philosophical anarchism which rejects all government interference.

Political Justice brought Godwin widespread renown, which *Caleb Williams* (1794), his most successful novel, confirmed. By the end of the decade, however, he had fallen victim to the loyalist reaction – a fate he partly invited by his frank memoir of his deceased wife, Mary WOLLSTONECRAFT (1798). While he continued to write until his death, he never regained his reputation.

2 Ethics

Godwin's moral position as expressed in *Political Justice* is complex because he endorses two potentially conflicting moral principles. In the chapter 'Of Justice' (II.2), he uses his most famous moral example, 'The Famous Fire Cause'. He argues that when faced with a situation in which I can save either Fenelon (see FENELON, F.), the illustrious Archbishop of Cambrai, or his chambermaid, I should save Fenelon, even if the chambermaid is my mother. This is justified not on grounds of desert, but because of the benefit which Fenelon will confer on humankind. This argument encapsulates Godwin's more general claim that we should act to maximize utility, motivated wholly by disinterested benevolence, and unaffected by familial or other attachments.

Godwin's argument involves a most demanding conception of personal rectitude (albeit softened by changes in later editions of *Political Justice* and elsewhere). His position rests on three elements: that we can all come to recognize the same or similar moral or ethical principles upon which to base our conduct; that we will act on the basis of these principles without incentives from self-interest or coercion; and that we will order every aspect of our lives, public and private, in accordance with these principles. The first premise derives from Godwin's background in rational dissent, coupled with a more general enlightenment optimism, which assumed convergence in matters of belief. The second rests on an understanding of necessitarianism derived initially from David HARTLEY, Jonathan Edwards and Joseph PRIESTLEY, which held that when feeling contends with moral truth the understanding experiences this as a contention of ideas, and will resolve in favour of the more general and powerful (a view also indebted to Price's Platonism). The third has its origins both in Godwin's classical reading, with its ideal of the virtuous citizen, and in his theological training, in which subordination to God is equally demanding of public and private life.

Godwin's endorsement of the utility principle is qualified by two arguments: that the happiness of another can best be promoted indirectly, by enlightening the understanding; and that pleasures differ qualitatively, with wisdom and benevolence affording infinitely superior pleasure to sensual gratification. His utilitarianism is, then, indirect and ideal (see UTILITARIANISM).

Godwin's second basic moral principle is the right of private judgment. Morality requires that we act wholly upon the dictates of the understanding. We have a duty to justice, but our only route to justice is through the full and free exercise of private judgment.

Private judgment is best seen as a right for Godwin, despite his rejection (most forcefully in the first edition of *Political Justice*) of the language of rights. It is not reducible to utility because its exercise is both an indefeasible duty and the highest form of existence we can attain. Clearly, there is utility to be gained from respecting private judgment, but we cannot abrogate an individual's judgment for the sake of utility – not least because there is no infallible standard for what utility demands. This suggests that Godwin's position is best characterized as perfectionist: the true end of moral action is the progressive improvement of our moral and intellectual faculties.

Godwin's position is distinctive because he combines an act-centred conception of moral duty – act so as to maximize overall benefit – with an agent-centred, perfectionist conception of moral agency and virtue – according to which action is only fully moral when intention and outcome are brought together in a fully rational will. Neither government nor individuals may legitimately transgress another's private judgment. We have a right to remonstrate with them, but we have a duty to respect their considered judgment. Behind this account lies a deeper theory, driven by the doctrine of necessity and by the belief that mind is potentially sovereign over desire and feeling, which sees the apex of human perfection as a life lived in the light of truth. It is not difficult to recognize here the residual effect of Godwin's Dissenting inheritance.

Godwin's philosophical position underwent a number of changes at the end of the 1790s and after: his rationalism ebbed, and he endorsed a sentiment-based theory of moral judgment and moral motivation. Yet, even while making the changes, Godwin insisted that they did not touch the central tenets of his position. This is not an easy claim to assess. The later editions of *Political Justice* (1796, 1798) advance a more tepid doctrine of progress than the first. In *The Enquirer: Reflections on Education, Manners and Literature* (1797) sympathy is clearly rehabilitated, as is feeling more generally. It is also possible to identify a more nuanced doctrine of moral motivation, in which the love of fame or distinction is accorded a more positive role than in *Political Justice*. The emphasis on stimulating the imagination, rather than on reason, and the suggestion that the imagination is the basis for moral sense can be recognized in both *The Enquirer* and the later *Letter of Advice* (1818). Moreover, *Thoughts on Man* (1831) contains arguments which seem wholly at odds with his earlier egalitarianism.

3 Anarchism and liberalism

There is, nonetheless, a consistent core to Godwin's work. His philosophical speculations are best understood as speculations, not foundations. What is foundational is his basic conviction that private judgment and public discussion are the essential means to the development of moral and political truth, and that we become fully human only by coming to live wholly in accord with the dictates of the understanding. To do less is to be less – less rational, less individual, less worthy and less human. Godwin's novels, and much of his other writing, explore how we come to be less than we might be; and it is in these accounts, and in the swingeing attack on monarchical and aristocratic regimes in *Political Justice*, that he takes to task the world of aristocratic power and privilege in which he lived. His religious writings perform much the same role with respect to the other central institution of imposture and fraud, the Christian Church. Indeed, the separation of his works into disciplinary categories misses the point that in nearly everything he wrote Godwin was concerned to further the moral and intellectual development of his fellow men and women, and to reveal to them the extent to which they have been misled and imposed upon by the political, social and religious institutions of their society.

Political Justice remains Godwin's most forceful expression of this position. Despite its eccentricities and occasional extremism, it is a work of considerable philosophical originality and power. Sixty years before John Stuart Mill's *On Liberty* (1859), Godwin synthesized an indirect and ideal utilitarianism with a conception of individual wellbeing and a rights-based doctrine of private judgment, which is in many respects more compelling than Mill's. Moreover, where Mill hedges liberty against the masses, Godwin shares the eighteenth-century view that the greatest threat is from government. His anarchism simply takes this distrust to its ultimate conclusion. Liberals have tended to dismiss Godwin as an extremist and utopian, yet by combining his commitment to utility as a principle of justice with an equal commitment to private judgment as an indefeasible adjunct principle of right, he offers us a radical vision set within impeccably liberal constraints.

See also: ANARCHISM

List of works

Godwin, W. (1993) *The Political and Philosophical Writings of William Godwin*, ed. M. Philp, London: Pickering & Chatto. (Volumes 1 and 2 contain Godwin's political writings, from his first published work, a biography of Pitt the Elder, and a number of pamphlets from the 1780s, through to his defence of the radicals charged with Treason in 1794 and his replies to the critics – notably Samuel Parr and Thomas Malthus. Volume 3 reprints the 1793 edition of *An Enquiry Concerning Political Justice* (Godwin's major philosophical work); while volume 4 contains variant material from the manuscript and from the second edition of 1796 and the third edition of 1798, together with Godwin's manuscript comments on the development of his views. Volume 5 contains Godwin's essays and educational writings, notably *The Enquirer* which develops less formally many of the themes of his *Political Justice*; volume 6 his *Thoughts on Man*, his last major philosophical work, and volume 7 his religious writings which range from Sermons first delivered in the early 1780s through to a substantial but uncompleted manuscript denouncing Christianity which was published posthumously. (The extended introduction to volume 1 of this contemporary series provides an overview of Godwin's central contribution.)

—— (1992) *The Collected Novels and Memoirs of William Godwin*, ed. M. Philp, 8 vols, London: Pickering & Chatto. (The extended introduction to volume 1 of this contemporary series provides an overview of Godwin's central contribution.)

—— (1793) *An Enquiry Concerning Political Justice*, London: Robinson; revised 1796, 1798. (Godwin's major philosophical treatise in which he develops a philosophical anarchism which looks forward to the increasing perfection of the human race through the development of mind.)

—— (1794) *Things as They Are: Or the Adventures of Caleb Williams*, London: Robinson (Godwin's most successful novel. A tale of domestic despotism and of flight and pursuit which makes original use of a flawed first person narrator.)

—— (1797) *The Enquirer: Reflections on Education, Manners and Literature*, London: Robinson. (A collection of diverse essays in which some of the themes of his *Enquiry Concerning Political Justice* are analysed less formally, resulting in some modification of his philosophical position with respect to equality.)

—— (1798) *Memoirs of the Author of a Vindication of the Rights of Woman*, London: J. Johnson; in W. Goodwin (1992), vol. 1. (Godwin's affectionate and candid memoir of his wife, Mary Wollstonecraft.)

—— (1818) *Letter of Advice to a Young American*, London: M.J. Godwin; in W. Goodwin (1993), vol. 5. (A synopsis of Godwin's beliefs about the appropriate philosophical education.)

—— (1831) *Thoughts on Man*, London: Effingham Wilson; in W. Goodwin (1992), vol.6. (Godwin's last major philosophical work, which largely confirms his continuing commitment to the central doctrines of his *Enquiry Concerning Political Justice*.)

References and further reading

Barry, B. (1955) *Justice as Impartiality*, Oxford: Clarendon Press. (A defence of impartialist ethics which discusses Godwin's relevance to our understanding of the character of impartiality in chapter 9.)

Clark, J.P. (1977) *The Philosophical Anarchism of William Godwin*, Princeton, NJ: Princeton University Press. (A sophisticated reading of Godwin's political philosophy, which regards him as a utilitarian.)

Locke, D. (1980) *A Fantasy of Reason: The Life and Thought of William Godwin*, London: Routledge & Kegan Paul. (A major biography with substantial philosophical commentary.)

* Mill, J.S. (1859) *On Liberty*, London: J.W. Parker and Son. (A seminal defence of liberty in all its forms in which the only justification for constraint is the avoidance of harm to others.)

Philp, M. (1986) *Godwin's Political Justice*, London: Duckworth.(A contextual study of Godwin's work 1789–1800 which advances a perfectionist interpretation of his moral philosophy.)

MARK PHILP

GOETHE, JOHANN WOLFGANG VON (1749–1832)

Goethe was a statesman, scientist, amateur artist, theatrical impresario, dramatist, novelist and Germany's supreme lyric poet; indeed he provided the Romantic generation which followed him with their conception of what a poet should be. His works, diaries and about 12,000 letters run to nearly 150 volumes. His drama Faust *(1790–1832) is the greatest long poem in modern European literature and made the legend of Dr Faust a modern myth. He knew most of the significant figures in the philosophical movement of German Idealism (though he never met Kant), but he was not himself a philosopher. His literary works certainly addressed contemporary philosophical concerns:* Iphigenie auf Tauris (Iphigenia in Tauris) *(1779–86) seems a prophetic dramatization of the ethical and religious autonomy Kant was to proclaim from 1785; in his novel* Die Wahlverwandtschaften *(The Elective Affinities) (1809) a mysterious natural or supernatural world of chemistry, magnetism or Fate, such as 'Naturphilosophie' envisaged, seems to underlie and perhaps determine a human story of spiritual adultery; in* Faust, *particularly* Part Two, *the tale of a pact or wager with the Devil seems to develop into a survey of world cultural history, which has been held to have overtones of Schelling, Hegel or even Marx. But whatever their conceptual materials, Goethe's literary works require literary rather than philosophical analysis. There are, however, certain discrete concepts prominent in his scientific work, or in the expressions of his 'wisdom' – maxims, essays, autobiographies, letters and conversations – with which Goethe's name is particularly associated and which are capable of being separately discussed. Notable among these are: Nature and metamorphosis (Bildung), polarity and 'intensification' (Steigerung), the 'primal phenomena' (Urphänomene), 'the daemonic' (das Dämonische) and renunciation (Entsagung).*

1   **Life and works**
2   **Goethe and the philosophers**
3   **Some Goethean ideas**

1   Life and works

Johann Wolfgang Goethe was born on 28 August 1749 in Frankfurt am Main, then a self-governing free city within the Holy Roman Empire. His father lived off his capital and his mother was the daughter of the city's principal official. He studied law in Leipzig, where he met J.C. Gottsched, the literary reformer and interpreter of Leibniz, and then in Strasbourg, where he met J.G. HERDER, who opened his eyes to the merits of folk poetry and Shakespeare. Goethe's first great literary success was the Sentimentalist novel in letters, *Die Leiden des jungen Werthers* (*The Sorrows of Young Werther*) (1774). Its story of a young intellectual who falls in love with a married woman and commits suicide made him a European celebrity. The mid-1770s were a period of great fertility for Goethe, and in about 1773 he began *Faust*, the work which was to occupy him throughout the rest of his life. In 1775 he accepted an invitation from the young Duke of Weimar, a sovereign prince, to visit his court and then to become a Privy Councillor of the duchy. Goethe did not return to Frankfurt and remained permanently in the Weimar administration. At first he had a heavy load of official work and his responsibility for the (unproductive) Weimar silver-mines led him to an interest in geology and other branches of natural history. In 1782 he was ennobled, becoming 'von Goethe', but his literary powers seemed to be languishing. However, after he had spent a sabbatical period from 1786–8 in Italy (where he met the aesthetician K.P. Moritz), the Duke allowed him to concentrate on writing and on managing the Weimar theatre. A fragmentary version of *Faust* was published in the first authorized edition of his collected writings (1787–90), which also contained some other noteworthy plays, such as *Iphigenie auf Tauris* (*Iphigenia in Tauris*), *Egmont* and *Torquato Tasso* (believed to be the first tragedy with a poet as its hero), and the first collection of his lyric poems. In 1790 he published a brief general theory of botany, *Versuch, die Metamorphose der Pflanzen zu erklären* (*Essay in Elucidation of the Metamorphosis of Plants*).

Already in 1776 Goethe had arranged for Herder to come to Weimar as the head of the Lutheran Church in the duchy, and in 1789 he recommended Friedrich SCHILLER for a chair in history at the local university of Jena. After his return from Italy, Goethe became increasingly involved in the affairs of the university, paying particular attention to the appointments in the natural sciences and in philosophy, where he followed a policy of encouraging young talent and especially the new Kantian school (already established in Jena by Reinhold). He had some part in the successive appointments of FICHTE, SCHELLING and HEGEL, and after he had established a close friendship in 1794 with Schiller, who was just completing the major aesthetic essays of his Kantian period and with whom he undertook various joint editorial ventures, Goethe spent as much time in the university world of Jena and in the circle of Romantic writers centred on F. Schlegel as in the court world of Weimar. During this period he published a long novel, *Wilhelm Meisters Lehrjahre* (*Wilhelm Meister's Years of Apprenticeship*), which had been in the making for twenty years, and his interests in natural history were displaced by a passion for the theory of colour, of which he had become convinced Newtonian optics gave a perversely false account (see COLOUR AND QUALIA). His reactions to the French Revolution, which threatened to overturn the world he had grown up in, were expressed in the play *Die Natürliche Tochter* (*The Natural Daughter*) (1803). From 1799 Schiller's mature plays provided the Weimar theatre with the centrepiece of a programme for raising theatrical and literary standards throughout Germany, but the German Romantic movement was already well under way and Goethe's Italianate and Hellenizing tastes already seemed old-fashioned. In 1805 Schiller died, and the following year Napoleon put an end to the old German order and the Holy Roman Empire itself at the battle of Jena. The university of Jena had already begun to decline with the controversial departure of Fichte and then Schelling, and after a period of closure could not recover its position as a centre of philosophical innovation.

Goethe marked the new epoch in his life that began in 1806 by marrying Christiane Vulpius, with whom he had lived since 1788 and who had borne him several children, of whom only one survived infancy. (Having ceased to be a communicant Christian at the age of 21, Goethe gave his refusal to undergo a church ceremony as his reason for postponing marriage so long.) 1806 also saw the completion of *Faust. Part One*, though publication was delayed until 1808. *Die Wahlverwandtschaften* (*The Elective Affinities*) (1809) was a kind of reckoning with a decade of Romantic culture, and in 1810, after a long gestation, *Zur Farbenlehre* (*On the Theory of Colour*) appeared. Much of the next ten years Goethe devoted to autobiographical writings, notably *Dichtung und Wahrheit* (*Poetry and Truth*) and *Italienische Reise* (*Italian Journey*), but from 1814 to 1817 there came a remarkable resurgence of lyric poetry, in imitation of the medieval Persian poet Hafiz, *West-östlicher Divan* (*The West-Eastern Divan*). A more sober atmosphere prevailed after the death of Christiane in 1816, and Goethe began to publish, rewrite and reinterpret his earlier studies in natural science. He remained hostile to the Christianizing tendencies in Romantic literature and art, resisted Schelling's proposed election to a chair in philosophy in Jena in 1816, since Schelling wished to combine it with a chair in theology, and favoured instead the appointment of Fries. Schopenhauer and his mother, who had settled in Weimar, were both close friends at this time.

For twenty years Goethe was a regular visitor to the Bohemian spas. At the age of 74, when in Marienbad, he proposed marriage to Ulrike von Levetzow, then 19 years old, and on being refused by her family gave up travelling and spent the last nine years of his life in Weimar preparing the final collected edition of his works. A stream of visitors – including Victor Cousin and Hegel – kept him in touch with European culture, and his list of correspondents – Byron and Carlyle among them – became immense. His last works, in which the theme of renunciation is increasingly prominent, show a concern with problems of world-historical dimensions: the nature of education and culture, the relation of America and Europe, the impending industrial revolution, 'world-literature' (*Weltliteratur*, a term he invented) and the preservation of humane values in a changing world. In addition to rounding off his autobiographical works he wrote a sequel to his major novel, *Wilhelm Meisters Wanderjahre* (*Wilhelm Meister's Years of Wandering*), and in his last five years wrote most of *Faust. Part Two*, which was not published until after his death. At his own suggestion, many aphoristic remarks scattered among his papers were collected together as his *Maximen und Reflexionen* (*Maxims and Reflections*) and published posthumously by his amanuensis J.P. Eckermann, whose *Gespräche mit Goethe in den letzten Jahren seines Lebens* (*Conversations with Goethe in the Last Years of his Life*) were described by Nietzsche as 'the best German book there is'.

2   Goethe and the philosophers

The philosophical orthodoxy prevailing at all German universities in Goethe's youth was the Wolffian version of Leibnizianism, and throughout his life it is possible to find in his literary and scientific works characteristically Leibnizian traits: in a conversation of 1813 he expressed a preference for 'the Leibnizian term' monad as a description of 'the ultimate primal components of all beings' (see LEIBNIZ, G.W. §§4,5). None the less it was long fashionable to regard SPINOZA as the main philosophical influence on Goethe, despite Goethe's own admission that Spinoza – whom he found 'abstruse' – had an effect on him like Shakespeare and Linnaeus, that is, he showed him the way he could not himself follow. A fragmentary essay of 1784–5, dubbed by its editors 'Studie nach Spinoza' ('Spinozan Study') has little in it that is certainly Spinozan and much that is probably Leibnizian.

Asked by Eckermann in 1827 who was pre-eminent among the modern philosophers, Goethe replied 'Kant...without any doubt'. He first sought help from REINHOLD in studying the new system in 1789, and made an attempt at reading the first *Critique*. In 1790, immediately after its publication, he made a careful study of the *Critique of Judgment*, which he ever after regarded as Kant's most important work, particularly the 'Critique of Teleological Judgment' (see KANT, I. §12). In 1794, when his closer acquaintance with Schiller was only beginning, he read Fichte's first systematic writings and could summarize them to their author's entire satisfaction (see FICHTE, J.G. §§12–13). Goethe was aware of, and to a great extent accepted, the Copernican revolution which founded the Idealist period of German philosophy – no one in the world of learning, he wrote in 1805, could ignore it with impunity.

From 1797, after Schiller had turned back to drama, Schelling and F.I. Niethammer were Goethe's main informants about contemporary philosophical developments, and for a while it seemed to Goethe that Schelling might be the man to heal the division between mind and nature which the new philosophy had opened up. Despite some admiration for J.W.

Ritter, however, Goethe's attitude to '*Naturphilosophie*' was consistently sceptical. He had less personal contact with Hegel than with Schelling, but had a high opinion of his character and abilities. Given the rapidly changing nature of scientific understanding, though, he doubted whether it was prudent for Hegel to incorporate so much empirical material into his philosophy, and objected to Hegel's continual recourse to the categories of the Christian religion (see HEGEL, G.W.F. §8). Goethe thought world history 'the most absurd thing there is', but his relations with Hegel in the last years of his life were genial.

3   Some Goethean ideas

A poem Goethe wrote in 1826 ends:

> What greater gain can a human being have from life than that God-or-Nature should reveal herself to him? – how she dissolves firm material into spirit; how she firmly preserves what spirit has produced.
>
> (1988: 1, 367)

Goethe early became familiar with the Spinozan tag 'Deus sive natura', and throughout his life 'Nature' was to him an expression of what is most perfect and most worthy of veneration. The content of the concept changed considerably: at first, in Rousseauist manner, it was an antithesis to the 'artificial' and was referred to an almost personal, creative and arbitrary power; later, as Goethe's scientific studies began, Nature was distinguished from the human world by being 'unfeeling', an impersonal repository of passionless order, contrasted with the turmoil of human emotions; later still, once Goethe had absorbed the implications of the Kantian revolution, he regarded the works of the human mind, which to his contemporaries seemed to transcend Nature, as, rather, her supreme product. In so far as this is the position of what Fichte called a 'realist', Goethe could be said never to have deviated from a Kantian belief in the independent reality of things in themselves, though, as he remarks in the essay 'Einwirkung der neueren Philosophie' ('Influence of Modern Philosophy'), his views appeared to Kant's disciples to be 'an analogy of Kantian conceptions, but a strange one'.

The most important single concept in Goethe's understanding of natural processes was that of 'metamorphosis'. (The term 'formation', '*Bildung*', probably borrowed from J.F. Blumenbach, is largely synonymous, but more indeterminate and multivalent.) Early in his botanical studies Goethe gave up the notion that all plants could be related to an ideal type, or 'primal plant' ('*Urpflanze*'), and substituted for it the notion that all vegetable shapes could be understood as the consequences of an ordered but unending series of transformations of a single fundamental organ, called 'the leaf'. An attempt to transfer this concept to vertebrate zoology was abandoned in 1795, under the influence of Kantian criticism, but Goethe's name remained associated with 'metamorphosis' – seen as an early form of evolutionary theory – in nineteenth-century biological textbooks. In Goethe's later years this (Leibnizian) conception of transformation in accordance with an innate rule was associated with two concepts for which he was particularly, though not wholly, indebted to Schelling: 'polarity' (*Polarität*) and 'intensification' (*Steigerung*). Not only is polar opposition held to be fundamental to the natural order (in colour theory, for example, the opposition of blue and yellow), but through 'intensification' opposites have a tendency to transform themselves jointly into a third term on a higher level (in colour theory: red).

However, at least from the time when he began reading Kant, Goethe thought of science not simply as speculation about the order of things, but as the attempt to understand human experience. Natural science was not concerned with an unobservable, mathematically constructed substratum to things (as Newton's optics seemed to imply), but with the material offered to us in and by our senses. The theories of natural science simply sought to make explicit an order already implicitly present in our observations. Experiments therefore were not devices for confirming or disproving hypotheses, but were the very material of science, and should consist of a large series of observations arranged so as to manifest all aspects of the phenomenon concerned. The ultimate constituents of our knowledge (never completely isolated in practice) are therefore 'primal phenomena' (*Urphänomene*), which are utterly simple manifestations to our senses of what is, and of which no explanation is possible (for any explanation would take us away from our senses into a merely imagined world). An example of the approach to such a 'pure' or 'primal' phenomenon would be the revelation of colour when a prism is held up against a boundary between light and dark.

Writing to Hegel, Goethe called the 'primal phenomena' 'daemonic' (*dämonisch*), which he later glossed as meaning 'which cannot be resolved by the understanding or the reason'. In the Kantian terms of this definition, the 'daemonic' is identical, therefore, with things as they are in themselves. The word, however, which has been the subject of much scholarly controversy, is also applied to personal individuality, especially when strongly marked, and to the operations of chance, of an unfathomable

providence (benign or malign) and of some animals (notably, bats and parrots). Although therefore Goethe might at first sight seem to share Hegel's principle that the noumenon is present to us in our experience, he also clearly refuses to identify the noumenon with our own spirit and insists that it is something *given*: human experience – and so human history – is not to be interpreted simply as the realm of the rational. The achievements of Hellenic civilization, for example, are extraordinary gifts of good fortune, not part of some inevitable process – not least because that might imply that their loss was inevitable too. But for Goethe the combination of ethical and sensual perfection in the Greek world can always in principle be recovered in uncovenanted moments of fulfilment, of which works of art are the principal monuments. Our normal lot, of course, is to do without such fulfilment, and to suffer our deprivation, and the absurd disorder of most of what is called world-history, in a spirit of renunciation (*Entsagung*). But that is the mirror-image of our tacit but never abandoned hope that the perfect order will one day be restored.

See also: GERMAN IDEALISM; NATURE, AESTHETIC APPRECIATION OF; NATURPHILOSOPHIE; POETRY; ROMANTICISM, GERMAN

List of works

Goethe's main works have been mentioned in the text, and most, it will be plain, are at least indirectly relevant to philosophy. The following is a selection of non- or semi-fictional works of more directly philosophical interest (the titles are often editorial, and may be misleading).

Goethe, J.W. von (1887–1919) *Goethes Werke, herausgegeben im Auftrage der Großherzogin Sophie von Sachsen (Weimarer Ausgabe)*, Weimar: Hermann Böhlaus Nachfolger. (Other, more fully annotated, editions exist, or are in progress, but this is, and is likely to remain, the only historical-critical edition. It is available on CD-ROM as *Goethes Werke auf CD-ROM*, Cambridge, Chadwyck-Healey, 1995, supplemented by Goethe's conversations and the letters not included in the edition of 1887–1919.)

—— (1988) *Johann Wolfgang von Goethe. Werke. Hamburger Ausgabe in 14 Bänden*, Munich: C.H. Beck, 1988. (A popular students' edition, with commentary. Volume 14 has a comprehensive bibliography; for Goethe and philosophy, see 618–19. Four volumes of selected letters, and two of letters to Goethe, are uniform with the works.)

—— (1983–9) *Goethe: Collected Works*, Cambridge,

MA: Suhrkamp Publishers Inc., Suhrkamp Edition, 12 vols. (An extensive collection of modern translations, with some notes, and including two volumes of essays, maxims and scientific writing.)

—— (1772) 'Brief des Pastors zu ** an den neuen Pastor zu **' (Letter from the pastor of ** to the new pastor of **), in Goethe (1988), vol. 12, 228–39. (Theology of toleration.)

—— (1784) 'Über den Granit' (On Granite) in Goethe (1983–9), vol. 12, 131–4. (Goethe's geological study.)

—— (1784–5) 'Studie nach Spinoza' (A Study Based on Spinoza), in Goethe (1983–9), vol. 12, 8–10. (Goethe's theory of knowledge.)

—— (1790a) *Versuch, die Metamorphose der Pflanzen zu erklären* (Essay in Elucidation of the Metamorphosis of Plants), in Goethe (1983–89), vol. 12, 76–97. (Goethe's principal work on botany.)

—— (1790b) 'Versuch einer allgemeinen Vergleichungslehre' (Toward a General Comparative Theory), in Goethe (1983–9), vol.12, 53–6. (His first attempt at a general morphology.)

—— (1792) 'Der Versuch als Vermittler von Objekt und Subjekt' (The Experiment as Mediator between Object and Subject), in Goethe (1983–9), vol. 12, 11–17. (Titled in 1823; despite the title the thinking is almost pre-Kantian)

—— (1795) 'Plato als Mitgenosse einer christlichen Offenbarung' (Plato as Party to a Christian Revelation), in Goethe (1983–9), vol. 3, 200–3. (Against Christian exclusivism.)

—— (1798a) 'Einleitung in die Propyläen' (Introduction to the *Propylaea*), in Goethe (1983–9), vol. 3, 78–90. (Art theory in a historical context.)

—— (1798b) 'Erfahrung und Wissenschaft' (Empirical Observation and Science), in Goethe (1983–9), vol. 12, 24–5. (His theory of 'empirical' and 'pure' phenomena.)

—— (1799) 'Der Sammler und die Seinigen' (The Collector and his Circle), in Goethe (1983–9), vol. 3, 121–59. (Aesthetic theory in a fictionalized form.)

—— (1805) 'Letzte Kunstausstellung. 1805' (Final Art Exhibition, 1805) in Goethe (1887–1919), part 1, vol. 36, 265–7. (Retrospect on Weimar art competitions.)

—— (1817) 'Geistesepochen' (Stages of Man's Mind), in Goethe (1983–9), vol. 3, 203–4. (Goethe's philosophy of history.)

—— (1817–20) 'Einwirkung der neueren Philosophie' (The Influence of Modern Philosophy), in Goethe (1983–9), vol. 12, 28–30. (Goethe's assessment of the influence on him of contemporary philosophers.)

—— (1827) 'Nachlese zu Aristoteles' Poetik' (On interpreting Aristotle's *Poetics*), in Goethe (1983–9), vol. 3, 197–9. (Goethe's interpretation of 'catharsis'.)

—— (1828) 'Erläuterung zu dem aphoristischen Aufsatz "Die Natur"' (A Commentary on the Aphoristic Essay 'Nature'), in Goethe (1983–9), vol. 12, 6–7. (General theory of Nature – the essay 'Die Natur' (Nature) is not by Goethe but by G.C. Tobler.)

References and further reading

Boyle, N. (1991) *Goethe: The Poet and the Age. Volume One: The Poetry of Desire (1749–1790)*, Oxford: Oxford University Press. (Includes the historical and philosophical background.)

* Bruford, W.H. (1962) *Culture and Society in Classical Weimar: 1775-1806*, Cambridge: Cambridge University Press. (Good accounts of Herder, Schiller and Fichte, as well as Goethe.)

Goethe-Jahrbuch (1994) Weimar: Hermann Böhlaus Nachfolger. (Papers read in 1993 at the 73rd Congress of the International Goethe Society, which together constitute the most comprehensive study of Goethe's thinking about history.)

Heller, E. (1952) *The Disinherited Mind*, Cambridge: Bowes & Bowes. (Classic essays on Goethe's place in the modern German tradition.)

Moln r, G. von (1993) *Goethes Kantstudien*, Weimar: Hermann Böhlaus Nachfolger. (Facsimiles and analysis of all Goethe's marginalia to the First and Third Critiques.)

Nisbet, H.B. (1972) *Goethe and the Scientific Tradition*, London: Institute of Germanic Studies. (Particularly useful on Goethe's view of Bacon.)

Rabel, G. (1927) *Goethe und Kant*, Vienna: privately printed, 2 vols. (A very thorough, if slightly obsessional, compilation, regrettably under-used by later writers.)

Reed, T.J. (1984) *Goethe*, Oxford: Oxford University Press. (Excellent summary account of life and works.)

Wells, G.A. (1978) *Goethe and the Development of Science: 1750–1900*, Alphen aan den Rijn: Sijthoff & Noordhoff. (A Darwinian-rationalist critique, which is extremely well-informed, both about the science and about Goethe's writings.)

NICHOLAS BOYLE

GOLDMAN, EMMA

see FEMINISM (§4)

GOOD AND RIGHT *see* RIGHT AND GOOD

GOOD, THEORIES OF THE

'Good' is the most general term of positive evaluation, used to recommend or express approval in a wide range of contexts. It indicates that a thing is desirable or worthy of choice, so that normally, if you have reason to want a certain kind of thing, you also have reason to prefer a good *thing of that kind.*

A theory of the good may consist in a general account of the good, which is meant to apply to all good things; or in a definition of 'good', an account of how the term functions in the language. Theories of the good have metaphysical implications about the relations of fact and value. Many ancient and medieval philosophers believed in the ultimate identity of the real and the good. Modern philosophers reject this identification, and have held a range of positions: realists, for example, hold that the good is part of reality, while certain moral sense theorists hold that when we call something good we are projecting human interests onto reality; and emotivists hold that we use the term 'good' only to signify subjective approval.

Theorists of the good also categorize different kinds of goodness and explain how they are related. Good things are standardly classified as ends, which are valued for their own sakes, or means, valued for the sake of the ends they promote. Some philosophers also divide them into intrinsic goods, which have their value in themselves, and extrinsic goods, which get their value from their relation to something else. Various theories have been held about the relation between these two distinctions – about whether an end must be something with intrinsic value. Philosophers also distinguish subjective goods – things which are good for someone in particular – from objective goods, which are good from everyone's point of view. Views about how these kinds of goodness are related have important implications for moral philosophy.

Usually, a theory of the good is constructed in the hope of shedding light on more substantive questions, such as what makes a person, an action, or a human life good. These questions raise issues about the relation between ethical and other values. For example, we may ask whether moral virtue is a special sort of goodness, or just the ordinary sort applied to persons. Or, since actions are valued as 'right' or 'wrong', we may ask how these values are related to the action's goodness or badness. We may also pose the question of whether a life that is good in the sense of being happy *must also be* a morally good *or virtuous life. This last question has occupied the attention of philosophers ever since Plato.*

1 History and metaphysics of the good

Almost anything may be assessed as 'good' or 'bad'. This ubiquity of 'good' and its cognates in other languages has suggested nearly opposite conclusions about the metaphysics of goodness to different philosophers. At one extreme we find Plato's view that the good is the fundamental principle of reality. Through works such as the *Republic*, Plato expounded his view that the reality of an object consists in its 'participation' in a 'Form'. A Form is both an archetype or pattern, and an ideal, a perfect version, of the things of which it is the Form. Each Form, because it is perfect, in turn participates in the Form of the Good. A thing is real, then, to the extent that it participates in the Form of the Good.

In *Nicomachean Ethics*, Aristotle criticizes Plato's account for not telling us anything about particular kinds of goodness (see ARISTOTLE §§21–6). Yet Aristotle's own metaphysics retains a version of the equation of goodness and reality. The essential nature of each thing, according to Aristotle, consists in its characteristic activity or function, and it is both most perfect and most real when it performs that function well (see PERFECTIONISM).

These metaphysical views may seem remote from our everyday employment of the idea of goodness. Yet most philosophers agree that the basic insight behind Aristotle's account throws important light on many uses of 'good'. To say that a thing is good is to say that it is a well-functioning thing of its kind, and its well-functioning is related to its reality: a good heart is one that pumps blood well, and a heart that ceases to pump blood altogether ceases to be a heart. This functional account of goodness applies most clearly to things that have purposes – instruments and tools, biological organs, parts of machines, crafts and professions – and it has the advantage of making it clear why we care about having things that are good. But when we say that happiness, or beauty, or freedom, is good, we do not seem to be talking about the performance of a function. Efforts have therefore been made to extend the basic idea of the functional account to things which are not clearly purposive, like people and lives. In *A Theory of Justice* (1971), Rawls proposes that 'a good x' means 'an x that has the properties it is rational to want in an x'. A good life, for example, has the properties it is rational to want in a life. The goodness of pleasure, freedom, or beauty may then be interpreted in terms of the role these things play in good lives.

The relinquishment of the view that the good coincides with the real marks the transition from the ancient and medieval to the modern world. Modern thinkers confront a value-neutral world, the world of matter and motion described by physics. Modern 'realists', although they reject the general equation of the real and the good, still believe that goodness is an objective property of certain objects (see MORAL REALISM). Other modern philosophers believe that goodness is not a property that exists independently of the human mind, but rather some sort of projection or construction out of the needs, desires, and interests of human or sensate beings.

Philosophers of the seventeenth and eighteenth centuries distinguished between the 'naturally good' and the 'morally good'. The naturally good is what is pleasant or desirable or makes us happy. Some early modern philosophers believed that the morally good is constructed out of the naturally good. For example, natural law theorists like Hobbes and Pufendorf thought that naturally good actions become morally obligatory when we are commanded to perform them by God or a sovereign (see NATURAL LAW), while sentimentalists, such as Hutcheson and Hume, held that naturally good dispositions – pleasant or useful character traits – are rendered moral virtues by the fact that we approve of them (see MORAL SENSE THEORIES). Rationalists such as Clarke and Price, on the other hand, believed that certain actions have a special kind of moral value which is independent of natural goodness, namely rightness.

By the late eighteenth century the distinction between natural and moral goodness began to blur, but from two opposed directions. Kant (1788) argued that moral goodness is the necessary condition of natural goodness. Happiness purchased by immoral action, for example, is not good at all (see KANTIAN ETHICS; KANT, I. §§9–11). The utilitarians, by contrast, made natural goodness the source of all value, arguing that morally right actions are simply those that produce the maximum amount of the natural good, happiness or pleasure (see UTILITARIANISM).

The claim that happiness or pleasure *just is* the good puzzled Moore, who, in the early years of the twentieth century, pointed out that 'good' certainly does not *mean* 'pleasant' (see MOORE, G.E. §1). Moore argued (1903) that any attempt to identify 'good' with a natural property is an instance of the 'naturalistic fallacy', and that we must therefore

suppose that 'good' is a 'non-natural' property (see NATURALISM IN ETHICS §3). This attempt to establish value-realism on linguistic grounds set off a discussion of what the word 'good' means, or how it is used. Does it describe some property of objects, or is it used just to prescribe or recommend? The most extreme view is that of the emotivists, who stand in diametric opposition to Plato. Emotivists believe not only that goodness is not the fundamental principle of reality, but that strictly speaking the word 'good' does not refer to anything real at all. Its ubiquity, they think, can be explained only by the supposition that 'good' is used merely to express the speaker's subjective approval, like a squeal of delight (see EMOTIVISM).

2 Distinctions in goodness

The most obvious distinction in goodness is that between things which are valued as means, or instrumental goods, and things which are valued as ends, or final goods (see VALUES). This distinction is often confused with the distinction between intrinsic and extrinsic value. To say that something is intrinsically good is to say that it is good in virtue of what it is – in virtue of its own intrinsic nature; while to say that something is extrinsically good is to say that it is good in virtue of the relations it stands to things outside of itself. Means, for instance, are obviously extrinsically valuable, because their goodness springs from the fact that they promote other good things. Ends, by contrast, are often characterized as intrinsically good. In fact, however, it is an open question whether in order to be an end – to be valued or valuable for its own sake – an object must have intrinsic value.

Early twentieth-century moral philosophers debated this question. Empiricists argued that for something to be a final good is just for it to be desired for its own sake; philosophers in the idealist tradition, in contrast, believed that to be a final good is to be the object of a rational will. On both accounts, final goods are extrinsically valuable, deriving their value from the desires or volitions of human beings. But Moore argued that because 'good' does not mean 'desired' or 'willed', it is always an open question whether something desired or willed is good. Final goods, he thought, must therefore be intrinsically valuable. Moore suggested that in order to ascertain whether something is intrinsically good we should use a test of isolation: we consider whether the object has value apart from its relations to other things. He claimed that when we used this method, we would discover that value belongs to complex states of affairs which he called 'organic unities', such as a person's contemplating a beautiful object, or two friends enjoying each other's company.

One of Moore's aims in advancing this theory was to oppose hedonism, the view that pleasure is the good (see HEDONISM). Yet the theory that final goods must be intrinsically valuable may push one towards hedonism, as we can see by applying Moore's isolation test. A beautiful painting must surely be a good thing, yet if we imagine it existing in isolation from all viewers who might enjoy it, it seems to be without value. So we may decide that the value belongs instead to an organic unity consisting of someone's enjoying the beautiful painting. This line of thought led Moore to conclude that human experiences, especially pleasant ones, are an element in most intrinsically valuable organic unities. But the same idea – that a thing's goodness cannot be completely independent of its relation to human or sensate experiences and concerns – led utilitarians to suppose that pleasure must be the good.

The categories of value which Kant adopted suggest a different way of thinking about the relation between value and human concerns. Kant distinguished unconditional and conditional value, a distinction that resembles the intrinsic/extrinsic distinction. According to Kant (1785), a thing has unconditional goodness if we value it under any and all conditions, whereas it is conditionally good if the value we accord it depends on circumstances. The only thing we value unconditionally, he argued, is a good will, and human beings as the possessors of the capacity for good will. Yet the things people desire and care about do have conditional value – they are valuable because they matter to people, who have value. In this way, all values are related to human concerns.

If value must be related to human concerns, then we might think that anything that is good must be good *for* someone. Goodness for someone is sometimes characterized as 'subjective' or 'agent-relative' goodness, as opposed to 'objective' or 'agent-neutral' goodness, which pertains to everyone. If something is subjectively good for me, then I have reason to promote it and care about it; while if something is objectively good, then everyone has reason to promote it and care about it.

Twentieth-century philosophers have debated the question of the relation between these two kinds of goodness. Some think that goodness is inherently subjective, and people have reason to pursue common objects only when their interests happen to coincide. Others think that subjective values always give rise to objective ones, so that if it is (subjectively) good *for* me to have something, then it is objectively good *that* I should have it. Still others think that some subjective values – say, the ones associated with needs – give rise to objective ones, while others do not. And finally, at the other extreme, there are philosophers who think that subjective values are derived *from* objective ones. According to these philosophers, I cannot claim that something is good for me 'because it makes me happy', unless I consider my happiness to be, independently of my personal interest in it, an objectively good thing.

3 The goodness of people

When we call a person 'good' are we using 'good' in the ordinary sense? Sometimes it seems clear that we are. A person may be good *at* things – talented at sports or crafts, or master of an intellectual discipline. A person may also be good in certain roles – a good mother or teacher, for instance. Aristotle's functional account of goodness, or something like it, seems to apply to these cases: a good teacher is good at carrying out the functions of a teacher, or has the qualities that it is rational to want in a teacher. But what about when we say that a person is good, just as a person?

In fact there are two different ways in which people are said, just as people, to have value. Ordinarily, when we say of a particular person that they are 'a good person', we mean that they are morally good or virtuous. Aristotle applied his functional account of goodness to moral virtue in a straightforward way. He identified reason as the human function, meaning that what is distinctive of human beings is the use of reason to govern our activities. Virtues are qualities that foster the good performance of this function. Both Plato and Aristotle compared moral virtue to health: it is a way of being in good psychological condition. The functional account has also been used in a more broadly social way to explain moral goodness. On this view you are morally good if you are good at the performance of all of your various social roles, or if you have the qualities it is rational for your friends and fellow citizens to want in a friend and fellow citizen; or, as in certain sentimentalist theories, if you are an object of moral approval because you have these qualities (see VIRTUES AND VICES §§2–3).

Those accounts identify moral goodness with the possession of certain dispositions – character traits – that influence a person's conduct. Philosophers who favour such accounts usually suppose that your actions issue directly from your character. But other philosophers claim that human beings have a power distinct from and more directly related to actions than character traits are, namely the will (see WILL, THE). The will enables you to act freely, even to the point of doing what is 'out of character'; and it makes you responsible for your actions, even when they seem to be determined inevitably by your character. Kant, accordingly, recognized a form of moral goodness distinct from virtue or the goodness of character traits, namely goodness of the will or *moral worth*, which pertains to the well-functioning of the will itself, either as it is exercised in particular actions, or as a standing disposition. Kant famously claimed that you may achieve moral worth even if you have temperamental qualities which make it hard for you to do what duty demands (see SELF-CONTROL). This claim raises important questions about how the will and character are related.

The second way in which people are considered to be valuable just as people, enshrined in many religious and philosophical systems, involves the thought that every human being as such has a fundamental value which it is wrong to deny or overlook. The religious view that we are all God's children, the political view that all human beings are created equal, and the Kantian moral view that every human being is an end-in-itself are all expressions of this idea. There are various views about what makes people valuable in this way – freedom of the will, rationality, consciousness, the possession of identifiable interests, the capacity for pleasure and pain, or simply life itself – and so what treatment is called for. Some of these options raise the question whether other living things should also be accorded such value (see MORAL STANDING §§1–3). This kind of value is different from that which we attribute to particular people when we say they are morally good, for one need not be an especially good person to lay claim to the political rights or the moral respect due to every human being. But the two ideas are sometimes related by the thought that it is the capacity for moral goodness, or the capacity that makes us capable of moral goodness, that gives us this fundamental value (see RESPECT FOR PERSONS).

4 The right and the good

Good is a ubiquitous term, applying to almost any sort of thing, but actions, policies and laws are also praised as being 'right' or 'just'. Right actions are those which are required by morality or, more extensively, those not forbidden by morality, not 'wrong'. So a question arises about the relation between these two kinds of value, the right and the good. Consequentialists think that the relation is simple: right actions are those which tend to maximize good results, so that rightness is actually a form of instrumental goodness (see CONSEQUENTI-ALISM). Yet we sometimes seem to care about doing

the right thing independently of, or even in the teeth of, the consequences that it produces. We may decide that we will uphold someone's rights, or obey the law, or keep a promise, though we know the results will be bad, because, as we say, 'it is the principle of the thing'. Consequentialists think this attitude is either an acknowledgement of the especially important consequences that result from the observance of certain rules, or else a misguided form of rule-worship. But 'deontologists' believe there is something valuable about doing the right thing apart from the good results it may or may not produce (see DEONTOLOGICAL ETHICS).

Since deontologists deny that rightness is merely an instrumental value, we might be tempted to say they think of rightness as either a final good or a special kind of intrinsic value, characteristic of actions. But this does not completely capture the deontological intuition. Final and intrinsic values, as they are often conceived, may be weighed in with other values, so on this view we might sometimes endure wrongdoing, as we sometimes endure pain, for the sake of the larger benefits it brings. But deontologists deny that such values as freedom, justice, or fidelity may be traded off for other goods. They also believe that the way in which right actions serve these values is not by producing or causing them, but instead is direct or constitutive. For example, a deontologist may think that it is right to keep a promise, not because fidelity to promises is thereby efficiently produced (for we can imagine circumstances in which one person's keeping a promise will induce others to break theirs), but because it is an act of fidelity. And we respect human rights, not because this produces freedom, but because this is what freedom consists in – living in a world in which human rights are respected.

The question of the relation between the right and the good therefore gives rise to deep questions about the relations between actions and the values they serve. But these questions belong more properly to a discussion of the right (see RIGHT AND GOOD).

5 The good life

One of the oldest questions of moral philosophy is what the best life is for a human being. A standard view in ancient Greek philosophy was that there are three types of life: a contemplative or philosophical life; a life of virtuous political activity; and a hedonistic or money-making life. Plato and Aristotle agreed that the contemplative life is best and the political life second best; in their view, only those who do not know the true pleasures of contemplation and virtuous action resort to hedonistic pursuits (see EUDAIMONIA; HEDONISM).

The idea that so specific a life can be identified as best may seem paradoxical. If there is a best life for human beings, does that mean it is the best life for any human being, regardless of personal endowments or natural tastes? On this view, lives are like looks: there may be a best way for each person to look, but the best way for you to look may not, unfortunately, be the best way to look. Some philosophers argue that this makes no sense: how can a certain way of life be better for you, if there is no way in which you could enjoy, appreciate, or be interested in such a life and still be *yourself*?

What sorts of arguments might be used to show that one type of life is best? Plato favoured a test of experience: we should take as authoritative the preferences of those people who have experienced the kinds of activities central to all three types of life. John Stuart Mill (1861) suggested that this test could be used to identify those pleasures whose 'quality' is so high as to outweigh considerations of 'quantity,' and so which belong in the best life (see MILL, J.S. §9). Aristotle appealed to his own idea of function: if human beings have a function, the person who performs the human function well must lead the best life. But Aristotle also thought we could identify certain criteria which any good life must meet, and rate lives by the extent to which they fulfil these criteria: the pursuits central to a good life must be active, pleasant, self-sufficient, and done for their own sake alone. Moore's theory suggests a simpler account: the good life is one that consists of intrinsically valuable states and activities, such as appreciating beauty, having friends, and seeking knowledge.

Perhaps the most common strategy is to appeal to human psychology, to what people actually care about. Classical utilitarians argued that human beings care about only two things: getting pleasure and avoiding pain. The best life must therefore be the one with the greatest balance of pleasure over pain. Others claim that the goodness of your life is a function of how many of your desires are satisfied and the strength of those desires. But the content of your desires and their strength may be determined in unfortunate ways by the limitations of your knowledge or imagination, and this has led some philosophers to adopt an idealized version of this account: the good life for you is the one you *would* choose under conditions of perfect knowledge and imaginative reflection.

But we must also ask whether the *good* life and the *happy* life are the same. The early modern philosophers' distinction between moral and natural goodness brought this question sharply into focus. They thought of happiness as a natural good and many of them believed that reason demands the pursuit of happiness just as obviously as it demands the practice of virtue. Yet virtue does not always bring happiness. Are human beings then subject to conflicting demands of reason? Ancient Greek philosophers had raised a parallel question, whether being virtuous is a good thing for the virtuous person. But ancient and modern solutions are different in an important way. For the Greeks, the answer lay in demonstrating that the qualities we ordinarily regard as moral virtues really are qualities that make us good at the performance of the human function – qualities without which we would be incapable of choosing and acting well. Once this is established, it is evident that a virtuous person will necessarily have a better life. Modern philosophers, however, are more inclined to believe that happiness and virtue are independent. Many modern philosophers have therefore tried to produce what Rawls calls 'congruence' arguments: arguments that show that the pursuit of virtue will also bring happiness, and so that the two kinds of good, although independent, come together in practice. But others have drawn a more austere conclusion, namely that a life which is both morally good and happy is open to us only in favourable circumstances – circumstances which must be secured by divine arrangements or, more optimistically, by political action.

See also: EVIL; HAPPINESS; PRACTICAL REASON AND ETHICS; RIGHT AND GOOD; XUNZI

References and further reading

Anderson, E. (1993) *Value in Ethics and Economics*, Cambridge, MA: Harvard University Press. (Categorizes different ways in which we value things and examines the moral and other consequences of these categorizations; especially concerned to show that not every form of value may be handled properly by the mechanisms of the market.)

* Aristotle (*c.* mid 4th century BC) *Nicomachean Ethics*, in *The Complete Works of Aristotle*, ed. J. Barnes, Princeton, NJ: Princeton University Press, 1984, esp. books I 6–7, X. (Criticizes Plato's lack of guidance on particular kinds of goodness, gives a functional account of goodness, and discusses the three kinds of life: contemplative, political and hedonistic.)

—— (*c.* mid 4th century BC) *Metaphysics*, in *The Complete Works of Aristotle*. ed. J. Barnes, Princeton, NJ: Princeton University Press, 1984, esp. books VII–X, XII. (Outlines the connections between goodness, function and reality.)

Ayer, A.J. (1936) *Language, Truth, and Logic*,

London: Gollancz; 2nd edn, 1946, ch. VI. (The founding statement of emotivism.)

Butler, J. (1726) *Fifteen Sermons Preached at the Rolls Chapel*, Sermons I, II, III, XI, XII; repr. in S. Darwall (ed.) *Five Sermons Preached at the Rolls Chapel and A Dissertation Upon the Nature of Virtue*, Indianapolis, IN: Hackett Publishing Company, 1983, Sermons XI, XII. (The most influential 'congruence' argument of the eighteenth century, to the effect that self-love favours the practice of virtue; later adopted by David Hume and others.)

Foot, P. (1961) 'Goodness and Choice', *Proceedings of the Aristotelian Society*, supplementary vol.; repr. in *Virtues and Vices and Other Essays in Moral Philosophy*, Berkeley, CA: University of California Press, 1978. (An influential twentieth-century presentation of the functional account of goodness.)

Griffin, J. (1986) *Well-Being*, Oxford: Clarendon Press. (One of the most complete presentations of the view that the good is what we would desire under ideal conditions of knowledge and reflection.)

* Kant, I. (1785) *Grundlegung zur Metaphysik der Sitten*, trans. and ed. M. Gregor, *Groundwork of the Metaphysics of Morals*, Cambridge: Cambridge University Press, 1997. (Introduces the ideas of unconditional value and of goodness of will; argues for the unconditional value of humanity and the good will.)

* —— (1788) *Critik der practischen Vernunft*, trans. L.W. Beck, *Critique of Practical Reason*, Upper Saddle River, NJ: Prentice Hall, 1993. (Part 1, book I, ch. 2 deals with the relation between moral and natural goodness; part 1, book II deals with the relation between virtue and happiness.)

Korsgaard, C.M. (1996) *Creating the Kingdom of Ends*, New York: Cambridge University Press. (Chaps 4, 8 and 9 concern the concept of unconditional value; ch. 10 discusses various theories of the relation between subjective and objective value.)

Lewis, C.I. (1946) *An Analysis of Knowledge and Valuation*, La Salle, IL: Open Court. (Critical exploration of the concept of intrinsic value; introduces a new category, inherent value, in response to problems with the former category.)

* Mill, J.S. (1861) *Utilitarianism*, ed. G. Sher, Indianapolis, IN: Hackett Publishing Company, 1979, chaps II, IV. (Uses Plato's test of experience to identify the 'higher' pleasures, and provides a 'proof' that pleasure and the avoidance of pain are the only desirable things.)

* Moore, G.E. (1903) *Principia Ethica*, Cambridge: Cambridge University Press, 1971. (Argues that goodness must be an intrinsic non-natural property, and explains the idea of 'organic unities'.)

* —— (1912) *Ethics*, Oxford: Oxford University Press, chaps IV, VII. (Presents Moore's theory of the good in the context of a theory about right and wrong.)

* —— (1922) 'The Conception of Intrinsic Value', in *Philosophical Studies*, London: Kegan Paul. (Argues that final goods must be intrinsically valuable.)

Nagel, T. (1970) *The Possibility of Altruism*, Oxford: Clarendon Press, reprinted Princeton, NJ: Princeton University Press, 1978. (The most important examination of the relation between subjective and objective value written in the twentieth century, in which it is argued that all subjective values have objective correlates.)

—— (1986) *The View From Nowhere*, Oxford: Oxford University Press, chaps VIII, IX. (Modifying his earlier position, this work argues that only some subjective values have objective correlates.)

Perry, R.B. (1926) *General Theory of Value: Its Meaning and Basic Principles Construed in Terms of Interest*, Cambridge, MA: Harvard University Press. (An influential work in twentieth-century American value theory, proposing that to be valuable means to be the object of any interest.)

* Plato (*c*.380–367 BC) *Republic*, trans. G.M.A. Grube, revised by C.D.C. Reeve, Indianapolis, IN: Hackett Publishing Company, 1992. (Presents the Theory of Forms and an account of the fundamental role of the Form of the Good.)

* Rawls, J. (1971) *A Theory of Justice*, Cambridge, MA: Harvard University Press, part III. (Ch. 7 argues that for a thing to be good is to have the properties it is rational to want in a thing of that kind; ch. 9 presents an argument for the 'congruence' of happiness and justice.)

Stevenson, C.L. (1944) *Ethics and Language*, New Haven, CT: Yale University Press. (The most complete and systematic development of the emotivist theory of evaluative language.)

CHRISTINE M. KORSGAARD

GOODMAN, NELSON (1906–)

Nelson Goodman is an American philosopher who has written important works in metaphysics, aesthetics and epistemology. Throughout his work runs a concern with the ways that the symbols we construct inform the facts that we find and structure our understanding of them. Different symbol systems yield irreconcilable structures. So there is no one way things really are. There are, he concludes, many worlds if any. Moreover, worlds are made rather than found, for the categories we construct fix the criteria of identity for the individuals and kinds we recognize. Thus they determine what objects and kinds constitute a world.

Goodman argues that the arts as well as the sciences make and reveal worlds. Aesthetics as he construes it is a branch of epistemology. He analyses a variety of modes of symbolization, literal and metaphorical, and shows how they contribute in the arts and elsewhere to the advancement of understanding.

Goodman's 'new riddle of induction' reveals that the problem of induction runs deeper than philosophers had thought. He defines the predicate 'grue' as 'examined before future time t *and found to be green or not so examined and blue.' All emeralds examined to date have been both green and grue. What justifies our expecting future emeralds to be green rather than grue? Inductive validity, the new riddle shows, turns not only on the constitution of an evidence class, but also on its characterization. The question then is what favours one characterization over its rivals. The fact that 'green' has been used far more often than 'grue' in induction, Goodman contends, provides the answer – not because it increases our odds of being right, but because of its pragmatic advantages.*

1 **Metaphysics**
2 **Aesthetics**
3 **Induction**

1 Metaphysics

Nelson Goodman (1906–) has made groundbreaking contributions to aesthetics, epistemology, metaphysics and the philosophy of science. In his youth he ran an art gallery. Throughout his life he has been an avid and eclectic collector of art. He founded the Harvard Summer Dance programme and Project Zero, an ongoing research programme in arts education at the Harvard Graduate School of Education. As graduate students at Harvard, he and Henry Leonard developed a version of mereology that they dubbed 'the calculus of individuals'. Elaborated in *The Structure of Appearance*, it forms the basis for Goodman's nominalism. As Goodman construes it, the difference between mereology and set theory lies in the sorts of constructions they permit. Set theory admits infinitely many distinct entities – sets of sets of sets of sets... – all composed of the same basic elements. Mereology holds that the same basic elements are parts of but a single whole. Goodman's nominalism consists in a refusal to recognize more than one entity comprised of the same basic elements. It says nothing about the

metaphysical constitution of the elements. The decision of whether to countenance abstract or concrete, immaterial or material, mental or physical entities requires more than a commitment to nominalism.

The constructionalism Goodman espouses in *The Structure of Appearance* is a methodology for systematizing a body of pretheoretical beliefs. Such beliefs tend to be inchoate, vague, even inconsistent. By devising an interpreted formal system that derives them from or explicates them in terms of a suitable base of primitives, we can bring them into logical contact with each other, eliminate inconsistencies and disclose unanticipated logical and theoretical connections. Were such a system required to reflect all our relevant pretheoretical beliefs exactly, it would simply replicate received errors and confusions. But, Goodman argues, the regimentation constructionalism countenances involves judicious correction, refinement and even repudiation of presystematic convictions in the interests of simplicity, coherence, theoretical tractability and the like.

Multiple, divergent systems do justice to the same range of pretheoretical beliefs. One system might identify a geometrical point with the intersection of two non-parallel lines. Another might identify it with the limit of a sequence of nested spheres. Neither invalidates the other, for each provides a geometrically acceptable definition of a point. Here lies the root of Goodman's relativism. Relative to each acceptable system, the constitution of a point is determinate. But absolutely and independently of the systems we construct, it is indeterminate.

In *Ways of Worldmaking*, Goodman provides a less formal treatment of the same themes. Worlds and the objects that comprise them are made, he contends, not found. The members of any group are alike in some respects, different in others. So mere inspection cannot settle whether two manifestations are of the same thing or of the same kind. To answer such questions we require a category scheme or system of classification that distinguishes differences that matter from differences that do not. Such schemes are not dictated by nature, but are human constructs. We draw the lines. Lines can be drawn in various places, resulting in divergent but equally viable world versions. One person might count a newspaper with a new publisher and a radically revised editorial stance as the same newspaper it always was. Another might count it as a different newspaper. One might classify a black hole as a star, another as the residue of an extinguished star. Relative to its own world version, each is right. Relative to its rival's, each is wrong. Neither is absolutely right or wrong.

If all overlapping world versions were reducible to

or supervenient on a single base, such divergences would be insignificant. But, Goodman insists, such is not the case. In *The Structure of Appearance* he develops a phenomenalist constructional system whose primitives are qualia – phenomenal individuals out of which enduring perceptibles are constructed. He does not claim that this is the only viable form of phenomenalism and he recognizes that it neither underwrites nor reduces to a physicalist system. But it is none the worse for that. Rather, he urges that physicalist and phenomenalist systems are distinct, valid constructions of independent interest and importance. Neither is parasitic on the other.

If the proliferation derives from the availability of clashing category schemes, why not take it to show simply that there are multiple conceptualizations? Then we could retain our pretheoretical conviction that there exists exactly one world underlying them. Were the analytic/synthetic distinction tenable, such a strategy might work. But as Goodman, W.V.O. Quine, and Morton White demonstrated, it is not. Although statements depend on both meaning and fact, the dependence on meaning cannot be separated from the dependence on fact. There is thus no way to make sense of the claim that the difference between clashing world versions derives from different ways of conceptualizing the same facts. Category schemes dictate the criteria of identity of their objects, so mutually irreducible schemes do not treat of the same things. Since a world is the totality of things that comprise it, irreducible schemes define distinct worlds. There are, Goodman concludes, many worlds if any.

Still, it is not the case that just anything goes. Goodman describes his position as relativism under rigorous restraints. Consistency, coherence, suitability for a purpose, as well as accord with past practice and antecedent convictions are among the restraints he recognizes. Fitting and working are the marks of a successful version. A world version must consist of components that fit together; it must fit reasonably well with our considered judgments about the subject at hand, and must work to further our cognitive objectives. A version that is internally incoherent, is inconsonant with our antecedent considered judgments or impedes the advancement of understanding is unacceptable. Worldmaking need not be deliberate. *Ways of Worldmaking* discusses how, with only sparse cues, the visual system constructs the apparent motion it discerns. Nor is worldmaking exclusively the province of science – the arts as well as the sciences make worlds.

2 Aesthetics

Works of art, Goodman contends, are symbols. As such, they require interpretation. The aesthetic attitude, then, is not one of passive contemplation, but of active cognitive engagement; its main goal is understanding, not pleasure. Aesthetics, as Goodman conceives it, is a branch of epistemology.

Languages of Art characterizes a range of symbol systems used in the arts and elsewhere, and identifies the syntactic and semantic structures that give rise to their powers and limitations. The basic modes of reference are denotation and exemplification. Denotation is the relation of a name to its bearer, a predicate to the members of its extension, a picture to its subject. 'Charles I', 'the father of Charles II' and a Van Dyck portrait all denote Charles I. Fictional symbols lack denotata. Their significance, Goodman maintains, derives from symbols that denote them. Although the term 'unicorn' fails to denote, the terms 'unicorn-description' and 'unicorn-picture' denote a variety of symbols that collectively constitute the meaning of the term 'unicorn'. Many works of art – abstract art, most instrumental music and much dance – do not even purport to denote. They refer, Goodman maintains, by means of exemplification. In exemplification, a symbol points up and hence refers to features it serves as a sample or example of. Thus, a commercial paint sample exemplifies its colour and sheen; a late Mondrian painting exemplifies squareness. Exemplification is widespread not only in the arts but also in science, commerce and pedagogy – indeed wherever samples and examples are used.

Denotation and exemplification are not mutually exclusive. Denoting symbols in the arts typically also exemplify. A portrait by Whistler denotes his mother and exemplifies a seemingly infinite spectrum of shades of grey. Seventeenth-century Dutch still lifes denote opulent arrangements of flowers and fruit and exemplify ambivalence about worldly success. Symbols, particularly aesthetic ones, often perform a variety of interanimating referential functions.

Symbols normally do not operate in isolation. They belong to schemes that collectively sort the objects in a realm. In metaphor a scheme that normally sorts one realm is imported to effect a re-sorting of another. New groupings emerge as items that belong to disjoint literal categories are classed together under a single metaphorical label and affinities between literal and metaphorical referents of a term are brought to light. In calling a plumber a virtuoso, for example, we import a scheme that literally sorts musicians to effect a sorting of craftsmen. New patterns and distinctions emerge as we recognize the delicacy, dexterity and skill displayed by some few members of the several crafts. Because they draw their lines where no literal label does, metaphors resist paraphrase. No literal label quite captures what all and only the virtuosi in the building trades have in common with one another or with literal virtuosi.

Figurative reference is real reference, Goodman maintains, and figurative truth is real truth. 'Feline cunning' genuinely if metaphorically denotes some scheming politicians. 'The walls of the Alhambra are made of lace' is genuinely if metaphorically true, and Michelangelo's *Pietà* genuinely if metaphorically exemplifies incalculable sorrow.

Expression, he contends, is metaphorical exemplification by a work of art functioning as such. The *Pietà* then expresses the incalculable sorrow it metaphorically exemplifies. But expression is not limited to emotions. A work of art, functioning as such, expresses any feature it metaphorically exemplifies. Thus, for example, Brancusi's *Bird in Space* expresses fluidity and flight. There is, evidently, no limit on the range of features that works of art can express.

Reference is not always direct. In indirect reference, one symbol refers to another by means of a chain consisting of denotational and exemplificational links. Rembrandt's *Night Watch* alludes to the history of the militia it depicts by portraying its subjects wearing costumes that exemplify important periods of the militia's history. In *Reconceptions* Goodman construes variation as a form of indirect reference, where a variation must in some respects resemble its theme and must differ from it in others. But every two passages do that, and not every passage is a variation on every other. A symbol functions as a variation on a theme when it uses the resemblances and differences as routes of reference to the theme. It exemplifies features it shares with the theme, contrastively exemplifies features it does not share with the theme, and effects reference back to the theme via both exemplification and contrastive exemplification. On Goodman's analysis, variation is not restricted to music. Nor need a variation occur in the same work as the theme on which it is a variation.

Scientific symbols tend to be attenuated, symbolizing along comparatively few dimensions, whereas aesthetic symbols are relatively replete. For example, the same configuration might serve as an electrocardiogram or a line drawing. In an electrocardiogram, only its shape is significant, whereas in a line drawing, the exact colour and thickness of the line, the precise shade of the background, the size and shape of the paper, the position of the line on it and even the texture of the paper may be significant. The electrocardiogram is referentially austere denoting a pattern of heartbeats and perhaps exemplifying a certain symptomatology. The drawing, however, is apt

to perform a variety of interanimating referential functions.

Whether the symbol is an electrocardiogram or a drawing depends on its function. It counts as a work of art as long as it functions as an aesthetic symbol. And it may do so intermittently. The crucial question for Goodman is not 'What is art?' but 'When is art?', that is, 'Under what circumstances does an object function as an aesthetic symbol?' He gives no criterion, but identifies five symptoms of the aesthetic: syntactic density, semantic density, relative repleteness, exemplification and complex and indirect reference. A symbol system is syntactically dense when the finest differences between signs constitute a difference between symbols, that is, when it can mark the finest differences between items in its domain. Symptoms, Goodman acknowledges, are neither necessary nor sufficient conditions. But they are good, if defeasible, indications of the presence of a condition.

Interpretation requires discovering what symbols constitute a work, how they function, what they refer to and what they achieve. The richness and complexity of aesthetic symbols means that the task may be interminable and that multiple, irreconcilable interpretations may be correct. But not every interpretation is correct. Only those that make maximally good sense of the work's symbolic functions are to be accepted. Goodman's pluralism consists in his recognition that more than one interpretation can often do so.

3 Induction

Symbol systems are artefacts. Their syntactic and semantic features are not dictated by the domain but result from decisions about how the domain is to be organized, which can be done in an enormous number of divergent ways. Acceptability of a symbol system depends on its suitability for the purposes at hand.

In empirical science and elsewhere the purpose is often inductive – a matter of projecting from limited evidence to a wider class of cases. The traditional problem of induction is to say when and to what extent a limited evidence-class warrants such an inference. How many emeralds need be examined and from what sources need they be drawn before we are justified in inferring that all emeralds are green? In *Fact, Fiction, and Forecast*, Goodman shows that the problem runs deeper. It is a matter not just of the composition of the evidence class, but also of its characterization. He defines novel predicates 'grue' and 'bleen' as follows:

x is 'grue' = x is examined before future time t

and is found to be green, or x is not so examined and is blue.

x is 'bleen' = x is examined before future time t and is found to be blue, or x is not so examined and is green.

All emeralds examined to date have been grue as well as green, for the extensions of the two predicates do not yet diverge. Yet we confidently expect emeralds found after t to be green, not grue. What, if anything, is our justification?

We can't dismiss 'grue' as derivative from 'green', for 'green' can be defined in terms of 'grue' and 'bleen', just as 'grue' is defined in terms of 'green' and 'blue':

x is 'green' = x is examined before future time t and found to be grue, or x is not so examined and is bleen.

Which predicate is basic and which is derivative depends entirely on where we start. Nor can we dismiss 'grue' on the grounds that it makes essential reference to a specific time t. For whether 'grue' or 'green' makes reference to t again depends on which is taken as primitive. One might argue that 'green' marks a more natural kind than 'grue' does. Then it is, in some sense, essentially more primitive. But in the absence of an acceptable standard of naturalness that does not presuppose the very differences in projectibility we are trying to account for, this claim rings hollow. For we neither know what it means, nor how to tell whether one predicate is more natural than another.

The solution, Goodman maintains, lies in entrenchment. What favours 'green' over 'grue' is the brute fact that 'green' and its cognates have been successfully projected far more often than 'grue'. The fact that up to now 'grue' would have worked as well is irrelevant. The decision favours the predicates that were actually successfully used.

Induction provides no guarantees. Goodman recognizes that we currently have no way of knowing whether future emeralds will be grue, green or something else entirely. The problem as he sees it is how to proceed in the absence of such knowledge. He argues that entrenched predicates are to be preferred, not because they have any lien on the future, but because they have served us well so far, and their continued use enables us to make efficient use of available cognitive resources and habits of thought. But the presumption in favour of entrenched predicates evaporates as soon as counterexamples emerge. When the first non-green emerald is found, 'All emeralds are green' loses its claim on our epistemic allegiance.

The emphasis on entrenchment does not preclude innovation. Novel predicates can be projected when entrenched hypotheses are violated. Thus, for example, the Michelson-Morley experiment, by violating Newtonian generalizations, opened the way for the projection of novel, relativistic predicates. New predicates can also be introduced at interstices where no entrenched predicate prevails. A term like 'quark' can be introduced to denote phenomena that previously lacked a label. Such terms, Goodman maintains, derive their projectibility from related terms such as 'subatomic particle'. Novel predicates thus become projectible by fitting into working inductive systems or into replacements for systems that do not work.

See also: ANALYTICITY; FICTIONAL ENTITIES §2; INDUCTION, EPISTEMIC ISSUES; NOMINALISM; REFERENCE; RELATIVISM

List of works

Goodman, N. (1951) *The Structure of Appearance*, Boston, MA: Reidel, 3rd edn, 1977. (This work uses devices of formal logic to construct systems that solve or dissolve perennial problems in epistemology. It argues that the availability of multiple, divergent constructional systems is a virtue rather than a flaw.)

—— (1954) *Fact, Fiction, and Forecast*, Cambridge, MA: Harvard University Press, 4th edn, 1984. (This work poses the new riddle of induction, and proposes a solution to it. It argues that only by looking at past inductive practice do we have the resouces for precluding the induction of 'All emeralds are grue'.)

—— (1968) *Languages of Art*, Indianapolis, IN: Hackett Publishing Company. (A development of a general theory of symbols and an application to the arts.)

—— (1972) *Problems and Projects*, Indianapolis, IN: Hackett Publishing Company. (A collection of papers on a variety of issues including art, meaning, induction and simplicity.)

—— (1978) *Ways of Worldmaking*, Indianapolis, IN: Hackett Publishing Company. (This work argues that worlds are made through the construction and deployment of symbol systems, and that there are many worlds if any.)

—— (1984) *Of Mind and Other Matters*, Cambridge, MA: Harvard University Press. (A collection of papers on metaphysics, aesthetics and the theory of reference.)

Goodman, N. and Elgin, C.Z. (1988) *Reconceptions in Philosophy and Other Arts and Sciences*, Indianapolis, IN: Hackett Publishing Company. (This book reconceives the ends and means of philosophy, taking understanding and rightness of symbols rather than knowledge and truth as central notions.)

Goodman, N. (1990) *A Study of Qualities*, New York: Garland Publishing Company. (Goodman's Ph.D. dissertation. A precursor to the position developed more fully in The Structure of Appearance.)

References and further reading

Elgin, C.Z. (1983) *With Reference to Reference*, Indianapolis, IN: Hackett Publishing Company. (An explication and elaboration of Goodman's theory of symbols, which also extends it to the philosophy of language.)

Hellman, G. (1977) 'Introduction' to N. Goodman *The Structure of Appearance*, 3rd edn, Boston, MA: Reidel. (An excellent, accessible introduction to the main themes in Goodman's technical work.)

Schwartz, R. (1986) 'I'm Going to Make You a Star', *Midwest Studies in Philosophy* 11: 427–39. (A discussion of the metaphysical position Goodman adopts in *Ways of Worldmaking*.)

Stalker, D. (ed.) (1994) *Grue*, Chicago, IL: Open Court. (An anthology of papers on the new riddle of induction. Contains an excellent annotated bibliography.)

CATHERINE Z. ELGIN

GOODNESS, PERFECT

The concept of perfect goodness had a central place in ancient Greek and medieval philosophy, and is still frequently discussed in contemporary natural theology. Medieval philosophers adopted the idea from the philosophies of Plato and Aristotle, with the difference that they identified perfect goodness with a personal God. In ancient and medieval philosophy the concept is primarily a metaphysical one, since goodness was thought to be extensionally equivalent to being, but it is secondarily a moral concept referring to the distinctive sort of goodness appropriate to those beings that have wills. Thus it is fundamental to a long tradition on the metaphysical basis of value which lasted from Plato until at least the sixteenth century.

In Plato, perfect goodness is the Form of the Good, upon which everything that has being is ontologically and causally dependent. In Aristotle, the good is identified with the end or purpose of a natural being. The good is that towards which all things move for the

fulfilment of their natures. By the time of Aquinas, medieval philosophers had identified the good in both the Platonic and Aristotelian senses with the Christian God and had argued that God is both the perfectly good creative source and the perfectly good end of all beings other than himself.

The concept of a perfectly good being in Christian philosophical theology faces two major kinds of difficulty. One is the problem that perfect goodness appears to be incompatible with the divine attributes of omnipotence and freedom of the divine will. And if a perfectly good being does not have a will that is free in a morally significant sense, that being seems to lack goodness in the moral sense of goodness. The second kind of problem is that the existence of a being who is both omnipotent and perfectly good seems to be incompatible with the existence of evil. In spite of these problems, there is a strong attraction to the idea of a perfectly good God in contemporary philosophical theology. The category of perfect goodness is therefore one of the most persistent of the concepts in the Platonic legacy.

1   **Perfect goodness in Greek and medieval philosophy**
2   **The possible incompatibility of perfect goodness with other divine attributes**
3   **Perfect goodness and the problem of evil**

1   Perfect goodness in Greek and medieval philosophy

In Plato's metaphysics it is the Form of the Good, not the Form of Being, which is at the pinnacle of the realm of the Forms (see PLATO §14). Since any object of kind K is real to the extent that it approximates perfect K-ness, the better an object is as a K, the more real it is. The source of the being of any individual object of kind K is the Form K, and the individual Forms themselves derive their being from the Form of the Good. In Plato, then, perfect goodness is ultimately the source of the being of everything else. In the *Republic*, Plato asserts the dependency of everything on the Form of the Good by the relation of participation. In the *Timaeus*, Plato develops the theory of Forms into a cosmological theory according to which all things in the physical world are caused to be by emanation from the Form of the Good, and ultimately return to it.

ARISTOTLE (§§9, 16–17) introduced the connection between the idea of the good and the notion of an end. Each thing of kind K has an end or purpose (*telos*) which is the fulfilment of the nature of things of kind K, and an individual is good to the extent to which its nature is actualized. Since desires are related to ends, the notion of an end gives desire a role in achieving an end. Aristotle's teleological theory of nature therefore includes a teleological view of human psychology. Aristotelian natural teleology had a significant impact on the treatment of the concept of the good in later philosophy.

One of the most important features of the concept of goodness arising from Greek philosophy was the identification of goodness with being. The idea that everything is good in so far as it exists leads to the position taken explicitly by AUGUSTINE (§§7, 9) in the *Confessions* that evil is only the privation of being. This means that good and evil are not ontologically on a par and, with certain other assumptions deriving from Greek metaphysics, it led to the view that perfect goodness can and, in fact, must of necessity be actualized, whereas perfect evil cannot be. Furthermore, on the view that everything is good in so far as it has being and evil is only a privation of being, it seems to follow that evil is metaphysically necessary if anything exists besides a perfect being. The doctrine that evil is only a privation of being, therefore, suggests a way out of the problem of evil (see §3 below).

BOETHIUS (§2) defended the thesis that everything is good in so far as it exists in the first of his five theological treatises, which became known as *De hebdomadibus*. There he explains how substances can be good in virtue of the fact that they have being even though they are not good in virtue of their substance or nature. Goodness does not constitute the substance of created substances, but constitutes the substance only of God, from whom all things proceed. Every created substance is therefore good in that it flows from the first and perfect good.

Thomas AQUINAS (§§2, 9) synthesized a number of elements of the pre-existing tradition on perfect goodness. Like Plato, he believed that creatures are good by virtue of participation in divine perfect goodness; the created universe is an outpouring of the goodness of God. As Aquinas reads Aristotle, in every genus there is something highest that is the cause of the other members of the genus. Aquinas employs this view in his 'Fourth Way' of proving the existence of God:

> That which is said most of all to be such and such in some genus is the cause of all the things that belong to that genus. In this way fire, which is hot to the highest degree, is the cause of all hot things, as is said in Metaphysics, Bk II. Therefore there exists something that is the cause of being and goodness and any perfection in all things; and this we call God.
>
> (*Summa theologiae* Ia, q.2, a.3)

In another work he says, 'Therefore, the highest good [*summum bonum*], which is God, is the cause of goodness in all things' (*Summa contra gentiles* III, 17: 2). Aquinas follows Aristotle in identifying the good of a thing with its complete being and its end as the achieving of its complete being. And he follows Aristotle's view of the will as naturally directed towards the proper end of the willer, which is the good for the willer. He follows Augustine and Boethius in identifying good with being and perfect goodness with pure being, in which there is no potentiality unactualized.

After its high point in late medieval philosophy, there was a decline of interest in the concept of perfect goodness. But in the later twentieth century there has been both a resurgence of interest in medieval philosophy and a renaissance in the philosophy of religion. Part of the work in these areas has focused on an approach to theology in which the concept of a perfectly good being occupies the centre of attention. Some of this work aims at reworking medieval philosophy into the contemporary milieu. Other work aims at defending the concept of perfect goodness from the kinds of objection many contemporary philosophers find compelling. Some of the puzzles most commonly addressed will be the subject of the next two sections.

2 The possible incompatibility of perfect goodness with other divine attributes

The idea of a God who is the personification of perfect goodness creates problems when combined with some of the other traditional attributes of the deity. In particular, three problems of compatibility have been discussed in the recent literature, and some of them have a long history.

First, there is the alleged incompatibility of perfect goodness and omnipotence. A perfectly good being was traditionally understood to be one whose will is so fixed in goodness that he is actually incapable of willing anything other than good, a property sometimes called 'impeccability'. An omnipotent being is one who has maximal power, and while there are many different accounts of what maximal power entails, it has often been understood to involve the power to do anything possible (see OMNIPOTENCE §§1, 5). But since sinning or doing evil is a possible thing to do, if a perfectly good being lacks the power to do evil, such a being lacks the power to do something possible and hence is not omnipotent. This puzzle has recently been articulated by Pike (1969), but it was also known to Aquinas and other medieval philosophers.

Aquinas' way out of this problem was to deny that the power to do evil is a power in the true sense (*Summa theologiae* Ia, q.25, a.3, ad.2), and many philosophers subsequently have taken some version of this approach. To be successful, this approach must elucidate a plausible concept of power which includes what is intuitively desired in the powers of the deity but excludes what is not desired. A different approach is to argue that God *can* do evil, but simply does not. Reichenbach (1982) maintains a position of this kind. Clearly, this move uses a different notion of the nature of perfect goodness from one in which perfect goodness is entailed by God's very nature. Taking this approach involves weakening the metaphysical connection between God's nature and being, on the one hand, and his goodness, on the other. A third solution to the problem is to claim that God has the power to do anything possible, including the things which are, in fact, evil, but if he were to do such things, they would not be evil. This approach utilizes the 'divine command' theory, according to which God's will and God's nature are prior to morality, although perhaps not prior to good in the metaphysical sense of good as pure being (see RELIGION AND MORALITY §1; VOLUNTARISM). Divine command theories claim that what is morally right (or good) is made to be right (or good) by God's will. A frequently mentioned problem with this approach is that it makes God's will appear to be arbitrary. This is because God cannot have a moral reason for willing as he does, since it is his will that determines what counts as a moral reason. In addition, a divine command theory seems to make the concept of perfect goodness vacuous. That is, there is no content to the property of goodness other than this: goodness is whatever it is that God is, and rightness is whatever it is that God wills.

The reasoning behind the alleged incompatibility of perfect goodness and omnipotence leads to a second difficulty. Under the assumption that a perfectly good being is incapable of doing wrong or willing anything but good, the will of such a being does not appear to be free in any morally significant sense (see FREEDOM, DIVINE). On a common interpretation of the conditions for moral praise and blame in the human case, persons are morally praised because they choose good when they could have chosen evil instead, and they are morally blamed because they choose evil when they could have chosen good instead. The understanding of the conditions of moral praise and blame as entailing the ability to do otherwise was not stressed prior to the modern era, but it is also one which many philosophers think important (see FREE WILL; PRAISE AND BLAME §4). But then, on the understanding of perfect goodness as involving the inability to will evil, a perfectly good being is not free in a morally significant sense. And it then seems to follow from that that a perfectly good being cannot be praised in the moral sense of praise because he lacks morally significant freedom, and so cannot be good in the moral sense of good. This leads to a third and even more serious problem. If the concept of perfect goodness is intended to include moral goodness and yet the concept of perfect goodness is inconsistent with the concept of moral goodness, as allegedly demonstrated by the foregoing argument, it seems to follow that the concept of perfect goodness is self-inconsistent.

An interesting attempt has been made to use the Thomistic doctrine of divine simplicity (see SIMPLICITY, DIVINE) to resolve the above puzzles about the compatibility of perfect goodness with other divine attributes. According to Aquinas' concept of simplicity, there is no composition in God at all, so God does not even have attributes, even though it is necessary for us to think of God as having attributes because of the limitations of our finite minds. As this doctrine is described by Stump and Kretzmann (1985), the actual referent of such terms as 'divine omnipotence', 'divine goodness' and 'divine being' is the (simple) divine nature, and so there can be no conflict in reality between any pair of attributes.

3 Perfect goodness and the problem of evil

Even if the problem of the alleged inconsistency of perfect goodness and omnipotence can be resolved, there is still another difficulty. The combination of these two attributes leads to one of the most intractable of all theological problems, the problem of evil (see EVIL, PROBLEM OF). This problem has a number of forms, but it most directly threatens the concept of perfect goodness by way of the following argument: (1) a perfectly good being would be motivated to eliminate all evil; (2) an omnipotent being would be able to eliminate all evil; (3) if a being is both motivated to eliminate evil and is able to do so, he would do so; (4) so if there was a perfectly good and omnipotent being, evil would not exist; (5) but evil does exist; therefore, (6) there is no being who is both perfectly good and omnipotent.

Defences of the compatibility of evil with divine omnipotence and perfect goodness generally focus on modifying either premise (2) or premise (3) of the above argument, or on interpreting them in such a way that (4) does not follow. It is virtually always taken for granted that a perfectly good being is motivated to prevent or to eliminate evil, and so premise (1) is usually accepted by all sides of the discussion. Theists looking for ways out of the dilemma then typically look for reasons why a perfectly good God would permit evil for the sake of some good – often the good of free will or, in general, the good of the world and its creatures. The idea is that a certain kind and amount of evil is a logically necessary prerequisite for obtaining such good.

But there are ways of understanding the concept of perfect goodness which are both faithful to the tradition of reflection on the concept and which lead to the denial of (1) in the sense intended in this dilemma. One is suggested by the divine command theory mentioned in §2. Since divine command theories maintain that what is right or good is determined to be right or good by the will of God, they maintain (1) only in the trivial sense that since good just is what God wills, and since it is trivially true that God is motivated to will what he wills and is not motivated to will what he does not will, then God is motivated to will good and not to will evil. Such an interpretation of (1) does not generate the problem of evil. A modification of this approach is to attempt to ground God's perfect goodness in those conditions of his nature out of which his will arises, but without making his will primary. One way this might be done is to make motivations the primary good. If God's motivations are an intrinsic feature of his nature and hence good in the primary sense, it follows that good is not something against which the motivations of a good being are to be measured. Instead, the dependency goes the other way. What is good is good because a perfectly good being is motivated to bring it about. It is not the case that a being is good in part because his motivations are to do or to bring about good. On this approach there is no independent conception of good for the sake of which a perfectly good being derives its motivations and for the sake of which he permits some independent conception of evil. This approach could be called a 'divine motivation' theory rather than a divine command theory.

Another way out of the problem of evil raises one of the deepest questions on the metaphysics of value. This is the view that evil does not exist at all. This approach has been favoured at various times in the history of philosophy, but the present era is not one of them. Both inside and outside professional philosophy, many persons believe that the twentieth century has been especially evil and that it is no longer tenable to maintain that evil is a subjective reaction to the undesirable rather than an active and virulent force in history and human life. This attitude threatens the viability of the concept of perfect goodness to the extent that on the traditional conception, a perfectly good being does not *compete* with evil or evil beings. Unlike some of the religions of the East, Western philosophy and religion have never understood good and evil to be on the same level, either ontologically or practically (see EVIL). For this

reason the concept of perfect goodness has been able to exert a hold on the philosophical imagination far greater than it would have done if evil had been supposed to be an equal combatant.

See also: GOD, CONCEPTS OF §§1–6

References and further reading

* Aquinas, T. (1266–73) *Summa theologica*, trans. Fathers of the English Dominican Province, Westminster, MD, 1981, Ia, q.5, a.1; q.25, a.3. (Aquinas' treatment of the connection between being and goodness appears in many places in his work. These passages are among the more important. Other references appear in Stump and Kretzmann (1991).)
* —— (1259–65) *Summa contra gentiles*, trans. A.C. Pegis, J.F. Anderson, V.J. Bourke and C.J. O'Neil, Notre Dame, IN: University of Notre Dame Press, 1975. (Divided into four books, of which the first three deal with natural theology and the last with revealed theology. The *Summa contra gentiles* has a more philosophical purpose than the *Summa theologiae* since it is directed towards non-believers.)
* Augustine (397–401) *Confessions*, trans. with commentary by H. Chadwick, Oxford and New York: Oxford University Press, 1991, bk VII. (An important book in the history of the Christian concept of the relation between being and goodness, frequently cited throughout the medieval period.)
* Boethius (early 6th century) *De hebdomadibus*, trans. S. MacDonald, in S. MacDonald (ed.) *Being and Goodness*, Ithaca, NY: Cornell University Press, 1991. (The third of Boethius' *Opuscula sacra* (Theological Tractates), this aims to discover 'how substances are good in that they have being, yet are not substantial goods'.)
Kretzmann, N. (1991) 'A General Problem of Creation: Why Would God Create Anything at All?' and 'A Particular Problem of Creation: Why Would God Create This World?', in S. MacDonald (ed.) *Being and Goodness*, Ithaca, NY: Cornell University Press. (In this pair of papers, Kretzmann poses a serious puzzle for the idea that God is free in choosing to create the world. He traces two different lines – a Platonistic necessitarian one and a libertarian one – running through the theology of the medieval period, and finds Aquinas' position inconsistent.)
MacDonald, S. (ed.) (1991) *Being and Goodness*, Ithaca, NY: Cornell University Press. (This collection provides an up-to-date treatment of the metaphysics of goodness as it appears in medieval

philosophy broadly construed. It includes a translation of Boethius' *De hebdomadibus* in the appendix.)

Morris, T.V. (1987) 'Duty and Divine Goodness', 'The Necessity of God's Goodness' and 'Perfection and Power', in *Anselmian Explorations*, Notre Dame, IN: University of Notre Dame Press. (Good examples of contemporary work attempting to resolve puzzles about the connection between divine goodness and certain other attributes.)

* Pike, N. (1969) 'Omnipotence and God's Ability to Sin', *American Philosophical Quarterly* 6 (3): 208–16. (The most important contemporary article on this puzzle.)

* Plato (*c.*380–367 BC) *Republic*, trans. G.M.A. Grube, Indianapolis: Hackett Publishing Company, 1974. (This is a classic of political philosophy as well ethics and metaphysics, and its influence on theology has been considerable.)

* —— (*c.*366–360 BC) *Timaeus*, trans. B. Jowett, in E. Hamilton and H. Cairns (eds) *The Collected Dialogues of Plato*, New York: Pantheon Books, 1961. (This work exerted a profound influence on the medieval mind. It is the account in mythical form of Plato's cosmology.)

* Reichenbach, B.R. (1982) *Evil and a Good God*, New York: Fordham University Press. (An example of the idea that God has the ability to do evil, but simply does not.)

* Stump, E. and Kretzmann, N. (1985) 'Absolute Simplicity', *Faith and Philosophy* 2 (3): 353–82. (This paper explores the Thomistic concept of divine simplicity as a way of resolving a number of puzzles about the divine attributes.)

—— (1991) 'Being and Goodness', in S. MacDonald (ed.) *Being and Goodness*, Ithaca, NY: Cornell University Press, 98–128. (This paper explicates Aquinas' conception of the relation between being and goodness and argues that this position can be used to solve some problems discussed in contemporary ethics.)

LINDA ZAGZEBSKI

GORDON, A.D. *see* ZIONISM

GORGIAS (late 5th century BC)

The most important of the fifth-century BC Greek Sophists after Protagoras, Gorgias was a famous rhetorician, a major influence on the development of artistic prose and a gifted dabbler in philosophy. His display speeches, Encomium of Helen of Troy *and* Defence of Palamedes, *are masterpieces of the art of making a weak case seem strong, and brilliant exercises in symmetrical and antithetical sentence structure. Of philosophical importance is his treatise* On Not-Being, or On the Nature of Things, *an elaborate reversal of the metaphysical argument of Parmenides, showing: (1) that nothing exists; (2) that if anything exists, it cannot be known; and (3) if anything can be known, it cannot be communicated. This nihilistic tour de force is probably a caricature rather than a serious statement of a philosophical position. Gorgias is a master of the persuasive use of* logos *(discourse), understood both as eloquence and as argumentative skill.*

1 Career
2 Teaching
3 Philosophical work

1 Career

Born in Leontini in Sicily, Gorgias came under the influence of the Sicilian philosopher Empedocles as well as the local school of rhetoric associated with the names of Corax and Tisias. In 427 BC Gorgias led a delegation from Leontini to Athens, where his new oratorical style proved to be a great success. His lessons were very highly paid, and as a teacher he travelled throughout Greece. He gave public speeches at Olympia (where he urged the Greeks to unite against the Persians), at Delphi and elsewhere. His written works, such as the epideictic or model speeches *Encomium of Helen of Troy* and *Defence of Palamedes*, created a new, elaborate prose style which profoundly influenced the development not only of oratory but of literary prose generally. His pupil Isocrates founded the first school of rhetoric and the first institution of higher learning in Athens.

Gorgias lived to be over one hundred years old, and he is said to have read with amusement Plato's dialogue named *Gorgias* (written c.395–387 BC) and remarked: 'How well Plato knows how to make fun of people!'.

2 Teaching

Unlike PROTAGORAS (§2) and many later Sophists (see SOPHISTS), Gorgias made no claim to train students in moral and political virtue, but only to make them skilful public speakers. He developed both the theory and practice of persuasive speech (logos) as a technique of power (see LOGOS §1). Comparing the effect of speech on the soul to the action of drugs on the body, Gorgias describes how 'some speeches cause grief, some cause delight, some produce fear in the hearers while others produce confidence, and some by an evil persuasion drug and bewitch the soul' (*Helen* 14, fr.11). Hence in legal and political competitions 'a single *logos* delights and persuades a great crowd, because it is written with art, not because it is spoken with truth' (*Helen* 13, fr.11). In the dialogue *Gorgias*, Plato calls attention both to the power and to the lack of moral responsibility involved in Gorgianic training in rhetoric. And by presenting as followers of Gorgias the subsequent speakers Polus and CALLICLES, who systematically attack traditional Greek notions of morality, Plato's dialogue clearly implies that 'Gorgias' teaching is the seed of which the Calliclean life is the poisonous fruit' (Dodds 1959: 15).

Gorgias' own conception of 'writing with art' produced a highly ornamental prose style, where balanced clauses and euphonious word choice dazzle the ear and titillate the mind in sentence after sentence. We can still appreciate this effect in the extant *Encomium of Helen* and *Defence of Palamedes*, two display pieces that were apparently written as models for his students to memorize and imitate. A later taste finds this style artificial and exaggerated, but as a sheer technical exploit Gorgias' compositions made such an impression on his contemporaries that the art of writing in prose was permanently changed. Agathon's speech in Plato's *Symposium* (194e–197e) is one of the more elegant examples of direct Gorgianic influence. Gorgias' most distinguished pupil, Isocrates, established the classical style in Greek oratory with milder, less mechanical forms of parallelism and antithesis in sentence structure, which Cicero was later to reproduce in Latin.

3 Philosophical work

It is not clear that Gorgias made any major contribution to the development of Greek philosophy. Whether or not he was personally a pupil of Empedocles, as an ancient tradition reports, he was certainly familiar with the new natural philosophy which had come from Ionia to Sicily by the middle of the fifth century BC, and he made use of it in his teaching. Thus Meno, who is represented by Plato as a pupil of Gorgias, is fond of physical explanations of sensory perception in the style of Empedocles (*Meno* 76c–e) (see EMPEDOCLES §6). To this extent, as a popularizer of the new science Gorgias was (like the other Sophists) a typical representative of the fifth-century Enlightenment. His own, more personal, achievement is represented by a treatise *On Not-Being or On the Nature of Things*, which has come down to us in two later summaries, one in the Aristotelian corpus (the pseudo-Aristotelian text *On Melissus,*

Xenophanes and Gorgias, 979a–980b) and another version given by Sextus Empiricus (*Against the Professors* VII 65–87).

It would seem that the title of this treatise is already a joke, since it equates a discussion of nonentity or nothingness (the Parmenidean notion of not-being) with the Ionian investigation of the nature of things (*peri physeōs*) (compare PARMENIDES §2). Even if the intention of the author is not entirely serious, the text is of considerable historical interest, on several counts. It contains the longest example of continuous argumentation that has reached us from the fifth century BC. The closest precedent is provided by the poem of Parmenides and the paradoxes of ZENO OF ELEA. Gorgias' argument is in fact a direct inversion of Parmenides' reasoning in favour of being, which, according to Parmenides' argument, is the only subject that can be known and described in rational language. By contrast, Gorgias argues: (1) that nothing exists, or that there is no being at all; (2) that if anything exists, it cannot be known; and (3) if anything can be known, it cannot be communicated in language. Gorgias' reversal of Parmenides' reasoning follows the original so carefully that it has permitted modern scholars to reconstruct some features that are badly preserved in Parmenides' text. Gorgias' reasoning is indirect in form, like Parmenides', and it has benefited from the additional subtlety introduced by Zeno's paradoxes. Gorgias' work thus served to popularize not only natural philosophy but also Eleatic logic.

This treatise is, like the *Encomium of Helen*, a *paignion* or plaything. But what Gorgias is playing with is Parmenidean ontology and Zenonian dialectic. Consider the argument for the first thesis, 'that nothing exists' or 'that there is nothing'. (Translation is difficult, since in Greek the verb *esti*, 'is', and the participle *on*, 'being', cover both existence and predication; the notion of being represents a fusion of the two.) In the version of the argument given by Sextus, the proof of this thesis begins with a trilemma, echoing the three Paths of Parmenides' discourse on Truth. 'If something exists, then either Being (*to on*) exists or Not-being (*to mē on*) exists or both Being and Not-being exist'. The three options are then eliminated *seriatim*. First of all, 'Not-being is not (does not exist). For if Not-being exists, it will at the same time be and not be. Understood as Not-being, it will not be. But insofar as Not-being exists it will also be. But it is utterly absurd for something at the same time to be and not to be. Therefore Not-being does not exist'. The proof that being also does not exist begins again with a trilemma: 'If Being exists, it is either eternal or generated or both'. All three possibilities are then refuted.

The arguments to show (2), that, if anything exists, it is unknowable, and (3), that, if anything is known, it cannot be communicated, are of philosophical interest inasmuch as they emphasize the gap between thought and reality on the one hand, and between thought and language on the other. But the preserved arguments seem grossly fallacious. They are good illustrations of the later notion of sophistry as making use of specious argument. On the other hand, the general form of the reasoning is reminiscent of the dialectical second part of Plato's *Parmenides*. Since we do not have Gorgias' own wording, it is difficult to know whether Plato is imitating Gorgias or whether our text has been reshaped under the influence of later, more sophisticated argumentation.

Besides displaying the virtuoso skills of its author, Gorgias' treatise seems designed to discredit ambitious philosophical reasoning of the sort initiated by Parmenides and Zeno. This is in any case the conclusion drawn by Isocrates (Gorgias fr. 1): if these theses can be logically argued for, why should we take any such arguments seriously? In a more light-hearted way, but with greater technical sophistication, Gorgias thus joins the attack on Parmenidean dogmatism that was launched by Protagoras with his 'Man-the-measure' thesis.

References and further reading

* Anon. (date unknown) *On Melissus, Xenophanes and Gorgias*, trans. W. S. Hett, *Aristotle, Minor Works*, Loeb Classical Library, Cambridge, MA: Harvard University Press and London: Heinemann, 1936. (Although spuriously attributed to Aristotle, and of uncertain date, it is an important source on Gorgias' *On Not-Being*, omitted from Diels and Kranz (1954); includes Greek text with English translation.)
Cole, T. (1991) *The Origins of Rhetoric in Ancient Greece*, Baltimore, MD, and London: Johns Hopkins University Press. (Strikingly original view of Gorgias' place in the development of rhetoric and written prose.)
* Dodds, E.R. (1959) *Plato, 'Gorgias', A Revised Text with Introduction and Commentary*, Oxford: Oxford University Press. (Masterful discussion of the relation between Plato's dialogue and the historical figure of Gorgias.)
Gorgias (late 5th century BC) Fragments, in H. Diels and W. Kranz (eds) *Die Fragmente der Vorsokratiker* (Fragments of the Presocratics), Berlin: Weidemann, 7th edn, 1954, vol. 2, 271–307. (The standard collection of the ancient sources; includes Greek texts with translations in German.)
Guthrie, W.K.C. (1969) *A History of Greek Philosophy*, vol. 3, Cambridge: Cambridge University Press. (A full, scholarly account.)
Kerferd, G.B. (1981) *The Sophistic Movement*, Cambridge: Cambridge University Press. (A briefer, more personal interpretation than that of Guthrie (1969).)
* Plato (c.395–387 BC) *Gorgias*, trans. T. Irwin, Oxford: Oxford University Press, 1979. (Includes commentary.)
* —— (c.386–380 BC) *Meno*, trans. W.K.C. Guthrie, Harmondsworth: Penguin, 1956. (Presents Meno as a pupil of Gorgias.)
* —— (c. 386–380 BC) *Symposium*, trans. A. Nehamas and P. Woodruff, Indianapolis, IN and Cambridge: Hackett Publishing Company, 1989. (Contains display speech in Gorgianic style.)
* Sextus Empiricus (c.200 AD) *Against the Professors*, trans. R.G. Bury, *Against the Logicians*, vol. 1, *Against the Physicists, Against the Ethicists*, vol. 2 and *Against the Professors*, vol. 3, Loeb Classical Library, Cambridge, MA: Harvard University Press and London: Heinemann, 3 vols, 1935, 1936, 1949. (Contains summary of *On Not Being*.)
Sprague, R.K. (ed.) (1972) *The Older Sophists*, Columbia, SC: University of South Carolina Press, 30–67. (Full translation of the fragments.)

CHARLES H. KAHN

GOTAMA *see* GAUTAMA, AKṢAPĀDA

GOURNAY, MARIE DE
see FEMINISM (§2)

GRACE

Grace is a gift of personal relationship with God surpassing the powers of nature. Such relationship presupposes the relation every creature has with God as immediately dependent on him for its very existence and continuance, but goes beyond it in its distinctive personal character and the resulting more intimate dependence.

Such personal relationship necessarily depends upon some will or expression of will. The development of the relationship must be free in relation to what has gone before – it must in no way be necessitated. Therefore, if the relationship arises within some established natural system involving some degree of conformity to law at some levels of description (physical or otherwise), such a system and laws must leave some degree of indeterminacy. This allows the possibility that free actions, physically and psychologically contingent, should be among the ultimate determinants of what unfolds. For the workings of grace must always be free or contingent in relation to such a system of nature, concordant with and fulfilling nature, but working according to distinct principles – grace and nature are both equally God's gift, but always distinct.

The notion of grace has no place outside some kind of theism. Implicit in Judaism, its explicit development has been in Christian theology, which sees human beings as radically dependent upon God not only for redemption from personal sin, but for any personal or 'supernatural' relationship to God at all. This emphasis on grace is peculiar to Christianity, although the general conception seems implicit in most theistic religions; it can perhaps be found in the more theistic forms of Hindu devotion, although it is absent from Buddhism and the stricter forms of Hinduism.

1   Grace and nature
2   Grace essentially related to loving personal relationship with God
3   Grace within the human framework
4   Grace and creation

1   Grace and nature

In considering grace, there are questions which spring from a need for logical clarification and questions arising from real theological disagreement. Differences in philosophical framework often make applying this distinction difficult. The same formulation may disguise real differences, while opposed forms of words sometimes conceal agreement.

The first distinction to be made is between what belongs to God's unconstrained will simply by his being and nature (for example, his existence and his delight in it, and, in Christian understanding, the relationships of Father, Son and Holy Spirit, none of which are by free choice) and what arises from his free will. Creation and grace both belong to his free overflow of love, entirely without necessity.

Grace is a gift of God constituting or expressing a supernatural relationship (analogous to friendship) or relational disposition (personal goodwill directed towards such friendship): many of the words for 'grace' in different languages signify 'being favoured', either as a steady state or as a possibly temporary disposition. As such, it arises in connection with created persons, not just as created beings but precisely as persons. In the human case, these persons begin in the womb and mature in stages. In Christian

understanding, their relationship is to God as three persons, Father, Son and Holy Spirit, united in one single act of being. The word 'supernatural' in this context means something essentially geared to such a relationship or possibility of relationship, freely given and entered into. As such, it is entirely distinct from the merely 'preternatural', a word which refers to what is coeval with nature even if interfering with it, such as poltergeists and other supposed paranormal phenomena, and any supposed activities of spirits, devils or disembodied souls not directed to assisting or resisting divine activity.

However, God's special favours towards individuals have sometimes been conceived solely in terms of his providing some special created happiness (such as envisaged in portrayals of paradise as an earthly garden), or special help in dealings in this life (such as described in some of the Psalms), or special prophetic knowledge. This is compatible with a way of thinking which regards virtue pleasing to God, and even perseverance so as to attain heaven (identified with paradise), as within human power, perhaps assisted by the imitation of moral examples such as Jesus. This view is represented in the fifth-century British monk Pelagius as well as in modern exemplarist theories of the atonement, such as that of Hastings Rashdall (see PELAGIANISM §1).

Such approaches led Western Christian theology, following AUGUSTINE (§13), to give primary emphasis to the necessity of grace for any state, act or virtue pleasing to God, for any repentance and any perseverance in virtue. Augustine conceived mankind as having forfeited all right to friendship with God by a primeval choice preferring lesser goods (for, since God had created mankind to be a family in solidarity with one another, the sin of one affected all) (see SIN §2). Hence, the first role of grace was to undo the effects of this 'original sin'. Accordingly, the primary role of Jesus' redeeming action tended to be seen as the undoing of this negative effect so as to reopen the possibility of supernatural friendship with God.

But such a negative conception of grace, as necessary simply to undo the effects of sin, obscures the absolutely basic Christian presumption that any act of love towards God appropriate to the kind of friendship God intends is beyond human power alone. In this conception, such acts of love would have been beyond human power even if there had been no sin – indeed they are equally beyond angelic power, so that even the angels depend on grace. Such love requires the coaction of God within our act, and it is this which makes the kind of friendship concerned essentially 'supernatural'. This principle was plain in John's Gospel, Augustine and many other Christian 'Fathers' long before being given Thomas Aquinas' careful articulation, according to which any act meriting salvation has to be moved by charity (*Summa theologiae* IaIIae, q.109; q.114, aa.2, 4), which is explained as a God-empowered mutual friendship involving God's co-working in us (IIaIIae, q.23, aa.1–2; compare a.7; on co-working, IaIIae, q.111, a.2).

Many other theists share this general conception, but Christian teaching gives it special emphasis. Christianity envisages a relationship which enables us to pray 'Abba, Father' ('Abba' being an intimate word like 'papa' or 'daddy'). Such prayer expresses some intimate sharing in the life of the Godhead alongside Jesus, a sharing that gives hope of the vision of God. Such intimacy and such vision are not within natural human power.

2 Grace essentially related to loving personal relationship with God

Historically we find two different accents in the treatment of grace. First, there is an accent on grace as God himself, under the aspect of giving himself in some kind of divine indwelling, and under this aspect referred to as 'uncreated grace'. Second, there is an accent on created grace, grace considered as involving alteration in the created person and their intellect and will. Eastern Christian tradition has always emphasized uncreated grace, that is, God himself, sometimes speaking of this as an uncreated divine energy, and regarding this as primary. By contrast, Western tradition has commonly treated the real alteration of created persons, their transformation into new creatures, as most important. This created grace has been conceived as going to the root of the person's being, but also as co-working within their faith and love and their particular acts of faith and love.

The insistence on grace as something real in the creature (on created grace), has been especially evident in Roman Catholic teaching; for example, it is found in Aquinas' rejection of the idea that grace consists only in an attitude of God (of 'favour') towards someone, rather than in a gift of God to that person making them pleasing to God (equally, Aquinas rejects the idea that the remission of sins involves only imputing justice to people rather than effecting a real change in them, rendering them actually just and pleasing; see *Summa theologiae* IaIIae, q.110, a.1, q.113, a.2). This has sometimes generated the picture of grace as being like a liquid poured upon us or into us, it then being mistakenly conceived of as something which, once given to us by God, we possess neither more nor less independently of him than we possess his natural created gifts; this picture is often associated with the (mistaken) belief

that medieval thinkers supposed the sacraments to communicate grace by created human power (contrary to the Catholic insistence that God alone causes grace and is the principal agent in the sacraments). LUTHER revolted against such notions, insisting on speaking of justification as something imputed rather than imparted, and rejecting the supposed conception of the sacraments as human works causing grace. In such a context, the Reformers unsurprisingly preferred such translations as 'highly favoured' to 'full of grace' as descriptions of the Virgin Mary.

Hans Küng (1964) interprets Luther's texts in a way seemingly compatible with regarding the grace of being justified as internal to the person justified, it being wrong to suppose that what God regards as just he could so regard if he did not in the same act make it actually just. Whether or not Küng's own explanations are satisfactory, granted the obscurities of his phenomenological/existentialist idioms, clearly many other points of dispute between Catholic and Protestant conceptions are terminological rather than real. Standard logical distinctions have to be taken into account: for example, whether or not someone is courageous is a matter of fact, not a matter of degree, whereas how courageous someone is is a matter of degree. Thus, in the standard Protestant idiom, 'the grace of justification' refers to the matter of fact and 'sanctification' to what has degrees – whereas the standard Catholic idioms for the same matter of fact are 'being in a state of sanctifying grace' or 'being in communion with God', and 'the grace of justification' and 'sanctification' are treated as the same reality, distinct only in the aspect described, both equally having degrees.

John OMAN (1917) indicates how the underlying problem is to be resolved by recovering the full implications of conceiving grace relationally. His explanation is reminiscent of Aquinas' treatment of the supernatural ('theological') virtue of charity as involving essential mutuality, mutuality deeper than in normal human friendship. Aquinas' explanation of this depth is that this friendship is only established by the love of God first giving us the requisite faith and goodwill towards him, and that the acts belonging to it essentially involve, on the human side, God's co-working in us. The general problem is how to give an adequate explanation of the particular way in which grace in the creature has no existence independently of relationship with God. It is the peculiar way in which personal relationship is internal to grace that makes it intrinsically supernatural.

Karl RAHNER (§5) uses ideas from Aquinas to explain how God dwelling in us (uncreated grace) is specially internal to the transformation of the creature (created grace), noting that Aquinas regarded the sanctifying grace required for charity towards God in this life as having the same ontological presuppositions as the immediate vision of God (Rahner 1961). Only God (Jesus, the Word of the Father) dwelling in the soul could be the principle of this beatific vision – God is related to it as the impression or concept shaping our seeing or understanding of something is related to that seeing or understanding. God the Father and Son, with the Spirit breathed by them, make themselves, as it were, the internal principles of the workings of our own heart and mind. It is this presence which makes us 'new creatures', adapted to God's co-working in us in this love and vision, things whose possibility is known only through revelation.

In Catholic and Orthodox thinking, grace always perfects nature, never abolishes it. It has to be the very same human being, previously sinful, who is now in love with God: continuity in individual identity depends on some continuity of nature. Nature is not of itself capable of grace, nor is the finite of itself capable of the infinite, but created nature can be enhanced by grace so as to be able, with God's co-working, to reach the love and vision spoken of. However, this still involves not just an addition to or strengthening of the powers of the human soul or person, but a change at a logically deeper level. For, as the difference between a human being and an amoeba is not just that additional powers are added to a nature which is the same, but that the possession of these additional powers reflects a richer nature of which these powers are only an expression, so the difference between a person supposed to be without grace and a person in a state of grace involves an enlargement of a person's nature. A person's power to know and love God in the way appropriate to the friendship opened out by faith presupposes such enlargement. Therefore, grace has the same logical relation to the powers and activities which it makes possible as human nature has to natural human powers and activities, and it is in this sense that it belongs to the essence of the soul rather than being a mere accident external to it – that is, it constitutes a real transformation at the root of the human being, making a person, in St Paul's words, 'a new creature'.

3   Grace within the human framework

The phrase 'the economy of grace' traditionally signified the household provision for the distribution of grace among the human race as a historically ramified family (subject to no restrictions of scarcity such as the modern use of the word 'economy' suggests). In the traditional Christian conception, every giving of grace in God's providence is preceded by some preparedness for the receiving of the grace concerned (some 'prevenient' grace). Thus, in each individual's life, some remnants of the original good in human nature give them some openness to truth and desire for relationship in their heart with God. More particularly, before giving any special gift, God tends first to raise up the desire and then even the will and prayer for it. In this conception, the whole law of God's working towards humanity is not that he imposes his will, but that he waits on human readiness, consent and cooperation, each as appropriate to the degree of maturity of the human beings concerned.

In Jewish as well as Aristotelian thinking, human beings are essentially social by nature – an inseparable consequence of their bodiliness and biological nature (in scholastic thinking, putting human beings in contrast with the angels, whose sociality is supposedly differently rooted). This essential sociality is the key to Mersch's explanation of 'original sin' (Mersch 1951): God allowed the sin of one to affect all, preserving human solidarity, because he was intent on human beings coming to salvation as one community, so that in Jesus' becoming man the same solidarity should become the means of opening up a new way to salvation, the obedient love of one being effective for all. It also explains how the prayer or consent of one person or group, or the Church, can avail for others, so that none need be too immature, too weak or even too proud (since pride can be broken) to be outside the scope of grace – and none too ignorant by reason of their historical or geographical situation.

In common Christian thinking, grace restoring human beings to fellowship with God ('freeing them from original sin') has been made available to every human being throughout time. Thus, before the coming of Christ, independently of historically received knowledge of his redemptive suffering and death on the cross (his 'passion'), human beings received grace in anticipation of this redemptive work. All this is conceived as geared to a plan of God for the whole of mankind; so, for example, the fact that Old Testament prophets, and, in Catholic and Orthodox belief, the Virgin Mary in an especially complete way, should have received grace and grown in friendship with God from early in their lives was part of God's wider plan, each stage of the unfolding of which should wait upon appropriate human preparation, consent and cooperation.

It accords with this conception that, within this plan, the immature (for example, the infants massacred in Bethlehem) with a place in the prayer of Israel or of other God-inspired religious company (in the case of infant baptism by the prayer of the Church), and all young or old who suffer 'for the sanctification of the Name' (Jews, notably in the Holocaust, and Christians and others in other martyrdom), are in reach of salvation – and, along with these, everybody who, although mature, lacks effective explicit knowledge of God's desire and plan (whether through living in times and places too early or remote to have heard the gospel, or through accidents of culture affecting response to the gospel). All these stand as people waiting, waiting to enter salvation in one company with those to whom Christ's coming, the Church, Scripture and history make a more fully human response possible in this life. 'Fully human' means fully relational, personal and communal, fully intellectual with appropriate bodily and social expression by sign and voice. In this conception, such waiting is absolutely required if the salvation into which all who are willing are to enter is to be as fully humanly unified and complete as the work of Christ makes possible: bodiliness and historicality necessarily involve such a structured communal entry into salvation. In this conception, a person can be excluded from such salvation only by their own decision of heart and will. Tradition and different theologians have indicated so many different ways God might prepare human beings so as to be able to receive grace that it has become increasingly obscure whether a doctrine of limbo is necessary at all – so long as grace is only in anticipation of Christ's work and salvation is completed only in being joined in community with Christ and waiting 'to reach their perfection only in company with us' (Hebrews 11: 40) (see LIMBO).

St Paul tells us that God desires the salvation of all human beings. Not all have interpreted Paul in the way sketched above (Aquinas outlines the three traditional alternatives in *Summa theologiae* Ia, q.19, a.6, ad.1). For some, grace seemed inaccessible to the unbaptized and even to all the immature, as well as to virtuous heathen ancient or modern. Others made the human will seem almost irrelevant by considering all salvation to depend upon God's determination in giving the graces of conversion and perseverance to an effective extent, either predestining only some (Calvin's tendency) or by predestining all ('universalism'). Modern theological history is littered with controversies in this area, with views associated with CALVIN (§§3–4) and Jansen (tending in one direction), and MOLINA (§§2–3) and Arminius (tending in the other) all seeming one-sided or unacceptable to some, while Dominicans and Jesuits were restrained from controversy even in the supposed middle ground. In short, the problems of conceding a genuine reality to time and a real coauthorship in history between God and human beings in the giving and receiving of grace have proved more difficult than those concerning God's foreknowledge.

There has been much confusion between foreordination to salvation and knowledge of it (called 'assurance'). Aquinas argued that none have certain knowledge of their damnation (such knowledge would make them worse) and that few have certain knowledge of their salvation (knowledge tending to generate arrogance), regarding this as a special gift reserved for a few (*Disputed Questions on Truth*, q.6, a.5); many Protestants, however, regard it as the norm, and this has been presented as one of the defining features of Methodism.

4 Grace and creation

One problem with conceiving grace negatively as simply undoing the effects of sin was discussed in §1 above. A second defect in this conception is that it obscures the logical point that the good gained in redemption may be greater than that lost through sin. Christian theology requires not just that this may be so, but is so, for, as AUGUSTINE (§9) says, God only permits evil because through it he may bring greater good: Adam consorted with God in the first paradise but, after the death and ascension of Jesus the Son, the whole Godhead, Father, Son and Holy Spirit, are to come together to live in those who abide in the Son's love – God not only with us but within us. The Roman Catholic Easter liturgy even refers to Adam's sin as 'happy fault, necessary sin, to gain for us so great a Redeemer'.

Medieval theologians asked whether Jesus, God the Son, became incarnate only to undo the effects of sin, further benefits being accidental, or whether he would have adopted this solidarity with mankind anyway, independently of sin. Aquinas, regarding Scripture as making sin the only certain reason for the Incarnation, left it open that God might still have willed the Incarnation even if there had been no sin. By contrast, Duns Scotus, relying on the principle that what is fitting must be true (a principle Aquinas did not regard as giving proof in revealed theology), envisaged the willing of the Incarnation as unconditional, a way followed by many modern theologians, especially those influenced by Karl Barth; it is echoed by de Lubac (1984) and Rahner (1961), who both represent 'nature' as a mere abstraction, historically never free of the supernatural, but always already laden with grace. They refuse to envisage the plan of creation as established first, with grace arising only as a special response to a contingency within it; instead they regard the whole history of creation as set within the context of the order of grace rather than vice versa, so that it is essentially, not just incidentally, a

Heilsgeschichte (conventionally translated as 'Salvation History'). Within such a perspective, the greater good arising in response to a foreknown Fall is conceived as foreordained.

See also: JUSTIFICATION, RELIGIOUS; PREDESTINATION; PROVIDENCE; REPROBATION; SACRAMENTS; SANCTIFICATION

References and further reading

* Aquinas, T. (1266–73) *Summa theologiae*, London: Blackfriars, 1961–70, Ia, q.19, a.6; IaIIae, qq.109–14; IIaIIae, q.23, aa.1–3. (These are the key questions respectively on the distribution of grace; grace and merit; and on charity.)
* —— (1256–9) *Disputed Questions on Truth*, Chicago, IL: Regnery, 1952. (Also commonly referred to as *QD. de veritate*; on predestination and the relation of foreknowledge and foreordination, see q.2, a.12; q.5, a.5; and q.6, aa.3, 5.)
* Küng, H. (1964) *Justification: The Doctrine of Karl Barth and a Catholic Reflection*, London: Burns & Oates. (The then Catholic theologian's attempt to reconcile Protestant and Catholic views of justification.)
* Lubac, H. de (1984) *A Brief Catechism on Nature and Grace*, San Francisco, CA: Ignatius. (Presents the idea that human nature's orientation towards grace is a datum of human existence; see also his *The Mystery of the Supernatural*, London: Chapman, 1967.)
* Mersch, É. (1951) *The Theology of the Mystical Body*, St Louis, MO: Herder. (Chapter 7, on original sin, explains the notion in terms of our understanding of salvation, rather than vice versa.)
* Oman, J. (1917) *Grace and Personality*, Cambridge: Cambridge University Press. (Presents the idea of explaining 'grace' in terms of relationship.)
* Rahner, K. (1961) *Theological Investigations*, London: Darton, Longman & Todd, vol. 1, chaps 9–10. (Chapter 9, 'Concerning the Relationship between Nature and Grace', presents 'nature' as an abstraction rather than an empirical reality, the possibility of grace being the context of any human existence; chapter 10, 'Some Implications of the Scholastic Concept of Uncreated Grace', shows how the concept of created grace appears to be ultimately dependent on the concept of uncreated grace, that is, on special ways of God's being personally present.)

DAVID BRAINE

GRAMSCI, ANTONIO (1891–1937)

An Italian Marxist theorist and activist, Gramsci's main contribution lies in his critique of dialectical materialism. This school treated both the power of the bourgeois state and the prospects for its revolutionary overthrow and replacement by a stateless communist society as necessary consequences of the autonomous development of the economic forces of production. In contrast, Gramsci emphasized the relatively independent role played by politics and culture in upholding the authority of the state and in organizing popular resistance to it. A canonical figure of Western Marxism, he is credited with formulating a strategy applicable to all communist parties operating in the democratic states of advanced industrial societies. However, the posthumously published Quaderni del carcere *(Prison Notebooks) elaborate on theoretical questions that had preoccupied Gramsci throughout most of his political career and which reflect peculiarities of the Italian political situation and traditions.*

1 Life
2 Historical materialism and Crocean historicism
3 Hegemony
4 The New Order
5 An Italian theorist

1 Life

Born in Sardinia, Gramsci won a scholarship to study at the university of Turin in 1911. He became involved in the Socialist Party and eventually gave up his studies to become a full-time journalist for various Party newspapers. The journal *L'Ordine Nuovo* (New Order), which he edited with the future communist leader Palmiro Togliatti, provided the main theoretical inspiration for the occupation of the factories in the Turin region in September 1920. Dissatisfaction with the Socialist Party and union support for the movement led him to join the secession to form the Communist Party of Italy (PCd'I) in 1921. However, his unorthodox Marxism and his advocacy of workers' democracy and the formation of an alliance between proletariat and peasants were initially just as out of favour here. Mussolini's seizure of power in 1922 led to a change of Party policy. In 1924 Gramsci was elected to Parliament. He returned from Moscow, where he had acted as the PCd'I's representative and met his wife Julia Schuct, and was appointed General Secretary of the Party. In 1926, however, he was arrested, and in 1928 sentenced to twenty years imprisonment. In spite of the Fascist prosecutor's desire 'to stop this brain functioning', enforced withdrawal from politics enabled him to reflect upon it: between 1929 and 1935, when chronic illness sapped even his intellectual willpower, he filled thirty-three exercise books with some 2,848 pages of notes. He had suffered from ill health all his life which was exacerbated by prison conditions and died a week after his commuted term ended.

2 Historical materialism and Crocean historicism

The distinctiveness of Gramsci's thought stems from his critique of the positivist Marxism of his day. He began by attacking the materialist and associationist psychologies employed by certain versions of historical materialism. While matter might be the essence of things, such theories ignored humanity's capacity to control natural processes and mould them to its will. He criticized the crude empiricism of certain positivist Marxists on similar grounds: facts do not speak for themselves but only make sense within some theory that provides criteria for their selection and significance. He then built on these criticisms to dispute the claim that the economic base determined in a mechanical manner the ideological and political superstructure (see MARX, K. §7). As before, such a statement ignored the independent role played by human consciousness. Gramsci pointed out that institutions and belief systems had internal dynamics of their own, which had no direct connection with economic developments. More important, the influence of the base was mediated through particular superstructures, and we engage with the structure and partially constitute it through our activity and ideologies. In one of his most famous early articles, he contended that the Russian Revolution could only be understood in this way. The collapse of the Tsarist regime and Lenin's ability to seize his opportunity had been to a large extent superstructural. The Soviet Union's task was now to build the economic conditions from which a true communist society could emerge. As such it was a 'Revolution against *Capital*', at least as economistic Marxists interpreted this work.

Gramsci's critique drew on the ideas of the idealist philosophers CROCE (§3) and GENTILE (§3), both of whom had written important studies of Marxism. Particularly influential were Croce's denial of a priori principles and his identification of philosophy with historical judgment, and Gentile's thesis of self-constitution through the unity of theory and practice. However, Gramsci was keen to rebut the charges of idealism and voluntarism that had been levelled against him, and a major section of the *Quaderni del carcere* (Prison Notebooks) is devoted to pointing out

Croce's errors. Gramsci argued that just as materialists treated matter as a metaphysical entity that determined all human action, so Croce had a tendency to attribute all human thought to the unfolding of a mystical ideal entity – spirit. He charged Croce with treating history as the product of the internal dynamics of thought, and ignoring the interplay of theory and action in the practical task of engaging with and changing the world. Gentile's actualism might seem more promising in this respect, but Gramsci believed he committed the even graver error of emotivism, which culminated in the conclusion that might is right, as his allegiance to Fascism demonstrated only too clearly.

Thus, Gramsci contended that in different ways both materialism and idealism resulted in passivity. Materialism encouraged the masses to regard revolution as an inevitable product of changes to the economic base to which they need not contribute. However, the existence of the objective conditions for revolution was not in itself sufficient: 'One must "know them" and how to use them. And want to use them' (*Quaderni*: 1338). Idealism led to an uncritical acceptance of prevailing ideas and a failure to relate them to economic and social circumstances. Going back to Marx's 1857 'Preface' and the *Theses on Feuerbach*, Gramsci argued that the true Marxist message was that the economic base constrained rather than determined the superstructure. The superiority of Marxism over other social philosophies lay in its claim to be able to make the most of existing circumstances so as to benefit humanity at large – a goal Gramsci largely associated with the achievement of the maximum productivity possible with the available techniques. However, this claim had to be sustained by engaging with existing ideologies and persuading the masses to act on the basis of Marxist principles.

3 Hegemony

Gramsci's emphasis on the role of will and consciousness fed into what most commentators regard as his chief contribution to philosophy – his concept of hegemony. Gramsci employed this term in two related ways. First, he used it to denote the consensual and ideological, as opposed to the coercive, basis of a political system. The state consisted of two elements. On the one hand, there was the coercive apparatus comprising the police, army and judiciary who could uphold the authority of the ruling class through force. On the other hand, there were the various institutions of civil society, such as the media, schools, churches, clubs, parties and trade unions. These organizations were the instruments of hegemony, the means whereby the dominant class obtained the spontaneous adherence of the rest of the population to its rule. Hegemony would allow a ruling group to hang on to power long after it had ceased to be the leading economic class. This point was vital to understanding the resilience of liberal democracies during the economic crisis following the First World War. Gramsci claimed that civil society was infinitely more developed within advanced industrial societies. In contrast to Russia, which was comparatively backward, in these countries revolution could not take the form of a direct military assault on the forces of coercion until the battle for civil society had been won and the masses convinced that their true interests lay in overthrowing the old order. In Gramsci's terminology, it was necessary to fight a 'war of position' to capture or supplant the institutions of hegemonic power before turning to a 'war of manoeuvre' and violent revolutionary action.

This leads to Gramsci's second usage of 'hegemony'; this time referring to the cultural and educative task of the Party in the formation of a coherent moral awareness and political will among the proletariat. The building of this new hegemony went through numerous phases. At the most basic level, it involved the political organization of the proletariat and making them conscious of their class and economic interests. However, to be truly hegemonic it was necessary to go beyond this stage and persuade other groups, particular the peasantry and the petit bourgeoisie, to identify their interests with those of the proletariat. Gramsci believed that the bourgeoisie in the UK and France had successfully universalized their point of view in this manner, convincing workers of the validity of capitalist economics and getting them to adopt bourgeois aspirations.

While Gramsci believed that this strategy had to have some foundation in economic reality to be plausible, it was an essentially political task. The Party had to constitute itself as an alternative civil society, offering schools, clubs and a focus for social life. A particularly important role would be played by intellectuals, who had the job of mediating between the Party leadership and ordinary people. Gramsci distinguished between 'traditional' and 'organic' intellectuals. The first were self-styled 'detached' scholars such as Croce. The second, in contrast, did not see themselves as a class apart. They acknowledged their membership of a particular social group and sought to lead its members to greater self-awareness. Gramsci did not think that the masses could ever be totally deluded by bourgeois ideology. The seeds of dissent from hegemonic views always existed in embryonic form if these failed to correspond to real interests. Organic leadership simply consisted of making the masses aware of this fact and getting them to relate their dissatisfaction to those of others. The result was to be the formation of a collective will for change.

Gramsci rejected Lenin's view that the Party cadres had to form an elitist vanguard and dictate to the people what they ought to believe and do by referring to scientific laws of history (see LENIN, V.). He opposed 'democratic centralism', that brought together leaders and led 'organically' to 'bureaucratic centralism' that operated 'mechanically' on the basis of directives sent from above. A Party organized in this fashion would always be a 'policing organ' rather than 'a deliberative body' (*Quaderni*: 1691–2). However, his theory was not without a sinister side of its own. The moral and intellectual revolution within people's consciences was to be so complete that the Party was to take the place of 'the Divinity or the categorical imperative' in their minds, with all acts judged good or bad to the extent that they benefited the Party (*Quaderni*: 1561).

4 The New Order

Gramsci believed that a cultural consensus around a shared moral vision would make the coercive force of the state redundant under communism. Drawing on Lenin's somewhat idealized account of the soviets, his own experience of worker's self-management during the occupation of the Turin factories, and his reading of accounts of the introduction of Frederick Taylor's management techniques by Henry Ford, he argued that factory production provided the economic and social preconditions for the autonomous organization of workers. He believed that the industrial system was potentially self-regulating. All that was required to ensure that production was related to the needs of the producers and that supply exactly matched demand, was to raise each individual worker's consciousness of their role within the productive process and their relationship to the rest of the global economy. This goal could be achieved through a worldwide network of factory and peasants councils that was hierarchically organized according to trade and region, and which culminated in an international administration that supervised the world's resources in the interests of all humanity. This network would serve as a vast information system through which workers both channelled their requirements and modified them to take into account those of others. In this way, a collective will gradually came into being that was linked to the maximal employment of the productive system. In so arguing, however, Gramsci risked justifying as total a subordination of the individual to the demands of technological development as he accused deterministic Marxists of proposing. His theory has no place for the traditional Marxist concern with alienation, concentrating rather on the removal of anomie through the assimilation of norms most suited to the regulation of production (see ALIENATION §§3–5).

5 An Italian theorist

Gramsci's ideas grew out of his reflections on the relatively backward nature of Italian capitalism and liberal democracy, and his attempts to account for the failure of revolutionary action and the triumph of fascism in the aftermath of the First World War. In addressing these problems, Gramsci was influenced as much by certain themes of the Italian political tradition as he was by his reading of Marx and Lenin. The machiavellian view that politics involves the mobilization of consent as well as the judicious employment of force, which was taken up in very different ways by contemporary Italian political sociologists such as Mosca and Pareto, and idealist philosophers such as Croce and Gentile, was particularly important in this regard. Indeed, Gramsci significantly referred to the Party as the Modern Prince (see MACHIAVELLI, N. §6).

In common with a long tradition of nineteenth- and twentieth-century Italian writers, Gramsci believed that the unification of Italy had been incomplete. As a Sardinian, he was all too aware that the Piedmontese state had succeeded in imposing political unity upon the region but had failed to assert its hegemony so as to 'make Italians'. Gramsci thought Fascism had arisen in Italy in part because the capitalist class had not become hegemonic and so had had to rely on more directly coercive methods. A successful and enduring social revolution would have to make good this failure. Gramsci's emphasis on consent and cultural consciousness, therefore, resulted in part from reading Marx from the perspective of a characteristic Italian concern with moral unity in order to construct a *via italiana* to communism.

See also: MARXISM, WESTERN

List of works

Gramsci, A. (1913–17) *Cronache torinese* (Turin Diary), ed. S. Caprioglio, Turin: Einaudi, 1980. (Contains Gramsci's earliest journalism.)
—— (1917–18) *La città futura* (The Future City), ed. S. Caprioglio, Turin: Einaudi, 1982. (Contains Gramsci's reaction to the Russian Revolution and the First World War.)

—— (1919–20a) *Il nostro Marx* (Our Marx), ed. S. Caprioglio, Turin: Einaudi, 1984. (Contains his shift towards a redefinition of Marxism in more cultural terms.)
—— (1919–20b) *L'Ordine Nuovo* (The New Order), ed. V. Gerratana and A.A. Santucci, Turin: Einaudi, 1987. (Contains the articles written during the occupation of the factories.)
—— (1921–2) *Socialismo e fascismo: L'Ordine Nuovo, 1921–22* (Socialism and Fascism), Turin: Einaudi, 1966. (Contains Gramsci's analysis of fascism and his work on the split of the Communists from the Italian Socialist Party.)
—— (1923–6) *La costruzione del Partito communista* (Building the Communist Party), ed. S. Caprioglio, Turin: Einaudi, 1971. (Contains articles written as leader of the Communist Party on the strategy they should adopt.)
—— (1926–37) *Lettere dal carcere* (Prison Letters), ed. S. Caprioglio and E. Furbini, Turin: Einaudi, 1965; trans. R. Rosenthal and ed. F. Rosengarten, *Prison Letters*, New York: Columbia University Press. (Written while imprisoned by Fascist authorities, these letters are an invaluable source for the evolution of Gramsci's thought at this time; definitive English translation.)
—— (1948–51) *Quaderni del carcere* (Prison Notebooks), ed. V. Gerratana, Turin: Einaudi, 4 vols, 1975; trans. J. Buttigieg and A. Callari, *Prison Notebooks*, New York: Columbia University Press, 1992–. (The former is the standard Italian edition of the *Prison Notebooks*; the latter is a translation of the Gerratana edition, of which vol. 1 has so far appeared.)
—— (1992) *Lettere, 1908–26* (Letters), ed. A.A. Santucci, Turin: Einaudi. (Collects together the relatively few surviving letters from Gramsci's early years.)
—— (1993) *Pre-Prison Writings*, trans. V. Cox, ed. R. Bellamy, Cambridge: Cambridge University Press. (Contains a wide-ranging selection of Gramsci's journalism, Party memoranda and letters, taken from the seven volumes of pre-prison writings and letters listed above.)

References and further reading

Adamson, W.L. (1980) *Hegemony and Revolution*, Berkeley, CA: University of California Press. (A good piece of intellectual history.)
Bellamy, R. and Schecter, D. (1993) *Gramsci and the Italian State*, Manchester: Manchester University Press. (Situates Gramsci's thought in the contemporary debate between various shades of liberals,

fascists and socialists about the nature and future of the Italian state.)

Clark, M. (1977) *Antonio Gramsci and the Revolution that Failed*, New Haven, CT, and London: Yale University Press. (An excellent study of the occupation of the factories.)

Femia, J. (1981) *Gramsci's Political Thought*, Oxford: Clarendon Press. (Best analysis of the concept of hegemony outlined in Gramsci's *Prison Notebooks*.)

Fiori, G. (1977) *Antonio Gramsci: Life of a Revolutionary*, trans. T. Nairn, London: Verso. (The standard biography.)

RICHARD BELLAMY

GRATITUDE *see* RECTIFICATION
AND REMAINDERS (§4)

GREEK PHILOSOPHY
see ANCIENT PHILOSOPHY

GREEK PHILOSOPHY: IMPACT ON ISLAMIC PHILOSOPHY

During the Hellenistic period (323–43 BC), classical Greek philosophy underwent a radical transformation. From being an essentially Greek product, it developed into a cosmopolitan and eclectic cultural movement in which Greek, Egyptian, Phoenician and other Near Eastern religious and ethical elements coalesced. This transformation is best symbolized by the role Alexandria played as the hub of diverse currents of thought making up the new philosophy.

When the Abbasid Caliphate was founded in Baghdad in 750 AD, the centre of learning gradually moved to the Abbasid capital, which became in due course the heir of Athens and Alexandria as the new cultural metropolis of the medieval world. About two centuries later Cordoba, capital of Muslim Spain, began to vie with Baghdad as the centre of 'ancient learning'. From Cordoba, Greek–Arabic philosophy and science were transmitted across the Pyrenees to Paris, Bologna and Oxford in the twelfth and the thirteenth centuries.

The initial reception of Greek–Hellenistic philosophy in the Islamic world was mixed. It was frowned upon at first as being suspiciously foreign or pagan, and was *dismissed by conservative theologians, legal scholars and grammarians as pernicious or superfluous. By the middle of the eighth century AD the picture had changed somewhat, with the appearance of the rationalist theologians of Islam known as the Mu'tazilites, who were thoroughly influenced by the methods of discourse or dialectic favoured by the Muslim philosophers. Of those philosophers, the two outstanding figures of the ninth and tenth centuries were al-Kindi and al-Razi, who hailed Greek philosophy as a form of liberation from the shackles of dogma or blind imitation (*taqlid*). For al-Kindi, the goals of philosophy are perfectly compatible with those of religion, and, for al-Razi, philosophy was the highest expression of man's intellectual ambitions and the noblest achievement of that noble people, the Greeks, who were unsurpassed in their quest for wisdom (*hikma*).*

1   The rise of Neoplatonism
2   Arabic translations of Greek philosophical texts
3   Eclecticism and the systematization of philosophical ideas
4   The legacy of Aristotle
5   Presocratic and post-Aristotelian philosophers

1   The rise of Neoplatonism

Neoplatonism has been described as the final summation or synthesis of the major currents in Greek philosophy, Pythagoreanism, Stoicism, Platonism and Aristotelianism, into which an oriental religious and mystical spirit was infused (see NEOPLATONISM). Its founder, PLOTINUS, was born in Lycopolis in Egypt, studied at Alexandria and lectured in Rome. He studied with Ammonius Saccas and was a classmate of ORIGEN, who became a Christian. Plotinus was so profoundly interested in oriental religions that he joined the abortive expedition of the Roman Emperor Gordian to Persia, as we are told by PORPHYRY, Plotinus' disciple and biographer, in search for 'the ways and beliefs of the Persians and Indians'. When the Emperor died on the way and the expedition came to grief, Plotinus sailed to Rome in AD 244, where he achieved great success as a teacher.

The other great representative of Neoplatonism was Diadochus PROCLUS, whose metaphysical outlook, like that of Plotinus, marks the final phase in the struggle of Greek paganism against Christianity at Athens, where he taught, and Alexandria, where he studied under Olympiodorus. It also marked that version of Greek philosophy which exerted a particular fascination upon Muslim minds. Other representatives of Neoplatonism during the Byzantine period include Syrianus, the teacher of Proclus,

155

Damascius, Proclus' pupil, SIMPLICIUS and PHILO-PONUS. All those philosophers or commentators were known to the Arabs and some of their writings, sometimes lost in Greek, were translated into Arabic.

In AD 529 the Byzantine Emperor Justinian ordered the school of Athens, the last bastion of Greek paganism, to be closed. Seven of its teachers, including Syrianus and Damascius, emigrated to Persia and were well received by the Emperor Chosroes I, who was an admirer of Greek learning and the founder, in AD 555, of the School of Jundishapur which was destined to become a major centre of Greek medical and scientific studies (see NEOPLATONISM IN ISLAMIC PHILOSOPHY §1). Subsequently, due to its proximity to Baghdad and the close political links between the Abbasids and the Persians, Jundishapur served as a staging station in the process of transmitting Greek medical and scientific learning into the Islamic world.

However, the first phase in the process of transmitting Greek learning into the Near East was the translation of theological treatises, such as Eusebius' *Ecclesiastical History* and Clement's *Recognitiones*, into Syriac. As a prelude, a series of logical texts were also translated into Syriac, including the *Isagōgē* of Porphyry, Aristotle's *Categories*, *De interpretatione* and *Prior Analytics*. Beyond these, for theological reasons, the Syriac translators were not allowed to proceed.

2 Arabic translations of Greek philosophical texts

The Arab conquest of Syria and Iraq in the seventh century did not, on the whole, interfere with the academic pursuits of Syriac scholars at Edessa, Nisibis, Qinnesrin and other centres of Syriac–Greek learning. To these Christian centres should also be added Harran in Northern Syria, home of a sect of star-worshippers known in the Arabic sources as the Sabaeans and alleged to have been founded by Alexander the Great. Throughout the eighth and ninth centuries (second and third centuries AH), a new impetus was given to the translation movement thanks to the enlightened patronage of three of the early Abbasid caliphs at Baghdad, al-Mansur, Harun and his son al-Ma'mun, who founded the House of Wisdom in Baghdad to serve as a library and institute of translation. It was during the reign of al-Ma'mun that the translation of medical, scientific and philosophical texts, chiefly from Greek or Syriac, was placed on an official footing. The major translators who flourished during al-Ma'mun's reign include Yahya ibn al-Bitriq, credited with translating into Arabic Plato's *Timaeus*, Aristotle's *On the Soul*, *On the Heavens* and *Prior Analytics* as well as the *Secret*

of Secrets, an apocryphal political treatise of unknown authorship attributed to Aristotle.

However, the shining star of al-Ma'mun's reign was the Nestorian Hunayn ibn Ishaq (d. AH 264/AD 873), who hailed from al-Hirah in Iraq and, jointly with his son Ishaq (d. AH 299/AD 911), his nephew Hubaysh and other associates, placed the translation of Greek medieval and philosophical texts on a sound scientific footing. The chief interests of Hunayn himself were medical, and we owe to him the translation of the complete medical corpus of Hippocrates and GALEN, but Hunayn and his associates were also responsible for translating Galen's treatises on logic, his *Ethics* (the Greek original of which is lost) and his epitomes of Plato's *Sophist*, *Parmenides*, *Cratylus*, *Euthydemus*, *Timaeus*, *Statesman*, *Republic* and *Laws*. (Only the epitomes of the *Timaeus* and the *Laws* have survived in Arabic.)

The interest of Hunayn and his school in Galen, the outstanding Alexandrian physician and Platonist, is noteworthy and this philosopher-physician is a major figure in the history of the transmission of Greek learning into Arabic. Not only his sixteen books on medicine but a series of his logical and ethical writings were translated and played an important role in the development of Arabic thought. Apart from the epitomes of Plato's *Dialogues* already mentioned, his *Pinax* (list of his own writings), *That the Virtuous can Profit from Knowing Their Enemies*, *That One Should Know His Own Faults* and especially his *Ethics* have influenced moral philosophers from Abn Bakr AL-RAZI to IBN MISKAWAYH and beyond.

Of the works of Aristotle, Hunayn's son Ishaq is responsible for translating the *Categories*, *De interpretatione*, *On Generation and Corruption*, the *Physics*, *On the Soul*, the *Nicomachean Ethics* and the spurious *De Plantis*, written by the Peripatetic philosopher Nicolaus of Damascus (first century BC). By far the most important Aristotelian treatise to be translated into Arabic during this period is the *Metaphysics*, known in the Arabic sources as the *Book of Letters* or the *Theologica* (al-Ilahiyat). According to reliable authorities, a little-known translator named Astat (Eustathius) translated the twelve books (excluding M and N) for al-Kindi, as did Yahya ibn 'Adi a century later. However, Ishaq, Abu Bishr Matta and others are also credited with translating some parts of the *Metaphysics*.

Equally important is the translation by Ibn Na'imah al-Himsi (d. AH 220/AD 835) of a treatise allegedly written by Aristotle and referred to in the Arabic sources at *Uthulugia* or *Theologia Aristotelis*. This treatise, which consists of a paraphrase of Plotinus' *Enneads* IV–VI, made by an anonymous Greek author (who could very well be Porphyry of

Tyre), together with Proclus' *Elements of Theology* (known as the *Pure Good* or *Liber de causis*), thoroughly conditioned the whole development of Arab–Islamic Neoplatonism (see NEOPLATONISM IN ISLAMIC PHILOSOPHY). Al-Kindi is said to have commented on the *Theologia Aristotelis* as did Ibn Sina and others, and al-Farabi refers to it as an undoubted work of Aristotle. A series of other pseudo-Aristotelian works also found their way into Arabic, including the already mentioned *Secret of Secrets, De Plantis, Economica* and the *Book of Minerals*.

Among other translators of Greek philosophical texts, we should mention Qusta ibn Luqa (d. AH 300/ AD 912), Abu 'Uthman al-Dimashqi (d. AH 298/AD 910), Ibn Zur'ah (d. AH 398/AD 1008) and Ibn al-Khammar (d. AH 408/AD 1017), as well as the already-mentioned Abu Bishr Matta (d. AH 328/AD 940) and his disciple Yahya IBN 'ADI. None of those translators made any significant or original contribution to Arabic philosophical literature, although they laid the groundwork for subsequent developments and served as the chief purveyors of Greek philosophy and science into the Islamic world. However, there were noteworthy exceptions: Abu Bishr Matta was a skilled logician, and the Jacobite Yahya ibn 'Adi stands out as the best-known writer on Christian theological questions and on ethics in Arabic. The Harranean Thabit ibn Qurra (d. AH 289/AD 901) was an outstanding mathematician and astronomer as well as a translator.

3 Eclecticism and the systematization of philosophical ideas

AL-KINDI, already mentioned in connection with the translation of Aristotle's *Metaphysics* and the apocryphal *Theologia Aristotalis*, should be regarded as the first genuine writer on philosophical subjects in Islam. He appears from bibliographical sources to have been a truly encyclopedic writer on every philosophical or scientific subject; his works total around three hundred, of which only a small number have survived in Arabic or Latin. He was profoundly interested in Greek thought as well as Indian religious ideas, and was a professional astrologer. His extant works, however, give the impression of eclectic and hasty composition, reflecting the influence of Socrates, Plato and Aristotle in an undefined manner. We owe to him however the first treatise on philosophical terms and definitions, modelled on Aristotle's Book Delta of the *Metaphysics*, which became in due course the model of almost all subsequent parallel treatises (see ARISTOTELIANISM IN ISLAMIC PHILOSOPHY).

The first genuine system-builder in Islam, however, was al-Farabi. He was the first outstanding logician of Islam, who commented on or paraphrased the six books of Aristotle's Organon, together with the *Rhetoric* and the *Poetics*, which formed part of the Organon in the Syriac–Arabic tradition and to which the *Isagōgē* of Porphyry, also paraphrased by al-Farabi, was added. He also wrote several original treatises on the analysis of logical terms, which had no parallels until modern times. He defended Aristotelian logic against the Arabic grammarians who regarded logic as a foreign importation, doubly superfluous and pernicious (see LOGIC IN ISLAMIC PHILOSOPHY). He also laid down the foundations of Arab–Islamic Neoplatonism in a series of writings, the best-known of which is *al-Madina al-fadila* (Opinions of the Inhabitants of the Virtuous City). This treatise is inspired by the same utopian ideal as Plato's *Republic* (see PLATO §14), but is essentially an exposition of the emanationist world-view of PLOTINUS to which a political dimension has been added. In that latter respect, it had hardly any impact on political developments in Islam, but it did inspire subsequent writers on political philosophy such as IBN BAJJA. Another great champion of the emanationist world-view was Abu 'Ali al-Husayn IBN SINA (Avicenna), who was a confessed spiritual disciple of al-Farabi.

The only great Platonist of Islam was Abu Bakr AL-RAZI, the greatest medical author and practitioner of the third and fourth centuries AH (ninth and tenth centuries AD). Both in ethics and in metaphysics, al-Razi exhibits a profound veneration for Plato, 'the master of the philosophers and their leader', as well as to the great Alexandrian doctor and philosopher GALEN, whose epitomes of Plato's *Dialogues*, as we have mentioned, formed the basis of the Arabic translations of Plato's works in the third century AH (ninth century AD). Although a Manichean or Harranean influence is discernible in his thought, the 'five eternal principles' which form the substance of al-Razi's metaphysics and cosmology, namely the Creator (*al-Bari'*), the soul, prime matter (*al-hayula, hyle*) space and time, can be shown to derive from Plato's *Timaeus* and his other dialogues. The other noteworthy Platonist, especially in the realms of ethics and psychology, was a fellow Persian philosopher, IBN MISKAWAYH, the best known ethical philosopher of Islam (see ETHICS IN ISLAMIC PHILOSOPHY §4; PLATONISM IN ISLAMIC PHILOSOPHY).

4 The legacy of Aristotle

As already mentioned, all the works of Aristotle were translated into Arabic with the exception of the

Politics, which for some obscure reason remained unknown to the Arabs. In addition a large number of apocryphal writings, including the *Secret of Secrets*, the *Economica*, *De plantis*, *De mundo*, the *Theologia* and the *Liber de causis* were also attributed to Aristotle. Of these works, the Organon, *On the Soul*, the *Nicomachean Ethics*, the *Physics*, the *Metaphysics*, *On Generation and Corruption* and *On the Heavens* played a decisive role in the development of logical and metaphysical ideas in Islam. However, chiefly due to the influence of the apocryphal *Theologia Aristotalis*, the tendency of early Muslim philosophers was to interpret Aristotle in Neoplatonic terms; a basic premise of this interpretation was the total agreement of Plato and Aristotle on all major issues alleged to separate them. (A famous treatise of al-Farabi entitled *al-Jam' bayn ra'yay al-hakimayn* (The Reconciliation of Plato and Aristotle), probably modelled on Porphyry's lost work of the same title, illustrates this point.)

The picture radically changed with the appearance on the philosophical scene of the greatest Arab Aristotelian, IBN RUSHD of Cordoba, known in Latin as Averroes. Ibn Rushd continued the tradition of commenting on Aristotle's works initiated in Arab Spain by IBN BAJJA (Avempace) and in the East by al-Farabi. Ibn Rushd, however, produced the most extensive commentaries on all the works of Aristotle with the exception of the *Politics*, for which he substituted the *Republic* of Plato. These commentaries, which have survived in Arabic, Hebrew or Latin, earned him in the Middle Ages the title of the Commentator, or as Dante put it in *Inferno* V. 144, 'che'l gran commento feo' (he who wrote the grand commentary). Ibn Rushd actually wrote three types of commentaries, known as the large, middle and short commentaries, on the major Aristotelian treatises, notably the *Physics*, the *Metaphysics*, the *Posterior Analytics*, *On the Soul* and *On the Heavens*. In addition, he defended Aristotle against the onslaughts of AL-GHAZALI, the famous Ash'arite theologian, in a great work of philosophical debate entitled the *Tahafut al-tahafut* (Incoherence of the Incoherence), a rebuttal of al-Ghazali's *Tahafut al-falasifa* (Incoherence of the Philosophers).

5 Presocratic and post-Aristotelian philosophers

The records of the early Greek philosophers in Arabic, such as al-Sijistani's *Siwan al-hikma* (Vessel of Wisdom) and al-Shahrastani's *al-Milal wa'l nihal*, usually begin with the Seven Sages, followed by a list of the Presocratics, including THALES, ANAXAMINES, ANAXIMANDER, DEMOCRITUS, PYTHAGORAS and HERACLITUS, with very brief accounts of their views,

which are invariably given a religious and mystical twist. This is particularly true of Empedocles and Pythagoras, who are said to have received 'wisdom' (*hikma*) from Semitic sources, notably Luqman and Solomon, and to have asserted as genuine Muslims *avant la lettre* the unity of God, the creation of the world and the resurrection.

Of the post-Aristotelian philosophers, CHRYSIPPUS is almost the only Stoic philosopher mentioned; ZENO OF CITIUM is almost unknown, despite the significant influence of Stoicism both in logic and in ethics on the early philosophers and theologians. Diogenes the Cynic (see DIOGENES OF SINOPE), often confused with Socrates, is represented as a key moral and ascetic figure, but of the latter Stoic philosophers such as CICERO, EPICTETUS and MARCUS AURELIUS, no mention is made in the classical Arabic sources. Of the materialists, only the names of DEMOCRITUS and EPICURUS are mentioned. The impression one gains from reading these sources is that Greek philosophy had, according to the authors, reached its zenith with Aristotle, who superseded his predecessors in such a way as to render them superfluous. Ibn Bajja, for instance, in his paraphrase of the *Physics* of Aristotle, justifies his total omission of the views of the Presocratics on the grounds that Aristotle had refuted their 'dialectical' views and therefore it was unnecessary to dwell on them, a position which al-Ghazali had also adopted in his *Tahafut al-falasifa*. As his target, al-Ghazali chose Aristotle to the exclusion of all others, on the ground that 'he (Aristotle) had refuted all his predecessors, including his teacher, whom they nickname Plato the Divine. Then he excused himself for disagreeing with his teacher, saying: "Plato is a friend and the truth is a friend, but truth is a greater friend than Plato"' (an obvious paraphrase of *Nicomachean Ethics* I). Of Aristotle's Greek commentators, the Arab historians of ideas and philosophers refer frequently to, or quote from, the writings of ALEXANDER OF APHRODISIAS, THEMISTIUS, Olympiodorus, SIMPLICIUS, PHILOPONUS and Nicolaus of Damascus (first century BC). The earliest commentators, such as THEOPHRASTUS (d. 288 BC) and STRATO (d. *c.*269 BC), were virtually unknown to the Arabs.

The chief historical significance of the Muslim–Spanish phase in the rise and development of Muslim philosophy is that it served as a major link in the transmission of Greek philosophy to Western Europe. The Muslims had been the custodians of that philosophy, which had been almost completely forgotten in Western Europe since the time of BOETHIUS, who was responsible chiefly for translating the Aristotelian logic into Latin. By the end of the twelfth century, the translation of Arabic philosophical, scientific and medical works into Hebrew or Latin by such eminent scholars as GERARD OF CREMONA, Michael Scot and Herman the German (see TRANSLATORS) had wrought a genuine intellectual revolution in learned circles. The most influential Muslim philosopher to leave a lasting impression on Western thought was Ibn Rushd (Averroes). During the thirteenth century, philosophers and theologians split into two rival groups, the Latin Averroists with SIGER OF BRABANT and BOETHIUS OF DACIA at their head, and the anti-Averroist group led by ALBERT THE GREAT and Thomas AQUINAS (see AVERROISM). The confrontation between these two groups became so violent that in the second half of the thirteenth century the Bishop of Paris, Étienne Tempier, had to intervene and in 1270 and 1277 issued ecclesiastical condemnations of a total of 219 propositions which were of Aristotelian or Averroist inspiration (see ARISTOTELIANISM, MEDIEVAL). It should be noted, however, that it was thanks to the Latin translations of Ibn Rushd's commentaries that the rediscovery of Aristotle in Western Europe and the concurrent emergence of Latin Scholasticism, one of the glories of late medieval thought, were made possible.

See also: ARISTOTELIANISM IN ISLAMIC PHILOSOPHY; HELLENISTIC PHILOSOPHY; ISLAM, CONCEPT OF PHILOSOPHY IN; ISLAMIC PHILOSOPHY: TRANSMISSION INTO WESTERN EUROPE; NEOPLATONISM IN ISLAMIC PHILOSOPHY; PLATONISM IN ISLAMIC PHILOSOPHY

References and further reading

Badawi, A.-R. (1987) *La transmission de la philosophie grecque au monde arabe* (The Transmission of Greek Philosophy into the Arab World), Paris: Vrin. (Contains useful information on manuscripts and Greek–Arabic texts or translations.)

Duval, R. (1970) *La littérature Syriaque* (Syriac Literature), Amsterdam: Philo Press. (First published in 1899, this is a detailed account of the Syriac translations of philosophical texts.)

Madkour, I. (1969) *L'Organon d'Aristote au monde arabe* (The Organon of Aristotle in the Arab World), Paris: Vrin. (First published in 1934, an important review of the stages through which Aristotelian logic passed in the Arab world.)

Peters, F. (1996) 'The Greek and Syriac Background', in S.H. Nasr and O. Leaman (eds) *History of Islamic Philosophy*, London: Routledge, ch. 3, 40–51. (Discussion of some of the important features of Greek and Syriac culture as sources of Islamic philosophy.)

Pines, S. (1986) *Studies in Arabic Versions of Greek Texts*, Jerusalem: Hebrew University and Brill. (The first part consists of a series of important Greek texts in Arabic translation, with valuable comments and information.)

Shayegan, Y. (1996) 'The Transmission of Greek Philosophy into the Islamic World', in S.H. Nasr and O. Leaman (eds) *History of Islamic Philosophy*, London: Routledge, ch. 6, 98–104. (Detailed account of how the transmission took place, paying particular attention to the Persian background.)

Steinschneider, M. (1960) *Die Arabischen Übersetzungen aus dem Griechischen* (The Arabic Translations of Greek Writings), Graz: Akademische Druck U. Verlagsanstalt. (First published 1889, this is the earliest authoritative review in a European language of the Arabic translation of Greek texts.)

Vacherot, E. (1846–51) *Histoire critique de l'École d'Alexandrie* (Critical History of the Alexandrian School), Paris. (The most comprehensive history of philosophical developments during the Alexandrian period.)

Walzer, R. (1962) *Greek into Arabic*, Cambridge, MA: Harvard University Press. (A collection of studies dealing with the transmission of Greek philosophy to the Arabs, by an eminent classical scholar and Arabist.)

MAJID FAKHRY

GREEN ETHICS *see* ENVIRONMENTAL ETHICS

GREEN POLITICAL PHILOSOPHY

All the major political philosophies have been born of crisis. Green political philosophy is no exception to this general rule. It has emerged from that interconnected series of crises that is often termed 'the environmental crisis'. As we enter the third millennium and the twenty-first century it seems quite clear that the level and degree of environmental degradation and destruction cannot be sustained over the longer term without dire consequences for human and other animal species, and the ecosystems on which all depend. A veritable explosion in the human population, the pollution of air and water, the over-fishing of the oceans, the destruction of tropical and temperate rain forests, the extinction of entire species, the depletion of the ozone layer, the build-up of greenhouse gases, global warming, desertification, wind and water erosion of precious topsoil, the disappearance of valuable farmland and wilderness for 'development' – these and many other interrelated phenomena provide the backdrop and justification for the 'greening' of much of modern political thinking.

The task of outlining and summarizing the state of green political philosophy is made more difficult because there is as yet no agreement among 'green' political thinkers. Indeed there is, at present, no definitive 'green political philosophy' as such. The environmental or green movement is diverse and disparate, and appears in different shades of green. These range from 'light green' conservationists to 'dark green' deep ecologists, from ecofeminists to social ecologists, from the militant ecoteurs of Earth First! to the low-keyed gradualists of the Sierra Club and the Nature Conservancy. These groups differ not only over strategy and tactics, but also over fundamental philosophy.

While there is no single, systematically articulated and agreed-upon green political philosophy, however, there are none the less recurring topics, themes, categories and concepts that are surely central to such a political philosophy. These include the idea that humans are part of nature and members of a larger and more inclusive 'biotic community' to which they have obligations or duties. This community includes both human and non-human animals, and the conditions conducive to their survival and flourishing. Such a community consists, moreover, not only of members who are alive but those who are as yet unborn. A green political philosophy values both biological and cultural diversity, and views sustainability as a standard by which to judge the justness of human actions and practices. Exactly how these themes might fit together to form some larger, systematic and coherent whole is still being worked out.

1 **Political philosophy and green political philosophy**
2 **A green theory of value**
3 **Green political agency**
4 **Green economic thought**
5 **Conclusion**

1 Political philosophy and green political philosophy

Green political philosophy is the attempt to think clearly and systematically about the political and ethical aspects of environmental issues and problems. Just as political philosophy is a sub-species of philosophy, so green political philosophy is a sub-species of political philosophy. Political philosophy is the attempt to think systematically about the ethical and political problems that arise in the course of

living together (see POLITICAL PHILOSOPHY, NATURE OF). Green political philosophy is the attempt to think systematically about those problems and prospects as they are reflected and refracted through the lens of an 'ecological' or 'environmental' perspective.

An environmental perspective places the natural environment at the centre of attention and concern. It sees human beings as one of many species, and views all as interdependent and dependent on the integrity, stability and carrying capacity of the ecosystems that sustain human and non-human animals alike. Humans are members of a community whose boundaries are both wider than and different from those of conventional political communities. As Aldo Leopold puts the point in his now-classic *A Sand County Almanac* (1949: 240): 'a land ethic changes the role of *Homo sapiens* from conqueror of the land-community to plain member and citizen of it. It implies respect for his fellow-members, and also respect for the community as such'. An environmental perspective also recognizes that there are natural limits to human activity and endeavour. Thus one may not, for example, extract more energy from an ecosystem than is required to sustain it, that is, without that ecosystem ceasing to function well, or at all. 'Sustainability' thus becomes a standard for assessing the rightness or wrongness of human activities, practices and interventions in natural processes. As Leopold observes: 'A thing is right when it tends to preserve the integrity, stability, and beauty of the biotic community. It is wrong when it tends otherwise' (1949: 260). (Whether this is to commit the 'naturalistic fallacy' of deriving 'ought' from 'is', is discussed in Callicott (1989).)

An environmental or green political philosophy questions a number of conventional philosophical views. It is especially critical of the anthropocentric or 'humanist' bias of much of Western philosophy, that puts human beings at the apex of creation. Whether it is because we humans are created in God's image, or are alone capable of rational thought and speech, or belong (as Kant put it) to the kingdom of ends, we have set ourselves apart from, and above, nature and its myriad species. On the conventional view, nature and non-human animals are means to human ends and endeavours. Many Western (and some non-Western) thinkers have held humans to be superior to 'lesser' creatures and have seen the natural environment as a cornucopia of 'resources' for our use and enjoyment.

If this is the conventional view, then green thinking is, by implication, unconventional. It offers alternative ways of thinking about nature and our species' place in – and responsibility for – the natural world. Much of modern green philosophizing takes the form of a critique of conventional ways of thinking about nature, as a prelude to thinking anew about our species' place in the natural order (see ECOLOGICAL PHILOSOPHY §3). Let us consider several specific ways in which we are asked to think anew about these matters.

2 A green theory of value

The green theory of value holds that the worth of some things does not derive solely from human assessments of their utility or beauty, and still less from their price or market value (see §5 below). Some things have intrinsic value; that is, they are valuable in and of themselves, quite apart from any human estimate of their worth or any value they might have as means to some other end. This is especially true, some greens argue (see for example Goodin 1992: 30–41), of certain natural objects or entities. For example, wilderness *per se* has no instrumental value; indeed, it is often called 'wasteland'. LOCKE put the point well in the second of his *Two Treatises of Government* (1690: para 42): 'land that is left wholly to nature, that hath no improvement or pasturage, tillage, or planting, is called, as indeed it is, waste; and we shall find the benefit of it amount to little more than nothing'. Nor of course is Locke alone in taking this view; he merely articulates a pervasive – and decidedly anthropocentric – view of the value of cultivated versus uncultivated land. Against Locke and other like-minded thinkers, environmentally minded philosophers maintain that wilderness has value in itself, and for the non-human creatures whose haven it is. Likewise, many of these species – the northern spotted owl, for example – have no instrumental or market value; they are not a means to any human end, nor are they sold or traded in any market. And yet all are valuable and worth protecting, for all have a place and a function in their respective ecosystems.

Greens tend to reject, with widely varying degrees of rigour, the anthropocentric view that human needs and wants supply the only standard of value or worth. They opt instead for one or another version of the biocentric view that the health and wellbeing of the biotic community – for example, an ecosystem and the myriad species it sustains – takes precedence over any of its individual members. This amounts to a conception of value that is both naturalistic and holistic; that is, it takes nature – and not one of its creatures, namely man – as the source and measure of value; and it views all creatures as part of a larger, life-sustaining whole. Some dark green thinkers, especially those calling themselves 'deep ecologists', say that this new way of thinking requires a radical shift in perspectives – roughly, from a hierarchical pyramid with humans at the apex, to an interdependent web in which humans are but one species amongst many (Devall and Sessions 1985) (see ENVIRONMENTAL ETHICS).

Not all green thinkers agree, however. Indeed, some – including 'social ecologists' such as Murray Bookchin (1990) – are highly critical of any attempt to make *Homo sapiens* merely one species among many. Such a view would, they contend, diminish the value of human beings more than it would re-value nature. And such a view would fail to recognize that, like it or not, human beings, because of their knowledge and technology, have a disproportionate power over nature and its creatures, and therefore disproportionate responsibility for the health and wellbeing of both. To see the human species as co-equal with other species is to be blind to this exceedingly important – and indeed unique – aspect of human existence.

This in turn introduces another 'green' theme: the use and abuse of scientific knowledge and technology. Much of Western thought since the scientific revolution of the seventeenth century has tended to celebrate the increasing power of the human species over nature. Sir Francis Bacon and other seventeenth-century philosophers saw science and technology as means of mastering or dominating nature for human ends (Leiss 1972). Variations on this view can be found among later thinkers. Karl Marx, for one, looked forward to the pacification or 'humanization' of nature which modern science made possible. The productive forces – roughly, natural resources and the technology used to turn them into objects useful to humans – that were developed under capitalism have transformed nature beyond all recognition, and that, Marx thought, was a commendably progressive development (see MARX, K.).

Right and left, capitalist, communist, conservative or liberal, Western political philosophers have for the most part embraced and celebrated the 'conquest' or 'pacification' of nature for human purposes. Green political philosophers have, by contrast, been highly critical of any philosophy that views nature only as a 'resource base' or a means to human ends and is, in consequence, heedless of the conditions conducive to the health and wellbeing of nature's myriad species.

In different ways and with different emphases, green political philosophers generally subscribe to what one might call a 'systemic' or 'ecological' view of value. Some things, as noted already, have intrinsic value as ends in themselves. Others, by contrast, have value by virtue of the contribution they make to a larger whole. The value of such a thing is determined by its place in, and contribution to, some larger

161

functional whole – an ecosystem or (in Leopold's phrase) a biotic community. Thus, for example, certain predator species – for example wolves – have value not only in themselves but because of their function within the ecosystem of which they are an integral part. Wolves cull sick, lame or deformed deer; by preventing the weaker members of the deer population from reproducing, wolves actually benefit that species. And by controlling the deer population wolves protect the larger ecosystem which both share with other species. This green view of value is directly contrary to the conventional view – long established in law and public policy in North America – that wolves and other predator species should be trapped or shot (and bounties paid to trappers and hunters) because predation is cruel, wanton, wasteful and without value to human beings.

But what, exactly, is 'political' about predators and prey, about anthropocentric versus biocentric conceptions of value, and the like? The most obvious answer, of course, is that laws, rules, regulations and government policies on environmental matters must be made on the basis of our beliefs about nature and its creatures. These include laws and public policies concerning mining and forestry, tourism and economic development, land use and property rights, motorway construction, parks and recreation, reforestation, the preservation of wilderness, the protection of endangered species, and many other matters. Some of the most heated and hard-fought political battles of the modern age have been concerned with these and other broadly environmental issues.

These matters are also 'political' in a second, and much older, sense. For politics is concerned (as Aristotle famously put it) with the good life and the conditions conducive to it. But while Aristotle was concerned with the good life as lived by (some) human beings, modern greens cast their net more widely, to include non-human creatures and the biotic communities they share with human beings. And still, in our day as in Aristotle's, what constitutes or counts as the good life is hotly disputed amongst philosophers.

Contemporary political debates and divisions over environmental issues are, as often as not, based on philosophical differences over value (anthropocentric versus biocentric; instrumental versus intrinsic), over what counts as the good life, over the proper place and role of human beings in the natural order, over obligations to non-human creatures and future humans, and so on. A green political philosophy is simply the attempt to articulate and justify a biocentric view of the good life for human beings and for other creatures with whom they share a common planet.

What will count as the good life for fish will of course differ from what counts as the good life for monkeys. But what all creatures share is an interest in a healthy habitat. Fish and frogs have an interest in clean or unpolluted water, monkeys in intact tree canopies, whales in plankton, koala bears in eucalyptus trees, and so on. They need not know or be consciously cognizant that they have an interest in these things in order to actually have an interest, since being aware that one has a need for or interest in X is not a necessary condition for having an interest in X (see NEEDS AND INTERESTS §1).

Humans are of course able to know, as non-human animals are not, what is required to sustain non-human species. This confers upon humans the 'epistemic responsibility' that comes with knowing what members of other species do not or cannot know. Our knowing what conditions are conducive to some species' survival and flourishing confers upon our species an added measure of responsibility. More specifically, it requires that we recognize, and not wantonly disregard, the interest such a species has in the conditions conducive to its survival and flourishing (Johnson 1991, ch. 6). Our ever-expanding knowledge of the natural world brings with it an expanded responsibility to recognize the interests (some greens go further, and say 'rights') of other creatures. And while we may not always be able to promote these interests, we must, as moral and political agents, at least accord them serious consideration (see ANIMALS AND ETHICS).

A green political philosophy expands the circle of value and moral concerns not only spatially, so to speak – to include non-humans – but also temporally, to include generations of human beings who are as yet unborn. A green political philosophy – and a green theory of value in particular – places posterity on a par with people now living. Our distant descendants are our moral equals, their happiness and wellbeing as valuable as our own (see FUTURE GENERATIONS, OBLIGATIONS TO).

3   Green political agency

If the green theory of value sets the ends, the green theory of political agency offers an account of the means to achieve those ends. A theory of agency operates at two levels. The first, and more fundamental, level is individual agency, which specifies the characteristics of individual agents; the second, and derivative, level is that of collective agency, which describes the main features of organizations and institutions within which individual agents work. Taken together, these two features of a theory of agency supply an account of the kinds of actors and institutions that would be required to achieve the ends stipulated by a green theory of value (Goodin 1992, ch. 4). Two questions are particularly pertinent. The first is: what kinds of agents – that is, political actors or citizens, consumers and so on – are best suited for realizing green ends? The second is: what kinds of political organizations or institutions, what form of government, and what strategies and tactics are most likely to implement green values?

First, at the individual level: green agents or political actors must be motivated by a love of and respect for the natural world, of which they are a small but important and morally responsible part; their satisfactions and pleasures will not, in the main, be materialistic; their wants will be satisfiable in sustainable ways; they will act in nonviolent ways; their time horizon will typically extend further than their own and one or two adjoining generations.

There is, as some have noted, nothing all that new or novel in this picture of green political agency. It is a picture painted, with many minor variations, by philosophers from Plato onward, of the good man and the good citizen motivated by a vision of the good life (O'Neill 1993, ch. 1). The good life for humans consists of appreciating the superiority of spiritual and intellectual satisfactions over material ones, of getting outside ourselves, as it were, to care about something larger and longer-lived than our own mortal selves. And how better to do this, greens ask, than recognizing our place in, and responsibility to care for, the natural world? (Passmore 1980).

A second set of questions concerns collective agency. What kinds of political organizations, institutions and strategies might best achieve green goals? Here again green thinkers differ amongst themselves. Most greens tend to believe that the most desirable and effective institutions are broadly democratic, decentralized and participatory (see for example Porritt 1984; Dobson 1990). Others are more sceptical, suggesting that solutions to environmental problems require the kind of coordination that can come only through the modern state, its allied agencies and cooperation between states (for example, Ostrom 1991; Goodin 1992). Others are more sceptical and despairing still, arguing that environmental crises are apt to be so numerous, so pervasive and so severe as to require the harsh interventions of an authoritarian, hierarchical, and not necessarily democratic, state (for example Heilbroner 1975; Ophuls 1977; Catton 1980). Such dire predictions and prescriptions, in combination with the radical beliefs of some militant environmentalists, have led some critics to suggest that there is a historical, if not a logical, link between green political thought and fascist or Nazi-like political practice (Bramwell 1989; Pois 1986).

This last criticism relies for its force on a single historical case. Certainly it is true that some Nazis did indeed embrace green themes, values, beliefs and attitudes not unlike those held by some amongst the more militant and mystical greens (nature goddess worship, a marked hostility toward the natural sciences and so on). And this fact should give self-critical and reflective greens some pause. But it does not follow, of course, that anyone who subscribes to green values is a Nazi. To claim otherwise is analogous to arguing that: 'Nazis loved dogs; therefore dog-lovers are Nazis.'

A more serious set of questions concerns the shape and structure of green political institutions. For example, are the interest-group politics of Western liberal democracy well-suited to achieving environmental ends? Ought greens to organize themselves into parties and pressure groups? If so, should they nominate candidates for election to public office and lobby on behalf of their green agenda? Or should greens remain a broad-based movement, aloof from party politics and pressure-group tactics?

Such questions admit of no easy answers and are hotly debated amongst greens. In two-party systems such as the USA, third parties have little hope of success, and the best bet might be to try to influence the platforms and policies of the major parties. In multi-party parliamentary systems, by contrast, it might be more rational to organize green political parties – as has been done in the UK and Germany, for example, albeit without notable electoral success.

Some of the more militant greens hold that conventional party politics will not suffice and that direct action – civil disobedience, protest marches and demonstrations, even 'ecotage' or 'monkey-wrenching' – is required (see CIVIL DISOBEDIENCE §2). Such action is politically and morally justifiable, its defenders say, if it is nonviolent. Thus, for example, motorway construction and the destruction of wildlife habitat may be slowed or stopped by nonviolent civil disobedience. By drawing public attention to such issues, protestors hope to educate or 'raise the consciousness' of their fellow citizens so as to put pressure on their political representatives, planners and policy makers. Some more militant green activists advocate such tactics as monkey-wrenching (the disabling of machinery), the destruction of surveyors' stakes, the 'spiking' of old-growth trees to prevent their being cut. The arguments for and against such measures have been a lively topic of political and philosophical debate amongst environmentalists (Goodin 1992: 133–5).

Arguments about strategies, tactics, and institutions are arguments about agency, both individual and collective, and constitute an important aspect of green political philosophy.

4 Green economic thought

A green view of economic relations is an integral part of a green political philosophy, its theory of value, and its theory of individual and collective agency. In the main, green economic thinking represents a critique of, and a challenge to, much of conventional market-based economic thought – especially in so far as such thinking forms the basis and justification for present-day policies regarding energy and other broadly environmental issues.

What is wrong with modern economic thought, green critics contend, is that it knows the price of everything and the value of nothing. Or, perhaps more accurately, it is mistaken in assuming without argument that everything has a price, even if some things are not actually traded in any market. Three features of green economic thought merit special mention. The first is its critique of, and alternative to, the practice of assigning 'shadow prices' to goods not traded in markets. The second concerns the practice of 'discounting' the welfare of future generations via a 'social discount rate'. And the third is the green questioning of the use of cost–benefit analysis in making and justifying political decisions and policies.

Conventional economic thinking translates the question, 'What is the value of X?' into another question, 'What is the price of X?' That is, what would X be worth in monetary terms, if it were to be traded in a market? Now clearly, since some things are not bought and sold, some way must be found for determining their price. Some economists contend that so-called 'shadow prices' can be assigned to such goods as clean air, scenic beauty, the preservation of a particular species, and so on. The hypothetical price is determined by asking people what they would be 'willing to pay' to (for example) preserve the Grand Canyon or to prevent the extinction of an entire species of plant or animal. By this means it should be possible to ascertain the economic value of these and other 'environmental' goods.

The problem with the practice of shadow pricing, say critics (see for example Sagoff 1988), is that it cheapens things that are beyond price, that is to say, literally priceless. To ask what someone would be willing to pay for being treated with respect would thereby demean the very idea of kindness and respect. Some things actually lose value (and, arguably, all meaning) when they are bought and sold. Such is the case, critics argue, when a price, even a hypothetical one, is put on species, ecosystems and other natural entities.

A second, and scarcely less controversial, practice is that of discounting the wellbeing of future generations by means of the social rate of discount. Roughly, the idea is this: just as individuals discount their own future, so too does an entire society at some time discount its future members' welfare at all later times. And, just as it is rational for individuals to discount their own future wellbeing, so it is rational for one generation to discount the welfare of future generations.

The green critique of social discounting is easily summarized. It is one thing to discount one's own future wellbeing; it is a morally much more questionable matter to discount other people's wellbeing. I am not entitled, rationally or morally, to discount your future wellbeing at my personal rate of discount. And yet that is precisely what defenders of social discounting attempt to do. One's moral worth does not vary according to one's place in the temporal order of succession. I am not entitled to discount your wellbeing, whether you are my contemporary or my very distant descendant. The practice of social discounting, its critics claim, works to the distinct disadvantage of future generations and is clearly unjust (Cowen and Parfit 1992; Cowen 1992; O'Neill 1993, ch. 4).

The practice of social discounting, when combined with other economic tools or techniques, such as cost–benefit analysis, further disadvantages future people (O'Neill 1993, chs 4 and 5). Consider, by way of example, the claim that nuclear power is preferable to other alternatives because it has a higher benefit-to-cost ratio. In practice, however, the benefits – including access to cheap and plentiful electricity – accrue to those now living, whilst the costs will be borne by future people, in the form of increased risk of radiation exposure. To measure the benefits over the short term and the costs over the longer term is systematically to disadvantage future people.

It is important to note that this is not an argument against cost–benefit analysis *per se* or in principle, but against taking a too-constricted time horizon over which to measure costs and benefits. If the wellbeing of future people is not discounted, and the benefits not enjoyed exclusively by one generation while the costs are borne by another, then cost–benefit analysis can be a useful tool of analysis, even for environmentally minded policy analysts, legislators and concerned citizens.

Greens tend to be critical of conventional economic thinking, and particularly of the view that market allocations of valued goods are always fair or necessarily just. This does not mean, however, that all greens are therefore socialists of one or another stripe (although some certainly are). Green economic thought is at present more critical than constructive – more articulate about what is wrong with modern market economics than what alternative system might be devised (see MARKET, ETHICS OF THE).

5 Conclusion

The task of a green political philosophy is twofold. It is critical in that it aims to expose and criticize the flaws, fallacies and contradictions that lurk in conventional ways of thinking about human beings and their proper place in the natural world. And it is constructive in that it aims to sketch the contours and outline the institutions of a society that values the natural world, practises sustainability and concerns itself with the longer-term consequences of present-day policies and practices. Much of the critical groundwork has now been laid, but the task of constructing a coherent, systematic and persuasive political philosophy has only just begun, and remains a task for the twenty-first century.

See also: ECOLOGY; ENVIRONMENTAL ETHICS

References and further reading

Berry, W. (1981) *The Gift of Good Land*, San Francisco, CA: North Point Press. (A thoughtful, provocative and beautifully written book about agriculture, conservation, and human community and responsibility.)

* Bookchin, M. (1990) *Remaking Society: Pathways to a Green Future*, Boston, MA: South End Press. (A philosophical and programmatic statement by a leading social ecologist.)

* Bramwell, A. (1989) *Ecology in the 20th Century: A History*, New Haven, CT: Yale University Press. (A very critical history.)

* Callicott, J.B. (1989) *In Defense of the Land Ethic*, Albany, NY: State University of New York Press. (A collection of essays on issues and topics deriving from Leopold's 'land ethic'. Includes an account of American Indian environmental ethics.)

* Catton, W.R. (1980) *Overshoot: The Ecological Basis of Revolutionary Change*, Urbana, IL: University of Illinois Press. (Argues that overpopulation threatens to exceed or 'overshoot' the earth's carrying capacity.)

* Cowen, T. (1992) 'Consequentialism Implies a Zero rate of Intergenerational Discount', in P. Laslett and J.S. Fishkin (eds), *Justice Between Age Groups and Generations*, 'Philosophy, Politics, and Society', series 6, New Haven, CT, and London: Yale University Press, ch. 8. (Argues on consequentialist

grounds against applying any social rate of discount.)

* Cowen, T. and Parfit, D. (1992) 'Against the Social Discount Rate', in P. Laslett and J.S. Fishkin (eds), *Justice Between Age Groups and Generations*, 'Philosophy, Politics, and Society', series 6, New Haven, CT, and London: Yale University Press, ch. 7. (A critique of the very idea of a social rate of discount.)

* Devall, B. and Sessions, G. (1985) *Deep Ecology*, Salt Lake City, UT: Peregrine Smith Books. (A wide-ranging critique of anthropocentrism and a defence of a 'deep ecology' ethic.)

* Dobson, A. (1990) *Green Political Thought*, London: Unwin Hyman. (A useful introduction.)

Foreman, D. (1993) *Confessions of an Eco-Warrior*, New York: Crown. (A passionate and sometimes amusing analysis of a number of issues by a leading radical environmentalist.)

* Goodin, R.E. (1992) *Green Political Theory*, Cambridge: Polity Press. (A clear and systematic account of what a rationally reconstructed green political philosophy might look like.)

* Heilbroner, R.L. (1975) *An Inquiry into the Human Prospect*, New York: W.W. Norton; revised 1975. (An economist's sombre inquiry into the trends and tendencies that are likely to lead to environmental disaster and political repression.)

* Johnson, L.E. (1991) *A Morally Deep World: An Essay on Moral Significance and Environmental Ethics*, Cambridge: Cambridge University Press. (Argues that animal species and ecosystems have morally considerable interest that humans must take into account.)

* Leiss, W. (1972) *The Domination of Nature*, New York: George Braziller. (Explores the theme of the domination or 'conquest' of nature in Western thought.)

* Leopold, A. (1949) *A Sand County Almanac*, Oxford and New York: Oxford University Press; repr. New York: Ballantine Books, 1970. (The concluding section – 'The Land Ethic' – is widely considered to be a modern classic of environmental thinking.)

* Locke, J. (1690) *Two Treatises of Government*, repr. Cambridge: Cambridge University Press, 1992. (Propounds a theory of property according to which ownership and value are determined by the labour expended in obtaining and transforming land and other natural goods.)

* O'Neill, J. (1993) *Ecology, Policy and Politics: Human Well-being and the Natural World*, London: Routledge. (A sophisticated and wide-ranging analysis of a variety of issues ranging from green value theory to green economics.)

* Ophuls, W. (1977) *Ecology and the Politics of Scarcity:*

Prologue to a Theory of the Steady State, San Francisco, CA: W.H. Freeman. (A defence of no-growth or 'steady-state' economy and society.)

* Ostrom, E. (1991) *Governing the Commons*, Cambridge: Cambridge University Press. (Analyses strategies for bringing those resources we have in common under rational and responsible collective control.)

Partridge, E. (ed.) (1981) *Responsibilities to Future Generations*, Buffalo, NY: Prometheus Books. (An excellent anthology.)

* Passmore, J. (1980) *Man's Responsibility for Nature*, London: Duckworth, 2nd edn. (Defends the view that humans have a special species-specific responsibility to protect and preserve the natural environment.)

* Pois, R.A. (1986) *National Socialism and the Religion of Nature*, London: Croom Helm. (A historical exploration of 'environmental' themes in Nazi theory and practice.)

* Porritt, J. (1984) *Seeing Green: The Politics of Ecology Explained*, Oxford: Blackwell. (A useful primer on the political theory and practice of the green movement.)

* Sagoff, M. (1988) *The Economy of the Earth: Philosophy, Law, and the Environment*, Cambridge: Cambridge University Press. (A wide-ranging critique of conventional 'economic' thinking about environmental issues.)

Worster, D. (1994) *Nature's Economy: A History of Ecological Ideas*, Cambridge: Cambridge University Press, 2nd edn. (A useful survey of key themes and thinkers.)

TERENCE BALL

GREEN, THOMAS HILL (1836–82)

Green was a prominent Oxford idealist philosopher, who criticized both the epistemological and ethical implications of the dominant empiricist and utilitarian theories of the time. He contended that experience could not be explained merely as the product of sensations acting on the human mind. Like Kant, Green argued that knowledge presupposes certain a priori categories, such as substance, causation, space and time, which enable us to structure our understanding of empirical reality. Physical objects and even the most simple feelings are only intelligible as relations of ideas constituted by human consciousness. However, unlike Kant, he did not draw the conclusion that things in themselves are consequently unknowable. Rather, he argued that reality itself is ultimately spiritual, the product of an eternal consciousness operating within both the world and human reason. Green adopted a similarly anti-naturalist and holistic position in ethics, in which desires are seen as orientated towards the realization of the good – both within the individual and in society at large. In politics, this led him to criticize the laissez-faire individualist liberalism of Herbert Spencer and, to a lesser extent, of J.S. Mill, and to advocate a more collectivist liberalism in which the state seeks to promote the positive liberty of its members.

1 Life and works
2 Critique of empiricism and naturalism
3 Ethics and politics

1 Life and works

Green was born in Birkin, Yorkshire, on 7 April 1836, the fourth child of the Reverend Valentine Green. His evangelical religious views played a profound part in his later philosophy, alienating the orthodox but having a great appeal for those seeking a rational basis for Christianity that was compatible both with Darwinism and the new historical scholarship, which were then calling traditional beliefs into question, and which issued in a broadly humanist social ethic. He was educated first by his father and then, from the age of 14, at Rugby School, where the future Cambridge philosopher Henry Sidgwick was also a pupil. He went up to Balliol in 1855, coming under the influence of Benjamin Jowett, who introduced him to German as well as Greek philosophy. He took a First in Greats in 1859, and was elected to a college fellowship the following year. In 1863 he refused the editorship of the *Times of India* and in 1864 was an unsuccessful candidate for the chair in philosophy at the University of St Andrews, largely due to his religious opinions. He served as an assistant to the Schools Inquiry Commission in 1865 and 1866, and was later involved in the founding of Oxford School for Boys. From 1866, he became heavily involved in college business and was the first Tutor not to be enrolled in holy orders. Together with Jowett, he played a prominent role in the university reforms that were to orientate the curriculum towards the needs of modern society and to professionalize academia. Green has been described as the first professional philosopher in the modern sense, and he influenced the emergence of a new kind of hard-working undergraduate, who viewed a degree as a qualification for a career, with Greats in particular becoming a training for politics or the imperial civil service.

The Philosophical Works of David Hume, edited with T.H. Gross, appeared in 1874–5. Green's long introduction contained his critique of empiricism and naturalism in LOCKE and HUME, an argument that was extended to J.S. Mill, Spencer and Lewes in subsequent articles. He had failed to get elected as Waynflete Professor in 1867, but in 1878 became Whyte's Professor of Moral Philosophy. He took his lecturing duties seriously and his best known books, the *Prolegomena to Ethics* (1883) and the *Lectures on the Principles of Political Obligation* (1886), were both published posthumously on the basis of his lecture notes. Many of his other essays, including the important 'On the Different Senses of "Freedom" as Applied to Will and to the Moral Progress of Man', similarly originated as lectures and likewise only appeared with the publication of his collected works after his death.

Green played an active part in radical liberal politics, supporting John Bright and the cause of the North in the American Civil War. He was a prominent member of the temperance movement from 1872, and in 1876 was the first Oxford academic to be elected to the city council as a representative of the town rather than the University. Together with his wife Charlotte Symonds, whom he married in 1871, he participated in the University extension movement and in attempts to open up higher education to women. His lecture *Liberal Legislation and Freedom of Contract* (1881) has often been taken as providing the philosophic basis for the shift from *laissez-faire* to social liberalism at the turn of the century. He died prematurely on 26 March 1882.

2 Critique of empiricism and naturalism

Green first presented his own theory in terms of a critique of the native empiricist tradition of Locke, Hume and their nineteenth-century followers. For Green, the heart of the empiricist project lies in the contention that ideas arise from sensation. According to this thesis, at least as Green understood it, a distinction is made between those 'simple' ideas that the mind passively receives through the sensory mechanisms, and 'complex' ideas that result from reflection upon these basic notions and the combinations which the mind performs between them. The crux of Green's criticism consisted in denying the validity of this distinction. Drawing on Kant, he claimed that what he calls 'formal conceptions', such as subject and object, or cause and effect, cannot be derived from simpler ideas stemming directly from sensation because even our most basic notions presuppose these more complex concepts. For example, knowledge of cause and effect cannot be acquired (as Green held that Locke maintained) through reflection on the circumstances under which things

come to exist, because the very idea of an external thing can only be derived from sensations if we already conceive of them as being caused by outer objects. A conception of causation is therefore intrinsic to our knowledge of those very objects from which we are supposed to obtain it. Green found additional evidence of the circularity of the empiricist argument in the tendency to equivocate over whether simple ideas are the result of mere feelings or feelings that already have certain properties built into them, such as notions of space or blueness. If the latter, then the empiricist has simply assumed what needs to be explained. If the former, then there remains the difficulty that the simple ideas from which we allegedly develop our more complex ideas seem to require such notions for us to be able to conceive of them in the first place.

From this critique, Green drew the conclusion that conscious experience could not be accounted for in terms of a succession of passively received feelings that act upon us in much the same way as certain climatic or chemical changes act on a plant and cause it to pass through a number of different physical states. Mind or consciousness had to be ascribed an active role from the beginning. On this view, feelings or sensations can only be experienced in the relevant sense of constituting knowledge if they are present to a self-conscious mind that is distinct from them and is capable of relating them to each other. Green insisted that one could not even conceive of a present and immediate sensation without relating it to other general notions of immediacy, presentness and sensation that denied its particular character.

This emphasis on relations is vital to Green's argument and was later taken up by F.H. Bradley (see BRADLEY §5). For Green, 'formal conceptions' or any kind of general notion are essentially relations. However, this does not imply that there are ideas or objects that exist independently of relations. Thought does not simply relate things that are already there. His thesis is essentially holistic, in which a single self-consciousness mind is regarded as constituting the world as part of a unified system of mutually related and entailed elements. Thus, particulars always stand in relation to something else, and are real only in so far as they form part of those relations. Likewise, general categories exist only in so far as they comprise relations. This inter-relatedness of universal and particular is generally known as the doctrine of the concrete universal.

Much of Green's argument can be characterized as broadly Kantian. Indeed, Green identified his principle of consciousness with Kant's synthetic unity of apperception. However, he went beyond Kant in denying that there are 'things-in-themselves' that mind plays no role in constituting (see KANT, I. §5). Green believed that in this respect Kant had failed to take his critique of Humean empiricism far enough. He held that Kant regarded the noumenal world as totally inaccessible to thought, and charged this position with incoherence on the grounds that such a world would be unknowable and so it would be impossible to say whether it existed and hence was antithetical to thought in the first place. Denial of the noumenal world, however, raises the problem of solipsism. If mind constitutes reality, does that mean that there are as many worlds as there are individual minds? Or do our individual minds somehow collaborate together to create the phenomenal world? Green rejected both these suggestions to argue that reality itself is the product of a single, eternal self-conscious mind which manifests itself, albeit incompletely, in individual human minds. Green's religious beliefs play a major role in his argument at this point – in particular, the view that the essence of Christianity is that human beings partake in some measure in the divine spirit. As we saw, Green contended that this single eternal Mind unifies the whole of reality, relating every part to every other part. No single element exists or can be known, therefore, except in relation to everything else. As a consequence, human knowledge will always be incomplete, although for the divine consciousness, which is omniscient, all relations are known and hence, Green believed, necessary.

3   Ethics and politics

Green's ethics follows on from his critique of naturalism. Here his target is utilitarianism, which he regarded as intimately bound up with empiricist epistemology and a hedonist psychology. A utilitarian morality of this kind holds that human beings are motivated by the pursuit of pleasure and the avoidance of pain. However, Green argued that even those forms of happiness that originated in purely animal wants or impulses could only become objects of conscious human desire if they are related to an ideal of self-perfection describing the sort of person one ought to be and a corresponding conception of the good. We cannot derive our view of morality from pleasure, any more than we can acquire other forms of knowledge from different kinds of sensations. The experience of pleasure presupposes notions of good and bad in exactly the same way as different sensations are bound up with other 'formal conceptions'.

Green maintained that we can only conceive of and actively pursue self-perfection within a society, for our sense of personal identity arises out of our relations with others, for instance in the various professional, familial and other social roles which we perform or to which we aspire. As a result, the goals which we come to pursue will be similarly tied up with how we relate to others. The only good that can foster and preserve the relations between individuals is a common good which is non-competitive in nature and the attainment of which by each promotes that of everyone else. Such a good cannot be conceived in material terms but is rather a state of mind or character. Toleration provides an example of what Green had in mind, since tolerance is a good that can only be understood as a social relation between two or more persons, and each individual's aiming to be tolerant fosters the ability of everyone else to be so.

The origins of this argument are firmly located in his metaphysics and his holistic account of reality as a system of necessary relations. It is important to stress that Green never treats society as a collective subject. He regarded any suggestion that society and the common good might be distinct from or superior to its individual members and their particular goods as being as meaningless as attempts to establish the converse.

Green's conception of positive liberty, his main contribution to political philosophy, is closely tied to his ethics. Green associated a purely negative conception of freedom, as the absence of external physical constraints, with a naturalistic view of human beings as driven by innate impulses and appetites which they sought to satisfy in the pursuit of various material goods. As we have seen, he disputed this conception of human motivation. He also believed that it issued in an atomistic and ultimately incoherent view of society, since it failed to offer a satisfactory account of social relations. Negative liberty was the freedom of Hobbes's state of nature, of the war of all against all. Positive freedom, in contrast, was the attempt to secure the conditions for the self-realization of all. It was orientated towards a common, moral good, rather than purely individual, material goods. Green noted that both negative liberties and certain material conditions formed preconditions for the attainment of this moral freedom. A moral action had to issue from a free will and be voluntarily performed on Green's somewhat Kantian account, so that individuals needed to be protected from undue coercion by others. However, he also claimed that some obstacles were insurmountable by individual action alone, so that public education and welfare legislation were also necessary.

In this way, Green's ethical theory fed into a progressive liberal politics, and he defended measures such as the Factory Acts, regulating conditions at work, on these grounds. He argued that properly understood freedom of contract entailed a mutual recognition of positive rights guaranteeing certain standards of safety, remuneration and limiting hours rather than just the negative right to sell and hire labour freely. He rejected both the minimal state of *laissez-faire* liberals such as Spencer and the conception of the state as the monopoly holder of force, which he associated with Hobbes and J. Austin (see LIBERALISM §1). Rather, he argued that the state's role consists in coordinating the complex relations between the various institutions and individuals that comprise it. Our obligation to the state is moral and stems from a consciousness of its function in promoting certain common ends. Rights are neither natural properties of individuals nor positive enactments of the sovereign power, but grow out of a mutual awareness of those common goods necessary for the fullest degree of self-realization by all. He held that our understanding of the nature and purposes of the state has steadily broadened, as our consciousness of the common good and the resulting rights stemming from the relations between individuals has developed. Some governments may move more slowly than others in responding to this greater awareness among the people, and in such cases civil disobedience or even revolution might be justified. Green used these arguments to support the North in the American Civil War, Giuseppe Mazzini's movement for national liberation in Italy, and the campaign for suffrage reform in Britain.

Critics, such as Isaiah BERLIN , have complained of two major problems with Green's advocacy of positive liberty. First, they have argued that there are a number of different moral goals that it may be rational to pursue and these are not always compatible or commensurable with each other. Second, they have noted that the welfare goods advocated by Green are capable of being objects of competition. Education, for example, can give someone a positional advantage when it comes to getting a given job. Both these objections suggest that social relations are liable to be less harmonious than Green supposes and that an attempt to coordinate all forms of self-realization will either prove incoherent or totalitarian. Green disputed the validity of these sorts of criticism at both a metaphysical and a practical level. While he asserted that ultimately all forms of genuine human self-perfection prove mutually supportive, he insisted that full consciousness of these relations was only accessible to God. However, he did believe that human beings were capable of making progressive steps towards such a perfected state. Nevertheless, moves in this direction always had to come from below, since morality could not be imposed.

It is undeniable that an optimistic teleology underlies his thesis, in which the widening area of state action and social cooperation results from the gradual diffusion of reason and self-consciousness among the general public. The ambivalences of Green's position come out clearly when the people failed to move in the direction he desired. One prime example is temperance reform, for which Green ultimately abandoned schemes for voluntary abstinence and advocated the compulsory prohibition of alcohol.

Green's political writings had an important impact at the time, influencing a whole generation of British liberal politicians and theorists, such as L.T. Hobhouse and J. Hobson. His arguments, however, are deeply embedded in a metaphysics the religious assumptions of which came to seem increasingly dated and questionable.

See also: EMPIRICISM; FREEDOM AND LIBERTY §3; HEGELIANISM §5; NATURALISM IN ETHICS

List of works

Green, T.H. (1883) *Prolegomena to Ethics*, ed. A.C. Bradley, Oxford: Clarendon Press. (This book is not contained in the complete works.)

—— (1997) *Works*, ed. P. Nicholson, 5 vols, Bristol: Thoemmes Press. (Volumes 1–3 reproduce the Nettleship edition of the Works, volume 4 the 1883 edition of the Prolegomena to Ethics, which was not included in Nettleship's Works, and volume 5 reprints all previously uncollected published material, including letters and selections from Green's papers, plus a new bibliography and an introduction by the editor.)

—— (1885–8) *The Works of Thomas Hill Green*, ed. R.L. Nettleship, London: Longman's, Green, 3 vols. (Volume 3 contains a valuable 'Memoir' by the editor.)

—— (1986) *Lectures on the Principles of Political Obligation and Other Writings*, ed. P. Harris and J. Morrow, Cambridge: Cambridge University Press. (The definitive edition of the *Lectures*, corrected against the original manuscript, together with extracts from the *Prolegomena* that have been similarly checked, and some previously unpublished essays and other important political articles.)

References and further reading

Bellamy, R.P. (1990) 'T.H. Green and the Morality of Victorian Liberalism', in R.P. Bellamy (ed.) *Victorian Liberalism: Nineteenth-Century Political Thought and Practice*, London: Routledge. (Locates Green's thought in the context of his times, arguing that he was not so innovative or radical as is often thought.)

—— (1992) 'T.H. Green, J.S. Mill, and Isaiah Berlin on the Nature of Liberty and Liberalism', in H. Gross and R. Harrison (eds), *Jurisprudence: Cambridge Essays*, Oxford: Clarendon Press. (Defends Green against the criticisms of Berlin.)

* Berlin, I. (1969) 'Two Concepts of Liberty', in *Four Essays on Liberty*, Oxford: Oxford University Press. (Explicit criticism of Green is found on 133 and 150, but he associates him with the errors of the concept of positive liberty in general.)

Hylton, P. (1990) *Russell, Idealism and the Emergence of Analytical Philosophy*, Oxford: Clarendon Press, ch. 1. (A fine account of Green's critique of naturalism, which forms the basis of §2 above.)

Nicholson, P.P. (1990) *The Political Philosophy of the British Idealists*, Cambridge: Cambridge University Press, Studies 2–5. (A critical defence of various aspects of Green's political thought.)

Pucelle, J. (1961, 1965) *La Nature et l'esprit dans la philosophie de T.H. Green* (Nature and Mind in the Philosophy of T.H. Green), Paris and Louvain: Beatrice Nauwellaerts Editions, 2 vols. (The most extensive study of Green's epistemology.)

Richter, M. (1964) *The Politics of Conscience: T.H. Green and his Times*, London: Weidenfeld & Nicolson. (A classic work of intellectual history, particularly good at tracing the origins of Green's views to his evangelical background.)

Thomas, G. (1987) *The Moral Philosophy of T.H. Green*, Oxford: Clarendon Press. (A recent analysis and defence of Green's ethics.)

Vincent, A. (ed.) (1986) *The Philosophy of T.H. Green*, Aldershot: Gower. (Contains articles covering all aspects of Green's activity and thought, together with a very useful bibliography.)

RICHARD BELLAMY

GREGORY OF RIMINI
(*c*.1300–58)

Gregory of Rimini was for a long time known primarily for his doctrine of predestination and for his notion of 'the complexly signifiable' in the semantics of propositions. However, he also provides an interesting alternative to William of Ockham among medieval nominalists. His chief work was his Lectura super primum et secundum Sententiarum *(Lectures on Books I and II of Peter Lombard's* Sentences*).*

Born in Rimini in Italy, Gregory began studies in theology at Paris in 1323 and attained the rank of lector there in 1329. He then taught at Augustinian houses of study in Bologna, Padua and Perugia, before returning to Paris in 1341 or 1342 to prepare for his lectures on the *Sentences* of Peter LOMBARD as a baccalaureus from 1342–3 or 1343–4. Gregory returned to his native Rimini as regent of the Augustinian *studium* (house of studies) in 1351 and taught there until 1357. He replaced Thomas of Strasbourg as General Prior of the Augustinians in 1357, but died a year later.

Gregory's chief work was his *Lectura super primum et secundum Sententiarum* (Lectures on Books I and II of Peter Lombard's *Sentences*). Through it he helped introduce to Paris many new English philosophers, including WILLIAM OF OCKHAM, Walter CHATTON, Adam WODEHAM, Richard Fitzralph and, to a lesser degree, Thomas BRADWARDINE, Richard KILVINGTON, William HEYTESBURY, Thomas Buckingham and Robert of Halifax. He had encountered the works of some of these authors during his many years of teaching in Italy, and of others during his preparatory year in Paris. Gregory's own doctrinal positions were carried back to the Augustinian house of studies at Oxford in the 1350s by John Klenkok. His philosophical works, *Tractatus de intensione et remissione formarum corporalium* (Treatise on the Intension and Remission of Corporeal Forms) and *De quattuor virtutibus cardinalium* (On the Four Cardinal Virtues) are complemented by a number of scriptural commentaries, theological treatises and his administrative records.

Although Gregory was portrayed by Joannes Aventinus (John Thurmayr) in 1517 as 'the standard-bearer of the nominalists', some historians have considered him to be a leader of the anti-nominalists and promoter of the condemnations touching John Mirecourt in 1347. To evaluate the tag of nominalism is a complex affair, especially in the fourteenth century, when it swelled from a denial of real entities corresponding to our universal concepts to include a dozen other points. The most recent editors of his *Lectura* label him 'a nominalistic alternative to William of Ockham'.

Gregory is known for his staunch allegiance to AUGUSTINE: he criticizes Peter AUREOL in particular for imprecise Augustinian quotations and argues against Thomas AQUINAS and for the intellectual knowledge of singulars by citing chapter after chapter of Augustine's *De libero arbitrio* (On Free Choice). Experience plays a very strong role in Gregory's philosophy as it did in Augustine's, since there are many things that we experience both within and outside ourselves that we cannot deny even though we also cannot explain them in terms of universal scientific knowledge. The intellect, according to Gregory, knows singulars directly before it knows universals: 'a universal is not some thing outside the mind but is rather a concept created (*fictus*) or formed by the soul that is common to many things' (*Lectura*, I, 396). This *fictum* theory of the concept was defended earlier by HENRY OF HARCLAY and William of Ockham, but it was challenged by Walter Chatton and seemingly abandoned by Ockham in his later works.

Gregory argues against Ockham that the object of science cannot be identified as the conclusion of a demonstration. Yet he does not agree with Walter Chatton's claim that things outside the mind are the objects of science:

> since if this were the case, many sciences would be about contingent things that could be different than they are, whereas for strict science the object must be eternal and necessary. Every being, however, besides God is contingent and not necessary. If things outside the mind were the objects of the sciences, then many sciences, physical and geometrical, and many others, would be about things other than God, and therefore about contingent things.

> (*Lectura* I, 6)

Following the lead of Adam Wodeham, Gregory found a middle path between the positions of Ockham and Chatton and located the eternal and necessary knowledge of science in the total over-all meaning or significate (the *complexe significabile*) of the conclusion of a syllogism. Thus, the total significate of the proposition 'God is eternal' is neither the proposition 'God is eternal', nor God, nor eternity, but the *dictum* (which might be expressed as God's-being-eternal). The total significate of 'God is eternal' or the state of affairs expressible as God's-being-eternal is the object of our scientific knowledge (see LOGIC, MEDIEVAL; WODEHAM, A.).

Gregory accepts with little alteration many claims of Ockham's natural philosophy. Gregory, like Ockham, employs a razor to establish that motion, time and sudden change are not distinct and definable entities in themselves. 'Sudden change', for example, does not signify some thing over and above the permanent things involved in the change, that is, over and above the subject which is changed and the form gained which the subject did not have previously, or the form lost which it previously had. Gregory stresses the contingency of the natural world. Since God is the only necessary being, all creatures and thus the whole created universe are contingent. The laws of nature have been freely chosen by God and have no absolute necessity of their own (see NATURAL PHILO-SOPHY, MEDIEVAL).

If Gregory welcomes a great deal of Ockham's logic, scientific theory and physics, especially as adjusted by the latter's pupil, Adam Wodeham, his anthropology is quite critical of these Englishmen and he accuses both of being modern Pelagians in their appreciation of man (see PELAGIANISM). He stresses the weakness of fallen human nature both in our ability to know what we should choose and what we should shun and in our ability to carry out our will in the proper direction even if we had the right knowledge.

In his scientific methodology, in his interest in questions of logic and language and in his natural philosophy, Gregory brings a new form of Augustinianism to Paris and to the Augustinian Order elsewhere. The form of Augustinianism initiated in the late thirteenth century by GILES OF ROME was not long-lasting and was without great difficulty replaced by Gregory's stronger, English-influenced approach to philosophical and theological questions.

See also: AUGUSTINIANISM; AUREOL, P.; CHATTON, W.; WILLIAM OF OCKHAM; WODEHAM, A.

List of works

Gregory of Rimini [Gregorius Ariminensis] *Lectura super Primum et Secundum Sententiarum* (Lectures of Books I and II of Peter Lombard's *Sentences*), ed. A. Damasus Trapp *et al.*, Berlin: de Gruyter, 1979–87. (These volumes replace the Venice edition of 1522, reprinted St Bonaventure, NY: The Franciscan Institute, 1952. The introduction to Volume I provides a description of the manuscripts for Book I, the principles of the edition and the distinction between the final text and the additions, which paradoxically are pre-Parisian elements that are subtracted in the Parisian *Lectura*. The introduction to Volume IV provides a description of the manuscripts for Book II, a comment on marginal notes and sources and doctrinal reflections called 'Themes and Problems'.)

References and further reading

Courtenay, W.J. (1978) *Adam Wodeham: An Introduction to his Life and Writings*, Leiden: Brill, 123–33. (Provides the *curriculum vitae* of Gregory.)

dal Pra, M. (1956) 'La Teoria del 'significato totale' della proposizione nel pensiero di Gregorio da Rimini' (The Theory of the 'Complete Significate' of the Proposition in the Thought of Gregory of Rimini), *Rivista critica di storia della filosofia* XI: 287–311. (On the significate of a proposition.)

de Muralt, A. (1991) *L'enjeu de la philosophie médiévale* (What is at Stake in Medieval Philosophy), Studien und Texte zur Geistesgeschichte des Mittelalters XXIV, Leiden: Brill. (Gregory's theory concerning the object of knowledge.)

Eckermann, W. (1978) *Wort und Wirklichkeit: Das Sprachverständnis in der Theologie Gregors von Rimini und sein Weiterwirken in der Augustinerschule, Cassiacum* (Word and Reality: The Understanding of Language in the Theology of Gregory of Rimini and its Effects in Augustinianism), Würzburg: Augustinus-Verlag. (On the theory of language and its relation to reality.)

Gál, G. (1977) 'Adam Wodeham's Question on the *complexe significabile* as the Immediate Object of Scientific Knowledge', *Franciscan Studies* 37: 66–102. (Shows the dependence of Gregory on Adam Wodeham regarding the significate of a proposition.)

Kölmel, W. (1955) 'Von Ockham zur Gabriel Biel. Zur Naturrechtslehre des 14. und 15. Jahrhunderts' (From Ockham to Gabriel Biel: Natural Law Theory in the Fourteenth and Fifteenth Centuries), *Franziskanische Studien* 37: 767–87. (On the influence of Gregory on Gabriel Biel and Suárez concerning natural law.)

Kretzmann, N. (1970) 'Medieval Logicians on the Meaning of the *Propositio*', *The Journal of Philosophy* 67: 767–87. (Discusses the medieval debate on propositions.)

Kretzmann, N., Kenny, A. and Pinborg, J. (eds) (1982) *Cambridge History of Later Medieval Philosophy*, Cambridge: Cambridge University Press. (Passages of interest include G. Nuchelmans on the significate of propositions, 203–6; C. Normore on future contingents, 376–80; and J.E. Murdoch on infinites, 572–3.)

Marmo, C. (1990) 'Gregory of Rimini: *notitia intuitiva*, *species* and Semiotics of Images', in S. Knuuttila, R. Työrinoja and S. Ebbesen (eds) *Knowledge and the Sciences in Medieval Philosophy (Proceedings of the Eighth International Congress of Medieval Philosophy, SIEPM*, Helsinki: Publications of Luther–Agricola Society B 19, II: 257–64. (Conference paper on Gregory's logic and language.)

Leff, G. (1961) *Gregory of Rimini: Tradition and Innovation in Fourteenth Century Thought*, Manchester: Manchester University Press. (Full survey of Gregory's life and works.)

Miccolo, L. (1987) 'L'oggetto della conoscenza scientifica nel Prologo del Commento alle Sentenze di Gregorio da Rimini' (The Object of Scientific Knowledge in the Prologue to Gregory of Rimini's Commentary on the *Sentences*), *Journal Philosophique* 13: 86–109. (Analysis of the opening question of Gregory's prologue to Book I, concerning the object of scientific knowledge.)

Oberman, H.A. (ed.) (1981) *Gregor von Rimini. Werk und Wirkung bis zur Reformation* (Gregory of Rimini: His Work and its Influence on the Reformation), Spätmittelalter und Reformation Texte und Untersuchungen 20, Berlin: de Gruyter, 1–126, 127–94, 241–300. (Passages of interest include M. Schulze, an overview of Gregory's accomplishments, 1–126; V. Marcolino on the so-called 'additions' to Gregory's commentary, 127–94; and V. Wendland on the theory of scientific knowledge, 241–300.)

Paqué, R. (1970) *Das Pariser Nominalistenstatut: Zur Entstehung des Realitätsbegriffs der neuzeitlichen Naturwissenschaft* (The Parisian Statute Regarding Nominalism: the Origin of the Concept of Reality in Modern Natural Science), Berlin: de Gruyter. (Discusses the 1347 Paris condemnations of John Mirecourt, in which Gregory reputedly played a major role.)

Tachau, K.H. (1988) *Vision and Certitude in the Age of Ockham*, Leiden: Brill. (Treats Gregory in passing, especially on pages 357–71 and 373–7.)

Thijssen, J. (1985) 'Het continuum-debat bij Gregorius van Rimini (1300–1358): Wijsbegeerte en theologia in de 14de eeuw' (Gregory of Rimini (1300–58) the Debate over the Continuum: Science and Theology in the Fourteenth Century), *Algemeen Nederlands Tijdschrift voor Wijsbegeerte* 77: 109–19. (A detailed study of Gregory's discussion concerning the nature of a continuum.)

Trapp, A.D. (1956) 'Augustinian Theology of the 14th Century', *Augustiniana* 6: 146–274. (Gregory is treated in great detail on pages 182–213.)

Worek, J. (1964) 'Agustinismo y aristotelismo tomista en la doctrina gnoseológica de Gregorio Ariminense' (Augustinianism and Thomistic Aristotelianism in the Epistemological Theory of Gregory of Rimini), *La Ciudad de Dios* 177: 435–68, 635–82. (A treatment of the more traditional elements in Gregory's philosophy and theology.)

STEPHEN F. BROWN

GRICE, HERBERT PAUL (1913–88)

Grice was a leading member of the post-war Oxford group of analytic philosophers. His small body of published work, together with an oral tradition, has been deeply influential among both philosophers and theoretical linguists. His outline of general rules of conversation began a new era in pragmatics. Grice's analysis of speaker's meaning explicates semantic notions in terms of the psychological concepts of intention and belief. His theory of conversation is based on the nature of language as a rational, cooperative activity. His account of conversational rules gave him a tool that he applied to a wide class of philosophical problems. Although Grice is most famous for his work on language and meaning, his interests cover a full range of philosophical topics, including ethics, moral psychology and philosophical psychology.

1   Life

Paul Grice was born on 15 March 1913 in Birmingham, England. A fellow and tutor at St John's College, Oxford, from 1938 to 1967, except when serving in naval intelligence during the Second World War, he was a member of a group of young Oxford philosophers who met under the leadership of J.L. Austin (see AUSTIN, J.L. §2). He became Professor of Philosophy at the University of California at Berkeley in 1967, and died in Berkeley in 1988. Since he published reluctantly, much of his considerable influence came from the seminars and lectures he gave as a visitor to numerous universities and from his collaborative work. Grice was interested in a wide range of philosophical problems; more than most of his contemporaries of his rank he studied the great philosophers of the past, especially admiring Aristotle and Kant. He was exacting in presenting a problem, and lucid in exposing underlying issues and questions of methodology. Although his texts are often difficult to read, they are filled with wit, occasional irreverence and an exuberance which comes from his love of ideas.

Grice is most famous as a philosopher of language. His views on ethics, moral psychology and philosophical psychology, to some extent presented in public lectures, are mainly unpublished. The lectures, along with notebooks, are available in the Archives of the University of California.

2   Language and meaning

Meaning, Grice argued, does not result from conventions but is a function of what users do – with sounds and gestures as well as sentences and words. It is to be analysed in terms of intentions, on

the part of an utterer, to produce a particular response in an audience. Utterer's meaning provides the basis for an analysis of utterance-type meaning, the meaning of words or sentences. The analysis explicates the stable truth-functional content of meaning – what, in Grice's terms, is 'said' by a speaker. But utterers may use language to mean more than what they say. Grice's theory of conversational implicature, propounded in 1967 in his William James lectures (1989), explains how this is possible (see LANGUAGE, PHILOSOPHY OF §1).

3   Utterer's meaning

The meaning in general of a sign is to be explained in terms of what users of the sign mean by it on particular occasions. Grice's core idea is simple; the difficulties lie in the details. He begins by suggesting that 'x meant something' would be true if x was intended by its utterer to induce a belief in some audience. To say what the belief was would be to say what U meant. But there is more to meaning that Jones is a murderer than acting so as to get someone to believe Jones to be a murderer: you could do that by leaving his handkerchief at the scene of the crime. Grice added nested intentions: you do something, meaning by it that p, if you do it intending to get someone to think that p, and intending to produce this result partly through the person's realizing that that is what you are up to ([1957] 1989). The idea seems obvious: meaning something by an utterance is distinguished from causing someone to believe something (or have some other propositional attitude) by the utterers' using their audience's *recognition* of their intention. The task of unpacking the idea is quite complex. The 'openness' of an utterer's intentions would later become an issue of considerable debate.

In his essay 'Utterer's Meaning and Intentions' ([1968] 1989), Grice proceeded to analyse utterer's meaning in two stages: (1) what it is for an individual to mean something; (2) what it is to mean that p. The interesting case, (2), is explained in terms of (1).

(1) 'By uttering x, U meant something' is true if and only if, for some audience A, U uttered x intending:

  (i) A to produce some particular response r,
  (ii) A to recognize that U intends (i), and
  (iii) As recognition that U intends (i) to function, in part, as a reason for (i).

To specify what U meant is to specify the nature of the intended response: where x is an indicative utterance, the response is A's believing something, and where x is an imperative type the response is A's intending to do something.

(2) 'By uttering x, U meant that p' is true if and only if for some audience A, U uttered x intending:

(i) A to believe that p,
(ii) and (iii) above.

This type of complex intention is called an 'M-intention'. In a series of articles Grice revised this structure of nested intentions using more formal apparatus. He directed his attention to the meaning of imperative-type utterances, to a large range of speech-act types, and to meeting various counterexamples that he and others had proposed.

One series of issues concerns the 'openness' of meaning. A threatening infinity of intentions emerged in response to a case in which the three conditions for (2) – 'By uttering x, U meant that p' – are fulfilled. I do something (i) intending to get you to think that p, and (ii and iii) intending this to come about through your realizing that this is what I am up to, but *not* (iv) intending you to realize that (ii and iii) is what I am up to. For example, a man wants to ingratiate himself with his boss by letting him win at bridge. He does not wish to be blatant, but he does wish his boss, who likes such self-effacement, to know he wants him to win. To get this effect, he produces a smile when he has a good hand, intending this to be recognized as a simulation of a spontaneous response. Conditions i–iii of (2) are then fulfilled, but as Grice uses the idea of meaning, the employee did not mean by smiling that he had a good hand.

The problem, in the words of P.F. Strawson (1964), is that the employee's intentions are not *wholly overt*; indeed, given that the employee does not wish to be crude, partial concealment is required. Utterer's meaning requires openness; how is this to be conveyed in the analysans? Strawson proposed that Grice add a further condition, that the utterer U should utter x not only, as already provided, with the intention that U intends to obtain a certain response from A, but also with the intention that A should think that U has the intention just mentioned. This excludes the bridge-playing employee who wished his boss to take the smile as a spontaneous giveaway. With enough ingenuity, however, the same sort of counterexample can still be generated, and then a fifth clause will be needed, then a sixth, and so on.

Grice proposed to block an infinite regress by adding a condition which prevents 'sneaky intentions'. Although there is continued debate about the extent of transparency required, as well as the form of its expression in the analysans, Grice himself felt that 'the sneaky intention' condition is ad hoc. Returning much later to the topic, he discussed what general conditions might legitimate our 'deeming' a speaker, given the absence of a sneaky intention, to have an infinity of intentions, and so to mean p. He worried about the legitimacy of 'deeming' someone to have an unrealizable intention.

The considerations which intrigued Grice, sketched in 'Meaning Revisited' ([1983] 1989) and in his 'Reply to Richards' (Grandy and Warner 1986), include his views on the nature of rational capacities, their connection to pre-rational states, and what he called value-oriented terms, that is, terms referring to a capacity or property such that attribution depends on proper or good specifications of that property. No completed account exists and much of the material is unfortunately unpublished. Some of his work on reasoning was however presented in the Locke/Kant lectures (1977, 1979).

4 Conversational implicature

Conversational implicature is not just a theory about language, but a tool to be applied to a wide class of philosophical problems. The theory simplifies semantics both by providing a single sense for the many uses of a word and by permitting a truth-functional analysis of ordinary language. Grice's argument against the trenchant criticisms of P.F. Strawson would return us, in some ways, to Bertrand Russell's conception of the relation between logic and language.

A person communicates more than what is said. Much of what is communicated is implied in one way or another. In the William James lectures Grice sketched the main types of implication, roughly characterized them, and proposed rules of conversation or communication which were specifications of a most general 'cooperative' principle. These rules govern a central class of implicatures, but they are not semantic in nature. They guide our conversations because they are rational, efficient ways to achieve common ends. Grice's work inaugurated a new era in what is now called pragmatics (see PRAGMATICS §§1, 3).

Grice's most general rule, the Cooperative Principle, requires that an individual's conversational contribution be such as is required, at the stage at which it occurs, by the accepted purpose or direction of the talk exchange. More specific maxims (and their submaxims) articulate this rule: they enjoin truthfulness, informativeness, relevance and clarity.

Speakers conversationally imply that which they must be assumed to think if we are to suppose them to observe the conversational maxims, or at least the Cooperative Principle. Conversational implicatures are brought within Grice's general account of meaning in terms of speaker's intentions by the further condition that it is known (and known to be known) by both audience and speaker that the audience is capable of working out the assumption required.

Grice illustrates how implicature works. One example, in which no maxim is violated, is of such a recognizably common nature that we can also see the pervasiveness of conversational implicatures. A man stands by an obviously immobilized car and says to an approaching stranger 'I am out of petrol'. The stranger replies, 'There is a garage around the corner'. He implies that he thinks the garage is open, has petrol to sell and so on, for otherwise the relevance maxim would be infringed.

Grice's most arresting examples concern speakers who deliberately flout a subordinate maxim while adhering to the overarching Cooperative Principle. These are used to show how tautologies and figures of speech can be meaningful. In general, speakers may flout a subordinate maxim in order to introduce into the exchange something they do not want to say explicitly. Here is one of Grice's examples: a tutor, writing a testimonial for a pupil who is a candidate for a philosophy job, says only that the candidate's command of English is excellent, and his attendance at tutorials regular. Given his knowledge of his pupil, the tutor must be wishing to impart information that he is reluctant to write down, namely that his pupil is no good at philosophy.

The William James lectures ([1967] 1989) display the sensitivity to nuances of ordinary language that made Grice such a notable practitioner of 'Ordinary Language' philosophy. He did think that what he called linguistic botanizing, as practised in that tradition, was essential. He also regarded himself as part of that philosophical tradition that wished to defend common sense. None the less, he criticized both the practices of common-sense philosophers and the lack of theoretical justification in much ordinary language philosophy. In his analysis of perception and when treating the logical stucture of ordinary English, Grice protested against those who would block a philosophical analysis whenever its key terms were used in ways that were out of line with common speech. Oddness was to be distinguished from the truth or falsity of an utterance. Grice used his general theory of conversational implicature to explain the oddness, and in this way defended the unfashionable causal theory of perception. Similarly, in discussing Strawson's thesis that certain expressions, such as 'not', 'and', 'or', 'if', 'all', 'some' and, famously, the definite description operator 'the', diverge in meaning from their counterparts in formal logic, Grice held that both the advocates of truth-functional analyses

and their opponents fail to attend to the conditions governing conversation (see ORDINARY LANGUAGE PHILOSOPHY, SCHOOL OF §3).

5 Value

Grice's views on value are subtle. Value is constructed by us, but objective. His lectures, 'The Conception of Value' ([1983] 1991) attempt to provide a metaphysical basis for value. Grice depicts an Aristotelian world in which objects and creatures are characterized in terms of what they are supposed to do, thus enabling us to evaluate by reference to function and finality. But he argues that the legitimacy of these evaluative judgments rests on an argument for absolute value. He makes the same claim for explanations in terms of purposiveness. Vitalistic phenomena can also be explained by mechanistic, cybernetic notions; these threaten the irreducibility of finality features unless there is a domain of objects in which attribution of finality has no substitute. Rational beings, or persons, are said to furnish such a domain.

Grice's attempt to secure our evaluations takes as its first task understanding the concept of value, whose hybrid nature – describing and motivating – needs to be made intelligible. He begins by utilizing a device called 'Humean Projection'. Hume attributed to the mind a tendency 'to spread itself upon objects'; values start off as human attitudes, features of our minds or psychological states, but are projected onto the world. Motivation comes via our own attitudes, description from their projection. What served Hume as a diagnosis of one source of illusion becomes, under conditions Grice carefully specified, a legitimating procedure.

Humean projection was first used in an address, 'Method in Philosophical Psychology (from the Banal to the Bizarre)' ([1975] 1991), to justify the attribution to creatures of concepts which were unavailable to their predecessors. It offers a partial explanation of what it is to be a more developed psychological creature, by describing greater internalization or representational capacity in a creature. Internalized expressions include connectives, quantifiers, temporal modifiers, mood indicators, modal operators and names of psychological states, such as 'judge' and 'will'. The specific benefit of the procedure when applied to value is that judgments of value are not translatable back into preferences or imperatives or any other approving or volitional attitudes from which they are being constructed. Non-translatability does not, however, guarantee objectivity for value judgments. Grice thought that objectivity required the provision of 'something like' truth conditions for their expression. The lectures on value present a story, which Grice intended as the analogue of truth-conditions.

Objective value is attributed to the end-products of Humean projection if those who do the projecting are themselves of absolute value and can thus 'transmit' it – an adaptation of Aristotle's 'what seems good to the good man *is* good'. Two moves are thought to legitimate this attribution of value. First, Grice argues for the propriety of conceiving of human beings as persons. He introduces an operation flauntingly named Metaphysical Transubstantiation, a procedure for the redistribution but not the invention of properties. What was accidental becomes essential, and rationality, which attaches only accidentally to humans, becomes, via this construction routine, an essential property of persons. As persons, Grice claims, we will have a 'rational demand for absolute value'. Grice's second move is to invoke a 'metaphysical principle of supply and demand' which allows us to believe what can in a 'trouble-free' manner satisfy a rational demand. Despite his persuasive defence of these ideas, Grice recognized that, rather than offering a systematic account, he was sketching a story of value 'bristling with problems'.

See also: ANALYTICAL PHILOSOPHY §3; COMMUNICATION AND INTENTION; VALUE, ONTOLOGICAL STATUS OF

List of works

Grice, H.P. (1941) 'Personal Identity', *Mind* 50: 330–50. (Grice states and defends a form of Logical Construction theory, offering a modification of Locke's memory-based theory of personal identity.)

Grice, H.P. and Strawson, P.F. (1956) 'In Defence of a Dogma', *Philosophical Review* 65: 141–58. (Grice defends the analytic-synthetic distinction, which had been criticized by W.V. Quine in 'Two Dogmas of Empiricism'.)

Grice, H.P. (1969) 'Vacuous Names', in D. Davidson and J. Hintikka (eds) *Words and Objections*, Dordrecht: Reidel, 118–45. (Grice presents an account of referential usage and defends Russell's Theory of Descriptions; he argues against the charge that definite descriptions are ambiguous between Russellian and referential readings.)

——(1970) 'Lectures on Language and Reality', delivered at University of Illinois, Urbana, Illinois, unpublished: Archives, University of California, Berkeley, CA. (Lecture IV, 'Presupposition and Conversational Implicature', published in *Studies in the Way of Words*, presents Grice's defence of Russell and his attack on the notion of presupposition.)

—— (1971) 'Intention and Uncertainty', *Proceedings of the British Academy* 57: 263– 79. (Grice rejects his earlier (unpublished) view, which understood intention as a form of belief. He defends the thesis that there is a special attitude of willing distinct from belief and desire. Intentional action results from this special form of willing, which can occur in the absence of intention, but is a component of intention, where intention is present.)

—— (1977) 'The Immanuel Kant Lectures', delivered at Stanford University, revised and presented as the John Locke lectures at the University of Oxford as 'Aspects of Reason' (1979), unpublished: Archives, University of California, Berkeley, CA. (These lectures on reasons and reasoning also contain material which bears importantly on a problem raised in connection with meaning. Grice's analysis of meaning features utterers and audience guided implicitly by procedures. The difficulty is in understanding of what it is to be *implicitly* guided by procedures.)

Grice, H.P. and Baker, J. (1985) 'Davidson on Weakness of the Will', in B. Vermazen and M. Hintikka (eds) *Essays on Davidson: Actions and Events*, Oxford: Oxford University Press, 27–50. (Grice analyses and criticizes the account of weakness of will offered by Donald Davidson.)

Grice, H.P. (1986) 'Reply to Richards', in R.E. Grandy and R. Warner (eds) *Philosophical Grounds of Rationality*, Oxford: Clarendon Press. (Grice offers a general reply to the authors of the essays in his honour and a statement of his philosophical views.)

—— (1986) 'Actions and Events', *Pacific Philosophical Quarterly* 67: 1–35. (Grice's discussion focuses on, but is not confined to, Davidson's views on this topic. Grice offers an alternative account of actions and events.)

—— (1988) 'Aristotle on the Multiplicity of Being', *Pacific Philosophical Quarterly* 69: 175–200. (Grice discusses a well-known cluster of Aristotelian theses about the connection of semantic multiplicity and the notion of being. He discusses the different ways in which semantic multiplicity becomes unified – recursive, focal and analogical.)

—— (1989) *Studies in the Way of Words*, Cambridge, MA, and London: Harvard University Press. (Collected essays, some previously published in journals but not listed above, written 1946–88. Includes 'Meaning' (1957), 'The Causal Theory of Perception' (1967), the first complete publication of The William James Lectures (1967) and 'Utterer's Meaning and Intentions' (1969).)

—— (1991) *The Conception of Value*, Oxford: Clarendon Press. (Includes 'The Carus Lectures on the Conception of Value' (1983), which attempts to provide a metaphysical basis for value, 'Method in Philosophical Psychology (From the Banal to the Bizarre)' (1975) and 'Reply to Richards' (Final Section) (1986).)

References and further reading

Baker, J. (1991) 'Introduction', in H.P. Grice, *The Conception of Value*, Oxford: Clarendon Press. (An expansion of the material of §5 of this entry.)

Bennett, J. (1976) *Linguistic Behaviour*, Cambridge: Cambridge University Press. (Bennett's project is influenced by the Gricean programme. He develops a view of language in general as a matter of systematic communicative behaviour and offers a rationale for the primacy of utterer's meaning.)

* Grandy, R. and Warner, R. (eds) (1986) *Philosophical Grounds of Rationality*, Oxford: Clarendon Press. (This is a Festschrift honoring Paul Grice and includes an overview of his work by Grandy and Warner, as well as essays by P. Suppes, 'The Primacy of Utterer's Meaning', and A. Kemmerling, 'Utterer's Meaning Revisited', defending Grice's account. Kemmerling's article is technical. See 'On Defining Relevance' by D. Wilson and B. Sperber for discussion of the conversational maxims.)

Levinson, S. (1983) *Pragmatics*, Cambridge, MA: Harvard University Press. (A good introduction to pragmatics and to Grice's contribution to the field.)

Loar, B. (1981) *Mind and Meaning*, Cambridge: Cambridge University Press. (Influenced by Grice's account of meaning, the chief concerns of the book are in the foundations of the theory of meaning and are directed towards understanding the contents of belief and linguistic meaning. Somewhat technical.)

Neale, S. (1992) 'Paul Grice and the Philosophy of Language', *Linguistics and Philosophy* 15: 509–59. (A comprehensive, critical commentary on the development of Grice's work on language and meaning as displayed in Grice 1989. Excellent bibliography.)

Schiffer, S. (1972) *Meaning*, Oxford: Clarendon Press. (Schiffer presents objections to Grice's account of speaker meaning and discusses what must be added for a satisfactory analysis. Schiffer attempts to cut off the threat of an infinite regress of intentions by appealing to mutual knowledge. Somewhat technical.)

* Strawson, P.F. (1964) 'Intention and Convention in Speech Acts', *Philosophical Review* 73: 439–60. (Strawson proposes a modification to Grice's account of utterer's meaning in order to resolve a

problem he attributes to the openness of utterer's intentions.)

JUDITH BAKER

GROSSETESTE, ROBERT (*c.*1170–1253)

Grosseteste's thought is representative of the conflicting currents in the intellectual climate of Europe in the late twelfth and early thirteenth centuries. On the one hand, his commitment to acquiring, understanding and making accessible to his Latin contemporaries the texts and ideas of newly discovered Arabic and Greek intellectual traditions places him in the vanguard of a sweeping movement transforming European thought during his lifetime. His work in science and natural philosophy, for example, is inspired by material newly translated from Arabic sources and by the new Aristotelian natural philosophy, especially the Physics, On the Heavens *and* Posterior Analytics *(Aristotle's treatise on the nature of scientific knowledge). Similarly, in his work in metaphysics, ethics and theology Grosseteste turns to ancient sources previously unknown (or incompletely known) to Western thinkers, prominent among which are Aristotle's* Ethics *and the writings of Pseudo-Dionysius. His work as a translator of and commentator on Aristotle and Pseudo-Dionysius places Grosseteste among the pioneers in the assimilation of these important strands of the Greek intellectual heritage into the mainstream of European thought.*

On the other hand, Grosseteste's views are in significant respects conservative. His greatest debt is to Augustine, and his most original ideas – such as his view that light is a fundamental constituent of all corporeal reality – are extensions of recognizably Augustinian themes. Moreover, although his work on Aristotle is groundbreaking, his approach is judicious and measured, lacking any hint of the crusader's zeal that marks the work of the later radical Aristotelians. In general his practice conforms to the traditional Neoplatonist line, viewing Aristotle as a guide to logic and natural philosophy while turning to Platonism – in Grosseteste's case, Augustinian and Pseudo-Dionysian Platonism – for the correct account of the loftier matters of metaphysics and theology.

1 **Life and works**
2 **Augustinian psychology and epistemology**
3 **Light as the first corporeal form**

1 Life and works

Grosseteste was born probably shortly before 1170 in Suffolk, England. There is little evidence of his activities until the mid-1220s, when he would have been already well over fifty years old. In 1225 he was lecturing in theology at Oxford, where he also served for a time as chancellor of the university. In 1230 he left his post in Oxford's secular schools to become the first lecturer at the newly established house of studies for the Oxford Franciscans. He remained there until 1235 when he was elected bishop of Lincoln, England's largest diocese, which then included Oxford. He served in that position until his death in 1253.

We know little about Grosseteste's formal training or career prior to his appearance at Oxford in 1225. He may have begun his studies at Oxford or Cambridge in the 1180s, receiving the degree of Master of Arts by the end of that decade. He seems to have had an administrative career in the household of the Bishop of Hereford until perhaps 1198. It may have been in Hereford, an early centre of interest in scientific speculation, that Grosseteste developed his deep interests in natural philosophy, astronomy and mathematics. His earliest works, dating from about 1200–20, deal with subject matter of this sort: they include *De cometis* (On Comets), *De artibus liberalibus* (On the Liberal Arts), *De generatione sonorum* (On the Generation of Sounds), *De sphaera* (On the Sphere) and *De impressionibus aeris* (On the Influences of Air). Shortly after 1220 Grosseteste seems to have begun serious reflection on Aristotle. His *Commentarius in Posteriorum analyticorum libros* (Commentary on Aristotle's *Posterior Analytics*), perhaps the first complete medieval commentary on that text, probably dates to the early 1220s. The earliest of his notes on Aristotle's *Physics* (which have been gathered together as the *Commentarius in VIII libros Physicorum*) may date from the same period. It is unclear whether Grosseteste ever studied at Paris or whether he spent time in Paris during the suspension of studies at Oxford in 1209–14, as many English academics did.

During the 1220s at Oxford, the study and teaching of theology moved to the center of Grosseteste's attention. As part of his study of the Bible and the Church Fathers, Grosseteste began learning Greek, an undertaking that would yield remarkable fruit in his late-blooming career as a philosophical theologian. The writings in philosophical theology that belong to the period from 1225–30 include *De veritate* (On Truth), *De veritate propositionis* (On the Truth of the Proposition), *De libero arbitrio* (On Free Choice) in two recensions, *De scientia Dei* (On God's Knowledge) *De statu causarum* (On the Finitude of Causal Series), *De intelligentiis* (On Intelligences) and *De unica forma* (On the Single Form).

Grosseteste's growing theological occupations did not displace his work in natural philosophy, however, and in the period from 1225 to about 1240 he continued to write on natural philosophy, weaving together his scientific and mathematical interests with his theological work. He continued to lecture on Aristotle's *Physics* into the early 1230s, and composed his treatise on the six days of creation, *Hexaemeron*, in 1230–5 as well as several treatises on broadly scientific matters, including *De impressionibus elementorum* (On the Influences of the Elements), *De motu supercaelestium* (On the Motion of What is Above the Heavens), *De motu corporali et luce* (On Corporeal Motion and Light), *De lineis* (On Lines), *De natura locorum* (On the Nature of Places), *De iride* (On the Rainbow), *De colore* (On Colour), *De calore solis* (On the Heat of the Sun), *De operationibus solis* (On the Activities of the Sun, an exposition of Ecclesiasticus 43: 1–5), *De finitate motus et temporis* (On the Finitude of Motion and Time) and *De differentiis localibus* (On the Differentiae Associated with Place). Central to Grosseteste's scientific reflections in this period is his developing account of the nature of light and its fundamental role in both natural and divine causality. That account reaches its fullest development in *De luce* (On Light).

The crowning scholarly achievements from the years in which Grosseteste was Bishop of Lincoln result from monumental projects involving translation of and commentary on Greek philosophical and theological texts. In the mid-1230s he revised a twelfth-century translation of John Damascene's *De fide orthodoxa* (On the Orthodox Faith) (see JOHN OF DAMASCUS) and produced the first Latin translations of the remainder of Damascene's corpus, *De logica* (On Logic), *De centum heresibus* (On the Hundred Heresies), *Elementarium dogmatum* (Introduction to Doctrine) and *De hymno Trisagion* (On the Hymn 'Holy, Holy, Holy'). Shortly thereafter he began the largest of his scholarly endeavours, the production of translations of and commentaries on each of Pseudo-Dionysius's four major treatises: *De caelesti hierarchia* (On the Celestial Hierarchy), *De ecclesiastica hierarchica* (On the Ecclesiastical Hierarchy), *De divinis nominibus* (On the Divine Names) and *De mystica theologia* (On Mystical Theology) (see PSEUDO-DIONYSIUS). By 1243 this massive undertaking was complete, and Grosseteste turned next to Aristotle's *Ethics* (see ARISTOTLE). By the late 1240s he had finished the first Latin translation of the complete text of the *Ethics*. To accompany his translation Grosseteste produced translations of the ancient Greek commentators on the *Ethics* and his own glosses on the text. Apparently in the last years of his life, at close to eighty years of age, Grosseteste began studying Hebrew.

2 Augustinian psychology and epistemology

Following AUGUSTINE, Grosseteste appeals to the nature and behaviour of light to explain the fundamental nature of reality and human cognition of it. God is the first and highest light, and all creatures depend on God in the way rays of light depend on the light source from which they radiate. The eternal ideas in God act as principles in creation (*creatrices*) insofar as they are the formal exemplar causes of created things. Creatures have their being, and hence are 'true' (in the sense of 'true friend') to the extent to which they conform or are 'adequated' to the eternal ideas.

Grosseteste holds that since the eternal ideas in God are the exemplars of created things, knowledge of creatures depends on illumination from God:

Since the truth of each thing is its conformity to the idea of it in the eternal Word, it is clear that every created truth is seen only in the light of the highest truth.... All created truth, therefore, is clear insofar as the light of its eternal idea is present to the observer, as Augustine testifies. Nor can anything be seen to be true in its created truth alone, just as a body cannot be seen to be coloured solely in its colour apart from the illumination of an extrinsic light.

(*De veritate*)

Grosseteste believes that our cognitive dependence on God's illumination is a function of our weakness. Just as the weak eyes of the body cannot look at the sun itself, despite their depending on sunlight for seeing coloured bodies, the weak eyes of the mind cannot look on the highest truth itself, though the mind depends for its vision of truth on the light streaming from it. By contrast, pure intellects – the divine intellect, the separate intelligences and purified human intellects (in heaven) – have knowledge by virtue of their direct awareness of the eternal ideas and of the highest light itself (*De veritate; Commentarius in Posteriorum analyticorum libros* I.7, I.14).

In Grosseteste's view, our cognitive weakness is explained in part by the soul's embodiment:

If the highest part of the human soul – the so-called intellective part which is not the actuality of any body and needs no corporeal instrument for its proper activity – were not clouded and weighed down by the weight of the corrupt body, it would have complete knowledge without the aid of sense-perception through an irradiation received from a higher light, just as it will have when the soul has cast aside the body.... But because the purity of the eye of the soul is clouded and weighed down by the weight of the body, all the powers of the rational soul are oppressed from birth by the weight of the body so that they cannot act, and so are in a certain way drowsy.

(*Commentarius in Posteriorum analyticorum libros* I.14)

Our embodiment also accounts for the indispensable role sense-perception plays in our acquisition of knowledge: 'In the course of time, as sense-perception acts through its many encounters with sensible things, reason (which is intermingled with the senses and is, as it were, ferried to sensible things by the senses as in a boat) is awakened' (*Commentarius in Posteriorum analyticorum libros* I.14). Once awakened, reason begins to function, drawing distinctions and abstracting until it arrives at cognition first of universals, then of necessary truths and finally of the sorts of demonstrations that provide the strictest kind of knowledge.

Human cognitive weakness results not only from the soul's embodiment but also from the soul's misdirected love:

The cause of the soul's sight's being clouded through the weight of the corrupt body is that the soul's affection and vision (*affectus et aspectus*) are not distinct, and it attains its vision only by that by which it attains its affection or its love. Therefore since the soul's love and affection are directed toward the body and bodily enticements, it necessarily drags the soul's vision behind it and directs it away from its light.

(*Commentarius in Posteriorum analyticorum libros* I.14)

In our present state, turned away from the light, we must make our way toward truth starting from vestiges of light discovered in the external senses; but to the extent that our love is directed away from corruptible things, our cognitive gaze will be directed toward its own light until, purified of bodily distractions, it will look on the light itself.

3 Light as the first corporeal form

Some of Grosseteste's most original ideas result from his extension of the Augustinian metaphor of illumination to issues in natural philosophy. He is captivated by a particular characteristic of light, namely, its essential ability to multiply and diffuse itself instantaneously (as he thought) in all directions.

He saw in this feature the mechanism of an ambitious account of the generation of the physical universe (see ILLUMINATION).

The problem, as Grosseteste sees it, is to account for the three-dimensional extension of bodies and of the corporeal universe in general. This is because the ultimate principles of corporeal things are prime matter and bodily form, each of which is in itself simple and utterly dimensionless. Prime matter must be dimensionless because its possessing dimensions would entail its being informed in some way; and bodily form, considered just as form, must be wholly immaterial and cannot therefore be spatially extended. Hence the combination of simple, unformed matter with simple form cannot give rise to quantitative extension. Moreover, no finite multiplication of a simple form in matter can give rise to quantitative extension because no aggregation of a finite number of extensionless entities can constitute anything extended. Grosseteste's solution to this problem is to identify light with the primary corporeal form:

I judge that the first corporeal form, which some call corporeity, is light. For light, of itself, diffuses itself in every direction so that from a point of light, a sphere of light as great as you please is generated instantaneously.... But corporeity is that from which the extension of matter into three dimensions necessarily follows.... But it was impossible for form, which in itself is simple and dimensionless, to introduce dimensions into matter in every direction – since matter is likewise simple and dimensionless – except by multiplying and diffusing itself instantaneously in every direction and by extending matter, in its diffusion. For form itself could not leave matter behind, since it is not separable.

(De luce)

In its instantaneous infinite multiplication light, as it were, stretches the matter it informs into a three-dimensional quantity. Grosseteste holds that this generation of extended matter occurs instantaneously at the beginning of time when God creates the first corporeal form in prime matter, which God also creates simultaneously. Moreover, he holds that since the infinite multiplication of something simple yields something finite (because what is produced by the infinite multiplication of something infinitely exceeds that by the multiplication of which it was produced), light's instantaneous infinite multiplication of itself yields finite corporeal extension in every direction. The full extent of that finite extension defines a sphere coextensive with the whole of the corporeal universe (*machina mundi*).

Grosseteste's reflections on the generation of the corporeal universe lead him to two particularly interesting corollaries. First, he reasons that if in general the infinite multiplication of something simple is required to produce a thing of finite quantity, then it must be that there are infinities of different magnitudes, the difference in the magnitude of the infinities accounting for the quantitative difference in objects of different sizes:

Now, it is possible that an infinite aggregation of numbers is related to another infinite aggregation in any numeric ratio (and even in any non-numeric ratio), and [so] there are infinities that have more [elements] than other infinities and infinities that have fewer than others. (The aggregation of all the numbers, both even and odd, is infinite, and it is thus greater than the aggregation of all the even numbers, which is nevertheless infinite.) ... It is clear therefore that by its infinite multiplication, light extends matter into smaller finite dimensions and into larger finite dimensions in any ratio whatever.

(De luce)

Thus, the first corporeal form – light – explains not only how there can be a three-dimensional corporeal world but also how there can be bodies in it of different sizes.

Second, Grosseteste supposes that since light is the first corporeal form and as such is intrinsic and fundamental to all corporeal reality, understanding the behaviour of light is fundamental to understanding all natural phenomena. Mathematics, therefore, and in particular geometry and optics (the science of refraction), are indispensable tools for natural philosophy: 'The consideration of lines, angles, and figures is especially useful since it is impossible to have knowledge of natural philosophy without them' (*De lineis*). Grosseteste's lifelong commitment to these disciplines provides the foundation for an enduring tradition of mathematical and scientific speculation at Oxford in the later Middle Ages (see NATURAL PHILOSOPHY, MEDIEVAL; OXFORD CALCULATORS).

See also: ARISTOTELIANISM, MEDIEVAL; AUGUSTINE; AUGUSTINIANISM; BRADWARDINE, T.; PLATONISM, MEDIEVAL; PSEUDO-GROSSETESTE; TRANSLATORS

List of works

Grosseteste, R. (*c.*1170–1253) *Opera Roberti Grosseteste Lincolniensis*, ed. J. McEvoy, Corpus Christianorum Continuatio Medievalis, Turnhout: Brepols. (A number of volumes are projected, including volumes devoted to Grosseteste's work on the

Pseudo-Dionysian corpus. To date, only the first volume has appeared, containing Grosseteste's Pauline commentaries and his *Tabula*.)

—— (*c*.1200) *De cometis* (On Comets), ed. S. Thomson, 'The Text of Grosseteste's *De cometis*', *Isis* 19, 1933: 19–25.

—— (1200–10) *De artibus liberalibus* (On the Liberal Arts), ed. L. Baur in *Die Philosophischen Werke des Robert Grosseteste*, Münster: Aschendorff, 1912, 1–7.

—— (1200–10) *De generatione sonorum* (On the Generation of Sounds), ed. L. Baur in *Die Philosophischen Werke des Robert Grosseteste*, Münster: Aschendorff, 1912, 7–10.

—— (*c*.1215) *De sphaera* (On the Sphere), ed. L. Baur in *Die Philosophischen Werke des Robert Grosseteste*, Münster: Aschendorff, 1912, 10–32.

—— (1215–20) *De impressionibus aeris* (On Atmospheric Pressures), ed. L. Baur in *Die Philosophischen Werke des Robert Grosseteste*, Münster: Aschendorff, 1912, 41–51.

—— (1220–32) *Commentarius in VIII libros Physicorum Aristotelis* (Commentary on Aristotle's *Physics*), ed. R. Dales, Boulder, CO: University of Colorado Press, 1963.

—— (early 1220s) *Commentarius in Posteriorum analyticorum libros* (Commentary on Aristotle's *Posterior Analytics*), ed. P. Rossi, Florence: Olschki, 1981. (Translation by S. Macdonald, *Commentary on the Posterior Analytics*, New Haven, CN: Yale University Press, forthcoming.)

—— (1225–30) *De veritate* (On Truth), ed. L. Baur in *Die Philosophischen Werke des Robert Grosseteste*, Münster: Aschendorff, 1912, 130–43; trans. R. McKeon in *Selections from Medieval Philosophers*, New York: Charles Scribner's Sons, 1929, vol. 1, 263–81.

—— (1225–30) *De veritate propositionis* (On the Truth of a Proposition), ed. L. Baur in *Die Philosophischen Werke des Robert Grosseteste*, Münster: Aschendorff, 1912, 143–5; trans. R. McKeon in *Selections from Medieval Philosophers*, New York: Charles Scribner's Sons, 1929, vol. 1, 282–4; trans. N. Lewis in 'Time and Modality in Robert Grosseteste', Ph.D. dissertation, University of Pittsburgh, 1988, 427–9. (Lewis' dissertation also contains a corrected version of Baur's edition on pages 380–4.)

—— (1225–30) *De libero arbitrio* (On Free Will), ed. N. Lewis, 'The First Recension of Robert Grosseteste's "De libero arbitrio"', *Mediaeval Studies* 53, 1991: 1–88; trans. N. Lewis in 'Time and Modality in Robert Grosseteste', PhD. dissertation, University of Pittsburgh, 1988, 391–424.

—— (1225–30) *De scientia Dei* (On the Knowledge of God), ed. L. Baur in *Die Philosophischen Werke des Robert Grosseteste*, Münster: Aschendorff, 1912, 145–7; trans. R. McKeon in *Selections from Medieval Philosophers*, New York: Charles Scribner's Sons, 1929, vol. 1, 285–7; trans. N. Lewis in 'Time and Modality in Robert Grosseteste', PhD. dissertation, University of Pittsburgh, 1988, 425–6. (Lewis' dissertation also contains a corrected version of Baur's edition on pages 377–9.)

—— (1225–30) *De statu causarum* (On the State of Causes), ed. L. Baur in *Die Philosophischen Werke des Robert Grosseteste*, Münster: Aschendorff, 1912, 120–6.

—— (1225–30) *De intelligentiis* (On Intelligence), ed. L. Baur in *Die Philosophischen Werke des Robert Grosseteste*, Münster: Aschendorff, 1912, 112–20. (This treatise is the second part of a single letter composed by Grosseteste; *De unica forma* is the first part.)

—— (1225–30) *De unica forma* (On the Unity of Forms), ed. L. Baur in *Die Philosophischen Werke des Robert Grosseteste*, Münster: Aschendorff, 1912, 106–12. (This treatise is the first part of a single letter composed by Grosseteste; *De intelligentiis* is the first part.)

—— (1230–5) *Hexaemeron*, ed. R. Dales and S. Gieben, London: Oxford University Press, 1982; trans. C. Martin, *Robert Grosseteste: On the Six Days of Creation*, London: Oxford University Press, 1996.

—— (1230–5) *De impressionibus elementorum* (The Impressions of the Elements), ed. L. Baur in *Die Philosophischen Werke des Robert Grosseteste*, Münster: Aschendorff, 1912, 87–90.

——_ (1230–5) *De motu supercaelestium* (On the Motion of What is Above the Heavens), ed. L. Baur in *Die Philosophischen Werke des Robert Grosseteste*, Münster: Aschendorff, 1912, 92–101.

—— (1230–5) *De motu corporali et luce* (On Corporeal Motion and Light), ed. L. Baur in *Die Philosophischen Werke des Robert Grosseteste*, Münster: Aschendorff, 1912, 90–2.

—— (1230–5) *De lineis* (On Lines), ed. L. Baur in *Die Philosophischen Werke des Robert Grosseteste*, Münster: Aschendorff, 1912, 59–65. (This treatise and *De natura locorum* are two parts of a single treatise.)

—— (1230–5) *De natura locorum* (On the Nature of Places), ed. L. Baur in *Die Philosophischen Werke des Robert Grosseteste*, Münster: Aschendorff, 1912, 65–72. (This treatise and *De lineis* are two parts of a single treatise.)

—— (1230–5) *De iride* (On the Rainbow), ed. L. Baur in *Die Philosophischen Werke des Robert Grosseteste*, Münster: Aschendorff, 1912, 72–8.

—— (1230–5) *De colore* (On Colour), ed. L. Baur in *Die Philosophischen Werke des Robert Grosseteste*, Münster: Aschendorff, 1912, 78–9.

—— (1230–5) *De calore solis* (On the Heat of the Sun), ed. L. Baur in *Die Philosophischen Werke des Robert Grosseteste*, Münster: Aschendorff, 1912, 79–84; trans. A.C. Crombie in D.A. Callus (ed.) *Robert Grosseteste: Scholar and Bishop*, Oxford: Clarendon Press, 1955.

—— (1230–5) *De operationibus solis* (On the Activities of the Sun), ed. J. McEvoy, 'The Sun as "Res" and "Signum": Grosseteste's Commentary on Ecclesiasticus ch. 43, vv. 1–5', *Recherches de théologie ancienne et médiévale* 41, 1974: 38–91.

—— (1230–5) *De finitate motus et temporis* (On the Finitude of Motion and Time), ed. R. Dales, 'Robert Grosseteste's Treatise "De finitate motus et temporis"', *Traditio* 19, 1963: 245–66.

—— (1230–5) *De differentiis localibus* (On the Differentiae Associated with Place), ed. L. Baur in *Die Philosophischen Werke des Robert Grosseteste*, Münster: Aschendorff, 1912, 84–7.

—— (1235–40) *De luce* (On Light), ed. L. Baur in *Die Philosophischen Werke des Robert Grosseteste*, Münster: Aschendorff, 1912, 51–9; trans. C. Riedl, *Robert Grosseteste on Light*, Milwaukee, WI: Marquette University Press, 1942.

—— (1238–43) *Notulae in De caelesti hierarchia* (Glosses on Pseudo-Dionysius' *On the Celestial Hierarchy*), chs 1–9 ed. and trans. J. McQuade in 'Robert Grosseteste's Commentary on the "Celestial Hierarchy" of Pseudo-Dionysius the Areopagite', Ph.D. dissertation, Queen's University of Belfast, 1961; chs 10–15 ed. and trans. J. McEvoy, 'Robert Grosseteste on the *Celestial Hierarchy* of Pseudo-Dionysius', MA dissertation, Queen's University of Belfast, 1967. (These two editions are scheduled to appear in *Opera Roberti Grosseteste Lincolniensis*.)

—— (1238–43) *Notulae in De ecclesiastica hierarchia* (Glosses on Pseudo-Dionysius' *On the Ecclesiastical Hierarchy*), ed. C. Taylor Hogan, 'Robert Grosseteste, Pseudo-Dionysius, and Hierarchy: A Medieval Trinity', Ph.D. dissertation, Cornell University, 1991. (Editions of Grosseteste's work on the Pseudo-Dionysian corpus are scheduled to appear in *Opera Roberti Grosseteste Lincolniensis*.)

—— (1238–43) *Notulae in De divinis nominibus* (Glosses on Pseudo-Dionysius' *On the Divine Names*), chs 1 and 4 ed. F. Ruello, 'La Divinum Nominim Reseratio selon Robert Grosseteste et Albert le Grand', *Archives d'histoire doctrinale et littéraire du moyen âge* 34, 1959: 99–197. (Editions of Grosseteste's work on the Pseudo-Dionysian

corpus are scheduled to appear in *Opera Roberti Grosseteste Lincolniensis*.)

—— (1238–43) *Notulae in De mystica theologia* (Glosses on Pseudo-Dionysius' *On Mystical Theology*), ed. U. Gamba, *Il Commento di Roberto Grossatesta al 'De Mystica Theologia' del Pseudo-Dionigi Areopagita*, Milan, 1942. (Editions of Grosseteste's work on the Pseudo-Dionysian corpus are scheduled to appear in *Opera Roberti Grosseteste Lincolniensis*.)

—— (1240–7) *Notulae in Ethicam Nicomacheam* (Glosses on Aristotle's Nicomachean Ethics), ed. H. Merken, *The Greek Commentaries on the Nicomachean Ethics of Aristotle in the Latin Translation of Robert Grosseteste*, Leiden: Brill, 1973–, 5 vols. (Vol. I containing Grosseteste's translations of the Greek commentators on Books I–IV of the *Ethics* appeared in 1973; vol. III containing the translations of the Greek commentators on Books VII–X appeared in 1991; vol. II containing the translation of the commentators on Books V–VI, vol. IV containing indices for vols 1–III, and vol. V containing an edition of Grosseteste's glosses have not to date been published.)

References and further reading

Callus, D.A. (ed.) (1955) *Robert Grosseteste: Scholar and Bishop*, Oxford: Clarendon Press. (Six seminal essays on Grosseteste's life and thought.)

Crombie, A.C. (1953) *Robert Grosseteste and the Origins of Experimental Science 1100–1700*, Oxford: Clarendon Press; 2nd edn, 1962. (An ambitious argument, in some respects now qualified by more recent scholarship, for Grosseteste's fundamental significance for the development of the experimental method in Western science.)

Gieben, S. (1969) 'Bibliographia Universa Roberti Grosseteste ab an. 1473 ad an. 1969', *Collectanea Franciscana* 39: 362–418. (Bibliography supplementing and extending Thompson (1940).)

—— (1995) 'Robertus Grosseteste: Bibliographia 1970–91', in J. McEvoy (ed.) *Robert Grosseteste: New Perspectives on His Thought and Scholarship*, Steenbrugge: Brepols. (The continuation of Gieben (1969).)

McEvoy, J. (1982) *The Philosophy of Robert Grosseteste*, Oxford: Clarendon Press. (A compendious study of Grosseteste's philosophical ideas with valuable biographical and bibliographical resources. The appendix to this masterful work updates the bibliographical work of Thomson (1940).)

—— (ed.) (1995) *Robert Grosseteste: New Perspectives on His Thought and Scholarship*, Steenbrugge:

Brepols. (A collection of nineteen essays on a wide range of issues, presenting a synoptic view of the current state of Grosseteste scholarship.)

Southern, R.W. (1986) *Robert Grosseteste: The Growth of an English Mind in Medieval Europe*, Oxford: Clarendon Press; 2nd edn, 1992. (A provocative reassessment of Grosseteste's intellectual development and historical significance. The biographical material presented in this article for the most part follows Southern's account.)

Thomson, S.H. (1940) *The Writings of Robert Grosseteste, Bishop of Lincoln 1235–1253*, Cambridge: Cambridge University Press. (A pioneering catalogue and scholarly assessment of the manuscripts and published editions of Grosseteste's works identified prior to 1940.)

SCOTT MacDONALD

GROTE, JOHN (1813–66)

From 1855 Grote was Knightbridge Professor at Cambridge. His literary legacy was largely posthumous. Often seen as unsystematic, he was in fact a penetrating thinker who forcefully criticized utilitarianism and positivism and ably argued that 'all that we call existence is for us a thought of ours'; his was a seminal British idealism, stressing both the gulf between philosophical inquiry and the sciences and the difficulty of distinguishing the necessary from the contingent.

Grote's views derived from Plato, Aristotle, Cicero, Christianity, Kant and the Cambridge Moralists. *An Examination of the Utilitarian Philosophy* exposes the gap between J.S. Mill's abstract utilitarian principle and concrete guidance, and shows how Mill failed to justify utilitarian benevolence over egoism or the demands of special relations – 'family, order, class, friends, country' (see MILL, J.S.). Though the ideal of happiness needs an intuitive ground, utilitarianism is partly right. What it misses is the more basic viewpoint of human agency: what we ought to do. Virtue and duty, requiring benevolent and distributivist action, are distinct demands, better addressing the basic ethical question: 'How different is moralized human nature to be from human nature unmoralized and as it is a subject of simple observation?' *A Treatise on the Moral Ideals* develops this system of 'Eudaemonics and Aretaics'; the former engages our sentient nature, that pain is undesirable to suffer, the latter our active nature, that pain ought not to be inflicted, though their common source is the claim that existence is driven by 'want' – a want to be, know,

do and realize ideals. Positivism and utilitarianism miss the ideality or 'aspiringness' of thought, or how imagination constitutes our world. Ultimately, Eudaemonics is subordinate to Aretaics, which includes Deontics, and is differentiable into a plurality of other ideals with independent value – for example, justice, generosity, perfection, courage. The theistic faith that all these ideals cohere in an orderly universe is one 'we instinctively and intuitively have'.

Exploratio Philosophica develops Grote's original epistemology, critically engaging J.F. FERRIER but intricately demolishing a host of others for not keeping philosophical inquiry into truth separate from scientific inquiry into causes. For Grote, knowledge involves both propositions and judgments about what is 'given' immediately in experience, and progresses by 'distinction, not aggregation', discerning parts of a 'previously conceived whole'. He introduces the distinction between knowledge by acquaintance and by description, but for him, immediacy and reflection are continuous, complementary aspects of experience, whereby mind, via philosophy, traces itself in the order and purpose there. It is a basic truth that 'we know' and are free; we 'cannot superadd the idea of knowledge to that of existence and *then* analyse the knowledge' without disintegrating the idea of existence presupposed, just as the 'idea of freedom or choice of action will not superadd itself to that of a state of things independent of it, without pulling this latter to pieces'. Moreover, as 'one word of a language implies the whole system of it, so does one particular of knowledge involve thought of the, as yet unparticularized, universe'. 'On Glossology' (1872, 1874) also seeks the origins of knowledge in language, as speech, looking not to etymology but to what we 'wish to express, by the words' and 'what the person whom we address will understand by them'.

J.B. Mayor rightly noted not only Grote's 'freshness of thought', but also his 'fearlessness in the use of neologisms' – notably 'personalism', 'hedonics', and 'relativism'. Yet, however knotty his style, Grote foreshadowed much that was to come in idealistic, analytic and linguistic philosophy.

See also: COMMON SENSE SCHOOL; EPISTEMIC RELATIVISM; GOOD, THEORIES OF THE; HEDONISM; INTUITIONISM IN ETHICS; MORAL KNOWLEDGE

List of works

The following list is limited to Grote's philosophical works, and does not include various other works. The best archival source is the Grote/Mayor Papers in the Wren Library, Trinity College, Cambridge.

Grote, J. (1865) *Exploratio Philosophica, Part I*, Cambridge: Deighton, Bell. (Published under his supervision, this work gives the substance of Grote's own idealist epistemology and ontology, which are elaborated through a conversational engagement with the work of such contemporaries as Ferrier, Whewell, Hamilton and J.S. Mill.)

—— (1867) 'What is Materialism?', *Macmillan's Magazine* 15: 371–81. (Forming chapters 1–3 of *Exploratio Philosophica, Part II*, this work criticizes the development of psychology by a comparative analysis of the logical coherence of materialist physiology, associational psychology, philosophical epistemology and idealism.)

—— (1870) *An Examination of the Utilitarian Philosophy*, ed. J.B. Mayor, Cambridge: Deighton, Bell. (A brilliant assessment of utilitarianism, arguing that J.S. Mill's revision of the doctrine is at odds with the earlier tradition and incoherent in itself.)

—— (1871) 'Thought versus Learning', *Good Words* 12: 818–23. (Argues that the best strategy in adult education is to encourage thinking via engagement in conversation, rather than to impose learning via the digestion of books.)

—— (1871) 'On a Future State', *Contemporary Review* 18: 133–40. (Attacks the appeal to supposed knowledge of the afterlife and the threat of damnation as a means of inculcating religious observance.)

—— (1872) 'On Glossology', *Journal of Philology* 4: 55–66, 157–81; also in *Journal of Philology* 1874 (5): 153–82. (Grote's linguistic prolegomena to philosophy and ethics, which in opposition to the philologists argues that the meaning of words is best established by the study of everyday usage.)

—— (1876) *A Treatise on the Moral Ideals*, ed. J.B. Mayor, Cambridge: Deighton, Bell. (Being the positive statement of Grote's moral philosophy, this text unites what is valid in both consequentialism and deontology in the systems of Eudaemonics and Aretaics, and grounds both of these in the experience of 'want' while also elaborating the plurality of moral ideals.)

—— (1877) 'Pascal and Montaigne', *The Contemporary Review* 30: 285–96. (A careful comparison of Pascal and Montaigne on the human condition.)

Grote, J. and Sidgwick, H. (1889) 'A Discussion Between Professor Henry Sidgwick and the Late Professor John Grote, on the Utilitarian Basis of Plato's *Republic*', *The Classical Review* 3: 98–102. (A reconstruction of an earlier debate on ethics between Grote and his younger colleague, cast in the form of a dialogue involving Thrasymachus, Adeimantes, Glaucon, Socrates and George Grote.)

Grote, J. (1900) *Exploratio Philosophica, Part II*, ed. J.B. Mayor, Cambridge: Cambridge University Press. (Elaborates and further illustrates Grote's epistemology, nicely articulating the idealist theory of the development of knowledge and the controversy between idealism and positivism.)

References and further reading

Bosanquet, B. (1902) 'Review: *Exploratio Philosophica*', *Archiv für Systematische Philosophie* 8: 128–30. (A vital source on how a major Oxford idealist recognized Grote as an objective idealist.)

Cunningham, G.W. (1933) *The Idealistic Argument in Recent British and American Philosophy*, New York: The Century Co. (Good chapter on Grote's *Exploratio*, stressing the Hegelian elements in his idealism.)

Gibbins, J. (1997) *John Grote, Cambridge University and the Development of Victorian Ideas*, Edinburgh: Edinburgh University Press. (This book locates Grote in the context of his day, analyses his original theories of history, politics and language, and provides photographs and an up-to-date bibliography of manuscripts and references to Grote. Argues that while developing an idealist position, Grote also set a new direction for Cambridge philosophy and brings out his influence on or affinities with such later figures as J. Ward, C.D. Broad, M. Oakeshott, J.A. Smith and H.W.B. Joseph.)

Lasson, G. (1878) 'Review: *Treatise on the Moral Ideals*', *Zeitschrift für Philosophie* u.k.r. 84: 149–54. (As the editor of Hegel's Works, Lasson provides a review that indicates the German and idealist response to Grote.)

Macdonald, L. (1966) *John Grote, A Critical Estimate of His Writings*, The Hague: Martinus Nijhoff. (Good bibliography, but seems to have been unable to track down various writings. Densely written, it interprets Grote as a personal idealist and is good on the originality of Grote's distinction between knowledge by description and by acquaintance, but contains less on his moral philosophy and very little on his views on history, politics and language.)

Mayor, J.B. (1870, 1876, 1900) Editorial introductions to *An Examination*, *Moral Ideals*, and *Exploratio Philosophica, Part II*. (These introductions are essential for understanding Grote's development and significance, and the last noted work, which contains the index for the whole, explains how H. Sidgwick and H. Joseph were instrumental in helping Mayor publish it at last.)

Quinton, A. (1973) *Utilitarian Ethics*, New York: St Martin's Press. (One of the few relatively recent introductory surveys of utilitarianism to pay Grote his due, with a short section summarizing his objections to Mill.)

Schneewind, J.B. (1977) *Sidgwick's Ethics and Victorian Moral Philosophy*, Oxford: Clarendon Press. (A splendid overview of philosophical developments in the half-century leading up to Sidgwick's *Methods of Ethics*. Relates Grote more to the earlier conflict between intuitionism and utilitarianism than to the growth of idealism – a key source of controversy in Grote studies.)

Seth, J. (1912) *English Philosophy and Schools of Philosophy*, London: J.M. Dent. (Detailed examination, identifying Grote, along with T.H. Green, as a typically English philosopher in both his procedures and his concern with the experiential basis of knowledge.)

Sidgwick, H. (1877) 'Review: *A Treatise on the Moral Ideals*', *Mind* 2: 239–44. (Sidgwick's various reviews of Grote tend towards the ungenerous in accusing Grote of being unsystematic and, consequently, unphilosophical.)

Whitmore, C.E. (1927) 'The Significance of John Grote', *Philosophical Review* 36: 307–37. (A very helpful overview.)

JOHN GIBBINS
BART SCHULTZ

GROTIUS, HUGO (1583–1645)

Scholar, lawyer and statesman, Grotius contributed to a number of different disciplines. His reputation as the founder both of a new international order and of a new moral science rests largely on his De iure belli ac pacis *(The Law of War and Peace) (1625). Though the tendency today is to regard Grotius as one figure among others in the development of the concept of international law, he is increasingly regarded as one of the most original moral philosophers of the seventeenth century, in particular as having laid the foundations for the post-sceptical doctrine of natural law that flourished during the Enlightenment.*

Of several striking epithets applied to Grotius, the earliest was that of Henry IV, who called him 'the miracle of Holland'. When only 15 years old Grotius had been taken on a diplomatic mission from the United Provinces to France, where he astonished the King with his prodigious learning. As a classicist, poet, historian, theologian and jurist he continued to impress his contemporaries throughout his life. He also continued to participate in international diplomacy during a period of almost constant conflict. For some twenty years he served the United Provinces until, on the fall of his patron Jan van Oldenbarnevelt in 1619, he was imprisoned for life. After a dramatic escape two years later he once again left The Netherlands for France, this time permanently. From 1634 until his death he acted as ambassador to France for Queen Christina of Sweden.

His interest in international relations earned Grotius another remarkable epithet, 'the father of international law'. As early as 1605 he wrote a treatise in defence of Dutch incursions in the East Indies, of which one chapter was published as *Mare liberum* (The Freedom of the Seas) in 1609. The treatise as a whole did not appear in print until 1864 as *De iure praedae* (The Law of Plunder), but in 1625 Grotius provided a fuller and somewhat revised statement of his ideas in the work on which his reputation chiefly rests, *De iure belli ac pacis*. In the first of its three books Grotius examined the notion of a just war, before moving on in the second to review the causes of just wars and in the third to consider how wars were justly waged.

The *De iure belli* did much to promote the idea of a society of states bound together by the common recognition of a set of rules governing relations between them. None the less, Grotius' reputation as the founder of an international legal order has not survived intact, partly because he wrote on only some aspects of international law, partly because his views were largely derivative. By contrast, his reputation as the founder of a new moral science has been rehabilitated. Although he wrote in the apparently familiar language of the natural law tradition, Grotius is believed to have established a new basis for ethical inquiry by tracing everything back to the one tenet of natural law that even sceptics would not deny, the idea that men were entitled to preserve themselves. From this foundation he – and to a greater degree his successors – reconstructed an elaborate body of natural law doctrine on a mathematical model (see NATURAL LAW §§4–5).

See also: LAW, PHILOSOPHY OF; PUFENDORF, S.; RIGHTS; ROMAN LAW §3; WAR AND PEACE, PHILOSOPHY OF

List of works

Grotius, H. (1609) *Mare liberum* (The Freedom of the Seas), trans. R. Magoffin, Oxford: Oxford University Press, 1916. (Translation printed along with a facsimile of the 1633 edition.)

—— (1625) *De iure belli ac pacis* (The Law of War and Peace), trans. F.W. Kelsey, Oxford: Oxford University Press, 1925. (Translation printed along with a facsimile of the 1646 edition.)

—— (1864) *De iure praedae* (The Law of Plunder), trans. G.L. Williams, Oxford: Oxford University Press, 1950. (Translation printed along with a facsimile of Grotius' original manuscript, replete with interesting alterations.)

References and further reading

Bull, H., Kingsbury, B. and Roberts, A. (eds) (1990) *Hugo Grotius and International Relations*, Oxford: Clarendon Press. (Contains essays reappraising Grotius' role in the history of international relations, with a useful bibliography.)

Grotiana (1928–47) and *Grotiana*, new series (1980–) Assen: Grotiana Foundation. (Devoted to Grotian studies, with bibliography updated in the latter.)

Knight, W.S.M. (1925) *The Life and Works of Hugo Grotius*, London: Sweet and Maxwell. (The most detailed biography.)

Onuma, Y. (ed.) (1993) *A Normative Approach to War*, Oxford: Clarendon Press. (Provides reliable accounts of Grotius' central concepts.)

Tuck, R. (1993) *Philosophy and Government, 1572–1651*, Cambridge: Cambridge University Press. (Assigns Grotius a pivotal position in the development of seventeenth-century moral and political thought.)

J.D. FORD

GUANZI

The Guanzi, *or 'Book of Master Guan', is an eclectic work including textual materials dating from the fourth century BC to the first century AD, drawing on themes from Daoism, the science of government, yin–yang and the Five Phases, Legalism, Confucianism, the art of war, economics and the Huang–Lao movement. Its pragmatic outlook is founded on a kind of objective realism that is the signature of the famous fourth-century BC Jixia academy in the principality of Qi. It was this academy that consolidated several different schools of thought.*

Historians have for the most part regarded the *Guanzi* as a treatise on political economy, and have not appreciated its philosophical side. This is because it has come down to us in an incomplete, corrupt and reworked form. The current version was reputedly compiled by Liu Xiang (76–6 BC) and includes various kinds of texts, from short maxims and popular

sayings to philosophical discourses and historical moralizings. Some chapters apparently were originally separate works, while others look like commentaries. The two main strains in the work seem to be the thought of Guan Zhong (the prime minister and architect of the economic dominance of the principality of Qi in the seventh century BC) and that of his anonymous disciples of the Han imperial epoch (second century BC to the second century AD).

Some of the ideas found in the *Guanzi* are reminiscent of legalism, including government by impersonal and invariable law, the concepts of 'profit' and 'propitious dates', the supreme position of the prince, the notion that one must adapt to circumstances with 'non-action' and that one must follow the will of Heaven as an impersonal, predetermined natural order (see LEGALIST PHILOSOPHY, CHINESE). Then there are other, more Confucian concepts: a respect for rituals that ensure social order by assigning a place to each person reflective of the inevitable differences in social status (the knowledge of how to allocate the places equitably being the mark of the Sage); a respect for unchanging, cosmic moral rules, the 'just way' (*dao*) and the cultivation of a 'sense of shame', along with a concern for the welfare of the people as necessary to the maintenance of good order (see CONFUCIAN PHILOSOPHY, CHINESE). In the *Guanzi*, Legalism is tinted by Confucian ideas while at the same time, Confucianism is influenced by Legalism and marked by a centralizing and authoritarian tendency closer to XUNZI than to CONFUCIUS. The two tendencies merge, respecting both the authority of the prince and the desires of the people.

The role of the prince is primary since he determines each person's rank and function, establishes laws and moral rules and hands out rewards and punishments. Being the central authority, he must exercise power by himself, maintaining rituals and dispensing law and punishments while also enforcing respect for political institutions. The prince must be a moral example, inspiring his people. His 'love' for the people is not purely humanitarian; it derives from the fact that the people, in their complete obedience, serve him and ensure his continued power without having any of their own. This contrasts with Confucius' insistence on the people's right and duty to give counsel, and Mencius' conception of the people's right to revolt against tyranny (see MENCIUS). In the *Guanzi*, the people need not be considered when their wants are individual and short-term; only the prince can decide how to evaluate the collective desires of his subjects and determine how to satisfy their deeper, long-term wishes.

The economic ideas in the *Guanzi*, with its insistence on the need to pay attention to prices and to seek a mean between poverty and excessive wealth, favour productivity and suggest some real commercial influence (see ECONOMICS, PHILOSOPHY OF). One famous chapter on 'the light and the heavy' is the first exposition of the need to watch over the circulation and amount of goods. However, the work also favours agriculture as a basic activity, ranking it higher than the occupations of craftsmen and merchants. The land itself constitutes the basis of government and its tax system. Emphasis is placed on the fair distribution of land, with attention to territorial organization and precise administrative boundaries, as well as to the nature of the soil and propitious dates. In this context there are several calendars, and a chapter on maps.

Alongside the notion of a Confucian-style *dao* or moral path and some Daoist-like ideas which had been rejected by the Daoists themselves, we also find chapters redolent of psycho-physiological Daoism, with ideas of non-action and the interior void that constitutes purity and receptiveness (see DAOIST PHILOSOPHY). In this vein there is also the idea of a metaphysical *dao*, ineffable and impossible to place, omnipresent as an all-encompassing void and as such, the source of all life. Paradoxically, a Confucian-like discussion on 'correcting names' is linked with a treatise on the Daoistic silence that the Sage must observe, a silence which allows for the establishment of an indispensable, exact terminology.

See also: CONFUCIAN PHILOSOPHY, CHINESE; DAOIST PHILOSOPHY; DAO; HUAINANZI; LEGALIST PHILOSOPHY, CHINESE; POLITICAL PHILOSOPHY, HISTORY OF; SMITH, A.

References and further reading

* *Guanzi* (4th century BC–1st century AD), trans. W. Allyn Rickett, *Kuan-tzu, a Repository of Early Chinese Thought*, Hong Kong: University of Hong Kong Press, 1965; trans. W. Allyn Rickett, *Guanzi: Political, Economic, and Philosophical Essays from Early China*, Princeton, NJ: Princeton University Press, 1985. (Two translations of the *Guanzi*.)

Haloun, G. (1951) 'Legalist Fragments: Part I; *Kuan-tsï* 55 and Related Texts', *Asia Major*, new series 2 (1): 85–120. (A translation of Chapter XVIII, 55 of the *Guanzi* with a study of the transmission of the text and its various editions.)

ISABELLE ROBINET

GUEVARA, ERNESTO 'CHE'
see MARXIST THOUGHT IN LATIN AMERICA

GUIFENG ZONGMI *see* ZONGMI

GUILT *see* MORAL SENTIMENTS; RECTIFICATION AND REMAINDERS (§5)

GURNEY, EDMUND (1847–88)

Edmund Gurney was an English psychologist and musician. His major work, The Power of Sound, *is a vast treatise on musical aesthetics, ranging from issues in the physiology of hearing to the question of the relation of music to morality, but is mostly devoted to central questions of form, expression and value in music. It is the most significant work of its kind in the latter half of the nineteenth century.*

Commentators often couple Gurney with Hanslick as a supporter of musical formalism, but his views on the expressive dimension of music are neither as restrictive nor as doctrinaire as Hanslick's. Hanslick insisted on denying specific emotional content to music, allowing it only to convey dynamic features, which emotions, among other things, might exhibit. Gurney, on the other hand, grants that some music possesses fairly definite emotional expression, and discusses at length the grounds of such expression; he is primarily concerned to deny that musical impressiveness, or beauty, is either the same as or depends on musical expressiveness.

Gurney maintains that overall form in music is not of primary relevance to the appreciation of music. This is because the central feature of musical comprehension is the grasping of individual parts as they occur, and the grasping of connections to immediately neighbouring parts, whatever the overarching form of a piece might be. The value of a piece is directly a function of the pleasurableness of its individual parts and the cogency of sequence exhibited at the transitions between them, not a function of its global architecture.

1 Form, understanding and value in music
2 Beauty and expression in music

1 Form, understanding and value in music

A cornerstone of Gurney's view of music is the

contrast between the temporal art of music and the static visual art of two dimensions. He is struck by the difference between the apprehension of music and the apprehension of a linear arabesque or an architectural façade. While one can have a single sweeping perception of the whole of an arabesque or façade, a musical work allows one only a series of perceptions of its parts as it unfolds in time, never a single perception of the work in its entirety. The experience of music is fundamentally a matter of individual, overlapping impressions of short duration.

Despite the successiveness of our apprehension of them, however, moments of music often group themselves into extended units that we seem to grasp as a whole, though we cannot literally perceive them at one time. We find that some sequences of minute, heard events cohere together strongly when sequentially perceived, so that we hear them as single, unified movements. This is the phenomenon of melody, a string of successive auditory impressions somehow yielding a single impression comprising them all. When a sequence of notes constitutes a melody, the notes together display a certain minimum rightness. This rightness can be understood counterfactually, in terms of the effects, usually deleterious, of changing a single note. The special quality or character of a given melody is dependent on every note that comprises it; change any one and invariably the result is either no melody or another melody. The general outline or contour of a melody gives practically no sense of it at all; its essence lies in the specific notes that make it up, and not in anything more general that may be abstracted from them. No pitch or rhythm sequence, furthermore, possesses any inherent goodness in itself, and there are in fact no necessary and sufficient conditions discoverable for what constitutes a good melody.

Gurney later supplements this counterfactual criterion of melody with one that is more directly phenomenological. It is a mark of a melody that one is familiar with, that when one is strictly only hearing one part of it, it is *as if* one is also hearing the whole thing; one is in some way aware of the remainder while hearing any one part. 'When a melody is familiar to us we realize it by a gradual process of advance along it, while yet the whole process is in some real manner present to us at each of the successive instants at which only a minute part of it is actually engaging our ears' (1880: 165). It is this that Gurney famously labels 'Ideal Motion', noting that it is as much a characteristic of the process by which we perceive melody as of melody itself. The peculiarity of audible as opposed to visible form, of which melody is the paradigm, is that it is both formed, implying completeness, and at the same time moving or developing, implying incompleteness. Though Ideal Motion bears some analogy to physical motion, and often induces the latter in sympathetic listeners, it is a distinct phenomenon, neither reducible to nor proportional to the other. Gurney also notes a related feature of familiar melodies, namely that in listening to them one seems to construct them, with their characteristic tensions and overall flavour, in the very act of listening.

The emergence of melody is thus the chief way in which the moment-to-moment nature of musical apprehension is tempered and, to an extent, transcended. Gurney does, however, admit the existence of larger unities (musical paragraphs, for example) provided the components are bound together in a certain way. Although such paragraphs, unlike melodies, are not experienced as wholes, they can be internally unified in such a fashion that their successive parts do not strike a listener as unconnected to each other. What is required for this Gurney names 'organicity' or 'cogency of sequence' – the one and only adequate criterion of effective musical form, the *sine qua non* of well-formedness at any level. It is possessed by the succession of unprepossessing two- and three-note fragments that make up a melody, and by the succession of melodic and transitional passages that make up a unified musical paragraph. In the first case, one has parts, the individual tones, which are not themselves impressive, combined into a unit that is; in the second, the parts are already independently impressive, though they yield a whole that is impressive as well. In discussing what it is for a musical paragraph to constitute a form in the strict sense, Gurney offers a characterization of cogency of sequence in which its additional application to melody is plain: 'any paragraph which is to be musically valuable must satisfy the test that each bit shall necessitate, as it were, and so enter into organic union with, the one next to it' (1880: 204).

A sequence is cogent, then, when each part – whether motive, phrase, melody or paragraph – leads convincingly to the next, each consequent appearing, upon familiarity, to be the natural and inevitable continuation of its antecedent. Where there is cogency of sequence, there is resistance to any imagined substitution for any part in the musical chain, the test of cogency being precisely 'the feeling of resentment ... with which the ear, after sufficient acquaintance, would receive changes or omissions' (1880: 212). Cogency of sequence admits of degrees, however. It reaches its apex within single melodies, tying together component motives or phrases, and can run fairly high in a paragraph composed of several melodic or quasi-melodic passages. But it is usually on the wane within extended movements made up of several sections, and generally approaches zero between the movements of large-scale works.

For Gurney, cogency of sequence – including unity of melody, which is a species of it – is a purely *intuitive* matter, judged by an autonomous musical faculty. It cannot be assessed or demonstrated by rational means; no formulable rules of repetition, contrast or balance can guarantee the presence of cogency or organicity. The musical faculty, in accord with the experiential criteria that have been mentioned, is the ultimate arbiter of musical form and effectiveness.

Gurney insists that the essential sequentiality of musical apprehension, and our inability to take in an extended portion of music as a whole at one stroke, entails the absolute primacy of the *parts* of a musical composition with regard to musical form, musical enjoyment and musical worth. The real form of a piece of music is wholly exhausted by the constitution of the smallest independent units out of formless elements, and the specific manner in which each independent unit leads on to the next. There is in no important sense an overall form to an extended piece of music; there is only form within and between parts that are successively apprehended. Musical enjoyment is likewise grounded entirely in the grasp of individual moments of various lengths and the transitions between them. 'The whole is a combination of parts successively enjoyed, and can only be impressive so far as the parts are impressive' (1880: 97). The parts, even taken out of context, are often of exceptional value; the whole comprising all the parts in order, on the other hand, carries no additional value of its own. As for relations which a given part may bear to other parts distant from it, these may affect one's experience of the given part, but attention remains fixed on the part being heard, and not on any skein of relations encompassing the piece as a whole in which the part abstractly figures. Furthermore, though awareness of such relations may enhance one's pleasure in what is then being heard, there is no distinct pleasure to be had in the relations themselves.

This view, which emphasizes the concrete detail of musical surface and its quality and connectedness from moment to moment, is clearly inimical to that to which music theorists often implicitly subscribe – namely, that elucidation and awareness of large-scale structural relations is of primary relevance to the understanding and evaluation of musical works, and that the whole is indeed as important as the parts, if not more so. Nevertheless, it seems that Gurney is fundamentally right in this respect. The simple insight at the root of his thought, and one that promoters of overall form tend to forget, is that music consists of a series of successive events which can never be apprehended simultaneously in a single perceptual act. The parts of a façade can be taken in more or less in one sweep, unlike the parts of a symphony. Of course, earlier portions of a musical work can be abstractly reviewed in memory as listening proceeds, or later portions entertained in anticipation, but that is not the same as the perceptual experience of a whole. What is crucial, according to Gurney, is involvement in local movement from phrase to phrase, and not architectonic vistas beyond aural experience.

Gurney distinguishes finally between two modes of listening to music, the 'definite' and the 'indefinite'. His conclusions concerning musical form, value and enjoyment all presuppose listening that occurs in the definite mode. Someone listening definitely attends to the specific features of the melodic and harmonic motion of the music as it passes, registers the individuality of what they hear, and typically acquires a recognitional capacity for those parts of form as a result. Definite listening is active, alert, participatory and particularizing. Someone listening indefinitely, on the other hand, is mainly aware of a succession of sounds, and reacts to and registers only gross changes in the overall sound-image.

2 Beauty and expression in music

Gurney is a musical formalist in the following respects. First, he posits an autonomous musical faculty, whose charge is the grasping and assessing of musical forms. This faculty derives from the apprehension of 'impressive' forms, that is, ones that can be synthesized as wholes in the short span, and which thus exhibit Ideal Motion, a distinct and *sui generis* pleasure. Second, he maintains that the impressiveness of musical forms – their purely musical beauty – is not different from but entirely independent of whatever 'expressiveness' they possess. But Gurney, unlike Hanslick, clearly accepts the phenomenon of musical expressiveness and devotes considerable attention to it (see HANSLICK, E). He begins, in anticipation of Goodman's claim that expressive properties are only metaphorically possessed, by observing that a thing does not express its central or defining attributes, but rather its incidental (or 'occasional') ones, for only the latter display sufficient separability from the thing to allow them to be expressed. Gurney's specific analysis of musical expressiveness is thus: 'when a particular feeling in ourselves is identified with a particular character in a particular bit of music, then we say without hesitation that such a particular bit *expresses* the quality or feeling' (1880: 313). This formulation can evidently be construed in both an arousalist and a cognitivist way, depending on how the phrase 'a particular feeling in ourselves' is understood; indeed Gurney seems to waver between the two in subsequent discussion. On the first construal, what is expressed by music is necessarily some feeling evoked in us as we listen. On the second construal, what is expressed is a feeling that we have experienced and are familiar with, and which we are disposed to relate to the character of the part being heard, but this is not necessarily something we are then experiencing; it is a feeling the music suggests to us, rather than awakens in us.

An additional complication in Gurney's account is that although the 'feeling in ourselves' by which the expressiveness of the music is gauged is in most cases the same as the quality we ascribe to the music, it is in some cases rather the feeling that *contemplation* of the quality ascribed is apt to induce in us. Thus, while the special feelings corresponding to melancholic or joyful music are melancholy and joy, those corresponding to humorous and terrible music, that is, music expressive of humour and terror, are amusement and fear, not wittiness or menace. Unfortunately, Gurney gives no principled criterion for when the relationship between expressed feeling and feeling in listeners conforms to the direct, as opposed to the indirect, model.

Gurney holds that the grounds of musical expressiveness are to be found in the resemblances between music and human behaviour that is expressive of emotion. Musical motion, in its pace, rhythm and shape, echoes that exhibited in the gestures, movements and vocal inflections that outwardly manifest human feeling. Gurney holds that a certain asymmetry obtains when accounting for expressiveness, which partly parallels the absence of criteria for impressiveness. When a moment or section of music expresses an emotion, it is always possible to find structural features of the music that, by underpinning a resemblance to standard expressive behaviour, are largely responsible for the expressiveness, and thus explain it; but we cannot reverse this procedure and dependably predict, on the basis of its structural features, the emotion that a moment or section of music will express.

Gurney's arguments concerning impressiveness and expressiveness have a variety of targets and are of varying soundness. Some are designed merely to underline the difference between impressiveness and expressiveness, some are aimed at denying any dependence of impressiveness on expressiveness, and some are concerned with the different bearing of the two on musical worth.

Gurney notes that in much impressive music 'definable expression' is absent and that much music with 'definable expression' fails to be impressive. Thus – on the assumption that definable expression and

expressiveness are the same – expressiveness is distinct from, and neither necessary nor sufficient for, impressiveness. And reinforcing for Gurney the nonidentity of expressiveness and impressiveness is the fact that assessments of expressiveness often vary widely for different listeners, while judgments of impressiveness roughly coincide. But Gurney goes on to assert that musical features that are intended to bring about the definite expression of some emotion will only do so if the music is impressive as well – suggesting that impressiveness, far from depending on expressiveness, may even be a necessary condition of it.

Gurney notes that pieces with equivalent expressiveness are often musically valuable in different ways, so that we would not be content to keep one and not the other. He concludes that the musical value of such pieces must be independent of the expressiveness they have in common, and observes that emotions are expressed by human behaviour even more directly and unequivocally than by music, yet the former is not seen as a source of aesthetic satisfaction; again, the aesthetic worth of music cannot rest merely on its capacity to express emotion.

Reviewing the above, it is evident that Gurney does not sufficiently consider the possibility that *part* of a piece's value might reside in its expressiveness, even if its expressiveness is shared with other pieces, and even if a concomitant impressiveness is required for that value to be realized; nor does he consider that value might reside in the particular *way* in which music, as opposed to ordinary behaviour, is expressive of emotion; nor that the *interplay* of expressiveness and impressiveness in a given piece might be a focus of interest.

It is sometimes ventured that music, through its almost infinite variety of forms, might have the ability to convey correspondingly fine nuances of feeling, and thus might outstrip what word or gesture can accomplish in expressive capacity. However, if one holds with Gurney that the only way in which music is expressive is in its reflection of the normal, behavioural expression of emotion, then the idea that music will be able to express finer shades of emotion than are already differentiated in the full range of human behaviour necessarily comes to grief. On this hypothesis, the emotional suggestions of musical form and content can be no more finely-grained than pre-existing correlations of behaviour with emotion, by reference to which such suggestions are accomplished at all.

Finally, Gurney examines with devastating results the thesis that expressive music expresses the emotions of its creator. First, there is the gross implausibility of the claim that an extended piece might track the regularly fluctuating feelings of the composer;

second, music expressive of a feeling is clearly composable by one who is not experiencing that feeling and has perhaps never experienced it; and third, observation gives no support even to any rough rules connecting the expressive character of a piece and a composer's contemporaneous state. A more plausible thesis, according to Gurney, proposes only that the dominant character of a composer's music, as evidenced in their entire *oeuvre* or a significant portion thereof, reliably reflects the composer's characteristic psychological condition.

See also: ART, UNDERSTANDING OF; EMOTION IN RESPONSE TO ART; ARTISTIC EXPRESSION; FORMALISM IN ART; MUSIC, AESTHETICS OF §§6, 10

List of works

Gurney, E. (1880) *The Power of Sound*, New York: Basic Books, 1966. (His major work, an important contribution to aesthetics of music in the nineteenth century.)

—— (1887) *Tertium Quid*, London. (A collection of essays.)

References and further reading

Budd, M. (1985) *Music and the Emotions*, London: Routledge, ch. 4. (Discusses Gurney's views on the roots of musical affect and the nature of musical expressiveness.)

Cone, E. (1966) 'The Power of *The Power of Sound*', intro. to *The Power of Sound*, New York: Basic Books, 1966. (Contains biographical and anecdotal material, and contrasts Gurney's view of musical form with those advanced by other theorists of music.)

Hospers, J. (1982) *Understanding the Arts*, Englewood Cliffs, NJ: Prentice Hall, ch. 4. (Discusses Gurney's arguments concerning musical expressiveness.)

Levinson, J. (1993) 'Edmund Gurney and the Appreciation of Music', *IYYUN, The Jerusalem Philosophical Quarterly* 42: 181–205. (An elaboration of the material of the first part of this article, on musical understanding.)

—— (1997) *Music in the Moment*, Ithaca, NY: Cornell University Press. (A monograph that defends an account of musical comprehension based on Gurney's ideas about music listening.)

JERROLD LEVINSON

GYELTSAP DARMA RINCHEN
see rGYAL TSHAB DAR MA RIN CHEN

H

HA'AM, AHAD (1856–1927)

Ahad Ha'am (Asher Hirsch Ginzberg) was one of the most remarkable Jewish thinkers and Zionist ideologists of his time. Born in the province of Kiev in the Ukraine, he moved in 1884 to Odessa, an important centre of Hebrew literary activity. In 1907 he moved on to London, and in 1922 settled in the young city of Tel Aviv. He attended the universities of Vienna, Berlin and Breslau but did not pursue any regular course of study and was primarily an autodidact. Never a systematic philosopher, Ginzberg, who wrote in Hebrew and adopted the pen name Ahad Ha'am, 'one of the people', became a first-rate and widely read essayist and polemicist. He engaged in controversies over the practical problems of the early Jewish settlements in Palestine, his opposition to Theodore Herzl's drive to create a Jewish state, and numerous problems of Hebrew culture, tradition and literature. No single principle or theme stands out as the guiding idea of his thought. Indeed, his ideas are sometimes inconsistent. But his writings preserve the flavour of his values and commitments. Although his outlook never became the main road of Zionist ideology, its impact on Zionist thought was powerful, especially after the establishment of the State of Israel.

1   Jewish nationhood
2   The spiritual centre

1   Jewish nationhood

Ahad Ha'am's thinking was strongly influenced by nineteenth-century evolutionism and the philosophy of Herbert SPENCER. Unlike most other Jewish thinkers of his time, he was more under the spell of English and French than German philosophers, but he applied his eclectic thinking most concertedly to the complex of difficulties known in his time as 'the Jewish problem'. Jewish nationality, like any other, he argued, is acquired naturally – unlike the moral idea of humanity, which is derived from abstract reasoning. It is grounded in a spontaneous sentiment of national belonging, akin to family ties and needs no theoretical justification. For the sense of national belonging is prior to consciousness itself; it springs from a kind of biological impulse and is felt as an emotion, rather than reasoned like a universal moral truth.

A people, like any organism, Ahad Ha'am reasoned, strives for self-preservation. This national 'will to live' is the resultant of every individual's will to live. But its demands take precedence over individual survival, since the nation will endure long after the individual's death. Indeed, the national 'urge to survive' is not merely a Darwinian biological concept but a cultural and social imperative. Following up on a Hegelian idea elaborated by the Jewish philosopher Nachman KROCHMAL in the 1840s, Ahad Ha'am maintained that every nation has its own distinctive spiritual character. This spiritual factor, and no mere political fact like statehood, was the true expression of peoplehood and the true basis of national survival. Diverging from his positivist and evolutionary bent, Ginzberg turned here towardss ideas influenced by German idealism and romanticism. Every national spirit, he observed, has its sources in the past. In Judaism the national idea is inspired by the moral teaching of the Hebrew prophets. Thus the core of the Jewish spirit is not ultimately a matter of religion but of ethics (see COHEN, H.). Unlike many previous thinkers, Ahad Ha'am found the core message of Jewish ethics in turn not at the individual but at the social level, in the prophet's uncompromising insistence on objective justice, not mere love or compassion. What matters is the act, not the agent or the intention. He drew this theme from his reading of the Jewish sources, but he did not restrict it to Judaism. He conceived of the quest for justice as the universal human quest and thus found a world historical mission in the particularities of Jewish history. But the enduring message and the enduring bond were not those of religion. Monotheism and messianism, to be sure, had played their parts historically in upholding the national will to existence. But with the rise of secularism the Jewish religion could no longer unify the Jewish people. The historico-religious bond had crumbled. Ahad Ha'am himself had become a secular Jew, and he looked forward to the emergence of a new Judaism that would take over the unifying role once played by religion. Modern Judaism will respect the Jewish religion as the most significant creation of the Jewish people; but it can no longer accept that religion's imperatives. For these are not divine commands but historical expressions of peoplehood. These ideas of Ahad Ha'am's were later taken up by the American Jewish philosopher Mordecai KAPLAN.

2 The spiritual centre

Despite the Hegelian and romantic essentialism at the root of his ideas of the Jewish spirit, it was in a Spencerian vein that Ahad Ha'am addressed the Jewish urge for survival, arguing, in effect, that there is no Jewish national problem, any more than there is a French or English problem. The peculiarity of the Jewish question derives only from the complexity of the Jewish situation. Assimilation, long identified as a critical issue for the Jews of the diaspora, is the most portentous of the problems faced in that situation. In his famous essay 'Hikkuj ve-Hitbollelut' (Imitation and Assimilation) (1893), Ahad Ha'am defines assimilation as the disappearance of the natural will for national survival. This contretemps is seen by him as a danger to Jews only as individuals. Surprisingly, it need not threaten Jewish peoplehood. For Judaism, he reasoned, could be saved by the establishment of a spiritual centre in Palestine. The message of Judaism emanating from this centre to the Jewish periphery – the message oriented by the moral exhortations of the Hebrew prophets – will strengthen national consciousness in the diaspora and endow spiritual life with a true national content. It will thereby constitute an effective barrier against assimilation, without need of a state, as called for by the political Zionists of Theodore Herzl's movement (see ZIONISM).

The question remained, of course, whether the Jews to be influenced by the centre would willingly follow those who hoped to influence them. Clearly Ahad Ha'am's schema of spokes and a wheel more adequately reflects present-day relations between Israel and world Jewry than did the maximalist ideology that often characterized political Zionism. Yet, contrary to his hopes, even the State of Israel and the activity of its emissaries in the diaspora, not to mention the many cultural and educational institutions it shelters, have only partially arrested the trend towards assimilation among Jews in their countries of residence. The Jews of those lands have not come to see Israel as their capital; and Israel itself, in an ironic commentary on Ahad Ha'am's vision, is fully subject to the same forces that drive much of the assimilation of diaspora Jewry.

Ahad Ha'am's cultural Zionism was his alternative to assimilation on the one hand and political Zionism on the other. Unlike Pinsker and Herzl, whose Zionism was triggered by the collision of Jews with their social and political environment, and especially by the growth of anti-Semitism, Ha'am believed the Jewish predicament to consist in growing to feel too much at home in that environment and becoming estranged from the Jewish national heritage. His sensitivity to the problem of assimilation indeed tended to blind him to the threat of tragedy that hung over the diaspora Jewry in the form of anti-Semitism.

See also: NATION AND NATIONALISM; ZIONISM

List of works

Ahad Ha'am (1946) *Ahad Ha'am: Essays, Letters, Memoirs*, ed. and trans. L. Simon, Oxford: East and West Library. (Broad translated collection of Ahad Ha'am's writings in various forms.)
—— (1950) *Kol Kit've Ahad Ha'am* (Complete Works of Ahad Ha'am), Tel Aviv: Dvir. (The essays deal with Judaism, Zionism and the issues of the Zionist movement and colonization of Palstine.)
—— (1970) *Selected Essays by Ahad Ha'am*, ed. and trans. L. Simon, New York: Atheneum. (A presentation of Ahad Ha'am's life, public activity in the Zionist movement, his controversy with Herzlian Zionism, and his literary and publicist work.)
—— (1893) 'Hikkuj ve-Hitbollelut' (Imitation and Assimilation), trans. and ed. L. Simon, in *Ahad Ha'am: Essays, Letters, Memoirs*, Oxford: East and West Library, 1946, 71–5. (Points out the positive aspects of cultural assimilation and the negative aspects of abandoning the Jewish heritage for its sake.)

References and further reading

Fraenkel, J. (1963) *Dubnow, Herzl and Ahad Ha'am*, London: Ararat. (Three monographs on a great non-Zionist Jewish scholar and two Zionist thinkers with divergent views on the aim of Zionism.)
Simon, L. (1960) *Ahad Ha'am Asher Ginzberg: A Biography*, New York: Herzl Press. (Biography of Ahad Ha'am.)

ZE'EV LEVY

HABERMAS, JÜRGEN (1929–)

Jürgen Habermas, German philosopher and social theorist, is perhaps best known for his wide-ranging defence of the modern public sphere and its related ideals of publicity and free public reason, but he has also made important contributions to theories of communication and informal argumentation, ethics, and the foundations and methodology of the social sciences. He studied in Göttingen, Zurich and Bonn, completing a dissertation on Schelling's philosophy in 1954. After working for a short time as Theodor Adorno's research assistant at the Institute for Social

Research in Frankfurt he held professorships in Heidelberg and Frankfurt and, from 1971 to 1981, was co-director of the Max Planck Institute in Starnberg. With the publication of Knowledge and Human Interests *(1968) he became widely recognized as the leading intellectual heir to the Frankfurt School of Critical Theory, a variant of Western Marxism that included such figures as Adorno, Max Horkheimer and Herbert Marcuse. His two-volume* The Theory of Communicative Action *(1981) is a major contribution to social theory, in which he locates the origins of the various political, economic and cultural crises confronting modern society in a one-sided process of rationalization steered more by the media of money and administrative power than by forms of collective decision-making based on consensually grounded norms and values.*

1   **Early work**
2   *The Theory of Communicative Action*
3   **Discourse ethics**
4   **Politics and law**
5   **Habermas as polemicist**

1   Early work

In his first book, *The Structural Transformation of the Public Sphere* (1962), Habermas traces the emergence of a bourgeois public sphere which, at least for a time, offered the prospect of an arena that would mediate between state and society. Rooted in the social and economic conditions of liberal capitalism, the 'bourgeois public sphere' refers to those sociocultural institutions that arose in the eighteenth century in opposition to the absolutist powers of the state – private clubs and coffeehouses, learned societies and literary associations, publishing houses, journals, and newspapers. Taken as a whole these institutions constituted a 'public realm of reasoning private persons' that was partially secured through the enactment of various constitutional rights and liberties. In theory and (to a more limited extent) in practice, this public sphere was distinct both from the private sphere of the market and the family and from the political authority of the state. It designated a sphere that comes about whenever private persons reason collectively about their common interests, and its function was both to restrain and legitimate the political power exercised by the administrative state.

Habermas' thesis, however, is that this idea of the public sphere had a very limited lifespan. At the level of theory, the idea of a 'reasoning public' was treated with suspicion by conservatives and progressives alike and, in liberal theory, the defence of a public sphere was often limited to the formal guarantee of a narrow set of 'natural' civil and political rights. As an historical phenomenon, the bourgeois public sphere suffered an equally unfortunate fate. In connection with what he refers to as the 'refeudalization' of civil society during the latter part of the nineteenth century, Habermas traces the commercialization of civil society, the bureaucratization of political and non-political authority, and the growth of a manipulative or propagandistic mass-media. A 'repoliticized social sphere' erodes the real distinction between state and society that is a necessary social condition for the bourgeois public sphere, and a society oriented to consumption and a politics based on the competition and bargaining between interest groups emerges in the place of a public sphere formed by an enlightened citizenry. Although Habermas never abandons the normative claims expressed in the bourgeois ideal, the conclusion of *The Structural Transformation of the Public Sphere* is extremely cautious about the possibility for a renewed public sphere under the altered conditions of late capitalist society. Only thirty years later in *Between Facts and Norms* (1992) does Habermas return, on a more optimistic note, to the prospects for democracy in complex, pluralist societies.

In the 1960s and 1970s, Habermas pursued a number of related issues. He sharply criticized the 'scientization of politics' and increase in 'technocratic consciousness' he discerned in contemporary societies. For Habermas the growth of technocracy was not inevitable but the result of a failure to preserve (albeit by other means) the classical distinction between theory and practice, and between practical wisdom (*phronēsis*) and technical skill (*technē*). In a series of influential essays, many of which are collected in *Theory and Practice* (1963), he traced the loss of these distinctions in modern political theory (from Hobbes to Hegel) as well as in Marx whose own concept of praxis blurred a related and equally important distinction between labour (*Arbeit*) and modes of social interaction based on shared interpretations of the world. Thus, contra Marx, Habermas argues that the end of alienated labour does not alone ensure social emancipation.

During this same period, Habermas also pursued a more systematic critique of positivism, found in his contributions to the so-called 'positivist dispute' in German sociology and in his popular study, *Knowledge and Human Interests* (1968). The latter work traces the 'dissolution of epistemology' from its origin as a critical enterprise with Kant to its status as a relatively uncritical 'theory of science' in the first half of this century. Positivism (or scientism), for Habermas, is the insistence that only the sciences constitute genuine knowledge together with the belief that science does not need any further critical analysis or justification. It refers less to the practice of the sciences than to their 'scientistic self-misunderstanding'. Habermas challenges this view (which was still popular at the time) and attempts to secure an independent basis for critique by arguing that all forms of knowledge are rooted in fundamental human interests. He identifies three 'quasi-transcendental' or 'anthropologically deep-seated' cognitive interests with reference to which distinct forms of knowledge can be delineated: the natural sciences correspond to a technical interest; the historical-hermeneutic sciences, to a practical interest; and the critical sciences (for example, Marxism and psychoanalysis when each is freed from its own 'scientistic self-misunderstanding'), to an emancipatory interest. Thus, through a kind of continuation of epistemology by social theory, Habermas sought to complete a critique of positivism and provide a 'prolegomenon' for a critical social theory. Though he quickly became dissatisfied with the anthropological underpinnings of this initial attempt, there are already hints of the 'linguistic turn' in his later theory, evident, for example, in his remark that 'the human interest in autonomy and responsibility is not mere fancy, for it can be apprehended a priori. What raises us out of nature is the only thing whose nature we can know: language' (1968: 314) (see POSITIVISM IN THE SOCIAL SCIENCES).

2 The Theory of Communicative Action

The Theory of Communicative Action (1981), Habermas' magnum opus, is a major contribution to social theory which in its aim and structure resembles Max WEBER's *Economy and Society* and Talcott Parson's *The Structure of Social Action*. Like those works, it presents metatheoretic reflections on the basic concepts of social theory along with observations on the methodology of the social sciences and quasi-empirical hypotheses about modernization as a process of societal rationalization. However, in contrast particularly to Weber, Habermas does not regard rationalization as a process that inevitably culminates in the loss of meaning and freedom in the world, but as an ambivalent process that also opens up a potential for societal learning and new levels of human emancipation.

Like Weber and Parsons, Habermas begins with a set of metatheoretic reflections that yields a typology of action. His basic distinction is between 'consent-oriented' (or communicative) and 'success-oriented' (or purposive-rational) actions; within the latter he distinguishes further between strategic and instrumental action. Instrumental actions are goal-oriented

interventions in the physical world. They can be appraised from the standpoint of efficiency and described as the following of technical rules. Strategic action, by contrast, is action which aims at influencing others for the purpose of achieving some end. It too can be appraised in terms of its efficiency and described with the tools of game theory and theories of rational choice (see RATIONAL CHOICE THEORY). Many instrumental actions can also be strategic, and some forms of strategic action may be instrumental. Communicative action, however, constitutes an independent and distinct type of social action. The goal or 'telos' of communicative action is not expressed or realized in an attempt to influence others, but in the attempt to reach an agreement or mutual understanding (*Verständigung*) about something in the world. Thus, while all action is teleological or goal-oriented in a broad sense, in the case of communicative action any further ends the agent may have are subordinated to the goal of achieving a mutually shared definition of the agent's lifeworldly situation through a cooperative process of interpretation. In acting communicatively, individuals more or less naïvely accept as valid the various claims raised with their utterance or action and mutually suppose that each is prepared to provide reasons for them should their validity be questioned. In a slightly more technical (and controversial) sense, and one tied more specifically to modern structures of rationality, Habermas also holds that individuals who act communicatively aim at reaching understanding about something in the world by relating their interpretations to three general types of validity claims that are constitutive for three basic types of SPEECH ACTS: a claim to truth raised in constative speech acts, a claim to normative rightness raised in regulative speech acts, and a claim to truthfulness raised in expressive speech acts (1981, vol. I: 319–).

At a methodological level, this analysis of social action underlines the need for an interpretive or *Verstehende* approach in the social sciences. The requirement of *Verstehen* arises because the objects that the social sciences study – actions and their products – are embedded in 'complexes of meaning' (*Sinnzusammenhänge*) that can be understood by the social inquirer only as he or she relates them to his or her own pre-theoretical knowledge as a member of the lifeworld. This, in turn, gives rise to the 'disquieting thesis' that the interpretation of action cannot be separated from the interpreter's taking a position on the validity of the claims explicitly or implicitly connected with the action. The process of identifying the reasons for an action unavoidably draws one into the process of assessment in which the inquirer must adopt the perspective of an (at least virtual) participant. Understanding the reasons for action requires taking a position on the validity of those reasons according to our own lights, and that means (at least initially) setting aside an external or 'third person' perspective in favour of an internal or 'first person' perspective in which both agent and interpreter belong to the same 'universe of discourse'. It is in this way that Habermas is able to connect the notion of rationality generally with his more specific claims that reason is a capacity to test validity claims.

However, despite his emphasis on social (or communicative) rationality with its ties to criticizable validity claims, Habermas does not think that society can be viewed as a sort of large-scale debating club. On the one hand, agents' interpretations are generally taken for granted and form part of an implicit background of knowledge and practices that constitute what he calls (following Edmund Husserl and Alfred Schutz) the 'lifeworld'. On the other hand, social integration can also be achieved in large measure by relegating tasks of action coordination to social institutions that operate, so to speak, 'behind the backs' of social agents. In fact, Habermas' distinction between society as lifeworld and society as system reflects a trend toward differentiation that is yet another feature of modern societies.

Beyond these metatheoretic and methodological concerns, *The Theory of Communicative Action* presents an interpretation of modern society as the outcome of a process of rationalization and societal differentiation. Rationalization, as in Weber, refers most generally to the extension of the criteria of rational choice and purposive-rational action to ever more aspects of social life (for example, science, law, business, and even religion and the arts). Differentiation in modern societies is reflected, first, in a (functional) separation of the economic and political subsystems from society as a whole and, second, within the lifeworld, in the division among institutional complexes devoted, respectively, to the tasks of the transmission of knowledge and interpretive patterns (culture), social integration ('society' in the narrower sense of normative orders), and socialization (personality). Finally, within culture one can also trace a differentiation among the three values spheres of science and technology, law and morality, and art and aesthetic criticism as each becomes independent of the other and develops its own internal standards of critique and evaluation. This interpretation of modern society as a process of rationalization is, of course, not new. However, in contrast to the classical theorists who generally viewed it as a threat to social life – Weber's 'iron cage', Marx's thesis of reification, DURKHEIM's analysis of anomie – Habermas emphasizes the potential for emancipation also made

available. Thus, social pathologies are not an inevitable consequence of rationalization *per se* but result rather from a one-sided process in which the market and administrative state invade the lifeworld, displacing modes of integration based on communicative reason with their own form of functional rationality. Habermas dramatically describes this as the 'colonization of the lifeworld'. The primary task of a critical theory is to draw attention to this process of colonization and indicate the ways in which various social movements are a response to it (see SOCIAL SCIENCES, PHILOSOPHY OF).

3 Discourse ethics

Habermas' development of a discourse (or communicative) ethics is an important corollary of his theory of communicative action and represents his formulation of a post-conventional moral theory as an alternative to utilitarianism and Kantian theories. Its basic idea is expressed in a principle of universalizability, analogous to the categorical imperative of KANT, which is intended to function as a rule of argumentation for testing the legitimacy of contested norms. The principle reads:

> Every valid norm must satisfy the condition that all affected can accept the consequences and the side effects its general observance can be anticipated to have for the satisfaction of everyone's interests (and these consequences are preferred to those of known alternative possibilities).
>
> (Habermas 1983: 65)

Habermas' strong claim is that this principle can be derived from the general pragmatic presuppositions of communication and argumentation. His strategy runs roughly as follows: In making utterances, speakers at least implicitly raise different types of validity-claims – for example, claims to truth, normative rightness, and sincerity or truthfulness. These validity-claims, in turn, point to the notion of an ideal speech situation freed from all external constraints and in which nothing but the force of the better argument prevails. The principle of universalizability represents an attempt to formulate this counterfactual ideal as a constitutive rule of argument for moral-practical discourses: norms or maxims of action are only morally legitimate if, when contested, they could be justified in a moral-practical discourse (see COMMUNICATIVE RATIONALITY).

Discourse ethics shares several features with other broadly Kantian moral theories. It is a formalistic ethic in the sense that it does not presuppose substantive moral content (beyond the idea of practical reason) but rather specifies a formal procedure which any norm must satisfy if it is to be morally acceptable. It is also a cognitivist ethic, not in the sense that it supposes an independent order of moral facts, but in its insistence that there exists a sufficient analogy between moral discourse and scientific discourse to make it possible to speak, for example, of progress in learning or of a comparable notion of 'good reason' or argument in both. Finally, discourse ethics is a deontological moral theory in two senses. It assumes the priority of the right over the good. The basic moral principle must be specified in a way that does not presuppose a specific conception of the good life since that would violate the liberal commitment to a plurality of conceptions of the good. In a further sense the distinction between deontological and teleological theories is closely related to Kant's distinction between categorical and hypothetical imperatives, a distinction strongly contested in contemporary analytic moral philosophy. Habermas sides with those who argue that morality consists of categorical imperatives (imperatives that do not require non-reason-based interests or desires), but agrees with critics that Kant's defence of such imperatives was not successful. In his own theory, Habermas accounts for the obligatory character of moral norms in terms of their relation to communicative action: valid norms are morally binding because of their intimate connection with processes of social interaction and communication out of which one cannot easily (or even rationally) choose to step (1983: 109).

At the same time, discourse ethics differs from Kant's moral theory in some important respects. It breaks with Kant's two-world metaphysics (phenomenal/noumenal) and rejects his exclusively monological interpretation of the categorical imperative in favour of an intersubjective or communicative version of the principle of universalizability. Of course, Kant's categorical imperative – especially in its 'Kingdom of Ends' formulation – already has an intersubjective dimension to it. However, it is only because of his two-world metaphysics that Kant is able to equate what one person can consistently and rationally will with what everyone could consistently and rationally agree to. Only because interests, desires and inclinations are set over against reason and purged from the Kingdom of Ends can Kant assume a harmony between the individual and the collective rational will. In communicative ethics, by contrast, such simulated thought experiments should ideally be replaced by practical discourses. Even though any actual discourse will always be limited by constraints of space and time and will thus fall short of their ideal, virtual dialogues carried out by a few on behalf of others are not an adequate substitute.

It is perhaps still too soon to tell whether discourse ethics represents a distinct alternative in contemporary moral theory. On the one hand, it must respond to some of the same challenges that confront other impartialist theories and it has to make good its claim that a notion of rational consensus or rational acceptability (distinct from the Hobbesian sort) provides the best general account of more ordinary moral intuitions. On the other hand, discourse ethics does seem to capture central insights that have made utilitarian and Kantian theories attractive: It regards respect for individual integrity (or 'autonomy') and concern for the welfare of others (or 'solidarity') as two aspects of the abstract notion of equal respect implicit in the idea of communicative action (see KANTIAN ETHICS; UTILITARIANISM).

4 Politics and law

In *Between Facts and Norms* (1992) Habermas returns to the political questions that guided his early studies and outlines in greater detail some of the implications of *The Theory of Communicative Action* for democratic theory and practice. A central claim of the work is that the common contrast between democracy (or popular sovereignty) and constitutionalism (with its emphasis on individual rights) is overdrawn since each is conceptually dependent on the other. Popular sovereignty and basic rights are co-original (*gleichursprünglich*) in that each derives from an ideal implicit in the notion of communicative reason: the right not to be bound to norms other than those to which one could give uncoerced rational consent. Moreover, by stressing the procedural dimensions of communicative reason Habermas offers a model of 'deliberative politics' that steers between the alternatives of liberalism and republicanism (or communitarianism). In particular, with the republican model, it rejects the vision of the political process as primarily a process of competition and aggregation of private preferences. However, more in keeping with the liberal model, it regards the republican vision of a citizenry united and actively motivated by a shared conception of the good life as unrealistic in modern, pluralist societies. By contrast, as he puts it, 'the success of deliberative politics depends not on a collectively acting citizenry but on the institutionalization of the corresponding procedures and conditions of communication, as well as on the interplay of institutionalized deliberative processes with informally constituted public opinions' (1992: 298). Central to this model is not only the institutionalization of different forms and levels of discourse that, taken together, allow for (a reasonable expectation of) a rational public opinion and will-formation, but, as the quotation indicates, a 'two-

197

track' process in which there is a division of labour between 'weak publics' – the informally organized public sphere ranging from private associations to the mass media located in 'civil society' – and 'strong publics' – parliamentary bodies and other formally organized institutions of the political system. In this division of labour, 'weak publics' assume a central responsibility for identifying, interpreting and addressing social problems. Decision-making responsibility, however, as well as the further 'filtering' of reasons via more formal parliamentary procedures, remains the task of a strong public (for example, the formally organized political system).

Within legal theory Habermas also resists the sharp contrast between positivism ('law as the will of the sovereign' (see LEGAL POSITIVISM)) and natural law theories (see NATURAL LAW). Legitimate law must in some meaningful sense be construed as the will of the people or demos, yet a democratic process itself requires legal regulation. 'The idea of the rule of law [or 'constitutional state' (*Rechtsstaat*)] sets in motion a spiralling self-application of law' (1992: 39). Habermas' response to this paradox is twofold. At an institutional level he pursues a strategy of differentiation: legal discourses are but one (albeit important) form of discourse that must simultaneously constrain yet be pervious to other forms of practical discourse. This leads to a reformulation of the classical separation of powers in discourse-theoretic terms. At a normative level, he advocates a 'public reasons' approach similar to the recent proposal by John RAWLS: ordinary law-making is subject to a higher law of 'constitutional essentials' (Rawls 1993: 227), but these essentials are themselves ultimately justified in terms of their ability to realize effectively citizens' basic moral powers – Habermas speaks of their 'public' and 'private' autonomy – and give expression to an ideal of free public reason (see LIBERALISM; REPUBLICANISM).

5 Habermas as polemicist

Throughout his career Habermas has been a frequent participant in cultural and political debates as well as more narrowly academic discussions. In fact, his reputation, at least in Germany, may be due as much to these interventions in public life as to his academic writings. From the 1950s when he challenged HEIDEGGER's willingness to publish his 1935 lectures, Introduction to Metaphysics, without any apology for its support of fascism, through his spirited debates with radical students in the 1960s, his response to neoconservatism and the 'historian's debate' in the 1980s (which concerned the public use of revisionist historical interpretations of the 'final solution' for

politcal purposes), and his reflections on nationalism and European identity in the 1990s, Habermas has exemplified in practice the ideals of the public sphere he has defended in his academic writings.

One of the more widely discussed of these debates is his engagement with postmodernism. In *The Philosophical Discourse of Modernity* (1985) Habermas argues that much of postmodern thought (from its roots in NIETZSCHE and Heidegger through to its representatives in FOUCAULT and DERRIDA) rests ironically on a failure to break sufficiently with the modern philosophy of consciousness (or *Bewußtseinsphilosophie*) against which so much of its criticism is directed. Within this tradition, the (knowing and acting) subject is regarded either as one object among others in the world (and thus, too, as something to be dominated) or as a 'transcendental' subject whose conscious activity, while always presupposed, can itself never be consciously apprehended. Most modern and contemporary philosophy – including postmodernism or deconstructionism – oscillates between these alternative positions, thereby rendering incoherent their own normative claims and critical positions. Habermas argues (as he did in *The Theory of Communicative Action*) that one can escape the bottlenecks of the philosophy of consciousness only by making a 'paradigm shift' to a model of communicative action in which subjectivity is first approached through the intersubjective relations individuals establish with one another in the medium of language. Autonomy, for example, is then less a property that the individual agent obscurely possesses than it is a set of competencies that actors mutually ascribe to one another in specific forms of social interaction. Habermas' aim, once more, is to show that the positive achievements of modernity can be salvaged from their shaky metaphysical foundations without, however, requiring that one relinquish a rational (or reasonable) grounding for normative criticism. Modernity thus remains for Habermas an 'unfulfilled project', though one that should not be abandoned (see POSTMODERNISM).

See also: FRANKFURT SCHOOL; MODERNISM; ADORNO; MARCUSE

List of works

Habermas, J. (1962) *Strukturwandel der Öffentlichkeit*, Darmstadt: Hermann Luchterland Verlag; trans. T. Burger, *The Structural Transformation of the Public Sphere*, Cambridge, MA: MIT Press, 1989. (Traces the history and ideology of the 'bourgeois public sphere' from its emergence in the eighteenth century to its decline in the twentieth century.)

—— (1963) *Theorie und Praxis*, Darmstadt: Hermann Luchterhand Verlag; trans. J. Viertel, *Theory and Practice*, Boston, MA: Beacon Press, 1973. (Contains important essays on modern political theory, including several on Hegel.)

—— (1968) *Erkenntnis und Interesse*, Frankfurt: Suhrkamp; trans. J. Shapiro, *Knowledge and Human Interests*, Boston, MA: Beacon Press, 1971; Oxford: Polity Press, 1987. (An important interpretation of philosophy from Kant to the pragmatists arguing that epistemology must now be pursued as social theory. Part 1 contrasts Hegel's critique of knowledge with that of Kant and Marx.)

—— (1970) *Zur Logik der Sozialwissenschaften*, Frankfurt: Suhrkamp; trans. S. Nicholsen and J. Stark, *On the Logic of the Social Sciences*, Cambridge, MA: MIT Press, 1988. (An early sketch of Habermas' interpretive approach and his critique of Gadamer's philosophical hermeneutics.)

—— (1971) *Theorie und Praxis*, Frankfurt: Suhrkamp, 4th edn; trans. J. Viertel, *Theory and Practice*, Oxford: Polity Press, 1973. (Contains several influential essays on Hegel.)

—— (1973) *Legitimationsprobleme im Spätkapitalismus*, Frankfurt: Suhrkamp; trans. T. McCarthy, *Legitimation Crisis*, Boston, MA: Beacon Press, 1975. (An important and influential early formulation of Habermas' critical analysis of modern society.)

—— (1976) *Zur Rekonstruktion des historischen Materialismus*, Frankfurt: Suhrkamp; trans. T. McCarthy, *Communication and the Evolution of Society*, Boston, MA: Beacon Press, 1979. (The abridged English translation contains essays on Habermas' theory of social evolution and an important essay on the linguistic grounding of normative critique, 'What is Universal Pragmatics?'.)

—— (1981) *Theorie des kommunikativen Handelns*, Frankfurt: Suhrkamp, 2 vols; trans. T. McCarthy, *The Theory of Communicative Action*, Boston, MA: Beacon Press, 1984/1987. (His two-volume magnum opus, a systematic treatise on the foundations of social theory and one-sided process of rationalization in modern societies.)

—— (1983) *Moralbewußtsein und kommunikatives Handeln*, Frankfurt: Suhrkamp; trans. C. Lenhardt and S. Nicholsen, *Moral Consciousness and Communicative Action*, Cambridge, MA: MIT Press, 1990. (A collection of five essays, including a central essay on 'discourse ethics'.)

—— (1985) *Der philosophische Diskurs der Moderne*, Frankfurt: Suhrkamp; trans. F. Lawrence, *The Philosophical Discourse of Modernity*, Cambridge, MA: MIT Press, 1987. (Series of polemical lectures, ranging from Hegel to Derrida and Foucault, in which Habermas challenges the postmodern turn in philosophy.)

—— (1985/1987) *Kleine Politische Schriften*, vols. V and VI, Frankfurt: Suhrkamp; trans. S. Nicholsen, *The New Conservatism: Cultural Criticism and the Historians' Debate*, Cambridge, MA: MIT Press, 1989. (A collection of essays on politics and culture, including the 'historians' debate' on the memory of the Holocaust, Heidegger's politics, and an essay on Henrich Heine and the role of the intellectual in Germany.)

—— (1988) *Nachmetaphysisches Denken*, Frankfurt: Suhrkamp; trans. W. Hohengarten, *Postmetaphysical Thinking*, Cambridge, MA: MIT Press, 1992. (Collection of philosophical essays defending his 'postmetaphysical' position from both traditional philosophy of consciousness and its postmodern alternative.)

—— (1992) *Faktizität und Geltung*, Frankfurt: Suhrkamp; trans. W. Rehg, *Between Facts and Norms*, Cambridge, MA: MIT Press, 1996. (A discourse-theoretic interpretation of law and democracy, and their interconnection.)

References and further reading

Benhabib, S. and Dallmayr, F. (eds) (1990) *The Communicative Ethics Controversy*, Cambridge, MA: MIT Press. (Contains translations from the German discussion and a lengthy 'Afterword' by Benhabib.)

Bernstein, R. (ed.) (1985) *Habermas and Modernity*, Cambridge, MA: MIT Press. (Contains essays on Habermas' later work and his debate with postmodernism.)

Calhoun, C. (ed.) (1992) *Habermas and the Public Sphere*, Cambridge, MA: MIT Press. (An excellent collection devoted to *The Structural Transformation of the Public Sphere*.)

Dews, P. (ed.) (1986) *Habermas: Autonomy and Solidarity – Interviews with Jürgen Habermas*, London: Verso. (An important collection of interviews with Habermas, including the 'Dialectics of Rationalization' with Axel Honneth.)

Honneth, A. and Joas, H. (eds.) (1991) *Communicative Action*, Cambridge, MA: MIT Press. (A valuable collection of essays on *The Theory of Communicative Action*.)

Ingram, D. (1987) *Habermas and the Dialectic of Reason*, New Haven: Yale University Press. (Full-length study focused primarily on *The Theory of Communicative Action*.)

McCarthy, T. (1978) *The Critical Theory of Jürgen Habermas*, Cambridge, MA: MIT Press. (A thorough study of Habermas' development prior to *The Theory of Communicative Action*.)

McCarthy, T. and Hoy, D. (1994) *Critical Theory*, Cambridge, MA: Blackwell. (An exchange between a leading exponent of Habermas' theory and a 'postmodern' critic.)

* Parsons, T. (1937) *The Structure of Social Action*, New York: McGraw-Hill. (Classic survey of foundations of empirical social science.)

* Rawls, J. (1993) *Political Liberalism*, New York: Columbia University Press. (Includes Rawl's articulation of the role of a just constitution within a pluralist society.)

Rehg, W. (1994) *Insight and Solidarity: The Discourse Ethics of Jürgen Habermas*, Berkeley, CA: University of California Press. (A full-length study of Habermas' discourse ethics.)

Thompson, J. and Held, D. (1982) *Habermas: Critical Debates*, Cambridge, MA: MIT Press. (An early but important collection of critical essays exploring various aspects of Habermas' work, including a 'Reply' by Habermas.)

* Weber, M. (1925) *Wirtschaft und Gesellschaft*, Tübingen: J.C.B. Mohr; revised 4th edn, J. Winckelmann, 1956; trans. as *Economy and Science*, ed. G. Roth and C. Wittich, New York: Bedminster Press, 1968. (Classic theory of social and economic structures.)

White, S. (1995) *The Cambridge Companion to Habermas*, New York: Cambridge University Press. (A volume dealing primarily with Habermas' political theory and postmodernism.)

KENNETH BAYNES

HAECKEL, ERNST HEINRICH (1834–1919)

Haeckel was the leading German Darwinist. His evolutionary philosophy of monism differed substantially from the views of Darwin or of British evolutionary philosophers such as Herbert Spencer or the dualist T.H. Huxley. Haeckel's monism asserted the unity of physical and organic nature, and included mental processes and social phenomena. Its initial form was mechanistic, seeking to reduce vital processes to physicochemical laws and substances. However, his efforts to construct the history of life meant that Haeckel became preoccupied with historical processes. In its final form, his monism was pantheistic. Although Haeckel has been regarded as a forerunner of national socialism, a contextual reading of his works does not support this interpretation.

Haeckel studied medicine and zoology. His approach to biology should be contrasted with the reductionist biophysics programme of the physiologists Hermann HELMHOLTZ , Emil DU BOIS-REYMOND and Rudolf Virchow. During the 1850s Virchow (for whom Haeckel was assistant) moved away from reductionism to a belief in distinct organizational properties of life – notably in the cell. Haeckel was influenced by Virchow's theories of cellular organization and by the vitalist comparative anatomist and physiologist, Johannes Müller. More distant influences included Goethe's concept of morphology (see GOETHE, J.W.) and the *Naturphilosophen* Lorenz OKEN and Friedrich SCHELLING.

Darwin's *Origin of Species* inspired Haeckel to advance Darwinism scientifically and as a popular form of materialist ethics (see DARWIN, C.). This coincided with Max Schultze's protoplasmic theory of the cell, which gave Haeckel the idea that the cell substance or 'Plasma' was equivalent to the first-formed life. All organisms were plasmatic bodies differing only in degrees of organization. In linking cell theory to evolutionary theory, Haeckel was not a conventional Darwinist. Natural selection assumed only a limited role, being circumscribed by environmental and historical forces: Haeckel endorsed Lamarckian factors, such as the direct effects of the environment.

In reconstructing the history of life, Haeckel adopted a causal and mechanistic approach: in the 1870s he developed the 'biogenetic law' that ontogeny (the development of an individual organism) recapitulated phylogeny (the evolution of the species). The Gastraea Theory of 1874 deduced an extinct primitive organism (the Gastraea) that explained the early stage of embryological development, which Haeckel termed 'gastrulation'. Past evolutionary history provided a causal explanation of development.

Haeckel's monism was first developed in the *Generelle Morphologie* (General Morphology) of 1866. It implied that there was no essential difference between organic and inorganic nature, life differing from inorganic nature only in its higher organization. Atoms had immanent properties of irritability. Substance united matter and spirit. Haeckel liked to evoke the image of 'crystal minds' (*Kristalseelen*) to convey the link between matter and mind. There were two fundamental laws of substance: that of energy and material as constant throughout the world, and that of evolution from the unformed to the fully formed. Similarly there was no fundamental difference between animals and the human species. All mental powers were derived from sensitivity and movement. Ethics was based on the natural sciences, particularly the evidence of the social instincts of animals. The advance of science had the consequence of making mankind more aware of the rationale of the new morality. Certain aspects of modern civilization could be condemned as degenerative.

Haeckel drew on non-Darwinian concepts of division of labour in order to demonstrate that a centralized nervous system was an essential feature of the evolution of higher organisms. Following Spencer, he argued that the more an organism was differentiated the greater its need of centralized coordination and control. He applied Virchow's egalitarian concept of a 'cell state' in a hierarchical fashion to argue that higher organisms manifested greater centralization, just as empires were higher than republics.

Haeckel condemned Christianity, and especially Roman Catholicism, as a primitive superstition, accusing Christianity of despising nature. Monism should replace religion as the basis of education in the newly united nation. At the same time he denied liberal notions of free will, which led to controversy with Virchow in 1877. Virchow viewed Darwinism only as an hypothesis, whereas for Haeckel it was a proven law. This was the first of a number of disputes over the processes of development and heredity that left Haeckel scientifically isolated. His increasing popularity compensated for this, as his ideas contributed to the development of psychology, sociology and psychoanalysis. In 1906 Haeckel was a founder of the Monist League, in which he encountered opposition to his pantheism, particularly from the physicist Wilhelm Ostwald.

It has been suggested that Haeckel's monism supplied the scientific roots of National Socialism (Gasman 1971). He certainly endorsed eugenics, and from 1905 he was an honorary member of the German Society for Racial Hygiene. Although on occasion personally anti-Semitic, Haeckel's monistic philosophy did not support anti-Semitism. However, his anthropology was based on progression from 'primitive races' to Europeans. While for primitive races the survival of the fittest had been a historical factor, higher civilized races were immune from its workings. In 1872 he argued that the death penalty was necessary for irredeemable criminals, and ascribed 'less value' to weak and sick persons. Haeckel noted that euthanasia of the malformed and crippled new-born children had served to maintain the military prowess of the Spartans, but that it had no place in modern, civilized society. This would suggest that certain Social Darwinist tenets were redundant in higher societies. While the Nazis venerated Haeckel, it was on the basis of a very selective reading of his ideas. On the other hand, Haeckel was much appreciated for furthering materialism, by Lenin and by German socialists such as Walther Ulbricht. Although this was also a distortion, it gave Haeckel an honoured place under communism. His evolutionary ethics interested a variety of thinkers, including Sigmund Freud, Magnus Hirschfeld (the campaigner for homosexual rights) and many authors and artists.

See also: EVOLUTION AND ETHICS; EVOLUTION, THEORY OF

List of works

Haeckel, E.H. (1866) *Generelle Morphologie der Organismen* (General Morphology), Berlin: G. Reimer. (Integrates Darwinism with cell theory and embryology.)
—— (1868) *Natürliche Schöpfungsgeschichte*, Berlin: G. Reimer; trans. E.R. Lankester, *The History of Creation*, London: Routledge, 1876. (Applies evolutionary theories to explain the development of life, culminating in human evolution.)
—— (1899) *Die Welträthsel*, Bonn: E. Strauss; trans. J. McCabe, *The Riddle of the Universe*, London: Watts, 1929. (A popular evolutionary cosmology.)

References and further reading

* Gasman, D. (1971) *The Scientific Origins of National Socialism. Social Darwinism in Ernst Haeckel and the Monist League*, London: MacDonald. (Links monism and Nazism; now superseded.)
Holt, N.R. (1971) 'Ernst Haeckel's Monistic Religion', *Journal of the History of Ideas* 32: 265–80. (On Haeckel's later pantheism.)
Sandmann, J. (1990) *Der Bruch mit der humanitären Tradition* (The Break With Humanitarian Tradition), Stuttgart: Gustav Fischer. (A careful exposition of Haeckel's ideas, although it over-emphasizes selectionism.)
Weindling, P.J. (1989) 'Ernst Haeckel, Darwinismus and the secularisation of nature', in Moore, J.R. (ed.) *History, Humanity and Evolution*, Cambridge: Cambridge University Press, 311–29. (A contextualized exposition of Haeckel's changing views.)
—— (1989) *Health, Race and German Politics between National Unification and Nazism*, Cambridge: Cambridge University Press. (A contextualized analysis of Social Darwinism and eugenics.)

PAUL WEINDLING

HÄGERSTRÖM, AXEL ANDERS THEODOR (1868–1939)

Hägerström was professor of philosophy at Uppsala University, Sweden, from 1911 until 1933, and together with his pupil Adolf Phalén founded the Uppsala school of conceptual analysis. He first came to the attention in 1902 with a study of Kant's ethics, but his main claim to fame rests upon the anti-metaphysical and emotivist positions which he developed during the years 1905–39. Thus the two fundamental theses of his moral philosophy are that moral valuations are neither true nor false, and that the proper task of moral philosophy itself is only descriptive and not normative. In this connection he argued that the philosophical ideas of objective moral values and of absolute rights have created fanaticism and sharpened conflicts in human history. He is also well known for his work in jurisprudence as the founder of Scandinavian legal realism. Here again his thought is predominantly antimetaphysical, and he criticized many legal concepts for their metaphysical and magical elements.

1   Kant research
2   Ontology and epistemology
3   Moral philosophy and theory of value
4   Legal philosophy
5   Philosophy of religion

1   Kant research

Hägerström's *Kants Ethik* (1902) is in part an attempt to find a coherent line of thought in Kant's ethics. But the first part of the book is a penetrating analysis of Kant's epistemology in general. Hägerström sharply criticizes the prevalent psychologistic interpretation of Kant (such as that of VAIHINGER) according to which the central line of thought in *The Critique of Pure Reason* is a psychological theory of the causes of human knowledge; according to Hägerström's logistic interpretation it should be understood instead as a logical analysis of the reasons of knowledge (see KANT, I.; NEO-KANTIANISM).

2   Ontology and epistemology

The motto of Hägerström's *Selbstdarstellung* (Self-description) (1929) is '*Praeterea censeo metaphysicam esse delendam*' (Besides, it is my opinion that metaphysics ought to be destroyed). According to Hägerström metaphysics rests on a deep misunderstanding of the concept of reality: in metaphysics, reality (the universal concept) is conceived as itself something

real. This error is a result of a confusion that is natural to the human mind; it is implied by the common-sense conception of temporal and spatial facts; it is connected, Hägerström argues, with the idea that the past is unreal, an idea which belongs to common sense but which, like many other common-sense ideas, is absurd.

By an abstract argument Hägerström tries to show that the real world must be identical with the spatiotemporal continuum of experience. But the concept of reality is not derived from experience; on the contrary, it is a presupposition of all experience (and a presupposition of every judgment). This is one of the rationalistic ingredients of Hägerström's epistemology. Another important ingredient is the criticism of subjectivism, that is, of the idea that the only thing immediately given for a subject is that subject itself and its perceptions. Hägerström's picture of reality is strictly deterministic, the principle of causality being a logical condition of all empirical knowledge. He rejects the conventionalist opinion that the principle of causality is just a postulate stipulated by science; nor does he share Kant's opinion that it is a synthetic a priori judgment. He argues instead that it is deducible from the logical principle of the self-identity of reality.

3   Moral philosophy and theory of value

The main thesis of Hägerström's famous inaugural lecture of 1911, *Om moraliska föreställningars sanning* ('On the Truth of Moral Ideas'), is that moral valuations are neither true nor false. Even such moral valuations as are usually expressed by declarative sentences lack the character of judgment; the value predicate is an expression of emotion, and in every valuation an emotion is a constituent element. Hägerström was one of the first philosophers to hold a no-truth-value theory about moral valuations, and one of the first to propose an emotive theory that did not take a moral valuation as a judgment about an emotion, but as itself constituted by an emotion. Emotive theories must explain the existence of abstract value sentences (such as 'Honesty is something good'), since emotions are evoked by particular phenomena such as individual actions or persons, not by universal concepts. Similarly, it is also a problem for an emotive theory to explain the existence of inferences having a value sentence as a premise, since emotions cannot enter into an inference. As early as the 1910s Hägerström was conscious of these and similar problems, and gave interesting solutions.

The moral valuations are the primary elements of morals, but in addition there are, in common types of morality, important elements which, according to

Hägerström, are false judgments. The idea of free will, which is absurd according to Hägerström's determinism, plays an enormous role in the history of morals, and so does the idea of objective values, which again is false. Several metaphysical ideas are false ingredients of many kinds of morals: for example, a metaphysical concept of person is presupposed by many deontological norms and in the doctrine of human dignity; a metaphysical assumption is also presupposed by the idea of absolute values. Hägerström gave a complex analysis of the idea of duty and found certain absurd conceptions involved in it. Thus Hägerström combined his emotive theory of the primary elements in morality with an error theory about other elements. Hägerström was influenced in certain ways by Meinong, Westermarck and Nietzsche, but on the whole his moral theory is an original achievement (see EMOTIVISM; MORALITY AND EMOTIONS).

4 Legal philosophy

According to Hägerström several of our fundamental legal concepts are metaphysical and magical, and hence absurd. An example is the concept of ownership: a person's ownership is an intermediary link between its legal ground (for instance, a gift or a purchase) and its legal consequences. This link cannot be identified with any empirical fact; it is a metaphysical entity, or, more precisely, a metaphysical force or power. Thus, the transfer of an ownership between persons is a transfer of a metaphysical force, that is, a magical procedure. (Hägerström's strong interest in the social and cultural role of magic was stimulated by Frazer's celebrated *The Golden Bough* (1911–15). Hägerström's view on the essence of magic was not identical with Frazer's, but he was much influenced by his scheme of classifications and by certain details in Frazer's work.)

Hägerström made a thorough and comprehensive inquiry into certain central themes of Roman law, paying great attention to its magical elements. He analysed the connection between Roman law and the doctrine of Natural law. He rejected this doctrine in all its forms, and urged that even many modern authors who explicitly disavow the principles of Natural law have nevertheless resorted to such ideas. He also rejected the will theory and Kelsen's pure theory of law (see KELSEN, H.). He was the founder of the school of Scandinavian legal realism, according to which it is a main task of legal science to give a description of legal phenomena in strictly empirical terms, without any metaphysical or ethical ingredients (see LEGAL REALISM).

5 Philosophy of religion

In his lectures of the 1920s, Hägerström developed a theory of religion which resembles, in an important respect, his theory of morality. The primary element in religion, as in morality, is something which is constituted by emotions, and which is neither true nor false. With this element, however, are combined false ideas of different kinds, and in religious dogmatics such false ideas are of essential importance (for example, the idea of God as an objective reality and the common conceptions of the effects of prayer or sacramental acts); an important factor in the formation of these ideas is the objectification of the contents of religious emotions.

Hägerström made thoroughgoing psychological investigations of these false religious ideas, of their relations to the emotive element, to morals and to magic. His psychological views about emotions and about self-consciousness are very complex, and this is especially evident in his philosophy of religion. He analysed both positive religion and metaphysical religiosity. In his treatment of positive religion, Hägerström utilized his great classical learning by taking examples from Greek and Roman religion, but he also referred to the religions of India, to primitive religion and, most often, to Christianity. An important detail is his investigation of the relation between magic and religion in the Lutheran doctrine of justification by faith; another, his analysis of different forms of the consciousness of sin. In his treatment of metaphysical religiosity he dealt with Plotinus, Eckhart, Spinoza and others, analysing how mysticism passes over into scholasticism and scholasticism into mysticism (see MYSTICISM, NATURE OF).

See also: SCANDINAVIA, PHILOSOPHY IN

List of works

Hägerström, A. (1902) *Kants Ethik im Verhältnis zu seinen erkenntnistheoretischen Grundgedanken systematisch dargestellt* (Kant's Ethics Systematically Expounded with Reference to the Basic Ideas of his Theory of Knowledge), Uppsala: Almqvist & Wiksell. (An accurate and detailed interpretation (not a critical examination) of Kant's ethics and parts of Kant's epistemology.)

—— (1908) *Das Prinzip der Wissenschaft. Eine logischerkenntnistheoretische Untersuchung. I. Die Realität* (The Principle of Science: A Logical and Epistemological Inquiry, vol. 1, The Reality), Uppsala: Humanistiska Vetenskapssamfundet. (Hägerström called this his most important work.)

—— (1911) *Om moraliska föreställningars sanning,*

203

Stockhom: Bonniers; trans. T. Mautner, *'On the Truth of Moral Ideas'*, Canberra: The Australian National University, 1971. (Hägerström's inaugural lecture; also included in Hägerström 1964.)

—— (1927–41) *Der römische Obligationsbegriff im Lichte der allgemeinen römischen Rechtsanschauung I–II* (The Roman Concept of Obligation in the Light of General Roman Jurisprudence), Uppsala: Humanistiska Vetenskapssamfundet; trans. R.T. Sandin, in *Philosophy and Religion*, London: Allen & Unwin, 1964.

—— (1929) 'Axel Hägerström', in R. Schmidt (ed.) *Die Philosophie der Gegenwart in Selbstdarstellungen* (The Philosophy of the Present in Self-Descriptions), Leipzig: Felix Meiner, vol. 7; trans. R.T. Sandin, in *Philosophy and Religion*, London: Allen & Unwin, 1964. (The major part of this Selbstdarstellungen is mainly an account of Hägerström's ontology and his criticism of metaphysics.)

—— (1939) *Socialfilosofiska uppsatser* (Studies in Social Philosophy), Stockholm, 1966. (Eight papers on moral and political philosophy and on philosophy of law.)

—— (1948) 'Lectures on So-called Spiritual Religion', trans. C.D. Broad, *Theoria* 14: 28–67. (A central text in Hägerström's philosophy of religion.)

—— (1953) *Inquiries into the Nature of Law and Morals*, ed. K. Olivecrona, trans. C.D. Broad, Uppsala: Humanistiska Vetenskapssamfundet. (Contains a selection from Hägerström's philosophy of law.)

—— (1964) *Philosophy and Religion*, trans. R.T. Sandin, London: Allen & Unwin. (Selected writings on moral philosophy and philosophy of religion.)

—— (1987) *Moralfilosofins grundläggning* (The Foundation of Moral Philosophy), ed. T. Mautner, Uppsala: Humanistiska Vetenskapssamfundet. (Contains a summary in English.)

References and further reading

Broad, C.D. (1951) 'Hägerström's Account of Sense of Duty and Certain Allied Experiences', *Philosophy* 26. (A discussion of Hägerström's moral philosophy.)

—— (1964) 'Memoir of Axel Hägerström', in A. Hägerström, *Philosophy and Religion*, trans. R.T. Sandin, London: Allen & Unwin. (A biographical sketch, mainly based on a biography published in Swedish in 1961 by Hägerström's daughter Margit Waller.)

Dahlquist, T. (1976) 'Some Pages from the History of Philosophy in Uppsala', in *Uppsala University: 500 Years*, Uppsala, vol. 5. (Discusses Hägerström's role in founding the Uppsala school of philosophy.)

Ehnmark, E. (1956) 'Religion and Magic – Frazer, Söderblom, and Hägerström', *Ethnos* 21. (An account of Hägerström's use of Frazer.)

Frazer, J.G. (1911–15) *The Golden Bough: A Study in Magic and Religion*, ed. R. Fraser, Oxford: Oxford Paperbacks, 1994. (Frazer's twenty-five year study of primitive customs, magic and superstitions around the world.)

Hedenius, I. (1941) *Om rätt och moral* (On Law and Morals), Stockholm. (A book of central importance for the Scandinavian debate on Hägerström's moral and legal philosophy.)

Marc-Wogau, K. (1968) *Studier till Axel Hägerström s filosofi* (Studies in the Philosophy of Axel Hägerström), Falköping. (An important critical discussion by one of Hägerström's former students.)

—— (1972) 'Axel Hägerström's Ontology', in *Contemporary Philosophy in Scandinavia*, ed. R.E. Olson and A.M. Paul, Baltimore, MD, and London. (Discusses Hägerström's attack on metaphysics.)

Mautner, T. (1994) *'Vägledning till Hägerström studiet'* (Guide to Hägerström Research), Uppsala: Humanistiska Vetenskapssamfundet. (Includes a complete bibliography and a list of extant manuscripts.)

Passmore, J. (1961) 'Hägerström's Philosophy of Law', *Philosophy* 36: 143–60. (Lucid exposition and critical discussion.)

Petersson, B. (1973) *Axel Hägerström värdeteori* (The Value Theory of Axel Hägerström), Uppsala: Uppsala University Philosophy Department. (A lucid analysis of Hägerström's moral philosophy and value theory. Contains a summary in English.)

Sandin, R.T. (1962) 'The Founding of the Uppsala School', *Journal of the History of Ideas* 23: 496–512. (A largely historical account.)

THORILD DAHLQUIST
ANN-MARI HENSCHEN-DAHLQUIST

HALAKHAH

The central ideal of rabbinic Judaism is that of living by the Torah, that is, God's teachings. These teachings are mediated by a detailed normative system called halakhah, which might be translated as 'the Way'. The term 'rabbinic law' captures the form of halakhic discourse, but not its range. Appropriate sections of halakhah have indeed served as the law of Jewish communities for two millennia. But other sections relate to individual conscience and religious observance and are enforceable only by a 'heavenly court'.

Although grounded in Scripture, halakhah*'s frame of reference is the 'oral Torah', a tradition of interpretation and argument culminating in the twenty volumes of the Talmud. God's authority is the foundational norm, but it is only invoked occasionally as superseding human understanding. Indeed, the rabbis disallowed divine interference in their deliberations, asserting, in keeping with Scripture, that Torah is 'not in heaven' (Bava Metzia 59b, citing Deuteronomy 30: 12).*

Given the lack of binding dogma in Judaism, halakhic *practice has often been regarded as the common denominator that unites the Jewish community. The enterprise of furnishing 'reasons of the commandments' (*ta'amei ha-mitzvot*), central to many thinkers in Judaism, accordingly reveals a great diversity of orientations. These range, in medieval Judaism, from esoteric mystical doctrines to Maimonides' rational and historical explanations; and among modern writers, from moral positivism to existentialism.*

1 **Interpreting biblical law**
2 **Rabbinic Judaism:** *halakhah***'s classical era**
3 **Post-Talmudic Judaism: decentralized** *halakhah*
4 **Contemporary** *halakhah*
5 **Philosophies of** *halakhah*

1 Interpreting biblical law

Of the twenty-four books canonized in the Hebrew Bible, *halakhah* accords strictly binding status only to the norms recognized as having been promulgated in the five books of Moses, the Pentateuch. Revered as the document of God's revelation, these constitute Torah in its narrow sense, and are regarded as the core of Torah (instruction) in the broad sense, which encompasses all valid teachings in Judaism through to the present (see BIBLE, HEBREW).

The Pentateuch contains not only laws, but also their setting: the story of creation and of God's relationship with humankind in general and with the Israelite people in particular. This relationship is consummated in the Sinai Covenant, whose human partners become committed to God's commandments (*mitzvot*). Much of the Torah is indeed composed of laws, typically introduced by 'The Lord spoke to Moses'.

This divine legislation differs from familiar legal codes in both scope and form. Its scope extends to issues which in the modern West belong not to law but more typically to the realms of religious practice or personal morality. This broad scope is characteristic of *halakhah* throughout its history. Some contempor-

ary scholars have therefore proposed to treat Jewish law as a subcategory of *halakhah* relating to those issues generally included in the realm of law. As to form, the legal passages in the Pentateuch hardly read as a coherent system of law. They contain many duplications, gaps and inconsistencies; and their texts are traced by Bible scholars to a variety of circles and periods between the times of Moses (thirteenth century BC) and the first exile (sixth century BC). While some of these biblical teachings undoubtedly embody ancient Israelite legal practices, others seem to enunciate utopian legislation, a prescriptive parallel to the social criticism of the post-Mosaic prophets.

Since all Scriptural verses are, in the *halakhic* system, equally holy, the biblical heritage, from the outset, called for extensive interpretation and harmonization. For example, according to Exodus 21: 1–7, a fellow-Israelite bought as a slave must be set free at the seventh year; but if he formally refuses this option he remains a slave 'forever'. Leviticus 25: 39–43 restricts slavery in a rather different way: it makes no mention of a seventh-year release, but prohibits gruelling labour, and proclaims freedom for all Israelite slaves in the Jubilee year. Jeremiah 34: 8–16 suggests that neither legal scheme had the impact that the imperatives seem to expect. But the *halakhah* accepted both, offering a liberal harmonization: the slave could not be forced into gruelling labour, *and* was to be offered his freedom on the seventh year. Even if he chose servitude, 'forever' was interpreted as 'until the Jubilee'.

The Second Commonwealth (fifth century BC to first century AD) saw a great increase in reinterpretations and enhancements of Torah for diverse reasons, in particular among the 'Pharisees'. By contrast with their rivals, the Sadducees (the priestly party, who put primary emphasis upon the temple rituals), the Pharisees gave greater weight to personal spirituality. Inspired by biblical passages like Leviticus 19: 2 ('You shall be holy, for I the Lord thy God am holy'), they sought to direct everyday life and behaviour towards an ideal of pervasive holiness. After the destruction of the Second Temple (70 AD), the Pharisees became, perforce, the preservers of Jewish norms and ideals. They and their heirs became known as 'the rabbis' (masters or teachers), and their work defines classical 'rabbinic Judaism', the socio-cultural context of *halakhah*.

2 Rabbinic Judaism: *halakhah*'s classical era

In the definitive work of early rabbinic Judaism, the Mishnah (compiled by Rabbi Judah the Prince in the Galilee, *c.*200 AD), some sections closely follow biblical law; others boldly modify it, not through outright rejection or explicit amendment, but through a mode of qualifications and reinterpretations, called midrash (exposition or explication) (see MIDRASH). The rabbis recognized the great disparity between rabbinic and biblical law, and emphasized that the 'written Torah' must be accompanied and complemented by the 'oral Torah'. Indeed, they came to describe the oral Torah as a historical concomitant of the written Torah and even claimed normative primacy for the oral law: 'God's covenant with Israel was in regard to the oral *torah*' (Gittin 60b) (see THEOLOGY, RABBINIC §5).

A fine example of rabbinic boldness is the Mishnah's treatment of capital punishment. Detailed codification of the many capital offences prescribed in biblical law is combined with a procedural policy explicitly aimed at making executions virtually impossible. The Mishnah's discussion of capital punishment concludes by citing Rabbi Akiba, widely considered the greatest of the rabbinic sages: 'Were [I] in the Sanhedrin [the High Court], no person would ever be put to death' (*Mishnah Makkot* 1: 7). The rabbinic policy expressed here reflects a pervasive religious humanism, harking back to the dictum of Genesis that humanity, and so each individual human being, is created in God's image.

The Mishnah faithfully preserves the record of disagreements among the rabbinic sages, but it typically omits mention of their argumentation and much more. Its condensed legal clauses became focal points for elaboration, explanation and enhancement. These afford much of the bulk of the Gemara, by which the Mishnah is expanded to form the Talmud. The Talmud seeks to leave no issue unexplained; indeed, its redactors seem committed to overexplanation, sometimes advancing three or four alternative answers to each of the questions it raises, or offering strings of arguments and counterarguments to render plausible each side of its myriad of debates. The Talmud's interest in reasons and ideas, rather than in mere legal pronouncements, is further reflected in the fact that perhaps a third of it consists of *aggadah*, that is, narrative material – stories and parables, expositions of the non-legal parts of the Bible, theological and moral homilies, and the like.

3 Post-Talmudic Judaism: decentralized *halakhah*

After the redaction of the Talmud (in Mesopotamia, *c.*500 AD – hence the name 'Babylonian Talmud', as distinct from the earlier and less influential 'Jerusalem Talmud'), Judaism saw a shift away from a single cultural centre. The commitment of Jewish communities throughout the diaspora to the *halakhah* canonized the Talmud with its complex dialectic

form, where hardly any debate ends with an explicitly stated definitive conclusion. Practical rulings in moral, legal, and ritual matters of *halakhah* came to rest in the hands of local courts or individual rabbinic scholars, masters in the art of Talmudic interpretation. Jewish communities had a considerable measure of legal autonomy as tolerated minorities, and through their various internal processes endowed such courts and scholars with *halakhic* authority.

This reality fit well with the classical rabbinic application of the dictum of Deuteronomy that the Torah is 'not in heaven': God's will is to be determined not by prophecy or oracles but by study and interpretation. Thus, despite the system's ultimate grounding in revelation, post-Talmudic Halakhists rarely appeal to Scripture – let alone to revelation – in arguing or deciding points of *halakhah*. Instead, they focus on the oral Torah, God's word as mediated by tradition, precedent and practical reason (*sevara*). When Moses MAIMONIDES sought to offer, in his monumental *Mishneh Torah*, a univocal codification of Talmudic law, his code was widely respected but not accepted as final or binding. One central criticism was that he had written 'like a prophet', failing to support his rulings or to quote and engage alternative opinions and interpretations. Despite the recognized usefulness of Maimonides' code, and others as well, then, the most important repository of *halakhic* sources from medieval and early modern times was and remains the Responsa literature: wide ranging and unsystematic collections of reasoned rulings, resembling court opinions, issued by eminent scholars in response to written queries.

4 Contemporary *halakhah*

Halakhic authority reached a watershed with the political changes of the eighteenth and nineteenth centuries, which greatly undermined the jurisdiction of *halakhic* courts. For Orthodox Jews, *halakhah* continues to function as a system of religious law: through contemporary Responsa, essays and monographs, it addresses a broad spectrum of issues in modern life. Conservative, Reform, Reconstructionist, and many other Jews relate in their own ways to *halakhah* as a less binding framework, which nevertheless informs their normative thinking. In the state of Israel, *halakhic* courts have limited jurisdiction, primarily in matters of personal and family law. The contemporary Jewish scene thus reflects an unprecedented diversity of perspectives regarding *halakhic* concepts and norms.

For example, an issue of major contention concerns defining the Jewish community itself. In rabbinic Judaism, joining the community from without was perceived as a transformation of religious identity. The national and religious communities were one and the same, and the convert joined the Jewish people through a ritual defined by religious law. In the modern setting, however, many Jews (both in Israel and in the diaspora) see themselves as members in a national or ethnic collectivity rather than as adherents of a religion. While the Orthodox continue to require ritual immersion for those who wish to become Jewish, and (for males) circumcision, accompanied by (at least an overt) commitment to *halakhah*, and overseen by a rabbinic court of three men, other circles, drawing on Talmudic sources, have adopted alternative criteria and procedures.

5 Philosophies of *halakhah*

Philosophical discourse on the *halakhah* has traditionally focused on two main problems: rationality and coherence.

The rationality of *halakhah* is problematic in light of the numerous details, mainly in ritual law, which may seem alien to the dictates of reason. The rabbis were prepared to grant, on occasion, that particular commandments were 'divine decrees', unfathomable demands of the divine Sovereign. But to medieval religious philosophers, who had come to share Aristotelian traditions, a much greater segment of *halakhah* appeared hard to justify. Starting with SAADIAH GAON Al-Fayyumi, some offered a distinction between 'commandments of reason' and 'commandments of obedience'; even the latter, however, were in principle justifiable – for example, by the value (intrinsic or instrumental) of obedience itself.

The second issue in the philosophy of *halakhah* relates to the system's formal coherence, rather than to the substance and sense of its particular elements. The rabbinic idea of norms grounded in God's revealed words, but subject to extensive midrashic remoulding, seems to pose a fundamental paradox: If the autonomy of human reasoning is upheld against the divine author's intention, has not the commitment to revelation become insincere? This challenge was posed most poignantly by the Karaites, a powerful movement in medieval Judaism radically opposed to midrash and to the entire project of an oral law (see KARAISM).

Rabbinic responses in this case diverge into two different tracks. Some play down the scope of innovation in *halakhah*, insisting that the entire oral law was revealed at Sinai. Others seek to distinguish between an unchanging core of divine law and a supple, growing body of human teachings.

Some views of Judaism emphasize elements outside of *halakhah*; they may contain a philosophy of *halakhah* but do not make it their main subject. This is true of Maimonides' philosophy, as presented in his *Guide to the Perplexed*, which views the entirety of the divine law as a means to an end, the attainment of human perfection through the realization of the inner human propensity to become Godlike. It is equally true of various systems of Jewish mysticism (see KABBALAH). In their different ways, both rationalists of the Maimonidean persuasion and mystics of Kabbalistic inclination have seen intimate knowledge of God as the focus of religious life and have gauged the import of *halakhah* from that standpoint. The work of Franz ROSENZWEIG represents a modern counterpart to such approaches.

See also: BIBLE, HEBREW; LAW, PHILOSOPHY OF; LEIBOWITZ, Y.; MAIMONIDES, M.; THEOLOGY, RABBINIC

References and further reading

Berkovits, E. (1983) *Not in Heaven*, New York: Ktav. (Restatement of the traditional doctrine regarding the primacy of the oral Torah and the role of human reason in *halakhah*.)

Elon, M. (1994) *Jewish Law: History, Sources, Principles*, trans. B. Auerbach and M.J. Sykes, Philadelphia, PA: Jewish Publication Society. (A comprehensive description and analysis of the *halakhic* legal system: its constitution, textual sources, and evolution.)

Jacob, W. and Zemer, M. (eds) (1991) *Progressive Halakhah: Essence and Application*, Tel Aviv and Pittsburgh, PA: Freehof Institute of Progressive Halakha. (Essays on the problems of 'Liberal' (Reform) Jewish Law.)

Roth, J. (1986) *The Halakhic Process: A Systemic Analysis*, New York: Jewish Theological Seminary. (Well-documented, systematic presentation of modes of *halakhic* change.)

NOAM J. ZOHAR

HALEVI, JUDAH (before 1075–1141)

Physician, philosopher and perhaps the greatest Hebrew poet since the Psalms, Judah Halevi studied the Neoplatonic Aristotelianism widespread in Islamic Spain, but his loyalty to Judaic traditions, love of Israel and poetic empathy for the sufferings and aspirations of his people made him a powerful critic of that philosophical tradition. His philosophical masterpiece, the Kuzari, is a fictional dialogue set at the court of the king of the Khazars, a people of the Volga basin whose leaders had converted to Judaism in the early ninth century. Reports of the Khazar realm sparked Halevi's imagination and gave him the backdrop for this effort to celebrate and shape his ancestral faith.

Beyond heartening his fellow Jews in times of upheaval, Halevi confronted philosophical questions that conventional thinkers often begged or ignored. He found the erudite Neoplatonism of his day too confining to God, too speculative and a priori. Tellingly, he condemns Neoplatonism for cultural vacuity, moral sterility and spiritual escapism: while Christians and Muslims, with the highest spiritual intentions, earnestly set about one another's murder, the philosophers fail to differentiate one faith from another. What is needed, Halevi reasons, is not a still more spiritual intellectualism but a historically and geographically rooted tradition concretely directed by God's love.

Halevi did not, as romantics often suppose, simply turn his back on reason, or on philosophy generically. Rather, he used his own philosophical gifts and poetic tact to retune philosophy to the ground notes of Jewish experience. He retained but structurally adapted the Neoplatonic linkage of God to the world via emanation, replacing the elaborate hierarchy of star souls with the simple manifestation of God's word, the 'Amr. Like Philo's Logos, Halevi's 'Amr was at once an attribute of God, his wisdom and a manifestation of God immanent in nature. Since the 'Amr is an imperative, it connotes power, volition and command, not just logical entailment or necessitation. Since it is immanent, it allows fuller appropriation than was possible for many philosophers and many of the pietists and mystics in their wake, of the material side of nature, including human nature: language, material culture – including agriculture and other economic activities – law and politics belong to realm of God's expression. Particularity is not isolated from God. Poetry and works of imagination can be expressions of the divine, not just stepchildren mediating the ever more abstract and abtruse flights of the intellect. Zion could be acknowledged as the land where the divine afflatus was most clearly articulated as a way of life. Longing for Zion need no longer be sublimated in prayer; rather, Israel's songs of longing for the robust life of the land of God's grace would voice a spiritual imperative that demanded practical expression and historical realization.

1   Life
2   The Kuzari: the basis of commitment
3   The Kuzari: idea and embodiment

1   Life

Born in Toledo and broadly educated in Arabic and Hebrew letters and sciences, Judah Halevi became a physician and poet in the Spain of the early Reconquista period. His poems speak of love, wine, gardens, friendship and the death of friends, of spiritual quest, devotion and the love of God, his Hebrew reluctantly attuned to Arabizing rhymes and cadences; but the ruined campsite that once prompted elegies for lost loves in pre-Islamic odes, is now the ruined Temple mount. Alienation gives edge to Halevi's poetry and thought. Philosophy, as he finds it, shows deep rifts between ideals and practice. Medicine is wanting both technically and spiritually. The Christian rulers of Northern Spain seem inhuman taskmasters, with the Jews their ministering slaves: 'we heal Babel, but it will not be healed' (letter to David Narboni, in Diwan, Brody 1974: 224).

Leaving Castile and settling in Cordova, Halevi saw the streams of Jewish refugees who fled the Almoravids and the Christian plundering and destruction of Jewish towns, and he learned of the terrors of the First Crusade. 'How can I savour what I eat', he wrote, '... When Zion is in Christian chains, and I in the shackle of Islam?' ('Libbi be-Mizrah', in Diwan, Brody 1974: 2). The smouldering scenes of a medieval Guernica, etched in his verses, made Halevi a proto-Zionist. Moving between Christian and Muslim Spain, protected by Jewish courtiers who prized his poetic and medical skills, Halevi saw no respite for his people.

Restless and troubled, he longed for Zion: 'My heart is in the East, but I am in the farthest West' ('Libbi be-Mizrah', in Diwan, Brody 1974: 2). The East here was more than geographical. The very direction held a spiritual significance for Halevi, conveyed in ideas of light, life and enlightenment. But could the East even in that sense exclude the earthly land of Israel, the land where the people of Israel had lived their earliest history and fullest life as a nation? Could even the spiritual East be less than Zion? How could one mourn the lost Jerusalem and pray for its restoration, yet remain in exile? Friends might urge complaisance, but as Halevi's historic vision deepened and darkened, his friends seemed drunk. Casting them in the stock role of the 'reproacher' of Arabic love lyrics, he turned on them: 'Is it good for a pure and honest man to be led about like a captive bird in the hands of children?' Halevi expanded on such questions in his Kuzari, an Arabic philosophical dialogue (the full title of the work is Kitab al-radd wa 'l-dalil fi 'l-din al-dhalil (A Defence and an Argument on behalf of the Abased Religion).)

2   The *Kuzari*: the basis of commitment

Written between 1130 and 1140, the *Kuzari* reflects a striking episode of Jewish history. In the early ninth century, Bulan, King of the Khazars, a people of the Volga basin, along with four thousand of his nobles, had adopted Judaism. Under Byzantine and Muslim pressure, the king sought his own monotheistic faith. Granted religious freedom, most Khazars probably never became Jews; but until the Khazars were swept away in the Tatar invasion of 1237, Judaism was the state religion. Hasdai ibn Shaprut, wazir of 'Abdu 'l-Rahman III of Cordova, thrilled to hear of a powerful Jewish state in the East, wrote to the Khazar monarch around 960. Replying, King Joseph told of the Khazar conversion and described his kingdom.

The conversion had followed a debate among Christian, Jewish and Muslim spokesmen, which Halevi fictively reconstructed. The king has dreamt that his intentions, but not his practices, are pleasing to God. He consults a philosopher but hears only a disappointingly intellectualist Neoplatonic Aristotelianism. 'If philosophers say that God created you, that is metaphorical, of course. For He is the Cause of all the causes that conspire in the creation of all things' (*Kuzari* 1.1).

The philosopher argues smoothly, with many therefores and an almost equally smooth stream of disembodied intellects through which God's act reaches the world: 'The world is eternal. Human beings have always arisen one from another, their forms compounded and their characters formed by those of their fathers and mothers, and by their environment – airs, lands, foods and waters – along with the influences of the spheres, constellations and signs of the Zodiac' (*Kuzari* 1.1). Man's goal is to purify the soul, for the perfect may reunite with the nearest hypostasis, the 'active intellect' – which the perfect man, ignoring mere limbs and organs, already is. Religion is a valuable moral conditioner, especially for the masses. Once its function is grasped, however, it may be moulded at will.

The king finds the philosopher's argument 'impressive', but unhelpful. He still seeks a way of life pleasing to God. Christians and Muslims divide the world; with the highest intentions, they earnestly pursue one another's murder. Philosophy seems to wish to stand above the fray, deeming all monotheists to be truth seekers. But how can these enemies all be right? The philosopher's affirmation, 'In the faith of the Philosophers there is no such killing, since we foster the mind' (*Kuzari* 1.1), betrays a stunning innocence. The highest intentions, it seems, do not differentiate acts of heroism from obscene atrocities. Ethos is grotesquely under-determined by ideology.

Khalas (sincerity) must be given a material, not merely formal sense; devotion must extend to action, not just in cultivating personal virtues but communally. Neoplatonists, pietists and ascetics still must address the embodiment of their ideals and the delicate, dangerous nexus between ethos and ethnicity. The philosophers have paid too little mind to history.

The king grows curious about Christians and Muslims: 'Surely one of these two ways of life is the pleasing one' (*Kuzari* 1.1). The obvious abasement of the Jews seems to exclude theirs. A Christian and a Muslim speak, appealing, respectively, to the divinity of Christ and the inimitable language of the Qur'an. The king's responses vividly signal Halevi's outlook: a little philosophy would not hurt the Christian case. 'Not having grown up in these beliefs', the king feels no need to seek credibility for them. Logic will accommodate experience, but that is because experience takes root in the heart (*Kuzari* 1.5).

Like Muhammad, the Muslim spokesman avoids appeal to miracles, except the Qur'an, whose every verse Muslims call a portent. Again the Khazar answers existentially:

If one hopes for guidance from God's Word and hopes to be convinced, against his own scepticism, that God does speak to mortals, things ought to be manifest and incontrovertible. Even then one would hardly credit that God spoke to a man. If your book is miraculous, being written in Arabic its uniqueness and inimitability are indiscernible to a non-Arab like me. When read to me, it sounds like any other Arabic book.

(*Kuzari* 1.6)

Since both Christian and Muslim cite Jewish history, the Khazar summons a rabbi, called a *Haver* or Fellow of a Talmudical academy. The rabbi opens not with a cosmological credo but an invocation of the God of Abraham, Isaac and Jacob. He avoids proofs like the design argument:

'If you were told that the ruler of India was a virtuous man whom you should hold in awe and whose name you should revere, but his works were described to you in reports of the justice, good character and fair ways of the people of his land, would that bind you to him?'

'How could it, when the question remains whether the people of India act justly of their own accord and have no king at all, whether they do so on account of their king, or whether both are true?'

(*Kuzari* 1.19–20)

Mere argument does not show whether the order and design of nature are the work of God, intrinsic to nature, or Neoplatonically imparted by God through the natures of things:

> 'But if a messenger came to you from that king with Indic gifts, that you were certain could be had only in India, and only in the palace of a king, and he brought you a written attestation that these came from the king, and enclosed medicines to treat your illnesses and preserve your health... would this not bind you to his allegiance?'
>
> (*Kuzari* 1.21)

Similarly, God confronts Pharaoh (Exodus 5: 1) not as the creator but as the ancestral help of Israel; at Sinai (Exodus 20: 2), he is the God who saved Israel from Egypt. What mattered then was not what God had done for the universe, but what he had done for them. Only Israel, the Rabbi argues, has a true and continuous tradition regarding the divine. India may be ancient, but its people have no coherent system of ideas, and they are polytheists. Greek philosophical originality is a *tour de force*, but it shows the unsteady gait of solecism. Aristotle has no tradition to keep him from going overboard, as when he ascribes intelligence to nature at large.

The religion of Israel, the *Haver* argues, uniquely combines the intimacy of God's unique historical relationship with Israel and the publicity of the entire nation's experience of God's act, receipt of his gifts and their written attestation, passed down undisrupted through the generations, preserving the certitude of God's ancient self-revelation. The true religion did not evolve like man-made faiths. Like creation, it was complete in a moment, when 600,000 Israelites experienced their redemption, and after wandering in the desert, somehow heard God's words, each individual directly and personally inspired.

Reacting to the palpable chauvinism (*ta'assub*) of the *Haver*'s claims, the king asks if the sin of the Golden Calf does not diminish the rabbi's all but insufferable pride. Every nation, the *Haver* replies, was full of idolaters at the time. Any philosophers who could prove that God was one would still have rationalized idolatry as symbolism mediating the divine to the masses. Israel's backsliding was grievous principally because the sin was theirs. The people sinned, but they were forgiven. What matters is that they were chosen. They preserved the perfection in which Adam was created. The perfect climate of the God-given land would prepare them to live by God's word. Prophecy will never leave them.

Israel's great gift is not the specious reward of a sensuous afterlife, or even a spiritual afterlife that no one really wants, but the abiding presence of the divine in this life. Philosophers imagine that only pure intellects are immortal; Muslims and Christians compound such exclusivism with superstitious notions that lipservice somehow confers immortality. But Jews believe that God rewards the righteous of all nations. What distinguishes Israel lies in this world. Jews do not spend their lives begging their king for safe conduct on the parlous journey that every mortal must undertake; they live confident that God, by whose word they live, will not forsake them.

Convinced that here must be the way of life his dream foretold, king and *wazir* embrace Judaism and gradually win over many of their nation. They study the Torah and gain great worldly success, honoring the Israelites among them as the first and most fully Jewish of their countrymen. Only after extensive study of the Torah does the king begin to inquire speculatively into its theology; existential commitment comes first.

3 The *Kuzari*: idea and embodiment

Through the dialogue, Halevi proposes that God is described in three ways: (1) negative predicates, indicative of perfection, as when we say 'the living God,' to distinguish him from the dead, false gods of idolaters; (2) relative predicates, expressing human attitudes toward God, as when we call him blessed and exalted; and (3) predicates of creativity, which speak of God's acts through some natural medium or agency, as when we say, 'making poor and rich' God's agency in nature is his will, the motive force behind all natural and supernatural events, and the source of the created glory that manifests God's grace on Israel in their land, the favoured place for its appearance. When Israel dwells on its soil in peace and justice, prophecy becomes possible among the pious. All true prophecy was either in or for the land of Israel, the centre of the globe and reference point of day and night, east and west. Its very air imparts wisdom. Thus the sages were not misled in saying that one who walks four yards there is assured of happiness in the world to come: such a person already tastes transcendence.

Surely then, the king responds, the rabbi is remiss in not returning to that land. For even if the Shechinah, God's immanence, is no longer present there, one should seek to purify the soul in such a holy place, if only because it once was there. The rabbi accepts the reproach, answering only that Israel's return has always depended on the people's willingness, for 'God's Word grants a man no more than he is capable of receiving' (*Kuzari* 2.24). Israel today is no longer a body but only dry bones. Yet these bones preserve a trace of life, which can return to them if the

Temple, which animated them, and made them vulnerable, is restored.

Adapting a thought that Plato had applied to philosophers, the Rabbi says that Israel is the heart among the nations, at once the most vital and the most vulnerable. Prophecy will return, but prophets and saints are not the same as hermits and ascetics. Mere renunciation does not achieve the intimacy with God that makes a nation the true seedbed of prophecy. Justice, not humility or spirituality, is the natural, rational and necessary foundation of a nation's life: 'The divine law cannot be fulfilled until the civil and rational laws are perfected.' Israel cannot survive and fulfil God's commandments as a soul without a body. Not withdrawal and asceticism are demanded but the full life of an economy and a state. It is as much a divine commandment to labour and cultivate the soil as it is to keep the Sabbath, for both celebrate God's act of creation and the liberation of Israel from Egypt.

Piety is not best shown by upturned eyes, meditative postures and gestures, or fine words that intend no action, but by genuine commitment and sincere intentions, manifested in demanding actions performed with dedication. What Halevi calls for here is not simply a return to Zion; not mere spiritual longing, but the reconstitution of the full, robust life of Israel in its land, under its laws. The members of the Sanhedrin, he argues, were responsible for knowledge of every science: the authentic sciences, to fulfill the intentions of the Law and preserve the health and welfare of the people; the conventional sciences, to perfect their use of language; and even the specious sciences, evidently to understand ambient superstitions. These sciences, whose relics still distinguish Jews, must be restored, along with the Hebrew language, which has fallen into decline since the days of the psalmists and has become the toy of lackeys and misfits.

Israel's aim is not otherworldliness. We love life and all its goods. True, a man who reaches moral perfection, like Enoch or Elijah, will grow uncomfortable in the world and will feel no isolation in solitude. Yet today, when there is no clear vision, the good man must be the guardian of his country. He must give all his powers their due, preparing them to serve when called on. The king is surprised at so political an idea of personal goodness, but the rabbi replies that human goodness is political for Plato's reason, that it rests on command over one's powers: 'The good man is the prince, obeyed by his senses, and by his spiritual and physical powers.... It is he who is fit to rule. For if he led a state, he would apply the same justice in it as he does in governing his own body and soul' (*Kuzari* 3.5).

Human rationality regulates the good man's life. However, God adds further refinements to the life of Israel, rendering specific the generic obligations of reason, and instituting the visible symbolisms that save the idea of a covenant with God from reduction to a mere abstraction. The good Israelite lives in the thought that God is ever-present; the world is not finished or abandoned but an ongoing creation, in which our own words and the songs that spring from our mouths at God's behest issue without our least knowledge of how the God-given powers of the body and creativity of the mind spring to his service.

Obedience, not zeal, is God's desire. Moderation, not excess, anchors God's plan. Just as only God, and no mere alchemist, knows the proportions needed to compound a living body, so no mere tinkerer can fashion a law of life. No individual can possibly replace the careful, systemic modulation of the good life. Halevi's target here is the Karaites, whose rejection of oral or Talmudic Law seemed to leave each individual to comprehend the Torah in isolation (see Karaism). Without an oral tradition, we would not even know how to vocalize or parse the text, let alone govern by it. True, the Karaites show originality, the product of their isolation. They are like foot soldiers in no man's land; the Rabbanites, secure in their traditions, seem as confident and lax as the populace of a walled city. But on Karaite principles, there would be as many codes as opinions.

The Oral Law is stricter than the Law of Moses, making a margin (*seyag*) around the Torah, but that allows the Rabbis to qualify and mitigate their rulings, guided by God's still present Word. We are not confined to the flickering light of reason but know God through our intercourse with him and the long history of our growing awareness, traceable in a tradition recorded by Scripture all the way back to Adam.

God's will is executed in nature without intermediaries, the *Haver* argues, with a sidelong glance at the Neoplatonic cosmos, clogged with disembodied intelligences. Like other critics, including AL-GHAZALI, Halevi finds the idea that emanation is the truth behind scriptural creation reductionistic. It treats God's creativity too much as a mechanism or a necessity of logic, placing God at a remove and setting the ideas of things between God and his creatures. Knowing that his battle is with intellectual authority, Halevi turns satirical, asking how it is that thought in disembodied intellects generates a sphere. When Aristotle reflected, no such sphere arose!

Dispensing with the entire complex disembodied apparatus, Halevi ascribes God's knowledge and governance of the world directly to his Word, preserving the double edged efficacy of the ancient

Philonic Logos: immanent in nature yet in no way separate from God, since it is His will. The *'Amr* or divine word of command is still, in a way, an emanation. For it does convey the divine idea and impress it upon the world, the Land and the prophets, who are recipients of inspiration. But the emergence of the Word from God in Halevi, like the initial differentiation of the First Essence in IBN GABIROL, is now volitional. The work of emanation is no longer conceived through a mystification of logic that makes entailment somehow a source or vehicle of creation. The impact is to immanentize divine volition. This approach has a long afterlife: in Maimonides' theory of angels as forms and forces, in Kabbalistic developments pioneered by NAHMANIDES, in Spinoza's *conatus*, Bergson's *élan vital*, Whitehead's creativity and beyond.

In dismissing intellectualist emanation, Halevi has not rejected logic or philosophy; he has rejected the specific product that prominent philosophers ascribed to logic. Only tradition can explain their reliance on arguments as suppositious as those behind the Neoplatonic ontology. However, Halevi faults the philosophers not for their logic but for their want of logic. The naturalism to which Halevi appeals in rejecting the idea that mere self-reflection or contemplation of the divine can entail spheres or angels into being is philosophic, although it is corrosive to the intellectualist assumptions of the prevalent philosophical school of his day.

Philosophers may say that love of God follows from knowledge of his omnipotence, but such inferences are too abstract to command the heart. Similarly, even the most impressive arguments of the philosophers find no following among the common people, not because the people are too crude, as the philosophers suppose, but because the philosophers are too far removed from life. Humans need language, images and rituals. What we need to know of theology is that the world is created, that it has a cause in God, who is eternal and unconditioned, incorporeal, omniscient and omnipotent, living and willing eternally, and that the human will, like God's, is free. Volition is delegated to human beings, just as natural dispositions are imparted to all things. For if an external determinism were true, 'a man's speaking would be compulsory, like his pulse' (*Kuzari* 5.20).

The *Haver* draws his teaching to a close with new thoughts of Zion, which has never been far from the aim of his argument. The life of Israel in her land and the will of God are of a piece. The rabbi dismisses the pious notion that Israel's sins debar return. The liturgical confession 'and for our sins were we exiled from our land' is hortatory and admonitory, not explanatory or normative. The Psalmist's lines (102:

14–15) 'Thou wilt arise and take pity on Zion, for the time to favour her is here, the time is come – since Thy servants delight in her stones and cherish her dust', mean that Jerusalem will be rebuilt when Israel so yearns for it as to cherish her very stones and dust. The gloss sums up the hearty rootedness that Halevi opposes to Neoplatonic intellectualism and pietist asceticism. Responding, the king offers a courtly opportunity for his teacher to take his leave: 'If this be so, it would be culpable to detain you' (*Kuzari* 5.28).

Acting on the same conclusion, Halevi left Spain in 1140, travelling to Egypt and on to Palestine. In legend, he lived to kiss the ground outside Jerusalem, where, as he spoke the words of his Ode to Zion, he was killed by an Arab horseman. But the meaning of his journey is best captured in the direction he took, encoded not in the poet's life but in his work and above all in the *Kuzari*, with its intellectually serious call for the reintegration of Israel, body and spirit, land, language and Logos, the freely imparted and freely chosen direction of God's eternal Idea.

See also: GOD, CONCEPTS OF; ZIONISM

List of works

Halevi, Judah (c.1130–40) *Kitab al-radd wa- 'l-dalil fi 'l-din al-dhalil (Kuzari)*(A Defence and an Argument on behalf of the Abased Religion), ed. D.H. Baneth, Jerusalem: Magnes Press; trans. H. Hirschfeld, London: Routledge, 1905; repr. New York: Schocken, 1974. (The Hirschfeld translation is misleadingly imprecise. A new translation is in preparation as part of the Yale Judaica series. Passages quoted here are translated by L.E. Goodman.)

—— (before 1141) *Diwan*, ed. H. Brody, *Jehuda Ha Levi, Die Sch'nen Versmasse*, Berlin, 1894–1930, 4 vols; ed. H. Brody, *Selected Poems of Jehudah Halevi*, Philadelphia, PA: Jewish Publication Society, 1974. (The Berlin edition is the classic four-volume edition of Halevi's poetry, which includes his secular poetry in vols 1 and 2 and his religious poetry in vols 3 and 4; selections from this edition are reprinted, with English translation by S. Bernstein in Brody's *Selected Poems*, which was first published in 1924.

—— (before 1141) 'Letter to Rabbi Haviv' (in Hebrew), ed. H. Ratzhaby, 'A Letter from R. Judah Halevi to R. Haviv', *Gilyonot* 28, 1953: 268–72. (Useful for biographical detail on Halevi.)

References and further reading

Allony, N. (1951) *Torat ha-Mishkalim – The Scansion*

of Medieval Hebrew Poetry: Dunash, Jehuda Halevi, and Abraham ibn Ezra, Jerusalem. (In Hebrew, this work discusses Halevi's theories of prosody and his attitudes towards meter in Arabic and Hebrew.)

Baer, Y. (1971) A History of the Jews of Christian Spain, trans. L. Schoffman, Philadelphia, PA: Jewish Publication Society. (Valuable exposition of the historical backgrounds.)

Baljon, J.M.S. (1958) 'The amr of God in the Koran', Acta Orientalia 23: 7–18. (Explores the Islamic logos theory that influenced Halevi's conception.)

Baneth, D.H. (1981) 'Judah Halevi and al-Ghazali', trans. G. Hirschler in A. Jospe (ed.) Studies in Jewish Thought: An Anthology of German Jewish Scholarship, Detroit, MI: Wayne State University Press, 181–99. (First published in German in 1924; important comparative study.)

Baron, S. (1960) A Social and Religious History of the Jews, Philadelphia, PA: Jewish Publication Society. (Includes detailed discussions of the poet and his times.)

Brann, R. (1991) The Compunctious Poet: Cultural Ambiguity and Hebrew Poetry in Muslim Spain, Baltimore, MD: Johns Hopkins University Press. (A study of the ambivalent reception of Arabic themes and methods by Hebrew poets.)

Davidson, H. (1972) 'The Active Intellect in the Cuzari and Hallevi's Theory of Causality', Revue des Études Juives 131: 351–96. (Explores Halevi's ideas on the metaphysics of emanation.)

Dunlop, D.M. (1954) The History of the Jewish Khazars, Princeton, NJ: Princeton University Press. (A scholarly review of the evidence avoiding the extravagant speculations of some popularizers.)

Goitein, S.D. (1967) A Mediterranean Society, Berkeley, CA: University of California Press. (Magisterial study of the Cairo Geniza materials, which preserve primary evidence for the life and times of Halevi.)

Hamori, A. (1985) 'Lights in the Heart of the Sea: Some Images of Judah Halevi's', Journal of Semitic Studies 30: 75–83. (Examines Halevi's use of Neoplatonic imagery in his poetry.)

Motzkin, A. (1980) 'On Halevi's Kuzari as a Platonic Dialogue', Interpretation 9: 111–24. (A Straussian reading.)

Neumark, D. (1929) 'Jehuda Hallevi's Philosophy', in S. Cohon (ed.) Essays in Jewish Philosophy, Cincinnati, OH: Central Conference of American Rabbis; repr. Amsterdam: Philo Press, 1971, 219–300. (Draws the connection between Halevi and Ibn Gabirol.)

Pines, S. (1960) Encyclopedia of Islam, London: Luzac, 1.29–30, s.v. 'amr. (This article connects Halevi's use of the term 'amr with the Islamic background and usage.)

—— (1980) 'Shiite Terms and Conceptions in Judah Halevi's Kuzari', Jerusalem Studies in Arabic and Islam 2: 165–219. (Further clarification of the Islamic background for Halevi's philosophical theology.)

Scheindlin, R. (1986) Wine, Women, and Death: Medieval Hebrew Poems on the Good Life, Philadelphia, PA: Jewish Publication Society. (Excellent survey (with translations) of the thematics of Hebrew poetry of Islamic Spain.)

—— (1991) The Gazelle: Medieval Hebrew Poems on God, Israel and the Soul, Philadelphia, PA: Jewish Publication Society. (Sequel to Scheindlin 1986.)

Silman, Y. (1995) Philosopher and Prophet: Judah Halevi, the Kuzari and the Evolution of his Thought, trans. L.J. Schramm, Albany, NY: State University of New York Press. (Analyses the Kuzari from a developmental perspective, showing how it embeds elements of the poet's early attachment to the Neoplatonic philosophical tradition and how the work grows beyond its original aim, as a riposte to Karaism.)

Spiegel, S. (1976) 'On Medieval Hebrew Poetry', repr. in J. Goldin (ed.) The Jewish Expression, New Haven, CN: Yale University Press. (A compact but wide-ranging survey of the medieval Hebrew poets, their themes and their relations with Biblical and post-Biblical poetry, liturgy and ideas.)

Strauss, L. (1952) 'The Law of Reason in the Kuzari', in Persecution and the Art of Writing, New York: Free Press, 95–141. (Classic study from the volume in which Strauss established the methodology of a still influential school of thought focused on the idea of indirection in the texts of philosophical past masters.)

L.E. GOODMAN

HAMANN, JOHANN GEORG (1730–88)

Hamann was one of the most important critics of the German Enlightenment or Aufklärung*. He attacked the* Aufklärung *chiefly because it gave reason undue authority over faith. It misunderstood faith, which consists in an immediate personal experience, inaccessible to reason. The main fallacy of the* Aufklärung *was hypostasis, the reification of ideas, the artificial abstraction of reason from its social and historical context. Hamann stressed the social and historical dimension of reason, that it must be embodied in society, history and language. He also emphasized the pivotal role of language in the development of reason.*

The instrument and criterion of reason was language, whose only sanction was tradition and use.

Hamann was a sharp critic of Kant, whose philosophy exemplified all the sins of the Aufklärung. *Hamann attacked the critical philosophy for its purification of reason from experience, language and tradition. He also strongly objected to all its dualisms, which seemed arbitrary and artificial. The task of philosophy was to unify all the various functions of the mind, seeing reason, will and feeling as an indivisible whole.*

Although he was original and unorthodox, Hamann's critique of reason should be placed within the tradition of Protestant nominalism. Hamann saw himself as a defender of Luther, whose reputation was on the wane in late eighteenth-century Germany.

Hamann was also a founder of the Sturm und Drang, *the late eighteenth-century literary movement which celebrated personal freedom and revolt. His aesthetics defended creative genius and the metaphysical powers of art. It marked a sharp break with the rationalism of the classical tradition and the empiricism of late eighteenth-century aesthetics.*

Hamann was a seminal influence upon Herder, Goethe, Jacobi, Friedrich Schlegel and Kierkegaard.

1 **Critique of reason**
2 **Philosophy of language**
3 **Aesthetics**
4 **Politics**

1 **Critique of reason**

Born into a middle class family, Hamann spent almost all of his life in Königsberg, Prussia. He formulated many of his ideas in exchanges with his friend and neighbour, Immanuel KANT. From 1762 to 1764 he was the tutor of Johann HERDER, who was profoundly influenced by him. For most of his life Hamann was a minor official in the Prussian bureaucracy, a position procured for him by Kant. Because of his mysticism and sibylline style he earned the sobriquet 'The Magus of the North'.

The starting point of Hamann's philosophy was his mystical experience and conversion, which took place in London in March 1758. Hamann went through a deep personal crisis that shattered his earlier allegiance to the *Aufklärung*. The solution to his crisis was a mystical experience, a rebirth through faith in Christ. During his experience Hamann had a vision of the divine omnipresence, of God dwelling within him and speaking to him through all the events of nature and history. The creation was the secret language of God, the symbolism by which he communicated his message of redemption to human beings. All of nature

consisted in hieroglyphs, secret symbols and puzzles, which could be interpreted through Scriptures alone. Hamann wrote down his experiences and reflections upon them in several early manuscripts, *Biblische Betrachtungen* (Scriptural Meditations), *Brocken* (Fragments), *Gedanken ueber meinen Lebenslauf* (Thoughts on My Life's Path), and *Gedanken ueber Kirchenliedern* (Thoughts on Hymns), which were all composed from March to May, 1758. Although it was deeply personal, Hamann's vision had its roots in a commonplace of the pietist tradition: that all the events portrayed in the Bible are a spiritual allegory, a metaphor for the soul's struggle for salvation (see PIETISM).

Hamann's reaction to the *Aufklärung* began with his defence of his new faith, which he set forth in his short tract *Sokratische Denkwürdigkeiten* (Socratic Memorabilia, 1759). This work was dedicated to Christoph Berens, Hamann's employer, and Immanuel Kant, who attempted to reconvert him to the cause of the *Aufklärung*. Its central thesis is that reason does not have the power to criticize faith. The jurisdiction of reason, Hamann argues, is limited to the assessment of the truth-value of propositions. Its task is to determine whether we have sufficient evidence for some statement. Faith therefore falls outside the sphere of reason, because faith consists in a living experience, which cannot be expressed in any proposition or statement. Just as reason cannot criticize our ordinary sensations, whose qualities are just given and indescribable, so it cannot detract from a mystical experience, whose qualities are no less present and ineffable.

In his defence of faith Hamann appealed to the scepticism of David HUME. According to Hamann, the Scottish philosopher had shown that reason cannot demonstrate or refute the existence of anything, and that we need faith to sustain us even in our ordinary life. Contrary to Hume's intentions, though, Hamann used his scepticism to *defend* religious belief itself. If reason cannot prove or disprove the existence of ordinary things, then *a fortiori* it cannot prove or disprove the existence of God. If we need faith in ordinary life, then why cannot we have it in religion too? In general, Hamann proved to be an important transmitter of Hume's ideas in Germany. His July 1759 letter to Kant refers to Hume, providing Kant with his first knowledge of the philosopher who would later awaken him from his 'dogmatic slumber'.

In many of his later writings – especially his *Kreuzzüge des Philologen* (Crusades of the Philologist, 1762), *Philologische Einfälle und Zweifel* (Philological Whimsys and Doubt, 1772) and *Metakritik ueber den Purismus der Vernunft* (Metacritique of the Purism of Reason, 1781) – Hamann deepened and broadened his attack upon the faith in reason of the *Aufklärung*. The chief target of Hamann's critique was the tendency of the *Aufklärung* to abstract reason from its social, historical and linguistic context. The *Aufklärer* treated reason as if it were a selfsufficient, autonomous faculty, operating independently of political interests, cultural traditions or subconscious desires. If, however, we are to avoid hypostasis, then we must raise the questions 'Where is reason?', 'In what particular things does it exist?' We can answer these questions, Hamann argues, only by identifying the embodiment or manifestation of reason in language, custom and action. Reason then proves to be not a special kind of faculty existing in some Platonic or noumenal realm but only a specific manner of speaking, writing and acting in concrete cultural circumstances. Accordingly, Hamann stressed the social and cultural dimension of reason, which had been much neglected in the eighteenth century. In this regard his teaching was influential upon Herder and anticipates the historicism of the nineteenth century.

When Kant's *Critique of Pure Reason* appeared in 1781, Hamann attacked it as a perfect example of the *Aufklärung*'s hypostasis of reason. The main fallacy of the *Critique*, as he described it, is 'the purism of pure reason', the abstraction of reason from its embodiment in language, tradition and experience. According to Hamann, Kant hypostasized reason by postulating a selfsufficient noumenal realm that exists apart from the phenomenal realms of language, history and experience. Kant commits a threefold hypostasis or purification of reason. He abstracts it from sense perception, tradition or custom, and – worst of all – language. What remains after all this abstraction is nothing but the purely formal transcendental subject=X, 'the talisman and rosary of a transcendental superstition which believes in all *ens rationis*'. In general, Hamann deplored Kant's dualisms in all their forms –noumena/phenomena, understanding/sensibility, concept/intuition – since they were nothing more than arbitrary and artificial abstractions. The central task of the philosophy of mind, in his view, is not to divide but to unite the various powers, showing how they stem from a single source. This single source, Hamann suggested, lay in words, the embodiment of thought in sensible marks and sounds. The central task for the critique of reason therefore lay in the examination and criticism of language itself.

Although Hamann's critique of reason made him a rebel against the prevailing ideology of the *Aufklärung*, it was not entirely new or original. To say that Hamann is without any known debt to anyone else is to ignore his broader intellectual context. Hamann's critique of reason should be placed firmly within the Protestant tradition, which had always insisted upon a sharp distinction between realms of faith and reason. It was Hamann's aim to defend this distinction, the integrity of the sphere of faith, against the incursions of the *Aufklärung*. His critique of hypostasis, his emphasis upon concrete experience, his insistence upon the linguistic embodiment of reason, and his claim that language consists only in convention and custom, all show his debt to the nominalism so characteristic of the Protestant tradition. It is indeed important that Hamann saw himself as the defender of LUTHER, whose reputation had waned at the close of the eighteenth century. Although Hamann's critique of reason moves within the broad contours of the Protestant tradition, it would be a mistake to regard him as an orthodox Lutheran or typical pietist. In the famous dispute between LESSING and Goeze, Hamann refused to side with the orthodox pastor, who had defended the literal truth of the Bible. Hamann's ultimate authority was mystical experience more than the Bible, which required a more metaphoric and spiritual interpretation. It is more accurate to place Hamann within the spiritualist tradition of Protestantism, among such radical reformers as Gottfried Arnold, Valentin Weigel, Jakob Boehme, Hans Denck and Sebastian Franck. Like Hamann, these thinkers stressed the importance of personal freedom and mystical experience.

It would be a mistake, too, to describe Hamann's critique of reason as a form of 'irrationalism', as if he were strongly prejudiced against reason and the sciences. Hamann frequently insisted that his critique was directed against only the *illegitimate extension* of reason beyond experience, and that reason had a perfectly valid use within the boundaries of ordinary experience. If we use the term 'irrationalism' strictly and accurately, then it applies to the acceptance of beliefs that are contrary to evidence, the attitude typified by Tertullian's famous maxim *credo quia absurdam* (I believe because it is absurd). But Hamann rejected any such 'leap of faith'. In this regard he was only keeping with the traditional Lutheran distinction between the heavenly and earthly realms, where the supernatural heavenly realm was the object of faith, the empirical earthly realm the domain of reason.

2 Philosophy of language

The most important aspect of Hamann's critique of reason was his philosophy of language, which he first sketched in his *Kreuzzüge* and then developed in many writings throughout his life. Hamann is one of the first thinkers in the modern tradition to stress the importance of language for thought. He denies the prevalent eighteenth-century view – common to both the empiricist and rationalist traditions – that there are clear and distinct ideas apart from their embodiment in language. Words are not just arbitrary signs for already formed ideas but the very medium by which ideas come into existence. Thinking is nothing more than the use of symbols. To talk about ideas or concepts apart from words is again to lapse into that old fallacy of the *Aufklärung*: hypostasis.

Hamann takes a very radical stand on the connection between ideas and signs, thoughts and words. It is not only that signs are the *medium of existence* of reason; they are also the criterion of its truth. True to the nominalism of the Protestant tradition, Hamann denies that a proposition is true because it corresponds to some special kind of entity, such as facts, universals or states of affairs. All that exists are particulars, which can be explained and classified in all kinds of ways, depending upon our interests. The main criterion for truth is only the correct use of language, which is determined by nothing more than convention and tradition. In making language the criterion of reason and use the sanction of language, Hamann flirted with relativism, though he never explicitly avowed it.

In 1772 Hamann became involved in the famous eighteenth-century controversy regarding the origin of language (see HERDER, J. §3). This debate, launched by CONDILLAC in 1746, concerned whether language had a merely human or a divine origin. Hamann criticized his erstwhile pupil, Herder, for his view that the origin of language could be explained purely naturalistically, as a product of human need and skill. Although Hamann is generally regarded as a defender of the divine origin view, his theory is much more complex and obscure. On at least one reading, Hamann does not deny that the origin of language can be explained naturalistically. Rather, he holds that language has *both* a divine and human, a supernatural *and* natural, source. Although language is created through natural means, by the use of native human powers, God is also coactive in the use of these powers. Since God acts through man, what man creates through his natural capacities is also what God creates through him. Sometimes, however, Hamann resorts to mystical and metaphorical expressions, as if God directly taught Adam how to use language after the creation.

3   Aesthetics

Hamann's historical significance lies in his aesthetics no less than his critique of reason. His main work in aesthetics is his *Aesthetica in nuce*, which appeared as part of his *Kreuzzüge des Philologen*. Its defence of artistic creativity and the metaphysical significance of art had a great influence upon the *Sturm und Drang* and ultimately Romanticism itself (see ROMANTICISM, GERMAN).

One of the main aims of Hamann's text is to liberate the artist from the shackles of conventions and norms. *Aesthetica in nuce* is a manifesto on behalf of artistic creativity, a paean to the genius who dares to break all the rules. Rather than aspiring to portray archetypes or models, the artist should dare to express his passions and reveal his personal vision. What makes a work of art beautiful, Hamann suggests, is its expression, the revelation of the personality of the artist.

Another objective of the *Aesthetica* is to reaffirm the metaphysical significance of art, the classical equation of truth and beauty. This significance had been denied or depreciated by most eighteenth-century aestheticians, who usually regarded aesthetic experience as little more than a pleasant sensation or an amusing illusion. According to Hamann, however, art is nothing less than the purest medium of truth. Our knowledge of life and reality comes through immediate experience, and only a non-discursive medium such as art reproduces such sensations and feelings. While philosophers must resign themselves to concepts, which are only artificial and arbitrary abstractions, artists deal with images, which capture all the vividness and richness of experience.

In defending the equation of truth and beauty, Hamann appears to return to the classical aesthetics of the seventeenth century. Indeed, he even retains the doctrine of imitation, so important for that tradition. But Hamann retained this doctrine in his own manner and for his own purposes. He reformulated it in accord with his empiricist and mystical epistemology, and so at odds with the more rationalist epistemology of classicism. He broke with classicism with regard to both the object and manner of imitation. What the artist should imitate, Hamann thinks, is the secret language of God, not the eternal archetypes of things, as in classicism; and he imitates this language not by following classical rules or norms but by creating images and symbols.

The *Aesthetica* appears to consist in two conflicting doctrines: an extreme subjectivism, which encourages artists to express their personal feelings and visions; and an extreme objectivism, which demands that they imitate nature and reveal the presence of God. What is central to, and characteristic of, Hamann's aesthetics, however, is precisely the synthesis of these doctrines. They come together in Hamann's mystical vision of the omnipresence of God. Since God is inside man, dwelling in man's inner heart, artists have only to reveal their innermost feelings to reveal God himself. Their personal symbols and images then become nothing less than the language of God.

4 Politics

Although not primarily a political thinker, Hamann made some important criticisms of the political doctrines of the *Aufklärung*. In *Golgotha und Scheblimini* (1784), a critique of Moses Mendelssohn's *Jerusalem*, he criticized the prevalent natural law doctrine (see MENDELSSOHN, M.). Since reason becomes determinate only in a specific cultural context, it is a false abstraction, Hamann argues, to seek some universal and eternal norm true for any culture. Natural law doctrine also assumes that people are rational outside society; yet it is only through society that they learn the use of language, restrain their appetites and conduct themselves according to rules.

In *Kreuzzüge des Philologen* Hamann attacked the individualism prevalent in the modern political tradition. He explicitly appealed to Aristotle's conception of man as a political animal to refute the notion that the individual is selfsufficient and born with natural needs. Freedom and reason are not properties inherent in each individual apart from society, Hamann contended, but only their manner of acting and speaking within it.

Because of his critique of the *Aufklärung* and the liberal values associated with it, Hamann has sometimes been portrayed as a reactionary, indeed as a founding father of the modern alliance of irrationalism and conservatism. But this interpretation is anachronistic, failing to consider the context in which Hamann lived and wrote. All his mature life Hamann was a passionate critic of the reigning Prussian monarch, Friedrich II, 'the philosopher king'. But his critique of Friedrich and the *Aufklärer* in Berlin is not a rejection of their liberal principles – toleration, freedom of press, equality before the law – but of the paternalism and authoritarianism of the absolutist Prussian state. Hamann too embraced these principles, and his critique of the *Aufklärung* is indeed motivated by them. He argued, however, that the *Aufklärer* had betrayed them through their intolerance toward revealed religion and through their alliance with the autocratic Prussian monarch. In his critical review of Kant's essay on enlightenment, Hamann attacked Kant not because he advocated emancipation – the right to think for oneself – but because he restricted it to the public sphere. By denying the people a right to think for themselves in their official duties, Kant had virtually sanctioned Friedrich's despotism, the old maxim 'Say what you like but obey'.

See also: ENLIGHTENMENT, CONTINENTAL; FAITH; JACOBI, F.; SCHLEGEL, F. VON

List of works

Nadler, J. (ed.) (1949–57) *Sämtliche Werke*, Vienna: Herder, 6 vols.
Includes the following:

Hamann, J.G. (1759) *Sokratische Denkwürdigkeiten* (Socratic Memorabilia).
—— (1762) *Briefwechsel*, Ziesemer, W. and Henkel, A. (eds) (1955–79), Wiesbaden and Frankfurt: Insel, 6 vols.
—— *Hamann's Socratic Memorabilia: A Translation and Commentary*, trans. O'Flaherty, J.C. (1967), Baltimore, MD: Johns Hopkins University Press.
—— *Golgotha and Scheblimini*, trans. Dunning, S.N. (1979), in *The Tongues of Men: Hegel and Hamann on Religious Language and History*, Missoula, MT: Scholars Press.
—— (1985) *Aesthetica in nuce 'Aesthetics in a Nutshell': A Rhapsody in Cabbalistic Prose*, trans. Crick, J.P., in H.B. Nisbet (ed.) *German Aesthetic and Literary Criticism: Winckelmann, Lessing, Hamann, Herder, Schiller, Goethe*, Cambridge: Cambridge University Press.

References and further reading

Alexander, W.M. (1966) *Johann Georg Hamann: Philosophy and Faith*, The Hague: Martinus Nijhoff.
Berlin, I. (1993) *The Magus of the North: J.G. Hamann and the Origins of Modern Irrationalism*, London: John Murray.
German, T. (1981) *Hamann on Language and Religion*, Oxford: Oxford University Press.
O'Flaherty, J.C. (1952) *Johann Georg Hamann*, Chapel Hill, NC: University of North Carolina.
Smith, R.G. (1960) *J.G. Hamann 1730–1788 A Study in Christian Existence, with Selections from his Writings*, London: Collins.

FREDERICK BEISER

HAMILTON, WILLIAM (1788–1856)

Sir William Hamilton was a leading exponent of the Scottish philosophy of 'common sense'. This philosophy had its origin in the works of Thomas Reid, but it was

217

through Hamilton that it achieved its most subtle form and exerted its greatest influence.

'Common-sense' philosophy, on a superficial view, may seem to hold that philosophical problems should be settled by appealing to the commonly accepted opinions of ordinary people. But that is not what it holds. The 'common sense' to which it refers are certain powers and beliefs natural to the mind and therefore common alike to the learned and vulgar. Hamilton holds that these powers and beliefs can neither be doubted nor justified. They carry their own authority. This view derives its significance from a point which has often been overlooked. When we doubt or justify a belief, we stand outside that belief and compare it with the world. But the power to compare a belief with the world itself presupposes beliefs about the world. We cannot step outside all our beliefs. That is why, according to Hamilton, certain powers and beliefs must carry authority.

Hamilton was educated in Glasgow and Oxford. After graduation he entered the legal profession, passing as advocate at the Scottish Bar in 1813. His chief interest, however, was in philosophy. Between 1829 and 1836 he published in the *Edinburgh Review* a series of articles which established his reputation, both in Britain and on the Continent. In 1826 he was appointed to a chair in philosophy at the University of Edinburgh, which he held until his death.

Hamilton wrote very little and was not a gifted writer. In this respect, he suffers in comparison with his predecessor Thomas REID and his associate Henry Mansel, both of whom were masters of English prose. But he was a deep thinker and a powerful teacher, greatly respected by his pupils. In his time, he exerted an influence on philosophy which extended throughout the English-speaking countries. In the colleges of America, for example, his was the predominant philosophy throughout the greater part of the nineteenth century.

His influence waned after the publication of J.S. Mill's *Examination of Sir William Hamilton's Philosophy* (1865). Mill took Hamilton to be the leading opponent of his own empiricism and therefore subjected his views to a severe criticism, which at the time was generally thought to be successful (see MILL, J.S.).

In logic, Hamilton is best known for his view that in the proposition 'All *A* is *B*', one may distinguish between 'All *A* is all *B*' and 'All *A* is some *B*'. This doctrine – known as the quantification of the predicate – served to reduce propositions to equations, thereby preparing the way for mathematical logic. Thus if the letters *X* and *Y* stand for classes, and

are regarded as universally quantified, then for 'All *X*s are all *Y*s' one may substitute '$X = Y$'.

Hamilton's more general philosophy may be taken in two parts. The first is a reworking of views he shared with Reid; the second a development of these into a subtle form of realism. The views he shared with Reid may be contrasted with idealism on the one hand and hypothetical realism on the other. The idealist criticism of realism is that it leads to scepticism. The realist holds that the world exists independently of our beliefs. How then can we ever be sure that our beliefs correspond to that world? The hypothetical realist argues that our beliefs may be justified by an argument to the best explanation: that there is an independent world corresponding to our beliefs is the best explanation for our having them. Both these views, however, have an assumption in common. The assumption is that we are not entitled to our beliefs unless they can be supported by reason. It is precisely this assumption, according to Hamilton, which leads to scepticism. If every belief has to be justified, every justification has itself to be justified. The regress is vicious and scepticism inevitable. Against this, Hamilton argued (anticipating the later Wittgenstein) that belief is primary: 'belief is the primary condition of reason and not reason the ultimate ground of belief'.

Hamilton's development of realism is made distinctive by his insistence that knowledge is relative. The essence of realism is that objects exist independently of being known. It follows, on the realist view, that they can be known only in so far as they enter into relations with the mind. But the *existence* of an object does not depend on the relations by which it is known. It is only knowledge which is thus relative, not the existence of the object itself. For example, unless an object reflects light, it cannot be seen; but it exists, whether or not it reflects light. Consequently we have no reason to suppose that what we know of the object, through its reflecting light, is exhaustive of the object itself. Moreover it is not simply our knowledge of the world which is thus relative; our conception of the world, so far as it is positive, must also be relative. For we have no such conception which does not depend on our knowledge. It follows that we have no positive conception of the world in its ultimate nature, but only of the world as it is in its relations to the mind. Moreover, Hamilton believed that this will always be so; the idea that we may obtain an absolute conception of the world is an aspiration without content and it forms no part of a coherent realism (see COMMON SENSE SCHOOL).

Modern readers who consider Mill's criticism of Hamilton may be inclined to suppose that its success was due not so much to its validity as to the prestige of Mill himself. They may note also that empiricism is no longer as dominant as it was in Mill's day and that there has been a revival of interest in views, such as those of Wittgenstein or the pragmatists, which are clearly related to Hamilton's.

See also: COMMONSENSISM; LOGIC IN THE 19TH CENTURY; REALISM AND ANTIREALISM

List of works

Hamilton, W. (1853) *Discussions on Philosophy and Literature, Education and University Reform*, London: Longman. (Hamilton's major work.)
—— (1858–60) *Lectures on Metaphysics and Logic*, Edinburgh: Blackwood, 4 vols. (Lectures to his students; they do not contain his fully developed views.)

References and further reading

Grave, S.A. (1960) *The Scottish Philosophy of Common Sense*, Oxford: Clarendon Press. (A modern survey of the Scottish school.)
Mansel, H. (1866) *The Philosophy of the Conditioned*, London and Edinburgh: Strachan. (A defence of Hamilton by his most famous associate.)
* Mill, J.S. (1865) *An Examination of Sir William Hamilton's Philosophy*, London: Longman and Green, 2 vols. (The most famous criticism of Hamilton.)
Veitch, J. (1888) *Hamilton*, Edinburgh and London: Blackwood. (Contains a defence of Hamilton against Mill.)

H.O. MOUNCE

HAN FEI/HAN FEI-TZU *see* HAN FEIZI

HAN FEIZI (*c.*280–233 BC)

Han Feizi was the pre-eminent Legalist philosopher. The work attributed to him, the Han Feizi, *is his conscious response to the general breakdown of civil order and the interminable inter-state struggle for survival and conquest during the Warring States period (463–222 BC). However, Han Feizi's work transcends the particular circumstances that gave rise to it and addresses perennial philosophical issues that continue to remain relevant.*

In the *Han Feizi*, the works 'Gufen' (Solitary Indignation), 'Wudu' (Five Vermin) and 'Shuonan' (Difficulties of the Way of Persuasion) constitute Han Feizi's response to the political pathology of his time. The central and compelling concern was political survival in the vortex of transformation precipitated by the systemic disintegration of what was left of the Zhou feudal order. This overriding political reality in large measure explains the way Han Feizi identified the outstanding political problems of his time: (1) 'learned celebrities' deluding the ruler with irresponsible eloquence so as to undermine the law; (2) itinerant speakers mouthing deceptive theories to serve their own interests; (3) private swordsmen violating the interdicts of government; (4) well-connected courtiers engaging in all manner of corruption; and (5) nonproductive tradesmen and craftsmen collecting useless luxuries and exploiting peasants. These are the 'Five Vermin' that undermine and ruin the state.

Han Feizi identified the root causes underlying these problems and called for a new prescriptive model of sociopolitical organization to remedy them. First, he called for the establishment of objective and impartial standards of human conduct, impersonal standards patterned after *dao* (the Way the natural world works) and free of subjective preferences (see DAO). The term *fa* means both prescriptive standards and penal law; *fa* is designed to remould human behaviour so that individual interest will 'naturally' dovetail with public interest (see FA). Moreover, it is *fa* alone, not moral suasion, that will serve as the guiding principle of sociopolitical behaviour. Second, authoritative power (*shi*) is 'well-ordered' when it is securely based on clearly established and objective *fa*. Thus, *shi* is the impersonal, institutionalized position of the rulership, rather than a charismatic power to inspire awe and obedience among the masses. Only when *shi* is 'well-ordered' will penal law function properly. Furthermore, *shi* cannot govern effectively without the organizational power of bureaucracy under the centralized control of the ruler. Thus, Han Feizi advocated a rational paradigm of bureaucratic accountability and merit-based functional specificity. The ruler needs to master the 'technique' (*shu*) of controlling bureaucracy by comparing 'word' (proposals) and actual 'performance'. If they tally, reward is in order; if not, then punishment is required. The ruler holds bureaucracy accountable not only by means of empirical verification but also by means of 'The Two Handles' of power over life and death.

Han Feizi elaborated on and synthesized the three interdependent pillars of the Legalist School: the *fa* of Shang Yang (390–338 BC), the *shi* of Shen Dao (*fl.* 310 BC) and the *shu* of Shen Buhai (d. 337 BC). In doing so, he produced a coherent and theoretically sophisticated Legalist philosophy.

See also: LEGALIST PHILOSOPHY, CHINESE; FA

List of works

Han Feizi (*c.*280–233 BC) *Han Feizi,* ed. Wang Xianshen, *Han Feizi jijie* (The Complete Works of Han Feizi with Collected Commentaries), 1896; ed. Chen Chiyu, *Han Feizi jishi* (Collected Explanations), Beijing: Zhonghua Book Co., 1958; ed. Chen Chitian, *Zengding Han Feizi jiaoshi* (Further Revisions of Collations and Explanations of Han Feizi), Taipei: Taiwan Commercial Press, 1972; trans. W.K. Liao, *The Complete Works of Han Fei Tzu,* London: Arthur Probsthian, vol. 1, 1938; vol. 2, 1959. (The work was in all probability written by Han Feizi himself with the exceptions of 'Interview with the King of Ch'in: A Memorial' and 'Having Regulations'. Jong Tsau-chu's *Textual Criticisms of Han Fei Tzu's Works* (Shanghai: Shanghai Commercial Press, 1936) notwithstanding, there is no convincing evidence that Han Feizi did not write 'Interpreting Laozi' , 'Illustrating Laozi' and other writings with Daoist contents: see Appendix I in H.P. Wang and L. Chang, *The Philosophical Foundations of Han Fei's Political Theory,* Honolulu, HI: University of Hawaii Press, 1986, 87–109. Of the editions given here, Wang (1896), Chen (1958) and Chen (1972) are extensively annotated. Liao remains the only complete translation of the work in English, although twelve chapters are translated by B. Watson in *Han Fei Tzu: Basic Writings,* New York: Columbia University Press, 1964.)

References and further reading

de Bary, W.T. (1960) *Sources of Chinese Tradition,* New York: Columbia University Press, vol. 1, 122–49. (A brief introduction to Han Feizi and Li Si for students.)

Fung Yu-lan [Feng Youlan] (1952) *A History of Chinese Philosophy,* trans. D. Bodde, Princeton, NJ: Princeton University Press, vol. 1, chap. 13. (A clear exposition of Han Feizi and Legalist philosophy with many excerpts from the original texts; for upper level undergraduates.)

Graham, A.C. (1989) *Disputers of Tao,* La Salle, IL: Open Court. (Erudite and evenhanded treatment of Legalist philosophy for advanced students.)

Schwartz, B.I. (1985) *The World of Thought in Ancient China: Philosophical Argument in Ancient China,* Cambridge, MA: Harvard University Press. (Sophisticated and insightful exposition of Legalist philosophy that transcends the stereotypical views.)

Wang, H.P. (1991) *Hsien Ch'in fa-chia ssu-hsiang shih lun* (Discourses on the Pre-Qin Legalist Thought), Taipei: Linking (Lien Ching) Publishing Co. (The most comprehensive and clear account of Legalist philosophy; see especially pages 267– 319.)

Wang, H. P. and Chang, L. (1986) *The Philosophical Foundations of Han Fei's Political Theory,* Honolulu, HI: University of Hawaii Press. (For graduate students.)

LEO S. CHANG

HAN WÔNJIN (1682–1751)

Han Wônjin was a major thinker of the Korean neo-Confucian tradition. One of the leading scholars of his time, he is especially remembered as a protagonist in the Horak controversy, which he ignited with the observation that ki *(in Chinese,* qi*) or 'material force' is present even when the mind is in a meditative, quiescent state.*

Neo-Confucian metaphysics is a dualistic monism in which the single *dao* or pattern running through all things is concretized and individualized in real beings only through *ki* (see QI). The patterning element, known as *i* and often translated as 'principle', also constitutes the innermost nature of all things; its presence as the substance of the human heart-and-mind accounts for our innate potential to respond appropriately to all things and situations (see XIN).

Han's observation that *ki* is always present is consistent with a metaphysics where *i* and *ki* are strictly interdependent and complimentary in function: any real existent always involves both. But in addition to individuation, imperfection or turbidity in *ki* also is a distorting element that accounts for our often imperfect response to things. A cornerstone of neo-Confucian self-cultivation was quiet-sitting, a meditative technique of mental quiescence understood as putting oneself in union with the perfection of *i*, the inner nature and substance of the heart-and-mind. By asserting that even in quiescence the imperfection of *ki* could not be considered absent Han aroused a storm of controversy. His monistic emphasis on absolute interdependence was metaphysically sound, but was problematic in the context of an ascetical system which was naturally more dualistic in emphasis in order to account for perfection and imperfection.

As the controversy unfolded it soon involved issues

related to understanding the unitary *i* of the universe as the nature of individual things. His opponent upheld the more conventional bifurcation: considered in itself, *i* is unitary, but considered as concretized and differentiated by *ki* it is the nature of single, individual beings. Han fastened onto the need for a differentiated normative nature: the norm for a cow is not the same as the norm for a human. The problem is that the normative nature conventionally is *i* in itself, unlimited and undistorted by imperfect *ki* – and hence evidently undifferentiated as well. Han introduced a threefold schema: between the unitary nature and the completely individuated one he proposed a unique level, '*i* as based on *ki*'. On this level, *i* would be differentiated as the nature of various species, but not concretely limited to imperfect individuals.

Han's novel doctrine was roundly criticized by opponents as being unintelligible, for the new level seemed neither to consider *i* in itself nor actually join it with *ki*. The controversy crystallized as the question whether the normative 'original' nature was the same or different for all species, and continued for generations without resolution (see XING). It calls attention to a deep seam in neo-Confucian thought, where the metaphysics of *i* and *ki* synthesize and mask quite different meanings of 'nature' from the Daoist and Buddhist traditions.

See also: CONFUCIAN PHILOSOPHY, KOREAN; NEO-CONFUCIAN PHILOSOPHY; YI KAN

List of works

Han Wônjin (1682–1751) *Namdang Chip* (The Collected Writings of Han Wonjin), Seoul: Ch'ae Insik, 1976. (Photo reprint.)

References and further readings

There is at present no further information on Han in Western languages.

MICHAEL C. KALTON

HAN YU (768–824)

Among the most important figures in the history of medieval Confucianism, Han Yu helped to redefine and adapt earlier Confucian teachings to the needs of his contemporary society. He strove to make Confucianism a more popular and comprehensive doctrine by devising a basic metaphysics and epistemology to complement the earlier Confucian emphasis on ethics.

Han Yu was a government official, writer, and scholar of the Tang dynasty (618–907) who played a central role in the medieval redefinition of the Confucian tradition. He was the major figure in the transition between the first state-supported formulation of Confucian ideology in the Han dynasty (206 BC–AD 220) and the later transformation of that tradition, known today as neo-Confucianism, in the Song dynasty (960–1279).

The centrepiece of this transformation was a new concept of the Confucian Sage. Whereas early Confucian teachings stressed the ethical dimension of the Sage, Han Yu and his Song dynasty successors worked to broaden this earlier concept of the Sage to include a metaphysical and epistemological dimension. According to most understandings of Chinese intellectual history, their effort resulted from the challenge and popularity of Buddhist and Daoist teachings in the Six Dynasties and early Tang dynasty (see BUDDHIST PHILOSOPHY, CHINESE; DAOIST PHILOSOPHY).

For Han Yu, the Sage was a person who had achieved a perfect integration in his own daily life between theory and action. In this process, the Sage becomes one with a metaphysical Absolute. This unity is described as *cheng*, translated as 'integrity, being true to oneself' (see CHENG). In forging this union, Han Yu sought to discover new epistemological values in the writings of pre-Han Confucian antiquity. In his writings, the phrase *gudao*, or 'way of antiquity', assumes an almost philosophical dimension as the source of positive human values.

To extract these values from the text of the Confucian canon, Han Yu espoused an interpretative method known as 'overall meaning', which rejected established commentary in favour of an intuitive understanding by direct appeal to the reader's 'mind'. The process attempted to make the old texts relevant to contemporary issues and resulted in a concentration on sections of the old canon that best lent themselves to such reinterpretation. One may see in the philosophical writings of Han Yu a concern with those texts that were later to become known as the Four Books: the *Analects*, *Daxue* (Great Learning), *Zhongyong* (Doctrine of the Mean) and *Mengzi* (see CONFUCIUS; DAXUE; ZHONGYONG; MENCIUS).

Han Yu also constructed for his rejuvenated Confucianism a lineage or progression of orthodox teachers from antiquity down to his own time. The contemporary Chan Buddhist system of master-disciple lineages probably stimulated Han Yu's thinking in this area, and the formation of such lineages became an important concern of later neo-Confucianism. Han Yu was known both in his own day and in later times primarily as a man of letters and creator of guwen, the 'literature of antiquity', a style of writing that was intended as a literary reflection of the 'way of antiquity'.

See also: CHENG; CONFUCIAN PHILOSOPHY, CHINESE; NEO-CONFUCIAN PHILOSOPHY

List of works

Han Yu (768–824) *Han Changli shi xinian jish* (The Poetry of Han Yu Arranged Chronologically with Collected Annotations), ed. Qian Zhonglian, Shanghai: Gudian wenxue chubanshe, 1957. (Standard modern edition of Han Yu's poetry.)

—— (768–824) *Han Changli wen ji jiaozhu* (The Prose Writings of Han Yu, Collated and Annotated), ed. Ma Chichang, Shanghai: Gudian wenxue chubanshe, 1957; partial trans. Liu Shih Shun, *Chinese Classical Prose: The Eight Masters of the T'ang-Sung Period*, Hong Kong: The Chinese University Press, 1979. (The Ma edition is the standard modern edition of Han Yu's prose writings; Liu has English translations of Han Yu prose texts. For translations of key Han Yu philosophical texts, see W.T. de Bary (ed.) *Sources of Chinese Tradition*, New York: Columbia University Press, 1964, 426–37.)

References and further reading

Hartman, C. (1986) *Han Yü and the T'ang Search for Unity*, Princeton, NJ: Princeton University Press. (The only attempt at a comprehensive study of Han Yu in a Western language; Chapter 3 is devoted to Han Yu's philosophical thought.)

CHARLES HARTMAN

HANSLICK, EDUARD (1825–1904)

Eduard Hanslick, a music critic for the popular Viennese press, is principally known as the author of Vom Musikalisch-Schönen *(1854). This is probably the most widely read work in the aesthetics of music for both philosophers and musicians, and remains the starting point for any discussion either of the place of emotion in music, or of the doctrine usually referred to as 'musical purism'. On the former, Hanslick maintained what he calls the negative thesis, which 'first and foremost opposes the widespread view that music is supposed to represent the feelings'; on purism, he proposed the positive thesis or antithesis, 'that the beauty of a piece of music is specifically musical, that is, is inherent in the tonal relationships without reference to an extraneous, extra-musical context'.*

1 Major arguments
2 Music and emotion

1 Major arguments

What was Hanslick denying? As becomes clear in the progress of his argument, the negative thesis denies that it is any part of the office of music, *qua* music, to arouse or represent 'feelings' of the kind I shall call 'ordinary', by which I mean feelings or emotions such as love, fear, hatred, anger and the like. Two further possibilities remain open: that music might arouse some other kind of feeling as part of its essential nature, and that it might arouse the ordinary emotions, but in an aesthetically irrelevant context. As we shall presently see, Hanslick affirmed both.

Hanslick presents three basic arguments in support of the negative thesis, all of which take the following general form. Music demonstrably does not (or cannot) arouse or represent the ordinary emotions in any aesthetically relevant way; therefore it cannot be any part of the aesthetic purpose of music to do so.

The first of these arguments, and certainly the most subtle, is this: 'The representation of a specific feeling or emotional state is not at all among the characteristic powers of music' because such feelings or emotional states 'depend upon ideas, judgments, and (in brief) the whole range of intelligible and rational thought to which some people readily oppose feeling' (1854 (1986): 9). In other words, emotions cannot either exist or be 'represented' in the absence of what contemporary philosophers, following Franz BRENTANO (§3), call 'intentional objects'. And music cannot in any way make those intentional objects available to the listener. Particularly in the latter form, the argument seems generally persuasive, although a possible response to each form of the argument might at least serve to qualify it. For it might be argued both that there are other ways that music can make up for lack of intentional objects in representing the emotions, and at least peripheral ways in which some emotions are perhaps aroused without them.

The second argument, which might be called the 'argument from disagreement', is directed specifically against the possibility that music can represent the ordinary emotions (although, if good, it would apply with equal force to their arousal). It is simply that, according to Hanslick, since there is no consensus at all in any individual case about which emotion a passage of music may represent, it cannot make sense to say that it can represent any at all. But anyone who has ever played passages with distinct emotive character to a typical listener or indeed has read any critical literature (including Hanslick's), will find Hanslick's premise of chaotic disagreement utterly false, and emotive consensus, at least within reasonable limits, fairly widespread. Nor, given the historical continuity of our musical materials, could this consensus come as a surprise to anyone who had not begged the question against it from the outset.

Hanslick's final argument is based on the growing awareness in the nineteenth century that composers of earlier times recycled their music, and in particular that they sometimes used the same music for different texts. It charges that if the same music can seem emotively appropriate to two texts of very different expression, one cannot say that the music has any particular emotive character at all. However, this is clearly a case of drawing an extreme and false conclusion from an undoubtedly true premise. And Hanslick's prime example, Handel's well-known use of music from his erotic love duets for sacred choruses in *Messiah*, simply shows that music expressive of melancholy or joy can seem appropriate both to the joy and melancholy of erotic love and to the joy and melancholy of the Christian religion, which is by no means surprising, and hardly proof that the music is not expressive both of joy and melancholy.

Of the positive thesis, little need (or can) be said here because, apart from some suggestive and, as it turned out, fruitful metaphors, Hanslick was able to give his concept of musical beauty little substantive content. The metaphor which is most remembered, and in the event proved most fruitful, is: 'The content of music is tonally moving forms' (1854 (1986): 29). Hanslick combined this recognition of absolute music (that is, instrumental music) as a formal structure in apparent motion with the equally important 'intuition' that the formal structure is not merely a kaleidoscopic pattern (another of his metaphors) but a quasi-syntactical one, bearing, in that respect, an analogy to language. Beyond such intriguing, though fragmentary, remarks Hanslick was not able to put forward a systematic musical purism.

2 Music and emotion

The question now remains of what role, if any, human feeling plays in Hanslick's musical philosophy. As regards the ordinary emotions, Hanslick does not deny them a role, but explicitly affirms that 'music can nevertheless excite such feelings as melancholy, gaiety and the like (can, not must)' (1854 (1986): 9–10). How is this consistent with the negative thesis? It is consistent because what the negative thesis asserts is that it is no part of the *aesthetic* significance of music

to arouse the ordinary emotions; it indeed *cannot* arouse them in an aesthetically meaningful way. What it can do is arouse such emotions in those who, by virtue of particular personal associations or a 'pathological' nervous condition, may be abnormally susceptible.

Are we to conclude, then, that Hanslick views a proper experience of music as completely 'cold' and 'unemotional'? Such a view would be hard to credit, but there is no need to impute it to him, for nothing he says implies it, and one intriguing passage, in the Foreword to the Eighth Edition (1891), suggests just the right response to the question. Hanslick writes: 'I share completely the view that the ultimate worth of the beautiful is always based on the immediate manifestation of feeling' (1854 (1986): 22). Can we not read this as an assertion of the undoubted truth that the beautiful always deeply moves us upon its recognition? And what is true of beauty *sans phrase* must also be true of musical beauty. Beautiful music can no more leave those who perceive it unmoved, unfeeling and emotionally untouched than beauty in any instance.

The weakness in Hanslick's position lies, then, not in his inability to accommodate an emotionally involved listener; rather, it involves his denial that music can sensibly be characterized in terms of the ordinary emotions. Apparently seeing emotive arousal or emotive representation as the only possible avenues to specific emotive description, and rejecting both for at least one of the right reasons, he was left with the implausible conclusion that calling music 'sad' or 'happy', 'angry' or 'yearning', is either figurative or foolish. But other ways in which music might 'embody' the ordinary emotions have been explored since Hanslick's time; and there is a growing consensus that this aspect of his negative thesis is in need of serious revision. Nevertheless, *Vom Musikalisch-Schönen* remains the starting point of the philosophical aesthetics of music and its first modern text, and suffices to keep Eduard Hanslick's name alive.

See also: EMOTION IN RESPONSE TO ART §4; EMOTIONS, PHILOSOPHY OF; ARTISTIC EXPRESSION; FORMALISM IN ART; MUSIC, AESTHETICS OF

List of works

Hanslick, E. (1854) *Vom Musikalisch-Schönen*, Wiesbaden: Breitkopf & Hartel, 1980; trans. G. Cohen, ed. M. Weitz, *The Beautiful in Music*, New York: The Liberal Arts Press, 1957; and trans. G. Payzant, *On the Musically Beautiful*, Indianapolis, IN: Hackett Publishing Company, 1986. (The twentieth edition of the German text, in paperback.

The 1957 edition uses the original, but still useful, English translation (1891), with an insightful philosophical introduction by Morris Weitz, while the 1986 translation is new and philosophically superior.)

—— (1846–99) *Music Criticisms 1846–99*, ed. and trans. H. Pleasants, Baltimore, MD: Penguin, 1950. (A valuable volume allowing a comparison of Hanslick's theory with practice.)

References and further reading

Budd, M. (1980) 'The Repudiation of Emotion: Hanslick on Music', *British Journal of Aesthetics* 20: 29–43. (A philosophically astute account of Hanslick's position.)

Kivy, P. (1990) 'What was Hanslick Denying?', *Journal of Musicology* 8: 3–18. (A careful philosophical analysis of the negative thesis.)

Wilkinson, R. (1992) 'Art, Emotion and Expression', in O. Hanfling (ed.) *Philosophical Aesthetics, an Introduction*, Oxford: Blackwell, 207–20. (A clear and accurate discussion of Hanslick's arguments.)

PETER KIVY

HANSON, NORWOOD RUSSELL (1924–67)

Hanson was a philosopher of science who introduced novel ways of relating logical, historical and linguistic analyses. His best-known book, Patterns of Discovery, *stressed the theory-ladeness of observational reports and argued that causality is a feature of inference systems, rather than of nature as such. He pioneered in combining historical and analytic analyses of significant breakthroughs in science. Though he clarified patterns of discovery he never succeeded in the project of developing a logic of discovery, or an account of the inferences leading from problematic situations to novel explanatory hypotheses. A man of many talents, he also made contributions to the history of science, aerodynamics and epistemology.*

Hanson was born in west New York, made his undergraduate studies at the University of Chicago, served as a marine fighter pilot in the Second World War, did further studies at both Oxford and Cambridge, where he became the first university lecturer in the philosophy of science. In 1957 he returned to the USA, set up the department of the history and logic of science at Indiana University, and vociferously opposed McCarthyism. In 1962 he accepted a

position as philosophy professor at Yale. He died when the beloved Bearcat he was flying crashed into a mountain near Cortland, New York.

Hanson was a baseball player, a Golden Gloves heavyweight boxer, a proficient classical trumpet player, an artist especially adept in illustrating Homeric heroes, a decorated fighter pilot (Air Medal, Distinguished Flying Cross) shot down over Japan, a gadget designer, a daredevil pilot who set speed records for propeller driven airplanes, and a prolific writer in both the philosophy and history of science. The tension and conflict that stimulated him were reflected in his way of doing philosophy. He introduced into logical positivism analytic methods developed by the later WITTGENSTEIN (see LOGICAL POSITIVISM §3). Though, with the positivists, he professed a belief that the history of science is irrelevant to the philosophy of science, he pioneered the use of critical historical reconstructions as a testing ground for philosophical accounts of science. His first, and most influential book, *Patterns of Discovery* (1958), treated the issues that were explored in his later writings.

Hanson popularized the term 'theory-laden observation' (see OBSERVATION §§3–4), which he intended in a rather Wittgensteinian sense. One cannot *see* something *as* an X unless one already has the concept of an X. Such 'seeing as' depends more on acquired skills than on formal theories. His emphasis played a historically significant role in undercutting the positivist ideal of reporting observations in a theory-neutral language. Hanson's treatment of facts and causes illustrates his fusion of positivism and analysis. A fact is something reported in a that-clause: the fact that... . This requires a classification of propositional types into necessary and contingent, a priori and a posteriori, general and particular. This positivistic technique was supplemented by an analytic insistence that the meaning of terms used to report facts depends on their use. Scientific breakthroughs occur when old presumptions are discarded in favour of new ways of observing and reporting. Hanson supplemented this analysis by detailed historical studies of how Kepler used ellipses as a tool to approximate distorted circular orbits and finally saw that the ellipses fit the data; and of how a protracted muddling through involving Galileo, Descartes and Beeckman, finally led to a correct account of free fall. He explained causality as a feature of our explanations of nature, rather than of nature itself. We introduce causes to explain phenomena. In experiments we try to develop causal chains, not because these chains really describe nature, but because they simplify inferences.

The most novel feature of Hanson's philosophy of

science was his protracted attempt to develop a logic of discovery. Detailed analysis of historical examples led to a general pattern of discovery. A curious iconoclast challenges traditional ways of reporting and explaining and comes to see accepted facts as involving problematic relationships. A tentative hypothesis, introduced to explain the newly perceived problem, must meet various criteria: initial plausibility, coherence with accepted background assumptions, logical and empirical constraints on testing hypothesis. A logic of discovery concerns inferring novel hypotheses from problematic situations.

This project encountered two chief difficulties. The first was the Newtonian precedent of rejecting any reliance on hypotheses. This Hanson tackled through his analytic approach to history. After distinguishing different senses of hypotheses he showed that Newton rejected the Scholastic type of subjunctive hypothesis and emphatically rejected any Cartesian-style metaphysical hypotheses. However, Newton repeatedly and fruitfully introduced his own type of hypothesis, a categorical proposition that, if true, would both explain phenomena and also lead to testable consequences. The second difficulty concerned the suitability of the term 'logic'. Here Hanson eventually distinguished between the precise hypothesis tested and inference from a problematic situation to a suitable type of hypothesis. This, he insisted, was a rational process although he could not formulate logical rules governing it.

Hanson championed the Copenhagen interpretation of quantum mechanics (see QUANTUM MECHANICS, INTERPRETATION OF §3). He supplemented his flying activities with studies of the history and physics of aerodynamics. He became proficient in celestial mechanics and used detailed analyses of historical examples to illustrate subtle differences between philosophical ideals of explanation and the types of explanation scientists are willing to accept. He defended atheism on the grounds that there is no good reason for believing in the existence of a personal God, and attacked agnosticism as a timid compromise.

Hanson readily provoked controversy and polarized conferences into his adversaries and his supporters. He never produced a school of disciples nor developed a general system. His talent was for attacking, rather than formulating, systems.

See also: DISCOVERY, LOGIC OF; GALILEI, G.; KEPLER, J.; SCIENTIFIC METHOD; THEORIES, SCIENTIFIC §4

List of works

Hanson, N.R. (1958) *Patterns of Discovery*, Cambridge: Cambridge University Press. (His basic work, reprinted in paperback in 1961.)

—— (1963) *The Concept of the Positron: A Philosophical Analysis*, Cambridge: Cambridge University Press. (A defence and analysis of the Copenhagen interpretation of quantum mechanics and the discovery of the positron.)

—— (1969) *Perception and Discovery: An Introduction to Scientific Inquiry*, ed. W.C. Humphreys, San Francisco, CA: Freeman, Cooper & Co. (Text constructed from Hanson's lecture notes.)

—— (1971) *Observation and Explanation: A Guide to the Philosophy of Science*, New York: Harper & Row. (An introductory work posthumously edited by Stephen Toulmin.)

—— (1972) *What I Do Not Believe, and Other Essays*, eds S. Toulmin and H. Woolf, Dordrecht: Reidel. (A 2-volume collection of Hanson's essays on philosophy of science, theology and the history of flight.)

—— (1973) *Constellations and Conjectures*, ed. W.C. Humphreys, Dordrecht: Reidel. (A copiously illustrated history of planetary theory from Plato to Kepler emphasizing the gap between explanation and prediction.)

References and further reading

Cohen, R.S. and Marx M.W. (eds) (1968) *Boston Studies in the Philosophy of Science*, vol. III, Dordrecht: Kluwer. (Contains tributes to Hanson and a list of his publications.)

Duhem, P. (1906) *La théorie physique. Son objet et sa structure*, Paris: Chevalier et Rivière; 2nd edn, 1914; trans. P.P. Wiener, *The Aim and Structure of Physical Theory*, Princeton, NJ: Princeton University Press, 1954. (The English version influenced Hanson's *Patterns of Discovery*.)

Feyerabend, P.K. (1960) 'Patterns of Discovery', *Philosophical Review* 59, 247–52.

—— (1961) 'Explanation, Reduction, and Empiricism', in H. Feigl and G. Maxwell (eds) *Minnesota Studies in the Philosophy of Science*, vol. III, Minneapolis, MN: University of Minnesota Press. (An early summary of the position of Hanson's primary opponent.)

Humphreys, W.C. (1968) *Anomalies and Scientific Theories*, Sudbury, MA: Jones & Bartlett. (An expanded version of a dissertation directed by Hanson.)

Wittgenstein, L. (1953) *Philosophical Investigations*, eds G.E.M. Anscombe and R. Rhees, trans. G.E.M. Anscombe, New York: Macmillan, and Oxford:

Blackwell. (Hanson was one of the earliest philosophers of science to adopt Wittgenstein's later ideas.)

EDWARD MacKINNON

HAPPINESS

In ordinary use, the word 'happiness' has to do with one's situation (one is fortunate) or with one's state of mind (one is glad, cheerful) or, typically, with both. These two elements appear in different proportions on different occasions. If one is concerned with a long stretch of time (as in 'a happy life'), one is likely to focus more on situation than on state of mind. If a short period of time, it is not uncommon to focus on states of mind.

By and large philosophers are more interested in long-term cases. One's life is happy if one is content that life has brought one much of what one regards as important. There is a pull in these lifetime assessments towards a person's objective situation and away from the person's subjective responses. The important notion for ethics is 'wellbeing' – that is, a notion of what makes an individual life go well. 'Happiness' is important because many philosophers have thought that happiness is the only thing that contributes to wellbeing, or because they have used 'happiness' to mean the same as 'wellbeing'.

What, then, makes a life go well? Some have thought that it was the presence of a positive feeling tone. Others have thought that it was having one's desires fulfilled – either actual desires (as some would say) or informed desires (as others would say). It is unclear how stringent the requirement of 'informed' must be; if it is fairly stringent it can, in effect, require abandoning desire explanations and adopting instead an explanation in terms of a list of good-making features in human life.

1 **The ordinary notion**
2 **The notion in philosophy**
3 **'Wellbeing', 'welfare', 'utility' and 'quality of life'**

1 The ordinary notion

'Happiness' is a central term – for some philosophers *the* central term – in ethics. It is also a term in everyday speech, and one should be aware of how the philosophical and the ordinary uses of the word are related.

'Happy' comes from the noun 'hap': what just happens, chance, luck. It came to mean having good hap, fortunate, lucky, a sense that it still retains (death

can be a happy release). Etymology is not meaning, but there is a large etymological residue in our current use of the word. In a very common use now, to be 'happy' is to be satisfied or contented with having a good measure of what one regards as important in life. In this use of the word, 'happy' has to do with one's situation; one is fortunate. It also has to do with one's state of mind; one is glad or cheerful. It typically has to do with both situation and state of mind (one has the latter because of the former), but the two elements can appear in very different proportions in different cases. At one extreme, a martyr can go happy to the stake, merely secure in the conviction of right. At another extreme, a person can be happy (cheerful) for a few moments before realizing how unfavourable the situation actually is. There are other current uses of the word as well; for example, 'happy' can mean 'productive of favourable results' (a happy intervention). There is no definition of 'happiness', in the sense of a list of essential properties. Few words in a natural language, especially words covering as much ground as 'happiness', allow definition in that form. We can use these words correctly; hence we know their meaning. But we know it by catching on to the use of the words, not by catching on to a set of defining properties.

'Happiness' does not mean the same as 'pleasure', despite J.S. Mill's definition (1861) (see MILL, J.S. §8; PLEASURE). He defined 'happiness' as 'pleasure, and the absence of pain'. But the words mark different features of life; the martyr who goes happy to the stake is unlikely to do so with pleasure. Nor does 'happiness' mean the same as 'wellbeing', if the latter term is used, as it often is, of one's actual situation. Because of the psychological element in the word, one may be 'happy' when things are going badly for one, if one is unaware that they are.

There are, as we have noted, two important strands to happiness, one's situation and one's state of mind. If it is a long stretch of time that one is interested in – say, 'a happy life' – one is likely to focus more on situation than on a flow of psychological states. If it is a short period, it is not uncommon to focus on psychological states. By and large philosophers are more interested in the long term use. Certain tensions can emerge in speaking of 'happy lives'. One's life is happy if one is content that life has brought one much of what one regards as important. The standard case is one in which one regards certain things as important because they *are* important and one thinks that life has brought them because it *has* brought them. But what happens to the use of the word 'happiness' if one or other of the standard conditions fails? Think, for instance, of a society in which women's expectations are very low. Aspirations are largely relative to expectations. A particular woman in that society might be pathetically content with a small improvement in her generally miserable lot. Would we say that she has a 'happy life' merely because she is content? There would be strain in saying so because there is some pull in these lifetime assessments towards a person's objective situation, and away from the person's subjective responses. People may have various views about what good fortune in life is, but when they explain their conception of a happy life they will describe what they regard as good fortune, not what they believe, justified or not, will produce states of contentment or cheerfulness. I have been speaking of a tension in our use of the word 'happiness'. There is also a troubling tension in our attempts to be happy. One route to happiness is to strive to achieve more of what is important in life. Another route is to be content with what one has already got. It is not easy, though just possible, to take both routes.

2 The notion in philosophy

'Happiness' is not the important notion in ethics; 'wellbeing' is – that is, a notion of good fortune, of what makes a life go well. 'Happiness' is important only if one thinks, as many philosophers of course have thought, that happiness is the only thing that contributes to wellbeing (a substantive claim), or if one uses 'happiness', as some philosophers have used it, to mean the same thing as 'wellbeing'. What we want, and what philosophers have generally been in search of, is an account of what it is for a life to go well.

Aristotle spoke of 'eudaimonia' (literally, 'good divine power' or 'good fortune'), normally translated in English as 'happiness' (see EUDAIMONIA). For him, it is the central term in ethics. 'What is the supreme good attainable in our actions? Well, so far as the name goes, there is pretty general agreement. "It is happiness," say both intellectuals and the unsophisticated, meaning by "happiness" living well and faring well' (*Nicomachean Ethics* 1095a). Aristotle's notion therefore is what I have called 'wellbeing' – what actually makes a life go well – and it is often thought that the prominent psychological element in the English word 'happiness' makes it an inappropriate translation for 'eudaimonia'. But even if 'eudaimonia' and 'happiness' do not mean quite the same, it does not follow that Aristotle, on the one hand, and anglophone philosophers who have used the term 'happiness' on the other, are talking about different things. For the reason given earlier, they are often both talking about wellbeing and, if they say different things about it, they may well be making contrary claims (see ARISTOTLE §§21–2).

It is a plausible thought that faring well in some way involves acting well. How are virtue and happiness related? Some, such as Socrates, Plato, and Aristotle on some interpretations, have held that virtuous action is necessary and sufficient for happiness (see PLATO §14; SOCRATES §4). On this view, all that matters for happiness is internal to one's will: happiness *is* being virtuous and nothing else. Others, including Aristotle on other interpretations, have held that, important though virtue is to happiness, it is not all there is to it; external conditions such as health, wealth and avoidance of disasters matter too. Still others have thought that virtue is generally inimical to happiness (Thrasymachus as depicted by Plato in the *Republic* and Thomas HOBBES on some interpretations). It is somewhat easier to argue that virtue is sufficient for happiness than that it is necessary. Some elements of a good life (say, accomplishing things such as creating great art or making major scientific discoveries) do not seem to lose their value just because the agent concerned is not virtuous. If we could resolve these issues in favour of the first option, we should have a powerful answer to the vexed question, 'Why be moral?' Because, we could then say, it is a (or the only) way to be happy.

The most prominent use of the term 'happiness' in modern philosophy is to be found in the work of utilitarians (see UTILITARIANISM). They hold that acts are right in virtue of the value of their consequences, and what makes consequences valuable, according to classical utilitarians, such as Jeremy BENTHAM, J.S. Mill and Henry SIDGWICK, is the presence of pleasure or happiness (see CONSEQUENTIALISM). This appeal to pleasure or happiness, although historically important in utilitarianism, is not essential to it. A utilitarian may say, and many modern utilitarians have said, that several irreducibly different things, perhaps including happiness, are valuable. The classical utilitarians put the term 'happiness' to various theoretical uses. Some of them used it in an empirical theory of action (psychological hedonism), which claims that pleasure or happiness is the only end which in fact we desire or at which we aim. They also used it in a normative theory of the ends of life (ethical hedonism), which claims that pleasure or happiness is the only thing worth acting for (see HEDONISM §2). Once 'happiness' is given these theoretical roles, it comes under pressure to grow to fill them. If happiness is what in fact we aim at, then the term 'happiness' must encompass all that in fact we aim at (for example, saving one's children at the cost of one's own life). If it is the only thing worth aiming at, then whatever is worth aiming at (such as saving one's children at the cost of one's own life) must be fitted under the term 'happiness'. It is not that the term cannot be stretched to include them; it is rather that once it includes them it may have become a technical term, and we should then need to know its technical sense. The natural elasticity of the word 'happiness' can easily lead to confusion. It is easy to be deceived by shifts of sense such as this: 'happiness is what makes a life good' (a substantive claim: happiness is the one and only end in life); 'happiness is what makes life good' (a tautology: 'happiness' means 'what makes a life good').

The classical utilitarians paid insufficient attention to the meaning of their central term. Jeremy Bentham seems to have thought of 'pleasure' or 'happiness' primarily as a positive feeling tone. But when he defined 'utility', he described it as 'that property in any object, whereby it tends to produce benefit, advantage, pleasure, good, or happiness (all this in the present case comes to the same thing)' (1789: 12), thus running together what improves one's situation and what produces certain mental states. J.S. Mill's approach was more complex. What links valuable states for him is that they are pleasurable, but this is not a case of there being any common positive feeling tone running through them all. In *Utilitarianism* (1861), he famously claims that pleasures differ in quality as well as quantity: states of higher quality are those that we prefer when sufficiently informed. Then, returning to differences in quantity, he observes that pleasures are not homogeneous, and that pleasure is always heterogeneous with pain. Informed preferences, he says, enter too in determining which is the greater of two pleasures or the worse of two pains. He may mean merely that the preference of the informed judge is a way for us to *learn* which pleasure is greater, but he sometimes seems to suggest that being the object of an informed preference is all that we can *mean* by a pleasure's being greater. Henry Sidgwick also adopted a preference account. He thought that the only things that we wanted for their own sakes were mental states, but that there was no single feeling tone running through all of them that gave them their unity. What unified them was that they were desired. The ultimate good, he concluded, was 'desirable consciousness' (1874: 397).

3   'Wellbeing', 'welfare', 'utility' and 'quality of life'

It is because 'wellbeing' (or 'welfare', 'utility', 'quality of life') is the important notion in ethics, not 'happiness', that most attention now goes to it (see WELFARE). What, then, makes a life go well? How one answers that question will depend on how many of the following arguments one finds persuasive.

Wellbeing is not simply a positive feeling tone. There is no one tone running through all the things that make a life go well. Wellbeing, one might instead say, taking a lead from Sidgwick, is the fulfilment of desires. However, despite what some economists say, it certainly could not be the fulfilment of one's actual desires; they can be fulfilled and one be worse off. It would have to be, as Sidgwick himself says, the fulfilment of informed desires. But 'informed' in what sense? Suppose we say that a desire is informed if it exists when I am aware of all relevant facts and I commit no logical error (Brandt 1979: 10). But an irrational desire might well survive criticism by facts and logic, and its mere survival is less than it takes to make one better off. For instance, a man might have a crazy aim in life – say, counting the blades of grass in various lawns (Rawls 1971: 432–3). He accepts, let us say, that no one is interested, that the information is of no use, and he makes no logical error. Still, it is unlikely that we would regard the fulfilment of this obsessive desire as, in itself, enhancing his life – apart, that is, from preventing anxieties or tensions that might be set up by frustrating the desire, which are not the point. Cases like this suggest that our standard of 'informed' is not stiff enough yet. To make it stiffer, though, we should have to make desires 'informed' in some such strong sense as 'formed in proper appreciation of the nature of their object'. But this makes the mere occurrence of desire much less important and the nature of the object of desire much more important.

We might say therefore, as many philosophers do, that there are many different things that enhance life: happiness, seen as a state of mind, might be one, but perhaps also accomplishing something in the course of one's life, knowledge of certain basic metaphysical and moral matters, deep personal relations, and so on. Wellbeing, we could say, consists in having good things (a list of which we could provide).

The list-account of wellbeing has the potential of being much broader than the happiness-account of classical utilitarianism. Philosophers now debate just how broad it can be. Sidgwick thought that nothing enhanced a life unless it entered consciousness or experience. One might call this the 'experience requirement'. But some think that the requirement is too restrictive. They say that we sometimes want things other than states of consciousness, and these things seem to make our lives better. For instance we may desire a good reputation among people we shall never know about, or posthumous fame, or to accomplish something with our lives. One way to clarify one's thoughts on this issue is to ask: supposing there were a foolproof machine that would give one any experience one wanted, would one plug in? What could matter except how life feels from the inside? Many would answer that what they want is to accomplish something with their lives (such as write a good novel, or discover a cure for AIDS), not to have the impression that they are. Many would say that they also want simply to be in touch with reality, even at a cost in desirable consciousness.

Some philosophers think that if, for these reasons, we drop the experience requirement, the list of things that make a life better will grow counter-intuitively large. Without the requirement, we seem to have to fall back on the view that wellbeing is the fulfilment of desires formed in proper appreciation of the nature of their object. I want our twenty-fifth century successors to flourish (any moderately decent person would), but surely the fulfilment of that desire centuries from now will not retroactively make my life better. The fulfilment of such desires has to be excluded, but the experience requirement is not the only way of doing it. The list-account of wellbeing will do it too. The list is composed by identifying what enhances life. Nothing enhances life but instances of items on that list: happiness, knowledge, accomplishment, personal relations, and so on. The fulfilment of my desire for our twenty-fifth century successors to flourish may be excluded simply because it does not fit under any of the headings on the list that we should eventually compile.

References and further reading

Annas, J. (1993) *The Morality of Happiness*, New York: Oxford University Press. (A history of ancient ethics, focused on the notions of virtue and happiness, from Aristotle onwards.)

* Aristotle (*c.* mid 4th century BC) *Nicomachean Ethics*, trans. with notes by T. Irwin, Indianapolis, IN: Hackett Publishing Company, 1985, books I, X. (Contains the core of his account of happiness.)

Austin, J. (1968) 'Pleasure and Happiness', *Philosophy* 43. (Examines the distinction.)

* Bentham, J. (1789) *An Introduction to the Principles of Morals and Legislation*, ed. J.H. Burns and H.L.A. Hart, revised F. Rosen, Oxford: Clarendon Press, 1996. (Classic expression of the view that happiness consists in pleasure.)

* Brandt, R.B. (1979) *A Theory of the Good and the Right*, Oxford: Clarendon Press. (Argues that rational persons would choose a utilitarian moral code, and provides important discussions of such issues as happiness, welfare and desire-satisfaction.)

Crisp, R. (1997) *Mill on Utilitarianism*, London: Routledge, chaps 2–3. (Discusses Mill's view of happiness.)

Den Uyl, D. and Machan, T.R. (1983) 'Recent Work on the Concept of Happiness', *American Philo-*

sophical Quarterly 20. (A survey of contemporary discussions.)

Glover, J. (ed.) (1990) *Utilitarianism and its Critics*, New York: Macmillan, part II. (Good selection of writings on happiness, with special relevance to utilitarianism.)

Griffin, J. (1986) *Well-Being*, Oxford: Clarendon Press, part I. (Examines different accounts of wellbeing in modern ethics.)

Hobbes, T. (1651) *Leviathan*, ed. C.B. Macpherson, Harmondsworth: Penguin, 1968. (Can be interpreted as arguing that virtue and happiness are in opposition.)

Kraut, R. (1979) 'Two Conceptions of Happiness', *Philosophical Review* 80. (Explores the similarities and differences in two conceptions of happiness, Aristotle's and our own.)

* Mill, J.S. (1861) *Utilitarianism*, ed. R. Crisp, Oxford: Clarendon Press, 1998, ch. 2. (Argues that happiness consists in both higher and lower pleasures.)

Parfit, D. (1984) *Reasons and Persons*, Oxford: Clarendon Press, appendix I. (Identifies different positions about what makes someone's life go well.)

Plato (*c.*380–367 BC) *Republic*, trans. G.M. Grube, revised by C. Reeve, Indianapolis, IN: Hackett Publishing Company, 1992. (Famous ancient argument for the identification of virtue and happiness.)

* Rawls, J. (1971) *A Theory of Justice*, Cambridge, MA: Harvard University Press. (In the course of developing a non-utilitarian theory of justice, presents important criticisms of utilitarianism.)

* Sidgwick, H. (1874) *The Methods of Ethics*, London: Macmillan; 7th edn, 1907. (The fullest and most closely argued version of classical utilitarianism.)

Sumner, L.W. (1996) *Welfare, Happiness, and Ethics*. (Rejects hedonism and desire accounts, and defends a close connection of wellbeing to happiness.)

J.P. GRIFFIN

HARE, RICHARD MERVYN (1919–)

R.M. Hare is the creator of the ethical theory called 'prescriptivism'. This holds that moral statements differ from purely factual ones in prescribing conduct; they differ from simple imperatives in invoking universal principles that apply to all similar cases. The theory has three aspects: prescriptivity and universalizability as formal features of moral statements; appeal to the Golden Rule (that we should do to others as we wish them to do to us) for selecting moral principles; two levels of practical thinking, critical and intuitive.

1 Prescriptivity and universalizability

Richard Hare is a British philosopher, educated at Oxford, who has held chairs in moral philosophy at Oxford and Gainesville, Florida. His best-known work, *The Language of Morals* (1952), introduces a distinction between prescriptive and descriptive meaning. Prescriptive meaning is defined in relation to imperatives: a statement is prescriptive if it entails, if necessary in conjunction with purely factual statements, at least one imperative; and to assent to an imperative is to prescribe action. Descriptive meaning is defined in relation to truth-conditions: a statement is descriptive to the extent that factual conditions for its correct application define its meaning. In this usage, the factual is that which is only contingently motivating: desire is no part of sincere assent to a purely factual statement. The meaning of a moral statement is prescriptive, but may also be partly descriptive. Thus '*A* [a person] ought to ϕ' entails the imperative 'Let $A\phi$', so that to assent to it sincerely is to have an overriding desire (which in application to oneself will amount, if its satisfaction is practicable, to an intention) that $A\phi$. If there are agreed reasons for ϕ-ing within a linguistic community, for example that it is enjoyable, '*A* ought to ϕ' may take on the descriptive implication 'ϕ-ing is enjoyable'. '*X* [a person, object or whatever] is a good *F* [a kind of thing]' prescribes choice within a certain range; it takes on a descriptive connotation if there are agreed standards for assessing *F*'s. Cases of failing to try to do what one admits one ought to do may involve psychological incapacity, or an off-colour use of 'ought' whereby it retains descriptive meaning but loses its prescriptive meaning. What the modal '*A* ought to ϕ' adds to the simple 'Let $A\phi$' is universalizability: one who assents to the former is implicitly accepting a universal principle that applies equally to anyone else whose condition and situation are identical in kind (see PRESCRIPTIVISM).

2 The Golden Rule

Freedom and Reason (1963) extracts from these features a mode of reasoning, the so-called 'Golden-Rule Argument', for selecting moral principles; this was subsequently clarified and fortified in writings leading up to *Moral Thinking* (1981). In wondering whether to assent to the statement '*A* ought to ϕ', I have to reflect whether I can prescribe that everyone should act in the same way in every possible world, whatever my role within that world. (This talk of possible worlds is useful, though Hare denies it to be essential.) 'I' connotes no essence (for example, human): I occupy every possible role in some possible world. But there is a prescriptive aspect to its meaning: to take a role within some possible but non-actual world as *my* role is to give weight to the desires of the occupant of that role as if they were actually my own. Hence, I can rationally assent to a particular 'ought'-statement only if it is derivable from some universal principle that I shall accept if I give impartial and positive weight to all preferences whose fulfilment would be affected by its fulfilment. Thus moral reflection generates a universalized prudence. Possibly it should also respect 'external' preferences, that is, the preferences of those (say the dead) who will *experience* no satisfaction; *Moral Thinking* leaves this as 'unfinished business'. Moral ideals register within this framework simply as universal preferences; to allow one's own ideals to override the stronger or more prevalent desires and ideals of others is a kind of egoism, and so excluded. The upshot is a variant of utilitarianism that aims at the maximization not of happiness, but of the satisfaction of preferences (see UTILITARIANISM §2). Human decision remains free, however rational and informed, because anyone can avoid the constraints of morality by declining to moralize; for this reason, 'is' still fails to entail 'ought'.

3 Critical and intuitive thinking

Reasoning according to the Golden Rule will ascribe maximum observance-utility to highly specific universal principles. However, a greater acceptance-utility may attach to more general principles that it is easier to apply without error or self-deception. *Moral Thinking* elaborates a distinction between a 'critical' level of thinking, conducted by 'archangels' with the use of the Golden-Rule Argument, and an 'intuitive' level, conducted by 'proles' with the use of simple principles (often articulating emotional responses) whose acceptance can be justified at the critical level. These two levels define not two social castes, but two roles between which each of us learns to alternate as appropriate. Intuitive objections to utilitarianism (such as that it neglects rights) can often be accommodated at the intuitive level, and then cease to be objections (see INTUITIONISM IN ETHICS §3).

Hare further argues that prescriptivism guarantees objectivity, while descriptivism collapses into relativism. How I can rationally apply the terms 'right' and 'wrong' is determined by what I can will universally, which rides free of the contingencies of my own tastes and intuitions. But if the correct application of such terms was determined by their descriptive meaning within some linguistic community, it would be relative to the culture and ideology of that community. Only a prescriptivist ethics can achieve moral universality. The theory has received much critical attention, and while few may accept it as a whole, the simplicity and fertility of its main ideas make it a paradigm of practical philosophy.

List of works

Hare, R.M. (1952) *The Language of Morals*, Oxford: Clarendon Press. (Discusses imperative inference, explains 'good' as a term of commendation, and relates 'ought' to imperatives.)
—— (1963) *Freedom and Reason*, Oxford: Clarendon Press. (Derives from prescriptive universalizability a Golden-Rule Argument for testing moral maxims.)
—— (1971a) *Essays on Philosophical Method*, London: Macmillan. (Essays, partly historical, exploring the proper goals and methods of philosophy, especially of moral philosophy.)
—— (1971b) *Practical Inferences*, London: Macmillan. (An important set of essays on imperative logic, practical reasoning, and meaning and speech acts.)
—— (1972a) *Applications of Moral Philosophy*, London: Macmillan. (Essays on practical issues originally intended for a non-professional audience. 'Nothing Matters' is a lucid and engaging statement of Hare's scepticism about the objective/subjective debate in ethics.)
—— (1972b) *Essays on the Moral Concepts*, London: Macmillan. (Partly polemical essays exploring the relation between moral and descriptive concepts.)
—— (1981) *Moral Thinking: Its Levels, Method and Point*, Oxford: Clarendon Press. (Distinguishes two levels of moral thinking as 'critical' and 'intuitive'. Importantly discusses the Golden-Rule Argument, alleging a prescriptive use of 'I' and 'my'.)
—— (1982) *Plato*, Oxford: Oxford University Press. (Introduces Plato's philosophy, especially as a response to the moral uncertainties of his time.)
—— (1989a) *Essays in Ethical Theory*, Oxford: Clarendon Press. (A valuable collection of essays, some polemical, others constructive, preparatory or accessory to *Moral Thinking*.)
—— (1989b) *Essays on Political Morality*, Oxford: Clarendon Press. (Essays on legal obligation, war and terrorism, rights, justice and the environment.)
—— (1992) *Essays on Religion and Education*, Oxford: Clarendon Press. (Essays on the relation of religion to morals, and on the nature of moral education from the viewpoint of a prescriptivist meta-ethics.)
—— (1993) *Essays on Bioethics*, Oxford: Clarendon Press. (Essays in medical ethics and related topics. Particularly important are discussions, in relation to abortion, of decisions about possible people.)
—— (1997) *Sorting out Ethics*, Oxford: Clarendon Press. (Recommends prescriptivism in the context of a mapping of the possible alternatives within meta-ethics.)

References and further reading

Fehige, C. and Meggle, G. (eds) (1995) *Zum moralischen Denken* (Towards Moral Thinking), Frankfurt: Suhrkamp. (Twenty-three essays, with replies by Hare, in German.)
Seanor, D. and Fotion, N. (eds) (1988) *Hare and Critics: Essays on Moral Thinking*, Oxford: Oxford University Press. (Contains concise comments by Hare; careful and sophisticated.)

A.W. PRICE

HARMONIA *see* PHILOLAUS; PYTHAGOREANISM

HARRINGTON, JAMES (1611–77)

Harrington was the premier English republican political theorist. His The Commonwealth of Oceana *(1656), published soon after the Civil War, analysed the collapse of monarchy and recommended institutions for a perfect commonwealth. He argued that forms of government were shaped by modes of land tenure; the decline of the feudal aristocracy and rise of the gentry rendered monarchy inviable. His proposed republic entailed regular elections for all public offices and secret ballots among a citizenry of independent gentlemen. Harrington influenced English, American and French radicals throughout the eighteenth century. Today he tends to be a talisman for those who would inject an aspect of 'civic republicanism' or 'public virtue' into contemporary politics, by contrast with the liberal rights theories of the natural jurisprudence tradition.*

1 Life and works
2 The argument of *Oceana*
3 Interpretations
4 Influence

1 Life and works

Born to a gentry family in Lincolnshire, Harrington studied at Oxford and the Middle Temple. In the 1630s he served as a volunteer in the Thirty Years War in Germany and undertook the Grand Tour, visiting France and Italy. He served King Charles I and accompanied him during his captivity: his republicanism was not grounded in personal animosity. His publishing career was brief. His chief work, *The Commonwealth of Oceana*, appeared in 1656, and was followed by a series of vindications. His notoriety was greatest in 1659–60 when the Rota Club met in a London coffeehouse to debate models of government. Harrington fell silent after the restoration of monarchy in 1660, and was briefly jailed. He died apparently insane.

Oceana is dedicated to Oliver Cromwell; its Legislator, called Olphaus Megaletor, is plainly an Oliverian figure. Like other republicans, Harrington saw Cromwell's Protectorate as a betrayal of the 'Good Old Cause', a return to quasi-monarchic rule, yet he appealed to Cromwell to act heroically as midwife to a utopian commonwealth. Sir Henry Vane's *A Healing Question* and Marchamont Needham's *The Excellency of a Free State* were published in the same year (1656). The Harringtonians were pervasively civic humanist in their language and committed to constructing republican institutions – unlike John Milton, whose 'republicanism' amounted to a defence of king-killing, couched in the language of natural jurisprudence (see REPUBLICANISM).

Harrington's mentors were Aristotle, who provided the concept of the self-sufficient gentlemanly household; Polybius, who celebrated the mixed and balanced polity; Machiavelli, who suggested the emphasis on arms and citizen militias; and John Selden, who documented English feudalism. Harrington admired the republics of ancient Rome and modern Venice, as well as Israel in the age of the Judges. His hero-lawgivers were those of the Renaissance humanists: Solon, Lycurgus, Numa, Romulus and (echoing Machiavelli) Moses. Harrington was transfixed by 'the archives of ancient prudence' and by Machiavelli, 'the only politician of later ages', whom he read as the republican idealist of the *Discourses*.

There is also a distinctive Platonist voice. Harrington's only essay in metaphysics was his *Mechanics of Nature* (written around 1662 and published posthumously in 1700). It shows him to have adopted a hylozoist and pantheist position. Behind nature and human polities lies the *anima mundi* or world-soul. More broadly, Harrington inclined towards Socinianism. Grace and charism have little place: the divine is fulfilled through natural virtue, and the Kingdom of God is no other than the perfect commonwealth.

2 The argument of *Oceana*

Oceana is divided into two parts, a diagnosis of contemporary England in 'The Preliminaries', followed by a description of the imagined commonwealth. 'The Preliminaries' are known for their doctrine that forms of government tend to follow the 'balance of property', and hence that the art of politics consists of 'the skill of raising such superstructures of government as are natural to the known foundations' (1656 (1977): 202). There are 'natural' (stable) and 'violent' (unstable) governments, those which accord with, or violate, their tenurial foundations. Harrington argues that the two centuries prior to the Civil War saw a drastic change in the balance of property. Crown and aristocratic lands were gradually distributed to the gentry. Without the support of a dominant nobility, or a standing army, kingship became unsustainable. Thus, the feudal or 'Gothic' polity, in which land was the reward for military service to the crown, was gone forever. Harrington's editor, John Toland, remarked, 'that empire [government] follows the balance of property, whether lodged in one, in a few, or in many hands, he was the first that ever made out; and is a noble discovery...the foundation of all politics' (1700a: preface).

The institutions of Oceana are grounded in the new circumstances of a gentry commonwealth. Oceana has a senate composed of 300 of the wealthier landholders, who have the power of debate, and an assembly of 1,050 smaller freeholders, who have the power of resolution. There is a three-year term of office, one-third of each house coming up for election annually. The citizen body – the electors – must be economically independent (not servants or poor), be over 30 years of age, and have served in the militia. There are four executive councils – of state, war, religion and trade – and members must stand down after two years in office. Olphaus Megaletor is the presidential figure. All offices, including religious and military, are elective, with regular rotation: 'They, who do command today, shall learn again tomorrow to obey'. The basic geographical unit remains the parish (rationalized into 10,000 in number), revitalized as the locus of civic life. There are counties and hundreds, but no boroughs: this is a resolutely rural commonwealth. Each year, one in five citizens compulsorily serves in the militia.

A crucial stipulation is the Agrarian Law, which, through the abolition of primogeniture and a ceiling of £2,000 worth of property, aimed to prevent the emergence of an overweening oligarchy. The Agrarian Law renders Oceana 'an immortal commonwealth', free from the instability of the Polybian cycles of rise and decline. It also inclines Oceana more towards the Athenian model of democracy than was customary among the Roman-inspired Renaissance republicans, although the presidential and senatorial elements sufficiently exemplify the traditional one-few-many formula.

The whole fabric is designed to ensure 'an empire of laws and not of men', a regime of reason and not of mere will. It is a commonwealth which nurtures civic virtue and service to the public. The landed gentleman governs himself and so is fit to govern the polity. The obverse of virtue is corruption: tyranny is that which serves private or factional interests rather than the public good (see CORRUPTION §§1, 3).

3 Interpretations

Modern interpretations of Harrington fall into three camps. One group, in the thrall of positivist political science, celebrates Harrington's empiricism and secularism, his grasp of the mechanics of power and the calculus of interest. A second group, Marxian-inspired (notably R.H. Tawney, Christopher Hill and C.B. Macpherson), finds in Harrington an economic determinist, the first theorist to offer a structural interpretation of the English Revolution, and a spokesman of the bourgeois gentry. The third group (J.G.A. Pocock and his followers) emphasizes the civic humanist character of Harrington's thought. Against the political scientists, the Pocockians point to his Platonic and occasionally millenarian language. Against the Marxians, they argue that Harrington was no determinist, and that his grasp of economics went no further than land tenure. His account of the transition from feudalism rested on the contingent political changes by which Henry VII and Henry VIII curtailed aristocratic estates and retinues, and redistributed monastic lands. The Agrarian Law manifestly limits a free market in land.

Some attention has been paid to Harrington's 'civil religion'. Clerics quickly attacked Oceana, and Harrington retorted with extensive discussion of ecclesiastical power. He was vehemently anticlerical, praising HOBBES (from whom he otherwise diverged) for his critique of the pretensions of papalists, prelatists and presbyterians. Harrington coined the word 'priestcraft'. Oceana is secular in the sense that it rejects divine right clericalism and embraces religious toleration within a broad church. Yet Oceana is a Christian commonwealth, indeed one in which the Church finds its apotheosis in the commonwealth itself. Harrington argues that it was so in Israel, and he explains that the Greek 'ecclesia' or 'congregation' meant only the civic assembly of the citizens. The ancient manner of choosing clergy by popular vote – chirotonia – was perverted by usurping ecclesiastics into the practice of clerical 'laying on of hands' – chirothesia. Harrington's millenarianism is most visible in his recommendation that Ireland be colonized by the Jews.

4 Influence

Harrington's republicanism was profoundly influential in the later seventeenth and eighteenth centuries. Oceana inspired a body of 'neo-Harringtonians', the True, Old, or Real Whigs, who provided a radical critique of England's monarchical polity, and later attacked the executive tyranny of prime ministerial and cabinet government. Harrington helped fuel assaults on standing armies, 'placemen' and irregular elections. Early examples are Plato redivivus (Plato Revived) (1680) by Harrington's friend Henry Neville, who also published an edition of Machiavelli's works; and An Essay upon the Roman Government (1698) by Walter Moyle. Toland published Harrington's collected Works in 1700. Eighteenth-century political analysts, such as Bolingbroke and Hume, deployed the idea of 'the balance of property', although they rejected the republican utopianism. Harrington's mark is also visible in some of the early constitutions of the American colonies, and among the rebels of 1776. It was said of General Warner, the hero of Bunker Hill, that 'like Harrington he wrote, like Cicero he spoke, like Hampden he lived, like Wolfe he died'. In 1779 it was proposed, albeit ironically, that Massachusetts be renamed Oceana. In 1795 Oceana was republished in revolutionary France and the Abbé Sieyès drew up a Harringtonian constitutional plan. In the nineteenth century George Grote found inspiration in Harrington for his campaign for the secret ballot.

List of works

Harrington, J. (1977) *The Political Works of James Harrington*, ed. J.G.A. Pocock, Cambridge: Cambridge University Press; abridged edn, *James Harrington: The Commonwealth of Oceana and A System of Politics*, ed. J.G.A. Pocock, Cambridge: Cambridge University Press, 1992. (Contains all of Harrington's political writings, the chief of which are listed separately.)

—— (1656) *Oceana*, in *The Political Works of James Harrington*, ed. J.G.A. Pocock, Cambridge: Cambridge University Press, 155–360. (England's premier republican text. Part 1 analyses the historical reasons for the collapse of the monarchy; part 2 sketches the spirit and institutions of an ideal agrarian republic.)

—— (1658) *The Prerogative of Popular Government*, in *The Political Works of James Harrington*, ed. J.G.A. Pocock, Cambridge: Cambridge University Press, 389–498. (Book 1 is a reply to Matthew Wren's *Considerations upon Mr Harrington's Commonwealth of Oceana*; book 2 is an anticlerical history of priestly ordination, directed against Presbyterians and Anglicans.)

—— (1659a) *The Art of Lawgiving*, in *The Political Works of James Harrington*, ed. J.G.A. Pocock, Cambridge: Cambridge University Press, 599–704. (Book 1 recapitulates arguments from *Oceana* about the 'foundations and superstructures of government'; book 2 discusses the commonwealth of ancient Israel; book 3 elaborates on the institutions needed in a republic.)

—— (1659b) *Aphorisms Political*, in *The Political Works of James Harrington*, ed. J.G.A. Pocock, Cambridge: Cambridge University Press, 761–80. (A short work consisting of 120 apothegms on government.)

—— (1700a) *The Mechanics of Nature*, in *Works*, ed. J. Toland, London. (A metaphysical essay of pantheist or neoplatonist leanings. The divine is embodied in the world soul and in natural virtue.)

Harrington, J. (1700b) *Works*, ed. J. Toland, London. (The neo-republican Toland provided the standard edition until the twentieth century and offered ammunition for the radical critique of English government during the eighteenth century.)

—— (1700c) *A System of Politics*, in J. Toland (ed.), *Works*; repr. in *The Political Works of James Harrington*, ed. J.G.A. Pocock, Cambridge: Cambridge University Press, 833–54. (Written around 1661 and published posthumously, in it Harrington analyses the art of government, reducing it to several hundred aphorisms.)

References and further reading

Goldie, M. (1987) 'The Civil Religion of James Harrington', in A. Pagden (ed.) *The Languages of Political Theory in Early Modern Europe*, Cambridge: Cambridge University Press. (Explores Harrington's religious thinking.)

* Moyle, W. (1698) *An Essay upon the Roman Government*, in *Works*, London, 1726. (Moyle used a discussion of the virtues and institutions, and the corruption and decline, of Rome as a warning for contemporary England.)

* Needham, M. (1656) *The Excellency of a Free State*, London. (After Harrington's *Oceana*, the principal republican work published during the interregnum. Comprises newspaper editorials published in 1651 and 1652 in *Mercurius Politicus*.)

* Neville, H. (1680) *Plato redivivius*, London. (An adaptation of Harrington's republican theories for the circumstances of the restored monarchy. Neville proposed to strip the crown of most of its executive powers.)

Pocock, J.G.A. (1975) *The Machiavellian Moment*, Princeton, NJ: Princeton University Press. (Places Harrington and the neo-Harringtonians in the context of civic humanism.)

Russell Smith, H.F. (1914) *Harrington and His Oceana*, Cambridge: Cambridge University Press. (Discusses Harrington's republican constitutionalism and its legacy.)

Tawney, R.H. (1942), *Harrington's Interpretation of his Age*, Oxford: Oxford University Press. (A Marxian emphasis on Harrington as a theorist of economy and polity.)

* Vane, Sir H. (1656) *A Healing Question*, London. (A work of 'godly' republicanism. The armed 'saints' have a duty to create a perfect commonwealth, protected by a righteous army.)

MARK GOLDIE

HART, HERBERT LIONEL ADOLPHUS (1907–93)

H.L.A. Hart, Professor of Jurisprudence at Oxford University, 1952–1968, is an outstanding representative of the analytical approach in jurisprudence and philosophy of law. He restated 'legal positivism' in the tradition of Jeremy Bentham and John Austin, differentiating between law's existence and its moral qualities. But he rejected the Benthamite identification of law with a sovereign's commands, advancing instead a theory of law as comprising a special, systematically organized, kind of social rules. He did this in a linguistic-analytical style, showing how attention to our way of speaking and thinking about rules can yield new insights into their nature.

Hart aimed to establish that legal obligation is intelligible in itself and yet conceptually distinct from moral obligation (see LAW AND MORALITY §3). This depends on differentiating different types of rules in the legal setting, showing how some impose requirements upon conduct, while others confer power over rules of the former, 'primary' type. Legal obligations are imposed by 'primary rules', but since these can be varied through application of 'secondary' power-conferring rules, they can and do differ in content from moral obligations. He also argued for the possibility of a moral critique of law as it is, aimed at reforming it in favour of liberty and tolerance. His work here had important practical influence. He offered a distinctive account of rights, including human rights, and argued that a 'minimum content of natural law' is present in all viable forms of human social order (see NATURAL LAW §5).

The Concept of Law (1961), Hart's outstanding work, explains law as a system of social rules distinct from the rules and principles of morality, whether conventional or ideal. Legal rules divide into 'primary rules' laying down duties to act (for example, in pursuance of the terms of a contract) or to abstain (for example, to avoid harming others or attacking them in body or in reputation, or defrauding them) and 'secondary rules' relating in a systemic way to primary rules. Some secondary rules ('rules of adjudication') regulate the ways in which primary rules can be implemented through courts and other agencies. Others are 'rules of change', either enabling legislatures to secure large-scale legal changes, or enabling private persons to exercise powers under, for example, the law of contract, or property law, or trust law, so as to make changes in individual legal relationships.

Finally, there is the 'rule of recognition' containing the criteria for validity of primary rules and other secondary rules. A legal system thus comprises a rule of recognition and all the other rules valid by reference to it. The existence of a rule of recognition, and thus of the legal system, depends on human practice, especially the practices of officials. Acceptance of a common public standard under which all persons have an obligation to respect and apply laws that are valid by that standard is constitutive of the existence of a rule of recognition (see LEGAL CONCEPTS §3).

This framework also accounts for rights, the legal position held by those who are able to act in their own interest to activate or enforce duties laid upon others by law. Related kinds of right, also characterized by the law's deference to individual choice, are the liberties enjoyed by those who are not duty-bound to act in a certain way, or the powers conferred by 'rules of change', particularly those conferring private powers. This leaves open the question whether there are any 'natural' or 'human' rights. Hart's answer was hypothetical: if there are any rights that are a morally required part of any social order, the first and central of them must be the equal right of all humans to be free (see RIGHTS §4). As for 'natural law', human nature makes restraints on violence and deception,

and provision of some sort about possession of and access to material things, essential to the existence of any viable society. But this is not a detailed blueprint for either law or conventional morality, and hence does not justify a restricted definition of law that excludes from it any grossly unjust rules.

Law, Liberty and Morality (1963) was his own statement on the limits of law. He demanded that law be used only to prevent harm to others or for some restricted forms of 'paternalism' restraining people from severely self-harming activity (see LAW, LIMITS OF §4). 'Positive morality', the conventional moral opinion of a community, is firmly differentiated from 'critical morality', rational and enlightened standards for criticizing or upholding norms of law or of positive morality. Hart rejected the use of law simply to enforce positive morality. *Punishment and Responsibility* (1968) was a collection of essays in which he developed a middle way between utilitarian and retributive principles of punishment, arguing that the latter ought to prevail in respect of distribution of punishments (only to those who deserve it, and in proportion to desert), while general deterrence remained the justifying aim of the system (see CRIME AND PUNISHMENT §2).

Causation in the Law (jointly with Tony Honoré, 1958) is an outstanding example of an effective combination of philosophical analysis and legal exposition, giving an account of the legally important idea of causality poised between common sense, science and law (see CAUSATION). Hart's collected essays were published in two volumes (*Essays on Bentham*, 1982; *Essays in Jurisprudence and Philosophy*, 1983) one blue and one brown. If there was here an allusion to Wittgenstein's 'blue book' and 'brown book' it was not inapt; for Hart above all brought to jurisprudence the linguistic-philosophical insights of Wittgenstein, J.L. Austin and Ryle (see ORDINARY LANGUAGE PHILOSOPHY).

Hart's elucidation of rules involves a hermeneutic approach examining conduct 'from the internal point of view' of a group's members (see LEGAL HERMENEUTICS). This owes much to Wittgenstein, and something also to Max Weber, but remains an original contribution to rule-analysis (see NORMS, LEGAL §2). Some critics have argued that one cannot start down this road without ending up in a fully 'natural law' approach. Others have argued that analysis of law purely in terms of conventional rules omits its essentially principled character, or that its sociological presuppositions are untenable. Hart's legal positivism, albeit highly persuasive, remains open to doubt.

See also: AUSTIN, J.; BENTHAM, J.; LAW, PHILOSOPHY OF

List of works

Hart, H.L.A. with Honoré, T. (1958) *Causation in the Law*, 2nd edn, Oxford: Clarendon Press, 1985. (A detailed study of causation, pursued first through general philosophical accounts and second, at considerable length, through analysis of case law dealing with causal problems. Accessible to the general reader.)

Hart, H.L.A. (1961) *The Concept of Law*, Oxford: Clarendon Press. (Hart's most celebrated work, originally intended as a high-level student's introduction to jurisprudence. A gracefully written book, deceptively easy to read.)

—— (1963) *Law, Liberty and Morality*, Oxford: Clarendon Press. (An accessible, well-argued account of the case for a liberal and anti-moralistic approach to legislation and law.)

—— (1968) *Punishment and Responsibility*, Oxford: Clarendon Press. (A collection of essays in which aspects of utilitarianism and of retributivism are reconciled.)

—— (1982) *Essays on Bentham*, Oxford: Clarendon Press. (A collection of papers mainly directed at positivism and utilitarianism, containing important revisions of Hart's earlier approach to jurisprudence.)

—— (1983) *Essays in Jurisprudence and Philosophy*, Oxford: Clarendon Press. (A collection of Hart's main contributions to discussions of basic jurisprudential issues, including critiques of his main rivals.)

References and further reading

Bayles, M. (1992) *Hart's Legal Philosophy: an Examination*, Dordrecht/Boston/London: Kluwer. (An extended account of Hart's theories and of objections to them; some telling criticisms carry the debate beyond Martin and MacCormick. Contains complete Hart bibliography.)

Cotterrell, R. (1991) *The Politics of Jurisprudence*, London: Butterworths. (Takes up a critical position on the style of philosophical jurisprudence developed by Hart and continued by various successors; a critique of Hartian (and other) legal philosophy from a critical sociological standpoint.)

MacCormick, N. (1981) *H.L.A. Hart*, London: Edward Arnold. (A relatively short intellectual biography and sympathetically critical account of Hart's main tenets; an essentially Hartian view of Hart.)

Martin, M. (1987) *The Legal Philosophy of H.L.A. Hart*, Philadelphia, PA: Temple University Press. (Longer and more detailed than MacCormick, and more distanced from Hart's own position.)

NEIL MacCORMICK

HARTLEY, DAVID (1705–57)

David Hartley commands a distinctive place in Enlightenment thinking for his attempt to establish an empiricist epistemology upon a foundation of ontological materialism – in other words, a philosophy of mind that incorporates a physiology of the brain. He also set forth an optimistic vision of human progress which was nonetheless cast within the framework of a transcendental theology. Though his views might seem to be a singular fusion of disparate strands, they nevertheless epitomized much liberal and advanced English thinking of the time, and exercised considerable influence upon the philosophical radicalism of subsequent generations.

1   Life and contacts
2   Physiological philosophy
3   Influence

1   Life and contacts

David Hartley was born the son of a poor Anglican clergyman in Armley, Yorkshire, probably on 30 August 1705. Both his father and mother died while he was still a child. He attended Bradford Grammar School before matriculating at Jesus College, Cambridge, as a sizar at the age of seventeen, at precisely the moment when a thoroughly modern synthesis of Newtonian natural philosophjy and Lockean philosophy was becoming the staple of the undergraduate curriculum. He graduated BA in 1726 and MA three years later, and held a fellowship at the college from 1727 until he married in 1730.

As his writings show, Hartley was a devout Christian; yet scruples against signing the Thirty-Nine Articles precluded him from taking orders, and he chose medicine as a career. Apparently without any medical degree or licence, he began to practise in Newark, moving on to Bury St Edmunds. After his wife's death, he remarried in 1735, and his second wife's wealth enabled him to settle just off London's fashionable Leicester Square (then the physicians' quarter); subsequently her ill-health induced the couple to move to Bath, where Hartley built up a successful medical practice.

A Fellow of the Royal Society, Hartley was able to move in the best intellectual and scientific circles. His friends included the physician Sir Hans Sloane (who became president of the Royal Society), the Revd Stephen Hales, famous for his pioneering physiological experiments, the evangelical William Law, and Joseph Butler, the leading rational Anglican theologian. Hartley had a part to play in major intellectual and philanthropic causes of the day, championing smallpox inoculation and John Byrom's shorthand system, and writing pamphlets to secure a parliamentary subvention for Mrs Joanna Stephens' lithontriptic nostrum against kidney and bladder stones (he had suffered from the disorder while still a young man). He died in Bath on 28 August 1757.

2 Physiological philosophy

Hartley is best remembered for his *Observations on Man, His Frame, His Duty, and His Expectations*, published in 1749 – a two-volume philosophical *tour de force* that systematized views set out in his earlier *The Progress of Happiness Deduced From Reason* (1734) and *Conjecturae quaedam de sensu, motu, et idearum generatione* (1746). The *Observations on Man* offered a comprehensive vision of the individual considered both as an earthly being and in regard to a future state. Emphasizing the view that all knowledge derives from experience, it drew heavily upon the empiricist theory of mental operations explicated in John Locke's *Essay Concerning Human Understanding* (1690; see LOCKE, J.). It also absorbed the innovative associationist utilitarianism of the Revd John Gay's *Preliminary Dissertation Concerning the Fundamental Principle of Virtue or Morality* (1731), which set out a pleasure and pain psychology as the key to the formation of opinions and to the philosophy of action. Like Locke and Gay, Hartley sought to refute nativist theories of cognition and morality (see NATIVISM), insisting that complex ideas were built up from simple imputs by repeated combinations of what Hartley called the 'sensations of the soul'. Hartley thus grounded thoughts and values upon the Lockean principle of the association of ideas.

Unlike Locke and Gay, however, Hartley aimed to set these epistemological and psychological observations upon concrete physical foundations – the anatomy of the nervous system and the physiology of 'motions excited in the brain'. For this he drew upon the theory of sensation suggested in the 'Queries' to Isaac NEWTON's *Opticks* (1704; see NEWTON, I.). Newton had shown how light vibrated in a medium; such vibrations had an impact upon the retina; having impinged upon the eye, Hartley argued, these corpuscular motions set off further vibrating waves that passed along the nerves to the brain. The Lockean notion of the association of ideas was thus

visualized and made material by Hartley in terms of reiterated vibrations in the white medullary matter of the brain and spinal cord, which resulted in lasting traces or vestiges that served as the physical substrate of complex ideas, memory and dispositions. Unlike the French *philosophes* like LA METTRIE, Hartley framed his materialist physiological psychology in terms of a Christian natural theology. In his view, materialism was not the slippery slope to atheism, precisely because it was the Christian God who, in His Wisdom, had endowed matter with all its powers and potentialities. The necessitarianism entailed by materialism was, in Hartley's opinion, the finest guarantee of the universal operation of cause and effect, hence of the uniformity of nature, and so of the boundless power of God.

As befitted a medical man, the first volume of *Observations on Man* explored major aspects of neurophysiology, discussing the human mind and appetites in terms of the evolution of complex ideas and habits from elementary sensations. Hartley demonstrated the formation of mental associations on the basis of the vibrations of particles in the nervous system which persisted in the form of the more minute 'vibratiuncles', which in turn provided the physical basis for memory, regarded in something of a rather Hobbesian way as decaying sense (see HOBBES, T.). Individual chapters explored the mental physics of feeling, taste, smell, seeing and hearing. The second volume extended the system to account for morality and the individual's prospects in a future state.

Unlike Stephen Hales, Hartley was less an experimenter than a systematizer, offering a comprehensive framework for interpreting the phenomena of life and mind. Among his followers, the *Observations on Man* came to be seen as the fountainhead of key biological, psychological and social doctrines. Hartley's tenets provided the framework for the associationist heritage in psychology – in particular, learning theory. His conjectures concerning the physiology of the nervous system offered suggestions for sensory-motor theories later influential in neurophysiology, and for the experimental localization of brain functions. Hartleian notions are the distant ancestors of Pavlovian notions of conditioned reflexes.

3 Influence

Hartley's particular neurophysiological theories proved erroneous, yet his work was of cardinal significance in the development of attempts to apply scientific concepts to the study of the individual as a social being and as a progressive creature. His was the first methodical elaboration of the explanatory principle (psychophysical parallelism) that came to play a role in the human sciences analogous to that played by the concept of gravity in the physical sciences. Though Hartley was personally devout, his unification of sensation, motion, association and volition within a mechanistic theory of consciousness and action created a framework of thinking that later supported more secular readings of the concepts of utility. His agenda was widely taken up in late Enlightenment and nineteenth-century doctrines as a means of accounting for cumulative ordered change through experience, changing responses being explained in terms of adaptation to pleasurable and painful consequences. Hartley put learning theory and moral judgment on a scientific basis.

Hartley had an influence on Samuel Taylor COLERIDGE, whose brief flirtation with his notions led to his first-born being baptised Hartley Coleridge. Joseph PRIESTLEY stressed Hartley's determinism, but omitted his materialist neurology in his edition of the *Observations on Man*, retitled [Hartley's] *Theory of the Human Mind* (1775). Priestley put his modified version of Hartley's theory at the service of a Unitarian philosophy of nature. Erasmus Darwin used Hartley's neurological mechanisms as the basis for his system of medical classification in *Zoonomia* (1794–6) and for his theory of evolution in the *Temple of Nature* (1803). In sociopolitical theory, the arguments advanced in William Godwin's *Political Justice* (1793) for inevitable human progress towards perfection were based on inferences from Hartley. The psychological, social, and political theories of James and John Stuart MILL and other English utilitarians were also based on Hartleian psychology and generalizations from it. In the nineteenth century, Hartley's fusion of corpuscular physics with empiricist epistemology and sensationalist psychology became reworked in more modern evolutionary terms to provide the foundations for theories in biology, neurophysiology, psychology, psychiatry, sociopolitical theory and to endorse a general faith in progress. Hartley's psychophysiological theory of learning underpins modern, evolutionary human science.

See also: HUMAN NATURE, 18TH CENTURY SCIENCE OF; UTILITARIANISM

List of works

Hartley, D. (1730) *Conjecturae quaedam de sensu, motu, et idearum generatione*, London; 2nd edn, Bath, 1746; repr. in S. Parr (ed.) *Metaphysical Tracts*, London, 1837. (The first statement of Hartley's interests in the physiological basis of perception and ideation.)

—— (1749) *Observations on Man, His Frame, His Duty, and His Expectations*, London: Leake & Frederick, 2 vols. (Hartley's *opus magnum*, subsequently edited in 'bowdlerized' form by Joseph Priestley, sets out a materialist theory of the activity of mind, understood in terms of Newtonian corpuscular theory and a Providential reading of Christianity.)

References and further reading

* Darwin, E. (1794–6) *Zoonomia*, London: J. Johnson, 2 vols; repr. New York: A.M.S. Press, 1974.
* —— (1803) *Temple of Nature*, London: J. Johnson; facsimile Menston: Scolar Press, 1973.
* Gay, J. (1731) *A Dissertation concerning the Fundamental Principle and Immediate Criterion of Virtue*, London: W. Thurlborn.
* Godwin, W. (1793) *An Enquiry Concerning Political Justice*, London: Robinson; revised 1796, 1798.
* Halévy, E. (1928) *The Growth of Philosophic Radicalism*, trans. M. Morris, London: Faber & Faber; rev. edn, London: Faber & Faber, 1934. (By far the best survey of the radical intellectual tradition of which Hartley formed a part.)
Oberg, B.B. (1976) 'David Hartley and the Association of Ideas', *Journal of the History of Ideas* 37: 441–54. (The best brief account of Hartley's psychology.)
Smith, C.U.M. (1987) 'David Hartley's Newtonian Neuropsychology', *Journal of the History of the Behavioral Sciences*, 23: 123–36. (This offers a lucid exegesis of the largely Newtonian physical theories underpinning Hartley's science.)
Webb, M.E. (1988) 'A New History of Hartley's Observations on Man', *Journal of the History of the Behavioral Sciences* 24: 202–11. (Insists upon the importance of the iatrophysical medical theories of the early eighteenth century as a major context for Hartley's doctrines.)
—— (1989) 'The Early Medical Studies and Practice of Dr David Hartley', *Bulletin of the History of Medicine* 63: 618–36. (Informative on Hartley's medical career.)
Young, R.M. (1972) 'David Hartley', *Dictionary of Scientific Biography* 6, New York: Scribner, 138–40. (An exposition of Hartley's views which stresses the debts of later theorists to him.)
—— (1973) 'Association of Ideas', *Dictionary of the History of Ideas*, ed. P.P. Wiener, New York: Scribner, 111–18. (A fine account of the post-Lockean tradition of associationism which stresses the major part played by Hartley.)

ROY PORTER

HARTMANN, KARL ROBERT EDUARD VON (1842–1906)

Eduard von Hartmann was born in Berlin and lived there for most of his life. He was a prolific writer of both scholarly and popular works on a wide variety of topics, including aesthetics, ethics, religion and politics. He forecast a gloomy future for Germany, insisting that the only way to rectify the problems of modernity was with a strong nationalistic Germany ruled by an educated elite.

After distinguishing himself as a student Hartmann joined the military, intending to become an officer in the Prussian army. However, a severe knee injury frustrated these plans. During his convalescence he began a two-year study of music and painting. Believing he lacked the 'creative genius' necessary for art he began an independent study of philosophy. In 1864 he began writing his best known work *Philosophie des Unbewußten* (*Philosophy of the Unconscious*). When this three-volume work appeared in 1869, it made Hartmann an overnight success. Some ten thousand copies were sold between 1869 and 1875. The eleventh edition was published posthumously. Hartmann's widow compiled a chronological overview of his writings with 400 entries. Hartmann died in Berlin.

Hartmann is perhaps best known as a philosophical pessimist, and is thus usually regarded as a disciple of SCHOPENHAUER. Indeed Hartmann acknowledged that Schopenhauer exerted an early influence on his philosophical development. However, he insisted that he was a follower of KANT, whom he regarded as the true father of pessimism. Hartmann offered his own version of pessimism in his many writings, but perhaps the best statement of his position is found in his *Philosophy of the Unconscious*. Most of the first volume deals with Hartmann's scientific and mathematical justifications for his belief that not only humans but all animals are prompted to actions by various unconscious motives; the 'Will' is the cause of everything that comes to be. He credits Kant with having discovered unconscious motives, but faults him for not having sufficiently appreciated the unconscious workings of the mind. In Hartmann's view, Kant shared this deficiency with most of the figures in the history of philosophy. Schelling and Hegel barely improved upon Kant's philosophy. It was Schopenhauer who began to grasp the fundamental importance of the unconscious, what he called the 'Will'. Unfortunately, Schopenhauer was too blinded by Eastern influences to appreciate sufficiently how the unconscious worked in the human

realm. (For Hartmann's view of his predecessors see the foreword to the tenth edition.)

There are, Hartmann maintained, three stages of the illusion regarding the state of happiness. In the first stage we believe that happiness is already attained in this life, yet there is far more pain than pleasure. In the second we believe that we will attain happiness in an afterlife. But happiness must be the concern of this life, and thus the second stage is a necessary transitional stage to the third stage, in which we believe in the progress of mankind. However, this concern with a future paradise on earth is also based on an illusion. Philosophical maturity comes in the realization that happiness is illusory.

Hartmann's pessimism did not lead him to agree with Schopenhauer that this was the worst of all possible worlds; instead he thought that Leibniz was actually closer to being correct in the belief that it was the best. However, he strongly rejected Leibniz's belief that we should consider evil to be a privation. Instead evil is manifest in this world. But it is part of the world's teleological nature, the striving towards the final completion of the world, which means its utter and total annihilation. Again, despite some similarities with Schopenhauer, Hartmann believes that this outcome is not tragic. Rather, it is the culmination of the strivings of the unconscious through the entire human race – the end will be the highest expression of the unconscious in human nature.

Hartmann's main debt is to Kant, whom he credits with emphasizing the subjective workings of the mind. According to Hartmann, Kant's metaphysics and epistemology are primarily a doctrine of categories (see KANT, I. §6; CATEGORIES §3). Kant's successors may claim to have continued Kant's work, but Hartmann insists that his own philosophy represents the first major improvement on Kant's epistemology. In his *Kategorienlehre* (Doctrine of Categories) (1896a), Hartmann attempted to show that categories apply not only to the mind and nature but also essentially to what he called the 'metaphysical sphere', that is, to the realm of the unconscious. He argued that there is not only intra-individual causality but also trans-individual causality, a kind of universal causality that organisms share at the biological level.

Hartmann sought to develop his theory of the unconscious and to apply it in many areas. Besides his attempt to rework Kant's categories, he also tried to build an ethics on his philosophy of the unconscious. He was also extremely interested in science, frequently using tables, graphs and calculations to illustrate his point. Yet he objected to the mechanical science of the day, occasionally singling out Darwin for special criticism.

He was, among other things, a historian of

philosophy, a preoccupation he shared with many of his fellow nineteenth-century German philosophers. In his two-volume *Geschichte der Metaphysik* (History of Metaphysics) (1899–1900) he traced the role of metaphysics from the pre-Socratics to Nietzsche. He emphasized the place of metaphysics in the German philosophical tradition.

Hartmann's popularity waned immediately after his death, and today he is generally ignored. When he is remembered, it is primarily as one of the last of the nineteenth-century German speculative philosophers who sought to extend Kant's subjective philosophy by showing that our minds work not only at the conscious level but also at the unconscious level, thus prefiguring some aspects of modern psychology.

See also: GERMAN IDEALISM

List of works

Hartmann, K.R.E. von (1869) *Philosophie des Un-bewußten. Versuch einer Weltanschauung* (Philosophy of the Unconscious: An Attempt at a World View), Berlin: Duncker, 11 editions; trans. W.C. Coupland, London: Macmillan, 1884; reprinted New York, Greenwood, 1972. (Hartmann's central work, and the best statement of his philosophical pessimism.)
—— (1876) *Gesammelte Studien and Aufsätze* (Collected Studies and Essays), Berlin: Duncker. (An early collection of essays.)
—— (1876) *Phänomenologie des sittlichen Bewußtens. Prolegomena zu jeder künftigen Ethik* (Phenomenology of Moral Consciousness. Prolegomena to any Future Ethic), Berlin: Duncker. (A copy of Kant's work, but intended to show how pessimism allows for ethics.)
—— (1887) *Philosophie des Schönen. Zweiter systematischer Teil der Aesthetik* (Philosophy of Beauty. Second Systematical Part of Aesthetic), Leipzig: Friedrich. (Hartmann's weak attempt at a theory of beauty and aesthetics.)
—— (1888) *Lotze's Philosophie*, Leipzig: Friedrich; reprinted Ann Arbor, MI: Books on Demand, 1990. (An investigation of an influential thinker.)
—— (1896a) *Kategorienlehre* (Doctrine of Categories), Leipzig: Haake. (An attempt to show how we unconsciously apply categories.)
—— (1896b) *Tagesfragen* (Questions of the Day), Leipzig: Haake. (Discussion of contemporary issues – of little interest today.)
—— (1899) *Ethische Studien* (Ethical Studies), Leipzig: Haake. (Connects with his attempt to show that pessimism 'makes' ethics possible.)
—— (1899–1900) *Geschichte der Metaphysik* (History of Metaphysics), Leipzig: Haake; reprinted Darmstadt, Wissenschaftliche Buchgesellschaft, 1969. (A difficult and rather biased history of metaphysics.)
—— (1885–1901) *Ausgewählte Werke* (Selected Works), Leipzig: various publishers, 13 vols. (A huge collection, reviewing all aspects of Hartmann's writings.)

References and further reading

Bavarian Academy of Sciences Historical Commission (1966) *Neue Deutsche Biographie* (New German Biography), Berlin: Duncker & Humblot, vol. 7: 738–40. (Contains biographical material.)
Caldwell, W. (1893) 'The Epistemology of Ed. V. Hartmann', *Mind* n.s. 11: 188–207. (Reviews and criticizes Hartmann's thought.)
—— (1899) 'Moral and Social Philosophy. 1: The Positive Ethic', *Philosophical Review* 8 (5): 465–83. (Further criticism of Hartmann, focusing on his ethical theory.)
—— (1899) 'Moral and Social Philosophy. 2: The Metaphysic', *Philosophical Review* 8 (6): 589–603. (Caldwell's final review of Hartmann's central ideas, dealing with his writings on metaphysics.)
Copleston, F. (1962) *A History of Philosophy; Modern Philosophy: Schopenhauer to Nietzsche*, Garden City, NY: Image Books, vol. 7, 2: 57–9. (Gives a brief, readable account of Hartmann's thought.)
Hall, G.S. (1912) *Founders of Modern Psychology*, New York and London: D. Appleton; reprinted Ann Arbor: University Microfilms, 1978, 178–242. (A readable introduction by one of Hartmann's acquaintances.)
Hartmann, A. von (1912) 'Chronological Overview of the Works of Eduard von Hartmann', *Kant Studien* 17: 501–20. (The best bibliography of Hartmann's writings.)
Loemker, L. (1967) 'Hartmann, Eduard von', in *Encyclopedia of Philosophy*, ed. P. Edwards, New York: Macmillan, vol. 3, 419–21. (A broad account of the main themes of Hartmann's philosophy.)
Ringer, F.K. (1969) *The Decline of the German Mandarins. The German Academic Community, 1890–1933*, Cambridge, MA: Harvard University Press, 128–30. (A very interesting account of the German professorial community. Ringer chronicles the decline of their importance.)

CHRISTOPHER ADAIR-TOTEFF

HARTMANN, NICOLAI (1882–1950)

Nicolai Hartmann's intellectual trajectory was similar to that of his contemporary, Heidegger. He abandoned his early Neo-Kantian concern with knowledge and its foundations in favour of 'ontology', a study of the being of entities. Unlike Heidegger he assigned no ontological priority to human beings. Human beings are the highest level of entities, perched precariously above the physical, organic and animal levels, but conferring meaning and value on an otherwise meaningless and Godless universe.

Hartmann was born in Riga and, after a period as a medical student, studied history, classics and philosophy at the university of Saint Petersburg. In 1905 he moved to Marburg, and gained a professorship there in 1920. He later held chairs successively at Cologne, Berlin and Göttingen, where he died. For some years he remained under the spell of the Neo-Kantians, COHEN and Natorp, but by 1921, he had awoken from his 'critical slumber'. He rejected transcendental idealism, the transcendental ego, the primacy of practical reason and many other Kantian doctrines (see KANT, I.; NEO-KANTIANISM). Knowledge does not produce or alter what is known. Epistemology is not, as some neo-Kantians believed, the sole preoccupation of philosophy. We must also consider being, the being of the objects known and of the knower.

Hartmann did not reject Kantianism *in toto*. Philosophers have constructed systems and they have also tackled problems, often reaching conclusions at odds with their chosen system. Systems must be rejected; they belong to the past. But problems are eternal, and philosophers have made enduring contributions to their solution. One such contribution was Kant's belief that our experience involves categories (see KANT, I. §6). Kant inferred that categories are subjective, supplied by us to our experience and inapplicable to things in themselves. Hartmann rejects this inference. Categories are involved both in our cognition and in things in themselves. On this basis, Hartmann constructed an ontology.

Entities form a hierarchy of levels. At the lowest level are physical entities, involving such categories as extension and causality. Above these are plants, which involve organic categories. Then, various forms of animal life, requiring such categories as consciousness and purpose. Finally there are human being with their social and cultural products, which Hartmann, following Hegel, calls 'objectivized spirit'. These levels

or regions of beings are related in such ways as these. Lower entities need not constitute higher entities. There are, for example, purely material entities forming no part of a plant, animal or human being. Conversely, a higher entity necessarily involves the lower levels and the corresponding categories. A human being consists of matter, is a self-maintaining organism in the way that a plant is, and shares the basic features of animals. A higher entity is not determined solely by the laws governing the lower entities on whose presence it depends; it has considerable free-play. An organism consists of matter, but not the same material particles throughout its life; it organizes the matter of which it successively consists according to biological laws that do not govern purely material entities. Humans have free will: their decisions are not undetermined, but determined by factors peculiar to their spiritual life, not by the laws governing matter, plants or animals.

There are values, but they do not (as Kant supposed) depend on the legislation of the rational will nor are they all encompassed by the moral 'ought'. They constitute a realm of objective essences, as do the truths of logic and mathematics, and can similarly be discovered a priori. Values form a complex hierarchical system, and the realization of higher values depends on the realization of lower values, that is, nonmoral values and rudimentary moral values. One cannot properly aspire to sainthood unless one first fulfils one's familial and civic duties. Values can conflict: appropriate action in specific situations requires a combination of different and often conflicting virtues. Hartmann explores the relations between the ancient and the Christian conceptions of virtue.

Values are not realized independently of human activity nor is there any providential power to guarantee their ultimate realization. The nonhuman world is devoid of value and 'sense'. If it were not, human freedom would be restricted. We could not realize values that are already realized or frustrate the realization of values the eventual triumph of which is assured by God. Efficient causality does not threaten freedom, since a causal system or sequence can be diverted by external intervention. But final or teleological causality undermines freedom. Hence Hartmann rejects attempts, theological or otherwise, to find value, meaning and purpose in the nonhuman world. The human being is free, and alone actualizes values, not only moral values, but also aesthetic. A work of art, like any other entity, is primarily a material thing. In it the artist realizes aesthetic value as a sort of superstructure. Hartmann explored the ontology of the work of art, as well as several other 'regional ontologies'. The priority of persons in the realm of value does not correspond to their ontological position. We are latecomers, resting on more fundamental levels of being.

Hartmann's work has much in common with that of other twentieth-century German philosophers. He believed, like SCHELER, in objective, non-formal values, and, like HEIDEGGER, that being is prior to knowledge and that philosophy goes hand in hand with history of philosophy. There are, however, differences. Scheler and Heidegger saw themselves as revolutionaries, changing the direction of philosophy. For Hartmann philosophy steadily advances in the solution of perennial problems. Philosophy is to be pursued for its own sake, not – as Heidegger sometimes suggests – as a prelude to life or *Existenz*. The 'subject' has no such ontological priority for Hartmann as 'Dasein' does for Heidegger. Hence Hartmann proceeds from lower ontological levels to higher, not, as Heidegger does, from the higher to the lower. For example, 'real time' is the uniformly flowing time in which physical objects and events occur; 'experience-time', the time of human awareness and agency, is located within real time but does not determine its nature. Hartmann lacks Heidegger's interest in *being as such*. This coheres with his other views. Our conception of being needs no radical overhaul; he largely accepts traditional categories, such as reality and value. He gives no priority to the human being, who (on Heidegger's view) needs an overall understanding of being in order to make possible the encountering of particular beings. Nor is he tempted to ask 'Why is there anything at all?' or 'Why are we in a world?' It is enough to describe systematically the wealth of beings we encounter.

Hartmann lacked sympathy with existentialism, and with such of its precursors as Nietzsche and Kierkegaard – though he had a close affinity to Hegel. Hartmann is overshadowed by his competitors, but has significant merits: an encyclopedic range, dispassionate rigour of argument, clarity of thought and style, and single-minded devotion to philosophy.

List of works

Hartmann, N. (1909) *Platos Logik des Seins* (Plato's Logic of Being), Giessen: Töpelmann. (The first of many works on ancient philosophy.)
—— (1921) *Grundzüge der Metaphysik der Erkenntnis* (The Basis of the Metaphysics of Knowledge), Berlin: de Gruyter, 2nd edn. 1925. (This work marks Hartmann's break with Neo-Kantianism.)
—— (1923, 1929) *Die Philosophie des deutschen Idealismus* (The Philosophy of German Idealism), vol.1 *Fichte, Schelling und die Romantik*, vol. 2 *Hegel*, Berlin: de Gruyter. (One of the best works

on the subject, combining scholarship with critical acumen.)
—— (1926) *Ethik*, Berlin: de Gruyter; trans as *Ethics*, London: Allen & Unwin, 1932, 3 vols. (Hartmann's main work on value was reviewed by J.S. Mackenzie in *Mind* 42 (1933–4):217–37.)
—— (1933) *Das Problem des geistigen Seins* (The Problem of Spiritual Being), Berlin: de Gruyter. (This deals with objectivized spirit.)
—— (1942) 'Neue Wege der Ontologie', in *Systematische Philosophie*, ed. N. Hartmann, Stuttgart and Berlin: W. Kohlhammer, 199–311; trans. as *New Ways of Ontology*, Chicago, IL: Regnery, 1953. (A clear, brief account of Hartmann's ontology.)
—— (1950) *Philosophie der Natur* (Philosophy of Nature), Berlin: de Gruyter. (Hartmann's last work on the philosophy of nature.)
—— (1953) *Ästhetik*, Berlin: de Gruyter. (A posthumous work on aesthetics.)
—— (1955–7) *Kleinere Schriften* (Shorter Writings), Berlin: de Gruyter, 2 vols. (These volumes contain Hartmann's diverse journal articles.)

References and further reading

Heimsoeth, H. and Heiss, H. (1952) *Nicolai Hartmann: Der Denker und sein Werk* (Nicolai Hartmann: The Thinker and his Work), Göttingen: Vandenhoeck & Ruprecht. (Fifteen essays by German philosophers, with a bibliography of works by and about Hartmann.)
Scheler, M. (1927/8) 'Idealismus – Realismus', *Philosophischer Anzeiger* 2: 255–324; repr. with additions in *Späte Schriften* (Late Works), Bern: Francke, 1976, 183–340; trans. as 'Idealism and Realism' in M. Scheler, *Selected Philosophical Essays*, Evanston, IL: Northwestern University Press, 1973, 288–356. (Criticizes Hartmann's metaphysics of knowledge, and compares him with Heidegger.)
—— (1929) *Philosophische Weltanschauung* (Philosophical Worldview), Bonn: Cohen. (Considers the anti-teleological atheism of Hartmann's *Ethics* together with other 'philosophical worldviews'.)

MICHAEL INWOOD

HASIDISM

Its name literally meaning pietism, Hasidism is a mystical renewal movement that originated in eastern Europe in the mid-eighteenth century. It has become one of the most important spiritual and social developments of Orthodox Judaism and has exerted an influence as well on non-Jews and Jews who are not Orthodox. Early Hasidic leaders claimed their spiritual authority on the basis of heavenly revelations and mystical awakenings. But they generally differed from the more esoterically minded Kabbalists, from whom they drew their earliest following, in seeking to present the fruits of mystical inspiration to the community. Hasidic teachings fostered specific spiritual and ritual innovations, which gave outward expression to the profound nexus that the Hasidic masters saw between mundane existence and the inner, mystical meaning of God's law. According to Hasidic thinking, the divine and the human formed a single, all-encompassing unity, and it was on this basis that the Hasidic rabbis found in acts of Jewish piety means of linking divine experience with human responsiveness. Notable for its vitality and continuity in diversity, Hasidism continues its influence on religious Jewry and beyond to the present day.

1   **Hasidic thought**
2   **The Hasidic ethos and worship**

1   Hasidic thought

Hasidism arises out of the tendency of Kabbalistic leaders to claim charismatic authority and mystical inspiration (see KABBALAH). The early Hasidic figures used such claims to set out original ideas about God and worship. They established new patterns of leadership based on a sense of immediate connection with the divine presence and the central relevance of that presence to all aspects of life. The founder of Hasidism, Rabbi Israel Ben Eliezer (1698–1760), known as the Ba'al Shem Tov or by the acronym BESHT, drew his following from the eastern European circles devoted to the Lurianic Kabbalah, a tradition of esoteric mysticism, ascetic seclusion, spiritual devotion and reliance on the efficacy of ecstatic prayer. The spiritual life organized by these charismatic leaders was routinized in a social structure grounded upon mystical leadership but capable of profound impact on broad circles of followers. The Ba'al Shem Tov sought to bring a similar structure to a much wider public.

Hasidic thought rests on the assumption that all things in this world are imbued with divine vitality. A hidden core of divine essence sustains all outward existence. God is omnipresent and manifest in all dimensions of existence, permeating every human act, every thought, and every material object (see OMNI-PRESENCE). Physical objects, seen in the light of the infinite, are illusory mantles, mere vessels for the divine presence (*shekhinah*). Reality, then, is a spiritual core enveloped by a physical exterior, a divine unity disguised within the multiplicity of

corporeality. The linked but opposing visages of the internal and external – the hidden divine substance and its material manifestation – condition one another. For the divine essence cannot be revealed except in its corporeal manifestation, but material existence has no actuality without the sustaining divine essence.

The matrix from which Hasidic worship springs is this assumption that the divine essence (*'ayin* – literally, 'nothingness') preconditions every mundane and spiritual phenomenon (*yesh* – literally, 'being') and that beyond perceived reality (*yesh*) abides a hidden truth (*'ayin*). Reality, then, is a dialectical whole composed from being and nothingness, in which all things are united with their opposites and combined with their inversions. The opposing elements annihilate, garb, sustain, transform and change one another from being into nothingness and from nothingness into being. The fullest expression of each spiritual element resides within its manifestation through inversion. The truth of reality is the struggle to achieve this reversal, abstraction and restoration of each thing to its source.

Hasidism strives to establish a connection both with the hidden divine element which vitalizes manifest concrete reality and with the divine presence beyond the material garment. Thus the paramount demand of Hasidic worship is for constant realization of the overwhelming presence of the divine and the acknowledgement of the inherent unity of opposites. Hasidic literature reflects this interest and is replete with expressions indicating the contemplative consciousness to which the *hasid* (devotee) is to aspire: *devekut* (literally, 'cleaving') devotion in study and contemplation of the incongruity between the divine essentiality and its physical manifestation is sought through the perception of the spiritual inwardness that lines material reality. Such awareness can lead to ecstatic union with the divine presence. *Bittul hayesh* – nullification of existence – is contemplation of divine reality through its corporeal garment, stripping away corporeality. *Avoda be-gashmiut* – service in corporeality – is the daily obligation to illuminate the mundane with its hidden divine essence. *Ha'alat nizozot* – literally, 'raising sparks' – is elevation of divine elements in one's consciousness in order to assess the true meaning of *yesh* and *'ayin*. All of these notions are adapted from the Kabbalah, but now qualified to accommodate the new theology.

2   The Hasidic ethos and worship

Hasidic efforts to achieve contemplative consciousness by abolishing sensory experience are called the subordination of the eyes of the flesh to the eyes of

243

the intellect. The goal is realization of the ultimate unreality of material existence. Only the all-pervasive divine presence is ultimately real. Existence and nothingness are no longer determined by empirical criteria but through contemplation. The transformation of human consciousness implies an obligation to lay bare the divine in all things and discover the unity behind the specious multifariousness of appearances. The separate existence of all things in thought must be nullified. The ultimate goal is proximity to God.

To remove all encumbrances to awareness, Hasidism proposes an ethos based on equanimity, worldly abnegation, and 'the nullification of existence'. Human thought is at the forefront of the spiritual struggle, since its creative and transformative powers and its capabilities of unifying opposites mark it clearly as the divine element in man. Although amorphous in itself, thought has the divine power to penetrate to the truth of things and illuminate the consciousness concealed and imprisoned within tangible externalities, to remove the barriers separating the divine presence from human contact, and so, ultimately, to achieve union with God.

The spiritual impetus that Hasidism founded upon transformative thought brought about a renewed appraisal of the means and ends of spiritual activity. Spiritual ascension, for example, had been pursued by Kabbalistic practitioners through penitential mortification and the cultivation of lofty spiritual and moral virtues arranged on a mystical ladder that led to God. This scheme was now discarded in favour of direct contact with a divine omnipresence that was freely accessible to all. Hasidic theology demanded only that human consciousness be directed towards devotion to God and proximity to his presence through contemplation of the dual visage of existence.

Hasidic dialectical assumptions made the mystic's focus on the inner, spiritual dimensions of religious life into a matter of public, communal concern. As one popular Hasidic saying has it, 'Because God is present in every place and human thought is present in every place about which one thinks, every act, every time and every place can serve as the point of departure for every man's contemplation of the divine inwardness of reality that lies beyond its physical garments'. In the Hasidic idiom this claim is finely honed by the radical pietist slogan 'In all your ways, know Him'.

The most conspicuous conclusion that Hasidism draws from this thought is an expansion of worship to include the most mundane and secular actions, by virtue of the thought and intentionality that illuminate and accompany them. 'Worship through corporeality' means that any mundane act may become divine service, if performed with the proper intention.

The sanctification of the mundane and the conversion of all aspects of life to divine service become core features of Hasidism. But these reflect the centrality of thought and intention in Hasidism. The claim for divine immanence and omnipresence, reiterated throughout Hasidic literature, entails an unfettered but also unbounded human obligation to seek and attain this immanence. Herein lies the deep conflict with the basic worldview of the Kabbalah. For not only is the Kabbalistic hierarchy denied but the very boundaries between heavenly and earthly existence are obliterated. The transcendental Godhead has been displaced by an immanent and accessible divinity, and the wall between esoteric and exoteric has been removed, allowing the attainment of divinity, in principle, by anyone (see GOD, CONCEPTS OF).

These changes had far-reaching social ramifications. Worship now extends far beyond the realm of accepted convention and common Kabbalistic interpretation. The often conventional reliance on acts alone as a standard of religious commitment is displaced as intention and consciousness move to the fore. Further, the assumption that the divine presence is the core within all fosters a substantial expansion of the social circles for whom a spiritual life on the highest order is accessible. All is God, and God is everywhere. Everyone, without exception, should approach the divine in all possible ways. The Hasidic mystical leader and his community become counterparts, envisaged through the polarity of *yesh ve-'ayin*. Detailed guidance in the worship of God and a sense of guardianship for the individual and the whole Jewish people led to the formation of a new spiritual agenda and new social affinities.

Opposition to the Hasidic movement was not slow to appear, focused on principled reservations to the doctrine of immanence but also aware of the broader significances of that idea. Controversy, infighting, schism, social conflict, denunciations to the ruling authorities of Russia and Poland, and a mountain of polemic marked the spread of Hasidism. The controversy, like the Hasidic ideas themselves, can still be felt within the Orthodox Jewish community today. On the other hand, Hasidism proved to be a source of inspiration to such thinkers as Martin BUBER.

The spiritual self perception of Hasidism is best represented in its voluminous homiletic literature, known as *Sifrut ha-Drush*, emerging in 1780 and continuing to the present. This literature shows the diversity and creativity of Hasidic mysticism and sheds light on its social ramifications. The major innovations of Hasidism are also represented in short tracts from the end of the eighteenth century, known as *Sifrut ha-Hanhagot*, which are abridgements of the homiletic literature. The controversial position of Hasidism is reflected in the polemical literature known as *Sifrut Hasidim ve-Mitnaggdim* and *Sifrut ha-Haskalah*, representing the controversies with Orthodox 'Opponents' of Hasidism on the one hand and with the exponents of the Jewish Enlightenment of the other (see ENLIGHTENMENT, JEWISH). The unique Hasidic social structure and the major role of the *Zaddik* (Hasidic mystical leader) are reflected in the Hasidic tale, a literary genre known as *Sifrut ha-Sipurim ha-Hasidit*.

See also: BUDDHIST CONCEPT OF EMPTINESS; GOD, CONCEPTS OF; KABBALAH; MYSTICISM, NATURE OF

References and further reading

Elior, R. (1988) 'Between Yesh and Ayin: The Doctrine of the Zaddik in the Works of Jacob Issac, the Seer of Lublin', in A. Rapoport-Albert and S. Zipperstein (eds) *Jewish History: Essays in Honour of Chimen Abramsky*, London: Peter Halban, 393–455. (A study of the mystical foundations of Hasidic social innovation.)

—— (1993) *The Paradoxical Ascent to God: The Kabbalistic Theosophy of Habad Hasidism*, Albany, NY: State University of New York Press. (A study of Lubavitch Hasidism, its mystical ideas and religious practice, in the late eighteenth and early nineteenth centuries.)

—— (1996) 'The Paradigms of Yesh and Ayin in Hasidic Thought', in A. Rapoport-Albert (ed.) *Hasidism Reappraised*, London: Littman Library. (An introductory essay on the foundations of Hasidic mysticism.)

—— (1997) *Israel Ba'al Shem Tov: Between Magic and Mysticism*, Jerusalem: Am Oved. (Comprehensive study of the BESHT and the innovative aspects of his mystical teaching.)

Etkes, I. (1988) 'Hasidism as a Movement: The First Stage', in B. Safran (ed.) *Hasidism, Continuity or Innovation*, Cambridge, MA: Harvard University Press. (Concise historical reappraisal of the emergence of Hasidism.)

Green, A. (1981) 'Hasidism: Discovery and Retreat', in P.L. Berger (ed.) *The Other Side of God*, Princeton, NJ: Princeton University Press. (A concise discussion of the major spiritual issues in Hasidism.)

Heschel, A.J. (1989) *The Circle of the Ba'al Shem Tov*, Chicago. IL: University of Chicago Press. (A study of the group that initiated the Hasidic movement in the first half of the eighteenth century.)

Loewenthal N. (1990) *Communicating the Infinite*, Chicago, IL: University of Chicago Press. (A study of the methods of propagating mystical ideas to broad circles in Lubavitch Hasidism in the nineteenth century.)

Rapoport-Albert, A. (1979) 'God and the Zaddik as Two Focal Points of Hasidic Worship', *History of Religion* 18 (4): 296–325. (A study on the Hasidic Tzaddik and his mystical and social role.)

Schatz-Ufffenheimer, R. (1968) *Hasidism as Mysticism, Quietistic Elements in Eighteenth Century Thought*, Princeton, NJ: Princeton University Press. (Comprehensive discussion of the mystical elements in Hasidic thought.)

Scholem, G. (1949–50) 'Devekut and Communion with God', in *Review of Religion* 14: 115–39. (A study of a major Hasidic mystical concept.)

Weiss, J. (1985) *Studies in Eastern European Jewish Mysticism*, Oxford: Oxford University Press. (Essays on various aspects of Hasidism, integrating phenomenological and historical approaches.)

RACHEL ELIOR

HASKALAH *see* ENLIGHTENMENT, JEWISH

HAYEK, FRIEDRICH AUGUST VON (1899–1992)

An Austrian-born British economist who turned political philosopher, Hayek was best known for his critique of socialism and the modern welfare state. Writing as an avowed classical liberal (he repudiated the label 'conservative'), he attempted to develop his account of the market as a mechanism facilitating economic coordination into a more general theory of law and politics.

Hayek's liberalism was first formulated as a response to totalitarianism, which he regarded as a tendency manifest in the regimes of Nazi Germany and Stalinist Russia, and inherent in proposals for central planning in society. This was the basis of his early opposition to socialism and his theory of limited constitutional government under the rule of law. The development of his political thought, however, saw him become increasingly critical of government and its interventions in the spontaneous evolution of society. Society was a 'spontaneous order' and not the product of human design. The threat to this order or civilization came from mankind's mistaken confidence in reason's capacity to take control of social processes to shape society in accordance with particular ideals. Socialism, as well as proposals for social justice, he regarded as variants of this tendency, which he labelled 'constructivist rationalism'. This social philosophy was underpinned by a philosophy of science which emphasized the subjective character of the data of the social sciences.

1 **Life**
2 **Economics and social philosophy**
3 **Political philosophy**

1 Life

Coming from a distinguished Austrian family of scientists and academics (he was a cousin of Ludwig Wittgenstein), Hayek entered the University of Vienna after serving in the First World War. Graduating with doctorates in law (1921) and political science (1923), he became a legal consultant in the civil service and, later, director of the Austrian Institute for Business Cycle Research. After a period as *Privatdozent* in Political Economy at the University of Vienna, Hayek accepted an invitation to lecture at the London School of Economics in 1931, and subsequently was appointed Tooke Professor of Economic Science and Statistics.

In the 1930s Hayek engaged in several important controversies in monetary economics, capital theory and business cycle research, taking issue with John Maynard KEYNES (§3) and Pierro Sraffa. He also played a leading role in debates over the possibility of economic calculation under socialism. With Ludwig von Mises, Hayek argued against economists such as Oskar Lange that, once prices in a market economy were recognized as carriers of information, it had to be conceded that central planning was impossible: command economies had no mechanisms for coordinating economic knowledge.

When he became a British citizen in 1938, Hayek's reputation as an economist rivalled that of Keynes. Yet it was the publication in 1944 of *The Road to Serfdom* that brought him to the attention of a wider public. Warning that economic planning would subvert the institutions of a free society, the book become a controversial bestseller and established Hayek's reputation as a critic of government economic intervention at a time when arguments for central planning were in the ascendant.

In 1950 Hayek moved to the University of Chicago as Professor of Social and Moral Sciences on the Committee on Social Thought. Most of the following decade was devoted to work on his political treatise, *The Constitution of Liberty* (1960), although he also published an important collection of the J.S.Mill–Harriet Taylor correspondence, and edited a collec-

tion of papers on *Capitalism and the Historians* (1954). In 1962 he retired from Chicago to the University of Freiburg and then, in 1967, to the University of Salzburg. In the 1970s he continued his work on the philosophy of law in his trilogy, *Law, Legislation and Liberty* (1973–9). Interest in his work revived following his award of the 1974 Nobel Prize for Economics. In the 1980s Hayek set out upon another ambitious project: a three-volume refutation of socialism. A single volume, *The Fatal Conceit: The Intellectual Error of Socialism*, appeared in 1989, three years before his death.

2 Economics and social philosophy

Hayek belonged to the Austrian school of economics. He studied under Friedrich von Wieser, but his work also bears the influence of Carl Menger and Ludwig von Mises. Hayek's economic theory offers a general account of economics as a coordination problem. The economic problem of society is not how to allocate given resources; it is, rather, 'how to secure the best use of resources known to any of the members of society, for ends whose relative importance only these individuals know'. Hayek's theory of capital, and his work on trade cycles and on money, attempt to account for failures of economic coordination, particularly over time. He rejected Keynes' economics which, he thought, ignored the temporal structure of production and so did not properly comprehend how market processes facilitated economic coordination over time. More generally, he objected to neoclassical equilibrium analysis which, he held, conflated individual choice at one point in time with market processes over time. Such models made assumptions about the knowledge possessed by economic agents which it was the task of economics to uncover.

Methodologically, these views have their origin in the Austrian school's subjective theory of value, which holds that value, far from being an inherent property of any object, is conferred upon goods by the subjective preferences of agents. Austrians such as Mises thus concluded that economics was an a priori or apodictic science: economic laws were deductions from a few basic axioms about human action. Hayek, however, rejected the radical subjectivism implicit in this conception of economic theory. In 'Economics and Knowledge' (1937) he articulated an empirical conception of the nature of economics as a body of testable theories; yet at the same time he rejected general equilibrium models of analysis.

The problem with such models, he thought, was that they were unable to explain how equilibrium (or a state of coordination of different individual purposes) was achieved. This was because the theory of perfect competition at their core ignored the adjustment process required to reach equilibrium. The standard assumptions of economic theory accepted as given: (1) complete knowledge on the part of economic agents; (2) the absence of costs or restraints upon the movement of goods and prices; and (3) a homogeneous commodity being supplied and demanded by many sellers and buyers. These assumptions were untenable because the economic world was a world in motion – one in which the process of coordinating economic plans took place despite the ignorance of economic agents, the existence of transaction costs and the subjective character of the individual valuation of commodities. Hayek thus rejected Lionel Robbins' influential interpretation of economics as the science that studied the allocation of scarce means among competing ends. This view presumed something false: that knowledge of those means and ends was given.

At the heart of Hayek's economics is a view of the nature of knowledge. This has two important aspects. First, Hayek distinguished two kinds of knowledge: theoretical or articulated knowledge, and tacit or unarticulated knowledge. Theoretical knowledge exists in the form of explicit statements and is the product of conscious reflection. Tacit knowledge, however, is unarticulated; it exists in the skills, instincts and dispositions of individuals and is also embodied in institutions and practices. (This distinction encompasses Gilbert Ryle's distinction between 'knowing that' and 'knowing how'; see RYLE, G.) Most knowledge, Hayek thought, was of the latter sort; and its existence was also, therefore, dependent upon context or local circumstances. Second, Hayek argued that much of human knowledge is not only dispersed but also, because it is unarticulated, is incapable of being collected.

This view had an important bearing upon Hayek's economic argument, particularly in the socialist calculation debates. Here Hayek extended Mises' analysis of the impossibility of rational calculation under socialism. Mises had criticized socialist economics for not recognizing that economic value was subjective. Valuation could only take place in terms of units, yet it was impossible that there should ever be a unit of subjective use-value for goods. Judgments of value did not measure but established grades or scales, and, in the exchange economy, the 'objective exchange-value' of commodities became the unit of economic calcuation. In a monetary exchange economy *money* was the good used as the unit in which exchange-values are defined. While the value of money might fluctuate as its value relative to other goods changed, monetary calculation enabled us to

judge the relative values of all goods and so to make production plans over time.

Hayek accepted Mises' argument that, without a pricing mechanism (given the defects of calculation in terms of labour rather than money), there could be no economic calculation. He pressed this critique of socialist economics further, however, by arguing that the fundamental problem was not calculational but epistemological. In 'The Use of Knowledge in Society' (1945) he argued that the problem to be solved when seeking to construct a 'rational economic order' is not a logical problem to be overcome using all relevant information concerning preferences and the factors of production. The data from which economic calculus begins are never given complete to a single mind which could work out their implications. The nature of the problem of a rational economic order is: 'determined precisely by the fact that the knowledge of the circumstances of which we must make use never exists in concentrated or integrated form but solely as the dispersed bits of incomplete and frequently contradictory knowledge which all the separate individuals possess' (Hayek 1945) (see SOCIALISM §2).

This division of knowledge Hayek thought to be the central problem of economics as a social science. However, investigating this problem meant moving away from the study of 'the economy' as a fixed domain marked by clear boundaries. Economies, in the strict sense in which households or enterprises can be called economies, consist of a complex of activities by which a given set of means is allocated in accordance with a unitary plan among the competing ends according to their relative importance. But the domain of human exchange encompasses not a single economy. What is commonly called a social or national economy is in fact a network of many economies. While such an order shares with an economy proper some formal characteristics, it does not share the most important one: its activities are not governed by a single hierarchy of ends. A better term for the extended order of human cooperation, Hayek suggests, is 'catallaxy': an order brought about by the mutual adjustment of many individual economies in a market. The task of economics is to investigate this order; but this also means that economics, ultimately, involves a more general investigation of social institutions.

Hayek's economics is therefore part of a larger social philosophy describing the extended order of society. The key to this account is his concept of 'spontaneous order'. For Hayek, an order is: 'a state of affairs in which a multiplicity of elements of various kinds are so related to each other that we may learn from our acquaintance with some spatial or temporal part of the whole to form correct expectations concerning the rest'. Order can be created by forces outside the system or it may be created from within as an equilibrium is generated by the interaction of elements whose natures impel them towards stable formations. This distinction is between an order that is 'made' and one that is formed spontaneously given the existence of particular elements in an environment. In the social world, the mind, language, law, and indeed society itself, should be understood as spontaneous orders.

In viewing society as a spontaneous order Hayek emphasizes that it is not the product of human design. While it is the result of human intention, it evolves without anyone controlling its development. This is partly because the knowledge possessed by any individual is so limited that no one could understand more than a fraction of the social environment. But it is also because not only society but also the individual is in a state of continuous evolution. Human nature – and mind and reason themselves – are not fixed but evolve with society (see ECONOMICS, PHILOSOPHY OF §3).

The important conclusion Hayek draws from this social philosophy is that individual reason is incapable of comprehending the social order in its entirety. Therefore, reason should not overreach itself by attempting to control or redirect the development of society. Such attempts would not only fail in their own terms but also threaten the progress of civilization, and the future evolution of reason itself. This concern about the 'abuse of reason' is the basis of Hayek's political philosophy.

3   Political philosophy

In his politics, Hayek defined himself as a classical liberal. He rejected socialism, but also denied that he was any sort of a conservative.

Hayek's liberalism stems from his social philosophy. His objection to socialism was that its aims, while noble, were unattainable. Its hope to bring about a planned society, organized in accordance with some common purpose, in which social forces were brought under human control, was in Hayek's view incapable of being fulfilled. The cost of the attempt, he argued, would be not only material impoverishment but also the gradual loss of individual liberty. The greatest danger to modern civilization came from the alliance of socialism with nationalism, which threatened to destroy the 'extended order of human cooperation' by drawing boundaries closing off societies in separate, controlled states.

Liberalism, for Hayek was a philosophy opposed to socialism and to nationalism. Its starting point was an understanding of society as a 'spontaneous' order. Any plausible answer to the question of what are the best social and political arrangements for human beings must be based upon this understanding. Hayek's answer is that human relations should be governed by arrangements which preserve liberty, with liberty understood as 'independence of the arbitrary will of another'. His political philosophy thus argues that a liberal society is one governed by the rule of law, and that justice is served only if law delimits the scope of individual freedom. In short, liberalism favours a 'free' society in which individual conduct is regulated by rules of justice, so that all may pursue their own purposes in peace (see LIBERALISM §2).

The ideal of equality has a place in this scheme only in so far as Hayek concedes that the aim of the struggle for liberty has been equality before the law. Individual differences do not justify different treatment. However, this will inevitably lead to inequality in the actual positions people occupy and to material inequality. In Hayek's view, the state is not justified in using coercion to try to reduce or eliminate such inequalities. His objection is not to equality as such but to any attempt to impose a chosen pattern of distribution.

For the same reason, he objects to attempts to distribute goods according to 'merit' (see DESERT AND MERIT). If the principle of reward according to merit were institutionalized, we would end up with attempts to control remuneration which would in turn require even more controls upon human activity. For Hayek, this would not make for a free society since authority would decide what individuals were to do and how they were to do it.

The fear of this outcome is also the basis of his rejection of demands for equal distribution based upon membership of a particular community or nation. Membership of a national community does not, in Hayek's liberalism, confer entitlements to any share of national wealth. The result of recognizing any such entitlement would be that, rather than admit people to the advantages that living in their country offers, a nation will prefer to keep them out altogether.

In his early political writings, which include *The Road to Serfdom* and *The Constitution of Liberty*, Hayek argued that liberalism required a constitutional regime of limited government (see CONSTITUTIONALISM §2). Government's essential function is to enforce the abstract rules of the society applying equally to all, although it is also charged with the task of preserving the market order. Beyond these, government also has a legitimate role to play in the administration of the resources of society to render some services to citizens, and also to provide a welfare safety net for the poor. It is not, however, any part of government's role to secure a particular distribution of income or wealth. This argument was developed at greater length in *The Mirage of Social Justice*, volume 2 of *Law, Legislation and Liberty*, which rejected the idea of social justice as not only unattainable but also 'meaningless'.

Yet while *The Constitution of Liberty* conceded a substantial – if limited – role for government in a constitutional regime, Hayek became progressively more critical of government as his political thinking developed. In *Law, Legislation and Liberty*, he began to criticize government's extensive legislative powers. This was an aspect of the development of his philosophy of law, which became increasingly critical of all forms of legal positivism (see LEGAL POSITIVISM). It also ushered in some interesting speculations about constitutional reform, although these sat uncomfortably with his growing scepticism about any kind of intervention in the spontaneous order of society by government.

This was the source of the fundamental difficulties in Hayek's political thought. As an intellectual who was genuinely concerned for the plight of post-war civilization, Hayek was a tireless advocate, arguing about the appropriate role of government and the conduct of policy. Yet his philosophical starting point was an emphasis upon human ignorance and the limits of reason, and the impossibility of humans controlling their social development. When, and for what reason, government could legitimately intervene in the processes of social evolution was thus difficult to establish.

Hayek's thought none the less is of interest as a liberal political philosophy. It is the most ambitious attempt in the twentieth century to develop a comprehensive liberal system of ideas. In its emphasis upon the danger of central control of knowledge, Hayek's thought also offers a liberalism whose core is strikingly postmodern.

See also: ECONOMICS, PHILOSOPHY OF; LIBERALISM

List of works

Hayek, F.A. von (1937) *'Economics and Knowledge'*, *Economica* 4 (new series): 33–54. (Hayek's first articulation of his economic theory.)
—— (1944) *The Road to Serfdom*, London: Routledge & Kegan Paul. (Hayek's polemical first political work, arguing against central planning.)
—— (1945) 'The Use of Knowledge in Society', *American Economic Review* 35 (4): 519–30. (On how to create a rational economic order in society.)
—— (1948) *Individualism and Economic Order*, Chicago, IL: University of Chicago Press. (Contains important economic essays, as well as his contributions to the socialist calculation debates.)
—— (1952) *The Counter-Revolution of Science*, Glencoe, IL: Free Press. (Develops Hayek's philosophy of science.)
—— (ed.) (1954) *Capitalism and the Historians*, Chicago, IL: University of Chicago Press. (A collection of revisionist essays defending capitalism, introduced by Hayek)
—— (1960) *The Constitution of Liberty*, London: Routledge. (A statement of Hayek's liberalism containing his theory of the rule of law.)
—— (1973–9) *Law, Legislation and Liberty*, London: Routledge, 3 vols. (Presents Hayek's later legal philosophy and also his arguments against social justice.)
—— (1989) *The Fatal Conceit: The Intellectual Error of Socialism*, London: Routledge. (The last statement of Hayek's critique of socialism.)

References and further reading

Barry, N. (1979) *Hayek's Social and Economic Philosophy*, London: Macmillan. (An expository account of Hayek's social and economic thought.)
Gray, J. (1986) *Hayek on Liberty*, Oxford: Blackwell. (A comprehensive review of Hayek's system of ideas with an extensive bibliography.)
Kukathas, C. (1989) *Hayek and Modern Liberalism*, Oxford: Oxford University Press. (A critical examination of Hayek's liberalism.)

CHANDRAN KUKATHAS

HEAVEN

In Christian theology, heaven is both the dwelling place of God and the angels, and the place where all who are saved ultimately go after death and judgment to receive their eternal reward. The doctrine of the resurrection of the body requires that heaven be a place because it must contain the glorified bodies of the redeemed, but heaven is more theologically important as a state than as a place. This state is traditionally described as involving the most intimate union with God without the elimination of the individual human personality (the beatific vision); it is a state of perfect bliss beyond anything possible on earth. In high medieval theology, the happiness of heaven is understood to be so great that it is even beyond the capability of human nature to enjoy without divine aid. There are varying views on the nature of heavenly society, however, with some theologians (Augustine, Aquinas, Bonaventure) arguing that perfect happiness will be derived from the love of God alone, while others (for example, Giles of Rome) stress the joy that will be derived from the company of the elect. More recently, interest in the nature of heaven has declined, and Christian theology has tended to play down its importance.

1   Heaven in the Bible
2   Heaven in salvation history
3   The beatific vision
4   The society of heaven
5   The decline of heaven in contemporary theology

1   Heaven in the Bible

The Hebrew word for heaven or the heavens (*samayim*) means 'that which is above the earth'; in particular, it refers to that which is above the firmament (*raqia*). This, in the book of Genesis, is a solid vault in the visible sky holding back the waters beyond (Genesis 1: 8; Psalms 148: 4–6); it contains windows that open to let rain fall on the earth (Genesis 7: 11; 2 Kings 7: 2, 19), and the stars are suspended from it (Genesis 1: 14). The heavens are God's handiwork, but are also the special domain of God himself. While it is vicious pride that leads human beings to attempt to reach heaven, as in the tower of Babel (Genesis 11: 1–9), the Hebrew tradition stresses the idea that while God is transcendent, he is also active in the history of his people and comes down repeatedly to intervene in human affairs; he is, in fact, omnipresent (Psalm 139: 8–10). In the New Testament, the ministry of Jesus begins with the heavens opening (Matthew 3: 16) in order that salvation might descend to earth. Christ returns to his Father in heaven (John 6: 62; 13: 1) and prepares a place for his followers (John 14: 3). The Ascension of Jesus into heaven (Mark 16: 19; Luke 24: 51; Acts 1: 9) led Christians to await the return of Christ, when both heaven and earth will be transformed (Isaiah 65: 17; Romans 8: 19–23; 2 Peter 3: 13; Revelation 21: 1). The Book of Revelation contains vivid imagery of resurrection, judgment and the City of God after the Second Coming.

2   Heaven in salvation history

In Hebrew thought, the belief that human beings were raised to heaven after death was not widespread. It was distinctive of Christian faith to interpret the crucifixion of Christ as a victory over death as well as over sin. Belief in a victory over death included not only belief in eternal life beyond the grave, but also

belief in a resurrection of the body. This doctrine was predicated on the resurrection of Jesus from the tomb and was connected with the early Christian concern with the end of history and the expectation of the Second Coming (the *Parousia*); at this time, Christ would return in glory, the dead would be raised, all would be judged, and those who were saved would be taken to heaven to enjoy eternal glory. Heaven is therefore the culmination of salvation history. But it has always been a part of Christian belief that even before the general resurrection at least some of the redeemed will be with Christ, although in traditional Roman Catholic teaching some are detained for a time in purgatory. It is possible, then, to enjoy the glory of heaven without the resurrected body, so it must be a place/state for which bodies are not necessary. Still, AQUINAS (§10) maintained that the enjoyment of heaven after the resurrection of the body will be greater than in the disembodied state. He argued that this must be the case because the operation of the soul united to a body is more perfect than the operation of the separated soul. Since happiness consists in an operation, he reasoned, the soul's happiness after bodily reunion will be greater than before (*Summa theologiae* IIIa, q.93, a.1, corpus). Heavenly bliss is therefore enhanced by the union of the human soul with the resurrected body (see ESCHATOLOGY §3).

Glorified bodies are said by Aquinas to have the qualities of impassibility, subtlety, agility and clarity (*Summa theologiae* IIIa, qq.82–5). Impassibility means that the glorified body does not suffer and does not need to preserve itself from wear or harm from within or without. Aquinas identifies subtlety with the power to penetrate. This was sometimes interpreted as the ability to pass through other bodies, but Aquinas identifies it with the perfect subjection of the body to the soul (*Summa theologiae* IIIa, q.83, a.1, corpus). Agility allows the glorified body to move about unimpeded and with great rapidity. Clarity makes the glorified body luminous and brilliant to behold even to the non-glorified eye.

In Roman Catholic theology, there is no official position on the spatial characteristics of heaven or its relationship to the physical universe, in part because of the problem of explaining how it can be the abode of non-physical beings. However, some fundamentalist Christians interpret the Bible as referring to heaven as a physical place. The Latter Day Saints (Mormons) believe that the Second Coming will usher in a thousand-year reign of Jesus on earth which will involve the physical transformation of the planet into a Garden of Eden. This belief in a thousand-year reign after the Second Coming (millenarianism) has appeared from time to time in Christian history, in such groups as the Gnostics, the Montanists, the Anabaptists and the Pietists. Millenarianism never dominated the Christian tradition, but many theologians, including Aquinas, maintained that after the general resurrection and last judgment the earth will be transformed in a way analogous to the glorification of the human body (*Summa contra gentiles* IV, ch. 96). Since it was generally thought that the renewed earth would become part of heaven, it followed that heaven, or some part of heaven, has at least quasi-spatial features. On the other hand, Aquinas thought that the transformed physical universe will have no temporal features, but will be permanent and changeless. At the end of time, the earth and all heavenly bodies will stand still (*Summa theologiae* IIIa, q.91, a.2). Heaven itself is a static state to which nothing can be added and nothing taken away.

3 The beatific vision

The essential element in the state of heavenly glory is the beatific vision, which was defined by Aquinas as the intuitive vision of God in his essence. The idea is inspired by Paul: 'We see now through a glass darkly, but then face to face' (1 Corinthians 13: 12). This doctrine is theologically important because it indicates that the enjoyment of God in heaven is not only a historical end, or the aim of the divine plan of human salvation, but constitutes the fulfilment of the nature of each individual human person. Adopting Aristotle's teleological view of nature, Aquinas describes human beings as incomplete and in a state of movement towards an end that fulfils that for which they were designed. Like ARISTOTLE (§21), Aquinas identifies the end of human life as happiness; happiness is what human beings by nature desire. But unlike Aristotle, Aquinas maintains that true happiness is not possible in this life (*Summa theologiae* IaIIae, q.5, a.3). He interprets the desire for happiness as a natural but obscure awareness in each human person that their goal is union with the supreme good. Since the supreme good is God, it follows that there is a natural but obscure desire for union with God, and this union is the supernatural end for which every human being was created. Aquinas thus combines Aristotelian metaphysics with the Christian theology of AUGUSTINE (§11), whose famous prayer 'Our hearts are restless until they rest in thee, oh Lord' expresses the failure of the fulfilment of human desires in this life.

The doctrine of the beatific vision raises interesting questions about the nature and limits of human knowledge. Aquinas was clearly concerned with the problem of whether a finite created being can actually know an uncreated infinite deity. He decided that it is

beyond the nature of created beings to do so, but supernatural help enhances the human and angelic intellects to make this possible. Aquinas calls this aid 'illumination'. In the beatific vision, Aquinas says, God himself is in direct contact with the human mind; this contact is not via images or concepts, which are the only ways human beings can have knowledge otherwise (*Summa theologiae* IIIa, q.92, a.1). As infinite truth, God alone is able to satisfy fully the human and angelic intellects, which are made for the possession of truth. As infinitely desirable, God alone is able to satisfy the desires of the human heart or the angelic will. The end for which human beings were created is thus a gratuitous gift of God, one which is fully satisfying, but which human beings would be incapable of enjoying without supernatural aid. The blessed in heaven will not all enjoy the beatific vision in equal measure, however. There will be degrees of happiness and union with God corresponding to the degrees of merit of persons at death (*Summa theologiae* IIIa, q.93, a.2–3).

The secondary object of the beatific vision is our continuing knowledge of the beings and events of creation. These will be known through the vision of the divine essence in whom all things are known. This raises a series of questions about the importance of contingent relationships to human happiness. Since human beings in heaven are self-conscious egos, it is reasonable to think that they do not lose their memories of the past or their attachment to particular persons. But what if certain persons loved while on earth are absent from heaven? Aquinas says that no unhappiness would result from this, since all delight is in God and in God there can be no attachment to evil or to evil persons. But as long as it is admitted that there is enjoyment in the company of the elect, it is reasonable to think that there would have been greater delight had certain loved ones been saved. Furthermore, it is difficult to believe that the blessed in heaven would want to observe the sufferings of the damned. Yet Aquinas not only maintains that they do, but that this enhances their bliss:

> Everything is known the more for being compared with its contrary.... Therefore in order that the happiness of the saints may be more delightful to them and that they may render more copious thanks to God for it, they are allowed to see perfectly the sufferings of the damned.
>
> (*Summa theologiae* IIIa, q.94, a.1, corpus)

4 The society of heaven

McDannell and Lang (1988) raise the problem of how happiness deriving from the particularity of human relationships is related to happiness deriving from the vision of God. They claim that there are two strands in the history of the idea of heaven in Christian thought, one theocentric and one anthropocentric, and that the two are in tension with each other. The dominant theocentric strand either ignores or at least downgrades social joys in heaven. Bonaventure, like Augustine, rejected any idea of individualized friendships in heaven. Likewise, Aquinas says that there will be no sexual love or enjoyment of food in heaven (*Summa contra gentiles*, ch. 83) – a view contrasting with the Islamic heaven – and that friendship is not necessary for perfect happiness: 'But if we speak of perfect Happiness which will be in our heavenly Fatherland, the fellowship of friends is not essential to Happiness, since man has the entire fullness of his perfection in God' (*Summa theologiae* IaIIae, q.4, a.8). Aquinas implies, though, that while the love of friends is unnecessary, it will still exist as derived from the love of God: 'And so if there were but one soul enjoying God, it would be happy, though having no neighbour to love. But supposing one neighbour to be there, love of him results from love of God' (*Summa theologiae* IaIIae, q.4, a.8, ad.3).

The other strand identified by McDannell and Lang emphasizes the joy of the company of the elect. This strand has appeared from time to time throughout the Christian era. While Aquinas was somewhat reticent about the extent of social life in heaven, his student Giles of Rome was not, and he speculated that the saints form a heavenly *societas perfecta*. During the nineteenth century, a conception of heaven as full of earthly delights, including all the pleasures of social relations, replaced the theocentric conception in the popular imagination and represented the apex of the anthropocentric view of heaven. Although this conception of heaven has largely been discarded in theology (with the exception of Mormon theology), it has not usually been replaced by a well-developed theocentric theology. With a few exceptions (for example, Hick 1976), heaven is not a significant topic in contemporary theology. Occasionally, however, some interesting new problems about heaven have been raised. Examples are the problem as to whether the unchangeability of heaven would make it boring, and the problem of there seeming to be a significant amount of luck involved in getting there. This is because part of what gets a person to heaven is what one does during life, but what one does during life is partly determined by such things as the kind of upbringing one has, the circumstances in which one makes choices, and even the timing of one's death (see Zagzebski 1994). There is also, of course, the traditional dispute over predestination (see PREDESTINATION).

5 The decline of heaven in contemporary theology

There has been a decline of interest in Christian theology regarding what were traditionally called the 'last things': death, judgment, the resurrection of the body, and heaven and hell. In the Roman Catholic Church, this may be partly due to embarrassment over the centuries of teaching the faithful to accept their lot in life, no matter how poor, on the grounds that the important thing was the next life. Heaven is mentioned only briefly in the documents of Vatican II, and the influential Jesuit theologian Karl Rahner said late in life that we have but one life and no continued existence after death (1975). Liberal Protestant theologians have little to say about heaven, and when it is mentioned, it is usually described in minimalist terms as a state which concerns our contact with God in the afterlife. There has been more speculation on the existence of hell; and since the traditional theology of heaven is the counterpart to the theology of hell (the former being associated with reward and the latter with punishment) changes in the conception of the latter will require some changes in the former.

See also: FAITH; HEAVEN, INDIAN CONCEPTIONS OF; HELL; JUSTIFICATION, RELIGIOUS; LIMBO; PURGATORY; RESURRECTION; SALVATION; SOUL, NATURE AND IMMORTALITY OF THE; TIAN

References and further reading

* Aquinas, T. (1266–73) *Summa theologica*, trans. Fathers of the English Dominican Province, Westminster, MD: Christian Classics, 1981, IaIIae, qq.1–5; sup. qq.91–6. (A very influential account of heaven.)

* —— (1259–65) *Summa contra gentiles*, trans. A.C. Pegis, J.F. Anderson, V.J. Bourke and C.J. O'Neil, Notre Dame, IN: University of Notre Dame Press, 1975, chaps 82–7, 92, 95–6. (One of the fullest and most influential treatments of the doctrine of heaven in Christian theology. The work of Aquinas is particularly important for those who wish to investigate the connection between the idea of heaven and philosophically important medieval views in ethics and metaphysics.)

Arendzen, J.P. (1951) *Purgatory and Heaven*, New York: Sheed & Ward. (A short and simple summary of traditional Roman Catholic teaching on judgment, the resurrection of the body, heaven and purgatory.)

Garrigou-Lagrange, R. (1952) *Life Everlasting*, trans. P. Cummins, St Louis and London: B. Herder Book Co. (A good explanation of Roman

Catholic theology on the traditional last things – death, judgment, heaven, hell and purgatory – by an important theologian of the era preceding Vatican II.)

* Hick, J. (1976) *Death and Eternal Life*, New York: Harper & Row. (An influential book by an important Christian theologian. A discussion of both Western and Eastern eschatologies is included.)

* McDannell, C. and Lang, B. (1988) *Heaven: A History*, New Haven, CT: Yale University Press. (A useful and interesting history of the idea of heaven in Western religion, with discussions of its treatment in imaginative literature and art, as well as theology and philosophy; not theologically technical.)

* Rahner, K. (1975) *Theological Investigations*, trans. D. Bourke, London: Darton, Longman & Todd. (Rahner was a leading twentieth-century Catholic theologian who attempted to work out a new teaching on heaven that did not include the idea of a continued personal life.)

* Zagzebski, L. (1994) 'Religious Luck', *Faith and Philosophy* 11 (3): 397–413. (Argues that certain Christian doctrines make the problem of moral luck, which has received a lot of attention in contemporary ethics, particularly critical for Christian moral theology. The focus of the problems is the doctrine of an eternal heaven and hell, particularly the latter.)

LINDA ZAGZEBSKI

HEAVEN, CHINESE CONCEPT OF *see* TIAN

HEAVEN, INDIAN CONCEPTIONS OF

Heaven is an important part of Indian religious cosmology and also figures strongly in Indian philosophical discourse. In the cosmologies of the early period of Indian thought, from the Ṛg Veda to the advent of the so-called heterodox schools of Jainism and Buddhism (c.1500–500 BC), heaven was conceived of in relatively simple terms, as a happy and permanent abode for both the deceased (particularly those who performed Vedic sacrifices) and the gods. In all three of the major religious systems of classical India, namely Hinduism, Buddhism and Jainism, heavenly realms

expanded in number, and were usually depicted in terms of the deities who inhabited them and the prevailing life-situations of the deceased. Geographically, the heavens of classical India were envisaged as either parallel, occupying separate, bounded, horizontal space, or vertical, existing on separate tiers of upper-level space. Philosophically, the existence and soteriological value of heaven were much debated, from the earliest Upaniṣads (c.500 BC) and philosophical sūtras of Vedānta and Pūrva Mīmāṃsā (the Brahmasūtra of Bādarāyaṇa and the Mīmāṃsāsūtra of Jaimini respectively) to the later logicians and systematizers of the standard philosophical systems (c.1500 and beyond). Religion and philosophy were always intimately linked in India, indeed were often barely distinguishable; thus the soteriology of a religious form would be logically supported and fully explicated by allied philosophical schools. Broadly, two points of view were represented: first, that heavenly realms did exist and were achievable for one's ultimate benefit, or, second, that they existed but were phenomena subject to decay, rather like ordinary reality, or (as the Buddhists thought) were mental constructs. In the second case, heaven was regarded as inferior to variously conceived states of enlightenment or liberation.

1   **Heaven in the Vedas**
2   **Heaven in classical Indian religious systems**
3   **Heaven in philosophical thought**

1   Heaven in the Vedas

In the religious and philosophical schools of India, notions and descriptions of heaven follow one of two paths: heavens are either permanent abodes of bliss and happiness based on earthly models, or they are (along with various hells) temporary states where good (or bad) karma (Pāli, *kamma*) is consumed during an all-but-eternal cycle of births and deaths (*saṃsāra*). In the Vedas and most of the religious and philosophical traditions that follow in their wake, the word that comes closest to 'heaven' is *svarga*, from *s(u)var* ('light', 'the sun', 'the realm of celestial light') and *ga*, from the Sanskrit verbal root *gam* ('to go'). Thus the etymological meaning of *svarga* is 'going to the realm of celestial light' (see Gonda 1966: 73–106). Other words are used occasionally in post-Vedic literature, such as *devaloka* or *devālaya*, 'the realm (or abode) of the gods'. *Svarga*, more explicitly, was an abode of religious merit identified with the celestial counterpart of the Vedic sacrificial ritual, located in the highest part of the vault which comprised the tripartite Vedic universe: the earth, mid-region and celestium. *Svarga* was a ritually replicated embodiment of 'Vedic man's desire to live in a pure, strong

253

and perfect "sphere" or "world"' (Gonda 1966: 73). It was connected to this world not just ideologically but physically. The *Ṛg Veda* (10.90.3–4) states that three feet of the archetypal cosmic being (*puruṣa*) obtain immortality in the divine celestium (*amṛtaṃ divi*), while the fourth foot 'is all beings'. This inspired the common Indian trope of the inverted tree, with its many roots in the sky and its leaves on earth, an image which envisages a connection of the world of the gods and the deceased with that of humanity (see Coomaraswamy 1938–9).

In order to grasp fully the significance of the idea of heaven in ancient and classical India, it is important to understand at least the broad outlines of the metaphorical uses of *svar* and *svarga* in the earliest Vedic texts. In the *Ṛg Veda* itself (7.90.6), the patrons of the sacrifice bring *svar*, 'celestial light', to the poets, presumed to take the form of worldly payment for services rendered. Gonda concludes: 'The ideas of sun, sunlight, celestial light are inextricably mixed up with those of well-being, good fortune, happiness, glory' (Gonda 1966: 78; see also Kirfel 1967: 22–).

Svarga is often thought of as the 'yonder world' to which the ritually perfected Vedic sacrificer travels after death to live in a state of happiness or bliss. It is the ultimate abode of the one 'who knows thus', the one who has acquired the esoteric meaning or connections of ritual performance. It is important to understand that this is not just armchair speculation or meditative cognition: ritual action and intent were considered essential to realizing and entering into the celestial region. This 'yonder world' was often identified as both the realm of the gods (*devalokaḥ*) and the realm of the deceased ancestors (*pitṛlokaḥ*), though these were just as often distinguished. *Svarga* was variously described as infinite (*ananta*), immeasurable (*aparimita*), undefined (*anirukta*), whole or complete (*sarva*, hence also identified with the year), immortal (*amṛta*), and as the sacrifice itself (*svargo vai loko yajñaḥ*, Kauṣītaki Brāhmaṇa 14.1). It was thus every bit as much an abstraction or symbol, an ideal of earthly life, as a paradisiacal abode of the dead. Indeed, the Vedas do not contain florid descriptions of *svarga*. It is merely described as full of pleasures and resplendent. Occasionally it is said to be in the east or northeast; 'up from the earth', according to two Vedic texts (Aitareya Brāhmaṇa 7.5, Śatapatha Brāhmaṇa 3.5.1.9). It is difficult to attain. One mounts or ascends to *svarga* as if on a chariot or ship. 'Becoming a hawk one flies to it' (Taittirīya Saṃhitā 5.4.11.1). The sacrifice, as a ship, was oriented towards the east, for when the priest 'walks towards the east, he steers that [ship] eastward toward the heavenly realm [*svargaṃ lokam*]. By this he attains

the heavenly realm' (Śatapatha Brāhmaṇa 2.3.3.16). Similarly, the eastern sacrificial fire (*āhavanīya*) is regarded as the world of heaven, so the sacrificer who is anointed near the *āhavanīya* attains this realm (Śatapatha Brāhmaṇa 9.3.4.11–13). Often *svarga* is associated with Brahman, which in the middle Vedic literature indicates the power of expansion that expresses all things superior in the Vedic universe. Thus this heavenly realm has both geographical and existential status: it is both 'a soteriological "world of heaven" (*svarga loka*) and a cosmological "world of the sky" (*svar, dyaus*)' (Smith 1994: 127).

2 Heaven in classical Indian religious systems

Heavenly or celestial realms multiply dramatically – they expand vertically as well as horizontally, which is to say they are multi-tiered and parallel – and receive much more detailed treatment in Jainism and Buddhism than in the Vedic literature, as well as in the Purāṇas and the Hindu *bhakti* traditions that grew out of it and which continue to dominate the Indian religious landscape. Much of the discourse on heaven is intimately connected with notions of karma and retribution. The general rule is that if one performs good actions, one attains a pleasant celestial abode, pleasant in a measure corresponding to the merit accruing from the good actions; but the abode can equally be destructive or frightening as a result of an overflow of bad actions. For example, the Buddhist cosmologies speak of pleasant heavenly realms of sensual pleasures, called *kāmadhātu*; realms in which gods are liberated from sensuality, called *rūpadhātu*; immaterial realms in which one may continue spiritual work, called *arūpyadhātu*; the abode of the 'satisfied' Bodhisattvas, called *tuṣita*; and finally the 'happy universe' or 'pure land', *sukhāvatī*, where blissful creatures are born from lotuses in the presence of the Buddha Amitābha, Avalokiteśvara and certain Bodhisattvas (La Vallée Poussin 1926; see also Hirakawa 1990: 170–; Kirfel 1967: 190–).

The Hindu Purāṇas have, in theory at least, five characteristic features (*pañcalakṣaṇa*), one of which is describing the knowledge of the cosmos (*sarga*, 'the creation'). Included in this cosmology are various heavenly realms (usually seven), which are usually ideal and paradigmatic, and mappable according to both physical, social and mythic notions, and ideas of psychological symmetry, order and justice. One of the common images (not always satisfactorily mapped) is the descent of the Ganges (and other rivers) from heaven. The Ganges, an artery of celestial water, connects the world of humans and the comparatively proximate world of the dead (*pitṛloka*) with the heavenly fountainhead of the gods. Thus, immersion of physical remains in rivers, especially the Ganges, connects the deceased (and the consequent offerings to them by the living) with the higher realms (see Witzel 1984; von Stietencron 1972; Lüders 1951: 138–61, 269–193; Kirfel 1967: 59–, 109–). Heavenly worlds in Jainism are every bit as elaborate as their Hindu and Buddhist counterparts, are equally dependent on notions of karma produced, and are populated by several levels of gods and exalted beings (see Kirfel 1967: 285–; Caillat and Kumar 1981).

Despite their splendour, these higher or heavenly worlds are, in post-Vedic India, almost invariably regarded as impermanent, subject to decay. Indeed, perhaps the most prominent feature of heavenly worlds, at least for Indian philosophical schools, is their ambiguity. The virtue which leads to residence in them and the rewards resulting from such residence are decidedly transitory, yet they represent progress towards emancipation. But it is a peculiar kind of progress, in that it that can be fully realized only when the denizens of heaven, from ordinary mortal souls to the highest of the gods, take rebirth once again in human form. On the whole, the philosophical schools recognize heaven as a reward of properly intended and performed ritual action, action performed for the explicit purpose of otherworldly reward. But as the merit and the corresponding participation in such worlds become exhausted, heavenly beings begin to lose their lustre in preparation for a fall. But the fall is deceptive: although it is a fall from certainty and near immortality in pleasant realms into the uncertainty and suffering of this mortal world, it is necessary and in the interest of the highest good because final liberating knowledge and experience can only be gained from decisively confronting the visage of mortality.

3 Heaven in philosophical thought

In India, philosophy was almost invariably a hand-maiden of religious doctrine. Thus, heaven, which was intimately associated with specific religious doctrines, became a point of contention in sectarian and inter-religious debate. In general, the classical schools of Indian philosophy argued against the ultimate value of the Vedic notion of heaven, a place to which deserving humans or even sacrificed animals ascended after death, regarding it as limiting and therefore inferior to the 'higher' goal of spiritual emancipation. Regardless, philosophers regularly appealed in establishing the truth of their respective positions to the authority or verbal testimony (śabdapramāṇa) of Śruti, which indicated either the Vedic corpus vaguely or the Upaniṣads specifically. The first question considered by the philosophical schools was the very

existence of heaven. This question was taken up because heaven is invisible and must therefore be proved to exist (the Cārvāka, or atheist, school declared that it is invisible and thus nonexistent). To this end the philosophers resorted to the authority of scripture. For example, UDDYOTAKARA (a sixth-century logician) says in his Nyāyavārttika that, based on descriptions in Vedic texts, heaven and the gods are perceptible, have specific location and exist for the sake of others, but are not eternal (see Potter 1977: 311). He declares that the Veda aims at heaven through ritual means, while self-knowledge can be attained only through understanding of the ontological categories presented in Nyāya-Vaiśeṣika, including, among others, the nature of substances, wholes, parts and proper reasoning (see NYĀYA-VAIŚEṢIKA §§4–5).

The philosophical system that most naturally defends the Vedic notion of heaven is Pūrva Mīmāṃsā (see MĪMĀṂSĀ). Śabara (c. second century AD) states in his commentary on Jaimini's Mīmāṃsāsūtra (6.1.1, c. second–third century BC) that svarga is a form of happiness, because that is the way people describe it. Only in a 'secondary figurative sense', he says, is it 'applied to the thing or substance that causes happiness' (Jha 1942: 270). It is a condition in which one is devoid of pain and in which the self alone is the object of consciousness. It is also, according to Pūrva Mīmāṃsā, the result of a desire that is fulfilled by ritual action. The connection between sacrificial action and later residence in heaven is established by the later philosophers of Pūrva Mīmāṃsā (beginning with Kumārila, seventh century) by the assumption of apūrva, 'a potency produced by the sacrifice which makes it possible that its fruits be reaped at a later time; it is a bridge between the actions and their promised results' (Halbfass 1980: 275).

The notion of desire, however, which most of the philosophical traditions associate with popular religion, is generally rejected as a causal factor in the acquisition of the highest state of existence. Most of the philosophical schools regard as naïve both the Vedic notion of heaven and the correlative notion of desire as a means to attain it, and replace them with more systematic paradigms of liberation and proper understanding of reality, usually accompanied with programmatic spiritual practice. Indeed, desire and sacrifice come to be regarded as antithetical to the 'higher' goal of enlightenment (mokṣa, mukti). The major (but partial) exceptions to this are some of the devotionally based schools of Vedānta, including, for example, the Śuddhādvaita of VALLABHĀCĀRYA (1479–1531), in which passionate attachment to Kṛṣṇa, to be sure a form of desire, can lead to final residence and near partnership in the archetypal realm of Kṛṣṇa's creative matrix. Vallabhācārya regards this blissful condition as superior to the state of enlightenment in which the individual self is absorbed into the abstract absolute (see VEDĀNTA §3).

One example of the classical Advaita Vedānta position is found in Śaṅkara's (early eighth century) commentary on Bṛhadāraṇyaka Upaniṣad 3.2–3, which discusses the question 'What is this "death" that the liberated man is freed from?' Śaṅkara concludes, against the views of his (rather unfairly represented) Pūrva Mīmāṃsā opponent, that ritual action cannot lead to liberation but only to heaven, that residence in heaven is not possible after the body has returned to its constituent elements after death, that dissolution cannot result in abidance in any 'state'. Indeed, liberation is characterized by destruction of ignorance (avidyā), the underlying cause of the world, and this is only possible through proper understanding of the relationship between the self and the absolute. And, he adds, it does not require dissolution of the physical body (see ŚAṄKARA).

One final position may be mentioned here which allows for both the Pūrva Mīmāṃsā and the Vedānta views. This is the view of the grammarians (vaiyākaraṇāḥ). Nāgeśa (seventeenth century) states in his commentary on Kaiyaṭa's Pradīpa on the Mahābhāṣya of PATAÑJALI (second century BC) that the study of grammar is useful for the attainment of both svarga and mokṣa; it results in correct understanding of Vedic texts, which enables one to perform rituals properly, leading to svarga, while it is also useful for understanding the Upaniṣads, which lead to mokṣa.

See also: COSMOLOGY AND COSMOGONY, INDIAN THEORIES OF; HEAVEN; HINDU PHILOSOPHY; JAINA PHILOSOPHY §1; KARMA AND REBIRTH, INDIAN CONCEPTIONS OF

References and further reading

* Caillat, C. and Kumar, R. (1981) *The Jain Cosmology*, New York: Harmony Books. (A 'coffee-table' book with a good introduction and excellent colour reproductions of Jaina paintings and manuscript pages.)
* Coomaraswamy, A.K. (1938–9) 'The Inverted Tree', *Quarterly Journal of the Mythic Society* (New Series) 29: 111–49; in R. Lipsey (ed.) *Coomaraswamy*, vol. 1, *Selected Papers: Traditional Art and Symbolism*, Bollingen Series 89, Princeton, NJ: Princeton University Press, 1977, 376–404. (An accessible and intriguing account of this important image.)
* Gonda, J. (1966) *Loka: World and Heaven in the Veda*, Amsterdam: North Holland Publishing Company. (A thorough, indispensible and highly philological account of heaven as it is represented in the early and middle Vedic literature.)
* Halbfass, W. (1980) 'Karma, *Apūrva*, and 'Natural' Causes: Observations on the Growth and Limits of the Theory of *Saṃsāra*', in W. Doniger O'Flaherty (ed.) *Karma and Rebirth in Classical Indian Traditions*, Berkeley, CA: University of California Press, 268–302. (An accessible article on a difficult topic.)
* Hirakawa, Akira (1990) *A History of Indian Buddhism from Śākyamuni to Early Mahāyāna*, ed. and trans. P. Groner, Honolulu, HI: University of Hawaii Press. (The section on Buddhist heavens is the most complete among general textbooks on early Buddhism.)
* Jha, G. (1942) *Pūrva-Mīmāṃsā in its Sources*, Varanasi: Banaras Hindu University. (This remains unsurpassed as a guidebook to early Pūrva Mīmāṃsā.)
* Kirfel, W. (1967) *Die Cosmographie der Inder*, Hildesheim: Georg Olms. (This indispensible book includes many important texts on 'heaven' from post-Vedic India, including Jaina, Buddhist and Purāṇic.)
* La Vallée Poussin, L. de (1926) 'Abode of the Blest (Buddhist)', in J. Hastings (ed.) *Encyclopedia of Religion and Ethics*, Edinburgh: T. & T. Clark, vol. 2, 687–9. (A good, but very brief, account of the subject.)
* Lüders, H. (1951) *Varuṇa*, vol 1, *Varuṇa und die Wasser* (Varuṇa and Water), Göttingen: Vandenhoeck & Ruprecht. (An excellent sourcebook, with much on the subject, as Varuṇa is a 'heavenly' deity.)
* Potter, K.H. (ed.) (1977) *Encyclopedia of Indian Philosophies*, vol. 2, *Indian Metaphysics and Epistemology: The Tradition of Nyāya-Vaiśeṣika up to Gaṅgeśa*, Princeton, NJ: Princeton University Press, and New Delhi: Motilal Banarsidass. (The editor's introduction includes a succinct account of heaven according to this system of Indian philosophy. The summaries of the texts also provide information on the subject.)
* Smith, B.K. (1994) *Classifying the Universe: The Ancient Indian Varṇa System and the Origins of Caste*, New York and Oxford: Oxford University Press. (This book provides considerable material on Vedic notions of heaven and their correspondences with the physical world.)
* Stietencron, H. von (1972) *Gaṅgā und Yamunā: zur*

symbolischen Bedeutung der Flussgöttinnen an indischen Tempeln (Gaṅgā und Yamunā: On the Symbolic Meaning of the River Goddesses on Indian Temples), Wiesbaden: Harrassowitz. (In India, rivers are said to originate in celestial or heavenly realms. This excellent book recounts both the mythology and the artistic representations of this notion.)

* Witzel, M. (1984) 'Sur le chemin du ciel' (On the Way to Heaven), *Bulletin d'Études Indiennes* 2: 213–77. (This innovative and philologically thorough article makes the case that the Vedic Sarasvatī is in fact the Milky Way.)

FREDERICK M. SMITH

HEDONISM

Hedonism is the doctrine that pleasure is the good. It was important in ancient discussions, and many positions were taken, from the view that pleasure is to be avoided to the view that immediate bodily pleasure is to be sought. More elevated views of pleasure were also taken, and have been revived in modern times. There are three varieties of hedonism. Psychological hedonists hold that we can pursue only pleasure; evaluative hedonists that pleasure is what we ought to pursue; reflective hedonists that it is what on reflection gives value to any pursuit. Arguments for psychological hedonism suggest that an agent's actions are a function of what they think will maximize their pleasure overall. Explaining altruism can lead such theories into truism. Similar arguments are used for reflective hedonism, and the same problem arises. The difficulty for evaluative hedonism lies in deciding how we can establish certain ends as desirable. The claim that pleasure is to be maximized seems immoral to many. Hedonism also faces problems with the measurement of pleasure.

1 **History and varieties of hedonism**
2 **Psychological, evaluative and reflective hedonism**
3 **Arguments for hedonism**
4 **Problems for hedonism**

1 History and varieties of hedonism

Hedonism is the doctrine that pleasure is the good (see PLEASURE; GOOD, THEORIES OF THE). It has usually been viewed as a doctrine of self-indulgence, and so morally suspect. In classical Greece the pre-philosophical picture of pleasure is given in the Myth of Prodicus, where Pleasure vies with Virtue in tempting Hercules. Among philosophers, some ad-vocated pursuit of immediate bodily pleasures (see CYRENAICS); some, hoping to show disreputable pleasures to be detrimental to overall pleasure, took the maximization of pleasure over one's life as the good (their hope is helped if non-bodily pleasures are included) (see DEMOCRITUS; PROTAGORAS); some (such as Plato in *Republic* and Aristotle in *Nicomachean Ethics*) held that at least the good life is the pleasantest, and perhaps that, if you understood about pleasure, arguing from hedonistic premises would lead you to the morally right conclusion (see PLATO; ARISTOTLE); some held that pleasure is to be avoided (see CYNICS). After Aristotle, EPICURUS and his followers advocated a life of physical pleasure unadulterated by pain, and of unanxious memory and anticipation of such pleasures. For a number of centuries they were an influential school. The Stoics, by contrast, considered pleasure to be a false belief in the agent's wellbeing (see STOICISM).

In the Middle Ages the topic did not arouse such excitement, although it was treated in commentaries on Aristotle. In post-Cartesian philosophy Claude-Adrien HELVETIUS was a proponent, and many of the British empiricists adopted some form of hedonism. This was developed into utilitarianism by Jeremy BENTHAM, James MILL and John Stuart MILL (see UTILITARIANISM). J.S. Mill (1861) distinguished higher from lower pleasures, declaring the former, more admirable, pleasures pleasanter. Hedonism received judicious consideration from Henry SIDGWICK and was vigorously attacked by G.E. MOORE, but has benefited from sophisticated development at the hands of Richard Brandt (1979).

Psychological hedonists hold that we can pursue only pleasure; evaluative hedonists that pleasure is what we ought to pursue; reflective hedonists that it is what on reflection gives value to any pursuit. Some have tried to be all three at once, usually through failure to notice the differences. The varieties of hedonism in the first paragraph above will match with types in these three to produce different forms of hedonism. Further variations may be introduced as follows: (a) while the pleasure in question is usually the agent's own, it may be that of any human or sentient being (see ANIMALS AND ETHICS); (b) different views of the nature of pleasure will yield different pictures of the goal in life (see EUDAIMONIA). For example, if pleasure is the realization of one's own good functioning, we get one picture (see PERFECTIONISM); if it is the satisfaction of desire, another (see DESIRE).

2 Psychological, evaluative and reflective hedonism

Whether this distinction holds depends on conclusions about the distinction between fact and value (see FACT/VALUE DISTINCTION). In classical Greek philosophy it was standard practice to argue from the supposed fact that something is the only thing wanted (or really wanted) by an individual or species, to the conclusion that it is the good of that individual or species. To show that everyone wants only pleasure was thought necessary and sufficient to show that pleasure is the human good, and so what humans ought to pursue. If it is invalid to argue from facts about what people do want to conclusions about what they ought to want, then there will be a clear difference between holding that we all do want pleasure and holding that we ought to. Indeed, it will be a waste of time telling people that they ought to want pleasure if pleasure is the only thing they are capable of wanting. Proponents of evaluative hedonism seem to suppose the falsity of the psychological variety.

Reflective hedonism is a halfway house. The thesis is that when we reflect on what is valuable in life, then only considerations of pleasure weigh; but in many of our pursuits we lose sight of this. Thus I may become overconscientious and in all my actions be ruled by considerations of duty; when I stand back and review my life, it is its dreary lack of pleasure which convinces me that it is all worthless. This is a psychological thesis about our reflective valuing which allows us to make sense of raising questions about the worth of what we actually pursue.

3 Arguments for hedonism

(a) Psychological hedonism. Arguments may be to the effect that all of every agent's actions are a function of what they consider will maximize their pleasure overall, or will be the pleasantest thing in itself of the available alternatives. It will depend on how the end of pleasure is conceived. Apparent exceptions, such as altruistic acts, will have to be shown nevertheless to be a function of the goal as specified. Two points are important here. First, suggesting a way in which an agent might see an act as maximizing pleasure is not showing that they do: hypotheses have to be substantiated. Second, showing that an act is a function of what the agent thinks the most titillating in prospect of the available alternatives is not showing it to be a function of what they think will maximize pleasure overall. In other words, one has to ensure that one has evidence for the hypothesis, and to be sufficiently precise about its formulation to be sure that the evidence tells in favour of it and not some other view.

Faced with apparent counterexamples, such as altruism, there is a temptation to claim that if the agent does not envisage some pleasure from their altruism, or view it with pleasure, then they do not really want to act as they do. This saves the thesis but at the cost of making it truistic; pleasure can no longer illuminate why we desire anything: if pleasure is absent we do not count as desiring.

In these arguments, not only is it important to beware the slide into making the thesis truistic; one must also take care about the relations between various explanations in terms of pleasure. If I am depressed, I may recoil from the prospect of going to a party which I know I should enjoy if I made the effort. Evidence about what I view with pleasure does not seem relevant to the question of what I think will produce pleasure, or conversely. It is necessary to argue the connection.

(b) Evaluative hedonism. The issue here depends on the possibilities for establishing the desirability of ends. Is it intuitively obvious that in some sense pleasure is (the) good? Or by some account of rationality is it the only rational thing to pursue? Or does pleasure alone make sense of our moral concerns? The argument is not now about actual pursuits, nor about what counts as wanting, but about how one might argue that pleasure ought to be pursued or desired.

(c) Reflective hedonism. Points paralleling those on psychological hedonism hold. First, there are arguments as to whether all our reflective valuing does in the last resort rely on appeal to hedonistic considerations; second, there is the possibility of arguing that we count as evaluating only if we refer to hedonistic grounds. There is the same risk of lapse into truism.

4 Problems for hedonism

Hedonism may be aimed at supplying either a rationale for morality, or an alternative to it. Since most forms of hedonism judge the worth of courses of action by their consequences in terms of pleasure, they encounter the problems, as rationales of morality, of consequentialism (see CONSEQUENTIALISM): moral judgments of worth seem often partly or wholly independent of consequences, certainly of pleasure, however long-term (see DEONTOLOGICAL ETHICS; INTUITIONISM IN ETHICS). For egoistic forms of hedonism, there is the problem of explaining the apparently anti-egoistic bias of morality (see EGOISM AND ALTRUISM).

Whether considered as a rationale of morality or an alternative, hedonism has problems with the measurement of pleasure. It is not clear what to make of the question whether a given episode of skating gave as much pleasure as the supping of a glass of wine. They seem incommensurable. If these problems can be surmounted, there remain problems, for non-egoistic hedonists, of comparing different people's pleasures.

See also: ASCETICISM; ECONOMICS AND ETHICS; EUDOXUS; HAPPINESS; MORAL MOTIVATION; RATIONAL CHOICE THEORY; SUFFERING

References and further reading

* Aristotle (*c.* mid 4th century BC) *Nicomachean Ethics*, trans. with notes by T. Irwin, Indianapolis, IN: Hackett Publishing Company, 1985. (Contains two important discussions of pleasure, 1152b–1154b and 1172a16–1176a29, which attempt to reconcile the hedonist and anti-hedonist insights of predecessors.)

Bentham, J. (1789) *An Introduction to the Principles of Morals and Legislation*, ed. J.H. Burns and H.L.A. Hart, revised F. Rosen, Oxford: Clarendon Press, 1996. (Central modern account, which gives a qualified hedonistic basis for utilitarianism.)

* Brandt, R.B. (1979) *A Theory of the Good and the Right*, Oxford: Clarendon Press. (Sophisticated contemporary discussion, which defends hedonism against modern criticisms.)

Gosling, J.C.B. (1969) *Pleasure and Desire*, Oxford: Clarendon Press. (Discusses the issues introduced in this entry, in §§2–4.)

Gosling, J.C.B. and Taylor, C.C.W (1982) *The Greeks on Pleasure*, Oxford: Clarendon Press. (Comprehensive discussion of the disputes in classical Greece up to Epicurus and the early Stoics.)

Mill, J.S. (1861) *Utilitarianism*, in J. Gray (ed.) *On Liberty and Other Essays*, Oxford: Oxford University Press, 1991. (Classic modern discussion of hedonistic utilitarianism.)

Moore, G.E. (1903) *Principia Ethica*, Cambridge: Cambridge University Press. (Contains spirited attack on hedonism, especially that of J.S. Mill.)

Plamenatz, J. (1958) *The English Utilitarians*, Oxford: Blackwell. (Treatment of some of the main figures in the British empiricist tradition.)

* Plato (*c.*380–367 BC) *Republic*, trans. G.M. Grube, revised by C. Reeve, Indianapolis, IN: Hackett Publishing Company, 1992. (Seeks to justify life of reason as most pleasant.)

Sidgwick, H. (1874) *The Methods of Ethics*, London: Macmillan; 7th edn, 1907. (Contains well-balanced and careful assessment of hedonism.)

JUSTIN GOSLING

HEGASIAS *see* CYRENAICS

HEGEL, GEORG WILHELM FRIEDRICH (1770–1831)

Hegel was the last of the main representatives of a philosophical movement known as German Idealism, which developed towards the end of the eighteenth century primarily as a reaction against the philosophy of Kant, and whose main proponents, aside from Hegel, include Fichte and Schelling. The movement played an important role in the philosophical life of Germany until the fourth decade of the nineteenth century. Like the other German Idealists, Hegel was convinced that the philosophy of Kant did not represent the final word in philosophical matters, because it was not possible to conceive a unified theory of reality by means of Kantian principles alone. For Hegel and his two idealistic predecessors, a unified theory of reality is one which can systematically explain all forms of reality, starting from a single principle or a single subject. For Hegel, these forms of reality included not only solar systems, physical bodies and the various guises assumed by organic life, for example, plants, animals and human beings, but also psychic phenomena, social and political forms of organization as well as artistic creations and cultural achievements such as religion and philosophy. Hegel believed that one of the essential tasks of philosophy was the systematic explanation of all these various forms starting from one single principle, in other words, in the establishment of a unified theory of reality. He believed this because only a theory of this nature could permit knowledge to take the place of faith. Hegel's goal here, namely the conquest of faith, places his philosophical programme, like that of the other German Idealists, within the wider context of the philosophy of the German Enlightenment.

For Hegel, the fundamental principle which explains all reality is reason. Reason, as Hegel understands it, is not some quality which is attributed to some human subject; it is, by contrast, the sum of all reality. In accordance with this belief, Hegel claims that reason and reality are strictly identical: only reason is real and only reality is reasonable. The considerations which moved Hegel to identify reason with reality are various. On the one hand, certain motives rooted in Hegel's theological convictions play a role. According to these convictions, one must be able to give a philosophical interpretation of the whole of reality which can simultaneously act as a justification of the basic assumptions of Christianity. On the other hand, epistemological convictions also have to be identified to support *Hegel's claim that reason and reality are one and the same. Among these convictions belong the assumptions (1) that knowledge of reality is only possible if reality is reasonable, because it would not otherwise be accessible to cognition, and (2) that we can only know that which is real.*

According to Hegel, although reason is regarded as the sum total of reality, it must not be interpreted along the lines of Spinoza's model of substance. Reason is rather to be thought of as a process which has as its goal the recognition of reason through itself. Since reason is the whole of reality, this goal will be achieved when reason recognizes itself as total reality. It is the task of philosophy to give a coherent account of this process which leads to self-knowledge of reason. Hegel conceived this process by analogy with the model of organic development which takes place on various levels. The basic presupposition governing the conception of this process is that reason has to be interpreted in accordance with the paradigm of a living organism. Hegel thought of a living organism as an entity which represents the successful realization of a plan in which all individual characteristics of this entity are contained. He called this plan the concept of an entity, and conceived its successful realization as a developmental process, in the course of which each of the individual characteristics acquires reality. In accordance with these assumptions, Hegel distinguished the concept of reason from the process of the realization of this concept. He undertook the exposition of the concept of reason in that section of his philosophical system which he calls the Wissenschaft der Logik *(Science of Logic). In this first part of his system, the various elements of the concept of reason are discussed and placed into a systematic context. He presented the process of the realization of this concept in the other two parts of his system, the* Philosophie der Natur *(Philosophy of Nature) and the* Philosophie des Geistes *(Philosophy of Spirit). Apart from their systematic function, which consists in demonstrating reason in the Hegelian sense as total reality, both parts have a specifically material function in each case. In the* Philosophy of Nature, *Hegel aims to describe comprehensively all aspects of natural phenomena as a system of increasingly complex facts. This system begins with the simple concepts of space, time and matter and ends with the theory of the animal organism. The* Philosophy of Spirit *treats of various psychological, social and cultural forms of reality. It is characterized by the assumption of the existence of something like genuine, spiritual facts, which cannot be described as subjective states of individual persons possessing consciousness, but which have an independent, objective existence. For Hegel, examples of such facts are the state, art, religion and history.*

In spite of the relatively abstract metaphysical background of his philosophy, which is difficult to reconcile with common sense, Hegel's insights in his analysis of concrete facts have guaranteed him a permanent place in the history of philosophy. None the less, for contemporary readers these insights are interesting hypotheses, rather than commonly accepted truths. Of lesser importance among these insights should be counted Hegel's results in the realm of natural philosophy, which soon suffered considerable criticism from practising natural scientists. The important insights apply more specifically to the spheres of the theory of knowledge as well as the philosophy of right, and social and cultural philosophy. Hegel is thus regarded as an astute and original representative of the thesis that our conception of objectivity is largely determined by social factors which also play a significant role in constituting the subject of cognition and knowledge. His criticisms of the seventeenth- and eighteenth-century concepts of natural law and his thoughts on the genesis and significance of right in the modern world have had a demonstrable influence on the theory of right in juridical contexts. Hegel's analysis of the relationship and interplay between social and political institutions became a constituent element in very influential social theories, in particular that of Marx. The same applies to his central theses on the theory of art and the philosophy of religion and history. Hegel's thoughts on the history of philosophy made that topic a philosophical discipline in its own right. Thus Hegel was a very influential philosopher. That his philosophy has none the less remained deeply contentious is due in part to the fact that his uncompromising struggle against traditional habits of thought and his attempt to establish a conceptual perspective on reality in contrast with the philosophical tradition of the time remains characterized by a large measure of obscurity and vagueness. Unfortunately these characteristics also infect every summary of his philosophy.

1　Life and works
2, 3　The development of the system
4–8　The system

1　Life and works

Hegel was born on 27 August 1770 in Stuttgart, son of a Württemberg official. In the autumn of 1788, after attending the local grammar school, he began a course of study at the Protestant Seminary in Tübingen in preparation for a career as a Protestant clergyman. Two of his fellow students and friends were F.W.J. SCHELLING and F. HÖLDERLIN. In autumn 1793, after successfully completing this period of study, Hegel became a private tutor in

Berne, Switzerland, and remained there until 1796. From January 1797 until the end of 1800 he was a private tutor in Frankfurt am Main, where he again came into contact with Hölderlin, who played an important role in the formation of Hegel's early philosophical convictions. Thanks to a legacy, Hegel was able to abandon his position as a tutor and pursue his academic ambitions. Early in 1801 he went to Jena. His student friend Schelling had become Fichte's successor and was lecturing in philosophy at the university there. With Schelling's energetic support Hegel qualified as a *Privatdozent* in the autumn of 1801 with a thesis on natural philosophy. Initially, Schelling and Hegel worked closely together, a fact which is documented by a philosophical periodical which they published jointly from 1802 (although it ceased publication following Schelling's departure from Jena in 1803). In 1805 Hegel was appointed Extraordinary Professor, but financial difficulties forced him to abandon his activities at the University of Jena in the autumn of 1806. A friend's intervention enabled him to take over as editor of a daily newspaper in Bamberg in March 1807. In November 1808 the same friend then ensured that Hegel was nominated rector and professor at a grammar school in Nuremberg. After a few years in this capacity, Hegel was able to return to university life. In 1816 he was called to the University of Heidelberg, which he left again in 1818 to take a chair at the University of Berlin, as Fichte's successor. There he revealed a considerable talent for academic teaching and succeeded in assuring a dominant position in contemporary discussions for his philosophical doctrines. Hegel died in Berlin during a cholera epidemic on 14 November 1831, at the height of his fame.

Hegel's works can be divided into three groups: (1) texts written by Hegel and published during his lifetime; (2) texts written by him, but not published during his lifetime; and (3) texts neither written by him nor published during his lifetime. Two texts from his early years in Frankfurt do not fit into this scheme. The first is the translation of a pamphlet by Cart, a Berne lawyer, on the political situation in the Canton of Vaud, which was translated and annotated by Hegel, and which he published anonymously in 1798. This is the first printed text by Hegel; the second is a fragment dating from the same period and known as the *Systemprogramm des deutschen Idealismus* (System-Programme of German Idealism). The text has survived in Hegel's handwriting, but his authorship remains controversial.

The earliest writings in the first group date from the beginning of Hegel's time in Jena. His first philosophical work is entitled *Differenz des Fich-*

te'schen und Schelling'schen Systems der Philosophie (The Difference between Fichte's and Schelling's System of Philosophy) (1801b). This was followed later during the same year by the essay which he had to submit in order to qualify as *Privatdozent, De Orbitis Planetarum* (*On the Orbits of the Planets*). In 1802–3 Hegel published various philosophical works in the periodical which he edited with Schelling, the *Kritisches Journal der Philosophie* (Critical Journal of Philosophy). The most important among these were *Glauben und Wissen* (Faith and Knowledge), *Verhältnis des Skeptizismus zur Philosophie* (The Relationship of Scepticism to Philosophy) and *über die wissenschaftlichen Behandlungsarten des Naturrechts* (On the Scientific Ways of Dealing with Natural Law). Immediately after his period as a university teacher in Jena and at the beginning of his period in Bamberg, Hegel published his first great philosophical work, the *Phänomenologie des Geistes* (Phenomenology of Spirit) (1807). During the eight years in which he taught at the grammar school in Nuremberg, Hegel published his three-volume *Wissenschaft der Logik* (Science of Logic) (1812, 1813, 1816). While in Heidelberg, the complete presentation of his system appeared for the first time, in his *Enzyklopädie der philosophischen Wissenschaften in Grundrisse* (Encyclopedia of the Philosophical Sciences in Outline) (1817), which was reprinted twice during his Berlin period in two completely revised editions (1827, 1830). Also during this period he published *Naturrecht und Staatswissenschaft im Grundrisse. Grundlinien der Philosophie des Rechts* (Natural Law and Politics in Outline. The Principles of the Philosophy of Right) (1821). Apart from these, Hegel published only minor writings during his lifetime. These were written partly in response to events at the time, although most articles were for the *Jahrbücher für wissenschaftliche Kritik* (Yearbooks of Scientific Criticism), which he co-edited from 1827. Among these is his final published work, *Über die englische Reform-Bill* (On the English Reform Bill) (1831).

The second group of texts includes those works which were written by Hegel but not published by him. Almost all these texts first became accessible in a more or less authentic form during the twentieth century. They can again be divided into three groups. The first group consists of the manuscripts which Hegel wrote between the end of his time as a student and the end of his time in Jena. Among the most important are the so-called *Theologische Jugendschriften* (Early Theological Writings), which were published in 1907 at the instigation of Wilhelm Dilthey by his pupil, H. Nohl. Today they are known as Hegel's *Frühschriften* (Early Writings). Further important texts from this period are the three *Jenaer*

Systementwürfe (Jena Drafts of a Philosophical System), written between 1803 and 1806, partly for publication and partly as lecture notes. The second group of writings not published by Hegel consists of works produced during his period in Nuremberg. Hegel's first biographer, K. Rosenkranz, presented excerpts from these writings as the *Philosophische Propädeutik* (Philosophical Propaedeutic) (1840). In this text Hegel attempted to present his philosophical views in a form suitable for use within the framework of his grammar-school teaching courses. The third group of texts comprises manuscripts and notes which he wrote in connection with his lectures in Heidelberg and Berlin. They are partly contained in the editions in which his pupils and friends published his works after his death.

The third major group of texts covers those works which were neither written nor published by Hegel. They form almost half the texts contained in the first complete edition of Hegel's works. Among them one finds Hegel's extremely influential lectures on aesthetics, the philosophy of history, the history of philosophy and the philosophy of religion. In the form in which they have become influential, these texts are the product of students, in most cases representing the result of notes compiled during Hegel's lectures. Insufficient attention has been paid to this remarkable fact, that is, that some of Hegel's most influential texts actually have the status of secondhand sources.

The first complete edition of Hegel's work, published during the years 1832–45, proved to be influential but highly unreliable both from a historical and a critical point of view. Since the beginning of the twentieth century several attempts have been made to produce a new edition. To date, none has reached a successful conclusion. Since 1968 a new historical and critical edition of Hegel's complete works has been in preparation. By the end of 1996 fifteen volumes had been published.

2 The development of the system: the early writings

The early years of Hegel's intellectual career were characterized less by philosophical ambitions than by interests in public enlightenment and public education. In contrast to his student friends Hölderlin and Schelling, whose activities were directly based on internal philosophical discussions, Hegel aimed in his early works to find ways 'to influence men's lives' (as he wrote to Schelling). He regarded as an appropriate starting point for these attempts the analysis of the role and consequences which must be attributed to religion, especially Christianity, for the individual and for the social context of a nation. In this early approach two different interests are at work. On the one hand, Hegel aims to show how religion had developed into a power hostile to life, which produces its effect through fear and demands submission. On the other hand, however, he would like to understand the conditions under which it can prosper as a productive element in the life of the individual and society. Hegel's investigations of religion under these two aspects were strongly influenced during the early years (1793–1800) by the cultural criticism and social theories of ROUSSEAU as well as the religious philosophy of KANT (§§11, 13), and by his critical assessment of the theological positions of his academic theology teachers in Tübingen (G.C. Storr and J.F. Flatt). The most important works during this period are represented by the texts which have been preserved as fragments, and which have become known under the titles *Die Positivität der christlichen Religion* (The Positivity of the Christian Religion) (1795–6) and *Der Geist des Christentums und sein Schicksal* (The Spirit of Christianity and its Fate), (1798–9).

Hegel's religious criticism centres on the concept of 'positive religion'. For Hegel, a positive religion is one whose fundamental content and principles cannot be made comprehensible to human reason. They thus appear unnatural and supernatural, and are seen to be based on authority and to demand obedience. For Hegel, the Jewish religion represents the paradigm of a positive religion. Hegel also considers that the Christian religion has been transformed into a positive religion during the course of its history, in other words into a religion which alienates human beings from themselves and from their fellow creatures (see ALIENATION §1). He tries to identify cultural and social developments as an explanation for this transformation. In direct opposition to positive religion, Hegel conceives what he calls 'natural religion', which he defines as one whose doctrines correspond with human nature: one which permits or even encourages people to live not only in harmony with their own needs, inclinations and well-considered convictions, but also without being alienated from other people. Hegel's belief in the value for mankind of harmony with oneself (and others), which is strongly influenced by the Stoic ethic (which also via Rousseau had an impact on Kant's practical philosophy), is grounded in a quasi-metaphysical conception of love and life. It owes a considerable debt to the philosophical approach of Hölderlin, with whom Hegel again associated closely during his Frankfurt period. According to this conception, there is a sort of moral emotion of love, which rises above all separations and conflicts, in which persons might be involved in relation to themselves and to others. It is this emotion of love which makes people aware of their unity with others and with themselves. It cannot be adequately thematized by philosophy, which is based on reflection and (conceptual) distinction. It demonstrates vividly, however – and here metaphysics enters – the true constitution of reality, which consists of a state of unity forming the basis for all separations and conflicts and making these possible. This reality, which has to be thought of as unity, Hegel calls 'Life' (*Leben*) and also 'Being' (*Sein*). Hegel's efforts at the end of his Frankfurt period are directed towards thinking of reality in these terms in a sufficiently differentiated manner. In doing so he pursues above all the goal of conceiving of life as a process which generates as well as reconciles oppositions, a dynamic unity of generation and reconciliation. To explain this complex structure, which he conceives what he calls 'life' to be, Hegel devised in the so-called *System-fragment von 1800* the formula 'Life is the connection of connection and non-connection'. This formula and the concept of life on which it is based already point clearly towards Hegel's later organicist metaphysics.

3   The development of the system: the Jena writings

The work of Hegel's Jena period (1801–6) can be divided into critical and systematic writings. Among the critical writings are his first philosophical publication, *The Difference between Fichte's and Schelling's Systems of Philosophy*, and most of the essays which he published during the years 1802–3 in the *Critical Journal of Philosophy*. In these essays, Hegel reveals himself as a critic of the philosophy of his age, especially of the positions of Kant, Jacobi and Fichte whom he accuses of practising a 'reflective philosophy of subjectivity' as he calls it in the sub-title of his essay *Faith and Knowledge* (1802). For Hegel, reflective philosophy is initially an expression of an age or historical situation. Such an age is subject to the dichotomies of culture (*Bildung*), which are the products of the understanding and whose activities are regarded as divisive and isolatory. Being subject to those dichotomies, it is impossible for such an age to overcome them and restore the harmony which the understanding has destroyed. A philosophy committed to such an age shares its fate, being also unable to remove, at least in theory, the conflicts which appear as the concrete forms of dichotomy. For even when philosophy strives to overcome these conflicts – according to Hegel, 'the only interest of reason' – and thus makes reference to a particular idea of unity or harmony, even then it remains committed to the conditions of its age and will achieve nothing except newer and even more acute conflicts. According to Hegel, we can characterize the

general form underlying the various conflicts as the conflict between subjectivity and objectivity. The attempts of reflective philosophy to overcome them fail, in Hegel's view, because they are largely abstract: that is, they fail to take into account either the subjective or the objective component of the conflict, and declare it to be resolved by neglecting or abstracting from either of these components. In abstracting from subjectivity, objectivity (in Hegel's terminology) is posited as absolute, which leads to the subordination of subjectivity. This way of reconciling the conflict between subjectivity and objectivity is characteristic of all religions describable as positive by Hegel's definition. If, on the other hand, abstraction is made from objectivity, and subjectivity is thus posited as absolute, then objectivity is regarded as being dependent on subjectivity. This one-sided absolutization of subjectivity is Hegel's objection to the philosophies of Kant, Jacobi and Fichte and the reason he describes their theories as forms of a reflective philosophy of subjectivity.

During his early years in Jena, in contrast to the philosophical attitudes which he criticized, Hegel assumes along with Schelling that the described conflict between subjectivity and objectivity can only be overcome by a philosophy of identity. A philosophy of identity is characterized by the preconditions (1) that for each opposition there is a unity which must be regarded as a unity of the opposing factors, and (2) that the opposing factors are nothing more than their unity under the description or *in the form* of the opposing factors. These preconditions suggest that one should understand the overcoming of the opposition between subjectivity and objectivity as a single process which *reconstructs* the unity underlying the opposing factors and makes them possible in the first place. Following the conceptual assumptions favoured by Hegel at the time, the unity to be reconstructed in a philosophy of identity is defined as the 'subject–object', and the subject and object themselves are characterized as 'subjective subject–object' or 'objective subject–object' respectively. The process of reconstruction of the subject–object by means of the assumptions of the philosophy of identity consists of recognizing the subjective and objective subject–object in their specific one-sidedness or opposition to each other, and thus gaining an insight into the internal structure of the subject–object as the unity which underlies the two conflicting factors and makes them possible in the first place. Although Hegel did not persist in using this terminology for long, for most of his time in Jena he nevertheless remained faithful to the project of the development of a unity which he considered to be comprehensive and which consists of its internal opposing elements. The various attempts at a formal description of a process which was aimed at a unity led Hegel to various system models. All of them contained – albeit with variations of terminology and detail – a discipline initially defined by Hegel as 'logic and metaphysics' as well as a so-called 'real philosophy' (*Real-Philosophie*), in other words a 'philosophy of nature' as well as what he later called a 'philosophy of spirit'.

The systematic works of the Jena period, apart from the *Phenomenology of Spirit*, principally include the three *Jena Drafts of a Philosophical System*. Of these (in some cases) comprehensive fragments, mainly the sections dealing with the philosophy of nature and of spirit are extant. As regards the philosophy of nature, in all the Jena versions of this part of Hegel's system the description of all natural phenomena, the analysis of their processes and their interrelationships is achieved by recourse to two essential factors, which Hegel calls 'Ether' and 'Matter' (*Materie*). 'Ether' describes something like a materialized absolute, which expresses and develops itself within the realm of space and time. This entity is now introduced by Hegel in connection with the development of the determinations of nature as absolute matter or alternatively as absolute being, and the task of philosophy of nature lies in interpreting the various natural phenomena – from the solar system and the laws governing its movements to illness and death of animal organisms – as different manifestations of this absolute matter. Hegel is concerned not merely to show that any particular natural phenomenon is in its peculiar way a specific expression of absolute matter. Above all, he is concerned to prove that nature is a unity ordered in a particular manner. As a specific expression of absolute matter, each natural phenomenon represents an element in the ordered succession of natural phenomena. The position of a natural phenomenon in the order of nature is laid down by the specific way in which absolute matter is expressed in it. A consequence of this approach is that here the natural order is understood as determined by certain postulates which result from the structural conditions of the absolute matter and the methodological maxims of the complete description of these conditions. Differences between the Jena versions of Hegel's philosophy of nature mainly result from the inclusion of new facts made available by current science; but they leave his basic assumptions untouched.

Things are different in the case of the Jena writings on the second part of real philosophy – the philosophy of spirit – initially still described by Hegel as the 'philosophy of ethical life' (*Philosophie der Sittlichkeit*). They reveal many changes, all linked to

modifications of his conception of spirit. Initially, he presents his philosophy of spirit as a theory of ethical life, which he then transforms into a theory of consciousness. For reasons linked to a renewed preoccupation with Fichte and certain new insights into the logical structure of self-consciousness, towards the end of his Jena period Hegel found himself obliged to present an approach which had occupied him since at least 1804–5. This approach enabled him to liberate the philosophy of spirit from its narrow systematic links to a conception of ethical life based on assumptions incompatible with his new conception of spirit. It assumes that only the formal structure of self-consciousness, which consists in its being a unity of generality and singularity, can provide the framework within which the logical-metaphysical determinations, the natural world and psychosocial phenomena unite to form a meaningful systematic context. For the philosophy of spirit this means in particular that as far as method is concerned it is better equipped for the implementation of its systematic task of being the representation of the processes of self-realization of what Hegel calls 'reason'. This insight into the formal structure of self-consciousness is the final achievement of his Jena period, and one which he never subsequently abandoned.

4 The system: metaphysical foundations

Hegel's systematic philosophy attempts to comprehend reality in all its manifestations as a self-representation of reason (*Vernunft*). His conception of what he calls 'reason' combines various specifically Hegelian connotations, both ontological and epistemological. For him, 'reason' is not merely the name for a human faculty which contributes in a specific manner to our gaining knowledge; he also uses 'reason' to describe that which is ultimately and eminently real. This is the ontological connotation. Reason is reality, and that alone is truly real which is reasonable. This programmatic credo, which has become famous from the foreword to Hegel's *Philosophy of Right*, is the basic precept determining the entire approach to his system.

At least three different convictions make up this basic precept of the ontological dignity of reason. The first is that the totality of that which in one sense or another is real must be considered as the differentiation and partial realization of a primary structure which forms the basis for all facts which are real in that specific sense. Hegel calls this primary structure 'the absolute' or 'reason'. He shares this conviction of the necessity of assuming a primary structure called 'reason' (interpreted ontologically) with Fichte, Schelling, Hölderlin and other members of the post-Kantian idealistic movement whose monistic approach is, indeed, defined by this assumption. For Hegel, therefore, this conviction does not require detailed philosophical justification. For him, it is justified because it alone offers a basis for systematic philosophical considerations, following the failure of all previous philosophical attempts to conceive of a unified and complete representation of the world.

This first conviction, which forms a part of Hegel's ontological conception of reason, is still too imprecise to provide a clue as to why exactly the concept 'reason' can be used to characterize the primary structure. Hegel's second important conviction, however, makes this clearer. It relates to the internal constitution of the structure which he characterizes as reason. He understands this structure to be a complex unity of thinking and being. The relevant motives for this conviction can be summarized as follows: the only philosophical approach which can organize the whole of reality into a unified and coherent picture accessible to knowledge is one which insists that everything taken to be real is only real inasmuch as it can be comprehended as the actualization of some specific structural elements of reason. This assertion of the essential reasonableness of all being, together with the first conviction of the necessity of assuming a primary structure, leads directly to the concept of this primary structure as a unity of thinking and being, understood in the very radical sense that thinking and being are one and the same, or that only thinking has being. If we now call this unity of thinking and being 'reason', and if, like Hegel, we are convinced that the requisite primary structure must be thought of as this unity of thinking and being, then reason will be declared on the one hand to represent what in the final analysis is ultimately real, and on the other that which alone is real. Since a monistic position is one in which a single entity is maintained as the ultimate and sole reality, Hegel's philosophical conception has rightly been called a 'Monism of Reason' (see MONISM).

The third conviction which enters into Hegel's basic assumption of reason as the primary structure constituting reality and thus being ultimately and only real is that this structure constitutes reality and thus its own objectivity in a teleological process which must be understood as a process of knowledge. It is this conviction which leads to the characteristically Hegelian dogma that there can be no adequate theory of reality without a dynamic or process-oriented ontology (see PROCESSES §5). The formula which Hegel uses to characterize this process from his early Jena works onwards shows very clearly the dominant role which he assigns to what he defines as 'reason' in

the systematic approach designed to elaborate his third conviction. This process is described as 'self-knowledge of reason' (*Selbsterkenntnis der Vernunft*). Hegel tries to integrate within this formula various aspects of his conception of reason. The first aspect is that it is necessary to take reason, understood as the primary structure, as something which is essentially dynamic. By this he means that the element of self-realization forms part of the moments which determine the primary structure. It is difficult to understand the way in which Hegel links this element of self-realization into his idea of reason as the unity of thinking and being. In order to get a rather over-simplified idea of the background for Hegel's claim, it might help to rely metaphorically on the theory of organism: just as an organism can be described as an entity whose development is linked to the concept or the structural plan of itself in such a way that the (more or less) successful realization of this concept or structural plan belongs to its being real, so we should think of Hegelian reason, understood as the ontologically relevant primary structure, as realizing in a quasi-organic developmental process the unity of thinking and being which characterizes its concept, thereby representing itself as real or as reality.

The second aspect Hegel has in mind when he speaks of 'self-knowledge of reason', describing a process which must indeed be understood as that of the self-realization of reason, is that this process represents a process of *recognition* for reason. It is apparently not sufficient for Hegel to embed his idea of reason as the ontological primary structure in a conception of realization based on the paradigm of the organism. Such a grounding seems to be too unspecific for him, because it does not show how to describe a process which is typical of *all* organisms in such a way that we understand more precisely and in detail what it means for the process to be one of self-realization of *reason*. The specific way in which reason realizes itself is to be characterized first of all as a process of recognition, because only this characterization takes into account the fact that that which is being realized, namely reason, must be thought of strictly as nothing more than thinking *qua* recognition. But even this way of conceiving the realization of reason is still too imprecise, unless one includes in the concept of realization the thesis that reason is the ultimately and only real ontological primary structure. The inclusion of this thesis then leads directly to the teleologically conceived description of the process of the realization of reason as a process of self-recognition. For if only reason – by which is meant the unity of thinking and being – is real, and if an integral part of this concept of reason is the conception of its realization in the form of a process of recognition, then this process can only be directed towards the recognition of reason itself, because nothing else exists. Since this process aims to make reason aware that it alone is real, the presentation of this process, in Hegel's view, must take on the form of a system in which each manifestation of reality documents its reasonable nature. His philosophy aims to elaborate this system.

The project of exhibiting reason not only as the basis for all reality, but also as the whole of reality itself, was Hegel's sole, lifelong philosophical goal. It took him some time to be able to formulate this project explicitly. This is linked to his intellectual development (see §2 above). He also considered various approaches to the realization and development of this project (see §3 above), but he never felt any need to question the project itself.

5 The system: *Phenomenology of Spirit*

The *Phenomenology of Spirit* (1807) is Hegel's most influential work. It serves as an introduction to his philosophical system by means of a history of the experience of consciousness. The *Phenomenology of Spirit* represents only one of a number of introductory attempts he made. In the Jena writings and system drafts, a discipline which Hegel calls 'logic' assumes this function. This logic is intended to fulfil its introductory function by raising our 'normal' thinking, which is characterized by its confinement to irreconcilable oppositions, to the level of 'speculation' – Hegel's term for philosophical thinking. Speculative thought is characterized by the knowledge of the reconcilability of oppositions and of the mechanisms of their coming about. That thinking, which by its insistence on oppositions simultaneously maintains their basic irresolvability, Hegel referred to at this time as 'reflection'. He regarded the elevation of this thinking to the position of speculation as a destruction of the structures which characterize reflection, and which together constitute the finiteness of reflection. 'Finiteness' of reflection or (used by Hegel as a synonym) of the understanding (*Verstand*) is initially a way of saying that thinking whose oppositions are irreconcilable moves within limits and must thus be regarded as finite. According to Hegel, it is now the task of logic to carry out the destruction of the finiteness of reflection or of the thinking of the understanding, thereby simultaneously leading to the standpoint of speculation or of the thinking of reason. Hegel sees the problem of a logic, which he understands as an introduction to philosophy, to be to carry out this destruction in such a way that not only the limitations of the thinking of the understanding and its preconditions are presented as mistakes and

absurdities, but also that during this destructive process those structures become clear which guarantee a reasonable (that is, an intrinsic speculative) insight into the basic structures of reality.

Towards the end of his Jena period, Hegel abandoned the project of developing a system of logic as an introduction to philosophy, and in its place presented a new discipline which he called the 'Science of the Experience of Consciousness' or 'Phenomenology of Spirit'. The declared goal of this discipline is twofold: on the one hand, it should destroy our supposedly natural picture of the world, and thus also our understanding of ourselves as the more or less consistent holders or subjects of this view, by demonstrating the contradictions which arise in our normal, complex view of the world. And second, it should thereby demonstrate that our view of the world as something which is both alien and different from us is not tenable, but that we and the world represent a structural unity with the essential characteristic of self-knowledge and thus being conscious of itself.

Hegel pursues this dual goal in a complex and ambitious thought-process, which attempts to combine and position within a comprehensive context a wide range of themes – historical, epistemological, psychological, meta-scientific, ideological-critical, ethical, aesthetical and religio-philosophical. This whole thought-process is based on two convictions which govern Hegel's entire construction: (1) It is possible to conceive of all epistemic attitudes of a consciousness towards a material world as relations between a subject termed 'cognition' (*Wissen*) and an object termed 'truth' (*Wahrheit*). That which is presented as cognition or truth is in each case determined by the description which the consciousness is able to furnish of its epistemic situation and its object corresponding to this situation. (2) 'Knowledge' (*Erkenntnis*) can only be taken to be that epistemic relation between cognition (subject) and truth (object) in which cognition and truth correspond with each other, which for Hegel is only the case if they are identical. A necessary, though not sufficient, condition for claiming this relationship of identity between cognition and truth is that what is regarded as cognition or as truth respectively is not formulated in a self-contradictory or inconsistent manner. For the Hegel of the *Phenomenology of Spirit*, and of the writings which were to follow, knowledge in the strict sense is thus really self-knowledge.

In characterizing the various epistemic attitudes of a consciousness to the world in the *Phenomenology of Spirit*, Hegel takes as his starting point something which he calls 'sense certainty'. He uses this term to describe an attitude which assumes that in order to know the true nature of reality we must rely on that which is sensually immediately present to us as a spatiotemporally given single object. Hegel demonstrates the untenability of this attitude by attempting to prove that in such an immediate reference to objects nothing true can be claimed of them. Moreover this immediate approach shows that any attempt to gain knowledge of what an object really is implies at the outset a different attitude towards objects. This attitude is determined by the assumption that what we are really dealing with if we refer to objects in order to know them is not the immediately given object, but the object of perception, which is characterized by Hegel as an entity defined through its qualities. According to Hegel, however, even this attitude is not tenable. Neither the perceiving consciousness nor the object perceived nor the relationship which is believed to exist between the two can be accepted in the manner in which they appear in this constellation: the subject, which aims to perceive the object of perception as that which it really is, can neither formulate a consistent concept of this object nor describe itself in unequivocal terms. The consciousness is thus led to a concept of an object which differentiates between what the object is in itself and what it appears to be. In order to differentiate in this manner, the consciousness must define itself as understanding, to which the inner constitution of the object in itself is disclosed as being constituted by its own laws, that is, by the laws of the understanding. Although, according to Hegel, this interpretation of the objective world through the cognizing subject also produces neither a truthful concept of the cognizing consciousness nor of the object in question, it none the less leads to the enforcement of an attitude according to which consciousness, when referring to an object, is referring to something which it is itself. The realization of this insight – that consciousness, when referring to objects, in reality relates to itself – converts consciousness into self-consciousness.

The various ways in which consciousness deals with itself and the objective manifestations corresponding with these ways as reason and spirit are comprehensively discussed by Hegel in the remainder of his *Phenomenology of Spirit*. It is in this context that he presents some of his most famous analyses, such as the account of the master–servant relationship, his critique of the Enlightenment and the French Revolution, his diagnosis of the strengths and weaknesses of the ancients' ideas of morality and ethical life and his theory of religion. The conclusion of the *Phenomenology of Spirit* forms what Hegel calls 'absolute knowledge'. Hegel characterizes this knowledge also as 'comprehending knowledge' (*begreifendes Wissen*), aiming thereby to highlight two ideas: (1) that this knowledge is only present when the subject of the knowledge knows itself to be identical *under every description* with the object of that knowledge. Comprehending knowledge therefore only occurs when the self knows itself to be 'in its otherness with itself', as Hegel puts it at the end of the *Phenomenology of Spirit*. He also aims to point out (2) that this type of identity of a subject with an object is that which constitutes the essence of that which he calls the 'Concept' (*Begriff*) of reason. The task of the *Science of Logic* is to develop this 'Concept' of reason in all its logical qualities. The goal of the *Phenomenology of Spirit*, the discipline which is to provide an introduction to logic, is achieved when it becomes evident to the consciousness that (Hegelian) truth only belongs to the (Hegelian) Concept.

But the *Phenomenology of Spirit* is not just an introduction to the system. From another point of view, Hegel describes the phenomenological process as 'self-fulfilling scepticism'. By means of this metaphor he attempts to establish a link to a subject closely connected with his critical assessment of his cultural and political environment, namely that of dichotomy (*Entzweiung*). For Hegel, the modern age is characterized by the fact that unity has disappeared from people's lives. The all-embracing unity of life can no longer be experienced, as people are no longer in a position to integrate the various aspects of their understanding of the world in a conflict-free context. So, for example, their moral convictions will force upon them a view of the world in which something like freedom and consequently something like the belief in the possibility to cause events based on free decisions occupies an irrefutable position. This view, based on moral convictions, stands in a conflicting and, finally, aporetic relationship to their scientific view of the world, which commits them to an understanding of the world in which there are no first causes or unconditioned facts, because each cause must itself be interpreted anew as an effect, whose cause can only be seen as determined by previous circumstances. In this view of the world there is apparently no place for freedom. The conflict between various aspects of the understanding of the world, cited here by way of example, is for Hegel by no means singular; instead, it runs like a leitmotif through the modern conceptualizations of all spheres of life. He initially interprets it wholly in the spirit of Rousseau as a product of culture and civilization. This conflict is what separates a human being from itself, so that it continues to be denied a coherent image of the world. As a creature living in dichotomies, the modern person is an example of what Hegel calls the 'unhappy consciousness'.

Modern consciousness now attempts to solve this conflict by making each in turn of the conflicting views into the dominant attitude of its entire interpretation of the world. In this way, however, it can only achieve a one-sided interpretation of reality, which is just as incapable of doing justice to the true nature of reality as to the need of human consciousness to integrate all aspects of reality into its understanding of the world as a coherent unity. According to Hegel, it is in this situation that the need for philosophy arises. It is philosophy's task to destroy these one-sided total interpretations of consciousness and in this destruction to lay the foundation for the true complete interpretation of reality. The *Phenomenology of Spirit* describes this process of destruction and foundation-laying. The consciousness experiences it as a process of permanent destabilization of all the convictions on which it has always based its one-sided interpretations of the world. In this sceptical approach it is forced to doubt everything and to abandon all its supposed certainties. While the phenomenological process thus concedes a philosophical value to scepticism, in Hegel's understanding it simultaneously overcomes this scepticism by claiming a truth-revealing function for it. It is also Hegel's intention that the *Phenomenology of Spirit* should in this respect be understood as a treatise on the cathartic effect of philosophical scepticism.

Two questions have often been raised in connection with Hegel's conception of the *Phenomenology of Spirit* as an introduction to his 'System of Science', especially his logic. The first is whether Hegel does not assume in advance certain central theses of the discipline to which the *Phenomenology of Spirit* is intended to provide an introduction. This question draws attention to a methodological problem which originates from Hegel's assertion that the process of consciousness described in the *Phenomenology of Spirit* is not guided by any preconditions external to this process. This assertion seems difficult to square with certain manoeuvres which Hegel makes during the course of the *Phenomenology of Spirit*. The second question is of a more intrinsic nature and concerns the categorical apparatus employed by Hegel in the *Phenomenology of Spirit*. In this context, in particular his phenomenological conception of negation and identity as well as his concept of knowledge aroused critical interest from the very beginning.

It is difficult to determine exactly how Hegel himself later assessed the success of the *Phenomenology of Spirit* as an introduction to the point of view which is assumed at the beginning of his *Science of Logic*. On the one hand, he seems to have allotted it a certain value throughout his entire life, not only as a history of consciousness but also as an introduction.

This is shown not only by the fact that he made arrangements for the publication of a second edition of the work immediately before his death, but also by later statements in the various editions of the *Science of Logic* and the *Encyclopedia of the Philosophical Sciences*. However, it is in precisely these statements that one finds Hegel expressing an increasingly critical attitude towards his project of a phenomenological introduction to the system. In this context it should also be recorded that by 1827 at the latest (that is, from the second edition of the *Encyclopedia of the Philosophical Sciences*) Hegel no longer has recourse to a version of phenomenology as 'a more detailed introduction, in order to explain and lead to the meaning and the point of view which is here allotted to logic', but for this purpose uses instead a discussion which deals with three different 'attitudes of thought to objectivity'.

6 The system: *Science of Logic*

The real centre of the Hegelian system is the discipline he described as 'Logic'. It contains his doctrine of the categories, to use traditional terminology (see CATEGORIES §1). Hegel dedicated his most comprehensive and complex work to this discipline, the *Science of Logic* (1812–16), later adding a much shorter version within the framework of the *Encyclopedia of the Philosophical Sciences*.

The starting point of the *Logic* is the insight, justified in Hegel's view by the result of the *Phenomenology of Spirit* (1) that all true knowledge is knowledge of oneself, and (2) that the subject of this knowledge, that is to say, that which knows about itself, is reason. Because Hegel – following Schelling – only considers that to be real which can also be known, he concludes from the results of the *Phenomenology of Spirit* that only reason is real. He thinks of this reason as, internally, an extremely complex entity. Hegel now distinguishes between the 'Concept' of reason and the process of its realization. The object of the *Science of Logic* is the conceptual, that is to say, for Hegel, the logical development of this Concept. Since this Concept is the Concept of that which alone is real, Hegel can maintain that his *Science of Logic* takes the place of traditional metaphysics, which concerned itself with the elucidation of the basic ways in which we can think of reality.

Since the object whose Concept is to be logically discussed is reason, understood to be the sum of reality, the Concept of reason must include not only those aspects which account for reason's character of reality or of being, but also those aspects which do justice to the peculiar character of reason as thinking. Hegel calls these aspects 'Determinations of the

Concept' (*Begriffsbestimmungen*). Those aspects of the Concept of reason which take into account its character of being are developed by Hegel in the section 'Objective Logic' in the *Science of Logic*. He presents those aspects which are intended to do justice to its thinking character in the section called 'Subjective Logic'. He further subdivides 'Objective Logic' into 'Logic of Being' and 'Logic of Essence'.

In his 'Objective Logic', Hegel tries to show how it is possible to generate from very simple, so-called 'immediate' determinations such as 'Being', 'Nothing' and 'Becoming' other categories of quality and quantity as well as relational and modal determinations, such as 'Cause–Effect', 'Substance–Accidence' and 'Existence', 'Necessity' and the like. As in the 'Subjective Logic', the basic strategy here for the creation of categories or determinations of the Concept, assumes that (1) for every category there is an opposing one which upon closer analysis reveals itself to be its true meaning, and that (2) for every two categories opposing each other in this manner there is a third category whose meaning is determined by that which makes the opposing categories compatible. Hegel considers these two assumptions justified because only they can lead to what in his eyes is a complete and non-contingent system of categories. Hegel himself, however, did very little to make their exact meaning clear, although he uses them with great skill. Immediately after his death this led to a confused and still inconclusive discussion regarding their interpretation. Many judgments concerning the worth or worthlessness of Hegel's philosophy are linked to this discussion, which has taken its place in the annals of Hegel research as a discussion concerning the meaning, significance and value of the so-called 'dialectical method'. (Hegel himself preferred 'speculative method'.)

In particular, Hegel's claims about the truth-generating function of contradiction have played a major role in the discussion of the 'dialectical method' described in the *Science of Logic*. Though highly praised by Hegel himself, his doctrine of the nature and methodological merits of contradiction has proved to be inaccessible and obscure. This may have been caused in part by Hegel's extremely concise and provocative formulations of this methodical maxim. The reader is reminded in this context not only of the succinct formulation which he chose to defend on the occasion of his Jena Habilitation – 'contradiction is the rule of truth, non-contradiction the rule of falsehood' – but also of his provocative version of the principle of contradiction, according to which 'everything is inherently contradictory'. The difficulties associated with the comprehension of the Hegelian conception of contradiction have perforce

a link with his particular unconventional concept of contradiction. Two points are particularly important, in that they differentiate his concept from the classical concept of contradiction of traditional logic: (1) A contradiction between two propositions cannot be confirmed solely on the basis of their ascription to a single subject of two contradictory predicates; it is also necessary to take into account the meaning of the subject of these propositions. If the contradictory predicates cannot meaningfully be attributed to the subject, then no contradiction arises. 'Legible' and 'illegible' are predicates which will only lead to contradiction if attributed to texts, but not, for example, to bananas. For Hegel, this means among other things that the relation of contradiction is dependent on the context. (2) Hegel thinks of contradictions as analogous to positive and negative determinations, which neutralize each other but without making that whose neutralizing determinations they are into a contradictory concept which has absolutely no meaning, which therefore means nothing (the Kantian 'Nihil negativum'). Rather, the way in which positive and negative determinations neutralize each other tells us something informative about the object to which the neutralizing determinations apply. For example, possession of DM100 neutralizes a debt of DM100, without thereby making the concept of property a contradictory concept. Instead, the way in which this neutralization takes place makes clear that the concept 'property' means something which must be thought of as of a quantifiable size. For Hegel this is a consequence of 'the logical principle that what is self-contradictory does not dissolve itself into a nullity, into abstract nothingness, but essentially only into the negation of its *particular* content'. Whether these two convictions are sufficient to justify Hegel's thesis that contradictions play a 'positive' role in cognition procedures is rightly controversial.

Hegel's 'Subjective Logic', the second part of the *Science of Logic*, contains not only his so-called 'speculative' interpretation of the objects of traditional logic, that is, his own doctrine of concepts, judgments and syllogisms, but above all his theory of the 'Concept'. This theory is deeply rooted in Hegel's critique of traditional metaphysics, and is thus most easily comprehended when placed in that context. He presents this critique most tellingly in the third edition of the *Encyclopedia of the Philosophical Sciences*. What matters in philosophy, and what philosophy aims at, is the 'scientific recognition of truth'. This means among other things that philosophy is concerned with the recognition of 'what objects really are'. According to Hegel, the question of what objects really are has been approached in philosophy from a variety of angles, but all the different modes in which the question has been answered to date are unacceptable because they are based on false premises. Traditional metaphysics is one of the ways of approaching the question of what objects really are. Hegel characterizes this approach as 'the *impartial method*', which is motivated by the assumption that 'through *thinking the truth becomes known*, what objects really are is brought to one's consciousness'. In contrast to other philosophical approaches that deal with the question posed, metaphysics, according to Hegel, is in principle certainly capable of contributing to the cognition of what things in truth are, because it starts from the correct assumption that 'the determinations of thought' are to be seen as 'the fundamental determinations of things'. But traditional metaphysics has not made a significant contribution to the cognition of truth, because it was only able to transform its correct initial assumption in a systematically erroneous manner.

According to Hegel, the crucial weakness of traditional metaphysics is to use the form of judgment *in an unreflective manner*, and this shows itself in various ways. First it shows in the unfounded assumption of traditional metaphysics that judgments provide a particular and direct insight into the constitution of reality or that which really exists. In Hegel's view this unfounded assumption has two consequences: the first is that it tends without reason to favour a particular ontological model of reality because it regards the subject–predicate form as the standard form of the judgment; the second consequence, in Hegel's view incomparably more problematic, consists of the unfounded tendency of traditional metaphysics to conclude from the unquestioned and assumed correspondence between the form of judgment and constitution of reality that one can express by means of judgments what objects really are. Hegel does not find problematic the assumption contained in this conviction that one can make judgments concerning objects. He believes that the problem lies rather in the fact that one can assume *without examination* that 'the form of the judgment could be the form of truth'. In Hegel's view, however, such an examination is essential because the traditional understanding of subject and predicate does not justify the assertion that a subject–predicate judgment actually contributes something to the determination of a real object. An additional problem lies in the fact that the unconsidered use of the form of judgment has led traditional metaphysics erroneously to use a 'natural' interpretation of the concepts of subject and predicate. The consequence of this interpretation is that judgments of the subject–predicate form can lay no claim to 'truth'.

Hegel's chief criticism of traditional metaphysics therefore lies in the lack of clarity associated with its interpretation of the form of the judgment. In particular he rejects its tendency to interpret the judgment 'naturally', which for him means to encourage a subjectivist interpretation of the judgment built on the concept of representation. Such a subjectivist interpretation cannot show how to guarantee for the judgment some sort of claim to truth or recognition of what something really is. Therefore the subjectivist metaphysical interpretation of the judgment is problematic at the very outset. Moreover, it becomes downright dangerous when one considers its ontological implications, for it leads erroneously to the assumption that the objects corresponding to the subjects of the judgment are to be thought of as substances to which are attributed the characteristics described by the predicate-concepts. The unreflective subjectivist interpretation implies or at least suggests what may be called a substance-ontology, according to which substances which are independent of each other are taken as the fundamental entities of reality, determined predicatively by accidental characteristics which are applicable or not applicable to them. It is this commitment to a substance-ontology which Hegel critically imputes to traditional metaphysics. From this criticism, he deduces that it is first necessary to reach an agreement as to what the object really is before one can adequately assess the function and the achievement of the judgment in the context of knowledge. To reach this agreement is the task of the Logic of the Concept.

The starting point of Hegel's theory of the Concept is the assumption which he imputes to traditional metaphysics as an insight which is in principle correct. This was the insight that only through thinking can one recognize what something really is. Since in Hegel's view thinking is concerned not with intuitions or representations, but with concepts, he identifies that which something in truth or really is with its Concept. Because of this identification, talk of the Concept acquires an ontological connotation. Hegelian Concepts must not be confused with the so-called general concepts of traditional logic. They are difficult to understand precisely and are characterized by the fact that they are (1) non-sensible – which means that they are a particular type of thought-object – and that they are (2) something objective as opposed to subjective. Regarded as these objective thoughts, these Concepts are determined in the sense that in them different relations of determinations of the Concept are to be encountered which occur as determinations of thinking or of thought (*Denkbestimmungen*). These determinations of thought can themselves be regarded as a kind of predicative characteristic. They make up the multitude of all those determinations on the basis of which the Concept of an object can be seen as completely fixed.

Now, in Hegel's view, not everything has a Concept which in one sense or another is ordinarily thought of as an object. A (Hegelian) Concept is only allotted to objects which can be thought of on the model of an organism. Hegel thus maintains that one can only regard those objects as real or as existing in truth for which there is a Concept which can be interpreted on the organic model. If, then, the 'scientific recognition of truth' consists in recognizing the Concept of something, and if a Concept is always a Concept of a organic-type object, then the question arises how one should conceive of such a Concept. For Hegel it is clear that in his concept of a Concept, he must include everything needed to describe an organism. This includes first of all what Hegel calls the subjective Concept, which one can best regard as the sum of all characteristics whose realization represents an organic-type object. For Hegel, in the case of the concept of reason, whose Concept the *Science of Logic* elaborates, these characteristics are exclusively logical data which can be presented in the form of determinations of concepts, judgments and syllogisms. Furthermore, Hegel's Concept must include the element of objectivity. 'Objectivity' here means more or less the same as reality or the state of being an object and suggests the fact that it is part of the Concept of an organism to realize itself. Since, however, Hegel holds that there is ultimately only one object which really exists, namely reason, the Concept of this object must include a characteristic which is exclusively applicable to itself. This characteristic must permit the justification of the claim that in reality there is only one Concept and therefore also only one object. Hegel calls this characteristic 'subjectivity'.

Although it is easy to see that the term 'subjectivity' describes a central element of Hegel's logical theory, it is very difficult to shed light upon its meaning and function therein. It is relatively obvious only that Hegel attributes the characteristic of subjectivity not just to his Concept, but also to entities such as 'I', 'self-consciousness' and 'spirit'. We are therefore on safe ground if we assume that the subjectivity which is to be attributed to the Concept is precisely that which is also attributed to the I, self-consciousness or spirit and which distinguishes them from other types of organism. The ground becomes more dangerous when it is a matter of stating what subjectivity actually means. This is not merely because Hegel distinguishes between different types of subjectivity, but also because the subjectivity which is constitutive of the Concept is tied to conditions which are difficult to state with any precision. In general it seems to be correct to say that subjectivity occurs when something recognizes itself as being identical with something else. If we follow the *Science of Logic*, then this relationship of identity known as 'subjectivity' can only be established between entities which themselves can be thought of as being particular complexes of relations of similar elements or moments. Subjectivity in this sense is thus intended to describe a certain form of self-reference or self-relationship. According to Hegel, there should be only one entity to which the term 'subjectivity' can be attributed as a characteristic in the sense which has just been explained – the Hegelian 'Idea'. He says of it, 'The unity of the Idea is subjectivity'. This Idea now forms the end of the *Science of Logic*, because through it the Concept of reason has been completely explicated. He also describes this Idea as the absolute method, for it is not only the result, that is, the Concept which comprehends all his moments, but also the complete and systematically generated series of these moments.

The results of the Logic of the Concept represent the justification for Hegel's belief that, apart from a system of logic, a complete system of philosophy must include a so-called 'real philosophy', which is divided into a philosophy of nature and a philosophy of spirit. Hegel undertakes this justification within the framework of the exposition of what characterizes the fully developed (Hegelian) Concept. This exposition only becomes comprehensible if one remembers that Hegel is a supporter of the organological paradigm in metaphysics, according to which that which really is must be regarded as a particular type of organism. Hegel describes the type of organism relevant to his metaphysics as an object which has realized or objectivized its Concept in such a way that it comprehends itself as the objectivization of this Concept of itself. On the basis of this conception, Hegel now develops the following consideration: the (Hegelian) Concept is something which is to be regarded as a unity of (in some ways incompatible) determinations of the Concept. Among these determinations also belong, as Hegel believes he can show, that of objectivity. By this he means that it is a part of the nature of a Concept to become objective, to manifest itself as an object. Now, the only object which is an adequate realization of the Concept is the one to which what Hegel calls 'subjectivity' can be attributed. 'Subjectivity' is the name of a relational characteristic which is present when something *knows* itself to be identical with something else. For Hegel, it follows from these stipulations that subjectivity can only be attributed to the object which knows itself to be identical with its Concept. To produce this knowledge is therefore a demand inherent in the nature of the Concept. Since it is the sole task of the *Science of Logic* to exhibit the Concept of reason, and since this Concept contains the demand for the production of a form of knowledge which can only be acquired when (1) the Concept objectivizes itself, that is, becomes an object, and (2) this object comprehends itself as being identical with its Concept, then it is already a demand inherent in the Concept of reason that reason should be discussed (1) from under the point of view of its objectivity or as an object, and (2) under the aspect of its known identity with its Concept. The first of these topics is the subject of a philosophy of nature; the second that of a philosophy of spirit.

7 The system: philosophy of nature

Hegel's philosophy of nature is an attempt to explain how it is possible that we can recognize nature as a complex whole standing under a set of laws. He thereby takes up the question, important in particular to both Kant and Schelling, of which epistemological and ontological preconditions underlie our conviction that nature can be known. Although Hegel had thought about the problems of a philosophy of nature since his time in Frankfurt, and although he produced several versions of a philosophy of nature during his Jena period, he only published this part of his system once, quite late, in his *Encyclopedia of the Philosophical Sciences*. Hegel's philosophy of nature is of interest mainly in three respects. The first concerns the way in which he transforms his logical theory into an interpretation of natural phenomena. The second relates to the question of how far Hegel's conceptions in the field of the philosophy of nature take into account the scientific theories current at the time. Finally, the third leads to the question of what we should make of Hegel's approach to a philosophy of nature within the framework of present-day philosophy of science. Since the philosophy of nature is that part of the Hegelian system which is traditionally regarded with the greatest suspicion and which for this reason has received the least scholarly attention, the assessment of the second and third aspects of this philosophy of nature has so far produced very few uncontroversial results.

As far as the construction of a philosophy of nature according to the requirements of the logical theory of the Concept is concerned, Hegel assumes in accordance with his organological conception of reason that we should think of nature '*in itself* as a living whole'. This living whole has to be conceived of primarily under three different determinations, which reproduce to a certain extent the central characteristics of the Concept of reason as developed by the logical process. According to the first of these determinations, nature is to be considered as a whole defined by space, time, matter and movement. This way of looking at nature makes it the object of what Hegel calls 'mechanics'. According to Hegelian mechanics, space, time, matter and movement, their characteristics and the laws of nature which describe their relationship are generated by the formal structural moments of the (Hegelian) Concept. The utilization of such a 'conceptual' procedure to gain and secure scientific results was never seen by Hegel himself as a direct alternative procedure to empirical scientific research. On the contrary, he was of the opinion that (for instance, by means of his philosophical mechanics) he only makes explicit the conceptual elements and secures for them a rational foundation which is implicitly contained in every scientific mechanical theory that acquires its data 'from experience and then applies the mathematical treatment'.

According to Hegel, his philosophical mechanics leads to the insight that we must think of the whole of physical nature as 'qualified matter', that is, as a totality of bodies with physical characteristics. This provides the second main determination by which nature is to be comprehended. Hegel ascribes to this way of comprehending nature a discipline which he calls 'physics', including under this heading everything which can in any way be linked with the material status of a body. Accordingly, from phenomena like specific weight, through those like sound, warmth, shape, electricity and magnetism, to the chemical reactions of substances, everything is described as being a consequence of and following from the constitution of the (Hegelian) Concept. He also adds theses concerning the nature of light and a doctrine concerning the elements earth, fire, water and air. It was this part of Hegel's philosophy of nature in particular which drove Hans Scholz, among others, to the following crushing judgment: 'Hegel's philosophy of nature is an experiment which set the philosophy of nature back several centuries instead of furthering its cause, returning it to the stage it had reached at about the time of Paracelsus'. Whether this dictum has substance, however, depends very much on what conception of nature and science one favours.

The third part of Hegel's philosophy of nature consists of the so-called 'organic physics' or 'organics'. In this section the characteristic of subjectivity, familiar from his logical theory, is the determination under which nature is to be regarded. Since in the context of the philosophy of nature, Hegel interprets subjectivity as an essential characteristic of organic life, this section of his philosophy of nature is concerned with nature as a hierarchy of organisms or as an 'organic system'. He distinguishes between three forms of organic life which are exemplified in three types of organism: the general form, which is represented by the geological organism, the particular, which is realized in vegetation, and the individual, which finds its expression in animal organisms. He regards these forms as hierarchically ordered by increasing degree of complexity. In some ways Hegel thematizes relations and conditions of dependence: just as vegetable life-forms presuppose geological structures and processes, so animal organisms presuppose a fully developed plant world. Hegel links this last part of his philosophy of nature to his philosophy of spirit by means of an analysis of the phenomenon of the death of an individual natural being. Here the leading idea is that although through death all natural determinations of the individual are removed, so that we can speak of the 'death of the natural element', none the less death does not annihilate the principle of life, that which is responsible for the essential unity of animal organization and which Hegel calls the 'soul'. Since Hegel interprets the soul as a form of spirit, and since according to his conception the soul is not destroyed by death, he can now postulate the reality of spirit independently of natural determinations as the result of his philosophy of nature, and investigate this reality in its various forms within the framework of a philosophy of spirit.

The question whether Hegel's philosophy of nature integrates in a relatively informed manner the state of science during his lifetime has provoked a number of fairly controversial answers, as has the question whether his approach can still provide any promising perspectives which are relevant today. During the nineteenth century, Hegel's philosophy of nature was broadly considered scandalous by the majority of scientists, an attitude which contributed in no small measure to the discrediting of his philosophy as a whole. This assessment also meant that Hegel's philosophy of nature has never really been taken seriously again. Since 1970, however, the situation has changed somewhat. Starting from and relying on recent investigations in the history of science regarding the development and state of the sciences during the early nineteenth century, increasing numbers of scholars are inclining towards the view that Hegel was indeed much more familiar with the science of his time and its problems than was generally believed during the nineteenth and most of the twentieth century. It seems advisable at present to refrain from passing final judgment on this matter. The same cannot, however, be said with regard to the present relevance. Here one cannot ignore the fact that Hegel's theses concerning philosophy of nature are, quite simply, meaningless for present-day scientific theory.

8 The system: philosophy of spirit

Hegel's philosophy of spirit is divided into a theory of subjective, objective and absolute spirit. The philosophy of subjective spirit contains Hegel's philosophical psychology; his philosophy of objective spirit is devoted to his theory of law and politics and his conception of world history; and his philosophy of absolute spirit presents his theory of art, religion and philosophy. Hegel presented his philosophy of subjective spirit and in particular his philosophy of absolute spirit to a wider public only in outline in a few paragraphs of the *Encyclopedia of the Philosophical Sciences*. He presented his philosophy of objective spirit not only in the *Encyclopedia*, but also in detail in a work which was already highly regarded during his lifetime, *Natural Law and Politics in Outline: The Principles of the Philosophy of Right* (1821). In this part of his system Hegel again relies on the principle developed in his logical theory that something – here the entity called 'spirit' – must experience a process of realization in order to be able to recognize its truth, or what it is.

The philosophy of subjective spirit contains an anthropology, a phenomenology of spirit and a psychology. In these sections Hegel describes and analyses all the phenomena that influence the somatic, psychophysical and mental characteristics, conditions, processes and activities of the individual. The gamut of subjects he covers runs from the natural qualities of the individual, expressed in temperament, character and physiognomy, via sensibility, feeling, awareness and desire, to self-awareness, intuition, representation, thinking and wanting. Here one finds Hegel's theory of language acquisition, of practical feeling, of the achievements and function of imagination, his defence of the life-preserving power of habit, his solution of the mind–body problem, his understanding of the origin and treatment of mental illnesses and many other subjects. In these analyses Hegel's aim is to replace the 'ordinary approach' of empirical psychology with a 'philosophical perspective' towards psychological phenomena. The dominant characteristic of this philosophical attitude, it is claimed, is that it permits an interpretation of the subject of psychic processes as the product of psychic activity and not as an object to be thought of as a substance possessing certain powers and capacities which are its characteristics.

While the philosophy of subjective spirit really only

attracted attention up to the middle of the nineteenth century, Hegel's philosophy of objective spirit, in other words his theory of law and politics, received a great deal of attention during the nineteenth and especially the twentieth century. This was not only because of the theory's great importance for the Marxist and other anti-liberalistic social theories (see MARX, K.; WESTERN MARXISM). It has also repeatedly been the object of violent controversy, especially because of its political implications. In all its versions, Hegel's political philosophy rests on three main convictions which he cherished from his early years and held for the rest of his life. The first is that every modern philosophy of law and politics must incorporate the conception of freedom which was central to the European Enlightenment, and in particular to that of Germany (see ENLIGHTENMENT, CONTINENTAL). The second is that, especially in the case of modern political philosophy, the insight that the whole takes priority over its separate parts, an insight formulated by ARISTOTLE in his *Politics*, must be maintained and brought up to date. Finally, the third conviction consists in an application of the principle which shapes Hegel's whole philosophical enterprise, namely, that political philosophy must play its part in the confirmation of the thesis that only reason is real. Hegel attempts to do justice to these three convictions within the framework of his theory of objective spirit by (1) introducing an extravagant conception of freedom, (2) identifying the whole of Aristotle with the phenomenon which he calls 'ethical life' and (3) declaring this phenomenon called 'ethical life' to be the 'reality of reason'.

Hegel fulfils his self-imposed demand for the integration of freedom by making the conception of free will the fundamental concept of his philosophy of the objective spirit; this is where his characteristic conception of freedom comes into play. According to Hegel, a will is free not because it can choose its ends from a virtually limitless number of objective alternatives; the truly free will is the will which only determines itself. For Hegel, self-determination means to refer willingly to oneself, that is, to will oneself. Thus he thinks of freedom as a case of self-reference and in this way assimilates it into his concept of cognition, which is also based on the idea of self-reference (see §5 above). This assimilation is utterly intentional on Hegel's part, because it gives him the opportunity to interpret the process of the systematic unfolding of the various determinations of the will not only as different ways of the realization of free will but also as a process of cognition (see FREEDOM AND LIBERTY; FREE WILL).

Against this background, Hegel first develops his theories of law and morality, which derive all legal relationships and the obligatory character of moral acts from the concept of free will. In his theory of law, Hegel makes his contribution to the discussion of the philosophical foundations of civil and criminal law. His basic thesis is that property, the acquisition and use of which is a presupposition for being able to act freely, is the necessary condition of law in all its different variations. In his theory of morality, Hegel discusses the moral behaviour of autonomous subjects under the aspect of the gaining of moral standpoints for the purpose of judging actions and of the conversion of moral goals into actions. According to Hegel, however, legal relationships and moral standards are *founded* in social institutions. He thinks of these institutions as forms of what he calls 'ethical life' (*Sittlichkeit*). In Hegel's language, ethical life as the basis for the possibility of law and morality is the truth of free will, that which free will really is. Since it is a characteristic of the truth of free will to be real, it follows that, for Hegel, ethical life is also the reality of free will. This reality is thus the 'presupposed whole', without reference to which the discussion of law and morality makes no sense at all. This thesis of the function of real ethical life as the basis for law and morality is intended to account for the Aristotelian maxim of the primacy of the whole in political philosophy (see LEGAL IDEALISM §§1–2).

For Hegel, ethical life appears in three institutional forms: family, bourgeois society and the state. The theory of the family contains his thoughts on the ethical function of marriage, his justification of monogamy, his views on family property and the laws of inheritance and his maxims for bringing up children. The theory of bourgeois society became well-known and influential, above all because of Hegel's diagnosis of the difficulties which will arise within a society based solely on economic interests and elementary needs of its individual members. This diagnosis is grounded in Hegel's analyses of a society founded solely on economic relationships. They owe much to the works on political economy by Adam Smith, J.P. Say and Ricardo, to whom Hegel often explicitly refers. According to Hegel, a bourgeois society considered as an economic community is defined by the fact that in it people can satisfy their needs through labour. The manifold nature of these needs means that they can only be satisfied by division of labour within the society. This leads economic subjects to join together into estates (*Stände*) and corporations whose members each undertake specific tasks with regard to the socially organized satisfaction of their needs. Hegel recognizes three estates: the peasant estate, which he calls the 'substantial estate'; the tradesmen's estate, among which he includes craftsmen, manufacturers and traders; and what he calls the 'general estate', whose members fulfil judicial and policing functions. Corporations are formed mainly in the tradesmen's estate. Although this entire realm of bourgeois society organized along these lines does involve legal restrictions, and is regulated by a civil and criminal legal code, it none the less cannot remain indefinitely stable. For it is not possible to prevent the polarization of the poor majority and the rich minority which leads to overpopulation, so that eventually the entire social wealth will not suffice to satisfy even the most elementary needs of all. The consequences are colonization and the formation of the 'proletariat'. Both will tend to destroy this bourgeois society.

If one follows Hegel's arguments, bourgeois society can only avoid this fate if its members act not according to their own particular interests and needs, but recognize the state as their 'general purpose', and direct all their activities to maintaining it (see CIVIL SOCIETY §1; STATE). Hegel thinks of the state as a constitutional monarchy with division of power. For Hegel, the constitution of a state is in no sense the product of some constitution-creating institution or the work of individual persons. It is 'absolutely essential that the constitution, although the product of past history, *should not be seen as a finished entity*'. A constitution is rather the manifestation of the spirit of a people, created during the course of history through their customs and traditions. This view permits Hegel to maintain on the one hand that each people has the constitution 'which is appropriate to it and fits it', and on the other to insist that there is not much leeway for the modification of constitutions. The constitutional form of a reasonably organized state must be a monarchy because its characteristic individuality can only be appropriately represented by a concrete individual to whom as a person the sovereign acts of the state can be attributed. Hegel also favours a hereditary monarchy, since he sees the process of determining a person as monarch by virtue of its origin as the method which is least dependent upon arbitrary decisions. Hegel's theory of the powers of the state (*Staatsgewalten*) recognizes, in addition to the princely power (*fürstliche Gewalt*) which represents the instance of ultimate decision-making within the constitutional framework, the governmental power (*Regierungsgewalt*) and the legislative power (*gesetzgebende Gewalt*). It is the task of the governmental power, which for Hegel also includes the judicial power, to pursue the general interests of the state, ensure the maintenance of right and enforce the laws. The legislative power is responsible for the 'further determination' of the constitution and laws. It is executed by an assembly of the estates which is divided into two chambers. The first chamber consists of a certain group of powerful landowners chosen by virtue of their birth; the second chamber comprises representatives of the corporate associations of the bourgeois society, who are sent to the assembly by their various corporations. Thus in Hegel's model state, both chambers are constituted without the direct political involvement of the population. Hegel's theory of the state provoked considerable controversy, particularly during his own time, because of its resolute defence of the hereditary monarchy and its strongly anti-democratic characteristics in all questions concerning the political representation of the citizens of the state. It was this section of his political philosophy in particular which, as early as the mid-nineteenth century, gave rise to the statement that Hegel was the philosopher of the Prussian state.

Hegel forges the link to his theory of the spirit, which contains his political philosophy, by interpreting what he calls 'ethical life' as the 'spirit of a people'. This allows him to elaborate his conception of history on the one hand and on the other to introduce his theory of the absolute spirit. The philosophy of history is introduced by the idea that ethical life as the reality of free will takes on different forms for different peoples. These forms differ from each other in the degree to which the different institutions of ethical life are actually developed. Now, Hegel believes that this development has taken place during the course of a historical process which he calls 'world history' (see HISTORY, PHILOSOPHY OF). This process of world history, which he sees as 'progress in the consciousness of freedom', can be divided into four distinct epochs, which correspond to four 'empires of world history'. Hegel describes this process of world history as beginning with the 'Oriental Empire', which is followed by the 'Greek' and then by the 'Roman' empires. The process is brought to a conclusion by the 'Germanic Empire', in which the 'Germanic peoples are given the task of accomplishing the principle of the unity of divine and human nature, of reconciling...objective truth and freedom'. Hegel now interprets this reconciliation as the conclusion of the process of the self-recognition of reason. The result of this process consists of the insight that reason *knows itself* to be the whole of reality. Thus Hegel links the theory of the objective spirit with his metaphysics of reason and can now concentrate on the various aspects of this self-knowledge of reason as a theory of absolute spirit.

Hegel's philosophy of absolute spirit contains his philosophy of art, his philosophy of religion and his theory of philosophy. Although from the very first all these subjects had a fixed place in Hegel's attempts at a system, and although his philosophies of art and religion were to become very influential (the one in the history of art and the theory of aesthetics and the other in theology), none the less these sections of Hegel's philosophy are relatively little elaborated in the works published by Hegel himself. Apart from a few sketch-like hints in his first work, *Difference between the Systems of Fichte and Schelling* (see §3 above), and the two final chapters of the *Phenomenology of Spirit*, Hegel devoted only a few paragraphs to these themes at the end of the *Encyclopedia of Philosophical Sciences*. We can gather from these paragraphs that there are three different ways in which reason, which knows itself, relates to itself; these are manifested in art, religion and philosophy. They differ from each other in the way in which in each of these ways reason knows itself. In art, reason relates to itself *intuitively* or, as Hegel says, *knows itself immediately*, while in religion this knowing relationship with itself realizes itself in the form of *representation*, which is linked with the sublation of the immediacy of knowledge. In philosophy, the self-reference of reason is accounted for in the mode of *cognition*. The theory of epistemic modes which underpins this functional analysis of art, religion and philosophy, though obviously relying on the results of the Hegelian theory of the subjective spirit, none the less contains a number of difficulties which are hard to unravel.

Against this background of different forms of knowledge, Hegel first reveals his theory of art in the form of a theory of styles of art (*Kunstformen*) and of individual arts (*Kunstarten*). He recognizes three different styles of art, which he calls symbolic, classical and romantic. They differ from each other in their various means of expressing the distinguishing characteristics of the spiritual, which belong to the sensible and therefore to the intuitive manifestations which reason gives itself. These styles themselves are characterized by the ways in which a spiritual content presents itself as the meaning of a sensible object. The symbolic style of art is thus the one in which the relationship between meaning and sensible appearance is relatively contingent, since it only arises through a randomly chosen attribute. By way of example Hegel takes the lion, which symbolizes strength. In the classical style of art the sensible appearance expresses adequately what it is intended to signify. For Hegel, the human figure serves as a paradigm for this adequate symbolization of the spiritual, especially in the way in which it is represented in sculpture and painting. Finally, the romantic style of art takes as its subject the representation of the 'self-conscious inwardness' of the spirit. In it, the emotional world of the subject is expressed by reference to sensible characteristics. Hegel interprets the various individual arts as

realizations of styles of art in various materials. Although each individual art can present itself in each style of art, there is for each individual art an ideal style, which he calls its basic type. The first individual art which Hegel discusses is architecture. Its task is to deal with nonorganic nature in an artful manner. Its basic type is the symbolic style of art. The second individual art is sculpture, the basic type of which is the classical style. Sculpture aims to transform nonorganic nature into the physical form of the human body. The remaining individual arts are painting, music and poetry, whose basic type is represented by the romantic style of art. Painting marks the beginning of the separation of the direct processing of natural materials and thus a certain intellectualization of matter, which makes it capable of representing feelings, emotions, etc. Music is the romantic style of art *par excellence*. Its material is sound, which is matter only in a figurative sense and is therefore particularly suitable for the representation of even the most fleeting affects. Finally poetry, the last of the romantic arts, has as its material only signs, which here play no part as material entities, but as bearers of meaning. These meanings refer to the realm of imagination and other spiritual content, so that in poetry a spiritual content can be presented in a manner appropriate to its spirituality. Hegel could not resist the temptation to use his theory of individual arts and styles of art as a model for the interpretation of the history of the development of art. His historicizing of individual arts and styles of art played a significant role in making the concept of an epoch an important tool in the history of art.

In the philosophy of religion Hegel holds that only in Christianity are the conditions fulfilled which are characteristic of the representational self-knowledge of reason. Philosophy of religion has as its subject not only God, but also religion itself, and for Hegel that means the way in which God is present in the religious consciousness. By this characterization he aims to distinguish philosophy of religion from the traditional *theologia naturalis*. On the basis of the two components which make up its nature, the philosophy of religion attempts in the first instance to characterize more closely the concept of God and the various kinds of religious consciousness which Hegel takes to be feeling, intuition and representation. This will be found in the first part of the philosophy of religion, which thematizes the 'concept of religion'. The second part of the philosophy of religion discusses what Hegel calls 'determinate religion'. Here, he is concerned with something resembling a phenomenology of religions, the exposition of their various forms of appearance and objectivizations. This exposition starts with so-called natural religion, which according to Hegel assumes three forms: the religion of magic, the religion of substantiality and the religion of abstract subjectivity. The specific characteristic of natural religion is that it thinks of God in direct unity with nature. Natural religion finds its historical concept in the Oriental religions. Hegel regards the 'religions of spiritual individuality' as a second stage; these assume the forms of the religion of sublimity, the religion of beauty and the religion of teleology. At this stage, God is regarded as the primary spiritual being, which is not only nature but which also rules over and determines nature. Hegel puts the Jewish, Greek and Roman religions in this category. Finally, the third stage represents the 'perfect religion', to the discussion of which he devotes the third section of his philosophy of religion. In it, God is presented as He in reality is, namely the 'infinite, absolute end in itself'. To the religious consciousness, the God of the perfect religion appears in the trinitarian form as the unity of the Father, Son and Holy Ghost. According to Hegel, this idea of religion was first realized adequately in Christianity. Hegel's philosophy of religion greatly influenced theological discussions and points of view. None the less, it was not without its critics, for whom it represented a theory which, as, for example, R. Haym claimed in the last century, contributed to the dissolution of the Godly in reason and of Piety in knowledge.

As far as philosophy is concerned, Hegel maintains that its distinguishing mode of knowledge, namely cognition, is present when something is seen to be necessary. Since reason within the sphere of the absolute spirit relates only to itself, the achievement of the cognitive reference of reason to itself lies in the fact that it understands the progress of its realization in logic, nature and spirit as a necessary process. Philosophy is the representation of this process in its necessity. This philosophical process also has its appearance in time in the form of the history of philosophy. For Hegel, the history of philosophy presents itself as a historical succession of philosophical positions in which in each case one of the essential characteristics of (Hegelian) reason is made the principle of a philosophical interpretation of the world in a one-sided and distorted way that is characteristic of its time. He sees the existence of political freedom as a necessary precondition for a philosophical interpretation of the world. Only in societies in which free constitutions exist can philosophical thought develop. Since, he claims, the concepts of freedom and constitution only arose as the products of Greek (that is, occidental) thought, philosophical discourse is really a specifically Western achievement. He therefore absolutely refuses to ascribe any philosophically relevant intellectual achievements to the Oriental world, the principle proponents of which are in his view China and India. All the doctrines of wisdom of the Orient can at most be accepted as codifications of religious ideas. If, for a Westerner, some of these doctrines none the less seem to express a philosophical thought, this is because they confuse the abstract generality of Oriental religious ideas with the generality which is applicable to the thoughts of reason engaged in thinking itself. Hegel divides Western philosophy into two main periods: Greek and Germanic philosophy. Up to a certain point, Greek philosophy also includes Roman, and Germanic philosophy includes not only German philosophy but that of other European peoples as well, since these peoples have 'in their totality a Germanic culture'. The difference between Greek and Germanic philosophy lies in the fact that Greek philosophy was not yet in a position to comprehend the conception of spirit in all its profundity. This only became possible through Christianity and its acceptance throughout the Germanic world. For only in this historical context was it possible for the insight to establish itself that the essence of spirit is subjectivity and hence knowledge of itself. Hegel regards it as a great merit of his philosophy that it adequately explains this, and thus reconciles reason with reality in thought. In the last analysis, his message consists of a single proposition: Reason is and knows itself to be the ultimate reality. His system is brought to a conclusion in what is, in his view, a successful justification of that proposition. Even during the nineteenth century, the optimism of reason underlying Hegel's system aroused criticism, for example, from Nietzsche and the representatives of Neo-Kantianism. It seems doubtful whether, at the end of the twentieth century, Hegel's indomitable faith in reason can continue to convince.

See also ABSOLUTE, THE; GERMAN IDEALISM; HEGELIANISM; NEO-KANTIANISM

List of works

German editions of major works

Hegel, G.W.F. (1968–) *Gesammelte Werke*, ed. von der Rheinisch-westfälischen Akademie der Wissenschaften, Hamburg: Meiner. (This is the historical-critical edition in progress which aims at completeness. Up to the end of 1996 fifteen volumes have appeared.)

—— (1832–45) *Werke. Vollständige Ausgabe durch einen Verein von Freunden des Verewigten*, 18 vols in 21, Berlin: Duncker & Humblot. (This is the first edition – inaugurated by an association of friends of

Hegel – which contains a large amount of material from Hegel's lectures. Of particular importance are vol. 9 *Lectures on the Philosophy of History*, vols 10, 1–3 *Lectures on Aesthetics*, vols 11–12 *Lectures on the Philosophy of Religion*, vols 13–15 *Lectures on the History of Philosophy*.)

—— (1970) *Werke in 20 Bänden (Theorie-Werkausgabe)*, ed. E. Moldenhauer and K.M. Michel, Frankfurt: Suhrkamp. (This is a modified and slightly enlarged reprint of the 1832–45 edition.)

—— (c.1793–1800) *Theologische Jugendschriften*, ed. H. Nohl, Tübingen: J.C.B. Mohr, 1907, reprinted 1968. (Collection of manuscripts and fragments written before 1801.)

—— (1801a) *De Orbitis Planetarum*, Jena: Seidler. (Hegel's Habilitation Essay.)

—— (1801b) *Differenz des Fichte'schen und Schelling'schen Systems der Philosophie*, Jena: Seidler. (Hegel's first philosophical publication.)

—— (1802) *Glauben und Wissen oder die Reflexionsphilosophie der Subjektivität*, in *Kritisches Journal der Philosophie*, ed. F.W.J. Schelling and G.W.F. Hegel, Tübingen: Cotta. (Contains his early criticism of Kant, Jacobi and Fichte.)

—— (c.1803–4) *Jenaer Systementwürfe I*, newly ed. K. Düsing and H. Kimmerle, Hamburg: Meiner, 1986. (Contains fragments of the first system draft.)

—— (c.1804–5) *Jenaer Systementwürfe II*, newly ed. R.P. Horstmann, Hamburg: Meiner, 1982. (Documents his early conception of logic and metaphysics and contains a fragmentary version of his philosophy of nature.)

—— (c.1805–6) *Jenaer Systementwürfe III*, newly ed. R.P. Horstmann, Hamburg: Meiner, 1987. (Incomplete versions of his philosophy of nature and of spirit.)

—— (1807) *System der Wissenschaft. Erster Theil, die Phänomenologie des Geistes*, Bamberg & Würzburg: Goebhardt. (The famous introduction to the system.)

—— (1812–16) *Wissenschaft der Logik*, Nürnberg: Schrag, 3 vols. (The most extensive elaboration of his metaphysical logic.)

—— (1821) *Naturrecht und Staatswissenschaft im Grundrisse. Grundlinien der Philosophie des Rechts*, Berlin: Nicolai. (Contains his theory of law and morality as well as his social and political philosophy.)

—— (1830) *Enzyklopädie der philosophischen Wissenschaften im Grundrisse. Dritte Ausgabe*, Heidelberg: Winter. (The last and most comprehensive version of his system.)

—— (1952–81) *Briefe von und an Hegel*, ed. J. Hoffmeister and F. Nicolin, Hamburg: Meiner, 4 vols. (A richly commented edition of his correspondence.)

—— (1983–) *Vorlesungen. Ausgewählte Nachschriften und Manuskripte*, Hamburg: Meiner. (Contains a large number of manuscripts which are based on student notes of Hegel's lecture courses. Many of these manuscripts have been discovered only recently.)

English translations

—— (1892–6) *Lectures on the History of Philosophy*, trans. E.S. Haldane and F.H. Simson, London: Kegan, Paul, Trench, Trübner, 3 vols; reprinted, Atlantic Highlands, NJ: Humanities Press, 1983. (Translation of vols 13–15 of Hegel (1832–45).)

—— (1948) *Early Theological Writings*, trans. T.M. Knox, Chicago, IL: University of Chicago Press. (Translation of Hegel (c.1793–1800).)

—— (1969) *Science of Logic*, trans. A.V. Miller, London: Allen & Unwin; repr. Atlantic Highlands, NJ: Humanities Press, 1993. (Translation of Hegel (1812–16).)

—— (1970a) *Phenomenology of Spirit*, trans. A.V. Miller, Oxford: Clarendon Press. (Translation of Hegel (1807).)

—— (1970b) *Philosophy of Nature*, trans. and ed. M.J. Petry, London: Allen & Unwin, 3 vols. (Translation of part 2 of the *Enzyklopädie der philosophischen Wissenschaften im Grundrisse* in the version presented as vol. 7, 1 in Hegel (1832–45). With informative introduction and excellent explanatory notes. Also translated by A.V. Miller, Oxford: Clarendon Press, 1970.)

—— (1975) *Aesthetics*, trans. T.M. Knox, Oxford: Clarendon Press, 2 vols. (Translation of vols 10, 1–3 of Hegel (1832–45).)

—— (1977a) *Faith and Knowledge*, trans. and ed. W. Cerf and H.S. Harris, Albany, NY: State University of New York Press. (Translation of Hegel (1802).)

—— (1977b) *The Difference between Fichte's and Schelling's System of Philosophy*, trans. and ed. H.S. Harris and W. Cerf, Albany, NY: State University of New York Press. (Translation of Hegel (1801).)

—— (1978) *Philosophy of Subjective Spirit*, trans. and ed. M.J. Petry, Dordrecht and Boston, MA: Reidel, 3 vols. (Contains a translation of the first section of part 3 of the *Enzyklopädie der philosophischen Wissenschaften im Grundrisse* in the version printed as vol. 7, 2 in Hegel (1832–45). With introduction and explanatory notes.)

—— (1984) *Letters*, trans. C. Butler and C. Seiler, Bloomington, IN: Indiana University Press. (Contains a selection from Hegel (1952–81).)

—— (1984–7) *Lectures on the Philosophy of Religion*, trans. C.P. Hodgson and R.F. Brown, Los Angeles, CA: University of California Press, 3 vols. (Translation of vols 3–5 of Hegel (1983–).)

—— (1986) *The Jena System of 1804–05: Logic and Metaphysics*, trans. J. Burbidge *et al.*, Kingston and Montreal: McGill-Queen's Press. (Contains part of Hegel (*c*.1804–05).)

—— (1988) *Introduction to the Philosophy of History*, trans. L. Rauch, Indianapolis, IN: Hackett Publishing Company. (Contains material from vol. 9 of Hegel (1832–45).)

—— (1990) *Encyclopedia of the Philosophical Sciences in Outline, and Critical Writings*, ed. E. Behler, New York: Continuum. (Contains a translation of the first edition of the *Encyclopedia*.)

—— (1991a) *The Encyclopaedia Logic*, trans. T.F. Geraets, W.A. Suchting and H.S. Harris, Indianapolis: Hackett Publishing Company. (Translation of part 1 of *Enzyklopädie der philosophischen Wissenschaften im Grundrisse* as printed in vol. 6 of Hegel (1832–45).)

—— (1991b) *Elements of the Philosophy of Right*, trans. H.B. Nisbet, ed. A. Wood, Cambridge: Cambridge University Press. (Translation of Hegel (1821).)

References and further reading

Beiser, F.C. (ed.) (1993) *The Cambridge Companion to Hegel*, Cambridge: Cambridge University Press. (Collection of essays on various topics of Hegel's philosophy.)

Dickey, L. (1987) *Hegel: Religion, Economics and Politics of the Spirit, 1770–1807*, Cambridge: Cambridge University Press. (Social, religious and political background of Hegel's early philosophy.)

Düsing, K. (1983) *Hegel und die Geschichte der Philosophie* (Hegel and the History of Philosophy), Darmstadt: Wissenschaftliche Buchgesellschaft. (Focuses on Hegel's interpretation of important positions in ancient and modern philosophy.)

Fulda, H.F. (1975) *Das Problem einer Einleitung in Hegels Wissenschaft der Logik* (The Problem of an Introduction to Hegel's Science of Logic), Frankfurt: Klostermann, 2nd edn. (An essay on the role of the *Phenomenology of Spirit* in Hegel's system.)

Hardimon, M. (1994) *The Project of Reconciliation: Hegel's Social Philosophy*, Cambridge: Cambridge University Press. (Hegel's views on the relation between the individual and the modern social world.)

Harris, H.S. (1972–83) *Hegel's Development*, vol. 1 *Toward the Sunlight 1770–1801*, vol. 2 *Night Thoughts. Jena 1801–1806*, Oxford: Oxford University Press. (Hegel's intellectual development in the light of his early writings.)

* Haym, R. (1857) *Hegel und seine Zeit* (Hegel and his Age), Berlin: Gärtner; reprinted, Darmstadt: Wissenschaftliche Buchgesellschaft, 1962. (Very important critical study of Hegel's system and its development.)

Henrich, D. (1971) *Hegel im Kontext* (Hegel in Context), Frankfurt: Suhrkamp. (Influential essays on logical themes.)

Horstmann, R.P. (1990) *Wahrheit aus dem Begriff* (Truth from the Concept), Frankfurt: Anton Hain. (Deals with metaphysical assumptions of Hegel's philosophy.)

Inwood, M. (1983) *Hegel*, London: Routledge & Kegan Paul. (Critical discussion of central topics.)

McTaggart, J. (1910) *A Commentary on Hegel's Logic*, Cambridge: Cambridge University Press. (Still very informative.)

—— (1922) *Studies in the Hegelian Dialectic*, Cambridge: Cambridge University Press. (A well-informed contribution to Hegel's methodology.)

Pinkard, T. (1994) *Hegel's Phenomenology. The Sociality of Reason*, Cambridge: Cambridge University Press. (A penetrating interpretation of the aim and the structure of Hegel's most influential book.)

Pippin, R.B. (1989) *Hegel's Idealism: The Satisfactions of Self-Consciousness*, Cambridge: Cambridge University Press. (Concentrates on Hegel's epistemology and its Kantian sources.)

Rosen, M. (1982) *Hegel's Dialectic and its Criticism*, Cambridge: Cambridge University Press. (Methodological problems of Hegel's metaphysics.)

* Rosenkranz, K. (1844) *Hegel's Leben* (Hegel's Life), Berlin: Duncker & Humblot. (The first biography of Hegel.)

* Scholz, H. (1921) *Die Bedeutung der Hegelschen Philosophie für das philosophische Denken der Gegenwart* (The Relevance of Hegel's Philosophy for Contemporary Philosophical Thought), Berlin: de Gruyter. (Contains a harsh criticism of Hegel's endeavour.)

Stern, R. (ed.) (1993) *G.W.F. Hegel: Critical Assessments*, London: Routledge & Kegan Paul, 4 vols. (A voluminous collection of essays on Hegel.)

Taylor, C. (1975) *Hegel*, Cambridge: Cambridge University Press. (The best and most comprehensive introduction to Hegel for the English speaking reader.)

Theunissen, M. (1978) *Sein und Schein. Die kritische Funktion der Hegelschen Logik* (Being and Appearance. The critical function of Hegel's Logic), Frankfurt: Suhrkamp. (A very detailed account of central ideas of Hegel's Logic.)

Wood, A. (1990) *Hegel's Ethical Thought*, Cambridge: Cambridge University Press. (A modern interpretation of Hegel's moral and social philosophy.)

Translated by Jane Michael-Rushmer

ROLF-PETER HORSTMANN

HEGELIANISM

As an intellectual tradition, the history of Hegelianism is the history of the reception and influence of the thought of G.W.F. Hegel. This tradition is notoriously complex and many-sided, because while some Hegelians have seen themselves as merely defending and developing his ideas along what they took to be orthodox lines, others have sought to 'reform' his system, or to appropriate individual aspects and overturn others, or to offer consciously revisionary readings of his work. This makes it very hard to identify any body of doctrine common to members of this tradition, and a wide range of divergent philosophical views can be found among those who (despite this) can none the less claim to be Hegelians.

There are both 'internal' and 'external' reasons for this: on one hand, Hegel's position itself brings together many different tendencies (idealism and objectivism, historicism and absolutism, rationalism and empiricism, Christianity and humanism, classicism and modernism, a liberal view of civil society with an organicist view of the state); any balance between them is hermeneutically very unstable, enabling existing readings to be challenged and old orthodoxies to be overturned. On the other hand, the critical response to Hegel's thought and the many attempts to undermine it have meant that Hegelians have continually needed to reconstruct his ideas and even to turn Hegel against himself, while each new intellectual development, such as Marxism, pragmatism, phenomenology or existential philosophy, has brought about some reassessment of his position. This feature of the Hegelian tradition has been heightened by the fact that Hegel's work has had an impact at different times over a long period and in a wide range of countries, so that divergent intellectual, social and historical pressures have influenced its distinct appropriations. At the hermeneutic level, these appropriations have contributed greatly to keeping the philosophical understanding of Hegel alive and open-ended, so that our present-day conception of his thought cannot properly be separated from them. Moreover, because questions of Hegel interpretation have so often revolved around the main philosophical, political and religious issues of the nineteenth and twentieth

centuries, Hegelianism has also had a significant impact on the development of modern Western thought in its own right.

As a result of its complex evolution, Hegelianism is best understood historically, by showing how the changing representation of Hegel's ideas have come about, shaped by the different critical concerns, socio-political conditions and intellectual movements that dominated his reception in different countries at different times. Initially, Hegel's influence was naturally most strongly felt in Germany as a comprehensive, integrative philosophy that seemed to do justice to all realms of experience and promised to preserve the Christian heritage in a modern and progressive form within a speculative framework. However, this position was quickly challenged, both from other philosophical standpoints (such as F.W.J. Schelling's 'positive philosophy' and F.A. Trendelenburg's neo-Aristotelian empiricism), and by the celebrated generation of younger thinkers (the so-called 'Young' or 'Left' Hegelians, such as Ludwig Feuerbach, David Strauss, Bruno Bauer, Arnold Ruge and the early Karl Marx), who insisted that to discover what made Hegel a truly significant thinker (his dialectical method, his view of alienation, his 'sublation' of Christianity), this orthodoxy must be overturned. None the less, both among these radicals and in academic circles, Hegel's influence was considerably weakened in Germany by the 1860s and 1870s, while by this time developments in Hegelian thought had begun to take place elsewhere.

Hegel's work was known outside Germany from the 1820s onwards, and Hegelian schools developed in northern Europe, Italy, France, Eastern Europe, America and (somewhat later) Britain, each with their own distinctive line of interpretation, but all fairly uncritical in their attempts to assimilate his ideas. However, in each of these countries challenges to the Hegelian position were quick to arise, partly because the influence of Hegel's German critics soon spread abroad, and partly because of the growing impact of other philosophical positions (such as Neo-Kantianism, materialism and pragmatism). Nevertheless, Hegelianism outside Germany proved more durable in the face of these attacks, as new readings and approaches emerged to counter them, and ways were found to reinterpret Hegel's work to show that it could accommodate these other positions, once the earlier accounts of Hegel's metaphysics, political philosophy and philosophy of religion (in particular) were rejected as too crude.

This pattern has continued into the twentieth century, as many of the movements that began by defining themselves against Hegel (such as Neo-Kantianism, Marxism, existentialism, pragmatism, post-structuralism and even 'analytic' philosophy) have then come to find unexpected common ground, giving a *new impetus and depth to Hegelianism as it began to be assimilated within and influenced by these diverse approaches. Such efforts at rapprochement began in the early part of the century with Wilhelm Dilthey's attempt to link Hegel with his own historicism, and although they were more ambivalent, this connection was reinforced in Italy by Benedetto Croce and Giovanni Gentile. The realignment continued in France in the 1930s, as Jean Wahl brought out the more existentialist themes in Hegel's thought, followed in the 1940s by Alexander Kojève's influential Marxist readings. Hegelianism has also had an impact on Western Marxism through the writings of the Hungarian Georg Lukács, and this influence has continued in the critical reinterpretations offered by members of the Frankfurt School, particularly Theodor W. Adorno, Max Horkheimer, Herbert Marcuse, Jürgen Habermas and others. More recently, most of the major schools of philosophical thought (from French post-structuralism to Anglo-American 'analytic' philosophy) have emphasized the need to take account of Hegel, and as a result Hegelian thought (both exegetical and constructive) is continually finding new directions.*

1 **The Hegelian School in Germany 1816–40**
2–3 **The critique of Hegelian idealism 1840–70**
4–5 **Hegelianism outside Germany in the nineteenth century**
6–7 **Hegelian influence in the twentieth century**
8 **Contemporary developments**

1 The Hegelian School in Germany 1816–40

Initially, Hegel's influence was naturally most strongly felt in Germany, and can be seen in the relatively rapid formation within the philosopher's lifetime of something like a 'Hegelian school'. The representatives of this school procured a considerable influence for themselves not only through the personal prestige of Hegel, but also through the foundation of important journals more or less expressly designed to propagate and disseminate the philosophical principles of Hegel himself and apply them to central theoretical and practical issues of the day. But the very comprehensiveness and richness of Hegel's systematic synthesis placed his more original students in an ambiguous and paradoxical position. Eduard Gans wrote 'Hegel has left behind a number of gifted students but no successor. For philosophy has now for the first time completed the cycle of its existence; further advance can only be expected as the further intelligent penetration of the material of knowledge.'

One of the earliest explicit champions of Hegel's thought was Georg Andreas Gabler (1786–1853), a student from Hegel's Jena period 1801–07, who later

succeeded to Hegel's chair in Berlin (1835) and was one of the few students to write intensively on (part of) the *Phenomenology*, with the *Kritik des Bewußtseins* (Critique of Consciousness) (1827). When Hegel moved to take up his first chair in Heidelberg in 1816 he also found an ardent supporter in the theologian Karl Daub (1765–1836), who expounded a thoroughly Hegelian approach to religious questions with *Die dogmatische Theologie jetziger Zeit* (The Dogmatic Theology of Our Times) (1833). But it was essentially during his final Berlin period (1819–31) that Hegel began to develop a proper 'School' around him, with the founding of a *Gesellschaft für wissenschaftliche Kritik* (Society for Scientific Criticism) in 1825 and the consequent launching of the journal *Jahrbücher der wissenschaftlichen Kritik* (Yearbook of Scientific Criticism) under the editorship of Hegel and his more prominent students. The journal explicitly began to disseminate a Hegelian line on contemporary philosophical and cultural issues and was soon dubbed the 'Hegel newspaper' by its opponents.

Other followers at this time who produced Hegelian interpretations in the fields of ethics, history of philosophy, speculative theology, law and political thought were Leopold von Henning (1791–1866) with his *Prinzipien der Ethik in historischer Entwicklung* (Principles of Ethics in Historical Development) (1824), Karl Ludwig Michelet (1801–93) with the *Geschichte der letzten Systeme der Philosophie in Deutschland* (History of the Most Recent Systems of Philosophy in Germany) (1837–38), Philipp Karl Marheinecke (1780–1846) with *Die Grundlehren der christlichen Dogmatik als Wissenschaft* (The Fundamental Doctrines of Christian Dogmatics as Science) (1827) and, one of the most interesting and original, Eduard Gans (1798–1839). Gans had become a friend of Hegel's in Heidelberg and strongly under his influence produced his major work *Das Erbrecht in weltgeschichtlicher Entwicklung* (The Law of Inheritance Considered in its World-Historical Development) (1824–35) which forcefully pursued Hegel's own criticism of the 'Historical School' of jurisprudence defended by Karl von SAVIGNY. Gans also lectured on the philosophy of world history from a liberal-progressive Hegelian perspective as well as upon law and may well have been a powerful influence upon the young Karl Marx who heard him lecture in Berlin in the mid-1830s (see MARX, K. §2). These early protagonists of Hegel's thought are sometimes described as the 'Old Hegelians' because they represented the first generation of the 'School', by contrast with the later so-called 'Young Hegelians' of the 1840s, but the label is often quite uninformative about the substance of their teachings or their political and religious persuasions.

Karl Rosenkranz (1805–1879) was another of these early disciples who remained perhaps most faithful to the original Hegelian vision but also showed himself an independent thinker in his wide-ranging oeuvre. Rosenkranz consciously strove to defend and re-articulate Hegel's position in all its dialectical complexity and, unlike most of Hegel's followers, laid particular stress upon Hegel's fundamental debt to Kant and aspects of the Enlightenment heritage. Rosenkranz expressed his faith in the Hegelian 'middle' in declaring that 'only all of his students taken together are the equal of Hegel; each one on his own account merely represents a one-sided moment of Hegel' (Rosenkranz 1840a: xxxv).

2   The Critique of Hegelian idealism 1840–70

Rosenkranz's preface to his biography of Hegel, *Hegels Leben* (Hegel's Life) (1844), reveals something of the fervent ideological climate of the early 1840s and reflects the various splits within the Hegelian school which had developed in the previous decade, not to mention the counter-reaction to Hegel's influence in the later work of Schelling, Hegel's former friend and collaborator (see SCHELLING, F.W.J. §4). For it was during the 1830s that the apparent solidity and impressive unity of Hegel's achievement gradually began to fissure and the potentially centrifugal tendencies of the system revealed themselves under the pressure of significant new social and cultural developments.

These divisions first appeared in theology and the philosophy of religion as Hegel's successors attempted to clarify the contemporary implications of Hegel's famous philosophical appropriation of Christianity as the 'consummate' religion corresponding to the 'absolute' perspective of the speculative system. Nevertheless, it was far from clear how much of what many of Hegel's contemporaries still took to be the essence of Christianity really was preserved and adequately reformulated in Hegel, especially traditional dogmatic beliefs concerning individual immortality and the afterlife, the personal and transcendent God of theism, the uniqueness of the incarnation and the entire eschatological dimension.

The figure who brought the interpretation of Hegel's philosophy of religion to a head under all these aspects was David Friedrich Strauss, whose *Das Leben Jesu, kritisch bearbeitet* (*The Life of Jesus, Critically Examined*) (1835–6) represents a watershed in nineteenth-century religious Protestant thought (see STRAUSS, D.F. §1). Hegel himself had spoken of religious language in terms of pictorial representation,

symbolism and on occasion myth, but it was Strauss who fearlessly subjected the received Gospel accounts to a 'demythologizing' technique and attempted to reveal the intelligible ethical and spiritual truths misleadingly couched in archaic symbolic form in the original texts of the tradition. He not only expressed doubts about the historical verisimilitude of the stories and discounted the miraculous and supernatural elements, but also reinterpreted the idea of special revelation in terms of an unfolding historical revelation and rejected traditional accounts of Christ's uniquely divine status. Thus Strauss brought latent tensions in Hegel's legacy into the open and considerably sharpened the ensuing debate. It is in this theological context that Strauss himself first made the distinction in his *Streitschriften zur Vertheidigung meiner Schrift* (Polemical Writings in Defence of My Work) (1837) between 'right', 'centre' and 'left' positions in the spectrum of Hegelian philosophy: the right held to orthodox tradition in emphasizing divine transcendence, personal deity and the doctrine of immortality; the left dissolved the radical uniqueness and sometimes even the historicity of Christ and adopted a progressive humanistic domestication of Christianity as a social creed not so far removed from the 'religion of humanity' of Auguste COMTE, (see §6); while the centre attempted the most difficult task of all, upholding the complexity of the original Hegelian 'middle' and avoiding alike the extremes of traditional theism, romantic pantheism or humanist reduction.

Some of those who attempted to negotiate this path in a sensitive and interesting way, apart from Rosenkranz, fell into neglect once the poles of the ensuing debate had ossified into fixed positions. Thus Ferdinand Christian Baur (1792–1860), although he never considered himself a strict adherent of the 'School' in any of its forms, developed in his *Die christliche Gnosis oder die christliche Religionsphilosophie in ihrer geschichtlichen Entwicklung* (Christian Gnosis, or the Christian Philosophy of Religion in its Historical Development) (1835) a kind of speculative hermeneutic of biblical texts and traditional dogmas that remained closer in certain important respects to Hegel's spirit than the investigations of Baur's pupil Strauss. And Strauss' friend Wilhelm Vatke (1806–82) brought a Hegelian perspective to the study of Judaic thought, a neglected subject at the time, with *Die Religion des alten Testaments* (The Religion of the Old Testament) (1835), and produced detailed work on central religio-philosophical questions with *Die menschliche Freiheit in ihrem Verhältniss zur Sünde und Gnade* (Human Freedom in its Relation to Sin and Divine Forgiveness) (1841). Alois Emanuel Biedermann (1819–1885) was another thinker who engaged with the theological debates on the left and later continued to exploit Hegelian ideas in the quest for a responsible modern Christology which would avoid the pitfalls of anthropological reduction and antiquated supranaturalism in his *Christliche Dogmatik* (Christian Dogmatics) (1868).

The traditional division between 'right' and 'left', with the 'centre' being largely ignored, is an extremely inadequate intellectual shorthand that threatens to obscure rather than illuminate the complexity of the central issues, especially in the 1830s. For it is really only with the development of a radically secular and increasingly naturalistic worldview in the next couple of decades that the earlier Hegelian positions could globally be labelled as 'right-Hegelian', and it is historically anachronistic to regard thinkers such as Gans and most of Hegel's earlier students as politically 'conservative'. In fact many representatives of the 'School' supported liberal-progressive causes and were not initially disappointed by the revolutionary events of 1848.

From the end of the 1830s and throughout the 1840s the ideological fronts sharpened radically in the context of social and political thought. Thus the continuing concern with 'saving' historical Christianity through philosophy on the part of nearly all the original Hegelians came increasingly to seem an antiquated and regressive debate with the growing importance of radical humanistic political thought as the primary site of opposition to entrenched and antiliberal state social policies in the period up to 1848. It was symptomatic of this trend when the Polish Count August von CIESZKOWSKI reinterpreted Hegel's philosophy of religion in terms of a secularized eschatological philosophy of history with practical intent in his *Prolegomena zur Historiosophie* (Prolegomena to the Wisdom of History) of 1838. He had concluded that the ultimate logic of Hegel's thought demanded not a contemplative or predominantly theoretical relation to reality but rather a 'philosophy of action' ('praxis'). If, as Hegel had claimed, the future could not be predicted, it could nevertheless be shaped with will and consciousness: the task therefore was no longer to recognize the supposed actuality of reason, but actively to procure a place for the emerging rationality of the future. In emphasizing the open and dynamic element of Hegel's thought, stressing the immanent negativity of the dialectical 'method' at the expense of the apparently static 'system', and in elevating the active will over purely retrospective thought, Cieszkowski epitomized the Young Hegelian approach to Hegel's philosophical legacy. A similar position was adopted by Moses HESS who also preached the transformation of traditional religious ideas into an ethical programme for the future with *Die heilige Geschichte der Menschheit* (The Sacred History of Humanity) (1837).

The remarkable intellectual career of Bruno BAUER vividly illustrates these developments since he began as a protagonist of the theological Hegelian right and subsequently progressed through the centre towards a radically atheistic stance: in his *Die Posaune des jüngsten Gerichts über Hegel den Atheisten und Antichristen* (*The Trumpet of the Last Judgement upon Hegel the Atheist and Antichrist*) (1841), Bauer ventriloquized strategically from an apparently orthodox theological perspective precisely in order to reveal the ultimately heterodox and destructive implications of Hegelian philosophy for traditional Christian belief. These radical developments within the Hegelian school were most clearly registered in the journal founded by Arnold RUGE and T. Echtermeyer in 1838, the *Hallische Jahrbücher für deutsche Wissenschaft und Kunst* (Halle Yearbook for German Science and Art). Although initially representatives of the whole spectrum of the school published articles in the journal, the general tenor of the contributions soon began to reflect the most advanced position of the left. In this respect the article 'Zur Kritik der Hegelschen Philosophie' (Towards a Critique of Hegelian Philosophy) (1839) by Ludwig proved symptomatic. Indeed it was Feuerbach's influential book *Das Wesen des Christentums* (*The Essence of Christianity*) (1841) which seemed in the eyes of many to draw the ultimate conclusions from Hegel's philosophy of religion and Strauss's development of it by 'unmasking' all theological discourse as an alienated and 'inverted' projection of human imagination and desire. He proposed to reveal through his 'transformational method' that the ultimate truth of theology is anthropology (in the sense that chemistry is the truth of alchemy). This interpretation of religion generally as a compensating 'ideology' has proved enormously influential in modern thought (see FEUERBACH, L.A. §2).

Feuerbach also turned his critique of religion against Hegel's philosophy itself, and in particular against his idealism, accusing speculative philosophy of making the same mistake as theology: it prioritizes the infinite over the finite, thought over sense, the abstract over the concrete, and so ends up as a panlogistic idealism which sets essence above existence. This nominalistic attack on Hegel exerted a great influence, and marks the beginning of a turn away from idealism towards a new materialist metaphysics, as the dominant philosophical outlook ceased to be speculative and became anthropological and naturalistic.

283

3 The critique of Hegelian idealism 1840–70 (cont.)

Under the influence of this critique of Hegel's idealism, those who succeeded Feuerbach among the so-called 'Young Hegelians' (such as Ruge, Friedrich ENGELS, Hess and the early Marx) extended it to include Hegel's political thought, while at the same time this turn towards naturalism was treated as a key to the reinterpretation and radicalization of some of Hegel's fundamental doctrines. Thus, in the first place, Ruge objected that Hegel's 'metaphysics of politics' lacks a proper critical standpoint because it 'would offer us the passing realities of history as eternal figures', and is thereby rendered 'impotent': 'Hegel undertook to present the hereditary monarch, the majority, the bicameral system, etc, as *logical necessities*, whereas it had to be a matter of establishing all these as products of history and of explaining and criticizing them as *historical existences*' (Ruge (1842: 763) 1983: 228). In a similar vein, Marx accused Hegel of 'logical, pantheistic mysticism', of attempting 'to provide the political constitution with a relationship to the abstract Idea, and to establish it as a link in the life-history of the Idea – an obvious mystification' (Marx 1975: 69–70). It is evident, therefore, how the turn against Hegel's idealism decisively influenced the Young Hegelians in their attitude to his Philosophy of Right and its place in the speculative system.

In the second place, the Young Hegelians saw the need (in Marx's famous phrase) to locate properly the 'rational kernel within the mystical shell' of Hegel's philosophy: to rescue what is valuable in Hegel from his idealistic metaphysics. So, for example, Engels argued that Hegel's dialectical procedure, while apparently based on an abstract logic of concepts, is (as Marx's work showed) nothing more than a *historical* method, 'which ultimately amounts to the discovery of the general laws of motion which assert themselves as the ruling ones in the history of human society' (Engels (1886) 1968: 612). Likewise, Marx himself took Hegel's analysis of the estrangement between man and nature, based on his conception of nature as the 'otherness of the idea', and interpreted this in anthropological terms, as the separation of man from the human process of productive activity. By approaching Hegel in this heterodox manner, the Young Hegelians hoped to recover the radical historicism, humanism and social critique that lay obscured in the empty abstractions of his metaphysical idealism.

If most of the Young Hegelians of radical political persuasion tended to substitute the idea of a new collective humanity or an appropriately transformed 'species being' for the spiritual teleology of Hegel's

thought, it was left to Max STIRNER (pseudonym of Johann Kaspar Schmidt) to develop the other individualistic extreme of the Hegelian mediation with *Der Einzige und sein Eigentum* (*The Ego and Its Own*) (1845), exalting the sovereign negativity of the singular ego in an almost proto-Nietzschean sense to create and recreate its own value systems and emancipate itself from all heteronomous givenness through tradition and previous history. In drawing the ultimate conclusions from the modern liberal emphasis upon subjective freedom Stirner's philosophy of the liberated 'self' represents the extreme counter-position to Feuerbach's and Marx's conception of the 'social individual'.

Alongside this revolt against idealism brought about by the turn towards naturalism and materialism by the Young Hegelians, Hegel's alleged panlogicism also came under attack from F.W.J. Schelling and his 'positive philosophy', which he adopted from around 1827 until his death in 1854. This position was explicitly conceived in contrast to the 'negative philosophy' Schelling claimed to find in Hegel, which is confined to concepts and essences, but neglects being or existence; as a result, it overlooks the fact that it cannot answer the fundamental question 'Why does anything exist at all? Why is there not nothing?', and so cannot make the transition from the Idea to nature. Schelling therefore insists that Hegel fails to surmount the 'nasty broad ditch' between the first and second parts of the *Encyclopedia*, because concepts are mere abstractions from the empirical world, and so cannot be treated as ideal forms from which the latter can be deduced; on the contrary, the limits of Hegel's rationalistic metaphysics are shown by the fact that existence must be taken (by us) to be an inexplicable *prius*. In attacking Hegel's idealism in this way, Schelling began an antirationalistic revolt against his panlogicism which has become one of the fundamental critical reactions to his thought.

Another significant strand in this broadly existentialist critique of Hegel's idealism which emerged in the 1840s lies in the assertion that Hegel is unable to grasp the reality of becoming, finitude and temporality, despite his talk of movement in his dialectical treatment of the categories. The claim (made, for example, by F.A. Trendelenburg (1802–72) and echoed by Kierkegaard) is that like all idealists, Hegel posits a world of abstract essences behind the world of time and transience, and so fails to give due weight to the reality of finite existence; where Hegel is deceptive, however, is in the way in which he attributes a dynamic interrelation to the categories, and talks in terms of 'transition', 'development' and 'movement'. Hegel's critics insisted, however, that this talk of movement can only be figurative, and that in fact it is senseless to talk of real change and development in connection with Hegel's Logic. Hegel's followers tried to respond to this wave of anti-idealist criticism: Rosenkranz, for example, insisted in vain that Hegel was not a Platonist, to be 'reproached with offering up the world of blooming life to the idea as to a desolate Hades' (Rosenkranz (1870: 125) 1993 I: 283–4); on the contrary, he argued, Hegel saw universals as more like souls that must be embodied in concrete particulars.

None the less, the effect of this materialist and existentialist critique meant that from around 1860 only the more moderate epistemological idealism of the Neo-Kantians was taken seriously as a systematic philosophy; among those self-confessed Hegelians who remained academically active, the scope of their operations was considerably narrowed, so that John Erdmann (1805–92), Eduard Zeller (1814–1908) and Kuno Fischer (1824–1907) are principally known as historians of philosophy. Another figure whose considerable output reflects something of the vicissitudes of the Hegelian tradition in Germany throughout this period is the prolific writer and critic Friedrich Theodor Vischer (1807–87). His earlier works, such as *Über das Erhabene und Komische* (On the Sublime and the Comic) (1837) and the monumental *Ästhetik oder Wissenschaft des Schönen* (Aesthetics or the Science of Beauty) (1845–57), express more or less total commitment to Hegel's philosophy as a whole; but his later contributions represent a progressive abandonment of all ambitious metaphysical claims for art and religion in the modern world in favour of an increasingly sceptical and critical relationship to social reality and to the classical Hegelian project of reconciliation as he had earlier understood it.

4 Hegelianism outside Germany in the nineteenth century: France, Northern Europe and Italy

While Hegelianism in Germany was gradually eclipsed, in several other countries it continued to have an impact into the second half of the nineteenth century. Although in its earlier stages, the reception of Hegel in these countries broke little new ground, none the less an inevitable diversification occurred as Hegel's ideas were taken up in different climates of thought, while Hegel was later read both as part of the broader development of German Idealism, and as closer in outlook to some of his critics. This process has continued into the twentieth century, and has yielded some profound reassessments of his ideas.

France. Although French Hegelianism is best known for its influence on European thought in the 1930s onwards (see §6 below), France was also one of the first countries outside Germany to feel the impact of Hegel's ideas in the nineteenth century, largely due to the efforts of Victor COUSIN. Having met Hegel in Heidelberg in 1817, Cousin became an enthusiastic admirer, returning several times to Germany thereafter. He helped give currency to Hegel's ideas through his lectures of 1828–9 at the École Normale in Paris, and with the advent of the July Monarchy in 1830, he was able to acknowledge Hegel's influence explicitly. In his later work, however, he was more guarded, partly due to his growing support for Schelling, and partly due to his increasingly conservative and conformist position. None the less, it was through Cousin that many in France came to know of Hegel's work (such as Pierre-Joseph PROUDHON), while he also encouraged others, such as the Italian Augusto Vera (1813–85), who later translated several of Hegel's works into French.

With the advent of the Second Empire in 1852, Cousin lost his official posts, while the growing influence of Auguste Comte meant that the outlook of many thinkers in France became increasingly positivisitic. As a result, Hegel came to be viewed in a new light, as attempts were made to find a fruitful synthesis of both positions, particularly by Ernest Renan (1823–92) and Hippolyte TAINE, both of whom had discovered Hegel in the 1840s. Renan sought to develop a less secularized positivism, using Hegel's conception of progress as bringing a divine consciousness into existence through the realization of reason. Taine was likewise attracted to Hegel's idea of a temporal development of reason, and tried to use it to give a historical dimension to the static metaphysics of Spinoza, while fusing the rationalism of the latter with a positivistic recognition of empirical knowledge and apparent contingency.

By the 1850s and 1860s there was a growing awareness of the critical debate surrounding Hegel that had developed in Germany, while Vera attempted to win disciples for the Hegelian cause in France with his *Introduction à la Philosophie de Hegel* (Introduction to the Philosophy of Hegel) (1855), though with little obvious success. Publications by Vera, Rosenkranz and Hegel's critic Rudolf Haym, were reviewed by Edmond Scherer in 1861, who commented that 'Hegel cannot begin to be known, and his philosophy assessed, since there are no longer any Hegelians' (Scherer 1861: 813). He himself offered an influential assessment of what was valuable in Hegel's thought, emphasizing broadly Left Hegelian themes (such as Hegel's notion of contradiction and historical change), and analysing his *Philosophy of Right* and philosophy of religion (which he considered in relation to D.F. Strauss' *Leben Jesu*). However, positive discussion and dissemination of Hegel's ideas was brought to a halt by the Prussian invasion of France in the 1870s, as (not for the first time) he was blamed for fostering the expansionist nationalism of his country.

The credit for subsequently rehabilitating Hegel in France is usually given to Lucien Herr (1864–1926), who wrote an article on him for the *Grande Encyclopédie* (1893–4). Moreoever, as librarian at the École Normale Superieure from 1886, Herr was able to introduce a large number of philosophy students to Hegel's ideas during this period. In his article, Herr emphasized and appreciated Hegel's systematic ambitions, and placed considerable emphasis on the *Logic*. Though he did not try to resolve any of the philosophical cruxes of his thought, Herr did none the less present a reasonably clear and appealing synopsis of Hegel's views. An equally sympathetic but more partisan view of Hegel, intended as a rebuttal of positivism and Neo-Kantianism, was offered by Georges Noël in his study of Hegel's *Logic*. It is significant, too, that by this time Hegel was being recognized as an important precursor of Marxist thought, and that this rapprochement led to a less panlogistic and quietistic reading of his work (as can be seen in René Bertholet's address to the French Philosophy Society of 1907).

Northern Europe. Around the middle of the nineteenth century, Hegelian ideas had an important impact on the intellectual life of several northern European countries.

In Denmark, the person most responsible for introducing these ideas was the dramatist and man of letters Johan Ludwig Heiberg (1791–1860). Heiberg met Hegel in Berlin in 1824, and in the same year he brought out his *Om den menneskelige Frihed* (On Human Freedom), in which he makes several references to Hegel, while using distinctly Hegelian ideas and terminology in his dispute with F.G. Howitz over this issue. Heiberg subsequently produced other works that established him as a spokesman for Hegelianism, and in June 1837 he began publication of *Perseus, Journal for den speculative Idee*. At the same time, Hegel's ideas were also being critically discussed by Poul Martin Moller (1794–1838) and Frederich Christian Sibbern (1785–1872). The former left Denmark to occupy a chair at Oslo University from 1826–31, and introduced the study of Hegel into Norway.

Among a slightly younger generation, Hegelian ideas were enthusiastically taken up by Hans Martensen (1808–84) and Rasmus Nielsen (1809–84). Martensen saw Hegel in much the same way as he presented himself – as attempting to bring modern philosophy to its highest standpoint by overcoming all previous one-sided approaches, and as therefore forming the culminating point of philosophical development. Martensen also argued that Christian orthodoxy had nothing to fear from Hegel, whom he followed in seeking to reconcile philosophy and theology by making the latter speculative, and applying the methods of philosophy to the received dogmas of the church. Nielsen also lectured and wrote extensively on Hegel, and his main work *Grundideernes Logik* (The Logic of Fundamental Ideas) of 1864–6 gave a full account of his Hegelian views in this area. None the less, he came under the influence of Kierkegaard's attack on Hegel's treatment of religion, and so criticized Martensen's position as being too complacent in this regard. In 1860, Nielsen was joined at Copenhagen as a professor by Hans Bockner (1820–75), who also thought and wrote as a Hegelian, principally on the history of philosophy.

As well as having an influence on Hegel's reception in Denmark, Kierkegaard is clearly the most philosophically significant thinker to have responded to his work in this country. While Kierkegaard attacked Hegel from a theistic perspective, his own form of Christianity was sufficiently radical to set him apart from any standard Right Hegelian approach; his critique can rather be seen as undermining Hegel's entire project, which was apparently to provide a systematic, rational and complete conception of the world, of the sort traditionally associated with a divine understanding. In rejecting this ambition as 'comic' and 'absurd', Kierkegaard therefore gave a very special twist to some of the themes found earlier in Schelling, and so deepened this existentialist reaction to Hegel's work. Kierkegaard came to this position out of a desire to save the religious outlook from the claim (made by Martensen, for example) that this Hegelian standpoint could give Christianity a rational basis. Kierkegaard argued that this was impossible, as philosophical speculation could never assimilate both the metaphysical and ethical paradoxes of true Christian faith: that God has become man, that religious knowledge can be based on subjective feeling, and that the religiously inspired individual (such as Abraham) may act out of a purely individual sense of the will of God. Kierkegaard therefore sets Christianity *against* the Hegelian conception of philosophy and philosophical reason, in order to demonstrate the limitations of the latter (see KIERKEGAARD, S.A. §2).

In Holland, Hegel's earliest follower was P.G. van Ghert (1782–1852), who was a student of his in Jena and later became his friend. A more significant spokesman for Hegelianism was G.J.P.J. Bolland (1854–1922), who, as professor at Leiden (from 1896), established a kind of Hegelian sect which later infiltrated all parts of Dutch intellectual life (J.

Hessing (1874–1944), J.G. Wattjes (1879–1944) and Esther Vas Nunes (1866–1929) being his most important pupils). However, this school lost its influence after the Second World War, due to the anti-Semitic views of Bolland himself, and the extreme right-wing affiliations of his pupils.

Italy. While GIOBERTI and ROSMINI drew in a general way on aspects of post-Kantian German Idealist metaphysics, Hegel's ideas were more explicitly introduced into mainstream Italian culture through the efforts of Augusto Vera and Bertrando Spaventa (1817–82), who founded an influential Hegelian school in Naples and expounded Hegel's social and political thought with his *Studi sull'etica hegeliana* (Studies on Hegelian Ethics) (1869). Hegelian ideas were also represented by Francesco de Sanctis (1817–83), whose classic literary history, *La storia della letteraria italiana* (*History of Italian Literature*) (1870–1) is much influenced by Hegel's aesthetics, and by Raffaele Mariano (1840–1912) and Pasquale d'Ercole (1831–1917). One of Spaventa's pupils was Antonio LABRIOLA, who later proved to be an independent Marxist thinker who appreciated the importance of Hegel for the evolution of historical materialism. He avoided the reductive positivist interpretation of Marxism which was currently being codified as a system of 'dialectical materialism' and was not inhibited from drawing freely on his Hegelian teachers and predecessors. For him as for them the living heritage of Hegel lay in his profoundly historical conception of social and political life, not in his metaphysical ambitions. In regarding Hegel as pre-eminently a great philosopher of culture Labriola anticipated much of the later Italian reception of Hegelian thought, by Marxists and non-Marxists alike. Labriola's expressly non-positivist interpretation of Marxism as essentially a 'philosophy of praxis' rather than a supposedly scientific and comprehensive worldview was a significant precursor of the Hegelian-Marxist approach that would emerge in Germany in the 1920s.

5 Hegelianism outside Germany in the nineteenth century: America and Britain

America. In the second half of the nineteenth century, Hegel's ideas came to play an important part in the intellectual life of the USA, where two centres of Hegelian thought began to develop. The first was a loosely associated group of friends and acquaintances based at this time in Cincinnati, Ohio, the most important of whom were John Bernard Stallo (1823–1900), August Willich (1810–78) and Moncure Conway (1832–1907). Broadly speaking, the Cincinnati Hegelians offered a left-wing interpretation of his views, which stressed his conception of a cosmos 'full of life and reason' (as Conway put it), in which scientific and social progress were possible, leading to a more liberal and rational political and religious order.

A similar outlook can be found in the second centre of Hegelian ideas at this time, in St Louis. The leading figures here were Henry Conrad Brokmeyer (1826–1906) and William Torrey Harris (1835–1909). After the Civil War, members of the Kant Club in St Louis formed the Philosophical Society, inaugurated in 1866 with Brokmeyer as president, Harris as secretary, and Denton Snider (1841–1925), G.H. Howison (1834–1916), A.E. Kroeger (1837–82) and Thomas Davidson (1840–1900) among its leading members. All were to contribute articles and translations to *The Journal of Speculative Philosophy*, which Harris edited from 1867 to 1893. The *Journal* had considerable influence in making Hegelian ideas part of the mainstream philosophical discussion in America, while Harris's own large output made a major contribution to the study of Hegel's works. Many of the St Louis Hegelians (including Brokmeyer and Harris) also had important institutional positions, in which they tried to apply his ideas in the fields of government and education.

Of this group, Harris was perhaps the most successful in developing a general philosophical outlook that is clearly Hegelian in character. He argued that in its highest stage, knowledge reveals 'independence and self-relation underlying all dependence and relativity' (Easton 1966: 481); and he used this structure, as Hegel had done, to develop a dialectical conception of 'identity-in-difference' that provided the basis for his account of the universe, God's relation to the world and the place of the individual in society.

By the end of the nineteenth century, many of the major academic posts in America were occupied by self-styled idealists, who accepted Hegel's central place in this tradition of thought. At this time, Hegel in particular and idealism in general were used to come to terms with the growing impact of Darwinian ideas on theology and philosophy, in part by using the notion of the dialectic to find reason in the process of evolution itself.

From the 1880s onwards, however, the claim by Hegel's earlier American disciples that he represented the highest point of German thought began to be challenged, as pragmatism started to make its mark in academic philosophical circles (see PRAGMATISM). This drew on a much broader range of idealist thinkers than just Hegel, who was no longer viewed as the culminating point of the tradition. Thus, for an influential figure such as William JAMES, the less rationalistic and metaphysical idealism of Kant, Schopenhauer and Lotze was more congenial to his pragmatic outlook. The central target of James' attack was Hegel's 'vicious intellectualism', to which he opposed his own radical empiricism (James 1909: 105). James argued that the concrete world of experience has a different structure from the world of thought, and that the particularity of things can never be adequately conceptualized. He criticized intellectualism for substituting 'a pallid outline for the real world's richness', and (like Kierkegaard) claimed that it sought to transcend becoming and temporality by abandoning the human point of view. In voicing these misgivings about Hegel's alleged essentialism, James was developing a familiar line of criticism, but in a way that was new in the American reception of Hegel's work.

The effect of this critique can be seen in the writings of James' Harvard colleague and contemporary, Josiah ROYCE. Unlike James, Royce was prepared to follow through the developments in idealism that led to Hegel, and so became his most sympathetic and sophisticated interpreter in this period, basing his conception of the Absolute on Hegel's account of the concrete universal as an organic unity of individual minds. In his posthumously published lectures on 'Aspects of Post-Kantian Idealism', delivered in 1906, Royce broke new ground by laying greater stress on the *Phenomenology of Spirit* than the *Logic*, emphasizing the voluntaristic aspects of the former, as showing that 'for Hegel, thought is inseparable from will' (1919: 145). By adopting this approach, Royce hoped to show that Hegel's real intention was to portray a 'logic of passion', and of the conflicts of the will, and not a system of abstract thought; this would demonstrate the continuity of Hegel's ideas with the outlook of pragmatism.

The other leading American pragmatists, C.S. Peirce and John Dewey were also influenced by their encounter with Hegel. While Peirce was quick to distance himself from American Hegelianism as a school (entering into a sharp critical exchange with W.T. Harris in 1868), he none the less acknowledged the affinities that existed between Hegel's outlook and his own, while more broadly he may be seen as a Neo-Kantian. The greatest convergence comes in Peirce's phenomenological deduction of the categories of Firstness, Secondness and Thirdness, and his demonstration that our immediate perceptual judgments (Firstness) and our relational judgments (Secondness) require mediation by reference to generalities (Thirdness); as Peirce admits in his *Lectures on Pragmatism* (1903), this deduction echoes Hegel's opening arguments in the *Phenomenology* (see PEIRCE, C.S. §7). None the less, Peirce complains that Hegel appears to reduce Firstness and Secondness to Thirdness, instead of recognizing that all three categories must be present in any coherent conception of the world. In Dewey, the influence of Hegel is more diffuse, as he was attracted more to his 'dissolution of hard-and-fast dividing walls', rather than any particular doctrine, although he was prepared to defend Hegel's criticisms of Kant in his important early essay 'Kant and Philosophic Method' (1884) (see DEWEY, J. §1).

Britain. If the pragmatists took Hegel seriously, this was not just because of his impact in America, but also because of the importance of Absolute Idealism in Britain in the 1880s and '90s, which represented the high point of Hegel's influence there.

In Britain, the initial reception of Hegel's work came relatively late. His ideas were given some limited attention in the writings of William HAMILTON and James FERRIER, and figured briefly in the historical accounts of German Idealism by J.D. Morrell and G.H. Lewes, while the first translation (of part of Hegel's *Logic*) appeared in 1855. It was not until J.H. Stirling's *The Secret of Hegel* (1865), however, that any substantial sympathetic treatment of Hegel's work became available, and it marks the real beginning of Hegel's influence. While he was aware of the sustained critique of Hegel as a Platonic idealist and essentialist that had gained currency in Germany in the 1840s and '50s, Stirling still adopted this reading, proclaiming that for Hegel 'organic Reason (is) a self-supported, self-maintained, self-moved life, which is the all of things, the ultimate principle, the Absolute' (Stirling (1865) 1898 I: 96).

Stirling's book was followed in 1874 by a translation of Hegel's *Encyclopedia Logic* by William Wallace (1844–97), together with a long introduction entitled *Prolegomena to the Study of Hegel's Philosophy*. Like Stirling, Wallace sought to use Hegel in the critique of positivism and scientific naturalism, and interpreted his idealism as a kind of thoroughgoing holism, while, like his American contemporaries, he sought to show how Hegel's notion of the dialectic might be used to bring out the rationality of Darwinian evolution. A similar set of concerns is reflected by Edward Caird (1835–1908) in his *Hegel* (1883), for whom 'the task of philosophy is to gain, or rather perhaps to regain, such a view of things as shall reconcile us to the world and to ourselves' (Caird 1892 I: 191). It was this search for unity that Caird found in Hegel's work, particularly in relation to the opposing claims of freedom and necessity, subject and object, God and the universe, and he therefore interpreted Hegel's Absolute as such a reconciling principle.

As well as these published accounts of Hegel's thought, a positive view of Hegel also began to emerge more indirectly, as he was taken up by the important group of idealist thinkers who were becoming increasingly influential at this time. One of the first of these was T.H. GREEN, who was led to read Hegel by his tutor and later colleague at Balliol, Benjamin Jowett. Green's critique of empiricism had both Kantian and Hegelian elements, while his account of self-consciousness as a single, actively self-distinguishing spiritual principle which expresses itself in temporal human intelligence reflected his understanding of Hegel's conception of *Geist*. None the less, Green declared himself unhappy with Hegel's method for arguing to this conception, stating that 'it must all be done again'. Likewise, while he was clearly helped to his own account of freedom by his reading of Hegel, he remained suspicious of what he took to be the latter's uncritical acceptance of the modern state, in which this freedom was to be realized.

This equivocal attitude is also reflected in the relation of one of the other leading British Idealists to Hegel, F.H. BRADLEY. Hegel's influence can be traced in Bradley's critique of Kantian ethics in his early *Ethical Studies* (1876); in his hostility to the classical empiricist's view of our experience of reality as divisible into discrete simple elements; in his treatment of judgment, the concrete universal and the problem of relations; and in his conviction that from the perspective of the Absolute, all *aporiai* in our understanding of reality would be overcome. None the less, Bradley remained critical of central aspects of Hegel's thought and method, famously dismissing his *Logic* as an 'unearthly ballet of bloodless categories', and with it the panlogist metaphysics this seemed to represent.

Bradley's contemporary Bernard BOSANQUET was less openly critical of Hegel, as he developed Bradley's Hegelian approach to the logical forms of thought (such as judgment and syllogism), in order to show how in these forms, all abstraction from the whole turns out to be incoherent. Bosanquet carried this holism over into what was seen as a Hegelian conception of the individual and society, claiming that for human beings 'their true individuality does not lie in their isolation, but in that distinctive act or service by which they pass into unique contributions to the universal' (Bosanquet [1899] 1923: 170). In his work on aesthetics, Bosanquet focused attention on this aspect of Hegel's system, with his translation of the introduction to Hegel's *Lectures on Aesthetics* (1886), and his account of Hegel in his influential *History of Aesthetics* (1892).

Bosanquet was not alone among the British Idealists in offering interpretative commentaries on Hegel's work, although towards the end of the 1880s, these became increasingly critical and critically informed. A decisive moment came in 1887, with the publication by Andrew Seth (later Andrew Seth Pringle-Pattison) (1856–1931) of *Hegelianism and Personality*, in which he followed Schelling, Trendelenburg and others, and criticized Hegel's apparent panlogicism; following the Left Hegelians, he gave this attack an ethical and political dimension, arguing that by hypostatizing universality, Hegel gives priority to the species over and above the individual, a move which Seth set out to oppose with his own so-called 'Personal Idealism'. For Hegel's followers in Britain Seth therefore represented a parallel to the existentialist critique of his system already developed in Germany, but which had not been properly addressed by the British Idealists before.

In response, interpretations of Hegel emerged which played down his apparent panlogism, and instead began to treat the *Logic* as a kind of category theory. For example, in an influential article on 'Darwin and Hegel' (1890–1), D.G. Ritchie (1853–1903) argued that Hegel does not have to be read as a speculative cosmologist; rather, 'we (will) find that his logic and the whole of his philosophy consist in this perpetual "criticism of categories", i.e. in an analysis of the terms and concepts which ordinary thinking and the various special sciences use as current coin without testing their real value' (Ritchie 1890–1: 61). This approach was most fully developed in the commentaries on Hegel's system by J.M.E. MCTAGGART. McTaggart argued that the aim of Hegel's dialectic was to show how the categories of ordinary thought provide only partial or imperfect conceptions of the truth, which point towards a highest form of thought – the Absolute Idea – in which these imperfections are finally overcome. Where McTaggart criticized Hegel was for underestimating the difficulty which we have, as limited intellects, in conceiving of the world in these terms, so that although he accepted the Hegelian claim that a resolution of all *aporiai* must be possible, he questioned whether such a view of reality was achievable by us. This approach to the reading of Hegel led McTaggart to emphasize the many apparent contradictions in how things appear to us (most famously, as events occuring in time), and to claim that therefore these appearances must be unreal, opening the way for him to indulge in extravagant metaphysical theorizing about ultimate reality at odds with our experience of the world.

By the beginning of the First World War, the taste for such theorizing had changed, as the Idealist's claims about the contradictory nature of how things appear to us seemed increasingly spurious, thereby disposing of the need to overcome these contradictions in a view of reality as somehow monistic, atemporal, changeless or immaterial. Anglo-Hegelian idealism was therefore increasingly viewed as irrelevant and poorly grounded by the leaders of the next generation of philosophical thinkers (such as Bertrand RUSSELL and G.E. MOORE), while at the same time the 'New Liberals' (such as J.A. Hobson and L.T. Hobhouse) submitted the idealist's theory of the 'organic' state to merciless attack, an attitude which hardened once the war against Germany had begun.

6 Hegelian influence in the twentieth century: Germany, Italy

While towards the end of the nineteenth century it may have appeared that Hegel's philosophy was destined to have only a marginal significance in twentieth-century thought, in fact its impact has been remarkable. This renewed interest in Hegel's position was made possible by a broader understanding of his project, which made many of the standard nineteenth-century criticisms (of panlogism, quietism, anti-individualism and theistic romanticism) appear crude and simplistic, reflecting a misconception of his work.

Germany. During a period in which various forms of positivist naturalism or Neo-Kantian schools dominated the German philosophical scene the Hegelian and idealist legacy generally had found some refuge within the traditional humanistic disciplines which escaped subjection to the methodological canons of the natural sciences. A broadly Hegelian approach thus survived in a largely non-systematic and non-metaphysical hermeneutic form which seemed to offer significant elements at least for the construction of an alternative methodology for the newly developing social and human sciences, the 'Geisteswissenschaften'. Wilhelm DILTHEY was particularly influential in reawakening interest in the world of early German Idealism with his path-breaking study of Hegel's early development, *Die Jugendgeschichte Hegels* (The Young Hegel) (1905). It was also under Dilthey's direct encouragement that his student Hermann Nohl first thoroughly edited and published most of Hegel's surviving early manuscripts of 1790–1800 as *Hegels theologische Jugendschriften* (*Hegel's Early Theological Writings*) in 1907, an event which inaugurated that German resurgence of interest in Hegel's philosophy during the first couple of decades of this century which culminated in the broad movement known as 'Neuhegelianismus'. Hegel's early writings challenged the image of the systematic rationalist metaphysician of tradition and seemed rather to reveal a thinker passionately

concerned with restoring a concrete sense of cultural wholeness and identification with the natural and historical world of lived experience.

The interest in Hegel and the tradition of German Idealism in general did not simply displace the still vigorous forms of Neo-Kantianism but rather entered initially into a complex symbiotic relationship with certain trends within that movement, especially the so-called Southwest School associated principally with Heinrich Rickert (1863–1936) and Wilhelm Windelband (1848–1915) (see NEO-KANTIANISM §4). Like Dilthey, these thinkers were attempting to develop an appropriate philosophical approach to the entire sphere of cultural and spiritual life as an autonomous domain alongside the sphere of the natural and the exact formal sciences. Many of them believed that the Kantian tradition required significant extension and supplementation to do justice to this dimension of experience and looked to Hegel in particular for intellectual resources adequate to the task. A symptomatic document for the period was Windelband's influential address of 1910, 'Die Erneuerung des Hegelianismus' (The Renewal of Hegelianism). Eventually a fully-fledged neo-Hegelian school began to form as part of a broader cultural project of German intellectual renewal, a process that was actually encouraged rather than weakened by the catastrophic experience of the First World War and the ensuing social and political instability.

An important figure in this development was Georg Lasson (1862–1932) who tirelessly promoted a strongly religious interpretation of Hegel's philosophy as the appropriate antidote to the disintegrative and sceptical tendencies and sense of cultural alienation of the time. The intrinsic philosophical significance of Lasson's work is negligible and often represents little but nationalistic edification, as in *Was heisst Hegelianismus?* (What is Hegelianism?) (1916), but he performed an extremely important role as an indefatigable editor of Hegel's works.

Other principal figures associated with or broadly sympathetic with *Neuhegelianismus* were Hermann Glockner (1896–1978), also important as an editor of Hegel, with his synoptic monograph *Hegel* (1929–40); Nicolai Hartmann (1882–1950), who drew strongly on Hegel in his own work and provided a classical ontological interpretation of the philosopher in his *Die Philosophie des deutschen Idealismus* (The Philosophy of German Idealism) (1923–9); Richard Kroner (1884–1974) perhaps the purest and most dedicated representative of the movement, who wrote a standard neo-Hegelian history of German Idealism *Von Kant bis Hegel* (From Kant to Hegel) (1921–4) but reverted in his later writings to a more Kantian position influenced by Kierkegaard; Theodor Litt

(1880–1962) who remained strongly influenced by Dilthey's philosophy of culture and Heidelberg Neo-Kantianism and later attempted to synthesize contemporary trends in a quasi-Hegelian fashion in *Denken und Sein* (Thought and Being) (1948), *Mensch und Welt* (Man and World) (1948) and *Hegel* (1953). Kroner helped to establish the journal *Logos* which functioned as the organ of the German neo-Hegelians and sympathetic Neo-Kantians during the 1920s. There were also a number of more important and original thinkers on the fringes of the movement who were profoundly influenced by the resurgence of interest in German Idealism and Hegel in particular. These included Georg SIMMEL, Ernst CASSIRER and Franz ROSENZWEIG, who all engaged with central Hegelian problems in their work and occupied something of an ambiguous and contested space between Kant and Hegel.

By the end of the 1920s, in the context of the German crisis of democracy and the rise of fascism, the vague romantic and undifferentiated aspiration to living 'wholeness' as a supposed alternative to social atomism readily lent itself to ideological mystification and exploitation. Some neo-Hegelians made uncritical appeal to the idea of '*Sittlichkeit*' or concrete ethical life as a model of organic community, but increasingly detached from its original context in Hegel's elaborate conception of the rational modern constitutional state as the climax of the philosophy of history and the evolution of the consciousness of freedom. The Hegelian notion of the '*Volksgeist*' or 'spirit of the people' was also interpreted more in the spirit of Savigny and the 'Historical School' than in that of Montesquieu or even Herder, and the resulting simplification was urged in support of an illiberal communitarian ideology. Certain tendencies in this direction are clearly discernible in the works of Lasson, Glockner and in the monumental study by Theodor Haering (1884–1964) of Hegel's development, *Hegel. Sein Wollen und sein Werk* (Hegel: His Project and his Work) (1929–38). In all these authors romantic over-interpretation and a celebration of the supposedly 'irrational' character of the dialectic almost completely effaces the universalist and rationalist dimension of Hegel's thought and minimizes the significance of his relationship to Kant and eighteenth-century thought. None the less, except for similar interpretations by fascistically inclined legal theorists such as Julius Binder and Karl Larenz the official ideology showed little interest in reclaiming Hegel for the cause of National Socialism.

The significant alternative to the repristination of Hegel under the sign of cultural philosophies of life and value during this entire period was provided by the intellectual renewal of Marxist thought and the emergence of what later became known generically as 'Western Marxism' and 'Critical Theory'. The early work of Karl Korsch (1886–1961), especially his *Marxismus und Philosophie* (Marxism and Philosophy) (1930) and of Georg LUKÁCS, with *Geschichte und Klaßenbewusstsein* (*History and Class Consciousness*) (1923), proved to be the initial stimulus for this development. Both rejected the positivist interpretation of Marxism as a scientific worldview supposedly in secure possession of the 'laws' of social and historical development and regarded the 'dialectics of nature' as a theoretical illusion and a practical irrelevance. Lukács extrapolated from Marx's mature work to his Hegelian origins and outlined a non-deterministic philosophy of praxis and potential self-liberation which owed much to Hegel's *Phenomenology*. Although Lukács later repudiated his earlier work in certain respects as 'idealist revisionism', he continued to emphasize the enduring significance of the Hegelian legacy in Marx against the Marxist-Leninist orthodoxy with *Der junge Hegel* (*The Young Hegel*) (1948), and drew equally heavily on Hegel in his own later works, like the massive study on aesthetics (*Die Eigenart des Asthetischen* (The Specificity of the Aesthetic)) (1963) and the unfinished treatise *Zur Ontologie des gesellschaftlichen Seins* (*The Ontology of Social Being*) (1971–2). The contemporary need to reinvestigate the entire relationship of Hegelian and Marxist thought was also stimulated during this period by the continual publication of previously unknown texts by both Hegel (especially the Jena writings then issued as his *Realphilosophie* in 1933) and Marx (particularly the *Economical and Philosophical Manuscripts* in 1932), writings which did much to confirm the insights of Lukács' contested interpretation of Marx's debt to Hegel.

Herbert MARCUSE was influenced in his early period by Diltheyan philosophy of life, Heidegger's existential phenomenology, and the rediscovery of Hegel's early work. After his study *Hegels Ontologie* (*Hegel's Ontology*) (1932), Marcuse turned explicitly to Marx whose thought he interpreted in a humanist manner in the light of the early Hegelian manuscripts, stressing like Lukács the key concept of alienation and the ineliminable moment of social subjectivity against more standard mechanistic interpretations. Marcuse also defended the Hegelian tradition directly against the charge of totalitarianism and articulated the deep continuity between the thought of Hegel and Marx in *Reason and Revolution* (1941). In his later work Marcuse focused on the question of the aesthetic dimension and its emancipatory potential as a prefiguring of a non-repressive relation to inner and outer nature, attempting to mediate the heritage of classical German philosophy with elements of Freudian thought.

Although Theodor-Wiesengrund ADORNO repeatedly made Hegel an object of privileged critique, as in the *Drei studien zu Hegel* (*Three Studies on Hegel*) (1963), he could also be regarded as the most profoundly Hegelian of modern thinkers in terms of the fundamental themes of his philosophy and its elaborate dialectical conceptuality. His major works, *Negative Dialektik* (*Negative Dialectics*) (1966) and *Ästhetische Theorie* (*Aesthetic Theory*) (1970) are a sustained critical engagement in a Marxist spirit with the tradition of Hegel and German Idealist thought and are unintelligible without constant reference to the concepts of totality and dialectic subject–object identity. Adorno sought to reclaim the concept of reconciliation (of social antagonism, spirit and nature, universal and particular) from its apologetic use in speculative philosophy and employ it as a critical measure of existing contradiction and unfreedom. He drew strongly on Hegelian patterns of argument to criticize other thinkers, such as Kierkegaard, Husserl and Heidegger.

Italy. At the turn of the century the tradition of neo-Hegelian thought in Italy was principally represented by Benedetto CROCE and Giovanni GENTILE. Croce's reception of Hegelian thought was selective and highly reconstructive, in some respects paralleling the initial German renewal of Hegelian studies in Dilthey's wake. Again it was not the metaphysical dimension of Hegel's thought, but rather the doctrine of concrete spiritual agency and its self-objectification in social and cultural life which attracted Croce, as can be seen from his *Ciò che è vivo e ciò che è morto nella filosofia di Hegel* (*What is Living and What is Dead of the Philosophy of Hegel*) (1907). However, Croce's aesthetics owes at least as much to Kant in its emphasis upon the priority of intuition and the total autonomy of the art work; he also rejected the concept of aesthetic genre which was central to Hegel's historical construction of art. He also repudiated the supposed 'death of art' thesis which he influentially took to be implied in Hegel's subordination of art to religion and philosophy. However, Croce entertained no qualms about the apparent supercession of the religious dimension in speculative philosophy and his appropriation of Hegel was thoroughly immanent and humanistic.

If Croce stressed the autonomy of the different domains of spiritual activity, his erstwhile friend and collaborator Gentile followed Hegel more directly in grasping all human activities as interrelated manifestations of creative spirit. Similarly in his philosophy of art Gentile defended a less formalist position than Croce. Gentile's philosophy generally is also marked by a strong voluntarist emphasis and an ardent educational idealism that has affinities with FICHTE. Croce finally broke with Gentile when the latter attempted to provide a Hegelian justification of the new, fascist 'Corporate State' as the concrete realization of ethical life. In spite of his political affiliations Gentile's thought continued to exercise a significant influence on Italian thought at both ends of the political spectrum. Hegel's influence was also strongly registered by the Marxist theoretician Antonio GRAMSCI through the contemporary example of Croce and Gentile. Gramsci developed a philosophy of praxis that closely paralleled Lukács' interpretation of Marx and rejected the quasi-naturalistic conception of dialectical materialism, seeking rather to transcend and preserve the heritage of bourgeois culture and philosophy and endow the Marxist perspective with the potential for cultural hegemony. As with the Western Marxists generally, Gramsci distrusted the mechanical application of any simple basis/superstructure distinction and attempted to grasp the complex mediation between social determinants and the collective self-consciousness of human agents in more dialectical fashion.

7 Hegelian influence in the twentieth century: Britain, America and France

Britain and America. The appropriation of Hegelian idealism by Croce and Gentile influenced R.G. COLLINGWOOD, who was one of Hegel's few sympathetic readers in Britain between the wars. Like the Italians, Collingwood believed that Hegel's Platonism had stopped him properly overcoming the opposition of art and logic, feeling and thought, and in his own method of question and answer he sought to present Hegel's dialectic in less panlogistic, more historicist terms, which did not seek to escape the 'absolute presuppositions' of its time. Moreover, in taking up a Crocean approach to the historical method (summed up in Croce's dictum that 'every true history is contemporary history'), Collingwood drew attention back to Hegel's philosophy of history, from which Croce's was a critical development.

In America in this period, direct interest in Hegel had also waned, although a continuing commitment to the idealist tradition can be found in the work of W.M. Urban (1873–1952) and Brand Blanshard (1892–1966), whose coherence theory of truth refers back to the British school of Absolute Idealism, and thus indirectly to Hegel.

France. As in Germany and Italy, the view of Hegel that emerged in France in the twentieth century no longer set him in opposition to the humanistic, non-metaphysical, anti-essentialist perspective of his critics, but instead treated him as an important precursor and source of this very perspective. Within French thought, the beginnings of this reassessment can be traced back to Jean Wahl's *Le Malheur de la Conscience dans la Philosophie de Hegel* (The Unhappy Consciousness in the Philosophy of Hegel) (1929). In this work, Wahl (1888–1974) attempted to uncover a side to Hegel's thought that was darker, more romantic and less rationalistic than had previously been noticed, and to cast fresh light on the whole direction of his philosophy. He was helped towards this reinterpretation by the publication of Hegel's early writings by Dilthey and Nohl, which revealed to Wahl that Hegel's real preoccupations and concerns were close to those of a Christian existentialist like Kierkegaard, a fact that had been obscured by the speculative approach of the later Encyclopedic system. Wahl was therefore led to look anew at the *Phenomenology of Spirit*, treating it not merely as a prolegomenon to the mature system, but as the highest expression of Hegel's troubled vision; at the centre of his reading of the *Phenomenology*, Wahl placed Hegel's treatment of the Unhappy Consciousness, in which (he argued) the sense of loss is epitomized. Thus, although Wahl himself was not prepared to call Hegel an existentialist, his influential study of the *Phenomenology* showed how existentialist themes could be uncovered in Hegel's thought (see EXISTENTIALISM).

In the wake of Wahl's study, the Hegel renaissance in France was taken further and given greater impetus by the work of Alexandre KOJÈVE and Jean Hyppolite (1907–68). Kojève gave an important series of seminars on the *Phenomenology* from 1933 to 1939 at the École Pratique des Hautes Études, which was attended by many who were to become leading luminaries of French intellectual life, as well as influential interpreters of Hegel in their own right, including Maurice MERLEAU-PONTY, Eric Weil (1904–77), Georges BATAILLE and Jacques LACAN. The text of these seminars was published in 1947, and it remains one of the most challenging readings of Hegel's thought. Equally important were the efforts of Hyppolite, who published the first volume of his magisterial translation of the *Phenomenology* in 1939 and the second in 1941, and in 1946 completed his commentary on the text, entitled *Genèse et structure de la Phénoménologie de l'esprit de Hegel* (Genesis and Structure of Hegel's Phenomenology of Spirit). Kojève made the master–slave dialectic the key to his treatment, into which he wove both Heideggerian and Marxist themes. He cites as an epigraph to his lecture on the *Phenomenology* Marx's comment that 'Hegel... sees *labour* as the *essence* of man, the self-confirming essence, of man' (Marx 1975: 386) and,

like Marx, identifies the work of the slave as an essential moment in self-objectification. At the same time, with Heidegger he emphasizes the slave's experience of death, and his recognition of finitude, out of which the slave also feels liberation from the natural world. Kojève therefore interprets Hegel's move to idealism in this light: it is an attempt to show how the human mind can overcome the material world of nature, by creating its own world through the power of speech, language and thought, an ideological realm in which we feel at home and free. This free creativity also has a more tragic aspect, however, as it is limited and defined by an awareness of finitude and death; at the same time the capacity to die represents our liberation from the control of any transcendent creative power, such as God, and is thus the dialectical expression of our highest freedom.

Perhaps Kojève's best-known and most remarkable contribution to the interpretation of Hegel arises directly from the conjunction of Marxist and existentialist aspects in his account: for, drawing on both Heidegger and Marx, Kojève argues that for Hegel history began with the sense of otherness, and can end in the universal satisfaction of the desire for recognition, putting a stop to our urge to negate and overcome all externality. Thus Kojève arrives at a non-metaphysical, secularized conception of Hegel's philosophical history, and reads the end of his system in anthropological, not theological terms; he therefore takes another step away from the nineteenth-century image of Hegelianism, and offers a new vision of this notoriously problematic aspect of Hegel's work.

For readers of Hegel, however, Kojève's interpretation raises almost as many problems as it solves, and many have felt (with Jean Wahl) that 'it is quite false but very interesting'. Hyppolite's approach is rather more judicious, while he too is influenced in his reading by existentialism and Marx. Like Wahl, he holds that 'unhappy consciousness is the fundamental theme of the *Phenomenology*.... The happy consciousness is either a naïve consciousness which is not yet aware of its misfortune or a consciousness that has overcome its duality and discovered a unity beyond separation. For this reason we find the theme of unhappy consciousness present in various forms throughout the *Phenomenology*' (Hyppolite 1946 I: 184; 1974: 190). Also like Wahl, Hyppolite argues that 'we find (Hegel) in his early works and in the *Phenomenology*, a philosopher much closer to Kierkegaard than might seem credible' (Hyppolite 1971 I: 93): although Hegel admittedly ends in Absolute Knowledge which seems to transcend all diremptions, the journey of consciousness is nevertheless characterized as 'the way of despair'. At the same time, Hyppolite emphasizes Hegel's foreshadowing of

Marx's account of alienation, and agrees with Kojève that recognition is capable of overcoming the tension between self and other. None the less, in his later writings on Hegel (such as *Logique et existence* (Logic and Existence) and 'Essai sur la *Logique* de Hegel' ('On the *Logic* of Hegel')), Hyppolite gave greater weight to the *Logic* than hitherto; for, he argues, the claim to Absolute Knowledge, and the transition to the *Logic* must be made, if 'the phantom of the thing-in-itself' is to be avoided, and with it the sense that we are out of touch with Being. Hyppolite acknowledges, however, that there is a tension between this return to the Logic and metaphysics, and the more humanistic, anthropological method of the *Phenomenology*, a tension which he sees as fundamental to Hegel's thought.

It is partly thanks to this reading of Hegel by Kojève and Hyppolite that Marxism and existentialism became so interlinked in the intellectual life of post-war France; and it is clear that they helped bring about a rapprochement between Hegel and Marx in this period by treating existentialism as a kind of common ground on which Hegelianism and Marxism could be reconciled. While some (such as ALTHUSSER) remained hostile to this development, existentialism also served to bring about the same kind of reconciliation outside France, as the themes of alienation, reification and estrangement from nature were discovered in both their works.

8   Contemporary developments

In the last third of the twentieth century, Hegel has continued to have a considerable influence on philosophical thought, both as a major figure within the canon of 'continental' philosophy, and (more recently) within Anglo-American 'analytic' and post-analytic philosophy.

France. Since the end of the 1960s the reception of Hegelian thought in France has been significantly determined by successive waves of intellectual reaction to the previously dominant philosophies. The structuralist movement which partially supplanted the phenomenological and existentialist tradition tended to minimize the Hegelian elements in Marx's thought and emphasize the radical incompatibility of 'idealist' and scientifically 'materialist' approaches to the constitution of social reality. The emergence of a genealogical mode of critical discourse in Michel FOUCAULT, the libidinal materialism of Gilles DE-LEUZE and the postmodern pluralism of Jean LYOTARD represented a decided antirealism and anti-foundationalism which questioned the central assumptions of the classical philosophical tradition and its metaphysics of truth. The pervasive influence

of Nietzsche and Heidegger, and the perceptible political retreat from a hitherto powerful Marxist tradition, has conspired in the French context to produce something resembling a regnant anti-Hegelianism as a negative mirror image of the era of Kojève, Merleau-Ponty and Sartre. The critique of the metaphysical tradition of ontology and its supposed prioritizing of self-presence has inspired the ethically oriented philosophies of alterity like those of Emanuel LEVINAS in *Totalité et Infini* (*Totality and Infinity*) (1961) and Jacques DERRIDA in *Glas* (1974) respectively. For both thinkers, though in subtly distinct ways, Hegel again represents an exemplary case of all-consuming totalizing discourse and consequently a privileged object of critical analysis. What is at stake here is the claim to articulate a logic which can grasp difference positively rather than in terms of opposition, and the rejection of dialectic as an appropriate conceptual resource for this task.

Italy. Since the 1970s, the influence of alternative models of radical philosophy like French structuralism, post-structuralism and deconstruction has partially eclipsed the previous Marxist monopoly on critical social thought in Italy, while as in France, the rejection of 'grand narratives' and supposedly totalizing metaphysical discourse has led to a developing critique of the idealist tradition as a whole, and Hegelian philosophy in particular. One result has been an increasingly scholarly and interpretative engagement with Hegel and the modern German tradition, but less evidence of any productive appropriation of dialectical thought.

Germany. After the neo-Hegelian movement of the pre-war period in Germany one cannot accurately speak of any Hegelian 'School' of thought. None the less, the significance of Hegel continued to make itself felt indirectly in the hermeneutic version of phenomenology developed by Martin HEIDEGGER. Heidegger's reading of the European metaphysical tradition, supposedly culminating in Hegel, exercised considerable influence upon the interpretation of Hegel's thought. If Heidegger's own attitude to Hegel was problematically ambivalent, his student Hans-Georg GADAMER developed a critical but productive relationship to Hegel mediated by his appropriation of Heidegger's thought as a universal ontological hermeneutics. In *Wahrheit und Methode* (*Truth and Method*) (1960) he drew especially on Hegel's account of experience and endorsed the anti-subjectivist thrust of Hegelian philosophy in his rejection of the psychologistic hermeneutics he associated with Schleiermacher and Dilthey.

It was also in the context of the hermeneutic tradition that a distinct renewal of theological interest in Hegel first arose after the war, a development that was subsequently intensified by the social turn in modern theology with the influence of the Frankfurt School and issues of Marxist-Christian dialogue. Although Karl BARTH had always emphasized the autonomy of theological discourse, his evolving thought eventually led him from an initial commitment to a paradoxical dialectic indebted to Kierkegaard towards a position of theological realism, a quasi-Hegelian insistence upon systematic objectivity grounded in the trinitarian nature of God's unreserved self-disclosure. A number of Barth's students and interpreters pursued the critical turn against exclusively existentialist emphasis upon individual subjectivity and an apparent neglect of social reality and historical revelation. Jürgen Moltmann (1926–) responded to impulses from Ernst Bloch and the Frankfurt School and adumbrated a dialectical theology of liberation with his *Theologie der Hoffnung* (*Theology of Hope*) (1965) and *Der gekreuzigte Gott* (*The Crucified God*) (1973). The work of Wolfhart Pannenberg (1928–) reflects the new confidence in systematic theology that draws comprehensively on the classical idealist tradition and Hegel's incarnational metaphysics in particular. Sharing Moltmann's insistence on an open dialectic with a liberatory eschatological dimension, Pannenberg has also attempted a qualified and critical re-appropriation of Hegelian insights. Although profoundly influenced by Heideggerean hermeneutics, Eberhard Jüngel (1934–) also pursues the arguably Hegelian insistence on the radical humanity of God in the later Barth and addresses the question of the 'death of God' through close engagement with German Idealism and the Left Hegelian tradition in his *Gott als Geheimnis der Welt* (*God as the Mystery of the World*) (1977). What unites these theologians, despite significant differences of emphasis, is the attempt to exploit the conceptual resources of the dialectical tradition to overcome the abstract antithesis of atheism and theism and restate the trinitarian character of spirit.

Naturally Hegel also remained a permanent point of reference for the more orthodox strains of Marxism in Germany throughout this period. None the less, the most significant and vital engagement with the Hegelian tradition was still to be found among the heirs of the Frankfurt School and those broadly sympathetic to the aspirations of Critical Theory. Thus Jürgen HABERMAS has responded intensively to aspects of Hegel's thought in his reformulation of an emancipatory social philosophy. While rejecting Hegel's supposed metaphysical philosophy of identity in favour of a quasi-transcendental account of irreducible constitutive interests, Habermas exploited Hegel's insights into the communicative dimension of social interaction and the centrality of the concept of recognition. In contrast with his predecessors, Habermas has attempted to reorient critical theory through the turn to intersubjectivity as an alternative to traditional philosophy of consciousness. In his later work, *Der philosophische Diskurs der Moderne* (*The Philosophical Discourse of Modernity*) (1985), Habermas recognizes Hegel's contribution to the formulation of the concept of modernity and pursues a postmetaphysical appropriation of aspects of the idealist tradition for a non-foundational universalist ethics.

Karl-Otto Apel (1922–) originally revealed the influences of Heideggerian hermeneutics, philosophical anthropology and Litt's neo-Hegelian idealist philosophy, subsequently modified by an increasing interest in Critical Theory. Like Habermas, Apel's critical relation to the tradition was motivated by the accommodations and failures of pre-war historicist philosophies of culture and ossified Marxism in the face of authoritarianism on right and left. Accepting fundamental features of Hegel's critique of Kant, he has drawn extensively on the American idealist and pragmatic tradition of Royce and Peirce in his *Transformation der Philosophie* (*Towards a Transformation of Philosophy*) (1973) to develop a social conception of the rational community as the ultimate normative presupposition of enquiry. Apel is committed to the dialectical mediation of abstract alternatives in contemporary philosophy and overcoming the opposition between rational grounding and practical ethical orientation in transcendental self-reflection, employing Kantian and Hegelian elements as mutual correctives of one another. The communicative turn and the question of intersubjectivity is also central for Michael Theunissen (1932–) who has interpreted and productively appropriated aspects of Hegel in sustained interaction with Kierkegaard and constant conjunction with developments in contemporary thought. In his attempt to relate the insights of dialogical and dialectical thought his work reflects all the different currents of existential phenomenology, theology and critical theory in which Hegel has been a latent presence or critical point of reference throughout the century.

Britain and North America. Until recently Hegel was left largely unread by those working within the 'analytic' tradition of Anglo-American philosophy, while the issues raised by Hegelian idealism were only discussed by those at the margins of this movement, such as J.N. Findlay (1903–87) and G.R.G. Mure (1893–1979). Since the 1970s, however, respect for Hegel's thought has grown, partly because of his influence on the communitarian and historicist ideas of Charles TAYLOR and Alasdair MACINTYRE, and partly because Hegel's attack on the Kantian division of 'form' and 'matter' in experience has been echoed by those (such as Donald DAVIDSON, Hilary PUTNAM and Richard RORTY) who question the scheme/content distinction in epistemology, and who thereby seek to go beyond Kant's 'subjective idealism' in a somewhat Hegelian manner.

Thus, as the 'continental' and 'analytic' traditions have come together over the question of how far metaphysics is possible after the Kantian turn, the current intellectual landscape is characterized by a continuing interest in examining, clarifying and exploiting the conceptual resources of the German Idealist tradition, for which the interpretation, appropriation and contestation of Hegelian philosophy will inevitably represent a permanent point of reference.

See also: ABSOLUTE, THE; AMERICAN PHILOSOPHY IN THE 18TH AND 19TH CENTURIES §2; DIALECTICAL MATERIALISM; FRANKFURT SCHOOL; GERMAN IDEALISM; HEGEL, G.W.F.; IDEALISM; ITALY, PHILOSOPHY IN; KYOTO SCHOOL; MARXIST PHILOSOPHY OF SCIENCE; ROSENZWEIG, F.; RUSSIAN HEGELIANISM; SCANDINAVIA, PHILOSOPHY IN; WESTERN MARXISM

List of works

For reasons of space, some of the works cited in the text are not given in the bibliography below, but are cited in the respective biographical entries of the particular author.

Primary literature

Stern, R. (ed.) (1993) *G.W.F. Hegel: Critical Assessments,* London: Routledge, 4 vols. (The first two volumes contain a selection of the main writings in Hegel's nineteenth- and twentieth-century reception.)

Germany

Apel, K.-O. (1973) *Transformation der Philosophie,* Frankfurt: Suhrkamp; trans. G. Adey and D. Frisby, *Towards a Transformation of Philosophy,* London: Routledge, 1980. (Extensive essay collection presenting Apel's attempt to mediate the extremes in contemporary philosophy by recourse to the hermeneutic and pragmatic traditions.)

Baur, F.C. (1835) *Die christliche Gnosis oder die christliche Religionsphilosophie in ihrer geschichtlichen Entwicklung* (Christian Gnosis, or the Christian Philosophy of Religion in its Historical Development), Tübingen: Osiander. (Traces the evolution of the Gnostic theological tradition up to and including Hegel and German Idealism.)

Biedermann, A.E. (1849) *Unsere junghegelianishe Weltanschauung oder der sogennante neueste Pantheismus* (Our Young Hegelian Worldview, or the so-called latest Pantheism), Zurich: F. Schultheiss. (A critical response to a theological polemic directed against the 'Tübingen School' and Hegel's influence.)

—— (1868) *Christliche Dogmatik* (Christian Dogmatics), Berlin: Georg Reimer; 2nd edn, 1884–5. (A late example of a broadly Hegelian and reconstructive exposition of traditional doctrines which questions the 'personality' of God.)

Daub, K. (1833) *Die dogmatische Theologie* (The Dogmatic Theology of Our Times), Heidelberg: J.B. Mohr. (A standard and cautious early Hegelian interpretation of traditional theological topics.)

Dilthey, W. (1905) *Die Jugendgeschichte Hegels* (The Young Hegel), Abhandlungen der Königlich Preussiche Akademie der Wissenchaften; repr. *Wilhelm Diltheys gesammelte Schriften,* vol. 4, Leipzig and Berlin: D.G. Teubner, 1921. (Led to an important reassessment of Hegel's early writings.)

Erdmann, J.E. (1834–53) *Versuch einer wissenschaftlichen Darstellung der Geschichte der neueren Philosophie* (Attempt at a Scientific Presentation of the History of Modern Philosophy), Leipzig: Riga & Dorpat, 6 vols. (One of the most comprehensive and magisterial Hegelian accounts of philosophy from Descartes to Hegel. Very incisively written.)

—— (1841) *Grundriß der Logik und Metaphysik* (Outline of Logic and Metaphysics), Halle: J.H. Lippert; 5th edn, 1875. (Succinct and careful restatement of the essential categories of Hegel's Logic.)

—— (1865–7) *Grundriß der Geschichte der Philosophie,* Berlin: Wilhelm Hertz, 2 vols; 4th edn, 1895–6.; trans. W.S. Hough, *A History of Philosophy,* London: Swan Sonnenschein, 3 vols, 1890. (Influential classic history of philosophy, thoroughly and carefully written from a Right Hegelian perspective.)

Fischer, K. (1852) *System der Logik und Metaphysik oder Wissenschaftslehre* (System of Logic and Metaphysics or Doctrine of Science), Stuttgart: C.P. Scheitlin; 3rd edn, 1909. (Lucid and brief exposition of Hegel's logical doctrines.)

—— (1852–77; 1897–1904) *Geschichte der neueren Philosophie* (History of Modern Philosophy), 10 vols in 11, Heidelberg: Carl Winters Universitätsbuchhandlung. (A classic, massively detailed history of philosophy from Descartes to Schopenhauer, with the concluding two-volume monograph on Hegel.)

Gabler, G.A. (1827) *Kritik des Bewußtseins* (Critique of Consciousness), Leiden: A.H. Adriani; 2nd edn, 1901. (One of the very few early examinations of Hegel's *Phenomenology*, written by Hegel's follower and successor in Berlin.)

Gans, E. (1824–35) *Das Erbrecht in weltgeschichtlicher Entwicklung* (The Law of Inheritance Considered in its World-Historical Development), vols 1 and 2, Berlin: Maurische Buchhandlung; vols 3 and 4, Stuttgart and Tübingen: Cotta. (The major Hegelian contribution to the history of law, written in conscious opposition to the 'Historical School'.)

Glockner, H. (1929–40) *Hegel*, Stuttgart: Frommann, 2 vols. (Typical expression of vitalist neo-Hegelianism, emphasizing the cultural concreteness and historical richness of Hegelian thought.)

—— (1931) 'Hegelrenaissance und Neuhegelianismus' (The Hegel Renaissance and Neo-Hegelianism), *Logos* 20; repr. with other contributions in *Hegel-Studien*, Beiheft 2, Bonn: Bouvier. (A historical account of the early twentieth-century Hegel revival in Germany by one of the leading participants.)

Haering, T. (1929–38) *Hegel. Sein Wollen und sein Werk* (Hegel: His Life and his Works), Leipzig and Berlin, 2 vols; repr. Aalen: Scientia, 1979. (Enormous genetic study of Hegel's thought from 1790–1807, stressing Hegel's practical and political concerns. Typical of the organic 'communitarian' interpretation of conservative neo-Hegelianism.)

Hartmann, N. (1923, 1929) *Die Philosophie des deutschen Idealismus* (The Philosophy of German Idealism), Berlin and Leipzig, 2 vols; 3rd edn, repr. Berlin: de Gruyter, 1974. (An important ontological and 'realist' reading of Hegel, emphasizing his systematic ambitions and debt to the classical tradition.)

Haym, R. (1857) *Hegel und seine Zeit* (Hegel and his Times), Berlin: Rudolph Gaertner. (Contains an influential attack on Hegel as an apologist for the Prussian Restoration.)

Henning, L. von (1824) *Prinzipien der Ethik in historischer Entwicklung* (Principles of Ethics in Historical Development), Berlin: Friedrich August Herbig. (A lucid brief outline of the history of ethics, dedicated to Hegel.)

Jüngel, E. (1977) *Gott als Geheimnis der Welt*, Tübingen: J.C.B. Mohr, trans. D.L. Guder, *God as the Mystery of the World*, Edinburgh: T. & T. Clark, 1983. (A magisterial contribution to philosophical theology, influenced by Barth and Heidegger, which engages seriously and productively with Hegel and the Left Hegelian tradition.)

Korsch, K. (1930) *Marxismus und Philosophie*, Leipzig: C.L.Hirschfeld, trans. F. Halliday, *Marxism and Philosophy*, London: New Left Books, 1970. (This work reopened the question of Marx's debt to Hegelian idealism.)

Kroner, R. (1921–4) *Von Kant bis Hegel* (From Kant to Hegel), Tübingen: Mohr Verlag, 2 vols; 3rd edn, repr. 1977. (The most substantial single product of neo-Hegelianism, interpreting Hegel as the fitting culmination of the entire tradition of classical and idealist thought from a Christian perspective.)

Lasson, G. (1916) *Was heißt Hegelianismus?* (What is Hegelianism?), Berlin: Reuther & Reichard. (An uncritical and enthusiastic neo-Hegelian manifesto from a rather nationalistic perspective.)

Litt, T. (1948) *Denken und Sein* (Thought and Being), Zurich: S. Hirzel. (Attempts to apply reformed Hegelian categories to central metaphysical and epistemological questions.)

—— (1948) *Mensch und Welt* (Man and World), Heidelberg: Quelle & Meyer, 1961. (A quasi-Hegelian reinterpretation of philosophical anthropology, strongly influenced by Dilthey.)

—— (1953) *Hegel*, Heidelberg: Quelle and Meyer. (An appreciative assessment and reconstruction of Hegel, but critical of allegedly panlogistic and totalizing elements.)

Löwith, K. (ed.) (1962) *Die Hegelsche Linke* (The Hegelian Left), Stuttgart: Frommann-Holzboog. (Selected texts by members of the Left Hegelian school.)

Lübbe, H. (ed.) (1962) *Die Hegelsche Rechte* (The Hegelian Right), Stuttgart: Frommann-Holzboog. (Selected texts by members of the Right Hegelian school.)

Lukács, G. (1963) *Ästhetik* (Aesthetics), Berlin: Luchterhand; repr. in *Werke*, Berlin: Luchterhand, 1968, vols 11–12. (The most sustained example of a Marxian appropriation of classical German Idealist aesthetics and the concept of 'mimesis'.)

Marheineke, P.K. (1819) *Die Grundlehren der christlichen Dogmatik als Wissenschaft* (The Fundamental Doctrines of Christian Dogmatics as Science), Berlin: F. Dummler; 2nd edn, Duncker & Humblot, 1827. (One of the first thoroughgoing applications of Hegel's thought to Christian theology as a whole.)

Marx, K. (1975) *Early Writings*, trans. R. Livingstone and G. Benton, Harmondsworth: Penguin. (A useful paperback edition, which contains Marx's posthumously published 'Critique of Hegel's Doctrine of the State' and 'Economic and Philosophical Manuscripts' and his (1844), as 'A Contribution to the Critique of Hegel's Philosophy of Right'.)

Michelet, K.L. (1837–8) *Geschichte der letzten Systeme der Philosophie in Deutschland von Kant bis Hegel* (History of the Most Recent Systems of Philosophy in Germany from Kant to Hegel),

Berlin: Dunker and Humblot, 2 vols. (A lucid history of German idealism by a representative of the liberal Hegelian 'centre'.)

Moltmann, J. (1965) *Theologie der Hoffnung*, Munich: Kaiser; trans. J.W. Leitch, *Theology of Hope*, London: SCM Press, 1967. (Indicative of reaction against existentialist dialectics and a renewed theological interest in the social dimension of the German Idealist tradition.)

—— (1972) *Der gekreuzigte Gott*, Munich: Chr Kaiser; trans. R.A. Wilson and J. Bowden, *The Crucified God*, London: SCM Press, 1974. (Approach to a liberation theology of the cross influenced by Marxist-Christian dialogue.)

Pannenberg, W. (1967) *Grundfragen systematischer Theologie* (Fundamental Questions of Systematic Theology), Gottingen: Vandenhoek & Ruprecht. (Draws on Hegel and idealist thought to articulate a rational philosophical theology and defend the concept of progressive historical revelation.)

Rosenkranz, J.K.F. (1837) *Psychologie, oder die Wissenschaft vom subjektiven Geistes* (Psychology, or the Science of Subjective Spirit), Königsberg: Bornträger. (A succinct outline of the Hegelian philosophy of mind.)

—— (1840a) *Kritische Erläuterungen des Hegelschen Systems* (Critical Exposition of the Hegelian System), Königsberg: Bornträger. (Interesting collection of sympathetic essays on various aspects of Hegel, reflecting many of the debates within the school in the 1830–40 period.)

—— (1840b) *Geschichte der Kantischen Philosophie* (History of Kantian Philosophy), Leipzig: Leopold Voss; repr. in J.K.F. Rosenkranz and F.W. Schubert (eds) *Immanuel Kants sämmtliche Werke*, vol. 12. (A supplement to Rosenkranz's edition of Kant's works indicating the 'completion' of Critical Philosophy in Hegelian idealism.)

—— (1844) *Hegels Leben* (Hegel's Life) (Berlin); repr. Darmstadt: Wissenschaftliche Buchgesellschaft, 1988. (Rosenkranz's official biography of Hegel.)

—— (1858–9) *Wissenschaft der logischen Idee* (Science of the Logical Idea), Köningsberg: Borntrager, 2 vols; repr. Osnabruck: Zeller, 1972. (A major critical reworking of Hegel's Logic.)

—— (1870) *Hegel als deutscher Nationalphilosoph* (Hegel as German National Philosopher), Leipzig: Duncker & Humblot; extracts translated in Stern (ed.) 1993, vol. 1, 256–297. (A contemporary study of Hegel's thought and influence.)

Stepelevich, L.S. (ed.) (1983) *The Young Hegelians*, Cambridge: Cambridge University Press. (An anthology of writings by Strauss, Cieszkowski, Feuerbach, Bruno Bauer, Ruge, Edgar Bauer, Engels, Marx, Stirner, Hess and Schmidt.)

Theunissen, M. (1970) *Hegels Lehre vom absoluten Geist als theologisch-politischer Traktat* (Hegel's Doctrine of Absolute Spirit as Theological-Political Treatise), Berlin: de Gruyter. (Major sympathetic exposition of Hegel's religious philosophy which attempts to undercut standard Left and Right interpretations.)

—— (1980) *Sein und Schein* (Being and Appearance), Frankfurt: Suhrkamp. (Pursues an 'intersubjective' approach to the claims of Hegel's Logic as a potential theory of communicative freedom.)

Trendelenburg, F.A. (1840) *Logische Untersuchungen* (Logical Investigations), Leipzig: S. Hirzel; 2nd edn, 1862. (An influential critique of Hegel's Logic.)

—— (1843) *Die logische Frage in Hegels System* (The Logical Question in Hegel's System), Leipzig: F.A. Brockhaus. (Further develops his critique of Hegel's Logic.)

Vatke, W. (1835) *Die Religion des alten Testaments* (The Religion of the Old Testament), Berlin: G. Bethge. (Important early treatment of the then-neglected area of Judaism from a Hegelian perspective.)

—— (1841) *Die menschliche Freiheit in ihrem Verhältniss zur Sünde und zur göttlichen Gnade* (Human Freedom in its Relation to Sin and Divine Forgiveness), Berlin: Bethge. (Applies Hegel's philosophy of spirit to elucidate classical theological questions concerning guilt and forgiveness.)

Vischer, F.T. (1837) *Über das Erhabene und Komische* (On the Sublime and the Comic), ed. W. Oelmüller, Frankfurt: Suhrkamp, 1967. (Reprinted with other essays, this essay gives a thoroughly humanistic Left-Hegelian approach to an area rather neglected by Hegel.)

—— (1846–54) *Ästhetik oder Wissenschaft des Schönen* (Aesthetics or the Science of Beauty), Reutlingen & Leipzig: Carl Mäckens, 6 vols. (The largest Hegelian contribution to aesthetics which supplements Hegel by examining the question of natural beauty and the psychology of imagination.)

Windelband, W. (1910) 'Die Erneuerung der Hegelianismus' (The renewal of Hegelianism', *Sitzungsberichte der Heidelberger Akademie der Wissenschaften* 1 (10); repr. in W. Windelband, *Präludien*, Tübingen: J.C.B. Mohr, 6th edn, 1919, 273–89. (An important expression of the German resurgence of interest in Hegel at the beginning of the twentieth century.)

Zeller, E. (1844–52) *Die Philosophie der Griechen* (Philosophy of the Greeks), 3 vols in 2, Tübingen: Friedrich Fues. (Very influential standard history of ancient philosophy from a Hegelian perspective which was widely studied and translated.)

France

Bataille, G. (1955) 'Hegel, le mort et le sacrifice' (Hegel, Death and Sacrifice), *Deucalion* 5: 21–43; trans. J. Strauss, in A. Stoekl (ed.) *On Bataille*, New Haven, CT: Yale University Press, 1990. (A response to Kojève's reading of Hegel.)

Bertholet, R. (1907) 'Thèse: Sur la nécessité, la finalité et la liberté chez Hegel' (Thesis: On Necessity, Finality and Liberty in Hegel), *Bulletin de la Société française de philosophie* 115–140; repr. in R. Bertholet, *Evolutionisme et platonisme*, Paris: Alcan, 1908. (Defends Hegel against the accusation of absolute determinism, integral optimism and panlogicism, and discusses Hegel's influence on Marx.)

Herr, L. (1894) 'Hegel', *La Grande Encyclopédie* 19: 997–1003; repr. in L. Herr, *Choix d'Écrits*, Paris: Les Éditions Ridier, 1932, vol. 2, 109–40. (Contains a lengthy summary of the Hegelian system, which revived interest in his philosophy in this period.)

Hyppolite, J. (1946) *Genèse et structure de la Phénoménologie de l'esprit de Hegel*, Paris: Aubier, 2 vols; trans. S. Cherniak and J. Heckman, *Genesis and Structure of Hegel's Phenomenology of Spirit*, Evanston, IL: Northwestern University Press, 1974. (Hyppolite's magisterial and influential commentary.)

—— (1948) *Introduction à la philosophie de l'histoire de Hegel* (Introduction to Hegel's Philosophy of History), Paris: Rivère; Paris: Editions du Seuil, 1983. (A collection of short studies stressing the relation between the early and later Hegel.)

—— (1953) *Logique et existence, essai sur la Logique de Hegel* (Logic and Existence: Essays on Hegel's Logic), Paris: Presses Universitaires de France. (Explores the contested issue of the relation of Hegel's *Logic* to the 'existential' dimension of the *Phenomenology*.)

—— (1955) *Études sur Marx et Hegel*, Paris: Rivière; trans. J.O. Neill, *Studies on Marx and Hegel*, London: Heinemann, 1969. (Stresses the place of Hegelian themes in Marx's early writings.)

—— (1971) *Figures de la Pensée Philosophiques*, Paris: Presses Universitaires de France, 2 vols. (Contains all of Hyppolite's articles on Hegel.)

Koyré, A. (1970) *Etudes d'histoire de la pensée philosophique* (Historical Studies of Philosophical Thought), Paris: Gallimard. (Contains the three most important essays by Koyré on Hegel: 'Note sur la langue et la terminologie hégélienne' ('Note on Hegelian Language and Terminology') (1931) 'Rapport sur l'état des études hégéliennes en France' ('Report on the State of Hegelian Studies in France') (1931) and 'Hegel à Iéna' ('Hegel in Jena') (1934).)

Nöel, G. (1897) *La Logique de Hegel* (Hegel's Logic), Paris: Alcan; repr. Paris: Vrin, 1933, 1938 and 1967. (A careful and sympathetic analysis of Hegel's *Logic*, which first appeared in instalments in the *Revue de métaphysique et de morale* from 1894 to 1896.)

Renan, E. (1876) *Dialogues et fragments philosophiques* (Dialogues and Philosophical Fragments), Paris: Calman Lévy. (Written between 1860 and 1871, Renan here attempts to combine Comtean positivism with religion, via an evolutionary reading of Hegel.)

Scherer, E. (1861) 'Hegel et l'hégélianisme' (Hegel and Hegelianism), *Revue des deux mondes* 31: 812–56. (Gives a reasonably sympathetic overview of the attitude to Hegel in this period.)

Vera, A. (1855) *Introduction à la philosophie de Hegel* (Introduction to Hegel's Philosophy), Paris: A. Franck. (A popular introduction to Hegel's thought.)

—— (1864) *Essais de philosophie hégélienne* (Essays on Hegelian Philosophy), Paris: G. Ballère. (The three essays are 'La peine de mort', 'Amour et philosophie', and 'Introduction à la philosophie d'histoire'.)

Wahl, J. (1929) *Le Malheur de la conscience dans la philosophie de Hegel* (The Unhappy Consciousness in the Hegel's Philosophy), Paris: Rieder, 2nd edn, 1951; repr. New York and London: Garland, 1984; 119–147 trans. R. Northey in Stern (ed.) (1993) vol. 2: 284–310. (An influential study, which treats Hegel's notion of the Unhappy Consciousness as a key to the reading of his work.)

—— (1938) *Études kierkegaardiennes* (Kierkegaardian Studies), Paris: Éditions Montaigne; 2nd edn, Paris: Vrin, 1949, 159–171. (A collection of articles, including 'Hegel et Kierkegaard' and 'La lutte contre l'hégélianisme'.)

Weil, E. (1950a) *Logique de la philosophie* (Logic of Philosophy). Paris: Vrin. (A major systematic appropriation of Hegel's thought as a comprehensive theory of categories.)

—— (1950b) *Hegel et l'état* (Hegel and the State) (Paris: Vrin. (An important defence of Hegel's political thought against accusations of conservatism.)

Northern Europe

Heiberg, J.L. (1824) *Om den menneskelige Frihed* (On Human Freedom), Kiel: Universitets Boghandlingen. (An early contribution by one of Hegel's students to the theory of the will.)

Martensen, H.L. (1850) *Den Christlige Dogmatik*,

trans. W. Urwick *Christian Dogmatics*, Edinburgh: T. & T. Clark, 1866. (Martensen's major work.)

Nielsen, R. (1864–6) *Grundidéernes Logik* (The Logic of Fundamental Ideas), Copenhagen. (An application of Hegel's Logic.)

Italy

Sanctis, F. de (1870–1) *La storia della letteraria italiana*, Naples: Domenico & Antonio Morano, 2 vols; trans. J. Redfern, *History of Italian Literature*, London: Oxford University Press, 2 vols, 1932. (Important document in the influence of Hegel's ideas in Italy, strongly influenced by Hegel's approach to aesthetics.)

Spaventa, B. (1869) *Studi sull'etica hegeliana* (Studies in Hegelian Ethics), *Proceedings of the Royal Academy of Moral and Political Sciences of Naples*, vol. 4; repr. in *Opere*, ed. G. Gentile, Florence: Sansoni, 1972, vol. 1, 611–801. (An important and influential early study.)

America

Dewey, J. (1884) 'Kant and Philosophic Method', *Journal of Speculative Philosophy* 18: 162–74; repr. in Stern (ed.) (1993) vol. 2, 151–61. (Presents a reading of Kant from a Hegelian perspective.)

—— (1930) 'From Absolutism to Experimentalism', in G.P. Adams and W.P. Montague (eds) *Contemporary American Philosophy*, New York, 1930, vol. 2, 13–27; repr. in R.J. Bernstein (ed.) *John Dewey, On Experience, Nature and Freedom*, New York: The Liberal Arts Press, 1960. (An autobiographical essay, in which Dewey expresses his attraction towards Hegelianism when a young man.)

Goetzmann, W. (ed.) (1973) *The American Hegelians: An Intellectual Episode in the History of Western America*, New York: Alfred A. Knopf. (Contains excerpts from the major works of main nineteenth-century American Hegelians, including Brokmeyer, Harris and Stallo.)

Harris, W.T. (1890) *Hegel's Logic, A Book on the Genesis of the Categories of the Mind: A Critical Exposition*, Chicago IL: S.C. Griggs; New York: Kraus Reprint Co., 1970. (The major work on Hegel by one of the most significant nineteenth-century Hegelians.)

Britain

Caird, E. (1883) *Hegel*, Edinburgh and London: Blackwood. (A short but well-respected study.)

—— (1892) *Essays on Literature and Philosophy*, Glasgow: James Maclehose, 2 vols. (Contains several essays with comments on Hegel, informed throughout by Hegelian ideas.)

Ritchie, D.G. (1890–1) 'Darwin and Hegel', *Proceedings of the Aristotelian Society* 1: 55–74; repr. in Stern (ed.) (1993) vol. 2: 41–59. (Attempts to defend Hegel against Seth's critique.)

Seth, A. (1887) *Hegelianism and Personality*, London: Blackwood. (Contains Seth's most developed and influential critique of Hegel.)

Stirling, J.H. (1865) *The Secret of Hegel*, London: Longman, Roberts & Green, 2 vols; 2nd edn, Edinburgh: Oliver & Boyd, 1898; repr. Bristol: Thoemmes, 1990. (The first major study on Hegel to appear in Britain.)

Wallace, W. (1874) *Prolegomena to the Study of Hegel's Philosophy*, Oxford: Oxford University Press. (Wide-ranging, sympathetic essays, trying to illuminate the background and content of Hegel's Logic.)

Secondary literature

Bellamy, R. (1987) *Modern Italian Social Theory*, Cambridge: Polity Press. (Contains chapters on Labriola, Croce, Gentile and Gramsci, and traces the roots of their thought back to the native idealist tradition.)

Bowie, A. (1993) *Schelling and Modern European Philosophy*, London: Routledge. (Chapter 6 provides a clear account of Schelling's critique of Hegel.)

Bradley, J. (1979) 'Hegel in Britain: A Brief Survey of British Commentary and Attitudes', *Heythrop Journal* 20: 1–24 and 163–82. (A useful survey of Hegel's reception in Britain.)

Brazill, W.J. (1970) *The Young Hegelians*, New Haven, CT: Yale University Press. (Discusses the origins and development of the Young Hegelian school.)

Butler, J. (1987) *Subjects of Desire: Hegelian Reflections in Twentieth Century France*, New York: Columbia University Press. (A specialized treatment of the impact of Hegel on twentieth century French thought.)

Cornehl, P. (1971) *Die Zukunft der Versöhnung* (The Future of Reconciliation), Göttingen: Vandenhoek & Ruprecht. (An outstanding study of the immediate theological reception of Hegel, focusing on the question of eschatology.)

Derbolav, J. (1969) 'Über die gegenwärtigen Tendenzen der Hegelaneignung in Deutschland' (On the Current Trends in Hegel Reception in Germany), *Hegel-Studien* 5: 267–91. (On the various forms of German Hegel reception since 1945.)

Descombes, V. (1980) *Modern French Philosophy*, Cambridge: Cambridge University Press. (Traces the importance of Kojève's Hegel reception and the eventual reaction to it for an entire generation of contemporary French thinkers.)

Easton, L. (1966) *Hegel's First American Followers: The Ohio Hegelians*, Athens, OH: Ohio University Press. (A useful discussion of Stallo, Kaufman, Conway and Willich, with extracts from their works.)

Fisch, M.H. (1974) 'Hegel and Peirce', in J.J. O'Malley, K.W. Algozin and F.G. Weiss (eds) *Hegel and the History of Philosophy*, The Hague: Martinus Nijhoff, 171–93. (Provides an account of Peirce's view of Hegel.)

Flower, E. and Murphey, M.G. (1977) *A History of Philosophy in America*, New York: Capricorn and Putnam, 2 vols. (Chapter 8 gives a very useful account of the St Louis Hegelians.)

Gasché, R. (1986) *The Tain of the Mirror. Derrida and the Philosophy of Reflection*, Cambridge, MA: Harvard University Press. (A philosophical presentation of Derrida's thought against a Hegelian background.)

Glockner, H. (1965) *Beiträge zum Verständnis und zur Kritik Hegels* (Contributions towards the Understanding and Critique of Hegel), *Hegel-Studien*, Beiheft 2, Bonn: Bouvier. (Contains 'Hegelrenaissance und Neuhegelianismus' and other relevant essays on neo-Hegelianism.)

Hodgson, P.C. (1966) *The Formation of Historical Theology: A Study of F.C. Baur*, New York: Harper & Row. (On F.C. Baur.)

Jacobitti, E.E. (1981) *Revolutionary Humanism and Historicism in Modern Italy*, New Haven, CT: Yale University Press. (A useful account of Hegel's influence in Italy, including details of his nineteenth-century reception.)

Jarvis, S. (1996) *Adorno*, Cambridge: Polity Press. (A comprehensive reading of Adorno which strongly emphasizes the Hegelian dimension.)

Jay, M. (1984) *Marxism and Totality: The Adventures of a Concept from Lukács to Habermas*, Cambridge: Polity Press. (Traces the legacy of the Hegelian emphasis upon totality in Western Marxism.)

Kelly, M. (1992) *Hegel in France*, Birmingham: Birmingham Modern Languages Publications. (A thorough survey of Hegel's reception in France from 1800 to the present, with a useful bibliography.)

Kortian, G. (1980) *Metacritique: The Philosophical Argument of Jürgen Habermas*, Cambridge: Polity Press. (Chapter 2 discusses Habermas's reception and engagement with Hegel.)

Löwith, K. (1941) *From Hegel to Nietzsche: The Revolution in Nineteeth-Century Thought*, trans. D.E. Green, London: Constable, 1965. (A classic study of the fate of the Hegelian system and the subsequent polarization of right and left interpretations.)

Mader, J. (1993) *Philosophie in der Revolte: das Ende des Idealismus im 19 Jahrhundert* (Philosophy in Revolt: The End of Idealism in the Nineteenth Century), Vienna: Universitätesverlag. (A recent account of the break-up of the Hegelian school in the nineteenth century.)

Muirhead, J.H. (1931) *The Platonic Tradition in Anglo-Saxon Philosophy*, London: Allen & Unwin, and New York: Macmillan. (A classic and still useful study of the development of British Idealism.)

Oelmüller, W. (1959) *F.Th. Vischer und das Problem der nachhegelschen Ästhetik* (Vischer and the Problem of Posthegelian Aesthetics), Stuttgart: Kohlhammer. (Provides a discussion of Vischer and the post-Hegelian legacy in aesthetics.)

Oldrini, G. (1973) *La cultura filosofica napoletana dell'ottocentro* (The Neapolitan Culture of the Nineteenth Century), Bari: Laterza. (The main Italian study of the Neapolitan Hegelians.)

Riedel, M. (1967) 'Hegel und Gans', in H. Braun and M. Riedel (eds) *Natur und Geschichte. Karl Löwith zum 70. Geburtstag*, Stuttgart: Kohlhammer, 257–73. (On Eduard Gans' relation to Hegel and Hegelianism.)

Roth, M. (1988) *Knowing and History: Appropriations of Hegel in Twentieth Century France*, Ithaca, NY: Cornell University Press. (A useful discussion of twentieth-century French Hegelianism.)

Sass, H.M. and Wartofsky, M.W. (eds) (1978) *Feuerbach, Marx and the Left Hegelians, The Philosophical Forum* 8: 1, 2 and 3. (A special issue on the Left Hegelians.)

Schmidt, A. (1962) *Der Begriff der Natur in der Lehre von Marx*, Frankfurt: Europäische Verlagsanstatt; trans. B. Fowkes, *The Concept of Nature in Marx*, London: New Left Books, 1971. (Analyses Marx's complex philosophical relation to Hegel and the Young Hegelians.)

—— (1962) *Geschichte und Struktur*, Munich: Carl Hanser; trans. J. Herf, *History and Structure*, Cambridge, MA: MIT Press, 1981. (Criticizes Althusser and the structuralist tendency to separate an early 'Hegelian' from a mature 'scientific' phase in Marx's thought.)

Stern, R. (1994) 'British Hegelianism: A Non-Metaphysical View?', *European Journal of Philosophy* 2: 293–321. (Examines the impact of Schelling on the readings of Hegel offered by the British Idealists.)

Thulstrup, N. (1967) *Kierkegaard's Relation to Hegel*,

trans. G.L. Stengren, Princeton, NJ: Princeton University Press, 1980. (A thorough account of Kierkegaard's acquaintance with Hegel's writings and those of his followers in Denmark.)

Toews, J. (1980) *Hegelianism: The Path Towards Dialectical Humanism, 1805–1841*, Cambridge: Cambridge University Press. (A study of the Hegelian movement before and after Hegel's death.)

Wartofsky, M.W. (1977) *Feuerbach*, Cambridge: Cambridge University Press. (Contains a thorough discussion of Hegel's place in Feuerbach's intellectual development.)

ROBERT STERN
NICHOLAS WALKER

HEGELIANISM, RUSSIAN

In Russian intellectual history the so-called 'remarkable decade' of 1838–48 (P.V. Annenkov's expression) could be characterized as a truly 'philosophical epoch'. Speculative philosophy was seen by then as directly relevant to all important questions of national existence. A similar situation obtained then, in exactly the same years, in the lands of partitioned Poland. In both countries all philosophical discussions revolved around Hegel, whose system was perceived as the culminating point in the development of Western philosophy. In Russia the fascination with Hegelianism was widespread and profound, reaching distant provincial centres and leaving its mark on literature. 'Philosophical notions', wrote Ivan Kireevskii in 1845, have become quite commonplace here now. There is scarcely a person who does not use philosophical terminology, nor any young man who is not steeped in reflections on Hegel'. Herzen provides an identical testimony. Hegel's works, he wrote,

> *were discussed incessantly; there was not a paragraph in the three parts of the* Logic, *in the two of the* Aesthetics, *the* Encyclopaedia *and so on, which had not been the subject of desperate disputes for several nights together. People who loved each other avoided each other for weeks at a time because they disagreed about the definition of 'all-embracing spirit', or had taken as a personal insult an opinion on the 'absolute personality and its existence in itself'.*

(Herzen [1853] 1968: 398)

This vivid reception of Hegelianism was a socially important phenomenon, meeting several deep-seated psychological demands of the young Russian intelligentsia. First, as in Germany, speculative idealism provided the intelligentsia with a sort of compensation for the paralysis of public life under authoritarian government. Second, Hegelian philosophy was welcomed as an antidote to introspective day-dreaming and attitudes of Romantic revolt; in this context Hegelianism was largely interpreted as a philosophy of 'reconciliation with reality'. Somewhat later this conservative interpretation of Hegelianism was replaced by a Left-Hegelian philosophy of rational and conscious action; at this stage Hegelianism came to be a powerful instrument in the struggle against Slavophile conservative Romanticism. Both as a philosophy of reconciliation and as a philosophy of action Russian Hegelianism was above all a philosophy of reintegration; a philosophy which helped young intellectuals in overcoming their feeling of alienation and in building bridges between their ideals and reality.

1 **From reconciliation with reality to philosophy of action**
2 **Belinskii's aesthetics and literary criticism**
3 **The Westernizing philosophies of Russian history**
4 **Hegelianism and Slavophilism**
5 **Russian Hegelianism in the second half of the nineteenth century**

1 From reconciliation with reality to philosophy of action

In the 1830s the chief centre of Russian Hegelianism was the Moscow circle of Nikolai Stankevich (1813–40). It counted among its members the literary critic Vissarion Belinskii, the future anarchist Mikhail Bakunin, the liberal historian Timofei Granovskii and even the future Slavophile Konstantin Aksakov; closely associated with the circle was the great Russian writer Ivan Turgenev.

Stankevich's intellectual evolution was a development from Schellingian pantheistic Romanticism (see SCHELLINGIANISM), combined with SCHILLER's militant 'subjectivism', to Hegelianism, interpreted initially as a philosophy of reconciliation. In the last year of his life he was greatly impressed by August Cieszkowski's *Die Prolegomena zur Historiosophie* (Prolegomena to the Wisdom of History) (Berlin, 1838) and tried to link Cieszkowski's idea of the 'translation of philosophy into action' (see CIESZKOWSKI, A.) with the Feuerbachian rehabilitation of feelings and senses (see FEUERBACH, L.). A similar pattern can be discerned in the intellectual evolution of Bakunin and Belinskii.

After Stankevich left Russia to study philosophy in Berlin (in 1837), the leadership in his circle was taken over by Mikhail BAKUNIN. His conversion to Hegelianism took place in 1838 and was heavily influenced by the mystical ideas of the German Romantics (see ROMANTICISM, GERMAN). In his 'Gimnazicheskie rechi Gegelia. Predislovie perevodchika' (Foreword to Hegel's School Addresses) (1838) Bakunin proclaimed 'the reconciliation with reality in all respects and all spheres of life'. He meant by this a radical overcoming of the abstract intellect (*Verstand – rassudok*) whose separation from the historical reason (*Vernunft – razum*) had caused the terrible modern disease of subjective revolt, finding expression in Schiller, Fichte and the rebellious poetry of Byron. The most advanced stage of this disease was embodied, in his view, by France – a country mortally sick of a barren revolutionary negation.

In 1840 Bakunin, following Stankevich, went to Berlin – the 'New Jerusalem' of the Russian idealists – and very soon became an extreme Left Hegelian, an apostle of a radical, revolutionary 'negation' of the 'old world'. In his article in 'Die Reaktion in Deutschland' (Reaction in Germany) (published under the pseudonym Jules Elysard in *Deutsche Jahrbücher für Wissenschaft und Kunst*) (1842) he elaborated a theoretical foundation for a revolutionary philosophy of action. It was one of the first serious attempts to make a radical 'Left-wing' interpretation of the Hegelian dialectic. In contrast to Hegel, Bakunin saw transcending (*Aufhebung*), in other words the final result of dialectic process, as a complete destruction of the past. The essence of contradiction, he argued, is not an equilibrium but 'the preponderance of the negative', whose role is decisive. Revolutionary negation includes within itself the totality of the contradiction and so alone has absolute legitimacy. The article ended with the words: 'The joy of destruction is also a creative joy'. Shortly thereafter Bakunin cut himself off from speculative philosophy and began his 'search for God' in revolutionary praxis.

The story of Vissarion Belinskii's involvement in Hegelianism was especially dramatic (see BELINSKII, V.). Before his acquaintance with Hegel he was influenced by the activist idealism of FICHTE, interpreted by him as a philosophy of heroic voluntarism. However, towards the end of 1837, he became struck by Hegel's famous thesis: 'What is real is rational, what is rational is real'. This led him to proclaim a philosophy of reconciliation, condemning all sorts of voluntaristic 'subjectivism' in the name of objective and rational laws of history. Unlike Bakunin, Belinskii was far from mystical idealism; hence he interpreted reconciliation in an empirical way, forcing himself to glorify tsarist autocracy and to accept the stifling social realities of Nicolaevan Russia. But this sort of self-indoctrination did not help him to overcome the painful feelings of alienation. In March 1841 he revolted against Hegel's historiosophical theodicy, vindicating the value of individual freedom and the heritage of the French Enlightenment. Initially it was a purely moral protest but very soon it became philosophically justified by a radical reinterpretation of the notion of 'rational reality', stressing the role of 'dialectical negation'. In this way Belinskii rejected conservative historicism, setting against it the idea of free, autonomous individuality, non-reducible to a mere instrument of 'vast impersonal forces' (Isaiah Berlin's expression). At the end of his life he sympathized with the philosophy of Feuerbach, in which he recognized a form of anthropocentrism liberating the individual from the despotic power of 'the absolute spirit' and rehabilitating the 'natural side' of human existence.

Unlike the members of Stankevich's circle, HERZEN was never tempted by the philosophy of reconciliation, seeing it as a form of moral suicide. In 1840 he embarked on a systematic study of Hegelianism with the aim of refuting its right-wing interpretation. He was helped in this endeavour by two Left-Hegelian thinkers: Cieszkowski (whose *Prolegomena* he read in 1838) and Feuerbach.

Herzen's philosophical essays of the 1840s, especially 'Buddizm v nauke' (Buddhism in Science) (1843) and 'Pis'ma ob izuchenii nauki' (Letters on the Study of Nature) (1845), develop the themes of the 'philosophy of action' and 'the rehabilitation of the natural', as two approaches to the problem of personal identity and freedom. In 'Buddizm v nauke' Herzen set his philosophy of action against the contemplative 'panlogism' of Hegel. He wrote: 'Action is the personality itself'. This meant that in order to become a personality man must get rid of his 'natural immediacy', raise himself to the 'Buddhist' realm of impersonal, abstract thought, get lost in the general and then (the third stage) regain his identity and express himself in free, conscious activity, changing the world in the desired direction. In 'Pis'ma ob izuchenii nauki' the problem of personality was shown against the background of the historical development of philosophical attitudes towards Nature. Their leitmotif was the demand for a reconciliation between naturalistic empiricism (identified with materialism) and idealism, with a strong insistence that it was to be realized not only for the sake of science but above all for the benefit of the human personality. Following Feuerbach, Herzen saw idealism as representing 'The General', at the expense of ignoring and annihilating the individual. 'Materialism', on the other hand, threatened to reduce human beings to their natural, immediate particularism. The future synthesis of both outlooks, Herzen concluded, should vindicate the rights of concrete individuals of flesh and blood but without losing the achievements of idealism, which had raised humans to the level of universalism.

An important theme in Herzen's critique of Hegel's philosophy of history was his protest against treating individuals and nations as mere instruments of the Reason of History. Nevertheless, before he went to the West (in 1847) he retained his faith in progress and Hegelian belief in the basic rationality of the historical process as a whole. This belief, however, did not survive the defeat of socialism in the revolutions of 1848. In his book *S togo berega* (*From the Other Shore*) (1850) Herzen definitely broke with Hegelianism, asserting that history was but a blind play of chances and refusing to make human sacrifices on the altar of illusionary progress.

2 Belinskii's aesthetics and literary criticism

As a literary critic Belinskii owed a great deal to the German Romantics while supporting the realist tendency in Russian literature. Hegelianism enabled him to overcome Romantic 'subjectivism' and to embrace instead the ideal of 'objective art'. In the period of 'reconciliation' he meant by this that writers should reflect objective reality in all its richness, putting aside their 'subjectivity' and refraining from value-judgments. The perfect embodiments of this ideal were for him the great 'Olympians', Goethe and Pushkin. The rejection of 'reconciliation' entailed a re-examination of this view – a rehabilitation of the artists' right to 'subjectivism'. At this stage, however, 'subjectivism' in art was no longer identified with Romantic whims; Belinskii stressed that legitimate subjectivism does not distort reality but reproduces it faithfully and judges it from the point of view of the forward-moving trend within society. In this way he justified and propagated the ideological commitment of realistic literature.

The influence of Hegel's aesthetics on Belinskii's thought is most visible in Belinskii's article 'The Idea of Art' (1841). It is very characteristic, however, that Belinskii corrected Hegel by placing art, defined as 'the immediate contemplation of truth', above religion, defined as an 'immediate representation of truth'. This correction reflected Belinskii's view that religious mythology was good only for the lowest, infantile stage of the human spirit, and that the development of literature was preparing society for the attainment of maturity in conscious, self-reflecting thought. In this way Belinskii justified his ardent belief in the emancipatory mission of Russian literature.

Belinskii emphasized that artistic generalization should not be confused with a 'logical syllogism' or 'schematic abstraction'. This would be transgressing against the very nature of art, since art was 'thinking in images'. But it was difficult to reconcile the autonomy of art with the conviction that artists, particularly writers, should serve the cause of historical progress. Hence a certain tension in Belinskii's views. In his series of articles on Pushkin (1843–6) he stated that poetry has no purpose beyond itself; in his other articles, however, he used to encourage the progressively minded writers by repeating that there is no such thing as pure art, since every work of art is tendentious. Thus, the legacy of Belinskii's literary criticism was somewhat ambivalent and subject to different interpretations.

3 The Westernizing philosophies of Russian history

Hegel's philosophy of history, as well as his philosophy of law, stressed the necessity and progressive function of the increasing rationalization of social bonds, which was directly relevant for the Russian controversy between Slavophiles and Westernizers. Hegelianism was incompatible with idealization of the Russian past and, for this reason alone, served the cause of Westernism.

The most consistent and prolific Westernizer of the 'remarkable decade' was Belinskii. His contribution consisted in applying to Russia the Hegelian conception of development from 'natural immediacy' to 'rational reality' and the Hegelian distinction between 'nonhistorical peoples' and 'historical nations'.

Pre-Petrine Russia, in Belinskii's view, was a nation in its natural, immediate and patriarchal state; hence it was not a nation in the modern sense of this term (*natsiia*) but only a people (*narod*), and its culture could not have any universal human significance. Only the reforms of Peter the Great raised Russia to the level of nationhood. The price for this was the radical negation of the natural immediacy of ancient Russia and the resulting cleavage between the Westernized 'society' and non-Westernized folk (*narod*). Owing to these reforms the Russian state could become an active subject of universal human history. However, in order to become a fully fledged 'historical nation' the Russians had to develop modern national consciousness and create a national literature of a truly world-historical significance. The decisive step in this direction was made by Pushkin. Thus, the Westernization of Russia laid foundations for its truly national development.

Another Hegelianizing interpretation of Russian history was provided by the young Moscow historian Konstantin Kavelin, a disciple of T. Granovskii. In his study 'Vzgliad na iuridicheskii byt v drevnei Rossii' (A Brief Survey of Juridical Relations in

Ancient Russia) (1847) he developed the argument that the Russian historical process consisted in the gradual dissolution of patriarchal bonds and their replacement by the juridical order of the centralized state, which made room for individual freedom. From this perspective Peter the Great appeared as the first completely emancipated individual in Russian history. The historical process in Russia led, therefore, to the emancipation of the individual through the rationalization of social relations by means of law. According to Kavelin, the emergence of the centralized Muscovite state played an important part in this process. This view – which sprang from Kavelin's interpretation of the Muscovite autocracy in terms of the rationalistic Hegelian state – was later to be developed by the 'etatist school' of Russian historiography. Its representatives, including the Hegelian philosopher Boris Chicherin, argued that in Russia the state had always been the chief organizer of society and the main agent of progress (see LIBERALISM, RUSSIAN §2).

4 Hegelianism and Slavophilism

The leading Slavophile thinkers, Ivan Kireevskii and Aleksei Khomiakov, were definitely opposed to Hegelianism. They saw Hegelian philosophy as the culmination of the anti-ontological tendency in Western rationalism, which transformed living reality into a dialectic of incorporeal notions. They passionately rejected Hegel's view that the meaning of universal history was the necessary process of the rationalization of society; according to them this was true of the West but did not apply to Russia. On theoretical grounds, against Hegelian dialectical historicism they set a conservative-Romantic historicism, enshrining uninterrupted historical continuity and condemning sudden breaks with the past as a betrayal of 'historicity'.

Nevertheless, two younger Slavophile thinkers – Konstantin Aksakov and Iurii Samarin – tried for some time to combine Slavophilism with Hegelianism, thus giving rise to a curious phenomenon known as 'Orthodox-Christian Hegelianism' (Herzen's expression). The main documents of this trend are two books written as master's dissertations for the University of Moscow: Aksakov's *Lomonosov in the History of Russian Language and Literature* (published 1846) and Samarin's *Stepan Iavorskii and Theophan Prokopovich* (defended 1844). The first of them was an ingenious interpretation of the history of Russian language and literature as a process raising the particular to the universal and then overcoming abstract universality. The second developed the view that the lack of rational scholastic theology was in

fact the great merit of Orthodox Christianity because, as Hegel had shown, religious truths should not be rationally defined and presented in the form of a quasi-scientific system.

However, Slavophile Hegelianism did not stand the test of time. The two Slavophile Hegelians soon realized that in fact Hegelian philosophy supported the standpoint of the Westernizers and that attempts to make it consonant with Slavophilism were futile and doomed to failure (see SLAVOPHILISM).

5 Russian Hegelianism in the second half of the nineteenth century

The 'philosophical epoch' in Russia ended abruptly in 1848. The revolutionary events of the European Springtime of the Peoples pushed the tsarist government in the direction of the most severe repression of intellectual life. Philosophy, seen as a source of dangerous disease, was banished from universities and the new censorship rules made it impossible even to mention in print the names of Hegel, Feuerbach, or Belinskii. This gloomy period of repression ended only after Russia's defeat in the Crimean War and the unexpected death of Nicholas I. The first symptom of the forthcoming political 'thaw' was the public defence of Chernyshevskii's master's dissertation *'Ésteticheskie otnosheniia iskusstva k deistvitelnosti'* (The Aesthetic Relations Between Art and Reality), in the University of St Petersburg in May 1855 (see CHERNYSHEVSKII, N.G.).

The content of Chernyshevskii's thesis was directly linked with the philosophical discussions of the 'remarkable decade'. Without mentioning the prohibited names, Chernyshevskii discussed in it Hegelian idealism, Feuerbachian anthropological materialism and Belinskii's views on art: he accused Hegel of establishing 'the tyranny of the universal', praised Feuerbach for rehabilitating nature and developed Belinskii's view in a consistently utilitarian direction, stressing especially the didactic function of literature. His utilitarian approach to art, further radicalized by Nikolai Dobroliubov and Dmitrii Pisarev, aroused indignation among the so-called Aesthetic Critics (V. Botkin, P. Annenkov and A. Druzhinin) and caused them to defend Hegelian aesthetics, philosophical idealism in general, and the legacy of the Russian intellectuals of the 1840s. Owing to this Hegelianism came to be associated with the liberal aestheticism, characteristic of the older generation and opposed by the young radicals, who chose to be seen as intransigent enemies of all idealism and aesthetics. This conflict between the two generation of Russian intellectuals is shown in Turgenev's novel *Fathers and Sons*.

In contrast to the younger radicals, Chernyshevskii himself did not see Hegel's philosophy as entirely obsolete and worthless. He made a distinction between Hegel's system and Hegel's dialectical method, rejecting the first but trying to save the second through giving it a naturalistic interpretation. For this reason Soviet philosophers treated him as a precursor of dialectical materialism (see RUSSIAN MATERIALISM: 'THE 1860S' §3).

Philosophical naturalism and positivistic scientism, which dominated Russian intellectual life after the 1860s, were, of course, deeply inimical to Hegelian idealism. Nevertheless, the Hegelian tradition survived in Russia, although in a marginalized and defensive form. Thus, for instance, Pavel Bakunin, brother of Mikhail Bakunin, elaborated a religious, Romantic interpretation of Hegelianism and presented it in his two books: *Zapozdalyi golos sorokovykh godov* (A Belated Voice of the Forties) (1881) and *Osnovy very i znzniia* (Foundations of Faith and Knowledge) (1886). Another religious reinterpretation of Hegelianism was offered by Nikolai Debolskii, professor at the St Petersburg Theological Academy, whose *Filosofiia fenomenal'nogo formalizma* (Philosophy of Phenomenalistic Formalism) (2 vols, 1892–5) tried to reconcile Hegelian rationalism with traditional Christian theism.

The greatest representative of the Hegelian tradition in the second half of the century was Chicherin, who also tried to reconcile philosophy and religion by identifying universal Reason with a personal God. In his political philosophy he combined Hegelian emphasis on the need of a strong state with conservative liberalism, making use of the Hegelian concept of civil society as a sphere of civil liberties (as distinct from political freedom) and free play of particularistic economic interests. Evgenii Trubetskoi, author of the classical monograph on Vladimir Solov'ëv saw Chicherin as the living bridge between the 'philosophical epoch' of 1838–48 and the Religious-Philosophical Renaissance of the twentieth century.

The legacy of the Russian Hegelians of the 1840s, especially the legacy of Belinskii, was claimed also by a thinker representing the opposite pole of the ideological spectrum: Georgii PLEKHANOV, 'father of Russian Marxism'. He was greatly impressed by Hegelian dialectical historicism, particularly the concept of rational historical necessity, seeing in it an effective antidote to populist 'subjective sociology' and all sorts of social utopianism. Due to his efforts interest in Hegelian dialectics, in a materialistic interpretation, became a characteristic feature of Russian and Soviet Marxism.

See also: HEGELIANISM; IL'IN, I.A.

References and further reading

* Bakunin, M.A. (1838) 'Gimnazicheskie rechi Gegelia. Predislovie perevodchika' (Foreword to Hegel's School Addresses), in Iu.M. Steklov (ed.), *Sobranie sochinenii i pisem 1828–76*, Moscow: AN SSSR, 1934–5, vol. 2, 166–78. (Referred to in §1.)

* Belinskii, V.G. (1841) 'The Idea of Art', in J.M. Edie *et al.* (eds), *Russian Philosophy*, Chicago: Quadrangle Books, 1969, vol. 1, 285–95. (Referred to in §2.)

Berlin, I. (1979) 'A Remarkable Decade', in H. Hardy and A. Kelly (eds), *Russian Thinkers*, New York: Viking Press. (An excellent general account of the 'remarkable decade' in Russian intellectual history.)

Billig, J. (1930) *Der Zusammenbruch des deutschen Idealismus bei den russischen Romantikern. Belinskii, Bakunin* (The Collapse of German Idealism among the Russian Romantics. Belinskii, Bakunin), Berlin. (A valuable study of Belinskii and young Bakunin, in the context of the crisis of absolute idealism in Germany.)

* Chernyshevskii, N.G. (1855) 'Ėsteticheskie otnosheniia iskusstva k deistvitelnosti' (The Aesthetic Relations Between Art and Reality), in J.M. Edie *et al* (eds), *Russian Philosophy*, Chicago: Quadrangle Books, 1969, vol. 2, 16–28. (An abridged translation of Chernyshevskii's master's thesis)

Chizhevskii, D.I. (1939) *Gegel' v Rossii* (Hegel in Russia), Paris. (The first comprehensive history of Hegelianism in Russia.)

* Cieszkowski, A. von (1838) *Die Prolegomena zur Historiosophie* (Prolegomena to the Wisdom of History), Berlin: Viet. (A dominant influence on Herzen's early Hegelianism.)

* Herzen, A.I. (1843) 'Buddizm v nauke'; trans. 'Buddhism in Science', in J.M. Edie *et al.* (eds) *Russian Philosophy*, Chicago, IL: Quadrangle Books, 1969, vol. 2, 16–28.

* —— (1850) *S togo berega*, Paris; trans. M. Budberg, *From the Other Shore*, London: Weidenfeld & Nicolson, 1956. (Herzen's break with the Hegelian belief in the rationality of the historical process.)

* —— (1853) *Byloe i dumy*, London; trans. C. Garnett, *My Past and Thoughts. The Memoirs of Alexander Herzen*, revised by H. Higgens, introduced by I. Berlin, London: Chatto & Windus, 1968, 4 vols. (See ch. 24, vol. 2 for the reception of Hegel in Russia.)

Jakowenko, B. (1938) *Geschichte des Hegelianismus in Rußland* (History of Hegelianism in Russia), vol. 1, Prague. (Covers the period 1835–60.)

Koyré, A. (1950) *Études sur l'histoire de la pensée philosophique en Russie* (Studies in the History of Philosophical Thought in Russia), Paris, 103–70. (A good presentation of Russian Hegelianism of the 'remarkable decade'.)

Planty-Bonjour, G. (1974) *Hegel et la pensée philosophique en Russie 1830–1917*. (Hegel and Philosophical Thought in Russia 1820–1917), La Haye: M. Nijhoff. (The most recent comprehensive history of the reception of Hegelian ideas in Russia.)

Volodin, A.I. (1973) *Gegel' i russkaia sotsialisticheskaia mysl' xix veka* (Hegel and Russian Socialist Thought of the Nineteenth Century), Moscow: Mysl'. (Includes bibliography.)

Walicki, A. (1975) *The Slavophile Controversy. History of a Conservative Utopia in Nineteenth-Century Russian Thought*, Oxford: Clarendon Press. (Contains a detailed analysis of the ideas of the 'Slavophile Hegelians' (287–335) and also two chapters dealing with the role of Hegelianism in the controversy between Slavophiles and Westernizers (335–455).)

—— (1991) 'Alexander Herzen, August Cieszkowski, and the Philosophy of Action', in *Russia, Poland, and Universal Regeneration. Studies on Russian and Polish Thought of the Romantic Epoch*, Notre Dame, IN: University of Notre Dame Press, 73–106. (An analysis of Cieszkowski's influence on Herzen, as well as a comparative study of both thinkers in a broader context.)

ANDRZEJ WALICKI

HEIDEGGER, MARTIN (1889–1976)

Martin Heidegger taught philosophy at Freiburg University (1915–23), Marburg University (1923–8), and again at Freiburg University (1928–45). Early in his career he came under the influence of Edmund Husserl, but he soon broke away to fashion his own philosophy. His most famous work, Sein und Zeit *(Being and Time) was published in 1927. Heidegger's energetic support for Hitler in 1933–4 earned him a suspension from teaching from 1945 to 1950. In retirement he published numerous works, including the first volumes of his* Collected Edition. *His thought has had strong influence on trends in philosophy ranging from existentialism through hermeneutics to deconstruction, as well as on the fields of literary theory and theology.*

Heidegger often makes his case in charged and dramatic language that is difficult to convey in summary form. He argues that mortality is our defining moment, that we are thrown into limited worlds of sense shaped by our being-towards-death, and that finite

meaning is all the reality we get. He claims that most of us have forgotten the radical finitude of ourselves and the world we live in. The result is the planetary desert called nihilism, with its promise that an ideally omniscient and virtually omnipotent humanity can remake the world in its own image and likeness. None the less, he still holds out the hope of recovering our true human nature, but only at the price of accepting a nothingness darker than the nihilism that now ravishes the globe. To the barely whispered admission, 'I hardly know anymore who and where I am', Heidegger answers: 'None of us knows that, as soon as we stop fooling ourselves' ([1959a] 1966: 62).

Yet he claims to be no pessimist. He merely wants to find out what being as such means, and Being and Time *was an attempt at this. He called it a fundamental ontology: a systematic investigation of human being (Dasein) for the purpose of establishing the meaning of being in general. Only half of the book – the part dealing with the finitude and temporality of human being – was published in 1927. Heidegger elaborated the rest of the project in a less systematic form during the decades that followed.*

Heidegger distinguishes between an entity (anything that is) and the being of an entity. He calls this distinction the 'ontological difference'. The being of an entity is the meaningful presence of that entity within the range of human experience. Being has to do with the 'is': what an entity is, how it is, and the fact that it is at all. The human entity is distinguished by its awareness of the being of entities, including the being of itself. Heidegger names the human entity 'Dasein' and argues that Dasein's own being is intrinsically temporal, not in the usual chronological sense but in a unique existential sense: Dasein ek-sists (stands-out) towards its future. This ek-sistential temporality refers to the fact that Dasein is always and necessarily becoming itself and ultimately becoming its own death. When used of Dasein, the word 'temporality' indicates not chronological succession but Dasein's finite and mortal becoming.

If Dasein's being is thoroughly temporal, then all of human awareness is conditioned by this temporality, including one's understanding of being. For Dasein, being is always known temporally and indeed is temporal. The meaning of being is time. The two main theses of Being and Time *– that Dasein is temporal and that the meaning of being is time – may be interpreted thus: being is disclosed only finitely within Dasein's radically finite awareness.*

Heidegger arrives at these conclusions through a phenomenological analysis of Dasein as being-in-the-world, that is, as disclosive of being within contexts of significance. He argues that Dasein opens up the arena of significance by anticipating its own death. But this event of disclosure, he says, remains concealed even as it opens the horizon of meaning and lets entities be understood in their being. Disclosure is always finite: we understand entities in their being not fully and immediately but only partially and discursively; we know things not in their eternal essence but only in the meaning they have in a given situation. Finite disclosure – how it comes about, the structure it has, and what it makes possible – is the central topic of Heidegger's thought. 'Time is the meaning of being' was only a provisional way of expressing it.

Dasein tends to overlook the concealed dimension of disclosure and to focus instead on what gets revealed: entities in their being. This overlooking is what Heidegger calls the forgetfulness of the disclosure of being. By that he means the forgetting of the ineluctable hiddenness of the process whereby the being of entities is disclosed. He argues that this forgetfulness characterizes not only everyday 'fallen' human existence but also the entire history of being, that is, metaphysics from Plato to Nietzsche. He calls for Dasein resolutely to reappropriate its own radical finitude and the finitude of disclosure, and thus to become authentically itself.

1 **Life and works**
2 **Temporality and authenticity**
3 **Being-in-the-world and hermeneutics**
4 **Dasein and disclosure**
5 **Hiddenness, *Ereignis* and the Turn**
6 **Forgetfulness, history and metaphysics**
7 **The work of art**

1 Life and works

Martin Heidegger was born on 26 September 1889 in Messkirch, Southwest Germany, to Roman Catholic parents of very modest means. From 1899 to 1911 he intended to become a priest, but after two years of theological studies at Freiburg University a recurring heart condition ended those hopes. In 1911 he switched to mathematics and the natural sciences, but finally took his doctorate in philosophy (1913) with a dissertation entitled *Die Lehre vom Urteil im Psychologismus* (The Doctrine of Judgment in Psychologism) (1914). Hoping to get appointed to Freiburg's chair in Catholic philosophy, he wrote a qualifying dissertation in 1915 on a theme in medieval philosophy, *Die Kategorien- und Bedeutungslehre des Duns Scotus* (Duns Scotus' Doctrine of Categories and Meaning) (1916). However, the job went to someone else, and in the autumn of 1915 Heidegger began his teaching career at Freiburg as a lecturer.

At this time Heidegger was known as a Thomist, but his 1915 dissertation was strongly influenced by the founder of phenomenology, Edmund HUSSERL. When Husserl joined the Freiburg faculty in the spring of 1916, Heidegger came to know him personally, if not well. Their relation would blossom only after the First World War. Heidegger was drafted in 1918 and served as a weatherman on the Ardennes front in the last three months of the war. When he returned to Freiburg his philosophical career took a decisive turn. In a matter of weeks he announced his break with Catholic philosophy (9 January 1919), got himself appointed Husserl's assistant (21 January), and began lecturing on a radical new approach to philosophy (4 February).

Many influences came to bear on Heidegger's early development, including St Paul, Augustine, Meister Eckhart, Kierkegaard, Dilthey and Nietzsche. But the major influences were Husserl and Aristotle. Heidegger was Husserl's protégé in the 1920s, but he never was a faithful disciple. He preferred Husserl's early work, *Logische Untersuchungen* (Logical Investigations) (1900–1), to the exclusion of the master's later developments. Moreover, the things that Heidegger liked about *Logical Investigations* were generally consonant with the traditional scholastic philosophy he had been taught.

First, Husserl's early phenomenology considered the human 'psyche' not as a substantial thing but as an act of revealing (intentionality), one that revealed not only *what* is encountered (the entity) but also the *way in which* it is encountered (the entity's being). Second, the early Husserl held that the central issue of philosophy was not modern subjectivity but rather 'the things themselves', whatever they might happen to be, in their very appearance; and he provided a descriptive method for letting those things show themselves as they are. Third, phenomenology argued that the being of entities is known not by some after-the-fact reflection or transcendental construction but directly and immediately by way of a categorial intuition. In short, for Heidegger, phenomenology was a descriptive method for understanding the being of entities as it is disclosed in intentional acts (see PHENOMENOLOGICAL MOVEMENT).

As Heidegger took it, all this contrasted with Husserl's later commitment to pure consciousness as the presuppositionless 'thing itself' that was to be revealed by various methodological 'reductions'. Heidegger had no use either for the Neo-Kantian turn to transcendental consciousness that found expression in Husserl's *Ideen* (Ideas) (1913) or for his further turn to a form of Cartesianism. Against Husserl's later theory of an unworldly transcendental ego presuppositionlessly conferring meaning on its objects, Heidegger proposed the historical and temporal situatedness of the existential self, 'thrown' into the world, 'fallen' in among entities in their everyday meanings, and 'projecting' ahead towards death.

In the 1920s Heidegger began interpreting the treatises of ARISTOTLE as an implicit phenomenology of everyday life without the obscuring intervention of subjectivity. He took Aristotle's main topic to be 'disclosure' (*alētheia*) on three levels: entities as intrinsically self-disclosive; human *psyche* as co-disclosive of those entities; and especially the human disclosure of entities in discursive, synthetic activity (*logos*), whether that be performed in wordless actions or in articulated sentences. Going beyond Aristotle, Heidegger interpreted this discursive disclosure as grounded in a kind of movement that he named 'temporality', and he argued that this temporality was the very essence of human being.

Using this new understanding of human being, Heidegger reinterpreted how anything at all appears to human beings. He argued that humans, as intrinsically temporal, have only a temporal understanding of whatever entities they know. But humans understand an entity by knowing it in its being, that is, in terms of how it happens to be present. Therefore, as far as human being goes, all forms of being are known temporally and indeed *are* temporal. The meaning of being is time.

Heidegger developed this thesis gradually, achieving a provisional formulation in *Sein und Zeit* (Being and Time) (1927). In public he dedicated the book to Husserl 'in respect and friendship', but in private he was calling Husserl's philosophy a 'sham' (*Scheinphilosophie*). Meanwhile, in 1923 an unsuspecting Husserl helped Heidegger move from a lecturer's job at Freiburg to a professorship at Marburg University; and when Husserl retired in 1928, he arranged for Heidegger to succeed him in the chair of philosophy at Freiburg. Once Heidegger had settled into the new job, the relationship between mentor and protégé quickly fell apart. If *Being and Time* were not enough, the three works Heidegger published in 1929 – 'Vom Wesen des Grundes' ('On the Essence of Ground'), *Kant und das Problem der Metaphysik* (Kant and the Problem of Metaphysics), and *Was ist Metaphysik?* (What is Metaphysics?) – confirmed how far apart the two philosophers had grown.

Heidegger's career entered a new phase when the Nazis came to power in Germany. On 30 January 1933 Adolf Hitler was appointed Chancellor, and within a month the German constitution and all-important civil rights were suspended. On 23 March Hitler became dictator of Germany, with absolute power to enact laws, and two weeks later, harsh anti-Semitic measures were promulgated. A conservative nationalist and staunch anti-Communist, Heidegger supported Hitler's policies with great enthusiasm for at least one year, and with quieter conviction for some ten years thereafter. He was elected rector (president) of Freiburg University on 21 April 1933 and joined the Nazi Party on May 1, with the motive, he later claimed, of preventing the politicization of the university. In his inaugural address as rector, *Die Selbstbehauptung der deutschen Universität* (The Self-Assertion of the German University) (27 May 1933), he called for a reorganization of the university along the lines of some aspects of the Nazi revolution. As rector he proved a willing spokesman for, and tool of, Nazi policy both foreign and domestic.

Heidegger resigned the rectorate on 23 April 1934 but continued to support Hitler. His remarks in the classroom indicate that he backed the German war aims, as he knew them, until at least as late as the defeat at Stalingrad in January 1943. The relation, or lack of it, between Heidegger's philosophy and his political sympathies has long been the subject of heated debate.

Heidegger published relatively little during the Nazi period. Instead, he spent those years rethinking his philosophy and setting out the parameters it would have, both in form and focus, for the rest of his life. The revision of his thought is most apparent in three texts he published much later: (1) the working notes from 1936–8 that he gathered into *Beiträge zur Philosophie. Vom Ereignis* (Contributions to Philosophy: On Ereignis), published posthumously in 1989; (2) the two volumes of his *Nietzsche*, published in 1961, which contains lecture courses and notes dating from 1936 to 1946; and (3) 'Brief über den Humanismus' ('Letter on Humanism'), written in the autumn of 1946 and published in 1947.

After the war Heidegger was suspended from teaching because of his Nazi activities in the 1930s. In 1950, however, he was allowed to resume teaching, and thereafter he occasionally lectured at Freiburg University and elsewhere. Between 1950 and his death he published numerous works, including the first volumes of his massive *Gesamtausgabe* (Collected Edition). He died at his home in Zähringen, Freiburg, on 26 May 1976 and was buried in his home town of Messkirch. His literary remains are held at the German Literary Archives, at Marbach on the Neckar.

Heidegger, a Catholic, married Elfride Petri (1893–1992), a Lutheran, on 21 March 1917. They had two sons, both of whom served in the *Wehrmacht* during the Second World War and were taken prisoner on the Eastern Front. In February of 1925 Heidegger began a year-long affair with his then student, Hannah Arendt. In February of 1950 they resumed a strong but often stormy friendship that lasted until Arendt's death.

2 Temporality and authenticity

Heidegger was convinced that Western philosophy had misunderstood the nature of being in general and the nature of human being in particular. His life's work was dedicated to getting it right on both scores.

In his view, the two issues are inextricably linked. To be human is to disclose and understand the being of whatever there is. Correspondingly, the being of an entity is the meaningful presence of that entity within the field of human experience. A proper or improper understanding of human being entails a proper or improper understanding of the being of everything else. In this context 'human being' means what Heidegger designates by his technical term 'Dasein': not consciousness or subjectivity or rationality, but that distinctive kind of entity (which we ourselves always are) whose being consists in disclosing the being both of itself and of other entities. The being of this entity is called 'existence' (see §4).

Heidegger argues that the structure of human being is comprised of three co-equal moments: becoming, alreadiness and presence. (These are usually, and unfortunately, translated as: 'coming towards itself', 'is as having been' and 'making-present'.) As a unity, these three moments constitute the essence of human being, which Heidegger calls 'temporality': opening an arena of meaningful presence by anticipating one's own death. Temporality means being present by becoming what one already is.

Becoming. To be human means that one is not a static entity just 'there' among other things. Rather, being human is always a process of becoming oneself, living into possibilities, into one's future. For Heidegger, such becoming is not optional but necessary. He expresses this claim in various co-equal formulas: (1) The essence of human being is 'existence' understood as 'ek-sistence', an ineluctable 'standing out' into concern about one's own being and into the need to become oneself; (2) the essence of human being is 'factical', always already thrust into concernful openness to itself and thus into the ineluctability of self-becoming; and (3) the essence of being human is 'to be possible' – not just able, but above all needing, to become oneself.

The ultimate possibility into which one lives is the possibility to end all possibilities: one's death. Human beings are essentially finite and necessarily mortal, and so one's becoming is an anticipation of death. Thus, to know oneself as becoming is to know oneself, at least implicitly, as mortal. Heidegger calls this mortal becoming 'being-unto-death'.

Alreadiness. Human being consists in becoming; and this becoming means becoming what one already is. Here the word 'already' means 'essentially', 'necessarily' or 'inevitably'. 'Alreadiness' (*Gewesenheit*) names one's inevitable human essence and specifically one's mortality. In becoming the finitude and mortality that one already is, one gets whatever presence one has.

Presence. Mortal becoming is the way human being (a) is meaningfully present to itself and (b) renders other entities meaningfully present to itself. To put the two together: things are present to human being in so far as human being is present to itself as mortal becoming. In both cases presence is bound up with absence.

How human being is present to itself. Since mortal becoming means becoming one's own death, human being appears as disappearing; it is present to itself as becoming absent. To capture this interplay of presence and absence, we call the essence of human being 'pres-abs-ence', that is, an incomplete presence that shades off into absence. Pres-abs-ence is a name for what classical philosophy called 'movement' in the broad sense: the momentary presence that something has on the basis of its stretch towards the absent.

Pres-abs-ence is an index of finitude. Any entity that appears as disappearing, or that has its current presence by anticipating a future state, has its being not as full self-presence but as finite pres-abs-ence. The movement towards death that defines human being is what Heidegger calls 'temporality'. The quotation marks indicate that 'temporality' does not refer to chronological succession but rather means having one's being as the movement of finite mortal becoming.

How other things are present to human being. Other entities are meaningfully present to human being in so far as human being is temporal, that is, always anticipating its own absence. Hence the meaningful presence of things is also temporal or pres-abs-ent – always partial, incomplete and entailing an absence of its own. Not only is human being temporal but the presence of things to human being is also temporal in its own right.

All of Heidegger's work argues for an intrinsic link between the temporality or pres-abs-ence that defines human being and the temporality or pres-abs-ence that characterizes the meaningful presence of things. But the meaningful presence of things is what Heidegger means by being. Therefore, Heidegger's central thesis is this: as far as human experience goes, all modes of being are temporal. The meaningful presence of things is always imperfect, incomplete, pres-abs-ential. The meaning of being is time.

Heidegger argues that this crucial state of affairs – finite human being as an awareness of the finitude of all modes of being – is overlooked and forgotten both in everyday experience and in philosophy itself. Therefore, his work discusses how one can recover this forgotten state of affairs on both of those levels.

As regards everyday life, Heidegger describes how one might recall this central but forgotten fact and make it one's own again. The act of reappropriating one's own essence – of achieving a personal and concrete grasp of oneself as finite – is called 'resolution' (in other translations, 'resoluteness' or 'resolve'). This personal conversion entails becoming clear about the intrinsic finitude of one's own being, and then choosing to accept and to be that finitude.
Awareness of one's finitude. Human being is always already the process of mortal becoming. However, one is usually so absorbed in the things one encounters ('fallenness') that one forgets the becoming that makes such encounters possible. It takes a peculiar kind of experience, more of a mood than a detached cognition, to wake one up to one's finitude. Heidegger argues that such an awakening comes about in special 'basic moods' (dread, boredom, wonder and so on) in which one experiences not things but that which is not-a-thing or 'no-thing'. Each of these basic moods reveals, in its own particular way, the absential dimension of one's pres-abs-ence.

Heidegger often uses charged metaphors to discuss this experience. For example, he describes dread as a 'call of conscience', where 'conscience' means not a moral faculty but the heretofore dormant, and now awakening, awareness of one's finite nature. What this call of conscience reveals is that one is 'guilty', not of some moral fault but of an ontological defect: the fact of being intrinsically incomplete and on the way to absence. The call of conscience is a call to understand and accept this 'guilt'.
Choosing one's finitude. One may choose either to heed or to ignore this call of conscience. To heed and accept it means to acknowledge oneself as a mortal process of pres-abs-ence and to live accordingly. In that case, one recuperates one's essence and thus attains 'authenticity' by becoming one's proper (or 'authentic') self. To ignore or refuse the call does not mean to cease being finite and mortal but rather to live according to an improper (inauthentic or 'fallen') self-understanding. Only the proper or authentic understanding of oneself as finite admits one to the concrete, experiential understanding that all forms of being, all ways that things can be meaningfully present, are themselves finite.
Summary. The essence of human being is temporality, that is, mortal becoming or pres-abs-ence. To overlook mortal becoming is to live an inauthentic temporality and to be a fallen self. But to acknowl-

edge and choose one's mortal becoming in the act of resolution is to live an authentic temporality and selfhood. It means achieving presence (both the presence of oneself and that of other entities) by truly becoming what one already is. This recuperation of one's own finite being can lead to the understanding that what conditions *all* modes of being is finitude: the very meaning of being is time.

3 Being-in-the-world and hermeneutics

In *Being and Time* Heidegger spells out not only the reasons why, but also the ways in which, things are meaningfully present to human being.
Being-in-the-world. In contrast to theories of human being as a self-contained theoretical ego, Heidegger understands human being as always 'outside' any supposed immanence, absorbed in social intercourse, practical tasks and its own interests. Evidence for this absorption, he argues, is that human being always finds itself caught up in a mood – that is, 'tuned in' to a given set of concerns. The field of such concerns and interests Heidegger calls the 'world'; and the engagement with those needs and purposes and the things that might fulfil them he calls 'being-in-the-world' (or equally 'care').

Heidegger's term 'world' does not mean planet earth, or the vast expanse of space and time, or the sum total of things in existence. Rather, 'world' means a dynamic set of relations, ultimately ordered to human possibilities, which lends meaning or significance to the things that one deals with – as in the phrase 'the world of the artist' or 'the world of the carpenter'. A human being lives in many such worlds, and they often overlap, but what constitutes their essence – what Heidegger calls the worldhood of all such worlds – is the significance that accrues to things by their relatedness to human interests and possibilities. Although being-in and world can be distinguished, they never occur separately. Any set of meaning-giving relations (world) comes about and remains effective only in so far as human being is engaged with the apposite possibilities (being-in). Being-in holds open and sustains the world.

In *Being and Time* Heidegger studies the world that he considers closest to human beings: the world of everyday activity. The defining moment of such a world is practical purposes ordered to human concerns – for example, the need to build a house for the sake of shelter. A group of things then gets its significance from the direct or indirect relation of those things to that goal. For example, these specific tools get their significance from their usefulness for clearing the ground, those trees get their significance from being suitable for lumber, these plants from their serviceability as thatch. A dynamic set of such relations (such as 'useful to', 'suitable as', 'needed for'), all of which refer things to a human task and ultimately to a human possibility, constitutes a 'world' and defines the current significance that certain things (for example, tools, trees and reeds) might have.

The significance of things changes according to the interplay of human interests, the relations that they generate, and the availability of material. For example, given the lack of a mallet, the significance of a stone might be its utility for pounding in a tent peg. The stone gets its current significance as a utensil from the world of the camper: the desire for shelter, the need of something to hammer with, and the availability of only a stone. (When the camper finds a mallet, the stone may well lose its former significance.)

Hermeneutical understanding. Heidegger argues that the world of practical experience is the original locus of the understanding of the being of entities. Understanding entails awareness of certain relations: for example, the awareness of this *as* that, or of this *as for* that. The 'as' articulates the significance of the thing. In using an implement, one has a practical understanding of the implement's relation to a task (X as useful for Y). This in turn evidences a practical understanding of the being of the implement: one knows the stone as *being* useful for pounding in a tent peg. In other words, prior to predicative knowledge, which is expressed in sentences of the type 'S is P', human beings already have a pre-theoretical or 'pre-ontological' understanding of the being of things (this as *being for* that).

Since the 'as' articulates how something is understood, and since the Greek verb *hermeneuein* means 'to make something understandable', Heidegger calls the 'as' that renders things intelligible in practical understanding the 'hermeneutical as'. This 'hermeneutical as' is made possible because human being is a 'thrown project', necessarily thrust into possibilities (thrownness) and thereby holding the world open (project).

Hermeneutical understanding – that is, pre-predicatively understanding the 'hermeneutical as' by being a thrown project – is the kind of cognition that most befits being-in-the-world. It is the primary way in which humans know the being of things. By contrast, the more detached and objective 'apophantic' knowledge that expresses itself in declarative sentences ('S is P') is evidence, for Heidegger, of a derivative and flattened-out understanding of being.

Summary. As long as one lives, one is engaged in mortal becoming. This becoming entails having purposes and possibilities. Living into purposes and possibilities is how one has things meaningfully present. The ability to have things meaningfully present by living into possibilities is called being-in-the-world. Being-in-the-world is structured as a thrown project: holding open the possibility of significance (project) by ineluctably living into possibilities (thrownness). This issues in a pre-predicative, hermeneutical understanding of the being of things. Thus mortal becoming *qua* being-in-the-world engenders and sustains all possible significance. In another formulation: temporality determines all the ways that things can have meaningful presence. Time is the meaning of all forms of being.

4 Dasein and disclosure

Heidegger calls human being 'Dasein', the entity whose being consists in disclosing and understanding being, whether the being of itself or that of other entities. In so far as Dasein's being is a disclosure of its *own* being, it is called 'existence' or 'ek-sistence': self-referential standing-out-unto-itself. Dasein's very being consists in being related, with understanding and concern, to itself.

But Dasein is not just related to itself. Existence occurs only as being-in-the-world; that is, the openness of human being to itself entails the openness of the world for other entities. One of Heidegger's neologisms for 'openness' is 'the there' (*das Da*), which he uses in two interrelated senses. First, human being is its own 'there': as a thrown project, existence sustains its own openness to itself. And second, in so doing, human being also makes possible the world's openness as the 'there' for other entities. Human being's self-disclosure makes possible the disclosure of other entities.

Heidegger calls human being in both these capacities 'being-the-there' – Dasein, or sometimes Da-sein when it refers to the second capacity. In ordinary German *Dasein* means existence in the usual sense: being there in space and time as contrasted with not being at all. However, in Heidegger's usage Dasein means being disclosive of something (whether that be oneself or another entity) in its being. In a word, Dasein is disclosive. And since human being is radically finite, disclosure is radically finite.

The Greek word for disclosure is *alētheia*, a term composed of the privative prefix *a-* (un- or dis-) and the root *lēthē* (hiddenness or closure). Heidegger finds the finitude of dis-closure inscribed in the word *a-lētheia*. To disclose something is to momentarily rescue it from (*a-*) some prior unavailability (*lēthē*), and to hold it for a while in presence.

Heidegger discusses three levels of disclosure, ranging from the original to the derivative, each of which involves Dasein: (1) disclosure-as-such, (2) the disclosedness of entities in their being, and (3) disclosure in propositional statements. Heidegger's chief interest is in the first. There, disclosure/*alētheia* is the original occurrence that issues in meaningful presence (being).

Heidegger argues that levels 1 and 2 are distinct but inseparable and, taken together, make possible level 3. The word 'truth' properly applies only at the third level, where it is a property of statements that correctly represent complex states of affairs. Therefore, to the question 'What is the essence of truth?' – that is, 'What makes the truth of propositions possible at level 3?' – Heidegger answers: Proximally, the disclosure of entities in their being (level 2); and ultimately, disclosure-as-such (level 1). His argument unfolds as follows.

Level 1. Disclosure-as-such is the very opening-up of the field of significance. It is the engendering and sustaining of world on the basis of Dasein's becoming-absent. In so far as it marks the birth of significance and the genesis of being, disclosure-as-such or world-disclosure is the reason why any specific entity can have meaningful presence at all.

There are three corollaries. First, the disclosure of world never happens except in Dasein's being; indeed, without Dasein, there is no openness at all. The engendering and sustaining of the dynamic relations that constitute the very possibility of significance occurs only as long as Dasein exists as mortal becoming. And conversely, wherever there is Dasein, there is world. Second, disclosure-as-such never happens apart from the disclosedness of *entities* as being this or that. In speaking of disclosure 'as such', Heidegger is naming the originating source and general structure of all possible significance that might accrue to any entity at all. The result of disclosure-as-such is the fact that referral-to-mortal-Dasein (that is, significance) is the basic state of whatever entities happen to show up. Third, disclosure-as-such is always prior to and makes possible concrete human action in any specific world. Such concrete actions run the risk of *not* being disclosive (that is, being mistaken about the meaning of something). By contrast, world-disclosure is *always* disclosive in so far as it is the opening-up of the very possibility of significance at all.

Alētheia/disclosure-as-such – how it comes about, the structure it has, and what it makes possible – is the central topic or 'thing itself' of Heidegger's thought. He sometimes calls it the 'clearing' of being. He also calls it 'being itself' or 'being-as-such' (that is, the very *engendering* of being). Frequently, and inadequately, he calls it the 'truth' of being.

Level 2. What disclosure-as-such makes possible is the pre-predicative availability of entities in their current mode of being. This pre-predicative availability constitutes level 2, the basic, everyday disclosedness of entities as meaningfully present. This disclosedness is always finite, and that entails two things.

First, what disclosure-as-such makes possible is not simply the being of an entity but rather the being of that entity as or as not something: for instance, this stone as not a missile but as a hammer. I know the stone only in terms of one or another of its possibilities: the entity becomes present not fully and immediately but only partially and discursively. Thus the entity's being is always finite, always a matter of synthesis-and-differentiation: being-as-and-as-not. Second, disclosure-as-such lets an entity be present not in its eternal essence but only in its current meaning in a given situation; moreover, it shows that this specific entity is not the only one that might have this meaning. For example, in the present situation I understand this stone not as a paperweight or a weapon but as a hammer. I also understand it as not the best instrument for the job: a mallet would do better.

Even though it is a matter of synthesis-and-differentiation, this pre-predicative hermeneutical understanding of being requires no thematic articulation, either mental or verbal, and no theoretical knowledge. It usually evidences itself in the mere doing of something. Nevertheless, in a more developed but still pre-predicative moment, such a hermeneutical awareness might evolve into a vague sense of the entity's being-this-or-that ('whatness'), being-in-this-way-or-that ('howness'), and being-available-at-all ('thatness'). Still later, these vague notions might lose the sense of *current* meaningfulness and develop, at level 3, into the explicit metaphysical concepts of the essence, modality and existence of the entity.

The second level of disclosure may be expressed in the following thesis: within any given world, to be an entity is to be always already disclosed as something or other. This corresponds to the traditional doctrine of metaphysics concerning a trans-generic (transcendental) characteristic of anything that is: regardless of its kind or species, every entity is intrinsically disclosed in its being (*omne ens est verum*).

Heidegger argues that while it is based on and is even aware of this second level of disclosure, metaphysics has no explicit understanding of disclosure-as-such or of its source in being-in-the-world. What is more, he claims that the disclosedness of entities-in-their-being (level 2) tends to overlook and obscure the very disclosure-as-such (level 1) that originally makes it possible. He further argues that there is an intrinsic hiddenness about disclosure-as-such, which makes overlooking it virtually inevitable (see §6).

Level 3. Being-in-the-world and the resultant pre-predicative disclosedness of entities as being-thus-and-so make it possible for us to enact the predicative disclosure of entities. At this third level of disclosure we are able to represent correctly to ourselves, in synthetic judgments and declarative sentences, the way things are in the world. A correct synthetic representation of a complex state of affairs (a correct judgment) is 'true', that is, disclosive of things just as they present themselves. Such a predicative, apophantic sentence ('S is P') is able to be true only because world-disclosure has already presented an entity as significant at all and thus allowed it to be taken as thus and so. This already disclosed entity is the binding norm against which the assertion must measure itself.

At level 3, however, it is also possible to *mis*represent things in thought and language, to fail to disclose them just as they present themselves in the world. At level 1 Dasein is always and only disclosive. But with predicative disclosure at level 3 (as analogously with hermeneutical disclosure at level 2) Dasein's representing of matters in propositional statements may be either disclosive or non-disclosive, either true or false.

One of Heidegger's reasons for elaborating the levels of disclosure is to demonstrate that science, metaphysics and reason in general, all of which operate at level 3, are grounded in a more original occurrence of disclosure of which they are structurally unaware. This is what he intends by his claim 'Science does not think'. He does not mean scientists are stupid or their work uninformed, nor is he disparaging reason and its accomplishments. He means that science, by its very nature, is not focused on being-in-the-world, even though being-in-the-world is ultimately responsible for the meaningful presence of the entities against which science measures its propositions.

5 Hiddenness, *Ereignis* and the Turn

Hiddenness. Heidegger claims that disclosure-as-such – the very opening up of significance in Dasein's being – is intrinsically hidden and needs to remain so if entities are to be properly disclosed in their being. This intrinsic concealment of disclosure-as-such is called the 'mystery'. Since Heidegger sometimes calls disclosure-as-such 'being itself', the phrase becomes 'the mystery of being'. The ensuing claim, that the mystery of being conceals itself while revealing entities, has led to much mystification, not least among Heideggerians. Being seems to become a higher but hidden Entity that performs strange acts

that only the initiated can comprehend. This misconstrual of Heidegger's intentions is not helpful.

How may we understand the intrinsic concealment of disclosure-as-such? One way is to understand the paradigm of 'movement' that informs Heidegger's discussion of revealing and concealing. Taken in the broad philosophical sense, movement is defined not as mere change of place and the like, but as the very being of entities that are undergoing the process of change. This kind of being consists in anticipating something absent, with the result that what is absent-but-anticipated determines the entity's present being. Anticipation *is* the being of such entities, and anticipation is determined from the absent-but-anticipated goal. For example, the acorn's being is its becoming an oak tree; and correspondingly the future oak tree, as the goal of the acorn's trajectory, determines the acorn's present being. Likewise, Margaret *is* a graduate student in so far as she is in movement towards her Ph.D. The still-absent degree *qua* anticipated determines her being-a-student.

The absent is, by nature, hidden. But when it is anticipated or intended, the intrinsically hidden, while still remaining absent, becomes quasi-present. It functions as the 'final cause' and *raison d'être* that determines the being of the anticipating entity. That is, even while remaining intrinsically concealed, the absent-as-anticipated 'gives being' (*Es gibt Sein*) to the anticipating entity by disclosing the entity as what it presently is. This pattern of absence-dispensing-presence holds both for the disclosure of Dasein and for the disclosure of the entities Dasein encounters.

It holds pre-eminently for Dasein. Dasein's being is movement, for Dasein exists by anticipating its own absence. Dasein's death remains intrinsically hidden, but when anticipated, the intrinsically hidden becomes quasi-present by determining Dasein's being as mortal becoming. The absent, when anticipated, dispenses Dasein's finite presence.

The same holds for other entities. The anticipated absence determines Dasein's finite being. But Dasein's being is world-disclosive: it holds open the region of meaningful presence in which other entities are disclosed as being-this-or-that. Hence, the intrinsically hidden, when anticipated, determines the presence not only of Dasein but also of the entities Dasein encounters.

Therefore, the very structure of disclosure – that is, the fact that the absent-but-anticipated determines or 'gives' finite presence – entails that its ultimate source remain intrinsically hidden even while disclosing the being of entities. This intrinsic hiddenness at the core of disclosure is what Heidegger calls the 'mystery'. Heidegger argued that the 'mystery' is the ultimate issue in philosophy, and he believed HERACLITUS had said as much in his fragment no. 123: 'Disclosure-as-such loves to hide' (Freeman 1971: 33).

Ereignis. The paradigm of movement also explains why Heidegger calls disclosure-as-such '*Ereignis*'. In ordinary German *Ereignis* means 'event', but Heidegger uses it as a word for movement. Playing on the adjective *eigen* ('one's own'), he creates the word *Ereignung*: movement as the process of being drawn into what is one's own. For example, we might imagine that the oak tree as final cause 'pulls' the acorn into what it properly is, by drawing the acorn towards what it is meant to be. This being-pulled is the acorn's movement, its very being. Likewise, Dasein is 'claimed' by death as its final cause and 'pulled forth' by it into mortal becoming. This being-drawn into one's own absence, in such a way that world is engendered and sustained, is what Heidegger calls 'appropriation'. It is what he means by *Ereignis*.

The word '*Ereignis*', along with the image of Dasein being appropriated by the absent, emerges in Heidegger's thought only in the 1930s. However, this later language echoes what Heidegger had earlier called Dasein's thrownness, namely, the fact that Dasein is thrust into possibilities, anticipates its self-absence, and so is 'already' involved in world-disclosure. Both the earlier language of thrown anticipation *of* absence, and the later language of appropriation *by* absence, have the same phenomenon in view: Dasein's alreadiness, its constitutive mortality that makes for world-disclosure.

The paradigm of movement also helps to clarify Heidegger's claim about the concealing-and-revealing, or withdrawing-and-arriving, of being itself (that is, of disclosure-as-such). In a quite typical formulation Heidegger writes: 'Being itself withdraws itself, but as this withdrawal, being is the 'pull' that claims the essence of human being as the place of being's own arrival' (1961: vol. 2, 368). This sentence, which describes the structure of *Ereignis*, may be interpreted as follows:

The 'withdrawal' of disclosure-as-such

(that is, the intrinsic hiddenness of world-disclosive absence)

maintains a relation to Dasein

(which we may call either 'appropriation' or 'thrown anticipation')

that claims Dasein

(by appropriating it into mortal becoming)

so that, *in* Dasein's being,

(in so far as Dasein's being is the openness that is world)

being itself might arrive

(in the form of the relations of significance whereby entities have being-as this-or-that).

The Turn. One can notice a certain shift within Heidegger's work beginning around 1930, both in his style and in the topics he addresses. As regards style, some have claimed that his language becomes more abstruse and poetic, and his thinking less philosophical than mystical. As regards substance, he seems to introduce new topics like 'appropriation' and the 'history of being'.

The problem is to discern whether these and other shifts count as what Heidegger calls the Turn (*die Kehre*). Some argue that beginning in the 1930s Heidegger radically changed his approach and perhaps even his central topic. The early Heidegger, so the argument goes, had understood being itself (that is, disclosure-as-such) from the standpoint of Dasein, whereas the later Heidegger understands Dasein from the standpoint of being itself. But to the contrary it is clear that even the early Heidegger understood Dasein only from the standpoint of being itself.

Heidegger clarifies matters by distinguishing between (1) the Turn and (2) the 'change in thinking' that the Turn demands, both of which are to be kept distinct from (3) the various shifts in form and focus that his philosophy underwent in the 1930s. The point is that, properly speaking, the Turn is not a shift in Heidegger's thinking nor a change in his central topic. The Turn is only a further specification of *Ereignis*. There are three issues here.

First, the 'Turn' is a name for how *Ereignis* operates. *Ereignis* is the appropriation of Dasein for the sake of world-disclosure. For Heidegger, this fact stands over against all theories of the self as an autonomous subject that presuppositionlessly (that is, without a prior world-disclosure) posits its objects in meaning. In opposition to that, *Ereignis* means that Dasein must already be appropriated into world-disclosive absence before anything can be significant at all.

Ereignis also means that Dasein's appropriation by, or thrownness into, world-disclosive absence is the primary and defining moment in Dasein's projection of that disclosure. This reciprocity (*Gegenschwung*) between appropriation/thrownness on the one hand and projection on the other – with the priority going to appropriation/thrownness – constitutes the very structure of *Ereignis* and is what Heidegger calls the Turn. The upshot of this reciprocity is that Dasein must be already pulled into world-disclosive absence (thrown or appropriated into it) if it is to project (that is, hold open) disclosure at all. In a word, the Turn *is Ereignis*.

Second, the 'change in thinking' refers to the

personal conversion that the Turn demands. To become aware of the Turn and to accept it as determining one's own being is what Heidegger had earlier called 'resolution' and what he now describes as 'a transformation in human being'. This transformation into an authentic self consists in letting one's own being be defined by the Turn.

Third, the shifts in Heidegger's work in the 1930s – and especially the development and deepening of his insights into thrownness and appropriation – are just that: shifts and developments within a single, continuing project. Important as they are, they are neither the Turn itself nor the change in personal self-understanding that the Turn requires.

6 Forgetfulness, history and metaphysics

Heidegger sees a strong connection between the forgetting of disclosure-as-such, the history of the dispensations of being, and metaphysics.

Forgetting disclosure-as-such. Because disclosure-as-such is intrinsically hidden (this is what is meant by the mystery), it is usually overlooked. When the mystery is overlooked, human being is 'fallen', that is, aware of entities as being-thus-and-so, but oblivious of what it is that 'gives' being to entities. Fallenness is forgetfulness of the mystery. Another term for fallenness is 'errancy', which conveys the image of Dasein 'wandering' among entities-in-their-being without knowing what makes their presence possible. Since disclosure-as-such is sometimes called 'being itself', fallenness is also called 'the forgetfulness of being'.

However, disclosure-as-such need not be forgotten. It is possible, in resolution, to assume one's mortality and become concretely aware of disclosure-as-such in its basic state of hiddenness. Such awareness does not undo the intrinsic hiddenness of disclosure-as-such or draw it into full presence. Rather, one accepts the concealment of being itself (this is called 'letting being be') by resolutely accepting one's appropriation by absence.

The history of the dispensations of being. Heidegger's discussions of the 'history of being' sometimes verge on the anthropomorphic, and he often uses etymologies that are difficult to carry over into English. Nevertheless, his purpose in all this is clear: to spell out the world-historical dimensions of fallenness.

As we have seen, disclosure-as-such 'gives' the being of entities while the 'giving' itself remains hidden; and this happens only in so far as Dasein is appropriated by absence. When one forgets the absence that appropriates Dasein, and thus forgets the hidden giving that brings forth the being of entities, fallenness and errancy ensue. Fallen Dasein

then focuses on the given (entities-in-their-being) and overlooks the hidden giving (disclosure-as-such). None the less, the hidden giving still goes on giving, but now in a doubly hidden way: it is both intrinsically hidden *and* forgotten. When the hiddenness is forgotten, a disclosure is called a 'dispensation' (*Geschick*) of being. The word connotes a portioning-out that holds something back. A certain form of the being of entities is dispensed while the disclosing itself remains both hidden and forgotten.

In German, 'dispensation' (*Geschick*) and 'history' (*Geschichte*) have their common root in the verb *schicken*, 'to send'. Playing on those etymologies, Heidegger elaborates a 'history' of being, based on the 'sendings' or 'dispensations' of being. (The usual translations of *Geschick* as 'fate' or 'destiny' are not helpful here.) In Heidegger's view each dispensation of being defines a distinct epoch in the history of thought from ancient Greece down to today. He calls the aggregate of such dispensations and epochs the 'history of being'. Because the whole of these dispensations and epochs is correlative to fallenness, Heidegger seeks to overcome the history of being and return to an awareness of the hidden giving.

Heidegger believes the parameters of each epoch in the history of being can be glimpsed in the name that a major philosopher of the period gave to the being of entities in that age. A non-exhaustive list of such epoch-defining notions of being includes: *idea* in Plato, *energeia* in Aristotle, act in Aquinas, representedness in Descartes, objectivity in Kant, Absolute Spirit in Hegel, and will to power in Nietzsche. What characterizes each such epoch is (1) an understanding of being as some form of the presence of entities and (2) an oblivion of the absence that bestows such presence. None the less, even when forgotten the absence is never abolished, and thus traces of it remain in the various dispensations. Therefore, in studying the texts of classical philosophy Heidegger searches for and retrieves the unexpressed absence (the 'unsaid') that hides behind what the text actually expresses (the 'said').

Metaphysics. The various ways that presence or being has been dispensed, while absence has been overlooked, are called in their entirety 'metaphysics'. Heidegger argues that metaphysics as a philosophical position began with Plato and entered its final phase with Nietzsche.

The Greek philosophers who preceded Socrates and Plato were, in Heidegger's view, *pre*-metaphysical in so far as they had at least a penumbral awareness of disclosure-as-such and at least named it (Heraclitus, for example, called it *logos*, *alētheia*, and *physis*). However, none of these thinkers thematically addressed disclosure-as-such or understood the correlative notions of ek-sistence and Dasein. Heidegger calls the penumbral awareness of disclosure-as-such among archaic Greek thinkers the 'first beginning'. And he hoped that a 'new beginning' would follow the end of metaphysics. If the first beginning was not yet metaphysical, the new beginning will be no longer metaphysical. Heidegger considered his own work a preparation for that new beginning.

But metaphysics persists. The history of the dispensations of being has reached its fullness in the present epoch of technology. As Heidegger uses the word, 'technology' refers not to hardware or software or the methods and materials of applied science. Rather, it names a dispensation in the history of metaphysics, in fact the final one. It names the way in which entities-in-their-being are disclosed today.

Heidegger maintains that in the epoch of technology entities are taken as a stockpile of matter that is in principle completely knowable by human reason and wholly available for human use. With this notion metaphysics arrives at its most extreme oblivion of disclosure-as-such. In our time, Heidegger says, the presence of entities has become everything, while the absence that brings about that presence has become nothing. He calls this nil-status of absence 'nihilism'. *Overcoming metaphysics.* None the less, Heidegger sees a glimmer of light in the dark epoch of nihilism. In this final dispensation of metaphysics, the hidden giving does not cease to function, even when it is completely forgotten. It continues dispensing presence – paradoxically even the nihilistic presence which obscures the absence that gives it. Because the hidden giving goes on giving even when it is forgotten, we can still experience it today (in a mood not unlike dread) and retrieve it. This recovery of world-disclosive absence requires resolution or, as Heidegger now calls it, 'the entrance into *Ereignis*'. To enter *Ereignis* today is to experience a different kind of *nihil* ('nothing') from the one that defines nihilism. The absence that bestows presence is itself a kind of 'nothing' (not-a-thing). This absence is no entity, nor can it be reduced to the being of any specific entity or be present the way an entity is. That is why it is so easily overlooked. Its 'nothingness' is its intrinsic hiddenness.

To enter *Ereignis* is to become aware of and to accept the disclosive *nihil* that rescues one from nihilism. Thereupon, says Heidegger, metaphysics as the history of the dispensations of being ceases and a new beginning takes place – at least for those individuals who achieve authenticity by way of resolution. But metaphysics will continue for those who remain inauthentic, because dispensation is correlative to fallenness.

Summary. The forgetting of disclosure-as-such is metaphysics. Metaphysics knows entities-in-their-being but ignores the very giving of that being. The aggregate of the epochs of metaphysics is the history of the dispensations of being. The history of these dispensations culminates in the epoch of technology and nihilism. But world-disclosive absence can still be retrieved; and when it is retrieved, it ushers in (at least for authentic individuals) a new beginning of ek-sistence and Dasein.

7 The work of art

One of Heidegger's most challenging essays is 'The Origin of the Work of Art', originally drafted in 1935 and published in an expanded version only in 1950. There he distinguishes between the work of art as a specific entity (for example, a poem or a painting) and art itself, the latter being understood not as a collective name for, but rather as the essence and origin of, all works of art. Heidegger asks what art itself is, and he answers that art is a unique kind of disclosure.

Dasein is disclosive of the being of an entity in many ways, some of them ordinary and some of them extraordinary. An outcome common to both kinds of disclosure is that the disclosed entity is seen as what it is: it appears in its form. Examples of ordinary, everyday ways of disclosing the being of entities include showing oneself to be adept at the flute, or moulding clay into a vase, or concluding that the accused is innocent. Each of these ordinary cases of praxis, production and theory does indeed disclose some entity as being this or that, but the focus is on showing what the *entity* is rather than on showing how the entity's *being* is disclosed. On the other hand, extraordinary acts of disclosure bring to attention not only the disclosed entity but above all the event of disclosure of that entity's being. Extraordinary acts of disclosure let us see the very fact that, and the way in which, an entity has become meaningfully present in its being. In these cases not only does an entity appear in its form (as happens in any instance of disclosure) but more importantly the very disclosure of the being of the entity 'is established' (*sich einrichten*) in the entity and is seen there as such.

Heidegger lists five examples of extraordinary disclosure: the constitution of a nation-state; the nearness of god; the giving of one's life for another; the thinker's questioning as revealing that being can be questioned; and the 'installation' (*Sich-ins-Werk-Setzen*) of disclosure in a work of art. Each of these cases discloses, in its own particular way, not just an entity but the very disclosure of that entity's being. Heidegger seeks to understand the particular way in which art itself discloses disclosure by 'installing' disclosure in the work of art.

In his essay Heidegger refers mainly to two works of art: van Gogh's canvas 'Old Shoes', painted in Paris in 1886–7 and now hung in the Stedelijk Museum, Amsterdam; and the 5th century BC Doric Temple of Hera II – the so-called Temple of Poseidon – at Paestum (Lucania), Italy. Let us consider the temple at Paestum as we attempt to answer two questions: what gets disclosed in a work of art and how does it get disclosed?

(1) *What gets disclosed in a work of art?* Heidegger gives three answers. First, a work of art lets us see disclosure in the form of 'world' and 'earth'. A work of art discloses not just an entity or an ensemble of entities but the whole realm of significance whereby an ensemble of entities gets its finite meaning. The temple at Paestum not only houses (and thus discloses) the goddess Hera, but more importantly lets us see the social and historical world – rooted as it was in the natural setting of Lucania – that Hera's presence guaranteed for the Greek colonists. A work of art, Heidegger argues, reveals the very event of disclosure, which event he calls the happening of world and earth, where 'earth' refers not only to nature and natural entities but more broadly to all entities within a specific world.

Second, a work of art lets us see the radical tension that discloses a specific world of significance. Heidegger understands being-in-the-world as a 'struggle' (*Streit* or *polemos*) between a given world and its earth, between the self-expanding urge of a set of human possibilities and the rootedness of such possibilities in a specific natural environment. Here, 'struggle' is another name for the event of disclosure whereby a particular world is opened up and maintained. What a specific work of art discloses is one particular struggle that discloses one particular world – for instance, the world of the Greek colonists at Paestum.

Third, a work of art shows us disclosure-as-such. The movement of opening up a particular world is only one instance of the general movement of *alētheia*: the 'wresting' of being-at-all from the absolute absence into which Dasein is appropriated. Thus a work of art not only shows us a particular world-disclosive struggle (the way the temple of Hera shows us the earth–world tension at Paestum) but also lets us see the 'original struggle' (*Urstreit*) of disclosure-as-such, whereby significance is wrested from the double closure of intrinsic hiddenness and fallenness.

In short, what a work of art reveals is disclosure in three forms: as world and earth; as the struggle that opens up a specific world and lets its entities be meaningful; and as the original struggle that structures all such particular disclosures.

(2) *How does a work of art disclose disclosure?* The specific way that art discloses disclosure is by 'installing' it in a given work of art. Here, 'to install' means to bring to stability; and 'to install disclosure' means to incorporate it into the physical form of a work of art. There are three corollaries:

What the installing is not. Heidegger does not claim that the work of art 'sets up' the world and 'sets forth' the earth for the first time. That is, installing the disclosure of earth and world in the work of art is not the only or even the first way that earth and world get disclosed. The sanctuary of Hera was not the first to open up the world of Paestum and disclose the fields and flocks for what they are. Tradesmen and farmers had been doing that – that is, the disclosive struggle of world and earth had been bestowing form and meaning – for at least a century before the temple was built.

What the installing is and does. Art discloses, in a new and distinctive way, a disclosure of earth and world that is already operative. Heidegger argues that the temple as disclosive (a) captures and sustains the openness of that world and its rootedness in nature, and (b) shows how, within that world, nature comes forth into the forms of entities while remaining rooted in itself. Heidegger calls these two functions, which happen only in art, the 'setting up' of world and the 'setting forth' of earth.

The work of art lets us see – directly, experientially and in all its glory – the already operative interplay of human history's rootedness in nature and nature's emergence into human history. In Heidegger's words, art 'stabilizes' (*zum Stehen bringen*) the disclosive struggle of world and earth by 'installing' it in a particular work of art, such that in and through that medium, disclosure 'shines forth' brilliantly in beauty.

The two ways art discloses disclosure, and their unity. Art itself is a specific and distinctive way in which Dasein is disclosive: it discloses disclosure by installing disclosure in the physical form of a work of art. This installation has two moments: the creation and the preservation of the work of art.

Creation is an artist's Dasein-activity of incorporating disclosure – the world-openness that is already operative – into a material medium (stone, colour, language and so on). This incorporation of disclosure is carried out in such a way that the material medium is not subordinated to anything other than disclosure (for example, it is not subordinated to 'usefulness'). Rather, the medium becomes, for whoever experiences it, the immediate disclosure of disclosure.

Preservation is the corresponding Dasein-activity of maintaining the power of disclosure in the work of art by resolutely letting disclosure continue to be seen there. Creation and preservation are the two ways that Dasein 'projects' (holds open and sustains) the disclosure that is installed in the work of art. The unity of creation and preservation is art itself, which Heidegger calls *Dichtung* – not 'poetry' but *poiesis*, the creating-and-preserving installation of disclosure in a disclosive medium.

Disclosure is the central topic of all Heidegger's philosophy, and this fact shines brilliantly through his reflection on the origin of the work of art. Art, both as creation and as preservation, is a specific and distinctive Dasein-activity: the disclosure of disclosure in a medium that is disclosive. In the work of art, as in Heidegger's own work, it's *alētheia* all the way down.

See also: HERMENEUTICS §4; KUKI SHŪZŌ; PHENOMENOLOGICAL MOVEMENT §§4–5; WATSUJI TETSURŌ

List of works

Heidegger, M. (1975–) *Gesamtausgabe* (Collected Edition), Frankfurt: Vittorio Klostermann. (The standard edition of Heidegger's works. Over 80 volumes are projected, of which more than forty appeared by 1997. English translations of individual volumes are given at the end of the list of works below.)

—— (1914) *Die Lehre vom Urteil im Psychologismus. Ein kritisch-positiver Beitrag zur Logik* (The Doctrine of Judgment in Psychologism: A Critical-positive Contribution to Logic), Leipzig: Barth. (Heidegger's doctoral dissertation.)

—— (1916) *Die Kategorien- und Bedeutungslehre des Duns Scotus* (Duns Scotus' Doctrine of Categories and Meaning), Tübingen: J.C.B. Mohr (Paul Siebeck). (Heidegger's Habilitationsschrift, the qualifying dissertation required for teaching at a university.)

—— (1927) 'Sein und Zeit', *Jahrbuch für Philosophie und phänomenologische Forschung* 8: 1–438; *Sein und Zeit*, Halle an der Salle: Max Niemeyer; trans. J. Macquarrie and E. Robinson, *Being and Time*, New York: Harper & Row, 1962; trans. J. Stambaugh, *Being and Time*, Albany, NY: State University of New York Press, 1996. (Heidegger's most famous work, which treats the structure of Dasein as being-in-the-world and as temporal. The unpublished second half of the work was to have shown that the meaning of being is time.)

—— (1929a) 'Vom Wesen des Grundes', *Jahrbuch für Philosophie und phänomenologische Forschung*, supplement 71–100; trans. T. Malick, *The Essence of Reasons*, Evanston, IL: Northwestern University Press, 1969; trans. W. McNeill, 'On the Essence of Ground', in *Pathmarks*, New York: Cambridge University Press, 1997. (An essay on truth, transcendence and ground, written in honour of Edmund Husserl's 80th birthday, April 1929.)

—— (1929b) *Kant und das Problem der Metaphysik*, Bonn: Friedrich Cohen; trans. R. Taft, *Kant and the Problem of Metaphysics*, Bloomington, IN: Indiana University Press, 1990. (Originally conceived as part of the second half of *Sein und Zeit*, this work argues that the hidden meaning of the transcendental imagination in the 'A' version of Kant's *Critique of Pure Reason* is the temporality of Dasein as presented in *Sein und Zeit*.)

—— (1929c) *Was ist Metaphysik?*, Bonn: Friedrich Cohen; trans. D.F. Krell, 'What is Metaphysics?', in D.F. Krell, *Basic Writings*, revised edn, San Francisco: Harper, 1993; and in *Pathmarks*, New York: Cambridge University Press, 1997. (Heidegger's inaugural address as Husserl's successor at Freiburg University. It discusses boredom as a 'basic mood' and broaches the topic of being as 'the nothing' or 'not-a-thing'.)

—— (1933) *Die Selbstbehauptung der deutschen Universität*, Breslau: Wilhelm Gottlieb Korn; trans. K. Harries, 'The Self-Assertion of the German University', *Review of Metaphysics* (1985) 38: 470–80. (Heidegger's controversial inaugural address as rector of Freiburg University, 27 May 1933.)

—— (1942) 'Platons Lehre von der Wahrheit', *Geistige Überlieferung* 2: 96–124; trans. J. Barlow, 'Plato's Doctrine of Truth', in W. Barrett (ed.) *Philosophy in the Twentieth Century*, New York: Random House, 1962, vol. 2; trans. T. Sheehan, 'Plato's Doctrine of Truth', in *Pathmarks*, New York: Cambridge University Press, 1997. (This close reading of Allegory of the Cave in Plato's *Republic* argues that Plato inaugurates the metaphysical notion of truth as correspondence.)

—— (1943a) *Vom Wesen der Wahrheit*, Frankfurt: Vittorio Klosterman; trans. J. Sallis, 'On the Essence of Truth', in D.F. Krell (ed.) *Basic Writings*, revised edn, San Francisco: Harper, 1993; and 'On the Essence of Truth', in *Pathmarks*, New York: Cambridge University Press, 1997. (Originally drafted in 1930, the essay discusses the levels of disclosure: propositional truth, the manifestness of entities, and disclosure-as-such or *aletheia*.)

—— (1947) 'Brief über den Humanismus', in *Platons Lehre von der Wahrheit. Mit einem Brief über den Humanismus*, Bern: Francke; trans. F.A. Capuzzi, 'Letter on Humanism', in D.F. Krell (ed.) *Basic Writings*, revised edn, San Francisco: Harper, 1993; and in *Pathmarks*, New York: Cambridge University Press, 1997. (Written as an open letter to Jean Beaufret, Heidegger's first publication after the

Second World War reveals the shifts his thinking had undergone in the 1930s.)

—— (1950) *Holzwege* (Forest Paths), Frankfurt: Vittorio Klosterman. (A collection of essays dating from 1936 to 1946.)

The following six references are the translations into English of all the essays contained in *Holzwege*. Dates within parentheses indicate the original redaction of the German text.

—— (1935) 'The Origin of the Work of Art', trans. A. Hofstadter, in D.F. Krell (ed.) *Basic Writings*, revised edn, San Francisco: Harper, 1993. (Originally delivered as a lecture in 1935, the essay argues that art, taken as the essence of any work of art, consists in disclosing disclosure by 'installing' it in the physical medium of the work.)

—— (1938) 'The Age of the World Picture', in W. Lovitt (trans. and ed.) *The Question Concerning Technology and Other Essays*, New York: Harper & Row, 1977. (Originally delivered as a lecture in 1938, the essay discusses, among other things, the birth of modernity with Descartes' view of thinking as the representation of entities by the subject as unshakable foundation.)

—— (1942–3) *Hegel's Concept of Experience*, trans. J.G. Gray, New York: Harper & Row, 1970. (Drawn from seminars Heidegger gave in 1942–3, the essay presents Hegel as the culmination of subject-centred metaphysics.)

—— (1943b) 'The Word of Nietzsche "God is Dead"', in W. Lovitt (trans. and ed.) *The Question Concerning Technology and Other Essays*, New York: Harper & Row, 1977. (Originally presented in 1943 (but drawing on lecture courses dating from 1936 to 1940), the essay interprets no. 125 of Nietzsche, *The Gay Science*, and other texts, in order to present Nietzsche's thought as the culmination of Western metaphysics.)

—— (1946a) 'What Are Poets For?', trans. A. Hofstadter, in D.F. Krell (ed.) *Poetry, Language, Thought*, New York: Harper & Row, 1971. (Given as a lecture to commemorate the twentieth anniversary of Rainer Maria Rilke's death, the essay argues that the poet was both subject to Nietzschean nihilism and attempted to overcome it by recovering the authentic sense of language.)

—— (1946b) 'The Anaximander Fragment', trans. D.F. Krell, in D.F. Krell and F.A. Capuzzi (eds) *Early Greek Thinking*, New York: Harper & Row, 1975. (Dating from 1946 but drawing on work done as early as 1932, this essay provides a close reading of Anaximander's Fragment 1 and offers some remarks on the history of being.)

—— (1951a) *Erläuterungen zu Hölderlins Dichtung*

(Elucidations of Hölderlin's Poetry), Frankfurt: Vittorio Klostermann; 4th expanded edn, 1971. (Six essays on Hölderlin's poetry.)

Two of these essays on Hölderlin's poetry have been translated into English and are given below. Dates within parentheses indicate the original redaction of the German text.

—— (1936) 'Hölderlin and the Essence of Poetry', in W. Brock (ed.) *Existence and Being*, Chicago: Henry Regnery, 1949. (Delivered as a lecture in Rome in 1936 and first published the following year, the essay presents Hölderlin as the 'poet of poetry' and reflects on *poiēsis* as the 'establishment' of disclosure.)

—— (1943c) 'Remembrance of the Poet', in W. Brock (ed.) *Existence and Being*, Chicago: Henry Regnery, 1949. (Given as a lecture in June 1943, at the centenary celebration of Hölderlin's death, the essay interprets the poet's elegy 'Heimkunft/An den Verwandten' ('Homecoming/To the Kinsmen') and reflects on the poet's relation to disclosure-as-such, here called 'the holy'.)

—— (1953a) *Einführung in die Metaphysik*, Tübingen: Max Niemeyer; trans. R. Manheim, *An Introduction to Metaphysics*, New Haven, CT: Yale University Press, 1959. (A lecture course from 1935, treating among other things Heidegger's interpretation of the meaning of being in Parmenides and Heraclitus.)

—— (1954) *Vorträge und Aufsätze* (Lectures and Essays), Pfullingen: Günter Neske. (A collection of eleven essays, ranging in date from 1936 to 1954.)

Ten of the eleven essays in *Vorträge und Aufsätze* have been translated into English and are given below. Dates within parentheses indicate the original redaction of the German text.

—— (1936–46) 'Overcoming Metaphysics', in J. Stambaugh (trans. and ed.) *The End of Philosophy*, New York: Harper & Row, 1973. (Thirty-eight brief notes, dating from 1936 to 1946, on the overcoming of metaphysics.)

—— (1943d) 'Aletheia', trans. F.A. Capuzzi, in D.F. Krell and F.A. Capuzzi (eds) *Early Greek Thinking*, New York: Harper & Row, 1975. (Drawing on Heidegger's 1943 course, 'The Beginning of Western Thinking (Heraclitus)', the text, first published in 1954, interprets Heraclitus' Fragment 16 in the light of what Heidegger calls 'the clearing'/disclosure-as-such.)

—— (1944) 'Logos', trans. D.F. Krell, in D.F. Krell and F.A. Capuzzi (eds) *Early Greek Thinking*, New York: Harper & Row, 1975. (Drawing on Heidegger's 1944 course 'Logic (Heraclitus' Doctrine of *Logos*), the text interprets Heraclitus' Fragment 50 in the light of the relation between disclosure-as-such and Dasein's correspondence to it.)

—— (1949a) 'The Thing', trans. A. Hofstadter, in D.F. Krell (ed.) *Poetry, Language, Thought*, New York: Harper & Row, 1971. (Written in 1949, delivered as a lecture in June 1950, and first published in 1951, the essay offers a phenomenological description of a wine-pitcher as a way of reflecting on the 'nearness' of things.)

—— (1949b) 'The Question Concerning Technology', in W. Lovitt (trans. and ed.) *The Question Concerning Technology and Other Essays*, New York: Harper & Row, 1977. (Written and delivered as a lecture in 1949 under the title 'Das Gestell', ('The Enframing'), then delivered under its present title, 'Die Frage nach der Technik', in 1953 and published in the following year, the text argues that technology is not primarily something instrumental (a means to an end) but a form of disclosure, and that modern technology, as the demand for complete disclosure, is intrinsically nihilistic.)

—— (1951b) 'Building Dwelling Thinking', trans. A. Hofstadter, in D.F. Krell (ed.) *Poetry, Language, Thought*, New York: Harper & Row, 1971. (Delivered as a lecture in 1951 and first published in the following year, the text meditates on the 'nearness' of things in terms of the 'bringing-forth' (*poiesis*) of things.)

—— (1951c) '... Poetically Man Dwells ...', trans. A. Hofstadter, in D.F. Krell (ed.) *Poetry, Language, Thought*, New York: Harper & Row, 1971. (Delivered as a lecture in October 1951 and first published in 1954, the text reflects on Hölderlin and on poetry as a bringing-forth (*poiesis*) of things.)

—— (1952) 'Moira', trans. F.A. Capuzzi, in D.F. Krell and F.A. Capuzzi (eds) *Early Greek Thinking*, New York: Harper & Row, 1975. (Originally planned as part of Heidegger's 1951–2 lecture course 'Was heißt Denken?' the text interprets Parmenides' Fragment 8, lines 34–41, and specifically the word '*moira*', as referring to the togetherness of Dasein and disclosure-as-such.)

—— (1953b) 'Science and Reflection', in W. Lovitt (trans. and ed.) *The Question Concerning Technology and Other Essays*, New York: Harper & Row, 1977. (Delivered as a lecture in 1953, the text probes the thesis that science is the theory of the real and raises the question of disclosure as the concealed essence of science.)

—— (1953c) 'Who is Nietzsche's Zarathustra?', trans. D.F. Krell, in *Nietzsche*, New York: Harper & Row, 1984, vol. 2. (Delivered as a lecture in May 1953, the essay interprets some major themes in Nietzsche – time and revenge, nihilism, eternal recurrence, will to power – and suggests that Zarathustra represents

the togetherness of eternal recurrence and superman.)

—— (1956) *Was heißt Denken?*, Tübingen: Max Niemeyer; trans. F. D. Wieck and J.G. Gray, *What Is Called Thinking?*, New York: Harper & Row, 1968. (The text of Heidegger's wide-ranging, two-semester lecture course, 1951–2.)

—— (1957a) *Der Satz vom Grund*, Pfullingen: Günther Neske; trans. R. Lilly, *The Principle of Reason*, Bloomington, IN: Indiana University Press, 1991. (The text of Heidegger's lecture course, 1955–6.)

—— (1957b) *Identität und Differenz*, Pfullingen: Günther Neske; trans. J. Stambaugh, *Identity and Difference*, New York: Harper & Row, 1969. (Two lectures from 1957, one on the principle of identity, the other on the ontotheological structure of metaphysics.)

—— (1958) 'Vom Wesen und Begriff der Φύσις Aristoteles Physik B 1', *Il Pensiero* 3: 131–56; 265–90; trans. T. Sheehan, 'On the Being and Conception of PHYSIS in Aristotle's *Physics* B, 1', *Man and World* (1976) 9: 221–70; and in *Pathmarks*, New York: Cambridge University Press, 1997. (Based on Heidegger's 1940 seminar, the text examines Aristotle's understanding of *physis* (nature) and argues that *physis* originally meant disclosure-as-such.)

—— (1959a) *Gelassenheit*, Pfullingen: Günther Neske; trans. J.M. Anderson and E.H. Freund, *Discourse on Thinking*, New York: Harper & Row, 1966. (Two occasional pieces, one an imaginary dialogue dating from 1944, the other a speech commemorating the eighteenth-century composer Conradin Kreutzer, dating from 1955.)

—— (1959b) *Unterwegs zur Sprache*, Pfullingen: Günther Neske; trans. P.D. Hertz and J. Stambaugh, *On the Way to Language*, New York: Harper & Row, 1971. (Four essays and one dialogue, ranging in date from 1950 to 1958, dealing with the question of language.)

—— (1961) *Nietzsche*, Pfullingen: Günther Neske, 2 vols; trans. D.F. Krell and F. Capuzzi, *Nietzsche*, New York: Harper & Row, 1979–87, 4 vols. (Lecture courses and notes on Nietzsche, dating from 1936 to 1946.)

—— (1962) *Die Frage nach dem Ding. Zu Kants Lehre von der transzendentalen Grundsätzen*, Tübingen: Max Niemeyer; trans. W.B. Barton and V. Deutsch, *What Is a Thing?*, Chicago, IL: Henry Regnery, 1967. (The text of Heidegger's lecture course of 1935–6, which includes a substantial discussion of the 'Analytic of Principles' in Kant's *Critique*.)

—— (1967, 1976) *Wegmarken*, Frankfurt: Vittorio Klostermann; trans. and ed. D.F. Krell, W. McNeill and J. Sallis, *Pathmarks*, New York: Cambridge University Press, 1997. (A collection of fourteen of Heidegger's most important essays, ranging in date from 1919 to 1961. The essays include Heidegger 1929a, 1929c, 1942, 1943, 1947 and 'Zur Seinsfrage' ('The Question of Being') (1955).)

—— (1969) *Zur Sache des Denkens*, Tübingen: Max Niemeyer; trans. J. Stambaugh, *On Time and Being*, New York: Harper & Row, 1972. (Four shorter texts dating from 1961 to 1964, including the 1962 lecture 'Zeit und Sein' ('Time and Being').)

—— (1970a) *Heraklit. Seminar Wintersemester 1966/ 1967*, Frankfurt: Vittorio Klostermann; trans. C.H. Seibert, *Heraclitus Seminar 1966/67*, Tuscaloosa, AL: University of Alabama Press, 1979. (The text of the seminar Heidegger conducted in tandem with Eugen Fink, 1966–7.)

—— (1970b) *Phänomenologie und Theologie*, Frankfurt: Vittorio Klostermann; trans. J.G. Hart and J.C. Maraldo, *The Piety of Thinking*, Bloomington, IN: Indiana University Press, 1994. (Two essays, dated 1927 and 1964 respectively, on the possible relation between theology and Heidegger's thinking.)

—— (1971) *Schellings Handlung Über das Wesen der menschlichen Freiheit (1809)*, Tübingen: Max Niemeyer; trans. J. Stambaugh, *Schelling's Treatise On the Essence of Human Freedom*, Athens, OH: Ohio University Press, 1985. (The text of Heidegger's lecture course of 1936.)

—— (1972) *Frühe Schriften* (Early Writings), Frankfurt: Vittorio Klostermann. (This volume reprints most notably Heidegger's Ph.D. dissertation of 1914, and his qualifying dissertation of 1916.)

—— (1976) 'Nur noch ein Gott kann uns retten', *Der Spiegel* 23: 193–219; trans. W.J. Richardson, 'Only a God Can Save Us: The *Spiegel* Interview', in T. Sheehan (ed.) *Heidegger, the Man and the Thinker*, New Brunswick, NJ: Rutgers University/Transaction Publishers, 1981. (In this posthumously published interview Heidegger attempts to explain, among other things, his relation to the Nazi regime in 1933–4.)

—— (1977a) *Vier Seminare* (Four Seminars), Frankfurt: Vittorio Klostermann; 2nd seminar trans. as 'A Heidegger Seminar on Hegel's *Differenzschrift*', *Southwest Journal of Philosophy* (1980) 11. (The records of four informal seminars that Heidegger conducted with friends and colleagues between 1966 and 1973.)

English translations of works in the Collected Edition

Heidegger, M. (1975) *Die Grundprobleme der Phäno-menologie*, in *Gesamtausgabe*, vol. 24; trans. A. Hofstadter, *The Basic Problems of Phenomenology*, Bloomington, IN: Indiana University Press, 1982. (Lecture course, summer 1927.)

—— (1977b) *Phänomenologische Interpretation von Kants Kritik der reinen Vernunft*, in *Gesamtausgabe*, vol. 25; trans. P. Emad and K. Maly, *Phenomenological Interpretation of Kant's Critique of Pure Reason*, Bloomington, IN: Indiana University Press, 1997. (Lecture course, winter 1927–8.)

—— (1978) *Metaphysische Angangsründe der Logik*, in *Gesamtausgabe*, vol. 26; trans. M. Heim, *The Metaphysical Foundations of Logik*, Bloomington, IN: Indiana University Press, 1984. (Lecture course, summer 1928.)

—— (1979) *Prolegomena zur Geschichte des Zeitbe-griffs*, in *Gesamtausgabe*, vol. 20; trans. T. Kisiel, *History of the Concept of Time: Prologomena*, Bloomington, IN: Indiana University Press, 1985. (Lecture course, summer 1925.)

—— (1980) *Hegels Phänomenologie des Geistes*, in *Gesamtausgabe*, vol. 32; trans. P. Emad and K. Maly, *Hegel's Phenomenology of Spirit*, Bloomington, IN: Indiana University Press, 1988. (Lecture course, winter 1930–1.)

—— (1981) *Aristoteles, Metaphysik 1–3*, in *Gesamtausgabe*, vol. 33; trans. W. Brogan, *Aristotle, Metaphysics 1–3: On the Essence and Actuality of Force*, Bloomington, IN: Indiana University Press, 1996. (Lecture course, summer 1931.)

—— (1982) *Parmenides*, in *Gesamtausgabe*, vol. 54; trans. A. Schuwer and R. Rojcewicz, *Parmenides*, Bloomington, IN: Indiana University Press, 1992. (Lecture course, winter 1942–3.)

—— (1983) *Die Grundbegriffe der Metaphysik. Welt – Endlicheit – Einsamkeit*, in *Gesamtausgabe*, vol. 29/ 30; trans. W. McNeill and N. Walker, *The Fundamental Concepts of Metaphysics: World, Finitude, Solitude*, Bloomington, IN: Indiana University Press, 1995. (Lecture course, winter 1929–30.)

—— (1984a) *Grundfragen der Philosophie. Ausge-wählte 'Probleme' der 'Logik'*, in *Gesamtausgabe*, vol. 45; trans. R. Rojcewicz and A. Schuwer, *Basic Questions of Philosophy: Selected 'Problems' of 'Logic'*, Bloomington, IN: Indiana University Press, 1994. (Lecture course, winter 1937–8.)

—— (1984b) *Hölderlins Hymne 'Der Ister'*, in *Gesamtausgabe*, vol. 53; trans. W. McNeill and J. Davis, *Hölderlin's Hymne 'The Ister'*, Bloomington, IN: Indiana University Press, 1996. (Lecture course, summer 1942)

—— (1989) *Beiträge zur Philosophie (Vom Ereignis)*, in *Gesamtausgabe*, vol. 65; trans. P. Emad and K. Maly, *Contributions to Philosophy: On Ereignis*,

Bloomington, IN: Indiana University Press, 1989. (Working notes, 1936–8.)

—— (1991) *Grundbegriffe*, in *Gesamtausgabe*, vol. 51; trans. G.A. Aylesworth, *Basic Concepts*, Bloomington, IN: Indiana University Press, 1993. (Lecture course, summer 1941.)

References and further reading

* Freeman, K. (ed.) (1971) *Ancilla to the Pre-Socratic Philosophers*, Cambridge, MA: Harvard University Press. (Heidegger interprets Heraclitus' word *physis* as meaning disclosure-as-such.)
* Husserl, E. (1900–1) *Logische Untersuchungen*, Halle an der Salle: Max Niemeyer, 2 vols; trans. J.N. Findlay, *Logical Investigations*, London: Routledge & Kegan Paul, 1970, 2 vols. (Husserl's foundational work in phenomenology.)
* —— (1913) *Ideen zu einer reinen Phänomenologie und phänomenologischen Philosophie*, vol. 1, *Jahrbuch für Philosophie und phänomenologische Forschung* 1: 1–323; Halle an der Salle: Max Niemeyer; trans. F. Kersten, *Ideas Pertaining to a Pure Phenomenology and to a Phenomenological Philosophy*, The Hague: Nijhoff, 1982. (Earliest published evidence of Husserl's turn to transcendental phenomenology and his use of the reductions.)

Kisiel, T. (1993) *The Genesis of Heidegger's Being and Time*, Berkeley, CA: University of California Press. (Exhaustive treatment of Heidegger's development, 1915–26.)

Pöggeler, O. (1987) *Martin Heidegger's Path of Thinking*, Atlantic Highlands, NJ: Humanities Press. (Lucid overview by the leading German commentator.)

Richardson, W.J. (1963) *Heidegger: Through Phenomenology to Thought*, The Hague: Nijhoff. (The classical presentation of the entire *oeuvre* by the pre-eminent Heidegger scholar.)

Sallis, J. (1986) *Delimitations: Phenomenology and the End of Metaphysics*, Bloomington, IN: Indiana University Press; 2nd expanded edn, 1995. (Groundbreaking essays by a major American interpreter.)

Sass, H.-M. (1982) *Martin Heidegger: Bibliography and Glossary*, Bowling Green, OH: Philosophy Documentation Center. (The most comprehensive bibliography in English, but needing to be supplemented by materials found in Sass 1968, 1975.)

—— (1968) *Heidegger-Bibliographie*, Meisenheim am Glan: Anton Hain. (First comprehensive bibliography of primary and secondary sources up to 1967.)

—— (1975) *Materialien zur Heidegger-Bibliographie 1917–1972*, Meisenheim am Glan: Anton Hain.

(This compliments and revises the information in the previous entry.)

Schürmann, R. (1987) *Heidegger on Being and Acting: From Principles to Anarchy*, Bloomington, IN: Indiana University Press. (Comprehensive interpretation and an argument for postmetaphysical anarchy.)

Taminiaux, J. (1991) *Heidegger and the Project of Fundamental Ontology*, Albany, NY: State University of New York Press. (Essays on Heidegger's early philosophy.)

Van Buren, J. (1994) *The Young Heidegger: Rumor of the Hidden King*, Bloomington, IN: Indiana University Press. (Thorough account of Heidegger's early development.)

Zimmermann, M. (1990) *Heidegger's Confrontation with Modernity: Technology, Politics, Art*, Bloomington, IN: Indiana University Press. (Focuses on the connection between Heidegger's relation to Nazism and his views on technology.)

THOMAS SHEEHAN

HEIDEGGERIAN PHILOSOPHY OF SCIENCE

Heidegger's importance in the philosophy of science stems less from his scattered remarks about science than from the larger conception of intentionality and ontology that informs them. Heidegger's earliest major work, Being and Time *(1927), displayed everyday practical purposive activity as the most fundamental setting for the disclosure of things in the world. Heidegger claimed that the traditional epistemological conception of a subject who represents objects was derivative from and dependent upon such ongoing everyday practical engagement with one's surroundings. Science was then supposed to be the practice that allows things to show themselves shorn of their significance within the 'in-order-to-for-the-sake-of' structure of everyday activity; nevertheless, the sense of scientific claims remained dependent upon the everyday interactions from which they were abstracted.*

Shortly after writing Being and Time, *Heidegger revised his project in ways that also transformed his account of science. His overall project shifted from describing the transcendental structure of the meaning of being, to interpreting the 'history of being'. Science was reinterpreted as an activity ('research') closely allied with machine technology, and oriented towards more extensive and intensive manipulation and ordering of things. Understood as such, science for Heidegger was an essential manifestation of the modern age.*

Whereas, earlier, Heidegger thought that science presupposed a philosophical ontology, Heidegger eventually portrayed science and technology as the conclusion of the philosophical tradition. While philosophical metaphysics and epistemology were thus naturalized, Heidegger was concerned with the possibility of a way of thinking outside this convergence of scientific and philosophical metaphysics.

1 **Science in Heidegger's early work**
2 **Science in later Heidegger**
3 **Contemporary issues in Heideggerian philosophy of science**

1 Science in Heidegger's early work

Heidegger followed Edmund Husserl's phenomenology in describing the meaning structures through which beings become manifest or *evident* (see PHENOMENOLOGICAL MOVEMENT §5). His inquiry into the 'meaning of being' accepted Husserl's claim that any intentional directedness also incorporates a 'categorial intuition' of being, as an understanding of what could fulfil that intending. For Husserl, however, perception or intuition was the model for intentional fulfilment (see HUSSERL, E. §§2–5); Heidegger argued instead that using equipment to realize an end was more basic. This shift had several important consequences. Heidegger argued that equipment is encountered holistically: understanding and using one instrument requires understanding others, and what we encounter foremost in successful practice is an interrelated equipmental setting. Equipment use is also not mediated: one encounters the tool itself rather than a representation of it. Finally, using equipment is socially normative. Equipmental complexes are organized around what one does with them and what they are for, and are governed by the enforcement of norms of correct use. Heidegger argued that the subjects of everyday practice are not individuated knowers, but anonymous, undifferentiated doers of what 'one' does.

The most basic form of intentionality is thus not consciousness but agency. We encounter the world as already organized around available *possibilities* for action that make sense of ourselves and our surroundings. We *interpret* the world and ourselves by enacting some of the possibilities disclosed by understanding the world as a setting for action. For Heidegger, one interprets something most appropriately as, for example, a hammer by hammering with it, not by perceiving it or making assertions; one also thereby interprets nails and boards, oneself as a builder, and one's surroundings as a setting in which hammering makes sense. Heidegger thus takes the

'hermeneutical circle' as a general structure of all meaningful activity, and not just of the interpretation of texts. Intentionality is thus fundamentally temporal: present activity is directed towards a future by working out possibilities made available by having been already 'thrown' into a meaningful situation.

Heidegger portrayed science as a distinctive kind of interpretive engagement with the world. Although science also uses equipment for locally intelligible purposes, he ascribed to these local performances a characteristic end, namely the interpretation of things in the world as 'present-at-hand', shorn of their practical significance. For example, Heidegger suggested that 'mass' acquires its sense as a physical property by gradual abstraction from the practical contexts in which things are 'too heavy' or 'too light'. This changeover from a practical to a theoretical understanding can supposedly be initiated whenever equipment is broken, missing or in the way. What can eventually result is an altogether different sense of what it means to be: beings are understood within a mathematized theoretical framework rather than local contexts of practical activity. Heidegger thought that the intelligibility of this theoretical projection of nature nevertheless presupposed an understanding of the world as practical setting.

This attempt to understand science as decontextualizing things and overlooking their practical significance confronts serious difficulties. First, Heidegger never convincingly described the *genesis* of this ontological shift. The momentary breaking of practical absorption when things malfunction normally results in re-engagement with the equally practical tasks of repair, replacement or removal. Heidegger does not indicate *how* such practical problem-solving yields to decontextualized theorizing. Moreover, Heidegger does not describe how the practical tasks of science (experiment, instrumental manipulation, theoretical problem-solving and calculation) are connected to the disclosure of things as present-at-hand (see EXPERIMENT; SCIENTIFIC METHOD). Philosophers who emphasize these practical dimensions of science may well find a more adequate account of scientific practice in Heidegger's overall account of everyday practical understanding and interpretation, than in his initial understanding of science as abstracting from practical engagement with local equipmental complexes.

2 Science in later Heidegger

Heidegger's philosophical development in the 1930s had striking consequences for his understanding of science. In that later understanding science ceases to be an intelligible possibility whenever one disengages from practical absorption in the world and frames things theoretically. Instead, science makes sense only within the modern age. Science is not opposed to everyday practice, but rather is taken to manifest more clearly what is happening throughout the modern world. This distinctively modern phenomenon of science is still understood as a theoretical (and ultimately mathematical) projection of nature which permits diverse changing phenomena to be understood as instantiations of necessary unchanging laws. But instead of being accomplished all at once by disengagement from practical absorption in the world, this theoretical projection is itself situated within the ongoing activity of scientific research. Research aims to extend the domain within which facts can be exhibited as regulated by law, by working on and with the laws already articulated. This elucidation of scientific laws both extends their scope and justifies earlier laws by displaying their fruitfulness (see LAWS, NATURAL §1).

What is distinctive about modern scientific experimentation for Heidegger is its guidance by and conformity to this theoretical projection of nature as lawful:

> experiment begins with the laying down of a law as a basis. To set up an experiment means to represent or conceive the conditions under which a specific series of motions can be made susceptible of being followed in its necessary progression.
>
> (Heidegger [1952] 1977: 121)

Research and experimentation continually and characteristically open up new possibilities for research. The achievements of scientific research are then adapted as resources for further research. Thus for Heidegger science aims at the continual *expansion* of research as ongoing activity; its continuing successful extension to new domains legitimates its prior achievements.

Heidegger connected the expansion of science's capacities for theoretical calculation with the development of machine technologies. Science does not just use machines to produce, measure and interpret phenomena. Heidegger thought that the *theoretical* framework of modern science projected Nature from the start as calculable and manipulable: 'modern science's way of representing pursues and entraps nature as a calculable coherence of forces'. (Heidegger [1954] 1977: 21)

Nature is thus manifest neither as Greek *physis*, nor as independent substances, nor as a significant equipmental complex, but instead as a stockpile of interchangeable resources (for example, of energy, chemicals, genes, labour or population).

Heidegger also connected the development of scientific research and machine technology, and the interpretation of Nature as 'stock', to the metaphysical conception of 'world pictures'. The scientific concern to represent the world objectively requires the right *approach*, so it can show itself unchanged by inquiry. Objectivity thus requires the right method, theories or attitudes, in short, the right kind of *subjectivity*. This shift from correct appearance to correct viewing in turn suggests the possibility of alternative views or pictures of the world. What Heidegger found questionable, however, is the underlying metaphysics of the world as depicted by a subject. Heidegger thought that understanding ourselves as subjects representing and manipulating objects is not itself a picture to accept or reject, or a position to take up, but a disturbing and questionable historical situation we find ourselves in.

Heidegger's questioning of the metaphysics of the world picture was not intended to develop an alternative metaphysics. Heidegger accepted that naturalized metaphysics and epistemology are the appropriate culmination of the philosophical tradition stemming from classical antiquity. He nevertheless asked whether there might still be a way of thinking apart from scientific or philosophical metaphysics. Such thinking would not determine what there is or what we should do, although he thought it might manifest what is at stake in our situation. Heidegger's remarks about thinking are enigmatic. Many commentators emphasize his association of thinking with the poetry of Hölderlin or the fragments of the pre-Socratics. Others argue that his later thinking attempted to purify transcendental inquiry of any metaphysical implications. On either reading, Heidegger associated such thinking with the possibility of salvation from the nihilism he ascribed to the limitless expansion of scientific and technological control. To realize these possibilities willfully, however, would self-defeatingly try to overcome willfulness. Hence the indirection and apparent quietism of Heidegger's later reflections upon science, technology and the modern world.

3 Contemporary issues in Heideggerian philosophy of science

Heidegger's work encourages attention to the local, circumspective understanding of the world manifest in scientific experiment and instrumental work, without reducing that understanding to explicit theoretical representations. Yet Heidegger also emphasizes the theory-ladeness of science. One possible reading of this latter point suggests continuity with early postpositivist emphases upon theory: all understanding and observation are guided by specific theoretical preconceptions (see OBSERVATION). Another reading, not incompatible with the first, highlights a specific presumption within scientific practices, that a calculable order in nature is more fully realizable by an interplay between theoretical modelling and the experimental and technological reconstruction of the world.

Heidegger's work challenges both scientific realism and its empiricist and constructivist critics, by questioning the representationalist conception of scientific knowledge that both presuppose (see SCIENTIFIC REALISM AND ANTIREALISM; CONSTRUCTIVISM). Perhaps science and technology are better understood as practical engagement with and intervention in the world, rather than systematic representation of its underlying causal structures or their empirical or social manifestations. To some philosophers this Heideggerian perspective suggests a modest and pluralist realism, for which science accurately describes real causal powers in the world without precluding other true descriptions for different purposes. Others take it to undercut the questions that realism and antirealism alike attempt to answer, and shift attention to the cultural and political significance of scientific engagement with the world.

Heidegger also encourages a new perspective on epistemological naturalism (see NATURALIZED EPISTEMOLOGY; NATURALIZED PHILOSOPHY OF SCIENCE). Later Heidegger entertains no doubts of science being understood biologically, psychologically or sociologically; he also accepts that such perspectives offer the best answer to traditional epistemological and metaphysical questions about the sciences. He nevertheless wants to formulate another kind of question that naturalized philosophy of science perhaps cannot address, concerning what is at issue and what is at stake in the historical development of scientific practice.

Heidegger's attempt to move beyond naturalized philosophy of science has encouraged some reconsideration of the relation between the natural and the human sciences (see UNITY OF SCIENCE). Heidegger's account of understanding and interpretation rejects traditional hermeneuticist defences of the methodological uniqueness of the human sciences, since he takes the hermeneutical circle to characterize all understanding, and not just the interpretation of texts and human action. Some philosophers, however, have used Heidegger's work to distinguish human science from natural science on different grounds. They draw upon Heidegger's account of human existence (*Dasein*) either to argue for methodological constraints upon adequate interpretations of the meaningful world of human interaction, or to argue that a theoretically stable or predictively successful

human science is impossible. Others have argued that such adaptations of Heidegger commit a paralogism: they interpret transcendental conditions upon the possibility of interpretation as objective characteristics of interpreters. If this argument is right, Heidegger's hermeneutics imposes no distinctive methodological constraints upon the human sciences. Heideggerian philosophy of science may then suggest, however, that the significance of scientific interpretation of nature cannot be disentangled from what is at stake (culturally or politically) in specific historical practices.

The transition in Heidegger's thinking about science contributes to the historicizing of the philosophy of science. His concern is not to display the essential structure of science as a form of knowledge or inquiry, but instead to inquire into the historical emergence and future prospects of a particular set of practices whose goals and achievements are at issue in their ongoing development. Heidegger's account of science thereby contributes to the philosophical discourse of modernity, that is, reflection upon how our 'modern' world differs from its predecessors. In Heidegger's own thinking, this interpretation of science sustained a reactionary anti-modernism. Heidegger's work has nevertheless influenced philosophers who take quite different philosophical and political stances toward characteristic features of the modern world.

The connection between Heidegger's reflection upon science and his criticisms of modernity nevertheless raise disturbing questions about the relation between philosophy and political life. The shift in Heidegger's thinking which identified science and technology as essential phenomena of the modern age coincided with his overt identification with National Socialism in Germany in the 1930s. Heidegger's influence upon subsequent philosophy of science can certainly be detached from his personal philosophical allegiance to the Nazis even if his own philosophical project cannot. What cannot be so readily set aside, even today, is the urgency of critical reflection upon the political uses of philosophical work and the dangers as well as hopes attached to politically engaged philosophical reflection upon the modern world.

See also: HEIDEGGER, M.; PRAGMATISM

References and further reading

Heidegger's works involve extensive technical terminology that present considerable additional difficulties in translation. All other works listed are straightforwardly readable and clearly explicate the technical terms used.

Blattner, W. (1995) 'Decontextualization, Standardization, and Deweyan Science', *Man and World* 28: 321–39. (Assesses different readings of Heidegger's early philosophy of science, and develops parallels to Dewey's pragmatism.)

Caputo, J. (1986) 'Heidegger's Philosophy of Science: The Two Essences of Science', in J. Margolis, M. Krausz and R. Burian (eds) *Rationality, Relativism and the Human Sciences*, Dordrect: Nijhoff, 43–60. (Argues for Heidegger's early philosophy of science as better suited for what is valuable in his later critique of modernity.)

Dreyfus, H. (1986) 'Why Studies of Human Capacities Modeled on Ideal Natural Science Can Never Achieve their Goal', in J. Margolis, M. Krausz and R. Burian (eds) *Rationality, Relativism and the Human Sciences*, Dordrect: Nijhoff, 3–22. (Develops a Heideggerian distinction between natural and human sciences.)

—— (1991) 'Heidegger's Hermeneutic Realism', in D. Hiley, J. Bohman and R. Shusterman (eds) *The Interpretive Turn*, Ithaca, NY: Cornell University Press. (Heidegger as a realist about science.)

* Heidegger, M. (1927) 'Sein und Zeit', *Jahrbuch für Philosophie und phänomenologische Forschung* 8: 1–438; trans. J. Stambaugh, *Being and Time*, Albany, NY: State University of New York Press, 1996. (Heidegger's first and most important work, and principal presentation of his early philosophy of science.)

* —— (1952) 'Die Zeit des Weltbildes', in *Holzwege*, Frankfurt: Vittorio Klostermann; trans. W. Lovitt, 'The Age of the World Picture' in *The Question Concerning Technology and Other Essays*, New York: Harper & Row, 1977. (Most detailed discussion of Heidegger's later philosophy of science.)

* —— (1954) 'Die Frage nach der Technik', in *Vorträge und Aufsätze*, Pfullingen: Gunther Neske; trans. W. Lovitt, 'The Question Concerning Technology', in *The Question Concerning Technology and Other Essays*, New York: Harper & Row, 1977, 3–35. (Heidegger's most extended later discussion of the relation between science and technology.)

Ihde, D. (1991) *Instrumental Realism*, Bloomington, IN: Indiana University Press. (Develops a Heideggerian interpretation of science emphasizing instrumentation and the relation of science to technology; usefully connects Heidegger to more recent philosophy of science.)

Rouse, J. (1985) 'Heidegger's Later Philosophy of Science', *Southern Journal of Philosophy* 23: 75–92. (Expansion of material of §§1–2 of this entry.)

—— (1987) *Knowledge and Power*, Ithaca, NY: Cornell University Press. (Draws extensively upon Heidegger to emphasize the practical and political aspects of science, while opposing both realism and antirealism.)

Zimmerman, M. (1990) *Heidegger's Confrontation with Modernity*, Bloomington, IN: Indiana University Press. (Critically situates Heidegger's discussion of science and technology within his criticism of modernity and his political engagement with National Socialism.)

JOSEPH ROUSE

HEISENBERG, WERNER (1901–76)

One of the most outstanding of twentieth-century physicists, Werner Heisenberg is famous for the uncertainty, or indeterminacy, principle of quantum mechanics, widely interpreted as implying an irreducibly indeterministic conception of nature. The main proponent of the Copenhagen interpretation after Bohr, Heisenberg conceived of the quantum description as referring not to objective spacetime realities, but merely to the probable outcomes of measurements. Heisenberg's philosophy, containing contradictory positivistic and realistic strands, is best understood in the context of his creative scientific theorizing.

In 1925 Heisenberg developed the foundations for quantum mechanics, proclaiming that a consistent atomic theory should contain only relations between experimentally observable quantities. Heisenberg replaced such 'unobservables' as electrons' positions by an ordered set of data related to the 'directly observable' frequencies and intensities of emitted radiation. An analysis of Heisenberg's work reveals that he used this positivistic principle not as a heuristic guide, but as an a posteriori justification of the successful technical method that *de facto* eliminated electronic positions. Heisenberg's approach, rather than being positivist, is akin to what he defined as 'practical realism'. A 'practical realist' does not resign from the quest for the underlying reality, yet dispenses with those realistic notions which cease to be theoretically fruitful.

In 1927, in an attempt to provide an 'intuitive' interpretation of the abstract quantum formalism, Heisenberg reversed his opinion about the unobservability of electrons' positions. By declaring that the meaning of concepts is identical with the procedure of their measurement, Heisenberg demonstrated agreement between the operational definition of spacetime concepts in thought experiments and the mathematically derived uncertainty formulas. Heisenberg concluded that the precise simultaneous specification of canonically conjugate variables, such as positions and momenta, is impossible in principle. Rather, they are subject to uncertainty relations: $\Delta p \Delta q \sim h$, where Δp, Δq are indeterminacies in the position and momentum measurements, and h is Planck's constant. A similar relation, $\Delta E \Delta t \sim h$, holds between energy and time. These formulas imply that in the atomic domain, as opposed to the classical one, the spacetime and energy–momentum descriptions are mutually exclusive, or 'complementary'.

Heisenberg's operational approach in the deduction of the uncertainty principle is often interpreted as a direct continuation of his earlier positivistic stand. Yet we witness here a fruitful epistemological about-face: if in 1925 the directly observable data determined the structure of the theory, in 1927 the theory dictated the possibilities of observation. In 1925 Heisenberg eliminated classical spacetime concepts; in 1927 he resurrected them, restricting their simultaneous applicability. In both cases Heisenberg aimed to secure the acceptance of an unconventional and abstract theory. This strategy of persuasion, which elevated local epistemological moves into overarching principles of knowledge, is a source of confusion in interpretations of Heisenberg's philosophy.

Heisenberg explored the philosophical implications of the uncertainty principle in relation to two central issues: 'indeterminism' and 'objective reality'. Heisenberg declared that the uncertainty principle, necessarily introducing probability into the definition of a system's state, implies a conclusive renunciation of causality. In principle, we cannot know the present with enough precision in order to predict the future with certainty.

Heisenberg's initial explorations of uncertainty contain ambiguities. He did not make clear whether uncertainty signified an epistemological limitation on measurability, or is of an ontological nature – the later Copenhagen stand. Heisenberg did not carefully distinguish between acausality and indeterminism (see DETERMINISM AND INDETERMINISM §2), nor did he provide cogent reasons why the uncertainty principle necessarily applies to an individual system, rather than to the statistics of an ensemble of similar systems – a less radical interpretive option.

Another implication of uncertainty concerns the physicist's notion of reality. The probability function does not describe what happens between observations in classical visualizable terms. The physical description, Heisenberg maintained, is no longer about the objective course of nature. Rather than describing 'nature in itself', physicists only specify nature's responses to questions put in experimental set-ups.

Despite positivistic overtones, Heisenberg's position is not identical with Bohr's prohibitions on inquiring about the reality 'behind the phenomena' (see BOHR, N.). Heisenberg describes his position as a neo-Platonic one, which identifies genuine reality with the underlying mathematical forms. Heisenberg's position that the 'primal' reality is mental is revealed by his introduction of a conscious observer into physical description. According to Heisenberg, it is the experiment that 'forces' an atom to indicate a definite property. While the transition from the 'possible' to the 'actual' occurs during measurements, the discontinuous change in the system's probability function takes place only when a conscious observer registers measurement results (see QUANTUM MEASUREMENT PROBLEM).

Even though Heisenberg and Bohr often presented a united front against the opponents of the Copenhagen interpretation, they differed on many crucial issues. Their disagreement about Bohr's doctrine of the indispensability of classical concepts – the heart of complementarity philosophy – is a most notable example. Contrary to Bohr, Heisenberg did not believe that a consistent interpretation of the microdomain is possible by using only classical concepts, without recourse to the quantum formalism. Heisenberg's endorsement of Bohr's arguments alongside his own dissenting views, resulted in numerous contradictions in Heisenberg's philosophical writings.

Heisenberg's philosophy was not formed in an attempt to erect a consistent structure. It was developed in numerous talks to different audiences in changing sociopolitical circumstances. Brilliant and intellectually fearless, Heisenberg was not constrained by logical inconsistencies. Pauli, Heisenberg's closest collaborator, criticized Heisenberg at the beginning of his scientific career for being 'very unphilosophical' (Hermann et al. 1979). Many years later, Pauli singled out Heisenberg's philosophical opportunism as a major source of his astounding scientific creativity.

See also: LOGICAL POSITIVISM §4; OPERATIONALISM; QUANTUM MECHANICS, INTERPRETATIONS OF

List of works

Heisenberg, W. (1930) *Die Physikalischen Prinzipien der Quantentheorie* (Physical Principles of the Quantum Theory), Leipzig: Hirzel; trans. C. Eckart and F.C. Hoyt, Chicago, IL: University of Chicago Press, 1930. (A presentation of the foundations of the quantum theory and its interpretation in the 'Copenhagen Spirit'.)

—— (1952) *Philosophic Problems of Nuclear Science*, New York: Pantheon Books. (A collection of Heisenberg's lectures in the 1930s and 1940s, including those to audiences in the occupied territories during the Second World War.)

—— (1958) *Physics and Philosophy: The Revolution in Modern Science*, New York: Harper & Row. (A collection of philosophical essays which covers Heisenberg's main interpretive contributions.)

—— (1969) *Der Teil and das Ganze: Gespräche im Umkreis der Atomphysik* (Physics and Beyond: Encounters and Beyond), Munich: Piper; trans. A.J. Pomerans, New York: Harper & Row, 1971. (Heisenberg's memoirs, presented in the form of dialogues, describing the development of atomic physics and its philosophical interpretations.)

—— (1984–9) *Gesammelte Werke* (Collected Works. Series A, B and C) , eds W. Blum, H.-P. Dürr and H. Rechenberg, Munich: Piper, and Berlin: Springer. (Contains all Heisenberg's published works, with series A devoted to original scientific publications, series B containing review articles, lectures and books, and series C containing philosophical and popular writings.)

References and further reading

Beller, M. (1983) 'Matrix Theory Before Schrodinger: Philosophy Problems, Consequences', *Isis* 74: 469–91. (An analysis of Heisenberg's original understanding of the new quantum theory, with an emphasis on the elimiantion of spacetime and its justification by the principle of elimination of unobservables.)

Cassidy, D.C. (1992) *Uncertainty. The Life and Work of Werner Heisenberg*, New York: Freeman. (The only comprehensive biography of Heisenberg, this book traces Heisenberg's intellectual and personal life in the changing sociopolitical context.)

* Hermann, A., Meyenn, K.v. and Weisskopf, V.F. (eds) (1979) *Wolfgang Pauli: Wissenschaftlicher Briefwechsel mit Bohr, Einstein, Heisenberg u.a, Band I: 1919– 1929* (Scientific Correspondence with Bohr, Einstein, Heisenberg and others. Volume I: 1919–1929), Berlin: Springer. (Contains Heisenberg's letters to Pauli during crucial phases of the creation and interpretation of quantum mechanics.)

Home, D. and Whitaker, M.A.B. (1992) 'Ensemble Interpretations of Quantum Mechanics. A Modern Perspective', *Physics Reports* 210: 224–317. (A comprehensive review and re-evaluation of ensemble interpretations of quantum physics as compared to the orthodox version of Heisenberg and Bohr.)

Jammer, M. (1974) *The Philosophy of Quantum Mechanics. The Interpretation of Quantum Mechanics in Historical Perspective*, New York: Wiley. (Contains an analysis of Heisenberg's uncertainty paper, as well as numerous discussions on the relevance of the uncertainty principle to different interpretations of quantum physics.).

Stapp, H.P. (1972) 'The Copenhagen Interpretation', *American Journal of Physics* 40: 1098–116. (This attempt of a systematic presentation of philisophy of Heisenberg and Bohr is more faithful to Heisenberg's thought than it is to Bohr's.)

MARA BELLER

HELL

The ancient idea that the dead go to a dark subterranean place gradually evolved into the notion of divinely instituted separate postmortem destinies for the wicked and the righteous. If the former lies behind the Psalms, the latter version appears in apocalyptic works, both canonical and deutero- or non-canonical, and is presupposed by numerous passages in the New Testament. Through the patristic and medieval periods the doctrine gradually achieved ecclesiastical definition, stipulating eternal torment (both physical and spiritual) in a distinctive place for those who die in a state of mortal sin. Most reformers recognized biblical authority for this doctrine. Philosophically, the notion of postmortem survival raises many questions in the philosophy of mind about personal identity. Recent discussion, however, has concentrated on the specialized version of the problem of evil to which the doctrine gives rise.

1 The problem of hell
2 Varieties of goodness
3 Free-will defences of hell
4 Pragmatic arguments
5 Alternative destinies

1 The problem of hell

The doctrine of hell gives rise to a specialized version of the problem of evil because it can be argued that the propositions:

(I)   God exists and is essentially omnipotent, omniscient and perfectly good; and

(II)   some created persons will be consigned to hell forever,

are logically incompossible, as follows:

(1) if God existed and were omnipotent, he would be able to avoid (II);

(2) if God existed and were omniscient, he would know how to avoid (II);

(3) if God existed and were perfectly good, he would want to avoid (II);

(4) therefore if (I), not (II).

Premise (1) seems obvious because an omnipotent creator could falsify (II) either by altogether refraining from making persons, or by annihilating created persons any time he chose. Further, some traditional theologians (for example, Augustine, Duns Scotus, William of Ockham and Calvin) take divine sovereignty over creation – both nature and soteriology – to imply divine freedom with respect to soteriological policy. For example, God could have legislated annihilation at death for human persons, or temporary purgatory followed by everlasting utopia for all sinners. Premise (2) follows because an omniscient God would know the scope of his powers. Premise (3) rests on the twin intuitions that a perfectly good God would want to be good to any persons he created, whereas hell means decisive ruin for its inhabitants.

The most straightforward solution is to reject either (I) or (II). The problem is that each is deeply entrenched in Christian belief. The Bible represents Christ as teaching that the disobedient and unfaithful will be 'cast into outer darkness', where there is 'weeping and gnashing of teeth' (Matthew 13: 42, 50; 22: 13), or thrown into the 'unquenchable fire' that is 'prepared for the devil and all his angels' (Matthew 13: 42, 50; 18: 8–9; 22: 13; see also 3: 10). If faith in Christ implies a belief that the teachings of Christ are true, then such texts seem *prima facie* to commit Christians to (II). Hermeneutical ingenuity will be required to reject (II) without eroding the epistemological foundation for faith in Christ itself. A minority of universalists (who believe that everyone will be saved) and annihilationists (who hold that the wicked will be annihilated at death or after a finite period of postmortem suffering) have shouldered that burden and declared (II) false.

2 Varieties of goodness

The argument in (1)–(4) above will convict Christians of contradiction, however, only if they understand the attribute terms and the doctrine of hell in something like the above-mentioned ways. In fact, Scripture and tradition contain a range of interpretations of divine goodness (see GOODNESS, PERFECT §3) and specify a variety of reasons why God might not falsify (II).

Global approaches. Some say that divine goodness finds its expression in the world as a whole, that universal republic for the good of which the wellbeing of individuals may be sacrificed. Thus, some medieval and Reformation theologians affirm that – whether because of the ontological incommensurability of the infinite relative to the finite, or because God is creator and governor of all else – God has no obligations to creatures and so cannot be deemed to be unjust to them, no matter what he does. Whether in fact or by natural necessity, God orders the world as a whole to advertise his goodness and manifest his glory. Given the Fall, Aquinas explains, God predestines some to show his mercy and damns others to declare his justice. It is certainly epistemically possible that a maximally perfect ordering of the world as a whole should include hell for some created persons.

Metaphysical goodness. Christian Platonist that he is, Augustine assumes that to be is to be good, because it is either to be God (who is goodness itself) or to be somehow God-like. He concludes not only that God is good to any creature simply by conferring the gift of existence, along with other natural endowments, but also (in apparent contradiction of Matthew 26: 24) that the value of such goods to their created possessor trumps any disvalue constituted by deprivations of its wellbeing. Thus, even the damned in hell have reason to give thanks and praise to God!

Conditional goodness to created persons. More intuitive, because more concrete, is the notion that divine goodness to created persons involves God's guaranteeing to each that their life is a great good to them on the whole and in the end. Yet many defenders of the doctrine of hell (Swinburne 1983; Stump 1986; Craig 1989; Walls 1992) insist that taking created freedom seriously forces the qualification 'except through some fault of their own' – which is enough to falsify (3) in the argument in §1.

3 Free-will defences of hell

Since much biblical talk of heaven and hell functions to make ante-mortem created free choices seem momentous, many defend the logical compossibility of (I) and (II) on the basis of the following assumptions:

(A1) created free will is a very great good, whether intrinsically or as a necessary means to God's central purposes in creation;

(A2) God cannot fulfil his purposes for and with free creatures without accepting the possibility that (II) some will qualify for damnation.

(A1) is variously explained in terms of alleged divine desires to confer on created persons the dignity of self-determination with respect to their own (eternal) destinies, or to enter into mutual relations of beatific intimacy with created persons in which their 'yes' to God is their own. (A2) rests on multiple philosophically controversial assumptions. First, it presupposes that created freedom is incompatible with divine determinism; otherwise God could avoid damning creatures simply by causing them to make choices that qualify them for heaven. Second, even granting libertarian or incompatibilist freedom, (A2) holds only if either God lacks middle knowledge (see PROVIDENCE §3) of what free creatures would do in which circumstances prior in the order of explanation to the divine decision to actualize them in those or other circumstances, or it is logically possible that some creatures are 'transworld damned', in the sense that no matter what circumstances God actualized them in, and no matter what helps of grace compossible with their freedom God furnished, their choices would qualify them for damnation. For if God had such middle knowledge and no creatures suffered from transworld damnation, God could falsify (II) by solving the coordination problem and actualizing created persons only in those circumstances in which none would qualify for hell. SUÁREZ (§1), who is an advocate of divine middle knowledge, affirms the necessity of divine resourcefulness – necessarily, for any possible person and any situation in which it can exist, there are some helps of grace that would (should God supply them) win the creature over without compromising its incompatibilist freedom – and so would pronounce transworld damnation impossible and (A2) false.

Third, (A2) assumes that, given sufficiently sinful exercise of created freedom, God does not have the option of waiving the consequence of damnation. For if (as Duns Scotus and William of Ockham suppose) worthiness of damnation were a statutory policy created by free and contingent divine legislation, it would be within God's power to spare all incompatibilist-free creatures no matter what they did. Even if hell were understood not as external and arbitrarily contrived punishment, but as the intrinsic and natural consequence of ante-mortem sinful choices, divine omnipotence would be as able miraculously to obstruct them as to prevent fire from burning the three young men in the furnace (Daniel 3: 13–20). To defend the impossibility claim in (A2), one would have to maintain that God necessarily owes it to himself to punish such sinners in one of those ways. Otherwise additional reasons will be required to explain God's free and contingent choice.

Contemporary free-will defenders of the doctrine of hell (notably Swinburne, Stump, Craig and Walls) meet this demand by reasserting (A1), the intrinsic value of created freedom and/or the importance of its unfettered exercise to God's purposes. Postmortem miracles transforming the sinner's character to make beatific intimacy with God possible and desirable would rob the creature of the dignity of self-determination with respect to its relationships and destiny. Although the creature would remain metaphysically the same person, the miraculous disruption would produce such discontinuities that it would be difficult for the post-conversion self to identify with the projects and purposes of the ante-mortem character. God pays his respects to created personality precisely by not effecting such miraculous changes, but regretfully giving the creature over to the consequences of its choices and allowing it to remain the person it has become.

By contrast, medieval theologians refused to hold God to a postmortem non-interference policy. They reasoned that if rational creatures were as free to accept or reject God after death as before, the blessed might fall again and the damned might repent. To prevent both, God was said to confirm them in their choices by making it causally impossible for them to deviate from their 'deathbed' orientations. With the elect, the value of divine interference was glossed in terms of a traditional equivocation which saw freedom on the one hand as a self-determining power for opposites, and on the other as an orientation towards intrinsic value for its own sake (see ANSELM OF CANTERBURY §6). Ante-mortem careers in which created freedom imitated God with respect to self-determination were brought to rest in a higher freedom that mimicked God's stable orientation to the good. Applying – as they did not – their estimate of the value of libertarian freedom to the fate of the damned, it might seem that if hell is bad enough, the failed effort 'to do it oneself' – like a child's attempt to put a toy aeroplane together – might come to rest in assisted success. Moreover, the transformation could be gradual, carefully engineered by God to approximate the continuity with difference found in dramatic ante-mortem conversions.

Whether divine non-interference constitutes respect for created agency depends on the strength of human agency and the perniciousness of hell. Toning down vivid biblical imagery, some (notably Swinburne and Stump) contend that hell does not rob life of all positive meaning because abandonment to the natural consequences of ante-mortem choices is compatible with many and diverse satisfactions – some perverse (for example, rebellion for its own sake) and all minuscule (for example, debating with Milton's fallen angels the compossibility of divine foreknowledge and created free will) in comparison to the joys of divine company. Others (for example M.M. Adams) reason that since humans were made to find ultimate satisfaction in God, persistent turning away from

God, cemented in vice, will eventually unravel the personality into madness, the pain of which is only faintly anticipated by ante-mortem schizophrenia and depression. Could God really respect our dignity by standing idle while we degrade ourselves? Yet if God intervenes to put a floor under our fall, why not to turn us – by a continuity-preserving process – to himself?

A sober look at the reality of human life raises the question whether the vast majority of human beings were ever up to the challenge of deciding their own eternal destinies, of taking it upon themselves to give a final 'yes' or 'no' to God. Humans begin life ignorant, weak and helpless, psychologically so lacking in self-concept as to be incapable of choice. We learn to 'construct' a picture of the world, ourselves and other people only with difficulty over a long period of time and under the extensive influence of non-ideal choosers. We emerge from the long, messy developmental process with entrenched neuroses that colour our cognitive as well as affective 'takes' on the world and thus impair our freedom, while we unconsciously 'act out' doing harm to self and others. Our grasp of hell's grim torments, as of heaven's bliss, is radically inadequate. Even if we could experience either for a short time (for example, burning fire, deep depression, consuming hatred; St Teresa's joyful glimpse of the Godhead), we are unavoidably unable to experience their cumulative effect in advance, and so unable more than superficially to appreciate what is involved in either. The apparent conclusion is that human agents are unavoidably unable to exercise their free choice with fully open eyes, the way free-will defenders sometimes suggest.

The evaluation of ante-mortem human agency is something about which Christians have disagreed for centuries. What may be the majority report tries to reconcile empirical realities with its free-will defence of the doctrine of hell by appealing to the doctrine of Adam's Fall. Adam and Eve, the primordial human couple, had the robust agency required to make the momentous choice. Our damaged agency is an inherited consequence of their sin (see SIN §2). Nevertheless, whether because of a doctrine of collective responsibility (according to which it is just that all members of a family participate in the punitive consequences and/or the guilt of the deeds of its head) or because the damages are alleged not to be disabling, such impairments do not excuse us from the task or the consequences of making our own momentous decision.

4 Pragmatic arguments

Closely coupled with free-will defences of the doctrine of hell is the pragmatic or moral argument that the threat of hell is a powerful incentive to religious fidelity and moral diligence. Kantians, who may themselves believe in some sort of postmortem retribution, counter that the motive of punishment avoidance undercuts the moral enterprise, which enjoins duty for duty's sake. Moralists of other stripes allow threats a place in the early stages of moral pedagogy or grant moral legitimacy to the self-concerned desire to be rightly related to God, the good, the moral law, and so on. Still others charge that pragmatic arguments cut both ways: the notion that the governor of the universe will consign sinners to the eternal consequences of their choices might just as easily produce rebellion (as, for example, in the case of J.S. Mill), or combine with a pessimistic appraisal of human nature to foster despair!

5 Alternative destinies

While many take biblical apocalyptic language at face value, others see the rhetorical context of exhortation and poetic imagery as opening hermeneutical loopholes that leave the fate of persistent sinners scripturally underdetermined. Positions can be seen to vary along the following five dimensions: the degree of divine initiative involved in setting up and consigning people to hell; whether death is the 'deadline' at which qualifications are assessed, or whether there is a temporary or indefinite period of postmortem opportunity; the duration of hell – whether it begins immediately after death or only after the Last Judgment, and whether it lasts forever or whether souls consigned there eventually wither away; whether the suffering is psychospiritual only or also physical; and whether the fate is irreversible.

See also: ESCHATOLOGY; EVIL, PROBLEM OF; HEAVEN; LIMBO; PREDESTINATION; PURGATORY; REPROBATION; RESURRECTION; SOUL, NATURE AND IMMORTALITY OF THE

References and further reading

Adams, M.M. (1993) 'The Problem of Hell: A Problem of Evil for Christians', in E. Stump (ed.) *Reasoned Faith, A Festschrift for Norman Kretzmann*, Ithaca, NY: Cornell University Press, 301–27. (Defends universalism in preference to doctrines of hell or annihilation.)

* Craig, W.L. (1989) 'No Other Name: A Middle Knowledge Perspective on the Exclusivity of

Salvation through Christ', *Faith and Philosophy* 6 (2): 172–88. (Uses middle knowledge and the hypothesis of transworld damnation to mount a free-will defence of the doctrine of hell.)

Hick, J. (1966) *Evil and the God of Love*, San Francisco: Harper & Row, 2nd edn, 1978, 87–9, 91–2, 107–14, 177, 341–5. (Argues against traditional doctrines of hell in favour of indefinite postmortem opportunities and eventual universal salvation.)

* Stump, E. (1986) 'Dante's Hell, Aquinas' Theory of Morality, and the Love of God', *Canadian Journal of Philosophy* 16: 181–98. (Develops a free-will defence of Dante's hell and defends divine goodness in setting it up.)

* Swinburne, R. (1983) 'A Theodicy of Heaven and Hell', in A. Freddoso (ed.) *The Existence and Nature of God*, Notre Dame, IN: University of Notre Dame Press, 37–54. (Offers a free-will defence of annihilation or benevolent alternative environments for those who die with characters unfit for heaven.)

* Walls, J. (1992) *Hell: The Logic of Damnation*, Notre Dame, IN: University of Notre Dame Press. (Offers a free-will defence of a 'Methodist' hell modified by the hypothesis that God gives disadvantaged agents a postmortem opportunity to make a decisive choice.)

MARILYN McCORD ADAMS

HELLENISTIC MEDICAL EPISTEMOLOGY

During the Hellenistic period (323–31 BC), there arose, largely in Alexandria, a profound debate in medical methodology. The main participants were the Empiricists, committed to an anti-theoretical, practical medicine based on observation and experience and the various Rationalists, such as Herophilus, Erasistratus, and Asclepiades, who held that general theories of physiology and pathology were both attainable and essential to proper medical understanding and practice. Dispute about the nature of scientific inference and the status of causal explanation mirrored and to some extent conditioned the contemporary debate between Stoics and sceptics about epistemology.

1 Rationalists and Empiricists
2 Methodists

1 Rationalists and Empiricists

In the medicine of the post-Classical period, the empiricism already discernible among the Hippocratic doctors (see HIPPOCRATIC MEDICINE) gathers strength. Diocles of Carystus (*fl. c.*350 BC) denied that explanation was in all cases possible or even desirable; some things simply have to be accepted as though they were first principles, while experience is the best guide to therapy. The main function of theoretical explanations (in terms of the balance of humours, or whatever) is simply to convince the patient of the doctor's competence.

This empirical approach was taken up by Herophilus (*fl. c.*260 BC), who held that 'the appearances should be stated first even if they are not first' (fr. 50a), and that causes should be accepted 'only hypothetically' (fr. 58). He devised a set of dilemmatic arguments against the existence of causes (fr. 59), for example: causes must be either (a) corporeal of corporeal effects; (b) incorporeal of incorporeal effects; (c) corporeal of incorporeal effects; or (d) incorporeal of corporeal effects; but none of (a)–(d) is possible; hence there are no causes. He performed dissections and vivisections (perhaps even on human subjects: frs 63–74), discovering the distinction between motor and sensory nerves, and described four basic 'powers' responsible for human physiological functioning (frs 131, 184).

His contemporary, Erasistratus, another brilliant anatomist, doubted whether so-called antecedent causes (such as the excessive exposure to sunlight which presages fever) were properly causes at all, since they are not invariably followed by their supposed effects (a view countered by GALEN (§3). While paying lip-service to teleology, he developed a severely mechanistic physiology, rejecting specific organic 'faculties' (for example, of attraction for urine by the bladder) to explain particular functions, in favour of a fluid dynamics based on the principle of *horror vacui* (see STRATO §3).

Philinus (*fl. c.*250 BC) and Serapion (*fl. c.*225 BC), a pupil of Herophilus, adopted this cautious, empirical attitude and gave it a full-bloodedly sceptical twist, founding the school of medical Empiricism, the fullest account of which is given in Galen's *Outline of Empiricism*. They held that all theoretical knowledge (of the micro-structures of the body, and of causal powers) was unattainable, and in any case unnecessary for successful medical practice, which required only the accumulation of large amounts of empirical data of regular connections between phenomenally observable types of events, in regard both to the prognosis of the course of a disease and its therapy (*Outline of Empiricism* 2). Such evidence was to be gained primarily by personal observation, supplemented by second-hand reports whose reliability was itself subject to empirical testing (*Outline of Empiricism* 3, 8).

Possible remedies might be suggested by inspiration or luck, or the observation of a fortuitously therapeutic set of circumstances (*Outline of Empiricism* 2). Such initially successful therapies must then be subjected to further empirical testing, for 'experience' (a suitably large set of such congruent concatenations) to produce a 'theorem' (an empirically-based therapeutic generalization, for example, 'pomegranates cure diarrhoea'). A third, controversial, feature of their method was 'transition to the similar', a form of analogical reasoning which some of the Empiricists allowed to suggest therapies for hitherto unobserved conditions (*Outline of Empiricism* 4): thus, confronted with an unprecedented ankle-ailment, noting that ankles resemble wrists, one might apply some previously tested wrist-remedy.

The status and applicability of transition was much disputed. It was not emphasized by the earliest Empiricists, and their successors disagreed as to whether it was a proper part of medical practice (hence requiring theoretical justification), or whether doctors simply found themselves using it (*Outline of Empiricism* 4). Some later Empiricists, notably Cassius 'the Sceptic', refused to allow transition any role at all, and tried to re-establish Empiricism in its original pristine form, unsullied by any such Rationalist accretions.

'Rationalist' here is an umbrella-term for anyone committed to any theoretical physiology and pathology; thus Herophilus, Erasistratus, the Pneumatists (who held that the condition of the *pneuma*, modified inspired air (see PNEUMA), was fundamental to health and disease), and the followers of Asclepiades (second century BC), who held that disease was caused 'by the lodgement of theoretical particles in the theoretical pores' (Sextus Empiricus, *Against the Professors* VIII 220) and developed a theory of the internal fluid dynamics of the body on the basis of the principle of 'movement towards the rarefied' (compare Erasistratus' *horror vacui*), are all Rationalists. However disparate their views, they all believed in the possibility of inferring from surface phenomena to the underlying structural reality of things, by a process known as *analogismos*. By contrast, the Empiricists restrict themselves to *epilogismos*, inference from one evident phenomenon to another with which it is regularly associated (*Against the Professors* VIII 7; compare Sceptic and dogmatist on signs: see PYRRHONISM §4).

Galen wrote an early treatise *On Medical Experience* presenting the anti-Empiricist arguments of Asclepiades and the replies of Menodotus (*fl. c.* AD 150), the most sophisticated Empiricist of his day. Asclepiades argues that Empiricists cannot avoid theoretical commitment: their syndromes are supposed to consist of concatenations of phenomena that have been observed to occur similarly in many cases. But what is similarity? Everything both resembles and is distinct from everything else in innumerable ways. What is required is some concept of *relevant* similarity: but that is already a theoretically-laden notion (*On Medical Experience* 4–6). Moreover, how many cases are enough? The Rationalist deploys a Sorites argument (see VAGUENESS §2) to undermine the coherence of such a concept (*On Medical Experience* 7).

Both charges are answered. First, the Empiricist requires no *theory* of relevant similarity; he is simply guided by the way things appear. He need not say *why* things appear to be alike – they just do. And experience itself shows that this is the way to acquire practical abilities (*On Medical Experience* 9–11). Moreover, although the Rationalists claim to be able to infer from the phenomena to the hidden natures of things, they disagree radically among themselves as to what those natures are – and these disagreements are, by their very nature, undecidable (*On Medical Experience* 12–13). Finally, there is no determinate answer to the question how many cases are enough: that varies from case to case, doctor to doctor. If serious, the Sorites is quite general and will destroy the coherence of innumerable everyday concepts (*On Medical Experience* 16–17, 21). But this is of no concern to the Empiricist, who has no time for such theoretical niceties.

2 Methodists

In the first century AD there arose a third medical sect, that of the Methodists. They held that all disease was reducible to either excessive constriction or excessive dilation of the pores of the body, or to some combination of these conditions. These 'communalities' are directly evident to suitably-trained observation, and require no theoretical inferences. Thus the Methodists agreed with the Empiricists in eschewing theory, but parted company with them over the issue of causes. Rationalists were united by the belief that proper physiology and pathology (and hence proper therapy) demanded a theoretical understanding of the hidden causal mechanisms of nature. Empiricists rejected such speculation about the hidden structure of things as being both inherently ungroundable and therapeutically useless, but were prepared to allow into their syndromes reference to items which the Rationalists at least would describe as antecedent, evident causes. Methodists rejected even appeal to antecedent causes, holding that all that mattered was the current condition of the patient's body, a condition whose aetiology was quite irrelevant.

References and further reading

Deichgräber, K. (1965) *Die griechische Empiri-kerschule: Sammlung der Fragmente und Darstellung der Lehre* (The Greek Empiricist School: Collection of Fragments and Teachings of the School), 2nd edn, Berlin: Weidmann. (Fragments of the Empiricist school.)

Edelstein, L. (1967) *Ancient Medicine*, Baltimore, MD: Johns Hopkins University Press. (Fine collection of papers, several of which are relevant to the themes of this article.)

Frede, M. (1987) *Essays in Ancient Philosophy*, Oxford: Oxford University Press. (Contains several important essays on medical epistemology.)

* Galen (*c.* AD 150–90) *On the Sects, Outline of Empiricism*, and *On Medical Experience*, trans. M. Frede, *Galen: Three Treatises on the Nature of Science*, Indianapolis, IN: Hackett Publishing Company, 1985. (Includes an excellent introduction.)

Hankinson, R.J. (1987) 'Causes and Empiricism', *Phronesis* 32: 329–48. (Analysis of the Empiricist attitude to antecedent causes.)

* Herophilus (*fl. c.*260 BC) Fragments, in H. von Staden, *Herophilus: The Art of Medicine in Early Alexandria*, Cambridge: Cambridge University Press, 1989. (Fine edition – from which the fragments of Herophilus are cited – with translation and discussion.)

Vallance, J. (1990) *The Lost Theory of Asclepiades of Bithynia*, Oxford: Oxford University Press. (Good account of Asclepiades' medical system.)

R.J. HANKINSON

HELLENISTIC PHILOSOPHY

The Hellenistic schools dominated the Greco-Roman world from c.300 BC to the mid first century BC, making it an era of great philosophical brilliance. The principal doctrinal philosophies were Stoicism and Epicureanism, but this was also the age in which scepticism emerged as a philosophical movement. The central issues of debate were the nature and origin of the world, the means to attaining truth and the ethical goal.

The Hellenistic age is defined negatively, as the interregnum between two empires. It starts with the death of Alexander the Great in 323 BC and the collapse of his empire, and ends with the battle of Actium in 31 BC, the official start of the Roman Empire. Its main positive feature is the 'Hellenization' of – that is, the spread of Greek culture to – much of the Mediterranean world, especially the East. A high proportion of the converts to the Hellenistic philosophical schools flocked to Athens from the cities of western Asia, and a sense of excitement about Greek culture was one factor in the emergence of new philosophical schools. A favoured alternative explanation is that the collapse of the old Greek *polis*, or city state, had left people feeling lost and in need of philosophical succour, but it is doubtful whether that hypothesis, even if sustainable, could account for more than a fraction of the new converts.

Although Alexandria eclipsed it as a centre of learning, Athens remained the headquarters of philosophy almost throughout the era. Hence in many ways Hellenistic philosophy would better be dated from 306 BC, when Epicurus founded his school in Athens, to 88 BC, when the Athenian schools were badly weakened in war, never fully to recover their institutional supremacy. The succeeding era was marked by a philosophical diaspora throughout the Roman Empire.

A Hellenistic doctrinal philosophy was a complete system, which had to offer: (1) an understanding of the world's origins, components and organization, and of our place in it; (2) a methodology of discovery, which included in particular naming one or more 'criteria of truth'; (3) an account of what the 'goal', happiness (see EUDAIMONIA), consists in. These three areas correspond to what had become the standard tripartition of philosophy into (1) physics, (2) logic and (3) ethics.

The main two doctrinal Hellenistic philosophies can be studied in the entries on EPICUREANISM and STOICISM. The sceptical philosophers of the New Academy constituted a third main movement, which provided constant critiques of its doctrinal rivals (see ARCESILAUS; CARNEADES). Pyrrhonist Scepticism made a brief appearance at the beginning of the era (see PYRRHO; TIMON), but did not become a formal movement until its refoundation by Aenesidemus towards the end of it (see AENESIDEMUS; PYRRHONISM). Nevertheless, Pyrrhonism is commonly counted as a Hellenistic philosophy.

'Hellenistic' is in any case not a purely chronological label. Aristotelianism survived in some form throughout the period (see THEOPHRASTUS; STRATO; PERIPATETICS), but did not really become distinctively Hellenistic. The philosophy of the period is sometimes called *post*-Aristotelian. However, although Aristotle did happen to die within a year of Alexander the Great, this label is misleading: it is unclear how far the philosophers of the period recognized Aristotle as a major philosopher to whom they were obliged to respond. Aristotle's real revival occurred only at the very end of the Hellenistic age.

On the other hand, the main spokesman of Pyrrhonism today is SEXTUS EMPIRICUS, who is often therefore treated as a Hellenistic thinker, despite his probable date in the second century AD. Likewise, Stoics of the first two centuries AD are commonly thought of as Hellenistic (see SENECA; MUSONIUS RUFUS; EPICTETUS; MARCUS AURELIUS).

Plato remained a philosophical influence throughout the era, but there was no genuine doctrinal Platonism between c. 265 and c. 50 BC. In the early first century BC ANTIOCHUS advertised a return to Platonism, but his philosophy is in fact characteristically Hellenistic in its terminology and concepts.

Apart from some short writings of EPICURUS, no Hellenistic philosophical treatises have survived intact. It has been the task of modern scholarship to reconstruct the systems and debates from secondary sources. The most important of these are the Latin philosophical dialogues of CICERO, and the third-century AD *Lives of the Philosophers* by DIOGENES LAERTIUS.

See also: ACADEMY; ARISTON OF CHIOS; CHRYSIPPUS; CLEANTHES; HELLENISTIC MEDICAL EPISTEMOLOGY; LUCRETIUS; PANAETIUS; PHILO OF LARISSA; PHILODEMUS; POSIDONIUS; ZENO OF CITIUM

References and further reading

Annas, J. (1992) *Hellenistic Philosophy of Mind*, Berkeley, CA: University of California Press. (The best study of the topic.)

—— (1993) *The Morality of Happiness*, Oxford: Oxford University Press. (Major study of issues surrounding eudaimonism in Aristotle and Hellenistic philosophy.)

Barnes, J., Brunschwig, J., Burnyeat M. and Schofield, M. (eds) (1982) *Science and Speculation*, Cambridge: Cambridge University Press. (Collection of articles on Hellenistic philosophy of science.)

Barnes, J. and Mignucci, M. (eds) (1988) *Matter and Metaphysics*, Naples: Bibliopolis. (Collection of articles on Hellenistic metaphysics.)

Brunschwig, J. (1994) *Papers in Hellenistic Philosophy*, Cambridge: Cambridge University Press. (Magisterial anthology of articles.)

Brunschwig, J. and Nussbaum, M.(eds) (1993) *Passions and Perceptions*, Cambridge: Cambridge University Press. (Collection of articles on Hellenistic psychology.)

* Cicero (mid 45 BC) *On the Ends of Good and Evil*, trans. H. Rackham, Loeb Classical Library, Cambridge, MA: Harvard University Press and London: Heinemann, 1914. (A dialogue in which Hellenistic ethical theories are defended and criticized; includes Latin text.)

* —— (late 45 BC) *On the Nature of the Gods*, trans. H. Rackham, Loeb Classical Library, Cambridge, MA: Harvard University Press, and London: Heinemann, 1933. (A dialogue in which Hellenistic theologies are defended and criticized; includes Latin text.)

* —— (mid 44 BC) *On Fate*, trans. R.W. Sharples, Warminster: Aris & Phillips, 1991. (A classic source on the Hellenistic debate about determinism; includes Latin text.)

* Diogenes Laertius (c. early 3rd century AD) *Lives of the Philosophers*, trans. R.D. Hicks, *Diogenes Laertius Lives of Eminent Philosophers*, Loeb Classical Library, Cambridge, MA: Harvard University Press and London: Heinemann, 1925, 2 vols. (Covers the lives and work of most major Hellenistic philosophers.)

Flashar, H. (ed.) (1994) *Die Philosophie der Antike, 4: Die hellenistische Philosophie* (Philosophy in Antiquity, 4: Hellenistic Philosophy) Basle: Schwabe. (Monumental survey, with comprehensive bibliography.)

Frede, M. (1987) *Essays in Ancient Philosophy*, Oxford: Oxford University Press. (Contains several seminal papers on Stoicism and Scepticism.)

Griffin, M. and Barnes, J. (eds) (1989) *Philosophia Togata: Essays on Philosophy and Roman Society*, Oxford: Oxford University Press. (Series of studies on the place of Hellenistic philosophy in Roman life and thought.)

Inwood, B. and Gerson, L.P. (1988) *Hellenistic Philosophy, Introductory Readings*, Indianapolis, IN: Hackett Publishing Company. (Includes a large body of primary texts, in translation.)

Laks, A. and Schofield, M. (eds) (1995) *Justice and Generosity*, Cambridge: Cambridge University Press. (Collection of articles on Hellenistic political philosophy.)

Long, A.A. (1974) *Hellenistic Philosophy*, London: Duckworth. (Superbly accessible and engaging introductory account.)

Long, A.A. and Sedley, D.N. (1987) *The Hellenistic Philosophers*, Cambridge: Cambridge University Press. (Volume 1 contains sources in translation, with commentary; volume 2 contains the original texts.)

Nussbaum, M. (1994) *The Therapy of Desire*,

Princeton, NJ: Princeton University Press. (An eloquent comparison of the different Hellenistic schools' treatments of the emotions.)

Schofield, M., Burnyeat, M. and Barnes, J. (eds) (1980) *Doubt and Dogmatism*, Oxford: Oxford University Press. (Collection of articles on Hellenistic epistemology.)

Schofield, M. and Striker, G. (eds) (1986) *The Norms of Nature*, Cambridge: Cambridge University Press. (Collection of articles on Hellenistic ethics.)

Scott, D. (1995) *Recollection and Experience*, Cambridge: Cambridge University Press. (Contains invaluable analyses of Stoic and Epicurean cognitive psychology.)

Sedley, D. (1977) 'Diodorus Cronus and Hellenistic philosophy', *Proceedings of the Cambridge Philological Society* 203: 74–120. (On the dialectical background to the main Hellenistic philosophies.)

* Sextus Empiricus (c. AD 200) *Against the Professors*, Books VII–XI trans. R.G. Bury, Loeb Classical Library, Cambridge, MA: Harvard University Press and London: Heinemann, 1935–6. (Contains extensive comparative reports of Hellenistic philosophical positions and arguments.)

Sharples, R.W. (1996) *Stoics, Epicureans and Sceptics*, London: Routledge. (The best short introduction to Hellenistic philosophy.)

Striker, G. (1996) *Essays on Hellenistic Epistemology and Ethics*, Cambridge: Cambridge University Press. (A set of important studies.)

DAVID SEDLEY

HELMHOLTZ, HERMANN VON (1821–94)

In physiology, physics, mathematics, aesthetic theory and epistemology, Helmholtz intervened, and innovated. He contributed to the physiology of perception through work on the central nervous system, followed by work on optics and acoustics. He invented instruments, such as the opthalmoscope and introduced the mathematical principle of the conservation of energy to physics. For geometry, Helmholtz elaborated on the concept of an n-dimensional manifold. He secured the influence of the 'Berlin physics', introduced Faraday and Maxwell to Germany, refined the theory of electrodynamics and reflected on the role of discrete entities in physics. Having become the most influential representative of German science and its uncontested spokesperson, he repeated the importance of the connection between education and research and the necessity not to separate the natural sciences (Naturwissenschaften) from the social sciences (Geis-Geisteswissenschaften). This monumental body of work is experiencing a revival of interest today as historians of both science and culture consider it in a new light. But the question remains of how to characterize what we might call 'the Helmholtz effect' in philosophy. Why was Helmholtz equally influential not only on Cassirer, Husserl, Schlick, Meyerson and Freud, but also on the principal founders of contemporary physics; Einstein, Bohr and Heisenberg? To grasp this, we must understand the constant interaction between science and philosophy which characterized, even permitted, the extraordinary developments in mathematics, physics and physiology in Germany at that time. Here the connection between Helmholtz and Kant is fundamental, since 'the Helmholtz effect' transformed the Kantian heritage. Helmholtz did not write a systematic philosophical work, but in redefining fundamental epistemological concepts and constructing a large part of the conceptual structure in which both philosophy and relativistic and quantum physics developed during the early twentieth century, he modified the very problems of epistemology.

1 Epistemology after Kant
2 Sensation/intuition, categories, schema/symbol: redefinitions
3 Conclusions

1 Epistemology after Kant

In its usual nineteenth-century German, philosophical sense, the term epistemology (*Erkenntnistheorie*) designates the theory of knowledge or cognition with a view to the determination of objectifying acts: how can the subject transform *phenomena*, which are given to it, into *objects* of cognition? In this sense epistemology, in the nineteenth century, appeared less as a particular doctrine, as it had been for Immanuel KANT, than as a problem: the problem of 'objectification', which the Kantian critique had recast at the centre of a philosophy founded on the concept of *Vorstellung* (representation). Epistemology was, as Harald Höffding repeated in 1925, the most exact part of philosophy, in contrast with the diverse forms of *Lebensphilosophie* (philosophy of life). But it was, for the followers of Kant, something not only to be repeated (against the idealism of Hegel or Schelling) but also something to be adapted (to the advancement of knowledge) and modified.

Helmholtz clearly indicated that the aim of all his work had been to elaborate a general conception of representation which would permit him to establish 'the sources and the degree of legitimacy of our cognitions', adding that no area of learning could ignore this question with impunity. The *Handbuch der physiologischen Optik* (Treatise on Physiological Optics) (1856, 1860, 1867) already stemmed from his ambition to develop the Kantian transcendental aesthetic in the domain of the natural sciences. The famous lecture of 1878, Die Tatsachen in der Wahrnehmung (Facts in Perception) made clear that the basic problem of the natural sciences is the same as that of epistemology: the problem of knowing in what sense our representations correspond to *das Wirkliche* (the actual real; that is to say, for Kant, that which accords with the material conditions of experience). And in the preface to the 1884 edition of his *Vorträge und Reden* (Lectures and Talks), Helmholtz wrote: 'I was a committed Kantian at the beginning of my career and I still am'. To understand where our representations come from and how they are organized, Helmholtz wanted to continue Kant's work. But, in so doing, he radically transformed Kantianism.

2 Sensation/intuition, categories, schema/symbol: redefinitions

Perhaps nothing is more difficult to grasp in the history of philosophy than the operation which consists of preserving a problematic while displacing its centre (or its scaffolding), and of changing the concepts of a language without changing its words. It is exactly this operation which defines 'the Helmholtz effect'. To understand this, we will rely upon the internal architecture of Kantian critique by noting the three questions that Helmholtz found in it.

The first question concerns the apprehension of phenomena. How is that which is given in phenomenal manifestations given to us? Kant had answered this question by distinguishing purely subjective conscious *Empfindung* (perception) from objectively conscious perception or intuition, and by defining pure intuition as the combination of two a priori forms of sensibility (which are thus anterior to all experience): space, the form of external intuitions, and time, the form of internal intuitions. Kant wished, above all, to limit dogmatic metaphysics and to do away with onto-theology; he did not aim to provide the foundation for a psychology and was thus uninterested in analysing sensations. Furthermore, he seemed to assume that the basic constitution of spatiality was correctly described by the axioms of Euclidean geometry; in this sense, whenever a phenomenon is given to us, it is on condition of its localization in ordinary space and time (see KANT, I. §5).

Now, by returning to the questions of sensation and intuition, Helmholtz was first led to recognize the existence of a process of objectification at the level of perception, and then radically to enlarge the concept of intuition. First, with regard to the 'analysis of sensations', until then overshadowed by the transcendental aesthetic, Helmholtz (following his first professor of physiology, J. Müller) showed that sensations are not reflections of real, objective properties of things, but depend essentially on the appropriate sensory receptor, the field of perception, and so on. Extended objects in space only appear to us, in reality, as 'enveloped' in sensations produced by our nervous system. In sensation, there is no relation of resemblance with things, but rather a construction of signs (for example, in depth perception). Correspondence with the external world becomes a matter of *learning* by accumulating 'unconscious inferences'. Second, concerning space and time, Helmholtz showed that what is at issue again are progressively constructed forms of experience. Proposing a new type of empiricism in philosophy of mathematics, he links the structure of spatial intuition to the experience of the free mobility of rigid bodies (this idea of the kinaesthetic constitution of the concept of space was taken up by Edmund HUSSERL) and he anchors the structure of temporal intuition in that of counting and in the concept of ordinal numbers. From that moment on, the forms of sensibility cease to be a priori, while Euclidean geometry and the axioms of arithmetic lose their transcendental status. Conversely, the concept of intuition must be expanded: for the construction of intuition, it suffices that the impressions of the senses, which may correspond to any mode of observation (including the imaginary), be specified in a determinate and nonambiguous manner. This expanded intuition, which Helmholtz sees as the basis of non-Euclidean geometries, paves the way for Husserlian 'categorial intuition'. In addition, we should note that, for their part, Niels BOHR and Werner HEISENBERG adopt the redefinition literally when they come to describe the 'intuitive character' of the new quantum mechanics. In every case, we thus see in Helmholtz a radical displacement of Kantian concepts. For Kant, intuition was an immediate and a priori presentation of phenomena and a specification of the general concept of *Vorstellung* (representation). For Helmholtz, representations become modes of *acquired* presentation, through unconscious inferences (sensations) and systematic work (symbolic languages) at the same time. In addition, intuition, broadly conceived, appears as *interpretation*, which depends simultaneously on the natural environment, the subject's history, the historical condition of languages and forms of thought, and so on.

We can easily see how Helmholtz will transform the

second question he takes from Kant: that of the pure concepts of the understanding, the Categories. For Kant, the basic cognitive process is objectification, and objectification takes place by subsuming our intuitions of phenomena under pure (a priori) concepts. The list of these concepts is closed and ahistoric, for the simple fact that it is derived, at least in principle, from general logic. In scientific cognition, the principles of causality (*Ursache und Wirkung*), of the permanence of substance and of reciprocal action are thus the constitutive principles which allow the transformation of phenomena into objects (see KANT, I. §6). Without going into the details, we can say that Helmholtz imposes upon these principles an essential limitation, while interpreting them as simple, *invariant*, methodological rules *and* introducing historicity into them. Helmholtz, in effect, replaces causality with the idea of *Gesetzlichkeit* (lawfulness), that is to say, the requirement that certain relations amongst certain processes have a nomological character (see LAWS, NATURAL §2). Lawfulness is, in fact, the only possible 'object' for cognition. In science, we do not know the imminent properties of real objects, but only the nomological regularity of recurring relations. There is no isomorphism between the external world and human cognition; simply put, cognition can only develop by presupposing the existence of a sort of parallelism of lawfulness (Heinrich HERTZ develops this idea in his introduction to *Die Prinzipien der Mechanik* (The Principles of Mechanics) (1894), via the concept of a model). On the other hand, in place of the concept of substance, Helmholtz puts that of an invariant element. Most notably, he dissociates substantiality from materiality, which permits him to introduce in 1881 the 'elementary quantum of electricity' (the electron) as a nonmaterial, invariant quantity – a number, not a thing. What we know of the real is what we perceive as invariant, in a manner which is, every time, historically determined, but without our ever being able to found science on a closed system of pure concepts.

Finally, the third 'Kantian question' which is fundamentally reformulated in Helmholtz concerns the *relation* between intuition and concept. For Kant, this relation was established in two different ways, depending on whether the subject matter was, on the one hand, science, or, on the other hand, art, language, religion or teleology. In scientific cognition (the domain of determinative judgments), what made it possible to link intuitions and concepts was the Schematism, the transcendental imagination's 'hidden work' (see KANT, I. §7). In the altogether different domain of reflective judgments – of taste (where the subject relates only to itself and where there cannot be any direct presentation of concepts in sensible intui-

tion), only what Kant called the Symbolism was operative: an indirect mode of knowledge formation, which proceeds by analogy (see KANT, I. §12). This distinction shaped the entire subsequent history of the relationship between the exact and the human sciences during the nineteenth century in Germany (see UNITY OF SCIENCE). It was, however, challenged by the increasingly open suggestion that, in science, as in art or language, there is only one single cognitive process. In this development, which leads from Wilhelm von HUMBOLDT to SCHLICK, CASSIRER and WITTGENSTEIN, Helmholtz plays an essential role because he wants to provide a general theory of signs and symbols – that is, a general theory of cognition in which the Kantian distinction disappears. To be sure, he did no more than propose this: the hints we find in his various articles, and even the lecture of 1878, merely indicate the direction to be followed. But in 1910, Cassirer, in *Substance and Function*, claimed to have found in this theory of signs the idea that, in cognition, humans deal only with 'functional correspondences of one structure to another' – thus making Helmholtz the inspiration for the notion of 'symbolic forms'. And it is difficult not to see the influence of Helmholtz in the generalization of the concept of symbol for twentieth-century philosophers and scholars, from Husserl and Schlick to Bohr and Heisenberg – or even Granger and GOODMAN.

3 Conclusions

Helmholtz stands at a crossroads of research and ideas of diverse origin. He maintained, in a certain sense, the spirit of the Enlightenment in post-Hegelian Germany. But 'the Helmholtz effect' went beyond this. He touched upon the problems and the language of philosophy in a style both new and enduring, a style which has been clandestinely propagated well into the present. In his effort to reflect on each element of the Kantian account of cognition, Helmholtz accomplished, in effect, an unexpected dissolution of the Kantian critique. He analysed sensations, introduced the idea of unconscious memory and reduced intuition to its elementary processes: this reduction put the *body* in the foreground of the formation of all cognition and by so doing subjected geometry and arithmetic to the human *experience* of movement. Furthermore, Helmholtz expanded the concept of intuition and restricted that of causality by substituting for it the idea of lawfulness: this gives the formation of mathematical or physical concepts complete *freedom* with regard to the constraints of objectification via the tetralogy space-time-causality-continuity (which Bohr later used to define 'classical' physics). In addition, by generalizing the concept of symbol, Helmholtz abolished the fundamental Kantian distinction between science on the one hand and merely analogical knowledge on the other: this opened the way to a global conception of cognition as a construction of systems of signs. For those who read Helmholtz, cognition became a learning process anchored in bodily experience. At the same time, it was freed from the illusion in which concepts reflected stable and objective properties of things, and could thus turn towards the simple search for invariance. Finally, cognition emerged everywhere as a symbolic construction (sensations, language, sciences, art or religions), as a historically determined interpretation of that which is perceived as given for a particular epoch. Helmholtz not only brought the nineteenth century to a close, he set the stage for the twentieth in nearly every discipline.

See also: GEOMETRY, PHILOSOPHICAL ISSUES IN §4; LOGICAL POSITIVISM §1; NEO-KANTIANISM; SCIENCE, NINETEENTH CENTURY PHILOSOPHY OF; SPACE; TIME

List of works

Helmholtz, H. von. (1847) *Über die Erhaltung der Kraft: eine physikalische Abhandlung*, Berlin: G. Reimer; trans. R. Taylor, *H. von Helmholtz, Scientific Memoirs*, London: Tyndall & Francis, 1853. (Introduction of the mathematical principle of conservation of energy.)

—— (1856, 1860, 1867) *Handbuch der physiologischen Optik*, Leipzig: Leopold Voss, 3 vols; 3rd edn, 1909–11; trans. J.P.C. Southhall, *Helmholtz's Treatise on Physiological Optics*, New York: Optical Society of America, 1925; repr. New York: Dover, 1962. (The translation is of the 3rd edn of 1867.)

—— (1863) *Die Lehre von den Tonempfindungen als physiologische Grundlage für die Theorie der Musik*, Brauschweig: Vieweg; trans. A. Ellis, *On the Sensations of Tone as a Physiological Basis for the Theory of Music*, London: Longmans, 1875, 1885; repr. New York: Dover, 1954.

—— (1882–95) *Wissenschaftliche Abhandlungen*, Leipzig: J.A. Barth, 3 vols. (With a bibliography.)

—— (1883) *Vorträge und Reden*, Braunschweig: Vieweg, 2 vols; 3rd edn, 1884; 5th edn, 1903. (See especially, on the philosophy of mathematics, 'Über die Tatsachen die der Geometrie zugrunde liegen', 1868, 'Über den Ursprung und die Bedeutung der geometrischen Axiome', 1870 and 'Zählen und Messen', 1887; reprinted in M. Schlick and P. Hertz (eds) *Schriften zur Erkenntnistheorie*, Berlin: Springer, 1921; translation by M. Lowe *Epistemo-*

logical Writings, Dordrecht: Reidel, 1977. See also, on the general philosophy of knowledge, 'Die Tatsachen in der Wahrnehmung'.)

Kahl, R. (ed.) (1971) *Selected Writings of H. von Helmholtz*, Middletown, CT: Wesleyan University Press. (Recent compilation.)

References and further reading

Cahan, D. (ed.) (1993) *Hermann von Helmholtz and the Foundations of XIX Century Science*, Berkeley, CA: University of California Press. (Good synthesis of Helmholtz. Includes an overall bibliography of secondary literature.)

Koenigsberger, L. (1902–3) *Hermann von Helmholtz*, Braunschweig: F. Vieweg und Sohn, 3 vols; abridged English trans. F.A. Welby, Oxford, 1906; repr. New York, 1965. (The standard biography.)

Turner, S. (1970–80) 'Hermann von Helmholtz', in C. Gillispie (ed.) *Dictionary of Scientific Biography*, New York: Charles Scribner's Sons, 16 vols. (Short treatment of his life and scientific work.)

Translated by J. Maskit

CATHERINE CHEVALLEY

HELMONT, FRANCISCUS MERCURIUS VAN (1614–98)

Although he lived in the seventeenth century, van Helmont belongs more to late Renaissance than to modern intellectual culture. He was a larger-than-life figure who, in his prime, had an international reputation as an alchemist and a physician. His metaphysical interests came increasingly to the fore, however, and he became particularly associated with Kabbalistic doctrines. A friend of Locke and Henry More, he was also closely connected with Anne Conway and Leibniz, with whom he shared many intellectual affinities. It is these connections that make his philosophy – in particular, his theodicy and his monadology – of enduring interest.

Franciscus Mercurius van Helmont was born at Vilvoorde, near Brussels. His father, Jean-Baptiste van Helmont, was a famous Paracelsian medic who made a significant contribution to the history of chemistry, especially to the theory of gases. Like his father, Francis became famous as both doctor and alchemist. He too was harassed by the Inquisition, from whom he escaped only by giving up the estate he had inherited. Later, in the freer context of the Protestant Netherlands, he was able to publish many of his father's writings that had been previously suppressed. Indeed he became a publisher of many religiously heterodox works and, with characteristic courage, allowed his name to be associated with some whose actual author was anonymous. For this reason a number of works were mistakenly attributed to him. Even those of which he was the author were often produced by collaboration, or written up by others on the basis of conversations with him.

Van Helmont's first book was concerned with developing the idea of an alphabet of nature, a natural rather than a conventional language originally spoken by Adam. He made practical proposals arising from his theory for teaching those born deaf to speak and to understand speech, which some implemented with success. Over time, however, he became less interested in experiments and more metaphysical than his father had ever been, partly through the influence of Knorr von Rosenruth with whom he collaborated on a German translation of Boethius' *De Consolatione Philosophiae*. He also assisted him in collecting together the mostly Hebrew texts made available for the first time in the Latin *Kabbala denudata* in 1677 and 1684, to which he contributed writings which include his *Cabbalistical Dialogue*, a classic defence of Kabbalistic metaphysics.

Van Helmont was physician to Lady Anne CON-WAY from 1670 until her death in 1679. They came to share not only a commitment to Kabbalistic metaphysics and Biblical interpretation but also an involvement with the Quaker movement. He saw to the publication of her Platonic/Kabbalist *Principles of the Most Ancient and Modern Philosophy*. Although outside the mainstream of Modern philosophy, he became a good friend of LOCKE whom he met at the Lantern Club in Rotterdam and with whom he spent the winter of 1693–4 during his last visit to England. Like van Helmont, Locke was also a physician, but the bond between them seems to have been a sceptical and liberal attitude concerning speculative matters of religious importance.

Of greater philosophical significance was his friendship with Leibniz, with whom he was associated in the early 1670s and again in the late 1690s. The extent to which they belonged to the same intellectual tradition is shown by their accounts of evil and of matter. For van Helmont and others there is a puzzle as to how God, a wholly perfect being, could have created pain and suffering, supposing these to be evils. There is also a problem of how, if God is pure spirit, he could have produced something as alien to himself as matter. Van Helmont's solution to the first problem lay in a form of optimism in which God is claimed to allow no more suffering than is necessary. As to belief in hell, all punishment is 'medicinal' and no soul is

ultimately lost. His opposition to the arbitrary and vindictive god of some of the major Christian denominations is reflected in this view. He also followed the Lurianic Kabbalah in adopting the doctrine of the evolution of human souls through twelve lives, linked to belief in the eventual progress of every soul to eternal happiness. He managed to secure quite a following for this view among the English Quakers, until it was quashed in a revival of orthodoxy in the early 1690s.

Van Helmont's solution to the problem of the existence of matter is analogous to his treatment of the problem of evil, with the counterpart to optimism being a form of idealism, that is an affirmation that only spirit is ultimately real. Matter, being antithetical to God's nature, cannot result from that nature, and so is not so much a reality as a privation. A philosophy, such as Aristotelianism, that affirms the reality of matter must, he thought, deny the existence of a spirit creator. According to van Helmont's Neoplatonic-Kabbalistic theory, the monads emanate as pure spirits from the divinity. But these sparks of divinity eventually become 'dull' and 'sluggish', coalescing to form what is called matter. Yet the monads, though they are in a degenerate state of 'privation', do not entirely lose their individual or spiritual character, which *'fundamentally'* and *radically'* they retain. Their material state is only transitory, according to van Helmont, and they will eventually return 'to a more loose and free state'.

Leibniz's solutions to these problems, though they have affinities, are more complex and less obviously open to objection (see LEIBNIZ, G.W. §§2–6). Between the early 1670s, when van Helmont impressed Leibniz in long and deep discussions, and the 1690s, when he visited Hanover as an old man, Leibniz himself had changed. He had become too much of a Modern not to be embarrassed by van Helmont. The work published in his friend's name often lacked rigour, sophistication and paid no attention to recent developments in the sciences. Van Helmont was fluent in Dutch and German but not in Latin or English, and so could only produce works in these languages by recruiting the support of people whose versions of his thought did not, in Leibniz's view, do him justice. This may be partly why Leibniz himself was willing to help in the production of van Helmont's last Kabbalistic work on the Book of Genesis, being entirely responsible for the Latin and even being to some extent a co-author. It was shortly after this collaboration that van Helmont returned to the Brabant to settle his affairs. After his death his niece turned to Leibniz for an epitaph, but appears to have ignored his plea to publish some of her uncle's literary remains.

See also: KABBALAH

List of works

Helmont, F.M. van (1667) *Alphabeti vere naturalis Hebraici brevissima Delineatio*, Sultzbach. (Van Helmont's theory of a natural 'Adamic' language.)

—— (1682) *A Cabbalistical Dialogue in Answer to the Opinion of a Learned Doctor in Philosophy and Theology that the World was Made of Nothing*, London. (English translation from the Latin edition of Part I of the *Kabbala denudata* which includes *A Rabbinical and Paraphrastical Exposition of Genesis I*. This is the most concise statement of van Helmont's Kabbalistical theory of the origin of matter.)

—— (1684) *Two Hundred Queries Moderately Propounded concerning the Doctrine of the Revolution of Humane Souls and Its Conformity to the Truths of Christianity*, London. (The main account of van Helmont's theory of transmigration.)

—— (1697) *Quaedam praemeditatae et consideratae cogitationes super quatuor priora capita libri primi Moysis*, Amsterdam; trans. as *Some Premeditate and Considerate Thoughts on the first four Chapters of the first book of Moses called Genesis*, London, 1701. (A Kabbalistic interpretation of the Biblical story of the creation.)

References and further reading

Brown, S. (1989) 'Leibniz and More's Cabbalistic Circle', in S. Hutton (ed.) *Of Mysticism and Mechanism: Tercentenary Studies of Henry More (1614–1687)*, Dordrecht: Nijhoff. (Develops affinities between Leibniz's monadology and those of van Helmont and others.)

—— (1997) 'F.M. van Helmont: his philosophical connections and the reception of his later Cabbalistic philosophy (1677–1699)', in *Oxford Studies in Seventeenth Century Philosophy*, ed. M.A. Stewart, Oxford: Oxford University Press. (Includes accounts of van Helmont's relationships with both Locke and Leibniz, as well of his extensive publications in English.)

Coudert, A. (1975) 'A Cambridge Platonist's Kabbalist Nightmare', *Journal of the History of Ideas* 36: 633–52. (A good account of Henry More's involvement with van Helmont.)

—— (1978) 'Some Theories of a Natural Language from the Renaissance to the Seventeenth Century', *Studia Leibnitiana Sonderheft* 7: 56–114. (Focuses particularly on the context of van Helmont's *Alphabet of Nature*.)

—— (1995) *Leibniz and the Kabbalah*, Dordrecht: Kluwer. (Argues that van Helmont was an important influence on Leibniz.)

STUART BROWN

HELP AND BENEFICENCE

Which people are we morally required to help, and to what extent? In a world where the basic needs of many millions remain unmet, this is a philosophical question of great practical urgency. A minimal position is that while it is always praiseworthy to help someone, we are morally required to help only those to whom we stand in some special relation. In addition to the objection that it is too minimal, this view faces difficulties in accounting for emergency cases, in which one could, for example, save a stranger's life at little cost to oneself. More stringent views that place no restrictions on the range of people to be helped do not have these difficulties; they do, however, raise the intractable problem of how much we must sacrifice for the sake of others.

1 **Principles of beneficence**
2 **The problem of demands**

1 **Principles of beneficence**

A requirement to help or benefit a person to whom one stands in some special relation (such as a family member) is a 'special obligation'. A requirement to benefit people generally is a 'principle of beneficence'. Some principles of beneficence require us to promote other possible aspects of 'the good' in addition to human wellbeing, but our focus is on this central case. Further, as our topic is the general form principles of beneficence might take, we will not consider different possible accounts of wellbeing (see EUDAIMONIA; HAPPINESS), though of course any actual principle of beneficence requires such an account. Nor will we discuss the problems that arise when a person who could genuinely be helped opposes the intervention (see AUTONOMY, ETHICAL; PATERNALISM).

The idea of a general principle of beneficence, as distinct from special obligations, has roots in the West in Judaism and Stoicism, and was developed in Christianity in the form of the virtue of charity (see CHARITY). We should note here that possession of a virtue involves a certain motivational state, whereas following a duty or obligation need not (see VIRTUES AND VICES §§4–5; DUTY §3). The scope of this entry, however, does not extend to the question of ethically appropriate motives, nor to the question of the 'natural' motivational sources of beneficent action (see MORAL MOTIVATION).

Locke understood charity as requiring us to meet the serious needs of any person (1690); this is a more stringent requirement than the duty of beneficence Kant argued for (1797) (see §2). But the modern moral philosophers who take beneficence most seriously are the utilitarians: the whole of morality, on their view, consists in a requirement to promote – indeed to maximize – the good (see UTILITARIANISM). And the utilitarian tradition has no doubt influenced many non-utilitarians in their attitude to beneficence. It is notable, for example, that W.D. Ross (1930), who argued strongly against the reduction of all of morality to beneficence, accepted, as part of morality, a duty of beneficence of the same stringent maximizing form as the utilitarian principle.

Recognition of a principle of beneficence of some form continues to be common in moral philosophy in the late twentieth century, even among philosophers who reject the primacy of duty and obligation: 'virtue theorists' are likely to discuss a virtue of charity or benevolence (see VIRTUE ETHICS). There is, however, an important school of thought, with historical roots in parts of the social contract tradition, that relegates beneficence to the realm of the supererogatory (that is, morally good but not morally required) (see SUPEREROGATION §§4–6). This position is at its most plausible in the context of a liberal egalitarian theory of justice, such as that of John Rawls (1971) (see RAWLS, J.). The idea is not merely that a just institutional scheme will remove the need for individual acts of beneficence, but that on a proper moral understanding, requirements of justice exhaust the normative domain claimed for requirements of beneficence. An important objection to this view is that it leaves it unclear what is required of a well-off individual in an unjust society; this problem is especially serious in the international sphere, where the prospect for institutions that promote distributive justice is remote. Advocates of the view could reply that unmet human needs do indeed raise an urgent moral issue, but that it is extravagant to respond to this issue by attributing responsibility for the well-being of all humanity to each moral agent (see §2). Rather, we should see the responsibility of individuals as mediated: they are required to support reform of the institutional structures that allow the needs to remain unmet.

There is a further difficulty for a moral account in which beneficence is supererogatory. While 'ordinary' moral thought is by no means settled on the issue of beneficence generally, it does seem to be so on the special case of easy assistance in emergency situations. That it would be wrong to walk away from a child drowning in a shallow pond seems so uncontroversial a claim that some philosophers, notably Peter Singer (1972), have seen in such 'rescue' cases firm intuitive foundations for an argument for a general principle of beneficence. This argument could be blocked by offering some principled distinction between rescue and non-rescue cases and by suggesting that the former generate some kind of special obligation. It is by no means clear, however, that a principled distinction is available.

2 The problem of demands

A principle of beneficence makes each of us responsible, in some sense and to some degree, for the wellbeing of everyone else. As we have noted, this can seem to be an extravagant position. The underlying worry here is simply that principles of beneficence require too much from individuals. Applied to utilitarianism, this 'over-demandingness objection' is long-standing, going back at least to Henry SIDGWICK. But the issue of over-demandingness has received most attention since the 1970s, stimulated in part by a more general attack on modern moral theories that has centred around the work of Bernard WILLIAMS.

It might be thought that the cause of the extreme demands of the utilitarian principle is that it requires us to promote all aspects of the wellbeing of others, and that a more plausible principle of beneficence would require us to meet only the most basic of human needs, such as those for food, shelter, and health care. A principle of beneficence, however, that requires us to do whatever we can to meet even just these needs remains, in the circumstances of the late twentieth century, extremely demanding on individuals. The principle would, of course, be much less demanding if all or most people complied with it, but clearly we cannot assume ideal levels of compliance when assessing actual demands. (That the utilitarian principle is extremely demanding is sometimes denied on the grounds that an individual is rarely in a position to make great sacrifice that will be beneficial on the whole; this claim is typically based on scepticism about, for example, the effectiveness of humanitarian aid programmes.)

The real cause of the extreme demands of the utilitarian principle is its maximizing form: it requires individuals to promote the good up to the point where further sacrifice would burden them as much as it would benefit others. If extreme demands are objectionable, then a possible plausible principle of beneficence would seem to be one that requires sacrifice only up to a certain point. As an example there is the Judaeo-Christo-Islamic idea of giving up a 'tithe' or tenth of what one produces or earns. The problem, however, is to identify the criteria that would justify any particular limit to demands. Indeed it is on reflection difficult to accept that there could be a limit to required sacrifice that remains fixed whatever the changes in circumstances.

Other non-maximizing principles are possible. Thus Kant's duty of beneficence, on some interpretations, requires agents to adopt a 'maxim' of benefiting others, where this is compatible with acting to benefit others only rarely and in minor ways. For someone who takes beneficence seriously, this will be an unacceptably minimal principle. Likewise, the suggestion that no particular degree of beneficence is morally required, that all we need say is 'the more the better', will be seen as too close to the view that beneficence is supererogatory. A third view is motivated by a concern not with the extent of the demands of a maximizing principle, but with the way it imposes demands when not everyone is complying with it. As we have noted, a maximizing principle typically demands more of a complying agent as the number of other people complying decreases; this is to make agents responsible not just for their own 'share' of the demands of beneficence, but also for the shares of everyone else. If this is objectionable we could consider a principle of beneficence that requires agents to sacrifice only as much as it would be optimal for them to sacrifice under full compliance. Among other problems, it is not clear that this suggestion can account for rescue cases.

See also: CONSEQUENTIALISM; EGOISM AND ALTRUISM; SUFFERING; VULNERABILITY AND FINITUDE; IMPARTIALITY

References and further reading

Aiken, W. and La Follette, H. (eds) (1996) *World Hunger and Morality*, Upper Saddle River, NJ: Prentice Hall. (Useful introductory collection on the topic.)

Cohen, J. (1981) 'Who is Starving Whom?', *Theoria* 157: 65–81. (Defends a principle of beneficence requiring people to do only their 'fair share'.)

Kagan, S. (1989) *The Limits of Morality*, Oxford: Clarendon Press. (Defends a maximizing principle of beneficence.)

* Kant, I. (1797) *Metaphysische Anfangsgründe der Tugendlehre*, trans. J.W. Ellington, *Metaphysical Principles of Virtue*, Indianapolis, IN: Hackett Publishing Company, 1964. (Advocates less stringent principle of beneficence.)

* Locke, J. (1690) *Two Treatises of Government*, ed. P. Laslett, Cambridge: Cambridge University Press, 1963. (Suggests we are required to meet the serious needs of any person.)

Murphy, L. (1993) 'The Demands of Beneficence', *Philosophy and Public Affairs* 22 (4): 267–92. (General discussion of the problem of demands and defence of a principle of beneficence requiring people to sacrifice only as much as it would be optimal to sacrifice under full compliance.)

Nagel, T. (1986) *The View From Nowhere*, New York: Oxford University Press, ch. 10. (Influential general discussion of the problem of demands.)

O'Neill, O. (1989) 'The Great Maxims of Justice and Charity', in *Constructions of Reason*, Cambridge: Cambridge University Press. (Defends a broadly Kantian approach, and includes a very helpful discussion of the liberal egalitarian interpretation of benficence.)

Paul, E.F., Miller, F.D. and Paul, J. (eds) (1987) *Beneficence, Philanthropy and the Public Good*, New York: Blackwell. (Collection devoted to beneficence, offering a variety of approaches.)

Paul, E.F., Miller, F.D. and Paul, J. (eds) (1993) *Altruism*, New York: Cambridge University Press. (Collection featuring different perspectives on altruism.)

* Rawls, J. (1971) *A Theory of Justice*, Cambridge, MA: Harvard University Press. (Influential contemporary theory of justice.)

* Ross, W.D. (1930) *The Right and the Good*, Oxford: Clarendon Press; repr., Indianapolis, IN: Hackett Publishing Company, 1988. (Advocates the principle of beneficence as one among others.)

Scheffler, S. (1992) *Human Morality*, New York: Oxford University Press. (Defends limits to required sacrifice.)

* Singer, P. (1972) 'Famine, Affluence, and Morality', *Philosophy and Public Affairs* 1 (3): 229–43; repr. in W. Aiken and H. La Follette (eds) *World Hunger and Morality*, Upper Saddle River, NJ: Prentice Hall, 1996. (Influential article, claiming that morality requires us to sacrifice our interests for those in the developing world.)

Unger, P. (1996) *Living High and Leting Die*, New York: Oxford University Press. (Extensive discussion of the difficulty of distinguishing between rescue cases and non-rescue cases, and defence of a stringent requirement to help those in need.)

Williams, B. (1981) 'Persons, Character and Morality', in *Moral Luck: Philosophical Papers 1973–80*, Cambridge: Cambridge University Press. (Criticism of the strict impartiality of modern moral theory.)

LIAM B. MURPHY

HELVÉTIUS, CLAUDE-ADRIEN (1715–71)

Helvétius was one of the most noteworthy and notorious figures of the French Enlightenment. In common with his fellow philosophes, *he asserted that all philosophical discussions should be based on the empiricism of Locke's* Essay on Human Understanding *(1689). But unlike Voltaire, d'Alembert, and the other members of 'the party of humanity', Helvétius took literally the notion that each person is a* tabula rasa *at birth – he boldly argued the case for unabashed environmental determinism. We are what our surroundings have made us, and nothing more.*

Immediately after Helvétius published De l'Esprit *in 1758, the Catholic authorities cited his book as definitive proof that the* philosophes *were out to destroy religion, throne, family, and all that is sacred. Only the struggle between court and parliament over control of censorship, along with his ties to Madame de Pompadour and the Duc de Choiseul, saved Helvétius. After suffering the indignity of three recantations, he decided upon posthumous publication of his second major work,* De l'Homme *(1773).*

Not a single philosophe *accepted Helvétius' view that the mind is a completely passive recipient of data received through the senses; nor did any of his comrades second his constantly reiterated claim that all sensibility may be reduced to physical sensations. Some privately expressed their exasperation that Helvétius published so much that seemed to vindicate every charge the Church lodged against them: that they were materialists, advocates of free love, and champions of a scandalous hedonism. Nevertheless at least a few of the* philosophes, *after setting aside the philosophical suppositions of* De l'Esprit, *came to appreciate that the larger concern of Helvétius was with their own search for the social and political preconditions of an independent intelligentsia, the would-be agents of Enlightenment.*

1 Philosophy
2 Politics and the Arts
3 Conclusion

1 Philosophy

An empiricist, a materialist, and a utilitarian, Helvétius was in every respect a son of the French Enlightenment, yet his fellow *philosophes* remained wary of his writings, which they regarded as a *reductio ad absurdum* of their own.

When Helvétius began his studies with the announcement that all the faculties of the human mind – memory, imagination, judgment, reason – can be reduced to sensation, he undoubtedly believed he was merely repeating what CONDILLAC had set forth in his celebrated *Treatise on Sensations* (1754). Neither Condillac nor any of the *philosophes* had anything but praise for Locke's attack on innate ideas (see LOCKE, J.). Where Locke went wrong, in Condillac's estimation, was in his retention of the notion of innate mental faculties. Conducting one of the most memorable thought-experiments of the century, Condillac slowly brought a hypothetical statue-man to life, first by endowing it with one sense after another, then by showing how one sense comes to the aid of another, until a being emerges whose mind possesses all the higher mental faculties.

To the *philosophes* the *Treatise on Sensations* was a method of research; it provided the means to disprove all notions of innate ideas, especially as used by the Church to place its views beyond the reach of criticism. Alone among their numbers, and much to their dismay, Helvétius transformed Condillac's method into a system of reductionist philosophy. No longer did the investigation end when painstaking analytical and genetic procedure slowly uncovered the hidden sensual roots of a given faculty of mind. Rather, the books of Helvétius begin with the dogmatic assertion that none of the faculties is anything more than the passive product of sense experience.

No support was forthcoming for the position staked out by Helvétius, not even – as the response of DIDEROT attests – from other materialists. Overwhelmingly in the eighteenth century, French materialists grounded their position in the newly emerging sciences of life. Sensitive matter, to Diderot, acts on its surroundings no less than the environment shapes matter. Where Helvétius denied the significance of organic constitution, Diderot believed that much of an individual's character is given from the beginning, and will ultimately win out regardless of environmental circumstances. To Helvétius a new environment makes a new person; to Diderot criminals cannot be rehabilitated because it is impossible to override heredity and physical organization.

In ethics Helvétius was a hedonist and a utilitarian, so it is understandable that BENTHAM regarded *De l'Esprit* and *De l'Homme* as forerunners of his work, all the more so since on more than one occasion Helvétius uttered words virtually identical to Bentham's formula of 'the greatest good of the greatest number'. But had Bentham taken a closer look, he might well have rejected the notion that Helvétius was his predecessor; for hedonism as understood by Bentham had only the slightest connection with sexual liberation and was in every respect the opposite of a heroic ethic. How shocked, then, Bentham would have been to realize that the primary objective of Helvétius was to recreate the heroic values of antiquity in the modern world, a goal the Frenchman sought to pursue through the lure of sexual rewards.

Surprisingly, it was to ancient Sparta that Helvétius looked for a model of a sexually liberated social existence. Previously Sparta had been regarded as the home of a repressive civic virtue, a city whose citizens were forced to be free, forced to live in accordance with the dictates of their 'higher selves'. Self-denial and self-overcoming, a constant and painful effort to put the public good above private interest − these themes, long associated with Sparta, were sometimes admired by the *philosophes* but always rejected, because the virtue of Spartans sounded too much like the monkish virtue they despised. Altogether different was the Sparta depicted by Helvétius. Drawing upon Plutarch's life of Lycurgus, Helvétius conjured up a Sparta in which men eagerly engaged in noble deeds for their country because the greatest citizens were granted the sexual favours of the most beautiful women. 'Lycurgus made love one of the principal springs of legislation' (1758, II: 15); he understood that it is great passions that lead to great actions, and was wise enough to stir up grand emotions through the custom of having naked young women dance in front of youthful soldiers, praising the brave men and shaming the cowards.

All the *philosophes* agreed that the reverse side of denying original sin was an affirmation of the joys of sexuality. They also concurred that virtue and self-interest should not be set in opposition to one another; their shared view was that society should be so ordered that everyone has an interest in acting virtuously. However, it was one thing for Diderot to praise the free sexuality of Tahitians in an unpublished essay and quite another for Helvétius to publish and sign his name to an equally audacious proposal, and to imply, unlike Diderot, that his findings were directly applicable to the Europe of his day. The official Diderot, the public spokesman for the cause of enlightenment, was the author of *The Natural Son* (1757) and *The Father of the Family* (17??), two plays that endorsed conventional familial ideals in language that could not have been more exclamatory.

Diderot complained that Helvétius spent so much time attempting to prove that his kennelman, if placed in the proper environment, could have written *De l'Esprit*; he gasped in disbelief when he saw that Helvétius, in reducing everything to physical sensibility, was forever trying to explain the accomplishments of a genius in terms of copulation and defecation. Still, that did not prevent Diderot from

placing *De l'Esprit* 'among the great books of the century'.

What was it that Diderot and some of the other *philosophes*, for all their misgivings, admired in the writings of Helvétius? Above all, they gained a political education from his works; his conviction, that only through better legislation would humans ever have an interest in being virtuous, became theirs as well. 'Morality is only a frivolous science unless blended with politics and legislation', wrote Helvétius (1758, II: 15), 'from which I conclude that, to be useful to the world, philosophers must consider objects from the viewpoint of the legislator'. Originally Diderot and many of the *philosophes* showed very little interest in forms of government; it was from Helvétius, a political thinker from the outset, that they learned how intimately their concerns about literature and the arts were tied to questions about politics.

2 Politics and the Arts

Both *De l'Esprit* and *De l'Homme* are primarily studies of the social situation of the *gens de lettres*, the intellectuals, under different political regimes. The maturity or childishness of the audience, its willingness or refusal to be instructed as well as entertained, the popularity of certain literary genres and the irrelevance of others, the inspiration or desperation of the writer − these matters and more hinge on the type of political regime that rules a country, argued Helvétius.

Helvétius adapted his study of the links between politics and the arts from MONTESQUIEU. But before taking anything from the *Spirit of the Laws* (1748), Helvétius deleted Montesquieu's chapters on climate. Why rule out in advance the possibility that the peoples of some parts of the world can ever hope to live under better conditions, inquired Helvétius, when political and social explanations suffice to account for their present predicament?

Although he rejected climate as a causal explanation, Helvétius kept intact the entirety of Montesquieu's typology of political regimes, the division of governments into feudal monarchies, Oriental despotisms, and republics ancient and modern. Sparta, as we have seen, was the ancient republic most frequently cited by Helvétius; England, called by Montesquieu a 'republic hiding under the form of a monarchy', was the country Helvétius constantly alluded to when he wished to draw a contrast between the monarchy France was and the republic he desired it to be.

The constant complaint of Helvétius was that 'our [French] mores and the form of our government do not permit us to deliver ourselves to strong passions'.

Under monarchy, petty intrigue at court to enhance one's reputation takes the place in politics that under a republic is filled by the ambition of citizens to win fame for doing great deeds for their country. Wherever monarchy is triumphant, there are subjects rather than citizens, and the socially best-placed of these subjects care only for their personal advantage and that of their family name. A good aristocratic father in France will use all his influence to secure a public office for his incompetent son. How different was the world of republican Rome wherein Brutus did not hesitate to sacrifice his sons for the sake of preserving the public good.

From top to bottom of the social scale Helvétius found nothing to admire and much to condemn in the France of his day. So downtrodden were the peasants, so dehumanized were they by the brutality of the nobles, that Helvétius deemed the life of savages preferable to that of the simple folk living in the French countryside. Nor, for that matter, was the existence of Parisians as admirable as foreign visitors were wont to believe. Beneath the glamour and brilliance of operas, dramas, and salons lay a disturbing human reality. To be successful in social life, Helvétius noted, a man must have a pliable character that assumes as many shapes as the number of mansions he visits. Perhaps it is no accident that it was shortly after the publication of De l'Esprit that Diderot penned a memorable depiction of a 'man without character', who had 'no greater opposite than himself', in Rameau's Nephew (1762–74).

The novelty of Helvétius lies in his efforts to apply Montesquieu's sociopolitical models to the study of literature and the arts. Each type of political regime, the despotic, the monarchical, and the republican, shapes culture in its own image, Helvétius believed. Montesquieu had hinted as much: he had gone so far as to suggest that satirical writings cutting the powerful down to size thrive in England because in that nation society no longer revolves around feudal privilege and legally sanctioned class hierarchy. It was left for Helvétius to convert Montesquieu's passing suggestions into a systematic treatise on politics and the arts.

About Oriental despotism Helvétius had relatively little to say. He was willing, however, to risk a few statements on the subject of politics and the arts in the non-Western world. It was his contention that Oriental authors, if they ever told the truth, had to present their thoughts in coded form. 'Under submission to arbitrary power,... it is certain that writers must insensibly contract the habit of thinking allegorically' (1758, III: 29). Since the historians of despotic countries, unlike the poets, cannot hide behind a veil of allusions and symbols, their account of the past is inevitably a pack of tricks the living play on the dead.

For the most part Helvétius concentrates his energies on drawing a series of sharp contrasts between the vitality of the arts and letters in republican England and the waning of literary glory in monarchical France. Living in a nation that is not politically free, looking up to grands who are idle, spoiled, and vain, the French are 'the most gallant, the most loveable, but the most frivolous people of Europe' (1758, II: 20). Boileau, repeating Horace, had indicated that the calling of the writer is to instruct as well as to please; Helvétius, however, complained bitterly that the French, 'by the form of our government, have less need of instruction than of amusement' (1758, II: 20). Love affairs, flirtations, coquetry, changes of fashion in clothing, and other private matters, none capable of stirring great passions, are the concerns of monarchical subjects. One trivial preoccupation supplants another with remarkable rapidity in France because persons confined to the pettiness of private lives are readily bored. For years the explicit objective of the philosophes had been to mould the new phenomenon they referred to as 'public opinion'; Helvétius' response was to point out that a public exists only where there is a republic.

'In London it is a merit to be instructed; in Paris it is ridiculous' (1758, II: 20). Inevitably, then, the English writer is inspired, the French writer diminished, by the audience.

In a free state a man conceives the highest thoughts and can express them as vividly as they enter his mind. Such is not the case in monarchical states: in these countries the interest of certain corporations, that of various powerful individuals, and most of all a false and small politics, thwart the élans of genius.

(De l'Esprit, IV, ch. 4)

Helvétius was typically French in his belief that drama is the highest of the arts, and he was typical of his century in his conviction that the theatre of his day was inferior to that of the grand siècle. But he sounded a new note when he offered a political explanation of the decline of French drama. In republican England, he suggested, the grandeur of the tragic genre still holds sway; by contrast, in monarchical France the pettiness of comedy dominates the stage. Tragedies similar to those written by Corneille during a period of sedition and grand passions continue to be well received in England; but in France, beginning with Racine, the corrupted audience has become as indifferent to uplifting public themes as it is eager for love stories.

I say that in every country where the inhabitants have no part in the management of public affairs, where the words *patrie* and *citoyen* are rarely cited, one does not please the public except in representing on the stage passions agreeable to [private] individuals, such as those of love.

(*De l'Esprit*, II, ch. 19)

Romantic love makes us small; love of country enhances our stature, and there is no better way to promote great civic passion than through offering sexual rewards which satisfy the cravings of physical sensibility. Greek tragedies were as replete with civic lessons as they were devoid of the motif of romantic love. Modern playwrights may yet return to the model set by Sophocles, provided modern legislators precede them in copying the political strategies of Lycurgus. In the posthumous *De l'Homme* Helvétius proposed to convert France into a federation of thirty republics, each animated by civic passion.

3 Conclusion

One of the favourite topics of the *philosophes* was the question of how the intellectuals could become independent and influential voices for enlightenment in a social world based on privilege, wealth and patronage. It was Helvétius who convinced at least a few of the *philosophes*, especially those who remained outside the academies, that only a political solution would suffice. In a civic society writers will be inspired by an enlightened audience and rewarded for their creative efforts. Until the dawn of the new era, the best book will be the one that champions the republican cause.

Evidence of what some *philosophes* eventually borrowed from Helvétius, as well as what they chose to repudiate, may be found in the *Système social* of the Baron d'Holbach, published fifteen years after *De l'Esprit* and at virtually the same time as *De l'Homme*. Almost word for word Holbach repeated the arguments of Helvétius against dramas revolving around the theme of romantic love and in favour of tragedies modelled on those of ancient Greece. Again echoing Helvétius, Holbach complained that the French were a frivolous people, the women especially because they had been miseducated by erotic paintings and literature, in consequence of which the favourite pastime of the *grands* was adultery.

When it came to women Helvétius and Holbach could not have been more similar in their diagnosis, nor more different in their solutions. Holbach advocated that women withdraw from high society to the privacy of their families. Motherhood, fidelity, and a restoration of traditional familial virtues was

his message. Only if women accept the sanctity of marriage will men recover from their socially induced corruption. Helvétius, in dramatic contrast, would abolish the remnants of feminine modesty so that 'the favours of women, becoming more common, will appear less precious' (1758, II: 20). Long ago Plato had made a similar suggestion, and Lycurgus – Helvétius believed – had transformed theory into practice.

Helvétius was not a great thinker, but he was surely one of the most daring writers of his age.

See also: D'ALEMBERT, J.; ENLIGHTENMENT, CONTINENTAL; VOLTAIRE, F.-M. A. DE

List of works

Helvétius, C.-A. (1758) *De l'Esprit*, Paris: Arthème Fayard, 1988.
—— (1773) *De l'Homme*, Paris: Arthème Fayard, 1989, 2 vols.
(The English translations date from the eighteenth century and are unreliable.)

References and further reading

Andlau, B. (1939) *Helvétius, Seigneur de Voré*, Paris: Fernand Sorlot. (For information about his life and family.)
Smith, D.W. (1965) *Helvétius, a Study in Persecution*, Oxford: Clarendon Press. (For the politics of censorship.)
(A good study of the thought of Helvétius has yet to be written.)

MARK HULLIUNG

HEMERKEN, THOMAS
see THOMAS À KEMPIS

HEMPEL, CARL GUSTAV (1905–)

Hempel's defence of Carnap's and Neurath's physicalism testifies to the presence of certain 'postmodern' themes in logical empiricism (or logical positivism): (1) a textualist turn to sentences from the facts or reality they are said to report; (2) a pragmatic turn from truth to inclusion in the text as the basic scientific concern; and (3) a descriptive turn from logic to empirical sociology of science.

Throughout his philosophical writings Hempel held that the question of what truth-claims mean should be replaced by the question of what criteria we use in deciding whether or not to call sentences true. Granted that 'Whales are mammals' is true if and only if whales are mammals, the question remains of how observation reports bear on whether or not to include a sentence in the text of current knowledge, and how received observation sentences may be dropped from it. For Hempel, then, the problem of analysing the concept of confirmation of sentences by sentences is either the heart of the problem of truth or the successor to that problem. Like Carnap, in 1945 he thought such an analysis necessary to connect the terms 'logical' and 'empiricism'; but four decades later he would conclude that, after all, one must 'leave the decision in matters of confirmation to the intuitive appraisal of the scientist' (1945b: 98).

1   **Life**
2   **Confirmation**
3   **Law and explanation**
4   **Theoreticity and cognitive significance**
5   **The career of logical positivism**

1   Life

Born in Oranienburg of Prussian stock, Carl Gustav Hempel (called 'Peter' since his school days) studied mathematics, physics and philosophy at Göttingen, Heidelberg, Vienna and Berlin, where he received the Ph.D. in 1934 for work with Hans REICHENBACH, lately dismissed from his professorship on account of his Jewish ancestry. In Brussels (1934–7) he was employed by his fellow exile Paul Oppenheim as a philosophical tutor-collaborator. When Oppenheim left Belgium in anticipation of a German invasion, CARNAP obtained a research grant for Hempel, taking him to Chicago (1937–8). In time he found teaching posts at City and Queens Colleges (New York, 1939–48) and Yale (1948–55). Much courted, he then taught at Princeton (1955–75) and other universities, notably Pittsburgh (1977–85), and lectured widely (for example, in Beijing in 1982), before finally retiring to Princeton. He has received countless honours, including nine honorary doctorates and is much loved.

2   Confirmation

Hempel's paradox of the ravens has been a persistent challenge for theories of confirmation. Adumbrated (1937: 222) in a critique of Reichenbach's treatment of the probability of laws, it emerged as an illustration of the 'paradox of confirmation' (1945a). The sentences

(1) 'All ravens are black' and (2) 'All non-black things are non-ravens' are logically equivalent; each simply denies the existence of non-black ravens. But if reports of black ravens confirm (1), then on the same showing, reports of non-black non-ravens confirm (2). Therefore, since any report confirming a sentence equally confirms any logically equivalent sentence, we have a seeming paradox: reports of non-black non-ravens (for instance, white shoes) confirm the hypothesis that all ravens are black.

Hempel's own account of the conditions under which observation-sentences confirm general sentences (1943, 1945a) can be summarized as follows. Consider an observation report in which certain names appear – perhaps, in the ravens case, just 'a' and 'b', where the report is the pair of sentences: 'a is a black raven', 'b is a non-black non-raven'. This report is said to *directly* confirm (1) because it logically implies the restriction of (1) to the individuals mentioned in it; and it is said to *indirectly* confirm all other logical consequences of sentences it directly confirms. In the present example the restriction of (1) to 'a' and 'b' is the sentence (0) 'If a is a raven then a is black and if b is a raven then b is black'; and since the report does logically imply (0), it directly confirms (1), and indirectly confirms (2).

This purely classificatory analysis of confirmation makes no distinction between white shoes and black ravens as sources of confirmation for (1); but perhaps that is because those two sorts of evidence confirm (1) to very different degrees. Hosiasson suggested that while reports of black ravens and white shoes both confirm (1), the latter confirm it to a much lower degree, in the light of our background beliefs about the rarity and homogeneity of ravens (Hosaisson 1940).

Hempel and Oppenheim (1945b) propose a quantitative account of degree of confirmation of hypotheses H by evidence-sentences E. If the language in which H and E are stated can classify members of the (finite) population into non-overlapping, exhaustive categories, then a statistical distribution is an assignment to these categories of definite proportions in the population. Relative to different distributions, a sentence of the language may have different probabilities. Now the degree of confirmation of H given E is defined as the probability that H and E are both true divided by the probability that E is true – both probabilities being determined by a 'maximum likelihood' distribution, that is, a distribution making E as probable as any distribution can (1945b: 112).

In Carnap the role of the maximum likelihood distribution in this definition is played by the average of all possible distributions (Carnap 1950: appendix). Carnap's degrees of confirmation then satisfy all laws of probability, including one violated by the Hempel–Oppenheim definition, namely, the 'multiplication principle', according to which the probability that A and B, given E, is the degree of confirmation of A, given E, times the degree of confirmation of B, given that E and A are both true. Hempel and Oppenheim preferred their definition to Carnap's on grounds of empiricism; where Carnap assigns equal a priori probabilities to all possible distributions, they choose a distribution by reference to the evidence sentence E. They offer their definition as establishing fair betting-odds on H given E, thus accounting for one aspect of confirmation. Other aspects – number and variety of instances reported in E – remain to be accounted for by some other concept, which would determine the amount it would be fair to stake in bets at those odds (1945b: 114). But that view was hard to maintain in the face of Ramsey's and de Finetti's 'Dutch book' arguments for the multiplication principle, showing that 'If anyone's mental condition violated [it], his choice would depend on the precise form in which the options were offered him, which would be absurd' (Ramsey 1931: 182). This would be part of Hempel's later disenchantment with the project of an inductive logic (see CONFIRMATION THEORY §1; PROBABILITY THEORY AND EPISTEMOLOGY §1).

3 Law and explanation

From FREGE (1879: §12) and MACH (1883: ch. 4, §4.3) through the various phases of logical empiricism, scientific laws were taken to have the same logical form as other factual generalizations; especially, the suggestion was resisted that scientific laws are marked by modal operators, as in 'Necessarily, all Ps are Q' or 'Being P makes things Q'. Where Mach put this as a metaphysical claim – 'In nature there is no cause, no effect; nature is only there once' (1883: 455) – the logical empiricists put it as a decision about the language of science; it is to be extensional. But they saw the function of laws and theories as the systematization of otherwise unwieldy bodies of particular empirical claims, that is, data compression, Mach's 'economy of science'. This would accord well with the puzzling character of fundamental physics that emerged with increasing clarity during the twentieth century, with quantum theory providing predictions of unprecedented accuracy, explicable only as being what the theory provides. Here Hempel's 'covering-law model' of explanation matched the consensus of physicists that accurate systematization is all we can reasonably ask in the way of explanation – 'understanding' being a secondary psychological state that may come with familiarity (see LAWS, NATURAL §1; LOGICAL POSITIVISM §§2–3).

Hempel identifies laws as those truths of the forms 'Every physical object is so-and-so' and 'Every space-time point is so-and-so' that make no essential reference to particular physical objects or space-time regions (1965: 271). The seemingly limited generalization 'All ravens are black' is really a universal generalization in which 'so-and-so' stands for 'black if a raven' and 'if' is read extensionally, as 'or not'. If that generalization is a law, 'raven' must be definable without essential reference to the planet Earth, as is presumably the case if biology is reducible to physics.

A deductive explanation of an event is a logical deduction of an 'explanandum' sentence, asserting that the event happens, from premises (the 'explanans') which are either general laws or statements of antecedent conditions (1965: 249). Hempel thought that this put explanation on a par with prediction, the difference being attributed to the timing of the explanandum-event, that is to say, after or before the act of prediction or explanation, respectively. In inductive explanations the requirement of logical deductibility is weakened to high logical probability of the explanandum, given the explanans. Since the conditional probability of a statement is highest (that is, 1) given statements that logically imply it, deductive explanations are also inductive explanations – of the strongest sort (see EXPLANATION §§1–2).

4 Theoreticity and cognitive significance

Explanation is systematization. Hempel proposes a measure of the power of a theory T to systematize putative data S (1965: 287). The idea is that the content of a sentence is determined by the possibilities it rules out, so the content of a sentence is represented by its denial, and the common content of two sentences by the sentence 'Both are false'. Measuring contents by logical probabilities of denials, Hempel then measures T's power to systematize S by the ratio of the measure of their common content to the measure of S's content, that is, by the logical probability of T's falsity, given S's. The idea is applied to 'the theoretician's dilemma': if theoretical terms and laws do their work of deductive systematization in linking observational antecedents to observational consequents, they are otiose, for functionally equivalent rules in a purely observational vocabulary can then establish exactly the same inferential transitions; but this overlooks the role of theoretical terms and principles in *inductive* systematization of observational sentences (1965: 186, 122).

Following WITTGENSTEIN (1922), logical empiricists rejected metaphysics as empty of cognitive content. Early on, this was derived from the so-called verifiability criterion, identifying the content of a sentence or a system with the set of ways in which it might be refuted by experience. Like tautologies, such as 'What will be, will be', metaphysical sentences were thought to be unfalsifiable, and so to be empty of cognitive content. Hempel famously chronicled and sharpened the problems and changes attending attempts at logical definition of this concept, for example, the replacement of the verifiability requirement by confirmability (1965: 101–22). He concludes: 'cognitive significance in a system is a matter of degree: Significant systems range from those whose entire extralogical vocabulary consists of observation terms, through theories whose formulation relies heavily on theoretical constructs, on to systems with hardly any bearing on potential empirical findings' (1965: 117).

5 The career of logical positivism

Logical empiricism was meant to be scientific philosophy, applying the new logic to the structure and methods of all the sciences, as Whitehead and Russell had to mathematics in *Principia Mathematica* (1910–25). The products would be purely logical definitions – of confirmation, explanation, systematic power and so on – but their selection or design would be determined pragmatically, by the needs of science. That was Carnap's view, anyway; and Hempel's, for nearly half a century. But where Carnap's hopes were steady to the end, Hempel's eventually turned from logical analysis to Neurath's old project of *Gelehrtenbehavioristik* (empirical sociology of science) – in loose alliance with KUHN (1962, 1970), but with fresh concern for the justification of scientific norms.

See also: MEANING AND VERIFICATION §4

List of works

Hempel, C.G. (1934) *Beiträge sur logischen Analyse des Wahrscheinlichkeitsbegriffs* (Contributions to the Logical Analysis of the Concept of Probability), Jena. (Hempel's Berlin Ph.D. thesis.)

—— (1935a) 'On the Logical Positivists' Theory of Truth', *Analysis* 2: 49–59. (Exposition and defence of Carnap's and Neurath's physicalism, presented as a quasi-coherence theory of truth.)

—— (1935b) 'Analyse logique de la psychologie', *Revue de Synthèse* 10: 27–42; trans. 'The Logical Analysis of Psychology', in H. Feigl and W. Sellars (eds) *Readings in Philosophical Analysis*, New York: Appleton Century; Crofts, 1949, 373–84. ('Psychology is an integral part of physics.')

—— (1937) 'Le problème de la vérité' (The Problem of Truth), *Theoria* 3: 206–46. (An accessible bridge from the early work on probability and truth to the mature work on confirmation.)

—— (1943) 'A Purely Syntactical Definition of Confirmation', *Journal of Symbolic Logic* 8: 122–43. (Non-quantitative confirmation as a relation between sentences; a narrowly technical preamble to Hempel 1945a.)

—— (1945a) 'Studies in the Logic of Confirmation', in *Aspects of Scientific Explanation*, London: Collier-Macmillan, 1965. (Hempel's classical discussion of non-quantitative confirmation and its paradoxes.)

Hempel, C.G. and Oppenheim, P. (1945b) 'A Definition of Degree of Confirmation', *Philosophy of Science* 10: 98–115. (Quantitative confirmation of one sentence by another.)

Hempel, C.G. (1952) *Fundamentals of Concept Formation in Empirical Science*, International Encyclopedia of Unified Science 2, Chicago, IL: University of Chicago Press. (A readable account of the logical empiricist line at the time on definition, reduction and types of measurement.)

—— (1960) 'Science and Human Values' in R. Spiller (ed.) *Social Control in a Free Society*, Philadelphia, PA: University of Pennsylvania Press, 39–64. (Interactions and parallels between scientific and value judgment.)

—— (1962) 'Rational action', *Proceedings and Addresses of the American Philosophical Association* 35, Yellow Springs, OH: Antioch, 5–23. (American Philosophical Association presidential address; explanatory uses of the concept of rational action.)

—— (1965) *Aspects of Scientific Explanation*, London: Collier-Macmillan, and New York: Free Press. (Reproduces some fifteen previously published essays, with commentary, blending and revision. The title essay is original.)

—— (1966) *Philosophy of Natural Science*, Englewood Cliffs, NJ: Prentice Hall. (A lucid introduction, from a broadly logical empiricist standpoint.)

—— (1970) 'On the "Standard Conception" of Scientific Theories', in M. Radner and S. Winokur (eds) *Minnesota Studies in the Philosophy of Science* 4, Minneapolis, MN: University of Minnesota Press, 142–263. (How do new theoretical terms get their meanings? Old answers are faulted – as is the question itself.)

—— (1977) *Aspekte wissenschaftlicher Erklarung*, Berlin: de Gruyter. (Translation and revision of Hempel 1965, with a new section on statistical explanation.)

—— (1979) 'Scientific Rationality: Analytic vs Pragmatic Perspectives', in T. Geraets (ed.) *Rationality Today/La rationalité aujhourd'hui*, Ottawa, Ont.: University of Ottawa Press, 46–58. (Critique of

Kuhn and others, issuing in a view of rational explanation as Janus-headed, at once explanatory and normative.)

—— (1983) 'Schlick und Neurath: Fundierung *vs.* Koharenz in der wissenschaftlichen Erkenntnis', *Gratzer philosophische Studien*, 16/17: 1–18. (Schlick and Neurath: foundation versus coherence in scientific knowledge. A debate, in Vienna in the 1930s, resonating with Hempel 1979.)

—— (1988) 'On the Cognitive Status and the Rationale of Scientific Rationality', *Poetics Today* 9: 5–27. (Pragmatic perspectives on induction; methodology as both descriptive and prescriptive.)

—— (1990) 'The Significance [misprinted 'Signification'] of the Concept of Truth for the Critical Appraisal of Scientific Theories', *Nuova civilita delle macchine* 8: 109–13. (Watered-down title; the manuscript said 'Irrelevance', not 'Signification'.)

—— (1993) 'Empiricism in the Vienna Circle and in the Berlin Society for Exact Philosophy, Recollections and reflections', in F. Stadtler (ed.) *Scientific Philosophy: Origins and Developments*, Dordrecht: Kluwer. (An eyewitness report.)

References and further reading

* Carnap, R. (1928) *Der logische Aufbau der Welt*, Berlin: Felix Meiner; trans. R. George, *The Logical Structure of the World*, Berkeley: University of California Press, 1969. (Phenomenalism formalized; the book that brought Hempel to Vienna.)
* —— (1934) *Logische Syntax der Sprache*, Vienna; trans. A. Smeaton, *The Logical Syntax of Language*, London: Kegan Paul, Trench, Trubner & Co, 1937. (Physicalism formalized.)
* —— (1950, 1962) *Logical Foundations of Probability*, Chicago, IL: University of Chicago Press. (Probability as a logical magnitude. Crititique of Hempel 1943 and 1945a on pages 468–82.)
* Frege, G. (1879) *Begriffsschrift*, Halle: Louis Nebert. (The ultimate source of the logic in logical empiricism.)
Heijenoort, J. van (ed.) (1967) *From Frege to Gödel*, Cambridge, MA: Harvard University Press. (A valuable source book.)
Horwich, P. (ed.) (1993) *World Changes*, Cambridge, MA: MIT Press. (New light on Kuhn, Hempel and Carnap.)
* Hosiasson, J. (1940) 'On confirmation', *Journal of Symbolic Logic* 5: 136–41. (Probabilistic resolution of Hempel's paradoxes of confirmation. Hosaisson was killed by the Gestapo in 1942.)
* Kuhn, T. (1962, 1970) *The Structure of Scientific Revolutions*, Chicago, IL: University of Chicago Press. (The book that killed logical empiricism?)

* Mach, E. (1883) *Die Mechanik in ihrer Entwickelung*, Leipzig: F.A. Brockhaus; trans. T. McCormack , *The Science of Mechanics*, La Salle, IL: Open Court, 1893. (The economy of science: ch. 4, §4.)
Neurath, O. (1983) *Philosophical Papers 1913–1946*, Dordrecht: Reidel. (Far-left wing of the Vienna Circle.)
* Ramsey, F.P. (1931) *The Foundations of Mathematics*, London: Routledge. ('Truth and Probability' is one of many gems here. See page 182 for the 'Dutch' book.)
* Reichenbach, H. (1935) *Wahrscheinlichkeitslehre*, Leyden: A.W. Sijthoff; trans. *The Theory of Probability*, Berkeley, CA: University of California Press, 1949. (Hempel (1934) was largely concerned with this theory.)
Russell, B.A.W. (1940) *An Inquiry into Meaning and Truth*, London: Allen & Unwin, and New York: Norton, 139–49. (Caricature of Hempel and Neurath on truth.)
Stadtler, F. (ed.) (1993) *Scientific Philosophy: Origins and Developments*, Dordrecht: Kluwer. (Essays relating to the Vienna Circle, with useful references.)
* Whitehead, A.N. and Russell, B. (1910–25) *Principia Mathematica*, Cambridge: Cambridge University Press. (The immediate source of the logic in logical empiricism.)
* Wittgenstein, L. (1922) *Tractatus Logico-Philosophicus*, London: Routledge. (Mysticism and logic. It electrified the Vienna Circle.)

R. JEFFREY

HENRICUS REGIUS (1598–1679)

Henricus Regius supported many of Descartes' doctrines, such as the distinction between mind and body, but disagreed with Descartes' arguments for that distinction, and rejected metaphysics. Their differences led to a celebrated public dispute which lasted until Descartes' death.

Henricus Regius (Hendrik De Roy), one of Descartes' first Dutch disciples, also studied in France and Italy. In 1638 he was appointed professor of Theoretical Medicine and Botany at the University of Utrecht. Through Henricus Reneri he became deeply influenced by Descartes' *Discourse* and *Essays* of 1637, meeting Descartes in 1638 (see DESCARTES, R. §§1, 8). When Reneri died in 1639, Regius became the primary representative of Cartesianism at Utrecht.

Regius first presented his natural philosophy in a series of disputations in 1641, published as *Physiologia sive cognitio sanitatis*. It incurred the wrath of the Theological Faculty and of the University rector, Gisbertus Voetius. Most controversial were his denial of the scholastic doctrines of matter and form, and his assertion that the human being is an accidental unity. With Descartes' advice, Regius replied to the attacks in 1642. This elicited a formal condemnation of Descartes' philosophy at the University, and Regius was forbidden to teach physics. Descartes responded in the 'Letter to Father Dinet' (1642), which appeared with the Amsterdam edition of his *Meditations* publicly attacking Voetius, who then focused his attention on Descartes.

Throughout this time, Regius was summarizing his own natural philosophy. Descartes disagreed with certain crucial aspects of it and urged him not to publish, but *Fundamenta physices* appeared in spring 1646, followed by *Fundamenta medicinae* in 1647. Descartes consequently denounced Regius in the preface to the new French edition of the *Principles of Philosophy* (1647). Regius responded with *Explicatio mentis humanae* (1647b), emphasizing his points of difference. Descartes retorted with *Notae in programma quoddam* (1648), and finally Regius published *Brevis explicatio mentis humanae sive animae rationalis* (1648).

Bitter as these exchanges were, Descartes is thought to have forgiven Regius before his death in 1650, and Regius continued to be identified as a Cartesian. He remained at Utrecht until his death, a person of some importance in the University. Although he did not write anything new after the 1640s, he published later editions of the *Fundamenta physices* in 1654 and 1661.

Regius rejected scholastic philosophy, embracing a version of the new mechanical philosophy. Like Descartes he distinguished between mind, a thinking substance, and body, an extended substance. The details of his general physics, for example his conception of the laws of nature, are similarly indebted to Descartes, as are his views on human physiology. But there are also notable differences. Descartes' physics was grounded in metaphysics, in God, the human soul and in the validation of reason. Regius rejected metaphysics, beginning his philosophy directly with physics. He also disagreed with the Cartesian arguments for the distinction between mind and body: in the *Fundamenta physices* he argued that the real distinction can be known only by Biblical revelation. In the *Explicatio* (§2), he went farther still: 'so far as the nature of things is concerned... mind could be either a substance or a certain mode of corporeal substance'.

Regius also attacked Descartes' proof of the external world. According to Descartes, God gave us a strong inclination to believe that bodies cause sensations, and no means to correct this strong inclination. Therefore, he would be a deceiver if there were none. Apart from the fact that God might deceive us to punish us, Regius did not think God would be a deceiver if no bodies existed, since we are capable of withholding our assent to their existence, viewing our sensations as mere appearances which may not have bodies as their causes. Again, it is revelation that assures the existence of the external world. Finally, Regius rejected Descartes' innate ideas and all ideas of pure intellection; we have only sensation, imagination and memory – all our ideas come to us from experience. Pierre GASSENDI is a possible source of some of Regius' non-Cartesian theses.

See also: MEDIEVAL PHILOSOPHY

List of works

Regius, H. (1641) *Physiologia sive cognitio sanitatis* (Physiology, or, knowledge of health), Utrecht. (Collection of disputations which contain the earliest presentation of Regius' natural philosophy.)

—— (1646) *Fundamenta physices* (Foundations of physics), Amsterdam. (Regius' main presentation of his natural philosophy.)

—— (1647a) *Fundamenta medicinae* (Foundations of medicine), Utrecht. (A further presentation of Regius' natural philosophy.)

—— (1647b) *Explicatio mentis humanae* (Explanation of the human mind) in *The Philosophical Writings of Descartes*, ed. and trans. J. Cottingham, R. Stoothoff, D. Murdoch, and A. Kenny, Cambridge: Cambridge University Press, vol. 1, 1984–91, 294–6. (Reprinted here with Descartes' response *Notae in programma quoddam*.)

—— (1648) *Brevis explicatio mentis humanae sive animae rationalis... a Notis Nobil. Cartesii vindicata* (Brief explanation of the human mind or rational soul... vindicated from the notes of Descartes), Utrecht. (A response to Descartes' *Notae in Programma*.)

—— (1654) *Philosophia naturalis...* (Natural philosophy), Amsterdam. (A second edition of the *Fundamenta physices*.)

—— (1661) *Philosophia naturalis...* (Natural philosophy), Amsterdam. (A third edition of the *Fundamenta physices*.)

References and further reading

Adam, C. and Tannery, P. (1964–74) 'Descartes et

Regius', *Oeuvres de Descartes*, vol. 11, ed. C. Adam and P. Tannery, Paris: CNRS/Vrin, new edn, 11 vols. (A detailed discussion of Descartes' relations with Regius, and Regius' treatment of Descartes and his thought in the *Fundamenta physices*.)

* Descartes, R. (1642) 'Letter to Father Dinet', *The Philosophical Writings of Descartes*, vol. 2, (partial trans.), ed. and trans. J. Cottingham, R. Stoothoff, D. Murdoch and A. Kenny, Cambridge: Cambridge University Press, 1984–91. (First published in the 1642 second edition of the *Meditations*. Although mostly a response to perceived Jesuit attacks against him, it also includes a defence of Regius against Voetius.)

* —— (1647) 'Author's letter to the translator of the book which may here serve as a preface', *Principles of Philosophy*, Paris; repr. in *The Philosophical Writings of Descartes*, vol. 1, ed. and trans. J. Cottingham, R. Stoothoff, D. Murdoch and A. Kenny, Cambridge: Cambridge University Press, 1984–91. (This preface to the French translation of the *Principles* denounces Regius' *Fundamenta physices*.)

—— (1959) *Lettres à Regius et remarques sur l'explication de l'esprit humain*, ed. G. Rodis-Lewis, Paris: Vrin. (Contains the correspondence between Regius and Descartes, both in Latin and in French, the *Notae*, as well as excerpts from others of Regius' writings, an extensive introduction and helpful notes.)

Farina, P. (1977) 'Il corpuscolarismo di Henricus Regius: materialismo e medicina in un Cartesiano olandese del Seicento', in Ugo Baldini *et al.* (eds) *Ricerche sull'Atomismo di Seicento: Atti del Convegno di Studio di Santa Margharita Ligure (14–16 ottobre 1976)*, Florence: La Nuova Italia, 119–78. (A discussion of Regius's physics and medical theories.)

Verbeek, T. (1988) *La querelle d'Utrecht*, Paris: Les impressions nouvelles. (The documents connected with Descartes' troubles in Utrecht, translated into French, with copious commentary.)

—— (1992) *Descartes and the Dutch*, Carbondale, IL: Southern Illinois University Press. (A short but engaging account of Descartes' troubles in Utrecht and Leiden, containing a good account of his relations with Regius.)

—— (1994) 'Regius's Fundamenta Physices', *Journal of the History of Ideas* 55: 533–51. (An account of the history of Regius' main work in natural philosophy.)

—— (ed.) (1993) *Descartes et Regius. Autour de l'explication de l'esprit*, Amsterdam: Rodopi. (A collection of essays concerning Descartes and Regius on the mind, focusing on Regius' *Explicatio* and Descartes' response.)

Vrijer M.J.A. de (1917) *Henricus Regius: een 'Cartesiaansch' hoogleeraar aan de Utrechtsche Hoogeschool*, The Hague: Nijhoff. (Though somewhat dated, still the most complete account of Regius's life and thought currently available.)

DANIEL GARBER

HENRY OF GHENT
(early 13th century–1293)

Perhaps the most influential theologian between Thomas Aquinas and Bonaventure in the third quarter of the thirteenth century and John Duns Scotus at the beginning of the fourteenth century, Henry of Ghent stands at a turning point in scholastic philosophy. He was a defender of traditional Neoplatonic positions and has often been seen as the epitome of thirteenth-century Augustinianism. Yet his convoluted metaphysics and a theory of knowledge weaving together Neoplatonic and Aristotelian strands inspired novel philosophical trends in the fourteenth century, particularly among Franciscan thinkers. His work thus constituted the point of departure for scholastic giants like Duns Scotus and William of Ockham, who not only used him as a foil against which to articulate their own system of thought but also absorbed much of his fundamental philosophical outlook and terminology.

Characteristic of Henry's metaphysics was an essentialism so pronounced that critics accused him of positing a realm of essences separate from worldly actuality. In his defence, Henry insisted that essences, though prior to actual existence, were separate only as grounded in the divine exemplars of things, but the Platonism of his approach struck his contemporaries as extraordinary nonetheless. Ironically, Henry's understanding of essence as congruent with intellectual coherence provided an opening for a more logic-based analysis of modality, especially possibility, in succeeding thinkers such as Duns Scotus.

The emphasis on essence re-emerged in Henry's theory of knowledge, and at least in his early writings he offered a vision of knowing truth through divine illumination often taken as paradigmatic of medieval Augustinianism. Even his later attempts to cast epistemology in a more Aristotelian light retained the insistence that true knowledge somehow entails access to the exemplary essences in God's mind. The same essentialism led Henry to formulate what he called an a priori proof for God's existence, best approximation in the thirteenth century to Anselm's ontological argu-

ment. Again, however, Henry's Augustinianism provided an unintended springboard for innovation, leading to Duns Scotus' theory of the univocity of being and metaphysical proof of God's existence.

1   Life and writings

Henry was born in Ghent early in the thirteenth century, but we know little about his life before 1275 or 1276, when he assumed a secular chair as master of theology at the University of Paris. By this time he was already working his way up the ladder of ecclesiastical politics in the Low Countries, having been appointed canon at the wealthy episcopal see of Tournai; soon after he was named archdeacon of Bruges, and finally in 1278 or 1279, archdeacon of Tournai. In 1277, Bishop Etienne Tempier of Paris included him in the commission of theologians assigned to examine the orthodoxy of doctrines being taught at the University. Their report led to the list of 219 proscribed propositions in philosophy and theology issued in Tempier's famous condemnation of 1277 (see AVERROISM; BOETHIUS OF DACIA; SIGER OF BRABANT).

By this point, Henry had become aligned with conservative thinkers fearful of the influence of a radical Aristotelianism among Parisian masters of arts and alarmed even by the moderate Aristotelianism of AQUINAS and his followers in the school of theology (see ARISTOTELIANISM, MEDIEVAL). Members of this group rallied to the banner of Augustine, and because of the prominence of Franciscans within their ranks they have often been characterized as proponents of a peculiarly Franciscan Augustinianism (see AUGUSTINIANISM). Ironically, Henry was a bitter opponent of the Franciscans in the political disputes of the late thirteenth century over the conflicting rights and privileges of regular and secular priests.

Henry died in 1293 after an illustrious career at the centre of intellectual debate. His chief works are a series of fifteen *Quodlibeta*, the carefully revised redactions of public disputations which he held nearly annually at the university from 1276 to his withdrawal from academic life the year before his death, and his *Summa* – more properly, *Quaestiones ordinariae* (Ordinary Questions) – a massive compilation of edited classroom debates on questions of philosophy and theology that he left only half finished. Although the latter presents itself as a self-contained and independent work, it was laboriously put together over the same span of time as the *Quodlibeta* and parallels them in chronicling the development of Henry's ideas throughout his career.

2   Metaphysics

Like many of his contemporaries, Henry began with the conviction, promoted by Aquinas, that the most fundamental divide in reality lay between essence and existence. In contrast to Aquinas he interpreted the division so as to give priority to essence. Going back to Avicenna (see IBN SINA), he claimed that the broadest way of conceiving of an object was as 'thing' (*res*), a concept shorn of all consideration of the conditions of being, particular or universal, mental or extramental, actual or hypothetical. Void of ontological significance, 'thing' was thus the marker of essentiality alone, and its intelligible content could be represented solely by essential or quidditative descriptions, pointing to the 'what' of objects exclusive of the 'whether' or 'how' of their existence.

Yet despite their formal opposition to being, quidditative descriptions varied according to how dense their 'thingness' was: in other words, how suitable they were to represent actual existing objects. The most tenuous – least 'real' – kind of thing included all that could be described, even barely imaginable constructs which would not withstand scrutiny for logical coherence. This was the vast domain of 'thing', opposed only to that which was absolutely nothing at all. Henry called it *res a reor reris*, by which he meant 'thing' insofar as it embraced any content that could be grasped by mind or imagination and which we might translate as 'imaginable object'. Less thin was 'thing' that was not only imaginable but also internally consistent enough to be suitable for becoming an object in the real world. The domain of this kind of 'thing' was of course less extensive than *res a reor reris*, since it contained only objects more truly 'thing-like' or 'real' and thus more worthy of being denominated by the terms 'essence', 'nature' or 'quiddity' in their proper sense. Henry called such objects *res a ratitudine* – that is, 'things' as disposed to rational analysis – and among them he located Avicenna's absolute essence, which he understood to be essence separated from existence but opposed to the less-than-absolute nothingness of incoherent figments of imagination. Finally – and least thin – was the realm of 'things' in the world, objects not only inherently suited to existence but in fact existing. This field of things was naturally the narrowest, but it was denser or more 'real' than either of the other two. Henry called its constituents actually existing things (*res existentes in actu*) or things of nature (*res naturae*).

Such a hierarchical vision of 'thing' was more intricately articulated than any consideration of essence produced before, and in order to accommodate it Henry had to introduce distinctions on the other side of the divide, in the category of 'being.' According to him, there were two kinds of being. First was being of essence (*esse essentiae*), a state less than actuality, characterizing objects at the level of *res a ratitudine* and constituting that which separated them from more nothing-like imaginary objects that could not bear logical scrutiny. Second was being of existence (*esse existentiae*), the full being of actuality possessed by all real objects in the temporal present and therefore proper to *res existentes in actu*. From this it followed that there was a two-fold composition of being and essence, the first a combination of absolute essence with the special being distinguishing it from the purely ephemeral whatness of imaginable fictions, the second the joining of such essence with actual existence (see EXISTENCE).

The result was that Henry, while maintaining the being-essence distinction, had managed to undermine its radical duality, shifting the analytical balance strongly to the side of essence. By his scheme essences, even when considered 'absolutely', already possessed a sort of being that lifted it into the domain of non-fictive things, so that even on a conceptual level essence was never completely denuded of implications of being. Furthermore, essence, taken along with its special sort of being, was clearly prior to existence. One might almost describe it as 'resident' in an essential realm ready to receive the actual existence that, in Henry's words, 'came to it' and accounted for its presence in actuality. For Henry, then, being was more like a variable quality of essence in its different states than a fundamental constituent of reality, as it had been for Aquinas. GILES OF ROME, Henry's contemporary at Paris and an extreme defender of the Thomistic real distinction between essence and being, continually attacked Henry on this score. Henry's response was to invent a distinction intermediate between the purely conceptual and the real – what he called an intentional distinction – and to insist that essence and its two kinds of being were 'intentionally' distinct. This tour de force of metaphysical compromise fed into the similarly controversial 'formal distinction' of DUNS SCOTUS.

Already strongly Neoplatonic in his essentialism, Henry exaggerated the tilt in his metaphysics by tying his theory of essence to Augustine's exemplarism. What made an essence an essence, Henry claimed – what explained its being more coherent than an imaginary object and a bearer of being of essence –

was the fact that it corresponded to a formal ideal in the divine mind. Essence was essence because it was exemplified, because it was the image of a conceptual exemplar in God. Indeed, the being of essence was reducible to the relation between the exemplified and its exemplar. God's knowledge made essences what they were, and each was a sort of participation in the divine being.

Henry took this idea so far as to approach a Platonism astonishing even among thirteenth-century Augustinians (see PLATONISM, MEDIEVAL). Contemporaries such as GODFREY OF FONTAINES accused him of positing a world of essences, eternal and separate from God, since by Henry's terms each essence had its own being of essence different from the existence of a created thing in the actual world. Indeed, it is hard not to read some of his statements about exemplified essences as implying what Godfrey claimed. Yet Henry vigorously rebutted such accusations, insisting that being of essence was not an attribute things could have without also possessing being of existence and thus not a separate state of being. It was rather the metaphysical purchase on actuality that a coherent essential content had as something suitable for existence. In the case of objects not actually existing in the external world, essence was manifested, and possessed its being of essence, just insofar as it was actualized in the intelligible processes of an existing mind. This could be the mind of an intelligent creature, like a human being, considering the essence abstracted from any particular instances external to its thought; it could also be the mind of God. Of course, before creation it was only in God's mind that essence could thus take shape. Eternal essences fell back completely on the ontic grounding of God's eternally active mind and so were identical with the divine ideas, thus substantially identical with God (on this controversial point see Marrone 1985: 122–7).

A system of this sort, isolating essence as an absolute in itself but also grounding it eternally in God, required considerable philosophical elasticity to accept, but it paid handsome metaphysical dividends. For Henry, essences were not purely fictive constructs on the level of *res a reor reris*, but quidditative contents that could be made existent. They constituted, therefore, all simple possibles. Besides providing an exposition of the relation between God and the rest of reality, Henry's theory of essence thus promised to lay bare the foundations of modality as well. In this connection it must be remembered that in Henry's words what made an essence an essence – what constituted it as a possible – was, first, its being represented by an idea in God's mind but, second, its possessing a coherent intelligible content, formally entailed in its corresponding to a divine idea. In the end, Henry was suggesting that what separated possibles on the essential level of *res a ratitudine* from fictive impossibles on the level of *res a reor reris* was internal consistency, with all essences being made up of logically compatible parts. Despite the fact that Duns Scotus criticized Henry's ontology of essence as unworkable and implausible, it provided a major inspiration for his own innovative ideas about modality, which were formally quite similar to those Henry had laid down.

3   Theory of mind and knowledge

Henry's epistemology is often taken as emblematic of thirteenth-century Augustinianism, but it was likewise the area of his thought in which he did most to bring new elements of Aristotelianism into a more traditional Neoplatonic base. This was the side of his philosophy most subject to development throughout his career, where it is especially important to pay attention to the chronology of his ideas.

In the early sections of his *Summa*, Henry laid out a theory of knowledge dependent on a notion of truth as rightness deriving from ANSELM and insistent on the inadequacy of the unaided human intellect to achieve fully reliable knowledge without God's help, traditionally described in Neoplatonic terms as an illumination from the divine intelligible light (see NEOPLATONISM). This first statement of his views about knowledge and truth constitutes the most detailed thirteenth-century exposition of the theory of divine illumination and was taken as the paradigm of illuminationism by later Augustinians such as Duns Scotus, who criticized any such theory as philosophically unsustainable. According to Henry's position, human intellect begins with the data of sensation and works its way by purely natural means to an approximate understanding of an object's essential composition, an understanding neither completely clear nor precise. Henry called this 'knowledge of the true' (*verum*). Only after it had reached this point could the mind call upon its reflexive capacities and God's aid to refine its understanding until it was fully clear and adequate to the theoretical requirements for certain knowledge of the truth.

The first step in the refining process involved taking the cognitive representation of the object achieved in the initial understanding – which Henry identified at that stage of his career as an intelligible species – and comparing it to the external thing again as known through the senses, critically reshaping it into a precise image of the object's essential characteristics. The results of this comparison, Henry said, were preserved in the mind as what he called an expressed concept or 'word' (*verbum*), and it was with this 'word' that mind first reached a grade of cognition worthy of being called knowledge of the truth (*veritas*) and sufficient for the beginnings of scientific thought. From simple truths gathered in this way, one could construct a system of intellection adequate to the standards ARISTOTLE had established for science in his *Posterior Analytics*.

Yet such truth, and such science, was still imperfect, because the human mind working on its own was subject to error. For absolute certitude, and perfect science, the intellect had to turn to God, calling upon an illumination from above to confirm its insights and correct its mistakes. Although Henry described this second step in various ways, his preference was to see it as a comparison drawn by the mind between the word of truth established at the lower boundaries of science and the eternal exemplar rendered intelligible by God through illumination (see ILLUMINATION). The expressed concept, rectified to suit the contours of the divine ideal, was now fashioned into a vehicle for knowledge of the 'full truth, pure and simple' (*sincera veritas*), upon which could be constructed an absolutely reliable system of knowledge.

Already evident in this early view was Henry's intention to make room for Aristotle and the epistemology of the *Analytics* in the rarefied world of illuminationism and exemplarism. Yet in the years 1279–81 he took far greater steps to amplify his commitment to an Aristotelianizing theory of knowledge. In Quodlibets IV and V and in Article 34 of the *Summa*, Henry revisited his description of the process by which intellect moves from apprehension of the true to an understanding of truth worthy of science. He now insisted that the initial apprehension constituted genuine knowledge of the quiddity or essence of an object, although not a precise articulation of all quidditative parts. The way the mind worked its way from this imperfect knowledge to the truth was by applying the Aristotelian procedures of composition and division – what Henry called 'the art of definition' (*ars definitiva*) – progressing by means of analysis to a description of essence precise enough to provide the foundation for apodictic science. This precise description, an authentic Aristotelian definition, was manifested in the intellect by what Henry characterized as the refined mental concept or word, which he now conceded to be indicative of the pure truth he had previously reserved for understanding illuminated by God.

At the same time, Henry took parallel steps in his theory of mind. For all his early illuminationism, he had always rejected the notion, advanced by Augustinians like Roger BACON in the mid-thirteenth century, that God was the agent intellect responsible for human cognition, or the equally Augustinian view that the ideas of things were impressed by God on the mind at its creation. Instead, he held to what he took to be authentic Aristotelianism: the claim that the human intellect possessed its own active power to generate knowledge from sensory data. In these middle years he fleshed out his understanding of this power by combining an Augustinian conviction that the mind was autonomously active and capable of producing knowledge on its own with an understanding of the mechanics of mind drawn from Averroes (see IBN RUSHD). The most striking feature of this synthesis was the notion of a possible intellect rendered active by its initial reception of the concept of the quiddity and working to turn out higher forms of cognition, an idea Henry consciously patterned after Averroes' 'speculative intellect'.

Henry carried the emphasis on intellectual activity so far as to reject entirely the notion of intelligible species, which he now saw as tokens of a passivity unworthy of the dynamism of the human soul (Nys 1949). Instead, all knowledge from the very start was contained in his 'expressed concepts' or 'mental words', products of the immanent agency of intellect as it reached out to grasp the essences of objects, and which could be regarded as those very essences residing in the mind as understood by it. Such a notion of intellectual immediacy was unusual in Henry's day, but it prepared the ground for the idea of intellectual intuition found later in Duns Scotus as well as the even more radical theories of intellectual agency developed by OCKHAM and his followers.

Such views enabled Henry, by the end of his career, to find a way of reaffirming the divine presence in human cognition conveyed by his early epistemology of illumination. If mental words were nothing less than the essences of objects brought onto the mind's cognitive field, they were then the perfect expression of Avicennian absolute essence, shorn of external existence and instantiated solely by the actuality of an intellect's active consideration. But, of course, absolute essences were eternally present in divine cognition. Here the profound essentialism of Henry's ontology emerged in full force, leading him to assert that the essence the human mind knew and the essence known by God were the very same on the rarefied level of being of essence. Thus every intelligent agent touched on things at just the point at which they participated in the divine mind, so that knowing the definitive truth in Aristotelian terms was, in a real sense, knowing the object as it bore an ideal relation to God. Henry's mature understanding of the divine role in human intellection caught Duns Scotus' attention as much as the literally illuminationist views

of Henry's early years, and he took aim against this as well in his criticism of traditional Augustinian theories of knowledge.

4 Transcendentals and proof of God's existence

The essentialism of Henry's metaphysics and the exemplarism lurking behind even his most Aristotelianizing versions of a theory of knowledge encouraged him to make extraordinary use of the emerging doctrine of transcendentals (see LANGUAGE, MEDIEVAL THEORIES OF). Although he had insisted that 'thing' was the broadest term which could be used to describe an object, Henry agreed with his scholastic predecessors that the first and most general concept available to the human intellect was that of being (ens or esse). This term, transcendental in the sense that it was logically prior to the generic division of things into the ten categories, brought the mind face to face with the participationist foundations of reality.

Like all thinkers before Duns Scotus, Henry conceded that 'being' at its most general was strictly equivocal, disjunctively applicable to the irreducibly distinct realities of God's being and the being of creatures. Yet although these two 'beings' had nothing really in common, they were similar enough – related by means of analogy – to give rise to concepts that were extremely close. Indeed, Henry said that in its initial perception of being, the mind was so deluded by this similarity as to mistake the two concepts referring to the being of God and that of creatures for a single concept.

The mind's confusion on this point looked to Henry like a most fruitful mistake. After all, his account of the conceptualization of being did not mean simply that the mind took two different concepts or terms to be the same. It actually stipulated that from the start the human intellect was confronted with a dual object: the unlimited being of God and the finite being of creation. From this, Henry concluded that every human intellect had a natural knowledge of God: not a knowledge impressed on the mind at creation, but rather one springing naturally from its very first act of understanding.

Implausible as this position might appear from an Aristotelian point of view, it was fully in line with the cognitive implications of Henry's own metaphysics, which opened the mind to a world of essence vibrant with the participatory relation between creature and creator. Moreover, it allowed Henry to support what he said was Avicenna's opinion that the human intellect could naturally construct an a priori proof for the existence of God. Such a proof would be a priori not in the sense that its foundations preceded sensory perception but rather because it arose from a primitive quidditative understanding of the divine being and did not have to be argued a posteriori from the evidence of created existence. If in its first, imprecise efforts to grasp 'being' conceptually the mind formed two general concepts so vague and indeterminate as to appear identical, upon reflection it would realize that what it took to be one idea was in fact two. First would be the concept of the 'negatively indeterminate' divine being, inherently incompatible with any limitation whatsoever; second, there would be the concept of a 'privatively indeterminate' created being, not yet reduced to any genus or species but necessarily determined in that way in every real case outside the mind. For all its vagueness, the first of these two concepts was in fact quidditative and proper to God, adequate to the demands of a priori demonstration.

With this assertion Henry left contemporary theologians behind, most of whom were content with an a posteriori proof for God modelled on the Aristotelianizing inclinations of Aquinas or Averroes. Yet his ideas impressed the following generation. For all his criticism of Henry, Duns Scotus' radical position on the univocity of the concept of being and the way he worked from it to develop a quidditative argument for God's existence were inspired by his predecessor's a priori proof (Marrone 1983: 49–56) (see GOD, ARGUMENTS FOR THE EXISTENCE OF).

5 Theory of will

Henry is generally credited with a voluntarist notion of moral action, in contrast to intellectualism of either the robust variety found in Godfrey of Fontaines or the mitigated strain of Aquinas and Giles of Rome. Although in fact no thinker of Henry's day was voluntarist to the extent of completely severing the will's choice from the practical intellect's judgment, it is true that his philosophical position placed the autonomous power of will in sharp relief. For him, will retained free choice even after judgment, its actions entirely uncoerced by what intellect had decided. Although this did not mean that a free will would arbitrarily disregard intellect's advice, Henry believed it did demand a distinctly non-Aristotelian account of causality in voluntary acts. The will could not act until it was presented with an object by the mind, but it was not the object, the mind's judgment or any affect triggered by the intellect that caused the will to act as it did. Instead, the will was entirely self-moved, endowed by God with an immanent power to go from potency to act (see FREE WILL).

Henry went so far as to reject the Thomistic distinction between a primary freedom to act (*libertas exercitii*), independently available to the will, and a secondary freedom to act in a specific way (*libertas specificationis*), constrained by intellect's judgment. Instead, he claimed that the will was always free not just to act or not to act but also to specify the act it would perform. Anything short of this he took to be intolerably deterministic (Macken 1977b: 146–7, 158–9). As with other areas of his philosophy, Henry's vision of the will laid the groundwork for several Augustinian currents in the fourteenth century, feeding into the quite distinct moral theories of Duns Scotus and Ockham.

List of works

Henry of Ghent (*c*.1275–93) *Opera omnia* (Complete Works), Louvain: University Press, 1979–. (Published to date are *Quodlibeta* I, II, VI, VII, IX, X, XII, XII q. 31, XIII; *Summa* art. 31–40; *Lectura ordinaria super Sacram Scripturam* (Ordinary Lectures on the Bible).)

—— (1275–93) *Summa quaestionum ordinariarum* (Collected Ordinary Questions), Paris: Badius, 1520; St. Bonaventure, NY: Franciscan Institute, 1953, 2 vols. (Intended as an exhaustive exposition of Henry's philosophy and theology; never completed.)

—— (1276–92) *Quodlibeta*, Paris: Badius, 1518; Louvain: Bibliothèque S.J., 1961, 2 vols. (A translation of selected questions appears in R.J. Teske (1993) *Quodlibetal Questions on Free Will*, Milwaukee: Marquette University.)

References and further reading

Bérubé, C. (1983) *De l'homme à Dieu selon Duns Scot, Henri de Gand et Olivi* (The Path from Man to God According to Duns Scotus, Henry of Ghent and Olivi), Rome: Istituto Storico dei Cappuccini. (Essays on the historical relation between Henry and some of his contemporaries and successors.)

Dumont, S. (1984) 'The quaestio si est and the Metaphysical Proof for the Existence of God according to Henry of Ghent and John Duns Scotus', *Franziskanische Studien* 66: 335–67. (Compares metaphysical foundations of Henry's and Scotus' theory of knowledge with that of Aristotle.)

Gómez Caffarena, J. (1958) *Ser participado y ser subsistente e la metafÚsica de Enrique de Gante* (Participated Being and Subsistent Being in the Metaphysics of Henry of Ghent), Rome: Pontificia Università Gregoriana. (Detailed analysis of Henry's ontology.)

Hödl, L. (1964) 'Neue Nachrichten über die Pariser

Verurteilungen der thomasischen Formlehre' (New Findings Concerning the Parisian Condemnations of Thomas' Theory of Form), *Scholastik* 39: 178–96. (On Henry's position in early debates over Thomas Aquinas.)

Macken, R. (1972) 'La théorie de l'illumination divine dans la philosophie d'Henri de Gand' (The Theory of Divine Illumination in the Philosophy of Henry of Ghent), *Recherches de Théologie Ancienne et Médiévale* 39: 82–112. (On the development of Henry's theory of knowledge.)

—— (1973) 'Les corrections d'Henri de Gand à ses Quodlibets' (Henry of Ghent's Corrections to his Quodlibets), *Recherches de Théologie Ancienne et Médiévale* 40: 5–51. (Critical for understanding textual tradition of Henry's works.)

—— (1977a) 'Les corrections d'Henri de Gand à sa Somme' (Henry of Ghent's Corrections to his Summa), *Recherches de Théologie Ancienne et Médiévale* 44: 55–100. (Critical for understanding textual tradition of Henry's works.)

* —— (1977b) 'Heinrich von Gent im Gespräch mit seinen Zeitgenossen über die menschliche Freiheit' (Henry of Ghent in Dialogue with his Contemporaries over Human Freedom), *Franziskanische Studien* 59: 125–82. (Detailed analysis of Henry on the will, comparing him with contemporaries.)

* Marrone, S.P. (1985) *Truth and Scientific Knowledge in the Thought of Henry of Ghent*, Cambridge, MA: Medieval Academy. (On the relation between Henry's changing theory of knowledge and his metaphysics.)

* —— (1988) 'Henry of Ghent and Duns Scotus on the Knowledge of Being', *Speculum* 63: 22–57. (Ties Henry's views on natural knowledge of God to Scotus' position on univocity of being and proof for God's existence.)

* Nys, T.V. (1949) *De werking van het menselijk verstand volgens Hendrik van Gent* (The Action of the Human Intellect According to Henry of Ghent), Louvain: Nauwelaerts. Abbreviated Latin version: *De psychologia cognitionis humanae secundum Henricum Gandavensem*, Rome: Pontificia Università Gregoriana. (Traces Henry's abandonment of intelligible species.)

Paulus, J. (1935–6) 'Henri de Gand et l'argument ontologique' (Henry of Ghent and the Ontological Argument), *Archives d'Histoire Doctrinale et Littéraire du Moyen Age* 10–11: 265–323. (On metaphysical implications of Henry's proof for existence of God.)

—— (1938) *Henri de Gand. Essai sur les tendances de sa métaphysique* (Henry of Ghent: Essays on the Contours of his Metaphysics), Paris: Vrin. (Most complete study of Henry's metaphysics.)

Porro, P. (1990) *Enrico di Gand. La via delle proposizioni universali* (Henry of Ghent: The Proof from Universal Propositions), Bari: Levante. (Analysis of ontological and theological significance of Henry's views on natural knowledge of God.)

STEVEN P. MARRONE

HENRY OF HARCLAY (*c.*1270–1317)

An English philosopher of the early fourteenth century, Harclay moved away from the position of Duns Scotus on the extramental existence of universals and towards the more conceptualist or nominalist stance of William of Ockham. On questions of infinity and continuity, Henry was strongly anti-Aristotelian, holding that there were numbers that were actually infinite and not all equal to each other, and that a continuum was composed of an actual infinity of indivisibles, by which it was properly measured. His position came under powerful mathematical attack.

Henry of Harclay, a member of a noble family from the North of England, received his education in arts at Oxford University and afterwards studied theology at Paris. He was much influenced by Duns Scotus, then teaching at Paris. In 1312, having returned to Oxford, he was elected and confirmed (by the Bishop of Lincoln) as Chancellor of the University. In this capacity in 1317 he journeyed to the papal court at Avignon in pursuance of a university dispute with the Dominican order, where he died.

In his commentary on the *Sentences* of Peter LOMBARD, representing his lectures at Paris in the course of attaining his theological qualifications, Harclay's teaching was very close to that of Duns Scotus, and he is counted among the first of Scotus' expositors. Later he adopted a more independent position, which has been seen as leading him in the direction of WILLIAM OF OCKHAM. His later thought is revealed in a number of disputed questions, whose contents have been rather spasmodically preserved in different manuscript codices. In one codex, pride of place is taken by a question as to whether astrologers or other 'calculators' can foretell the time of Christ's Second Coming. In this, Henry may be seen as upholding the claims of rational philosophy against the more mystical and inspirationist views of Arnald of Villanova, although he still allowed that the prophetic abbot JOACHIM OF FIORE had made some true predictions.

On the vexed question of universals, Henry was

concerned to diminish their extramental existence (see UNIVERSALS). He held that each individual thing outside the mind could move the intellect to conceive it either confusedly or distinctly. By the latter conception the mind could distinguish Plato from Socrates, but from the former it received the general notion of man. Harclay's somewhat woolly, if not confused, view was attacked from the realist side by Walter BURLEY, and from the nominalist camp by William of Ockham, who said that the opinion was false, unintelligible, and neither true nor logical. In the case of relations also, Henry veered towards conceptualism, holding that, if *A* was related to *B*, this did not mean that the relation *inhered* in *A*. This in turn implied that God could be really related to his creatures, since no change was entailed in him. On the question of the univocality of being, Harclay held that there is one kind of being in both God and creatures, and in this he was close to Scotus (although with several differences of nuance) and fervently opposed to Thomas AQUINAS, whose positions he often explicitly attacked.

It was in his views on continuity, however, that Henry went most strongly against the mainstream of scholastic philosophy. In these views, Henry built on the opinions of Robert GROSSETESTE, who had held that a line was properly measured by the number of points that it contained (and it would seem, although some scholars disagree, of which it was composed). To humans such numbers were infinite, but to God they were finite, and they could have between them both rational and irrational ratios. Harclay developed his views in two questions on the eternity of the world, concerning respectively its beginninglessness and its endlessness. Quite probably no schoolman held the heretical position that the world had actually existed from eternity, but there was controversy as to whether the opposite position could be proved by natural reason (see ETERNITY OF THE WORLD, MEDIEVAL VIEWS OF). Those who held that it was impossible for there to have been an infinite past time were wont to cite paradoxes, such as that, if there had been an infinite past time, then there would have been the same number of past revolutions of the Sun as of the Moon, and in general that a whole would be equal to its part. Harclay's principal strategy in rebutting these claims was to assert that there could be actually infinite numbers, and that one of these could be greater than another. This was contrary to the conventional view that numbers were only potentially infinite, in the sense that there was no limit to how far one could go on counting; the question of comparing different infinite numbers did not then arise.

Harclay extended his arguments into questions concerning the structure of continua, holding that each was composed of an infinite number of indivisibles, so that a line was made up of an infinite number of points. This again was opposed to the more holistic Aristotelian view that a continuum was infinitely divisible potentially (again in the sense of unlimited acts of division), but always into finite parts. It was certainly not composed of indivisibles, and was only measured by fictive indivisibles, as in treating feet as indivisibles for the measurement of lines. Harclay's position, like that of those who would compose continua out of finite numbers of indivisibles, gave rise to a host of difficulties. Among these was the question of how indivisibles could touch each other, for as Aristotle said, 'Since indivisibles have no parts, they must be in contact with one another as whole with whole' (*Physics* VI.1, 231b3). If that was the case, however, it was hard to see how they could compose something continuous bigger than themselves. Harclay's reply was that they did touch whole to whole, but according to a different position (*secundum distinctum situm*). Not surprisingly, such responses did not convince everyone, and among many attacks on indivisibilist positions, a devastating mathematically-based critique was made by Thomas BRADWARDINE, who cited Henry by name. However, Bradwardine did admit that he himself could be accused of a *petitio principii* by assuming the truth of the principles of Euclidean geometry.

See also: CANTOR'S THEOREM §1; DUNS SCOTUS, J.

List of works

Henry of Harclay (before 1310) *Commentarius in I et II (?) Sententiarum* (Commentary on Books I and [perhaps] II of the *Sentences* of Peter Lombard). (A discussion, in Latin, with refererence to the manuscript basis, can be found in C. Bali¢, (1959) 'Henricus de Harcley et Ioannes Duns Scotus', *Mélanges offerts à Étienne Gilson*, Toronto, Ont.: Pontifical Institute of Mediaeval Studies, and Paris: Vrin, 93–121.)

—— (*c.*1313) *Utrum mundus potuit fuisse ab eterno* (Whether the World Could Have Existed From Eternity), ed. R.C. Dales, 'Henricus de Harclay: Quaestio "Utrum Mundus Potuit Fuisse ab Eterno"', *Archives d'Histoire Doctrinale et Littéraire du Moyen Age* 50, 1983: 223–55.

—— (*c.*1313) *Utrum universale significet aliquam rem extra animam, aliam a singulari vel supposito* (Whether a Universal May Signify Some Thing Outside the Soul Other Than a Singular or Suppositum), ed. G. Gál, 'Henricus de Harclay: Quaestio de Significato Conceptus Universalis',

Franciscan Studies 31, 1971: 178–234. (Includes Latin discussion of the text.)

—— (*c*.1313) *Utrum praedestinatio aeterna qua Deus praedestinavit aliquem ad gloriam et reprobatio aeterna qua Deus aliquem reprobavit ponant in praedestinato vel in reprobato necessitatem aliquam respectu salutis vel repectu damnationis* (Whether the Eternal Predestination by which God Predestined One to Glory, and the Eternal Condemnation by which God Condemned Another, imply any Necessity in the Predestined or in the Condemned with Respect to Salvation or Damnation), ed. M.G. Henninger, 'Henry of Harclay's Questions on Divine Prescience and Predestination', *Franciscan Studies* 40, 1980: 167–243. (Henninger provides editions of this and the following question.)

—— (*c*.1313) *Utrum in praedestinato sit aliqua causa praevisa a Deo quare iste sit praedestinatus et ille reprobatus* (Whether in the Predestined there is any Cause Foreseen by God Whereby One should be Predestined and the other Condemned), ed. M.G. Henninger, 'Henry of Harclay's Questions on Divine Prescience and Predestinatio', *Franciscan Studies* 40, 1980: 167–243. (Henninger provides editions of this and the previous question.)

—— (*c*.1313) *Utrum Dei ad Creaturam sit Relatio Realis* (Whether there is a Real Relation of God to a Creature), ed. M.G. Henninger, 'Henry of Harclay's Question on Relations', *Mediaeval Studies* 49, 1978: 76–123. (Edition of the question.)

—— (*c*.1313) *Utrum Deo et creaturis aliquid sit commune univocum* (Whether Anything is Univocally Common to God and Creatures). (A discussion, without edition, may be found in A. Maurer, 'Henry of Harclay's Question on the Univocity of Being', *Mediaeval Studies* 16, 1954: 1–18.)

—— (*c*.1313) *Utrum aliud a Deo sit simpliciter necesse est* (Whether Anything other than God Exists in an Unqualifiedly Necessary Way), ed. A. Maurer, 'Henry of Harclay's Questions on Immortality', *Mediaeval Studies* 19, 1957: 79–107. (Edition includes two questions on immortality.)

—— (*c*.1313) *Utrum anima intellectiva sit immortalis* (Whether the Intellective Soul is Immortal), ed. A. Maurer, 'Henry of Harclay's Questions on Immortality', *Mediaeval Studies* 19, 1957: 79–107. (Edition includes two questions on immortality.)

—— (*c*.1313) *Utrum ad hoc quod Deus cognoscat alia a se oportet ponere in Deo relationes rationis ad absoluta cognita, quae sunt ideae* (Whether for God to Know Things other than Himself it is Necessary to Posit in God Relations of Reason to Things Absolutely Known, which are Ideas), ed. A. Maurer, 'Henry of Harclay's Questions on the

Divine Ideas', *Mediaeval Studies* 23, 1961: 163–93. (Edition includes two questions on divine ideas.)

—— (*c*.1313) *Utrum ad distinctam cognitionem quam habet Deus ab aeterno de rebus creabilibus requiruntur in eo distinctae rationes cognoscendi, per quas cognoscit ipsas res creabiles* (Whether for the Distinct Cognition that God has from Eternity of Creatable Things there are Required in Him Distinct Reasons of Knowing, by which He Knows those Creatable Things), ed. A. Maurer, 'Henry of Harclay's Questions on the Divine Ideas', *Mediaeval Studies* 23, 1961: 163–93. (Edition includes two questions on divine ideas.)

—— (*c*.1313) *Utrum in homine sit aliqua forma sustantialis praeter intellectivam* (Whether there is any Substantial Form in the Human Being besides the Intellective), ed. A. Maurer, 'Henry of Harclay's Disputed Question on the Plurality of Forms', in J.R. O'Donnell (ed.) *Essays in Honour of Anton Charles Pegis*, Toronto, Ont.: Pontifical Institute of Medieval Studies, 1974, 125–159. (Edition of Henry's question on the plurality of forms.)

—— (*c*.1313) *Utrum mundus potuit fuisse ab eterno* (Whether the World could have Existed from Eternity). (Discussion of the manuscripts and extensive analysis of the doctrines can be found in J.E. Murdoch, 'Henry of Harclay and the Infinite', *Studi sul XIV Secolo in Memoria di Anneliese Maier*, ed. A. Maierù and A. Paravicini Bagliani, Rome: Storia e Letteratura, 1981, 219–261.)

—— (*c*.1313) *Utrum mundum poterit durare in eternum a parte post* (Whether the World could Endure to Eternity Hereafter). (Discussion of the manuscripts and extensive analysis of the doctrines can be found in J.E. Murdoch, 'Henry of Harclay and the Infinite', *Studi sul XIV Secolo in Memoria di Anneliese Maier*, ed. A. Maierù and A. Paravicini Bagliani, Rome: Storia e Letteratura, 1981, 219–261.)

—— (*c*.1313) *Utrum astrologi vel quicumque calculatores possint probare secundum adventum Christi* (Whether Astrologers or any Calculators could Prove the Second Coming of Christ), ed. F. Pelster, 'Die Quaestio Heinrichs von Harclay über die Zweite Ankunft Christi und die Erwartung des baldingen Weltendes zu Anfang des XIV Jahrhunderts', *Archivio Italiano per la Storia della Pietà* 1, 1951: 27–82. (Edition of the question.)

References and further reading

Adams, M.M. (1982) 'Universals in the Early Fourteenth Century', in N. Kretzmann, A. Kenny and J. Pinborg (eds) *The Cambridge History of Later Medieval Philosophy*, Cambridge: Cambridge University Press, 411–39. (Places Henry's views on universals in the context of late medieval debates.)

Aristotle (*c*.mid 4th century BC) *Physics*, trans. R.P. Hardie and R.K. Gaye in W.D. Ross (ed.) *The Works of Aristotle Translated into English*, Oxford: Clarendon Press, 1930, vol. 2. (Includes Aristotle's writings on indivisibles, discussed by Harclay.)

Dales, R.C. (1984) 'Henry of Harclay on the Infinite', *Journal of the History of Ideas* 45: 295–302. (Discusses the issue with reference to the traditions from which Henry drew.)

Henninger, M.G. (1989) *Relations: Medieval Theories 1250–1325*, Oxford: Clarendon Press. (Devotes a chapter to Henry's views on the subject.)

Maier, A. (1964) *Ausgehendes Mittelalter: Gesammelte Aufsätze zur Geistesgeschichte des 14. Jahrhunderts* (The Closing of the Middle Ages: Collected Articles on the Intellectual History of the Fourteenth Century), Rome: Storia e Letteratura, vol. I. (Chapter 2 is concerned with early fourteenth-century discussions of the actual infinite, and Chapter 11 contests Balič's ascription of a commentary on Book II of the *Sentences* to Henry.)

Murdoch, J.E. (1982) 'Infinity and Continuity', in N. Kretzmann, A. Kenny and J. Pinborg (eds) *The Cambridge History of Later Medieval Philosophy*, Cambridge: Cambridge University Press, 564–91. (Valuable for placing Henry's views on the subject in their historical context.)

Pelster, F. (1924) 'Heinrich von Harclay, Kanzler von Oxford, und seine Quaestionen' (Henry of Harclay, Chancellor of Oxford, and His Questions), *Miscellanea Francesco Ehrle*, Rome: Biblioteca Apostolica Vaticana, vol. I, 307–56. (Still the fundamental overall study.)

Thijssen, J.M.N.H. (1990) 'The Response to Thomas Aquinas in the Early Fourteenth Century: Eternity and Infinity in the Works of Henry of Harclay, Thomas of Wilton and William of Alnwick OFM', in J.B.M. Wissink (ed.) *The Eternity of the World in the Thought of Thomas Aquinas and his Contemporaries*, Leiden: Brill, 82–100. (Pays particular attention to Henry's stance towards Aquinas.)

GEORGE MOLLAND

HERACLIDES OF PONTUS
(4th century BC)

Heraclides, a pupil of Plato, was roughly contemporaneous with Aristotle. Best known in antiquity as a writer of dialogues on moral and religious themes, he also held interesting views about cosmology and the structure of matter. Only fragments of his works survive.

Heraclides was probably born before 385 BC at Heraclea Pontica, on the Black Sea coast of modern Turkey, and lived into the penultimate decade of the fourth century. He received his philosophical training in Plato's Academy, where he may also have been influenced by Speusippus and Aristotle. Heraclides seems to have remained at the Academy under Plato's successor Speusippus, but retired to his home town after being defeated in the contest to succeed him.

Like Aristotle and other pupils of Plato, Heraclides made a transcript of Plato's lecture *On the Good* and wrote independent works on 'dialectic', moral and political philosophy, and religion, as well as literary and historical subjects. Today he is best known for two of his scientific theories. First, he combined a belief in the infinity of the universe with a system of planetary movements partly anticipating that of Tycho Brahe (see KEPLER, J.): the earth rotates about its axis from west to east in one synodic day; the sun circles the earth from west to east in a year, presumably in the plane of the ecliptic; and the inner planets, Mercury and Venus, revolve about the sun on epicycles. We are not told his views on the movements of the outer planets.

Second, he believed that matter is made up of two kinds of particle separated by microvoids: 'corpuscles' (*onkoi*) and 'fragments'. Corpuscles themselves are constituted of 'fragments' (*thrausmata*) and may be broken down into fragments; fragments, however, cannot be broken down any further. The corpuscles have at least some of the sensible qualities of macroscopic bodies, but the fragments do not; thus the corpuscles are analogous to the atoms of modern chemistry, the fragments to protons and electrons.

Both theories were inspired by Plato's Timaeus (see PLATO §16). In this text, the movements of Mercury and Venus were described, but not explained (38d); an axial rotation of the earth was thought by many to be mentioned at 40b–c; and Plato introduced a theory according to which each of the four elements consists of minimum particles shaped like one of the regular solids, and these in turn are constituted of and can be broken down into two kinds of triangle (54d–57c). Heraclides substituted three-dimensional 'fragments' for Plato's two-dimensional triangles; instead of seeing the elementary particles as geometrical constructs, he treated them as aggregates of matter. But his postulating two stages of aggregation distinguished his theory from other contemporary atomic doctrines, and this came to him from Plato.

There was a similar development in his doctrine of

the soul. Like Plato, he believed that the soul is immortal and subject to reincarnation, but whereas Plato regarded it as incorporeal, Heraclides taught that it is constituted of 'light', the finest kind of matter; between incarnations, souls not wicked enough to be sent to hell congregate in one part of the heavens, where they form the Milky Way. With this doctrine we leave the field of science and come to that on which Heraclides' popularity rested: ethical and religious dialogues. His outlook was puritanical. He believed that the desire for pleasure corrupts both individuals and societies, with dire results; for the gods observe human behaviour and ensure that crimes are punished. His dialogues were full of such stories, and also revelations, including eschatological ones, miracles and sermons by ancient wise men including Empedocles, Pythagoras and the Scythian *shaman* Abaris. They were heady stuff and found readers until the end of antiquity.

Heraclides left no school. CICERO (§1) admired his style and used his writings as a model for his own dialogues, but the only reader to take his ideas seriously was the physician Asclepiades of Bithynia (see HELLENISTIC MEDICAL EPISTEMOLOGY). Asclepiades work was based on Epicurean conceptions, but he adopted Heraclides' corpuscular theory; presumably he found it useful for explaining physiological processes.

References and further reading

Gottschalk, H.B. (1980) *Heraclides of Pontus*, Oxford: Clarendon Press. (Includes English translations of most of the important fragments and a full bibliography; in the appendices some new texts are added and others are shown to be spurious.)

* Plato (c. 366–60 BC) *Timaeus*, trans. F.M. Cornford, *Plato's Cosmology*, London: Routledge & Kegan Paul, 1937. (Plato's theory of elements is at 53b–6c, his astronomical system at 34a–40d.)

Wehrli, F. (1953) *Die Schule des Aristoteles* (The Aristotelian School), vol. 7, Basle: Schwabe; repr., 2nd edn, 1969. (Greek text of Heraclides' main fragments, bibliography and German commentary.)

H.B. GOTTSCHALK

HERACLITUS (*c.*540–*c.*480 BC)

No Greek philosopher born before Socrates was more creative and influential than Heraclitus of Ephesus. Around the beginning of the fifth century BC, in a prose that made him proverbial for obscurity, he criticized conventional opinions about the way things are and attacked the authority of poets and others reputed to be wise. His surviving work consists of more than 100 epigrammatic sentences, complete in themselves and often comparable to the proverbs characteristic of 'wisdom' literature. Notwithstanding their sporadic presentation and transmission, Heraclitus' sentences comprise a philosophy that is clearly focused upon a determinate set of interlocking ideas.

As interpreted by the later Greek philosophical tradition, Heraclitus stands primarily for the radical thesis that 'Everything is in flux', like the constant flow of a river. Although it is likely that he took this thesis to be true, universal flux is too simple a phrase to identify his philosophy. His focus shifts continually between two perspectives – the objective and everlasting processes of nature on the one hand and ordinary human beliefs and values on the other. He challenges people to come to terms, theoretically and practically, with the fact that they are living in a world 'that no god or human has made', a world he describes as 'an ever-living fire kindling in measures and going out in measures' (fr. 30). His great truth is that 'All things are one', but this unity, far from excluding difference, opposition and change, actually depends on them, since the universe is in a continuous state of dynamic equilibrium. Day and night, up and down, living and dying, heating and cooling – such pairings of apparent opposites all conform to the everlastingly rational formula (logos) that unity consists of opposites; remove day, and night goes too, just as a river will lose its identity if it ceases to flow.

Heraclitus requires his audience to try to think away their purely personal concerns and view the world from this more detached perspective. By the use of telling examples he highlights the relativity of value judgments. The implication is that unless people reflect on their experience and examine themselves, they are condemned to live a dream-like existence and to remain out of touch with the formula that governs and explains the nature of things. This formula is connected (symbolically and literally) with 'ever-living fire', whose incessant 'transformations' are not only the basic operation of the universe but also essential to the cycle of life and death. Fire constitutes and symbolizes both the processes of nature in general and also the light of intelligence. As the source of life and thought, a 'fiery' soul equips people to look into themselves, to discover the formula of nature and to live accordingly.

The influence of Heraclitus' ideas on other philosophers was extensive. His reputed 'flux' doctrine, as disseminated by his follower Cratylus, helped to shape Plato's cosmology and its changeless metaphysical foundations. The Stoics looked back to Heraclitus as the inspiration for their own conception of divine fire, identifying this with the logos *that he specifies as the world's explanatory principle. Later still, the neo-Pyhrronist Aenesidemus invoked Heraclitus as a partial precursor of scepticism.*

1 **Life and work**
2 **Methodology**
3 **Unity of opposites and perspectivism**
4 **Cosmology**
5 **Psychology, ethics and religion**
6 **Influence**

1 Life and work

Heraclitus appears to have spent his life in Ephesus, which had been founded as a Greek colony some 200 years before his birth. According to ancient biography he was an arrogant and surly aristocrat, given to eccentric behaviour, but these anecdotes are largely a fictional construction built out of his own words, in which the tone he adopts in relation to other people is contemptuous. Rather than viewing this as a psychological trait, it is better to treat it as an extreme instance of the way early Greek poets and sages claimed authority for their work. Heraclitus, however, is exceptional in the explicit contempt he expresses for such hallowed authorities as Homer and Hesiod, and also for the contemporary intellectuals Xenophanes, Hecataeus and Pythagoras. He may have been on bad terms with his fellow citizens for political reasons, including perhaps support he received from King Darius of Persia, and it is likely that he was opposed to the democratic constitutions some Greek communities were beginning to adopt.

Although Heraclitus presents himself as uniquely enlightened, he was clearly familiar with the leading thinkers of his time. He draws attention to the relativity of judgments and the difference between humans and animals in ways that recall Xenophanes' critique of religious beliefs (see XENOPHANES §3). He almost certainly knew and rejected Pythagoras' doctrine of the transmigration of souls (see PYTHAGORAS §2). His cosmology is both indebted to and a criticism of Milesian science: the criticism appears particularly in his denial of the world's beginning, but his focus on the law-like processes of nature has clear affinities with Anaximander's celebrated doctrine of cosmic justice (see ANAXIMANDER §4).

Heraclitus' work does not survive as a continuous whole. What we have instead is a collection of more than 100 independent sentences, most of which are *ad hoc* citations by authors from the period AD 100–300. Plato and Aristotle rarely cite Heraclitus directly, but their interpretations of him, which are influenced in part by their own preconceptions, shaped the ancient tradition of Heraclitus as exponent of universal flux and of fire as the primary material. Interpretation of Heraclitus is further complicated by the work of his professed follower CRATYLUS, and still more so by the way Stoics and Pyrrhonists looked back to him as a precursor of their own philosophies (see §6). This afterlife is important as an indication of Heraclitus' complexity and capacity to influence a range of very different thinkers, but modern interpretation of him rightly treats it as secondary to the evidence of his own words.

Heraclitus is credited with writing a book, *On Nature*, and depositing it in a temple of Artemis. Some scholars believe that the book was a later compilation of sayings that he never wrote down, but while many of the fragments are well suited to oral delivery, this scarcely applies to the longest one, with which he is said to have begun his book:

> Of this formula (*logos*) that is so always people are uncomprehending, both before hearing it and once they have heard it. For although all things come to pass in accordance with this formula, people seem lacking in experience even when they experience such words and deeds as I expound, when I distinguish each thing according to its nature and explain how it is. But other people are oblivious of what they do awake just as they forget what they do asleep.
>
> (fr. 1)

2 Methodology

Heraclitus presents himself as the deliverer of a *logos* (see LOGOS). Any speaker could make a similar claim, but Heraclitus' *logos* is not his personal message or thought. Rather, Heraclitus views himself simply as a conduit for *the logos, the* means by which his audience will learn the objective truth about everything. In characterizing the *logos*, Heraclitus claims that 'it is so always'; it is the world's rationale or determining formula, the key to each thing's nature.

The *logos* is accessible to thought and linguistic expression because it is 'common' or 'public'; but 'most people live as though their thinking were private'. Heraclitus uses this contrast, and the contrast between waking and sleeping, to signal the gap between experience people have in common and the erroneous or purely subjective opinions they typically base on that experience. Taken as a set of general truths, the *logos* includes such propositions as the following: 'All things are one', 'All things are an exchange for fire, and fire for all things', 'Nature loves to hide', 'War is father of all and king of all',

'The way up and down is one and the same', 'God is day night, winter summer, war peace, satiety hunger'. Heraclitus does not present arguments for these cryptic statements, nor does he elucidate them. His Delphic style is a deliberate provocation of thought, a way of rousing his audience to solve his riddling account of nature and to discover the *logos* for and in themselves. In order to do so, he suggests, they need to rid themselves of naïve empiricism, to 'expect the unexpected', to connect things that they normally keep separate, to practise self-scrutiny, self-knowledge – in short, they need to discover the 'depth of the soul's own *logos*', which presumably signifies the mind's unlimited capacity to arrive at a complete understanding of the *logos* of nature.

In addition to general statements of the kind illustrated above, Heraclitus uses many other kinds of sentence. These include comments on the lack of wisdom manifested by the supposedly learned as well as by ordinary people, graphic statements concerning the 'unity of opposites' and the relativity of values, instruction concerning the 'measures' of physical change, characterizations of the soul, and numerous injunctions about the wisdom, lawfulness and piety requisite for a good life. One ancient commentator described his book as consisting of three topics: the universe, politics and theology. Another called it 'a guide to conduct', and it was also described as being about 'society, with the treatment of nature being metaphorical'. Such attempts at systematizing Heraclitus are anachronistic, but they have the merit of recognizing his complexity. He was, as he describes himself, an inquirer into the 'nature' of things, but it would be no less correct to call him a moralist and psychologist; what he derived from his inquiry was an urgent message about the need for human beings to refashion their values and their outlook in accordance with the implications of the *logos*.

3 Unity of opposites and perspectivism

In emphasizing the 'unity of all things', Heraclitus was not saying, as his Milesian predecessors had done, that every natural object is the manifestation of a single material nature such as water or air (see ANAXIMENES). Nor was he denying the obvious phenomenal difference between hot and cold, light and dark, living and dead, up and down. Heraclitus' world includes the normal range of things that are different from one another. What makes all things one is the fact, as he sees it, that a common formula (*logos*) is at work in everything to which we attribute spatial and/or temporal identity and continuity. Such opposites as those just enumerated are not separate or separable from one another but are co-dependent

contributors to the identity of things. In any day (regarded as twenty-four hours), light and dark are combined, as are up and down in any road. Nothing can be alive that will not die, and nothing can be dead that has not lived. If one of these opposites is removed, the other must go too.

Apart from cases where the co-presence or successive presence of opposites is *obviously* essential to things, Heraclitus drew support for the unity of opposites from examples where it could be inferred even though it was less obvious. In the bow and the lyre, he said, there is a 'back-stretched structure' (or 'back-turning structure' on an alternative reading). The effectiveness of both instruments depends upon tension between a piece of wood and a taut string. These components pull in opposite ways, and thereby they generate the unitary objects, lyre and bow. His famous image, 'You can't step twice into the same river', is probably to be interpreted in a similar way. What gives the river its identity is the continuous flow of successively different water. If 'All things flow' is a statement that Heraclitus approved, it is best interpreted as his image for the claim that even apparently stable beings depend for their identity on the interchange or succession of their constituent parts or on conflicting forces. The image need not, and probably should not, be regarded as a claim that nothing has a stable identity, but rather that such stability as things do have is derived from the equipollence of their constitutive opposites.

The unity of opposites formula is also applicable to Heraclitus' account of the way physical processes occur in the world at large. Changes of temperature and liquidity are constantly taking place, but they do so according to measure and balance. In the cosmic context, 'All things are one' obtains because a single thermodynamic principle (as it might be called now) is operative throughout the system: 'an ever-living fire, kindling in measures and going out in measures' (fr. 30). Another name for this principle, and another view of the unity of opposites, are evident in the statement that 'God is day night, winter summer, war peace, satiety hunger. He alters as when [fire] mingled with spices is named according to each person's pleasure' (fr. 67). Two implications might be drawn from this passage. One is that, from a divine perspective, the contrary evaluations normally accorded to day *or* night, to war *or* peace, are transcended. The other is that human discriminations between these opposites are purely arbitrary.

Heraclitus certainly endorsed the first implication, but did so for the second only with qualification. The passage does indeed suggest a radical difference between the divine and the human, but Heraclitus' point is probably that people need to adjust those of their perspectives that are purely personal or subjective and bring them into line with the objective way things are: it will always be the case that sea water is fair *and* foul, 'fair for fish and foul for human beings' (fr. 61). It is equally and necessarily the case that non-human animals have different preferences from humans. Yet the unity of opposites is a principle that also requires radical reordering of conventional opinions. Because the world is a dynamic interplay of opposing forces, 'people must realize that war is common and justice is strife' (fr. 80). In this difficult saying, Heraclitus is not recommending belligerence and the breakdown of civil society. His point is rather that people must come to terms with the fact that conflicting forces are basic to the way the world is structured – are in fact essential to its balance and order. That is how inanimate physical powers interact. He seems to have inferred, by analogy, that competition, involving winners and losers, is no less essential when accounting for the differences of status within his own day-to-day world. Hence the assertion that: 'War is father of all and king of all; and some he has shown as gods, others as humans; some he has made slaves and others free' (fr. 53).

4 Cosmology

Judging from the extant fragments, Heraclitus devoted only a small fraction of his philosophy to cosmology and explanation of physical phenomena. Many of his ancient interpreters, however, starting with Aristotle, interpreted him as if this were his main purpose. Working from texts in which Heraclitus refers to the transformations of 'ever-living' fire, they concluded that he endorsed the following doctrines: first, that fire is the underlying principle of all things; second, that particular phenomena are composed of and resolved into fire by rarefaction and condensation; and third, that the world as a whole is an everlastingly repeated sequence of temporally limited cycles, each of which emerges out of fire and ends in fire. These 'doctrines', or at least the first and the third of them, are generally treated today as anachronistic attempts to fit Heraclitus' ideas into a pattern more applicable to other thinkers. Although this modern diagnosis is justified in part, ancient philosophers were clearly right in thinking that Heraclitus regarded fire as the world's primary and most explanatory phenomenon. The problem is to understand what he intended by this claim.

Some of his statements suggest that fire is what one should start from and end with in any reflection on natural change. He certainly thought that what would later be called elements or elementary qualities (hot, cold, moist and dry) are interdependent phases of a continuous cycle. Hence his use of statements such as 'The cold gets warm, the warm gets cold, the moist gets dry, the dry gets damp' (fr. 126). This kind of insight is obviously suitable as an illustration of the way 'All things flow' and the unity of opposites, but it does not explain why he said that 'All things are an exchange for fire, and fire for all things, as goods for gold and gold for goods' (fr. 90). What is it that privileges fire in the cycle of change and makes it the one appropriate exchange symbol for everything else?

The answer, authorized by the Aristotelian tradition, is that fire is *the* underlying principle or *the* element. An underlying principle or element should be the unchanging foundation of everything that changes, but Heraclitus explicitly denies that fire is like this. Rather, it is continuously changing, 'kindling in measures and going out in measures'. What is unchanging about Heraclitus' fire is the *way* it changes – according to 'measures'. Heraclitus uses the term 'measures' to indicate cosmic order, balance, proportionality, natural law. He probably inferred by observation that, of all natural phenomena, fire is not only the most dynamic but also the one that is most obviously self-regulating. A fire consumes all the material that is available to it, nothing more and nothing less. What it consumes it also changes. It lives, as it were, by destroying something else; or, viewed from another perspective, it destroys itself by creating something else.

Heraclitus' fire, then, is not merely *one* phase in the cycle of natural changes. As the world's 'currency' or exchange symbol, the sum of fire's activity is completely commensurate with the sum of everything else. Fire's gain is everything else's loss and vice versa. The reciprocity or exchange between fire and the rest of things is Heraclitus' principle of cosmic order. There is a clear similarity here to Anaximander, who invoked 'crime and retribution' as the model to explain how change (hot to cold, wet to dry, and so forth) is balanced and reciprocal. Heraclitus was clearly impressed by his predecessor's bold appeal to 'justice' as the regulating principle of natural processes. But he was entirely original in treating fire as the primary process of nature. Given the conceptual resources available to him, nothing could have served him better as the way to indicate that nature is a dynamic system, that apparently stable things are also processes, that apparent unities are also polarities.

This, then, appears to be what Heraclitus meant by premising his cosmology on 'ever-living fire, kindling in measures and going out in measures'. He probably did not think, as ancient interpreters supposed, that our world is everlastingly recreated and destroyed, but rather, that nothing exists outside the system of fire and its exchanges. The system is self-regulating, and because there is nothing to interrupt its rhythm it persists for ever. Heraclitus is the earliest Greek thinker to postulate an everlasting world, and he is also probably the earliest to apply the term *kosmos* (meaning 'beautiful structure') to the world (see however PYTHAGORAS §2).

Did Heraclitus identify his cosmic fire with the god to whom he sometimes referred? Did he also think of these as the physical correlate or referent of his *logos* formula? Precise answers to these questions are scarcely possible, but his Stoic interpreters were probably not far wrong in answering affirmatively for him. Although he evidently took a huge step in the direction of treating the universe as an autonomic field of counterbalancing forces, he probably also thought of it as a mind-directed system. Some of the fragments seem to allude to a divine plan or purposiveness. Still more suggestive are connections he drew between fire, soul, life and intelligence.

5 Psychology, ethics and religion

No fewer than ten of the fragments are statements about the PSYCHĒ. In its primary Greek usage this term signifies a human being's life, but Heraclitus uses the word not only in this way but also to signify mind and intelligence. He made a major contribution to the idea (immensely important to Greek philosophy from Socrates and Plato onward) that cultivation of the *psychē* is the prerequisite for living well.

'Eyes and ears', he said, 'are poor witnesses to those who have barbarian *psychai*' (fr. 107). In this dense statement Heraclitus likens the unenlightened majority to 'barbarians' – that is, foreigners, who lack the language and culture of genuine Greeks. In order to live authentically, one needs a *psychē* that can interpret empirical evidence correctly – a *psychē* that understands the truths expressed by Heraclitus' *logos*. The *psychē* as such, he suggests, has unlimited resources, but in order to draw on them it is necessary, as he has done, to 'inquire into oneself'. Such observations indicate that Heraclitus' philosophy was simultaneously outward-and inward-looking: his *logos* is both the formula of nature's processes and the account of a mind or a self thinking and understanding that formula.

Heraclitus forges a link between these two aspects of his *logos* by invoking fire in remarks about the *psychē*. He associates life, intelligence and excellence with fire and dryness; by contrast, it is 'death for souls to become water', and a drunken man (that is, someone who has lost his bearings) 'has a soul that is moist'. We are probably intended to take these statements both literally and symbolically. This complex reading fits Heraclitus' statements about fire

in cosmological contexts, where fire is both a constituent of nature and the currency for understanding all processes. It is also relevant in the case of the *psychē*. Living beings derive their vitality from the ever-living fire, but what a fiery soul contributes to humans is not merely life but the 'light' of intelligence. It is entirely in Heraclitus' manner to exploit the multiple resonance of words, and to demand interpretation that is metaphorical as well as literal.

The intelligence that Heraclitus seeks to kindle should, he suggests, make people rethink their beliefs about life, death, religion and society. He attacks the folly of religious rituals, especially blood sacrifice; he recommends strict respect for civic law and order; he contrasts 'the best', who seek immortal fame, with the bovine satisfactions of the majority. He particularly emphasizes people's inability in general to come to terms with death, suggesting that the way one dies has a bearing both on one's worth as a person and also on one's postmortem condition. Does this last point refer to some kind of postmortem existence or simply to a person's reputation after death? The latter seems the more likely, given his emphasis upon the cyclical phases of natural processes. Nothing seems to have mattered more to Heraclitus than persuading people to regard themselves as integral parts of an ineluctable cosmic order. From this perspective, we should organize our lives in the realization that we are mortal but intelligent phases in the cosmic life of ever-living fire.

6 Influence

Heraclitus' influence on subsequent philosophers was large and complex. It is probably first evident in PARMENIDES (§§3–8), whose argument for a wholly changeless and homogeneous reality reads often like a direct echo and refutation of Heraclitus. In response to the Heraclitean philosopher Cratylus, Plato was impressed by the thesis that phenomena are in constant flux, but he rejected this as an account of 'intelligible' reality on the grounds that what is in constant flux cannot be known. Aristotle, taking Heraclitus' combinations of opposites to be a flagrant breach of the principle of non-contradiction, interpreted him as 'making all statements true'. It seems not to have occurred to either Plato or Aristotle that Heraclitus' *logos* could be interpreted as the changeless and knowable formula of a world that is incessantly but regularly changing.

Heraclitus' most penetrating and positive interpreters were the early Stoic philosophers. He inspired basic features of their cosmology, especially their identification of the world's 'active principle' with divine fire, and they also gave their own slant to the

Heraclitean *logos*, which they interpreted as the 'rationality' embodied in divine fire (see CLEANTHES; STOICISM §3). A reading of Cleanthes' *Hymn to Zeus* is the best way to view Heraclitus' influence on Stoicism. In that text, Cleanthes reflects Heraclitus not only in his references to fire and *logos* but also in the way he presents the divine principle as reconciling opposites and embodying the laws of nature.

A further aspect of Heraclitus' influence is to be seen in AENESIDEMUS, the founder of neo-Pyrrhonist philosophy. Aenesidemus was in the habit of citing Heracliteanism as 'a route to scepticism', basing this claim on Heraclitus' way of predicating opposites of the same subject.

See also: PRESOCRATIC PHILOSOPHY

References and further reading

Barnes, J. (1982) *The Presocratic Philosophers*, London: Routledge & Kegan Paul, chaps 4 and 7. (A vigorous treatment, often critical of Heraclitus' logical acumen.)

* Cleanthes (*c.*331–232 BC) *Hymn to Zeus*, in A.A. Long and D.N. Sedley, *The Hellenistic Philosophers*, Cambridge: Cambridge University Press, 1987, vol. 1, 326–7, vol. 2: 326–7. (Greek text and translation.)

Guthrie, W.K.C. (1962) *A History of Greek Philosophy*, vol. 1, Cambridge: Cambridge University Press, 6 vols. (Volume 1, chapter 7 gives a detailed and balanced treatment.)

* Heraclitus (*c.*540–480 BC) Fragments, in H. Diels and W. Kranz (eds) *Die Fragmente der Vorsokratiker* (Fragments of the Presocratics), Berlin: Weidemann, 6th edn, 1952, vol. 1, 139–82. (The standard collection of the ancient sources; includes Greek texts with translations in German.).

Hussey, E. (1972) *The Presocratics*, London: Duckworth, ch. 3. (Excellent study comparing Heraclitus to Wittgenstein.)

—— (1982) 'Epistemology and Meaning in Heraclitus', in M. Schofield and M. Nussbaum (eds) *Language and Logos*, Cambridge: Cambridge University Press, 33–60. (Subtle analysis of Heraclitus' interpretative methodology.)

Kahn, C. (1979) *The Art and Thought of Heraclitus*, Cambridge: Cambridge University Press. (Text, translation and commentary; a fundamental exposition, taking the condition of mortality to be Heraclitus' real subject.)

Kirk, G.S. (1962) *Heraclitus: The Cosmic Fragments*, Cambridge: Cambridge University Press. (Classic study, particularly valuable for assessing the authenticity of key fragments.)

Kirk, G.S., Raven, J.E. and Schofield, M. (1983) *The Presocratic Philosophers*, Cambridge: Cambridge University Press, 2nd edn. (A valuable survey of Presocratic philosophy, including texts and translations; Heraclitus is discussed in chapter 6.)

Long, A.A. (1975–6) 'Heraclitus and Stoicism', *Philosophia* 5–6: 133–56; repr. in A.A. Long, *Stoic Studies*, Cambridge: Cambridge University Press, 1996, 35–57. (Chapter 2 is a study of Heraclitus and Stoicism.)

McKirahan, R.D. (1994) *Philosophy Before Socrates*, Indianapolis, IN: Hackett. (Contains translation and helpful discussion of the fragments in chapter 10.)

Marcovich, M. (1967) *Heraclitus, Greek Text with a Short Commentary*, Merida: Los Andes University Press. (Important scholarly tool.)

Mondolfo, R. and Tarán, L. (1972) *Eraclito: Testimonianze e imitazioni* (Heraclitus: Testimonies and Imitations), Florence: La Nuova Italia. (Contains and comments on Greek texts referring to and imitative of Heraclitus.)

Robinson, T.M. (1987) *Heraclitus, Fragments*, Toronto, Ont.: Toronto University Press. (Includes Greek text of the fragments, with translation and commentary.)

Vlastos, G. (1955) 'On Heraclitus', *American Journal of Philology* 76: 337–68; repr. in *Studies in Greek Philosophy*, Princeton, NJ: Princeton University Press, 1995, vol. 1, 127–50. (Important study of the 'river' fragments.)

Wiggins, D. (1982) 'Heraclitus' Conceptions of Flux, Fire and Material Persistence', in M. Schofield and M. Nussbaum (eds) *Language and Logos*, Cambridge: Cambridge University Press, 1–32. (Sympathetic study by a major modern philosopher.)

A.A. LONG

HERBART, JOHANN FRIEDRICH (1776–1841)

From 1798, Herbart developed a 'realistic' alternative to the idealistic philosophy of Kant, Fichte, Schelling and Hegel. His theoretical philosophy, which centres around metaphysics and psychology, is sharply critical of the idealistic concept of subjectivity. His practical philosophy rests on ethics and educational theory, each of which presumes the existence of the other.

Herbart laid the foundations for his philosophy by

369

critically examining Fichte's philosophy in the late 1790s. Like Kant, Fichte had distinguished between theoretical and practical philosophy. Unlike Kant, however, he believed he could pinpoint the factor uniting them. Fichte called this uniting factor 'the ego', 'pure, absolute self-consciousness' (see FICHTE, J.G. §§3–5).

Herbart responded by stating that it is true that we understand the ego to be identical with self. It is also true that this term suggests itself forcibly to us. However, we cannot conceive of the ego as constituting an identity of this kind, because it is a contradictory concept in itself. If the ego is to be comprehended as an act of 'conceiving of oneself' or as 'conceiving of one's ego', it should be possible for us to know *that* the ego is conceiving something, but not *what* it is conceiving. Fichte's concept of the absolute ego is therefore circular and incomplete.

This leads on to the theoretical part of Herbart's philosophy and into the realms of metaphysics and psychology. For Herbart, metaphysics consists first of a search for and analysis of concepts which are given but not conceivable, because they are contradictory in themselves. Contradictions of this kind present themselves not merely in terms of the concept of 'ego', but also in the concept of an individual thing with many characteristics (the problem of inherence), the concept of change (the problem of causality), and in the concept of matter. In Herbart's view, the second task of metaphysics is to map out a path showing how such contradictions in thinking can be resolved. This task is performed by methodology. In general terms, an attempt is made to demonstrate that the given contradiction in concepts (for example, identity of ego subject and ego object) rests on manifold, composite premises. While these premises are not apparent in the given concepts, the concepts refer to them as a part or outcome. Herbart calls this analysis the 'relations method'. Finally, his view of metaphysics incorporates ontology and 'synechology'. The task of ontology as the science of being is to cast light on the characteristics and structure of being, in other words to determine what is real in the appearances of things. While scepticism may prevail in respect of what we perceive or experience in the world, the fact that we do actually experience something cannot be denied or arbitrarily declared invalid. Experience as a state cannot be negated. For Herbart this implies that being means at any one time an 'absolute position'. Being is positive, *per se* simple, and beyond all relationship. The world we know is based on a multiplicity of simple entities, the 'reals', which are self-sufficient and react to change ('pressure') by seeking self-preservation. Synechology, then, determines the metaphysical manifestations in time and

space of the multitude of individual reals which are in themselves simple (line, level, space; movement, speed).

By drawing on the essentials of metaphysics, Herbart was at the same time able to lay the foundations for his psychology. The 'true' basis of the concept of the ego, which is recognized as being contradictory, resides in the fact that Fichte's formula of the conceiving ego being identical with the conceived ego actually refers to a multiplicity of changing states, for which the formulas must be presumed. Herbart's explanation of self-consciousness as the essential task of 'realistic' psychology is as follows. Human consciousness is a mass of different interacting presentations. A study of their interaction gives rise to 'statics and dynamics' of the mind. The conscious separation of the act of conceiving from what is conceived is important for the development of self-consciousness. These two series of 'presentations' are joined by the concept of 'self' which presents itself, above all, in linguistic terms. Just as we say that water carves out its river bed 'for itself', we also project ourselves as the 'subject' of the act of conceiving onto a 'self' in which the conceiving and the conceived ego are deemed to be one and the same thing.

Herbart's practical philosophy also flows from his criticism of ego. Just as there can be no pure ego, there can equally be no pure, transcendentally free will (see FICHTE, J.G. §§3–5; KANT, I. §11). A pure will would be a will which does not desire anything. That is a contradiction, however, since we always want something.

Herbart deduces from this that reason does not express itself as will, but rather as an aesthetic judgment. In the sphere of ethics, reason does not pass judgment on natural or artistic beauty, but on the well-balanced nature of human decisions. The fundamental judgment here is that human beings should gain an insight into what is good by dint of their will. This judgment leads to the 'idea of inner freedom' as consisting of a unity between insight and will. Herbart answers the question of which insight is good by presenting four more aesthetic ideas: perfection, benevolence, right and equity. These five ideas are directed at the individual. Similarly, Herbart derives five other ideas for society. In passing its judgment on aesthetic grounds, reason cannot induce morality (as a unity between insight and will). The fact that individuals can follow the judgments of reason is not a matter for moral philosophy or reason itself, but for educational theory. The primary task of educational theory – of 'educative instruction' – is to ensure that the child gains an insight. Its second task is to strengthen the will of the child and lead it to follow its insights – the task of 'discipline'. Ethics is ineffectual without educational theory and is devoid of any moral reality, while educational theory without ethics is devoid of any goal or reason.

See also: EDUCATION, HISTORY OF PHILOSOPHY OF §8; GERMAN IDEALISM

List of works

Herbart, J.F. (1887–) *Sämtliche Werke in chronologischer Reihenfolge* (Complete Works), ed. K. Kehrbach, Langensalza: Beyer. (The standard complete works.)

—— (1806a) 'Hauptpunkte der Metaphysik' (Chief Points of Metaphysics), in Herbart, 1887, vol. 2: 175–226. (Herbart's answer to the question put by Kant in his *Critique of Pure Reason*: 'How is cognition possible?'. A very compact survey of Herbart's theoretical philosophy.)

—— (1806b) 'Allgemeine Pädagogik aus dem Zweck der Erziehung abgeleitet' (General Pedagogy Derived from the Aim of Education), in Herbart, 1887, vol. 2: 1–139. (Herbart's solution of the practical problem of how to make moral ideas real – by education.)

—— (1808) 'Allgemeine praktische Philosophie' (General Practical Philosophy), in Herbart, 1887, vol. 2: 329–458. (Herbart's proposal concerning the practical question of what, in an ethical sense, is the good.)

—— (1824, 1825) 'Psychologie als Wissenschaft neu gegründet auf Erfahrung, Metaphysik und Mathematik' (Psychology as a Science Newly Based on Experience, Metaphysics and Mathematics), Part 1 in Herbart, 1887, vol. 5, 177–402; Part 2 in Herbart, 1887, vol. 6, 1–338. (Herbart's fundamental work on the theoretical concept of the self.)

References and further reading

Dunkel, H.D. (1970) *Herbart and Herbartianism: An Educational Ghost Story*, Chicago, IL, and London: University of Chicago. (A systematic introduction to Herbartian pedagogy.)

Frank, M. (1991) 'Fragmente einer Geschichte der Selbstbewu tseinstheorien von Kant bis Sartre' (Historical Fragments of the Theory of the Self from Kant to Sartre), in *Selbstbewu tseinstheorien von Fichte bis Sartre* (Theories of the Self from Fichte to Sartre), ed. M. Frank, Frankfurt am Main: Suhrkamp, 413–599. (A critical discussion of the concepts of the self since Kant.)

Langewand, A. (1991) *Moralische Verbindlichkeit oder Erziehung. Herbarts frühe Subjektivitätskritik und die Entstehung des ethisch-edukativen Dilemmas* (Moral Obligation or Education. Herbart's Early Critique of Subjectivity and the Rise of the Dilemma Between Ethics and Education), Munich and Freiburg: Alber. (A study of the genesis of Herbart's theoretical and practical philosophy.)

ALFRED LANGEWAND

HERBERT, EDWARD (BARON HERBERT OF CHERBURY) (*c.*1583–1648)

Responding, on the one hand, to religious conflicts over the question of the locus and interpretation of authority for deciding what constitutes authentic belief and, on the other hand, to general philosophical scepticism, Herbert of Cherbury wrote De Veritate *(On Truth) in an attempt to determine the character and circumstances of true understanding. In this work, first published in 1624, he sought to enable people to decide for themselves, by the use of their reason, what they ought to hold. According to his thesis the touchstone for such decisions is provided by certain fundamental truths, the 'common notions', which all people recognize to be true once they have become aware of them. In two later works,* De Religione Gentilium *(On the Religion of the Heathens) (1663) and* A Dialogue between a Tutor and his Pupil *(1768), both published after his death, Herbert attempted to show that his position is not falsified by the evidence of wide differences among religions. His other writings include an important history of Henry VIII based on research into state papers, an autobiography that tells the story of his life up to 1624, and some poems. While this courtier, adventurer and diplomat was something of a failure as a public figure, and while he is commonly held to have essayed views about innate notions that were to be refuted by Locke's* Essay, *his writings provide pioneering studies in England in the genres of metaphysics, comparative religion and autobiography. Religiously he has been persistently maligned as 'the father of English deism' although closer consideration suggests that this reputation is not justified. He is, rather, to be considered an independent thinker who wanted to identify a form of religious belief that was rationally warranted and universally perceivable.*

1 Life

Edward Herbert, the son of Richard Herbert of Montgomery Castle, was probably born in 1583. His mother was a close friend of John Donne. In 1596 he matriculated at Oxford where he is said to have established a reputation for learning. He attended the court of Queen Elizabeth and was knighted at the accession of James I in 1603. In 1608 he began a series of visits to the continent where, as a courtier and soldier, he observed the consequences of religious disputes. In 1619 he became English ambassador to the French Court. While involved in diplomatic and social duties, he completed his major philosophical treatise, *De Veritate* (On Truth) and, encouraged by Hugo GROTIUS and Daniel Tilenus, had it printed in Paris in 1624. During that year he was recalled to England and dismissed, probably because his sensible advice to the king was disliked. James I and Charles I failed to reimburse Herbert for the debts that he incurred while ambassador, seeking to satisfy him with titles, first with the Irish peerage of Castle Island in 1624 and then with the barony of Cherbury in 1629. In fruitless attempts to regain royal favour he wrote two historical studies, the first an attempt to vindicate Buckingham's expedition to the Île de Rhé and the other a deservedly respected study of the reign of Henry VIII (both published posthumously, in 1656 and 1649 respectively).

In 1639 Herbert attended the King at Alnwick and in 1640 argued in the Council against a peace treaty with the Scots. Thereafter, however, although his sons served on the royalist side, Herbert's own main aims seem to have been to preserve his property and to continue his studies. In 1644, under threat that his library in London would be seized, he surrendered Montgomery Castle to Parliamentary forces. He moved to London and was given a pension by Parliament. In 1645 he published a revised and enlarged edition of *De Veritate*, copies of which often include his *De Causis Errorum* (Concerning the Causes of Errors) and other pieces, a collection that was also published separately in the same year. In 1647 he visited Pierre GASSENDI in Paris. On his deathbed he asked Archbishop Ussher, an old friend, to bring him the sacrament but his request was made in a less than wholly reverential way. Ussher consequently refused and Herbert died in London on 5 August 1648.

2 Metaphysics

Although respected, as well as criticized, by Grotius, Gassendi, DESCARTES and Locke, Herbert of Cherbury's work has largely been neglected since the beginning of the eighteenth century. This is partly because of the mixture of notions that provide the background to his insights (as well as being widely read in classical works, scholastic literature and works of Renaissance Humanism, he was influenced by Hermetic notions of universal harmony to the extent of suggesting a 'judicial' use of astrology), partly to a lack of order and precision in developing his ideas, and partly to the fact that his work does not allow historians of thought to fit him easily into some school or pattern of development. If, however, he is to be linked to any contemporary intellectual tradition, it probably should be to that of seventeenth-century Platonism (see CAMBRIDGE PLATONISM; PLATONISM, RENAISSANCE). Herbert himself, however, was not interested in either supporting or rebutting the views of others. While he culled his ideas from a wide range of sources, he regarded himself as an independent thinker who philosophized 'freely' (*libere*) and who considered 'right reason' (*recta ratio*) as the only authority, although, as Gassendi points out, in some respects his originality may lie more in his terminology than in the content of his thought.

The primary aim of Herbert's philosophical and theological works is well expressed in the full title of his pioneering study *De Veritate, Prout Distinguitur a Revelatione, a Verisimili, a Possibili, et a Falso* (On truth in distinction from revelation, probability, possibility, and error). His intention in this work is not to develop a new doctrine but to clarify the meaning of 'true' and to determine how any normal person may identify what is true. His method is to assert the canon of 'right reason' in contrast to the appeal to supposed authorities that characterized the religious disputes of his time. Although he sometimes suggests that the assertion of the ultimate status of reason may be justified by reference to God's creative benevolence and overall providence, on the whole he simply presupposes that reason is the indisputable final judge of what is true. He is aware, however, that people differ about what is true. Hence, while he holds that people should trust their own natural instinct (*instinctus naturalis*), he also asserts that their findings should be tested against the standard of universal consent since this is, for him, a sure and available criterion for determining what reason perceives to be true.

Herbert's understanding of how we grasp the truth is based on a doctrine of the faculties. According to his thesis, all people possess a vast number of potential faculties, each of which is 'an internal power of the mind' that corresponds to a differentiable object, whether intellectual or physical, and provides a distinct way of perceiving it. Truth is accordingly defined in relational terms as conformity between objects and their appropriate faculties. Human knowledge of the truth is consequently limited by the range of the available 'faculties' but the existence of a 'faculty' is held to show the existence of a corresponding object. Agreement about what can be known to be true and how it may be so known thus depends upon determining the range, character and proper application of the 'faculties'. This is what Herbert investigates in *De Veritate*, distinguishing between four classes of truth (truth of things as they are in themselves, of the appearance of things, of conceptual distinctions, and of judgments about the correctness of the deliverances of the faculties) and attempting to identify the conditions for the perception of what is true in each class.

Herbert's doctrine of the 'faculties' means that, whereas Locke was to suggest that ideas of objects are basically the product of passive experiences, and whereas Kant's 'critical' revolution was to maintain that objects as known are fashioned by our modes of cognition, Herbert presented a third alternative, namely that there is a fundamental correspondence between what is actually the case and our latent modes of apprehension (see KANT, I. §§4–6). He thus puts forward what may be described as a 'common sense' view of 'truth' according to which the mind has an active role in grasping the reality of what it 'truly' apprehends. In this way, then, Herbert rejects on the one hand the view that the mind is a clean sheet or *tabula rasa* on which objects make their own impressions and which, consequently, receives its ability to deal with objects from objects themselves; on the other hand he accepts the principle that nothing is in the intellect which has not first been in the senses, provided that it is also appreciated that the mind deals with its experiences according to the structures prefigured by the 'faculties'. Contrary to what Locke may suggest, what are innate for Herbert are not propositions but the 'faculties' as pre-established potential modes of thought. The harmonious world system, however, entails that the interaction of the faculties with experiences produces true understanding of reality. Furthermore, Herbert claims that people are so constituted that what he describes as 'the common sense of the inner senses' is only satisfied when the 'faculties' are correctly adjusted to what they are seeking thereby to know. When, therefore, they attempt to apprehend something by what is not the correct corresponding 'faculty', Herbert holds that they experience a particular kind of corrective sensation which tells them that they are falling into error.

As well as holding that a person feels when the correct faculty is not being used to apprehend something, Herbert also maintains that among the intellectual objects represented by the faculties are certain fundamental 'common notions'. These are normative principles implanted by God in every person to ensure that they can distinguish what is true and good from what is false and bad. Accordingly they are to govern understanding and action. Since they are apprehended by natural instincts, they are found in every normal person. The six characteristic qualities of the common notions are *prioritas, independentia, universalitas, certitudo, necessitas* and *modus conformationis* (priority, independence, universality, certainty, necessity – in the sense of being required for human preservation, and immediacy –in that they do not need to be warranted by discursive reasoning). What is *common* about the 'common notions' is that they are latently present in the mind of every person. Individuals only explicitly apprehend them when their minds have been suitably stimulated. Once they have become aware of them, however, normal people everywhere immediately recognize them to be true.

3 Views on religious belief

According to Herbert, certain 'common notions' provide the proper basis for judging what is true in matters of religious belief, including claims about what is held to have been divinely revealed. In *De Veritate* he discusses five 'common notions' that, in his judgment, constitute the foundation of and norm for the true Catholic or universal Church that is the only source of salvation. They are:

1 Some supreme deity exists
2 This supreme deity ought to be worshipped
3 Virtue joined with piety... is and always has been held to be the principal part of religious practice
4 Vices and crimes must be expiated by repentance
5 There is reward or punishment after this life

Herbert does not deny that some truths may have been revealed by God, including ones that may in principle be discovered naturally. He insists, however, that care must be taken to make sure that any alleged revelation is authentic and, furthermore, that no alleged revelation can be regarded as authentic if it contradicts (rather than reasserts or augments) what is laid down in the 'common notions' of religion.

In *De Religione Laici* Herbert develops his understanding of the common notions 'divinely transcribed in the mind itself' to hold that any lay person may, can and should decide between rival systems of religious belief by determining, through the use of reason, which set of doctrines and practices is the closest to those implied by the 'common notions'. Moreover, where beliefs involve claims about what happened in the past, they cannot escape the uncertainty that belongs to all such claims. As for the authority of the Bible, Herbert maintains that each individual has the right to judge the significance of its contents and to accept as 'the very Word of God' needed for salvation only those parts which agree with 'our Catholic Truths, which are like indubitable utterances of God, and matters recorded in the inner court' – by which he means the truths that are contained in the 'common notions' and, as such, that are engraved in the conscience by providence. The products of priestcraft are similarly to be subjected to these criteria. Herbert, however, does not see such an approach to doctrines and practices as hostile to authentic religion, but as upholding it.

While Herbert's views raise questions about unwarranted (and unwarrantable) claims to divine revelation and about the perversion of authentic religion by priestcraft, and while he proposes 'right reason' as the way to determine what is to be believed, it is misleading to describe him (as is widely done) as 'the father of English Deism' (see DEISM). Herbert's own remarks and religious practice suggest that he was convinced not only of the actuality of God but also of the gracious activity of God in the lives of individuals, of the possibility of divine revelations, of the efficacy of prayer and of the reality of personal immortality. Moreover, there is little evidence that he was a significant influence on others given the unclear and confusing title of 'deists', despite his treatment as the first English 'deist' in early attacks on 'deism' by Thomas Halyburton (1714), Philip Skelton (1749) and John Leland (1754) in confessedly apologetic works which have provided the basic canon for later studies of this aspect of religious thought in the late seventeenth and eighteenth centuries.

4 Other religions

Two principles guide Herbert's approach to the various religions of the world. The first is his conviction that universal providence is the highest attribute of God. Hence God's benevolence must be regarded as concerned for all people, and salvation as available to all. The second is the need to show empirically that the 'common notions' of religion are indeed universally recognized.

Herbert meets the first principle by holding that atonement for sin is obtained through repentance. This means that neither a believing response to a particular event (such as the death of Jesus as the Christ) nor assent to a particular set of doctrines nor the fulfilment of prescribed rites is necessary for a person to be saved. The knowledge of what is necessary for salvation is, always has been and always

will be available to all people since it is contained within the 'common notions' of religion. Thus God does not unfairly limit saving knowledge to only part of humankind. The providential grace of God extends to all.

The second principle is met by arguing, both in *De Religione Gentilium* and in *A Dialogue between a Tutor and his Pupil*, that, in spite of what the evidence of the doctrines and practices of the world's faiths may seem to indicate, all people do basically recognize the 'common notions' of religion. Herbert deals with apparent evidence to the contrary in three ways. First, he suggests that some reports about the beliefs and practices in other religions have simply been misunderstood, particularly because of ambiguity in the language used. Second, he holds that sometimes symbolic usages have been misinterpreted as literal references. Third, he admits that some doctrines and rites found in other faiths do conflict with the 'common notions' of religion, but only because they have been corrupted by priestcraft. Priests are charged with distorting and perverting religion for their own selfish advantage. Herbert thus maintains that both in principle and practice the religions of the world fundamentally support his understanding of the actuality of the universal providence of God, and that the basic truths of religion are found in the non-Christian religions.

See also: GRACE; HERMETISM

List of works

Herbert, Edward, Baron of Cherbury (1624) *De Veritate, Prout Distinguitur a Revelatione, a Verisimili, a Possibili, et a Falso* (On Truth in Distinction from Revelation, Probability, Possibility, and Error), Paris; 3rd edn, London, 1645; partial trans. M.H. Carré, Bristol: University of Bristol, 1937; repr. London and Kinokuniya, Tokyo: Routledge/Thoemmes Press, 1992. (Written in a somewhat unusual Latin and completed while Herbert was ambassador in France, this seeks to identify 'the common nature of the search for truth which exists in every normal human being'. The revised edition of 1645 is best.)

—— (1645) *De Causis Errorum: Una cum Tractatu de Religione Laici, et Appendice ad Sacerdotes, nec non quibusdam Poematibus* (Concerning the Causes of Errors: with a Treatise on the Religion of the Laity, and a Supplement to Priests, also certain Poems), London, 1645; ed. and trans. H.R. Hutcheson as *Lord Herbert of Cherbury's De Religione Laici*, New Haven, CT: Yale University Press, 1944. (Copies of the 1645 London edition of *De Veritate* often also contain this work which was also published separately. The Hutcheson translation contains a useful discussion of Herbert's life and thought and a bibliography.)

—— (1649) *The Life and Raigne of King Henry the Eighth*, London, 1672. (Written between 1632 and 1639, this was long regarded as the standard history of the reign.)

—— (1656) *Expeditio in Ream Insulam* (The Expedition to the Island of Rhé), ed. and Latin trans. T. Baldwin, London; original English text ed. Lord Powis, London: Philobiblon Society, 1860. (Completed in 1630, this attempts the difficult task of justifying the conduct of the Duke of Buckingham as leader of an unsuccessful attempt to relieve the Hugenots in La Rochelle in 1627.)

—— (1663) *De Religione Gentilium* (On the Religion of the Heathens), ed. I. Vossius, Amsterdam; trans. W. Lewis as *The Antient Religion of the Gentiles*, London, 1705. (Attempts to show that the basic truths of religion are found, albeit sometimes using indirect modes of expression, in non-Christian religions. To date the only English translation is that by Lewis.)

—— (1764) *The Life of Edward Lord Herbert of Cherbury written by himself*, Strawberry Hill; ed. with notes, appendices and later life, S.L. Lee, London, 1886; ed. with notes, J.M. Shuttleworth, London: Oxford University Press, 1976. (This pioneering work in autobiography (it stops at 1624) is amusing, sometimes frivolously teasing, as well as informative. The edition by Lee includes a useful addition that covers his life after 1624; Shuttleworth takes account of Herbert's corrections and notes significant variant readings.)

—— (1768) *A Dialogue between a Tutor and his Pupil*, London. (Authorship disputed, but probably at least largely by Herbert. Seeks to show that basic religious truths are recognized by all religions in spite of corruptions due to priestcraft.)

References and further reading

Bedford, R.D. (1979) *The defence of truth: Herbert of Cherbury and the seventeenth century*, Manchester: Manchester University Press. (Readable and comprehensive work that perhaps exaggerates the influence of hermetic ideas upon Herbert. Select bibliography.)

* Halyburton, T. (1714) *Natural religion insufficient; and revealed necessary to man's happiness*, Edinburgh. (Chapter 13 includes an early, brief and hostile 'account' of Herbert as 'the first inventor' of the deist 'religion'.)

Harrison, P. (1990) *'Religion' and the religions in the English enlightenment*, Cambridge: Cambridge University Press, 61–73. (Short but perceptive account, primarily concerned with Herbert's religious ideas and his relationship to 'deism'.)

* Leland, J. (1754) *A view of the principal deistical writers*, London: B. Dod, vol. 1, 1–39. (Although hostile to 'deism' and holding Herbert to be 'justly regarded as the most eminent of the deistical writers' (page 4) this is reasonably fair in its critical appraisal of his thought.)

Pailin, D.A. (1983) 'Herbert of Cherbury and the deists', *The Expository Times* 94: 196–200. (Outlines Herbert's religious views and practices to defend him against the charge of being a 'deist'.)

—— (1988) 'Herbert von Cherbury', in J.-P. Schobinger (ed.) *Grundriss der Geschichte der Philosophie, Band 3: Die Philosophie des 17. Jahrhunderts*, Basel: Schwabe, 224–39, 284–5. (Brief survey in German of Herbert's ideas and of major responses to them.)

Remusat, C.F.M. de (1874) *Lord Herbert de Cherbury. Sa vie et ses oeuvres ou les origines de la philosophie du sens commun et de la théologie naturelle en Angleterre* (Lord Herbert of Cherbury. His life and works, or the origins of the philosophy of common sense and of natural theology in England), Paris. (An old but still useful study in French.)

Rossi, M.M. (1940) 'The nature of truth and Lord Herbert of Cherbury's inquiry', *The Personalist* 21: 243–56, 394–409. (Critical of Herbert's attempt to deal with the question of truth, accusing him of presenting a patchwork of incompatible views.)

—— (1947) *La vita, le opere, i tempi di Eduardo Herbert di Chirbury* (The life, work and times of Edward, Herbert of Cherbury), Florence: G.C. Sansoni, 3 vols. (Major, comprehensive study in Italian, if somewhat unsympathetic to its subject.)

* Skelton, P. (1749) *Deism revealed or, the attack on christianity candidly reviewed*, London: A. Millar, 2 vols. (Response to what is said to be deism's attack on Christianity that was approved for publication by David Hume and that, in vol. 2, 240–1, describes Herbert as the one whom 'later deists' imitate.)

Sorley, W.R. (1894) 'The philosophy of Herbert of Cherbury', *Mind* n.s. 3: 491–508. (Largely descriptive and balanced account of Herbert's theory of knowledge.)

Webb, C.C.J. (1915) *Studies in the history of natural theology*, Oxford: Clarendon Press, 344–58. (Sound and sympathetic interpretation of Herbert's views.)

DAVID A. PAILIN

HERBRAND'S THEOREM

According to Herbrand's theorem, each formula F of quantification theory can be associated with a sequence F_1, F_2, F_3, ... of quantifier-free formulas such that F is provable just in case F_n is truth-functionally valid for some n. This theorem was the centrepiece of Herbrand's dissertation, written in 1929 as a contribution to Hilbert's programme. It provides a finitistically meaningful interpretation of quantification over an infinite domain. Furthermore, it can be applied to yield various consistency and decidability results for formal systems. Herbrand was the first to exploit it in this way, and his work has influenced subsequent research in these areas. While Herbrand's approach to proof theory has perhaps been overshadowed by the tradition which derives from Gentzen, recent work on automated reasoning continues to draw on his ideas.

Herbrand's theorem says that each formula F of quantification theory can be associated with a sequence $F_1, F_2, F_3, ...$ of quantifier-free formulas such that F is provable just in case F_n is truth-functionally valid for some n. If F is prenex – that is, consists of a quantifier-free matrix G preceded by a string of quantifiers – then each F_i will be a disjunction of instances of G obtained by substituting terms for free variables. To simplify the exposition we consider only prenex formulas F. With each such F we can associate an existential formula F^H as follows: (1) substitute new constants for the free variables of F; (2) remove each universal quantifier $\forall x$ and replace the resulting free occurrences of x by a term $f(y_1, ..., y_m)$, where f is a new function symbol and $y_1, ..., y_m$ are all the variables bound by existential quantifiers to the left of $\forall x$ in F. For example, applied to $\forall x \exists y \forall z R(x,y,z)$ (with R quantifier-free) this procedure yields $\exists y R(c,y,f(y))$.

Although Herbrand would not have described their relationship in these terms, F^H can be said to express the meaning of F in the sense that F is true under an interpretation $\mathbb{I}$ just in case F^H is true under any expansion of $\mathbb{I}$ to the new constants and function symbols in F^H. To see this, consider our example. Let α, β range over the domain of $\mathbb{I}$, ϕ over functions on this domain and let 'x_α' indicate that the value α is assigned to the variable x. Then the following are equivalent:

$\forall x \exists y \forall z R(x,y,z)$ is true under $\mathbb{I}$.

There is no α such that for all β $\exists z \neg R(x_\alpha, y_\beta, z)$.

There is no α and no function ϕ such that for all β $\neg R(x_\alpha, y_\beta, z_{\phi(\beta)})$.

For every α and every function ϕ there is some β such that $R(x_\alpha, y_\beta, z_{\phi(\beta)})$.

No matter which individual α is chosen to interpret c and which function ϕ to interpret f, $\exists y R(c,y,f(y))$ is true under $\mathbb{I}$.

This means, in particular, that F is true under every interpretation iff F^H is; the latter is called the validity functional form of F.

We can use the functional terms appearing in F^H to generate a series of finite domains $\mathbf{D}_i$. These will consist of constants which can themselves be substituted into the quantifier-free matrix G^H of F^H. For convenience, let $\mathbf{D}_1$ consist of a single constant d, $\mathbf{D}_2$ of a distinct constant (its 'denotation') for each term obtained from one occurring in G^H by substituting d for its free variables; in particular, constants occurring in G^H are assigned denotations in $\mathbf{D}_2$. In general, $\mathbf{D}_{n+1}$ consists of distinct denotations for each term obtained from one occurring in G^H by substituting members of $\mathbf{D}_n$ for its free variables. F_n, the Herbrand expansion of F of order n, is a disjunction whose disjuncts represent all possible ways of substituting members of $\mathbf{D}_n$ for the variables of G^H and replacing functional terms, where possible, by their values in $\mathbf{D}_n$. For example, if we allow each closed term to denote itself, then the first three domains generated by our earlier formula will be $\{d\}$, $\{d,c,f(d)\}$ and $\{d,c,f(d),f(c),f(f(d))\}$. The Herbrand expansions of orders 1, 2 and 3 are:

$$R(c,d,f(d))$$
$$R(c,d,f(d)) \lor R(c,c,f(c)) \lor R(c,f(d),f(f(d)))$$
$$R(c,d,f(d)) \lor R(c,c,f(c)) \lor R(c,f(d),f(f(d)))$$
$$\lor R(c,f(c),f(f(c))) \lor R(c,f(f(d)),f(f(f(d)))).$$

Notice that F_n is not an interpretation of the quantifiers of F^H in $\mathbf{D}_n$ in the usual sense because some of the terms occurring in F_n only acquire a denotation in $\mathbf{D}_{n+1}$.

Now, for provable F, Herbrand showed how to compute a number n such that F_n would be a tautology. He argued by induction on the proof of F. The only axioms in his system are the quantifier-free tautologies, so his method is to analyse each rule of inference and show how the order of a tautologous expansion of its conclusion can be calculated from the order(s) of such expansions of its premises. Conversely, he showed how to construct a proof of F from any tautologous F_n. Because the only rules required here are forms of generalization and simplification (in particular, *modus ponens* is not used), this yields a normal form for proofs in quantification theory analogous to Gentzen's cut-elimination theorem and lends itself to many of the same applications. It allows a bound to be placed on the complexity of formulas appearing in a normal proof depending on the complexity of its conclusion (and assumptions, if any).

Herbrand's proof contains ideas of great interest but, in contrast to Gentzen's, it is not easily adapted to non-classical systems. Furthermore, it is difficult to follow and turns out to contain a defect. Although this has been repaired by Dreben and his collaborators, the proof has not been reproduced and nowadays the theorem (for prenex formulas only) is often established as a corollary to a refinement of the cut-elimination theorem. (Since a cut-free proof of a prenex formula can be separated into a truth-functional and a quantificational part, by working back from the conclusion we can discover a truth-functionally valid formula from which it follows.)

While he accepted set-theoretic arguments in mathematics, Herbrand was committed to using finitary methods in metamathematical investigations. His work was influenced by Löwenheim (1915), but he rejected the naïve notion of satisfiability in an infinite domain the latter assumed. In fact, Herbrand claimed that his result was just a more rigorous version of Löwenheim's famous theorem to the effect that a sentence is satisfiable if and only if it is satisfiable in a denumerable domain. It would be more accurate, however, to describe it as a finitist variant thereof. To understand why this is so, notice that we can reformulate Herbrand's theorem using a construction dual to the above. We remove existential quantifiers from F, replacing the newly freed variables by functional terms to obtain a universal formula (the satisfiability functional form of F), which can then be expanded as a series of finite conjunctions F'_n over the $\mathbf{D}_n$. The theorem then states that F is irrefutable iff F'_n is truth-functionally satisfiable for every n. (This is the original theorem expressed as a criterion for the non-provability of $\neg F$.) Constrained by his finitist scruples, Herbrand explicated validity in terms of provability and, a fortiori, satisfiability in terms of irrefutability. He also suggested that F's having truth-functionally satisfiable expansions F'_n for every n could serve as a constructive account of what it means for F to be satisfiable in a (denumerable) domain. Replacing the informal set-theoretic notions in the statement of Löwenheim's theorem by their finitist analogues transforms it into a statement of Herbrand's theorem – even though the theorems themselves remain distinct.

Herbrand's ideas have yielded numerous metamathematical applications. The normal form for proofs mentioned above supplies a tool for obtaining consistency proofs. Furthermore, the elimination of quantifiers in favour of functional terms suggests how to exhibit the constructive content of the theorems of a formal theory – as in the 'no counterexample' interpretation of arithmetic, for example (Kreisel 1951). Herbrand's theorem also allows us to prove a theory consistent by approximating a model for it, that is, by establishing that, for every (finite) conjunction F of the theory's axioms, F'_n is truth-functionally satisfiable for every n. Herbrand himself gave a consistency proof for a fragment of arithmetic along these lines, and his methods have been extended to yield proofs for the full system (see Dreben and Denton 1970, Scanlon 1972). These proofs, while no less complex than Gentzen's, yield directly the sort of constructive interpretations alluded to above.

Finally, Herbrand's theorem supplies an approach to the decision problem for classes of quantificational formulas, that is, to discovering an algorithm which, for any formula in the class, computes whether or not it is satisfiable. The idea here is to investigate the relationship between syntactic properties of quantificational formulas and the structure of their expansions, and to discover properties of the latter which ensure the existence of a decision procedure (see Dreben and Goldfarb 1979). His theorem and the methods introduced in its proof are relevant not only to theoretical decidability results, but also to the design of implementable automated reasoning procedures. These employ unification algorithms to improve the efficiency of testing quantifier-free expansions for satisfiability, and Herbrand is credited with being the first to devise such an algorithm (Snyder 1991).

See also: HILBERT'S PROGRAMME AND FORMALISM; LOGICAL AND MATHEMATICAL TERMS, GLOSSARY OF; PROOF THEORY

References and further reading

Andrews, P.B. (1986) *An Introduction to Mathematical Logic and Type Theory: To Truth Through Proof,* New York: Academic Press. (§35 contains an interesting discussion of Herbrand's theorem, focusing on its significance for decision problems and automated theorem proving, as well as a proof of one version of it.)

Buss, S.R. (1995) 'On Herbrand's Theorem', in D. Leivant (ed.) *Logic and Computational Complexity,* Berlin: Springer, 195–209. (An up-to-date exposition of the theorem from a proof-theoretic perspective which also sets it in the context of Herbrand's dissertation.)

* Dreben, B. and Denton, J. (1970) 'Herbrand-Style Consistency Proofs', in J. Myhill, R.E. Vesley and A. Kino (eds) *Intuitionism and Proof Theory,* Amsterdam: North Holland, 419–33. (Building

on ideas to be found in Herbrand, the authors sketch a proof of the consistency of arithmetic and discuss some of its corollaries.)

* Dreben, B. and Goldfarb, W.D. (1979) *The Decision Problem: Solvable Classes of Quantificational Formulas*, Reading, MA: Addison-Wesley. (This monograph offers a unified treatment of solvable cases of the decision problem by way of an approach that can be traced back to Herbrand.)

Goldfarb, W.D. (1979) 'Logic in the Twenties: The Nature of the Quantifier', *Journal of Symbolic Logic* 44 (3): 351–68. (A very readable discussion of the background to Herbrand's work.)

Heijenoort, J. van (1985) 'Jacques Herbrand's Work in Logic and its Historical Context', in *Selected Essays*, Naples: Bibliopolis, 99–121. (A readable informal survey of Herbrand's work.)

Herbrand, J. (1968) *Écrits logiques*, Paris: Presses Universitaires de France; trans. *Logical Writings*, ed. W.D. Goldfarb, Cambridge, MA: Harvard University Press, 1971. (All of Herbrand's logical writings, with extensive annotations, needed corrections and a helpful introduction by the editor.)

Hilbert, D. and Bernays, P. (1939) *Grundlagen der Mathematik* (Foundations of Mathematics), vol. 2, Berlin: Springer, 2nd edn, 1970. (A standard reference; Herbrand's theorem is derived from the first ε-elimination theorem and its metamathematical applications detailed.)

* Kreisel, G. (1951, 1952) 'On the Interpretation of Nonfinitist Proofs', *Journal of Symbolic Logic* 16 (4): 241–67, 17 (1): 43–58. (The methods of Hilbert and Bernays (1939) are utilized to impart a finitist sense to proofs in arithmetic and a subsystem of analysis.)

* Löwenheim, L. (1915) 'Über Möglichkeiten im Relativkalkül', *Mathematische Annalen* 76: 447–70; trans. S. Bauer-Mengelberg, 'On Possibilities in the Calculus of Relatives', in J. van Heijenoort (ed.) *From Frege to Gödel: A Source Book in Mathematical Logic, 1879–1931*, Cambridge, MA: Harvard University Press, 1967. (A seminal paper which, because its results are stated and proved in terms of Schröder's calculus of relatives, is accessible only with difficulty to the modern reader.)

* Scanlon, T.M. (1972) 'The Consistency of Number Theory via Herbrand's Theorem', *Journal of Symbolic Logic* 38 (1): 29–58. (This paper presents in some detail an improved and slightly more general version of the proof given by Dreben and Denton (1970).)

Schwichtenberg, H. (1977) 'Proof Theory: Some Applications of Cut-Elimination', in J. Barwise (ed.) *Handbook of Mathematical Logic*, Amsterdam: North Holland, 867–95. (Herbrand's theorem is derived from the cut-elimination theorem and some of its proof theoretic applications are sketched.)

Shoenfield, J. (1967) *Mathematical Logic*, Reading, MA: Addison-Wesley. (Chapter 4 includes an accessible and enlightening proof of Herbrand's theorem for the predicate calculus with equality.)

* Snyder, W. (1991) *A Proof Theory for General Unification*, Boston, MA: Birkhäuser. (A specialized monograph which describes an abstract framework within which to understand different kinds of unification.)

A.M. UNGAR

HERDER, JOHANN GOTTFRIED (1744–1803)

Herder was a central figure in the German intellectual renaissance of the late eighteenth century. His achievement spanned virtually every domain of philosophy, and his influence, especially upon Romanticism and German idealism, was immense. In social and political philosophy he played a prominent role in the development of historicism and nationalism. In metaphysics he developed the doctrine of vitalist pantheism, which later became important for Goethe, Schelling and Hegel. In the philosophy of mind he formulated an organic theory of the mind-body relationship, which was crucial for Schelling and Hegel. And in aesthetics he was among the first to defend the value of ethnic poetry and the need for the internal and historical understanding of a text.

Herder's main aim was to extend the powers of naturalistic explanation to the realm of culture, so that characteristic human activities, such as art, religion, law and language, could be included within the scientific worldview. But he also wanted to avoid reductivistic forms of explanation that viewed such activities as nothing more than matter-in-motion or stimulus-response mechanisms. He insisted that explanation in the cultural sphere had to be holistic and internal as well as mechanical and external. An action had to be understood in its historical context and according to the intention of the agent and not simply as another instance of a causal regularity between events. Herder's programme, then, was to develop naturalistic yet non-reductivistic explanations for the realm of culture. He attempted to realize this programme in many spheres, especially language, history, religion and the mind.

1 Intellectual ideals and background
2 Theory of language

1   Intellectual ideals and background

Born into a middle-class family in Mohrungen, East Prussia, Herder spent most of his life as a Lutheran pastor in the provincial cities of Riga, Bueckeburg and Weimar. Herder's intellectual development was dominated by one central fact: during his formative university years in Königsberg from 1762 to 1764, he was the student of both KANT and HAMANN. To the same degree, they were a profound influence upon him. But such a rich legacy also proved problematic, for Kant and Hamann represented opposing intellectual movements. While Kant was a champion of the *Aufklärung*, the German Enlightenment, Hamann was a founder of the *Sturm und Drang* (lit: Storm and Stress), the German literary movement of the 1760s and 1770s that proclaimed personal freedom and glamorized revolt. Although these movements had some common values – individual emancipation, the essential goodness of human nature, contempt for aristocratic privilege and clerical prejudice, hatred of superstition and intolerance – they also had some conflicting ones. The *Aufklärung* stressed the sovereignty of reason, the value of the arts and sciences, and the virtues of cosmopolitanism; the *Sturm und Drang* emphasized the rights of feeling and imagination, the problems of civilization, and the value of local and ethnic identity. Herder struggled to reconcile these opposing ideals. His philosophy could be described as a rich synthesis – or unstable mixture – of these antithetical movements. We might best describe Herder with oxymorons: a turbulent *Aufklärer*, a rational *Stürmer und Dränger*.

What, more specifically, did Herder learn from Kant? All his life Herder adhered to the young Kant's conception of the aim and method of philosophy: its purpose is to develop intellectual autonomy; and its method should be 'analytic', beginning from experience and ascending to general principles. In his later works Herder applied these early Kantian ideals –much to the chagrin of the mature Kant, who regarded them as a relapse into metaphysical dogmatism. Of all Kant's works Herder was most influenced by the *Allgemeine Naturgeschichte und Theorie des Himmels* (Universal Natural History and Theory of the Heavens, 1755). This work was important for Herder for two reasons: (1) its idea of a natural history, that the apparently eternal and static structure of nature is really the product of historical development; (2) its suggestion that human beings are

part of nature and also have a natural history. Herder's historicism arose from his application of Kant's idea of natural history to the social, religious and historical spheres.

What, more precisely, did Hamann teach Herder? There were many influential ideas: the value of cultural diversity, the vitality of folk poetry, the power of the passions, the importance of language for reason and of custom for language, and the need to examine the social and historical context of reason. Hamann also impressed upon Herder the limitations of the *Aufklärung*: that religious experience cannot be criticized by reason, that the mind-body relationship is inexplicable by mechanism, and that human beings are indivisible wholes not neatly analysed into faculties.

The guiding ideal behind Herder's intellectual development was a synthesis of Kant and Hamann. Throughout his career Herder's aim was to develop naturalistic and historical explanations for characteristic human activities, such as art, religion, language, law and morality. He wanted to extend the powers of natural explanation, so that all forms of humanity would be brought within the scientific worldview. In this regard he revealed himself as a loyal follower of Kant and the *Allgemeine Naturgeschichte*. Yet there was something unique about Herder's programme that broke from the heritage of Kant and the *Aufklärung*. Herder insisted that naturalistic explanations do not reduce human activities to matter-in-motion or stimulus-response mechanisms. His critique of mechanism, and his demand for a more holistic and internal form of understanding, betrays the influence of Hamann. Herder's programme for naturalistic yet non-reductivistic explanation attempted to do justice to the legacy of both Kant and Hamann. We shall now see how Herder attempted to fulfil this programme in virtually every field of philosophy.

2   Theory of language

In 1769 the Berlin Academy of Sciences announced a prize competition for the best essay on the questions 'If human beings were left with their natural faculties, would they be able to invent language? And, if so, by what means could they invent it?' Competitors were invited to disagree with a late member of the Academy, J.P. Süssmilch, who argued that a perfect and complete language could have only a divine origin. This quaint question raised an important and broader issue: to what extent is reason, which depends on language, explicable according to natural laws? Should human intelligence be brought within the scientific worldview?

Inspired by the question, Herder wrote a short tract to answer it in December 1770, *Ueber den Ursprung der Sprache* (On the Origin of Language). This marks the starting point of his philosophical programme, the attempt to provide naturalistic yet non-reductivistic explanations of characteristic human activities. Herder takes a firm stand on behalf of naturalism, dismissing Süssmilch's theory as so much nonsense. He puts forward two specific theses, each of which is necessary to prove his naturalism. (1) Human reason is sufficient to create language. Since, however, reason itself might have a supernatural or divine origin, he adds a second thesis. 2) The use of reason is natural and necessary because it is the means by which human beings acquire the skills and information necessary for survival. Hence if reason is sufficient to create language, and if its use is natural, then the creation of language will be natural too.

To defend his first thesis, Herder argues that the function of reason is to direct, control and organize our experience. Such a function involves what he calls 'reflection' (*Besonnenheit*), the capacity to be self-conscious of our sensations by identifying or remembering them. We can exercise this capacity only by giving signs to specific features of experience; only through the use of signs are we able to identify, remember and control our sensations. In employing signs, though, we have already created language.

To support his second thesis Herder develops a proto-Darwinian account of why reason, and indeed language, is necessary for survival. Since men, unlike animals and insects, do not have instincts to guide them, they must learn how to survive. If each new generation is not to be exposed to the same dangers and perils as past ones, its ancestors must teach them the skills and facts necessary for survival. The most effective means of doing so is, of course, language.

The aim of Herder's tract is not simply to develop a naturalistic theory of the origin of language. That had been done before by such eminent thinkers as Rousseau and Condillac. Herder's specific aim is to develop a naturalism that is not reductivist. He rejects the theories of Rousseau and Condillac precisely because they were reductivist, failing to explain the characteristic functions of human reason. In his second *Discours* (1755) Rousseau argued that language originates with the expression of feeling; the first words were cries or ejaculations (see Rousseau, J.-J. §2). In his *Essai sur l'origine des connaissances humaines* (1746) Condillac maintained that language begins with convention, the agreement between speakers about the referents of sounds (see Condillac, É.B. De §2). The purpose of language is to communicate; but people can do this only by agreeing about the meaning of sounds. Herder rejects Rousseau's theory because it treats human beings as if they were animals, ignoring what is most distinctive about human language, its cognitive dimension. He dismisses Condillac's theory for its circularity: primitive people cannot make conventions unless they already have a sophisticated concept of language. Both theories are inadequate because they do not consider the characteristic nature of man – reason. Either they reduce reason to man's animal nature (Rousseau) or they assume it without explaining it (Condillac). Yet it is human rationality, Herder contends, that holds the key to the origin of language. Since men alone possess rationality, and since they also are unique in having language, we must seek its origin in their characteristic nature. That, Herder says, is the guiding assumption behind his whole investigation.

3 Philosophy of mind

In 1774 Herder wrote another treatise for an academic prize, his *Vom Erkennen und Empfinden der menschlichen Seele* (On the Knowledge and Sensation of the Human Soul), which was eventually published in 1778. He again attempted to answer a question posed by the Academy of Sciences: 'What is the nature of, and relationship between, the two basic faculties of the soul, knowledge and sensation?' This question too raised a wider problem: the relationship between the mind (the source of knowledge) and the body (the source of sensation).

Herder began by criticizing some of the current theories about the mind-body relationship. In the late eighteenth century these usually took two forms: they were dualistic, making the mind into a special substance distinct from the body, or materialistic, explaining the mind as if it were a complicated machine. Herder rejects dualism because it makes the interaction of mind and body mysterious (see Dualism); and he dismisses materialism since it reduces the mind down to a mere stimulus-response mechanism (see Materialism in the philosophy of mind). What is required, he contends, is a theory that avoids both these pitfalls. It should remove the mystery of mind-body interaction while not reducing one to the other. In other words, it must be naturalistic yet non-reductivist. The main task of his tract is to sketch just such a theory.

The central thesis of Herder's organic or vitalist theory is that the mind and body are not heterogeneous substances, nor more or less complicated machines. Rather, they are simply different degrees of organization and development of a single living power. The essence of power consists in self-generating and self-organizing activity, which gradually develops from lower to higher forms of organization and structure. The difference in mind and body is therefore not in kind but only in degree: the mind is organized and developed, the body is amorphous and inchoate, power. Such a theory easily explains interaction since mind and body are both aspects of a single force; but it also does not reduce one to the other because they are different degrees of organization and development.

Herder develops his theory by questioning the fundamental premise behind both dualism and materialism: that matter consists in extension alone. It was this assumption that forced the dualist to separate the mind from the body and that compelled the materialist to reduce it to a machine. If, however, we reject this assumption, then we escape the whole dilemma between materialism and dualism. According to Herder, the latest work in the natural sciences permits us to do just this. The recent discoveries of electricity and magnetism, the phenomenon of irritability investigated by Albrecht von Haller, the concept of *vis viva* developed by Hermann von Boerhaave, and the critique of preformation by Thomas Needham and P.L. Maupertuis, all seem to show that the essence of matter is not extension but force, power or energy. In general, Herder stressed the importance of empirical research for the philosophy of mind. No psychology could succeed, he stressed, unless it followed physiology at every step.

4 Philosophy of history

The most influential aspect of Herder's thought was his philosophy of history, which laid the foundation for much of the historicism of the nineteenth century. He developed his philosophy of history in two main works, *Auch eine Philosophie der Geschichte der Menschheit* (Another Philosophy of History of Humanity, 1774) and *Ideen zur Philosophie der Geschichte der Menschheit* (Ideas for a Philosophy of History of Humanity, 1784–91).

Crucial for the development of Herder's historical thought was his 'genetic method', which he first sketched in his *Fragmente* (1767). This was originally conceived as a method for the proper understanding of a work of literature; but Herder eventually extended it to all human actions and creations. This method consists in two basic principles. (1) To understand an action or creation, it should be seen within its historical context, as the product of a specific time and place. (2) It is necessary to understand the action or creation from within, according to the intention of the agent or creator, and not merely from without, according to its external causes or some purported universal rules. With the first guideline Herder attempted to satisfy the demand for natural

explanation; he was applying the general lesson he had learned from Kant's *Allgemeine Naturgeschichte*, that what appears given and eternal is really the product of history. With the second guideline he stressed the need for non-reductive explanation. Here Herder's immediate target was those literary critics who attempted to evaluate a work according to their own standards without attempting to grasp the purpose of the author.

In his *Auch eine Philosophie der Geschichte* Herder criticized the historiography of the *Aufklärung* and stressed the importance of an internal understanding of the past. The historians of the *Aufklärung*, he claimed, were guilty of ethnocentrism. They judged the past and alien cultures in the light of their own, as if the values of their age are universal and eternal and the very end of history itself. They failed to judge each epoch in its own terms, according to its own values and ideals. If the historian is to comprehend an alien culture or epoch, then he must suspend his preconceptions and feel himself into the standpoints of the agents themselves. In this regard Herder was one of the first to stress the need for a more sympathetic understanding of the Middle Ages, which had been dismissed as an age of darkness, superstition and fanaticism.

Herder's critique of Enlightenment historiography raises the question whether he is admitting, or even advocating, relativism. In several places of his tract he openly states that the values of different cultures are incommensurable, and that each culture is valid in its own terms. Indeed, he argues that the apparently universal and eternal standards of the *Aufklärung* are really only invalid generalizations from their own age.

Nevertheless, despite his flirtations with cultural relativity, Herder was anxious to claim that there are some universal values in history. In an early fragment – *Von der Verschiedenheit des Geschmacks und der Denkart unter den Menschen* (On the Difference in Taste and Thinking among Human Beings, c.1765–8) – he reveals a deep concern to refute sceptical arguments for cultural relativism. In the 1774 tract, he expressly maintains that his aim is to show how, amid all the diversity of cultures, there is still 'progress in a higher sense' and how 'humanity still remains humanity'. Herder's aim, then, was to find some middle path between ethnocentrism and relativism. A closer reading of the 1774 tract indeed shows that Herder stresses the individual worth of each culture not because all values are relative but because each has the value appropriate to humanity *at that stage of its development*. In other words, cultures have *sui generis* values because what is appropriate for a lower stage of development is not so for a higher, just as what is good for a child is not so for an adult. This is not relativism but the very opposite: the belief that all cultures can be graded on a scale of progress and development. There remains in Herder's philosophy of history, then, a profound teleological dimension, an abiding belief in progress and providence. In the 1774 tract, however, Herder is reluctant to identify the goal of history. Such hesitation is understandable, given that any specific definition invites ethnocentrism.

Herder's main work in the philosophy of history is his massive, but still incomplete *Ideen*, which appeared in instalments from 1784 to 1791. It consists in four parts. The first two discuss natural history, human anatomy and anthropology. Only in the third part does Herder begin to treat recorded history, whose course is followed until the Roman Empire. The fourth part continues the history to 1500 AD. The fifth part, which was to conclude with the present age, was never written. Conceived on a grand scale, the *Ideen* attempts to examine all of world history, giving equal weight to the cultures of Egypt, China, India and Greece, and the place of humanity within the cosmos.

The *Ideen* was the crowning work of Herder's philosophical programme. Its aim was to bring human history within the naturalistic worldview. Herder wanted to see history as part of the cosmos as a whole, and to formulate its natural laws. But his naturalism was, again, non-reductivist. He conceived the laws of historical development in organic rather than mechanical terms. For Herder, to explain a culture naturalistically meant to see it as an organism, having a purpose and stages of growth.

The first books of the *Ideen* begin with a grand survey of the whole order of nature. Herder locates the place of the earth in the solar system, then the place of man on earth. Following his dynamic view of matter, he sees all of nature as a hierarchy, as so many stages of organization and development of living force. At the summit is man, the culmination of all the powers of nature. It is a central claim of the *Ideen* that there is no distinction between the realms of culture and nature. A culture is portrayed as a continuous development from nature, a unique adaption to specific natural circumstances, such as terrain and climate. Human rationality is also placed within this naturalistic framework. It is seen as the tool by which man learns the skills and information necessary for survival.

The foundation of Herder's concept of history is his anthropology, which he sketches in the first two parts. Herder stresses that the characteristic feature of mankind is plasticity, the ability to adapt to the most diverse circumstances. While an insect or animal can live in only a specific climate and terrain, mankind can live almost anywhere upon earth. This plasticity also means that a person is shaped by society. Reason, feeling and volition are determined by education, by assimilating a cultural tradition. With this anthropology, Herder broke with the assumptions of a universal human nature, which were so endemic within the seventeenth and eighteenth centuries.

Although he stresses human plasticity, the formative role of culture and nature in shaping our identity and rationality, Herder again refuses to draw relativistic conclusions. As in the 1774 tract, he maintains that there is a single goal to world history, which each culture attempts to realise in its unique way. Now, however, he is more explicit about the nature of this goal. It is what he calls 'humanity' (*Humanität*). This is Herder's ideal of human perfection, the realization of all characteristic powers, the development of reason, feeling and will into a harmonious whole. Such a vague concept was, however, a mere stopgap against relativism. Although he tries to avoid it, Herder faces the dilemma of relativism or ethnocentrism. If he defines his ideal more specifically, he invites the danger of ethnocentrism; but if he leaves it general and abstract, different cultures can realise it in incompatible ways.

The reception of the *Ideen* was marked by controversy. The first two parts were harshly reviewed by Kant, who saw his erstwhile pupil as a rival. Kant felt that Herder had refused to learn the main lessons of his new critical philosophy. He accused Herder of indulging in metaphysics, for there cannot be any empirical verification for the concept of an organic power. He also took strong exception to Herder's naturalistic conception of rationality, which threatened the noumenal/phenomenal dualism of the critical philosophy. Herder was not without his supporters, however, who wrote counter-reviews to Kant. He was defended by K.L. Reinhold, who later became a prominent spokesman for Kant, and Georg Forster, the German explorer and naturalist. This debate about the limits and validity of an organic concept of nature proved to be an important stimulus for Kant's *Kritik der Urteilskraft* (*Critique of Judgment*, 1790).

5   Metaphysics

Herder's most explicit statement of his general metaphysical views is his *Gott, Einige Gespräche* (God, Some Conversations), which appeared in 1787. This work is essentially an attempt to rehabilitate Spinozism by interpreting it in organic or vitalist terms (see SPINOZA, B. DE). It is Herder's contribution to the famous 'pantheism controversy', which dominated German intellectual life in the late 1780s.

This controversy began in 1786 when JACOBI

published his *Briefe über Spinoza* (Letters on Spinoza). Jacobi argued that Spinozism ends in atheism and fatalism. Since he regarded Spinoza's naturalism as the paradigm of a rational or scientific worldview, he was in effect pointing out the dangerous consequences of reason or science for morality and religion.

Herder's tract was a defence of Spinoza, and indeed scientific naturalism, against Jacobi's criticisms. Herder agreed with Jacobi that Spinoza's philosophy represents the spirit of scientific naturalism; but he denied that it ends of necessity in atheism and fatalism (see JACOBI, F. §§2,4). Such a conclusion follows, he argued, only for Jacobi's very orthodox concepts of God and freedom. If we regard God as personal and supernatural, then Spinozism is indeed atheism, for Spinoza thinks that that God is the whole of nature. And if we assume that freedom involves the power of acting otherwise, then Spinozism is also fatalism, since Spinoza also holds that everything is determined to act of necessity. But, Herder insists, we should reject these concepts of God and freedom in the first place, which are nothing more than relics of mythology. To think of God as transcendent is to make him irrelevant to human concerns; and to ascribe personality to him is to anthropomorphize him, making the infinite merely finite. Like Spinoza, then, we should view God as immanent and impersonal, not as transcendent and personal. Similarly, freedom should be understood not as a mysterious power to act contrary to nature, but as 'acting according to the necessity of our own nature alone', just as Spinoza defines it. Given such an interpretation of the concepts of God and freedom, Spinozism does not undermine but supports morality and religion. Indeed, the great attraction of Spinozism for Herder, and many thinkers of his generation, such as Goethe, Schleiermacher, Hölderlin and Novalis, was that it seemed to reconcile science with religion and morality. Spinozism seemed to be the religion of science, the science of religion.

Herder's account of Spinozism ultimately rested upon his organic or vitalist conception of nature. Since naturalism for Herder means organicism, he interprets Spinoza's naturalism too in vitalist terms. Accordingly, he sees Spinoza's God not as a static substance but as an active force, the force of forces or primal force. If God is such a living force, then, Herder thinks, we can attribute ends to his activity. This will salvage the concept of providence, removing any further traces of fatalism from Spinoza's system.

Of course, such an interpretation was hardly orthodox Spinozism. Although Spinoza had a dynamic view of substance, he banished teleology and understood explanation in purely mechanical terms.

Herder has to admit, therefore, that he is transforming Spinoza more than interpreting him. But he insists that he is only trying to make Spinoza's naturalistic spirit consistent with the latest scientific research. All the results of its investigations – the new chemistry, the concepts of electricty and magnestism, Boerhaave's revival of *vis viva* – show that matter is not extension but force. Spinoza's mechanical conception of nature was simply the legacy of his Cartesianism and the physics of his day. If Spinoza were only alive today, Herder suggests, then he too would have an organic conception of God.

The net result of Herder's *Gott* was his vitalistic pantheism or pantheistic vitalism. Whether this was orthodox Spinozism was merely a side issue. By injecting life into Spinoza's static universe, Herder made Spinozism much more appealing for his generation. The revival of Spinozism in late eighteenth-century Germany is a flowering more of vitalistic pantheism than Spinozism proper. That vital pantheism has much of its roots in Herder's *Gott*.

6 Political thought

Although Herder was not a systematic political thinker, political issues were at the very heart of his concerns. His views are scattered in several writings, especially in various passages of his historical works. The first version of *Briefe, die Humanität betreffend* (Letters concerning Humanity), written in 1792 but never published, examined the issues raised by the French Revolution.

Herder's most important contribution to modern political thought lay in his nationalism. Although he was not the first spokesman for this doctrine, he did play a prominent part in its formulation and transmission. The essence of Herder's nationalism is his model of government and political association. The foundation of both should be, in Herder's view, not a centralized state but the nation, the culture of a people. The people should be joined together by laws that express their common language, religion, customs and history. Their government should represent and defend, not repress or merely tolerate, their distinctive values and way of life.

Herder's nationalism arose from his profound dissatisfaction with the absolutist states of late eighteenth-century Europe, such as Prussia, Russia and Austria. These states held together people of the most diverse cultures by sheer political force, a centralized bureaucracy run according to the whim of the monarch. The cosmopolitan ideals of these states, Herder firmly believed, were often nothing more than a mask for their oppression. In making the nation rather than the state the basis of political order, Herder's motive was largely populist and democratic. He believed that a government based on the culture of a nation reflected the will of the people.

Although Herder was a pioneer of modern nationalism, his views differ from more recent versions in three fundamental respects. (1) Herder saw the nation as the alternative to, rather than foundation for, the centralized bureaucratic state. (2) He believed in the equal value of all cultures and despised all forms of chauvinism or jingoism. (3) Herder's concept of a nation (*Volk*) is based not on race but culture, whose essential component is language.

In wishing to replace the state with the nation, Herder sometimes leaned toward anarchism. He firmly believed that the people could govern themselves and that the modern state was a persistent threat to that right. The most noble end of the state, he wrote in a censored passage of the *Ideen*, is to become superfluous and disappear. His anarchist sentiments became especially apparent in his polemic against Kant in the *Ideen*. He flatly denies Kant's thesis that the purpose of history is to form a perfect state, insisting instead that its purpose is for the state to disappear. He also takes strong exception to Kant's statement that man is an animal in need of a master; in his view, the very opposite is the case: a man in need of a master is an animal.

Although Herder wanted to abolish the state, he never denied the need for some form of government. All that he opposed is the centralized, bureaucratic modern state. True to the Aristotelian tradition, he insisted that man is a political animal with a natural need for government. That some form of authority is necessary to bridle unruly passions and to arbitrate disputes he fully recognized. He admitted the need, therefore, for written laws and a representative body to administer civic affairs. Yet the form such authority should take is local self-government, because that alone gives the people maximal opportunity to govern themselves about issues that affect them most. This belief in the value of local self-government appears in Herder's admiration for some of the old German city-states, such as Riga and Hamburg.

In the spectrum of late eighteenth-century German politics, Herder belongs firmly to the left wing. He admired the Revolution in France and embraced its ideals of liberty, equality and fraternity. Like many French radicals, he insisted upon the need for a broad franchise and the responsibility of the government to ensure a minimal standard of welfare and education for the people. All his life he had a contempt for the aristocracy and the royalty of the *ancien régime*. Yet Herder was no radical, still less a revolutionary. He became disillusioned with the Revolution after the execution of Louis XVI. His disillusionment stemmed not from any love for the monarchy, but from his hatred of the Jacobins, who, he rightly feared, wanted to establish another form of centralized bureaucratic state. Like many of his contemporaries, he stressed the need for more education and enlightenment as a precondition of social change.

See also: HISTORY, PHILOSOPHY OF; NATION AND NATIONALISM; ROMANTICISM, GERMAN; VICO, G.

List of works

Herder, J.G. (1881–1913) *Sämtliche Werke*, ed. B. Suphan, Berlin: Weidmann. (The standard edition, which contains all works mentioned in the text.)
—— *Briefe, Gesammtausgabe*, ed. W. Dobbek and G. Arnold, Weimar: Bohlausnachfolger, 1979.

References and further reading

Barnard, F.M. (1965) *Herder's Social and Political Thought*, Oxford, Clarendon Press.
Berlin, I. (1976) *Vico and Herder. Two Studies in the History of Ideas.* London, Hogarth Press.
Clark, R.C. (1955) *Herder. His Life and Thought*, Berkeley, CA: University of California Press. (The most comprehensive study in English).
Haym R. (1877–85) *Herder nach seinem Leben und seinen Werken dargestellt*, Berlin: Gaertner. (The most complete and authoritative study).
Norton, R.E. (1991) *Herder's Aesthetics & the Enlightenment*, Ithaca, NY: Cornell University Press.

FREDERICK BEISER

HERMENEUTICS

Hermeneutics, the 'art of interpretation', was originally the theory and method of interpreting the Bible and other difficult texts. Wilhelm Dilthey extended it to the interpretation of all human acts and products, including history and the interpretation of a human life. Heidegger, in Being and Time *(1927), gave an 'interpretation' of the human being, the being that itself understands and interprets. Under his influence, hermeneutics became a central theme of continental philosophy. Hermeneutics generates several controversies. In interpreting something do we unearth the author's thoughts and intentions, imagining ourselves in his position? Or do we relate it to a wider whole that gives it meaning? The latter view gives rise to the hermeneutic circle: we cannot understand a whole (for example, a text) unless we understand its parts, or the parts unless we understand the whole. Heidegger discovered another circle: as we inevitably bring presuppositions to what we interpret, does this mean that any interpretation is arbitrary, or at least endlessly revisable?*

1 **The beginnings of hermeneutics**
2 **Schleiermacher**
3 **Dilthey**
4 **Heidegger**
5 **After Heidegger**

1 The beginnings of hermeneutics

The Greek *hermeneuein* means to express, explain, translate or interpret; *hermeneia* is interpretation and so on, often the interpretation of a sacred message. Plato called poets the *hermenes* – interpreters – of the gods. Philosophers interpreted Homer allegorically. Augustine interpreted the Old Testament as allegory, using Neoplatonic concepts and recording the rise of the soul above the literal and the moral senses of the text to its spiritual sense. Allegorical interpretation remained the norm throughout the Middle Ages. With the Reformation, especially in Germany, *hermeneia* became more explicit and systematic. The word *hermeneutica*, the 'art of interpretation', appeared in the title of J.C. Dannhauer's 1654 work *Hermeneutica sacra sive methodus exponendarum sacrarum litterarum*. Protestants had to interpret the Bible properly; they appealed to it against Roman Catholicism. They rejected allegorical interpretation and insisted on the letter of the text, hoping to retrieve its meaning from distortions introduced by the Church and by scholasticism. Biblical exegesis did not remain isolated from interpretation of other texts. Spinoza, in *Tractatus theologico-politicus* (1670 ch. VII: §94), affirmed that the 'standard of biblical exegesis can only be the light of reason common to all'. For Spinoza, biblical exegesis became biblical criticism, and this involved history. Since reports of miracles fall short of rational standards of belief, we must explain why the authors of the Bible and their contemporaries believed in miracles (see SPINOZA, B. DE §14).

Johann Ernesti declared in his manual of hermeneutics (1761: 7) that the 'verbal sense of Scripture must be determined in the same way in which we ascertain that of other books'. Other texts in need of interpretation were legal documents and the works of classical antiquity, and these disciplines also contributed to hermeneutics. Significant advances were made by two classicists, Friedrich Ast and Friedrich August Wolf. Ast, in *Grundlinien der Grammatik, Hermeneutik und Kritik* (Elements of Grammar, Hermeneutics and Criticism) (1808), distinguished

different levels of understanding a text. The first is 'historical', establishing the authentic text by comparing different manuscripts and deploying knowledge of the history and other writings of the period; to this understanding corresponds the 'hermeneutics of the letter'. The second is grammatical, corresponding to the 'hermeneutics of the sense': we understand the meaning of the words and sentences in the text. The third is spiritual: we ascend from the literal meaning to the spirit (*Geist*) of the author and of their society ('spirit' means 'outlook', 'mentality' or 'worldview'; it need have no theological or psychological connotation). In his lectures on the 'encyclopaedia of classical studies' from 1785 to 1807, Wolf defined hermeneutics as the 'science of the rules by which the meaning of signs is discerned' (1831: 290). Its aim is to 'grasp the written or even merely spoken thoughts of someone else just as he would have them grasped' (1831: 293). This involves not only knowledge of the language of the text, but also historical knowledge, a knowledge of the author's life, of the history and geography of their country. An interpreter should ideally know everything known by the author. Wolf proposed many rules for handling problems of interpretation, but insisted that an interpreter needs a 'lightness of soul' that 'quickly attunes itself to foreign thoughts' (1831: 273). Knowing rules is not enough; we need a skill in applying rules which no rule can guarantee.

2 Schleiermacher

Friedrich SCHLEIERMACHER welded these partial theories into a single discipline, embracing the interpretation of all texts, regardless of genre and doctrines (he interpreted Heraclitus and Plato as well as the Bible.) At each level of interpretation we are involved in a hermeneutical circle. We cannot know the correct reading of a passage in a text unless we know, roughly, the text as a whole; we cannot know the text as a whole unless we know particular passages. We cannot know the meaning of a word unless we know the meanings of surrounding words and of the text as a whole; knowing the meaning of the whole involves knowing the meaning of individual words. We cannot fully understand the text unless we know the author's life and works as a whole, but this requires a knowledge of the texts and other events that constitute his life. We cannot fully understand a text unless we know about the whole culture from which it emerged, but this presupposes a knowledge of the texts and so on that constitute the culture. Not only is there circularity within each level of interpretation, but also between levels. We cannot decide on the correct reading of a particular passage unless we already know something of its meaning and also of the author's life or culture. But how are we to acquire this knowledge, if not from such texts as this?

The hermeneutic circle is less mysterious than often supposed. A text need not be uniformly problematic. A hopelessly corrupt manuscript (or misprinted book) may be undecipherable. But if the manuscripts are reliable over the bulk of the text, the interpreter brings the knowledge of this part to bear on those parts where the manuscripts are corrupt. Not all words and sentences are equally obscure; the relatively transparent supply a clue to the relatively opaque. Again, understanding is a matter of degree. I cannot fully understand a text unless I fully understand each word and sentence, and I cannot fully understand any word or sentence unless I understand the whole. If full understanding and blank incomprehension were the only alternatives, I could not understand a text of any length or complexity. But understanding is not like that: I can roughly understand a text without fully understanding it, and rough understanding enables me to decipher particular parts.

In 1813 Schleiermacher wrote: 'Essentially and inwardly, thought and its expression are completely the same' (1959: 21). This suggests that what we understand is the literal meaning of a text, what the words mean or meant. In 1819 he wrote: 'The art can develop its rules only from a positive formula, and this is: the historical and divinatory, objective and subjective reconstructing of a given utterance' (1959: 87). This suggests that there may be more to an author's thought than the meaning of their words, and that the interpreter has to unearth the thought. The thought may differ from the meaning of the words for several reasons: authors may express themselves badly, a slip of the pen or the tongue, a lack of verbal facility or malapropism. (When someone speaks of 'mitigating against' or writes 'It is worth nothing that...', we assume that they meant 'militating against' and 'It is worth noting that...'.) To understand an utterance fully, we often go beyond the meaning of the words and ask about its author's intentions: Did the author mean it seriously or as a joke? Did they mean the word in this sense or in that? Was the author implicitly criticizing so-and-so? Conversely we may discern more in an author's words than we can plausibly attribute to their conscious thoughts, and invoke their unconscious thoughts or the 'spirit' of the author or his culture. Or we may appeal to the audience. The question 'What does this text mean?' can be expanded in two ways: (1) 'What does/did the author mean by the text?', (2) 'What does/did the text mean to its audience?' These expansions can in turn be interpreted in different

ways. What constitutes the author and their meaning? We may restrict this to the author's conscious thoughts and intentions, or we may include their subconscious thoughts and intentions, or even the spirit of their age, implicitly granting this a share in their authorship. Who are the audience? It may be the author's contemporaries, or a later audience such as ourselves. The answers to the two questions are unlikely to coincide, if author and audience belong to different times or cultures. What Shakespeare meant by *Hamlet* is not what *Hamlet* means to a modern audience, unless that audience consists of skilful hermeneuticists. The answers are most likely to coincide if the audience is contemporary with the author; then author and audience share the same 'spirit', even if they do not have the same creative ability.

When Schleiermacher aimed to reconstruct the verbal meaning of a text, in the belief that 'thought and its expression' are identical, he was answering the question 'What did the text mean to its contemporary, cultivated audience?' When he tried to reconstruct the author's thought, in the belief that this need not be the same as its expression, he was answering the question 'What did the author mean by the text?' How can we know what Shakespeare meant (that is, what he had in mind)? Can we know it in much the same way as we know what a contemporary with whom we are conversing has in mind? Our minds are not wholly different from Shakespeare's; there is a 'spiritual affinity' between us. If we acquire sufficient knowledge of his life and works, we can imaginatively step into his shoes, reproducing his thought. It is possible so to step into someone else's shoes; novelists often do it. It is doubtful whether we need to do this to know what someone is thinking: I may know that a dog wants a bone without imaginatively reproducing this want in myself.

3 Dilthey

Wilhelm DILTHEY owed his acquaintance with hermeneutics to his theological training, but he used it to answer the question 'How do the social or human sciences differ from the natural sciences?' While the natural sciences explain (*erklären*), the social sciences understand (*verstehen*). They understand not simply texts and utterances, but any meaningful 'objectification' or 'expression' of human life: gestures, actions, one's own or another's life, paintings, institutions, societies, past events. There are two types of understanding. First, the understanding of simple expressions such as an utterance, an action or a gesture of fear. Here there is no gulf between the expression and the experience expressed: we understand immediately with no inference. Such understanding presupposes a medium 'common to the I and the You', an 'objective spirit' within which expression and understanding occur: a shared language and culture. Secondly, there are 'higher forms of understanding', dealing with complex wholes, such as a life or a work of art. A part has a meaning (*Bedeutung*) grasped by elementary understanding, the whole has a sense (*Sinn*) resulting from the ordered composition of its parts and grasped by higher understanding. Higher understanding is often provoked by a failure of elementary understanding. If I cannot immediately understand a person's action, I explore their culture or their life as a whole. If I cannot understand a sentence, I may interpret the whole book.

Often when elementary understanding fails, this is because a person – the author of a text, a gesture or an action – is unusual, and cannot be understood by the normal canons of objective spirit. To understand what the author says or does, we need to understand them in their individuality. Thus, higher understanding usually involves the understanding of individuals, not simply the general understanding appropriate for daily life. I also understand myself: by elementary understanding I know immediately that I am hungry, jealous and so on without recourse to my expressions. By higher understanding I make sense of myself, of my life as a whole. Higher understanding may again be stimulated by a failure of immediate understanding: how can I be jealous, I wonder, or how can I have done this? In higher understanding of myself, I become aware of my individuality, of what differentiates me from others.

In the 1890s Dilthey regarded psychology as the foundation of the social sciences. Later, hermeneutics displaced psychology. What interests the social sciences is not the 'soul', an individual's psychological processes, but 'spirit', the shared cultural world. The meaning of a play is independent of its author's 'soul'. Even if a work expresses joy or grief, they are states not of the author but of the 'ideal person' in whose mouth he puts his experience. Psychological life, even one's own, is known by the interpretation of its expressions: 'Man knows himself only in history, never by introspection' (1981: 348). Interpretation of history does not capture the essence of humans in a formula. It reveals to us the diverse possibilities of humanity, liberating us from the confines of the present.

4 Heidegger

Historical studies depend, Dilthey held, on our awareness of a human life as a coherent, 'historical' whole, embedded in a historical context. Martin Heidegger also connected questions about the meaning of historical texts with questions about the meaning of life. Texts like St Paul's letters cannot be understood from dictionaries and grammar-books alone; we need to understand the lives and situation of the author and his audience. In the case of any text, but especially those of a difficult philosopher such as Aristotle, we need to explore our 'hermeneutical situation', the situation, shaped by the past, which imposes on us the presuppositions we bring to the understanding of the text. Are the terms in which we interpret Aristotle appropriate? If not, how can we account for this apparent degeneration in our conceptual apparatus? These are questions about the present, and not just about contemporary philosophy, but about contemporary life and our tendency to misconstrue the past. So Heidegger moves on, in his lectures of 1923, to a 'hermeneutic of facticity', an interpretation of the human being ('Dasein') and everyday life.

Heidegger's *Being and Time* (1927) is a 'hermeneutic', in several ways. It explores Dasein's own understanding and interpreting: Dasein understands and interprets, not incidentally and sporadically but essentially and constantly. It understands – it knows its way around in the world as a field for its own activities. It interprets entities within the world – it sees a table as a table, a chair as a chair (see DE RE/DE DICTO). Such understanding and interpretation are prior to the sciences. Before I interpret a document I see it as a document; before I do geology I see rocks as rocks. Interpretation involves presuppositions: to interpret something as a book I must be familiar with a world in which books have a place, a world of rooms, furniture, shelves, readers. Dasein also interprets itself. It regards itself, for instance, as a cobbler or a sailor. It regards its own life in a certain way. Implicitly in everyday life, more explicitly in philosophy, Dasein misinterprets itself – as a rational animal, a thinking substance, or a machine.

Heidegger describes Dasein's essential features, including interpretation and self-interpretation. Since philosophers themselves are Dasein, they display the same tendencies as Dasein in general. Hence, in studying Dasein, they understand and interpret it, continuing, on a higher, conceptual, plane, the self-interpretation that is an inescapable feature of all Dasein. Like all interpretation, Heidegger's involves presuppositions: a preliminary understanding of Dasein such as all Dasein has, a certain way of viewing Dasein (with regard to its 'being', rather than, say, its biological characteristics), and concepts to be applied to it, such as 'existence'.

The interpretation of Dasein and of being in general involves interpretation of texts. Since Dasein misinterprets itself, we must peel away layers of misinterpretation to see it as it is. These misinterpretations occur in their original purity in such philosophers as Kant, Descartes and Aristotle. We study them to see what they got right and where they went astray, to disclose and assess their influence on our hermeneutical situation and, where appropriate, to free ourselves of their influence. Heidegger interpreted such texts mainly in later works, but *Being and Time* foreshadows his procedure. Words do not have fixed, univocal meanings independently of their use and application. Meanings accrue to words from the significant interrelationships that constitute our world. A 'hammer' is not simply an 'implement for banging': the meaning of the word derives from the context of bench, nails, wood, workshop and customers that constitutes the 'world' of the craftsman. What a word means depends on the world of its user: by 'transport', 'freedom' or 'education', Aristotle does not mean the same as we do since he inhabited a different world. To understand a text we need to go beyond dictionaries and grammars to reconstruct the world of its author and the 'possibilities' it offered.

Later, Heidegger avoided the word 'hermeneutics'. But he continued to interpret texts, poetical as well as philosophical, in his quest for the 'meaning of being'. He equivocates on the question whether we can interpret a text definitively. Our interpretations of the past are bound to our hermeneutical situation and open to future revision. *Being and Time* implies that the meaning of an event or of a life, if not of a text, is what it means *for* us/me, depending on the significance we/I confer on it by and in our/my decisions for the future. Conversely, he claims – for all his 'violence' to the literal text – to unearth the meaning of, for example, Aristotle, with scarcely a hint that his own interpretation might later be seen, with equal justification, as yet one more misinterpretation. At all events, the hermeneutical circle now embraces interpreters and their presuppositions, as well as the text, the author and their culture. The prior understanding of the whole, that Schleiermacher and Dilthey saw as required for the interpretation of a part, can come only from the interpreter's own presuppositions. These may however be revised in the course of the interpretation.

5 After Heidegger

Heidegger's hermeneutics has been exploited by BULTMANN, RICOEUR and DERRIDA, but his closest follower is GADAMER. Gadamer also insists that we recapture the context in which an author wrote, taking into account the intended audience and the questions the author was answering. Interpretation presupposes a historically determined 'pre-understanding', a 'horizon'; it involves a 'fusion of horizons', the horizons of the past and of the present. We cannot be sure that our interpretation is correct, or better than previous interpretations. Our interpretation, and our verdict on previous interpretations, is open to future revision. In interpreting a past text we explore our own pre-understanding as much as the text itself.

With Gadamer and others, hermeneutics has returned to its ancient and medieval roots. We no longer seek what the author meant by a text, but what the text means to, or for, us. The medieval justification of this is that God, the ultimate author of the text, can inscribe in it any meaning he chooses, however allegorical or anachronistic. The moderns justify it by appeal to the non-existence, indeterminacy, inaccessibility, or irrelevance of an author's intentions, or to the historically variable presuppositions of interpretation. Dilthey's extension of hermeneutics to lives and to historic events supports this trend. The 'meaning' of the French Revolution cannot be what its author(s) meant by it, or even what it meant to its contemporary audience. It is what it 'means' to successive later audiences or even what they make of it by their own plans and decisions. Few argue, however, that the interpretation of a text is entirely at the whim of the interpreter. This would subvert the communicability of the hermeneuticist's scepticism by allowing opponents to interpret its expression as they please.

See also: CHINESE CLASSICS; HERMENEUTICS, BIBLICAL; LEGAL HERMENEUTICS; MIDRASH; VEDĀNTA

References and further reading

* Ast, F. (1808) *Grundlinien der Grammatik, Hermeneutik und Kritik* (Elements of grammar, hermeneutics and criticism), Landshut: Thomann. (Outlines a universal hermeneutics, based on a single spirit running through human history. It contains the first formulation of the hermeneutic circle.)

Bruns, G.L. (1992) *Hermeneutics Ancient and Modern*, New Haven, CT: Yale University Press. (A good introduction to the subject, covering the whole history of hermeneutics.)

* Dannhauer, J.C. (1654) *Hermeneutica sacra sive methodus exponendarum sacrarum litterarum* (Sacred hermeneutics: the method of expounding holy scripture), Strasbourg: J. Städel. (Apart from its innovative use of the word 'hermeneutica' this work proposes rules for the sound interpretation of the Bible.)

Dicenso, J. (1990) *Hermeneutics and the Disclosure of Truth: A Study in the Work of Heidegger, Gadamer and Ricoeur*, Charlottesville, VA: University of Virginia Press. (A sound work on these important figures.)

* Dilthey, W. (1981) *Der Aufbau der geschichtlichen Welt in den Geisteswissenschaften* (The construction of the historical world in the human sciences), ed. M. Reidel, Frankfurt am Main: Suhrkamp. (Dilthey's main work on the application of hermeneutics to history.)

* Ernesti, J.A. (1761) *Institutio interpretis Novi Testamenti*, Leipzig: Weidmann; trans. M. Stuart as *Elements of Interpretation*, Andover: M. Newman, 1827: trans. C.H. Terrot as *Principles of Biblical Interpretation*, Edinburgh: T. Clark, 1832–3. (A work of biblical interpretation which helped to refine grammatical analysis and influenced Schleiermacher's early lectures on hermeneutics.)

Gadamer, H.-G. (1960) *Wahrheit und Methode*, Tübingen: J.C.B. Mohr; trans. W. Glen-Doepel as *Truth and Method*, London: Sheed & Ward, 1975. (Surveys modern aesthetics and the theory of historical understanding, and presents Gadamer's own 'philosophical hermeneutics'.)

—— (1976) *Philosophical Hermeneutics*, trans. D. Linge, Berkeley, CA: University of California Press. (A selection of Gadamer's essays on hermeneutics, phenomenology and Heidegger.)

Grondin, J. (1994) *Introduction to Philosophical Hermeneutics*, New Haven, CT: Yale University Press. (A wide-ranging historical introduction that considers the major hermeneuticists from antiquity to Habermas.)

—— (1995) *Sources of Hermeneutics*, Albany, NY: State University of New York Press. (A difficult but rewarding work on the contributions to hermeneutics of Heidegger and Gadamer.)

* Heidegger, M. (1927) *Sein und Zeit*, Halle an der Salle: Max Niemeyer; trans. J. Macquarrie and E. Robinson as *Being and Time*, New York: Harper & Row, 1962; trans. J. Stambaugh, Albany, NY: State University of New York Press, 1996. (Heidegger's first major work, which initiated the modern interest in philosophical hermeneutics.)

—— (1988) *Ontologie (Hermeneutik der Faktizität)* (Ontology (Hermeneutics of facticity)), ed. K. Bröcker-Oltmans, Frankfurt am Main: Vittorio Klostermann. (Volume 63 of Heidegger's collected works contains his lectures from the summer of 1923, in which he examines Dasein's self-interpretation.)

Laks, A. and Neschke, A. (eds) (1990) *La naissance du paradigme hermeneutique: Schleiermacher, Hum-* boldt, Boeckh, Droysen (The birth of the hermeneutical paradigm: Schleiermacher, Humboldt, Boeckh, Droysen), Lille: Presses universitaires de Lille. (Collection of essays focusing on the lesser known hermeneuticists, especially the linguist Wilhelm von Humboldt.)

Mueller-Vollmer, K. (ed.) (1986) *The Hermeneutics Reader*, Oxford: Blackwell. (A judicious selection of hermeneutical writings in translation, from Schleiermacher to the present.)

Palmer, R.E. (1969) *Hermeneutics: Interpretation Theory in Schleiermacher, Dilthey, Heidegger and Gadamer*, Evanston, IL: Northwest University Press. (A good historical introduction, which also discusses the philosophical problems in hermeneutics.)

* Schleiermacher, F.D. (1959) *Hermeneutik*, ed. H. Kimmerle, Heidelberg: Carl Winter, Universitätsverlag; trans. J. Duke and J. Forstmann as *Hermeneutics: The Handwritten Manuscripts by F.D. Scleiermacher*, Missoula, MT: The Scholars Press, 1977. (The definitive edition of Schleiermacher's manuscripts on universal hermeneutics.)

* Spinoza, B. de (1670) *Tractatus Theologico-politicus* (Theological-Political Treatise), in *The Chief Works of Benedict de Spinoza*, vol. 1, trans. R.H.M. Elwes, New York: Dover, 1951. (A pioneering work of rational interpretation and criticism of the Old Testament.)

Tully, J. (ed.) (1988) *Meaning and Context: Quentin Skinner and his Critics*, Cambridge: Polity Press. (A collection of essays by and about Skinner, concerned with interpretation in political philosophy and the history of ideas.)

* Wolf, F.A. (1831) *Vorlesung über die Enzyklopädie der Altertumswissenschaft* (Lectures on the encyclopedia of classical studies), ed. J.D. Gurtler, Leipzig: Lenhold. (A great classical scholar's ideas about the interpretation of ancient texts.)

MICHAEL INWOOD

HERMENEUTICS, BIBLICAL

Hermeneutics has traditionally been defined as the theory of interpretation. Biblical hermeneutics concerns the interpretation of biblical texts. But 'interpretation' tends to reflect the nature of the discipline only from ancient times to about 1960. Increasingly it has come to be seen not as a tool used for difficult or obscure texts, or even for the application of such texts to the present, but as a theory of understanding in the broadest sense. It currently also relates to views of contextual theories

389

of meaning and truth, in contrast to formalist approaches.

From ancient times until about 1800, philosophy played a minimal role in biblical hermeneutics. The subject concerned theology in the context of grammatical, philological, historical and linguistic inquiry. With the work of Schleiermacher in the early years of the nineteenth century, however, hermeneutics entered a new phase. It became a transcendental discipline, seeking to explore the conditions under which the understanding of texts becomes possible at all. In the era following Schleiermacher, theorists drew on the work of Dilthey and Heidegger, among others.

A third phase began with the work of Hans-Georg Gadamer in the early 1960s. Gadamer replaced the Enlightenment preoccupation with 'method' in the context of 'science' and 'reason' with a hermeneutics which took full account of the interpreter's prior situatedness within a given historical tradition. This angle of approach was developed further by Habermas, who noted the role of 'interest' in understanding, and by Ricoeur, who, in dialogue with Freud and others, stressed the role of 'suspicion' as well as 'listening' in hermeneutics. Barthes and Derrida challenged the very notion of a 'given' text, shifting emphasis to construals by society and by readers which reflect motivations not immediately apparent from the supposed messages of texts.

This raises a multitude of fundamental questions for biblical hermeneutics and theology. If texts are no more than shifting constructs, what may still be said about divine grace or revelation? Do sacred texts merely mediate idolatrous constructs? How may hermeneutics serve to unmask interests which interpreters bring to the text and tempt them to use texts manipulatively?

1   The ancient world
2   Medieval, Reformation and post-Reformation
    issues
3   Schleiermacher and Dilthey
4   The turn to existentialism
5   Issues raised by Gadamer, Habermas, Ricoeur and
    Derrida
6   Post-Gadamerian biblical hermeneutics

1   The ancient world

Processes of interpretation of earlier biblical texts were already at work in parts of the Hebrew Bible. But hermeneutics entails conscious reflection on what it is to interpret, and in Hebrew tradition this did not explicitly emerge until the era of rabbinic theology, from 70 AD onwards. In the absence of the Temple and its institutions, reflection about the application of ancient biblical texts to the present became a matter

of detailed concern. The so-called 'rules of interpretation' of Rabbi Hillel, though, were little more than rule-of-thumb rabbinic procedures (see HILLEL BEN SAMUEL OF VERONA).

Among the ancient Greeks, more conscious hermeneutical reflection arose over the issues of whether the 'classic' text of Homer could be interpreted allegorically, in such a way that stories of the exploits of the gods could be read as information about the world – about the properties of different substances, for example, or about virtues, vices and values. In the *Republic*, Plato expresses reservations about such allegorical 'under-meaning' (*hyponoia*), but many of the Stoics interpreted Homer allegorically and Zeno of Citium read parts of Hesiod in this way. The Jewish writer PHILO OF ALEXANDRIA drew on this tradition to interpret the Old Testament allegorically. For example, God cannot 'plant a garden' (Genesis 2: 8); the verse signifies God's 'planting' of virtue. Philo thus smoothed away both anthropomorphisms and time-bound regulations to open a path to the Hebrew Scriptures for educated Greek and Roman readers.

Whether, or in what way, the New Testament writers interpret the Old Testament allegorically remains a matter of controversy. Certainly they use typology (correspondence of events); it is debatable whether they use allegory (correspondence of ideas). Paul's interpretation of Genesis 16: 15 and 21: 2 in Galatians 4: 24–6 offers one of the most probable examples of allegory, although some insist that it is typology. In the sub-apostolic 1 Clement (c. AD 95), the scarlet thread in the house of Rahab (Joshua 2: 18, 21) is seen as an allusion to the blood of the cross. Gnostic writers used allegorical interpretation extensively, not least because it seemed to offer a secret key for initiates. This drove some of the Church Fathers, notably ORIGEN (§1–2), to the first explicitly Christian hermeneutical reflections on method. The difficult question of the status of the Hebrew Old Testament as Christian scripture was among those considered, not least because Marcion had rejected it in the second century.

2   Medieval, Reformation and post-Reformation issues

Origen argued that although the interpreter began with the literal (that is, semantic, grammatical or lexicographical) meaning, it was legitimate to proceed to a 'spiritual' meaning for pastoral purposes. An ambivalence towards allegorical interpretation emerged in Christian tradition. Origen's reason for being willing to go 'beyond the letter' was different from that of the Gnostics, although an intermediate and ambivalent position was held by CLEMENT OF

ALEXANDRIA. Origen recognized the importance of the public domain rather than 'secret' meanings, and was concerned that 'the rude vessel of words' should be 'brought to life'. Here he anticipated the late twentieth-century turn from author to reader. In the School of Antioch, however, the fourth-century writer John Chrysostom approached interpretation as a matter of disclosing 'the mind of the writer'. Hence, although he also used allegorical interpretation, he did so mostly in sermons, and to a much lesser extent in didactic expositions. On the other hand, the contrast between Alexandria (Origen and those who shared his method) and Antioch (Chrysostom and others, especially Theodore of Mapsuertia) is often exaggerated in popular works. By the time of Gregory the Great of Rome, in the second half of the sixth century, the notion of 'three senses of Scripture' (literal, moral and spiritual) associated with Origen had become the Gregorian tradition of four senses: the literal (semantic and historical); the allegorical (a theological or spiritual extension); the moral (an ethical application); and the anagogical (that which embraces the future).

The medieval period witnessed the rise of the *Glossa ordinaria* (Standard Gloss), which provided a brief explanatory comment on a given chapter or verse. Among some less learned or more manipulative writers these glosses were sometimes arbitrary or without due historical understanding. But some major thinkers, notably HUGH OF ST VICTOR, contributed commentaries (for example, on Lamentations) and biblical homilies (for example, on Ecclesiastes) which placed a renewed emphasis on the historical understanding of the text. Reading based on historical and textual study led on to meditation or spiritual reflection. The ultimate aim, however, was to combine such reading with purity of life, to seek loving contemplation of divine thoughts behind Scripture.

Thomas Aquinas discussed linguistic issues, such as the status of metaphor, raised by the biblical text. He was aware that the Gregorian 'fourfold sense' had the capacity to confuse readers unless its logic was clear. However, since he held that scripture reveals both God's being and God's will and purpose, Aquinas supported the notion of moral, allegorical and anagogical (eschatological) meanings in addition to the semantic or literal meaning, even if this last remained primary. Thus he lent his authority to the prevailing methods of medieval writers.

The Reformers reacted against these 'four senses' with grave suspicion. In his early writings, LUTHER (§6) followed medieval tradition. But he moved away from it for two main reasons: first, positively, because of his engagement with the linguistic and rational tools of Renaissance learning; and second, negatively, because of his perception that supposed 'spiritual' meanings could be used in manipulatory ways to serve the interests of ecclesiastical authority and to give the Bible 'a wax nose' to be pushed into any shape. In his middle and later years, he regarded all but the 'plain' meaning as 'nothing but rubbish'. For CALVIN (§2) even more, the hermeneutical goal is to apprehend 'a true single [*simplex*] sense'.

The post-Reformation era witnessed a steady growth of works on hermeneutics. It seems that the term 'hermeneutics' first explicitly appeared as a title for a work in 1654, with J.C. Dannhauer. Major scholars of the eighteenth century included J.A. Turretinus, J.M. Chladenius, J.A. Ernesti and J.S. Semler.

3 Schleiermacher and Dilthey

SCHLEIERMACHER (§9) was nurtured in the tradition of Moravian pietism and became associated with the blossoming Romantic movement. He accepted the transcendental challenge of Kant's three *Critiques*, and perceived clearly the inadequacy and circularity of any system of hermeneutics that served some prior doctrinal understanding of texts. He asked two transcendental questions: how is Christian theology possible? And how do processes of understanding become possible?

Schleiermacher was the first theorist to perceive that the problem of hermeneutics lay in holding together each side of three sets of issues: how understanding in its 'divinatory' or trans-rational dimension interacts with the critical, rational appeal to patterns or regularities of criteria; how understanding the elements or components of texts relates to a more intuitive anticipation of the text as a whole; and how understanding what is to be understood links or engages with a prior or provisional understanding of that to which the subject matter of the text relates. This last issue became known as the problem of 'pre-understanding', for which the German *Vorverständnis* became a technical term in later hermeneutics. As understanding of the text begins to develop, the revised or fuller understanding feeds back into the 'pre-understanding' to produce more appropriate questions and a better readiness to understand.

Simultaneously, understanding parts of the text depends on a provisional, quasi-intuitive leap into an anticipatory understanding of the whole, but at the same time corrects it, while the reverse process of correction and revision also takes place. Both of these processes constitute different versions of 'the hermeneutical circle'.

In biblical studies this hermeneutical approach had several effects. First, it underlined both the importance and the limits of the rational or 'scientific' aspect of enquiry. DILTHEY, writing at the beginning of the twentieth century, took up this issue in his appeal to 'life' rather than to mere 'thought' as the key category in hermeneutical understanding. In his exposition of Schleiermacher, he took up and developed the latter's 'psychological' axis of hermeneutics, namely the need to stand in the shoes of 'the other' in order to understand the other on the basis of shared life and shared humanity. In his criticism of rationalism and empiricism, Dilthey argued that in the veins of the knowing subject (as defined by Locke, Hume and even Kant), no real blood flowed.

Second, the hermeneutical approach led to an emphasis on historical reconstruction in biblical studies, which cohered with the rise of biblical criticism. However, against many popular misunderstandings of Schleiermacher, it must be stressed that this arose not from preoccupation with 'genetic origin', but from the Romantic concern with capturing the living vision of which the textual remainder was a mere deposit. It was for this reason, and not out of mere antiquarian curiosity, that Schleiermacher worked backwards from the text to what lay behind it. It was a side effect in biblical studies that this fostered an approach to texts which used them as mere sources for historical reconstruction. This hermeneutical reductionism and instrumentalism would not have been endorsed by Schleiermacher, who is frequently blamed for it. The level of complexity and sophistication which characterizes his work is vigorously defended in Thiselton (1992).

4 The turn to existentialism

Martin HEIDEGGER (§§2–3) took up and developed further the notions of 'the hermeneutical circle' and a prior 'life relationship' to that which the interpreter seeks to understand. But whereas Dilthey saw 'life' as part of a common humanity, Heidegger stressed the historical finitude and unique 'givenness' or situatedness of the interpreter within pre-given horizons of orientation and practical purpose. In continuity with Kierkegaard and Nietzsche, he called attention to the close connection between finite *Existenz* and the directionality of human will towards its own goals.

In the field of New Testament studies, Rudolf BULTMANN (§§2–3) viewed this perspective as fruitful for a hermeneutical engagement with texts. New Testament texts, he argued, are not to inform neutral curiosity, but to challenge the human will. The interpreter may be misled by what appears to speak descriptively of God, Christ or human persons. For this, according to Bultmann, is the language of 'myth', which obscures its genuine purpose. Neither God nor Christ nor persons are to be 'objectified' as being or substance as such. Rather God addresses humanity through the pseudo-descriptive language only to summon humanity from inauthentic existence orientated towards the past and under law and bondage, to an authentic mode of existence made possible through the event of Christ (see EXISTENTIALIST THEOLOGY §3).

The relation between operative linguistic function and historical states of affairs for Bultmann remains a complex and controversial issue. 'Right-wing' critics accuse him of too readily collapsing the Bible into Christian existentialism; 'left-wing' critics accuse him of arbitrarily clinging to the factual reality of the cross, or of failing to carry through his 'demythologizing' by exposing 'God' to be no more than a functionally useful linguistic cipher. For this reason, 'the Bultmann School' broke apart in different directions. Ernst Fuchs, for example, provides a bridge between Heidegger and Gadamer, since Fuchs, with Ebeling, identifies the creative eventfulness of language as the key issue in hermeneutics.

5 Issues raised by Gadamer, Habermas, Ricoeur and Derrida

The publication of Hans-Georg Gadamer's *Truth and Method* in 1960 constitutes the most important turning point for the subject since Schleiermacher, who founded the modern discipline (see GADAMER, H.-G.). The term 'method' in the title stands in a negative, or at least ironic, relation to 'truth'. Gadamer attacks as an artificial abstract construct the pure 'reason' and 'method' of Enlightenment thought in Descartes (as opposed to Vico) and in all thinkers who naïvely assume that methods of science can disclose all truth. He agrees with his teacher Heidegger that the individual thinker is shaped by their situatedness within historical tradition. He writes: 'The self-awareness of the individual is only a flickering in the closed circuits of historical life' ([1960] 1989: 276). But this does not exclude the possibility of understanding, for 'pre-judgments' (*Vorurteile*) constitute a 'historical reality' in which the interpreter participates.

Gadamer clarifies the issue by drawing on the analogy of games. The presuppositional stance (that is, the ways in which the rules of the game determine goals and what counts as an appropriate move or strategy) determines 'meaning' and 'reality' for players more than their own conscious reflection. Thus a tradition of 'effective-history' (*Wirkungsgeschichte*) lies beneath the distinctive and indeed unique 'performances' which characterize each game, or each interpretive or communicative event. Gadamer has thus transposed the relation between the whole and the parts which occupied Schleiermacher and Dilthey into a post-Hegelian rather than post-Kantian key. All understanding, he believes, is hermeneutical, not value-neutral. This is what he means by 'the universality of the hermeneutical problem'.

HABERMAS (§§1–2) was quick to identify a lack of critical social awareness in Gadamer's hermeneutics. Where Gadamer spoke of 'pre-judgment', Habermas spoke of 'interest'. What determines the horizons of understanding, he argues, is social interests (which include power interests) on the part of interpreters and, more especially, their communities of interpretation. But Habermas refuses, as against Richard Rorty, to reduce this to social pragmatism. Through a carefully elaborated theory of communicative action, he denies that communities of interpretation are so radically conditioned by social and historical context that no trans-contextual criteria of meaning and understanding can remain operative. Thus his earlier work, *Knowledge and Human Interests* (1978), leads on to his more complex and valuable work, *The Theory of Communicative Action: The Critique of Functionalist Reason* (1984).

Paul RICOEUR moved from work on human will and fallibility to theories of symbol, and then through hermeneutics to a dialogue between hermeneutics and structuralism, ending with a dialogue between hermeneutics, metaphor and narrative theory. His later work returns to the relation between hermeneutics and personal agency. He is probably best known for his aphorism that 'the symbol gives rise to thought'. His work on hermeneutics led him to explore the phenomena of self-deception and 'double meaning' in Freud's *Interpretation of Dreams*. The element of disguise and deception led to his formulation of 'a hermeneutic of suspicion'. He writes that Freud's work 'compelled me to enlarge my first concept of hermeneutics beyond a mere semantic analysis of double-meaning expressions' ([1975] 1978: 318).

While Ricoeur rejects the 'reductionism' of Freud's theories as an explanation of human life, including religion, he accepts Freud's emphasis on the capacity of the self for self-deception. Hermeneutics, therefore, in Ricoeur's view, performs the double task of 'destroying idols' (that is, unmasking the wishes that condition interpretation and cause projection of one's own desires into texts) and 'listening to symbols'. The first entails a 'vow of rigour', the second a 'vow of obedience'. The symbolic level of meaning appears as metaphor in relation to sentences, and as the projection of narrative-worlds in relation to sentences

which combine together to present a structured whole. Some of the more controversial aspects of his hermeneutics concern the 're-figuration' or 'construal' of narrative, and a readiness to speak at times of 'the death of the author' (1976: 29–30).

This attempt to speak of 'the death of the author' for interpreting written texts stems primarily from Roland BARTHES. Barthes' semiotics, in turn, paved the way for DERRIDA. Jacques Derrida stresses that writing (in contrast to oral speech) entails 'the absence of the signatory' and even 'the absence of the referent' ([1967] 1976: 40–1). Further, no text is a 'finished' product or a 'given'. Allegedly on the basis of a theory of semiotics and textuality, he sees textual meaning as endlessly 'deferred'. On the basis of a legacy drawn partly from Freud, Husserl, Nietzsche and Heidegger, he proposes a hermeneutic that has affinities with postmodernism and articulates deconstructionism. In effect, it seems to reduce texts to an ever-shifting flux, which is constantly subject to new forms as new conventions and societal assumptions re-contextualize what on the surface appears to count as meaning and truth.

6 Post-Gadamerian biblical hermeneutics

Two aspects of Gadamer's work have been of particular importance in the field of biblical studies. First, while he rightly insists that the interpreter must respect the distinctive horizon of the text, Gadamer urges that understanding works towards the goal, at least in principle, of a fusion of the two horizons of meaning and understanding. Second, his work stresses the distinctiveness and uniqueness of each 'performance' as an actualization of interpretation. His emphasis on the 'radical finitude' of each performance must be understood against the background of Hegel and especially Heidegger. Hence, issues of polyvalency of meaning arise. In biblical studies this engages with work on the 'narrative-worlds' of parables and raises questions about a reappraisal of 'tradition' and 'effective-history' as against Enlightenment reason alone.

The unmasking by Habermas of the role of 'interest' in interpretation coheres well with attacks on those interpretations of the Bible that function primarily to serve the interests of oppressive or 'establishment' groups. Thus it adds to the hermeneutical resources of feminist and liberation hermeneutics (see FEMINIST THEOLOGY; LIBERATION THEOLOGY §3). At the same time, however, the insistence of Habermas that trans-contextual criteria of meaning or truth also have some place firmly separates him from the social pragmatism of Richard Rorty and Stanley Fish. If Rorty's approach is accepted, it invites the oppressed to wield the same kind of instrumental tools as the oppressors, in which case hermeneutics comes to depend on the force of contextual rhetoric, not trans-contextual truth. But if Christian theology is to embody any universal truth-claim, this approach becomes difficult to sustain. Habermas offers a middle ground on which a socially sensitive hermeneutic may operate with intellectual integrity.

Ricoeur has illuminated symbol, metaphor and narrative for biblical hermeneutics. In particular, he constructively stresses both the creative power of 'double-meaning' language in biblical texts and rightly urges suspicion concerning the interpreter's own desire to manipulate them. He has also called attention to the importance of hymnic, narrative and wisdom modes of biblical discourse alongside the prophetic, didactic and directive modes.

It is too soon to chart the ultimate effects of the work of Derrida and deconstructionism on biblical interpretation. Some have attempted to view his approach as an iconoclastic tool which coheres with a 'silent' or 'negative' articulation of divine transcendence. But Derrida's work offers more than a tool. He himself is drawn towards the 'unfinished' vision associated with apocalyptic writings. But interpreters of the Bible have used deconstructive strategies of reading effectively, to date, only on such untypical literature as Ecclesiastes, Job and possibly some parables of reversal which serve only to break the spell of some established view. The best example with regard to the Old Testament is D.J.A. Clines' work on Job: Job 'undermines the... hierarchical oppositions on which it relies' (1990: 65). The most influential examples of work on the New Testament come from J.D. Crossan, who argues that parables subvert the very 'worlds' which they project.

The emphasis on polyvalency in textuality and the role of narrative and of active readers has led to an unprecedented interest in literary theory in biblical hermeneutics. In some quarters, this has led to a partial abandonment of necessary concerns about biblical languages and biblical history. In others, a genuine attempt is made to hold together the best in mainstream methods of enquiry with newer insights which, in some cases, have yet to prove their value fully. At all events, the shift of perspective in biblical interpretation has been considerable over the last twenty years, and biblical hermeneutics has come to occupy a necessary place, after long neglect, in most research universities. Very recently, attention is being given to the ethics of hermeneutics (Patte 1995), the hermeneutics of the self (Ricoeur 1990; Thiselton 1995) and speech-act theory (Wolterstorff 1995), all

against the background of the challenges of post-modern thought.

See also: DECONSTRUCTION; HERMENEUTICS; MIDRASH; POSTMODERN THEOLOGY; POSTMODERNISM; THEOLOGY, RABBINIC

References and further reading

Aquinas, T. (1266–73) *Summa theologiae* Ia, ed. H. McCabe, Oxford: Blackfriars Press, 1964, vol. 3: 47–107. (Q.13, aa.1–12 discuss the language of God.)

Bartsch, H.-W. (1962, 1964) *Kerygma and Myth*, London: Society for Promoting Christian Knowledge. (A sample of debate about existential interpretation and demythologizing, including the classic essay by Bultmann on this subject.)

Bultmann, R. (1964–5) *Glauben und Verstehen* (Faith and Understanding), 4 vols, Tübingen: Mohr; vol. 2 trans. as *Essays Philosophical and Theological*, London: SCM Press, 1955; vol. 1 trans. as *Faith and Understanding*, London: SCM Press, 1969. (A collection of classic essays; of particular interest is 'The Problem of Hermeneutics' in volume 2.)

* Clines, D.J.A. (1990) 'Deconstructing the Book of Job', in M. Warner (ed.) *The Bible as Rhetoric*, London: Routledge, 65–80. (A sample of 'post-modern' hermeneutics.)

* Derrida, J. (1967) *Of Grammatology*, Baltimore, MD: Johns Hopkins University Press, 1976. (A difficult text on hermeneutical theory.)

* Dilthey, W. (1976) *Selected Writings*, ed. H.P. Rickman, Cambridge: Cambridge University Press. (This contains translations of parts of volumes 5 and 7 of the standard collected works, in which the ideas described in §3 are developed.)

Fuchs, E. (1964) 'The New Testament and the Hermeneutical Problem', in J.M. Robinson and J.B. Cobb (eds) *New Frontiers in Theology*, vol. 2, *The New Hermeneutic*, New York: Harper & Row, 111–45. (The easiest essay by this complex writer; the other essays in the volume offer a useful critique of his work.)

—— (1970) *Hermeneutik*, Tübingen: Mohr, 4th edn. (A classic, although difficult, exposition of the so-called new hermeneutic, which applies perspectives from the late Heidegger and Gadamer to New Testament interpretation.)

* Gadamer, H.-G. (1960) *Truth and Method*, London: Sheed & Ward, 2nd English edn, 1989. (A complex but influential work.)

—— (1966) 'The Universality of the Hermeneutical Problem', in his *Philosophical Hermeneutics*, Berkeley, CA: University of California Press, 1975.

(Attacks suppositions about the scope of 'reason' or 'science'.)

* Habermas, J. (1978) *Knowledge and Human Interests*, London: Heinemann, 2nd edn. (A classic exposition of his earlier thought prior to more sophisticated work on hermeneutics and language. The appendix to the second edition contains seminal ideas on 'interest', later developed more fully in *The Theory of Communicative Action*.)

* —— (1981) *The Theory of Communicative Action: The Critique of Functionalist Reason*, Cambridge: Polity Press, 1984. (Combines critical hermeneutical views with socio-linguistic theory and social philosophy.)

Jeanrond, W.G. (1991) *Theological Hermeneutics, Development and Significance*, London: Macmillan. (An intermediate-level introduction to the subject.)

Morgan, R. and Barton, J. (1988) *Biblical Interpretation*, Oxford: Oxford University Press. (A basic introduction to some general issues.)

* Patte, D. (1995) *Ethics of Biblical Interpretation*, Louisville, KY: Westminster–Knox. (Discusses ethical dilemmas in first-person mode.)

* Ricoeur, P. (1975) *The Rule of Metaphor*, London: Routledge & Kegan Paul, 1978. (Reflects the turn to double-meaning in sentences, with useful autobiographical reflectins at the end.)

* —— (1976) *Interpretation-Theory Discourse and the Surplus of Meaning*, Fort Worth, TX: Texas Christian University Press. (A succinct exposition of Ricoeur's views in mid-development.)

—— (1983–5) *Time and Narrative*, 3 vols, Chicago, IL: Chicago University Press, 1984–8. (Ricoeur's *magnum opus* on the hermeneutics of narrative. A work of great stature.)

* —— (1990) *Oneself as Another*, Chicago, IL: Chicago University Press, 1992. (His crowning work on the hermeneutics of the self.)

* Schleiermacher, F.D.E. (1977) *Hermeneutics: The Handwritten Manuscripts*, ed. H. Kimmerle, Missoula, MT: Scholars' Press. (Taken from manuscripts written between about 1805 and 1831, this is the best source for Schleiermacher's hermeneutical ideas.)

Schneiders, S.M. (1991) *The Revelatory Text: Interpreting the New Testament as Sacred Scripture*, San Francisco, CA: Harper. (Applies hermeneutical theory to some biblical material.)

Tate, W.R. (1991) *Biblical Interpretation: An Integrated Approach*, Peabody, MA: Hendrickson. (Elementary textbook covering only part of the ground.)

Thiselton, A.C. (1980, 1993) *The Two Horizons: New Testament Hermeneutics and Philosophical Description*, Carlisle: Paternoster, and Grand Rapids, MI: Eerdmans. (Detailed exposition and bibliography, with special studies of Heidegger, Bultmann, Gadamer and Wittgenstein.)

* —— (1992) *New Horizons in Hermeneutics – The Theory and Practice of Transforming Biblical Reading*, London: HarperCollins, and Grand Rapids, MI: Zondervan. (A detailed critical discussion of the subject, with a comprehensive bibliography; extensive chapters on Schleiermacher, Gadamer, literary theory and specific biblical texts.)

—— (1995) *Interpreting God and the Postmodern Self: On Meaning, Manipulation and Promise*, Edinburgh: T. & T. Clark. (This work addresses postmodern tendencies to translate truth-issues into issues of rhetoric and social power. It also includes a hermeneutic of selfhood on pages 47–79. In the final part (121–64) it offers a hermeneutic of biblical and theological approaches to hope and to Trinitarian theology.)

Watson, F. (1994) *Text, Church and World: Biblical Interpretation in Theological Perspective*, Edinburgh: T. & T. Clark. (A useful interactive discussion drawing together biblical studies, theology and postmodernity.)

* Wolterstorff, N. (1995) *Divine Discourse*, Cambridge: Cambridge University Press. (A Yale philosopher of religion uses speech-act theory to evaluate the plausibility of the claim that God speaks through the Bible.)

ANTHONY C. THISELTON

HERMENEUTICS, LEGAL

see LEGAL HERMENEUTICS

HERMETISM

A primarily religious amalgam of Greek philosophy with Egyptian and other Near Eastern elements, Hermetism takes its name from Hermes Trismegistus, 'thrice greatest Hermes', alias the Egyptian god Thoth. Numerous texts on philosophical theology and various occult sciences, ascribed to or associated with this primeval figure, were produced in Greek by Egyptians between roughly AD 100 and 300, and are a major document of late pagan piety. Reintroduced into Western Europe during the Renaissance, they provided considerable inspiration to philosophers, scientists and magicians of the fifteenth and sixteenth centuries.

Hermetic literature can be divided into *philosophical*

treatises, on God, the world and man, and *technical* writings on astrology, alchemy and other branches of occult science. The philosophical Hermetica comprise principally: (1) the *Asclepius* or *Perfect Discourse*, a longish work surviving in a Latin translation; (2) the *Corpus Hermeticum* proper, a Byzantine collection of fourteen treatises, translated into Latin by Marsilio Ficino in 1462–3 and published in 1471 under the title *Pimander* (after *Poemandres*, its first and most important treatise), to which three further pieces were later added; and (3) some twenty-nine extracts in the anthology compiled in the fifth century AD by John Stobaeus. The Stobaeus *Hermetica* vary in length from single sentences (12, 27, 28) to an important extract (23, from the *Korē Kosmou* or *Pupil of the Cosmos*) as long as anything in the *Corpus Hermeticum*.

The philosophical treatises take the form of dialogues, or rather, since disputation and argument are notably absent from them, of expositions, usually although not always by Hermes himself, to one or more trusting disciples. Their scenery and *dramatis personae* – Hermes, his son Tat, Asclepius (alias Imouthes or Imhotep), King Ammon and so forth – are Egyptian and ancient, investing these treatises, like so many other writings of the period, with the authority of primeval revelation. Their philosophy – that is, their cosmology and metaphysics – is a contemporary 'Middle Platonism' (see PLATONISM, EARLY AND MIDDLE), the only philosophical idiom available in late antiquity to anyone attempting a non-mythological treatment of these subjects. (There are also gnostic and Jewish elements, notably in *Poemandres* and *Corpus Hermeticum* III.) Their purpose, however, is not strictly philosophical. A treatise may start with some standard question of school philosophy – for example, motion (II), death (VIII), or intellection and sensation (IX). But the answer, often garbled, is seldom more than a starting point for meditation and homily. The aim is not to offer some new, coherent and discussible account of God, the world and man so much as to satisfy a religious need, common enough in this period, for a saving 'gnostic' illumination. The purpose of the Hermetist teacher – and the treatises tend to be stylized as lessons in a course of ever more esoteric instruction – is to generate a *gnōsis*, an intuitive knowledge of god and self, vouchsafed to very few, an answer in cosmic terms to the perennial question 'What am I here for? What am I?'. The instruction finds its fulfilment in intellectual illumination, as the pupil becomes aware of being a particle of divine life and light (*Poemandres* 21) and the teacher can say 'You have come to know yourself and our common Father' (*Corpus Hermeticum* XIII 22).

In this context, doctrinal consistency and lucid theory are minor considerations. There are numerous contradictions between the treatises – one text admits as much (*Corpus Hermeticum* XVI 1). Some of these go back to Plato's own works, to the contrast there between the *Timaeus*, with its picture of mankind placed in a good world by a good god – an optimism strongly endorsed by the *Asclepius* and by *Corpus Hermeticum* II, V–VI, VIII–XII, XIV, XVI – and the gloomier account of our human condition in the *Phaedo* and the *Phaedrus*, reflected in the severe pessimism of *Poemandres*, *Corpus Hermeticum* IV, VII, XIII and *Korē Kosmou*, when they dismiss the material world as a 'totality of evil' (*Corpus Hermeticum* IV 6), into which the soul has fallen as a punishment for original sin (*Korē Kosmou* 24), or in consequence of some primeval blunder (*Poemandres* 14). But the inconsistencies hardly matter. The Hermetic treatises are documents of spirituality, not philosophy. Scholarship has come increasingly to see them as translations, as products of a native Egyptian religious tradition (the very fact that they are attributed to Hermes-Thoth is confirmation of their author's religious loyalties) rewritten in the language of Middle Platonism.

Thoth was, among other things, the god of wisdom, knowledge and science. In Roman Egypt numerous works were ascribed to Hermes Trismegistus on technical subjects such as astrology, alchemy and the hidden properties of plants. His name is constantly invoked in magical papyri. These disciplines all rested on a principle, widely held in late antiquity and briefly sketched in the *Asclepius* (2–7, 19), of cosmic 'sympathy'. Linking things on earth to each other and to things in heaven is a nexus of largely hidden sympathies and antipathies which can be used to explain, predict and manipulate the course of events. The philosophical Hermetica, where mentioning these occult sciences, give them a high religious colouring. Magic and philosophy alike, says the *Korē Kosmou* (68), nourish the soul. Both are ways to salvation.

Hermes was remembered as a magician, and also as a primeval sage, a younger contemporary of Moses, who foretold the coming of Christianity. During the Middle Ages, numerous works in Arabic and Latin were produced under his name. The arrival of *Corpus Hermeticum* in the West created something of a sensation: Ficino interrupted his life's work on Plato and Plotinus to translate it. A vastly older figure than Plato and a vastly purer exponent of the 'original theology' (*prisca theologia*), Hermes lent authority and respectability to the active interest which FICINO, PICO DELLA MIRANDOLA and others took in magic. The broad Hermetic vision of the world as a network of hidden forces waiting to by discovered and exploited by the magus was to be an inspiration to such luminaries of sixteenth-century science as Paracelsus, whose experiments in alchemy led to the discovery of laudanum, and Giordano Bruno, whose Hermetic interests ended with him burnt at the stake. The antiquity, and hence the authority, of Hermes Trismegistus received a fatal blow in 1614 when Isaac Casaubon demonstrated, on linguistic and other grounds, that the Hermetic writings could only be a late forgery. Hermes still had admirers and readers in the seventeenth century, including the Cambridge Platonists and even Isaac Newton. But Casaubon remained unrefuted; and the Hermetic writings lost their appeal to all save lovers of the occult and, in the twentieth century, historians of religion.

See also: Gnosticism; Mystical philosophy in Islam §2; Renaissance philosophy

References and further reading

Copenhaver, B.P. (ed.) (1992) *Hermetica: The Greek 'Corpus Hermeticum' and the Latin 'Asclepius'*, Cambridge: Cambridge University Press. (English translation, with notes and a useful introduction.)

Festugière, A.-J. (1944–54) *La révélation d'Hermès Trismégiste*, Paris: Gabalda, 4 vols. (Indispensable in-depth study.)

Fowden, G. (1986) *The Egyptian Hermes*, Cambridge: Cambridge University Press. (Important for the historical and social background of the *Hermetica*.)

Grafton, A. (1983) 'Protestant Versus Prophet: Isaac Casaubon on Hermes Trismegistus', *Journal of the Warburg and Courtauld Institutes* 46: 78–93. (On Casaubon's seminal redating of the *Corpus Hermeticum*.)

Kingsley, P. (1993) 'Poimandres: The Etymology of the Name and the Origins of the Hermetica', *Journal of the Warburg and Courtauld Institutes* 56: 1–24. (Seeks to vindicate as authentically Egyptian the main content of the treatises.)

Nock, A.D. and Festugière, A.-J. (eds) (1945–54) *Hermès Trismégiste*, Budé series, Paris: Belles Lettres, 4 vols. (Text, French translation and notes.)

Yates, F.A. (1964) *Giordano Bruno and the Hermetic Tradition*, London: Routledge & Kegan Paul. (Important study of the Renaissance tradition.)

JOHN PROCOPÉ

HERRERA, ABRAHAM COHEN DE (*c*.1562–*c*.1635)

Herrera was a philosophically oriented Kabbalist who combined Neoplatonism and Kabbalistic knowledge learned from Israel Sarug, a disciple of Isaac Luria. In his Spanish works Puerta del Cielo *(The Gate of Heaven), and* Casa de la Divinidad *(The House of Divinity), he considered Kabbalah as the source of the ancient truth.*

Herrera believed that as the intellect is the highest epistemic grade, one must rely on philosophy to reach the divine secrets. He dealt with the concept of Ensoph (his own spelling of Eyn Sof – the Infinite) in terms of its Thomistic and Renaissance definitions – the Infinite that excludes limit. Tzimtzum is the voluntary Contraction of Ensoph, which prepares space for worlds to be created. The space opened up is metaphorically called Adam Kadmon (Primordial Man), the first emanation of which is the Intelligible World and the Tetragrammaton, the principle that shapes the Chain of Being around the Pythagorean number four. Neoplatonically, Adam Kadmon is the Intelligible World. Herrera's account incorporates further complex ideas about First and Second Causes of creation.

In 1699, Herrera drew the attention of Johan Georg Wachter, who, on the basis of Knorr von Rosenroth's Latin translations of Herrera's works in Kabbala Denudata, *blamed him for inspiring Spinoza's supposed pantheistic heresy.*

1 Life, writings and sources
2 Philosophy and Kabbalah
3 Legacy

1 Life, writings and sources

Born to a *converso* family, probably in Italy, Abraham Cohen (Alonso Nuñez) de Herrera worked in the commercial service of the Sultan al-Mansur of Morocco. In 1596 he was taken prisoner by the Earl of Essex at Cadiz and brought to London, but was finally freed after extended diplomatic negotiations. He met Israel Sarug in Ragusa and delved into Lurianic Kabbalah (see Kabbalah). In Amsterdam he belonged to the synagogue which Spinoza attended in his youth, continued in business, and headed the committee that approved Joseph del Medigo's *Sefer Elim* (Book of Deities) for publication by Menasseh ben Israel. In the latter's own *Conciliador* (Conciliator), the imprimatur calls him *Philosopho, Theologo y Cabalista* (philosopher, theologist and Kabbalist).

Between 1620 and 1632 Herrera wrote *Casa de la*

Divinidad and *Puerta del Cielo*, to introduce other ex-Conversos to Lurianic mysticism. Isaac Aboab da Fonseca translated the works into Hebrew (1655), but lacked his master's philosophical background and failed fully to capture the letter and spirit of the Spanish originals, especially when pagan or Christian sources came into play. To these two works Herrera added two auxiliary booklets, *Epitome de la Logica o Dialectica* (Summary of Logic or Dialectics) and *Libro de Diffiniciones* (Book of Definitions).

Herrera's library included the chief medieval philosophers, such as AQUINAS and other scholastics, but he favoured Marsilio FICINO, Giovanni PICO DELLA MIRANDOLA and their Neoplatonic followers. Besides MAIMONIDES, ALBO and Leone Ebreo, he cites Kabbalist sources, including Hayyim Vital's unprinted tractates and sayings heard from Sarug. But he never cites such writings attributed to Sarug as *Limudei Atzilut* (Studies of Emanation) and does not ascribe to him the doctrines of the *malbush* (garment) or the *shi'ashua* (the delighting motion), which are central in his own thought. Indeed, he relies not on Sarug but on Moses Cordovero (1522–70) in dealing philosophically with Kabbalah.

2 Philosophy and Kabbalah

Herrera viewed Kabbalah, stemming from Adam or Abraham, as the fount of *prisca theologia* (ancient theology), standing above philosophy and even theology. He saw no conflict among the three, nor between Lurianic and Cordoveran Kabbalah, but relied on philosophy for aid in deciphering the enigmatic language of the Lurianic Kabbalah, just as Pico deciphered the gnomic symbolism of Plato.

Puerta del Cielo opens with reflections on the Kabbalistic Infinite, here equated with the First Cause of the scholastics. The Ensoph (Infinite) (so transcribed by Herrera himself) was a subject Lurianic Kabbalists avoided, loath to conceptualize God's transcendence. But Herrera gained support from scholastic works like Aquinas' *Summa contra gentiles* and *Quaestiones disputatae* and their Renaissance interpreters. Thus he adopts Aquinas' and Ficino's distinction between the privative infinity of matter, which longs for limit, and the negative infinity of the First Cause, which excludes limit. Infinity verges towards limit in Tzimtzum, the Contraction of the Ensoph. Adapting Aristotle's principle (*Physics* VII) that every cause is present in its effect, the transcendence of the Ensoph is rendered immanent (see ARISTOTLE). Following Pico's tripartite ontology, Herrera calls the First Cause 'eminent' or 'causal'; the Sephirot (as with Ensoph, his own transliteration of Sefirot – Numerations), or primal hypostases,

'formal' or 'proper'; and the Lower Worlds 'remote' or 'participative'.

Unlike some Kabbalists, Herrera does not imagine Tzimtzum in cathartic, mythical or eschatological terms but conceptualizes it as a voluntary act of Ensoph, preparing space for worlds to be created. What had been a convulsive event within the Divinity, is now a metaphor of the transition to finitude. The space opened up in the Ensoph is metaphorically called Adam Kadmon. This first creation by, from and within Ensoph is the ultimate substrate of potentiality and the first form or actuality.

Herrera treats the doctrine of Adam Kadmon as a central Lurianic theme and labours to find it in pre-Lurianic authorities – the *Sefer Yetzirah* (Book of Creation), the *Zohar* (Book of Splendour), Cordovero – arguing that the Keter Eyon (Supernal Crown) is, in fact, Luria's Adam Kadmon. He equates the distinction in *Tikkunei Zohar* between the 'Cause of All Causes' and the 'Cause of Causes' with that between Ensoph and Adam Kadmon. Two generations later this conclusion had dramatic consequences in the theology of the followers of Shabtai Tsvi (Sabbatai Sevi, as the name is sometimes transliterated), which sharply distinguished the First Cause from the Second and equated the latter with the God of Israel.

In a remarkable collation of medieval and renaissance sources, Herrera identifies the Adam Kadmon as a primal hypostasis with the Tetragrammaton, shaping the entire Chain of Being around the Pythagorean number four as the Ineffable name does. Neoplatonically, Adam Kadmon is the Intelligible World and thus the abode of the Sephirot. Responding to the problematics of emanation, Herrera presents the first perfect effect as the first link in an emanative chain, above which no higher perfect effect is possible.

In Cordovero, the Ensoph begins the emanative process by taking pleasure in God, either intellectually or somehow more concretely. But Herrera ascribes the doctrine of *shi'ashua* to Luria and interprets it metaphorically: the delighting motion of sexual congress within the Ensoph leads to a cosmic pregnancy and the birth of the finite from the infinite. Herrera interprets this imagery in terms of an intellectual process within the First Cause that gives definition to its future effects.

Herrera considers the Sephirot, or hypostatic numbers, as the cornerstone of the Kabbalah, which sets numerous hypostases between Ensoph and the Lower Worlds. Relying on the medieval scholastic Cardinal Pierre d'Ailly, he suggests that the First Cause acts the better through Secondary causes. The Sephirot are representations of Ensoph, the world of beauty surrounding the supreme good (see Plato's *Second Letter*) and the formal mode of being that provides our epistemic access to the First Cause. They are thus the *malbush* or garment of Ensoph, but they emanate from Adam Kadmon and lie below it, not at the top of the ontic hierarchy, like the *malbush* in Sarug. As a secondary cause, each Sefira is the supreme perfection of its own genus, heading a certain order of perfections, a supreme *henad*. This Proclean excursion leads Herrera to the audacious description of the Sephirot as secondary deities – a conception that influenced the Sabbatean subordination of the God of Israel.

Transposing the dynamism of Luria's divine lights into the language of ideas, Herrera interprets the Kabbalistic *Mot ha-Melachim* (Death of the Kings) and *Shevirat ha-Kelim* (Breaking of the Vessels) as metaphors for the Platonic fall of the soul into the body. Following Ficino's *Theologia platonica* (Platonic Theology), he explains that when our soul inclines towards the body it forgets the divine intelligibles. *Tikkun* (restoration) is the return of divine intellects to their former perfection. Intellection, like biological generation, results from the union of the (male) intelligible with (female) intellectual receptivity. The Broken Vessels are restored not by additional light or power but by heightened intellectual receptivity.

In Kabbalistic emanation the soul is represented as a circle, a space produced by the self-contraction of the Infinite. The intellect is a straight line descending through that space. Discussing this idea with Sarug, Herrera had wondered why the circle, a curved line, takes precedence over a straight line. Sarug suggested that Luria's circle was in fact a single point, preceding the line as the principle of life. The line penetrating soul-space descends to produce more and more circles, conjoining soul and intellect, ultimately even in the lowest worlds (see SOUL, NATURE AND IMMORTALITY OF THE).

The psychological chapters of *Casa de la Divinidad* elaborate a doctrine of prophecy based on reconciling Lurianic with other Kabbalistic, scholastic and Renaissance ideas. Prophecy, Herrera concludes, is the highest grade of intellection granted by the divine will. Herrera adopts Aquinas' view and rejects that of Maimonides, which finds prophecy only in the most intellectually prepared. Here Herrera's intellectualism bends towards tradition.

3 Legacy

Herrera's conclusions were not wholly accepted, even by his few disciples. By the later seventeenth century his school had become quite unfamiliar with scholas-

tic arguments, and those arguments themselves grew increasingly obsolete. Yet several prominent Kabbalists did adopt the conclusions of Herrera's metaphorical hermeneutic, rejecting in particular the notion that Tzimtzum was a real event within the divinity. Among these Kabbalists were the Sabbatean Miguel Cardoso and such anti-Sabbateans as Joseph Ergas and David Nieto. Herrera's strong opponents on this issue included the Sabbatean Nehemia Hayoun. Most of Herrera's adversaries disliked his reliance on philosophy, and even disciples like Aboab and Zakuto were unfamiliar with Herrera's more technical writings and confined themselves to quoting sayings from his doctrine of the soul. Yet the Hasidic thinker Baruch of Kosov is influenced by Herrera's findings, and the implicitly philosophical discourse of the Kabbalist Moshe Luzatto shows Herrera's distinctive influence.

The influence on SPINOZA sometimes ascribed to Herrera is harder to detect. Many modern scholars assume, because of some terminological similarities, that Spinoza knew Herrera's writings, perhaps from his youth. Herrera's Sephirot, for example, each perfect in its own genus, have been linked with Spinoza's theory of God's attributes. Closer analysis shows that this and similar presumed parallels, for example, those regarding creation, reflect a common Judaeo-Spanish background and the influence of the scholastic and Renaissance literature that both men read but each used in his own way.

See also: FICINO, M.; KABBALAH; PLATONISM, RENAISSANCE

List of works

Herrera, A. Cohen de (c.1620–32) *Puerta del Cielo* (The Gate of Heaven), Amsterdam: Jewish-Portuguese Seminary, Ets Haim Library, manuscripts EH 48 A 16 and EH 48 B 19; The Hague: Royal Library, manuscript 131 C 10; New York: Library of Columbia University, manuscript X 86-H 42 Q; Hebrew trans. I.A. da Fonseca, *Sha'ar ha-Shamayim*, Amsterdam, 1655; Latin trans. C. Knorr von Rosenroth, *Kabbala Denudata seu Doctrina Hebraeorum, Apparatus in Librum Sohar, Pars Tertia et Quarta, Quorum prior est Liber Sha'ar ha-Shamayim Seu Porta Coelorum* (The Kabbalah Unveiled or the Doctrine of the Hebrews. A Work on the Book of Splendour the third and fourth parts being what was entitled before The Gate of Heaven), Sulzbach, 1678; German trans. F. Hausermann with introduction by G. Scholem, *Das Buch Sha'ar ha'Shmayim oder Pforte des Himmels*, Frankfurt am Main: Suhrkamp Verlag, 1974; ed. K.

Krabbenhoft, *Puerta del Cielo* (text abridged from manuscript 131 C 10), Madrid: Fundación Universitaria Española, 1987. (Herrera's remarkable effort to translate Lurianic Theosophy – the mystical Kabbalah taught in the sixteenth century by Rabbi Issac ben Shlomo Luria (the ARI) – into philosophical and metaphorical terminology. The work deals mainly with the Divinity, namely the highest ontological hypostases of the Chain of Being and the Intelligible World. These grades can be partially approached with the help of our intellectual efforts.)

—— (*c*.1620–32) *Casa de la Divinidad* (The House of Divinity), Amsterdam: Jewish-Portuguese Seminary, Ets Haim Library, manuscript H 48 A 20; Jerusalem: Jewish National and University Library, Varia 106; Hebrew trans. I.A. da Fonseca, *Beit Elohim*, Amsterdam, 1655; Latin trans. C. Knorr von Rosenroth, *Kabbala Denudata Partis Tertiae Tractatus 1 cui nomen Bet Elohim seu Domus Dei* (The Kabbalah Unveiled. The name of the first tractate of the third part is The House of Divinity) Frankfurt, 1684. (The second main work of Herrera deals with other aspects of Lurianic Kabbalah and their philosophical interpretations: angelology and the Upper Worlds under the Divinity; demonology and the Lower Worlds, including our material one; and the epistemic and psychological ways of Kabbalah and philosophy that can help us to reach the divine secrets. His analysis of prophecy favours Aquinas' conclusion that it is a gift of divine grace rather than an inwardly grounded intellectual gift.)

—— (*c*.1632–5) *Epitome de la Logica o Dialectica* (Summary of Logic or Dialectics), published originally with *Libro de Diffiniciones* as one booklet, Amsterdam: Rosenthalania (library). (This auxiliary work was written for those contemporaries of Herrera who had returned to Judaism after leaving the Iberian peninsula. Its aim is that of teaching them the rules of philosophy.)

—— (*c*.1632–5) *Libro de Diffiniciones* (Book of Definitions), published originally with *Epitome de la Logica o Dialectica* as one booklet, Amsterdam: Rosenthalania (library). (As with the *Epitome*, this handbook was written following the Aristotelian method of preparing a philosophic *organan*, for those of Herrera's contemporaries who had returned to Judaism.)

References and further reading

Altmann, A. (1982) 'Lurianic Kabbalah in a Platonic Key: Abraham Cohen Herrera's *Puerta del cielo*', *Hebrew Union College Annual* 80: 1–38. (Excellent introduction to Herrera's thought regarding his Platonic and Neoplatonic sources.)

Krabbenhoft, K. (1982) 'The Mystic in Tradition: Abraham Cohen Herrera and Platonic Theology', unpublished Ph.D. dissertation, New York: New York University. (Deals with the Platonic and Neoplatonic influences on Herrera's work.)

Scholem, G. (1978) *Abraham Cohen Herrera ba'al Sha'ar ha-Shamayim – Hayav, Yetsirato vehashpa'ato* (Abraham Cohen Herrera, Author of the Puerta del Cielo: His Life, Writings, and Influence), Jerusalem: Mossad Bialik Publishing House. (Spinoza was accused by eighteenth-centruy philosophers, mainly in Germany, of pantheistic heresy and some of them, Wachter being the first, accused him of following Herrera's Kabbalah into this heresy. Scholem describes brilliantly this polemical debate, which lasted almost a century.)

Saccaro Battisti, G. (1985) 'Herrera and Spinoza on Divine Attributes', *Italia* 4: 21–58. (Finds traces of Herrera's thought in Spinoza's philosophy.)

—— (1986) 'La cultura filosofica del Rinascimento italiano nella *Puerta del cielo* di Abraham Cohen Herrera', *Italia Judaica* 2: 295–334. (Analyses some of Herrera's Renaissance sources.)

Yosha, N. (1993) 'Abraham Cohen de Herrera: An Outstanding Exponent of *Prisca Theologia* in Early Seventeenth Century Amsterdam', *Dutch Jewish History* 3: 117–26. (Analyses the Renaissance *Prisca Theologia* theory in thought of Herrera, who considered Kabbalah to be the source of the common and eternal truth.)

—— (1994) *Mytos u-metaforah – ha-parshanut ha-filisofit shel Abraham Cohen Herrera le-kabbalat ha-Ari* (Myth and Metaphor: Abraham Cohen Herrera's Philosophical Interpretation of the Kabbalah of the ARI (R. Isaac ben Solomon Luria)), Jerusalem: The Magness Press. (In this Hebrew work with an English summary, Yosha addresses Herrera's philosophic interpretation of Lurianic Kabbalah, referring in detail both to Herrera's Kabbalistic and philosophical sources and to its influence on later thinkers.)

NISSIM YOSHA

HERTZ, HEINRICH RUDOLF (1857–94)

Heinrich Hertz demonstrated the existence of radio waves in research between 1887 and 1888, opening the way for Marconi to develop long distance radio communication. Hertz's results confirmed Maxwell's electromagnetic theory, and sealed the fate of action-at-a-distance in physics. His theoretical analysis included the famous dictum: 'Maxwell's theory is Maxwell's system of equations'. Hertz also developed a new formulation of Newtonian mechanics using the concepts of mass, length and time, but not force. He presented mechanics as the axiomatic consequence of a single fundamental law: 'every free system persists in its state of rest or of uniform motion in a straightest path'. Hertz's ideas influenced later philosophers of science but were most important as a source for Wittgenstein's Tractatus Logico-Philosophicus, *which influenced logical positivism. Hertz's proposal to eliminate the concept of force in physics was an important contribution to the twentieth-century ideal of a philosophical method that does not solve, but rather dissolves, philosophical problems.*

Heinrich Hertz began studies under H. VON HELMHOLTZ at Berlin in 1878. At that time there was no general agreement on the nature of electricity or its fundamental laws. For Wilhelm Weber electrical currents were counterflows of positive and negative electric particles, with forces between them depending on both their positions and their motions. F.E. Neumann used potential functions and avoided electrical particles. J.C. MAXWELL also used potentials, but believed that motions in a universal ether underlay electricity and magnetism (see ELECTRODYNAMICS). Helmholtz constructed a synthetic theory that led to all three alternatives as special cases. He believed, with Weber and Neumann against Maxwell, that forces acted instantaneously at a distance. He criticized Weber's theory on conceptual grounds – it violated conservation of energy – but failed to produce experimental results that would distinguish between the theories.

In 1879 Hertz showed that the 'inertia' of electricity was either nonexistent or impossibly small, providing the first strong experimental evidence against Weber's theory. A later series of experiments (1887–8) made all theories except Maxwell's untenable. Hertz showed that electrical oscillations in open circuits generated electromagnetic waves in the surrounding space which travelled at the speed of light, and could be refracted, reflected, polarized and diffracted. None of this could be reconciled with forces acting at a distance (Buchwald 1994). Development of Maxwell's theory led directly to Lorentz's classical electron theory (from 1892), which was superseded in turn by quantum mechanics and relativity, in the early twentieth century (Jungnickel and McCormmach 1986).

In the last years of his short life Hertz turned his attention to another theory that existed in several different versions: classical mechanics. As it was impossible to distinguish the versions experimentally, Hertz fell back on philosophical analysis, and it is to this work that he owes his main philosophical influence.

In the introduction to his *Principles of Mechanics* (1894) Hertz compared three 'representations': the traditional version of mechanics presented by Newton and refined by Lagrange; the contemporary Energeticist formulation; and Hertz's own. Each version differed mathematically, and employed different fundamental concepts. Newton and Lagrange employed the concepts of space, time, mass and force. The Energeticists replaced mass and force with the concept of energy. Hertz proposed to eliminate force but to introduce no new concepts. These different representations of mechanics were compared by three standards called by Hertz 'permissibility', 'correctness' and 'appropriateness'. In modern terms these requirements might be expressed as logical adequacy, empirical adequacy and perspicuity. Hertz maintained that the mechanics of Newton and Lagrange had yet to be presented in a form that avoided contradictions, and might therefore be impermissible. Energeticist mechanics was either incorrect or inappropriate. To be appropriate a representation should not exclude anything essential ('distinctness'), and should not include anything inessential ('simplicity').

To maximize 'appropriateness' it was important to eliminate 'empty relations' – concepts with no counterparts in the real world. Examples were the 'idle wheels' introduced by Maxwell in his 1862 theory, to allow cells of ether spinning in opposite directions to rotate freely. Equally 'permissible', 'correct' and 'distinct' representations that did not contain a concept showed it to be superfluous. In Hertz's analysis, 'force' was such a concept. This served Wittgenstein as a model for the elimination of signs from language that fail to mirror the world.

Wittgenstein's picture theory of meaning (see WITTGENSTEIN, L. §3) extends Hertz's account of scientific theories as representations to language as a whole. The critical method of the *Tractatus Logico-Philosophicus* follows Hertz in attempting to eliminate 'empty relations' and to define its domain of inquiry from within. Wittgenstein's 'objects', and the technique used to place awkward questions outside the domain so they need no answers, are also influenced by Hertz (Barker 1980; Hamilton 1994). The account of science in the *Tractatus* 6.3 covers many issues treated by Hertz in his analysis of mechanics (Barker 1979).

In the *Philosophical Investigations* Wittgenstein continues Hertz's programme of conceptual reform based on scrutiny of our mode of representation, developing methods of dissolving philosophical problems by bringing his audience to see that certain linguistic elements do not deserve their accustomed status. Throughout his mature work Wittgenstein refers to concepts that fail philosophical scrutiny as 'idle wheels'. Thus, Hertz not only provided one of the starting points for philosophy of science, in his account of theory choice, but, through the work of Wittgenstein, Hertz's call to eliminate force from physics contributed to twentieth-century philosophers' attempts to dissolve philosophical problems by eliminating conceptual confusions.

See also: FIELD THEORY, CLASSICAL; MECHANICS, CLASSICAL

List of works

Hertz, H.R. (1892) *Untersuchungen über die Ausbreitung der Electrischen Kraft*, Leipzig: Barth; *Gesammelte Werke*, vol. 2, Leipzig: Barth, 1894. (See *Electric Waves*, translated by D.E. Jones, London: Macmillan, 1893. Reprinted in 1962, New York: Dover. The main papers on electromagnetic waves. The introduction is an autobiographical account of their discovery, followed by a searching analysis of Maxwell's theory.)

—— (1894) *Die Principien der Mechanik*, Leipzig: Barth; *Gesammelte Werke*, vol. 3, Leipzig: Barth, 1894. (See *The Principles of Mechanics*, translated by D.E. Jones and J.T. Walley, London: Macmillan, 1899. Reprinted in 1956, New York: Dover. The introduction is Hertz's main contribution to philosophy.)

—— (1895) *Schriften vermischten Inhalts*, Leipzig: Barth; *Gesammelte Werke*, vol. 1, Leipzig: Barth, 1896. (See *Miscellaneous Papers*, translated by D.E. Jones and G.A. Schott, London: Macmillan, 1896.)

—— (1927) *Erinnerungen, briefe, tagbücher*, ed. J. Hertz, Leipzig: Akademische verlagsgesellschaft; repr. M. Hertz and C. Süsskind (eds) *Heinrich Hertz: Memoirs, Letters, Diaries*, San Francisco: San Francisco Press, 1977, 2nd edn, enlarged. (Biographical material, much with scientific content, prepared by one of Hertz's daughters. The 1977 edition contains additional material and has a parallel text translation with German and English on facing pages.)

Hertz, H.G. and Doncel, M. (1995–6) 'Heinrich Hertz's Laboratory Notes of 1887', *Archive for History of Exact Sciences* 45: 149–270. (A facsimile, with transcription and translation, of newly discovered notes from a key period in Hertz's experiments on electromagnetic waves.)

Mulligan, J. (ed.) (1994) *Heinrich Rudolf Hertz*

(1857–94): A Collection of Articles and Addresses, New York: Garland. (English versions of most of Hertz's important papers, including the introductions to *Electric Waves* and *Principles of Mechanics*, and remarks on Hertz by Helmholtz, Planck and others.)

References and further reading

With the exception of the first two, which are written for people already familiar with Wittgenstein's *Tractatus*, these items presuppose some knowledge of basic physics, but no special philosophical background.

* Barker, P. (1979) 'Untangling the Net Metaphor', *Philosophy Research Archives* 5: 184–99. (Relates Wittgenstein's account of science, Tractatus 6.3, to Hertz's discussion of mechanics.)

* —— (1980) 'Hertz and Wittgenstein', *Studies in History and Philosophy of Science* 11: 243–56. (Establishes connections between Hertz's *Principles of Mechanics* and Wittgenstein's *Tractatus*.)

* Buchwald, J.Z. (1994) *The Creation of Scientific Effects: Heinrich Hertz and Electric Waves*, Chicago, IL: University of Chicago Press. (An important historical study of Hertz.)

* Hamilton, K. (1994) *Hertz and Wittgenstein: The Philosophical Significance of Wittgenstein's Scientific Training*, Ph.D. dissertation, University of Notre Dame, IN. (Presents new historical information about Wittgenstein in a full-length study of his debt to Hertz.)

* Jungnickel, C. and McCormmach, R. (1986) *Intellectual Mastery of Nature: Theoretical Physics from Ohm to Einstein*, vol. 1, *The Torch of Mathematics, 1800–1870*, vol. 2, *The Now Mighty Theoretical Physics, 1870–1925*, Chicago, IL: University of Chicago Press. (Presents the theoretical, experimental and institutional development of German physics. Volume 1 ends with Helmholtz's early researches. Volume 2 covers the whole career of Hertz, and the development of physics up to the founding of quantum mechanics and relativity theory.)

McCormmach, R. (1983) *Night Thoughts of a Classical Physicist*, New York: Avon Books. (A recreation of the world of physics at the time of Hertz, in the form of a short novel.)

PETER BARKER

HERVAEUS NATALIS (d. 1323)

The French scholastic philosopher and theologian Hervaeus Natalis was not only one of the most influential early Thomists, but was also an original thinker who made an important contribution to the medieval debate on intentionality. He examined carefully the ontological question of what intentional objects are, and discussed the epistemological problem of how they are generated in a cognitive act. Hervaeus argued that intentional objects are 'third entities' that cannot be reduced to extramental or mental entities, a thesis that sparked controversy in the fourteenth century.

Hervaeus Natalis (Hervé Nédellec, or Nédélec) was born in Brittany in the middle of the thirteenth century and entered the Dominican Order in 1276. He commented on the *Sentences* of Peter Lombard at the University of Paris in 1301–2, obtained the degree of Master in Theology in 1307 and acted as *magister regens* until 1309. From 1309 to 1318 he headed the French province of the Dominican Order, and was elected Master General of the Order in 1318. He died in 1323, shortly before the canonization of Thomas AQUINAS.

Hervaeus eagerly defended and developed Aquinas' theology and philosophy. In his *Defensa doctrinae D. Thomae* (Defence of Saint Thomas' Teaching) he expounded Aquinas' theological methodology, and in his *Quodlibeta* he defended the Thomistic epistemology against the objections of HENRY OF GHENT. Yet he did not slavishly follow Aquinas. In his philosophy of mind, he distinguished himself as an original thinker who exerted a considerable influence on fourteenth-century debates, both on the Continent and in England.

Hervaeus discussed extensively the question of the nature of intentional objects, that is, the objects of directed cognitive acts (see INTENTIONALITY). In his *Tractatus de secundis intentionibus* (Treatise on Second Intentions), the first medieval treatise dealing exclusively with the problem of intentionality, he claimed that these objects are not the extramental things that have real existence, because even if one directs a cognitive act towards a nonexistent object (for example, a chimaera) or towards a not actually existing object (for example, the dead Caesar), the act is directed toward something. Nor are these objects 'intelligible species', that is, representational entities produced by the intellect and existing in the intellect; these species are only the means by which the intellect has access to the intentional objects, but not the objects themselves. Rather, intentional objects are peculiar things with 'objective existence': they have existence only *qua* objects of the intellect and cannot be reduced to the species of things having 'subjective existence', that is, the kind of existence a quality has in a subject. Thus, although several people cognizing a table have their own individual species, which subjectively exist in their individual intellects, all these people are directed toward one and the same intentional table.

Hervaeus emphasized that every intentional object of a cognitive act has objective existence. All that varies is the foundation of such an object. If one is having a cognition of an existing table, the intentional table is immediately founded upon the real table. If, however, one is having a cognition of a chimaera, the intentional chimaera is founded upon the combination of three kinds of real animals. Of course, the cognition of a nonexistent thing is more complex than that of an existing thing because it involves the combination of various real things and the formation of several intelligible species; but the important point is that in cognizing a nonexistent thing, one does have an immediate intentional object.

Hervaeus held that in addition to particular intentional objects (so-called 'first intentions') there are also universal intentional objects. Having cognized a particular thing, such as a human being, one is also able to cognize the universals 'human being' (species) and 'animal' (genus). These universals are abstracted on the basis of particular intentional objects and function as higher-level intentional objects (so-called 'second intentions'). Such an abstraction is possible because universals are instantiated in particular things. This claim makes it clear that Hervaeus' theory of second intentions is closely linked to a realist theory of universals (see UNIVERSALS).

Hervaeus' introduction of intentional objects with a peculiar ontological status sparked an intense discussion among some of his fourteenth-century contemporaries and successors, including Peter AUREOL, WILLIAM OF OCKHAM, Walter CHATTON and Adam WODEHAM. Ockham, in his *Ordinatio*, adduced two main arguments against Hervaeus' theory of intentionality. First, the introduction of intentional objects threatens direct realism: if one only has immediate cognition of intentional objects, one never has direct access to extramental reality. Second, if intentional objects are really distinct from the extramental things, entities will be multiplied without necessity; for each thing with real existence there will be a corresponding thing with objective existence. This doubling of the world is superfluous, Ockham claimed, because the cognitive act is by itself directed toward the extramental thing, without there being any need for an intermediary entity.

403

Yet, in evaluating Ockham's famous criticism, one should take into account the fact that Hervaeus did not aim to refute direct realism or to posit superfluous entities. Rather, he intended to point out that the thing *qua* cognized thing is not simply the extramental thing, which in itself has no linkage with the intellect, but something founded upon the extramental thing that somehow hooks the intellect up to this thing and determines the cognitive act. Thus, his theory of intentional objects should be understood as an attempt to understand what the content of a mental act is – an attempt that had an impact not only on late medieval discussions, but also on Brentano's philosophy of mind (see BRENTANO, F.C.).

List of works

Hervaeus Natalis (before 1323) *Tractatus de secundis intentionibus*, Venice, 1508. (More or less reliable text; there is no critical edition and no English translation of this treatise.)
—— (before 1323) *Defensa doctrinae D. Thomae*, in E. Krebs, *Theologie und Wissenschaft nach der Lehre der Hochscholastik an der Hand der bisher ungedruckten Defensa Doctrinae D. Thomae des Hervaeus Natalis mit Beifügung gedruckter und ungedruckter Paralleltexte*, Beiträge zur Geschichte der Philosophie des Mittelalters 11, Münster: Aschendorff, 1912. (The edition of the *Defensa* is included along with an analysis of Hervaeus' theory of science.)
—— (before 1323) *De intellectu et specie* (On the Intellect and the Intelligible Species), ed. P. Stella, 'La prima critica di Hervaeus Natalis O.P. alla noetica di Enrico di Gand', *Salesianum* 21 (1959): 125–70. (Edition of *De intellectu et specie* with commentary.)
—— (before 1323) *Quodlibeta* (Quodlibetal Questions), Venice, 1513. (No modern editions or translations exist at present.)

References and further reading

Allen, E.B. (1960) 'Hervaeus Natalis. An Early 'Thomist' on the Notion of Being', *Mediaeval Studies* 22: 1–14. (Critical analysis of a key term in Hervaeus' metaphysics.)
Hedwig, K. (1978) 'Der scholastische Kontext des Intentionalen bei Brentano' (The Scholastic Context of the Intentional in Brentano), *Grazer Philosophische Studien* 5: 67–82. (Study dealing with the possible sources of Brentano's thesis that psychic phenomena have an 'intentional inexistence'.)

Käppeli, T. (1970) *Scriptores Ordinis Praedicatorum Medii Aevi* (Writers of the Dominican Order in the Middle Ages), Rome: S. Sabina, vol 2, 231–. (A comprehensive list of Hervaeus' works, including all the manuscripts and Renaissance editions.)
Kelley, F.E. (1978) 'Some Observations on the *Fictum* Theory in Ockham and its Relation to Hervaeus Natalis', *Franciscan Studies* 38: 260–82. (Detailed analysis of Hervaeus' objective existence' theory and Ockham's critique.)
Roensch, F.J. (1964) *Early Thomistic School*, Dubuque, IA: The Priory Press. (Short presentation of Hervaeus' life and intellectual activity.)
Schöllgen, W. (1927) *Das Problem der Willensfreiheit bei Heinrich von Gent und Herveus Natalis* (The Problem of Freedom of the Will in Henry of Ghent and Hervaeus Natalis), Dusseldorf: Pädagogischer Verlag Schwann; repr. 1975. (Introduction to Hervaeus' philosophical psychology and its impact on the problem of freedom.)
Senko, W. (1961) 'Les opinions d'Hervé Nédellec au sujet de l'essence et l'existence' (Hervaeus Natalis' Opinions on Essence and Existence), *Mediaevalia Philosophica Polonorum* 10: 59–74. (Presentation of a fundamental metaphysical issue and comparison with Thomas Aquinas' treatment of this problem.)
* William of Ockham (1317–19) *Ordinatio*, Book I, in G. Gál *et al.* (eds) *Opera Theologica*, St Bonaventure, NY: The Franciscan Institute, vol. IV. (Dist. 27 includes a critique of the thesis that intentional objects are a kind of 'third entities'.)

DOMINIK PERLER

HERZEN, ALEKSANDR IVANOVICH (1812–70)

Lauded by Nietzsche as 'a man of every distinctive talent' and admired by Lenin as the founder of the Russian revolutionary movement, Herzen eludes all neat categorizations. As a moral preacher he stands alongside Tolstoi and Dostoevskii (who praised him as a poet). As a philosopher, he was the principal interpreter and popularizer of Hegel's thought in Russia in the first half of the 1840s, while the rebellion against metaphysical systems in his mature work has led him to be seen as a precursor of existentialism. Through the Russian press that he founded in emigration he helped to shape the beginnings of a public opinion in his country and played a major role in debates on Russia's political future on the eve of the emancipation of the serfs, while laying the foundations of the Russian populist movement through his writings on Russian socialism. He is best known in the West for his memoirs, Byloe i dumy *(My Past and Thoughts) (1861, 1866), which rank among the great works of Russian literature, and for* S togo berega *(From the Other Shore) (1850), the most brilliant and original of the works in which he expresses his rejection of all teleological conceptions of history.*

1   **Life and works**
2   **Philosophy of history**
3   **Russian socialism**
4   **Herzen's legacy**

1   Life and works

Aleksandr Herzen owed his surname to an affair of the heart between a rich and cultivated Russian landowner, Ivan Iakovlev, and the daughter of a minor German official whom he met when travelling in Europe. Although his parents never married, Aleksandr enjoyed the status of a pampered only son. He received a rounded education in European culture from foreign tutors, and was especially drawn to Rousseau, Voltaire, Schiller and the history of the French Revolution. His illegitimacy undoubtedly contributed to his precocious sense of independence and spirit of protest against the existing order. He identified with the heroes of the Decembrist Revolt of 1825 and (an event celebrated in the history of the Russian revolutionary movement) made a vow with his cousin Nikolai Ogarev at the age of 16 to devote their lives to the struggle against despotism in their country. Like other Russians of his generation, he channelled his frustrated urge for political action into philosophical speculation and was much attracted to the historiosophical schemata of German Idealism. But in an essay written as a student of natural sciences at the University of Moscow he points out that the 'one-sidedness' of pure speculation had been demonstrated by Francis Bacon: only by linking 'the rational method with the empirical' (a combination which Herzen later, in an echo of Feuerbach, calls 'speculative empiricism') would mankind finally achieve an approach to knowledge that would reconcile the claims of the particular and the universal, the individual and the social whole. Such a reconciliation was to be the main concern of Herzen's later thought. It drew him to doctrines of palingenesis and to the humanistic socialism of the Saint-Simonians, whose theories he adopted with Ogarev and their circle in 1833: an event that has been seen as marking the birth of socialism in Russia.

The following year the circle was arrested on suspicion of spreading subversive ideas. Herzen spent nearly a year in prison, followed by five in provincial exile, when (for the last time in his life) he plunged into romantic introspection and religious mysticism. In 1840 he was allowed to return to Moscow, where Hegel's influence was at its peak. He embarked on a systematic study of Hegel's philosophy (during which he was exiled for another year), which resulted in two long cycles of essays: 'Diletantizm v nauke' (Dilettantism in Science) (1842–3) and 'Pis'ma ob izuchenii prirody' (Letters on the Study of Nature) (1845). The most important critique of Hegel to appear in Russia in that decade, Herzen's essays were much influenced by the left Hegelian 'philosophy of action' and the anthropocentrism of Feuerbach, which had greatly excited him. In Hegel's vision of dialectical becoming he saw a justification of his own hopes of a socialist transformation. As he put it in the Aesopian language of his essays, in Hegel's philosophy abstract thought had reached its highest achievement by liberating men's minds from the transcendent authorities of the past. The next stage was liberation in life, the move from philosophy to action (see HEGELIANISM, RUSSIAN).

Herzen's vision of the path that action would take was shaped in particular by Proudhon's anarchism, which promised the kind of reconciliation of individual freedom with social harmony that he sought. Unable to discuss political theories in print in Russia, he directed his efforts to fostering the inner moral independence which he saw as the precondition of political liberty, through essays that criticized the human tendency to seek moral direction from external authorities and norms. After 1845 he turned from philosophy to fiction, exploring the problem of moral freedom in short stories and a semi-autobiographical novel *Kto vinovat? (Who is to Blame?)* dealing with a love triangle. In 1847, finding his talents stifled in his country, he emigrated with his family to the West.

His historical optimism was shattered by the European upheavals of 1848. Observation of political events in France from 1847 until 1850 convinced him that parliamentary democracy was a palliative that did not address fundamental issues of social injustice, and he accused both liberals and radical republicans of a worship of political forms combined with indifference to the real needs and aspirations of the masses. In *From the Other Shore*, his philosophical summing-up of the lessons of 1848, he attacked the utopianism of the European left as both empirically unfounded and morally pernicious in subordinating the self-fulfilment of living individuals to the empty abstraction of progress.

With the disappointment of his own utopian hopes of imminent social transformation in the West, Herzen turned his attention to the socialist potential of Russia. The theoretical foundations of Russian populism were laid between 1849 and 1852 in a series of essays (such as 'Ruskii narod i sotsializm' (The Russian People and Socialism), addressed to Jules Michelet) in which Herzen sought to acquaint progressive Europeans with the existence of a radical intelligentsia in Russia and the potential of the peasant commune. (His own interest in the commune had been aroused by discussions with the Slavophiles in the early 1840s). He pointed out that its democratic structure, guaranteeing the right of all its members to the use of a share of its land, contained the seeds of a solution to the problems of pauperization and social atomization currently facing the West.

In 1851–2 Herzen's personal life was shattered by a series of tragedies beginning with the revelation of an affair between his wife and an intimate family friend, the German radical poet Georg Herwegh. After she ended the affair, Herwegh circulated his version of events among the European radical community with the intention of discrediting Herzen, who vainly sought to be publicly vindicated through a revolutionary 'court of honour'. In the midst of these betrayals and humiliations his mother and younger son were drowned at sea. His wife, her health destroyed by the succession of calamities, died a few months later.

The effect of these tragedies was to intensify Herzen's sense of alienation from the West and turn his full attention back to Russia. He began his memoirs, *Byloe i dumy* (*My Past and Thoughts*), 'to get into communication with my people', and in 1853 embarked on a new phase of his life with the founding of a Russian Press in London to act as his people's 'uncensored voice' in exerting pressure on the Russian government for reform. In 1856 Ogarev arrived from Russia to join him, and became co-editor of his celebrated periodical *Kolokol* (The Bell).

Herzen emphasized that his press was not to be the vehicle for a particular political programme or ultimate ideal (his memoirs record that his personal tragedy had destroyed the last remnants of his early utopianism and forced him to accept the dominant role of chance in human affairs). While not renouncing his hopes of a future 'Russian socialism' he saw his political role as mobilizing opinion within Russia to exert pressure for immediate concrete reforms (in particular, emancipation of the serfs, freedom of speech and the end of corporal punishment), and providing a forum for discussion about further steps, in the hope of reaching a consensus on the social form most capable of combining individual liberty with social cohesion. What such a form would be, he stressed, depended on contingent circumstances and could not be predicted in advance.

While *Kolokol* played a major role in shaping public opinion in Russia on the eve of the Great Reforms, after the Emancipation Herzen's open-mindedness on the paths of progress brought him into sharp conflict both with the Russian liberals (who wished Russia to follow a Western path to constitutional democracy), and the radicals who preached an immediate transition to socialism through revolution. Herzen's preference for evolution over revolutionary violence alienated him from the left, while his refusal to exclude revolution as a means of progress was condemned by the liberals.

In a number of essays (notably 'Robert Owen', and those found in 'Kontsy i nachala' (Ends and Beginnings) and 'K staromu tovarishchu' (To an Old Comrade)), Herzen developed his view of the open-endedness and unpredictability of the historical process against what he saw as the deterministic utopianism of most Russian progressive thought.

Herzen's complex vision of the historical process met with little sympathy or understanding among the Russian intelligentsia. In 1863 he moved to Geneva in order to have closer contact with the growing population of Russian radical émigrés, but his relations with them soon soured. *Kolokol* ceased publication in 1867 (although it was briefly revived in a French edition), and Herzen's political isolation became complete. His last years were embittered by a stormy relationship with Ogarev's wife Natalie who bore him three children. 'Probably everyone in Russia will say that Herzen should have died sooner, that he outlived his reputation', Turgenev wrote on his death: but from a historical perspective the isolation of Herzen's last years can be attributed to the fact that his vision was far in advance of his time.

2 Philosophy of history

'Do not look for solutions in this book', Herzen warns the reader of *From the Other Shore*: 'in general, modern man has no solutions.... We do not build, we destroy; we do not proclaim a new revelation, we eliminate the old lie' ([1850] 1956: 3). To a critic who asked him to explain his system, he retorted that his philosophy of history was no system, only 'a scourge to be used against absurd theories...a fermenting agent, no more'. It was, however, systematically consistent in its attack on all systems, dogmas and political eschatologies that claimed to justify or explain the oppression of human beings by reference to idealized abstractions such as freedom, progress, humanity or the common good.

Like most radicals of his time, Herzen was deeply indebted to the anthropocentrism of the Left Hegelians, from whose perspective he approached

406

Hegel's dialectic as 'an algebra of revolution'. But (like PROUDHON, who influenced his thought in this respect), he rejected the secular eschatology which substituted Universal Reason for Divine Providence as the guiding force of the historical process, accusing both Hegel and his radical interpreters of evading the logical consequence of his historicism: the denial of all suprahistorical absolutes and universal historical goals.

In his major professions of philosophical faith (*From the Other Shore*, 'Robert Owen', 'Ends and Beginnings'), Herzen defines what NIETZSCHE would call the 'craving for metaphysical comfort' as the principal obstacle to the fulfilment of human potential in the historical world. He points out that observation and experience do not support the view that history is an ascent towards a final goal, whether pre-programmed by the Creator or inherent in the rational structure of the universe. 'Life has its own embryogenesis which does not coincide with the dialectic of pure reason' ([1850] 1956: 31). It was more like nature than was commonly believed: chance and 'dark forces' constantly triumphed over rational intention, killing off promising beginnings or unpredictably rerouting them into new channels. No ideal could ever be realized in the way in which it had been conceived, no model of human society could be more than a provisional experiment whose life expectancy would depend largely on chance. Herzen attributes the reluctance of mankind to face this truth to the dualism pervading human judgments. Anticipating Nietzsche's critique of otherworldly values that degrade the world of experience, he notes that all the great moral systems have been built on the assumption that process, chance and change are less real than timelessness and stasis, singular events less significant than universal laws and norms. All our images, all our metaphors, are imbued with a dualism that 'sides with one shadow against another, granting spirit the monopoly over matter, species the monopoly over the particular, sacrificing man to the state, the state to humanity' ([1850] 1956: 136). The Enlightenment had replaced Christianity with 'the *Religion des Diesseits*, the religion of science, or universal, hereditary, transcendental Reason'. We seek (against the empirical evidence) to impose a libretto on history; yet if there were such a libretto, we would be mere wheels in a machine. By denying us the consolations of self-transcendence, history maximizes the possibilities of self-creation. Instead of seeking to escape our contingency we should cease to allow preoccupation with an unknown future to distract us from self-fulfilment in the present; but to do so we must revise all our notions about the relation of the individual to himself, society and the state.

Herzen believed that the traditional vocabulary of philosophy was inimical to the perception of reality that was born with Hegel's historicism. He stresses that it is not just a question of revising our categories of ultimate goals and purposes; we must cease to derive the significance of the individual and the contingent from its place in some larger scheme of things. To the '*memento mori*' of metaphysics he opposes the '*memento vivere*' of nature and art. 'Thought must take on flesh': we must counter our tendency to rationalize and universalize by cultivating an aesthetic receptivity to the transient and unrepeatable manifestations of life which will allow us maximally to exploit the multiplicity of possibilities for self-creation.

Herzen's writings on this theme seem to anticipate Nietzsche's notion of *amor fati*: the demand that we face up to the 'beautiful chaos' of contingent existence and joyfully accept the historicity of the human condition with its attendant suffering, finitude and mortality, by shaping random events into the aesthetic unity of a unique self. Herzen's famous claim that 'the truly free man *creates* his own morality' has been likened to Nietzsche's assertion that 'nothing is true, all is permitted': there is no reality independent of our shifting perspectives on it. But these parallels are misleading. Herzen did not live to engage with Nietzsche's irrationalism, but he unambiguously rejected the pessimism of Nietzsche's mentor, SCHOPENHAUER, arguing that the vision of the world as a chaotic battleground of blind forces was a petulant overreaction to the failure of unjustified idealist expectations, a muddled transitional stage on the way to understanding reality without metaphysical preconceptions. As a corrective both to comforting illusion and exaggerated pessimism Herzen recommends to the student of history a training in the natural sciences that will inculcate 'true nihilism', which he defines as 'science without dogmas...the unconditional submission to experience and the resigned acceptance of all consequences, whatever they may be, if they follow from observation, or are required by reason' ([1861, 1866] 1968: 1764).

Herzen intended his reflections on history to serve as an object-lesson in this approach, spelling out what he regarded as the inescapable, but by no means wholly negative, consequences of the observable parallels between historical development and the chanciness of evolutionary processes. Against the pessimist he argues that experience reveals that chance operates within a framework of laws which allow us to calculate probabilities, to direct and control events within narrow boundaries, and even to progress, although not to utopia. When the anarchist (and former Left Hegelian) Bakunin pronounced the will to destroy as the creative force that would lead mankind to 'absolute liberty', Herzen accused him of a Romantic's disregard for the 'physiology' of historical and social development, the painful slowness of processes of growth in real time (see BAKUNIN, M. §2).

The shock and disbelief that greeted *On the Origin of Species* (1859), a decade after Herzen published *From the Other Shore*, testifies to the novelty and daring of Herzen's ideas on the dominant role of chance in nature and human life. In the furore over Darwin's opus, Herzen was among the first to grasp clearly the importance of the challenge that it posed to teleological thinking in all branches of intellectual activity, recommending it to Russian readers as an antidote to the extreme conservatism of most contemporary European thought.

Herzen's historical method owed much to the inspiration of an earlier innovator: Francis Bacon. In his philosophical writings of the 1840s he had stressed the significance of Bacon's analysis of those tendencies of the human mind that had to be corrected if knowledge were to be advanced, in particular the 'Idols of the Tribe' – the tendency to impose on external reality an order and a regularity that comes from the human intellect and does not belong to the world itself (see BACON, F. §5). In his writings on history Herzen frequently cites Bacon's aphorisms on method, his demand that metaphysics be separated from science and his insistence on the barrenness of research into final causes, the *'magnum ignotum'* beyond the realm of knowledge. In 'Sur le libre arbitre' (On Free Will), his philosophical *prise de position* (in the form of a letter to his son) on the question of free will, it is Bacon ('an honest thinker') whom he cites in support of his attack on the dogmatically reductionist materialism of mid-nineteenth-century biological scientists. By declaring our sense of moral freedom to be an illusion, he argues, they had exceeded their competence: it was at the very least, an 'anthropological reality', without which we could not function as social beings. The dominance of dualistic systems had ensured that we possessed neither the words nor the categories to discuss the nature of choice in the nexus of contingency and invariant laws. But the purpose could be served by aesthetic metaphor: Herzen expresses the relationship between physical determinism and moral freedom through the distinction between a sound in isolation (a physical phenomenon subject to the laws of acoustics) and a sound in a musical phrase, where it 'acquires for us another value (or existence, if you like)'. This existence does not exempt it from the physical laws to which it is subject – the string may break and the sound will disappear, 'but as long as the

string remains unbroken, the sound belongs not just to the realm of vibrations, but also to the realm of harmony where it exists as an aesthetic reality, functioning in a symphony which allows it to resound, dominates and absorbs it, and then abandons it in its wake'.

This unfinished symphony is the historical process, for which Herzen uses a related image in a fine passage in 'Robert Owen':

> having neither programme, set theme nor unavoidable *denouement*, the dishevelled improvisation of history is ready to walk with anyone; anyone can insert into it *his* line of verse and, if it is sonorous, it will remain his line until the poem is torn up, so long as the past ferments in its blood and memory.
> ([1861, 1866] 1968: 1245)

This notion of moral freedom bears little resemblance to Nietzsche's concept of the lonely Superman, asserting his will in defiance of history and human societies, which he identifies with the life-denying values of the herd. Herzen believed that as social animals, human beings could achieve freedom only through a constant adjustment of their demand for self-fulfilment with their need for social solidarity – a model of freedom that has close parallels with Schiller's treatise *On the Aesthetic Education of Man* (1795). Like Schiller, Herzen believed that one should seek to govern one's conduct not by universal rational precepts but by the cultivation of an aesthetic sense of relationships that would allow one to respond to the demands of specific situations without either rigidly adhering to principle or blindly obeying the compulsion of instinct (see SCHILLER, J.C.F.).

Herzen pronounced Schiller's treatise 'a prophetic work...far in advance of its time'. One of its central themes – the 'fear of freedom' that drives individuals to seek to regulate their conduct by reference to transcendent authorities and universal norms – is the leitmotif of Herzen's writings on the nature of history. It is 'frightening' to abandon religious and secular concepts of predestination, to accept the ominous truth that it is absurd to apply our 'petty household rules', our human demands for intentionality and purpose, to the economy of the universe. The demystification of the world was a deeply painful process: but only those who had passed through that furnace, he maintained, could regard themselves as 'truly modern'.

3 Russian socialism

Herzen's interest in the structure and potential of the Russian peasant commune has been variously, but in general negatively, interpreted by historians. His belief that the commune contained the seeds of an advanced form of socialism has been represented as a messianic faith in flat contradiction with his critique of utopian thought, while his concern in the 1850s and 1860s with such matters as the methods of repartitioning land in the existing village commune has been described as a descent from the sublime to the ridiculous, from the great philosophical issues of *From the Other Shore* to the petty minutiae of peasant life.

Both types of charge were made against Herzen in his lifetime: the first by liberals who interpreted his faith in the commune's potential as a form of Slavophile messianic nationalism, and the second by socialists who demanded of him an inspiring vision of an ideal future. Herzen's response to both groups was to defend his view of the commune as wholly consistent with his view of freedom and the historical process.

Against the liberals he argued that, unlike the Slavophiles, he approached the commune not as a sign of Russia's superior destiny, but as a chance historical survival which might (although only if developed with the aid of Western technology and political theories) offer a solution to the most urgent problems facing both Russia and Europe: how to combine individual liberty with social cohesion, and to achieve economic development without mass pauperisation. While the commune might provide a way for Russia to pass to socialism without the trauma of mass industrialization, there was no guarantee that it would: socialism might be achieved both in Russia and the West by some quite different path, or not at all. He contrasts his 'prosaic' approach, focused on how best to balance individual aspirations and social needs at a given historical juncture, with the doctrinairism of the Russian liberals (who held that Russia's historical destiny was to discard the commune and follow the West along a common path to parliamentary democracy), and of those radicals who lived in expectation of a revolutionary leap to an ideal freedom. In the contempt of many progressive intellectuals for the primitive outlook of the Russian peasant and the imperfections of the existing commune he saw an instance of the teleological thinking that had been the principal target of his philosophical essays. He accused his critics of devaluing all aspects of contemporary experience that did not lead to their chosen goal, and respecting history and human liberty 'only in the future'. In 'K staromu tovarish-chu', sometimes described as his political testament, he declares that his aim is to understand the size of the human pace in the present and, by substituting 'tact and inspired improvisation' for doctrinal con-

sistency, 'to keep up with it, not falling behind, but not going so far ahead that it will not follow'.

4 Herzen's legacy

Herzen frequently remarked that his writings consisted of the constant repetition of a few simple truths, but that these truths were so repugnant to his contemporaries that they persisted in misconstruing them.

His message – that there were no ultimate solutions to the fundamental problems of human existence – has proven equally repugnant to Russian intellectuals in this century, leading to interpretations of his work that he would have repudiated. His ideas did not find favour among representatives of the Russian religious and philosophical renaissance of the early 1900s such as S.N. BULGAKOV, who argued that his rejection of a transcendent world order had led him ultimately (and inevitably) to a despairing nihilism. This view is echoed in V.V. Zenkovsky's authoritative history of Russian philosophy, which describes Herzen's thought as a philosophy of 'despair, hopelessness and disbelief'. Exceptions to this consensus were P.B. Struve (see SIGNPOSTS MOVEMENT), who saw in Herzen 'one of our national heroes of the spirit' and the precursor of a new humanism, and Tolstoi, who noted in his diary that Herzen 'awaits his readers in the future. He imparts his thoughts far above the heads of the present crowd to those who will be able to understand him'.

The understanding of Herzen in his own country was not advanced by Lenin's canonization of him as the founder of the Russian revolutionary movement, an interpretation that was faithfully echoed by generations of Soviet historians. In the West his reputation has been slow to grow. As Isaiah Berlin argued in essays that brought Herzen to the attention of a wide English-speaking public, a condescending classification of his views 'as yet another variant of early socialism' left out the attack on utopian systems that was his most arresting contribution to political theory. At the end of the twentieth century we are better placed than Herzen's contemporaries to grasp the significance of that contribution. Herzen was among the first to predict a process with whose consequences we are only beginning to come to terms: the erosion of that faith in a purposeful universe in which all the basic assumptions of the great optimistic systems of his time (including Marxism) were grounded. He was more than just a precursor: his work remains relevant to contemporary debates in philosophy and cultural theory on the effect that the collapse of the 'grand narratives' of progress has had on traditional views of society, morality and the self. Herzen offers a clear alternative to two of the most common philosophical approaches to an inherently contingent world: Schopenhauerian pessimism and Nietzschean aesthetic immoralism. He has been compared to contemporary hermeneutic philosophers who argue that the historicity of the self does not render moral generalizations meaningless, and detect in history the unifying thread of a spiritual quest: the search to articulate our intuitive sense of the good. To those who felt themselves cast adrift in an unprogrammed world, he responded with the invigorating message that not only are freedom and moral responsibility possible in such a world: they are not possible in any other.

See also: LIBERALISM, RUSSIAN; SLAVOPHILISM

List of works

Herzen, A.I. (1954–65) *Sobranie sochinenii* (Collected Works), Moscow: AN SSSR, 30 vols. (The most complete edition to date, with copious notes and commentaries.)

—— (1845) *Kto vinovat?*, trans. M.R. Katz, *Who is to Blame?*, Ithaca, NY and London: Cornell University Press, 1984. (Herzen's most important fictional work.)

—— (1850) *S togo berega*, Paris; trans. M. Budberg, *From the Other Shore*, with an introduction by I. Berlin (ed.), London: Weidenfeld & Nicolson, 1956.

—— (1852) 'Russkii narod i sotsializm', trans. R. Wollheim, *The Russian People and Socialism*, with an introduction by I. Berlin (ed.), London: Weidenfeld & Nicolson, 1956. (One of Herzen's most important texts.)

—— (1858) *Letters from France and Italy, 1847–1851*, trans. and ed. J.E. Zimmerman, Pittsburgh, PA: University of Pittsburgh Press, 1995. (Extended reflections on contemporary Europe, a source of much of Herzen's later thought.)

—— (1861, 1866) *Byloe i dumy*, vols 1 and 2, London; vols 3 and 4 France; first complete publication Berlin: Slovo, 1921, 5 vols; trans. C. Garnett, *My Past and Thoughts. The Memoirs of Alexander Herzen*, revised by H. Higgens, with an introduction by I. Berlin, London: Chatto & Windus, 1968, 4 vols. (Written between 1852 and 1867. Fourth volume includes important essays.)

References and further reading

Acton, E. (1979) *Alexander Herzen and the Role of the Intellectual Revolutionary*, Cambridge: Cambridge University Press. (Focuses on the years 1847–63.)

Berlin, I. (1978) *Russian Thinkers*, London: The Hogarth Press. (Contains two seminal essays on Herzen's view of liberty.)

Carr, E.H. (1968) *The Romantic Exiles. A Nineteenth-Century Portrait Gallery*, Harmondsworth: Penguin. (A study of Herzen, Ogarev and their families in exile.)

Kelly, A. (forthcoming) *Towards Another Shore: Russian Thinkers between Necessity and Chance*, New Haven, CT and London: Yale University Press. (Includes five essays on Herzen as a precursor of developments in twentieth-century thought.)

Labry, R. (1928a) *Alexandre Ivanovic Herzen, 1812–1870: Essai sur la formation et le développement de ses indées (Aleksandr Ivanovic Herzen, 1812–1870: Essay on the Formation and Development of his Ideas)*, Paris: Bossard. (A good general study.)

—— (1928b) *Herzen et Proudhon*, Paris: Bossard. (On the most important foreign influence on Herzen's ideas.)

Lampert, E. (1957) *Studies in Rebellion*, London: Routledge. (Includes a chapter on Herzen.)

Malia, M. (1961) *Alexander Herzen and the Birth of Russian Socialism, 1812–1855*, Cambridge, MA: Harvard University Press. (A detailed study of Herzen's formative period.)

Shpet, G. (1921) *Filosofskoe mirovozzrenie Gertsena* (Herzen's Philosophical Outlook), Petrograd: Kolos. (An exceptionally perceptive study of Herzen's philosophy, which the author describes as 'historical realism'.)

AILEEN KELLY

HESCHEL, ABRAHAM JOSHUA (1907–72)

Born in Warsaw and educated there and in Berlin, Abraham Joshua Heschel moved to the USA in 1940, where he lived and taught for the rest of his life. His elegantly written books and essays and his striking personality made him a key figure in American Jewish philosophical theology after the Second World War. Written in German, English, Hebrew and Yiddish, his books reflect widely on the Hebrew Bible, Talmud and midrash, and on Jewish mystical writings, continuously engaging with contemporary philosophy and theology.

Born in Warsaw, the scion of a major Hasidic dynasty, Abraham Joshua Heschel was educated thoroughly in Bible, rabbinics, Kabbalah and Hasidism in his youth. After a brief period in Vilnius (Vilna, as it was known in Jewish letters), he studied philosophy at the

University of Berlin and taught at the Hochschule für die Wissenschaft des Judentums in Berlin. He moved to the USA in 1940 and first taught at Hebrew Union College (the Reform rabbinical seminary) in Cincinnati and after 1945 at Jewish Theological Seminary (the Conservative rabbinical seminary) in New York for the rest of his life.

In his Berlin doctoral dissertation on prophetic consciousness, *Die Prophetie* (Prophecy) (1937), Heschel creatively used the methods of phenomenology, especially as applied to religious concerns by Max Scheler, to develop the concept of divine pathos that was to be a leitmotif of his subsequent thought. Where many medieval Jewish thinkers had adopted Hellenic ideas of God, most prominently those of ARISTOTLE that assume divine eternity and impassivity, Heschel found the chief emphasis of the Hebrew Bible in God's concern for humanity (see BIBLE, HEBREW). Timelessness and perfection seemed to preclude any real divine concern with what is essentially temporal and imperfect. But in the God of the Hebrew Scriptures Heschel saw a pathos that was of the essence of prophetic consciousness and its inner sympathy with God's relation to the world.

Heschel's first major English work, *The Sabbath* (1951a), applied his phenomenological method at the core of Jewish piety, pointing out the primacy of time consciousness over space consciousness in Judaism. Heschel showed how the Sabbath addresses sacred time rather than sacred space. Out of step with the more pragmatic and worldly approach of many writers on religion, especially at the time of his writing, Heschel did not seek the value of the Sabbath in its worldly utility. Rather than appeal to secular values by describing the benefits of the Sabbath as a humane institution or a vehicle of socio-cultural continuity, Heschel introduced his readers to the spiritual needs that the Sabbath can address. Pressing the point, he went on to argue that the Sabbath is the only true antidote to the dehumanizing effects of unlimited technology.

In his next English book, *Man Is Not Alone* (1951b), Heschel sought to show the necessity of taking revelation seriously (see REVELATION). The opening to this concern was what he called the sense of radical amazement: that is, the human realization that existence itself, our own and that of the world, cannot simply be taken for granted. Only when one sees that the world does not supply the answer to our most basic existential question 'Why is there something and not nothing?' can one be ready for the answer to that question that comes from the Source of the world, who radically transcends its being and all the categories devised to explicate its immanent processes. In thinking along these lines, Heschel

shows especially the influence of his long philosophical friendship with Martin BUBER.

Heschel's next major book, *God In Search of Man* (1955), contains the most significant statement of his thought and shows Heschel as the theologian he basically was. *Man Is Not Alone* was subtitled A *Philosophy of Revelation*, but the subtitle of *God In Search of Man* is A *Philosophy of Judaism*. He calls his method here 'depth theology', by which he means confrontation of the most basic human questions that religion addresses rather than the presentation of a dogmatic system. Following the fundamental assumption of phenomenology that all thought is about something other than itself, that thought is reflective not self-creative, Heschel presents the key doctrines and norms of classical Judaism as Israel's way of orienting itself towards God. Thus, in discussing the relations between Jewish law (*halakhah*) and reflection (*aggadah*), he argued, too many traditionalists see the law as an end in itself and adopt what Heschel called 'religious behaviourism'. They fail to realize that the religious obligations are part of the human response to the revelation of the transcendent God. Too many liberals, by contrast, see the Law as something arbitrary, to be supplanted in large part by inner religious attitudes. In a striking variation of Kant's famous dictum, Heschel writes: 'Halakha without aggada is dead, aggada without halakha is wild' (see HALAKHAH). Throughout his career, Heschel portrayed Judaism as a complex of transcendent intent with immanent content. The categories he developed in *God In Search of Man* have lent themselves to a wide range of applications by later Jewish thinkers.

During his lifetime, Heschel was often described and sometimes dismissed as a mystic. If this means someone who claims to have unusual personal experience of the divine, then calling Heschel a mystic is empty and misleading. But Heschel certainly was influenced by the esoteric Jewish tradition of Kabbalah (see KABBALAH). He incorporated in his mature outlook much of the Kabbalah he learned in his youth, especially the Hasidic versions of it that stressed the human experience of the intimate presence of God, more than the esoteric theosophy of the earlier Kabbalah (see HASIDISM). Although in his adult life he was no longer a Hasid in the strict sense of the word, Heschel was always deeply beholden to his spiritual roots. Indeed, his last book was the closest he came to returning to that world. It was a study, in Yiddish, his first spoken and literary language, of the thought of the outspoken nineteenth-century Hasidic master Rabbi Menachem Mendel of Kotsk.

One fundamental Kabbalistic idea that played a key role in Heschel's thought is that of 'divine needs':

God not only wills that there be a world, he actually desires it and wants an ongoing relationship with it, as is manifest in the history of the people of Israel. The ultimate source of this divine need is a mystery beyond human ken, but it is the basis of God's reaching out to create. Thus humanity's response to God (through keeping the commandments of the Torah) answers not just to human needs but to those of God. Heschel's recourse to this classic Kabbalistic theme (see NAHMANIDES) allows him to offer insightful and spiritually moving explanations of many Jewish practices that some liberals found merely bizarre and that many traditionalists simply accept with a dulling kind of positivism.

See also: BIBLE, HEBREW; HASIDISM; KABBALAH

List of works

Heschel, A.J. (1975) *Between God and Man: An Interpretation of Judaism*, ed. F. Rothschild, New York: Free Press. (An anthology of some of Heschel's more important writings along with a general introduction and shorter introductions to the sections of the anthology.)
—— (1937) *Die Prophetie* (Prophecy), Warsaw: Polish Academy of Sciences. (Heschel's doctoral dissertation, a phenomenology of prophetic consciousness.)
—— (1951a) *The Sabbath*, New York: Abelard-Schuman. (Theological reflections on the spiritual significance of this cornerstone of Jewish religious life.)
—— (1951b) *Man Is Not Alone*, Philadelphia, PA: Jewish Publication Society. (Lays the theological groundwork for his more philosophical works.)
—— (1954) *Man's Quest for God*, New York: Charles Scribner's Sons. (Heschel's chief reflection on the Jewish liturgy.)
—— (1955) *God in Search of Man*, New York: Farrar, Straus & Cudahy. (Heschel's major work in philosophical theology.)
—— (1962) *The Prophets*, Philadelphia, PA: Jewish Publication Society. (An expanded version of *Die Prophetie* with more extensive illustrations from biblical texts but not developing philosophically the core phenomenological project of the earlier work.)
—— (1965) *Who Is Man?*, Stanford, CA: Stanford University Press. (Lectures on philosophical anthropology.)
—— (1966) *The Insecurity of Freedom*, Philadelphia, PA: Jewish Publication Society. (A collection of essays on social, political and religious issues, reflecting his social activism.)

References and further reading

Merkle, J.C. (1985) *The Genesis of Faith: The Depth Theology of Abraham Joshua Heschel*, New York: Macmillan. (The most extensive analysis of Heschel's philosophical theology.)
—— (ed.) (1986) *Abraham Joshua Heschel: Exploring his Life and Thought*, New York: Macmillan. (A collection of essays by Jewish, Catholic and Protestant scholars.)

DAVID NOVAK

HESIOD (*c.*700 BC)

*One of the earliest surviving Greek poets, Hesiod was a direct precursor of the first philosophers. He composed one poem on mythic cosmogony and cosmology (*Theogony*) and another on work and justice in human life (*Works and Days*).*

Little is known of Hesiod's life, beyond what he tells us: his father emigrated from Asia Minor to Ascra in Boeotia and left him a share of an inheritance over which he quarrelled with his brother Perses, he won first prize in a poetic contest and the Muses themselves initiated him into poetry while he was tending sheep. The *Theogony* and *Works and Days*, which survive intact, are undoubtedly by him. Numerous other works were attributed to him in antiquity.

At least in part because Aristotle systematically distinguishes Hesiod as one of the earlier, mythical, philosophically unserious 'theologians' from the later, more rational and philosophically interesting thinkers he calls 'physicists,' most accounts of Greek philosophy tend to separate Hesiod from the Presocratics, assigning Hesiod's poetry to the primitive phase of mythic thought and locating in Thales the beginning of genuine philosophical reflection in Europe. Yet Hesiod's questions – What are the origin and structure of things? How can humans achieve success and happiness in their lives? – are the same ones that concern all later philosophers; and his answers, despite their often mythical form, remain of considerable interest.

In the *Theogony*, Hesiod attempts to unify many divergent local versions of Greek mythology by systematizing them all in terms of a coherent account of the origin and legitimacy of the current moral structure of the universe, identified with the rule of Zeus. Conceptual relations like implication, entailment or association are expressed mythologically as procreation or consanguinity, opposition or contradiction as warfare. Although Zeus' rule was founded upon violence and crime in a succession of divine generations, it is now characterized by justice and order and is a welcome improvement upon earlier conditions. Human beings are a small but not quite negligible part of an extraordinarily complex and by now fairly stable world in which all natural and moral phenomena, including those viewed in a negative light, have a fixed place; cosmic forces of potential disorder remain, but they are at least temporarily under control and the threat of primitive anarchy they represent is remote.

Human existence becomes the central theme in Hesiod's later *Works and Days*. Once again he uses myths to explain the origins of its permanent features: because of Prometheus labour is necessary; because of Pandora many evils plague human life; the sequence of gold, silver, bronze, heroic, and iron races demonstrates the relation between work, responsibility, and success. Now he adds numerous direct precepts and admonitions concerning social behaviour, religious practice and agriculture, and analyses the concept of *eris* (contention) to show that it can be not only baneful, when it leads to strife and war, but also beneficial, when it provides the impetus towards economic competition. It is Zeus' rule of justice that distinguishes us from the animals and that ensures that, even though we are obliged to labour incessantly and to worry about an uncertain future, we can console ourselves with the reasonable hope that we not only will survive, but may even flourish, if we choose to face this obligation responsibly rather than try to prosper by immoral means.

See also: PRESOCRATIC PHILOSOPHY

List of works

Hesiod (*c.*700 BC) *Theogony*, in M.L. West (ed.) *Hesiod. Theogony*, Oxford: Clarendon Press, 1966; H.G. Evelyn-White (ed. and trans.) *Hesiod, The Homeric Hymns and Homerica*, Loeb Classical Library, Cambridge, MA: Harvard University Press and London: Heinemann, 1914, 78–155. (The Evelyn-White edition provides Greek text with an English prose translation.)

—— (*c.*700 BC) *Works and Days*, in M.L. West (ed.) *Hesiod. Theogony*, Oxford: Clarendon Press, 1978; H.G. Evelyn-White (ed. and trans.) *Hesiod, The Homeric Hymns and Homerica*, Loeb Classical Library, Cambridge, MA: Harvard University Press and London: Heinemann, 1914, 2–65. (The Evelyn-White edition provides Greek text with an English prose translation.)

—— (*c.*700 BC) *Fragments*, in R. Merkelbach and

M.L. West (eds) *Fragmenta Hesiodea*, Oxford: Clarendon Press, 1967. (A scholarly edition, without translation, of the Greek texts deriving Hesiod's other works than the *Theogony* and the *Works and Days* and surviving in citations or on papyri.)

References and further reading

Cornford, F.M. (1952) *Principium Sapientiae. The Origins of Greek Philosophical Thought*, ed. W.K.C. Guthrie, Cambridge: Cambridge University Press. (Provides in part 2 pages 159–256 a very stimulating although uneven analysis of the relation between philosophical cosmogony and myth and ritual.)

Kirk, G.S., Raven, J.E. and Schofield, M. (1983) *The Presocratic Philosophers*, Cambridge: Cambridge University Press, 2nd edn. (The discussion of Hesiod at pages 34–46 concentrates on the *Theogony*, with attention to Near Eastern parallels.)

Most, G.W. (1997) 'Hesiod's Myth of the Five (or Three or Four Races)', *Proceedings of the Cambridge Philological Society*. (Interprets the structure of Hesiod's myth of the races in terms of his view on time, responsibility, and the conditions and chances for human success in the world in which we live.)

Rowe, C.J. (1983) '"Archaic" Thought in Hesiod', *Journal of Hellenic Studies* 103: 124–35. (Argues against the idea of a linear evolution from mythic to philosophical thought.)

Solmsen, F. (1949) *Hesiod and Aeschylus*, Ithaca, NY: Cornell University Press. (Provides a useful general account at pages 3–100, focusing on Hesiod's relation to his predecessors.)

Stokes, M.C. (1962–3) 'Hesiodic and Milesian Cosmogonies', *Phronesis* 7: 1–37, and 8: 1–34. (A careful comparison between mythical and philosophical cosmogonies.)

GLENN W. MOST

HESS, MOSES (1812–75)

Hess was a socialist philosopher, closely connected with the Young Hegelians, who influenced the initial philosophical development of Karl Marx, and later articulated, in the context of a critique of European bourgeois society, one of the first calls for the re-establishment of a Jewish commonwealth in Palestine.

Hess was born to a Jewish family in Bonn, Germany. At an early age he repudiated the religious teachings of his parental home and under the influence of Spinozist, Young Hegelian and Feuerbachian ideas developed a highly original, though philosophically eclectic, socialist philosophy (see FEUERBACH, L.A.; HEGELIANISM §2).

His first book, *Die heilige Geschichte der Menschheit* (The Holy History of Mankind) (1837) proposes a three-stage philosophy of history (God the Father, God the Son and the Holy Spirit) based on the changing relationship between politics and ethics, to culminate in a new, socialist 'New Jerusalem'. This new order, based on the abolition of private property, will reintroduce into politics those ethical elements banished from human life due to the Christian dichotomy between the material and the spiritual which enabled the emergence of individualist capitalism. In a further publication, *Die Europäische Triarchie* (The European Triarchy) (1841) he sees the cultures of France, Germany and England symbolizing, respectively, radical political, philosophical and industrial innovation, as the foundation of a new progressive alliance against the conservative post-1815 reality in Europe.

Active in the radical intellectual movement which included also Marx and Engels, Hess went into exile, to Belgium and France. In numerous essays, such as *Die Philosophie der Tat* (The Philosophy of the Deed) (1843), *Über das Geldwesen* (On Money), *Über die sozialistische Bewegung in Deutschland* (On the Socialist Movement in Germany) (1845) and *Die letzten Philosophen* (The Recent Philosophers) (1845), he continued to develop his brand of 'ethical' socialism, slowly differentiating his approach from the 'materialistic' approach of Marx and his followers.

After a short return to Germany during the 1848–9 revolution, Hess spent the rest of his life in Paris. There, under the impact of the rise of national movements in Germany and Italy in the wake of the failure of 1848, he also developed his own thoughts on the future of the Jews and Jewish civilization. In his earliest writings he expressed the view that the socialist revolution will also integrate Jewish life into the new revolutionary Europe; but Hess always recognized the salience of national identity in the course of world history. The rise of nationalism in Europe led him to the conclusion that only the renewal of Jewish political life in the ancestral land of Israel could guarantee both an adequate social solution to the Jewish problem and the survival of Jewish culture. Greatly influenced by Mazzini's ideas of a universalist, harmonious nationalism, Hess developed these ideas in his book *Rom und Jerusalem* (Rome and Jerusalem) (1862). The socialist structure of this Jewish commonwealth would be based both on universalist principles and on the strong socially-orientated precepts which Hess, despite his religious agnosticism, found underlying

much of the historical Judaic biblical legislation. His book – rather idiosyncratic and hardly noticed at the time of publication – was later to become one of the major intellectual texts of Zionism, especially in its socialist variation.

In his later years Hess tried to develop, on Spinozist lines, a modern philosophy of science with radical, socialist-activist implications; but the work was never finished. He died in Paris on 6 April 1875 and was later to become the only thinker revered by both the socialist and Zionist movements.

Because of his philosophical eclecticism, Hess never produced a systematic body of work comparable to that of other socialist thinkers, such as Saint-Simon or Marx. Yet his interpretation of Spinoza's monism and pantheism can be seen as the mainstay of both his socialist and proto-Zionist ideas (see SPINOZA, B. DE). Similarly, because of this lack of a systematic doctrine, Hess was more receptive to a pluralist interpretation of history, which gave a role to issues of national identity and cultural tradition, generally overlooked by more systematic thinkers like Marx.

The unity of matter and spirit which Hess discerns in Spinoza serves him as the foundation of his ethical socialism: economic life cannot be divorced from ethical considerations, nor can ethics be relegated to a separate compartment ('religion'), purely focused on an other-worldly redemption (which Hess saw as the main characteristic of Christianity). That the historical Jewish legislation institutionalized this unity of politics and ethics in the concept of a 'holy nation' Hess saw (when shorn of its ethnocentric connotations) as the specifically socialist element embedded in Judaism, in contrast to the dichotomies of Christianity, which have led to competitive individualism, alienation and capitalism.

Many of Hess' ideas on alienation in modern industrial society, on money as 'reified' power dominating the lives of human beings who created it, found their way, via Marx, into the general canon of socialist critique. But because of his eclecticism Hess was free from the reductionist flaws of Marxian thought. Similarly, his recognition of both the autonomy and intrinsic value of culture as embedded in specific national memory and identity saved him from the abstractedness and lack of understanding for national problems which characterized much of socialist thought. Echoes of Hess' thought can be found among the so-called 'Austro-Marxist' thinkers, in the Yugoslav attempt, under Tito, to combine socialism with a multi-ethnic reality, and in socialist Zionism.

See also: ALIENATION; SOCIALISM; ZIONISM §1

List of works

Hess, M. (1961) *Philosophische und sozialistische Schriften* (Philosophical and Socialist Writings), ed. A. Cornu and W. Mönke, Berlin: Akademie Verlag. (Includes 'The Holy History of Mankind', 'The European Triarchy' and all of Hess' socialist writings until 1850.)

—— (1843) 'Die Philosophie der Tat', trans. 'The Philosophy of the Deed', in A. Fried and R. Saunders (eds) *Socialist Thought*, Garden City, NY: Doubleday, 249–75, 1964. (The major essay in which Hess develops his 'philosophy of praxis' as a critique of classical German Idealist philosophy, which he depicts as quietistic, passive and hence politically reactionary.)

—— (1845) 'Die letzen Philosophen', trans. 'The Recent Philosophers', in L. Stepelevich (ed.) *The Young Hegelians*, Cambridge: Cambridge University Press, 355–75, 1982. (A critique of idealist philosophy as a secular version of traditional Christian duality between 'spirit' and 'matter' which is, according to Hess, at the root of the development of European capitalist society.)

—— (1862) *Rom und Jerusalem*, selections trans. as *Rome and Jerusalem*, in A. Hertzberg (ed.) *The Zionist Idea*, New York: Atheneum, 119–39, 1969. (Hess' major proto-Zionist work, in which he criticizes the failure of Jewish emancipation in Europe and calls for the establishment of a Jewish commonwealth in Palestine, to be founded on socialist precepts drawn both from the international socialist movement as well as for the socially oriented content of traditional Judaic law as seen by him.)

—— (1962) *Ausgewählte Schriften* (Selected Writings), ed. H. Lademacher, Köln: Melzer Verlag. (Includes a selection of his early writings, and the full text of *Rome and Jerusalem*, with all its notes, appendices, etc.)

References and further reading

Avineri, S. (1985) *Moses Hess: Prophet of Communism and Social Zionism*, New York: New York University Press. (A detailed study of the development of Hess' thought, based on his writings throughout his life. Contains extensive quotations from the writings and a bibliography.)

Berlin, I. (1980) 'The Life and Opinions of Moses Hess', in *Against the Current*, New York: Viking. (The best concise résumé of Hess' work in relation to that of Marx).

McLellan, D. (1969) *The Young Hegelians*, London: Macmillan, 137–59. (Places Hess in the context of his contemporaries among the Young Hegelians.)

Weiss, J. (1960) *Moses Hess – Utopian Socialist*, Detroit, MI: Wayne State University Press. (A comprehensive study of Hess' critique of capitalist society and his vision of an ethically based socialism.)

SHLOMO AVINERI

HESSEN, SERGEI IOSIFOVICH (1887–1950)

Sergei Hessen, a disciple of Rickert, has been described as 'the most brilliant and philosophically gifted' representative of Neo-Kantian transcendentalism in Russia on the eve of the Revolution. A co-editor of the St Petersburg-based philosophical journal Logos, *he represented a distinctively Westernizing trend, critical in many respects of the openly metaphysical religious idealism of the 'religious-philosophical renaissance' in Russia. However, he readily acknowledged the existence of an ineradicable metaphysical need in human beings and stressed the metaphysical relevance of his philosophy of moral and cultural values. B.V. Iakovenko attributed to him a pronounced 'ontological aspiration' and Hessen's philosophical evolution led him beyond 'pure anthropologism', towards a religiously tinged Platonism.*

Like many Russian philosophers, Hessen concentrated on philosophical problems which had direct relevance for practice. His main fields were philosophical pedagogy, which he defined as 'applied philosophy', and political philosophy, with particular emphasis on philosophy of law. Like many other Russian philosophers, he was forced to emigrate, moving from one country to another, which did not help his professional career. Nevertheless, his work Osnovy pedagogiki *(Foundations of Pedagogy) (published in Berlin, 1923) was translated into many languages and won him international recognition as the main author of the 'pedagogy of culture'. His original conception of 'rule-of-law socialism' (which deserves to be regarded as the last link in the legal philosophy of Russian liberalism) was much less known, and the manuscripts of his two books on political philosophy perished in the Warsaw uprising of 1944. Still, the UNESCO Committee on the Philosophic Basis of Human Rights invited him to contribute to the preparation of the Universal Declaration of Human Rights of 1948. His article for UNESCO, together with his writings on political philosophy published posthumously in Italy, were a*

Russian contribution to the philosophy of human rights in modern, liberal democratic states.

1   **Philosophy of values**
2   **Rule-of-law socialism**
3   **Human rights and philosophy of law**

1   Philosophy of values

Sergei Iosifovich Hessen was a son of a Russian lawyer who became the editor of the St Petersburg journal *Pravo* (Law) and a prominent member of the Kadet Party. Owing to this Hessen grew up surrounded by the best representatives of Russian liberalism and the legal profession (P. Miliukov, L. Petrażycki and others). He studied philosophy in Germany under the direction of Heinrich Rickert (see NEO-KANTIANISM §§6–8). His doctoral thesis, *Individuelle Kausalität* (Individual Causality), was defended *summa cum laude* in 1908 and published in Kantstudien. Having returned to Russia, he edited *Logos* (together with F. Stepun) and lectured at St Petersburg University (see NEO-KANTIANISM, RUSSIAN §6). In 1917 he was a personal secretary of PLEKHANOV. After the Revolution he served for four years as a professor of philosophy in Tomsk but the increasing ideological pressure made it impossible for him to continue his work in Russia. He emigrated to Berlin and then to Prague, where he lectured in the Russian Pedagogical Institute. In 1935 he moved to Poland, on the invitation of the Free University in Warsaw. During the war he took an active part in the underground university courses in Warsaw. After the war he resumed his professional duties in the newly created University of Łódź.

The intellectual situation of the early twentieth century was defined by Hessen as a double crisis: the crisis of philosophy and the crisis of liberalism, both caused by the undermining of the belief in the objectivity of truth and in the objectivity of values. He wanted to overcome this philosophical and political crisis without returning to naïve scientific and moral dogmatism, and without resuscitating the rationalistic and class-bound illusions of classical liberalism.

In his efforts to do this Hessen made use of a peculiar variant of dialectical method. He attributed its discovery to Plato. In his interpretation dialectic was a means of combating relativism and saving values from destruction: it enabled him to detect continuity and permanence in historical change, to see in the realm of the relative a reflection of the absolute. 'Dialectical comprehension' was to him a combination of the historical approach with phenomenological 'eidetic insight', and the ontological foundation of

dialectics was, in his view, the Neoplatonic idea of 'All-Unity' – an idea which, thanks to SOLOV'ËV, became strongly embedded in Russian religious philosophy.

Under the influence of Roman Jakobson's Linguistic Circle in Prague (see STRUCTURALISM IN LINGUISTICS §2), Hessen turned his attention to structuralism and made 'the principle of structure' an integral part of his dialectical method. His concept of structure was composed of three elements: (1) the idea of wholeness, levelled against nineteenth-century atomism; (2) the idea of a 'hierarchy of layers', levelled against genetic reductionism; and finally (3) the idea of autonomy, levelled against naturalism and psychologism. All these components were combined in a dialectical relationship which prevented the distorting isolation and absolutization of any, thereby removing the danger of interpreting wholeness as totalism and autonomy as autarchy.

In his *Osnovy pedagogiki* (Foundations of Pedagogy) (1923) Hessen developed a conception of personality as rooted in objective, universal values. Personality, he claimed, is discovered only by participation in suprapersonal tasks. Without having physical existence, values have, nonetheless, 'universal validity'; hence, their mode of being is independent both from the individual psyche and from the supra-individual collective consciousness. Their objectivity and universality consists in their 'inner quality' which can be neither deduced from social conditions nor made dependent on their subjective recognition by a social group. In contrast to the norms of social life, cultural values act not by means of pressure but by means of 'appeal' – an appeal directed to people as free spiritual beings or personalities. The world of values is a hierarchical, multilayered structure; the higher values 'glow through' the lower ones and the lower values are both negated and preserved in the higher. History is a process of realizing values but the 'inner quality' of values is independent of changing historical situations. Philosophy is the self-consciousness of man as a value-realizing or – which means the same – a culture-producing being. The practical application of philosophy is pedagogy, or the science of education.

In later years Hessen tried to transcend this 'purely cultural' standpoint by developing the idea of a supracultural level of human existence. The first outline of this new conception appeared in his book *O sprzecznościach i jedności wychowania* (On Contradictions and Unity in Education) (1939). It divided human existence into four levels: biological, social, cultural (spiritual), and the level of grace. Hessen explained that the highest level was equivalent to the 'Kingdom of God' in the conception of such religious philosophers as Solov'ëv and August CIESZKOWSKI.

The appearance of a religious perspective in Hessen's thought resulted from his deep interest in Russian religious thinkers, above all Solov'ëv and DOSTOEVSKII. From Solov'ëv he took the idea of 'All-Unity', setting it against both atomistic pluralism and ossified monism; his criticism of isolating and absolutizing certain elements of a dialectical whole was directly related to Solov'ëv's criticism of 'abstract principles'. Dostoevskii was for him the greatest Russian thinker, whose works, especially *The Brothers Karamazov*, provided the formulation and intuitive solution of the deepest problems of modern ethics.

Hessen's articles on Dostoevskii and Solov'ëv show both his relative closeness to the broadly conceived 'religious-philosophical renaissance' in Russian thought (see RUSSIAN RELIGIOUS-PHILOSOPHICAL RENAISSANCE) and the peculiarity of his standpoint, clearly distinguishing him from other Russian thinkers inspired by Solov'ëv's philosophy. In his interpretation of Solov'ëv Hessen was a resolute Westernizer, having nothing to say on the 'Russian Idea'. He minimized the importance of Solov'ëv's theocratic utopianism, stressing instead the presence of Kantian motives in his philosophy and crediting him with overcoming utopian tendencies. Similarly, Hessen saw in Dostoevskii not a messianic utopian but rather a profound critic of utopianism, a thinker who powerfully and prophetically foretold the inevitable totalitarian consequences of utopian thinking.

In his essay 'Krushenie utopizma' (The Breakdown of Utopianism) (1924) Hessen defined utopianism as 'absolutization of the relative': attributing absolute significance to the realization of certain relative values and setting them against the entire historical tradition. This explained, in particular, the nihilistic and purely instrumental attitude towards law, so characteristic of the utopian mentality.

2 Rule-of-law socialism

In Hessen's view, the most important modern utopia was, of course, socialism. He brilliantly analysed the destructive nature of socialist utopianism but stressed, at the same time, that socialism should not be reduced to its utopian features. In the serialized book *Problema pravovogo sotsializma* (The Problem of Rule-of-Law Socialism) (1924–7) he argued for the possibility of overcoming socialist utopianism from within, through combining socialist ideas with the liberal principle of the rule of law.

The first phase of socialism – 'Utopian socialism as the abstract negation of capitalism' – was a reaction against the juridical worldview of the French Revolution. It rejected the rule-of-law state as legalized anarchy, accused the law of sanctifying social

atomization and set against it the principle of the Good. According to Saint-Simon and his disciples law was necessarily subjectivist, pluralist and purely formal, whereas the good was objective, monistic and had a concretely definable content. Socialism, therefore, was conceived not as yet another political system, yet another legal order, but as an organic industrial system in which political power is replaced by the administration of things, and law, as a means of delimiting subjective, egoistic interests, gives way to organic social ties.

The second phase of socialism – classical Marxism – was described as a 'real' negation of liberal-capitalist order. It was real, and not merely abstract, because of the scientific character of Marxian analyses of the real contradictions of capitalist development. However, this scientific side of Marxism coexisted with a pronounced hostility towards the rule of law, defined as bourgeois hypocrisy, and with a strong strain of utopianism, culminating in the idea of the 'withering away of state and law'. Another side of the Marxist utopia was the idea of the disappearance of economy or, rather, its replacement by a purely technical scientific organization of labour.

Russian revolutionary communism represented, in Hessen's view, the quintessence of Marxist utopianism. Its inner nature was revealed by 'War Communism', that is, the subordination of all spheres of life to the militarized control of those in power. The degradation of law in the Soviet state revealed another aspect of the communist utopia: its striving by all possible means to realize an arbitrarily defined and absolutized ideal of positive Good.

The next part of the book is devoted to those currents of socialist thought, both Marxist and non-Marxist, in which the negation of capitalism was not only 'real', that is, derived from an analysis of real social contradictions, but also 'transforming' and 'constructive'. Following P.I. Novgorodtsev (see NEO-KANTIANISM, RUSSIAN §4), Hessen discussed in this part both individual thinkers, such as Lassalle, Proudhon and Bernstein, and entire movements, such as French Syndicalism and German social-democratic revisionism. He presented them as different dialectical phases of the process by which the socialist Good was permeated by the principle of law.

In the last part of the book Hessen discussed the views of the British 'guild socialists' who defined their socialist ideal as 'the New Middle Ages'. He welcomed this ideal with important qualifications, stressing that 'the truth of liberalism' had to be preserved. Referring to Chicherin (see LIBERALISM, RUSSIAN §2) he pointed out that law should not be confused with morality, as had been the case in the 'Old Middle Ages', and assured his readers that in the new medievalism the 'impenetrability of the person' and inviolable rights of the individual would be fully respected.

The essence of the new medievalism would consist in the sovereignty of law and plurality of legal orders mutually limiting each other. Law would no longer be identified with the official laws of the state and the state itself would undergo a process of 'devolution'. Social atomization would be abolished, individuals would participate in the life of different communities without losing their individual autonomy. Property would lose its alienated character and become personalized, conditional and divided. The economy would be 'bridled' by law while preserving its autonomy and spontaneity. Human dignity would gain enormously because being dependent on law, rather than on arbitrary political power or blind economic forces, is not a humiliating relationship. In this way socialism would at last fully overcome its utopianism and reveal itself as a new and higher form of the rule of law.

3 Human rights and philosophy of law

In his works written under the Nazi occupation and under the communist rule in Poland (such as his UNESCO article and the booklet *Modern Democracy*) Hessen gave up his idealization of the pluralist legal order of the Middle Ages but further developed his conception of socialism as the last stage in the development of human rights and the rule of law.

In the first stage, represented by the absolute state, human rights took the form of the security of law, which implied the inviolability of the citizen's person, property and dwelling. In the second stage, that of classical liberalism, security of law was transformed into the liberal principle of limited government, safeguarding the existence of a private sphere in which individuals were free from any interference by the state. The third stage – the modern democratic state – broadened the scope of governmental activity by endowing the state with the task of securing for its citizens certain forms of 'positive freedom'. This provided justification for welfare policies, universal compulsory education and different kinds of social insurance. Socialism represented the fourth stage in this development. Its task was the further extension of 'positive freedom' and democratic rights through endowing all individuals with economic rights and safeguarding their implementation. Its highest principle was to be freedom from exploitation or the right of everyone to be treated in economic life as a person, not a mere commodity.

The Soviet system, in Hessen's view, was a product of the destructive spirit of communist utopianism. Nevertheless he saw in it an encouraging phenomenon: the gradual overcoming of its initial utopianism, the vindication of some measure of autonomy for the economic sphere, the restoration of law and an increasingly positive attitude towards the historical heritage. He expected therefore that sooner or later the Soviet Union would develop into a democratic and law-respecting socialist state.

Hessen's views on the current state of affairs in the liberal-democratic West stemmed from his conviction that liberalism had entered the phase of its final, insoluble crisis. The Western countries, he argued, had abandoned the Puritan values of the fathers of liberalism; hence the prevalence of consumerist attitudes, a special kind of tolerance, expressing not respect for persons but indifference towards truth, and the peculiar infantilism of mass culture. Hessen saw these phenomena as symptoms of a dangerous, destructive process. It seemed to him that the overcoming of such a crisis could be expected only from an overall regeneration: from religious revival on the one hand and from socialist reconstruction on the other.

Hessen's conception of the changing content of human rights was linked to his general philosophy of law, elaborated in his unpublished book 'On the Essence and Calling of Law'. It placed law between two levels of human existence: the social level and the spiritual/cultural level. Law is below the spiritual level because it lacks *eros* and *caritas*: it replaces moral values by commands, attraction by pressure, autonomy by heteronomy. On the other hand, however, law stands above the social level of existence, since it is a means by which spiritual life influences its social basis. Without law members of a social group cannot become individualized persons. Absolutization of the legalistic outlook leads to atomism but disregard for law in the name of higher moral principles results, as a rule, in descent to the animal level.

In the last two years of his life Hessen was a victim of the enforced Stalinization of Polish intellectual life. He was subject to increasing ideological pressure and forced thereby to withdraw from teaching philosophy and pedagogy, becoming instead a teacher of Russian. After his death several of his works were translated into Italian and influenced Italian educational policies.

List of works

S.I. Hessen (1909) *Individuelle Kausalität. Studien zum transzendentalen Empirismus* (Individual Causality. Studies in Transcendental Empiricism), *Kantstudien*. Ergänzungsheft 15, Berlin.

—— (1910) 'Mistika i metafizika' (Mysticism and Metaphysics), *Logos*, 1. St Petersburg.
—— (1912, 1913) 'Filosofiia nakazaniia' (The Philosophy of Punishment), *Logos*, 1–2. St Petersburg.
—— (1917) *Politicheskaia svoboda i sotsializm* (Political Freedom and Socialism), Petrograd.
—— (1923) *Osnovy pedagogiki: Vvedenie v prikladnuiu filosofiiu* (Foundations of Pedagogy: Introduction to the Applied Philosophy), Berlin; trans. Fondamenti della Pedagogia come Filosofia Applicata, introduction by G.L. Radice, Florence, 1936. (Also translated into Latin, Bulgarian, Polish, Serbian and Czech.)
—— (1924) 'Krushenie utopizma' (The Breakdown of Utopianism), in *Sovremennye zapiski*, Paris, vol. 19.
—— (1924–7) 'Problema pravovogo sotsializma' (The Problem of Rule-of-Law Socialism), in *Sovremennye zapiski*, Paris, vol. 22 (1924), vol. 23 (1925), vols 27–9 (1926), vol. 30 (1927).
—— (1931) 'Bor'ba utopii i avtonomii dobra v mirovozzrenii F.M. Dostoevskogo i Vl. Solov'ëva' (The Struggle Between Utopia and the Autonomy of Good in the Worldview of F.M. Dostoevskii and V. Solov'ëv), in *Sovremennye zapiski*, Paris, vols 45–6.
—— (1938) *Szkola i demokracja na przelomie*, Warsaw.
—— (1939) *O sprzecznościach i jedności wychowania* (On Contradictions and Unity in Education), Lwów-Warsaw.
—— (1949) 'The Rights of Man in Liberalism, Socialism and Communism', in *Human Rights. Comments and Interpretations. A Symposium* edited by UNESCO with an introduction by J. Maritain, New York.
—— (1952) *Le virtù platoniche et le virtù evangeliche* (Platonic and Evangelical Virtues), Rome: Armando Armando.
—— (1957) *Democrazia moderna* (Modern Democracy), Rome: Armando Armando.
—— (1958) *Diritto e morale* (Law and Morality), Rome: Armando Armando.
—— (1968) *Studia z filosofii kul'tury* (Studies in the Philosophy of Culture), ed. A. Walicki, Warsaw: PWN. (Contains a comprehensive bibliography of Hessen's works.)

References and further reading

Broccolini, G. (1966) *Mito e realtà nel pensiero di Sergio Hessen* (Myth and Reality in the Thought of Sergius Hessen), Rome. (A brief but comprehensive outline of Hessen's philosophy of culture.)
Walicki, A. (1987) 'Sergius Hessen: A Post-Revolutionary Synthesis', in A. Walicki, *Legal Philosophies of Russian Liberalism*, Oxford: Clarendon Press,

404–70. (An outline of Hessen's philosophy and a detailed presentation of his philosophy of law.)
Zenkovsky, V.V. (1948–50) *Istoriia russkoi filosofii*, Paris: YMCA-Press, vol. 2; 2nd edn 1989; trans. G.L. Kline, *A History of Russian Philosophy*, London: Routledge & Kegan Paul and New York: Columbia University Press, 1953, vol. 2, 697–702. (The author presents Hessen as the best, most original representative of the Neo-Kantian current in Russian philosophy.)

ANDRZEJ WALICKI

HEYTESBURY, WILLIAM (before 1313–1372/3)

William Heytesbury, an English logician of the mid-fourteenth century, is, with Richard Kilvington, Richard Swineshead, Thomas Bradwardine and John Dumbleton, one of several philosophers known as the Oxford Calculators. In his works, Heytesbury examined mathematical topics related to motion and the continuum as well as paradoxes of self-reference and problems arising from intentional contexts, all within the context of terminist logic, through the resolution of sophismata. He is most noted for developing the mathematics of uniform acceleration, and for his contributions to developing the mathematical treatment of physical qualities such as heat.

William Heytesbury became a fellow of Merton College in 1330. He was a foundation fellow of Queen's College in 1340, but soon returned to Merton, becoming a doctor of theology there in 1348. He served as Chancellor of Oxford University in 1371–2, just before his death. All of his works concern logic and were written in Merton College during his Regency in Arts (1331–9). His writings were particularly popular in fifteenth-century Italy.

Heytesbury's logical investigations centered on sophismata, as his two major works, *Sophismata* and *Regulae solvendi sophismata* (Rules for Solving Sophismata) reveal in their titles. A sophisma is not a sophistical argument, but a statement the truth of which is at issue, given certain assumptions specified within a disputation (see LANGUAGE, MEDIEVAL THEORIES OF). The respondent must take a position on the statement's truth, and answer his opponent's questions for a certain time without being driven into absurdity or contradiction. Medieval sophismata were intended to be of logical interest, and may pose important philosophical problems.

Regulae solvendi sophismata has six chapters. The

first deals with 'insoluble' sentences, self-referential paradoxes such as 'what I am now uttering is false'. The second, 'On knowing and doubting', deals with sentences involving intentional contexts, such as 'You know the king is seated', when the king is seated, and 'you know that sentence A (asserting this) is true, but you do not know what A asserts'. The third chapter deals with sophismata involving relative pronouns, and the fourth with sentences involving the terms 'begins' and 'ceases'. The fifth, 'On maxima and minima', deals with sentences concerning the limits of capacities measured on linear continua, and the sixth with sentences about change and motion.

The first three types of sophismata raise logical questions, but the rest border on mathematics and physical theory in their discussion of continua and motion. Heytesbury first makes a sophisma's logical form clear, using a variety of tools, and then applies the conditions specified to the determination of its truth. As an example, take 'Socrates ceases to know ten propositions', given that he now forgets one of the propositions but continues to know the other nine. The logical form of the sophisma is unclear on the surface, but William 'exposits' it as 'Socrates knew ten propositions immediately before now, but does not know ten propositions now'. Given that exposition, the sophisma follows. The objection that he ceases to know only one proposition, and continues to know the other nine, is handled by pointing out that 'ceases' imposes a compounded, not a divided, sense on 'ten propositions', since it precedes that phrase. The sophisma is not 'ten propositions (each) cease to be known by Socrates', which involves the divided sense and would receive a different exposition.

Again, take a proposition stated in the chapter on relative pronouns, 'Now there begins to be some instant which after the present instant will begin to be'. The exposition yields 'Now there is no instant which after the present instant will begin to be, and immediately after now there will be some instant which after the present instant will begin to be', and so the sophisma is true. The second part of the exposition is taken to mean 'there is no instant after the present instant such that at no instant between it and the present instant there is some instant which after the present instant will begin to be'. In his *De sensu compositio et diviso* (Compounded and Divided Senses), an important summary of the state of the question on the issues it discusses, and on which medieval logicians afterwards relied, Heytesbury denies that from 'immediately after this there will be some instant', one may conclude that 'there will be some instant immediately after this', relying, as he often does, on word order to make his distinctions. In the first case, 'immediately' comes before 'some

instant', and renders its supposition confused, so that what is said is 'there is no instant after the present instant such that at no instant between it and the present instant *there is some instant*'. In the second case 'immediately' comes after 'some instant', so that its supposition is not confused, and the sentence means that, for some specific instant I, 'there is no instant after the present instant such that at no instant between it and the present instant *I is*'. Thus, whereas the first is true, the second is false.

Heytesbury's central concern is often the logic of continua and infinite divisibility, a pursuit we nowadays regard as a part of mathematics. In constructing his sophismata, he makes free use of whatever can happen *secundum imaginationem*, that is, any set of conditions or events involving no formal contradiction, whether or not it is physically or metaphysically possible. (Thus the reductionism characteristic of his nominalism is disabled, and Heytesbury neither attempts to explain how an instant is really identical with things in motion, nor avoids speaking of instants merely because they are not really distinct from such things.) Despite their abstraction, these investigations contributed to the development of the natural sciences. In Aristotelian physics only space, time and motion are considered amenable to mathematical treatment. However, William's sophismata conceive qualities such as heat and whiteness in quantitative terms, while avoiding any metaphysical difficulties in such a conception by proceeding *secundum imaginationem*. As thinkers became used to the notion that anything lying along a continuous range could, in principle, be spoken of quantitatively, the search for a way to measure such things as heat became possible, and so mere logic laid the groundwork for a broadened application of mathematics to the physical world.

In the sixth chapter of his *Regulae*, Heytesbury developed the mathematics of uniform acceleration, proving the mean–speed theorem, in other words that a uniformly accelerated body will, over a given period of time, traverse a distance equal to the distance it would traverse if it were moved continuously in the same period at its mean velocity (one-half the sum of the initial and final velocities) during that period. He derives from this the conclusion that a uniformly accelerated body will, in the second equal time interval, traverse three times the distance it does in the first. Domingo de SOTO observed the applicability of the theorem to free fall in 1555. Galileo, although he probably was not acquainted with Heytesbury's work, would have benefitted from the medieval background of which Heytesbury was a part (see GALILEI, G.).

See also: BRADWARDINE, T.; KILVINGTON, R.; LOGIC, MEDIEVAL; NATURAL PHILOSOPHY, MEDIEVAL; OXFORD CALCULATORS

List of works

William Heytesbury (1331–9) Works, in *Tractatus de sensu composito et diviso, Regulae solvendi sophismata, et cetera*, Venice: Bonetum Locatellum, 1494. (This includes also *Sophismata* and *De veritate et falsitate propositionis* (On True and False Propositions) and commentaries by Gaetano of Thienne. See Wilson (1960) for additional editions and manuscripts.)

—— (1331–9) *Sophismata asina* (The Asinine Sophismata), ed. F. Pironet, Paris: Vrin, 1944. (An early collection of sophismata each of which proves the proposition, 'You are a donkey' (*Tu es asinas*). Edition, commentary and full manuscripts; the only modern edition of any of Heytesbury's works.)

—— (1331–9) *De sensu composito et diviso* (The Compounded and Divided Senses), trans. in N. Kretzmann and E. Stump, *The Cambridge Translations of Medieval Philosophical Texts*, Vol. 1: *Logic and the Philosophy of Language*, Cambridge: Cambridge University Press, 1988. (An accurate and logically sensitive translation with a brief introduction.)

—— (1331–9) *De probationibus conclusionum tractatus regularum solvendi sophismata* (On the Proofs of Conclusions from the Treatise of Rules for Resolving Syllogisms), Pavia, 1483. (Includes work on the speed of uniformly accelerated bodies.)

—— (1335) *Regulae solvendi sophismata* (Rules for Solving Sophisms): Chapter 1 trans. P.V. Spade, Toronto, Ont.: Pontifical Institute of Medieval Studies, 1979; Chapter 2 trans. 'The Verbs "Know" and "Doubt"', in N. Kretzmann and E. Stump, *The Cambridge Translations of Medieval Philosophical Texts*, Vol. 1: *Logic and the Philosophy of Language*, Cambridge: Cambridge University Press, 1988; Chapter 5 trans. J. Longeway in *William Heytesbury: On Maxima and Minima. Chapter 5 of Rules for Solving Sophismata with an anonymous fourteenth-century discussion*, trans. J. Longeway, Dordrecht: Kluwer, 1984. (Chapter 1 deals with self-referential paradoxes; Spade's translation and commentary is intelligent and well-informed. Chapter 2 deals with, among other things, logical problems raised by internal contexts; not much commentary, but the translation is accurate and logically astute. The translation of Chapter 5 contains a study and extensive analytical notes, arguing especially for the mathematical character of the work.)

References and further reading

Sylla, E. (1971) 'Medieval quantifications of qualities: the "Merton school"', *Archive for History of Exact Sciences* 8: 9–39. (An excellent introduction treating Heystesbury within the context of his school.)

Weisheipl, J. (1968) 'Ockham and some Mertonians', *Mediaeval Studies* 30: 163–213. (A biographical discussion of the Mertonian School, including Heytesbury.)

—— (1969) 'Repertorium Mertonense', *Mediaeval Studies* 31: 174–224. (A listing of the works of the Mertonian School, including Heytesbury.)

Wilson, C. (1960) *William Heytesbury: Medieval Logic and the Rise of Mathematical Physics*, Madison, WI: University of Wisconsin Press. (An excellent study of the last three chapters of the *Regulae solvendi* sophismata with complete information on Heytesbury.)

JOHN L. LONGEWAY

HIEROCLES (2nd century AD)

The Stoic philosopher Hierocles lectured and wrote on ethics. He is important for his defence of the theory of oikeiōsis *(affiliation), a form of self-perception and self-love which becomes the foundation for human commitment to rationality and virtue. Observation of animal and human behaviour, he argues, shows that* oikeiōsis *is innate, rather than learned.*

Little is known of Hierocles' life. He should, however, be distinguished from the later fifth-century Neoplatonist of the same name. When von Arnim demonstrated the common identity of the author of a papyrus text (known now as *Foundations of Ethics*) and the author of ethical excerpts preserved in a late ancient anthology by Stobaeus, it became apparent that Hierocles was active as a philosophical lecturer, in Asia Minor and/or Athens, in the second century AD (a date confirmed by the dating of the papyrus). The excerpts, of which more than a dozen survive, are from discourses on topics in practical ethics (for example, family relations, marriage, civic duty, household management) and on religion, and resemble lectures by other Stoics such as MUSONIUS RUFUS and Antipater. *Foundations of Ethics* deals in a more technical manner with the doctrines of self-perception and *oikeiōsis* (affiliation) (see STOICISM §14) and provides philosophical arguments for the view that self-perception is the basis for our affiliation to ourselves.

Foundations preserves evidence about Stoic views

421

on perception and self-awareness, the nature of the soul, and the 'self' as a complex relation of soul to body. It also sheds light on the problem of reconciling the self-directed inclinations of humans (self-love, the natural desire for one's own virtue to thrive) with the social inclinations which are the basis of the other-regarding virtues. Hierocles recognizes three affiliations: to oneself, to other humans, and to appropriate external objects.

One of the discourses (which can be found in von Arnim and Schubart, 1906: 61–2) also sheds light on our relations with others. People should be thought of as being arranged around us (that is, our mind) in a series of concentric circles. In the first and closest circle is our own body and the external things which help to fulfil its needs. The second circle contains our immediate relatives: parents, siblings, wife, children. The next two circles contain other relatives in order of closeness. The circles which follow include the various degrees of civic relationship (deme, tribe, city). Last is the circle of the entire human race. Hierocles proposes that social relations will be improved if we try to treat each group as though it were closer to us than it really is. He also suggests addressing remote relatives by more intimate labels (calling our cousins brothers, for example) in order to demonstrate and to strengthen our feeling for other people. The goal of this exercise is not to treat all human beings as we treat ourselves, but rather to 'reduce, through our own effort, the remoteness of our relationship with each set of people'. Hierocles' theory aims to achieve the closest possible bonds between people, but he falls short of calling for genuine altruism or impartialism.

List of works

Hierocles (2nd century AD) *Foundations of Ethics*, ed. G. Bastianini and A.A. Long, *Corpus dei papiri filosofici greci e latini*, part 1, *Autori Noti*, Florence: Olschki, 1992, vol. 1, 268–451. (Italian translation and commentary; includes excellent introduction and bibliography.)

—— (2nd century AD) Fragments, ed. H. von Arnim and W. Schubart, *Hierokles: Ethische Elementarlehre*, Berliner Klassikertexte, Heft 4, Berlin: Weidmann, 1906. (Contains the fragments preserved in Stobaeus' anthology; also contains the now obsolete first edition of the papyrus text.)

References and further reading

* Inwood, B. (1984) 'Hierocles: Theory and Argument in the Second Century AD', *Oxford Studies in Ancient Philosophy* 2: 151–83. (Discussion of date, identity and nature of argument.)

Isnardi Parente, M. (1989) 'Ierocle Stoico. Oikeiosis e doveri sociali' (Hierocles the Stoic. *Oikeiōsis* and Social Duties), in W. Haase (ed.) *Aufstieg und Niedergang der römischen Welt*, Berlin and New York: de Gruyter, II 36: 3, 2201–26. (A survey of Hierocles' identity, doctrines and relation to other schools.)

Praechter, K. (1901) *Hierokles der Stoiker*, Leipzig: Dieterich. (Basic work on identity and date.)

BRAD INWOOD

HIGH-ORDER LOGICS

see SECOND- AND HIGHER-ORDER LOGICS

HILBERT'S PROGRAMME AND FORMALISM

In the first, geometric stage of Hilbert's formalism, his view was that a system of axioms does not express truths particular to a given subject matter but rather expresses a network of logical relations that can (and, ideally, will) be common to other subject matters.

The formalism of Hilbert's arithmetical period extended this view by emptying even the logical terms of contentual meaning. They were treated purely as ideal elements whose purpose was to secure a simple and perspicuous logic for arithmetical reasoning – specifically, a logic preserving the classical patterns of logical inference. Hilbert believed, however, that the use of ideal elements should not lead to inconsistencies. He thus undertook to prove the consistency of ideal arithmetic with its contentual or finitary counterpart and to do so by purely finitary means.

In this, 'Hilbert's programme', Hilbert and his followers were unsuccessful. Work published by Kurt Gödel in 1931 suggested that such failure was perhaps inevitable. In his second incompleteness theorem, Gödel showed that for any consistent formal axiomatic system T strong enough to formalize what was traditionally regarded as finitary reasoning, it is possible to define a sentence that expresses the consistency of T, and is not provable in T. From this it has generally been concluded that the consistency of even the ideal arithmetic of the natural numbers is not finitarily provable and that Hilbert's programme must therefore fail.

Despite problematic elements in this reasoning, post-Gödelian work on Hilbert's programme has generally accepted it and attempted to minimize its effects by proposing various modifications of Hilbert's programme. These have generally taken one of three forms: attempts to extend Hilbert's finitism to stronger constructivist bases capable of proving more than is provable by strictly finitary means; attempts to show that for a significant family of ideal systems there are ways of 'reducing' their consistency problems to those of theories possessing more elementary (if not altogether finitary) justifications; and attempts by the so-called 'reverse mathematics' school to show that the traditionally identified ideal theories do not need to be as strong as they are in order to serve their mathematical purposes. They can therefore be reduced to weaker theories whose consistency problems are more amenable to constructivist (indeed, finitist) treatment.

1 **The formalism of the geometric period**
2 **Axiomatization and the ideal method**
3 **The formalism of the arithmetical period**
4 **The consistency of arithmetic**

1 The formalism of the geometric period

Hilbert's conception of mathematics during the period of his work on the foundations of geometry was 'formalist' in the sense that it viewed an axiomatic system as providing not a family of truths specific to a particular subject matter but, rather, a 'theory-form' or hypothetico-deductive framework which potentially and, indeed, preferably served as the form for a variety of different particular sciences.

This doctrine has two distinct moments that it is important to distinguish. One is a 'rigourist' moment which maintains that, for the sake of achieving rigour in mathematical reasoning, axiomatic systems must be formalized to the point of emptying their distinctively mathematical concepts of all intuitional or distinctly mathematical content so that they become mere 'positions' in a network of logical relations. The other moment is a 'schematist' one which says that even for the sake of achieving truth in one's axioms, the non-logical terms in an axiomatic theory do not have to be tied to any particular intuitive content. Conceived in this way, the mathematical terms of an axiomatic theory become 'variables' of a sort (that is, terms that range over a variety of different intuitive contents) rather than 'constants' (that is, terms that signify a unique particular content).

Historically, the rigourist moment had its origins in the seventeenth-century discovery that various proofs in Euclid's *Elements* relied upon assumptions not stated in his axioms, postulates and definitions. In the eighteenth century, Lambert (1766: 162) proposed a remedy for such failures of rigour. He reasoned that

since they occur when one makes tacit use of geometric intuition while conducting an inference in a proof, they ought to be eradicable by forcing all inferences to be validated without appeal to geometric intuition. This, he maintained, could be accomplished by requiring the validation of inferences to proceed in abstraction from the intuitive meanings of the mathematical terms involved and to be warranted solely on the basis of their 'symbolic characteristics'. Axioms would thus be treated like 'algebraic equations' in which mathematical terms are manipulated according to the logical positions laid down for them in the axioms and not according to their intuitive meanings.

This, essentially, was the conception of rigour that Pasch (1882) and Hilbert (1899a) put into effect in their axiomatizations of geometry a century later.

Inference, however, is only one part of mathematical practice and rigour, therefore, only one of its goals. Traditionally, it has also been required that the theorems, and, hence, the axioms, be true. To satisfy this goal, however, would seem to require treating the mathematical terms occurring in the axioms from the point of view of their intuitive meanings or contents. Such, at any rate, is the traditional view. The schematist moment of Hilbert's formalism challenges this view by maintaining that, ideally, a system of axioms should have a number of different (important) realizations and that these different realizations should be obtainable from one another by relatively simple schemes of interchange of the meanings of the non-logical terms in the axioms. What is most important, then, is for a system of axioms to have not one particular realization but a variety of different ones.

This interesting view is sometimes distorted and misrepresented by saying that Hilbert defined truth as consistency or that he advocated mere consistency rather than truth (as ordinarily defined) as the goal of mathematical theorizing. Hilbert sometimes said things that encourage such readings (1899b: 39–40, 1900: 448, 1905: 125, 1922: 157). However, more careful consideration of the ideas that influenced his views together with a balanced reading of the texts themselves (1922: 162–5, 1923: 179–80; Hilbert and Bernays 1934: §1) indicates that this was not his position.

This type of formalist view was suggested by a striking phenomenon of nineteenth-century geometry – the so-called 'dualities' that emerged in projective geometry. Generally speaking, a duality is a pair of theorems one of which can be obtained from the other by a simple and uniform scheme of substitution of geometric terms. Among the simpler examples are the following pairs of propositions:

(1)   For every two distinct points, there is exactly one line which is incident with both.

(1′) For every two distinct lines, there is exactly one point which is incident with both.

(2)   For every three points that are not incident with the same line, there is exactly one plane with which they are all incident.

(2′) For every three planes that are not incident with the same line, there is exactly one point with which they are all incident.

(1′) results from (1) by interchanging 'point' and 'line'. They illustrate a general principle – the principle of duality for the projective plane – that covers many more instances. Similarly, (2) and (2′) illustrate the principle of duality for projective space. (Statements (1′) and (2′) are not true for ordinary or 'metric' geometry, of course, but only for geometries in which the usual elements are augmented by various ideal elements such as points and lines at infinity.)

In addition to these simple and basic dualities, there are many others, some quite striking. They include a duality linking theorems of the Riemannian geometry of the plane to theorems of the Euclidean geometry of the sphere under interchange of the terms 'straight line' and 'great circle', and a duality linking theorems concerning lines in Euclidean three-dimensional geometry to theorems concerning points in Euclidean space of four dimensions under replacement of 'line' with 'point'.

Hilbert, however, was more taken with a duality that had been observed to exist between geometry – specifically, the axioms of linear congruence in Euclidean geometry – and a wholly non-geometric subject – namely, the laws governing proportions of trait-couplings in mutations of certain varieties of fruit flies (Hilbert 1922/1923: 84–6). This duality suggested to Hilbert the idea that certain non-logical 'forms' of thought might be so basic or useful to our thinking that they would belong to even its most widely disparate parts (intuitively speaking). He therefore described it as 'more wonderful' than anything imagined in even the 'boldest fantasy' (Hilbert 1930: 380). Others, too (see Weyl 1927: 26–7, 1944: 635), were moved by dualities between remote subject matters.

The importance of the dualities for understanding Hilbert's formalist view is twofold. First, they suggest that in an axiom system, the mathematical terms do not function as constants but rather as variables of some sort. This in turn suggests that axiom systems are not to be seen as designed to capture a single, favoured interpretation that we think of as 'the truth'. Rather, they are to be seen as structuring a number of

different subject matters. They are not designed to serve as theories of a particular subject matter but as 'theory-forms' – 'empty frames' (Pasch 1915: 11), 'logical moulds', 'hypothetico-deductive frameworks' (Weyl 1927: 25–6) – which provide a logical framework for the description of a variety of different subject matters (Hilbert 1899b: 40–1; see Detlefsen 1993 for more).

2   Axiomatization and the ideal method

The second respect in which the dualities of nineteenth-century projective geometry shed light on Hilbert's formalism is in their reliance upon the use of so-called 'ideal' or 'imaginary' elements. These are elements that (need) have no intuitional or perceptual basis and whose sole justification is the simplifying or generalizing effects they have on our thinking about a given subject. Their use is well-illustrated by the duality between (1) and (1′) above. This depends upon the use of 'points at infinity' to serve as the points of incidence of pairs of parallel lines. (Without such ideal points, the duality between (1) and (1′) would have to be reduced to one in which 'exactly' were replaced by 'at most'.)

Hilbert embraced the use of ideal elements in axiomatic theorizing. Indeed, he essentially identified the axiomatic method with the method of ideal elements (1926: 383). Specifically, he took the conditions for justified use of the ideal method to be the same as those for justified use of the axiomatic method; namely, that it be consistent with the underlying contentual practice to which it is applied and that it bring simplicity or efficiency to the production of mathematical knowledge (1926: 370, 372–3).

In Hilbert's view, then, the justification of an axiomatic system depends upon more than its mere consistency. It depends as well upon its promotion of 'epistemic efficiency', which is what use of the method of ideal elements has to offer. The geometric dualities illustrate this point well; for every contentual proof, they yield not one but two theorems – one directly provided by the contentual proof, the other by application of the substitution scheme of the duality. One thus, roughly speaking, obtains two theorems for the 'price' (that is, the genuine proof) of one. The second, 'free' theorem will, of course, imply not only real propositions but also ideal or imaginary propositions (for example, the intersections of parallel lines at infinity). Not everything that it covers thus constitutes a gain in real knowledge. Nevertheless, a great part of what it covers does, and it produces this with superior ease or efficiency.

Hilbert described the axiomatic or ideal method as the expression of an important intellectual freedom –

namely, the freedom to create and use imaginary elements. This freedom could be taken as far as one wanted to take it provided that it did not clash with an associated body of contentual practice and that it promoted simplicity or efficiency in the production of real knowledge (1900: 439–40, 1905: 135–6, 1926: 372, 379). Dedekind also spoke of the 'freedom' of the axiomatic method. However, he understood it in a sense importantly different from Hilbert's – namely, as a freedom that contrasts axiomatic thinking not with contentual thinking, but with genetic thinking. Dedekind observed that genetically constructed objects (for example, the finite cardinals constructed as set-theoretic objects) inevitably take on features (for example, the infinity of the individual cardinals thus constructed) that are not relevant to their mathematical functioning. In Dedekind's view, the axiomatic method provides an alternative by giving us the freedom simply to declare that a set of items has exactly the properties laid down for them in a given set of axioms. Items introduced in this way are 'free creation(s) of the human intellect' (1888: §73) which retain only the relevant features of their genetically constructed counterparts.

Axiomatic freedom according to Hilbert, on the other hand, was the freedom to introduce admittedly non-real, imaginary entities into our thinking when doing so increases efficiency (over against purely contentual reasoning) in the production of contentual knowledge (1926: 370–73, 379, 392). He thus assigned ideal elements a role similar to that which Kant assigned the so-called 'ideas of reason' in his critical philosophy. Kant saw ideas of reason as non-descriptive, regulative, conservative devices for the efficient development of the judgments of the understanding (*Critique of Pure Reason*, B85–6, 362, 385, 536–7, 825–7). We are free to use them so long as we do not confuse them with objective, descriptive laws applying to an external reality (which confusion leads to inconsistency). Hilbert saw ideal elements as a psychologically efficient (perhaps even indispensable) means of developing our real or contentual knowledge: we are free to use them so long as doing so does not lead to inconsistencies with contentual thinking (1905: 135–6; 1926: 383, 392; 1928: 471).

3 The formalism of the arithmetical period

This basic conception of the ideal or axiomatic method was a key ingredient of Hilbert's thinking in both the foundations of geometry and the foundations of arithmetic.

Hilbert's work in the foundations of arithmetic – his so-called 'programme' – was, indeed, nothing other than a defence of a particular application of the ideal method. What distinguished it from his work in the foundations of geometry was that the ideal elements used had a peculiarly 'logical' character, and that the consistency demand for use of these ideal elements could not be satisfied by reducing it to that of some more basic application of the ideal method.

The ideal elements that Hilbert proposed to defend in arithmetic were not imaginary mathematical items (for example, points at infinity, ideal numbers and the like) but imaginary *logical* items – what he referred to as 'ideal propositions'. These are not genuine propositions. They have neither meaning nor truth-value in the ('absolute') sense in which contentual propositions do. They are, rather, imaginary constructions (*Ideenbildungen*) that function only as symbolic or 'algebraic' devices for securing a desirable logic – namely, classical logic – for arithmetical reasoning. (See Hilbert 1922: 164–5; 1923: 179–80; 1926: 379–81; 1928: 467, 469–71; Hilbert and Bernays 1934: §1; see Hallett 1990 for a different interpretation.)

Examples that Hilbert gave of ideal propositions included, on the one hand, denials of true contentual generalizations (for example, '$\neg\forall x(x+1=1+x)$'), and, on the other, unbounded existential generalizations (for example, '$\exists x(\mathrm{Prime}(x)\,\&\,x>p)$', where p is some selected natural number) which follow classically from bounded, contentual existential generalizations (for example, '$\exists x(\mathrm{Prime}(x)\,\&\,x>p\,\&\,x<p!)$'). The former are 'ideal' because they do not bound the search for a counter-example to the generalization denied; the latter because they do not bound the search for a witness of the type they assert to exist. However, both help to preserve classical logic as the logic of arithmetical thinking; the first by protecting the law of the excluded middle for true contentual generalizations, the second by protecting the classically valid inference-form from '$\exists x(\phi x\,\&\,\psi x)$' to '$\exists x(\phi x)$', where the former is a contentual truth.

Hilbert's claim is neither that there is no logic of finitary or contentual reasoning nor that, though there is, we cannot know it. Rather, it is that even if such a logic were to be given, we would not want and, perhaps, psychologically speaking, would not be able to use it. For even if given, it would diverge from that logic according to which we most naturally and efficiently reason towards truth in contentual arithmetic (1926: 379–80, 1928: 470–2).

Hilbert thus introduced ideal propositions as purely formal or algebraic instruments for preserving (on a formal level) the desirable patterns of classical logical inference. But this purely formal conception of the ideal propositions induced a similarly formal character for arithmetic as a whole (1926: 376–83, 1928: 467–70; Hilbert and Bernays 1934: §1) – the

425

logical terms as well as the arithmetical terms. The logical terms occur in purely formal devices (namely, ideal propositions) and must therefore themselves be treated from a purely formal point of view. Hilbert's formal conception of ideal propositions thus drove his formalization of arithmetic beyond where his formalization of geometry had gone – namely, to the inclusion of logical as well as non-logical terms (see Detlefsen 1993).

4 The consistency of arithmetic

As we will now see, this radical formalization of ideal arithmetic is what motivated Hilbert's belief in the possibility of a direct or finitary proof of its consistency.

Reasoning from the radical formalization of ideal arithmetic, Hilbert offered a purely syntactic formulation of its consistency problem; namely, to show the non-existence of a formal proof whose endformula is '$0 \neq 0$', or some similarly contentually refutable formula. In like spirit, he believed that there ought to be a purely finitary, contentual resolution of this problem. The problem is to search for a certain type of 'formal object'. The negative resolution of such a problem would, it would seem, lie as much within the province of finitary reasoning as, say, the task of proving the nonexistence of two numerals a and b satisfying the equation '$a^2 = 2b^2$', a task which is finitarily manageable (1926: 383, 1928: 471).

Hilbert therefore undertook to give such a proof. It would, he believed, fill the final gap in the foundational enterprise by founding elementary ideal arithmetic. It would do so because it would be founded upon the 'absolute' truths of finitary judgment – judgments which neither need nor admit of any more basic justification (1926: 376–7, 1922: 163; Hilbert and Bernays 1934: 20–1), and because the consistency of the other theories of ideal mathematics (most particularly those in analysis and geometry) can be reduced to that of ideal arithmetic (together with some basic set-theoretic apparatus).

This 'programme' of Hilbert's came under heavy attack in 1930–1 with the discovery of Gödel's incompleteness theorems. The second of these (G2), in particular, was important in this connection (see GÖDEL'S THEOREMS §6; PROOF THEORY §2). It showed, for any formal axiomatic system T containing a fragment of arithmetic, how to construct a sentence Con_T of the language of T which seemingly 'expresses' the claim that T is consistent. It then went on to show that Con_T cannot be proved in T so long as T is consistent. If, therefore, T is rich enough to express all finitary proofs, it would follow that Con_T cannot be proved finitarily. From this it has generally been inferred that a finitary consistency proof is not possible for virtually any interesting portion of classical mathematics. Hilbert's programme therefore fails.

Whether such reasoning is correct depends, of course, upon whether Con_T really does 'express' the consistency of T in the appropriate sense. This, therefore, is one issue that must be resolved before the argument against Hilbert's programme from G2 can be conclusively evaluated. However, even if it is granted that Con_T does express the consistency of T, a further serious question arises: namely, whether the properties of Con_T that make for its unprovability in T (for example, the so-called derivability conditions of Hilbert–Bernays–Löb, or the RE condition of Feferman – see GÖDEL'S THEOREMS §5) are also properties that are indispensable to its ability to 'express' the consistency of T. Only if they are can the unprovability in T of Con_T be taken as showing the finitary unprovability of T's consistency.

This deep and difficult problem has received little attention in the literature on Gödel's theorems and Hilbert's programme. But there are exceptions – see Detlefsen (1986: ch. 4) for a critical discussion of them. Detlefsen (1986, 1990) discusses what an adequate solution to the problem would look like and establishes the main features of two different types of negative solutions to it. Auerbach (1992) continues this discussion. In the end, the problem leads to fundamental questions concerning the nature of formal systems and to the perhaps even more fundamental question of what should be regarded as the basic unit of epistemic commitment in mathematics (see Detlefsen 1990 for further discussion).

Gödel's first incompleteness theorem (G1) has also been used against Hilbert's programme (see Kreisel 1976; Smorynski 1977, 1985, 1988; Prawitz 1981; Simpson 1988). The usual argument here begins with the basic premise that ideal arithmetic should be required to be a conservative extension of finitary or real arithmetic. G1 is then used to argue that this requirement cannot be met. The reasoning proceeds as follows: G_T (the undecidable sentence for a given ideal system of arithmetic T) can be proved by ideal but not by finitary methods; the ideal system in which G_T is provable is therefore not a conservative extension of finitary arithmetic; hence, by the basic premise of the argument, Hilbert's programme cannot be carried out. Detlefsen (1990) critically examines this argument, questioning, in particular, whether Hilbert's programme is rightly seen as requiring that ideal arithmetic be a conservative extension of real arithmetic. See also Webb (1980) for an argument that G1 actually confirms a formalist position like Hilbert's.

The Gödelian challenge to Hilbert's programme has also called forth other types of responses (see PROOF THEORY §§3–4) – responses that concede the legitimacy of the arguments from G1 and G2, but which maintain that Hilbert's programme can none the less survive in a suitably modified form. For the most part, these arguments have taken one of two basic forms. In the first, the key element is weakening the evidential standards for consistency proofs to something less restrictive than Hilbert's original finitary demand. Some in this group (for example, Gentzen, Ackermann and Gödel) have argued that there are types of evidence having the same basic epistemic virtues as finitary evidence that extend well beyond the (traditionally identified) boundaries of finitary reasoning. Others (see Kreisel 1958; Feferman 1988; Sieg 1988) have argued not so much for a reconsideration of what should count as admissible evidence in a consistency proof as for a liberalization of our concept of what a consistency proof should do. They argue that the basic obligation of a consistency proof is to bring about some epistemic gain, and that there are epistemically gainful means of proving the consistency of ideal arithmetic that are not finitary. They therefore urge the replacement of the finitary/non-finitary distinction by a more refined hierarchical scheme that distinguishes grades of constructivity. Doing so, they believe, allows a significant partial realization of Hilbert's programme (see PROOF THEORY §§2–4).

The other main type of response to Gödel's challenge is that represented by the so-called 'reverse mathematics' school of Friedman, Simpson and others. Instead of arguing for an extension of the types of reasoning to be allowed in consistency proofs, it aims at reducing the strength of the systems of ideal reasoning whose consistency needs proving. It begins by identifying more exactly those parts of traditional ideal mathematics that are truly indispensable to the distinctive achievements of classical mathematics. It then seeks axiomatizations that are 'equivalent to' these core parts and that therefore eliminate the extraneous elements of the usual axiomatizations. The idea is that the consistency of these diminished bodies of ideal reasoning might be susceptible to proof of a type to which that of their stronger standard counterparts is not. So far, significant success has been achieved along these lines (see Simpson 1988; PROOF THEORY §4).

See also: ARITHMETIC, PHILOSOPHICAL ISSUES IN; CONSTRUCTIVISM IN MATHEMATICS; GEOMETRY, PHILOSOPHICAL ISSUES IN; INTUITIONISM; KRONECKER, L.; LOGICAL AND MATHEMATICAL TERMS, GLOSSARY OF; MATHEMATICS, FOUNDATIONS OF

References and further reading

* Auerbach, D. (1992) 'How to Say Things with Formalisms', in M. Detlefsen (ed.) *Proof, Logic and Formalization*, London: Routledge. (Detailed defence of the view that G2 refutes Hilbert's programme.)
* Dedekind, R. (1888) *Was sind und was sollen die Zahlen?*, Braunschweig: Vieweg; trans. W.W. Beman (1901), 'The Nature and Meaning of Numbers', in *Essays on the Theory of Numbers*, New York: Dover, 1963. (§73 includes an interesting statement of Dedekind's philosophical conception of the axiomatic method and its relationship to the older, genetic method.)
* Detlefsen, M. (1986) *Hilbert's Program: An Essay on Mathematical Instrumentalism*, Boston, MA, and Dordrecht: Reidel. (Detailed examination of the arguments from Gödel's incompleteness theorems against Hilbert's programme. Focuses primarily on the arguments from G2 and the question of what is required of formulas that are to express consistency.)
* —— (1990) 'On an Alleged Refutation of Hilbert's Program using Gödel's First Incompleteness Theorem', *Journal of Philosophical Logic* 19: 343–77. (Critical appraisal of the arguments against Hilbert's programme from G1.)
* —— (1993) 'Hilbert's Formalism', *Revue internationale de philosophie* 47: 285–304. (Attempt to clarify Hilbert's 'formalist' conception of mathematics and its relation to Kant's views.)
* Feferman, S. (1988) 'Hilbert's Program Relativized: Proof-Theoretical and Foundational Reductions', *Journal of Symbolic Logic* 53: 364–84. (Useful introduction to the author's conception of a workable and interesting modification of Hilbert's original programme.)
* Hallett, M. (1990) 'Physicalism, Reductionism and Hilbert', in A. Irvine (ed.) *Physicalism in Mathematics*, Dordrecht: Kluwer. (Argues for a non-instrumentalist reading of Hilbert.)
* Hilbert, D. (1899a) *Grundlagen der Geometrie*, Leipzig: Teubner, 7th edn, 1930; 2nd edn trans. L. Unger and P. Bernays, *Foundations of Geometry*, La Salle, IL: Open Court, 1971. (Influential treatment of geometry from the widely held formalist perspective of the late nineteenth century.)
* —— (1899b) letters to Frege of 12 and 29 December 1899, trans. H. Kaal, in G. Gabriel *et al.* (eds) *Gottlob Frege: Philosophical and Mathematical Correspondence*, Chicago, IL: University of Chicago Press, 1980. (Basic statement of Hilbert's formalist view of theories as logical frameworks of concepts/relations.)

* —— (1900) 'Mathematische Probleme. Vortrag, gehalten auf dem internationalen Mathematiker-Kongreß zu Paris 1900', *Nachrichten von der königlichen Gesellschaft der Wissenschaften zu Göttingen, mathematisch-physikalische Klasse* 253–97; trans. 'Mathematical Problems', *Bulletin of the American Mathematical Society* 8: 437–79, 1902. (Includes a number of interesting remarks concerning the nature of mathematical truth and the axiomatic method.)

* —— (1905) 'Über die Grundlagen der Logik und der Arithmetik', in A. Krazer (ed.) *Verhandlungen des dritten internationalen Mathematiker-Kongreßes in Heidelberg vom 8. bis 13. August 1904*, Leipzig: Teubner, 174–85; trans. 'On the Foundations of Logic and Arithmetic', in J. van Heijenoort (ed.) *From Frege to Gödel: A Source Book in Mathematical Logic, 1879–1931*, Cambridge, MA: Harvard University Press, 1967, 130–8. (Early statement of Hilbert's developing views on the foundations of arithmetic. Perhaps most important for its statement of the 'creative principle' (135–6), which provides an important insight into his conception of the axiomatic method.)

* —— (1922) 'Neubegründung der Mathematik. Erste Mitteilung' (New Foundations for Mathematics: Part 1), *Abhandlungen aus dem mathematischen Seminar der Hamburgischen Universität* 1: 157–77; repr. in *Gesammelte Abhandlungen*, vol. 3, Berlin: Springer, 1935. (Perhaps the clearest technical statement of Hilbert's programme for the foundations of arithmetic prior to the statement in Hilbert and Bernays (1934).)

* —— (1922/1923) 'Wissen und mathematisches Denken. Vorlesungen 1922/23' (Knowledge and Mathematical Thinking), lecture notes taken by W. Ackermann; repr. Göttingen: Mathematisches Institut, 1988. (Largely philosophical discussion of Hilbert's foundational ideas.)

* —— (1923) 'Die logischen Grundlagen der Mathematik' (The Logical Foundations of Mathematics), *Mathematische Annalen* 88: 151–65. (Includes Hilbert's distinction between the kind of truth – 'absolute truth' – that characterizes contentual thinking and the 'truth' that pertains to axiomatic or ideal thinking.)

* —— (1926) 'Über das Unendliche', *Mathematische Annalen* 95: 161–90; trans. 'On the Infinite', in J. van Heijenoort (ed.) *From Frege to Gödel: A Source Book in Mathematical Logic 1879–1931*, Cambridge, MA: Harvard University Press, 1967. (Perhaps the fullest and philosophically most revealing of Hilbert's writings on the foundations of arithmetic. Points out certain connections

between Hilbert's and Kant's philosophies of mathematics.)

* —— (1928) 'Die Grundlagen der Mathematik', *Abhandlungen aus dem mathematischen Seminar der Hamburgischen Universität* 6: 65–85; trans. 'The Foundations of Mathematics', in J. van Heijenoort (ed.) *From Frege to Gödel: A Source Book in Mathematical Logic, 1879–1931*, Cambridge, MA: Harvard University Press, 1967. (Mature statement of Hilbert's views regarding the foundations of arithmetic. Includes an important philosophical characterization of the central philosophical motive of his proof theory (page 475).)

* —— (1930) 'Naturerkennen und Logik' (Logic and the Knowledge of Nature), *Die Naturwissenschaften* 18: 959–63; repr. in *Gesammelte Abhandlungen*, vol. 3, Berlin: Springer, 1935. (Philosophically revealing statement of Hilbert's mature thinking on the foundations of arithmetic. Points out respects in which Hilbert's philosophical thinking represents a modification of Kant's.)

* Hilbert, D. and Bernays, P. (1934) *Grundlagen der Mathematik* (Foundations of Mathematics), vol. 1, Berlin: Springer, 2nd edn, 1968. (Classic work of mathematical logic; includes valuable statements of Hilbert's conception of the axiomatic method and finitary reasoning.)

* Kreisel, G. (1958) 'Hilbert's Programme', *Dialectica* 12: 346–72; revised version in P. Benacerraf and H. Putnam (eds) *Philosophy of Mathematics: Selected Readings*, Cambridge: Cambridge University Press, 2nd edn, 1983. (Reflections of a leading contemporary foundational thinker on Hilbert's programme. Interesting postscript added in 1978.)

* —— (1976) 'What Have we Learnt from Hilbert's Second Problem?', in *Proceedings of Symposia in Pure Mathematics*, vol. 28, Providence, RI: American Mathematical Society. (Discussion of what recent developments in mathematical logic (especially proof theory) have to teach us about Hilbert's programme.)

* Lambert, J.H. (1766) 'Theorie der Parallellinien' (Theory of Parallel Lines), *Magazin für reine und angewandte Mathematik* 2: 137–64, 3: 325–58, 1786; repr. in P. Stäckel and F. Engel (eds) *Theorie der Parallellinien von Euclid bis auf Gauss*, Leipzig: Teubner, 1895.

* Pasch, M. (1882) *Vorlesungen über neuere Geometrie* (Lectures on Modern Geometry), Leipzig: Teubner; 2nd edn Berlin: Springer, 1926. (Influential modern statement of the view that rigour requires that the inferences in a proof be formalized.)

* —— (1915) *Mathematik und Logik*, Leipzig: Engelmann, 2nd edn, 1924. (Further statements of

Pasch's views regarding the formalization of inference in mathematical proof.)

* Prawitz, D. (1981) 'Philosophical Aspects of Proof Theory', in G. Fløistad (ed.) *Contemporary Philosophy: A New Survey*, vol. 1, The Hague: Martinus Nijhoff. (Useful discussion of the bearing of Gödel's theorems on Hilbert's programme.)

* Sieg, W. (1988) 'Hilbert's Program Sixty Years Later', *Journal of Symbolic Logic* 53: 338–48. (Discussion of the progress and changes in Hilbert's programme since its formulation in the 1920s.)

* Simpson, S. (1988) 'Partial Realization of Hilbert's Program', *Journal of Symbolic Logic* 53: 349–63. (Survey of the progress made towards realizing the aims of Hilbert's programme via the approach of 'reverse' mathematics.)

* Smorynski, C. (1977) 'The Incompleteness Theorems', in J. Barwise (ed.) *Handbook of Mathematical Logic*, Amsterdam: North Holland. (Survey of some of the technical material pertaining to Gödel's theorems.)

* —— (1985) *Self-Reference and Modal Logic*, New York: Springer. (Includes a clear statement of an argument that G1 destroys Hilbert's programme.)

* —— (1988) 'Hilbert's Programme', *Centrum voor Wiskunde en Informatica Quarterly* 1 (4): 3–59. (Fullest presentation of Smorynski's argument that G1 refutes Hilbert's programme.)

* Webb, J. (1980) *Mechanism, Mentalism, and Metamathematics: An Essay on Finitism*, Boston, MA: Reidel. (Insightful discussion of various of Hilbert's philosophical ideas and the bearing of Gödel's theorems upon them.)

* Weyl, H. (1927) 'Philosophie der Mathematik und Naturwissenschaft', in *Handbuch der Philosophie*, Munich: Oldenbourg; revised and expanded trans. *Philosophy of Mathematics and Natural Science*, Princeton, NJ: Princeton University Press, 1949. (Excellent introduction to foundational concerns in mathematics and the natural sciences by one of the most profound thinkers of the twentieth century.)

* —— (1944) 'David Hilbert and his Mathematical Work', *Bulletin of the American Mathematical Society* 50: 612–54. (Survey of Hilbert's work including comments on his foundational ideas.)

MICHAEL DETLEFSEN

HILDEGARD OF BINGEN (1098–1179)

Hildegard of Bingen saw herself as a prophet sent by God to awaken an age in which great troubles were besieging the Church and people no longer understood Scripture. She tried to alleviate the first problem by writing letters to secular and religious leaders and preaching against those she saw as the culprits, and to this end she undertook preaching tours throughout Germany, preaching in cathedrals, monasteries and synods. Her writings, primarily interpretations of her own visions, address the second problem by trying to cast a new light on Christian revelation through illustrating it with original vivid imagery and personifications of abstract concepts. Though her works are not, for the most part, clearly philosophical, Hildegard does show philosophical insight.

Hildegard of Bingen was born to a noble family in Bermersheim in Germany. At the age of eight, she entered a hermitage which soon became a full Benedictine convent (whose abbess she became in 1136). She seems to have had more than the average education given to a noble-born Benedictine nun; she received regular instruction in Latin from the vulgate Bible from the abbess, and was further taught by one of the monks. Nevertheless, Hildegard repeatedly describes herself as ignorant and unschooled. Perhaps she says this to give legitimacy to her own writings: if she was unschooled, then whence could her elaborate texts and interpretations of Scripture come, if not directly from God?

Her claim of divine origin for most of her writings was supported by Bernard of Clairvaux and Pope Eugenius III in 1146–7. Their support launched her public career as a prophetess, and her influence and reputation grew steadily throughout Germany and all of Europe. As a woman receiving visions from God, she advised, admonished and criticized political and religious leaders, and undertook at least three preaching tours through Germany (1160–3). This growing influence enabled her to found her own convent at Mount St Rupert, near Bingen, where she died in 1179.

Hildegard's three major works, *Scivias* (Know the Ways) (1141–51), *Liber vitae meritorum* (Book of the Rewards of Life) (1158–63) and *Liber divinorum operum* (Book of Divine Works) (1163–73) all consist of extremely detailed accounts of her visions followed by allegorical commentaries on them, as well as commentaries on relevant passages of Scripture. *Scivias* and the *Liber divinorum operum* are organized in the same general way: they follow the history of salvation from the creation of the universe and human beings, the fall of the devil, the devil's temptation of Adam and Eve, the fall from Eden, redemption first through the law, the prophets and the synagogue, and then through Christ, the church and the sacraments to the end of times. Although Hildegard organizes her visions around the chronology of the history of salvation, within her interpretation of any single vision her method is to explain every detail of the vision in the order in which it was first described, without regard for thematic organization. The *Liber vitae meritorum* is an examination of thirty-five vices contrasted with their corresponding virtues, stemming from visions of various monsters personifying the different vices. Hildegard also wrote scientific and medical texts, lives of saints, and the music and text for a number of liturgical songs collected under the title *Symphonia*. She believed that all music (vocal and instrumental) brings the human soul back to the original praise Adam raised to God in Eden and which was lost in the Fall.

Hildegard's work is best characterized as theology of an unphilosophical sort. She does not explain Christian doctrine discursively, but rather illustrates it with images and comparisons which she only very rarely explains. For instance, when she discusses virtues and vices she does not explain what they are, nor does she provide the defining characteristics of individual virtues or vices (see VIRTUES AND VICES). She also seems oblivious to contradictions; throughout her work, for example, she hesitates between the view that the human body is essentially and incurably evil and the soul necessarily good (forced to sin unwillingly by the body), and the view that the body can be made good (as the tabernacle of the soul) and the soul evil (responsible for sin). Hildegard sometimes does make philosophical distinctions (for example, between different faculties of the human soul: the intellect, the will, reason, passions), and sometimes too she asks distinctly philosophical questions. For instance, in *Scivias* she considers the problem that divine foreknowledge poses for human freedom, but her reply is a heated denunciation of the prideful who suspect God of injustice. However, in her answers to two letters inquiring about fine points of theology, Hildegard gives philosophical characterizations of eternity as timeless existence and of simplicity as indivisibility, and she distinguishes between God's simple eternal nature, and a human being's understanding of God, which is composite and temporal (see ETERNITY; SIMPLICITY, DIVINE).

It often seems that Hildegard is fettered by her method of 'vision-commentaries', which leads to difficult and disorganized texts, contradictions and a general lack of clarity in her thought. It was her visions, however, which gave her an authority uncommon to medieval women, and without the visions as legitimizers of her thought, she may not have been able to write as freely and originally as she did. Paradoxically, Hildegard often claimed divine authority for her visions from the fact that she was a 'weak little woman', and that God chooses those who have the appearance of weakness as his prophets, in an age in which those who have the appearance of strength are corrupted. Thus her gender also helped her to establish her claim of divine inspiration.

See also: MYSTICISM, HISTORY OF; NATURAL PHILOSOPHY, MEDIEVAL §4; SOUL, NATURE AND IMMORTALITY OF

List of works

Hildegard of Bingen (1098–1179) *Opera omnia*, ed. J.-P. Migne, *Sanctae Hildegardis Abbatissae Opera Omnia*, Patrologia Cursus Completus Series Latina, vol. 197, Paris, 1855; repr. Turnhout: Brepols, 1976.

—— (1141–51) *Scivias* (Know the Ways), ed. A. Führkötter and A. Carlevaris, *Hildegardis Scivias*, Corpus Christianorum: continuatio mediaevalis 43 and 43a, Turnhout: Brepols, 1978; trans. Mother Columbia Hart and J. Bishop, *Scivias*, New York: Paulist Press, 1990. (Barbara Newman's introduction to this volume is an excellent introduction to important themes in Hildegard's thought, and more especially to the *Scivias*.)

—— (1158–63) *Liber vitae meritorum* (Book of the Rewards of Life), ed. A. Carlevaris, *Liber vitae meritorum*, Corpus Christianorum, Continuatio Medievalis 90, Turnhout: Brepols, 1995; trans. B. Hozeski, *The Book of the Rewards of Life*, New York: Garland, 1994. (Although Hildegard's descriptions of each vice and its corresponding virtue do not include philosophical definitions, they include insightful diagnoses of the psychological conditions that lead to behaviour characteristic of the vices, and of the ways in which someone might justify such behaviour to oneself or to others.)

—— (1163–73) *Liber divinorum operum* (Book of Divine Works), ed A. Derolez and P. Dronke, *Liber divinorum operum*, Corpus Christianorum, Continuatio Mediaevalis 92, Turnhout: Brepols, 1996; trans. (abridged) R. Cunningham, ed. M. Fox, *Book of Divine Works with Letters and Songs*, Santa Fe, NM: Bear & Company, 1987. (Throughout this work, Hildegard hesitates between a dualist view of sin (that is, it is the nature of the soul to be good while it is the nature of the body to be corrupt) and the more orthodox position which she holds, for example in the *Ordo virtutum*, that the soul is responsible both for good and evil. She also hesitates between a fideist view of human reason's ability to understand God, and a more rationalist account according to which God gave human beings reason in part so that they can come to understand him.)

—— (1098–1179) Letters, ed. L. Van Acker, *Hildegardis Bingensis Epistolarium*, Pars Prima, Corpus Christianorum, Continuatio Mediaevalis 91, Turnhout: Brepols, 1991; Pars Secunda, Corpus Christianorum, Continuatio Mediaevalis 91A, Turnhout: Brepols, 1993; trans. J. Baird and R. Ehrman, *The Letters of Hildegard of Bingen*, vol. 1, New York: Oxford University Press, 1994. (Some of the letters have clearer philosophical significance than do Hildegard's major works, as she is often asked to answer distinctly philosophical questions as well as pastoral and liturgical ones.)

References and further reading

Dronke, P. (1984) *Women Writers of the Middle Ages*, Cambridge: Cambridge University Press. (A study of Hildegard's understanding of herself in the context of the twelfth century, drawn from a somewhat eclectic selection of materials including biographical fragments, writings in the natural sciences and letters.)

Gössmann, E. (1989) 'Hildegard of Bingen', in M.E. Waithe (ed.) *A History of Women Philosophers*, vol. 2, Dordrecht: Kluwer. (A study of Hildegard as a philosopher and a theologian, with special attention to her views on the place of women.)

Gottfried of St Disibod and Dieter of Echternach (1177–81) *Vita Sanctae Hildegardis*, ed. M. Klaes, Corpus Christianorum, Continuatio Medievalis 126, Turnhout: Brepols, 1993; trans. J. McGrath, ed. M. Palmquist, *The Life of the Holy Hildegard*, Collegeville, MN: Liturgical Press, 1995. (A translation of the earliest life of Hildegard, which contains some important autobiographical fragments. The translation is from A. Führkötter's German, not the Latin text.)

Newman, B. (1987) *Sister of Wisdom, St. Hildegard's Theology of the Feminine*, Berkeley, CA: University of California Press. (A comprehensive study of feminine themes in Hildegard's work, from her scientific view of women's physiology and sexuality to the identification of some aspects of God as feminine, ranging through traditional themes such as Eve's special role in the Fall of Adam and Mary's role in the redemption of humankind. There are many insightful observations, but the arguments are sometimes unclear, and many of the conclusions are unsupported.)

CLAUDIA EISEN MURPHY

HILLEL BEN SAMUEL OF VERONA (*c.*1220–95)

Hillel played a crucial role in the response of the philosophers in the Jewish community to the attacks made upon them by their enemies. He stoutly defended Maimonides while at the same time opposing the allegorical interpretation of miracles. Far less radical than Maimonides or Averroes, he tended to follow the approach of Aquinas. He also translated many philosophical texts from Latin into Hebrew. He was influenced by scholastic ideas and especially by the anti-Averroistic controversy. His major work, Tagmule ha-Nefesh *(The Rewards of the Soul), completed in Forlì in 1291, deals with the nature of the soul and the intellect and with the spiritual requital of the soul after death. The chief purpose of this work is 'to explain the existence of the soul, its essence and its rational faculty, which continues to exist externally after death'.*

1 Life and works
2 *Tagmule ha-Nefesh*

1 Life and works

Hillel was a physician, translator, philosopher and Talmudic scholar. He studied medicine at the University of Montpellier and lived for three years (1259–62) in Barcelona. There he would have studied natural sciences. He would have been a pupil of the famous Talmudist Jonah Gerondi, an anti-Maimonidean thinker. Hillel also spent time in Rome, where he became acquainted with Zerahiah ben Isaac Gracian of Barcelona and Isaac ben Mordekhai (Maestro Gaio). He is known to have been in Naples and then in Capua (until after 1270), where he practised medicine and studied philosophy with Abraham Abulafia. After 1287 he retreated to Forlì, occasionally visiting Bologna and Ferrara. Between 1287 and 1289 he defended Maimonides. He sent two letters to that purpose to Maestro Gaio, at that time physician of Pope Nicholas IV. The occasion was the arrival at Ferrara of Solomon ben Abraham of Montpellier (Solomon Petit), the chief instigator of the anti-Maimonidean movement and teacher of Jonah Gerondi. Hillel requested that Maestro Gaio use his influence over the Jewish community of Rome to organize a synod at Alexandria, to which the Jewish communities of Germany and France would be asked to send representatives to discuss whether the reading of Maimonides' works should or should not be permitted. The final decision would be entrusted to a court of Babylonian rabbis.

Between 1289 and 1291 a controversy occurred

between Hillel and Zerahiah ben Isaac Gracian over the rationalistic interpretation of the Bible. Hillel supported the historical reality of the supernatural events described in Scripture, such as the encounter between Jacob and the angel and the speech of Balaam's ass, whereas Zerahiah, stressing the twofold sense of the Bible – literal for the masses and allegorical-philosophical for the learned – stated that the miracles had taken place in prophetic visions and hid a philosophical meaning.

2 *Tagmule ha-Nefesh*

Hillel's major work, *Tagmule ha-Nefesh* (The Rewards of the Soul), is divided into two parts, preceded by an introduction. The first part, divided into seven sections, deals with the nature of the soul and the intellect; the second, divided into three sections, addresses the question of the reward and punishment of the soul after death, addressing and relying for support on quotations from the Bible, the Talmud and midrash. In the introduction, based on the beginning of Aristotle's *De Anima* (On the Soul), Hillel states that he wishes to write a concise treatise on the soul, because it is 'the most beautiful possession that mankind has' and its happiness constitutes the ultimate purpose of man. By means of a compilation of writings by philosophers, Hillel intends to discuss the existence, nature and recompense of the soul, since it is the soul that defines the human being. He further aims to establish that retribution after death is not corporeal. According to Hillel, a literal interpretation of the Bible and the Talmud can lead to the erroneous conclusion that the retribution of the soul is corporeal, that the soul is a body and that the angels and God, the prime source of emanation, are also bodies.

In the first part (sections I–II) Hillel draws on Avicenna's *al-Nafs* (The Soul) and Dominicus Gundisalvi's *De Anima* (On the Soul). He then presents *Sheloshah Ma'amarim 'al ha-Sekhel* (Three Articles on the Intellect), his own Hebrew translation of *Tractatus de Animae Beatitudine* (On the Beatitude of the Soul), attributed to Averroes. Hillel holds that the soul exists (I) and is not an accident but rather an incorporeal substance. The soul is the substantial form of the human being. Its relation to the body is like that of form to matter. Its 'descent' into union with the body and its 'ascent', in separating from the body are not motions (II). The soul is immutable; furthermore, when united with the body, it is not subject to motion. It is indivisible and is a form between the specific and material forms, united through divine grace to the matter of the human body in order to perfect it (III). The soul emanates

from God through the mediation of the separate Intelligences. It represents the fourth stage in the emanatory process, directly after the 'active intellect'. The latter, one of the ten separate Intelligences, illuminates the rational soul during the cognitive process and is the cause of the passing of the mind from potentiality to actuality (IV). Hillel follows Averroes in asserting that there is only one eternal universal soul, one in substance and number, from which emanate the souls of individuals, like the rays from the sun; the plurality is accidental, a result of the number of subjects that receive it (V) (see IBN RUSHD; NEOPLATONISM).

The anti-Averroistic controversy, which inflamed the University of Paris in 1270 and 1277, exerted an important influence on *Tagmule ha-Nefesh*, in which special attention is paid to the Averroistic thesis of the oneness of the potential intellect for the whole of mankind (VI) (see AVERROISM). In order to refute this thesis, the adoption of which would lead to a doctrine of collective immortality, Hillel adapts a denial of faith, he adapts the first chapter of Aquinas' *De Unitate Intellectus contra Averroistas* (Article on the Unity of the Intellect against the Averroists) (VII): the soul is the form of the body, as the intellect is the form of the soul. From this Hillel infers that the rational part of every individual soul persists eternally after it leaves the body. Hillel states that he has not described the soul's faculties, except for the rational one, because 'the treatment of the other, corporeal faculties, such as the nutritive, the augmentative and the generative' is the object of medical science.

In the second part, Hillel states that the soul's reward or punishment after parting from the body is spiritual. The soul derives from a spiritual source to which it returns. Being incorporeal, the soul, cannot be subject to a corporeal reward or punishment (I). God granted humanity the possibility of attaining eternal happiness by means of the three intellects. Hillel describes them in detail, in particular the acquired intellect, which gives the intelligibles to the soul and is intermediary between the potential intellect and the active intellect. The latter watches over the human being in order that he may attain happiness. The quantity of the influence of the active intellect, exerted upon the rational and imaginative powers of the soul, varies with the nature of the individual. In addition to his imaginative and rational faculties, man must also correctly guide his sensitive and appetitive faculties, because on them depend the virtues and vices and the observation and violation of the divine precepts. The individual who has perfected the intellectual and ethical virtues can reach during his life the level of the active intellect and thereby acquire the ability to change the natural course of events by performing miracles. Such a soul, after the separation from the body, reaches a greater perfection than it had before the union. It is able to enjoy the happiness conferred by knowledge. The soul that has sinned, however, descends to a lower level. Through the imaginative power, which, like the intellective power, is immortal, such a soul will then imagine its punishments, and through the intellective power it will rationally know that it will not be able to enjoy spiritual happiness, because of its separation from the divine intellectual light, in accordance with the Avicennian tradition. In closing, Hillel hermeneutically divides the tales of the Rabbis into six classes and states that those passages which refer to corporeal retribution should not be interpreted literally.

See also: AVERROISM, JEWISH; MAIMONIDES, M.; SOUL, NATURE AND IMMORTALITY OF THE

List of works

Hillel ben Samuel of Verona (1291) *Tagmule ha-Nefesh* (*The Rewards of the Soul*), ed. J. Sermoneta, *Sefer Tagmulei ha-Nefesh le-Hillel ben Shmu'el mi-Verona*, Jerusalem: The Israel Academy of Sciences and Humanities, 1981. (His main philosophical work, which deals with the nature of the soul and the intellect, and with the spiritual requital of the soul after death.)

References and further reading

Davidson, H.A. (1988) 'Averrois Tractatus de Animae Beatitudine', in R. Link-Salinger (ed.) *A Straight Path: Studies on Medieval Philosophy and Culture. Essays in Honor of Arthur Hyman*, Washington, DC: The Catholic University of America Press, 57–73. (A study of the treatise *On the Beatitude of the Soul* attributed to Averroes.)

Elbogen, J. (1935–7) 'Hillel da Verona e la lotta per Mosè Maimonide', *Annuario di studi ebraici* 2: 99–105. (Hillel on the Maimonidean controversy.)

Sermoneta, G. (1962) *Hillel ben Shemuel of Verona and his Philosophical Doctrine*, Ph.D. dissertation, The Hebrew University of Jerusalem. (A monograph on Hillel's philosophy.)

—— (1974) 'Mappelet ha-Mal'akhim' (The Fall of the Angels), in S. Pines (ed.) *Studies in Memory of Jacob Friedman*, Jerusalem: The Hebrew University of Jerusalem, 155–203. (A study of Hillel's treatise on the fall of the angels.)

* Ibn Rushd (1169–98) *Tractatus de Animae Beatitudine* (On the Beatitude of the Soul), in *Aristotelis opera... cum Averrois Cordubensis variis in eosdem commentariis* (Commentaries of Averroes on Aristotle), vol. 9, Venice: Juntas, 1573; repr. Frankfurt: Minerva, 1962. (Commentary on the intellect, attributed to Ibn Rushd, as it appeared in Latin in Christian Europe.)

CATERINA RIGO

HINDU PHILOSOPHY

Hindu philosophy is the longest surviving philosophical tradition in India. We can recognize several historical stages. The earliest, from around 700 BC, was the proto-philosophical period, when karma and liberation theories arose, and the proto-scientific ontological lists in the Upaniṣads were compiled. Next came the classical period, spanning the first millennium AD, in which there was constant philosophical exchange between different Hindu, Buddhist and Jaina schools. During this period, some schools, such as Sāṅkhya, Yoga and Vaiśeṣika, fell into oblivion and others, such as Kashmir Saivism, emerged. Finally, after the classical period only two or three schools remained active. The political and economic disturbances caused by repeated Muslim invasions hampered intellectual growth. The schools that survived were the Logic school (Nyāya), especially New Logic (Navya-Nyāya), the grammarians and, above all, the Vedānta schools.

The central concerns of the Hindu philosophers were metaphysics, epistemological issues, philosophy of language, and moral philosophy. The different schools can be distinguished by their different approaches to reality, but all considered the Vedas (the sacred scriptures) authoritative, and all believed that there is a permanent individual self (ātman). They shared with their opponents (Buddhists and Jainas) a belief in the need for liberation. They used similar epistemic tools and methods of argument.

In contrast to their opponents, who were atheists, Hindu philosophers could be either theists or atheists. Actually we can observe an increased tendency towards theistic ideas near the end of the classical period, with the result that the strictly atheistic teachings, which were more philosophically rigorous and sound, fell into disuse. Hindu metaphysics saw ātman as part of a larger reality (Brahman).

Because these views of the world differed, they had to be proved and properly established. Accordingly, logical and epistemological tools were developed and fashioned according to the needs and beliefs of individual philosophers. Most agreed on two or three sources of knowledge: perception and inference, with verbal testimony as a possible third. In this quest for philosophical rigour, there was a need for precision of language, and there were important philosophical developments among the grammarians and the philosophers who explained the Vedas (the Mīmāṃsakas). A culmination of these linguistic efforts can be seen in the philosopher of language Bhartṛhari. One of his greatest accomplishments was the full articulation of the theory that a sentence as a whole is understood in a sudden act of comprehension.

It is customary to name six Hindu schools, of the more than a dozen that existed, thus lumping several into a single school. This is particularly the case with Vedānta. The six are listed in three pairs: Sāṅkhya–Yoga; Vedānta–Mīmāṃsā; Nyāya–Vaiśeṣika. This does not take account of the grammarians or Kashmir Saivism.

In their quest for freedom from rebirth, all the Hindu schools operated within the same framework. Their ultimate goal was liberation. How much they were truly engaged in the quest for liberation apart from their philosophical preoccupations is not always clear, yet they never doubted its real possibility.

1   **General presuppositions**
2   **Metaphysics**
3   **Epistemic concerns**
4   **Philosophy of language**
5   **Moral issues**
6   **Philosophical schools: Vedānta**
7   **Other philosophical schools**

1   General presuppositions

Hindu schools of philosophy developed in close, lively dialogue with other philosophical trends and schools. As early as 400–300 BC, both Pāṇini and the author of *Manusmṛti* (a third century BC book of laws) identified two major intellectual trends, one involving belief in the sacred texts known as the Vedas, and one involving their rejection. Those who considered the Vedas as their authority later developed into what we know as the Hindu schools.

With a few exceptions, most of the religious and philosophical movements aimed at liberation, complete freedom from life and rebirth. From about the eighth century BC, belief in rebirth was found among most philosophical and religious leaders. At first, the mechanism of rebirth was thought to be prompted by bad actions. It was also believed that by good actions a person became good and by evil actions a person became evil. Since with time this must have come to be perceived as rather simplistic, the idea of rebirth became more complex. A person was reborn just by acts, regardless of whether those acts were good or evil. Liberation from rebirth could be achieved by an absence of desire; desire of any sort, whether a craving

for food, say, or for a new thing, entangled a person in the worldly mechanism of repetition (see KARMA AND REBIRTH, INDIAN CONCEPTIONS OF).

The various thinkers and teachers were specifically concerned with effective ways of achieving liberation. This meant establishing the basic presuppositions of the theory, such as what it is that truly exists, how this could be proved, and how liberation was to be viewed, and, moreover, how to promulgate such beliefs. There were constant discussions, an ongoing search for better ways of arguing with opponents. The formal requirements for building an argument were much disputed; each school believed that only its tools for debate were necessary, and that any others were useless.

An axiom held by most followers of the Vedic tradition was that there is a self (*ātman*) which travels from life to life. The 'life' in question need not be human; it can also be that of an animal.

In the early philosophical sources, the Upaniṣads, there is little room for any sort of agency beyond individuals with selves. It is only later that we find the idea of God or gods actively creating the universe and directing individual persons towards liberation or towards realizing some sort of aspiration towards the divine. Sometimes both these aims were combined.

2   Metaphysics

The concept of *ātman* was crucial in many debates, because there were many who either had a different understanding of it or who claimed to need no such concept. Argument helped towards a more precise articulation of the term, although many Hindu thinkers held that knowledge of *ātman* is only a partial understanding of reality; the individual self is only a part of the larger scenario of the universe. The universe was thought to be an all-encompassing spiritual entity, of which *ātman* is a minute fragment. Experiencing this spiritually, through meditative practices, frees a person from the ordinary way of things: such a person is not reborn, and does not repeat the anguish, pain, disease, old age and death of ordinary mortals, but is instead forever free. This can be accomplished through one's own efforts, although often the guidance of a teacher, a guru, is needed. These efforts may need to be extended over several lifetimes in order to work off all the accumulated karmic impressions. Karmic impressions, which may result from physical activities, speech or mental acts, are what actually bind people to the revolving process of rebirth.

Gradually, notions of divine intervention in the process of liberation found their way into numerous teachings. It was a combination of one's own efforts plus divine grace which would grant final deliverance, which was now not only freedom from repeated cycles of lives, but also either an identification with the divine, or companionship with a god as a lover or eternal servant. Some Advaita philosophers postulated a single ultimate principle, whereas others argued for the existence of an ultimate cause of the universe, namely God. Yet the worship of a multitude of gods was still widely practised, as it is to this day (see GOD, INDIAN CONCEPTIONS OF).

UDAYANA (eleventh century), one of the most prominent thinkers of the School of Logic (Nyāya), constructed an elegant set of arguments for the existence of God. Put crudely, his claim is that this multifarious world must obviously be the effect of some cause, and that cause must be nothing other than God. On the other hand, not all thinkers felt a need to trace the world to one primary cause, even though most took it for granted that causal chains are of prime importance in interpreting the world. The nature of the causal relation was much debated. Some claimed that an effect somehow already exists in latent form in its cause, just as yoghurt is potentially already present in milk even before the milk turns sour. In the same way, this whole manifold world somehow pre-existed in an undifferentiated primeval watery mass, into which it will dissolve itself again at the end of its existence. There are repeated existences and dissolutions.

Other philosophers, such as Śaṅkara (eighth century), interpreted the relation between cause and effect in a slightly different way. The difference between the two is only apparent, because in reality the universe is only superimposed onto an unchanging, everlasting, universal and undifferentiated principle, the Brahman of the Upaniṣadic thinkers. We superimpose things out of ignorance. A favourite analogy is that of a man walking along the road, half-blinded by the brilliant sunshine at noon. Suddenly he jumps across an elongated shape in the road, out of fear that he may step on a snake. A passer-by laughs and asks, 'Are you afraid of a dirty old piece of rope?' The person who jumped with fear was superimposing a snake onto the old rope. In the same way, we superimpose the whole universe onto Brahman. In reality, there are no causal relations at all. We talk of such concepts to facilitate debate, but they have no place on the ultimate level.

3 Epistemic concerns

Philosophers differed in their views about the number and characteristics of the various means of knowledge (pramāṇas). The most widely accepted pramāṇa was perception. Inference and verbal testimony (such as an utterance by a competent speaker or a statement from the Vedas) were also considered important. Some schools added analogy and other special kinds of inference (see KNOWLEDGE, INDIAN VIEWS OF).

Because of their differing ontologies, schools also disagreed about the objects of knowledge. Nyāya held that these were self, body, sense organs, mind, rebirth, pain and freedom (mokṣa). Sāṅkhya linked the objects of cognition to the sense organs: the eye has colour as its object, the ear has sound, the tongue taste, and so on; inference has as its objects things beyond sensory perception, such as consciousness, the undifferentiated material stuff of the universe, and causal relations.

'Perception' was usually confined to sensory or external perception. Some thinkers also recognized a sort of mental perception for mental states (such as joy or anguish). This was sometimes classed as belonging to a larger category of internal perception which also included yogic perception. Yogic and other types of perception in turn could be classed as 'extraordinary', as in the Nyāya system, especially its later form (Navya-Nyāya, 'New Logic'). Precise definitions of perception varied widely. Some thought it was direct awareness of colour; others argued that it was a cognition arising from the relation of an object with the senses, which is not verbal and not erroneous, but definite. An exchange of ideas arose over whether perception is a direct experience, that is, non-propositional, and whether one can postulate a propositional level of perception. Nyāya and the classical Sāṅkhya of Īśvarakṛṣṇa claimed to understand perceptions of two levels: non-propositional (roughly what we call 'sense data') and propositional (naming and attaching concepts to the sense-data) (see SENSE PERCEPTION, INDIAN VIEWS OF).

Inference (anumāna) was the next most important instrument of knowledge. In the classical period, three kinds of inference were usually enumerated. Their definitions betray a certain confusion between old and new ideas of inference. Inference is used as a source of knowledge in cases where objects cannot be apprehended directly. The basis of inference is the consistent relation between the reason and the thing-to-be-proved (sādhya). This requires that we perceive the reason. Here is an example of an argument:

There is fire on the mountain. (Thesis)

Because there is smoke (which I see with my naked eye). (Reason)

Like in the kitchen. (Positive example)

Unlike in the lake. (Negative example)

Therefore there is fire on the mountain. (Conclusion)

The consistent relation is not explicitly stated in the

syllogism, although it is quite obvious: where there is smoke, there is fire (see INFERENCE, INDIAN THEORIES OF).

Verbal testimony was thought to be another decisive source of knowledge of things beyond sensory apprehension. A competent testifier is a reliable person who has direct knowledge, wants to communicate it and is also capable of expressing it. It was argued that the revealed sacred literature could be classed as testimony. There was also some discussion about whether to subsume this source of knowledge under inference. Other suggested *pramāṇas* were analogy and presumption. An example of presumption is the following: it is observed that Devadatta is fat; nobody sees him overeating during the day; so (the presumption is that) he must eat all night. Indian philosophers also discussed an argument known as *tarka*, a kind of reasoning that we call *reductio ad absurdum*.

4 Philosophy of language

From the earliest times, there was a preoccupation with language in Indian culture. 'Language' here means Sanskrit. A concern with the power and limitations of language is already clear in the *Ṛg Veda*. Of the six theoretical branches of learning listed in the Vedas, four are closely related to language: grammar, etymology, lexicography and poetry. The level of accomplishment eventually attained in these is demonstrated in Pāṇini's descriptive grammar, the *Aṣṭādhyāyī*. Patañjali's commentary on this, the *Mahābhāṣya* (second century BC) can be thought of as a kind of a bridge between grammatical and philosophical concerns (see PATAÑJALI).

The fifth-century philosopher BHARTṚHARI stands out among those who studied language. In his *Vākyapadīya*, he considers the faculty of speech to be an instinct or intuition. He compares it to animal instinct and does not believe that language is learned. Language, according to Bhartṛhari, accompanies cognition – there is no cognition without language. His understanding of language is rather metaphysical, as he equates language with Brahman.

Bhartṛhari is particularly associated with the theory of *sphoṭa*, although the notion had been formulated some centuries before him. According to this theory, a sentence is an integral unit. Analysing a sentence in terms of phonemes, morphemes or words is useful for learning purposes, but the whole sentence alone is meaningful. When those who know a language hear an utterance in that language, they hear a sentence, not single words or phonemes; only those who do not know the language will hear individual bits of sound. As for the relation between word and meaning, Bhartṛhari holds that it is permanent and natural, not based on convention.

Althought all schools of philosophy were concerned with language, perhaps the earliest was Mīmāṃsā. The followers of this school were concerned with the interpretation of the Vedas, and in particular with the problem of the relation between words and sentences. The Mīmāṃsakas argued that, for a word to be intelligible, each utterance of it has to be identical with an earlier utterance that is now remembered. By extrapolation, words must be eternal. In the same way, the meaning of words is eternal, as is the relation between word and meaning.

Pāṇini had seen the need for a capacity for mutual connection between the meanings of words, and the Mīmāṃsakas similarly developed a set of conditions for meaningful and correct sentences. They named the capacity for mutual connection between the meanings of words 'mutual expectancy'. For example, 'he rides an elephant' fulfils the condition of mutual syntactic expectancy, but a string of words such as 'elephant, house, riding' does not. But according to this condition, the sentence 'he rides a house' is also a sentence. So another condition, 'semantic compatibility', was added. In a sentence like 'he rides a house', the semantic compatibility is absent. The Mīmāṃsakas also required that the condition of 'contiguity' be fulfilled: words must not be spoken at long intervals or be separated by other words. Another condition was 'the intention of the speaker', about which there were varying opinions.

Each of the main branches of the Mīmāṃsā school developed its own theory regarding the semantic relationship between words and sentences. The adherents of Prābhākara believed that the meaning of a sentence arises directly from its collection of words. Conversely, words convey meaning only in the context of a sentence. Each word in a sentence conveys both its isolated meaning and the syntactic meaning. On the other hand, Kumarila Bhāṭṭa and his followers believed that the meaning of a sentence arises indirectly. Each word gives its individual meaning, and this uses up its significative power; therefore the syntactic relation must be obtained by means of a secondary significative power. This view was also shared by the Advaita Vedāntins, who, in order to be able to express truths about the Absolute, could not always use words with their primary meaning, but had instead to use the secondary meaning.

Of course, the Advaitins were not the only ones who distinguished between the primary and secondary meanings of words. This practice was well known among other philosophers, grammarians, and especially literary critics. In his *Mahābhāṣya*, Patañjali distinguished primary and secondary meanings, while Bhartṛhari discussed transfer of meaning (*upacāra*) through such tropes as simile, metonymy, synecdoche and so on. By the ninth century, Ānandavardhana, in his exposition of literary criticism, was discussing the 'suggestive power' of words. He observed that a text does not yield its full meaning to every reader, since the ideal reader must be trained in the symbolism and conventions of a text, and familiar with the realities to which the text refers. Such a reader has an intuitive grasp of the text that untrained readers lack.

The school of Nyāya was at first primarily concerned with theories of the relation between a word and its meaning. The Naiyāyikas did not consider this relation to be natural, but saw it as just a matter of convention. This conventional relation is called 'significative power' (*śakti*). *Śakti* applies to primary meaning only; although secondary meaning is accepted, it is considered only in terms of its relation to the primary meaning and can apply only to single words, not to whole sentences.

The Naiyāyikas and the grammarians stayed active for many centuries, in the course of which their teachings were transformed. The Naiyāyikas especially developed new terminology and techniques of argument; this change was reflected in their adoption of a modified name, Navya-Nyāya (New Logic) (see GADĀDHĀRA; GAṄGEŚA; LANGUAGE, INDIAN THEORIES OF).

5 Moral issues

Two important principles govern Indian moral philosophy: karma and *dharma*. The theory of karma was articulated early in Upaniṣadic times (which are usually placed from 700 BC onwards, but were possibly earlier). It concerns the causal relation between acts and their results, although neither was always understood in a uniform way. In general, the workings of karma were not interpreted as a fatalistic mechanism. With the exception of a few schools, most Indian thinkers came to conceive of karma in terms of a kind of naturalistic law of causation. The best-known philosopher of the Upaniṣads, Yājñavalkya, was the first one to teach karma, which soon became discernible in almost all intellectual developments, as well as being a governing principle in everyday ethics.

The principle of *dharma* is closely connected with karma. *Dharma* literally means 'to uphold what is correct', what we may call today 'morality'. The precise translation of the term depends on the context. For example, we can translate *dharma* as 'justice' in cases where something that was unlawfully taken away is to be regained. Thus, in the epic *Mahābhārata*, it is justice for the Pāṇḍavas to regain

their kingdom, which was illegally taken from them by their cousins, the Kauravas. There is also *dharma* as 'individual duty', according to a person's social and economic status in society. This could be compared to a certain extent with the Kantian idea of duty (duty for duty's sake). Then there is general *dharma* which applies to society as a whole, a guide in moral and social issues.

An important ideal in Hindu moral philosophy, that of the stages of life, is described in the body of literature known as the Dharmaśāstras. This endorses the determination of social status by birth, and prescribes for each individual (at least, each male of the two highest classes, namely priests and royalty) the various stages to progress through in life. The prescribed sequence is as follows: first, the socially responsible person should study and abstain from sexual relations; next, he should marry, bring up offspring and accumulate material possessions; third, he should become a religious seeker, leaving behind the comforts of home, family and riches (although his wife may still provide some familiar comfort); finally, he should leave the companionship of his wife and roam alone as an ascetic until death. Two value systems, one socially engaged, the other with an ascetic tendency, appear to be combined here (see DUTY AND VIRTUE, INDIAN CONCEPTIONS OF). Closely related are the four aims of human life (*puruṣārtha*): material wellbeing, pleasure and enjoyment, morality and social responsibility, and, the ultimate goal, liberation from repeated birth. Here, too, two value systems are combined: the first three aims guide the socially engaged, whereas the last is the aim of a person in the final stage of life.

6 Philosophical schools: Vedānta

When speaking of Indian philosophy, it has become a convention to count six schools in the Hindu tradition. This division is rather artificial, especially since it involves putting the schools together in three pairs: Sāṅkhya–Yoga; Vedānta–Mīmāṃsā; Nyāya-Vaiśeṣika. In fact, by the fourteenth century we find sixteen philosophical schools discussed in Mādhava's *Sarvadarśanasaṃgraha* (Survey of the Major Philosophical Systems). Among these are schools opposed to the Hindu ones, such as Buddhism, Jainism and materialism. MĀDHAVA places the materialists at the beginning of his treatise and culminates it with the Vedānta school to which he himself belongs. Including the different schools of Vedānta, we can count about a dozen Hindu schools.

Vedānta still survives and is the most influential school of modern times, having great intellectual and political figures among its adherents. 'Vedānta' describes several schools and numerous thinkers, and means 'the appendage to the Vedas', referring in this way to the body of texts known as the Upaniṣads. The Upaniṣads have been a source of inspiration and dogma since their beginnings around 700 BC. Embedded in them are ideas that came to dominate Indian thought, namely karma, rebirth, and liberation from the ever-revolving cycle of rebirth. The means of liberation is to experience the identity of the individual self (ātman) with a larger cosmic entity (Brahman). Individual thinkers each had a different interpretation of these tenets, but all essentially agreed on the means of liberation. Curiously, the development of Vedānta did not take place until more than a millennium after the earlier Upaniṣads. The most influential thinker of whom we know today was ŚAṄKARA.

Śaṅkara, like other Vedāntins, built on an earlier tradition. The work to which they all responded was Badarāyaṇa's *Brahmasūtra* (or *Vedāntasūtra*) of around AD 50. It stimulated many interpretive commentaries, which gave occasion for new schools to arise. The most prominent interpretation of the *Brahmasūtra* is known as Advaita Vedānta. It focuses on Brahman, which is understood as identical with *ātman*. Out of ignorance, the material world is superimposed on the ultimately empty Brahman; this superimposition is sometimes described as an illusory projection (*māyā*). The first prominent name in this tradition is Gauḍapāda, who taught Śaṅkara's teacher.

Śaṅkara was prolific in his philosophical output. He commented on all the major Upaniṣads and the *Bhagavad Gītā* ([Upaniṣad, or Secret Teaching] Recited by the Lord Krishna), and a number of other works are ascribed to him. His Advaitism can be characterized as a strict nondualism: there is nothing other than Brahman, either real or unreal, and the goal is to know this through a trance-like experience which grants liberation (*mokṣa*) from rebirth. Were it not for this experience of truth, which is the vision of identity between *ātman* and Brahman, we would always superimpose this colourful world on transparent Brahman. This superimposition is an act of mistaking an unreal object for a real one, just as we superimpose silver on a piece of a glittering shell or a snake on a rope (see §2). If we could lift the superimposed object away from the real one, underneath we would find something altogether different.

This doctrine is austere and diminishes the importance of a personal God. It failed to stimulate the imagination of many people, and with time there was a strong reaction to such an abstract portrayal of reality. The form of Vedānta that flourished subsequently tended to have a more theistic cast. The earliest work of theistic Vedānta was Bhāskara's interpretation of the *Brahmasūtra*, whereby the individual self is both different and not different from God (Brahman). This doctrine was called 'the teaching of difference with no difference' (Bhedābhedavāda).

The *Brahmasūtra* was often seen in the light of theology devoted to the god Viṣṇu. The eleventh-century philosopher RĀMĀNUJA, commenting on the *Brahmasūtra* in his *Śrībhāṣya*, claims that everything is Brahman, yet acknowledges the reality of individual selves and the material world. This teaching is called 'qualified monism' (Viśiṣṭādvaitavāda) because Brahman is described as Knowledge and as being merciful, all-powerful and all-pervading. Everything that exists is contained in Brahman, understood as a personal God who should be approached with constant devotion. Other interpreters of the *Brahmasūtra* postulated devotion to God; to many of them, he was some form of Viṣṇu, which indicates that they too had a problem with absolute monism. Therefore they introduced a modified monism: Nimbārka, for instance, combined both dualism and nondualism (Dvaitādvaitavāda).

The extreme position of disavowing monism was taken in the thirteenth century by MADHVA (not to be confused with Mādhava), who claimed that there is an absolute difference between Brahman and individual selves (Dvaitavāda). Another extreme position was expressed by VALLABHACĀRYA in his teaching of pure nondualism (Śudhādvaitavāda). Still other thinkers with other interpretations, such as Caitanya (1486–1534) of the Bengal Vaiṣṇavism, did not leave a corpus of literature behind them (see GAUḌĪYA VAIṢṆAVISM; BRAHMAN; MONISM, INDIAN).

7 Other philosophical schools

Sāṅkhya and Vedānta are similar with respect to epistemology and some ontological issues. Sāṅkhya was an old dualistic school reaching back to the ontologies of Upaniṣadic times. It postulated an irreducible duality of consciousness and material stuff. Originally, the material stuff existed in an undifferentiated form, until it was disturbed by an intangible prodding of consciousness. Once disturbed, it produced twenty-three parts of the universe, with the human individual's parts in preponderance. Altogether, with consciousness and the undifferentiated material stuff, there are twenty-five things that exist. The goal of Sāṅkhya was to experience the basic duality in a trance-like state, to discriminate between 'spirit' and 'matter'. Perhaps this dualism reflected vacillation between idealistic/metaphysical tendencies and naturalistic/materialistic tendencies.

Another old school was Vaiśeṣika, which in some respects was close to Sāṅkhya. Like Sāṅkhya, it strove to list all the things that exist in reality, to name everything there is. Such a proto-scientific enumeration of categories marks the antiquity of these systems. The number of ontological categories according to the classical Vaiśeṣika of Praśastapāda is six. Other philosophers enumerated as many as ten, others only seven. Among these categories, such as substance, quality and activity, we find a category of relation, inherence. Inherence is a relation between things that do not exist in isolation. It holds between qualities and substances, and between particulars and universals; a quality inheres in its substratum, a substance, so that, with a red apple, the red colour is a quality of the substance apple. This red colour cannot exist on its own, but always has to inhere in something, whether an apple or a hibiscus flower. The Vaiśeṣikas are known as the Indian atomists. Motion inheres in the atoms, which, in their varying compositions as whole objects, are the substratum of motion (see ONTOLOGY IN INDIAN PHILOSOPHY).

The Vaiśeṣika school is frequently lumped together with the Nyāya ('Logic') school. The reason for this might be that later Nyāya philosophers took it upon themselves to comment upon and revise the old atomistic school. The word *nyāya* is often used for a maxim or an example in an argument, which is perhaps why it was adopted for the Logic school; earlier, however, it was used to refer to the system of Mīmāṃsā, yet another school.

The Nyāya school also had a list of basic categories. Their sixteen categories are quite obviously the parts of a rigorous argument: for example, instruments of knowledge, objects of knowledge, doubt, purpose, example, and so on. Thus the list consists of epistemological or proto-epistemological tools. The main preoccupation among the Naiyāyikas was to build proper arguments. They used a five-member syllogism based on the constant relation between logical reason and thing-to-be proved (*sādhya*). This relation came later to be known as concomitance or pervasion (*vyāpti*). The Naiyāyikas also tried to safeguard against possible mishaps in argument by distinguishing three kinds of fallacy in reasoning.

The early Mīmāṃsakas were completely engaged in interpreting the scriptures, which conveyed injunctions for ritual actions such as sacrifices and ceremonies. These actions should be performed because the Vedas say so – the Vedas are authoritative. Other pursuits, such as acquiring knowledge of oneself or engaging in philosophical debates about God, serve no purpose. Furthermore, any philosophical pursuit may give rise to doubts, and

the doubts may extend to the authority of the Vedas. It was centuries before Mīmāṃsā was freed from such dogmatism, by the philosophers Kumārila and Prabhākara (both seventh century). They maintained atheistic positions, and made fun of inconsistencies in arguments for the existence of God. Prabhākara put forward a theory of the self-verifying nature of simple (non-propositional) perceptual knowledge which was heavily criticized by philosophers of other schools.

Yoga was a practical discipline of physical postures, breathing techniques and meditation whose origin we are unable to trace to any precise time, place or event. It went hand-in-hand with the ascetic life, no matter what the value system or outlook of its practitioners. Yoga is classically grouped with Sāṅkhya. There may be two reasons for this. First, both systems date back to the ancient encounter in Indian history between Aryan nomadic conquerors and a settled agricultural people (which lasted several centuries from 1500 BC onwards). There are speculations that Sāṅkhya developed within the newcomers' tradition, whereas Yoga was practiced among the original inhabitants. Perhaps just as the worldviews of these groups grew together, so were the schools assimilated one to the other. The second reason may have been that Yoga needed a theoretical background to become a system. Sāṅkhya is the oldest recognizable proto-philosophical bundle of ideas. But what Sāṅkhya and Yoga share is not really significant in view of the fact that many other schools adopted Yoga techniques.

According to the *Yogasūtra*, the aim of Yoga is to be able to attain a state of deep concentration (*samādhi*) by stopping the activity of the mind. Yoga differs significantly from Sāṅkhya in requiring the grace of God for liberation. Yoga can be seen as a practical discipline capable of being adapted by various theoretical systems, especially those whose adherents are supposed to undergo spiritual experiences to achieve liberation from pain, anguish, longing and rebirth.

See also: BUDDHIST PHILOSOPHY, INDIAN; JAINA PHILOSOPHY; MĪMĀṂSĀ; NYĀYA-VAIŚEṢIKA; SĀṄKHYA; VEDĀNTA

References and further reading

Chattopadhyaya, D. (1964) *Indian Philosophy: A Popular Introduction*, Delhi: People's Publishing House; repr. 1972. (Lucid and accessible survey of Indian philosophical schools.)

Coward, H.G. and Kunjunni Raja, K. (eds) (1990) *Encyclopedia of Indian Philosophies*, vol. 5, *The Philosophy of the Grammarians*, Princeton, NJ: Princeton University Press. (A useful handbook.

Contains a historical résumé and discussion of the main philosophical concerns. Summaries of works by language philosophers and grammarians comprise most of the volume.)

Larson, G. and Bhattacharya, R.S. (eds) (1987) *Encyclopedia of Indian Philosophies*, vol. 4, *Sāṅkhya: A Dualist Tradition in Indian Philosophy*, Princeton, NJ: Princeton University Press. (A handbook containing a historical survey and discussion of Sāṅkhya philosophy. Most of the volume consists of summaries of the work of Sāṅkhya thinkers.)

Halbfass, W. (1991) *Tradition and Reflection: Explorations in Indian Thought*, New York: State University of New York Press. (Asks new questions and develops novel ideas about important issues. The approach combines history, philology and hermeneutics.)

—— (1992) *On Being and What There is: Classical Vaiśeṣika and the History of Indian Ontology*, New York: State University of New York Press. (A comprehensive study which includes a broad range of texts by the best classical thinkers.)

Mohanty, J. (1992) *Reason and Tradition in Indian Thought: An Essay on the Nature of Indian Philosophical Thinking*, Oxford: Clarendon Press. (A modern philosopher trained in Western phenomenology and analytical philosophy interprets Indian philosophy, with reference to the original sources, for contemporary thinkers.)

Phillips, S.H. (1995) *Classical Indian Metaphysics: Refutations of Realism and the Emergence of 'New Logic'*, La Salle, IL: Open Court. (This book juxtaposes realists and idealists, focusing primarily on the systems of Old and New Logic, and gives responses to the arguments that the idealists directed against the Logicians.)

Potter, K.H. (1963) *Presuppositions of India's Philosophies*, Englewood Cliffs, NJ: Prentice-Hall. (Discusses issues in Indian philosophies, identifying liberation as the ultimate goal for most schools. In a very useful diagram, philosophers are arranged according to their stances on liberation.)

—— (ed.) (1977) *Encyclopedia of Indian Philosophies*, vol. 2, *Indian Metaphysics and Epistemology: The Tradition of Nyāya-Vaiśeṣika up to Gaṅgeśa*, Princeton, NJ: Princeton University Press. (An account of the historical background and an excellent discussion of the main issues form the introduction to summaries of works.)

—— (ed.) (1981) *Encyclopedia of Indian Philosophies*, vol. 3, *Advaita Vedānta up to Śaṃkara and his Pupils*, Princeton, NJ: Princeton University Press. (A historical overview is followed by a discussion of the main philosophical issues. Most of the volume consists of summaries of a comprehensive collection of texts.)

Potter, K.H. and Bhattacharyya, S. (eds) (1993) *Encyclopedia of Indian Philosophies*, vol. 6, *Indian Philosophical Analysis: Nyāya-Vaiśeṣika from Gaṅgeśa to Raghunātha Śiromaṇi*, Princeton, NJ: Princeton University Press. (A short historical survey is complemented by a table of fifty philosophers and their works. A brief discussion of the philosophical ideas accompanies the summaries of the works.)

EDELTRAUD HARZER CLEAR

HIPPARCHIA *see* CYNICS

HIPPIAS (late 5th century BC)

The Greek Sophist Hippias of Elis is a familiar figure in Plato's dialogues. He served his city as ambassador, and he earned a great deal of money from his lectures. His unusually wide range of expertise included not only rhetoric but also history, literature, mnemonics, mathematics and natural philosophy.

As a contemporary of Socrates, Hippias of Elis appears (as a rather self-important character) in several dialogues of Plato. Because of his learning and eloquence, he served as ambassador for Elis, and he lectured with great success at Athens and elsewhere. His intellectual range was very wide. Plato depicts him as lecturing on Homer (*Hippias Minor* 363a–b) and on astronomy and natural philosophy (*Protagoras* 315c). He also composed poems in several genres, and is credited with an important discovery in geometry, the *quadratrix*, a curve for trisecting angles and squaring the circle. He was one of the earliest specialists in mnemonics, and is reputed to have been able to memorize fifty names at first hearing. His historical research included compiling a list of Olympic victors (an important basis for Greek chronology) and collecting information on genealogies, tribes, famous or legendary persons and the foundation of cities.

Hippias' energy and versatility must have been extraordinary. Plato makes fun of him for appearing once at Olympia dressed in his own handiwork from head to foot, including his home-made signet ring, ornamental belt and sandals. He offered to answer questions on any subject, and he seems to have a prepared speech ready for any occasion (*Protagoras* 347b; *Hippias Minor* 363a–d, 369c).

The most original work of Hippias was a book from which we have the opening sentence:

Some of these things have perhaps been said by Orpheus, some by Musaeus briefly here and there, some by Hesiod and Homer and other poets, as well as by prose authors, both Greek and barbarian. I will compose a novel and manifold discourse by combining the most important and similar items from all these.

(fr.6)

The book seems to have been an allegorical work in which doctrines from Presocratic philosophy were attributed to the early poets. Hippias is apparently the authority Plato and Aristotle are following when they find the doctrines of Thales and Heraclitus in verses from Homer, Hesiod and Orpheus. It is likely that he was Aristotle's primary source for information on Thales. Hippias thus appears as the first doxographer and hence as the remote precursor for ancient and modern historians of philosophy (see DOXOGRAPHY).

Plato's satirical presentation suggests that he found Hippias' vanity great and his learning superficial. Nevertheless, of all the Sophists Hippias was apparently the most universal in his intellectual activity, a fifth-century precedent for Aristotle.

Hippias is the title of two dialogues in the Platonic corpus, the shorter of which (*Hippias Minor*) is surely by Plato. The authenticity of the longer dialogue (*Hippias Major*) is contested.

See also: SOPHISTS

References and further reading

Guthrie, W.K.C. (1969) *A History of Greek Philosophy*, vol. 3, Cambridge: Cambridge University Press. (A full, scholarly account.)
* Hippias (late 5th century BC) Fragments, in H. Diels and W. Kranz (eds) *Die Fragmente der Vorsokratiker* (Fragments of the Presocratics), Berlin: Weidemann, 7th edn, 1954, vol. 2, 326–34. (The standard collection of the ancient sources; includes Greek texts with translations in German.)
Kerferd, G.B. (1981) *The Sophistic Movement*, Cambridge: Cambridge University Press. (A briefer, more personal interpretation than Guthrie (1969).)
Patzer, A. (1986) *Der Sophist Hippias als Philosophiehistoriker* (The Sophist Hippias as Historian of Philosophy), Freiberg and Munich: Verlag Karl Alber. (An ambitious, largely convincing reconstruction of Hippias' doxographical work, the *Synagōgē* or 'Gathering-together', as source for many passages in Plato and Aristotle where early poetical texts are cited as anticipations of later philosophical views.)
* Plato (c.395–387 BC) *Hippias Minor*, trans. H.N. Fowler, Loeb Classical Library, Cambridge, MA: Harvard University Press and London: Heinemann, 1926. (Short conversation between Socrates and Hippias on Achilles and truthtelling.)
* —— (c.386–380 BC) *Protagoras*, trans. C.C.W. Taylor, Oxford: Oxford University Press, 2nd edn, 1991. (Hippias appears in a gathering of famous Sophists and speaks on several subjects.)
* —— (c.380–367 BC) *Hippias Major*, trans. P. Woodruff, Oxford: Blackwell, 1982. (Longer conversation between Socrates and Hippias on the nature of the beautiful; Platonic authorship is dubious.)
Snell, B. (1976) 'Die Nachrichten über die Lehren des Thales und die Anfänge der griechischen Philosophie- und Literaturgeschichte' (Reports on the doctrines of Thales and the beginnings of Greek history of philosophy and literature), in C.J. Classen (ed.) *Sophistik*, Darmstadt: Wissenschaftliche Buchgesellschaft, 478–90. (The basic scholarly paper on Hippias as authority for Plato and Aristotle; in German only.)
Sprague, R.K. (ed.) (1972) *The Older Sophists*, Columbia, SC: University of South Carolina Press, 94–105. (Full English translation of the fragments and testimonia from Diels and Kranz (1954).)

CHARLES H. KAHN

HIPPOCRATIC MEDICINE

The Hippocratic corpus is a disparate group of texts relating primarily to medical matters composed between c.450 and c.250 BC and dealing with physiology, therapy, surgery, clinical practice, gynaecology and obstetrics, among other topics. The treatises are (for the most part) notable for their sober naturalism in physiological theory, their rejection of supernatural explanations for disease, and their insistence on the importance of careful observation. Although embodying a variety of different physiological schemes, they are the origin of the enormously influential paradigm of humoral pathology. In antiquity, the authorship of the entire corpus was mistakenly ascribed to the semilegendary doctor Hippocrates of Cos (fl. c.450 BC).

1   The Hippocratic corpus
2   Naturalism

1 The Hippocratic corpus

The collection known as the Hippocatic corpus comprises some sixty or more texts, of greatly varying styles, subject matters, lengths and probable origins, written in terse and unattractive Greek. The earliest may date from the mid-fifth century BC; the latest are certainly third century BC. The corpus contains the first treatises in Western rational medicine; and the best of them display the fruits of meditation not only upon practical problems in therapy but also upon fundamental methodological questions in science.

It is unclear how many if any of the Hippocratic texts can be associated with Hippocrates himself. Some of the treatises are clearly working notes of practising doctors (*Epidemics*); others are attempts to supply theoretical frameworks within which such practical medicine may flourish (*Prognosis*). Some treat the nature and aetiology of specific diseases (*On the Sacred Disease*), others the impact of certain environmental features on general epidemiology (*Airs, Waters, Places*); others still are devoted more to practical therapeutics (*Regimen in Acute Diseases*). Some are surgical (*On Joints*), while others (notably the late text *On the Heart*) deal with anatomy; yet others are ethical in nature, notably the famous *Oath* (and *On Decorum*), while some (*On Breaths, On the Art*) were written to justify the practice of medicine against its detractors. Also important was the influential anti-theoretical account of medicine in *On Ancient Medicine*, as well as important groups of texts on general pathology, gynaecology and obstetrics.

2 Naturalism

Prominent among the texts is a commitment to sober clinical observation and an attempt to account for diseases on the basis of a naturalistic approach to physiology, epidemiology and therapeutics, eschewing accounts of disease as the results of divine visitation, on the model of Apollo's plague at the beginning of the *Iliad*.

In the opening chapter of *On the Sacred Disease* (*c.*420 BC), which deals with epilepsy and related seizures, the author affirms roundly that, however terrifying and numinous its appearance, this ailment is no more nor less sacred than any other. He exposes the claims of the 'purifiers' that it is divinely sent (and hence requires apotropaic ritual treatment) to a cogent and systematic critique. Their 'account' is simply an attempt to conceal their own ignorance, their 'treatments' ritual mumbo-jumbo; they take the credit if patients recover, while arming themselves with excuses when they do not. Their taboo prohibition on goat products suggests that people who

associate more with goats (such as the Libyans) should be more prone to the disease (which they are not), and that the causes of the disease are implicitly non-supernatural. Moreover, anatomical investigation of afflicted creatures shows them to be suffering from a superfluity of plegm, which suggests that the disease is caused by phlegm (which is cold and moist) blocking crucial pathways in the brain.

This text, which is typical of the corpus, is remarkable for the acuity of its criticism of the opposing model, but equally for the cavalier manner in which its author erects his own preferred physiological model on the flimsiest of evidential bases. Equally optimistic extrapolations from inadequate evidence may be found in *Airs, Waters, Places*, whose author attributes the prevalence of particular types of ailment in certain locales to their aspect, the type of water available, and their prevailing atmosphere. The notion that such environmental influences play some role in epidemic and endemic diseases is no doubt sound and empirically based: the theory that seeks to integrate that evidence is not.

The physiological theories espoused by Hippocratic texts are various, but in general they seek to explain health and disease in terms of the interplay of basic internal elements. Thus *On Regimen* makes fire and water the primary constituents of the human body, the various ratios between them being responsible for different individuals' differing physiology and psychology, with serious imbalances among them producing disease. By contrast, *On Breaths* makes air fundamental: internal air regulates the body, inspired air nourishes it, noxious air harms it.

On the Nature of Man, rejecting element theory as too remote from the actual facts of human physiology, outlines the theory of the 'four humours' inextricably associated with Hippocrates' name. The four basic physiological constituents are blood, phlegm, yellow bile and black bile, a preponderance of any of which yields one of the four basic character types (sanguine, phlegmatic, bilious, melancholic), and excesses of which cause disease. Cures are thus effected by redressing the balance (almost all of Hippocratic therapeutic theory is allopathic in form, 'opposites cure opposites' being a constantly recurring aphorism). The theory purports to rest upon solid empirical foundations: yet black bile is a theoretical construction, answering (despite its enviable conceptual longevity) to no actual bodily fluid.

In reaction against this type of theorizing, *On Ancient Medicine* takes issue with 'new-fangled hypotheses' as being empirically undeterminable and therapeutically pointless. Medicine consists of seeing what sorts of regimen produce what kinds of illness, and what functions best in their treatment. This text thus anticipates medical Empiricism (see HELLENIS-TIC MEDICAL EPISTEMOLOGY).

Equally, the case histories of the *Epidemics* are apparently untheoretical: they record the onset and progress of diseases, merely noting causal relevant features, such as overwork, fatigue, overheating, over-indulgence in food, drink or sex, as well as location and regimen. But these are precisely the sorts of things that might be expected to disturb a delicate internal humoral balance, not factors to be associated with an infectious model of disease transmission (whom the patient had visited, and so on) which is utterly absent from the Hippocratic corpus (even though Thucydides, for example, was well aware that the great Athenian plague was contagious). The Hippocratics do occasionally point to cuts and wounds as being relevant to the development of certain diseases, although they have little idea how such septic mechanisms might operate. But the notion that pathogens might be directly transmitted from one person to another is implicitly rejected as being incompatible with the dominant model of health and disease as depending upon the state of internal equilibrium or otherwise.

See also: GALEN

References and further reading

* Hippocratic corpus (*c.*450–250 BC) in *Hippocrates*, trans. W.H.S. Jones, E.T. Withington and P. Potter, Loeb Classical Library, Cambridge, MA: Harvard University Press and London: Heinemann, 6 vols, 1923, 1931, 1987. (Good selection of the basic Hippocratic texts with parallel Greek/English translation.)

Lloyd, G.E.R. (1979) *Magic, Reason and Experience*, Cambridge: Cambridge University Press. (Magisterial account of the nature of Greek science; chapter 1 is largely devoted to Hippocratic medicine.)

Longrigg, J. (1994) *Greek Rational Medicine*, London: Routledge. (Generally reliable introductory survey.)

R.J. HANKINSON

HISTORICISM

Historicism, defined as 'the affirmation that life and reality are history alone' by Benedetto Croce (1938: 65), is understood to mean various traditions of historiographical thinking which developed in the nineteenth century, predominantly in Germany. Historicism is an insistence on the historicity of all knowledge and cognition, and on the radical segregation of human from natural history. It is intended as a critique of the normative, allegedly anti-historical, epistemologies of Enlightenment thought, expressly that of Kant. The most significant theorists and historians commonly associated with historicism are Leopold von Ranke, Wilhelm Dilthey, J.G. Droysen, Friedrich Meinecke, Croce and R.G. Collingwood.

The main antecedents for the development of historicism are to be found in two key bodies of work. J.G. Herder's Outlines of a Philosophy of the History of Man *(1784) argues against the construction of history as linear progress, stating rather that human history is composed of fundamentally incomparable national cultures or totalities. G.W.H. Hegel's* The Philosophy of History *(1826) insists on the historical situatedness of each individual consciousness as a particular moment within the total progression of all history towards a final goal. The shifting fusion of these ideas provides the foundation for both the strengths and the problems of historicism. Historicism follows both Herder, in attempting to do justice to objective history in its discontinuity and uniqueness, and Hegel, in attempting to determine general patterns of historical change. Indeed, historicism can perhaps be best termed a Hegelian philosophy of history without an all-encompassing notion of progress.*

Rather than constituting a unified intellectual movement, historicism is best known for its elusiveness. Its multifarious quality can be inferred from the variety of critical positions taken up against it. Influential critiques of historicism have been written by Friedrich Nietzsche, Friedrich Rickert, Ernst Troeltsch, Walter Benjamin, Karl Löwith and Karl Popper. Critical engagement with historicism has focused on its alleged relativism, its alleged particularism, its alleged claims to totality, its alleged subjectivism and its alleged objectivism. More positive debates with historicism have significantly influenced the thought of Martin Heidegger, Edmund Husserl and Hans-Georg Gadamer.

1 Historicity and knowledge
2 Totality and particularity

1 Historicity and knowledge

For much of the nineteenth century historicism was broadly linked with the great historian, Ranke, whose formulated intention was to describe history 'as it actually happened'. In this, historicism moves close to simple empiricism. However, later readings of historicism have moved substantially away from this conception.

Karl Heussi has argued in one of the most significant critiques of historicism, *Die Krisis des*

Historismus (The Crisis of Historicism) (1932), that it possesses four main characteristics: (1) it is historical writing without cognitive analysis; (2) it incorporates a sceptical belief that history cannot lead us to certain judgments; (3) it claims that scientific knowledge is only possible within its own boundaries; and (4) it attempts to reach philosophical and theological truths through an immanent study of history. In contrast, George G. Iggers (1969) has argued that historicism possesses three chief characteristics: (1) the tendency to view the nation-state as an end in itself; (2) a hostility to ethical normativity, that is, the imputation of value to all historical information; and (3) a hostility to conceptuality in historical analysis, that is, an emphasis on intuitive or non-rational means of understanding. Similar points have been made more positively by Friedrich MEINECKE in his *Historicism* (1936), the most significant twentieth-century defence of historicism.

These observations, despite clear distinctions, concur in suggesting a definition of historicism as a radical shift away from Enlightenment understandings of history. All of these traits can be viewed as counterpoints to key assumptions of Enlightenment thought: primarily to the identification of personal and national interest with higher morality (natural law) and to the faith in universal norms, both ethical and cognitive (see ENLIGHTENMENT, CONTINENTAL).

The vitalist, interested approach which both Heussi and Iggers attribute to historicist thought also derives from a critique of the Enlightenment. It rests on the following assumptions: that humanity has no nature, only history: that is, that experience and cognition are conditioned solely by history; that laws determining human life are not naturally prescribed, but are the products of specific historical contexts; and that the truth-content of cognition is dependent not on categorial logic, but upon its situatedness in, and constant attentiveness to, history. Implicit in this is the suggestion that the historian and the object of historical study are situated in the same totality of experience and shared history. Historicism thus replaces epistemology and normativity with a notion of a shared, historically shaped, experiential horizon, through which all knowledge must be processed. It has often been claimed, not without justification, that this conception lends itself readily to specifically national historiography, as the experiential totality of history can be easily narrowed to national history (Iggers 1969: 272).

These assumptions have been variously expressed. For example, J.G. Droysen (1858) argues that historian and historical personality both constitute totalities of experience, and that through their interaction the historian may reconstruct the totality of the historical personality through an understanding of surviving expressions and data. In this conception, the norms of historical analysis and value are derived from a process of immanent critique. The immanence of this process is underscored by the assumption of the shared human, expressly not natural, quality of history and historian.

The vitalist or essentialist undercurrent in this historiography is articulated as a hermeneutic procedure by Wilhelm DILTHEY (§3) in *Introduction to the Human Sciences* (1883). Here the moment of historical perception is called *Erlebnis* (experience). In this process, the task of the historian is the actualization of the general quality of a particular history through experiential communication with it. For Dilthey, the boundless stream of life is objectified in all historical personalities and artefacts, and can be reactivated by, and for, the present experience and interest of the historian. Historicism thus treats its reflections as context-embedded insights, constantly to be reworked in a cultural synthesis for the historian. The vitalist subjectivism of this construct resurfaces in Georg Simmel's *Problems of the Philosophy of History* (1892) (see SIMMEL, G.) and, in the context of English thought, in R.G. Collingwood's *The Idea of History* (1946) (see COLLINGWOOD, R.G.). For Collingwood, history and narrative literature have near identity: 'Both the novel and the history are self-explanation, self-justifying, the product of an autonomous or self-authorizing activity; and in both cases this activity is the a priori imagination' (Collingwood 1946: 246). Collingwood's 'a priori imagination' or 're-enactment' echoes the historical thought of Croce, in which historiography and aesthetics are also linked: 'Every serious history, and every serious philosophy, ought to be a history and a philosophy "for the occasion", as Goethe said of genuine poetry, though the occasion of poetry is in the passions, that of history in the conduct of life and in morality' (Collingwood 1946: 36).

It is in this radical historicization of knowledge that historicism has achieved its most durable philosophical impact. In the post-historicist thought of Martin HEIDEGGER and Hans-Georg GADAMER (§3), the analytical complexities of historicism are transposed into an ontology of historicity in which the earlier methods of *Verstehen* (understanding) and *Erlebnis* (experience) are assimilated into a universal hermeneutic process, structured around language.

2 Totality and particularity

Particularly in the English-speaking world, historicism is better known for various critiques of its methods than for its own character. However, it is notable that the major critiques of historicism address significantly conflicting ideas of what historicism may mean. Indeed, these critiques are often articulated from positions themselves associated with historicism.

Perhaps the most influential of all critiques of historicism, Nietzsche's *Untimely Meditations* (1876) (see NIETZSCHE, F.), attacks historicism as an unselective objectivizing reading of the past which is detrimental to the vital impulses of the present. Walter BENJAMIN, particularly in his 'Theses on the Philosophy of History' in *Illuminations* (1940), rejects historicism as mere reproduction of the oppressive forces of homogenous (capitalist) history. Both these readings clearly see in historicism an early form of historical empiricism. Both, however, launch their attack from within the vitalist tradition of historicist thought.

In *Die Probleme der Geschichtsphilosophie* (The Problems of the Philosophy of History) (1924), the Neo-Kantian Henrich Rickert condemns historicism as 'nihilism' for its supposed lack of ethical values and norms. Karl Löwith, in *Meaning in History* (1949), denounces historicism as a secular product of occidental eschatology. Both these critiques attack radically different notions of historicism. Both however – Rickert in his attempt to ground historical hermeneutics, Löwith in his opposition to redemptive history – are rooted in a territory which historicism, in various guises, has already claimed. Even the theologian Ernst TROELTSCH (1922), who proposes a reading of history underpinned by the supremacy of the evangelical church as a counterpoint to ethical relativism in historicism, remains caught within that which he seeks to undermine.

The most famous critique of historicism in twentieth-century philosophy, Karl Popper's *The Poverty of Historicism* (1957), attacks a construct of historicism overshadowed by the conception that German historical writing, from Hegel through Marx to the 1930s, is sworn to totality (and totalitarianism). Like Löwith, although for wholly different reasons, Popper links historicism with theological, 'utopianist' conceptions of history. In his critique, Popper asserts a theory of historical causality which concentrates on the deduction of specific historical results from specific conditions, and is not reliant on any claim to totalizing perspectives on historical trends or broad-ranging experiential tendencies. Rather, the theory attempts to reintegrate the methodologies of the human and natural sciences. This critique is in fact a reiteration of two different repudiations of historicism, both common in the nineteenth century, on account of its supposed totalizing intention and its supposed historical relativism. Popper's argument culminates in the following: 'I wish to defend the view, so often attacked as old-fashioned by histori-cists, that history is characterized by its interest in actual, singular, or specific events, rather than in laws or generalizations' (1957: 143).

While Popper's critique certainly proved influential in the English-speaking world, and undoubtedly addressed key general problems of historiography, it is difficult to view this position as a comprehensive investigation into the character of historicism. Popper's analysis has two key deficiencies: (1) it focuses on a tradition of totalizing thought to which much historicism is expressly opposed; (2) it is itself bound into a framework of individualizing empiricism which certain traditions of historicist thought have always sought to make their own. Paradoxically, Popper condemns in historicism precisely what Nietzsche suggests as an alternative to it (see POPPER, K. §4).

This diversity both in the defence and critique of historicism can clearly be seen to derive from an aporia implicit in the term itself. The terrain covered by historicism in its protean changes not only evades definition, it encompasses the ground from which antidotes to historicism can be administered. However, it is helpful to understand this aporia as conditioned by the general development of historical thought in the nineteenth century. Indeed, the tensions and contradictions within both pro- and anti-historicist thought can be viewed as energies released by nineteenth-century critique of the Enlightenment. As historicism is articulated as a loose corrective both to the perceived neglect of Enlightenment thought for the non-rational life of the individual subject and to its schematic way of dealing with particular objectivity, it is hardly surprising that historicism should fluctuate between (or seek to reconcile) the extremes of the empiricist particularism and the totalizing subjectivism of early vitalism – both positions seek to guarantee a critical perspective on the Enlightenment. It is within the tensions of critical engagement with the Enlightenment that historicism can be best understood, if not synthetically defined.

See also: HISTORY, PHILOSOPHY OF

References and further reading

* Benjamin, W. (1940) 'Theses on the Philosophy of History', in *Illuminations*, London: Cape, 1970. (Recently established as a major work on historical philosophy.)
* Collingwood, R.G. (1946) *The Idea of History*, Oxford: Clarendon Press. (Major work in the tradition of English historicism.)
* Croce, B. (1938) *History as the Story of Liberty*, London: Allen & Unwin, 1941. (Major work in the tradition of Italian historicism.)

D'Amico, R. (1989) *Historicism and Knowledge*, New York and London: Routledge. (Excellent for its critique of Popper.)

* Dilthey, W. (1883) *Introduction to the Human Sciences*, ed. R.A. Makkrees and F. Rodi, Princeton, NJ, and Oxford: Princeton University Press, 1989. (Seminal work in the tradition of philosophical historicism ; makes links with hermeneutics.)

* Droysen, J.G. (1858) *Historik: Vorlesungen über Enzyklopädie und Methodologie der Geschichte* (Historics: Lectures on Encyclopedism and the Methodology of History), Munich: Oldenbourg. (Liberal historicism; closely associated with early German parliamentarianism.)

Engel-Jánosi, F. (1944) *The Growth of German Historicism*, Johns Hopkins University studies in historical and political sciences, series 62, no. 2, Baltimore, MD: Johns Hopkins University Press. (A clear overview.)

Gumley, J.E. (1989) *History and Totality: Radical Historicism from Hegel to Foucault*, London and New York: Routledge. (Interesting scrutiny of emancipatory historicism; imprecise on the definition of historicism.)

* Hegel, G.W.H. (1826) *Lectures on the Philosophy of World History*, Cambridge: Cambridge University Press, 1975. (Elaborates history as dialectical teleology; weakest work of a great philosopher.)

* Herder, J.G. (1784) *Outlines of a Philosophy of the History of Man*, London: Johnson, 1800. (Seminal work of pre-Hegelian philosophy of history; especially influential in nineteenth-century national theory.)

* Heussi, K. (1932) *Die Krisis des Historismus* (The Crisis of Historicism), Tübingen: Mohr. (Influential critique; not available in translation.)

* Iggers, G.G. (1969) *The German Conception of History: The National Tradition of Historical Thought from Herder to the Present*, Middletown, CT: Wesleyan University Press. (Indispensable critique, although rather weak on emancipatory dimensions to historicism.)

* Löwith, K. (1949) *Meaning and History: The Theological Implications of the Philosophy of History*, Chicago, IL: Chicago University Press. (Outstanding and original work of critical philosophy.)

* Meinecke, F. (1936) *Historicism: The Rise of a New Historical Outlook*, London: Routledge, 1972. (The most extensive defence of historicism ever written.)

* Nietzsche, F. (1876) *Untimely Meditations*, Cambridge: Cambridge University Press, 1983. (Most famous of all critiques of historicism; criticizes historicism as the debilitation of the present.)

* Popper, K. (1957) *The Poverty of Historicism*, London: Routledge. (Enormously influential, but theoretically misinformed reading of historicism.)

Reill, P.H. (1975) *The German Enlightenment and the Rise of Historicism*, Berkeley and Los Angeles, CA, and London: University of California Press. (Illuminating survey of earliest historicist writings.)

* Rickert, H. (1924) *Die Probleme der Geschichtsphilosophie* (The Problems of Historical Philosophy), Heidelberg: Winter. (Neo-Kantian theory of concept formation, applied to history.)

Schnädelbach, H. (1974) *Geschichtsphilosophie nach Hegel: Die Probleme des Historismus* (Historical Philosophy After Hegel: The Problems of Historicism), Freiburg and Munich: Karl Alber. (Excellent analysis of the development of nineteenth-century historiography.)

* Simmel, G. (1892) *The Problems of the Philosophy of History: An Epistemiological Essay*, New York: Free Press, 1977. (Relatively minor work of a great sociologist.)

* Troeltsch, E. (1922) *Der Historismus und seine Probleme* (Historicism and its Problems), Tübingen: Mohr. (Most painstaking account of historicism. Extremely illuminating exemplification of difficulties experienced by early twentieth-century thinkers in their attempts to overcome historicism; not available in English.)

CHRISTOPHER THORNHILL

HISTORY, CHINESE THEORIES OF

The beginnings of Chinese historical writing can be seen in the works of several early thinkers of the sixth through third centuries BC. The various features which we see in their nascent form in early classical sources were developed, synthesized and found their first mature expression in the composition of what came to be known as the Standard or Official Histories, notably the Spring and Autumn Annals*, the* Shiji *(Records of the Historian) and the* Hanshu *(History of the Former Han Dynasty).*

Much has been made of the purported 'cyclical' nature of Chinese views of time and the implications this has had on everything from Chinese views of history to the development of science. It is alleged that there was no notion of historical progress among the Chinese, who purportedly held a fatalistic view of infinitely repeating cycles of alternating political order and chaos, beyond human control. However, Chinese thinkers have held a wide range of different views about the pattern and flow of history.

While the amount of historical writing in China is truly staggering, Chinese thinkers have paid relatively little attention to the systematic study of the methodology and nature of history. However, there have been notable exceptions in both critical and speculative history. Critical historians at different times modified and made further suggestions regarding the form and content of the Official Histories. They also criticized the methods by which material for the Official Histories was gathered and controlled, and offered a variety of opinions regarding other forms of historical writing. Chinese philosophers of history developed elegant and sophisticated theories of history which purport to reveal the significance and structure of historical processes.

The nineteenth century marks the beginning of modern Chinese views of history, when Chinese intellectuals were first deeply influenced by Western views on the nature of history and historical method. This was also a time when Chinese society was shaken to its foundations by Western colonialism. Chinese historians of this period responded with impressive syntheses of traditional and western views. Traditional notions – for example the idea that history must fulfil a moral purpose – were recast in terms of the emerging phenomenon of Chinese nationalism. At the same time, new ideas about how objective factors, such as economic forces, shape historical events and the global scale on which these events take shape were incorporated into novel Chinese conceptions of history. This process continued into the early twentieth century when Marxist views became most influential. Early Chinese Marxist theories of history reveal a remarkable mixture of the strange and the familiar. However, Stalinist ideology quickly came to dominate more subtle forms of Marxism. As a result, Chinese Marxist views of history soon became ossified and uninspired. Little new or interesting can be found after the early 1950s.

1 Views of history in the pre-Qin period
2 The Official Histories
3 Chinese views of historical pattern and flow
4 Theories of history in traditional China
5 Modern views of history

1 Views of history in the pre-Qin period

The Chinese have shown a remarkable reverence for their past and have expended tremendous effort to record and preserve their history. This intense interest in history may have arisen, at least in part, from the practice of ancestor worship. The early Chinese sought guidance from their ancestors by divining with shell and bone, and engraved their queries and the received responses upon these materials. K.C. Chang (1983: 90) suggests that these inscriptions may have been saved for future reference, thus contributing to the notion that a *record* of past events can serve as a *guide* to proper future action, a central idea in Chinese philosophy of history. E.G. Pulleyblank (Dawson 1964: 144) has noted that ancestor worship required the maintenance of detailed genealogies and that the need to announce important state decisions to royal ancestors may have led to the keeping of state chronicles, one of the earliest forms of history found in China. These chronicles were maintained by court officials called *shi* (scribes), the same character that came to mean 'historian' and 'history'.

These early 'historians' were renowned for unswerving dedication to their calling. Several are said to have died insisting, against the wishes of their lords, that events be fully and accurately set down. These early paragons also purportedly embraced the notion that the historian's ultimate goal is to ensure the just distribution of 'praise' and 'blame'. The deeds of worthy individuals must be preserved, assuring them a kind of immortality and affording uplifting examples to later generations. Despicable acts too must be recorded and their agents held up for perpetual contempt and as a warning to future generations. Chinese history was thus seen as an accurate record of the intentions and actions of human beings, primarily those prominent in the central government, which served as a witness to good and bad deeds and a guide to future generations. These ideas about the proper role of history explain why biography played such a prominent role in Chinese historical writing, and why these biographies largely concern issues of character.

CONFUCIUS believed in a Golden Age brought into being by a series of world-ordering sages, from which subsequent ages had devolved and to which his own age needed to return (see CONFUCIAN PHILOSOPHY, CHINESE). He saw his personal mission as preserving and restoring the beliefs, practices and institutions of this past age (see *Analects* 9.5). He himself was merely the messenger, someone who 'transmits but does not create' (*Analects* 7.1). In these respects, he can be seen as a figure who epitomizes the ideal of the historian as custodian of a record of ethical guidance, handed down from sagely ancestors.

The Mohists, chief rivals of the Confucians, criticized the traditionalism of the former (see MOHIST PHILOSOPHY). In a chapter entitled 'Against Confucians', a Mohist points out that the Confucian teaching of 'transmitting but not creating' is self-contradictory, for the divine sages who *created* the culture the Confucians claim to preserve and revere did not themselves practice this ideal. However, the Mohists too appealed to their own version of an idealized past. While they recognized and advocated technological progress, they believed that the proper forms and institutions of society had been discovered by past sages, and these simply needed to be revived.

A third representative of this general belief in a lost Golden Age is the later Daoist thinker Laozi, purported author of the *Daodejing* (see DAODEJING). In Chapter 38 of this work, Laozi describes the devolution of the *dao* (way) (see DAO). Human history is the story of the rise of ethical self-consciousness, with a corresponding and proportional loss of innocence and simplicity, resulting in chaos and strife. While the Daoist Golden Age is very different from that of either Confucians or Mohists, the goal – to return to it – is the same. However, unlike the latter, Laozi makes no appeal to written records. In the ideal state, people do not employ writing at all; they keep their accounts by use of 'knotted cords'. For Laozi, the Way lies in certain pre-rational intuitions that cannot be captured in words. During the time of the Golden Age, people embraced *pu* (unadulterated simplicity), were *wuzhi* (without knowledge) and *wuwei* (without action), living spontaneous lives in accord with natural patterns and tendencies (see DAOIST PHILOSOPHY). The revival of such a state would seem to entail the end of 'history'.

Another major thinker of this period is the Confucian MENCIUS, who presents an interesting collection of views regarding history. While he is a strong defender of the Confucian vision, unlike Confucius, he relies more on intuition than tradition and expresses scepticism regarding even revered historical sources: 'It would be better not to have the *Book of Documents* than to completely trust in it' (*Mengzi* 7B3). Mencius also seems to have believed in an alternating five-hundred-year cycle of order and chaos (*Mengzi* 2B13). However, it is not clear the degree to which he believed this was an immutable pattern or simply an account of the interval between traditional sage–kings.

A contemporary Daoist thinker, ZHUANGZI, recognized that different times and circumstances employ and indeed require different actions and policies. Things ebb and flow in human history but lack any set pattern or structure. Zhuangzi concluded that there was no discernable pattern in history, devolutionary, cyclical or progressive. The one thing one could learn from history is that to insist on patterning oneself on the ways of past sages is a recipe for failure. Thus the records of even the most gifted sages are nothing but their 'chaff and dregs'.

The next great Confucian of this period, XUNZI, strongly criticized Mencius for believing that human nature contains innate moral tendencies. Xunzi saw this belief as not only wrong but also a threat to the status of the traditional wisdom of the founding Confucian sages. Xunzi regarded the insights of these sages as discoveries that had been achieved through a long and difficult process of experimentation. The founding sages had discovered how to organize society just as potters had discovered how to produce exquisite pottery, through a process of trial and error. Xunzi thus strongly implies an early period in which the *dao* evolved through successive stages until it resulted in the Golden Age whose plan Confucius preserved.

One of Xunzi's disciples, HAN FEIZI, ultimately broke with the Confucian tradition, a move which required, and perhaps was in part caused by, his rejection of the Confucian view of history. Han Feizi argued that human history was progressive, moving from more primitive to more advanced stages. He mocked the Confucian call to study the 'ways of the ancients' and used historical examples primarily to illustrate the folly of such an attempt (*Han Feizi* 49). Han Feizi did show a strong sympathy with the Daoist belief in a primitive past utopia, but rejected the idea that this state of affairs could be revived. The world had become nastier since then: people were now too numerous and goods too scarce. All that remained were selfish human desires, which could only be controlled through a system of strict rewards and punishments (see LEGALIST PHILOSOPHY, CHINESE; LAW AND RITUAL IN CHINESE PHILOSOPHY). Hence, while technology and certain social institutions would need continually to evolve, the evolution of human beings had come to a halt after an initial fall from innocence.

2 The Official Histories

The *Spring and Autumn Annals*, along with its various commentaries, served as the earliest models for Chinese historical writing. The text itself is taken to be the court record of Confucius' native state, covering the years 722–481 BC. Confucius purportedly edited it in order to insure that 'praise' and 'blame' were properly assigned. This and another, later classic, the *Shujing* (Book of Documents), existed in some form during the early period of Chinese philosophy (see §1). Traditional accounts describe the *Shujing* as a 'record of words' – in other words, official proclamations – in contrast to the *Spring and Autumn Annals* which was 'a record of deeds', that is, the actions of officials. The form and theory of the Official Histories was greatly influenced by these two texts and early views regarding them.

A major development with profound and enduring consequences for Chinese views of history and methods of historiography was the writing of the

Shiji (Records of the Historian). Its author, Sima Qian (145?–90? BC), completed the work begun by his father, Sima Tan. Both had held the office of *taishi* (grand scribe) but their project was a private, family enterprise. The *Shiji* was a world history, seeking to provide an account of all of Chinese history down to the time of its composition. It presents the past primarily in terms of the lives of important families and individuals, largely though not exclusively those involved directly in the government, relying upon vivid and lively descriptions of their actions and intentions. Its narrative style is designed to allow historical events to speak for themselves; however, the author clearly embraced the 'praise' and 'blame' model of historical writing and believed strongly in the didactic value of history.

The composition of the *Shiji* was followed by another family production when Ban Gu (AD 32–92) completed the *Hanshu* (History of the Former Han Dynasty). Ban Gu laboured to complete a project begun by his father, and his sister, Ban Zhao, helped to complete the work after his own death. While its structure is largely based upon the *Shiji*, Ban Gu's work differed in being a history of a single dynasty. This affected not only the structure of the work but the view that history should be seen as a unified whole: history now was presented in terms of the rise and fall of a single dynasty. Another difference between this later work and the *Shiji* is that while both began as private family projects, Ban Gu's work was co-opted by the government and received official support and sanction in its later stages. Thus it was the first truly official history, creating a model which began a series of later works that continued until the end of the imperial period in 1911.

While the different official histories vary in detail, they share a remarkable number of general features. As mentioned above, with the exception of the *Shiji*, all concern a single dynastic period; taken together, they present history as a series or, in some conceptions, a repeating cycle of imperial reigns. All rely, almost exclusively, on literary sources to construct their account of the past and employ a cut-and-paste method to arrange these materials into a coherent narrative. Again with the exception of the *Shiji*, all the official histories are retrospective, written by people from succeeding dynasties. By the time of the Tang dynasty (618–906) institutions were in place whereby the reigning dynasty prepared material intended to serve as the primary source for their own future history. Also beginning with the Tang, with the single exception of the *Xin Wudai shi* (New History of the Five Dynasties) by Ouyang Xiu (1007–72), official histories were the product of a team of historians assigned by the government to complete the task.

It was not long before historical writings came to be seen as a distinct and important genre. In the fourfold classification that became standard in the third century, history is ranked immediately after the classics, coming before both philosophy and *belles lettres*. It might seem strange that history was ranked ahead of philosophy, since historical writing owed much of its esteem to its ethical value. However, history, being a record of actual conduct was generally regarded as superior to philosophy, which was by its very nature abstract and speculative. This view was widely held throughout the tradition and precedents for it can be found in texts as early as the the *Zhongyong* (see ZHONGYONG) and the *Shiji*.

3 Chinese views of historical pattern and flow

We have seen that early Chinese thinkers expressed a wide range of different views concerning the pattern and direction of history (see §1). Some saw history as a repeating cycle of periods of human flourishing and decline. Others believed that history had evolved in earlier periods but that in at least certain important respects – specifically in terms of social institutions and practices – it had reached a stage of completion. Yet other thinkers denied that there was any discernable pattern or rhythm to the flow of history. The most widely held view was that history was a process of devolution from a past Golden Age to present turbid times. The exact nature of the lost Golden Age and the causes of its decline varied widely among different thinkers, but those who advocated such views all advanced an accompanying appeal to revive past institutions and practices in order to return to the Golden Age. This idea was further developed during the succeeding Han dynasty and found clear expression in texts like the *Liji* (Book of Rites), particularly in the chapter *Liyun* (Evolution of the Rites) (see CHINESE CLASSICS), and the *Huainanzi*, particularly Chapter 2 (see HUAINANZI). It is important to note that while such views hoped for a revival of the Golden Age, they also clearly entailed the idea that one can fall out of such a state as well as regain it. In other words, these were not millennial movements that saw an end to history in some final, ideal utopia. Some Chinese thinkers did express views like this: for example, the popular Daoist uprisings of the Red Eyebrows in the first century AD and the Yellow Turbans in the second century AD and the Taiping movement of 1851–64 were all founded on such a belief. The modern thinker Kang Youwei (1858–1927) also espoused a similar view (see §5).

Those who believed in a past Golden Age, as well as those who tended to see this age only as a future possibility, often described history in terms of set phases either devolving from or evolving into an age of good order, prosperity and peace. In some cases, such phases were seen as repeating historical cycles. Mencius may have held a view like this and the Han Confucian DONG ZHONGSHU, possibly developing ideas of an earlier thinker named Zou Yan (*fl.* 4th century BC), described history as a repeating cycle of five elemental phases: wood, fire, earth, metal and water, each of which exerts the dominant influence in their respective age.

Under the influence of Buddhism, later Chinese thinkers developed elaborate cosmic histories (see BUDDHIST PHILOSOPHY, CHINESE). For example, SHAO YONG presented a complex scheme which describes history in terms of the coming into being of the universe, the emergence of living things, the flourishing of human society, the eventual decline of society and human beings, the ultimate end of all life and the extinction of this world system. The process then begins anew. ZHU XI espoused a similar though much less articulated view, believing that the universe arose out of and would eventually devolve back into a state of undifferentiated *qi*, out of which a new universe would gradually coalesce and take shape (see QI).

4 Theories of history in traditional China

Liu Zhiji (661–721) composed the first treatise on the writing of history in China, the *Shitong* (Survey on History). Liu embraced most traditional notions concerning the purpose of historical writing and the idea that history should be viewed in terms of separate dynastic units. However, he criticized the degree to which the bureaucratization of the process of producing the Official Histories had come to influence their accuracy and objectivity. He also offered specific recommendations regarding the form and content of the Official Histories, suggesting that some of the traditional *zhi* (monographs) be dropped and others added. For example, he argued that the monographs on astronomy be eliminated since they concerned a topic that was timeless and hence inappropriate for inclusion in a historical work. He also argued that a new monograph on cities be added, thus expanding the range of material that was to be considered in the official histories. His ideas regarding the incorporation of local material in the writing of the Official Histories and his view that a historian had to possess the specific virtues of insight, literary skill and learning in order to perform his task, influenced Zhang Xuecheng (see below).

While Liu's *Shitong* was a treatise on the theory of historiography, the *Zizhi tongjian* (A Comprehensive Mirror for Aid in Government) of Sima Guang (1019–86) was a world history in chronicle form, covering the period 403 BC–AD 959. In the process of composing this great work, Sima Guang developed and refined his own ideas on the nature and practice of historical writing. As the title of the work suggests, the *Zizhi tongjian* had a very traditional goal: to provide a collection of historical examples of good and bad government that could serve as a resource for contemporary rulers. Sima Guang drew upon a wide variety of different sources for this work, going well beyond those normally used in composing the Official Histories. He began with a vast collection of material organized by period, which he then whittled down in successive drafts. One of his most significant methodological developments was his effort to verify the authenticity of his sources and the events they recorded. He carefully examined the texts he drew upon and subjected them to strict philological and textual analysis. He would not accept the validity of any purported event if it conflicted with objective facts – such as a firmly established date – or if it failed to cohere with reliable collateral evidence and the dictates of common sense. He developed and maintained the rigorous critical standards of a scientific historian.

The greatest Chinese philosopher of history is undoubtedly Zhang Xuecheng (1738–1801). He made significant contributions to historiography; for example, he wrote and promoted *fangzhi* (local gazetteers) as an important historical genre. However, as he said of himself, his greatest insights concerned not the method of history but its significance. Zhang is renowned for his claim that, 'the six classics are all history'. By this he meant several things, all related to his grand speculative theories concerning history.

Like HEGEL, Zhang believed history went through distinct and necessary stages of development. The *dao* (way) came into being as a response to historical necessities. However, unlike Hegel, Zhang believed that the process of historical development – specifically the evolution of social institutions and practices – had reached its highest point in the distant past. The *dao* had attained full form in the Golden Age of the Duke of Zhou. At that point in time, society had become a perfect and harmonious whole in which what we now regard as the separate functions of officials and teachers were united; there were no individual disciplines or schools of learning and all writing was anonymous and *gong* (public), being in the service of some branch of government. Later history has meandered around this lost ideal, with successive ages dominated by an excess of 'philosophy', 'philology' or 'literature'.

Confucius is unique in having been born at the historical moment when the *dao* crested and began to decline. He realized that his historically determined mission was to preserve a record of this ideal society. Later ages wrongly regard the texts he preserved as 'records of the *dao*', but in fact they are simply the records of various official agencies of this ideal time. The *dao* itself cannot be seen or described, only its traces, like the tracks of an invisible passing wheel (see DAOIST PHILOSOPHY §2; DAO). The *dao* takes shape and is revealed in the playing out of historical processes and so the classics, like all texts, are 'history'.

People of later ages also fail to see that their historical situations differ from that of Confucius and mistakenly attempt to emulate him by writing books about the *dao* instead of doing whatever their own historical moment requires. Their true task lies in discerning which of the three errant tendencies is in ascendance in their own age and working to counteract it. In order to succeed at this task, one must be able to read events in the world properly. This requires one to be a certain *kind* of historian. In addition to the three virtues described by Liu Zhiji, one needs to have the *virtue* of a historian: a kind of faculty or sense that allows one to discern how historical events fit into the grand pattern of the *dao*. Zhang's philosophy of history raises history to preeminent status: it is the way – the only true way – to understand the dao.

5 Modern views of history

The story of modern Chinese views of history remains incomplete. However, its opening chapter was written by Kang Youwei (1858–1927). Kang was both a highly respected traditional scholar and one of the first Chinese intellectuals to have a firm grasp and appreciation of Western ideas regarding the nature of history and historical method. This combination led him to propose a revolutionary view of history and in particular, Confucius' role in it. In his *Datongshu* (Book of Great Unity), Kang rejected the traditional notion of a past Golden Age and the idea that Confucius had merely 'transmitted' its *dao* to later ages. Drawing on and modifying earlier Chinese views of history, such as those found in the *Liyun* (Evolution of the Rites) chapter of the *Liji* (see §2) and the *Gongyang* commentary to the *Spring and Autumn Annals* (see CHINESE CLASSICS), and combining these with ideas taken from Buddhism, Christianity and Confucianism, Kang developed a highly original speculative philosophy of history. His view is based upon his theory that the history of the world consists of 'three ages': the past age of Chaos, the present age of Approaching Harmony and future age of Great Harmony. Kang attempted to trace this idea

back to early Chinese sources. However, while certain similar ideas can be found in early texts, particularly among the writings of DONG ZHONGSHU, Kang differed in seeing history as evolutionary and not cyclical. His theory of the three ages described a philosophy of historical progress culminating in a future grand utopia; the Golden Age lay not behind but ahead of us. Moreover, Kang claimed that this was Confucius' real view as well and argued that Confucius, aware of how revolutionary his message was, had cleverly presented his vision of the future as a form of traditionalism.

Kang's student Liang Qichao (1873–1929) eventually distanced himself from most of his teacher's views of history. Liang turned to less speculative projects and wrote the *Zhongguo lishi yanjiu fa* (Methodology for the Study of Chinese History). This work of practical, critical history attacked traditional Chinese historical method from a western perspective. However, in doing so it relied heavily on earlier Chinese critics of traditional methods, several of which have been discussed above.

Neither Kang nor Liang broke free from the traditional idea that history was to serve a higher moral purpose. Both were trying to relate their philosophies of history to the immediate and pressing concerns of contemporary Chinese nationalism. This led them and their successors to a broader examination of Chinese culture and a much greater appreciation of its variety and richness, particularly its more popular forms, which traditionally had been almost wholly neglected. This development had a profound effect on thinkers like Hu Shi (1891–1962) and Lu Xun (1881–1936) who advocated and contributed to the history and promulgation of popular literature.

The rise and eventual dominance of Chinese Marxism both contributed to and later constricted the development of modern Chinese views of history (see MARXISM, CHINESE). The Marxist explanation of history as the playing out of economic forces across vast spans of time, helped to introduce new ideas about the role of objective and enduring factors in human history. This broadened the scope and range of Chinese conceptions of history and worked to break down the dynastic view. It also encouraged a more synthetic approach to historical problems. However, cruder forms of Marxist historicism became dominant and the older dynastic view came to be replaced by an equally Procrustean scheme of 'slave' and 'feudal' periods. Debates then raged as to whether Confucius had lived during a 'slave' or 'feudal' period. A great deal was seen to turn on this issue: since Confucius defended the 'feudal system', if he lived in a slave period he should be viewed as a progressive, someone moving history forward on the 'inevitable' course toward its communist future. If however, it turned out that Confucius lived in a feudal period, then he should be viewed as a reactionary, someone holding back the future Golden Age.

In many respects, the Chinese Marxist view of history is both strange and familiar. Its moral temper and utopian nature are familiar features of traditional Chinese conceptions of history; and while its particular content is surely new, its general form and the trajectory it describes can be found in several of the sources and thinkers discussed above. The persistence of these traditional themes suggests that the story of modern Chinese views of history is still being written.

See also: CHINESE CLASSICS; LEGALIST PHILOSOPHY, CHINESE; MARXISM, CHINESE; CHINESE PHILOSOPHY; CONFUCIAN PHILOSOPHY, CHINESE; DAOIST PHILOSOPHY; HISTORY, PHILOSOPHY OF; LAW AND RITUAL IN CHINESE PHILOSOPHY; MENCIUS; XUNZI; ZHUANGZI

References and further reading

Beasley, W.G. and Pulleyblank, E.G. (eds) (1962) *Historians of China and Japan*, London: Oxford University Press. (The best anthology available. In particular, see the contributions of van der Loon, Pulleyblank, Demieville and Gray.)

* Chang, K.C. (1983) *Art, Myth and Ritual: The Path to Political Authority in Ancient China*, Cambridge, MA: Harvard University Press. (A study of very early Chinese culture from an archaeological perspective.)

* Dawson, R. (ed.) (1964) *The Legacy of China*, Oxford: Clarendon Press, 1964. (Solid introduction to Chinese culture.)

Feuerwerker, A. (ed.) (1968) *History in Communist China*, Cambridge, MA: MIT Press. (A collection of articles on various aspects of Marxist historiography.)

Hartwell, R.M. (1971) 'Historical Analogism, Public Policy and Social Science in Eleventh and Twelfth-Century China', *American Historical Review* 76 (3): 690–727. (On the role reasoning from historical analogy and precedent played in the formation of governmental policy and how this affected the development of a social scientific approach.)

Grieder, J.B. (1970) *Hu Shih and the Chinese Renaissance*, Cambridge, MA: Harvard University Press. (Intellectual biography of this important modern Chinese philosopher, social activist and intellectual.)

* Kang Youwei (1902) *Datong shu* (Book of Great Unity), trans. L.G. Thompson, *Ta t'ung shu: The One-world Philosophy of K'ang Yu-wei*, London:

Allen & Unwin, 1958. (The definitive statement of Kang's utopian vision.)

Levenson, J.R. (1953) *Liang Ch'i-ch'ao and the Mind of Modern China*. Cambridge, MA: Harvard University Press. (Intellectual biography of Liang Qichao, one of modern China's leading thinkers.)

Liji (Book of Rites) (2nd century BC–2nd century AD), trans. J. Legge, *Li Chi: Book of Rites*, New York: University Books, 1967, 2 vols. (The most important source for traditional ritual practice.)

Needham, J. (1965) *Time and Eastern Man*, Royal Anthropological Institute Occasional Paper 21, Glasgow: The University Press. (Thorough exploration of this topic.)

Nivison, D.S. (1966) *The Life and Thought of Chang Hsüeh-ch'eng (1738–1801)*, Stanford, CA: Stanford University Press. (The definitive work on Zhang Xuecheng and his thought.)

Shujing (Book of Documents) (5th–4th century BC) trans. J. Legge, *The Shoo King or The Book of Historical Documents*, vol. 3 of *The Chinese Classics*, Hong Kong: Hong Kong University Press, 1970. (Translation with facing Chinese text.)

Sima Qian (2nd–1st century BC) *Shiji* (Records of the Historian), trans. B. Watson, *Records of the Grand Historian of China*, New York: Columbia University Press, 1961, 2 vols. (Selective translation of China's first official history.)

Watson, B. (1963) *Ssu-ma Ch'ien, Grand Historian of China*, New York: Columbia University Press. (A thorough study of the *Shiji* and its author, Sima Qian.)

Zuozhuan (Zuo Annals) (2nd–1st century BC), trans. J. Legge, *The Ch'un Ts'ew with the Tso Chuen*, vol. 5 of *The Chinese Classics*, Hong Kong: Hong Kong University Press, 1970.

PHILIP J. IVANHOE

HISTORY, EXPLANATION IN
see EXPLANATION IN HISTORY AND SOCIAL SCIENCE

HISTORY, HOLISM AND INDIVIDUALISM IN *see* HOLISM AND INDIVIDUALISM IN HISTORY AND SOCIAL SCIENCE

HISTORY, PHILOSOPHY OF

Philosophy of history is the application of philosophical conceptions and analysis to history in both senses, the study of the past and the past itself. Like most branches of philosophy its intellectual origins are cloudy, but they lie in a refinement of 'sacred' histories, especially those of Judaism and Christianity. The first major philosopher to outline a scheme of world history was Immanuel Kant in The Idea of a Universal History from a Cosmopolitan Point of View *(1784), and German Idealism also produced Hegel's* Lectures on the Philosophy of World History *(1837), a much longer and more ambitious attempt to make philosophical sense of the history of the world as a whole. According to Hegel, history is rational, the working out, in fact, of philosophical understanding itself.*

The accelerating success of natural science in the nineteenth century gave rise to a powerful combination of empiricism and logical positivism which produced a philosophical climate highly unfavourable to Hegelian philosophy of history. The belief became widespread among philosophers that Hegel, and Marx after him, had developed a priori theories that ignored historical contingency in favour of historical necessity, and which were empirically unfalsifiable. Karl Popper's philosophy of science was especially influential in converting philosophy of history to a new concern with the methods of historical study rather than with the shape of the past. Two rival conceptions of historical method existed. One tried to model explanation in history on what they took to be the form of explanation in science, and argued for the existence of 'covering laws' by which historians connect the events they seek to explain. The other argued for a distinctive form of explanation in history, whose object was the meaning of human action and whose structure was narrative rather than deductive.

Neither side in this debate was able to claim a convincing victory, with the result that philosophers gradually lost interest in history and began to concern themselves more generally with the nature of human action. This interest, combined with a revival of nineteenth-century German hermeneutics, the study of texts in their social and cultural milieu, in turn revived interest among analytical philosophers in the writings of Hegel and Nietzsche. The impact of continental influences in philosophy, art criticism and social theory was considerable, and reintroduced a historical dimension that had been largely absent from twentieth-century analytical philosophy. In particular, the formation of fundamental philosophical ideas began to be studied as a historical process. The Enlightenment came to be seen as a crucial period in the development of philosophy, and of modernity more generally, and with this understanding came the belief that the contemporary Western world is postmodern. In this way, social theory and the philosophy of culture in fact returned, albeit unawares, to the 'grand narrative' tradition in philosophy of history.

1 **Origins**
2 **Philosophical history**
3 **Analytical philosophy of history**
4 **History and the understanding of action**
5 **The return of 'grand theory'**

1 Origins

Is there a logic of history? Is there, beyond all the causal and incalculable elements of the separate events, something that we may call a metaphysical structure of historic humanity, something that is essentially independent of the outward forms – social, spiritual and political – which we see so clearly? ... Does world-history present to the seeing eye certain grand traits, again and again, with sufficient constancy to justify certain conclusions?

(Spengler 1918, vol. 1: 3)

So writes Oswald Spengler at the start of his monumental book *The Decline of the West* (1918). Spengler thought that the sort of interest in history which he proposed to take was novel, and to be contrasted with an interest in the 'elements of separate events'. This implies that hitherto (that is before Spengler) all history was concerned with the mere recording of what actually happened, in fact the desire to have a knowledge of the past entirely for its own sake and without practical or theoretical aims, is a relatively sophisticated, and relatively late, intellectual accomplishment. Most historical writing is characterized by a less detached view. Arguably all cultures which lend importance to an awareness of their own past have tried to ascertain within it some meaning, significance or purpose, to cast light upon present events and speculate successfully upon the future. Generally, interest in the past of this practical sort has prevailed over the more academic concern of the study of what has been called 'scientific history'. Scientific history here means the attempt simply to arrive at an accurate account of past events based upon sufficient evidence, without regard to learning lessons or predicting the future course of events. To say that a 'practical' interest in the past has overshadowed a more academic one is not to deny that traces of scientific history can be found in the ancient world; there is reason to regard Herodotus as one of its earliest and in some ways finest practitioners, and it was this sort of detachment from ultimate meaning that led St AUGUSTINE (§15) to regard the 'pagan' history of his own time as seriously inadequate. But more strikingly, and even earlier in Western culture, we find a broader intellectual ambition that can be described as the attempt to look beneath the surface of events and find their inner or ultimate meaning.

The most familiar histories of this kind have been religious. A marked feature of Judaism, for instance, is a belief in the revelatory power of the past to disclose, and to confirm, a relationship between a people and their god. The Jewish religion, as its sacred books reveal, is coloured by the desire to formulate a sacred history. Many of the books of the Old Testament try to move behind such historical events as the Exodus from Egypt or the removal of the Jews to Babylon and detect in them the purposes of God. In Isaiah, for example (which is generally agreed to be the work of at least two authors), the first prophet's principal interest is in explaining the conquests, invasions and natural disasters to which Judea was subjected at one point in its history as the actions of a God highly displeased by the moral and religious waywardness of his chosen people and unmoved by the ritualistic sacrifices they made it their practice to offer (see HERMENEUTICS, BIBLICAL §1).

Jewish theology is sacred history *par excellence*, but in this it is not unique. It has provided a model on which other religions have sought to improve. This is most obviously true of Christianity, which picks out a special set of events from the general flow of the past as the reference points around which a story of divine intentions may be told. This set of events includes many of those from Jewish history, but adds the central event of the Incarnation of God in Jesus, a historical figure of first-century Palestine, through whose life and teaching God can be seen to act directly in a historical time. Among the Church Fathers it is St Augustine who first makes Christian sacred history explicit; indeed we owe the term 'sacred history' to him. But much of the general idea is present in early Christian writings. These make extensive use of historical typology – of patriarch, prophet and messiah, for example.

2 Philosophical history

The idea of a 'sacred history' has its origins in these two religions, and their prominence in Western culture has made its conceptions highly influential in the subsequent development of historical and cultural self-understanding. However, histories of this rather grand sort need not always be concerned with the purposes of God, or even with the invocation of supernatural agencies. Subsequent, secular, thinkers have taken up the same ambition, but transformed it

in essentially non-religious ways. The intellectual Enlightenment in the eighteenth century was a considerable stimulus to this. Among the writers who began this process the most notable were J.G. HERDER (§4), author of *Outlines of a Philosophy of the History of Man* (1800), and the Marquis de Condorcet, who wrote a *Sketch for an Historical Picture of the Progress of the Human Mind* (1795). Immanuel KANT, was the first major philosopher to formulate explicitly 'The Idea of a Universal History from a Cosmopolitan Point of View' (1784). In this essay Kant maintains that though the empirical study of historical phenomena is essential to understanding the human past, in itself it is insufficient, since the plans of individuals, however rational, cannot on their own explain the emergence of developing forms of thought and civil association. There are, Kant contends, general trends to be observed in the history of humankind. These cannot plausibly be attributed to the purposes of individuals, even in concert, and thus any serious intellectual concern with the past has to supply a different explanation. Their explanation, Kant believed, must impute to the historical process a natural teleology, a purpose or end which nature or providence (he uses both terms) develops through the rational agency of human beings.

Kant's essay is merely an outline of a possible form of inquiry, and in it he looks to the emergence of an equivalent in this sphere of a Kepler or a Newton in physical science, someone intellectually equipped to compose a genuinely universal history which will reveal the underlying rationale of the past in the way that Kepler and Newton uncovered the underlying rationality of the physical universe. Such a figure as Kant anticipates might be thought to have been found in his celebrated successor G.W.F. HEGEL (§8), whose *Lectures on the Philosophy of World History* (1837) probably constitute the most sustained effort ever made in this aspect of philosophy. Though Hegel believed himself to be providing a rational exposition of the truths obscurely contained in Christianity, the outcome of his reflections on 'world history' was one in which theological categories were systematically replaced by philosophical conceptions. Thus the work of divine agency is in Hegel converted into the activity of 'reason' itself, and the end of history is not the kingdom of God but the manifestation of absolute mind or spirit.

There remain some mystical elements in Hegel's view, and he himself did not intend that the religious dimension should be eliminated; it was, rather, to be rationalized by philosophy. But even if Hegel retains some of the essential characteristics of sacred history, during the course of the nineteenth century successor histories of the same 'grand' sort emerged which had no place for religious meaning or the divine. The best known of these is that of Karl MARX (§8). Set out in brief in the *Communist Manifesto* (1848), co-authored with Friedrich Engels, and elaborated at much greater length in the unfinished three-volume work *Capital* (vol. 1, 1867), Marx's theory of history self-consciously abandons religious aspirations as products of false-consciousness and seeks their replacement with purely material (largely economic) alternatives. Marx does not invoke divine intentions but rather historical laws governing economic change – from feudal to capitalist to socialist – and the communistic classless society to which he looks as the future ideal is not a world constituted and governed by universal acknowledgement of divine rule, but one waiting to be created by imaginative human endeavour freed from the constraints of economic necessity.

Marx is not alone with his secular alternative to sacred history. Better known in their own day were those of Auguste COMTE and Herbert SPENCER. For Comte, regarded by some as the founder of modern sociology, the categories of religious thought which traditional sacred histories employed, represented a primitive 'theological' stage of mind, that the philosophical rationalism of the seventeenth and eighteenth centuries had replaced and hence rendered redundant. This rationalism, which Comte referred to as the 'metaphysical' stage of human history, was in its turn being replaced by the scientific advances of the 'positivist' period in which he was writing. Spencer also saw contemporary science as containing the means of remedying the inadequacies of religious understanding, and set about deploying, as he saw them, the insights of evolutionary theory for the purposes of constructing a new world history.

The accounts of the past elaborated by Comte, or Spencer, have attracted little serious attention in this century, but, no less than Marx's more famous contention that 'all history is the history of class struggle', they exemplify an attempt that has often been made to formulate a grand narrative of human history without the assistance, or restrictions, of revealed religion. These attempts retain a continuity with those that they sought to replace. Between the older sacred histories and their newer secular rivals there are marked differences. Yet there remains in them the same aspiration of looking behind the surface appearances of history, and the same belief that we need not rest content with merely recounting sequences of events in chronological order, but may properly seek to discern a meaningful direction within them.

Alternatives to sacred history, such as those of Hegel, Marx and Comte, have been called 'grand narratives', and in them we find the origins of philosophy of history, to be contrasted with history

simpliciter. These various and familiar conceptions all illustrate the nature of 'philosophical' as opposed to 'scientific' history. They contend that behind the miasma of historical chance and change, the past has a shape or a direction or a meaning. The task of discerning this shape has attracted various labels. Sacred history is one, grand narrative, world history, philosophical history and universal history are others. But whatever the variety of terms, it is here that philosophy of history proper begins.

3 Analytical philosophy of history

The foregoing is philosophy in rather a grand sense, the sense in which many people who do not know a great deal about philosophy expect it to be conducted. But from an early stage philosophers, especially in the analytical tradition, were sceptical of the ambitions of Hegel and his successors. In fact Hegelian philosophy of history, and with it the whole endeavour to produce a universal history, fell out of favour relatively quickly, and never attracted very widespread support in the English speaking world. There were several reasons for this, one of which was that Hegelian philosophy came to be associated with totalitarianism. A more deep-seated philosophical reason, however, had to do with the success of natural science and the philosophical dominance of the positivistic, empirical conceptions of knowledge to which this success gave rise. The positivist idea that our knowledge can only comprise plain, empirically ascertainable fact is, by its nature, unsympathetic to conceptions of hidden or underlying 'meanings' (see POSITIVISM IN THE SOCIAL SCIENCES §1). This is as true of history as of other disciplines.

The most influential elaboration of these doubts for the philosophy of history is to be found in Karl Popper's celebrated book *The Open Society and its Enemies* (1945), in which he develops a line of thought similar to that found in earlier British critics of Hegel, notably L.T. Hobhouse and Bertrand Russell (see POPPER, K. §4). In an earlier work Popper had developed a criterion of proper science, by which we should take him to mean real knowledge. This is the falsifiablity criterion. A theory counts as a genuine contribution to knowledge if it can in principle be falsified by empirical observation, and has withstood attempts to falsify it. According to Popper, Hegel's philosophy of history, like its less philosophical successor, Marxism, is vitiated by its manipulation of evidence to avoid falsification. Rather than the theory being answerable to the facts scientific history uncovers, the 'facts' are determined by the theory. Hegel and Marx do not tell us how the past was, but how, in the light of their theories, it must have been.

In this way, though they masquerade as historians, they in fact pass beyond the realms of empirical history, and the claims they make, though they may superficially look like historical theories, are actually unfalsifiable a priori assertions. Thus, when Hegel considers the histories of India or China, which do not fit the general conception with which he is working, they are not taken as refutations, but explained away as aberrations.

In a later book, *The Poverty of Historicism* (1957), Popper applied this criticism to theories of history more broadly, and his attack on what he labelled 'historicism' has generally been regarded as both innovative and effective. Marx raises the very same criticism against Hegel, and Hegel himself is not only aware of it, but tries to answer it. Whatever the justice of the criticism, or the cogency of Hegel's original reply, Popper's charge stuck for some considerable time, and this caused the philosophy of history to take a different turn.

If the construction of grand narratives is no longer respectable, what interest can philosophy take in history? The answer is 'methodology'. In this respect philosophy of history in the twentieth century followed the path of philosophy of science a century earlier. With the divorce between natural philosophy and empirical science, philosophers in the nineteenth century ceased to concern themselves directly with explaining the phenomena of the natural world, as philosophers of an earlier period had tried to do, and focused instead upon the methods by which empirical science did this. This is a large part of the purpose of John Stuart Mill's *System of Logic* (1843), for instance, which has had great influence on philosophers of science, whose aim increasingly became that of making explicit the methods of science (see MILL, J.S.). In a similar fashion, philosophers tried to articulate the methods and presuppositions of empirical history.

Once the subject turned in this direction it was inevitable that comparisons would be drawn between science and history, and hence for a time the predominant ambition was to give history a status equivalent to that of science. Thus, for instance, against a background assumption that natural scientists are value-neutral with respect to their subject matter, it became a question as to whether historians could likewise achieve neutrality with respect to the events they recounted. The attempt to answer this question positively was allied by a movement among historians themselves to abandon 'Whig' interpretations of history, according to which the past was conceived as a struggle between the 'good' forces of enlightenment and the 'bad' forces of reaction.

The high point of philosophy of history modelled

on philosophy of science was a famous essay by Carl Hempel, 'The Function of General Laws in History' (1942). Having earlier set out a logic of scientific explanation, showing it to require only empirical observation and logical validity, Hempel argued that the same pattern could be found in the investigations of historians, and that the explanation of historical events required general 'covering laws' no less than that of physical events. However, Hempel's application of natural scientific models to history was convincing only so long as it was thought that he had really uncovered the logic of science. In fact, philosophers of science, including Hempel himself, found serious difficulties with the basic model, which, being a purely logical structure, had difficulty in accommodating temporal order and causal dependence. It could, for instance, as easily accommodate the idea that the length of a shadow explains the height of the sun, as that the height of the sun explains the length of a shadow.

4   History and the understanding of action

Despite several attempts like Hempel's, the difficulty of establishing a convincing parallel between history and natural science raised more serious sceptical doubts: do historians actually explain events? Is an objective knowledge of the past possible at all? These questions drew philosophers of history into yet more general questions of epistemology and metaphysics. What is knowledge? What sort of existence does the past really have? In turn, this prompted an examination of alternative philosophies of knowledge and understanding and, at the hands of philosophers such as Isaiah Berlin, attention began to be paid to German thinkers of the nineteenth century, notably Herder and DILTHEY (§3). It also drew attention to the earlier and hitherto neglected author of *The New Science*, the Italian philosopher Giambattista VICO (§6), whose principal intellectual endeavour had been to capture the distinctiveness of cultural study.

This movement away from the scientific analogy was strengthened by those philosophers of history who had remained convinced that the attempt to model history on science was mistaken. One important thinker in this regard was R.G. COLLINGWOOD, an Oxford philosopher, also a distinguished historian in his own right, who had remained in the idealist tradition, largely unaffected by the major currents of the positivistic philosophy of his time. Collingwood's *The Idea of History* (1946) was not published until after his death, but it set out in an influential way both the history of history and a striking alternative account of historical understanding to that of the scientific model.

Collingwood argues, in common with many German philosophers of the nineteenth century, that there is a radical difference between natural processes and historical events. What distinguishes the latter from the former is that they have meaning. That is to say, natural processes, such as volcanoes or chemical reactions, have no significance for the objects or materials which undergo them. This leaves scientists who study them free to identify and order in accordance with their theoretical and explanatory purposes. But the actions of which history is composed are quite different. These have significance and meaning for the agents who performed them; their nature is determined by the cultural context and individual thought that gives rise to them. In the strict sense, natural processes can only be explained; there is nothing about them that requires understanding. By contrast, the events of history have to be understood, and Collingwood marked this difference by saying the historical events have an inner meaning as well as an outer form. The task of the historian, accordingly, is to rethink the thought of the historical agent.

Among philosophers in the analytical tradition, the writer who brought Collingwood's ideas to greatest prominence was W.H. Dray. In his book *Laws and Explanation in History* (1957), Dray directly confronted the Hempel-inspired conception of historical explanation, and argued for a more humanistic conception. In the same spirit, W.H. Walsh argued in favour of 'colligatory' explanations that brought to prominence the idea of historical explanation as narrative. For a time these alternatives fought a vigorous battle in a large number of books and articles. The argument was extended, in fact, into the philosophy of the social sciences, where the gulf between empirical, positivistic theories and hermeneutic, interpretative conceptions of the understanding of human behaviour widened (see SOCIAL SCIENCE, METHODOLOGY OF §4).

However, no clear victory emerged on either side, and the dispute rather suddenly ground to a halt. Interest in Vico, Collingwood and hermeneutics all grew, but explicit interest in the philosophy of history itself declined.

5 The return of 'grand theory'

With the demise of its analytical version, philosophy of history appeared almost to disappear. But this was largely a matter of mere appearance. In other branches of philosophy the introduction of a historical element became increasingly important. In Richard Rorty's *Philosophy and the Mirror of Nature* (1980), for example, the thesis was advanced that the central problems of metaphysics and especially epistemology had to be understood, and resolved, in the context of a historically specific ambition (see RORTY, R.M.). And Alasdair MacIntyre's *After Virtue* (1981) applied the same sort of thinking to the problems of moral philosophy. According to MacIntyre, the philosophical difficulties encountered by attempts to render morality coherent were the outcome of a long historical process of cultural disintegration (see MACINTYRE, A.). Charles Taylor, in *Sources of the Self* (1989), was another influential thinker who sought philosophical illumination from the history of ideas (see TAYLOR, C.).

Rorty, MacIntyre and Taylor, though closely concerned with the analysis and resolution of philosophical problems, all took an approach that set them in the broader context of the general sweep of the past. Their concern was with what had happened to the human mind in the course of developing its ideas. None, with the possible exception of Taylor, were self-consciously followers of Hegel, but the Hegelian character of their approach to philosophy and its past is unmistakable. This powerful movement in analytical philosophy thus found common ground with hitherto alien continental philosophy, which, having always been more historical in its orientation, had gradually focused around the idea that the collapse of Enlightenment rationalism was the key to the demise of the modern mind, or modernity, fashioned by two hundred years of theorizing, and to understanding a postmodern, relativistic world in which values, including even knowledge itself, were in constant flux. Among the most prominent continental theorists are Martin Heidegger, Michel Foucault, Emmanuel Levinas and Jacques Derrida.

These trends in philosophy have been highly influential in legal and social theory, literary criticism and anthropology. They are not always self-consciously philosophical, however, and still less have they been seen as a revival of speculative philosophy of history. Yet this is what they are – the application of philosophical concepts and analysis to history, and especially cultural history, in the belief that an adequate understanding of contemporary thought requires the mutual illumination of the two. The difference from Hegel's philosophy of world history is in substance rather than style. Whereas Hegel believed that the world of ideas he inhabited was the culmination of rational processes, one in which the human mind had finally arrived at its own intelligibility, postmodernist thinkers, Rorty and MacIntyre no less than continental philosophers such as Foucault and Derrida, generally think of the modern mind as a fragmentary residue of past ideas, and incapable of sustaining the sort of rational intelligibility the Enlightenment aspired to. They are thus 'grand theorists' no less than Herder, Kant or Hegel, though whereas the latter were rationalists and progressivists, the ideas of the former are broadly relativist and pessimistic.

The question therefore arises as to whether these modern grand theories are susceptible once more to the sorts of criticism that turned philosophy in a more methodological direction. And, in a slightly disguised form, this is indeed the direction in which the subject has moved. It is not the illegitimate deployment of the a priori in history that is the chief concern, but whether these new theorists can escape the intellectually crippling implications of radical relativism, and whether indeed they offer a real prospect of genuine knowledge and understanding. If all is in flux, is there any Archimedean point from which this judgment itself is to be made?

In this way philosophy of history, in common with many other branches of philosophy, is best understood as a series of repeated attempts to organize knowledge and insight into a coherent whole, one characterized by a constant dialectic between philosophical criticism and historical understanding.

See also: HERMENEUTICS; HISTORICISM; HISTORY, CHINESE THEORIES OF; KYOTO SCHOOL §5

References and further reading

Atkinson, R.F. (1978) *Knowledge and Explanation in History*, London: Macmillan. (A good introduction to analytical philosophy of history.)

Augustine (413–26) *The City of God Against the Pagans*, trans. G.E. McCracken, London: Heinemann, 1957. (In this monumental work are the origins of philosophical history.)

* Collingwood, R.G. (1946) *The Idea of History*, Oxford: Clarendon Press. (The most influential elaboration of an idealist conception of historical understanding in English-speaking philosophy.)

Comte, A. (1890) *Introduction to Positive Philosophy*, ed. F. Ferré, Indianapolis, IN: Bobbs-Merrill, 1970. (Comte's positivism is not now well regarded.)

* Condorcet, A.N. de (1795) *Sketch for an Historical Picture of the Progress of the Human Mind*, trans. J. Barraclough, London: Library of Ideas, 1955. (A good example of the intellectual ambitiousness of the French *philosophe*.)

Croce, B. (1921) *History: Its Theory and Practice*, trans. D. Ainslee, New York: Harcourt Brace. (The influence of this prominent Italian philosopher on philosophy of history is largely through the writings of Collingwood.)

Danto, A.C. (1965) *Analytical Philosophy of History*, Cambridge: Cambridge University Press. (Arguably the high point of analytical philosophy of history.)

* Dray, W.H. (1957) *Laws and Explanation in History*, Oxford: Clarendon Press. (The most influential rejection of the 'covering law' theory of historical explanation.)

Gardiner, P. (1952) *The Nature of Historical Explanation*, Oxford: Clarendon Press. (A useful introduction to the central debate among analytical philosophers of history.)

—— (1959) *Theories of History*, New York: Free Press. (A useful collection of extracts from classic works and essays in analytical philosophy of history.)

* Hegel, G.W.F. (1837) *Lectures on the Philosophy of World History*, trans. H.B. Nisbet, Cambridge: Cambridge University Press, 1975. (The best translation of the high point of philosophical history.)

* Hempel, C.G. (1942) 'The Function of General Laws in History', *Journal of Philosophy* 38 (1): 35–48. (The definitive statement of the 'covering law' theory of historical explanation.)

* Herder, J.G. (1800) *Outlines of a Philosophy of the History of Man*, trans. T.O. Churchill, abridged F.C. Manuel, London: University of Chicago Press, 1968. (This translation originally appeared in 1803.)

* Kant, I. (1784) 'The Idea of a Universal History from a Cosmopolitan Point of View', in *Kant on History*, trans. L.W. Beck, R.E. Anchor and E.L. Fackenheim, Indianapolis, IN: Bobbs-Merrill, 1963. (The *locus classicus* of philosophical history shorn of its theological origins.)

* MacIntyre, A.C. (1981) *After Virtue*, London: Duckworth. (One of the most influential books in moral and social philosophy in the twentieth century.)

* Marx, K. (1867) *Capital*, trans. B. Fowkes, Harmondsworth: Penguin, 1976. (The outcome of Marx's many years of intellectual labour, only the first volume was published in his lifetime.)

* Marx, K. and Engels, F. (1848) *The Communist Manifesto*, in *Selected Works in Two Volumes*, Moscow: Foreign Languages Publishing House, 1951. (A brilliantly short résumé of the historical materialist theory of history.)

* Mill, J.S. (1843) *System of Logic: Ratiocinative and Inductive*, in *Collected Works of John Stuart Mill*, Toronto, Ont.: University of Toronto Press, vols 7 and 8, 1991. (Mill's account of scientific method held impressive sway for almost a hundred years.)

* Popper, K.R. (1945) *The Open Society and its Enemies: Volume 2: The High Tide of Prophecy*, London: Routledge. (A celebrated, though somewhat misguided, attack on Hegel.)

* —— (1957) *The Poverty of Historicism*, London: Routledge & Kegan Paul. (Widely regarded as a conclusive refutation of historicist philosophy.)

* Rorty, R. (1980) *Philosophy and the Mirror of Nature*, Oxford: Blackwell. (An important modern attempt to dissolve philosophical problems through historical understanding.)

* Spengler, O. (1918) *The Decline of the West*, trans. C.F. Atkinson, London: Allen and Unwin, 2 vols, 1926. (Possibly the most ambitious work in philosophical history ever attempted.)

* Taylor, C. (1989) *Sources of the Self*, Cambridge: Cambridge University Press. (Taylor may be ranked with Rawls and MacIntyre as among the most influential moral philosophers of the late twentieth century.)

* Vico, G. (1744) *The New Science*, trans. T.G. Bergin and M.H. Fisch, Ithaca, NY: Cornell University Press, 1948. (Sir Isaiah Berlin discovered in this hitherto obscure Italian writer the founder of the human sciences.)

Walsh, W.H. (1967) *Introduction to Philosophy of History*, London: Hutchinson, 3rd revised edn. (For many years the standard introduction to the subject.)

GORDON GRAHAM

HOBBES, THOMAS (1588–1679)

Among the figures who were conscious of developing a new science in the seventeenth century, the Englishman Hobbes stands out as an innovator in ethics, politics and psychology. He was active in a number of other fields, notably geometry, ballistics and optics, and seems to have shown considerable acumen as a theorist of light. His contemporaries, especially in Continental Europe, regarded him as a major intellectual figure. Yet he did not earn a living as a scientist or a writer on politics. In 1608 he entered the service of Henry Cavendish, First Earl of Devonshire, and maintained his connections with the family for more than seventy years, working as tutor, translator, travelling companion, business agent and political counsellor. The royalist sympathies of his employers and their circle determined Hobbes' allegiances in the period preceding and during the English Civil War. Hobbes' first political treatise, The Elements of Law *(1640), was not intended for publication but was meant as a sort of long briefing paper that royalists in parliament could use to justify actions by the king. Even* Leviathan *(1651), which is often read as if it is concerned with the perennial questions of political philosophy, betrays its origins in the disputes of the pre-Civil War period in England.*

For much of his life the aristocrats who employed Hobbes brought him into contact with the intellectual life of Continental Europe. He found not just the ideas but also the spokesmen congenial. Perhaps as early as 1630 he met Marin Mersenne, then at the centre of a Parisian network of scientists, mathematicians and theologians that included Descartes as a corresponding member. It was to this group that Hobbes attached himself in 1640 when political events in England seemed to him to threaten his safety, causing him to flee to France. He stayed for ten years and succeeded in making a name for himself, particularly as a figure who managed to bring geometrical demonstration into the field of ethics and politics. His De cive, *a treatise that has much in common with the* Elements of Law, *had a very favourable reception in Paris in 1642.*

By the time De cive *appeared, Hobbes had taught himself enough natural philosophy and mathematics to be taken seriously as a savant in his own right. He had also conceived the plan of producing a large-scale exposition of the 'elements' of philosophy as a whole – from first philosophy, geometry and mechanics through to ethics and politics.* De cive *would be the third volume of a trilogy entitled* The Elements of Philosophy. *These books present Hobbes' considered views in metaphysics, physics and psychology against the background of a preferred scheme of science.*

Metaphysics, or first philosophy, is primarily a definitional enterprise for Hobbes. It selects the terms whose significations need to be grasped if the principles of the rest of the sciences are to be taught or demonstrated. Foremost among the terms that Hobbes regards as central are 'body' and 'motion'. According to Hobbes, the whole array of natural sciences can be organized according to how each treats of motion. Geometry is the first of these sciences in the 'order of demonstration' – that is, the science whose truths are the most general and on which the truths of all the other natural sciences somehow depend. Mechanics is next in the preferred order of the sciences. It considers 'what effects one body moved worketh upon another'. Physics is the science of sense and the effects of the parts of bodies on sense. Moral philosophy or 'the science of the motions of the mind' comes next, and is informed by physics. It studies such passions as anger, hope and fear, and in doing so informs civil philosophy. Starting from the human emotional make up, civil philosophy works out what agreements between individuals will form commonwealths, and what behaviour is required within commonwealths to make them last.

The behaviour required of the public in order to maintain a commonwealth is absolute submission to a sovereign power. In practice this means abiding by whatever a sovereign declares as law, even if those laws appear to be exacting. Law-abiding behaviour is required so long as, in return, subjects can reasonably expect effective action from the sovereign to secure their safety and wellbeing. With minor variations, this is the theme of all three of Hobbes' political treatises – the Elements of Law, De cive *and* Leviathan. *Government is created through a transfer of right by the many to the one or the few, in whom an unlimited power is vested. The laws of the sovereign power may seem intrusive and restrictive, but what is the alternative to compliance? Hobbes' answer is famous: a life that is solitary, poor, nasty, brutish and short. This conception of life without government is not based on the assumption that human beings are selfish and aggressive but, rather, on the idea that if each is their own judge of what is best, there is no assurance that one's safety and one's possessions will not be at the mercy of other people – a selfish few, a vainglorious minority or even members of a moderate majority who think they have to take pre-emptive action against a vainglorious or selfish few. It is the general condition of uncertainty, in conditions where people can do anything they like to pursue their wellbeing and secure their safety, that Hobbes calls 'war'.*

1   **Life**
2   **Science and human improvement**
3   **The elements of philosophy: logic and metaphysics**
4   **Geometry, optics and physics**
5   **Ethics**
6   **Politics: the state of nature**
7   **Politics: the commonwealth**
8   **Problems with Hobbes' political theory**
9   **The scientific status of Hobbes' ethics and politics**

1   Life

Hobbes was born in Westport, a parish of the town of Malmesbury in Wiltshire, England. His mother came from a yeoman family; his father was a poorly educated vicar who seems to have left his parish in disgrace, deserting his family after having come to blows with another clergyman early in Hobbes' childhood. Hobbes' uncle subsequently supported the family, and it was he who paid for Hobbes' university education. Hobbes was lucky to receive good schooling locally, and he showed an early talent for the classical languages.

In 1602 or 1603, Hobbes began study towards an arts degree at Magdalen Hall, Oxford. From his criticisms of the universities in his published writings, it is sometimes inferred that he disliked his college days, or at least that he disliked the scholasticism of

Oxford at that time. (Scholasticism – the fusion of Christian with ancient Greek thought, especially the thought of Aristotle – dominated the curricula of the schools and universities of Europe in the sixteenth and early seventeenth centuries – see MEDIEVAL PHILOSOPHY §§3–4.) Certainly he disliked the university curriculum in retrospect, as chapter 46 of *Leviathan* (1651) makes clear.

Hobbes completed his degree in 1608, and entered the service of William Cavendish, First Earl of Devonshire, as companion and tutor for his son. Although Hobbes was about the same age as the young Cavendish, he was put in charge of his purse as well as his education. He was the earl's representative at meetings of the Virginia Company, in which the Devonshire family had a considerable financial stake. He also accompanied the earl's son on a grand tour of the Continent in 1610, which allowed Hobbes to improve his command of French and Italian. According to some accounts, he also became acquainted then with criticisms of scholasticism current among Continental intellectuals.

It is unclear how long this grand tour lasted, but Hobbes had returned to England by 1615. At some point during these travels Hobbes seems to have met Fulgenzio Micanzio, the friend and personal assistant of the Venetian writer and politician Paolo Sarpi. He must also have met Marc Antonio de Dominis, who was involved in the translation of Bacon's writings into Italian and who also had connections with Sarpi. Hobbes' own contact with Bacon may have had its stimulus in the requests of the newly befriended Venetians for more details of the Baconian philosophy. The young Cavendish began a correspondence with Micanzio after returning to England in 1615. Hobbes translated this correspondence and through it would have been exposed to Sarpi's theory of the supremacy of temporal rulers rather than spiritual authorities. The theory went against the Papal interdict of 1606, which asserted Rome's right to overrule the decisions of local monarchs and which had encountered much criticism in England. There are apparently strong echoes of this anti-Papal line in Hobbes' own writings.

During his first twenty years of service to the Devonshires, Hobbes seems to have spent his free time immersed in classical poetry and history. His employers had a good library, and Hobbes made use of it. The first fruit of this regrounding in the classics was a translation into English of Thucydides' *History of the Peloponnesian Wars*, published in 1628. Hobbes believed that Thucydides had lessons for those who overvalued democracy and did not see the strengths of monarchy, and it may have been the Petition of Right of 1628 that led to the publication of the translation. The Petition called on Charles I not to levy taxes without the consent of Parliament, not to imprison subjects without due cause, not to billet soldiers in private homes and not to put civilians under martial law.

In 1628 Hobbes chose history as the medium for a political message. Later, in writings like *Leviathan*, he thought science or philosophy was the better vehicle. In the writing of history it is possible for the conventions of the genre to interfere with the communication of wisdom; in the writing of science, he came to believe, the communication of wisdom is assured, if the audience is prepared to pay attention and able to follow a demonstration. He struggled throughout his intellectual life with the problem of combining political rhetoric with political science, and some of his best writings are experimental solutions to this problem. The translation of Thucydides is important as the first of many such experiments.

The year 1628 was a kind of turning-point in Hobbes' career. Apart from publishing the translation of Thucydides, he had to contend with the death of the second earl at the age of 43, resulting in his loss of employment with the Devonshires. Hobbes took up a new post in the house of Sir Gervase Clifton, not far from Hardwick Hall, the home of the Devonshires. Once again he was engaged as a companion on a grand tour, this one lasting from 1629 to 1631. During this journey Hobbes looked for the first time at Euclid's *Elements*, and fell in love with geometry. There is plenty of evidence in Hobbes' writings that he regarded Euclid's book as one of the supreme examples of a scientific presentation of a subject. Perhaps also during this second journey to the Continent Hobbes was present at a discussion among some well-educated gentlemen about the nature of sense-perception, in which it emerged that none of the participants could say what sense-perception was. Both episodes are significant, because they seem to mark the beginning of Hobbes' transformation from man of letters to man of science.

Perhaps the stimulus for the change was not the second grand tour alone. After his return, Hobbes went back into the service of the Devonshires and became tutor to the young third earl. At about the same time, he came into contact with a branch of his master's family who lived at Welbeck, near Hardwick Hall. The Welbeck Cavendishes were interested in science. The Earl of Newcastle is known to have sent Hobbes on an errand to London to find a book of Galileo's in the early 1630s. The earl's younger brother, Charles, had an even greater interest in science: he acted as something of a patron and distributor of scientific writings. Hobbes was one of those who looked at and gave his opinion of these writings. Charles Cavendish also had contacts among Continental scientists, including Marin MERSENNE, a friar in Paris who was at the centre of a circle of scientists and philosophers that included Descartes.

Hobbes' scientific development continued when he embarked with the third earl on yet another grand tour from 1634 to 1636. During this journey he is supposed to have met Galileo in Italy, as well as Mersenne and some members of his circle in Paris in 1636. Hobbes had probably become acquainted with Mersenne five years earlier on the second tour. It is said that on the third grand tour Hobbes was much preoccupied with the nature and effects of motion, and that he started to see for the first time how many natural phenomena depended upon it.

On his return to England, Hobbes kept up with some of the scientific work being produced in Mersenne's circle. Descartes' *Discourse and Essays* were published in 1637. Hobbes was sent a copy and seems to have made a careful study of the first of the *Essays* – on optics – perhaps taking time himself to write something of his own on the same subject. But he was not keeping abreast solely of scientific ideas. Through his association with a circle of clergy, lawyers and aristocrats at Great Tew, near Oxford, he was able to follow the continuing debates surrounding the troubles of Charles I. In 1634 the king started to raise funds for a navy by a ship-money tax levied county by county. This tax-raising met opposition, particularly in non-coastal counties. Besides the ship-money dispute, Charles I had to reckon with the consequences of trying, in 1637, to bring the Scottish Presbyterian prayer book into line with its Anglican counterpart. This provoked a National Covenant in Scotland expressing wholesale opposition to ecclesiastical innovations from England. In 1639 and 1640 the Scots raised armies to back up their opposition, and Charles was forced to recall a parliament he was used to ruling without, and which was extremely hostile to him. When Parliament acted against Stafford, a minister of the King associated with the Earl of Newcastle, Hobbes worked on arguments that could support the royalist position in parliamentary debates. The arguments were produced in a treatise, *The Elements of Law* (1640), not intended for publication but which, in fact, contains much of the doctrine of Hobbes' political philosophy. Fearing that he would be prosecuted for giving the royalists their arguments, he fled to Paris and joined the circle of philosophers and scientists around Mersenne.

Some years after 1640 Hobbes wrote that he had recently conceived a plan for expounding, in three parts, the elements of philosophy or science in

461

general. His exposition would begin with the nature of body and the elements of what we now call physics. It would go on to discuss human nature, in particular perception and motivation, and the third part would be a discussion of moral and civic duty. Perhaps he had already drawn up this plan, and even executed some of it, by the time he reached Paris. What *is* certain, however, is that the first part of the exposition to be published was the last of the three in his outline – the part on morals and politics. Hobbes called this part of his exposition *De cive* and published a very limited edition of it in Latin in 1642.

Hobbes seems to have enjoyed good relations with most of Mersenne's circle. He was at odds with Descartes, however, whose *Meditations* he criticized in a set of 'Objections' – the anonymous 'Third Set' (see DESCARTES, R. §§4, 6). From 1641 until Mersenne's death in 1648, Hobbes applied himself to the composition of the rest of his three-part exposition of the elements of science. He produced some of the material for the first part of the exposition – on body, the part published in 1655 as *De corpore* – and took up topics that would later occupy the middle part of the exposition. In 1643 he wrote a critical commentary on *De Mundo*, a treatise written by Thomas WHITE (another Englishman in Paris at that time) which was sympathetic to scholasticism. In 1646 Hobbes composed some arguments about the respects in which freedom is compatible with causal necessitation in nature, arguing once more on this occasion against scholastic positions. He suffered a serious illness in 1647 and almost died. While on his sickbed he rebuffed an attempt by Mersenne to convert him to Roman Catholicism.

In 1648 Mersenne died and the philosophical and scientific activity that had gone on around him ceased to have a focal point. Hobbes now had a place among the royalists in exile, but he was on poor terms with churchmen around England's exiled Charles II in Paris and was receiving his pay rather irregularly. By the autumn of 1649 he seems to have formed the intention of going home.

Leviathan, in which Hobbes attempted to derive from his now well-worked-out political principles the right relation of Church to state, was written at the end of the 1640s, when church government in England began to run on lines of which he approved and at a time when the influence of bishops in the English royal court-in-exile in Paris was, in Hobbes' eyes, too great. In any case, the fact that the theory in the book vindicated Cromwell's policy on church government does not mean that it was a partisan work in favour of Cromwell, calculated to ease Hobbes' return to England. If that had been so, Hobbes would not have made a special presentation copy for the future Charles II. Instead, it seems that the doctrine in *Leviathan* favoured the concentration of all authority in any *de facto* sovereign power, whether republican or royal. To the Paris royalists, mostly strong Anglicans in favour of political powers for bishops, the new book was highly offensive.

By the end of 1651 Hobbes was back in London and all three statements of his political philosophy were available in some form in English. These political works were widely known and read before his exposition of the elements of science was complete. Even though *De cive* had been planned to complete a sequence of three treatises on these elements, it did not depend on the other treatises in order to be understood, and it has always had a readership of its own. When the other two works in the sequence appeared in the 1650s, they did not match *De cive* in quality. The treatise on which Hobbes had been working longest was the opening work of the sequence, *De corpore*, published in 1655. In it Hobbes tried to show how the mature sciences of geometry, mechanics and physics were concerned with the effects of different kinds of motion in matter. Politically motivated critics soon exposed the weaknesses in the mathematical sections of the book, and Hobbes' attempt to vindicate his work involved him in years of fruitless polemic. *De homine*, the second volume of his *Elements* and undoubtedly the least well-integrated of the three, was published in 1658. It was never widely read, and a modern English translation of it has only recently appeared.

In 1660 the monarchy was re-established in England, and on the coat-tails of Charles II there returned to political power many who regarded Hobbes as a traitor to the royalist cause. Charles himself was not hostile, however, and other influential people were also well-disposed towards him. Nevertheless, in 1666 and 1667, Parliament came close to passing a bill outlawing Christian heresy and atheism, and *Leviathan* was specifically investigated as a source of heretical and atheistic views. The danger of imprisonment and exile did not dissipate until the end of the decade. The threats to Hobbes were reflected in additions that he made to an edition of his works published in 1668. He argued that punishment for heresy was illegal under English law and that his materialism was compatible with Christian faith. Two significant works from the 1660s were applications of his political philosophy. There was a history of the English Civil War, *Behemoth* (1668), and the *Dialogue between a Philosopher and a Student of the Common Laws of England*. By the time these works were composed, Hobbes was not permitted to publish, and though he busied himself with some translations of the classics and a few other minor writings of his own in the 1670s, he had come almost to the end of his working life.

In his ninetieth year, Hobbes returned to physics. His *Decameron Physiologicum* (1678) restates some of the methodology and principal results of the physical sections of *De corpore*. For the preceding three years Hobbes had divided his time between the two Devonshire houses of Chatsworth and Hardwick. In December 1679 he died of a urinary complaint. His remains are buried in a small parish church near Hardwick.

2 Science and human improvement

Hobbes' writings are those of an advocate and practitioner of a new science, a system of knowledge of causes that could, as he believed, greatly benefit human life. Yet he formed his ideas during a period when human intellectual powers, including the ability to develop science, were commonly thought to be limited. According to some theories prevalent in the late sixteenth and early seventeenth centuries, the whole human race was involved in a quite general and unstoppable process of natural decay, so that all the best achievements of human beings belonged to a long-lost golden age. It was a way of understanding things that was consistent with, if not inspired by, the Biblical story of the Fall of Adam and Eve, and the loss of paradise. According to some understandings of that story, Adam's expulsion from paradise cost him not only a life of ease in harmony with God and the rest of nature, but also the gift of a natural insight into the natures of all the things he could name. Regaining the knowledge of those natures might never be possible. In France, in the late sixteenth and early seventeenth centuries, recently popularized Greek sceptical arguments against dogmatism reinforced the view that human intellectual possibilities were limited (see SCEPTICISM, RENAISSANCE §§1, 4). The arguments were directed not only against the traditional learning of the schools but against the idea that any human learning – even untraditional or anti-traditional learning – could amount to a system of genuine knowledge. Hobbes' philosophy of science stands in opposition to much of this gloomy theorizing. It stands in opposition to philosophical scepticism, to the theory of the decay of nature as applied to the human intellect and, to a lesser extent, to pessimistic interpretations of the intellectual costs of the Fall.

Although Hobbes had close friends and intellectual influences among French thinkers who took sceptical arguments seriously, there is little if any solid evidence in his own writing that he studied these arguments closely or took their conclusions to heart. He seems never to have doubted the soundness or scientific status of Euclid's geometry, and he was an early enthusiast for the applied mathematics of Copernicus, Kepler and GALILEO. He was also proud of the judgment of some early readers of *De cive* that this book ushered in a demonstrative science of ethics. Hobbes called himself the inventor of civil science and thought that his politics deserved a place alongside Galileo's mechanics. The newly founded natural and moral sciences he regarded not only as great intellectual achievements, but as distinctively modern ones. Contrary to the theory of the decay of nature as applied to the human intellect, natural and civil science had not ceased with the ancients, but had only properly begun with the work of the mathematical astronomers and his own work in *De cive*. However, Hobbes also held that human beings were badly adapted by nature to do science of this kind, and that they had to work very hard to be capable of it. He thus disagrees both with the Cartesian idea that God benignly creates us with the ingredients of science latent in our minds *and* with the Aristotelian idea that knowledge of the natures of things is the unforced and inevitable by-product of repeatedly looking and seeing. To a very significant extent, according to Hobbes, our capacities for natural science are made by us rather than given to us. This position concedes something to both scepticism and the theory that life will always be difficult for Fallen Man. Although sceptics are wrong to claim that we are incapable of science, they would not be wrong to claim that we lack native scientific ability. Neither would they be wrong to deny that human beings are capable of an exalted sort of knowledge, the knowledge of what necessitates effects. For Hobbes, the scientific knowledge of which we are capable rarely rises to the level of knowledge of how effects *must* have been brought about, and it is not taken to extend to all effects. Again, although Hobbes believed that the scientific achievements of his contemporaries and himself were important, and that the then nascent sciences of nature and politics would develop further, he did not, with Descartes, suppose that we might one day complete science. Finally, while he claimed that even in their undeveloped state the sciences had delivered considerable benefits, Hobbes did not expect a more developed science to be the answer to all our problems. Like Bacon he believed that science could not entirely repair the Fall, that it could only act to relieve some of what was bad in human existence. Whatever one did, life would continue to have 'incommodities', but with the development of science life would contain fewer of them.

Science is not, then, for Hobbes, a means of regaining Eden. At best, it is our only way of cutting the costs of losing Eden. In paradise, Adam enjoyed the gift of immortality in conditions of ready abundance. Everything he could properly want was there for the taking. Punished for eating from the tree of knowledge Adam lost his immortality. He lived, as Hobbes puts it in *Leviathan*, under a death sentence ([1651] 1839 III: 438). Adam also lost the abundance of Eden. Banished to a place outside paradise, he had for the first time to work for a living, and to do so in a relatively inhospitable environment. Had they stayed in Eden, Adam and Eve would not have reproduced their kind continually or perhaps at all ([1651] 1839 III: 440). When they left they came under a necessity to multiply that worsened the life of their kind still further. Adam's descendants, the rest of humanity, inherit from him not only their mortality but also life outside Paradise. Thanks to Adam's transgression, human beings in general live in a world that demands ingenuity and hard work for survival. And thanks to human carnality, Adam's descendants have to eke out a living in the company of, and often in competition with, many others of their own kind. These facts of life do not make it easy to do well. In order to flourish in a sometimes harsh physical environment people have to know which effects they observe are beneficial and which are harmful, and they have to learn to reproduce the beneficial ones and prevent, or at least avoid, the harmful ones. In order to flourish in a heavily populated environment people have to know how to co-operate with one another. Moreover, these problems have to be coped with simultaneously.

As things naturally are, however, the problems are too great for creatures like us. For, being descended from Adam, human beings inherit the cognitive and conative capacities of someone designed to live in paradise, not the harsh world outside. If things had gone according to God's plan, Adam would not have needed to get causal knowledge of nature; he could have satisfied himself with contemplating the diversity and order in nature. Adam would not have had to make nature supply his needs. He would not have had to cope with overpopulation and the demands of co-operation. Made for a life without problems, Adam lacked the means – that is, the science – to solve problems. As Hobbes points out in *Leviathan*, there is no evidence in scripture that Adam had the vocabulary to do science ([1651] 1839 III: 19), and yet without the vocabulary to do science we should be no better off than savages or beasts (1640 pt I, ch. 5: iv; 1658 ch. 10: ii, iii). Either people reconcile themselves to living at the mercy of the elements and of one another – Hobbes thought that this was the course taken by Native Americans – or else they take the long and difficult road to a better life through science. Neither the better life nor the means to it are out of

bounds to human beings, but both involve a kind of human reform. To get access to the degrees and varieties of motion that are required to understand nature, human beings need to acquire concepts more general and universal than those for everyday experience, and they need to apply principles involving these concepts in tasks of measurement and manufacture. To solve the problems of peaceful co-operation they need to be able to recognize the consequences of everyone's trying to get what they want. This means more than knowing what moral precepts to follow. It means being able to see what overall good the moral precepts promote – something revealed by Hobbes' civil science – and adjusting one's practical reasoning to the pursuit of that good rather than something nearer and more gratifying.

Although human beings cannot live well without science, science does not come naturally to them. Science depends on the ability to impose names aptly, to join names into propositions, and to join propositions into syllogisms, but not even these prescientific linguistic skills are natural to people. People come into the world being able at most to form sensory representations of things, and to learn from experience. But experience is a far cry from science. In its raw state experience is either a disorganized stream of representations or else a coherent sequence. If it is a coherent sequence, then, according to *Leviathan*, it is 'regulated' by some design or plan, or by curiosity about an observed body's effects ([1651] 1839 III: 13). Regulated in either way, a train of experience is only regulated as past experience allows it to be. Going by its past associations of observed phenomena, the mind will focus on a means to some goal or purpose in hand, or will suggest properties it is accustomed to conjoin with other properties it is now curious about. Once there are words for the things of which the mind has conceptions – words that can be used to signify the elements of experience – the possible ways of juxtaposing the words significantly, of analysing them and drawing consequences, introduce ways of ordering the elements that are not foreshadowed in previous experience.

New ways of regulating thought become possible because, for one thing, it is not necessary for a body spoken about to be present or remembered in order for a train of thought about it to be created. The train of thought can be generated instead by exploiting logical relations or analytic truths to get from one speech or thought to another. Reasoning can thus introduce new possibilities of combining things given separately in experience; it can also introduce ways of taking apart or separating things confounded in experience. Nor are the possibilities confined to the powers of one man's reasoning. Speech enables investigation and reasoning to be carried on co-operatively, and allows one person's explanations to be tested for clarity and coherence by others. The reasonings or explanations of one person can be preserved over time and made the model for those of many other people. A method can even be extracted from the findings of the most successful or conclusive pieces of reasoning, so that conclusive reasonings and explanations – in a word, science – can deepen and spread.

Hobbes believed that science as a whole could be divided into two principal parts, one concerned with natural bodies, the other with bodies politic. Each part of science arrives by reasoning at the causes of the properties of its subject matter; and demonstrates effects, with a view to making the relevant subject matter useful and beneficial to human beings. But the two types of bodies are very different from one another, and pose different scientific problems. Natural bodies are not made by us, and so the causes of their properties have to be worked out by reasoning from the appearances they present. Since the maker of natural bodies, God, is omnipotent and able to bring about effects in more ways than can be dreamed of in our explanations, only possible causes can be assigned to the appearances they present. Bodies politic *are* made by us – they are human artefacts and so at least in principle we can be certain of the causes of *their* properties. But the philosophical challenge they present is not primarily that of knowing their causes: it is that of knowing how they should be designed so that they last. This means setting out rules by which those involved in the commonwealth – those in government on the one hand and those subject to government on the other – can conduct themselves so that civil peace is ensured. It is doubtful whether the statement of these rules is really a science of a kind of body, as is natural science, and probably the differences between natural and civil science are to be taken more seriously than the supposed analogies. Hobbes claims that civil science is not only more certain, but more widely needed, and more accessible than natural science. On the other hand, natural science is the more fundamental of the two parts of science: its explanatory concepts are more general than those of civil science and are needed if a scientific understanding of the passions and actions of agents in civil life is to be acquired from the 'first and few' elements of science as a whole.

3 The elements of philosophy: logic and metaphysics

The relative positions of the two parts of science – natural and civil – are reflected in the organization of

Hobbes' trilogy on the elements of philosophy. The first volume, *De corpore*, expounds first philosophy, geometry, mechanics and physics. It is followed by *De homine*, which is half optics and half psychology; this volume in turn is supposed to prepare the ground for the exposition of the elements of ethics and politics in *De cive*.

The account of the 'elements' of science starts in *De corpore* with chapters on the ways in which philosophy depends on names, propositions and methods of reasoning. For Hobbes, logic is nothing more than the right ordering and joining of significant propositions into chains of reasoning. Propositions in turn are no more than coherent concatenations of names with significations of different extents. A name signifies an idea – whatever idea it conveys in the context of a speech to a hearer. But the idea is not what the name refers to or stands for: it refers to or stands for an object. To make a proposition, names have to be put together coherently, and coherent concatenations are concatenations of the same category of name – names of bodies with names of bodies, names of names with names of names. The 'extent' of the signification of a name has a bearing on the truth of propositions. The signification of a proper name will extend to an individual, that of a universal name – 'man', 'horse', 'tree' – to each of a plurality of individuals. In the propositions of natural science, names are universal names of bodies. Truth in the propositions of natural sciences is a matter of the inclusion of the extent of a universal subject-term within the extent of a universal predicate-term. Demonstrations are chains of syllogisms, and syllogisms are the stringing together of trios of propositions that share appropriate subjects and predicates. In a sense, then, logic is a technique for working out the consequences of relations between the significations of universal names or their extents. There are also methods belonging to logic for analysing the significations of names, and for arriving at the most general of these significations from a starting point in everyday universal names. Logical analysis of this kind is what is required to locate the terms fundamental to the various branches of science; it also has a role in making scientific questions amenable to resolution. Metaphysics or first philosophy sets out, ideally by means of definitions, the concepts necessary for conducting fruitful enquiries concerning natural bodies and for communicating the results. The relevant concepts include those of body, motion, time, place, cause and effect.

Hobbes composed no full-scale treatise on logic, and no work of his is concerned with metaphysics alone. *De corpore* contains the nearest approximation to a full first philosophy, and even here he is not entirely clear about the borderline between that 'prior' science and geometry. There is a chapter on 'syllogism', but it is not comprehensive and its relation to traditional syllogistic is never spelled out. As for the chapters on first philosophy, they are more significant for what they deny than for what they affirm. They deny that it makes sense to study 'being' in the abstract; they deny that species or genera are things; they deny that 'substance' can mean something very different from 'body'; and they deny that other predicables are more than varieties of sensory appearance caused by bodies. In short, they deny much standard Aristotelian doctrine, including the doctrine defining the subject matter of metaphysics itself – the doctrine that metaphysics studies being *qua* being. As will become clear, the chapters on first philosophy can also be understood to register disagreements between Hobbes and some of the *moderns* – Descartes and GASSENDI, among others.

Hobbes' first philosophy starts with a thought experiment. He imagines that the external world has been annihilated – all that remains is a single thinker and the traces in memory of the world he previously sensed and perceived. Hobbes claims that the disappearance of the external world would not take away conditions for thought or reasoning, even about the physical world. The annihilation of the world would not even *alter* conditions for such thought and reasoning, since the medium of thought and reasoning is never things themselves but only appearances or phantasms. Hobbes thinks that the annihilation of the external world leaves only the mind and its phantasms in existence. There is no third world of things that exist outside the mind but outside the physical world as well. So Hobbes denies that there exist without the mind abstract natures such as Descartes claims to discover in Meditation V; and, contrary to Gassendi in the *Syntagma*, he does not think that space and time are real independently of the mind. He derives the idea of space from the memory images or phantasms presenting things as if from outside the mind. He derives the idea of time from imagined motion, from succession without existence. He derives the idea of an existing thing from the imagination of an empty space suddenly getting an occupant. Existence is thus restricted to existence in space, which is in turn identified with corporeal existence. These resources allow for only a straitened conception of cause or power, and certainly not for an Aristotelian conception. There are no forms or purposes in nature; but the makings of a conception of efficient cause are available, and that is the only sense of 'cause' recognized by Hobbes' first philosophy.

Most of the concepts that Hobbes thinks are needed for natural science have now been indicated.

In Part Two of *De corpore*, after defining 'time' and 'place', he thinks he is in a position to define 'body' and its most general accidents. He then deals with magnitude or real space-occupation, and the spatial relations of continuity and contiguity. Against this background he defines 'motion', and in terms of motion the ideas of length, depth and breadth. After the three spatial dimensions are explicated, he defines quantitative identity and difference for motions and bodies, and then discusses the conditions of qualitative difference between bodies over time. He goes on to consider the causes of qualitative change, concluding with a demonstration of the thesis that all change is motion, that motion is the only cause of motion, and that power (*potentia*) is nothing but motion in so far as it is a cause of motion.

Definitions dominate Hobbes' first philosophy and, officially at least, their purpose is to fix ideas necessary for the business of science proper. Hobbes thought that the mark of a prescientific branch of learning was controversy, and he traced controversy to a failure to define terms and to proceed in orderly fashion from definitions to conclusions. The task of first philosophy is to provide insurance against controversy. It does not do this by coming up with substantive truths that command assent. Instead, Hobbes describes first philosophy as a necessary *preliminary* to the demonstration of substantive truths, where demonstrator and learner are put on one another's wavelength and attach the same significations to their terms, but where their agreement is terminological rather than doctrinal. As Hobbes puts it in the *Six Lessons*, 'he that telleth you in what sense you are to take the appellations of those things which he nameth in his discourse, teacheth you but his language, that afterwards he may teach you his art. But teaching of language is not mathematic, nor logic, nor physic' ([1656b] 1839 VII: 225).

That 'the teaching of language' underdescribes what Hobbes does in practice in stating his first philosophy, and that it suppresses entirely the revisionary character of some of his definitions when compared with Aristotelian ones (and so the controversial nature of the devices that are supposed to pre-empt controversy), should already be clear. But, up to a point, Hobbes' first philosophy is genuinely unassuming. It takes for granted no exotic powers or substances, God included, and it postulates no exotic human capacities for acquiring the concepts that are the key to natural science. The point is not just that Hobbes keeps the relevant concepts to a small number, so that he is economical in the concepts he uses and also in his assumptions about the types of real things there have to be for these concepts to be applicable. Hobbes' first philosophy is also *naturalis-*

tic. Nothing supernatural is assumed to exist in order for natural science to be acquired; indeed, nothing besides matter in motion is postulated. What remains after the annihilation of the world in Hobbes' thought experiment is not the immaterial self of Descartes, but the corporeal body or perhaps the brain, and the motions conserved in its internal parts from past impacts of the external world on the sense-organs.

The denial of immaterialism in Hobbes' first philosophy is anticipated in his Objections to Descartes' *Meditations*. An objection that Hobbes directs at Meditation II sets the tone (see DESCARTES, R. §5). He accepts that from the fact that I am thinking it follows that I exist, but he wonders whether Descartes can properly conclude, as a corollary, that the I is a mind or an intelligence or a thinking thing. For all the *Cogito* shows, Hobbes says, the I could be corporeal. And not only does the *Cogito* leave open the possibility of the I being corporeal, he goes on, the later wax argument actually *shows* that the I is corporeal:

We cannot conceive of jumping without a jumper, or knowing without a knower, or of thinking without a thinker.

It seems to follow from this that a thinking thing is something corporeal. For it seems that the subject of any act can be understood only in terms of something corporeal or in terms of matter, as the author himself shows later [in] his example of the wax: the wax, despite the changes in its colour, hardness, shape and other acts, is still understood to be the same thing, that is, the same matter is the subject of all of these changes.
(Hobbes [1641] 1985 vol. 2: 122)

Descartes' reply concedes that acts need subjects, that it is a *thing* that is hard, changes shape and so on, and also a *thing* that thinks, but he insists that 'thing' in this sense is neutral between the corporeal and the spiritual. He insists, too, that he is non-committal about the nature of the thing that thinks in Meditation II, a claim borne out by his responding agnostically in Meditation II to the question of whether he might be a structure of limbs or a thin vapour. If Hobbes misses that, it may be because he misunderstands the rules of the method of doubt. While implementing the method of doubt, Descartes does assume rather than prove that there is no body for the thinking thing to be or for the thought to inhere in. But this is not a case of begging the question, for the belief in the existence of bodies is reinstated in Meditation VI, and with that the question of whether the subject is essentially immaterial or material.

Hobbes comes at Descartes' immaterialism from another, more revealing direction when he tries to suggest that it is not needed to underpin the distinction between imagination and conception by the mind. In his fourth objection, Hobbes equates imagination in Descartes' sense with having an idea of a thing, and conception in Descartes' sense with reasoning to the conclusion that something exists. Descartes already agrees that imagination is a partly corporeal process resulting from action on the sense organs, but his text suggests that conception by the mind is an altogether different operation. Hobbes puts forward a suggestion that allows the explanation of conception and imagination to be linked, without the postulation of immaterial things. He proposes that reasoning is the process in which labels attached to various things are concatenated into sentences according to conventions agreed by humans.

Reasoning will depend on names, names will depend on the imagination, and imagination will depend (as I believe it does) merely on the motions of our bodily organs; and so the mind will be nothing more than motion occurring in various parts of an organic body.
(Hobbes [1641] 1985 vol. 2: 126)

The compatibility of this proposal with mechanistic explanation appeals to Hobbes; but Descartes raises some powerful doubts about Hobbes' idea that names alone come into reasoning. Contrary to Hobbes, Descartes takes it that reasoning is a matter of linking together the significations of names, not just the names themselves, and also that the significations of some names cannot be imaged.

As in the case of his objection concerning the subject of the thinking, which seems to overlook the constraints of the method of doubt, Hobbes' objection to Descartes on imagination and conception seems to miss the point. Descartes is not trying to explain the workings of the faculties that result in science, only to find that he has to explain them on immaterialistic principles. He is trying to show that science is possible, that real knowledge of the physical world is possible, because not all of our faculties can coherently be held to be unreliable. Conception by the mind is a case in point. It cannot be held to be unreliable, because it is autonomous and independent of unreliable sense-perception. Hobbes does not see that it is the objectivity of conception rather than the process of conception that Descartes is concerned with. And doubting the objectivity of conception himself, Hobbes does not seek to reconstruct conception as reasoning that might be guaranteed to lead to true conclusions; he wants only to reconstruct it in ways that will not multiply entities beyond those required by mechanistic explanation. The point is that a proof of the objectivity of the conceptions arrived at by science may legitimately be demanded of a metaphysics, and Hobbes' metaphysics does little if anything to meet the demand. The metaphysical economy of materialism will not impress someone who is sceptical of the existence of the external world: the undeniability of the *Cogito* might. One cost of Hobbes' naturalistic approach is that it never attempts the task of legitimizing the scientific enterprise in general, and is probably incapable of doing so.

4 Geometry, optics and physics

First philosophy is a preliminary to natural science proper, and the first of the natural sciences is geometry. Geometry is a natural science for Hobbes, because it studies the effects of moving bodies. It studies the properties of straight lines, for instance, and straight lines are the effects of the motion of a small material thing – a point. He rejects the idea that the geometrical point is an abstraction distinct from some small material mark or other. Being a body, a geometrical point is divisible and not, as Euclid had it, 'that which hath no part'. A point could no more lack quantity than a line could lack breadth and be constructed by motion. The bodies whose motions geometry studies may not have much quantity, and the quantity may not be relevant to what is being demonstrated of them, but they are bodies all the same. Though geometry is a science of bodies, it is also in a sense an a priori certain science, as physics is not, for the effects are produced by us, and we know in advance by what means they are produced. In this, Hobbes believed, geometry is like politics. In a sense, too, geometry is a very basic science – basic not in the sense that the objects it studies are higher or more real than those in nature, but in the sense that it studies bodies and motion at a very high level of generality, with much that is specific about the bodies left out of account. Hobbes thinks that geometry is also basic in another sense, for its methods of demonstration and analysis are the inspiration for the methods of the other demonstrative sciences.

Hobbes was self-taught in mathematics, and his friend and biographer, John Aubrey, says he did not encounter Euclid until he was middle-aged. Nevertheless, he was taken seriously by very able geometers in Mersenne's circle, and is even credited with inspiring a proof by Roberval of the equality of arcs of a parabola and an 'Archimedean' spiral. He is much better known, however, as a mathematical failure whose attempts at expounding geometry in *De corpore* were ridiculed by the English mathematician John Wallis. Wallis' attack was motivated by a wish to discredit the anticlerical passages in *Leviathan*, and its attack on the universities. In correspondence with Huygens, Wallis said that Hobbes 'took his courage' from mathematics, and so it 'seemed necessary for some mathematician to show him how little he understands'. Wallis' attack succeeded – it focused on Hobbes' doomed enterprise of producing a quadrate of the circle – and was made the more effective by Hobbes' persistent refusal to concede errors.

Although the geometrical parts of *De corpore* were supposed to present some new results, Hobbes did not claim any great stature for himself in geometry. In optics, on the other hand, he regarded himself as a major figure. It was certainly a subject he turned to early in his transformation from man of letters to man of science. As early as 1636, optical questions were featuring in his correspondence with the Earl of Newcastle, and the treatment of the sensible qualities was mechanical: 'whereas I use the phrases, the light passes, or the colour passes or diffuseth itselfe, my meaning is that the motion is onely in the medium, and light and colour are but the effects of that motion in the brayne'. Perhaps more accurately, these effects were supposed to be the effects of the motion of the medium transmitted to the animal spirits in the brain.

Exactly how early Hobbes arrived at his conception of the workings of light is not entirely clear. A short treatise dated to 1630 and originally attributed to Hobbes is now thought by some scholars to be the work of someone else in the Cavendish circle. It contains doctrines different from writings that are more certainly ascribed to Hobbes, and which probably belong to the 1640s: the *Tractatus Opticus* I and II. It also contains as 'principles' formulations that these later optical writings present as mere hypotheses. Whether the writings of the 1640s represent only a change of mind or whether they are Hobbes' first extended publications in optics, they show him adopting a mediumistic theory of the propagation of light based on the idea of continuously expanding and contracting light sources. These displace contiguous parts of an ethereal medium of uniform density and set up a chain reaction to the eye. A resistance in the eye caused by a countervailing motion from the brain produces a phantasm of a luminous object – that is, in Hobbes' terminology, light. Light is propagated instantaneously, as both luminous object and medium expand simultaneously. The account does without the postulation of an emission by luminous objects of species or replicas of themselves which subsequently inform the senses and permit perception. Instead, luminous objects illuminate by radiation: they, so to speak, send out rays or, more precisely, displace the medium along paths called 'rays'. In their passage from luminous objects to the eye, rays are supposed to describe parallelograms. Hobbes used the properties of other geometrical figures described by rays of light passing through different densities to account for refraction. Colour he regarded as light perturbed by the internal motions of rough or coarse bodies on its way to the eye. The differences between the colours on the spectrum from blue to red he accounts for as the product of refraction plus restraint or reinforcement of the lateral motion of rays of light that goes with refraction.

At no point in the process that starts with the motion of the luminous objects and ends in the production of the phantasm does Hobbes depart from a mechanical model of the causes of sense-perception. His mature theory of optics is through and through an account in terms of matter and motion. But between the *Tractatus Opticus I* and the *Tractatus Opticus II*, he seems to have revised his ideas about the organs of sensory perception. Phantasms are said to come from the heart, rather than to result from the clash of incoming motions with motions from the brain. By 1646, when Hobbes produced *A Minute or First Draught of the Optiques*, the most polished of his optical treaties, the main lines of his doctrine were settled. In addition to material on light and its propagation, refraction and reflection, there are accounts of various kinds of sensory error.

Physics, understood as the theory of the causes of appearances to sense and of the nature of the objects of sense, is in part an offshoot of optics. It is expounded at the end of *De corpore*. By an 'object' of sense Hobbes means an external body that registers in experience as being the subject of certain qualities, and that sets off the process culminating in an 'act of sense'. The object of sense is not an idea or a sense-datum or a mental image, though such a thing may be the medium in which the object of sense is registered. The greatest of the objects of sense is the world itself, as registered from some point within it. But only a few intelligible questions can be asked about the world, and these cannot be conclusively answered. One can ask whether it is of finite or infinite magnitude, whether it is full or contains empty space, and how long it has lasted. Only the second of these questions is open to a scientific answer, and even then only to a probable conclusion, while the others are for lawfully appointed churchmen to discuss. Hobbes thinks that probably there is no vacuum, that the world is full, but that some of the bodies that make it up are invisible: thus the ether and 'the small atoms disseminated through the whole space between the earth and the stars'. He adopts Copernican and Galilean hypotheses in chapter 26 of *De corpore* to explain the order,

motion and relative position of the planets. He also infers explanations of, among other things, the passage of the seasons, the succession of day and night and 'the monthly simple motion of the moon'.

Hobbes goes on to consider the bodies between the earth and the stars. Foremost among these is 'the most fluid ether', which he proposes to regard as if it were first matter. He supposes that its parts only receive motion from bodies that float in them, and impart none of their own. The bodies in the ether are supposed to have some degree of cohesion or hardness and to differ from one another in shape, figure and consistency. Any more specific hypotheses about them Hobbes adopted only to explain particular phenomena. He is, however, willing to venture that many such bodies are 'unspeakably little' or minute, since God's infinite power includes a power infinitely to diminish matter. Assumptions about intersidereal bodies inform his theories of the phantasms appropriate to the different senses, not only light but also heat, sound and odour.

5 Ethics

'After *physics*,' Hobbes writes in chapter 6 of *De corpore*, 'we must come to *moral philosophy*; in which we are to consider the motions of the mind, namely, *appetite, aversion, love, benevolence, hope, fear, anger, emulation, envy &c*; what causes they have and of what they be causes' ([1655] 1839 I: 72). The use of the term 'moral philosophy' for the doctrine of the motions of the mind is unfortunate; elsewhere Hobbes says that the precepts of his natural law doctrine add up to a moral philosophy. 'Ethics' is another label he sometimes uses, and it is preferable. The reason ethics comes after physics is that the motions of the mind 'have their causes in sense and imagination, which are the subjects of physical contemplation'. What Hobbes means is that when a body registers in a sensory representation – when, for example, a person sees something – the thing imparts motion to the innermost part of the organ of sight. One effect of the motion is to set up an outward reaction which produces visual experience. But there can be a further after-effect. As Hobbes puts it in chapter 8 of *Elements of Law*, the 'motion and agitation of the brain which we call conception' can be 'continued to the heart, and there be called passion'. The heart governs 'vital motion' in the body, that is the circulation of the blood. In general, when motion derived from an act of sense encourages vital motion, the sentient creature experiences pleasure at the sight, smell or taste of the object and is disposed to move its body so as to prolong or intensify the pleasure. If the object of the pleasure is at a distance, then the creature will typically move towards it. There is a symmetrical account of displeasure. This is an after-effect of the act of sense consisting of a hindrance of vital motion. A creature experiencing a hindrance of vital motion will try to counteract it, typically by retreating from the object of sense. Aversion consists of the small inner movements that initiate the evasive action, just as 'appetite' names the internal beginnings of approach behaviour.

The pursuit of pleasure and the avoidance of pain are the basic drives recognized by Hobbes' psychology, and they determine the systems of valuation of different individuals. The individual takes as good what it has learned to pursue and regards as bad what it has learned to avoid. In developing a system of valuation, a creature is not discovering an objective distinction in nature between things that are good and things that are bad. Nothing is good or bad independently of its effects on creatures, and the effects may vary from creature to creature. At most, things are good or bad *to* individuals, not good or bad 'simply and absolutely'. In the same vein, Hobbes denies that in the sphere of good and bad things there is one that is the highest and whose attainment constitutes happiness. Instead, there are many different goods for many different individuals. Becoming happy in life is not a matter of being successful in the pursuit of one favoured good, but of being continually successful in the pursuit of many.

Hobbes' account of the constraints on the pursuit of human happiness is the connecting link between his theory of the motions of the mind and his moral and political philosophy proper. To attain happiness, people need to know what goods to pursue and how to pursue them. But in the absence of a science of good and evil, pleasure is their main criterion of the good, displeasure the main criterion of bad. Both pain and pleasure, however, are unreliable guides to the good and bad. A person may find a thing pleasant on one occasion and call it 'good', only to change their mind later. Two people can react differently to the same thing, so that it produces pleasure in one and pain in the other, and is called 'good' and 'not good' simultaneously. Pleasure biases judgment in favour of the nearer and more intense good, even if the cost of pursuing this good is displeasure later, and so on. Part of the correction to these distortions is to judge the good of various things not by how they feel when they are enjoyed or shunned, but by the consequences of enjoying or shunning them. If the costs of the consequences outweigh the present benefits, then a supposed good may be merely an apparent good. Again, if someone detached from the pursuit or avoidance of a thing can judge it good or bad, then it may really be so; while if no-one else can see the

attraction or repugnance, it may be illusory. Hobbes thinks only science can supply knowledge of the consequences of actions needed to counterbalance valuations derived from pain and pleasure; and he thinks science does not come naturally to people. Abiding by the value judgments of arbitrators does not come easily either, since people are attached to their valuations and unwilling to lose face by deferring to the judgments of others.

6 Politics: the state of nature

Despite the inconsistency in individual value judgments over time, and between the value judgments of different people at the same time, Hobbes thinks that there are some evils that are so large, and that interfere so markedly with everyone's pursuit of happiness, that practically no-one would knowingly pursue a course of action that resulted in them. War is such an evil, and Hobbes thinks he can show that if everyone makes themselves their own judge of what to pursue in the name of happiness, everyone will be involved in war. His argument to this conclusion is at the same time an argument for people to be guided by a judgment other than their own about what is best for them, the judgment of an existing civil power if they live in an existing commonwealth, the judgment of an as-yet-to-be designated civil power if they live outside any commonwealth.

The argument for the inevitability of war starts with assumptions about what is useful to the achievement of any goal. What is useful, no matter what good is being pursued, no matter whether the good is real or merely apparent, is power – that is, present means to future ends. 'Power' covers the physical capacities of individual agents, and also friends, riches and reputation. Not only is power in any form useful, but there can never be, according to Hobbes, too much power at the disposal of an agent in the nature of things. The reason is not that each agent naturally has an insatiable hunger for power, but that each agent is in competition with other agents for other goods, and any advantage one competitor temporarily has over another can, in principle, be overcome. The naturally strong can be toppled by a number of weak people who join forces; the man who has no enemies can be made into an object of hate with a well-judged campaign of character assassination; the wealthy can be robbed or swindled of their riches, and so on. Not only is it useful to acquire more and more power, but people cannot be blamed for doing so if all that organizes their activity in life is the pursuit of felicity.

Felicity is continual success in one's undertakings, whatever they may be. If what one undertakes is to do down one's competitors, then any means that helps to achieve it will be permissible. Or if, as is more likely, one aims at something else, doing down one's competitors can still often promote one's goal. Even the moderate man who wants only a small share of the good life can have reason to resort to foul means if he thinks he will lose everything by playing fair with rivals. And he cannot be sure he does not risk losing everything if he plays fair. In general, the goal of felicity requires one to get an advantage and keep it. Disabling others is a means of keeping the advantage; the outright elimination of competitors is even surer. Because these facts can be discovered by everyone, everyone who pursues felicity must bargain for severe insecurity and even worry about survival. Struggling for survival is far removed from felicity, but the pursuit of felicity, no holds barred, can quickly turn into a struggle for survival. Or to put it Hobbes' way, in the state of nature, people who pursue felicity are in a condition of war.

The argument does not depend on the idea that every human being is naturally selfish. It is true that in *De cive* Hobbes paints an unflattering picture of ordinary human behaviour, emphasizing the tendency of people to look out for themselves, to say one thing to other people's faces and another thing behind their backs, the tendency to think very well of their own opinions, but poorly of the views of others, and to fight over trivialities. This is all ordinary human behaviour, but it is not the behaviour of absolutely every human being. That it is so ordinary is enough, in Hobbes' view, to overturn the Aristotelian idea that human beings are by nature fit for society, but he is not claiming that human beings are uniform, or that their behaviour is uniformly antisocial. Hobbes recognizes a variety of temperaments in human beings, and his state of nature encompasses the vainglorious as well as the moderate. The vainglorious will seek to dispossess others because having more than anyone else is an end in itself. Moderates will go on to the attack because they want only a little and fear that the greedy will take even that. Others again will be at odds because they want something that cannot be shared. Whatever the cause, the general effect will be insecurity, and with insecurity goes many unattractive things – not only feelings of fear, but loss of society, loss of production, loss of technology, loss of art, loss of everything that enables human beings to rise above a life of bare subsistence and savagery. Life in the state of war is, in Hobbes' famous phrase, 'solitary, poor, nasty, brutish, and short'.

Is there no such thing as virtue to keep people from pursuing felicity ruthlessly? Hobbes thinks that precepts enjoining the moral virtues – what he calls 'the laws of nature' – are discoverable even in the state of nature, but people are not morally obliged to act on them if they run the risk of dying as a result: the most basic law of nature is to preserve oneself, and there is an inalienable 'right of nature' to be one's own judge of how to secure one's own preservation and well-being. This right may be laid down in the interest of self-preservation, but never at the cost of self-preservation. So if one has reason to think that others will take advantage of one's keeping agreements, or of showing gratitude, of not being judge in one's own cause, of being forgiving and so on through the rest of the virtues, one is not obliged to behave in those ways. One is not obliged to act in a way which will advertise one's vulnerability to the unscrupulous. It is enough that one is willing to behave virtuously if it is not too dangerous.

7 Politics: the commonwealth

The answer to the problems of life in the state of nature is an agreement by most in it to delegate their right of nature to a person, or body of persons, empowered to secure the many against physical attack and against the severe deprivations of the state of nature. That person or body of persons is empowered by a collective submission of the wills of the many to the will of the one or few. The many agree to be guided in their behaviour by the laws of a sovereign, on the understanding that this is a more effective way of securing their safety than individual action in the state of nature. The many lend their wills to the sovereign both as potential enforcers of the law against law-breakers and as an army of defence against foreign invasion. They lend their wills by doing only what is permitted by the sovereign's law and refraining from what the law prohibits. The law in turn expresses the sovereign's judgment regarding who should own what, who should teach what, how trade may be conducted, how wars should be waged, who should be punished and by what method of punishment, and who should be rewarded and the scale of the reward given.

The sovereign's judgment prevails because it, uniquely in the commonwealth, is still allied to a right of nature. Everyone who is subject to the sovereign thereby delegates their right of nature to the sovereign, but not in return for any forfeit or transfer of right by the sovereign himself. It is true that the commonwealth dissolves – that the obligation not to retract the right of nature lapses – if the sovereign is not able to secure the many against life-threatening incursion. But short of a reversion to the state of nature, the state in the person of the sovereign has a claim to expect the compliance of the many. The many owe it to one another to comply, because they agree between themselves to be law-abiding in return for safety if everyone else is law-abiding. They also owe it to the sovereign, at least for the time that he succeeds in making and keeping the peace, because they voluntarily and publicly submit to the sovereign, signifying to him that they will do what he decrees should be done for their safety.

Hobbes' idea that the sovereign's law can justly reach into every sector of public life had clear application to the questions being debated during the Civil War period in England. Those who complained that it was wrong for Charles I to appropriate property, to billet troops at will, to raise taxes without the consent of parliament, were given a theory that legitimized those actions. According to the theory, the limitations on a king's powers indicate that a state of nature, with its potential for open war, still prevails. Either the powers of government are separated (in which case the contention between, say, king and parliament reproduces the contention between individuals in the pre-political condition), or else the powers of government are not separated, but are limited by the rights of the subjects (in which case the right of nature has not really been transferred, and people are still liable to prefer their own judgment about what is best for them to the judgment that they have agreed to be guided by, with the same potential for slaughter).

Hobbes' theory permits the sovereign to regulate public life very stringently, but his message to sovereigns – there is no doubt that *Leviathan* in particular was intended to be read by heads of state – was not that it was *wise* to regulate public life very stringently. To begin with, there were limits to what laws could do: belief could not be commanded, so a certain tolerance of freedom of thought was inevitable. Again, people could not be expected to risk their lives in order to obey the law, as that would leave them no better off in the state than outside it. So laws that impoverished people to such an extent that they were starving, having to steal in order to live, were ill-conceived. Likewise forced military service, if it were likely to lead to death, might reasonably be seen as unacceptable according to the terms of Hobbes' social contract. Even a regime of law that secured most people from theft and common assault, but that confiscated all income above a measly minimum, could be seen as a failure by the sovereign to come up with what the many bargained for in entering the state. What the many bargain for is safety and, as Hobbes explains in chapter 30 of *Leviathan*, 'safety' signifies more than a 'bare preservation': it means a modicum of wellbeing over and above survival.

The arguments from prudence against overregulation by the sovereign are also arguments against

iniquitous practice by the sovereign. Hobbes distinguishes between iniquity and injustice. The sovereign does no injustice to his subjects if he decides to claim as his own all the land in a particular county or all the houses in a village: in creating the sovereign, his subjects give him the power to decree who is the owner of what. For all that, the sovereign may act iniquitously in the sense that he allows his own appetites and interests to count for more than those of anyone else, and so makes himself, for selfish reasons, the owner of more land than anyone else. There is a law of nature against iniquity, and therefore a law that decrees that the sovereign has to *try* to be equitable. But efforts are one thing; actual behaviour is another. The law of nature is not binding on the sovereign's behaviour, since he retains the right of nature and is authoritative about what to do for the best. If, in his opinion, it is for the best to behave iniquitously, then no other free agent, still less one of his subjects, can blame him for behaving accordingly. But the fact that his iniquitous acts are in this sense blameless does not mean that they are wise. If appropriating everyone's land makes people rebellious, albeit unjustly rebellious, then appropriating other people's land may have greater costs than benefits: it is subversive of the sovereign's power, which depends on the willingness of others to obey him.

Regarding the practice of religion, the relationship between church and state is a central preoccupation of *Leviathan*. Hobbes insists there that it is for the sovereign to decide whether people can join together for purposes of worship – that is, whether a given church can lawfully exist in the commonwealth. And he appears not to have been in favour of the establishment of a plurality of churches:

> But seeing a Common-wealth is but one Person, it ought also to exhibite to God but one Worship; which then it doth, when it commandeth it to be exhibited by Private men, Publiquely. And this is Publique Worship; the property whereof, is to be *Uniforme*: For those actions that are done differently, by different men, cannot be said to be a Publique Worship. And therefore, where many sorts of Worship be allowed, proceeding from the different Religions of Private men, it cannot be said there is any Publique Worship, nor that the Commonwealth is of any Religion at all.
>
> (Hobbes [1651] 1839 III: 354)

He goes on to say that 'whereas there be an infinite number of Actions and Gestures, of an indifferent nature; such of them as the Common-wealth shall ordain to be Publiquely and Universally in use, as signes of Honour, and part of Gods Worship, are to be taken and used for such by the Subjects'. It is hard to gather from these passages even tacit approval for a pluralistic form of national religious life. On the contrary, it is strongly implied that unless all members of the commonwealth worship in the same way, it will be doubtful not merely which religion the commonwealth observes but whether it observes any. It is as if Hobbes thinks that in a babble of different religious rites there will be no clear sign of honour from the commonwealth to God. For a clear signal to be sent, the same thing must be transmitted by everyone in the commonwealth. This 'clear-signal' justification for uniformity is not as anti-tolerationist as a justification that holds that all but the appointed religious rites are idolatrous, but it lends support all the same to a highly restrictive form of public religious worship.

As chapter 12 of *Leviathan* shows, Hobbes was aware that people living together but worshipping differently could ridicule or belittle one another's ceremonies and come into conflict. This is another reason for the secular authority to regulate public worship. It is also a reason for worshippers to take religious ceremony out of the public arena altogether, and preserve their differences in private. Hobbes has no quarrel with this sort of privatization of religious practice, so long as it is thoroughgoing: driving it out of the public arena means driving it well out. To obviate regulation, worship must be not only be private (that is, practised openly by a private person) but practised by a private person in secret. As Hobbes says in chapter 31 of *Leviathan*, private worship 'when secret, is Free; but in the sight of the multitude, it is never without some restraint, either from the Laws, or the opinion of men, which is contrary to the nature of Liberty'.

Not only actions required by religious rites can be driven underground if they might disturb the peace; freedom of action in matters indifferent to religion can also be open to regulation, as chapter 31 of *Leviathan* makes clear. Arguably it is indifferent whether prayers are said in Latin or in English; arguably it is indifferent whether services are conducted by married or by celibate men; but notoriously, these are things that people look askance at or insist upon, and about which they can come to blows. For this reason, if for no other, there is a reason for the sovereign to declare what the language shall be, and who shall preside at services.

What is in the sight of the multitude and in the control of the religious is one thing; what is out of sight and uncontrollable is another: 'Internal faith is in its own nature invisible, and consequently exempted from all humane jurisdiction', Hobbes says in chapter 42 of *Leviathan*. Humane jurisdiction is not just secular jurisdiction, but also that of a body charged by a church with the inquisition of believers.

Beliefs in general are not subject to the will he says in *De Politico Corpore*, a pirated edition of part two of the *Elements of Law* (1839 IV: 339). And although salvation depends on believing some things and not others, it is hard to be sure which things have to be believed beyond an uncontroversial minimum. For all of these reasons Hobbes is against the policing of religious belief, and against preferment for any one creed. It is in connection with the policing of belief rather than religious practice that his views come close to those of Independents, who in seventeenth-century England favoured a relatively loose, relatively tolerant organization of religious life, in particular a life outside a unitary Church of England. For when he appears in *Leviathan* (chapter 47) to side with the Independents in the Primitive church it is over each person deciding whose preaching to follow, not over many different religions being openly practised ([1651] 1839 III: 695). And in countenancing a variety of religious persuasions Hobbes is not so much showing tolerance as denying the importance to civil order of what goes on below the threshold of visible action.

8 Problems with Hobbes' political theory

In order to legitimize the powers of sovereigns, Hobbes invites his readers to think of sovereigns and states as the creations of free, self-interested people. The condition of subjection to a sovereign, even if it is not entered into by an original contract, can nevertheless be freely endorsed by each subject, since there is a good argument from self-interest for the condition. The argument says that the alternative to subjection is a dangerous chaos, which is infinitely worse than an intrusive but protective civil power. This is the argument directed against people who are already subjects; is the same argument effective when directed at people who do not yet belong to a state, who are in a state of nature? The issue can be sharpened by pointing out that the process of trading the state of nature for the commonwealth involves each person giving something now for the sake of a benefit later. Each person agrees to lay down their right of nature if everyone else will do likewise for the sake of peace. Granting that the condition of peace is better for each than the condition of war, is it not even better for anyone who can get away with it, to retain their right of nature while others give away theirs? Is it not better to pretend to lay down that right and then to take advantage of those who genuinely do so? If the answer to this question is 'Yes', how can the best outcome, from the point of self-interest, be one in which everyone performs and lays down their right of nature?

The question is taken up in a famous passage in chapter 15 of *Leviathan* where Hobbes replies to the fool who pretends that there is no such thing as justice. Commentators have likened it to the question posed by 'prisoners' dilemmas' where, for example, the outcome that would be best for each of two prisoners is for the other to confess and solely take a punishment for a crime, but where it turns out to be rational for each to confess and receive a punishment less severe than the maximum. The question is how this 'lesser' outcome can be the better one. In the case of the opportunistic non-performer of covenants discussed by Hobbes, the answer is that there is more security in the performance than in the non-performance of covenants. Someone who takes advantage of another's laying down the right of nature can only do so once and expect to get away with it. And the temporary advantage they gain may in any case not counterbalance what they will lose by being opposed by all those whose trust is threatened or betrayed.

Another problem with Hobbes' theory turns on the supposed moral urgency of each person's laying down the right of nature. Hobbes thinks that the biggest threat to the stability of states is the existence of too much scope for private judgment. The more each person is entitled to think for themselves in matters of wellbeing, the worse it turns out for everyone. This implication is supported in Hobbes' theory by a supposedly scientific understanding of the diversity of the passions and the way that the passions get the better of judgment in human beings. By delegating their power of judgment to someone who is not affected by the individual passions of the people ruled over, people actually get access to a more effective (because more dispassionate) means of securing themselves than their own individual judgments. But, by the same token, they forgo any intellectual contribution to public life. They do not contribute to the state as citizens but as subjects only: political life for the many consists solely of submission to law. It is by their passivity rather than by the application of their powers of judgment that people promote the public good. This may have seemed persuasive in a time when the Biblical example of Adam and Eve would have been widely understood to illustrate the dangers of private judgment of good and evil, but to contemporary sensibility it verges on the paranoid. In fact, Hobbes' point is not quite that the judgments of human beings about their wellbeing can never be trusted, but rather that their *prescientific* judgments cannot be trusted. Prescientifically, people are moved by their feelings of pleasure and displeasure to call things 'good' and 'bad' – few have either the resources or the circumstances to be taught any better. But there is a better conception to be inculcated: Hobbes

indicates that it consists of showing how things that are genuinely good, as opposed to pleasant, promote peace or self-preservation, while things that are genuinely bad, as opposed to unpleasant, are conducive to war and self-destruction.

9 The scientific status of Hobbes' ethics and politics

The main lines of Hobbes' political philosophy include the idea that the commonwealth is a solution to the ever-present threat of war in the passionate make-up of human beings, and that the commonwealth is made by delegating the right of nature to a sovereign power with unlimited power. This summarizes a theory worked out in very great detail, a theory Hobbes always regarded as ushering in the scientific treatment of morals and politics. What made the theory scientific? A number of answers get support from Hobbes' writings. The scientific status of politics is sometimes said to be owed to its derivation, in some sense, from Hobbes' natural science. Again, Hobbes' use in civil philosophy of a method applicable to natural bodies and bodies politic alike is sometimes thought to be crucial to its scientific status. These answers are consistent with some texts but sit uneasily with others. First, although Hobbes thought that there was a way of approaching the principles of morals and politics from a starting point in the workings of sense and imagination (which were treated of by physics), he consistently denied that civil science *had* to be approached by way of physics. In chapter 6 of *De corpore* he says that people entirely innocent of physics, but who enjoy introspective access to their own passionate states, are able to see in themselves evidence for the truth of the theory of human nature in the civil science. Something similar is said in the Introduction to *Leviathan*. In the same vein there is the explanation of his having been able to publish *De cive*, the third volume in his trilogy, without having first expounded the principles of parts of philosophy that were prior to politics. Hobbes said that this was possible because civil philosophy depended on principles of its own. What ties together all of these remarks is a belief in the autonomy of civil science, a belief that is not seriously called into question by his saying that the two principal parts of civil philosophy were alike in applying a certain sort of method to the investigation of bodies – bodies politic on the one hand and natural bodies on the other.

When Hobbes says that each part of philosophy deals with bodies, he makes clear that the two kinds of bodies are 'very different' from one another. And there is no evidence that 'body', when applied in the phrase 'body politic', is supposed to mean 'space-occupying thing existing without the mind'. In other words, there is no evidence that bodies politic are bodies in any more than a metaphorical sense. Finally, it is not clear that Hobbes thought that the scientific status of his politics was made more credible by an analogy between bodies politic and natural bodies. It is not as if he thought that natural bodies were well-understood scientifically, and that bodies politic might in principle be as well understood if the methods of physics were applied to them. On the contrary, Hobbes always thought that the properties of human artefacts, such as bodies politic, were much better understood than the properties of natural bodies, which had God's inscrutable will behind them.

It would be a mistake, however, to think that civil science for Hobbes was primarily an exercise in the investigation of the properties of bodies. It was an exercise in putting our judgments about what we ought to do on grounds that were far more solid than pleasure and pain. Good and bad were a matter of what conduced or interfered with self-preservation or peace, not how it felt to do or get this or that. The core of Hobbes' civil science is an attempt to recast the precepts of morality – the laws of nature – as instruments of peace, and to show how the ingredients of war are latent in any project for the pursuit of happiness. The scientific status of the doctrine of the laws of nature – the ground of its claim to be called moral philosophy – was its conforming to the pattern of a deductive system, based on two fundamental laws of nature and the rest derivative. Similarly with the deduction of the rights of sovereigns from the goal of peace. The scientific status of the argument for the inevitability of war consisted in its proceeding from principles about the passions. But these principles were by no means the property of physics or physicists; they were available in each person's introspective self-knowledge.

See also: HUMAN NATURE; JUSTICE; PUBLIC INTEREST

List of works

A new edition of Hobbes' works is currently in preparation. Until it is complete, the standard edition will remain that of Sir William Molesworth, which omits many manuscripts and a great deal of Hobbes' correspondence.

Hobbes, T. (1839) *The English Works of Thomas Hobbes*, ed. W. Molesworth, London: John Bohn, 11 vols. (The spelling and punctuation are modernized in this collection.)

—— (1845) *Opera Latina*, London: John Bohn, 5 vols. (Hobbes' works in Latin.)

—— (1628) *Thucydides' History of the Pelopennesian Wars*; repr. ed. R. Schlatter, New Brunswick, NJ: Rutgers University Press, 1975. (The Petition of Right of 1628 may have led to the publication of this translation.)

—— (1630?) *The Short Tract*, in *The Elements of Law Natural and Politic*, ed. F. Tonnies, London: Simpkin & Marshall, 1889. (This work, which appears as Appendix I, is attributed by Tonnies to Hobbes.)

—— (1640) *The Elements of Law Natural and Politic*, ed. F. Tonnies, London: Simpkin & Marshall, 1889. (The correct and intact edition of material also reproduced as *Human Nature* and *De Corpore Politico* in Molesworth, volume 4.)

—— (1641) *The Third Set of Objections to Descartes Meditations*, in *The Philosophical Writings of Descartes*, vol. 2, trans. J. Cottingham, R. Stoothoff and D. Murdoch, Cambridge: Cambridge University Press, 1985. (Hobbes wrote these objections as a member of Mersenne's circle in Paris.)

—— (1642) *De cive*, in *The English Works of Thomas Hobbes*, vol. 2, ed. W. Molesworth, London: John Bohn, 1839. (Molesworth follows an English translation, not by Hobbes, of the original Latin.)

—— (1643) *Thomas White's De Mundo Examined*, trans. H Jones, Bradford: Bradford University Press, 1976. (A recently discovered early foray into metaphysics.)

—— (1646) *A Minute or First Draught of the Optiques.* (The most polished of Hobbes' optical treaties)

—— (1651) *Leviathan, or the Matter, Form and Power of Commonwealth, Ecclesiastical and Civil*, in *The English Works of Thomas Hobbes*, vol. 3, ed. W. Molesworth, London: John Bohn, 1839; repr. ed. R. Tuck, Cambridge: Cambridge University Press, 1991; repr. ed. E. Curley, Chicago, IL: Hackett Publishing Company, 1994. (Hobbes' masterpiece.)

—— (1654) *Of Liberty and Necessity*, in *The English Works of Thomas Hobbes*, vol. 4, ed. W. Molesworth, London: John Bohn, 1839. (Classic discussion of freedom and determinism.)

—— (1655) *De corpore*, in *The English Works of Thomas Hobbes*, vol. 1, ed. W. Molesworth, London: John Bohn, 1839. (Follows an English translation of 1656.)

—— (1656a) *The Questions concerning Liberty, Necessity and Chance, Clearly Stated and Debated between Dr Bramhall, Bishop of Derry, and Thomas Hobbes of Malmesbury*, in *The English Works of Thomas Hobbes*, vol. 4, ed. W. Molesworth, London: John Bohn, 1839. (Bramhall had accused Hobbes of atheism and irreligion.)

—— (1656b) *Six Lessons to the Professors of Mathematics... in the University of Oxford*, in *The*

English Works of Thomas Hobbes, vol. 7, ed. W. Molesworth, London: John Bohn, 1839. (Testy reply to some Oxford antagonists.)

—— (1658) *De homine*; trans. and abridged B. Gert, T. Scott-Craig and C.T. Wood as *On Man*, in *Man and Citizen*, New York: Humanities Press, 1972. (A complete translation of *De homine* is in preparation at Cambridge University Press.)

—— (1668) *Behemoth, or the Long Parliament, Dialogue of the Civil Wars of England*, in *The English Works of Thomas Hobbes*, vol. 6, ed. W. Molesworth, London: John Bohn, 1839. (Hobbes' own history of the English Civil War.)

—— (1678) *Decameron Physiologicum*, in *The English Works of Thomas Hobbes*, vol. 7, ed. W. Molesworth, London: John Bohn, 1839. (Restates some of the methodology and principal results of the physical sections of *De corpore*.)

—— (1681) *Dialogue between a Philosopher and a Student of the Common Laws of England*, in *The English Works of Thomas Hobbes*, vol. 6, ed. W. Molesworth, London: John Bohn, 1839. (A discussion of political philosophy.)

References and further reading

Aubrey, J. (1898) *Brief Lives, Chiefly of Contemporaries, Set Down by John Aubrey between the Years 1669 & 1696*, ed. A. Clark, Oxford, 2 vols. (Contains an early biographical sketch of Hobbes.)

Johnston, D. (1986) *The Rhetoric of Leviathan*, Princeton, N.J: Princeton University Press. (A study of the tensions between the scientific pretensions of some of Hobbes' political writings and their persuasive purpose.)

Mintz, S. (1970) *The Hunting of Leviathan*, Cambridge: Cambridge University Press. (Deals with the context and early reception of *Leviathan*.)

Peters, R. (1956) *Hobbes*, Harmondsworth: Penguin. (A clearly written study of all Hobbes' philosophy.)

Rogers, G.A.J. and Ryan, A. (eds) (1988) *Perspectives on Thomas Hobbes*, Oxford: Clarendon Press. (A collection of mostly accessible papers about Hobbes' metaphysics, philosophy of science and politics, published to mark the four-hundredth anniversary of his birth.)

Sommerville, J. (1992) *Thomas Hobbes: Political Ideas in Historical Context*, London: Macmillan. (A very clear and comprehensive account of the historical context of Hobbes' political writings.)

Sorell, T. (1986) *Hobbes*, London: Routledge. (A study of Hobbes' metaphysics and politics against the background of his philosophy of science.)

—— (ed.) (1995) *The Cambridge Companion to Hobbes*, Cambridge: Cambridge University Press.

(Articles on all aspects of Hobbes' thought, including his mathematics, optics and his theories of law and religion. Contains an authoritative biographical account by Noel Malcolm.)

Tuck, R. (1989) *Hobbes*, Oxford: Oxford University Press. (A short study claiming the importance for Hobbes' thought of philosophical scepticism.)

Zarka, Y. (1987) *La décision métaphysique de Hobbes – Conditions de la politique*, Paris: Vrin. (A study of Hobbes' system, bringing to bear the great sophistication of French scholarship on Hobbes. The author is editor of the Vrin edition of Hobbes.)

TOM SORELL

HOHFELD, WESLEY NEWCOMB (1879–1918)

W.N. Hohfeld, US law professor and proponent of analytical jurisprudence, was responsible for one of the most influential analyses of the concept of a right in legal and moral philosophy. He offered to resolve all complex legal relations into a few simple and elementary ones, often confusedly referred to as 'rights'.

For Hohfeld, 'right' in its strict sense necessarily correlates with an identical duty owed by a second party. Rights differ from 'privileges' (where a person is not duty-bound), from 'powers' (where a person is legally enabled to bring about change in some legal relationship) and from 'immunities' (where a person is legally protected from another person's purported exercise of legal power designed to effect some change in a given legal relationship).

Hohfeld constructs two sets of interrelated 'correlatives' and 'opposites'. The first set comprises 'right' or 'claim' (sometimes 'claim-right' in the subsequent literature), with its correlative 'duty' and its opposite 'no-right'; 'privilege' (or, preferably according to most commentators, 'liberty') is in turn the opposite of duty and the correlative of no-right. These always concern some action or abstention by a person. One has a duty to act, for example, to make a payment, for another; then, correlatively, that other has a (claim-) right to the payment. The opposite would be if the second party had no right to be paid by the first – and in that case the first would be at liberty to, or would have the privilege to, withhold payment.

The second set concerns power and its correlative 'liability' and opposite 'disability'. Legal power always refers to some legal relationship, for example, a contractual right of A to some payment by B. In this case, the law may enable A in some way to vary the existing legal relationship, for example by voluntarily renouncing right to payment. Then B has as correlative the liability to have the privilege of non-payment conferred on them by A. In the opposite case, we consider the possibility of an absence of power. For example, B normally lacks power to revoke unilaterally A's contractual right. B thus has a 'disability' to bring about this change; A correlatively enjoys an immunity from it.

Notable in this analysis is the atomistic character of each legal relationship; everything is brought down to single relationships of distinct persons in respect of specific actions or abstentions, or particular (purported) power-exercising acts. Hohfeld indeed argues that more complex situations, such as those we encounter in property-ownership or in corporate relations, are resolvable without residue into aggregate sets of simple atomic relationships belonging to his categories; hence his claim that these are the 'fundamental' legal conceptions. This claim has been challenged, and along with it the claim that Hohfeld's analysis merely clarifies or purifies existing legal usages; Hohfeld was more a reformer than an analyst of current legal usage. For those purposes for which it is useful exhaustively to investigate the totality of relations between single individuals for some legal purpose, the analysis provides a valuable tool. But it is less valuable for other purposes, such as elaborating a catalogue of fundamental human or constitutional rights, or constructing a theory of property.

See also: Law, philosophy of; Legal concepts §3; Rights §2

List of works

Hohfeld, W.N. (1919) *Fundamental Legal Conceptions as Applied in Judicial Reasoning*, ed. W.W. Cook, New Haven, CT: Yale University Press, 1966. (Hohfeld's basic statement of position, comprising a series of highly influential and attractively written articles from learned journals.)

References and further reading

Paton, G.W. (1972) *A Text-book of Jurisprudence*, ed. G.W. Paton and D.P. Derham, Oxford, Clarendon Press, 4th edn. (Chapters on rights (18–21) give a good account of Hohfeld in the light of forerunners and successors.)

White, A.R. (1984) *Rights*, Oxford: Clarendon Press. (Contains a root-and-branch critique of Hohfeld and those who have been tempted to follow his doctrines, written in the spirit of linguistic-analytical philosophy.)

NEIL MacCORMICK

HOLCOT, ROBERT (*c.*1290–1349)

Earlier scholars labeled Robert Holcot a sceptic, a nominalist and an Ockhamist. In fact, the work of this English Dominican friar is too complex and original for any simple label. What can be said with justice is that Holcot belongs among philosophers who work not at developing their own systematic philosophies but at criticizing the speculative efforts of their predecessors. Holcot questions the scope of Aristotelian logic, the extent of theological knowledge and even the extent to which we can have knowledge of the world around us.

Holcot studied theology at Oxford, delivering his commentary on Peter Lombard's *Sentences* over two academic years there, beginning probably in 1331. This was a fruitful period for philosophical theology at Oxford. Holcot's lectures overlapped with those of William CRATHORN, a fellow Dominican but nevertheless a fierce rival, and the influential Franciscan Adam WODEHAM. Holcot himself was highly influential, and his biblical commentaries, especially his commentary on the Book of Wisdom, were widely circulated throughout the later Middle Ages and beyond.

Besides the works just mentioned, Holcot also composed a series of quodlibetal questions. The first of these quodlibets is an ideal introduction to Holcot's philosophical views. In it he asks whether theology is a science. His surprising answer is that it is not, or at least not one we can naturally acquire in this life. He means that there are no theological truths we can know naturally with the sort of certainty required for *scientia*; that is, no theological truths are demonstrable (by us, on our own, in this life). First and foremost, we cannot demonstrate that God exists; cosmological arguments rest on contingent facts that are not themselves demonstrable. Moreover, to prove God's existence, one must prove the existence of a thing that satisfies all the articles of the faith: this God must be shown to be infinite, triune, the creator, and so on (see God, arguments for the existence of). Anselm's ontological argument comes in for careful criticism at this point because it takes off from a richer conception of God, one from which many divine attributes might be derived.

In this quodlibet, Holcot notes rather casually that

he would extend these claims to all incorporeal things, including the human soul. There is therefore no science of the human soul, and (presumably) we cannot demonstrate even that we have souls. Holcot's discussion of God's causal powers suggests even more strongly that he is a thoroughgoing sceptic. There he acknowledges (as it seems any Christian philosopher must) that God can intervene in the natural order, causing fire to stop giving heat or, as he luridly puts it, causing the entire structure of the world to take on the appearance of a fly. Such possibilities lead Holcot to claim that there is always an element of uncertainty in our empirical beliefs, and in his commentary on the *Sentences* he goes on to conclude that there can be no scientia regarding them.

Much has been made of these claims, and if *scientia* is translated as 'knowledge' then Holcot appears to be a quite radical sceptic. However, his position is more subtle than this. The remainder of his argument makes it clear that Holcot does not believe our empirical beliefs lack all warrant: 'It is sufficiently established [*persuasum*], to me, that God has not made such alterations' (*In quatuor libros Sententiarum* IV q.3 ad1); 'that A is the cause of B is held with probability' (*Determinationes* 3). From the fact that such beliefs are not held with complete certainty, we cannot infer that they should not be held at all, and Holcot insists that we have good reasons for believing as we do about the world. He does not go on to ask the questions a modern reader would like to have answered, such as what exactly those good reasons are and whether such beliefs can still count as knowledge. Nevertheless, Holcot is clearly not entirely the thoroughgoing sceptic he might seem to be.

Relatively little of Holcot's work is concerned with establishing the limits of *scientia*. Indeed, he argues in his first quodlibet that theology is still very much worth studying, even if it is not a science, because through it we can acquire a stronger, broader and more explicit faith. True to his words, Holcot involves himself in a wide range of theological and philosophical controversies. One of his more distinctive claims, and one with far-ranging implications, is his rejection of any sort of metaphysical distinction other than a 'real' distinction. This point receives special attention in his discussion of the divine perfections and the Trinity. Following WILLIAM OF OCKHAM and John DUNS SCOTUS, Holcot rejects out of hand the suggestion of Thomas AQUINAS that conceptual distinctions (distinctions 'of reason') account for the differences between, for example, divine wisdom and divine goodness. However, Holcot also rejected the proposals of Scotus and Ockham, each of whom in his own way analysed the divine essence in terms of

'formal' distinctions. 'All that are formally distinct are distinct things,' Holcot charges (*Determinationes* 10). By rejecting all non-real distinctions, Holcot places himself in a difficult position as regards the Trinity (see TRINITY). Church doctrine was very clear in rejecting any real distinction among the divine Persons, and so Holcot was committed to saying that there are no distinctions at all within the Trinity. If so, however, then the following syllogism should be valid: 'The Divine Essence is the Father, and the Divine Essence is the Son; therefore, the Son is the Father.' This syllogism is not valid: the premises are true and the conclusion false. The threat that looms, then, is that Aristotle's 'entire syllogistic form would be defective' (*Determinationes* 10). Holcot's reply is to claim that Aristotelian logic is not universally applicable: 'the logic of the faith has to be different from natural logic' (*In quatuor libros Sententiarum* I q.5, ad1). However, this striking pronouncement, once developed, turns out to be less interesting than it sounds. Holcot does not offer anything like an alternative logic: what he gives us instead are fairly obvious rules for excluding terms that stand for 'many things and also each one of them' (*Determinationes* 10), a restriction that rules out terms that stand for God.

See also: KNOWLEDGE, CONCEPT OF; NATURAL PHILOSOPHY, MEDIEVAL

List of works

Many of the *Quodlibets* do not have definite numbers assigned to them, as the order of the questions is highly uncertain. Editions of several *Quodlibets* are given here. See also Molteni (1968) and Kennedy (1993) in the list of references and further reading.

Holcot, Robert (1331–3) *In quatuor libros Sententiarum* (Commentary on the Four Books of *Sentences*), Lyons, 1518; repr. Frankfurt: Minerva, 1967. (Remains the only printed source for most of Holcot's philosophical work, including a dozen questions from *Quodlibet* I, printed here as *Determinationes*.)

—— (1332) *Sex articuli* (Six Articles), ed. F. Hoffmann, *Die 'Conferentiae' des Robert Holcot O.P. und die akademischen Auseinandersetzungen an der Universität Oxford 1330–1332*, Beiträge zur Geschichte der Philosophie und Theologie des Mittelalters NF 5, Münster: Aschendorff, 1993. (Edition of the philosophically rich *Sex articuli*, also known as the *Conferentiae*.)

—— (1333) *Sermon*, ed. J.C. Wey, 'The *sermo finalis* of Robert Holcot', *Mediaeval Studies* 11, 1949:

219–23. (A humorous sermon delivered at the end of his Oxford lectures.)

—— (1333) *Quodlibet*, ed. J.T. Muckle, '"Utrum Theologia Sit Scientia". A Quodlibet Question of Robert Holcot O.P.', *Mediaeval Studies* 20, 1958: 127–53. (Edition of *Quodlibet* I q.1.)

—— (1333–4) *Quodlibet*, ed. W. Courtenay, 'A Revised Text of Robert Holcot's Quodlibetal Dispute on Whether God is Able to Know More Than He Knows', *Archiv für Geschichte der Philosophie* 53, 1971: 1–21. (Edits *Quodlibet* I q.6, which contains a detailed discussion of Holcot's interesting view that the objects of knowledge and belief are not things in the world, but individual tokens of a proposition.)

—— (1333–4) *Quodlibets*, ed. H.G. Gelber, *Exploring the Boundaries of Reason: Three Questions on the Nature of God*, Toronto, Ont.: Pontifical Institute of Medieval Studies, 1983. (Edits *Quodlibeta* I qq.2–4, in which Holcot rejects all non-real distinctions and argues for limitations on the applicability of Aristotelian logic.)

—— (1333–4) *Quodlibets*, ed. P. Streveler *et al.*, *Seeing the Future Clearly: Questions on Future Contingents*, Toronto, Ont.: Pontifical Institute of Medieval Studies, 1995. (Edits *Quodlibeta* III qq.1–3, as well as corresponding material from the *Sentences* commentary. K. Tachau's introduction presents important new historical research.)

References and further reading

Gelber, H.G. (1974) 'Logic and the Trinity: A Clash of Values in Scholastic Thought, 1300–1335', PhD thesis, University of Wisconsin. (Never published, but extremely valuable as a survey of the ways in which scholastics from Bonaventure through Holcot attempted to reconcile the Trinity with standard principles of logic.)

Hoffmann, F. (1972) *Die theologische Methode des Oxforder Dominikanerlehrers Robert Holcot* (The Theological Method of the Oxford Dominican Scholar Robert Holcot), Beiträge zur Geschichte der Philosophie und Theologie des Mittelalters NF 5, Münster: Aschendorff. (A detailed look at Holcot's philosophical and theological method, with particular attention to his views on the status of theology as a science.)

Kennedy, L.A. (1993) *The Philosophy of Robert Holcot, Fourteenth-Century Skeptic*, Lewiston, NY: Mellen. (Valuable for the passages that it collects and translates, and for the seven quodlibetal questions it edits.)

Molteni, P. (1968) *Roberto Holcot, O.P. Dottrina della grazia e della giustificazione con due questioni*

quodlibetali inedite, Pinerolo: Editrice Alzani. (Edits *Quodlibeta* I q.9, III q.7.)

Moody, E.A. (1964) 'A Quodlibetal Question of Robert Holkot, O.P., on the Problem of the Objects of Knowledge and of Belief', *Speculum* 39: 53–74. (The text has been superseded by Courtenay's edition, but Moody's analysis remains well worth reading.)

Oberman, H. (1963) *The Harvest of Medieval Theology: Gabriel Biel and Late Medieval Nominalism*, Cambridge, MA: Harvard University Press. (Perhaps the best starting point for an overview of Holcot's philosophical tendencies.)

—— (1966) *Forerunners of the Reformation: The Shape of Late Medieval Thought*, New York: Holt, Rinehart & Winston. (Translates passages from the Wisdom Commentary concerning grace and justification.)

Schepers, H. (1970–2) 'Holkot contra dicta Crathorn' (Holcot Against the Claims of Crathorn), *Philosophisches Jahrbuch* 77: 320–54; 79: 106–136. (Assesses the philosophical dispute between Crathorn and Holcot, with particular reference to their dispute over the objects of knowledge. In German.)

Smalley, B. (1960) *English Friars and Antiquity in the Early Fourteenth Century*, New York: Barnes & Noble. (Offers a colourful account of Holcot's life and literary methods.)

ROBERT PASNAU

HÖLDERLIN, JOHANN CHRISTIAN FRIEDRICH (1770–1843)

An outstanding German poet, Hölderlin is now widely recognized as one of the most important writers and thinkers of his time. After an initial period of critical neglect and relative public indifference, he eventually came to enjoy a privileged status in German cultural life at the beginning of the twentieth century, and has continued to exercise a profound influence on modern literature and critical thought. Hölderlin's work emerged within the context of Kant's Critical Revolution and developed in constant interaction with the German Idealist speculation this subsequently provoked, against the background of the French Revolution and the fundamental issues raised in its wake for an entire generation. Hölderlin was personally acquainted with many of the leading figures of the period, including Schiller, Goethe, Herder, Novalis, Fichte, Schelling and Hegel. His writings reflect and respond to many of the

central philosophical concerns and themes of his time,
in a highly original and prescient fashion. However, it is
only since Wilhelm Dilthey that the importance of his
specific influence on the intellectual development of
Schelling and Hegel in particular has been fully
recognized, so that he has even been described as the
'Doctor Seraphicus' of German Idealism. His work
subsequently provided a frequent point of reference for
the Frankfurt School's engagement with the heritage of
German Idealism and the problem of the relationship
between aesthetics, ethics and politics. More recently,
Hölderlin has become a major presence in much
contemporary critical and deconstructive theory, largely
through the pervasive influence of Martin Heidegger.

1   Life and writings
2   Fundamental themes

1   Life and writings

Hölderlin grew up in a sheltered, intensely Pietist
domestic environment. His mother directed his
education towards a career in the ministry, a later
source of much psychological conflict since he never
subsequently gained the financial independence necessary to pursue his chosen literary career. In 1788
Hölderlin entered the Tübingen Stift, ostensibly to
study theology, but was soon preoccupied with
developments in contemporary literature and philosophy, and the beginnings of the French Revolution.
He shed his earlier orthodox religious beliefs under
the influence of KANT and the classicizing humanism
of Friedrich SCHILLER, and became friends with his
fellow-students SCHELLING and HEGEL. His early
poetry celebrated humanistic ideals using a rhyming,
hymnic style indebted largely to Schiller. Hölderlin
encapsulated his central interests at this time: 'Kant
and the Greeks are my only reading' (1946–85 vol. 6:
128). His attempts to mediate his Graecophile
enthusiasm with the rigorous republicanism of
FICHTE, and with the latter's radicalization of
Kantian ethics, is documented in the mid 1790s
through the various evolving versions of his first
major work, the novel *Hyperion* (1798–9).

Almost alone among his writings *Hyperion* enjoyed
a certain celebrity in Hölderlin's lifetime, becoming
something of a 'sentimental' classic, not entirely
unlike Goethe's *Werther*, by which it was probably
influenced. Set in the contemporary context of the
Greek struggle for national independence, the structure of the first-person epistolary narrative presents
the spiritual evolution of its idealistic eponymous
protagonist, combining the personal theme of transforming love with broader concerns for the nature of
genuine political freedom. The hero moves from an
initial pantheistic identification with the totality of
life, through painful but educative experiences of
failure and disappointment with a recalcitrant human
reality, towards a more mediated and differentiated
relationship between self and world. *Hyperion* contains numerous allusions to contemporary debates
concerning the possibilities of revolutionary social
transformation and the appropriate means for its
realization. But the narrator also undergoes a process
of personal transformation in the act of narration
itself, culminating in an emancipatory vision of what
it means to become an artist dedicated to the
projection of a human future free of despotic
coercion. The lyrical, poetic prose celebrates a
religio-aesthetic conception of the world as an
intrinsically harmonious totality that requires no
external theological legitimization, and recognizes
the experience of mortality and finitude as a necessary
moment of the life of the whole, concluding upon a
prospective rather than a resigned note of chastened
aspiration.

Hölderlin's next major project, a tragedy on the
death of Empedocles, continued and deepened many
of these central themes. Hölderlin never brought the
play to a satisfactory conclusion, but three fragmentary versions survive, together with an exceedingly
compressed and obscure related prose study known as
the *Grund zum Empedokles* (The Groundplan of
Empedocles), all composed between 1797 and 1799.
Here, too, he concerns himself with the possibility of
revolution and the necessity of an accompanying
moral-spiritual reformation. But a newer note is also
struck through emphasis upon the theme of tragic
hubris on the part of the protagonist, and the poet's
increasing concern with the dangers of human
identification with the divine – the seductions of
pantheism – and the concomitant tendency to exalt
human power in a unilaterally dominating relationship with the natural world and other human beings.
This arguably represents an incipient critique of the
'Promethean' tendencies of Fichtean idealism and its
subordination of nature as object to the subject as free
power of total self-determination. None the less,
Hölderlin equally emphasizes the importance of
'maturity' and autonomy in the Kantian sense if the
potentially authoritarian excesses of revolutionary
despotism are to be avoided. If Hölderlin originally
conceived his drama as a contribution to contemporary political enlightenment and an encouragement to
social renewal, it is unsurprising that he finally
abandoned work on it when Napoleon became First
Consul in 1799 and the hopes of a peaceful 'German'
Revolution receded dramatically.

In the poetry written between 1800 and his
apparent mental collapse in 1806, Hölderlin turned

increasingly to more explicit engagement with the decisive actualities of European history, particularly the ambivalent relationship between the classical heritage and the claims of the Christian tradition. The implicit and semi-secularized eschatological dimension of Hölderlin's thought now comes insistently to the fore, and he concentrates upon the aporias of the poet's proclamation in a barren age characterized by a thankless and essentially instrumental attitude to the world. The concern with preserving a sense of proper limitation is reflected in the constant reference to 'mortals' and the powerful apocalyptic tone of the final hymns. After his breakdown (arguably exacerbated if not actually precipitated by drastic contemporary 'treatment') Hölderlin was taken under benevolent care until his death. In this last phase he reverted to a more detached and naïve style of composition in which the tensions and problems of his earlier life and work seem fictively resolved and dissolved into an eerie catatonic calm.

2 Fundamental themes

If poetry is 'made of words not ideas', there is an obvious danger in abstracting selected themes from their complex aesthetic context. But Hölderlin 's work articulates rather than illustrates a developing and penetrating body of coherent concerns and a distinctive mode of spiritual perception. In the first instance, it aesthetically prefigures a comprehensive reconciliation of the great polarities and disabling dualisms bequeathed by Kantian thought, principally the bifurcation between subject and object, spirit and nature. Yet the anti-identitarian, literally 'anti-monarchical', moment of Hölderlin's thought also resists the institution of a single controlling principle, that would suppress diversity and differentiation, in favour of an ontology of reciprocal interaction (1946–85 vol. 6: 300–1). The rehabilitation of finitude and fragility, of an acknowledged interdependence of subject and object, art and nature, is typically connected with an ethics of gratitude that is more than an ideology of subservience or deference. Many poems express the thought of an intrinsic dependency of the 'divine' dimension upon the sphere of mortal experience if it is to find fulfilment through an appropriate human 'correspondence' which constitutes neither an identity nor an antithesis. Despite the repudiation of a traditional metaphysical concept of an infinite creator-God independent of the created world, there remains a permanent 'theological' residue, a sublimated Christian element, in Hölderlin's recognition of our inherent 'creatureliness' within the economy of nature, our privileged vocation as the finite site for

the self-manifestation and self-enjoyment of life through the indispensable, cultivating addition of human 'art' (1946–85 vol. 6: 326–30). Perhaps Hölderlin's most lasting significance lies in this powerful utopian vision of reconciled dwelling, rooted in a conception of art as liberating praxis that has only become central in our own time. This work is less a unique subjective and personal expression – though it is also that – than a compelling articulation of universal human aspirations for a transformed relationship to inner and outer nature. Aesthetic formalist tendencies can arguably do little justice to work which 'aesthetically' questions the supposed 'autonomy of the aesthetic' as a subjective and sequestered sphere of private experience, and implicitly challenges some of our most cherished modern philosophical assumptions.

See also: GERMAN IDEALISM; ROMANTICISM, GERMAN

List of works

Hölderlin, J.C.F. (1946–85) *Sämtliche Werke (Große Stuttgarter Ausgabe)*, ed. F. Beissner and A. Beck, Stuttgart: Kohlhammer, 8 vols. (The standard critical edition of Hölderlin's writings with extensive commentary and accompanying documentation – an indispensable reference source.)

—— (1975–) *Sämtliche Werke (Frankfurter Ausgabe)*, ed. D.E. Sattler, Frankfurt: Verlag Roter Stern. (A recent edition of Hölderlin's writings which attempts to present the evolving stages of his poems with less editorial intervention in favour of the supposedly 'final' closed text.)

—— (1798) *Hyperion*, trans. W.R. Trask in E.L. Santer (ed.) *Friedrich Hölderlin. Hyperion and Selected Poems*, New York: Continuum, 1994. (English translation of Hölderlin's novel, adapted by D. Schwarz, and bilingual selection of mainly later poems translated by various hands.)

—— (1799) *Empedocles*, trans. M. Hamburger in *Hölderlin. Poems and Fragments*, London: Anvil Poets Press, 3rd edn, 1994. (Excellent bilingual edition with representative selection of poems, including the second and third versions of *Empedocles* and the commentated translations of Pindar.)

—— (1988) *Friedrich Hölderlin. Essays and Letters on Theory*, ed. and trans. T. Pfau, Albany, NY: State University of New York Press. (Contains the philosophical fragments and essays, the remarks on Greek tragedy and relevant excerpts from the correspondence.)

References and further reading

Adorno, T.W. (1965) 'Parataxis', in *Noten zur Literatur III*, Frankfurt: Suhrkamp, 156-209; trans. S.W. Nicholsen in *Notes to Literature*, New York: Columbia University Press, vol. 2, 109–49, 1992. (Critical of attempts, like those of Heidegger, to minimize Hölderlin's debt to the context of German Idealism.)

Dastur, F. (1992) *Hölderlin, Tragédie et Modernité* (Hölderlin: tragedy and modernity), Fougères: Encre Marine. (A concentrated and elegant introduction to Hölderlin's thought, focusing on his understanding of the relation between the ancients and moderns.)

Dilthey, W. (1905) 'Hölderlin', in *Das Erlebnis und die Dichtung*, Leipzig: Teubner Verlag, 349–459; trans. J. Ross, in R.A. Makkreel and F. Rodi (eds) *Poetry and Experience*, Princeton, NJ: Princeton University Press, 303–83, 1985. (The first important study of Hölderlin's importance in the evolution of idealist philosophy, with an emphasis upon the earlier works.)

Heidegger, M. (1981) *Erläuterungen zu Hölderlins Dichtung*, vol. 4 of *Gesamtausgabe*, Frankfurt: Klostermann; trans. W. McNeill and J. Davis as *Hölderlin's Hymn to the 'Ister'*, Bloomington and Indianapolis, IN: Indiana University Press, 1996. (Penetrating and influential readings of the poetry in terms of the author's central philosophical preoccupations.)

Henrich, D. (1992) *Der Grund im Bewusstsein, Untersuchungen zu Hölderlins Denken (1794–1795)* (Foundations in consciousness. Studies in Hölderlin's thought), Stuttgart: Klett Cotta. (Detailed philosophical analysis of Hölderlin's role in developing a new theory of self-consciousness in relation to Fichte and Schelling.)

—— (1997) *The Course of Remembrance and other Essays on Hölderlin*, Stanford: Stanford University Press. (Contains a detailed study of one of Hölderlin's late poems, and other essays on Hölderlin in the context of German idealist thought.)

Hölderlin-Jahrbuch (1944–), Tübingen: Verlag Metzler. (Leading journal which continuously reviews the international secondary literature and publishes articles on all aspects of Hölderlin.)

Kurz, G. (1975) *Mittelbarkeit und Vereinigung. Zum Verhältnis von Poesie, Reflexion und Revolution bei Hölderlin* (Mediation and unification: the relationship of poetry, reflection and revolution in Hölderlin), Stuttgart: Metzler. (General study of Hölderlin in the historical context of early idealism

from the perspective of the Frankfurt School of critical theory.)

Ryan, L. (1960) *Hölderlin Lehre vom Wechsel der Töne* (Hölderlin's theory concerning the modulation of tones), Stuttgart: Metzler. (Detailed study of Hölderlin's aesthetic reflections on poetic genre and register.)

—— (1965) *Hölderlins 'Hyperion': Exzentrische Bahn und Dichterberuf* (Hölderlin's 'Hyperion': eccentric path and poet's vocation), Stuttgart: Metzler. (Important systematic reading of *Hyperion* which explores Hölderlin's response to idealist thought and stresses the philosophical structure of the novel.)

Taminiaux, J. (1977) *La nostalgie de la Grèce à l'aube de l'idéalisme allemand, Kant et les Grecs dans l'itinéraire de Schiller, de Hölderlin et de Hegel* (The yearning for Greece and the origin of German idealism: Kant and the Greeks in the intellectual development of Schiller, Hölderlin and Hegel), The Hague: Martinus Nijhoff. (Differentiated study of the relationship between early idealist reception of Kant's third Critique and the cult of classical antiquity in Hölderlin, Schiller and Hegel.)

Unger, R. (1975) *Hölderlin's Major Poetry. The Dialectics of Unity*, Bloomington, IN: Indiana University Press. (General study stressing the tension between pantheistic intention and literary realization; good bibliographical references to the entire field.)

Warminski, A. (1987) *Readings in Interpretation: Hölderlin, Hegel, Heidegger*, Minneapolis, MN: University of Minnesota Press. (Comparative analysis of Hölderlin in the light of contemporary deconstructive criticism.)

NICHOLAS WALKER

HOLISM AND INDIVIDUALISM IN HISTORY AND SOCIAL SCIENCE

Methodological individualists such as Mill, Weber, Schumpeter, Popper, Hayek and Elster argue that all social facts must be explained wholly and exhaustively in terms of the actions, beliefs and desires of individuals. On the other hand, methodological holists, such as Durkheim and Marx, tend in their explanations to bypass individual action. Within this debate, better arguments exist for the view that explanations of social phenomena without the beliefs and desires of agents are deficient. If this is so, individualists appear to have a distinct edge over their adversaries. Indeed, a consensus exists among philosophers and social scientists that holism is implausible or false and individualism, when carefully formulated, is trivially true.

Holists challenge this consensus by first arguing that caricatured formulations of holism that ignore human action must be set aside. They then ask us to re-examine the nature of human action. Action is distinguished from mere behaviour by its intentional character. This much is uncontested between individualists and holists. But against the individualist contention that intentions exist as only psychological states in the heads of individuals, the holist argues that they also lie directly embedded in irreducible social practices, and that the identification of any intention is impossible without examining the social context within which agents think and act. Holists find nothing wrong with the need to unravel the motivations of individuals, but they contend that these motivations cannot be individuated without appeal to the wider beliefs and practices of the community. For instance, the acquiescence of oppressed workers may take the form not of total submission but subtle negotiation that yields them suboptimal benefits. Insensitivity to social context may blind us to this. Besides, it is not a matter of individual beliefs and preferences that this strategy is adopted. That decisions are taken by subtle strategies of negotiation rather than by explicit bargaining, deployment of force or use of high moral principles is a matter of social practice irreducible to the conscious action of individuals.

Two conclusions follow if the holist claim is true. First, that a reference to a social entity is inescapable even when social facts are explained in terms of individual actions, because of the necessary presence of a social ingredient in all individual intentions and actions. Second, a reference to individual actions is not even necessary when social facts are explained or understood in terms of social practices. Thus, the individualist view that explanation in social science must rely wholly and exhaustively on individual entities is hotly contested and is not as uncontroversial or trivial as it appears.

1   Introduction
2   Ontological reasons
3   Epistemological reasons
4   Individualist intentional explanation
5   The holist challenge

1   Introduction

Several commentators have noted the extraordinarily muddled character of the debate that ensued in the 1950s between individualists and holists. Why this has been so is one of the enigmas of social science. The main issue was repeatedly derailed, peripheral issues were given singular pre-eminence, different versions of the doctrine remained entangled, and deeper philosophical issues in the philosophy of science were never adequately probed. What is worse, both sides persistently knocked down the weakest, most caricatured formulation of the opponent's views. Retrospectively, the battle does give the appearance of possessing a large element of sham. No wonder then that when the dust settled, many of the issues that once provoked so much controversy were resolved; motivated prejudice against the other was acknowledged, and soon, more concessive versions, plainly indistinguishable from each other, were formulated. A careful analysis of the debate can identify points of agreement between the two and, more importantly, that something significant and contentious between the two sides persists, therefore the battle is likely to rage in the future. This shall be demonstrated by first unearthing the principal assumptions of individualism and then showing that they can be challenged from a non-individualist viewpoint.

Any further exploration of the subject must begin with a warning: it is unwise to be tempted by the view that a worthy political cause or great moral ideal is at stake in contending methodologies. The passion that Popper (1960) and Hayek brought into the debate immobilized it rather than provided the fresh impetus it badly needed. On this point SCHUMPETER was right: an advocacy of methodological individualism entails no commitment to liberalism. Likewise, opposing it does not imply abandoning political liberalism or denying the moral value of the individual. So it is not just that methodological individualism should not be confused with political, moral or religious individualism but, more importantly, it must not be seen automatically to enlist itself behind any of them.

It is equally important to remind ourselves that the term 'methodological' must be understood here in the broadest sense possible to include at least three distinct but related ingredients. The first, epistemological, concerns the understanding and explanation of social and individual entities. The second, ontological, turns on whether or not social entities are anything beyond a collection of individual entities. The third, semantics, is about the meaning of words: can a term referring to a social entity be analysed without remainder into terms that refer only to individual entities? The literature on the subject abounds with attempts to turn methodological individualism and holism into purely explanatory doctrines, but disputes over the relevant type of explanatory variable or over correct explanatory form have frequently turned into sharp controversies on ontological and semantic matters. This is hardly surprising, because an explanatory doctrine presupposes or entails ontological and semantic commitments. Therefore, individualism and holism are best viewed as comprehensive strategies with all the three components mentioned above.

2 Ontological reasons

This much clarified, it must be noted that a particular dispute, over one form of semantic individualism, is entirely settled. There are no takers any more for a project inspired by logical constructionism recommending that every single term referring to social entities be analysed as a collection of individual terms. However, for individualists, this failure has no ontological or explanatory ramifications. Second, one ontological dispute must be set aside. Encouraged by careless formulations and deep misunderstanding, it was once thought that holists believed in supra-substances hovering over and above all individuals; that they were carrying forward the Cartesian legacy of substance-dualism by introducing yet another substance called the social. This is unfair to the holist who must be seen instead to be advocating property pluralism and emphasizing the distinctive causal efficacy of social properties.

We may compare this point with an issue in the natural sciences. Non-reductionists in biology often argue that biological organisms display teleological properties that are best understood as irreducible to but supervenient upon physical properties (see SUPERVENIENCE). The principle of supervenience views the world as stratified, with properties at one level dependent for their existence in a non-causal way on properties lying at the more basic level. However, this relation of ontological dependence is non-reductive because the two sets of properties are never identical. Thus, teleological properties presuppose the existence of physical properties without being reducible to them.

It is in this sense that social properties are said to be supervenient on physical and biological ones. This much ought to be beyond dispute. What is not clear, however, is that this entails a supervenience of the social on the individual. For much depends on what we mean by the individual. If the term 'individual' refers to a single identifiable biological organism, then the statement is true. But surely, it is not the pure and abstract biological individual in focus here; rather what concerns us is the individual with distinctive human properties. The key question then is whether these distinctive human properties emerge only when individuals come together or if they already exist,

independent of any relations between them. Similarly, it is fairly incontrovertible to claim that any social process is supervenient on the physio-biological movement of individual organisms. Durkheim, as good a non-individualist as any, said so much: 'It is very true that society comprises no active force other than individuals' (1982: 251). The holist argument contends only that the specific pattern of this dynamic process is not reducible to the movement of individual biological organisms taken aggregately (see further §5 below).

Another vital issue to register is this: the individualist/holist controversy is not identical to the structure/agency debate in the social sciences, for a number of reasons. First, individualism does not entail a commitment to free human agency. The individualist may believe agency to be restricted too, but locate all constraints on it within the individual psyche. Individualism is compatible with internal constraints and therefore with a full-blooded determinism. Second, it is simply false to assume that anything external to the individual agent is thereby constraining. External structures are not just constraining but also enabling. Indeed a robust view of free and active human agents is compatible with the claim that such capacities depend on the presence of relevant external structures. More importantly, individualists can develop not only a conception of internal but also of external constraints. They too can account for the very constitution of external structures, of rules, norms and conventions constraining human action. Likewise holists can develop a perfectly cogent account of free human action. If this is so, the principal dividing line between the two sides cannot be drawn at the level of free agency and external constraint.

This is not the dominant understanding of those engaged in this debate. Holists accused individualists of ignoring the relations of the individual to the larger social context. Individualists, on their part, blamed holists for treating individuals as mere cogs in the social wheel. One was charged with ultra-voluntarism, the other reproached for supra-determinism. At the end of a long and unsavoury controversy, however, each side realized what should have been obvious from the very start: that neither agency nor the context within which it occurs can be ignored.

Let us identify the points where agreement is undeniable. Holists do not believe in supra-individual, social substances. They emphasize social relations and their undeniable constraining effects. Individualists cannot fault these claims. Individualists, likewise, highlight human agency and show that societies consist in or are a result of people acting. Holists can hardly object to this. Furthermore, both accept that the social does not think; it is individuals who do the thinking. We appear then genuinely to arrive at a consensus on a set of statements so truistic that an explanatory strategy must be deemed mistaken if it fails to incorporate or is incompatible with it.

However, a plausible holist contention is that this agreement is at the price of an even greater intellectual muddle. The seemingly uncontroversial character of these statements obscures the fact that they are open to rival interpretations, one that antecedently shifts the entire balance in favour of the individualist and another which obdurately refuses to do so. The claim that individualism is trivially true may well be a rhetorical device that conceals deeper ontological and methodological issues that divide rival camps. All the dimensions of the debate are not unravelled unless another vital issue, forced upon us less by ontological than by epistemological reasons, is addressed. Sharp differences between holists and individualists are often believed to lie precisely at this point. Close analysis reveals, however, a thicker consensus on this issue. Contentious issues lurk in the background, despite this agreement.

3 Epistemological reasons

The correct move here would first be to identify the relevant explanatory form and then try and show it as ontologically neutral, usable by individualists and non-individualists alike. But contestants in the debate have not approached the issue in this way nor found it easy to identify the correct explanatory form. One reason for this is their insensitivity to another major controversy in social science, namely, the argument between naturalists and anti-naturalists. Each side has often assumed not only the absolute validity of their preferred model of scientific explanation but their monopoly over it. The second reason is the wholly opposite error of identifying the individualist/holist debate with the naturalist/anti-naturalist controversy, as if the settlement of the first dispute rests solely on the successful resolution of the second. By assuming that holism entails scientism and that therefore their victory flows automatically from the defeat of positivist naturalism, individualists such as Hayek (1973) have been prone to this mistake. Clearly, many individualists are no less dogmatic about the claim that human affairs must be studied strictly with the methods of natural science. Conversely, holists can be equally steadfast in their advocacy of a distinctive method for social science. So it is important to see both the relevance of the naturalist/non-naturalist dispute to the individualist/holist issue and not to identify them (see NATURALISM IN SOCIAL SCIENCE).

The other related difficulty is that the debate is conducted without disentangling different explanatory forms. We may begin by distinguishing five versions of individualist and holist explanatory strategies. Three of these deploy the deductive nomological model of explanation (see EXPLANATION §2). The first attempts to explain particular social facts by deducing them from laws of individual action. The second, known as explanatory reduction, explains not particular social facts but social laws by deducing them from laws pertaining to individuals (see REDUCTION, PROBLEMS OF). Since this reduction is achieved with the help of bridge statements which in turn can take two forms, we obtain two forms of reductionist strategies. The first requiring correlatory laws may be called correlatory reduction; the second, requiring identity statements is called identity-reduction. Identity-reduction is also referred to as micro-reduction because here a macro-entity (the social) is identified with all the micro-entities (the individuals) that compose it.

The difference between each must be maintained because arguments that work against one kind of individualist strategy do not necessarily work against the other. For example, if laws are deemed essential for explanations, and if it is shown that only laws pertaining to individual action can be formulated, then the first non-reductionist deductive-nomological version of individualism is vindicated. Holism fails because no social laws exist to explain particular social facts. Mandelbaum believed precisely this to be the target of individualist attack and therefore tried to establish the existence of social laws (1973). But an argument establishing social laws does not invalidate individualism because by deducing them from laws pertaining to individuals, one version of individualism is still exonerated. Similarly, showing the impossibility of correlatory laws does not defeat reductionist individualism because the absence of correlatory laws may indicate not the impossibility of reduction but the prior realization of a successful identity-reduction.

A large part of the debate has been traditionally obsessed with these issues. However, this intellectual effort may have been futile if laws pertaining to individuals do not exist. For all these strategies depend not just on the presence of social laws but on general laws concerning individuals. And it is doubtful if such laws of human action exist. Notice that the laws in question must capture the precise features individuating human action. The same entity when subsumed under other descriptions may indeed yield laws but these would be utterly irrelevant. Reductionists are not pursuing laws of physical movement or bodily behaviour. The laws they are after must refer to actions, and therefore, to the beliefs and desires of individuals. However, as Davidson has shown, precisely such strict laws that explain or predict mental phenomena are impossible to obtain (1980). If valid, this is a decisive argument against all deductive-nomological versions of individualism. To revive this aspect of the debate, one has either to defeat this argument or give a conception of laws different from the one normally accepted (see EXPLANATION IN HISTORY AND SOCIAL SCIENCE §§1, 3).

Two conclusions may follow from this. First, that explanations in social science are not possible, and second, more importantly, that laws are not necessary for explanation. Therefore we may explore explanatory forms unconnected with the deductive-nomological model. Forms that do not rely on the deductive-nomological model are intentional explanation and intentional understanding. The first, without invoking general laws or theoretical syllogism, explains action by showing that the behaviour of individuals is guided by beliefs and desires (intentions). The second, intentional understanding stresses the pivotal significance of understanding the beliefs and desires of agents. These strategies can be combined to give one overarching model for social science in which the understanding of beliefs and desires go hand in hand with the explanation of action. In what follows, the term 'intentional explanation' refers to this model.

4   Individualist intentional explanation

The formal structure of intentional explanation is simple and, up to a point, relatively uncontroversial: A desires X; A believes that doing Y will get him X; A does Y. The action, Y, is explained by deducing it, via a practical syllogism, from the given beliefs and desires. A crucial feature of beliefs and desires, of all intentional states generally, is that they are directed towards a real or imaginary object and that therefore they have an intentional content. Since these states are complex and in large measure linguistically constituted, we may say that they possess a linguistic content or meaning. Their ascription always involves the use of a 'that'-clause. For example, A does not just believe or desire; A believes that the world is menacing and ugly or desires that it be beautiful. Clearly, the individuation of beliefs and desires depends on the meaning of words in these clauses. This presupposes that we capture the oblique occurrence of these expressions, where the oblique occurrence of expression is one in which the substitution of coextensive expression affects the truth-value of the whole containing sentence. For example, if 'water' occurs obliquely in 'A believes water to be the most refreshing drink in the world', then replacing it with 'H$_2$O' will alter the truth-value of the whole sentence.

This feature of obliqueness of expressions is of great significance for intentional explanation. Actions are individuated by their appropriate description, the description under which agents subsume their behaviour. To grasp their perspective or point of view, we must get right the description of their beliefs and desires, and this depends in turn on getting hold of obliquely occurring expressions. Likewise, a situation on which agents hold a view plays no direct role in characterizing their mental states or actions; it contributes to the explanation of actions only as it occurs obliquely, mediated by their points of view. This much is uncontroversial. But contrary to appearance, this by itself does not lead to individualism. The individualist turn comes with the further ontological assumption that these intentional states exist internal to agents, only in their heads. The individualist interpretation appears even more invincible with the second assumption that the meaning of beliefs and desires, their content, is individuated wholly internally, without reference to the external environment of the agent. These Cartesian assumptions turn action into a wholly individualist entity, bolstering the individualist belief that if the correct explanatory form in the social science is intentional explanation, then it just has to imply a victory of the individualist over the non-individualist.

5 The holist challenge

The widespread acceptance of these assumptions has generated the illusion of consensus. The holist challenge shatters it. It is levelled on two fronts, one at individualist theories of meaning, the other at individualist theories of action. Arguments developed by Putnam and Burge help reinvigorate a non-individualist theory of meaning. Here one begins by the standard disambiguation of meaning into (a) extension and (b) intension (see SENSE AND REFERENCE). Then one shows that traditional theories of meaning are characterized by two assumptions. First, that intension determines extension. This can mean many things but it means at the very least that it helps to fix extension. Also, that sameness of intension always entails sameness of extension. Let us call this the functional character of intension. The second is the ontological assumption, already mentioned, that intension is a psychological entity that exists in the heads of individuals. So, we possess in our heads mental entities or representations that fix extensions of terms.

Putnam's thought experiment about two different substances on earth and twin earth, identical in all respects but their chemical structure, involves a long and complicated argument the conclusion of which, on one possible interpretation, is this: that the functional and the ontological assumptions cannot both be true (1975). Since identical mental states refer to different extensions, we must abandon either the view that meaning is a psychological entity or the claim that intension determines extension. Arguably, Putnam offers sound reasons for dropping the first and retaining the second. In other words, if the conclusion forced by Putnam's thought experiment is true, we must infer that meaning is not a psychological entity in the head of individuals. What then is it? Several answers exist but perhaps the one that challenges the individualist most is the view that it is fixed by an interlocking system of beliefs and actions necessarily involving several individuals. If so, meaning is a social not an individual entity. A related argument developed by Burge shows first that a difference in extension also affects oblique occurrences in 'that'-clauses, and therefore, the contents of mental states, and second, that 'communal practice is a factor in fixing and interpreting the words and attitudes of a person' (1979: 85). In the individuation of beliefs we must refer not just to the internal environment of agents but also to their external context, particularly to relevant social practices. If meanings are inescapably social, then, given that beliefs are individuated by meanings, beliefs too are social, and further, given that beliefs are analytic to action, so are actions. We began by attempting to explain a social entity wholly and exclusively in terms of individual entities, namely actions, beliefs and desires, we now find that all these are inescapably social. A social fact is then explained by another social fact. Individualism is challenged quite fundamentally. Also, holists do not abandon intentional explanation; they give it a non-individualist interpretation. There is no necessary dispute between individualists and non-individualists over which explanatory form is suitable for human affairs.

So, this is the crux of the matter. For individualists, beliefs, desires, intentions and actions are intrinsically individual. This is implausible for the holist because the intention of one person already makes reference to the intention of another; beliefs, desires and actions are already social. But what of the individualist view wherein intentions exist as internal states in the heads of individuals? And what about the ontology of irreducible social practices? To answer this, the holist opens the second front of attack, this time on the traditional theory of action. Put simply, the individualist theory of action is the widely accepted causal view according to which action can be analysed into three components: behaviour, intentional states and the relation of causality that binds them (see ACTION §1). Action is behaviour caused by intentions. An alternative theory refuses to reduce action to anything

more basic. Intentional states separate from behaviour do not exist; rather, agents intend something by their behaviour. On this view, intentions lie directly embedded in behaviour so that we see behaviour as action. Action then is a basic ability of human beings quite independent of the ability to form representations in their heads. The holist accepts this and asks us to go further. If intention can directly inhabit the bodily behaviour of one individual, it can also occupy the bodily behaviours of several individuals.

This ontological issue has consequences for explanatory strategy as well. First, the identification of beliefs and intentions of an individual, crucial for intentional explanation, requires sensitivity to the interlocking intentions of a community of agents. The perspective of the agent, the oblique expressions in which it is embedded, is still crucial but the holist holds no presumption that it is available only or completely to the agent. Second, a grasp of social practice is necessary to situate individual beliefs, desires and actions. This is less a function of mental operations in individual heads and more of practical know-how. Without practical understanding, as anthropologists testify and as philosophers who have worked on problems of translation and cross-cultural understanding know only too well, intellectual effort, no matter how sincere, is puerile.

See also: INTENTION; METHODOLOGICAL INDIVIDUALISM; SOCIAL LAWS

References and further reading

Bhargava, R. (1992) *Individualism in Social Science*, Oxford: Clarendon Press. (Expansion of 2–5 of this entry.)

* Burge, T. (1979) 'Individualism and the Mental', in P. French, T. Uhelling and H. Wittestein (eds) *Midwest Studies in Philosophy* 4: 73–121. (Sophisticated defence of holist theory of meaning.)

* Davidson, D. (1980) *Essays on Actions and Events*, Oxford: Clarendon Press. (Particularly sophisticated piece against the possibility of psychological laws and on the causal theory of action.)

* Durkheim, É. (1982) *The Rules of Sociological Method*, ed. S. Lukes, trans. W.D. Halls, Basingstoke, Macmillan. (Classic sociological defence of holist explanations.)

Elster, J. (1985) *Making Sense of Marx*, Cambridge: Cambridge University Press. (Short statement of methodological individualism known for its defence of an individualist Marxism.)

Garfinkel, A. (1981) *Forms of Explanation*, New Haven, CT: Yale University Press. (Pragmatist defence of holistic explanation.)

* Hayek, F.A. (1973) 'From Scientism and the Study of Society', in J. O'Neill (ed.) *Modes of Individualism and Collectivism*, London: Heinemann, 27–67. (Passionate defence of individualism on grounds that holism is committed to scientism.)

James, S. (1984) *The Content of Social Explanation*, Cambridge: Cambridge University Press. (Interprets the individualist/holist controversy as an agency/structure debate.)

Lukes, S. (1973) 'Methodological Individualism Reconsidered', in A. Ryan (ed.) *The Philosophy of Social Explanation*, Oxford: Oxford University Press, 119–29. (One of the best commentaries on the debate of the 1950s–60s.)

* Mandelbaum, M. (1973) 'Societal Laws', in J. O'Neill (ed.) *Modes of Individualism and Collectivism*, London: Heinemann, 235–47. (Defends holism on the grounds that irreducible social laws exist.)

Manninen, J. and Tuomela, R. (eds) (1976) *Essays on Explanation and Understanding*, Dordrecht: Reidel. (Fine pieces on the structure of intentional explanation.)

O'Neill, J. (ed.) (1973) *Modes of Individualism and Collectivism*, London: Heinemann. (Best anthology of the individualist/holist controversy in the 1950s–60s.)

* Popper, K.R. (1960) *The Poverty of Historicism*, London: Routledge & Kegan Paul. (Passionate defence of methodological individualism. One of the principal originators of the debate.)

* Putnam, H. (1975) *Philosophical Papers: Mind, Language and Reality, Vol. 2*, Cambridge: Cambridge University Press. (Particularly original attack on traditional theories of meaning, can be deployed for holist purposes.)

Ruben, D.-H. (1985) *The Metaphysics of the Social World*, London: Routledge & Kegan Paul. (Sophisticated analysis of group/individual relation and supervenience.)

Ryan, A. (1970) *The Philosophy of Social Explanation*, London: Macmillan. (Useful introduction to the main issues in the philosophy of social science, including the individualist/holist controversy.)

Taylor, C. (1985) *Philosophy and the Human Sciences*, Cambridge: Cambridge University Press. (Original and suggestive pieces on holist theories of meaning and action.)

Wright, G.H. von (1971) *Explanation and Understanding*, London: Routledge & Kegan Paul. (Classic study of the difference between nomological explanation and human understanding.)

RAJEEV BHARGAVA

HOLISM: MENTAL AND SEMANTIC

Mental (or semantic) holism is the doctrine that the identity of a belief content (or the meaning of a sentence that expresses it) is determined by its place in the web of beliefs or sentences comprising a whole theory or group of theories. It can be contrasted with two other views: atomism and molecularism. Molecularism characterizes meaning and content in terms of relatively small parts *of the web in a way that allows many different theories to share those parts. For example, the meaning of 'chase' might be said by a molecularist to be 'try to catch'. Atomism characterizes meaning and content in terms of* none *of the web; it says that sentences and beliefs have meaning or content independently of their relations to other sentences or beliefs.*

One major motivation for holism has come from reflections on the natures of confirmation and learning. As Quine observed, claims about the world are confirmed not individually but only in conjunction with theories of which they are a part. And, typically, one cannot come to understand scientific claims without understanding a significant chunk of the theory of which they are a part. For example, in learning the Newtonian concepts of 'force', 'mass', 'kinetic energy' and 'momentum', one does not learn any definitions of these terms in terms that are understood beforehand, for there are no such definitions. Rather, these theoretical terms are all learned together in conjunction with procedures for solving problems.

The major problem with holism is that it threatens to make generalization in psychology virtually impossible. If the content of any state depends on all others, it would be extremely unlikely that any two believers would ever share a state with the same content. Moreover, holism would appear to conflict with our ordinary conception of reasoning. What sentences one accepts influences what one infers. If I accept a sentence and then later reject it, I thereby change the inferential role of that sentence, so the meaning of what I accept would not be the same as the meaning of what I later reject. But then it would be difficult to understand on this view how one could rationally – or even irrationally! – change one's mind. And agreement and translation are also problematic for much the same reason. Holists have responded (1) by proposing that we should think not in terms of 'same/different' meaning but in terms of a gradient of similarity of meaning, (2) by proposing 'two-factor' theories, or (3) by simply accepting the consequence that there is no real difference between changing meanings and changing beliefs.

1   The doctrines

Semantic holism is the view that the meaning of a sentence is determined by its place in the web of sentences comprising a whole theory. Mental holism is the corresponding view for belief content – that the identity of a belief content is determined by its place in the web of beliefs comprising a theory. Sometimes holists advocate a more sweeping view in which the identity of a belief is determined by its relations to a body of theories, or even *the whole of a person's belief system*. In what follows, mental and semantic holism are treated as two aspects of a single view.

Holism can be contrasted with two other views: molecularism and atomism. Molecularism characterizes meaning and content in terms of a relatively small part of the web that many different theories may share. For example, the meaning of 'bachelor' might be said by a molecularist to be 'man who has never married'. And the meaning of 'and' might be given by a molecularist version of inferential role semantics via specifying that the inference from 'p and q' to 'p', and from 'p', 'q' to 'p and q' has a special status (for example, it might be 'primitively compelling', in Peacocke's terms; see SEMANTICS, CONCEPTUAL ROLE). Atomism characterizes meaning and content in terms of none of the web; it says that sentences and beliefs have meaning or content independently of their relations to any other sentences or beliefs and, therefore, independently of any theories in which they appear.

Note the contrast between the semantic issues that are of concern here and those that concern particular phenomena in particular languages. Semantics in the present sense is concerned with the fundamental nature of meaning and what it is about a person that makes their words mean what they do. We might call the present sense the 'metaphysical' sense. Semantics in the other sense – what we might call the 'linguist's' sense – concerns the issues of how meanings of words fit together to determine the semantic properties and internal structures of sentences. Semantics in the linguist's sense concerns such issues as how many types of pronouns there are and why it is that 'The temperature is rising' and 'The temperature is 60 degrees' does not entail that 60 is rising. There are interactions among the two enterprises, but semantics in the linguist's sense can proceed without taking much notice of the issue of semantic holism.

2   Motivations for holism

The best-known motivation for semantic/mental holism involves Quine's doctrine of *confirmation holism*, according to which 'Our statements about the external world face the tribunal of sense experience not individually but only as a corporate body' (1953: 41). This view gains its plausibility from the logic of theory revision. An experimental datum confirms (verifies; gives us some reason to believe) a statement only in conjunction with a great number of theoretical ideas, background assumptions about the experiment, and assumptions from logic and mathematics, any one of which could be (and in the history of science often has been) challenged when problems arise (see CONFIRMATION THEORY). If we combine this confirmation holism with the logical positivist doctrine that the meaning of a sentence is its method of verification or confirmation (see LOGICAL POSITIVISM; MEANING AND VERIFICATION), that is, if we combine the doctrine that meaning is confirmation with the claim that confirmation is holistic, we get semantic holism. And this implies that talk of the meaning of a sentence in isolation from other sentences makes no more sense than talk of the meaning of 'of' apart from the contexts in which it occurs.

Positivism and confirmation holism are not the only roads to semantic/mental holism. Another route proceeds from considering how people learn actual scientific theories. For example, one does not learn definitions of 'force', 'mass', 'kinetic energy' or 'momentum' in terms that are understood beforehand, for there are no such definitions. Rather, these terms are learned together (in conjunction with procedures for solving problems). As Quine (1954) and Putnam (1965) argued, local 'definitions' in a scientific theory tend to be mere passing expository devices of no lasting importance for the theory itself. And this is quite ubiquitous in theories, where there is a circle of interdefined theoretical terms none of which is definable in terms outside the theory. This fact motivates Lewis' proposal that scientific terms can be defined functionally in terms of their roles in a whole theory.

3   Must functionalism lead to holism?

Functionalism has become a popular approach in the philosophy of mind generally (see FUNCTIONALISM). For example, the difference between the belief that one will win the lottery and the desire that one will win the lottery is plausibly a functional difference (a difference in the roles of the states), since one but not the other leads to test-driving a Ferrari. But functionalists go further, claiming that the common *content* of these propositional attitudes can also be functionally defined (in terms of the cognitive roles of states which have these contents in the psychological economy, including links to inputs and outputs). It has often been supposed that the most important feature of the functional role of a belief in determining its content is its role in inference, and for that reason functionalism about content or meaning is sometimes called 'inferential role semantics'. The functional role of a thought includes all sorts of causes and effects that are non-semantic, for example, perhaps depressing thoughts can lower one's immunity, causing one to become ill. Conceptual roles are functional roles minus such non-semantic causes and effects.

A functional theory of the whole mind must make reference to any difference in stimuli or responses that can be mentally significant. The difference between saying 'damn' and 'darn' can be mentally significant (for example, one can have a policy of saying one rather than the other). Your pains lead to 'darn', mine to 'damn', so our pains are functionally different, and likewise our desires to avoid pain, our beliefs that interact with those desires, and so on. So if we functionally define 'pain' in terms of a theory of the whole mind, we are naturally led to the conclusion that two individuals who differ in this way share no mental states. This is why functionalism can lead to holism.

Molecularists object that if you have a fine-grained way of categorizing, you can just coarsen it. But which causes and effects of pain are constitutive and which are not? The form of a solution could be: 'pain = the state constituted by the following causal relations...', where the dots are replaced by a specification of a subset of the mentally significant causal relations into which pain enters. Putnam suggested we look for a normal form for a computational description of pain, and Lycan (1988) and Rey (1997) have suggested that we construct functional theories at different levels, one of which would be suitable to define 'pain' without distinguishing between 'damn' and 'darn'. But after years of discussion, there is no real solution, not even a proposal of something functional common to all and only pains. Lycan and Rey expect the issue to be settled only by an empirical psychology. Moreover, even if one is optimistic about finding a functional definition of pain, one cannot assume that success will transfer to functionalist accounts of meaning. Success in the case of meaning would seem to require an analytic/synthetic distinction which many have found independently to be problematic.

4 Problems with the analytic/synthetic distinction

Another route to holism arises from considerations involving the analytic/synthetic distinction, that is, the distinction between claims that are true solely in virtue of meaning and claims that depend also on the way the world is. Quineans often hold that the analytic/synthetic distinction is confused. Some philosophers have argued from the idea that there is something wrong with analyticity to holism. We can put the argument in terms of conceptual role semantics. It seems that some inferences (for example, from 'bachelor' to 'unmarried') are part of meaning-constitutive inferential roles, but others (for example, from 'bachelor' to 'dislikes commitment') are not. However, if there is no analytic/synthetic distinction, then there is no principled way to draw a line between inferences that constitute meaning and those that do not (see ANALYTICITY). So, the argument concludes, if some inferences are part of meaning-constitutive inferential rules, *all* inferences are part of meaning-constitutive inferential roles, and this is a form of holism (Fodor and LePore 1992; Devitt 1995).

This argument is of course fallacious. A bald man can have some hairs, and there is no principled way of drawing a line between the number or distribution of hairs on a bald man and on a non-bald man. But one would not conclude that everyone is bald. Failure to find a principled way of drawing a line need not require one or the other extreme.

Still, the argument is onto something. How would the molecularist choose those inferences which are meaning-constitutive if the meaning-constitutive must be analytic rather than synthetic but there is no such distinction? In fact, the problem is more general, and far from being an argument *for* holism, it casts doubt on holism too. If meaning-constitutivity entails analyticity, any view – molecularist or holist – that postulates anything meaning-constitutive is in trouble if there is no such thing as analyticity.

One response to this argument has been to 'challenge' the principle that a statement or inference that is meaning-constitutive is thereby analytic (Block 1993). There are two very different points of view which see a gap between meaning-constitutivity and analyticity.

One approach to finding a gap between meaning-constitutivity and analyticity derives from the views of Quine and DAVIDSON, on which there is no clear difference between a change of meaning and a change of belief (see RADICAL TRANSLATION AND RADICAL INTERPRETATION). The other appeals to narrow contents (see CONTENT: WIDE AND NARROW). Narrow contents are contents that are necessarily shared by 'twins', people who are internally as similar as you like, even though their environments differ. Consider the influential example of Putnam's 'twin earth' which is a planet identical to earth in every respect except that wherever earth has H_2O, it has a superficially similar but chemically different substance, XYZ. Arguably, I and my twin on Putnam's twin earth share a narrow content for 'water' despite the different referents of our words. If meaning is narrow in this sense, it is false that meaning-constitutive sentences or inferences are thereby analytic if meaning is narrow. The narrow contents which constitute meaning *themselves* are neither *true* nor *false* and hence cannot be true in virtue of meaning. For example, let us suppose that my twin and I accept the propositions that we express with 'Water contains hydrogen'. My belief has a true wide content, my twin's has a false wide content, but the narrow content has to be the same (since we are twins) and is therefore neither true nor false (see PUTNAM, H. §3). Further, we can even imagine a twin earth in which a putative meaning-constitutive inference is invalid. If there is any inference that is a good candidate for analytically defining 'water', it is the inference from 'water' to 'liquid'. But consider a twin earth on which 'water' is used as here to refer to H_2O, but where water is very rare, most of the substances referred to as 'liquids' being granular solids that look like liquids. So 'Water is a liquid' as said by on this twin earth is *false*, even though it is true in our mouths. Perhaps it will be said that what is analytic is not 'Water is a liquid' but 'Water has a liquidish look and feel'. But it is easy to imagine circumstances in which the look and feel of water changes. Perhaps what we should be looking for is not a narrow content that is *true* in virtue of meaning but one that is only *assertible* in virtue of meaning. But it is part of our commitment in the use of natural kind terms that the world plays a part in determining truth-values, so we must regard any appearance of warrant solely in virtue of meaning as superficial.

5 The problem of disagreement and translation

Holism has some weird-sounding consequences. Suppose we say that all of a sentence's inferential links (within a theory or body of theories) are included in its set of meaning-constitutive inferential roles. But what sentences I accept influences what I infer, so how can I reason so as to change my own mind? If I accept a sentence, say, 'Bernini stole the lead from the Pantheon', and then later reject it, I thereby change the inferential role of that sentence, so the meaning of the sentence that I accept is not the same as the one that I later reject. So how can I reason about which of my beliefs should be given up? Along similar lines, one can argue that no two people ever agree or disagree, and that we can never translate anything perfectly from one language to another. The holist owes us a way to reconcile such conclusions with common sense. This section will explore three holistic responses.

Harman (1973) and Block (1986) have argued that we can avoid the problem by replacing the dichotomy between agreement and disagreement with a gradient of similarity of meaning, perhaps multi-dimensional. If I first accept and then reject 'Bernini stole the lead from the Pantheon', it is not as if I have rejected something *utterly unrelated* to what I earlier accepted. This position profits from the analogy with the ordinary dichotomy between believing and disbelieving. Reasoning with this dichotomy can lead to trouble, trouble that is avoided if we substitute a graded notion for the dichotomy. For example, I can have a low degree of belief in a long conjunction even though I have a high degree in each of the conjuncts. But if we put this in terms of the dichotomy between believing and disbelieving, we say that I could believe each conjunct while disbelieving the conjunction, and that is a contradiction. The proposal, then, is that we substitute a graded notion of similarity of meaning for the ordinary notion of same/different meaning. It must be conceded, however, that there are no specific suggestions as to what the dimensions of similarity of meaning are or how they relate to one another.

This approach can be combined with the aforementioned 'two-factor theory', according to which meaning consists of an internal holistic factor and a non-holistic purely referential factor (see SEMANTICS, CONCEPTUAL ROLE §2). For purposes of translation and communication, the purely referential factor plays the main role in individuating contents. For purposes of psychological explanation, the internal factor plays the main role (see Loar 1987).

There is another (compatible) holistic response to the problem of disagreement which is associated with the views of Quine, Davidson and Putnam, namely that there is something wrong with the terms in which the problem is posed. They explicitly reject the very distinction between disagreeing and changing the subject that is presupposed by the statement of the problem. Putnam (1988) and Stich (1983) have argued, along these lines, that translation is not an objective process; it depends on subjective value-laden decisions as to how to weigh considerations of similarity in reference and social and functional role. It is controversial whether this Quinean response avoids the problem of disagreement only by rendering meaning something unsuitable for science.

Another holistic response is exemplified by Lewis' observation (1995) that there is no need to suppose that a satisfier of a functional description must fit it perfectly – fitting *most* of it is good enough. Lewis proposes that in framing the functional roles, we replace the set of inferences that are the basis for a functionalized account of belief with the disjunction of all the conjunctions of most of them. Thus, if we think there are three inferences, *A*, *B* and *C*, that are closely linked to the meaning of 'if', we might define 'if' as the relation that satisfies either *A* & *B* or *A* & *C* or *B* & *C*. (Of course, we thereby increase the danger that more than one relation will satisfy our definition.) Then disagreement will be possible between people who accept most of the inferences that define their subject matters.

I have just been canvassing holistic responses to the problem, but of course atomism and molecularism are also responses. Fodor's version of atomism (1987) construes meanings as purely referential. Fodor goes so far as to insist that there could be punctate minds; minds that have only one belief. This view must, however, find some way of accommodating the insights that motivate holism.

6 Psychological laws

FODOR and LePore (1992) object to holistic accounts of mental content on the ground that they would preclude psychological laws, for example, the belief that one is in immediate danger causes release of adrenaline. According to holism, there is no such thing as 'the' belief that one is in immediate danger because the belief that you designate in this way is not quite the same as the belief that I designate in this way. Beliefs are too fine-grained to be referred to in this way (see BELIEF; PROPOSITIONAL ATTITUDES). One strategy for dealing with this issue is to observe that many candidate psychological laws can generalize about contents without actually specifying them. Consider this candidate for a law: for *any* action *a* and any goal *g*, if one wants *g* and also believes that *a* is required for *g*, then one will try to do *a*. This is a universally quantified law (because of the role of 'any'), albeit a trivial one. Universally quantified laws are a good scientific bet, and these can involve holistic content. By quantifying over goals, one can state laws without committing oneself to two agents ever having exactly the same goal. The point just made says that the holist can allow one kind of psychological law (the quantified kind) but not another (the kind that mentions specific contents such as the belief that one is in danger). But the holist may go further,

arguing that there is something wrong with the putative laws of specific contents. The point is that 'The belief that one is in immediate danger causes release of adrenaline' stands to psychological law as 'Large slippery rocks on mountain-tops can damage cars on roads below' stands to physical law. Laws should quantify over such specific items, not mention them explicitly (see LAWS, NATURAL; EXPLANATION).

However, Fodor and LePore are right that any particular type of holistic state will exist only rarely and transiently. In this respect, holistic mental states are like the states of computers (see MIND, COMPUTATIONAL THEORIES OF). A total computer configuration as specified by the contents of every register in the internal memory and every cell on the hard disk will occur only rarely and transiently. There are deterministic laws of the evolution of total computer states, but they deal with such transient states. So psychological explanation will have to be seen by holists as like explanation of what computers do, in part a matter of fine-grained laws of the evolution of systems, in part coarse-grained accounts of how the systems work that do not have the status of laws.

7 Narrow-content holism

There is a great deal of controversy about whether there is such a thing as narrow content or meaning, but if narrow content exists, there is good reason to think it is holistic. We have already seen one reason having to do with the fact that there is no analytic/synthetic distinction for narrow content. But there is another reason as well that focuses on change of narrow content with learning. Putnam (1983) and Block (1994) give an argument that uses some relatively uncontroversial premises about identity and difference in narrow content at a single time to squeeze out a conclusion to the effect that one's narrow contents can be expected to change whenever one receives substantial new information, however trivial. The argument depends on a variant of the famous 'twin earth' example. Consider twins who grow up in different communities where 'grug' is used to denote different substances, beer in one and whisky in the other, but the difference has not made any difference to the twins. At the age of 10, they are as similar as you like, and so the narrow contents of their 'grugs' are the same. By the age of 12, they know as much about 'grug' as teenagers normally know, including the (different) translations of 'grug' into English. One knows that 'grug' in his language is beer, the other that 'grug' is whisky. The argument motivates the claim that their 'grugs' differ in narrow content at 12 despite being the same at 10, so the information that they have acquired (which is designed to be run-of-the-mill) has changed the narrow contents. (But see Devitt 1995 for a reply.)

Issues about holism continue to be at the heart of debate in philosophy of language and mind. In the mid-1960s, it was widely assumed that to be a holist was to be a sceptic about any science of meaning or content, but thirty years later there has been a spirited debate about whether cognitive science can tolerate it.

References and further reading

* Block, N. (1986) 'Advertisement for a Semantics for Psychology', in P.A. French *et al.* (eds) *Midwest Studies in Philosophy*, vol. 10, *Studies in the Philosophy of Mind*, Minneapolis, MN: University of Minnesota Press. (Discussion of inferential role semantics.)
* —— (1993) 'Holism, Hyper-Analyticity and Hyper-Compositionality', *Mind and Language* 8 (1): 1–27. (Defence of holism from a critique by Fodor and LePore.)
* —— (1994) 'An Argument for Holism', *Proceedings of the Aristotelian Society*, new series, 94: 151–69. (Concludes that one's narrow contents can be expected to change whenever one receives substantial new information.)
* Devitt, M. (1995) *Coming to Our Senses: A Naturalistic Program for Semantic Localism*, Cambridge: Cambridge University Press. (Spirited defence of molecularism.)
* Fodor, J.A. (1987) *Psychosemantics: The Problem of Meaning in the Philosophy of Mind*, Cambridge, MA: MIT Press. (Defence of an atomistic view of content and meaning.)
* Fodor, J.A. and LePore, E. (1992) *Holism: A Shoppers' Guide*, Oxford: Blackwell. (Critique of arguments for holism.)
* Harman, G. (1973) *Thought*, Princeton, NJ: Princeton University Press. (Defence of a language of thought. Uses a functionalist point of view.)
* Lewis, D. (1995) 'Lewis, David: Reduction of Mind', in S. Guttenplan (ed.) *A Companion to Philosophy of Mind*, Oxford: Blackwell. (Summary and defence of Lewis' views on mind and meaning.)
* Loar, B. (1987) 'Social Content and Psychological Content', in R. Grimm and D. Merrill (eds) *Contents of Thought: Proceedings of the 1985 Oberlin Colloquium in Philosophy*, Tucson, AZ: University of Arizona Press. (Argument that narrow content is the only content.)
* Lycan, W. (1988) *Judgment and Justification*, Cambridge: Cambridge University Press. (Includes a defence of empirical functional definitions of psychological terms.)
* Putnam, H. (1965) 'The Analytic and the Synthetic', in *Philosophical Papers*, vol. 2, *Mind, Language and Reality*, Cambridge: Cambridge University Press, 33–69. (Discussion of the (in)significance of the analytic/synthetic distinction in science.)
* —— (1983) *Philosophical Papers*, vol. 3, *Realism and Reason*, Cambridge: Cambridge University Press. (A rich development of a conceptual role semantics.)
* —— (1988) *Representation and Reality*, Cambridge, MA: MIT Press. (Critique of cognitive science views of mind and meaning.)
* Quine, W.V. (1953) 'Two Dogmas of Empiricism', in *From a Logical Point of View*, Cambridge, MA: Harvard University Press. (The classic argument against the analytic/synthetic distinction.)
* —— (1954) 'Carnap and Logical Truth', in *The Ways of Paradox and Other Essays*, Cambridge, MA: Harvard University Press, 2nd edn, 1976, 70–132. (Rich examination of the role of definition in logic, mathematics and science.)
* Rey, G. (1997) *Contemporary Philosophy of Mind: A Contentiously Classical Approach*, Oxford: Blackwell. (Defends the prospect of empirical functional definitions of many mental states.)
* Stich, S. (1983) *From Folk Psychology to Cognitive Science*, Cambridge, MA: MIT Press. (Argument against appealing to content in psychological explanation.)

NED BLOCK

HOLMES, OLIVER WENDELL, JR (1841–1935)

The most famous judge in the history of the USA, Holmes was also one of the most important US legal theorists. Within US jurisprudence, his work prefigured and stimulated the development of a general distrust of abstractions. Holmes emphasized that, in so far as logical deductions and abstract principles play any role at all in the law, they are side-effects of the ways in which struggles among different interests have been varyingly resolved. For him, the life of the law was not logic but experience; and experience was too diverse and conflict-ridden to be controllable on the basis of any sweeping formulae.

Born in Boston, Massachusetts, Holmes attended Harvard as an undergraduate and (after service in the American Civil War) as a law student. He then practised law for sixteen years, towards the end of which he published his most famous work, *The Common Law* (1881). After a very brief stint as

Professor of Law at Harvard, Holmes became a Justice on the Massachusetts Supreme Judicial Court, where he remained for two decades. In 1902 he moved to the United States Supreme Court, where he served as a Justice for three decades.

Having befriended William James, C.S. Peirce and other like-minded men at Harvard, Holmes infused his jurisprudential writings with the spirit of pragmatism and legal positivism. Perhaps the most striking expression of that spirit in Holmes' work was the predictive theory of law which he developed in his famous essay 'The Path of the Law' (1897) and elsewhere. Although Holmes there spoke somewhat strangely of rights and duties as predictions, his analyses make clear that he viewed our *ascriptions* of rights and duties – rather than the rights and duties themselves – as predictive. To ascribe a legal right to someone is to predict that the person will (if necessary) be protected by the coercive power of the state in specified ways. Conversely, to ascribe a legal duty to someone is to predict that the person will (if necessary) be authoritatively punished for performing a forbidden act or for declining to perform a required act. Far from being mysterious entities, rights and duties are positions which people occupy in varying configurations; specifically, rights are positions of protectedness, and duties are positions of threatenedness.

Not only one's attributions of rights and duties, but also any other statements within and about the law, are essentially predictive. Laws and analyses of laws amount to forecasts of the consequences that attend disobedience. Such, at least, is the view which 'The Path of the Law' declares: 'The prophecies of what the courts will do in fact, and nothing more pretentious, are what I mean by law' (1897: 461). This famous assertion did not bespeak a cynical 'anything goes' attitude towards legal decision-making, but simply flowed from Holmes' legal-positivist belief that official pronouncements and actions – as opposed to extra-legal standards – are the keys to the content and indeed to the very existence of law. Such a positivist stance can perfectly well square with the fact that what judges do in any of the liberal democracies is usually to interpret statutes or other legal materials (including past judicial decisions, of course) in an effort to find and apply relevant laws rather than create them entirely afresh. Though the distinction between finding and creating law is highly problematic, and though the particular means by which any legal system distinguishes finding from creating are decidedly variable, the judicial role in liberal democracies is based on such a distinction. Hence, a reduction of law to 'what courts do in fact' is fully compatible with the thesis that judges apply existent laws scrupulously.

Holmes' affinities with the pragmatists and his emphasis on predictability turn up further in his insistence that the relevant standards of evaluation within the law – standards such as reasonableness – are fundamentally external. Holmes pointed to two kinds of externality. First, the legal standards are brought to bear on people's behaviour rather than on their inner capacities and convictions. The law requires people to tailor their conduct to comply with the norms that regulate their interaction; if some people cannot live up to those norms (because of unintelligence, for example), they will usually be held responsible none the less. Outward deeds, as opposed to inward sentiments, are the overriding concern of the law. A second and partly related way in which the law's standards are external is that they typically flow from the *mores* of the general public rather than from the preferences of a wrongdoer or from the preferences of the decision-maker who passes judgment on the wrongdoer. A judge or a juror should seek to decide cases not on the basis of personal predilections but on the basis of ideals and expectations that are widely shared throughout the community in which the cases arise.

Holmes consistently exhibited a pragmatist distrust of abstractions. With his predictive theory of law, for instance, he explicated the abstractions of legal parlance by reference to their concrete functioning. There are two basic complaints against a reliance on abstractions in his writings. First, he believed that such a reliance was pointlessly ineffectual. As *The Common Law* proclaims: 'An answer cannot be obtained from any general theory.... The grounds of decision are purely practical, and can never be elicited from grammar or from logic' (1881: 264). Abstract principles in themselves are empty and boundless, and they therefore simply distract us from our genuine problems. Furthermore, even if abstractions could yield determinate guidance, an adherence to them would be undesirable. As Holmes stated: 'To rest upon a formula is a slumber that, prolonged, means death' (1915: 3). Anyone who conjures with abstract formulations is attempting to lock the flux of reality into static moulds. For Holmes, who perceived human existence as a constant and highly salutary struggle among vying interests, the quest for overarching legal/ethical guidelines that could transcend all divisions was a denial of progress and of life itself.

See also: COMMON LAW §3; LAW, PHILOSOPHY OF; LEGAL POSITIVISM; LEGAL REALISM §2; PRAGMATISM

List of works

Holmes, O.W., Jr (1881) *The Common Law*, Boston, MA: Little, Brown. (Holmes' *magnum opus*.)
—— (1897) 'The Path of the Law', *Harvard Law Review* 10: 457–78. (Predictive theory of law.)
—— (1915) 'Ideals and Doubts', *Illinois Law Review* 10: 1–4. (Short article on political idealism.)
—— (1918) 'Natural Law', *Harvard Law Review* 32: 40–44. (Doubts about natural law.)
—— (1995) *Collected Works*, 3 vols, ed. S. Novick, Chicago, IL: University of Chicago Press. (Thorough collection of Holmes' writings.)

References and further reading

Gordon, R. (ed.) (1992) *The Legacy of Oliver Wendell Holmes, Jr*, Stanford, CA: Stanford University Press. (Collection of essays.)
Grey, T. (1989) 'Holmes and Legal Pragmatism', *Stanford Law Review* 41: 787–870. (Highly readable account.)
—— (1992) 'Holmes, Pragmatism, and Democracy', *Oregon Law Review* 71: 521–42. (A lucid analysis highlighting Holmes' political views as well as his pragmatism.)
Rosenblatt, R. (1975) 'Holmes, Peirce, and Legal Pragmatism', *Yale Law Journal* 84: 1123–40. (Introductory-level exposition.)

MATTHEW H. KRAMER

HOLOCAUST, THE

The specific, tragic event of the Holocaust – the mass murder of Jews by the Nazis during the Second World War – raises profound theological and philosophical problems, particularly problems about the existence of God and the meaning of Jewish existence. Among the thinkers who have tried to wrestle with the conceptual challenge posed by the destruction of European Jewry, three who have presented original arguments that can be termed, in a relatively strict sense, philosophical are Richard L. Rubenstein, Emil Fackenheim and Arthur A. Cohen.

Rubenstein has formulated an argument that turns on the theological difficulties raised by the realities of the evil of Auschwitz and Treblinka in a world putatively created and ordered by a benign God. For him, such evil decisively refutes the traditional theological claim that a God possessed of goodness and power exists, and entails the conclusion that 'there is no [traditional] God'. In working out this conceptual position, he uses an unsatisfactory empirical theory of
verification concerning religious propositions and too narrow a notion of evidence, both historical and ethical, that ultimately undermines his counterclaims and 'Death of God' affirmations.

Fackenheim seeks not to defend a religious 'explanation' of the Holocaust, but rather to provide a 'response' to it that maintains the reality of God and his continued presence in human, and particularly Jewish, history. To do so, he uses Martin Buber's understanding of dialogical revelation, asserting that revelation is an ever-present possibility, and formulates his own moral-theological demand to the effect that after the Holocaust, Jewish survival is the '614th commandment' (there are 613 commandments in classical Judaism). Fackenheim's defence of this position, however, is philosophically problematic.

Cohen probvides a 'process theology' argument as an explanation of the Holocaust; that is, the Holocaust requires a revision in our understanding of God's nature and action. It forces the theological conclusion that God does not possess the traditional 'omni' predicates; God does not intervene in human affairs in the manner taught by traditional Western theology. However, Cohen's working out of a process theological position in relation to the Holocaust raises as many philosophical problems as it solves.

1 **Richard Rubenstein**
2 **Emil Fackenheim**
3 **Arthur A. Cohen**
4 **Conclusion**

1 Richard Rubenstein

Rubenstein has been attempting to make sense of the Holocaust since the 1960s, when he published his well-known collection of essays *After Auschwitz* (1966). The theological position he articulated in this first work has changed little over the years: Auschwitz and Treblinka decisively refute any belief in the existence of God or that life is made meaningful by a transcendent source. Had God existed, he would not have permitted the Death Camps, he would have put a stop to the slaughter (see EVIL, PROBLEM OF). Since God does not exist, the universe is a meaningless conglomeration of circumstances without transcendental direction, purpose or warrant. Accordingly, Rubenstein rejects all such traditional Jewish beliefs as the sanctity of the Torah, the normativity of the *mitzvot* (commandments), and divine creation, covenant, revelation and redemption.

Beginning with this series of negations, Rubenstein, like such atheist existentialists as Jean-Paul SARTRE, formulates an existential affirmation that creates human meaning without assistance, and so redeems human life from absurdity – to the extent that this is possible. In a world without inherent value, all we have is ourselves and each other; self-confirmation and communal belonging become ultimate values. The living Jewish community, in particular, is not rejected, but it is fundamentally redefined. In place of the divinely chosen, covenanted people of tradition, we find in the Jewish Community a human fellowship that is socially and psychologically supportive despite the denial of its ancient theological message.

Rubenstein gives essentially empirical grounds for his denial of the existence of God: propositions about God are to be straightforwardly confirmed or disconfirmed by appeal to empirical events in the world. On the basis of these events Rubenstein judges that 'God is dead'. The Holocaust becomes the critical empirical test, demonstrating God's nonexistence. In effect Rubenstein argues: there is too much evil in the world, there was too much at Auschwitz, to allow us any longer to affirm that God, as conceived in Judaism, can exist (see ATHEISM).

Respecting this challenge as an important one, too often lightly dismissed by theologians, and respecting Rubenstein's authentic existential response to an overwhelming reality, one needs to recall that empirical falsifiability is not generally definitive in theological matters and does not provide the unimpeachable criterion that Rubenstein seeks. History provides evidence both for and against the existence of God, since there is both good and evil in history. The issue may turn on the questionable coherence of verificationism itself. But even one who accepts Rubenstein's assumption that theological judgments can be grounded in historical events, might dispute what counts as crucial empirical or experiential evidence. The State of Israel is also an empirical datum, and some argue that if Auschwitz is evidence against the 'God-Hypothesis', the re-establishment of the State of Israel is evidence in its favour. Neither position is decisively provable but both are equally meaningful.

In recent works like *The Cunning of History* (1975), *The Age of Triage* (1983), and the new edition of *After Auschwitz* (1992), Rubenstein has increasingly turned away from narrowly theological and philosophical concerns to a broader comparative sociological form of inquiry that draws on the thinking of HEGEL and Max WEBER and emphasizes the important role of the historical development of bureaucracy, technology and capitalism in deciphering not only the Holocaust but modernity at large. Rubenstein now sees the Holocaust as the culmination of a variety of negative processes that have increasingly defined modern European history since the sixteenth century. The Nazi Death Camps, he now contends, were an extension of the logic of New World black slavery, a rational and bureaucratic exploitation of labour taken to the ultimate extreme. The murder of European Jewry was the maximal application of modern notions of surplus population control. These sociological and historical claims have met with considerable critical resistance.

2 Emil Fackenheim

Emil FACKENHEIM is perhaps the best-known philosophical respondent to the Holocaust. Careful to insist that his work be understood as a 'response' to the Death Camps and not as an explanation of them, he vehemently rejects the notion that suffering is the result of sin (a classical Jewish doctrine sometimes applied to the Holocaust: that is, that it was God's way of punishing Israel for its sins). Fackenheim has sought principally to provide reasons for Jewish survival, to give meaning to ongoing Jewish communal life, after the Holocaust.

He begins with what he acknowledges to be a Buberian model of revelation: revelation is the ever-present possibility of divine–human relationship that speaks anew in every historical and inter-human context. This existential possibility is not subject to objective or public proof, any more than is the existence of God. But, taken on faith, this Buberian dogma, that God cannot be proven but can be met, undergirds Fackenheim's mature reflections on a post-Holocaust Judaism (see BUBER, M.).

We witness God's presence in history, Fackenheim argues, in the experience of the people of Israel throughout its existence, and this in two ways: in the 'root experiences' of the people of Israel, and in 'epoch-making events'. The first are creative, extraordinary historical happenings that decisively form the character and continue to influence all future 'presents' of the Jewish people, forever legislating in every future generation of the nation. The Exodus from Egypt, for example, is a historical movement relived every Passover; its power affects each new generation, continually revealing in its yearly re-enactment the saving activity of God. Because past root experiences are lived through as present reality, Jews in every age are 'assured that the past saving God saves still'.

'Epoch-making events' are not formative for Jewish collective consciousness. They are historical challenges to the root experiences, demanding an answer to new and often unprecedented conditions. The occurrences encompassing the destruction of the First and Second Temples were such events. They tested the foundations of Jewish life, specifically the existence of the saving power and commanding providence of God, as previously revealed in the Exodus and at Sinai. But they did not shatter them, as the survival of the Jewish people testifies. The traditional interpretive paradigm has always shown its resiliency, absorbing and surviving the catastrophes that shook its foundations.

What, then, of Auschwitz? Can it be assimilated to Fackenheim's ancient and rather midrashic model? Fackenheim's answer is an unreserved 'yes'. Even Auschwitz does not destroy the 'root experiences' of Israel's faith. God is present even in the Kingdom of Night, commanding Israel still, from within the eye of the storm itself. This extreme reply of unwavering affirmation, in the face of the unprecedented terrors of Auschwitz, is the core of Fackenheim's response and that of others who follow his lead: a Jew cannot, dare not, must not, reject God. Auschwitz itself is revelatory, commanding, and one must learn to sense what God would reveal to Israel even there.

The commanding word of Auschwitz, which Fackenheim, in a now famous phrase, called the 614th commandment, is this: 'Jews are forbidden to hand Hitler posthumous victories!'. After Auschwitz, Jews are under a sacred obligation to survive; Jewish existence is itself a holy act; Jews have a duty not only to remember the martyrs but to remain open to the possibility of redemption. To succumb to cynicism is to abdicate responsibility for the here and now and to deliver the future over to the forces of evil. Above all, Jews are 'forbidden to despair of the God of Israel, lest Judaism perish'. Hitler's demonic passion was to eradicate Israel from history. For the Jew to despair of the God of Israel as a result of Hitler's monstrous actions would be to do Hitler's work and by a dreadful irony to aid in the accomplishment of Hitler's goal.

The Jewish will for survival is natural enough, but Fackenheim invests it with transcendental significance: precisely because others would eradicate Jews from the earth, Jews are commanded to resist annihilation. Hitler makes Judaism after Auschwitz a necessity. To say 'no' to Hitler is to say 'yes' to the God of Sinai; to say 'no' to the God of Sinai is to say 'yes' to Hitler. Since 1945, every person who has remained a Jew has, from Fackenheim's perspective, responded positively to the commanding voice of God heard at Auschwitz.

What Fackenheim affirms here is only half of the traditional content of Judaism: the God of biblical faith is a commanding as well as a saving God. The crossing of the Red Sea is as central to Jewish history as the revelation at Sinai; both are 'root experiences'. Fackenheim has made much of the commanding presence of Auschwitz, but where is the saving power of the God of the Exodus? Without the crossing of the Red Sea there is no Sinai, as Fackenheim knows. He also knows that to talk of a God of deliverance, no matter how tentatively, after the Holocaust is highly problematic, since God did not work his kindness there and then. The continued existence of the people of Israel, however, and specifically the re-establishment and survival of the State of Israel, allow Fackenheim to risk speaking of hope and the possibility of redemption. The destruction of European Jewry and the birth of the State of Israel are, for him, inseparably linked (see ZIONISM). What the Holocaust seems to deny, the new state, at least tentatively, affirms, a living testimony to God's continued presence in history that reconfirms the 'root experience' of salvation essential to the survival of Jewish faith.

Despite its interest and wide appeal, Fackenheim's response is not philosophically unproblematic. At least three issues need to be raised: (1) Is Buber's 'I–Thou' dialogical theology an adequate basis for a post-Holocaust religious commitment (see BUBER, M. §§3–4)? Can it ground Fackenheim's particular project? (2) What exactly can Fackenheim mean, in light of his Buberian starting point, by referring to a 614th commandment? That is, what are the meaning and force of the notion of a commandment in this context? (3) How can Fackenheim confront the issues of meaning, verification and disconfirmation that are raised but not adequately addressed by his important work?

While raising the level of discussion as regards the philosophical significance of the Holocaust, Fackenheim leaves us with a position that is not entirely conceptually compelling.

3 Arthur A. Cohen

Four highly ramified theses lie at the root of Arthur Cohen's philosophical reflections on the Holocaust, as expressed in his work *The Tremendum* (1981): (1) the Holocaust is unique, and its uniqueness entails particular theological consequences; (2) human thought cannot grasp the enormity of Auschwitz; (3) no 'meaning' is to be found in this genocidal carnage; (4) evil is more real, more consequential, than many, including Cohen himself, had heretofore allowed. These four radical reflections lead Cohen to recognize a need to return to the traditional questions of theology with a new uncertainty, to ask again concerning 'the reality of evil and the existence of God, the extremity of evil and the freedom of man, the presentness of evil and the power of God' (Cohen 1981: 97). They lead him to ask, still more concretely, if,

like our ancestors we are obliged to decide whether (national) catastrophes are compatible with our traditional notions of a beneficent and providential God. The past generations of Israel decided that they were. The question today is whether the same conclusion may be wrung from the data of the *tremendum*.

(Cohen 1981: 86)

Cohen's reply is that the traditional Jewish 'God concept' cannot survive the Holocaust but requires radical revision along the lines suggested by Alfred North WHITEHEAD and Charles Hartshorne (see PROCESS THEISM). God is neither to be blamed for the Holocaust nor censured for not stopping the murder. But the idea of God and of God's relationship to the world needs to be reinterpreted in what Cohen calls a 'di-polar' manner. God, on this redefinition, though loving, is respectful of human freedom and, whether by choice or metaphysical necessity, does not interfere in human history.

Provocative as it is, Cohen's position raises a host of philosophical and theological questions. Is God still God if he is no longer an agent of providence? If he lacks the power to enter history vertically through miracles? Is the dipolar Absolute still the God to whom one prays, the God of salvation? Is the non-interfering God 'whom we no longer fear and from whom we no longer demand' still, as Cohen would have it, worthy of our 'love and honour?' Is this God now reduced to the status of Plato's Demiourgos (see PLATO §16), or perhaps closer still to the innocuous and irrelevant God of the Deists (see DEISM)? Such a God, it could be argued, makes no difference in how we act and plays no role at all in how history revolves or transpires. If God is indeed so absent from our life and from the historical record, what difference remains for us between this God and no God at all?

Furthermore, the proposed metaphysical reconstruction is founded on no direct phenomenological or experiential procedure, but fashioned, in the present instance, in response to the Holocaust. If so, belief in the dipolar God requires as great a 'leap of faith' as do the theistic affirmations of the ancient Jewish tradition – greater, perhaps, since the new God lacks the support of history and tradition.

It is difficult to see why one would turn towards dipolar theism, given the tragedy of the Holocaust, unless one were already committed to theism to start with. But Cohen has not shown why we should begin with this assumption. The moral dimension of theodicy remains to be dealt with, moreover. For Cohen's dipolar God appears, of necessity, indifferent to human suffering and acts of evil. In short, Cohen's revision of the 'God-concept', and the whole process-theology response to the Holocaust, raises at

least as many questions as it answers (see GOD, CONCEPTS OF).

4   Conclusion

The Holocaust has shown itself to be an extremely difficult matter to philosophize about. This is because of the enormity and complexity of the issues it raises for all human reflection and for Jewish philosophical deliberation in particular. It has not been shown that the *Shoah* (Holocaust) disconfirms all pre-Holocaust metaphysical and theological systems; but, given the reality that is the *Shoah*, it is correct to require that all philosophical and theological judgments be called upon to measure their conceptual adequacy against the circumstances of Auschwitz and Treblinka.

See also: ANTI-SEMITISM; EVIL, PROBLEM OF; FACKENHEIM, E.L.; JEWISH PHILOSOPHY, CONTEMPORARY

References and further reading

* Cohen, A.A. (1981) *The Tremendum*, New York: Crossroad Publishing. (An interesting, if ultimately unsatisfactory, attempt to rework post-Holocaust Jewish thought in a Whiteheadian mode.)

Fackenheim, E.L. (1967) *The Religious Dimension in Hegel's Thought*, Bloomington, IN: University of Indiana Press. (A basic, informed study of Hegel's religious thought by one of the most prominent philosophers to focus on the Holocaust. Highly recommended.)

—— (1968) *Quest for Past and Future*, Bloomington, IN: University of Indiana Press. (A collection of Fackenheim's essays.)

—— (1970) *God's Presence in History*, New York: New York University Press. (Argues that we witness God's presence in history through the experiences of the people of Israel.)

—— (1982) *Encounters between Judaism and Modern Philosophy*, New York: Basic Books. (A series of important essays on major modern philosophers including Kant, Hegel and Sartre in relation to Judaism.)

—— (1978) *The Jewish Return into History*, New York: Schocken. (A second valuable collection of essays.)

—— (1994) *To Mend the World*, Bloomington, IN: University of Indiana Press. (Fackenheim's most sustained, but only partially successful, effort to write a post-Holocaust theology.)

Katz, S.T. (1983) *Post-Holocaust Dialogues: Critical Studies in Modern Jewish Thought*, New York: New

York University Press. (Essays on key modern Jewish thinkers.)

—— (1992) *Historicism, The Holocaust, and Zionism: Critical Studies in Modern Jewish Thought and History*, New York: New York University Press. (Essays on the basic issues surrounding the Holocaust and Zionism.)

—— (1994) *The Holocaust in Historical Context*, New York: Oxford University Press, vol. 1; vols 2 and 3 forthcoming. (Discusses the uniqueness of the Holocaust in comparative historical perspective.)

* Rubenstein R.L. (1966) *After Auschwitz*, Indianapolis, IN: Bobbs-Merrill; 2nd revised edn, Baltimore, MD: Johns Hopkins University Press, 1992. (Core essays on theology after the Holocaust.)

—— (1968) *The Religious Imagination*, Indianapolis, IN: Bobbs-Merrill. (Studies the relationship between psychoanalysis and Jewish theology and examines Jewish theology from a psychoanalytic perspective.)

* —— (1975) *The Cunning of History*, New York: Harper & Row. (An important theoretical effort to situate the Holocaust within the stream of Western history, using a Weberian model.)

* —— (1983) *The Age of Triage*, Boston, MA: Beacon Press. (Offers an explanation of the Holocaust within the context of modern culture in general and modern mass murder in particular.)

Schweid, E. (1994) *Wrestling Until Day-Break: Searching for Meaning in the Thinking on the Holocaust*, Lanham, MD: University Press of America. (A valuable critical study of post-Holocaust Jewish theology.)

Tiefel, H.O. (1976) 'Holocaust Interpretations and Religious Assumptions', *Judaism* 25: 135–49. (A helpful introductory evaluation of several post-Holocaust thinkers.)

Wyschogrod, M. (1971) 'Faith and the Holocaust', *Judaism* 20: 286–94. (Well-known critical appraisal of Emil Fackenheim's work.)

STEVEN T. KATZ

HOME, HENRY (LORD KAMES) (1696–1782)

Henry Home (better known as Lord Kames, his title as a Scottish judge of the Courts of Session and Justiciary) was an important promoter of and contributor to the Scottish Enlightenment. His philosophy was a search for causes which could serve as the bases of policies to improve most aspects of Scottish life and thought. His writings, like his involvements in clubs, *government bodies and improving economic activities, were all means to enlightened and improving ends. Kames was perhaps the most typical thinker of the Scottish Enlightenment, uniting interests in philosophy, science,* belles lettres, *history, education and practical improvements of every sort.*

Born in Eccles, Berwickshire, Henry Home, Lord Kames' parentage related him to the Jacobite and Whig gentry but also to the professional classes. Unfortunately, gentility did not confer wealth. Kames' notable interests in improvements were made necessary by his relative poverty which lasted until *circa* 1766 when his wife, Agatha Drummond, inherited the Blair Drummond estate in Stirlingshire. By the end of his career he had been honoured by societies or academies in Manchester, Philadelphia and Berne; he had also been attacked by Voltaire. At home his philosophic views seemed to many overly naturalistic and secular, even atheistic in their tendencies. Such conclusions were relatively easy to draw because Kames tended to deny free will, criticized Newtonian physics (the great prop to design arguments for the existence of God) (see NEWTON, I.) and extended the scope of sense and reason beyond what the religious were prepared to accept. He never produced a system based on the methods and views of his favourite philosophers – Francis Bacon, Isaac Newton, John Locke, the Third Earl of Shaftesbury and Joseph Butler – but in his works he laid out views which foreshadowed Scottish Common Sense philosophy (see COMMON SENSE SCHOOL).

Kames, like David HUME, Thomas REID and other Scots, thought that all knowledge and belief had to be related to human nature, that is the structure and capacities of the mind. His clearest statements of this belief are found in *Essays on the Principles of Morality and Natural Religion* (1751, revised 1758 and 1779), but they are not lacking in other works. Kames found his great guides in sense and feeling. Belief comes from a simple, unanalysable feeling not identical with Hume's 'vivacity of perception' or other modes of awareness. If we have the feeling, we are caused and determined to believe in what we have perceived or remembered or what the critically evaluated testimony of others induces us to believe. Experience shows us a world in which causation is perceived – in ourselves as we will and act, in matter as objects at rest or in motion collide or move in determinable ways apparent to our senses of touch and sight. We do not know why or how objects move, but *motion, rest, power, cause* and *effect* are simple ideas derived from our experiences and requisite to the establishment of both morality and physics.

Kames differed from Newtonians in believing

matter to be active and self-moving but bound by God to rules of motion which Newton's physics defined. Surveying nature revealed a lawful and designed world, a beautiful system of related causes and effects. Taken as a whole, it was an effect which led irresistibly to a belief in a creative and benevolent God. Sensations and feelings may mislead us but they do not regularly do so when inductions are carefully made. Moreover, we find in them signs of the substances whose qualities sensations reveal and of which they are correlatives. Through the external senses we perceive external objects; through the external and internal senses we know ourselves and others as enduring and identical persons.

The internal senses are important to Kames' morals and aesthetics. Morality, he thought, rests on instincts, feelings of pleasure and pain and sensations of right or wrong, propriety and impropriety, all of which are produced because we possess moral senses, 'the voice of God within us' (*Essays*, 1751: 63) (see MORAL SENSE THEORIES). This view owes more to Joseph Butler than to the Earl of SHAFTESBURY, Francis HUTCHESON or George TURNBULL. Kames may well have developed it independently, and prior to the publication of David Hume's earlier works.

Kames extended these views to law. Criminal laws rest on a sense of impropriety, upon the perception of the improper actor as guilty and one whose actions we resent and try to punish. Sympathy allows us to participate in the feelings of revenge raised in other injured parties. Laws in the various stages of society express all this in ways which depend upon levels of civility. Civil law rests in like manner upon changing notions of property, contract, society and of the wrongness of their violation. The laws of all peoples will, Kames believed, eventually converge, which led him to hope for a more perfect union between England and Scotland.

Kames developed his views of aesthetics in a somewhat similar fashion. A work of art evokes in our internal sense feelings of beauty, sublimity, grandeur, novelty and propriety. Understanding how this comes about and judging the means to their production are the functions of aesthetics and criticism. Kames did this so well that his *Elements of Criticism* (1767) remained a useful textbook in America until the mid-nineteenth century.

Kames' views were unacceptable to many. John Stewart, the pious Edinburgh Newtonian, attacked his science and metaphysics because it allowed for a Godless, self-acting, self-designing world of mere matter. Kames' denial of free will (1751) was condemned by Church courts in 1757 – an event which showed some of the limits to Scottish enlightened thought. His views on law were severely criticized by utilitarians, although the historicism with which they were associated survived (see HISTORICISM). Indeed, his historical views resonated well into the nineteenth century, touching many fields such as sociology and anthropology and contributing to more general views of progress. In philosophy his work set out strategies pursued by the Scottish Common Sense philosophers, who more skilfully defended views he had held. When Lord Kames died many Scots mourned the man who, for contemporaries, was Scotland's most notable philosopher.

See also: ENLIGHTENMENT, SCOTTISH; HUMAN NATURE, SCIENCE OF IN THE 18TH CENTURY

List of works

Home, H. (Lord Kames) (1751) *Essays on the Principles of Morality and Natural Religion*, Edinburgh: Kincaid & Donaldson; revised London: Hitch & Hawes and Dodsley, Rivington, Fletcher & Richardson, 1758; Edinburgh: Bell & Murray, 1779.

—— (1754) 'Essays on the Laws of Motion', *Essays and Observations, Physical and Literary*, Philosophical Society, vol.1, 1–69. (In the same volume see the reply to Kames' views by John Stewart, 'Some Remarks on the Laws of Motion and the Inertia of Matter', 70–140.)

—— (1756) *Objections against the Essays on Morality and Natural Religion Examined*, Edinburgh. (This work contains passages which are thought to be by Hugh Blair and/or Robert Wallace, as well as by Home.)

—— (1758) *Historical Law Tracts*, Edinburgh: Kincaid & Bell and London: Millar, 2 vols; revised and enlarged, Edinburgh: Bell & Creech and London: Cadell, 1776.

—— (1761) *Introduction to the Art of Thinking*, Edinburgh: Kincaid & Bell.

—— (1762) *Elements of Criticism*, Edinburgh: Kincaid & Bell and London: Millar; 6th edn with Kames' last additions and corrections, Edinburgh: Bell & Creech and London: Cadell & Robinson, 1785.

—— (1774) *Sketches of the History of Man*, Edinburgh: Creech and London: Strahan & Caddell, 2 vols; 3rd edn with Kames' last additions and corrections, Edinburgh: Creech and London: Strahan & Cadell, 1778. (This has sections on the historical evolution of morals and philosophy generally.)

—— (1781) *Loose Hints upon Eduction, Chiefly concerning the Culture of the Heart*, Edinburgh and London: Bell & Murray.

References and further reading

Barfoot, M. (1983) 'James Gregory (1753–1821), and Scottish Scientific Metaphysics, 1750–1800', unpublished Ph.D. dissertation, University of Edinburgh. (Best discussion of Kames' scientific and metaphysical views).

Emerson, R.L. (1991) 'Henry Home, Lord Kames', ed. D.T. Siebert, *Dictionary of Literary Biography*, vol. 104, *British Prose Writers, 1660–1800*, vol. 104, Detroit, MI: Gale Research International. (Most recent short general account with a bibliography and note on manuscript sources.)

McGuinness, A.F. (1970) *Henry Home, Lord Kames*, New York: Twayne Publishers. (General discussion of Kames' aesthetic and critical views.)

Norton, D.F. (1982) *David Hume: Common-Sense Moralist, Sceptical Metaphysician*, Princeton, NJ: Princeton University Press. (This contains an excellent discussion of Kames' views and their background.)

Ross, I.S. (1972) *Lord Kames and the Scotland of His Day*, Oxford: Clarendon Press. (Currently the best biography.)

Stocking, G.W., Jr (1975) '"Scotland as the Model of Mankind": Lord Kames's Philosophical View of Civilization', in T.H.H. Thoresen (ed.) *Towards a Science of Man: Essays in the History of Anthropology*, The Hague: Mouton, 65–89. (Interesting discussion of Kames' place in the history of social thought).

ROGER L. EMERSON

HOMER (*fl. c.*700 BC)

Author of the Iliad *and* Odyssey*, the Greek poet Homer is probably the earliest surviving, and certainly among the greatest, of European poets. Down to the Renaissance he was considered the source of all scientific and philosophical wisdom; and he still supplies fruitful material for philosophical discussion of moral issues.*

For ancient, and many modern, thinkers Homer was most interesting philosophically for the rather primitive cosmological views he no doubt took over from Greek popular belief. 'The Shield of Achilles' (*Iliad* XVIII), with its even-handed depiction of the totality of human life – war and peace, city and country, youth and age, birth and death, dance and trial – all encompassed within nature's temporal cycle of the seasons and the spatial horizon of the heavens and all-surrounding Ocean, sets the bloodily narrow-minded action of the Trojan War in a larger, humanizing context; this image of the largest sources and limits of our human world is filled out by scattered references elsewhere to the brazen heavens, to Ocean, the origin of all things, and to Night's primordial power. Familiarity with an allegorical interpretation of divine myths is implied already in some passages in Homer himself (for example, 'the Battle of the Gods', *Iliad* XX, XXI); this technique went on to become a central way of reinterpreting his authoritative text for later needs: in part fostered by Homer's role as a major author read in schools, this long-lived tradition could claim that numerous philosophical and scientific doctrines were anticipated and legitimized by the poet's words.

In modern times, philosophical attention has tended to focus instead upon Homer's narrative account of human action and responsibility. Homer's poetry, although written, is the culmination of an oral epic tradition, in which many generations of poets gradually refined and improved an inherited body of traditional legendary tales. Homer seems to have inherited stories of divine determination and blood-thirsty war but himself to have preferred to tell them, at least in part, in terms of moral responsibility and humane compassion: the *Iliad*, whose first word is 'wrath', turns out in the end to be no less concerned with pity. The generic tension produced by an oral epic evolving over time through incrementally quite different ethical conceptions ended by posing for Homer the fundamental question to what extent freedom of choice, individual responsibility and feelings of guilt were compatible with the determinative influence of seemingly external factors like gods, oracles, destiny and temporary infatuation. His answer takes the form not of stringent argument but of compelling narrative and, above all, of direct speech in which characters lay bare the wellsprings of their action with breathtaking clarity: external factors turn out always to be involved and to affect the outcome of choice and action, but they never prevent human agents from choosing freely, erring irremediably and being regarded, by themselves and by others, as fully culpable – at least until they choose to accept their human limitations and to acknowledge their culpability in the eyes of their society and, especially, in the eyes of those they have wronged.

List of works

These cannot be dated securely, but the *Iliad* is generally regarded as earlier than the *Odyssey*.

Homer (*c.*700 BC) *Iliad*, in D.B. Monro and T.W. Allen (eds) *Homeri Opera*, vols 1 and 2, Oxford: Clarendon Press, 3rd edn, 1920; A.T. Murray (ed.

and trans.) *Homer, The Iliad*, Loeb Classical Library, Cambridge, MA: Harvard University Press and London: Heinemann, 1924, 2 vols. (Monro and Allen provide the scholarly edition; Murray gives Greek text with an English prose translation.)
—— (*c*.700 BC) *Odyssey*, in T.W. Allen (ed.) *Homeri Opera*, vols 3 and 4, Oxford: Clarendon Press, 2nd edition, 1917–19; A.T. Murray (ed. and trans.), revised by G.E. Dimock, *Homer, The Odyssey*, Loeb Classical Library, Cambridge, MA: Harvard University Press and London: Heinemann, 1995, 2 vols. (Monro and Allen provide the scholarly edition; Murray gives Greek text with an English prose translation.)

References and further reading

Adkins, A.W.H. (1960) *Merit and Responsibility. A Study in Greek Values*, Oxford: Clarendon Press. (The first four chapters provide one of the most influential and controversial accounts of Homeric ethics.)
Buffière, F. (1956) *Les Mythes d'Homère et la pensée grecque* (Homer's Myths and Greek Thought), Paris: Les Belles Lettres. (The standard survey of ancient allegorical interpretations of Homer's myths.)
Dodds, E.R. (1951) *The Greeks and the Irrational*, Berkeley and Los Angeles, CA: University of California Press. (Chapter 1 pages 1–27 is a widely influential study of irrational behaviour in Homer in terms of psychology and anthropology.)
Gaskin, R. (1990) 'Do Homeric Heroes Make Real Decisions?' *Classical Quarterly* 84, new series, 40: 1–15. (A careful analysis of Homeric decision-making.)
Hernandez-Galiano, M., Heubeck, A. and Russo, J. (1988–92) *A Commentary on Homer's Odyssey*, Oxford: Clarendon Press, 3 vols. (The commentary is uneven but comprehensive.)
Kirk, G.S. (1985–93) *The Iliad: A Commentary*, Cambridge: Cambridge University Press, 6 vols. (The commentary is uneven but comprehensive.)
Kirk, G.S., Raven, J.E. and Schofield, M. (1983) *The Presocratic Philosophers*, Cambridge: Cambridge University Press, 2nd edn. (Pages 7–17 provide a brief but balanced treatment of Homeric cosmology.)
Lamberton, R. (1986) *Homer the Theologian. Neo-platonist Allegorical Reading and the Growth of the Epic Tradition*, Berkeley and Los Angeles, CA, and London: University of California Press. (A general survey of one important aspect of the tradition of allegorical interpretation of Homer.)
Lamberton, R. and Keaney, J.J. (eds) (1992) *Homer's Ancient Readers. The Hermeneutics of Greek Epic's Earliest Exegetes*, Princeton, NJ: Princeton University Press. (A useful collection of essays ranging from Homer to the Renaissance.)
Snell, B. (1953) *The Discovery of Mind*, trans. T.G. Rosenmeyer, Oxford: Oxford University Press. (Chapter 1 is a widely influential presentation of a 'primitivist' view of Homeric psychology and ethics.)
Williams, B. (1993) *Shame and Necessity*, Berkeley and Los Angeles, CA, and Oxford: University of California Press. (An eloquent defence of the sophistication of Homer's views on the self and action.)

GLENN W. MOST

HONOUR

Honour consists in living up to the expectations of a group – in particular, in keeping faith, observing promises, and telling truth. This restriction to a particular group is not easy to justify against the background of universalist theories of ethics, and neither does honour accord readily with the central modern concepts duty and utility. Honour requires a social context in which individuals can bind themselves, and has tended to be restricted to free, adult males, who alone have been thought to have the capacity to bind themselves in this way. Older traditions, however, regarded honour as the goal of all virtuous action; and newer thinkers have been rediscovering attractions in this view.

Honour is the disposition to fulfil promises and commitments, whether explicit or implicit, made to other members of a group. Honour has traditionally been important in public affairs, with political and commercial life resting on the notion that commitments must be 'honoured' even without explicit obligation by the person concerned.

Even thieves have honour, however, which seems to show that honour's compatibility with dubious principles makes it a crude guide to moral action. In many respects, indeed, it looks morally atavistic. Hobbes' disquisition about the nature of honour (1651) seems to voice only the crude principles of a society at war (compare Reiner 1972). Today, almost all functional applications of honour have been individualized and legalized. Nobody today fights duels; attempts to vindicate feminine honour would most often, if not always, meet with scorn; politicians no longer tend to resign; conduct in commercial organizations and other traditional concerns of honour are regulated by law. Only at the margins does scope for honour remain, for example *vis-à-vis* gambling debts, which are not recoverable by legal action.

Most modern philosophers would regard honour as superficial to the proper concerns of moral philosophy. Kant's contrast between honour and 'what is in fact useful or dutiful' is probably typical ([1785] 1903: 398). Utilitarianism finds honour inexplicable, for the value of honourable behaviour is not rationally determined by its consequences (see Utilitarianism; Consequentialism). For deontology, the relativity of honour condemns it as cynical (compare the thieves) (see Deontological ethics).

None the less, Aristotle, in *Nicomachean Ethics*, called honour the 'end of virtue' (1115b13); modern virtue ethics more or less explicitly follows this tradition (see, for instance, MacIntyre 1980, Solomon 1993); and even consequentialists seem to be rediscovering its appeal (expressly in Hollis 1992). What has mainstream ethical individualism, with its bare choice between consequentialism and deontology, overlooked?

The structure of honour seems to be as follows. At its heart is a comparatively formal disposition, namely 'fidelity, the observing of promises, and telling truth' (Hume 1741/2: 294). The commitments entered into are not contractual in nature and do not presuppose reciprocal utility. Honour involves a context in which others also assume comparably onerous roles; but despite this background, individuals who assume a role bind in the first instance only themselves.

Only agents considered to have full capacity can bind themselves in this way. Historically, and to a degree even now, children, slaves and women cannot bind themselves, and hence commitments in relation to their roles have to be taken over by proxies (usually males of full age and capacity). Capacity is a condition for the possession of honour.

The content of the commitments assumed by the agent is dependent on social context – which is why thieves can still be honourable. The commitments may coincide with duty (deontologically conceived) or even utility; but they may equally be virtues of a kind not always directly reconstructible in this way, such as continence, bravery, generosity and so forth. They are not generalizable or absolute; the content of honour varies with the honourable society, and is subject to no universal codes.

The fact and degree of honour, by contrast, are amenable to general ascertainment, for the quantity of commitments satisfied is a measure of the agent's capacity. Honour is most evident in those with the means to fulfil conspicuous promises. This is why princes and 'magnificent persons' are favourite illustrations of honour (in Aristotle and Hobbes), and why incapacities such as illness or poverty, even when undeserved, diminish honour. For Hobbes, honour is by its very nature a display of *power*, and 'to honour' is to acknowledge that power in others.

Honour is the final goal and completion of the virtues, which thus do not have value independently of the moment when they are undertaken in commitment to an honourable life (*Nicomachean Ethics* 1115b13; compare also 1122b7).

There are several obvious difficulties connected with the concept of honour. First, it is sometimes argued that honour is primarily a matter of status or of passively acquired reputation. If, however, honour is the sum of a person's virtues, then personal merit must be involved to a degree. So contrary to Solomon's view (1993), honour does depend on what one has done, or is taken to be prepared to do; simply being 'a member of the group in good standing' is a defective form of honour.

A second problem is the apparent connection between honour and uncritically affirmed collectives, as in 'the honour of the school', and so on. However, although honour requires an interpersonal context, only individuals possess it. Honour is the sum and goal of an individual's virtues; it is not properly attributable to groups (football teams, nations, religions, or even, in the final degeneration of this kind of thinking, races). Commitment to the interests of some specific group, while no doubt essential to honour, does not entail conferring personality on it.

Third, honour reflects the interests and concerns of its social context, and other societies' notions of honour can seem alienating or downright immoral. Nonetheless honour is a formal concept and can in principle be adapted to 'enlightened' concerns. Its central structural motif, that value resides not in individual acts or dispositions, but in their participation in an interpersonally directed whole, is present in a number of modern ethical systems. It is most obvious in Nietzsche, who in his doctrine of the 'will to power' institutes the same equivalence between honour and power as does Hobbes, while at the same time allowing for the virtues to be completed by power in a broader, nonpolitical sense (see Nietzsche, F. §11). It also emerges in G.E. Moore's insistence that virtues have value only when practised for the sake of a higher 'organic unity' (1903: 225, 238; compare *Nicomachean Ethics* 1115b13) (see Moore, G.E.).

It remains an open question, perhaps, whether the nonuniversalism of systems founded on honour is not too restrictive for the scope of modern ethical intuitions, notably in such areas as international human rights (see UNIVERSALISM IN ETHICS §1). This is a difficulty for all nonuniversalist doctrines such as virtue ethics and communitarianism (see COMMUNITY AND COMMUNITARIANISM).

See also: BUSHI PHILOSOPHY; DESERT AND MERIT; VIRTUES AND VICES

References and further reading

* Aristotle (*c.* mid 4th century BC) *Nicomachean Ethics*, trans. with notes by T. Irwin, Indianapolis, IN: Hackett Publishing Company, 1985. (Classic ancient discussion of honour and the virtues.)
* Hobbes, T. (1651) *Leviathan*, ed. R. Tuck, Cambridge: Cambridge University Press, 1991. (Discusses honour in a society at war.)
* Hollis, M. (1992) 'Honour Among Thieves', in M. Hollis and W. Vossenkuhl (eds) *Moralische Entscheidung und rationale Wahl*, Oldenbourg: Scientia Nova. (Considers honour in a consequentialist context.)
* Hume, D. (1741/2) *Political Essays*, ed. K. Haakonssen, Cambridge: Cambridge University Press, 1994. (Discusses honour and fidelity.)
* Kant, I. (1785) *Grundlegung zur Metaphysik der Sitten*, in *Kants gesammelte Schriften*, ed. Königlichen Preußischen Akademie der Wissenschaften, Berlin: Reimer, vol. 4, 1903; trans. with notes by H.J. Paton, *Groundwork of the Metaphysics of Morals* (originally *The Moral Law*), London: Hutchinson, 1948; repr. New York: Harper & Row, 1964. (References made to this work in the entry give the page number from the 1903 Berlin Akademie volume; these page numbers are included in the Paton translation. The work provides a classic exposition of a deontological standpoint.)
* MacIntyre, A. (1980) *After Virtue*, London: Duckworth. (Influential rejection of the dichotomy between deontology and consequentialism.)
* Moore, G.E. (1903) *Principia Ethica*, ed. T. Baldwin, Cambridge: Cambridge University Press, 1994. (Discusses value in 'organic unities'.)
* Reiner, H. (1972) 'Ehre', in *Historisches Wörterbuch der Philosophie*, vol. 2, Darmstadt: Wissenschaftliche Buchgesellschaft. (Includes discussion of Hobbes on honour.)
* Solomon, R. (1993) *Ethics and Excellence*, Oxford: Oxford University Press, esp. 222. (A recent application of virtue ethics.)

JULIAN ROBERTS

HOOKER, RICHARD (1554–1600)

Hooker's Of the Laws of Ecclesiastical Polity (1593–1662) is the first major work of English prose in the fields of philosophy, theology and political theory. After setting out an entire worldview in terms of the single idea of law, Hooker attempted to justify – and, arguably, to transform – the religious and political institutions of his day. Hooker's work contributed to later, more narrowly political, political thought (Locke cited 'the judicious Hooker' at crucial points in his Second Treatise of Civil Government), but the Laws is chiefly significant for articulating the ideal of a society coherent in and through its religion, a body politic which succeeds in being – not merely having – a church. In Hooker's England this meant that royal authority in religion was extensive, but derived from the community and limited by law. Modern separations of politics from religion and of philosophy from edification have made him difficult to assimilate. More recent critiques of Enlightenment secularism and purely technical philosophy help make him again intelligible.

1   Life
2   The kinds of law and other principles
3   The public duties of religion
4   Supreme authority in religion

1   Life

Hooker was born in England, near Exeter. With the help of Bishop John Jewel, the first official apologist for the Elizabethan religious settlement of 1559, Hooker attended Corpus Christi College, Oxford, where he later taught logic and Hebrew. In 1585 his appointment as Master of the Temple made him chief pastor of an important centre of legal studies. His surviving sermons, all from this period or earlier, show notable concern for the crises of faith experienced by reflective Christians during the Reformation. In 1591 he resigned from the Temple to work on *Of the Laws of Ecclesiastical Polity*. The preface and first four books were published in 1593, Book V in 1597. Hooker died in 1600. The politically sensitive last three books were published, in unfinished form, between 1648 and 1662.

2   The kinds of law and other principles

Although formally addressed to Puritan critics of the Elizabethan religious establishment, *Of the Laws of Ecclesiastical Polity* is also directed to the large number of Hooker's compatriots who were reluctant or unwilling to participate in the life of the English church after Pius V's excommunication of the Queen in 1570. Hooker's aim in Book I was thus to lay out normative principles acceptable to the broadest possible range of Christians at a time when violent accentuation of differences was more usual.

The scheme of laws Hooker set forth in Book I comprises (1) a twofold eternal law, in accordance with which (a) God's own voluntary actions are carried out and (b) creatures are directed to their various ends; this second eternal law subdivides, in application to the different kinds of creatures, into (2) a law governing the lives of the angels; (3) laws of purely 'natural' (that is, non-rational) agents; (4) principles of individual and social morality rationally discoverable by human beings; (5) laws made by humans themselves, consisting of (a) 'mixedly' human laws, which set down what we are already obliged to do on rational grounds, and (b) 'merely' human laws, which make obligatory actions which had not previously been obligatory; and (6) divine law, the supernatural law of biblical revelation, by which God directs fallen human nature to eternal blessedness.

It is a mark of Hooker's success in constructing a generally acceptable normative context for his later discussion of disputed issues that Book I can be read as an extraordinarily eloquent but unoriginal distillation of the wisdom of the ages. There is more to it than that. Hooker weaves together some quite diverse past wisdoms, and his elaboration of at least three particular points has substantive significance. First, in defining law as any rule directing to goodness of action, Hooker explicitly refrains from making imposition by a superior essential to law. Further, he argues that human beings are naturally equal with respect to political association. Accordingly, he urges the necessity of consent as a basis for governmental authority and, particularly, for legislative authority (see AUTHORITY §3).

The presentation of a lawful cosmos in Book I of the *Laws* has commonly been taken to be Hooker's greatest claim to philosophical merit. Other, more overtly polemical, parts of his work also deserve attention. Before undertaking his account of 'laws and their several kinds in general' in Book I, Hooker had found it necessary to gain breathing space from the Puritan contention that God's law, revealed in the Bible, uncompromisingly commanded major changes in church and society. The preface he composed for this purpose includes an astute analysis of what Hooker presents as an implicitly revolutionary movement, as well as discussion of the comparative authority of conscience and consensus.

Following his attempt to set out acceptable general norms in Book I, Hooker sought in Books II–IV to refute three principles he saw as underlying the numerous particular Puritan complaints. These principles were (1) that the Bible is the sole rule for everything to be done in this life; (2) that the Bible must of necessity contain full directions for church government; and (3) that the adequacy of a church's reformation could be measured by its distance from the practices of the Roman church. Against (1) Hooker defended (partly on biblical grounds) the competence of human reason. Against (2) he defended the competence of individual national churches to govern their own affairs. Against (3) he developed a historically contextualized account of the scandalous and the edifying in religion.

3 The public duties of religion

The fifth and longest book of the *Laws* is primarily a defence of particular features of the Elizabethan Book of Common Prayer, which was thought by Puritans to be insufficiently Protestant. Hooker begins the book's two main sections, however, with general discussions of the contributions of religion to social well-being. Even in its details, Hooker's championing of public worship as the central setting for personal participation in the life of God is of philosophical interest. It challenges the widespread modern assumption that faith is purely an inward matter or, at its most external, one component of individual ethics – in any case something private rather than public. (Hooker's account of the 'virtue' and 'discipline' of repentance in Book VI also negotiates the border between the subjective and outward sides of religion and does so with a sensitivity unusual in a defender of law and order.)

4 Supreme authority in religion

In the three last books of the *Laws* Hooker turned to the weightiest political problem of his day, the location of supreme human authority in religion. Three positions concerned him: the Presbyterianism advocated by some Puritans as divinely ordained; the papal supremacy advocated as divinely ordained by, among others, Jesuits clandestinely active in England after 1570; and the supremacy of the English crown asserted in parliamentary acts under Henry VIII and Elizabeth I.

Some of Hooker's case against Presbyterianism can be gathered from earlier books, from the preface, and from his defence of episcopal authority in Book VII, but his chief objection both to Presbyterianism and to papal jurisdiction independent of national authority is put most cogently in the first chapter of Book VIII: both positions assume an untenable dualism of 'church' and 'commonwealth' even when the membership of both is identical.

With reliance on ARISTOTLE (§§27–8), Hooker argued that the aims of political association included psychological goods (goods of the soul) and that, since the most important of these was religion, every body politic properly 'cared' for religion. Given the assumption, uncontested in his circumstances, that Christianity is the true religion, Hooker concluded that a commonwealth of Christians is a church, a body politic distinguished from other bodies politic, not by religion but by truth of religion: 'We say that the care of religion being common unto all *Societies* politic, such *Societies* as do embrace the true religion, have the name of the *Church* given unto every of them for distinction from the rest' ([1593–1662] 1989: VIII 1.2).

On this analysis, a royal supremacy of some kind was one way for a (national) community of Christians to care for its Christianity. Hooker's emphasis on the theoretically optional, communally chosen character of the royal supremacy is noteworthy. It may indeed explain why Book VIII was not published during the heyday of divine right monarchy under the early Stuarts. Besides grounding the crown's authority in communal consent, Hooker was also more insistent than any contemporary English author in construing that authority as legally limited. And further, as his recently discovered notes for Book VIII reveal, he intended to conclude the book with a substantial discussion of whether and how a community might correct an errant supreme ruler.

Although Hooker defended a supremacy in religious affairs granted to the civil ruler of the land, the limitations he placed on the royal supremacy, at a time when absolutism was budding in both theory and practice, suggest that Locke's use of Hooker to support the authority of community and law over regal power has more to be said for it than is often supposed. However, while Hooker could still envisage an agreed integration of spiritual and civil life as a feasible social goal, Locke saw the achievement of such coherence as a problem for individuals, who were likely to solve it in fundamentally different ways.

See also: BODIN, J.; LAW, PHILOSOPHY OF; LAWS, NATURAL; LOCKE, J.; NATURAL LAW; POLITICAL PHILOSOPHY, HISTORY OF; SOVEREIGNTY

List of works

Hooker, R. (1582–91) *Tractates and Sermons*, in W.S. Hill (ed.) *The Folger Library Edition of the Works of Richard Hooker*, vol. 5, Cambridge, MA: Harvard University Press, 1990. (Hooker's preaching on issues of faith and conscience that were of central concern during the Reformation.)

—— (1593–1662) *Of the Laws of Ecclesiastical Polity*, in W.S. Hill (ed.) *The Folger Library Edition of the Works of Richard Hooker*, vols 1–3, Cambridge, MA: Harvard University Press, 1977–81; vol. 6, Binghamton, NY: Medieval & Renaissance Texts & Studies, 1993. (Volumes 1–3 provide the main text; volume 6 gives discursive introductions and detailed commentary. The Preface and Books I–V of the *Laws* (published 1593–7) criticize the origins and tactics of the Puritans (including their exclusive reliance on biblical authority and unqualified opposition to Roman Catholicism), lay out Hooker's comprehensive normative framework, and defend the forms of public religious life prescribed and embodied in the Elizabethan Book of Common Prayer. Books VI–VIII (published posthumously between 1648–62) discuss the spiritual jurisdiction claimed for lay-elders by those pressing for a Presbyterian church polity, the authority and honour of bishops, and the power of ecclesiastical 'dominion' granted to the crown by English law.)

—— (1593–1662) *Of the Laws of Ecclesiastical Polity: Preface, Books I and VIII*, ed. A.S. McGrade, Cambridge Texts in the History of Political Thought, Cambridge: Cambridge University Press, 1989. (Hooker's address to Puritan critics of the Elizabethan religious establishment (with an analysis of their movement), the scheme of norms he proposed as a basis for adjudicating disputed issues, and his reformative defence of the royal supremacy in the English church.)

References and further reading

Hill, W.S. (ed.) (1972) *Studies in Richard Hooker: Essays Preliminary to an Edition of his Works*, Cleveland, OH: Case Western Reserve Press. (Bibliography; includes a perceptive, in the end critical essay by W.D.J. Cargill Thompson on Hooker as a political thinker.)

Kirby, W.J.T. (1990) *Richard Hooker's Doctrine of the Royal Supremacy*, Leiden and New York: Brill. (Argues for Hooker's fidelity to the Magisterial Reformation of Luther and Calvin; see also A.S. McGrade's review in *Journal of Ecclesiastical History* 44 (1993): 315–9.)

Lake, P. (1988) *Anglicans and Puritans? Presbyterian and English Conformist Thought from Whitgift to Hooker*, London: Unwin, Hyman. (Argues for Hooker's originality in relation to previous defenders of the Elizabethan religious settlement.)

McGrade, A.S. (ed.) (1997) *Richard Hooker and the*

Construction of Christian Community, Tempe, AZ: Medieval & Renaissance Texts & Studies. (Bibliography; papers on different sides of central issues concerning Hooker's historical and current significance.)

Shuger, D.K. (1990) *Habits of Thought in the English Renaissance: Religion, Politics, and the Dominant Culture*, Berkeley, CA: University of California Press. (Sensitive to tensions within, as well as between, establishment and anti-establishment thought.)

A.S. McGRADE

HOPE

In Christian theology 'hope' has a central role as one of the three theological virtues. As theology has gradually become separated from moral theory, the inclusion of 'hope' within a theory of ethics has become rare. Hope can be either intentional or dispositional. The former is a specific hope for something, whereas the latter is a state of character. Kant gave a central place to intentional hopes in his moral theory with his doctrine of the postulates. Hope also played an essential role in the moral and political writings of Ernst Bloch and Gabriel Marcel. Bloch regarded hope as concerned with a longing for utopia, whereas Marcel regarded hope as a disposition to rise above situations which tempt one to despair. In each of these writers the Christian connection between hope, on the one hand, and faith and love, on the other, remained, although Kant and Bloch did not oppose these categories to reason, but sought to 'subsume' them under it.

1 Historical outline
2 The concept of hope
3 Hope in Kant's moral philosophy
4 Hope in Bloch's thought
5 Marcel on hope

1 Historical outline

Hope first plays a significant role within Augustine's theory of morality where it appears as one of the three theological virtues – faith, hope and charity, or love (see AUGUSTINE §8; THEOLOGICAL VIRTUES). According to Augustine, the virtue of hope is subordinate only to faith, and on a level footing with love: 'there is no love without hope, no hope without love, and neither love nor hope without faith' (*Enchiridion*).

As morality became separated from theology during the Enlightenment hope became less impor-

tant in ethics. There are, however, three notable exceptions to this general trend: Immanuel Kant, Ernst Bloch, and Gabriel Marcel (see §§3–5). In each of these writers the connection between hope, on the one hand, and morality, religion and faith, on the other, is as tight as it was for Augustine. However, both Kant and Bloch interpret religion and faith neither as revealed nor as metaphysically proven, yet as reasoned, while Marcel contrasts both hope and faith to human desiring and calculating, that is, to instrumental rationality.

2 The concept of hope

Hope can be either intentional or dispositional (see INTENTIONALITY). Intentional hope is oriented to some desired state of affairs which is believed to be attainable. Hobbes describes such hope as an '*appetite with an opinion of attaining*' (1651: 123; original emphasis). Dispositional hope is a state of being hopeful. This state should be distinguished from optimism and wishful thinking.

A philosophical formulation of optimism is given in Leibniz's work (1710). For Leibniz, the thought that God could have created anything less than the best of all possible worlds is self-contradictory, since it would mean that God would not be the most perfect being, and hence would not be God (see LEIBNIZ, G.W. §§3, 7). Consequently, we can be certain that present suffering is for the greater good and that the future will be as good as it can be (see EVIL, PROBLEM OF §2). This confidence that everything is for the best was famously, and justifiably, ridiculed in Voltaire's *Candide* (1759). But, unlike optimism, being hopeful is not based on the certainty that things will get better. Hope, unlike optimism, presupposes a degree of uncertainty. Descartes noted this when he pointed out that '[w]hen hope is extreme, it changes its nature and is called "confidence" or "assurance"' (1649: 351) (see also Spinoza 1677: 106–7).

Hope should also be distinguished from wishful thinking. It is as impossible to hope legitimately for something which is impossible as it is inappropriate to hope for something which is certain. All wishful thinking is by its nature illusory, whereas only illegitimate hopes are illusory.

3 Hope in Kant's moral philosophy

Like Augustine, KANT held that hope and love presuppose faith. Kant, however, viewed faith as moral faith. Moral faith, unlike what he called ecclesiastical faith, is not based upon belief in metaphysical truth or contingent historical fact, and so available only to those who know of this truth or fact, but is a reasoned corollary of the moral law, and available to all (1793: 93–4). For Kant, the ultimate hope is no longer a hope for union with God, but a hope to attain the highest good (*summum bonum*) which is demanded by the moral law. The three postulates of pure practical reason, as laid out in the *Critik der practischen Vernunft* (*Critique of Practical Reason*) (1788), namely the hope for the existence of God, for immortality and for the attainment of perfect freedom, are all subordinate to this super-ordinate hope, and ultimately to the moral law.

Kant describes the assumption of the validity of the three postulates as 'a need of reason' (1788: 149). The use of the term 'need of reason' is not meant to suggest that the hope for the existence of God, immortality and freedom are necessary illusions. These postulates are both possible from a theoretical point of view, and objectively justified from a practical point of view by the fact that they are necessary corollaries of the moral law, which itself is based on reason (1788: 127). Since the postulates are the necessary and unavoidable conditions of the possibility of the *summum bonum*, every rational being ought (morally) to hope for the existence of God, immortality and freedom (1788: 149).

This moral argument for the belief (or hope) in God and immortality, has been subjected to a great deal of criticism. Nevertheless it has had an important influence on certain figures in twentieth-century critical theory. Walter Benjamin held that the historical materialist cannot abandon hope for those who have suffered past injustice, and therefore, cannot regard the past as closed. To do so would be implicitly to side with the victors and betray their victims (see §5 for an account of hope as a relation of communion or love).

Peukert also takes up this Kantian/Benjaminian approach to hope in *Science, Action and Fundamental Theology* (1984). Here he argues that utopianism requires hope (see UTOPIANISM). Utopian existence would be destroyed if the individuals who participate in it were burdened with the memory of unredeemed suffering. He asks: 'How can one hold on to the memory of the conclusive, irretrievable losses of the victims of history – to whom one owes one's entire happiness – and still be happy?' (1984: 209). If Peukert's argument is sound, the very idea of utopia is incoherent without hope for immortality, for the redemption of the victims of history, and the hope that God exists.

4 Hope in Bloch's thought

Ernst BLOCH takes a Hegelian approach to religion. He conceives God not as radically opposed to the human subject, as the absolutely Other, in the way Kierkegaard does (1844: 44–5), but as a human ideal. Bloch interprets faith in God as a hypostatized longing for a utopian form of existence. Once this hypostatization is recognized for what it is, the concept of 'God becomes the kingdom of God, and the kingdom of God no longer contains a god' (1954–9: 1196). God is recognized as embodying the hope for an ideal but thoroughly human kingdom.

Bloch's anthropological interpretation of religion owes a great deal to FEUERBACH. He was, however, deeply critical of Feuerbach for eliminating all traces of the transcendent from religion. The human perfection which Feuerbach saw man as projecting onto God is not reappropriated in the recognition of this projection, but is recognized as the promise of reappropriation – that is, as the promise of human perfection. This promise of perfection is the transcendent element which remains in religion, even after its anthropologization (1954–9: 1284–8).

Bloch's main critics included orthodox Marxists such as Manfred Buhr (1970), who were deeply suspicious of religious utopias. They see religion as tranquillizing, and socially stabilizing, as the 'opium of the people'. Bloch acknowledged this conservative tendency within religion, but also interpreted the revolutionary tendency of religious hope as the most extreme manifestation of dissatisfaction with, and rebellion against, the present. For Bloch, religious utopias, especially the Christian utopia of the king-dom of God, express revolutionary hope for an utterly different and better form of existence (1954–9: 1193). They are not merely tranquillizing, but in principle transforming.

5 Marcel on hope

For MARCEL, hope is a way of overcoming the trials of life. These trials can take the form of, for example, illness, separation, exile or slavery. 'Hope is situated within the framework of the trial, not only corre-sponding to it, but constituting our being's veritable *response*' (1945: 30; original emphasis). Such trials are a potential cause of despair in which subjects 'go to pieces' or lose themselves (1945: 37). So there is no hope without the temptation to despair, and hope is understood by Marcel as 'the act by which this temptation is actively or victoriously overcome' (1945: 36).

Marcel is concerned not with intentional hopes, but ultimately with a particular form of dispositional hope which he expresses as 'I hope in thee for us' (1945: 60). To place one's hope in somebody is not the same as to hope for something, that is, for some desired object, although it is usually related to such a hope. I do not want the person in whom I have placed my hope (although I may hope to gain some desired object by placing my hope in another person).

Hope is here understood as trust without self-interest. It is not like the hope of patients who place their hope in the psychiatrist, which can be expressed as 'I hope in thee *for me*'. Such hope is still bound up with self-interest. Marcel sees the fundamental form of hope as expressing human dignity as the ability to transcend one's own desires and to hope for a shared project. Here hope transcends self-interest: my relation to the other person (or persons) in whom I have placed my hope is not instrumental, but a collaborative, ethical relation of communion (1945: 67). Marcel locates such hope against a background of faith in God (1945: 60–1), rather than seeing it as Kant did against the background of the moral law.

Although the 'thou' in whom I hope is, for the most part, another person or group, Marcel maintains that we can regard reality itself as a thou. We do this when we cease to regard it as something which can be described exhaustively in terms of a catalogue of facts, and of what can be inferred from these facts, and regard it as an open process, that is, as full of real possibilities which are unconstrained by what is or has been the case. Marcel distinguishes between an objective judgment based on the facts, such as the judgment that there is a chance that I will see my son again, and the simple affirmation, 'You are coming back', which is expressed in hope (1945: 66). The former is constrained by the evidence and by what can legitimately be inferred from this, whereas the latter is not so constrained. Such hope is not based upon a calculation, or miscalculation, of probabilities, and hence is not governed by the norms of such calculation. It is rather a refusal to calculate, a refusal to regard the future as wholly delimited by the past and the present. Thus, when hope takes this form, it is beyond objective criticism. It is, however, only beyond objective criticism in so far as it is an expression of love, rather than desire (1945: 66).

See also: VIRTUES AND VICES

References and further reading

* Augustine (421) *Enchiridion*, trans. M. Dods, in *The Works of Aurelius Augustinus*, Edinburgh: T. & T. Clark, 1871–6; this translation repr. in V.J. Bourke (ed.) *The Essential Augustine*, New York: New American Library, 1964, 173. (A handbook, or manual, covering the manner in which God is to be worshipped; among the last of Augustine's works.)
* Bloch, E. (1954–9) *Das Prinzip Hoffnung*, Frankfurt: Suhrkamp Verlag, 2 vols; trans. N. Plaice, S. Plaice and P. Knight, *The Principle of Hope*, vol. 3: Oxford: Blackwell, 1986. (Bloch's major, encyclopedic work expressing his views about hope.)
* Buhr, M. (1970) 'A Critique of Ernst Bloch's Philosophy of Hope', *Philosophy Today* 14: 259–71. (Example of the orthodox Marxist response to Bloch's philosophy.)
Day, J.P. (1969) 'Hope', *American Philosophical Quarterly* 6: 89–102. (Clear analysis of goal-directed hope.)
* Descartes (1649) *La passions de l'âme*, trans. J. Cottingham, R. Stoothoff and D. Murdoch, *The Passions of the Soul*, in *The Philosophical Writings of Descartes*, Cambridge: Cambridge University Press, 1985. (This work grew out of the correspondence with Princess Elizabeth of Bohemia and addresses the question of how mind and body can interact given that they share nothing in common.)
Godfrey, J.J. (1987) *A Philosophy of Human Hope*, The Hague: Martinus Nijhoff. (An excellent account of different types of hope, and an overview of its role in the writings of Kant, Bloch and Marcel. It is better on Bloch and Marcel than on Kant.)
—— (1987) 'Appraising Marcel on Hope', *Philosophy Today* 31: 234–40. (Economical introduction to Marcel on hope.)
* Hobbes, T. (1651) *Leviathan*, Harmondsworth: Penguin, 1982. (Hobbes' major work on political philosophy, in which he argues for the absolute power of the sovereign.)
* Kant, I. (1788) *Critik der practischen Vernunft*, trans. L.W. Beck, *Critique of Practical Reason*, New York: Macmillan, 1985, book II, ch. 2, sections IV, V and VI. (Kant's second major work on ethics, containing his doctrine that there are three postulates of practical reason: hope that God exists, hope for immortality and hope for the attainment of perfect freedom.)
* —— (1793) *Die Religion innerhalb der Grenzen der blossen Vernunft*, trans. T.M. Greene and H.H. Hudson, *Religion Within the Limits of Reason Alone*, New York: Harper & Row, 1960. (A late work by Kant which offers a moral interpretation of religion and further develops the role of hope in his philosophy.)
* Kierkegaard, S. (1844) *Philosophiske Smuler*, trans. H.V. Hong and E.H. Hong, *Philosophical Fragments*, Princeton, NJ: Princeton University Press, 1985. (An important work by Kierkegaard in which he argues against any attempt to arrive at faith by means of argument, or objective thinking.)
Leibniz, G.W. (1710) *Essai de Theodicée sur la bonté de Dieu, la liberté de l'homme, et l'origine du mal*, trans. E.M. Huggard, *Theodicy: Essays on the Goodness of God, the Freedom of Man, and the*

Origin of Evil, London: Routledge & Kegan Paul, 1952. (An attempt to reconcile God's perfection with the fact that there is evil in the world.)

* Marcel, G. (1945) 'Sketch of a Phenomenology and Metaphysic of Hope', in *Homo Viator: prolégomènes à une métaphysique de l'espérance*, Paris: Aubier; trans. E. Crauford, *Homo Viator: Introduction to a Metaphysic of Hope*, New York: Harper & Row, 3rd edn, 1965. (Marcel's most comprehensive statement of his views on hope and its relation to faith and love.)

McCarthy, T. (1986) 'Philosophical Foundations of Political Theology', in L. Rouner (ed.) *Civil Religion and Political Theology*, London: Notre Dame, 23–40. (Makes interesting connections between Kant's defence of the three postulates from Wizenmann's criticism and debates within critical theory.)

Moltmann, J. (1964), *Theologie der Hoffnung*, Munich: Chr. Kaiser Verlag; trans. J.W. Leitch, *Theology of Hope*, London: SCM Press, 1967. (Hard reading for the uninitiated. Good introduction.)

* Peukert, H. (1984) *Science, Action and Fundamental Theology: Toward a Theology of Communicative Action*, Cambridge, MA: MIT Press. (Develops a theology based on Jürgen Habermas' critical theory, in which it is argued that that the utopian element in Habermas' thought commits one to a hope for the redemption of the victims of history.) *Philosophy Today* 14 (1970). (This volume has a number of clear, short, introductory articles on Bloch's philosophy of Hope.)

Ricoeur, P. (1970) 'Hope and the Structure of Philosophical Systems', *Proceedings of the American Catholic Philosophical Association* 44: 55–69. (Interesting and lucid use of Moltmann's *Theology of Hope* to relate philosophy and theology.)

* Spinoza, B. (1677) *Ethica Ordine Geometrico Demonstrata* (Ethics Demonstrated in a Geometrical Manner), trans. E. Curley, *Ethics*, Harmondsworth: Penguin, 1996. (Spinoza's philosophical system presented according to the geometrical method covering God, the mind, the affects, human subjection and human freedom.)

* Voltaire, F.M.A. de (1759) *Candide*, trans. D.M. Frame, in *Candide, Zadig and Selected Stories*, New York: New American Library, 1961. (Voltaire's famous satire of Leibniz's optimism.)

PHILIP STRATTON-LAKE

HORKHEIMER, MAX (1895–1973)

One of the initiators and founders of the Institute for Social Reasearch in Frankfurt, Germany, Max Horkheimer's philosophical importance derives from his programmatic essays of the 1930s in which he conceptualized the Institute's project of interdisciplinary research, and his later collaboration with Theodor W. Adorno in writing Dialectic of Enlightenment *(1947). Horkheimer's vision of a 'critical theory' of society was intended as a reformulation of Marxist theory in which empirical research would be combined with philosophical reflection.*

Born near Stuttgart, Max Horkheimer was the only son of a wealthy Jewish family. He studied philosophy at the then new Frankfurt University, writing both his doctoral thesis and *Habilitationsschrift* on Kant's *Critique of Judgment*. He became the director of the newly founded Institute for Social Research in Frankfurt in 1930, and organized the Institute's move first to Geneva and then New York City in 1934. Throughout the 1930s he edited the Institute's innovative journal *Zeitschrift für Sozialforschung* (Journal for social research), in which appeared important and characteristic essays by Theodor Adorno, Herbert Marcuse and Walter Benjamin. Horkheimer re-established the Institute in Frankfurt after the war, and served as rector of the Frankfurt University from 1951 to 1953. After retiring, he moved to Italy.

Beneath the surface, and in all periods of his work, Horkheimer's philosophy was shaped by the attempt to align Karl Marx's materialist critique of bourgeois society with Arthur Schopenauer's pessimistic vision of human suffering in the midst of a meaningless universe (see Marx, K.; Schopenhauer, A.). Human suffering, the experience of which is the ground of creaturely solidarity, cannot for Horkheimer be transfigured or redeemed; even a future utopian society would carry the curse of the countless victims of history. While compassion for the suffering of other living beings and individuals' longing for happiness form the ethical core of Horkheimer's thought, his most distinctive contribution to philosophy emerges in his attempt to formulate a new Marxist theory of society which would overcome what he saw as the dogmatism and failures of the original.

In his essay 'Traditional and Critical Theory' (1937) Horkheimer attempts to elaborate how the interdisciplinary research programme of the Institute is to be separated from the then standard paradigm of scientific knowledge as a theoretical representation of a wholly independent object domain. What traditional theory overlooks is that both the activity of knowing itself and its (social) objects are historically formed. Because the categories of human existence are historically formed, philosophy needs to be supplemented by social scientific research. Because those same social categories are the bearers of human significance, they require philosophical elucidation. Hence, only a complex interdisciplinary programme integrating philosophy and the social sciences (sociology, history, economics, social psychology and psychoanalysis) can do justice to the complex problems facing contemporary society. While both the actual programme of interdisciplinary research and the hopes for it had faded for Horkheimer by the end of the 1930s, the project was re-launched by Jürgen HABERMAS, the leading second-generation exponent of critical theory.

For Horkheimer, what makes critical theory 'critical' is its combining of the Marxist 'critique of political economy' with the Kantian 'critique of pure reason'. The importance of the latter for Horkheimer should not be underestimated. In criticizing traditional theory, Horkheimer is assuming the Kantian, 'critical' distinction between the causal understanding of theoretical reason (*Verstand*) and the ends-oriented, holistic thinking of practical reason (*Vernunft*) (see KANT, I. §6). In Horkheimer's lexicon the former appears as 'subjective' or 'instrumental' reason, the latter as 'objective' reason. While in his original programme for critical theory Horkheimer intended the whole complex interdisciplinary practice to be a surrogate for objective reason, with the waning of any hope for radical social change his philosophy became a relentless critique of instrumental reason.

Written with Adorno, *Dialectic of Enlightenment* (1947) was intended to provide a theoretical and historical generalization of the critique of enlightenment found in Hegel's *Phenomenology of Spirit* (see HEGEL, G.W.F. §5). The core claim of the *Dialectic* is that myth is already a form of enlightened, instrumental reason – an attempt to control hostile nature – and that the enlightenment critique of myth and superstition reverts to myth. By this latter claim Adorno and Horkheimer mean that the wholly disenchanted modern world is itself under a mythic curse or spell, in which individuals become anonymous ciphers within a wholly functional system. Instrumental rationality pervades the world – as the rationality of capitalist economy right through to the 'culture industry', and as the reason of a positivistically understood science. Because instrumental rationality is only a part of reason pretending to be the whole of reason, it becomes irrational. It is this thought that lies behind the exorbitant claim

that the whole (of society) is untrue (see ADORNO, T.W. §3)

In *Eclipse of Reason* (1947), originally presented as lectures at Columbia University in 1944, Horkheimer presented a reprise of the central arguments of *Dialectic of Enlightenment* in a slightly simpler form. Only now is the insistent negativity of his collaborative work softened; throughout history, he claims, myth, religion and philosophy have presented versions of objective reason that have only slowly and recently been 'eclipsed' by subjective reason. While independent thought cannot renew the worn-out ideals of objective reason, it can find equivalents in the affinity of nature and human nature. Alas, these equivalents, given through art, cannot provide the pivot Horkheimer requires for a renewal of reason. At the end Horkheimer was left with only compassion and pity for suffering life, and the longing for sensuous happiness, that had been throughout the mainsprings of his thought.

See also: CRITICAL THEORY; FRANKFURT SCHOOL

List of works

Horkheimer, M. (1930–8) *Between Philosophy and Social Science: Selected Early Essays*, trans. G. F. Hunter, M.S. Kramer and J. Torpey, London: MIT Press, 1993. (This selection includes most of Horkheimer's most important essays from the 1930s on moral philosophy, the philosophy of history, and methodology.)

—— (1932–41) *Critical Theory: Selected Essays*, trans. M.J. O'Connell *et al.*, New York: Seabury Press, 1972. (Some overlap with the above, but importantly includes 'Traditional and Critical Theory' and 'Authority and the Family'.)

Adorno, T.W. and Horkheimer, M. (1947) *Dialectic of Enlightenment*, trans. J. Cumming, London: Allen Lane, New York: Herder & Herder, 1972. (The classic text of first generation Critical Theory, arguing that Enlightenment rationalisation collapses into pure instrumental rationality and a new form of mythology.)

Horkheimer, M. (1947) *Eclipse of Reason*, New York: Continuum, 1992. (Originally given as lectures at Columbia University, a somewhat more accessible version of the previous item, with a more fully articulated conception of objective, subjective and instrumental reason.)

References and further reading

Benhabib, S., Bonß, W. and McCole, J. (eds) (1993) *On Max Horkheimer: New Perspectives*, London:

MIT Press. (An excellent collection of fifteen essays covering in detail the most important aspects of Horkheimer's thought. All are worth reading.)

Wiggerhaus, R. (1986) *The Frankfurt School*, trans. M. Robertson, Oxford: Polity Press, Cambridge, MA: MIT Press, 1994. (An authoritative history of the Frankfurt School, which provides a useful account of Horkheimer's activities in relation to the Institute for Social Research.)

J. M. BERNSTEIN

HSIN (HEART AND MIND)

see XIN (HEART-AND-MIND)

HSIN (TRUSTWORTHINESS)

see XIN (TRUSTWORTHINESS)

HSING *see* XING

HSÜN TSU/HSÜN TZU

see XUNZI

HUAI-NAN TZU *see* HUAINANZI

HUAINANZI (179–122 BC)

Huainanzi is both the honorific name of Liu An, the second king of Huainan and the title of the philosophical work for which he was responsible. The most important surviving text of the academy he established at his court, it consists of twenty-one essays that form a compendium of knowledge the Daoist ruler needs to govern effectively. In this work, the universe is a well-ordered, dynamic and interrelated whole, interfused by the unifying principle of the dao, *that develops according to patterns and processes comprehensible to self-realized human beings. The ruler must cultivate himself fully so that he comprehends these patterns and processes and must establish human society in harmony with them. Embracing the best ideas of earlier philosophers within a Daoist framework, the* Huainanzi *represents the fullest flowering of the Huang–Lao thought that dominated the early Han dynasty.*

Huainanzi is the honorific name sometimes given to

Liu An, a Chinese philosopher-king who was the grandson of Liu Bang, founder of the Han dynasty (206 BC–AD 220). After his father, Liu Chang, was punished for *lèse majesté* and died on the way to exile, Liu An was enfeoffed as the second king of Huainan, a vassal state in what was then considered the southern part of China, today mostly in Anhui province. This area, previously part of the old state of Chu, had long been associated with hermit-mystics and shamans and still retained in the early Han a culture distinct from that of the north, where the new central government resided. By about 150 BC, Liu had established an academy at his court wherein Daoist and Confucian thinkers mingled with scholars of the esoteric arts (*fangshi*), proponents of the 'naturalist' cosmology of *yin* and *yang* and the five phases of *qi*, systematized a century earlier by Zou Yan (see YIN–YANG; QI). Among the many literary products of Liu's academy, the principal survivor is a text called the *Huainanzi*, which Liu presented to his nephew, Emperor Wu, in 139 BC. In 122 BC Liu was accused of sedition and he perished, along with many of his courtiers and his rival cultural centre, at the hands of imperial troops sent to quell his alleged rebellion.

The *Huainanzi* is a work of twenty-one essays on a wide range of topics that was intended to be a compendium of all the knowledge a Daoist sovereign needed to govern effectively. Its topics include cosmology and cosmogony, astronomy and astrology, seasonal ordinances, human nature, psychology and physiology, political theory and the theory of strategic warfare, and mystical self-transformation. Although a few scholars have maintained single authorship by Liu, the predominant opinion is that Liu edited, compiled and arranged the essays and wrote the final essay, which summarizes each of the others and rationalizes their arrangement in the text.

Although initially categorized by bibliographers as an eclectic work because of its selective use of the non-Daoist ideas of such earlier schools as the Confucians and Legalists, the *Huainanzi* is increasingly being recognized as a product of the Daoist syncretism of the early Han that many identify with the Huang–Lao lineage of thought. 'Huang' stands for Huangdi, the mythical Yellow Emperor, and 'Lao' stands for Laozi, the legendary author of the foundational Daoist text, the *Daodejing* (see DAODEJING). In light of the mythical connotations of each figure and the ideas associated with this lineage, in the appellation 'Huang–Lao', Huangdi probably symbolizes the coordination of the political with the cosmological and Laozi probably symbolizes the mystical self-realization of the enlightened ruler. Taken together, we find the advocacy of a strong central government whose institutions, daily rituals, and organization of human society parallel greater patterns in the universe of which human beings form an integral part. This government is presided over by a benevolent ruler who is both philosopher and mystic and who is fully self-realized according to Daoist meditation techniques. During the first seven decades of the Han dynasty, the imperial court was dominated by Huang–Lao philosophy, a domination that was coming to an end when Liu An presented his *Huainanzi* to Emperor Wu. As a last-ditch attempt to convince the emperor to abandon the Confucian ideology he eventually chose, the *Huainanzi* represents the final flourishing of the Huang–Lao syncretism that adapted the best ideas of earlier thinkers into a Daoist philosophical framework.

In the cosmology of the *Huainanzi*, the universe is a well-ordered, intricately interrelated and constantly changing dynamic whole, governed by regular patterns and processes (*li*) that can be understood by exceptional human beings (see LI). Precise parallelisms exist between the basic levels of this universe. For example, the roundness of the human head parallels that of heaven, the squareness of the human feet parallels that of earth, heaven's four seasons parallel the four human limbs and so on. All phenomena are constituted of varying densities of *qi*, the vital energy/matter, and each has an inherent nature that determines its physical form and provides the spontaneous tendencies for growth, development and response that arise during its lifetime (see QI). Because each thing has a characteristic type of *qi*, one of its 'five phases', it resonates (*ganying*) with other things of the same phase and is thus impelled to develop or act in certain ways when acted upon by other things; when the seasons change, as the planetary bodies revolve and so on. All phenomena, processes and events within the universe on both macrocosmic and microcosmic levels are included in this grand 'correlative' scheme. While all act spontaneously, responses are never random and chaotic; they occur according to the regular and predictable patterns that govern the cosmos. Finally, the entire cosmos is interfused by a singular dynamic force called the *dao* (Way), which is inherent in each phenomenon as its ultimate unifying and guiding principle (see DAO).

Because human beings and their societies are integral parts of this dynamic, interrelated whole, they are subject to its same governing principles. Hence the ruler must know these principles and how the various levels parallel and interact with one another, and must set up governmental and societal institutions to accord with them. Furthermore, after establishing a hierarchical bureaucracy filled by officials whose deeds correspond to their titles, the ruler must cultivate a profound tranquility through meditation that enables him to become unified with the *dao*. Emerging from this mystical unity, the ruler has developed a totally unbiased clarity of mind that enables him to 'take no action (*wuwei*) and leave nothing undone'. With his mental acuity and metaphysical insight into cosmic patterns and inherent natures, the ruler can develop suitable tasks and appropriate customs for his subjects that enable them to realize the fullest potential of their inherent natures, transform his subjects through a mysterious resonance of *qi*, and more generally govern in a benevolent and unbiased manner that brings order and harmony throughout the land. This is how things were in the distant past of the sage-rulers, but the world lost this harmony because people lost the understanding of the value of – and the ability to effect – this profound coordination of the cosmological with the political. The *Huainanzi* was written to provide the ruler with the means to restore this harmony.

See also: CHINESE PHILOSOPHY; CONFUCIAN PHILOSOPHY, CHINESE; DAOIST PHILOSOPHY; GUANZI; LEGALIST PHILOSOPHY, CHINESE; LI; MACHIAVELLI, N.; POLITICAL PHILOSOPHY, HISTORY OF; QI

List of works

Liu An [Huainanzi] (179–122 BC) *Huainanzi*, Sibu congkan edition, Shanghai: The Commercial Press, 1920; ed. Haruki Kusuyama, *Enanji*, Shunyaku kambun taikei edition, Tokyo: Meiji Shoin, 1979–88, 3 vols; ed. D.C. Lau and Chen Fong Ching in *A Concordance to the Huainanzi*, The Institute of Chinese Studies Ancient Chinese Texts Concordance Series, Hong Kong: The Commercial Press, 1992. (There are over eighty-five complete and thirty partial editions of the *Huainanzi* in Chinese and Japanese; details are given in Roth (1992). Of the three mentioned here, the Sibu congkan edition is the best of the traditional Chinese editions and is ultimately based on an eleventh-century printed edition of the text. Kusuyama contains an excellent critical Chinese edition together with a modern Japanese translation. Lau and Chen provide a computer-coordinated concordance of all the words in the text as well as one of the best new critical editions. English translations of portions of the Huainanzi are to be found in various works; see Ames 1983, Larre, Robinet and Rochat 1993, LeBlanc 1985, Major 1993, Wallacker 1962.)

References and further reading

Ames, R. (1983) *The Art of Rulership: A Study in Ancient Chinese Political Thought*, Honolulu, HI: University of Hawaii Press. (A careful and readable translation of *Huainanzi* 9, the essay on political theory, that contains a valuable analysis of the philosophical background of its key ideas.)

Graham, A.C. (1986) *Yin–Yang and the Nature of Correlative Thinking*, IEAP Occasional Paper and Monograph Series 6, Singapore: Institute for East Asian Philosophies. (This is a comprehensive and sophisticated analysis of the correlative thinking that produced the cosmology of *yin* and *yang* and the five phases of *qi* that is so important to the *Huainanzi*.)

Larre, C., Robinet, I. and Rochat de la Vallée, E. (1993) *Les grand traités du Huainan zi*, Paris: Les Éditions du Cerf. (Contains translations of the *Huainanzi* chapters 1, 7, 11, 13 and 18.)

LeBlanc, C. (1985) *Huai-Nan Tzu: Philosophical Synthesis in Early Han Thought*, Hong Kong: Hong Kong University Press. (A heavily annotated translation of *Huainanzi* 6, 'Peering Into the Mysterious', that contains an excellent discussion of the concept of resonance).

Major, J.S. (1993) *Heaven and Earth in Early Han Thought*, Albany, NY: State University of New York Press. (This is an annotated translation of the three most technical essays in the *Huainanzi*, 3, 4 and 5, on the topics of astronomy, geography and seasonal ordinances, accompanied by excellent introductory chapters on the philosophy of the *Huainanzi* in the context of Huang–Lao thought and on early Han cosmology.)

Roth, H.D. (1991) 'Psychology and Self-Cultivation in Early Taoistic Thought', *Harvard Journal of Asiatic Studies* 51 (2): 599–650. (An analysis of the *Huainanzi*'s theories on self-cultivation and their background.)

—— (1992) *The Textual History of the Huai-nan Tzu*, Ann Arbor, MI: Association for Asian Studies Monograph 46. (A comprehensive study of the history and transmission of the text of the *Huainanzi* that includes an introduction to its thought and the circumstances of its creation.)

Wallacker, B. (1962) *Huai-nan Tzu, Book Eleven: Behavior, Culture, and Cosmos*, New Haven, CN: The American Oriental Society. (This is a translation of the *Huainanzi* essay on social customs and human nature with a brief introduction.)

H.D. ROTH

HUET, PIERRE-DANIEL (1630–1721)

Huet was a French Catholic bishop who wrote important works in theology, philology and literary criticism. In philosophy, he defended an apologetic interpretation of scepticism and opposed Cartesianism, which he thought to be a fanatical form of rationalism. For Huet, faith must guide reason since only the former, received from God, can provide absolute certainty, whereas human knowledge is inevitably fallible. A moderate scepticism is therefore the most appropriate attitude for a philosopher, since it tempers the ambitious claims of reason and extricates the mind from prejudices and false certainties, thus preparing it to receive the divine gift of faith.

1 Life
2 Anti-Cartesianism
3 Scepticism

1 Life

Pierre-Daniel Huet was considered one of the most learned men of his time. Born in Normandy, he was educated by the Jesuits and acquired a remarkable knowledge of Latin, Greek and mathematics while still very young. In Paris, he studied Hebrew and became deeply interested in the philosophy of DE-SCARTES. In 1652, he travelled with his friend Samuel Bochart to Holland and Sweden, where the latter had been invited by Queen Christina, and had the opportunity to meet Henricus REGIUS, Claude Saumaise and Isaac Vossius. After his return to Paris, he became acquainted with GASSENDI, and in 1661 he founded a scientific academy in Caen which is still active. At the age of forty, Huet was elected tutor of the Dauphin Louis, son of Louis XIV, under Jacques Bossuet's direction. He began to edit the famous series of Classics *ad usum Delphini* and became member of the *Académie Française* in 1674. Ordained two years later, he was bishop of Avranches from 1689 when he published the *Censura philosophiae cartesianae*, a meticulous critique of Descartes' philosophy. In 1690, he published the *Alnetanae quaestiones de concordia rationis et fidei*, a theological treatise in which he argues that no truth or ultimate certainty can be reached without the help of faith. This was preparatory to the most famous of Huet's philosophical books, the *Traité philosophique de la faiblesse de l'esprit humain* (1723), which he seems to have considered his best work. Huet died in Paris, and his collection of more than 8,000 volumes, many bearing his annotations, later became part of the Bibliothèque

Nationale. His anti-Cartesianism attracted much attention and, soon after his work was published, defences of Cartesianism were written against him by Andreas Petermann, Pierre-Sylvain RÉGIS, Joannes Schotanus, Burchard de Volder and, in 1745, by Lodovico Antonio Muratori.

2 Anti-Cartesianism

Huet treats Cartesianism as merely another philosophical school attempting to restore the old mistakes of dogmatism. The importance Descartes ascribes to the sceptical approach is highly valuable, but his positive principles are all erroneous. First, the firmness of the 'Ego cogito, ergo sum' is deceptive for a number of reasons:

1 It is a mere tautology – either the 'ego' in the expression 'ego cogito' is meaningless, or it refers to something that already exists. But then the whole statement says nothing more than 'I exist and I am something that thinks; whatever exists and is something that thinks, exists; therefore I exist', and this is of course a true, but non-informative tautology.
2 It is not logically prior to, or more simple than, any other form of knowledge – it requires, at least, that one understands the principle 'whatever thinks, exists', and may be capable of using it as the premise of the relevant syllogism.
3 Its acceptance is inconsistent with the strategy of radical and systematic doubt – if Descartes can use the natural light to grasp the truth that whatever thinks exists, then why can the natural light not be employed to affirm other principles equally obvious, as that the whole is bigger than the part?
4 It is not immediate – the *Cogito* is a syllogism, and hence to be formulated requires a process of successive inferences, the correct application of logical principles and a reliable memory.

Second, the criterion of truth is established only via a vicious circle (see DESCARTES, R. §§5–7). We can trust that our clear and distinct ideas lead from the certainty of a belief to its truth if and only if there is a veridical God, but we can prove as true the existence of a veridical God only by relying on the certainty of our clear and distinct ideas.

Third, it is false that we know the mind before, and better than, the body, since the two are united, and Descartes' intellectualism (we are our minds, not our bodies) is wrong because mind and body are indivisible. The body, and not the mind, perceives the physical objects, and the mind without the perceptual experience of the body would be empty, since we have no innate ideas, but only particular ideas made more general by abstraction.

Fourth, God's existence cannot be proved by reason. We possess only a finite and imperfect collection of ideas about God's nature, acquired via a negative procedure of amplification of what we know to be positive and exclusion of what we know to be negative in the world. We cannot rise from this inadequate description, whose origin is thoroughly dependent on our minds, to the necessary existence of its reference, with the certainty of a logical proof.

3 Scepticism

The Cartesian edifice therefore collapses and can be replaced by a moderate form of scepticism, to which Huet ascribes an apologetic function. The process of knowing consists of four stages: the Understanding receives perceptual impressions from physical objects, transforms them into image-like ideas, compares ideas and objects, and evaluates their correspondence. We know the truth when we know both the idea and that the idea perfectly corresponds to the object. Thus the level of certainty of our knowledge depends on the level of reliability of each of the previous stages, which Huet claims to be rather low, again for several reasons:

1 Since there is a gap between a physical object, as the source of knowledge, and its idea, as a mental product, knowledge of things is only indirect. Yet (a) everything changes constantly, including the known object, the impressions, and the knowing Understanding; (b) the senses are unreliable; (c) the Understanding is fallible; and (d) the Understanding modifies the impressions coming from the senses (Huet himself anatomized some animals, concluding that the nerve-channels are such that they must modify the impressions when they run through them.) Therefore, it is impossible to verify that internal ideas really correspond to external objects, and any description of the physical world remains at most verisimilar, but is never utterly certain.
2 It is impossible to demonstrate, by mere reflection, that the Understanding is capable of certainties, without falling into a *petitio principii*; but we can analyse the Understanding only by relying on the Understanding itself, thus falling into a vicious circle.
3 Knowledge of something *per genus et differentiam* (for example, to know man as the rational animal) is impossible. We know the genus of x if and only if we know both its essence and how it is similar to y, where y belongs to a different species but the same

genus (for example, man and horse are two species belonging to the same genus, animal). Therefore, in order to provide the definition of x it is necessary to begin by knowing the essence of both x and y, but for this purpose it is necessary to know the genus of both, thus falling into a vicious circle. The same applies to the use of the notion of difference: in order to establish that x is different from y, we must first know both x and y, but such knowledge is based on the possibility of applying the notion of difference in order to have a definition of both.

4 Nobody can be certain that everybody else has the same impressions, or the same ideas on the same things. Moreover, the very notion of evidence is relative. People in different states (ill, drunk, sleeping, hungry, worried and so forth) perceive the world in different and irreconcilable ways. Perhaps Descartes was right: we do not know whether God – whose omnipotence is interpreted as boundless – has wished to create us so imperfect as to err always. What seems clear is that there is total disagreement about the nature of knowledge and truth even among the Dogmatists.

5 In order to know x adequately, we must also know the causes of x, but this leads to an infinite regress, for everything depends on something else, and the Understanding is incapable of omniscience.

6 We have no objective and uncontroversial criterion of truth. Huet distinguishes three meanings of criterion: the *criterium duquel* (the knowing subject); the *criterium par lequel* (the senses and the Understanding); and the *criterium selon lequel* (the action of the Understanding, when it applies the *criteria par lequel* in the search of truth.) But we have seen that human nature is unreliable, the senses and the Understanding are not sources of certainty and, with respect to the *criterium selon lequel*, if the faculties are unreliable then so is their action. The problem is that in order to find a proper criterion of truth we must already possess one.

7 Reasonings are always uncertain, and even simple syllogisms beg the question. For example, from the two premises 'all men are rational animals' and 'Peter is a man' we infer that 'Peter is a rational animal', but the first premise depends on inductive reasoning – every man examined so far has been a rational animal. So the inference is hypothetically certain (given the premise the conclusion follows necessarily), but the knowledge so achieved is still questionable, for God could create a man who is not rational. Syllogisms remain the best weapons of the dogmatists, but they become harmless if one rejects their premises.

From all these arguments, Huet concludes that all forms of *human certainty* – in descending order, the certainty provided by God's words, mathematical certainty, perceptual certainty, and finally moral certainty (the certainty we have about what we have not experienced personally) – are inevitably bound within the limits of our capacities, and relative to our subjective condition. The Understanding can formulate plausible beliefs, but it necessarily remains unknown whether they represent true knowledge. It is possible to achieve total certainty only when there is direct and complete access to the intrinsic nature of things, but this happens only to the blessed souls who, illuminated by God, know with divine certainty and reassurance what, in the best case, we can believe only with limited confidence. While awaiting the acquisition of such a spiritual state, a probabilistic form of scepticism remains the most desirable attitude for a human being. As the origin of all philosophy, scepticism teaches us how to avoid epistemic errors, makes us more critical and independent of intellectual authorities, helps us to accept from every past philosopher whatever looks more acceptable and probable (eclecticism) and, above all, prepares the mind for the divine gift of faith.

Huet is aware of the classic arguments against scepticism. To the philosophers (Plato, Proclus and Descartes) who defend the presence of innate knowledge in the Understanding, he replies that they forget that nothing is in the mind which was not previously in the senses (see PLATO §13; PROCLUS). Universals are acquired from particular ideas: sometimes one particular idea is elected as a general prototype (one particular triangle stands for all triangles), sometimes a general idea is the result of a process of abstraction from a collection of particular ideas (as happens with the idea of movement), but in any case we have no innate knowledge and no ultimate certainties. It is often argued, on the ethical side, that scepticism makes life impossible, is irreligious – because it suggests that God is deceitful, since he makes us incapable of knowledge – and undermines the possibility of developing any sort of belief, including faith in God, thus advancing the moral corruption of man. Huet rejoins that scepticism inclines us to avoid fanaticism and to follow the customs and habits of our time, without fully committing ourselves to anything but a reasonable trust in Christian religion. God has created us limited and weak, but free to give or withhold our assent to opinions. It is only our fault if we give precipitous assent to superficial opinions, and hence err. Scepticism does not lead to atheism. On the contrary, the recognition of the limits of our Understanding helps us to acquire faith. Since knowledge of God is not discursive, acquired by the Understanding with a spontaneous act, but intuitive and given by God to the soul as a free and generous gift, it is not epistemic and hence remains unaffected by sceptical doubts. This explains why, according to Huet, Christian religion appreciates scepticism, although it must be noted that most of the passages he quotes – from Wisdom, Ecclesiastes, Paul, Augustine, Aquinas, and many others – were meant to undermine intellectual pride, not human confidence in ordinary knowledge. Scepticism can be criticized on the epistemological side because it undermines all sciences, the greatest human achievement; because it either begs the question – since it presupposes a criterion to distinguish what is certain from what is only probable, and what is true from what is false, so, after all, the sceptic knows something – or it is self-contradictory, for it denies all knowledge and discredits the validity of all possible reasonings, including its own; and finally, because it does not lead to a systematic philosophy. Huet retorts that faith, not science, is the greatest human achievement, and the sceptic is not to be blamed because he reveals the embarrassing weakness of the Understanding. The dogmatist is hopeless, for he seeks truth through science, whereas the sceptic is happy with his probable opinions, makes no mistakes and is open to the religious message. Indeed, many people have become dogmatists rather than sceptics only because they are lazy, wishing to enjoy their ignorance without searching further. Descartes is one of them. He is ambitious and – although he has taken most of his ideas from ancient philosophers – he has ostracized erudition, cultural tradition and historical knowledge, thus removing the only basis for the collaborative construction of a body of verisimilar opinions. Scepticism is not self-contradictory either, because it eliminates even its own certainties, and follows only the most likely appearances. The sceptic is like Samson, who destroys the temple of dogmatic presuppositions and himself. Finally, scepticism does not give rise to an ordinary sect, but to the 'philosophy of not philosophizing', as Lactantius called it, which can nevertheless become fairly systematic, as SEXTUS EMPIRICUS showed.

See also: PASCAL, B.; PYRRHONISM; SCEPTICISM, RENAISSANCE

List of works

Huet, P.D. (1679) *Demonstratio evangelica*, Paris; 2nd edn, 1680. (An attempt to prove the principles of Christian religion by means of an axiomatic apparatus. 'Praefatio' section 3, and 'Axiomata' IV sections 2 and 3 contain an interesting, sceptical philosophy of mathematics. The revised 1680 edition is more important.)

—— (1689) *Censura philosophiae cartesianae*, Paris; repr. Hildesheim, New York: G. Olms, 1971. (The sceptical reply to Descartes' *Meditations*. The first edition was printed by Kampen in 1690, but the work was printed and re-edited several times. The fourth revised and augmented edition of 1694 is the most important.)

—— (1690) *Alnetanae quaestiones de concordia rationis et fidei*, Paris; repr. Leipzig, 1692. (This work, which takes its name from Alnay, Huet's abbey, is a bridge from Huet's anti-Cartesianism as a form of dogmatic and impious rationalism, to his moderate scepticism, in which the process of systematic doubt becomes preparatory to the acquisition of faith.)

—— (1692) *Nouveaux mémoires, pour servir à l'histoire du cartésianisme*, Paris; important 3rd edn, Paris: R. Mazieres, 1711. (Published under the name of Gilles de l'Aunay, this is a satire in which Huet presents a caricature of Descartes and derides, rather wittily but superficially, his philosophical positions.)

—— (1718) *Commentarius de rebus ad eum pertinentibus*, Amsterdam; trans. as *Memoirs of the life of Peter Daniel Huet, bishop of Avranches, written by himself*, London: Longman, Hurst, Rees, & Orme, and Cadell & Davies, 2 vols, 1810. (Huet's autobiography.)

—— (1723) *Traité philosophique de la faiblesse de l'esprit humain*, Amsterdam; repr. Hildesheim, New York: G. Olms, 1974; trans. as *An essay concerning the weakness of the Human Understanding*, London, 1725; and as *A philosophical treatise concerning human understanding*, London, 1729. (Written in 1690 but published posthumously, this combines ancient, sceptical arguments with the anti-intellectualist perspective of the Pauline tradition and the Neoplatonist distrust of empirical knowledge, to attack Cartesianism as the latest form of dogmatism.)

References and further reading

Alberti, A. (1978) 'Lo Scetticismo Apologetico di Pierre Daniel Huet', *Giornale Critico della Filosofia Italiana* 9: 210–37. (Suggests, but does not develop, the thesis that the *Censura*, the *Alnetanae Questiones* and the *Traité* are three parts of a unique anti-Cartesian and apologetic project. The comparison of Huet's position to Mersenne's gives too little space to the former.)

Aubry, D. (1944) *Daniel Huet*, Paris: La Bonne Presse. (An odd companion, in which Huet's remarks on his life, studies and ideas are selected and reorganized alphabetically and by topic.)

Brown, H. (1934) *Scientific Organization in 17th century France*, Baltimore, MD: Russell & Russell, repr. 1967. (Pages 216–27 discuss Huet's scientific interests.)

Cabeen, D.C. and Brody, J. (eds) (1961) *A Critical Bibliography of French Literature*, vol. 3, *The Seventeenth Century*, ed. N. Edelman, Syracuse, NY: Syracuse University Press. (Some of the most important works published on Huet before 1960 are listed with comments.)

Dini, A. (1987) 'Anticartesianesimo e apologetica in Pierre-Daniel Huet', *Rivista di Storia e Letteratura Religiosa* 23: 222–39. (A well-documented analysis of Huet's interest in Descartes and of his later *Censura*, which subordinates Huet's scepticism to his anti-Cartesianism.)

Flottes, J.B.M. (1857) *Étude sur Daniel Huet, évêque d'Avranches*, Montpellier: F. Seguin. (Credibly defends Huet from the charge of being a Pyrrhonian. It summarizes Huet's *Démonstration*, *Censure*, *Questions* and *Traité*, attempting to present him as a systematic writer.)

Guellouz, S. (ed.) (1994) *Pierre-Daniel Huet, 1630–1721: Actes du Colloque de Caen 12–13 novembre 1993*, Biblio 17, *Suppléments aux Papers on French Seventeenth Century Literature*, Paris. (Includes twenty-two contributions, covering many aspects of Huet's biography, interests, intellectual production and latter fortune, it includes an extended and updated bibliography.)

Henry, C. (1879) *Un érudit homme du monde, homme d'église, homme de cour*, Paris: Librairie Hachette. (A selection of Huet's correspondence.)

Malbreil, G. (1985) 'Les droits de la raison et de la foi, la dissociation de la raison, la métamorphose de la foi, selon P.D. Huet', *Dix-septieme Siècle* 147: 119–33. (Reconstructs various interpretations of Huet's philosophy and, by focusing on the *Alnetanae Quaestiones*, defends an apologetic rather than a fideistic view of his Christian scepticism.)

—— (1991) 'Descartes censuré par Huet', *Revue Philosophique de la France et de l'Etranger* 116: 311–28. (Accurate, historical study of Huet's critique of Descartes, as presented in the *Censura* and the *Nouveaux memoires*, with ample references to the debate between Huet and Regis.)

Massimi, J.-R. (1985) 'Vérité et histoire chez P.D. Huet', *Dix-septieme Siècle* 147: 167–8. (A review of the Demonstratio suggesting that, for Huet, truth is discovered by investigating the sources of our present beliefs and customs in the past.)

McKenna, A. (1985) 'Huet and Pascal', *Dix-septieme Siècle* 147: 135–42. (A philological and comparative study based on Huet's remarks on the margins of his copy of Pascal's *Pensées*. It focuses mainly on the *Demonstratio*.)

Neto, J.R.M. and Popkin, R.H. (1995) 'Bishop Pierre-Daniel Huet's Remarks on Pascal', *British Journal for the History of Philosophy* 3: 147–60. (The first half of the paper presents a standard summary of Huet's scepticism interpreted in terms of religious fideism; the second half contains a more interesting analysis of Huet's *marginalia*. The authors conclude that Huet's humanistic and naturalistic Christianity presents a vision of the human situation that is both existentially and religiously much less dramatic than Pascal's Augustinianism.)

Rodis-Lewis, G. (1985) 'Huet lecteur de Malebranche', *Dix-septieme Siècle* 147: 169–89. (Much information on Huet's library, especially the philosophical books, together with a philological collection and reconstruction of his remarks on Malebranche.)

Sciacca, G.M. (1968) *Scetticismo Cristiano*, Palermo: Palumbo. (Reconstructs Huet's cultural milieu, and provides two long paraphrases of his *Traité* and Muratori's attack.)

Tolmer, L. (1949) 'Pierre-Daniel Huet (1630–1721) humaniste, physicien', *Mémoires de l'Académie nationale des sciences, arts et belles-lettres de Caen*, Nouvelle série, vol. 11. (Probably the most complete intellectual biography written so far, includes a wealth of interesting details on Huet's studies, his cultural milieu and his scientific activities.)

LUCIANO FLORIDI

HUGH OF ST VICTOR (d. 1141)

Hugh of St Victor initiated the teaching programme that distinguished the Parisian abbey of St Victor during the twelfth century. His teaching combined an ambitious programme of biblical exegesis with the construction of theological syntheses and the detailed subordination of a comprehensive philosophy to both. Hugh's principal works in theology are biblical commentaries of different kinds and a theological overview based on the notion of sacrament. His philosophical work include Epitome Dindimi in philosophiam *(Dindimus' Epitome of Philosophy) and, most importantly, the* Didascalicon de studio legendi *(Didascalion, or On the Study of Reading). This last book attempts to show how all human knowledge can be used as preparation for the study of the Christian Bible, which in turns leads to the contemplation of God.*

Hugh of St Victor initiated the project of teaching and writing that came to distinguish the abbey of St Victor in Paris during the twelfth century. He is, in that sense, the first 'Victorine' theologian. His teaching combined an ambitious program of biblical exegesis with the construction of theological syntheses and the detailed subordination of philosophy to both.

The abbey of St Victor grew out of the community founded by WILLIAM OF CHAMPEAUX on his retreat from the Parisian schools of theology in 1108. William brought to the community customs of learning, but no distinctive theological or philosophical project. On his consecration as bishop in 1113, William secured for the small group a significant endowment and a royal charter permitting the free election of an abbot.

When Hugh entered the abbey sometime between 1115 and 1118, it had already begun a thorough reform of monastic life under its first real leader, Gilduin. It was thus ready to receive the kind of intellectual definition Hugh's work and his legacy would bring. Indeed, Hugh was a pioneer in each of the several fields that would become distinctive of the abbey, even as he brought it considerable renown as a school. Hugh himself served as the abbey's prior from 1133, and he died in 1141 within the community.

Hugh's study and teaching ranged widely. Indeed, he could be admired by someone such as BONAVENTURE just for the breadth of his education. One important group of his writings consists of scriptural interpretations. Hugh wrote three works in which he unfolded the image of Noah's ark into a paradigm of the stages of contemplation. Since the image of the ark is treated in enormous detail as a visual image, Hugh's tropological reading may also have had some influence on the aesthetics of Gothic art. However, Hugh also practised a kind of literal interpretation that put a premium on historical accuracy and made ample use of contemporary Jewish exegesis. One instance of his literal interpretation is a *Chronica* (Chronicle) in which he outlines the rational order of Hebrew history. This style of reading would be carried forward by Hugh's student, Andrew of St Victor. Hugh further undertook the construction of a unified or 'systematic' theology in his *De sacramentis christianae fidei* (On the Sacraments of the Christian Faith). This impulse to theological construction was continued by another of Hugh's followers, Richard of St Victor, who knew of Hugh only through his writings. Hugh also produced a number of spiritual writings in more traditional genres, as well as sermons and letters.

Hugh produced several works that can be counted philosophical. There are, for example, introductory treatises on the liberal arts. One of these, *Epitome*

Dindimi in philosophiam (Dindimus' Epitome of Philosophy), is a short dialogue that lays out definitions and divisions of philosophy for the beginner. It can serve to show how broadly Hugh understands philosophy. He divides philosophy into four parts: logic, ethics, theory and mechanics. Logic comprises grammar and the rule of inference (*ratio disserendi*), which is in turn divided into probable, necessary and sophistical reasoning. Ethics comprises the solitary or individual, the domestic or economic and the public or political. Theory covers mathematics, physics and theology, which here means not Christian doctrine but the study of immaterial beings. In last place, Hugh incorporates what he calls 'mechanics'. Here he means not only technologies such as weaving or techniques such as navigation, but medicine and even theatre. Hugh seems the first Latin author to make 'mechanics' a part of philosophy (see NATURAL PHILOSOPHY, MEDIEVAL).

The disposition of the parts of philosophy and their subordination to Christian ends is accomplished more fully in Hugh's *Didascalicon de studio legendi* (Didascalion, or On the Study of Reading), which must be regarded as his masterpiece in philosophy. In accord with current taste, Hugh borrows for his title the Greek term *didascalicon*, which he probably takes to mean the art of teaching. His *Didascalicon* is, indeed, a work that teaches what, when, and how to read for the sake of a well-formed wisdom. The *Didascalicon* is divided into two parts, each of which has three Books. The first part concerns philosophy and all its parts, which are distinguished much as they were in the *Epitome*. The second part, which finds no correspondence in the *Epitome*, concerns the reading of 'holy writings', which are principally but not exclusively found in the Christian Bible.

The treatment of philosophy in the *Didascalicon* is considerably more detailed than in the *Epitome*. Here Hugh provides not just descriptions of each part of philosophy, but remarks on their founders or principal authors and on the sequence of study. Throughout, he follows traditional sources. He seems mostly uninfluenced by the pieces of Arabic science that were beginning to find their way into Latin learning (see TRANSLATORS). More importantly, Hugh here reiterates an Augustinian account of how the various moments in the study of philosophy adumbrate a unified wisdom in which 'the form of the complete good' is grasped (see AUGUSTINIANISM). This wisdom is, of course, Christian. The study of 'holy writings' both completes and corrects the study of philosophy. Hugh introduces the second part of the *Didascalicon* by comparing the writings of philosophers to a whitewashed wall that covers over the clay of error with seeming truth. The Christian Bible, by contrast, is like a honeycomb: dry on the outside, filled with sweetness within.

The second part of the *Didascalicon* is in this way something more than an introduction to biblical study. It does contain a number of chapters on the levels of scriptural meaning, as on the canon and the rules for resolving ambiguous interpretations. However, it directs these materials to a practice of meditation in which scriptural reading is enacted as communion with God. This communion is the Christian's philosophy. Indeed, the person whom Hugh calls the 'Christian philosopher' turns out to be a monk reading scripture prayerfully. 'The monk's simplicity is his philosophy', and the monk's 'philosophizing' is not academic disputation, but delight in learning from scripture the life of virtue.

See also: RICHARD OF ST VICTOR

List of works

Hugh of St Victor (1118–25?) *Practica geometriae* (Practice of Geometry), in R. Baron (ed.) *Hugonis de Sancto Victore Opera propaedeutica*, Notre Dame, IN: University of Notre Dame Press, 1966; trans. F.A. Homann, *Practical Geometry*, Milwaukee, WI: Marquette University Press, 1991. (An introduction to applied plane geometry.)

—— (1118–25?) *De grammatica* (On Grammar), in R. Baron (ed.) *Hugonis de Sancto Victore Opera propaedeutica*, Notre Dame, IN: University of Notre Dame Press, 1966. (An introduction to the elements of Latin grammar.)

—— (1118–25?) *Epitome Dindimi in philosophiam* (Dindimus' Epitome of Philosophy), in R. Baron (ed.) *Hugonis de Sancto Victore Opera propaedeutica*, Notre Dame, IN: University of Notre Dame Press, 1966. (An introduction to the scope and rudimentary principles of philosophy most broadly conceived.)

—— (1120–5) *Didascalicon de studio legendi* (Didascalicon, or On the Study of Reading), ed. C.H. Buttimer, Washington, DC: Catholic University of America Press, 1939; trans. J. Taylor, *Didascalicon: A Medieval Guide to the Arts*, New York: Columbia University Press, 1961. (Taylor's translation contains an ample introduction and very rich notes.)

—— (1130–3) *De sacramentis christianae fidei* (On the Sacraments of the Christian Faith), Patrologia Latina 176: 173–618; trans. R.J. Deferrari, *On the Sacraments of the Christian Faith*, Cambridge, MA: Mediaeval Academy of America, 1951. (Hugh's magisterial survey of the foundations of Christian faith and life.)

—— (before 1141) *Chronica* (Chronicle), partial edn in L.B. Mortensen, 'Hugh of St Victor on Secular History: A Preliminary Edition of Chapters from His *Chronica*', *Cahiers de l'Institut du Moyen Âge Grec et Latin* 62, 1992: 3–30. (An edition of a portion of Chapter 3 and Chapter 9 from a single manuscript.)

References and further reading

Baron, R. (1957) *Science et Sagesse chez Hugues de Saint-Victor* (Knowledge and Wisdom in Hugh of St Victor), Paris: Lethielleux. (A general introduction to Hugh's writings.)

Châtillon, J. (1992) *Le mouvement canonial au Moyen Age: Réforme de l'Église, spiritualité et culture* (The Movement of Canons in the Middle Ages: Reform of the Church, Spirituality and Culture), ed. P. Sicard, Paris and Turnhout: Brepols. (An anthology of earlier essays, several of them devoted to Hugh.)

Ehlers, J. (1973) *Hugo von St Victor: Studien zum Geschichtsdenken und der Geschichtsschreibung des 12. Jahrhunderts* (Hugh of St Victor: Studies on the Concepts of History and Historiography in the Twelfth Century), Wiesbaden: Steiner. (Studies of Hugh's concept of history and practice of historiography.)

Girolimon, M.T. (1994) 'Hugh of St Victor's *De sacramentis Christianae fidei*', *Journal of Religious History* 18 (2): 127–138. (A useful introduction to the intention of Hugh's work on the sacraments.)

Goy, R. (1976) *Die Überlieferung der Werke Hugos von St Viktor* (The Transmission of the Works of Hugh of St Victor), Stuttgart: Hiersemann, 1976. (A very detailed scholarly study of the authenticity of the corpus attributed to Hugh.)

Illich, I. (1993) *In the Vineyard of the Text: A Commentary to Hugh's Didascalicon*, Chicago, IL: University of Chicago Press. (A free meditation on Hugh's *Didascalicon*; not to be used as an accurate paraphrase of the text.)

Van den Eynde, D. (1960) *Essai sur la succession et la date des écrits de Hugues de St-Victor* (Essay on the Sequence and Date of Writings of Hugh of St Victor), Rome: Pontificium Athenaeum Antonianum. (A carefully reasoned hypothesis about the chronology of Hugh's writings; not universally accepted.)

MARK D. JORDAN

HUMAN NATURE

Every political philosophy takes for granted a view of human nature, and every view of human nature is controversial. Political philosophers have responded to this conundrum in a variety of ways. Some have defended particular views of human nature, while others have sought to develop political philosophies that are compatible with many different views of human nature, or, alternatively, which rest on as few controversial assumptions about human nature as possible. Some political philosophers have taken the view that human nature is an immutable given, others that it is shaped (in varying degrees) by culture and circumstance. Differences about the basic attitudes of human beings toward one another – whether selfish, altruistic or some combination – have also exercised political philosophers. Although none of these questions has been settled definitively, various advances have been made in thinking systematically about them.

Four prominent debates concern: (1) the differences between perfectionist *views, in which human nature is seen as malleable, and* constraining *views, in which it is not; (2) the* nature/nurture *controversy, which revolves around the degree to which human nature is a consequence of biology as opposed to social influence, and the implications of this question for political philosophy; (3) the opposition between* self-referential *and* other-referential *conceptions of human nature and motivation – whether we are more affected by our own condition considered in itself, or by comparisons between our own condition and that of others; and (4) attempts to detach philosophical thought about political association from all controversial assumptions about human nature.*

1 Perfectionist versus constraining views of human nature
2 The nature/nurture controversy
3 Self-referential versus other-referential conceptions of human nature
4 'Political' versus 'metaphysical' conceptions of human nature

1 Perfectionist versus constraining views of human nature

The most celebrated proponent of perfectionist views of human nature is ARISTOTLE, and his most elaborate discussion of the question appears in *The Nicomachean Ethics* (perhaps *c.*330 BC). Aristotle's view developed there is sometimes described as teleological because it was defined by reference to a fundamental contrast between untutored or brute

human nature on the one hand, and human nature as it could be if we realized our essential nature or *telos* on the other. Ethics, for Aristotle, is the science that instructs us how to get from the one to the other. When correctly employed, ethical precepts thus have the potential to transform human beings from their rude and untutored states into the best kinds of beings they can become.

Although there is both room and need for human nature to develop and change on Aristotle's view, his is a *naturalist* one in that both the accounts of brute human nature and perfected human nature are rooted in a philosophical psychology, a theory of natural human needs and potentials. Naturalist views are generally distinguished from *anti-naturalist* accounts, in which the sources of meaning and value for human beings are externally given, whether in Platonic forms, transcendental arguments about the nature of knowledge and obligation, or some other extrinsic origin. On anti-naturalist views what is good or right is good or right regardless of actual human needs and desires, whereas for naturalists the gulf between 'is' and 'ought' is bridged via an account of human needs or psychology (see NATURALISM IN ETHICS; NEEDS AND INTERESTS). Naturalist perfectionism can be secular or theologically-based; indeed, much medieval Christian Aristotelianism rested on the adaptation of the story of the Garden of Eden, the Fall from Grace, and the possibility of redemption to Aristotle's ethical categories. Marxism, on the other hand, is a secular version of naturalist perfectionism. For Marx, human beings as we find them are alienated from their 'true' selves, their potential stunted by a variety of malevolent forces. But these forces are in some sense artificial impediments to human flourishing that can be understood and ultimately vanquished, opening the way for authentic human development (Marx 1875) (see ALIENATION §6).

Although perfectionist views can be naturalist or anti-naturalist, constraining views of human nature are invariably naturalist in character. Proponents of constraining views regard human nature as an immutable given, holding that social and political institutions must take account of it but that have no effect on it. Perhaps the most extreme proponent of this view in the history of Western philosophy was Jeremy BENTHAM (§3), who made it an axiom of his utilitarian system that nature: 'has placed mankind under the governance of two sovereign masters, *pain* and *pleasure*' (1948: 125). For Bentham, pleasure seeking and pain avoidance 'govern us in all we do, in all we say, in all we think: every effort we can make to throw off our subjection, will serve but to demonstrate and confirm it' (1948: 125). Bentham believed that the utilitarian system he advocated was uniquely scientific in that it recognized our inescapable subjection to the pleasure/pain calculus.

Although Bentham offers one of the most forthright and clear accounts of a constraining view of human nature, his is by no means the first or the only such view in the history of Western political theory. In their modern form such views are traceable at least to Hobbes' insistence, *contra* Aristotle, that human nature is rigidly fixed. For Hobbes human beings are inescapably driven by a primordial fear of death, which produces in them a 'relentless desire for power after power'. Basic human impulses can be channelled in more and less productive ways, and to some extent people can be educated to see that certain political allegiances are better than others given their basic impulses, but the impulses themselves cannot be altered (Hobbes 1651) (see HOBBES, T. § 6).

Utilitarians since Bentham have generally regarded human nature as given and external to the operations of political and cultural institutions. Even if utilitarians have differed greatly from one another concerning the content of human nature and even how much we can reasonably aspire to know about its content, they have generally accepted Hume's dictum that 'reason is the slave of the passions'. Whereas Hume, like Bentham, thought we are all driven by the same passions in the same ways, neoclassical utilitarians of the late nineteenth and early twentieth centuries (such as Pareto 1970) questioned this assumption, taking a view of human nature that was perhaps most decisively stated by the emotivist philosopher Charles Stevenson in his critique of Hume: that even if we are convinced that all human beings are driven by needs for gratification of some sort, there is no decisive reason to think we all have the same such needs, or even that we can intelligently compare different desires experienced by different individuals with one another (Stevenson 1944). This is the standard view in modern economics and rational choice theories of politics: Preferences are thought of as exogenously determined, but the possibility of meaningful interpersonal comparisons of preferences across individuals is denied (see UTILITARIANISM; ECONOMICS AND ETHICS).

2 The nature/nurture controversy

Since time immemorial scientists and philosophers have debated the question whether human nature is biologically given or rather the result of contingencies of cultural and historical circumstance, and these debates have been thought to be pregnant with political significance. ROUSSEAU (§2), for example, was the first in a long line of political theorists who have argued that Hobbes' political system was based on a confusion of parochial traits that were the product of seventeenth-century English life with enduring features of the human condition. In Rousseau's view, Hobbes wrongly thought the impulse toward self-preservation was incompatible with a desire to preserve others: 'because of [his] having improperly included in the savage man's care of self-preservation the need to satisfy a multitude of passions which are the product of society' (1964: 129). Rousseau's own account of the state of nature has been criticized on analogous grounds however. Indeed it has become a standard move in modern political argument to question every assertion about natural human traits and propensities, however qualified or historicized, by arguing that the traits in question are socially produced or 'socially constructed'. Such debates can become exceedingly heated when they become embroiled in discussions of the determinants of intelligence and such things as ethnic, racial and gender differences (see SOCIOBIOLOGY).

The nature/nurture controversy is often confused with the issue of whether or not human nature is alterable by human design. It is often said, for instance, that much or all of human nature is socially constructed rather than naturally given, and that for this reason it should not be regarded as immutable. In fact, whether a given human characteristic is a product of nature or culture may have little to do with the degree to which it is alterable by conscious human design. On the one hand, there are many features of the natural world that human beings have effectively altered and will alter more in the future; the science of genetic engineering, for example, is presumably in its infancy. On the other hand, there are many pieces of human reality that, while indisputably the product of human action, we often seem powerless to influence. Ethnic hatred may be learned, for example, yet it may be impossible to get people to unlearn it or even to stop them passing it on to the next generation.

It is sometimes thought that cultural creations can be more easily understood than natural creations because they are the products of the human will. This view was common in the seventeenth century, for example, where philosophers like Hobbes and Locke, under the strong influence of the Cartesian idea that the reflective individual has privileged access to the contents of their own mind, held that only this individual can really know 'the ghost in the machine' in Gilbert Ryle's memorable phrase. Knowing one's own motivations and understanding one's behaviour guarantees nothing, however, about one's understanding of the complexities of human interaction in the social and political arena. In any case, in a post-Freudian age the Cartesian view must be regarded as questionable. We might be confused, or wrong, or we might deceive ourselves about our motivations and purposes. For all we know Bentham might have been right when he insisted that, 'it is with the anatomy of the human mind as with the anatomy and physiology of the human body: the rare case is, not that of a man's being unconversant, but of his being conversant with it' (1954, vol. III: 425). In short, the human capacity to shape human nature is a product of how well we can understand and control the causal mechanisms that lead human traits to be what they are. This is contingently related, if it is related at all, to whether a particular trait is a product of biology, culture, some combination of the two, or some third thing.

For all the attention it has received from political philosophers over the centuries, the nature/nurture controversy is a red herring in a second respect as far as politics is concerned. Since human beings are naturally conventional creatures who often achieve biological adaptation through social learning, the distinction between what is natural and what is cultural in human behaviour is not merely difficult to pin down in practice, but impossible to get at in principle. Perhaps partly for this reason, in recent years much of the discussion in Anglo-American political and moral philosophy has turned away from the nature/nurture debate and towards requiring principled justifications for any differences among persons that have political consequences, regardless of their origin. John RAWLS is perhaps more responsible for this than any other single figure. In *A Theory of Justice* (1971) he makes the case that differences in talents and abilities among persons, whether natural or cultural in origin, are 'morally arbitrary'; that is, they are products of luck either in the genetic lottery or in the milieu into which one happens to be born. In either case, the differences are not chosen or produced by actions for which the relevant agents can reasonably be held responsible. By the same token, it seems unfair that benefits should accrue to persons differentially in virtue of differences in their talents and abilities, whether such differences are rooted in nature, culture or both.

Making the Rawlsian move has the effect of socializing human capacities regardless of their origins (at least as a normative matter), and although it is exceedingly difficult to find a principled basis on which to resist his reasoning, it generates problems that are in many ways as difficult as those that it resolves. A person might find it both rationally undeniable and psychologically impossible to accept that nothing they do or achieve is the autonomous result of their own efforts. Analogously, it might be

argued that for both individual and species some fictions about individual responsibility for different outcomes may be required for human reproduction and wellbeing, even if we know them to be fictions. Such beliefs may be indispensable to the basic integrity of the human psyche and necessary for generating and sustaining the incentive to work on which human beings are, after all, critically reliant. As a result, although facts about moral luck and socially produced productive capacities conspire – when confronted – to enfeeble the idea of individual responsibility for outcomes, people may none the less be powerless to abandon it (see RESPONSIBILITY). One interesting strand of modern scholarship by Ronald Dworkin, Amartya Sen, Richard Arneson and others attempts to grapple with the issues raised by Rawls' discussion of moral arbitrariness, but it has not converged on any single or compelling conclusion (see DWORKIN, R.).

3 Self-referential versus other-referential conceptions of human nature

A third dimension along which conceptions of human nature vary concerns the degree to which people's interests are linked to the fortunes and perceptions of others. Contrast Ronald Reagan's 1984 election slogan: 'Are you better off now than you were four years ago?' with an employee who says to his employer 'I don't care what I get paid, so long as its more than Jones down the corridor'. The Reagan slogan is based on a *self-referential* conception of human nature; it assumes that people are interested in improving their own fortunes without any necessary reference to anyone else. The latter example is *other-referential*: a person's perception of their interests is intrinsically reliant on the welfare of others. We cannot make a judgment about their welfare without reference to the welfare of others. The distinction between self- and other-referential views operates independently of whether one is a subjectivist and of the basic metric of value along which welfare is judged. For instance, Marx's measure of exploitation is radically other-referential in that it is critically reliant on the proportion of the social surplus that the workers receive as compared with employers. Thus his technical measure of the rate of exploitation may increase even if real wages are increasing and the worker's subjective sense is that his welfare is improving. Rawls, on the other hand, works with a hybrid of self- and other-referential views of human nature in that he argues that rational people will always want to improve the lot of the worst-off individual in society, relative to what it was before, even if this means that who is the worst off changes.

523

Whether one thinks human nature is basically self- or other-referential has substantial implications for politics and distributive justice. Utilitarians, both classical and neoclassical, tend to think of people as self-referential maximizers who want to get on as high an indifference curve as possible without reference to anyone else, although there is no necessary reason that this be so. Aristotelians like Alasdair MacIntyre (1981), on the other hand, are necessarily committed to other-referential views. For them what people value above all is to be valued by others whom they value (see MACINTYRE, A.; RECOGNITION). 'She's a cellist's cellist' is an appellation we intuitively grasp, and to the extent that it captures something fundamental about what motivates people, models of individual maximization that ignore it will be descriptively misleading and morally unsatisfying. In this connection it is worth noting that in Hegel's (1807) *Phenomenology* the argument is made that slavery is an unstable set of social arrangements not merely because the slave can eventually be expected to resist oppression, but also because the master will find it unsatisfying; he needs recognition from someone whom he values (see HEGEL, G.W.F.).

Whether and to what extent human nature is substantially self-referential is not to be confused with whether and to what degree people are selfish. Although self-referentially motivated people may typically be indifferent – at best – to the fortunes of others, other-referential motivations may be more or less selfish. The demand to be paid 'more than Jones', 'the same as Jones' or 'less than Jones' are all other-referential in character, although they vary considerably on the dimension between selfish and altruistic motivation. Sadists and rapists exhibit what economists refer to as 'interdependent negative utilities' in that their wellbeing is intrinsically linked to the suffering of others; so too does the divorcing spouse whose utility increases if a dollar is taken out of the pocket of their spouse and burned. These are all other-referential types of motivation, no more or less than are the motivations of those who seek and experience increased happiness at another's happiness or success. In short, the self-referential/other-referential dimension refers to the structure of human psychology rather than its content. This is not to say that the structure has no implications for content. In particular, to the extent that people are other-referentially motivated, their behaviour and aspirations will tend not to be captured by rational agent models adapted from microeconomics, which rest exclusively on self-referential assumptions about human psychology. People who find arguments based on rational agent models unsatisfying descriptively or morally tend to be sceptical of the extent to which

self-referential assumptions capture important dimensions of the human condition. Whether or not such scepticism is warranted is in the end an empirical question; it will not be settled by armchair reflection (see RATIONAL CHOICE THEORY).

4 'Political' versus 'metaphysical' conceptions of human nature

Given the enduring – perhaps endemic – disagreements about human nature it is perhaps unsurprising that some political philosophers have sought to develop political theories assuming as little as possible about it. One strategy that has been extensively explored since the 1960s is to try to seek political principles that are neutral between different views of human nature and conceptions of the human good. Some of Rawls' earlier formulations of his project were understood thus, and Bruce Ackerman, Charles Larmore and others subsequently attempted to formulate different neutrality arguments (see NEUTRALITY, POLITICAL §§1, 4). By the 1990s a fairly broad consensus had begun to emerge that neutrality arguments fail, that there is no set of political principles that can be genuinely neutral among different conceptions of human nature and the human good, and that a little digging into allegedly neutral arguments will inevitably bring their assumptions to the surface.

A subtler response to the problem is to abandon the search for neutral political standards, but retain the ambition to develop political principles that may be compatible with as many different views of the human condition as possible. Here the key idea is to try to limit what one might reasonably expect of justification in political theory, and in particular to abandon all aspirations to get at the true or right theory of human nature. This is the strategy adopted by the later Rawls (1992), who asks: which political principles does it make most sense to agree on, given that we know we will never all agree on basic metaphysical questions about the human condition? The answer to which he is drawn is the one that tolerates as many conceptions of the human good as possible, consistent with a 'like liberty for all'. This approach explicitly abandons the agenda of coming up with right answers to questions about human nature, seeking only to tolerate as many answers as possible. It courts the possibility that it may actually lead us not to tolerate the 'true' view of human nature if, for instance, this is embedded only in a fundamentalist religion that also requires that no other views be tolerated. On a 'political not metaphysical' approach, we are not expected – as political theorists – to take any view on the question whether the fundamentalist view is correct; for all we know it might be. However, since we can never know that it is the correct view and we do know that there will always be competing views, it is never rational to accept it as governing our politics. Various difficulties confront this and other attempts to move in the 'political not metaphysical' direction, and some will find the philosophical abdication implied by this strategy impossible to live with. But in a world in which assumptions about human nature are both indispensable to politics and endemically controversial, it is difficult to see how the impulse to turn to institutional, rather than philosophical, solutions to the problems it creates can reasonably be resisted.

See also: XING; POLITICAL PHILOSOPHY, NATURE OF

References and further reading

* Aristotle (perhaps c.330 BC) *The Nicomachean Ethics*, trans. J.A.K. Thompson, Harmondsworth: Penguin, 1977. (The most mature and elaborate statement of Aristotle's ethical naturalism. A difficult work.)
Arneson, R. (1989) 'Equality and Equal Opportunity for Welfare', *Philosophical Studies* 56 (1): 77–93. (A utilitarian response to the moral arbitrariness inherent in the distribution of natural capacities. Moderately difficult.)
Ashcraft, R. (1987) *Locke's Two Treatises of Government*, London: Allen & Unwin. (An accessible introduction to Locke's views on human nature and natural law.)
* Bentham, J. (1948) *A Fragment on Government and An Introduction to the Principles of Morals and Legislation*, Oxford: Blackwell. (The *locus classicus* of Bentham's utilitarianism. Contains a programmatic statement of his assumptions about human nature, as well as applications in the fields of politics, law and economics. Easy to read despite arcane English.)
* —— (1954) *Jeremy Bentham's Economic Writings*, ed. W. Stark, London: Allen & Unwin, 3 vols. (The complete collection of all Bentham's writings on economics and economic psychology. Accessible.)
* Hegel G.W.F. (1807) *Phenomenology of Spirit*, trans. A.V. Miller, Oxford: Oxford University Press. (Chapter 4 contains the famous discussion of 'Lordship and Bondage' commented on in §3. A difficult work.)
* Hobbes, T. (1651) *Leviathan*, London: Pelican, 1968. (Part one contains the fullest statement of Hobbes' views about human nature. Easy to read despite arcane English.)
Locke, J. (1690) *Two Treatises of Government*, ed. P.

Laslett, Cambridge: Cambridge University Press, 1960. (The most elaborate statement of Locke's views on human nature and politics. Reasonably accessible.)
* MacIntyre, A. (1981) *After Virtue: An Essay in Moral Theory*, London: Duckworth. (A neo-Aristotelian theory of politics and human nature. Reasonably accessible.)
* Marx, K. (1875) *Critique of the Gotha Program*, Beijing: Foreign Language Publishers, 1972. (Contains Marx's most mature and elaborate attempt to distinguish human needs from human wants, and to develop the implications of this distinction for distributive justice under capitalism, socialism and communism. An accessible work.)
* Pareto, V. (1970) *Manual of Political Economy*, New York: Augustus Kelly. (The most elaborate statement ever developed of the logical bases of neoclassical utilitarianism. An exceedingly difficult work.)
* Rawls, J. (1971) *A Theory of Justice*, Cambridge, MA: Harvard University Press. (The most elaborate statement of Rawls' theory. The pertinent discussion of assumptions about human nature appears in chapter 7. A difficult work.)
* —— (1992) *Political Liberalism*, New York: Columbia University Press. (Contains Rawls' attempt to detach his theory more completely than in his earlier work from controversial assumptions about human nature. A difficult work.)
Riley, P. (1982) *Will and Political Legitimacy*, Cambridge, MA: Harvard University Press. (A useful and accessible survey of different views of the human will, and their implications for politics, in the Western tradition since the seventeenth century.)
* Rousseau, J.-J. (1964) *The First and Second Discourses*, ed. R. Masters, New York: St Martin's Press. (Contains Rousseau's celebrated critique of Hobbes' view of human nature as fixed, and defence of a developmental view in its stead.)
Shapiro, I. (1986) *The Evolution of Rights in Liberal Theory*, Cambridge: Cambridge University Press. (A history of changing conceptions of human nature in the Anglo-American tradition since the seventeenth century, and their implications for liberal theories of individual rights. Moderately accessible.)
—— (1991) 'Resources, Capacities and Ownership: The Workmanship Ideal and Distributive Justice', *Political Theory* 19 (1): 47–72. (A discussion of the origins and implications of the 'socialization of human capacities' discussed in this entry. Moderately accessible.)
* Stevenson, C.L. (1944) *Ethics and Language*, New Haven, CT: Yale University Press. (A critique of

Hume's assumption that human nature is invariant across individuals, developed in the course elaborating the controversial view that ethical propositions are no more than expressions of emotion. A moderately difficult work.)

IAN SHAPIRO

HUMAN NATURE, SCIENCE OF, IN THE 18TH CENTURY

Eighteenth-century speculation on human nature is distinguishable by its approach and underlying assumptions. Taking their cue from Francis Bacon and Isaac Newton, many philosophers of the Enlightenment endeavoured to extend the methods of natural science to the moral sciences. Perhaps the most explicit of such endeavours was David Hume's ambition for a 'science of man', but he was not alone. There was a general convergence on the idea that human nature is constant and uniform in its operating principles – that is, its determining motives (passions), its source of knowledge (sense experience) and its mode of operation (association of ideas). By virtue of this constancy human nature was predictable, so that once it was scientifically understood, then social institutions could be designed to effect desired outcomes.

David Hume regarded his proposed 'science of man' as fundamental because upon it depended not only logic, morals, criticism and politics but also even mathematics, natural philosophy and natural religion. Hence he believed that if that science is conquered then a relatively easy victory over the others can be expected. We know from Hume's own *Abstract* (1740) of the *Treatise of Human Nature* (1739–40) that he himself thought the most original element was the use made of the principle of the association of ideas. Hume identified three principles of association – resemblance, contiguity and causation (see HUME, D. §2). Starting from the Lockean premise that any inquiry into human nature must rely entirely upon experience, these principles operate uniformly for humans to bind the universe together. Just as there is, accordingly, a general course of nature with respect to the sun and climate, so there is in human actions; and just as there has been great success in the understanding of natural phenomena, so Hume aimed to emulate that success in the moral sciences through adopting its 'experimental' procedures. While this was Baconian in provenance (see BACON, F.), it was Newton's achievements that were more generally paradigmatic (see NEWTON, I.).

Newton himself had indicated the appropriateness of the endeavour when in Question 31 (1953: 179) of the *Opticks* (1730) he remarked that if the analytical method of natural philosophy is perfected then 'the bounds of moral philosophy will also be enlarged'. Since for Newton the key to natural philosophy lay in mathematics, one characteristic of the eighteenth-century attempt to establish a science of human nature was to subject the phenomena of human nature to quantification. Francis HUTCHESON, whom Hume identified as one of his predecessors in the scientific quest, flirted with this when he developed a calculus derived from certain simple axioms whereby $M = B \times A$ or the moment of good equals benevolence times ability (see Hutcheson 1725).

Although Hutcheson excised this calculus from later editions of the *Inquiry*, this quantitative and calculative concern persisted. Jeremy BENTHAM stated that we are governed by the two sovereign principles of pleasure and pain, and that it is the principle of utility that recognizes this subjection and employs it as the foundation of a system. The object of this system is to promote felicity, and to achieve that end with precision it is necessary to calculate which policies will produce a net balance of pleasure over pain. Armed with this scientific knowledge, the legislator will be able to pass laws that can be guaranteed to further the interests of the community. The view that this science should be useful is typical. Cesare Beccaria, in his argument for a reformed penal system (see Beccaria 1764), held that punishment should be determined with geometric precision, and that the probability of guilt amounts to moral certainty – something humans necessarily presuppose in daily life. The computation of such probability was undertaken by the Marquis de CONDORCET, by far the most sophisticated eighteenth-century social scientist.

Condorcet stands at the end of a significant French tradition, which, although there is a Cartesian ingredient, has a similar genealogy to that of the British. This is evident in Etienne Bonnot de CONDILLAC, the most systematic French writer. He too believed that moral reasoning was susceptible to the same exactitude as geometry, and also identified the association of ideas as the key to the study of human nature. Condillac sought to trace all 'ideas' to sensation thus rendering Locke's 'ideas of reflection' derivative. In his *Traité des sensations* (Treatise of Sensations) of 1754 he traced the development of a statue, such that by the addition of each of the senses in turn it came to possess the full range of human mental ability.

Any account of human nature seemingly has to distinguish the nature of humans from that of animals. Georges, Comte de BUFFON, who wrote the fullest scientific natural history (1749–89) in the eighteenth century, thought humans resembled animals materially but differed by virtue of possessing a soul, reason and language. It was a common task of the science of human nature to account for language 'naturally' by tracing its evolution from onomatopoeic interjections to grammatical abstractions, without recourse to divine interposition or rational direction. While Buffon retained a traditional account of human differentia, Julien Offroy de LA METTRIE argued that if animals were machines then, contrary to DESCARTES, there was no need to withhold that designation from humans. More explicitly Newtonian, David HARTLEY attempted to provide a physiological foundation for the association of ideas.

Leaving aside Hartley's own particular, ultimately religious, agenda, there is no reason to think Hume would find any incompatibility between that attempt and his own ambitions for a science of human nature; and it is those same ambitions that lie at the roots of contemporary social science.

See also: ENLIGHTENMENT, CONTINENTAL; ENLIGHTENMENT, SCOTTISH; HUMAN NATURE

References and further reading

Aarsleff, H. (1974) 'The Tradition of Condillac', in H. Hymes (ed.) *Studies in the History of Linguistics*, Bloomington, IN: Indiana University Press, 93–156. (An excellent survey of eighteenth-century speculation on language.)

Baker, K.M. (1975) *Condorcet: From Natural Philosophy to Social Mathematics*, Chicago, IL: University of Chicago Press. (Not only the best book on Condorcet but one of the richest on Enlightenment thought in general and social science in particular.)

* Beccaria, C. (1764) *On Crimes and Punishment*, trans. H. Paolucci, Indianapolis, IN: Library of Liberal Arts, 1963. (Most influential work on penology in the eighteenth century, especially for its attack on the death penalty and torture.)

* Bentham, J. (1789) *An Introduction to the Principles of Morals and Legislation*, ed. W. Harrison, Oxford: Blackwell, 1948. (His first attempt at systematizing and applying the 'principle of utility' to the end of social reform.)

Berry, C.J. (1982) *Hume, Hegel and Human Nature*, The Hague: Nijhoff. (Chapter 1 & Part II discuss respectively the account of human nature propounded by the Enlightenment and by Hume.)

* Buffon, G.L. de (1749–89) *Natural History: General and Particular*, trans. W. Smellie, London, 1812, 20 vols. (A compendium of data with the emphasis on description which is critical of Linnaean classification.)

* Condillac, E.B. de (1740) *Essai sur l'origine des connoissances humaines* (Essay on the Origin of Human Knowledge), in G. Le Roy (ed.) *Oeuvres Philosophiques de Condillac*, Paris: Presses Universitaires de France, 1947. (The first systematic French development of Locke's empiricism.)

* —— (1754) *Traité des Sensations* (Treatise on Sensations), in G. Le Roy (ed.) *Oeuvres philosophiques*, Paris: Presses Universitaires de France, 1947. (A more rigorous advance on the argument of the Essay and expounds a thoroughgoing sensationalist psychology.)

Gay, P. (1967–70) *The Enlightenment*, London: Weidenfeld & Nicolson, 2 vols. (The most generally informative and readable treatment of the Enlightenment, the second volume deals with issues closest to this article; both volumes contain lengthy bibliographic essays.)

* Hartley, D. (1749) *Observations on Man, His Frame, His Duty and His Expectations*, London: Leake & Frederick, 2 vols. (Expounds a physiological theory of the mind with changes in the brain in form of vibrations corresponding to changes in ideas.)

* Hume, D. (1739–40) *A Treatise of Human Nature*, ed. L.A. Selby-Bigge, revised P.H. Nidditch, Oxford: Clarendon Press, 1978. (One of philosophy's great books that Hume himself later dismissed in preference for his subsequent writing.)

* —— (1740) *An Abstract of a book lately published entitled A Treatise of Human Nature*, repr. in *An Inquiry concerning Human Understanding*, 1748, ed. C. Hendel, Indianapolis, IL: Library of Liberal Arts, 1955. (Hume's own anonymous review of the *Treatise*.)

* Hutcheson, F. (1725) *An Inquiry into the Original of our Ideas of Beauty and Virtue: in Two Treatises*, London and Dublin. (Contains his first formulation of the philosophy of moral sense.)

Knight, I.F. (1968) *The Geometric Spirit: The Abbé Condillac and the French Enlightenment*, New Haven, CN: Yale University Press. (A good exposition of Condillac's thought and the fullest available in English.)

* La Mettrie, J.O. de (1758) *Man and Machine*, trans. and ed. G. Bussey, La Salle, IL: Open Court Press, 1912. (An uncompromising enunciation of materialism.)

* Newton, I. (1730) *Opticks*, 4th edn, in H. Thayer (ed.) *Newton's Philosophy of Nature*, New York: Hafner Library of Classics, 1953. (Contains selections of the *Opticks*, which along with his *Principia Mathematica* (1687) established Newton's reputa-

tion, especially once experiments supported his calculations rather than Descartes.)

CHRISTOPHER J. BERRY

HUMANISM

The philosophical term 'humanism' refers to a series of interrelated concepts about the nature, defining characteristics, powers, education and values of human persons. In one sense humanism is a coherent and recognizable philosophical system that advances substantive ontological, epistemological, anthropological, educational, aesthetic, ethical and political claims. In another sense humanism is understood more as a method and a series of loosely connected questions about the nature and character of human persons.

From the fourteenth century to the end of the nineteenth century, humanism minimally meant: (1) an educational programme founded on the classical authors and concentrating on the study of grammar, rhetoric, history, poetry and moral philosophy; (2) a commitment to the perspective, interests and centrality of human persons; (3) a belief in reason and autonomy as foundational aspects of human existence; (4) a belief that reason, scepticism and the scientific method are the only appropriate instruments for discovering truth and structuring the human community; (5) a belief that the foundations for ethics and society are to be found in autonomy and moral equality. From the end of the nineteenth century, humanism has been defined, in addition to the above, by the way in which particular aspects of core humanist belief such as human uniqueness, scientific method, reason and autonomy have been utilized in such philosophical systems as existentialism, Marxism and pragmatism.

1   **The problem of humanism**
2   *Studia humanitatis, Humanista* and *Humanismus*
3   **Enlightenment humanism**
4   **Modern humanism**

1   The problem of humanism

Like other terms that have had parallel careers in philosophy, intellectual history and popular usage (for example, liberalism or idealism), the concept of humanism suffers from an overabundance of definitions such that when considering them together it is not uncommon to ask whether there is anyone who is not a humanist. One can, for instance, define humanism by historical period: classical humanism, Renaissance humanism, Enlightenment humanism.

Or one can adopt a definition that links humanism with a particular philosopher or philosophical movement, such as Marxist humanism, Heideggerian humanism or existentialist humanism. Or again one might, like the 1928 *Oxford English Dictionary*, approach the task of defining humanism by its constituent themes or claims: humanism centred on humane virtues like benevolence, humanity – independent persons as opposed to persons conceived within a transcendent divine order – and humane learning as structured within the classical *studia humanitatis*.

In each of these definitional approaches there is a risk of producing an account either so general as to be unhelpful or so particular as to contradict other legitimate usages. Thus, because of the ambiguity and controversy surrounding such terms as 'Renaissance' and 'Enlightenment', it is doubtful whether it helps in defining humanism to speak of Renaissance or Enlightenment humanism. Similarly, to speak of humanism in Pope's sense as 'the proper study of mankind is man' is to bring everything – scientific, non-scientific, religious, anti-religious, for instance – within its orbit. Nor is it apparent that we make any significant gain by talking about Marxist or Christian humanism as if they shared any substantial resemblance. In short, to be helpful, a definition of humanism must be as much alive to what it excludes as to what it includes.

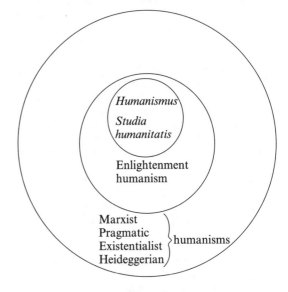

Figure 1

Such an overabundance of definitional signposts, many of them pointing in different directions, suggests that humanism is as much a series of interrelated definitional and methodological questions as of substantive questions about the plausibility of a particular set of philosophical doctrines. This means that perhaps the most coherent understanding of humanism can be found by thinking about it in terms of a series of concentric circles in which the innermost and smallest circle contains the most limited and unproblematic sense of the term, the next and larger circle contains a more comprehensive and contested sense, and the outer and largest circle contains the most recent and controversial usages of the concept (see Figure 1).

2 *Studia humanitatis*, *Humanista* and *Humanismus*

At the centre of the humanist circle are two definitions, one modern, the other originally ancient and subsequently revived in the Italian Renaissance, both of which define humanism in terms of an educational programme, *studia humanitatis*.

The word 'Humanismus' was created to differentiate the classical curriculum of secondary education with its emphasis on Greek and Latin from the modern obsession with scientific, mathematical and practical education. The word was then borrowed by nineteenth century historians (see George Voigt's 1859 *The Revival of Classical Antiquity* or *The First Century of Humanism*) to describe the educational and cultural programme of a group of Renaissance writers, historians and philosophers, such as PETRARCH, VALLA, FICINO, and POMPONAZZI.

Humanismus is thus derived from *humanista* or humanist, which along with its equivalents in English, French and Italian referred to teachers in schools or universities and students of the humanities. Paul Kristeller (1961: 9) suggested that 'to judge from its earliest appearance known so far, [the word] seems to have originated in the student slang of the Italian universities, where the professor of the humanities came to be called *umanista*, after the analogy of his colleagues in the older disciplines'. The Renaissance term *Humanista* is itself derived from a more ancient usage *studia humanitatis*, the educational programme of the Greeks and Romans that centred on grammar, rhetoric, history, poetry and moral philosophy. It is important to note that the *studia humanitatis* did not include logic, natural philosophy, metaphysics or mathematics. *Humanismus*, *humanista* and *studia humanitatis* refer not to some philosophical doctrine but to a broad cultural and educational programme that focused, through close study of the ancients, on the development of elegant writing and speaking.

3 Enlightenment humanism

In the second and wider circle one finds Enlightenment humanism which is closest to the sense that commonly attaches today to the terms 'secular' or 'scientific' humanism. By Enlightenment humanism one means the men of letters, philosophy and science (for instance, VOLTAIRE, ROUSSEAU, MONTESQUIEU, DIDEROT, D'ALEMBERT, LOCKE, HUME, CONDORCET and, more problematically, KANT) who lived in the seventeenth and eighteenth centuries and believed that the central concern of human existence was not the discovery of God's will, but the shaping of human life and society according to reason. For these thinkers, human dignity was not a function of man's allegedly divine origin, but of the ordering and rational possibilities of earthly existence. The end of persons is neither the immediate adoration of God nor the heavenly city of the blessed, but rather the realization of those projects appropriate to this world, suggested by both reason and imagination.

What drives the project of Enlightenment humanism is the attempt to replace the traditional belief that the concept of a human person makes sense only within the context of talk about created souls, a transcendent, divine order and faith, with the conviction that the idea of persons is correctly to be understood within the context of reason, freedom for self-creation and fundamental scepticism. Enlightenment humanism is at foundation the re-defining of the nature of persons within a conceptual framework of their own making rather than one imposed from the outside. In this sense to speak of Christian humanism seems to be a fundamental contradiction inasmuch as it assumes a prior ontology of divinity within and against which the essence of human persons must be situated. For the Enlightenment humanist there is no such framework, no such transcendent God, no such pre-ordered account of the good life of individual persons or human societies.

To this general focus on the world of self-creating persons must be added a second feature of Enlightenment humanism, namely its conception of reason. Though immensely diverse in both interests and intellectual programme, in substance and nuance, what unites the Enlightenment humanists in a way quite different from either Renaissance humanists or subsequent modern humanism is their enormous confidence in the power of human reason to describe and order the world, and in their ready acceptance of responsibility for the consequences of reason's ordering.

This confidence and its consequences are frequently caricatured. Enlightenment reason and Enlightenment humanism are often portrayed as cold, passionless, abstract and inappropriately systematic. But this is to mistake the mask for the face. At its core what drives reason for the Enlightenment humanist is passion, a passion for exposing error, for facts based on sound observation and for the coherent ordering of those facts in a fashion that would produce not so much a system as genuine insight into the character of existence even if the product of such insight were not so much illumination as perplexity. As d'Alembert put it in his summation of the eighteenth century 'everything has been discussed and analysed, or at least mentioned. The fruit or sequel of this general effervescence of minds has been to cast new light on some matters and new shadows on others' (1759 (4): 5–6).

Reason, for the Enlightenment humanist, is driven by criticism and scepticism, and if we are to find the most consistent feature of Enlightenment reason it would be its insistence that all claims are falsifiable, and that no one has a privileged position in determining truth by virtue of their authority. For the humanist, sceptical reason thus ensures that all knowledge claims are publicly tested and that no person or institution can claim infallibility. For the Enlightenment humanist the importance of science lies primarily not in its advances in knowledge but in the energy, force and universality of its method.

Reason is central for the Enlightenment humanist not merely because of its critical and sceptical force but equally because of its objective character. Unlike revelation and dogma, which links truth to a particular authoritative person, reason for the humanist acquires its power precisely because the persons advancing knowledge claims are in a crucial sense interchangeable. Reason has the capacity, the humanist argues, to produce a truth that is quite literally subject-free: its claims hold only if they are accessible and make sense to all. Reason in this sense is genuinely emancipatory in at least three ways. First, it liberates individuals from what Kant termed the tutelage of others, the imposed dictates of external authority. Second, it opens up the process of truth to everyone, for truth is not a function of position or perspective. Third, it has the capacity to liberate persons from their own subjectively imposed prejudices by forcing them to abandon the inadequacy of their merely private viewpoints for the widest, most objective perspective. Reason is thus an instrument of emancipation – it produces not just truth but also autonomy and equality. And it is this connection with autonomy and equality that provides the foundation for the moral and political content of Enlightenment humanism.

As with the Enlightenment humanists' account of reason, so with their conceptions of ethics and politics

there is a strong temptation to reduce an enormous diversity and complexity to the simplicity of caricature. Thus some accounts of Enlightenment humanism find within its central tenets sweeping accounts of historical progress, grand schemes for educational reform and radical changes for political institutions. While there are elements of such beliefs and programmes in certain humanists of this period, the general content of humanist ethical and political thought is more restrained.

What emerges most clearly from the humanist emphasis on autonomy and equality is the open, tolerant and diverse character of humanist society. If reason is genuinely the gift of all and if criticism and scepticism and the public search for truth are the task of all, then the number of absolute truths that will structure the social life of society is very small and the circle of those competent to participate actively in the life of running society is very large – humanist reason serves to decrease the amount of societal certainty while increasing the number of qualified members of a political society. Questions of the good personal and collective life are by definition questions that people will solve, as autonomous beings, in different and (in some instances) competing ways. Enlightenment humanism comes closest to agreement in its ethical and political maxims in its commitment to the discipline of reason in which truth must emerge, both publicly and privately, not through dogma but through argument and counter-argument, and in its commitment to the virtues of beneficence and non-malfeasance. In this sense it is not incorrect to claim that much of what today is described as a liberal society – basic liberties, free institutions, diversity and tolerance, the sense, to use Bertrand Russell's phrase, of 'order without authority' – can plausibly be traced to the Enlightenment humanist's conception of reason.

Enlightenment humanism can be approached from any number of directions to come to terms with its intellectual and emotional core: through its compassion for humanity and social reform, through its interest in material and intellectual progress, through its championing of literary freedom, its interest in the classical past, or its belief in the centrality of science and scientific method. At the end, however, its defining characteristic is its confidence in and celebration of human autonomy, an autonomy secure through the critical and creative powers of reason.

4   Modern humanism

There are at least four modern versions of humanism, three of which claim some affinity with the themes of Enlightenment humanism, and one which explicitly disavows any connection with it. These four, Marxist humanism, pragmatic humanism, existentialist humanism and Heideggerian humanism, do not exhaust the humanisms of the modern age, for in popular usage one will frequently find reference to scientific humanism, Christian humanism and secular humanism.

Of the four, pragmatic humanism is closest to the humanism of the Enlightenment (see PRAGMATISM). Rooted in the American philosophy of pragmatism as developed by Charles PEIRCE, William JAMES, John DEWEY and F.C.S. SCHILLER, pragmatic humanism shares the Enlightenment humanist concerns for human primacy, the validity of the scientific method and the incompatibility of human dignity with religious belief. While championing the humanist themes of dubitability and scepticism, pragmatic humanism is at odds with Enlightenment humanism on the belief that reason is an unchanging and defining essence of human nature and on the nature of human freedom. Most pragmatic humanists would extend their scepticism to the claim that there is a human essence, and certainly to the belief that reason occupies a privileged place in defining 'humanness'. These humanists would prefer to speak of persons being what they do, with the anthropological emphasis placed squarely on the changing ensemble of environmental conditions that create persons. Similarly, such pragmatists are uncomfortable with the confident Enlightenment talk of human freedom and autonomy, though they do speak of freedom in terms of variation, innovation and foresight.

Closely aligned with pragmatic humanism in its denial of a universal human essence is existentialist humanism, particularly as formulated by J.-P. Sartre in his lecture 'Existentialism is a Humanism' (1946) (see EXISTENTIALISM). Inasmuch as 'existence precedes essence', according to Sartre, there is no objective and permanent thing called human nature. It is nothing else than what persons do, how they choose to act. There is no paradigm of human against which action can be measured. But while concurring with the pragmatic humanists with respect to the essence of human persons, and registering, unlike Enlightenment humanists, a fair degree of scepticism about the capabilities of reason itself, existentialist humanism shares unreservedly in the Enlightenment humanist's celebration of human autonomy. While existentialists like Sartre would allow, at one level, that natural explanations of human actions are appropriate, at another level they would insist that human actions, individual and collective, must be subject to another type of explanation – the explanation of freedom or self-causation. Of the first two types of modern humanism, each has accepted but part of the Enlightenment humanist programme.

Whereas pragmatic humanism concurs with the Enlightenment's celebration of human reason but rejects its emphasis on human freedom, existentialist humanism makes human freedom central to its affirmation of humanness but doubts the Enlightenment's emphasis on the primacy of reason.

Any discussion of Marxist humanism labours under the considerable disadvantage of having to come to terms with a complicated variety of Marxes and Marxism (see MARX, K.). Despite this, the general outline of Marxist humanism seems relatively clear with respect to the paradigm of Enlightenment humanism. Although Marx often used the word humanism during 1843–4, it occurs very rarely in his post-1845 works. The reason for this is that Marx came to three insights that subsequently led to his rejection of much of Enlightenment humanism: first, that the development of history is really the constant creation of human nature; second, that if we can speak of a real essence of persons it can be nothing more than the complete ensemble of an individual's social relations; and third, that humanism in the traditional sense is simply another ideology that masks the true nature of social relations by conferring a spurious legitimacy on the status quo. Thus, while accepting Enlightenment humanists' rejection of theism, and their instrumental rationality, Marxist humanism is not prepared to accept their essentialist reading of human nature.

Equally problematic for the Marxist humanist is the Enlightenment's emphasis on individual autonomy, for there is a strong deterministic, or at least inevitabilist element within much Marxist thought. Perhaps the most significant contribution of Marxist humanism, however, is its attempt to give concrete definition to the social ideals that are often only given the vaguest mention in Enlightenment humanism. Apart from its claims about the ideological character of humanism, the unique character of Marxist humanism lies in its practical attention to the Enlightenment's ideas of autonomy and equality.

The other variety of modern humanism is that of Martin HEIDEGGER in his famous Letter on Humanism (1947). The letter is a wide-ranging analysis of the humanisms of the past, particularly those of Marx and Sartre. Heidegger's thesis is that traditional humanism (including Enlightenment humanism) in what he calls metaphysical humanism, mistakenly locates human essence in the rational animality of persons, and thus fails to recognize that the genuine source of human essence is in existence, in the human's primordial relationship with Being. Heidegger's rejection of traditional humanism is not based simply on the fact that such rooting of human essence is wrong but that it necessarily corrupts

531

humanism by investing it with a metaphysical character. The goal is thus to 'think the truth of Being at the same time... to think the humanity of *homo humanus*. What counts is *humanitas* in the service of the truth of Being, built without humanism in the metaphysical sense' ([1947] 1977: 21). Heideggerian humanism thus explicitly rejects metaphysical humanism, yet retains both reason and thinking as central to its account of persons and Being. At the same time, however, as this rejection of metaphysical humanism occurs, there is a residual concern for 'meditating and caring, that man be human and not inhumane' ([1947] 1977: 200), in effect an ethical concern, that is surprisingly consistent not only with Enlightenment and every other type of metaphysical humanism, but with every other modern humanism as well.

See also: HUMANISM, RENAISSANCE; ENLIGHTENMENT, CONTINENTAL

References and further reading

While many of these works require both some knowledge of the history of philosophy and the development of intellectual history and a facility for often difficult argument, they do not require any technical knowledge.

Cassirer, E. (1951) *The Philosophy of the Enlightenment*, Boston, MA: Beacon Press. (A philosophically sophisticated and at times difficult work which centres on the coherence of Enlightenment humanism.)

* D'Alembert, J. (1759) 'Élements de Philosophie', in *Mélanges de littérature, d'historie et de philosophie*, novelle édition, Amsterdam, 6 vols. (One of the best introductions to what might be termed the 'mind of the mid-eighteenth century'. Particularly useful in that it provides an analysis of the development of Enlightenment thought in the context of the three hundred years preceding the eighteenth century and the critical perspective of the author's own philosophy.)

Gay, P. (1959) *The Party of Humanity*, New York: Norton. (An elegant discussion of the Enlightenment concept of humanism described in §3 above.)

—— (1966) *The Enlightenment: An Interpretation*, New York: Vintage Books, 1969. (One of the best accounts of the development, scope and logic of Enlightenment humanism in all of its dimensions.)

Goicoechea, D., Luik, J. and Madigan T. (eds) (1991) *The Question of Humanism: Challenges and Possibilities*, Buffalo, NY: Prometheus Books. (A comprehensive analysis, by a collection of authors, of the career of humanism from the ancient world to the twentieth century.)

* Heidegger, M. (1947) *Letter on Humanism*, trans. J.G. Grey and F.A. Capuzzi, New York: Harper & Row, 1977. (Like much of Heidegger, a very dense work that demands some understanding both of the development of humanism and of Heidegger's general philosophy.)

Kant, I. (1784) *What is Enlightenment?*, trans. L. White Beck, New York: Bobbs-Merrill, 1963. (A classic account of the tenets of an Enlightenment humanist.)

* Kristeller, P.O. (1961) *Renaissance Thought: The Classic, Scholastic and Humanist Strains*, New York: Harper & Row. (Examines the humanism discussed in §2 above.)

—— (1965) *Renaissance Thought II: Papers on Humanism and the Arts*, New York: Harper & Row. (As with the previous work, examines the humanism discussed above in §2.)

Manuel, F. and Manuel, F. (1979) *Utopian Thought in the Western World*, Boston, MA: Harvard University Press. (Humanism within the context of the larger issues of utopianism and human perfectability.)

Marx, K. (1932) *Economic and Philosophical Manuscripts*, trans. R. Livingstone and G. Benton, Harmondsworth: Penguin, 1975. (A difficult discussion of the basis of Marx's humanism.)

Passmore, J. (1970) *The Perfectibility of Man*, New York: Scribner. (Humanism within the context of the larger issues of utopianism and human perfectibility.)

Petrosyan, M. (1972) *Humanism: Its Philosophical, Ethical and Sociological Aspects*, Moscow: Progress. (A contemporary explication and defence of Marxist humanism which presupposes a fair understanding of Marxist texts and interpretation.)

* Sartre, J.-P. (1946) *L'Existentialisme est un humanisme*, Paris: Nagel; trans. B. Frechtmen as *Existentialism*, New York: Philosophical Library, 1947. (A key text of existentialist humanism but one which requires some persistence.)

* Voigt, G. (1859) *The Revival of Classical Antiquity* or *The First Century of Humanism*; reprinted in D. Goicoechea, J. Luik and T. Madigan (eds) *The Question of Humanism: Challenges and Possibilities*, Buffalo, NY: Prometheus, 1991. (Mentioned above in §2.)

JOHN C. LUIK

HUMANISM, RENAISSANCE

The early nineteenth-century German educator, F.J. Niethammer, coined the word 'humanism', meaning an education based on the Greek and Latin classics. The Renaissance (for our purposes, Europe from about 1350 to about 1650) knew no such term. The Renaissance had, instead, the Latin phrase studia humanitatis (literally 'the studies of humanity'), best translated 'the humanities'. The Renaissance borrowed the phrase from classical antiquity. Cicero used it a few times, but it was the later grammarian Aulus Gellius who clearly equated the Latin word humanitas with Greek paideia, that is, with the classical Greek education of liberal learning, especially literature and rhetoric, which was believed to develop the intellectual, moral and aesthetic capacities of a child (pais in Greek; hence paideia).

Renaissance humanists understood by studia humanitatis a cycle of five subjects: grammar, rhetoric, poetry, history and moral philosophy, all based on the Greek and Latin classics. A humanist was an expert in the studia humanitatis. The dominant discipline was rhetoric. Eloquence was the highest professional accomplishment of the Renaissance humanists, and rhetorical interests coloured humanists' approach to the other parts of the studia humanitatis. The Renaissance humanists were the successors of the medieval rhetorical tradition and the resuscitators of the classical rhetorical tradition. Renaissance humanism was, in the words of P.O. Kristeller, 'a characteristic phase in what may be called the rhetorical tradition in Western culture' ([1955] 1961: 11).

Renaissance humanism was neither a philosophy nor an ideology. It reflected no fixed position towards religion, the state, or society. Rather it was a cultural movement centred on rhetoric, literature and history. Its leading protagonists held jobs primarily as teachers of grammar and literature. Outside academia, they served as secretaries, ambassadors and bureaucrats. Some were jurists. The Renaissance humanists reasserted the importance of the humanities against the overwhelming dominance of philosophy and science in medieval higher education. As humanism penetrated the wider culture, it was combined with other disciplinary interests and professions so that one found humanist philosophers, physicians, theologians, lawyers, mathematicians and so forth.

Ideologically humanists were a varied lot. Some were pious, some were not. Some were interested in philosophy, most were not. Some became Protestants, others remained Catholic. Some scorned the vernacular while others made important contributions to it. Humanism influenced virtually every aspect of high culture in the West during the Renaissance. Depending on the humanist under discussion, one can legitimately speak of Christian humanism, lay humanism, civic humanism, Aristotelian humanism and other combinations.

Humanism had a profound effect on philosophy. Writing outside the philosophical establishment, humanists sought to make philosophy more literary in presentation and more amenable to rhetorical concerns. No less importantly, they recovered and translated into Latin a large reservoir of Greek classical texts unknown or ignored in the Middle Ages. Platonism, Stoicism, Epicureanism and scepticism all experienced revivals. The humanists challenged medieval Aristotelianism by offering new Latin translations of Aristotle that in some respects amounted to fresh interpretations. They also significantly enriched the Aristotelian corpus by translating the Poetics and the late ancient Greek commentators on Aristotle.

Renaissance humanism arose out of the peculiar social and cultural circumstances of thirteenth-century Italy. It came to maturity in Italy in the fifteenth century and spread to the rest of Europe in the sixteenth. It gradually lost its vitality in the seventeenth and eighteenth centuries as its focus on Latin eloquence became out of date in a world increasingly won over to the vernacular literatures and new science. In the nineteenth century, it did not so much die as become metamorphosed. Renaissance humanism sloughed off its rhetorical impulse and became modern scholarly classicism. Today the word humanism has taken on new connotations, but the heritage of Renaissance humanism runs deep in our culture. As long as we continue to value literature and history, and the functional skills and cultural perspective attached to these disciplines, every educated person by training will be a humanist in the Renaissance sense.

1   Origins
2   Francis Petrarch
3   A name and an image
4   Language
5   Learning: the classical heritage
6   Learning: philology
7   Evolution of humanism

1   Origins

Education reflects the culture that it serves. In antiquity, it was not philosophers and scientists but rhetoricians who provided the most common form of higher education. Literary-rhetorical training sufficed to qualify one as an educated person. In the cultural disasters that marked the passing of antiquity, monasteries became for a while the main depositories of learning in the West. But in the great medieval resurgence of the eleventh and twelfth centuries, cathedral schools in northern and central France emerged as centres for the education of the clergy. They were, in modern terminology, seminaries. These schools taught the seven liberal arts, a curriculum in which the core subject was grammar and the main reading the classical Latin authors. Thus, at one point in the Middle Ages literary studies constituted, as they had once before in antiquity, the basis of professional education.

Towards the end of the twelfth century, however, the medievals began to find logic and the newly translated Aristotelian corpus, especially the *Physics*, far more valuable (see ARISTOTELIANISM, MEDIEVAL). By the early thirteenth century, a new institution had emerged in northern Europe, the university, where the fundamental faculty was that of arts, and where arts meant the study of Aristotelian logic, philosophy and science. Arts graduates, having received this scientifico-philosophic education, could then proceed to one of the three professional faculties: law, medicine or theology. At no time in Western history have science and philosophy dominated educated culture to the degree they did in the later Middle Ages.

Italy differed from the rest of Europe. North of Rome it was a land not of agrarian feudal principalities, but of city states. Urban interests and urban culture dominated, and the universities differed accordingly from their counterparts elsewhere. Italy's first university, Bologna, began at the end of the twelfth century as a law school; an arts faculty dominated by the medical faculty quickly followed. The Bolognese two-faculty university became the standard form of Italian universities: in medieval Italian universities the two secular professions of law, with its own faculty, and medicine, within the arts faculty, achieved hegemonic status.

One subject closely connected with law but found in the arts faculty was the *ars dictaminis*, the art of letter writing. This *ars* had emerged in the eleventh century to answer a functional need of the new burgeoning urban society of Italy. The manuals provided instruction on how to write different kinds of letters to different classes of people, along with a generous dose of sample letters, salutations and formulas. The practitioners and teachers of the *ars dictaminis* were the *dictatores*. Their business was eloquence and persuasion. They were medieval rhetoricians, hired by chanceries all over Italy. By the early thirteenth century, *dictatores* were teaching in the arts faculty of the University of Bologna.

Medieval Italy also created another practical form of secular rhetoric, the *ars arengandi*, the art of haranguing. Public speeches played a role not only in politics, but also in a variety of social functions, such

as weddings and the awarding of a university degree. In the thirteenth century, Bolognese *dictatores* began to produce model speeches for public occasions; the first extant *artes arengandi* date from the end of the century. Medieval Italy produced a rich literature of *arenge* (secular speeches in Latin) and *dicerie* (secular speeches in Italian). The *ars dictaminis* spread to the rest of Europe, but the *ars arengandi* remained unique to Italy, and in combination with the *ars dictaminis* set medieval Italy apart as the home of a lively culture of secular oratory and rhetoric.

During the thirteenth century, *dictamen* entered into the training of notaries by being linked to the *ars notaria*. The *ars notaria* focused on document writing. Even more than lawyers, notaries gained fame, especially through their skill in composition. Notaries filled the Italian chanceries and the most skilled of them rose to be chancellors of Italian governments and secretaries of popes.

Thus, by the thirteenth century, Italy had a large class of lay professionals associated with law who took a special interest in eloquence and rhetoric. Not by chance, notaries, lawyers and bureaucrats loom inordinately large in the development of medieval Italian literature. The first school of Italian poetry arose in the chancery of Emperor Frederick II (1215–50), one of whose leaders was Giacomo 'the Notary'. Two of the most eminent Italian poets before Dante were Guittone of Arezzo, chancellor of his home town, and the Bolognese judge Guido Giunicelli. The earliest extant examples of Italian literary prose are the model speeches found in a work of the late thirteenth-century *dictator* Guido Faba. Of the three great fourteenth-century Florentine authors, Dante was a nobleman enrolled in the apothecary guild (see ALIGHIERI, DANTE), but Petrarch (see PETRARCA, F.) was the son of a notary and was himself trained in law at Bologna, while Boccaccio actually took a law degree.

In the thirteenth century, the Italian rhetorical tradition began to absorb the classicism of the dying cathedral school culture of France. The wellsprings of Latin eloquence, it was believed, lay in the Latin classics. Commentaries on classical rhetoric that were no longer being copied in France, began to be copied in Italy in the thirteenth century. By the fourteenth century, Italians were writing their own commentaries. *Dictatores*, such Giovanni del Virgilio at Bologna, a correspondent of Dante, began to lecture on classical authors at the universities. Late in the century, the Paduan judge Lovato de'Lovati studied the metre of Seneca and gathered about himself a circle of lawyers interested in classical studies. A younger contemporary, the notary Albertino Mussato became chancellor of Padua and gained eminence because of his Latin histories and epic poem *Ecernis*. In 1315 the Paduans crowned him poet laureate.

This classicization of the medieval Italian rhetorical tradition produced Renaissance humanism. The person who made the movement self-conscious was the Florentine expatriate Petrarch (1304–74).

2 Francis Petrarch

Read today by the general public almost exclusively for his Italian poetry, Petrarch was the greatest classical scholar and Latinist of his time. He was also a cultural icon. Popes at Avignon tried to make him a papal secretary. The republic of Venice furnished him with a free house in the vain hope of acquiring his library. The despots of Parma, Padua and Milan gave him hospitality, and for these princely patrons he several times indited letters and wrote orations in the tradition of the medieval *dictatores*. He had himself crowned poet laureate at Rome in 1337, but not before having the King of Naples 'test' him and give him a diploma (probably written by Petrarch himself) qualifying him as a poet and a historian.

Petrarch promoted the ideal of classical eloquence. The embodiment of that eloquence, he believed, was Cicero. In 1333 Petrarch inaugurated the Renaissance's reappropriation of classical oratory with the discovery at Liège of Cicero's oration *Pro Archia*. In 1345 at Verona he discovered Cicero's *Letters to Atticus*. Petrarch's interests extended to Greek literature. He acquired a Greek codex of Plato's dialogues and another of Homer, though he never learned to read Greek.

Imitating his classical models, Petrarch composed moral treatises and biographies of classical heroes, wrote an introspective dialogue (entitled *The Secret*), produced several collections of his Latin letters, drafted and delivered orations, gained fame as a Latin poet, exposed medieval forgeries of classical documents, and worked on correcting the corrupted texts of classical authors. Petrarch shared the medieval admiration for St Augustine, but reflecting his new cultural perspective, the Augustine he admired was not the theologian but the psychologist and doctor of souls he found in the *Confessiones* (Confessions).

The contrast between Petrarch's humanist perspective and the philosophico-scientific culture regnant in the universities emerges with special clarity in his invective *De Sui Ipsius et Multorum Ignorantia* (On His Own Ignorance and the Ignorance of the Many) (completed 1371). About 1366, already a cultural icon, Petrarch met four young Venetians who decided, it later transpired, that Petrarch was a good man, but

ignorant. If one grants their premise, that learning is defined by the scientific and philosophical interests of the medieval university, then, despite Petrarch's classical learning and literary greatness, the young men were right. In their naïvety, they had accurately drawn the line between humanism and the medieval scientific culture. Petrarch's defence was pretty weak. Apart from using Socratic ignorance as a rhetorical stratagem ('at least I know that I am ignorant'), what he had to say was more a programme than an argument. He denigrated the value of scholastic learning, noted Aristotle's less than dominant position in antiquity, expressed his preference for Plato as being more in harmony with Christianity, and portrayed himself as a true Christian in opposition to the contemporary Aristotelians who worshipped the pagan Aristotle and his Arab commentator Averroes. Petrarch did not even have a name for the outlook he espoused. His successors would remedy this failing and make good his programme (see PETRARCA, F.).

3 A name and an image

In the first half of the fifteenth century the new movement had established itself in all the major cultural centres of Italy. Its image-conscious exponents came up with an attractive name for it: the *studia humanitatis* ('the humanities'), and gave its products a new appearance: roman and italic script.

Coluccio Salutati, an Italian notary and a great admirer of Petrarch, was using the phrase *studia humanitatis* as early as the 1360s. Salutati is important because he eventually became the chancellor of Florence and gathered about himself a brilliant circle of younger humanists. The most illustrious were the notaries Leonardo Bruni and Poggio Bracciolini, who became in turn not only famous humanists, but also chancellors of Florence. Salutati did not identify a fixed set of subjects as constituting 'the studies of humanity', but by the 1440s Tommaso Parentucelli (the future Pope Nicholas V) could draw up for Cosimo de'Medici, the political leader of Florence, a plan for an ideal library collection in which he defined the *studia humanitatis* as works of grammar, rhetoric, history, poetry and moral philosophy. These five subjects were in fact those which the humanists taught and on which they wrote with professional competence.

The word *humanista* originated as student slang at the Italian universities in the late fifteenth century as the name of teachers who taught the *studia humanitatis*. No component of the new humanistic programme was in itself new. Ethics was the one part of philosophy which had special relevance to students of literature and rhetoric (see ARISTOTELIANISM, RENAISSANCE §7). In the case of history the humanists were innovative in that they were the first to make it an academic subject, not just a literary genre. (Significantly, Petrarch wished to have his diploma qualify him as a historian, not just a poet.) Furthermore, they gave grammar, rhetoric and poetry the quite specific meaning of classical grammar, rhetoric and poetry. The humanists despised medieval Latin. They strove to recover classical Latin and they studied classical Greek. They cultivated neoclassical Latin in their own writings and assiduously imitated classical literary forms. Ironically, a purist humanist would not use the word *humanista* because it was an unclassical neologism.

Along with the name, humanism also acquired a script. Poggio Bracciolini created the new hand in the early fifteenth century under the misconception that in rejecting the angular, densely abbreviated gothic script of the later Middle Ages, he was restoring antique script. He was in fact imitating not Roman manuscripts, but Carolingian manuscripts of the early Middle Ages. Nonetheless, Bracciolini called his creation *littera antiqua*, and we have gone along with his misnomer by calling his new hand 'roman'. Italic seems to have been the brainchild of Bracciolini's associate in the Salutati circle Niccolò Niccoli, who sought a cursive version of Bracciolini's new humanist script. When at the end of the fifteenth century the internationally famous press of Aldo Manuzio began using this humanist cursive in its books, the new script gained the name by which it is known in many languages: 'italic'. Humanism thus acquired a distinctive look to go along with its propaganda-laden name.

4 Language

Language was at the heart of the humanist movement (see LANGUAGE, RENAISSANCE PHILOSOPHY OF). Indeed, the distinguishing mark of the humanists was not any philosophy or ideology but their desire for eloquence based on a classicizing Latin. A humanist incapable of writing neoclassical Latin was a contradiction in terms. Humanists enthusiastically revived the classical prose genre of the oration and the letter. They imitated as best they could classical poetic forms such as the epic and the epigram. They composed neoclassical tragedies and comedies. And they wrote manuals of poetics, oratory, history and epistolography with classical models constantly in mind.

Petrarch complained about medieval Latin, but by the early fifteenth century even his Latin no longer met humanist standards. Leonardo Bruni became the new model of contemporary Latin scholarship and

others would follow, such as the great philologist Angelo Poliziano (d. 1494) at the end of the century and the Christian humanist Desiderius ERASMUS (d. 1536) in the first half of the sixteenth century. Since the humanists took over the teaching of Latin, they achieved near total victory over medieval Latin. Early in the sixteenth century, medieval Latin grammars ceased to be printed. Eventually the only Latin one could learn in the schools was the neoclassical Latin of the humanists. Medieval Latin survives today mainly in specialized vocabulary encountered outside the Latin class, for example, the phrase *a priori* in philosophy, which should be written *a priore* according to classical grammar.

It would be a mistake to think that the humanists collectively were hostile to the vernacular. Some were, but many (starting with Petrarch) wrote in the vernacular as well as in Latin. In the case of Thomas More, his Latin *Utopia* was a far more original work than any of his English writings (see UTOPIANISM), whereas some humanists, such as Pietro Bembo (1470–1547), were actually instrumental in formulating the standards of vernacular literature. Michel de MONTAIGNE, the greatest French author of the second half of the sixteenth century, even had Latin as his first language, because his father would only let him hear Latin until he was old enough to go to school. In general, however, the replacement of Latin by the vernacular as the standard language of literature and learning continued apace in the Renaissance. But even into the eighteenth century, Latin remained an important medium for literary and scientific expression.

Humanist literary values transferred not merely to the vernacular, but also to non-humanistic disciplines. In the Renaissance science and philosophy became more literary in presentation and increasingly vernacular in language. By the mid-seventeenth century, it was hardly scandalous that Galileo published his most substantial scientific works in the form of vernacular dialogues and that Descartes would describe his method of philosophy in a consciously limpid style of French. The *philosophes* of the Enlightenment are in this sense the heirs of the Renaissance humanists, and every academic discipline today presumes at least some minimum literary standard in expository writing.

Petrarch had intuited the importance of Greek for Latin literature. His successors put that intuition into effect. The first decisive moment came in 1397 when the city of Florence hired the Byzantine teacher and sometimes diplomat Manuel Chrysoloras to satisfy the desire of Coluccio Salutati and his circle to learn Greek. Some humanists, such as the famous educator Guarino Veronese, travelled in the other direction to learn Greek by living in Constantinople. Very rapidly in the fifteenth century it was established that excellence as a humanist demanded a thorough knowledge of Greek. Only a minority of humanists ever achieved this ideal, though all praised it. Oddly enough, when other Byzantine scholars followed Chrysoloras to Italy, such as GEORGE OF TREBIZOND of Crete about 1416 and Theodore Gaza of Constantinople about 1439, they initially had little impact on Greek learning in Italy. Some of the scholars that arrived after the fall of Constantinople in 1453, especially Johannes Argyropoulos at Florence, did become important cultural forces, but these later Greeks did not shape what had already become a mature humanist movement. They simply served its interests.

5 Learning: the classical heritage

The impulse that drove the humanists to recover the classical languages also drove them to discover lost or unknown classical texts. The Middle Ages had experienced a transformatory infusion of classical texts, but nothing on the scale of the Renaissance revival. Petrarch's discoveries have already been mentioned, but the most spectacularly successful discoverer was Poggio Bracciolini, who in series of forays into German and French libraries during the Council of Constance (1414–7) unearthed a breathtaking number of classical Latin texts. The process of discovery was ongoing from the fourteenth century into the seventeenth century. By the mid-seventeenth century, the Renaissance had recovered the overwhelmingly larger part of the classical literary heritage available now, and in the process had transformed Western learning and literature.

In the case of Latin texts, the humanists essentially discovered manuscripts copied in the early Middle Ages and ignored thereafter. Among their more notable finds were the historians Tacitus and Ammianus Marcellinus as well as new decades of Livy, the poets Catullus and Lucretius, new comedies of Plautus, the architectural authority Vitruvius, the orations, letters and some of the major rhetorical works of Cicero, the complete text of Quintilian, the cookbook of Apicius, the *Astronomicon* of Manilius, the medical author Celsus Cornelius and ten books of the letters of Pliny the Younger.

As varied as these Latin finds were, they pale in comparison to the great mass and riches of the Greek classical heritage exposed by the humanists. Greek texts involved the further difficulty that they had be translated in addition to being found. By the midseventeenth century the humanists had put into Latin virtually every Greek text known to them. Some of

these translations have remained the only one in any language up to today. Leonardo Bruni, the star pupil of Chrysoloras in Florence, led the way in the first decades of the fifteenth century with his very popular translations of Plato, Aristotle, Demosthenes, Plutarch and St Basil the Great (see ARISTOTELIANISM, RENAISSANCE §7; PLATONISM, RENAISSANCE §§1, 4). His work proved to be only the beginning of a huge expansion of translation from the Greek during the Renaissance.

Translating became, in fact, a major enterprise of the humanists. As classroom teachers they focused on the humanities, but as translators and classical scholars they took in the whole of the Christian as well as pagan classical heritage. They recovered and translated for the first time not only works by the Greek orators, dramatists, historians, poets, rhetoricians, literary critics (including the *Poetics* of Aristotle) and essayists, but also the Greek mathematicians, astronomers, geographers, philosophical writers (especially Plato, Plotinus, Sextus Empiricus and the commentators on Aristotle), medical authors and military tacticians. They retranslated virtually every Greek scientific and philosophical text known in the Middle Ages, including Aristotle. They also set about finding and translating the vast number of writings left by the Greek church fathers, retranslating the Bible itself and publishing it in its original languages. The humanists created a patristic and biblical renaissance in addition to a pagan literary renaissance.

Before the West could surpass antiquity, it had to know and make available what the ancients knew and did. Bringing that about in literature, science, philosophy and theology was one of the great achievements of the Renaissance humanists (see ARISTOTELIANISM, RENAISSANCE; PLATONISM, RENAISSANCE).

6 Learning: philology

The humanists did much more than introduce classical texts: they came to understand them better. They could do so, first, because of their superior knowledge of classical history and languages. The first landmark work in this regard was Lorenzo Valla's *Elegantiae Linguae Latinae* (The Fine Points of the Latin Language) completed in the 1440s, where Valla taught the West to understand many of the words, idioms, phrases and grammatical constructions of classical Latin correctly(see VALLA, LORENZO §1). Second, the humanists began to become professionally concerned with the emendation of texts. The key event here was the printing press.

Before printing, the reproduction of a text meant

copying. Any substantial copying invariably corrupted the text and, were copying to be repeated often enough or carelessly enough, such corruption could become serious indeed. The early humanists were acutely aware of the need to emend the classical texts they cherished. Petrarch and Valla, for instance, attempted to emend the text of Livy. In the 1440s at Naples, Valla even became involved in a quarrel with other humanists concerning the emendation of Livy.

The introduction of printing into Italy in the late 1460s transformed this situation. Whereas every manuscript copy of a text was different from every other, every copy of a printed edition was at least theoretically identical with every other. Humanists quickly became editors and correctors of classical texts for the new presses. They also began to argue furiously about the principles and practice of textual emendation. One humanist, Niccolò Perotti, at Rome in 1470, even urged the pope to censure the printing of books not for the purposes of religion but for the purpose of maintaining quality control in the reproduction of classical texts.

Humanists had found a new professional outlet; they had become philologists, the editors and correctors of texts. The most sophisticated of them early on was Angelo Poliziano (1454–94), whose *Miscellanea* summed up many of the principles developed by previous humanists (for example, going back to the Greek models of Latin texts, understanding the linguistic habits of an author, and seeking out the oldest manuscripts) and added some new ones (including the need to understand the genealogy of a manuscript and historical sources, and the need to cite sources precisely).

Lorenzo Valla provided a prime example of how this emerging philological sophistication could be put to use for more than purely grammatical purposes. In his clamorous *Oratio de falso credita et ementita Constantini Donatione* (Oration on the Falsely Believed and Fabricated Donation of Constantine) of 1440, he investigated the authenticity of a document that had been cited for centuries to prove that the Emperor Constantine gave the whole western half of the empire to the papacy. Using linguistic, historical and numismatic evidence Valla proved that it was in fact a medieval forgery. This sort of historical and philological knowledge had a wide application. In law it meant a reinterpretation of Justinian's *Corpus Iuris Civilis*, which had served as the basic text of secular law in the universities. The medieval commentators had frequently made the *Corpus* applicable to the new society of medieval Europe by interpreting it anachronistically. The new historical methods of the humanists totally undermined this medieval approach. Ironically, the humanist historical understanding of the *Corpus* failed to take hold in Italy, where the traditionalists, called the Bartolists (after the famous medieval jurist Bartolo of Sassoferrato), were able to retain control of the law faculties. Instead the Italian historico-philological approach to law received the name *mos Gallicus* ('the French custom') because it was the sixteenth-century French jurists who appropriated it and took the lead in applying it.

The new humanist philology had an even greater impact on religion. The Italian humanists translated many Greek church fathers, especially under the influence of Pope Nicholas V (1447–55), formerly Tommaso Parentucelli (see §3). The Florentine businessman turned humanist Gianozzo Manetti (d. 1459) made a fresh translation of the New Testament from the Greek and the Psalms from the Hebrew. In the 1440s, Lorenzo Valla prepared a comparison of the Greek text of the New Testament with the current Latin translation, called the Vulgate, and found the latter faulty in hundreds of places. Manetti's and Valla's work had little resonance in Italy because as a group Italian humanists took no professional interest in theology. In the sixteenth century, however, the discovery of Valla's *Annotationes in Novum Testamentum* (Annotations on the New Testament) inspired the humanist religious reformer Desiderius ERASMUS (§6) of Rotterdam to become a scripture scholar, and in 1516 he published the first printed Greek edition of the New Testament. He also made a new Latin translation and wrote a commentary where he drew theological conclusions from his philological and historical understanding of the Greek text. Humanist philology when applied to religion had resulted in scriptural theology. Humanists now clearly had a professional role to play in theology alongside the traditional doctrinal theologians.

Erasmus' timing could not have been better. The year after his edition, the appearance of Luther's Ninety-Five Theses ushered in the Reformation. Protestants made Scripture the sole source of religious authority. Martin LUTHER was in many ways a very traditional dogmatic theologian, but he learned Greek and translated the New Testament into German from Erasmus' edition. Henceforth humanist philological knowledge was necessary in any serious treatment of the text of Scripture on the Catholic as well as the Protestant side of the struggle. Moreover, since both sides claimed continuity with the early church and wished to harness to their positions the authority of the church fathers, the historical and linguistic expertise of the humanists became all the more crucial to official religion, as reflected in not only biblical scholarship, but also the myriad editions of the church fathers and the monumental cooperative historical projects, such as *The Magdeburg Centuries* of the Protestants and the *Acta Sanctorum* of Jean Bolland and his fellow Jesuits.

Philosophy also began to blend with humanism, most notably with regard to Platonism. As we have seen, Petrarch expressed preference for Plato. Leonardo Bruni considered himself an Aristotelian, but his translation of some of Plato's dialogues inaugurated the Renaissance reception of Plato. The process culminated in the great Renaissance Platonist Marsilio FICINO who combined competence in Greek and humanist literary interests with the profession of a philosopher. Only such a combination allowed Ficino to make Platonism a powerful element in Renaissance philosophy. Similarly, the humanistically trained Gianfrancesco Pico della Mirandola was able to introduce classical scepticism into Renaissance philosophical discourse because his anti-Aristotelian *Examen vanitatis doctrinae gentium* (An Examination of the Emptiness of Pagan Learning) of 1520 incorporated large tracts of the then still untranslated works of Sextus Empiricus. The humanists Cosma Raimondi and Lorenzo Valla became the chief proponents of Epicureanism in the fifteenth century.

Humanism combined less significantly with Aristotelianism (see ARISTOTELIANISM, RENAISSANCE; LOGIC, RENAISSANCE §3). Early on, several important humanists, such as Leonardo Bruni, GEORGE OF TREBIZOND, and Theodore Gaza, were avowed Aristotelians. Bruni and Gaza consciously strove to replace in their translations the traditional terminology of medieval Aristotelianism. By the early sixteenth century one of the leading traditional Aristotelians in Italy, Agostino NIFO, thought it necessary to learn Greek. By the later sixteenth century humanistic Aristotelianism had become a powerful force, as documented by the popularity of the bilingual Aristotelian editions of Giulio Pace (1550–1635) and most of all by the bilingual editions and commentaries of the Jesuits of the Portuguese University of Coimbra (see COLLEGIUM CONIMBRICENSE).

7 Evolution of humanism

Different humanists had different interests and served different masters. Petrarch at times did the bidding of tyrants and sang the praises of the solitary life. In fifteenth-century Italy, the tyrants, popes and Aragonese kings of southern Italy had large numbers of humanists serving them. So did the republics of Florence and Venice. Leonardo Bruni, even before he became chancellor of Florence, glorified participation in the republic and has been hailed in more recent times as the founder of civic humanism (a brand of humanism that stressed republican

values). Some humanists, such as Giannozzo Manetti, Bartolomeo Fazio and Erasmus emphasized the moral freedom of humans while others, such as Coluccio Salutati, Lorenzo Valla and all Lutheran humanists denied or severely limited the range of human free will. The Aristotelian George of Trebizond launched a crusade against Platonism at Rome in the 1450s and 1460s on the eve of the emergence of Florentine Platonism under Marsilio Ficino. Petrarch and Valla attacked medieval Aristotelianism in order, they said, to defend Christianity. Most Italian humanists, on the other hand, did not involve themselves with theology. Starting in the early sixteenth century, under the leadership of Erasmus, Christian humanism became a potent force for religious reform. In the religious crisis of the sixteenth century, humanists could be found on all sides of the theological arguments. Eventually Catholics as well as the major Protestant churches made humanism the basis of their respective educational curricula. Humanists vented their fury on matters of Latin style. Some, such as George of Trebizond, Paolo Cortese, Pietro Bembo and the Jesuit schoolmasters insisted on the imitation of Cicero. Others, such as Angelo Poliziano, Erasmus and Petrus RAMUS (§2) bitterly opposed the Ciceronians and called for an eclectic approach to imitation. Other models were also proposed: Valla favoured Quintilian, Cortese towards the end of his life converted to the imitation of Apuleius, and late in the sixteenth century Justus LIPSIUS popularized the imitation of Seneca. In short, apart from their commitment to Latin eloquence and classical literature, Renaissance humanists could differ considerably on philosophical, religious and cultural issues.

The people involved with humanism also changed over time. As the fifteenth century advanced, the link between notaries and humanists in Italy faded with the humanists becoming a distinct group of educated professionals, mainly occupied with teaching. The prototypical fifteenth-century Italian Renaissance educators had been Vittorino da Feltre and Guarino Veronese who ran humanist schools for the princely courts of Mantua and Ferrara respectively. But humanists also made careers in secular governments and the church. A few were businessmen, such as Niccolò Niccoli (d. 1437), a great collector of books. After Niccoli's death, Cosimo de'Medici took control of his library (in return for paying his debts) and made it the nucleus of the first public library since antiquity, the Biblioteca Laurenziana in Florence. Some humanists were even businessmen, such as Aldo Manuzio, whose printing press at Venice from the 1490s onwards became famous for its editions of the Greek and Latin classics. The Aldine Press remains today the best-known publishing house of the Renaissance.

Almost all humanists were men, but some women were also involved. The first female humanist of importance was Isotta Nogarola (1418–66), a noblewoman of Verona, whose Latin writings fill two volumes in their modern edition. At the other end of the chronological and geographical spectrum the pious Dutchwoman Anna Maria van SCHURMAN (1607–78) was significant; she was best known for her treatise defending the education of women and extraordinary for her command of languages (Latin, Greek, Hebrew, Aramaic, Syrian, Arabic, Turkish, Ethiopian, Dutch, Spanish and English). The problem for women in the Renaissance was that they were denied access to the universities and learned professions.

Towards the end of the fifteenth century humanism began to penetrate northern Europe, which differed from Italy in some important respects. The north lacked Italy's tradition of secular oratory, and its universities were more involved in preparing students for a clerical career than those of Italy. Consequently, though northern Europe had its share of secular-minded humanists, it is no accident that Christian humanism became a movement first in the north and that the first humanist manuals for sacred oratory emanated from northern humanists. As in Italy, the vast majority of northern humanists were by profession teachers, along with a significant number of lawyers (including Thomas More), diplomats, bureaucrats and clergymen.

In the course of the sixteenth century a revolution took place in education (see MELANCHTHON, P.). The Jesuit colleges and the Protestant academies established a system of secondary schools, unknown to the Middle Ages. The basis of these new schools was the humanist curriculum. They were popular because they worked. Their students were better prepared for the university than those students who did not attend them. By the mid-seventeenth century, the victory of humanism was virtually complete. To be educated meant that one had received along the way a humanistic education.

That victory cost Renaissance humanism dearly. The humanists had captured the grammar schools and the new secondary schools and lost the universities. By the mid-seventeenth century, humanists had come to be mainly primary and secondary school teachers. In Catholic countries, for lay humanists even this career path was limited by the Jesuit colleges. Furthermore, in a world where the language of learning and letters had become the vernacular and where science and philosophy had left behind the classical systems, Renaissance humanist education appeared increasingly irrelevant and provoked calls for educational reform. Paradoxically, this turn away from Renaissance humanism proved liberating. In the nineteenth century, humanism was able to slough off its Renaissance rhetorical mission and become instead a training in culture and taste. The educated public rediscovered antiquity as a source of aesthetic and cultural values. No less importantly, the new humanist became a scientific discoverer, that is, the university professor opening up new frontiers of knowledge. The new humanism emanating from Germany had its own professional education, scientific methods and prestigious *cursus honoris*. Humanism once again took the lead in innovative learning. It engendered the research seminar and made research the standard for promotion within higher education. Indeed, as humanism became scientific classicism, it showed the way for the vernacular literatures and the arts to become in their own right academic subjects at all levels of education. The Renaissance *studia humanitatis* had evolved into the modern humanities.

See also: ARISTOTELIANISM, RENAISSANCE; LANGUAGE, RENAISSANCE PHILOSOPHY OF; MESSER LEON; PETRARCA, F.; PLATONISM, RENAISSANCE; RENAISSANCE PHILOSOPHY; SCEPTICISM, RENAISSANCE

References and further reading

Baron, H. (1966) *The Crisis of the Early Italian Renaissance: Civic Humanism and Republican Liberty in an Age of Classicism and Tyranny*, Princeton, NJ: Princeton University Press. (Revised edition of the 1955 publication; responsible for popularizing the notion of civic humanism.)

Chomarat, J. (1981) *Grammaire et rhétorique chez Erasmus* (Erasmus' Grammar and Rhetoric), Paris: Les Belles Lettres, 2 vols. (The fundamental work on the humanism of the most important northern humanist of the Renaissance.)

Ferguson, W.K. (1948) *The Renaissance in Historical Thought*, Cambridge, MA: Harvard University Press. (The best study on the idea of the Renaissance with many references to humanism.)

Hankins, J. (1990) *Plato in the Renaissance*, Leiden: Brill, 2 vols. (A wide-ranging study of an important cultural current.)

Ijsewijn, J. (1990) *Companion to Neo-Latin Studies*, Louvain: Peeters, 2nd edn. (The best survey of Neo-Latin authors and literature.)

Kraye, J. (ed.) (1996) *The Cambridge Companion to Renaissance Humanism*, Cambridge: Cambridge University Press. (A collection of essays covering scholarship, teaching, the Bible, political thought, dialectic and science. Good bibliography, organized by topic.)

Kristeller, P.O. (1956–85) *Studies in Renaissance Thought and Letters*, Rome: Storia e Letteratura, 2 vols. (Contains many of Kristeller's important articles.)

* —— (1955) 'The Humanist Movement', in *Renaissance Thought: The Classic, Scholastic, and Humanistic Strains*, New York: Harper, 1961, 3–23. (This was the first of Kristeller's celebrated Martin Classical Lectures of 1954 (published in 1955). The lecture also appears in *Renaissance Thought and Its Sources* on pages 21–32.)

—— (1979) *Renaissance Thought and Its Sources*, New York: Columbia University Press. (The handiest collection of Kristeller's 1945 article 'Humanism and Scholasticism in the Italian Renaissance' and his 1954 Martin Classical Lectures, which are the classic expositions of his interpretation of Renaissance humanism, presented in this entry. Also contains his magisterial overview of rhetoric and philosophy from antiquity to the Renaissance.)

Rabil, A., Jr (ed.) (1988) *Renaissance Humanism: Foundations, Forms, and Legacy*, Philadelphia, PA: University of Pennsylvania Press, 3 vols. (A rich collection of articles by many specialists.)

Rose, P.L. (1975) *The Italian Renaissance of Mathematics*, Geneva: Droz. (A study of the importance of humanism to a non-humanistic discipline in the Renaissance.)

Schmitt, C.B. (1983) *Aristotle and the Renaissance*, Cambridge, MA: Harvard University Press. (Brings out the significance of humanistic Aristotelianism.)

Seigel, J.E. (1968) *Rhetoric and Philosophy in Renaissance Humanism: The Union of Eloquence and Wisdom, Petrarch to Valla*, Princeton, NJ: Princeton University Press. (A polemical assertion of the Kristeller thesis and an attack on the Baron thesis of civic humanism.)

Trinkaus, C. (1970) *In Our Image and Likeness*, Chicago, IL, and London: University of Chicago Press, 2 vols. (Extensive discussion of major humanist thinkers.)

Voigt, G. (1893) *Die Wiederbelebung des classischen Alterthums* (The Revival of Classical Antiquity), ed. M. Lehnerdt, Berlin: Reimer, 3rd edn, 2 vols; Italian trans. of 2nd edn, G. Zippel (ed.) and D. Valbusa (trans.) *Il risorgimento dell'antichità classica*, Florence: Sansoni, 1888–97, 3 vols. (The first great study of Renaissance humanism; it has not yet lost its usefulness.)

Weinberg, B. (1961) *A History of Literary Criticism in the Italian Renaissance*, Chicago, IL: University of Chicago Press, 2 vols. (A fundamental study of a major interest of the humanists.)

Weiss, R. (1969) *The Renaissance Discovery of Classical Antiquity*, Oxford: Blackwell. (A guide to humanist antiquarian researches.)

JOHN MONFASANI

HUMBOLDT, WILHELM VON (1767–1835)

Along with Schiller and Goethe, Humboldt was one of the chief representatives of Weimar classicism, a movement that aspired to revive German culture along the lines of ancient Greece. Humboldt's philosophical significance resides mainly in two areas: political theory and the philosophy of language. In political theory he was one of the founders of modern liberalism; and in the philosophy of language, he was among the first to stress the importance of language for thought, and of culture for language.

Born into an aristocratic family in Prussia, Humboldt received a private education by some luminaries of the Berlin Enlightenment (see ENLIGHTENMENT, CONTINENTAL). As a young man he frequented the literary salons of Rahel Levin and Henriette Herz, where he cavorted with some of the leaders of the romantic movement. Humboldt spent much of his career in the service of the Prussian state. From 1802 to 1810 he was the Minister of Education in the Prussian Reform Administration of Baron von Stein; and from 1813 to 1815 he acted as Prussian representative at the Congresses of Prague and Vienna. His most important achievements were as Minister of Education. In this role he founded the University of Berlin, and created the first unified school system in Germany, whose broad outlines still exist.

Like Kant, F.H. Jacobi and Georg Forster, Humboldt was one of the founders of German liberalism. His *Ideen zu einem Versuch, die Gränzen der Wirksamkeit des Staats zu bestimmen* (*The Limits of State Action*), which was written in 1792 but not published until 1851, later became a classic of the liberal cause. Strictly speaking, it is anachronistic to regard Humboldt as a spokesman for liberalism, given that liberalism was not a self-conscious and organized movement in Germany until the 1840s. Nevertheless, his ideas proved influential for later liberals. The *Ideen* inspired much of J.S. Mill's *On Liberty* and Edouard Laboulaye's *L'État et ses limites* (The State and Its Limits).

The distinguishing feature of Humboldt's liberalism is its humanism, its ethic of perfection, the development of individuality (*Eigentümlichkeit*) and wholeness. Humboldt contended that the main aim of the state should not be to promote happiness, but excellence or individuality. The central argument of the *Ideen* is that the best state to achieve this end is the minimal one that permits everyone to do whatever they want, as long as they do not interfere with a similar liberty for others. Since the chief condition of individuality and excellence is freedom of choice, the best state is the smallest.

It is important not to confuse Humboldt's view with other doctrines later associated with liberalism. Unlike most German liberals of the 1840s, Humboldt had little sympathy for democracy, and held that the best government for the protection of liberty is a constitutional monarchy. Although Humboldt approved of a market economy, his liberalism was also not a defence of *laissez-faire*. He deplored the doctrine that the main aim of the state should be to create wealth or prosperity, for he feared that such materialism undermined the pursuit of excellence. Finally, unlike later liberalism, Humboldt's individualism was not at the expense of communal values, because he insisted that people develop their powers only through cooperation with others.

Humboldt's role in the development of the modern philosophy of language has been the subject of dispute. It is too much to claim that he is 'the father of modern linguistics' (Ernst Cassirer), since this ignores the many earlier contributions to this field (F. Bopp, J. Degerando, E. Condillac, F. Schlegel and J. Herder). Humboldt's philosophy synthesized, however, many of the most advanced ideas on the nature of language in the early nineteenth century. At the very least, Humboldt was one of the leading figures behind the development of comparative linguistics, the detailed study of the different forms of language.

The characteristic conception behind Humboldt's theory is his view of language as an organism. Like many early nineteenth-century thinkers, Humboldt believed that human activities are best explained in organic rather than mechanical terms. He held that language, like any organism, is an indivisible whole. It is a whole in two respects: the main unit of meaning is not the word but the sentence; and each language is unique, having a distinctive meaning that cannot be completely translated into another language. Humboldt also maintained that, like any living thing, language is dynamic. We cannot understand it simply as a static collection of rules and words, because it is an activity, the attempt to express thoughts in symbols. Because it is an activity, language is constantly evolving and changing.

Rejecting the older rationalist view that words are only arbitrary symbols to designate already fixed concepts, Humboldt stressed the unity of thought and language. He insisted that we discover, define and develop our concepts only through words. Thinking consists in a dynamic interchange between words and concepts. After expressing an idea in a sign, that sign takes on an existence of its own that also partially determines the shape of our ideas. Both concept and sign shape each other until there is at least an approximate correspondence between them.

Humboldt also emphasized the cultural dimension of language. Each language is a unique form of thought, expressing the whole way of life of a people. This view led him to a doctrine of linguistic relativity, which he never fully explored. According to this doctrine, there are as many ways of thinking about the world as there are cultures.

The most controversial aspect of Humboldt's philosophy of language is his typology, which evaluates languages according to the degree that their matter is subordinate to form. He imagined a hierarchy beginning with the purely agglutinative languages, where matter dominates form, and ending with the inflected languages, where form subjugates matter. Such a typology, however, presupposes that there is some ideal or universal language, which is incompatible with the cultural dimension of language. It also clashes with two facts: that some peoples who have an agglutinative language have a highly developed culture (the Chinese); and that some inflected languages, such as English, tend to become formless by losing their endings. Humboldt attempted to meet these difficulties by revising and refining his typology. In the end, however, he never perfected his theory, which remains scattered in many unfinished writings spanning several decades.

See also: LIBERALISM

List of works

Humboldt, W. (1903–36) *Gesammelte Schriften* (Complete Works), ed. Prussian Academy of Sciences, Berlin: Behrs Verlag. (The most complete and authoritative edition of Humboldt's works.)

—— (1981) *Werke in Fünf Bänden* (Complete Works, in Five Volumes), ed. A. Flitner and K. Giel, Darmstadt: Wissenschaftliche Buchgesellschaft. (The most accessible and commonly used edition.)

—— (1792) *Ideen zu einem Versuch, die Gränzen der Wirksamkeit des Staats zu bestimmen* (Ideas for an Essay to Determine the Limits of State Activity), in *Gesammelte Werke* (Complete Works), ed. C. Brandes, Berlin: Reimer, 1851, (7), 1–197; trans. J.W. Burrow, *The Limits of State Action*, Cambridge: Cambridge University Press, 1969. (Humboldt's central work of political philosophy, in which he emphasizes the importance of the minimal state in the promotion of individuality and excellence.)

—— (1963) *Humanist without Portfolio: An Anthology of the Writings of Wilhelm von Humboldt*, trans. M. Cowan, Detroit, MI: Wayne State University Press. (Selected translations of Humboldt's writings.)

—— (1973) *Schriften zur Sprache* (Writings on Language), ed. M. Böhler, Stuttgart: Reclam. (A useful anthology of all the essential writings.)

—— (1988) *On Language: The Diversity of Human Language-Structure and its Influence on the Mental Development of Mankind*, trans. P. Heath and with intro. by H. Aarsleff, Cambridge: Cambridge University Press. (A good anthology and translation of Humboldt's writings on the philosophy of language, with a useful introduction.)

References and further reading

Beiser, F. (1992) *Enlightenment, Revolution and Romanticism*, Cambridge, MA: Harvard University Press, 111–37. (A detailed summary of Humboldt's early political theory.)

Brown, R. (1967) *Wilhelm von Humboldt's Conception of Linguistic Relativity*, Hague: Mouton, Janua linguarum, series minor 65. (A clear explanation of Humboldt's philosophy of language.)

Haym, R. (1856) *Wilhelm von Humboldt: Lebensbild und Charakteristik* (Humboldt: His Life and Character), Berlin: Gaertner. (The classic biography of Humboldt.)

Kaehler, S.A. (1927) *Wilhelm von Humboldt und der der Staat* (Humboldt and the State), Munich: Oldenbourg. (A detailed account of Humboldt's politics.)

Lammers, W. (1936) *Wilhelm von Humboldt's Weg zur Sprachforschung 1785–1801* (Humboldt's Path towards the Investigation of Language 1785–1801), Berlin: Junker & Dünnhaupt. (A detailed account of the development of Humboldt's philosophy of language.)

Leroux, R. (1932) *Guillaume de Humboldt. La formation de sa pensée jusqu'en 1794* (Humboldt: The Development of His Thought up to 1794), Paris: Vrin. (The clearest and most detailed account of his early intellectual development.)

FREDERICK BEISER

HUME, DAVID (1711–76)

Hume's philosophy has often been treated as the culmination of the empiricist tradition of Locke and Berkeley, but it can also be seen to continue the sceptical tradition, and, even more strikingly, the naturalist tradition of Epicurus, Lucretius, Hobbes and Spinoza. Hume challenges orthodox religious conceptions of human nature. He presents us as part of a larger nature, sharing our basic cognitive and affective capacities with the higher animals. Our 'reason' is not some God-given privileged access to truth, but simply our language-affected variant of 'reason in animals'. The negative, anti-rationalist arguments of his first work, A Treatise of Human Nature, where he attacks the views of theistic rationalists, are more muted in his later writings, but the anti-religious arguments become ever more explicit. The importance of his philosophy lies in the thoroughness of his naturalistic project. He tries to show that neither knowledge nor ethics nor the political order needs any sort of religious foundations, and also to explain why so many thinkers had mistakenly held that they did.

To the end of his life Hume called himself a sceptic, but his scepticism was in the service of his secular reform of culture, and always 'mitigated' by his recognition that a 'true sceptic' would be as diffident of his doubts as of his convictions. Sceptical arguments are found useful, however, to cut down the pretensions of dogmatic religious and rationalist claims. His essay 'The Sceptic', although purporting only to portray one sort of philosopher, is often read as a self-portrait.

His first and now most famous work, his Treatise, *was 'of human nature', which he takes to include our understanding, our passions, and what drives our moral and political life. Much of Book I of the* Treatise, *'Of the Understanding', is devoted to showing how many of our beliefs are owing to our 'imagination', rather than to our 'reason'. Book II analyses our passions, their foundation in pleasure and pain, their various idea 'causes' and 'objects', and their communication by sympathy. One of its most famous claims is that passions are needed to motivate action. Hume, whose project is similar to that of Hobbes in* Human Nature *or the Fundamental Elements of Policy, follows him in taking will to be simply the transition from belief-informed passions to action, and takes voluntary human action to be in principle predictable, like everything else. Book III examines our moral evaluations of actions and passions.*

In the Abstract *of the* Treatise *Hume underscores the importance of psychological association in our passions, our belief formation, and, more generally, in the workings of our imagination. Where John Locke*

543

and Francis Hutcheson had found associative thinking a disease of the mind, Hume makes it the norm. Association of ideas by 'resemblance', by temporal and spatial 'contiguity', and by 'causation' gently guides our minds in our spontaneous thinking and fantasizing, and association by causation guides us less gently in our inferences. Like Locke, Hume takes it for granted that 'anatomists' will have some explanation, say in terms of our nervous system and the physical proximity of memory traces in the brain, to account for the psychological phenomena.

Hume emphasizes the influence of experienced repetition on our beliefs and our passions. His famous account of causal inference, which Immanuel Kant claimed woke him from his 'dogmatic slumber', makes it the more or less instinctive extrapolation into the future of regularities and frequencies that have been experienced in the past, along with a tendency to project the felt 'determination of the mind', in its causal inferences, onto the subject matter of those inferences, giving us the idea of causal necessity. Even when made explicit in language, our causal inferences cannot be made into 'demonstrations', in which the conclusion follows with logical necessity from premises known to be true. Hume is credited with discovering 'the problem of induction', although Pascal may have helped in that discovery. Problematic or not, induction is relied on in Hume's own account of our nature. Indeed he believed that, unless we did rely on it in ordinary life, we would 'perish and go to ruin'.

Hume's general theory of human nature, and of the basic capacities and passions which we share with other mammals, is put to work in his account of what is distinctive to us, namely morality, religion, art, politics, and criticism. Like Shaftesbury and Hutcheson before him, he takes morality to involve a special pleasure taken in some human character traits. As moral judges, we find various character traits pleasing and displeasing, and we evaluate forms of social, cultural, and political organization which express or encourage such traits. Our moral sense is a reflexive form of our more basic capacity to take pleasure and displeasure in a range of different things. Morality, as Hume analyses it, is in no way dependent on that other distinctively human phenomenon, religion.

In his writings on religion he gave great offence to believers of his day, both by his diagnosis of the causes of religious fervour, and by his claims about its 'pernicious' effects. Like Pascal, he saw the basic cause of religion to lie in our anxiety about our own fate, but unlike him, did not endorse the religious response to this anxiety. Our ability to think about the future, combined with the limits of our success in finding natural causes for events that affect our happiness, and the intensity of our concern for that, lead us to postulate gods, invisible intelligent causal forces, super-persons, whom we try to please and placate by our prayers and devotions. Different religions and different forms of monotheism naturally develop, and religious persecution and religious wars are the result.

This entirely naturalistic account of reason, morality, politics, culture, and religion made Hume a hero for later Darwinians, such as Huxley, and the toast of the free-thinking Paris salons of his day. But in Britain, despite the fact that his political views are often taken to be conservative, his views on religion were seen by his contemporaries as dangerously radical, as an attack on the very foundations of his own culture.

1   Life and reputation
2   Hume's account of knowledge
3   Human passions and human actions
4   Ethics
5   Political and social philosophy
6   Philosophy of religion

1   Life and reputation

Hume was born in Edinburgh on 26 April 1711. He left us his own brief account of his life, where he highlights the 'good family' he came from (lawyers and landowners on both sides of the family), his 'slender' patrimony from his father, Joseph Home of Ninewells, who died in his infancy, the devotion of his mother, Katherine Falconer, to her three children, his own disinclination to study law, as was thought suitable for him as younger son, and his life-long 'passion for literature'.

After study at Edinburgh University, and beginning the study of law, he began working on what became the Treatise of Human Nature while living at Ninewells (Chirnside, near Berwick, Scotland) with his mother, brother and sister. His mother's only recorded comment about her famous son, 'Our Davie is a fine gude-natured crater [creature], but uncommon wake-minded [weak-minded, or weak of will]', may have its explanation in his failure to stick to his law studies. He left home in 1734 and completed the Treatise in La Flèche, 'a country retreat' in France, where he had the use of the library of the Jesuit college (where Descartes had been educated), and could try out his arguments about miracles on the priests. The book was published in London in 1739–40, and Hume was bitterly disappointed by its reception. He published essays during the next few years, and his Essays Concerning Human Understanding (later the Enquiry Concerning Human Understanding), which restates some themes of the Treatise, in 1748. He had written to his friend Francis HUTCHESON that the Treatise would offend the religious, but he still seems to have been dismayed when the offence it gave ruled him out as an applicant for the chair of Moral Philosophy at Edinburgh University in 1745. His radical views also cost him the Chair of Logic at Glasgow; the only teaching position he ever held was as tutor to a mad English nobleman, for one year, 1745–6. Later he served as a military and diplomatic secretary, as librarian to the Advocates' Library in Edinburgh (while he was working on his *History of England*), and as an Undersecretary of State in London, 1767–9. As Secretary to the British Ambassador in Paris, 1763–6, he met many French intellectuals and earned the title 'le bon David'. On his return journey he escorted Rousseau to England to escape persecution in France and Switzerland. This brief acquaintance ended in a famous falling out.

During the 1750s he had published the *Enquiry Concerning the Principles of Morals*, which Hume believed was his best work, the *Political Discourses*, and the *Four Dissertations* (containing his controversial *Natural History of Religion*), as well as volumes of his *History of England*. It was chiefly as a historian and essayist that he achieved fame in his lifetime. In 1769 he retired to Edinburgh, built a house in the new St Andrews Square, and could live 'opulently' on his earnings. He never married, but had several close friendships with women, and took a great interest in the education of the children of his older brother and of some of his friends. He and his sister entertained a large circle of Scottish friends (including Adam SMITH, the architects Robert and James Adam, William Robertson, Adam FERGUSON, Hugh BLAIR, and many ministers of the Church of Scotland), and occasional guests from overseas, such as Benjamin FRANKLIN, who stayed with Hume for a month. Until his death in 1776 Hume continued adding corrections to new editions of his published writings and polishing his *Dialogues Concerning Natural Religion*, published posthumously in 1779. As he was dying he was visited by James Boswell, curious to find out if, when death was close at hand, the 'great infidel' could preserve his calm Epicurean acceptance of the view that death was annihilation. (His publisher, William Strahan, also expressed the same curiosity in a letter.) Hume joked with Boswell about death and the possibility of an afterlife, and then changed the subject to recommend that Boswell read Smith's *Wealth of Nations*. Boswell left 'with impressions which disturbed me for some time'.

Hume continued to disturb the religious from the grave. Leslie Stephen, writing in 1876, remarked that Hume's writings were so subversive to religion that the general reluctance to face up to their arguments had led to a neglect of his philosophy. However Thomas REID and Immanuel KANT had not neglected it, and

nor had Jeremy BENTHAM and John Stuart MILL. T.H. HUXLEY saw Hume as an ally in the cause of a naturalistic science of human nature, and even T.H. GREEN, who found in his philosophy little except an object lesson in the errors of subjectivism and empiricism, did him the valuable service of re-editing his writings.

To his first biographer, T.E. Richie, Hume was a great historian who had dabbled in philosophy in his youth. For much of the twentieth century he was seen as a great sceptical philosopher who, having shown how little philosophy could hope to do, turned away from philosophy and passed his time writing a sort of '1066 and all that'. Increasingly he is coming to be seen as a scientist of human nature whose 'science' included studying the origins and development of his own culture. His *History* is found to be interestingly philosophical, his philosophy from the start to have been intent on 'a cautious observation of human life... men's behaviour in company, in affairs, and in their pleasures' (*Treatise: xix*). The sceptical strain in his thought, especially when combined with his ambitions as a scientist of human nature, continues to fascinate commentators. Increasing attention is being paid to Hume's essays and later work, and to their relationship to his earlier more 'abstruse' writings.

Strahan, in a letter to Hume's nephew who was arranging the posthumous publication of the *Dialogues Concerning Natural Religion*, wrote that this long-delayed publication 'will probably make some noise in the world; and its tendency be considered in different lights by different men'. Not only the *Dialogues*, but the entire corpus of Hume's writings continues to make some noise in the world, and the tendency of his thought continues to be considered in different lights by different interpreters of it.

2 Hume's account of knowledge

Knowledge and probability. In Hume's early works, the term 'knowledge' is restricted to what is certain, and the term 'probability' (in a wide sense) is used in the *Treatise* for all factual beliefs which might get revised. (Later Hume is more willing to talk with the vulgar, and use 'knowledge' less strictly, 'probability' more narrowly.) Knowledge in the strictest sense is confined to current sense impressions, along with 'intuitions' about the relations between currently sense-perceived qualities, and certain 'relations of ideas', namely those that are 'demonstrably certain'. 'Demonstration' shows that some claims must be affirmed if we are to avoid self-contradiction. Factual claims are never of this 'demonstrated' sort. They are either, if restricted to current sense certainties, known immediately, or, if they make a claim about what goes beyond the evidence of current sensation, then they will be less than certain. Some past tense factual claims will be based on memory (and we can of course misremember), but most factual claims depend upon some inference which takes us from the evidence of current sense impressions and memories to a belief about what we have not, or not yet, ourselves observed. Hume's main concern in Book I of the *Treatise* and in the *Enquiry Concerning Human Understanding* is to examine these latter inferences, and distinguish the relatively well-supported from the less well-supported of them. Of particular interest to him are those that involve reliance on other people's testimony, and his famous discussion of the acceptance of reports of miracles (*Enquiry Concerning Human Understanding*: X) puts all the main principles of his epistemology to work. (This discussion was originally intended for inclusion in the *Treatise*.)

Impressions and ideas. Hume's most general epistemological principle is that all 'ideas', the contents of our thought, derive from more lively 'impressions', the contents of our sense experience and emotional experience. This is put forward at first as an empirical thesis, but it is also used as a normative principle. Impressions are either 'of sense' or, like passions, 'of reflection'. Ideas for which impression-credentials cannot be produced are dubbed 'false', 'imagined', or 'pretended' ideas. Hume takes this line with the idea of a vacuum, and of duration without change. We may *think* we have such ideas, he argues, but we cannot really have them. It is as if ideas, simply by being ideas, make some implicit claim to having impressions as their source, and, if such claims cannot be made good, they are dismissed as false pretenders. Ideas which go well beyond their impression data are termed 'fictions'. These include the idea of the continuous existence through time of physical things we have only intermittently observed, and of the identity of our own minds, with their everchanging perceptions. In accepting such ideas we 'disguise the variation' and 'remove the interruption' (*Treatise*: 254) in the data on which such ideas are based. This constructive contribution of the human mind, in its interpretation of the data of its experience, was highlighted also by Immanuel Kant, who promoted Hume's 'fictions' into a priori 'categories'.

Abstract ideas. Hume follows BERKELEY in taking every idea to be fully particular or 'individual', and to refer to something of which we have had or might have an impression. Abstractness and generality get into ideas by the use to which they are frequently put in our thinking. A particular idea becomes general, on a given occasion for a given thinker, if, for the

purposes in hand, any other idea from a certain set could be substituted for it – if it is serving as a representative of that group of resembling ideas. The words of the thinker's language label these sets (are 'annexed' to them), and fix the sort of 'resemblance' determining their membership. So if our purpose is to consider a claim about all triangles, we will begin with an 'image' before our minds of, say, an equilateral triangle, but we may and should substitute other ideas of other types of triangles to test the claim. As Hume puts it, it is as if the thinker had 'a whole intellectual world of ideas' available to them, all of them ideas of particulars, but 'collected together' in groups and 'plac'd under a general term with a view to that resemblance which they bear to each other'. We show a capacity to 'pick out such as were most proper for our purpose' (*Treatise*: 24). Hume terms this instinct for relevance 'a kind of magical faculty in the soul'. At times he speaks as if the crucial resemblances are recognized before the resembling ideas are 'plac'd under a general term'; at other times it seems as if the prior availability of such terms is crucial to the operation of abstraction, as he analyses it. To treat language as a great aid to abstraction and generalization, rather than an indispensable precondition, would sit better with Hume's views about the role of generalization in causal inference, since he attributes causal inference to animals who lack language. He says that 'men...surpass animals in reasoning', and that 'books and conversations enlarge the sphere of one man's experience and thought' (*Enquiries*: 107).

Causal inference to new beliefs. Hume defines belief as 'a strong and lively idea deriv'd from a present impression related to it' (*Treatise*: 105). The derivation is by causal inference; the relation is causation. The inference is a move of the mind from some impression of sense (or memory) to a conclusion about what is not (or not yet) observed. The conclusion inherits liveliness, 'vivacity', or 'the belief feeling' from its impression-premise. An inference such as 'this is bread, so it will nourish' is never a 'demonstration', since there would be no logical self-contradiction in affirming the premise but denying the conclusion. Memory may assure us that in the past bread has nourished us, and current sense impressions may assure us that this seems to be bread, but what assures us that this bread will act on us as past bread has acted? We can try to convert the causal inference 'this is bread; past bread has nourished us; so this will nourish us' into a 'demonstration' by supplying an extra premise claiming that 'instances of which we have no experience must resemble those of which we have had experience' (*Treatise*: 89); but to claim that we *know* this, that it is certain, would be false pretence. It itself cannot be 'demonstrated'. Moreover, if we try to make it a matter of 'probability', itself a conclusion of an inference whose premise is that *in the past* instances which we had not yet experienced turned out to resemble those we had already experienced, we would have an inference of the same form as the original one, from evidence about the observed to a conclusion about the unobserved. To try to support the 'presumption' that 'the course of nature always continues uniformly the same' by pointing out that it *has* so continued is to give an answer that 'gives still occasion to a question of the same kind, even *in infinitum*' (*Treatise*: 91). We cannot turn our original inference into a sound demonstration. Either we add a premise about what nature 'always' does, which is merely dogmatically asserted, and so get a valid demonstration one of whose premises is a mere 'presumption', or we add less general premises for which we can provide empirical verification, but which leave the inference non-demonstrative in form.

Hume in *Enquiry Concerning Human Understanding* presents this argument as if it provides 'sceptical doubts concerning the operations of the understanding'. In the *Treatise* it is simply a phase of a longer positive argument to the conclusion that ''tis only so far as it [causation] is a natural relation, and produces an union among our ideas, that we are able to reason upon it, or draw any inference from it' (*Treatise*: 94). This is the substance of what the *Enquiry Concerning Human Understanding* calls the 'sceptical solution' to the 'sceptical doubts'. For Hume the scientist of human nature it is simply a fact about us, and a fortunate one, that like other animals we do make causal inferences; unlike them, however, we are able to realize exactly what we are doing, and to formulate rules to help us do it better, so that our predictions will be less often falsified.

The *Treatise* account of our belief formation through causal inference is not only explanatory but also normative, since it ends in rules for improving our inferences. Hume shows how we can see causal inferences as cases of mental association, and explains just what is special about association by 'causation'. Originally in the *Treatise* (Bk I, Pt I, Sec. IV, he had simply listed causation as one of the three 'natural relations' or associative principles. But its effects are found to be special. Only causation, among the forms of association, can form a new belief – not merely, like the other principles of association, revive an old one, or make it more vivid. Hume undertakes to analyse the causal relation as we perceive it, so as to show how it can guide inference to new factual beliefs. He takes it to require contiguity, rather than distance, in space (one of the other principles of association), contiguity in time in the form of immediate priority in time, and

some other more mysterious element that we perceive as 'necessary connexion'.

It is not until near the end of his long account that Hume can demystify that important ingredient in our idea of cause, although 'hints' had been given eight sections earlier, when Hume had 'discover'd' a 'new relation betwixt cause and effect, ... *Constant Conjunction*' (*Treatise*: 87; original emphasis). Although 'from the mere repetition of any past impression [or successions of impressions?], even to infinity, there never will arise any new original idea, such as that of necessary connexion', he had written, 'it wou'd be folly to despair too soon', and in the end it turns out, on his story, that the experience of constancy of temporal conjunction does produce something from which the idea of necessity can be derived, namely inference, or constrained belief, what Hume calls 'the determination of the mind'. His prediction that 'Perhaps t'will appear in the end, that the necessary connexion depends upon the inference, instead of the inference's depending on the necessary connexion' (*Treatise*: 88) turns out to be correct. Necessity 'lies only in the act of the understanding' (*Treatise*: 166). Causal necessity has been reduced to the inferability of one member of a constantly conjoined pair of events from the other. So Hume then offers us two alternative definitions of causation, one as constant conjunction, the other as inferability.

In Section V of the *Enquiry Concerning Human Understanding* Hume says that the 'custom' that determines our causal inferences has 'equal weight and authority' with the 'reason' which is at work in demonstrative inferences. Yet he calls his naturalistic solution 'sceptical', and in Section XII of the *Enquiry Concerning Human Understanding* refers to the sceptic's 'triumph' in such an analysis of causal inference. In the *Treatise* the 'rules' offered for improving our causal inferences are characterized as having the status only of 'unphilosophical probability', or prejudice, albeit a reflexive case of prejudice. Sceptics may be pleased, Hume writes, when they observe 'a new and signal contradiction in our reason ... the following of general rules is a very unphilosophical species of probability; and yet 'tis only by following them that we can correct this, and all other unphilosophical probabilities' (*Treatise*: 150). Scholars continue to disagree about the sense of 'sceptic' in which Hume sees himself as one of these sceptics, and about what most pleased him in his account of causal reasoning.

Testimony, credulity, and miracle reports. Hume's descriptive account covers bad as well as good causal inferences and probability estimations, and it is as part of his attempt to separate the better from the worse inferences that he looks at our reliance on

547

human testimony, the inference from the fact that someone says they witnessed something to the conclusion that they did witness it, or, more generally from the fact that they say that they believe something, and have good evidence to do so, to the conclusion that they do believe it, and do have the evidence they claim for it. A large part of what we call 'education', Hume says, is simply believing what we are told, especially if it is repeated over and over again. (This for him confirms how sensitive we are to repetition.) Such uncritical credulity is out of conformity to Hume's epistemic rules. 'The wise man...proportions his belief to the evidence' (*Enquiries*: 110). The evidence on human lying, and on human error, should give us pause before believing all we hear. When what we hear goes counter to the most widely established 'constant conjunctions', when it is something that it suits someone's purpose that we believe, when it caters to our own suspect 'inclination to the marvellous', and especially when all these factors are present, the wise person is on their guard. Miracles, claimed violations of laws of nature on which religions are founded, do combine all these factors. 'What greater temptation than to appear a missionary, a prophet, an ambassador from heaven?' (*Enquiries*: 125). Self-delusion and 'pious frauds' are to be expected in such cases, from both reporter and hearer of the report. To anyone who looks calmly at the human record of miracle reports and at the rival religions founded on such reports, and who then weighs the probability that a reporter of such a miracle is lying or deluded against the 'proof' (constancy of conjunction), which is the support for the 'law of nature' that supposedly has been violated, the conclusion will be clear. 'We may conclude that the Christian Religion not only was at first attended by miracles, but even at this day cannot be believed by any reasonable person without one.' Hume here does his typical reflexive turn – as he applies causal reasoning to itself, so he here applies his account of belief in miracles to that very belief itself. (This idea is celebrated in the title of a modern challenge to theism, John Mackie's *The Miracle of Theism*.)

Bodies and minds. Book I, Part IV of the *Treatise* explores 'sceptical and other systems of philosophy'. The influence of Berkeley is apparent in Hume's discussion of our belief in lasting physical things, but Hume, unlike Berkeley, cannot appeal to God's notions of physical things to explain their individuation and identity. Belief in lasting bodies pervades our interpretation of current sensations, and so infects the terminology in which most of our causal inferences are formulated. So if these beliefs are, as Hume claims, mere 'fictions', based on 'false suppositions' (*Treatise*: 217), then our causal inferences will also be contaminated. Belief in lasting material objects ('bodies'), Hume claims, helps us to shore up our belief in constant conjunctions, since we just assume that although we may not have observed some particular cause or effect, it nevertheless happened. Lasting things serve as homes for unperceived events, and we need to believe in them to sustain our faith in 'nature's' regular course of action. But some uses of causal analysis, in particular those used to examine the causal relation between physical stimuli and our sense organs, and the supposed relation of 'secondary' to 'primary' properties, can seem to destroy our belief that in sense perception we get reliable information about lasting bodies. There is an unstable relation between our trust in causal inference and our presumption that there are lasting physical things that are involved in causal relations with one another, and with our minds. The first part of the conclusion to Book I of the *Treatise* explores this instability.

Hume's account in the *Treatise* (Bk I, Pt IV, Sec. VI) of what we believe about the identity of our own minds over time, an account supplemented in Book II of the *Treatise*, when he turns to personal identity 'as it regards our passions' (*Treatise*: 253), is less sceptical than the account of belief in lasting mind-independent bodies. However, in the 'Appendix' he reports that his hopes that a contradiction-free account could be given of our self-conceptions and the sort of identity we have reason to ascribe to ourselves (*Treatise*: 633) had been dashed when he realized that, in the section on personal identity, he had involved himself in a 'labyrinth'. Commentators do not agree on just what the perceived difficulty was. He had rejected the idea of a simple self, possessor of its perceptions, since there is no impression from which such an idea could be derived. The 'true idea' of any human mind is of a 'system of different perceptions or different existences, which are link'd together by the relation of cause and effect, and mutually produce, destroy, influence, and modify each other' (*Treatise*: 261). The identity of a mind is 'only a fictitious one, and of a like kind to that which we ascribe to vegetables and animal bodies' (*Treatise*: 259). The most proper analogy, however, is not to bodies but to a 'republic or commonwealth...as the same individual republic may not only change its members, but also its laws and constitution; in like manner the same person may vary his character and disposition, as well as his impressions and ideas, without losing his identity' (*Treatise*: 261). This account of the 'fiction' we tell ourselves about our (and our nation's) identity, and of the factual supports which give it believability, had seemed a satisfactory substitute for the rejected rationalist view that we know ourselves to be simple thinking substances, with an unchanging essence, persisting uninterruptedly through time. But the 'Appendix' finds the account given of 'the principle of connexion' that binds the 'different existences' together to be 'very defective'. Hume's 'scepticism' (*Treatise*: 633) about his original account of the achievable coherence and empirical well-groundedness of our ideas of ourselves continues to spawn a wealth of interpretative literature.

On Hume's own account, if it takes very 'refin'd and elaborate' or 'metaphysical' reasonings (*Treatise*: 268) to see the difficulties the philosophical sceptic finds, then even the mind that has seen them usually 'quickly forgets' them. His own purported attitude to our questionable beliefs about the world and ourselves is, by the end of the conclusion of Book I of the *Treatise*, that of the 'true sceptic', who, while not forgetting his philosophical doubts, is nevertheless as diffident about them as about his earlier convictions. In both cases he defers to his readers to point out to him any errors they find in his reasoning. Plenty of readers have taken up Hume's invitation, especially when it comes to his *Treatise* writings on personal identity. In the *Enquiry Concerning Human Understanding* he dropped this 'difficult' topic, and very much curtailed his treatment of belief in lasting bodies and a 'material world' (Sec. XII, Pt I). 'A blind and very powerful instinct of nature' is said to make us have and preserve a belief in lasting external objects, and trust our own senses to give us reliable information about such objects. 'The profounder and more philosophical sceptics' will be able to shake our blind faith, producing 'momentary amazement and confusion', but if we ask the sceptic 'what he proposes by all these curious researches?' 'if any durable good or benefit to society could ever be expected to result' (*Enquiries*: 159) from dwelling on his arguments, then, Hume says, the sceptic is the one who will be embarrassed.

Social epistemology. Hume's discussions of human knowledge in his essays and in the *History of England* keep the question 'Do you expect durable good and benefit for society to come from your epistemological researches, or are you merely amusing yourself?' very much in the forefront of their author's mind. His question becomes 'When and how do various branches of knowledge grow?' not 'Is knowledge possible?' Where his earlier epistemology was 'abstruse', analytical, and general, his later epistemology is much less general, and not at all abstruse. His interest shifts to social epistemology. Do the sciences thrive better in a republic than in a monarchy? What sort of representation does a guinea make, and would it make a different representation if it were made of copper, not gold? What relation is there between commercial trade between nations and exchange of ideas? What has the invention of the printing press done to the life of the mind, and what other inventions make or might make comparable changes? Epistemology merges into social philosophy and ethics.

3   Human passions and human actions

Passions and sentiments. Hume takes us to share our basic passion-repertoire, as well as our ability to learn from experience, with the higher animals. They may lack moral, aesthetic, religious, and philosophical 'sentiments', but they do, if Hume is right, love, hate, feel pride and shame, as well as desire, enjoy, suffer, hope, and fear. Their passions have the same sorts of objects that ours do, and we can sympathize with some of their passions, as some of them can with some of ours. 'Passions', with the exception of a few instinctive appetites, are 'impressions of reflection', reactions of pleasure or displeasure to some perception of our situation.

All passions have 'objects', what BRENTANO called 'intentional directedness' and others have termed 'aboutness' (see INTENTIONALITY). 'Direct' passions, such as desire, joy, sorrow, hope and fear, are caused by their 'objects'. What Hume calls the 'indirect' passions, such as pride, involve both the thought of something that pleases, such as a fine cloak, and also the recognition of that good thing as belonging to a particular person, bringing a consequent pleasure in that person. Should the particular person be oneself, the pleasure one feels will be pride. Should it be another person, the pleasure will be affection or esteem for that person. So the basic 'causes' of all passions are 'agreeable' pleasure and 'uneasy' pain or distress, and thoughts about their causes or occasions. Since they are 'impressions *of reflection*', they are equally founded on our thoughts about what has given or would give us such pleasure and pain. Throughout Parts I and II of Book II of the *Treatise*, Hume traces 'the double relations of impressions and ideas' which are responsible for the varieties of pride and humility, love and hate, and various mixtures of them. He invokes association by resemblance to explain the transitions in our emotional life from one pleasure to another (from being pleased by some witticism to being pleased with the friend who uttered it), and he invokes association of more varied sorts to explain the thought transitions involved in such sequences of passions.

When Hume rewrote his account of human passions, as given in Book II of the *Treatise*, in one of his *Four Dissertations*, 'Of Passions', he blunted the distinction between direct passions such as joy and indirect passions such as pride, but he is still fairly boastful about the explanatory power of his principles of association. The *Dissertation* reverses the order of treatment in the *Treatise*, beginning with hope and fear and moving on to pride, humility, love, and hate, which he terms not 'indirect', but simply 'passions of a more complicated nature', ones which 'imply more than one view or consideration'. The substance of the account is largely unaltered, and the 'mechanics' of association are still very prominent, but the order of treatment and the terminology have changed.

In both *Treatise* and *Dissertation* a distinction is drawn between 'calm' and 'violent' passions. This cuts across the distinction between relatively simple (or 'direct') passions and relatively complicated ones. Any passion can become violent. A passion, say a desire, is said to be violent when it produces 'sensible emotion' (*Treatise*: 417) or 'sensible agitation'. Passions tend to become violent when one 'swallows up' another, thereby getting 'new force and violence', when a passion encounters opposition or delay in gratification, when uncertainty produces 'agitation' in the mind, including the case where the object of a passion is temporarily absent, or partially concealed or veiled. Although violence is not the same as strength, still the 'force' it involves usually strengthens a passion, so that 'when we wou'd govern a man, and push him to any action, t'will commonly be better policy to work upon the violent than the calm passions' (*Treatise*: 419). Custom, by giving us 'facility', can strengthen a passion despite the fact that it removes some causes of violence, namely agitating novelty, challenge, and uncertainty. Hume ends the *Dissertation* with the expressed hope that he has shown that 'in the production and conduct of the passions, there is a certain regular mechanism, which is as susceptible of as accurate a disquisition, as the laws of motion, optics, hydrostatics, or any part of natural philosophy'. (Here he seems to echo Spinoza in his preface to *Ethics* III.) The 'mechanics' of violence in passions, however, seems a little less than fully systematised by Hume. Since, in the *Treatise*, he wants to explain the errors of rationalists in ethics in part by the hypothesis that they confuse calm passions with reason, any inadequacies in his account of calm and violence has repercussions for his case against the rationalists.

Sympathy. All passions can be and often are communicated from one animal or person to another, through their understood bodily expression and our response to that in what Hume calls 'sympathy'. Sympathy enlivens a mere idea of another's passion into an impression. 'The howlings and lamentations of a dog produce a sensible concern in his fellows' (*Treatise*: 398). It is not only distress which is thus communicated, but any expressed passion, or even opinion. 'This is not only conspicuous in children,

who implicitly embrace every opinion propos'd to them; but also in men of the greatest judgment and understanding, who find it very difficult to follow their own reason or inclination, in opposition to that of their friends and daily companions' (*Treatise*: 316). We spontaneously imitate the expressed state of mind of those around us, Hume believes, and this communication of feeling, along with its extension by our ability to imagine what others would feel, in various circumstances, is essential for the possibility of 'the moral sentiment'. But there is also a 'principle', or basic tendency, which interferes with the workings of sympathy. This is 'comparison', which leads us to ask if we are doing better or worse than others. We can welcome another's misfortune, rather than feel compassion for them, if that misfortune points up our own better fortune. 'Comparison' is invoked by Hume to explain malice and envy. He treats remorse as a case of malice against oneself, 'an irregular appetite for evil'. He finds envy to be typically felt for those close in position to ourselves, and to be felt even when we are 'superior', should our inferiors be perceived to be advancing.

Sympathy can be blocked by the operation of 'comparison', but is facilitated by the perception of any sort of 'natural relation' between ourselves and others. 'Similarity in our manners, or character, or country, or language...facilitates the sympathy' (*Treatise*: 318). (Blood ties, and spatial contiguity also facilitate it.) Sympathy is sharing the feelings of others perceived to be like ourselves, or related to us, and so is felt differentially. Hume takes the moral sentiment to correct for such natural partialities in our sympathy.

The will, passion, and action. Hume includes an account of the will, and its freedom or lack of it, in Book II of the *Treatise*. Although he takes will to be the transition from thought and passion to action, it is discussed in his book on the passions, since 'the full understanding of its nature and properties is necessary to the understanding of them [the passions]' (*Treatise*: 399). The 'mechanical' nature of human passions is found to be corroborated by the 'uniformity and regularity' of human conduct. Our decisions and behaviour are just as predictable (in principle) as what happens in inanimate matter. We have at best 'the liberty of spontaneity', on those occasions when our behaviour has determining causes internal to us as persons, rather than 'violent' external causes, overriding our own conscious wishes. In the *Enquiry Concerning Human Understanding* Hume defines liberty as 'the power of acting or not acting according to the determinations of the will', (*Enquiries*: 94) and the will's determinations are taken themselves to have their own psychological determining causes. This makes liberty a property not of the will, but of the agent (see WILL, THE). In this, as in his determinism, Hume agrees with HOBBES.

His account of our motivation, then, is that the complicated play of our passions, closely affected as they are by our memories, beliefs, and imaginings, lead to our intentions, 'the determinations of our will'. These, as long as we are at liberty and do not forget or change our minds, get realized in our actions. Because passions are 'impressions', they are active psychological causes, sufficient to cause action. Because they are 'impressions of reflection', they incorporate the information about our situation that our memory, our beliefs, our reason and our reflection have given us. They need not be blind, however partial their 'views' often are. Hume's account of the passions which motivate us makes them intrinsically reflective and thought-informed.

Because Hume takes our passions to determine our actions, the sort of conversation and company we provide, and the sorts of institutions, books, and artworks we are likely to produce, the evaluation of our passions becomes very important. His essays 'Of Tragedy', and 'Of the Standard of Taste' explore the passions literature arouses, our pleasure in it, and evaluation of it. Moral evaluation, he holds, is always the evaluation of 'character', of 'principles in the mind and temper' (*Treatise*: 477). His careful exploration of different sorts of sensitivity or 'delicacy', in the essay 'Of the Delicacy of Taste and Passion', like his investigations into relative 'violence' in passions, and into the role played in our passions by sympathy and by 'the principle of comparison', as well as his discussion of liberty and necessity, all feed into his account of moral evaluation.

Hume's 'moral psychology' bears a striking similarity to Spinoza's. Whether he had read Spinoza's *Ethics* or just Bayle's version of it, he certainly shows agreement with Spinoza's deterministic version of our psychology, and with particular points of detail, such as the effects of vacillation. His account of the effect of opposition on the violence of a passion (so that we naturally 'desire what is forbid') and his negative treatment of remorse, also repeat theses that Spinoza had advanced (see SPINOZA, B. DE; BAYLE, P.).

4 Ethics

The virtues. Hume takes it to be agreed that moral judgment is primarily a judgment about human character traits, a recognition of 'virtues' and 'vices' (see VIRTUES AND VICES). He has some controversial views both about what enlightened moral judges will and will not include in their lists of virtues, and about how they do their judging.

In his 'catalogue of virtues' he distinguishes the 'natural virtues' from what in the *Treatise* he calls 'artificial', or convention-dependent, virtues. The latter consist in conformity to some beneficial social scheme of cooperation, such as a particular form of government. The artificial virtues, for him, include 'justice' (taken to include respect for traditional property rights, and 'fidelity to promises'), 'allegiance' (to magistrates), female modesty and chastity (preparation for and conformity to the role given to women in the artifice of marriage), and the duties of sovereign states to keep treaties, to respect each others' territorial boundaries, to give protection to ambassadors, and otherwise conform to 'the law of nations'. All the artificial virtues will be expected to take different specific forms in different societies and historical conditions.

In contrast to the artificial virtues, the 'natural' virtues are expected to be fairly invariant across cultures. Hume includes among the natural virtues compassion, generosity, gratitude, friendship, fidelity, charity, beneficence, clemency, equity, prudence, temperance, frugality, industry, courage, ambition, due pride (duly concealed so as not to offend others), due modesty (awareness of one's weaknesses), due self-assertiveness, good sense, wit and humour, perseverance, patience, courage, parental devotion, good nature, cleanliness, articulateness, responsiveness to poetry, decorum, and 'a certain *je-ne-sais-quoi* of agreeable and handsome', which 'render a person lovely or valuable' (*Treatise*: 611–12). The controversial features of his catalogue lie in part in the substitution of pride for humility, in part in the inclusion of qualities which do not depend on their possessor's will, and in part in the particular glosses he gives to traditional virtues such as courage and charity.

Courage is to be exercised, if possible, in non-military contexts, so that it need not involve killing or 'the sack of cities'. About charity Hume says:

> Giving alms to common beggars is naturally praised; because it seems to carry relief to the distressed and indigent: but when we observe the encouragement thence arising to idleness and debauchery, we regard that species of charity rather as a weakness than a virtue.
>
> (*Enquiries*: 180)

From the truly beneficent person, the hungry may indeed 'receive food, the naked clothing', but mainly because from such a person they will also receive 'skill and industry' (*Enquiries*: 178). Hume's later essays on economics develop this theme.

Hume's list of virtues is a self-conscious rejection of a puritan morality, and to some extent of Christian morality. Not only, as he wrote to Francis Hutcheson, does he not take his 'catalogue of virtues' from *The Whole Duty of Man* (a Protestant religious tract he had been encouraged to read as a child), but he finds some of the virtues listed there to be vices, from the point of view of a morality which has freed itself from 'the delusive glosses of superstition and false religion'. Hume's ethics are avowedly hedonist (see HEDONISM). All virtues, he generalizes, are qualities that please from a moral point of view either because they prove 'agreeable' (tend to bring pleasure) to their possessors or to others, or else because they are seen to have 'utility' for their possessors or for others. 'Celibacy, fasting, penance, mortification, self denial, humility, silence, solitude, and the whole train of monkish virtues' are, he finds, neither agreeable nor useful; they 'stupify the understanding and harden the heart, obscure the fancy and sour the temper' (*Enquiries*: 270). *The Whole Duty of Man* had included, in its list of breaches of duty, various breaches of the duty of humility, and such other sins as 'eating too much', 'heightening of lust by pampering the body', 'not labouring to subdue it by Fasting, and other Severities', and 'not assigning any Set or Solemn time for Humiliation and Confession, or too seldom'. It was not merely the 'monks' whom Hume was opposing when listing the virtues, but the Calvinists who had preached to him, and the other Protestant divines whose tracts he had been given as a child to help him learn to recognize vice.

But there are very many of the duties listed in *The Whole Duty of Man* that Hume includes in his catalogue, and that repeat those listed in Cicero's *Offices*, which he told Hutcheson was his preferred source book on morals (see CICERO). 'Not loving peace', and 'going to law on slight occasion', as well as theft, ingratitude, lying, malice, and oppression are all condemned in *The Whole Duty of Man*, and Hume would have little quarrel with these disapprobations. He told Boswell that, as a child, he skipped such things as theft and murder, in the list of sins provided by the *Whole Duty*, 'having no inclination to perform them'. As far as murder goes, not only did he omit to think about it, when examining his conscience as a child, but he omitted to consider it carefully enough in his moral philosophy. After citing parricide as a 'horrid crime' which rationalist moralists may have difficulty explaining, he then proceeds to say all but nothing in his own voice about what is wrong with homicide (as distinct from cruelty). He defends suicide (in the posthumously published 'Of Suicide'), and discusses varying tolerance of it and of tyrannicide in 'A Dialogue', (published with *Enquiries Concerning the Principles of Morals*) but gives us no extended discussion either of any artifice-grounded

right to life, or of any natural virtue consisting of respect for human life.

Which forms of killing are vicious, and why? The rationalist answer may well have weaknesses, or even incoherencies, but Hume gives us no explicit answer. At most he gives us hints, such as 'While we are ignorant whether a man were an aggressor or not, how can we determine whether the man who killed him be criminal or innocent?' (*Enquiries*: 290). There are also many discussions of particular killings in the *History of England*, where Hume charts the shifting penalties for murder, their variation depending on the rank and sex of the victim, and the various degrees of cruelty in methods used by official or semi-official killers. (See his accounts of the killing of the exiled Queen Elgiva, of King Edward II, of Joan of Arc, as well as of the followers of Wycliff and other martyrs at the hands of various church and state authorities.)

Hume calls it a verbal matter that he includes among the virtues qualities of mind, such as wit and good sense, and 'involuntary' as well as 'voluntary' abilities. But it is no *merely* verbal matter that he refuses to call the 'involuntary' excellences 'talents', and to separate them from moral virtues. A sharp distinction between the voluntary and the involuntary is needed, he wrote in the *Treatise*, only by those who are handing out rewards and punishments, hoping thereby to regulate voluntary actions (*Treatise*: 609). But expressed moral approbation and disapprobation, as he understands them, are not deliberate reward and punishment, nor need they be preludes to reward and punishment. They are the more or less spontaneous expression of moral sentiments, themselves no more wholly voluntary than their objects. 'Philosophers, or rather divines under that disguise, treating all morals on a like footing with civil laws, were necessarily led to render this circumstance, *voluntary* or *involuntary*, the foundation of their whole theory' (*Enquiries*: 322). Hume does not treat morals this way, and so he is just as 'necessarily led' to resist the restriction of moral judgment to the voluntary.

Artificial virtues: justice. The part of morals that Hume does treat as being on a like footing with civil laws, and so as sanction-backed, is the area covered by 'the artificial virtues'. These consist in conformity to some generally beneficial convention, where the benefit accrues not act by act, but from the 'whole scheme of actions'. Since general conformity is needed for the benefit to be obtained, pressure is deliberately brought to bear, on adults as on children, to get them to show honesty in matters of property, to keep their promises, to show allegiance to lawful magistrates, and to show chastity and marital fidelity, at least if they are women.

'Justice', as rendering each their due, is taken by

Hume to be primarily respect for property rights. His brief discussion of what we would call retributive justice is to be found in his discussion of liberty of the will (and throughout the *History of England*), not in his account of what he calls 'justice'. Although he frequently refers to equity, it is not clear what relation he took it to have to justice. (He includes it in a list of natural virtues.) What he argues about 'justice', in his sense, is that we need to have a convention establishing property, and establishing particular property rights, before anything could count as respect for such rights. Similarly, he will argue, we must have the social institution of promise (or contract, taken as mutual promise) before anything could count as keeping or breaking promises, and must have the institution of government before anyone can count as a superior, to whom allegiance is owed. To get the needed distinctions between possession and property, or between telling someone what one will do and promising to do it, or doing what one is told and showing allegiance to one's rightful superior, we must be able to turn to some social 'convention' which promotes some cases of possession into ownership, some transfers into barter, gifts, loans or sales, some statements of intention into promises, some issuing of sentences in the imperative mood into lawful commands.

In the *History of England*, when reporting John Ball's 'seditious preaching' in the late fourteenth century, Hume describes the popularity of Ball's doctrine of 'the first origin of mankind in one common stock, their equal right to liberty and to all the goods of nature, the tyranny of artificial distinctions'. He says that such doctrines are bound to be popular since they are 'so conformable to ideas of primitive equality, which are engraven in the hearts of all men' (Ch. XVII). His own story, which he owes to LUCRETIUS, about the origins of justice is not so different from Ball's, except that he emphasizes the inevitability of 'artifice', and does not regard it as necessarily bringing tyranny. The 'primitive equality' he recognizes lies in the need to get the agreement of each person to limiting the equal access of all to 'all the goods of nature'. Until there is a general agreement ending the primitive scramble to grab what one can from the goods of nature, then nothing will count as theft, as unjust taking, as wrongful possession. On Hume's story, only when every person sees, or seems to see, that they will be better off if present possession is frozen into rightful possession, into property, and only when there is an agreement to take only with owner's consent, can it cease to be all right for people to take what they please and can. Hume's story, like Ball's and like Hobbes' before him, and like that of ROUSSEAU after him, presupposes the

postulation of a primitive equality and liberty. The 'convention' needed to create private property rights, Hume writes, depends upon a 'general sense of common interest', on the perception that although any single property-respecting act may not bring advantages, indeed may involve loss, still 'the whole system of actions, concurr'd in by the whole society, is infinitely advantageous to the whole and to every part' (*Treatise*: 498). Unlike the Lollards and Levellers, however, Hume thought that rational and long-sighted convenors would see that equality of property, however theoretically desirable, is impracticable: 'Render possession ever so equal, men's different degrees of art, care, and industry will immediately break that equality. Or, if you check these virtues, you reduce society to the most extreme indigence' (*Enquiries*: 194). 'The most rigorous inquisition too is requisite to watch every inequality on its first appearance, to punish and redress it...so much authority must soon degenerate into tyranny' (ibid.). Where Ball saw inequality to depend upon tyranny, Hume sees the threat of tyranny to accompany the attempt to prevent inequality. But his sympathy with the egalitarians' ideals is as clear as his disagreement with them concerning the costs of equality.

Artificial virtues: fidelity to promises. Hume's analysis of promises and promissory rights follows the same lines as the analysis of property and property rights. Until a convention fixes which assurances are binding assurances, there will be no promises or contracts. The fixing, as in the case of property, will contain some elements of arbitrariness. Societies vary in such matters as the need for witnesses, for the contract to be written and signed, for there to be some 'consideration'. Hume takes the function of promise to be to extend security in transfers of goods and services to include future delivery and future services. He takes there to be a special form of words, 'I promise...' used when such binding assurances are given, and he takes their force to include the promisor's acceptance of the appropriateness of penalty in the form of withdrawal of trust (and thus disablement as a party to binding agreements) if the promise is broken. This informal enforcement of the sacredness of promissory obligations gives promises their verbal magic. Hume likens them to the priest's words in the mass, to the magic of transubstantiation, with the significant difference that 'the obligation [binding force] of promises is an invention for the interest of society', while 'priestly inventions...have no public interest in view' (*Treatise*: 524).

Hume denies that promises need to be given when any convention is accepted. Because he regards the obligation to keep promises and contracts as itself 'artificial', it would be absurd, he finds, to rest all artifice on promise. 'We are not surely bound to keep our word because we have given our word to keep it' (*Enquiries*: 306). Hume likens the conventions on which property and promissory rights rest to the tacit agreement we give to the conventions of our native language, or to the use of the monetary currency we find in use around us as 'measures of exchange', and to the agreement of rowers who both want to get in one boat across a river, and so coordinate their strokes. Recent contractarians have claimed Hume as one of them, despite his explicitly dismissing as absurd the suggestion that the agreement on which the obligations of justice rest could possibly itself be a mutual promise, and his rejection, both in the *Treatise* and in his essay 'Of the Original Contract', of the view that the authority of magistrates must rest on some promise or contract tying governor to governed. He agrees with the contractarians that the origins of justice lay in some sort of agreement that it was in everyone's interest to make with everyone else, but he would probably reject the label 'contractarian', and he certainly would not agree with those who try to make all of morality, not only justice, rest on a hypothetical self-interested agreement (see CONTRACTARIANISM).

Artificial virtues: chastity and modesty. Hume includes the virtues of female modesty and chastity among the artificial virtues, since he sees them to depend upon the existence of the institution of marriage, and in particular on the 'agreement' that husbands should not be expected to contribute to the upbringing of children they did not father. The only way men can have any confidence that the children born to their wives are 'really their own' (*Treatise*: 571) is by taking as wives only those women trained from childhood to an unnatural 'modesty', 'some preceding backwardness or dread' of sexual activity, and then by imposing the 'punishment of bad fame or reputation' on any wives suspected of infidelity. Hume stresses the 'unnaturalness', not just the social contrivance and usefulness, of these demands made on wives and would-be wives. It is in the interests of children that they receive care from a male as well as a female parent, and in general men can only be 'induc'd' to contribute to the care of children whom they take to be 'their own', so it becomes 'reasonable, and even necessary, to give them some security in this particular'. All men, Hume notes, including 'batchelors, however debauch'd', are shocked at 'lewdness or impudence in women', or at least in marriage-bent women. Is there irony in his account of the 'reasonableness' of a double standard? His early essays 'Of Love and Marriage', 'Of Polygamy and Divorces', and 'Of Moral Prejudices', continue his examination of the forms of marriage with which he was familiar,

but readers do not agree on what these discussions reveal of Hume's own views.

How artificial virtue is inculcated. Hume takes it that we have a self-interested motive to adopt the policy of respecting property and keeping our promises and marriage vows since these 'inventions' are so designed that general conformity to their rules does bring advantages to 'the whole and every part' of society. And we have good moral reason to approve of such conformity. But, especially with property rights as they develop over a long period of time, and are affected by the transfers that have occurred through contract and through the invention of money, it is easy for a person to lose sight of the 'remote' and long term interest they may have in respect for established property rights. 'The artifices of politicians' may be needed to bolster their motivation. But Hume believes that we will usually see well enough what is wrong with disrespect for property rights when we are the victims of it. We see such disrespect as a 'vice', and feel disapprobation. We feel sympathy with other victims of theft, and our 'sympathy with public interest' leads us to condemn all breaches of property rights, however 'obscure' it may have become just what personal advantage we each get from a policy of honesty in preference to occasional judicious dishonesty. Hume grants that there may be no convincing answer to the 'sensible knave', who successfully conceals his dishonesty, and believes he does better than the scrupulously honest person. If educators, moralists and politicians have failed to give him 'an antipathy to treachery and roguery', if all he cares about is 'profit or pecuniary advantage', then no argument the moralist can provide is likely to change his mind. The moralist, on behalf of 'the party of humankind' (some of whom the clever knave is cheating and defrauding), may sincerely believe that the knaves are 'the greatest dupes', since they 'have sacrificed the invaluable enjoyment of a character, with themselves at least, for the acquisition of worthless toys and geegaws' (*Enquiries*: 283), but the knave will have his own sincere views about what is and is not worthless, and who are the dupes.

The moral sentiment, moral points of view. Hume takes virtues to be recognized as such by the moral sentiment, a special pleasure taken in agreeable and useful character traits, when these are surveyed from a 'general and steady' point of view. One of his most famous theses is that moral distinctions are not made by 'reason alone', but by the special sort of pleasure and displeasure we take in character traits and in the 'manners', or ways of behaving, that express them. Our approbation and disapprobation are what makes the approved traits virtues, the disapproved ones vices. 'We do not infer a character to be virtuous, because it pleases: But in feeling that it pleases after such a particular manner, we in effect feel that it is virtuous' (*Treatise*: 471). The 'particular manner' in which character traits must please to be virtues stems from the special 'point of view' which must be taken, and which we take in order to 'converse together on any reasonable terms' (*Treatise*: 581) about human merit. It is a 'steady and general' point of view which we have reason to expect others to be able to take, and from which agreement is in theory possible. In order to 'overlook our own interest', and get such a 'general' view, we must be capable both of sympathizing with other people's private viewpoints, and of correcting for natural bias in our sympathy. We consider how a given trait, say our own ambition, affects others, and try to see it as they see it. We do not ignore our own interest, but we look beyond that to the interests and concerns of everyone affected. When what we are judging is some military leader's courage, we will sympathetically consider both its effects on the armies he led, and his own nation, and also its effects on those against whom he led his forces, 'the subversion of empires, the devastation of provinces, the sack of cities' (*Treatise*: 601). Moral approbation is a pleasure taken in a character trait, all things considered, and much preparation, including fact-finding, is needed to get to a point of view which really can claim to be general, which can expect to be 'steady', and expect to be shared.

Moral disagreement. Our expectation that our moral judgment will be shared with other moral judges is usually tempered by experience of moral controversy. Can Hume account for apparent moral disagreement? Even when we try to speak for 'the party of humankind', rather than just for ourselves, our class, or our nation, we often find other would-be representatives for humankind contradicting us.

Hume discusses apparent moral disagreement in 'A Dialogue'. 'Of the Standard of Taste' addresses what he sees as the closely similar topic of apparent disagreement about literary merit. In both these discussions Hume explains away the appearance of disagreement as due to some confusion, or lack of proper preparation or competence in some of the disagreeing judges. 'In moral decisions, all the circumstances and relations must be previously known; and the mind, from the contemplation of the whole, feels some new impression of affection or disgust, esteem or contempt, approbation or blame' (*Enquiries*: 290). Since very many judgments which purport to be moral are based on imperfect knowledge of circumstances, on narrow sympathies, on a contemplation of much less than 'the whole', it is not surprising that there is less than unanimity in such judgments. Whereas Hume takes all of us to be

capable of becoming competent moral judges (if we are able and willing to rid our minds and hearts of 'the illusions of religious superstition and philosophical enthusiasm'), he took literary criticism to be a more elite skill, requiring both a 'delicacy of taste' and an extensive reading which not all could be expected to have. One interesting feature of his specification of the competent literary critic is that they show due allowance for difference of religion from writer to writer, so not condemn a book simply because of the false religion it presents, but show no such toleration on moral matters. The critic will be justly 'jealous' of their moral standards.

The arguments against the rationalists. Hume, in the *Treatise*, tries to refute the claims of rationalists such as Samuel CLARKE that moral distinctions can be discerned by pure reason. His argument has two main parts. The first is that the conclusions of reason are 'ideas', but only 'impressions' can motivate, and moral distinctions are supposed to motivate. This argument relies on the sharp contrasts, drawn earlier in the *Treatise*, between impressions and less vivacious ideas, and between sense impressions and the passions they would need to 'concur' with, in order to motivate. Hume suggests that the rationalist may be mistaking calm passions, which do not agitate us, for passionless reason. The rationalist who disagrees with Hume's distinctions will be unmoved by his first argument.

The second part of the argument is that, in any case, there do not seem to be any rationally discernible facts or relations which would establish the sort of conclusion which the rationalist moralist expects to be able to draw, for example that certain sorts of behaviour (incest, killing a parent) are wrong if done by human beings, but not if done by animals or plants. This argument attempts to show that the wrongness of murder or incest is not a matter of rationally discernible relations. Hume cites the supposedly exhaustive list of 'philosophical' (cognitively discernible) relations of ideas given in Book I of the *Treatise*, and the claim of the *Treatise* (Bk I, Pt III, Sec. I) that only four of these, resemblance, contrariety, degrees in quality, and proportion in quantity or number, can be traced by 'demonstration'. Hume challenges any rationalist who disputes the completeness of his list of 'demonstrable relations' to point out the extra morally relevant relation. He requires that such a relation relate inner actions or states of mind to mind-external 'objects' (since he takes it that we all agree that moral judgment is restricted to expressed character traits), and that such a relation or relations determine what is 'forcible and obligatory' for all those capable of discerning them, that is for all rational beings. He takes it that, in order to found obligations, the relations would have to be shown to have a necessary effect on the will of all those who are obligated, and he seems to think that no rationalist could meet this challenge.

He adds, to his main anti-rationalist arguments, a famous 'observation' which he thought would 'subvert all the vulgar systems of morality' (*Treatise*: 470). This observation is that those who want to move from some factual claim to some conclusion about how we ought to behave owe us an explanation of how to derive the 'ought' of the conclusion from the 'is' of the premise (see FACT/VALUE DISTINCTION). This is a challenge similar to that issued earlier to the rationalist who wants to found obligations on rationally discernible relations – to show a connexion to the will of the obligated, to show why that relation, or that fact, should fix for them what to do. He has not shown, nor does he claim to have shown, that there is no adequate answer to his challenges. 'Vulgar' rationalist systems may be subverted by his observations, along with other vulgar systems, but more refined versions of such systems can be depended upon to find a way around the 'difficulties' which he challenges them to face.

5 Political and social philosophy

Nature and point of government. In the *Treatise* governmental authority is a social 'artifice', added to those of property, promise, and marriage. For it to come to exist, there must be a felt need that it satisfies, some 'convention' creating the right to govern, and bestowing it on some person or some group of persons. The need for government arises, Hume believed in the *Treatise*, only when other artifices, such as promise and contract, have enabled some people to accumulate so much property that they cannot adequately guard it against marauders, and to acquire it in ways suspected of fraudulence, so that others resent their possession of it. 'Acts of injustice' become frequent, and those who continue to respect property and promissory rights fear becoming 'cullies of their integrity'. What becomes needed is some security for the 'just' against exploitation by the 'unjust'. By creating a special job, that of 'magistrates', who will be responsible for 'the execution and decision of justice', such security is provided. The security is not only for the just against the unjust, but for the just impulses in any person against any temptation to injustice and inequity. Hume follows Hobbes in finding it a universal human weakness to see the attractions of the good that is close more easily than the attractions of 'remoter' goods, even when they are real and often greater. Without enforcement of property rules and contracts, 'the consequences of every breach of equity seem to lie very remote, and are

not able to counterballance any immediate advantage, that may be reap'd from it' (*Treatise*: 535). The remedy, Hume writes, is to create rule-enforcers, so that there will come to be an immediate interest (avoiding punishment) as well as a remote interest (good character and reputation for it, social order and the benefits one gets from it) in avoiding acts of injustice. 'We are, therefore, to look upon all the vast apparatus of our government as having ultimately no other object or purpose but the distribution of justice, or, in other words, the support of twelve judges' (*Essays*: 27). These are Hume's words in 'Of the Origin of Government', a relatively late essay. In the *Treatise* he gave magistrates an additional role, namely coordinating new beneficial cooperative schemes which private enterprise might have neither motive to embark on nor the needed supervisory ability to bring to completion. Hume became more of a prophet for limited government as he grew older, but even in his late works he saw it as the governors' task not merely to declare and protect rights which pre-existed their own right to govern, but 'to point out the decrees of equity, to punish transgressors, to correct fraud and violence, and to oblige men, however reluctant, to consult their own real and permanent interests' (*Essays*: 38).

Who should govern. Hume is, of course, acutely aware of the difficulty of finding competent and reliable 'magistrates' or governors. In the *History of England* he praises the 'mixed' character of the English government, even in its earliest days providing some protection against tyranny. To avoid tyranny, powers must be balanced against each other, and the main tasks of politics as a 'science' are to find the best such balance, to design institutions that work well even when bad people are office-holders, and to provide for orderly transitions of power. The party system, the different roles of electorate, of the legislature, of monarch or other executive, of the judiciary, of the press, all should contribute to the goal of providing an ongoing government that really does serve the real interests of the governed.

Hume emphasizes that there is some inevitable arbitrariness in the selection of governors. 'The magistrate may often be negligent, or partial, or unjust in his administration', and yet be a lawful magistrate, who is owed allegiance. The right to govern, like a property right, can be based on any of several different grounds. The hypothetical first magistrate might well have derived his authority from the consent of the governed, who might well have promised him allegiance:

But when government has been establish'd on this footing for some considerable time, and the separate interest, which we have in submission, has produc'd a separate sentiment of morality, the case is entirely alter'd.

(*Treatise*: 554)

The same interest, therefore, which causes us to submit to magistracy, makes us renounce itself in the choice of our magistrates, and binds us down to a certain form of government, and to particular persons, without allowing us to aspire to the utmost perfection in either. The case is here the same as in that law of nature concerning the stability of possession.

(*Treatise*: 555)

As the initial property rights were, Hume supposes, determined by 'present possession', to which in time get added 'prescription' or 'long possession', 'accession', 'succession', and 'transfer by consent' from former owners, so with governmental authority – a parallel plurality of grounds can be taken to establish it. What our 'interest' in government dictates is that the transitions from one governor to the next be smooth and nonviolent, and this paramount interest means that laws dictating how the next governor is to be selected are usually in place. 'Positive law', as well as 'original contract', 'long possession', 'present possession', and 'succession' can select the magistrates.

In his essay 'Of the Original Contract', in other essays, and throughout the *History of England*, Hume continues this *Treatise* discussion of the dangerousness and impracticality of being determined to 'aspire to the utmost perfection' in government, especially given widely different opinions of what method of selecting a magistrate is the more perfect. Consent or 'original contract' can get government started, but once any of the original contractors (subjects or sovereign), dies, or new subjects are born, it is wildly impractical and dangerous to demand renewed contracts. 'Did one generation of men go off the stage at once, and another succeed, as is the case with silkworms and butterflies, the new race...might voluntarily, by general consent, establish their own form of civil polity, without any regard to the laws and precedents, which prevailed among their ancestors' (*Essays*: 476). Hume has no quarrel with those who believe that 'the consent of the people' is 'the best and most sacred' of any claim to authority (*Essays*: 474), just as he has no quarrel with those who believe that equality would be the ideal distribution of property. In both cases, it is the means of trying to sustain the ideal state that pose the problems and the dangers. Even when nations do not aim so impossibly high as to found their governments on the consent of each and every subject, but appeal, as England did, to royal 'succession', disputes easily arise, and such

disputes provide Hume with much of the storyline of the *History of England*. Hume's political philosophy is realistic and pragmatic in character. Sympathetic though he is with the ideals of equality and government by consent, he sees the dangers of violence, disorder, and tyranny very vividly, and sees them to be the usual costs of aspiring to perfection in government. He did however write one very interesting essay on 'The Idea of a Perfect Commonwealth' in which his own republican ideals are developed, and he supported the cause of independence for the American colonies.

Hume's later writings do not significantly alter his *Treatise* account of the function and authority of governments. They add mainly reflections on the relative wisdom of different governors and rebels against them, rather than any new points about the basis of governmental authority. The *History of England* tries to rebut the Whig claim that the English constitution, protecting their 'ancient liberties', dated from the Magna Carta. Hume describes a slow evolution of the 'plan of liberty' which eighteenth-century Britons enjoyed, with many periods of great but tolerated tyranny (under Edward III, under Elizabeth), some periods of lesser tyranny which nevertheless led to civil war and the king's execution (the reign of Charles I), with rebellions occurring for all sorts of reasons and on all sorts of pretext, sometimes leading to improvements, sometimes to worse tyranny, sometimes to unintended advances in the direction of 'a regular and equitable plan of liberty'. The study of English history, he wrote at the end of his discussion of the reign of Richard III, shows 'the great mixture of accident which commonly concurs with a small ingredient of wisdom and foresight, in erecting the complicated fabric of the most perfect government'.

Social philosophy. There is virtually nothing that Hume wrote, after Book I of the *Treatise* that could not properly be classed as 'social philosophy'. Even the *Enquiry Concerning Human Understanding*, mainly concerned with fairly 'abstruse' epistemological topics, keeps its eye on the social role of the epistemologist, and the social use made of, say, miracle reports. 'Man is a sociable, no less than a reasonable being' (*Essays*: 8), and Hume expresses the hope that even relatively abstruse philosophy may 'diffuse itself throughout the whole society', so that, among other effects, 'the politician may acquire greater foresight and subtility, in the subdividing and balancing of power' (*Essays*: 10). His essays on economics combine fairly detailed discussion of particular aspects of the then current economic policy in Britain with discussions of the highest generality about the role of money, the determinants of its value at a given time, the unimportance of what metal or non-metal is used as currency, the importance of a national debt. The *History of England* is crammed with interesting observations on such matters as the changing attitude to usury, what was being imported and exported, what taxes were being levied and with what purported authority, what role the church was playing, what the relationship was between canon law and civil law.

6   Philosophy of religion

Causes and effects of religion. Hume believes that religions, especially primitive religions, spring from the 'trembling curiosity' with which men, 'agitated by hopes and fears', scrutinize the 'course of future causes' affecting their life. Prominent among these fears is the fear of death and what may lie beyond it, and so it is part of Hume's proposed cure for what he sees as the evils of 'religion as it has been commonly found in the world' that this fear be conquered, that he persuade us both that death is 'annihilation', which 'entirely destroys this self', and that the thought of such future annihilation need be no more repugnant than the thought that, before conception and birth, we were nothing. Hume here repeats EPICURUS.

The 'trembling curiosity' into future causes affecting our life gets its anxious quality in part from the intensity of the hopes and fears which are involved, in part from uncertainty, in part from the sort of causes which are postulated. Religion involves 'belief of invisible intelligent power'. 'Invisible' signalizes our lack of real understanding of this power; 'intelligent' signalizes our determination to make it comprehensible, to treat it as if it were a person, one to whom we can make petitions, who might be placated by our praises and sacrifices. It is our 'curiosity about causes', and its imperfect satisfaction by our empirical inquiries, which is the cognitive component of the religious impulse. It is our concern for our own welfare which provides the affective component. Religion evidences both our will to know the causes affecting our welfare, and our only partial success in discovering the determinants of our happiness and misery by natural means, let alone in controlling them.

As scientific understanding of these causal factors increases, religion might be expected to have a less vital role to play, but then, if Hume is right, religion's role is never purely cognitive. It is our anxiety that needs a palliative, and uncertainty is only part of the cause of our anxiety. There is also our concern for our own future, and science may fail to cater to that. Hume sees the natural development of religion, once natural knowledge grows, to be a shift from polytheism to more 'rational' monotheism. Monotheism fits better with a more or less unified account of an orderly universe, whose regularities can be regarded as divine laws. But when one all powerful God is substituted for the many gods of more primitive religions, the reasons for fear of this God are increased, not diminished. Belief in one all-powerful God 'is apt, when joined to superstitious terrors, to sink the human mind into the lowest submission and abasement' (*The Natural History of Religion*: 52). What is more, different religious traditions develop slightly different versions of this one God, who becomes a jealous God, requiring his worshippers not merely to abase themselves, but to go to war against the infidel, and to burn the heretic. Hume sees monotheistic religions to be intellectually less 'ridiculous' than the polytheism from which they develop, but to be, morally speaking, much worse. The roots of religion are our ignorance of causes affecting our happiness, our tendency to anthropomorphism, and our desperate fears for our own future. To the extent that ignorance of causes is reduced, without any abatement of our fear of death or our infantile wish that some super-person be in charge of our fate, religion will simply adapt itself to scientific knowledge, not be banished by it. Hume's thesis in the *Treatise*, that reason serves the passions, gets special application in the *Natural History*, where he tries to diagnose the particular passions served by theology and by religious beliefs, and finds that 'the love of truth' is 'too refined' a motive to explain such beliefs. They are not caused nor can they be cured by rational argument, however refined. If the roots of religion lie as much in our anxious passions and in our will to anthropomorphism as in our interest in causal forces at work in the world, then, to counter religion, more than science and argument will always be needed. The clever arguments put into the sceptic Philo's mouth in the *Dialogues on Natural Religion*, and not answered by stronger counterarguments, seem in the end not to convince even Philo himself.

Argument from design. 'The argument from design' is put forward in the *Dialogues* by Cleanthes, a very calm and enthusiasm-free believer, who is of the opinion that 'religion, however corrupted, is better than no religion at all', (*Dialogues Concerning Natural Religion*: 219) and who defends the hypothesis that the universe, with the order it displays to our eyes and minds, is the work of an intelligent creator. Philo argues, against Cleanthes, that the hypothesis of an intelligent cause of the universe is only one of several that intelligent human thinkers have come up with, and has no better empirical support than the others. No hypothesis about a supposedly unique cause of a unique effect can have support of the usual inductive sort. Since the universe was not formed under our eye, all we can do is speculate and suggest analogies, taken from the 'corner' of the universe we have observed. We know by experience that an orderly effect (that is, one that strikes us as well-ordered) can come about in several ways. It may, like a building, have an intelligent builder as its cause. It may, like a spider's web, be spun instinctively from the belly of an insect. It may, like a well-formed calf, have come to be by animal 'generation'. It may, like a well shaped turnip, have grown from seeds, by 'vegetation'. It may, like patterns in the sand on the beach, have come about by sheer chance. All these local causes of 'order' could be used as analogies to explain the order we perceive in the whole universe (or as much of it as we have any knowledge of). None of these known causes of local order are known as ultimate causes. In particular human thought is not. The builder's plans may have come into his head by observing and imitating natural order, or by copying earlier builders' work, and by cooperation with his workmates. Orderly thought itself calls for a causal explanation. Thought is often disorderly, and human designs are often botched. So our thought provides a very dubious analogy on which to model a worship-worthy universe-cause. 'What peculiar privilege has this little agitation in the brain which we call thought, that we must thus make it the model of the whole universe?' (*Dialogues Concerning Natural Religion*: 148).

Philo eventually answers his own question. Thought has privilege because the question of the cause of the universe arises only for thinkers. So 'a purpose, an intention, a design strikes everywhere the most careless, the most stupid thinker' (*Dialogues on Natural Religion*: 214). Our incurable anthropomorphism, what Hume in the *Treatise* called our mind's propensity to spread itself on external objects, ensures the privilege of thought among the many equally well- or ill-founded hypotheses about the cause of the universe. Philo's conclusion about what human reason can establish is 'one simple, though somewhat ambiguous, or at least undefined proposition, *that the cause or causes of order in the universe probably bear some remote analogy to human intelligence*' (*Dialogues on Natural Religion*: 227; original emphasis). The analogy is not said to be less remote than the others which Philo had proposed. 'Human intelligence' is undefined. It may still be being taken as a matter of agitation in the brain. And 'cause or causes' is carefully noncommital – reason cannot even establish monotheism over polytheism, let alone establish one intelligent *and just* cause of order in the universe. The remote analogy is to human intelligence, not to human benevolence or justice.

After this estimate of how little human thought at its least careless and stupid can conclude about the cause or causes of an orderly universe, and after a vivid catalogue of the 'pernicious consequences' of 'religion as it has commonly been found in the world', Philo purports to fly for alleviation of his ignorance to the revealed truths of Christianity (which, in the *Natural History*, Hume had argued was effectively polytheistic). Shortly before his dramatic flight, Philo had asked, 'When we have to do with a man, who makes a great profession of religion and devotion; has this any effect on those who pass for prudent, than to put them on their guard, lest they be cheated and deceived by him?' (*Dialogues Concerning Natural Religion*: 221). We have been put on our guard, but, as readers of Hume's *Dialogues*, we are still left in reasonable doubt about how to interpret the intentions of his characters, let alone of their author. Hume left his readers with a real enigma in the character of Philo, and, more generally, in these *Dialogues* and in the *Natural History*. As he wrote to Adam Smith when trying, shortly before his death, to arrange for the publication of the *Dialogues*, 'nothing can be more cautiously and more artfully written', and as he wrote at the end of the *Natural History*, 'the whole is a riddle, an aenigma, an inextricable mystery'.

Our prospects. In the *Natural History*, Hume's optimistic hypothesis was that 'the first religious principles must be secondary', or derivative. In some or even most conditions, human nature leads to religion, to varying religions, and so to religious zeal, religious persecution, religious wars. But religious belief and devotion are not 'so universal as to admit of no exceptions', and so do not spring from 'an original instinct', as Hume believed that, say, 'love of progeny' does. His aim was to diagnose the 'first principles' which in so many conditions had religion as their 'secondary' manifestation. Part of what we can see him to be doing in his *History of England* is studying the actual variations in religious (or irreligious) sentiment in one country's history, as a supplement to the less historical (more 'natural-historical') treatment of the varieties of religion that he gives us in the *Natural History*. His work as a scientist of human nature combined, in his lifelong attention to human religions, with his advocacy of the cause of 'the party of humankind', whom he saw to be so threatened by 'sacred zeal and rancor'. He spoke occasionally of the 'true religion'. Analogously to 'true scepticism', which turns scepticism on scepticism, this can be taken to refer to whatever benign reflection-improved form can be taken by the 'primary principles' that get their pathological secondary expression in superstition and in religious enthusiasm.

Hume is no optimist about the human condition. He is well aware of our bloodthirsty history, our record of inhumanity, and in his *History* he contributes to its recording. Where the Christians see religious devotion as the proper response to acknowledgment of the radical evil in our natures, Hume sees religion itself to be a near-inevitable evil propensity in our natures, one that increases our capacity for cruelty and inhumanity, and calls for some secular salvation. This turning of the tables yields a perhaps over-simplified diagnosis of the main causes of human misery, but its originality, its daring, and its considerable explanatory power can scarcely be gainsaid.

See also: ARTISTIC TASTE; CAUSATION; COMMON SENSE SCHOOL; EMPIRICISM; ENLIGHTENMENT, SCOTTISH; INDUCTION, EPISTEMIC ISSUES IN; MIRACLES; MORAL SENSE THEORIES; NATURAL THEOLOGY; NATURALISM IN ETHICS; RATIONALISM; SCEPTICISM; TESTIMONY

List of works

Hume, D. (1875) *The Philosophical Works of David Hume*, ed. T.H. Green and T.H. Grose, London: Longman, Green, 4 vols. (At present the most complete edition of Hume's philosophical writings. It contains 'A Dialogue', and all the following works except the *History of England*, the 'Abstract' of the *Treatise*, and *The Letter from a Gentleman*. A new edition of Hume's writings, to be published by Clarendon Press, is in progress, edited by T.L. Beauchamp, D.F. Norton and M.A. Stewart.)

—— (1739–40) *A Treatise of Human Nature*, ed L.A. Selby-Bigge and P.H. Nidditch, Oxford: Clarendon Press, 1975. (Includes the *Abstract*.)

—— (1740) *Abstract of A Treatise of Human Nature*, ed. J.M. Keynes and P. Sraffa, Cambridge: Cambridge University Press, 1938.

—— (1741–77) *Essays, Moral, Political and Literary*, ed. E.F. Miller, Indianapolis, IN: Liberty Classics, 1985.

—— (1745) *A Letter from a Gentleman to His Friend in Edinburgh: Containing Some Observations on A Specimen of the Principles Concerning Religion and Morality, said to be maintain'd in a Book lately publish'd, intituled, A Treatise of Human Nature*, ed. E.C. Mossner and J.V. Price, Edinburgh: Edinburgh University Press, 1967.

—— (1748, 1751) *Enquiries Concerning Human Understanding and Concerning the Principles of Morals*, ed. L.A. Selby-Bigge and P.H. Nidditch, Oxford: Clarendon Press, 1978. (Does not contain 'A Dialogue'. Page references in the entry given as *Enquiries* refer to the 1978 joint edition.)

—— (1754–62) *The History of England, from the Invasion of Julius Caesar to the Revolution in 1688*, Edinburgh and London, 6 vols. (Most easily obtainable now from Indianapolis, IN: Liberty Classics, 1983.)

—— (1757) *The Natural History of Religion*, ed. H.E. Root, Stanford, CA: Stanford University Press, 1957.

—— (1779) *My Own Life*, in T.H. Green and T.H. Grose (eds) *Works*, vol. 3, London: Longman, Green. (Also titled *The Life of David Hume, Written by Himself*.)

—— (1779) *Dialogues Concerning Natural Religion*, ed. N.K. Smith, London: Collier Macmillan Publishers; New York: Macmillan Publishing Company, 1947.

—— (1932) *The Letters of David Hume*, ed. J.Y.T. Greig, Oxford: Clarendon Press, 2 vols.

—— (1954) *New Letters of David Hume*, ed. R. Klibansky and E.C. Mossner, Oxford: Clarendon Press.

References and further reading

(Anthologies are not included.)

Árdal, P.S. (1966) *Passion and Value in Hume's 'Treatise'*, Edinburgh: Edinburgh University Press. (An important study of Book II of the *Treatise* in relation to Book III.)

Baier, A.C. (1991) *A Progress of Sentiments: Reflections on Hume's 'Treatise'*, Cambridge, MA: Harvard University Press. (Emphasizes the dialectical unity of the *Treatise*.)

Beauchamp, T.L. and Rosenberg, A. (1981) *Hume and the Problem of Causation*, New York: Oxford University Press. (The standard work on Hume's views about the causal relation.)

Box, M.A. (1990) *The Suasive Art of David Hume*, Princeton, NJ: Princeton University Press. (A study of Hume's changes of style after what he saw as the failure of the *Treatise* to convey his message.)

Bricke, J. (1996) *Hume's Moral Psychology*, New York: Oxford University Press. (Emphasizes Hume's account of motivation, and relates his views to those of Donald Davidson.)

Capaldi, N. (1989) *Hume's Place in Moral Philosophy*, New York: Peter Lang. (Takes Hume to have effected a 'Copernican revolution' in ethics by turning away from the 'I think' perspective of his predecessors to a more social and pragmatic 'we do' perspective, from which cultural practice commands attention.)

Danforth, J.W. (1990) *Hume and the Problem of Reason: Recovering the Human Sciences*, New Haven, CT: Yale University Press. (A study of Hume's philosophy of culture.)

Deleuze, G. (1953) *Empiricism and Subjectivity*, trans.

C.V. Boudas. London; New York, 1980. (Emphasizes the importance of Hume's account of the imagination, and the influence of general rules. Not for beginners.)

Flew, A. (1961) *Hume's Philosophy of Belief*, New York: Humanities Press. (A close examination of the *Enquiry Concerning Human Understanding*)

Fogelin, R.J. (1985) *Hume's Skepticism in the 'Treatise of Human Nature'*, London, and Boston, MA: Routledge & Kegan Paul. (A vivid presentation of Hume's *Treatise* sceptical arguments, taken to include his account of moral judgment.)

Forbes, D. (1975) *Hume's Philosophical Politics*, Cambridge: Cambridge University Press. (A mine of information about the complex background of Hume's political philosophy.)

Gaskin, J.C.A. (1978) *Hume's Philosophy of Religion*, New York: Macmillan. (The standard work on Hume's views on religion.)

Hall, R. (1978) *Fifty Years of Hume Scholarship: A Bibliographical Guide*, Edinburgh: Edinburgh University Press. (Supplementary updates are published in *Hume Studies*, the journal of The Hume Society.)

Hendel, C. (1925) *Studies in the Philosophy of David Hume*, Princeton, NJ: Princeton University Press. (Sympathetic and scholarly reading of some themes in Hume's writings, a good counterweight to T.H. Green's treatment, in his and Grose's edition of Hume's works.)

Huxley, T.H. (1894) *Hume with Helps to the Study of Berkeley*, London: Macmillan. (Of some historical importance. Hume's views on liberty and necessity are highlighted, as are his views about religion. Hume is praised for the 'sagacity' of treatment of human capacities as continuous with those of the higher animals. A brief but beguiling biography is included.)

Ikeda, S. (1986, 1988) *David Hume and Eighteenth Century British Thought*, Tokyo: Chuo University Library, 2 vols. (A valuable bibliography.)

Jones, P. (1982) *Hume's Sentiments: Their Ciceronian and French Context*, Edinburgh: Edinburgh University Press. (The book lives up to its title.)

Kemp Smith, Norman (1941) *The Philosophy of David Hume*, London: Macmillan. (Emphasizes the influence of Hutcheson, the priority of Hume's moral over his epistemological interests, and of his naturalism over his scepticism. A landmark work.)

Laird, J. (1932) *Hume's Philosophy of Human Nature*, London: Methuen. (A good critical survey of Hume's philosophy. Broad in coverage of topics, fair in criticism.)

Lecaldano, E. (1991) *Hume e la nascita dell'etica contemporanea* (Hume and the Origin of Modern Ethics), Laterza. (Relates Hume's ethics and social

philosophy to the contemporary contractarian tradition.)

Livingston, D. (1984) *Hume's Philosophy of Common Life*, Chicago, IL: University of Chicago Press. (Emphasizes the importance of Hume's treatment of time, and the 'narrative structure' of thought.)

Mackie, J. (1980) *Hume's Moral Theory*, London: Routledge & Kegan Paul. (An acute analysis and sympathetic criticism of Hume's moral theory.)

Malherbe, M. (1976) *La Philosophie Empiriste de David Hume* (The Empiricist Philosophy of David Hume), Paris. (A general introduction.)

Miller, D. (1981) *Philosophy and Ideology in Hume's Political Thought*, Oxford: Clarendon Press. (A helpful introduction not only to Hume's political theory, but to his philosophy in general.)

Mossner, E.C. (1954) *The Life of David Hume*, Oxford: Clarendon Press. (Goes well beyond the earlier biographies by T.E. Richie (1907), John Hill Burton (1846), and J.Y.T. Greig (1931) in the wealth of fascinating information offered.)

Norton, D.F. (1982) *David Hume: Common-Sense Moralist, Sceptical Metaphysician*, Princeton, NJ: Princeton University Press. (Discusses Hume's relation to Hutcheson, and the restrictions of his scepticism.)

—— (ed.) (1993) *The Cambridge Companion to Hume*, New York: Cambridge University Press. (Essays on all aspects of Hume's thought, with extensive bibliography.)

Noxon, J. (1973) *Hume's Philosophical Development: A Study of His Methods*, Oxford: Clarendon Press. (About the only study of Hume's philosophical development.)

Passmore, J.A. (1952) *Hume's Intentions*, Cambridge: Cambridge University Press. (A clear and scholarly book which stresses the many different strains in Hume's thought, including associationism, positivism, scepticism.)

Pears, D. (1990) *Hume's System: An Examination of the First Book of His 'Treatise'*, Oxford: Oxford University Press. (Particularly helpful on Hume's *Treatise* account of causal inference.)

Penelhum, T.H. (1975) *Hume*, London: Macmillan. (A short clear book, especially interesting and influential on personal identity.)

—— (1992) *David Hume: An Introduction to His Philosophical System*, West Lafayette, IN: Purdue University Press. (A very helpful commentary on selected texts from Hume's *Enquiries*. Contains a fine bibliographical guide.)

Phillipson, N. (1989) *Hume*, London: Weidenfeld & Nicolson. (A study of Hume as historian, emphasizing his criticisms of religion as a social force.)

Price, H.H. (1940) *Hume's Theory of the External*

World, Oxford: Clarendon Press. (A close examination of Book I, Part IV of the *Treatise*. Ingenious, influential, idiosyncratic.)

Snare, F. (1991) *Morals, Motivation and Convention: Hume's Influential Doctrines*, Cambridge: Cambridge University Press. (A close critical scrutiny of Hume's *Treatise* views in social philosophy and their relevance for contemporary discussion.)

Stewart, J.B. (1992) *Opinion and Reform in Hume's Political Philosophy*, Princeton, NJ: Princeton University Press. (Challenges the view that Hume is a 'conservative' in his politics.)

Strawson, G. (1989) *The Secret Connexion: Causation, Realism, and David Hume*, Oxford: Clarendon Press. (Challenges the usual reading of Hume's views about causes in nature.)

Streminger, G. (1994) *David Hume: Sein Leben und Sein Werk* (David Hume: His Life and Work), Paderborn-München-Wien-Zürich: Ferdinand Schöningh. (A lavishly illustrated comprehensive account of Hume's life and writings, particularly good on the cultural background.)

Stroud, B. (1977) *Hume*, London: Routledge & Kegan Paul. (A deeply philosophical exploration of the interplay of scepticism and naturalism in Hume's philosophy.)

Whelan, F.G. (1985) *Order and Artifice in Hume's Political Philosophy*, Princeton, NJ: Princeton University Press. (Has become the standard work on Hume's political philosophy in the *Treatise*.)

Wright, J. (1983) *The Sceptical Realism of David Hume*, Manchester: Manchester University Press. (Helpful on Hume's debt, in his epistemology and metaphysics, to Descartes and Malebranche.)

Yandell, K.E. (1990) *Hume's 'Inexplicable Mystery': His Views on Religion*, Philadelphia, PA: Temple University Press. (Relates Hume's views on religious belief to his *Treatise* account of belief in general.)

ANNETTE BAIER

HUMOUR

What is meant by saying that something is humorous or funny? It is clear that humorousness must be elucidated in terms of the characteristic response to humour, namely humorous amusement, or mirth. It is plausible to define humour in this way: for something to be humorous is for it to be disposed to elicit mirth in appropriate people through their awareness or cognition of it, and not for ulterior reasons. But this invites the question, 'What is mirth?' The three leading ideas in philosophical theories of humour are those of incongruity, superiority and relief or release. Although the perception of incongruity is often involved in finding something funny, and the resolution of a perceived incongruity plays an important role in good humour, none of these, in themselves or combined with others, is capable of capturing the concept of mirth. Mirth is not identical with the pleasurable perception of an incongruity, pleasure in feeling superior, the relief of tension or release of accumulated mental energy, or any combination of these elements. A better account of mirth is that it is a certain kind of pleasurable reaction which tends to issue in laughter if the reaction is sufficiently intense. So something is funny if it in itself pleases appropriate people through being grasped, where the pleasure is of the sort that leads, though not inevitably, to laughter.

1   **The main question**
2   **Traditional theories of humour**
3   **The analysis of humour**
4   **Incongruity reconsidered**
5   **Other issues**

1   The main question

What is humour? Or alternatively, what makes something funny? This basic query can be interpreted as a call for either conceptual elucidation or causal explanation. Taken the first way, the question asks, 'What does it mean to say, or what are the truth conditions of saying, that a given item is humorous or funny?' In other words, how is 'humorous' or 'funny' to be defined in a philosophically rigorous fashion? Taken the second way, the question becomes, 'What is it about a humorous or funny item that is responsible for its being humorous or funny?' On the first construal, we seek to understand exactly when something counts as humorous; on the second, we seek to ascertain in virtue of what a given item succeeds in being humorous. These questions have not been sharply separated in traditional theories, which sometimes seem concerned to address the one and sometimes the other. Whether in the last analysis the questions *can* be sharply separated, though, is not entirely clear. Ultimately it comes down to asking whether the identifying response to humorousness can itself be identified without specifying what occasions it, either externally, in terms of features of the occasioning item, or internally, in terms of features of the subject's representation of the item. This identifying response is usually labelled 'amusement', but 'amusement' is here to be understood in its specifically humour-related sense, and not in the sense of general entertainment or diversion.

Although the basic query has here been formulated

in the objective mode – that is, it asks what it is for something to *be* humorous – there is, perhaps, the prior question, in the subjective mode, of what it is for someone to *find* something humorous. These, however, can be plausibly related as follows: something is humorous if and only if it is found humorous by appropriate (or intended) audiences under favourable conditions, including cognitive, attitudinal and emotional ones. The context should make clear under which of these modes the basic question is being pursued at a given point. Some objectivity about humour – some degree of true-or-false-ness in the attributions of humour – is presupposed in considering the question in the objective mode, but this appears to be justified: items are regularly and sustainedly classified as humorous, and not just as humorous to a particular person on a particular occasion. Humour, though patently a response-dependent phenomenon, seems to have at least as much objectivity as, for example, the properties of beauty or virtue.

2 Traditional theories of humour

There are three main philosophical traditions of accounting for humour: the incongruity tradition, the superiority tradition and the relief or release tradition.

The hallmark of incongruity theory is that it locates the humorous in some incongruity presented by or perceived in some item. The humorous item may be itself incongruous, relative to some assumed other object, or it may involve or contain incongruity. There have been various interpretations of the incongruity of items or elements, ranging from logical impossibility or paradoxicality, to absurdity and irrelevance, to unexpectedness and general inappropriateness.

Incongruity theorists include Schopenhauer, Hazlitt, Kierkegaard, A. Koestler, D.H. Monro and perhaps KANT. Kant held the humorous to consist in 'the sudden transformation of a strained expectation into nothing' (1790). The incongruity here, if any, is between the expectation, or what it points towards, and its deflation, or what it issues in. Schopenhauer gave incongruity theory a clearer, perhaps canonical, formulation: the essence of the ludicrous, he claimed, lies in the incongruity between concepts, the vehicles of abstract thought, and concrete objects, apprehended in perception, when the incongruity is grasped of a sudden. The mismatch of thought and perception can appear from either of two directions: a single concept can be applied to two very different objects, which only awkwardly encompasses them both ('wit'), or two objects originally ranged under a given concept can be subsequently realized to be fundamentally

disparate ('folly'). Koestler's version of incongruity theory, a descendant and elaboration of Schopenhauer's, holds that humour arises from the bisociation (double association) of an item in respect of two different and incompatible reference frames or interpretive matrices at once.

Recent incongruity theorists have generally held the perception of incongruity to be the core of the response to something as humorous, but not the whole of it. Perceived incongruity is taken as necessary, but not sufficient, for the occurrence of humorous amusement, and the reasons for this are manifest. Incongruity is on the face of it an undesirable property and its confrontation usually fails to elicit pleasure straightforwardly; anxiety or bewilderment, or at best curiosity, are more likely to result. In addition, not all pleasure taken in incongruity appears to constitute amusement, as opposed to aesthetic or other forms of satisfaction.

What more, then, is required? Some theorists hold that the perceived incongruity must be enjoyed for its own sake, some that it must be enjoyed as such but not aesthetically, some that it must not give rise to negative emotions (such as fear or disgust), some that it not engage practical concerns (as for knowledge or safety), and some that it must have a tendency to issue in laughter. Some stress the temporal structure needed for perceived incongruity to be found humorous, while others insist it is not perceived incongruity itself that is the source of amusement, but only the consequent resolution of such incongruity. Still others underline the fulfilment of background conditions, such as being in fun, or the absence of egoistic or sympathetic concern for the object of humour.

Nevertheless, we may be justifiably sceptical of the claim that all intuitively accountable instances of humour, for example, mimicry, satire, sarcasm, slapstick or sexual ribaldry, turn on the perception of incongruity. It has not been demonstrated that properties other than incongruity cannot sensibly figure as what one is explicitly amused by. Thus, doubt remains over whether the incongruity theory, however qualified or supplemented, can be correct as a conceptual elucidation of humour.

Superiority theorists, who include ARISTOTLE, Thomas HOBBES, Alexander Bain and Henri BERGSON (§6), construe humour as rooted in the subject's awareness of superiority, in some respect, to the humorous object. Hobbes famously declared humorous laughter to be the result of a 'sudden glory' in one's eminence or fortune, in contrast with another or one's former self. Bergson (1899) theorized the comic as essentially 'the encrustation of the mechanical on the living' – a falling-off from the human ideal of flexibility, suppleness and accommodation. The observer of this, for Bergson, accordingly feels superior, takes pleasure in so feeling, and manifests their pleasure naturally in laughter at the imperfectly human. Comedy and emotion are held to be incompatible, since comic engagement by its very nature short-circuits emotional involvement. In addition, Bergson maintains that comic laughter is a social corrective that chastises and hopefully reforms the socially undesirable rigid behaviour at which it is directed.

Spencer and Freud, the most well-known relief theorists, locate the essence of the humorous in the relief from psychic constraint or the release of accumulated mental energy that it affords (see FREUD §4). Spencer (1911) felt it important to investigate not only the features of humour, but why it is specifically laughter that humour induces, thus necessitating a physiological explanation. The explanation he offers emphasizes nervous tension and its bodily manifestation when suddenly excessive or redundant. Freud's striking account of the pleasure taken in jokes, influenced by Spencer's, is well worked out, as is his extensive typology of jokes in terms of their structures and techniques. Freud (1905) viewed the enjoyment of jokes as rooted in an economy of psychic energy, namely, that of inhibition or repression. With innocent jokes, the inhibition is against nonsense and pure play, while with tendentious jokes, the inhibition is against a display of aggression or sexuality, but in both cases the energy of inhibition thus freed up manifests itself as pleasure.

Whatever truth they contain, superiority and release theories lack the generality of incongruity theory. In addition, they seem more concerned with concomitants or mechanisms of the humorous reaction than with its conceptual core. Thus these competitors of incongruity theory are currently seen as even less able to provide an adequate answer to the basic question.

The above classification of theorists involves a good deal of oversimplification, for strands of each of the three guiding traditions of reflection on humour can be uncovered in almost every major theorist. Thus, Kant might just as easily be called a relief theorist as an incongruity theorist, in virtue of the stress he placed on the animation of the body through the quick release of tension built up in expectation of what does not arrive. Bergson could justifiably be classified as an incongruity theorist rather than a superiority theorist. The incongruity that defines the comic in his analysis is posited between a human or human-like being and various quintessentially anti-human automatisms and rigidities with which they are afflicted. Schopenhauer's account (1844), though obviously bringing incongruity to the fore, also includes a strain of superiority theory; for Schopenhauer, the phenomenon of humour exemplifies an important truth that we have independent reasons for acknowledging, namely, the superiority of perceptual to conceptual modes of knowing the world. Part of our pleasure in humour is in direct consequence of its affirmation of this truth. Spencer's account, which conceives the humorous reaction as a sudden release of nervous energy, also posits that this results from a 'descending incongruity', in a manner reminiscent of Kant. Koestler's account (1964), borrowing from Spencer, combines the postulation of a collision of incompatible frames or matrices – a form of the incongruity idea – with the notion of an emotional mass and its explosive diversion as laughter when deserted by thought, in the tradition of release theories.

3 The analysis of humour

A number of considerations must be borne in mind when formulating an adequate analysis of humour, that is, an answer to the question 'What is humour?' construed conceptually. Most of these concern the proper relationship of humour to other phenomena, such as laughter, emotion, pleasure and aesthetic appreciation. First, humour and laughter are not coextensive, that is, not all laughter, by any means, is occasioned by humour. Laughter can result from, among other things, tickling, nitrous oxide, organic disorder, joy, embarrassment or vengeful exultation. Second, not all humour is productive of laughter, even in appropriate subjects; humour may engender amusement without any behavioural manifestation, or with only the lesser one of smiling. Third, humour does not always produce amusement, its characteristic pleasure, even in appropriate subjects; certain background conditions of mood or psychic preparedness also need to be met. Fourth, humour seems to have both a cognitive and an affective component, which are bound up together in the response.

It might be thought that incongruity theory is clearly aimed at answering the conceptual query, while release theory is clearly aimed at the causal one: noticing incongruity at least appears explicative of what finding something funny consists in, whereas the release of tension seems to concern the mechanism whereby finding something funny generates pleasure or some other effect. Perceived incongruity is a plausible intentional object of amusement – what it is directed upon – while release of tension is not.

But what of superiority theory? Though one is surely not amused at a quick release of nervous energy, it seems not impossible that one might be amused at one's evident superiority to some less fortunate person, when it is suddenly noted, in addition to or as opposed to whatever incongruity such misfortune may present. It is not clear that the pleasure I take in someone's accidentally slipping on a banana skin without serious harm cannot be accounted part of humorous enjoyment as such, but only as something distinct. It is not clear that an item's reinforcement of one's good fortune, or its deflation of expectations, or its presentation of ambiguity, or its surprisingness, or its strangeness, or some other more specific property, cannot itself be what is relished, and even the whole of what is relished, in certain cases of amusement. If so, then it may be a mistake to regard perceived incongruity as conceptually requisite to humorousness.

Hence there seem to be two choices for proceeding with the analysis. On one hand, if all cases of humour can be demonstrated to involve perceived incongruity, and to do so non-accidentally, then perceived incongruity should figure in an elucidation of the notion of humour, with apparent cases of humour without incongruity being shown to be cases either of non-humour or of humour in which non-humorous pleasure, derived from other sources, overshadows what proper humour-pleasure is present. On the other hand, if apparent cases of humour without incongruity are to be accepted as genuine instances of humour, then an analysis is needed which elucidates humour without reference to perceived incongruity. Perhaps the only plausible way of doing so would be in terms of a distinctive and recognizable effect on perceivers and one arising through cognition of the item in question. On such a perspective, apparent incongruity would be the most common, but not the necessary, focus of humorousness; other properties might so figure, on other occasions.

Suppose, believing that even incongruity theory unjustifiably limits the possible objects of amusement, we begin with this general idea: the humorous is that which makes one laugh by thinking or perceiving it. Then a natural refinement would be as follows: an item x is humorous (or funny) if and only if x has the disposition to elicit, through mere cognition of it, and not for ulterior reasons, a certain kind of pleasurable reaction in appropriate subjects generally (that is, informationally, attitudinally and emotionally prepared subjects), where this pleasurable reaction (amusement or mirth) is identified by its own disposition to induce, at moderate or higher degrees, a further phenomenon, namely, laughter. Thus described, the humorous cannot be detached from all felt inclination, however faint, toward the convulsive bodily expression we call laughing. The propensity of the state of amusement to issue in laughter is arguably what is essential to its identity,

and underpins the widespread intuition that humour and laughter, though not coextensive, are nevertheless intimately related. The connection between amusement and laughter, then, would be this: the mental state of amusement is partly identified by its disposition (universal in humans, if ultimately contingent) to issue in laughter if sufficiently intense.

What of the idea that amusement is not amusement unless it both arises in a certain way and has a certain intentionality? The present analysis acknowledges this in its own fashion, for it entails that a reaction to x is not amusement unless, in addition to being pleasurable and characteristically leading to laughter, it comes about in virtue of cognition of x, and is also directed on x. However, *pace* certain theorists, such as Clark (1970), amusement may not have a formal object – a description under which an object must be seen if it is to amuse – beyond the minimal 'that which is amusing'.

'What makes x funny?', when taken as a question about why speakers count x as funny, is directly answered by such an analysis. Roughly, x is funny in that, or because, the cognition of x amuses people with an appropriate mental set, that is, pleases them in such a way that they have some inclination to laugh at x. But 'What makes x funny?', taken as a question regarding what it is about x that underwrites or contributes to its being funny or eliciting amusement, can be answered only by empirical investigation or reflective survey. There may be many factors that enter into the explanation of an item's possessing the power of humorousness, though we can be confident that presenting appearances of incongruity will figure largely among them.

It may then be useful to recognize two analyses of humorousness: one 'thin', one 'thick'. The 'thinner' analysis, which we have just been sketching, denies there is any necessary focus or intentional object of humour, and holds an item's humorousness to be merely its power to raise via cognition a certain pleasurable effect, identified through its connection with laughter, in appropriate subjects. The 'thicker' analysis assumes that all cases of humour can be shown conceptually to involve the perception of incongruity, and so adds that to the specification of the thought through which a humorous item must cause a pleasurable effect or produce enjoyment. But as we have seen, adopting an analysis of that sort runs the danger of prematurely foreclosing on the possible objects of amusement, a reaction that may well be characterizable without recourse to a focus on incongruity.

4 Incongruity reconsidered

Even if incongruity is not a necessary condition or component of humorousness, no account of humour can fail to accord it a special status. Beyond being the most common focus of humour, its special status may consist in the following. First, there is reason to think that superior forms of humour – those which are most satisfying, intellectually and emotionally – all rely on incongruity in one way or another. Second, there may be categories of humour (jokes, for instance) that are inconceivable in the absence of incongruity, even if there are categories (farce, perhaps) that have another basis. Third, the quality of incongruity-based humour may be tied to a further feature, one obviously presupposing such incongruity, namely, the nature and extent of the resolution of the incongruity that the humorous item embodies or presents.

The pleasure afforded by incongruity-based humour characteristically seems to require that the apparent incongruity be in some sense *resolved* by the subject. Such resolution can be an object of conscious awareness on the subject's part, and can take various forms, including justification, rationalization, unification, or dissolution, but is perhaps best understood as the *grasping* of the rationale of the incongruity the humorous item presents. The appreciation of incongruity-based humour can be likened to the solution of a puzzle, though a puzzle where insight is attained in a relatively immediate and effortless way. The resolution of a joke's incongruity is easily related to or identified with the experience known as 'getting' the joke. In good incongruity humour – a clever pun, for example – one is made to see the 'why' of the incongruity in addition to the 'what'.

The idea of grasping the incongruity in an instance of humour might be taken further: to resolve the incongruity in an item of humour and thus to be in a position to appreciate its humorousness is to grasp the basis of the incongruity involved, and, at the same time, an aspect of congruity as well often residing in the humorous vehicle itself. Without such a double grasp, of both the 'fit' and the 'non-fit' involved in a piece of humour, amusement of a high order is unlikely. Good incongruity-humour offers 'the pleasure of finding connections where none were thought to exist' (Monro 1951).

We may thus propose that model instances of incongruity-humour involve an underlying unification of their disparate contents, a tying together in the humorous vehicle of incongruous elements, rather than just their brute juxtaposition. In other words, the best such humour always has a pivot on which the humour turns, which rationalizes the apparently incongruous elements that have been brought together.

5 Other issues

Other issues of philosophic interest involving humour include: the status of amusement *vis-à-vis* emotion; the relation of humour and aesthetic experience; the relation between producing and consuming humour; the role or use of humour in human life; the nature of the sense of humour; the distinctive features of jokes; humour and society; humour and seriousness; humour and creativity; the ethics of humour.

See also: COMEDY; EMOTION IN RESPONSE TO ART

References and further reading

* Bergson, H.-L. (1899) *Le rire: essai sur la significa- tion du comique*, Paris; trans. 'Laughter', in W. Sypher (ed.) *Comedy*, Garden City, NY: Double- day, 1956. (The most fecund and imaginative of traditional theories of humour, combining elements of the superiority and incongruity traditions, and paying special attention to the social dimensions and purposes of humour.)

Carroll, N. (1991) 'On Jokes', *Midwest Studies in Philosophy* 16: 280–301. (Criticizes Freud's account of jokes and proposes an alternative account in terms of puzzle-solving.)

* Clark, M. (1970) 'Humour and Incongruity', *Philo- sophy* 45: 20–32. (A seminal essay that analyses humour as involving the enjoyment of perceived incongruity for its own sake.)

Cohen, T. (1983) 'Jokes', in E. Schaper (ed.) *Pleasure, Preference, and Value*, Cambridge: Cambridge Uni- versity Press: 120–36. (Explores some of the presuppositions and implications, including ethical ones, of making and enjoying jokes.)

Dauer, F.W. (1988) 'The Picture as the Medium of Humorous Incongruity', *American Philosophical Quarterly* 25: 241–51. (Argues that pictures, not propositions, are the fundamental vehicle of hu- mour.)

* Freud, S. (1905) *Der Witz und seine Beziehung zum Unbewussten*, Leipzig/Vienna: Dueticke; trans. J. Strachey, *Jokes and their Relation to the Uncon- scious*, Harmondsworth: Penguin, 1956. (Presents an elaborate categorization of jokes and a unified account of their functioning, with the pleasure of all jokes based on an economy of psychic energy.)

Hartz, G. (1991) 'Humor: The Beauty and the Beast', *American Philosophical Quarterly* 28: 299–309. (Argues that humour is a special sort of emotion, akin to aesthetic emotions.)

* Kant, I. (1790) *Kritik der Urteilskraft*, Berlin: Lagarde; trans. J.H. Bernard, *Critique of Judgment*, New York: Hafner, 1951. (Kant offers a compressed, though suggestive, proposal along incongruity lines, seeing the essence of humour in a sudden deflation of expectation.)

Kierkegaard, S.A. (1846) *Concluding Unscientific Postscript*, trans. D.F. Swenson, Princeton, NJ: Princeton University Press, 1941. (A particular version of incongruity theory, relating issues about humour to the demarcation of the aesthetic, the ethical and the religious.)

* Koestler, A. (1964) *The Act of Creation*, New York: Macmillan. (Perhaps the most sophisticated recent form of incongruity theory, coupled with elements of relief theory.)

Kulka, T. (1990) 'The Incongruity of Incongruity Theories of Humour', *IYYUN, The Jerusalem Philosophical Quarterly* 39: 223–35. (Argues that humour derives from resolution of incongruity, as opposed to incongruity itself.)

LaFollette, H. and Shanks, N. (1993) 'Belief and the Basis of Humor', *American Philosophical Quarterly*, 30: 329–39. (Relates the problem of humour to others more central in current philosophy.)

McGhee, P. (1979) *Humor: Its Origin and Development*, San Francisco, CA: W.H. Freeman. (A comprehensive survey of its questions by a leading psychologist of humour.)

Martin, M.W. (1983) 'Humour and the Aesthetic Enjoyment of Incongruities', *British Journal of Aesthetics* 23: 74–84. (Argues that enjoyment of perceived incongruity for its own sake is insufficient for humorous amusement.)

* Monro, D.H. (1951) *The Argument of Laughter*, Melbourne: Melbourne University Press. (Comprehensive classification and survey of theories of humour.)

Morreall, J. (1983) *Taking Laughter Seriously*, Albany, NY: State University of New York Press. (Monograph by the most prominent contemporary philosophical writer on humour, which explains laughter as the result of a pleasant psychological shift.)

—— (1983) 'Humor and Emotion', *American Philosophical Quarterly*, 20: 297–304. (Argues that amusement is not usefully categorized as an emotion, but should be contrasted with it.)

—— (1989) 'Enjoying Incongruity', *Humor*, 2: 1–18. (Explores evolutionary reasons for the development of the sense of humour in humans.)

Mulkay, M. (1988) *On Humour*, Oxford: Blackwell. (General survey of the topic from a sociological point of view.)

Raskin, V. (1985) *Semantic Mechanisms of Humor*, Dordrecht: Reidel. (An impressive treatise bringing to bear insights from linguistics and communication theory.)

Santayana, G. (1896) *The Sense of Beauty*, New York: Charles Scribner's Sons. (Offers criticisms both of incongruity and superiority theories.)

* Schopenhauer, A. (1819, 1844) *Die Welt als Wille und Vorstellung*, vols 1 and 2, Leipzig: Brockhaus; trans. E.F.J. Payne, *The World as Will and Representation*, vols 1 and 2, New York: Dover, 1966. (An early and influential formulation of incongruity theory, which sees humorous incongruity as invariably rooted in the discrepancy between the concreteness of percepts and the abstractness of concepts.)

Scruton, R. (1982) 'Laughter', *Proceedings of the Aristotelian Society*, supplementary vol. 56: 197–212. (Questions whether humour necessarily focuses on incongruity, stressing instead its devaluational or demolitional aspect.)

Sousa, R. de (1987) *The Rationality of Emotion*, Cambridge, MA: MIT Press. (§11 explores the ethics of 'dark' humour and laughter.)

* Spencer, H. (1911) 'The Physiology of Laughter', in *Essays on Education, Etc.*, London: Dent. (Formulation of the relief theory, in terms of 'mental hydraulics'.)

Swabey, M. (1961) *Comic Laughter*, New Haven, CT: Yale University Press. (Defends an incongruity account of humour of broad scope.)

JERROLD LEVINSON

HUNGARY, PHILOSOPHY IN

The situation of Hungarian philosophy can be best illustrated by two sayings: 'there are Hungarian philosophers, but there is no Hungarian philosophy', and 'a certain period of Hungarian philosophy stretches from Descartes to Kant'. The two ideas are closely connected. Thus on the one hand, there is such a thing as Hungarian philosophy: there are scientific-educational institutions in philosophical life and there are philosophers working in these institutions. On the other hand, there is no such thing as Hungarian philosophy: it is a history of adoption, largely consisting of attempts to introduce and embrace the great trends of Western thought.

After some preliminaries in the medieval and early-modern periods, Hungarian philosophy started to develop at the beginning of the nineteenth century. As a result of the reception of German idealism – the so-called Kant debate and Hegel debate – the problems of philosophy were formulated as independent problems

567

for the first time, and a philosophical language began to evolve. After an attempt to create a 'national philosophy' – and after some outstanding individual achievements – the institutionalization of Hungarian philosophy accelerated at the end of the century. The early years of the twentieth century brought the first heyday of philosophy to Hungary, with the rapid reception of new idealist trends and notable original contributions. In the period between the two wars the development stopped: many philosophers were forced to emigrate, and Geistesgeschichte *(the history of thought) became prevalent in philosophical life. Following the communist take-over, the institutions of 'bourgeois' philosophy were eliminated, and Marxism-Leninism, which legitimated political power, took a monopolistic position. During this period, the only significant works created were in the tradition of critical Marxism and philosophical opposition. The changes in 1989 regenerated the institutional system, and the articulation of international contemporary trends – analytic philosophy, hermeneutic tradition and postmodernism – came to the fore.*

Besides some works by thinkers in exile, Hungarian philosophy has produced only one achievement which can be considered significant at an international level: the oeuvre *of György (Georg) Lukács.*

1   **The beginnings**
2   **Debates and achievements**
3   **The establishment and functioning of the institutional system**
4   **Decades of communism**
5   **After 1989**

1   The beginnings

The origins of Hungarian philosophical thinking can be traced back to the Middle Ages. The products of the Latin-speaking culture of the age were defined by scholasticism. Following a number of anonymous or insignificant authors, the only important and influential thinker appeared on the scene in the fifteenth century: Pelbárt Temesvári, Franciscan theologian, was a philosopher of European standard, representative of the medieval spirit. His collection of sermons, containing drafts of speeches, based on the strict logical order of the scholastic division-system and illustrated by literary stories, became highly popular both within and outside the country.

In the Hungarian history of ideas, the influence of scholasticism continues well beyond the Middle Ages: it was the predominant philosophy until the nineteenth century, taught in Catholic high-schools. The effects of the different trends of Renaissance, Enlightenment and German Idealism found their place within

this tradition (see RENAISSANCE PHILOSOPHY; ENLIGHTENMENT, CONTINENTAL; GERMAN IDEALISM).

The author of the first Hungarian philosophical work, János Apáczai Csere, was the most prominent among the Protestant students who had been educated at Western universities. His main work, the *Magyar encyclopaedia* (Hungarian Encyclopedia, 1655) printed in Utrecht, summarizes the scholarship of the age for the school curriculum. Its significance for cultural history comes from the fact that this was the first work to expound the ideas of the time (through Cartesian epistemology) in Hungarian. Apáczai's attempt, however, did not have followers and Hungarian philosophy showed no notable development for another hundred years.

2   Debates and achievements

After these sporadic and isolated preliminaries, real development was initiated at the beginning of nineteenth century. The starting point was the reception of German Idealism, with the two debates spanning through the first half of the century: the Kant and the Hegel debates (see KANT, I.; HEGELIANISM).

The two important features of the Kant debate were the lack of an autonomous philosophical milieu on the one hand, and the reductive character of the Kant interpretation on the other. The debate of Protestant ministers – who had visited German universities and become acquainted with Kantianism – was a philosophical debate at a time when no philosophical life was to be found. The reception of philosophical thought, therefore, lacked an independent sphere, and its treatment was defined by different – mainly moral and political – dimensions. Kantians saw Kant as a supporter of religion, morals and political status quo; anti-Kantians viewed his work as an attack on these. Accordingly, the discussion was seriously deformed: Kant's *oeuvre* was reduced to ethical-theological aspects. The fact that the epistemological and logical aspects of the critical philosophy took precedence over the ethical-ideological aspects both genetically and structurally was hardly acknowledged.

The Hegel debate was also mainly conducted by Protestant ministers, but was effected less by denominational characteristics. Its driving force was the awakening of national spirit, typical of the early romantic age, whose main purpose was to promote scholarship – including philosophizing – in the national language. The Hegelian participants of the debate attempted to introduce the most influential contemporary philosophy, namely Hegelianism, to Hungary; the anti-Hegelians, however, judged the abstract Hegelian system of categories to be alien to the national spirit. The discussion had a dual result. On the one hand, this was the first time that a philosophical debate gained broader publicity: following articles in literary journals, Hegelianism became a widespread topic of discussion. On the other hand, the discussion initiated a considerable development in Hungarian philosophical language as the translation of Hegelian terms contributed to the establishment of Hungarian philosophical terminology.

The Hegel debate forms the background to the evolution of the so-called 'reconciliation' school of philosophy, which had a dominant role from the late 1830s until the mid-1850s. The school set itself the task of creating a characteristically Hungarian 'national philosophy'. Although its representatives took sides against German Idealism, their philosophy was in fact nothing but the adoption of ideas of some German thinkers – mainly those of Krug and FRIES, who interpreted Kant from an empirical-psychological point of view. The significance of the eclectic, rather low-level reconciliation school is to be found not so much in its intellectual contribution as in its culture-founding role. Following the example of the conventional school, the next century brought several more attempts to create a 'national philosophy' as an answer to the challenge which arose from the consciousness of both national and philosophical underdevelopment.

Around the middle of the century, two thinkers did significant work. János Erdélyi, aesthete and littérateur, represented Hegelianism on the *niveau* of the age. His polemical treatise, *A hazai bölcsészet jelene* (The Present State of Domestic Philosophy) (1857) criticizes the national philosophy of the reconciliation school by appealing to the universal character of philosophy. His monograph about the early history of Hungarian philosophy has been the most useful summary on the topic ever since. Writer and politician József Eötvös's reflections on liberal ideas yielded quite modern insights in contemporary terms. His monograph, *Der Einfluß der herrschenden Ideen des 19. Jahrhunderts auf den Staat* (The Influence of the Predominant Ideas of the Nineteenth Century on the State) (1851–4) (published originally in German), analysed the concepts of liberty, equality and nationality in sociological terms, and thereby became one of the first manifestations of a conservative reinterpretation of liberalism (see EQUALITY; FREEDOM AND LIBERTY; LIBERALISM; NATIONS AND NATIONALISM).

3 The establishment and functioning of the institutional system

The full development of the institutional system of Hungarian philosophy started in the last third of the nineteenth century. The infrastructure of philosophizing became consolidated, and philosophy secured an autonomous position within intellectual life.

Bernát Alexander, a prominent figure of the turn of the century, played a major role in this process. The author of some eclectic works in the history of philosophy, psychology, aesthetics and literary studies, using mainly elements of positivism and Neo-Kantianism (see NEO-KANTIANISM), his significance is due to his activity as organizer of philosophical life. He had a considerable influence as a teacher, an editor and publicist, and he translated many works into Hungarian. He was the editor of the series called 'Collection of Philosophical Writers', published in twenty-nine volumes between 1881 and 1919 by the Hungarian Academy of Science. This series played a fundamental role in spreading philosophical scholarship in Hungary: for the first time, many classics of the history of philosophy – including the works of PLATO and ARISTOTLE, BRUNO, DESCARTES, PASCAL, SPINOZA, HUME, DIDEROT and KANT – were published in Hungarian, and some of these translations are still in use today.

The first Hungarian philosophical periodical was the *Magyar Philosophiai Szemle* (Hungarian Philosophical Review), founded in 1882; from 1892, it was replaced by *Athenaeum*. The Hungarian Philosophical Society was founded in 1901, first as an opposition to official philosophical scholarship, then becoming a part of the status quo.

Supported by the institutional bases, a significant flowering occurred in philosophy at the beginning of the twentieth century, and especially after 1910: this was the first heyday of Hungarian philosophy. The somewhat late positivist orientation was followed by the reception of various directions of new idealism. Axiological Neo-Kantianism, Diltheyian philosophy of life, Bolzano's logic, Husserlian phenomenology and Meinongian theory of objects all soon found supporters (see DILTHEY, W.; BOLZANO, B.; HUSSERL, E.; MEINONG, A.). Two groups played a determining role in introducing the new idealist paradigm: the Böhm-students around the turn of century, and the Lukács-circle in the 1910s. Károly Böhm first tried to find a compromise between positivism and Neo-Kantianism, then worked on an axiology-based philosophy, akin to the efforts of the Baden school of Neo-Kantianism. His students at Kolozsvár – members of the 'Transylvanian School' – exemplified a specifically Hungarian branch of Neo-Kantianism. The young Lukács, with his short-lived journal *A Szellem* (The Spirit) and his intellectual group, the Sunday Circle, represented an ethical idealism embedded in a partly Kantian, partly philo-

sophy-of-life-based conceptual framework (see Lukács, G.). Some members of the Circle subsequently
emigrated from Hungary and made a name for
themselves, such as art historian Frigyes Antal, art
sociologist Arnold Hauser, and the founder of
sociology of knowledge, Károly (Karl) Mannheim.
The intellectual prosperity of the beginning of the
century formed the background of the early intellectual development of both the philosopher of economics Károly (Karl) Polányi and the philosopher of
science Mihály (Michael) Polányi (see POLÁNYI, M.).

After the First World War and the revolution,
development stopped. Many figures who had been
important at the beginning of the century were forced
to emigrate. The most significant character between
the two wars was Ákos Pauler. Beginning as a
positivist, then embracing the different tendencies of
new idealism, Pauler built a system that reflected the
Platonism of pure logic. His works – the two most
important being the *Bevezetés a filozífiába* (Introduction to Philosophy) (1920) and *Logika* (Logic) (1925)
– still breathe an air of cold perfection, but they were
considered somewhat anachronistic even in their time.

The dominant trend of the period was the
Geistesgeschichte approach which transformed new
idealism into philosophy of history and culture. Its
most prominent representative, Lajos Prohászka,
combined this direction with neo-Hegelianism. His
work on national characterology *A vándor és a bujdosó*
(The Wanderer and the Exile) (1934), born under
German influences, became the major philosophical
bestseller of the age. Beside the broadly interpreted
Geistesgeschichte tendency, all other schools lacked
influence: this was the case with Neo-Kantianism,
which had gradually lost ground, as well as with
German existentialism, which occasionally appeared
in Hungary.

4 Decades of communism

Following the few years of democratic digression
immediately after the end of the Second World War,
Hungary was ruled by communist regimes for about
four decades. This essentially determined the institutional system, the dominant direction and the
achievements of Hungarian philosophy.

The institutional system underwent a radical
transformation. The traditional 'bourgeois' institutions of philosophy were closed. The Hungarian
Philosophical Society fell apart, and the publication
of *Athenaeum* stopped. The institutional field of
philosophical activity was provided by the system of
Marxism-Leninism departments (a compulsory subject at all universities), and by the Philosophical
Institute founded within the Hungarian Academy of

Sciences (see MARX, K.; DIALECTICAL MATERIALISM;
MARXISM, WESTERN). The only periodical which was
devoted entirely to philosophical scholarship was the
Magyar Filozófiai Szemle (Hungarian Philosophical
Review, started in 1957). The philosophical life which
developed within the institutional system was usually
at a very low level, was imbued with ideology, and yet
functioned with shared subjects, a set terminology
and a unified audience.

The dominant philosophical trend was Soviet-
Marxism, which commanded a monopolistic position
at the beginning of the period but lost force after 1956
in the post-Stalinist period (see MARXIST PHILO-
SOPHY, RUSSIAN AND SOVIET). As for its function,
this was the ideology that served as legitimization of
political power. Its tenets were to refer to the works of
Marx and Engels, and were called 'scientific'; any
criticism of the official worldview was condemned as
'revisionist' or 'anti-scientific'. It consisted of two
parts: dialectical materialism – the ontology providing
cosmology and natural philosophy; and historical
materialism, the history of philosophy yielding a
teleological explanation of history.

In this period, there were considerable philosophical accomplishments, but mainly on the margins and
outside official philosophy. The former case is
exemplified by the activity of the Budapest School,
which formed around the later György Lukács. The
critical Marxist group's watchword was 'the renaissance of Marxism', announced by Lukács in the 1960s
(see LUKÁCS, G.). They produced notable works
which, however, eventually resulted not so much in
the renewal, but rather in the deconstruction of
Marxism. Of the circle, Ágnes Heller published
ethical works; Ferenc Fehér wrote aesthetic studies;
György Márkus attempted to introduce analytic
philosophy and expounded the notion of human
essence in the works of the young Marx; and Mihály
Vajda worked on the Marxist reception of phenomenology and on an analysis of fascist movements. The
book *Hogyan lehetséges kritikai gazdaságtan?* (How
Can Critical Economics be Possible?) (1970–72) –
written by Márkus with his students, György Bence
and János Kis and not published at the time –
criticizes the foundations of Marxian socialism.
Another book, *Dictatorship over Needs* (1981), co-
authored by Márkus, Heller and Fehér after their
emigration, provides a critical Marxist explanatory
theory of Soviet socialism. The philosopher of science
Imre LAKATOS who became famous after his emigration, was also a member of the circle for some time.
Two works outside official philosophy deserve mention. Political thinker István Bibó attempted to
reconcile liberalism and socialism (see SOCIALISM).
He was generally condemned to silence, but at the

time of the postcommunist transition his writings served as the most influential ideological reference. The philosopher Béla Hamvas, who started with a philosophy of crisis and ended up with a new sacral metaphysics, also relied on oriental traditions. His enigmatic essays, published years after they had been written, were a major inspiration to literary philosophical essay-writing.

5 After 1989

As far as philosophy is concerned, the changes of 1989 were preceded by earlier developments. In the last decade, the dominance of Marxist-Leninist philosophy became merely apparent. There was no opportunity for open criticism of official ideology, but members of the philosophical elite all joined contemporary Western trends. The significance of the changes in 1989 is due to the fact that these endeavours could become public within the new institutional system.

During the 1980s, ideological research was no longer compulsory in the Institute of Philosophy, and the Institute finally became a place for ideology-free philosophizing in official terms. In 1987, the social organization for philosophy, the Hungarian Philosophical Society, was reorganized. Since 1989, Marxism-Leninism has not been a compulsory subject at the universities; the departments that had earlier taught dialectic and historical materialism here started to give courses on the history of philosophy, introductions to philosophy and applied philosophy adjusted to the profile of their university. The publication of philosophical periodicals also was revitalized. About a dozen new philosophy-oriented periodicals were founded, the most important of which being the *Athenaeum*, which contains collections of translations on given topics, and *Gond*, which publishes philosophical essays. To compensate for the loss of several years a number of new editions of older translations have been published, together with new translations of classic and contemporary works and the writings of Hungarian authors blacklisted for ideological and political reasons. Following the renewal in the institutional system, there has been a renaissance in philosophy: philosophy seems to have become a significant area of contemporary Hungarian intellectual life.

The three most important schools in the country today appear to be analytic philosophy, hermeneutics and the postmodern approach (see ANALYTIC PHILOSOPHY; HERMENEUTICS; POSTMODERNISM). Scholars of analytic philosophy are interested in the philosophy of language, the philosophy of science and the history of philosophy. They are primarily influ-

enced by WITTGENSTEIN and KUHN. Those who work in the hermeneutic tradition are mainly attached to HEIDEGGER, and to GADAMER in aesthetic research. The most prominent representatives of postmodernism are members of the former Budapest School who returned from external or internal emigration, and (following some US and French examples) renewed the tradition of philosophical essay-writing. The rediscovery of a Hungarian philosophical tradition is an important element of this philosophical renaissance.

References and further reading

Alexander, B. (1896) 'Magyar filozófia története' (History of Philosophy in Hungary), in *Pallas Nagy Lexikona* (Pallas Great Encylopedia), vol. XII, Budapest: Pallas, 16–22. (Relevant to §§1–3. (A concise and useful summary about the development to the beginning of the twentieth century.)

* Apáczai, Cs.J. (1655) *Magar encyclopaedia* (Hungarian Encylopedia), Utrecht: Ex officina Joannis Waesberg; Bucharest: Kriterion Könyvkiadó, 1977. (The first philosophical work in Hungarian.)

Bence, Gy., Kis, J. and Márkus, Gy. (1970–2) *Hogyan lehetséges kritikai gazdaságtan?* (How Can Critical Economics be Possible?), Budapest: T-Twins-Lukás Archívum, 1992. (Critical analysis of the foundations of Marxian socialism.)

* Eötvös, J. (1851–4) *Der Einfluss der herrschenden Ideen des 19. Jahrhunderts auf den Staat* (The Influence of the Predominant Ideas of the Nineteenth Century on the State), Vienna: Jasper Hügel u Manz, 1851; Leipzig: Brockhaus, 1854; Budapest: Magyar Helikon, 1981. (One of the first manifestations of a conservative reinterpretation of liberalism in contemporary terms.)

* Erdélyi, J. (1857) *A hazai bölcsészet jelene* (The Present State of Domestic Philosophy), Sárospatak: Főiskolai Nyomda; reprinted in *Filozófiai és esztétikai írások* (Philosophical and Aesthetical Writings), Budapest: Akadémiai Kiadó, 1981, 25–102. (A polemical treatise representing Hegelianism on the niveau of the age.)

—— (1981) *A hazai bölcsészet múltja'* (The Past of Domestic Philosophy) in *Filozófiai és esztétikai írások* (Philosophical and Aesthetical Writings), Budapest: Akadémiai Kiadó, 142–299. (Relevant to §1. Written in the nineteenth century, but still the most thorough account of the early history of philosophy in Hungary today.)

* Fehér, F., Márkus, G. and Heller, Á. (1981) *Dictatorship over Needs: An Anaylsis of Soviet Societies*, Oxford: Blackwell, 1983. (A critical Marxist explanatory theory of Soviet socialism.)

Hanák, T. (1976) *Die marxistische Philosophie und Soziologie in Ungarn* (Marxist Philosophy and Sociology in Hungary), Stuttgart: Ferdinand Enke Verlag. (Relevant to §4, a characterization of the institutional system and achievements of official Marxism.)

—— (1982) *Az elfelejtett reneszánsz. A magyar filozófiai gondolkodás századunk elsö felében* (The Forgotten Renaissance: Hungarian Philosophical Thinking in the First Half of This Century), Bern: EPMSZ. (Relevant to §3, a monograph on the non-Marxist philosophy.)

—— (1990) *Geschichte der Philosophie in Ungarn. Ein Grundriß* (History of Philosophy in Hungary: An Outline), Munich: Dr Rudolf Trofenik Verlag. (The most up-to-date monograph on the subject.)

Hanák, T. and Lendvai, L.F. (1996) 'Ungarn' (Hungary), in H. Dahm and A. Ignatow (eds) *Geschichte der philosophischen Traditionen Osteuropas* (The History of Eastern European Traditional Philosophy), Darmstadt: Wissenschaftliche Buchgesellschaft, 451–513. (An overall view of non-Marxist philosophical development.)

Hermann, I. (ed.) (1982) *A magyar filozófiai gondolkodás a két világháború között* (Hungarian Philosophical Thinking Between the Two World Wars), Budapest: Kossuth Könyvkiadó. (A collection of essays on topics related to §3.)

Kiss, E. and Nyíri, K. (eds) (1977) *A magyar filozófiai gondolkodás a századelön* (Hungarian Philosophical Thinking at the Beginning of the Century), Budapest: Kossuth Könyvkiadó. (A collection of essays on topics related to §3.)

Kornis, Gy. (1907) 'A magyar bölcseleti münyelv fejlödése' ('The development of Hungarian philosophical terminology'), *Magyar Nyelv* (Hungarian language) III: 97–104, 145–53, 193–201, 241–50, 301–7, 348–56. (Relevant to §§1–2. The history of the formation of Hungarian philosophical terminology.)

Kovesi, J. (1967) 'Hungarian Philosophy', in P. Edwards (ed.) *The Encyclopedia of Philosophy*, vol. 4, New York and London: Macmillan, 93–5. (A short summary in English.)

Nyíri, J.C. (1986) 'Österreich und Ungarn: Eine philosophisch-soziologische Skizze' (Austria and Hungary: a Socio-philosophical Account), in *Gefühl und Gefüge. Studien zum Entstehen der Philosophie Wittgensteins* (Feeling and Construct: Studies in the Origination of Wittgenstein's Philosophy), Amsterdam: Editions Rodopi, 11–30. (Relevant to §3. An interpretation of developments at the turn of the century from the point of view of the sociology of knowledge.)

—— (1994) 'Tradition and Bureaucratic Lore: Lessons from Hungary', in B. Smith (ed.) *Philosophy and Political Change in Eastern Europe*, La Salle, IL: The Monist Library of Philosophy. (Relevant to §5; an apt characterization of post-Marxist tendencies.)

* Pauler, Á. (1920) *Bevezetés a filozófiába* (Introduction to Philosophy), Budapest: Pantheon. (The main work of the most significant thinker between the two world wars.)

* —— (1925) *Logika* (Logic), Budapest: Eggenberger. (A Platonistic work of pure logic.)

Perecz, L. (1994) 'Két kísérlet. Az egyezményesek és Alexander Bernát a nemzeti filozófiáról' ('Two attempts: the reconciliation school and Bernát Alexander on the national philosophy'), *Gond* (Care) 5–6: 104–28. (Relevant to §2. A sketch of the history of the 'national philosophy' idea.)

—— (1995) 'Az elsö másfél évtized. A Magyar Filozófiai Társaság indulása' ('The first one and a half decades: the beginning of the Hungarian Philosophical Society'), *Magyar Tudomány* (Hungarian science) CII: 735–42. (Relevant to §3. A description of the foundation of the Hungarian Philosophical Society as a part of the institutionalization of Hungarian Philosophy.)

* Prohászka, L. (1936) *A vándor és a bujdosó* (The Wanderer and the Exile), Budapest: Dunántúli Pécsi Egyetemi Könyvkiadó éd Nyomda; reprinted Szeged: Universum Kiadó, 1990. (A national characterology, conceived under German influences.)

Rácz, L. (1928) 'Die Ungarische Philosophie' ('Hungarian Philosophy') in K. Oesterreich (ed.) *Friedrich Ueberwegs Grundriß der Geschichte der Philosophie, Fünfter Teil, Die Philosophie des Auslandes*, Berlin: Mittler & Sohn, 348–57. (Relevant to §§1–3, a summary with much information.)

Sándor P. (1973) *A magyar filozófia története, 1900–1945* (The History of Philosophy in Hungary), vols I–II, Budapest: Magvetö Könyvkiadó. (Relevant to §3. Describes the philosophy of the first half of the twentieth century, with much information but with an ideologically biased view.)

Steindler, L. (1988) *Ungarische Philosophie im Spiegel ihrer Geschichtsschreibung* (Hungarian Philosophy Through its Historical Writings), Freiburg and Munich: Verlag Karl Alber. (An up-to-date monograph on research of the history of philosophy in Hungary.)

Tamás, G.M. (1994) 'A filozófia és az új Magyarország' ('The philosophy of the new Hungary'), in *Másvilág* (Other-world), Budapest: Új Mandátum Kiadó, 211–18. (Relevant to §§4–5, a witty account of Marxist and post-Marxist philosophy.)

Tankó, B. (1934–5) 'Hungarian Philosophy', *Acta literarum ac scientiarum Regiae Universitatis Hun-*

gariae Francisco Josephinae, Sectio Philosophica, V: 119–36. (Relevant to §§1–3, an account in English from a *Geistesgeschichte* approach.)

Veres I. and Mezei B. (eds) (1994) *Gondolatok gondolatokról. Elöadások a magyarorsz gi filozófia történetéről* (Ideas on Ideas: Lectures on the History of Philosophy in Hungary), Miskolc: Felsömagyarország Kiadó. (A collection of papers with the most recent results of research into the history of Hungarian philosophy.)

LÁSZLÓ PERECZ

HUS, JAN (*c.*1369–1415)

From his appointment as rector of the Bethlehem chapel in Prague in 1402 until his execution at the Council of Constance in 1415, Jan Hus advanced the goals of an ecclesiastical reform movement with Czech national overtones. Hus' ministerial and academic posts provided a broad platform for his leadership. He preached tenaciously against clerical abuses. At the University of Prague he taught philosophical and ecclesiological doctrines which, his opponents charged, were taken from the radical Oxford reformer, John Wyclif. Whereas Wyclif's philosophical realism (for example, the indestructibility of 'being', led him to adopt several positions, condemned as heretical, Hus' polemic, in which he castigated the fiscalization and bureaucratization of the papacy, sprang more from his ideals of evangelical minority and apostolic poverty.

Hus came from Husinec in southern Bohemia. He was trained at the University of Prague, earning his BA in 1393 and his MA in 1396. Divisions in the university faculty ran along national origins, German and Czech, and were reflected in schools of philosophy. Hus sided with his compatriots who adhered to the realism of WYCLIF as opposed to the nominalism embraced by the German counterparts. Along with his teaching duties, Hus preached in the large Bethlehem chapel. He followed in the footsteps of John Milic of Kromeríz and Matthew of Janov, forerunners of the Czech reform effort, committed to the reformation of the church according to the ideal of the early apostolic community.

The conflict between the faculties escalated into denunciations of heresy. Accused of Wycliffite errors, Hus and his fellow Czech academics responded by overturning the university voting procedure which had favoured the German students. After King Wenceslaus IV of Bohemia confirmed this reversal by mandate in 1409, the Germans left *en masse* for other German universities, where they continued to challenge the 'Wycliffites' by seeking their condemnation at the imperial court and the Roman Curia. Moreover, Hus encountered stiff resistance from the indigenous clerical hierarchy, stung by his strident accusations of careerism and moral laxity. Ultimately, he broke with the archbishop of Prague, Zbynek Zajíc, over the papal election at the Council of Pisa in 1409. The archbishop, although at first sympathetic to reform, maintained obedience to Pope Gregory XII of Rome, while Hus supported the newly elected Alexander Zbynek; in return the Pisan pope decreed that preaching cease in all Prague chapels. Hus ignored the pope's prohibition; even more, he publicly defended condemned articles of Wyclif. Outraged at Hus' defiance, Zbynek declared him excommunicate.

Hus alienated King Wenceslaus when Alexander's successor, John XXIII, called for a crusade in 1411 against the supporters of Gregory XII. The campaign was to be financed by the sale of indulgences, the profits of which Wenceslaus shared. Hus decried the crusade as fratricide; the King withdrew his protection for Hus. Meanwhile, Hus' antagonists at the Pisan curia secured papal excommunication against him, extended by an interdict on Prague.

In deference to his sovereign, Hus left the city in 1412 and found refuge among nobles in southern Bohemia. From there he defended his position in Latin and Czech treatises, the most important titled *Tractatus de ecclesia* (On the Church). Like Wyclif before him, Hus defines the universal Church as the 'totality of the predestined'. The Church on earth consists of the elect and those foreknown by God to be damned. This militant Church includes the Roman Church with the pope and the cardinals who form 'the chief part of its dignity', provided they adhere to Christ's example. Hus rejects papal claims to headship; Christ alone remains head of the Church. Anyone not prepared to follow Christ in word and deed is a 'disciple of the Antichrist'.

When summoned to appear before the general council at Constance (1414–18), Hus received from the emperor Sigismund a guarantee of safe conduct to and from Constance. Instead of being allowed to present his case, Hus was imprisoned. Confronted with a series of loose quotes, deemed Wycliffite, that were gleaned from his works, Hus responded that he would abandon any position if it could be proven heretical on the basis of the Scriptures. Herein lay the main cause for his condemnation: Hus repudiated all pronouncements, either papalist or conciliarist, formulated without scriptural foundation. Refusing to recant, Hus was burned as a heretic on 6 July 1415. His death rallied his Czech countrymen and ignited a broad-based reform movement. Its conservative wing wrested major concessions from the Council of Basel in 1431–49, which were acknowledged in the Compacts of Prague (1436).

See also: LUTHER, M.; WYCLIF, J.

List of works

Jan Hus (*c.* 1393–1415) *Magistri Iohannis Hus, Opera Omnia*, ed. V. Flajshans, Prague: J. Bursík and J.R. Vilímek, 1903–7, 8 vols. (A collection of Hus' academic works including his commentary on Lombard's *Sentences*.)
—— (*c.*1393–1415) *Documenta Magistri Johannis Hus*, ed. F. Palacky, Prague: F. Tempsky, 1869. (Collection of correspondence and documents related to Hus' career.)
—— (1413) *Tractatus de ecclesia* (On the Church), ed. S.H. Thomson, *Magistri Johannis Hus, Tractatus de Ecclesia*, Boulder, CA: University of Colorado Press, 1956. (The critical edition of Hus' most significant and controversial work.)

References and further reading

De Vooght, P. (1960) *L'hérésie de Jean Huss* (The Heresy of Jan Huss), Louvain: Publications Universitaires de Louvain. (For a counter-balancing perspective.)
Kaminsky, H. (1967) *A History of the Hussite Revolution*, Berkeley and Los Angeles, CA: University of California Press. (For further study of the Czech revolution after Hus' execution.)
Novotný, V., and Kybal, V. (1919–31) *M. Jan Hus, Zivot a UcenÙ* (The Life and Teachings of Master Jan Hus), Prague: J. Laichter, 5 vols. (The foundational biography for any in-depth study.)
Spinka, M. (1968) *John Hus, a Biography*, Princeton, NJ: Princeton University Press. (Well-written but partisan.)

CURTIS V. BOSTICK

HUSSERL, EDMUND (1859–1938)

Through his creation of phenomenology, Edmund Husserl was one of the most influential philosophers of our century. He was decisive for most of contemporary continental philosophy, and he anticipated many issues and views in the recent philosophy of mind and cognitive science. However, his works were not reader-friendly, and he is more talked about than read.

Husserl was born in Moravia, received a Ph.D. in mathematics while working with Weierstraß, and then turned to philosophy under the influence of Franz Brentano. He was particularly engaged by Brentano's view on intentionality and developed it further into what was to become phenomenology. His first phenomenological work was Logische Untersuchungen *(Logical Investigations) (1900–1). It was followed by* Ideen *(Ideas) (1913), which is the first work to give a full and systematic presentation of phenomenology. Husserl's later works, notably* Vorlesungen zur Phänomenologie des inneren Zeitbewusstseins *(On the Phenomenology of the Consciousness of Internal Time) (1928),* Formale und transzendentale Logik *(Formal and Transcendental Logic) (1929),* Kartesianische Meditationen *(Cartesian Meditations) (1931) and* Krisis der europäischen Wissenschaften und die transzendentale Phänomenologie *(Crisis of the European Sciences) (partly published in 1936), remain largely within the framework of the* Ideas. *They take up topics that Husserl only dealt with briefly or were not even mentioned in the* Ideas, *such as the status of the subject, intersubjectivity, time and the lifeworld.*

Brentano had characterized intentionality as a special kind of directedness upon an object. This leads to difficulties in cases of hallucination and serious misperception, where there is no object. Also, it leaves open the question of what the directedness of consciousness consists in. Husserl therefore endeavours to give a detailed analysis of those features of consciousness that make it as if of an object. The collection of all these features Husserl calls the act's 'noema'. The noema unifies the consciousness we have at a certain time into an act that is seemingly directed towards an object. The noema is hence not the object that the act is directed towards, but is the structure that makes our consciousness be as if of such an object.

The noemata are akin to Frege's 'third world' objects, that is, the meanings of linguistic expressions. According to Husserl, 'the noema is nothing but a generalization of the notion of meaning [Bedeutung] to the field of all acts' ([1913] 1950: 3, 89). Just as distinguishing between an expression's meaning and its reference enables one to account for the meaningful use of expressions that fail to refer, so, according to Husserl, can the distinction between an act's noema and its object help us overcome Brentano's problem of acts without an object.

In an act of perception the noema we can have is restricted by what goes on at our sensory surfaces, but this constraint does not narrow our possibilities down to just one. Thus in a given situation I may perceive a man, but later come to see that it was a mannequin, with a corresponding shift of noema. Such a shift of noema is always possible, corresponding to the fact that perception is always fallible. These boundary conditions, which constrain the noemata we can have, Husserl calls 'hyle'. The hyle are not objects experienced by us, but are experiences of a kind which we typically have when our sense organs are affected, but also can have in other cases, for example under the influence of fever or drugs.

In our natural attitude we are absorbed in physical objects and events and in their general features, such as their colour and shape. These general features, which can be shared by several objects, Husserl calls essences, or 'eidos' (Wesen). Essences are studied in the eidetic sciences, of which mathematics is the most highly developed. We get to them by turning our attention away from the concrete individuals and focusing on what they have in common. This change of attention Husserl calls 'the eidetic reduction', since it leads us to the eidos. However, we may also more radically leave the natural attitude altogether, put the objects we were concerned with there in brackets and instead reflect on our own consciousness and its structures. This reflection Husserl calls 'the transcendental reduction', or 'epoché'. Husserl uses the label 'the phenomenological reduction' for a combination of the eidetic and the transcendental reduction. This leads us to the phenomena studied in phenomenology, that is, primarily, the noemata.

The noemata are rich objects, with an inexhaustible pattern of components. The noema of an act contains constituents corresponding to all the features, perceived and unperceived, that we attribute to the object, and moreover constituents corresponding to features that we rarely think about and are normally not aware of, features that are often due to our culture. All these latter features Husserl calls the 'horizon' of the act. The noema is influenced by our living together with other subjects where we mutually adapt to one another and come to conceive the world as a common world in which we all live, but experience from different perspectives. This adaptation, through empathy (Einfühlung), was extensively studied by Husserl.

Husserl emphasizes that our perspectives and anticipations are not predominantly factual: 'this world is there for me not only as a world of mere things, but also with the same immediacy as a world of values, a world of goods, a practical world' ([1913] 1950: 3, 1, 58). Further, the anticipations are not merely beliefs – about factual properties, value properties and functional features – but they also involve our bodily habits and skills.

The world in which we find ourselves living, with its open horizon of objects, values, and other features, Husserl calls the 'lifeworld'. It was the main theme of his last major work, The Crisis of the European Sciences, *of which a part was published in 1936. The lifeworld plays an important role in his view on justification, which anticipates ideas of Goodman and Rawls.*

1 **Life**
2 **Intentionality**
3 **Noema**
4 **Hyle; filling; evidence**
5 **Intuition**
6 **The reductions; phenomenology**
7 **The past**
8 **Values; practical function**
9 **Horizon**
10 **Intersubjectivity**
11 **Existence**
12 **The lifeworld**
13 **Ultimate justification**
14 **Influence**

1 Life

Edmund Gustav Albrecht Husserl was born of Jewish parents in Prossnitz (now Prostejov in the Czech Republic) in Moravia, in what was then Austria-Hungary on 8 April 1859. He was thus of the same age as Dewey and Bergson.

Husserl's early interests lay in the direction of mathematics and science. In 1876 he began studying mathematics and astronomy at the University of Leipzig. After three semesters he transferred to the University of Berlin in order to study with Weierstraß, Kronecker and Kummer, a trio that made Berlin a centre in the mathematical world during that period. After three years in Berlin he left for Vienna, where he received his doctorate in January 1883. He then returned to Berlin in order to become an assistant for Weierstraß. However, Weierstraß became ill, and after just one semester in Berlin Husserl entered military service for a year, spending most of it in Vienna. A growing interest in religious questions made him decide in 1884 to study philosophy with Franz BRENTANO in Vienna, who inspired him to go into philosophy full-time and exerted a decisive influence on his later phenomenology.

Husserl studied with Brentano until 1886, when Brentano advised him to go to Halle, where one of Brentano's earlier students, Carl Stumpf, was teaching philosophy and psychology. Husserl habilitated in Halle in 1887 and remained there as a *Privatdozent* until 1901, when he became Associate Professor (*außerordentlicher Professor*) in Göttingen, and in 1906 Full Professor. In 1916 he went to Freiburg, where he taught until he retired in 1928. He died in Freiburg on 27 April 1938.

Husserl's first philosophical work was his

Habilitation dissertation, *On the Concept of Number*, which was printed, but not published, in 1887. This was incorporated into the first three chapters of his *Philosophy of Arithmetic*, whose first volume was published in 1891. A second volume was announced, but never came. Instead, Husserl underwent a radical philosophical reorientation. He gave up his main project in *Philosophy of Arithmetic*, which had been to base mathematics on psychology. Instead, he developed his lasting philosophical achievement, phenomenology, which was first presented in *Logische Untersuchungen* (*Logical Investigations*), arriving in two volumes in 1900 and 1901. In 1905–7 he introduced the idea of a transcendental reduction and gave phenomenology a turn towards transcendental idealism. This new version of phenomenology was expounded in *Ideen* (*Ideas*) (1913), and is the most systematic presentation of phenomenology.

Husserl's notable later works were *Vorlesungen zur Phänomenologie des inneren Zeitbewusstseins* (*On the Phenomenology of the Consciousness of Internal Time*) (1928), *Formale und transzendentale Logik* (*Formal and Transcendental Logic*) (1929), which Husserl characterized as his most mature work, and *Kartesianische Meditationen* (*Cartesian Meditations*) (1931). The first part of his *Krisis der europäischen Wissenschaften* (*Crisis of the European Sciences*) was published in 1936, but the main part of this work and about 40,000 pages of manuscripts were left after his death. These manuscripts, together with Husserl's family and his library, were rescued from Germany by the Belgian Franciscan Van Breda, who established the Husserl Archive in Louvain, where the material is now accessible to researchers. Copies of the manuscripts are kept in other Husserl archives in various parts of the world. Gradually, the most important parts of Husserl's papers and scholarly editions of his published works are being published in the series *Husserliana*. In addition, *Erfahrung und Urteil* (*Experience and Judgment*) was prepared by Husserl's assistant Ludwig Landgrebe in consultation with Husserl, and appeared shortly after Husserl's death in 1938. Husserl's main works are available in good English translations.

2 Intentionality

The central theme of phenomenology is intentionality. All of phenomenology can be regarded as an unfolding of the idea of intentionality (see INTENTIONALITY). Husserl's interest in intentionality was inspired by his teacher, Franz Brentano. However, there are many differences between Husserl's treatment of this notion and that of Brentano. This section deals first with these differences, then goes on to

further features of Husserl's notion of intentionality reaching beyond the issues considered by Brentano.

Husserl retains the following basic idea of Brentano's: 'We understand by intentionality the peculiarity of experiences to be "consciousness of something"' ([1913] 1950: 3, 1, 188; Husserl's emphasis). Husserl's formulation comes close to Brentano's oft-quoted passage from *Psychology from an Empirical Point of View*:

> Every mental phenomenon is characterized by what the scholastics in the Middle Ages called the intentional (and also mental) inexistence of an object, and what we could also call, although in not entirely unambiguous terms, the reference to a content, a direction upon an object.
> (1874: 1, 2, 85)

However, there is already an important difference between Brentano and Husserl at this starting-point. While Brentano says straightforwardly that for every act there is an object towards which it is directed, Husserl focuses on the 'of'-ness of the act. There are two reasons for this difference: First, Husserl wants to get around the difficulties connected with acts that lack an object. Second, he aims to throwing light on what it means for an act to be 'of' or 'about' something. Let us begin by discussing these two differences.

Acts that lack an object. Brentano's thesis may seem unproblematic in the examples Brentano considered: just as when we love there is somebody or something that we love, so there is something that we sense when we sense, something we think of when we think, and so on. However, what is the object of our consciousness when we hallucinate, or when we think of a centaur? Brentano insisted that even in such cases our mental activity, our sensing or thinking, is directed towards some object. The directedness has nothing to do with the reality of the object, he held. The object is contained in our mental activity, 'intentionally' contained in it. And Brentano defined mental phenomena as 'phenomena which contain an object intentionally'.

Not all of Brentano's students found this lucid or satisfactory, and the problem continued to disturb both them and Brentano. Brentano struggled with it for the rest of his life, and suggested, among other things, a translation theory, giving Leibniz credit for the idea: when we describe an act of hallucination, or of thinking of a centaur, we are only apparently referring to an object. The apparent reference to an object can be translated away in such a way that in the full, unabbreviated description of the act there is no reference to any problematic object. There are two weaknesses of Brentano's proposal. First, unlike

Russell later, Brentano does not specify in detail how the translation is to be carried out (see RUSSELL, B. §9). Second, if such a translation can be carried out in the case of hallucinations and so on, then why not carry it out everywhere, even in cases of normal perception? What then happens to the doctrine of intentionality as directedness upon an object?

One of Brentano's students, Alexius MEINONG (§§2–4), suggested a simple way out. In his *Gegenstandstheorie* Meinong maintained that there are two kinds of objects, those that exist and those that do not exist. Hallucinations, like normal perception, are directed towards objects, but these objects do not exist. Brentano was not happy with this proposal. He objected that, like Kant, he could not make sense of existence as a property that some objects have and others lack.

Husserl's solution was, as noted, to emphasize the 'of'. Consciousness is always consciousness *of* something. Or better, consciousness is always *as if of* an object. What matters is not whether or not there is an object, but what the features are of consciousness that makes it always be as if of an object. These three words, 'as if of' are the key to Husserl's notion of intentionality. To account for the directedness of consciousness by saying only that it is directed towards an object leaves us in the dark with regard to what that directedness is. This leads us to the second reason for why Husserl diverged from Brentano. Husserl wanted to throw light on just this issue: what does the directedness of consciousness consists in? He made it a theme for a new discipline: the discipline of phenomenology.

What is directedness? To get a grip on what the directedness of consciousness consists in – to understand better the word 'of', which Husserl emphasized in his definition of intentionality quoted at the beginning of §2 above – let us note that for Husserl intentionality does not simply consist in consciousness directing itself towards objects that are already there. Intentionality for Husserl means that consciousness in a certain way 'brings it about' that there are objects. Consciousness 'constitutes' objects, Husserl said, borrowing a word from the German Idealists, but using it in a different sense. Above, the phrase 'bringing about' was put in quotation marks to indicate that Husserl does not mean that we create or cause the world and its objects. 'Intentionality' means merely that the various components of our consciousness are interconnected in such a way that we have an experience as of one object. To quote Husserl:

an object 'constitutes' itself – 'whether or not it is actual' – in certain concatenations of consciousness which in themselves bear a discernible unity in so far as they, by virtue of their essence, carry with themselves the consciousness of an identical X.

([1913] 1950: 3, 1, 313; translation emended)

Husserl's use, here and in many other places, of the reflexive form 'an object constitutes itself', reflects his view that he did not regard the object as being produced by consciousness. Husserl considered phenomenology as the first strictly scientific version of transcendental idealism, but he also held that phenomenology transcends the traditional distinction between idealism and realism, and in 1934 he wrote in a letter to Abbé Baudin: 'No ordinary "realist" has ever been as realistic and concrete as I, the phenomenological "idealist" (a word which by the way I no longer use)' (Kern 1964: 276). In the preface to the first English edition of the *Ideas* (1931), Husserl stated:

Phenomenological idealism does not deny the factual [*wirklich*] existence of the real [*real*] world (and in the first instance nature) as if it deemed it an illusion .... Its only task and accomplishment is to clarify the sense [*Sinn*] of this world, just that sense in which we all regard it as really existing and as really valid. That the world exists...is quite indubitable. Another matter is to understand this indubitability which is the basis for life and science and clarify the basis for its claim.

(1950: 5, 152–3)

To see more clearly what Husserl is after, consider Jastrow and Wittgenstein's duck/rabbit picture. In order to come closer to Husserl we should modify the example and consider not a picture, but a silhouette of the real animal against the sky. When we see such a silhouette against the sky, we may see a duck or a rabbit. What reaches our eyes is the same in both cases, so the difference must be something coming from us. We structure what we see, and we can do so in different ways. The impulses that reach us from the outside are insufficient to determine uniquely which object we experience; something more gets added.

3 Noema

The structure that makes up the directedness of consciousness, Husserl called the 'noema'. More accurately, the noema has two main components. First, the 'object meaning' that integrates the various constituents of our experience into experiences of the various features of *one* object, and second, the 'thetic' component that differentiates acts of different kinds, for example, the act of perceiving an object from the act of remembering it or thinking about it. The thetic component is thereby crucial for the reality-character which we ascribe to the object.

Our consciousness structures what we experience (see KANT, I.). How it structures it depends on our previous experiences, the whole setting of our present experience and a number of other factors. If we had grown up surrounded by ducks, but had never heard of rabbits, we would have been more likely to see a duck when confronted with the duck/rabbit silhouette; the idea of a rabbit would not have occurred to us.

The structuring always takes place in such a way that the many different features of the object are experienced as connected with one another, as features of one and the same object. When, for example, we see a rabbit, we do not merely see a collection of coloured patches, various shades of brown spread out over our field of vision (incidentally, even seeing coloured patches involves intentionality, since a patch is also a kind of object, but a different kind of object from a rabbit). We see a rabbit, with a determinate shape and a determinate colour, with the ability to eat, jump and so on. It has a side that is turned towards us and one that is turned away from us. We do not see the other side from where we are, but we see something which has another side.

That seeing is intentional, or object-directed, means just this, that it is as if of an object: the near side of the object we have in front of us is regarded as a side of a thing, and the thing we see has other sides and features that are co-intended, in the sense that the thing is regarded as more than just this one side. The object meaning of the noema is the comprehensive system of determinations that gives unity to this manifold of features and makes them aspects of one and the same object.

It is important at this point to note that the various sides, appearances or perspectives of the object are constituted together with the object. There are no sides and perspectives floating around before we start perceiving, which are then synthesized into objects when intentionality sets in. There are no objects of any kind, whether they be physical objects, sides of objects, appearances of objects or perspectives of objects without intentionality. And intentionality does not work in steps. We do not start by constituting six sides and then synthesize these into a die; we constitute the die and the six sides of it in one step.

We should also note that when we experience a person, we do not experience a physical object, a body, and then infer that a person is there. We experience a fully fledged person, we are encountering somebody who structures the world, experiences it from their own perspective. Our noema is a noema of a person; no inference is involved. Seeing persons is no more mysterious than seeing physical objects, and

no inference is involved in either case. When we see a physical object we do not see sense-data or the like and then infer that there is a physical object there, but our noema is the noema of a physical object. Similarly, when we see an action, what we see is a fully fledged action, not a bodily movement from which we infer that there is an action.

The word 'object' must hence be taken in a very broad sense. It comprises not only physical things, but also, as we have seen, animals, and likewise persons, events, actions and processes, and sides, aspects and appearances of such entities.

Essences. Husserl distinguishes between physical objects and processes, which are temporal and normally also spatial, and essences (*Wesen*) or eidos, which are features that the object can share with other objects, such as the triangularity of a triangle or the greenness of a tree. For Husserl, an object's essence is therefore not something unique to that object, as it is for many other philosophers. Mathematics is the most highly developed study of essences.

Noema and meaning. The features of the noema that we have mentioned, in particular the role it plays in the analysis of acts without objects and the way it accounts for the object-directedness of acts, make it natural to compare the noema to the meaning of linguistic expressions. This comparison and the ensuing way of reading Husserl has been contested. However, it is well supported by textual and systematic considerations, and it is now often regarded as the standard way of interpreting Husserl. One factor contributing to this has been Husserl's own statement, in a manuscript, that 'the noema is nothing but a generalization of the notion of meaning (*Bedeutung*) to the field of all acts' ([1913] 1950: 5, 89).

Noesis. The noema is an abstract structure that can in principle be the same from act to act, in the unlikely case that at two different occasions we should have the same kind of experience of the same object from the same point of view, with exactly the same anticipations, and so on. An act has a noema in virtue of comprising a kind of experience that Husserl calls a 'noesis'. The noema is the meaning given in an act, Husserl says, while the noesis is the meaning-giving aspect of the act. There is hence a close parallelism between noema and noesis. The relation between noema and noesis bears some similarity to the type/token relation in Peirce (see TYPE/TOKEN DISTINCTION). The noesis is a temporal process, in which the noema 'dwells'.

4 Hyle; filling; evidence

In acts of perception, the noema that we can have is restricted by what goes on at our sensory surfaces, but the restriction does not narrow our possibilities down to just one. Thus in a given situation I may perceive a man, but later come to see that the man was a mannequin, with a corresponding shift of noema. Such a shift of noema is always possible, corresponding to the fact that perception is always fallible. These boundary conditions, which constrain the noemata we can have, Husserl calls 'hyle'. The hyle are not objects experienced by us, but are experiences of a kind which we typically have when our sense organs are affected, but also can have in other cases, for example, under the influence of fever or drugs.

In the case of an act of perception, its noema can also be characterized as a very complex set of expectations or anticipations concerning what kind of experiences we will have when we move around the object and perceive it, using our various senses. We anticipate different further experiences when we see a duck and when we see a rabbit. In the first case we anticipate, for example, that we will feel feathers when we touch the object, while in the latter case we expect to find fur. When we get the experiences we anticipate, the corresponding component of the noema is said to be 'filled'. In all perception there will be some filling: the components of the noema that correspond to what presently 'meets the eye' are filled, and similarly for the other senses.

Such anticipation and filling is what distinguishes perception from other modes of consciousness, such as imagination or remembering. If we merely imagine things, our noema can be of anything whatsoever. In perception, however, our sensory experiences are involved; the noema has to fit in with our sensory experiences. This eliminates a number of noemata which I could have had if I were just imagining. In your present situation you can probably not have a noema corresponding to the perception of an elephant. This does not reduce the number of perceptual noemata you can have just now to one, for example, of having a book in front of you.

It is a central point in Husserl's phenomenology that I can have a variety of different perceptual noemata that are compatible with the present impingements upon my sensory surfaces. In the duck/rabbit case this was obvious, for we could go back and forth at will between having the noema of a duck and having the noema of a rabbit. In most cases, however, we are not aware of this possibility. Only when something untoward happens, when I encounter a 'recalcitrant' experience that does not fit in with the anticipations in my noema, do I start seeing a different object from the one I thought I saw earlier. My noema 'explodes', to use Husserl's phrase, and I come to have a noema quite different from the previous one, with new anticipations. This is always

possible, he says. Perception always involves anticipations that go beyond what presently 'meets the eye', and there is always a risk that we may go wrong, regardless of how confident and certain we might feel.

When some components of the noema are filled, we have 'evidence'. Evidence comes in degrees, depending on how much of the noema is filled. Husserl discusses two kinds of perfect evidence: 'adequate' evidence, where every component in the noema is filled, with no unfilled anticipations, and 'apodictic' evidence, where the negation of what seems to be the case is self-contradictory. After some vacillation Husserl ended up holding that we can never attain any of these kinds of perfect evidence – we are always fallible.

5   Intuition

Husserl uses the term 'intuition' (*Anschauung*) for any act where an object is experienced as 'given', that is, as really there. Earlier philosophers have used the word 'intuition' in a variety of ways, mostly about some sort of direct, non-inferential insight. Perception has usually been classified as a kind of intuition. A key issue in medieval philosophy as well as in rationalism and empiricism was whether there are other sorts of such insight. Kant defined 'intuition' as a representation which 'relates immediately to its object and is singular' (*Critique of Pure Reason* 1781/87: A320; B376–7). Bernard BOLZANO developed this idea with great precision. For Husserl, an intuition is an act where we are constrained in how we constitute its objects, such as we typically are in perception, which is one of his two varieties of intuition. He calls the other variety 'essential insight' (*Wesensschau*). The object is here a general feature, an essence. For Husserl, as for Kant, intuition is a key kind of evidence in mathematics. This, then, is what Husserl means by the mysterious-sounding term '*Wesensschau*'. One might still claim that there is no such thing, but it is difficult to reject the notion once one agrees that the object of an act is underdetermined by what reaches our senses, and one accepts the correlated idea of intentionality.

6   The reductions; phenomenology

Husserl distinguishes between several so-called 'reductions'. First, there is the 'eidetic' reduction, which we perform each time we pass from focusing on an individual physical object to focusing on one of its essences (eidos). This kind of reduction has been carried out in mathematics since its beginning, and Husserl conceived of other eidetic sciences in addition to mathematics. Second, a reduction that is distinctive for phenomenology is a special kind of reflection.

Instead of focusing on the normal objects of our acts, be they physical objects, actions, persons or general features that many objects can have in common, we reflect on the structures of our own consciousness and study the noemata, the noeses or the hyle. The noemata, the noeses and the hyle have two important features: we are normally not aware of them, and they are a *sine qua non* for the appearance of a world. Entities with these two features are called 'transcendental'. The reduction that leads to them, where the ordinary objects are bracketed, is therefore called the 'transcendental' reduction. Husserl also calls it the 'epoché', using a word that the ancient sceptics used for refraining from taking a stand. We study the features of the act that make it seem to have an object and do not ask whether or not it actually has one. Husserl got the idea of the transcendental reduction in 1905. It marks the transition from the early phenomenology of the *Logical Investigations* to the 'idealist' phenomenology of the *Ideas* and later works.

The 'phenomenological' reduction, finally, is the combination of the eidetic reduction and the transcendental reduction. That is, it is a reduction that leads us from acts directed towards physical objects via acts directed towards essences to acts directed towards the noema, noesis and hyle of acts directed towards essences. Husserl sometimes takes the two steps in the inverse order, starting with a transcendental reduction and then focusing on the essential traits of the noema, noesis and hyle. The end product is not quite the same, but the phenomenological reduction can presumably be either.

Phenomenology is the study of the transcendental elements in our experience that are uncovered through the phenomenological reduction: the noema, the noesis and the hyle. In phenomenology, all these three elements are studied, with emphasis on the noematic/noetic structures. Husserl carried out detailed analyses of temporal structures and how they are constituted, in *On the Phenomenology of the Consciousness of Internal Time*, on the structures that are basic to logic and mathematics, in *Formal and Transcendental Logic* and *Experience and Judgment*, and on intersubjectivity and the processes whereby we come to constitute a common world, in *Cartesian Meditations* and in thousands of pages of manuscripts, the most important of which have been collected by Iso Kern in *Husserliana*, vols 13–15.

For Husserl, phenomenology is a study of the subjective perspective. In science one aims for objectivity and endeavours to arrange observations and experiments in such a way as to minimize differences between different observers. Phenomenology focuses on the subjective, on the manner in which each subject structures or 'constitutes' the world differently, on the basis of different experiences and cultural background, but also on the basis of adaptation to other subjects through interaction and communication.

7 The past

We constitute not only the different properties of things, but also the relation of the thing to other objects. If, for example, I see a tree, the tree is conceived of as something which is in front of me, as perhaps situated among other trees, as seen by other people than myself, and so on. It is also conceived of as something which has a history: it was there before I saw it, it will remain after I have left, or perhaps it will eventually be cut down and transported to some other place. However, like all material things, it does not simply disappear from the world.

My consciousness of the tree is in this way also a consciousness of the world in space and time in which the tree is located. My consciousness constitutes the tree, but at the same time it constitutes the world in which the tree and I are living. If my further experience makes me give up the belief that I have a tree ahead of me because, for example, I do not find a tree-like far side or because some of my other expectations prove false, this affects not only my conception of what there is, but also my conception of what has been and what will be. Thus in this case, not just the present, but also the past and the future are reconstituted by me. To illustrate how changes in my present perception lead me to reconstitute not just the present, but also the past, Husserl uses an example of a ball which I initially take to be red all over and spherical. As it turns, I discover that it is green on the other side and has a dent:

> the sense of the perception is not only changed in the momentary new stretch of perception; the noematic modification streams back in the form of a retroactive cancellation in the retentional sphere and modifies the production of sense stemming from earlier phases of the perception. The earlier apperception, which was attuned to the harmonious development of the 'red and uniformly round', is implicitly 'reinterpreted' to 'green on one side and dented'.
>
> (1938: 96)

Husserl held that time and space are constituted. In *On the Phenomenology of the Consciousness of Internal Time* and various manuscripts that have been published in Volume 10 of *Husserliana* he gives a highly interesting analysis of the way objective time is constituted (Miller 1984).

8 Values; practical function

So far we have focused on the factual properties of things. However, things also have *value* properties, and these properties are constituted in a corresponding manner. The world within which we live is experienced as a world in which certain things and actions have a positive value, others a negative. Our norms and values, like our beliefs, are subject to change. Changes in our views on matters of fact are often accompanied by changes in our evaluations.

Husserl emphasizes that our perspectives and anticipations are not predominantly factual. We are not living a purely theoretical life. According to Husserl, we encounter the world around us primarily 'in the attitude of the natural pursuit of life', as 'living functioning subjects involved in the circle of other functioning subjects' (1950: 4, 375). Husserl says this in a manuscript from 1917, but he has similar ideas about the practical both earlier and later. Thus in the *Ideas* he says: 'this world is there for me not only as a world of mere things, but also with the same immediacy as a world of values, a world of goods, a practical world' ([1913] 1950: 3, 1, 58).

In later manuscripts, particularly from 1917 onwards, Husserl focused more and more on the role of the practical and the body in our constitution of the world. Just as he never held that we first perceive sense-data, or perspectives or appearances, which are then synthesized into physical objects, or that we first perceive bodies and bodily movements and then infer that there are persons and actions, so it would be a grave misunderstanding of Husserl to attribute to him the view that we first perceive objects that have merely physical properties and then assign a value or a practical function to them. Things are directly experienced by us as having the features – functional and evaluational as well as factual – that are of concern for us in our natural pursuit of life.

In our discussion of the hyle we characterized the noema of an act of perception as a very complex set of expectations or anticipations concerning what kind of experiences we will have when we move around the object and perceive it. We should note that these experiences depend not only on our sensory organs, but also on the movements of our body, on our bodily skills and our familiarity with various kinds of practical activities. In numerous passages Husserl talks about practical anticipations and the role of kinesthesis in perception and bodily activity (Føllesdal 1979).

9 Horizon

When we are experiencing an object, our conscious-ness is focused on this object, and the rest of the world and its various objects are there in the background as something we 'believe in' but are not presently paying attention to. The same holds for most of the inexhaustibly many features of the object itself. All these further features of the object, together with the world in which it is set, make up what Husserl calls the 'horizon' of that experience. The various features of the object, which are co-intended, or also-meant, but not at the focus of our attention, Husserl calls the 'inner horizon', while the realm of other objects and the world to which they all belong, he calls the 'outer horizon'.

The horizon is of crucial importance for Husserl's concept of justification, which we shall discuss later. What is particularly significant is the hidden nature of the horizon. As we noted, the horizon is that which is not attended to. Take as an example our 'expectation' that we will find a floor when we enter a room. Usually, we have not even thought about there being a floor. Typically, we cannot even recall when we first acquired the corresponding 'belief' or 'anticipation'. According to Husserl, there may never have been any occasion when we actually judged there to be a floor in some particular room. Still we have come to 'anticipate' a floor, not in the sense of consciously expecting one, but in the sense that if we entered the room and there were none, we would be astonished. In this example we would easily be able to tell what was missing, in other cases our 'anticipations' are so imperceptible that we just may feel that something has gone awry, but not be able to tell what it is.

Words like 'belief' and 'anticipate' are clearly not the proper ones here, since they have overtones of something being conscious and thought about. Both English and German seem to lack words for what we want to get at here: Husserl uses the words '*antizipieren*', '*hinausmeinen*' and '*vorzeichnen*'.

10 Intersubjectivity

Throughout his life, Husserl emphasized that the world we intend and thereby constitute is not our own private world, but an intersubjective world, common to and accessible to all of us. Thus in the *Ideas* he writes:

I continually find at hand as something confronting me a spatiotemporal reality [*Wirklichkeit*] to which I belong like all other human beings who are to be found in it and who are related to it as I am.
([1913] 1950: 3, 1, 61)

Husserl's studies of intersubjectivity focus in particular on the processes by which we experience others as experiencing subjects, like ourselves, and adapt our anticipations to those that we take them to have. Thanks to this, our way of constituting the world is not solipsistic, but we constitute the world as a shared world, which we each experience from our different perspective. A notion of objectivity arises, we may come to regard ourselves as deviant, for example, as colour-blind or as cognitively biased, and we also experience ourselves as confronted with a reality to which our beliefs and anticipations have to adapt. In works that remain largely unpublished, Husserl started to develop an ethics based in part on a study of the objectifying processes whereby objective ethical principles and norms arise from our subjective likes and dislikes.

Husserl stresses the shared, intersubjective nature of the world, particularly in §29 of the *Ideas*, which he entitles 'The "Other" Ego-subjects and the Inter-subjective Natural Surrounding World'. There he says:

> I take their surrounding world and mine Objectively as one and the same world of which we are conscious, only in different ways [*Weise*] .... For all that, we come to an understanding with our fellow human beings and together with them posit an Objective spatiotemporal reality.
>
> ([1913] 1950: 3, 1, 60)

In the later works one finds similar ideas, particularly in the many texts that have been collected by Iso Kern in the three volumes of the *Husserliana* devoted to intersubjectivity, but also in many other works, for example in the *Crisis*:

> Thus in general the world exists not only for isolated men but for the community of men; and this is due to the fact that even what is straightforwardly perceptual is communal.
>
> (1936, 1954: 6, 166)

Husserl discusses in great detail empathy and the many other varieties of intersubjective adaptation that enable us to intend a common, intersubjective world. (See the three volumes on intersubjectivity referred to above.)

11 Existence

The passages quoted in §10 above express a further feature of Husserl's notion of intentionality which is rarely discussed, in spite of its importance: intentionality does not just involve directedness upon an object, but also a 'positing' of the object, corresponding to the two components of the noema discussed in §3 above. The object is experienced as real and present, as remembered, or as merely imagined, and so on. In the passages just quoted, Husserl said, 'I

continually find at hand as something confronting me a spatiotemporal reality', and 'we come to an understanding with our fellow human beings and together with them posit an Objective spatiotemporal reality'. The same point is stressed also when he discusses the lifeworld in the Crisis:

> the lifeworld, for us who wakingly live in it, is always there, existing in advance for us, the 'ground' of all praxis, whether theoretical or extratheoretical. The world is pregiven to us, the waking, always somehow practically interested subjects, not occasionally but always and necessarily as the universal field of all actual and possible praxis, as horizon. To live is always to live-in-certainty-of-the-world.
>
> (1936, 1954: 6, 145)

Husserl discusses this *thetic* character of intentionality, and, correspondingly, of the noema, in many of his books and manuscripts. He was particularly concerned with what gives reality-character to the world. Like William James, whom he had read already when he made the transition to phenomenology in the mid-1890s, he stressed the importance of the body, and the inflictions upon our body, for our sense of reality. As James put it: 'Sensible vividness or pungency is then the vital factor in reality' (1890: 2, 301). Husserl could also have subscribed to James's observation that 'the *fons et origo* of all reality, whether from the absolute or the practical point of view, is thus subjective, is ourselves' (1890: 2, 296–7).

This latter passage from James gets a double meaning in Husserl which expresses the core of his view of the reality of the world: the subjective (ourselves) is the *fons et origo* of all reality in two senses, a transcendental and an empirical: we constitute the world as real through our intentionality, and the reality-character we give it is derived from our being not merely transcendental subjects, but empirical subjects with a body immersed in a physical world.

12 The lifeworld

The idea of Husserl's that has become most widely known is that of the lifeworld. In particular, the word 'lifeworld' (*Lebenswelt*) itself has gained wide currency. It was used by Simmel and others before Husserl. After the Second World War it became a favourite word of many social scientists, who used it in many different senses. Several of them refer to Husserl without seeming to have studied his philosophy and therefore without knowing the many important features that the lifeworld has in his thought.

The first place Husserl uses the word 'lifeworld' in print is in his latest work, the *Crisis*, of which the first two parts were published in 1936. The rest of this unfinished work, containing the important third part, with the main discussion of the lifeworld, was not published until 1954, but it was known to some of Husserl's students and followers, including Maurice MERLEAU-PONTY, who came to the Husserl Archives in Louvain to study this part in April 1939.

Interpreters of Husserl differ widely in their views on the lifeworld. It is often thought that it constitutes a major break in Husserl's development, from the 'early' Husserl of the *Ideas* to the 'late' Husserl of the *Crisis*. Is it such a break? And second, what exactly is the lifeworld and what role does it play in phenomenology? On the former question the answer is a definite 'No'. The lifeworld is fully compatible with Husserl's earlier philosophy, and there is even a definite place for it in his phenomenology from its beginning. Husserl touches upon the lifeworld repeatedly in his earlier work and he gradually deepens and modifies his views on it, as he did with everything else in his phenomenology. Instead of regarding the lifeworld as a break with Husserl's earlier philosophy, we should view it as intimately connected with the other main themes in phenomenology. Properly to understand the lifeworld with all its nuances it is important to appreciate fully the connection between it and the rest of Husserl's philosophy.

The lifeworld arises from the distinction between the natural attitude and the transcendental or phenomenological attitude, which Husserl introduced in 1905. The first appearance of the notion for which he later introduced the term 'lifeworld' occurs shortly thereafter, in his lectures 'Fundamental Problems in Phenomenology' in 1910–11, that is, already before the *Ideas*. Husserl begins these lectures with an extended discussion of 'the natural attitude and the "natural world concept"'. Here he says:

> It could also be shown that philosophical interests of the highest dignity require a complete and comprehensive description of the so-called *natural world concept*, that of the natural attitude, on the other hand also that an accurate and profound description of this kind is not easily carried out, but on the contrary would require exceptionally difficult reflections.
>
> (1950: 13, 124–5)

Husserl here borrows the phrase 'natural world concept', which he emphasizes, from Richard AVENARIUS, whom he discusses later in the lecture. In a manuscript from 1915, Husserl describes this world in the following way (following Avenarius):

> All opinions, justified or unjustified, popular, superstitious, scientific, all relate to the already *pregiven world*. . . . All theory relates to this immediate givenness and can have a legitimate sense only when it forms thoughts which do not offend against the general sense of the immediately given. No theorizing may offend against this sense.
>
> (1950: 13, 196; emphasis added)

In the following years, Husserl repeatedly returns to this and related themes, using various labels that sometimes allude to other philosophers who had propounded similar ideas, such as Nietzsche. Quite often he uses Avenarius' phrase 'natural world'. In a manuscript from 1917, which appears to be the first place where he uses the word 'lifeworld', he introduces this new word as equivalent to the former: 'The lifeworld is the natural world – in the attitude of the natural pursuit of life are we living functioning subjects involved in the circle of other functioning subjects' (1950: 4, 375; the manuscript dates from 1917, but was copied during the first half of the 1920s, and it is possible that the word 'lifeworld' appeared then).

Gradually during the 1920s and especially in the 1930s the lifeworld becomes a central theme in Husserl's writings, until his discussion culminates in the *Crisis* in 1936. One aim of this work was to provide a new and better access to phenomenology, through the notion of the lifeworld. The lifeworld is for Husserl our natural world, the world we live in and are absorbed by in our everyday activities. A main aim of phenomenology is to make us reflect on this world and make us see how it is constituted by us. Through the phenomenological reduction phenomenology will take us out of our natural attitude where we are absorbed by the world around us, into the phenomenological, transcendental attitude, where we focus on the noemata of our acts – on our structuring of reality.

Pregivenness. In the passage just quoted from Husserl's 1915 manuscript, Husserl says that the world is pregiven (*vorgegeben*). This point is also discussed in the *Ideas*, where Husserl notes that

> In my waking consciousness I find myself in this manner at all times, and without ever being able to alter the fact, in relation to the world which remains one and the same, though changing with respect to the composition of its contents. It is continually 'on hand' for me and I myself am a member of it.
>
> ([1913] 1950: 3, 1, 58)

and a few pages later the passage that was quoted earlier, in the section on intersubjectivity:

I continually find at hand as something confronting me a spatiotemporal reality [*Wirklichkeit*] to which I belong like all other human beings who are to be found in it and who are related to it as I am.

([1913] 1950: 3, 1, 61)

Also the passage from §37 of the *Crisis* that was quoted in the section on existence above expresses this same idea:

The lifeworld . . . is always there, existing in advance for us, the 'ground' of all praxis, whether theoretical or extratheoretical. The world is pregiven to us . . .

(1936, 1954: 6, 145)

Science and the lifeworld. A contested point in Husserl scholarship is the relation between the lifeworld and the sciences. Many interpreters of Husserl like to find an opposition to the sciences in the lifeworld. However, such a disdain for the sciences is out of character with Husserl's background in and continued interest in mathematics and science. It also accords poorly with the texts, which give us a different and more intriguing picture. According to Husserl, the lifeworld and the sciences are intimately connected, in three different ways:

(1) The sciences are *part* of the lifeworld. This comes out most explicitly and clearly in *Experience and Judgment*, where Husserl says:

everything which contemporary natural science has furnished as determinations of what exists also belong to us, to the world, as this world is pregiven to the adults of our time. And even if we are not personally interested in natural science, and even if we know nothing of its results, still, what exists is pregiven to us in advance as determined in such a way that we at least grasp it as being in principle scientifically determinable.

(1938: 39)

Similar statements are also found elsewhere in Husserl's work, for example in the *Crisis*: 'Now the scientific world – [the subject matter of] systematic theory – . . . like all the worlds of ends "belongs" to the lifeworld' (1936, 1954: 6, 460).

(2) Scientific statements get their *meaning* by being embedded in the lifeworld. This was stressed by Husserl already in the manuscript from 1915, quoted in §12 above:

All opinions, justified or unjustified, popular, superstitious, scientific, all relate to the already pregiven world. . . . All theory relates to this immediate givenness and can have a legitimate *sense* only when it forms thoughts which do not offend

against the general sense of the immediately given. No theorizing may offend against this sense.

(1950: 13, 196; emphasis added)

(3) The sciences are *justified* through the lifeworld. There is an interplay between this point and point (1) above; the sciences are justified because they belong to the lifeworld, and at the same time they belong to the lifeworld because they are conceived of as describing the world, as claiming to be true:

Though the peculiar accomplishment of our modern objective science may still not be understood, nothing changes the fact that it is a validity for the lifeworld, arising out of particular activities, and that it belongs itself to the concreteness of the lifeworld.

(1936, 1954: 6, 136)

And similarly:

all these theoretical results have the character of validities for the lifeworld, adding themselves as such to its own composition and belonging to it even before that as a horizon of possible accomplishments for developing science. The concrete lifeworld, then, is the grounding soil [*der gründende Boden*] of the 'scientifically true' world and at the same time encompasses it in its own universal concreteness.

(1936, 1954: 6, 134)

13 Ultimate justification

This brings us to the final theme of this presentation of Husserl's phenomenology: the role of the lifeworld in justification (see JUSTIFICATION). The traditional interpretation of Husserl attributes to him a 'foundationalist' position: he is alleged to hold that we can reach absolute certainty with regard to a number of matters, particularly in philosophy. However, there is considerable evidence that Husserl had a view on justification similar to that of Goodman and Rawls (Føllesdal 1988). An opinion is justified by being brought into 'reflective equilibrium' with the *doxa* of our lifeworld. This holds even for mathematics: 'mathematical evidence has its source of meaning and of legitimacy in the evidence of the lifeworld' (1936, 1954: 6, 143).

A major puzzle that many see in this idea of justification is, 'How can appeal to the subjective-relative doxa provide any kind of justification for anything? It may help to resolve disagreements, but how can it serve as justification?' Husserl answers by pointing out that there is no other way of justifying anything, and that his way is satisfactory:

What is actually first is the 'merely subjective-relative' intuition of prescientific world-life. For us, to be sure, this 'merely' has, as an old inheritance, the disdainful colouring of the *doxa*. In prescientific life itself, of course, it has nothing of this; there it is a realm of good verification and, based upon this, of well-verified predicative cognitions and of truths which are just as secure as is necessary for the practical projects of life that determine their sense. The disdain with which everything 'merely subjective and relative' is treated by those scientists who pursue the modern ideal of objectivity changes nothing of its own manner of being, just as it does not change the fact that the scientist himself must be satisfied with this realm whenever he has recourse, as he unavoidably must have recourse, to it.

(1936, 1954: 6, 127–8)

So far, this is a mere claim. However, Husserl elaborates his view in other parts of his work. His key observation, which is an intriguing contribution to our contemporary discussion of ultimate justification, is that the 'beliefs', 'expectations' or 'acceptances' on which we ultimately fall back are unconsidered, and in most cases have never been considered. Every claim to validity and truth rests upon this 'iceberg' of unconsidered prejudgmental acceptances discussed earlier. One would think that this would make things even worse. Not only do we fall back on something that is uncertain, but on something that we have not even thought about, and have therefore never subjected to conscious testing. Husserl argues, however, that it is just the unconsidered nature of the lifeworld that makes it the ultimate ground of justification. 'Acceptance' and 'belief' are not attitudes that we decide to have through any act of judicative decision. What we accept, and the phenomenon of acceptance itself, are integral to our lifeworld, and there is no way of starting from scratch, or 'to evade the issue here through a preoccupation with aporia and argumentation nourished by Kant or Hegel, Aristotle or Thomas' (1936, 1954: 6, 134). Only the lifeworld can be an ultimate court of appeal: 'Thus alone can that ultimate understanding of the world be attained, behind which, since it is ultimate, there is nothing more that can be sensefully inquired for, nothing more to understand' ([1929] 1974: 17, 249) (see PHENOMENOLOGY, EPISTEMIC ISSUES IN).

14 Influence

Husserl's phenomenology has been a major influence on philosophy in our century, primarily on the continent, but since the 1970s also in the United States, Britain and several other countries. Husserl's immediate successor in Freiburg, Martin HEIDEGGER, conceived of *Being and Time* (1927) as a phenomenological study and dedicated it to Husserl. Also Jean-Paul SARTRE received strong impulses from Husserl, particularly from Husserl's idea that our material surroundings do not uniquely determine our noema. Sartre developed this idea into a philosophy of freedom, notably in *Being and Nothingness* (1943), which has the subtitle 'A Phenomenological Essay on Ontology'. Also Emmanuel LEVINAS, Paul RICOEUR and several other French philosophers were heavily influenced by Husserl. A new generation of young French and German philosophers is now combining Husserl scholarship with work on systematic issues in epistemology, philosophy of language and philosophy of mind.

Husserl's conception of the lifeworld become important for the so-called 'new hermeneutics' (Heidegger and GADAMER; see HERMENEUTICS) and for the methodology of the humanities and the social sciences (SCHÜTZ, Luckmann), largely because it provides a framework for discussing the subjective perspective and the many features of our way of structuring the world of which we are unaware and that often reflect the culture in which we have grown up. The issues connected with intersubjectivity and Husserl's exploration of the various ways in which we adapt to one another and come to conceive the world as a common world were pursued by several of his students, notably Edith Stein, in her dissertation *On the Problem of Empathy* (1917). His ideas about the role of the body, of kinesthesis and of practical activity recur in different versions in Heidegger's existentialism and in Merleau-Ponty's phenomenology. MERLEAU-PONTY in particular is generous in the credit he gives Husserl.

Husserl's many students and followers explored a number of other themes in Husserl and applied his ideas in a variety of fields. Thus Roman INGARDEN used them in aesthetics, Aron Gurwitsch and several others in the study of perception. Husserl's views have led to new developments in psychology and psychotherapy. They have influenced philosophers of mathematics, including GÖDEL (see Føllesdal 1995), and they are beginning to have an impact on the philosophy of mind and on cognitive science.

See also: PHENOMENOLOGICAL MOVEMENT

List of works

Husserl, E. (1950–) *Husserliana*, ed. H.L. Van Breda, The Hague: Nijhoff; since 1989, Dordrecht: Kluwer. (The standard critical edition of Husserl's work. References to Husserl's works are by volume, page number and line number in this edition.)

—— (1891) *Philosophie der Arithmetik. Logische und psychologische Untersuchungen*, vol. 1, in *Husserliana*, vol. 12, 1970. (Husserl's first book, where he attempted to found arithmetic on psychology. He gave up this project, and the planned second volume of the work never appeared.)

—— (1900–1) *Logische Untersuchungen*, in *Husserliana*, vols 18–19, 1950; trans. J.N. Findlay, *Logical Investigations*, London: Routledge & Kegan Paul, 2 vols, 1970. (Husserl's first phenomenological work. Volume 1 is a criticism of psychologism, volume 2 consists of six studies of key themes in phenomenology.)

—— (1913) *Ideen*, 3 vols, in *Husserliana*, vols 3–5, 1950; revised edn in two parts, 1976; *Ideas*, vol. 1, trans. F. Kersten, The Hague: Nijhoff, 1982; vol. 2, trans. R. Rojcewicz and A. Schuwer, Dordrecht: Kluwer, 1989; vol. 3, trans. T.E. Klein and W.E. Pohl, Dordrecht: Kluwer, 1980. (Husserl's main systematic presentation of phenomenology. Difficult, but *the* book to read if one should read only one book by Husserl.)

—— (1928) *Vorlesungen zur Phänomenologie des inneren Zeitbewußtseins*, in *Husserliana*, vol. 10, 1966; trans. J.B. Brough, *On the Phenomenology of the Consciousness of Internal Time (1893–1917)*, The Hague: Nijhoff, 1991. (Husserl's main texts on time and time-consciousness.)

—— (1929) *Formale und transzendentale Logik*, in *Husserliana* vol. 17, 1974; trans. D. Cairns, *Formal and Transcendental Logic*, The Hague: Nijhoff, 1969. (This book, which Husserl characterized as one of his most mature works, aims at providing a phenomenological foundation for formal logic.)

—— (1931) *Kartesianische Meditationen*, in *Husserliana* vol. 1, 1950; 2nd edn, 1973; improved edn, ed. E. Ströker, *Philosophische Bibliothek*, vol. 291, Hamburg: Felix Meiner, 1977; trans. D. Cairns, *Cartesian Meditations*, The Hague: Nijhoff, 1960. (A 'Cartesian' approach to phenomenology. Focuses especially on the ego and on intersubjectivity. Easiest to read among Husserl's later works.)

—— (1936, 1954) *Krisis der europäischen Wissenschaften und die transzendentale Phänomenologie*, in *Husserliana* vol. 6, 1954; trans. D. Carr, *The Crisis of European Sciences and Transcendental Phenomenology*, Evanston, IL: Northwestern University Press, 1970. (Presents Husserl's theory of the lifeworld.)

—— (1938) *Erfahrung und Urteil. Untersuchungen zur Genealogie der Logik*, ed. L. Landgrebe, Prague: Akademia Verlagsbuchhandlung; trans. J.S. Churchill and K. Amerik, *Experience and Judgment*, Evanston, IL: Northwestern University Press, 1973. (Compiled by Husserl's assistant Ludwig Landgrebe, this work throws light on the lifeworld and several of the themes dealt with in *Formal and Transcendental Logic*.)

Schuhmann, K. and Schuhmann, E. (eds) (1994) *Edmund Husserl Briefwechsel*, The Hague: Nijhoff, 10 vols. (A critical edition of Husserl's correspondence.)

References and further reading

Avenarius, R. (1891) *Der menschliche Weltbegriff*, Leipzig: Reisland. (One source of Husserl's concept of the lifeworld.)

Bell, D. (1990) *Husserl, The Arguments of the Philosophers*, London: Routledge. (Good on the early Husserl.)

Bernet, R., Kern, I. and Marbach, E. (1993) *An Introduction to Husserlian Phenomenology, Studies in Phenomenology and Existential Philosophy*, Evanston, IL: Northwestern University Press. (A good introduction to phenomenology by three eminent Husserl scholars.)

Boehm, R. (1968, 1981) *Vom Gesichtspunkt der Phänomenologie*, in *Phenomenologica* 26 and 83, The Hague: Nijhoff, 2 vols. (Two collections of essays on the epoché and other central topics in Husserl by a most knowledgeable Husserl editor and scholar.)

* Brentano, F. (1874) *Psychologie vom empirischen Standpunkt* (Psychology from an Empirical Point of View), Leipzig: Duncker & Humblot. (This work by Husserl's main teacher had a strong influence on Husserl and many of his contemporaries.)

Dreyfus, H. (ed.) (1982) *Husserl, Intentionality and Cognitive Science*, Cambridge, MA: MIT Press. (A selection of articles on Husserl and cognitive science.)

Føllesdal, D. (1969) 'Husserl's Notion of Noema', *Journal of Philosophy* 66: 680–7. (This and the following two articles present evidence for the interpretation of Husserl on which this entry is based.)

* —— (1979) 'Husserl and Heidegger on the Role of Actions in the Constitution of the World', in E. Saarinen, R. Hilpinen, I. Niiniluoto and M. Provence Hintikka (eds) *Essays in Honour of Jaakko Hintikka*, Dordrecht: Reidel, 365–78.

* —— (1988) 'Husserl on Evidence and Justification', in R. Sokolowski (ed.) *Edmund Husserl and the Phenomenological Tradition: Essays in Phenomenology* (*Studies in Philosophy and the History of Philosophy*, vol. 18), Washington, DC: Catholic University of America Press, 107–29.

* —— (1995) 'Gödel and Husserl', in J. Hintikka (ed.) *From Dedekind to Gödel: Essays on the Development of the Foundations of Mathematics*, Dordrecht: Kluwer, 427–46.

Gurwitsch, A. (1966) *Studies in Phenomenology and Psychology*, Evanston, IL: Northwestern University Press. (Collection of significant articles, particularly on consciousness and on perception.)

Haaparanta, L. (ed.) (1994) *Mind, Meaning and Mathematics. Esssays on the Philosophical Views of Husserl and Frege*, Dordrecht: Kluwer. (Brings together several contributions on the interesting relationship between Frege and Husserl.)

Heidegger, M. (1927) *Being and Time*, trans. J. Macquarrie and E. Robinson, *Being and Time*, New York: Harper & Row, 1962. (Heidegger's main work, a phenomenological study dedicated to Husserl.)

Ingarden, R.W. (1931) *The Literary Work of Art*, Evanston, IL: Northwestern University Press, 1973. (The first of Ingarden's many influential studies of the philosophy of art.)

* James, W. (1890) *The Principles of Psychology*, New York: Holt. (Husserl studied this work in the 1890s and felt that James had said what he himself wanted to say.)

* Kern, I. (1964) *Husserl und Kant*, in *Phenomenologica* 16, The Hague: Nijhoff. (*The* book on Husserl's study of Kant and on the similarities and differences between Husserl's philosophy and that of Kant.)

Künne, W. (1986) 'Edmund Husserl: Intentionalität', in J. Speck (ed.) *Grundprobleme der großen Philosophen, Philosophie der Neuzeit IV*, Göttingen: Vandenhoeck & Ruprecht, 165–215. (A lucid presentation of Husserl's thought by a philosopher who combines systematic insight with scholarship.)

Lapointe, F.H. (1980) *Edmund Husserl and His Critics. An International Bibliography (1884–1979)*, Bowling Green, OH: Philosophy Documentation Center. (The most comprehensive bibliography on Husserl. However, literature on Husserl is growing rapidly, and bibliographies quickly become outdated.)

Marbach, E. (1993) *Mental Representation and Consciousness. Towards a Phenomenological Theory of Representation and Reference*, Dordrecht: Kluwer. (A discussion of Husserlian notions that have a bearing on cognitive science.)

* Meinong, A. (1904) 'Über Gegenstandstheorie', in A. Meinong (ed.) *Untersuchungen zur Gegenstandstheorie und Psychologie*, Leipzig: Barth, 1–50; trans. and ed. R.M. Chisholm, 'The Theory of Objects', in *Realism and the Background of Phenomenology*, Atascadero, CA: Ridgeview, 1982, 76–117. (Presents Meinong's theory of objects. Meinong's ideas also became influential in the English-speaking world through Russell's generous review articles in *Mind* (1894) of Meinong's *On Assumptions* (1902).)

* Miller, I. (1984) *Husserl, Perception, and Temporal Awareness*, Cambridge, MA: MIT Press. (A clear and pedagogical discussion of Husserl's view on perception and its relation to time.)

Mohanty, J. (1989) *Transcendental Phenomenology: An Analytic Account*, Oxford: Blackwell. (One of several books by a prominent Husserl scholar who is also familiar with other traditions in philosophy.)

Sartre, J.-P. (1943) *Being and Nothingness: An Essay of Phenomenological Ontology*, New York: Philosophical Library, 1956. (Sartre's first major philosophical work, with the subtitle *An Essay on Phenomenological Ontology*, reflects his study of phenomenology, notably in Germany in 1933–4, encouraged by Raymond Aron.)

Schuhmann, K. (1973) *Die Dialektik der Phänomenologie*, in *Phenomenologica* 56/7, The Hague: Nijhoff, 2 vols. (Two collections of essays by the editor *of Husserl-Chronik* and Husserl's *Briefwechsel*, as well as of the new, improved edition of the *Ideen*.)

—— (1977) *Husserl-Chronik. Denk- und Levensweg Edmund Husserls*, The Hague: Nijhoff. (A detailed chronology of Husserl's life and activities.)

Smith, D. and McIntyre, R. (1982) *Husserl and Intentionality: A Study of Mind, Meaning and Language*, Dordrecht: Reidel. (Relates Husserl's work to other recent approaches to intentionality. It was the most cited Husserl book during the first years after it was published.)

Smith, B. and Woodruff Smith, D. (eds) (1995) *The Cambridge Companion to Husserl*, Cambridge: Cambridge University Press. (Essays by several prominent Husserl scholars on various aspects of Husserl's thought, followed by useful bibliographies.)

Sokolowski, R. (1970) *The Formation of Husserl's Concept of Constitution*, in *Phenomenologica* 18, The Hague: Nijhoff. (A classic study in English of one of the key notions in phenomenology.)

—— (ed.) (1988) *Edmund Husserl and the Phenomenological Tradition: Essays in Phenomenology (Studies in Philosophy and the History of Philosophy, vol. 18)*, Washington DC: Catholic University of America Press. (The essays stem from a lecture series at the Catholic University of America in the Fall of 1985.)

Spiegelberg, H. (1960) *The Phenomenological Movement: A Historical Introduction*, in *Phenomenologica* 5/6, The Hague: Martinus Nijhoff, 2 vols; 3rd edn, 1982. (The standard historical survey of the development of the phenomenological tradition from Brentano and Stumpf through Husserl to its mid-century representatives.)

Stein, E. (1917) *Zum Problem der Einfühlung*, Halle; trans. W. Stein, *On the Problem of Empathy*, The Hague: Nijhoff, 1970. (The dissertation of Edith Stein, Husserl's assitant, who later became a Carmelite nun and died in Auschwitz in 1942.)

Ströker, E. (1993) *Husserl's Transcendental Phenomenology*, Stanford, CA: Stanford University Press. (A presentation of the development of Husserl's thought by a leading Husserl scholar.)

DAGFINN FØLLESDAL

HUTCHESON, FRANCIS (1694–1746)

Francis Hutcheson is best known for his contributions to moral theory, but he also contributed to the development of aesthetics. Although his philosophy owes much to John Locke's empiricist approach to ideas and knowledge, Hutcheson was sharply critical of Locke's account of two important normative ideas, those of beauty and virtue. He rejected Locke's claim that these ideas are mere constructs of the mind that neither copy nor make reference to anything objective. He also complained that Locke's account of human pleasure and pain was too narrowly focused. There are pleasures and pains other than those that arise in conjunction with ordinary sensations; there are, in fact, more than five senses. Two additional senses, the sense of beauty and the moral sense, give rise to distinctive pleasures and pains that enable us to make aesthetic and moral distinctions and evaluations.

Hutcheson's theory of the moral sense emphasizes two fundamental features of human nature. First, in contrast to Thomas Hobbes and other egoists, Hutcheson argues that human nature includes a disposition to benevolence. This characteristic enables us to be, sometimes, genuinely virtuous. It enables us to act from benevolent motives, whereas Hutcheson identifies virtue with just such motivations. Second, we are said to have a perceptual faculty, a moral sense, that enables us to perceive moral differences. When confronted with cases of benevolently motivated behaviour (virtue), we naturally respond with a feeling of approbation, a special kind of pleasure. Confronted with maliciously motivated behaviour (vice), we naturally respond with a feeling of disapprobation, a special kind of pain. In short, certain distinctive feelings of normal observers serve to distinguish between virtue and vice. Hutcheson was careful, however, not to identify virtue and vice with

these feelings. The feelings are perceptions (elements in the mind of observers) that function as signs of virtue and vice (qualities of agents). Virtue is benevolence, and vice malice (or, sometimes, indifference); our moral feelings serve as signs of these characteristics.

Hutcheson's rationalist critics charged him with making morality relative to the features human nature happens at present to have. Suppose, they said, that our nature were different. Suppose we felt approbation where we now feel disapprobation. In that event, what we now call 'vice' would be called 'virtue', and what we call 'virtue' would be called 'vice'. The moral sense theory must be wrong because virtue and vice are immutable. In response, Hutcheson insisted that, as our Creator is unchanging and intrinsically good, the dispositions and faculties we have can be taken to be permanent and even necessary. Consequently, although it in one sense depends upon human nature, morality is immutable because it is permanently determined by the nature of the Deity.

Hutcheson's views were widely discussed throughout the middle decades of the eighteenth century. He knew and advised David Hume, and, while Professor of Moral Philosophy at Glasgow, taught Adam Smith. Immanuel Kant and Jeremy Bentham, among other philosophers, also responded to his work, while in colonial America his political theory was widely seen as providing grounds for rebellion against Britain.

1   Life and works
2   The foundations of morality and the moral sense
3   Practical ethics and influence

1   Life and works

Francis Hutcheson was born on 8 August 1694 near Saintfield, County Down, Ireland. Although often taken to be the founder of the Scottish Enlightenment, he always considered himself an Irishman. Hutcheson studied first at a classical school in Saintfield, then at an academy in Killyleagh, and finally, for two years, at Glasgow College. Ordained as a minister in the Presbyterian Church of Ireland, Hutcheson followed instead an academic career. In the early 1720s he established a dissenting academy in Dublin, where he remained until called to Glasgow as Professor of Moral Philosophy in 1729. This position he held until his death, having in 1745 declined an offer of a similar position at Edinburgh.

In Dublin, Hutcheson came under the influence of Robert Molesworth, himself a philosophical disciple of the Third Earl of Shaftesbury. In the mid 1720s Hutcheson published papers outlining some of his own views, and others criticizing Thomas Hobbes and Bernard Mandeville, as well as his first book, *An*

Inquiry into the Original of our Ideas of Beauty and Virtue (1725a). This work he initially described as a defence of SHAFTESBURY against an attack by MANDEVILLE. His *Essay on the Nature and Conduct of the Passions and Affections: with Illustrations on the Moral Sense* appeared in 1728. His next work was probably *A System of Moral Philosophy*, written by 1738 but published only posthumously in 1755. His last major work was his *Philosophiae moralis institutio compendiaria* (1742a), a translation (Hutcheson himself was probably the translator) of which, *A Short Introduction to Moral Philosophy*, appeared in 1747, the year of his death.

Hutcheson corresponded with, and probably met, David Hume, and gave HUME advice, some of which he took, regarding the third volume of his *Treatise of Human Nature*. Notwithstanding these connections, Hutcheson apparently opposed Hume's efforts to be appointed (in 1745) to the chair of moral philosophy in Edinburgh. Hutcheson's students at Glasgow included Adam SMITH, author of *The Theory of Moral Sentiments* (1759) and *The Wealth of Nations* (1776).

2 The foundations of morality and the moral sense

Much of Hutcheson's early work may be seen as a contribution to a long-standing debate about the foundations of morality. For over a century before Hutcheson joined the debate, moral theorists had offered fundamentally incompatible accounts of the origin and nature of morality. Every participant in this debate accepted the fact that there are moral phenomena to explain. No participant denied, for example, that there is a set of moral terms (such terms as, in English, 'good', 'evil', 'virtue', 'vice', 'right', 'wrong', 'just', 'unjust') that are competently used by ordinary speakers. Even those philosophers who were said to have denied that morality has a foundation assumed that it is to rational beings (principally humans) and their actions that this set of terms applies, and supposed that ordinary humans do so apply the terms, however much they may disagree about which term to use in any given situation. The controversy raged, however, over the proper characterization of such moral phenomena. For many writers, it was not merely a matter of providing a causal explanation of these phenomena. Even cynics and sceptics could do that. Rather, these writers, who tended to think of themselves as moral realists, demanded that a proper understanding of morality be a part of this explanation. Having concluded that moral differences are both real and unique, they insisted that one could be said to have given an account of the foundations of morality only if one could trace these real and unique moral differences to

some set of objective and unique natural or transcendental features adequate to ground such differences in a non-reductive way.

Hutcheson's work illustrates this latter demand. In a preview of his influential *Inquiry*, he says that his new work will include an essay on the foundations of morality, a needed antidote to the socially poisonous views of those (most notably HOBBES, Samuel PUFENDORF and John LOCKE, as we later learn) who suppose that the 'foundation of virtue' is nothing more than fear of punishment. In the *Inquiry* itself Hutcheson develops his criticism of these 'selfish moralists' (egoists, as we would say), and also makes explicit his deeply felt objections to Mandeville's claim that what is called virtue is simply 'the Political Offspring which Flattery begot upon Pride' (1724a).

Although his philosophy owes much to Locke's empiricist approach to ideas and knowledge, Hutcheson was far from satisfied with Locke's account of our moral ideas and our moral psychology. According to Locke, our normative ideas – of beauty and virtue, for example – are complex ideas of mixed modes, and, although formed out of the materials of experience, have no objective reference. These ideas, Locke says, are constructed by our minds, and are neither copies of anything real, nor even made according to the pattern of any real existence. Hutcheson found this anti-realist account of the origin of our moral ideas seriously flawed. Moreover, he also complained that Locke's account of human pleasure and pain was too narrowly focused. Locke had failed to note that there are pleasures and pains other than those that arise in conjunction with ordinary sensations. Indeed, Locke had failed to note that there are more than five senses, and that our additional senses – the sense of beauty and the moral sense – give rise to distinctive pleasures and pains (to approbations and disapprobations) that enable us to make moral distinctions and moral evaluations. Human nature is considerably more complex than Locke had supposed.

As to Hutcheson's disagreement with Hobbes and Mandeville, Hutcheson can be seen to have rejected their pessimistic, cynical view of human nature – in effect, that humans are inherently corrupt – and to have adopted in its place the more optimistic view that human nature incorporates a substantial element of goodness. More particularly, while Hobbes and Mandeville argue that all human acts are motivated by self-interest, Hutcheson argues that humans have, and actually do act from, other-regarding motives, and that the 'selfish theory' – the view that all motivations are self-interested – cannot account for many features of our moral experience. Hutcheson sees the selfish theorists as maintaining that we act only from a regard for our own pleasure, and hence that those things that we call 'good' are simply those things that give us pleasure, and that the actions we call 'morally good' or 'just' are simply those actions that correspond to whatever laws politicians happen to have promulgated. As a matter of pure speculation these claims may be comprehensible, but a more careful survey of our moral evaluations shows them to be false.

Hutcheson notes in the *Inquiry*, for example (1) that although both a generous action and a productive field give us pleasure, there is a significant difference in the pleasures derived from these two things. Our approbation of them differs in such a way that we would think it quite odd or senseless to say that the field is virtuous, but entirely sensible to say that the action is virtuous (1725a: 114–5, 119, 140–41); (2) that while reading history we learn of temporally distant individuals who cannot contribute to our interests or pleasure, and that, as the actions of these individuals vary, so do our responses: we feel approbation toward some, and disapprobation or indifference toward others; (3) that while we benefit from the actions of an individual who treasonously betrays his country to ours, we none the less morally disapprove of that individual and his actions; (4) that while we ourselves may be bribed to perform an action which we think to be morally wrong, we cannot be bribed to *feel* that this same action is right or that we are right to undertake it; (5) that we sometimes feel a moral indignation toward a person who has caused us no injury at all, while on other occasions we find that, although someone has acted in such a way as to injure us, we feel no moral indignation.

Facts of this sort, Hutcheson concludes, establish beyond doubt that the selfish theory is mistaken. They show that there are natural (immediate and unlearned) differences in our responses to actions or events, differences that cannot be accounted for by this theory. Our moral approvals and disapprovals are more subtle than these philosophers have thought. We find that we naturally and routinely make reliable distinctions (1) between *natural good* and *moral good*; (2) between *moral good* and *moral evil*; and (3) between things that are *immediately good* and those only 'advantageous' or *instrumentally good*. Given these important facts, the question becomes, as Hutcheson typically frames it: 'What feature of human nature is presupposed by the fact that we can and do make these distinctions?' His answer: 'The moral sense'. Had we, he writes in the *Inquiry*, no moral sense enabling us to perceive the moral qualities of agents and actions, we could not respond to them as we do. Without a moral sense we might have developed an abstract idea of virtue, but we would not, as we do, actively approve and esteem those who reveal themselves to be virtuous. Had we 'no Sense of moral Good in Humanity... Self-Love, and our Sense of natural Good' would cause us, contrary to fact, always to approve, for example, of the traitor who benefits our cause, and always to disapprove the courageous patriot who harms our cause. But that is not the case; the facts do not fit the egoists' theory. Rather, such facts reveal that 'there is in human Nature a disinterested ultimate Desire of the Happiness of others', an inherent benevolent, and hence moral, concern.

Humans have also an inherent cognitive power that enables them to respond differently to benevolence and self-interest. The human mind is formed in such a way that it can approve or condemn actions or agents without concern for its own pleasure or interest. Just as the Creator has 'determin'd us to receive, by our external Senses, pleasant or disagreeable Ideas of Objects, according as they are useful or hurtful to our Bodies ... [so] he has given us a moral Sense, to direct our Actions, and to give us still nobler Pleasures'. Thus if two individuals contribute in similar ways to our wellbeing, but the one acts 'from an ultimate Desire of our Happiness, or Good-will toward us; and the other from Views of Self-Interest, or by Constraint', we have, we find, significantly different responses to these two individuals and their acts. In response to the one we feel gratitude and approbation; to the other we are indifferent. Or, if we know that an individual has benevolent dispositions but has been prevented from exercising them, we count that individual as morally good even though they have not been able to act – even though they have done nothing to benefit us. The nature and complexity of these responses show that we must have a perceptual power, a moral sense, for without such a sense we would assess fields and agents or patriots and traitors only with regard to our own interests and wellbeing.

In the third edition (1729) of the *Inquiry* Hutcheson explicitly denied that he meant to identify virtue and vice with feelings or sentiment. The moral sense relies upon feelings to distinguish virtue or vice, but moral qualities are themselves independent of the observer who feels approbation or disapprobation of them. The 'admired Quality', he says, is a quality of the agent judged, and entirely distinct from the approbation or pleasure of either the approving observer or the agent, and the moral perceptions (the idea or concept) involved 'plainly represents something quite distinct from this Pleasure'. Feelings play a cognitive and a motivating role, but virtue is constituted by the benevolent disposition that gives rise to approbation, and vice by the malevolent or sometimes indifferent dispositions that give rise to disapprobation.

Gilbert Burnet and John Balguy, two early

rationalist critics, pronounced themselves satisfied with Hutcheson's good intentions and even with his fundamental conclusion, namely that virtue and vice are, contrary to Hobbes, Locke, and Mandeville, fundamentally real. Burnet, in his Letter to the *London Journal* (1969–71, vol. 7: 6) could not agree, however, that Hutcheson had found 'the true and solid foundation' of morality, while Balguy (1728–9), all praise for Hutcheson's good nature and good sense, regrets that he makes serious mistakes – mistakes that 'lie at the Foundations of Morality, and like Failures in Ground-work, affect the whole Building'.

Burnet's fundamental complaint is that Hutcheson's account of moral good and evil explains these notions only relatively – only as good or evil things relate to us or affect us – and gives us no guarantee that good and evil have an immutable foundation in the nature of things. Balguy objected that Hutcheson had rested virtue or morality on two features of human nature, a natural affection (a concern for others) and an instinct (the moral sense). These are, he granted, features of humankind, and it is right of Hutcheson to try to represent virtue as something that flows 'unalterably from the Nature of Men and Things'. But, he went on, Hutcheson portrays morality as something arbitrary, dependent upon human features 'that might originally have been otherwise, or even contrary to what they now are; and [that] may at any time be alter'd, or inverted, if the Creator pleases' (1728: 292). Moreover, in Hutcheson's hands morality is resolved into 'mere *Instinct*'. If we are motivated to what we call virtuous acts by an instinct, of what moral merit are the resulting actions? These actions seem to be necessitated, while virtuous acts are always free acts. If Hutcheson should reply that these instincts do not '*force* the Mind, but only *incline* it', then, says Balguy, it will be reason, and not the moral sense, that decides our actions and thus serves as the foundation of morality.

Hutcheson undertook to meet these objections in a series of letters to the *London Journal* (1725b) and in the second part of his *Essay* of 1728. As an ordained clergyman of the Westminster Confession, Hutcheson was unwilling to deny the creative freedom of the Deity. Consequently, he could not in one sense deny that his theory of the moral sense made morality dependent upon the free choice of the Deity. But he could and did argue that, were the Deity's basic nature not in its own way similar to our kindest affections and best moral nature, then he would not have been motivated to create us in the particular manner in which he did actually create us. On the other hand, if we suppose that the Deity does have an analogously kind and moral nature, then we see at once that this would have motivated him to create us as he did. As long as we are satisfied that the Deity is unchanging, and that his is the best nature possible, we can see that our own natures are nothing like the merely arbitrary result of some divine whim. Our natures are, in any relevant sense, necessary and necessarily fixed or unchanging.

To the charge that he had made morality dependent on an instinct that effectively eliminates the free choice required of moral behaviour, Hutcheson replied by distinguishing between instincts of body and certain mental powers or 'affections'. The latter, he insists, are no more destructive of morality than is the '*Determination to pursue Fitness*' that, according to his opponents, characterizes the divine will. Virtue, Hutcheson argues, can be real and meritorious even though perceived by a sense, and chosen because of an affection or instinct. It is not necessary that reason play these roles. Hutcheson's critics were not satisfied by these replies (Richard Price (1758) was to pose similar objections some thirty years later; see PRICE, R.), but Hutcheson's responses show how far he was from being the moral noncognitivist some commentators have supposed. He undertook to determine the origin of our moral ideas in order 'to prove what we call the *Reality of Virtue*' (1725a: xi). That his inquiry led him to argue that our moral concerns and evaluations depend on certain fundamental dispositions and feelings – that morality has its origin in certain senses and affections found in human nature – should not prevent us from recognizing this realist intent.

3 Practical ethics and influence

Although Hutcheson's later works, his *System* and his *Short Introduction*, reveal his continuing commitment to the moral sense theory and all that presupposes, these works more noticeably reflect his need, after 1729, to offer lectures on a broad range of moral issues – issues of practice as well as principle – to largely adolescent audiences. Making extensive use of writers in the modern natural law tradition (Grotius, Pufendorf, and Richard Cumberland, for example), as well as of Cicero, Hutcheson in these works focuses principally on such practical issues as our duties to God, to humanity, and to ourselves; the law of nature and the rights of individuals; property and contracts; marriage and parenting; and civil government.

Hutcheson's contemporaries and students remembered him as earnestly concerned with civil and religious liberty. He was, for example, an outspoken critic of the Aristotelian or classical theory of slavery, and also of the justification of slavery by conquest.

Arguing that there are no natural slaves nor ought there to be slaves by conquest, Hutcheson insists that the *'natural equality of men'* consists chiefly in the fact that 'natural rights belong equally to all', and that the laws of God and nature prohibit even the most powerful from depriving the least powerful of their rights, or from inflicting any harm on them. The least talented humans have the use of reason and thus have vastly greater capacity for happiness or misery than do animals. All humans 'have strong desires of liberty and property, have notions of right, and strong natural impulses to marriage, families, and offspring, and earnest desires of their safety.... We must therefore conclude, that no endowments, natural or acquired, can give a perfect right to assume powers over others, without their consent'. This, he adds, 'is intended against the doctrine of Aristotle, and some others of the ancients, "that some men are naturally slaves"' (1755, I: 299–301). Equally abhorrent is the view that those taken prisoner in a just war may be justly enslaved as punishment or security against further offence. No 'damage done or crime committed can change a rational creature into a piece of goods void of all right, and incapable of acquiring any [rights]' (1755, II: 202–3). Those who claim that Africans were better off as slaves than they would have been if left in Africa have let custom and the prospect of profit stupefy their consciences until they have lost all sense of natural justice (1755, II: 84–5).

At the heart of Hutcheson's political theory is his endorsement of the principle that the safety of the people is the supreme law. He insists that there are specifiable limits to the powers of the state, and that citizens retain the right to resist the excesses of any form of government and even the right to overthrow and replace a government. Consequently, any government that fails to function for the 'safety and happiness of the whole body' can be legitimately abolished (1742b: 303). Hutcheson explicitly applied these principles to colonies. Colonial subjects also have a right to legitimate – that is, beneficial – government. If they fail to receive such government, and are oppressed, they may justly overthrow their oppressor: 'the people's right of resistance is unquestionable' (1742b: 292).

Hutcheson's writings had a substantial influence in the eighteenth century. His claim that ill-governed colonies have the right to rebel was widely and effectively repeated in colonial north America, and may rightly be taken as having provided many patriots with a philosophical rationale for rebellion. His published views on natural equality and natural rights were reprinted in colonial Philadelphia, where they added philosophical weight to the anti-slavery movement. His moral sense ethics, although much criticized by rationalists, gained partial allegiance from David Hume. His best-known student, Adam Smith, learned from him both moral and economic theory, and credits Hutcheson as 'being the first who distinguished with any degree of precision in what respect all moral distinctions... are founded upon immediate sense and feeling' (Smith 1759: 321). Even Immanuel KANT, a moralist so apparently different, was initially attracted by, and always respectful of, Hutcheson's contributions to moral theory. And if Jeremy BENTHAM thought the theory of the moral sense was simply totally unconvincing, he none the less adopted as fundamental to his utilitarian theory a principle that Hutcheson had enunciated, namely 'that Action is best, which procures the greatest Happiness for the greatest Numbers' (1725a: 181).

See also: BEAUTY; EGOISM AND ALTRUISM; ENLIGHTENMENT, SCOTTISH; HUME, D.; MORAL SENSE THEORIES; SHAFTESBURY; SLAVERY; VIRTUES AND VICES

List of works

Hutcheson, F. (1969–71) *Collected Works*, ed. B. Fabian, Hildesheim: Olms, 7 vols. (A facsimile edition of the works listed below, with the exception of the items found in (1724).)

—— (1724) 'Reflections on the Common Systems of Morality', *The London Journal*; repr. in *Francis Hutcheson: Two Texts on Human Nature*, ed. T. Mautner, Cambridge: Cambridge University Press, 1993. (The two texts are Hutcheson's brief account of the systems of morality (1724), and a translation of his inaugural lecture on the social nature of man (1730).)

—— (1725a) *An Inquiry into the Original of our Ideas of Beauty and Virtue; In Two Treatises*, London and Dublin; revised 1726, 1729, 1738. (The two treatises are: I, *An Inquiry concerning Beauty, Order &c.* and II, *An Inquiry concerning Moral Good and Evil*. These constitute Hutcheson's initial attempt to show that we are equipped with aesthetic and moral senses that enable us to recognize beauty and virtue.)

—— (1725b) Letters to *The London Journal*. (Hutcheson's letters of June and October were in response to critical letters by Gilbert Burnet the Younger, who objected to Hutcheson's attempt to found morality in human nature. The complete exchange is reprinted in *Collected Works*, 1969–71, vol. 7.)

—— (1725) 'Reflections upon Laughter', *The Dublin Weekly Journal*. repr. in *Collected Works*, 1969–71, vol. 7. (Three letters criticizing Hobbes' account of laughter and of human nature.)

—— (1725d) 'Remarks upon the Fable of the Bees', *The Dublin Weekly Journal*; repr. in *Collected Works*, 1969–71, vol. 7. (Three letters criticizing Mandeville's egoistic account of morality.)

—— (1728) *An essay on the Nature and Conduct of the Passions and Affections: With Illustrations on the Moral Sense*, London and Dublin, revised, 1728, 1730, 1742. (Hutcheson's account of the passions and a further explication and defence of the moral sense theory.)

—— (1730) *De naturali hominum Socialitate Oratio Inauguralis* (Inaugural Lecture on the Social Nature of Man), Glasgow; repr. in *Francis Hutcheson: Two Texts on Human Nature*, ed. T. Mautner, Cambridge: Cambridge University Press, 1993. (1993 is a recent translation, with helpful notes.)

—— (1742a) *Metaphysicae synopsis: ontologiam et pneumatologiam complectens* (Synopsis of Metaphysics: Comprising ontology and pneumatology), Glasgow; repr. in *Collected Works*, vol. 7, 1969–71. (Apparently lecture notes from Hutcheson course on metaphysics, published without his consent; revised by Hutcheson 1744–5.)

—— (1742b) *Philosophiae moralis institutio compendiaria*, Glasgow; trans. *A Short Introduction to Moral Philosophy*, Glasgow, 1747. (A comprehensive survey, based on Hutcheson's lectures, of the elements of ethics and the law of nature. The translation is thought most likely to be by Hutcheson or his colleague and friend James Moor.)

—— (1755) *A System of Moral Philosophy*, Glasgow. (Written by 1738, but published posthumously by Hutcheson's son, Francis the Younger. A comprehensive account of morality in three books. Includes discussions of human nature, the supreme good, and of our natural and civil duties.)

References and further reading

* Balguy, J. (1728–9) *The Foundation of Moral Goodness: or a Further Inquiry into the Original of our Idea of Virtue*, London, 1728; Part II 1729; facsimile repr. Part I and Part II, New York: Garland Press, 1976. (Includes Balguy's objections to Hutcheson's moral theory as well as his alternative rationalist account of the foundations of morality.)

Frankena, W. (1955) 'Hutcheson's Moral Sense Theory', *Journal of the History of Ideas* 16: 356–75. (Argues that Hutcheson is an emotivist.)

Haakonssen, K. (1990) 'Natural Law and Moral Realism: The Scottish Synthesis', in *Oxford Studies in the History of Philosophy I* (*Studies in the Philosophy of the Scottish Enlightenment*), 61–85.

(Important effort to assess the character of Hutcheson's moral realism.)

Henrick, D. (1957) 'Hutcheson und Kant', *Kant-Studien* 49: 49–69. (An account of Kant's interest in, and disagreements with, Hutcheson.)

Hope, V. (1989) *Virtue by Consensus: The Moral Philosophy of Hutcheson, Hume, and Smith*, Oxford: Clarendon Press. (An essentially comparative study of Hutcheson, Hume and Adam Smith.)

* Hume, D. (1739–40) *A Treatise of Human Nature*, London. (Book III, a classic work of moral theory, was revised in response to Hutcheson's criticisms.)

Jensen, H. (1971) *Motivation and the Moral Sense in Francis Hutcheson's Moral Theory*, The Hague: Martinus Nijhoff. (Aims to show the problems arising from Hutcheson's accounts of motivation and the moral sense.)

Kivy, P. (1976) *The Seventh Sense: A Study of Francis Hutcheson's Aesthetics and its Influence in 18th-century Britain*, New York: Franklin. (A comprehensive study of Hutcheson's aesthetic theory.)

Leidhold, W. (1985) *Ethik und Politik bei Francis Hutcheson* (Ethics and Politics in Frances Hutcheson), Munich: Alber. (A comprehensive study of Hutcheson's moral philosophy.)

* Mandeville, B. (1714–23) *The Fable of the Bees: or, Private Vices Publick Benefits*, London. (Includes several works supportive of Mandeville's cynical, egoistic account of the origins of morality.)

Moore, J. (1990) 'The Two Systems of Francis Hutcheson: On the Origins of the Scottish Enlightenment', in *Oxford Studies in the History of Philosophy I* (*Studies in the Philosophy of the Scottish Enlightenment*), 37–59. (Argues for a distinct change of view between Hutcheson's earlier and later writings.)

—— (1994) 'Hume and Hutcheson', in M.A. Stewart and J.W. Wright (eds) *Hume and Hume's Connexions*, Edinburgh: Edinburgh University Press. (A somewhat speculative account of the relationship between Hutcheson and Hume.)

Norton, D.F. (1974) 'Hutcheson's Moral Sense Theory Reconsidered', *Dialogue* 12: 3–23. (A rebuttal of Frankena's emotivist interpretation of Hutcheson.)

—— (1976) 'Francis Hutcheson in America', *Studies in Voltaire and the Eighteenth Century* 151 (5): 1547–68. (A discussion of Hutcheson's influence in colonial north America.)

—— (1982) *David Hume: Common-Sense Moralist, Sceptical Metaphysician*, Princeton, NJ: Princeton University Press, 1982. (Chapter 2 discusses Hutcheson; Chapter 3 includes a comparison of important aspects of the moral theories of Hutcheson and Hume.)

—— (1985) 'Hutcheson's Moral Realism', *Journal of the History of Philosophy* 23: 397–418. (Argues against Winkler (1984) that Hutcheson is plausibly interpreted as one kind of moral realist.)

* Price, R. (1758) *A Review of the Principal Questions in Morals*, London. (Includes criticisms of Hutcheson's account of the foundations of morality.)

Raphael, D.D. (1947) *The Moral Sense*, Oxford: Oxford University Press. (Includes a chapter on Hutcheson's moral theory.)

Robbins, C. (1954) 'When it is that Colonies May Turn Independent: An Analysis of the Environment and Politics of Francis Hutcheson', *William and Mary Quarterly*, 3rd series, 11: 214–51. (On Hutcheson's political philosophy and its influence in colonial America.)

Scott, F.R. (1900) *Francis Hutcheson: His Life, Teaching and Position in the History of Philosophy*, Cambridge: Cambridge University Press. (Outdated, but the only substantial biography of Hutcheson available.)

* Smith, A. (1759) *The Theory of Moral Sentiments*, London. (A much-modified account of the moral sense, by Hutcheson's most famous student.)

Smyth, D. (ed.) (1992) *Francis Hutcheson, Fortnight* 308, supplement, Belfast. (Includes brief articles by D.D. Raphael, J. Moore, D.F. Norton, and seven others, on Hutcheson's life, philosophy and influence.)

Winkler, K. (1984) 'Hutcheson's Alleged Realism', *Journal of the History of Philosophy* 23: 179–94. (Criticism of Norton's realist interpretation of Hutcheson.)

DAVID FATE NORTON

HUXLEY, THOMAS HENRY (1825–95)

Huxley, an English zoologist with strong philosophical interests, originally influenced by K.E. von Baer's embryological typology, became an authority first in invertebrate zoology and then in vertebrate palaeontology. After the publication of Darwin's On the Origin of Species, *he proclaimed his acceptance of the theory of evolution, but disagreed on important points and applied common descent – but not natural selection – in his scientific works only after reading Ernst Haeckel's* Generelle Morphologie *(1866). He published extensively in anthropology, ethnology, philosophy, religion, politics and ethics, and was a great popularizer of science.*

Thomas Henry Huxley, a leading exponent of nineteenth-century evolutionism, was born in Ealing, near London. After studying medicine he sailed, in 1846, as assistant surgeon on board HMS *Rattlesnake* in the southern hemisphere. His brilliant voyage observations would further his scientific career, but he secured a stable job only in 1854 at the School of Mines in London. His fame and authority grew with time and by 1883 he was President of the Royal Society, but had to resign in 1886 because of a breakdown.

The traditional view of Huxley as a staunch Darwinist was challenged by scholars in the 1970s, and now he is generally seen as an evolutionist but not of the Darwinian kind. An admirer of German culture and conversant with the language, he interpreted morphology in the light of Baer's embryological typology – animal forms classified according to four separate structural plans determined through embryological development.

Desirous to combat both the Platonic interpretation of animal type and the influence in scientific circles of Richard Owen, the leading British morphologist of the time, Huxley and he were often at odds. Before the publication of Darwin's *On the Origin of Species* (1859) Huxley opposed evolutionary views, both Lamarck's and those of Robert Chambers, the 'anonymous' author of the popular *Vestiges of the Natural History of Creation*.

When the *Origin* appeared, Huxley wrote two predominantly positive reviews of it, after which he often assumed in public the role of official spokesman ('bulldog', he called it) of Darwin's group. He saw two reasons for supporting Darwin's views: (a) it identified a vera causa of the production of species; (b) it was a valid hypothesis of the order of nature based on natural processes. But it was a hypothesis and not yet the theory of species, since there was no decisive experimental proof that natural selection had produced, from one species, another infertile with it. Huxley conceived the value of a theory as 'absolute'; a theory can be isolated and individually assessed in a context of truth and falsity provided by experimentally ascertained facts. For Darwin, on the other hand, if the consequences of a hypothesis are in accordance with a number of facts to be explained, the hypothesis gains explanatory power which justifies its retention. Huxley constantly played down natural selection, and never accepted Darwin's gradualism, but supported a saltatory view of evolution, probably a remnant of his originally discontinuous view of type organization. After his famous Oxford clash with Bishop Wilberforce on human descent in 1860, Huxley became popularly known as a champion of Darwinism, but his scientific production does not show any deployment of evolutionary reasoning until

1868. Even his 1863 *Man's Place in Nature*, though showing anthropomorphic apes morphologically closer to humans than to lower primates, and thus providing evidence for Darwin's views, made little reference to evolution, being mainly an attack on Owen's systematics. Only after reading Haeckel's *Generelle Morphologie* (1866), which presented a reinterpretation of embryological typology in evolutionary terms and emphasized descent rather than natural selection, did Huxley introduce evolutionism into his science (see HAECKEL, E.H.). Thus Huxley related evolution to the scientific tradition to which he belonged.

In ethnology, Huxley denied a role for philology in human taxonomy, and fought the polygenic view of human origins. Huxley popularized science and devoted much time to teaching. He followed with interest philosophical debates, and wrote on Descartes with appreciation for his view of knowledge and of animals as automata. He respected Mill, but loathed the positivist movement, both French and British. Possibly it was through his acquaintance with Darwin's views that he approached Hume's philosophy, on which he wrote (1878). He applauded Hume's view of the connection between common sense and scientific discourse, and of the untenability of the evidence for miracles (see HUME, D. §2), a subject on which Huxley argued with Gladstone. The term 'agnostic' was coined by Huxley to denote the scientific refusal to make statements in fields which, like theology, were outside the scope of his research. His latter publications concerned the debate on evolution and ethics, in which he opposed Spencer's naturalistic ethics (see SPENCER, H.), arguing for a complete separation of knowledge from values, opposing *laissez-faire* policy in favour of state intervention, but critical at the same time of socialism. He was concerned at the extreme individualism of his time and believed that only through science was the progress of humankind possible; that human suffering could not be explained or justified scientifically. Huxley thought that in the course of evolution, higher degrees of consciousness had arisen with humankind, and with them, a higher awareness of suffering.

See also: DARWIN, C.R.; EVOLUTION AND ETHICS; EVOLUTION, THEORY OF; PHILOSOPHY OF SCIENCE IN THE 19TH CENTURY

List of works

Huxley, T.H. (1893–4) *Collected Essays*, London: Macmillan, 9 vols. (Huxley edited these volumes that contained most of his works. Specifically from the text: (1859) *The Darwinian Hypothesis*, in volume 2, 1–21; (1860) *The Origin of Species*, in volume 2, 22–79; (1863) *Evidence as to Man's Place in Nature*, in volume 7, 1– 208. This collection of papers, sprang from Huxley's controversy with Owen. (1863) *On Our Knowledge of the Causes of the Phenomena of Organic Nature*, in volume 2, 303–475; (1874) *On the Hypothesis that Animals are Automata, and its History*, in volume 1, 199–250; (1878) *Hume*, in volume 6, 3-240; (1889) *Agnosticism*, in volume 5, 209–62.)

—— (1898–1903) *The Scientific Memoirs of Thomas Henry Huxley*, eds G. Foster and E.R. Lankester, London, 4 vols and supppplement. (Contains original writings; *On the Anatomy and Affinities of the Medusae*, in volume 1, 9–32; (1853) *On the Morphology of the Cephalous Mollusca, as illustrated by the Anatomy of Certain Heteropoda and Pteropoda collected during the Voyage of HMS Rattlesnake in 1846–50*, in volume 1, 152–93; (1857–9) *On the Theory of the Vertebrate Skull*, in volume 1: 538–606.)

References and further reading

Bartholomew, M. (1975) 'Huxley's Defence of Darwin', *Annals of Science* 32: 525–35. (Huxley did not apply Darwin's theory to his scientific works.)

* Chambers, R. (1844) *Vestiges of the Natural History of Creation*, London: Churchill. (Published anonymously, a popular book which propounded a progressive view of evolution.)

Collie, M. (1991) *Huxley at Work*, London: Macmillan. (Huxley's methods and results.)

* Darwin, C. (1859) *On the Origin of Species*, London: Murray. (Darwin's celebrated book on the origin of species by natural selection.)

Desmond, A. (1994, 1996) *Huxley, The Devil's Disciple*, London: Michael Joseph, 2 vols. (A biography of Huxley in his social and political context.)

Di Gregorio, M.A. (1984) *T.H. Huxley's Place in Natural Science*, New Haven, CT, and London: Yale University Press. (The contents and significance of Huxley's science.)

* Haeckel, E. (1866) *Generelle Morphologie der Organismen* (The General Morphology of Organisms), Berlin: Reimer, 2 vols. (On evolutionary morphology.)

Huxley, L. (1900) *The Life and Letters of Thomas Henry Huxley*, London and New York: Macmillan, 2 vols. (Huxley's biography based on his correspondence arranged by his son.)

Jensen, J.V. (1991) *Thomas Henry Huxley: Commu-*

nications for Science, Newark, NJ: University of Delaware Press. (The cultural aspects of Huxley's work.)

Paradis, J.G. (1978) *T.H. Huxley: 'Man's Place in Nature'*, Lincoln, NE, and London: University of Nebraska Press. (Huxley in his Victorian milieu).

MARIO A. DI GREGORIO

HYPATIA (*c.* AD 370–415)

The Greek philosopher Hypatia was a Neoplatonist. She was famous for her public talks on philosophy and astronomy, and her forthright attitude to sex. Although concerned with higher knowledge, she was also a political animal and had a keen sense of practical virtue. She was killed by a Christian mob, and has remained since a martyr to the cause of philosophy.

Hypatia was born in Alexandria around AD 370. However, according to one source she was 'aged' (*palaia*) in AD 415, which has led some to propose she was born around AD 355 (Dzielska 1995: 68). She was educated by her father Theon, who wrote important treatises on mathematical astronomy. But in what field did she flourish? This presents the first of several fascinating problems of interpretation. The works ascribed to her (none survives) are exclusively mathematical commentaries: *On Diophantus* (a third-century Alexandrian mathematician and the first to use algebra), *On the Conic Sections of Apollonius* and *On the Astronomical Canon* (of Ptolemy). Furthermore, when Damascius (a sixth-century Alexandrian Neoplatonist, who became head of the Athenian school) compared her to his teacher, he deemed her to be 'much different from him, not only as woman is to man, but also as a geometer is to a real philosopher' (Damascius, *Life of Isidore*, fr. 164.1–2). On the other hand, 'she was more courageous than her father and was not content with her mathematical education but boldly reached up to the other philosophy' (*Suda*, U166.13–5). (For this passage from astronomy to knowledge of the Forms, see Plato, *Republic* 529a9.) 'She outdid the philosophers of her time.... Those interested in philosophy run to her from everywhere' (Socrates, *Ecclesiastical History* 7.15), and for Hypatia's eminent student, Synesius (first pagan, then Christian bishop of Cyrene and statesman), she surpassed the Athenian 'sophists' (Synesius, *Letters* 136.17–21). So, her intellectual home may have been the mathematical quadrivium – traditionally part of Platonism – but she dared to do exceptionally well in metaphysics.

What was her philosophy? According to one statement, 'she succeeded to the Platonic school that descended from Plotinus' (Socrates, *Ecclesiastical History* 7.15.5). According to another, 'she explained Aristotle or Plato or some other philosopher' (*Suda* U166.17–9). Furthermore, 'the woman wore a rough mantle (*tribōn*) and made public appearances at the centre of the city' (U166.16). However, the last two tell nothing special. The rough mantle, although originally of the Cynics, was often the habit of the plain-living philosopher (for example, the Stoics). Interpretation of Aristotle, Plato or others was carried out by most philosophers, including the Neoplatonists and Ammonius Saccas, the Alexandrian teacher of Plotinus. So, Hypatia must have followed Neoplatonism, probably as a result of Porphyry's dissemination (see NEOPLATONISM). Her students included both pagans and Christians.

What was her stand on gender issues? Men extolled her 'exceptional' beauty, her flair for public speaking and her capacity to do things unexpected of a woman in that society. Male followers were enamoured of her intellectually and emotionally. How did she cope? On one celebrated occasion, to temper a love-sick student she removed her bloody sanitary towel, threw it at him and told him 'this is what you really want, young man, and it is no good' (Damascius, *Life of Isidore* 102). This agrees with other descriptions of her as 'solemn' and 'virgin/unmarried to the end'. But, these were the very attitudes cultivated equally by select male philosophers (see, for example, PROCLUS §1). Hypatia upheld the Platonic, or generally philosophical, freedom from bodily concerns, to rise above sex altogether.

These elements, and others, are brought into sharp focus when the possible reasons for her gruesome murder are considered. Some jealousy was to blame, fuelled by her political prominence when secular civic authority was being challenged by the ambitious bishop Cyril. Was the acrimony purely local? Was it intellectual or religious (shared belief in astrology and paganism)? Was it personal (the result of Hypatia's friendship with the city's Governor)? Whatever the complex truth, Hypatia soon came to be seen as martyr in the hands of the Christian mob. In modern times, criticism of the Victorian novel *Hypatia* by C. Kingsley (London, 1853) has brought to the fore the gender aspects, and, more recently, 'Hypatia' has become the name of two philosophy journals on feminism.

References and further reading

* Damascius (*c.* AD 462–540) *Life of Isidorus*, ed. C. Zintzen, *Damascii vitae Isidori reliquiae*, Hilde-

sheim: Olms, 1976. (Greek text; a source for many late Neoplatonists.)

* Dzielska, M. (1995) *Hypatia the Alexandrian*, Cambridge, MA: Harvard University Press. (Extensive account of Hypatia's life, historical and ideological context.)

* Kingsley, C. (1853) *Hypatia: or: New Foes with an Old Face*, London: Parker. (A morality novel by the chaplain to Queen Victoria.)

* Socrates (5th century AD) *Socrates' Ecclesiastical History*, ed. W. Bright, Oxford: Clarendon Press, 2nd edn, 1893. (The church historian Socrates is the main source for Hypatia's life.)

* *Suda* (10th century AD) *Suidae Lexicon*, ed. E. Adler, Leipzig: Teubner, 1931; repr. Stuttgart, 1967. (Greek text of the dictionary; often the only place where ancient fragments survive; for Hypatia.)

* Synesius (4th century AD) *Letters of Synesius of Cyrene*, trans. A. Fitzgerald, Oxford: Clarendon Press, 1926. (For Hypatia, see letter 54.)

Wider, K. (1986) 'Women Philosophers in the Ancient Greek World: Donning the Mantle', *Hypatia* 1: 21–62. (Women philosophers and gender bias in the reports about them.)

LUCAS SIORVANES

HYPPOLITE, JEAN
see HEGELIANISM

I

IAMBLICHUS (*c.* AD 242–327)

The late ancient philosopher Iamblichus was, alongside Plotinus and Porphyry, a founder of Neoplatonism. He established a new curriculum for the teaching of philosophy and formulated many distinctions that pervaded later Neoplatonic metaphysics. He began to mathematize all fields of philosophical concern. Most of all, he asserted that acts of transcendence, not contemplation, secure union with the divine, because it can only be reached by an equally divine faculty, which is present in every individual. Matter, soul and mind contain images of the divine and so are genuine participants in salvation.

Details of Iamblichus' life are scant. He was born at Chalcis, a descendant from an ancient line of priest-kings of Syria. In the AD 270s he studied at Caesarea (where many Christian theologians flourished). Perhaps he was still there when he heard of PORPHYRY, and may have visited him in Italy. They split in the AD 290s over theurgy, and Iamblichus' chief surviving work, *On the Mysteries*, is a record of their disagreement. He went to teach philosophy at Apamea (Syria), where the Neo-Pythagorean Numenius, and more recently Plotinus' chief follower Amelius, had flourished. The school he set up became very popular. From Pergamum his envoys converted the emperor Julian from Christianity, influencing the Athenian school of philosophy, and through it the Alexandrian school.

Iamblichus took further the programme of 'harmonization' of Greek philosophies that had been started by Porphyry: Aristotle agreed with Plato even on the Theory of Forms and on learning as recollection. He designed a curriculum for the teaching of Plato which had Aristotle as a prerequisite (see NEOPLATONISM §2). He also wrote grand commentaries on the two philosophers. However, he considered Pythagoras the supreme authority. Iamblichus saw number as the essence of Forms and things, and promised to make philosophy and

theurgy scientific. His many treatises on Pythagoreanism mark a revival of the movement. Eight or so titles of his large number of works survive, along with reports in Proclus, Damascius and Simplicius. Later Neoplatonists were wary of Iamblichus' claims about Aristotle and Plato, but maintained his curriculum, his metaphysical distinctions and his emphasis on mathematics.

Iamblichus introduced radical revisions to Plotinus' philosophy, multiplying the ranks of being (see PLOTINUS §§3–4). Plotinus saw the metaphysical levels as areas of the soul's activity, with flexible and sometimes conflicting properties. Iamblichus separated psychology from ontology, and looked for distinct properties and substances in the anatomy of things. He also distinguished the 'imparticipable' from the 'participated'. Every class of things has a first principle, which retains its pure definition by being exempt from its members.

The Neoplatonic One was inferred by stripping away all attributions, but was also the first cause of being. How could the same thing transcend its products, and also be in a causal relation to them? Iamblichus promptly introduced two Ones (later Neoplatonists reverted to a single One). At the level of intellect (see NOUS), he distinguished the acts of thought – the 'intellective' – from their objects – the 'intelligible'. At the level of soul (*psychē*), he separated the individual soul from the higher: in contrast to Plotinus, for Iamblichus the individual soul descends entire into the body (see PSYCHĒ). Similarly Iamblichus distinguished not only between time and timelessness, but also between a pure, eternal time and ordinary time, which is flowing.

To describe the essential nature of things, and the 'flow' or 'procession' from unity to diversity, Iamblichus turned to Neo-Pythagorean metaphysics of number. He believed that things are organized by number and relate to each other in mathematical proportion. The 'divine numbers' distribute the unity of the One to things and render them coherent. The 'intelligible numbers' stand as paradigms of the many species of reality. Intellect is organized by 'intellective numbers'. Soul exemplifies the 'mathematical numbers'. Last are the 'physical numbers', the forms immanent in matter.

Iamblichus' conclusion that the soul descends entire into matter had profound consequences.

Individual souls are dominated by physical necessities (which fits with Aristotle's definition of soul as the form of biological body). But soul is still essentially divine and rational. So the embodied soul presents an uncomfortable mystery. It contains an immortal, intelligent, divine nature, but is genuinely part of a mortal, concrete, imperfect domain. The personal soul has lost touch with its deeper nature and has become self-alienated.

Iamblichus' analysis was that the transcendent cannot be grasped with mental contemplation, because the transcendent is supra-rational. Theurgy, literally 'divine-working', is a series of rituals and operations aimed at recovering the transcendent essence by retracing the divine 'signatures' through the layers of being. Education is important for comprehending the scheme of things as presented by Aristotle, Plato and Pythagoras but also by the Chaldaean Oracles (see CHALDAEAN ORACLES). The theurgist works 'like with like': at the material level, with physical symbols and magic; at the higher level, with mental and purely spiritual practices. Starting with correspondences of the divine in matter, the theurgist eventually reaches the level where the soul's inner divinity unites with God.

See also: NEO-PYTHAGOREANISM

List of works

Iamblichus (late 3rd century AD) *On the Mysteries*, ed. E. des Places, *Jamblique. Les mystères d' Égypte*, Paris: Les Belles Lettres, 1989; trans. T. Taylor, *On the Mysteries*, London, 1821; repr. Hastings: Chthonios Books, 1989. (The former is parallel Greek text and French translation; the latter is English translation of old edition.)

—— (late 3rd century AD) *On the Pythagorean Life*, trans. E.G. Clark, Liverpool: Liverpool University Press, 1989. (English translation and annotation.)

—— (early 4th century AD) *Commentaries on Plato*, ed. J.M. Dillon, *Iamblichi Chalcidensis in Platonis dialogos commentariorum fragmenta*, Leiden: Brill, 1973. (Greek text with English translation of the fragments and extensive notes.)

—— (early 4th century AD) *Exhortation: Protrepticus*, ed. L. Pistelli, Leipzig: Teubner, 1888; repr. Stuttgart, 1975; trans. and ed. E. des Places, *Jamblique: Protreptique*, Paris: Les Belles Lettres, 1989; trans. T. Johnson, 1907; repr. in S. Neuville (ed.), *Iamblichus. Exhortation to Philosophy*, Grand Rapids, MI: Phanes Press, 1988. (The former is parallel Greek text and translation; Neuville is an English translation of Johnson.)

—— (early 4th century AD) *Common Mathematical*

Theory, ed. N. Festa, *Iamblichi de communi mathematica scientia*, Leipzig: Teubner, 1891; repr. Stuttgart, 1975. (Greek text.)

References and further reading

Blumenthal, H.J. and Clark, E.G. (eds) (1993) *The Divine Iamblichus*, London: Bristol Classical Press. (Collection of articles, including some on soul, political theory and theurgy.)

Finamore, J.F. (1985) *Iamblichus and the Theory of the Vehicle of the Soul*, Chico, CA: Scholars Press. (Covers aspects of Iamblichus' psychology, metaphysics and mysticism.)

Gersh, S. (1978) *From Iamblichus to Eriugena*, Leiden: Brill. (Detailed account of later Neoplatonic metaphysics and the transition to medieval theology, including pseudo-Dionysius; major themes are illustrated with diagrams.)

Larsen, B.D. (1972) *Jamblique de Chalcis*, Aarchus: Aarchus University. (Comprehensive study of Iamblichus' thought, and treatment of Plato and Aristotle, including the scale of virtues.)

O'Meara, D.J. (1982) *Pythagoras Revived: Mathematics and Philosophy in Late Antiquity*, Oxford: Clarendon Press. (Important study on the programme of mathematization and relation to metaphysics and epistemology.)

Plass, P.C. (1977) 'Timeless Time in Neoplatonism', *Modern Schoolman* 55: 1–19. (On Iamblichus' conception of time.)

Saffrey, H.D. (1990) *Recherches sur le néoplatonisme après Plotin* (Studies of Neoplatonism After Plotinus), Paris: Vrin. (Collected articles about Porphyry, Iamblichus and Proclus on theological themes, by a leading scholar in the field.)

Shaw, G. (1995) *Theurgy and the Soul*, University Park, PA: Pennsylvania State University Press. (A new account of the religious value of theurgy, and the relation of soul to matter.)

Steel, C. (1978) *The Changing Self: A Study on the Soul in Later Neoplatonism: Iamblichus, Damascius, Simplicius*. Brussels: Royal Academy. (Seminal study of Iamblichean psychology.)

LUCAS SIORVANES

IBN 'ADI, YAHYA (893–974)

Following in the footsteps of the Greek philosophers, Ibn 'Adi concerned himself with the ultimate human end, happiness, which he found in knowledge. However, he was primarily occupied with defending the compat-

ibility between the concept of God's unity and that of the trinity. He reasoned that a thing can be one in one respect and many in another. Therefore, there is no inconsistency in holding that God is both one and three. Ibn 'Adi can best be described as the Christian philosopher of unity, as he devoted most of his career and used all his logical skills to defend the concept of God's unity and its consistency with the concept of trinity.

Ash-Shaykh Abu Zakariyya' Yahya ibn 'Adi was a Jacobite Christian who lived in Iraq. Born in Takrit, he moved as a youth to Baghdad, one of the most important centres of learning in the tenth century. Of Syriac origin, he was Arabized like many other Syriacs at that time. He learned logic and philosophy with the well-known logicians, Abu Bishr Matta ibn Yunis and AL-FARABI, and after their deaths he became the leading logician of his time. He translated Greek philosophical works from Syriac into Arabic, wrote a number of logical, philosophical and theological treatises – the most important of which are *Tahdhib al-akhlaq* (Refinement of Character) and *Maqala fi at-tawhid* (Essay on Unity) – and established the Aristotelian school at Baghdad. His students, a mixture of Muslims and Christians, included IBN MISKAWAYH, Ibn al-Khammar, who wrote a treatise on the harmony between philosophy and dogma (which may have influenced Ibn Rushd in his treatment of the same subject), and Ibn Zur'a.

In *Tahdhib al-akhlaq*, Ibn 'Adi sets out his ethical philosophy along Greek lines (see ETHICS IN ISLAMIC PHILOSOPHY). It is based on his view of the human soul, which is divided into three parts or souls: the appetitive, the courageous and the rational. The first is the lowest and is shared by humans with other animals. The last is the noblest and the distinguishing mark of being human. To follow the first is to fall into ignorance and evil; to follow the last is to adhere to goodness and happiness. While all human beings have the natural capacity for reasoning, some have the skill to reason and some do not. Those who do not may acquire it by learning the rational sciences.

Ibn 'Adi's concern with God's unity, however, was his main preoccupation. He identifies the meaning of the word 'one' as it applies to God, and investigates whether God is one in all respects or one and many. Asserting that the one is that in which there is no otherness inasmuch as it is one, he classifies six things as one: the genus, the species, the relation, the continuous, the indivisible and the definition. He then offers arguments to show that God cannot be one except in the sense of definition (definition being a descriptive statement of the essence of a thing, in that it gives the essence as it is). Since every definition mirrors an essence, God must also be one in essence.

Most Greek and medieval philosophers considered God indefinable. A definition, they say, includes a genus and a difference, such as 'animality' and 'rationality' for 'humanity'. God, being simple, cannot be included in any genus because there is nothing above him. But if he has no genus, he cannot have any difference, for the difference is what differentiates a genus. Without a genus and a difference, God cannot be defined. While agreeing that a definition requires a genus and at least one difference, Ibn 'Adi believes that God is definable because he falls under the genus 'substance', for like every substance he does not reside in anything. This is interesting because it places something, the genus 'substance', above God and makes him the cause of the substance out of which he is made. This follows from Ibn 'Adi's view that the genus is caused by its members and that God is the cause of everything. The difficulty then arises that there was a time when God had no substance.

Ibn 'Adi asserts that God is one in one respect and multiple in another. As stated earlier, God is one in definition and in essence. However, a definition is a statement, and every statement has its parts. Such parts signify separate meanings. As such, these parts are separate definitions. Thus there is no contradiction between saying that God is one in definition and multiple in definition. The multiple definitions of God signify the three attributes, goodness, power and wisdom, referred to in Ibn 'Adi's later works as intellect, act of intellection and object of intellection, respectively. Goodness signifies the Father; power signifies the Holy Spirit; and wisdom signifies Christ. The same thing may be reflected in two mirrors differently, in one as a cause and in the other as an effect. Similarly, God and the Trinity are one in essence but different as individuals. Observation of God's creatures demonstrates these attributes.

The third century AH (ninth century AD) Muslim philosopher AL-KINDI wrote a treatise attempting to refute the Christian concept of the Trinity purely on the basis of logical reasoning. This treatise is, as far as we know, preserved only in the writings of Ibn 'Adi. Al-Kindi asserts that, according to Christianity, the three figures of the Trinity share substance or essence, but each is an individual by virtue of a specific property. The substance plus this property makes every one of them a composite. However, every composite is caused, and whatever is caused cannot be eternal. Ibn 'Adi responds that it is true that the three figures are composite individuals by virtue of their substance and properties, but their being composite does not make them caused, because it is possible for a thing to be composite eternally if the parts were not separate before the composition.

See also: ETHICS IN ISLAMIC PHILOSOPHY; GOD, CONCEPTS OF; LOGIC IN ISLAMIC PHILOSOPHY; TRINITY

List of works

Ibn ʿAdi (893–974) *Tahdhib al-akhlaq* (Refinement of Character), ed. N. at-Takriti, Beirut: ʿUweidat, 1978. (An Arabic edition of *Tahdhib al-akhlaq* and a critical study of this treatise, showing the significant impact it had on Christian and Islamic circles. Unfortunately, the English sections suffer from a number of typographical errors and inaccuracies, and must therefore be read with caution.)

—— (893–974) *Maqala fi at-tawhid* (Essay on Unity), ed. S. Khalil, Juni: Al-Maktaba al-Bulisiyya; Rome: al-Maʿhad al-Babawi ash-Sharqi, 1980. (The best and most comprehensive treatise of Ibn ʿAdi on the concept of God's unity.)

—— (893–974) *Maqalat Yahya Ibn ʿAdi al-falsafiyya* (Yahya ibn ʿAdi's Philosophical Essays), ed. S. Khulayfat, ʿAmman: Manshurat al-Jamiʿa al-Urduniyya, 1988. (Includes twenty-four of Ibn ʿAdi's essays carefully edited and annotated. The introduction examines Ibn ʿAdi's general thought and its influence on various students and later philosophers. This work is a fairly reliable source for Ibn ʿAdi's logical, philosophical and theological thought.)

References and further reading

Endress, G. (1977) *The Works of Yahya Ibn ʿAdi: An Analytical Inventory*, Wiesbaden: Reichert. (The best available classification of Ibn ʿAdi's works.)

Platti, E. (1983) *Yahya Ibn ʿAdi, théologien chrétien et philosophe arabe: sa théolgie de l'Incarnation* (Yahya Ibn ʿAdi, Christian Theologian and Arab Philosopher: His Theology of the Incarnation), Orientalia Lovanensia analecta vol. 14, Leuven: Departement Orientalistiek. (Deals with a major theme in Ibn ʿAdi's thought.)

SHAMS C. INATI

IBN AL-ʿARABI, MUHYI AL-DIN (1164–1240)

Ibn al-ʿArabi was a mystic who drew on the writings of Sufis, Islamic theologians and philosophers in order to elaborate a complex theosophical system akin to that of Plotinus. He was born in Murcia (in southeast Spain) in AH 560/AD 1164, and died in Damascus in AH 638/AD 1240. Of several hundred works attributed to him the most famous are al-Futuhat al-makkiyya (The Meccan Illuminations) and Fusus al-hikam (The Bezels of Wisdom). The Futuhat is an encyclopedic discussion of Islamic lore viewed from the perspective of the stages of the mystic path. It exists in two editions, both completed in Damascus – one in AH 629/AD 1231 and the other in AH 636/AD 1238 – but the work was conceived in Mecca many years earlier, in the course of a vision which Ibn al-ʿArabi experienced near the Kaaba, the cube-shaped House of God which Muslims visit on pilgrimage. Because of its length, this work has been relatively neglected. The Fusus, which is much shorter, comprises twenty-seven chapters named after prophets who epitomize different spiritual types. Ibn al-ʿArabi claimed that he received it directly from Muhammad, who appeared to him in Damascus in AH 627/AD 1229. It has been the subject of over forty commentaries.

Although Ibn al-ʿArabi was primarily a mystic who believed that he possessed superior divinely-bestowed knowledge, his work is of interest to the philosopher because of the way in which he used philosophical terminology in an attempt to explain his inner experience. He held that whereas the divine Essence is absolutely unknowable, the cosmos as a whole is the locus of manifestation of all God's attributes. Moreover, since these attributes require the creation for their expression, the One is continually driven to transform itself into Many. The goal of spiritual realization is therefore to penetrate beyond the exterior multiplicity of phenomena to a consciousness of what subsequent writers have termed the 'unity of existence'. This entails the abolition of the ego or 'passing away from self' (fana) in which one becomes aware of absolute unity, followed by 'perpetuation' (baqa) in which one sees the world as at once One and Many, and one is able to see God in the creature and the creature in God.

1 Epistemology

While still an unbearded youth, Ibn al-'Arabi was introduced by his father to the celebrated philosopher IBN RUSHD, who eagerly questioned him about his spiritual experiences. Ibn al-'Arabi describes the interview as follows:

He said, 'How did you find the situation in unveiling and divine effusion? Is it what rational consideration gives us?' I replied, 'Yes and no. Between the yes and the no spirits fly from their matter and heads from their bodies.'

(al-Futuhat al-makkiya I.154, in Chittick 1989: xiii)

This cryptic answer, which reputedly made the philosopher turn pale and tremble, implies the existence of divinely-bestowed knowledge which is superior to knowledge gained by 'rational consideration' (nazar). But what precisely is the relationship between them? Elsewhere, Ibn al-'Arabi speaks not of two levels of knowledge, but of three (for example, in al-Futuhat al-makiyya I.31). First, there is 'knowledge based on reason' ('ilm al-'aql), that is, knowledge which can be acquired by rational consideration. Here he probably has in mind the principal tenets of Muslim theology rather than the a priori self-evident propositions of logic and mathematics. Second, there is knowledge based on states ('ilm al-ahwal), which is what we would call empirical knowledge. He gives as examples the sweetness of honey, the bitterness of aloes and the pleasure of sexual intercourse, none of which can be known without 'tasting' them. Third, there is 'knowledge of mysteries' ('ulum al-asrar) – sometimes called 'gnosis' (ma'rifa) – which is specific to prophets and saints and is akin to Spinoza's scientia intuitiva (see SPINOZA, B. DE) It is futile to strive for this third type of knowledge, for it lies concealed in every man but is only unveiled when the divine light is effused into the hearts of those who are predisposed to receive it. 'Knowledge of mysteries' includes knowledge of the first type, except that it is acquired without reflection, and knowledge of the second type but pertaining to higher states not experienced by lesser mortals; potentially it embraces everything except the unknowable Essence. It is nothing short of divine knowledge for, in the words of the celebrated hadith qudsi (extra-Qur'anic revelation), when God loves his servant he becomes 'the hearing with which he hears, the sight with which he sees'.

The distinctly subordinate role given to reason in Ibn al-'Arabi's epistemology appears at first to be out of step with the Qur'an, which repeatedly urges man to engage in 'rational consideration' and 'reflection'

(see EPISTEMOLOGY IN ISLAMIC PHILOSOPHY). In his view however, there is no real tension because the main purpose of considering and reflecting is to lead man to the realization that he cannot reach knowledge of God through his unaided reason. This is illustrated in Chapter 167 of al-Futuhat al-makkiyya (The Meccan Illuminations), in which the progressive journey of the gnostic and the philosopher towards the truth is depicted in terms of a heavenly ascent akin to that experienced by Muhammad (the mi'raj). As they pass through each of the celestial spheres the gnostic is addressed by their spirits – the prophets who inhabit each sphere – and perceives their inner reality. The philosopher, on the other hand, learns only the phenomenal or apparent and becomes increasingly perplexed and sceptical until he finally becomes a Muslim and follows the path of the gnostic (see GNOSTICISM).

2 Theology

Although Ibn al-'Arabi has often been labelled a pantheist, he was far too subtle a thinker to have subscribed to the doctrine that God is everything and everything is God (see PANTHEISM). He believed that God per se – whom he called 'the Real' (al-Haqq) or 'the Essence' (al-dhat) – is absolutely unknowable because he transcends all humanly conceivable qualifications. God's 'names' (asma') or 'attributes' (sifat), on the other hand, are the relationships which can be discerned between the Essence and the cosmos. They are known to God because he knows every object of knowledge, but they are not existent entities or ontological qualities, for this would imply plurality in the godhead. It may help to understand the status of the 'names' (which of course must not be confused with 'the names of the names' known to us from the Qur'an and Islamic tradition) if we draw an analogy with the complex web of interpersonal human relationships. One and the same individual may be known to others variously as teacher, pupil, friend, enemy, father, son, brother, husband, lover and so forth. A man who knows another as his friend genuinely knows him, but does not necessarily know him as his teacher or his father and cannot know him as he is in himself without regard to others. Similarly, to know God as the All-Merciful, for instance, does not entail knowing him as the Vengeful or the Abaser, nor does it mean knowing his Essence even though each of the names denotes the Essence. The analogy must not be pressed, however, because unlike human beings, whose relationships are temporal, God has possessed the divine names from all eternity.

Thus far Ibn al-'Arabi's theology remains within the confines of Islamic kalam, although he seems in some ways to have more affinity with the Mu'tazila than with the Ash'ariyya (see ASH'ARIYYA AND MU'TAZILA; ISLAMIC THEOLOGY). However, he differs markedly from both in holding that, not withstanding the fact that in his Essence, God is independent of the cosmos, his names none the less seek the creation, for without it they would remain virtualities. The cosmos as a whole is the locus of their manifestation and it is only through it that their properties can be seen and understood. Moreover, since all the creatures in the cosmos and everything which they make or do are God's 'acts' (af'al), God is present everywhere and the all-inclusive name Allah may be used to denote the sum total of all things: divine Essence, divine names and divine acts. Nevertheless, since creatures have only relative existence (see §3), it also has to be said that he is nowhere to be found (see GOD, CONCEPTS OF).

3 Ontology

In agreement with the Islamic philosophers, Ibn al-'Arabi distinguishes between the essence or 'quiddity' (mahiyya, literally the 'what is it?') of a thing and its 'existence' (wujud, literally its 'being found'), holding that the former is mentally separable from the latter. That is, one can define the nature of things (unicorns, pink elephants and so forth) regardless of whether or not they are actually found as phenomena. He also accepts the distinction between necessary being (wajib al-wujud), impossible things and possible things. The necessary being is God, the one reality who cannot not exist because his quiddity is being (see BEING). Impossible things are things which cannot exist as phenomena although they may subsist in the imagination (see §5). Possible things are things which become 'existent entities' (a'yan mawjuda) when God chooses to give them existence; their existence or nonexistence at any given time depends on his will. They have, however, been known to him eternally as 'immutable entities' (a'yan thabita). This latter term is rendered by Affifi (1938: 47) as 'fixed prototypes' and Izutsu (1983: 159) as 'permanent archetypes', expressions which suggest that like the Platonic Ideas they are the original models of which objects in the phenomenal world are multiple copies (see UNIVERSALS). Chittick (1989: 84) objects to this on the grounds that although the 'immutable entities' actually become the 'existent entities', they are the things themselves prior to their being given existence in the world. Although I have adopted his translation as closer to the meaning of the Arabic, I have reservations about his interpretation, for there are passages in Ibn al-'Arabi's writings which seem to imply that some of the immutable entities are

universals. Nevertheless it may well be the case that Ibn al-'Arabi's views on this subject were not entirely consistent.

Another problem area is Ibn al-'Arabi's lack of precision in using the word wujud to mean both 'existence' and 'Being'. It was stated above that possible things become existent entities when God gives them existence, but it must be stressed that the existence which he gives them is relative existence. They become the 'loci of manifestation' (mazahir) of the names of God, who, as Essence, is alone Being in the strict sense. Another way of putting it is to say that each entity becomes a receptacle for Being, but that since entities differ from one another, they differ also in their capacity to function as vehicles of his self-manifestation.

4 The 'perfect man' and the Muhammadan reality

The first chapter of the Fusus al-hikam (The Bezels of Wisdom) is entitled 'The Wisdom of Divinity in the Word of Adam'. It begins with the assertion that the Real created the cosmos as an all-inclusive object in which he could contemplate the entities of his names, but that until he created Adam and breathed his spirit into him, the cosmos remained like an unpolished mirror. Here Ibn al-'Arabi's idea seems to be that the cosmos as a whole – the totality of existent entities – manifests all the divine names but does so in a diffuse way, whereas man, as a microcosm endowed with consciousness, brings them into sharp focus as a unity. Potentially every man is a microcosm, but in practice men differ in their polishing of the cosmic mirror, with only a select few realizing their primordial nature. These are the prophets and saints, all of whom belong to the category of 'the perfect man' (al-insan al-kamil). They alone assume the character traits of God, which are latent in all human beings, and manifest them in perfect equilibrium.

Muhammad is the 'perfect man' par excellence. Basing his argument on the hadith (sayings of the Prophet), 'I was a prophet when Adam was between water and clay', Ibn al-'Arabi propounds the view that as 'the Muhammadan reality' (al-haqiqa al-Muhammadiyya), Muhammad is identical with 'the first intellect' (al-'aql al-awwal), the eternal principle unifying the immutable entities. All the other prophets, beginning with Adam, only became prophets during their historical mission; each was the bearer of a fragment of this Muhammadan reality in a particular place and time, a bezel in which a jewel of the divine wisdom was displayed. None the less, after their mission the prophets continued to exert an influence through the saints who were their spiritual heirs.

5 Imagination and mysticism

The *al-Futuhat* contains a good deal of autobiographical material in anecdotal form, some of which strains credulity. For instance Ibn al-ʿArabi, who was in no doubt that he himself was one of the most important saints in the history of Islam, tells us that he met and conversed with the prophets of old including Moses, Jesus and Muhammad. On one moonlit night, when on board a ship in the port of Tunis, he allegedly encountered Moses' spiritual guide al-Khidr, who came to him walking on the water without getting his feet wet, before going off to a lighthouse over two miles away, which he reached in two or three steps (*al-Futuhat al-makkiyya* I: 186). It is tempting to dismiss these visions as hallucinations induced by extreme ascetic practices or illness – on the occasion when he saw al-Khidr he had gone to the side of the ship because of a stomach pain which prevented him from sleeping – but Ibn al-ʿArabi offers a different explanation based on his perception of the nature of the cosmos.

In his view, the cosmos comprises a hierarchy of three distinct worlds or levels: the 'world of spirits', 'the world of images' and 'the world of bodies'. The second of these – 'the world of images' (*ʿalam al-amthal*), also called 'the world of imagination' (*ʿalam al-khayal*) – plays a key role because of its intermediate position. It is the isthmus (*barzakh*) between the world of spirits and the world of bodies, the realm in which spirits are corporealized and bodies are spiritualized. The world of images is a really existent world, but in the waking state we are generally unaware of it; in our dreams, when our souls are no longer distracted by sensory input from the world of bodies, we function at this level, conversing with the departed and with those normally separated from us by geographical distances. What ordinary human beings experience only in their dreams, the mystic may experience at other times. Thus for example, when al-Khidr appeared to Ibn al-ʿArabi, this took place in the world of images, al-Khidr – who belongs to the world of spirits – being corporealized for the occasion.

The supposition of this intermediate world of images also furnishes the key to understanding both the miracles performed by prophets and saints and some of the more bizarre descriptions of the hereafter in the *hadith*. As regards the miracles, Ibn al-ʿArabi's starting point is the observation that we all can create things in our imagination or imagine things happening as we would like them to happen. The 'perfect man' is in addition endowed with extraordinary spiritual energy or *himma*, which enables him to bring the creatures of imagination out of the world of images into the world of bodies thus giving them existence. However, far from acting like a superman, he exercises restraint only employing his miraculous powers when commanded by God to do so. As regards the traditional descriptions of the hereafter, Ibn al-ʿArabi maintains that they should be understood as comparable to dream imagery. In a celebrated dream, the Prophet was given a cup of milk to drink, which in the waking state he subsequently interpreted as knowledge. What is impossible in the world of bodies – the corporealization of milk as knowledge – is perfectly possible in the world of images. Similarly in the hereafter, our works will be weighed in the scales and death will be brought in the form of a salt-coloured ram. We who are resurrected will really see these things, but we will see them in the world of images.

6 Assessment

In view of the volume of Ibn al-ʿArabi's work, much of which is still unpublished, any assessment of his philosophy must remain highly tentative. Although he was influenced by earlier Sufis and was conversant with the works of the *falasifa* and the disputes between the Muʿtazila and Ashʿariyya, the dominant influence on his thought seems to have been the Neoplatonism of PLOTINUS as mediated by the *Epistles* of the Brethren of Purity (Affifi 1938: 174–94) (see IKHWAN AL-SAFAʾ; NEOPLATONISM IN ISLAMIC PHILOSOPHY). Nevertheless he differs from them in at least two important respects. First, despite his use of emanationist language, it is clear that for him 'emanation' (*fayd*) is a figure of speech for what is more accurately described as self-revelation. Second, he does not simply take from the Qurʾan and hadith convenient pegs on which to hang his doctrine, but rather offers what amounts to a profound esoteric commentary on both.

See also: ISLAMIC THEOLOGY; MYSTICAL PHILOSOPHY IN ISLAM

List of works

Ibn al-ʿArabi (after 1229) *Fusus al-hikam* (The Bezels of Wisdom), ed. A. Affifi, Cairo, 1946; trans. R.W.J. Austin, *The Bezels of Wisdom*, New York: Paulist Press, 1980. (A late work which contains the quintessence of Ibn al-ʿArabi's spiritual doctrine in the form of twenty-seven brief chapters named after prophets who epitomize different spiritual types.)
—— (c.1231–8) *al-Futuhat al-makkiyya* (The Meccan Illuminations), Cairo, 1911; partial trans. M. Chodkiewicz *et al.*, *Les Illuminations de la Mecque:*

The Meccan Illuminations, Textes choisis/Selected Texts, Paris: Sindbad, 1988. (The definitive synthesis of Ibn al-'Arabi's teaching, comprising 560 chapters which deal with every aspect of mystical knowledge.)

References and further reading

Addas, C. (1989) *Ibn 'Arabi ou La quête du Soufre Rouge* (Ibn al-'Arabi and The Quest for Red Sulphur), Paris: Gallimard; trans. P. Kingsley, *Quest for Red Sulphur: The Life of Ibn 'Arabi*, Cambridge: Islamic Texts Society, 1993. (Critical biography.)

* Affifi, A.E. (1938) *The Mystical Philosophy of Muhyid Din-Ibnul Arabi*, Cambridge: Cambridge University Press. (Pioneering work, still useful although polemical and somewhat dated.)

Austin, R.W. J. (1971) *Sufis of Andalusia*, London, George Allen & Unwin. (Biographical essay and partial translations of *Ruh al-quds* and *al-Durrat al-fakhirah*, which give valuable insight into the spiritual milieu of Ibn al-'Arabi's early years.)

* Chittick, W.C. (1989) *The Sufi Path of Knowledge: Ibn al-'Arabi's Metaphysics of Imagination*, Albany, NY: State University of New York Press. (Exposition of Ibn al-'Arabi's thought, based primarily on *The Meccan Illuminations* with extensive excerpts translated by the author.)

—— (1996a) 'Ibn 'Arabi', in S.H. Nasr and O. Leaman (eds) *History of Islamic Philosophy*, London: Routledge, ch. 30, 497–509. (Clear and perceptive discussion of Ibn al-'Arabi.)

—— (1996b) 'The School of Ibn 'Arabi', in S.H. Nasr and O. Leaman (eds) *History of Islamic Philosophy*, London: Routledge, ch. 31, 510–23. (Discussion of Ibn al-'Arabi's school.)

Chodkiewicz, M. (1992) *Un océan sans rivage: Ibn al-'Arabi le livre et la loi* (An Ocean Without Shore: Ibn al-'Arabi, the Book and the Law), Paris, Seuil; trans. D. Streight, *Ocean Without Shore*, Albany, NY: State University of New York Press, 1993. (A study of the hermeneutical principles which govern Ibn al-'Arabi's approach to the Qur'an.)

* Izutsu, T. (1983) *Sufism and Taoism*, Los Angeles, CA: University of California Press. (Pages 1–283 contain the classic account of Ibn al-'Arabi's ontology, based primarily on *The Bezels of Wisdom* as interpreted by early Muslim commentators. The book is a revised version of *A Comparative Study of the Key Philosophical Concepts in Sufism and Taoism*, 1966–7.)

NEAL ROBINSON

IBN 'ARABI *see* IBN AL-'ARABI, MUHYI AL-DIN

IBN BAJJA, ABU BAKR MUHAMMAD IBN YAHYA IBN AS-SAY'IGH (d. 1138)

Ibn Bajja's philosophy may be summed up in two words; al-ittisal (conjunction) and al-tawahhud (solitude). Conjunction is union with the divine realm, a union that reveals the eternal and innermost aspects of the universe. Through this union or knowledge, one is completed as a human being, and in this completion the ultimate human end, happiness, is achieved. Solitude, on the other hand, is separation from a society that is lacking in knowledge. Once united with the eternal aspects of the universe, one must isolate oneself from those who are not in the same state, who may therefore distract one from the supernatural realm through their ignorance and corruption.

1 Life and works
2 The human soul
3 Intelligible forms
4 The state of conjunction
5 Solitude

1 Life and works

Abu Bakr Muhammad ibn Yahya ibn as-Say'igh, known as Ibn Bajja (or Avempace in the West), was born in Saragossa, Spain, at an unknown date and died in Fez in North Africa in AH 537/AD 1138. In *Akhbar al-hukama'* (Information About Wise People), al-Qifti mentions that Ibn Bajja died from being poisoned by rivals in the field of medicine. He was the teacher of Ibn al-Imam and IBN RUSHD (Averroes). His prominence was the result of his being the first in the West to show deep understanding of the views of some of his predecessors, such as PLATO, ARISTOTLE, AL-FARABI, IBN SINA (though Ibn Bajja never directly mentions him) and AL-GHAZALI. Thus he served as a link between the East and the West.

Ibn al-Imam edited his teacher's works in AH 534/AD 1135. They include medical works, commentaries on Aristotle and al-Farabi and original philosophical treatises. The most important of these treatises are *Tadbir al-mutawahhid* (Management of the Solitary), *Risalat al-wada'* (Essay on Bidding Farewell) and *Risalat al-ittisal al-'aql al fa''al bil-insan* (Essay on the Conjunction of the Intellect with Human Beings).

In spite of the criticism directed against Ibn Bajja by some of his contemporaries, such as IBN TUFAYL, he was highly regarded even by those critics themselves. Ibn Tufayl described him as possessing 'the sharpest mind', 'the soundest reasoning' and 'the most valid opinion' of those following the first generation of thinkers. The reference here is to the Arab/Spanish thinkers who lived from the earlier part of the second half of the tenth century to the end of the eleventh century, which marks the emergence of the second generation of Arab/Spanish thinkers. The first generation is characterized by interest in learning about ancient logic and philosophy; the second, beginning with Ibn Bajja, is characterized by originality of philosophical writings. His student Ibn al-Imam describes him as the marvel of his time in depth of philosophical knowledge.

2 The human soul

The two most essential pillars on which Ibn Bajja's philosophy rests are *al-ittisal* (conjunction) and *al-tawahhud* (solitude or union). *Al-ittisal* is that of the philosopher with the agent intellect (the lowest celestial intelligence and home to the universals), and *al-tawahhud*, when used in the sense of solitude, is that of the philosopher in society. *Al-tawahhud* is also used in the sense of *al-ittisal* (union). Like his Eastern predecessors, al-Farabi and Ibn Sina, Ibn Bajja was most concerned with the ultimate human objective, the intellectual or philosophical ideal, which in turn is in conjunction with the agent intellect through grasping the universals (see UNIVERSALS). This conjunction results in self-completion, which is the same as happiness. To understand the ultimate human objective and the instruments through which it is attained, Ibn Bajja first traces the development of the human soul, the only means to conjunction.

The human soul, he believes, develops from the plant to the animal and finally to the rational life. The plant life is the embryonic life, which provides one with nourishment and growth. With the progress from the plant to the animal life, which is the sensitive life, one moves from mere vegetation to sensation, movement and desire. Sensation is acquired either by the five external senses or by the internal senses, the common sense, the imagination and memory. By acquiring thought, or the highest human state, one rises to the level of rational speculation. While the human soul incorporates these three states, human nature or essence as such is described as *'aql* (reason or intellect). In the tradition of AL-FARABI and IBN SINA, Ibn Bajja teaches that the intellect is either potential or actual. When it is potential, it has the capacity for acquiring its proper object, the intelligible

form (*as-sura al-'aqliyya*) or, as Ibn Bajja is fond of calling it, the spiritual form (*as-sura ar-ruhaniyya*), the form that belongs to the soul. When it is actual, it is identified with its object (see SOUL IN ISLAMIC PHILOSOPHY).

3 Intelligible forms

Four types of intelligible forms in themselves are distinguished: those of the bodies that have an eternal circular motion; those of the agent and acquired intellects (the acquired intellect being the highest level of the human intellect, which results from conjunction with the agent intellect); those of the material world, which are stripped by the external senses from external particular things; and those in the internal senses. The first are in all respects immaterial, that is, lacking any necessary relation to matter. The second are in themselves immaterial; they have only an inessential relation to matter, the agent intellect by virtue of causing the material forms and the acquired intellect by virtue of completing them. The third are essentially linked to matter; they exist in matter and are made intelligible only through the mediation of the external senses. The fourth lie between the second and the third and are therefore in part material and in part not. Since, to Ibn Bajja, immateriality necessitates universality and materiality necessitates particularity, the following conclusion is drawn: the first, second and, in part, fourth types of intelligible forms are universal, while the third and, in part, fourth are particular.

Along Greek and Islamic lines, Ibn Bajja insists that the completion of every nature is the best for that nature and its highest objective. However, the completion of a nature requires that nature to acquire its proper objects. Since the nature of being human is reason, and since the proper objects of reason are the separate forms or universals which reside in the agent intellect, to acquire these objects is to complete human nature. A human being grasps the purely material forms through the external senses and benefits from them, and grasps the forms that are somewhat purified from matter through the internal senses and also benefits from them. Grasping the separate forms through reason is, however, the most befitting to human nature, and hence is best for it. On the basis of the kind of power one uses to grasp the intelligibles, Ibn Bajja divides people into three groups: the multitudes, the theorists and the philosophers. The multitudes grasp the intelligibles with the external senses, the theorists grasp them with the internal senses and the philosophers grasp them with reason. Only the philosophers can be classified as happy, for they acquire the universals in themselves, the objects of reason.

In *al-Ittisal*, Ibn Bajja states that it is as if the multitudes grasp the sun as reflected in the mirror after its having been reflected in water. The theorists grasp it as reflected in water; the philosophers grasp it in itself. He compares the multitudes to people in a cave in which the sun never shines. If they are in the very inside of the cave, objects appear to them in a state of darkness; if instead they are at the entrance of the cave, objects appear to them in the shade. As the people of the cave, regardless of their place, have no idea of what it means to see the sun, so also the multitudes have no idea of what it means to grasp the intelligibles rationally. He compares the theorists, on the other hand, to those who have gone out of the cave, where they can see the sun shedding its light on things and making the colours of things visible in themselves. He does not believe, however, that the happy ones can be compared to any beings with physical vision 'since they and the thing they grasp become one'. Being in the happy state is like having vision itself transformed into light. In other words, the multitudes grasp the reflection of the reflection of a thing, the theorists grasp the reflection of a thing and the philosophers grasp the thing itself.

4 The state of conjunction

To be a philosopher, or to have conjunction with the universals in the agent intellect, is to have ultimate human happiness and to experience 'witnessing' of the truth. The happy ones are incorruptible, eternal and 'numerically one with no difference among them in themselves whatsoever'. Their instruments, or their bodies, are the only things that differentiate them from each other. They are incorruptible and eternal because the intelligibles with which they are identified are so, and are numerically one because they are all identified with the same intelligibles.

Ibn Bajja rejects the Sufi concept that the ultimate human end is the pleasure (*al-ladhdha*) which results from witnessing (*mushahadat*) the divine world internally, in a higher sensible form as presented by the common sense, imagination and memory. According to him, this amounts to saying that 'having pleasure internally is the ultimate objective of knowing the Truth through the internal senses'. However, this is not the case since this pleasure is not sought for its own sake. In support of his view, Ibn Bajja mentions among other things that if pleasure of the internal senses were the ultimate human end, then reason (which is a higher power than the internal senses) as well as its knowledge would be superfluous and futile.

Because knowledge of the internal senses is higher than that of the external senses, the objects of the former being more enduring than those of the latter, the pleasure of the internal senses is higher than that of the external senses. The assertion that the former objects are more enduring than the latter is demonstrated by the fact that one can imagine the existence of something that has ceased to exist externally. However, even knowledge of the internal senses still falls short of reaching the sublimity of the knowledge of reason since the objects of the former do not endure as much as those of the latter. Only the objects of the latter endure permanently, unaffected by the forgetfulness or even the removal of their subject. Knowledge of these permanent objects gives the knower a permanent status since the knower and the known in this case are one. It also gives the highest and most permanent pleasure. The state of happiness is one which cannot be described in language, owing to its nobility, pleasure, beauty and goodness. When human beings reach this ultimate end, they become simple intellects of which it is true to say that they are nothing but divine.

5 Solitude

The knower, or happy person, may exist in society in either a virtuous or a nonvirtuous city. A virtuous city is one whose members are all complete in knowledge, while in a nonvirtuous city the contrary is the case.

If perfected people exist in a nonvirtuous city, they must live in isolation from the rest of society, for their complete knowledge makes them 'strangers' or 'weeds', that is, those whose true opinions are contrary to the opinions of society. While isolation from society is not natural or essential for a human being in the natural or virtuous city, it is accidental to one's nature and must be practised in order to preserve oneself from the corruption of the nonvirtuous cities.

See also: EPISTEMOLOGY IN ISLAMIC PHILOSOPHY; ETHICS IN ISLAMIC PHILOSOPHY; SOUL IN ISLAMIC PHILOSOPHY

List of works

Ibn Bajja (before 1138) *Rasa'il ibn Bajja al-ilahiyya* (Ibn Bajja's Metaphysical Essays), ed. M. Fakhry, Beirut: Dar al-Jil, 1992. (The best available collection of Ibn Bajja's sociopolitical and metaphysical treatises. It includes the most important of such treatises, *Tadbir al-mutawahhid* (Management of the Solitary), *al-Ittisal al-'aql al-fa''al bil-insan* (Essay on the Conjunction of the Intellect with Human Beings) and *Risalat al-wada'* (Essay on Bidding Farewell).)

—— (before 1138) Commentary on Aristotle's *Physics*, ed. P. Lettinck, *Aristotle's Physics and Its Perception in the Arabic World with an Edition of the Unpublished Parts of Ibn Bajja's Commentary on the Physics*, Leiden: Brill, 1994. (Includes a survey of Ibn Bajja's commentary on Aristotle's *Physics*, his longest commentary, and its influence on Ibn Rushd.)

References and further reading

Al-'Alawi, J.D. (1983) *Mu'allafat Ibn Bajja* (Ibn Bajja's Works), Beirut: Dar ath-Thaqafa. (The best available classification of Ibn Bajja's works, including a discussion of the sources and influences of their ideas.)

Goodman, L. (1996) 'Ibn Bajjah', in S.H. Nasr and O. Leaman (eds) *History of Islamic Philosophy*, London: Routledge, ch. 21, 294–312. (Discussion of the thinker and his period, describing in detail the cultural context within which he worked.)

Ibn Rushd (1126–98) *Talkhis kitab an-nafs* (Summary of the Book on the Soul), ed. A.F. al-Ahwani, Cairo: Maktabat an-Nahda, 1950. (Includes Ibn Bajja's *Risalat al-ittisal*. Useful, not only in offering Ibn Bajja's view on the soul, but also in comparing it with those of Ishaq ibn Hunayn, al-Kindi and Ibn Rushd.)

* al-Qifti, A. (*c.*1172) *Akhbar al-hukama'* (Information About Wise People), ed. J. Lippert, Leipzig: Maktabat al-Mutanabbi, 1903. (Includes a section on Ibn Bajja's life and works.)

Zainaty, G. (1979) *La morale d'Avempace* (The Ethics of Avempace), Paris: Vrin. (Useful overview of Ibn Bajja's metaphysics, psychology and ethics.)

SHAMS C. INATI

IBN CRESCAS, HASDAI

see CRESCAS, HASDAI

IBN DAUD, ABRAHAM (c.1110–C.1180)

Ibn Daud was born in Cordoba and died in Toledo. In Jewish texts he is known as Rabad, an acronym of his Hebrew name, Rabbi Abraham ben David. He was known to medieval Christian philosophers by a variety of names, including Avendauth and possibly John of Spain as well. His Sefer ha-Kabbalah *(The Book of Tradition), regarded by some scholars as the first comprehensive study of Jewish history, is an extended argument for the authority of rabbinic Judaism on the grounds that it is an unbroken tradition of authentic sources, from the Mosaic origins through the first two Jewish commonwealths, the exile, and down to the author's time. His major work in philosophy is Al-'Aqida al-Rafi'a (The Exalted Faith), composed in 1160 in Judaeo-Arabic, the form of Arabic written in Hebrew characters that was commonly used by Jewish scholars and thinkers in the Muslim milieu. It survives only in two late fourteenth-century Hebrew translations, one by Samuel Motot, entitled* Ha-Emunah ha-Nissa'ah, *and the other, better known, by Solomon ibn Labi, entitled* Ha-Emunah ha-Ramah.

1 Aristotelianism
2 *Ha-Emunah ha-Ramah*
3 Influence

1 Aristotelianism

Abraham ibn Daud was the first philosopher to apply the diverse elements of Aristotelian philosophy to forge a philosophy of Judaism. He initiated a new direction in Jewish philosophy that continued in the writings of MAIMONIDES (1135–1204) and culminated in the philosophy of GERSONIDES (1288–1344). The relationship of these Jewish Aristotelians might be compared to that of Locke, Berkeley and Hume in British philosophy. If Ibn Daud is not always as rigorous as Maimonides or Gersonides, it is because they build on the foundations he laid down. But no Jewish Aristotelian's work is as comprehensive as Ibn Daud's, and on many topics his treatment is more thorough or philosophically more sophisticated than that of Maimonides. For example, the concept of the soul and its faculties is of central importance to Maimonides in the *Dalalat al-Ha'irin* (Moreh Nevukhim, Guide to the Perplexed). Yet he presents no clear theory of the soul in the *Dalalat al-Ha'irin* (Moreh Nevukhim, Guide to the Perplexed); and, where he does deal with psychology at length, as in *Shemonah Perakim* (Eight Chapters), many of his assertions become clear only with the aid of Ibn Daud's discussions in *Ha-Emunah ha-Ramah*. For instance, Maimonides states that while souls have multiple powers there are not multiple souls in each individual; and a particular faculty in one species is not the same as the corresponding faculty in another, even though the faculties bear the same name. Thus, both animals and humans exercise nutritive functions and have nutritive 'souls', but the term names a faculty, not a separate being; and the nutritive function in animals is not the same as that of humans.

Ibn Daud develops and defends these views at length; Maimonides merely asserts them.

2 Ha-Emunah ha-Ramah

Ha-Emunah ha-Ramah comprises three books. The first explains the presuppositions of Aristotelianism. The intended audience consists of those cultured Jews who know of, but little about, the new Aristotelian science. In the Western lands of Muslim civilization that science was now displacing the older atomism of the *kalam* (see ISLAMIC THEOLOGY). In the second book Ibn Daud lists six basic principles of Judaism and explains them in the light of the new science. In the third book he applies to ethics the presuppositions and principles he has laid out.

The status of the third book, entitled *Barefuah ha-Nafshiyah* (The Healing of the Soul), within the whole is problematic. Ibn Daud tells us that his goal in composing the entire work was to solve the problem of human choice and determinism. That question was dealt with directly in the final chapter of the second book. Given his stated intention, this is where *Ha-Emunah ha-Ramah* should end. Everything that goes before can be seen as material arrayed in support of this final discussion; but the internal structure of all the material presented in every known manuscript of the third book is incoherent. For example, it is supposed to comprise two chapters, but all the existing manuscripts contain only a first chapter that deals with a potpourri of issues in ethics. At best Book Three is an addendum, and one that has an unfinished look compared to the organized state of what went before. For these reasons the following summary is limited to the first two books.

Book One contains eight chapters. The first three define key technical terms in the new Aristotelian science: substance, accident, and the ten categories (ch. 1), form and matter (ch. 2), and motion (ch. 3). There follow two chapters on physics. Here Ibn Daud spells out the theses that material bodies possess neither actual nor potential infinity (ch. 4) and that all motion comes from a mover and requires a first mover (ch. 5). In two chapters on rational psychology he describes the nature and powers of the soul (ch. 6) and defends the claim that the rational power is nonphysical (ch. 7). The last chapter deals with astronomy. Here Ibn Daud argues for the claim, critical to his solution of the problem of determinism, that the heavens are rational, living organisms, their motion intentional.

Book Two uses the ideas of the first book to explain what Ibn Daud deems to be the basic principles of the Jewish faith and religious law (see HALAKHAH). The first four principles address the existence and nature of God. The fifth defends the authority of the rabbinic tradition. The sixth turns to the target Ibn Daud specified in his introductory abstract, the problem of human choice.

The first two principles are that God is a necessary being and that he is one. Only a necessary being can be truly one (ch. 1). God's unity is essential, not accidental and admits no plurality of any kind (ch. 2). Ibn Daud's third principle is that all affirmative characterizations of God, even the ascription to him of unity and necessity, are equivocal, bearing different senses from those of ordinary usage. As applied to God, they express either a negation or a relation. Like Maimonides, then, Ibn Daud espouses a negative theology (see NEGATIVE THEOLOGY). But his acceptance of relational statements about God saves him from the kind of attack that Maimonides' theology later received from such Aristotelians as Thomas AQUINAS and Gersonides.

Ibn Daud's fourth principle explains divine actions in terms of the mediation of the beings that Scripture calls angels. Ibn Daud identifies them with the separate intellects of Aristotelian cosmology. He devotes two chapters to proofs of their existence. The first argues from epistemology and the powers of the soul. The second is based on physics and astronomy. A third chapter surveys the entities in the universe and the kinds of angels/separate intellects who govern them on behalf of God.

The fifth principle is that the Hebrew Scriptures as interpreted by the rabbis (not the Karaites, Muslims or Christians) are an authoritative source of truth. An introductory abstract defends the general thesis that authentic traditions can make veridical claims. The next two chapters argue that rabbinic Judaism is such a tradition. The first of these deals with the nature of the prophecy recorded in Scripture and categorizes its degrees, laying a foundation for the argument that the prophecy of Moses, as recorded in the Torah, is an unimpeachable witness to the word of God. The second argues that the transmission of Moses' report through the early and later rabbinic sages was faithful to his original testimony. Thus statements in the rabbinic tradition preserve the same epistemic status as direct reports of sense experience or reliable traditions of such reports. This chapter recaps the more extended argument of Ibn Daud's earlier work on the continuity of Jewish ideas, *Sefer ha-Kabbalah* (The Book of Tradition).

The final principle is that human choice is not obviated by divine or natural necessity. The problem as Ibn Daud states it: if God rules over all things, no human being would have any choices. But that cannot be. For God issues commands and punishes disobedience, and no one can be justly punished for acts that were not free. Nor can one be commanded to do where one has no choice. So God's rule does not exclude human choice. But how can there be anything over which God does not have dominion? Scripture only exacerbates the dilemma. For some texts seem to say that God determines everything, while others imply that we do have choices.

Ibn Daud devotes two chapters to the problem. The first grounds his solution in his earlier discussion of God's attributes. Since all terms predicated of God are equivocal, no statements about divine power and rule can be understood literally. The second chapter presents Ibn Daud's answer. Everything is determined by God through his ordering of the universe, but this ordering allows us to make choices. So people are morally responsible and are subject to divine providence, punishment and reward.

Ibn Daud does not list creation as a fundamental principle of Judaism, although his predecessor, SAADIAH GAON al-Fayyumi (882–942), made it the cornerstone of Jewish belief. Perhaps Ibn Daud omitted creation because it was the one central belief in Judaism that could not be explained or defended from the standpoint of the new Aristotelianism. The conflict between Aristotelian eternalism and biblical creationism was to become a central theme in the philosophies of Maimonides and Gersonides.

3 Influence

Beyond their intrinsic worth and interest as contributions to philosophy, Ibn Daud's ideas had a powerful impact on later Jewish thought. While everything he said was rooted in rabbinic tradition, his formulations, applications and syntheses were highly original and presaged the issues that were to dominate the history of Jewish Aristotelianism. A key example is his understanding of the relationship between religion and science. For Ibn Daud and his Jewish Aristotelian successors, there is no conflict between religious and scientific truth. Truth is one. Religion no less than science makes truth claims; and these claims, if true, must cohere with those of science. Furthermore, since Jewish faith cannot be confined to one part of one's life, no understanding of Judaism that excludes the insights of science can be 'Torah true'. This challenging model of the relationship between science and religion allowed Ibn Daud to incorporate the new Aristotelian science into the outlook of rabbinic Judaism and set the agenda for later Jewish philosophers from Maimonides through Gersonides. The synthesis he inaugurated survived until its eventual overthrow by Hasdai CRESCAS (1340–1412) and Benedict de SPINOZA (1634–77), when Aristotelianism was itself surpassed.

See also: ARISTOTELIANISM, MEDIEVAL; HALAKHAH; MAIMONIDES, M.

List of works

Ibn Daud, A. (1160) *Sefer ha-Kabbalah*, trans. G.D. Cohen, *The Book of Tradition*, Philadelphia, PA: Jewish Publication Society, 1967. (An attack on the contentions of Karaism and a justification of rabbinical Judaism by the establishment of a chain of traditions from Moses to the author's own time.)

—— (1160) *Ha-Emunah ha-Ramah*, trans. N.M. Samuelson, ed. N.M. Samuelson and G. Weiss, *The Exalted Faith*, Rutherford, NJ: Fairleigh Dickinson University Press, 1986. (Written originally in Judaeo-Arabic as *Al-'Aqida al-Rafi'a*. The work is now known by the title cited here, which is that of the Hebrew translation made in the late fourteenth-century by Solomon ibn Labi. The translated Hebrew title of the third part of the work is *Barefuah ha-Nafshiyah* (The Healing of the Soul). The work introduced the phase of Jewish philosophy that led to Maimonides. This phase differs from earlier ones in its more thorough systematic from derived in large measure from Aristotle.)

References and further reading

Arfa, M. (1954) 'Abraham ibn Daud and the Beginnings of Medieval Jewish Aristotelianism', unpublished Ph.D dissertation, New York: Columbia University, 1954. (An interesting read.)

Elbogen, I. (1915) 'Abraham ibn Daud als geschichtsschreiber', in *Festschrift zum Siebzigsten Geburtsage Jabok Guttmanns*, Leipzig: G. Fock. (An examination of the importance of Ibn Daud as a historical writer.)

* Maimonides, Moses (1168) *Shemonah Perakim* (Eight Chapters), trans. with notes by J. Gorfinkle, *The Eight Chapters of Maimonides on Ethics*, New York, 1912; repr. New York: AMS, 1966. (Part of Maimonides' commentary on the Mishnah, *Kitab al-Siraj* (translated into Hebrew as *Sefer ha-Maor, hu Perush ha-Mishnah*). The work forms a thematic introduction to the mishnaic collection of ethical aphorisms known as *Pirkei Avot* (The Sayings of the Fathers).)

* —— (c.1190) *Dalalat al-Ha'irin* (Moreh Nevukhim, Guide to the Perplexed), ed. S. Munk, *Le Guide des Égarés*, Arabic text, critically edited, with annotated French translation, Paris, 1856–66, 3 vols; repr. Osnabrück: Zeller, 1964; trans. S. Pines, with an introductory essay by L. Strauss, *The Guide of the Perplexed*, Chicago, IL: Chicago University Press, 1963, 1969, 2 vols. (Maimonides' best-known

work, which takes the form of a letter to a disciple who is confused by the seeming disparity between biblical and scientific/philosophical ideas.)

Samuelson, N.M. (1977) 'Ibn Daud's Conception of Prophecy', *Journal of the American Academy of Religion* 45: 883–900.

—— (1979) 'Causation and Choice in the Philosophy of ibn Daud', in *The Solomon Goldman lectures*, vol. 2, Chicago, IL: Spertus College. (A study of Ibn Daud's account of free will and determinism.)

—— (1982) 'Ibn Daud and Franz Rosenzweig on Other Religions: A Contrast Between Medieval and Modern Jewish Philosophy', in *Proceedings of the Eighth World Congress of Jewish Studies, Division C: Talmud and Midrash, Philosophy and Mysticism, Hebrew and Yiddish Literature*, Jerusalem: World Congress of Jewish Studies, 75–80. (A comparative study of what these two major Jewish philosophers have to say as Jewish thinkers about other religions.)

NORBERT M. SAMUELSON

IBN EZRA, ABRAHAM (1089–1164)

The philosophy of Ibn Ezra attained broad influence in Jewish literature through his Bible commentaries, included to this day in rabbinic Bibles. Born in Tudela, Spain, he was forced in later life (1140 until his death) to wander widely, at length settling in Rome and Lucca, where he composed some of his greatest works. A friend and, by some traditions, son-in-law of the poet-philosopher Judah Halevi, whom he mentions occasionally, he was himself a poet and wrote prolifically on grammar, exegesis, philosophy, medicine, astronomy and astrology. The many editions and manuscripts of his works attest their popularity, and some, especially on astronomy and astrology, were translated into Latin and then into French, Spanish, English and German.

Neoplatonic in orientation, with a Neo-Pythagorean fascination with numerology, Abraham ben Meir ibn Ezra's philosophy is often difficult to follow, since most of his works are unsystematic in exposition and elliptical in style. Frequently he engages in technical issues of grammar or literary analysis. His commentaries sometimes note 'this is a mystery (*sod*)' or 'the intelligent (*maskil*) should keep silent'. Such comments can signal the profundity of an issue, but at times Ibn Ezra seems deliberately to mute his radical conclusions.

Reason (*sekhel*) for Ibn Ezra is at the core of revelation, which is not just a historical event but a rational process. A proper understanding of Scripture thus demands a rational exegetical method grounded in Hebrew grammar and seeking the plain sense (*peshat*) of the text, not subordinate to homiletics or allegories. Yet revelation cannot contradict reason. So when a literal interpretation contradicts our rational or empirical knowledge, we must read nonliterally. Ibn Ezra generally upholds rabbinic tradition, but he is critical of rabbinic homiletical liberties (for example, in reconciling the variant wordings of the Decalogue in Exodus 20 and Deuteronomy 5) and of Karaite literalism (regarding the *lex talionis* in Exodus 21, for instance). Of both he says, 'reason cannot tolerate (*ein ha-da'at sovelet*)' such views. For 'reason is implanted in the heart by divine wisdom.... The judgement of reason is the foundation, and the Torah was not given to those who lack reason. The angel between man and his God is his reason'.

SPINOZA, who founded modern critical readings of Scripture, saw Ibn Ezra as his forerunner in the belief that 'it was not Moses who wrote the Pentateuch, but someone who lived long after him'. 'Aben Ezra,' he writes (1670), '... a man of enlightened intelligence, and no small learning, who was the first, so far as I know, to treat of this opinion, dared not express his meaning openly, but confined himself to dark hints' (1670: ch. 8).

Ibn Ezra does question such passages as Genesis 12: 6, 22: 14, 36: 31–6, Exodus 6: 28, Numbers 21: 1–3, Deuteronomy 1: 2, and 34: 1–12, but his conclusion is not Spinoza's. Faithful to rabbinic tradition, he affirms as revealed the authority of the later prophets, the 'Oral Torah' of the rabbis and even the textual work of the medieval Masoretes (see HALAKHAH). Occasional interpolations do not undermine the authority of revelation but prove it, since revelation must make sense, and it would be absurd to ascribe, say to Moses, statements he could not meaningfully have made.

Ibn Ezra's interest in astrology was shared by some Jewish philosophers like Abraham BAR HAYYA and Levi Ben Gershom (see GERSONIDES) but vigorously opposed by others such as MAIMONIDES. For Ibn Ezra astrology can explain terrestrial phenomena and, so, some biblical phenomena scientifically (see Commentaries on Genesis 31: 19, 1 Samuel 19: 13, and Numbers 21: 8). Thus, unlike Maimonides, Ibn Ezra draws no sharp line between scientific astronomy and judicial astrology.

His Neoplatonic assumption that the terrestial realm is subject to influences from the incorruptible celestial spheres, which in turn are governed from the supernal realm of the rational soul (*neshamah*) and the angels, all under the sovereignty of God, the 'absolute One' (see Commentary on Exodus 3: 15, and 6: 3), prompts Ibn Ezra to seek astral explanations of terrestial, especially human, affairs. But he stoutly rejects star worship. The celestial bodies are 'servants' (*mershartim*), without independent will or conscious purpose; their activity is mechanical (see Commentary on Exodus 33: 21, citing the Epistles of the Sincere Brethren of Basra) (see IKHWAN AL-SAFA').

Ibn Ezra mitigates the determinism of astrology by arguing that astral influence is not merely a function of the celestial configuration (*ma'arekhet*) but also of the physical consititution (*toledet*) of the recipient (*meqabbel*) of influence (Introduction to Ecclesiastes). This explains why one astral agent can produce diverse terrestrial effects. It also leaves room for free will. Indeed, it is the predictability of astral effects that enables one to take measures to avoid their impact. The event will occur, but those who understand can escape its effect. Reason, after all, transcends the intermediate realm of the stars.

The Torah, deriving from the supernal rational realm, affords a systematic avenue of escape from astral determinations to those Jews who observe it. Building on the Talmudic dictum 'Israel has no constellar sign (*mazal*)', Ibn Ezra reasons: 'it is well established that every nation has a known star or constellation. But God gave Israel a great superiority, since He rather than a star is their guide – for "Israel is God's portion"' (Commentary on Deuteronomy 4: 19). The Torah imparts knowledge to its adherents, enabling them to escape astral influences. They do so naturalistically, not theurgically.

For Ibn Ezra revelation and reason are ultimately perfectly congruent. His critical reading of the biblical text and his astrological interpretations of some biblical passages arise from his consistent application of a naturalistic and rationalistic exegetical method and express his commitment to the view that rationality is inherent in revelation itself.

See also: COSMOLOGY; HALAKHAH; NEOPLATONISM IN ISLAMIC PHILOSOPHY

List of works

Ibn Ezra, A. (1970) *Kitvei R. Avraham ibn Ezra*, Jerusalem: Makor, 4 vols. (Collected free-standing works edited by several hands in the nineteenth century and photomechanically reprinted here.)

—— (1975) *The Religious Poems of Abraham Ibn Ezra*, Jerusalem: Israel Academy of Sciences and Humanities, 2 vols. (A critical, annotated edition.)

—— (1985) *Abraham Ibn Ezra Reader*, ed. L. Israel, New York and Tel Aviv: Israel Matz. (In the original Hebrew, this collection comprises valuable annotated texts of selected works, including poetry, Bible commentaries, philosophy and theology.)

—— (1986) *Ibn Ezra's Commentaries on the Pentateuch*, ed. A. Weiser, originally published as a separate volume; repr. in *Humash Torat Hayyim*, Jerusalem: Mosad ha-Rav Kook, 1986. (In Hebrew. Although not without errors, this edition is far more reliable than the standard texts printed in traditional rabbinic Bibles.)

—— (before 1164) *Perush Rabbenu Avraham ibn Ezra al Yishayahu* (Commentary of Ibn Ezra on Isaiah), ed. M. Friedländer, *The Commentary of Ibn Ezra on Isaiah*, London: Society of Hebrew Literature, Truebner and Co., 1873. (Classic presentation of an important text, with English translation and commentary.)

—— (before 1164) *Reshit Hokhmah* (The Beginning of Wisdom), ed. and trans. R. Levy and F. Cantera, *The Beginning of Wisdom: An Astrological Treatise by Abraham ibn Ezra*, Baltimore, MD: Johns Hopkins University Press, 1939. (An important study of Ibn Ezra's astrological theories.)

—— (before 1164) *Sefer ha-Yesodot* (Book of Foundations), French trans. J. Halbronn, *Le Livre des Fondements Astrologiques*, Paris: Retz, 1977. (An important study of Ibn Ezra's astrological theories.)

References and further reading

Assaf, S. *et al.* (1969) 'Ibn Ezra, Abraham', in *Encyclopedia Hebraica*, Jerusalem: Encyclopedia Publishers, vol. 1, 210–15. (A study of Ibn Ezra's life, thought and contributions to biblical exegesis, Hebrew poetry and grammar.)

Assaf, S. *et al.* (1972) 'Ibn Ezra, Abraham', in *Encyclopedia Judaica*, Jerusalem: Keter, vol. 8, 1163–70. (Account of Ibn Ezra's life, beliefs and contributions to Hebrew poetry, grammar and biblical exegesis.)

Cohen, J. (1983) *Mishnato ha-pilosofit Datit Shel Rabbi Avraham ibn Ezra* (The Philosophical-Religious Teaching of Rabbi Abraham ibn Ezra), unpublished Ph.D. dissertation, Israel: Bar Ilan University. (The most comprehensive recent overview of Ibn Ezra's philosophy; with many valuable references.)

Bacher, W. (1904–12) 'Ibn Ezra, Abraham', in *Jewish Encyclopedia*, New York: Funk and Wagnells, vol. 6, 520–4. (Still a useful survey of Ibn Ezra's life and works.)

Esteban, F.D. (ed.) (1990) *Abraham ibn Ezra and His Age: Proceedings of the International Symposium*, Madrid: Association Espanola de Orientalistas. (An important collection of recent international scholarship on diverse aspects of Ibn Ezra's work and thought.)

Friedländer, M. (1877) *Essays in the Writings of Abraham ibn Ezra*. (Despite a conservative approach to Ibn Ezra's philosophy and to his critical approach towards biblical exegesis, this remains the most complete treatment of his life and work.)

Goldstein, D. (ed.) (1971) *The Jewish Poets of Spain: 900–1250*, Harmondsworth: Penguin, 153–62. (Selected poems by Ibn Ezra in English translation.)

Guttman, J. (1964) *Philosophies of Judaism*, New York: Holt Rinehart, Winston, 118–20. (Places Ibn Ezra's work in its Jewish philosophical context.)

Halbronn, J. (1985) *Le Monde Juif et l'Astrologie*, Milan: Arche Milano. (Includes examination of Ibn Ezra's astrological ideas.)

Jospe, R. (1994) 'The Torah and Astrology According to Abraham ibn Ezra', *Proceedings of the Eleventh World Congress of Jewish Studies* (Division C) 2: 17–24; a much fuller version, in Hebrew, appears in *Da'at* 32–3: 31–52. (A study of the place of the Torah in Ibn Ezra's astrological theory.)

—— (1996) 'Biblical Exegesis as a Philosophical Literary Genre: Abraham ibn Ezra and Moses Mendelssohn', in E. Fackenheim and R. Jospe (eds) *Jewish Philosophy and the Academy*, Rutherford, NJ: Fairleigh Dickinson University Press. (Discusses philosophic issues in Ibn Ezra's exegesis.)

Kiener, R. (1987) 'The Status of Astrology in the Early Kabbalah: From the Sefer Yesirah to the Zohar', in *Jerusalem Studies in Jewish Thought* 6: 1–42. (Places Ibn Ezra's astrology in the context of the medieval Jewish astrological tradition.)

Simon, U. (1985) 'Ibn Ezra Between Medievalism and Modernism: The Case of Isaiah XL–LXVI', in *Supplements to Vetus Testamentum* 36: 257–71. (Important treatment of Ibn Ezra's exegetical methods.)

—— (1982) 'Bible: Exegesis, Abraham Ibn Ezra', in *Encyclopedia Biblica*, Jerusalem: Bialik Institute, vol. 8, 671–80. (A study of Ibn Ezra's methodology as a Bible exegete.)

Sirat, C. (1985) *A History of Jewish Philosophy in the Middle Ages*, Cambridge: Cambridge University Press, 93–112. (Valuable especially because it makes use of manuscript materials; includes discussion of Ibn Ezra's astrological interests.)

* Spinoza, B. (1670) Tractatus Theologico-politicus (Theological-Political Treatise), in *The Chief Works of Benedict de Spinoza*, vol. 1, trans. S. Shirley, Leiden: Brill, 1991. (Spinoza regarded Ibn Ezra highly and credited him with being the first critic of the traditional religious view of Moses as the author of the entire Pentateuch.)

Twersky, I. and Harris, J. (eds) (1993) *Rabbi Abraham ibn Ezra: Studies in the Writings of a Twelfth Century Jewish Polymath*, Cambridge, MA: Harvard University Press. (An up-to-date collection of papers by leading scholars on the thought and work of Ibn Ezra.)

Wolfson, E. (1990) 'God, the Demiurge and the Intellect: On the Usage of the Word *Kol* in Abraham ibn Ezra', in *Revue des Études Juives* 149 (1–3): 77–111. (Philosophical cosmology in the exegetical writings.)

RAPHAEL JOSPE

IBN EZRA, MOSES BEN JACOB (*fl.* 1055–1135)

Ibn Ezra was an exegete, Jewish scholar and one of the foremost Hebrew poets of medieval Spain. Although none of his systematic biblical commentaries have been preserved, two important works survive in Judaeo–Arabic prose, both dealing with biblical literary theory, rhetoric and philosophy. The literary dimension of his work makes Ibn Ezra a forerunner of modern biblical criticism. His speculative system, deeply influenced by Neplatonism, was to have a profound impact on the early Spanish Kabbalists.

Born in Granada into a family of government officials, Ibn Ezra was a disciple of the famous Talmudist Isaac ibn Ghiyath (1038–88) at Lucena, where he received a thorough Hebrew and Arabic education. In his youth, Ibn Ezra befriended the foremost literati of his time, especially the poet and philosopher Judah HALEVI, whose creative talent he encouraged. During the Almoravid invasion of Granada in 1090 he fled to Christain Spain, where he led a life of exile, constantly pining for his native Andalusia, which he never regained. Ibn Ezra is rightly considered one of the greatest Hebrew poets of the Andalusian Golden Age. His Arabic prose works, containing his views on literary history, theory and criticism, rhetorics and philosophy are not as well known. Yet his *Kitab al-muhadara walmudakara* (Book of Conversation and Discussion) and his *Maqalat al-hadiqa fi ma'na l-magaz walhaqiqa* (The Treatise of Garden on Metaphorical and Literal Meaning) rank amongst the classics of Judaeo–Arabic literature. The former is divided into eight chapters, containing a discussion of the nature of poetry and a treatise on Jewish literary history. The last and longest chapter examines the figures of thought and expression used to embellish Hebrew poetry. In addition to its didactic – and even polemical – content as a kind of Hebrew *ars poetica*, the book has recently been described as an attempt to provide biblical legitimation to the 'profane' Hebrew poetry of the Andalusian school. Its application of rhetoric to Scripture is an early step towards the modern literary criticism of the Hebrew Bible.

The *Maqalat al-hadiqa fi ma'na l-magaz wal-haqiqa* (The Treatise of Garden on Metaphorical and Literal Meaning), although not a systematic philosophical treatise in the strict sense, contains much speculative material. Inititially conceived of as a disquisition on the biblical use of metaphorical language, the work is divided into two parts, the first of which proposes a variety of philosophical themes for the consideration of the reader. Suffused with anecdotes, poetic quotations, wise sayings and scientific observations, the work preserves important extracts of works now lost, such as the Arabic original of Ibn Gabirol's *Fons Vitae*. It adopts a genuinely humanistic perspective, expressed in part in its anthropocentrism. The book as a whole reflects both the influence of the Mu'tazilite school and the strong Neoplatonic current that entered Spain with the works of the Brethren of Purity (see ASH'ARIYYA AND MU'TAZILA; IKHWAN AL-SAFA'). The eleven chapters of the first part discuss the fundamental themes of Mu'tazilite theodicy, coloured with Neoplatonic insights: divine unity and unknowability, negative and apophatic theology, creation, revelation, nature, intellect and the human soul. Drawing on the Neoplatonic systems of Pseudo-Empedocles, Isaac ISRAELI, Dunash ben Tamim, IBN GABIROL and, above all, the Brethren of Purity, Ibn Ezra adopts the doctrine of emanation and makes the 'active intellect' the first divine creation, an entity that by his account proceded from the divine Will. This intellect is a pure and simple substance containing the forms of all existents (see NEOPLATONISM). The author also adopts Ibn Gabirol's hylomorphism. On the Greco–Arabic side, besides the ancient authors, such as pseudo-Aristotle, Plato and Hippocrates, the most often quoted are the Brethren of Purity and AL-FARABI, mentioned here for the first time in Jewish philosophy.

The second part takes the form of a glossary of terms designating humanity, viewed from physical and spiritual perspectives, and examines their literal and figurative use. Ibn Ezra's exegesis belongs to the Andalusian rationalistic tradition. The Hebrew version of the philosophical section of the book, translated in the Middle Ages by the celebrated poet and translator, Judah al-Harizi, was to have an abiding impact even among Kabbalists, who used it in the development of their speculative systems. It was an important link in the transmission of Neoplatonic elements to the early Spanish Kabbalah (see KABBALAH). However, the work is important more as a transmittor than as a fount of original thinking.

See also: IKHWAN AL-SAFA'; NEOPLATONISM

List of works

Ibn Ezra, M. (*c*.1055–1135) *Kitab al-muhadara wal-mudakara* (Book of Conversation and Discussion), ed. A.S. Halkin, Jerusalem: Mekize Nirdamim, 1975. (Edition of original Arabic text with a modern Hebrew translation of this pioneering medieval work on Biblical poetics.)

—— (*c*.1055–1135) *Maqalat al-hadiqa fi ma'na l-magaz wal-haqiqa* (The Treatise of Garden on Metaphorical and Literal Meaning), ed. P. Fenton, Jerusalem: Mekize Nirdamim, 1989. (Edition contains the original Arabic plus a modern Hebrew translation. Long extracts in French can also be found in Fenton (1997a).)

References and further reading

Dana, J. (1982) *Poetics of Mediaeval Hebrew Literature according to Moshe Ibn Ezra*, Jerusalem–Tel Aviv: Dana, Dvir. (Analysis, in Hebrew, of the *Muhadara* in the light of Arabic rhetoric.)

Diez Macho, A. (1953) 'Mose Ibn Ezra como poeta y preceptista' (Moses ibn Ezra as a Poet), Madrid–Barcelona. (Introduction to the poetry of Ibn Ezra with a biographical essay.)

Fenton, P. (1976) 'Gleanings from Moseh Ibn 'Ezra's *Maqalat al-hadiqa*', *Sefarad* 36: 285–98. (An account of an important philosophical text.)

—— (1997a) *Philosophie et exégèse dans le Jardin de la Métaphore de Moïse Ibn 'Ezra* (Philosophy and Exegesis in Moses ibn Ezra's *Garden of Metaphor*), Leiden: Brill. (Analysis of the philosophical and exegetical material in the *Maqalat al-hadiqa*, including extensive passages in French translation, and an edition of Arabic extracts from the *Fons Vitae*.)

—— (1997b) 'Traces of Moses Ibn 'Ezra's *'Arugat ha-bosem* in the Writings of the Early Spanish Qabbalists', in I. Twersky (ed.) *Studies in Medieval Jewish History and Literature III*, Cambridge, MA: Harvard University, Center for Jewish Studies. (His links with the Kabbalists.)

Pinès, S. (1957) 'Fragments of the Arabic Original of *Fons Vitae* in Moses Ibn 'Ezra's *'Arugat ha-bosem*', *Tarbiz* 27: 218–33. (Study, in Hebrew, of the quotations in the *Maqalat* from the lost Arabic original of Ibn Gabirol's *Fons Vitae*.)

PAUL B. FENTON

IBN FALAQUERA, SHEM TOV (1223/8–after 1290)

A prolific author with a clear and precise Hebrew style, Ibn Falaquera wrote both original works and Hebrew translations of Arabic works of philosophy and science. His writings include encyclopedias, Bible commentaries, the first commentary on Maimonides' Guide to the Perplexed and, by his own account, some twenty thousand verses of poetry. Unlike Maimonides, who wrote for the intelligentsia, Ibn Falaquera wrote most of his works with the stated aim of raising the cultural level of the Jewish people. Most of his prose works survive, many in multiple editions or manuscripts and several in European translations, a testimony to their popularity. A consistent theme in his works is the harmony of faith and reason.

Shem Tov ben Joseph ibn Falaquera was born in Spain between 1223 and 1228; his last known work refers to events in 1290. Various etymologies have been suggested for the name Falaquera, for which we have diverse spellings in Hebrew and European languages, and which was the name of a prominent Jewish family in Tudela. Most of his prose works survive, and many can be found in multiple editions or manuscripts. More than half of his youthful poetry was lost, he tells us, and in later life he abandoned his poetic career but continued to intersperse poetry, some of it humorous, with his prose works.

We know of eighteen works by Ibn Falaquera. In probable chronological order they are:

(1) *Batei Hanhagat Guf ha-Bari, Batei Hanhagat ha-Nefesh* (Verses on the Regimen of the Healthy Body and Soul);

(2) *Iggeret ha-Musar* (Epistle on Ethics), a *maqama* (prose narrative interspersed with verse) replete with with Jewish and Arabic ethical maxims, recounting the adventures of a youth in search of wisdom;

(3) *Zeri ha-Yagon* (Balm for Sorrow), another *maqama*, containing rabbinic and philosophic consolations;

(4) *Megillat ha-Zikkaron* (The Scroll of Remembrance), a lost work, presumably chronicling Jewish sufferings;

(5) *Iggeret ha-Vikuah* (Epistle of the Debate), a debate between a pious traditionalist Jew and a philosopher, demonstrating that philosophy is the twin sister of Torah and fully harmonious with Judaism;

(6) *Reshit Hokhmah* (The Beginning of Wisdom), an introduction to the sciences, including much material based on the works of AL-FARABI;

(7) *Sefer ha-Ma'alot* (Book of Degrees), an ethical work on the corporeal, spiritual and divine degrees of human perfection (*ma'alot* (degrees) is the Hebrew term for the virtues);

(8) *Sefer ha-Mevaqqesh* (Book of the Seeker), composed in 1263, when Ibn Falaquera says he was past 35 and approaching 40, a *maqama* expanding on the theme of the youthful seeker after wisdom, surveying the arts, professions and sciences, culminating in philosophy;

(9) *De'ot ha-Philosofim* (The Opinions of the Philosophers), a voluminous encyclopedia of the sciences intended to propagate philosophy among Jews and quoting extensively from the Arabic sources;

(10) *Sefer ha-Nefesh* (Book of the Soul), the first systematic Hebrew work of psychology;

(11) *Shelemut ha-Ma'asim* (The Perfection of Actions), based on the *Nicomachean Ethics* and Arabic ethical literature;

(12) *Iggeret ha-Halom* (Treatise of the Dream), on physical and spiritual well-being;

(13) *Sefer ha-Derash* (The Book of Interpretation), no longer extant, probably a commentary on *aggadic* passages in the Talmud and midrash;

(14) *Perush* (Bible Commentary); only fragments (often philosophical in orientation) survive, in citations by later authors;

(15) *Moreh ha-Moreh* (Guide to the Guide), completed in 1280, the first commentary on Maimonides' *Guide to the Perplexed*, including original Hebrew translations of the passages discussed, and comparing Maimonides (sometimes critically) to numerous classical, Arabic and Jewish philosophers;

(16) *Liqqutim mi-Sefer Meqor Hayyim*, selections from the *Fons Vitae* in Hebrew translation, eliminating the dialogue format of Ibn Gabirol's original (see IBN GABIROL);

(17) *Liqqutim mi-Sefer ha-'Azamim ha-Hamishah* (Selections from the Book of the Five Substances), Hebrew translation of passages from a Pseudo-Empedoclean work;

(18) *Mikhtav 'al Devar ha-Moreh* (Letter on the Matter of the *Guide*), Ibn Falaquera's last known work, a defence of Maimonides' *Guide* against anti-philosophical critics.

A consistent theme in Ibn Falaquera's works is the harmony of faith and reason. Philosophy and Torah, when both are properly understood, are 'sisters' and 'twins'. The rabbinic saying, 'Rabbi Meir found a pomegranate; he ate what was within and discarded the peel' (Hagigah 15b), means that one must accept what is true and concordant with Torah in philosophy. Reason can verify religious truth, and faith perfects reason.

To reject philosophy because some philosophers have erred is like denying water to a person dying of thirst, just because some people have drowned. A Jew must learn the truth from any source, as one takes honey from a bee. For 'all nations share in the sciences; they are not peculiar to one people' (*Sefer ha-Ma'alot*). Thus: 'Accept the truth from whoever utters it; look at the content, not the speaker' (*Sefer ha-Ma'alot*). Since true human perfection is intellectual, dissemination of philosophy in Hebrew and rebuttal of its detractors serve a religious as well as a cultural need.

Ibn Falaquera's rationalism is manifest throughout his works, including his Biblical exegesis and his specific theses. He equates his Platonizing doctrine of creation with the account of Genesis, and he reads his intellectualism into Biblical ethics to derive an extreme asceticism which does not stop short of misogyny: ethical and social commitments are 'impediments' to true, intellectual fulfillment. Ibn Falaquera combines his deep concern for the education of his people with the belief that genuine felicity is attained by the individual who is 'solitary' (*mitboded*), isolated not physically but spiritually from the external distractions of society and the internal promptings of the appetites. Knowledge of God begins with self-knowledge, knowledge of one's own soul: 'Know your soul, O man, and you will know your Creator'. Psychology is thus prior to all other sciences: 'Knowledge of the soul is prior to the knowledge of God, and . . . is the most excellent form of knowledge after the knowledge of God' (*Sefer ha-Nefesh*; *De'ot ha-Philosofim* VI:A:1).

Ibn Falaquera was not an original thinker of the first order, but the breadth and depth of his knowledge of Judaism, philosophy and science make him an important figure in the history of Jewish philosophy. The pioneering philosophical efforts of earlier luminaries attained an enduring impact through their consolidation and popularization by philosophers like Ibn Falaquera, whose contribution is no less

important for the fact that their light was often a reflected one.

See also: MAIMONIDES, M.

List of works

Most of Falaquera's works exist in nineteenth or twentieth century Hebrew editions; some, accompanied by introductions or translations into European languages. See Jospe 1988: 485–97 for a more detailed bibliography.

Ibn Falaquera, Shem Tov (1223/8–after 1290) *Sefer ha-Ma'alot* (Book of Degrees), ed. L. Venetianer, Berlin, 1894; photo repr. in *Kitvei Rabbi Shem Tov Falaquera*, Jerusalem: Maqor, 1970. (An ethical work on the degrees of human perfection.)

—— (1223/8–after 1290) *Sefer ha-Nefesh* (Book of the Soul), Warsaw, 1924; photo repr. in *Kitvei Rabbi Shem Tov Falaquera*, Jerusalem: Maqor, 1970; ed. and trans. R. Jospe in *Torah and Sophia: The Life and Thought of Shem Tov ibn Falaquera*, Cincinnati, OH: Hebrew Union College Press. (The first systematic Hebrew work on psychology.)

—— (1223/8–after 1290) *Shelemut ha-Ma'asim* (The Perfection of Actions), ed. R. Jospe in *Torah and Sophia: The Life and Thought of Shem Tov ibn Falaquera*, Cincinnati, OH: Hebrew Union College Press. (Ethical work based on the *Nicomachean Ethics* and Arabic ethical literature.)

—— (1223/8–after 1290) *Zeri ha-Yagon* (Balm for Sorrow), trans. R.K. Barkan, 'Shem Tob ben Joseph ibn Falaquera's *Sori Yagon* or "Balm for Assuaging Grief"', Its Literary Sources and Traditions', Ph.D. thesis, Columbia University, 1971; repr. Ann Arbor, MI: University Microfilms, 1981. (A valuable study of the sources in classical and Arabic consolation literature.)

—— (1223/8–after 1290) *Iggeret ha-Vikuah* (Epistle of the Debate), ed. A. Jellinek, Vienna, 1875; photo repr. in *Kitvei Rabbi Shem Tov Falaquera*, Jerusalem: Maqor, 1970; ed. G. Dahan, 'Epistola Dialogi: Une Traduction Latine de L'*Igeret Ha-Vikuah* de Shemtov ibn Falaquera. Étude et Edition', *Sefarad* 39 (1979): 1–112; trans. S. Harvey, *Falaquera's Epistle of the Debate: An Introduction to Jewish Philosophy*, Cambridge, MA: Harvard University Press, 1987. (Dahan is a study of the Latin version of this popular work. Harvey is a clear annotated English translation with valuable appendices.)

—— (1223/8–after 1290) *Reshit Hokhmah* (The Beginning of Wisdom), ed. M. David, Berlin, 1902; photo repr. in *Kitvei Rabbi Shem Tov Falaquera*, Jerusalem: Maqor, 1970; trans. I. Efros in 'Palquera's *Reshit Hokmah* and Alfarabi's *Ihsa al'Ulum*', *Jewish Quarterly Review*, new series 25, 1934–5: 227–35. (An important annotated translation of this major work, citing Arabic sources.)

—— (1223/8–after 1290) *Perush* (Bible Commentary), fragments trans. R. Jospe and D. Schwartz, 'Shem Tov ibn Falaquera's *Lost Bible Commentary*', *Hebrew Union College Annual* 64, 1993: 167–200. (New manuscript material with English translation and notes.)

—— (1223/8–after 1290) *Iggeret ha-Halom* (Treatise of the Dream), ed. H. Malter, 'Shem Tob ben Joseph Palquera: His Treatise of the Dream', *Jewish Quarterly Review*, new series 1, 1910–11: 451–501; photo repr. in *Kitvei Rabbi Shem Tov Falaquera*, Jerusalem: Maqor, 1970. (A useful edition of this work.)

—— (1223/8–after 1290) *De'ot ha-Philosofim* (The Opinions of the Philosophers), introduction ed. M. Zonta, 'Un Dizionario Filosofico Ebraico del XIII Secolo: L'introduzione al 'Sefer De'ot ha-Filosofim' di Shem Tob ibn Falaquera', Turin: Silvio Zamorani Editore, 1992. (A carefully annotated presentation of the Introduction to Falaquera's unpublished philosophic encyclopedia.)

—— (1263) *Sefer ha-Mevaqqesh* (Book of the Seeker), ed. M. Tamah, The Hague, 1778; photo repr. in *Kitvei Rabbi Shem Tov Falaquera*, Jerusalem: Maqor, 1970; trans. M.H. Levine, *Falaquera's Book of the Seeker*, New York: Yeshiva University Press, 1976. (English translation, revised from the author's 1954 Columbia University Ph.D. thesis, which is still worth consulting in its own right (published Ann Arbor, MI: University Microfilms, 1971).)

—— (1280) *Moreh ha-Moreh* (Guide to the Guide), ed. Mordecai Leib Bislisches, Pressburg, 1837; photo repr. in *Sheloshah Qadmonei Mefarshei ha-Moreh*, Jerusalem, 1961; ed. Y. Shiffman, 'Rabbi Shem Tov ben Joseph Falaquera's *More ha-More*: A Philosophical and Philological Analysis', unpublished Ph.D. thesis, Hebrew University of Jerusalem, 1990. (Shiffman is the definitive, annotated critical edition of Ibn Falaquera's Commentary on Maimonides' *Guide to the Perplexed*, focusing on his Arabic sources.)

References and further reading

Harvey, S. (1992) 'Falaquera's Epistle of the Debate and the Maimonidean Controversy of the 1230s', in R. Link-Salinger (ed.) *Torah and Wisdom: Studies in Jewish Philosophy, Kabbalah, and Halacha: Essays in Honor of Arthur Hyman*, New York: Shengold, 75–86. (A helpful study of Ibn Falaquera

in the context of the controversy over philosophy in the century after Maimonides.)

Jospe, R. (1986) 'Rejecting Moral Virtue as the Ultimate Human End', in W.M. Brinner and S.D. Ricks (eds) *Studies in Islamic and Judaic Traditions*, Atlanta, GA: Scholars Press, 185–204. (A study of Ibn Falaquera's ethical theory, including his tendency towards asceticism, in light of tensions within Maimonides' thought.)

—— (1988) *Torah and Sophia: The Life and Thought of Shem Tov ibn Falaquera*, Cincinnati, OH: Hebrew Union College Press. (The most complete study to date of Ibn Falaquera's life and philosophy, including a critical edition and anotated translation of *Sefer ha-Nefesh* and a critical edition of *Shelemut ha-Ma'asim*.)

Malter, H. (1910–11) 'Shem Tob ben Joseph Palquera: A Thinker of the Thirteenth Century', *Jewish Quarterly Review*, new series 1: 151–81. (A still useful early study of Ibn Falaquera.)

Melamed, A. (forthcoming) *The Philosopher King in Medieval and Renaissance Jewish Political Thought*, Atlanta, GA: Scholars Press. (Includes an important study of Ibn Falaquera in the context of classical, Arabic and Western political philosophy.)

Munk, S. (1857) *Mélanges de Philosophie Juive et Arabe*, Paris; repr. Paris: Vrin, 1927. (A pioneering study of Ibn Falaquera on the basis of which Munk identified Solomon ibn Gabirol as the Avicebrol of the Latin *Fons Vitae*, until then known only as a translation from the Arabic.)

Sirat, C. (1985) *A History of Jewish Philosophy in the Middle Ages*, Paris: Éditions de la Maison des Sciences de l'Homme; Cambridge: Cambridge University Press, 234–8. (Includes much previously unpublished manuscript material and recent scholarship.)

Sitskin, L. (1979) *Eight Jewish Philosophers in the Tradition of Personalism*, New York: Feldheim, 134–40. (Treats Ibn Falaquera as a significant figure in the history of Jewish philosophy.)

Zonta, M. (1995) *Un Interprete Ebreo della Filosofia di Galeno: Gli Scritti Filosofici di Galeno Nell'opera di Shem Tob ibn Falaquera* (A Hebrew Interpretation of Galen's Philosophy According to the Works of Shem Tov ibn Falaquera), Turin: Silvio Zamorani. (A careful study of Ibn Falaquera in the medieval tradition of Galen's philosophy.)

RAPHAEL JOSPE

IBN GABIROL, SOLOMON (1021/2–57/8)

Ibn Gabirol was an outstanding exemplar of the Judaeo–Arabic symbiosis of medieval Muslim Spain, a poet as well as the author of prose works in both Hebrew and Arabic. His philosophical masterwork, the Mekor Hayyim *(Fountain of Life), was well known to the Latin scholastics in its twelfth century Latin translation, the* Fons Vitae. *The work presents a Neoplatonic conception of reality, with a creator God at the apex. The universal hylomorphism that pervades the created order, both spiritual and corporeal, has divine will as the intermediary between God and creation, allowing Ibn Gabirol to avoid the rigidly determinist emanationism of his Greek predecessors. The* Fons Vitae *challenged such philosophers as Thomas Aquinas and Duns Scotus to critical reflections regarding individuation and personal immortality.*

1 Life and writings
2 Philosophical thought
3 Influence

1 Life and writings

Solomon ben Judah Ibn Gabirol was born in Malaga, Spain, and reared in Saragossa. He spent his brief life under the enlightened reign of the Umayyad caliphate in Saragossa, Granada and finally Valencia, where he died between 1054 and 1070, most likely in 1057/8. Within a century of his death less tolerant regimes would hold sway, but for the moment Jews took an active part in the heady intellectual and literary life of Andalusia. Ibn Gabirol's poetry addresses both religious and secular themes. His *Keter Malkhut* (Kingly Crown) is a paean to God and creation. Its vivid expression of the poet's philosophical cosmology continues in use in some traditions of Jewish liturgy. Two philosophical prose works survive, both written originally in Arabic: the *Mekor Hayyim* (Fountain of Life), translated into Latin as *Fons Vitae*, and the *Tikkun Middot ha-Nefesh* (On the Improvement of Moral Qualities). The latter, written in 1045, survives in a fourteenth century Judaeo–Arabic manuscript; the former is represented in its original form only fragmentarily, but the twelfth-century Latin version is extant and was influential in Christian circles.

2 Philosophical thought

Ibn Gabirol's Neoplatonism is influenced by the Liber de causis, a ninth-century Arabic composition based

on Proclus' *Elements of Theology* (see LIBER DE CAUSIS). More proximately, his work is influenced by the writings of Isaac ISRAELI and the pseudo-Empedoclean *Book of the Five Substances*. His philosophical poetry is expressive of Neoplatonic themes such as the soul/body dualism that undergirds what might be called Ibn Gabirol's rational mysticism: corporeal existence is devalued, in so far as it is deemed to block the path to knowledge and true felicity.

The *Tikkun Middot ha-Nefesh* comprises five parts, each of four chapters. It traces the development of some twenty moral traits to roots in specific physical senses. Pride and humility are assigned to sight; love and hate, to hearing; joy and sorrow, to taste; anger and jealousy, to smell; liberality and niggardliness, to touch. The connections are hardly perspicuous, and Ibn Gabirol does not explain them thoroughly except by introducing biblical passages suggestive of his theme. Yet it is clear that for him the body as well as the soul plays a role in the formation of virtue and thus in the attainment of happiness, which depends on achieving the proper balance among the bodily humours.

Ibn Gabirol's interest in the duality of body and soul is equally marked in the *Mekor Hayyim*, with its central polarity of matter and form. Written as a dialogue between master and pupil, the five books or treatises of the work propose a Neoplatonic cosmology and ontology along with a complementary epistemology that makes knowledge of the external world (and thus natural science) not merely dependent on self-knowledge but in fact a recapitulation of our self-awareness. As in Plotinus (*Enneads* 1.6: 8–9), the macrocosm is contained within the microcosm.

Ibn Gabirol's ontology is triadic: God, the divine will and the hylomorphic substances are its prime components. All created substances, whether spiritual or corporeal, are conjuncts of matter and form. Spiritual substances are individuated by intelligible matter; and corporeal substances, by virtue of their place in the hierarchy of being, are composed of a plurality of forms. Both doctrines, that of intelligible matter and that of the plurality of forms, occasioned controversy among the Christian scholastics. Intelligible matter, upheld by some to account for the individuation of incorporeal entities and to differentiate such entities from God, seemed to others an incoherent notion that collapsed the very duality upon which Neoplatonic metaphysics is based. The plurality of forms, required by the emanationist programme and intended to account for the essence of corporeal entities, seemed to endanger the *unity* of the individual. A question arose whether living beings are composed of one soul or many; and if the latter, as

Ibn Gabirol held, it was asked, how can such a composite being can be a unitary entity?

Just as the Greek Neoplatonists link the One to nature via Mind (see NEOPLATONISM), Ibn Gabirol links God to the world through a series of emanations, via the divine will. The relation of this will to God, the so-called first essence, remains somewhat problematic. For this will is the creative power of God, and as such is *in* God and inseparable from his being; yet it is also the first emanation from God and so would seem to be not an attribute but a separate hypostasis. In either case, however, the divine will is the cause of all created substances, both spiritual and corporeal.

Ibn Gabirol's reliance on the creative role of the divine will and thus on the voluntariness of creation contrasts dramatically with the tactics of his Greek philosophical predecessors, whose emanationism seemed excessively deterministic to philosophers of a monotheistic stamp. Ibn Gabirol and many of his Jewish successors exalt the voluntariness of the creative act, divine or human. They see the world not as a sequence of predetermined steps or a 'timeless flowing forth of necessity', as a recent commentator has put it (Goodman 1992), but as the free act of God. Ibn Gabirol's postulation of a will that created the world is a Jewish Neoplatonist's way of safeguarding the divine from the necessitarianism of Neoplatonic emanationism. One corollary of this rejection of reductionism is the corresponding safeguarding of human freedom. If creation itself is an act of divine free will, human freedom need not be reduced to the mere product of a rigidly deterministic causal sequence. The freedom of the microcosm recapitulates that of the macrocosm.

Within the created order, matter and form are irreducible to one another (see MATTER). They emanate ultimately from different sources and are present at all levels of creation. Indeed, Ibn Gabirol (like Proclus) gives a striking and un-Aristotelian priority to matter, whose ultimate source is God, the first essence. Form derives from the divine will; its source is thus one rung removed from the deity. There is a fine irony here, in giving matter, the almost canonical source of evil, an immediate divine origin. However, the priority and divine origin of matter are driven by the assumption that matter is a genus made determinate by the imposition of successive differentiae.

3 Influence

Ibn Gabirol's philosophical work was destined to have comparatively little direct influence on later Jewish thinkers. Within a century of his death, Aristotelian trends interpenetrated with, altered and displaced Neoplatonic ones. Ibn Gabirol's philosophical influence waned, although it is strikingly visible among some later Jewish Neoplatonists and in Kabbalistic circles. His influence on Christian thinkers, however, was great. Translated into Latin by John of Spain (who may be the Jewish writer IBN DAUD) in collaboration with Dominicus Gundissalinus, the *Fons Vitae* was read and criticized by the Dominican Aristotelians Albertus Magnus (see ALBERT THE GREAT) and Thomas AQUINAS, who rejected outright its doctrine of intelligible matter on the grounds noted above. Franciscans such as BONAVENTURE and DUNS SCOTUS were more sympathetic, and Ibn Gabirol's hylomorphism seems to have fed the classic scholastic debates on identity and individuation, specifically over whether personal immortality presupposes intelligible matter, or whether form by itself can individuate particulars.

Ibn Gabirol's influence, however, was all but anonymous. His text bore no biblical or rabbinic citations as a sign of its Jewish authorship, and it came down under the (Arabicized) name of Avicebrol (or Avicebron or Avencebrol), a corruption of Ibn Gabirol. The identity of its author with the well-known Hebrew poet was rediscovered only in the nineteenth century by the French scholar Salomon Munk, who recognized fragments quoted from the work in the writings of Shem Tov IBN FALAQUERA. Perhaps by historical accident, Ibn Gabirol's philosophy becomes a paradigm of philosophical ecumenism.

See also: NEOPLATONISM; PLATONISM, MEDIEVAL

List of works

Ibn Gabirol, S. (1045) *Tikkun Middot ha-Nefesh* (On the Improvement of Moral Qualities), ed. and trans. S. Wise, *The Improvement of the Moral Qualities*, New York: AMS Press, 1966. (Hylomorphism in the context of moral philosophy.)

—— (before 1057/8?) *Mekor Hayyim* (Fountain of Life), Latin trans. *Fons Vitae*, ed. C. Baeumker, *Beiträge zur Geschichte der Philosophie des Mittelalters* 1, parts 2–4, Münster: Aschendorff, 1892–5. (The standard edition of the surviving Latin translation of Ibn Gabirol's philosophical masterwork.)

—— (before 1057/8?) *Keter Malkhut* (The Kingly Crown), trans. I. Zangwill in I. Davidson (ed.) *Selected Religious Poems of Solomon ibn Gabirol*, New York: Arno Press, 1973; trans. R. Loewe in R. Loewe, *Ibn Gabirol*, New York: Grove Weidenfeld, 1990. (A prayer to God, creator of the universe, and a celebration of divine creation.)

References and further reading

Brunner, F. (1965) *Platonisme et Aristotelisme: La Critique d'Ibn Gabirol par St. Thomas d'Aquin* (Platonism and Aristotelianism: the Critique of Ibn Gabirol by St Thomas Aquinas), Louvain: Publications universitaires de Louvain. (Details Aquinas' virulent critique of Ibn Gabirol's Neoplatonism.)

* Goodman, L.E. (ed.) (1992) *Neoplatonism and Jewish Thought*, Albany, NY: State University of New York Press. (See especially Goodman's introduction and the papers by J. Dillon, B. McGinn and A. Hyman.)

Guttmann, J. (1933) *Philosophies of Judaism*, New York: Schocken Books, 2nd edn , 1973, 101–17. (A good brief account of the *Fons Vitae* in a standard history of Jewish philosophy.)

Husik, I. (1916) *A History of Medieval Jewish Philosophy*, New York: Athenaeum, 2nd edn, 1976, 59–79. (A good brief account of both the *Fons Vitae* and the *Tikkun Middot ha-Nefesh*.)

Rudavsky, T. (1978) 'Conflicting Motifs: Ibn Gabirol on Matter and Evil', *New Scholasticism* 52: 54–71. (An important recent article detailing Ibn Gabirol's disparate, perhaps inconsistent views on matter and its relation to evil.)

Schlanger, J. (1968) *La Philosophie de Salomon ibn Gabirol*, Leiden: Brill. (The most important recent and comprehensive study.)

Sirat, C. (1985) *A History of Jewish Philosophy in the Middle Ages*, Cambridge: Cambridge University Press, 68–81. (A short account that focuses on the metaphysics of both the *Fons Vitae* and the philosophical poem *Keter Malkhut*.)

DANIEL H. FRANK

IBN HAZM, ABU MUHAMMAD 'ALI (994–1063)

Ibn Hazm was the originator of a school of interpretation which based its understanding of religious texts on the apparent meaning of scriptural concepts as opposed to their hidden meaning. He argued that there is a place for reason in the understanding of scripture, but that it has to be used within the context of revelation and is severely limited in terms of what it can demonstrate. His approach is based on the idea that the language and context of religious texts are sufficient for their readers to understand them, and that there is no need to use concepts such as analogy.

Abu Muhammad 'Ali ibn Hazm was born into an important Andalusian family and went on to have a rather tumultuous political career, being imprisoned three times and banished from Cordoba on several occasions. He is best known for his writings on jurisprudence, and also for his charming *Tawq al-hamama* (The Dove's Neck Ring), which deals with the concept of love. In it he analyses the concept and differentiates between divine love, which is placed at the highest level, and affection, which is the lowest. Clearly influenced by Plato's *Phaedrus* and *Symposium*, he regards love as the coming together of otherwise incomplete beings (see PLATO). Genuine love occurs when the lover sees beneath the surface of the appearance something which presents an idea of his own nature, and thus becomes strongly attracted by it. Weaker forms of affection result when the individual is limited to the form of the appearance, but perceives nothing deeper beyond it (see LOVE).

Ibn Hazm is the leading exponent of the Zahirite school of jurisprudence. This school adheres to the exoteric or apparent (*zahir*) meaning of the religious text, in accordance with the principles of grammar, the *hadith* (traditions) of the Prophet and the consensus (*ijma'*) of the community. The main opponents of this view are those Muslims who appeal to the esoteric meaning – such as the Isma'ilis, for example – because they think that one needs to look beyond the surface of the text to discover what it really means, and also the philosophers, who insist that reason is a vital means of gaining access to the meaning of scripture. This is more than a dispute about jurisprudence; it affects the understanding of the way in which texts are to be interpreted. Ibn Hazm attacks the notion that one can understand the meaning of a text by using principles such as analogy, as the Mu'tazilites do, to acquire some grasp of the nature of God. The latter argue that we can understand the *sifat*, the names or qualities of God, by analogy from our understanding of our own characteristics; so, for example, we can grasp what it means for God to be just if we understand what human justice is (see ASH'ARIYYA AND MU'TAZILA). According to Ibn Hazm, however, God is a unique being whose qualities cannot be grasped rationally but have to be accepted through faith. There is no objective standard of justice with which God has to concur. He could have obliged us to act in impossible ways, and set out to punish angels and reward the evil. To deny this is to anthropomorphize the concept of God, which is going beyond the nature of the language in Islam about God. The Zahirite uses reason to get an accurate view of the language of the relevant texts and the supplementary hermeneutical material, and stops there (see GOD, CONCEPTS OF; ISLAMIC THEOLOGY).

What role does reason play, then, in Ibn Hazm's understanding of the meaning of important concepts? Reason is important, and essential in any understanding of the facts. We have to use reason to work out what the facts of a particular situation are, but we cannot use it to identify its ethical or religious character. Within the context of revelation, reason has a role to play, but it is an essentially subsidiary role. In comprehending religious language we have to use reason to interpret the text, but we must be aware of the dangers of overelaborating and departing from the apparent meaning. Sometimes people are impressed with the ability of reason to delve into the mysteries of reality, yet all that emerges are disputes about what texts mean and what the nature of the law is. We can avoid this, according to Ibn Hazm, if we stick to the apparent meaning of the text and maintain the autonomy of God. God can do anything at all, he is absolutely free, and we are very limited in our ability to use reason to encompass him. We can use the laws of logic, Arabic grammar and the evidence of our senses, but that is all.

By the time of his death, Ibn Hazm had succeeded in establishing the Zahiri school of interpretation, which followed his particular approach to hermeneutics and which was solidly within the Asha'rite and Sunni tradition. The most distinguished follower of this form of thought was AL-GHAZALI, who was clearly heavily influenced by Ibn Hazm.

See also: ASH'ARIYYA AND MU'TAZILA; GOD, CONCEPTS OF; ISLAMIC THEOLOGY; LAW, ISLAMIC PHILOSOPHY OF

List of works

Ibn Hazm (994–1063) *Tawq al-hamama* (The Dove's Neck Ring), trans. A. Arberry, *The Ring of the Dove*, London: Luzac, 1953. (A systematic treatment of love and affection, combining metaphysics, social commentary and psychology.)

—— (994–1063) *al-Fisal fi'l milal wa'l ahwa' wa'n nihal* (Treatise on Religions and Schools of Thought), Cairo: Maktabat al-Khanji, no date; trans. M. Asín Palacios, *Abenhάzam de Córdoba y su historia crítica de las ideas religiosas*, Madrid: Real Academica de la Historia, 1927–32. (A treatise on the religions and beliefs which presents the first comparative work of its kind in Arabic.)

—— (994–1063) *Mudawat an-nufus* (Character and Behaviour), ed. and trans. N. Tomiche, Beirut, 1961; trans. M. Asín Palacios, *Los caracteres y la conducta, tratado de moral práctica por Abenházam de Córdoba*, Madrid: Junta para ampliación de estudios y investigaciones científicas, 1916. (Ibn Hazm's philosophical psychology, and an account of ethical development, with many interesting comments on contemporary Andalusian society.)

References and further reading

Arnaldez, R. (1984) *Grammaire et théologie chez Ibn Hazm de Cordoue: essai sur la structure et les conditions de la pensée musulmane* (The Grammar and Theology of Ibn Hazm of Cordoba: Essay on the Nature and Structure of Muslim Thought), Paris: Vrin. (A brilliant analysis of Ibn Hazm's philosophy of language as the key to his thought.)

Chejne, A. (1982) *Ibn Hazm*, Chicago: Kazi Publications. (A general account of his life and thought.)

Goldziher, I. (1884) *Die Zahiriten, ihr Lehrsystem und ihre Geschichte: Beitrag zur Geschichte der muhammedanischen Theologie* (The Zahirites, their School and its History: Contribution to the History of Islamic Theology), Leipzig: O. Schulze. (Still a very useful source of information about the school of theology which Ibn Hazm founded.)

Hourani, G. (1985) 'Reason and Revelation in Ibn Hazm's Ethical Thought', in G. Hourani (ed.) *Reason and Tradition in Islamic Ethics*, Cambridge: Cambridge University Press, 167–89. (Detailed exposition of the philosophical basis of Ibn Hazm's ethics.)

Pavlin, J. (1996) 'Sunni *Kalam* and Theological Controversies', in S.H. Nasr and O. Leaman (eds) *History of Islamic Philosophy*, London: Routledge, ch. 7, 105–18. (Account of some of the most important Sunni theologians, including Ibn Hazm.)

OLIVER LEAMAN
SALMAN ALBDOUR

IBN KAMMUNA (d. 1284)

Physician and man of letters, Ibn Kammuna left a number of writings on philosophy and religion. His treatise comparing Judaism, Christianity and Islam caused major rioting in Baghdad, forcing him to flee that city in secret. His commentary on al-Suhrawardi's Talwihat, *the major text of Islamic Illuminationist philosophy remains one of the clearest and most thorough expositions of that branch of thought.*

1 **Comparative religion**
2 **The Ishraqi tradition**
3 **Impact**

1 Comparative religion

Of the major writings of 'Izz al-Dawla Sa'd bin Mansur ibn Kammuna, only the two that compare the views of religious communities have been published thus far. The longer one, the *Tanqih al-abhath fi akhbar al-milal al-thalath* (An Overview of Investigations into the Views of the Three Faiths) is *sui generis* in medieval literature. It begins with a extended investigation of prophecy, aiming to establish in a manner acceptable to adherents of all faiths (not just the prophetic ones) that revelation does occur. Here as elsewhere, Ibn Kammuna combines ideas culled from highly diverse sources including Moses MAIMONIDES, Judah HALEVI, AL-GHAZALI and Fakhr al-Din AL-RAZI. The next next three sections examine the most important prophetic traditions: Judaism, Christianity and Islam. Each section opens with an exposition of the basic tenets of the faith concerning its revealed Scripture, followed by a series of queries or objections, and the answers that a defender of that faith may be expected to give.

The presentation is dispassionate and eschews any polemical tone. Ibn Kammuna perhaps hoped that philosophical commitments shared by readers from the different faiths, and the unique political situation – the rulers were pagan Mongols bearing allegiance to none of the three faiths – would allow a calm examination of the scriptures sacred to each. The rioting against his book was perhaps incited by religious leaders, but it is not hard to understand why both Christians and Muslims were moved to write refutations of the book. It gives considerably more space to criticism of the sacred scriptures of the two 'daughter religions' than to the Torah, and it dwells on sectarian and other internal differences in Christianity and Islam but not in Judaism – although elsewhere Ibn Kammuna wrote an entire treatise on the differences between Rabbanites and Karaites.

It is not clear whether Ibn Kammuna attempted to formulate positions reflecting an actual consensus within each community (which would lend even greater historical interest to his text), or whether he forged his own synthesis from a melange of doctrines taken from existing literature. His fusion of the Halevi's chronicle of divine revelation from Adam onwards with Maimonides' rationalistic explanation of the ancient Israelite temple cult is not attested from other sources. It suggests that the book displays an original concatenation rather than an empirical study of views then normative in the three communities.

The treatise on the two major trends within Judaism in his day is considerably shorter. It devotes about twice as much space to Rabbanite views as to the Karaites, leading Leon Nemoy to conclude that, 'dispassionate critic though he was, his sympathies nevertheless remained with the mother synagogue' (Nemoy 1968: 109).

2 The Ishraqi tradition

Ibn Kammuna's commentary on Ibn Sina's *al-Isharat wa 'l-tanbihat* is essentially a paraphrase, reflecting in a few places a somewhat different structure than the published text of IBN SINA. Among its distinctive features are its division of the sciences, particularly the characterization of mathematical sciences as 'proto-physical' (*ma qabla al-tabiy'a*), balancing the accepted term for metaphysics, as 'what comes after the physics'. Ibn Kammuna offers his own interpretation of the story of Ibn Sina's Salman and Absal (the former symbolizes the rational soul, the latter the speculative intellect) and offers other unusual insights into the gnosis which Ibn Sina sketches in the third part of the book.

Ibn Kammuna's commentary on al-Suhrawardi's *Talwihat* is his longest work and, to judge from the number of surviving manuscripts, his most widely read. It seems to have played no small role in the development the 'illuminationist' (*ishraqi*) school of philosophy. Corbin noted the value of its exposition as well as its critical importance for establishing the text of the *Talwihat*. Nonetheless, about all that is available in print of this work are some brief quotations in Corbin's study and translations of selected passages by Shlomo Pines in footnotes to his studies of Abu 'l Barakat AL-BAGHDADI. The commentary is encyclopaedic, its discussions much fuller than those in the commentary on Avicenna. It promises to be a rich source for the exposition of Ishraqi philosophy and for a broad range of topics debated by thinkers of the period. The legitimacy of the so-called fourth figure of the syllogism, the possibility of alchemical transmutation of metals, and the nature of time are among the topics on which Ibn Kammuna offers lengthy disquisitions.

3 Impact

We know from manuscript catalogues that Ibn Kammuna wrote a number of other treatises in addition to those discussed above, but the only one published thus far is a short work on the immortality of the soul, a typically thorough survey. His impact on Jewish thought was minimal at best. Only his treatises on comparative religion and al-Suhrawardi were transcribed into Hebrew characters, none was widely diffused, and no citations of his writings have been found in the work of any other Jewish thinker. His works seem to have addressed the general, rather than the Jewish, public; the most influential of them, as noted, being his commentary on al-Suhrawardi.

See also: ILLUMINATIONIST PHILOSOPHY; AL-SUHRAWARDI

List of works

Ibn Kammuna (before 1284) *The Arabic Treatise on the Immortality of the Soul by Sa'd ibn Mansur ibn Kammuna, facsimile reproduction of the only known manuscript... with a bibliographical note by Leon Nemoy*, ed. L. Nemoy, New Haven, CN: Yale University Library, 1944; trans. L. Nemoy, 'Ibn Kammuna's Treatise on the Immortality of the Soul', in S. Löwinger, A. Scheiber and J. Somogyi (eds) *Ignace Goldziher Memorial Volume*, Jerusalem: Rubin Mass, 1958, part II, 83–99. (The original Arabic work had no title: 'Treatise on the Immortality of the Soul' is the title given to the work by Nimoy.)

—— (before 1284) *Tanqih al-abhath fi akhbar al-milal al-thalath* (An Overview of Investigations into the Views of the Three Faiths), ed. M. Perlman, *Ibn Kammuna's Examination of the Inquiries into the Three Faiths*, Berkeley, CA: University of California, 1967; trans. M. Perlman, *Ibn Kammuna's Examination of the Three Faiths*, Berkeley, CA: University of California, 1971. (The 1971 translation contains Arabic text and English translation, both with a short introduction, and brief notes.)

—— (before 1284) Commentary on Ibn Sina's *al-Isharat wa 'l-tanbihat*. (No studies of this work have been undertaken and there are at present no editions; it exists as a manuscript in the British Library, I.O. Loth 484.)

—— (before 1284) 'Ibn Kammunah's Treatise on the Differences between the Rabbanites and the Karaites', ed. L. Nemoy, *Proceedings of the American Academy for Jewish Research* 36, 1968: 107–65. (Text, transcribed into Arabic characters, translation, and introduction. The original work had no title; 'Treatise on Differences' is the title given to the work by Nemoy.)

References and further reading

Corbin, H. (1945) *Şihabaddin Yahya as-Suhrawardi Opera Metaphysica et Mystica* (Metaphysical and Mystical Works of al-Suhrawardi), Istanbul: Maarif Matbaasi, vol. 1, pp. lxii–lxxiii. (Extensive discussion of the commentary on *al-Talwihat*, especially with regard to the establishment of the text.)

Baneth, D.H. (1925) 'Ibn Kammuna', *Monatsschrift für Geschichte und Wissenschaft des Judenthums* 69: 295–311. (Thorough refutation of Steinschneider's contention that Ibn Kammuna converted to Islam; contains many additional insights.)

* Nemoy, L. (1968) 'New Data for the Biography of Sa'd ibn Kammunah', *Revue des études juives* 123: 507–10. (Some biographical facts, with additional confimation that Ibn Kammuna never abandoned Judaism.)

Steinschneider, M. (1902) *Die arabische Literatur der Juden* (The Arabic Literature of the Jews), Frankfurt: J. Kaufman, 239–40. (List of works and manuscripts.)

Y. TZVI LANGERMANN

IBN KHALDUN, 'ABD AL-RAHMAN (1332–1406)

Ibn Khaldun's work on the philosophy of history is a landmark of social thought. Many historians – Greek, Roman, Muslim and other – had written valuable historiography, but here we have brilliant reflections on the meaning, pattern and laws of history and society, as well as profound insights into the nature of social processes and the interconnections between phenomena in such diverse fields as politics, economics, sociology and education. By any reckoning, Ibn Khaldun was the outstanding figure in the social sciences between Aristotle and Machiavelli, and one of the greatest philosophers of history of all time.

His most important philosophical work is the Muqaddima, *the introduction to a much longer history of the Arabs and Berbers. In this work, Ibn Khaldun clearly defines a science of culture and expounds on the nature of human society and on political and social cycles. Different social groups, nomads, townspeople and traders, interact with and affect one another in a continuous pattern. Religion played an important part in Ibn Khaldun's conception of the state, and he followed al-Ghazali rather than Ibn Rushd as a surer guide to the truth.*

1 Life and cultural context
2 Philosophy of history
3 Critique of Islamic philosophy

1 Life and cultural context

Abu Zayd 'Abd al-Rahman ibn Khaldun al-Hadrami was born in Tunis in AH 732/AD 1332. He was deeply rooted in his Islamic background, occupying high government posts in Granada, Morocco, Algeria, Tunisia and Egypt. He spent four years among the Bedouins, and negotiated with both Pedro the Cruel of Spain in Seville and with Timur Lenk (Tamurlane) on the outskirts of Damascus. He was deeply versed in Arabic literature, theology, historiography, jurisprudence and philosophy, and was particularly influenced in the latter by Averroes or IBN RUSHD. He died in Cairo in AH 808/AD 1406.

Ibn Khaldun lived at a time when it was possible to reflect upon a long and profound period of Islamic thought, and he seems to have felt that part of his function as a writer was to sum up this period, with the further aim of pointing towards the future of Islamic intellectual enquiry. As one would expect, he used the terms and concepts of his time, and some have argued that he was a culturally-specific phenomenon (al-Azmeh 1981), so that any attempt at interpreting his thought in Western terms must distort it fatally. This is an error. Like all great thinkers, Ibn Khaldun's thought contains both specific and universal elements, and the latter can readily be conveyed to modern readers with no more than the usual difficulties of translation from one cultural and historical period to another.

2 Philosophy of history

The work on which Ibn Khaldun's reputation chiefly rests is the *Muqaddima*, the introduction to his great history of the Arabs and Berbers, the *Kitab al-'ibar*, which is divided into a further six books. In the first book he presents a general account of sociology, in the second and third a sociology of politics, in the fourth a sociology of urban life, in the fifth a sociology of economics and in the sixth a sociology of knowledge. The whole work is studded with brilliant observations. Thus in the field of economics, Ibn Khaldun understands very clearly the supply and demand factors which affect price, the interdependence of prices and the ripple effects on successive stages of production of a fall in prices, and the nature and function of money and its tendency to circulate from country to country according to demand and the level of activity. In his writings on public finance, he shows why at the beginning of a dynasty taxation yields a large revenue from low rates of assessment, but at the end a small revenue from high rates of assessment. Elsewhere his observations on the evolution of the Arabic language and script are masterly

examples of sociological analysis, and his remarks on the difference between acquiring a skill in a language and learning its grammar, and on the use of intuition as opposed to logic in solving difficult problems, can still be read with profit.

However, it is Ibn Khaldun's views on the nature of the state and society which reveal most clearly both his profundity and the originality that marks him off so sharply from his Muslim predecessors and successors. Ibn Khaldun fully realised that he had created a new discipline, *'ilm al-'umran*, the science of culture, and regarded it as surprising that no one had done so before and demarcated it from other disciplines. This science can be of great help to the historian by creating a standard by which to judge accounts of past events. Through the study of human society, one can distinguish between the possible and the impossible, and so distinguish between those of its phenomena which are essential and those which are merely accidental, and also those which cannot occur at all. He analysed in detail the sources of error in historical writings, in particular partisanship, overconfidence in sources, failure to understand what is intended, a mistaken belief in the truth, the inability to place an event in its real context, the desire to gain the favour of those in high rank, exaggeration, and what he regarded as the most important of all, ignorance of the laws governing the transformation of human society. Ibn Khaldun's attitude to the study of social phenomena is suffused with a spirit which has caused several commentators to call him the founder of sociology. His attempt at creating a theoretical structure for the analysis of history is a very impressive contribution to the philosophy of history (see HISTORY, PHILOSOPHY OF; SOCIETY, CONCEPT OF).

For Ibn Khaldun, human society is necessary since the individual acting alone could acquire neither the necessary food nor security. Only the division of labour, in and through society, makes this possible. The state arises through the need of a restraining force to curb the natural aggression of humanity. A state is inconceivable without a society, while a society is well-nigh impossible without a state (see POLITICAL PHILOSOPHY IN CLASSICAL ISLAM). Social phenomena seem to obey laws which, while not as absolute as those governing natural phenomena, are sufficiently constant to cause social events to follow regular and well-defined patterns and sequences. Hence a grasp of these laws enables the sociologist to understand the trend of events. These laws operate on masses and cannot be significantly influenced by isolated individuals. There is very little talk of 'great men' in Ibn Khaldun's books; while individuals do affect the course of events, their influence is very limited.

The overwhelming impression given by Ibn Khaldun's writings is that society is an organism that obeys its own inner laws. These laws can be discovered by applying human reason to data either culled from historical records or obtained by direct observation. These data are fitted into an implicit framework derived from his views on human and social nature, his religious beliefs and the legal precepts and philosophical principles to which he adheres. He argues that more or less the same set of laws operates across societies with the same kind of structure, so that his remarks about nomads apply equally well to Arab Bedouins, both contemporary and pre-Islamic, and to Berbers, Turkomen and Kurds. These laws are explicable sociologically, and are not a mere reflection of biological impulses or physical factors. To be sure, facts such as climate and food are important, but he attributes greater influence to such purely social factors as cohesion, occupation and wealth. This comes out very clearly in his discussion of national characters, for example of Arabs, Persians and Jews, where he is careful to point out that what are regarded as characteristic features can be explained by sociological factors such as nomadism, urbanization and oppression. Similarly, different social groups, such as townspeople, nomads and traders, have their own characteristics derived from their occupations.

Ibn Khaldun sees the historical process as one of constant cyclical change, due mainly to the interaction of two groups, nomads and townspeople. These form the two poles of his mental map; peasants are in between, supplying the towns with food and tax revenue and taking handicrafts in return. Nomads are rough, savage and uncultured, and their presence is always inimical to civilization; however, they are hardy, frugal, uncorrupt in morals, freedom-loving and self-reliant, and so make excellent fighters. In addition, they have a strong sense of 'asabiya, which can be translated as 'group cohesion' or 'social solidarity'. This greatly enhances their military potential. Towns, by contrast, are the seats of the crafts, the sciences, the arts and culture. Yet luxury corrupts them, and as a result they become a liability to the state, like women and children who need to be protected. Solidarity is completely relaxed and the arts of defending oneself and of attacking the enemy are forgotten, so they are no match for conquering nomads.

Ibn Khaldun then traces very clearly the political and social cycle. Nomads conquer territories and their leaders establish a new dynasty. At first the new rulers retain their tribal virtues and solidarity, but soon they seek to concentrate all authority in their own hands. Increasingly they rule through a bureaucracy of clients – often foreigners. As their former supporters lose their military virtues there is an increasing use of mercenaries, and soldiers come to be more important than civilians. Luxury corrupts ethical life, and the population decreases. Rising expenditure demands higher taxes, which discourage production and eventually result in lower revenues. The ruler and his clients become isolated from the groups that originally brought them to power. Such a process of decline is taken to last three generations, or about one hundred and twenty years. Religion can influence the nature of such a model; when 'asabiya is reinforced by religion its strength is multiplied, and great empires can be founded. Religion can also reinforce the cohesion of an established state. Yet the endless cycle of flowering and decay shows no evolution or progress except for that from the primitive to civilized society.

Ibn Khaldun does occasionally refer to the existence of turning points in history, and thought that he was himself witnessing one of them. The main cause for this great change was the Black Death, which had a profound effect upon Muslim society, together with the Mongol invasions; and he may also have been impressed by the development of Europe, whose merchants and ships thronged the seaports of North Africa and whose soldiers served as mercenaries in the Muslim armies. He suggests that a general change in conditions can produce an entirely new social and political scene, rather as if a new world had been created.

3 Critique of Islamic philosophy

Ibn Khaldun wrote on other topics apart from history, although in his autobiography he is rather coy about admitting it. In his *Shifa' al-sa'il* (The Healing of the Seeker), he responds to the question as to whether it is possible to attain mystical knowledge without the help of a Sufi master leading the novice along the path. Ibn Khaldun tends to follow AL-GHAZALI (§3) in reconciling mysticism with theology, but he goes further than the latter in bringing mysticism completely within the purview of the jurisprudent (*faqih*) and in developing a model of the Sufi *shaykh*, or master, as rather similar to the theologian. The fourteenth century, in which Ibn Khaldun was working, was very strongly influenced by what Fakhry (1970) calls 'neo-Hanbalism', which brought with it a strong suspicion of the claims of both mysticism and philosophy. Philosophy was regarded as going beyond its appropriate level of discourse, in that 'the intellect should not be used to weigh such matters as the oneness of God, the other world, the truth of prophecy, the real character of the divine attributes, or anything else that lies beyond the level of the intellect' (*Muqaddima* 3, 38). He refers to the intellect as like a balance which is meant for gold, but which is sometimes inappropriately used for weighing mountains. Logic cannot be applied to this area of enquiry, and must be restricted to non-theological topics (see LOGIC IN ISLAMIC PHILOSOPHY).

Ibn Khaldun is also critical of Neoplatonic philosophy (see NEOPLATONISM IN ISLAMIC PHILOSOPHY). The main object of his criticism is the notion of a hierarchy of being, according to which human thought can be progressively purified until it encompasses the First Intellect which is identified with the necessary being, that is, God. He argued that this process is inconceivable without the participation of revelation, so that it is impossible for human beings to achieve the highest level of understanding and happiness through the use of reason alone. Interestingly, the basis of his argument here rests on the irreducibility of the empirical nature of our knowledge of facts, which cannot then be converted into abstract and pure concepts at a higher level of human consciousness.

Ibn Khaldun also had little respect for the political theories of thinkers like AL-FARABI (§4), with their notions of rational government being based upon an ideal prophetic law. He saw little point in using theories which dealt with ideals that have nothing to do with the practicalities of contemporary political life. Although Ibn Khaldun rarely agrees with IBN RUSHD, there is no doubt that his thought is strongly marked by the controversy between him and al-Ghazali, the latter being acknowledged as the surer guide to the truth. The basis of Ibn Khaldun's critique of philosophy is his adherence to the notion of the state. Religion has a vital role in society, and any argument that it can be identified with either reason or contact with God is to threaten that function. This is doubtless the basis of his attack on Islamic philosophy and on mysticism.

Although Ibn Khaldun is hostile to a version of Islamic philosophy, his discussion of society is full of observations and ideas which clearly have as their source philosophical distinctions. For example, his account of the three stages in the development of the state, from the nomadic to the militant and finally to the luxurious and decadent is modelled on the three types of soul in Greek thought (see SOUL IN ISLAMIC PHILOSOPHY §2), as is his notion of 'asabiya, of the spirit of cohesion, as a point of equilibrium between different aspects of the soul. One of the features of Ibn Khaldun's work which makes it so thought-provoking is the tension, which he never finally resolved, between a concern to acknowledge the facts of historical change while at the same time bringing those facts under very general theoretical principles. His contribution to the philosophy of history is outstanding.

See also: CULTURE; HISTORY, PHILOSOPHY OF; POLITICAL PHILOSOPHY, HISTORY OF; POLITICAL PHILOSOPHY IN CLASSICAL ISLAM

List of works

Ibn Khaldun (1332–1406) *Shifa' al-sa'il li-tahdib al-masa'il* (The Healing of the Seeker), ed. M. al-Tanji, 1957; trans. R. Pérez, *La voie et la loi ou le maître et le juriste*, Paris: Sindbad, 1991. (Ibn Khaldun's work on Sufism.)

—— (1332–1406) *Muqaddima*, ed. and trans. F. Rosenthal, *The Muqaddimah*, Princeton, NJ: Princeton University Press, 1967. (Outstanding translation of this key introduction to Ibn Khaldun's history of the Arabs and Berbers, the *Kitab al-'ibar*.)

References and further reading

* al-Azmeh, A. (1981) *Ibn Khaldun in Modern Scholarship: A Study in Orientalism*, London: Third World Centre. (A lively defence of the view that most previous commentators have misunderstood Ibn Khaldun.)

—— (1990) *Ibn Khaldun: An Essay in Reinterpretation*, London: Routledge. (A guide to the general thought of Ibn Khaldun.)

* Fakhry, M. (1970) *A History of Islamic Philosophy*, New York: Columbia University Press; repr. 1985. (A useful account of Ibn Khaldun's position in Islamic philosophy as a whole.)

Issawi, C. (1986) *An Arab Philosophy of History*, Princeton, NJ: Princeton University Press. (Translation and commentary on some important texts.)

—— (1994) *Ibn Khaldun on Roman History: A Study in Sources*, Princeton, NJ: Princeton Papers in Near Eastern Studies. (Ibn Khaldun's treatment of Roman history.)

Lakhsassi, A. (1996) 'Ibn Khaldun', in S.H. Nasr and O. Leaman (eds) *History of Islamic Philosophy*, London: Routledge, ch. 25, 350–64. (Comprehensive guide to Ibn Khaldun's thought, emphasizing the links between his social theories and philosophical ideas.)

Mahdi, M. (1957) *Ibn Khaldun's Philosophy of History*, London: Allen & Unwin. (A study of the philosophical foundations of his theory of culture.)

Rosenthal, E. (1956) 'The Theory of the Power-State: Ibn Khaldun's Study of Civilization', in E. Rosenthal, *Political Thought in Medieval Islam*,

Cambridge: Cambridge University Press. (A masterly summary of Ibn Khaldun's political philosophy.)

CHARLES ISSAWI
OLIVER LEAMAN

IBN MAIMON, MUSA *see*
MAIMONIDES, MOSES

IBN MASARRA, MUHAMMAD IBN 'ABD ALLAH (883–931)

Muhammad ibn Masarra is said to be responsible for the first structuring of Andalusian Spanish Muslim philosophy. The thrust of his philosophy was to show the agreement between reason and revelation. The two paths taken by honest philosophers and prophets lead to the same goal of reaching the knowledge of the oneness of God. We can only know that God exists but not what His nature is. Ibn Masarra held that the divine attributes of knowledge, will and power are a distinct aspect of the simple and ineffable essence of God, and the Neoplatonic theory that all beings have emanated from him through the First Intellect and are either invisible or apparent. There are two sciences, one of the invisible, transcendental world, the other of the apparent and sensible world. The inner meanings in the sciences can be learned through the science of letters. By studying the enigmatic letters at the beginning of the Qur'anic surahs, one can decipher the secret knowledge of the truth symbolized by them.

1 **Life and times**
2 **Doctrines**
3 **God's attributes**
4 **God's creation**
5 **Esoterism and mysticism**

1 Life and times

Muhammad ibn 'Abd Allah ibn Masarra was born in Cordoba, Spain, in AH 269/AD 883 and died in AH 319/AD 931. In a hermitage he had founded for his friends and disciples in the Sierra of Cordoba, Ibn Masarra undertook to instruct them in his doctrines, to initiate them into the use of esoteric knowledge and to practice *zuhd* (asceticism) through acts of penance and devotion. His success came from a Socratic style of pedagogy as well as a charismatic personality and skill in communication. After his death the jurists carried out a veritable persecution of his disciples; who had formed themselves into an ascetic order, the Masarriya, in Cordoba and later in Almeria.

Two of Ibn Masarra's four works, *Kitab al-i'tibar* (On Reflection) and *Kitab khawass al-huruf* (Characteristics of Letters), were published in 1982. Both are short tracts which have provided a better understanding of his thought, but because of their conciseness they raise new questions. It is still not possible to reconstruct his philosophical system until the remaining works are found, especially his *Tawhid al-muqinin* (The Certain Profession of the Oneness of God), where he discussed God's attributes.

2 Doctrines

M. Asín Palacios, the Spanish scholar who first reconstructed an integral account of Ibn Masarra's life and thought, concluded that he was the first Andalusian to structure Spanish Islamic philosophy (*hikma*) and that he conveyed his doctrines in a series of *batini* (inward) esoteric images and symbols (Asín Palacios 1972). The centrepiece of Asín's thesis, however, was the elaboration of a whole theory of Ibn Masarra's inspiration from a pseudo-Empedocles, who had developed a peculiar form of Plotinian ideas on the One and the five eternal substances of Primal Matter, Intellect, Soul, Nature and Secondary Matter. According to Asín, Ibn Masarra was the founder of a philosophical–mystical school which influenced Jewish, Christian and Muslim medieval philosophers. Andalusian Sufism from Isma'il al-Ru'ayni (d. AH 555/AD 1268) to IBN AL-'ARABI by way of Ibn al-'Arif (d. AH 536/AD 1141) sprang from the Masarri school.

The thrust of Ibn Masarra's philosophy is to demonstrate the agreement of reason and revelation. Each takes a different path leading to the same goal, *al-tawhid*, the knowledge of the oneness of God. By using *'aql*, the intellect with which God endowed human beings, they reflect on God's signs and rise step by step to the knowledge of the Truth. Those who ascend by way of reason proceed from the bottom up and discover the same truth the Prophets have brought down from on high. In fact, the Qur'an invites us to reflect on the signs of his creation. Reflection (*i'tibar*) only confirms prophecy; what is learned by authority (*sama'*) is confirmed by investigation. Ibn Masarra admits, however, that the philosophers and the ancients had attained the knowledge of the true One well before the age of prophecy and without its mediation, a position not acceptable to the religious scholars.

Ibn Masarra conceives of two sciences both created by God. One, the science of the invisible and

627

intelligible reality (*'ilm al-ghayb*), which cannot be grasped by the senses, is created whole, entire and at once. The other is the science of the apparent and sensible reality (*'ilm al-shahada*) (Surah 6: 73). The Qur'an, the speech of God, is one whole in its divine essence, but diversified (*mufassal*) with respect to creation. It displays three aspects, each the subject of a different science: the science of divinity (*rububiya*), its signs, evidences and certainty; the science of prophecy with its demonstrative arguments, signs and necessity; and the science of tribulation (*mihna*) with its laws, promises and threats.

3 God's attributes

God transcends all human thought and all we can know about his nature is that he exists. His attributes are distinct from him, that is, from his essence (*dhat*). They are, however, related to each other. Strangely enough, Ibn Masarra concludes from that relationship the finitude or creation of the attributes. Like many Mu'tazilite theologians of his time in the East, he distinguished between the attributes of the essence, which are eternal, and the attributes of action, which are created. This was a way to which the Mu'tazilites resorted in order to assert the oneness and ineffability of God while maintaining human free will and responsibility. God's knowledge is only of universals; were he to know particulars, his oneness would be jeopardized and our moral responsibility denied.

In making the distinction between God's essence and his action, Ibn Masarra established three hierarchical attributes, the highest of which is connected to God's essence and the other two to his actions. These are divinity (*aluhiya*), royalty (*mulk*) and grace (*ni'ma*) or creation (*khalq*), through which God the Artificer (*al-sani'*) is manifested. This hierarchy is reflected in the way human society is organized.

4 God's creation

All beings are divided into four categories, some nobler than others in accordance with the following scheme. First, there is the Being, or essence of God (*dhat*), separate, unique, ineffable, infinite and motionless; it is the ultimate, the visible and the invisible. The remaining beings are the signs that point to Him. Second is the Universal Intellect (*al-'aql al-kulli*), which is the conception or idea of things. It is spiritual by nature and permanent. It is the Mother of the Book (*umm al-kitab*) (Surah 3: 6), and the Preserved Tablet (*al-lawh al-mahfuz*) (Surah 85: 21) on which all things are inscribed. The totality of what is in the Book is the idea (*mithal*, Eidos) of the universe,

whatever was, is or shall be. It is also the Throne (Surah 10: 2) which incites motion in response to God's volition and will. The relationship of the Intellect to God is similar to the relation of the sun's light to the sun. Third is the Great Soul (*al-nafs al-kubra*) that carries the body of the universe. The relation of the Soul to the Intellect is like the light of the moon to that of the sun. Through this Soul, immersed in materiality, Royalty (*mulk*) is constituted and the celestial spheres are held. To Royalty are predicated government and politics. Finally, lower than the Great Soul is the Physical Soul (*al-nafs al-tabi'iya*), which is completely immersed in corporeality and is the efficient cause of corporeal beings. The Throne encloses the invisible world (*'alam al-ghayb*) and the Great Soul encloses the visible (*'alam al-shahada*).

The origination of the cosmos has been achieved in time by the command 'Be' (*kun*), expressing the volition and will according to knowledge. When the One wants to do something, he causes it to appear in the Preserved Tablet. This in itself is the command (*amr*) to set the idea into action by his willing. God, according to him, is concealed from creation by two veils from the perspective of his creation, inasmuch as nothing can conceal him from the perspective of his essence. Motion is then set by the Throne, since no action *ad extra* can be attributed to the One.

Unlike the pseudo-Empedocles, who conceived of love and discord as the driving force of creation, Ibn Masarra talked about capacity and power designating them as truth (*haqq*) (Surah 2: 72). In the final analysis God is the Aristotelian unmoved mover, but in Neoplatonic style all creation emanates from him. Unlike PLOTINUS, Ibn Massara finds that the processes of emanation and creation are the results of God's will (*irada*) and deliberate action. Both he and Plotinus agree on the intermediary roles played by the Intellect and the Soul in the creation of the material world, but whereas Plotinus believed in involuntary emanation, Ibn Massara retained the Islamic view of voluntary creation (see NEOPLATONISM; NEOPLATONISM IN ISLAMIC PHILOSOPHY).

The principles from which all creatures have come are fourteen in number, ten of which are in the sublunar world: chaos (*al-'ama*), primordial dust (*al-haba'*), which is considered by some as the *materia prima*, air, wind, atmosphere, water, fire, light, darkness and clay. The remaining four, the Pen (*qalam*), the Tablet, the Command and the Spiritual locus (*makan*) exist in the world above. From the fourteen are made the Throne, paradise, hell, the seven heavens, the earth, the angels, the jinn, human beings, animals and vegetation.

5 Esoterism and mysticism

In his work *Kitab khawass al-huruf* (Book of the Characteristics of Letters), Ibn Masarra appears as an esoteric (*batini*) philosopher investigating the esoteric meanings of the *nuraniya*, the fourteen separate letters which introduce certain surahs of the Qur'an, basically following the tradition of Islamic gnosis. The mysterious letters, according to the Batini school, represented the universe so that its entirety is a book whose letters are God's words. The 'science of letters' followed by Ibn Masarra had nothing to do with divination or magic; it is merely a path to the discovery of the truths hidden behind the symbols. In this he was inspired by the work of Sahl al-Tustari (d. AH 283/AD 896), the author of a similar work on the science of letters.

Reflection (*i'tibar*) allows us to decipher the principles of all beings. The basic idea is to show that the different degrees that constitute beings in general correspond to the surah's *fawatih* (opening letters) as well as to the order of being. The letters are twenty-eight in number, equal to the length of the lunar phases. Fourteen are exoteric and the remaining fourteen are esoteric. These are used by God to manifest his knowledge: their secret meanings have been bestowed upon the Prophet Muhammad as expressed in the Qur'an, and consequently the Qur'an is the source of all knowledge, old and new. The steps leading to paradise and salvation are equal in number to the Qur'anic verses and to the number of God's beautiful names, excepting the great name of Allah.

The first letter, *alif*, is the alpha and omega of all letters inasmuch as it represents the principle of all things. It is the first manifestation of God and his will; it is a metaphor for the production of things (*takwin*), the emergence of justice and the permanent and unchanging primordial decree (*al-qada' al-awwal*). It never rests and continuously causes generation and corruption. This decree has two aspects. A prior aspect (*sabiq*) is connected to the Preserved Tablet, the tablet of the Universal Intellect where all things are inscribed. This is a decree that does not respond to invocation. The second aspect, the diversifier (*mufassil*), particularizes all things that are not permanent. Like the other attributes, the two decrees manifesting God's knowledge and power are other than God, although they are not created in time. The concept of *huduth*, or coming to be, is realized only in time; but God's knowledge, according to Ibn Masarra, whether it is knowledge of the universals or particulars, is not in time. Coming to be in time is the particularization of beings found in a locus performed by that decree that particularizes things and responds to invocation.

Human salvation can be achieved through either the *via reflectiva* or the *via prophetica*, an idea considered heretical by most Muslim theologians (see ISLAMIC THEOLOGY). In both cases, individuals have to follow certain rules in order to free their souls from the bondage of materiality. Ibn Masarra distinguishes clearly between the soul (*ruh*) and spirit (*nafs*), with the latter being the prototype (*mithal*) of the first.

There is a tradition in Andalusian literature to the effect that Ibn Masarra enjoyed great respect and veneration in spite of the fact that his teachings were criticized and refuted. On the other hand, his disciples were persecuted. Transformed into an ascetic society, his disciples first in Cordova and later in Almeria put into practice his Sufi and esoteric teachings. He is certainly one of the first mystical–philosophical Andalusians. His Sufi teachings as well as his works continued to circulate and to be studied for centuries. His influence on IBN AL-'ARABI is attested by the many references to him in the latter's works and by similarity in a number of ideas, especially in the continuous use of similes of light and illumination to describe the essence of God.

See also: IBN AL-'ARABI; MYSTICAL PHILOSOPHY IN ISLAM; NEOPLATONISM IN ISLAMIC PHILOSOPHY

List of works

Ibn Masarra (883–931) *Kitab al-i'tibar* (On Reflection), ed. M.K. Ja'far, *Min al-turath al-falsafi li-ibn Masarrah: 1. Risalat al-i'tibar, 2. Khawass al-huruf*, Cairo, 1982. (One of Ibn Massara's two surviving works.)

—— (883–931) *Kitab khawass al-huruf* (Characteristics of Letters), ed. M.K. Ja'far, *Min al-turath al-falsafi li-ibn Masarrah: 1. Risalat al-i'tibar, 2. Khawass al-huruf*, Cairo, 1982. (One of Ibn Massara's two surviving works.)

References and further reading

Addas, C. (1992) 'Andalusi Mysticism and the Rise of Ibn Arabi', in S.K. Jayyusi (ed.) *The Legacy of Muslim Spain*, Leiden: Brill. (A well-written study on Sufism in Spain including a sizeable section on Ibn Masarrah's mystical teachings.)

* Asín Palacios, M. (1972) *The Mystical Philosophy of Ibn Masarra and His Followers*, trans. E.H. Douglas and H.W. Yoder, Leiden: Brill. (Still the major work on Ibn Masarra, although some of the conclusions have been challenged.)

Arnaldez, R. (1960) 'Ibn Masarra', in *The Encyclopedia of Islam*, 2nd edn, vol. 3: 868–72. (Concise account of Ibn Masarra's life and thought.)

Cruz Hernández, M. (1981) 'La Persecución anti-Masarri durante el reinado de 'Abd al-Rahman al-Nasir li-Din Allah según Ibn Hayyan' (The Anti-Masarri Persecution During the Reign of 'Abd al-Rahman According to Ibn Hayyan), *al-Qantara* II (182): 51–67. (An analysis of the account of Ibn Hayyan's *al-Muqtabas* concerning the persecution of the disciples of Ibn Masarrah, concluding that it does not differ substantially from that of Asín.)

Goodman, L. (1996) 'Ibn Masarra', in S.H. Nasr and O. Leaman (eds) *History of Islamic Philosophy*, London: Routledge, ch. 20, 277–93. (The role of Ibn Masarra in creating a distinctive philosophy and form of mysticism in al-Andalus.)

Stern, S.M. (1983) 'Ibn Masarra, Follower of Pseudo-Empedocles – An Illusion', in F. Zimmerman (ed.) *Medieval Arabic and Hebrew Thought*, London: Variorum. (A criticism of Asín's theory.)

Ternero, E. (1993) 'Noticia sobre la publicación de obras inéditas de ibn Masarra' (Review of the Publication of Ibn Masarra's Unedited Works), *al-Qantara* XIV: 47–64. (A summary of the two works of Ibn Masarra, published for the first time in 1982.)

GEORGE N. ATIYEH

IBN MISKAWAYH, AHMAD IBN MUHAMMAD (*c.*940–1030)

Like so many of his contemporaries in the fourth and fifth centuries AH (tenth and eleventh centuries AD) Ibn Miskawayh was eclectic in philosophy, basing his approach upon the rich variety of Greek philosophy that had been translated into Arabic. Although he applied that philosophy to specifically Islamic problems, he rarely used religion to modify philosophy, and so came to be known as very much an Islamic humanist. He represents the tendency in Islamic philosophy to fit Islam into a wider system of rational practices common to all humanity.

Ibn Miskawayh's Neoplatonism has both a practical and a theoretical side. He provides rules for the preservation of moral health based on a view of the cultivation of character. These describe the ways in which the various parts of the soul can be brought together into harmony, so achieving happiness. It is the role of the moral philosopher to prescribe rules for moral health, just as the doctor prescribes rules for physical health. Moral health is based upon a combination of intellectual development and practical action.

1 Metaphysics
2 Ethical writings
3 Practical ethics and humanism

1 Metaphysics

Like so many of his philosophical contemporaries, Ahmad ibn Muhammad ibn Miskawayh, born in Rayy in Persia *c.*AH 320/AD 940, combined an active political career with an important philosophical role. A historian as well as a philosopher, he served as a Buwayhid official at Baghdad, Isfahan and Rayy. He was a member of the distinguished group of intellectuals including AL-TAWHIDI and AL-SIJISTANI. He died in AH 421/AD 1030. Although not an important figure on the creative side of Islamic philosophy, he is a very interesting adaptor of existing ideas, especially those arising out of the Neoplatonic tradition in the Islamic world (see NEOPLATONISM IN ISLAMIC PHILOSOPHY).

Ibn Miskawayh wrote on a wide variety of topics, ranging from history to psychology and chemistry, but in philosophy his metaphysics seems to have been generally informed by a version of Neoplatonism. He avoids the problem of reconciling religion with philosophy by claiming that the Greek philosophers were in no doubt concerning the unity and existence of God. He goes so far as to suggest that Aristotle's identification of the creator with an unmoved mover is a powerful argument in favour of a creator acceptable to Islam, since the very distinct nature of such a being prevents our normal categories of description from making sense. Such a creator can only be described in terms of negative concepts, an interesting prefiguration of the tradition of the *via negativa* in philosophy. He has an unusual account of emanation, wherein the deity produces the active intellect, the soul and the heavens without intermediaries, making one suspect that he did not have a firm grasp of the distinction between emanation and creation. The normal Neoplatonic account of emanation then current in Islamic philosophy used the notion of a scale of being that separates these different divine products far more radically. It is difficult to see how Ibn Miskawayh really reconciles metaphysical difficulties at this point.

2 Ethical writings

Ibn Miskawayh's work on ethics, however, is of a much higher order, and does show evidence of considerable conceptual complexity. In his *Taharat al-a'raq* (Purity of Dispositions), better known as *Tahdhib al-akhlaq* (Cultivation of Morals) – which is not to be confused by the work of the same name by

Yahya IBN 'ADI – he sets out to show how we might acquire the right dispositions to perform morally correct actions in an organized and systematic manner.

The basis of his argument is his account, adopted from PLATO, of the nature of the soul, which he sees as a self-subsisting entity or substance, in marked contrast to the Aristotelian notion (see SOUL, NATURE AND IMMORTALITY OF THE). The soul distinguishes us from animals, from other human beings and from things, and it uses the body and the parts of the body to attempt to come into contact with more spiritual realms of being. The soul cannot be an accident (or property of the body) because it has the power to distinguish between accidents and essential concepts and is not limited to awareness of accidental things by the senses. Rather, it can apprehend a great variety of immaterial and abstract entities. If the soul were only an accident it could do none of these things, but could only perform in the limited way of the physical parts of the body. The soul is not an accident, and when we want to concentrate upon abstract issues the body is actually an obstruction that we must avoid if we are to make contact with intelligible reality. The soul, then, is an immortal and independent substance that controls the body. It has an essence opposite to that of the body, and so cannot die; it is involved in an eternal and circular motion, replicated by the organization of the heavens. This motion takes two directions, either upwards towards reason and the active intellect or downwards towards matter. Our happiness arises through upwards movement, our misfortunes through movement in the opposite direction.

Ibn Miskawayh's discussion of virtue combines Aristotelian with Platonic ideas (see VIRTUE ETHICS). Virtue is the perfection of the aspect of the soul (that is, human reason) that represents the essence of humanity and distinguishes it from lower forms of existence. Our virtue increases in so far as we develop and improve our ability to deliberate and apply reason to our lives. We should do this in accordance with the mean, the point most distant from two extremes, and justice results when we manage to achieve this. Ibn Miskawayh combines the Platonic division of virtues with an Aristotelian understanding of what virtue actually is, and adds to this the idea that the more these virtues can be treated as a unity, the better. This is because, he argues, that unity is equivalent to perfection, while multiplicity is equivalent to a meaningless plurality of physical objects. This idea is not just based upon a Pythagorean aesthetic (see PYTHAGOREANISM). Ibn Miskawayh argues further that the notion of justice when it deals with eternal and immaterial principles is a simple idea, while human justice by contrast is variable and depends upon the changing nature of particular states and communities. The law of the state is based upon the contingent features of the time, while the divine law specifies what is to be done everywhere and at every time.

Ibn Miskawayh uses the notion of friendship to distinguish between those relationships that are essentially transitory and variable (in particular those based upon pleasure) and those based upon the intellect, which are also pleasurable but not in a physical way. Our souls can recognize similarly perfected souls, and as a result enjoy intense intellectual delight. This is very different from the normal kind of friendship, in which people form relationships with each other because they want to get something out of it. Still, even those capable of the most perfect form of relationship have to involve themselves in the less perfect levels of friendship, since they must live in society if they are to achieve perfection, and so must satisfy at least some of the expectations of society (see FRIENDSHIP). The highest form of happiness exists when we can abandon the requirements of this world and are able to receive the emanations flowing from above that will perfect our intellects and enable us to be illuminated by divine light. The eventual aim seems to be the throwing off of the trappings of our physical existence and following entirely spiritual aims in mystical contemplation of the deity.

3 Practical ethics and humanism

This mystical level of happiness seems to rank higher than mere intellectual perfection, yet Ibn Miskawayh is particularly interesting in the practical advice he gives on how to develop our ordinary capacity for virtue. He regards the cultivation of our moral health in a very Aristotelian way as akin to the cultivation of physical health, requiring measures to preserve our moral equilibrium (see ARISTOTLE §§23–6). We ought to keep our emotions under control and carry out practices that help both to restrain us on particular occasions and also to develop personality traits that will maintain that level of restraint throughout our lives. To eradicate faults, we must investigate their ultimate causes and seek to replace these with more helpful alternatives. Take the fear of death, for example: this is a baseless fear, since the soul is immortal and cannot die. Our bodies will perish, but they must do so since we are contingent; to acknowledge that contingency and also to wish that we were not thus contingent is some sort of contradiction. If we are worried by the pain involved in dying, then it is the pain we fear, not death itself. Ibn

Miskawayh argues, along with AL-KINDI (§3) and the Cynics and Stoics who no doubt influenced him on this issue, that to reconcile ourselves to reality we have to understand the real nature of our feelings (see CYNICS; STOICISM). We have to use reason to work out what we should do and feel, since otherwise we are at the mercy of our feelings and the varying influences that come to us from outside ourselves (see DEATH).

This emphasis upon the capacity of the human mind to use reason to help us determine what we should do and who we are has led the most distinguished commentator on Ibn Miskawayh, Mohammed Arkoun (1970), to call him a humanist and part of the general humanist movement of his time. It is certainly true that religion plays a small part in Ibn Miskawayh's writings, and when he does consider Islam he often gives its religious practices a rather instrumental rationale. AL-GHAZALI (§5) was infuriated by Ibn Miskawayh's suggestion that the point of communal prayer is to base religion upon the natural gregariousness of human beings in society. This seemed to al-Ghazali to disparage the religious enterprise, since he argued that the significance of religious rituals is that they are specified by the religion, and there can be no other reason. Their rationale is that they are unreasonable. God indicates the huge gap that exists between him and us by setting us unpleasant and difficult tasks. For Ibn Miskawayh, the reason for the ritual is that it has a part to play in helping us adapt to religious life, using the dispositions that are natural to us, so that the rules and customs of religion are essentially reasonable. A whole range of authorities may be consulted to help us understand our religious duties concerning how we are to live and what we are to believe; some of these are Islamic, while others are not. Ibn Miskawayh seems on the whole to accord greater respect to Greek rather than specifically Islamic authorities.

Ibn Miskawayh's thought proved to be influential. His style, combining abstract thought with practical observations, is attractive and remained popular long after his death. Sometimes he merely presents aspects of 'wisdom' literature from previous cultures; sometimes he provides practical comments upon moral problems that are entirely unanalytical. At its best, however, his philosophy is highly analytical and maintains a high degree of coherence and consistency. The fact that he mixes together aspects of Plato, Aristotle, Pythagoras, Galen and other thinkers influenced by Greek philosophy is not an indication of cultural looting but rather a creative attempt at using these different approaches to cast light upon important issues.

Ibn Miskawayh shows how possible it is to combine a Platonic conception of the soul with an Aristotelian account of moral development. The idea of a still higher realm of being at which the soul comes into contact with divine reality is a perfectly feasible addition to the account he gives of social and intellectual life. He never imports the notion of revelation to resolve theoretical difficulties, and we have seen how his approach both annoyed and stimulated al-Ghazali. It is perhaps the combination in Ibn Miskawayh of elegance of style, practical relevance and philosophical rigour that prolonged his influence in the Islamic world.

See also: ETHICS IN ISLAMIC PHILOSOPHY; NEOPLATONISM IN ISLAMIC PHILOSOPHY; SOUL IN ISLAMIC PHILOSOPHY

List of works

Ibn Miskawayh (before 1030) *Tahdhib al-akhlaq* (Cultivation of Morals), ed. C. Zurayk, Beirut: American University of Beirut Centennial Publications, 1966; trans. C. Zurayk, *The Refinement of Character*, Beirut: American University of Beirut, 1968. (A summary of Ibn Miskawayh's ethical system. This work is also known as *Taharat al-a'raq* (Purity of Dispositions).)

References and further reading

Arkoun, M. (1961–2) 'Deux épîtres de Miskawayh' (Two Treatises of Miskawayh), *Bulletin d'Études Orientales* (Institut Français de Damas) 17: 7–74. (A clear account of Ibn Miskawayh's general metaphysics as well as his ethics.)

* —— (1970) *Contribution à l'Étude de l'humanisme arabe au IVe/Xe siècle: Miskawayh, philosophe et historien (320/325–421) = (932/936–1030)* (Contribution to the Study of Arab Humanism in the 4th/10th Century: Miskawayh, Philosopher and Historian), Paris: Vrin; revised 2nd edn, 1982. (The standard exegesis of Ibn Miskawayh's contribution to philosophy and history.)

Fakhry, M. (1975) 'The Platonism of Miskawayh and its Implications for his Ethics', *Studia Islamica* 43: 39–57. (A careful account of the Platonic and Neoplatonic influences on Ibn Miskawayh.)

Goodman, L. (1996) 'Friendship in Aristotle, Miskawayh and al-Ghazali', in O. Leaman (ed.) *Friendship East and West: Philosophical Perspectives*, Richmond: Curzon, 164–91. (A range of views on friendship, and their philosophical significance explained.)

Kraemer, J. (1984) 'Humanism in the Renaissance of

Islam: a Preliminary Study', *Journal of the American Oriental Society* 104 (1): 135–64. (An account of Ibn Miskawayh's place in the culture of Islamic humanism.)

Leaman, O. (1996a) 'Ibn Miskawayh', in S.H. Nasr and O. Leaman (eds) *History of Islamic Philosophy*, London: Routledge, 252–7. (An account of the context within which Ibn Miskawayh worked and the influence of his views.)

—— (1996b) 'Islamic Humanism in the Fourth/Tenth Century', in S.H. Nasr and O. Leaman (eds) *History of Islamic Philosophy*, London: Routledge, 155–61. (Survey of a group of thinkers including Ibn Miskawayh, al-Tawhidi and al-Sijistani.)

—— (1996c) 'Secular Friendship and Religious Devotion', in O. Leaman (ed.) *Friendship East and West: Philosophical Perspectives*, Richmond: Curzon. (Account of Ibn Miskawayh's notion of friendship and comparison with contrary views.)

OLIVER LEAMAN

IBN PAQUDA, BAHYA
(*fl.* early 12th century)

Bahya ibn Paquda, the chief exponent of Jewish pietism, gave that ecumenical strand of thought and practice a markedly philosophical cast, preferring the intellectual to the fideistic side of pietist tradition, and embracing rationalism as the ally of faith rather than rejecting it as an enemy. Drawing selectively from Muslim as well as Jewish sources, Bahya's spiritual vademecum, *al-Hidaya ila fara'id al-qulub (The Book of Guidance to the Duties of the Heart), was widely studied ever since its composition, especially in its medieval Hebrew translation, and parts of it are even included in the liturgical meditations of the Ten Days of Penitence. In it, Bahya thematizes his materials carefully, using his own sense of the reasonable to structure pietism as a philosophical system, controlling the monistic penchant of mysticism and disciplining the ascetic tendencies of the devotional cast of mind. Maimonides found Bahya's asceticism excessive and rejected Bahya's related leanings towards predestinarianism and resignation; but he quietly adopted Bahya's moral and intellectual interpretation of the mystic quest for unity with God, fell into step with his predilection for spiritual immortality as distinguished from bodily resurrection, echoed his affirmation of God's absolute unity and simplicity, and concurred in his admiration for negative theology, the theology of divine transcendence.*

1 General character of Bahya's thought
2 The duties of the heart

1 General character of Bahya's thought

Born in the later eleventh century, Bahya ibn Paquda flourished in Saragossa and served as a rabbinic judge. He is the probable author of some twenty Hebrew *piyyutim*, or hymns, extant under the name Bahya, but his best known work is the fountainhead of Jewish philosophical pietism, *al-Hidaya ila fara'id al-qulub* (The Book of Guidance to the Duties of the Heart), widely circulated since medieval times in the Hebrew translation (1161) of Judah ibn Tibbon and thus familiar to traditional Jews as *Hovot ha-Levavot*. This version, although its struggle for literalism sacrifices the fluidity of the original, was widely copied and abstracted in manuscript and first printed at Naples in 1489, again at Venice in 1548, and more critically at Mantua in 1559. It attracted Hebrew commentaries by various hands including those published in 1691, 1774, 1790, 1803 and 1836, and was translated into Portuguese, Italian, German, Spanish, Ladino, Yiddish, Arabic(!), French and English.

Steeped in Biblical and Rabbinic learning and the philosophy of SAADIAH GAON, Bahya also knows the Greek philosophers and Galen in their Arabic texts. He draws upon *kalam* and Sufi writers and the Shi'ite group known as the Sincere Brethren of Basra (see IKHWAN AL-SAFA'), whose cosmopolitan and humanistic pietism is akin to his own. Bahya does not seem to know the work of Avicenna; he shows numerous affinities to the writings of AL-GHAZALI, but exhibits a milder spirit and far greater confidence in the philosophical tradition. It is no longer believed that al-Ghazali was a source for him; rather, the two seem to share common sources in Sufi literature.

2 The duties of the heart

Complaining of the externalism prominent in Jewish religiosity, attention to the 'duties of the limbs' rather to the detriment of the inward or spiritual 'duties of the heart', Bahya announces at the outset of his magnum opus that he intends to redress the balance. The heart here is our spiritual identity, celebrated by PASCAL but named as early as the charge in Deuteronomy that we must love God with all our hearts. As Bahya's Muslim contemporary al-Ghazali carefully notes, the heart in this instance is not the physical organ. Bahya does not contrast reason with the promptings of the heart. On the contrary, the heart for him includes the mind. He argues dialectically that external obligations depend for their motivation on the commitment of the heart and that intention, which is rooted in heart, is of essence in determining the status of our acts, even at so behavioural a level as in the determination of the difference between murder and manslaughter. But the roots of sound intention must lie in understanding, and those who would attain the ideal of obedience to God's commandments must therefore pursue wisdom.

Wisdom comprises physics, mathematics and theology, the three canonical branches of philosophical exploration. It is theology that is crucial in religion and that makes philosophy a religious obligation. The weak-minded rightly rely on tradition and authority to frame their outlook, but those of more penetrating mind have an obligation to explore the foundations of faith and action, lest their actions be at odds with their intentions, through the incoherency or inadequacy of their understanding. In matters of law, it was long ago established that the majority decision of the learned is determinative of practice; here, convention, grounded in scriptural revelation, will suffice. But in theology we must probe the tradition, seeking not merely uniformity but the comprehension that will inform our lives. The argument is a pietist's counterpart to the Socratic thesis that the unexamined life is not worth living (see SOCRATES §4).

Bahya organizes his treatise around ten pietist virtues, a thematic easily lost sight of if we translate the title of the first of his ten chapters as 'On the Unity of God'. The title, *Tawhid*, in fact means monotheism, the affirmation of God's unity, and it is here in the first instance that Bahya seeks to bring philosophy to the aid of piety by clarifying the content of monotheistic belief. Such belief is to be affirmed by the heart, not merely uttered by the tongue. Its affirmation is our primal religious obligation, because from it flow all the rest. But if commitment to God is to be a ground of our intentions, that commitment must be conceptually lucid and firmly understood. Ordinary Israelites may content themselves with the apologetics of *kalam* (dialectical theology), but those who are capable of the understanding ordained by Deuteronomy (4: 39, 'lay it to heart') are obliged to delve beneath rote faith. They must seek deeper understanding not only for the sake of countrymen who need philosophical aid, but also for the nations of the world. In this way they contribute to the fulfilment of the prophecy (Isaiah 2: 3) that God's word will issue forth from Zion.

Such inquirers will find grounds for their belief in the beauty and order of the cosmos and in the recognition that nothing can create itself. Rather, the whole ontic hierarchy, the architecture of heaven and earth rises to the utter simplicity of God and the primal source of differentiation, in his will. To Moses, God revealed himself conceptually as 'I am that I am', but to lesser minds, he is revealed as a figure of

tradition, 'God of Abraham, God of Isaac, and God of Jacob'.

The second virtue is reflectiveness (*'i'tibar*), leading to fruitful meditations on creation and God's grace toward it. The study of nature is not merely a way of recognizing God's creative powers but also a way of exercising our own God-given potential, raising ourselves above the animal level. When Isaiah (40: 26) exhorts us 'Lift up your eyes on high and behold who created these things', we can learn from rabbinic teaching (Shabbat 75a) that one who is able to study astronomy but does not is among those who 'regard not the work of the Lord' (Isaiah 5: 12).

The boundedness of nature, the microcosm of human anatomy, the utility of the human faculties, the usefulness of all creatures in sustaining the world at large and ourselves in particular, the system of the arts and sciences, and the beauties of God's law are all objects of intellectual wonder, instruction and delight that draw the mind upward toward God. Man is the chief but not the sole object of creation, and it is through self-examination, as practised in philosophy that we gain our clearest apprehension of God's work and grace in nature.

The third virtue is obedience to God, a reasonable response to the grace we have received. Even if our performance is imperfect, we should try to make our intentions pure, although God alone acts entirely without self-interest. Human nature rests on a deep duality that generates inevitable tensions. We have a desire and appetite to populate the earth. However, we reach understanding only through self-denial, that is, denial of the lower self, the ego, which pietists sharply distinguish from the seat of pure intentions, the heart. The Law provides the discipline we require in mediating the demands of our earthly natures and our heaven-bound souls, so ill at ease in this world. However, study of the Law also fortifies the mind and is itself a spiritual ladder.

We may manifest our obedience to God through acts of submission expressive of fear and dread or through words of praise and glorification. External acts are significant enough to be subject to reward and punishment, but only inner devotion is truly free and sincere. The finite obligations of the Law are thus only the gateway to the open-ended obligations of the heart, the preparatory discipline for a rise typified by the infinite scope that opens in the quest for understanding, which grows 'day unto day' (Psalms 19: 3).

External duties are precisely specified; they discipline the appetites of both the many and the wise, but to follow the Law solely for the sake of a reward is tantamount to polytheism. The wisest follow God's commands for his sake, not their own; that is, they entrust their all to God, not for any gain but simply from the love of God.

The mind's persuasion is God's inspiration, Bahya argues. He illustrates this thesis by inserting a dialogue into his text in which the mind teaches the soul the nature of the obedience she owes God and shows her that philosophy can strengthen her resolve in ways that tradition cannot. Continuing their dialogue, the mind shows the soul that the conflict between free will and predestination is insoluble by reason or scriptural authority. The pious need not resolve this antinomy. They will, as their character calls upon them to do, accept full responsibility with regard to their own moral and spiritual obligations and treat all worldly outcomes as decrees of divine wisdom. Our 'inclination' urges just the opposite, pressing us to assume control in worldly matters (to take credit when they succeed, to feel anxiety when they hang in the balance, and to suffer regret when they fail) but to abdicate our moral and spiritual obligations by pleading the excuse of destiny, fate or nature. Pursuing a pietist stance, Bahya has here accurately pinioned much that passes for metaphysical discussion of the problem of free will (see FREE WILL; PIETISM).

The fourth virtue is reliance upon God alone. Bahya interprets this important pietist virtue as an appeal against worldliness and in behalf of peace of mind. He contrasts the pious man with the alchemist, whose Faustian desire for control drives him to hermetic studies, unending travels, and the constant worldly anxieties of *homo faber*. Mitigating the anti-causal doctrine of Islamic occasionalists, Bahya argues that natural causes are too weak to produce their effects but must be deemed to act at God's behest (see OCCASIONALISM). God works through nature, not despite it. So it is permissible for us to exert ourselves in our own behalf, paradigmatically, by the use of medicine. But we must constantly remember that it is God on whom we are reliant. We must keep our eye on the Source, not the instrumentality through which grace is manifested.

The fifth virtue is *ikhlas*, purity of intention. This sincerity is a material rather than a mere formal virtue; that is, sincerity here means focus on the highest ideal, direction of all our actions towards God. It is not a matter of mere faithfulness to our own intentions. The tranquillity that comes from trust, the clarity that comes to philosophical monotheism, and the perfect absence of hypocrisy that was Bahya's original goal are all products of the virtue of *ikhlas*. It is the essence of self-rule, and thus of freedom.

The sixth virtue is humility, necessary to counter the pride that might beset even our piety. Humility manifests itself bodily in softspokenness, clemency and self-restraint. It is attained through reflection on our fragility and abjectness before God and manifested in patience, benevolence and forbearance, modesty in the face of well-founded praise, and firm demurral in the face of unfounded praise. Mastery belongs only to God, and one cannot attain any part of piety without first abandoning all claims to mastery.

The seventh virtue is penitence, a special gift from God in recognition of the inadequacy of human deeds. The key to penitence is self-knowledge; thus the eighth virtue is self-scrutiny. This, like any intellectual virtue, imposes obligations that vary in accordance with our intellectual capacities. At its lowest it means simply reflection on the wretchedness of the human body and its vile origins. At a higher level, it involves reflections on God's grace; but ultimately it means constant, probing examination of our own intentions and the adequacy of our pursuit of the highest of them, allying ourselves firmly with others who can aid us in that pursuit.

The ninth virtue is abstemiousness (*zuhd*), a Sufi virtue and part of the legacy that all three monotheistic religions inherit from Hellenistic asceticism. All living beings, Bahya argues, need asceticism as a check upon their appetites and impulses, an inner counterpart to the economic and social discipline of the polity. Every nation has its own specialization in one or another art or science, through which it contributes to the world. Asceticism, which fosters the mind's dominance over the entire soul, is Israel's forte, allowing its people to overcome their powerful appetites and passions and become the spiritual physicians for the world, as it is said, 'The fruit of the righteous is a tree of life' (Proverbs 11: 30). Restoring the ideal of renunciation to its Platonic roots in the conception of sophrosyne, Bahya follows up on Sufi and other pietist elaborations of the ascetic ideal to find Jewish application for the notion of abstemiousness in the social sphere, through a cheerful and gentle comportment towards others; in the bodily sphere, through the discipline of the Torah's ritual laws, with their complex system of permitted and forbidden pleasures, where we are urged to progress to the point where we regard permitted pleasures as on a par with forbidden ones (but not to the point that we harm ourselves) and in the inward or spiritual sphere, through the conquest of covetousness and worldly ambition.

The final virtue is the love of God, the summation of all that has gone before, a sincere desire to cleave to God, in gratitude, penitence and awe, pursuing a mystic intimacy attained not by ecstatic exercises but by meditations on one's own history, on Scripture and on nature, by practice of the divine commandments, acceptance of God's sovereignty, and living the life of the pious and abstemious. Those who truly love God will give up property, body and soul for him, as Abraham did, first by placing his worldly goods at the service of his guests, so as to draw them to God; second by undergoing circumcision; and third by his willingness to sacrifice Isaac in obedience to God's command. The last is a superhuman piety, accessible to us only through God's aid. Fasts and vigils are part of intimacy with God; but so are justice, neighbourly reproof and the public institution of justice, as we read in *Avot* 5.18: 'Moses was meritorious and made the many meritorious, and the merit of the many came to them through him, as it is written, 'he worked the justice of the Lord and His righteousness with Israel' (Deuteronomy 33: 21). That is, Moses shared in God's attribute of justice by becoming its instrumentality in the world.

See also: PIETISM; VIRTUES AND VICES

List of works

Ibn Pakuda, Bahya (before 1161) *al-Hidaya ila fara'id al-qulub* (The Book of Guidance to the Duties of the Heart), ed. A.S. Yahuda, Leiden: Brill, 1912; trans. M. Mansoor, *The Book of Direction to the Duties of the Heart*, London: Routledge, 1973. (Judah ibn Tibbon's medieval translation is edited with English translation by M. Hyamson, New York, 1925–47, 5 vols; repr. Jerusalem: Boys Town Publishers, 1965.)

References and further reading

Eisenberg, Y. (1981) 'Reason and Emotion in *Duties of the Heart*', *Daat* 7: 5–35. (Examines the interplay of rationality with the heart in Bahya's pietist psychology.)

Goodman, L.E. (1983) 'Bahya on the Antinomy of Free Will and Predestination', *Journal of the History of Ideas* 44: 115–30. (Explores the pietist approach to the philosophical problem of free will and determinism and parallels between Bahya's approach and that of Kant.)

Vajda, G. (1937) 'Le Dialogue de l'âme et de la raison dans les *Devoirs des Coeurs* de Bahya Ibn Paquda' (The Dialogue of the Soul and Reason in Bahya ibn Paquda's *Duties of the Heart*), *Revue des Études Juives* 102: 93–104. (Deals with Bahya's literary device of setting up an internal device between reason and the soul.)

—— (1947) *La Théologie Ascetique de Bahya ibn Paquda* (The Ascetic Theology of Bahya ibn Paquda), Paris: Cahiers de la Société Asiatique,

vol. 7. (Surveys Bahya's efforts to create a balanced asceticism on the foundations of his pietist spirituality.)

L.E. GOODMAN

IBN AR-RAWANDI (*c*.910?)

A highly enigmatic and controversial figure in the history of Islamic thought, Ibn ar-Rawandi wavered between a number of Islamic sects and then abandoned all of them in favour of atheism. As an atheist, he used reason to destroy religious beliefs, especially those of Islam. He compared prophets to unnecessary magicians, God to a human being in terms of knowledge and emotion, and the Qur'an to an ordinary book. Contrary to Islamic belief, he advocated that the world is without a beginning and that heaven is nothing special.

Medieval biographical dictionaries agree that Ibn al-Husain Ahmad ibn Yahya ibn Ishaq ar-Rawandi lived in Baghdad, but differ as to the form of his name and the date of his death, and indicate that he was intellectually unstable and that very little was known about his real thought. While he is best known as ar-Rawandi, he is also referred to as ar-Rindi, ar-Rawindi and ar-Riwindi. Also he is said to have died at a number of different dates, ranging from AH 243 to AH 301. The most accepted view is that he died about AH 245/AD 910 at the age of forty.

Islamic sources mention that Ibn ar-Rawandi was first a Mu'tazilite, then a Shi'ite and later an atheist. The same sources indicate that the Jews had warned Muslims that, as his father converted to Islam from Judaism after trying to refute the Torah, Ibn ar-Rawandi would attempt to refute the Qur'an after abandoning Islam. These sources agree that this happened, and that he wrote books for the Jews, Christians and even dualists (idolators) in which he attacked Islamic beliefs. He was said to have told the Jews to inform Muslims that Moses had said that there will not be any prophet after him. With the exception of Ibn al-Murtada (d. AH 436/AD 1044) and Ibn Khallikan (d. AH 680/AD 1283), Muslim authors distanced themselves from him and many called him 'the cursed', including Abu al-Hayyan AL-TAWHIDI and Abu al-'Ala' al-Ma'arri (d. AH 449/AD 1057), who themselves were considered as atheists in Islamic religious circles.

The reasons for his abandoning Mu'tazilism and later Islam entirely were a matter of controversy. Some believed that poverty pushed him to earn some money by writing books for the opponents of

Mu'tazilism and Islam in general. The *Ma'ahid at-tansis* (Known Citations) of al-'Abbasi (d. AH 960/AD 1556) mentions that for four hundred dirhams Ibn ar-Rawandi wrote a book for the Jews, criticizing Islam. After he received the money he wished to refute it, but agreed not to do so after receiving one hundred dirhams more. Others were of the opinion that he abandoned Mu'tazilism because he did not reach the high positions in Mu'tazilite circles to which he aspired. Still others contended that the sense of rejection and loneliness he felt after having been isolated by the Mu'tazilites forced him to seek refuge in their opponents' circles. He himself claimed that he affiliated himself with different schools of thought, including atheism, in order to familiarize himself with their doctrines and learn from them.

Ibn ar-Rawandi's real thought remained somewhat unknown primarily because in the Middle Ages the authorities discouraged the reading of his books and banned their circulation. Most of the one hundred and fourteen books he wrote have been lost. Only parts of three of his works are extant. *Fadihat al-mu'tazila* (The Scandal of the Mu'tazilites) was preserved almost in its entirety and responded to by al-Khayyat (d. AH 300/AD 912) in *Kitab al-intisar* (The Book of Victory). *Fadihat al-mu'tazila* is a response to *Fadilat al-mu'tazila* (The Virtue of the Mu'tazilites), a work by al-Jahiz (d. AH 254/AD 868), in which the latter pointed out the vices of their opponents in addition to the virtues of the Mu'tazilites themselves. Following the heyday of the Mu'tazilite movement during the early Abbasid rule of al-Ma'mun, al-Mu'tasim and al-Wathiq (see ASH'ARIYYA AND MU'TAZILA), the movement felt the need to defend itself against attacks by various opponents; al-Jahiz was one of its defenders. In *Fadihat al-mu'tazila*, Ibn ar-Rawandi presents the views of all the major Mu'tazilite thinkers and tries to show that they suffered from inconsistencies. Many fragments of *ad-Damigh* (A Refutation), another work of Ibn ar-Rawandi, are extant in Ibn al-Jawzi's *al-Muntazam fi at-tarikh* (Organization in History). In *ad-Damigh*, Ibn ar-Rawandi attacks the Qur'an. Finally, parts of *az-Zumurrud* (Diamond) are also extant in the *Majalis* (Councils) of al-Mu'ayyad fi al-Din (d. AH 369/AD 979). In *az-Zumurrud*, Ibn ar-Rawandi focuses on proving the falsehood of prophets and prophecy, which he rejects in Islam and in general.

Ibn ar-Rawandi's tremendous courage in pursuing a rational path in religious debates forced him to reach conclusions not accepted by mainstream Islam. Thus he was attacked severely by the major Muslim thinkers as early as the fourth century AH (tenth century AD), including AL-KINDI, al-Khayyat, Abu al-Hasan al-Ash'ari, Abu 'Ali al-Jubba'i and AL-FARABI.

In most of his later works, Ibn ar-Rawandi advocated rejection of religious doctrines, which he considered unacceptable to reason. Thus, he attacked the prophets and certain traditional interpretations and concepts of the Qur'an. Among his teachings were the ideas that prophets make the same kind of claims that magicians make, and that the world is eternal and its events do not prove that they have a first cause. The Qur'an, in his view, is not the eternal word of God, nor is its language miraculous; some human beings, such as al-Aktham ibn Saifi, made better statements than some of those found in the Qur'an. God was without knowledge until he created his knowledge: God is like an angry enemy who can remedy things only by imposing punishment on others and who is capable of wrongdoing. Since he can do these things directly, he needs no holy book and no prophet. However, a God who treats his creatures in this way is not wise. His lack of wisdom is also revealed in his requiring his creatures to obey him when he knows that they will not do so, and in placing them in hell for eternity if they disobey him. Heaven, as described in the Qur'an, has nothing desirable.

Ibn ar-Rawandi had a gloomy outlook on life. This is best expressed in some of his verses where he says: 'The calamities of life are numerous and continuous. Its joy, on the other hand, comes to you as do holidays.'

See also: ASH'ARIYYA AND MU'TAZILA

List of works

Ibn ar-Rawandi (before 910?) *Fadihat al-mu'tazila* (The Scandal of the Mu'tazilites). (What remains of this work can be found in al-Khayyat, *Kitab al-Intisar war-radd 'ala Ibn ar-Rawandi al-Mulhid*, ed. H.S. Nyberg, Cairo: Matba'at al-Kutub al-Masriyya, 1925; trans. A.N. Nadir, *Le livre du triomphe et de la réfutation d'Ibn al Rawandi l'hérétique*, Beirut: Catholic Press, 1957. This also contains al-Khayyat's response to the work. This is the best primary source for understanding the debates between Ibn ar-Rawandi and the Mu'tazilites.)

—— (before 910?) *ad-Damigh* (A Refutation). (Portions of this work can be found in Ibn al-Jawzi, *al-Muntazam fi tarikh al-muluk wal-umam*, ed. M.A.Q. 'Ata and M.A.Q. 'Ata, Beirut: Dar al-Kutub al-'Ilmiyya, 1992.)

—— (before 910?) *az-Zumurrud* (Diamond). (Parts of this work can be found in al-Mu'ayyad fi al-Din, *al-Majalis al-mu'ayyadiyya lil-Mu'ayyad fi ad-Din ash-Shirazi*, ed. M.A.Q. 'Abd al-Nasir, Cairo: Dar ath-Thaqafa, 1975.)

References and further reading

* al-'Abbasi (before 1556) *Ma'ahid at-tansis* (Known Citations), ed. M. 'Abd al-Hamid, Cairo: Matba'at as-Sa'ada, 1947. (Includes a brief account of Ibn ar-Rawandi's life, works and poetry.)

al-A'sam, A. (1975) *History of Ibn Ar-Riwandi the Heretic*, Beirut: Dar al-Afaq al-Jadida. (A collection of the most important medieval Islamic sources, including those of Ibn al-Jawzi and al-Mu'ayyad fi ad-Din, that mention Ibn ar-Rawandi. It shows that the majority of Muslim thinkers in the Middle Ages rejected his views and tried to distance themselves from him.)

—— (1978–9) *Ibn ar-Riwandi fi al-maraji' al-'arabiyya al-haditha* (Ibn ar-Rawandi in Modern Arabic Sources), Beirut: Dar al-Afaq al-Jadida. (Another collection of Islamic sources, dating from the fourteenth century to the present. It reveals that Muslim thinkers continued to consider Ibn ar-Rawandi a heretic. Like the above work of al-A'sam, it is helpful in presenting the most important views about Ibn ar-Rawandi, as they circulated in chronological order.)

* al-Mu'ayyad fi al-Din (before 979) *al-Majalis al-mu'ayyadiyya lil-Mu'ayyad fi ad-Din ash-Shirazi* (The Mu'ayyadiyya Councils by al-Mu'ayyad fi ad-Din of Shiraz), ed. M.A.Q. 'Abd al-Nasir, Cairo: Dar ath-Thaqafa, 1975. (Includes parts of the *az-Zumurrud* of Ibn ar-Rawandi.)

* Ibn al-Jawzi (before 1201) *al-Muntazam fi tarikh al-muluk wal-umam* (Organization in the History of Kings and Nations), ed. M.A.Q. 'Ata and M.A.Q. 'Ata, Beirut: Dar al-Kutub al-'Ilmiyya, 1992. (Includes portions of the *ad-Damigh* of Ibn ar-Rawandi.)

Stroumsa, S. (1985) 'The Barahima in Early Kalam', *Jerusalem Studies in Arabic and Islam* 6: 229–41. (Offers a non-traditional interpretation of Ibn ar-Rawandi's thought, which helps in drawing attention to his early views that are usually neglected by the majority of Islamic sources.)

SHAMS C. INATI

IBN RUSHD, ABU'L WALID MUHAMMAD (1126–98)

Ibn Rushd (Averroes) is regarded by many as the most important of the Islamic philosophers. A product of twelfth-century Islamic Spain, he set out to integrate Aristotelian philosophy with Islamic thought. A common theme throughout his writings is that there is no incompatibility between religion and philosophy when both are properly understood. His contributions to philosophy took many forms, ranging from his detailed commentaries on Aristotle, his defence of philosophy against the attacks of those who condemned it as contrary to Islam and his construction of a form of Aristotelianism which cleansed it, as far as was possible at the time, of Neoplatonic influences.

His thought is genuinely creative and highly controversial, producing powerful arguments that were to puzzle his philosophical successors in the Jewish and Christian worlds. He seems to argue that there are two forms of truth, a religious form and a philosophical form, and that it does not matter if they point in different directions. He also appears to be doubtful about the possibility of personal immortality or of God's being able to know that particular events have taken place. There is much in his work also which suggests that religion is inferior to philosophy as a means of attaining knowledge, and that the understanding of religion which ordinary believers can have is very different and impoverished when compared with that available to the philosopher.

When discussing political philosophy he advocates a leading role in the state for philosophers, and is generally disparaging of the qualities of theologians as political figures. Ibn Rushd's philosophy is seen to be based upon a complex and original philosophy of languages which expresses his critique of the accepted methods of argument in Islamic philosophy up to his time.

1   **Commentaries**
2   **God and the world**
3   **The soul**
4   **Moral and political philosophy**
5   **The role of philosophy**
6   **Philosophy of language**

1   Commentaries

Abu'l Walid Muhammad ibn Ahmad ibn Muhammad ibn Rushd, often known as Averroes (the Latinized version of his name), was born in AH 520/AD 1126 in Cordoba. He came from a distinguished line of jurists and theologians, who like him served as public officials. As a result of royal patronage he became both royal physician and *qadi* (judge) of Cordoba in succession to his father. Due to the political turmoil in Andalus (Islamic Spain) at the time, he was not always in favour, and was banished to North Africa when he was seventy during a period of persecution of philosophy. He died in AH 595/AD 1198 after having been rehabilitated, but his religious orthodoxy still seems to have been suspected by the public.

There is a famous story that when Ibn Rushd was about forty-two there was a meeting between the caliph and Ibn Rushd, at which the latter was asked to summarize the works of Aristotle in order that the ideas of that thinker might be better understood by the caliph himself, and no doubt also by the intellectual community. Ibn Rushd's reported nervousness at accepting this commission was well-founded, since changing political circumstances had in the past – and would in the future – put Aristotle and those influenced by him under a theological cloud; the interest of a ruler in philosophy could quite easily turn into hostility. Over the next twenty-six years, however, Ibn Rushd wrote commentaries on most of Aristotle's works. These commentaries took a variety of forms. Often he would write a summary, medium commentary and long commentary of the same text, thus presenting the ideas of Aristotle to a variety of audiences; those who were seeking a detailed discussion of the whole text would look to the long commentary, while those who wanted just to get a flavour of the original could be satisfied with the paraphrase. As Aristotle's *Politics* was not available to him, he used Plato's *Republic* instead for his commentary on a political text.

The remarkable feature of these commentaries is the way in which Ibn Rushd tried to get back to the original arguments of Aristotle, cleansed of the Neoplatonic accretions which had developed. This was very difficult to do, since a long and well-developed tradition of Neoplatonic commentary had very much set the agenda over the previous centuries in the Islamic world (see NEOPLATONISM IN ISLAMIC PHILOSOPHY). However, Ibn Rushd was often able to distinguish between the points which Aristotle was trying to make and those which had been imposed upon him by the commentators. He certainly respected some of the classical commentators such as ALEXANDER OF APHRODISIAS and THEMISTIUS, as well as some of the Islamic philosophers and especially his own countryman IBN BAJJA, but the style of his commentaries is to try to understand the text anew and to reconstruct the Aristotelian argument in a way which represents Aristotle's original view. Sometimes he is more successful than at others, and he was not averse to adding his own comments on the text when he felt this would be useful. The paraphrases are certainly a very loose summary of the originals, and often give Ibn Rushd the opportunity to express his own views on an Aristotelian theme. However, the long commentaries are very impressive analyses of the text, especially given the nature of the translations with which Ibn Rushd was working, and they came to wield great influence in the Christian and Jewish worlds (see AVERROISM; AVERROISM, JEWISH.)

2 God and the world

Although Ibn Rushd did discuss theological topics in his commentaries on occasion, he usually reserved them for his more polemical works, where he has a more contemporary philosopher in mind. His *Tahafut al-tahafut* (Incoherence of the Incoherence) is a response to an earlier attack upon philosophy, the *Tahafut al-falasifa* (Incoherence of the Philosophers) written by AL-GHAZALI, who had argued in this work that there are two major problems with Islamic philosophy. The first problem is that it misapplies the very philosophical techniques which it advocates; that is, its arguments fall foul of the criteria for validity which philosophy itself advocates. The other problem is that the conclusions of philosophy go against the principles of Islam, which the philosophers pretend they are supporting. Al-Ghazali produced accurate descriptions of philosophical arguments and then set about demolishing them, using the same philosophical principles which his opponents try to employ. He argued that although the philosophers purport to prove that philosophy is merely a more sophisticated analysis of the nature of reality than that available to ordinary Muslims, the philosophers are in fact involved in dismantling the religious notion of God, the afterlife and creation in the guise of merely analysing these ideas. Although the object of his attack is primarily the work of AL-FARABI and IBN SINA, Ibn Rushd perceived that the whole peripatetic approach to philosophy was being challenged by al-Ghazali, and he rushed to its defence.

The nub of al-Ghazali's attack on philosophy is what he regards as its misguided interpretation of the relationship between God and the world. The Qur'an is full of references to the creation of the world and to its eventual destruction should the deity feel it appropriate, yet Islamic philosophy tends to argue that the world is eternal. If God really is an agent, al-Ghazali asks, why cannot he just create the world *ex nihilo* and then later destroy it? Ibn Rushd replies that temporal and eternal agents act very differently. We can decide to do something, we can wait for a certain time before acting, we can wonder about our future actions; but such possibilities cannot arise for God. In his case there is no gap between desire and action, nothing stands in the way of his activity; and yet we are told by al-Ghazali that God suddenly created the world. What differentiates one time from another for God? What could motivate him to create the world at one particular time as opposed to another? For us, different times are different because they have different qualitative aspects, yet before the creation of the world, when there was nothing

639

around to characterize one time as distinct from another, there is nothing to characterize one time over another as *the* time for creation to take place (see ETERNITY §4).

Al-Ghazali argues that such a response is evidence of mental laziness. Even we can choose between two alternatives which appear to be identical in every respect except position. He gives the example of a hungry man being confronted by only two dates, where he is able to take just one. Since they are to all intents and purposes identical, it would seem to follow that if the philosophers are right he must just stand there and starve since there is no difference between them. Ibn Rushd criticizes this analogy, since it is not really about a choice as to which date to eat but about a choice between eating and not eating. What al-Ghazali is trying to do is establish some scope for divine action and decision-making which represents God as a real agent and not just as a cipher for natural events which would take place anyway. Ibn Rushd comments that the difficulty lies in distinguishing between the divine will and knowledge. Since an omniscient God knows exactly how the universe should be organized to produce the optimal arrangement, Ibn Rushd insists that there is no point in thinking of a gap in time existing between that conception and its instantiation. An omnipotent God does not need to wait for the appropriate moment to create the universe since nothing exists which could oblige him to wait, and he does not require time to bring about the creation. Ibn Rushd argues that given God's nature, we cannot think of his acting in any different way from that represented by the organization of the world. This does not imply a lack of freedom or ability to choose, but is merely a reflection of God's perfect nature (see OMNIPOTENCE).

Al-Ghazali followed the Ash'arites in being so concerned to emphasize the power and ubiquity of God that he refused to accept that the ordinary world really consists of stable material objects between which there are relationships of natural necessity (see ASH'ARIYYA AND MU'TAZILA §5; CAUSALITY AND NECESSITY IN ISLAMIC THOUGHT §2). Ibn Rushd claims that this theory leads to a denial of the possibility of knowledge of the world. Since al-Ghazali accepts causality as a practical guide to our everyday lives, one might wonder what point Ibn Rushd is trying to make here. The point is that the nexus between a term and its causal properties is not merely contingent, but is really one of meaning. Al-Ghazali gives the example of a decapitated person acting just like an ordinary human being, except for the absence of a head. No such event has ever taken place, but if God wills it it

could happen, because God is omnipotent and we can imagine such a possibility. If God wants to activate a headless person, he could do so. This shows that the connection between having a head and being an active human being is merely contingent, without necessity. Ibn Rushd wonders whether this change to our conceptual scheme is really possible. There are some properties which are significant aspects of the meaning of the thing of which they are the properties, and there is a necessary relationship between what a thing is and what it does. The advantage of Ibn Rushd's response is that it provides an account of how naming is possible. We can set about naming things because we can identify relatively stable entities with lawlike patterns of behaviour with other things. We may often go awry in our naming, but if we could not be sure that on the whole our names correspond with stable and fixed essences, naming itself would be an empty procedure.

Along with his insistence that the deity is a real agent, al-Ghazali was concerned to provide God with real knowledge of the everyday events of the world he created. IBN SINA argued that God is limited to knowing only very general and abstract features of the world, since any other sort of knowledge would diminish him as an eternal and immaterial being. Al-Ghazali objects that any God which is acceptable to Islam must know the everyday events of our world. Ibn Rushd suggests that on the contrary, this would make God into someone very like his creatures and would provide him with knowledge that is beneath his dignity. God's knowledge is superior and unique because he is not limited to receiving information from the world, as is the case with finite creatures like human beings. He is the creator of the objects in the world, and he knows them in a more perfect and complete way than we can hope to attain. This suggests that God cannot know individuals as such. The best knowledge is abstract and universal, and this is the sort of knowledge which God can be thought to enjoy.

One might expect Ibn Rushd to share Ibn Sina's view that God's knowledge is limited to universal judgments, but he does not adopt this line, arguing rather that God's knowledge is neither universal nor individual, although it is more like the latter than the former. Our knowledge is the result of what God has brought about, whereas God's knowledge is produced by that which he himself has brought about, a reality which he has constructed. The organization of the universe is a reflection of God's thought, and through thinking about his own being he is at the same time thinking about the organization of the world which mirrors that essence. He cannot really be identical with contingent and accidental phenomena, yet his essence is not totally unconnected with such phenomena. They represent contingent aspects of the necessary and essential relationships which he has established. To take an example, God knows which physical laws govern the universe, but he does not need to observe any moving objects to understand the principles of movement. Such observations are only appropriate objects of knowledge of sentient creatures with sensory apparatus and are far beneath the dignity of the creator. Ibn Rushd argues that this is not to diminish God's knowledge, but rather emphasizes the distinctness of the deity from his creatures and their ways of finding things out (see GOD, CONCEPTS OF).

3 The soul

Another charge which al-Ghazali brought against philosophy was that it fails to allow the physical resurrection of human beings and the provision of physical rewards and punishments appropriate to their behaviour during their lives. He has in mind here the Aristotelian notion of the soul, which makes the idea of an afterlife difficult to grasp. This is because the soul is the form of the living being, an aspect of the being itself, and there is no point in talking about the matter existing without the form when we are considering living creatures. Persons are combinations of soul and body, and in the absence of the latter there are no persons left (see SOUL IN ISLAMIC PHILOSOPHY).

Ibn Rushd appears to argue that as we become more involved with immortal and eternal knowledge, and with universal and abstract principles, our mind becomes identical to a degree with those objects of knowledge. So, once we have perfected ourselves intellectually and know everything that there is to know about the formal structure of reality, there is no longer really any 'us' around to do the knowing. Ibn Rushd regards our progress in knowledge as equivalent to a lessening of our ties with our material and individual human characteristics, with the radical result that if anything survives death, it must be the species and not the individual. Temporal and finite creatures are destructible, but as members of a species we are permanent, although only the species itself is entirely free from destruction.

This seems even more incompatible with the traditional religious view of the afterlife than the position which al-Ghazali attacks. Ibn Rushd follows this with a political account of the function of the religious language, describing the afterlife as providing ordinary believers with a motive for virtuous action and dissuading them from immorality. He does not entirely rule out the possibility of the sort of physical afterlife on which al-Ghazali insists, but it is clear from his work that he regards such a possibility as wildly unlikely. The only meaning which can be given to such a notion is political, and there is nothing irreligious about such an interpretation, according to Ibn Rushd. It is difficult for unsophisticated believers to understand that it is worthwhile to act well and avoid evil, or that their actions have a wider reference than the immediate community of acquaintances, so any religion which is able to motivate them must address them in ways that they comprehend and in a language which strikes an emotional chord. Richly descriptive accounts of the afterlife, of God seeing everything which happens and of his creation of the world out of nothing, help adherence by the majority to the principles of religion and are the only sort of language which most members of the community can understand. The arguments which Ibn Rushd presents for hedging in the notion of the immortality of the individual soul would not mean much to the unsophisticated believer, while the more intellectually alert are expected by Ibn Rushd to understand how that notion fits in with the basic principles of Islam.

4 Moral and political philosophy

Ibn Rushd presents a firm critique of the Ash'arite theory of moral language, which interprets rightness and wrongness entirely in conformity with the commands of God. The purpose of that theory is to emphasize the power and authority of the deity over everything, even over the meaning of ethical terms (see ETHICS IN ISLAMIC PHILOSOPHY). What we ought to do then is simply equivalent to God's commands, and we ought to do it because God has commanded it, so that everything we need to know about moral behaviour is encapsulated in Islam. Ibn Rushd argued that on the contrary, a distinction should be drawn between moral notions and divine commands. Here he follows an Aristotelian approach. Since everything has a nature, and this nature defines its end, we as things also have natures and ends at which our behaviour is directed. The purpose of a plant is to grow and the aim of a saw is to cut, but what is the purpose of a human being? One of our ultimate aims is to be happy and to avoid actions which lead to unhappiness. It is not difficult here to align Islamic and Aristotelian principles: moral virtue leads to happiness since, if we do what we should in accordance with our nature, we will be able to achieve happiness. This happiness may be interpreted in a number of ways, either as a mixture of social and religious activities or as an entirely intellectual ideal.

However, the latter is possible only for a very few, and neither religion nor philosophy would approve of it as the ultimate aim for the majority of the community. There is an essential social dimension to human happiness which makes the identification of happiness with correct moral and religious behaviour much easier to establish. It is conceivable that someone would try to live completely apart from the community to concentrate upon entirely intellectual pursuits, but this way of living is inferior to a life in which there is a concentration upon intellectual thought combined with integration within the practices of a particular society.

One might expect that a thinker such as Ibn Rushd, who was working within an Islamic context, would identify happiness and misery with some aspect of the afterlife, but as we have seen, he was unable to accept the traditional view of the afterlife as containing surviving individuals like ourselves. What the notion of the afterlife is supposed to achieve is an understanding that the scope of personal action is wider than might immediately appear to be the case. Without religious language and imagery, ordinary believers may find it difficult to grasp that our moral actions affect not only ourselves but the happiness of the whole community, not just at a particular time or in a particular place but as a species. When we behave badly we damage our own chances of human flourishing, and this affects our personal opportunities for achieving happiness and growing as people. It also affects our relationships with other people, resulting in a weakening of society. While it is possibly true that the misery consequent upon evil-doing may not follow us personally after our death, it may well follow the community. The importance of the notion of an afterlife is that it points to the wider terms of reference in which moral action has life.

In his commentary on Plato's *Republic*, Ibn Rushd modifies Plato in terms of his own Aristotelian views and applies the text to the contemporary state. He uses Plato's idea of the transformation and deterioration of the ideal state into four imperfect states to illustrate aspects of past and contemporary political organization in the Islamic world (see POLITICAL PHILOSOPHY IN CLASSICAL ISLAM). He takes mischievous pleasure in comparing the theologians of his own time, the *mutakallimun*, to Plato's sophists (see ISLAMIC THEOLOGY §2). He describes the theologians as a genuine danger to the state and to the purity of Islam, and suggests to the ruler that a ban on the publicizing of their activities is advisable. In this and many of his other works, Ibn Rushd stresses the importance of a careful understanding of the relationship between religion and philosophy in the state. Revelation is superior to philosophy in that it makes its message more widely available than is possible for philosophy. The prophet can do things which the philosopher cannot, such as teaching the masses, understanding the future, establishing religious laws and contributing to the happiness of the whole of humanity. Through divine revelation or inspiration, the prophet establishes laws which make it possible for people to attain an understanding of how they should behave. The credentials of the prophet are to be established by political skill. Miracles are irrelevant here; only legislative abilities count.

The philosopher has all the theoretical knowledge which the prophet has, but only the latter can embody this knowledge in a law and persuade the general public that this is a law which must be obeyed (see LAW, ISLAMIC PHILOSOPHY OF). What the prophet has is practical knowledge as well as the theoretical knowledge which he shares with the philosopher, and so the content of the prophetic law (*shari'a*) is no different from the content of the philosophical law (*namus*). The prophet is much better at putting this content across to the community, and can transform abstract ideas about human happiness into political ideas and social norms which then are capable of regulating the life of the community. However, it is worth emphasizing that the only advantage which religion has over reason is that the former involves a practical form of knowledge which is not necessarily possessed by the latter. The issue of the relationship between philosophy and religion fascinated the Islamic philosophers (see EPISTEMOLOGY IN ISLAMIC PHILOSOPHY §5), and Ibn Rushd was no exception in this respect. He tried to refine this issue time and time again throughout his works.

5 The role of philosophy

The role of the philosopher in the state was a topic of continual interest for Ibn Rushd. He noticed that ARISTOTLE (§26) seemed to hesitate between the view that the prime constituent of the good life is intellectual thought and the alternative, based upon a broader collection of virtues. These two alternatives have very different implications, especially within the context of a religious philosophy. The identification of a more social notion of happiness as living in accordance with a general mixture of virtues would make happiness more generally available to the public, since it would mean that the unsophisticated but dutiful believer could achieve a high level of perfection in their life. The idea that intellectual excellence is the highest form of human wellbeing or happiness implies that the great majority of the community, unable or disinclined to concentrate completely on intellectual issues, is thereby deprived of the very best form of life. No religion such as Islam with its claims to universality could tolerate such a confining restriction on human happiness. Ibn Rushd thinks he can avoid this dilemma. The basis to his solution is the argument that religion and philosophy are not incompatible. Islam is a rational system of beliefs and it requires its adherents to attend to rational arguments concerning how they are to behave and think. The rational arguments are there in the Qur'an and other places for those who can follow them, and for those who cannot there are other forms of presentation of the truth which are easier to understand.

This might seem a patronizing way to describe the faith of the ordinary believer, but Ibn Rushd suggests that if we look at examples from law and medicine we shall see how acceptable it is. Lawyers may study in detail the principles behind legislation, yet most of the community just follows the law without thinking deeply about its rationale. Those who work in medical fields have a good understanding of how the body works and how different forms of treatment affect the health of the individual. The ordinary person does not understand much of this, and just goes along with what they are told by the medical experts. There is nothing wrong with this; there is no necessity for everyone in the community to be either a lawyer or a doctor. Different people have different attitudes to both the law and medicine, some based upon real understanding and some based upon casual acquaintance, and these differences do not interfere with the ability of everyone in the community to live in an organized and healthy society.

Any religion with claims to general acceptability must present its message in a suitable form for the particular audience it is addressing. Ibn Rushd argues that Islam is an especially excellent religion because it has the ability to present the important issues to the greatest variety of people. Some people will be attracted to Islam and strengthened in their faith if the philosophical arguments for being a Muslim are pursued and developed. Others, perhaps the majority, cannot really understand such arguments but can understand simpler arguments and parables which describe in simple terms what is wrong with other religions and why Islam is superior to them. Still others will not even be able to grasp such simple arguments and so must be persuaded by rhetorical devices, which include a grain of logical force but mainly consist of persuasive imagery and exhortation. The way in which Ibn Rushd makes this distinction has led some commentators to think that his real view is that philosophy alone reveals the truth, and religion is only suitable for the intellectually weak who have to be satisfied with stories and doctrines which are,

strictly speaking, false. Such a disingenuous interpretation is not required, however. Ibn Rushd is trying to highlight the fact that there are a variety of ways of coming to know something, some of which are surer than others, but all of which are acceptable. Once the object of knowledge is acquired then it is known, however that knowledge has been achieved. We know religious truths in different ways, but we really do know exactly the same thing.

One of the excellences of Islam, according to Ibn Rushd, is its accessibility to a wide range of adherents. In many of his works, and especially in his *Fasl almaqal* (Decisive Treatise), he argues that the highest form of demonstrative reasoning cannot clash with the principles of religion. He claims here that philosophers are best able to understand properly the allegorical passages in the Qur'an on the basis of their logical training, and that there is no religious stipulation that all such passages have to be interpreted literally. Where demonstrative reasoning appears to conflict with the sense of Scripture, then those capable of demonstration (the philosophers) know that the passages must be interpreted allegorically so as to cohere with the demonstrative truths. Philosophers should be careful when they do this not to offend the religious sensibilities of the less sophisticated, in sharp contrast with the practice of the theologians. The latter frequently interpret such passages so crudely that they either throw doubt on religion itself, or threaten the pursuit of philosophy by raising doubts in people's minds concerning the orthodoxy of the conclusions reached by the philosophers. Language should be seen as a sophisticated vehicle for communicating information to different categories of audience. Religion is a means for the easy comprehension of the majority of the people, and where a hidden meaning exists it is up to the philosophers to discover it and keep it to themselves, while the rest of the community must accept the literalness of Scripture.

6 Philosophy of language

Ibn Rushd is in a difficult position when trying to respond to al-Ghazali's attacks upon philosophy, since the former tried at the same time to distance himself from the sort of Neoplatonic approach to theoretical issues which Ibn Sina advocated, and it was Ibn Sina who was the direct object of al-Ghazali's critique. One of the most significant methodological disputes between Ibn Rushd and Ibn Sina lies in their differing analyses of the relationship between essence and existence, and this has an important influence upon Ibn Rushd's approach to meaning. Ibn Sina held that a state of affairs is possible if and only if something else acts to bring it into existence, with the sole exception of the deity. Ibn Rushd characterizes this view, quite correctly, as one in which possible states of affairs are nonexistent in themselves, until their existence is brought about by some cause. The possible is that whose essence does not include its existence and so must depend upon a cause which makes its actuality necessary, but only necessary relative to that cause. In this modal system there are really only two kinds of being, that necessary through another and that necessary in itself (that is, God), so that the realm of the possible becomes identical with both the actual and the necessary.

Both Ibn Rushd and Ibn Sina maintain that there is a logical distinction between essence and existence, but the former accuses the latter of conflating the order of thought with the order of things, the logical order with the ontological order. Ibn Sina does indeed start with the logical distinction between essence and existence and then proceeds via his theory of emanation to show how existence comes to essence from the necessarily acting Necessary Being (see NEOPLATONISM IN ISLAMIC PHILOSOPHY §3). The occasionalism of AL-GHAZALI is like the theory of emanation of IBN SINA, in that both doctrines interpret the contingent world as radically dependent upon something else. The account of essence and existence provided by Ibn Sina is perfectly acceptable to al-Ghazali, with the proviso that direct divine intervention is required to bring existence to the essences. Ibn Sina divides up the world into existing things and essences, into what we can think about and what really exists, and into things which are necessary through another and are possible in themselves. These distinctions throw doubt on the sort of realism and emphasis upon substance that is so important for Ibn Rushd and his form of Aristotelianism. This latter is based upon a model of the world as one entity, as a single order of nature with no impenetrable barriers to human understanding and investigation. This leads Ibn Rushd to argue that although a logical distinction can be drawn between the existence and essence of a thing, there is nonetheless a necessary relationship between existence and essence. Without such a relationship, one could conceive of all sorts of things happening to essences without regard to how they are actually instantiated – the sorts of thought-experiments which al-Ghazali advocates – which Ibn Rushd argues seriously misrepresents the nature of philosophy. The meaning of the name of a thing is intimately connected with the way in which it is instantiated, and it is a radical error in the philosophy of language to separate essence and existence (see EXISTENCE; MEANING IN ISLAMIC PHILOSOPHY §3).

To understand Ibn Rushd's account of a variety of paths to the truth, we have to grasp his theory of meaning. He emphasizes the importance of notions such as equivocation and ambiguity in language because he thinks it is important to be able to explain how names can be used in similar ways in different contexts. Ibn Rushd agrees with Aristotle that there can be no priority or posteriority within the same genus, and so he develops an account of meaning which is based upon the *pros hen* rather than the genus–species relation. If the latter were used, meaning would come out as univocal and al-Ghazali would be entirely justified in expecting the philosophers to account for God and his activity in the same sort of language as we use to describe ourselves. If meaning is expressed in terms of *pros hen* equivocals (*bi nisba ila shay' wahid*), then we can look for some similarity in the objects which form the basis to the sharing of the name, but we do not have to insist that exactly the same name be used in its different contexts with precisely the same meaning. We can also insist that the different contexts in which a name is used have to be taken into account when we come to ask for the meaning of the name. For al-Ghazali, abstract terms have a meaning which is independent of their reference in the external world. The meaning of such terms is equivalent to the series of pictures or images in which the events they describe are characterized in particular ways. All that we have to do to conceive of God miraculously creating something out of nothing is to imagine it happening, and so it is possible. Ibn Rushd argues that, on the contrary, it is not enough to have a series of images in one's mind to establish the meaningfulness of that combination of images. A meaningful use of language is possible only through the connection of linguistic terms and ideas with a framework in which they make sense, and such a framework is connected to the varying uses of the terms and to the way in which the world is.

The concept which Ibn Rushd wants his account of language to characterize is that of a point of view. In Ibn Rushd's thought there is a continual contrast between different points of view, not just a distinction between God's point of view and the human point of view, but also a differentiation of the standpoints of the whole of humanity based upon their forms of reasoning. For example, in the *Fasl al-maqal* he talks about demonstrative, dialectical, rhetorical and sophistical people, all of whom are using similar language to discuss what is important to them, namely their faith, morality, the next life and so on. This language is not identical regardless of the way in which it is used, nor is it completely equivocal. There are connections between different applications of the same name, and these connections are strong enough for it to make sense to say that these uses are of the same name; so we can talk about there being a variety of routes to the same destination, a variety of views based upon the same ideas and beliefs, and a variety of ways of living which together add up to a morally and religiously desirable form of life.

Ibn Rushd extends the use of the notion of *ijma'* (consensus) from its theological role of establishing what is acceptable within Islam to an even more important role, that of establishing what words mean. If there is agreement in the community that particular scriptural passages are clear, then they are clear and that is the end of the matter. If it is felt by some that there is ambiguity in some passages, then there is ambiguity which has to be resolved in some way if practice is not to suffer. Those who feel that there is ambiguity have to try to resolve that ambiguity in a way which enables them to follow the route to salvation. They must do this without challenging the views of the rest of the community, since to do so would threaten the ordinary meanings of the terms which are being used. Ibn Rushd suggests that if the theologians publicize their confused thoughts about the meaning of the Qur'an, ordinary believers would doubt that they understood the texts they originally thought they knew. If doctors were to do this sort of thing, then their patients would come to think that there is no such thing as health and illness.

Ibn Rushd argues that we know from our everyday experience that there exists health and illness, and that religious texts contain important information as to how we should behave. We also have to pay attention to the different ways in which different people relate to these facts. There exists a whole variety of different views on a particular issue, and this variety of views is represented by the variety of language which is available to describe this continuum of views, ranging from the entirely demonstrative to the purely poetic and expressive. Equivocation in language is not something to be challenged; rather it is to be accepted, since it represents a feature of our lives as different people living in a community with a whole range of ends and purposes. We should respect the different uses of the same word because they represent different points of view, different perspectives on the same thing. When Ibn Rushd tries to reconcile apparently contradictory views his approach is to argue that all these views are acceptable as different aspects of one thing. Throughout his philosophy he tries to show how it is possible for one thing to be described in a variety of ways.

See also: ARISTOTELIANISM IN ISLAMIC PHILOSOPHY; AVERROISM; AVERROISM, JEWISH; AL-GHAZALI; IBN SINA; ISLAMIC PHILOSOPHY: TRANSMISSION INTO WESTERN EUROPE; MEANING IN ISLAMIC PHILOSOPHY; NEOPLATONISM IN ISLAMIC PHILOSOPHY

List of works

Some of Ibn Rushd's works are now only extant in Hebrew or Latin, and some not at all. The most useful bibliography is Rosemann, P. (1988) 'Ibn Rushd: A Catalogue of Editions and Scholarly Writings from 1821 onwards', *Bulletin de philosophie médiévale* 30: 153–215.

Ibn Rushd (1169–98) Commentaries on Aristotle, *Aristotelis opera... cum Averrois Cordubensis variis in eosdem commentariis*, Venice: Juntas, 1562–74; repr. Frankfurt: Minerva, 1962. (Ibn Rushd's commentaries as they appeared in Latin and formed part of the approach to Aristotle in Christian Europe.)

—— (c. 1174) Middle Commentaries on Aristotle, ed. C. Butterworth, *Averroes' Middle Commentaries on Aristotle's Categories and De Interpretatione*, Princeton, NJ: Princeton University Press, 1983. (Translation and commentary on two of Ibn Rushd's major works on philosophical logic and language.)

—— (before 1175) Short Commentaries on Aristotle, ed. C. Butterworth, *Averroes' Three Short Commentaries on Aristotle's 'Topics', 'Rhetoric' and 'Poetics'*, Albany, NY: State University of New York Press, 1977. (A translation and commentary on three of Ibn Rushd's main discussions of different forms of language.)

—— (1179–80) *Fasl al-maqal* (Decisive Treatise), ed. G. Hourani, *Averroes on the Harmony of Religion and Philosophy*, London: Luzac, 1961; repr. 1976. (Translation and discussion of the *Fasl al-maqal* and two other short pieces on the same topic.)

—— (1180) *Tahafut al-tahafut* (The Incoherence of the Incoherence), ed. S. Van den Bergh, *Averroes' Tahafut al-Tahafut (The Incoherence of the Incoherence)*, London: Luzac, 1954; repr. 1978. (The standard translation of Ibn Rushd's response to al-Ghazali, incorporating the latter's text.)

—— (c. 1190) Long Commentary on Aristotle's *Metaphysics*, ed. C. Genequand, *Ibn Rushd's Metaphysics*, Leiden: Brill, 1984. (A translation and commentary of Ibn Rushd's commentary on Aristotle's *Metaphysics*, Book Lambda.)

—— (1194) Middle Commentary on Plato's *Republic*, ed. R. Lerner, *Averroes on Plato's 'Republic'*, Ithaca, NY: Cornell University Press, 1974. (The most modern translation with extensive commentary of Ibn Rushd's commentary on Plato's *Republic*.)

References and further reading

Allard, M. (1952–4) 'Le Rationalisme d'Averroès d'après une Étude sur la création' (Averroes' Rationalism in his Study on the Creation), *Bulletin d'Études Orientales* 14: 7–59. (An account of some of the stresses between the philosophical and theological approaches to creation.)

Fakhry, M. (1958) *Islamic Occasionalism and Its Critique by Averroes and Aquinas*, London: Allen & Unwin. (The way in which Ibn Rushd's approach to the topic of causality became part of wider philosophical thought in Christian Europe.)

Hayoun, M.-R. and Libera, A. de (1991) *Averroès et l'averroïsme*, Paris: Presses Universitaires de France. (A concise but comprehensive description of Ibn Rushd's thought and its philosophical impact through the Averroist movement.)

Kogan, B. (1985) *Averroes and the Metaphysics of Creation*, Albany, NY: State University of New York Press. (Comprehensive treatment of Ibn Rushd on causal necessity, miracles, God's knowledge and emanation.)

Leaman, O. (1988) *Averroes and His Philosophy*, Oxford: Clarendon Press; 2nd edn, Richmond: Curzon, 1997. (A general account of his philosophy.)

—— (1994) 'Was Averroes an Averroist?', in F. Niewöhner and L. Sturlese (eds) *Averroismus im Mittelalter und in der Renaissance*, Zurich: Spur Verlag, 9–22. (A discussion of the links between the thought of Averroes and the Averroist movement.)

—— (1995) 'Averroes', in F. Niewöhner (ed.) *Klassiker der Religionsphilosophie*, Munich: Beck, 142–62. (Concise account of the contribution of Averroes to philosophy.)

—— (1996) 'Averroes and the West', in M. Wahba and M. Abousenna (eds) *Averroes and the Enlightenment*, New York: Prometheus, 53–67. (The links between Ibn Rushd and Averroism should be acknowledged as close, as should the role of Ibn Rushd in the growth of modernity in the West.)

Urvoy, D. (1991) *Ibn Rushd (Averroes)*, London: Routledge. (An account of his thought which lays particular emphasis upon contemporary events in Andalus.)

—— (1996) 'Ibn Rushd' in S.H. Nasr and O. Leaman (eds) *History of Islamic Philosophy*, London: Routledge, 330–45. (General account of his thought, with particular attention to the context within which he was writing.)

Wolfson, H. (1961) 'The Twice-Revealed Averroes', *Speculum* 36: 373–92. (A highly influential and suggestive summary of Ibn Rushd's standing in the history of philosophy.)

OLIVER LEAMAN

IBN SAB'IN, MUHAMMAD IBN 'ABD AL-HAQQ (1217–68)

Ibn Sab'in is well-known in Islamic philosophy for presenting perhaps the most radical form of Sufism. He argued that everything is really just one thing, part of the deity, and that breaking up reality into different units is to deny the nature of creation. He was hostile as a result to the attempts of the philosophers who were inspired by Aristotle to develop logic as a means to understand reality. The best way to attain the truth is the mystical path, and this is achieved by appreciating the unity of everything, not by analysing reality into separable concepts.

Ibn Sab'in came from Murcia (southeast Spain) and embraced the same type of philosophical thinking and writing as the main mystic of the twelfth century, Ibn al-'Arabi. Ibn Sab'in moved to Mecca after the year AH 642/AD 1245, where he remained until he put an end to his life. His pre-eminence in Sufi circles won him the title 'Qutb ad-Din' (the Pole of Religion). He belongs to a school of Sufism which views existence, both in its divine and worldly forms, as one indivisible unit. An important work is *Asrar al-hikma al-mashriqiyya* (The Secrets of Illuminationist Philosophy). The most important source of Ibn Sab'in's philosophy, however, is his book *Budd al-'arif* (Escape of the Gnostic) which deals with the path to knowledge, which he wrote in AH 643/AD 1245 after moving from Spain to Morocco. In this book, Ibn Sab'in poses the fundamental question of how a Sufi can reach truth and prepare for the reception and comprehension of divine perfection. In answering these questions, he discusses the opinions of the philosophical schools that preceded him, proving the inability of those schools to reach the truth.

In his writings, Ibn Sab'in attempted to enter the realm of Sufism by way of philosophy, explaining in his presentation of the history of Islamic thought that such disciplines as philology, scholastic theology (*kalam*) and philosophy are but milestones along the Sufi's path to perfection. Thus the discipline of the Sufi who has achieved perfection is the essence of all the other disciplines. In his attempt to determine the manner in which a Sufi attains unity with God, Ibn Sab'in examines the manner in which a person achieves knowledge. By knowledge, he means the discipline of logic and the ability of such a discipline to help one to achieve divine knowledge (see LOGIC IN ISLAMIC PHILOSOPHY). He then deals with a host of concepts with a special focus on the 'intellect' and the 'self' as being the tools for achieving knowledge and as having a primary role in bringing the Sufi closer to God. Ibn Sab'in is close to most Muslim Sufi thinkers in their initial emphasis on other disciplines that a Sufi should master, particularly logic. He differs from them, however, in his conclusions about the role of logic. Whereas most philosophers, particularly the Aristotelians, view logic as a tool which helps us to know the world and which founds the theory of knowledge (see ARISTOTELIANISM IN ISLAMIC PHILO-SOPHY), Ibn Sab'in views the role of logic as being random and worthless, since for him knowledge is only knowledge of God. Such knowledge is subject in its meaning to one consideration, a consideration of the internal experience based on our stimulation and sensations, sensations with standards and bases superior to the standards and methods of logic.

Since according to Ibn Sab'in the unity of existence is the criterion for understanding existence, examination of the various phenomena in existence would be incompatible with such unity and hence would mean the postulation of the idea of a God superior to and separate from his creations. In Ibn Sab'in's concept of absolute unity of existence, following that of IBN AL-'ARABI, the separation of God from his creation is inadmissible. He presents the 'intellect' and the 'self' as the means which lead us to the divine Being. In this theory, Ibn Sab'in is critical of his predecessors who viewed the mind or intellect as no more than a means for the acquisition of knowledge; he views the intellect as being of divine origin. His defence of this theory is based on the Prophetic *hadith* (tradition) that 'the first thing God created was the intellect; God then told it to come forward which it did, and then told it to go away which it also did.' Ibn Sab'in's attempt to demonstrate the possibility of the intellect contacting the divine is based on this relationship, namely that the intellect is a divine creation and as such the mind can directly and without any mediation communicate with its origin. The philosophers' attempt to reach a higher level of knowledge through making contact with the active intellect is a less ambitious attempt than that of the Sufis, who make unity with God their chief concern.

Like the intellect, the self is not merely a means by which perception takes place but should rather be perceived as a goal in itself, a goal which constitutes the knowledge that the Sufi seeks. In Ibn Sab'in's theory the self, like the intellect, is a divine creation. The path that leads to unification with God, then, is based on the discovery of the self or, more correctly,

discovery of the secret which God has entrusted to us. Unification with God is thus an internal experience which does not follow the philosophers' accounts. For whereas the philosophers saw the path to God as a matter of proof, Ibn Sab'in saw such a path as a matter of experience based on a particular discovery through which the truth becomes evident, so that the Sufi feels that God is closer to him than his own jugular vein.

See also: MYSTICAL PHILOSOPHY IN ISLAM

List of works

Ibn Sab'in (1217–68) *Budd al-'arif* (Escape of the Gnostic), ed. G. Kattura, Beirut: Dar al-Andalus, 1978. (Most complete summary of Ibn Sab'in's critique of philosophy and defence of Sufism.)

—— (1217–68) *Asrar al-hikma al-mashriqiyya* (The Secrets of Illuminationist Philosophy). (There is no published edition of this work.)

—— (1217–68) *al-Kalam 'ala'l masa'il al-siqliyyah* (Philosophical Correspondence with the Emperor Frederick II Hohenstaufen), ed. S. Taltkaya, *Correspondance philosophique avec l'Empereur Frédéric II de Hohenstaufen*, Paris, 1943. (His discussions with the king of Sicily, the Emperor Frederick II, about the main principles of Aristotelianism.)

References and further reading

Taftazani, A. and Leaman, O. (1996) 'Ibn Sab'in', in S.H. Nasr and O. Leaman (eds) *The History of Islamic Philosophy*, London: Routledge, 346–9. (General account of Ibn Sab'in's thought and times.)

ELSAYED M.H. OMRAN

IBN SINA, ABU 'ALI AL-HUSAYN (980–1037)

Ibn Sina (Avicenna) is one of the foremost philosophers in the Medieval Hellenistic Islamic tradition that also includes al-Farabi and Ibn Rushd. His philosophical theory is a comprehensive, detailed and rationalistic account of the nature of God and Being, in which he finds a systematic place for the corporeal world, spirit, insight, and the varieties of logical thought including dialectic, rhetoric and poetry.

Central to Ibn Sina's philosophy is his concept of reality and reasoning. Reason, in his scheme, can allow progress through various levels of understanding and can finally lead to God, the ultimate truth. He stresses the importance of gaining knowledge, and develops a theory of knowledge based on four faculties: sense perception, retention, imagination and estimation. Imagination has the principal role in intellection, as it can compare and construct images which give it access to universals. Again the ultimate object of knowledge is God, the pure intellect.

In metaphysics, Ibn Sina makes a distinction between essence and existence; essence considers only the nature of things, and should be considered apart from their mental and physical realization. This distinction applies to all things except God, whom Ibn Sina identifies as the first cause and therefore both essence and existence. He also argued that the soul is incorporeal and cannot be destroyed. The soul, in his view, is an agent with choice in this world between good and evil, which in turn leads to reward or punishment.

Reference has sometimes been made to Ibn Sina's supposed mysticism, but this would appear to be based on a misreading by Western philosophers of parts of his work. As one of the most important practitioners of philosophy, Ibn Sina exercised a strong influence over both other Islamic philosophers and medieval Europe. His work was one of the main targets of al-Ghazali's attack on Hellenistic influences in Islam. In Latin translations, his works influenced many Christian philosophers, most notably Thomas Aquinas.

1   **Biography**
2   **Reason and reality**
3   **Theory of knowledge**
4   **Metaphysics**
5   **The existence of God**
6   **The soul**
7   **Reward and punishment**
8   **Poetry, character and society**
9   **Links to the West**

1   Biography

Ibn Sina was born in AH 370/AD 980 near Bukhara in Central Asia, where his father governed a village in one of the royal estates. At thirteen, Ibn Sina began a study of medicine that resulted in 'distinguished physicians ... reading the science of medicine under [him]' (Sirat al-shaykh al-ra'is (The Life of Ibn Sina): 27). His medical expertise brought him to the attention of the Sultan of Bukhara, Nuh ibn Mansur, whom he treated successfully; as a result he was given permission to use the sultan's library and its rare manuscripts, allowing him to continue his research into modes of knowledge.

When the sultan died, the heir to the throne, 'Ali

ibn Shams al-Dawla, asked Ibn Sina to continue as vizier, but the philosopher was negotiating to join the forces of another son of the late king, Ala al-Dawla, and so went into hiding. During this time he composed his major philosophical treatise, *Kitab al-shifa'* (Book of Healing), a comprehensive account of learning that ranges from logic and mathematics to metaphysics and the afterlife. While he was writing the section on logic Ibn Sina was arrested and imprisoned, but he escaped to Isfahan, disguised as a Sufi, and joined Ala al-Dawla. While in the service of the latter he completed *al-Shifa'* and produced the *Kitab al-najat* (Book of Salvation), an abridgment of *al-Shifa'*. He also produced at least two major works on logic: one, *al-Mantiq*, translated as *The Propositional Logic of Ibn Sina*, was a commentary on Aristotle's *Prior Analytics* and forms part of *al-Shifa'*; the other, *al-Isharat wa-'l-tanbihat* (Remarks and Admonitions), seems to be written in the 'indicative mode', where the reader must participate by working out the steps leading from the stated premises to proposed conclusions. He also produced a treatise on definitions and a summary of the theoretical sciences, together with a number of psychological, religious and other works; the latter include works on astronomy, medicine, philology and zoology, as well as poems and an allegorical work, *Hayy ibn Yaqzan* (The Living Son of the Vigilant). His biographer also mentions numerous short works on logic and metaphysics, and a book on 'Fair Judgment' that was lost when his prince's fortunes suffered a turn. Ibn Sina's philosophical and medical work and his political involvement continued until his death.

2   Reason and reality

Ibn Sina's autobiography parallels his allegorical work, *Hayy ibn Yaqzan*. Both clarify how it is possible for individuals by themselves to arrive at the ultimate truths about reality, being and God. The autobiography shows how Ibn Sina more or less taught himself, although with particular kinds of help at significant moments, and proceeded through various levels of sophistication until he arrived at ultimate truths.

Such progress was possible because of Ibn Sina's conception of reality and reasoning. He maintains that God, the principle of all existence, is pure intellect, from whom other existing things such as minds, bodies and other objects all emanate, and therefore to whom they are all necessarily related. That necessity, once it is fully understood, is rational and allows existents to be inferred from each other and, ultimately, from God. In effect, the totality of intelligibles is structured syllogistically and human knowledge consists of the mind's reception and grasp of intelligible being. Since knowledge consists of grasping syllogistically structured intelligibles, it requires the use of reasoning to follow the relations between intelligibles. Among these intelligibles are first principles that include both concepts such as 'the existent', 'the thing' and 'the necessary', that make up the categories, and the truths of logic, including the first-figure syllogistics, all of which are basic, primitive and obvious. They cannot be explained further since all explanation and thought proceeds only on their basis. The rules of logic are also crucial to human development.

Ibn Sina's stand on the fundamental nature of categorical concepts and logical forms follows central features of Aristotle's thought in the *Prior Analytics* (see ARISTOTLE §§4–7). Borrowing from Aristotle, he also singles out a capacity for a mental act in which the knower spontaneously hits upon the middle term of a syllogism. Since rational arguments proceed syllogistically, the ability to hit upon the middle term is the ability to move an argument forward by seeing how given premises yield appropriate conclusions. It allows the person possessing this ability to develop arguments, to recognize the inferential relations between syllogisms. Moreover, since reality is structured syllogistically, the ability to hit upon the middle term and to develop arguments is crucial to moving knowledge of reality forward.

Ibn Sina holds that it is important to gain knowledge. Grasp of the intelligibles determines the fate of the rational soul in the hereafter, and therefore is crucial to human activity. When the human intellect grasps these intelligibles it comes into contact with the Active Intellect, a level of being that emanates ultimately from God, and receives a 'divine effluence'. People may be ordered according to their capacity for gaining knowledge, and thus by their possession and development of the capacity for hitting on the middle term. At the highest point is the prophet, who knows the intelligibles all at once, or nearly so. He has a pure rational soul and can know the intelligibles in their proper syllogistic order, including their middle terms. At the other end lies the impure person lacking in the capacity for developing arguments. Most people are in between these extremes, but they may improve their capacity for grasping the middle term by developing a balanced temperament and purity of soul (see LOGIC IN ISLAMIC PHILOSOPHY §1).

In relation to the older debate about the respective scopes of grammar and logic, Ibn Sina argues that since logic deals with concepts that can be abstracted from sensible material, it also escapes the contingencies of the latter. Language and grammar govern sensible material and therefore have a different domain; indeed, languages are various and their rules of operation, their grasp of sensible material, are likewise articulated variously (see LANGUAGE, PHILOSOPHY OF). Nevertheless, languages make available the abstracted concepts whose operation is governed by logic; yet if language deals with contingencies, it is not clear how it can grasp or make available the objects of logic. At times, as for example in *al-Isharat*, Ibn Sina suggests that languages generally share a structure.

3 Theory of knowledge

In his theory of knowledge, Ibn Sina identifies the mental faculties of the soul in terms of their epistemological function. As the discussion of logic in §2 has already suggested, knowledge begins with abstraction. Sense perception, being already mental, is the form of the object perceived (see SENSE AND REFERENCE §1). Sense perception responds to the particular with its given form and material accidents. As a mental event, being a perception of an object rather than the object itself, perception occurs in the particular. To analyse this response, classifying its formal features in abstraction from material accidents, we must both retain the images given by sensation and also manipulate them by disconnecting parts and aligning them according to their formal and other properties. However, retention and manipulation are distinct epistemological functions, and cannot depend on the same psychological faculty; therefore Ibn Sina distinguishes faculties of relation and manipulation as appropriate to those diverse epistemological functions (see EPISTEMOLOGY IN ISLAMIC PHILOSOPHY §4).

Ibn Sina identifies the retentive faculty as 'representation' and charges the imagination with the task of reproducing and manipulating images. To conceptualize our experience and to order it according to its qualities, we must have and be able to reinvoke images of what we experienced but is now absent. For this we need sensation and representation at least; in addition, to order and classify the content of representation, we must be able to discriminate, separate out and recombine parts of images, and therefore must possess imagination and reason. To think about a black flag we must be able to analyse its colour, separating this quality from others, or its part in the image from other images, and classify it with other black things, thereby showing that the concept of black applies to all such objects and their images. Imagination carries out this manipulation, allowing us to produce images of objects we have not seen in fact out of the images of things we have experienced, and thereby also generating images for intelligibles and prophecies.

Beyond sense perception, retention and imagination, Ibn Sina locates estimation (*wahm*). This is a faculty for perceiving non-sensible 'intentions that exist in the individual sensible objects'. A sheep flees a wolf because it estimates that the animal may do it harm; this estimation is more than representation and imagination, since it includes an intention that is additional to the perceived and abstracted form and concept of the animal. Finally, there may be a faculty that retains the content of *wahm*, the meanings of images. Ibn Sina also relies on a faculty of common sense, involving awareness of the work and products of all the other faculties, which interrelates these features.

Of these faculties, imagination has a principal role in intellection. Its comparison and construction of images with given meanings gives it access to universals in that it is able to think of the universal by manipulating images (see UNIVERSALS). However, Ibn Sina explains this process of grasping the universal, this emergence of the universal in the human mind, as the result of an action on the mind by the Active Intellect. This intellect is the last of ten cosmic intellects that stand below God. In other words, the manipulation of images does not by itself procure a grasp of universals so much as train the mind to think the universals when they are given to the mind by the Active Intellect. Once achieved, the processes undergone in training inform the mind so that the latter can attend directly to the Active Intellect when required. Such direct access is crucial since the soul lacks any faculty for retaining universals and therefore repeatedly needs fresh access to the Active Intellect.

As the highest point above the Active Intellect, God, the pure intellect, is also the highest object of human knowledge. All sense experience, logic and the faculties of the human soul are therefore directed at grasping the fundamental structure of reality as it emanates from that source and, through various levels of being down to the Active Intellect, becomes available to human thought through reason or, in the case of prophets, intuition. By this conception, then, there is a close relation between logic, thought, experience, the grasp of the ultimate structure of reality and an understanding of God. As the highest and purest intellect, God is the source of all the existent things in the world. The latter emanate from that pure high intellect, and they are ordered according to a necessity that we can grasp by the use of rational conceptual thought (see NEOPLATONISM IN ISLAMIC PHILOSOPHY). These interconnections become clearer in Ibn Sina's metaphysics.

4 Metaphysics

Metaphysics examines existence as such, 'absolute existence' (*al-wujud al-matlaq*) or existence so far as it exists. Ibn Sina relies on the one hand on the distinction in Aristotle's *Prior Analytics* between the principles basic to a scientific or mathematical grasp of the world, including the four causes, and on the other hand the subject of metaphysics, the prime or ultimate cause of all things – God. In relation to the first issue, Ibn Sina recognizes that observation of regularities in nature fails to establish their necessity. At best it evinces the existence of a relation of concomitance between events. To establish the necessity implicated in causality, we must recognize that merely accidental regularities would be unlikely to occur always, or even at all, and certainly not with the regularity that events can exhibit (see CAUSALITY AND NECESSITY IN ISLAMIC THOUGHT). Thus, we may expect that such regularities must be the necessary result of the essential properties of the objects in question.

In developing this distinction between the principles and subject of metaphysics, Ibn Sina makes another distinction between essence and existence, one that applies to everything except God. Essence and existence are distinct in that we cannot infer from the essence of something that it must exist (see EXISTENCE). Essence considers only the nature of things, and while this may be realized in particular real circumstances or as an item in the mind with its attendant conditions, nevertheless essence can be considered for itself apart from that mental and physical realization. Essences exist in supra-human intelligences and also in the human mind. Further, if essence is distinct from existence in the way Ibn Sina is proposing, then both the existence and the non-existence of the essence may occur, and each may call for explanation.

5 The existence of God

The above distinctions enter into the central subject matter of metaphysics, that is, God and the proof of his existence. Scholars propose that the most detailed and comprehensive of Ibn Sina's arguments for God's existence occurs in the 'Metaphysics' section of *al-Shifa'* (Gutas 1988; Mamura 1962; Morewedge 1972). We know from the *Categories* of Aristotle that existence is either necessary or possible. If an existence were only possible, then we could argue that it would presuppose a necessary existence, for as a merely possible existence, it need not have existed and would need some additional factor to bring about its existence rather than its non-existence. That is, the possible existence, in order to be existent, must have been necessitated by something else. Yet that something else cannot be another merely possible existence since the latter would itself stand in need of some other necessitation in order to bring it about, or would lead to an infinite regress without explaining why the merely possible existence does exist. From this point, Ibn Sina proposes that an essential cause and its effect will coexist and cannot be part of an infinite chain; the nexus of causes and effects must have a first cause, which exists necessarily for itself: God (see GOD, ARGUMENTS FOR THE EXISTENCE OF §1).

From his proof of God's existence, Ibn Sina goes on to explain how the world and its order emanates from God. Whereas ARISTOTLE (§16) himself did not relate the Active Intellect that may be implied in *On the Soul* III with the first, ever-thinking cause of the universal found in Book XII of his Metaphysics, later commentators on his work (for example, ALEXANDER OF APHRODISIAS) identified the two, making the Active Intellect, the principle that brings about the passage of the human intellect from possibility to actuality, into the first cause of the universe. Together with this is the proof of God's existence that sees him not only as the prime mover but also as the first existent. God's self-knowledge consist in an eternal act that results in or brings about a first intelligence or awareness. This first intelligence conceives or cognizes the necessity of God's existence, the necessity of its own existence, and its own existence as possible. From these acts of conception, other existents arise: another intelligence, a celestial soul and a celestial body, respectively. The last constitutes the first sphere of the universe, and when the second intelligence engages in its own cognitive act, it constitutes the level of fixed stars as well as another level of intelligence that, in turn, produces another intelligence and another level of body. The last such intelligence that emanates from the successive acts of knowing is the Active Intellect, that produces our world. Such emanation cannot continue indefinitely; although being may proceed from intelligence, not every intelligence containing the same aspects will produce the same effects. Successive intelligences have diminished power, and the active intellect, standing tenth in the hierarchy, no longer possesses the power to emanate eternal beings.

None of these proposals by Ibn Sina give grounds for supposing that he was committed to mysticism (for an opposing view, see MYSTICAL PHILOSOPHY IN ISLAM §1). His so called 'Eastern philosophy', usually understood to contain his mystical doctrines, seems to be an entirely Western invention that over the last two hundred years has been read into Ibn Sina's work (see Gutas 1988). Nevertheless, Ibn Sina combines his Aristotelianism with a religious interest, seeking to explain prophecy as having its basis in a direct openness of the prophet's mind to the Active Intellect, through which the middle terms of syllogisms, the syllogisms themselves and their conclusions become available without the procedure of working out proofs. Sometimes the prophet gains insight through imagination, and expresses his insight in figurative terms. It is also possible for the imagination to gain contact with the souls of the higher spheres, allowing the prophet to envisage the future in some figurative form. There may also be other varieties of prophecy.

6 The soul

In all these dealings with prophecy, knowledge and metaphysics, Ibn Sina takes it that the entity involved is the human soul. In *al-Shifa'*, he proposes that the soul must be an incorporeal substance because intellectual thoughts themselves are indivisible. Presumably he means that a coherent thought, involving concepts in some determinate order, cannot be had in parts by different intellects and still remain a single coherent thought. In order to be a coherent single unity, a coherent thought must be had by a single, unified intellect rather than, for example, one intellect having one part of the thought, another soul a separate part of the thought and yet a third intellect having a third distinct part of the same thought. In other words, a coherent thought is indivisible and can be present as such only to an intellect that is similarly unified or indivisible. However, corporeal matter is divisible; therefore the indivisible intellect that is necessary for coherent thought cannot be corporeal. It must therefore be incorporeal, since those are the only two available possibilities.

For Ibn Sina, that the soul is incorporeal implies also that it must be immortal: the decay and destruction of the body does not affect the soul. There are basically three relations to the corporeal body that might also threaten the soul but, Ibn Sina proposes, none of these relations holds true of the incorporeal soul, which therefore must be immortal. If the body were a cause of the soul's existence, or if body and soul depended on each other necessarily for their existence, or if the soul logically depended on the body, then the destruction or decay of the body would determine the existence of the soul. However, the body is not a cause of the soul in any of the four senses of cause; both are substances, corporeal and incorporeal, and therefore as substances they must be independent of each other; and the body changes and decays as a result of its independent causes and substances, not because of changes in the soul, and therefore it does not follow that any change in the body, including death, must determine the existence of the soul. Even if the emergence of the human soul implies a role for the body, the role of this corporeal matter is only accidental.

To this explanation that the destruction of the body does not entail or cause the destruction of the soul, Ibn Sina adds an argument that the destruction of the soul cannot be caused by anything. Composite existing objects are subject to destruction; by contrast, the soul as a simple incorporeal being is not subject to destruction. Moreover, since the soul is not a compound of matter and form, it may be generated but it does not suffer the destruction that afflicts all generated things that are composed of form and matter. Similarly, even if we could identify the soul as a compound, for it to have unity that compound must itself be integrated as a unity, and the principle of this unity of the soul must be simple; and, so far as the principle involves an ontological commitment to existence, being simple and incorporeal it must therefore be indestructible (see SOUL IN ISLAMIC PHILOSOPHY).

7 Reward and punishment

From the indestructibility of the soul arise questions about the character of the soul, what the soul may expect in a world emanating from God, and what its position will be in the cosmic system. Since Ibn Sina maintains that souls retain their identity into immortality, we may also ask about their destiny and how this is determined. Finally, since Ibn Sina also wants to ascribe punishment and reward to such souls, he needs to explain how there may be both destiny and punishment.

The need for punishment depends on the possibility of evil, and Ibn Sina's examination maintains that moral and other evils afflict individuals rather than species. Evils are usually an accidental result of things that otherwise produce good. God produces more good than evil when he produces this sublunary world, and abandoning an overwhelmingly good practice because of a 'rare evil' would be a privation of good. For example, fire is useful and therefore good, even if it harms people on occasion (see EVIL, PROBLEM OF). God might have created a world in another existence that was entirely free of the evil present in this one, but that would preclude all the greater goods available in this world, despite the rare evil it also contains. Thus, God generates a world that contains good and evil and the agent, the soul, acts in this world; the rewards and punishments it gains in its existence beyond this world are the result of its choices in this world, and there can be both destiny and punishment because the world and its order are precisely what give souls a choice between good and evil.

8 Poetry, character and society

Identifying poetic language as imaginative, Ibn Sina relies on the ability of the faculty of imagination to construct images to argue that poetic language can bear a distinction between premises, argument and conclusion, and allows for a conception of poetic syllogism. Aristotle's definition of a syllogism was that if certain statements are accepted, then certain other statements must also necessarily be accepted (see ARISTOTLE §5). To explain this syllogistic structure of poetic language, Ibn Sina first identifies poetic premises as resemblances formed by poets that produce 'an astonishing effect of distress or pleasure' (see POETRY).

The resemblances essayed by poets and the comparisons they put forward in poems, when these are striking, original and so on, produce an 'astonishing effect' or 'feeling of wonder' in the listener or reader. 'The evening of life' compares the spans of a day and a life, bringing the connotations of the day to explain some characteristics of a lifespan. To find this use of poetic language meaningful, the suggestion is that we need to see the comparison as the conclusion of a syllogism. A premise of this syllogism would be that days have a span that resembles or is comparable to the progression of a life. This resemblance is striking, novel and insightful, and understanding its juxtaposition of days and lives leads subjects to feel wonder or astonishment. Next, pleasure occurs in this consideration of the poetic syllogism as the basis of our imaginative assent, paralleling assent in, for example, the demonstrative syllogism: once we have accepted the premise, we are led to accept the associations and imaginative constructions that result; once we accept the comparison between days and lives, we can understand and appreciate the comparison between old age and evening. Ibn Sina also finds other parallels between poetic language and meaningful arguments, showing that pleasure in imaginative assent can be expected of other subjects; assent is therefore more than an expression of personal preferences. This validity of poetic language makes it possible for Ibn Sina to argue that beauty in poetic language has a moral value that sustains and depends on relations of justice between autonomous members of a community. In his commentary on Aristotle's *Poetics*, however, he combines this with a claim that different kinds of poetic language will suit different kinds of characters. Comedy suits people who are base and uncouth, while tragedy attracts an audience of noble characters (see AESTHETICS IN ISLAMIC PHILOSOPHY).

9 Links to the West

Latin versions of some of Ibn Sina's works began to appear in the early thirteenth century. The best known philosophical work to be translated was his *Kitab al-shifa'*, although the translation did not include the sections on mathematics or large sections of the logic. Translations made at Toledo include the *Kitab al-najat* and the *Kitab al-ilahiyat* (Metaphysics) in its entirety. Other sections on natural science were translated at Burgos and for the King of Sicily. GERARD OF CREMONA translated Ibn Sina's *al-Qanun fi'l-tibb* (Canon on Medicine). At Barcelona, another philosophical work, part of the *Kitab al-nafs (Book of the Soul)*, was translated early in the fourteenth century. His late work on logic, *al-Isharat wa-'l-tanbihat*, seems to have been translated in part and is cited in other works. His commentaries on *On the Soul* were known to Thomas AQUINAS and ALBERT THE GREAT, who cite them extensively in their own discussions.

These and other translations of Ibn Sina's works made up the core of a body of literature that was available for study. By the early thirteenth century, his works were studied not only in relation to Neoplatonists such as AUGUSTINE and DUNS SCOTUS, but were used also in study of ARISTOTLE. Consequently, they were banned in 1210 when the synod at Paris prohibited the reading of Aristotle and of 'summae' and 'commenta' of his work. The force of the ban was local and only covered the teaching of this subject: the texts were read and taught at Toulouse in 1229. As late as the sixteenth century there were other translations of short works by Ibn Sina into Latin, for example by Andrea Alpago of Belluno (see ARISTOTELIANISM, MEDIEVAL §3; ISLAMIC PHILOSOPHY: TRANSMISSION INTO WESTERN EUROPE; TRANSLATORS).

See also: AESTHETICS IN ISLAMIC PHILOSOPHY; ARISTOTELIANISM IN ISLAMIC PHILOSOPHY; EPISTEMOLOGY IN ISLAMIC PHILOSOPHY; LOGIC IN ISLAMIC PHILOSOPHY; SOUL IN ISLAMIC PHILOSOPHY; ISLAMIC PHILOSOPHY: TRANSMISSION INTO WESTERN EUROPE

List of works

Ibn Sina (980–1037) *Sirat al-shaykh al-ra'is* (The Life of Ibn Sina), ed. and trans. W.E. Gohlman, Albany, NY: State University of New York Press, 1974. (The only critical edition of Ibn Sina's autobiography,

supplemented with material from a biography by his student Abu 'Ubayd al-Juzjani. A more recent translation of the Autobiography appears in D. Gutas, *Avicenna and the Aristotelian Tradition: Introduction to Reading Avicenna's Philosophical Works*, Leiden: Brill, 1988.)

—— (980–1037) *al-Isharat wa-'l-tanbihat (Remarks and Admonitions)*, ed. S. Dunya, Cairo, 1960; parts translated by S.C. Inati, *Remarks and Admonitions, Part One: Logic*, Toronto, Ont.: Pontifical Institute for Mediaeval Studies, 1984, and *Ibn Sina and Mysticism, Remarks and Admonitions: Part 4*, London: Kegan Paul International, 1996. (The English translation is very useful for what it shows of the philosopher's conception of logic, the varieties of syllogism, premises and so on.)

—— (980–1037) *al-Qanun fi'l-tibb* (Canon on Medicine), ed. I. a-Qashsh, Cairo, 1987. (Ibn Sina's work on medicine.)

—— (980–1037) *Risalah fi sirr al-qadar* (Essay on the Secret of Destiny), trans. G. Hourani in *Reason and Tradition in Islamic Ethics*, Cambridge: Cambridge University Press, 1985. (Provides insights into a neglected area of Ibn Sina's thought.)

—— (980–1037) *Danishnama-i 'ala'i* (The Book of Scientific Knowledge), ed. and trans. P. Morewedge, *The Metaphysics of Avicenna*, London: Routledge and Kegan Paul, 1973. (This is a translation of a metaphysical work in Persian.)

—— (c.1014–20) *al-Shifa'* (Healing). (Ibn Sina's major work on philosophy. He probably began to compose *al-Shifa'* in 1014, and completed it in 1020. Critical editions of the Arabic text have been published in Cairo, 1952–83, originally under the supervision of I. Madkour; some of these editions are given below.)

—— (c.1014–20) *al-Mantiq* (Logic), Part 1, *al-Madkhal* (Isagōgē), ed. G. Anawati, M. El-Khodeiri and F. al-Ahwani, Cairo: al-Matba'ah al-Amiriyah, 1952; trans. N. Shehaby, *The Propositional Logic of Ibn Sina*, Dordrecht: Reidel, 1973. (Volume I, Part 1 of *al-Shifa'*.)

—— (c.1014–20) *al-'Ibarah* (Interpretation), ed. M. El-Khodeiri, Cairo: Dar al-Katib al-'Arabi, 1970. (Volume I, Part 3 of *al-Shifa'*.)

—— (c.1014–20) *al-Qiyas* (Syllogism), ed. S. Zayed and I. Madkour, Cairo: Organisme Général des Imprimeries Gouvernementales, 1964. (Volume I, Part 4 of *al-Shifa'*.)

—— (c.1014–20) *al-Burhan* (Demonstration), ed. A.E. Affifi, Cairo: Organisme Général des Imprimeries Gouvernementales, 1956. (Volume I, Part 5 of *al-Shifa'*.)

—— (c.1014–20) *al-Jadal* (Dialectic), ed. A.F. Al-Ehwany, Cairo: Organisme Général des Imprim-

eries Gouvernementales, 1965. (Volume I, Part 7 of *al-Shifa'*.)
—— (*c.*1014–20) *al-Khatabah* (Rhetoric), ed. S. Salim, Cairo: Imprimerie Nationale, 1954. (Volume I, Part 8 of *al-Shifa'*.)
—— (*c.*1014–20) *al-Ilahiyat* (Theology), ed. M.Y. Moussa, S. Dunya and S. Zayed, Cairo: Organisme Général des Imprimeries Gouvernementales, 1960; ed. and trans. R.M. Savory and D.A. Agius, 'Ibn Sina on Primary Concepts in the *Metaphysics* of *al-Shifa'*, in *Logikos Islamikos*, Toronto, Ont.: Pontifical Institute for Mediaeval Studies, 1984; trans. G.C. Anawati, *La métaphysique du Shifa'*, Études Musulmanes 21, 27, Paris: Vrin, 1978, 1985. (This is the metaphysics of *al-Shifa'*, Volume I, Book 5.)
—— (*c.*1014–20) *al-Nafs* (The Soul), ed. G.C. Anawati and S. Zayed, Cairo: Organisme Général des Imprimeries Gouvernementales, 1975; ed. F. Rahman, *Avicenna's De Anima, Being the Psychological Part of Kitab al-Shifa'*, London: Oxford University Press, 1959. (Volume I, part 6 of *al-Shifa'*.)
—— (*c.*1014–20) *Kitab al-najat* (The Book of Salvation), trans. F. Rahman, *Avicenna's Psychology: An English Translation of Kitab al-Najat, Book II, Chapter VI with Historical-philosophical Notes and Textual Improvements on the Cairo Edition*, Oxford: Oxford University Press, 1952. (The pyschology of *al-Shifa'*.)

References and further reading

* Alexander of Aphrodisias (*c.*200) *De anima* (On the Soul), in *Scripta minora* 2.1, ed. I. Bruns, Berlin, 1887; ed. A.P. Fontinis, *The De Anima of Alexander of Aphrodisias*, Washington, DC: University Press of America, 1979. (Important later commentary on Aristotle.)
Davidson, H.A. (1992) *Alfarabi, Avicenna and Averroes on Intellect: Their Cosmologies, Theories of the Active Intellect, and Theories of the Human Intellect*, New York: Oxford University Press. (A thorough consideration of Ibn Sina's theory of the intellects in relation to Hellenistic and Arabic philosophers.)
Fakhry, M. (1993) *Ethical Theories in Islam*, 2nd edn, Leiden: Brill. (Contains material on Ibn Sina's ethical thought.)
Goodman, L. (1992) *Avicenna*, London: Routledge. (A useful introduction to central features of Ibn Sina's philosophical theories.)
* Gutas, D. (1988) *Avicenna and the Aristotelian Tradition, Introduction to Reading Avicenna's Philosophical Works*, Leiden: Brill. (An excellent account of the considerations that entered into the construction of Ibn Sina's *corpus*, the book contains translations of a number of smaller texts, a careful consideration of method and sharp criticisms of, among other things, ascriptions of mysticism to Ibn Sina. This is probably the most useful guide to an engagement with the philosopher's work currently available in English.)
Inati, S. (1996) 'Ibn Sina', in S.H. Nasr and O. Leaman (eds) *History of Islamic Philosophy*, London: Routledge, ch. 16, 231–46. (Comprehensive guide to his analytical thought.)
Janssens, J.L. (1991) *An Annotated Bibliography on Ibn Sina (1970–1989), Including Arabic and Persian Publications and Turkish and Russian references*, Leuven: University of Leuven Press. (An indispensible tool for study of Ibn Sina and recent work on the philosopher, though it will soon need to be updated.)
Kemal, S. (1991) *The Poetics of Alfarabi and Avicenna*, Leiden: Brill. (A philosophical study of Ibn Sina's philosophical poetics and its relation to epistemology and morality.)
* Mamura, M.E. (1962) 'Some Aspects of Avicenna's Theory of God's Knowledge of Particulars', *Journal of the American Oriental Society* 82: 299–312. (This paper, along with those of Morewedge (1972) and Rahman (1958), are seminal to contemporary understanding of Ibn Sina's thought.)
—— (1980) 'Avicenna's Proof from Contingency for God's Existence in the *Metaphysics* of *al Shifa'*, *Medieval Studies* 42: 337–52. (A clear exposition of the proof.)
* Morewedge, P. (1972) 'Philosophical Analysis and Ibn Sina's "Essence–Existence" distinction', *Journal of the American Oriental Society* 92: 425–35. (A welcome explanation of the implications of a distinction central to Ibn Sina's proof of God's existence.)
Nasr, S.H. (1996) 'Ibn Sina's Oriental Philosophy', in S.H. Nasr and O. Leaman (eds) *History of Islamic Philosophy*, London: Routledge, ch. 17, 247–51. (Concise and interesting defence of the idea that Ibn Sina really did have distinctive system of mystical philosophy.)
Rahman, F. (1958) 'Essence and Existence in Avicenna', *Medieval and Renaissance Studies* 4: 1–16. (A version also appears in *Hamdard Islamicus* 4 (1): 3–14. The paper considers the philosophical usefulness of the distinction of essence from existence.)

SALIM KEMAL

IBN TAYMIYYA, TAQI AL–DIN (1263–1328)

Ibn Taymiyya was a staunch defender of Sunni Islam based on strict adherence to the Qur'an and authentic sunna *(practices) of the Prophet Muhammad. He believed that these two sources contain all the religious and spiritual guidance necessary for our salvation in the hereafter. Thus he rejected the arguments and ideas of both philosophers and Sufis regarding religious knowledge, spiritual experiences and ritual practices. He believed that logic is not a reliable means of attaining religious truth and that the intellect must be subservient to revealed truth. He also came into conflict with many of his fellow Sunni scholars because of his rejection of the rigidity of the schools of jurisprudence in Islam. He believed that the four accepted schools of jurisprudence had become stagnant and sectarian, and also that they were being improperly influenced by aspects of Greek logic and thought as well as Sufi mysticism. His challenge to the leading scholars of the day was to return to an understanding of Islam in practice and in faith, based solely on the Qur'an and* sunna.

Ibn Taymiyya was born in Harran, Syria, and died in Damascus in AH 728/AD 1328. He lived in a time when the Islamic world was suffering from external aggression and internal strife. The crusaders had not been fully expelled from the Holy Land, and the Mongols had all but destroyed the eastern Islamic empire when they captured Baghdad in AH 656/AD 1258. In Egypt, the Mamluks had just come to power and were consolidating their hold over Syria. Within Muslim society, Sufi orders were spreading beliefs and practices not condoned by orthodox Islam, while the orthodox schools of jurisprudence were stagnant in religious thought and practice. It was in this setting of turmoil and conflict that Ibn Taymiyya formulated his views on the causes of the weakness of the Muslim nations and on the need to return to the Qur'an and *sunna* (practices) as the only means for revival.

Although Ibn Taymiyya was educated in the Hanbali school of thought, he soon reached a level of scholarship beyond the confines of that school. He was fully versed in the opinions of the four schools, which helped lead him to the conclusion that blind adherence to one school would bring a Muslim into conflict with the letter and spirit of Islamic law based on the Qur'an and *sunna*. Similarly, he had acquired a deep understanding of philosophical and mystical texts. In particular, he focused on the works of IBN SINA and IBN AL-'ARABI as examples of philosophical and mystical deviation in Islam, respectively. Both

of these trends had come to exert strong influence on Muslim scholars and lay people alike.

Ibn Taymiyya placed primary importance on revelation as the only reliable source of knowledge about God and about a person's religious duties towards him. The human intellect ('aql) and its powers of reason must be subservient to revelation. According to Ibn Taymiyya, the only proper use of 'aql was to understand Islam in the way the Prophet and his companions did, and then to defend it against deviant sects. When discussing the nature of God, he argued, one must accept the descriptions found in the Qur'an and *sunna* and apply the orthodox view of not asking how (bi-la kayf) particular attributes exist in God. This means that one believes in all of the attributes of God mentioned in the Qur'an and *sunna* without investigating the nature of these, because the human mind is incapable of understanding the eternal God. For example, one accepts that God is mounted upon a throne above the heavens without questioning how this is possible. This same attitude is held for all of God's attributes such as his sight, his hearing or his hand.

This view is very much opposed to the philosophical view of God as First Cause and as being devoid of attributes. Thus the philosophical argument that the oneness of God precludes a multiplicity of attributes was not acceptable to Ibn Taymiyya, because God says that he is one and that he has various attributes. This denial of the attributes of God based on rationalism was adopted by the Mu'tazila (see ASH'ARIYYA AND MU'TAZILA), of whom Ibn Taymiyya was especially critical. Even the more orthodox views of the Ash'aris, who accepted seven attributes basic to God, were criticized by Ibn Taymiyya. However, he did not go so far as to declare these two groups heretical, for they deviated only in their interpretation of God's nature. But he did not spare the label of apostate for those philosophers such as AL-FARABI and IBN SINA who, in addition to the denial of God's attributes, also denied the createdness of the world and believed in the emanation of the universe from God.

Ibn Taymiyya attacked the idea of emanation not only in its philosophical but also in its mystical context, as adopted by the Sufis (see MYSTICAL PHILOSOPHY IN ISLAM). He felt that the beliefs and practices of the Sufis were far more dangerous than were the ideas of the philosophers. The latter were a small elite group that had little direct effect on the masses. The Sufis, however, were widespread and had a large popular following. However, Ibn Taymiyya saw a link between the ideas of the philosophers and those of the Sufis, even though apparently they had little in common.

The main tenet of Sufi thought as propounded by Ibn al-'Arabi is the concept of the oneness of existence (*wahdat al-wujud*). Through this belief, Sufis think they are able to effect a merging of their souls with God's essence. That is, when God reveals his truth to an individual, that person realizes that there is no difference between God and the self. Ibn Taymiyya saw a link between the Sufi belief of *wahdat al-wujud* and the philosophical concept of emanation. Although the philosopher would deny that a human soul could flow into, and thus be, the First Cause, the mystical experience of the Sufis took them beyond the realm of intellectual discourse. According to the mystic, a merging occurred but could not be expressed in rational terms. For Ibn Taymiyya, both the philosopher and the mystic were deluded, the former by reliance on a limited human intellect and the latter by excessive emotions.

Ibn Taymiyya's argument against the Sufis is on two levels. First, there is the theological position that God has attributes and that one of these attributes is God as creator. Ibn Taymiyya believed that the Qur'an firmly establishes that God is the one who created, originated and gave form to the universe. Thus there exists a distinction between God the creator and the created beings. This is an absolute distinction with no possibility of merging. He then went on to say that those who strip God of his attributes and deny that he is the creator are just one step away from falling into the belief of *wahdat al-wujud*. This is the basis for the second part of his argument. Ibn Taymiyya believed that a Sufi is simply someone who is overcome by an outburst of emotion. For example, someone may deny God's attributes but could then be overwhelmed by a feeling of love for God. However, the basis of that person's knowledge is not the authentic information from the Qur'an, and so their weak intellectual foundation collapses with the onslaught of emotion. For according to Ibn Taymiyya, sense perception and emotions cannot be trusted, and the likelihood of being led astray by them is compounded when one has a basis of knowledge which is itself errant and deviant. One holds a proper belief in God and maintains a proper relationship with him, Ibn Taymiyya argued, by establishing a foundation of knowledge based on the Qur'an and authentic *sunna*.

See also: IBN AL-'ARABI; ISLAMIC THEOLOGY; LAW, ISLAMIC PHILOSOPHY OF; MYSTICAL PHILOSOPHY IN ISLAM; NEOPLATONISM IN ISLAMIC PHILOSOPHY

List of works

Ibn Taymiyya (1263–1328) *Mas'ala fi al-'aql wa al-*nafs (Concerning the Matter of the Intellect and the Soul), in A.A.M. Qasim and M.A.A. Qasim (eds) *Majmu' fatawa Shaykh al-Islam Ibn Taymiyya*, vol. 9, Riyad: Matba'ah al-Hukama, 1996. (This is a short essay in which Ibn Taymiyya summarizes his views on the relationship between the intellect and the soul.)

—— (1263–1328) *al-'Ubudiyya fi al-Islam* (The Concept of Worship in Islam), Cairo: al-Matba'ah al-Salafiyya. (This is one of Ibn Taymiyya's most important statements concerning issues of faith and belief in Islam. He speaks extensively on matters of predestination, love for God and Sufi concepts of the annihilation of the soul.)

—— (1263–1328) *al-Jawab al-sahih li-man baddala din al-masah* (The Correct Answer to the One Who Changed the Religion of the Messiah), trans. T.F. Michel, *A Muslim Theologian's Response to Christianity*, Delmar, NY: Caravan Books, 1984. (This is an abridged translation, with an excellent introduction to Ibn Taymiyya's polemics against various groups and an extensive bibliography.)

References and further reading

Bell, J.N. (1979) *Love Theory in Later Hanbalite Islam*, Albany, NY: State University of New York Press. (This work investigates the role of love in the thinking of Hanbali scholars and shows how they defined it in opposition to philosophers and mystics.)

Hallaq, W.B. (1993) *Ibn Taymiyya against the Greek Logicians*, Oxford: Clarendon Press. (An excellent translation of Ibn Taymiyya's most important arguments against Greek logic. The introduction and notes give depth and perspective to this very difficult topic. It also contains an extensive bibliography.)

Izutsu Toshihiko (1965) *The Concept of Belief in Islamic Theology: A Semantic Analysis of Iman and Islam*, Yokohama: Yurindo Publishing Company. (Although this work focuses on the concept of belief in early Islam, the author makes extensive use of Ibn Taymiyya's theories to explain how orthodox scholars came to understand this term.)

Pavlin, J. (1996) 'Sunni Kalam and Theological Controversies', in S.H. Nasr and O. Leaman (eds) *History of Islamic Philosophy*, London: Routledge, ch. 7, 105–18. (Includes a discussion of Ibn Taymiyya's view.)

JAMES PAVLIN

IBN TUFAYL, ABU BAKR MUHAMMAD (before 1110–85)

Ibn Tufayl's thought can be captured in his only extant work, Hayy Ibn Yaqzan *(The Living Son of the Vigilant), a philosophical treatise in a charming literary form. It relates the story of human knowledge, as it rises from a blank slate to a mystical or direct experience of God after passing through the necessary natural experiences. The focal point of the story is that human reason, unaided by society and its conventions or by religion, can achieve scientific knowledge, preparing the way to the mystical or highest form of human knowledge. The story also seeks to show that, while religious truth is the same as that of philosophy, the former is conveyed through symbols, which are suitable for the understanding of the multitude, and the latter is conveyed in its inner meanings apart from any symbolism. Since people have different capacities of understanding that require the use of different instruments, there is no point in trying to convey the truth to people except through means suitable for their understanding.*

1 Life and works
2 Ibn Tufayl's introduction to *Hayy Ibn Yaqzan*
3 Hayy's birth and rational progress
4 Harmony of Hayy's philosophy with revealed religion
5 Suitability of religion in its outward aspect to the majority of people

1 Life and works

Abu Bakr Muhammad Ibn 'Abd al-Malik Ibn Muhammad Ibn Muhammad Ibn Tufayl al-Qaysi is known to the West as Abubacer. It can be estimated that he was born in the first decade of the sixth century AH (twelfth century AD), based on the fact that he was in his sixties when he met Ibn Rushd in AH 564/AD 1169. Born in Wadi Ash (Guadix), a small town in Spain about sixty kilometres northeast of Granada, he died in Morocco in AH 581/AD 1185. Ibn Tufayl was the second most important Muslim philosopher in the West, the first being Ibn Bajja.

With the exception of some fragments of poetry, his only extant work is *Hayy Ibn Yaqzan* (The Living Son of the Vigilant). The title and names of characters of this work are borrowed from two of Ibn Sina's philosophical treatises, *Hayy Ibn Yaqzan* and *Salaman and Absal*, and its framework is borrowed from an ancient eastern tale, *The Story of the Idol and of the King and His Daughter*. The title is taken from the name of the main character, Hayy Ibn Yaqzan. In the

introduction and conclusion, the author addresses the reader directly; in other parts of the work, he uses a 'thin veil', a symbolic form, a story to express his philosophical views.

2 Ibn Tufayl's introduction to *Hayy Ibn Yaqzan*

In the introduction the author presents some of the views of his predecessors, al-Farabi, Ibn Sina, al-Ghazali and Ibn Bajja. AL-FARABI is strongly criticized for what is said to be his inconsistent view concerning the afterlife. No criticism of IBN SINA is given; on the contrary, it is said that Ibn Sina's oriental wisdom will be expounded in the rest of the work. Ibn Bajja's views are said to be incomplete, mentioning the highest speculative state but not the state above it, that of 'witnessing' or mystical experience (see IBN BAJJA). While al-Ghazali's mystical experience is not in doubt (see AL-GHAZALI), none of his works on mystical knowledge are said to have reached the author. The introduction is intended to announce the author's intention, namely the elaboration of Ibn Sina's oriental wisdom and to show how the work differs from those of his predecessors.

3 Hayy's birth and rational progress

The story of Hayy Ibn Yaqzan takes place on an equatorial island uninhabited by human beings. There Hayy is found alone as an infant. Philosophers were of the opinion that he was born spontaneously when the mixture of elements reached an equilibrium state, making it possible for this mixture to receive a human soul from the divine world. Traditionalists believed that he was the son of a woman who chose to keep her marriage to her relative, Yaqzan, secret from her brother who ruled a neighbouring island and did not find any man qualified to marry his sister. After breastfeeding Hayy well, she put him in a box and threw it into the waters, which took him to the uninhabited island.

A deer who had just lost her son and was still experiencing the feelings of motherhood heard Hayy's cries. She suckled him, protected him from harmful things and took care of him until she died when he was seven years of age. By then he had learned to imitate other animals in speech, and he covered parts of his body with leaves after noticing that those animal parts are covered with hair or feathers. The deer's death transformed Hayy's life from one of dependency to one of exploration and discovery.

In an effort to find out the reason for the deer's death, a reason which he could not locate by observing her appearance, he dissected her with sharp stones and dry reeds. Noticing that every bodily organ has a proper function and that the left cavity of her heart was empty, he concluded that the source of life must have been in this cavity, and must have abandoned it. He reflected on the nature of this vital thing, its link to the body, its source, the place to which it has departed, the manner of its departure and so on. He realized that it was not the body but this vital entity that was the deer and the source of its actions. With this realization he lost interest in the deer's body, which he then viewed as a mere instrument. While he could not decipher the nature of this vital thing, he observed that the shape of all deer was similar to that of his mother. From this he concluded that all deer were managed by something similar to the vital thing that managed his mother's life.

After his discovery of life, he came across a fire. He noticed that, contrary to other natural objects, which move downward, fire moves upward. This indicated to him that the essence of fire is other than that of natural things. He continued to investigate other parts of nature: animal organs, their arrangement, number, size and position, as well as the qualities that animals, plants and inanimate things have in common and those that are proper to each of them. Through continued reasoning he grasped the concepts of matter and form, cause and effect, unity and multiplicity, as well as other general concepts concerning the earth and the heavens. Concluding that the universe is one in spite of its multiple objects, he moved on to consider whether it is created or eternal. Through highly sophisticated reasoning, he found that neither the idea of creation nor that of eternity is immune to objection. Though he could not rationally decide whether the universe is created or eternal, he concluded that it must have a cause on which it remains dependent and that this cause or necessary being is non-physical and above it in essence, even if not in time.

He also concluded that the thing in him which knew this cause must also be non-physical. The more detached this non-physical thing in him was from sensory perceptions, the clearer was its vision of this cause, a vision that gave the highest joy. Even though sensations obstructed this vision, he felt obliged to imitate animals by experiencing sensations to preserve his animal soul, which would enable him to imitate the heavenly bodies. Imitating the heavenly bodies by doing things like circular movement provided him with continuous but impure vision, for attention in this type of imitation is still paid to the self.

By knowledge of the necessary being, Hayy sought to imitate this being's positive attributes; by an attempt to transcend the physical world, he sought to imitate the negative ones. Imitation of the necessary being for the sake of this being involved no attention to the self and hence provided him with pure vision. Not only was Hayy's self or essence obliterated in this state, but so also was everything other than the necessary being. No human sight, hearing or speech could grasp this state, as it lies beyond the world of nature and sense experience. Therefore no explanation of necessary being can be given, only mere signs, as Ibn Sina contends in *al-Isharat wa-'l-tanbihat* (Remarks and Admonitions). One who seeks an explanation of this state is like one who seeks 'the taste of colours inasmuch as they are colours'. Verification requires direct experience. Using human language, which is described as an inadequate instrument, to hint at the truth Hayy is said to have witnessed in this state, the necessary being is said to pervade the universe as sunlight pervades the physical world. Trying to express the inexpressible, the author says that Hayy realized in this state that the whole is one, even though unity and multiplicity, like other contraries, exist only for sense perception. The Neoplatonic pantheistic tendency is here obvious (see NECESSARY BEING; NEOPLATONISM).

4 Harmony of Hayy's philosophy with revealed religion

On a neighbouring island a group of people, including the king, Salaman, practised a religion which was sound yet provided the masses with symbols, not direct truths. Absal, a friend of Salaman, observed the rituals of this religion but, contrary to others who adhered to its literal meaning, he delved into its inner truths. Being naturally inclined to solitude, which was in agreement with certain passages of the Scripture, Absal moved to the island on which Hayy lived. When he encountered Hayy he was frightened, until Hayy made it clear that he intended no harm. Absal then taught Hayy human language by pointing to objects while uttering the corresponding words.

With the acquisition of language, Hayy was able to explain to Absal his development in knowledge. At hearing this, Absal realised that what Hayy had witnessed were the realities described in his own religion: God, the angels, the holy books, prophets, afterlife and so on. When Absal discussed the truths as detailed in his religion, Hayy too found these truths in agreement with what he had come to know. However, Hayy could not understand why Absal's religion resorted to symbols and permitted indulgence in material things.

5 Suitability of religion in its outward aspect to the majority of people

Hayy expressed interest in visiting the neighbouring island to explain to its people the pure truth. Absal, who knew their nature, reluctantly accompanied him. Addressing the most intelligent group on this island, Hayy was shown respect until he tried to go beyond the literal meaning of their Scripture. The people then shunned him, distracting themselves from the truth by commercial activity. Hayy understood then that such people are incapable of grasping the direct truth and that religion is necessary for their social stability and protection. Social stability and protection, however, in no way secure happiness in the afterlife. Only preoccupation with the divine, which is rare among people of this kind, can provide such security. In contrast, the preoccupation with this world in which the majority of people indulge results in darkness or hell. While the truths of reason and revelation are the same, the majority of those adhering to the latter do so for worldly success and hence achieve eternal misery. Realizing that an attempt to enlighten those incapable of vision will only destabilize them without preparing them for happiness, Hayy asked people to continue practising their religion, warning them only against indulgence in worldly matters. Hayy and Absal returned then to the deserted island to practise their mysticism in isolation.

Ibn Tufayl ends the work by describing it as 'containing a piece of discourse not found in a book nor heard in ordinary speech'. How is this to be understood when he had already told us in the introduction that the work is an elaboration of Ibn Sina's oriental wisdom? Perhaps the answer can be found in Ibn Tufayl's emphasis on the novelty of a certain 'discourse' or 'speech', not on the novelty of its content. If so, the originality of the work would seem to lie only in its form.

See also: IBN SINA, ABU 'ALI AL-HUSAYN; MYSTICISM IN ISLAMIC PHILOSOPHY; NECESSARY BEING; NEOPLATONISM IN ISLAMIC PHILOSOPHY

List of works

Ibn Tufayl (before 1185) *Hayy Ibn Yaqzan* (The Living Son of the Vigilant), ed. L. Gauthier, Beirut: Catholic Press, 1936; trans. L. Goodman, *Ibn Tufayl's Hayy Ibn Yaqzan, a Philosophical Tale*, New York: Twain Publishers, 1972. (Ibn Tufayl's only extant work, this book captures his main philosophical thought.)

References and further reading

Conradi, L.I. (ed.) (1996) *The World of Ibn Tufayl: Interdisciplinary Perspectives on Hayy Ibn Yaczan*, Islamic Philosophy, Theology and Sciences Series, vol. 24, Leiden: Brill. (Contains a large bibliography of works on Ibn Tufayl.)

Goodman, L. (1996) 'Ibn Tufayl', in S.H. Nasr and O. Leaman (eds) *History of Islamic Philosophy*, London: Routledge, ch. 22, 313–29. (Good examination of Ibn Tufayl's life and thought.)

Hawi, S. (1973) 'Ibn Tufayl's Hayy Ibn Yaqzan, Its Structure, Literary Aspects and Methods', *Islamic Culture* 47: 191–211. (Focuses on the most essential elements of the work, insisting that it is not a 'symbolic expression' but a 'philosophical discourse'.)

—— (1974a) *Islamic Naturalism and Mysticism: A Philosophical Study of Ibn Tufayl's Hayy Yaqzan*, Leiden: Brill. (Study of *Hayy Ibn Yaqzan*.)

—— (1974b) 'Beyond Naturalism: A Brief Study of Ibn Tufayl's Hayy Ibn Yaqzan', *Journal of the Pakistan Historical Society* 22: 249–67. (Lucid and shows a good grasp of Ibn Tufayl's view of mystical experience.)

—— (1976) 'Ibn Tufayl's Appraisal of His Predecessors and Their Influence on His Thought', *International Journal of Middle East Studies* 7: 89–121. (An attempt to show Ibn Tufayl's originality and the influence on him of al-Farabi and al-Ghazali, rather than Ibn Sina.)

Hourani, G. (1956) 'The Principal Subject of Ibn Tufayl's Hayy Ibn Yaqzan', *Journal of Near Eastern Studies* 15 (1): 40–46. (An excellent article, which reconsiders the principal subject of Ibn Tufayl's *Hayy Ibn Yaqzan*. It rejects Gauthier's thesis that the essential subject of the work is the harmony of religion and philosophy, arguing instead that it is the ascent of unaided human reason from elementary to mystical knowledge.)

SHAMS C. INATI

IBN TZADDIK, JOSEPH BEN JACOB (d. 1149)

Joseph ibn Tzaddik was a thinker firmly within the Neoplatonic tradition of Jewish philosophy. He argued that through knowledge of our own body we understand the natural world, and through knowledge of our soul the spiritual world. He identified prophecy with philosophy and suggested that we need to employ both philosophy and the religious commandments in order to worship God. Not everyone can understand philosophy, but everyone can follow the commandments and thus approach God. Human beings will receive their deserts in the next world. The pure soul will rise to the realm of spirituality, while the evil soul will be heavy and sink into matter, never achieving repose but continually caught up in the movement of the spheres.

1   **Life and works**
2   **Why human beings study themselves**
3   **The activity of the soul**
4   **The unity of God**
5   **Theodicy**

1   Life and works

Of Ibn Tzaddik's life we know very little. He seems to have been a well-known poet. From 1138 he was a rabbinical judge at Cordoba. He died in 1149. He was clearly influenced by Isaac ISRAELI and Solomon IBN GABIROL. His major work, *al-'Alam al-Saghir*, has survived only in an anonymous Hebrew translation entitled *Ha-Olam ha-Katan* (The Microcosm), a title indicative of the theme that unites the work. For Ibn Tzaddik follows Israeli's conception of philosophy as human self-knowledge. Man is a miniature of the world; and the world, in turn, a human being writ large. Humans are a microcosm because they have in themselves all elements of the universe.

The text is divided into four parts or discourses. The first deals with physics, the principles and constitution of the corporeal world. The second discourse, developing the idea that man is a microcosm of the larger world, deals with anthropology and psychology. Discourses three and four reflect the familiar concerns of *kalam* (dialectical theology), namely the existence, unity and attributes of God; theodicy; freedom of the will; and reward and punishment. Influenced by SAADIAH GAON, Bahya IBN PAQUDA, Ibn Gabirol and Islamic *kalam* theologians, Ibn Tzaddik combines familiar Jewish Neoplatonic themes along with Aristotelian and *kalam* influences. Two requisites are necessary for philosophic understanding: knowledge of God and performance of his will. But in order to acquire this level of philosophy, one must have a knowledge of everything else as well. And self-knowledge is the key to the requisite knowledge of all things.

2   Why human beings study themselves

Part One of the text starts with knowledge of the physical world, which ultimately reflects back upon the individual knower. Humans perceive things in two ways, through sense (*ha-regesh*) and through intellect

(*ha-sekhel*). The five senses yield knowledge of accidental qualities, or 'shells'; reason penetrates to the true nature or essence of a thing. Knowledge can be classified as either self-evident (immediate) or demonstrated (mediate). Correspondingly, there are four kinds of objects of knowledge: percepts of senses (*murgashot*); self-evident truths (*mefursamot*); traditions (*mekubalot*); and axioms (*muskalot*). According to Ibn Tzaddik, each of these can be traced back to either rational or sensory knowledge. The former is superior, for it distinguishes humans from animals.

The second discourse treats of ontology, and it displays the influence of both ISRAELI (§2) and IBN GABIROL (§2). Matter is the foundation (*ha-yesod*) and principle of all things (see MATTER). The common matter of the four elements is prime matter, which is endowed with the form of corporeality (*etzem gishmi*). Matter and form are relative to each other. Spiritual things are also composed of matter and form. In spiritual things, we may compare genus to matter, species to form, specific difference to efficient cause and individual to final cause. It is here that Ibn Gabirol's influence is most evident. Everything exists either in itself (*omed be'atzmo*) or in something else (*omed be-zulatto*). Thus matter exists in itself, whereas form exists in matter. After matter assumes a form, matter becomes an actual substance. However, matter and form can be separated only in thought, not in reality. Substance is is capable of bearing opposite and changing qualities. A substance can be the opposite of another only through its accidents. Absolute substance (*ha-etzem hamuhlat*) is pure and spiritual. It is what remains of a corporeal substance when we take everything away, and is similar to Ibn Gabirol's substance which supports the categories (see SUBSTANCE). Ibn Tzaddik then turns to the corporeal world (*ha-'olam hagishmi*), namely the spheres, the four elements and the three natures. The sphere (*galgal*) differs from other bodies in matter, form and qualities. Moving in a circle, the sphere has the most perfect of motions. For spherical motion has no beginning or end. The sphere also has knowledge of God. The four elements – fire, air, water, earth – are simple bodies and have no qualities. They can change into each other. The basis of the elements is a substance filling place as a result of its assuming the form of corporeality. The three natures – plant, animal and mineral – are composed of the four elements. The general process of the sublunar world is genesis and dissolution. Thus, the world is not permanent, for the basis of its processes is change. The human body corresponds to the corporeal world in that it too is subject to genesis and decay. It is composed of elements and has powers of growth and sustenance like plants. In true Neoplatonic fashion,

Ibn Tzaddik claims that humans are superior to all other beings in that they comprise all of them. In so far as the human is a 'celestial plant', its head is directed heavenward (see NATURAL PHILOSOPHY, MEDIEVAL).

3 The activity of the soul

Part Two of *Ha-Olam ha-Katan* deals with the different types of souls. Clearly combining Platonic and Aristotelian themes in an uncritical fashion, Ibn Tzaddik distinguishes three types of soul: the vegetative, the animal, and the rational (see PLATO §14). The faculty of the plant soul is appetition, and the seat of the faculty is the liver. All of its powers derive from universal powers in the upper world. The animal soul is seated in the heart; it is borne in the blood. Its functions are motion and sensation. Life is the effect of the animal soul. Death is the separation of rational soul (*ha-nefesh ha-chokhma*) from the body. Death results from an imbalance of the four humours in the heart, or by disease or injury to the brain. The rational soul is incorporeal; thus it is not located in the body. Like ARISTOTLE (§17), Ibn Tzaddik holds that the soul is a substance, not an accident, for it is permanent – reason is essential to humans. Moreover soul is superior to body, so it must be a spiritual substance, since the higher entity, it is reasoned, could not be a mere accident while the lower is a substance. All three souls are spiritual powers. The rational soul and the intellect have a common matter. When the soul is perfected it becomes intellect; the only difference between the two is one of degree and excellence, inasmuch as the intellect comes straight from God without intermediary. The activity of the rational soul is knowing, exploring the unknown. The rational soul of one who studies is destined for the spiritual world. In order to study, a person's animal impulses must be deadened. The person then comes to know first the corporeal world, then the spiritual world, and finally the Creator. Knowledge of God is the highest kind of knowledge and the basis of human perfection. Ibn Tzaddik states that those who have no such knowledge are doomed to error. The existence of many individual souls is evidence that there must be a universal or world soul. The universal soul is received into all living bodies; just as objects receive the sun's light, so too splitting of the world soul into many souls is due to the plurality of bodies which absorb it.

4 The unity of God

How do we achieve knowledge of God? Following Bahya IBN PAQUDA (§2), and contrary to the practitioners of *kalam*, Ibn Tzaddik argues that God's essence is unknowable. To know a thing, we must investigate its four causes, but with God we can only know whether he *is*, not what he is. Ibn Tzaddik offers a rudimentary proof for the existence of God as follows: if substance and accident are not eternal, something must have brought them into being. This something is God. Furthermore, since the cause of the many must be one, God is one. Ibn Tzaddik goes on to show, by means of *kalam* arguments, that there cannot be two eternal beings.

The troubling question is why God created the world at all. Clearly this is not because God lacked anything. For God is complete and needs nothing. Creation is an act of will, but Ibn Tzaddik regards God's will as eternal, not created. What then is the relation of God's will to God? As Guttman points out (1966: 131), Ibn Tzaddik's answer is ambiguous. Divine will is identical with divine essence, yet Ibn Tzaddik does not explain how this will and essence are compatible with God's immutability. According to Ibn Tzaddik, God is beyond space and time. So when we say that God's will created the world, we cannot mean either that creation is taking place now or that it took place at any definite time. Ibn Tzaddik simply declares that God created the world *ex nihilo* and that it is perfect. When he speaks of creation as a mystery, he suggests that not all men can understand the secrets of philosophy. Only a hint of these matters should be given, and intelligent individuals will comprehend of their own accord.

With respect to God's attributes, Ibn Tzaddik claims that they are different from all other attributes, in that they are all identical with his essence. The very notion of divine attributes can be applied only figuratively. The predicates assigned to God express either action or essence. But, in the end, both sorts are aspects of the same attribute. Divine attributes become models of moral action. We derive our knowledge of God from his effects, but ultimately we can apply them only negatively.

5 Theodicy

Ibn Tzaddik's distinction between rational and traditional commandments is similar to those of IBN PAQUDA (§2) and SAADIAH GAON (§2). These commandments are for our own good, so that we may be happy in the next life. Ibn Tzaddik's discussion of the four virtues (wisdom, courage, temperance and justice) is clearly influenced by Plato's four virtues. For Ibn Tzaddik, as for many of his contemporaries, knowledge of a suprasensual world is a prerequisite for eternal happiness. As recent scholars have pointed out, the identification of prophecy and philosophy causes problems because philosophy includes a number of sciences hard to envisage as having been revealed on Mount Sinai. Ibn Tzaddik attempts to resolve this problem by affirming that at the time of the Torah, God bestowed prophecy on the whole people, for such was his will; but since at the present time no one can attain philosophy, that is, prophecy, except through the mediation of science, all must successively acquire the various degrees of science. Science and the desire urging man towards God are common to all, but the aptitude for science depends essentially on climatic conditions. The good soul is knowledgeable and survives in the upper world. The bad soul loses its spirituality and revolves forever with the spheres in the world of fire. When the messiah comes, the saints will be brought back to life and never die again; the wicked souls will be rejoined to their bodies and burnt.

See also: IBN GABIROL; IBN PAQUDA; SAADIAH GAON; SOUL, NATURE AND IMMORTALITY OF THE

List of works

Ibn Tzaddik, Joseph ben Jacob (before 1149) *al-'Alam al-Saghir* (*Ha-Olam ha-Katan*, The Microcosm), ed. A. Jellinck, *Ha-Olam ha-Katan*, Leipzig, 1854; ed. S. Horovitz, *Sefer ha-Olam ha-Qatan*, Breslau: Druck von Th. Shatzky, 1903; trans. with notes and introduction by J. Haberman, *The Microcosm*, Doctoral Dissertation Series, no. 8676, Ann Arbor, MI: University Microfilms, 1954. (Written in Arabic, this work has survived only in an anonymous Hebrew translation. It is an eclectic Neoplatonic work with Aristotelian and *kalam* influences, written as a handbook for beginners.)

References and further reading

* Guttman, J. (1966) *Philosophies of Judaism*, New York: Anchor Books. (A history of Jewish philosophy.)

Vajda, G. (1949) 'La philosophie et la théologie de Joseph ibn Zaddiq', *Archives d'histoire doctrinale et littéraire du moyen âge* 24: 93–181. (An extensive, detailed examination of Ibn Tzaddik's cosmology.)

—— (1957) *L'Amour de Dieu dans la théologie juive du moyen âge* (The Love of God in Jewish Theology in the Middle Ages), Paris: Librairie Philosophique, J. Vrin. (A study of how medieval Jewish philosophers and theologians, including Ibn Tzaddik, viewed the love of God.)

Weinsberg, L. (1888) 'Der Mikrokosmos: Ein angeblich im 12, Jahrhundert von dem Cordubenser Josef ibn Tzaddik verfaßtes philosophisches Sys-

tem', repr. in S.T. Katz (ed.) *Jewish Neoplatonism*, New York: Arno Press, 1980. (A philosophical study of *Ha-Olam ha-Katan*.)

Wolfson, H.A. (1965) 'Joseph Ibn Saddik on Divine Attributes', *Jewish Quarterly Review* 55: 277–98. (Examination of the issue of divine predication.)

TAMAR RUDAVSKY

ICELAND, PHILOSOPHY IN
see SCANDINAVIA, PHILOSOPHY IN

I-CHING *see* YIJING

IDEALISM

Idealism is now usually understood in philosophy as the view that mind is the most basic reality and that the physical world exists only as an appearance to or expression of mind, or as somehow mental in its inner essence. However, a philosophy which makes the physical world dependent upon mind is usually also called idealist even if it postulates some further hidden, more basic reality behind the mental and physical scenes (for example, Kant's things-in-themselves). There is also a certain tendency to restrict the term 'idealism' to systems for which what is basic is mind of a somewhat lofty nature, so that 'spiritual values' are the ultimate shapers of reality. (An older and broader use counts as idealist any view for which the physical world is somehow unreal compared with some more ultimate, not necessarily mental, reality conceived as the source of value, for example Platonic forms.)

The founding fathers of idealism in Western thought are Berkeley (theistic idealism), Kant (transcendental idealism) and Hegel (absolute idealism). Although the precise sense in which Hegel was an idealist is problematic, his influence on subsequent absolute or monistic idealism was enormous. In the US and the UK idealism, especially of the absolute kind, was the dominating philosophy of the late nineteenth and early twentieth century, receiving its most forceful expression with F.H. Bradley. It declined, without dying, under the influence of G.E. Moore and Bertrand Russell, and later of the logical positivists. Not a few philosophers believe, however, that it has a future.

1   The general case for idealism
2   Berkeleian ontological idealism
3   Kantian transcendental idealism

1   The general case for idealism

As the term will be used here, a philosopher is an idealist if and only if they believe that the physical world exists *either* (1) only as an object for mind, *or* (2) only as a content of mind, *or* (3) only as something itself somehow mental in its true character, a disjunction we shall sum up as the thesis that the physical is derivative from mind. Particular idealists may go further and say that everything whatever is derivative from mind except mind itself, but this would not be affirmed by, for example, KANT, who believed in things-in-themselves which may be neither mental nor mind-derivative; neither, perhaps, would it be accepted by SCHOPENHAUER, for whom Kant's things-in-themselves become an unconscious cosmic Will. Moreover, there is no one view of the status of so-called abstract objects or universals which seems required of an idealist (see ABSTRACT OBJECTS).

The mind-dependence of the physical has been argued for and developed in widely varying ways. For example, the idealist may be a monist or a pluralist about the mind(s) from which the physical is derivative. Very significant too is the contrast between idealisms which are more ontological and those which are more epistemological in their approach. The two great exemplars of each are George BERKELEY and Immanuel Kant, the founding fathers of Western idealism and sources of most subsequent arguments in its favour.

Ontological idealism affirms that a certain view of reality, in which the physical is mind-dependent, is absolutely true, and regards such elements of common sense or science as seem to conflict with this either as wrong, or as only seemingly incompatible. Epistemological idealism is concerned, rather, to show that the most acceptable views of the physical world, which doubtless include the claim that it is not mind-dependent, are, indeed, only true-for-us, but that truth-for-us is the only kind of truth it makes sense to seek. (A more qualified epistemological idealism may allow that chinks of a more absolute truth may suggest themselves and be important, but hardly belong to the main body of what we should call knowledge.) Thus, for idealism of the second kind, the mind-dependence of the physical is not so much a claim as to what is true about it, as about the sort of truth which truth about it is.

2   Berkeleian ontological idealism

According to Berkeley, there are only two types of existent – spirits (or minds) and ideas. Physical objects, as we ordinarily conceive them, are collections of sensory ideas (sense impressions). Thus an apple is simply a collection of such sensory appearances as we are immediately aware of when we say that we are perceiving it (including the sensation of eating it). As for things, or those aspects of things, which are not perceived by any finite mind, they are there *either*: in the secondary sense that they would come into our minds if we took appropriate steps (gave ourselves appropriate impressions of moving in certain ways) to have a look at them, a sniff of them or whatever; *or* they are being perceived by an infinite mind. The second alternative brings in God immediately, the first is only explicable by saying that they are ideas which God would produce in us as a result of our taking those steps. Either way, the idealist truth that physical objects are collections of ideas, taken together with the obvious fact that everything is as though they continued their existence when unobserved by finite minds, appears to Berkeley an incontestable proof of God's existence.

Two of the main reasons why Berkeley thought that the physical world must consist of ideas were:

1   It is only if physical objects are conceived as collections of ideas which hang together in experience that we have any empirical evidence for their existence.

2   It is generally admitted that the so-called secondary qualities of physical things only exist as ideas in our minds (see PRIMARY–SECONDARY DISTINCTION). Moreover, it could be proved by the way in which secondary qualities vary with the state of the observer, and the way in which they are inseparable from sensations of pleasure and pain. But the considerations which show that secondary qualities are mind-dependent show equally that the primary ones are too. (Presented shape varies with conditions of observation as much as colour.) Moreover, no one can conceive of primary qualities existing in the absence of secondary qualities, so that they can only exist tied up with the admittedly mind-dependent.

It is usual to say that Berkeley's line of thought works only if one already accepts doctrines which he adopted uncritically from Locke (as he understood him), namely that all we ever perceive are ideas, and that secondary qualities are mind-dependent. It is, therefore, worth emphasizing that arguments of an essentially Berkeleian sort can be presented, and have been influential, which do not depend upon this Lockean inheritance.

The core of these arguments will be: physical objects, as they present themselves to our senses, do so with qualities which we cannot suppose to exist except for a perceiving mind. Indeed, we cannot even conceive them lacking all such qualities. These qualities, with which things present themselves to the senses, include what we may call all their perspectival qualities (the thing is given with features which reflect the position from which it is seen or the way in which it is felt and so on), also hedonic and aesthetic qualities, and finally an organization of the perceptual field into foreground and background, and into certain *Gestalten*. However much you try to imagine a thing as it is in itself, apart from any observer, you will find yourself imagining it as having features which represent the rough position of an observer of it, how they feel about it, and how they organize their perceptual field. In short you can only imagine it with features which it could only have as a presence to some observer. Such reasoning continues to persuade those of a Berkeleian cast of mind that one cannot form any genuine conception of a physical world existing except as an object for an observer.

All this is likely to invite two objections. First, it may be said that you should distinguish between the representation (such as an image in your mind) and what that representation represents for you. Only certain features of the image serve a representative function. Now the fact that the image may have some of the features which an actual sense impression of it would have only if the thing were perceived in a certain way, does not mean that these features must be regarded as belonging to what is represented. To this it may be replied by the idealist that they do not deny that, by ignoring certain features of the image, you can regard only the others as playing a role in picturing the object; and that these need not include those which obviously imply presence to a subject. What they deny, in contrast, is that one can form any sort of representation which will, so-to-speak, positively depict the thing as existing without subject-implying features. And unless one can do this one has no real sense of what an unperceived thing could be like.

The second objection is that one can conceive what one cannot imagine. Surely you can *conceive* a physical thing without these subject-implying features even if you cannot *imagine* it. To this the idealist may reply that you do not really understand what you are thinking if you only think about it in words (and doubtless this is what the objector means by conceiving it). Really to bring before your mind the character of the situation you believe in requires that, using the

expression broadly, you must *imagine* it, and this you cannot do except by imagining it as it would present itself to a certain observer.

Such a line of thought, though not precisely Berkeley's in detail, is Berkeleian in spirit and inspiration and it is likely to be a main plank of an ontological idealism which claims that unperceived physical reality is an impossibility. What positive view of the world can be based upon such reflections? For Berkeley it showed that there must be a God who is responsible for those ideas which (after acting in a certain way) we have no choice but to experience and who keeps the whole system of ideas available to each individual spirit in conformity with a universal system of laws determining the appearances available to each.

However, there have been philosophers who put forward a phenomenalism supposed not to imply the existence of God. According to them, one can speak meaningfully of physical things as existing unperceived. However, these only exist in a secondary sense as compared with those which are actually perceived, and their existence in this secondary sense is only the fact that they are available for perception. That is, there are definite facts for each of us (according to what we would ordinarily call our position in space) which determine what perceptions are available or compulsory for us in response to what we do or suffer (what sensations of movement we give ourselves or are given). There is no need to suppose that there is some explanation for this; it must just be accepted as a brute fact.

This phenomenalism is often not classed as idealist because its reductive account of the physical is divorced not only from theism, but from any other conception of the world as shaped by Reason or other higher forms of Mind. It is a puzzle of intellectual history that some of those most influenced by Berkeley's views of physical reality have been among the most atheistic and, in the popular sense, most 'materialist' of thinkers (for example, T.H. HUXLEY, A.J. AYER and, with qualifications, J.S. MILL).

3 Kantian transcendental idealism

A simple version of Kant might present him as a phenomenalist who supplemented his phenomenalism with the admission that there must be some explanation of why the sense experiences available to us are what they are, yet who regarded this explanation as unavailable to us except as the thesis that they result from unconscious operations which we (as we really are rather than as we appear to ourselves) conduct upon things-in-themselves of whose real character we can know nothing (except that it cannot be that of anything properly called physical). However, Kant's reasoning for his transcendental idealism is largely different from those deriving from, or inspired by, Berkeley (see KANT, I. §5).

For Kant there are two striking facts about our knowledge of the world which only his transcendental idealism can explain ('transcendental' means 'having to do with our cognitive powers'). First, we have a great deal of 'synthetic a priori' knowledge about it (see A PRIORI; ANALYTICITY). Thus we know that arithmetic and the axioms of Euclid apply to the physical world as a whole, that every physical or mental process occurs in conformity with universal causal laws, and that change requires a permanent substratum of matter which remains quantitatively the same. Second, neither a priori nor empirical knowledge can answer the great questions of human destiny, such as whether God exists and whether we are immortal. The only possible explanation of our synthetic a priori knowledge about the physical and, indeed, mental worlds is that it is really our knowledge of our own cognitive nature. Space and time are the forms of our perceptual intuition and the categories of causation, substance and accident and so on are the categories by which we construct the unitary world of our actual and possible experience out of unconscious stimuli which reach the hidden self from things-in-themselves (or 'noumena'), of whose character we must remain ignorant. And it is because we are ignorant of things-in-themselves that we cannot *know* the answers to the questions about God and immortality, for these concern absolute truth rather than that truth-for-us which is all that is available for knowledge. On the other hand, just because we cannot *know* the answers to these questions, we may have *faith* that they would suit our moral natures and show that, in spite of the causal determinism holding in the phenomenal world, we are responsible at some 'noumenal' level for our own adherence or otherwise to the categorical imperatives of morality.

Some of the details of Kant's theory are outmoded by the fact that science seems no longer committed to some of his supposedly synthetic a priori truths such as the axioms of Euclid and the universality of causation. However, the idea that the world as we know it owes, to an incalculable extent, its general character to our particular modes of perception and thought still has great force. In Berkeley there was no suggestion that what we know is created by our knowledge of it. The ideas which constitute the physical world are simply the ones which God has chosen to give himself and us and to organize in a certain way. Our knowledge of those we perceive is a fully accurate knowledge by direct acquaintance and

the existence and character of others, as actualities or possibilities, is known by induction. In Kant, knowledge itself to a great extent creates its objects by unconscious operations upon unconscious stimuli reaching us from things-in-themselves whose real nature it leaves in darkness.

The distinction is somewhat subtle, since both the Berkeleian and Kantian, in effect, regard facts about the physical world as facts about the perceptions we may obtain through sensations of movement in certain directions. However, the Berkleyan inheritance has mainly been to insist on the way in which the physical world cannot be conceived without sensory qualities which can only occur as contents of experience, while the Kantian inheritance has mainly been to insist on the way in which our cognition of the physical world interprets it by concepts which it *brings to* experience rather than *abstracts from* it.

In fact, Kant's position is nearer to Berkeley's than he himself allowed. According to Kant his idealism is transcendental, whereas Berkeley's is empirical. What this comes to is that Berkeley's idealism professes to give the absolute truth about the physical world, as a corrective to a realism which regarded it as existing independently of mind, while Kant accepted such realism, but claimed that it was only true for us, and that, as for the absolute truth about things which underlie it, we know nothing beyond the mere fact that there must be such an absolute truth (in the moral and theistic significance of which we may have faith).

4 German absolute idealism

The great figures in German absolute idealism were J.G. FICHTE, G.W.F. HEGEL and F.W.J. VON SCHELLING (see ABSOLUTE, THE). (The character of their considerable political influence cannot be considered here.) In effect, each agreed with Kant that ordinary common sense and 'scientific' (in our usual sense, not theirs, in which it referred to their own philosophic conclusions) truth about the physical world is only truth for us. But they went beyond Kant in holding that philosophy can put this in the context of an absolute and rationally demonstrated truth about an essentially spiritual world. In fact, Kant's attempt to close the door on attempts to know the ultimate truth of things opened it to some of the most robust claims ever made to have probed the mysteries of the universe.

For Kant the physical world only exists for us, and our knowledge of it is only truth for us. However, we can recognize that there must be two hidden determinants of it, modes of cognition which take place in our own hidden depths, and the unconscious non-physical stimuli from mysterious things-in-them-selves out of which they make the familiar physical world. Fichte thought the postulation of such things-in-themselves quite unnecessary. If the knowable physical world is something whose form we construct unconsciously why should not the matter be some-thing we determine unconsciously too? Thereby we avoid the nebulous hypothesis of things-in-themselves, and are left simply with our own indubitable existence and hidden depths thereof, of which we dimly sense the presence. Of course there is an external world or non-ego, but it exists only as something which the ego posits and does so for reasons the general character of which can be deciphered. For the ego wants to live a life of moral worth and this it can only do if it has obstacles to overcome; thus the external world it posits consists precisely in those obstacles whose over-coming is most morally valuable at its current stage of development.

But how is it that each ego shares a non-ego, as it evidently does, with other egos? Fichte has two related answers. One is that moral development is something which can only occur in a community, so that the different egos need to posit a shared non-ego giving them a common environment in which to work out their moral destiny. Second, as his thought developed, Fichte became clearer that the ego which is working out its moral destiny in each of us is really a single world-spirit living out an apparent multiplicity of lives. Fichte developed this account by way of a dialectical method which became the hallmark of German idealism (inspired by Kant for whom, however, it was rather a source of illusion than a means to truth) in which apparently opposed truths are successively reconciled in higher syntheses until absolute truth is reached. Thus was born absolute idealism, in which the reality behind both nature and finite mind is a single absolute mind or self in process of self-discovery or development. However, Fichte's brand of absolute idealism is sometimes also called 'subjective idealism', because it regards the natural world as existing only for the subjective experience of finite individuals, expressions of a single world self though they may be.

Schelling was originally a follower of Fichte, but his continually shifting versions of idealism tended to become more 'objective' or at least more positively concerned with nature for its own sake. The Absolute or universal self does not simply dream the physical world as the scene of moral endeavour but rather expresses itself in a parallel dialectic, both 'really' in the nature from which the mind arises and 'ideally' in the mind for which nature exists. The two come together eventually in philosophical understanding and, more concretely, in art.

Absolute idealism, and the dialectical method and ontology, reached its historically most important form in the philosophy of Hegel. For Hegel, the world consists in a series of terms each surpassing its (only sometimes temporal) predecessors by incorpor-ating what was satisfactory in them, in a manner which reconciles in a higher synthesis that in which they contradicted each other. The series begins with pure concepts, leading on to actual natural and then humanly historical processes and terminates in a community in the free service of which each individual can find themselves fulfilled and in the consciousness, in the minds of philosophers, of its total nature. Thus, everything exists as path to, and as fodder for, a rich communal spiritual life, but how far this means that nothing really exists except as a component within or object for consciousness or spirit, is controversial. Therefore, it is unclear how far Hegel was an idealist in our sense (as opposed to the broader sense mentioned parenthetically above).

Hegel and Schelling had originally seen themselves as partners in developing a new philosophy, but Hegel soon surpassed his at first better known associate in fame and influence. However, Schelling had his turn again on Hegel's death, developing a new so-called positive philosophy in which he rejected the high a priori road to the nature of existence which both thinkers had taken previously. Absolute idealism must appeal partly to empirical features of the world rather than merely cite them sometimes as illustrations of what reason can independently prove must be so. This more traditionally Christian philosophy sought to give God and man a freedom effectively denied them by Hegelianism. Its somewhat bizarre ontology also seemed to many to show German idealism in its death throes.

In different ways Fichte, Schelling and Hegel each held that the world could only be understood through realizing that it is the concrete actualization of concepts whose proper home is in the mind. This binds them to Kant, but they sought to go beyond him in explaining why the relevant categories are just as they are and why there is a real unity of experience common to apparently different minds: namely that, in the end, the world is the construction of one universal Mind or Reason. Each saw himself as drawing on SPINOZA as well as Kant, but as substituting an ultimate self or subject for Spinoza's substance.

Standing quite apart from these absolute idealists is the lonely but immensely influential figure of Arthur SCHOPENHAUER. Arguably the closest metaphysically, if not in mood, to Kant, and accepting in the main his transcendental idealism, he claimed to have discov-ered the true nature of the realm of things-in-themselves, regarding them as aspects of a single universal Will, manifesting itself as object for a subject (which was its own self fallen into a state of wretched self-assertion), from which it can escape only by a culmination of that denial of the will to live, characteristic, as he saw it, of sainthood.

5 Anglo-American absolute idealism

As German philosophers moved away from idealism in the later part of the nineteenth century, idealism of an essentially absolute kind became the dominant mode of philosophy in the UK and the USA (where, however, there were more serious rivals to it). This was motivated partly by the search for a form of religious belief which would be less vulnerable to Lyell and Darwin than traditional Christianity had been, and by an ethical viewpoint which would be rather nobler in its conception of the possibilities of human life than Benthamite utilitarianism. Some of these philosophers (for example John and Edward Caird, and William Wallace), were doctrinal Hegelians, utilizing Hegelianism to save Christianity.

More importantly original philosophers of an idealist persuasion during this period were T.H. GREEN and F.H. BRADLEY in the UK (also the very like-minded, though more Hegelian, Bernard BOSANQUET), and Josiah ROYCE in the USA. We can only mention in passing the very distinctive idealism already advanced by J.F. FERRIER in Scotland, which draws both on Berkeley and on German idealism. These thinkers were to various extents influenced by Kant and Hegel and the other German idealists, but in the case of Bradley, at least, something of the Berkeleian tradition is, perhaps unconsciously, present.

Green was anxious above all to show that the development of human life from animal origins could not be explained purely by way of natural selection, or indeed in any naturalistic way. Rather, must it be recognized as the gradual unfolding of the life of a universal spirit aspiring to fulfilment in an eventually virtuous form of human life. For empiricism and naturalism cannot explain the connectedness of the world, and the ability of the human mind to synthesize events of different times into a unitary history. This is only possible if the world is the expression of a single universal spirit of which each of us is an actualization in which it becomes aware of itself. The general upshot is quite Hegelian, but there is little use of Hegelian dialectic.

Bradley's metaphysics derives from two main reflections: first, that nothing is genuinely conceivable except experience with its various modes and contents; second, that what we describe as distinct things in relation to each other can only be adequately conceived as abstractions from a higher unity. In the end all things must, therefore, be abstractions from one single Cosmic Experience. With his denial of time's reality and his claim that Reality is really a single cosmic *Nunc Stans* whose ingredients only seem to be passing away in time, Bradley strikes a note which is perhaps more Platonic than Hegelian. Royce's absolute idealism has a good deal in common with Bradley, but whereas for Bradley God was only a rather superior 'appearance' along with the ordinary things of daily life, for Royce the Absolute was God, being personal in a way that Bradley's Absolute was not.

6 Panpsychism

One of the main charges against idealism is that of 'cosmic impiety' (Santayana). Its tendency is to make the vast realm of nature simply a representation in a mind observing or thinking of it. This can hardly do justice either to its obstinacy (surely not primarily of our own making, whatever Fichte may have thought) or to its wonderfulness. Such reflections have led some of those who are persuaded of the basic idealist claim that unexperienced reality is impossible, to hold the panpsychist position that nature is composed of units which feel their own existence and relation to other things, just as truly, if less articulately, as we do (see PANPSYCHISM). This was the view of Royce, and Bradley thought it might be true. It was a main plank, somewhat eccentrically developed, of the German idealist Gustav FECHNER (and is perhaps adumbrated in Schelling); also of LEIBNIZ, who in this respect can be called an idealist.

Panpsychism of this sort has been most fully developed in recent times in the work of A.N. WHITEHEAD and of Charles Hartshorne. It is sometimes regarded as a synthesis of realism and idealism; realist because it gives the ultimate units of nature (whatever they are) a reality in themselves (as what they are for themselves); idealist because it denies unexperienced reality. When the inner sentient life of (the rest of) nature is thought of as unified with the subjective life of humans and animals (as it must be for a Bradley or a Royce) in one absolute consciousness, we have a form of absolute or objective idealism which quite avoids the anthropocentric character it had in the work of thinkers such as Fichte.

7 Personal idealism

Many thinkers of an idealist persuasion in the English-speaking world bridled somewhat at the downplaying of individual persons by absolute idealism, especially Bradley and to a lesser extent Royce. This led to the development, as the nineteenth century closed, of some forms of personal idealism for which reality is a community of independently real spirits (with or without a God as a *primus inter pares*) and the physical world their common object or construction. There is no great figure here, with the possible exception of J.M.E. MCTAGGART who espoused a highly individual form of pluralistic idealism. Otherwise the main proponent of personal idealism was the US philosopher, G.H. Howison, although eight Oxford philosophers published a manifesto under this label in 1902 (see PERSONALISM).

Anglo-American idealism was, for a time, widely thought to have been refuted by the work of G.E. MOORE and Bertrand RUSSELL in the UK and such pragmatists as JAMES and DEWEY in the USA (though there were certainly idealist features to the thought of these two Americans), but a contrary judgement is now not uncommon. Edmund Husserl's phenomenology remains influential in some quarters, and some agree with his eventual view that it implies a form of transcendental idealism (see HUSSERL, E.). Some regard the antirealism associated with Michael DUMMETT as idealist in spirit (see REALISM AND ANTIREALISM), while some of the continuing school of Wittgensteinians regard the thought of WITTGENSTEIN as a form of social idealism. Much closer to traditional idealism, however, is the conceptual idealism of the important US philosopher Nicholas Rescher (which synthesizes idealism and pragmatism) and idealist positions (not, it must be admitted, so far very influential) advocated in the UK by John Foster and, if he may say so, by the author of this entry.

References and further reading

Berkeley, G. (1710) *A Treatise Concerning the Principles of Human Knowledge*, in *The Works of George Berkeley*, vol. 2, ed. T.E. Jessop, London: Thomas Nelson & Sons Ltd, 1949. (This and the following work give the complete statement of Berkeley's theistic idealism. Berkeley's introduction is essential reading.)

—— (1713) *Three Dialogues between Hylas and Philonous*, in *The Works of George Berkeley*, vol. 2, ed. T.E. Jessop, London: Thomas Nelson & Sons Ltd, 1949. (The second of Berkeley's two most important works. Many other satisfactory editions of these works exist.)

Bradley, F.H. (1897) *Appearance and Reality*, Oxford: Oxford University Press, 1930. (This work represents the high point of British idealism in the nineteenth century.)

Ferrier, J.F. (1854) *The Institutes of Metaphysics*, Edinburgh. (A fine, much-neglected work, presenting an idealism that lies somewhere between that of Berkeley and the German Idealists.)

Fichte, J.G. (1794, 1797) *The Science of Knowledge*, trans. P. Heath and J. Lachs, Cambridge: Cambridge University Press, 1982. (Develops Fichte's conception of the world as consisting of self and not-self, the latter a posit of the former as the scene for its ethical self-development.)

Findlay, J.N. (1970) *Ascent to the Absolute*, London: George Allen & Unwin. (Wide-ranging essays by an idealistically inclined philosopher.)

Foster, J. (1982) *The Case for Idealism*, London: Routledge & Kegan Paul. (A difficult but important argument for an idealist conception of the physical world.)

Green, T.H. (1883) *Prolegomena to Ethics*, Oxford: Oxford University Press. (Argues that a naturalistic, in particular Darwinian, account of the origin of mind in the universe can never explain how it can have anything beyond the momentary as its object. This ability shows that it is a stage in the self-realization of an infinite mind.)

Hartshorne, C. (1962) *The Logic of Perfection*, Peru, IL: Open Court. (A set of essays sufficient for a general grasp of Hartshorne's process philosophy which he regards as a form of idealism.)

Hegel, G.W.F. (1807) *Phenomenology of Spirit*, trans. A.V. Miller, Oxford: Oxford University Press, 1977. (Difficult like all Hegel's works, this charts the stages by which spirit or consciousness comes to consciousness of itself as the ultimate reality.)

Howison, G.H. (1901) *The Limits of Evolution, and Other Essays Illustrating the Metaphysical Theory of Personal Idealism*, New York: Macmillan. (Howison's personal idealism is presented as religiously more satisfactory than the then-still-dominant philosophy of absolute idealism.)

Husserl, E. (1913) *Ideas Pertaining to a Pure Phenomenology and to a Phenomenological Philosophy*, trans. F. Kersten, Dordrecht: Kluwer, 1982. (The first book is the most relevant. Shows that phenomenology is a route to transcendental idealism.)

Kant, I. (1781) *Critique of Pure Reason*, trans. N. Kemp Smith, London: Macmillan, 1933. (The classic statement of Kant's transcendental idealism, one of the greatest and most influential works in the history of philosophy.)

McTaggart, J.M.E. (1921, 1927) *The Nature of Existence*, Cambridge: Cambridge University Press, 2 vols. (The closely argued main statement of his doctrine of the Absolute as a society of spirits linked to each other by love.)

Schopenhauer, A. (1818) *The World as Will and Representation*, trans. E.F.J. Payne, New York:

Dover Publications, 1969, 2 vols. (The main work in which Schopenhauer develops his view that the natural world is the way in which the single World Will appears to itself at the level at which it actualizes itself as human consciousness.)

Royce, J. (1885) *The Religious Aspect of Philosophy*, Gloucester, MA: Peter Smith, 1965. (Royce's first work, perhaps the best statement of his form of absolute idealism.)

—— (1919) *Lectures on Modern Idealism*, New Haven, CT and London: Yale University Press, 1964. (Lectures delivered 1906: a perfect introduction to German Idealism.)

Schelling, F.W.J. (1797) *System of Transcendental Idealism*, trans. P. Heath, Charlottesville, VA: University Press of Virginia, 1978. (The classic statement of Schelling's idealism in one of its earlier phases.)

Sprigge, T.L.S. (1983) *The Vindication of Absolute Idealism*, Edinburgh: Edinburgh University Press. (Argues that the inner being of nature is experiential and that all experience is united in an absolute world consciousness.)

* Sturt, H. (ed.) (1902) *Personal Idealism: Philosophical Essays by Eight Members of the University of Oxford*, London: Macmillan. (Personal idealist manifesto against the submerging of the individual by absolute idealism. See especially the contributions of F.C.S. Schiller and Hastings Rashdall.)

Whitehead, A.N. (1929) *Process and Reality*, New York: The Free Press, 1978. (Classic statement of Whitehead's process philosophy which remains one of the great alternative conceptions of how things really are and purportedly combines what is true in realism and idealism.)

T.L.S. SPRIGGE

IDEALISM, GERMAN
see GERMAN IDEALISM

IDEALISM IN INDIAN PHILOSOPHY *see* BUDDHISM, YOGĀCĀRA SCHOOL OF

IDEALIZATIONS

Scientific analyses of particular phenomena are invariably simplified or idealized. The universe does not contain only two bodies as assumed in Newton's derivation of Kepler's laws, or only one body as assumed in Schwarzschild's relativistic update; real economic agents do not act exclusively to maximize expected utilities, the surfaces of ordinary plate condensers are not infinitely extended planes, and the sine of an angle is not equal in measure to the angle itself. There are many reasons for the use of such misdescriptions. First and foremost is the need to achieve mathematical tractability. Science gets nowhere unless numbers, or numerical constraints, are produced that can form the basis of predictions and explanations. Idealizations may also be required because of the unavailability of certain data or because of the absence of necessary auxiliary theories.

The philosophical problem is to make normative sense of this common but complex scientific practice. For example, how can theories be tested given that they connect to the world only through the intermediary of idealized descriptions? In what sense can there be scientific explanations if what is to be explained must be misdescribed before theory can be brought to bear? The fact that idealizations can often be improved, with corresponding salutary effect on the accuracy of prediction or usefulness of explanation, suggests that idealizations should be understood as part of some sort of convergent process.

1 **The falsity of idealizations**
2 **Idealizations as approximations**
3 **Monotonically convergent sequences and targets of approximation**
4 **Developments and consequences**

1 The falsity of idealizations

Idealizations are false. This much is clear. And not only false, but such that their use, by and large, must lead to incorrect observational consequences. In order to generate a numerical prediction, Michelson and Morley described their interferometer as being perfectly rigid and the optical media as being stable, even though they knew this not to be true. The example is not an isolated exception. This causes serious problems for conventional hypothetico-deductive and Bayesian views of theory confirmation (see CONFIRMATION THEORY). Let t represent some underlying or fundamental theory, i the idealizing assumptions made, and p some actually derivable prediction. Philosophical and scientific common sense has it that if p is found to be true there is confirmation, or at least the satisfaction of a necessary condition for confirmation, and if p is found to be false, disconfirmation. But the falsity of i blocks such inferences. Consider first disconfirmation. From the premises $t\&i \Rightarrow p$ and $\sim p$ all that follows is that $\sim (t\&i)$, which is equivalent to $\sim t\vee \sim i$ (that is, not t and/or not i). But this conclusion follows directly from the falsity of i. Therefore, there is no need to engage in the expense of experimentation if the conclusion sought is simply that either theory or idealizations are false. A similar problem holds for confirmation.

Bayesian accounts fare no better. Distinguishing, as above, between the underlying theory and the idealizations needed for an actual calculation, Bayes' theorem takes the form,

$$P(t\,\&\,i\,|\,e) = \frac{P(e\,|\,t\,\&\,i)P(t\,\&\,i)}{P(e)}$$

where e represents the empirical evidence. Because the idealizations are false, $P(t\,\&\,i) = 0$. Therefore, the evidence cannot affect the probability of $(t\,\&\,i)$. This is just the Bayesian analogue of the problem caused by the use of idealizations for hypothetico-deductivism. Consider also the typical case in science where the theory-produced prediction is false because of the distortion introduced by the idealizations. In such a case $P(e\,|\,t\&i)$ will be zero. So once again, there will be no change in the probability of $(t\,\&\,i)$. Trying to avoid such difficulties by separating i from t and conjoining it with e leads to similar disappointments for Bayesians.

2 Idealizations as approximations

One popular approach to idealizations is to view their use as a form of approximation. The basic idea is to think of individual idealizations as elements of some larger structure that is convergent on the truth. This way of thinking is naturally inspired by the existence in science of sequences, such as the following, of increasingly less idealized descriptive equations.

$$ml^2\frac{d^2\theta}{dt^2} = -mgl\theta \qquad (1)$$

$$ml^2\frac{d^2\theta}{dt^2} = -mgl\sin\theta \qquad (2)$$

$$ml^2\frac{d^2\theta}{dt^2} = -cl\frac{d\theta}{dt} - mgl\sin\theta \qquad (3)$$

These equations apply to simple pendulums where m is the mass of the pendulum bob, l the length of the suspension cord, g the gravitational strength, c the coefficient of resistance, and θ the angular displacement. A natural ordering exists insofar as (3) approaches (2) as the coefficient of resistance is made to approach zero, and (2) reduces to (1) if $\sin\theta$ is replaced by θ. Focusing first on the reduction of (2) to (1), the difference between $\sin\theta$ and θ will be 'small' if θ is itself 'small'. For example, if θ is 0.0873 radian, then $\sin\theta$ is 0.0872. And in general, as θ approaches zero the difference between $\sin\theta$ and θ also approaches zero. The hope therefore is that if θ is kept small, the difference in the solution to (1) will differ from that of (2) by a correspondingly small amount. And because this hope is satisfied, it can be said that θ approximates $\sin\theta$. The relationship between (2) and (3) is similar: if the coefficient of resistance c is small, then so too, one hopes, will be the difference between calculated periods. What is illustrated in these equations is a transformational sense of approximation: the substitution of some term or expression X' for X in a mathematical function or equation, where the effect of the transformation will be correspondingly small if the difference between X and X' is small. And if the transformations are made in the appropriate order, a sequence such as that illustrated is formed of increasingly less idealized and more realistic descriptive equations.

The above approach distinguishes between the process of idealization, the misdescription of things, and the hope that this misdescription will yield a successful transformational approximation. In the case of equation (2), the natural inclination is to say that a causal factor has been ignored or misdescribed, namely, the resistance. Examples such as this suggest that idealization involves the deliberate ignoring or misdescription of causally relevant factors. Whether or not such misdescriptions can be interpreted as yielding transformational approximations becomes a separate mathematical question. But as the approximation of $\sin\theta$ by θ suggests, there may be cases where the process of idealization seems motivated by exclusively mathematical considerations. It must also be kept in mind that the closeness of an original quantity and its idealized surrogate is by itself no guarantee that functional outputs or solutions will be correspondingly close. The specifics of the mathematics involved must be examined in order to determine whether closeness is preserved.

The construction of sequences that are increasingly less idealized is a major challenge for science. The pendulum example also illustrates an important experimental challenge. And that is the construction and development of experiments that more closely approach existing idealized analyses. So, for example, assuming the correctness of (3), eliminating the resistance and keeping the oscillations small is a way of making an actual pendulum approach its counterfactual cousins. There are two responses therefore that typically are made to the use of idealizations. First, one can try to bring the analysis to the phenomenon by making the analysis less idealized. Second, one can try to bring the phenomenon to the description by experimental refinement.

3 Monotonically convergent sequences and targets of approximation

In the case of the pendulum the identification of θ with $\sin\theta$ and the substitution of zero for resistance could be readily interpreted as transformational approximations because equation (3) served as a reference or target. But where do such targets come from? How completely need they be specified in order to determine that some idealization is a transformational approximation? Is the apparent convergence of a sequence of idealized analyses a reliable indication that a target exists? In order to appreciate the difficulties such questions pose, imagine that t is the true fundamental theory applicable in some domain of interest, and that there exists a sequence of input conditions and their idealizations $\langle i_1, \ldots, i_i, \ldots \rangle$ such that $t(langlei_1, \ldots, i_i, \ldots \rangle)$ is convergent on the actual effect. (Henceforth, the sequence will be denoted $\langle i_i \rangle$, and functional application as $t\langle i_i \rangle$.) So, for example, imagine that there are one hundred forces, f_1 through f_{100}, all aligned along a common axis, operating on some particle. And let the first ninety-nine be of equal magnitude but alternating direction, and the remaining force be twice the magnitude of the others. Now imagine that scientist S arrives on the scene, gradually learns of the existence of the forces in the sequence $\langle f_1, f_2, \ldots, f_i, f_{i+1} \rangle$, and applies standard Newtonian theory, that the acceleration of the particle will be equal to the product of its mass and the vectorial sum of the forces. (The complications that would result if S were to use idealized descriptions of the forces will be ignored.) The resultant summations can naturally be described as becoming increasingly more realistic and less idealized. Ss ongoing efforts, however, will be to little avail because improving things this way does not result in the gradual convergence of prediction to actual acceleration. Convergence occurs all at once when the enumeration is complete. The target becomes clear only once one has arrived and it is known that one has arrived. It must be known that the enumeration is complete. That $t\langle i_i \rangle$ is convergent is by itself not of much value because all that is assured is that if S works long enough, experimental fit will get better and remain so. But how long is long enough is not specified; only that there exists at least one such point. Consider the consequences of this observation for the testing of scientific theories. Say, for example, that S wishes to test whether the underlying Newtonian theory is true. Failure to achieve improvement of experimental fit by the use of increasingly more realistic idealizations would not be evidence of its falsity. By contrast, assume the existence of a world where the input can be ordered such that $t\langle i_i \rangle$ is strictly monotonic (that is, predictive

output is always getting better). In such a world, the use of t would be rewarded by constantly improving experimental fit as increasingly more realistic idealizations were employed – assuming, of course, that the appropriate input sequence is employed. If such continual improvement did not occur, then it would be known that the theory was not correct. So in a situation where strict monotonicity holds, disconfirmation is possible and the use of a correct theory will be rewarded in the sense that experimental fit will continually improve as increasingly more realistic idealizations are used. But only on the assumption that one has access to the strictly monotonic sequence of input conditions. How, though, is this to be assured? Or that such a sequence even exists? It is hard to see how such determinations could be made without assuming the truth of the very theory to be tested. Say, for example, that it is discovered that t and some set of idealizations, i_1, yield more accurate predictions than the combination of t and some other set i_2 of idealizations. Presumably, this lends some support for i_1 being placed later in the sequence than i_2. Such an appraisal, however, relies on the assumption that t is true. If so, then it is the idealizations that are being tested by means of experiment and not the theory itself! So it looks as though theories can be tested if it is assumed that idealizations are monotonically ordered, and idealizations can be ordered if the corresponding theory is assumed. But there seems no way to test experimentally both theory and idealizations.

One proposal for avoiding this result is to employ some sort of bootstrapping procedure. Briefly, the idea is to begin the confirmational process by using the theory along with experimentation to tentatively order the idealizations used in some particular domain of application. Attention is then shifted to a different domain or experimental situation, but it must be one that is not so different that the previously obtained measures of relative realism will not be expected to hold. If the new theoretical predictions do not retain the ordering of the original domain (assuming appropriate compensation can somehow be made for relevant differences), then suspicion is cast on the theory. So, for example, predictions of pendulum period are more accurate when hydrostatic effects are taken into account. This superiority is expected to continue in the case of compound pendulums. Sometimes enough is known about the interfering causes and the mathematical properties of possible idealizations that it can be formally shown that monotonically convergent sequences cannot exist for the theory in question. For example, with respect to the kinetic theory of gases, it was shown that the equipartition theorem entailed that making molecule descriptions more realistic (by adding more degrees of freedom) would lead to predicted values for specific heats that would be progressively worse than those predicted on the basis of simple models.

4 Developments and consequences

Systematic development of the themes presented above has proceeded along a broad front. Much effort has been expended to develop abstract but mathematically precise ways of characterizing scientific theories that will take into account idealizations and approximations. One of the anticipated benefits of such characterizations is being able to analyse theories themselves as idealizations or approximations of other theories. There has also been considerable formal development of appropriate measures for nearness or closeness of fit. The choice of such measures becomes problematic when more is involved than simply determining how far one number is from another and there are multiple criteria for successful fit. Another line of investigation involves understanding the scientific use of idealizations and approximations in terms of more general notions of computation. It has long been believed that there is a fruitful analogy to be developed between the development of science and finding equational solutions by means of successive approximations. Other subjects of active investigation include the differences between the uses of idealizations in the pure and applied sciences, the relevance of the use of idealizations for the debate among realists and instrumentalists (see SCIENTIFIC REALISM AND ANTIREALISM), and the importance of non-linear dynamics (see CHAOS THEORY) for understanding the successful use of idealizations and approximations.

See also: EXPERIMENT; MECHANICS, CLASSICAL; MODELS; THEORIES, SCIENTIFIC

References and further reading

Balzer, W., Moulines, C.U. and Sneed, J.D. (1987) *An Architectonic for Science: The Structuralist Program*, Dordrecht: Reidel. (Develops a formal taxonomy for scientific theories. See chapter VII for connections with approximation.)

Cartwright, N. (1983) *How the Laws of Physics Lie*, Oxford: Clarendon Press. (Discusses many interesting scientific cases and presents a very original view of the relevance of the use of idealizations for scientific realism and instrumentalism.)

—— (1989) *Nature's Capacities and their Measurement*, Oxford: Clarendon Press. (Further

developments of positions presented in her earlier book.)

Laymon, R. (1985) 'Idealizations and the Testing of Theories by Experimentation', in P. Achinstein and O. Hannaway (eds) *Experiment and Observation in Modern Science*, Boston, MA: MIT Press–Bradford Books, 147–73. (A general informal introduction to the subject. Contains many historical examples.)

—— (1990) 'Computer Simulations, Idealization and Approximation', in A. Fine, M. Forbes and L. Wessels (eds) *PSA 1990*, East Lansing, MI: Philosophy of Science Association, vol. 2, 519–34. (Develops connections with formal theories of computation and computer semantics. Discusses some of the implications of chaos theory.)

Niiniluoto, I. (1984) *Is Science Progressive?*, Dordrecht: Reidel. (Covers most of the items discussed in §4. Especially valuable is the work on measures of approximation. Also contains extensive literature reviews and bibliographies.)

RONALD LAYMON

IDEALS

Ideals are models of excellence. They can be moral or nonmoral, and either 'substantive' or 'deliberative'. Substantive ideals present models of excellence against which things in a relevant class can be assessed, such as models of the just society or the good person. Deliberative ideals present models of excellent deliberation, leading to correct or warranted ethical conclusions. Ideals figure in ethics in two opposed ways. Most centrally, ideals serve to justify ethical judgments and to guide people in how to live. Sometimes, however, ideals may conflict with moral demands, thereby testing the limits of morality.

Reliance upon ideals in the development of ethical theories seems unavoidable but raises difficult questions. How can the choice of a particular ideal be justified? How might conflicts between ideals and other values, especially moral demands, be resolved?

1 Substantive and deliberative ideals
2 Selecting ideals
3 Ideals and morality

1 Substantive and deliberative ideals

Substantive ideals delineate the features that something or someone must possess in order to be excellent in a specific regard. Such ideals can provide a highly detailed model or a more general framework.

Whether specific or general, however, substantive ideals logically imply certain evaluative judgments in conjunction with the facts about whether and to what degree something or someone possesses the relevant features. A person can hold universal ideals of human excellence or human social life, as well as more personal ideals regarding who to be and how to live. Common universal ideals include ideals of the just or virtuous person, ideals of human rationality, the liberal ideal of a free society, and hierarchical ideals of societies structured to realize human excellence. Prevalent personal ideals include those of being an exceptional parent, a connoisseur of high culture, a brave soldier or a devout follower of God.

Substantive ideals provide standards that guide the development of character and commitments, aims and attitudes, social relationships and institutions. When persons hold an ideal of human excellence, for instance, they regard it as central to their identity. They are normally motivated to cultivate the emotions, qualities and pursuits their ideal upholds, and they feel shame, guilt or self-contempt when they fail to live up to their ideal. To hold an ideal thus differs from merely wanting or preferring something. Because ideals provide a basis for assessment, holding an ideal is more akin to having a second-order desire, a desire to have or not to have certain other desires.

Each moral system or theory has its corresponding ideals, but whether each actually derives from an ideal is a matter of some controversy. Nevertheless, substantive ideals have historically been central to many different moral conceptions. In his *Republic*, Plato famously constructs a blueprint of the just state (see PLATO §14). Aristotle's account of human happiness in *Nicomachean Ethics* rests upon a substantive ideal of excellent human functioning (see ARISTOTLE §§22–7). G.E. Moore, in *Principia Ethica* (1903), presents an account of 'the Absolute Good or Ideal', which is made up of the intrinsic goods of personal affections and aesthetic enjoyments (see MOORE, G.E. §1). Other important substantive ideals include Kant's 'kingdom of ends' (1785), an ideal union between self-legislating rational beings (see KANT, I. §§9–10; KANTIAN ETHICS); Nietzsche's ideal of the 'overman' (*Übermensch*) (1883–5), the creative, self-determining man who lives without fear of himself or others (see NIETZSCHE, F. §10); and John Rawls' Kantian ideal of the person (1980) (see RAWLS, J.).

Substantive ideals continue to be important to ethical theorizing. But philosophers in the twentieth century have largely avoided explicit appeal to substantive ideals, perhaps in recognition of the apparent plurality of defensible values (see MORAL PLURALISM; VALUES). Instead, they often rely on deliberative ideals, seeking to develop a critical perspective on our ordinary desires and ethical assessments that is sensitive to value pluralism.

Deliberative ideals specify optimal conditions for reflection on ethical questions. They form the basis of broadly counterfactual accounts of moral and non-moral value, most notably, in 'ideal observer' theories and contractarian theories. The deliberative ideals developed in contractarian theories figure critically in attempted derivations of principles of justice or morality. But as employed in ideal observer theories, deliberative ideals do not logically support evaluative conclusions: evaluative conclusions are determined by an observer's reactions – usually some sort of 'pro' or 'con' attitude – under ideal conditions. In either case, though, deliberative ideals function to justify ethical conclusions by incorporating conditions designed to ensure both that a deliberator's conclusions or reactions have been subjected to rational, critical scrutiny and that they address the concerns of actual deliberators. Conditions are thereby also designed to preserve the recommending force of ethical judgments and the connection that normally holds between ethical judgment and motivation (see MORAL MOTIVATION §1). Deliberative ideals typically enhance the rationality of deliberators and either markedly increase or relevantly constrain their knowledge. They may also improve a deliberator's motivations, for instance, by eliminating emotional distortions (see MORALITY AND EMOTIONS §1).

Deliberative ideals are sometimes offered as analyses or reforming definitions of ethical terms. The paradigm ideal observer theory, developed by Roderick Firth (1952), analyses the meanings of ethical words in terms of the 'ethically significant reactions' of an ideal observer, one who is disinterested, dispassionate, omniscient, omnipercipient, consistent and 'otherwise normal'. Certain ethical naturalists, notably Richard Brandt (1979) and Peter Railton (1986), have offered structurally similar 'reforming definitions' of ethical terms. And R.M. Hare's account of 'critical thinking', based on the 'logic' of the moral concepts, parallels Firth's view in many respects (see HARE, R.M. §3).

John Rawls' account of the 'original position', in *A Theory of Justice* (1971), is perhaps the most famous contractarian deliberative ideal. According to Rawls, fair choice of principles of justice occurs when rational, self-interested, mutually disinterested persons select principles under conditions of limited shared information from behind a 'veil of ignorance'. Deliberative ideals related to Rawls' can be found in the contractarian views of Thomas Scanlon (1982) and David Gauthier (1986), for example, as well as in Jürgen Habermas' 'discourse ethics' (1990) (see

673

RAWLS, J.; CONTRACTARIANISM §9; HABERMAS, J. §3).

Deliberative ideals are often thought to avoid substantive evaluative commitments, at least controversial ones. Certain deliberative ideals, however, may reflect substantive ideals, as the deliberative ideal embodied in Rawls' original position reflects his Kantian ideal of the person. Thus, deliberative ideals may not be fully distinct from substantive ideals.

2 Selecting ideals

Given the important justificatory role of ideals in ethical theories, how might choice of a particular substantive or deliberative ideal be justified? Various answers have been given, each of which encounters difficulties.

Plato held that knowledge of the Forms of Goodness and Justice is innate and recovered through a process of recollection. But such claims regarding innate knowledge seem contradicted by ethical disagreement. We might, following Aristotle, look to human nature to support choice of ideals (see HUMAN NATURE §1). But we lack a convincing account of human nature, and the evident diversity of human talents and reasonable aims suggests that human nature will not support any single ideal. Moore determines the content of 'the Ideal' by considering items in complete isolation in order to ascertain their intrinsic value. This 'method of isolation', however, assumes implausibly that we can directly intuit an item's value. Firth claims to select the characteristics of an ideal observer 'by examining the procedures which we actually regard, implicitly or explicitly, as the rational ones for *deciding* ethical questions' (1952: 332; original emphasis). But our ordinary view of which procedures are rational may be faulty and less determinate than Firth supposes. Brandt's and Railton's reforming definitions incorporate purely epistemic ideal conditions, thereby apparently remaining neutral as between substantive ideals and desires. Yet conditions that are only epistemically ideal may lack normative force. For the reactions individuals would have under such conditions will depend, in part, on their own motivational systems, which may themselves warrant normative criticism. Finally, Rawls argues that his original position incorporates only weak and widely shared assumptions about what makes for a fair choice. Critics of Rawls have argued, however, that his assumptions are controversial.

Choice between ideals used to support competing conceptions of moral and nonmoral value can be settled to some degree by considering such things as the relative coherence and consistency of the ideals, as well as their compatibility with empirical information.

But as Samuel Scheffler regretfully remarks, there may be no 'ideal-independent, trans-theoretical moral perspective which condemns the ideal we abhor and favours the ideal we prize' (1979: 300) (see MORAL SCEPTICISM).

3 Ideals and morality

In some cases, conflicts may arise between a person's ideals (moral or nonmoral) and other values, in particular, alleged moral obligations (see DUTY). These conflicts reveal important questions about the divide between morality and nonmoral value and about what limits may exist to the demands of morality.

Bernard Williams has considered such conflicts (1973), arguing that utilitarianism in particular and impartial morality more generally may be destructive of individual integrity, since they demand that persons set aside their deepest commitments in favour of what morality may require (see IMPARTIALITY; WILLIAMS, B.A.O. §2). Williams does not use the language of ideals, but the commitments which give individuals a sense of what their lives are about will surely include commitments to particular ideals. The conflicts examined by Williams expose difficult questions about morality. Is it purely impartial or does it include 'agent-centred prerogatives' (Scheffler 1982)? If morality is purely impartial, are its demands always overriding? In answering these questions, we see how ideals may function not only to ground morality, but to fix its contours and limit its demands.

See also: AXIOLOGY; PERFECTIONISM; SOLIDARITY; VIRTUE ETHICS

References and further reading

Anderson, E. (1993) *Value in Ethics and Economics*, Cambridge, MA: Harvard University Press. (Develops a clear and accessible ideal-based theory of value.)

* Aristotle (c. mid 4th century BC) *Nicomachean Ethics*, trans. W.D. Ross, Oxford: Oxford University Press, 1975. (Aristotle's account of happiness and excellent human functioning.)

* Brandt, R. (1979) *A Theory of the Good and the Right*, Oxford: Clarendon Press. (Presents reforming definitions of ethical terms, such as 'good' and 'morally wrong', that employ deliberative ideals.)

* Firth, R. (1952) 'Ethical Absolutism and the Ideal Observer', *Philosophy and Phenomenological Research* 12: 317–45. (Classic example of a deliberative ideal offered as an analysis of ethical terms and judgments.)

* Gauthier, D. (1986) *Morals by Agreement*, Oxford: Clarendon Press. (Advanced. Argues that morality is a set of rational principles for choice that rational persons would accept in a fully voluntary *ex ante* agreement.)

* Habermas, J. (1990) 'Discourse Ethics: Notes on a Philosophical Program of Justification', in *Moral Consciousness and Communicative Action*, Cambridge, MA: MIT Press. (Explication and programmatic justification of discourse ethics, according to which the practical discourse that leads to valid norms involves communication that adequately approximates ideal conditions.)

Hare, R.M. (1963) *Freedom and Reason*, Oxford: Oxford University Press. (Contains discussion of conflicts between ideals and interests and how this may limit the scope of moral argument as Hare depicts it.)

—— (1981) *Moral Thinking: Its Method, Level, and Point*, Oxford: Oxford University Press. (Develops an ideal of moral reasoning based on Hare's account of the logic of moral concepts.)

* Kant, I. (1785) *Grundlegung zur Metaphysik der Sitten*, trans. with notes by H.J. Paton, *Groundwork of the Metaphysics of Morals* (originally *The Moral Law*), London: Hutchinson, 1948; repr. New York: Harper & Row, 1964, ch. 3. (Develops Kant's ideal of a kingdom of ends.)

* Moore, G. (1903) *Principia Ethica*, ed. T. Baldwin, Cambridge: Cambridge University Press, 1993, ch. 6. (Complex discussion of intrinsic goods and evils.)

* Nietzsche, F. (1883–5) *Also sprach Zarathustra*, trans. and ed. W. Kauffman, *Thus Spoke Zarathustra*, in *The Portable Nietzsche*, New York: Viking Penguin, 1982. (Presents Nietzsche's conception of the 'overman'.)

* Plato (*c*.380–367 BC) *Republic*, trans. P. Shorey, Cambridge, MA: Loeb Classical Library, Harvard University, 1930; repr. in *The Collected Dialogues including Letters*, ed. E. Hamilton and H. Cairns, Oxford: Oxford University Press, 1973. (Develops Plato's substantive ideals of justice in the state and in the individual.)

Railton, P. (1986) 'Facts and Values', *Philosophical Topics* 14: 5–31. (Develops a deliberative ideal as part of a reforming account of an individual's nonmoral good.)

* Rawls, J. (1971) *A Theory of Justice*, Cambridge, MA: Harvard University Press. (Main statement of Rawls' deliberative ideal and theory of justice.)

—— (1980) 'Kantian Constructivism in Moral Theory' (The Dewey Lectures), *Journal of Philosophy* 77: 515–72. (Advanced discussion of Rawls' Kantian ideal of the person.)

* Scanlon, T.M. (1982) 'Contractualism and Utilitarianism', in A. Sen and B. Williams (eds) *Utilitarianism and Beyond*, Cambridge: Cambridge University Press. (Presents a contractualist account of the nature of morality that incorporates a deliberative ideal.)

* Scheffler, S. (1979) 'Moral Scepticism and Ideals of the Person', *Monist* 62: 288–363. (Discussion of the connection between moral scepticism and ideals of the person.)

* —— (1982) *The Rejection of Consequentialism*, Oxford: Clarendon Press. (Addresses the challenge raised by Williams, defending the existence of 'agent-centred prerogatives'.)

—— (1982) 'Ethics, Personal Identity, and Ideals of the Person', *Canadian Journal of Philosophy* 12 (2): 229–62. (Suggests that moral theories rest on commitment to an ideal of the person, and offers this as a basis for replying to the sceptic.)

* Williams, B. (1973) 'A Critique of Utilitarianism', in J.J.C. Smart and B. Williams, *Utilitarianism For and Against*, Cambridge: Cambridge University Press. (Important critique of utilitarianism.)

CONNIE S. ROSATI

IDEAS, THEORY OF *see* PLATO

IDENTITY

Anything whatsoever has the relation of identity to itself, and to nothing else. Things are identical if they are one thing, not two. We can refute the claim that they are identical if we can find a property of one that is not simultaneously a property of the other. The concept of identity is fundamental to logic. Without it, counting would be impossible, for we could not distinguish in principle between counting one thing twice and counting two different things. When we have acquired the concept, it can still be difficult to make this distinction in practice. Misjudgments of identity are possible because one thing can be presented in many guises.

Identity judgments often involve assumptions about the nature of things. The identity of the present mature tree with the past sapling implies persistence through change. The non-identity of the actual child of one couple with the hypothetical child of a different couple is implied by the claim that ancestry is an essential property. Knowledge of what directions are involves knowledge that parallel lines have identical directions. Many controversies over identity concern the nature of the things in question. Others concern challenges to the orthodox conception just sketched of identity itself.

1   Exposition of a popular view
2   Alternatives

1   Exposition of a popular view

Identity is the relation that, necessarily, each thing has to itself and to nothing else. Thus Constantinople has the identity relation to Istanbul because Constantinople *is* Istanbul, the very same city. This relation is often called 'numerical' identity, to distinguish it from 'qualitative' identity, the relation of exact similarity. Although 'identical' twins might be qualitatively identical, they are not numerically identical, for there are two of them, not one. The formula '$x = y$' says that x and y are (numerically) identical.

Identity is governed by two basic logical principles, reflexivity and Leibniz's Law (see LEIBNIZ, G.W. §11). To say that the identity relation is reflexive is to say that for each thing x, $x = x$. Leibniz's Law says that if $x = y$ then whatever is true of x is also true of y; it is used in arguments such as 'Jack the Ripper was in Whitechapel last night, the Prince of Wales was not in Whitechapel last night; therefore Jack the Ripper is not the Prince of Wales'. Leibniz (1704) was not the first to formulate this law, which was known in antiquity. It is sometimes called the 'indiscernibility of identicals', not to be confused with Leibniz's principle of the 'identity of indiscernibles', a kind of converse, which says (implausibly) that qualitative identity implies numerical identity (see IDENTITY OF INDISCERNIBLES). Reflexivity and Leibniz's Law characterize identity uniquely: it is provably impossible for two non-equivalent relations to satisfy both principles. The two principles also entail that identity is symmetric (if $x = y$ then $y = x$) and transitive (if $x = y$ and $y = z$ then $x = z$).

If $a = b$, Leibniz's Law says that whatever is true of a is true of b. However, this permits the replacement of 'a' by 'b' only in contexts in which the expressions merely specify which thing is being talked about. For example, it is invalid to argue from 'Jocasta = the mother of Oedipus' and 'Oedipus knows that he married Jocasta' to 'Oedipus knows that he married the mother of Oedipus', for here 'the mother of Oedipus' does not merely specify a person; it specifies the description under which Oedipus is said to know that he married her (see PROPOSITIONAL ATTITUDES). Looking at photographs of a mature tree and a sapling, one cannot use Leibniz's Law to refute the hypothesis 'The mature tree = the sapling' on the grounds that 'The mature tree is tall' is true and 'The sapling is tall' is false. The noun phrases 'the mature tree' and 'the sapling' do not merely specify trees; they indicate the times with respect to which tallness is predicated. A correct understanding of Leibniz's Law is needed if identity through change is not to seem contradictory.

A genuine consequence of Leibniz's Law is the necessity of identity: things that are in fact identical could not have been distinct (see MODAL LOGIC, PHILOSOPHICAL ISSUES IN §4). For suppose that $x = y$. Since x could not have been distinct from itself, x could not have been distinct from y. Thus x and y cannot be contingently identical: they must be identical in all circumstances. A more complex argument concludes that they cannot be contingently distinct. They are either necessarily identical or necessarily distinct. Consequently, they are either always identical or always distinct. For example, if my headache is identical with an event in my brain, then that headache has to be that event; neither could exist without the other. Of course, a sentence such as 'Rome = the capital of Italy' is contingently true, but that is because the description 'the capital of Italy' need not have specified the city it actually specifies. The example is consistent with the necessity of identity, however, for it does not imply that one city could have been each of two.

An argument like that for the necessity of identity can be used to refute the idea that questions of identity need have no right answer. For example, it is sometimes held to be indeterminate whether a given mass of rock and ice is Everest (see VAGUENESS §1). However, it is determinate whether Everest is Everest. If Leibniz's Law and ordinary logic apply in this context, it follows that Everest is distinct from that mass, and the identity question has a right answer – a negative one. Thus the hypothesis of indeterminacy contradicts itself.

Statements of identity in natural languages often include a noun answering the question 'same what?', for example, 'Istanbul is the same city as Constantinople'. Since identity is uniquely characterized by its logic, the role of the noun is not to disambiguate 'same'; 'a is the same F as b' is equivalent to 'a is an F and $a = b$' (from which 'b is an F' follows by Leibniz's Law). Identity is not defined kind by kind. Rather, we use the pregiven notion of identity in defining kinds. For example, we explain the difference between rivers and collections of water molecules by saying that the same river contains different collections of water molecules at different times.

A 'criterion of identity' for a kind is a necessary and sufficient condition for members of the kind to be identical. Frege's criterion of identity for directions is that the directions of lines are identical if and only if the lines are parallel (1884). The criterion of identity for numbers is that the number of F things is the number of G things if and only if there is a one-to-one correlation between the F things and the G things. In such cases, members of the kind can be presented in various guises: directions as the directions of various lines; numbers as the numbers of various pluralities. The criterion of identity states the condition for two guises to be guises of one member of the kind. Without a grasp of these conditions, one would not know what directions or numbers were.

A criterion of identity for a spatiotemporal kind is expected to give the condition for a member of the kind at one place and time to be identical with a member of the kind at another place and time: for example, it may have to follow a continuous trajectory between these space-time points. An account may also be required of an object's identity across hypothetical circumstances. For example, one may hold that a member of the kind could not have originated at different places and times in different possible worlds. Spatiotemporal objects can be exactly similar without being identical, for they can originate at different times or places. In contrast, purely abstract objects cannot be exactly similar without being identical.

2 Alternatives

Every aspect of the preceding view has been questioned. Although it is popular, the philosophers who accept it all may be in a minority.

That identity is a relation has been denied, both on metaphysical grounds (it cannot relate two things) and on grammatical grounds (some assimilate 'is' in 'Constantinople is Istanbul' to the 'is' of predication as in 'Constantinople is crowded'). However, the logic of '=' does single out a unique class of ordered pairs of objects to which it applies, which suffices to make identity a relation in some minimal sense.

The contrast between identity and indiscernibility has been challenged, on the grounds that indiscernibles satisfy the same descriptions and since a satisfies the description 'identical with a', so does anything indiscernible from a. The obvious reply is that indiscernibles merely satisfy the same *intrinsic* descriptions, but it is hard to explain what 'intrinsicness' is.

Many applications of Leibniz's Law are problematic. Some deny its applicability to contexts that treat non-actual possibilities or even non-present times, thus excluding the derivation of the necessity or permanence of identity. The intention is, for example, to permit a pot to be contingently identical with the clay of which it is made, or the clay to be temporarily identical with the pot. One question is whether the envisaged restrictions on Leibniz's Law

are *ad hoc*. They would not be if so-called identity between objects in different possible worlds or at different times could not be taken at face value but was somehow reducible to relations of qualitative similarity among counterpart objects each of which was confined to a single possible world or time. Such views have been supported by appeal to the difficulty of specifying what is essential to an object, for example, to what extent a particular ship could originally have been made from different planks of wood, or how much it could change without ceasing to exist. However, the proposed reductions are both complex and hard to reconcile with ordinary assumptions about the nature of everyday objects.

Identity has also been regarded as sometimes indeterminate. Although it is usually conceded that if things are identical then it is determinate whether they are identical, in some nonstandard logics it does not follow that if it is indeterminate whether they are identical then they are not identical. Such logics postulate an intermediate status that propositions can have between truth and falsity. One challenge to this view is to explain what it means for a proposition to be not true without being false.

Yet another nonstandard view is the doctrine that identity is always relative to an answer to the question 'same what?'. For example, if a and b are copies of *Middlemarch*, this view disputes the inference from 'a is the same edition as b' and 'a is a copy' to 'a is the same copy as b'. The relation of being the same edition will not satisfy Leibniz's Law unrestrictedly, but the view needs to show that no other relation (for example, being the same copy) could satisfy Leibniz's Law unrestrictedly, for such a relation would be a case of non-relative identity.

Many disputes about criteria of identity for particular kinds of entity (see PERSONAL IDENTITY) concern the nature of those entities, not of identity itself. But even the concept of a criterion of identity is itself problematic. For example, can one give an adequate criterion of identity for events by saying that events are identical if and only if they have the same causes and effects? The problem is that the causes and effects of events include other events. The criterion is in some sense circular, but it is hard to state the requirement of non-circularity clearly. Even if that could be done, it is unclear why every kind of object should have a non-circular criterion of identity. There may be nothing more basic than identity to which identity could be reduced. The standard logic of identity demands no such reduction.

Perhaps identity will come to be regarded as a logical constant, no more problematic than, say, conjunction. If so, many of the issues mentioned above will remain difficult, but their difficulty will concern the nature of various kinds of object, not the relation of identity.

See also: CONTINUANTS §1; LOGICAL AND MATHEMATICAL TERMS, GLOSSARY OF

References and further reading

* Frege, G. (1884) *Die Grundlagen der Arithmetik: eine logisch mathematische Untersuchung über den Begriff der Zahl*, trans. J.L. Austin, *Foundations of Arithmetic*, Oxford: Blackwell, 2nd edn, 1980, §§64–73. (On criteria of identity.)

Kripke, S.A. (1980) *Naming and Necessity*, Oxford: Blackwell. (A basic work on the connection between identity and necessity.)

* Leibniz, G.W. (1704) *New Essays on Human Understanding*, trans. and ed. P. Remnant and J. Bennett, Cambridge: Cambridge University Press, 1981, bk 2, ch. 27. (Gives Leibniz's view of identity and contrasts it with that of John Locke.)

Noonan, H.W. (ed.) (1993) *Identity*, Aldershot: Dartmouth. (Collects many relevant articles.)

Wiggins, D.R.P. (1980) *Sameness and Substance*, Oxford: Blackwell. (On Leibniz's Law and the 'same what?' question.)

Williamson, T. (1990) *Identity and Discrimination*, Oxford: Blackwell. (On supposed cases of indeterminate identity.)

TIMOTHY WILLIAMSON

IDENTITY AND MORALITY

see MORALITY AND IDENTITY

IDENTITY OF INDISCERNIBLES

The principle of the identity of indiscernibles states that objects which are alike in all respects are identical. It is sometimes called Leibniz's Law. This name is also frequently used for the converse principle, the indiscernibility of identicals, that objects which are identical are alike in all respects. Both principles together are sometimes taken to define the concept of identity. Unlike the indiscernibility of identicals, which is widely accepted as a logical truth, the identity of indiscernibles principle has frequently been doubted and rejected. The principle is susceptible of more precise formulation in a number of ways, some more dubitable than others.

1 Leibniz's principle

In his metaphysics, Leibniz frequently stated a principle that no two separate individual things could differ only numerically, that is, resemble one another in all their properties or 'intrinsic denominations' and yet not be one and the same thing. According to various scholastics, two things may differ merely numerically, meaning they could have the same nature, but be distinguished by their matter. Immaterial individuals such as angels must each have a distinct nature, and Leibniz, rejecting matter, extended this view to all individuals. Sometimes he justified it theologically: God never does anything without a reason, and if two things were exactly alike, he would have no reason to create one rather than the other. Sometimes Leibniz referred to empirical evidence, recounting the story of the nobleman he set vainly to searching a castle garden to find two leaves exactly alike, though of course the mere failure to find a counter-instance on a restricted search is no serious test. LEIBNIZ used his principle to argue against empty space and time.

In his logical writings Leibniz defined a relation of sameness between terms as follows: 'Terms which can be substituted for one another whenever we please without changing the truth of any statement (*salva veritate*), are the same (*eadem*) or coincident (*coincidentia*)'. When terms are coincident they denote the same thing or things. Leibniz's definition covers general as well as singular terms, as his triangle/trilateral example makes clear. It would perhaps be better to say that the things are the same when their names are coincident, but Leibniz's meaning is clear.

Leibniz's definition of identity was adopted by Frege, who restricted it to singular terms. In second-order predicate logic, singular identity is often defined as follows:

$$a = b \equiv_{Df} \forall F(F(a) \equiv F(b)).$$

The left-to-right implication is uncontroversial, but needs careful formulation to exclude non-extensional contexts. For example, in 'John believes that *x* defeated Mark Antony', substituting the names 'Octavian' and 'Augustus' for *x* may yield different truth-values if John does not realize that Augustus and Octavian are the same person, yet his ignorance does not impugn their identity (see PROPOSITIONAL ATTITUDES). *F* is taken to range over properties or predicate extensions determined by extensional sentential contexts only. It is thus important to distinguish the substitution principle, which is about expressions, and requires such restrictions, from the indiscernibility principle, which is about the properties of individuals (see IDENTITY §1).

It is the right-to-left implication that is the modern symbolic form of Leibniz's identity of indiscernibles, and this is the half of the definition that has attracted most criticism. There is a version of the principle which is trivially true. Assume $\forall F(F(a) \equiv F(b))$. Substituting '$a = x$' for '$F(x)$' we have $(a = a) \equiv (a = b)$, and since it is logically true that $a = a$, it follows that $a = b$.

Leibniz hardly intended his principle to be understood thus: had it been a logical triviality, he would not have laboured it; indeed he did not consider it a logical truth. This version of the principle is not in doubt. To rescue it from triviality and make it fit to define identity, we must screen off identity and all properties involving it from consideration. Call properties that pass the supposed screening-off test 'material' properties. The most obvious material properties are qualities, so a more substantive version says that no two distinct individuals have all their qualities in common. This is closer to Leibniz's intentions, but readily refuted. For very simple and numerous individuals such as fundamental particles the qualities attributable to them are few, and it is unlikely that two such particles are never exactly alike with respect to the few qualities they do have.

Even allowing that a particle has a history and may change its qualities, we cannot exclude the possibility of two particles having exactly similar qualitative histories. Even if two things never in fact resemble one another exactly, it is not logically impossible that two distinct things be exactly alike. So the qualitative version of the principle seems clearly false.

2 Temporal and modal versions

Evidently there are several indiscernibility principles, differing in plausibility. The question becomes: which one is neither so weak that it is trivial nor so strong that it is false, but just strong enough to characterize identity?

Two objects may be 'temporarily' indiscernible and yet be distinct because they are discernible at some other time. A golden cup and the gold out of which it is made occupy the same place, have the same weight, thermal conductivity, stand in the same spatial and causal relations to other contemporaneous things, and so on. But the gold existed before the cup was fashioned out of it.

Suppose two objects came into being simultaneously and have been always indiscernible to date.

Are they identical? Not if their histories diverge later. If a cat C and the mereological sum of its body and tail $B + T$ have been indiscernible until now, but later the cat loses its tail, then the histories of C and $B + T$ diverge, for C loses T as a part but $B + T$ does not (it either becomes scattered or ceases to exist), so C was not identical with $B + T$: they were merely indiscernible prior to the loss of the tail. The property by which they differed was future-related, just as the history of the gold before it came to constitute the cup is past-related.

Neither temporary indiscernibility nor indiscernibility to date suffice for identity, but if individuals are 'permanently' indiscernible, that is, exist and have the same properties at the same times, are they identical? It seems not. For suppose C never loses its tail. C remains coincident and indiscernible from $B + T$ at all times it exists. But C, unlike $B + T$, could have lost T and carried on existing: cats, unlike body–tail sums, can exist without tails. So it seems that C is 'modally' discernible from $B + T$. (See ESSENTIALISM §4.)

Does identity require indiscernibility in all modal properties? This seems too strong. For example, it is necessary to the first Roman Emperor that he have subjects, but not necessary to Octavian that he have subjects, although Octavian was the first Roman Emperor. This example is inconclusive, since 'the first Roman Emperor' is a definite description and the necessity is *de dicto*: it is not necessary *de re* to the Emperor, that man, that he have subjects (see DE RE/DE DICTO §1; DESCRIPTIONS §2). This may seem to rebound on the cat example: '$B + T$' is also a definite description, 'the sum of B and T', so the fact that C might not have coincided with $B + T$ does not entail that they are distinct, since by the theory of descriptions 'C = the A' just means

$$\forall x(x \text{ is an } A \equiv (x = C)).$$

But the cases differ, for while it is true of Octavian that he was an emperor, it is not obviously true of the cat that it is a sum of body and tail. The difference is again modal: no emperor is essentially an emperor, but sums are essentially sums, and C is not essentially a sum (see ESSENTIALISM §4).

This gives us a more precise modal version: if a and b are indiscernible with respect to all their non-modal properties and all their 'essential' properties then $a = b$. What then is an essential property? One which a must have if it exists. But being identical with a is such a property, so triviality is again a problem. Furthermore, deciding whether a property is essential or not may turn on deciding identity questions. While this indicates that matters of essence are closely connected with identity, we have to restrict attention to material properties again, and modality muddies considerations.

3 Relations and thought experiments

Once we admit relational properties, that is, consider how individuals stand in relation to others, we radically enlarge the range we quantify over and enhance what can be discerned. Though two electrons might be qualitatively indiscernible, if one is 1 metre away from a third particle while the other is not, they are distinguished by this relational property. The Thomistic view that matter individuates bodies which are alike in nature is also relational: $a \neq b$ because m is a's matter and not b's.

This suggests a more promising non-modal version: individuals which are 'materially' indiscernible, that is, indiscernible with respect to all material properties (monadic and relational), are identical. Can there be two distinct materially indiscernible individuals? Take the two electrons mentioned above. If the third particle is a proton and the electron that is not 1 m from it is 1 m from no other proton, then the electrons differ in their material relations. If both were 1 m from qualitatively indiscernible protons the electrons would not thereby differ materially, for though this electron is 1 m from this proton and that electron 1 m from that proton, we can no longer use this information to discern them, since it turns on this proton's being distinct from that one.

To find numerically distinct but materially indiscernible individuals, philosophers have concocted thought experiments with symmetrical universes. Max Black (1952) envisaged a universe consisting solely of two qualitatively indistinguishable spheres with indiscernible histories. Each sphere and each part of a sphere is materially indiscernible from a numerically distinct sphere or part of a sphere. Except for symmetrical individuals, every part of the universe has a numerically distinct *doppelgänger*. Black's universe appears possible, so either the spheres would have to be merely formally distinct, violating the principle, or there would have to be some haecceitas or individualizer to distinguish the spheres, each being uniquely related to its own haecceitas. But to posit such unobservable things seems unacceptably metaphysical.

Those who uphold the principle of material indiscernibility argue by *modus tollens* that there can be no symmetrical universe, for the spheres would be one sphere, and since the sphere is spherically symmetrical it would 'collapse' to a line, whose points, being identical, would collapse to a point: the only symmetrical universe would be monistic.

Since our universe is apparently not symmetrical, it is hard to know how to resolve this dispute.

4 Empirical counterexamples

Harder and more disturbing evidence against Leibniz's principle in almost all versions comes from physics. Two electrons in an atomic shell are discernible from one another while both are in it, having opposite spins, but if an electron enters the shell and an electron later leaves it, there is no way to answer the question whether the same electron left as previously arrived. It is not merely that we cannot observe the proceedings closely enough: there is seemingly no fact of the matter. But electrons are fermions and so must always be discernible at a point in time by their quantum states. The Leibnizian may therefore retreat to holding that identity for electrons is only synchronic, and that they are only momentary, though lone electrons seem to persist happily, only gregarious ones 'losing their identity'. The case is worse for photons, which are bosons and so can be temporarily indiscernible in all their material properties, as well as their position and relations. They can become superposed 'soup': a laser is just very homogeneous photon soup. Yet the intensity of a laser beam depends on how many photons are in it: coincident photons do not collapse into one. A Leibnizian can rescue indiscernibility here only by denying that photons are individuals: talk of photons must then be a physicist's dispensable *façon de parler*.

So although there is dispute about what the indiscernibility of identicals amounts to, and whether in this or that version it is true, we appear comfortable conceiving of things as individuals only to the extent that they are in some sense discernible.

See also: LOGICAL AND MATHEMATICAL TERMS, GLOSSARY OF

References and further reading

* Black, M. (1952) 'The Identity of Indiscernibles', *Mind* 61: 153–64. (A famous dialogue on the spheres example.)

Brody, B.A. (1980) *Identity and Essence*, Princeton, NJ: Princeton University Press. (Tenaciously defends and exploits the trivial version of Leibniz's principle.)

Fraassen, B.C. van (1991) *Quantum Mechanics: An Empiricist View*, Oxford: Clarendon Press. (See chapters 11, 12 for a logically astute philosopher's discussion of the 'problem of identical particles' in physics.)

Leibniz, G.W. (1956) *Philosophical Papers and Letters*,

ed. L.E. Loemker, Dordrecht: Reidel, 1975. (Follow the index entries under 'Identity'.)

Mates, B. (1986) *The Philosophy of Leibniz: Metaphysics and Language*, New York: Oxford University Press. (Chapter 7, §3 discusses the identity of indiscernibles principle in Leibniz.)

Wiggins, D. (1980) *Sameness and Substance*, Oxford: Blackwell. (Chapter 2, §2 discusses (and rejects) the identity of indiscernibles principle amid a general theory of identity.)

PETER SIMONS

IDENTITY OF PERSONS
see PERSONAL IDENTITY

IDENTITY, POSTMODERN THEORIES OF *see* ALTERITY AND IDENTITY, POSTMODERN THEORIES OF

IDENTITY THEORY OF MIND
see MIND, IDENTITY THEORY OF

IDEOLOGY

An ideology is a set of ideas, beliefs and attitudes, consciously or unconsciously held, which reflects or shapes understandings or misconceptions of the social and political world. It serves to recommend, justify or endorse collective action aimed at preserving or changing political practices and institutions. The concept of ideology is split almost irreconcilably between two major senses. The first is pejorative, denoting particular, historically distorted (political) thought which reinforces certain relationships of domination and in respect of which ideology functions as a critical unmasking concept. The second is a non-pejorative assertion about the different families of cultural symbols and ideas human beings employ in perceiving, comprehending and evaluating social and political realities in general, often within a systemic framework. Those families perform significant mapping and integrating functions.

A major division exists within this latter category. Some analysts claim that the study of ideology can be non-evaluative in establishing scientific facts about the way political beliefs reflect the social world and propel people to specific action within it. Others hold that ideology injects specific politically value-laden meanings into conceptualizations of the social world which are inevitably indeterminate, and is consequently a means of constructing rather than reflecting that world. This also applies to interpretations undertaken by the analysts of ideology themselves.

1 **Marxist approaches**
2 **Generalizing ideology and the problem of knowledge**
3 **Ideology, political science and culture**
4 **Words, concepts and interpretation**

1 Marxist approaches

The study of ideologies initially arose from the attempt of the French writer Antoine Destutt de Tracy to create a systematic science of ideas, distinct from prejudices. That meaning of 'ideology' is no longer of importance in contemporary debate. Of far greater consequence was the Marxist conception of ideology, which has had a significant impact on the inquiry into, and understanding of, ideology, as well as directing its analysis into an intellectual cul-de-sac. In the nineteenth century Karl MARX (§§6, 7), assisted by Friedrich ENGELS, converted 'ideology' into a critical concept (Marx and Engels 1846). The great value of Marx's contribution lay in relating ideology decisively to the socio-economic practices from which it sprang – specifically to capitalist production – and in pointing out how effective its thought edifices could be in (mis)directing human energies and shaping human institutions. Ontologically, ideology could be contained in Marx's foundational materialist axiom that being conditions consciousness. Epistemologically, it emerged as a special case when human consciousness reflected the alienated, dehumanized and partial existence of human beings, through a distorted representation of that existence (see ALIENATION §§3, 5). Hence not all thought was ideological. Ideology arose historically as an inverted reflection of the material contradictions of the capitalist mode of production and denoted only one type of socially produced thought, albeit a very pervasive one. The misrepresentation of the real character of social relations, 'the distorted language of the actual world', was thus both a historical necessity – because of the conditioned nature of human thought – and a function of ideology (now interpreted as concealment). In identifying this latter aspect, Marx emphasized ideology as a reflection, and in itself a form, of the power and exploitation embedded in the social contradictions to which material conditions give rise.

681

The dominant class – the bourgeoisie – was the beneficiary of ideology, precisely because ideology served its interest – namely, the maintenance of its domination – through inverting the real facts about capitalism. Originally Marx employed the analogy of the mirror image of the *camera obscura* to illustrate that distortion and to distinguish ideology from error or illusion. However, his analysis was more sophisticated in that he did not see ideology as a direct reflection of a distorted reality but as an inversion of that distortion, so that the repressive elements of capitalism, such as entrapping people in commodity exchange relationships, could be presented as free trade.

One consequence of Marx's analysis of ideology lies in its opposition to true consciousness. The function of ideology is concealment, but its critical identification as such is a crucial step towards its overcoming. Ideology is hence an ephemeral phenomenon, and once the practices which give rise to it are negated, it too will disappear. A second consequence is its association with power and domination; indeed, for many analysts the 'dominant ideology' thesis locates its central feature in the superimposition of a class or particular world view on a society. Thus for the Italian Marxist Antonio GRAMSCI (§3), ideologies were superstructures, consolidated by intellectuals (Gramsci 1971). This replaced the need for a forced class rule through providing an integrating culture in the broadest sense. Such ideologies included art, religion, literature and law, avoiding reduction to economic analysis. They ensured the hegemony of a dominant class over the masses by means of a consensual historical bloc. The important notions of practice and action – the organizational attributes of ideology – are incorporated in this view which, at the same time, loses its ephemeral link to specific historical circumstances.

Louis ALTHUSSER further encouraged Marxists to analyse ideology on its own merits (Althusser 1984). He retained its dissimulative function but emphasized its integrative one, 'interpellating' individuals and bestowing on them a subjective (ostensibly free), as well as subjected, identity within their society. Thus recognition and misrecognition operate side by side to sustain a given society. All classes produce ideology, which is now seen as a permanent material phenomenon in societies, existing objectively in the form and substance of social practices and their rituals. In that sense, ideology is neither a distortion nor an illusion. It is an 'imaginary' representation of the real, yet also a 'lived' relation between individuals and their conditions of existence, a 'new reality'. Elaborating on earlier Marxist analyses, the state in particular was seen to employ 'ideological state apparatuses' in order to ensure the dominance of the established order and its relations of production.

2 Generalizing ideology and the problem of knowledge

The limitations of the Marxist family of theories in respect of ideology lay in restricting it to a highly specific mode of thinking about politics and society. The concept of ideology thus became attached to a number of perspectives: to a reflection in thought of historically situated classes; to an inverted or misperceived form of consciousness, detached from social and material reality; and to the pejorative converse of social truth, which would either replace ideology or existed, as scientific knowledge, in parallel to it. Although none of these perspectives was unequivocally held by any one thinker in the Marxist tradition, all were used to some effect within more 'vulgar' *marxisant* discourses about ideology. Outside the Marxist tradition, although in partial reaction to it, these themes were picked up or discarded in different measures. Althusser importantly recognized the relative detachment of ideology from a material base, a move which has both been welcomed and deplored. His views thus coalesced with those who were analysing ideology as a phenomenon worthy of study in its own rights rather than merely as an epiphenomenon.

Karl Mannheim had already been taking a similar direction, although for him it grew out of dissatisfaction with some of the problems incumbent in Marxism. In his seminal *Ideology and Utopia* (1929) he retained the Marxist insight into the social and historical origins of thought, linking the meaning of an idea not to the laws of logic but to its genesis. However, rather than subscribing to the view that ideology was a reflection of a particular historical distortion, Mannheim suggested that it was a pluralistic product of diverse social groups undergoing common experiences. Knowledge was a cooperative process, but political discussion was further characterized by an unmasking of rationalized situational motivations which were attributes of a collective unconscious. These could adopt two forms: ideology and utopia. Ideology referred to the interest-bound thought of ruling groups and had conservative, stabilizing consequences. It was divided into two conceptions: a particular conception, primarily on the psychological level, in which ideology is consciously recognized as a lie or an error; and a total conception, on a socio-historical level, in which the entire *Weltanschauung* of a group is involved. Utopia referred to an emphasis on the transformation of a society and, unwittingly, on misdiagnosing it by identifying only its negative features (see Utopianism §1). Mannheim's distinction is itself debatable, as both ideology and utopia could be complementary forms of an unconscious, action-oriented interpretation of a historical reality.

Mannheim raised the problem of analysing ideology as a fundamental methodological issue of the social sciences. Having abandoned the Marxist ontology of a true consciousness which would emerge once social contradictions were negated, and having unmasked Marxism itself as ideological in the total sense, Mannheim's general theory of ideology paved the way for a new epistemology expressing the notion that 'all historical knowledge is relational knowledge, and can only be formulated with reference to the position of the observer' (1929: 71). The problem became how to overcome the relativism implicit in the recognition that all social points of view were ideological, while eschewing any adherence to ultimate values (see Relativism). That was made especially difficult because an older epistemology was still attached to relativism, an epistemology which assessed each assertion from the intrinsic perspective of the logical and universal truths it contained. By replacing relativism with relationism – an appreciation, influenced by the holism of psychological Gestalt theory, of the systemically reciprocal interconnections among all historically and spatially located thinking – an evaluative procedure could emerge which surmounted the limitations of ideology. Intellectuals, those who were able to cut loose from their historical and social situatedness, could incorporate conflicting viewpoints in a flexible and dynamic relationism, assessing their scope and validity. An initially non-evaluative relativism, incapable of discriminating among various static and eternal views, would make way for an inescapably evaluative sociology of knowledge. The latter would embrace a more modest conception of truth, critically held and approximate, based on the multiple perspectives in a given society and seeking comprehensiveness and fruitfulness of understanding (see Sociology of knowledge).

3 Ideology, political science and culture

Ultimately, Mannheim too sought to transcend ideology, accepting its inevitability but arguing, somewhat unsatisfactorily, for a new objectivity alongside it. Mid-twentieth-century political scientists, while heavily influenced by Mannheim's concentration on ideology as an ubiquitous social and political given, had no such epistemological and critical aspirations, and approached their subject-matter both as a conscious, empirically ascertainable

product of politico-social groups, and as capable of rational assessment by external analysts. Furthermore, the location of ideology as the product of groups in specific historical situations was played down through employing a neo-positivist, individualist methodology. In particular, US political science adopted a functional approach, concentrating on the concrete phenomenon of ideologies rather than the category of ideology, and regarding them as necessary, often socially beneficial, and distinguishable from other types of thinking about society or in society (see Functionalism in social science §2). Political scientists, however, exhibited two different interpretations of ideologies. One, as exemplified in the work of Daniel Bell (1960) and Giovanni Sartori (1969), restricted them to doctrinaire, highly consistent and closed systems of ideas cum 'social levers', usually infused with extremist passion. These rationalist, deductive constructs, frequently having rhetorical purposes, were contrasted with pragmatic and empirical political belief systems. Given that distinction, it was possible to foresee the 'end of ideology' as passion and imperviousness to temporal and spatial influences apparently gave way, at least in the West, to pluralism and an exhaustion with the great 'isms'. This approach underplayed both the ideological components of so-called 'pragmatism' and the emotive elements endemic to political argument.

The second and more prevalent interpretation conceived of ideologies as a general and omnipresent category encompassing all relatively coherent sets of cultural symbols – ideas, beliefs and attitudes – that are action-oriented, and whose function it is to interpret the political system and to direct and justify public policy aimed towards preserving or changing political institutions and processes. That approach emphasizes ideologies as consciously-held views of aggregates of individuals or of ruling groups who impose them on such aggregates. Individual conduct is thus organized and integrated by cognitive rational constructs – regarded as simplified selection rather than distortion – abetted by evaluation of the options for action in the social world. This return to the scientific study of ideology as a value-free activity differs from the Marxist juxtaposition of ideology and science, because the truth–distortion dimension is removed from the consideration of ideology, and science is employed to comprehend, not to replace, ideology. Such a concrete and empirical view of ideologies involves typologies frequently based on a left–right continuum, ranging from communism through socialism, social democracy, liberalism, conservatism and fascism. Newer belief systems such as feminism, nationalism or ecologism fit uneasily into that rubric, nor can they always claim the comprehensiveness expected of systemic political ideologies. Others, such as anarchism or libertarianism, cut across conventional boundaries. Psychological offshoots of this approach relate to the formation of attitudes and their classification.

The structural anthropology of Claude LÉVI-STRAUSS (§6) and cultural anthropology of Clifford Geertz (1964) demonstrate affinity, although not identity, with such systemic, self-substantiating conceptions of ideology, as does Althusser's analysis. For Lévi-Strauss myths, and ideology as modern myth, manifest an internal, self-contained logic and are endowed with unconsciously held meaning. Unlike Althusser, he regarded ideology as a 'thought-of' order external to objective reality, but like Althusser, he argued that they made sense only in their relationships with 'lived-in' orders. For Geertz, an ideology is an ordered system of cultural symbols, both cognitive and expressive, that is interpenetrated by social and psychological processes and in turn organizes them into patterns of meaning. Its systemic features are 'maps of problematic social reality' which enable purposive action and perform an integrative function, irrespective of whether those maps are accurate or not. The relationship of an ideology to the real world is no longer as centrally challenging, methodologically speaking, as it is for Marxist theories. It is primarily assessed as a cultural whole performing necessary functions.

4 Words, concepts and interpretation

In the USA political science developed its conceptions of ideology in almost complete isolation, not only from a consideration of the unconscious elements of ideology which separate political actors and their thoughts from the perception of the analyst, but also from hermeneutic arguments which were beginning to affect the concept of ideology through a denial of the very epistemological validity of such separation. Hermeneutics transformed the view of ideology by refusing to ask questions concerning how to gain access to reality, or how to avoid the illusions of human perception (see HERMENEUTICS). Instead, social and historical actions and utterances are seen as bereft of objective meaning, and are to be experienced through the interpretive medium of the observer. The polysemy of words necessitates an appreciation of the dual contexts of both their authors and their readers or consumers in attaching a determinate meaning to texts. In allowing for a socio-cultural decontextualization of texts 'as wordless and authorless' objects, and for the 'surplus of meaning' that words carry, theorists such as Paul RICOEUR recognize the function of ideology as

effecting an inevitable closure of interpretation without which consciousness, self-representation and meaning, as well as social integration, are unattainable. Although it is possible to achieve critical distance from ideological closure, it will always – echoing Mannheim – be incomplete. The treatment of ideology is now virtually detached from the circumstances of its production, but is enriched by a sophisticated appreciation of the coexistence of intentional and unconscious import. Here, ideological unconsciousness is not necessarily distorted consciousness, the permanence of ideologies represents the infinite variety of the human imagination, yet the tentativeness of understanding is underlined by a consciousness of its own value-laden temporality.

The relationship of hermeneutics to the examination of language is crucial. The analysis of ideology was advanced by a harnessing of the insights of Ludwig WITTGENSTEIN (§11) and Ferdinand de SAUSSURE. Wittgenstein's notion of language games assisted in crystallizing the view that words could shape, rather than reflect, reality, albeit within a network ineluctably reflecting grammatical rules. Saussure's semiology – the study of signs – likewise suggested that the relationship between signs and meaning was arbitrary, but that meaning could be imposed on words by organizing them in specific patterns. In this systemic perspective, the mutual proximity of words established their meanings. The critical function of ideology was diminished by regarding it as a socially produced text in which meaning was related to usage and to form, impacting on, not merely representing, practices in the 'real' social and historical world. However, ideology was itself re-established as a symbolic human practice of direct interest to scholarship. Discourse analysis concentrates on these findings, but also links the study of language as a social phenomenon with the Marxist theme of ideology as domination. Successful closures of meaning in language reflect the power relationships of its users, and language is hence a medium through which political legitimacy may be accorded to groups, overtly or frequently through unconscious dissimulation. This method can be applied not only to the broad ideological families that attempt to control public policy making but to a wide range of discourse situations in which meanings are exchanged and displaced in specific, everyday, conversational contexts (see DISCOURSE SEMANTICS).

From the perspective of political theory it is possible to combine the focus of political scientists on the overt and systemic contents of ideological debate, with an interest in language and meaning and in the decoding of unconscious ideological messages. W.B. Gallie's notion of the essentially contested nature of political concepts presented them as indeterminate because of the impossibility of agreeing on their normative components (Gallie 1955–6). However, they are also indeterminate due to their inability to contain all their logically entailed meanings simultaneously. Hence, ideologies may be seen as clustered patterns of a wide spectrum of political concepts, such as liberty, justice or power, each of which is necessarily decontested, reflecting a specific set of historical and spatially located social meanings without which political decision making cannot be effected. A potentially unrestricted universe of meanings is also limited by logical and morphological constraints operating in all ideological systems, as political concepts are decontested by their users through deliberately or unconsciously arranging their proximity to other political concepts. Different conceptual patterns may be produced by any social group, although these still may be usefully classed according to loose family resemblances that approximate major ideological traditions such as liberalism, conservatism or socialism. Decontesting also expresses the inevitability of political power which, importantly, need not be exploitative. Ideologies hence complete over their claims to confer legitimate meanings on political concepts and words, and map and recommend thought practices which in turn affect political action. Ideology nevertheless is not coterminous with political thought, but is one of its analytical dimensions: a particular interpretive handling of political concepts which are suspended between logical indeterminacy and cultural determinacy.

References and further reading

* Althusser, L. (1984) *Essays on Ideology*, London: Verso. (Referred to in §1. A significant reappraisal of ideology within the Marxist tradition.)
* Bell, D. (1960) *The End of Ideology: On the Exhaustion of Political Ideas in the Fifties*, Glencoe, IL: Free Press. (The most prominent statement on the subject.)
  Freeden, M. (1996) *Ideologies and Political Theory: A Conceptual Approach*, Oxford: Clarendon Press. (An elaboration of the argument in §4.)
* Gallie, W.B. (1955–6) 'Essentially Contested Concepts', *Proceedings of the Aristotelian Society* 56: 167–98. (A seminal analysis of political concepts referred to in §4.)
* Geertz, C. (1964) 'Ideology as a Cultural System', in D.E. Apter (ed.) *Ideology and Discontent*, New York: Free Press, 47–76. (A groundbreaking article, referred to in §3.)
* Gramsci, A. (1971) *Selections from Prison Notebooks*, ed. Q. Hoare and G. Newell-Smith, London: Lawrence & Wishart. (The influential text on ideology as hegemony.)
  Larrain, J. (1979) *The Concept of Ideology*, London: Hutchinson. (A sophisticated overview, supportive of the critical function of ideology.)
* Mannheim, K. (1929) *Ideology and Utopia*, London: Routledge, 1936. (A modern classic on the subject, despite a confusing usage of terminology.)
* Marx, K. and Engels, F. (1846) *The German Ideology*, ed. C.J. Arthur, London: Lawrence & Wishart, 1974. (The foundational Marxist analysis of ideology.)
  Mullins, W.A. (1972) 'On the Concept of Ideology in Political Science', *American Political Science Review* 66: 498–510. (A good illustration of the approach of contemporary political science.)
* Sartori, G. (1969) 'Politics, Ideology, and Belief Systems', *American Political Science Review* 63: 398–411. (An example of confining ideology to closed, non-empirical systems.)
  Thompson, J.B. (1984) *Studies in the Theory of Ideology*, Oxford: Polity Press. (A perceptive assessment of a range of current views on ideology.)

MICHAEL FREEDEN

IKHWAN AL-SAFA'

The philosophy of the group of Arab philosophers of the fourth or fifth century AH (tenth or eleventh century AD) known as the Ikhwan al-Safa' (Brethren of Purity) is a curious but fascinating mixture of the Qur'anic, the Aristotelian and the Neoplatonic. The group wrote fifty-two epistles, which are encyclopedic in range, covering matters as diverse as arithmetic, theology, magic and embryology. Their numerology owes a debt to Pythagoras, their metaphysics are Aristotelian and Neoplatonic and they incorporate also a few Platonic notions into their philosophy. The latter, however, is more than a mere synthesis of elements from Greek philosophy, for it is underpinned by a considerable Qur'anic substratum. There are profound links between the epistemology and the soteriology (doctrine of salvation) of the Ikhwan, and it would not be an exaggeration to say that the former feeds the latter. In the history of Islamic philosophy the Ikhwan illustrate a group where the Aristotelian and the Neoplatonic clash head-on and where no attempt is made to reconcile competing and contradictory notions of God, whom the Epistles treat in both Qur'anic and Neoplatonic fashion. The final goal of the Ikhwan is salvation; their Brotherhood is the ship of that salvation, and they foster a spirit of asceticism and good living accompanied by 'actual knowledge' as aids to that longed-for salvation.

1 Life and works
2 Metaphysics
3 Epistemology
4 Soteriology

1 Life and works

The Arabic name Ikhwan al-Safa' has been translated as both 'Brethren of Purity' and 'Brethren of Sincerity'. Both are possible, though the former is probably to be preferred because of the emphasis throughout the group's writings on the concept of purity achieved via a life of asceticism and virtuous living.

Little firm information is available about their exact identities, their lives and the precise time during which they flourished. Most scholars agree, however, that they lived in Basra in the fourth or fifth century AH (tenth or eleventh century AD); beyond that there has been much diverse speculation. Their own thought and philosophy is enshrined in fifty-two epistles (*rasa'il*) of varying lengths which are encyclopedic in their scope and cover a vast number of topics. Formally, these epistles divide into four major sections: the first fourteen deal with the mathematical sciences, the next seventeen are on the natural sciences, a further ten deal with the psychological and rational sciences and the final eleven come under the heading of theological sciences. It should be noted that the Ikhwan's usage of these divisions is much broader in range than might be expected at first sight. For example, the last of the epistles grouped under the heading 'theological sciences' deals with magic and related subjects. What may broadly be said to link all the epistles, however, is a mixed Aristotelian and Neoplatonic substratum, though it must be stressed here that the epistles of the Ikhwan al-Safa' are more than just a synthesis of Aristotelian and dominant Neoplatonic themes. The incorporation by the Ikhwan of syncretic philosophical and theological themes, motifs, elements and doctrines in their writings was done with a particular soteriological purpose (see §4). Their eclectic borrowing was done with a view to bolstering the doctrine of purity which their name so neatly reflects.

2 Metaphysics

The metaphysics of the Ikhwan al-Safa' are built upon those of ARISTOTLE and PLOTINUS, though it must be emphasized that it is a Middle Eastern version of Aristotelianism and Neoplatonism which we encoun-

ter when we read the *rasa'il* of the Ikhwan. In the first place, their terminology is infused with such terms as matter and form, substance and accidents, the four causes and potentiality and actuality. Their usage of such terms, however, does not always adhere to the classical Aristotelian paradigm or usage. The development of terminology is often in a Neoplatonic direction. For example, the Ikhwan held in one place that substance was something which was self-existent and capable of receiving attributes. We recognize here a description akin to Aristotle's usage of the word 'substance' in the *Metaphysics*. But elsewhere, confusingly, form is divided into two kinds, constituting and completing; constituting forms are called substances and completing forms are called accidents. Similarly, the Ikhwan adopted a fourfold terminology of causes – material, formal, efficient and final – but the shades of astrology and Neoplatonism hang heavily over at least two of the examples of these four causes which they provide. They say that the material cause of plants is the four elements of fire, air, water and earth, and that their final cause is to provide food for animals: both of these ideas are recognizably Aristotelian in their orientation, but the Ikhwan then go on to suggest that the efficient cause of plants is the power of the Universal Soul and that their formal cause has complicated astral elements!

It is, however, the Neoplatonic elements which dominate the articulation of all thought in the writings of the Ikhwan al-Safa' and their metaphysics are no exception. The latter are imbued in particular with the Neoplatonic concepts of emanation and hierarchy. By contrast with the simple triad of Plotinus, which comprised the three hypostases of The One or The Good, Intellect and Soul, with the lower eternally emanating from the higher entity, the Ikhwan elaborated this into an emanationist hierarchy of nine 'members', hypostases or levels of being, as follows: the Creator, the Intellect, the Soul, Prime Matter, Nature, the Absolute Body, the Sphere, the Four Elements and the Beings of this world in the three divisions of mineral, plant and animal. In such a hierarchical profusion we can perhaps see the ghosts of IAMBLICHUS and PROCLUS, who also multiplied the hypostases about which they wrote. It is noteworthy that for the Ikhwan, and in contrast to the view of Plotinus, matter becomes a full part of the emanationist hierarchy and is regarded in a positive light. Furthermore, and this time in a very Neoplatonic way, God in the Ikhwan's scheme entrusts the movement of the world and the spheres to the Universal Soul, and it is the latter which channels God's gifts finally into Matter itself (see NEOPLATONISM).

The Neoplatonic dimensions of the thought of the Ikhwan have profound implications for their view of

God. The picture which they present of the deity in their epistles is a confused and ultimately contradictory one. No attempt is made to reconcile what is in fact irreconcilable. On the one hand, the Ikhwan present a God at the top of a complex emanationist hierarchy who is unknowable in the classic Neoplatonic sense. On the other hand, the Ikhwan present a Qur'anic God who is a guide and a help, and who is invoked at the end of many of the epistles as one who will grant success in correct action and show his people the path of righteousness. The majority of epistles also invoke God with the traditional Islamic *basmala*, 'In the name of God, the Merciful, the Compassionate'. However, God's power, as noted above, seems to be 'shared' in some way when it is exercised via the Universal Soul. To what extent, one may reasonably ask, does that compromise the traditional Islamic view of God? Furthermore, to what extent do the recognizably Islamic features in the Ikhwan's portrait of God prevent that deity being considered as a total mirror of Plotinus' One?

The metaphysics of the Ikhwan al-Safa' must therefore be regarded as *sui generis*. Their mixing of Aristotelian and Neoplatonic elements had profound implications both for their theology and the coherence of their philosophy. Contradictions abound; if reasons be sought for this, it is worth remembering one theory, promulgated by A.L. Tibawi (1955), that the epistles are akin to the minutes taken during the deliberations of a learned society, meeting on many occasions over a period of years. This would account for both contradiction and repetition. We know from the epistles themselves that the authors urged their brothers to meet specially at set times, in closed sessions.

3 Epistemology

Thus far in this article, nothing has been said about the impact of Platonic thought on the epistles of the Ikhwan. This is because the Brethren revere the Platonic *hero* rather more than they revere purely Platonic *philosophy*. SOCRATES is admired as a great and wise philosopher who knew how to meet death bravely. However, some Platonic imagery does permeate the epistles (see PLATONISM IN ISLAMIC PHILOSOPHY). The most notable image is that of the body constituting a prison for the soul. The Ikhwan indeed compare the soul in the body to the state of a man imprisoned inside a lavatory: the body's blemishes and sins are like the filth in the lavatory. It is clear that the Ikhwan were familiar with Plato's doctrine of Forms or *ideai*, since they quote a speaker saying that the different types of animal in the world simply mirror those in the world of the spheres and the

heavens (see PLATO). However, this is not a doctrine for which the Ikhwan seem to have had much use, for they neither discuss nor elaborate upon it.

It is, therefore, unsurprising that the Ikhwan's epistemology differs quite radically from that of Plato. The latter looked forward to a state of real knowledge achieved when the soul was separated from the body; but in the soteriology and epistemology of the Ikhwan, one could gain some knowledge of the divine in this world to help one reach Paradise. Indeed, they present their epistles to the world as a body of just such knowledge. For them, learning was much more than mere recollection or reminiscence. They held that the soul was 'potentially knowledgeable' and, with instruction, could become 'actually knowledgeable'. That instruction should be via the senses, the intellect and logical deduction, and they stressed that we could know nothing without the senses. This is indeed a far cry from Plato's well-known suspicion of evidence or knowledge gleaned via the senses, and his overwhelming exaltation of the intellect.

4 Soteriology

The mass of information – philosophical, theological and other – adumbrated in such an encyclopedic manner in the epistles of the Ikhwan al Safa' is probably incomprehensible as a totality unless one bears in mind the driving force which lies at the heart of the epistles themselves. The Ikhwan did not compile the epistles from a pure love of knowledge and for no other reason. The magpie eclecticism with which they surveyed and utilized elements from the philosophies of Pythagoras, Plato, Aristotle and Plotinus, and religions such as Christianity, Judaism and Hinduism, was not an early attempt at ecumenism or interfaith dialogue. Their accumulation of knowledge was ordered towards the sublime goal of salvation. To use their own image, they perceived their Brotherhood, to which they invited others, as a 'Ship of Salvation' that would float free from the sea of matter; the Ikhwan, with their doctrines of mutual cooperation, asceticism and righteous living, would reach the gates of Paradise in its care.

What, then, did it mean for the Ikhwan al-Safa' to 'do philosophy'? It did not mean to throw off the religious constraints of the Qur'an and to become pure rationalists. Though they often use the Qur'an as a cloak to disguise their Neoplatonism, one cannot ignore the massive Qur'anic substratum elsewhere in their writings, which has no such intent. 'Doing philosophy' did not mean either the uncritical acceptance of the data from a variety of sources such as Pythagoras, Plato and Aristotle, not to mention Plotinus, even though they were profoundly influenced by at least three of these four ancient masters and it is no misnomer to describe the Ikhwan as 'Muslim Neoplatonists'. Philosophy, for the Ikhwan, was still the handmaiden of a precise theological goal: salvation for the soul. Their eclecticism and tolerance provided them with a unique methodology for the achievement of that goal. Thus they searched out the texts of other creeds and the philosophies of non-Muslim sages in search of materials which might bolster their own ethics of purity and asceticism. Their intellectual heroes were Socrates and Jesus as well as Muhammad. Above all, knowledge and philosophy were always soteriological tools and never ends in themselves.

See also: ISLAMIC THEOLOGY; MYSTICAL PHILOSOPHY IN ISLAM; NEOPLATONISM IN ISLAMIC PHILOSOPHY

References and further reading

Diwald, S. (1975) *Arabische Philosophie und Wissenschaft in der Enzyklopädie Kitab Ihwan as-Safa' III: Die Lehre von Seele und Intellekt* (Arab Philosophy and Science in the Book of the Brethren of Purity III: Teachings on the Soul and the Intellect), Wiesbaden: Harrassowitz. (A German translation of the third section of the *Rasa'il* with extensive notes.)

Goodman, L.E. (1978) *The Case of the Animals versus Man Before the King of the Jinn*, Boston, MA: Twayne Publishers. (An English translation of a major portion of the second section of the *Rasa'il* with extensive introduction and notes.)

* Ikhwan al-Safa' (1957) *Rasa'il Ikhwan al-Safa'* (Epistles of the Brethren of Purity), Beirut: Dar Sadir, 4 vols. (The complete text of the fifty-two epistles in the original Arabic.)

Marquet, Y. (1975) *La philosophie des Ihwan al-Safa'* (The Philosophy of the Brethren of Purity), Algiers: Société Nationale d'Édition et de Diffusion. (A major study by France's leading expert in the field.)

Nasr, S.H. (1978) *An Introduction to Islamic Cosmological Doctrines*, revised edn, London: Thames & Hudson. (Contains a major section on the cosmology of the Ikhwan.)

Netton, I.R. (1982) *Muslim Neoplatonists: An Introduction to the Thought of the Brethren of Purity (Ikhwan al-Safa')*, London: Allen & Unwin; paperback edn, Edinburgh: Edinburgh University Press, 1991. (A major introduction in English to the thought of the Ikhwan.)

—— (1996) 'The Brethren of Purity', in S.H. Nasr and O. Leaman (eds) *History of Islamic Philosophy*, London: Routledge, ch. 15, 222–30. (Concise and clear outline of their views.)

* Tibawi, A.L. (1955) 'Ikhwan as-Safa' and Their Rasa'il: A Critical Review of a Century and a Half of Research', *Islamic Quarterly* 2 (1): 28–46. (A very useful and neat survey of Ikhwan scholarship up to 1955.)

IAN RICHARD NETTON

IL'ENKOV, EVAL'D VASIL'EVICH (1924–79)

Eval'd Il'enkov advanced a distinctive brand of Hegelian Marxism that was influential in the rejuvenation of Soviet philosophy after Stalin. Il'enkov draws on Hegel and Marx to argue that non-material phenomena can exist as genuine features of objective reality independent of the consciousness and will of individuals. Il'enkov argues that the existence of such phenomena, conceived as objectifications of human social activity, is central to the explanation of the nature and possibility of the human mind. The world becomes a possible object of thought through its 'idealization' by activity, and children attain mental capacities in the full sense only through the appropriation of the ideal as it exists objectified in 'humanity's spiritual culture'.

Il'enkov's defence of the reality of culture represents a critique of positivism and scientism, a critique he pursued in many other writings. A tireless opponent of reductionist theories of mind and 'biological determinist' theories of human development, he advanced a view of persons as socially constituted beings and stressed socialism's obligation to create the circumstances in which human beings may develop their almost limitless potential. Like many in the post-Stalin era, his criticism of the Soviet philosophical establishment takes the form of a call for a genuinely orthodox form of Marxism, faithful to the spirit of Marx's thought.

1 Life
2 Dialectics
3 The problem of the ideal
4 Popular and polemical writings

1 Life

Perhaps the most inventive of Russian Marxist philosophers, Eval'd Il'enkov made a significant contribution to the renewal of Soviet philosophy after the Stalin period. He advanced a form of Hegelian Marxism that stressed the active powers of human beings to transform themselves and their world through the objectification of culture. He was a relentless critic of reductionism and scientism, which he believed fed the dehumanizing elements of Soviet ideology, and his works upheld the importance of critical philosophical reflection in opposition to dogma.

Il'enkov was born in Smolensk, though he lived most of his life in Moscow. He was educated at the Moscow Institute of Philosophical and Literary Studies (IFLI) and Moscow State University (MGU), where he defended his 'candidate's dissertation' in 1954. During the 'thaw' in the early 1960s, he published the works which established him as a leading voice in the Soviet philosophical community. They include a treatise on Marx's method, *Dialektika abstraktnogo i konkretnogo v 'Kapitale' Marksa* (*The Dialectics of the Abstract and the Concrete in Marx's 'Capital'*) (1960), and an influential essay, 'Ideal'noe' (The Ideal) (1962), in which Il'enkov argues that non-material phenomena are genuine constituents of objective reality and advances a distinctive account of the relation of mind and world. Il'enkov continued to explore these themes in many subsequent writings spanning a variety of fields, including history of philosophy, education and aesthetics. Like many of his contemporaries, Il'enkov experienced political difficulties. Accused of the heresy of 'epistemologism', he lost his position at MGU in 1955. The rest of his career was spent at Moscow's Institute of Philosophy, though he continued to have an uneasy relation with the Soviet philosophical establishment, which was suspicious of the critical and humanistic elements of his work. He died in 1979, by his own hand.

2 Dialectics

Il'enkov's early work on dialectics develops the so-called 'method of ascent from the abstract to the concrete' sketched by Marx in his 'Introduction to a Critique of Political Economy'. Il'enkov argues that in both natural- and social-scientific inquiry, the objects of cognition are 'organic' wholes, consisting of parts standing in relations of mutual determination. These wholes develop through the tensions, or dialectical contradictions, between their parts. Il'enkov argues that cognition proceeds by isolating the 'principle of development' of the whole. This phenomenon – the 'cell' or 'unit' – represents the part, the evolution of which necessitates the development and mutual determination of the other parts. The 'unit' is thus a 'concrete universal' that explains the whole's development through the necessary interrelations of its developing parts. Cognition therefore represents a movement from the *abstract*

(from the abstraction of the unit) to the *concrete* (to a conception of the whole as a 'unity in diversity' of essentially related components). In this process, historical and logical analyses coincide, for to represent the history of the object is to chart the necessary logic of its evolution. Il'enkov argues that Marx's analysis of capitalism in *Capital* illustrates this method. By isolating the concept of commodity and tracing its development, Marx reconstructs the logic of capitalism, the principles of its existence and necessary transformation.

Such esoteric epistemology may seem an unlikely focus for scholars seeking to reanimate Marxism in Eastern Europe. But for Il'enkov (and others such as A.A. Zinov'ev and the Czech philosopher Jindřich Zelený), the analysis of 'Marx's logic' was an important catalyst because it demanded that Marx be treated, not as an authoritative source of state ideology, but as a philosopher whose ideas could be understood only through a critical engagement with the history of Western traditions in philosophy. Approaching Marx this way showed the virtues of scholarship, rather than partisanship. In addition, Il'enkov's work on dialectics had a political subtext. Il'enkov contrasts Marx's approach with empiricism. The latter typically construes the knowing subject as arriving at a conception of the world by a movement from concrete to abstract: the subject makes sense of perceptual data through the formation and application of abstract concepts and general laws that facilitate the organization and prediction of experience. Il'enkov was convinced that empiricist conceptions, often ill-conceived and poorly articulated, were prevalent in Soviet philosophy and contributed to positivistic infatuations with science as an all-powerful force. Il'enkov's work on method thus represents a critique of empiricism in Soviet thought and scientism in Soviet culture.

3 The problem of the ideal

Il'enkov's most original contribution to philosophy is his treatment of 'the problem of the ideal'. What place should a materialist find for meaning, value and universals in the material world? Many of Il'enkov's Soviet contemporaries portrayed such phenomena as mental in kind and argued that mental states were ultimately reducible to physical states of the brain: everything seemingly non-material is in the head. In contrast, Il'enkov maintains that ideal phenomena can have a supra-individual existence as aspects of the world as it is independent of individual consciousness. Drawing on Hegel and Marx, Il'enkov insists that there is nothing mystical in the objective existence of the ideal, for ideal phenomena are objectifications of human activity. In the course of the transformation of nature by human action, meaning and value are written into nature:

'Ideality' is like a peculiar stamp impressed on the substance of nature by social human life activity; it is the form of the functioning of a physical thing in the process of social human life activity. All things incorporated into the social process acquire a new 'form of existence', an ideal form, quite distinct from their physical nature.

(1979: 148)

Il'enkov argues that our natural environment is organized or 'humanized' by activity: our world is full of physical entities – artefacts, signs, symbols, models – made meaningful through action. The edifice of objectified ideality represents (in Marx's words) humanity's 'inorganic body' or 'spiritual culture', embodied in our environment as 'thought in its otherness':

Outside the individual and independently of his consciousness and will exists not only *nature*, but also the socio-historical environment, the world of things, created by human labour, and the system of human relations, formed in the process of labour. In other words, outside the individual lies not only nature as such ('in itself'), but also *humanized* nature, nature re-made by human labour. From the point of view of the individual, 'nature' and 'humanized nature' merge together into the 'surrounding world'.

(1964: 41–2)

This view is part of a dynamic vision of human beings creating themselves through the creation of culture. Transformed by activity, our environment confronts us as rich with significance; in virtue of this significance, we act further to transform our world, endowing it with new meaning and precipitating further transformations. Human beings must constantly adapt to their changing environment, acquiring skills necessary to orientate themselves within it. And in this dialectic, human beings gradually understand and harness the forces which define them and their world. Il'enkov sees communism as the project of attaining control over these powers.

Il'enkov's account of ideality is intended to solve fundamental issues of the relation of mind and world. He argues that 'nature "as such" is given to the individual only insofar as it is transformed into an object [*predmet*], into the material or means of production of material life' (1964: 42). There is thus a sense in which all of nature is 'idealized' by human activity: no object speaks to us unless it is brought within the compass of humanity's spiritual culture.

The primary object of thought is thus nature humanized or idealized.

In addition, Il'enkov's position yields a distinctive view of thought itself, which is conceived as the capacity to inhabit an idealized environment: a thinking body is one which shapes its activity to the norms that constitute our humanized environment. Thought is thus construed as a species of movement, the ability to conform to and manipulate meanings as they are formed in the flux of social being. Il'enkov significantly does not represent this ability as innate in the individual: it is as socially constituted as the environment the thinking thing inhabits. Human children become thinking things in so far as they acquire the ability to orientate themselves in their environment by internalizing the forms of activity of their community (note here the continuity with Vygotskii's psychology – see VYGOTSKII, L.S. §2). Thus, in contrast to the individualism of traditional epistemology, Il'enkov does not believe that each individual mind finds the world anew for itself. We enter a world which history has made cognizable and learn to find our way through the agency of others who help us appropriate our spiritual culture.

Il'enkov's solution to the problem of the ideal may thus be seen to follow from the application of his dialectical method to the question of the relation of thinking and being. For Il'enkov, human activity plays the role of the 'unit', the exploration of which reveals the nature and possibility of both halves of the cognitive relation – object (nature humanized by activity) and subject (the 'thinking body' that inhabits the humanized environment). Each is born of activity and their unity is sustained in and through activity.

4 Popular and polemical writings

Il'enkov believed that philosophers should be moralists, and he produced a significant number of popular and polemical writings. Many address questions of education. Developing his view that human individuals are socially constituted beings, he argued that a socialist government has an overriding responsibility to create a culture which nurtures the abilities of all individuals. Il'enkov was critical of the trend towards specialization in the Soviet education system, arguing that it should be guided by Marx's vision of the 'all-round individual' whose capacities are universal in nature. Some of Il'enkov's most striking writings on education were inspired by Aleksandr Meshcheriakov's work on the education of blind–deaf children, which Il'enkov took to illuminate the social construction of cognitive processes, as well as the duties of a radical education system.

As fascination with the 'scientific-technological

revolution' grew in the USSR through the 1960s and 1970s, Il'enkov's hostility to positivism became yet more pronounced. He was scathingly critical of thinkers who portray our mental lives as nothing more than a series of events in our brains, and he attacked the idea that the talents and aptitudes of human beings are genetically determined. The thirst to represent human beings as sophisticated machines, he suggested, was a symptom of the increasing technologization of social life. The latter was supposedly to be the theme of his final book, *Leninskaia dialektika i metafizika positivizma* (*Leninist Dialectics and the Metaphysics of Positivism*) (1980), which was to argue that although Soviet philosophers constantly reiterated Lenin's critique of the Russian empiriocriticist, Aleksandr Bogdanov, the technocratic vision of social organization advanced by Bogdanov in fact pervaded Soviet culture. Unfortunately, this message was obscured when the book was cut for posthumous publication.

Il'enkov's popular and polemical writings have aged badly, and though they have historical interest, they are not philosophically deep. Moreover, not all of these texts can be portrayed as progressive in orientation. His Hegelian attacks on formal logic, for example, provoked censure from thinkers anxious to animate Soviet philosophy by forging links with the analytic tradition. However, despite this, and the strident tone of much of his writing, with its call for a return to true orthodoxy after the perversions of Stalinism, there is no doubting the depth of Il'enkov's philosophical vision, particularly in his early work, and his importance in preserving a cultural tradition of philosophical criticism in Soviet Russia.

See also: MARXIST PHILOSOPHY, RUSSIAN AND SOVIET

List of works

Il'enkov, E.V. (1960) *Dialektika abstraktnogo i konkretnogo v 'Kapitale' Marksa*, Moscow: Akademiia nauk; trans. S. Syrovatkin, *The Dialectics of the Abstract and the Concrete in Marx's 'Capital'*, Moscow: Progress, 1982. (Il'enkov's influential work on Marx's method; said to have been heavily censored before publication.)

—— (1962) 'Ideal'noe' (The Ideal), in *Filosofskaya éntsiklopediia* (Philosophical Encyclopedia), Moscow: Sov'etskaya éntsiklopediia, vol. 2, 219–27; amended repr. in Il'enkov (1974), 183–210; and (1991), 212–28. (The first presentation of Il'enkov's philosophical anthropology in which the concept of activity is invoked to explain the very possibilty of the relation between subject and object.)

—— (1964) 'Vopros o tozhdestve myshleniia i bytiia v domarksistskoi filosofii' (The Question of the Relation of Thinking and Being in Pre-Marxist Philosophy), in *Dialektika – Teoriia poznaniia* (Dialectics – The Theory of Knowledge), Moscow: Nauka, 21–54. (A history of conceptions of the relation of mind and world from Descartes and Spinoza through the German idealists to Marx.)

—— (1968) *Ob idolakh i idealakh* (Of Idols and Ideals), Moscow: Politizdat. (A collection of previously published writings, popular in tone. After attacking scientism in the opening chapters, Il'enkov develops a humanistic philosophy of education.)

—— (1974) *Dialekticheskaia logika*, Moscow: Politizdat; 2nd edn, revised and enlarged, 1984; 1st edn trans. H. Campbell-Creighton, *Dialectical Logic*, Moscow: Progress, 1977. (A history of philosophy from Descartes to Marx; akin to the materialist phenomenology of spirit.)

—— (1979) 'Problema ideal'nogo' (The Problem of the Ideal), *Voprosy filosofii* (Questions of Philosophy), 6: 145–58; 7: 128–40; amended repr. as 'Dialektika ideal'nogo' (The Dialectic of the Ideal) in Il'enkov (1984), 8–77; and (1991), 229–70; abridged trans. R. Daglish, 'The Concept of the Ideal' in *Philosophy in the USSR: Problems of Dialectical Materialism*, Moscow: Progress, 1977: 71–99. (Il'enkov's fullest statement of his conception of activity and its role in the constitution of the non-material.)

—— (1980) *Leninskaia dialektika i metafizika positivizma*, Moscow: Politizdat; trans. B. Pearce, *Leninist Dialectics and the Metaphysics of Positivism*, London: New Park, 1982. (An account of Lenin's controversy with Bogdanov, from an unfinished manuscript. Intended as a critique of scientism and technologism in Soviet culture, though heavy censorship obscures this theme.)

—— (1984) *Iskusstvo i kommunisticheskii ideal* (Art and the Communist Ideal), Moscow: Iskusstvo. (A collection of writings on art, ideality and ideals; includes Il'enkov's notes on Wagner, his favourite composer.)

—— (1991) *Filosofiia i kul'tura* (Philosophy and Culture), Moscow: Politizdat. (A comprehensive anthology of Il'enkov's writings; annotated.)

References and further reading

Bakhurst, D.J. (1991) *Consciousness and Revolution in Soviet Philosophy. From the Bolsheviks to Evald Ilyenkov*, Cambridge: Cambridge University Press, 1991. (An account of Il'enkov's thought, set in the context of the history of the Soviet philosophical tradition.)

Korovikov, V.I. (1990) 'Nachalo i pervyi pogrom' (The Beginning and the First Pogrom), in *Voprosy filosofii* 2: 65–8. (A description of the climate in which Il'enkov's career began at MGU.)

Mikhailov, F.T. (1990) 'Slovo ob Il'enkove' (A Word about Il'enkov), in *Voprosy filosofii* 2: 56–64. (A discussion of the significance of Il'enkov's contribution by a friend and colleague.)

Novokhat'ko, A.G. (1991) 'Fenomen Il'enkova' (The Phenomenon of Il'enkov), in Il'enkov (1991) 5–16. (A detailed account of Il'enkov's life and work.)

DAVID BAKHURST

IL'IN, IVAN ALEKSANDROVICH (1883–1954)

Educated in law and philosophy in the first years of the twentieth century at Moscow University and several Western European universities, Il'in produced an important two-volume commentary on Hegel's philosophy (1918), and a number of substantial works in political and legal theory, ethics and religious thought, aesthetics and literary criticism in later years. As a resolute foe of the Bolsheviks before and after the Revolution of 1917, he was exiled by them in 1922, living in Berlin until 1938, and subsequently in Switzerland until his death. Throughout his exile he remained deeply devoted to his Russian homeland, circulating extensive proposals for the eventual reconstruction of the Russian state, Church and society following the collapse of the Soviet regime (see Nashi zadachi *(Our Tasks) (1956a)). He developed his own distinctive theory of monarchy as an ideal political form, grounded in a doctrine of natural right, and advocated it as the most appropriate choice for Russia in the best case, though he withheld judgment as to whether it would prove historically possible to implement it in the conditions prevailing after the demise of the Soviet system. His writing also focused to a significant extent upon moral and spiritual discipline and renewal, for societies as well as individuals, as necessary conditions of the well-ordered state and the well-lived life.*

1 Life
2 Commentary on Hegel
3 Political theory
4 Ethics, aesthetics and religious thought

1 Life

Il'in was born in Moscow; his father was a native Muscovite, and his mother was of German descent. He completed gymnasium in the spring of 1901, and entered the Faculty of Law of Moscow University in autumn of the same year, receiving his diploma in 1906. In the Faculty of Law he encountered two unusually inspiring philosopher-jurists, Pavel I. Novgorodtsev (from the beginning) and Prince Evgenii N. Trubetskoi (from the end of 1905), among his professors. They provided a solid grounding in the history of philosophy in addition to legal studies. Novgorodtsev conveyed a lively interest in natural right and the rule of law to his students, a lesson which Il'in absorbed thoroughly but interpreted in a distinctive way. Upon completion of his diploma Il'in was retained at the university (on the recommendation of both Novgorodtsev and Trubetskoi) to undertake the programme of studies leading to the master's degree, was appointed *privat-dozent* in the Faculty of Law (1909) and eventually (1918) received both the master's and the doctoral degrees at once for the two volumes of his dissertation on HEGEL.

Il'in undertook an intense study of Hegel beginning in 1908 and continuing until 1916, by which time his dissertation was essentially completed. During this period he spent two years (1911–12) engaged in study and research in Germany, Italy and France, including periods of work at Heidelberg (with Jellinek), Freiburg (with Rickert), Göttingen (with Husserl and Nelson) and Berlin (with Simmel).

With the outbreak of the First World War, Il'in began to take an active role in advocating the defence of tsarist Russia from enemies within and without. Following the events of February and October 1917 he became a particularly vigorous and public opponent of the Bolsheviks who arrested him six times between 1918 and 1922, finally exiling him in September 1922, under threat of execution, along with many other scholars, philosophers, theologians and writers irreconcilably opposed to the new regime.

Settling in Berlin, he became a professor at the newly opened Russian Academic Institute and taught there until the Nazis removed him in 1934 for refusal to cooperate with their propaganda aims. Forbidden all employment in Nazi Germany, deprived of the right to speak publicly, and watched by the Gestapo, he finally succeeded in leaving Germany for Switzerland in July 1938, where he remained until his death. During the difficult years of exile he produced a substantial number of highly original works on ethics, political theory, aesthetics, religion, and moral and spiritual discipline (see Poltoratzky 1989; Lisitsa 1993).

2 Commentary on Hegel

Il'in's commentary, *Filosofiia Gegelia kak uchenie o konkretnosti Boga i cheloveka* (The Philosophy of Hegel as a Doctrine of the Concreteness of God and Man) (1918) was published in two volumes and its structure reflects its intended purpose as a dissertation to be submitted to the Faculty of Law of Moscow University. Volume 2, *Uchenie o cheloveke* (The Doctrine of Man) was, broadly speaking, a study of Hegel's theory of the state, while volume one, *Uchenie o Boge* (The Doctrine of God), provided an overview of Hegel's philosophical position. Il'in declined to engage in the most usual form of Hegel commentary, the *explication de texte* retracing the author's exposition section by section through a single work. His commentary is rather a *reconstruction*, theme by theme, of the major distinctive elements of Hegel's position, often drawing simultaneously on several of Hegel's texts, while duplicating the rhetorical structure of none of them.

Volume 1 of *Logic*. It is of special interest in that Il'in explicated Hegel's doctrine of *speculative concreteness* with a degree of clarity and detail unmatched by any commentator before him. This volume of the commentary is itself structured in terms of the distinctive doctrine of speculative concreteness, and demonstrates that this doctrine, and the criterion of reality formulated in terms of it, also structure the central claims of Hegel's *Logic* as a whole.

The second volume of Il'in's commentary offers an extended reflection upon the central themes involved in Hegel's *Philosophy of Right*; thus 'freedom', 'will', 'right', 'morality' and 'the ethical' are all treated in separate chapters there, as well as 'humanity' and 'the state'. In this study, Il'in focused significant attention on Hegel's concept of God, most especially arguing that in Hegel's conception, the divine nature as a whole is subject to Becoming, thus capable of undergoing the tragic experience of suffering and death. Il'in himself held to the traditional doctrine of the divine nature as impassible, and so he personally rejected the view he ascribed to Hegel. He argued that in working out the details of his ethical and political doctrine Hegel was forced to 'compromise' the original intent of his philosophy which, according to Il'in, was above all to produce a theodicy (see Grier 1997).

Both volumes taken together constitute a profound, subtle and sustained reflection on the theological implications of Hegel's philosophy, and the influence of Il'in's commentary has been greatest in this area. Both Hans Küng's *Menschwerdung Gottes* (1970) (translated as *The Incarnation of God* (1987))

and Cyril O'Regan 's *The Heterodox Hegel* (1994) were significantly influenced by Il'in's commentary.

It should be pointed out, however, that it is only the drastically shortened German translation, *Die Philosophie Hegels als kontemplative Gotteslehre* (1946) produced by Il'in himself, that has been known to non Russian-speaking scholars. Owing to Il'in's failing health and his extreme reluctance to take time away from other unfinished projects, eight of the ten chapters of the original Russian volume 2 were left out of this edition.

3 Political theory

In formulating his own theory of right, authority, law and the state Il'in demonstrated the originality and independence of his thought to a striking extent. He departed from the settled paths and terms of modern European political theory to such a degree that all of his works on the subject must be read attentively in their entirety to avoid misunderstanding. He set aside the wisdom of the post-Lockean liberal democratic synthesis (which he labels generically 'the republican principle') as a conception aspiring merely to avoid the worst excesses of governmental tyranny, always threatened by degeneration into an unmanageable anarchy of extreme individualism (1979, chs 6, 7). In its place he offered a theory of maximum aspiration, a conception in which the ultimate justification of state authority would be the development in the citizenry of a moral, legal and spiritual culture in which the requirements of natural right would be so widely exemplified in human conduct as to make genuine self-government a reality. He conceives of 'monarchy' (in his own distinctive meaning of the term) as the most appropriate form for the realization of such a state (1979, chs 1–3).

'Pravosoznanie', from *pravo* (right or law) and *soznanie* (consciousness), is Il'in's distinctive term for an awareness (and acceptance) by the individual of the system of obligations and rights specified in natural (and positive) law. Conduct guided by *pravosoznanie* is necessary for any human community that provides the conditions for the emergence of spiritual life, the highest good for the individual, and *pravosoznanie* is itself one of the constituent elements of that highest good. A rational system of positive law would reflect the structure of natural law (1956b, chs 5, 6).

The development of *pravosoznanie* in the population remains a fundamental obligation and goal of state authority. The obligations laid upon the monarchical state itself by *pravosoznanie* are conceived as fundamental, and where the monarch fails to meet these obligations Il'in sees not merely a right, but an *obligation* of disobedience on the part of the population (1979: 222–3). The authority of the monarch is thus strictly limited by natural law, but within those bounds is depicted as properly autocratic, patriarchal, grounded in spiritual authority, and giving rise to gradations of rank among the population. Paradoxically, the ultimate justification of monarchical authority lies in the fulfilment of its obligation to render itself superfluous by the development of *pravosoznanie* to the point of genuine self-governance by the population. He supposed not that the ideal of such a state would be appropriate for every nation, but that it articulated something essential to the original Russian idea, a critically important ideal, he believed, if that nation was ever to be rescued from Bolshevism and reconstructed.

4 Ethics, aesthetics and religious thought

In 1925 Il'in published the very controversial *O soprotivlenii zlu siloiu* (On Opposing Evil with Force), carefully reviewing the fundamental tenets of Christian moral theory and defending the claim that under certain circumstances one's Christian duty might include using the sword to oppose evil. Having satisfied himself that the argument for this conclusion was sound, he forcefully and scornfully attacked the Tolstoian doctrine of non-resistance to evil so popular among many turn-of-the-century Russian intellectuals, characterizing it as a product of intellectual inadequacy and moral weakness of will and arguing that it was responsible in significant measure for the failure of the Russian state to defend itself against Bolshevism. The publication of this work produced a furore in the Russian émigré community, causing a division of opinion for and against Il'in that endured for many years (Il'in 1925, Poltoratzky 1975).

His principles of aesthetic criticism were first presented in *Osnovy khudozhestva: O sovershennom v iskusstve* (Fundamentals of Art: On Perfection in the Arts)(1937), and applied to some of the major Russian émigré writers in *O t'me i prosvetlenii* (On Darkness and Illumination)(1959). He regarded art as a kind of spiritual service and source of joy for the artist as well as the audience, a mode of religious experience for those capable of truly participating in it. A collection of his occasional essays and lectures on Russian writers and other aesthetic topics has also been published (Il'in, 1973).

As a deeply religious thinker and individual, Il'in tended to see a connection between most aspects of successful human endeavour and an actively lived faith. Philosophy, art, morality, law, politics and government, even science – each of these dimensions of human activity needed to be understood in

connection with the divine in order to reach its perfected form. In this sense nearly all of Il'in's major writings touched on religion in some respect. Among those devoted more exclusively to the topic of religion various emphases can be seen, such as (1) numerous occasional writings on the fate of the Russian Orthodox Church; (2) instruction and inspirational writing on the life of spirit, such as *Put' dukhovnogo obnovleniia* (The Path of Spiritual Renewal) (1935), *Poiushchee serdtse* (The Singing Heart) (1958) and *Put' k ochevidnosti* (The Path to Manifest Truth) (1957); and (3) his monumental two-volume work on the fundamental presuppositions of religious experience *Aksiomy religioznogo opyta* (The Axioms of Religious Experience) (1953). In this last work Il'in sought to specify the objective requirements of the fundamental 'religious act' inherent in the Eastern Orthodox faith, and the specific 'structure of the soul' presupposed by it and developed in it. He felt that these elementary 'presuppositions' of faith had been left largely unexamined by theologians and were subject to degeneration and distorted comprehension in the contemporary world. Il'in's overriding concern in all of these works was to trace the spiritual roots of the general crisis affecting Western and Russian civilization in the twentieth century and point out paths to the restoration of spiritual health for individuals and for nations.

List of works

Il'in, I.A. (1993) *Sobranie sochinenii v desiati tomakh* (Collected Works in Ten Volumes), ed. Iu.T. Lisitsa, Moscow: Russkaia kniga. (Vol. 1 contains a bibliography listing about 350 publications by Il'in, including books, brochures, journal articles and newspaper articles, in three languages. A still more detailed and corrected bibliography can be found in vol. 2 of *Sochineniia v dvukh tomakh* (Works in Two Volumes) compiled by Iu.T. Lisitsa in the series *Iz istorii otechestvennoi filosofskoi mysli* published by Voprosy filosofii, Moscow: Medium, 1993, 1994.)

—— (1918) *Filosofiia Gegelia kak uchenie o konkretnosti Boga i cheloveka* (The Philosophy of Hegel as a Doctrine of the Concreteness of God and Man), vol. 1, *Uchenie o Boge* (The Doctrine of God), vol. 2, *Uchenie o cheloveke* (The Doctrine of Man), Moscow: Izd. G.A. Lemana i S.I. Sakharova. (The author himself translated all of vol. 1 and the last two chapters of vol. 2 of the original Russian edn into German and published it as a single volume: *Die Philosophie Hegels als kontemplative Gotteslehre* (The Philosophy of Hegel as a Contemplative Doctrine of God), Berne: A. Francke, 1946. The original 1918 Russian edition has recently been republished in its entirety as a single volume (St Petersburg: Nauka, 1994).)

—— (1925) *O soprotivlenii zlu siloiu* (On Opposing Evil With Force), Berlin: privately published; 2nd edn London, Canada: Zaria, 1975. (Il'in's argument that under certain circumstances Christian moral doctrine does justify the use of the sword to oppose evil, and his attack on Tolstoi's doctrine of non-resistance to evil, and its consequences.)

—— (1935) *Put' dukhovnogo obnovleniia* (The Path of Spiritual Renewal), Belgrade: Russkaia biblioteka, Kniga 43; 2nd edn Munich: privately published by N.N. Il'ina, 1962. (The original edition did not contain the last three chapters included in the second publication.)

—— (1937) *Osnovy khudozhestva: O sovershennom v iskusstve* (Fundamentals of Art: On Perfection in the Arts), Riga: Russkoe akademicheskoe izd. (The primary statement of Il'in's aesthetic doctrine, in which he holds that great works of art and literature contain a religious/spiritual dimension of which the artist may not have been fully conscious.)

—— (1953) *Aksiomy religioznogo opyta* (Axioms of Religious Experience), Paris: privately published, 2 vols. (Il'in's most important religious work; an exploration of the fundamental 'religious act' inherent in the Eastern Orthodox faith, and the specific 'structure of the soul' required by it.)

—— (1956a) *Nashi zadachi: Stat'i 1948–1954* (Our Tasks: Articles 1948–1954), Paris: Izd. Russkogo Obshche-Voinskogo Soiuza, 2 vols. (Il'in's proposals for the reconstruction of the Russian state, Church and society following the collapse of Soviet regime, originally circulated as a series of 215 anonymous 'bulletins' by a Russian émigré organization called the Russian Joint Military Union, which collected all of the bulletins and published them together after Il'in's death.)

—— (1956b) *O sushchnosti pravosoznaniia* (On the Essence of Consciousness of Right), Munich: privately published by N.N. Il'ina. (The initial version (1919) was revised throughout Il'in's life. This is a work of political and legal philosophy in which Il'in explained the doctrine of 'consciousness of right/law' and its connection with natural law as an essential element of the political/legal arrangements he thought appropriate as an ideal for a future Russian state.)

—— (1957) *Put' k ochevidnosti* (The Path to Manifest Truth), Munich: privately published by N.N. Il'ina. (An inquiry and guide into the problem of self-evidence, or what is required for penetrating to the objective essence of a problem – of knowledge, of ethics, of spiritual life – and avoiding the blindness induced by surface appearances.)

—— (1958) *Poiushchee serdtse. Kniga tikhikh sozertsanii* (The Singing Heart. A Book of Quiet Contemplations), Munich: privately published by N.N. Il'ina, 1943. (Il'in described this as 'devoted not to theology, but to a quiet, philosophical praising of God', to the development of a new philosophy, Christian in spirit and style.)

—— (1959) *O t'me i prosvetlenii: Kniga khudozhestvennoi kritiki. Bunin–Remizov–Shmelev* (On Darkness and Illumination: A Book of Aesthetic Criticism. Bunin–Remizov–Shmelev), Munich: privately published by N.N. Il'ina. (Il'in's commentary on these three important writers of the emigration, illustrating his own principle of aesthetic criticism. Written 1939.)

—— (1973) *Russkie pisateli, literatura i khudozhestvo: Sbornik statei, rechei i lektsii* (Russian Writers, Literature and Art: An Anthology of Articles, Speeches and Lectures), Redaktsiia, predislovie i primechaniia N.P. Poltoratskogo, Washington: Izd. Russkogo knizhnogo dela v SShA, Kamkin. (A collection of Il'in's brochures, lectures and speeches devoted to the literary genius of Pushkin, the spiritual art of Shmelev, literary criticism of Merezhkovskii, the Russian folktale, Russian poetry and the idea of Russia contained in it, and questions of artistic creativity.)

—— (1979) *O monarkhii i respublike* (On Monarchy and the Republic), Redaktsiia, predislovie i prilozhenie N.P. Poltoratskogo, New York: Sodruzhestvo. (This is Il'in's primary work on forms of the political state. Not completed in his lifetime, it was assembled and edited by Poltoratzky.)

References and further reading

Evlampiev, I.I. (1992) '"Drama mirotvoriashchego bozhestva": Bog i chelovek v filosofii Ivana Il'ina' ('The Drama of the Worldcreating Divinity': God and Man in the Philosophy of Ivan Il'in), *Stupeni*, 3: 66–89. (An attempt to identify distinct 'periods' in the development of Il'in's outlook.)

Grier, P.T. (1994) 'The Complex Legacy of Ivan Il'in', in *Russian Thought After Communism: The Recovery of a Philosophical Heritage*, ed. J.P. Scanlan, Armonk, NY: M.E. Sharpe, 165–86. (A discussion of the contemporary revival and reception of Il'in's writings in Russia.)

* —— (1997) 'The Speculative Concrete: I.A. Il'in's Interpretation of Hegel', in *Hegel, History and Interpretation*, ed. S. Gallagher, Albany, NY: State University of New York Press, 169–93. (An examination of distinguishing features of Il'in's interpretation of Hegel. Expansion of §2.)

Lisitsa, Iu.T. (1991) 'I.A. Il'in kak pravoved i

gosudarstvoved' (I.A. Il'in as a Theorist of Law and the State), *Voprosy filosofii* 5: 146–58. (A careful, reliable discussion of aspects of Il'in's political theory.)

* —— (1993) 'Ivan Aleksandrovich Il'in. Istoriko-biograficheskii ocherk' (Ivan Aleksandrovich Il'in. A Biographical and Historical Essay), in *I.A. Il'in. Sobranie sochinenii v desiati tomakh*, Moscow: Russkaia kniga, vol. 1, 5–36. (The most recent, authoritative biographical essay on Il'in. A source for §1.)

Offermanns, W. (1979) *Mensch, werde wesentlich! Das Lebenswerk des russischen religiösen Denkers Ivan Iljin für die Erneuerung der geistigen Grundlagen der Menschheit* (Man, Become Your Essence! The Lifework of the Russian Religious Thinker Ivan Il'in for the Renewal of the Spiritual Foundation of Humanity), Band 11 von OIKONOMIA, Quellen und Studien zur orthodoxen Theologie unter Mitarbeit von Erich Bryner und Karl Christian Felmy, Erlangen: Hrg. von Fairy v. Lilienfeld. (The most important monograph-length study of Il'in's religious thought to date.)

* Poltoratzky, N. (1975) *I.A. Il'in i polemika vokrug ego idei o soprotivlenii zlu siloiu* (I.A. Il'in and the Controversy Over his Idea of Opposing Evil with Force), London, Canada: Zaria; also published as an appendix to the second edition of *O soprotivlenii zly siloiu*, London and Canada: Zaria, 1975. (Poltoratzky's compilation and review of the critical reaction to Il'in's publication.)

—— (1979) *Monarkhiia i respublika v vospriiatii I.A. Il'ina* (Monarchy and the Republic in the Perception of I.A. Il'in), New York: Sodruzhestvo. (An authoritative overview of Il'in's political thought. A source for §3. Also published as an appendix to Il'in's *O monarkhii i respublike*.)

* —— (1989) *Ivan Aleksandrovich Il'in. Zhizn', trudy, mirovozzrenie. Sbornik statei* (Ivan Aleksandrovich Il'in. Life, Works, Worldview. A Collection of Articles), Tenafly, NJ: Ermitazh. (Nikolai Petrovich Poltoratzky (1921–90) was the literary executor for Il'in, the compiler of the Il'in papers at Michigan State University, and the leading authority on Il'in. An important biographical work; a source for §1.)

PHILIP T. GRIER

ILLOCUTIONARY ACT

see SPEECH ACTS

ILLOCUTIONARY FORCE

see PRAGMATICS; SPEECH ACTS

ILLUMINATI

Begun in 1776 in Bavaria, the Illuminati were an overtly political as well as morally orientated secret organization that imitated the forms of freemasonry. While masonic lodges forbade discussion of politics and religion at their meetings, the Illuminati did the reverse. They were openly yet paradoxically secret about their irreligion and their devotion to the radical French Enlightenment; and they wanted reform in the absolutist states of Central Europe. The authorities arrested and persecuted them, but their activism foreshadows the French Revolution and a desire for more representative systems of government in Continental Europe. Despite the notoriety of the Illuminati, no more than about 600 members have been identified.

Freemasonry always promised more than it delivered. Its rules and the constitutions of Grand Lodges throughout Europe spoke of all men meeting upon the level, and of merit as the only requirement for advancement. Yet in lodge after lodge, hierarchy and social position reasserted themselves, and the Grand Lodges were, without exception, led by aristocrats. In addition the masonic lodges, particularly in the German-speaking lands, had been used by enlightened absolutists as extensions of their social influence. Frederick II in Berlin, and later Joseph II in Vienna, openly used membership as a symbol of loyalty to themselves, and of a man's willingness to work for the interests of the state before those of the clergy or the local power of old elites. It is little wonder that someone, somewhere would adopt the form and ideology of freemasonry and radicalize both. That is precisely what the Illuminati did.

Founded, not accidentally, in 1776 – the year of revolutionary upheaval in the new world – by Weishaupt (1748–1830), a professor of law at the Bavarian university at Ingolstadt, the Illuminati were overtly and dangerously political. Unlike the lodges which forbade open discussion of politics – and then subtly assumed political personae – the lodges of the Illuminati openly called for political and philosophical discussions, less hierarchy, and attention to issues of reform. Weishaupt adopted the form of the masonic lodge, issued 'statutes' as would a lodge, embraced secrecy, and called for moral reform: '*Mocht sich die alten und neuern System der Moral, Philosophie als stoischen, epikureischen...*' ('you should embrace the old and new System of Morality, Philosophy such as the stoic and the epicurean...'). Thus Enlightenment paganism was harnessed to political reform. Lessing's masonic dialogue, *Ernst und Falk* (1778), may have been partly inspired by Illuminati ideals; certainly it argued for democracy and for a set of reforms that would make societies and states less hierarchical, less sectarian, and less bellicose (see LESSING, G.E.). Lessing's argument in the dialogue centred on the notion that all he was doing was bringing freemasonry to its logical conclusion. The masonic goal of virtue and individual moral improvement was turned outward, and the mirror reflected poorly upon the absolutist principalities or the clergy favoured in them.

Again, it was not accidental that Weishaupt had been educated by the Jesuits. There had long been tension between the order and the masonic lodges. In the 1740s the leading Amsterdam freemason, Jean Rousset de Missy said that masters of a lodge would admit any man – except a Jesuit. The Illuminati were quickly locked in combat with the Jesuits who spied in them another example of masonic evil. Weishaupt argued that his brothers should do as had the Jesuits, make themselves indispensable as servants of the state. The point of this infiltration, however, would be to drastically alter the state; not to support it as had the Jesuits. Other German intellectuals were attracted to his arguments, notably the freemason Adolf Freiherrn von Knigge, who became a theorist of illuminism. The debate begun by the Illuminati and the Jesuits can be found echoed or discussed by Fichte, Schiller, and Herder.

The League of the Illuminati were strongest in Munich where von Knigge sought to use it as a vehicle to reform freemasonry and to extend its influence throughout Germany. At the height of its fame the League had no more than 600 members of which most were court and administrative officials, clergymen and military officers. They swore an oath that said 'the sole aim of the League is education, not by declamatory means but by favouring and rewarding virtue. The order of the day is to put an end to the machinations of the purveyors of injustice'.

The goals of the League provoked fear on the part of the authorities who sought to infiltrate their ranks, and eventually they arrested and imprisoned their leaders. It was said that Jesuits were also attempting to spy on the Illuminati, and what began as a small effort by a young professor in Bavaria suddenly captured the attention of the European press. The Illuminati became symbol and reality of the crisis of absolutism seen in Berlin, Paris and Vienna during the 1780s. At its heart lay the contradictions within enlightened absolutism: How to reform the state

without unleashing uncontrollable forces or allowing potential revolutionaries to gain the upper hand? The Illuminati became the Anabaptists of their era, indeed Catholic propaganda openly compared them to the radicals of Münster. For their part the German freemasons moved to distance themselves from this new hybrid. The Bavarian response foreshadows by a decade the emergence of conspiracy theory during the French Revolution. As early as the autumn of 1789 the freemasons were being blamed for events in Paris, but the background lay in the furore caused by the Illuminati and the efforts made by the German states to exterminate them.

Something discernibly modern emerged in Bavaria in 1776, only to be suppressed by 1786: groups of young men intent upon planning for radical political reform that could include the dismantling of established political authority. Equally modern was the response: conspiracy theorists surfaced who defined the world as a place threatened by dark forces possessed of extraordinary power solely by virtue of their secrecy and silence. In the process the state had come to be seen as a human institution, made by the people and not by divine will. As early as 1780 Illuminati showed how fragile the authorities of the absolutist state perceived their power and control to be; the decade of the 1790s would prove their fears to have been justified.

See also: ENLIGHTENMENT, CONTINENTAL

List of works

Von Knigge, A.F. (1799) *Practical Philosophy of Social Life*, London.
—— (1788) *Sämtliche Werke* (Complete Works), Leichtenstein: KTO Press, 1978.
Weishaupt, A. (1788) *Über die Gründe der menschlichen Erkenntniss* (On the Foundations of Human Knowledge) Berlin; Brussels, 1969.

References and further reading

Abbott, S. (1991) *Fictions of Freemasonry and the German Novel*, Detroit, MI: Wayne State University Press. (A useful collection of primary source material.)
Jacob M.C., (1991) *Living the Enlightenment. Freemasonry and Politics in Eighteenth Century Europe*, New York: Oxford University Press. (A survey of European freemasonry from its foundation in England in 1717 to the French revolution.)
Neugebauer-Wölk, M. (1995) *Esoterische Bünde und Bürgerliche Gesellschaft, Entwicklungslinien zur modernen Welt im Geheimbundwesen des 18.*

Jahrhunderts (Esoteric Societies and Citizens' Groups, Lines of Development to the Modern World from the Secret Societies of the Eighteenth Century), Wolfenbüttel: Lessing Academie.

Van Dülmen, R. (1992) *The Society of the Enlightenment, The Rise of the Middle Class and Enlightenment Culture in Germany,* trans. Anthony Williams, Cambridge: Polity Press. (A solid historical work on the emergence of civil society in the eighteenth century.)

MARGARET C. JACOB

ILLUMINATION

The most influential theories of illumination explain certain features of our knowledge by developing an analogy with ordinary sensory vision and the role played in it by light. According to theories of this sort, our knowledge of necessary and immutable objects and truths requires the activity of a kind of intelligible light illumining objects that are purely intelligible, thereby making them 'visible' to our mind. Plato held that this light comes from the Form of the Good, Augustine that it comes from God, and others that it is intrinsic to reason itself.

The peculiar nature and behaviour of light has provided a model not just for theories of knowledge but also for philosophical accounts of fundamental features of reality. Neoplatonist cosmologies, for example, liken the genesis of the universe to the emanation of rays of light from a light source. Theories of illumination therefore can be metaphysical as well as epistemological. Both kinds of theory have their historical roots in Platonism broadly construed.

1   **Epistemological illuminationism**
2   **Metaphysical illuminationism**

1   Epistemological illuminationism

Platonist epistemologies characteristically focus on the fact that we understand certain immutable, eternal natures (for example, the objects of geometry, such as the circle and the triangle) and know certain necessary truths (for example, that the interior angles of a triangle are equal to two right angles). They argue that we cannot have acquired knowledge and understanding of this sort through sense perception since no objects of sense perception are of the right sort to account for the necessity and immutability distinctive of this sort of knowledge. They conclude that if such knowledge is to be possible, there must be necessary

and immutable objects epistemically accessible to us by means other than sense perception. Epistemologies of this sort hold that these objects are purely intelligible and that we make epistemic contact with them through reason, intellect or mind. Our understanding of the nature of a triangle (for example) and our certain knowledge that its interior angles are equal to two right angles are to be explained by our being (or having been) directly acquainted with the relevant purely intelligible object(s).

The model for this epistemically fundamental notion of direct intellective acquaintance is sensory vision. Our access to purely intelligible objects by means of reason or mind is analogous to our access to ordinary visible objects through sight. According to this analogy, there are three essential components in both the sensory and intellective cognitive processes. First, we must possess the relevant cognitive power (sight in the case of sensory vision; intellect in the case of intellective cognition). Second, there must be an appropriate object for that power (a coloured material body; a purely intelligible object). And third, there must be an agent whose activity enables the cognitive power and its object to make contact. In sensory vision, this third component – the enabling agent of cognition – is light: corporeal light (from the sun, for example) illumines material objects, making them not merely potentially but actually visible to us. In intellective cognition, there must be an analogous intellectual light whose activity makes intelligible objects actually and not merely potentially intelligible to us. Our direct acquaintance with the nature of a triangle (for example) depends essentially, therefore, not only on our intellective powers and the existence of the relevant intelligible object(s) but also on the activity of an intellectual light.

The analogy between intellectual understanding and sensory vision is superficially compelling (our ordinary ways of talking about knowledge and understanding rely heavily on it), but the metaphor of intellectual light gives rise to difficult philosophical questions. What exactly is the nature of this intellectual light? Is it something ontologically independent of us or is it identical with or merely a function of our intellectual powers and capacities? Plato's famous analogy of the sun suggests that the intellectual light has as its source the Form of the Good:

> Say, then, that it is the sun which I call the offspring of the Good, which the Good begot as analogous to itself. What the Good itself is in the world of thought in relation to the intelligence and things known, the sun is in the visible world in relation to sight and things seen.... [W]henever one's eyes are turned upon objects brightened by

sunshine, they see clearly.... So too understand the eye of the soul: whenever it is fixed upon that upon which truth and reality shine, it understands and knows, and seems to have intelligence.... Say that what gives truth to the objects of knowledge, and to the knowing mind the power to know, is the Form of the Good.

(*Republic VI, 508b–e*)

Later Platonists develop and extend what we might call the supernaturalist elements of Plato's analogy. AUGUSTINE (§4), for example, typically describes the source of intellectual illumination not as the Form of the Good but as Truth itself, which he identifies with God. He holds, then, that our knowledge depends essentially on God's activity in our souls. For this reason, his view is typically characterized as a doctrine of divine illumination.

By developing Plato's analogy in an explicitly theological direction, Augustine intended to deepen it and weave its epistemological elements into his broad, theistic account of reality. But medieval philosophers attracted by Augustine's Christian Platonism saw two general difficulties in his doctrine of divine illumination. First, Augustine had suggested that in so far as any particular truth is necessary, immutable and eternal, it must be, or in some way be a part of, God, since God alone is truly necessary, immutable and eternal. But in that case it seems that in grasping a truth of this sort, ordinary human knowers are in direct epistemic contact with the divine nature, a state that Christian doctrine takes to be virtually unattainable by human beings in this life. Second, in so far as Augustine's account identified illumination with God's activity within our minds, it seemed to make genuine knowledge a product of supernatural intervention in our cognitive lives, and so not genuinely human at all.

Medieval philosophers and theologians typically try to steer a middle course between an interpretation of Augustine's doctrine of divine illumination that is unacceptably supernaturalist and an interpretation that leaves no room at all for divine activity in human knowing. Many preserve the doctrine essentially intact, introducing minor distinctions designed to blunt the most serious objections. BONAVENTURE (§7), for example, argues that our grasp of the eternal natures that are in God can be a matter of degree:

Since, then, certain knowledge belongs to the rational spirit, insofar as it is the image of God, it follows that in this knowledge the spirit attains to the eternal reasons [that are in God]. But since, as long as it is in the wayfaring state, [the rational spirit] is not fully deiform, it does not attain to them clearly and fully and distinctly.... It is to be

granted, then, ... that in all certain knowledge those principles of knowledge are attained by the knower. They are reached in one way, however, by the wayfarer, and in another way by him who enjoys the vision of God [in the next life].

(*Disputed Questions Concerning Christ's Knowledge*, q.4)

But some important late medieval thinkers give the doctrine of divine illumination an essentially naturalistic interpretation; this is especially the case with those philosophers – such as Bonaventure's contemporary, Thomas AQUINAS (§11) – who are committed to an Aristotelian analysis of mind and cognition. Aquinas argues that the intellectual light that makes immutable natures actually intelligible to us must be identified with a power *in us*, otherwise the resultant knowing would not be ours. That power, Aquinas claims, is the Aristotelian agent intellect, the power of the human soul that abstracts universal natures from the material and individuating conditions that characterize the presentations of sense perception. He adapts the terminology of the doctrine of illumination to fit the structure of his Aristotelian account, calling the agent intellect a 'light' and thinking of its activity of abstracting universal forms as a kind of 'illumination'. In doing so, Aquinas preserves the letter of Augustine's position if not its entire spirit.

This naturalistic rendering of the doctrine of illumination survives into early modern philosophy in the work of philosophers such as René DESCARTES (§7). The foundational role he assigns to propositions that are clearly and distinctly perceived to be true (or that are shown to be true by the natural light of reason) marks Descartes' theory of knowledge as part of the legacy of Platonist epistemological illuminationism.

2 Metaphysical illuminationism

Light's seeming propagation of itself in all directions from its source provides the model for emanationist cosmologies and related metaphysical accounts. PLOTINUS (§§3, 5), for example, described the emanation of all reality from the single, unified source of being (the One) as like the emanation of rays of light from a light source. Medieval Christian philosophers, who rejected emanationism as an account of the genesis of the universe, nevertheless incorporated the notion of emanation into their explanations of various aspects of the relation between creatures and their creator. According to ALBERT THE GREAT (§4), for example, metaphysical universals are like rays radiating from God, the primary intelligence and creator of all forms. These universal forms, which are in themselves simple, fall on matter (producing particular individuals) and on souls (for which they are the principles of cognition). HENRY OF GHENT (§§2–3) argued that a creature's essence is related to its existence in the way a ray of sunlight is related to the light it possesses: the ray receives its light from the sun (and so is in that respect distinct from and dependent on it), but it receives it in such a way that the ray's very nature and essence is light (and so is in this respect not distinct from it). Accounts of this sort can be thought of as developing the metaphysical side of the metaphor of illumination.

See also: CHINUL; EPISTEMOLOGY, HISTORY OF §§1–4; GROSSETESTE, R. §3; ILLUMINATIONIST PHILOSOPHY; MEDIEVAL PHILOSOPHY

References and further reading

Albert the Great (1240s) 'On Universals' (*Liber de praedicabilibus*, tr. II, ch. 6), trans. S. MacDonald, *Cambridge Translations of Medieval Philosophical Texts*, vol. 2, *Metaphysics*, Cambridge: Cambridge University Press, forthcoming. (Albert shapes a Neoplatonist metaphysics of emanation to fit his theistic conception of God.)

Aquinas, T. (1266–73) *Summa theologica* Ia, trans. Fathers of the English Dominican Province, Westminster, MD: Christian Classics, 1981. (Questions 79 and 84 show Aquinas developing his own Aristotelian account of intellectual cognition with a clear awareness of the Augustinian Platonist tradition of illumination.)

Augustine (388, 391–5) *On Free Choice of the Will*, trans. T. Williams, Indianapolis, IN: Hackett Publishing Company, 1993. (Book II contains one of Augustine's more extended developments of his doctrine of divine illumination.)

* Bonaventure (1256) *Disputed Questions Concerning Christ's Knowledge* (*Quaestiones disputatae de scientia Christi*), q.4, trans. E.R. Fairweather, *A Scholastic Miscellany: Anselm to Ockham*, New York: Macmillan, 1970. (Bonaventure's Augustinian sympathies lead him to try to resolve difficulties inherent in Augustine's doctrine of illumination.)

Descartes, R. (1641) *Meditations on First Philosophy*, trans. G.E.M. Anscombe and P.T. Geach, *Philosophical Writings*, Indianapolis, IN: Bobbs-Merrill, 1971. (Descartes' epistemology extends the Augustinian heritage into modern philosophy.)

Henry of Ghent (1276) 'Is a Creature's Essence its Being?' (*Quodlibet* I, q.9), trans. S. MacDonald, *Cambridge Translations of Medieval Philosophical Texts*, vol. 2, *Metaphysics*, Cambridge: Cambridge

University Press, forthcoming. (Henry finds in what he takes to be peculiar features of the rays of light emanating from a light source a useful analogy for the relation between essence and existence.)

* Plato (*c.*390 BC) *Republic*, trans. G.M.A. Grube, Indianapolis, IN: Hackett Publishing Company, 1974. (Plato's parable of the sun, in book VI, is an enormously influential source of epistemological illuminationism.)

Plotinus (*c.*260) *Enneads*, trans. A.H. Armstrong, Cambridge, MA: Harvard University Press, 1966–88, 7 vols. (Plotinus develops Platonist themes into full-blown cosmological emanationism.)

SCOTT MacDONALD

ILLUMINATIONIST PHILOSOPHY

Illuminationist philosophy started in twelfth-century Persia, and has been an important force in Islamic, especially Persian, philosophy right up to the present day. It presents a critique of some of the leading ideas of Aristotelianism, as represented by the philosophy of Ibn Sina (Avicenna), and argues that many of the distinctions which are crucial to the character of that form of philosophy are misguided. Illuminationists develop a view of reality in accordance with which essence is more important than existence, and intuitive knowledge is more significant than scientific knowledge. They use the notion of light, as the name suggests, as a way of exploring the links between God, the Light of Lights, and his creation. The result is a view of the whole of reality as a continuum, with the physical world being an aspect of the divine. This sort of language proved to be very suggestive for mystical philosophers, and Illuminationism quickly became identified with Islamic mysticism.

1 Origins
2 Logic and semantics
3 Epistemology and ontology
4 Light
5 The character of Illuminationist philosophy

1 Origins

Illuminationist philosophy stems from the Arabic term *ishraq*, meaning 'rising', in particular the 'rising of the sun'. The term is also linked to the Arabic for 'East', and has come to represent a specifically Eastern form of philosophical thought. It is used, especially within the context of Persian poetic literature, to represent a form of thought which contrasts with cognitive reason (*'aql*); that is, it is taken to be intuitive, immediate and atemporal knowledge. The source of this form of thought is often identified with IBN SINA's 'Eastern Philosophy' (*al-hikma al-mashriqiyya*), a text about which there is a great deal of dispute and discussion, and which may never have actually existed. It is supposed to represent Ibn Sina's departure from Peripateticism and his attempt to construct a new and deeper philosophical system (see ISLAM, CONCEPT OF PHILOSOPHY IN §2).

The real originator of illuminationist philosophy is AL-SUHRAWARDI, a Persian philosopher of the twelfth century AD, who composed over fifty works but who is chiefly remembered for his brief *Hikmat al-ishraq* (The Philosophy of Illumination). In this book, al-Suhrawardi (in Persian, Sohravardi) adopts some of the main principles of Peripateticism (*al-falsafa al-mashsha'iyya*), but also sets out to challenge others. He criticizes Peripatetic approaches to a wide variety of topics, in particular quantification, the confusion between 'term' and 'utterance', the notion of amphiboly, petitio principii and many other issues (see ARISTOTELIANISM IN ISLAMIC PHILOSOPHY). There is a marked similarity between his critique and that of WILLIAM OF OCKHAM, who also identifies in his *Summa logicae* what he regards as ten fallacies in Aristotelian logic. Both al-Suhrawardi and Ockham rearrange the parts of the Organon and omit from their discussions some of the books.

2 Logic and semantics

Illuminationist philosophy challenges the Peripatetic position of the absolute, unchanging and universal validity of the truths discoverable by Aristotelian methodology (see PERIPATETICS). It sets out instead to construct a system applicable to the whole continuum of being, including what is called 'immediate knowledge'. Al-Suhrawardi rejects Aristotle's theory of definition, arguing that there is no criterion for the parts of a definition (the genus and the differentia), and so the species is defined in terms of something less known than itself. He goes on to claim that some of the Aristotelian categories are superfluous, since action and passion are modes of motion, and possession and posture are kinds of relation. Thus we need only five categories instead of ten, leaving substance, quantity, quality, relation and motion.

The basis of al-Suhrawardi's approach is really Stoic and Megaric (see STOICISM; MEGARIAN SCHOOL). According to this approach, the denotation (the external object) should be compared with the thing, the sign should be compared with the utterance

and what is signified should be compared with the meaning. These semantic notions are used to define the relation between the first atemporal act of thought and the second temporally-extended grasp of the thing known, its essence (Ziai 1990: 42–). This involves the development of a theory of types of signification, relation of class names to constituents of the class, types of inclusion of members in classes, and a well-defined theory of supposition.

In the illuminationist view of logic, a conclusion reached by using a formally established syllogism has no epistemological value as a starting point in philosophical construction. For a universal affirmative proposition to have philosophical value as a foundation of scientific knowledge, it must be 'necessary and always true'. Yet if we introduce the mode 'possibility' and give it an extension in time as in 'future possibility', the universal affirmative proposition cannot be 'necessarily true always'. This is because of the impossibility of knowing or deducing all possible future instances. The epistemological implication of this logical position is that formal validity ranks lower than the certitude obtained by the self-conscious subject who, when alerted to a future possible event through 'knowledge by presence', will simply 'know' it. The future event cannot be deduced at the present time *and* given universal validity (see LOGIC IN ISLAMIC PHILOSOPHY).

3 Epistemology and ontology

The crucial notion for Illuminationist epistemology is knowledge-by-presence (*al-'ilm al-huduri*). This identifies an epistemological position prior to acquired or representational knowledge (*al-'ilm al-husuli*). This has often been related to intuitive knowledge, and results in attempts to unravel the mysteries of nature not through the principles of physics but through the metaphysical world and the realm of myths, dreams, fantasy and truths known through inspiration. The distinction between scientific knowledge and knowledge-by-presence is crucial for AL-SUHRAWARDI, who claims that the essence of human beings lies in their self-awareness, through the luminosity of their own inner existence (see EPISTEMOLOGY IN ISLAMIC PHILOSOPHY; SCIENCE IN ISLAMIC PHILOSOPHY).

This approach also has implications for ontology. Illuminationism defends the 'primacy of quiddity'; it sets itself up against both ARISTOTLE and IBN SINA in upholding the priority of essence over existence. Some philosophers uphold the primacy of being or existence, and consider essence to be a derived mental concept, while those who adhere to the primacy of quiddity consider existence to be a derived mental concept. If existence has a reality outside the mind, then the real must consist of the principle of the reality of existence and the being of existence, which requires a referent outside the mind. Its referent outside the mind must also consist of two things, which can in turn be subdivided, and so on ad infinitum. That is, if 'existence' denotes an existent, then there must be another 'existence' connected to it which makes it real, and if so then this would also apply to the second 'existence', which leads to a vicious regress. To avoid this absurdity, we must regard existence as an abstract and derived mental concept; existence cannot signify an actual entity. If there were a distinction between a substance external to the mind and its existence, it would exist by accident, since two external substances must have different essences and cannot be distinguished by being existents. In that case, existence is nothing but a mental idea and cannot be defined. Since existence is attributable to many things, it must be mental (see EXISTENCE).

4 Light

Illuminationism is distinguishable from Peripateticism through its semantics, logic, epistemology, ontology, the priority of the intuitive over the purely noetic, and also its use of a language of light entities to describe the whole continuum of reality. The latter consists of four things: intellect, soul, matter and a fourth realm named the 'alam al-khayal, which is similar to Platonic Forms except that entities in it are continuous with the whole of reality. This fourth realm (translated by Corbin as the 'mundus imaginalis' (Corbin 1971)) is describable as that of 'things as ideas' prior to taking on shape, that is, before they receive 'luminosity' from the One Source, the Light of Lights. The light received is essentially the same, and the luminous thing differs from other light entities only in respect of degrees of intensity. Luminosity flows eternally, and gives shape to the forms, thus making the entity 'visible' and known. The difference between things, then, lies not in their essences but in terms of the degrees of intensity of the shared essences of the things. All luminous things constitute an aggregate whole and are coeternal with the Light of Lights. The Light of Lights is one, but is neither beyond being nor nonbeing, nor does it have a will. Everything in the continuum is generated from the Light of Lights and shares a degree of light similarity. The Light of Lights is one with respect to all possible modes, known or discovered subsequently.

These highly suggestive references to light were taken up by a large number of later thinkers who developed it in different but connected ways. According to Nasafi, the existence of God is an infinite light, the existence of which is equivalent to its essence, and everything which exists is a face or expression of this light. God is the ultimate reality of everything which exists in the universe. Baba Afdal Kashani argues that the notion of being is more general than the notion of existence, since we can wonder whether a thing actually exists; being is then prior to existence, and experience of the light of God's creation is comprehended solely through an internal illumination of the soul. This results not in knowledge of a fact or thing, but rather in a way of relating to God, a way which maintains one's status as part of the deity. One of the key aspects of Illuminationism is its disinclination to make a sharp distinction between God and that which God has produced. This is what has made Illuminationist philosophy seem so close to mysticism at times, and it leads to a sharp differentiation from aspects of Ash'arite thought, such as adherence to the atom as the basic constituent of physical reality.

5 The character of Illuminationist philosophy

The influence of Illuminationist philosophy on the Islamic world persists to this day. A wide range of important thinkers including Nasir al-Din AL-TUSI, Shams al-Din Shahrazuri, Sa'd IBN KAMMŪNA, Qutb al-Din al-Shirazi, Jalal al-Din AL-DAWANI, the School of Isfahan and, right up to our own day, Ha'iri Yazdi, are clearly within this tradition of philosophy. When it comes to issues of interpretation, there is a controversy as to how close this form of philosophy really is to mysticism. Some writers such as Izutsu (1971), Rahman (1975) and Ziai (1990), stress its links with analytical thought and deny that there is anything particularly mystical about it. It is certainly true that the greatest interest has been focused on a relatively small number of al-Suhrawardi's works which have more of an esoteric nature, while his more technical and strictly logical works have tended to be ignored.

The work of Henry Corbin (1971) and Seyyed Hossein Nasr (1964), on the other hand, emphasizes the mystical contribution which Illuminationism makes, and they see the esoteric aspects of this form of thought as being of leading significance. There is no doubt that the general use to which Illuminationist philosophy has been put often involves mysticism, and there is little difficulty in combining it with the thought of IBN AL-'ARABI, for example, which later philosophers were to do. It is certainly true that some of the leading texts by al-Suhrawardi are entirely technical and deal with issues of philosophy which have no mystical dimensions, but it must be admitted that when one examines his general approach to metaphysics, it clearly fits in with many of the ideas which mystics like to use. The terminology of light points to a view of the nature of reality which is far removed from that presented by the Peripatetics, or even from Ibn Sina in his more suggestive and mystical moods. Illuminationism is not just a critique of Aristotle and Ibn Sina, but it is also the development of an original metaphysical model which has subsequently proved very fruitful within the Islamic world.

See also: ARISTOTELIANISM IN ISLAMIC PHILOSOPHY; EPISTEMOLOGY IN ISLAMIC PHILOSOPHY; ILLUMINATION; ISLAMIC PHILOSOPHY, MODERN; MYSTICAL PHILOSOPHY IN ISLAM; al-SUHRAWARDI

References and further reading

* Corbin, H. (1971) *En Islam iranien* (Islam in Iran), Paris: Gallimard. (The main interpreter of illuminationism in the West and the esoteric approach to it.)

Ha'iri Yazdi, M. (1992) *The Principles of Epistemology in Islamic Philosophy: Knowledge by Presence*, Albany, NY: State University of New York Press. (Masterly analysis of this key notion in illuminationist philosophy, treated from the perspective of analytical philosophy.)

* Izutsu Toshihiko (1971) *The Concept and Reality of Existence*, Tokyo: Keio Institute. (Detailed discussion of the notion of existence in illuminationism.)

* Nasr, S.H. (1964) *Three Muslim Sages*, Cambridge, MA.: Harvard University Press. (Exposition of the Corbin form of interpretation with respect to illuminationism.)

Netton, I. (1989) *Allah Transcendent: Studies in the Structure and Semiotics of Islamic Philosophy, Theology and Cosmology*, London: Routledge. (Very clear account of the metaphysics of illuminationism.)

* Rahman, F. (1975) *The Philosophy of Mulla Sadra*, Albany, NY: State University of New York Press. (An account of how later thinkers took up and developed illuminationism.)

* al-Suhrawardi (1183–91) *Oeuvres philosophiques et mystiques*, vols I and II, ed. H. Corbin, Tehran and Paris: Adrien-Maisonneuve, 1976; vol. III, ed. S.H. Nasr, Tehran and Paris: Adrien-Maisonneuve, 1977. (A vitally important collection of the basic principles of illuminationism. An English translation of some of the works in Volume 3 can be found in *The Mystical and Visionary Treatises of Shihabuddin Yahya Suhrawardi*, trans. W. Thackston, London: Octagon Press, 1982.)

Walbridge, J. (1992) *The Science of Mystic Lights: Qutb al-Din Shirazi and the Illuminationist Tradition in Islamic Philosophy*, Cambridge, MA: Harvard

University Press. (A commentaary on al-Suhrawardi and Ibn Sina, with an excellent discussion of the leading principles of illuminationism.)

* Ziai, H. (1990) *Knowledge and Illumination: A Study of Suhrawardi's Hikmat al-Ishraq*, Atlanta, GA: Scholars Press. (Study of the more analytical parts of al-Suhrawardi's philosophy.)

—— (1992) 'Source and Nature of Authority: A Study of Suhrawardi's Illuminationist Political Doctrine', in C. Butterworth (ed.) *The Political Aspects of Islamic Philosophy*, Cambridge, MA: Harvard University Press, 304–44. (Discussion of the political implications of lluminationism.)

—— (1996) 'The Illuminationist Tradition', in S.H. Nasr and O. Leaman (eds) *History of Islamic Philosophy*, London: Routledge, ch. 29, 465–96. (A clear description of the topic, with the emphasis on the analytic aspect of illuminationism.)

HOSSEIN ZIAI
OLIVER LEAMAN

ILLUSION, ARGUMENT FROM *see* PERCEPTION, EPISTEMIC ISSUES IN (§5)

ILLUSION, INDIAN CONCEPTS OF *see* ERROR AND ILLUSION, INDIAN CONCEPTIONS OF

'ILM AL-KALAM *see* ISLAMIC THEOLOGY

IMAGERY

Most philosophers prior to the twentieth century thought of mental images as inner pictures, along lines suggested by introspection. But there are obvious differences between mental images and pictures. The former have no objective size or shape, for example. These differences have led some philosophers to argue that mental images are more like linguistic descriptions. The descriptional view of images is also taken by some cognitive psychologists. Other psychologists maintain that the pictorial conception of images provides the best explanation for the results of a number of intriguing experiments on imagery.

Are the front legs of a kangaroo shorter than its back legs? Questions like these typically prompt people to form mental images, which they then inspect before answering. But just what are mental images?

Introspection suggests that images are inner pictures. And that is how most philosophers prior to the twentieth century thought of them. According to this view, held by ARISTOTLE, DESCARTES and the British Empiricists, visual images are significantly like pictures in the way that they represent things in the world (see EMPIRICISM). Notwithstanding its widespread acceptance, the picture theory of mental images was left largely unexplained in the traditional philosophical literature. Images were taken somehow to resemble the things that they represent, but little more was said.

In the twentieth century the pictorial view of mental images has been the target of numerous philosophical objections. It has been noted that mental images are not seen with real eyes; they have no objective weight or colour. What, then, can it mean to say that images are pictorial? Moreover, mental images seem indeterminate in ways that pictures are not: for example, a mental image of a striped tiger need not represent any definite number of stripes. But an ordinary picture of a striped tiger must be determinate with respect to the number of stripes.

Finally, there have been attacks on the evidential underpinnings of the pictorial theory. The introspections on which belief in images is often based are taken to reveal much less about the mind than was traditionally supposed. In particular, it has been argued that what introspection really shows about visual images is not that they are pictorial, but only that what goes on in imagery is experientially much like what goes on in seeing (see Block 1983; INTROSPECTION, PSYCHOLOGY OF).

Perhaps the most influential alternative to the pictorial view in philosophy has been an approach that is now standardly known as 'descriptionalism'. The basic thesis of descriptionalism is that mental images represent in the manner of linguistic descriptions. They are complex representations, structurally like descriptions, within some neural code – representations that are the objects of computational procedures. So, descriptionalism about images is often taken to go hand in hand with the classical computational model of the mind (see LANGUAGE OF THOUGHT; MIND, COMPUTATIONAL THEORIES OF).

Descriptionalism remains popular in philosophy today (see, for example, Dennett 1981), and it also has significant support in contemporary psychology, where it has received its clearest articulation (see, for example, Pylyshyn 1981). Nevertheless in recent years the pictorial view has been making a comeback. In response to a large corpus of experimental data on imagery, psychologists such as Stephen Kosslyn (1980, 1994) have developed an empirical version of the pictorial view that seems more promising than any of its philosophical predecessors.

Kosslyn hypothesizes that the imagery medium, which he calls 'the visual buffer', is shared with visual perception. Each cell in the medium represents a tiny, just noticeable patch of object surface. He begins by conceiving mental images on the model of displays on a cathode ray tube screen attached to a computer. Such displays are generated on the screen by the computer from information that is stored in the computer's memory. This display is spatial and it is made up of a large number of basic units or cells, some of which are illuminated to form a picture. Analogously, according to Kosslyn, mental images may be regarded as functional pictures in a functional spatial medium made up of a large number of basic units or cells, that is, they function with respect to the representation of relative distance relations *as if* they were screen displays, even though, in reality, they need not be laid out in the brain with just the same spatial characteristics as real displays.

This last point is significant, if Kosslyn's view is to be properly understood. Even though the initial model for mental images is provided by screen displays, there is an important respect in which images are *not* like such displays. The displays make no difference to the functioning of the machine. If the screen is shattered, for example, the machine will go on computing just as it did before. The displays are there for *us*, not for the machine. But that is not the case for mental images. They are critical to many cognitive tasks. On Kosslyn's view, mental images are really more like the internal arrays or matrix-like representational structures that computers sometimes manipulate, rather than the external screen displays. So, according to Kosslyn, there is nothing in the computational model of mind that commands adherence to descriptionalism. To be sure, computers manipulate internal descriptions, but they also manipulate internal, picture-like representations too.

This view is motivated by many intriguing experiments, of which I can mention only two. Kosslyn found that when people are told to form mental images of a map, which they have studied carefully, and to focus on one part of the image, the time it takes for them to shift their focus to another part of the image increases linearly with the distance apart of the objects on the map corresponding to the image parts. Kosslyn claims that this experiment shows that mental images can be scanned at fixed speed. This, in turn, is taken to support the pictorialist hypothesis (see Tye 1991).

In another experiment, Shepard and Metzler (1971) discovered that when people were shown drawings of pairs of block figures at different orientations, and were asked whether the members of each pair were congruent, the time it took the subjects to respond increased linearly with the angular separation of the figures. This experiment strongly suggests that mental images can be rotated (again at fixed speeds). This also fits in nicely with the view of images as having a picture-like (or array-like) character.

Not all cognitive scientists agree with pictorialism, however. According to Pylyshyn, Kosslyn's experiments on imagery can be explained by reference to the task demands placed on subjects by the experimenter's instructions together with facts the subjects already tacitly know, for example, the fact that it takes longer to scan greater distances with the eyes. No inner picture-like entity is needed.

It is far from clear that the appeal to tacit knowledge can explain all the imagery data, contrary to Pylyshyn's claim (see Kosslyn 1981). There are, however, other descriptional theories of imagery that have no need of the doctrine of tacit knowledge (for example, Hinton 1979). These versions also do well in explaining the results of Shepard and Cooper's rotation experiment. So, descriptionalism cannot be refuted simply by attacking the doctrine of tacit knowledge.

See also: VISION

References and further reading

Block, N. (ed.) (1981) *Imagery*, Cambridge, MA: MIT Press. (Useful anthology of central papers on both the philosophy and psychology of images, including many of the papers referred to here.)

* —— (1983) 'Mental Pictures and Cognitive Science', *Philosophical Review* 92: 499–542. (Philosophically sophisticated discussion of the current imagery debate.)

* Dennett, D. (1981) 'The Nature of Images and the Introspective Trap', in Block (1981), 51–61. (Imaginative effort to undermine the introspective appeal of positing inner pictures.)

* Hinton, G. (1979) 'Some Demonstrations of the Effects of Structural Descriptions in Mental Imagery', *Behavioral and Brain Sciences* 3: 231–50. (Defence of descriptionalism without an appeal to tacit knowledge of facts about visual processing.)

* Kosslyn, S. (1980) *Image and Mind*, Cambridge, MA: Harvard University Press. (Early discussion by the major proponent in psychology of pictorial imagistic representations.)

* —— (1981) 'The Medium and the Message in Mental Imagery', in Block (1981), 207–44. (Pictorialist's reply to descriptionalism.)

* —— (1994) *Image and Brain: The Resolution of the Imagery Debate*, Cambridge, MA: MIT Press. (Recent defence of imagery in psychology.)

* Pylyshyn, Z. (1981) 'The Imagery Debate: Analog Media Versus Tacit Knowledge', *Psychological Review* 88: 16–45; repr. in Block (1981), 151–206. (Psychologist's defence of descriptionalism.)

* Shepard, R. and Metzler, N. (1971) 'Mental Rotation of Three-Dimensional Objects', *Science* 171: 701–3. (One of the earliest of the experiments adducing non-introspective evidence of pictorial representations.)

* Tye, M. (1991) *The Imagery Debate*, Cambridge, MA: MIT Press. (Summary of the debate between pictorialism and descriptionalism and elaboration of an intermediate position.)

MICHAEL TYE

IMAGINATION

'Imagination' and 'imagine' enjoy a family of meanings, only some of which imply the use of mental imagery. If I ask you to imagine a red flower, I will likely be inviting you to form an image. But if, for example, I say that I imagine that I will go to the party after taking a nap, I am not obviously giving voice to mental imagery. A variety of questions has arisen concerning imagination in its various forms, of which the following four are central. How do internal acts of imagining come to be about particular external objects and states of affairs, actual and non-actual? How are perceptual acts similar to and different from the central cases of imagining? To what extent does routine perception and cognition use similar cognitive resources to creative imagination? Are there any cognitive pursuits in which imagination can play a justificatory role?

1   The intentionality of imagination
2   Imagining and perceiving
3   The imaginative and the routine
4   The justificatory role of imagination

1   The intentionality of imagination

The noun 'imagination' and the verb 'imagine' have a family of meanings rather than a single, sharp, meaning. We may use 'imagination' to indicate an ability to form images of things. Alternatively, 'imagination' can take on a more normative use, to indicate a measure of inventiveness, as when we say that something was done with imagination. Turning to 'imagine', we sometimes use that verb to describe image formation, sometimes as an indication of speculation ('I'd imagine that Jack the Ripper was responsible'), sometimes as an expression of surprise ('Imagine!'), sometimes to attribute error ('He imagines that Mars is the planet closest to the sun'), sometimes interchangeably with 'conceive'. Clearly, not all of these uses directly connote the use of mental imagery.

Exercises of the imagination have intentionality – that is, they are about objects, events and situations, actual and non-actual. We can imagine our best friend, a golden mountain, falling off a ladder, or that Martians visit Earth in the year 3000 (see INTENTIONALITY). Imaginings have not taken centre stage in twentieth-century philosophy of mind, which, perhaps regrettably, has tended increasingly to focus on belief and desire in its discussions of intentionality. Yet philosophers directly concerned with imagination have typically felt the need to provide an account of its intentionality. Taking those exercises of imagination that involve mental imagery as central, some have tried to explain the intentionality of imaginings in terms of the intrinsic properties of mental images, usually their pictorial properties. This approach is widely recognized as problematic. Even those who are willing to reify mental images recognize, first, that one cannot explain their intentionality by appealing to pictorial properties – pictorial properties cannot explain my imagining *my* cottage rather than another one that looks exactly like it – and, second, that there are plenty of mental acts that we call imaginings where mental images do not seem to be at play at all. As a result, accounts of the intentionality of imaginings have, increasingly, appealed to features other then the intrinsic properties of images – some to intentions that lie behind images, some to the mental activity of entertaining propositions, some to similarities between episodes of imagining and episodes of seeing, so that one imagines x just in case one is in a situation that is relevantly similar to seeing x. Of course, since 'imagine' has a variety of meanings, we need not require or expect that a single account will cover all exercises of imagination.

Many imaginative actions also have intentionality. For example, we can, by acting a certain way, make believe that a broom is a horse. It is natural to think that private mental episodes of imagining are conceptually primary, and that we can understand the intentionality of such actions in terms of the private imaginative episodes that cause them. This natural view has not gone unchallenged, however. Those of a more behaviouristic bent tend to recoil at

the idea of private mental imaginings that are relatively inaccessible from a third person, and which could, in principle, be divorced from any link whatever to behaviour (see BEHAVIOURISM, ANALYTIC; PRIVACY). An important source of broadly behaviourist ideas, Gilbert Ryle's *Concept of Mind* (1949), offers a package that eschews the existence of mental images before the mind's eye and instead takes *activities* of make-believe and pretence as the starting point for an account of imagination.

2 Imagining and perceiving

Paradigmatic cases of imagining seem to be akin to the act of seeing something. Aristotle (*On the Soul*; *On Dreams*: c. 360s BC–320s BC) was sufficiently struck by the similarities between imagining and perceiving to claim that both were movements within the single faculty of sense perception.

One similarity that has drawn the attention of philosophers is that of perspective. Paradigmatically, we adopt a particular perspective when we imagine things. Just as it is difficult to see the front and back of a house at the same time, it is difficult to imagine the front and back of a house at the same time. This has been an important datum in discussions of imagination. It has been used in favour of the reification of mental images with pictorial properties, whereby the need for perspective in imagination can be likened to the need for perspective in a painting. And it has been used against the view that paradigmatic cases of imagining can be thought of as the mere entertaining of a set of propositions, for the reason that the entertaining of a set of propositions seems no more restricted to a single perspective than a set of architectural descriptions in a book.

While obviously similar, there are, equally obviously, differences between paradigmatic cases of imagining something and perception. The most obvious difference is external to the agent: when one perceives a thing, that thing will tend to figure in the explanation of the perceiving, but when one imagines a thing, it will typically be inappropriate to invoke that thing in an explanation of the imagining. But there are also differences of a phenomenological kind between imaginings and perceivings, differences that can be sensed from the first person point of view. One difference that has often been highlighted – by Aristotle (*On the Soul*; *On Dreams*), Sartre (1948) and Wittgenstein (1953), for example – is this: imaginings seem subject to the will, perceivings not. This point can be pushed too far. For there do seem to be cases where one's imagination runs riot (to the extent that one's imaginings may be involuntary), and yet there is something quite right about the idea that I can ask you to imagine something in a way that I cannot ask you to perceive or believe something. Other differences between imaginings and perception have been explored. A common idea is that imaginings involve the entertaining of thoughts that are neither affirmed or denied, whereas both perceiving and believing involve taking something as true. Sartre offers a rather different account. When one perceives x, he explains, the presence of x is posited by the perception. When one imagines x, not only is the presence not posited, but its *absence* is posited. For Sartre this contrast is an important clue to the nature of consciousness: the presence posited by perception is used to account for our sense of 'being-in-the-world', the posited absence by imagination being the fundamental exercise of freedom, whereby one withdraws from the world.

3 The imaginative and the routine

When a child comes to recognize dogs as dogs, does it use similar cognitive resources to those used by an artist who comes to see a cloud as a camel? An important theme among some philosophers of the imagination has been the idea that the cognitive faculties, skills or phenomena at work in our adventures of the imagination are also very much involved in the most routine episodes of cognition. In Hume, for example, ordinary categorization of things into kinds and the belief in independent continuous objects are attributed to the very faculty – imagination – that is responsible for storytelling. This faculty, we are told, makes faint copies of perceptions, recombining them in accordance with certain associative habits that Hume sets out to specify.

In Kant, the current theme is even more at work: perceptual experience cannot properly be thought of as a passive registering of information but, rather, requires that one actively apply concepts to sensation so as to see the world as this way or that, an activity for which imagination is responsible (though no implication of illusion is intended). Taking one's sensations as perceptions those of a dog is apparently treated by Kant as importantly analogous to the child's playfully seeing a broom as a horse. Kant's imagination has two species: reproductive, whereby one sees something as being of a kind with something one has previously seen; and productive, whereby a priori concepts are brought to bear upon experience.

In finding continuities between the creative and the routine, one should not obliterate that distinction. One particular kind of exercise of the imagination that calls out for special treatment is the aesthetic variety. While giving imagination an extremely broad role to play, Kant was well aware that there is something distinctive about the aesthetic exercise of the imagination and sought to explain what that was. His central idea was that aesthetic imagination, while thought-provoking, takes us beyond the cognitive domain provided by our concepts. This idea proved crucially important to those Romantic thinkers after Kant who sought to use the aesthetic imagination as the grounding for fundamental metaphysics (see ROMANTICISM, GERMAN §3).

Both Kant and Hume use 'imagination' in an extended and thus unusual way in order to emphasis the putative continuities between the creative and the routine. A number of later writers such as Peter Strawson (1970) and Mary Warnock (1976) have also, in various ways, explored the continuity of imagination with humdrum perception and cognition, though there has been a move away from the idea of explaining the continuity in terms of a single faculty – an organ of the mind – that does various sorts of creative and humdrum work.

4 The justificatory role of imagination

It is important to cognitive excellence that we cultivate imagination in all areas of inquiry. Even in science, it is clear that fruitful inquiry requires an ability to imagine what an explanation for some given phenomenon might look like, imaginatively to see familiar things as somehow representative of theoretical phenomena, and so on.

Granting that imagination is a source of cognitive inspiration, a further question concerns the extent to which an exercise of the imagination can *justify* various kinds of beliefs.

One interesting test case here is provided by geometry, where some thinkers, including Kant and J.S. Mill (1843), have accorded spatial imagination an important justificatory role, while others have insisted that it is merely a useful aid to the geometer.

Meanwhile, in discussions of possibility and necessity, considerable attention has been given to Hume's idea that whatever can be imagined is possible. Hume himself wielded this idea against any putatively necessary link between cause and effect, arguing that one can always at least imagine the cause without the effect. The crucial issue here is whether there is a sense of 'imagine' that can hold the various strands of the Humean view together. If 'imagine' means 'form a mental picture', as in a story, we can well doubt whether an ability to imagine something can justify our believing it possible, because the standards of propriety that we apply when telling stories are quite different to those we apply when the question of genuine possibility is at stake. We may also note in passing that it seems clear that there are possibilities we cannot picture. Meanwhile, there is a use of 'imagine' that is conceptually linked to possibility, but in that sense it is far from clear that I can imagine, say, eating every living creature on this planet.

Finally, in ethics, some (for example Johnson 1985) have suggested that an exercise in imagination is important to the rational evaluation of competing ethical claims. The idea is that the weighting and choice of values, as well as, perhaps, the concrete deployment of abstract or metaphorical moral principles, requires some sort of imaginative engagement with relevant possible situations.

See also: IMAGERY

References and further reading

None of these works is very technical. Russow and Strawson are recommended as introductory pieces.

* Aristotle (*c.*360s BC–320s BC) *On the Soul* and *On Dreams*, in (ed.) R.McKeon *The Basic Works of Aristotle*, New York: Random House, 1941, 535–603 and 618– 25. (Mentioned in §3.)
  Brann, E. (1991) *The World of Imagination*, Lanham, MA: Rowman & Littlefield. (An encyclopedic and cross-disciplinary study of our image-making ability.)
  Casey, E. (1976) *Imagining: A Phenomenological Study*, Bloomington IN: University of Indiana Press. (A prominent philosopher of imagination in the phenomenological tradition.)
* Hume, D. (1739–40) *A Treatise on Human Nature*, ed. L.A. Selby-Bigge. Oxford: Clarendon Press, 1978. (Discussed in §4 and 5. See especially book I, part I and book I, part IV, §2.)
  Johnson, M. (1985) 'Imagination in Moral Judgment', *Philosophy and Phenomenological Research* 46: 265–80. (Explores a topic mentioned in §5.)
* Kant, I. (1787) *Critique of Pure Reason*, trans. N. Kemp Smith, London: Macmillan, 1929. (Discussed in §4, mentioned in §5. See especially 'Transcendental Deduction of the Pure Concepts of Understanding'.)
* —— (1790) *Critique of Judgment*, trans. J.C. Meredith, Oxford: Clarendon Press, 1952. (Discussed in 4. Contains discussion of aesthetic deployment of imagination.)
* Mill, J.S. (1843) A System of Logic in *The Collected Works of J.S. Mill*, vol. 7, book II, ch.5. (Mentioned in §5.)
  Russow, L. (1978) 'Some Recent Work on Imagination', *American Philosophical Quarterly* 15: 57–66. (Useful survey and bibliography.)
* Ryle, G. (1949) *The Concept of Mind*, New York: Barnes and Noble, ch. 8. (Discussed in §2.)
* Sartre, J.-P. (1948) *The Psychology of Imagination*, New York: Philosophical Library. (Discussed in §3.)
* Strawson, P.F. (1970) 'Imagination and Perception' in L. Foster and J.W. Swanson (eds) *Experience and Theory*, 31–54. (Contains excellent discussion of Hume and Kant.)
* Warnock, M. (1976) *Imagination*, London: Faber & Faber. (Useful history of the concept of imagination from Hume to the twentieth century, aimed at bringing out the importance for education of cultivating the imagination.)
* Wittgenstein. L. (1953) *Philosophical Investigations*, trans. E. Anscombe, Oxford: Blackwell. (Mentioned in §3. A lot of suggestive and much-discussed material on imagination.)

J. O'LEARY-HAWTHORNE

IMMANUEL BEN SOLOMON OF ROME (*c.*1261–before 1336)

Immanuel of Rome wrote commentaries on the Bible and poems of a religious, philosophical or jocular nature, concerning the most varied themes. His main topics are conjunction with the 'active intellect' and the superiority of theoretical knowledge. He participated in many of the leading controversies of his time and is interesting for the ways in which he managed to express theoretical ideas poetically.

Immanuel ben Solomon ben Moses ben Jekhutiel was born in Rome and probably studied at the school (*bet midrash*) of Zerahiah ben Isaac Gracian of Barcelona. In 1290–1, during a controversy between Zerahiah Gracian and Hillel BEN SAMUEL OF VERONA on the origin of human language and the rationalistic interpretation of biblical miracles, he sided with the former, writing a polemical letter to Hillel. Following the loss of his property, he left Rome and lived in various towns including Ancona, Perugia and Camerino. At Fermo he found shelter at the house of a patron, who requested that he assemble his scattered verses in a book. After a short time, however, he left for reasons unclear. Immanuel's father-in-law, Rabbi Samuel, was a well-known representative of the Jewish community of Rome. He was probably part of the mission sent by the community to obtain from the Pope, based at that time in Avignon, revocation of the decree of expulsion of the Jews from the Church's territory. After the murder of Rabbi Samuel in 1321, Immanuel sojourned in the towns of Perugia, Orvieto and Ancona and also visited Gubbio and the court of Can Grande della Scala in Verona. Following the revocation of the papal decree, he passed several years in Rome and then returned in 1328 to the house of his patron in Fermo.

In his vast literary-exegetic production Immanuel displays an encyclopedic knowledge, from the biblical and rabbinic literature and the oldest Hebrew mystical works, to such disciplines as poetry, grammar, rhetoric, music, astronomy, mathematics, medicine and philosophy. Belonging to the Aristotelian school, although introducing certain ideas drawn from the Neoplatonists, he deals with the entire gamut of philosophical topics in his exegetic commentaries. If from a literary point of view he is influenced by his immediate environment, in particular the Italian school of *dolce stil nuovo*, be it in the ideas or in style, introducing the fourteen-line Petrarchian sonnet to Hebrew poetry (while applying Arabic metre to the Italian verse), from the philosophic point of view, as is seen in his vast exegetic production, he is part of the Maimonidean-Tibbonian movement.

In his exegetical works, he continues in the tradition of the Tibbonids, adopting some of the formal components of the European university teaching method of the twelfth and thirteenth centuries: a great part of each commentary is actually devoted to the work of previous scholars and only a small part to original exegesis of the text, in accordance with the fourfold division of the role of the writer defined by the Latin scholastics (*scriptor, compilator, commentator, auctor*). In his *Perush ha-Torah* (Commentary on the Pentateuch), Immanuel, under the influence of Abraham IBN EZRA's hermeneutical method, gives a fivefold interpretation of the verses: the Aramaic translation, a grammatical analysis, a literal interpretation, a philosophical interpretation, and a mystical or esoteric explanation. In his other biblical commentaries as well, he begins with a grammatical analysis of the verse, followed by an exposition of the literal and then the philosophical-allegorical meaning, frequently offering several interpretations for the same verse. In the philosophical section of *Perush le-be-Reshit* (Commentary on Genesis), Immanuel interprets the creation of the sublunar world naturalistically. He also addresses topics such as time, motion, the nature of the spheres, the nature of light as identified with the celestial matter (Aristotle's fifth element), the nature of the prime matter, the concept of the creation existing for the sake of man, the origin of human language, the

superiority of the Hebrew language, the doctrine of prophecy, and the role of the imagination in the prophetic revelations.

There are links between his poetical and exegetical-philosophical works. In his best-known literary work, *Machberot* (Compositions), he often expresses himself in allegorical language, characteristic of the Maimonidean-Tibbonian school, in order to convey the same philosophical themes that occupy much of his exegetical commentaries, such as the influence of the heavenly bodies, the cognitive process of the human rational soul and the immortality of the human soul. The *Machberot* are organized as a dialogue between the author and a prince. Scholars are inclined to see in the prince who converses with Immanuel a symbol signifying the 'active intellect', with which the potential intellect of the poet strives to unite. These topics return frequently in the exegetic writings, in which Immanuel repeatedly emphasizes the superiority of intelligible knowledge, of which the highest degree of perfection is represented by the conjunction of the potential intellect with the last of the separate intelligences, namely, the active intellect. It is precisely this conjunction of the potential intellect with the active intellect, allegorically symbolized by the union between the lover and the beloved, that constitutes the main topic of *Perush le-Shir ha-Shirim*, his philosophical commentary on the Song of Songs.

List of works

Immanuel ben Solomon of Rome (before 1328) *Perush le-be-Reshit* (Commentary on Genesis), trans. and ed. F. Michelini Tocci, *Il commento di Emanuele Romano al Capitolo I della Genesi*, Rome: Centro di studi semitici, Istituto di studi del vicino Oriente, 1963. (Immanuel's commentary on the first chapter of Genesis. This Italian edition is introduced by the editor.)

—— (before 1328) *Perush le-Megillat Shir ha-Shirim-ha-Cheleq ha-Filosofi* (Commentary to the Song of Songs – the Philosophical Part), ed. with notes by Y. Ravitzky, Jerusalem: Hebrew University, 1970. (Written as an MA thesis, this edition comprises the Hebrew text of the philosophical section of Immanuel's commentary on the Song of Songs and critical study of it.)

—— (before 1328) *Sefer Mishle 'im Perush Immanuel ha-Romi* (The Book of Proverbs with the Commentary of Immanuel of Rome), ed. D. Goldstein, Jerusalem: The Jewish National and University Library Press and The Magnes Press, 1981. (This edition, which is accompanied by an introduction by the editor, is a facsimile of the Naples edition, *circa* 1487. It is the only completely published edition of a commentary by Immanuel on a biblical text.)

—— (1328) *Machberot Immanuel ha-Romi* (The Compositions of Immanuel of Rome), ed. D. Jarden, Jerusalem: Mossad Bialik, 1957, 2 vols. (Critical edition of Immanuel's major literary work. Jarden provides an introduction to and commentary on the work, and a comprehensive bibliography.)

References and further reading

Cassuto, U. (1971) 'Immanuel (ben Solomon) of Rome', *Encyclopedia Judaica*, Jerusalem: Keter, vol. 8, 1295–8. (Account of his life and works.)

Goldstein, D. (1971) 'Longevity, the Rainbow and Immanuel of Rome', *Hebrew Union College Annual* 42: 243–50. (Analysis of two passages of Immanuel's commentary on Genesis.)

Ravitzky, A. (1981) 'Immanuel of Rome's Commentary on the Book of Proverbs – its Sources', *Kiryat Sefer* 56: 726–39. (Analysis of the sources of Immanuel's commentary on Proverbs.)

Schechterman, D. (1984) 'The Philosophy of Immanuel of Rome in Light of his Commentary on the Book of Genesis', unpublished Ph.D. dissertation, Jerusalem: Hebrew University. (A study of the philosophical section of Immanuel's commentary on Genesis.)

Sermoneta, G. (1965) 'La dottrina dell'intelletto e la "fede filosofica" di Jehudàh e Immanuel Romano', *Studi Medievali* series 3, 6 (2): 3–78. (Compares Immanuel's doctrine of conjunction with the active intellect with that of Judah ben Moses.)

—— (1976) 'Yehudah and Immanuel ha-Romi, "Rationalism Culminating in Mystical Faith"', in M. Hallamish and M. Schwarz (eds) *Revelation, Faith, Reason*, Ramat Gan: Bar Ilan University, 54–70. (Examines Immanuel's doctrine of conjunction with the active intellect.)

Shiloah, A. (1993) 'A Passage by Immanuel ha-Romi on the Science of Music', *Italia* 10: 9–18. (An analysis of a passage of Immanuel's on the science of music included in his commentary on Genesis.)

CATERINA RIGO

IMMORTALITY OF THE SOUL

see SOUL, NATURE AND IMMORTALITY OF THE

IMMUTABILITY

The doctrine of divine immutability consists in the assertion that God cannot undergo real change. Plato and Boethius infer divine immutability from God's perfection, Aristotle from God's being the first cause of change, Augustine from God's having created time. Aquinas derives divine immutability from God's simplicity, his having no parts or attributes which are distinct from himself. All of these arguments finally appeal to aspects of God's perfection; thus, the doctrine of divine immutability grew from a convergence of intuitions about perfection. These intuitions dominated Western thought about God well into the nineteenth century.

The doctrine's foes argue that God's power, providence and knowledge require its rejection. Their arguments contend that since the world does in fact change through time, this must entail change in God. If God responds to changing historical circumstances and to prayers, that would seem to require some sort of change in him (from not responding to responding). And if he does not intervene to prevent a war, for example, then after the war, he will have lost the power to prevent it (assuming, as many do, that God cannot alter the past), so again there is a change of state. Finally, it is argued that God's knowledge of tensed truths (for example, 'it is now noon') must change as what time 'now' is changes. Some responses to these arguments appeal to the claim that God is in some sense outside time.

1   Introduction
2   The case for immutability
3   The case against immutability

1   Introduction

From Philo of Alexandria to the nineteenth century, 'classical theism' ruled Western thought about God, at times without challenge. Prominent in classical theism was the doctrine of divine immutability, that God cannot change in nature, character, intentions, knowledge or any other respect. In such writers as Augustine and Aquinas, God is eternal because he is immutable, and eternality is God's distinctive mode of being. So the doctrine of divine immutability is at the roots of such writers' understandings of God's nature.

The doctrine consists in the assertion that God cannot undergo real change, such as the change involved in learning, growing or reddening. Divine immutability does not entail that God cannot begin or cease to exist, if these are not real changes in the thing which begins or ceases. Nor does it rule out purely extrinsic changes in God, changes such as becoming admired. A thing changes purely extrinsically when it gains a property due entirely to real change in some other thing (see CHANGE §1). The doctrine allows that God becomes creator of a new creature when Moses is born. But it insists that this change in God is purely extrinsic. God always willed that Moses be born at *t*. When *t* arrived, his will took effect in real changes in Moses, his parents, and so on. But the only change in God was that he came to deserve a new title, Creator of Moses.

The doctrine of divine immutability is distinct from the doctrine of divine impassibility. Nothing external can affect an impassible entity. Something could be impassible but mutable if it could change itself, but nothing else could change or affect it. Again, God could be immutable but not impassible. An unchangeable God could feel such responsive emotions as love, pity and compassion. But he would feel them without change and so always feel them. If temporal, such a God would pity our pain before, while and after we suffer. If timeless, such a God would pity our pain timelessly – but responsively, because of our pain. Thus, the doctrine of divine immutability need not 'depersonalize' God.

Western Scriptures insist that God is unchanging in some respects: if he makes a promise, he never alters his intent to keep it, and his basic character (benevolence, holiness, great power) never alters. But Western Scriptures seem to conflict with full divine immutability. Some scriptural texts depict human sin as saddening God and so changing his feelings (for example, Genesis 6: 6), then bringing God to new decisions – for example, to flood the world. According to John, 'the Word became flesh' (1: 14), that is, God took on a human nature he did not always have. The doctrine of divine immutability appears in theologies which take Western Scriptures as authorities. It thus is worth asking why Western theism has so strongly endorsed the doctrine, given that its scriptural roots seem to deny it.

2 The case for immutability

The answer lies in the philosophical sources and methods of Western religious thought. Western thinkers have largely followed the method of perfect-being theology, filling out the concept of God by ascribing to him the properties he must have to count as absolutely perfect (see GOD, CONCEPTS OF §§2–6). God's perfection seems to rule out many sorts of change. If perfect, God is all-knowing. If God learns something new, then before that he was not all-knowing. If God changes his plans, either he did not anticipate what makes him change them and so was not all-knowing, or he was not perfectly wise in making his plans, or he is not perfectly wise in changing them now. So if God is *necessarily* all-knowing and perfectly wise, God *cannot* change in these ways. More general arguments convince adherents of perfect-being theology that God cannot change in any way.

Plato's Theory of Forms inclined many to believe in divine immutability (see PLATO §§10–14). In the *Phaedo* and elsewhere, Plato takes the Forms to be perfect cases of themselves – for example, the Good is a perfectly good thing – and associates the Forms' perfection with their immutability. Theists' liking for Plato's views disposed them to see perfection Plato's way. Plato argues specifically that God cannot improve or deteriorate: if God is already perfect, God cannot change for the better, and being perfect includes being immune to change for the worse (*Republic* II 381b–c). Plato ignores value-neutral changes. But there may be some; is it good or bad to become a nanosecond older? Still, God would undergo value-neutral change either voluntarily or involuntarily. If involuntarily, then either God wishes not to change but cannot avoid it, or God does not care whether he changes, but is subject to forces or conditions he does not control. Either way, God's power seems less than perfect. If voluntarily, God is less than perfectly rational, since he does or undergoes something with literally no value, and hence for which there is no good reason. (If God creates time and thereafter grows older, the good for which he creates time is reason to let himself grow older, and so growing older is not value-neutral.)

Many medieval theists accepted Aristotle's 'cosmological' argument for God's existence (see ARISTOTLE §16; GOD, ARGUMENTS FOR THE EXISTENCE OF §1). Aristotle reasoned that if change occurs, change has a final source, an eternally unchanged changer (*Physics*). He also argued that something is eternally unchanged only if unchangeable (*De caelo*). Later theists thought the role of first cause of change too lofty not to be God's. Writers who took Aristotle's argument or its variants to prove God's existence found themselves committed to divine immutability.

AUGUSTINE (§§7–8) developed Plato's thoughts into an ontology of degrees of existence. As he thought that to exist is to be present, his ontology was also of degrees of presence. Augustine thought immutable things most present. For a thing which changes realizes its nature gradually and never at any point has all the attributes it ever has; a human gains adult stature only by losing the distinctive charms of childhood. A thing which *can* change never actually has all the attributes it possibly has. If a thing is immutable, its entire character and nature are present at any moment: it always is all it can be. Thus, it is more fully present than changing things. So if existence is presentness, immutable things have a higher degree of existence than mutable things. As only highest existence is appropriate to a perfect being, perfect-being theology thus led Augustine to divine immutability.

Augustine also argued specifically (in *The Literal Meaning of Genesis*) that by creating temporal things, God created time itself. As free creator of time, God is intrinsically outside time (as PHILO OF ALEXANDRIA (§5) too saw, in *On the Unchangeableness of God*). But only things which exist in time can change. Hence, if God is intrinsically beyond time, God is intrinsically changeless. Augustine's understanding of God's role as Creator, then, led him to divine timelessness and so to divine immutability. One might move to divine immutability via timelessness today from the widely accepted premises that God is not located in space and (on a standard reading of Special Relativity) things are in time only if in space (see TIME §3).

Temporal beings no longer live the past parts of their lives, losing them forever, and still lack the future parts of their lives. A.M.S. BOETHIUS (§5) saw these traits as defects. So he inferred via perfect-being theology that God has no past or future, living his life in a pure present (see ETERNITY). What has no past or future does not change. For what changes goes from what it was to what it then was going to be, and so has a past and a future. Hence, for Boethius, perfection required changelessness. If it does, necessary perfection – which is better than contingent perfection, and so by perfect-being theology is God's – requires being immutable.

Aquinas (like Augustine) derived divine immutability from the deeper classical theist doctrine of divine simplicity (*Summa theologiae* Ia 9.1). If God is simple, God has no parts of any sort, including distinct attributes. Something which changes becomes partly different (else there was no change) and stays partly the same (else there was not change in one selfsame surviving thing; instead, one thing disappeared and another replaced it). So only things with parts can change. If so, a simple God cannot change. Divine immutability's connection with divine simplicity and the classical theist theory of God's perfection which centres on divine simplicity is one of the deepest reasons for its broad historical appeal; hence one cannot fully explain what moved thinkers to accept it without also treating the motivation for the doctrine of divine simplicity (see SIMPLICITY, DIVINE).

The doctrine of divine immutability was accepted, then, as intuitions about God's perfection and creatorhood came together with the seeming availability of arguments proving an unchangeable First Cause's existence. This convergence of intuitions and arguments from varied sources was the equivalent in philosophy of confirmation from independent tests in science: it strongly warranted belief in divine immutability.

3 The case against immutability

Direct challenges to the doctrine of divine immutability have rested on Scripture and on God's providence, power and knowledge. Scripture depicts God as changing, and so some who read it literally reject divine immutability. Facing such texts, friends of the doctrine defuse the appearance of divine change by appeal to doctrines less speculative and theoretical than divine immutability. Thus, Philo argues from God's foreknowledge of the future and constancy of character that God cannot repent or feel regret, as the Flood story suggests (*On the Unchangeableness of God*). Divine immutability's friends also stress the strengths of the overall theory (classical theism) that includes the doctrine; theories' overall virtues can be good reason to interpret data in a way one might not otherwise consider.

Providence. Believers in divine providence think that God answers prayers and acts in history. Parting the Red Sea (for instance) was a new act in response to historical developments. God first was not doing it, then did it. Thus, God's providence seems to involve him in change, partly because he responds to changes (see PROVIDENCE §1).

Divine immutability's partisans again respond to this by appealing to less theoretical theistic doctrines. They argue that before making the world, God knew what would or might occur and what would or might be prayed if he made it. Thus, God never has new decisions to make. As all-wise, God had full plans to meet events even before making the world. So in creating the world, God built into it 'trigger' mechanisms, which would bring about the responses God willed given the right events. Thus, God made his providential contribution all at once, without changing himself. God willed changing providential responses without having to change his will. God was spontaneous and creative, but expressed his creativity all at once rather than sequentially. Does this mean (oddly) that God answered our prayers before we prayed them? Not if God is also timeless; a timeless God's actions are not *earlier than* anything.

The Incarnation was an especially knotty problem for divine immutability's Christian friends. In general, these argued that all the change it involved occurred in the human nature which God the Son assumed rather than in God; God was eternally ready to be incarnate, and eternally had those experiences of the earthly Christ which the Incarnation makes part of God's life. Through changes in Mary and the infant she bore, what was eternally in God eventually took place on earth (see INCARNATION AND CHRISTOLOGY §§1–2).

Power. Before the Ice Age, God could ensure that there would never be an Ice Age. God has this power now only if he can alter the past. Few think he can (see OMNIPOTENCE §§1, 3). So events seem to change God's power. (If they do, God also is passible; other things affect him. Further, if God once had and no longer has a power, God has a past, and so is in time.) Defenders of divine immutability reply that any change here is purely extrinsic. God has the intrinsic power he always has. He has lost a chance to use it, and so we no longer want to *call* his power a power to prevent an Ice Age. But God is intrinsically as able as ever to do so.

Omniscience. Tensed facts and truths are those we state in tensed sentences such as 'today is Christmas' or 'it is now noon'. An argument that divine immutability is incompatible with God's being omniscient and there being tensed facts and truths can be traced back at least to Islamic Mu'tazilite theologians and Ibn Sina. The argument is this: if God is omniscient, then he knows what time it is now. Now, at t, what God knows is that it is now t. Only at t can God know that it is now t, since only at t is this true. Later, at $t+1$, what God knows is that it is now $t+1$. God can know that it is now $t+1$ only at $t+1$. So the content of God's knowledge changes. So God changes (see OMNISCIENCE §2). In reply, some argue that:

(a) No truths are *irreducibly* tensed. Rather, 'it is now t' really reports (say) that 'at t, it is t'. The latter truth is tenseless. It is true at all times. So one can know it at all times, without change. If God knows tensed truth by knowing tenseless truths, he knows at each time what time it is, without changing.

(b) God can know in other ways the facts we express in irreducibly tensed truths. This is enough to qualify him as omniscient.

(c) What the tensed facts are depends on one's temporal standpoint. If so, then if God is not just immutable but timeless, his omniscience need encompass only tenseless facts plus whatever tensed truths there are in eternity. The latter do not change.

One may also wonder whether the nature of God's mind undercuts the argument. On some externalist theories of mental content, my knowledge that P is a complex consisting of my inner mental state plus certain items in the world. Those items are where and when they are, yet the knowledge is 'in my mind', and so (one presumes) where and when I am. If God is timeless and his mind's contents are as externalism suggests, his state of knowledge might be a complex consisting of his mental state plus temporal items; this knowledge might be 'where and when' God is – that is, timeless – and, as timeless, never change.

See also: ASH'ARIYYA AND MU'TAZILA §4; NEGATIVE THEOLOGY; PROCESS THEISM; NECESSARY BEING; NATURAL THEOLOGY

References and further reading

* Aquinas, Thomas (1266–73) *Summa theologiae*, New York: Benziger Brothers, 1948. (*Locus classicus* of classical theism.)
* Aristotle (mid 4th century BC) *De caelo*, trans. R. Hardie and R. Gaye, in R. McKeon (ed.) *The Basic Works of Aristotle*, New York: Random House, 1941. (A theory of physical change; argues that only what cannot change can be eternally changeless.)
* —— (mid 4th century BC) *Physics*, trans. J. Stocks, in R. McKeon (ed.) *The Basic Works of Aristotle*, New York: Random House, 1941. (Treats the nature of change, and argues for God's existence.)
* Augustine (401–15) *De genesi ad litteram* (The Literal Meaning of Genesis), trans. J.H. Taylor, New York: Newman, 1982, 2 vols. (Clear, interesting source for many aspects of his theology and metaphysics; asserts that God creates time (V.5.12).)
Boethius, A.M.S. (c.522–4) *The Consolation of Philosophy*, trans. H. Stewart, in H. Stewart and E.K. Rand (trans.) *Boethius: The Theological Tractates*, Cambridge, MA: Loeb Classical Library, Harvard University Press, 1936. (Includes his most extensive treatment of time, change and eternity.)
Gale, R. (1986) 'Omniscience–Immutability Arguments', *American Philosophical Quarterly* 23 (4): 319–35. (Very full statement of the argument, with intricate exploration of possible replies. Rigorous but not technical.)
Hallman, J. (1981), 'The Mutability of God: Tertullian to Lactantius', *Theological Studies* 42 (3): 373–93. (Historical survey, mostly on divine emotion; blurs the distinction between immutability and impassibility.)
Hartshorne, C. (1948) *The Divine Relativity*, New Haven, CT: Yale University Press. (Freewheeling, many-faceted critique of the doctrine of divine immutability, and an argument for divine passibility.)
Helm, P. (1988) *Eternal God*, New York: Oxford

University Press. (Includes a nice treatment of the omniscience–immutability issue.)

Kretzmann, N. (1966) 'Omniscience and Immutability', *Journal of Philosophy* 63 (14): 409–21. (Independent rediscovery of the medieval omniscience–immutability argument.)

Leftow, B. (1991) *Time and Eternity*, Ithaca, NY: Cornell University Press. (Treats divine immutability and related issues in defending divine timelessness. Rigorous but not technical.)

Mann, W. (1987) 'Immutability and Predication', *International Journal for Philosophy of Religion* 22 (1): 21–39. (Elegant defence; traces the doctrine of divine immutability to divine simplicity.)

* Philo of Alexandria (first half of 1st century AD) *On the Unchangeableness of God*, trans. F. Colson and G. Whitaker, in F. Colson and G. Whitaker (trans.) *Philo*, vol. 3, Cambridge, MA: Loeb Classical Library, Harvard University Press, 1960. (Pioneering defence of divine immutability in the face of recalcitrant scriptural texts.)

* Plato (*c.*386–380 BC) *Phaedo*, trans. G. Grube, Indianapolis, IN: Hackett, 1977. (Develops his theory of Forms.)

* Plato (*c.*386–380 BC) *Republic*, trans. G. Grube and C. Reeve, Indianapolis, IN: Hackett, 1992. (Treats Forms and divine immutability (II 381b–c) during a broad discussion of human nature and political theory.)

Sorabji, R. (1983) *Time, Creation and the Continuum*, Ithaca, NY: Cornell University Press. (Valuable, clear treatment of many issues related to divine immutability.)

BRIAN LEFTOW

IMPARTIALITY

On the one hand, most of us feel that we are permitted, even required, to give special consideration to the interests of ourselves and our loved ones; on the other hand, we also recognize the appeal of a more detached perspective which demands equal consideration for the interests of all. Among writers in the utilitarian tradition, some insist that the strictly impartial perspective is the only one that is ethically tenable, while others argue that a measure of institutionalized partiality can be justified as a means to maximizing welfare. An alternative tradition, stemming from Kant, sees the demand for impartiality as deriving from the importance of fairness and equal respect for persons, but tends to leave open the degree of partiality permitted. Finally, the Aristotelian conception of ethics offers a justification of partiality based on the structure of those virtuous dispositions of character (such as those involved in friendship and self-esteem) which are required for developing our distinctively human potentialities.

1   The conflict between impartiality and partiality
2   Utilitarian approaches
3   Impartiality, fairness and respect
4   The perspective of virtue ethics

1   The conflict between impartiality and partiality

Impartiality commands widespread approval. When an action is exposed as an instance of bias we disapprove precisely because the agent has allowed special ties to particular individuals or groups to affect what ought to have been a fair and impartial decision. Some philosophers, indeed, see impartiality as part of the essence of the moral outlook, believing that to adopt that outlook is, in Adam Smith's famous phrase (1759), to try to put oneself in the position of an 'impartial spectator' of mankind. Pulling in the opposite direction, however, are the special commitments that most human beings have towards their close friends and loved ones (see FAMILY, ETHICS AND THE; FRIENDSHIP; LOVE §2). For a parent to treat a child with no more than the impartial consideration owed to any human being seems cold and unloving. If morality is concerned with the good for humankind, then it must surely find a legitimate place for the development of those special, inherently partialistic relationships which are virtually inseparable from our human nature. A major task for moral philosophy is to examine, perhaps to try to resolve, the apparent conflict between those of our ethical intuitions which seem to demand an impartial stance, and those which apparently permit, or even require, a large measure of partiality.

The importance of impartiality in moral thinking is given force by the thought that although my own life may appear 'special' from my personal perspective, that specialness seems to evaporate from the wider perspective of humanity as a whole. In assessing the rightness of an action, by reference to its consequences for general welfare, Jeremy BENTHAM, as quoted by J.S. Mill (1861), insisted on the maxim 'everybody to count for one, nobody for more than one', which seems to rule out skewing the calculation in favour of particular individuals or groups. Hence if benefiting X produces a greater overall good than benefiting Y, it is right to benefit X; the fact that I have some special tie to Y (who could be, for example, my brother, or a member of my club, clan or race) ought presumably to make no difference. William

Godwin (1793) devised a famous case to illustrate this: if two people (a philanthropic archbishop and a chambermaid) are trapped in a burning building, and I can rescue only one, then I should rescue the one who can do most good for mankind as a whole. Given that this is the archbishop, then it is he who should be rescued; I should resolutely set aside the fact that the chambermaid happens to be my mother, for 'what magic is in the pronoun "my" that should justify us in overturning the decisions of impartial truth?' ([1793] 1985: 170). Such resolute impartialism offers a potentially salutary challenge to many of our unreflective patterns of conduct, but, for its critics, it risks setting an unrealistic standard for action which few if any are capable of incorporating systematically into their daily lives.

2   Utilitarian approaches

Utilitarians have sometimes seemed quite prepared to embrace the austere consequences of the impartialist perspective (see UTILITARIANISM). Thus Peter Singer (1979) suggests that if I am dishing out food to hungry children, then I should make my own children wait in line; though favouring them might be psychologically understandable, from the ethical point of view it is suspect. There are two serious objections to any approach which yields this result. The first has the form of a 'slippery slope' argument. If all personal favouritism is ethically dubious, then we are apparently required to forego any good whatsoever for ourselves and our loved ones when an assignment of the relevant resources to others would produce greater global utility. Yet this implies not just (as most of us might on reflection accept) that I should give up luxuries when the money might be spent on famine relief, but that even the decisions to spend time and money on providing a home for my family, or on working at my own chosen career, are ethically tainted. In short, the insistence on impartialism seems to entail the unbearably demanding result of uncompromising ethical 'globalism': as long as one surplus penny remains which could benefit those in greater need, nothing short of a life of near total self-sacrifice will stand up to ethical scrutiny (see HELP AND BENEFICENCE). Defenders of strict impartialism, such as Shelly Kagan (1989), would reply that the fact we feel uncomfortable with this result is no reason to reject the underlying theory, for who ever imagined that to act morally was supposed to be easy?

Here, however, a second objection comes to the fore. There seems a risk that what the impartialist apparently requires us to give up will include those very ties and commitments which make human life worth living, the personal projects (raising a family,

developing long-term friendships, organizing a career) which are the very key to realizing our human potentialities. The point goes beyond the empirical observation that all these projects in fact require an enormous expenditure of time and energy on localized and individual (as opposed to general and global) welfare. For it appears, as Bernard Williams (1973) has argued persuasively, that our very individuality, our integrity as persons, depends largely on a self-oriented conception of ourselves (and by extension our loved ones) as special. Without that sense of specialness, and the partiality towards ourselves and those near to us which it implies, our very humanity is threatened: a being who lacked this orientation would be a mere worker bee in the utility hive, not a recognizable human being (see MORALITY AND IDENTITY §4).

These observations pave the way for a response structured by an indirect (institutional or 'rule') version of utilitarianism. If human happiness indeed requires us to develop self-oriented projects and ties, then the way to maximize global utility will turn out to be not to require austerely impartial behaviour from all, but rather to allow humans to develop those institutions, practices and relationships which permit them to fulfil their human nature (see UTILITARIANISM §§3, 5). The argument will then run in a way analogous to that which led Adam Smith to suggest that the pursuit of individual self-interest is in fact the best way to secure general happiness. Given this framework, the utilitarian may well recommend that each of us devote time and attention to self-oriented projects, such as raising families and forming close personal relationships; but at a more general and abstract level, the justification for such social structures will still be a firmly consequentialist one, namely that the fostering of relevant institutions is the best way for global happiness to be secured. Such an approach has the advantage of providing a critical framework for trying to distinguish those types of partiality which are permissible from those which are not. Thus, public institutions which foster cronyism, nepotism and patterns of preference based on gender or race may be condemned as diminishing the prospects for the long-term maximization of global happiness, while family loyalties and ties of friendship may be seen as benign. A further advantage is to allow room for preserving intuitions about the appeal of impartiality as an ethical ideal; for the 'benign' nature of those institutions which are justified by this type of argument will hinge precisely on the fact that they are the kinds of institution which would be approved by an impartial and detached spectator of the global human predicament.

3 Impartiality, fairness and respect

A problem with trying to link the value of impartiality to the demands of welfare maximization is that it seems possible to imagine that global utility might be maximized by partialistic institutions of an (intuitively) objectionable kind. A master race might secure enormous benefits by preserving entrenched institutions according systematic preferential treatment to their own kind; and the resulting highly partialistic system might be one which would have to commend itself to an impartial spectator interested in global utility. This line of thought suggests the need for a conception of impartiality that goes beyond purely aggregative and utilitarian concerns. On one such conception, a truly impartial evaluator would require not just the best overall result, but one that would be recognized by all parties as acceptable, irrespective of their position in the social order. This is the thought behind John Rawls' device of the 'veil of ignorance' (1971), designed to secure fairness by ensuring that social institutions are ones we could in principle approve of even if we had to change places with the least advantaged of our fellow citizens (see RAWLS, J. §1). It is not, however, clear that the application of these conditions yields one uniquely 'rational' choice. Just as two equally impartial judges might favour, respectively, stern retribution and maximum leniency, so one impartial deliberator might prescribe highly competitive social institutions which allowed the weak to go to the wall, while another might favour heavy taxation to fund lavish welfare benefits. Pure impartiality, in short, appears to be merely a 'meta-requirement', demanding consistency in the application of rules to all concerned, but not providing clear decisions about the ethical credentials of various possible social institutions.

The approach of Rawls owes much to the tradition in ethics started by Kant (1785), which, with its stress on respect for persons, would prohibit any action or institution which treats individuals merely as a means to an end (see KANTIAN ETHICS; RESPECT FOR PERSONS). Although this 'categorical imperative' is silent on the ethical status of personal ties and commitments, it suggests room for a compromise between partialistic ethics and impersonal duty: love and other partialistic emotions and patterns of conduct are permitted, so long as they do not violate (impartially defined) Kantian rules of justice and respect for others. But while such a compromise might operate satisfactorily in an economy of abundance, the preferential assignments demanded by the partialist will, in an economy of scarcity, inevitably raise questions about our ethical obligations to relieve suffering elsewhere. In devoting resources to myself and my loved ones, perhaps I may not formally be violating Kantian rules against treating others without respect, but I am certainly reserving for myself goods which might be used to enable others to reach the level of dignity and self-respect which I take for granted in pursuing my own partialistic concerns and projects. The conflict between the autocentric perspective of the partialist and the more universal stance of both deontological and consequentialist ethics seems inescapable (see DEONTOLOGICAL ETHICS).

4 The perspective of virtue ethics

The tradition of so-called 'virtue ethics' approaches these questions from a rather different standpoint (see VIRTUE ETHICS). For Aristotle, the dispositions of character to be fostered are those which develop our potentiality for human fulfilment, and though impartial virtues such as justice figure importantly in the resulting blueprint for the good life, many of the other virtues, most notably those connected with love and friendship, seem inherently partialistic, involving special commitments to those to whom I am bound by close personal ties (*Nicomachean Ethics*) (see ARISTOTLE §§25–6; VIRTUES AND VICES). Aristotle draws several interesting comparisons between my attitude to my friends and my attitude to myself, and it is striking that he allows a perfectly legitimate ethical space for self-love, or self-esteem. Aristotelian virtue thus allows me, in the assignment of goods, to give special preference to a particular individual, myself. Several twentieth-century philosophers have laid great stress on universalizability as a test for morality, holding that there is no place in ethics for principles which contain an ineliminable reference to particular individuals (see UNIVERSALISM IN ETHICS). It seems, though, that there is nothing to stop the advocate of Aristotelian-style partialism allowing that every human being is entitled to accord special preference to themselves and their loved ones, so that there is a sense in which the ethics of partiality do, after all, pass the test of universalizability. The difficulty remains, however, that the assignment of time and resources necessary to develop a rich and fulfilling life for myself and my close friends will inevitably mean that less remains for those outside the charmed partialistic circle; Aristotle himself was largely unbothered by slavery. That said, it remains an attractive feature of the Aristotelian approach that it allows due ethical value to those deep personal concerns and emotional commitments that appear to be crucial ingredients in any plausible recipe for a good human life. Ethical excellence, is, Aristotle insisted, concerned with feelings as well as actions; a significant part of our fulfilment lies in the cultivation of harmonious and enriching habits of feeling (see MORALITY AND EMOTIONS §3). Since so much that is of value in our emotional life seems to have an ineradicable dimension of particularity and partiality, any system of morality which fails to allow scope for that dimension risks being seriously defective.

See also: EQUALITY; FEMINIST ETHICS; JUSTICE; MORALITY AND IDENTITY §2

References and further reading

* Aristotle (*c.* mid 4th century BC) *Nicomachean Ethics*, trans. with notes by T. Irwin, Indianapolis, IN: Hackett Publishing Company, 1985, books II, VIII, IX. (Book II sets out the framework for virtue ethics, while books VIII and IX are particularly concerned with its application to friendship and self-love.)

Becker, L. *et al.* (1991) 'Symposium on Impartiality and Ethical Theory', *Ethics* 101 (4). (A collection of papers discussing various aspects of the debate between partialists and impartialists. Contributors include Lawrence Blum, Barbara Herman, Marcia Baron and John Cottingham.)

* Godwin, W. (1793) *An Enquiry Concerning Political Justice*, London: G.G. and J. Robinson, 3rd edn, 1798; 3rd edn, ed. I. Kramnick, Harmondsworth: Penguin, 1985, book II, ch. 2. (Introduces the dilemma of whether to rescue a philanthropic archbishop or a chambermaid, who happens to be my mother, from a burning building.)

Hare, R.M. (1981) *Moral Thinking*, Oxford: Oxford University Press, ch. 8. (Discusses the various levels at which moral thinking occurs, contrasting a ground floor level at which partialistic commitments might operate with a more detached perspective where impartiality is paramount.)

* Kagan, S. (1989) *The Limits of Morality*, Oxford: Clarendon Press. (Uncompromising impartialism defended from a consequentialist perspective.)

* Kant, I. (1785) *Grundlegung zur Metaphysik der Sitten*, trans. H.J. Paton, *Groundwork of the Metaphysics of Morals* (originally *The Moral Law*), London: Hutchinson, 1948; repr. New York: Harper & Row, 1964, ch. 2. (Presents the highly influential theory of the 'categorical imperative' and the principle of respect for persons.)

* Mill, J.S. (1861) *Utilitarianism*, ed. M. Warnock, London: Fontana, 1962, 319. (Mill here cites Bentham's dictum 'everybody to count for one, nobody for more than one'.)

Nagel, T. (1991) *Equality and Partiality*, New York: Oxford University Press. (A compelling account of the conflict between the impersonal and the personal perspectives in ethics.)

* Rawls, J. (1971) *A Theory of Justice*, Cambridge MA: Harvard University Press, part I. (Outlines the 'veil of ignorance' as a device for ensuring ethical principles are decided from an impartial perspective.)

* Singer, P. (1979) *Practical Ethics*, Cambridge: Cambridge University Press; 2nd edn, 1993, chaps 1, 8. (Strict impartiality defended as a fundamental feature of the ethical point of view. For the 'bowl of rice' example, which suggests that if a person is dishing out food to hungry children, then they should make their own children wait in line like all the others, see the 2nd edn, 233.)

* Smith, A. (1759) *The Theory of Moral Sentiments*, ed. D.D. Raphael and A.L. Macfie, Oxford: Clarendon Press, 1976, part I, section I, ch. 5, part II, section I, ch. 2. (Identifies the moral perspective with that of the 'impartial spectator'.)

* Williams, B. and Smart, J.J.C. (1973) *Utilitarianism, For and Against*, Cambridge: Cambridge University Press, part II. (Debate between a supporter and a critic of Utilitarianism. For Williams' objection that our integrity as persons depends largely on a self-oriented conception of ourselves, see section 5, 108–18.)

JOHN COTTINGHAM

IMPERATIVE LOGIC

Imperatives lie at the heart of both practical and moral reasoning, yet they have been overshadowed by propositions and relegated by many philosophers to the status of exclamations. One reason for this is that a sentence's having literal meaning seems to require its having truth-conditions and 'Keep your promises!' appears to lack such conditions, just as 'Ouch!' does. One reductionist attempt to develop a logic of imperatives translates them into declaratives and construes inferential relations among the former in terms of inferential relations among the latter. Since no such reduction seems fully to capture the meaning of imperatives, others have expanded our notion of inference to include not just truth- but also satisfaction-preservation, according to which an imperative is satisfied just in case what it enjoins is brought about.

A logic capturing what is distinctive about imperatives may shed light on the question whether an 'ought' is derivable from an 'is'; and may elucidate the claim that morality is, or comprises, a system of hypothetical imperatives. Furthermore, instructions, which are often

717

formulated as imperatives ('Take two tablets on an empty stomach!'), are crucial to the construction of plans of action. A proper understanding of imperatives and their inferential properties may thus also illuminate practical reasoning.

1 **Jörgensen's dilemma and Ross's 'paradox'**
2 **Reductionist approaches**
3 **Non-reductionist approaches**

1 Jörgensen's dilemma and Ross's 'paradox'

Any attempt to codify the logical properties of imperatives must grapple with the following dilemma, first formulated by Jörgensen (1938). On the one hand there appear to be cogent inferences involving imperatives, as in:

> Keep your promises!
>
> This is a promise of yours.
> _____
> Keep this promise!

On the other hand, the only widely agreed-upon conception of good inference is in terms of truth-preservation: a set of sentences Γ implies a sentence ϕ just in case there is no possible situation in which all members of Γ are true and ϕ is false. Yet evidently this conception of cogency in terms of truth-preservation cannot be used to assess the validity of arguments utilizing imperatives, for imperatives are not, *prima facie*, either true or false. Hence either we deny, implausibly, that there are good inferences involving imperatives; or we grant it and then face the question, to what conception of inference are we appealing?

This challenge is to be distinguished from another, less urgent concern first formulated by Ross (1944) and echoed by Williams (1963). According to the classical logic of truth functions, any proposition P implies $P \vee Q$, for any Q. Similarly, it would seem that even the most conservative imperative logic would countenance the inference

> Post this letter!
> _____
> Post this letter or burn it!

Demanding that the auditor either post the letter or burn it may be seen as granting permission to do either. But then if anyone committed to the premise is thereby committed to the conclusion above, it may seem that demanding that the auditor post the letter is implicitly granting permission to burn it. This reasoning vacillates on the concept of commitment. We may distinguish between commitment to the content of a sentence and commitment to performing the speech

act of uttering that sentence with its characteristic illocutionary force. One who utters the premise of the above inference is not thereby committed to performing the speech act of demanding that the auditor either post the letter or burn it, just as one who asserts P is not thereby committed to asserting $P \vee Q$. (Asserting P merely commits one to the truth of $P \vee Q$.) Yet it is only the performance of the speech act of uttering an imperative that grants permission to the auditor to satisfy that sentence by satisfying any disjunct that it contains: commitment merely to the content of that sentence does not suffice to grant permission of any kind.

To others a logic of imperatives may seem trivially simple. It is common to distinguish between two elements in an imperative sentence, one of which is shared with indicative sentences and the other not: from both 'Shut the door!' and 'The door is shut' we can abstract a reference to the state of affairs of the door's being shut. The former sentence enjoins that state of affairs while the latter asserts that it obtains. Following Stenius (1967), let us say that what is common to the two sentences is the 'sentence-radical', while what distinguishes them is their 'modal element'. One might urge that the validity of arguments involving imperatives should be understood just in terms of sentence-radicals, since these require no modification in our 'truth-preservation' conception of validity. But this leaves us with no account of when and where modal elements can occur in valid arguments. It is unclear, for instance, how without *ad hoc* postulation we are to avoid countenancing:

> Shut the door!
> _____
> The door is shut.

Approaches to the logic of imperatives may be seen as grappling with one or other horn of Jörgensen's dilemma.

2 Reductionist approaches

Reductionist approaches attempt to show that there is no good inference that crucially involves imperatives; at best, any inference that seems to involve imperatives can be replaced with an equivalent one comprising only indicatives, to which the truth-preservation conception of validity applies. To the objection that only propositions appear to be truth-bearers, reductionists might reply that the difference in grammatical mood between imperatives and declaratives is an idiosyncrasy of idiom; a mere reflection of the fact that these two types of sentence are typically used to perform different kinds of speech acts. The difference of mood need be of no more interest to the logician than is the difference between the active and passive voice in declarative propositions.

So with what propositions are imperatives to be identified? On one proposal, 'Shut the door!' is equivalent to 'You will shut the door'. This equation is perhaps suggested by the fact that the latter type of sentence is often used to convey a command; if correct then imperative inference may be understood in terms of inferential relations among statements in the future tense (see TENSE AND TEMPORAL LOGIC). Yet this identification falls foul of our ability to make predictions without formulating any kind of directive: a parole officer might say to a repeat offender, 'You will steal again', without enjoining him to crime. Others have contended that 'Shut the door!' is equivalent to 'I want you to shut the door'; here imperative inference is a direct consequence of the logical properties of attitude locutions (see PROPOSITIONAL ATTITUDE STATEMENTS §§1–2). But one can, and may have to, command something one does not want. Furthermore, recipes and instructions are often formulated with imperatives but appear not to be reports of anybody's desires.

It has also been proposed that 'Shut the door!' is equivalent to 'Either you are going to shut the door, or X will happen', where X is something bad for the person being addressed. Yet a speaker might reasonably utter an imperative such as 'Keep your promises!' knowing full well that no harm will come the auditor if they fail to obey. Second, the theory implies that for any action Y, either 'Do Y!' or 'Don't do Y!' is true. A distinct, 'performative' analysis of the imperative has it that 'Shut the door!' is equivalent to 'I order you to shut the door' (see PERFORMATIVES). This proposal requires an imperative to be as multiply ambiguous as there are distinct illocutionary acts that can be performed with that sentence; on a given occasion of utterance the same sentence might mean, 'I request that you shut the door'. This theory is thus committed to a multiplication of senses for what seem to be univocal sentences.

The most popular reduction may be traced to Kant (1785) and equates 'Shut the door!' with the 'deontic' proposition 'You should (or ought to) shut the door'. On this approach imperative inference is a matter of inferential relations among deontic locutions (see DEONTIC LOGIC). We may distinguish between two species of imperative – fiats and directives – only the latter of which are directed to a particular person or group of persons. Clearly, directives are the much more common form and for these it would seem that being directed to a particular individual is part of their content. This is perhaps why imperatives are so naturally issued with vocatives, as in 'Mary, make sure

John does his homework'. In contrast to an imperative, the truth of a deontic proposition does not, as such, lay obligations upon any one person rather than another. 'It is obligatory that A' does not discriminate among the various people who might be obliged to make it the case that A. This even holds for 'John should see to it that A': a speaker might want to lay responsibility on Mary for making John see to it that A, but will not be able to do so with just deontic propositions. A deontic reduction lacks the resources to capture the directedness of imperatives.

3 Non-reductionist approaches

Grappling with the other horn of Jörgensen's dilemma involves formulating a notion of inference to include things other than truth-bearers. Since validity as here characterized is a semantic notion, an account of valid reasoning with imperatives would require assigning semantic values to imperative sentences. One proposal stems from Lemmon (1965), according to whom the basic semantic value of an imperative is to be that of its being 'in force' (or not). Thus when a commanding officer says, 'Clean the latrine!' to a soldier, the command is typically in force, whereas if the soldier were to say the same to the commanding officer this would typically not be the case. This suggests the following criterion of validity:

> An argument is valid if and only if, given that all the directive premises are in force and all the declarative premises are true, then the conclusion is in force if it is a directive and true if it is a declarative.

This definition of validity sheds no light on the question whether, for instance, the being in force of 'Take all the boxes!' implies the being in force of 'Take this thing!' when the speaker is unaware that this thing is one of the boxes. Lemmon's proposal is thus a mere schema for a definition. A more explicit proposal flows from the work of Hofstadter and McKinsey (1939), Rescher (1966) and Sosa (1967). Say that an imperative is 'satisfied' just in case its sentence-radical (see above) is true. One might suggest that an argument is valid if and only if, whenever its imperative premises are satisfied and its indicative premises are true, then its conclusion is satisfied if imperative and true if indicative. This definition would explain the apparent validity of the inference with which §1 of this entry began. On the other hand, it countenances the inference from 'Shut the door!' to 'The door is shut'.

Sosa attempts a definition in terms of satisfaction-preservation for arguments consisting only of imperatives, some of which may be hypothetical in form.

Let us say that imperatives such as 'If it rains, close the window!' are 'satisfied' if it rains and the window is closed; 'violated' if it rains and the window is not closed; and 'neutral' if it does not rain. (All imperatives can be construed as hypothetical if we imagine $P \lor \sim P$ as antecedent when none is otherwise specified.) We now say:

> A directive argument is valid just in case (1) if its premises are satisfied then the conclusion is satisfied and (2) if the conclusion is violated then at least one of its premises is violated.

This definition can account for the validity of

> If you read this book, come to see me!
>
> Read this book!
> _____
> Come to see me!

On the other hand, the definition renders invalid the apparently correct

> If it rains, close the window!
> _____
> If it rains and thunders, close the window!

A cognate definition given by Rescher founders on its inability to treat the relation 'is validly inferable from' as being transitive.

There is today no accepted account of imperative inference. Instead research focuses upon the semantics of imperatives while stopping short of formulating a calculus. Yet if these semantic questions can be answered it may be hoped that new proposals for understanding imperative inference may grow in the light the answers shed. Until that time reductionist approaches will continue to be attractive.

See also: EMOTIVE MEANING; LOGICAL AND MATHEMATICAL TERMS, GLOSSARY OF; PRAGMATICS; QUESTIONS; SPEECH ACTS

References and further reading

Austin, J.L. (1962) *How to Do Things with Words*, Oxford: Clarendon Press. (A classic work in the theory of speech acts. Defends a version of the 'I order you to...' species of reduction.)

Beardsley, E. (1944) 'Imperative Sentences in Relation to Indicatives', *Philosophical Review* 53: 175–85. (Early proponent of non-reductionism.)

Belnap, N. (1989) 'Declaratives Are Not Enough', *Philosophical Studies* 59: 1–30. (Attacks the sentence-radical/modal element distinction as failing to capture the distinctive content of imperatives.)

Bohnert, H. (1945) 'On the Semiotic Status of Commands', *Philosophy of Science* 12: 302–15. (Argues for the reduction of imperatives to sen-tences of the form 'Either you conform or something bad will happen'.)

Castañeda, H.-N. (1975) *Thinking and Doing: The Philosophical Foundations of Institutions*, Dordrecht: Reidel. (Wide-ranging study of imperatives, particularly their semantics and their role in practical reasoning.)

Chellas, B. (1969) 'Imperatives', *Theoria* 37: 114–29. (Formulates a logic for imperatives, treating them as reducible to deontic propositions.)

Frege, G. (1892) 'Über Sinn und Bedeutung', *Zeitschrift für Philosophie und philosophische Kritik* 100: 25–50; trans. M. Black, 'On Sense and Reference', in *Translations from the Philosophical Writings of Gottlob Frege*, ed. P.T. Geach and M. Black, Oxford: Blackwell, 2nd edn, 1960. (Historically important formulation of a distinction between illocutionary force and semantic content.)

Hamblin, C.L. (1987) *Imperatives*, New York: Blackwell. (Best full-length treatment to date of the grammar, semantics and pragmatics of imperatives. Includes an extensive bibliography.)

Hare, R.M. (1952) *The Language of Morals*, Oxford: Clarendon Press. (Propounds the centrality of imperatives in ethical discourse. Distinguishes between phrastic and neustic.)

* Hofstadter, A. and McKinsey, J.C.C. (1939) 'On the Logic of Imperatives', *Philosophy of Science* 6: 446–57. (Mentioned in §3. Early formulation of the notion of satisfaction as a distinctive semantic value for imperatives.)

Huntley, M. (1984) 'The Semantics of English Imperatives', *Linguistics and Philosophy* 7: 103–33. (Sophisticated defence of a semantic treatment of imperatives as differing from propositions in lacking an indexical element.)

* Jörgensen, J. (1938) 'Imperatives and Logic', *Erkenntnis* 7: 288–98. (Mentioned in §1. Explains the central challenge facing attempts to formulate an imperative logic.)

* Kant, I. (1785) *Grundlegung zur Metaphysik der Sitten*, trans. H.J. Paton, *Groundwork of the Metaphysics of Morals*, London: Harper Perennial, 1989. (Mentioned in §2. Defends a reduction of imperatives to deontic propositions.)

* Lemmon, E.J. (1965) 'Deontic Logic and the Logic of Imperatives', *Logique et Analyse* 8: 39–71. (Mentioned in §3. Sketches a conception of imperative inference in terms of the concept of an imperative's being in force.)

Lewis, D.K. (1970) 'General Semantics', repr. in *Philosophical Papers*, vol. 1, Oxford: Oxford University Press, 1983. (A classic paper in the philosophy of language. Defends a version of the 'I order you to...' species of reduction.)

* Rescher, N. (1966) *The Logic of Commands*, London: Routledge & Kegan Paul. (Mentioned in §3. Highly readable general treatment of imperative logic as well as an excellent introduction to the topic. Defends a notion of imperative inference in terms of satisfaction-preservation.)

* Ross, A. (1944) 'Imperatives and Logic', *Philosophy of Science* 11: 30–46. (Mentioned in §1. Argues for the impossibility of a non-trivial imperative logic.)

Searle, J.R. and Vanderveken, D. (1985) *Foundations of Illocutionary Logic*, Cambridge: Cambridge University Press. (Develops some logical features of devices used to indicate illocutionary force and inferential relations among various types of speech act.)

* Sosa, E. (1967) 'The Semantics of Imperatives', *American Philosophical Quarterly* 4: 57–64. (Mentioned in §3. Defends a notion of imperative inference in terms of satisfaction-preservation.)

* Stenius, E. (1967) 'Mood and Language-Game', *Synthese* 17: 254–74. (Mentioned in §1. Defends a distinction between the sentence-radical and modal element.)

* Williams, B.A.O. (1963) 'Imperative Inference', *Analysis*, supplement 23: 30–6. (Mentioned in §1. Following Ross, argues for the impossibility of an imperative logic.)

MITCHELL GREEN

IMPLICATURE

A term used in philosophy, logic and linguistics (especially pragmatics) to denote the act of meaning or implying something by saying something else. A girl who says 'I have to study' in response to 'Can you go to the movies?' has implicated (the technical verb for making an implicature) that she cannot go. Implicatures may depend on the conversational context, as in this example, or on conventions, as when a speaker says 'He was clever but poor', thereby implying – thanks to the conventional usage of the word 'but' – that poverty is unexpected given intelligence. Implicature gained importance through the work of H.P. Grice. Grice proposed that conversational implicatures depend on a general principle of rational cooperation stating that people normally try to further the accepted purpose of the conversation by conveying what is true, informative, relevant and perspicuous. The extent and nature of the dependence, and the precise maxims involved, are matters of controversy. Other issues include whether certain implications are implicatures rather than presuppositions or parts of the senses (literal meanings) of the words used.

1 Speaker meaning and implication
2 Speaker implicature
3 Utterance and sentence implicature
4 Conventional versus conversational implicature
5 Conversational maxims and the cooperative principle
6 Theoretical importance

1 Speaker meaning and implication

H.P. GRICE (1989: chaps 5, 6 and 14) drew an important distinction between what a speaker means or implies, and what a sentence or other expression means or implies. The sentence 'The aeroplane is a mile long' means that the aeroplane is 5,280 feet long, and implies that it is over 3,279 feet long. Nevertheless, it would be most unlikely for a speaker uttering the sentence to mean or imply such things unless he were joking. More likely, the speaker would be exaggerating, meaning simply that the plane is enormous compared with typical planes. A speaker using the sentence in a coded message might mean something completely unrelated to its English meaning.

As a first approximation, word meaning may be characterized as *conventional* speaker meaning. Whereas we could conceivably use 'bachelor' to mean just about anything, we conventionally mean 'unmarried male', which is what the word means. Speaker meaning is determined by the intentions of the individual speaker (see COMMUNICATION AND INTENTION). While the exact intentions required are a matter of controversy, it is plausible that a speaker S means that the plane is enormous only if S used the sentence to express the belief that the plane is enormous. Typically, S would intend to produce that belief in the audience. Speaker implication is *indirect* speaker meaning: meaning one thing (for example, that one cannot go out) by meaning another (that one has to study).

2 Speaker implicature

Grice was the first to systematically study cases in which speaker meaning differs from sentence meaning. He introduced the verb 'implicate' and the cognate noun 'implicature' as technical terms denoting 'the act of meaning or implying something by saying something else' (Grice 1989: chaps 2 and 3). Consider the following dialogue:

(1)   Ann: Where can I get petrol?

        Bob: There's a petrol station around the corner.

We may suppose Bob to have implied that Ann can get petrol at the petrol station. Nevertheless, Bob did not actually say that Ann can get petrol there. So Bob has 'implicated' it. What Bob said, and therefore did not implicate, is just that there is a petrol station around the corner. By 'saying', Grice meant not mere uttering, but saying *that* something is the case. (As Grice realized, 'say' can be used more or less narrowly. The less speakers are counted as saying, the more they are counted as implicating.)

Example (1) shows that saying is more closely related to conventional meaning than to speaker meaning. The implication that Ann can get petrol at the petrol station is no part of the meaning of 'There's a petrol station around the corner'. If '*e*' means that *p* on a given occasion, then the speaker says that *p*. The converse fails for several reasons. First, a speaker who utters 'Jack and Jill went up the hill' has said that Jack went up the hill; but that is only part of what the sentence means. Second, a speaker who utters 'He is liberal' might have said that President Clinton is liberal; but (being indexical) 'He is liberal' does not mean 'President Clinton is liberal', even on that occasion (see DEMONSTRATIVES AND INDEXICALS). In general, though, an implicature may be described as something the speaker means or implies that is not part of what the sentence literally means.

If '*e*' means that *p*, or if *S* says that *p* by uttering '*e*', then '*p*' is a truth-condition of '*e*', either in general, or as used on that occasion. Truth-conditions are logical or a priori implications. Assuming particular interpretations, '*p*' is a truth-condition of sentence '*e*' if and only if it is absolutely impossible for '*e*' to be true without '*p*' being true. 'There is a petrol station' is a truth-condition of 'There's a petrol station around the corner'. For the latter cannot be true unless the former is true. But 'Ann can get petrol at the petrol station' is not a truth-condition of 'There's a petrol station around the corner'. The petrol station might be out of petrol or closed. It follows that an implicature need not be a truth-condition of the sentence uttered. The two notions are not mutually exclusive, however, as the following dialogue between an auditor and tax payer illustrates.

(2)   Alan: Is it true that you or your spouse is 65 or older or blind?

   Bill: I am 67.

By saying 'I am 67', Bill implicated (he implied but did not say) that he or his spouse is 65 or older or blind. Furthermore, he could not be 67 unless he or his spouse were 65 or older or blind. So *S*'s implicature is also a truth-condition of the sentence *S* uttered on that occasion.

Empirically necessary conditions, let us say, are 'natural' implications. 'The power is on' is a natural implication of 'The lights are on'. If '*e*' naturally implies '*p*', then '*e*' means that *p* in Grice's natural sense. Whether natural implications are implicatures depends on the speaker's intentions. In dialogue (3), we would expect Beth to have implicated that the power is on.

(3)   Alice: Is the power on?

   Beth: The lights are on.

But if Beth does not know what power is, and gives that answer out of desperation, then she would not have implicated that the power is on.

Speakers who know that an implicature is false have misled their audience. But they have not lied unless the implicature happens to be a truth-condition. If Bob knows there is no petrol at the petrol station, then he has misled Ann in dialogue (1). But Bob has not lied, since he did not actually say that there was petrol there. However, if Bill knows that what he has implicated is false in dialogue (2), then he has to be lying.

3   Utterance and sentence implicature

An utterance implicates whatever the utterer implicates. Thus in (1), Bob's utterance implicated that Ann can get petrol. A sentence implicates, roughly, what speakers following linguistic conventions would normally use it to implicate. Despite what Bob implicated in (1), the sentence Bob used does not itself implicate 'Ann can get petrol at the petrol station'. For in most contexts, there would be no impropriety in using 'There's a petrol station around the corner' without that implicature. In contrast, (4a) itself implicates (4b):

(4a) Bill is sick, so he should rest.

(4b) Bill's being sick implies that he should rest.

For a speaker could not properly use (4a) without implicating (4b). And (5a) implicates (5b):

(5a) Some died.

(5b) Not all died.

For speakers would normally use (5a) with that implicature.

4   Conventional versus conversational implicature

Implicatures generated by the conventional meaning of the words uttered, as in (4), are classified as 'conventional' (see, for example, Grice 1989: 25–6). Non-conventional implicatures, as in (5), are termed 'conversational', since they depend on the conversational context. Normally, if one uses a sentence aware of the falsity of some of its conventional implicatures or logical implications, one uses the sentence improperly. If one uses a sentence aware of the falsity of a conversational implicature, one's utterance is at most misleading. Conversational implicatures differ further in being cancellable. The implicature of (5a) can be explicitly cancelled by adding 'indeed, all did'. 'some died, indeed all did' is perfectly consistent, and does not imply 'Not all died' in any way. In contrast, since 'All died' logically implies 'some died', 'All died, indeed none did' is self-contradictory. 'Bill is sick, so he should rest, but Bill's being sick in no way implies that he should rest' is incoherent in a different way. Conventional implicatures can also be implicitly cancelled by the context. Thus (5a) would not have its customary implication if uttered in full view of a garden in which every single plant was obviously dead. Conversely, conversational implicatures are reinforceable. Conjoining a sentence with one of its conversational implicatures is not redundant, and logically implies what the original sentence implicates; witness 'some died, but not all did'; in contrast, 'All died, and some did' is redundant.

5 Conversational maxims and the cooperative principle

Besides identifying the phenomenon of implicature, Grice formulated a theory in terms of which he classified different sorts of conversational implicature, and tried to explain how they arise and are understood. It is common knowledge, he asserted, that people generally follow certain rules for efficient communication. Grice's rules (1989: 26–9) included one general 'principle of cooperation', and four 'maxims' specifying how to be cooperative:

The cooperative principle. Contribute what is required by the accepted purpose of the conversation.

The maxim of quality. Make your contribution true, so do not convey what you believe false or unjustified.

The maxim of quantity. Be as informative as required, neither more nor less so.

The maxim of relevance. Be relevant.

The maxim of manner. Be perspicuous, so avoid obscurity and ambiguity, and be brief and orderly.

Generalizations of these rules govern rational, cooperative behaviour in general. If I am helping a man change the oil, I will hand him a can of oil rather than a jack (relevance), a barrel of oil (quantity), or fake oil (quality), and I will not take all day doing it (manner). The maxims do not, therefore, have the characteristic arbitrariness of linguistic conventions. Much of the literature is devoted to clarifying and strengthening the maxims, relating them, and extending the list. But Grice's formulations are still dominant.

To sketch how the principles are thought to explain the way implicatures arise and are understood, consider (1). Bob would have infringed the maxim of relevance unless he believed Ann could get petrol at the petrol station. Since Bob was trying to cooperate, his utterance indicated that belief. Thus Bob could imply that Ann can get petrol there and expect Ann to recognize that implication. Speakers using (5a) would violate the maxim of quantity if they knew that all died. So by not making the stronger statement, they can imply that not all died, and expect hearers to recognize the implication. Unlike conventional implicatures, conversational implicatures are cancelled when the maxims are in abeyance. Under cross-examination of an uncooperative witness, (5a) would not implicate (5b).

Some implicatures depend on flouting the maxims, Grice proposed (1989: 30–1). This occurs when what a cooperative speaker says so obviously fails to obey the maxims that the hearer must assume the speaker to be meaning something different. Irony and metaphor appear to depend on flouting the maxim of quality. Hearing 'Fine day, isn't it?' in the middle of a blizzard, we would recognize that the speaker cannot really believe it to be a fine day, and means the opposite. Hearing 'The music danced lightly on his ears', we would recognize that the speaker believes no such thing, and is using metaphor. The speaker who says 'The singer produced a series of sounds closely corresponding to the score of *Oklahoma*', thereby meaning that the singing was terrible, is flouting the maxim of manner.

Many of Grice's theoretical claims about the exact role played by the maxims in implicature are implausible. For example, Grice suggested that S conversationally implicates 'p' only if: (i) S is presumed to be observing the cooperative principle ('cooperative presumption'); (ii) the supposition that S believes 'p' is *required* to make S's utterance consistent with the cooperative principle ('determinacy'); and (iii) S believes or knows, and expects the hearer H to believe, that S believes H is able to determine that (ii) is true ('mutual knowledge'). The cooperative presumption would fail if, as is possible, Beth implied what she did in case (3) in defiance of Alice's mistrust, or if Beth implicated that she cannot answer the question by saying 'I'm late for an appointment'.

Determinacy fails outright in case (1), as presumably does mutual knowledge: the assumption that

Bob believed Ann could at least learn where to get petrol would also reconcile his utterance with the maxims, as would the more fantastic assumption that Bob believed the petrol station was giving away new diesel Volvos. Indeterminacy is of legendary proportions in figures of speech. Mutual knowledge may even fail independently. In (3), for example, Beth may have contemptuously implied that the power is on, believing that Alice would not be smart enough to figure it out. Some authors have nevertheless strengthened the mutual knowledge condition to say that S knows that H knows that S knows that H knows *ad infinitum*, a requirement both psychologically unrealistic and theoretically unnecessary.

While the maxims undeniably provide insight into conversational implicature, their predictive and explanatory power is extremely limited. Consider the account of irony. Grice suggests that S implicates 'It is a lousy day' when saying 'Fine day, isn't it?' because otherwise S would be violating the maxim of quality and thereby the cooperative principle. But S is still violating that principle, by violating the maxim of manner: figures of speech are seldom the most perspicuous ways of communicating information. Consider quantity implicatures. If (5a) implicates (5b) because of the maxim of quantity, then why does (5a) not implicate 'It is not the case that two per cent died'? Why does 'The repairs will take some time' not implicate 'They will not take a long time'? Why does 'Ann said Bill was responsible' not implicate 'Ann did not insist (or predict, or argue, or shout, or . . .) that Bill was responsible'? Consider finally the sequential interpretation of conjunctions. Grice explained why a conjunction like (6a) implies (6b) in terms of the submaxim 'Be orderly'.

(6a) Bill fell ill and saw the doctor.
(6b) Bill fell ill and therefore saw the doctor.
(6c) Bill saw the doctor and therefore fell ill.
(6d) It is more likely that Bill fell ill than that he saw the doctor.
(6e) Bill did not see the doctor because he fell ill.

But reverse temporal or causal order is just as orderly as forward order (witness 'Bill died; he had cancer'). So why should (6a) not imply (6c)? It would also be quite orderly to express the conjuncts from most to least probable. So why is (6d) not implied? And since 'B because A' is stronger than 'A and B', why is (6e) not implied in virtue of the quantity maxim? (For a comprehensive critique of Gricean theory, see Davis 1998.)

6 Theoretical importance

Difficulties in Gricean theory do not cast doubt on the existence or theoretical importance of implicature. Speakers cannot be fully understood without knowing what they implicate. It does not suffice to know the truth-conditions (or in some cases even the meaning) of all the sentences uttered, or what is said. Implicature must be considered even in truth-conditional semantics. Here are two examples.

Ambiguity. Readily available evidence suggests that the word 'and' is ambiguous in English, having a strong sense (literal meaning) connoting temporal or causal order in addition to the weak sense connoting joint truth alone. But before this can be accepted, the competing hypothesis that the sequential connotation is merely an implicature must be rejected (see AMBIGUITY §3). Many facts support implicature over ambiguity. For example, 'Bill fell ill and saw a doctor, but not necessarily in that order' does not have a contradictory reading. Furthermore, 'It is not the case that Bill fell ill and saw a doctor' would be interpreted as false when 'Bill fell ill' and 'Bill saw a doctor' are both true, no matter what the sequence of events.

Grice (1989: 47–50) proposed a version of 'Ockham's razor' according to which 'senses are not to be multiplied beyond necessity'. But the same can be said for implicatures. It is often claimed that since implicatures can be accounted for in terms of general psycho-social principles of conversation, the postulation of senses rather than implicatures results in a more complex overall theory. But this overstates the explanatory powers of any known principles of conversation.

Presupposition. 'e' is said to (semantically) 'presuppose' 'p' provided the truth of 'p' is necessary for 'e' to be either true or false (see PRESUPPOSITION). Following P.F. Strawson, and opposing Bertrand Russell, many have argued that a sentence like (7a) presupposes (7b):

(7a) Your crimes are inexcusable.
(7b) You have committed crimes.
(7c) Your crimes are not inexcusable.

The presupposition hypothesis is plausible since (7c) seems to imply (7b) just as strongly as (7a) does. Accepting presuppositions seriously complicates logical theory, however. For example, if some declarative sentences are neither true nor false, then standard formulations of the 'law of excluded middle' must be modified. One strategy for avoiding these complications hypothesizes that the implication of the negation is merely a conventional implicature (see, for example, Karttunen and Peters 1979). On this view, (7c) conventionally implicates (7b) without logically implying it. The fact that a sentence may be true when an implicature is false allows the Russellian to account for the felt implications, while insisting that

INCARNATION AND CHRISTOLOGY

(7c) is true and (7a) false when (7b) is false. Supporting Strawson, though, is the strong intuition that 'Are your crimes excusable or not?' is a loaded question, which cannot be answered if you are innocent. An outstanding problem for either approach is to describe how implications of complex propositions (whether presuppositions or implicatures) are related to those of their components.

Implicature has also been invoked in accounts of lexical gaps, language change, indirect speech acts, textual coherence, discourse analysis and even syntax.

See also: MEANING AND COMMUNICATION; PRAGMATICS; SEMANTICS; SPEECH ACTS

References and further reading

Blakemore, D. (1992) *Understanding Utterances*, Oxford: Blackwell. (A readable introduction to the theory of implicature developed in Sperber and Wilson (1986).)

Davis, W.A. (1998) *Implicature: The Failure of Gricean Theory*, Cambridge: Cambridge University Press. (A comprehensive critique of Grice's theory of implicature, and of similar theories. Argues that conversational implicatures arise not from conversational principles, but from intentions and conventions.)

Gazdar, G. (1979) *Pragmatics: Implicature, Presupposition, and Logical Form*, New York: Academic Press. (Attempts a partial formalization of conversational implicatures, focusing on quantity implicatures, and uses it to provide a pragmatic theory of presupposition.)

* Grice, H.P. (1989) *Studies in the Ways of Words*, Cambridge, MA: Harvard University Press. (Contains all of Grice's work on meaning and implicature, plus an introduction and retrospective epilogue.)

Harnish, R.M. (1976) 'Logical Form and Implicature', repr. in S. Davis (ed.) *Pragmatics: A Reader*, Oxford: Oxford University Press, 1991, 316–64. (Presents many problems for Gricean theory, suggesting solutions and extensions.)

Horn, L.R. (1989) *A Natural History of Negation*, Chicago, IL: University of Chicago Press. (A remarkably comprehensive and detailed account of negation, focusing *inter alia* on its effect on implicature, and explanation of a wide variety of linguistic facts about negation in terms of implicature.)

Karttunen, L. and Peters, S. (1979) 'Conversational Implicature', in C.-K. Oh and D.A. Dinneen, *Syntax and Semantics*, vol. 11, *Presupposition*, New York: Academic Press, 1979, 1–56. (A detailed,

compelling argument that different sorts of presupposition can be accounted for as different types of implicature, plus a representation of conventional implicature using model-theoretic semantics, specifically, Montague grammar.)

Leech, G. (1983) *Principles of Pragmatics*, London: Longman. (A leading introduction to pragmatics stressing implicature. Develops Grice's suggestion that another maxim is 'Be polite', showing that it motivates many implicatures.)

Levinson, S.C. (1983) *Pragmatics*, Cambridge: Cambridge University Press. (A leading introduction to pragmatics, with an extensive discussion of conversational implicature and presupposition from a Gricean point of view.)

Martinich, A.P. (1984) 'A Theory for Metaphor', *Journal of Literary Semantics* 13: 35–56; repr. in S. Davis (ed.) *Pragmatics: A Reader*, Oxford: Oxford University Press, 507–18. (An extended Gricean treatment of metaphor.)

Sadock, J.M. (1978) 'On Testing for Conversational Implicature', in S. Davis (ed.) *Pragmatics: A Reader*, Oxford: Oxford University Press. (Points out problems with all of Grice's tests for conversational implicature.)

Sperber, D. and Wilson, D. (1986) *Relevance: Communication and Cognition*, Oxford: Blackwell. (Develops a theory of implicature in terms of a single 'principle of relevance' quite distinct from Grice's 'maxim of relevance'.)

WAYNE A. DAVIS

INCARNATION AND CHRISTOLOGY

It is a central and essential dogma of Christianity that Jesus of Nazareth, who was crucified in Judea during the procuratorship (AD 26–36) of Pontius Pilate, and God, the eternal and omnipresent creator of the universe, were in some very strong sense 'one'. The department of Christian theology that is devoted to the study of the nature and implications of this 'oneness' is called Christology. Orthodox Christology (unlike certain heretical Christologies) sees this oneness as a oneness of person, as consisting in the co-presence of two natures, the divine and the human, in one person, Jesus Christ. To speak plainly, orthodox Christology holds that there is someone, Jesus Christ, who is both divine and human. Because God pre-existed and is superior to every human being, orthodox theologians have found it natural to speak of the union of the divine and human natures in the person of Jesus Christ as

725

something that happened to *the pre-existent divine nature: at a certain point in time, at the moment of the conception of Jesus, it 'took on flesh' or 'became incarnate'; in the words of the Athanasian Creed, the union of the two natures was accomplished 'not by conversion of the Godhead [divinitas] into flesh, but by taking of the manhood into God'. This event, and the continuing union it established, are called 'the Incarnation'. The Incarnation was not, according to Christian teaching, undone by Christ's death (his corpse – a* human *corpse – continued to be united with the divine nature by the same bond by which the living man had been united) or by his 'Ascension' (his 'withdrawal' from the everyday world of space and time forty days after the Resurrection), and it will never be undone: the Incarnation is eternal.*

The primary statements of the dogma of the Incarnation are the Definition issued by the Council of Chalcedon (AD 451) and the Athanasian Creed (fifth century; its origins are obscure). The creed issued by the Council of Nicaea (AD 325) and the longer, revised version of this creed that is today used liturgically (and commonly called 'the Nicene Creed') contain nothing of substance that is not found in the two later statements.

1 **The doctrine of the Incarnation**
2 **Logical problems**
3 **Attributive solutions**
4 **Predicative solutions**

1 The doctrine of the Incarnation

Books present portraits, generally inadvertent, of their authors and their intended audiences. The New Testament presents a portrait of Christians who were not quite sure what to say about the relation between Jesus Christ and God. On the one hand, the earliest Christians could hardly deny that Christ was a man (had he not frequently referred to himself as 'the Son of Man'?), a human being who had been born and had died (albeit he was not dead for very long), who ate and drank and spoke and slept and left prints in the dust of Palestine. On the other hand, they could hardly speak of Christ without mentioning God in the same breath, they called him 'the Son of God', and they were unreflectively willing to ascribe to him honours held traditionally in their cultures to be due to God alone. Explicit statements about the relation between Christ and God are rare in the New Testament. There are, however, a few passages in which this relation is described, and all of these imply, or come very close to implying, a 'high' Christology – a Christology that in some sense identifies Christ with God. Thus

(the translations are those of the New American Standard Bible):

In the beginning was the Word [*logos*], and the Word was with God, and the Word was God. He was in the beginning with God. All things came into being by him, and apart from him nothing came into being that has come into being.... And the Word became flesh and dwelt among us, and we beheld his glory...

(John 1: 1–3, 14)

He [Christ] is the image of the invisible God, the first-born of all creation [that is, has an authority over the created world comparable to that which, under Jewish law, a first-born son had over his living father's estate]. For by him all things were created, both in the heavens and on earth, visible and invisible, ... – all things have been created by him and for him. And he is before all things and in him all things hold together [*sunistemi*].... For in him all the fullness of Deity dwells in bodily form.

(Colossians 1: 15–17; 2: 9)

In these last days, [God] has spoken to us in his Son, whom he appointed heir of all things, through whom also he made the world [literally: 'made the ages']. And he is the radiance of his [God's] glory, and the exact representation of his nature, and upholds all things by the word of his power.

(Hebrews 1: 2, 3)

It should also be noted that in John 8: 58, and possibly in John 10: 22–38, the author represents Jesus as affirming his own deity, and that in John 20: 28, the apostle Thomas addresses the risen Jesus as 'My Lord and my God'.

The New Testament, although it is rich in Christological suggestion, contains no systematic Christology. The development of a systematic Christology was the work of the first five Christian centuries. The relevant biblical passages – those quoted above, and a few others, such as Philippians 2: 5–11 – have been treated by most theologians not as explicit statements of doctrine but as data to which explicit statements of doctrine must be responsible. The 'developed' doctrine, the doctrine of the fifth century, is contained in the following two passages.

...we all unanimously teach that we should confess that our Lord Jesus Christ is one and the same Son, the same perfect in Godhead and the same perfect in manhood, truly God and truly man, the same of a rational soul and body, consubstantial with the Father in Godhead, and the same consubstantial with us in manhood, like us in all things except sin; begotten from the Father before the ages as regards his Godhead, and in the last days, the same, because of us and because of our salvation begotten from the Virgin Mary, the *Theotokos* [God-bearer], as regards his manhood; one and the same Christ, Son, Lord, only-begotten, made known in two natures without confusion, without change, without division, without separation, the difference of the natures being by no means removed because of the union, but the property of each nature being preserved and coalescing in one *prosopon* [person] and one *hypostasis* [subsistence], not parted or divided into two *prosopa*, but one and the same Son, only-begotten, divine Word, the Lord Jesus Christ, as the prophets of old and Jesus Christ himself have taught us about him and the creed of our fathers has handed down.

(Definition of Chalcedon; see Kelly 1960)

...[N]ow the right faith is that we should believe and confess that our Lord Jesus Christ, the Son of God, is equally both God and man.

He is God from the Father's substance, begotten before time; and he is man from his mother's substance, born in time. Perfect God, perfect man composed of a rational soul and human flesh, equal to the Father in respect of his divinity, less than the Father in respect of his humanity.

Who, although he is God and man, is nevertheless not two but one Christ. He is one, however, not by the transformation of his divinity into flesh, but by the taking up of his humanity into God; one certainly not by confusion of substance but by oneness of person. For just as rational soul and flesh are a single man, so God and man are a single Christ.

(Athanasian Creed; see Kelly 1964)

These passages seem to say, and rather insistently, that there is a single *prosopon* or *hypostasis* or *persona*, Jesus Christ, who both has a beginning in time and has no beginning in time. More generally, he has all of the properties – attributes, features or characteristics – appropriate to a (sinless) human being, and at the same time has all of the properties that the Christian faith ascribes to God.

In order to grasp the orthodox doctrine expressed in these statements, it is advisable to have some conception of unorthodoxy, of the great Christological heresies of the first five Christian centuries, for these heresies were present in the minds of the framers of the statements and are to a large extent responsible for the details of the wording. The most important heresies for this purpose are the following three.

Nestorianism denies that the two natures belong to the same person: according to Nestorianism – if not to the eponymous Nestorius (d. *circa* 451), who may not actually have held this – the divine Christ and the human Christ are numerically distinct persons. That is, however intimate the union – or 'conjunction' (*sunápheia*), the word preferred by the Nestorians – of the human and the divine Christs, there is no one who can say truly both 'I am God' and 'I am a human being'. According to Nestorians, the 'conjunction' of the divine and the human natures was effected between God and a pre-existent human being. Since God and Jesus each existed before the conjunction, and each was then who he was, there could not have been only one person 'present' after the conjunction unless the human person had somehow ceased to be – which is obviously unacceptable. (Orthodox Christology holds that the human being Jesus of Nazareth did not exist before the Incarnation, and that, in modern terminology, there is no possible world in which he exists, even for the briefest instant, without God's being incarnate in him.)

Monophysitism ('one-naturism') holds that there is only one nature, the divine nature, in the incarnate Christ. The human attributes of Jesus of Nazareth are somehow taken up into or made to be contained within the divine nature; at any rate, they do not constitute a distinct, subsistent human nature – that is, a human being. (It should be noted that early Christological writings do not always make it clear whether 'a nature' (*physis, natura*) is a 'predicable', like the *attributes* divinity and humanity, or a 'first substance', an impredicable subject of predication, like God and Jesus of Nazareth. Some authors write as if the distinction did not exist or was of no importance; others seem perversely to take their opponents to mean one of these things when they should pretty clearly be taken to mean the other.)

Apollinarianism (after Apollinarius (*c.*310–*c.*390)) holds that Christ did not have a human mind or spirit or rational soul – that he lacked something that is essential to human nature – and that God or some 'aspect' of God (such as the divine *logos*) was united to the human body of Jesus of Nazareth in such a way as to 'be a substitute for' or perform the function of the human mind or soul or spirit. This is perhaps the most important of the heresies for the task of understanding orthodoxy: it is certainly very frequently suggested by the language of popular Christianity. Orthodoxy insists, however, that whatever is present in our common human nature (other than sin) is present in Christ. The reason for this, briefly, is that the saving work of Christ is to heal our ruined human nature, and (in the words of Gregory of Nazianzus), 'what [Christ] has not assumed he has not healed' (Letter 101, *Patrologia Graeca*, vol. 37). The conviction that 'what he has not assumed he has not healed' is one of the main pressures that guided the development of the orthodox 'Chalcedonian' Christology. It was this conviction that made 'fully human' to be for the 'Chalcedonian' party what in the 1960s was called a 'non-negotiable demand'.

At the same time, other pressures made 'fully divine' non-negotiable for most of the parties, including the Chalcedonian party, to the great Christological controversies. One might cite (1) the conviction that the situation of fallen humanity was so desperate that any effective saviour of humanity must be divine, (2) the fact that from the earliest days of Christianity, Christians had offered honours to Christ that it would be blasphemous to offer to a creature, and (3) the realization that the biblical texts quoted above – which at the very least seem to represent Christ as 'very like' God – could not be interpreted as describing Christ as a being who was close to being God but was not quite God, or even as a being who was ontologically intermediate between God and man: no such 'not quite God', no such intermediate, is possible, because any being who is not God is finite, and any finite being must be infinitely closer ontologically to any other finite being than it is to God.

2 Logical problems

The main philosophical problems facing the doctrine of the Incarnation are logical: the doctrine implies, or seems to imply, that there is an object that has various pairs of incompatible properties – or worse (if worse is possible), that there is an object and a property such that that object both has and does not have that property. (God is eternal; Jesus is not eternal; God is identical with Jesus; hence there is something that both is and is not eternal.) Some theologians have held, apparently, that the doctrine does have these features and is therefore internally inconsistent, but is nevertheless to be believed. Having said this, they proceed to deprecate 'merely human logic'. Their point is not that the doctrine *seems* to be inconsistent owing to the deficiencies of merely human logic; it is rather that it is only because of the deficiencies of merely human logic that inconsistency (at least in theology) seems objectionable (see Morris 1986: 24–5 for a nice selection of quotations on this subject). This position has (to be gentle) little to recommend it. It perhaps rests on a failure to see clearly that a truth cannot be inconsistent with a truth.

It would, of course, be possible to maintain that although the orthodox doctrine of the Incarnation seems to be inconsistent, it is in fact consistent, the explanation of the fact that it is, despite appearances, consistent being beyond human understanding. This position will not be discussed in the present entry, for the simple reason that there is little if anything that can be said about it. Rather, various attempts to solve the problem that faces orthodox Christology owing to the *prima facie* inconsistency of the properties it ascribes to the incarnate Christ will be discussed. Philosophically promising solutions will be examined, but with no attempt to trace their historical roots. These solutions are (as perhaps any solution must be) of one or the other of two types:

(1) The orthodox doctrine does not imply all the statements it appears to imply. One or the other of each of the mutually contradictory pairs of statements the doctrine appears to imply it does not in fact imply. (For example, the doctrine appears to imply that Christ began to exist when Herod was king in Judea, and also appears to imply that Christ's existence had no beginning. But it in fact implies only the latter. Those who have concluded that the doctrine implies the former statement have reached this conclusion on the basis of a superficial understanding of what is contained in the concept of humanity.)
(2) The doctrine does imply all the statements it appears to imply, but these statements are not, as they appear to be, inconsistent. (For example, the doctrine implies that Christ began to exist when Herod was king in Judea, and also implies that Christ's existence had no beginning. But these two statements are consistent. Those who have concluded that they are inconsistent have reached this conclusion on the basis of a superficial understanding of their logical form.)

We shall call solutions of the former type 'attributive' and solutions of the latter type 'predicative'. These words are no more than convenient labels. Neither corresponds to any school or division in the history of theology.

3 Attributive solutions

Is it not possible that we sometimes read more into certain of the attributes that orthodoxy ascribes to Christ than is really there? We tend to assume that a human being must have a beginning in time, and that this is part of the concept of a human being. But what justifies this assumption? We tend to assume that whatever is a human being is essentially a human being. But, again, what justifies this assumption? Even if Solomon and Catherine the Great and all other 'ordinary' human beings have a temporal origin – even if they all have this property essentially – and even if they are all essentially human, does it follow that there could not be an eternal being who acquired the attribute of humanity at a certain point in time? Is there something about the concept of humanity that makes the idea of such a being a conceptual impossibility? Or is there something about the attribute of humanity that makes the idea of such a being a metaphysical impossibility? We may think so – but how do we know? Are we prepared to assert confidently that an alleged divine revelation that implied the existence of such a being would have to be judged a fraud or fantasy of merely human origin? (No doubt we ought to be prepared to assert this in respect of an alleged divine revelation that implied that the walls of the New Jerusalem would be both square and circular.) Or consider omnipresence. A human being must be locally present somewhere, but does it follow that a human being cannot be omnipresent? We must remember that local presence and omnipresence are two different modes of presence. It is indeed impossible for one and the same being to be both locally present everywhere (like the luminiferous ether) and locally present only at a certain spot on the shores of the Sea of Galilee – but omnipresence is not local presence everywhere (see OMNIPRESENCE §4). Again: is it really impossible for a human being to be omnipotent? If an omnipotent being took on a set of properties such that whatever had those properties would be human, it would thereby acquire a certain set of powers or abilities, a set that might be the whole set of the powers had by an 'ordinary' human being; but might this set not be simply a (rather small) subset of the set of all its powers – might that being not continue to be omnipotent? Might it not continue to be able to move mountains? (Only, of course, in the way it had been able to move mountains before it took on its 'new' set of properties and powers: it would be unable to move mountains by using its limbs to exert physical pressure on them, even as Solomon and Catherine were unable to do this.) Similar questions can be asked in respect of omniscience.

If a human being can indeed be omnipresent, omnipotent and omniscient, then one might address the problem of the apparent logical inconsistency of the doctrine of the Incarnation simply by denying it reality and asserting, without qualification, that Jesus of Nazareth was omnipresent, omnipotent and omniscient. Whether this solution is philosophically coherent could be debated interminably. But there is also the question whether it is in fact usable by Christians (who are, of course, the only people who have a use for it), for it is certainly arguable that it is inconsistent with the data of the New Testament, in which Jesus is sometimes represented as unable to do certain things and as learning things of which he had hitherto been ignorant and, in one case, as simply not knowing the exact day and hour of the end of the age (Matthew 24: 36; Mark 13: 32). It would no doubt be

possible to insist that the passages in the New Testament that represent Jesus as subject to many of the limitations of ordinary human existence can be reconciled with the thesis that he is omnipotent, omniscient and omnipresent – rather as many have found it possible to insist that the doctrine of a timeless, impassible God can be reconciled with the narratives of the Pentateuch. But it would seem that a solution to the problem would be more attractive to most Christians if it allowed Jesus to share our human limitations.

There is an attributive solution that claims to have this feature. It is called *kenoticism*, from the Greek *kenosis* ('emptying'), an account of the nature of the Incarnation that is based on the statement (Philippians 2: 7) that, in becoming incarnate, Christ 'emptied' himself. Whatever the correct interpretation of the difficult passage in which this statement occurs may be, kenoticism holds that, in becoming incarnate, Christ relinquished omnipotence, omniscience, omnipresence and various other of what are commonly called the divine attributes (although it continued to be true of him that he was morally perfect, had no beginning in time and was not a created being). Kenoticists do not, however, hold that when Christ had become incarnate *no one* was omnipotent and omnipresent. This entry has not so far touched on the relation of the doctrine of the Incarnation to the doctrine of the Trinity, but the two doctrines intersect on the following point: it was the second person of the Trinity alone, God the Son, who became incarnate. According to the kenotic theory, God the Son 'emptied himself' of omnipotence and omnipresence, but God the Father and God the Holy Spirit continued to possess these attributes.

Kenoticism, it will be noted, requires a 'rethinking' of divinity and various of the divine attributes as well as of humanity. We are inclined to think that a being that had attributes such as omniscience and omnipotence would have to have them essentially – and hence that that being could not relinquish them. But how, the kenoticist asks, do we know this? We are also inclined to think that a being who was not omniscient or omnipotent at t would not be at t a divine being. But how do we know this? How do we know that, for example, omnipotence is really a divine attribute, really entailed by divinity? Might it not be that it is not strictly omnipotence that is entailed by divinity, but rather some 'weaker' attribute – perhaps 'omnipotence unless omnipotence is voluntarily relinquished'?

It is very doubtful whether kenoticism can be reconciled with orthodoxy. The following two difficulties are apparent. First, the theory does not mesh well with orthodox Trinitarian theology, for it seems to imply that the persons of the Trinity are distinct substances, distinct *beings*, and hence to imply tritheism (see TRINITY §§1–2). Second, the theory allows the incarnate Christ to be divine only by considerably 'weakening' the concept of divinity. The incarnate Christ can indeed say truly 'I am a divine being', but only because, for the kenoticist, it is possible to be a divine being at a certain moment without then being omnipotent, omniscient or omnipresent. It is doubtful whether kenoticism can be reconciled with the following two requirements: 'the property [that is, defining properties or essential features] of each nature being preserved' (Definition of Chalcedon); 'not by the transformation of his divinity into flesh' (Athanasian Creed). Even if kenoticism can, by artful interpretations of their language, be reconciled with the letter of the two documents, it certainly cannot be reconciled with their spirit. (Kenoticism is a nineteenth-century invention and did not, therefore, influence the wording of the Definition or the Creed. There can be no real doubt that they would have been so worded as to exclude it if it had existed in the fifth century.)

Thomas Morris (1986) has defended an attributive solution that both takes into account the biblical data concerning the human limitations of Christ and retains a robust concept of divinity. Morris accounts for the biblical data by suggesting that Christ, in becoming incarnate, acquired a human mind without thereby relinquishing his divine mind. (The divine mind that Christ retains is not, according to Morris, 'divine' only in some etiolated, kenotic sense: it remains, for example, omniscient.) Between the two minds there exists an 'asymmetrical accessing relation': only a minuscule segment of what is present in the divine mind is accessible to the human mind. Christ's human limitations are to be traced to the limitations of his human mind, and it is this mind whose thoughts and sufferings are recorded in the Gospels.

Morris' solution is certainly to be preferred both to the 'unqualified' solution and to kenoticism. One might wonder, however, whether it is not a form of monophysitism. (This point could also have been brought against the 'unqualified' solution.) Morris' solution represents Christ's human mind as a 'subsystem' of his divine mind – which is, after all, really just his mind, his mind *simpliciter*. And although Christ has (on the physical side) weight and shape and local presence – all the physical properties that someone needs to be fully human – these are simply properties that God has acquired, 'additions' to the properties that he had before the Incarnation. It would seem, therefore, that Morris' solution inherits the following feature of the 'unqualified' solution: it

represents the incarnate Christ as a single substance, a divine substance that, by becoming incarnate, acquired certain properties that would otherwise belong only to created beings. Morris would certainly vigorously affirm the presence of two natures in the incarnate Christ, but his account of what this means seems to be very like the account given by those monophysites who were willing to accept the 'two natures' terminology: 'It is the claim of orthodoxy that Jesus had all of the [essential] properties of humanity, and all the [essential] properties of divinity, and thus existed (and continues still to exist) in two natures' (Morris 1986: 40). The definitional statements that an advocate of Morris' solution would have to pay special attention to are these: 'made known in two natures without confusion [without running together]' (Definition of Chalcedon); 'not by confusion of substance' (Athanasian Creed).

4 Predicative solutions

Predicative solutions concede that pairs of predicates like 'is eternal' and 'was born of a human mother in 6 BC' are inconsistent. But advocates of these solutions maintain that the real logical form of some or all sentences of the superficial form 'Christ is *F*' is not what that superficial form suggests. There are two, or perhaps three, ways a sentence of this form can be construed: 'Christ is *F qua* God (as regards his divinity)', 'Christ is *F qua* man', and, possibly, 'Christ is *F* without qualification (*simpliciter*)'. Predicative solutions contend, moreover, that pairs of sentences like 'Christ is eternal *qua* God' and 'Christ was born of a human mother in 6 BC *qua* man' are consistent. (It would seem natural to suppose that proponents of predicative solutions – since they concede that 'is eternal' and 'was born...' are inconsistent – must regard 'Christ is eternal *simpliciter*' and 'Christ was born of a human mother in 6 BC *simpliciter*' as inconsistent. Indeed, it would seem natural to suppose that they would have to say that it was false that Christ had either his 'exclusively divine' or his 'exclusively human' attributes *simpliciter*, and would allow only that he had each of them *qua* God or *qua* man, as appropriate – although they might hold that Christ had certain attributes, such as moral perfection, *simpliciter*. But some 'predicativists' may refuse to recognize the '*simpliciter*' mode of predication. And at least one 'predicativist' author explicitly treats such pairs of sentences as consistent, for reasons that will be given below.)

'Predicativism', so understood, is unquestionably orthodox. But it is doubtful whether it constitutes a solution to the problem of the apparent inconsistency of orthodox two-natures Christology. A satisfactory predicative solution must supplement the abstract theses of the preceding paragraph with some sort of reply to the following challenge:

Where F and G are incompatible properties, and K_1 and K_2 are 'kinds', what does it mean to say of something that it is F *qua* K_1 but G *qua* K_2? – or that it is F *qua* K_1 but is not F *qua* K_2? And can any more or less uncontroversial examples of such pairs of statements be found?

R.T. Herbert (1979) has offered an example of such a pair of statements. Consider ambiguous figures, like the familiar 'duck-rabbit'. One could point at such a figure and say truly both, 'That has ears *qua* rabbit' and 'That has no ears *qua* duck'. But this example immediately suggests a question: what does the word 'that' refer to? Certainly not to the ambiguous figure. The *figure* belongs neither to the kind 'rabbit' nor to the kind 'duck', and therefore, presumably, has no properties *qua* rabbit or *qua* duck. (And if 'that' does not refer to the figure, what does it refer to?) It may be true that the figure has the property 'representing something with ears' *qua* rabbit-representation and lacks this same property *qua* duck-representation. If so, this would be an example of a pair of '*qua*' statements of the forms the above challenge has demanded. But it does not seem that this example will be of use in Christology, for the property the figure has '*qua* something' and lacks '*qua* something else' is a representational property, and Christ, not being a drawing or a statue, has no representational properties. (It is not accidental to the example that the property it involves is representational, and the example provides the inquirer with no clue as to how to construct an example involving a property that is not representational.) It is true that one biblical quotation describes Christ as 'the exact representation [*charaktér*] of [God's] nature' (Hebrews 1: 3). But this means that Christ is a 'perfect copy' of God, and does not imply that any of Christ's properties is a representational property. (A daughter who is the 'spit and image' of her mother is not a representation of her mother in the way a portrait of her mother is.) Peter van Inwagen (1994) has presented a very comprehensive and general predicative solution to the problem of the apparent inconsistency of the doctrine of the Incarnation. It has been observed by several authors that Peter Geach's thesis of the 'relativity of identity' can be employed to solve the 'Leibniz's Law' problems faced by the doctrine of the Trinity (see TRINITY §3). Van Inwagen has shown that the techniques employed in this solution can be extended to solve the similar problems faced by the doctrine of the Incarnation. The following is a simplified version of van Inwagen's solution.

Suppose that, although God is not (of course) the same substance or being as the human being Jesus of Nazareth, he is nevertheless the same *person* – the same 'I' or 'thou' or 'he'. (This assumption has two closely related presuppositions: that it is possible for x to be the same person as y but not the same substance; and that if x is the same person as y, and x has the property F, it does not follow that y has F.) Let the adjective 'Nazarene' represent some conjunction of 'human' properties that uniquely identify the human being Jesus of Nazareth. We may now offer the following three definitions:

Jesus Christ is F *simpliciter*:

Something x is such that: something divine is the same person as x; and something Nazarene is the same person as x; and x is F.

Jesus Christ is F *qua* God:

Something x is such that: something divine is the same person as x; and something Nazarene is the same person as x; and x is divine; and x is F.

Jesus Christ is F *qua* man:

Something x is such that: something divine is the same person as x; and something Nazarene is the same person as x; and x is human; and x is F.

The two latter definitions have the expected and desired consequences. The following two consequences of the first, however, although not unorthodox, are certainly somewhat counterintuitive: Jesus Christ is eternal *simpliciter* (since something divine and something Nazarene are the same person, and the former is eternal), and Jesus Christ had a beginning in time *simpliciter* (since something divine and something Nazarene are the same person, and the latter had a beginning in time). Using constructions like those illustrated in the three definitions, van Inwagen has shown how to correlate each statement endorsed by the orthodox doctrine of the Incarnation with a statement in a formal language comprising only the two 'relative identity' predicates 'is the same being as' and 'is the same person as' and a small stock of additional predicates. (The formal language contains no names or descriptions; it contains no terms but variables.) He has shown that the set of statements in the formal language that are correlated with the set of statements that orthodoxy endorses are formally consistent (given a certain explicitly stated set of rules that defines valid inference in the formal language). This 'solution' to the problem of the apparent logical inconsistency of the doctrine of the Incarnation, unlike the other solutions we have examined, has no ontological content. Van Inwagen makes no attempt at a metaphysical analysis of divinity or humanity; his project is simply to set out a formal representation of the orthodox doctrine that is provably formally consistent.

His solution raises at least two serious questions (if, indeed, metaphysically empty as it is, it is proper to call it a solution). First, do the two 'closely related presuppositions' mentioned above (that it is possible for *x* to be the same person as *y* but not the same substance; and that if *x* is the same person as *y*, and *x* has the property *F*, it does not follow that *y* has *F*) really make any logical sense? Second, van Inwagen's constructions represent the statements of traditional Incarnational theology as having very different logical forms from those they appear to have. (For example, given the appropriate theological assumptions, the sentence 'Jesus Christ is eternal *qua* God' is true on his analysis – but not because 'Jesus Christ' is a singular referring expression that denotes an object that has, on those assumptions, the property expressed by the predicate 'is eternal *qua* God'.) In view of this fact, can these constructions plausibly be held to represent the intended content of the traditional statements?

See also: ATONEMENT; IDENTITY; IMMUTABILITY §3; SIMPLICITY, DIVINE

References and further reading

Bettenson, H. (ed.) (1963) *Documents of the Christian Church*, Oxford and London: Oxford University Press, 2nd edn. (A useful collection. Contains materials relating to Apollinarianism, Nestorianism and – under the heading 'Eutychianism'– monophysitism.)

Geach, P.T. (1977) *Providence and Evil*, Cambridge: Cambridge University Press. (An interesting discussion of the logic of 'predication *qua*', with applications to Christology; see especially pages 24–8.)

* Gregory of Nazianzus (mid-to-late 4th century) 'Letter 101', in J.P. Migne (ed.) *Patrologia Graeca*, vol. 37, Paris, 1857–66, 162 vols; also in A.E. McGrath (ed.) *The Christian Theology Reader*, Oxford: Blackwell, 1995, 141–2. (The source for the quotation discussed in §1, a famous line standardly quoted in discussions of Apollinarianism. McGrath's book contains an English translation of relevant parts of Gregory's letter.)

* Herbert, R.T. (1979) *Paradox and Identity in Theology*, Ithaca, NY: Cornell University Press. (An excellent discussion of the logical problems of the Incarnation, which contains Herbert's 'ambiguous figure' model; see especially chapter 4, 'The Absolute Paradox: The God-Man'.)

* Kelly, J.N.D. (1960) *Early Christian Doctrines*, London: A. & C. Black, 2nd edn. (The source of the translation of the Definition of Chalcedon quoted in the text; see especially pages 339–41.)

* —— (1964) *The Athanasian Creed*, London: A. & C. Black. (The source of the translation quoted in the text; see especially pages 19–20.)

McGrath, A.E. (1994) *Christian Theology: An Introduction*, Oxford: Blackwell. (Recommended for readers with no background in theology or Church history. Clear and reliable. See especially chapter 9, 'The Doctrine of the Person of Christ'.)

* Morris, T.V. (1986) *The Logic of God Incarnate*, Ithaca, NY: Cornell University Press. (The most important recent work on the Incarnation by a philosopher at time of writing. Contains discussions of most of the issues addressed in this article, as well as a presentation of Morris' 'two minds' Christology. May be consulted for references to a wide range of recent philosophical work on the Incarnation.)

* Van Inwagen, P. (1994) 'Not by Confusion of Substance, but by Unity of Person', in A.G. Padgett (ed.) *Reason and the Christian Religion: Essays in Honour of Richard Swinburne*, Oxford: Clarendon Press. (An application of the 'logic of relative identity' to the problems of Christology. Contains what could be described as an analysis of '*qua* God' and '*qua* man' in terms of relative identities.)

PETER VAN INWAGEN

INCOMMENSURABILITY

When one scientific theory or tradition is replaced by another in a scientific revolution, the concepts involved often change in fundamental ways. For example, among other differences, in Newtonian mechanics an object's mass is independent of its velocity, while in relativity mechanics, mass increases as the velocity approaches that of light. Earlier philosophers of science maintained that Einsteinian mechanics reduces to Newtonian mechanics in the limit of high velocities. However, Thomas Kuhn (1962) and Paul Feyerabend (1962, 1965) introduced a rival view. Kuhn argued that different scientific traditions are defined by their adherence to different paradigms, *fundamental perspectives which shape or determine not only substantive beliefs about the world, but also methods, problems, standards of solution or explanation, and even what counts as an observation or fact. Scientific revolutions (changes of paradigm) alter all these profoundly, leading to perspectives so different that the meanings of words looking and sounding the same become utterly distinct in the pre- and post-revolutionary traditions. Thus, according to both Kuhn and Feyerabend, the concepts of mass employed in the Newtonian and Einsteinian traditions are incommensurable with one another, too radically different to be compared at all. The thesis that terms in different scientific traditions and communities are radically distinct, and the modifications that have stemmed from that thesis, became known as the thesis of incommensurability.*

1 **Early phase of the debate**
2 **Criticisms of early forms of the thesis**
3 **Later phase of the debate**

1 Early phase of the debate

The thesis of incommensurability stemmed from new historical research indicating to some that 'once current views of nature were, as a whole, neither less scientific nor more the product of human idiosyncrasy than those current today' (Kuhn 1962: 2). Transitions from one theory to another seemed no longer understandable as resulting from new evidence forcing the rejection of one theory and the acceptance of a new one. The positivistic idea of evidence common to the rejected view and its replacement, of observations which remained invariant under theoretical change, had become suspect. More radical sorts of change seemed involved, implicating even scientific standards, methods and goals.

In the introduction to *The Structure of Scientific Revolutions* (1962) Kuhn framed the incommensurability claim in terms of 'paradigms', bodies of 'universally recognized scientific achievements that for a time provide model problems and solutions to a community of practitioners'. However, the paradigm itself is more 'global' than formulations in terms of particular theories or achievements. During its period of dominance, the paradigm governs research, shaping the community's 'methods, problem-field, and standards of solution' (1962: 102). Different paradigms shape different conceptions of all these, and also of observations or facts, methods, goals of science, and therefore the definition of the corresponding science. There remain no extra-paradigmatic criteria in terms of which two different paradigms can be compared or judged. Consequently, despite the retention in successive paradigms of many of the same terms (for example, 'mass' in Newtonian and Einsteinian physics), the concepts (presumably, the meanings of the terms) are so different as to be incomparable. Different paradigms are 'not only incompatible but often

actually incommensurable with that which has gone before' (1962: 102). Communication between adherents of different paradigms is impossible (see KUHN, T.S.).

Feyerabend's (1962, 1965) formulation of the thesis is similar to Kuhn's in many respects. He speaks of 'high-level background theories', rather than more 'global' paradigms, which shape the way science is done, and is more explicit than Kuhn in asserting that high-level background theories lie behind languages. Nevertheless, he agrees with Kuhn that at least some fundamental theories are incommensurable. Whereas the early Kuhn was at best ambivalent about the extent of incommensurability between paradigms (see §3), Feyerabend throughout his career asserted that incommensurability is rare, occurring only under special circumstances, the nature of which he never clarified. (Kuhn later came to agree that incommensurability is only 'local'.) The major difference between the two is that while Kuhn believed a scientific community or tradition to be governed by a common paradigm, Feyerabend argued that scientists should try to develop alternative hypotheses, the more radically different from the accepted one the better (see FEYERABEND, P.K.).

2 Criticisms of early forms of the thesis

These early forms of the incommensurability thesis were criticized on four general grounds.

First, the thesis as presented is vague and ambiguous. There are problems with the claim itself and what it has to do with. As to the claim itself, it relied on the vague terms 'paradigm' and 'high-level background theory'; but what is a paradigm exactly, especially if it is more 'global' than any attempted formulation of it? (Masterman (see Lakatos and Musgrave 1970) pinpoints twenty-one different uses of the word 'paradigm' in Kuhn's 1962 edition of *Scientific Revolutions*.) How, precisely, does it shape or determine the ways members of a tradition or community think – the standards, methods, and so on? Are the ways of thinking deduced from the paradigm, or does the paradigm exercise merely a psychological (rather than logical) control? These and other vagaries infected the incommensurability thesis, and were only aggravated by Kuhn's frequent but never-explained qualifications of his more radical contentions. Thus he declared, without further comment, that it is only 'often' that paradigm changes result in incommensurability. Elsewhere he maintained that 'proponents of competing paradigms practise their trades in different worlds...[and] see different things when they look from the same point in the same direction' (1962: 150). Yet he also alleged that they 'see different things' in 'different areas', presumably of the same world.

The thesis is also unclear about what it is about different paradigms that is incommensurable. Kuhn himself spoke of three types of incommensurability: conceptual, observational and methodological. Much discussion, both on Kuhn's part and that of his critics, has centred on the first of these: how is the claim of conceptual incommensurability to be understood? Much of Kuhn's talk suggests that it has to do with terms like 'mass' and their incomparability in different paradigm traditions. But what is it about such terms that is incommensurable? Is it their *meanings* that are so radically different, or their *referents*? Focusing on their meanings (for reference, see §3), what is supposed to be part of the incomparable meaning of a term? There are obviously similarities between the Newtonian and Einsteinian meanings of 'mass'; if the meanings themselves are held incomparable, the similarities are presumably relegated to the non-meaning portions of their use. Kuhn does not discuss this distinction. Further, are all the terms of a paradigm tradition incommensurable with all those of another, or does incommensurability arise only for some of the terms? Certainly Feyerabend believed that 'the meaning of every term we use depends upon the theoretical context in which it occurs' (1965: 180). Kuhn, too, sometimes wrote as if proponents of different paradigms are 'always at cross-purposes', that communication across paradigms is 'inevitable', though sometimes he qualified this claim by saying that they are only 'partially' so, 'in some areas' (1962: 149). But which is it, partial in all areas, complete in some areas, or both? Also, if the paradigm logically *entails* all the ways of thinking within a tradition, everything, presumably including all meanings, will be affected by the profound differences between paradigms; and even if determination by paradigm is only psychological rather than logical, the limits, if any, of such determination are left unclear. We are left wondering what it is that is incomparable, and whether there is anything that is not, and why.

Second, the thesis is incoherent, even self-contradictory. Feyerabend defines 'incommensurability' as: 'Two theories will be called incommensurable when the meanings of their main descriptive terms depend on mutually inconsistent principles' (1965: 227). This definition is puzzling, since for two propositions to be inconsistent with one another is for one to assert A and the other not A; but this is to share A and be comparable. In general there is ambiguity as to whether two fundamental theories *compete with*, *contradict* one another, or are strictly incomparable. This ambiguity also occurs in Kuhn when he claims that different paradigms explain in different ways; for this claim seems to require meta-paradigmatic criteria for identifying what counts as an explanation in each of the two paradigms – for saying that they differ in how they do something that can be compared, namely explain.

Third, the thesis leads to relativism – and merely through its vagueness and ambiguity, not through the revelations of its case studies. If a paradigm determines, in some sense, the standards, methods, goals, meanings of terms, and so on, used in a tradition or community, and if two paradigms are incommensurable with regard to these, then what criteria are left for assessing the relative merits of two different paradigms? *Reasons* become paradigm-relative, and there remain no paradigm-transcending reasons to accept one paradigm over another. Furthermore, these relativist consequences follow merely from the fact that paradigm scope and control are left so ambiguous. Much of the text suggests that paradigms control in the sense of determining, either logically or psychologically, all that goes on within a paradigm tradition. If, as Kuhn claimed in later years, this was never his intent, what he did want to say on these points was far from clear (see EPISTEMIC RELATIVISM).

Fourth, the thesis is falsified by actual science and its history. A host of historical case studies have purported to refute (or confirm) the incommensurability thesis. Many such studies, however, uncritically take it for granted that the thesis is clear and unambiguous, and that it need only be confronted with solid historical evidence to be refuted or confirmed.

3 Later phase of the debate

To the 1970 edition of *The Structure of Scientific Revolutions*, Kuhn appended a 'Postscript' replacing the term 'paradigm' with 'disciplinary matrix' and distinguishing four components of this matrix: 'symbolic generalizations', 'metaphysical paradigms', 'values' and 'exemplars' (1970: 182–6). These are transparadigmatic and can be used in comparison and evaluation of paradigms. The 'values' include 'accuracy of prediction...; the balance between esoteric and everyday matter; and the number of different problems solved' (1970: 205–6). However, 'such reasons function as values and ... they can thus be differently applied ... by men who concur in honoring them' (1970: 199–200). Thus they appeared to be agreed-on standards of comparison in name only, doing little to clarify and defend the thesis of incommensurability.

Kuhn's later writings (for example, 1983) speak

decreasingly of paradigms and increasingly of theories and languages. Otherwise, these later papers alter his previous ideas in at least three major respects. First, he advocates a theory of *local incommensurability*, according to which, rather than all meanings changing in revolutions, 'Only for a small subgroup of (usually interdefined) terms and for sentences containing them do problems of translatability arise' (1983: 670–1). Second, he distinguishes a 'narrow sense' of translation, piecemeal if not word-for-word, from 'interpretation', in which piecemeal translation is impossible. Third, combining these first two points, he argues that the interdefined concepts cause translation problems because they divide the world up in distinctive ways, different from the structurings of other theories or languages. This structuring can only be grasped holistically, by becoming familiar with the whole network of interrelations between the concepts and with the assumptions about the world which are made in that interlocked network. This constitutes *interpretation*, through which it is possible to gain an understanding of radically different theories even though *translation in the narrow sense* is impossible. Some critics maintain that the allegedly indissoluble connections of concepts can be disentangled in one way or another, for example, by attending to similarities and differences in the uses of *tokens* of terms (Kitcher) or by introducing a notion of *partial denotation* (Field). Kuhn's response to such arguments is that recognizing similarities and differences of denotation is only a first step in gaining adequate understanding of the alien theory or language. In any case, either on Kuhn's view or the views of such critics, this claim that two different theories can be mutually intelligible removes most of the sting that originally accompanied the charge of incommensurability. Understanding and communication are possible, even perhaps to a degree approximating that attainable through translation.

Other critics remain convinced that incommensurability in some radical sense holds for the *content of belief* of different traditions or fundamental theories, and have therefore turned to other aspects of the total scientific picture for ways of comparing and judging theories. Thus Laudan (1977: 143–5) has emphasized relative problem-solving ability, rather than factual disagreement, as the basis of theory comparison and evaluation. However, Laudan's view requires some unprovided principle of individuation for counting problems, and for giving them different weights on the basis of relative importance, ease of solution, and so on. Other writers have had recourse to formal and evaluative standards or internal consistency.

In recent years, attempts to resolve problems of

incommensurability by utilizing the causal theory of reference has been the most influential approach to the incommensurability claim. The causal theory of reference holds that the reference of a term is established not by a set of descriptive conditions having to do with the meaning of the term, but by ostension (roughly, pointing) in an original 'baptismal' ceremony, which reference is passed on to succeeding generations (see REFERENCE §4). Such constant reference can then serve as the basis for saying that very different traditions are continuous and comparable with one another, 'talking about the same thing', despite radical differences that may have come about between their descriptive concepts. There are many variations on this theme. Some writers have suggested that many successive 'baptismal events' can take place for a particular term, adding to or otherwise changing the original reference and extension; again, it has been objected that the references of theoretical terms in science cannot usually be established by pointing, and that some important types of reference must appeal to descriptive criteria. Sankey (1994) incorporates these and other modifications in a version of the causal theory that is consistent with incommensurability but allows comparability, thus harmonizing with Kuhn's later views. Again, however, this is an extremely weak version of incommensurability. In any case, the near-mythical nature of the baptismal event, the possibility of a succession of these, and the difficulties of satisfactorily interpreting theoretical terms along the lines of the causal theory of reference, all make it unlikely that appeal to that theory can help resolve disputes about the continuity or discontinuity of science.

A further possible solution of worries about incommensurability (Shapere 1989) consists in an analysis of the *reasons* advanced for altering a reference-fixing condition (for example, the particular shape of a track in a cloud chamber under particular conditions) or for making changes in attributions of descriptive properties to theoretical entities (for example, neutrinos). On this view, changes come about in understandable ways, and can be in either reference or meaning. This approach places the burden of analysis on the concept of a reason, rather than on meaning or reference, but it is perhaps closer to the ways scientists actually proceed.

References and further readings

* Feyerabend, P.K. (1962) 'Explanation, Reduction and Empiricism', in H. Feigl and G. Maxwell (eds) *Minnesota Studies in the Philosophy of Science*, Minneapolis, MI: University of Minnesota Press, vol. III, 28–97. (One of two early papers in which

Feyerabend presented his views of incommensurability.)

* —— (1965) 'Problems of Empiricism', in R.G. Colodny (ed.) *Beyond the Edge of Certainty*, Englewood Cliffs, NJ: Prentice Hall, 145–260. (The second of two early papers in which Feyerabend presented his views of incommensurability.)

Field, H. (1973) 'Theory Change and the Indeterminacy of Reference', *Journal of Philosophy* 70: 462–81. (Argues that there may be 'denotational refinement' of terms in transitions from one theoretical context to a later one.)

Gutting, G. (ed.) (1980) *Paradigms and Revolutions: Applications and Appraisals of Thomas Kuhn's Philosophy of Science*, Notre Dame, IN: Notre Dame University Press. (Articles on Kuhn, including both critical reviews and case studies.)

Hacking, I. (ed.) (1981) *Scientific Revolutions*, London: Oxford University Press. (Useful collection of articles.)

Hoyningen-Huene, P. (1993) *Reconstructing Scientific Revolutions: Thomas S. Kuhn's Philosophy of Science*, Chicago, IL: University of Chicago Press. (Careful study of Kuhn's views, usually interpreting him in a favourable light. Comprehensive bibliography.)

Kitcher, P. (1978) 'Theories, Theorists and Theoretical Change', *The Philosophical Review* 87: 519–47. (Approaches incommensurability problem via a distinction between types and tokens of a term.)

* Kuhn, T.S. (1962, 1970) *The Structure of Scientific Revolutions*, Chicago, IL: University of Chicago Press. (Second edition contains the important 'Postscript' in which Kuhn clarifies – or alters – his concept of a paradigm.)

* —— (1983) 'Commensurability, Comparability, Communicability', in P.D. Asquith and T. Nickles (eds) *PSA 1982*, East Lansing, MI: Philosophy of Science Association, vol. 2, 669–88. (Contains comments by P. Kitcher and M. Hesse with responses by Kuhn. Symposium discussion revealing evolution of Kuhn's thought.)

* Lakatos, I. and Musgrave, A. (eds) (1970) *Criticism and the Growth of Knowledge*, Cambridge: Cambridge University Press. (Post-*Structure* Kuhn and his critics, with an initial and a final article by Kuhn from the same period as the 'Postscript' to *Structure*. See especially the article by Masterman mentioned in §2.)

* Laudan, L. (1977) *Progress and its Problems*, Berkeley, CA: University of California Press. (See §3.)

* Sankey, H. (1994) *The Incommensurability Thesis*, Sydney: Averbury Press. (Critical review of attempts to deal with the problem, with the author's own views. Comprehensive bibliography.)

* Shapere, D. (1989) 'Evolution and Continuity in Scientific Change', *Philosophy of Science*, 419–37. (Scientific change and continuity seen in terms of reasons rather than in terms of linguistic categories of meaning and reference.)

—— (1971) 'The Paradigm Concept', *Science* 172: 706–9. (Review of the second edition of *Structure*, focusing on the 'Postscript' and on Kuhn's papers in Lakatos and Musgrave 1970, and supplementing this author's review reprinted in Gutting 1980.)

DUDLEY SHAPERE

INCONTINENCE *see* AKRASIA

INDETERMINACY OF MEANING AND TRANSLATION *see* RADICAL TRANSLATION AND RADICAL INTERPRETATION

INDETERMINISM *see* DETERMINISM AND INDETERMINISM

INDEXICAL CONTENT *see* CONTENT, INDEXICAL

INDEXICALITY *see* CONTENT, INDEXICAL; DEMONSTRATIVES AND INDEXICALS

INDIAN AND TIBETAN PHILOSOPHY

The people of South Asia have been grappling with philosophical issues, and writing down their thoughts, for at least as long as the Europeans and the Chinese. When Hellenistic philosophers accompanied Alexander the Great on his military campaigns into the Indus valley, on the western edge of what is now the Republic of India, they expressed delight and amazement upon encountering Indians who thought as they thought and lived the sort of reflective life that they recommended living.

Nearly all philosophical contributions in India were made by people writing (or speaking) commentaries on already existing texts; to be a philosopher was to interpret a text and to be part of a more or less well-defined textual tradition. It is common, therefore, when speaking of Indian philosophers, to identify them as belonging to one school or another. To belong to a school of philosophy was a matter of having an interpretation of the principal texts that defined that school. At the broadest level of generalization, Indians of the classical period were either Hindus, Buddhists or Jainas (see BUDDHIST PHILOSOPHY, INDIAN; HINDU PHILOSOPHY; JAINA PHILOSOPHY). In addition to these three schools, all of which were in some sense religious, there was a more secular school in the classical period, whose tenets were materialistic and hedonistic (see MATERIALISM, INDIAN SCHOOL OF). The end of the classical period in Indian philosophy is customarily marked by the arrival of Muslims from Turkey and Persia at the close of the first millennium. The contributions of Indian Muslims added to the richness of Indian philosophy during the medieval period (see ISLAMIC PHILOSOPHY).

Writing was introduced into Tibet not long after the arrival of Buddhism from India in the seventh century. The earliest literature of Tibet was made up mostly of Buddhist texts, translated from Indian languages and from Chinese. Eventually, ideas associated with Bon, the indigenous religion of Tibet, were also written down. Tibetan philosophers followed the habit of Indians in that they made their principal contributions by writing commentaries on earlier texts (see TIBETAN PHILOSOPHY). Key Buddhist philosophers from Tibet are SA SKYA PAṆḌITA (1182–1251), TSONG KHA PA BLO BZANG GRAGS PA (1357–1419), RGYAL TSHAB DAR MA RIN CHEN (1364–1432), MKHAS GRUB DGE LEGS DPAL BZANG PO (1385–1438) and MI BSKYOD RDO RJE (1507–54).

1 Hindu philosophy

The philosophical schools associated with what we now call Hinduism all had in common respect for the authority of the Veda ('Knowledge'), scriptures accepted as a revealed body of wisdom, cosmological information and codes of societal obligations. The textual schools that systematized disciplines derived from the Veda were the Mīmāṃsā, the Nyāya, the Vaiśeṣika, the Sāṅkhya and the various Vedānta schools (see MĪMĀṂSĀ; NYĀYA-VAIŚEṢIKA; SĀṄKHYA; VEDĀNTA). Concerned as all these schools

were with correct interpretation of the Veda, it is natural that questions of language were of paramount importance in Indian philosophy (see LANGUAGE, INDIAN THEORIES OF; MEANING, INDIAN THEORIES OF). These involved detailed investigation into how subjects are to be defined and how texts are to be interpreted (see DEFINITION, INDIAN CONCEPTS OF; INTERPRETATION, INDIAN THEORIES OF).

Closely related to questions of language were questions of knowledge in general and its sources (see EPISTEMOLOGY, INDIAN SCHOOLS OF; KNOWLEDGE, INDIAN VIEWS OF). The two most important sources of knowledge that Indian philosophers discussed were sensation and inference, the theory of inference being important to the development of logic in India (see SENSE PERCEPTION, INDIAN VIEWS OF; INFERENCE, INDIAN THEORIES OF). Another topic about which Indian thinkers had much to say was the problem of how absences are known (see NEGATIVE FACTS IN CLASSICAL INDIAN PHILOSOPHY). Because of the importance of scriptures and religious teachers, epistemologists in India discussed the issue of the authority of texts and the question of the reliability of information conveyed through human language (see TESTIMONY IN INDIAN PHILOSOPHY). The questions associated with epistemology are in Indian philosophy often closely connected with questions of human psychology (see AWARENESS IN INDIAN THOUGHT; ERROR AND ILLUSION, INDIAN CONCEPTIONS OF).

Most schools of Indian philosophy offered not only an epistemology but also an ontology (see ONTOLOGY IN INDIAN PHILOSOPHY). Many posited a personal creator god or an impersonal godhead (see GOD, INDIAN CONCEPTIONS OF; BRAHMAN; MONISM, INDIAN). Just how particular things come into being through creative agency or through impersonal natural laws was a matter of considerable debate (see CAUSATION, INDIAN THEORIES OF; COSMOLOGY AND COSMOGONY, INDIAN THEORIES OF). Indian thinkers also debated the precise nature of matter, the ontological status of universals, and how potentials become actualities (see MATTER, INDIAN CONCEPTIONS OF; UNIVERSALS, INDIAN THEORIES OF; POTENTIALITY, INDIAN THEORIES OF).

In addition to epistemology and metaphysics, a third area that Indian systematic philosophers nearly always commented upon were issues concerning the nature of the human being (see SELF, INDIAN THEORIES OF; MIND, INDIAN PHILOSOPHY OF). This included thoughts on a variety of ethical questions and the rewards for living an ethical life (see DUTY AND VIRTUE, INDIAN CONCEPTIONS OF; KARMA AND REBIRTH, INDIAN CONCEPTIONS OF; FATALISM, INDIAN; HEAVEN, INDIAN CONCEPTIONS OF). While most thinkers dealt with individual ethics, some also gave attention to the question of collective behaviour and policy (see POLITICAL PHILOSOPHY, INDIAN).

The Hindu tradition produced a number of important individual philosophers. Among the earliest extant philosophers from India are the political theorist KAUṬILYA (fourth century BC) and the grammarian and philosopher of language PATAÑJALI (second century BC). The legendary founder of the Nyāya school, Akṣapāda GAUTAMA, is traditionally regarded as the author of a set of aphorisms that modern scholars believe were composed in the second or third century. These aphorisms present the basic ontological categories and epistemological principles that were followed not only by the Nyāya school but by many others as well. The philosopher of language BHARTṚHARI (fifth century) developed the intriguing idea that the basic stuff of which all the universe is made is an intelligence in the form of a readiness to use language. VĀTSYĀYANA (fifth century) and UDDYOTAKARA (sixth century) were both commentators on Gautama. The Vedānta systematist ŚAṄKARA (eighth century) wrote that realizing the underlying unity of all things in the form of Brahman could set one free. The aesthetician ABHINAVAGUPTA (tenth–eleventh century) made the education of the emotions through the cultivation of aesthetic sensitivity the basis of liberation from the turmoil of life. UDAYANA (eleventh century) of the Nyāya school developed important arguments for the existence of God. RĀMĀNUJA (eleventh–twelfth century) and MADHVA (thirteenth century), both Vedāntins, offered systems that became serious rivals to Śaṅkara's monism. The work of the logician GAṄGEŚA (fourteenth century), who revised the classical system of logic and epistemology, became the foundation for an important new school of thought, Navya-Nyāya ('New Nyāya'). MĀDHAVA (fourteenth century) and VALLABHĀCĀRYA (fifteenth–sixteenth century) made important contributions to Vedāntin philosophy. GADĀDHARA (seventeenth century) continued making advances in logical theory by building on the work of Gaṅgeśa. Also important in the sixteenth century were several thinkers who commented upon the religious thinker Caitanya (see GAUḌĪYA VAIṢṆAVISM). Finally, there were several thinkers and movements in the nineteenth and twentieth centuries, a period during which Indian intellectuals struggled to reconcile traditional Indian ways of thinking with European and especially British influences (see AUROBINDO GHOSE; GANDHI, M.K.; RADHAKRISHNAN, S.; TAGORE, R.; ARYA SAMAJ; BRAHMO SAMAJ; RAMAKRISHNA MOVEMENT).

2 Buddhist and Jaina philosophy

As was the case for Hindu philosophy, Buddhist and Jaina Philosophy in India tended to proceed through commentaries on already existing texts. Jainism was founded by MAHĀVĪRA and is best known for its method of seeing every issue from every possible point of view (see MANIFOLDNESS, JAINA THEORY OF). The principal Buddhist traditions that incorporated significant philosophical discussions were those that tried to systematize doctrines contained in various corpora of texts believed to be the words of the Buddha (see BUDDHISM, ĀBHIDHARMIKA SCHOOLS OF; BUDDHISM, MĀDHYAMIKA: INDIA AND TIBET; BUDDHISM, YOGĀCĀRA SCHOOL OF). An important issue for Buddhist thinkers, as for most Indian philosophers, was analysing the causes of discontent and suggesting a method for eliminating unhappiness, the cessation of suffering being a condition known as *nirvāṇa* (see SUFFERING, BUDDHIST VIEWS OF ORIGINATION OF; NIRVĀṆA). A doctrine of special interest to the Mādhyamika school was that everything is conditioned and therefore lacking independence (see BUDDHIST CONCEPT OF EMPTINESS). Some Buddhists developed the view that the conditioned world is so transitory that it disappears and is recreated in every moment (see MOMENTARINESS, BUDDHIST DOCTRINE OF). In the area of epistemology and philosophy of language, some Buddhists repudiated the Hindu confidence in the authority of the Veda (see NOMINALISM, BUDDHIST DOCTRINE OF).

The Buddhist tradition gave India a number of important philosophers, beginning with the founder of the religion, the BUDDHA (fifth century BC). The first important Buddhist philosopher to write in Sanskrit and the man traditionally regarded as the founder of the Mādhyamika school was NĀGĀRJUNA (second century). A key commentator in both the Ābhidharmika schools and in the Yogācāra school was VASUBANDHU (fifth century). Two key Buddhist epistemologists and logicians were DIGNĀGA (fifth century) and DHARMAKĪRTI (seventh century). Buddhism disappeared from northern India in the twelfth century and from southern India a few centuries later. In the twentieth century, there has been an effort to revive it, especially among the community formerly known as 'untouchables'. A remarkable leader of this community was Bhimrao Ramji AMBEDKAR.

3 Pronunciation of Sanskrit words

Sanskrit is an Indo-European language, closely related to Greek and Latin. In India, it is written in a variety of phonetic scripts, and in the West it is customary to write it in roman script. Many letters used to write Sanskrit are pronounced almost as they are in English; k, g, j, t, d, n, p, b, m, y, r, l, s and h can be pronounced as in English without too much distortion. The sound of the first consonant in the English word 'church' is represented by a simple 'c' in Sanskrit. In addition to these consonants there is a class of retroflex consonants, so called because the tongue is bent back so that the bottom side of the tongue touches the roof of the mouth. These sounds are represented by letters with dots under them: ṭ, ḍ, ṇ and ṣ. As in English, some consonants are heavily aspirated, so that they are pronounced with a slight puff of air. These consonants are represented by single letters in Indian scripts but by two-letter combinations in roman script; thus 'kh' is pronounced as the 'k' in English 'kill', 'th' as 't' in 'tame' (never as 'th' in 'thin' or 'there'), 'dh' as in 'mudhouse', and 'ph' as 'p' in 'pat' (never as 'ph' in 'philosophy'). The letter 'ś' is approximately like 'sh' in 'shingle'. The letter 'ṅ' is like 'ng' in 'finger' or 'nk' in 'sink', while 'ñ' is approximately like 'ny' in 'canyon'.

Vowels are pronounced approximately as in Spanish or Italian. Vowels with a macron over them (ā, ī and ū) are pronounced for twice as much time as their unmarked equivalents. The vowel 'ṛ' is pronounced with the tip of the tongue elevated towards the roof of the mouth, very much like the 'er' in the American pronunciation of 'carter'. The diphthongs 'ai' and 'au' are pronounced as 'i' in 'kite' and 'ou' in 'scout' (or almost as 'ei' and 'au' are pronounced in German) respectively. Accent tends to be on the third syllable from the end; thus the name 'Śaṅkara' sounds like 'SHANG-ka-ra', not 'shang-KA-ra'. If the second syllable from the end is long, then it is accented; 'Dignāga' is pronounced 'dig-NAA-ga'.

4 Pronunciation of Tibetan words

Tibetan is a language of the Sino-Tibetan family, which includes various languages spoken in China as well as Burmese and Thai. It is written in a phonetic alphabet derived from the Brahmi script of India, from which most modern Indian scripts, as well as the alphabets used to write Sinhalese, Thai and Mon, are also derived. There are many different systems commonly used by Europeans to transliterate the spelling of Tibetan words. In this encyclopedia, the system designed by T. Wylie is used for transliteration, and a system used at the University of Virginia is used to indicate approximate pronunciation of names.

The spelling of Tibetan words was fixed over a millennium ago and has not changed since. Pronunciation, however, has shifted. Unfortunately, it has not shifted in exactly the same way in every region of Tibet, with the result that the same written word may

be pronounced quite differently in the east of Tibet from the way it is pronounced in the west and the central region. The University of Virginia system of indicating pronunciation captures the dialects of central Tibet, which have shifted the greatest distance from the pronunciations of a millennium ago. Consequently, many combinations of letters are not pronounced at all as they once were, and numerous letters have become silent in modern central Tibetan dialects. Given all these changes, the pronunciation of some Tibetan words can be surprisingly different from what one might expect from their spelling.

Many single letters and combinations are pronounced about as in Sanskrit, as described above; so k, kh, g, ṅ, c, j, ñ, t, th, d, n, p, ph, b, m, y, r, l, s and h can be pronounced as described there. The pairs of letters 'ts' and 'dz' represent single letters in the Tibetan alphabet and are pronounced as they would be in English 'cats' and 'adze' respectively. The letters 'tsh' represent a single Tibetan letter that is pronounced like an aspirated version of 'ts'. The combination 'sh' is used to represent a Tibetan letter that is pronounced about like 'sh' in 'show'. Some combinations of Tibetan letters are no longer pronounced as they were when spelling was fixed. Examples of this are 'kr', 'tr' and 'pr', all of which are now pronounced the same way, approximately as the 'tr' in 'trick'. Similarly, 'gr', 'dr' and 'br' are all pronounced about like 'dr' in 'drink'. When the letters 'g', 'b', 'm', 'r', 'l' and 's' occur at the beginning of a syllable and are followed immediately by any consonant other than 'r' or 'l', they are usually silent. The letter 's' at the end of a syllable is usually silent. Thus 'bsdigs' is pronounced somewhere between English 'dig' and 'dick'.

The Tibetan script does not have upper-case and lower-case letters, so there is no custom of writing proper names any differently from ordinary words. In roman transliteration, however, it is customary to capitalize the first pronounced letter of a name. In the name 'rGyal tshab', for example, the silent 'r' is not capitalized. Similarly, in 'mKhas grub' the silent 'm' is not upper case.

Tibetan consonants are pronounced with no trace of aspiration or with heavy aspiration. To the English ear attuned to hearing aspiration about midway between that used in Tibetan consonants, Tibetan 't' can sound like English 'd' and vice versa. Similarly, Tibetan 'k' and 'p' can sound like English 'g' and 'b' respectively. At the end of words, Tibetan 'g' and 'b' may sound like English 'k' and 'p' respectively. It is for this reason that the Virginia phonetic system renders 'Tsong kha pa' as 'Dzong-ka-ba' and 'rGyal tshab' as 'Gyel-tsap'. In the name 'mKhas grub rje' we can see many of the principles discussed above represented in its Virginia rendering as 'kay-drup-jay'.

See also: BUDDHIST PHILOSOPHY, CHINESE; IQBAL, M.; MYSTICISM, HISTORY OF; REINCARNATION; SALVATION; SHAH WALI ALLAH (QUTB AL-DIN AHMAD AL-RAHIM)

Further reading

Mohanty, J.N. (1992) *Reason and Tradition in Indian Thought. An Essay on the Nature of Indian Philosophical Thinking*, Oxford: Clarendon Press. (A thoughtful exploration of the principal issues of Indian philosophy.)

Powers, J. (1995) *Introduction to Tibetan Buddhism*, Ithaca, NY: Snow Lion Publications. (A useful survey of the main schools of Tibetan Buddhism, as well as of the Bon tradition.)

Raju, P.T. (1985) *Structural Depths of Indian Thought*, Albany, NY: State University of New York Press. (A good survey of the different schools of Indian philosophy from ancient times to the present.)

RICHARD P. HAYES

INDIAN ISLAMIC PHILOSOPHY *see* IQBAL, MUHAMMAD; SHAH WALI ALLAH (QUTB AL-DIN AHMAD AL-RAHIM)

INDICATIVE CONDITIONALS

Examples of indicative conditionals are 'If it rained, then the match was cancelled' and 'If Alex plays, Carlton will win'. The contrast is with subjunctive or counterfactual conditionals, such as 'If it had rained, then the match would have been cancelled', and categoricals, such as 'It will rain'.

Despite the ease with which we use and understand indicative conditionals, the correct account of them has proved to be very difficult. Some say that 'If it rained, the match was cancelled' is equivalent to 'Either it did not rain, or the match was cancelled'. Some say that the sentence asserts that the result of 'adding' the supposition that it rained to the actual situation is to give a situation in which the match was cancelled. Some say that to assert that if it rained then the match was cancelled is to make a commitment to inferring that the match was cancelled should one learn that it rained.

This last view is often combined with the view that indicative conditionals are not, strictly speaking, true or false; rather, they are more or less assertible or acceptable.

1   **Indicative and material conditionals**
2   **Possible worlds treatments**
3   **Adams and Lewis**

1   Indicative and material conditionals

In general an 'indicative conditional' has the form 'If A then C', where A is called the antecedent and C the consequent. A central issue is the relationship between the truth-value of a conditional and the truth-values of its antecedent and consequent. This much is immediately plausible: if A is true and C is false, then the conditional is false. If I say 'If it rained, the match was cancelled', and what happened was that it rained but the match went ahead, then what I say is clearly false. There are three other possibilities: A and C are both true, A is false and C is true, and A and C are both false. There are a number of arguments designed to show that in each of these cases the conditional is true. Here is one. 'If A then C' is intuitively equivalent to the disjunction 'Either not-A, or A and C'. (Instead of saying that if it rained the match was cancelled, I could have said 'Either it did not rain, or it did and the match was cancelled'.) But the latter is true in all three cases: in each, either the first disjunct ('not-A') or the second disjunct ('A and C') is true. A conditional that is false when its antecedent is true and its consequent false, and true in all other cases, is called a 'material conditional', and is symbolized '$A \supset C$' (read 'A hook C'). '$A \supset C$' is definitionally equivalent to 'Not-A or C'. Hence the argument's conclusion is that indicative conditionals are equivalent to material conditionals. This conclusion has the virtue of validating the two most obviously valid inferences governing conditionals – *modus ponens*: 'A, if A then C, therefore, C', and *modus tollens*: 'Not-C, if A then C, therefore, not-A'.

Despite the appeal of the argument, there are serious problems for the equivalence thesis that indicative conditionals are material conditionals. It entails that any conditional with a false antecedent is true regardless of its consequent, that is, the account validates 'Not-A, therefore, if A then C'. This is implausible. 'If I live in London then I live in Scotland' strikes us as false (it is rather 'If I live in London then I do not live in Scotland' which is true), but because I do not live in London, it is true on the equivalence thesis. Also, it entails that any conditional with a true consequent is true: the account validates

'C', therefore, if A then C'. But 'If I live in London, then I live in Australia' strikes us as false even after we learn that I do in fact live in Australia. These two results are known as the paradoxes of material implication ('material implication' being the name of the relation between A and C when '$A \supset C$' is true).

2 Possible worlds treatments

An obvious response to the paradoxes is to insist that more than the truth of '$A \supset C$' is required in order for 'If A then C' to be true; that the truth of '$A \supset C$' is a necessary but insufficient condition. One way to do this is to require a connection between antecedent and consequent; to hold that part of what makes 'If it rains, the grass will grow' true is the connection between rain and grass growing. This blocks the paradoxes. However, we sometimes use conditionals precisely to deny that there is a connection between antecedent and consequent. A doctor who says that if you go to bed and take an aspirin you will get better in a week, whereas if you go to work it will take seven days, is saying that there is no connection between going to bed and getting better.

A more promising approach is to require that the material conditional not only be true the way things actually are, but be true in the closest possible worlds where the antecedent is true (see SEMANTICS, POSSIBLE WORLDS). Roughly, the account is: 'If A then C' is true iff '$A \supset C$' is true, that is, true the ways things actually are *and also* true in the closest possible worlds where A is true. Another way of saying the same thing is: 'If A then C' is true iff the closest worlds in which A is true are worlds in which C is also true. (This is because any world where A and '$A \supset C$' are true is a world where C is true.) The appeal of this approach derives from the appeal of the idea that when we evaluate a conditional we look at the way things actually are and 'in imagination' add the antecedent and then see whether, with only the changes forced by adding the antecedent, the consequent comes out true.

This approach is very attractive for subjunctive or counterfactual conditionals (see COUNTERFACTUAL CONDITIONALS) but faces a problem when applied to indicative conditionals. (Interestingly, one architect of the possible worlds approach to conditionals, David LEWIS (1973), only ever intended it to apply to subjunctive conditionals. Robert Stalnaker, the other architect (1968), intended it to apply to both.) It construes indicative conditionals as being in part about the way things might have been but are not in fact. That seems exactly right for subjunctives. When I say that had I invested in Western Mining ten years ago, I would now be rich, I am saying how things are

in some possible but regrettably non-actual world. Indeed, I might express this by saying that had I invested in Western Mining ten years ago, things would now be different – and better – than they actually are. But I cannot say this in the indicative mood: 'If I invested in Western Mining ten years ago, things are different from the way they actually are' is nonsense. Or consider the difference between 'If Oswald had not shot Kennedy, Kennedy would have won a second term' and 'If Oswald did not shoot Kennedy, Kennedy won a second term'. The reason we reject the second, despite accepting the first, is that we know that the way things actually are Kennedy did not live to win a second term. Subjunctive conditionals typically concern non-actual worlds, whereas indicative conditionals concern the actual world under various hypotheses about what it is like. Thus we say that if Oswald did not shoot Kennedy, someone else did, because that is the only thing to think about the actual world (in which we know that Kennedy was shot) given that Oswald was not responsible.

3 Adams and Lewis

What about the acceptance or justified assertion conditions, as opposed to truth-conditions, for indicative conditionals? Many, including particularly Ernest Adams (1975), have urged that it is justified to assert 'If A then C' to the extent that C is probable given A. Because the probability of C given A – in symbols, $Pr(C|A)$ – is (roughly) the probability we ascribe to C on learning A (see PROBABILITY, INTERPRETATIONS OF §5), this suggestion fits nicely with the plausible idea that one is prepared to assert 'If A then C' to the extent that one is prepared to infer C on learning A. It also explains our reluctance to assert together 'If A then C' and 'If A then not-C' when A is consistent, for when A is consistent, $Pr(C|A) = 1 - Pr(\text{not-}C|A)$, so they cannot be high together.

Can we explain this assertibility condition in terms of truth-conditions? David Lewis (1976) showed that it cannot be the case that the truth-conditions of 'If A then C' are such that $Pr(\text{If } A \text{ then } C) = Pr(C|A)$. For then this equality would hold for all probability functions Pr, and that leads to trouble as follows:

$$Pr(\text{If } A \text{ then } C) = Pr(\text{If } A \text{ then } C|C).Pr(C)$$
$$+ Pr(\text{If } A \text{ then } C|\text{not-}C).Pr(\text{not-}C),$$

by expansion by cases. But if $Pr(\text{If } A \text{ then } C) = Pr(C|A)$ holds for all Pr, then it holds for $Pr(-|C)$ and $Pr(-|\text{not-}C)$, as the class of probability functions is closed under conditionalization. This means that

741

$$Pr(\text{If } A \text{ then } C|C) = Pr(C|A.C)$$

$$Pr(\text{If } A \text{ then } C|\text{not-}C) = Pr(C|A.\text{not-}C)$$

(where $Pr(C|A.C)$ is the probability of C given the conjunction of A and C). Hence we have

$$Pr(\text{If } A \text{ then } C) = Pr(C|A.C).Pr(C)$$
$$+ Pr(C|A.\text{not-}C).Pr(\text{not-}C)$$
$$= 1.Pr(C) + 0.Pr(\text{not-}C)$$
$$= Pr(C)$$

But then, by the claim under discussion, $Pr(C) = Pr(C|A)$. This is a 'reductio', for in general the probability of C is not independent of that of A. (This is the essence of the simplest of the proofs Lewis offered. For the substantial developments see Lewis (1986).)

Many respond to this proof by holding that indicative conditionals do not have truth-conditions at all; they only have assertion or acceptance conditions. This theory undoubtedly has its attractions but faces two problems. What should be said about the powerful intuition that a conditional with a true antecedent and a false consequent is false? And how should the relevant notion of assertibility be elucidated? Not in terms of likelihood of truth, obviously.

An alternative strategy, called the supplemented equivalence theory, is to return to the equivalence thesis and argue that there is a convention governing the assertion of 'If A then C' to the effect that it should only be asserted when it would be right to infer C on learning A. This convention is like that governing the use of 'but'. 'A but C' has the same truth-conditions as 'A and C', but the use of the former conventionally implicates, in H.P. Grice's terminology, a contrast (see Grice 1975; IMPLICATURE). Likewise, runs the suggestion, 'If A then C' has the same truth-conditions as '$A \supset C$' but its use carries the implicature that my reasons for '$A \supset C$' are such that it would be right, on learning A, to infer C (that is, to use *modus ponens*). Now that will be the case just if the probability of '$A \supset C$' would not be unduly diminished on learning that A is true – otherwise it would not then be available as a probably true premise to combine with A on the way to inferring C. It follows that it will be right to assert 'If A then C' to the extent that (1) '$A \supset C$' is probable, and (2) '$A \supset C$' is probable given A. It is an elementary exercise in probability theory to show that this two-fold condition is satisfied to the extent that $Pr(C|A)$ is high. The supplemented equivalence theory therefore explains the assertibility condition noted by Adams.

What do supplemented equivalence theorists say about our earlier example 'If I live in London, then I live in Scotland', which comes out true on the equivalence theory and so on the supplemented equivalence theory? They say that it seems false not because it is false but because it has very low assertibility – Pr(I live in Scotland/I live in London) $= 0$ – and in general that our intuitions about truth and validity of inferences involving indicative conditionals are governed by responses to assertibility rather than truth.

Warning: almost everything about indicative conditionals is controversial, including whether they are well labelled by the term 'indicative', and some even deny the validity of *modus ponens*!

See also: LOGICAL AND MATHEMATICAL TERMS, GLOSSARY OF; RELEVANCE LOGIC AND ENTAILMENT

References and further reading

* Adams, E. (1975) *The Logic of Conditionals*, Dordrecht: Reidel. (A detailed defence of an approach to conditionals that denies them truth-conditions and shows how to develop a logic of conditionals based on his views about their assertibility.)

Appiah, A. (1985) *Assertion and Conditionals*, Cambridge: Cambridge University Press. (A detailed exposition of an account of indicative conditionals in terms of assertibility, set within the philosophy of mind.)

Edgington, D. (1995) 'On Conditionals', *Mind* 104: 235–329. (Excellent survey article that contains interesting material in its own right; includes a comprehensive and up-to-date reading list.)

* Grice, H.P. (1975) 'Logic and Conversation', in F. Jackson (ed.) *Conditionals*, Oxford: Oxford University Press, 1991. (Explains implicature and the distinction between conversational and conventional implicature.)

Jackson, F. (1987) *Conditionals*, Oxford: Blackwell. (A detailed defence of the supplemented equivalence theory with criticisms of various alternative accounts of indicative conditionals.)

* Lewis, D.K. (1973) *Counterfactuals*, Oxford: Blackwell. (The book which, along with Stalnaker's paper, launched the possible worlds approach to conditionals.)

* —— (1976) 'Probabilities of Conditionals and Conditional Probabilities', in F. Jackson (ed.) *Conditionals*, Oxford: Oxford University Press, 1991. (Gives the full version of the proof sketched in this entry.)

* —— (1986) 'Probabilities of Conditionals and Conditional Probabilities II', in F. Jackson (ed.)

Conditionals, Oxford: Oxford University Press, 1991. (More on the proof sketched in this entry.)

* Stalnaker, R. (1968) 'A Theory of Conditionals', in F. Jackson (ed.) *Conditionals*, Oxford: Oxford University Press, 1991. (The paper which, along with Lewis's book, launched the possible worlds approach to conditionals.)

FRANK JACKSON

INDIRECT DISCOURSE

Indirect discourse is a mode of speech-reporting whereby a speaker conveys the content of someone's utterance without quoting the actual words. Thus, if Pierre says, 'Paris est belle', an English speaker might truly say,

(1) Pierre said that Paris is beautiful.

In English, sentences of indirect discourse often have the form 'A said that s', where 'A' refers to a person and 's' is often called the 'content sentence' of the report.

Sentences of indirect discourse have been classed with attributions of belief (and other psychological states) in view of an apparent conflict with the 'principle of the intersubstitutability of coreferring terms', which states that the truth-value of a sentence does not alter if one term in a sentence is replaced with another referring to the same thing. If (1) is true and 'Paris' and 'the City of Light' refer to the same thing, (2) may still be false:

(2) Pierre said that the City of Light is beautiful.

1   Frege's theory
2   Davidson's theory

1   Frege's theory

In 'indirect discourse' a speaker reports someone's utterance without quoting the actual words used (often using the form 'A said that s'). Sentences of indirect discourse give rise to an apparent conflict with the 'principle of the intersubstitutability of coreferring terms', which states that the truth-value of a sentence does not alter if one term is replaced with another which refers to the same thing. Gottlob Frege (1892) put forward an important theory to deal with this problem. He proposed that 'said' alters what the words in the 'content sentence' ('s' above) refer to. For example, consider the following statements:

(1) Pierre said that Paris is beautiful.
(2) Pierre said that the City of Light is beautiful.

'Paris' and 'the City of Light' both usually refer to the actual city, Paris. The phrase 'is beautiful' usually refers to the set of beautiful things. But when words appear after the phrase 'said that', they refer to the meanings they normally express – which Frege called their 'senses' – which are not the same as their referents (see FREGE, G. §3).

The sense of an expression is a 'mode of presentation' of its referent. The sense associated with 'the City of Light' presents Paris in a particular way: as the City of Light. To understand an expression is to grasp its sense (see SENSE AND REFERENCE). Frege called the sense of a sentence a 'thought'. To have a propositional attitude is to stand in a certain relation to a thought. For example, to believe that Paris is beautiful is to stand in the believing relation to the thought that Paris is beautiful. Frege claimed that senses and thoughts are not psychological, mind-dependent things, but rather are Platonic, abstract objects. If two people believe that Paris is beautiful, then it is the very same thought that they both have. And this thought would exist even if there had been no minds (see FREGE, G. §4).

The Fregean theory explains away the apparent failures of intersubstitution: the 'senses' of 'Paris' and 'the City of Light' are different. Hence the words refer to different things in (1) and (2) and so no violation of the substitution principle occurs.

2   Davidson's theory

Donald Davidson (1968/1969) has provided a very different account of indirect discourse. Davidson proposed that, at the level of logical form (see LOGICAL FORM), the analysis of speech reports should be composed of two separate sentences, the first ending in the demonstrative pronoun 'that'. The analysis of (1) above would then be:

(3) Pierre said that. Paris is beautiful.

On Davidson's theory the two sentences are logically distinct (not connected by any logical particle, such as 'and'). However, on specific occasions of use the demonstrative 'that' ending the first sentence refers to the reporter's utterance of the second.

According to this theory, the direct object of the verb 'said' is the reporter's own token utterance. So, suppose that someone, A, utters (1). This speech act is composed of two token utterances: one of 'Pierre said that' and one of 'Paris is beautiful'. Call this latter utterance 'U'. Then, what Pierre would be reported as saying is U.

This feature is surprising, since it does not seem that Pierre could have said U (the reporter's utterance) itself. But Davidson provides an account of what 'said' means which addresses the difficulty. He introduces the notion of 'samesaying': roughly, two individuals are samesayers if and only if they produce utterances which have relevantly similar semantic contents. Davidson has provided a general theory of meaning and interpretation which underwrites his appeal to semantic contents in this context (1984). We are then to understand (1) along the following lines:

(4) There was some utterance, *u*, of Pierre's, and *u* and my next utterance make us samesayers. Paris is beautiful.

The idea is that the relation expressed by 'said' in *A*'s utterance of (1) can be understood in terms of the more complex relation spelled out in (4). But (4) is not intended to be any part of a technical semantic theory. It is just an informal, extra-theoretic guide to readers to help them understand the theory. In a semantic theory in Davidson's style (see DAVIDSON, D. §4), the axiom for 'said' might be:

(5) $(x)(y)$('said' is true of $\langle x, y \rangle$ iff x said y).

The point is that since 'said' is supposed to relate reportees to utterances of reporters, some informal explanation of this saying relation is required. (4) provides this explanation.

Davidson's theory explains the apparent failures of substitution such as that illustrated by (1) and (2). In an utterance of (1) the main verb is 'said' and its syntactic object is the demonstrative 'that'. The ensuing utterance of 'Paris is beautiful' only serves as a referent for the demonstrative. It is not in any other way a semantically relevant component of the report. An utterance of (1) and an utterance of (2) resemble each other in that each has the form 'Pierre said that'. But the referents of the two instances of 'that' are different utterances. So (1) does not entail (2). No violation of the intersubstitutability of coreferring terms occurs. The latter principle still applies to the content sentences of (1) and (2):

(6) Paris is beautiful.

(7) The City of Light is beautiful.

(6) does entail (7), given the coreference of 'Paris' and 'the City of Light'. But this has no direct bearing on the logical relations between (1) and (2).

Davidson's theory differs importantly from Frege's. The former does not entail any shifts of reference for the words in the content sentence, which has exactly the same semantic features as it would have if uttered in isolation. This feature of the theory implements a natural and elegant idea of how speech reporting works. When *A* reports on the speech of *B*, *A* produces a new sentence, *S*, as content sentence of the report. *S* in *A*'s mouth expresses the content of *B*'s speech act. The utterance of *S* then serves as a model of *B*'s original speech act. And this exhausts its role.

Various objections have been made to Davidson's proposal. Only two are discussed here. The first objection is due to Tyler Burge (1986). Burge points out that on Davidson's theory, an utterance of (8) below would be true only if there were some utterance of the reporter's and some utterance of Pierre's that made them samesayers:

(8) Pierre said something.

This result follows from the functioning of the word 'said' on the theory. But the result is wrong: I might utter (8) truly without myself ever making any utterance that would make Pierre and me samesayers. The objection is perhaps not conclusive. But Burge points out that a solution to the difficulty would be to allow the objects of speech reports to be abstract objects, rather than token utterances, and offers several further arguments that this solution is correct. It seems natural to take the relevant abstract objects to be sentence-types. If this suggestion is adopted, then Burge's objection forces no major revisions of Davidson's theory. The original account of 'said' in terms of samesaying no longer applies. But an analogous explanation of the functioning of 'said' remains available. Instead of understanding (1) along the lines of (4), we would understand it along the lines of:

(9) There was some sentence, *s*, which Pierre uttered, and *s* meant in Pierre's mouth then what the following means now in mine: Paris is beautiful.

The second objection is due to James Higginbotham (1986). On Davidson's account, (10) and (11) ought to have identical semantic features:

(10) Every girl said that her mother was kind.

(11) Every girl said that. Her mother was kind.

This is because (11) merely makes explicit the analysis that Davidson would attribute to (10). However, (10) and (11) are semantically distinguishable. (10) is ambiguous: on the first reading, (10) would be true if and only if each girl said of some specific contextually indicated person, *x*, that *x*'s mother was kind; on the second reading, it would be true if and only if each girl said that her own mother was kind. But (11) is only subject to the first reading. This objection shows that Davidson's theory is not correct as it stands, and will have to modified in very serious ways if it is to accommodate interactions between words inside and outside content sentences.

See also: LOGICAL AND MATHEMATICAL TERMS, GLOSSARY OF; PROPOSITIONAL ATTITUDE STATEMENTS

References and further reading

* Burge, T. (1986) 'On Davidson's "On Saying That"', in E. LePore (ed.) *Truth and Interpretation: Perspectives on the Philosophy of Donald Davidson*, New York: Blackwell, 191–208. (A critical article on Davidson's theory of indirect discourse.)
* Davidson, D. (1968/1969) 'On Saying That', *Synthese* 19: 130–46. (The classic work of Davidson's theory of indirect discourse, including criticisms of Frege's theory.)
* —— (1984) *Inquiries into Truth and Interpretation*, Oxford: Clarendon Press. (A collection of Davidson's articles in the philosophy of language, including some seminal works on the theory of meaning and interpretation.)
* Frege, G. (1892) 'Über Sinn und Bedeutung', *Zeitschrift für Philosophie und philosophische Kritik* 100: 25–50; trans. M. Black, 'On Sense and Reference', in *Translations from the Philosophical Writings of Gottlob Frege*, ed. P.T. Geach and M. Black, Oxford: Blackwell, 1962, 56–78; 3rd edn, 1980. (The first clear statement of the problems of apparent failures of intersubstitutability from the standpoint of technical semantic theory. One of the most influential articles in philosophy of language.)
Geach, P.T. (1957) *Mental Acts*, London: Routledge & Kegan Paul. (A general work in the philosophies of mind and language, including extended discussion of the relationship between saying and propositional attitudes such as believing or judging.)
* Higginbotham, J. (1986) 'Linguistic Theory and Davidson's Program in Semantics', in E. LePore (ed.) *Truth and Interpretation: Perspectives on the Philosophy of Donald Davidson*, New York: Blackwell, 29–48. (Argues for the incorporation of Davidson's main technical innovations in philosophical semantic theory into empirical linguistics and includes a sophisticated theory of indirect speech that retains some core aspects of Davidson's proposal but avoids the main objections to it.)
Scheffler, I. (1954) 'An Inscriptional Approach to Indirect Quotation', *Analysis* 10: 83–90. (An influential nominalist account of indirect discourse.)
Segal, G. and Speas, M. (1986) 'On Saying ð∋t', *Mind and Language* 1 (2): 124–32. (An article criticizing Davidson's theory of indirect discourse on empirical grounds.)
Quine, W.V. (1960) *Word and Object*, Cambridge, MA: MIT Press, 1964. (A general work in systematic philosophy including arguments critical of semantic theories, such as Frege's, that use a mentalistic or abstract notion of meaning; and discussion of various approaches to indirect discourse and propositional attitude statements.)

GABRIEL SEGAL

INDIVIDUALISM IN HISTORY AND SOCIAL SCIENCE

see HOLISM AND INDIVIDUALISM IN HISTORY AND SOCIAL SCIENCE

INDIVIDUALS *see* PARTICULARS

INDUCTION, EPISTEMIC ISSUES IN

Consider the following:

(1) Emeralds have been regularly dug up and observed for centuries; while there are still emeralds yet to be observed, every one observed so far has been green.

It is easy to see why we regard (1) as evidence, if true, that:

(2) Every emerald observed up until 100 years ago was green.

(1) logically implies (2): there is no way (1) could be true without (2) being true as well. It is less easy to see why we should think that (1), if true, is any evidence at all that:

(3) All hitherto unobserved emeralds are green as well.

(1) does not logically imply (3): it is consistent with (1) that (3) be false – that the string of exclusively green emeralds is about to come to an end. None the less, we do regard (1) as evidence, if true, that (3). What, if anything, justifies our doing so?

To answer this question would be to take a first step towards solving what is known as the 'problem of induction'. But only a first step. There is, at least on the surface, a wide variety of arguments that share the salient features of the argument from (1) to (3): their premises do not logically imply their conclusions, yet we

745

think that their premises, if true, constitute at least some evidence that their conclusions are true. A fully fledged solution to the problem of induction would have to tell us, for each of these arguments, what justifies our regarding its premises as evidence that its conclusion is true. Still, the question as to how this step might be taken has been the focus of intense philosophical scrutiny, and the approaches outlined in this entry have been among the most important.

1   **The presupposition approach**
2   **The pragmatic approach**
3   **The inductive approach**
4   **The probabilist approach**
5   **The reflective-equilibrium approach**
6   **The naturalist approach**
7   **The meaning approach**
8   **The ordinary-language approach**
9   **The Wittgensteinian approach**

1   The presupposition approach

Considering the above, one proposal that leaps immediately to mind is that what justifies our regarding (1) as evidence that (3) is that we presuppose that the world is so constructed that observed samples are representative of the populations from which they are drawn – in Hume's words, that 'the future is conformable to the past' or (as others have put it) that 'nature is uniform' (see HUME, D. §2). We can express the presupposition thus (where *F* and *G* are any predicates):

(4)   Whenever at least some *F*s are observed and *n* per cent of all the *F*s observed are *G*, *n* per cent of the remaining *F*s are *G*.

Given this presupposition, it is no more difficult to see why we should regard (1) as evidence that (3) than it is to see why we should regard (1) as evidence that (2): the conjunction of (1) and (4) logically implies (3). But there are three problems.

(a)   *(1) and (4) imply too much.* Let us say that an object is *grue* just if *either* it has been observed by now and is green *or* it has yet to be observed and is blue. By this definition, (1) logically implies that:

(5)   Emeralds have been regularly dug up and observed for centuries; while there are still emeralds yet to be observed, every one observed so far has been grue.

And, just as (1) and (4) logically imply (3), so (5) and (4) logically imply:

(6)   All the hitherto unobserved emeralds are grue as well.

Thus (1) and (4) logically imply *both* (3) and (6). But, given that there are emeralds yet to be observed, (6) is incompatible with (3): unobserved emeralds that are grue are, by definition, blue. Now, the predicate 'grue' seems so obviously jerry-rigged for the occasion that it looks easy to circumvent the difficulty just described. Simply distinguish between jerry-rigged predicates and the rest – between *unprojectible* predicates and *projectible* ones – and say that what we presuppose is that observed samples are representative, *with respect to projectible predicates*, of the populations from which they are drawn. That is:

(4′)   Where *F* and *G* are projectible, whenever at least some *F*s are observed and *n* per cent of all the *F*s observed are *G*, *n* per cent of the remaining *F*s are *G*.

But only in concert with a premise asserting that 'emerald' and 'green' are projectible predicates and 'grue' is not, will this modification work. On pain of being entirely *ad hoc* this premise would need the support of some principled way of distinguishing between projectible and unprojectible predicates – something that has proved extremely elusive. This much, however, is worth noting. The problem just outlined (known as the 'new riddle of induction' – see GOODMAN, N. §3) is not peculiar to the presupposition approach: it is a problem that any non-sceptical approach to the problem of induction will also have to solve.

(b)   *Observed samples are not, as a matter of fact, always representative of the populations from which they are drawn.* This is particularly common with small samples, but can and does occur even with large ones; nature sometimes throws us a curve. Most of this difficulty can be circumvented by moving to a yet more modest version of (4). For example, we can say that what we presuppose is that the world is so constructed that observed samples are *usually* representative of the populations from which they are drawn, that:

(4″)   Where *F* and *G* are projectible, it is typically the case that when at least some *F*s are observed and *n* per cent of all the *F*s observed are *G*, *n* per cent of the remaining *F*s are *G*.

Of course, (1) and (4″) do not logically imply (3). But it is open to us to claim that what justifies our regarding (1) as evidence that (3) is that, in so far as we think that (4″) is true, we think that the argument from (1) to (3) is an instance of an argument form whose instances typically have a true conclusion when the premise is true. And, while further modification would be required to allay fully the worry about small samples – (4″) does not seem very credible in a case in which only one F has been observed as an instance – this does not seem in principle impossible.

(c) *It is hard to see how, by the lights of the presupposition approach itself, we could be justified in believing (4″) (or (4′) suitably modified)*. (4″) makes a very strong claim about the world. (4″) says, not only that samples so far observed have typically been representative, with respect to projectible predicates, of the populations from which they are drawn, but also that samples not yet observed are typically representative in this way as well. This latter claim is just of the sort we presumably are not justified in believing except on the basis of evidence – in this case, evidence that samples so far observed typically have, indeed, been representative. But, given the justificatory scheme advanced by the presupposition approach, we cannot regard the claim that observed samples have typically been representative as evidence that unobserved samples are typically representative unless we already believe (4″). Thus it would seem that very claim to which the presupposition approach would have us appeal to justify our regarding (1) as evidence that (3), is one that both requires justification and is (given this approach) incapable of receiving any.

2 The pragmatic approach

But is it so important that we believe (4″)? Clearly, if (4″) is true then the following argument form will be reliable:

(7) At least some Fs have been observed and n per cent of them have been G (where F and G are projectible).

Therefore, n per cent of the remaining Fs are also G.

That is, an instance of (7) will typically have a true conclusion when it has a true premise. And just as clearly, if (4″) is false, (7) will be unreliable. But, some have (in effect) suggested, if (4″) is false, then *no* competing projective argument form (no other argument form that predicts what percentage of the remaining Fs are G from the percentage in the observed sample) will be reliable. More precisely, they have claimed that (for any projectible F and G where the number of Fs is infinite) if there is a limit to the relative frequency with which observed Fs are G (roughly, if there is a point in an infinite sequence of observations beyond which the percentage of observed Fs that are G remains fairly stable) then the repeated use of (7) will eventually predict that relative

frequency: that is, they have claimed that, in such a case, (7) will eventually find the true relative frequency if any projective argument form will. Thus the justification for our regarding (1), if true, as evidence that (3): the argument from (1) to (3) is an instance of (7), an argument form which is (in this sense) reliable if any projective argument form is (see REICHENBACH, H. §3). There are, however, the following problems:

(a) *The pragmatic approach justifies too much*. Consider the infinite number of variants of the following argument form:

(7′) At least some Fs have been observed and n per cent of them have been G (where F and G are projectible).

Therefore, $(n+f(m))$ per cent of the remaining Fs are also G,

where m is the number of Fs that have so far been observed and where the values of the function $f(m)$, while non-zero up to rather large finite values of m (in particular, for values of m large enough to represent accurately the number of emeralds that have in fact thus far been observed), converge towards zero as m approaches infinity. No less than (7), all these argument forms will find the true relative frequency if any projective form will. Yet, among them are argument forms that have, as an instance, the inference from (1) to:

(8) Fifty per cent of the hitherto unobserved emeralds are green as well.

(Suppose that n is the number of emeralds that have in fact been observed and $f(m) = -\frac{1}{2}$, where $m \leqslant n$ and $f(m)$ converges to zero thereafter.) We do not (indeed, it would seem positively counterinductive to) regard (1) as evidence that (8). Yet the pragmatist approach provides no justification for regarding (1) as evidence that (3) that is not readily available to justify our regarding (1) as evidence that (8).

(b) *Even were (7) the only argument form that will eventually find the true relative frequency if any projective argument form will, this could not justify our regarding (1) as evidence that (3)*. For there to be a limit to the relative frequency with which observed emeralds are green, there needs to be an infinite number of emeralds to observe. But the quantity of emeralds is, presumably, finite. Once we know there is no limit of the relative frequency, we know that (7)'s boast, that it will find the limit if there is one, is a boast which can be equally made by any argument form whatsoever. Under such circumstances, it is hard to see why we would think that the fact that inference from (1) to (3) is an instance of (7) justifies our regarding (1) as evidence that (3).

3 The inductive approach

Some have suggested another way of circumventing the third difficulty with the presupposition approach. It is not really necessary, in order for us to be justified in regarding (1) as evidence that (3), that we believe (4″). It will suffice that we believe that:

(9) (4″) is true when F and G predicate properties of physical objects.

This, of course, is not a modest claim; if (3) requires justification, then certainly (9) does as well. But (it has been argued) that justification is readily available from the fact that instances of (7) employing the sort of predicates described in (9) (call these *type 1 instances of (7)*) have been observed to be reliable in the past, and from our belief that:

(10) (4″) is true when F and G predicate properties of type 1 instances of (7).

And, since (9) and (10) are logically independent, no begging of the question is involved when we appeal to our belief in (10) to justify our belief in (9).

Of course, (10) itself stands as much in need of justification as (9) did. But this, too, is available in so far as we have observed that instances of (7) employing predicable expressions of the sort described in (10) (call these *type 2 instances of (7)*) have been reliable in the past and in so far as we believe that:

(11) (4″) is true when F and G predicate properties of type 2 instances of (7).

This justification, again, begs no question. And, by appeal to the track record of instances of the sort described in (11) and to the truth of (4″) when F and G predicate properties of such instances, (11) can in turn be justified. The sequence of ever higher-level justification can be extended indefinitely. But then there are the following difficulties:

(a) *The proposed justification can never be produced, since it involves an infinite regress of justifying beliefs.* To that extent, the inductive approach would seem to exchange the defect of circularity for another defect just as serious.

(b) *We can just as easily justify regarding (1) as evidence that not-(3).* Modify (4″) so that it reads, 'It is not the case that n per cent of the remaining Fs are G'; modify (7) so that its conclusion reads, '*It is not the case that n per cent of the remaining Fs are also G*'. Call the results (4″)* and (7)* respectively. Substitute (4″)* for (4″) and (7)* for (7) in the

foregoing, and what you get is every bit as good a justification for regarding (1) as evidence that not-(3). But (1) presumably can not be at the same time evidence that (3) *and* evidence that not-(3).

4 The probabilist approach

This approach differs from those so far canvassed in that, while it also seeks to show how we can be justified in regarding one hypothesis as evidence for the truth of another when the first does not logically imply the second, it does not rely on any appeal to (4″) or the reliability of (7). It appeals instead to the propriety of probabilism.

Probabilism is the view that (a) confidence comes in degrees, and (b) where Z is any set of hypotheses closed under truth-functional operations, your degree of confidence assignment to the hypotheses in Z (a measure of how confident you are in the truth of each of the hypotheses in Z) is open to rational criticism if it fails to satisfy the following axioms of probability: for any propositions P and Q in Z, (i) $\text{prob}(P) \geqslant 0$; (ii) if P is a tautology, $\text{prob}(P) = 1$; (iii) if P and Q are logically incompatible,

$$\text{prob}(P \vee Q) = \text{prob}(P) + \text{prob}(Q)$$

Suppose you have a degree of confidence assignment to the hypotheses in some such Z, where that assignment satisfies the foregoing axioms. For any hypotheses P and Q in Z, let us define your personal odds for P as against Q as just the ratio your degree of confidence in P bears to your degree of confidence in Q. Since your degree of confidence that P and your degree of confidence that not-P must sum to 1 (if they are to satisfy the Kolmogorov axioms), the greater your personal odds are for P as against not-P, the more confident you are that P.

Suppose, now, that for some P and Q in Z of whose truth values you are uncertain, your personal odds for P & Q as against not-P & Q are greater than your personal odds for P as against not-P – that is, your personal odds for P as against not-P are greater given Q than they are otherwise. Then, probabilists hold, you must surely be counted as regarding Q as a positive indication that P – as a hypothesis that (if true) is evidence that P. But if so, it is possible for us to say how we can be justified in regarding (1) as evidence that the conjunction of (1) and (3) is true – even though (1) does not logically imply that conjunction. It suffices that the conjunction logically implies (1). That is because, if P logically implies Q, then, so long as your degree of confidence assignment satisfies the foregoing axioms and you are certain neither of the truth-value of P nor of the truth-value of Q, your personal odds for P & Q as against not-P & Q must be greater than your personal odds for P as against not-P – you must regard Q as evidence that P (see PROBABILITY THEORY AND EPISTEMOLOGY). But, again, there are difficulties.

(a) *Probabilism, and its doctrine about the relation between personal odds and the assessment of evidential relevance, are controversial.* Critics have argued that confidence does not (nor is there epistemic reason why it should) always come in degrees; that there are difficulties both with the doctrine that degrees of confidence are open to criticism if they do not satisfy the foregoing axioms and with the arguments probabilists have offered in support of that doctrine; that the probabilist's account of the relation between personal odds and assessments of evidential relevance has counterintuitive consequences. Probabilists have powerful responses to all these criticisms (and, indeed, the proliferation of more modest variants of probabilism that do not presuppose that we have, or ought to have, precise degrees of confidence has rendered the first criticism moot), but not everyone is convinced.

(b) *Since (1) is logically implied by the conjunction of (5) and (6), probabilism requires us to regard (1) as evidence that this conjunction – which is equivalent to the claim that all emeralds are grue – is true.* Not that this is obviously a mistake. After all, given (1), both the conjunction of (1) and (3) and the conjunction of (5) and (6) are guaranteed to be right about the emeralds already observed; otherwise they are not. But it does indicate that only because the truth of (1) forecloses the possibility that these conjunctions are wrong about the emeralds that have already been observed are we bound to regard (1) as evidence in favour of the conjunctions. What colour the conjunctions attribute to the emeralds that are still unobserved has nothing to do with it.

(c) *Probabilism does not justify our regarding (1) as evidence that (3).* (3) does not logically imply (1). So, even granting the propriety of what probabilists say about evidence (that is, even granting that probabilists have succeeded in showing how we can in some cases be justified in regarding one hypothesis as evidence for another it does not logically imply – no mean feat), probabilism provides no justification for regarding (1) as evidence that (3).

5 The reflective-equilibrium approach

The reflective-equilibrium approach, like the probabilist one, also renounces any appeal to (4″). Advocates of this approach argue that the only way to go about justifying our regarding (1) as evidence that (3), is to appeal to some argument form such as (7). But, convinced that there is no cogent non-question-begging way to argue for the reliability of such an argument form, the advocates of the reflective-equilibrium approach hold that the best we can do to justify our appeal to the argument form is to show that each of its instances is acceptable to us, that each of its instances is such that we are prepared on reflection to regard its premise as evidence that its conclusion is true. That is, the best we can do to justify our regarding (1) as evidence that (3) is to show that the inference from (1) to (3) is an instance of an argument form with respect to which we are in *reflective equilibrium*. But there are the following worries:

(a) *There is nothing in the procedure for achieving reflective equilibrium with respect to an argument form that offers even the slightest guarantee that the argument form is not (unknown to us) entirely fallacious.* Consider a person who regards this coin's landing tails on the first ten tosses as evidence that it will land heads on the next. This person is, of course, quite mistaken. If the coin is fair, its performance on its first ten tosses is no evidence at all of how it will perform on the eleventh: the outcomes of the tosses are independent. But the fact that this person is mistaken is entirely compatible with their being able to achieve reflective equilibrium with respect to the following (fallacious) argument form:

(12) *C* is a fair coin that has landed heads on its first ten tosses.

Therefore, *C* will land tails on its eleventh toss.

The procedure for achieving reflective equilibrium with respect to an argument does not guarantee that the form is not fallacious – only that those who have achieved this reflective equilibrium do not *regard* the form as fallacious. It would thus be disappointing if the best we can do to justify our regarding (1) as evidence that (3) is to engage in such a procedure. One would have hoped we could do (and one might even think a true justification would require us to do) something better.

(b) *Achieving reflective equilibrium requires too much.* The task of furnishing the sort of justification called for by the reflective-equilibrium approach is an extremely ambitious one, involving the crafting of an argument form (of which the argument from (1) to (3) is an instance) that can survive an extensive test of its adequacy to our intuitions about its instances. A fully adequate argument form has yet to be articulated. But if this task of justification is thus not one we have yet actually accomplished, then whatever it is

749

that justifies our regarding (1) as evidence that (3), it cannot be that we have placed our so regarding (1) in reflective equilibrium with an argument form and its instances. We have done no such thing.

6 The naturalist approach

All the approaches canvassed so far assume that what justifies our regarding (1) as evidence that (3) is that there is available to us some sort of argument in favour of the claim that (1) is evidence that (3). But to some philosophers, this idea seems misguided. Humans constitute just one species of creatures whose survival depends upon their following inductive practices. The rest of these species are quite incapable of understanding *any* argument in support of such practices; no arguments are available to *them*. Yet (these philosophers maintain) it still seems perfectly appropriate to say of a dog that it is justified in regarding its master's picking up its leash as evidence that it is about to go for a walk. Thus (they conclude) the availability of argument is not necessary for justification: to the dog, there is no argument available.

Nor (they continue) does the mere availability of argument seem sufficient for justification. Consider a person who sets no store by our canons of good argument and only regards (1) as evidence that (3) because they like the sound of the utterance, '(1) is evidence that (3)'. It is compatible with this that there is just as good an argument available to them as there is to you or me for regarding (1) as evidence that (3). But surely (these philosophers maintain), given that they set no store by that argument, we can hardly want to call their regarding (1) as evidence that (3) *justified*.

What qualifies the dog's state of opinion as justified, but not the person's, has nothing to do with the availability of argument; it has to do, instead, with what caused their respective states of opinion. Whether a state of opinion is justified is determined entirely by features of the process that is causally responsible for being in that state – for example, the features (such as reliability in producing true beliefs) that make these processes conducive to our survival. What the holder of the state of opinion is in a position to *say* about the features of the process that causes their belief is, in general, beside the point (see RELIABILISM; INTERNALISM AND EXTERNALISM IN EPISTEMOLOGY). But, again, there are worries.

(a) *The claim that being able to offer a justification for one's opinion is neither necessary nor sufficient to render the opinion justified is difficult to square with our practice.* Were the claim true, it is hard to see why

we would care in the least whether we could offer even the most meagre justification for any of our beliefs.

(b) *If it is the aetiology of our opinions that determines whether they are justified, then we are ill-placed to tell, with respect to most of them, why they are worth holding.* We are not usually in any position to say by exactly what processes our opinions have been caused – consider, for example, beliefs in theories, beliefs held since childhood – let alone whether the processes that have caused them possess whatever features are necessary and sufficient for them to confer justification on the beliefs they produce. But, if so, by the lights of the naturalist approach it would seem that we are usually in no position to say that our opinions are justified – that they are any more worth holding than those we would acquire by reading tea leaves.

7 The meaning approach

All the foregoing approaches presuppose that our regarding (1) as evidence that (3) *requires* some substantive justification. But not all philosophers think that this is so. Some have argued that no justification is called for: it is simply part of what we *mean* by 'evidence' that (1) constitutes evidence that (3). This approach has some difficulties:

(a) *To use a meaning claim in this way seems dogmatic.* In the wake of work (by Quine and others) to the effect that there is no bona fide distinction to be drawn between true claims that are true by virtue of meaning and those that are not (see ANALYTICITY), this attempt to settle an apparently open question by appeal to meaning claims looks to be just a form of dogmatism.

(b) *The meaning claim, even if granted, is ineffective.* It may well be that, for at least some people, it is part of what they mean by 'evidence' that the failure of a fair coin to land heads on one toss is evidence that it will land heads on the next one. But that can hardly show that they are justified in regarding the coin's having landed tails the first time as evidence that it will land heads the next. And, if so, the fact (if it is a fact) that it is part of what *we* mean by 'evidence' that (1) constitutes evidence that (3) cannot show that *we* are justified in regarding (1) as evidence that (3).

8 The ordinary-language approach

But, to some, there is still something perverse in the claim that our regarding (1) as evidence that (3) requires justification. To say that an opinion is one that requires justification is to say that it is an opinion that a person ought not to hold unless they can produce justification. But we cannot seriously mean that until they can successfully produce the requisite justification for so regarding (1), a person should not regard (1) as evidence that (3). This is a condition that no ordinary person – and possibly no philosopher – can satisfy. Anyone who insisted upon its being met – anyone who habitually demanded of any person who asserts that (1) is evidence that (3) that they either justify that claim or withdraw it – would rightly be counted as mad. But there is the following problem:

The ordinary-language approach appears to mistake the context in which we mean to be saying that our so regarding (1) requires justification. Granted, in an ordinary context, it would indeed be perverse to say of a person who regarding (1) as evidence that (3), that their so regarding (1) requires justification. But it does not follow that it is a perverse thing to say when our purposes are philosophical – that is, when we are in the context of philosophical inquiry. Yet, it is precisely for such purposes, and in such a context, that we mean to be asking what, if anything, justifies our regarding (1) as evidence that (3). It is precisely for such purposes, and in such a context, that we mean to be saying that our so regarding (1) requires justification.

9 The Wittgensteinian approach

Of course, this reply to the advocates of the ordinary-language approach presupposes that language can be freely wrested from the ordinary context in which it is used and thrust into a philosophical context without cost. But some (and Wittgenstein in particular) have argued that it cannot.

To appreciate how their reasoning might apply to the case at hand, suppose we say, with the critics of the ordinary-language approach, that, while our regarding (1) as evidence that (3) requires no justification for ordinary purposes in an ordinary context, it does require justification for philosophical purposes in a philosophical context. How are we to tell whether an adequate justification has been produced? For example, are justifications that contain circular arguments or infinite regresses admissible? Were we free to consult the standards of justification we employ in ordinary circumstances, we could easily see that the answer to this last question is 'no'. But we are not. The whole point of our reply to the advocates of the ordinary-language approach is to say that those standards of justification – and their verdict that our regarding (1) as evidence that (3) does not require justification – are to be set aside in a philosophical context. But what other standards do we have? None.

We are thus faced with a dilemma. The standards of justification we employ in ordinary contexts forbid us to say that our regarding (1) as evidence that (3) requires justification. But if we turn our backs on the standards of justification we use in ordinary contexts, as it is imagined we do in the philosophical context, we deprive ourselves of any source of insight into what would *count* as justifying our regarding (1) as evidence that (3). What sustains philosophical attempts to say what justifies our regarding (1) as evidence that (3) thus looks like nothing more than a failure to face up to this dilemma. There is one major difficulty:

Wittgensteinian doctrines are very controversial. This is all the more true for the fact that the morals drawn from them so often place apparently respectable philosophical enterprises in a poor light. In this case, it may be difficult to see how a sophisticated, orderly philosophical inquiry of more than two centuries' duration could possibly be the intellectual sham the advocates of the Wittgensteinian approach make it appear. Of course, it is part and parcel of Wittgensteinian doctrine that one cannot expect those who have toiled in the philosophical enterprise criticized to find it easy to see, even once it is pointed out to them, the way in which that enterprise is fundamentally ill-conceived: language bewitches us. But this consideration has done little to convince the many philosophers who (rightly or wrongly) see Wittgensteinian approaches to philosophical problems (such as this one) as fundamentally anti-philosophical, as attempts to hold philosophy to such standards as would make philosophy impossible.

See also: CONFIRMATION THEORY; INDUCTIVE INFERENCE; MEANING, INDIAN THEORIES OF

References and further reading

Black, M. (1954) *Problems of Analysis*, Ithaca, NY: Cornell University Press. (Prominent defence of the inductive approach. Chapter 11 is especially relevant.)

Edwards, P. (1949) 'Russell's Doubts about Induction', *Mind* 68: 141–63. (Prominent example of the ordinary-language approach.)

Goodman, N. (1955) *Fact, Fiction and Forecast*, Indianapolis, IN: Hackett Publishing Company, 3rd edn, 1979. (The classic presentation of both the reflective-equilibrium approach and the new riddle of induction.)

Hume, D. (1739) *A Treatise of Human Nature*, 2nd edn, ed. L.A. Selby-Bigge, revised P.H. Nidditch, Oxford: Clarendon Press, 1978. (The problem of induction is first introduced, and the presuppositition approach to its solution is first put forward and criticized.)

Kaplan, M. (1996) *Decision Theory as Philosophy*, New York: Cambridge University Press. (Chapters 1 and 2 provide an introduction to – and defence of – a modest variant on – probabilism and a critical discussion of the probabilist approach.)

Kitcher, P. (1992) 'The Naturalists Return', *The Philosophical Review* 101: 53–114. (Survey and defence of the naturalist approach.)

Skyrms, B. (1975) *Choice and Chance*, Encino, CA: Wadsworth, 2nd edn, 1985. (Chapter 2 provides an excellent brief survey of the major approaches to the problem of induction.)

Salmon, W. (1963) 'Inductive Inference', in B. Baumrin (ed.) *Philosophy of Science: The Delaware Seminar*, New York: Interscience Publishers, 353–70. (Defence of the pragmatic approach.)

Strawson, P.F. (1952) *Introduction to Logical Theory*, New York: John Wiley & Sons. (A defence of the meaning approach is provided in chapter 9.)

Swinburne, R. (ed.) (1974) *The Justification of Induction*, Oxford: Oxford University Press. (Collection of important papers on the topic, particularly on the pragmatic, inductive and ordinary-language approaches.)

Travis, C. (1991) 'Annals of Analysis', *Mind* 100: 237–64. (Section 1 contains a defence of Wittgensteinian misgivings about our capacity to evaluate the truth and falsity of what is asserted outside of our ordinary contexts.)

Wittgenstein, L. (1953) *Philosophical Investigations*, New York: Macmillan, 3rd edn, 1958. (The source of the line of thought behind the Wittgensteinian approach.)

MARK KAPLAN

INDUCTIVE DEFINITIONS AND PROOFS

An inductive definition *of a predicate R characterizes the Rs as the smallest class which satisfies a* basis clause *of the form* $(\beta(x) \to Rx)$, *telling us that certain things satisfy R, together with one or more* closure clauses *of the form* $(\Phi(x, R) \to Rx)$, *which tell us that, if certain other things satisfy R, x satisfies R as well. 'Smallest' here means that the class of Rs is included in every other class which satisfies the basis and closure clauses.*

Inductive definitions are useful because of inductive proofs. To show that every R has property P, show that

the class of Rs that have P satisfies the basis and closure clauses.

The closure clauses tell us that if certain things satisfy R, x satisfies R as well. Thus satisfaction of the condition $\Phi(x, R)$ *should be ensured by positive information to the effect that certain things satisfy R, and not also require negative informative that certain things fail to satisfy R. In other words, the condition* $\Phi(x, R)$ *should be* monotone, *so that, if* $R \subseteq S$ *and* $\Phi(x, R)$, *then* $\Phi(x, S)$; *otherwise, we would have no assurance of the existence of a smallest class satisfying the basis and closure conditions.*

While inductive definitions can take many forms, they have been studied most usefully in the special case in which the basis and closure clauses are formulated within the predicate calculus. Initiated by Yiannis Moschovakis, the study of such definitions has yielded an especially rich and elegant theory.

1   **Inductive definitions in general**
2   **First-order positive inductive definitions**
3   $\prod_1^1$ **and inductively defined sets**
4   **Inductive and admissible sets**

1 Inductive definitions in general

Inductive definitions occur throughout mathematics. For example, one aspect of the reduction of classical mathematics to set theory has been to treat natural numbers as sets, identifying a natural number with the set of its predecessors, so that they comprise the smallest class such that:

$\emptyset$ is a natural number

If $x = y \cup \{y\}$, for some natural number y, x is a natural number.

Having this inductive definition, we can give proofs by *mathematical induction*. To show that every number has property P, show that $\emptyset$ has the property and that, if y is a natural number with property P, so is $y \cup \{y\}$.

One inductive definition begets others. We define 'is a sum of' as the smallest ternary relation such that:

If x is a natural number, x is a sum of x and $\emptyset$.

If u is a sum of y and v, $x = u \cup \{u\}$ and $z = v \cup \{v\}$, then x is a sum of y and z.

An inductive proof shows that this stipulation uniquely determines a binary operation on the natural numbers.

We can extend arithmetical methods beyond the finite, identifying a limit ordinal with the set of its predecessors, so that the ordinals are the smallest class such that:

$\emptyset$ is an ordinal.

If $x = y \cup \{y\}$, for some ordinal y, then x is an ordinal.

If the set x is a union of ordinals, x is an ordinal.

Again one inductive definition leads to another. Given a function G, to define a function F on the ordinals such that:

$$F(\alpha) = G(\alpha, F \mid \alpha)$$

(where $F \mid \alpha = \{ <\beta, F(\beta) > : \beta < \alpha\}$), take the smallest class of ordered pairs such that:

$< 0, G(0, \emptyset) >$ is in F.

If h is a function defined on the ordinals $< \alpha$ such that $< \beta, h \mid \beta >$ is in F, for each $\beta < \alpha$, then $G(\alpha, h)$ is in F.

Speaking abstractly, an inductive definition describes the smallest relation such that:

If $\beta(x_1, \ldots, x_n)$, then $Rx_1 x_n$.

If $\Phi_1(x_1, \ldots, x_n, R)$, then $Rx_1 \ldots x_n$.

. . . .

If $\Phi_m(x_1, \ldots, x_n, R)$, then $Rx_1 x_n$.

Here β is an n-ary relation, and the conditions $\Phi_1, \ldots, \Phi_m$ are monotone relations between n-tuples and n-ary relations.

Since the disjunction of two monotone conditions is a monotone condition, we can consolidate the basis and inductive clauses thus:

If $\beta(x_1, \ldots, x_n)$ or $\Phi_1(x_1, \ldots, x_n, R)$ or ... or $\Phi_m(x_1, \ldots, x_n, R)$, then $Rx_1, \ldots, x_n$.

Consequently, there will be no loss of generality if we only consider inductive definitions that describe the smallest class such that:

If $\Phi(x_1, \ldots, x_n, R)$, then $Rx_1, \ldots, x_n$,

where Φ is monotone.

Setting the example of the ordinals aside, let us restrict our attention to situations in which there is some set A such that, for each $x_1, \ldots, x_n$ and S, if $\Phi_1(x_1, \ldots, x_n S)$, then each $x_i \in A$. Then, we shall not have to be concerned about the existence conditions for proper classes.

It is only because of the requirement that Φ is monotone that we can be confident that there is a smallest class which satisfies the closure clause, as we can see if we try to find the smallest class such that:

If either $x = 0$ and $\neq R1$ or $x = 1$ and $\neq R0$, then Rx.

Because of the monotony requirement, however,

the intersection of all the sets which satisfy the closure clause satisfies the closure clause. It also satisfies the converse of the closure clause, so that (setting $n = 1$):

$$(\forall x)(Rx \leftrightarrow \Phi(x, R)).$$

We have inductive proofs: if we know $(\forall x)((Rx \wedge \Phi(x, P)) \to Px)$, we can conclude $(\forall x)(Rx \to Px)$.

Inductively defined classes are naturally arrayed in a well-ordered sequence of layers, for we can define the level of a member of R to be the number of applications of the closure clause that are needed to capture it. More precisely, we define, for each ordinal α, R_α to be $\{x : \Phi(x, \cup_{\beta < \alpha} R_\beta)\}$. Then the R_αs form a nonstrictly increasing sequence (that is, if $\beta < \alpha$, then $R_\beta \subseteq R_\alpha$); their union is R. Because we have stipulated that the R_αs are all contained within a set A, the sequence cannot be strictly increasing, since, if each R_α introduced new members of R, there would be as many members of R as there are ordinals. Consequently, there must exist an ordinal α with cardinality at most the cardinality of A such that $R_\alpha = R_{\alpha+1} = R$. The least such α is the *height* of the inductive definition.

2 First-order positive inductive definitions

An occurrence of a predicate R in a formula of the predicate calculus without '$\to$' or '$\leftrightarrow$' is *positive* if it occurs within the scope of an even number of negation signs. A first-order formula $\Phi(x_1, \ldots, x_n, R)$ in which R occurs only positively describes a monotone condition. *First-order positive inductive definitions*, in which the antecedent of the closure clause is a first-order formula in which the defined term occurs only positively, have been extensively and fruitfully studied.

Let $\mathfrak{A}$ be a model for a language $\mathcal{L}$ for the first-order predicate calculus, and let $\mathcal{L}_\mathfrak{A}$ be the language derived from $\mathcal{L}$ by adding a new constant $\underline{a}$ for each element a of the universe A of $\mathfrak{A}$. Apart from the predicate being defined, our first-order positive inductive definitions will consist of symbols of $\mathcal{L}_\mathfrak{A}$.

We can explicitly describe how an inductively defined set is built. Suppose C is inductively defined as the smallest set such that:

If $\Phi(x, R)$, then Rx.

Then a is in C if and only if $R\underline{a}$ is derivable from the axiom:

$$(\forall x)(\Phi(x, R) \to Rx)$$

in $\mathfrak{A}$-logic, that is to say, $R\underline{a}$ is derivable from the axiom together with atomic and negated atomic sentences true in $\mathfrak{A}$ by first-order logic supplemented

753

by the $\mathfrak{A}$-rule: from $\psi(\underline{a})$, for each a in A, to infer $(\forall x)\phi(x)$.

We shall restrict our attention to cases in which $\mathfrak{A}$ is *acceptable*, that is, $\mathfrak{A}$ contains an isomorphic copy of the natural number system and $\mathfrak{A}$ can describe the formation of finite sequences. Acceptability of $\mathfrak{A}$ will make it possible for $\mathcal{L}_{\mathfrak{A}}$ to describe its own syntax. We also suppose that $\mathcal{L}$ is built up from a finite vocabulary. Similar but more complicated analogues to the results described here hold without these restrictions.

It turns out that, to get a satisfactory theory, we need to look, not at the separate behaviour of individual inductive definitions but at their combinations. A relation C is *inductively definable* (or simply *inductive*) over $\mathfrak{A}$ if C can be defined in a language derived from $\mathcal{L}_{\mathfrak{A}}$ by adding one or more inductively defined predicates; in the formula defining C the new predicates are allowed to occur only positively. More concisely, C is inductively definable over $\mathfrak{A}$ if and only if there exist an $n+m$-ary relation D and members $b_1,\dots,b_m$ of the universe A of $\mathfrak{A}$ such that D is defined by a first-order positive inductive definition and C is equal to $<a_1,\dots,a_n>: \,<a_1,\dots,a_n,b_1\dots,b_m> \in D$. Showing this equivalence is a matter of seeing how several inductive definitions can be consolidated.

An inductively defined set whose complement is also inductively defined is *hyperelementary*.

A set C is inductive if and only if there is a finitely axiomatized theory Δ and formula $\psi(x)$ in a language extending $\mathcal{L}_{\mathfrak{A}}$ such that, for any a, a is an element of C if and only if $\psi(\underline{a})$ is derivable from Δ in $\mathfrak{A}$-logic. Just in case C is hyperelementary, we can arrange things so that, if a is in C then $\psi(\underline{a})$ is derivable from Δ, whereas if a is not in C, $\neg\psi(\underline{a})$ is derivable.

The results cited in the last paragraph would also obtain if the word 'inductive' were replaced by 'recursively enumerable', 'hyperelementary' by 'recursive' and 'derivable in $\mathfrak{A}$-logic' by 'derivable in first-order logic'. This observation illustrates a far-reaching analogy between structural properties of inductively definable and recursively enumerable sets.

Another example is the following: inductive sets, like recursively enumerable sets, enjoy the *reduction property*, that is, for any inductive sets B and C, there exist nonoverlapping inductive sets $B\prime \subseteq B$ and $C\prime \subseteq C$ with $B\prime \cup C\prime = B \cup C$. We get them by comparing the stages in the relevant inductive definitions at which the members of B and C are introduced, putting a member of $B \cap C$ into $B\prime$ just in case it is put into B before being placed into C.

Again, there are inductively defined sets C which are *complete*, meaning that, for each inductive set D, there is a hyperelementary function F such that, for any a, $a \in D$ if and only if $F(a) \in C$. The best-known complete set, at least among philosophers, is the minimal fixed point of Saul Kripke's theory of truth. The theory of truth is robust enough to encode every inductive definition.

There is a version of the recursion theorem for inductive sets. Also, one can do priority arguments (see Sacks 1990).

The height of the monotone operator which generates an inductively defined set is a measure of the complexity of the set. Indeed, the principal ideas of the theory of inductive sets originate in S.C. Kleene's investigations of how to extend the arithmetical hierarchy into the transfinite. The *order* of $\mathfrak{A}$, $o(\mathfrak{A})$, is the supremum of the heights of all first-order positive inductive definitions over $\mathfrak{A}$. This supremum is reached by the complete inductive sets, among others. A subset of A is hyperelementary if and only if it is defined by a first-order positive inductive definition whose height is less than $o(\mathfrak{A})$.

3 $\prod_1^1$ and inductively defined sets

An element a of A will be in the smallest class which satisfies the closure clause $(\Phi(x,R) \to Rx)$ just in case the sentence $(\forall R)((\forall x)(\Phi(x,R \to Rx) \to R\underline{a})$ is true. It follows that every inductive set is $\prod_1^1$, that is, it is definable by a formula consisting of initial second-order universal quantifiers followed by a first-order formula.

If A is countable, the converse holds. $(\forall R)\psi(R,\underline{a})$ is true if and only if the sentence $\psi(R,\underline{a})$ is a member of the smallest class of sentences which:

contains the atomic and negated atomic sentences true in $\mathfrak{A}$;

contains the theorems of first-order logic;

contains θ whenever it contains $(\chi \to \theta)$ and χ; and

contains $(\forall v)\chi(x)$ whenever it contains each $\chi(\underline{a})$.

Because $\mathfrak{A}$ is acceptable, so that it can represent its own syntax, this can be written as a first-order positive inductive definition.

One proves this by proving a completeness theorem, showing that, for A countable, $(\forall R)\theta(R)$ is true if and only if $\theta(R)$ is derivable in $\mathfrak{A}$-logic.

4 Inductive and admissible sets

To get a picture of the place of inductively defined sets within the universe of set theory, we look at sets that can be built up by taking the elements of A as basic building blocks or *urelements*:

$$V_0 = A.$$

$V_{\alpha+1}$ = the set of subsets of V_α.

$V_lambda = \cup_{\alpha < \lambda} V_\alpha$, for λ a limit.

The *constructible sets* form a subclass of the V_αs:

$L_0 = A$.

$L_{\alpha+1}$ = the set of subsets of L_α which are definable in the language derived from $\mathcal{L}_\mathfrak{A}$ by adding a predicate 'U', whose extension is A, a predicate '$\in$', whose extension is the elementhood relation, restricted to L_α, and names for all the members of L_α.

$L_\lambda = \cup_{\alpha < \lambda} L_\alpha$, for λ a limit.

We are interested in the initial stages of the constructible hierarchy. First, let us introduce a little more notation. The *bounded formulas* are those in which every universal quantifier takes the form $(\forall x)(x \in t \to \ldots)$, and every existential quantifier takes the form $(\exists x)(x \in t \wedge \ldots)$. The Σ_1 *formulas* are those obtained by prefixing one or more existential quantifiers to a bounded formula.

One can show that $L_{0(\mathfrak{A})}$ constitutes the smallest set which:

(1) contains A and the sets definable in $\mathfrak{A}$;

(2) contains x, y and the union of x whenever it contains x and y;

(3) satisfies the universal closure of the separation axiom schema, $(\exists y)(\forall z)(z \in y \leftrightarrow (z \in x \wedge \phi(z)))$, restricted to bounded formulas ϕ; and

(4) satisfies the universal closure of
$(\forall x)(x \in t \to (\exists z)\phi(x,z)) \to (\exists y)(\forall x)(x \in t \to (\exists z)(z \in y \wedge (x,z))$, for ϕ bounded.

Subsets of the class of V_αs which satisfy these four conditions are said to be *admissible* above $\mathfrak{A}$. The first-order axioms which describe, in a natural way, a well-founded set which satisfies conditions (2) through (4) are called 'KPU' (for 'Kripke–Platek set theory with urelements', after the thinkers who first studied admissible sets).

The Barwise–Moschovakis–Gandy theorem states that a subset of A is inductive if and only if it is definable by a Σ_1 formula on $L_{o(\mathfrak{A})}$. While the proof is complicated, it is possible to give a summary. To show that every inductively definable set is Σ_1 definable on $L_{o(\mathfrak{A})}$, show that, if there is a proof in $\mathfrak{A}$-logic of a given sentence, then such a proof exists in $L_{o(\mathfrak{A})}$. For the converse, show that, if S is Σ_1 definable, there is a formula σ such that $a \in S$ if and only if $\sigma(\underline{a})$ is derivable from KPU in $\mathfrak{A}$-logic.

It follows that a set is hyperelementary over $\mathfrak{A}$ if and only if it is an element of $L_{o(\mathfrak{A})}$.

The Barwise–Moschovakis–Gandy theorem explains the parallels between recursively enumerable and inductive sets. Recursively enumerable = Σ_1 definable in the smallest set admissible above $\emptyset$. Inductive over $\mathfrak{A}$ = Σ_1 definable in the smallest set admissible above $\mathfrak{A}$.

Admissible sets have found widespread applications to the study of infinitary logic, but here it is possible to do no more than refer to Barwise (1975).

The results cited here are standard, and proofs can be found in Moschovakis (1974) and Barwise (1975).

See also: CONSTRUCTIBLE UNIVERSE; DEFINITION; INFINITARY LOGICS; LOGICAL AND MATHEMATICAL TERMS, GLOSSARY OF; TURING REDUCIBILITY AND TURING DEGREES

References and further reading

* Barwise, J. (1975) *Admissible Sets and Structures: An Approach to Definability Theory*, Berlin and New York: Springer. (A clear and readable development of the theory of admissible sets, with particular attention to infinitary logic.)
* Moschovakis, Y.N. (1974) *Elementary Induction on Abstract Structures*, Amsterdam: North Holland. (This is the fundamental work on inductively defined sets. Lucid and readable.)
* Sacks, G.E. (1990) *Higher Recursion Theory*, New York: Springer-Verlag. (Uses the methods of recursion theory, particularly priority arguments, to describe the structure of inductively defined sets.)

VANN McGEE

INDUCTIVE INFERENCE

According to a long tradition, an inductive inference is an inference from a premise of the form 'all observed A are B' to a conclusion of the form 'all A are B'. Such inferences are not deductively valid, that is, even if the premise is true it is possible that the conclusion is false, since unobserved As may differ from observed ones. Nevertheless, it has been held that the premise can make it reasonable to believe the conclusion, even though it does not guarantee that the conclusion is true.

It is now generally allowed that there are many other patterns of inference that can also provide reasonable grounds for believing their conclusions, even though their premises do not guarantee the truth of their conclusions. In current usage, it is common to call all such inferences inductive. It has been widely thought that all knowledge of matters of fact that we have not observed must be based on inductive inferences from what we have observed. In particular, all knowledge of the future is, on this view, based on induction.

1 Paradigms of induction

The inference from 'all observed *A* are *B*' to 'all *A* are *B*', which was once taken to be the pattern for all inductive inference, is called (universal) *inductive generalization* or *enumerative induction*. A standard example is the inference from all observed ravens being black to all ravens being black. The fallibility of such inference is illustrated by the fact that, although all the swans seen by Europeans of the eighteenth century were white, black swans existed in Australia.

Some writers, such as J.S. Mill, argued that inductive generalization is the only legitimate kind of induction. However, as Mill was well aware, others have thought that there are other ways of making inferences from the observed to the unobserved. One method that has played an important role in philosophy of science is the method of hypothesis. In this method, the premises are that (i) hypothesis *H* implies a proposition *E* describing observable phenomena, and (ii) *E* is observed to be true; the conclusion is that *H* is true. In modern discussions this method is often called the hypothetico-deductive method, because *E* is supposed to be deduced from the hypothesis *H*.

The method of hypothesis is not deductively valid, since false hypotheses can have true consequences. Its defenders have argued that its premises can nevertheless make it reasonable to believe its conclusion. Descartes offered an example to support this position: if we find that a message in code makes sense when for each letter we substitute the following letter (B for A, C for B, and so on), we will be practically certain that this gives the true meaning of the message, especially if the message contains many words.

The method of hypothesis licenses conclusions that can never be reached by inductive generalization. For example, from the fact that observable phenomena are as they would be if matter consists of atoms, one may infer by the method of hypothesis that matter does consist of atoms. This conclusion could be reached by inductive generalization only if one had observed instances of matter composed of atoms, something that had not been done at the time that most scientists accepted the atomic theory of matter.

Other commonly recognized types of inductive inference are: (1) *statistical inductive generalization*, in which the premise is that *x* per cent of observed *A*s have been *B* and the conclusion is that about *x* per cent of all *A*s are *B*; (2) *predictive inference*, in which the premises are that *x* per cent of observed *A*s have been *B* and that *a* is *A*, the conclusion being that *a* is *B*; (3) *direct inference*, in which the premises are that *x* per cent of all *A*s are *B* and that *a* is *A*, the conclusion being that *a* is *B*; and (4) *inference by analogy*, in which the premises are that certain individuals have properties $F_1, \ldots, F_n$ and *a* also has $F_1, \ldots F_{n-1}$, the conclusion being that *a* also has F_n.

2 Induction in practice

It is generally allowed that the cogency of an inductive inference is greater the more observations have been made and the more varied these observations have been. Mill also stressed that the reliability of an inductive generalization is greatly increased by finding that other similar generalizations hold up; conversely, he maintained that our knowledge of the variability of bird-colouring undermined the inductive generalization to the conclusion that all ravens are black. But the relevance of such considerations means that inductive inferences are not adequately represented by the paradigm forms listed above, since relevant information ought to be included in the premises.

Even if we added to the paradigm forms the sort of information just mentioned, they would still not adequately represent the inductive inferences that are made in everyday life and in science. For example, consider the inductive generalization to the conclusion that all ravens are black. The premise was that all observed ravens have been black. But observed by whom? If we say observed by anyone, then we cannot be sure that the premise is correct, and this ought to affect our confidence in the conclusion, though the argument does not provide for that. If we say observed by me, then the premise leaves out the very relevant information of what I know from the testimony of others. Further, even when the premise is limited to my own observation, I cannot be sure it is true; I could very well have observed a white raven and mistakenly inferred from the fact that it was white that it was not a raven. Thus my confidence in the conclusion ought to depend on how closely I have examined both what I take to be ravens and what I take to be non-black things, though this is not reflected in the premise.

Another example: suppose we have weighed an object three times and obtained measurements of 4.9, 5.0 and 5.1 grams. From these results we might infer that the true weight of the object is between 4.7 and 5.3 grams. If this is to fit one of the standard forms, it will have to be the method of hypothesis. But the hypothesis that the true weight is between 4.7 and 5.3 grams does not entail that the weighings will give the results they did. In modern presentations of the hypothetico-deductive method it is commonly said that the premises include not only the hypothesis itself but also initial conditions, such as that the object was weighed three times, and auxiliary hypotheses, such as that the balance is accurate; but even with these additional premises the evidence does not follow deductively.

Since tests of hypotheses in science typically involve measurement, the preceding example is sufficient to show that science does not have much use for a method that is truly 'hypothetico-deductive'. But if the evidence only follows from the hypothesis with some probability, then it makes a difference what that probability is, though the method of hypothesis as usually presented does not include this information in the premises. As we will see below, it also makes a difference how probable the conclusion is on competing hypotheses, another relevant consideration that is not incorporated in the premises of the method of hypothesis as standardly conceived. Finally, our background information almost always gives us at least some relevant information; for example, we usually have some approximate idea what an object should weigh, and measurements that diverge too far from this will be taken to show that the balance is faulty. If the object that was weighed at 4.9, 5.0 and 5.1 grams was a loaded truck, we will conclude that there is something seriously wrong with the measurement process. The method of hypothesis does not provide a way to incorporate such relevant information.

3   Cogency

The premises of an inductive argument may provide more or less support for the conclusion. We would like to be able to identify the factors that determine the strength of this support. Some platitudes to this effect were mentioned above, but they have several defects. In particular, despite their vagueness, they are not true in general. For example, increasing the number of As that have been observed to be B does not always make it more probable that all A are B; thus a person who died at age 149 is a person who died before age 150, but evidence that there is such a person would *reduce* the probability that all people die before age 150. In any case, those platitudes are limited to the paradigm forms of inductive inference, which we have seen inadequate to represent actual inductive inferences. For these reasons, many contemporary theorists have looked for a more rigorous yet flexible framework for discussing the degree to which inductive premises support their conclusions. Probability theory has often been seen as providing such a framework.

Let H be a hypothesis and E some evidence. Let

$P(H)$ be the probability that H is true given the other information that we have besides E. Then the probability that we should give to H after learning E is the probability of H conditional on E, which we write as $P(H \mid E)$. A theorem of probability, called Bayes' theorem (see PROBABILITY, INTERPRETATIONS OF §5), says the following (where $\bar{H}$ means H is false):

$$P(H \mid E) = \frac{P(E \mid H)}{P(E \mid H)P(H) + P(E \mid \bar{H})P(\bar{H})}P(H)$$

We say that E *confirms* H if $P(H \mid E) > P(H)$. Assuming $P(H) > 0$, E confirms H just in case the fraction on the right hand side of the above equation is greater than 1. Assuming $P(H) < 1$, this condition will hold just in case $P(E \mid H) > P(E \mid \bar{H})$. Thus for evidence to confirm a hypothesis, it is not necessary that the evidence be entailed by the hypothesis, or even that the evidence be very probable given the hypothesis. Evidence that is quite improbable supposing the hypothesis to be true will confirm that hypothesis if the evidence is even less likely on the supposition that the hypothesis is false.

Another implication of the above equation is that even if evidence E does strongly confirm hypothesis H, it does not follow that the hypothesis has a high probability of being true, for its probability given other information may be quite low; that is, $P(H \mid E)/P(H)$ may be large and yet $P(H \mid E)$ small, because $P(H)$ is small. For example, when H is the hypothesis that a loaded truck weighs about 5 grams, $P(H)$ is infinitesimal.

Philosophers often refer to the method of hypothesis as 'inference to the best explanation'. This terminology has the merit of recording the fact that the inference depends not just on the relation between hypothesis and evidence but also on how other hypotheses relate to the evidence. However, it is wrong to suggest that *explanation* plays a fundamental role here; what is important in the connection between evidence and hypothesis is the probability of the evidence given the hypothesis, and this probability is not a measure of the degree to which the hypothesis explains the evidence (see EXPLANATION; INFERENCE TO THE BEST EXPLANATION). Furthermore, the terminology misleadingly suggests that the cogency of an inference is determined by the relation between the various hypotheses and the evidence, when in fact it depends also on the prior probability of the hypotheses.

4   Inference

Inductive inference has traditionally been understood as inference in the usual sense: on the basis of premises that are categorically accepted one comes to categorically accept another statement, the conclusion. For writers such as Bacon, Whewell and Mill, this conception was unproblematic. They thought that inductive inference could provide practical certainty on substantive matters of science and everyday life, and that where such certainty was lacking we should withhold assent. However, various factors, in particular the failure of such well-supported scientific theories as Newtonian mechanics, have convinced contemporary writers that substantive inductive conclusions always have some uncertainty, the best-supported scientific theories not excepted. This presents a dilemma: either we accept only those conclusions that are certain, in which case it seems we can accept very little and there will be almost no inductive inference, or else we accept conclusions that might be wrong.

Some writers on probability and induction, notably Carnap and Jeffrey, have embraced the first horn of this dilemma. They hold that induction should be conceived, not as a process by which we pass from some accepted statements to others, but rather as a process by which we assign probabilities to various hypotheses in the light of our evidence. On this view, we ought virtually never to make inductive inferences, as these have been traditionally conceived.

This rejection of inductive inference presupposes that acceptance of a hypothesis involves treating it as if it were certainly true. Some writers have argued that we can preserve the legitimacy of inductive inference by abandoning the assumption that someone who accepts a hypothesis must treat it as certainly true. A popular suggestion is that accepting a hypothesis is merely a matter of being highly confident of it, for example, of giving it a probability greater than some threshold. One objection to this view is that the set of propositions that have high probability is not consistent. For example, in a large unbiased lottery, the probability that any particular ticket will not win is high, though we also know that some ticket will win. Thus if we accepted every proposition with high probability we would accept an inconsistent set of propositions. This is called the 'lottery paradox' (see PARADOXES, EPISTEMIC). Another objection to equating acceptance with high probability is that informativeness is a reason for accepting a hypothesis but is not a reason for giving the hypothesis high probability.

Several writers have suggested that we ought to think of acceptance as a risky decision and use decision theory to evaluate when acceptance is rational (see DECISION AND GAME THEORY §2). The thought is that acceptance has a certain cognitive utility, which is greater if the proposition accepted is true than if it is false; acceptance of a hypothesis is

rational, at least so far as cognitive goals are concerned, if it maximizes expected cognitive utility. The cognitive utility of accepting a true hypothesis is higher the more informative the hypothesis is, and thus this account provides a place for both probability and informativeness in determining the rationality of inductive inference. Some versions of this approach take acceptance to imply certainty while others do not.

See also: CHINESE PHILOSOPHY §§1–2; CONFIRMATION THEORY; CONFUCIAN PHILOSOPHY, CHINESE §1; INDUCTION, EPISTEMIC ISSUES IN; LEARNING; RATIONALITY OF BELIEF; REICHENBACH, H. §3; SCIENCE, 19TH CENTURY PHILOSOPHY OF; SCIENTIFIC METHOD; STATISTICS

References and further reading

Bacon, F. (1620) *Novum Organum*; repr. ed. T. Fowler as *Bacon's Novum Organum*, Oxford: Clarendon Press, 1888; trans. P. Urbach and J. Gibson, La Salle, IL: Open Court, 1994 (Referred to in §4. Book I argues that a new inductive methodology is needed and the incomplete Book II attempts to provide it.)

Carnap, R. (1950) *Logical Foundations of Probability*, Chicago, IL: University of Chicago Press; 2nd edn, 1962. (Carnap's conception of inductive inference, referred to in §4 above, is presented in §44B.)

Descartes, R. (1644) *Principles of Philosophy*; trans. V.R. Miller and R.P. Miller, Dordrecht: Reidel, 1983. (Descartes' defence of the method of hypothesis, mentioned in §1 above, is in §205.)

Fraassen, B.C. van (1989) *Laws and Symmetry*, Oxford: Clarendon Press. (Chapters 6 and 7 discuss inference to the best explanation.)

Jeffrey, R.C. (1956) 'The valuation and acceptance of scientific hypotheses', *Philosophy of Science* 23: 237–46. (Jeffrey's argument against acceptance of uncertain conclusions, mentioned in §4.)

Levi, I. (1991) *The Fixation of Belief and its Undoing*, Cambridge: Cambridge University Press. (A version of the decision-theoretic account of rational acceptance referred to in §4, with acceptance taken to imply certainty.)

Maher, P. (1993) *Betting on Theories*, Cambridge: Cambridge University Press. (A version of the decision-theoretic account of rational acceptance referred to in §4, with acceptance taken to be compatible with uncertainty.)

Mill, J.S. (1843) *A System of Logic*, London: Longman; 8th edn, 1872. (Referred to in §§1, 2 and 4. Mill's theory of induction can be studied by reading the introduction, Chapter I of Book II, and Book III.)

Milton, J.R. (1987) 'Induction before Hume', *British Journal for the Philosophy of Science* 38: 49–74. (Second section surveys thought on induction from Aristotle to Locke.)

Skyrms, B. (1986) *Choice and Chance*, Belmont, CA: Wadsworth, 3rd edn. (An elementary contemporary introduction to induction, probability and decision theory.)

Whewell, W. (1840) *Philosophy of the Inductive Sciences*, London: Parker; 2nd edn, 1847. (Referred to in §4. Advocates the method of hypothesis; presents a conception of induction deeply influenced by Kant.)

PATRICK MAHER

INDUCTIVE PROOFS

see INDUCTIVE DEFINITIONS AND PROOFS

INFANT COGNITION

see COGNITION, INFANT

INFERENCE, INDIAN THEORIES OF

The use of argument in rational inquiry in India reaches almost as far back in time as its oldest extant literature. Even in very early texts, one finds the deliberate use of modus tollens, *for example, to refute positions thought to be false. In light of such practice, it is not surprising to discover that Indian thinkers came to identify certain forms of reasoning and to study them systematically.*

The study of inference in India is, as Karl Potter (1977) has emphasized, not the study of valid reasoning as reflected in linguistic or paralinguistic forms, but the study of the circumstances in which knowledge of some facts permits knowledge of another fact, and of when acceptance by one person of some state of affairs as a fact requires that that person accept another as a fact. Still, the form of inference which came to be systematically investigated in India can be given schematically (see below).

*At the core of the study of inference in India is the use of a naïve realist ontology. The world consists of individual substances or things (*dravya*), universals*

*(*sāmānya*), and relations between them. The fundamental relation is the one of occurrence (*vṛtti*). The relata of this relation are known as substratum (*dharmin*) and superstratum (*dharma*) respectively. The relation has two forms: contact (*saṃyoga*) and inherence (*samavāya*). So, for example, one individual substance, say a pot, may occur on another, say the ground, by the relation of contact. In this case, the pot is the superstratum and the ground is the substratum. Or a universal, say brownness, may occur in an individual substance, say a pot, by the relation of inherence. Here, brownness, the superstratum, inheres in the pot, the substratum. The converse of the relation of occurrence is the relation of possession.*

*Another important relation is the relation that one superstratum bears to another. This relation, known as pervasion (*vyāpti*), can be defined in terms of the occurrence relation. One superstratum pervades another just in case wherever the second occurs the first occurs. The converse of the pervasion relation is the concomitance relation. As a result of these relations, the world embodies a structure: if one superstratum H is concomitant with another superstratum S, and if a particular substratum p possesses the former superstratum, then it possesses the second. This structure is captured in this inferential schema:*

Pakṣa *(thesis): p has S.*

Hetu *(ground): p has H.*

Vyāpti *(pervasion): Whatever has H has S.*

Here are two paradigmatic cases of such an inference:

Pakṣa *(thesis): p has fire.*

Hetu *(ground): p has smoke.*

Vyāpti *(pervasion): Whatever has smoke has fire.*

Pakṣa *(thesis): p is a tree (that is, has tree-ness).*

Hetu *(ground): p is an oak (that is, has oak-ness).*

Vyāpti *(pervasion): Whatever is an oak (that is, has oak-ness) is a tree (that is, has tree-ness).*

1 **Inference and rational inquiry**
2 **Seeds of rational inquiry**
3 **Growth of rational inquiry**
4 **Appearance of the canonical inference**
5 **Formalization of the canonical inference**
6 **Developments after formalization**

1 Inference and rational inquiry

In tracing out the origin and development of the science of reasoning in general, and of inference (*anumāna*) in particular, one must be careful to distinguish the exercise and implicit recognition of forms of reasoning in thought and inquiry from their explicit articulation and systematic study. This distinction is well exemplified by classical Greek mathematicians: the forms of arguments used in their proofs far exceeded Aristotle's syllogistic and Stoic propositional logic combined. In a similar way, classical Indian thinkers did not articulate many forms of argument which they instinctively recognized as valid and routinely deployed in rational inquiry.

While such principles of logic as the law of non-contradiction, the law of double negation, the law of excluded middle, De Morgan's laws and the equivalence of a proposition and its contrapositive were widely and routinely used by Indian thinkers, their formulation was not taken up for systematic study. Hence, the use of these principles of logic is not discussed in the present entry. Instead, attention is confined to how Indian thinkers came to identify inference as captured in the inferential scheme and how they made such inferences the object of systematic study.

The history of thought in India can be divided into three periods: the pre-classical period (up to the fourth century BC), the classical period (up to the tenth century AD) and the scholastic period (from the eleventh century on). During the pre-classical period the practice of rational inquiry and debate developed, furnishing the raw material for the formulation of works on the science of reason – *hetu-śāstra* or *nyāya*, as the Indian thinkers called it – which appeared at the beginning of the classical period and played an important role in every major school of philosophical and empirical thought.

Rational inquiry comprises the search for reasons for publicly accepted facts, subject to public and rational scrutiny. It is an activity which involves people both severally and collectively. It involves people severally in so far as individual people are the locus of the exercise of reason. It involves people collectively in so far as the exercise of reason is sharpened by the scrutiny of others. Inference is central to both its individual and collective exercise.

Undoubtedly, the Indian science of reason has its origins in the emergence of rational inquiry and debate. However, the origins of rational inquiry and debate are not clear, the relevant literature being scant and the references therein scanty. None the less, a sketch of the earliest period can be constructed.

2 Seeds of rational inquiry

The seeds of rational inquiry in India are found in appendices to its earliest extant body of literature, the Vedas (Wisdom, Knowledge), composed between the thirteenth and eleventh centuries BC, and comprising four collections (*samhitās*): the *Ṛg Veda* (Wisdom of the Verses), hymns dedicated to the gods worshipped by the Indo-Aryans; the *Yajur Veda* (Wisdom of the Sacrificial Formulas), sacred formulas recited at rituals; the *Sāma Veda* (Wisdom of the Chants), an anthology of chants used by priests in their rituals; and the *Atharva Veda* (Wisdom of the Atharva Priests), a compendium of hymns, incantations and magic charms used by priests.

Their appendices include the Brāhmaṇas (Books Pertaining to Prayer, dating from between the eleventh and eighth centuries BC), and the Āràyakas (Books Studied in the Forest, from between the ninth and seventh centuries BC). In them one finds speculation about the causal relations involved in sacrificial rites. Thus, one encounters the concept of *ṛta*, the natural order of things, which underwrites the efficacy of sacrifice, that is, the capacity of the performance of sacrificial rites to bring about prescribed effects. One also encounters the concept of karma, whereby deeds performed at one point in one's life have consequences which manifest themselves in terms of pain and pleasure experienced later in one's life or in one's later life (see KARMA AND REBIRTH, INDIAN CONCEPTIONS OF). Moreover, speculation about the origins of the universe is also found in the Aitareya Āraṇyaka.

The kind of speculation just described appears to have become the object of public contests in which contestants showed off their knowledge of ritual and their proto-cosmological speculations as to its basis. Inevitably, the views of these contestants differed, and indeed conflicted. Such differences undoubtedly gave rise to questions of how to establish the correctness of one view and how to adjudicate between conflicting views. In this way, according to some scholars (for example, Witzel 1987), arose the practice of public debates, so common in the classical and scholastic periods.

In any event, over the course of time the range of objects of speculation grew to include not only questions of cosmology but also questions of metaphysics, especially the question of what there is, and the naturally ensuing question of how one knows or can justify one's claims about what there is. Thus, one finds views purporting to assist humankind in the alleviation of the unhappiness it suffers, views about what comprises happiness, what constitutes matter, whether or not there is an eternal soul, whether or not there is free will, and whether or not knowledge is possible. The diversity of views includes not only views defended in the Brahmanical literature, in particular the Upaniṣads (dating from the eighth to sixth centuries BC) and, in the Buddhist canon, the

Tipiṭika (Three Baskets, dating from after the sixth century BC), but also dissenting views reported in the same literature, such as those of the materialist and atomist Ajita Kesakambalin, of the determinist Makkhali Gosāla, and of the sceptic Sañjaya Belatthiputta.

Central to the pursuit of these questions is the concept of causation, which itself fell within the purview of rational inquiry. Thus, for example, in the Śvetaśvatara Upaniṣad (1.2), a number of views pertaining to causation are reported: determinism (*niyativāda*), indeterminism (*yadṛcchāvāda*) and latency (*svabhāva*).

While the range of rational inquiry increased, it also deepened, for rational inquiry (*anvīkṣikī, parīkṣā*) itself became the object of rational inquiry, that is, questions were raised about how facts are known. Thus, one finds as early as the Taittirīya Āraṇyaka enumerations of the sources of knowledge (*pramās*), namely perception (*pratyakṣa*), inference (*anumāna*), religious authority (*smṛti*) and tradition (*aitihya*).

In short, during the pre-classical period, three practices important to the development of the study of inference make their appearance. Rational inquiry into the causes of things, rational inquiry into how things are known, and public contests which perhaps anticipate public debates.

3 Growth of rational inquiry

By the fifth century BC, great social change was taking place in India and a period of intense intellectual activity began. Rational inquiry had taken hold and its topics were not confined to cosmology and soteriology. True, apart from Pāṇini's *Aṣṭādhyāyī*, the world's earliest extant grammar, no works devoted to such topics as agriculture, architecture, astronomy, grammar, law, mathematics, medicine, phonology and statecraft date from this period. None the less, scholars agree that this period contains the roots of many works not redacted until around the turn of the millennium, including *Kṛṣiśāstra* (Treatise on Agriculture), *Śilpaśāstra* (Treatise on Architecture), *Jyotiṣaśāstra* (Treatise on Astronomy), *Dharmaśāstra* (Treatise on Law), *Carakasamhitā* (Caraka's Collection, a medical treatise) and *Arthaśāstra* (Treatise on Wealth, a political treatise).

Allusions to questions about the number of sources of knowledge, their nature and their objects are found here and there in the Upaniṣads (for example, Maitrī Upaniṣad). Similar issues find elaboration in the Buddhist literature dating from the same period.

Many of the dialogues of the BUDDHA, Siddhārtha Gautama, show that some version of the law of non-contradiction is to be respected, that is, they show

adherence to the view that consistency is a necessary condition for truth. Moreover, many dialogues suggest that truth consists in correspondence to facts, independent of observers. Indeed, a persistent message of the Buddha is that knowledge is grounded in personal observation and inference, where observation is taken to include paranormal observation (though observation none the less). In addition, Buddhists of this period recognize that inference itself must be grounded in causal explanation.

Indeed, much energy is devoted to the development of causal explanations, not only with respect to grounding soteriological claims, for example, as reflected in the doctrine of dependent origination (*pratītya-samutpada*), but even more broadly. Thus, for example, the *Paṭṭhāna* (Causes), one of the seven works of the *Abhidhamma piṭaka* (Basket of Further Doctrine), itself one of the three 'baskets' making up the Buddhist canon, classifies intentional states in terms of twenty-four kinds of causal relations. Causal relations are invoked to explain perceptual states as well. Indeed causal relations are routinely presupposed in discussions of physical events and processes, such as how seeds give rise to shoots (see CAUSATION, INDIAN THEORIES OF).

Moreover, these thinkers not only used causal relations to construct explanations, they were clearly sensitive to the problem of how to establish the existence of causal relations. Passages in the Pāli Canon indicate awareness of the problem of drawing general conclusions from limited observations. Indeed, this period seems to have witnessed the formulation of Mill's method of agreement and difference, known to Indian thinkers as the method of *anvaya-vyatireka*. Such a method, as G. Cardona (1967) has shown, was clearly known to Kātyāyana (*fl.* third century BC), the author of the earliest extant commentary on the *Aṣṭādhyāyī*, and seems to have been known to the Lokāyatikas, who also date from this early period (see MATERIALISM, INDIAN SCHOOL OF).

Publicly organized debates (*pariṣad*) were commonplace, alluded to in various Upaniṣads (Chāndogya Upaniṣad 5.3.1; Bṛhadāraṇyaka Upaniṣad 6.2.1) and exemplified in over half of the thirty-four *suttas* of the Buddhist *Dīgha Nikāya* (Collection of Long Discourses), which are a part of the *Sutta Piṭaka* (Basket of Discourses), one of the three 'baskets' of the Buddhist canon. A better-known, but much later, example of such engagements is the Buddhist work *Milindapañho* (Questions of King Milinda).

The earliest example of protracted systematic rational inquiry into metaphysical issues is found in Moggalīputta Tissa's *Kathāvatthu* (Points of Controversy), a Buddhist work of the third century BC. It sets out the refutation of some two hundred propositions over which the Theravādins, one of the Buddhist schools, disagreed with other Buddhist schools. The treatment of each point comprises a debate between a proponent and an opponent. The refutations turn on demonstrating the inconsistency of a set of propositions.

Not only is the form of the debate canonical but the form of the reasoning is as well. Thus, for example, one finds the following pattern throughout Book 1, Chapter 1:

Proponent: Is *A B*?

Opponent: Yes.

Proponent: Is *C D*?

Opponent: No.

Proponent: Acknowledge defeat, since if *A* is *B*, then *C* is *D*.

It is clear that refutation hinges on inconsistency as exhibited by the following propositional schema: p, $\neg q$, $p \rightarrow q$. Though, as I. Bochenski (1956) has remarked, no propositional forms are identified as such, it is none the less clear that inconsistency of a certain form was considered a decisive refutation.

4 Appearance of the canonical inference

In the classical period, as stated above, begins the redaction of works codifying the results of systematic, rational inquiry begun earlier, not only into such fields as grammar, architecture, mathematics, law and politics, but also into the enduring philosophical questions, including the nature of rational inquiry itself. This is made clear in a brief passage in the *Arthaśāstra* (1.2), a work on statecraft attributed to KAUṬILYA (*fl.* fourth century BC).

The texts surviving from this period have diverse origins. There are two important passages in the *Carakasaṃhitā*, a medical text which was redacted in its current form in the first century AD. There are also texts from the philosophical literature, both Brahmanical and non-Brahmanical. The best-known texts pertaining to inference are in a work attributed to Akṣapāda Gautama, the *Nyāyasūtra*, a Brahmanical treatise on rational inquiry, whose actual redaction is thought to date to the third century AD (see GAUTAMA, AKṢAPĀDA). Another Brahmanical work touching upon inference is the *Vaiśeṣikasūtra*, a work on speculative ontology attributed to Kaṇāda; this was redacted in its current form perhaps at the beginning of the second century AD, though perhaps some of its passages date back to the second century BC. Still another Brahmanical work, which survives only in fragments (which have been collected by E. Frauwallner), is a Sāṅkhya one entitled *Ṣaṣṭitantra*

(Sixty Doctrines), attributed by some to Pañcaśikha (*fl.* second century BC) and by others to Varṣaṇya (*fl.* after second century AD).

The remaining texts are found in the Buddhist philosophical literature. To begin with, there are four passages in four works by the Buddhist idealist Asaṅga (*fl.* fourth century AD): one in his *Abhidharmasaṅgītiśāstra* (Treatise on the Proclamation of the Abhidharma), one in his *Abhidharmasamuccaya* (Compendium of the Abhidharma), one at the end of a chapter of his *Yogācārabhūmiśāstra* (Treatise on the Stages of Yogic Practice) and one in a work which survives only in Chinese translation, *Shun Zheng Lun* (Treatise on According with What is Correct). In addition, VASUBANDHU (*fl.* fifth century AD), another Buddhist idealist, thought to be the younger brother of Asaṅga, wrote at least three works on debate: *Ru Shi Lun* (Treatise on Resembling the Facts, reconstructed in Sanskrit as *Tarkaśāstra*, or Treatise on Reasoning), which survives only in Chinese translation, the *Vādavidhi* (Rules of Debate), whose Sanskrit fragments have been collected by E. Frauwallner, and the *Vādavidhāna* (Precepts of Debate). Finally, there are two other works of unknown author and unknown date which survive only in Chinese translation: *Fang Bian Xin Lun* (reconstructed in Sanskrit by G. Tucci as *Upāyahṛdaya*, or Essential Methods), and *Xian Zhang Sheng Jiao Lun* (reconstructed in Sanskrit by G. Tucci as *Prakaraṇāryavācāśāstra*, or Treatise on the Noble Words of Explanation).

With the notable exception of the *Vaiśeṣikasūtra*, which treats inference only as an epistemic process, the greater part of each text is devoted to inference as argument in debate. These texts typically enumerate, define or classify public discussions, propositions as they are used in public discussions, parts of arguments, qualities which either enhance or detract from a discussant's performance, and statements or actions by a discussant which warrant his being considered defeated, including the uttering of various fallacies.

These texts identify the form of argument used in debate. Thus, for example, the *Nyāyasūtra* (1.1.32), like the *Carakasaṃhitā* (2.8.31), defines an argument as having five parts: the thesis (pakṣa), or proposition (pratijñā); the ground, or reason (hetu); the corroboration (dṛṣṭānta); the application (upanaya); and the conclusion (nigamana). The *Carakasaṃhitā* furnishes the following example:

Thesis: The soul is non-eternal.

Ground: Because it is detectable by the senses.

Corroboration: It is like a pot.

Application: As a pot is detectable by the senses, and

is non-eternal, so is the soul detectable by the senses.

Conclusion: Therefore, the soul is non-eternal.

This form of argument clearly reflects the debate situation. First, one propounds a proposition, that is, one sets forth a proposition to be proved. One then states the ground or reason for the proposition. Next, one corroborates with an example the implicit connection between the property mentioned in the proposition and the property adduced as its ground. The immediately ensuing step, the application, spells out the analogy between the example and the subject of the proposition. Notice that this part of the argument retains vestiges of the analogical reasoning that is no doubt its predecessor. Finally, one asserts the proposition.

As was obvious to these thinkers, not all arguments of this form are good arguments. Not surprisingly, the texts catalogue bad arguments. Grounds adduced in arguments catalogued as bad are referred to as non-grounds (*ahetu*) or pseudo-grounds (*hetu-ābhāsa*). It is difficult to be sure what the basis of the classification was. In the case of the *Nyāyasūtra*, the author gives neither a definition nor an example. Even in cases where definitions and examples are given, as in the *Carakasamhitā*, the modern reader is not always sure what is intended. In all likelihood, included here are cases where the premises of the argument can be true but the conclusion false – formal fallacies – and cases where the argument, though formally valid, is none the less unpersuasive, for example, because its ground (*hetu*) is as controversial as its conclusion.

These very same texts, as well as the *Vaiśeṣikasūtra*, touch on inference as an epistemic process. While the examples of inference furnished all comprise expressions corresponding with the thesis (*pakṣa*) and the ground (*hetu*) of the inferential schema, not all the texts are equally explicit in identifying the form of inference. In particular, both the *Carakasamhitā* (1.11.21–2) and the *Nyāyasūtra* (1.1.5) define inference as knowledge of one fact on the basis of knowledge of another, leaving unmentioned any knowledge of a relation linking the two. Moreover, these texts classify inferences on the basis of characteristics completely extrinsic to the logical features of the inferences adduced. Inferences appear to be classified according to the temporal order of the occurrences of the properties corresponding with those in the thesis (*pakṣa*) and the ground (*hetu*) of the inferential schema.

5 Formalization of the canonical inference

Improved definitions, which mention not only what corresponds with the thesis (*pakṣa*) and the ground (*hetu*) of the inferential schema, but also what corresponds with its pervasion (*vyāpti*), are found in the *Ṣaṣṭitantra*, the *Vaiśeṣikasūtra* and the *Abhidharmasamuccaya* (Further Doctrine Collection), where knowledge of a relation is explicitly included in their definitions of inference. However, what corresponds with pervasion (*vyāpti*) in the inferential schema is not a formal relation, but one of a miscellany of material relations instead. The *Ṣaṣṭitantra* enumerates seven such relations, while the *Vaiśeṣikasūtra* (9.20) enumerates five: the relation of cause to effect, of effect to cause, of contact, of exclusion, and of inherence. In each of these texts, the miscellany of material relations serves to classify inferences. Thus, although in these three works the parts of an inference are made explicit, the formal connection between them remains implicit.

As Katsura (1986) has observed, the earliest extant texts to grapple explicitly with making the formal connection between the parts of an inference apparent are those of Vasubandhu. To begin with, in his *Vādavidhi*, Vasubandhu makes it clear that the relation, knowledge of which is necessary for inference, is not just any in a miscellany of material relations, but a formal relation, which he designates in some places as *avinābhāva* ('being a *sine qua non*') and in others as *nāntarīyakatva* ('being unmediated').

At the same time, Vasubandhu exploits the idea, ascribed by Asaṅga in his *Shun Zheng Lun* to an unknown school (thought by at least one scholar to be the Sāṅkhya school), that a ground (*hetu*) in an inference is a proper one if and only if it satisfies three conditions – the so-called *trirūpahetu*, or the grounding property (*hetu*) in its three forms. The first form is that the grounding property should occur in the subject of an inference (*pakṣa*). The second is that the grounding property should occur in those substrata similar to the subject in so far as they have the property to be established (*sādhya*). And third, the grounding property should not occur in any of those substrata dissimilar from the subject in so far as they lack the property to be established. The first form corresponds to the inferential schema's ground (*hetu*), while the second and the third correspond to its pervasion (*vyāpti*). With the formulation of the *trirūpahetu*, the formal nature of the classical Indian inference is at last fully circumscribed. This form is succinctly displayed by the following schema:

Pakṣa (thesis): p has S.

Hetu (ground): p has H.

Vyāpti (pervasion): Whatever has *H* has *S*.

An insightful distinction found in Vasubandhu's work is the one between inference for oneself and inference for others, which makes explicit what had previously been only implicit, namely that inference, the cognitive process whereby one increases one's knowledge, and argument, the device of persuasion, are but two sides of a single coin.

DIGNĀGA (*fl.* beginning of the sixth century), another Buddhist philosopher, consolidates and systematizes the insights into the formal basis of inference found in Vasubandhu's works. First, he makes the distinction between inference for oneself and inference for others the organizational cornerstone of his treatment of inference. Second, he undertakes to make the three forms of the grounding property, the so-called *trirūpahetu*, more precise, pressing into service the Sanskrit particle *eva* (only). And third, and perhaps most strikingly, he devises the *hetucakra* ('wheel of reasons'), a three-by-three matrix set up to classify pseudo-grounds in the light of the last two forms of the *trirūpahetu*. On the one hand, there are the three cases of the grounding property occurring in some, none or all of the substrata where the property to be established occurs. On the other hand, there are the three cases of the grounding property occurring in some, none or all of the substrata where the property to be established does not occur.

6 Developments after formalization

Dignāga's works set the framework within which subsequent Buddhist thinkers address philosophical issues pertaining to inference and debate. Thus, Śankarasvāmin (*fl.* sixth century) writes a brief manual of inference for Buddhists, called the *Nyāyapraveśa* (Beginning Logic), based directly on Dignāga's work. Not long thereafter, DHARMAKĪRTI (*c.*600–60), the great Buddhist metaphysician, also elaborates his views on inference and debate within the framework found in Dignāga.

Dharmakīrti makes at least two contributions to the treatment of inference. Recall that one of the developments found in Vasubandhu's work was the identification of the formal contribution of what corresponds with the inferential schema's pervasion (*vyāpti*), making it explicit that the corresponding relation is a formal one. One of Vasubandhu's terms for it, namely *avinābhāva*, or 'being a *sine qua non*', made it clear that inference involves some form of necessity. The question raised and systematically investigated by Dharmakīrti is: in what does this necessity consist? His answer is that it consists in two things: the causation relation (*tadutpatti*) and the identity relation (*tādātmya*). The second contribution by Dharmakīrti is his attempt to bring knowledge of absences, or roughly negative facts, within the purview of inference (see NEGATIVE FACTS IN CLASSICAL INDIAN PHILOSOPHY §§1–2).

Another important Buddhist thinker who treated inference is Dharmottara (*fl.* eighth century). He wrote a useful commentary on Dharmakīrti's widely read *Nyāyabindu* (Drop of Logic).

Dignāga not only had a profound influence on his Buddhist followers, he also influenced his non-Buddhist contemporaries and their followers. It would be wrong, however, to conclude that every adoption of ideas similar to those used by Dignāga in his works should be attributed to him. After all, we cannot be certain that his contemporaries did not arrive at similar ideas independently or get their ideas from sources common to them and Dignāga. Thus, for example, in his *Nyāyāvatāra* (Descent into Logic), the Jaina thinker Siddhasena Divākara (*c.* fifth century), a contemporary of Vasubandhu, also speaks of the formal relation *antarvyāpti*, or inner pervasion, which corresponds to *vyāpti*, or pervasion, in the inferential schema. In addition, Praśastapāda (*fl.* sixth century), an adherent of the Vaiśeṣika school and near contemporary of Dignāga, also defines inference in a way which not only makes clear its formal nature but also uses the quantificational adjective *sarva* (all) to make the formal connection precise.

At the same time, some authors of this period seem to have retained a view of inference akin to the one found in the *Ṣaṣṭitantra* and the *Vaiśeṣikasūtra*, in which the formal role of what corresponds with the inferential schema's pervasion (*vyāpti*) has yet to have been identified. This is true both of VĀTSYĀYANA (*fl.* fifth century), the author of the earliest extant commentary on the *Nyāyasūtra*, and of Śabara (*fl.* sixth century), the author of the earliest extant commentary on Jaimini's *Mīmāṃsāsūtra*.

However, it was not long before the advocates of both Nyāya and Mīmāṃsā adapted to the formal view of inference. On the one hand, one finds that the Mīmāṃsā thinker Kumārila Bhaṭṭa (*fl.* early seventh century) adopts, without special comment, the formal perspective. On the other hand, though the Nyāya thinker UDDYOTAKARA (*fl.* late sixth century) argues vigorously against many of Dignāga's views, he none the less advocates a view which presupposes the formalization found in them. For example, Uddyotakara rejects the suitability of the quantifying particle *eva* (only) in the formulation of the three forms of the grounding property (*trirūpahetu*), yet he himself introduces a classification of inference which presupposes Dignāga's formalization. Thus, Uddyota-kara classifies grounds (*hetu*) as: concomitant (*an-vaya*), where nothing distinct from a particular substratum *p* (in the inferential schema) fails to have the property *S*; exclusive (*vyatireka*), where nothing distinct from *p* has *S*; and both concomitant and exclusive, where some things distinct from *p* have *S* and some fail to have *S*. This classification becomes the standard classification for the adherents of Nyāya during the scholastic period.

The developments of the scholastic period are confined almost entirely to the so-called Navya-Nyāya school. Its contributors to the treatment of inference include GAṄGEŚA (*fl.* fourteenth century), perhaps the most outstanding of all the thinkers of this school, Raghunātha (*fl.* early sixteenth century), Jagadiśa (*fl.* later seventeenth century) and GADĀ-DHĀRA (1604–1709).

We conclude with two warnings. First, the treatment of Indian inference here has centred exclusively on tracing out the unfolding of the inferential schema in the history of Indian thought. It has only hinted at the rich philosophical debates that arose among those Indian thinkers eager to harmonize their insights into the formal nature of inference with their views pertaining to metaphysical and linguistic questions. Second, the treatment has not prepared the reader for the intricacies and pitfalls of the terminology used by Indian thinkers in their discussions of inference. The terminology is both ambiguous and inconstant, not just as one goes from the work of one thinker to that of another, but even within the work of a single thinker. Annoying as the contemporary reader may find such ambiguity, it is necessary to remember that this is an inevitable by-product of intellectual fermentation.

See also: DEFINITION, INDIAN CONCEPTS OF; KNOWLEDGE, INDIAN VIEWS OF; NYĀYA-VAIŚEṢIKA

References and further reading

Annambhaṭṭa (*c.*1600) *Tarkasamgraha*, trans. M.R. Bodas, Poona: Bhandarkar Oriental Research Institute, 1918. (A very clear manual of logic for the Nyāya school.)

* Bochenski, I.M. (1956) *Formale Logik*, trans. I. Thomas, *A History of Formal Logic*, Nôtre Dame, IN: University of Nôtre Dame Press, 1961. (Part 6 is a forty-page history of Indian inference.)

* Cardona, G. (1967) 'Anvaya and Vyatireka in Indian Grammar', *Adyar Library Bulletin* 5 (31–2): 313–52. (The author describes the origins of Mill's method of agreement and difference in early Indian thought.)

* Dharmakīrti (*c.*650) *Nyāyabindu* (Drop of Logic), trans. M. Gangopadhyaya, Calcutta: Indian Studies Past and Present, 1971. (A good introduction to Dharmakīrti's metaphysics and logic.)

Dignāga (*c.*525) *Nyāyamukha* (Introduction to Systematic Reasoning), trans. G. Tucci, *The Nyāyamukha of Dignāga*, Heidelberg: Materialien zur Kunde des Buddhismus, 1930. (This very brief text summarizes Dignāga's views on inference and debate.)

Gillon, B.S. (1986) 'Dharmakīrti and his Theory of Inference', in B.K. Matilal and D. Evans (eds) *Buddhist Logic and Epistemology*, Dordrecht: Reidel, 77–87. (A self-contained explanation of how Dharmakīrti treats knowledge of absences as a form of inference.)

Gillon, B.S. and Hayes, R. (1982) 'The Role of the Particle *Eva* in (Logical) Quantification in Sanskrit', *Wiener Zeitschrift für die Kunde Süd-asiens* 26: 195–203. (The authors show how the Sanskrit particle *eva* ('only') is used to express logical quantification by Indian logicians.)

Gillon, B.S. and Love, M.L. (1980) 'Indian Logic Revisited: *Nyāyapraveśa* Reviewed', *Journal of Indian Philosophy* 8: 349–84. (The authors set out the logical and grammatical details of Indian inference as found in the *Nyāyapraveśa*.)

Hayes, R. (1980) 'Diṅnāga's Views on Reasoning (*Svārthānumāna*)', *Journal of Indian Philosophy* 8: 219–77. (A thorough and scholarly treatment of Dignāga's theory of inference.)

Jayatillike, K.N. (1963) *Early Buddhist Theory of Knowledge*, London: Allen & Unwin. (Thorough survey of the intellectual climate at the time of the Buddha.)

* Katsura Shoryu (1986) 'On the Origin and Development of the Concept of *Vyāpti* in Indian Logic', *Hiroshima Tetsugakkai* 38: 1–16. (The author traces the origin of the Indian form of inference.)

* Kauṭilya (4th century BC) *Arthaśāta*, ed. and trans. R.P. Kangle, Delhi: Motilal Banarsidass, 1988, 3 vols. (A work on statecraft.)

Matilal, B.K. (1985) *Logic, Language, and Reality: An Introduction to Indian Philosophical Studies*, Delhi: Motilal Banarsidass. (The first two chapters address many of the outstanding philosophical and philo-logical problems pertaining to the study of inference in Indian philosophy. This is a difficult but important work by one of the twentieth century's major contributors to Indian philosophy.)

Matilal, B.K. and Evans, D. (eds) (1986) *Buddhist Logic and Epistemology*, Dordrecht: Reidel. (A collection of articles by experts on Buddhist logic and epistemology.)

* *Milindapañho* (The Questions of King Milinda) (*c.*100

AD), The Sacred Books of the East 35–6, trans. T.W. Rhys-Davids, Oxford: Clarendon Press, 1890–4, 2 vols; repr. New York: Dover, 1963. (A work on Buddhist metaphysics set out as a dialogue between the senior Buddhist monk, Nāgasena, and the Indo-Greek king Menander.)

* Moggalīputta Tissa (c.255 BC) Kathāvatthu (Points of Controversy), trans. S.Z. Aung and C.A.F. Rhys Davids, London: The Pali Text Society, 1915. (The author sets out the refutation of some 200 propositions over which the Sthavīravādins, one of the Buddhist schools, disagreed with the Sarvāstivādins, another Buddhist school. The text illustrates both the canonical forms of debate and reasoning.)

Mokṣākaragupta (c.1000) Tarkabhāṣā, trans. G. Jhā, Poona: Oriental Book Agency, 1967. (A very clear manual of logic for Buddhists.)

* Nyāyasūtra (c.3rd century AD), trans. G. Jhā, Delhi: Motilal Banarsidass, 1984.(A fundamental work in the history of Indian inference.)

* Potter, K.H. (1977) 'Introduction to the Philosophy of Nyāya-Vaiśeṣika', in Encyclopedia of Indian Philosophies, vol. 2, New Delhi: Motilal Banarsidass. (Chapter 9 of Part 1 gives a clear thirty-page survey of the Nyāya theory of inference.)

* Śankarasvāmin (c.525) Nyāyapraveśa, trans. M. Tachikawa, Journal of Indian Philosophy 1: 111–45. (A clear and concise manual of logic for Buddhists.)

Staal, F. (1973) 'The Concept of Pakṣa in Indian Logic', Journal of Indian Philosophy 2: 156–66. (Useful and clear discussion of the difficulties of Indian inferential terminology.)

Stcherbatsky, T. (1931) Buddhist Logic, New York: Dover, 2 vols. (The first volume is a comprehensive introduction to Dharmakīrti's theory of knowledge and the second volume is a translation of Dharmakīrti's Nyāyabindu, together with the commentary by Dharmottara. The work is a remarkable achievement by one of the truly great scholars of the twentieth century. However, it is very difficult and somewhat dated.)

Uddyotakara (c.600) Nyāyavārttika, trans. G. Jhā, Delhi: Motilal Banarsidass, 1984. (Sets down one of the most important commentaries on the Nyāyasūtra.)

* Upaniṣads (8th–6th century BC), The Upaniṣads, The Sacred Books of the East 1, 15, trans. F. Max Müller, Oxford: Clarendon Press, 1879–84; repr. New York: Dover, 1962. (These texts record views pertaining to a variety of matters, including cosmological, soteriological and epistemological matters, and are ascribed to thinkers thought to have lived between 1000 and 500 BC.)

Vātsyāyana (c.450) Nyāyabhāṣya, trans. G. Jhā, Delhi: Motilal Banarsidass, 1984. (The author sets down the earliest extant commentary on the Nyāyasūtra.)

* Vaiśeṣikasūtra (1st century BC), ed. and trans. A.E. Gough, The Vaiśeshika Aphorisms of Kaṇāda, Varanasi: E.J. Lazarus, 1873; repr. Delhi: Munshiram Manoharlal, 1975. (The earliest extant work on speculative ontology within the Brahmanical tradition.)

Vidyabhusana, S.C. (1921) A History of Indian Logic, Delhi: Motilal Banarsidass, 1971, 2 vols. (This is the standard, though dated, reference on the history of Indian logic.)

Viśvanātha Pañcanana (c.1650) Bhāṣāpariccheda, trans. Mādhavānanda, Almora: Advaita Ashrama, 1940. (A widely used manual of logic for the Nyāya school.)

* Witzel, M. (1987) 'The Case of the Shattered Head', Studien zur Indologie und Iranistik 13/14: 363–415. (This article describes public contests which are thought to be the precursors of public debate.)

Yaśovijaya (c.1650) Jaina Tarkabhāṣā, trans. D. Bhargaya, Delhi: Motilal Banarsidass, 1973. (A manual of logic for Jainas.)

BRENDAN S. GILLON

INFERENCE TO THE BEST EXPLANATION

Inference to the best explanation is the procedure of choosing the hypothesis or theory that best explains the available data. The factors that make one explanation better than another may include depth, comprehensiveness, simplicity and unifying power. According to Harman (1965), explanatory inference plays a central role in both everyday and scientific thinking. In ordinary life, a person might make the inference that a fuse has blown to explain why several kitchen appliances stopped working all at once. Scientists also seem to engage in inference to the best explanation; for example, astronomers concluded that another planet must exist in order to account for aberrations in the orbit of Uranus. However, despite the suggestiveness of cases like these, the extent to which we do and should rely on inference to the best explanation is highly controversial.

1   The legitimacy of inference to the best explanation
2   Inference to the best explanation and enumerative induction
3   The scope and success of inference to the best explanation
4   Further issues

1 The legitimacy of inference to the best explanation

If inference to the best explanation is legitimate, then a person is entitled to accept a hypothesis provided it meets certain minimal standards in accounting for the relevant data, and explains the data better than any other hypothesis available. But, presumably, when we make an inference from a body of evidence, our goal is to arrive at a further or wider grasp of the truth. Inference to the best explanation will advance this goal only if the satisfaction of explanatory desiderata makes a hypothesis likelier to be true. The trouble is that explanatory virtues (like breadth or simplicity) and truth appear to be unrelated (see THEORETICAL (EPISTEMIC) VIRTUES). Under these circumstances, believing a hypothesis because of its explanatory value would not be much better than believing it because someone thought it up on your birthday. It seems that such a procedure will, if anything, hinder the search for truth, not promote it.

Proponents of inference to the best explanation may respond to this line of criticism in a number of ways:

(1) They could deny that truth is the goal of inquiry (see SCIENTIFIC REALISM AND ANTIREALISM §§1–2). This reply may become more difficult to sustain when inference to the best explanation is used in everyday life. For example, it would be uncomfortable to think that a jury which rejects a contention on explanatory grounds (say, for having too many loose ends) is not seeking the truth.

(2) Another response would be to deny that the goal of inquiry is *solely* to amass a body of truths. Rather, we seek (true) explanations of phenomena. Explanatory goodness thus stands alongside likelihood of truth as a distinct but legitimate basis for evaluating hypotheses. This suggestion, however, does not seem to dispel the concern that there may be a *conflict* between pursuit of truth and pursuit of explanatory goodness.

(3) Let us say that a hypothesis is *tested* in so far as it, or its consequences, is compared with observed data, and let us grant that the successful testing of a hypothesis by observations (*confirmation*) increases the likelihood that the hypothesis is true. One might then try to argue that better explanations are more testable by a body of data than inferior ones. In that event, the superior explanation will be better confirmed by the data, and favouring the superior explanation would at least indirectly further the pursuit of truth.

Consider, for illustrative purposes, the following all-too-crude way of linking simplicity and testability.

Suppose hypothesis *H* explains a given phenomenon by positing one mechanism *A*, while its competitor *H** accounts for the same phenomenon by positing the joint action of two different mechanisms *B* and *C*. The simpler hypothesis *H* will be more readily tested because we need evidence to support only one independent claim ('*A* is at work'), instead of two ('*B* is at work' and '*C* is at work'). A difficulty here is that one might just as well say that *H* is *less* testable than *H**, since *H** can be *disconfirmed* by finding evidence against either of its components. Friedman (1983) and others argue with much more sophistication and plausibility that: (a) explanatory hypotheses are ones that unify the data; and (b) to the extent that hypotheses participate in multifarious, unifying relations to the data, they are more thoroughly exposed to testing by that data. Hence, superior explanations are more strongly confirmed by observations, and have better claims to truth.

2 Inference to the best explanation and enumerative induction

Inference to the best explanation is *ampliative*. The conclusion one reaches is not a mere summary of the data on hand – one comes to believe something further which explains the data. We also recognize a pattern of ampliative inference called 'enumerative induction'. This is the extrapolation of observed regularities to universal generalizations or to conclusions about particular unobserved cases. Thus, given that every calico cat you have observed has been female, you may infer that the next calico cat you see will be female. This conclusion certainly goes beyond the data you possess, so enumerative induction is ampliative.

With these points in hand, we can consider a further response to the challenge raised in the previous section: (4) There is indeed no logical connection between the satisfaction of explanatory criteria and truth, but this gap does not impair the legitimacy of inference to the best explanation. For, arguably, no pattern of ampliative inference can be shown antecedently to lead to true conclusions (see INDUCTION, EPISTEMIC ISSUES IN). If the lack of such a guarantee were to make a pattern of ampliative inference illegitimate, it would be improper for us to rely on enumerative induction. Since this result is absurd, there can be no force to the demand that explanatory goodness be demonstrably associated with truth.

However, not all patterns of ampliative inference are reasonable or acceptable. Hence, (4) as such does not establish that inference to the best explanation, in particular, has anything to recommend it. The outcome would be more telling if inference to the best explanation could be more closely linked with enumerative induction. Proceeding along these lines, Gilbert Harman has argued forcefully that all enumerative induction really *is* inference to the best explanation (at least implicitly). If so, the legitimacy we accord to induction cannot be wholly denied to inference to the best explanation.

A difficulty for this view is that we seem to make inductive inferences that in no way serve to explain what has been observed. For example, you might notice that there have been fewer people in the supermarket on Tuesdays than on other days. You conclude by induction that Tuesday is in general the least crowded day at the market. Yet, you may have no explanation at all for what you have observed, no idea why the store has had fewer customers on Tuesdays. It is therefore difficult to see how inference to the best explanation enters into your inductive reasoning. This objection follows Ennis (1968).

Still, there is something suggestive about the notion that inference to the best explanation is of a piece with enumerative induction. Suppose that inference to the best explanation favours simple hypotheses. The inductive extrapolation of observed regularities to other times and places also displays a methodological preference for certain kinds of uniformity or simplicity. This point is highlighted by various cases which can equally well be treated as instances of explanatory inference or of enumerative induction. Suppose you are trying to determine the functional dependence of two quantities, X and Y, and you have collected data points like $(1,1)$, $(2.5, 2.5)$, $(4,4)$, and $(5,5)$. It would be natural and reasonable to suppose that the function is $X = Y$, representable as a straight line passing through the data points. Reaching the conclusion $X = Y$ can be thought of as a simple extrapolation from the data given, that is, as an example of enumerative induction. There are, however, indefinitely many wavier curves that pass through the given data points – for example, the graph of the function $Y = \sin (2 \pi X) + X$. The choice of a straight line to connect the points is sometimes cited as a paradigm of inference to the best explanation; one is opting for the simplest hypothesis (in this case, the simplest curve or function) that accounts for the data (see SIMPLICITY (IN SCIENTIFIC THEORIES)). If curve-fitting cases provide reason to think that enumerative induction and inference to the best explanation really merge or overlap, a critic will be unable to accept one wholeheartedly while rejecting the other across the board.

3 The scope and success of inference to the best explanation

The discussion to this point has treated the legitimacy of inference to the best explanation as an all-or-nothing affair. However, explanatory inference seems to raise the greatest doubts when it is used to support hypotheses about *theoretical* entities – that is, about entities that are unobservable in principle. The basic concern seems to be that theory is underdetermined by evidence: if you can formulate one theory about unobservables to account for a body of evidence, you can formulate indefinitely many others. Inference to the best explanation will select one theory from among these as the correct theory if it best meets our criteria of explanatory adequacy. How, though, are we ever to verify that this choice is in fact the correct one? The candidate theories agree in the observations they predict, so no evidence we can collect will settle the matter.

The reservation here would appear to be that the use of inference to the best explanation in theoretical contexts exacerbates the possibility that explanatory value and truth may diverge. For, if inference to the best explanation does lead us astray in some theoretical context, we will be unable to discover the error by observation, and we will have gone *hopelessly* astray. One response to this heightened concern would be retrenchment. For example, Reichenbach (1976) held that it is indeed proper to choose the simplest curve that fits one's data, as above – but only when that choice can be tested against additional data-points provided by observation. So, more generally, one might restrict the use of inference to the best explanation to non-theoretical contexts.

Another response by proponents of inference to the best explanation is to become more ambitious rather than less. Boyd (1991) and others maintain that science has historically demonstrated an impressive amount of *convergence*. That is, successor theories have tended to retain some important part of their predecessors' content. The best explanation of this fact is supposedly that our theories have become progressively more accurate. Now, if inference to the best explanation has had a large role to play in selecting scientific theories, the phenomenon of convergence provides evidence that inference to the best explanation leads to the truth, even in theoretical contexts.

Opinion about this ambitious line of thought has been sharply divided. One prominent objection is that, in so far as the argument purports to legitimate inference to the best explanation, it is unacceptably circular, as the thesis that inference to the best explanation reliably leads to the truth is itself established by inference to the best explanation (see SCIENTIFIC REALISM AND ANTIREALISM). Proponents of the argument deny that this circularity is objectionable. Also, altogether different defences of inference to the best explanation may sanction its use in theoretical settings.

4 Further issues

Bas van Fraassen (1989) and others have written critically about inference to the best explanation from a Bayesian or probabilist perspective. They hold that necessary and sufficient conditions for justified belief are provided by the probability calculus and the requirement that a subject's beliefs should be updated by the process of conditionalization (see PROBABILITY THEORY AND EPISTEMOLOGY §2). To the extent that inference to the best explanation imposes some further qualitative condition on the way one updates one's beliefs, such inference would lead one to accept, irrationally, bets that are guaranteed to lose. One way to try to meet this challenge would be to show how explanatory inference could be incorporated within a probabilist setting. Another response would be to argue that these critics have somehow misconstrued the way inference to the best explanation works.

There are various important aspects of inference to the best explanation that have not even been touched upon here. These include its implications for 'explanatory coherence' theories, the relation between inference to the best explanation and causal inference, and the utility of inference to the best explanation in responding to sceptical arguments (see the further reading suggestions offered below for references on these topics).

See also: RATIONAL BELIEFS; SCEPTICISM

References and further reading

* Boyd, R. (1991) 'Observations, explanatory power, and simplicity: toward a non-Humean account', in R. Boyd, P. Gasper and J.D. Trout (eds) *The Philosophy of Science*, Cambridge, MA: MIT Press. (Rich treatment of many of the issues discussed in this entry.)

Cartwright, N. (1983) *How the Laws of Physics Lie*, Oxford: Oxford University Press. (See especially chapters 4 and 5; against inference to the best explanation, with an interesting comparison to causal inference.)

* Ennis, R.H. (1968) 'Enumerative induction and best explanation', *Journal of Philosophy* 65 (18): 523–9. (Criticizes Harman's thesis that enumerative induction is implicitly inference to the best explanation.)

* Friedman, M. (1983) *Foundations of Space-Time Theories*, Princeton, NJ: Princeton University Press. (Advanced work, of which chapters 6 and 7 are most relevant; makes points that are both supportive and critical of inference to the best explanation.)

* Harman, G.H. (1965) 'The inference to the best explanation', *Philosophical Review* 74 (1): 88–95. (A seminal article.)

—— (1968) 'Enumerative induction as inference to the best explanation', *Journal of Philosophy* 65 (18): 529–33. (Harman's response to Ennis.)

Lipton, P. (1991) *Inference to the Best Explanation*, London: Routledge. (A good and approachable monograph.)

Peirce, C.S. (1960) *Pragmatism and Pragmaticism*, in *Collected Papers of Charles Sanders Peirce*, vol. 5, ed. C. Hartshorne and P. Weiss, Cambridge, MA: Harvard University Press. (Important source for Peirce's views about inference to the best explanation, which he calls 'abduction' or 'hypothesis'.)

Railton, P. (1989) 'Explanation and metaphysical controversy', P. Kitcher and W.C. Salmon (eds) *Scientific Explanation*, Minnesota Studies in the Philosophy of Science, vol. 13, Minneapolis, MN: University of Minnesota Press. (Masterly discussion of some issues raised in §3 above.)

* Reichenbach, H. (1976) *Experience and Prediction*, Chicago, IL: University of Chicago Press. (Classic treatment of induction, simplicity and the curve-fitting problem.)

Sellars, W.S. (1979) 'More on givenness and explanatory coherence', in G.S. Pappas (ed.) *Justification and Knowledge*, Dordrecht: Reidel. (Difficult but essential discussion of explanatory coherence.)

* van Fraassen, B.C. (1989) *Laws and Symmetry*, Oxford: Oxford University Press. (Advanced work that raises important objections from a probabilist perspective.)

Vogel, J.M. (1990) 'Cartesian skepticism and inference to the best explanation', *Journal of Philosophy* 87 (11): 658–66. (Discusses the use of inference to the best explanation to solve the problem of scepticism about the external world.)

JONATHAN VOGEL

INFINITARY LOGICS

An infinitary logic arises from ordinary first-order logic when one or more of its finitary properties is allowed to become infinite, for example, by admitting infinitely long formulas or infinitely long or infinitely branched proof figures. The need to extend first-order logic became pressing in the late 1950s when it was realized that many of the fundamental notions of mathematics cannot be expressed in first-order logic in a way that would allow for their logical analysis. Because infinitary logics often do not suffer the same limitation, they have become an essential tool in mathematical logic.

Traditionally, logic – considered as the analysis of valid human reasoning, or something intimately connected with it – was seen as having to be finitary in its expressions, inferences and proofs, owing to the finitude of the human mind. This situation began to change in the second half of the nineteenth century, for two principal reasons. First, in philosophy, the Neo-Kantian conception of '*Geltung*' (roughly, 'validity') gave rise both to a logical reconstructionist view in the philosophy of science – represented most prominently by Carnap – and to an anti-psychologistic strain of logical theory – represented most prominently by Frege. Second, in mathematics, although increased attention to foundations led to the elimination from analysis of a direct appeal to the infinite, it also led to increased emphasis on the infinite through the development of set theory.

In Löwenheim's proof of his famous theorem (1915), we find perhaps the first deliberate use of infinitely long formulas and strings of quantifiers (see LÖWENHEIM–SKOLEM THEOREMS AND NONSTANDARD MODELS). But development was interrupted for some thirty years by the influence of Hilbert, who stressed the finitary standpoint and focused on (the proof theory of) first-order logic and elementary recursion theory (see HILBERT'S PROGRAMME AND FORMALISM).

In the early 1950s older modes of research (for example, investigation by logical reconstruction relying on infinitary means whenever necessary) were knit together again and model theory became fruitful. However, with the success of first-order model theory the deficiencies of this language for the expression of mathematical concepts (for example, compactness arguments) also became apparent. Thus, by the end of the decade, an extended model theory which searched for stronger logics began to emerge. Infinitary logics (ILs), in addition to fragments of *n*th-order logic, new quantifiers, and so on, proved to be a useful tool in increasing the expressive power of logical language.

Karp, Henkin, Tarski and others pioneered the development of ILs. At roughly the same time, ILs were introduced into proof theory as a means of streamlining and extending known techniques for consistency proofs. Since the Lindström theorems (see Lindström 1969) showed that interesting properties of

first-order logic (for example, compactness; see Hanf 1964) must be lost if one tries to extend it, a new phase of research began when it was discovered that restriction to 'admissible' parts of a language not only preserves the usefulness of ILs but also yields suitable variants of lost properties (for example, Barwise compactness; see Barwise 1975).

Let $\mathcal{L}_{\kappa\lambda}$, with κ, λ (regular) infinite cardinals, denote an otherwise first-order language that allows for disjunctions (conjunctions) with fewer than κ disjuncts (conjuncts) and fewer than λ free variables (and hence fewer than λ quantifiers). (If κ or λ is arbitrary, we write ∞ instead.) Recall that ω is the cardinality of the natural numbers and ω_1 the least cardinal bigger than ω, that is, the cardinality of the reals in case the continuum hypothesis is true. In this notation ordinary first-order language $\mathcal{L}^1$, allowing for only finitely many disjuncts and free variables, becomes the finitary $\mathcal{L}_{\omega\omega}$.

Suppose we supplement a first-order language $\mathcal{L}_{\omega\omega}$ with an infinitary disjunctor, $\bigvee$, and add the formation rule: if Φ is a countable set of first-order formulas $\{\phi_n : n \in \omega\}$, then $\bigvee\Phi$ is a formula of $\mathcal{L}_{\omega_1\omega}$, being the countable disjunction of all $\phi \in \Phi$. Similarly for the infinitary conjunctor $\bigwedge\Phi$, though it might also be defined by De Morgan's law as $\neg\bigvee\{\neg\phi_n : n \in \omega\}$.

To obtain a semantics for $\mathcal{L}_{\omega_1\omega}$, add to the standard semantics the clause

$$\mathfrak{F} \models \bigvee\Phi \text{ iff there is some } \phi \in \Phi \text{ such that } \mathfrak{F} \models \phi$$

and the corresponding clause for $\bigwedge\Phi$. Complementing the deduction rules of $\mathcal{L}_{\omega\omega}$ with the obvious variants for $\bigvee$ (respectively, $\bigwedge$) results in a sound and complete calculus for $\mathcal{L}_{\omega_1\omega}$. Thus, for example, one might add the following rules:

(1) $\vdash \phi \rightarrow \bigvee\Phi$, for $\phi \in \Phi$

(2) If $\vdash \phi \rightarrow \psi$, for all $\phi \in \Phi$, then $\vdash \bigvee\Phi \rightarrow \psi$.

Two cautionary notes are in order here. First, completeness holds only with respect to the valid sentences and does not generally hold with regard to consequence (specifically, if the set of premises is not countable; see Scott 1965). Second, (2) shows that infinitely long derivations may occur, transforming the formal system into a semi-formal one.

In $\mathcal{L}_{\omega_1\omega}$ mathematical concepts that are not axiomatizable in ordinary $\mathcal{L}_{\omega\omega}$ become so. Simple examples include: the class of torsion groups, with the addition to the group axioms of the axiom

$$\forall x \bigvee \{\underbrace{x \circ \ldots \circ x}_{n \text{ times}} = e: 1 \leqslant n \in \omega\}$$

(where e denotes the neutral element of a group); the

class of fields with characteristic unequal zero, with the addition to the field axioms of

$$\forall x \bigvee \{\underbrace{1 + \ldots + 1}_{n\,\text{times}} = 0 : 2 \leqslant n \in \omega\};$$

and the class of structures isomorphic to the natural numbers, with the addition to the first two Peano axioms of

$$\forall x \bigvee \{\underbrace{S \ldots S}_{n\,\text{times}} 0 = x : 0 \leqslant n \in \omega\}$$

(where S denotes the successor function). Among the logical metatheorems, downward Löwenheim–Skolem holds. Thus, if a sentence $\phi \in \mathcal{L}_{\omega_1\omega}$ is satisfiable, then it is countably satisfiable. The upward theorem is more difficult, requiring the use of the Hanf number $\beth_\alpha$. If ϕ is satisfiable in all cardinalities $\beth_\alpha$, with $\alpha < \omega_1$ and $\beth$ a kind of superexponentiation of the alephs, then ϕ is satisfiable in all infinite cardinalities. Among other metatheorems that hold, Lopez-Escobar (1965), using a complete Gentzen system, was able to establish Craig's interpolation theorem and Beth's definability theorem (see also Karp 1964, Keisler 1971; BETH'S THEOREM AND CRAIG'S THEOREM).

For languages between $\mathcal{L}_{\omega_1\omega}$ and $\mathcal{L}_{\infty\infty}$, as expected, the expressive power increases as the language becomes more infinitary. Thus, for example, each well-ordering is characterizable up to isomorphism by a sentence ϕ of $\mathcal{L}_{\infty\omega}$ and the notion of well-ordering itself becomes definable in $\mathcal{L}_{\omega_1\omega_1}$. Large languages thus admit more applications to mathematics (especially in algebraic subjects), even though many fundamental second-order concepts (for example, the class of topological spaces) remain inexpressible in such a language as $\mathcal{L}_{\infty\infty}$. In addition, as the language becomes larger, the rather coherent framework of metatheoretic results that still hold for $\mathcal{L}_{\omega_1\omega}$ dissolves (see Dickmann 1975, 1985).

In proof theory, the Gentzen-type consistency proofs of the early 1950s (see PROOF THEORY) using ω-logic gained considerably in clarity by being reformulated in $\mathcal{L}_{\omega_1\omega}$ (see Tait 1968). Another kind of IL, ordinary $\mathcal{L}^1$ with infinitely long terms, was used to define functionals of finite type and was first employed by Tait (1965) to recast Gödel's *Dialectica* interpretation (producing a second link between infinitary logic and recursion theory in addition to that forged by the introduction of admissible sets; see INTUITIONISM §6).

See also: LOGICAL AND MATHEMATICAL TERMS, GLOSSARY OF

References and further reading

* Barwise, J. (1975) *Admissible Sets and Structures: An Approach to Definability Theory*, New York: Springer. (Reference work concerning infinitary logic and admissible set theory; accessible.)
—— (1980) 'Infinitary Logics', in E. Agazzi (ed.) *Modern Logic: A Survey*, Dordrecht: Reidel, 93–112. (A mostly historical survey, which complements Moore (1990); very readable.)
—— (1981) 'The Role of the Omitting Types Theorem in Infinitary Logic', *Archiv für mathematische Logik und Grundlagenforschung* 21: 55–68. (Surveys a metatheorem not treated here; useful.)
Barwise, J. and Feferman, S. (eds) (1985) *Model-Theoretic Logics*, New York: Springer, part A, chaps 2 and 3, and part C. (These first-rate surveys give ample information on infinitary logics in model theory, including a bibliography; advanced.)
* Dickmann, M.A. (1975) *Large Infinitary Languages: Model Theory*, Amsterdam: North Holland. (Textbook; advanced.)
* —— (1985) 'Larger Infinitary Languages', in J. Barwise and S. Feferman (eds) *Model-Theoretic Logics*, New York: Springer, 1985, 317–63. (Valuable survey; advanced.)
Ebbinghaus, H.-D. and Flum, J. (1995) *Finite Model Theory*, Berlin: Springer. (Textbook which also covers the use of infinitary logics in the growing field of finite model theory; very readable.)
Ebbinghaus, H.-D., Flum, J. and Thomas, W. (1984) *Mathematische Logik*, Heidelberg, Berlin and Oxford: Springer, 4th revised edn, 1996; trans. *Mathematical Logic*, Berlin: Springer, 2nd edn, 1994. (Introductory textbook including some infinitary logic and proofs of the Lindström theorems; very readable.)
Feferman, S. (1977) 'Theories of Finite Type Related to Mathematical Practice', in J. Barwise (ed.) *Handbook of Mathematical Logic*, Amsterdam: North Holland, ch. D4. (§8.3 provides some information on infinite terms; advanced.)
* Hanf, W. (1964) 'Incompactness in Languages With Infinitely Long Expressions', *Fundamenta Mathematicae* 53: 309–24. (A milestone proving that ordinary compactness is lost in infinitary logics; advanced.)
Henkin, L.A. (1961) 'Some Remarks on Infinitely Long Formulas', in *Infinitistic Methods: Proceedings of the Symposium on Foundations of Mathematics*, New York: Pergamon Press, 167–83. (One of the earliest papers on the subject; readable.)
Hugly, P. and Sayward, C. (1983) 'Can a Language Have Indenumerably Many Expressions?', *History*

and Philosophy of Logic 4: 73–82. (The authors claim not.)

* Karp, C. (1964) *Languages With Expressions of Infinite Length*, Amsterdam: North Holland. (The first textbook on the subject; proceeds algebraically. Austerely written.)

* Keisler, H.J. (1971) *Model Theory for Infinitary Logic: Logic With Countable Conjunctions and Finite Quantifiers*, Amsterdam: North Holland. (Proceeds along familiar model theoretic lines; very readable.)

* Lindström, P. (1969) 'On Extensions of Elementary Logic', *Theoria* 35: 1–11. (The paper in which the two famous Lindström theorems are proved; advanced.)

* Lopez-Escobar, E.G.K. (1965) 'An Interpolation Theorem for Denumerably Long Formulas', *Fundamenta Mathematicae* 57: 253–72. (Accessible.)

Moore, G.H. (1990) 'Proof and the Infinite', *Interchange* 21 (2): 46–60. (Survey of the history of infinitary logic from Aristotle to the early 1960s, which complements Barwise (1980); recommended.)

Pohlers, W. (1989) *Proof Theory: An Introduction*, Berlin: Springer. (Textbook using infinitary languages to obtain Gentzen-style consistency proofs; readable.)

* Scott, D. (1965) 'Logic With Denumerably Long Formulas and Finite Strings of Quantifiers', in J.W. Addison *et al.* (eds) *The Theory of Models*, Amsterdam: North Holland, 329–41. (Influential paper arguing convincingly to the effect that $\mathcal{L}_{\omega_1\omega}$ is the 'truest' first-order extension, whereas $\mathcal{L}_{\omega_1\omega_1}$ is already second-order logic in disguise.)

Scott, D. and Tarski, A. (1958) 'The Sentential Calculus With Infinitely Long Expressions', *Colloquium Mathematicum* 6: 164–70. (One of the earliest papers on the subject; readable.)

* Tait, W.W. (1965) 'Infinitely Long Terms of Transfinite Type', in J.N. Crossley and M.A.E. Dummett (eds) *Formal Systems and Recursive Functions*, Amsterdam: North Holland, 176–85. (Advanced.)

* —— (1968) 'Normal Derivability in Classical Logic', in J. Barwise (ed.) *The Syntax and Semantics of Infinitary Languages*, New York: Springer, 204–36. (Milestone introducing $\mathcal{L}_{\omega_1\omega}$ to proof theory; advanced.)

Tarski, A. (1958) 'Remarks on Predicate Logic With Infinitely Long Expressions', *Colloquium Mathematicum* 6: 171–6. (One of the earliest papers on the subject; readable. Note 5 gives some historical remarks.)

BERND BULDT

INFINITY

The infinite is standardly conceived as that which is endless, unlimited, immeasurable. It also has theological connotations of absoluteness and perfection. From the dawn of civilization, it has held a special fascination: people have been captivated by the boundlessness of space and time, by the mystery of numbers going on forever, by the paradoxes of endless divisibility and by the riddles of divine perfection.

The infinite is of profound importance to mathematics. Nevertheless, the relationship between the two has been a curiously ambivalent one. It is clear that mathematics in some sense presupposes the infinite, for instance in the fact that there is no largest integer. But the idea that the infinite should itself be an object of mathematical study has time and again been subjected to ridicule. In the nineteenth century this orthodoxy was challenged, with the advent of 'transfinite arithmetic'. Many, however, have remained sceptical, believing that the infinite is inherently beyond our grasp.

Perhaps their scepticism should be trained on the infinite itself: perhaps the concept is ultimately incoherent. It is certainly riddled with paradoxes. Yet we cannot simply jettison it. This is why the paradoxes are so acute. The roots of these paradoxes lie in our own finitude: it is self-conscious awareness of that finitude which gives us our initial sense of a contrasting infinite, and, at the same time, makes us despair of knowing anything about it, or having any kind of grasp of it. This creates a tension. We feel pressure to acknowledge the infinite, and we feel pressure not to. In trying to come to terms with the infinite, we are trying to come to terms with a basic conflict in ourselves.

1 **Early Greek thought**
2 **Aristotle**
3 **The rationalists and the empiricists**
4 **Kant**
5 **Post-Kantian metaphysics of the infinite**
6 **Modern mathematics of the infinite**
7 **Human finitude**

1 Early Greek thought

The Greek word *peras* is usually translated as 'limit' or 'bound'. *To apeiron* denotes that which has no *peras*, the unlimited or unbounded: the infinite. *To apeiron* made its first significant appearance in early Greek thought with Anaximander of Miletus in the sixth century BC (see ANAXIMANDER §2). He thought of it as the boundless, imperishable, ultimate source of everything that is. He also thought of it as that to which all things must eventually return in order to atone for the injustices and disharmony which result from their transitory existence.

Anaximander was something of an exception, however. On the whole, the Greeks abhorred the infinite (as the old adage has it). More typical of that era were the Pythagoreans, a religious society founded by Pythagoras (see PYTHAGOREANISM §2). They believed in two basic cosmological principles, *Peras* and *Apeiron*, the former subsuming all that was good, the latter all that was bad. They held further that the whole of creation was to be understood in terms of, and indeed was ultimately constituted by, the positive integers 1, 2, 3,...; and that this was made possible by the fact that *Peras* was continuously subjugating *Apeiron* (the integers themselves, of course, are each finite). The Pythagoreans were followed to some extent in these beliefs by Plato, who also held that it was the imposition of limits on the unlimited that accounted for all the numerically definable phenomena that surround us.

However, the Pythagoreans soon learned to their dismay that they could not simply relegate the infinite to the role of cosmic villain. This was because of Pythagoras' own discovery that the square on the hypotenuse of a right-angled triangle is equal to the sum of the squares on the other two sides. Given this theorem, the ratio of a square's diagonal to each side is $\sqrt{2} : 1$. There are some good approximations to this ratio: it is a little more than $7 : 5$, for example, and a little less than $17 : 12$. Indeed there are approximations of any desired degree of accuracy. Nevertheless, given the basic tenets of Pythagoreanism, it ought to be *exactly* $p : q$, for some pair of positive integers p and q. The problem was that they discovered a proof that it is not, which they regarded as nothing short of catastrophic. According to legend, one of them was shipwrecked at sea for revealing the discovery to their enemies. The Pythagoreans had stumbled across the 'irrational' within mathematics. They had seen the limitations of the positive integers, and had thereby been forced to acknowledge the infinite in their very midst.

At around the same time, Zeno of Elea was formulating various celebrated paradoxes connected with the infinite (see ZENO OF ELEA §6). Best known of these is the paradox of Achilles and the tortoise: Achilles, who runs much faster than the tortoise, cannot overtake it in a race if he lets it start a certain distance ahead of him. For in order to do so he must first reach the point from which the tortoise started, by which time the tortoise will have advanced a fraction of the distance initially separating them; he must then make up this new distance, by which time the tortoise will have advanced again; and so on *ad infinitum*. Such paradoxes, as well as having a

profound impact on the history of thought about infinity, did much to reinforce early Greek hostility to the concept.

2 Aristotle

Aristotle's understanding of the infinite was an essentially modern one in so far as he defined it as the untraversable or never-ending. But he perceived a basic dilemma. On the one hand Zeno's paradoxes, along with a host of other considerations, show that the concept of the infinite really does resist a certain kind of application to reality. On the other hand there seems to be no prospect of doing without the concept, as the Pythagoreans had effectively realized. As well as $\sqrt{2}$, time seems to be infinite, numbers seem to go on *ad infinitum*, and space, time and matter all seem to be infinitely divisible.

Aristotle's solution to this dilemma was masterly. It has dominated all subsequent thought on the infinite, and until very recently was adopted by almost everyone who considered the topic. Aristotle distinguished between the 'actual infinite' and the 'potential infinite'. The actual infinite is that whose infinitude exists, or is given, at some point in time. The potential infinite is that whose infinitude exists, or is given, *over* time. All objections to the infinite, Aristotle insisted, are objections to the actual infinite. The potential infinite is a fundamental feature of reality. It is there to be acknowledged in any process which can never end: in the process of counting, for example, in various processes of division, or in the passage of time itself. The reason why paradoxes such as Zeno's arise is that we pay insufficient heed to this distinction. Having seen, for example, that there can be no end to the process of dividing a given racecourse, we somehow imagine that all those possible future divisions are already in effect there. We come to view the racecourse as already divided into infinitely many parts, and it is easy then for the paradoxes to take hold.

Even those later thinkers who did not share Aristotle's animosity towards the actual infinite tended to recognize the importance of his distinction. Often, though, Aristotle's reference to time was taken as a metaphor for something deeper and more abstract. This in turn usually proved to be something grammatical. Thus certain medieval thinkers distinguished between categorematic and syncategorematic uses of the word 'infinite'. Putting it very roughly, to use the word categorematically is to say that there is something with a property that surpasses any finite measure; to use the word syncategorematically is to say that, given any finite measure, there is something with a property that surpasses it. In the former case the infinite has to be instantiated 'all at once'. In the latter case it does not.

The categorematic–syncategorematic distinction heralds another distinction, whose importance to the infinite is hard to exaggerate. This is the distinction between saying that there is something of kind X to which each thing of kind Y stands in relation R, and saying that each thing of kind Y stands in relation R to something of kind X (not necessarily the same thing each time). This is referred to below as the 'Scope Distinction' (see SCOPE).

But Aristotle himself was not thinking in these very abstract terms. He took the references to time in his own account of the actual–potential distinction quite literally, and this gave rise to his most serious difficulty. He held that time (unlike space) is infinite. He also held that time involves constant activity, as exemplified in the revolution of the heavens. When our attention is focused on the future, there is no obvious problem with this. Past revolutions, however, because they are past, seem to have an infinitude which is by now completely given to us, and hence which is actual. This difficulty, in various different guises, has been a continual aggravation for philosophers who have wanted to see the infinite in broadly Aristotelian terms.

3 The rationalists and the empiricists

For over two thousand years Aristotle's conception of the infinite was regarded as orthodoxy. Often this conception was motivated by a kind of empiricism: the actual infinite was spurned on the grounds that we can never encounter it in experience. But does the potential infinite fare any better in this respect? Is experience of an infinitude that is given over time any less problematic than experience of an infinitude that is given all at once? The more extreme of the British empiricists were hostile to the infinite in all its guises. Where Aristotle had felt able to accept that space and time were infinitely divisible, BERKELEY and HUME denied even that. They thought that the concept of the infinite was one that we could, and should, do without (see EMPIRICISM).

This was partly a backlash against their rationalist predecessors. The rationalists had argued that we could form an idea of the infinite, even though we could neither experience it nor imagine it. They thought that this idea was an innate one, and that it constituted, or helped to constitute, a vital insight into reality. They did not see any difficulty in this view. As Descartes put it, the fact that we cannot grasp the infinite does not preclude our touching it with our thoughts, any more than the fact that we cannot grasp

a mountain precludes our touching it (see RATIONALISM §2).

Descartes believed that our idea of the infinite had been implanted in our minds by God (see DESCARTES, R. §6). Indeed this was the basis of one of his proofs of God's existence. Only a truly infinite being, Descartes argued, *could* have implanted such an idea in our minds. Note here the assimilation of the infinite to the divine: this was a legacy of medieval thought which is nowadays quite commonplace. But when the assimilation was first made, at the end of antiquity – most famously, by the Neo-Platonist Plotinus – it marked something of a turning point in the history of thought about the infinite (see PLOTINUS §§3, 4). Until then there had been a tendency to hear 'infinite' as a derogatory term. Henceforth, it was quite the opposite.

The empiricists, meanwhile, needed to defend their rejection of the infinite against the charge that it invalidated contemporary mathematics. They had more or less sophisticated ways of doing this, though in the case of geometry, where the problem was at its most acute, Hume took the rather cavalier step of simply denying certain crucial principles which mathematicians took for granted. (Berkeley's chief concern was with the use of infinitesimals in the recently invented calculus. In fact, his reservations were perfectly justified: it was a century before they were properly addressed.)

4 Kant

Kant played his characteristic role of conciliator in the debate on the infinite (see KANT §§2, 5, 8). He had an empiricist scepticism about the infinite, based on the fact that we cannot directly experience it. Nevertheless, he sided with the rationalists by insisting that there are certain formal or structural features of what we experience, which are accessible a priori and which *do* involve the infinite. Thus he thought that space and time were infinite (both in the sense of being infinitely extended and in the sense of being infinitely divisible): it is written into the form of whatever we experience that there can also be experience of how things are further out, further in, earlier or later. These, on Kant's view, were mathematical truths, a priori and unassailable.

But there is a question about how the topology of space and time *can* be a priori. Kant's celebrated reply was that space and time are not features of 'things in themselves'; they are part of an a priori framework which we contribute to our experience of things. What then of the *contents* of space and time, the physical universe as a whole? This was different. Kant did not think that what was physical was constructed a priori.

Nor, on the other hand, did he think that it was ultimately real, that is to say real in a way that transcends any possible access we have to it. It had no features, on Kant's view, that exceed what we are capable of grasping through experience. So here the concept of the infinite did resist application. It still had what Kant regarded as a legitimate *regulative* use. That is, we could proceed *as if* the physical universe as a whole were infinite, thereby encouraging ourselves never to give up in our explorations. But we ultimately had no way of making sense of such infinitude. Kant was forced to take an extreme empiricist line by denying that the physical universe as a whole is infinitely big, that it has infinitely many parts and, going this time beyond Aristotle (thus bypassing the difficulty that had beset Aristotle himself), that it is infinitely old.

However, there was a dilemma. Kant was also forced to deny that the physical universe is *finite* in each of these three respects. Apart from anything else, to postulate infinite, empty space or time beyond the confines of the physical universe is itself to postulate that which exceeds what we are capable of grasping through experience.

This dilemma looks acute. Kant himself presented it in the form of a pair of 'antinomies'. These antinomies consisted of the principal arguments against the physical universe's being infinite in each of the specified respects, and the principal arguments against its being finite. But he believed that the dilemma contained the seeds of its own solution. If what is physical is not ultimately real – if there is no more to it than what we are capable of experiencing – then we are at liberty to deny that there is any such thing as the physical universe as a whole. There are only the finite physical things that are accessible to us through experience. The physical universe as a whole is neither infinite nor finite. It does not exist.

Kant's solution involved him in a direct application of the Scope Distinction (see §2 above). On the one hand he affirmed that any finite physical thing is contained within something physical. On the other hand he denied that there is something physical within which any finite physical thing is contained. Both of these, the affirmation and the denial, were grounded in the fact that there is nothing we can identify in space and time such that we cannot identify more. This is fundamentally a fact about us: the fact that we are finite. Our identifications are always incomplete. What Kant added, in an idealist vein, was that what we cannot identify does not exist. Here, as in so many other places, we see how deeply involved with human finitude Kant's philosophy was, and how seriously he took it.

5 Post-Kantian metaphysics of the infinite

Metaphysical thought about the infinite since Kant has continued to be just as deeply involved with human finitude. Existentialists in particular have been greatly exercised by it, especially in its guise of mortality. But they have also for the most part recognized an element of the infinite within us. This too is Kantian. Kant believed that we are free rational agents, and that when our agency is properly exercised, it has an unconditioned autonomy that bears all the hallmarks of the truly infinite. For Kant, this was something which exalts us. But for many of the existentialists, still preoccupied with the fundamental fact of human finitude, it is something which is responsible for the deepest tensions within us, and thus for the absurdity of human existence (see EXISTENTIALISM §2).

Hegel agreed with Kant that the truly infinite is to be found in the free exercise of reason (see HEGEL, G.W.F. §8). But he took this further than Kant. He argued that reason is the infinite ground of everything. Everything that happens, on Hegel's view, can be understood as the activity of a kind of world-spirit, and this spirit *is* reason.

This led Hegel to a very non-Aristotelian conception of the infinite. For Hegel, the infinite was the complete, the whole, the unified. Aristotle's conception of the infinite as the never-ending was in Hegel's view quite wrong. He explained this conception as arising from our finite attempts to assimilate the truly infinite. And he described Aristotelian infinity as a 'spurious', or 'bad', infinity – a mere succession of finite elements, each bounded by the next, but never complete and never properly held together in unity. Such 'infinitude' seemed to Hegel at turns nightmarish, then bizarre, then simply tedious, but always a pale, inadequate reflection of the truly infinite.

6 Modern mathematics of the infinite

Despite Kant's influence on Hegel, and despite his own commitment to infinite reason (as well as to infinite space), Kant certainly helped to propagate the Aristotelian tradition of treating the actual infinite with hostility and suspicion. As this tradition prevailed, the actual infinite came increasingly to be understood in the more general, non-temporal sense indicated in §2 above. Eventually, exception was being taken to any categorematic use of the word 'infinite'. The most serious challenge to this tradition, at least in a mathematical context, was not mounted until the nineteenth century, by Cantor, whose mathematical contribution to this topic is unsurpassed (see CANTOR, G.).

Objections to the actual infinite had tended to be of two kinds. The first kind we have already seen: objections based on the fact that we can never encounter the actual infinite in experience. Objections of the second kind were based on the paradoxes to which the actual infinite gives rise. These paradoxes fall into two groups. The first group consists of Zeno's paradoxes and their variants. By the time Cantor was writing, however, the calculus (which had then reached full maturity) had done a great deal to mitigate these. Of more concern by then were the paradoxes in the second group, which had been known since medieval times. These were paradoxes of equinumerosity. They derive from the following principle: if (and only if) it is possible to pair off all the members of one set with all those of another, then the two sets must have just as many members as each other. For example, in a non-polygamous society, there must be just as many husbands as wives. This principle looks incontestable. However, if it is applied to infinite sets, it seems to flout Euclid's notion that the whole is greater than the part. For instance, it is possible to pair off all the positive integers with those that are even: 1 with 2, 2 with 4, 3 with 6 and so on.

Cantor accepted this principle. And, consistently with that, he accepted that there are just as many even positive integers as there are positive integers altogether. Far from being worried by this, he defined precisely what is going on in such cases, and then incorporated his definitions into a coherent, systematic and rigorous theory of the actual infinite, ready to be laid before any sceptical gaze.

It might be expected that, on this understanding, all infinite sets are the same size. (If they are, that is not unduly paradoxical.) But much of the revolutionary impact of Cantor's work came in his demonstration that they are not. There are different infinite sizes. This is a consequence of what is known as Cantor's theorem: no set, and in particular no infinite set, has as many members as it has subsets. In other words, no set is as big as the set of its subsets. If it were, then it would be possible to pair off all its members with all its subsets. But this is not possible. Suppose there *were* such a pairing and consider the set of members paired off with subsets not containing them. Whichever member was paired off with *this* subset would belong to it if and only if it did not belong to it (see CANTOR'S THEOREM).

In the course of developing these ideas, Cantor laid down some of the basic principles of the set theory which underlay them; he devised precise methods for measuring how big infinite sets are; and he formulated ways of calculating with these measures. In short, he established transfinite arithmetic.

Even so, there are many who remain suspicious of his work and who continue to think of the infinite in broadly Aristotelian terms. Cantor himself was forced to admit that there are some collections, including the collection of all things, which are *so* big that they cannot be assigned any determinate magnitude (their members cannot be given 'all at once'). Concerning such collections, he even sometimes said that they are 'truly' infinite. There is in fact a real irony here: Cantor's work can in many ways be regarded as corroborating Aristotelian orthodoxy.

Brouwer believed that Cantor had gone wrong in not showing sufficient respect for the first kind of objection to the actual infinite: that we cannot encounter it in experience. All Cantor had done, in Brouwer's view, was to demonstrate certain tricks that can be played with (finite) symbols, without addressing the question of how these tricks answer to experience. The relevant experience here – the experience to which any meaningful mathematical statement must answer, according to Brouwer and other members of his intuitionistic school – is our experience of time. It is by recognizing the possibility of separating time into parts, and then indefinitely repeating that operation over time, that we arrive at our idea of the infinite. And such infinitude is potential, not actual – in the most literal sense (see INTUITIONISM §1).

There was a very different critique of Cantor's ideas in the work of Wittgenstein, though it led to similar results (see WITTGENSTEIN §14). Wittgenstein believed that insufficient attention had been paid (at least by those interpreting Cantor's work, if not by Cantor himself) to what he called the 'grammar' of the infinite, that is to certain fundamental constraints on what could count as a meaningful use of the vocabulary associated with infinity. In effect, Wittgenstein argued that the word 'infinite' could not be used categorematically.

7 Human finitude

Problems about the infinite, we have seen, are grounded in our own finitude. On the one hand our finitude prevents us from being able to think of anything, including the whole of reality, as truly infinite. On the other hand it also prevents us from being able to think of anything finite – anything to that extent within our grasp – as the whole of reality. One way to reconcile these would be to deny that there is any such thing as the whole of reality and to argue that there are only bits of reality, each a part of some other. Here once again we see application of the Scope Distinction: every bit of reality is a part of something, but there is nothing of which every bit of reality is a part. Aristotle, Kant and even to an extent Cantor played out variations on this theme.

But one of the most pressing questions of philosophy still remains: in what exactly does our finitude consist? Some of the most striking features of that finitude are conditioned by our temporality. In particular, of course, there is the fact of our death. How are we to view death? Among the many subsidiary questions that this raises, there are two in particular which are superficially equivalent but between which it is important to distinguish. Putting them in the crudest possible terms (their refinement would be a large part of addressing them): (1) Is death a 'bad thing'? (2) Would immortality be preferable to mortality?

It can easily look as if these questions must receive the same answer. True, no sooner does one begin refining them than one sees all sorts of ways in which a full, qualified response to one can differ from a full, qualified response to the other. But it is in any case important to see how, even at this crude level, there is scope for answering 'yes' and 'no' respectively. Putting it very roughly, death is a bad thing because it closes off possibilities, but immortality would not be preferable to mortality because mortality is what gives life its most basic structure and, therewith, the possibility of meaning.

To answer 'yes' to (1) and 'no' to (2) in this way is once again to invoke the Scope Distinction. It is to affirm that at each time there is reason to carry on living for longer, while denying that there is reason to carry on living forever. Meaning, for self-conscious beings such as us, can extend further than any given limits. But it cannot extend further than them all.

If it is true that, in some sense, at some level and with all the myriad qualifications that are called for, the answer to (1) is 'yes' and the answer to (2) is 'no', then, coherent though that is, it points to a basic conflict in us: while it would not be good never to die, it is nevertheless never good to die. That conflict is one of the tragedies of human existence. It is also a version of the original conflict which underlies all our attempts to come to terms with the infinite. In thinking about the infinite, we are thinking, at a very deep level, about ourselves.

See also: CONTINUUM HYPOTHESIS, THE §1; DEATH

References and further reading

My thanks are due to Dartmouth publishers for permission to re-use material from the introduction to my book *Infinity*.

Aristotle (*c.* mid 4th century BC) *Physics*, Books III and IV, trans. E. Hussey, Oxford: Oxford University Press, 1983. (Book III, sects 4–8, presents the main elements of Aristotle's account of the infinite.)

Benardete, J.A. (1964) *Infinity: An Essay in Metaphysics*, Oxford: Oxford University Press. (Entertaining and wide-ranging discussion of the infinite, with particular emphasis on its paradoxes.)

Bennett, J. (1971) 'The Age and Size of the World', in A.W. Moore (ed.) *Infinity*, Aldershot: Dartmouth, 1993. (Excellent discussion of Kant's antinomies.)

Bolzano, B. (1851) *Paradoxes of the Infinite*, trans. D.A. Steele, ed. F. Prihonsky, London: Routledge & Kegan Paul, 1950. (Anticipates some of Cantor's ideas, though with much less rigour. Historically significant.)

Brouwer, L.E.J. (1913) 'Intuitionism and Formalism', trans. A. Dresden, in P. Benacerraf and H. Putnam (eds) *Philosophy of Mathematics: Selected Readings*, Cambridge: Cambridge University Press, 1983. (Classic statement of some of the fundamental tenets of intuitionism.)

Cantor, G. (1895–7) *Contributions to the Founding of the Theory of Transfinite Numbers*, trans. P.E.B. Jourdain, New York: Dover, 1955. (Cantor's second major publication, in which he establishes transfinite arithmetic. Of ground-breaking importance, but very technical.)

Hegel, G.W.F. (1812–16) *Science of Logic*, trans. A.V. Miller, London: Allen & Unwin, 1969. (Pages 116–57 and 225–38 provide the main elements of Hegel's views.)

Heidegger, M. (1927) *Being and Time*, trans. J. Macquarrie and E. Robinson, Oxford: Blackwell, 1978. (*Locus classicus* of existential thought on human finitude, but exceedingly difficult.)

Hilbert, D. (1925) 'On the Infinite', trans. S. Bauer-Mengelberg, in J. van Heijenoort (ed.) *From Frege to Gödel: A Source Book in Mathematical Logic, 1879–1931*, Cambridge, MA: Harvard University Press, 1967. (A modern classic which defends 'finitism', a position according to which all references to the infinite are strictly meaningless though they can serve a useful function.)

Kant, I. (1781) *Critique of Pure Reason*, trans. N. Kemp Smith, London: Macmillan, 1933. (The section entitled 'Transcendental Dialectic' up to Book II, ch. 2 and omitting Book II, ch. 1 (A293/B349–A340/B398 and A405/B432–A567/B595) presents the antinomies and their solution.)

Lear, J. (1979–80) 'Aristotelian Infinity', in A.W. Moore (ed.) *Infinity*, Aldershot: Dartmouth, 1993. (Helpful and instructive account of Aristotle's views, including a superb discussion of the problem of infinite past time.)

Moore, A.W. (1990) *The Infinite*, London: Routledge.

(Introductory and partly historical study of all aspects of the infinite.)

—— (ed.) (1993) *Infinity*, Aldershot: Dartmouth. (Collection of the most important and influential articles on infinity published since 1950, with an extensive annotated bibliography and an introduction which expands on the material in this entry.)

Owen, G.E.L. (1957–8) 'Zeno and the Mathematicians', in A.W. Moore (ed.) *Infinity*, Aldershot: Dartmouth, 1993. (Thorough and scholarly discussion of Zeno's paradoxes.)

Rucker, R. (1982) *Infinity and the Mind: The Science and Philosophy of the Infinite*, Sussex: Harvester Wheatsheaf. (Lively and fascinating account of the more mathematical aspects of the infinite. Defends a kind of mysticism.)

Russell, B. (1926) *Our Knowledge of the External World as a Field for Scientific Method in Philosophy*, London: Allen & Unwin. (Chapters 5–7 provide a vigorous defence of Cantor.)

Salmon, W.C. (ed.) (1970) *Zeno's Paradoxes*, Indianapolis, IN: Bobbs-Merrill. (Collection of some of the best known articles on Zeno's paradoxes.)

Williams, B. (1973) 'The Makropulos Case: Reflections on the Tedium of Immortality', in A.W. Moore (ed.) *Infinity*, Aldershot: Dartmouth, 1993. (Superb defence of the ambivalent attitude to death advocated in §7 above.)

Wittgenstein, L. (1975) *Philosophical Remarks*, trans. R. Hargreaves and R. White, ed. R. Rhees, Oxford: Blackwell. (Section XII and pages 304–14 provide a good representative sample of Wittgenstein's views.)

A.W. MOORE

INFORMAL LOGIC *see* FORMAL AND INFORMAL LOGIC

INFORMATION AND COMPUTABILITY *see* COMPUTABILITY AND INFORMATION

INFORMATION TECHNOLOGY AND ETHICS

Information technology ethics is the study of the ethical issues arising out of the use and development of electronic technologies. Its goal is to identify and formulate answers to questions about the moral basis of individual responsibilities and actions, as well as the moral underpinnings of public policy.

Information technology ethics raises new and unique moral problems because information technology itself has brought about dramatic social, political, and conceptual change. Because information technology affects not only how we do things but how we think about them, it challenges some of the basic organizing concepts of moral and political philosophy such as property, privacy, the distribution of power, basic liberties and moral responsibility.

Specific questions include the following. What are the moral responsibilities of computer professionals? Who is to blame when computer software failure causes harm? Is computer hacking immoral? Is it immoral to make unauthorized copies of software? Questions related to public policy include: What constitutes just policy with respect to freedom of speech, association, and the exercise of other civil liberties over computer networks? What determines the extent and limits of property rights over computer software and electronic information? What policies adequately protect a right to privacy?

The list of questions shifts in response to developments in information technology. One noteworthy example is the rise in prominence of questions about communication and information in response to the explosive growth of high-speed digital networks. This shift has subsumed the field commonly called 'computer ethics' under the broader rubric of 'information technology ethics'.

1 **The philosophical study of information technology ethics**
2 **Property and information technology**
3 **Privacy and information technology**
4 **Risk and responsibility**
5 **Other issues**

1 The philosophical study of information technology ethics

Information technology gives rise to distinctive ethical questions. These questions challenge traditional moral concepts such as property, privacy, and responsibility, as described below by John Perry Barlow:

> Imagine a place where trespassers leave no footprints, where goods can be stolen an infinite number of times and yet remain in the possession of their original owners, where businesses you never heard of can own the history of your personal affairs, where only children feel completely at

home, where the physics is that of thought rather than things, and where everyone is as virtual as the shadows in Plato's cave.

(1991: 23)

In an influential essay, 'What is Computer Ethics?' (1985), James Moor characterized the challenge as a 'conceptual vacuum'. The vacuum is generated when ethical problems raised by information technology are inaccessible to concepts and principles of traditional theory (see MORALITY AND ETHICS). For example, Barlow's goods that 'can be stolen an infinite number of times' challenge a traditional understanding of property (see §2). In order to resolve problems in information technology ethics, according to Moor, one must not only deliberate about values, but also fill the conceptual vacuum; that is, one must develop ethical concepts and principles so that they cover novel situations. Philosophical work in the area of information technology ethics has been drawn particularly to these problems.

Below, three examples of problems calling for conceptual re-examination are discussed: ownership of computer software and digital information; privacy in the face of information technology; and risks and responsibilities in an age of computerization. Each has attracted considerable attention from philosophers and others writing about the social, ethical, and political impacts of information technology.

2 Property and information technology

Ownership of computer software and of digitalized information is a controversial matter. On the question of ownership over computer software some, like the computer scientist Richard Stallman, have argued that private ownership is morally indefensible. They contend that social welfare and progress in the field of computer science are both better served by allowing the free flow of ideas than by protecting the special interests of corporate and commercial developers with strong property rights (see PROPERTY). Like laws of physics and mathematical theorems, computer programs ought to remain in the public domain. A system of rewards and incentives could be devised, even in the absence of property rights, to motivate programmers to continue producing good work.

Most oppose Stallman's position in favour of at least some form and some degree of private ownership. They diverge, however, over the nature and extent of these ownership rights, puzzling over whether the existing legal framework for protecting intellectual ownership is appropriate to the unique metaphysical character of software. Some contend that one or another of the traditional categories of copyright and patent can and ought to be extended to cover software; others contend that a new *sui generis* form of ownership ought to be devised especially for it.

The growth of global, high-speed networks raises yet a different set of ownership issues, not only about computer programs but about all information in digital form, including computerized databases, creative works of writing and music, visual images, even computerized mailing lists and records of computerized transactions. Many have held that the electronic medium poses both a practical challenge to the exercise of traditional property rights, as well as a fundamental challenge to the very idea of ownership. These sceptics say that the digital electronic medium is importantly different because information can be reached via networks virtually instantaneously by vast numbers of people; it can be transmitted and copied with no deterioration in quality; and can be used and enjoyed by others without reducing access by owners. Some see this as a practical problem only. In time, the technical means will be devised to enable owners of digitally stored work to control access to it and exact payment. Others believe that applying old ideas of ownership to this new form of property is not only practically difficult, but morally indefensible. They suggest that society will be able to reap the full benefits of digital technology only by discarding the constraints of traditional intellectual ownership and encouraging the free flow of ideas and information. Strong proprietary holds may give a stranglehold to a few wealthy and powerful individuals over a valuable social resource and may even obstruct the right to free exchange of ideas by limiting quotation of copyrighted sources.

3 Privacy and information technology

Information technology enables the storage, retrieval, manipulation and communication of vast amounts of information. When the information is about persons, this raises serious and perplexing questions about personal privacy (see PRIVACY).

A great deal has been written about the effects of information technology on privacy. These works, which consider practical questions of immediate policy as well as theoretical questions about the moral foundations of privacy, have concentrated on two broadly defined areas. One deals with databases and 'information privacy', the other with electronic networks and 'communications privacy'.

Most discussions about information privacy concede that if individuals choose to live social lives in a civil society information about them is needed both for the effective running of government and for normal personal dealings. The type and extent of information required remains controversial. Information technology has made the question ever more urgent because of its capacities for storing and using information. Enhanced organization, communication, and retrieval mean that more information can be obtained and more sources tapped. No longer can we count on the *de facto* protections of privacy offered not only by the limitations of human memory but by inefficiencies in record-keeping and information-gathering practices in times before computers were commonly used for this.

In the 1960s, the greatest concern was with the role of governments in creating and using databases about citizens. Although record-keeping was not new to government, computerized records vastly enhanced the degree to which individuals could be tracked. Databases replaced existing paper records, multiplying in scope and magnitude as government agencies eagerly conceived new uses for them. The benefits of computerized databases were clear: greater efficiency, fairer allocation of benefits, and more effective control of crime, among others. Critics, by contrast, brandishing sinister images of 'Big Brother' from George Orwell's novel, *Nineteen Eighty-Four*, urged strict limits. They warned that unchecked collection of data threatened the privacy of individuals, as well as their autonomy and liberty (see FREEDOM AND LIBERTY). Through computerized databases, a government could acquire inordinate power over its citizens.

One way of placing limits is through legislation. In the United States, for example, the Privacy Protection Act of 1974 prohibited a centralized, comprehensive database, secret databases, and databases whose function is not explicitly stated and justified. Other countries have gone further, creating agencies with powers to regulate and enforce privacy protection in both government and the private sector. Nevertheless, many critics maintain that legislation has not gone far enough in protecting privacy.

As a consequence of technical improvements, greater ease of use, and a drop in prices, the private sector has played a growing role in creating personal databases. Information about persons has become a commodity of great value. Databases include comprehensive records of an individual's lifetime activities held by companies such as credit reporting agencies, medical insurance and mail order companies, as well as specialized databases containing one or two records. Because, in the private sector, political autonomy is not a driving force, the strength of the moral claims of privacy are less clear. One formulation of the dispute pits the rights of database subjects whose data is held frequently without their knowledge and against their will, against the rights claimed by owners of databases to create these databases and profit from them (see RIGHTS).

Philosophical discussion of privacy, suffering from Moor's 'conceptual vacuum', offers only partial insight. The connection some philosophers have demonstrated between personality development, autonomy, intimacy and liberty, on the one hand, and privacy, on the other, has helped justify special protection for confidential information and against invasive means of acquiring information. Philosophical images of privacy, however, remain insufficiently richly textured to draw fine distinctions between a general conception of morally allowable versus morally reprehensible intrusions on privacy.

On the separate question of communications privacy, discussion has focused on public policy. Some argue that it is reasonable to expect the very highest degrees of privacy, guaranteed by unlimited access to encryption technology. Others place interests, such as law enforcement and accountability for communications, above privacy. Progress in this area is likely to involve careful balancing of these competing interests and claims.

4 Risk and responsibility

As with other technologies, information technology introduces a risk of harm as a result of design, system failure or abuse. Because information technology is used so widely, such harm may be extensive and range from mere inconvenience to loss of wealth or even life, from loss of property to loss of reputation and peace of mind. Specialists in the field of computer system reliability have argued that the unique character of computer technology makes it dangerous in unique ways. 'Small' errors which are hard to detect can lead to disastrous outcomes; the enormous complexity of computer systems makes them opaque even to those who have created their components. Where security is not strong, information systems are attractive targets of abuse. The usual philosophical and moral problems of risk apply to information technology as well (see RISK).

Closely related to the problem of risk is that of responsibility (see RESPONSIBILITY). One set of questions about responsibility looks at the professional responsibility of the producers of information technology, including computer scientists, programmers, and engineers (see ENGINEERING AND ETHICS; PROFESSIONAL ETHICS). Themes raised in connection with computing overlap substantially with those prevalent in the context of other professions, such as the special responsibilities and privileges of computer professionals, the efficacy of codes of ethics as a means both to encourage and to enforce ethical behaviour, the problem of conflicting loyalties to clients, employers and society at large, and the duty of professional honesty. One consideration not typically an issue with traditional professions such as law and medicine is whether computer professionals are professionals in the full-blown sense at all.

Another set of questions about responsibility is concerned with moral blameworthiness for harms (see PRAISE AND BLAME). This is not an area unique to information technology ethics, but the technology makes an already thorny issue more complex. A tendency to accept the presence of errors (known as 'bugs') as a normal part of software because they are ubiquitous means they may not be considered as worthy of blame. Furthermore, because of the mystique of computers as intelligent machines, which carry out tasks performed previously by humans in positions of responsibility, there is a tendency to absolve humans from blame in computer-related incidents. Finally, because computer systems and the institutions responsible for producing them are large and complex, blame is easily obscured.

The advent of computer networks raises another set of issues mainly having to do with harms caused by certain uses and abuses of information. Examples include defamatory, offensive and abusive speech and unauthorized access to proprietary information and software. In response, philosophers, legal theorists, and social commentators have discussed morally and legally defensible lines of responsibility for these actions.

5 Other issues

Balancing the value of answerability for harms are other, sometimes conflicting, moral and political values, including civil liberties such as the freedoms of speech and association, and the right to anonymity (see FREEDOM OF SPEECH). Allowing users of computer networks to post anonymous notices on electronic bulletin boards, for example, creates the possibility of harmful speech for which there is no direct recourse. In another case, free association on-line enables the gathering of groups with immoral intent.

Also of considerable interest to computer ethics and computer law are activities known colloquially as 'hacking' and 'cracking'. These activities range from harmless pranks to unauthorized entry into computer systems to serious destruction of systems and data. Responses to hacking are varied. Some judge it immoral and say it should be outlawed, others not only tolerate forms of hacking that do not result in egregious harm but consider it worthy of both technical and ideological respect. They sympathize with the position frequently expressed by hackers that computing ought to be free and accessible and not hoarded by a privileged few.

The discussion of hacking ties into broader questions of distributive justice (see JUSTICE). Many commentators argue that just societies, in recognition of information technology as a substantial good, ought to guarantee to their citizens reasonable and equitable access to its benefits.

Another important approach to information technology ethics, distinct from the philosophical approach described in this entry, carves the area into quite different categories. It is organized around contexts rather than moral issues. Researchers taking this approach have, for example, examined the effects of computing on the workplace, on education, on social power and democracy, on communication, on information science, on cultures and on communities. Their work is descriptive as well as normative.

See also: APPLIED ETHICS; TECHNOLOGY AND ETHICS

References and further reading

* Barlow, J.P. (1991) 'Coming Into the Country', *Communications of the ACM* 34 (3): 19–21. (Suggestive short article on the unique nature of computing and information technology.)

Gavison, R. (1980) 'Privacy and the Limits of Law', *Yale Law Journal* 89: 421–71. (An article providing a definition of privacy useful for understanding information technology.)

Johnson, D.G. (1994) *Computer Ethics*, Englewood Cliffs, NJ: Prentice Hall. (Clear introductory text written from a philosophical perspective.)

Johnson, D.G. and Nissenbaum, H. (eds) (1995) *Computers, Ethics, and Social Responsibility*, Englewood Cliffs, NJ: Prentice Hall. (Comprehensive set of readings from various disciplines)

Mitcham, C. (1995) 'Computers, Information and Ethics: A Review of Issues and Literature', *Science and Engineering Ethics* 1 (2): 113–26 (Good historical review with wide-ranging bibliography.)

* Moor, J. (1985) 'What is Computer Ethics?', *Metaphilosophy* 16 (4): 266–75. (An essay defining the scope of computer ethics with special attention to its unique elements.)

Regan, P. (1995) *Legislating Privacy: Technology, Social Values and Public Policy*, Chapel Hill, NC: University of North Carolina Press. (A thorough discussion of contemporary privacy issues in the context of the United States.)

Westin, A.F. (1967) *Privacy and Freedom*, New York: Atheneum. (Classic work on the nature and value of privacy in a technological age.)

Weizenbaum, J. (1976) *Computer Power and Human Reason*, New York: W.H. Freeman and Company. (An early classic by a computer scientist which points to the dangers of over-dependence on computers.)

HELEN NISSENBAUM

INFORMATION THEORY

Information theory was established in 1948 by Claude Shannon as a statistical analysis of factors pertaining to the transmission of messages through communication channels. Among basic concepts defined within the theory are information (the amount of uncertainty removed by the occurrence of an event), entropy (the average amount of information represented by events at the source of a channel), and equivocation (the 'noise' that impedes faithful transmission of a message through a channel). Information theory has proved essential to the development of space probes, high-speed computing machinery and modern communication systems.

The information studied by Shannon is sharply distinct from information in the sense of knowledge or of propositional content. It is also distinct from most uses of the term in the popular press ('information retrieval', 'information processing', 'information highway', and so on). While Shannon's work has strongly influenced academic psychology and philosophy, its reception in these disciplines has been largely impressionistic. A major problem for contemporary philosophy is to relate the statistical conceptions of information theory to information in the semantic sense of knowledge and content.

1   The technical concept of information
2   Information channels
3   Two basic theorems of information theory
4   The entropy of information theory related to that of thermodynamics
5   Ramifications of philosophic interest

1   The technical concept of information

Information theory (less commonly called 'statistical communication theory') was first formulated systematically by Claude Shannon in 1948, in his paper 'A Mathematical Theory of Communication' (see Sloane and Wyner 1993). Its conceptual basis, however, was provided by previous engineering studies of efficiency in the transmission of messages over electrical channels. In 1924 Harry Nyquist proposed a logarithmic measure of speed in the 'transmission of

intelligence', and had shown that this variable depends both upon the speed of the signal and upon the number of different signal elements employed. R.V.L. Hartley used the same mathematical construct in 1928 as a quantitative measure of what he called 'information', and showed how this measure relates also to the frequency range of the transmitting medium. Shannon extended the theory to include other factors, such as the effects of noise, the statistical structure of the message and the reliability of the channel through which it is transmitted. His treatment was sufficiently rigorous to permit the derivation of several basic theorems that have proved essential to the design of present-day communication and computational systems.

The commonplace intuition upon which Hartley's measure was founded is that information is conveyed by relatively improbable events, and that the amount of information conveyed by an event (E) is inversely related to its probability. In order to make the information of associated events additive, the measure chosen was $\log 1/P(E)$ – that is, the logarithm of the reciprocal of the initial probability of the event in question. This measure admits further specification, inasmuch as logarithms may be based on any positive number. Three different bases have been used in the literature. When the base chosen is ten, the quantity $\log_{10} 1/P(E)$ is the unit of information, named a 'Hartley' in honour of the originator of the measure. Natural logarithms also have been used, with a unit called 'nat' for natural unit. Most commonly, however, logarithms to the base two are employed, with a unit called a 'bit' (for binary unit) following the usage of Shannon. One advantage of the latter is the intuitive understanding it provides of the mathematical measure $\log 1/P(E)$: the number of bits of information represented in the occurrence of a given E is equal to the number of times its initial probability must be doubled to reach unity. Thus the occurrence of heads in the flip of an unbiased coin (50 per cent probable) would yield one bit of information, the occurrence of an event initially 25 per cent probable would yield two bits, that of an event initially 60 per cent probable would yield 0.74 bits, and so on. Another advantage of a measure based on logarithms to the base two is its convenient application to factors involved in the design of digital computers. Logarithms to the base two will be assumed in the remainder of this entry.

Information, in the sense (henceforth called 'info(t)') germane to technical information theory, is the quantity measured by $\log 1/P(E)$. What is measured thereby is the difference between E's initial probability and the probability of 100 per cent that marks its actual occurrence. The difference between a probability before occurrence of 25 per cent and a probability upon occurrence of 100 per cent, as noted above, is a quantity characterized by two bits of information. The information thus characterized is just the difference in probability involved. Insofar as events can be characterized as statistically more or less uncertain prior to occurrence, info(t) is sometimes defined also as the amount of uncertainty removed by the occurrence of E. This conception of info(t) as the removal of statistical uncertainty is useful for interpreting the theory, but must be carefully guarded against psychological or 'subjective' connotations. Information in the relevant sense is entirely quantitative, and is defined with respect to a mathematical measure. Pending further discussion below, this in itself is enough to show that info(t) cannot be equated with either knowledge or semantic content.

2 Information channels

In its bare essentials, an information channel consists of two ensembles of statistically interrelated events. One is the *input ensemble*, consisting of events presented at the input of the channel. The other is the *output ensemble*, consisting of events at the terminus that are to some extent indicative of occurrences at the input. These two ensembles may be represented respectively as A, consisting of n symbols $a_1, a_2, \ldots, a_n$, and B, comprising m symbols $b_1, b_2, \ldots, b_m$. Both A and B are assumed to consist of mutually exclusive events, with combined probability of occurrence equal to unity. The relationship between input and output may then be described by a set of conditional probabilities $P(b_j/a_i)$, specifying for each output event b_j the probability of its occurrence in association with each input event a_i. This set of conditional probabilities characterizes the *channel* itself, in distinction from its input and output ensembles.

A typical realization of an information channel is a telephone circuit connecting two modems, with events at the sender and the receiver constituting A and B respectively, and their association through a physical medium represented by an appropriate set of conditional probabilities. Further characterization of the circuit might mention such features as the medium of transmission (satellite, fibre optics, and so on), the intervening switching mechanisms, and the temporal lag between events at input and output. Such features, however, are not essential to an information channel, and may be replaced by others in an equivalent physical system. It is even conceivable that there might be information channels without physically connecting media, such as in communication by 'mental telepathy'. The only general requirement for an information channel is two ensembles related by conditional probabilities.

The quantity of info(t) represented by the occurrence of an event a with probability $P(a)$ is $\log 1/P(a)$. Unless all input events are equiprobable, this quantity will vary for different members of the input ensemble. The average amount of info(t) represented by occurrences within the input ensemble is the sum of the quantities $\log 1/P(a)$ for individual events in A each multiplied by the probability of its occurrence. This average (which varies with different input distributions $P(a)$) is called the *entropy* of A, and is commonly designated '$H(A)$'. If the members of A are statistically independent (a 'zero-memory' input), its entropy is given by the formula:

$$H(A) = \sum_A P(a) \log 1/P(a)$$

A corresponding average $H(B)$ can be calculated for the ensemble of output events. In general, the closer the individual events within an ensemble approach equiprobability, the closer the entropy of that ensemble approaches maximum value.

The value of $H(A)$ does not reflect the statistical interaction between A and B in an information channel. Because of this interaction, the probability of a given event's occurring in A may be affected by the occurrence of an event in B, and vice versa. $H(A)$ thus is sometimes called the a priori entropy of A, in contrast to the a posteriori entropy of A conditional upon events in B. The a posteriori entropy of A given a particular b_j is the average info(t) represented by an event in A when b_j has occurred in B:

$$H(A/b_j) = \sum_A P(a/b_j) \log 1/P(a/b_j)$$

Summing $H(A/b_j)$ for all b_j, we then have the average a posteriori entropy of A:

$$H(A/B) = \sum_B P(b) H(A/b)$$

$$= \sum_B P(b) \sum_A P(a/b) \log 1/P(a/b)$$

$$= \sum_{A,B} (a,b) \log 1/P(a/b)$$

$H(A/B)$ is called the *equivocation* of A with respect to B. As this label suggests, the amount of uncertainty left in A given the occurrence of an event in B is a measure of the 'ambiguity' of A with respect to that event, where 'ambiguity' varies indirectly with the reliability of that event as an indication of events in A. The above equalities show how the equivocation of A with respect to B may be conceived as the average 'ambiguity' of A with respect to events in B. If we think of B as capable of yielding 'information about' A in proportion to its general reliability, then that capacity is inversely proportionate to $H(A/B)$.

There is an intuitive sense in which an information channel with low equivocation is characterized by a representation at the output of approximately the same occurrences as those presented at the input. Conversely, the higher a channel's equivocation, the less reliable are events at its output as representations of input occurrences. The capacity of a channel to convey info(t) thus varies inversely with the equivocation of input to output. This overall capacity also varies directly with the amount of info(t) that can be entered into the channel – that is, with the entropy of the input ensemble. The difference between the entropy of its input and the equivocation of its input with respect to the output thus measures the capacity of the channel as a reliable conveyor of info(t) given a particular input distribution $P(a)$. This quantity

$$I(A; B) = H(A) - H(A/B)$$

is called the *mutual information* of the information channel. *Channel capacity* in general is defined as the maximum of $I(A; B)$ over all possible input distributions.

Barring limiting cases, an information channel is characterized by equivocation in either direction, which is to say that both $H(A/B)$ and $H(B/A)$ possess positive values. One limiting case is the *noiseless channel*, in which each event at the output indicates a single input event with perfect reliability. A noiseless channel is one with $H(A/B) = 0$. A *deterministic channel*, on the other hand, is one in which each input event is associated invariably with a single event at the output, and in which accordingly $H(B/A) = 0$. A channel that is noiseless from input to output thus is deterministic in the opposite direction, and of course vice versa.

3 Two basic theorems of information theory

Practical use of an information channel typically involves both a sender (a source) and a receiver, and communication systems are usually designed with the needs of these users in view. Among factors influencing the design of such systems are considerations of efficiency in the coding of the sender's message. If the anticipated use of a digital communication system is to transmit alphabetically expressed messages, for example, then a system must be devised for coding the letters of the (Latin) alphabet into binary digital form. One such system would employ progressive series of 1s in combination to mark the ordinal place of each letter in the alphabet ('1' for a, '11' for b, '111' for c,

and so on), and with '0' to mark the end of a symbol. Simple calculations show that the code symbols assigned to letters in this system would average over thirteen digits in length. A much more efficient system would encode letters in terms of a progressive ordering of 1s and 0s in a five digit sequence ('00000' for a, '00001' for b, '00010' for c,..., '10000' for f, '10001' for g, and so on), with unambiguous decodability assured (independently of synchronization between input and output) by the fact that no complete symbol is a prefix of another symbol. The average symbol length in this system of course is five. One of Shannon's major results is the so-called 'noiseless coding theorem', which establishes limits in the efficiency of coding systems. According to this theorem, the average symbol length of a uniquely decodable coding system can be no less than the entropy of the message source (measured similarly to the input entropy). A special problem arises in the not uncommon case of a source that issues messages in a continuous (for example, not discrete) form, such as music and pictures involving variable pitch and colour. In order to code these messages in discrete binary symbols, their original form must be quantized into small discontinuous segments (as music is recorded on a compact disc). Shannon's noiseless coding theorem also quantifies the cost of fidelity in such transformations in terms of entropy characteristics of the quantized source.

Noise is constituted by any factor that contributes to equivocation $H(A/B)$, and thus prevents a channel from being noiseless from input to output. Communication engineers have various devices available for reducing noise, including coding systems incorporating redundancy and other 'error correction' features. A simple example of the latter is sheer repetition, as when a specific code element (0 or 1) is transmitted several times in sequence. An unavoidable by-product of such an expedient, however, is an increase in the time required to transmit a given message. Another basic theorem (Shannon's second, also called the 'noisy channel coding theorem') relates requirements of error correction to channel capacity and rate of message transmission through the channel. In very general terms, what this theorem states is that a (sufficiently long) sequence of messages can be transmitted with an error rate arbitrarily close to zero, as long as the rate of transmission is less than overall channel capacity.

4 The entropy of information theory related to that of thermodynamics

The entropy of an ensemble A can be expressed equivalently in the form:

$$H(A) = -\sum_A P(a) \log P(a)$$

which bears an oft-noted similarity to Boltzmann's formulation of thermodynamic entropy (S):

$$S = k \log_n P$$

Both H and S vary with the function $\log P$, where P measures the probability of a given system state. Their difference in sign, however, indicates that they are inversely related. An intuitive grasp of this relationship may be provided in terms of the conception of thermodynamic entropy as departure from order. According to the second law of thermodynamics, a closed system tends through time to increase in entropy, which is to lose energy capable of doing work or (equivalently) to lose structure in its overall configuration (see THERMODYNAMICS). Since order and structure are improbable conditions, this means that the detectable configurations (macrostates) in which the system actually exists from moment to moment become increasingly predictable, and that the initially improbable configurations (which provide structure and energy) become even less likely to occur. If we view the total set of possible macrostates (probable and improbable) as an ensemble with the properties of an information source, this means in turn that the possible configurations depart increasingly from equiprobability. Since an information source has maximum H when its states are equally probable, the result is that H decreases with an increase in S. This inverse relation between H and S has led some information theorists (for example, Brillouin 1962) to refer to info(t), along with energy and structure, as forms of negentropy.

Detailed technical discussions of the relation between H and S can be found in Brillouin and in Tribus (1961). An intriguing claim of the latter is that thermodynamics can be developed deductively from quantum physics by application of the methods of information theory.

5 Ramifications of philosophic interest

The term 'information' has various senses in ordinary discourse, including knowledge ('N's information about birds comes from actual experience') and propositional content ('N's report contained information that a golden eagle had been spotted'). Information in these senses has semantic features (call it 'info(s)'), such as reference and truth-value. In contrast with info(t), as already noted, info(s) is not quantitative and cannot be characterized mathematically. Another difference is that communication of info(s) is a three-term transaction, involving sender,

receiver and intended referent, whereas the communication of info(t) in relevant respects requires only sender and receiver. Another way of putting this point of difference is that intention is not a factor in the description of channels for communicating info(t).

Despite the insistence of information theorists (including Shannon) from the start that info(t) has nothing to do with semantics, there have been persistent attempts by philosophers and cognitive psychologists to found theories of semantic content on an information-theoretic basis. Shortly following Shannon's original paper, the physicist D.M. MacKay initiated a series of publications purporting to show that information theory deals with representation (a semantic relation; see the bibliography in *Information, Mechanism and Meaning*, 1969). MacKay's purported results stand behind subsequent influential work in information-processing psychology (for example, that of D.E. Broadbent and W.R. Garner), and may be in part responsible for the assumption found in recent cognitive psychology that information theory itself provides a theory of info(s).

An independent approach to semantic issues through information theory among professional philosophers began with D.M. Armstrong (1968) and D.C. Dennett (1969). This essentially materialist approach yielded, in F.I. Dretske (1981), a clearly articulated account of how info(s) might be produced by certain causal (hence, non-information-theoretic) properties of info(t)-processing systems. Apart from their other merits, however, none of these studies maintains fidelity to a precise understanding of information theory as developed by Shannon. An attempt to found an account of info(s) on a precise understanding of Shannon's theory is pursued in K.M. Sayre (1976).

See also: COMPUTABILITY AND INFORMATION; INFORMATION THEORY AND EPISTEMOLOGY

References and further reading

All except Brillouin (1962), Tribus (1961) and the Shannon collection (Sloane and Wyner 1993) can be read profitably without specialized training.

Abramson, N. (1963) *Information Theory and Coding*, New York: McGraw-Hill. (A standard introduction accessible to non-specialists.)

* Armstrong, D.M. (1968) *A Materialist Theory of the Mind*, London: Routledge & Kegan Paul. (An analysis of mind-making extensive use of the concept of information.)

* Brillouin, L. (1962) *Science and Information Theory*, New York: Academic Press. (Integrates thermo-

dynamics and information theory. Written for readers with broad interests.)

* Dennett, D.C. (1969) *Content and Consciousness*, New York: Humanities Press. (An early attempt to bring the concept of information to bear in philosophic analysis.).

* Dretske, F.I. (1981) *Knowledge and the Flow of Information*, Cambridge, MA: MIT Press. (A carefully argued and easily readable account of knowledge and related concepts, based on an interpretation of information theory deviating substantially from Shannon's.)

Hamming, R.W. (1980) *Coding and Information Theory*, Englewood Cliffs, NJ: Prentice Hall. (A more recent introduction of comparable difficulty to Abramson (1963). Hamming is a major contributor to information theory.)

* MacKay, D.M. (1969) *Information, Mechanism and Meaning*, Cambridge, MA: MIT Press. (A collection of essays documenting the author's influential efforts to inject 'meaning' into technical information theory.)

* Sayre, K.M. (1976) *Cybernetics and the Philosophy of Mind*, London: Routledge & Kegan Paul. (An attempt to establish a naturalistic view of the world on the basis of information theory.)

—— (1986) 'Intentionality and Information Processing: An Alternative Model for Cognitive Science', *Behavioral and Brain Sciences* 9: 121–65. (Tries to show how technical information theory can be employed as the basis of a theory of intentionality.)

* Sloane, N.J.A. and Wyner, A.D. (eds) (1993) *Claude Elwood Shannon: Collected Papers*, New York: IEEE Press. (A complete collection of Shannon's technical papers, including two delightful biographical essays.)

* Tribus, M. (1961) *Thermostatics and Thermodynamics*, Princeton, NJ: Van Nostrand. (A carefully executed attempt to relate quantum theory and thermodynamics by the statistical methods of information theory.)

KENNETH M. SAYRE

INFORMATION THEORY AND EPISTEMOLOGY

The mathematical theory of information (also called communication theory) defines a quantity called mutual *information that exists between a source, s, and receiver, r. Mutual information is a statistical construct, a quantity defined in terms of conditional probabilities between the events occurring at r and s. If* what happens at r depends on what happens at s to some degree, then there is a communication 'channel' between r and s, and mutual information at r about s. If, on the other hand, the events at two points are statistically independent, there is zero mutual information.

Philosophers and psychologists are attracted to information theory because of its potential as a useful tool in describing an organism's cognitive relations to the world. The attractions are especially great for those who seek a naturalistic account of knowledge, an account that avoids normative – and, therefore, scientifically unusable – ideas such as rational warrant, sufficient reason and adequate justification. According to this approach, philosophically problematic notions like evidence, knowledge, recognition and perception – perhaps even meaning – can be understood in communication terms. Perceptual knowledge, for instance, might best be rendered in terms of a brain (r) receiving mutual information about a worldly source (s) via sensory channels. When incoming signals carry appropriate information, suitably equipped brains 'decode' these signals, extract information and thereby come to know what is happening in the outside world. Perception becomes information-produced belief.

1 **Objective information**
2 **Pure and impure theories**
3 **How much information is enough?**

1 Objective information

The mathematical theory of information has its primary application to telecommunications systems. It deals exclusively with *amounts* of information, either the amount generated at a source – the more unlikely an event is the more information its occurrence generates – or the amount of mutual information existing between source and receiver. Mutual information between two points is just a useful measure of the statistical dependence of events occurring at these two points: the greater the independence between events occurring at r and s, the less mutual information there is between them (see INFORMATION THEORY).

If signals are understood to be information-carrying events (sounds, gestures, electric currents), then the mathematical theory is concerned with the statistical properties of these events, not with the information they happen to carry in any ordinary sense of the word 'information' (news or message). It is concerned with how probable or improbable these events are, not with what, if anything, they say or mean. For this reason it has sometimes been said that communication theory is not really a theory about information – *semantic* information – at all. There is some truth in this charge; mutual information is a statistical quantity and it must be carefully distinguished from the semantic content – the news or message – that events carry.

Nonetheless, though the theory is primarily concerned with the statistical properties of signals, not with the semantic information (if any) they carry, the statistical properties are relevant to a signal's capacity to carry semantic information. Unless there is, in a communication theory sense, a statistically reliable channel of communication between s and r, the signals reaching r from s cannot inform, tell or teach one what is happening at s. A broken instrument, one whose pointer (r) does not bear the right statistical relations to the quantity (s) it is supposed to measure, cannot convey semantic information about the value of that quantity. A broken clock cannot tell you the time of day even if it happens (coincidentally) to register the correct time. For the same reason, one receives little or no information from unpredictable liars even when they happen to be telling the truth. Hence, information theory, though not itself directly addressing semantic topics, does, it seems, formulate a possible objective condition on the flow of semantic information. No signal can carry semantic information unless it satisfies the appropriate statistical constraints of communication theory.

It is this fact about communication theory – that it can be interpreted as relating something important about the conditions that are needed for the transmission of information as ordinarily understood – that has tempted philosophers to use it in developing accounts of empirical knowledge. If coming to know p is equivalent to being 'informed' that p, and being informed that p is understood as a way of being made to believe that p by the information that p, then empirical knowledge is information-produced belief. If, in addition, information is taken to be constrained by, if not equivalent to, mutual information between world and believer, then one is close to having an objective theory of knowledge: knowing that p is being caused to believe that p by information-bearing signals arriving over a channel of communication.

Information-based accounts of knowledge, perception, memory and so on are variants of reliability theories of knowledge (see RELIABILISM). The basic idea behind such accounts of knowledge is that one knows if and only if one's belief – or (on some accounts) the evidence on which one's belief is based – exhibits a reliable connection with the conditions one believes to exist. Information theory is merely a convenient way of expressing these facts about the required reliability of the belief-formation process.

Information theory would not be useful in episte-mology if it embodied – implicitly – the very same ideas that philosophers use it to analyse. If it turned out that the probability relations used by this theory to define information were themselves ideas that presupposed – either in definition or application – knowledge and meaning, then it would be circular to use mutual information as a tool to analyse knowledge and meaning. For this reason, it is important to understand that the 'mutual information' that epistemology borrows from communication theory is supposed to be an objective commodity, one whose existence is independent of our knowledge or understanding. The probabilities defining mutual information cannot, therefore, be what are called *subjective* probabilities, probabilities that depend on what people know or believe about the likelihood of events at s given events at r (see PROBABILITY THEORY AND EPISTEMOLOGY §1). If mutual information is to serve as a useful tool in epistemological and semantic studies, then it must be conceived of as an objective measure of correlation or lawful dependency between events. No one need ever know, understand or believe that such correlations exist for them – and, hence, for *mutual* information – to exist.

2 Pure and impure theories

If epistemological concepts like knowledge, justification and evidence are interpreted in informational terms, one can distinguish pure and impure versions of such interpretations. An impure theory of knowledge, for example, would contain a mixture of conditions on knowledge, some involving information (to know that p one must stand in the right informational relation to the fact that p), others, perhaps, involving subjective conditions (to know that p, one must also be subjectively justified in thinking that the appropriate informational relations exist). A pure theory, on the other hand, forgoes all subjective requirements (except belief) and identifies knowledge of the facts with beliefs that stand in the appropriate informational relations to the facts. A pure theory, for example, identifies perceptual knowledge with beliefs aroused by information-carrying sensations. Subjects need not know or be justified in believing that their sensations do convey the requisite information. All that a pure theory requires is that sensations, in fact, carry the right information. In order to know, by perceptual means, that something is moving, one need not know, or be justified in believing, that one is receiving information. All that is required is that one *be* receiving it.

A pure theory of knowledge, in this sense, is most plausible in the case of direct observational knowledge. It enjoys greatest plausibility here because one seldom troubles to determine *how* reliable sensations are – and, thus, how much mutual information they carry – before one trusts them to 'inform' (give one knowledge about) the world one lives in. We see, and we promptly believe; there is precious little (if any) conscious thought, reasoning, justification or inference that comes between the seeing and the believing. We classify the resulting beliefs as knowledge – in both ourselves and animals – as long as we are convinced that the sensory mechanisms are operating reliably, as long as we believe they are channels of mutual information. According to its advocates, then, this is a strong endorsement of informationally pure theories of knowledge. If we do not, in actual everyday practice, require more than information-caused belief, then ordinary everyday knowledge requires nothing more, it is nothing more, than information-caused belief.

Advocates of a pure theory of knowledge also argue that it represents the best answer – indeed, according to some, the *only* answer – to philosophical scepticism. If knowledge of the world required not only information about the world but also that one had to somehow justify the claim that one's senses were providing genuine information, then the philosophical sceptic would be right: knowledge of the world would be impossible. For the only way we have of getting the information that we are, in fact, getting genuine information through the senses is through the very senses whose reliability is in question. This is a circle from which there is no escape. You cannot expect instruments to provide information about their own reliability (see SCEPTICISM §1).

Pure theories are at their weakest when applied to less direct forms of knowledge. When one comes to know that *p* by reasoning and inference, by using informants, instruments, tests and procedures, it seems implausible to suppose that one needs no information about the channels through which information arrives. Knowledge that *p* may not require knowledge that one is getting genuine information about *p*, but an impure theorist will insist that it requires some evidence, reason or justification for thinking one's instruments, methods and informants are reliable (see INTERNALISM AND EXTERNALISM IN EPISTEMOLOGY).

3 How much information is enough?

Since mutual information is a statistical quantity that comes in varying amounts, questions arise about how much of it is enough. Even cheap or badly calibrated instruments carry some mutual information about the quantities they are used to measure. Is it enough to know? Another way of putting this question is to ask how much mutual information a signal must carry about a condition at a source in order to carry the semantic information that that condition exists at the source.

Some philosophers have argued that perfect reliability is needed. If, given the sort of signals reaching *r* from source *s*, there is a chance, however small, that condition *q* rather than *p* exists at *s*, then the signals do not carry the information that *p* exists at *s* (though they might carry the information that *p* or *q* exists at *s*). The signals are equivocal – not reliable enough to enable someone at *r* to know that *p* exists at *s*. Others, assuming that such perfect reliability is seldom, if ever, achieved, have argued that to avoid scepticism, information and knowledge must be understood as requiring something less than a probability of 1. Otherwise, for any condition *p*, we would never get the information that *p* exists and, therefore (if knowledge requires information) never know that *p*.

Despite the apparent sceptical consequences of requiring perfect reliability for knowledge and information, there are theoretical reasons favouring this option. For if one could know that *p* when the informational sources are less than completely reliable, then knowledge would cease to 'add up' – one might know that *p* and know that *q* but fail to know that *p* and *q*. For suppose that a probability of only .98 was required to know. Then one might know that *p* (the probability of *p* being .98), know that *q* (probability also .98), but fail to know that *p* and *q* since the probability of *both p* and *q* is the product (.96) of their individual probabilities. This, however, seems like an unacceptable result. Knowledge (it is said) adds up: anyone who knows that *p* and knows that *q thereby* knows that *p* and *q*. Since the 'unacceptable' result occurs *whenever* the probability required for knowledge is less than 1, it seems that to avoid it, the probability required for knowledge must be set equal to 1.

For these and other reasons, some philosophers despair of finding general answers to questions about reliability conditions on knowledge. They argue that knowledge and semantic information are relative notions. What is *enough* depends on a context of inquiry. When a drug, if known to be safe, will be given to human infants, it takes more (mutual) information to know it is safe than it does when it will be administered to rats in a laboratory test. For the same reason, whether a newspaper contains semantic information about a death, for example, depends on whose death it is and what are the consequences of readers believing it.

See also: KNOWLEDGE, CAUSAL THEORY OF;
KNOWLEDGE, CONCEPT OF; NATURALIZED
EPISTEMOLOGY; PERCEPTION, EPISTEMIC ISSUES IN

References and further reading

Cherry, C. (1957) *On Human Communication*, Cambridge, MA: MIT Press. (Excellent history and exploration of the attempts to apply information theory in a variety of areas – including psychology.)

Dretske, F. (1981) *Knowledge and the Flow of Information*, Cambridge, MA: MIT Press. (Develops an information-based theory of knowledge, perception and meaning, and attempts to bridge the gap between mutual information (of communication theory) and semantic information. Contains an elementary exposition of the mathematical theory.)

—— (1983) 'Multiple book review of *Knowledge and the Flow of Information*', *Behavioral and Brain Sciences* 6 (1): 55–89. (Especially useful for criticisms and commentary by twenty philosophers and psychologists.)

Sayre, K. (1965) *Recognition: A Study in the Philosophy of Artificial Intelligence*, South Bend, IN: University of Notre Dame Press. (Early, interesting attempt by a philosopher to apply information-theoretical ideas to epistemology.)

Shannon, C. (1948) 'The mathematical theory of communication', *Bell Systems Technical Journal* 27: 379–423, 623–56; repr. with intro. by W. Weaver, Urbana, IL: The University of Illinois Press, 1949. (Mathematically demanding book, but the classic source for the engineer's concept of information.)

FRED DRETSKE

INFORMATIONAL SEMANTICS *see* SEMANTICS, INFORMATIONAL

INGARDEN, ROMAN WITOLD (1893–1970)

Ingarden was a leading exponent of phenomenology and one of the most outstanding Polish philosophers. Representing an objectivist approach within phenomenology he stressed that phenomenology employs a variety of methods, according to the variety of objects, and aspires to achieve an original cognitive apprehension of these objects. Its aim is to reach the essence of an object by analysing the contents of appropriate ideas and to convey the results of this analysis in clear language. Ingarden applied his methods in many areas of philosophy. He developed a pluralist theory of being and an epistemology which makes it possible to practise this discipline in an undogmatic manner and to defend the value of human knowledge. In the theory of values he developed an inspiring approach to the analysis of traditionally problematic areas. He was best known for his work in aesthetics, in which he analysed the structure of various kinds of works of art, the nature of aesthetic experience, the cognition of works of art and the objective character of aesthetic values. In general, he gave phenomenology a lucid and precise shape.

In the interwar period Ingarden was the main opponent in Poland of the dominant Lwów–Warsaw School (Polish Analytic School), which had a minimalistic orientation. The main lines of his own investigations emerged largely as a result of his regular debates with Husserl, in particular those concerning Husserl's transcendental idealism. Ingarden's best-known work, Das literarische Kunstwerk *(The Literary Work of Art) (1931a) has its origins in this debate.*

1   Life
2   Ontology
3   Aesthetics
4   Conclusion

1   Life

Roman Ingarden was born in 1893 in Cracow and died there in 1970. He studied in Lwów and Göttingen (1912–14), taking philosophy under Edmund HUSSERL, mathematics under David Hilbert and psychology under G.E. Müller. In 1916 he followed Husserl to Freiburg, where in 1918 he took a doctor's degree, then taught for some time at high schools in Lublin, Toruń and Lwów. He received his habilitation at Lwów University in June 1924, was appointed *dozent* there in 1925, and after Twardowski's retirement obtained the chair of philosophy in 1933. He stayed in Lwów until 1941; during the Soviet occupation he did not teach philosophy but German studies. He was also active in the Polish underground University. From 1945 to 1950, and from 1957 until his retirement in 1963, he was professor at the Jagiellonian University in Cracow.

Most of Ingarden's students from his Lwów period were either killed during the Second World War or became Marxists. After the war another group of his followers emerged in Cracow, though after Ingarden's death many of them questioned elements of his thought, some developing it, some reshaping it and others rejecting it.

2 Ontology

Ingarden held that philosophy divides into ontology and metaphysics. Ontology is an autonomous discipline in which we discover and establish the necessary connections between pure ideal qualities by intuitive analysis of the contents of ideas. This is an indispensable preparation for metaphysics, which aims to elucidate the necessary truths of factual existence. Each section of philosophy – theory of knowledge, philosophy of man, philosophy of nature and so on – has ontological and metaphysical aspects.

Ingarden argues that every being is a triple unity of matter (contents), form (of the matter) and existence (in a certain mode). Accordingly, ontology as a whole is divided into material, formal and existential ontology. Existence is neither a property nor one of the material or formal moments of an object; it is always the existence *of something* and what exists determines by its essence a mode of being which belongs to it. Modes of being are constituted from existential 'moments', of which Ingarden distinguishes the following opposite pairs: originality–derivativity, autonomy–heteronomy, distinctiveness–connectiveness and independence–dependence. Taking into account the modes of being thus constituted, there are four basic spheres of being: absolute (supratemporal), ideal (timeless), real (temporal – it has the most numerous forms) and purely intentional (atemporal, sometimes seemingly in time). Ingarden also draws a distinction between three domains: pure ideal qualities, ideas and individual objects. Each individual object is formally a subject of properties whose identity is determined by its constitutive nature. Individual objects of higher order, such as organisms, may be superstructured on autonomous individual objects. Ideas and purely intentional beings have a two-sided formal constitution – besides their own structure they also have contents (in the case of ideas it is constituted by constants and variables, and in the case of purely intentional beings by places of indeterminateness).

Analyses of being in time, of the stream of consciousness and of the world show that their existence is derivative and depends on their relation to original (absolute) being. The foundation of being is placed either in its essence (and ultimately in the content of some idea) or is purely factual in its character. In his analysis of the controversy over the existence of the world, Ingarden first formulates Husserl's transcendental starting point, and then demonstrates and states precisely its assumptions concerning the two elements of initial relation: the real world and the stream of consciousness, together with a subject which belongs to it (pure ego). These considerations lead Ingarden to reject both Husserl's solution and his way of setting the question.

What is real appears in three temporal phases: the future, the present and the past. Objects determined in time include objects enduring in time, processes and events. A human being is an object enduring in time and constituted by a soul, which comprises an ego together with a stream of consciousness, and a body (with a subsystem constituting 'the gate of consciousness'). Living on the border of two spheres, the real (nature, animality), and the ideal (values), human beings create a third sphere of culture. Thus their need to transcend this fragility by a process of self-formation that is subordinated to values makes them prone to tragedy.

3 Aesthetics

Ingarden gave special attention to questions concerning aesthetic and moral values. Art plays a significant role in human life, and Ingarden develops a complex theory of works of art: a work of art exists in a purely intentional manner, though on the basis of some physical foundation of its identity; it is formally two-sided (it has some contents, for example, a represented world in certain types of arts); it can be analysed in the respect of its phases and its 'layers'; it is given (in its contents) in quasi-perception or in imagining ('imagining-thinking'); if it is of linguistic character (such as a literary work), sentences in it form quasi-propositions, and not propositions in the sense of logic; because of its schematic character it allows for various interpretations, but its main aim is to make aesthetic interpretation (the construction of an aesthetic object) possible. Ingarden draws a distinction between artistic values, which belong to the work of art, and aesthetic values, which belong to the aesthetic object. A successful work of art may realize not only an aesthetic value but, in connection with this value, it may also 'flare-up' with a 'metaphysical' quality (that is, an existentially significant quality) and make visible an essential connection between some concrete situation in life (embodied in the represented world) and an existential quality or qualities. Aesthetic experience has many phases and it consists of various factors – perceptual, intellectual, imaginative, emotional and volitional, for instance. In a developed aesthetic experience there are four phases: the preliminary emotion, the adoption of an aesthetic attitude, aesthetic interpretation (the construction of an aesthetic object), and the approval or disapproval of the aesthetic value apparent in the aesthetic object. Ingarden maintains that there are many different aesthetic values (see ART, VALUE OF §1).

4 Conclusion

Ingarden contributed to many areas of philosophy, but his most significant achievements include the following: the formulation of conditions for practising an autonomous theory of knowledge, emphasizing the role in it of the immediate 'awareness of an experience'; the distinction between a 'mode of being' and an 'existential moment'; a new theory of ideas as two-sided structures (that is, containing 'constants' and 'variables') which allows him to refute arguments against 'general objects' as self-contradictory; an extensive analysis of the controversy over the existence of the external world as well as an analysis of Husserl's arguments on this subject; an account of the foundations of aesthetics by detailed studies of the structure and modes of existence of the main types of works of art and of the ways in which we perceive them (the theory of aesthetic experience); and the formulation of the concept of a relatively isolated object and its application to the theory of the physical world, the theory of organisms and the problem of the freedom of human action. Ingarden's understanding of the philosophy of language also led him to make a significant attack on the Vienna Circle in Prague in 1934. It was in aesthetics, however, that his influence proved to be deepest and most durable.

See also: PHENOMENOLOGICAL MOVEMENT §2

List of works

Ingarden, R.W. (1957–95) *Dzieła filozoficne* (Philosophical Works), Warsaw: PWN, 15 vols. (This edition contains all of Ingarden's important works.)
—— (1921) 'Über die Gefahr einer Petitio Principii in der Erkenntnistheorie' (On the Danger of a Petitio Principii in the Theory of Knowledge), *Jahrbuch für Philosophie und Phänomenologische Forschung* 4: 545–68. (An attempt to avoid the 'petitio principii' mistake by an appeal to the immediate awareness of experience.)
—— (1922) 'Intuition und Intellekt bei Henri Bergson. Darstellung und Versuch einer Kritik' (Intuition and Intellect by Henri Bergson), *Jahrbuch für Philosophie und Phänomenologische Forschung* 5: 286–461. (Contains critical analysis of Bergson's views and considerations on conditions for building a theory of knowledge.)
—— (1925) 'Essentiale Fragen. Ein Beitrag zum Problem des Wesens' (Essential Questions: A Contribution to the Problem of Essence), *Jahrbuch für Philosophie und Phänomenologische Forschung* 7: 125–304. (A new theory of ideas with reference to Husserl and Hering.)
—— (1929) 'Bemerkungen zum Problem "Idealismus–Realismus"' (Remarks on the Problem of 'Idealism–Realism'), *Jahrbuch für Philosophie und Phänomenologische Forschung*, supplement 10: 159–90. (Analysis of various aspects of the idealism–realism problem.)
—— (1931a) *Das literarische Kunstwerk*, Halle an der Saale: Niemeyer, 1960, 1965; trans. G.G. Grabowicz, *The Literary Work of Art*, Evanston, IL: Northwestern University Press, 1973. (Ingarden's classic work which began a revolution in aesthetics. It contains, among other things, analyses of four layers of literary work.)
—— (1931b) 'Niektóre założenia idealizmu Berkeleya' (Some Assumptions of Berkeley's Idealism), in *Księga Pamiątkowa Polskiego Towarzystwa Filozoficznego*, Lwów, 215–58. (A continuation of Ingarden 1929, and further preparation to Ingarden 1947–8, 'Controversy Over the Existence of the World'.)
—— (1935) 'L'essai logistique d'une refonte de la philosophie', *Revue Philosophique* 60 (120): 137–59. (French version of the debate with the Vienna Circle.)
—— (1937) *O poznawaniu dzieła literackiego*, Lwów; extended edn, Warsaw, 1976; German translation, *Vom Erkennen das literarischen Kunstwerk*, Tübingen, 1968; English trans., *The Cognition of the Literary Work of Art*, Evanston, IL: Northwestern University Press, 1973. (Supplements Ingarden 1931a, from the point of view of descriptive psychology.)
—— (1947–8) *Spór o istnienie świata* (The Controversy Over the Existence of the World), vols 1 and 2, Cracow, vol. 3, Warsaw, 1981; vol. 1 partially trans. H.R. Michejda, *Time and Modes of Being*, Springfield, IL, 1964; German trans. *Der Streit um die Existenz der Welt*, Tübingen, 1964, 1965, 1974. (Ingarden's fundamental work. After an outline of his conception of philosophy he begins systematic debate with Husserl's idealism using sophisticated analyses within existential and formal ontology. He gives theory of being, theory of world, theory of pure conciousness and its object.)
—— (1958) *Studia z estetyki* (Studies in Aesthetics), vols 1 and 2, Warsaw; vol. 3, Warsaw: PWN, 1970. (A series of analyses of various works of art (mainly literature, painting and music), aesthetic experience and the problem of values.)
—— (1957–8) 'The Hypothetical Proposition', *Philosophy and Phenomenological Research* 18 (4):

435–50. (Excellent analyses of hypothetical propositions.)

—— (1960–1) 'Aesthetic Experience and Aesthetic Object', *Philosophy and Phenomenological Research* 21 (3): 289–313. (Analysis of aesthetic experience and aesthetic object as opposed to the work of art.)

—— (1962) *Untersuchungen zur Ontologie der Kunst, Musikwerk, Bild, Architektur, Film* (Investigations into the Ontology of Art, Musical Works, Pictures, Architecture and Film), Tübingen: Niemeyer. (It undertakes the problem of the structure of various kinds of works of art.)

—— (1964) 'Artistic and Aesthetic Values', trans. H. Osborne, *British Journal of Aesthetics* 4 (3): 198–213. (It develops the distinction between the values of the work of art and the values of the aesthetic object.)

—— (1970) *Über die Verantwortung. Ihre ontischen Fundamente* (On Responsibility: Its Ontical Foundation), Stuttgart: Philip Reclam Jun. (An analysis of responsibility and its ontic fundaments. An outline of the theory of man.)

—— (1971) *U podstaw teorii poznania* (At the Foundation of the Theory of Knowledge), Cracow: Polish Academy of Sciences. (Critical analysis of psychophysiological theory of knowledge. It states the condition of possibility for a theory of knowledge.)

—— (1974) *Wstęp do fenomenologii Husserla* (Introduction to the Phenomenology of Husserl), Warsaw: PWN. (Short presentation of Husserl's views.)

—— (1989) *Wykłady z etyki* (Lectures in Ethics), Warsaw: PWN. (Lectures concerning the foundations of ethics.)

—— (1994) *Frühe Schriften zur Erkenntnistheorie*, ed. W. Galewicz (vol. 6, *Ingarden gesammelte Werke*, ed. R. Fieguth and G. Küng), Tübingen: Niemeyer. (Several articles concernign the conception and condition of possibility of a theory of knowledge.)

References and further reading

Dufrenne, M. (1953) *Phénomenologie de l'expérience esthétique*, Paris, vol. 1, 266–73. (Critical analysis of Ingarden's theory of aesthetic experience and aesthetic object.)

Galarowicz, J. (1983) 'U podstaw sporu Ingardena z Husserlem' (Foundations of the Controversy between Ingarden and Husserl), *Studia Filozoficzne* 3–4: 79–86; 5–6: 83–95. (An analysis of the controversy about the interpretation of Husserl's idealism.)

Gierulanka, D. (1989) 'Kształt metody fenomenologicznej w filozofii Romana Ingardena' (The Shape of Phenomenological Method in Ingarden's Philosophy), in J. Perzanowski (ed.) *Jak filozofować? Studia z metodologii filozofii*, Warsaw, 96–110. (An original analysis of Ingarden's method.)

Ingarden, R. (1964) *Szkice filozoficzne Romanowi Ingardenowi w darze*, various eds, Warsaw/Cracow. (Contains essays dedicated to Ingarden as well as a presentation of his philosophy and a bibliography of his works.)

—— (1990) 'Roman Ingarden – metafizyk wolności', *Studia Filozoficzne*, various eds, 2–3: 85–97. (An interesting interpretation of perspectives on metaphysics in Ingarden's late work.)

Kowalski, J. (1966) 'Romana Ingardena koncepcja materii i formy. Próba analizy krytycznej' (Ingarden's Conception of Matter and Form. A Critical Analysis), *Roczniki Filozoficzne* 14 (3): 99–123. (Detailed analysis of Ingarden's views in comparison with those of Aristotle and Aquinas.)

Półtawski, A. (1975) 'Ingarden's Way to Realism and His Idea of Man', *Dialectics and Humanism*, 2 (3). (An attempt to find a way to a realistic solution based on Ingarden's later remarks.)

Rudnick, H.H. (ed.) (1990) *Ingardeniana II*, Dordrecht; *Analecta Husserliana* vol. 30. (Contains an international primary and secondary bibliography of Ingarden's works by H.H. Rudnick, J.W. Wawrzycka, 225–96.)

Sosnowski, L. (ed.) (1993) *Estetyka Romana Ingardena. Problemy i perspektywy* (Ingarden's Aesthetics: Problems and Perspectives), Cracow. (An outline of Ingarden's aesthetic views.)

Stępień, A. (1976) 'Bemerkungen zu Ingardens Konzeption der Ontologie', in *S. Thomas Aquinas 700th Anniversary of His Death. Modern Interpretation of His Philosophy*, Lublin, 127–39. (Points out difficulties within Ingarden's ontology and problems connected with relation of ontology to metaphysics.)

Studia Filozoficzne (1972) 'Fenomenologia Romana Ingardena', special issue, Warsaw. (Contains a bibliography of Ingarden's works from 1915 to 1971, prepared by A. Półtawski, 19–54.)

Szczepańska, A. (1989) *Estetyka Romana Ingardena* (Roman Ingarden's Aesthetics), Warsaw. (An account of Ingarden's aesthetics.)

Tymieniecka, A.T. (1957) *Essence et existence. Étude à propos de la philosophie de Nicolai Hartman et Roman Ingarden*, Paris. (Comparative analysis of the two authors.)

—— (ed.) (1976) *Ingardeniana*, Dordrecht; *Analecta Husserliana* vol. 4. (Volume devoted to various aspects of Ingarden's thought.)

—— (ed.) (1990) *Ingardeniana III*, Dordrecht; *Ana-*

lecta *Husserliana* vol. 33. (Volume devoted to various aspects of Ingarden's thought.)

—— *et al.* (1959) *For Roman Ingarden: Nine Essays in Phenomenology*, S-Gravenhage. (Articles concerning various aspects of phenomenological thought.)

Wojtysiak, J. (1993) 'R. Ingardena koncepcja ontologii a koncepcja metafizyki tomizmu egzystencjalnego', *Studia metafilozoficzne*, Lublin, vol. 1, 167–211. (This article is a detailed examination of Ingarden's theory of being in comparison to ideas of Polish and American existential Thomists.)

Translated by Piotr Gutowski

ANTONI B. STĘPIEŃ

INGE, WILLIAM RALPH (1860–1954)

Inge, a philosopher and theologian, was a Christian Platonist. Platonic philosophy emphasized knowledge of necessary truths that it held to be grounded in abstract objects; its deity was a designer limited by the properties of a matter it did not create. Christian theology emphasizes a God who, both Creator and Providence, became incarnate in Jesus Christ. For Platonism, nothing historical could have ultimate significance or importance; for Christianity, the birth, death, and resurrection of Christ have ultimate significance. As his thought developed, Inge increasingly was able to retain much of Platonism while slowly coming to accept the consequences of the Christian emphasis on history.

William Ralph Inge was born in 1860 in Crayke, Yorkshire, and educated at Eton and Cambridge. He was a Fellow of Hertford College, Oxford, from 1889 to 1905, vicar of All Saints' Church, Knightsbridge, from 1905 to 1907, and became a professor of divinity at Cambridge in 1907. In 1911, he was appointed Dean of St Paul's Cathedral, from which he retired in 1934. The remaining twenty years of his life were spent in writing and reflection. He was influenced by the British neo-Hegelians (T.H. Green, Edward Caird, John Caird, F.H. Bradley and Bernard Bosanquet) and, especially, by Baron Friedrich von Hügel, whose emphasis on divine transcendence Inge entirely embraced. A bombastic speaker and writer, always a source of 'good copy', he defined pragmatism as an act of violence exercised by the will upon the intellect to make it accept what we find it helpful to believe, and replied by postcard to an invitation to an elaborate ecclesiastical ceremony planned in his honour, 'What do you think I retired for?'

Inge firmly identified himself as a Christian Platonist, belonging thereby to a tradition that extends from the first Christian century through Augustine to our own times. He held that any adequate view of the world must take modern science into account, and he spoke and wrote on social and moral issues. He consciously endeavoured to combine Platonic philosophy with Christian theology. Plato argued for the existence of Forms – abstract objects that are the truth conditions of necessary truths and the referent and ground of correct standards for moral and aesthetic values. There is, for Plato, also a deity who designs the world from matter whose recalcitrance limits his ability to form it exactly after the pattern provided by the Forms.

Inge held that religion involves belief in an eternal, spiritual, ideal world of which the natural, temporal world is an imperfect copy. Agreeing with Plato that there are eternal, unchangeable standards for truth, goodness and beauty, but holding to Christian monotheism, he held that Truth, Goodness and Beauty are not Forms, but attributes of a personal God who in no way depends for existence or perfection on the existence of a temporal world. The attributes themselves provide the only ontological basis for absolute values, and our awareness of these attributes provides us with the only knowledge of absolute values, which are discovered not made, ends and not means. Our wellbeing resides in awareness of, and conformity to, these ideals. Inge contrasted, then, the temporal world, in which evil is an inseparable condition of good, with the eternal world, which contains no evil. The hope that religion provides envisages our leaving the temporal world for the eternal.

Inge rejected natural theology, holding that there can be no successful inference from things that do exist but might not have existed to a being that exists with necessary independence. He also held that the doctrines of the virgin birth and bodily resurrection of Jesus Christ relate to scientific matters that are not of religious concern. The former entails that Mary bore a child without ceasing to be a virgin, and the latter entails that the dead body of Jesus was placed in a tomb and later restored to life, albeit as a body with powers not possessed by human bodies generally. Inge's Platonist, nonhistorical perspective led him to think of such things as biological and historical, not religious or theological. If Inge sometimes reshaped Platonism to fit his Christianity, here he arguably trimmed his Christianity to fit his Platonism.

In the *Outspoken Essays* (1922), Inge incautiously remarks that should the necessity arise, he could do without the Old Testament prophets and without Christ, and make do with just Plotinus. But in his Gifford Lectures, *The Philosophy of Plotinus*, he writes that:

> So far as I can see, nothing but a personal Incarnation, and the self-sacrifice of the Incarnate, could either adequately reveal the love of God for man, or call forth the love of man for God.... Vicarious suffering – the suffering of the sinless for the sinful – remained a stumbling block for the non-Christian world; and it is only in this doctrine that the sting of the world's sorrow and injustice is really drawn.
>
> (1918, vol. 2: 227)

The contrasting emphases of these remarks perhaps illustrate the conflicting perspective of a philosophy which can find no ultimate significance in anything not eternally true and a religion whose central doctrines make ineliminable reference to particular events and a particular historical person. At any rate, they illustrate the difficulty one who wishes to combine the two can have in doing so consistently.

List of works

Inge, W.R. (1899) *Christian Mysticism*, London: Methuen. (Contains Inge's Bampton Lectures; emphasizes the importance of religious experience as contrasted to texts and institutions.)

—— (1918) *The Philosophy of Plotinus*, London: Longmans, Green & Company. (Two series of Gifford Lectures, given in 1917 and 1918, by a sympathetic interpreter of Plotinus.)

—— (1919, 1922) *Outspoken Essays*, London: Longmans, Green & Company, two series. (Vintage, iconoclastic Inge.)

—— (1926) *The Platonic Tradition in English Religious Thought*, London: Longmans, Green & Company. (Inge's discussion of the tradition with which he was most in sympathy.)

—— (1930) *Christian Ethics and Moral Problems*, London: Hodder & Stoughton. (Gives Inge's distinctive perspective on issues in ethics.)

—— (1933) *God and the Astronomers*, London: Longmans, Green & Company. (Contains Inge's Wharburton Lectures concerning the problem of time, God in history, God and the world of nature, and the eternal world.)

References and further reading

Elliot-Binns, J.E. (1956) *English Thought 1860–1900: The Theological Aspect*, London: Longmans, Green & Company. (Discusses the historical, philosophical, theological and social setting of English theology in the indicated period.)

Horton, W.M. (date unknown) *Contemporary English Theology*, London: SCM Press. (Treats pre- and post-First-World-War English theology from a perceptive American perspective.)

Langford, T. (1969) *In Search of Foundations: English Theology 1900–1920*, Nashville, TN: Abington Press. (Presentation of English theological thought in its cultural and philosophical context; good bibliography.)

Mozley, J.K. (1951) *Some Tendencies in British Theology*, London: SPCK. (Discussion of British theology from *Lux Mundi* (1889) to the thought of John Oman.)

KEITH E. YANDELL

INNATE KNOWLEDGE

If innate knowledge exists, there must be innate beliefs and those beliefs must count as knowledge. In consequence, the problem of clarifying the concept of innate knowledge divides in two: to explain what it is for a belief to be innate and then to connect that account with a characterization of what knowledge is. Modern biology requires changes in traditional philosophical conceptions of innateness; and two quite different theories of knowledge entail that innate beliefs will often fail to count as knowledge.

1 **Innateness**
2 **Innateness and the a priori**
3 **Knowledge**

1 Innateness

Within some species of bird, individuals produce their characteristic song even if they are reared in silence. Among others, a bird sings its song only if it first hears that song performed. And among still others, a bird produces its characteristic song only if it hears some sort of song or other (Gould and Marler 1991). We are inclined to apply the concept of innateness to the first type of bird and to withhold it from the second. But what of the third? Should we say that these birds learn their songs by hearing any of a set of quite dissimilar songs? Or should we say that the song is innate – that it is 'in' the bird, only awaiting an environmental trigger for its release?

Both options seem unsatisfactory. How can a given song be learned from hearing a quite different song, if the target song would have emerged regardless of which song the bird had heard? The option of judging the song innate also has its pitfalls. What does it mean to say that the song is 'in' the bird from the start? This spatial metaphor sounds suspiciously like the pre-formationist doctrines of eighteenth century embry-ology, according to which foetal development simply involves an increase in size of the fully formed individuals found in newly fertilized eggs. Arguably, the song is 'in' the bird from birth no more than adolescent pubic hair is 'in' a new-born baby.

It is important not to confuse the claim that the song is 'in' the bird from birth with the much less controversial claim that the new-born bird is disposed to acquire the song once the bird passes various developmental landmarks and experiences various environmental cues. The latter claim does not entail the former. Indeed, the latter formulation offers a completely de-natured reading of the idea of innate-ness; it becomes trivially true that all beliefs are innate. Surely this formulation short-circuits the controversy rather than solving it.

(In *Notes on a Certain Program*, Descartes suggests that ideas are innate in precisely the same sense that diseases are sometimes innate; this does not mean that foetuses suffer from diseases *in utero*, but that individuals are born with a certain 'disposition' to contract them. The challenge to innatism, laid down by Locke in the *Essay Concerning Human Under-standing*, is to explain what 'disposition' means so that some traits, but not others, turn out to be innate. Leibniz takes up this challenge in the *New Essays*.)

Contemporary biology does not exploit the philo-sopher's traditional distinction between innate and learned. First of all, the biological opposite of innate is not 'learned', but 'acquired'. Learning is one way to acquire a characteristic, but there are others; sun-burns are acquired, but they are not learned. It is worth asking what distinguishes learning (and *mis-learning*) from other processes of belief acquisition; if beliefs could be acquired by swallowing pills, arguably that would not count as learning. In any event, the present point is that biologists do not think of 'innate' and 'learned' as exhaustive alternatives.

Perhaps the most important contrast between the biological and the traditional philosophical concept is that biology does not treat the difference between innate and acquired as a dichotomy; rather, it is a matter of degree. Traits differ with respect to how dependent their emergence is on environmental details. The three groups of birds described before can be arrayed on a continuum; there is no need to draw a line that separates two of them from the third.

It is also important to distinguish the initial appearance of a trait from its subsequent mainte-nance. A trait may emerge across a wide range of environments and yet be modifiable once in place. For example, an Egyptian vulture, when first confronted with an ostrich egg and a stone, will break the egg with the stone. However, if the vulture repeatedly discovers that the eggs it breaks open are empty, eventually it will stop breaking eggs (Pulliam and Dunford 1980). In this case, the behavioural disposi-tion might be termed innate. All the same, 'innate' does not mean 'unmodifiable'.

Yet another gap between the traditional philosophi-cal concept and modern biology concerns the issue of universality. Philosophers often expect innate beliefs to be universal in our species; they are part of 'human nature' and so should be present in all individuals who have enjoyed a normal development. (Thus we find Locke, in the *Essay* (bk I, ch. III, §§8–18), arguing that the idea of God is not innate because it is not found in children and 'savages'.) A related expectation is that if two people have a trait, then the trait must be innate for both if it is innate for either.

Neither of these assumptions is unproblematic. The biologist's concept of a 'norm of reaction' describes how the phenotype which a genotype will develop depends on the environment it experiences. For example, consider a particular fruitfly genotype; let us ask how that genotype's attainment of a particular phenotype (for example, bristle number) depends on some environmental variable (for example, nutrition). Different genotypes often exhibit different degrees of environmental contingency with respect to the same phenotype. One fruitfly genotype may produce the same bristle number regardless of variation in nutrition, whereas another may produce different numbers of bristles in response to different amounts of food. Because of this, it is quite possible for two flies to have the same number of bristles, but to have achieved that result by quite different developmental pathways. Bristle number may be 'innate' for one and 'acquired' for the other.

In view of all this, it is a reasonable hypothesis that the most that can be salvaged from the ancient concept of innateness is this: *a phenotypic trait is innate for a given genotype if and only if that phenotype will emerge in all of a range of developmental environments.* What counts as the appropriate range of environments is left open in this proposal. Perhaps there is a uniquely correct answer to this question; then again, maybe the range is determined pragma-tically. It is difficult to see how the latter conclusion can be evaded.

2   Innateness and the a priori

The above definition opens a large gap between the

concepts of innateness and a prioricity. A proposition is a priori if it can be known or justified independently of experience (see A PRIORI). A prioricity does not concern what causes an organism to formulate a belief; rather, it has to do with the status the belief enjoys once it is formulated. Arguably, the belief that all bachelors are unmarried is not innate; it emerges in some social and linguistic environments, but not in others. Still, once an individual has this belief, it may be true that the belief can be justified without appeal to experience.

Conversely, it is also possible for a belief to be both a posteriori and innate (see A POSTERIORI). Perhaps human cognitive development inevitably leads people to believe that a physical world exists external to their own minds. This is as natural and invariant a developmental outcome as the acquisition of pubic hair during adolescence. Yet, it remains for the philosopher to judge whether solipsism is a priori false. Perhaps our natural anti-solipsism is either unjustifiable or is justifiable as an inference to the best explanation; maybe the postulate of an external world makes sense because it explains regularities that obtain in the flow of experience. If so, we would have here the case of an innate belief that is a posteriori (see INFERENCE TO THE BEST EXPLANATION).

3 Knowledge

If we have beliefs whose emergence is relatively invariant across a range of developmental backgrounds, will those beliefs count as knowledge? To begin with, if S knows that p, then p must be true. Beyond that, what does knowledge require? Let us explore the suggestion that S's belief that p counts as knowledge only if S is justified in believing p.

The justification that S has for believing p presumably must come from other beliefs (or thoughts or sensations) that S has. In particular, it is not enough that those other beliefs (or other items) bear some abstract relation of justification to the proposition p; after all, it might be true that S believes q and that q is evidence for p even though S believes p for no reason at all or for bad reasons. What is required is that S's belief in p be related 'in the right way' to S's justifying belief in q.

What might this right way be? One possibility is that S's belief in q causes S to start believing p. Another is that S continues to believe in p because S believes q. A third is that S's belief in q makes it harder for S to stop believing p. The list could continue (see JUSTIFICATION, EPISTEMIC; KNOWLEDGE, CONCEPT OF §§1–6).

Regardless of how this condition is interpreted, it seems clear that innate true beliefs can fail to count as

knowledge. Consider a belief that people inevitably have and cannot abandon; perhaps our spontaneous anti-solipsism is an example. Such propositions may admit of inventive justifications, but this does not mean that philosophical pronouncements can influence whether ordinary folks believe in an external world.

Let us turn, instead, to a concept of knowledge that abandons the requirement of justification. Reliability theories of knowledge demand that the act of believing should be related to the world in the right way. If S knows that p, then it must be true that, in the circumstances that S occupied, S would not have believed p unless p had been true. If S knows that p, then the requirement is that the probability that p is true given that S believes that p, is equal to 1.0. S must be a perfectly reliable detector of the truth of p, if S's belief that p is to count as knowledge (Dretske 1981) (see RELIABILISM).

It is easy to see why an innate belief can evolve so as to violate the requirement that the probability that p is true given that S believes that p, is equal to 1.0. For example, suppose that snakes are usually, although not always, dangerous. An organism that confronts a snake thus faces a problem of decision-making under uncertainty. It can believe without further ado that the snake is dangerous; or, it can try to find some further observational evidence on which to base its decision. In the former case, the organism might have the innate belief that snakes are dangerous. In the latter, its opinion will depend on the details of present and past experience.

Imagine that the organism in question is not very good at determining from observable cues whether a snake is dangerous. Imagine further that the organism does better by erring on the side of caution (Stich 1990). If the snake is dangerous, it is very important to believe that this is so; but if the snake is not dangerous, it is of much smaller moment whether one realizes this fact. These assumptions all favour the evolution of the innate belief that snakes are dangerous. Innateness will be a better strategy than learning in this instance (Sober 1994).

Notice that the factors that predict the evolution of innateness provide no guarantee of the reliability of the resulting beliefs. The organism believes of each snake encountered that it is dangerous. The organism therefore has true beliefs only as often as snakes in fact are dangerous. This need not be a terribly high frequency; it clearly need not equal 100 per cent. For this reason, it is easy to see how innate beliefs can fail to count as knowledge from the point of view of the reliability theory of knowledge. Indeed, there is no guarantee that the belief must be true more often than not; pervasive error may be a consequence of the evolution of innate beliefs.

See also: COGNITIVE DEVELOPMENT; LANGUAGE, INNATENESS OF; NATIVISM; RATIONALISM §2

References and further reading

* Descartes, R. (1648) *Notes on a Certain Programme*, in *The Philosophical Works of Descartes*, trans. E.S. Haldane and G.R.T. Ross, Cambridge, Cambridge University Press, 1931, 431–50. (Descartes responds to various misunderstandings of his views, including his position on innate ideas.)
* Dretske, F. (1981) *Knowledge and the Flow of Information*, Cambridge, MA: MIT Press. (Elaboration of the reliability theory of knowledge.)
  Fodor, J. (1981) 'The Current Status of the Innateness Controversy', in *Representations*, Cambridge, MA: MIT Press, 257–316. (Argues that the dispute between empiricists and rationalists should be understood in terms of whether various simple beliefs are learned or triggered.)
* Gould, J. and Marler, P. (1991) 'Learning by Instinct', in D. Mock (ed.) *Behavior and Evolution of Birds*, San Francisco, CA: Freeman, 4–19. (Describes a variety of learning strategies that birds use to acquire their songs.)
* Leibniz, G.W. (1703–4) *New Essays Concerning Human Understanding*, trans. with notes by A.G. Langley, La Salle, IL: Open Court, 3rd edn. (Point-by-point commentary on Locke's essay by the greatest exponent of continental rationalism.)
* Locke, J. (1689) *An Essay Concerning Human Understanding*, ed. P.H. Nidditch, Oxford: Clarendon Press; New York: Oxford University Press. (The founding document of British empiricism, accessible to the general reader.)
* Pulliam, H. and Dunford, C. (1980) *Programmed to Learn*, New York: Columbia University Press. (Argues that different learning strategies will evolve depending on how the environment is structured.)
  Sober, E. (1993) *Philosophy of Biology*, Boulder, CO: Westview Press. (Clarifies concepts such as norm of reaction and heritability.)
* —— (1994) 'The Adaptive Advantage of Learning and *A Priori* Prejudice', in *From a Biological Point of View: Essays in Evolutionary Philosophy*, Cambridge: Cambridge University Press. (Presents an evolutionary model for predicting when a proposition will be an innate belief and when it will depend on experience for its emergence.)
  Stich, S. (1975) *Innate Ideas*, Berkeley, CA: University of California Press. (Anthology of historical and contemporary essays, some of which address issues concerning Chomskian linguistics. Of special interest are the essays by A. Goldman relating the causal theory of knowledge to the question of whether innate beliefs can count as knowledge; by W. Hart, arguing that innateness is irrelevant to the issue of a priori knowledge; and by S. Stich, which proposes a clarification of what innateness means.)
* —— (1990) *The Fragmentation of Reason*, Cambridge, MA: MIT Press. (Argues that evolutionary considerations make it plausible to suspect large amounts of irrationality and unreliability in belief formation.)

ELLIOTT SOBER

INNATENESS OF LANGUAGE
see LANGUAGE, INNATENESS OF

INNOCENCE

In its most general sense, innocence refers to the state of being without sin. A more restricted meaning is attributed to the word in the legal sphere, where people who are found not to be guilty of a particular crime are described as innocent. In official teaching of the Roman Catholic church, all direct killing of the innocent is forbidden. Here the word refers to people who are not harmful. Nowadays, this can be taken to mean 'non-aggressors'. According to Rousseau, humans possess original goodness. Corrupting influences come from outside them.

Innocence, in perhaps the oldest sense of the term, is the state of being sinless or unacquainted with evil (see EVIL; SIN). Within various branches of Christianity such is believed to have been the original state of the first humans. However, in view of the fact that nobody on this planet appears to be in such an immaculate condition now, the term 'innocence' usually has a more restricted meaning. It can be used thus in the sphere of ethics, although it would seem to be more commonly employed in legal circles, where people who are found not to be guilty of a particular crime are described as innocent. The fact that they may have committed innumerable other misdemeanours which do not fall within the ambit of the law is of no consequence in this regard. It is often said in such cases that the people concerned are not guilty of wrongdoing because they either did not perform a certain act, or, having indeed performed it, were not blameworthy in so doing. It is worth noting, however, that, in courts of law, the label 'innocent' can be, and often is, applied to people who have acted in accordance with the requirements of a particular law, even in cases in which, from an ethical point of view, breaking the law would have been the right thing to do. Nevertheless, there can also be innocence in the moral sense in such cases if the people concerned sincerely believe that they have acted rightly in obeying the law, unless, of course, their belief is based on culpable ignorance (see RESPONSIBILITY §2).

Having said that, it is worth noting that the term 'innocence' is, in fact, sometimes used to describe the state of people who are ignorant of certain evils. The adjective 'innocent' occasionally replaces 'naïve' in such cases. In spite of what has already been said about culpable ignorance, such innocence can be an endearing, although also dangerous, quality, as is often the case with small children who are open and trusting, never having been exposed to more than a few minor forms of malevolence. Here we can say that the state of ignorance or innocence results from a lack of experience of the harsh realities of life.

In some spheres of ethics, most notably in Roman Catholic moral theology, the term 'innocence' and its adjective have been attributed a good deal of importance in debate about the rightness or wrongness of killing people. According to official Roman Catholic teaching, no direct killing of the innocent can ever be condoned. Here again a restricted meaning is adopted. In current Catholic literature the word 'innocent' is used to refer to non-aggressors, an obvious example being noncombatants in time of war. One may kill an aggressor in a just war, or, even outside the war situation, in an act of self-defence or when acting in defence of a third party, provided that there is a proportionate reason for doing so. Non-aggressors (innocent people), however, may be killed only indirectly, in accordance with the requirements of the principle of double effect (see DOUBLE EFFECT, PRINCIPLE OF). This might happen during a just war, as a result of the bombardment of an enemy installation, near or in which are some noncombatants. Their deaths could be accepted as a regrettable but unavoidable side effect of the bombardment, provided that killing them was not the aim of those effecting the bombardment, that the good intended was not brought about by means of those deaths, and there was a proportionate reason for effecting the bombardment in the first place (see WAR AND PEACE, PHILOSOPHY OF §§2–3).

The same kind of thinking is applied in the sphere of medical ethics (see MEDICAL ETHICS §§2, 4). Official Catholic teaching prohibits all direct abortion, but permits such therapeutic procedures as hysterectomies performed on pregnant women suffer-ing from cancer of the uterus. The foetuses – described as innocent persons – are aborted indirectly. Something similar can be said about official Catholic teaching regarding euthanasia. Even a person who asks to be killed remains innocent in the sense under discussion, and may not, therefore, be killed directly. Analgesics, however, may be administered to such a person to relieve intolerable pain, even though it is foreseen that they will have the side effect of short-ening their life. Again, in this last case, an innocent person is killed, but indirectly.

A lack of innocence in this sense is also attributed to at least some people found guilty of murder. Official Roman Catholic teaching permits capital punishment in such cases, but only if less violent ways of protecting human life and public order from such aggressors are unavailable.

The unrestricted meaning of innocence would seem to be what is referred to in the writings of Jean-Jacques ROUSSEAU. In his opinion (1762), the fact that we see that people are wicked in no way conflicts with the fact that humans are naturally good, possessing original goodness. In their original state, there is not a single vice in their hearts, no perversity at all. Evil must have an external source. In bringing up our children, therefore, we need, according to Rousseau's way of thinking, to keep away from them all corrupting external influences in order that nature may be allowed to take its course. Children must have a natural education, that is, an education that interferes as little as possible with their free, natural development.

References and further reading

McCormick, R.A. (1989) *The Critical Calling: Reflections on Moral Dilemmas Since Vatican II*, Washington, DC: Georgetown University Press, ch. 12, esp. 220–32. (A detailed examination of the Roman Catholic teaching prohibiting direct killing of the innocent.)

Roche, K.F. (1974) *Rousseau: Stoic and Romantic*, London: Methuen, 39–51. (Explanation of Rous-seau's thought, as presented in his *Émile*.)

* Rousseau, J-J. (1762) *Émile: ou, de l'éducation*, trans. A. Bloom, *Emile: or, On Education*, Harmonds-worth: Penguin, 1991. (Rousseau claims that every child is born innocent.)

Seago, P. (1994) *Criminal Law*, London: Sweet & Maxwell, esp. 28–101. (A consideration of the general principles of criminal liability.)

BERNARD HOOSE

INSTITUTIONALISM IN LAW

'Institutionalism' is the name for an approach to the theory of law worked out in the late nineteenth and early twentieth centuries by a number of scholars from continental Europe, working mainly in independence from each other. Their common characteristics can be stated only in rather generic and negative terms. They are all critical of statalism, that is, too readily identifying law and state; of voluntarism, that is, treating will as an essential element of law; and of normativism, defining law as a body of norms. In positive terms, they have in common a generic emphasis on the social character of law, and a sense of the need to take a view of legal experience broader than that defined by its traditional boundaries, and to extend the 'official' catalogue of the sources of law.

Nowadays, there is new talk of institutionalism in the philosophy of law, but in a different sense, with reference to the idea of law as made up of institutional facts, that is, facts whose meaning depends on norms. This neo-institutionalism is normativist, analytical and hermeneutic in approach and has only the most tenuous links with classical institutionalism.

1 **Institutions and institutionalism in law**
2 **Maurice Hauriou**
3 **The development of French institutionalism: Renard and Gurvitch**
4 **Italian legal institutionalism: Santi Romano**
5 **Contemporary legal institutionalism: MacCormick and Weinberger**

1 Institutions and institutionalism in law

Legal institutionalism conceives of law as a kind of 'institution'. No less evasive a definition could be given without opening the question of the rival merits of the various institutionalist theories and of the notion of 'institution' that each adopts. 'Institution' is an intrinsically ambiguous term, used in a notably wide variety of senses, to the point of appearing useless to many thinkers. As well as being a term in general use, it is also a technical term in social science, particularly in sociology, where it is often simply a synonym for social organization or for some element of social structure; elsewhere, it has come to be used, in an equally general way, to denote any sort of conduct or belief sanctioned and practised in a stable way by a community. In a more restricted sense again, 'institution' is used to signify the normative aspect of social organizations; in this sense, for example, 'marriage' would be the institution corresponding to the family as a social order.

This variety of meanings is reflected, obviously

enough, in law. In legal culture, however, yet other senses of the term 'institution' are to be found. This expression is customarily used to signify appointment to an office, or constitution of an heir, or, in its substantive use, an entity or organization personified by the law. In the plural, one speaks of institutions to signify the fundamental elements of a discipline (here remembering the *Institutiones* of the Roman jurist GAIUS). Jurists in some linguistic traditions are accustomed to make a (somewhat variable) distinction between 'institution' and 'institute', often using the former to refer to underlying social regularities (for example, capitalist ownership) while the latter denotes a standard set of legal relations conceived in abstract terms (for example, property). This distinction highlights the normativism and formalism implicit in common juristic thought. It is no accident that it is a distinction given prominence by the neo-institutionalism discussed in §5 below.

'Classical' legal institutionalism is however more indebted to the sociological than to the juridical usage of the term 'institution'. Historically, institutionalism was a family of jurisprudential approaches that arose in the late nineteenth and early twentieth century in France and Italy. The historical phenomenon that most influenced its theoretical development was the swift transformation of the nineteenth-century liberal state through the rise of intermediate groups between individuals and the state, such as industrial corporations and trade unions. The concept 'institution', because of its very vagueness and ambiguity, has been found serviceable, in law and elsewhere, as the key to analysis and even justification of the changes in social relationships and power-relations that have taken place (see SOCIAL THEORY AND LAW §2).

Thus it is easy enough to determine the extension of the term 'legal institutionalism' by pointing out the approaches that have been called 'institutionalist'. What is not so easy is to determine its intension, by identifying the characteristics common to the various legal institutionalisms; some even doubt the possibility of doing so. A common characteristic does however exist, namely, a generically realist tendency, a propensity to regard the law as a social phenomenon (see LEGAL REALISM §2). The use by institutionalist approaches of the terminological apparatus thrown up by the nascent social sciences should not however deceive us into supposing that the theories in question sought to establish an empiricist view of law; on the contrary, legal institutionalism arose by and large from ethico-political impulses (this is particularly true of Renard and Gurvitch; see §3), and, even when driven by epistemological tenets, as in the case of Santi Romano (see §4), it was inspired more by a formalistic legal-science model than by sociological empiricism. Beyond the rather weak unifying element of a generic realism, one can go no further. For the institutionalist authors have neither a shared cultural formation nor shared philosophical reference points in the way of common ontological or epistemological ideas; nor have they even shared ethico-political attitudes.

2 Maurice Hauriou

Maurice Hauriou, French theorist of public law, has come to be regarded as the founding legal institutionalist. He set himself against two targets: extreme subjectivism fixated on the notions of will and of contract (here the critique is of Rousseau and certain nineteenth-century German theories of public law), and extreme objectivism premised on the notion of the rule of law (here criticized are Duguit and Durkheim) (see DURKHEIM, É.; ROUSSEAU, J.-.J.). For Hauriou, institutions are both social facts and legal configurations; they both pre-exist and produce law. They can be either institution-persons (corporate bodies such as the state, associations, companies) or institution-things (such as the standing rules of the law). His earlier work stresses power as the unifying factor of institutions, and he defines them in terms of power-relations (Hauriou 1910); later, he accords greater importance to what he calls the '*idée directrice*' ('directing idea') or '*idée d'oeuvre*' ('operative idea'). 'Among those interested in the idea there are produced manifestations of communion directed by its organs of authority and regulated by a definite procedure' (Hauriou 1925). The elements of the institution are thus the '*idée directrice*', the power organized through realization of the idea, and the communal activities which are produced in the social group as reflections of the idea and its realization. The profoundly mysterious notion of the 'directing idea' belongs to an organicist social theory, permeated with vitalism (the subtitle of Hauriou's best-known work is much to the point: 'an essay in social vitalism'); a theory in which the idea of institution remains nebulous and with the vaguest of boundaries. Hauriou's philosophical ideas are, to be sure, eclectic and unsystematic (Bergson's influence can be seen), and in any event they have the sound of *ex post* justifications for a theory that remains at base an essentially juristic one.

3 The development of French institutionalism: Renard and Gurvitch

Hauriou's work has aroused few echoes in common law countries, or in the German-speaking countries; yet it has been highly influential in the Hispanic and Italian worlds, and of course in France. In France, Georges Renard and Georges Gurvitch were both pupils of Hauriou's who reacted against voluntaristic dogmas and juridical individualism and statalism, and shared an ambition to broaden the horizons of legal experience.

A critic of voluntarism and of individualism, Renard (1876–1943) shared Hauriou's opposition to identification of law with enacted law. The essence of institutions in his view lies in the way in which activities cohere in the pursuit of a common aim, with a preordained internal structure; such a structure is always based on authority-relationships (Renard 1930). He tries to subsume this institutionalist conception of his, standing as it does midway between sociology and jurisprudence, under a Thomistic metaphysics. This leads Renard on the one hand to interpret the social philosophy of Aquinas as an institutionalist theory before its time, while on the other hand treating institutions as all essentially directed towards realization of the common good (see THOMISM; NATURAL LAW §§3–4).

Gurvitch (1894–1965), a Russian lawyer who became a naturalized French citizen, was a sociologist of law with social-democratic convictions. At the centre of his thought lay his idea of 'normative fact', which he treated as equivalent to Hauriou's 'institution'. Law was not founded on will or on some norm or norms, but on the very fact of union or of associational community, that is, on a 'normative fact'. Gurvitch (1932) also brings to bear on this pluralistic and anti-formalist conception of law a thoroughly value-laden philosophical approach, which he calls 'transpersonalism'. This is based on an exaltation of 'social law' and 'social rights', whose essential characteristic is found in integrative relationships, and which stand in opposition to individual rights, with their contrasting character of being coordinative and subordinative. Social rights, in Gurvitch's definition, are autonomous communitarian rights, which provide an objective integration of every really active collectivity, whether or not organized.

4 Italian legal institutionalism: Santi Romano

Santi Romano (1875–1947) was an Italian public lawyer and author of an institutionalist theory which enjoyed great currency in his own country, and was applied in several branches of law, including international law, ecclesiastical law and labour law. His thought was little if at all influenced by Hauriou's work, of which he had some knowledge and appreciation, but which he thought rather limited in scope and insufficiently jurisprudential. He was a pure jurist and the creator of a general theory that was rigorously anti-philosophical and pure of any sociological influence. Moreover, as against the French institutionalists, he was a critic of natural law and a defender of the thesis of the separation between law and morals; in this sense he can be considered a legal positivist (see LEGAL POSITIVISM §1).

Romano's polemical writings have as their targets normativism and the common definitions of law that are based on examples drawn from private law and hence inadequate for the explanation of the other branches of law (Romano 1917–18). This gives rise to his definition of law as a juridical order, a notion which in turn leads back to that of institution. Romano takes 'institution' to signify any social entity or body. This entails an extreme form of legal pluralism, and leads Romano to the point of treating as legal even organizations that are prohibited by state-law, and indeed to considering revolutionary organizations as juridical orders. Romano, for whom every social organization, however ephemeral and transitory, counted as a juridical order, tended to represent all social relations in a legal guise. Such an approach in the final analysis has the effect of blanking out social conflicts, since these come to be depicted as instances of relationships between orders, and the orders in their turn are seen as having a spontaneous tendency toward orderliness.

Romano's institutionalism won the approbation of the German legal thinker Carl SCHMITT, theorist of National Socialism, who saw in it an exemplification of his own conception of law as a concrete order. This conception, along with normativism and decisionism, in Schmitt's view constituted the three basic types of pure legal thought (Schmitt 1934). Extremist in thought as he was, Schmitt saw with perfect clarity that institutionalism, if carried to its logical conclusions, could not but end up in a radical realism in which the reality of the law becomes reduced to mere relations of power and of decision-making.

5 Contemporary legal institutionalism: MacCormick and Weinberger

The classical institutionalist theories were all ethico-political and were characterized in general by a holistic and organicist view of society and an aversion from conflict-models of society and law. Each emphasized the values of order, of neutralization of conflicts, of harmony and social integration.

Taken as legal theories in the strict sense, the varieties of institutionalism have the considerable merit of having neutralized the extremer versions of opposed opinions, and in particular normativism, though they did not refute it outright. In truth, the

anti-normativist polemics convince only in relation to a narrow Austinian notion of the legal norm, understood as the imperatival expression of an act of human will (see AUSTIN, J.). This notion is now completely discredited. Institutionalism in its moderate, non-Schmittian version cannot coherently be completely anti-normativist. For the very ideas of social organization on which it is founded presuppose norms that regulate and empower individuals (see NORMS, LEGAL). The anti-normativist polemics of the institutionalists have without doubt contributed to bringing legal theory up to date. In particular, the emphasis on the notion of organization has brought about general acceptance of a conception of the law as a normative order, and has led to the elaboration of a typology of norms better suited to representing law in terms of structured ordering, giving due recognition to organizational norms, or secondary norms.

Today, classical institutionalism has lost its innovative drive but jurists do still use many ideas drawn from institutionalist theories to give theoretical respectability to their own doctrinal writings. Suffice it here to mention the case of the *lex mercatoria*, or 'New Law Merchant', the so called 'common law of commerce', which has come to be construed as a form of legal order coexisting with the laws of the states and with international law (Osman 1992).

But at present there is also new talk of institutionalism on the part of two contemporary philosophers of law, Neil MacCormick in Scotland and Ota Weinberger the Czech scholar (see WEINBERGER, O.). MacCormick and Weinberger's neo-institutionalism however has declaredly little in common with classical institutionalism, on several counts. In truth theirs is a conception of law worked out not from the standpoint of the pure jurist nor from that of the sociologist of law, but from that of legal philosophy, indeed that of philosophers with an analytico-linguistic sensitivity and training. Its basis is a confessedly empiricist metaphysics. It is neither anti-statalist nor anti-formalist in its treatment of the sources of law; moreover, far from criticizing normativism, it treats norms as being at the core of the concept of an institution; and finally, it is a positivistic theory of law, critical of natural law theory (in this having affinity with the ideas only of Romano among the classical school).

The institutionalism of MacCormick and Weinberger starts out from the notion of 'institutional fact' and the related opposition between 'brute facts' and 'institutional facts' (Anscombe 1958; Searle 1969). The law is composed of institutions (contract, wills, statutes and so on) created through the implementation of legal rules. Such institutions are nothing other than abstract concepts through which it is possible to ascribe meaning to, and to interpret, congeries of human actions. Institutions in this sense belong, however, to a philosophical and semiotic notion, and have little in common with the various sociological notions of institution. The ideas of MacCormick and Weinberger (1986) do however disclose an institutional aspect in the classical sense to the extent that they give emphasis to the relationship that always exists between institutions in the philosophical sense and institutions as sociological realities. According to these authors the law is in fact always at the same time (1) an ensemble of abstract meaning-concepts; (2) an ensemble of institutional acts and facts understandable only in the light of the network of rules constitutive of the concepts; and (3) an ensemble of organizations in the sociological sense. However, to grasp the reality of the legal it is indispensable to adopt a hermeneutic outlook whereby it is possible to coordinate the contributions of lawyers, sociologists and philosophers of law (see LEGAL HERMENEUTICS).

Weinberger's work in particular brings together the notions of institutions and institutional facts and squares them with a more all-embracing philosophico-jurisprudential view, comprehending anthropology, ontology and a formal theory of action.

See also: HART, H.L.A.; LAW, PHILOSOPHY OF; LEGAL CONCEPTS; SOCIAL THEORY AND LAW §§1–3

References and further reading

* Anscombe, G.E.M. (1958) 'On Brute Facts', *Analysis* 18: 69–72. (A brilliant and concise pioneering treatment of the distinction between brute facts and institutional facts.)

Biscaretti di Ruffia, P. (ed.) (1977) *Le dottrine giuridiche oggi e l'insegnamento di Santi Romano*, Milan: Giuffré. (Particularly useful for anyone interested in the 'fate' of Romano's ideas in Italy; a collection of papers by philosophers and legal theorists, constitutional lawyers, administrative lawyers, international lawyers and ecclesiastical lawyers.)

Broderick, A. and Welling, M. (eds) (1970) *The French Institutionalists: Maurice Hauriou, Georges Renard, T. Delos*, Cambridge, MA: Harvard University Press. (Scholarly studies of French institutionalists from a standpoint broadly sympathetic to theirs; a helpfully constructive critique.)

* Gurvitch, G. (1932) *L'Idée du droit social. Notion et système du droit social. Histoire doctrinale depuis le XVIIe siècle jusqu'à la fin du XIXe siècle*, Paris: Sirey. (Contains a notable historical section reconstructing the idea of a social right from the time of Grotius onwards.)

* Hauriou, M. (1910) *Principes de droit public* (Principles of Public Law), Paris: Sirey, 2nd edn, 1916. (This little book on principles of public law is a student's introduction to the subject, in which Hauriou's theoretical approach is also introduced.)

* —— (1925) 'La Théorie de l'institution et de la fondation. Essai de vitalisme social' (On the Theory of the Institution and the Foundation), *Cahiers de la nouvelle journée* 4. (This essay is Hauriou's best-known theoretical statement; it is aimed more widely than at a purely juristic audience.)

Jennings, W.I. (1933) 'The Institutional Theory', in W.I. Jennings (ed.), *Modern Theories of Law*, London: Oxford University Press, ch. 5: 68–85. (An account of Hauriou and his school by the leading contemporary English public lawyer, considerably, and perhaps excessively, stressing the Catholic element in institutionalist thought.)

* MacCormick, N. and Weinberger, O. (1986) *An Institutional Theory of Law: New Approaches to Legal Positivism*, Dordrecht: Reidel. (This is the 'manifesto' of neo-institutionalism, comprising a collection of essays independently written by the two authors, together with a jointly-written introduction.)

* Osman, F. (1992) *Les Principes généraux de la lex mercatoria: contribution a l'étude d'un ordre juridique anational*, Paris: Librairie Générale de Droit et de Jurisprudence. (An application of Santi Romano's pluralistic theory of legal orders to the concept of the *lex mercatoria* or 'Law Merchant' in its modern form.)

* Renard, G. (1930) *La Théorie de l'institution. Essai d'ontologie juridique*, Paris: Sirey. (A prolix and sprawling piece of work, not an easy read.)

* Romano, S. (1917–18) *L'ordinamento giuridico* (Juridical Order), Florence: Sansoni, 2nd edn, 1946; 3rd edn, 1967. (This is Romano's chief work on 'juridical order', a concise and beautifully written account of his theory of the institution and its place in our understanding of legal order. The second edition is identical with the first, save for an updating note; the third is simply a reprint of the second.)

* Schmitt, C. (1934) *Über drei Arten des rechtswissenschaftlichen Denkens*, Hamburg. (A lucid and straightforward exposition of the fundamentals of Schmitt's decisionism, through an account of what he took to be the three basic types of purely legal thinking. Indispensable reading.)

* Searle, J.R. (1969) *Speech Acts: An Essay in the Philosophy of Language*, Cambridge: Cambridge

University Press. (This is the 'classical' account of institutional facts and constitutive rules.)

Translated by D.N. MacCormick

ANNA PINTORE

INSTRUMENTALISM

see CONVENTIONALISM; DEWEY, JOHN; FICTIONALISM; LAWS, NATURAL; SCIENTIFIC REALISM AND ANTIREALISM

INTELLECTUALS, RESPONSIBILITIES OF

see RESPONSIBILITIES OF SCIENTISTS AND INTELLECTUALS

INTENSIONAL ENTITIES

Intensional entities are such things as concepts, propositions and properties. What makes them 'intensional' is that they violate the principle of extensionality; the principle that equivalence implies identity. For example, the concept of being a (well-formed) creature with a kidney and the concept of being a (well-formed) creature with a heart are equivalent in so far as they apply to the same things, but they are different concepts. Likewise, although the proposition that creatures with kidneys have kidneys and the proposition that creatures with hearts have kidneys are equivalent (both are true), they are not identical. Intensional entities are contrasted with extensional entities such as sets, which do satisfy the principle of extensionality. For example, the set of creatures with kidneys and the set of creatures with hearts are equivalent in so far as they have the same members and, accordingly, are identical. By this standard criterion, each of the following philosophically important types of entity is intensional: qualities, attributes, properties, relations, conditions, states, concepts, ideas, notions, propositions and thoughts.

All (or most) of these intensional entities have been classified at one time or another as kinds of universals. Accordingly, standard traditional views about the ontological status of universals carry over to intensional entities. Nominalists hold that they do not really exist.

Conceptualists accept their existence but deem it to be mind-dependent. Realists hold that they are mind-independent. Ante rem realists hold that they exist independently of being true of anything; in re realists require that they be true of something.

1 History
2 Extensional reductions
3 Non-reductionist approaches

1 History

Contemporary use of the term 'intension' derives from the traditional logical doctrine that an idea has both an extension and an intension (or comprehension). This doctrine is explicit in most modern logicians of the nineteenth century, implicit in many medieval logicians and, arguably, present in Porphyry and Aristotle. Although there is divergence in formulation, most of these thinkers accept that the extension of an idea (or concept) consists of the subjects to which the idea applies, and the intension consists of the attributes implied by the idea. The Port Royalists (see Arnauld 1662) tell us, 'the comprehension of the idea of triangle includes extension, figure, three lines, three angles, and the equality of these three angles to two right angles, and so forth'. This yields the 'law of inverse ratio': the larger the intension, the smaller the extension. (Note that these traditional doctrines were expressed with the use of plurals and without explicit commitment to classes or sets.) If the extension consists of the individuals (as opposed to species) to which an idea applies, it is evident that two ideas could have the same extension but different intensions. This is the tie to Russell's subsequent notion of an intensional propositional function (1910–13) and leads to our contemporary usage of 'intensional entity' and 'extensional entity'.

In contemporary philosophy, it is linguistic expressions, rather than concepts, that are said to have intensions and extensions. The intension is the concept expressed by the expression, and the extension is the set of items to which the expression applies. On the standard picture, that set is the same as the set of items to which the concept applies, hence the standard view that intension determines extension. This usage resembles Mill's use of 'denotation' and 'connotation' and Frege's use of '*Bedeutung*' and '*Sinn*' (see MILL, J.S. §§2–3; FREGE, G. §3).

The systematic study of intensional entities has been pursued largely in the context of intensional logic; that part of logic in which the principle of substitutivity of equivalent expressions fails. For example, 'Necessarily, creatures with kidneys have kidneys' is true whereas 'Necessarily, creatures with hearts have kidneys' is false. Following Frege (1892), Whitehead and Russell (1910–13), Carnap (1947) and Church (1951), the now standard explanation of this failure of substitutivity is this: the truth-value of these sentences is determined, not (just) by the extension of 'creature with kidney' and 'creature with heart' (that is, the set of creatures with kidneys) but (also) by the intensions of these expressions, that is, by the intensional entities which they express (the concept of being a creature with a kidney and the concept of being a creature with a heart). Because these intensions are different, the sentences can have different truth-values.

This account yields a method for determining precise intensional identity conditions: intensional entities should be as finely discriminated as is necessary for explaining associated substitutivity failures in intensional logic. For example, this method has led most philosophers to hold that logically equivalent concepts can be distinct, and even that in a correct definition the definiens and the definiendum can express different concepts. This is not to say that the properties corresponding to those concepts would be distinct; on the contrary, the definition would be correct only if the properties were identical. Such considerations lead to the view that there are also more coarsely grained intensional entities (properties, relations, conditions in the world). Independent arguments in metaphysics, epistemology, philosophy of science and aesthetics seem to support the same conclusion (see, for example, Armstrong 1978, Bealer 1982, Lewis 1986). On this view, properties and relations (as opposed to concepts) play a primary role in the non-arbitrary categorization and identification of objects, in the constitution of experience, in description and explanation of change, in the theory of inductive inference, in the analysis of objective similarities and in the statement of supervenience principles. In the resulting picture there are both fine-grained intensions, which play the role of cognitive and linguistic contents, and coarse-grained intensions, which play a constitutive role in the structure of the world.

Systematic theories of intensional entities have often incorporated some form of extensional reductionism. The leading reductions (possible worlds, propositional complexes, propositional functions) are critically reviewed below; non-reductionist approaches to intensional entities are then discussed. At issue is the question of what intensional entities *are*. Are they identical to extensional functions, ordered sets, sequences and so on? Or are they *sui generis* entities, belonging to an altogether new category?

2 Extensional reductions

On the possible worlds reduction (see Lewis 1986; Stalnaker 1984), a proposition is either a set of possible worlds or a function from possible worlds to truth-values, and properties are functions from possible worlds to sets of possible (usually non-actual) objects (see SEMANTICS, POSSIBLE WORLDS §9). Many people find the possible worlds theory intuitively implausible. Are familiar sensible properties (for example, colours, shapes, aromas) really functions? When I am aware that I am in pain, is a set (function) of possible worlds really the object of my awareness? Besides this intuitive objection, there are familiar epistemological and metaphysical objections to a theory that is truly committed to the existence of things that do not exist actually. Finally, the possible worlds reduction implies that necessarily equivalent intensions are identical, but as seen above this is implausible in the case of concepts and propositions. Certain possible worlds theorists (for example, Cresswell 1985) have responded to this problem by holding that concepts and propositions are ordered sets (sequences, abstract trees) whose elements are possible worlds constructs. This revisionary view is a variation of the propositional-complex reduction.

According to this reduction (see Perry and Barwise 1983), concepts and propositions are nothing but ordered sets (sequences, abstract trees, partial functions) whose ultimate elements are properties, relations and perhaps individuals. For example, the proposition that you are running is the ordered set ⟨running, you⟩; the proposition that you are running and I am walking is

$$\langle conjunction, \langle running, you \rangle, \langle walking, me \rangle \rangle;$$

and so forth. As with the possible worlds theory, this theory clashes with intuition. When I am aware that I am in pain, is an ordered set the object of my awareness? When I see that you are running, do I see an ordered set? Furthermore, there is in principle no way to determine which ordered set I allegedly see. Is it ⟨running, you⟩? Or is it ⟨you, running⟩? The choice seems utterly arbitrary, but if the reduction were correct, there would have to be a fact of the matter.

A rather different kind of difficulty arises in connection with 'transmodal quantification'. Consider the following intuitively true sentence:

(1) Every x is such that, necessarily, for every y, it is either possible or impossible that $x = y$.

In symbols,

(2) $(\forall x)\square(\forall y)(\text{Possible } [x = y] \vee \text{Impossible } [x = y])$.

By the propositional-complex theory, this is equivalent to

(3) $(\forall x)\square(\forall y)($Possible $\langle x, \text{identity}, y\rangle$

Impossible $\vee\ \langle x, \text{identity}, y\rangle)$.

The singular term '$\langle x, \text{identity}, y\rangle$' may be thought of as a definite description, 'the ordered set whose elements are x, identity and y'. Accordingly, there are two ways to understand (3). On the first construal (corresponding to the narrow scope reading of the definite description), (3) implies

$(\forall x)\square(\forall y)(\exists v)v = \langle x, \text{identity}, y\rangle$.

However, by the principle that, necessarily, a set exists only if its elements exist, this implies

$(\forall x)\square(\exists v)v = x$.

That is, everything necessarily exists. A manifest falsehood. On the alternative construal of (3), corresponding to the wide scope reading of the definite description, 'the ordered set $\langle x, \text{identity}, y\rangle$', (3) implies that every x is such that, necessarily, for all y, there exists an actual set $\langle x, \text{identity}, y\rangle$. That is

$(\forall x)\square(\forall y)(\exists_{\text{actual}} v)v = \langle x, \text{identity}, y\rangle$.

But, by the principle that, necessarily, a set is actual only if its elements are actual, this implies

$\square(\forall y)y$ is actual.

That is, necessarily, everything (including everything that could exist) is already actual. Another manifest falsehood. So either way, (3) implies something false. But (3) is the propositional-complex theorists' way of representing the true sentence (2). So the propositional-complex theory appears unable to handle intuitively true sentences such as (2). (This style of argument can be exploited in a defence of *ante rem* realism.)

According to the propositional-function theory (see Whitehead and Russell 1910–13), a property is a function from objects to propositions, where propositions are taken to be primitive entities. For example, the property 'being red' is the function (λx)(the proposition that x is red). For any given object x, the proposition that x is red is the result of applying this function to the argument x. That is, the proposition that x is red is (λx)(the proposition that x is red)(x). But are the familiar sensible properties really functions? Once again, this is highly implausible and should be rejected on this ground alone if an acceptable alternative exists.

Besides this sort of intuitive difficulty, there are several technical difficulties. Consider an illustration involving properties of integers. Being even = being

an x such that x is divisible by two; and being self-divisible = being an x such that x is divisible by x. Given the propositional-function theory, the following identities hold:

that two is even $= (\lambda x)($that x is even$)($two$)$

$= (\lambda x)($that x is divisible by two$)($two$)$

$=$ that two is divisible by two

$= (\lambda x)($that x is divisible by $x)($two$)$

$= (\lambda x)($that x is self-divisible$)($two$)$

$=$ that two is self-divisible.

However, that two is even and that two is self-divisible are plainly different propositions: certainly someone could be consciously and explicitly thinking the former while not consciously and explicitly thinking the latter. Indeed, someone who is thinking that two is even might never have considered the concept of self-divisibility. (Analogous difficulties arise for Church's somewhat similar propositional-function theory of concepts (1951). Incidentally, since properties are not propositional functions, using function abstracts to denote them invites confusion. A growing practice is to use $\ulcorner[v: A]\urcorner$ to denote the property of being a v such that A, just as in set theory $\ulcorner\{v: A\}\urcorner$ denotes the set of things v such that A.)

3 Non-reductionist approaches

Each of the preceding problems arises from the attempt to reduce intensional entities of one kind or another to extensional entities; either extensional functions or sets. These difficulties have led some theorists to adopt non-reductionist approaches (see Bealer 1979, 1982). Consider the following truisms. The proposition that $A\&B$ is the conjunction of the proposition that A and the proposition that B. The proposition that not A is the negation of the proposition that A. The proposition that Fx is the predication of the property F of x. The proposition that there exists an F is the existential generalization of the property F, and so on. These truisms tell us what these propositions essentially are: they are by nature conjunctions, negations, singular predications, existential generalizations and so on. These are rudimentary facts which require no further explanation and for which no further explanation is possible. Until the advent of extensionalism, this was the standard view.

By adapting techniques developed in the algebraic tradition in extensional logic, one is able to develop this non-reductionistic approach. Examples such as those just given isolate fundamental logical operations: conjunction, negation, singular predication, existential generalization and so on. Intensional entities are then taken as *sui generis* entities; the aim is to analyse their behaviour with respect to the fundamental logical operations.

An intensional algebra is a structure consisting of a domain D, a set of logical operations and a set of possible extensionalization functions. The domain divides into subdomains: particulars, propositions, properties, binary relations, ternary relations and so on. The set of logical operations includes those listed above plus certain auxiliary operations. The possible extensionalization functions assign a possible extension to relevant items in the domain: each proposition is assigned a truth-value; each property is assigned a set of items in D; each binary relation is assigned a set of ordered pairs of items in D, and so on. One extensionalization function is singled out as the actual extensionalization function: the propositions which are true relative to it are the propositions which are actually true, and so on. (More formally, an intensional algebra is a structure $\langle D, \tau, K, G \rangle$. D divides into subdomains: $D_{-1}, D_0, D_1, D_2, \ldots$. D_{-1} consists of particulars; D_0, propositions; D_1, properties; D_2, binary relations, and so on. τ is a set of logical operations on D. K is a set of extensionalization functions. G is a distinguished function in K which is the actual extensionalization function.)

To illustrate how this approach works, consider the operation of conjunction, conj. Let H be an extensionalization function. Then, conj satisfies the following: for all propositions p and q in D, $H(\text{conj}(p, q)) = \text{true}$ iff $H(p) = \text{true}$ and $H(q) = \text{true}$. Similarly, if neg is the operation of negation, then for all propositions p in D, $H(\text{neg}(p)) = \text{true}$ iff $H(p) = \text{false}$. Likewise, for singular predication preds, which takes properties F in D and items y in D to propositions in D: $H(\text{pred}_s(F, y)) = \text{true}$ iff y is in the extension $H(F)$.

This non-reductionistic approach can be extended to more complex settings in which, for example, both fine-grained intensional entities (concepts, propositions) and coarse-grained intensional entities (properties, relations, conditions) are treated concurrently and in which a relation of correspondence between the two types of intensional entities can be characterized in terms of the fundamental logical operations. The non-reductionist approach can thus accommodate the fine-grained intensional entities which serve as cognitive and linguistic contents and also the more coarsely grained intensional entities which play a constitutive role in the structure of the world.

See also: NOMINALISM; INTENSIONAL LOGICS; LOGICAL AND MATHEMATICAL TERMS, GLOSSARY OF; MODAL LOGIC, PHILOSOPHICAL ISSUES IN; SECOND-ORDER LOGIC, PHILOSOPHICAL ISSUES IN; PROPERTY THEORY

References and further reading

Aczel, P. (1980) 'Frege Structures and the Notions of Propositions, Truth and Set', in J. Keisler, J. Barwise and K. Kunen (eds) *The Kleene Symposium*, Amsterdam: North Holland, 31–59. (Development of the propositional-function view.)

* Armstrong, D.M. (1978) *A Theory of Universals*, Cambridge: Cambridge University Press. (Study of coarse-grained intensional entities, discussed at close of §1.)

* Arnauld, A. (1662) *Logic, or the Art of Thinking: The Port-Royal Logic*, trans. T.S. Baynes, Edinburgh: Sutherland & Knox, 1850. (Presentation of the traditional doctrine of intension and extension, discussed in §1.)

* Bealer, G. (1979) 'Theories of Properties, Relations, and Propositions', *Journal of Philosophy* 76: 643–8. (Development of the non-reductionist view discussed in §3.)

* —— (1982) *Quality and Concept*, Oxford: Clarendon Press. (Expansion of the material in §1 and development of the non-reductionist view discussed in §3.)

* Carnap, R. (1947) *Meaning and Necessity*, Chicago, IL: University of Chicago Press. (Early presentation of the contemporary use of 'intension' and 'extension' and precursor to the possible worlds theory.)

* Church, A. (1951) 'A Formulation of the Logic of Sense and Denotation', in P. Henle, H.H. Kallen, S.K. Langer (eds) *Structure, Method, and Meaning: Essays in Honor of Henry M. Scheffer*, New York: Liberal Arts Press, 3–24. (Development of a Fregean version of the propositional-function view.)

* Cresswell, M.J. (1985) *Structured Meanings*, Cambridge, MA: MIT Press. (A combination of the possible worlds theory and the propositional-complex theory.)

* Frege, G. (1892) 'Über Sinn und Bedeutung', *Zeitschrift für Philosophie und philosophische Kritik* 100: 25–50; trans. M. Black, 'On Sense and Meaning', in *Translations from the Philosophical Writings of Gottlob Frege*, ed. P.T. Geach and M. Black, Oxford: Blackwell, 3rd edn, 1980. (Defence of the theory that meaningful expressions typically have both a sense and a reference.)

* Lewis, D.K. (1986) *On the Plurality of Worlds*, Oxford: Blackwell. (Defence of coarse-grained intensions and the possible worlds theory.)

Menzel, C. (1986) 'A Complete Type-Free "Second-

Order" Logic and its Philosophical Foundations', in *Report No. CSLI-86-40*, Stanford, CA: Center for the Study of Language and Information, Stanford University. (Development of the non-reductionist view discussed in §3.)

Parsons, T. (1980) *Nonexistent Objects*, New Haven, CT: Yale University Press. (Development of the non-reductionist view in combination with a Meinongian theory of nonexistent objects.)

* Perry, J. and Barwise, J. (1983) *Situations and Attitudes*, Cambridge, MA: MIT Press. (Development of the propositional-complex view.)

Salmon, N. (1986) *Frege's Puzzle*, Cambridge, MA: MIT Press. (Development of the propositional-complex view.)

* Stalnaker, R. (1984) *Inquiry*, Cambridge, MA: MIT Press. (Defence of the possible worlds view.)

Turner, R. (1991) *Truth and Modality for Knowledge Representation*, Cambridge, MA: MIT Press. (Development of the propositional-function view.)

* Whitehead, A.N. and Russell, B.A.W. (1910–13) *Principia Mathematica*, vol. 1, Cambridge: Cambridge University Press, 3 vols; 2nd edn, 1925–7. (A classic of mathematical logic, which includes a development of intensional logic based on the propositional-function theory.)

Zalta, E. (1988) *Intensional Logic and the Metaphysics of Intentionality*, Cambridge, MA: MIT Press. (Development of the non-reductionist view in combination with a Meinongian theory of nonexistent objects.)

GEORGE BEALER

INTENSIONAL LOGICS

Intensional logics are systems that distinguish an expression's intension (roughly, its sense or meaning) from its extension (reference, denotation). The purpose of bringing intensions into logic is to explain the logical behaviour of so-called intensional expressions. Intensional expressions create contexts which violate a cluster of standard principles of logic, the most notable of which is the law of substitution of identities – the law that from a = b and P(a) it follows that P(b). For example, 'obviously' is intensional because the following instance of the law of substitution is invalid (at least on one reading): Scott = the author of Waverley; *obviously Scott = Scott; so, obviously Scott = the author of* Waverley. *By providing an analysis of meaning, intensional logics attempt to explain the logical behaviour of expressions such as 'obviously'. On the assumption that it is intensions and not extensions*

which matter in intensional contexts, the failure of substitution and related anomalies can be understood.

Alonzo Church pioneered intensional logic, basing it on his theory of types. However, the widespread application of intensional logic to linguistics and philosophy began with the work of Richard Montague, who crafted a number of systems designed to capture the expressive power of natural languages. One important feature of Montague's work was the application of possible worlds semantics to the analysis of intensional logic. The most difficult problems concerning intensional logic concern the treatment of propositional attitude verbs, such as 'believes', 'desires' and 'knows'. Such expressions pose difficulties for the possible worlds treatment, and have thus spawned alternative approaches.

1 **Intension and extension**
2 **Possible worlds semantics**
3 **Montague's intensional logic**
4 **The problem of propositional attitudes**
5 **Alternative approaches**

1 Intension and extension

Gottlob FREGE believed that expressions of language have both an extension (reference, denotation) and an intension (sense, meaning; see SENSE AND REFERENCE). He distinguished intensions from extensions to explain a failure of the law of substitution of identity. From 'The author of *Waverley* = Scott' and 'John admires the author of *Waverley*' it does not follow that 'John admires Scott', for John may think that Scott wrote *Ulysses*, which he hates. (Frege illustrated the point with 'the morning star' and 'the evening star'.) One way out of the puzzle is to assume that the second sentence reports a relation (of admiration) between John and the meaning (or intension) of 'the author of *Waverley*', rather than a relation between John and the extension of 'the author of *Waverley*', that is, Scott. The fact that the meanings of 'Scott' and 'the author of *Waverley*' differ can help explain why substitution fails.

The failure of substitution in the preceding example is caused by the word 'admires'. Such intensional expressions violate several other standard principles of logic. A notable case is existential generalization: $P(a)$; therefore there exists an x such that $P(x)$. Existential generalization fails because, for example, 'John admires Superman' does not entail that Superman actually exists. The stock of intensional expressions of English is very large. It includes phrases such as 'it is necessary that', 'it used to be the case that', 'believes that', 'it ought to be the case that', and many more.

807

Under a broad construal, intensional logic includes any logic that accounts for the deductive behaviour of one or more of the intensional expressions. So modal logic, tense logic and logics of belief and obligation all count as intensional logics from this point of view. However, the term 'intensional logic' more commonly refers to those systems in which some explicit symbolic device is introduced for distinguishing intensions from extensions. These are the systems described here.

2 Possible worlds semantics

Despite its failings, possible worlds semantics has come to play a central role in intensional logic (see POSSIBLE WORLDS). The basic idea goes back to Rudolf Carnap. Why do the meanings (or intensions) of 'Scott' and 'the author of *Waverley*' differ? Because there are possible worlds where the author of *Waverley* was not Scott. We can imagine a world, for example, where it was James Joyce or Charles Dickens who wrote *Waverley*. If we consider the extensions that 'the author of *Waverley*' takes across different possible worlds, we will see variations from one world to the next. It makes sense, then, to identify the *intension* of the expression with the pattern of its *extensions* across different possible worlds. Seen in this way, its intension is a function that takes each possible world into a corresponding extension. The value of the function is Scott in the real world, Joyce in another world, and Dickens in another. The intension for 'Scott', on the other hand, is the constant function that has the value Scott in each possible world.

Intensions for sentences, predicates and expressions in other grammatical categories can be treated in a similar way. The extension of a sentence is its truth-value. The intension is identified with the pattern of truth-values the sentence takes across the different possible worlds. It is therefore a function that assigns to each possible world a corresponding truth-value. The same tactic can be used for predicates. The extension of the predicate 'is blue' is traditionally taken to be the set of objects that are blue. Its intension is a function that takes each of the possible worlds into a corresponding set of objects (the set of blue objects in that world).

3 Montague's intensional logic

Alonzo Church (1951) was the pioneer in intensional logic, basing it on his theory of types, but Richard Montague's work has been crucial to its widespread application in philosophy and linguistics (see Montague 1974). The system IL described here is a variant of Montague's approach, due to Gallin (1975). Intensions and extensions for sentences, names, predicates, adjectives, prepositions and so on are different sorts of things. Therefore we need to distinguish a rich variety of 'types' (grammatical categories or parts of speech). Most intensional logics are constructed from some form of type theory, a higher-order logic that allows a completely general formation of types (see THEORY OF TYPES; SECOND- AND HIGHER-ORDER LOGICS).

In IL there are two basic types: t for truth-values and e for entities (or objects). Extensions of sentences belong to type t and extensions of proper names belong to type e. An unlimited variety of complex types can be defined from the two basic types as follows. If α and β are types then (α, β) is another type, and if α is a type then so is (s, α), where the letter 's' is used to indicate the set of possible worlds (or situations). The type (α, β) is for the set of all possible functions which assign to each thing with type α a value with type β. For example, if α is the type for the extension of some expression, then (s, α) is the type for its intension.

Extensions and intensions for the different grammatical categories of English can be assigned one of these types in the following way. Extensions of sentences and proper names are of types t and e, respectively, and the types for their intensions are (s, t) and (s, e), respectively. The type for predicate extensions is (e, t): the type for functions that take entities into truth-values. The idea is that the extension for 'is blue' is a function that assigns the truth-value T (for true) to those entities that are blue and F (for false) to those that are not. This has the same effect as treating the extension of 'is blue' as a set of entities, but it simplifies the definition of the complex types. Extensions for transitive verbs should take a pair of entities (one for the subject and one for the object of the verb) into a truth-value, so transitive verb extensions are assigned to type $(e, (e, t))$. The types for intensions of intransitive and transitive verbs would be $(s, (e, t))$ and $(s, (e, (e, t)))$, respectively.

IL has both constants and variables in all the possible types. It also contains the logical symbols '$\equiv$', 'λ', '$^\wedge$', '$^\vee$', '[' and ']'. These symbols allow the construction of complex terms (or expressions). The symbols '$^\wedge$' and '$^\vee$' (called 'cap' and 'cup') indicate the intension and extension of a term, respectively. So when A has type α, $^\wedge A$ is the intension of A and must have type (s, α). When A has type (s, α), then $^\vee A$ is A's extension and belongs to type α. The symbol '$\equiv$' indicates identity. When A and B are two terms of the same type, the expression '$A \equiv B$' belongs to the t (truth-value) type, with the understanding that $A \equiv B$ is true if and only if A and B name the same thing.

[*A B*] indicates the result of applying the function that *A* names to whatever *B* names. So when *A* belongs to type (α, β) and *B* to type α, [*A B*] belongs to type β. For example, if *A* is 'runs' with type (e, t) and *B* is 'John' with type e, then [runs John] has type t, and symbolizes the extension of the English sentence 'John runs'. When x is a variable with type α, and *A* is an expression with type β, then $\lambda x A$ is an expression with type (α, β), indicating functional abstraction. For example, when $A =$ 'Mary loves x', $\lambda x A$ names the function that assigns to each entity o either T or F depending on whether Mary loves o or not. Hence, in this example, $\lambda x A$ corresponds to the predicate 'is loved by Mary'.

IL has strong expressive powers. All of the symbols of predicate logic can be defined in it – including propositional connectives (negation, conjunction and so on) and quantifiers in all the types. Furthermore, the presence of '$^\wedge$' ensures that an S5 strength modal operator '$\square$' (read 'it is necessary that') can be defined (for a description of S5, see MODAL LOGIC). IL is on a firm technical footing. Gallin has devised rules and axioms for IL and has shown how to provide a (generalized) semantics for this system for which IL is both consistent and complete.

Intensional logics such as IL have been applied to tenses, necessity, obligation and many other intensional constructions. The same ideas can be used to analyse indexicals such as 'I', 'it' and 'that', with the understanding that possible worlds include contexts of utterance that help fix the extensions of these terms. A hint at how IL is applied to language can be given by showing how to explain the failure of substitution in the case of John's admiring the author of *Waverley*. Assume that each of the words of English is assigned an appropriate type of IL. The verb 'admires' is intensional, meaning that the object of the verb is an *intension* of type (s, e). So the extension of 'admires' falls in type $(e, ((s, e), t))$, not $(e, (e, t))$. It follows that 'John admires Scott' is represented in IL by [[admires John] $^\wedge S$], where S abbreviates 'Scott'. The cap '$^\wedge$' makes it clear that it is the intension of 'Scott' that is at issue. Similarly, [[admires John] $^\wedge W$] represents 'John admires the author of *Waverley*'. The claim that Scott is the author of *Waverley* is written '$S \equiv W$'. Since $S \equiv W$ only says that S and W have the same *extension*, the inference from $S \equiv W$ and [[admires John] $^\wedge W$] to [[admires John] $^\wedge S$] is invalid. An identity involving S and W does not warrant substitution of $^\wedge S$ for $^\wedge W$.

4 The problem of propositional attitudes

While intensional logics in the style of IL appear to work nicely in the case of tense, necessity, obligation,

indexicals and the like, serious problems arise in certain cases when IL is applied to so-called propositional attitude verbs, such as 'believes', 'wants', 'knows' and 'admires' (see PROPOSITIONAL ATTITUDE STATEMENTS). The fundamental difficulty is that systems based on IL validate substitution of *necessary* identities: if expressions *A* and *B* have the same extensions in every possible world, then an occurrence of *A* in one expression may be replaced with an occurrence of *B* in another. But such substitution is not valid for propositional attitude verbs. For example, John can know that 17×3 is composite (not prime) but fail to know that 51 is composite, even though in every possible world $17 \times 3 = 51$.

The difficulty is more than a quirk about mathematical expressions. It is widely held that proper names and natural kind terms are rigid designators, that is, that they have the same extension (or none) in every possible world. So substitution of pairs of names ('Cicero', 'Tully') or natural kind terms ('water', 'H_2O') that have the same extensions should be correct in all contexts. However, John can admire Cicero without admiring Tully (even though Cicero *was* Tully), and he can know that water is safe to drink, without knowing that H_2O is safe to drink (even though water *is* H_2O). The distinctions between intensions defined by possible worlds semantics appear to be too crude to explain the failure of substitution in propositional attitude contexts.

5 Alternative approaches

Alternatives to the possible worlds approach in intensional logic have grown out of the desire to resolve problems including that of propositional attitudes. One natural reaction is to dispense with talk of intensions altogether, and to explain John's different reactions to the ideas that 17×3 and 51 are composite as due to his different relationships with the symbols '17×3' and '51'. However, 'John knows 17×3 is composite' cannot report a relation between John and the symbol '17×3', because this sentence can be true even when John has never seen the symbols '17×3'.

Max Cresswell's solution to the problem, following Carnap, is to bring in what he calls structured meanings (1985). The meaning of atomic expressions can be given by a possible worlds account. For example, the meaning of '51' can be the function that picks out 51 in every possible world. For complex expressions, such as '17×3', the meaning is a structure, $\langle \text{times}, 17, 3 \rangle$, composed of the meanings of the sub-expressions 'times', '17' and '3'. Note that $\langle \text{times}, 17, 3 \rangle$ is not itself a symbol, but does preserve the structure of '17×3', thereby allowing the meanings of '17×3' and '51' to differ.

Since neither 'Cicero' nor 'Tully' is complex, Cresswell must use different tactics to manage this case. One strategy he discusses is to analyse 'John admires Cicero' as 'John admires the person he calls Cicero'. (However, since Cresswell believes propositional attitude statements are essentially ambiguous, this is not his final word on the topic.)

Other approaches abandon entirely the possible worlds account of intensions. Anderson, for example, presents an intensional logic whose semantics is based on the notion of synonymy (1984). The idea is that the rules of a language allow us to define the class of synonyms for an atomic expression (that is, the set of expressions with the same intension), called its 'concept'. Concepts for complex expressions can be built up from the concepts for simple expressions. Expressions of the language are indexed so that A_1 indicates the concept for expression A. The problem of the failure of substitution of necessary identities in propositional attitude contexts is solved as follows. We assume that the verb 'admires' is intensional, so it must take expressions for concepts, not expressions for extensions. So 'Cicero is Tully' is represented by $c = t$, while 'John admires Cicero' is represented by Ajc_1, where the index 1 indicates that it is the *concept* of Cicero (c_1) that is at issue. But now Ajt_1 (for 'John admires Tully') does not follow, since $c = t$ does not warrant substitution of t_1 for c_1. On the plausible assumption that 'Cicero' and 'Tully' are not synonymous (that is, do not have the same intension), the substitution can be blocked as desired. Note, however, that ordinary intuitions rule that 'water' is synonymous with 'H$_2$O', and that '17×3' is synonymous with '51'. Hence the ordinary notion of synonymy cannot explain the failure of substitution in these cases. For a general solution to the problem, Anderson must employ a notion of synonymy that is at odds with ordinary intuitions.

Zalta (1988) lays synonymy aside, and introduces abstract objects to serve as the meanings of intensional expressions. Abstract objects may be thought of as visual images or other mental encodings used to represent features of the world. An extensional term c and its corresponding intensional term c_p belong to the same type, and the subscript p indicates which person does the encoding. Using this machinery, 'John admires Cicero' is represented by $A(j, c_j)$, where c_j indicates John's encoding of Cicero. Note that the encodings named by c_j ('Cicero') and t_j ('Tully') may be distinct. Since the notation for 'Cicero = Tully' ($c = t$) lacks the index j, this claim does not warrant substitution of t_j for c_j in $A(j, c_j)$.

See also: Intensional entities; Logical and mathematical terms, glossary of

References and further reading

* Anderson, C.A. (1984) 'General Intensional Logic', in D. Gabbay and F. Guenthner (eds) *Handbook of Philosophical Logic*, Dordrecht: Reidel, vol. 2, 355–85. (A clear and useful introduction to intensional logics, including an account of IL. See §§3, 5.)

Barwise, J. and Perry, J. (1983) *Situations and Attitudes*, Cambridge, MA: MIT Press. (An enjoyable introduction to situation semantics, an influential outgrowth of possible worlds semantics for intensional logic.)

* Church, A. (1951) 'A Formulation of the Logic of Sense and Denotation', in *Structure, Method, and Meaning*, New York: Liberal Arts Press. (The seminal work in intensional logic, mentioned in §3.)

* Cresswell, M.J. (1985) *Structured Meanings*, Cambridge, MA: MIT Press. (Referred to in §5. An accessible account of an intensional logic based on structured meanings.)

* Gallin, D. (1975) *Intensional and Higher-Order Modal Logic*, Amsterdam: North Holland. (The classic formulation of Montague's approach to intensional logic. Somewhat technical.)

* Montague, R. (1974) *Formal Philosophy: Selected Papers of Richard Montague*, ed. R.H. Thomason, New Haven, CT: Yale University Press. (A collection of Richard Montague's papers prefaced by a very helpful introduction describing the application of intensional logic to natural language.)

* Zalta, E.N. (1988) *Intensional Logic and the Metaphysics of Intensionality*, Cambridge, MA: MIT Press. (An accessible account of Zalta's approach to intensional logic described in §5.)

JAMES W. GARSON

INTENSIONALITY

The truth or falsity of many sentences depends only on which things are being talked about. Within intensional contexts, however, truth values also depend on how those things are talked about, not just on which things they are. Philosophers and logicians have offered different analyses of intensional contexts and the behaviour of terms occurring within them.

The extension of a term is the thing or things it picks out: for instance, the extension of 'the Big Dipper' is the stellar constellation itself. The intension of a term can be thought of as the way in which it picks out its extension. 'The Big Dipper' and 'the Plough' have the same extension – a particular constellation – but pick it out in different ways. The two terms have different intensions. There is much debate about how we should actually understand the notion of an intension (see INTENSIONAL ENTITIES).

For many classes of sentence, the substitution of one term for another with the same extension leaves the truth value unchanged, irrespective of whether the two terms also have the same intension. This is called intersubstitution *salva veritate* (preserving truth). For instance, if it is true that the Big Dipper consists of seven stars, then it is also true that the Plough consists of seven stars. In a number of important cases, however, terms with the same extension but different intensions are not intersubstituable *salva veritate*. Consider, for instance:

1 Tom believes that the Big Dipper consists of seven stars.
2 Tom believes that the Plough consists of seven stars.

It is quite possible that Tom mistakenly believes that 'the Plough' refers to a totally different constellation consisting of only six stars, in which case (1) could be true and (2) false. Co-extensive terms cannot be intersubstituted *salva veritate* within the scope of the verb 'believes'. Such contexts are called intensional.

Other verbs which, like 'believe', refer to propositional attitudes – verbs like 'hope', 'desire', 'fear' – also create intensional contexts (see PROPOSITIONAL ATTITUDE STATEMENTS). Propositional attitudes are *intentional* states (note the 't') which has led some to consider the possible connections between inten*S*ionality and inten*T*ionality (see INTENTIONALITY §2). The two must be distinguished carefully, however, not least because intensional contexts are also created by non-psychological terms, most importantly modal terms like 'necessarily' and 'possibly'. The intensionality of modal contexts leads to particular difficulties when they also involve quantification (see MODAL LOGIC, PHILOSOPHICAL ISSUES IN §3); these problems have led to controversies over the interpretation not only of modal terms but also of the quantifiers (see MODAL OPERATORS; QUANTIFIERS, SUBSTITUTIONAL AND OBJECTUAL §1).

The failure of intersubstitutability *salva veritate* raises questions about the behaviour of terms in intensional contexts. Frege (1892) argues that, in intensional contexts, the term 'the Big Dipper' in (1) refers not to the Big Dipper as usual but to its own intension (or, in Frege's terminology, its sense; see INDIRECT DISCOURSE §1; PROPER NAMES §5; SENSE

AND REFERENCE §5). Quine (1956, 1961) describes intensional contexts as *referentially opaque*, arguing that terms occurring within them do not refer at all (see PROPOSITIONAL ATTITUDE STATEMENTS §2; MODAL OPERATORS §1). Davidson's (1969) *paratactic* analysis of propositional attitude statements and of indirect discourse, another intensional context, tries to preserve our intuition that terms in intensional contexts work in the same way as in any other contexts (see INDIRECT DISCOURSE §2; PROPOSITIONAL ATTITUDE STATEMENTS §3).

Many philosophers think that logic should have nothing to do with intensions. But the intensionality of many natural language contexts is hard to deny, and the development of intensional logics suggests that a more tolerant attitude might well pay off (see INTENSIONAL LOGICS).

See also: CONCEPTS; REFERENCE; SEMANTICS, POSSIBLE WORLDS

References and further reading

* Davidson, D. (1969) 'On Saying That', *Synthese* 19: 130–46; repr. in D. Davidson and J. Hintikka (eds) *Words and Objections: Essays on the Work of W.V. Quine*, Dordrecht: Reidel, 158–74. (Davidson's paratactic analysis of indirect discourse.)
* Frege, G. (1892) 'Über Sinn und Bedeutung', *Zeitschrift für Philosophie und philosophische Kritik* 100: 25–50; trans. M. Black as 'On Sense and Reference', *Translations from the Philosophical Writings of Gottlob Frege*, ed. P.T. Geach and M. Black, Oxford: Blackwell, 1962, 56–78. (Frege's seminal discussion of failures of intersubstitution and distinction between sense and reference.)
* Quine, W.V. (1956) 'Quantifiers and the Propositional Attitudes', *The Ways of Paradox*, Cambridge MA: Harvard University Press, 1976. (Quine on referential opacity.)
* —— (1961) 'Reference and Modality', *From a Logical Point of View*, Cambridge, MA: Harvard University Press, 2nd edn, 1980; repr. in L. Linsky (ed.) *Reference and Modality*, Oxford: Oxford University Press, 1971. (Quine on the referential opacity of modal contexts. The Linsky collection contains some fairly difficult discussions.)
Searle, J.R. (1983) *Intentionality*, Cambridge: Cambridge University Press. (Chapter 1 contains a useful discussion of the relationship between inten*S*ionality and inten*T*ionality.)

SIMON CHRISTMAS

INTENTION

Suppose that Kevin intends to brush up on his predicate logic, and acts on this intention, because he wants to conduct a good tutorial and he believes that some preparatory revision will help him to do so. In an example like this, we explain why Kevin intends to revise his logic, and why he (intentionally) does revise it, by appealing to the belief and desire which provide his reasons both for his intention and his corresponding intentional action. But how does Kevin's intention to act, coming between his reasons and his action, help to explain what he does? Central questions in the theory of intention include the following: Are intentions distinct mental attitudes or are they analysable in terms of other mental attitudes – such as beliefs and desires? How is intending to do something related to judging that it is best to do it? What distinctive roles, if any, do intentions play in getting us to act? Are foreseen but undesired consequences of an intentional action intended?

1   Intention and belief

Is intending to act a belief that one (probably) will? The identification of intending to act in a certain way with a belief that one (probably) will so act is misguided since even the weaker thesis that intending to act in a certain way implies the belief that one (probably) will is too strong. Thus Kevin may intend to go to the gym (after revising his logic) while harbouring serious doubts about whether he will, which leave him agnostic about the future – for he may know only too well his tendency to balk at doing painful things when the time for action comes, or even to forget his good intentions in such cases. A principal motive for holding the thesis that intending to act implies believing that one (probably) will has been the concern to distinguish intentions from mere hopes or wishes, but such counterexamples show that the distinction will have to be drawn in some other way. Some philosophers hold that there is a minimal positive belief constraint on intention: intention implies the belief that one has some chance of achieving what one intends (see Davidson 1985). Others think that at most one can insist on a negative constraint: intention implies that one does not believe that one (probably) will not do as one intends. Still other philosophers prefer to interpret such a negative

belief constraint as a rationality condition on intention. It is not possible to adjudicate these issues here.

Even where an intention to act is matched by a belief that one (probably) will so act, the two are clearly not identical. Suppose an agent who intends to A actually does believe that they (probably) will A. The agent's belief (insofar as it is rational) will depend upon their estimate of their chances of A-ing given that they intend to A. So, in such examples, the agent's intention, as a cause of the belief about its presence, will belong, as a distinct item, in the causal background of the (tacit or explicit) reasoning which issues in their belief about what they (probably) will do. Some philosophers have thought that when an intention to act in a certain way corresponds to a belief about what one will do, the belief is not properly construed as based on evidence. Indeed, some even hold the belief in such cases to be noninferential. If the above account is correct, such a belief has perfectly familiar sorts of justifying grounds, namely evidential considerations that bear on one's chances of acting in a certain way, including (saliently) one's belief that one intends to act in that way.

2   Intention and desire

Is intending to do something the same as desiring most to do it? Every intention is or incorporates a desire or want in the broadest sense of these terms, since every intention is or incorporates a motivational state. This concession, however, raises a critical issue in the theory of intention. For some philosophers contend that intentions motivate actions because they are or essentially include predominant desires. This cannot be right since there can be intention without predominant desire, and the converse. Plausible examples here typically exploit a functional difference between intention and predominant desire: the former, unlike the latter, characteristically *settles* the question of what to do for an agent. Thus Kevin's intention may track what he thinks it is overall best to do despite his present strongest desire – as when he forms an intention to go to the gym, which he thinks it best to do, despite wanting most to go to the pub. And conversely, Kevin may continue to treat a question of what to do as open, and so not yet have formed an intention about what to do, despite his present strongest desire – as when he continues to wonder about whether to go to the gym, his predominant desire to go to the pub notwithstanding.

Once the conceptual wedge between intention and predominant desire is granted, however, there remains the issue of how to characterize the role of intentions as motivators of intentional actions, given that that role is not reducible to desire strength. A natural move, at this point, is to develop the notion that intentions settle for agents, or commit them on, questions of what to do. Such accounts suggest an intuitive contrast between intentions as executive desires and other mere desires. Intentions involve first-order dispositions to act (intentionally), whereas mere desires involve second-order dispositions to act (intentionally). That is, mere desires are or include dispositions to acquire such first-order dispositions to act as are involved in intentions.

Theories of intention which emphasize the notion that intentions settle for agents, or commit them on, questions of what to do have a further virtue. They are especially well-suited to do justice to the several important functional roles which mark out intentions as a group. These functions are that intentions initiate, sustain and guide intentional actions, are elements in coordinative plans, and prompt and terminate practical reasoning.

3 Intention and evaluation

Is intending to act an evaluative attitude? Donald Davidson (1978) construes desires and intentions as evaluative attitudes. Desires are conditional evaluations, the contents of which are expressible in judgments of the form: 'It is desirable for me to A insofar as my A-ing is F.' Thus the content of Kevin's desire to go to the gym would be expressible as (say): 'It is desirable for me to go to the gym insofar as my going to the gym will help me to keep fit.' Intentions are unconditional or all-out evaluations, the contents of which are expressible in judgments of the form: 'It is desirable (intention-worthy) for me to A.' Thus the content of Kevin's intention to go to the gym would be expressible as: 'It is desirable (intention-worthy) for me to go to the gym.' One of Davidson's chief concerns is how to set out schematically the form of practical reasoning, which contains a mix of cognitive and conative propositional attitudes. By distinguishing among the propositional expressions of attitudes, Davidson hopes to mark differences among the attitudes. His economical proposal is to let ordinary indicative sentences express the contents of 'factual' beliefs and to let indicatives with explicitly evaluative words express the contents of conative attitudes like desires and intentions. Intentions are then distinguished from mere desires by the all-out or unconditional form of the evaluative sentences which express them. On Davidson's account, the inferential step wherein an agent comes to have an intention (forms an all-out evaluation by detachment from a corresponding conditional one) is treated as analogous to the inferential step wherein a believer comes to have an inductive belief that a proposition is simply true or

false (by detachment from a corresponding subjective probability assessment).

Davidson's evaluative theory of intention has proved contentious. One issue is whether he is right about the logical form of evaluative sentences. For example, Davidson construes the conditional judgment that it is desirable for me to A insofar as my A-ing is F as having the logical form: 'It is prima facie desirable for me to A insofar as my A-ing is F', which he symbolizes as: pf (It is desirable for me to A, my A-ing is F) to bring out the point that these judgments are thought of as the result of applying a 'prima facie' operator to a pair of sentences related as evaluation and ground. Such judgments supposedly parallel probabilistic ones of the form: 'it is probable that it will rain insofar as rain is forecast.'

A second issue is whether, even if he is correct about logical form, Davidson is right to assimilate detached, unconditional evaluations to intentions to act. There are, in fact, good general reasons to resist the assimilation of conative attitudes to evaluative ones. Such reasons have to do with the explanatory value in philosophical psychology of being able to admit fractures between evaluation and corresponding desire or intention (see AKRASIA). Yet there is a need for caution here with respect to one of Davidson's chief preoccupations – namely, the issue of how to represent the form of practical reasoning. For, even if desires and intentions are different from evaluative attitudes, it remains a viable option that sentences expressing the latter are appropriate for marking the former in schematic representations of practical reasoning. The symmetrical line of thought here would be that just as sentences about what is true (belief-worthy) are appropriate for marking beliefs in theoretical cases, sentences about what is desirable in some way or intention-worthy are appropriate for marking conative attitudes in practical cases. Of course, a difference would also have to be conceded, once the difference between conative and evaluative attitudes was conceded. Sentences about what is true (or their equivalents) would count as expressing the contents of beliefs; whereas sentences about what is desirable or intention-worthy would count as expressing the contents of justifying evaluative judgments which corresponded to (without being identical with) conative attitudes.

4 Intentions as self-referential

Are intentions self-referential? When an agent intends to act in a certain way, does the content of the intention make essential reference to the intention itself?

On some proposals the self-referentiality thesis can

be characterized (roughly) as follows: an intention to *A* is the intention that, because of this very intention, one will *A*. So, if Kevin intends to brush up on his predicate logic, then (more fully) he intends that, as a result of this very intention, he will so act. Such proposals have an obvious curious feature: they tend to conflate standard cases of intending with special cases of self-control where an agent forms an intention with the higher-order intention of thereby bringing it about that they will act in a certain way.

One standard defence of the self-referentiality thesis is that it explains why some intended behaviour falls short of intentional action (see the discussion of deviant causal chains in ACTION; REASONS AND CAUSES §3). Consider just one kind of example. Suppose that Kevin intends to shoot an intruder. He aims his gun but, at the crucial moment, is startled by a moving shadow, which causes him to contract his finger, so that he shoots the intruder – but not intentionally. Advocates of self-referentiality have made claims like the following: Kevin does not shoot the intruder intentionally in such a case because he does not do what he intends – since his intention to shoot the intruder is the intention that that very intention will lead him to do the shooting at the crucial moment, which does not happen. Such a defence of the self-referentiality thesis is unconvincing since there is a clear, alternative reason why Kevin does not count as an intentional agent in the example, which has nothing to do with the supposed self-referentiality of intentions. Quite simply, the relevant bodily movement – Kevin's contracting his trigger finger (or perhaps better, the contracting of Kevin's trigger finger) – is not even an action; rather, it is an involuntary movement caused by Kevin's being startled. Or, if Kevin does contract his finger as an action, the action is not even caused by his intention to shoot – he contracts his finger as a result of being startled.

John Searle's version (Searle 1983) of the thesis that intentions are self-referential deserves special comment. Searle distinguishes between prior intentions (intentions that precede actions) and intentions in action (intentions that are contemporary with and part constituents of actions). On Searle's view, both prior intentions and intentions in action are self-referential. A prior intention (say) to raise one's arm has the content: that I perform the action of raising my arm by way of carrying out this intention. An intention in action, when one intentionally raises one's arm, has the content: that my arm go up as a result of this intention in action.

Searle's view that intentions are causally self-referential relies on the idea that the specification of the content of an intention should coincide with the specification of its conditions of satisfaction. But why should this be conceded? Searle seems merely to trade on the apparent coincidence of conditions of satisfaction and content in the case of certain other propositional attitudes (like beliefs and desires) and some speech acts (like statements).

Some philosophers have argued that, in the case of intentions, conditions of satisfaction go beyond content in that there is a distinct requirement on specifications of the former that they include a reference to intentions as causes. Alfred Mele (1992) advances a plausible alternative to the self-referentiality theory of content: the content of an agent's intention to *A* is identical with the intention's plan, and the plan simply consists in the agent's representation of their prospective *A*-ing and of the route, if any, that they intend to take. So the content (plan component) of Kevin's intention to revise his predicate logic simply is that he revise his predicate logic and that he do so by (say) working his way through the relevant chapters of his logic textbook.

5 Intention and intentional action

Is it the case that an agent intentionally *A*s only if the agent intends to *A*? Michael Bratman (1987) has dubbed the thesis that all intentional actions are intended 'the Simple View'. The thesis enjoys initial plausibility, though it does not survive scrutiny.

Sudden or impulsive intentional actions are held to provide counterexamples to the Simple View. The problem in such cases, supposedly, is that there is action without enough time for forethought. This difficulty, however, does not seem very serious. For just how long need it take to form (come to have) an intention? More serious is the problem raised by subsidiary actions, where routine action parts of encompassing intentional and intended actions – like the various steps one takes when walking to the theatre – are apparently intentional without being intended. Such examples do seem to defeat the Simple View.

Another objection concerns examples where rational agents apparently perform intentional actions which it would be irrational for them to intend to do straightout, given what they believe about the circumstances in which they act. I refer the reader to the debate between Bratman and McCann (1991). It is noteworthy that the examples in question raise several vexed issues. One of these issues is whether it can be rational to try to *A* without its being rational to intend to *A*. Another issue is whether one can intend to try to *A* (where the intention represents *A*-

ing as a desired goal, aim or purpose) without intending to *A*.

Consider, finally, the objection to the Simple View that there are intentional actions which are the foreseen, *non-intended* behavioural side effects of other intentional actions. Two concerns come into focus in evaluating this range of counterexamples. The first – and more basic – concern is: when, if ever, do expected behavioural side effects of intentional actions properly count as non-intended? For holists about intention urge that all foreseen side effects of an intentional action – or all seriously considered ones – properly count as intended. The second concern, which accepts that there are expected, *non-intended* behavioural side effects of intentional actions, is the following: when, if ever, are such side effects themselves intentional actions? A common view holds that when expected, non-intended side effects enter – or ought to enter – into one's practical reasoning as (significant) reasons against the action one settles on, such side effects count as intentional actions. On this view, for example, someone who foresees that leaving the party early will insult their host and reluctantly goes ahead – in order to get home to a sick friend by an agreed time – counts as intentionally insulting the host, even though they do not in the least intend to do this. If the common view in question is acceptable, the Simple View is false.

6 Intentions and reasons

When philosophers discuss reasons for intending to act, they normally concentrate on object-related considerations, such as ones which support the claim that the intention is an intention to do something which is of value in some way. Such reasons, which coincide with reasons for acting, do not exhaust the kinds of reasons there are for intending to act, however. For there are also attitude-related reasons, such as considerations that support the claim that the intention is one which it is in one's interest to have. This distinction between object- and attitude-related reasons applies across the range of propositional attitudes – as when, say, evidential reasons for believing are contrasted with prudential or hedonic ones. The distinction bears on rationality, since it suggests that, corresponding to the two broad kinds of reasons, the rationality of propositional attitudes like intentions can be assessed along two different dimensions.

See also: ACTION; BELIEF; COMMUNICATION AND INTENTION; DESIRE; PROPOSITIONAL ATTITUDES; RATIONALITY, PRACTICAL

References and further reading

Audi, R. (1986) 'Intending, Intentional Action, and Desire', in J. Marks (ed.) *The Ways of Desire*, Chicago, IL: Precedent. (A good representative of Audi's reductive theory of intention, which analyses intentions in terms of beliefs about what one (probably) will do and predominant desire. Relevant to §1–2.)

Bratman, M. (1985) 'Davidson's Theory of Intention' (with appendix), in E. LePore and B. P. McLaughlin (eds) *Actions and Events: Perspectives on the Philosophy of Donald Davidson*, Oxford: Basil Blackwell, 14–28. (Contains Bratman's criticisms of Davidson's evaluative theory of intention, together with his response to Davidson's rejoinder. Relevant to §3.)

* —— (1987) *Intention, Plans and Practical Reason*, Cambridge, MA: Harvard University Press. (For discussion relevant to: §1, see chapter 3; §2, see chapters 2 and 7; §5, see chapters 8 and 10.)

* Davidson, D. (1978) 'Intending', in *Essays on Actions and Events*, Oxford: Clarendon Press, 1980, 83–102. (Davidson's classic article on intentions as all-out evaluative judgments.)

* —— (1985) 'Replies to Essays I–IX', in B. Vermazen and M. Hintikka (eds) *Essays on Davidson: Actions and Events*, Oxford: Clarendon Press. (For discussion relevant to: §1, see 'Reply to David Pears'; §3, see 'Reply to Michael Bratman', 'Reply to Paul Grice and Judith Baker' and 'Reply to Christopher Peacocke'.)

Dunn, R. (1992) 'Akratic Attitudes and Rationality', *Australasian Journal of Philosophy* 70: 24–39. (Applies the distinction between object- and attitude-related reasons to an account of the rationality, and then of *akrasia*, of propositional attitudes like intentions. Relevant to §6.)

Hampshire, S. (1975) *Freedom of the Individual*, Princeton, NJ: Princeton University Press. (Argues for a contrast between non-inductive and inductive knowledge of the future – the former being had in virtue of one's having formed intentions to act. Relevant to §1.)

Harman, G. (1976) 'Practical Reasoning', *Review of Metaphysics* 79: 431–63. (Argues that intentions are self-referential. Relevant to §4.)

—— (1983) 'Rational Action and the Extent of Intentions', *Social Theory and Practice* 9: 123–41. (Criticizes the version of holism about intention which holds that all foreseen side effects of an intentional action properly count as intended. See §5.)

—— (1986) *Change in View*, Cambridge, MA: MIT Press. (Revised version of Harman (1983) appears as chapter 9. For discussion relevant to various sections in this entry, see also chapter 8.)

* McCann, H. (1991) 'Settled Objectives and Rational Constraints', *American Philosophical Quarterly* 28: 25–36. (A good representative of McCann's defence of the Simple View. Referred to in §5.)

* Mele, A. R. (1992) *Springs of Action*, New York: Oxford University Press. (Canvasses most central issues in the causal theory of intention and includes a comprehensive bibliography. For discussion relevant to: §1, see chapter 8; §2, see chapters 3, 8, 9 and 10; §4, see chapter 11; §5, see chapters 8 and 10.)

—— (1992a) 'Recent Work on Intentional Action', *American Philosophical Quarterly* 29: 199–217. (Excellent survey of important literature (1980–92) relating to most sections in this entry.)

Peacocke, C. (1985) 'Intention and Akrasia', in B. Vermazen and M. Hintikka (eds) *Essays on Davidson: Actions and Events*, Oxford: Clarendon Press, 51–73. (Includes Peacocke's criticisms of Davidson's 'pf' judgments. Relevant to §3.)

—— (1986) 'Intention and Practical Reasoning: A Reply to Donald Davidson', *Analysis* 46: 45–9. (Contains Peacocke's response to Davidson's rejoinder to Peacocke (1985). Relevant to §3.)

* Searle, J. (1983) *Intentionality*, Cambridge: Cambridge University Press. (Presents the theory that intentions are self-referential in chapter 3. See §4.)

ROBERT DUNN

INTENTION, ARTIST'S

see ARTIST'S INTENTION

INTENTIONAL FALLACY

see ARTIST'S INTENTION

INTENTIONALITY

Intentionality is the mind's capacity to direct itself on things. Mental states like thoughts, beliefs, desires, hopes (and others) exhibit intentionality in the sense that they are always directed on, or at, something: if you hope, believe or desire, you must hope, believe or desire something. Hope, belief, desire and any other mental state which is directed at something, are known as intentional states. Intentionality in this sense has only a peripheral connection to the ordinary ideas of intention and intending. An intention to do something is an intentional state, since one cannot intend without intending something; but intentions are only one of many kinds of intentional mental states.

The terminology of intentionality derives from the scholastic philosophy of the Middle Ages, and was revived by Brentano in 1874. Brentano characterized intentionality in terms of the mind's direction upon an object, and emphasized that the object need not exist. He also claimed that it is the intentionality of mental phenomena that distinguishes them from physical phenomena. These ideas of Brentano's provide the background to twentieth-century discussions of intentionality, in both the phenomenological and analytic traditions. Among these discussions, we can distinguish two general projects. The first is to characterize the essential features of intentionality. For example, is intentionality a relation? If it is, what does it relate, if the object of an intentional state need not exist in order to be thought about? The second is to explain how intentionality can occur in the natural world. How can merely biological creatures exhibit intentionality? The aim of this second project is to explain intentionality in non-intentional terms.

1 **The history of the concept of intentionality**
2 **The nature of intentionality**
3 **Intentionality as the mark of the mental**

1 The history of the concept of intentionality

The term 'intentionality' derives from the medieval Latin *intentio*. Literally, this means a tension or stretching, but it is used by scholastic philosophers of the thirteenth and fourteenth centuries as a technical term for a concept. This technical term was a translation of two Arabic terms: *ma' qul*, Al-Farabi's translation of the Greek *noema*; and *ma' na*, Avicenna's term for what is before the mind in thought (see AL-FARABI §3; IBN SINA §3). In this context, the terms *noema*, *ma' qul*, *ma' na* and *intentio* can be considered broadly synonymous: they are all intended as terms for concepts, notions or whatever it is which is before the mind in thought (see Knudsen 1982). Scholars translate *intentio* into English as 'intention' – but it should be borne in mind throughout that this is not meant to have the connotations of the everyday notion of intention.

Medieval logicians followed Al-Farabi in distinguishing between first and second intentions. First intentions are concepts which concern things outside the mind, ordinary objects and features of objects. Second intentions are concepts which concern other intentions. So, for example, the concept *horse* is a first intention since it is concerned with horses, but the concept *species* is a second intention, since it is concerned with first intentions like the intention *horse* (because of the nominalism prevalent at the time, the distinction between the concept/intention *horse* and the property of being a horse is not always clearly made). Many of the medieval philosophers, including Roger Bacon, Thomas Aquinas and John Duns Scotus, followed Avicenna in holding that second intentions were the subject matter of logic (see LOGIC, MEDIEVAL §4).

Some of these philosophers developed detailed theories about how intentions were connected to the things they concerned – what we would now call theories of intentionality. One of the most influential theories was that of Aquinas, whose starting point was Aristotle's theory of thought and perception. According to Aristotle, in thought and perception the mind takes on the form of the thing perceived, without receiving its matter. When I think about or perceive a horse, my mind receives the form of horse (see Sorabji 1991; see ARISTOTLE §18). Aquinas developed Aristotle's view. When I think about a horse, the form of horse exists in my mind. But the form has a different kind of existence in my mind than it does in a real horse. In a real horse, the form of horse has *esse naturale* or existence in nature; but in my thought of a horse, the form of horse has *esse intentionale* or intentional existence (see Anscombe and Geach 1961; Kenny 1984). The heart of Aquinas' view is that what makes my thought of an X a thought of an X is the very same thing which makes an X an X: the occurrence of the form of X. The difference is the way in which the form occurs (see AQUINAS, T. §11).

These scholastic terms largely disappeared from use during the Renaissance and the modern period. Empiricist and rationalist philosophers were of course concerned with the nature of thought and how it relates to its objects, but their discussions were not cast in the terminology of intentionality. The terminology was revived in 1874 by Franz BRENTANO, in his Psychology from an Empirical Standpoint. In a well-known passage, Brentano claimed that:

> Every mental phenomenon is characterized by what the scholastics of the Middle Ages referred to as the intentional (and also mental) inexistence of the object, and what we, although with not quite unambiguous expressions, would call relation to a content, direction upon an object (which is not here to be understood as a reality) or immanent objectivity.
>
> (Brentano [1874] 1973: 88)

A few clarifications of this passage are needed. First, Brentano is not particularly concerned to distinguish between a mental state's (or as he called it, a mental act's) relation to a content and its relation to an object – although as we shall see in §2, later writers find a related distinction useful. And second, intentional inexistence does not itself mean that the objects of thought need not exist – although as we shall see, this is a relatively uncontroversial feature of intentionality. What inexistence means is rather that one thing – the object of thought – exists in another, as the object of the mental state itself (see Bell 1990, ch. 1).

Brentano's account of intentionality was developed by his student Edmund HUSSERL, who reintroduced the Greek term *noema* (plural: *noemata*) for that which accounts for the directedness of mental states. *Noemata* are neither part of the thinking subject's mind nor the objects thought about, but abstract structures that facilitate the intentional relation between subject and object. So *noemata* are not the objects on which intentional states are directed, but it is in virtue of being related to a *noema* that any intentional state is directed on an object at all. In this respect the concept of a *noema* resembles Frege's concept of sense: senses are not what our words are about, but it is in virtue of expressing a sense that words are about things at all (see FREGE, G. §3). In other respects, however, senses and *noemata* differ – for instance, *noemata*, unlike Frege's senses, can be individuated in terms of perceptual experiences (see Dreyfus 1984). The point of Husserl's phenomenological reduction was to provide an account of the structure of *noemata* (see PHENOMENOLOGY, EPISTEMIC ISSUES IN).

A striking claim of Brentano's is that intentionality is what distinguishes mental from physical phenomena:

> This intentional inexistence is exclusively characteristic of mental phenomena. No physical phenomenon manifests anything similar. Consequently, we can define mental phenomena by saying that they are such phenomena as include an object intentionally within themselves.
>
> (Brentano [1874] 1973: 88)

However, it is important to stress that by 'physical phenomena', Brentano does not mean physical objects. Phenomena are what are given to the mind, and Brentano does not believe that physical objects are given to the mind (see Brentano [1874] 1973: 77–78). The distinction he is making is among the data of consciousness, not among entities in the world: among these data, mental phenomena are those which exhibit intentionality, and physical phenomena are those which do not.

However, in analytic philosophy in the second half of the twentieth century, Brentano's distinction came to be interpreted as a distinction between entities in the world. This was chiefly because of this period's prevailing realism. An important figure in this revival of interest in Brentano's notion of intentionality was R.M. CHISHOLM. In chapter 11 of Perceiving (1957), Chisholm argued against the behaviourism that was popular at the time by showing that it is not possible to give a behaviouristic account of, for example, belief, since in order to say how belief leads to behaviour one has to mention other intentional states (such as desires) whose connections with behaviour must themselves be specified in terms of belief and other intentional states (see BEHAVIOURISM, ANALYTIC). This suggests that we should postulate an irreducible category of intentional mental entities: reductive physicalism must be false. However, the argument can be taken in another way, as W.V. Quine argued: if we assume reductive physicalism, we can take the irreducibility of intentionality to demonstrate the 'baselessness of intentional idioms and the emptiness of a science of intention' (Quine 1960: 221). Work on intentionality in the analytic tradition in the 1980s and 1990s has attempted to resolve this dilemma. For example, Fodor (1987), Dretske (1980) and others have attempted to reconcile physicalism with the existence of intentionality by explaining it in non-intentional terms.

2   The nature of intentionality

Despite the interest in intentionality in twentieth-century philosophy, there is still controversy about how to characterize it. All writers agree that intentionality is the directedness of the mind upon something, or the aboutness of mental states, but the disagreements start when we try to explain these ideas in more detail.

To begin with, calling intentionality 'directedness' makes it look as if it is a relation between the mind and the thing on which the mind is directed. After all, if A is directed on B, then A and B are related – if an arrow is directed on a target, the arrow and the target are related. But if the arrow is genuinely related to the target, then the arrow and the target must exist. And similarly with other relations: if Antony kisses Cleopatra, Antony and Cleopatra must exist. But this is not so with intentionality, as Brentano observed (Brentano [1874] 1973: appendix). I can desire to possess a phoenix without there being any such thing. So what am I related to when I am in an intentional state?

One reaction is to postulate that intentional relations are relations to intentional objects. A phoenix is not the material object of my desire, but it is the desire's intentional object. However, it is not

obvious that this really solves any problems. For what are intentional objects? Are they real objects? Brentano and Husserl both thought so: intentional objects are just ordinary objects. But if this is so, then what does it mean to say that intentional objects need not exist? Alexius MEINONG, on the other hand, thought that intentional objects have a different kind of existence from real material objects. But this seems to misrepresent intentionality: if I want a phoenix, I want a real phoenix, with wings and feathers – not something with a different kind of existence. In any case, the idea that there are different kinds of existence is of dubious coherence. So whatever we say about intentional objects, they do not offer a satisfactory explanation of intentionality (see Scruton 1970–1).

A second important difference between intentionality and other relations is that with other relations, the way you describe the relata does not affect whether the relation holds. But with intentionality this is not so: you can believe that George Orwell wrote Animal Farm without believing that Eric Blair wrote Animal Farm, simply because you do not know that Orwell is Blair. But since Orwell is Blair, then your belief surely relates you to the same thing – so how can the obtaining of the relation (belief) depend on how the thing is described?

For these reasons, it seems impossible to regard intentionality as a relation at all. One way of avoiding these difficulties is to distinguish, as Brentano did not, between the intentional object of a state and its intentional content. Intentional content (like Husserl's noema or Frege's thought) is what makes it possible for a mental state to be directed on an object. Thus understood, intentional contents are not representations. Rather, they are what constitute something's being a representation: it is in virtue of the fact that a mental state has an intentional content that it represents what it does. It is in virtue of the fact that my belief that pigs fly involves some relation between me and an intentional content – the proposition or Fregean thought that pigs fly – that it represents what it does. This is what is meant by saying that intentional states, or propositional attitudes, are relations to propositions or contents (see PROPOSITIONAL ATTITUDES).

Although beliefs, desires and other intentional states are sometimes described in this way – as relations to propositions or contents – this idea should be sharply distinguished from the idea, just discussed, that intentional directedness is a relation. The intentional content expressed by the sentence 'Pigs fly' is not what my belief that pigs fly is directed on: the belief is directed on pigs and flying. Some have thought that all intentional directedness can ultimately be reformulated in terms of relations to intentional contents: an intentional state is directed on an object X in virtue of the fact that it is a relation to an intentional content concerning X. However, this thesis has difficulty dealing with certain intentional phenomena, most notably the phenomenon of loving: no one has given a satisfactory reformulation of the notion 'X loves Y' in terms of X's relations to intentional contents.

There is much controversy about exactly what intentional contents are and how we should individuate them (see Salmon and Soames 1988). Some philosophers attempt to clarify (or even sidestep) these ontological and epistemological difficulties by adopting what Quine calls 'semantic ascent': they examine sentences which report intentionality rather than intentionality itself. A distinctive feature of many sentences reporting intentional states is that their constituent words do not play their normal referential role. Part of what this means is that the apparently uncontroversial logical principles of existential generalization (from Fa infer $(\exists x)Fx$) and Leibniz's Law (from Fa and $a=b$ infer Fb) fail to apply to all sentences reporting intentionality. For example, from 'I want a phoenix' we cannot infer that there exists a phoenix that I want; and from 'Vladimir believes that Orwell wrote *Animal Farm*' and 'Orwell is Blair' we cannot infer that 'Vladimir believes that Blair wrote *Animal Farm*' (see PROPOSITIONAL ATTITUDE STATEMENTS).

Contexts where these two principles fail to hold are known as 'non-extensional' contexts – their semantic properties depend on more than just the extensions of the words they contain. They are also called 'intensional' contexts, or contexts which exhibit intensionality (see INTENSIONALITY). The connection between intensionality and intentionality is not merely typographical: the failure of existential generalization in intensional contexts is the logical or linguistic analogue of the fact that intentional states can be about things which do not exist. And the failure of Leibniz's Law is the logical or linguistic analogue of the fact that the obtaining of an intentional relation depends on the way the relata are characterized.

However, the notion of intensionality must be distinguished from the notion of intentionality, not least because there are intensional contexts which are nothing to do with the direction of the mind on an object. Prominent among these are modal contexts: for example, from 'Necessarily, Orwell is Orwell' and 'Orwell is the author of *Animal Farm*' we cannot infer 'Necessarily, Orwell is the author of *Animal Farm*'. Other concepts which can create intensional contexts are the concepts of probability, explanation and dispositionality. But it is very controversial to hold

that these concepts have anything to do with intentionality.

Another (more controversial) reason for distinguishing between intensionality and intentionality is that intentionality can be reported in sentences which are extensional. Some philosophers have argued that the context 'x sees y' is like this. Seeing seems to be a paradigm case of the direction of the mind on an object. But if Vladimir sees Orwell, then there is someone whom he sees; moreover, if Vladimir sees Orwell, then surely he also sees Blair, and he also sees the author of *Animal Farm*, and so on. So although seeing is intentional, 'x sees y' seems to be an extensional context.

3 Intentionality as the mark of the mental

Thus, the notion of intensionality cannot provide a purely logical or semantic criterion of intentionality. We should be content with the psychological criterion: intentionality is the directedness of the mind upon something. As I remarked earlier, Brentano thought that intentionality was the mark of the mental: all and only mental phenomena exhibit intentionality. In discussing this claim – often called Brentano's thesis – I shall follow analytic philosophers in ignoring Brentano's own quasi-idealistic use of the term 'phenomenon'. Brentano's thesis shall be taken as a thesis about the distinction between mental and physical entities in the world.

Is Brentano's thesis true? We can divide this question into two sub-questions: (1) Do all mental states exhibit intentionality? (2) Do only mental states exhibit intentionality?

(1) It is natural at first sight to think that there are many kinds of mental state which do not have any intentionality. For instance, there are states like undirected anxiety, depression and elation (see Searle 1983: 2). On what are these states directed? Well, I can be anxious without being anxious about anything in particular – but this anxiety is at least directed at myself. Other popular examples of supposedly non-intentional mental states are sensations like pain. But while it may be true that pains are not propositional attitudes – if propositional attitudes are states reportable by sentences of the form 'X φs that p', where φ is a psychological verb – this does not mean that pains are not directed on anything. I could have two pains, one in each hand, which felt exactly the same, except that one felt to be in my right hand, and the other felt to be in my left hand. This is a difference in intentionality – in what the mental state is directed on – so it is not true that pains exhibit no intentionality (see BODILY SENSATIONS §2).

However, there are properties of pains which do

819

seem to be wholly non-intentional, such as the nagginness of a toothache (see QUALIA). And these properties seem to be essential to pains. This shows that the distinction we need is between those mental states whose whole nature is exhausted by their intentionality, and those whose whole nature is not. Pains are in the latter category, since they seem to have essential non-intentional properties: there are elements of pains which are not exhausted by whatever intentionality those pains may have.

(2) So much, then, for the idea that all mental states exhibit intentionality. But is intentionality only exhibited by mental states? That is: is it true that if something exhibits intentionality, then that thing is a mind? Are minds the only things in the world that have intentionality?

To hold that minds are not the only things that have intentionality, we need an example of something that has intentionality but does not have a mind. This may seem easy. Take books: books contains sentences which have meaning and are therefore directed at things other than themselves. But books do not have minds.

The natural reply to this is to say that the book's sentences do not have intentionality in themselves – they do not have what some call 'original' intentionality – but only because they are interpreted by the readers and writer of the book. The intentionality of the book's sentences is derived from the original intentionality of the states of mind of the author and reader who interpret those sentences (for this distinction, see Haugeland 1990).

So we can reframe our question as follows: can anything other than minds exhibit original intentionality? One problem with this question is that if we encountered something that exhibited original intentionality, it is hard to see how it could be a further question whether that thing had a mind. The notion of intentionality is so closely bound up with mentality that it is hard to conceive of a genuine case of original intentionality that is not also a case of mentality. If, for example, we could establish that computers were capable of original intentionality, it would be natural to describe this as a case where a computer has a mind.

However, there is an interesting way in which original intentionality and mentality could come apart. Some philosophers want to locate the basis of intentionality among certain non-mental causal patterns in nature. So on this view, there would be a sense in which original intentionality is manifested by things other than minds. This is the hope of those philosophers who attempt to reduce the intentional to the non-intentional: the hope summed up by Jerry Fodor's quip that 'if aboutness is real, it must really be something else' (Fodor 1987: 97).

These philosophers are in effect trying to steer a course between the two horns of the dilemma presented by the passage from Quine's Word and Object quoted in §1: you can respond to the Chisholm–Brentano thesis of the irreducibility of intentionality either by accepting an autonomous theory of intentionality and rejecting physicalism, or by denying the reality of intentionality. There are those who are eliminative materialists and who deny the reality of intentionality (see ELIMINATIVISM), and there are those who are prepared to accept intentionality as an unanalysed, primitive phenomenon. But the orthodox line among late twentieth-century analytic philosophers is to reconcile the existence of intentionality with a physicalist (or naturalist) world view. This reconciliation normally takes the form of a theory of content: a specification in non-intentional terms of the conditions under which an intentional state has the intentional content it does, or concerns the object(s) it does. A common style of theory of content spells out these conditions in terms of hypothesized law-like causal relations between intentional states and their objects. The model here is the simple kind of representation or meaning found in nature: the sense in which clouds mean rain, and smoke means fire (see Dretske 1980). Causal theories of content hope to explain how the intentionality of mental states is underpinned by simple regularities like these. These theories have had great difficulty accounting for misrepresentation and the normative elements of mental states, and it is this problem that has received most attention in contemporary discussions of intentionality (see SEMANTICS, INFORMATIONAL; SEMANTICS, TELEOLOGICAL).

See also: BELIEF; DESIRE; INTENTION; PERCEPTION; IMAGINATION; EMOTIONS, NATURE OF

References and further reading

* Anscombe, G.E.M. and Geach, P.T. (1961) *Three Philosophers*, Oxford: Blackwell. (The chapter on Aquinas gives a very clear and nontechnical account of his views on intentionality.)

Bell, D. (1990) *Husserl*, London: Routledge (Clear and critical account of Husserl's philosophy. Chapter 1 is about Brentano.)

* Brentano, F. (1874) *Psychology from an Empirical Standpoint*, trans. A.C. Rancurello, D.B. Terrell and L.L. McAlister, London: Routledge & Kegan Paul, 1973. (The classic work that revived the concept of intentionality when it was first published in 1874. Difficult reading.)

* Chisholm, R.M. (1957) *Perceiving: A Philosophical Study*, Ithaca, NY: Cornell University Press.

(Chapter 11 contains the argument for the irreducibility of intentionality described in §1.)

* Dretske, F.I. (1980) 'The Intentionality of Cognitive States', in P.A. French *et al.* (eds) *Midwest Studies in Philosophy* V, Minneapolis, MN: University of Minnesota Press. (Useful and accessible summary of Dretske's reductive theory of content.)

* Dreyfus, H.L, with Hall, H. (eds) (1984) *Husserl, Intentionality and Cognitive Science*, Cambridge, MA: MIT Press. (Wide-ranging collection of essays on Husserl's ideas on intentionality and their relation to cognitive science.)

* Fodor, J.A. (1987) *Psychosemantics: The Problem of Meaning in the Philosophy of Mind*, Cambridge, MA: MIT Press. (Influential account of intentionality from a physicalist perspective. Chapter 4 contains Fodor's theory. Original but not excessively technical.)

* Haugeland, J. (1990) 'The Intentionality All-Stars', in J. Tomberlin (ed.) *Philosophical Perspectives 4: Action Theory and the Philosophy of Mind*, Atascadero, CA: Ridgeview. (Clear and readable survey of research in intentionality in the analytic tradition.)

* Kenny, A. (1984) 'Aquinas: Intentionality', in T. Honderich (ed.) *Philosophy Through Its Past*, Harmondsworth: Penguin. (A straightforward discussion of Aquinas' theory of intentionality and an attempt to relate it to Wittgenstein's views.)

* Knudsen, C. (1982) 'Intentions and impositions', in N. Kretzmann, A. Kenny and J. Pinborg (eds) *The Cambridge History of Later Medieval Philosophy*, Cambridge: Cambridge University Press. (Survey of the idea of an *intentio* as employed by the leading medieval philosophers.)

* Quine, W.V.O. (1960) *Word and Object*, Cambridge, MA: MIT Press. (Chapter 6 contains Quine's influential discussion of intentionality and intensionality discussed in §2. A classic, but a difficult work for the beginner.)

* Salmon, N. and Soames, S. (eds) (1988) *Propositions and Attitudes*, Oxford: Oxford University Press. (Useful collection of essays, many of them classics, on the notions of proposition and intentional content. Some technical logical material.)

* Scruton, Roger (1970–1) 'Intensional and Intentional Objects', *Proceedings of the Aristotelian Society* 92, 187–207. (Clear and thorough discussion of the notion of an intentional object.)

* Searle, J.R. (1983) *Intentionality*, Cambridge: Cambridge University Press. (A complete theory of intentionality, with material relating to the issues discussed in §§2–3. Chapter 1 is a good introduction.)

* Sorabji, R. (1991) 'From Aristotle to Brentano: The Development of the Concept of Intentionality', in H. Blumenthal and H. Robinson (eds.) *Oxford Studies in Ancient Philosophy*, supplementary vol. Oxford: Oxford University Press. (Informative discussion of how the concept of intentionality developed, particularly in later Greek philosophy, also with reference to Islamic and scholastic writers.)

Spiegelberg, Herbert (1976) '"Intention" and "Intentionality" in the Scholastics, Brentano and Husserl', trans. L. McAlister, in L. McAlister (ed.) *The Philosophy of Brentano* London: Routledge & Kegan Paul, 1976, ch. 9. (A standard source for the origins of the different uses of these terms.)

TIM CRANE

INTERESTS *see* NEEDS AND INTERESTS

INTERNALISM AND EXTERNALISM IN EPISTEMOLOGY

The internalism–externalism distinction is usually applied to the epistemic justification of belief. The most common form of internalism (accessibility internalism) holds that only what the subject can easily become aware of (by reflection, for example) can have a bearing on justification. We may think of externalism as simply the denial of this constraint.

The strong intuitive appeal of internalism is due to the sense that we should be able to determine whether we are justified in believing something just by carefully considering the question, without the need for any further investigation. Then there is the idea that we can successfully reply to sceptical doubts about the possibility of knowledge or justified beliefs only if we can determine the epistemic status of our beliefs without presupposing anything about which sceptical doubts could be raised – the external world for example.

The main objections to internalism are: (1) It assumes an unrealistic confidence in the efficacy of armchair reflection, which is often not up to surveying our entire repertoire of beliefs and other possible grounds of belief and determining the extent to which they support a given belief. (2) If we confine ourselves to what we can ascertain on reflection, there is no guarantee that the beliefs that are thus approved as justified are likely to be true. And the truth-promoting character of justification is the main source of its value.

Externalism lifts this accessibility constraint, but in its most general sense it embodies no particular positive view. The most common way of further specifying externalism is reliabilism, the view that a belief is justified if and only if it was produced and/or sustained by a reliable process, one that would produce mostly true beliefs in the long run. This is a form of externalism because whether a particular belief-forming process is reliable is not something we can ascertain just on reflection. The main objections to externalism draw on internalist intuitions: (1) If the world were governed by an evil demon who sees to it that our beliefs are generally false, even though we have the kind of bases for them we do in fact have, then our beliefs would still be justified, even though formed unreliably. (2) If a reliable clairvoyant (ones who 'sees' things at a great distance) forms beliefs on this basis without having any reason for thinking that they are reliably formed, those beliefs would not be justified, even though they pass the reliability test.

1   **Forms of the distinction**
2   **Justification internalism – pro and con**
3   **Justification externalism – pro and con**
4   **The distinction applied to knowledge**

1   Forms of the distinction

Although this entry is restricted to epistemology, the terms 'internalism' and 'externalism' are also used to mark distinctions in ethics and philosophy of mind (see CONTENT: WIDE AND NARROW; MORAL MOTIVATION §1). Within epistemology itself the terms are used variously. The most basic distinction is between views concerning the epistemic justification of belief and views concerning knowledge. As applied to either, *internalism* is construed variously – for example, as the irreducible normativeness of justification (knowledge), and as the view that justification or knowledge always depends on the subject's belief system. The most common understanding, however, is Access Internalism – the view that only what is cognitively accessible to the subject in some strong fashion can have any bearing on justification. We may think of *externalism* as simply the denial of this restriction. Strong cognitive access to a fact is variously conceived; the most common version is that the fact be ascertainable by the subject just by reflecting on the matter. If my justified belief that Susie is in Panama is to justify my belief that she will not be at the meeting tonight, then it must be that I can ascertain by armchair reflection that I justifiably believe that she is in Panama (Ginet 1975: 34; Pollock

1986: Ch. 5, §4.1 offers a quite different way of thinking of the internalist requirement.) Note that this constraint does not require that individuals actually have the knowledge that the alleged justifier obtains, but only that they be capable of acquiring it on reflection.

A crucially important, but usually ignored, distinction is between access to the justifier and access to the epistemic efficacy of the justifier. Consider the perceptual belief that there is snow in front of my house. The justifier, let us say, is my visual presentation as I look out the front window. That would seem unproblematically to satisfy the internalist constraint. But in order for me to know that the belief is justified, it is not enough that I know that my current visual presentation is of such-and-such a character. I must also know that this presentation suffices to justify the belief (that it possesses that 'justificatory efficacy'). And it is far from unproblematic that this is accessible just on reflection. Indeed, many philosophers have struggled in vain to show that our ordinary perceptual beliefs about the immediate environment are justified by the sensory experiences on which they are typically based. As we shall see, the most common arguments for accessibility internalism give equal support to both kinds of internalist constraint. If one advocates only one kind, we have a mixed view of the sort to be described below.

2   Justification internalism – pro and con

The most explicit arguments for accessibility internalism have proceeded from a deontological conception of justification, according to which a belief is justified only if having the belief does not violate any intellectual obligation or requirement, only if one is permitted to have the belief. In Ginet (1975) the argument goes as follows:

(1) One should believe that *p* only if one is (epistemically) permitted to do so.
(2) One is permitted to believe that *p* only if one has a justification for the belief.
(3) But a condition cannot be required for permission unless one is able to determine whether it obtains.
(4) Hence one can always determine whether one has a justification for a belief.

Note that this argument is designed to support both kinds of accessibility requirement. For to determine 'whether one has a justification for a belief' one must be able to spot both the allegedly justifying condition and also determine whether it suffices to do the job.

One trouble with this argument is that, even if cogent, it does not show that justification must be ascertainable simply on reflection. Its conclusion is only that the subject must be able to know of it somehow or other. In addition, there are serious questions about the deontological conception of justification on which the argument is based: it would seem to assume an unwarranted degree of voluntary control of beliefs (Alston 1989: 115–52).

To be sure, accessibility internalism has a strong intuitive appeal. It has seemed obvious to many philosophers through the centuries that we should be able to determine the epistemic status of our beliefs just by armchair reflection, and that has been the standard method, at least since Descartes shut himself up in a small room to determine whether there was anything he knew with certainty. But intuitive plausibility, even when combined with hallowed tradition, is not enough to bear the weight of so strong a restriction. Moreover, this plausibility stems partly from confusions, particularly that between the activity of justifying a belief and the state of being justified in believing that *p*. The former does seem to presuppose reflective access. At least I cannot adduce a support in justifying (arguing for) my belief that *p* unless I can become aware of that support. But we cannot infer from this that there is the same requirement for being justified in believing that *p*. Obviously, I am justified in many beliefs that I have never engaged in justifying. Otherwise I would have precious few justified beliefs, since I spend little time justifying my beliefs.

Another common motive for embracing internalism is the supposition that it removes an obstacle to giving an effective response to the sceptical denial or doubt that we have any knowledge or justified beliefs. If I have to rely on what I think I have learned from perception, induction, explanation or scientific theorizing, in order to show that certain of my beliefs are justified, then my attempt is open to sceptical challenges to those sources. If I only need to rely on reflection, it is supposed, I do not have this worry. But this line of thought deals only with certain kinds of scepticism. If my only appeal is to reflection, I am immune to challenge from scepticism about perception and induction. But that leaves scepticism about reflection. Though historically most sceptics have concentrated on perception, induction and high level reasoning, some of the classical sceptical arguments would apply to reflection as much as to anything else. Hence internalism provides only a limited guarantee against sceptical doubts (see SCEPTICISM).

The very features of internalism that make it attractive to many also give rise to some serious liabilities. For one thing the position would seem to be much too sanguine concerning the cognitive powers of mere reflection. Here the above distinction between access to the justifier and access to its justificatory efficacy is relevant. Claims to reflective access to the latter are very dubious. Some epistemologists (Chisholm [1966] 1989: 7, 76) exhibit confidence that, just by thinking about the matter, one can tell what justifies what, but I find this very questionable. It partly depends on how we think of justification. The deontological conception may seem more friendly to internalism here. It is easy to convince oneself that one can tell what is permitted to one or required of one just by carefully considering the matter. But if being justified in believing that *p* involves believing in such a way as to be in a strong position to get the truth, then we must deny, must we not, that we are generally able to determine *that* just by raising the question? Will that tell us, for example, how much and what kind of evidence will put us in a position to get the truth in our scientific theorizing or our religious beliefs?

This issue will recur in the second objection. For now we should note also that not everything is clear sailing *vis-à-vis* access to the justifier. For example, a common type of alleged justifier consists in other justified beliefs of the subject (my belief that my wife is not at home is justified because it is based on my justified belief that her car is not in the garage). But then to know that I have a justifier of this sort I would not only have to know that I have this belief (which may well be accessible on reflection) but also that it is justified. And that brings us back to justificatory efficacy again, namely the issue of what it takes to justify the belief that my wife's car is not in the garage. Again, suppose that a certain belief is justified only if my total evidence (the set of all my justified beliefs) renders that belief probable. Then we also run into the difficulty of determining just by reflection the entire range of my beliefs, and it is doubtful that I can accurately survey *all* my beliefs just by thinking about the matter.

The second objection involves the point just noted that it seems clearly wrong to suppose that we can determine by armchair reflection whether certain (allegedly justifying) conditions render a belief likely to be true. If a belief's being justified implies the probability of its truth, then it follows that anything we can ascertain by reflection will not amount to justification in this sense. And surely this implication of the probability of truth is an essential part of what makes it desirable and important that our beliefs be justified. If this implication is lacking why should we care whether our beliefs are justified? After all, the basic aim of cognition is to believe what is true and to avoid believing what is false. Thus internalism would seem disconnected from any understanding of justification that renders it a major epistemic desideratum.

In the face of these difficulties we should note that

there is a weaker brand of internalism on the market, according to which what bears on the justification of belief is restricted to the evidence, reasons or experiences of the subject, in contrast to what is external to the subject's cognitive states (Feldman and Conee 1985). This position is not subject to the objections we have been surveying. But the opposite side of that coin is that it cannot draw on the intuitive support we have seen to accrue to accessibility internalism.

3 Justification externalism – pro and con

In the most general sense, externalism is simply a rejection of the internalist constraint on access. (Externalism can allow reflectively accessible factors, but it denies that what affects justificatory status is *restricted* to them.) Externalism in this generic sense does not include any particular positive view of justification, but it is able to consider various possibilities that internalism blocks. In fact, externalism is always associated with 'strong position' conceptions of justification (believing in such a way as to be in a strong position to thereby get the truth). Since it can recognize conditions of justification that are not reflectively accessible, it is able uninhibitedly to carry out the idea that justification entails truth-conducivity.

The most prominent form of externalism is reliabilism, and in its most common form it holds that a belief is justified if and only if it was produced and/or sustained by a reliable belief-forming process (Goldman 1986) (see RELIABILISM §2). A particular perceptual belief, for example, is justified provided it was formed from sensory experience in such a way that when a belief with a content like that is formed from an experience related in that way to the belief content, it will usually be true. A belief formed by inferring a fact from observable indications (believing that a party is going on because one notes a lot of lights on and hears a lot of noise) is justified provided beliefs with that sort of content formed by indications like that will generally be correct. Since the truth-making tendency of a certain process is not something we can ascertain just on reflection, access internalists are not in a position to embrace reliabilism, but externalists are free to do so.

There are many problems one encounters in working out a reliabilist view in detail. For example, how does one assign a particular belief-forming process to a class or type of processes? (note the use of 'like that' in the above examples) (Feldman 1985). And is the reliability a matter of actual track record or a matter of what *would* happen in situations of certain kinds? I will just note here that some views

of this kind are formulated in terms of probability rather than in terms of processes. Thus the second example could be put in terms of the probability of a party occurring given that there is a lot of noise, and so on (Swain 1981; Dretske 1981) (see INFORMATION THEORY AND EPISTEMOLOGY; PROBABILITY THEORY AND EPISTEMOLOGY §1).

Since externalism amounts to a denial of internalism, it is to be expected that its main supports come from the difficulties in internalism. The main attraction of externalism lies in the facts that: (1) it enables us to retain the truth-conducivity implication of justification, as internalism does not; and (2) it does not require us to make exaggerated claims for the powers of rational reflection.

The chief criticisms of externalism are based on internalist intuitions and are typically directed against reliabilism. First, there is the consideration of 'demon worlds', worlds controlled by an evil omnipotent demon who sees to it that our beliefs are generally false, even when they seem most obviously true. In such a world one's perceptual, inductive, and mathematical beliefs are false even though one has the same bases for them that we have in the actual world. The denizens of this world believe that there is a tree in front of them when they seem to be seeing a tree in front of them. They believe that $3 + 2 = 5$ because it seems self-evident to them, and so on. There is a considerable tendency to judge that these unfortunates would be justified in their beliefs, just as much as we are in ours, even though they are formed in a very unreliable manner. Since they have the same grounds as we do, how can our beliefs be justified and theirs not? But then, reliability of formation is not necessary for knowledge (Foley 1987: Ch. 3). Although this argument is couched in terms of a fantastic scenario, the underlying idea is simple and sober. Since it is conceivable that we have what are recognized as very strong grounds for a belief even though it is not formed reliably, reliability cannot be *necessary* for justification.

Second, consider someone who forms beliefs in a reliable way but who has no, or insufficient, reason for supposing it to be reliable. Again, the argument is frequently presented in terms of *outré* examples like clairvoyance (BonJour: Ch. 3), but more standard cases will do as well. Suppose Jim infers emotional states from outward demeanour and behaviour in the standard way, but has no reason for thinking this to be a reliable way of making such judgments. There is a strong tendency to think that he has no justification for the beliefs so formed, given that this mode of belief formation could be completely unreliable so far as he can tell. But then the mere fact that the way of forming beliefs is reliable cannot be *sufficient* for justification.

The best counter-move for the reliabilist is to deny the 'intuitions' adduced by the critic. No doubt the demon world denizen has something going for them, epistemically, but, says the reliabilist, it is not *justification*, so long as there is nothing about the belief and the way it is formed or held that makes it likely to be true. And since the reliability condition is satisfied for Jim *vis-à-vis* beliefs formed in the usual way about the emotional states of others, that will suffice to render the beliefs justified, despite the lack of higher-level knowledge (justified belief) concerning how reliable that way is. This is to take truth-conducivity as both necessary and sufficient for justification and, as we have seen, this is the heart of epistemic justification from an externalist perspective.

What if Jim not only is not justified in supposing this way of forming beliefs to be reliable, but is justified in supposing it to be unreliable (even though it is reliable)? In that case the reliabilist could recognize Jim's beliefs about the emotional states of others to be *unjustified* – by taking reliability to be sufficient only for *prima facie* justified belief, belief that is justified provided the justification is not overridden in one way or another. In this case, Jim's justification for supposing that way of forming beliefs to be unreliable would be a sufficient overrider. To modify reliabilism in this way would not involve abandoning the basic thrust of the position. Reliability of belief formation would still be at the centre of the picture. It is just that other considerations are given a secondary role.

Various blends of internalism and externalism have been suggested. The distinction between 'justifier' and 'justificatory efficacy thereof' provides an obvious basis for such a combination. Thus Alston (1989: Ch. 9) develops a view ('Internalist Externalism'), according to which a condition can be a justifier only if it is the sort of thing that is typically available to reflection (this is the internalist part), but there is no such reflective access required for the justificatory efficacy of the condition. That efficacy depends on whether the alleged justifier is in fact a reliable indication of the truth of the belief in question (this is the externalist part).

4 The distinction applied to knowledge

As for knowledge, internalism would seem to be less plausible than in application to justification, while externalism is more plausible. This is because of doubts that justification of belief is a necessary condition of knowledge. The dominant view of knowledge in the twentieth century has been that it

consists of justified true belief. Since Gettier posed his famous difficulty for this view, those who take true justified belief to be at least sufficient for knowledge have tried to evade these difficulties by adding a fourth condition, but with indifferent success so far (see GETTIER PROBLEMS §§1–2). If justification were necessary for knowledge, then any constraint on the former would equally be a constraint on the latter, and so accessibility internalism could not be less plausible for knowledge than for justification. But if justification of belief is not necessary for knowledge, we have a different story. More than one prominent externalist has developed a conception of knowledge in which justification is not mentioned at all (Dretske 1981; Nozick 1981). Something like reliability, or probability of the belief on its grounds, is taken as sufficient to turn true belief into knowledge. For example, on Nozick's view the following four conditions are individually necessary and jointly necessary for S knowing, via method M, that p.

(1) p is true.
(2) S believes, via M, that p.
(3) If p were not true and S were to use M to arrive at a belief whether (or not) p, then S would not believe, via M, that p.
(4) If P were true and S were to use M to arrive at a belief whether (or not) p, then S would believe, via M, that p.

Nozick puts this by saying that a true belief counts as knowledge when it 'tracks' the truth, that is, when its being held or not varies with the truth value of the proposition believed. This form of externalism is cut loose from dependence on the right way of thinking of justification, though, of course, its success does depend on the right way of thinking of knowledge. (For some criticisms of Nozick's proposals see Luper-Foy 1987.)

See also: JUSTIFICATION, EPISTEMIC; KNOWLEDGE, CONCEPT OF; RATIONAL BELIEFS; REASONS FOR BELIEF

References and further reading

* Alston, W.P. (1989) *Epistemic Justification: Essays in the Theory of Knowledge*, Ithaca, NY: Cornell University Press. (Advanced essays on some of the main topics of current interest.)
* BonJour, L. (1985) *The Structure of Empirical Knowledge*, Cambridge, MA: Harvard University Press. (Accessible defence of coherence theory and excellent criticism of alternatives.)
* Chisholm, R.M. (1966) *Theory of Knowledge*, Engle-

wood Cliffs, NJ: Prentice Hall; 3rd edn, 1989. (Classic presentation of foundationalism.)

* Dretske, F.I. (1981) *Knowledge and the Flow of Information*, Cambridge, MA: MIT Press. (Major statement of an externalist theory of knowledge.)

* Feldman, R. (1985) 'Reliability and Justification', *The Monist* 68 (2): 159–74. (Classic presentation of the difficulty in determining the type to which to assign a particular belief-forming process.)

* Feldman, R. and Conee, E. (1985) 'Evidentialism', *Philosophical Studies* 48 (1): 15–34. (A moderate form of internalism.)

* Foley, R. (1987) *The Theory of Epistemic Rationality*, Cambridge, MA: Harvard University Press. (A relatively subjectivist form of internalism.)

* Gettier, E. (1963) 'Is Justified True Belief Knowledge?', *Analysis* 23 (6): 121–3. (The classic argument for a negative answer.)

* Ginet, C. (1975) *Knowledge, Perception, and Memory*, Dordrecht: Reidel. (Another outstanding version of internalism.)

* Goldman, A.I. (1986) *Epistemology and Cognition*, Cambridge, MA: Harvard University Press. (Definitive statement of reliabilism with connections to cognitive science.)

* Luper-Foy, S. (1987) *The Possibility of Knowledge: Nozick and His Critics*, Totowa, NJ: Rowman & Littlefield. (Collection of essays critical of Nozick's theory of knowledge.)

* Nozick, R. (1981) *Philosophical Explanations*, Cambridge, MA: Harvard University Press. (Influential version of externalism.)

* Pollock, J. (1986) *Contemporary Theories of Knowledge*, Totowa, NJ: Rowman & Littlefield. (Advanced textbook and presentation of an unusual form of internalism.)

* Swain, M. (1981) *Reasons and Knowledge*, Ithaca, NY: Cornell University Press. (Version of reliabilism in terms of probability.)

WILLIAM P. ALSTON

INTERNATIONAL LAW

see JUSTICE, INTERNATIONAL

INTERNATIONAL RELATIONS, PHILOSOPHY OF

The philosophy of international relations – or more precisely its political philosophy – embraces problems about morality in diplomacy and war, the justice of international practices and institutions bearing on economic welfare and the global environment, human rights, and the relationship between sectional loyalties such as patriotism and global moral commitments.

Not everyone believes that such a subject can exist, or rather, that it can have significant ethical content. According to political realism – a widely-held view among Anglo-American students of international relations – moral considerations have no place in decisions about foreign affairs and international behaviour. The most extreme varieties of realism deny that moral judgment can have meaning or force in international affairs; more moderate versions acknowledge the meaningfulness of such judgments but hold either that leaders have no responsibility to attend to the morality of their actions in foreign affairs (because their overriding responsibility is to advance the interests of their constituents), or that the direct pursuit of moral goals in international relations is likely to be self-defeating.

Leaving aside the more sceptical kinds of political realism, the most influential orientations to substantive international morality can be arrayed on a continuum. Distinctions are made on the basis of the degree of privilege, if any, extended to the citizens of a state to act on their own behalf at the potential expense of the liberty and wellbeing of persons elsewhere. 'The morality of states', at one extreme, holds that states have rights of autonomy analogous to those of individuals within domestic society, which secure them against external interference in their internal affairs and guarantee their ownership and control of the natural and human resources within their borders. At the other end of the continuum, one finds cosmopolitan views which deny that states enjoy any special privilege; these views hold that individuals rather than states are the ultimate subjects of morality, and that value judgments concerning international conduct should take equally seriously the wellbeing of each person potentially affected by a decision, whether compatriot or foreigner. Cosmopolitan views may acknowledge that states (and similar entities) have morally significant features, but analysis of the significance of these features must connect them with considerations of individual wellbeing. Intermediate views are possible; for example, a conception of the privileged character of the state can be combined with a conception of the international realm as weakly normative (that is, *governed by principles which demand that states adhere to minimum conditions of peaceful coexistence).*

The theoretical difference between the morality of states and a fully cosmopolitan morality is reflected in practical differences about the justifiability of intervention in the internal affairs of other states, the basis and content of human rights, and the extent, if any, of our obligations as individuals and as citizens of states to help redress the welfare effects of international inequalities.

1 The scope of the subject
2 Political realism and international scepticism
3 The morality of states and the domestic analogy
4 Cosmopolitan morality
5 Human rights

1 The scope of the subject

The philosophy of international relations is the branch of political philosophy devoted to the examination of principles of conduct for the international realm. Historically, such philosophical attention as has been paid to international relations has taken place mainly in three genres: (1) treatises on natural law, 'the law of nations' and international law; (2) the development of a doctrine of 'just' war (often in the context of the law of nations); and (3) the articulation of peace plans – that is, institutional schemes aimed at ending war. There are significant (albeit brief) passages concerning international relations in works devoted primarily to the political theory of the state by most of the important modern writers, including Machiavelli, Hobbes, Locke, Hume, Kant, Hegel, Bentham, Mill and Sidgwick. Among the few works of great stature devoted mainly to international relations, Kant's *Perpetual Peace* (1795) is arguably the most important, but its brevity and epigrammatic style render its normative content elusive.

The paucity of philosophical thought about international relations is not easy to explain, although the burden must fall on the central distinction of the international realm *vis-à-vis* the domestic – namely, the absence of a state-like structure, and consequently of an institutional focus for philosophical speculation. In recent decades there has been an increase in interest in the subject, doubtless reflecting the fundamental changes in the character of international politics and society that have occurred in the mid- and late twentieth century. An intensification of international and transnational activity, particularly in finance and trade, has given rise to a vast increase in the number of non-state participants in international affairs – including both international organiza-

tions (that is, organizations of states) and nongovernmental organizations. 'Total war' (characterized by the mobilization of entire societies) and the invention of chemical and nuclear weapons have rendered it virtually impossible to contain the harms of war to those who participate in combat, so that the traditional distinction between soldier and civilian has broken down (see WAR AND PEACE, PHILOSOPHY OF §6). The exploration of space, the exploitation of ocean resources and growing political concern about the environment have spawned policy issues which are essentially trans- (rather than inter-) national. For all of these reasons, the occasion for international philosophy is greater now than at any earlier point in the modern age.

Regarded as a normative enterprise, the philosophy of international relations might be seen as an outgrowth of speculation about the basis and content of the 'law of nations.' But this would convey an excessively narrow conception of the subject matter of international philosophy. The law of nations was a body of norms applicable to what was conceived as a society of states whose principal forms of interaction were diplomacy and war. International relations consists of more than the diplomatic and military engagements of states, however. The actors include international and transnational organizations (the latter composed of members which are not states), business firms, and sometimes individuals, and their forms of interaction extend well beyond diplomacy and war – they include commerce, financial transactions and the exchange of information and culture. Such variety gives rise to problems of choice of great complexity and potential moral significance. The consequences of transnational interactions for the global distribution of income and wealth, the movement of human capital in the form of immigration flows, and the quality of the global environment are of particular importance for human welfare. A normative philosophy of international relations adequate to its empirical referent would embrace all of these subject matters.

2 Political realism and international scepticism

Political realism is the name of a collection of views which are often traced to THUCYDIDES, MACHIAVELLI and HOBBES, but whose prominence in modern international thought is due largely to a small number of recent and contemporary students of international relations such as Hans Morgenthau (1946) and George Kennan (1951). The common element is a denial that moral considerations should carry weight in decisions about foreign policy.

The most impressive statement of the realist

position was given by Hobbes (1651), who compared the international realm with the state of nature in respect of the absence of a central authority, and concluded that states in international relations have the same freedom from the obligation to follow moral principles ('laws of nature') as do individuals in the state of nature. On the Hobbesian view, states are not obliged to comply with moral principles because they have no reason to do so in the absence of a common enforcement agency or effective conventions of reciprocal compliance. At the base of this view is a conception of morality as a mutual benefit scheme, in which individuals comply with principles restricting the direct pursuit of self-interest when and because general compliance with these principles is mutually beneficial in comparison to mutual noncompliance. In this extreme form, political realism is no more than a special case of a familiar type of moral scepticism, which denies that moral judgments can be either reasonable or motivationally efficacious if they are not backed up by considerations of advantage (see MORAL SCEPTICISM; MORAL MOTIVATION). If one were to reject this type of moral scepticism, then the form of political realism associated with it would fall by the wayside.

Another form of realism, found more often in the literature of policy than philosophy, holds that leaders of states are not obligated to follow higher-level moral principles because the controlling obligation of their office is to advance the state's interest. Views of this kind are likely to seem particularly plausible in democratic states, where leaders are elected by the people and their responsibilities are understood as the advancement of the interests of those for whom they act as agents. Unlike the form of political realism considered earlier, this version is not in any obvious sense a type of moral scepticism. Indeed, it acknowledges that leaders of states, and by inference, their constituents can have moral obligations. The challenge faced by anyone who wishes to defend this view is to explain why it should be thought that leaders of states may justifiably do for their constituents what their constituents, as a group, may not justifiably do for themselves.

Another non-sceptical kind of realism, and perhaps the most persuasive of all versions of the view, is best described as heuristic. It does not deny that outcomes in foreign affairs can be appraised in terms of the good and evil, or that actions and policies can be evaluated in terms of their rightness or wrongness. It holds, however, that outcomes which are desirable from a moral point of view are more likely to occur when foreign policy decisions are screened from the direct influence of moral considerations. The argument for this position is essentially historical:

typically, that moral considerations have tended to distort practical reasoning in foreign affairs in a more or less systematic way, and that reasoning which is blocked from the direct influence of such considerations, and whose scope is limited to considerations of interest, has more often led to morally desirable results. In his Lindley Lectures (1951) – a defining document of political realism – George Kennan made an argument of this kind with respect to US diplomacy between the wars. The historical thesis plainly cannot be examined here, but it is worth observing that, even if the thesis turns out to be true, there would be no theoretical challenge to the possibility of international philosophy.

3 The morality of states and the domestic analogy

Assuming that the sceptical challenge can be overcome, the most important problem in international philosophy is the moral status of the state and the character of its relationship to other agents in the world. This problem is implicated in most of the leading normative issues in international relations – for example, the meaning of sovereignty, the permissibility of intervention, the basis and content of human rights, the extent of acceptable restrictions on the movement of persons across borders, entitlements to natural resources, and the obligations of states and their people to provide material assistance to others.

Writing about immigration policy, SIDGWICK described a 'general conflict between the cosmopolitan and the national ideals of political organization'. According to the national ideal, foreign policy should 'promote the interests of a determinate group of human beings, bound together by the tie of a common nationality', according to the cosmopolitan ideal, it should strive impartially to promote the interests of everyone, regardless of location or citizenship (1919: 309). The distinction between 'national' and 'cosmopolitan' ideals is fundamental in contemporary discourse about international ethics.

The dominant view in modern political theory, enduring well into the twentieth century, has been one or another variation of Sidgwick's 'national ideal', or what we might more accurately call 'the morality of states'. This conception has four distinguishing features. First, the international realm is a 'society of states' in which states, rather than individuals, are the principal actors and therefore the subjects of the major rights and duties. Second, states have a moral status analogous to that of individuals in domestic society. In particular, states have rights of territorial integrity and political sovereignty, analogous to the right of individual liberty, which secure their governments against external interference in the exercise of political authority over their territories and populations. Third, states are not generally responsible for the circumstances of outsiders or of other states, and within limits set by the principle of sovereignty, any individual state is entitled to assign priority to advancing the wellbeing of its inhabitants in preference to the equal wellbeing of others. Fourth, there is a high level of tolerance for diversity within the international order: states are not held to a single standard of political legitimacy, and, except perhaps in extreme cases, neither individual states nor the international community are authorized to intervene to protect a state's people against their own government or to bring about domestic political reform.

The morality of states is a genuine morality: like individual liberty in the domestic case, sovereignty is hardly the same as licence (see SOVEREIGNTY). It is, however, peculiar in presuming that a discontinuity exists between the moral order among the individuals who cohabit a single domestic society and the more comprehensive moral order among all the individuals in the world. What can be said for this presumption?

We might begin with the picture of the international realm as a 'society' in which states play the roles played by persons in domestic society. This 'domestic analogy' is the most influential form in which the morality of states has been articulated, due mainly to the writings of eighteenth-century international jurists like Vattel (1758) and Wolff (1749) (see WOLFF §7). Many find the analogy persuasive even today; for example, it is the organizing principle of Michael Walzer's formulation of the doctrine of the just war (Walzer 1977).

Although influential, the domestic analogy faces notorious difficulties, among which the most serious is that individual persons and the collectivities to which they are compared are such fundamentally different kinds of entities. States, for example, lack the unity of consciousness and the capacity for moral personality which we presume individual moral persons to possess, and so cannot be said to be self-determining in the same sense as individuals. Indeed, as a general matter, states may not even be identified with the societies they presume to organize and govern; leaving aside the special (and historically unusual) cases of the representative democracies, an indigenous government may stand in as arbitrary a relationship to its own people as would a foreign conqueror. Because states and persons have such different properties, it would be a surprise if it turned out that the reasons for valuing *individual* autonomy also apply to the *state*; and if they do not, the domestic analogy will not do much philosophical work in justifying the morality of states (see STATE, THE).

Most contemporary writers who rely on the domestic analogy to describe an international order in which states have a privileged ethical status appeal to considerations other than the analogy itself to defend the view. Two contrasting approaches deserve particular attention: first, the liberal idea that states' rights of political sovereignty and territorial integrity derive from the underlying individual rights and liberties of their members; second, the communitarian argument that respect for sovereignty enables political communities to preserve their distinctive histories and cultures, and thus to serve the human interests of their inhabitants.

For the first of these arguments, it is necessary to describe the extent and character of the individual rights and liberties which are supposed to serve as the basis of the derivative rights of states. Such a view emerges most naturally from voluntaristic conceptions of the social contract, in which the state is pictured as a free association based on either a historical contract or an ongoing implicit agreement (see CONTRACTARIANISM). The state's authority to interfere in individual lives would, on such a view, be bounded by the terms of the underlying agreement; and the collective right against interference by outside forces in the internal life of the state would simply be the outward expression of the rights of its members not to be interfered with in their individual lives without their own consent. But the machinery of social contract theory is not really essential. Taking their lead from J.S. Mill (in 'A Few Words on Nonintervention', 1859), those who believe there is an important connection between individual liberty and the sovereignty of states need hold no more than that sovereignty makes individual liberty possible – if only because states serve as bulwarks against conquest by other states and protect a zone where free societies can flourish.

Liberal notions of the state's special status face two kinds of difficulties, which on examination reduce to one. Voluntaristic conceptions are open to the familiar criticism that very few actually existing states can realistically be described as voluntary associations; either the original contract lies too far in the past to exert any normative force in the present, or it is not possible to demonstrate that the prevailing terms of association are the object of a tacit or implicit agreement. Non-voluntaristic conceptions risk overgeneralizing by supposing that individual liberties are better protected through a system of more or less unconditional respect for the sovereignty of states than in a system in which the right of sovereignty is restricted.

The communitarian alternative links the moral status of the state with that of the underlying society.

The view develops in two stages. First, it is argued that individuals are unlikely to flourish (or to realize their goods) except as members of communities characterized by at least a minimum level of mutual identification and fellow-feeling. This is only in part because individual human good may involve intrinsically social elements; it is also because the instrumental values of society, such as stability of expectations, can only be realized when there is an unforced disposition to cooperate, and this in turn can only be sustained when individuals identify themselves and each other as members of a common enterprise. Second, it is claimed that individuals are not likely to develop or sustain the requisite level of mutual identification if they are not governed through institutions which they can regard as the political expression of their own community. Again, this is only in part because the motivational force of communal loyalty may arise from a conception of the autonomous community as having intrinsic value; it is also because a community's capacity to defend itself from others and to elicit the necessary degree of contribution from its members will certainly depend on the people's acceptance of their governing institutions (see COMMUNITY AND COMMUNITARIANISM; NATION AND NATIONALISM).

The communitarian view assumes that there is some meaningful sense in which states can be seen as expressions of the values of their underlying societies, but this is controversial. Particularly in societies without representative institutions, there may simply be no way to determine whether the existing institutions are expressions of widely shared political values or, instead, legacies of force and fraud. There is a further problem: the communitarian argument trades on an image of domestic societies as reflecting a moral consensus in their communities, a condition that is surely, today, more the exception than the rule. As David Luban has argued (1980), both the liberal and the communitarian accounts of the state's special status often seem to reflect a romantic idealization that obscures the diversity of state forms in the modern world and the great variation in their degrees of respect for individual rights and liberties.

A doctrine of international morality in which states occupy a privileged position might be defended without relying on any view about the morally special character of the state itself. In fact, some of the most influential views about international morality have this structure. They argue that a world order of states is more likely, on balance, to achieve values of general importance to human beings – a relatively high level of stability and conditions in which groups and societies will face the most favourable circumstances for their own prosperity. Such a generalization would

not necessarily be undermined by examples of states whose governments are repressively authoritarian or which enforce exploitative domestic economic arrangements, as long as these examples could be shown to be exceptional. Moreover, views as highly consequentialist as this would have no difficulty, in principle, accommodating principles establishing minimum global standards of political legitimacy such as those found in the international doctrine of human rights.

4 Cosmopolitan morality

Cosmopolitanism stands in contrast to the notion that the boundaries between states, nations or societies have deep moral significance. It holds that each person is equally a subject of moral concern (or, that in the justification of choices of action or policy, the interests of each person affected should be taken equally into account), and that spatial proximity or shared membership are not in themselves sources of moral privilege. On a cosmopolitan view, there is no fundamental moral discontinuity between domestic and international society because states *qua* states have no special standing; if individuals have more extensive responsibilities to their own compatriots than to foreigners, or if states are entitled to be treated with some special respect by others in the international arena, this should be explained in a way that is consistent with the basic conception of a single moral realm in which each individual is equally worthy of concern and respect (see IMPARTIALITY).

There is a strong *prima facie* case for cosmopolitanism. For one thing, ordinary morality appears to presuppose its essential premise. Cosmopolitanism applies to the world the maxim that what we should do, or what institutions we should establish, should be decided on the basis of an impartial consideration of the claims of each person who would be affected by our choices. In one or another form, this maxim, although not beyond philosophical criticism, is a mainstay of the political moralities found in virtually all contemporary democratic cultures. Moreover, as the discussion in §3 suggests, the morality of states – cosmopolitanism's major rival – is difficult to maintain as a distinct view once the special status assigned to the state is brought into question; indeed, the most plausible explanation of the right of sovereignty may be an application of cosmopolitan principle rather than an alternative to it.

Against these considerations, there are at least three sources of doubt about cosmopolitan moralities. First, such views can seem either pallid or otherworldly in their apparent failure to connect with recognizable sources of motivation (for example, local affiliations or patriotic loyalties). Second, and relatedly, cosmopolitanism can appear to be too demanding, imposing requirements on individual conduct which may properly be described as heroic. Finally, these views can appear politically innocent, inviting an effort to build global political structures (a 'world government') that would do more harm than good.

The most common reply to these doubts is to argue they rest on an excessively simple interpretation of cosmopolitanism. In response to the first point, for example, it might be noted that cosmopolitan views are no more remote than most other moral doctrines from recognizable sources of motivation; although there is certainly a question about the capacity of cosmopolitan reasons for action to influence the will, this question is not different or more complex than the same question raised about the more familiar versions of Kantianism and utilitarianism. It is not possible to reply to the second objection without considering the normative consequences of cosmopolitanism; but it is worth noting that the view need not be interpreted as a doctrine of individual conduct, and indeed, that its most natural interpretation is instead as a view (or family of views) about institutional policy, in which case the objection is out of place. Finally, cosmopolitanism need not make any assumptions at all about the best political structure for international affairs; whether there should be an overarching, global political organization, and if so, how authority should be divided between the global organization and its subordinate political elements, is properly understood as a problem for normative political science rather than for political philosophy itself. Indeed, cosmopolitanism is consistent with a conception of the world in which states constitute the principal forms of human social and political organization; the central question is whether this conception or some feasible alternative would be preferred when the matter is regarded from a perspective in which the interests of all are equally represented.

Although formally consistent with a state-based conception of world order, any plausible version of cosmopolitanism is likely to differ substantively from familiar versions of the morality of states. Consider, for example, the question of intervention. Because it assigns a high value to state sovereignty, the morality of states takes it as a settled matter that states, coalitions of states, and international agencies should refrain from interfering in the internal affairs of individual states, except in certain well-defined, exceptional cases, chief among which is intervention in self-defence. In the aftermath of Nuremberg, intervention to end shocking and egregious practices such as genocide has come to be accepted as well (although such an exception, because it presupposes an attenuated principle of sovereignty, fits uncomfortably with the morality of states). Cosmopolitanism, on the other hand, is likely to be less suspicious of intervention in principle, and to admit the possibility that intervention for protective and remedial purposes might be justified; on a cosmopolitan view, the most important questions about intervention are pragmatic, having to do with the chances that intervention would accomplish its legitimate purposes without doing unacceptable collateral harm.

Or consider the question of international distributive justice (see JUSTICE, INTERNATIONAL). In its traditional form, the morality of states must regard a state's involvement in the relief of material suffering elsewhere as a matter of charity or mutual aid. This is because the principle of sovereignty functions not only to protect a society against interference in its own political and social affairs, but also as a kind of collective property right: it secures a state against non-consensual deprivations of the resources and wealth to be found on (or under) its territory. Understood more abstractly, it conveys a conception of domestic societies as bearing the primary responsibility for their own development, and of social wealth as deriving more significantly from the collective efforts of previous generations in a single society than from that society's good fortune in the distribution of natural and genetic resources and in the favourable prior course of political and social history. A cosmopolitan view, again in contrast, would begin with a conception of the world as a single human community. It would be unlikely to regard states as having privileged claims to the accumulation of social wealth unless institutions embodying such a recognition were the best feasible means to realize the requirements of whatever principles of distributive justice, themselves global in their scope, would be preferred from a point of view in which everyone's interests were represented.

Between the morality of states and moral cosmopolitanism, a variety of intermediate positions might be identified. The most interesting of these are two-tiered views which combine acceptance of a minimum global standard of conduct with tolerance of substantial diversity above the minimum. Such views vary according to the content of the global minimum – whether, for example, it includes significant standards of domestic legitimacy (are states required to respect the human rights of their people?) or significant expectations of participation in schemes involving the international transfer of wealth (are states required to contribute to famine relief or international development efforts?) A good example of such a view is the revisionist doctrine of a 'law of peoples' recently set forth by John Rawls (1993).

5 Human rights

As an element of the discourse of international affairs, the doctrine of universal human rights is a legacy of the settlement of the Second World War. As a philosophical matter, however, the notion of a human right is ancient, its universalistic strand running to the Stoics and its deontological structure dating at least to the early modern notion of natural right.

The underlying idea is that all human beings, simply because they are human beings, are entitled to be treated according to certain minimum standards. Very extensive statements of the content of this doctrine can be found in the Universal Declaration of Human Rights, adopted by the United Nations in 1948, and in several human rights covenants adopted by the United Nations and various regional organizations. There is little dispute in contemporary public discourse about either the grounding or the content of human rights doctrine.

There is, however, very little agreement among philosophers about any of the major theoretical questions concerning human rights (see RIGHTS §5). Philosophers disagree, for example, about the grounding of human rights, particularly the sense in which these rights can be said to pertain to human beings 'as such'; their extent, particularly whether human rights include, in addition to the standard individual liberties, civil and political rights and rights to a minimum standard of living; about the priorities among human rights, a question which is especially vexed if their extent is taken to be relatively broad; and about the relationship between human rights and other moral values. The doctrine of human rights did not receive sustained theoretical attention until the late 1970s and 1980s; the most notable contributions are due to Henry Shue (1980) and R.J. Vincent (1986).

The doctrine of human rights is chiefly important in international philosophy as an embodiment of the notion that there are universal minimum standards of political legitimacy – that is, standards to which all societies are responsible. To put it slightly differently, the doctrine of human rights sets a limit to the extent of acceptable diversity among the political constitutions of states. As such, human rights doctrine might be seen from one perspective as the entering wedge of cosmopolitan thought, or, from another, as the price that statist conceptions must pay for their plausibility. Either way, human rights doctrine is the most familiar form in which two-tiered theories of international morality present themselves, and perhaps the most

likely avenue for the future development of international philosophy.

See also: STATE, THE

References and further reading

Beitz, C.R. (1979) *Political Theory and International Relations*, Princeton, NJ: Princeton University Press. (A critical analysis of political realism and the morality of states, and an effort to set forth a cosmopolitan theory of international justice; extensive bibliography.)

Brierly, J.L. (1963) *The Law of Nations: An Introduction to the International Law of Peace*, ed. Sir H. Waldock, Oxford: Oxford University Press, 6th edn. (Historical introduction to international law.)

Brownlie, I. (ed.) (1993) *Basic Documents on Human Rights*, 3rd ed. Oxford: Oxford University Press. (Comprehensive compilation of authoritative international documents on human rights.)

* Hobbes, T. (1651) *Leviathan. The English Works of Thomas Hobbes*, vol. 3, ed. Sir W. Molesworth, London: John Bohn, 1839. (Chapters 21 and 30 referred to in §2.)

* Kant, I. (1795) *Perpetual Peace*, trans. H. Nisbet in *Political Writings*, 2nd edn ed. H. Reiss, Cambridge: Cambridge University Press, 1991. (Referred to in §1.)

* Kennan, G. (1951) *American Diplomacy 1900–1950*, Chicago, IL: University of Chicago Press. (The Lindley Lectures referred to in §2 above; a defining document of American political realism.)

* Luban, D. (1980) 'Just War and Human Rights', *Philosophy & Public Affairs* 9 (2): 160–81, and 'The Romance of the Nation-State', *Philosophy & Public Affairs* 9 (4): 392–97. (Cosmopolitan critique of the morality of states.)

* Mill, J.S. (1859) 'A Few Words on Non-intervention', *Dissertations and Discussions: Political, Philosophical, and Historical*, London: Longmans, Green, Reader and Dyer, 1867, vol. 3, 153–78. (Historically important statement of the liberal theory of special status of the state; referred to in §3.)

* Morgenthau, H. (1946) *Scientific Man versus Power Politics*, Chicago, IL: University of Chicago Press. (Influential defence of political realism.)

Nardin, T. (1983) *Law, Morality, and the Relations of States*, Princeton, NJ: Princeton University Press. (Argues that the aim of international law and morality is to regulate a pluralistic international society consisting of states with differing internal moralities; comprehensive bibliography.)

Nickel, J.W. (1987) *Making Sense of Human Rights*, Berkeley and Los Angeles, CA, and London:

University of California Press. (Documentary appendix.)

* Rawls, J. (1993) 'The Law of Peoples', in S. Shute and S. Hurley (eds) *On Human Rights*, New York: Basic Books, 41–82. (Example of a 'two-tiered' view; referred to in §3.)

* Shue, H. (1980) *Basic Rights: Subsistence, Affluence, and U.S. Foreign Policy*, Princeton, NJ: Princeton University Press. (An argument for an expansive doctrine of universal human rights.)

* Sidgwick, H. (1919) *The Elements of Politics*, London: Macmillan, 4th edn. ('National' and 'cosmopolitan' ideals contrasted in connection with immigration policy; referred to in §3.)

* Vattel, E. de (1758) *The Law of Nations or the Principles of Natural Law*, trans C.G. Fenwick, The Classics of International Law no. 4, vol. 3, Washington, DC: The Carnegie Institution, 1916. (Important source of domestic analogy; referred to in §3.)

* Vincent, R.J. (1986) *Human Rights and International Relations*, Cambridge: Cambridge University Press, in association with the Royal Institute of International Affairs. (A survey of theoretical and political issues in human rights doctrine; extensive references.)

* Walzer, M. (1977) *Just and Unjust Wars*, New York: Basic Books. (Most influential contemporary work on morality in war, with extensive references; referred to in §3.)

* Wolff, C. (1749) *The Law of Nations Treated According to the Scientific Method*, trans. J.H. Drake, The Classics of International Law no. 13, vol. 2, Washington, DC: The Carnegie Institution, 1934. (Important source of domestic analogy referred to in §3.)

CHARLES R. BEITZ

INTERPRETATION, ARTISTIC

see ARTISTIC INTERPRETATION

INTERPRETATION, INDIAN THEORIES OF

Need for interpretation of texts was felt already during the ancient period of Vedic texts in India. Vedic texts were orally transmitted for over a thousand years. During this period, the change in locations of people reciting the texts and the mother tongues of the reciters led to a widening gap between the preserved sacred texts and their interpreters. Additionally, there was a notion that the sacred language was a mystery which was only partially understood by the common people. This led to the early development of exegetical tools to assist the interpretation of the sacred literature.

Later, grammarians and etymologists developed sophisticated exegetical tools and theories of interpretation. These generally led to a deeper understanding of the structure of language. The priestly tradition developed its own canons of interpretation, which are manifest in the system of Mīmāṃsā. Here we have the first fully developed theory of discourse and context.

The categories developed by Mīmāṃsā were used by other schools, especially by the school of Dharmaśāstra, or Hindu religious law. Both Mīmāṃsā and Dharmaśāstra created sets of hierarchical principles for authoritative guidance in interpretation. Other philosophical and religious traditions developed categories of their own to deal with problems of interpretation. A major problem was created when the literature accepted as authoritative by a tradition contained apparently contradictory passages. The traditions had to deal with this problem and find ways of explaining away those passages which did not quite fit with their own view of truth. For this purpose, a whole set of categories were employed. At a later period, several ingenious principles of interpretation were used for texts in general. Here, significant contributions were made by the traditions of Sanskrit grammar and poetics.

1 **Text and interpreter**
2 **Early tools to assist interpretation**
3 **Etymologists and grammarians**
4 **Mīmāṃsā principles of interpretation**
5 **Other philosophical traditions**
6 **Principles of interpretation in Hindu law**
7 **Generalized principles of textual interpretation**

1 Text and interpreter

Concern for the interpretation of the scriptural language was already being voiced in India from the earliest period of the Vedic scriptures (*c.*1500 BC). The primary reason for such concern lies in the real or perceived distance between the language of a sacred text and the contemporary language of the person trying to comprehend and use that text. Real distance between the language of a sacred text and the language of its interpreter or user can be caused by various factors, such as temporal and geographical distance, linguistic change in the sacred language, shifts in the mother tongues of the text's preservers, and corruption and loss in the text in the course of oral or written transmission. The middle Vedic texts already express a concern that the users of language are unable to pronounce proper accents. The loss of this ability contributed to improper use of sacred formulas, as well as to misinterpretation of their meaning. We are told a story about a demon who seeks a son who will kill the god Indra. He should ask for a son who will be *indraśatrú*, 'killer of Indra'. However, the ignorant demon uses a wrong accent and asks for a son who will be *índraśatru*, 'he whose killer is Indra'. This story is later repeated by Sanskrit grammarians and etymologists to illustrate the importance of a proper understanding of accents. Similarly, in the oral tradition, long stretches were memorized and recited in an unbroken fashion. Besides actual cases of mutilation and alteration of the text, such recitation resulted in multiple possibilities for dividing up the text.

Ideas regarding the nature of the sacred language contributed an additional feeling of distance between text and interpreter. The *Ṛg Veda* tells us that language, in reality, is measured in four quarters, all of which are known to the wise, insightful priests. However, three quarters of speech are hidden away from common people, who have access only to a single quarter. The goddess of speech is said to reveal her true form only to a person of her own choice. Another important notion is that the gods do not like the direct mode of expression (*pratyakṣa*). They would rather have sacred expressions in an indirect mode (*parokṣa*). Middle Vedic prose texts often explain the so-called indirect expressions by paraphrasing them with expressions which have structures more transparent to their audience.

2 Early tools to assist interpretation

In the middle (*c.* 1000 BC) and late (*c.* 700–500 BC) Vedic periods, we find a growing concern for proper understanding of older texts and the beginning of concerted efforts to develop technical tools towards that goal. For the Brāhmaṇa texts, the highest perfection (*rūpasamṛddhi*) of ritual results when the recited Vedic text matches the ritual action. This places a high premium on comprehending the meaning of the recited texts before one decides how and when they are to be used in ritual. The texts repeatedly state that the man who performs a ritual 'knowingly' (*ya evaṃ vidvān*) will be rewarded.

There was also a serious effort by priest-scholars such as Māṇḍūkeya and Śākalya to put together the Padapāṭhas, 'word-by-word' versions of Vedic texts. The late Vedic text *Aitareya-Āraṇyaka* speaks of *nirbhuja* ('unsegmented') versions versus *pratṛṇṇa*

('segmented', 'broken-down') versions. Later on, the segmented versions were used as the basis for reproducing continuous versions (*saṃhitā*) which were deemed to match the originals. These activities provided an enormous opportunity to build formal tools to assist interpretation, a task taken up later by the grammarians, etymologists and phoneticians of ancient India.

3 Etymologists and grammarians

The goal of the etymologists was to provide insight into the meaning of an expression (*nirvacana*) by providing an analytical breakdown of it. Yāska, the author of *Nirukta* (Analytical Exegesis, *c.* 500 BC), the only surviving ancient text on etymology, says that comprehension of meaning is the highest goal of his science. Without comprehension of meaning, one cannot break down a continuous Vedic text into its constituent words, nor can one know the proper ritual application for such a text. He criticizes the reciters of Vedic texts who do not care for meaning. He refers to Kautsa, who argued that the Vedas are devoid of meaning. Yāska refutes Kautsa's arguments and proposes a number of methods for etymology:

> Now we shall deal with etymology. In this context, words whose accent and grammatical form are regular and have a transparent modification of the formative elements should be explained in the regular manner. However, [for other words,] where the meaning is unclear and the modifications of the formative elements are not transparent, one should always analyse them by focusing on their meaning, by the analogy of some shared action [with another word]. If no such analogy is found, one should explain [words] even by the commonality of a single syllable or sound; but one should never give up an attempt at etymology.
>
> (*Nirukta* 2.1)

While the etymologists were busy offering a breakdown of difficult Vedic expressions, they were clearly aware of a different tradition, namely the tradition of grammar (*vyākaraṇa*). In Yāska's terminology, this reverse process, called *saṃskāra*, consists of building up words by fusing their formative elements and putting them through a series of modifications (*vikāra*). This is the pattern followed in the famous ancient grammar of Pāṇini. It extensively uses the term *artha*, 'meaning', and yet its goal is not interpretation *per se*. It is an encoding grammar rather than a decoding grammar. It begins with the meaning to be communicated and with morphological primes such as roots, stems and affixes. Through a series of steps involving affixation, substitution, modification, and so on, it builds up a surface expression in Sanskrit that corresponds to the intended meaning.

However, Pāṇini's successors, Kātyāyana and PATAÑJALI, clearly see the value of his grammar as a tool for the preservation and comprehension of the Vedic scriptures. They argue that the usage of Sanskrit backed by an understanding of grammar leads to success in life here and hereafter. The grammarians are dealing with a stage of Sanskrit when it is no longer a first language, and needs to be acquired by a deliberate study of grammar. Among the purposes of the study of Sanskrit grammar, Patañjali includes several which relate to one's ability to interpret the scriptural texts properly. One of these purposes is *asandeha*, 'removal of doubts'. Besides mentioning the old *indraśatrú* example, Patañjali cites one more case, *sthūlápṛṣatī*. This word describes a cow that is supposed to be sacrificed. If it is accented as *sthūlápṛṣatī*, then it can be interpreted as a Karmadhāraya compound to mean 'a cow that is fat and spotted'. However, if it is accented as *sthūlápṛṣatī*, then it becomes a Bahuvrīhi compound and means 'a cow that has fat spots'. A person who does not know the accents or what the difference in accent leads to will not be able to interpret the ritual prescription properly. For Patañjali, studying the Vedas without comprehending their meaning is as futile as throwing firewood away from fire. How can it possibly catch fire?

4 Mīmāṃsā principles of interpretation

The tradition of Mīmāṃsā systematizes the rules of interpretation as they apply to the ritual use of Vedic texts, as well as to the performance of ritual as understood from those texts. Here the term 'Veda' applies to both the mantras and the prose Brāhmaṇa commentaries. For Mīmāṃsā, the Vedas are entirely uncreated, not authored either by humans or by God, yet are fully meaningful and authoritative (see MĪMĀṂSĀ §3). Given this eternal innate authority of the Vedic texts, Mīmāṃsā provides a set of six hierarchical principles of interpretation, the earlier ones overriding the later ones: (1) direct statement (*śruti*); (2) word-meaning (*liṅga*); (3) syntactical connection (*vākya*); (4) context (*prakaraṇa*); (5) position in the text (*sthāna*); (6) name (*samākhyā*).

Let us consider the conflict between the first two guiding principles. Verse 8.51.7 of the *Ṛg Veda* describes the divinity Indra. On the basis of the word-meaning (*liṅga*), one would think that this verse should be used while making an offering to Indra. However, a direct statement (*śruti*) in the *Taittirīya-Saṃhitā* (1.5.8), another Vedic text, says that one

makes an offering to Gārhapatya fire by using a verse addressed to Indra. This direct statement overrides what one would otherwise decide on the basis of the meaning of the particular verse.

Besides these six principles, Mīmāṃsā also deals with numerous important issues relating to Vedic interpretation, such as cases where one finds seemingly contradictory statements in the Vedic corpus. How, for example, does one deal with a statement authorizing a Niṣāda chief to perform a certain sacrifice? The tribal people referred to by the term 'Niṣāda' are generally beyond the pale of those eligible to perform sacrifices to Vedic gods. If the word 'Niṣāda-chief' is taken to mean 'one who is a Niṣāda and a chief', this authorization conflicts with the general prohibition of low-caste people taking part in Vedic sacrifices. However, if it is taken to mean 'a chief of the Niṣāda', it could possibly apply to a person who is not a Niṣāda, yet is their chief. The Mīmāṃsakas try to resolve such issues. Where there is ultimately no way to choose between contradictory Vedic injunctions, Mīmāṃsā advises an optional choice, for example, between 'One uses the Ṣoḍaśī cup in the Atirātra sacrifice' and 'One does not use the Ṣoḍaśī cup in the Atirātra sacrifice'. Considering the entire Vedic corpus to be fully authoritative leads to rejection of its historical and geographical diversity. This rejection gives rise to many more instances of apparently contradictory statements.

5 Other philosophical traditions

Acceptance of the entire Vedic corpus as authoritative requires the reconciliation of a large number of apparently contradictory statements. However, the problem is not unique to Mīmāṃsā. Bādarāyaṇa, in his *Brahmasūtra*, uses the term *samanvaya* ('coordination', 'reconciliation') for the technique of reconciliation. While Mīmāṃsā deals largely with ritual injunctions, Bādarāyaṇa is concerned with the apparently divergent views regarding the ultimate reality of Brahman in the Upaniṣads. The commentators on the *Brahmasūtra* are faced with the same dilemmas, which get more complicated with every generation. Beginning with ŚAṄKARA, the tradition of Vedānta adopts the view that it is founded on three authoritative sources (*prasthānatrayī*), namely the Upaniṣads, the *Brahmasūtra* and the *Bhagavad Gītā*. The principle of *samanvaya* needs to be expanded to all these texts. With Rāmānuja and Madhva, the Purāṇas and the texts of the Pāñcarātra tradition are also added to this pool of authoritative texts. Commentators often create a deliberate hierarchy among different texts, or among different passages from the same text. Then they conveniently argue that some of these texts are to be taken literally (*mukhyārtha*), while others are to be interpreted metaphorically (*lakṣaṇā*). Another dichotomy among texts is stipulated by suggesting that different texts or passages are meant for different audiences, and that these audiences, having different intellectual and spiritual abilities, need suitably different teachings. Some teachings are meant for those who are truly capable, while others are meant to be provisional teachings for those who have not yet arrived at the same high level. Such distinctions are found also in the Jaina and Buddhist traditions (for example, the *upāya/upeya*, *vyāvahārika/pāramārthika* and *neyārtha/nītārtha* distinctions, all of which correspond respectively to 'provisional' and 'true'). With such tools, one can extract a uniformity of teaching from texts which apparently do not have it. The tradition of Dharmaśāstra, religious law, attempted to eliminate similar apparent conflicts between various texts by saying that some were restricted to certain periods of time, regions or social classes.

6 Principles of interpretation in Hindu law

Dharmaśāstra provides an important set of hierarchical guidelines for interpration. Authorities include the Vedas, the Smṛtis (law books), the behaviour of the elites in the community, and, finally, one's own judgment. According to this tradition, and most of the wider Indian tradition, the authority of the Vedic texts overrides that of the Smṛtis. While the Vedic texts are either uncreated or created by God, the Smṛtis are said to be authored by human scholars and are believed to be based on the Vedic texts. The behaviour of the elite leaders of the community is presumed to be based on the Vedas and the Smṛtis. When there is no access to any other authority, one has recourse to one's own conscience (see DUTY AND VIRTUE, INDIAN CONCEPTIONS OF §2).

In fact, some early Dharmaśāstra texts say that there were no prescriptions in the Vedas (*śrutyabhāvāt*) regarding the laws that govern different regional, caste and family traditions, and, for that reason, the ancient lawgiver Manu explained these topics. However, along with the tradition of Mīmāṃsā, Dharmaśāstra argues that this simply means that the Vedic texts dealing with such topics are lost, and not that they did not exist. The existence of lost Vedic texts (*anumitaśruti*) is inferred on the basis of statements in the Smṛtis. In general, while the Dharmaśāstra theory lays great emphasis on the Vedas as the ultimate basis for authority, in reality the interpretation of the Vedas gets pulled in the direction of contemporary beliefs and practices.

7 Generalized principles of textual interpretation

Coming back to the wider context of textual interpretation, we find a number of important initiatives. In the tradition of Sanskrit grammar and in the traditions relating to Brahmanical ritual and law, there is a large literature called Paribhāṣā, 'Maxims of Interpretation' (see Abhyankar 1968). In the context of rules of Sanskrit grammar, these maxims help account for the derivation of certain forms, by effectively extending or narrowing the scope of a rule through interpretation. Generally there is great reluctance to alter the wording of a rule or offer a new rule. The tradition would rather get a new ruling by reinterpreting an old one. In doing this, the commentators have recourse to a great many interpretive techniques (see Kielhorn 1887). Related to the Paribhāṣā literature is the device called *nyāya*. In this context, the term refers to a proverbial statement of colloquial (*laukika*) or technical (*śāstrīya*) wisdom. For example, when two events have no genuine relationship, but are merely coincidental, one cites the *kākatālīyanyāya*, which refers to a story of coincidences, such as the following: a person is resting under a palm tree; a crow flying over the tree comes and sits on a palm fruit; the weight of the crow causes the fruit to fall and crack the person's head. There are a large number of these traditional *nyāyas* (see Kane 1977).

The fifth-century grammarian BHARTṚHARI, in his *Vākyapadīya* (On Sentences and Words), provides a catalogue of many guiding principles of interpretation:

Meanings of words are differentiated on the basis of the sentence [in which they occur], the context, the meaning [of other words in the context], propriety, time and place [of utterance], and not merely on the basis of the form of a word. Connection, separation, association, opposition, meaning, context, indication, presence of another word, suitability, propriety, place, time, gender, and accent, etc. are the factors which help to determine a specific meaning, in the absence of [natural] clarity of meaning.

(*Vākyapadīya* 2.314–16)

Many of these ideas are carried over into the tradition of Sanskrit poetics, which aims at explaining how one understands the aesthetically pleasing significance of poetry. The notion of interpretation is crucial in all discussions in this tradition. While the lexical meaning of words may be taken for granted, there is a wide gap between lexical meaning and intended meaning. In discussing the phrase 'the cowherd colony is on the river Ganges', we are told that we move away from the literal meaning because of the difficulty of construing the literal meaning (*anvayānupapatti*) and the difficulty of justifying the literal interpretation in view of the intention of the speaker (*tātparyānupapatti*). Nudged by these two factors, we move to the meaning 'the cowherd colony is on the bank of the river Ganges'. Beyond this comes the level of implied or suggested meaning, which may or may not match the meaning intended by the speaker. A listener often understands far more than what the speaker intends. Such levels of suggested and implied meanings are further accounted for through the suggestive function of language and/or inference.

See also: LANGUAGE, INDIAN THEORIES OF; MEANING, INDIAN THEORIES OF

References and further reading

* Abhyankar, K.V. (ed.) (1968) *Paribhāṣāsaṃgraha: a Collection of Paribhāṣā Texts from Various Systems of Sanskrit Grammar*, Poona: Bhandarkar Oriental Research Institute. (A comprehensive collection of interpretive rules in different schools of Sanskrit grammar.)
* Bhartṛhari (5th century) *Vākyapadīya* (On Sentences and Words), ed. W. Rau, *Abhandlungen für die Kunde des Morgenlands* 42 (4), 1977. (A critical edition of the verse portion of the *Vākyapadīya*; there is no English translation of this, but see Iyer 1969.)
  Deshpande, M.M. (1992) *The Meaning of Nouns: Semantic Theory in Classical and Medieval India*, Dordrecht: Kluwer Academic Publishers. (The bulk of the book is an annotated translation of a seventeenth-century Sanskrit text on the meaning of nouns. The introduction covers the history of a number of semantic theories in Sanskrit grammar and philosophy.)
  Gächter, O. (1983) *Hermeneutics and Language in Pūrvamīmāṃsā*, Delhi: Motilal Banarsidass. (An important modern analysis of Mīmāṃsā theories of language and interpretation.)
  Iyer, K.A.S. (1969) *Bhartṛhari: A Study of the Vākyapadīya in the Light of the Ancient Commentaries*, Poona: Deccan College. (A very comprehensive study, though somewhat dated.)
* Kane, P.V. (1962) 'On Mīmāṃsā Principles and Rules of Interpretation in Relation to Dharmaśāstra', in *History of Dharmaśāstra*, Poona: Bhandarkar Oriental Research Institute, 2nd edn, 1977, vol. 5, part 2: 1283–1351. (A seminal study relating the interpretive rules of Mīmāṃsā to Hindu law.)
* Kielhorn, F. (1887) 'Notes on the Mahābhāṣya, No. 7, Some Devices of Indian Grammarians', *The Indian Antiquary* 16: 244–52. (A famous study of the principles of interpretation as used by Sanskrit grammarians.)
  Raja, K. (1963) *Indian Theories of Meaning*, Adyar Library Series 91, Madras: Adyar Library and Research Centre. (A somewhat dated, but still very useful, account.)
* Yāska (*c.*500 BC) *Nirukta* (Analytical Exegesis), ed. and trans. L. Sarup, *The Nighaṇṭu and the Nirukta: the Oldest Indian Treatise on Etymology, Philology and Semantics*, London: Oxford University Press, 1920. (Critical edition and translation of an important work attributed to Yāska.)

MADHAV M. DESHPANDE

INTERPRETATION, RADICAL

see RADICAL TRANSLATION AND RADICAL INTERPRETATION (§1–6)

INTERROGATIVES

see QUESTIONS

INTROSPECTION, EPISTEMOLOGY OF

If we wish to know what is going on in someone else's mind, we must observe their behaviour; on the basis of what we observe, we may sometimes reasonably draw a conclusion about the person's mental state. Thus, for example, on seeing someone smile, we infer that they are happy; on seeing someone scowl, we infer that they are upset. But this is not, at least typically, the way in which we come to know our own mental states. We do not need to examine our own behaviour in order to know how we feel, what we believe, what we want and so on. Our understanding of these things is more direct than our understanding of the mental states of others, it seems. The term used to describe this special mode of access which we seem to have to our own mental states is 'introspection'.

A view which takes its inspiration from Descartes holds that introspection provides us with infallible and complete access to our states of mind. On this view, introspection provides us with a foundation for our knowledge of the physical world. On this view we come to know the physical world by first coming to recognize certain features of our mind, namely, the sensations which physical objects excite in us, and then drawing conclusions about the likely source of these mental states. Our knowledge of the physical world is thus indirect; it is grounded in the direct knowledge we have of our own minds. The view that introspection provides an infallible and complete picture of the mind, however, is no longer widely accepted.

Introspection has also been called upon to support various metaphysical conclusions. Descartes argued for dualism on the basis of introspective evidence, and certain contemporary philosophers have argued in much the same spirit. Hume noted that introspection does not reveal the presence of an enduring self, but only a series of fleeting perceptions; some have concluded, therefore, that there is no enduring self.

Philosophers concerned with self-improvement, whether epistemological or moral, have frequently called upon introspection. Introspection has been thought to aid in forming beliefs on the basis of adequate evidence, and it has been used as a tool of self-scrutiny by those concerned to understand and refine their motivations and characters.

1   **The complete transparency view**
2   **Transparency and the contemporary scientific view of the mind**
3   **Cartesian projects in contemporary perspective**
4   **Introspection and the metaphysics of mind**
5   **Introspection and self-improvement**

1   The complete transparency view

Precisely what Descartes believed about introspection is a subject of some controversy (see DESCARTES, R.). Nevertheless, we may describe a view for which there is substantial textual support and which has historically played an important role. The powers of introspection, on this view, are considerable. First, introspection is held to be infallible. Thus, for example, if I believe that I am experiencing a mild headache, then I am experiencing a mild headache. Second, this infallibility is not merely a matter of psychological law, something which could have been otherwise; instead, it is a matter of necessity. The very idea of introspective error is incoherent. Finally, introspection provides one with a complete picture of the contents of one's mind. There can be nothing in the mind which may escape its notice. The picture one gets of one's mind when one introspects is thus both complete and completely accurate.

In all of these respects, introspection contrasts quite sharply with our ability to know the world outside our minds. We can and, of course, do make errors in our judgments about the world around us. We may sometimes think that a certain book is on the

shelf, but on trying to take it down discover that what seemed to be a book is merely an empty dust-jacket. When it comes to physical objects, appearances sometimes deceive. Our mental states, however, cannot fail to be precisely as they appear to us. By the same token, our picture of the world around us is fundamentally incomplete; we simply do not know everything there is to know about it. Our mental life, on the other hand, is wholly transparent to introspection. It would be incoherent, on Descartes' view, to suppose that one might be in a certain mental state without its being accessible to introspective attention.

Introspection is not merely superior to perception on Descartes' view, however; instead, introspection is a prerequisite for perceptual knowledge. We perceive the external world only indirectly. By way of introspection, we gain direct access to our mental states. Having made note of our mental states, we may then attempt to infer what external objects, if any, might have made such impressions upon us. The self-knowledge achieved through introspection thus forms an infallible foundation upon which we may attempt to build our understanding of the external world. The evidence we have for the existence and character of the external world is fully provided for us by way of introspection. Introspective knowledge is, on this account, epistemically prior to all knowledge of the external world.

This view of introspection gives rise to a number of epistemological problems which have been pursued with great vigour since the time of Descartes. First, and most obviously, there is the problem of explaining how it is that the knowledge we have of our own mental states can, by itself, provide sufficient evidence for beliefs about an external world of physical objects (see SCEPTICISM). Second, there is the problem of other minds, that is, the problem of explaining how the knowledge we have of the behaviour of others can provide sufficient evidence for beliefs about their mental states (see OTHER MINDS). Third, there is a problem about our knowledge of the past and the future. Since introspection provides us with knowledge of our current mental states alone, we must somehow find sufficient evidence in our knowledge of the present instant to ground claims about other times. Although Descartes raised and addressed only the first of these three problems, they are really variations on a common theme. In each case, there is thought to be only indirect access to certain potential objects of knowledge: in the first, physical objects; in the second, mental states of other people; in the third, the past and the future. One needs to develop hypotheses about these things, but the truth or falsity of one's hypotheses cannot be directly checked against the facts, since one has no direct access to them (see

INFERENCE TO THE BEST EXPLANATION). Some have argued that these problems are resolvable, that indirect evidence of the relevant facts is evidence enough. Others have argued that the problems are insurmountable, and that a very broad scepticism is thus forced upon us; we are left with knowledge of nothing but our current mental states. Still others have suggested that because the Cartesian approach inevitably leads to such radical scepticism, we should reject the premises which raised these difficulties in the first place.

2 Transparency and the contemporary scientific view of the mind

There are, however, problems for the transparency view in any case. It is quite clear that introspection does not give us total access to our current mental states. Moreover, once we recognize that the picture introspection presents is inevitably incomplete, it is but a small step to recognizing the fallibility of introspection as well.

The strengths and limitations of Descartes' view may best be understood by first examining a view which attributes even greater powers to introspection than did Descartes. Let us thus consider the view that mental phenomena are not merely accessible to introspection, but instead that they must actually be present to consciousness if they are to exist. On this very strong view, the idea that one might have memories (in the mind) which are not current objects of introspective awareness is a mistake. But how can one then account for the ability to recall past events? The simple phenomenon of memory retrieval becomes mysterious if one cannot allow for mental occurrences which are not conscious.

Far more plausible is Descartes' suggestion that mental phenomena are essentially introspectable, that is, that they are potential objects of introspection, rather than that they must actually be introspected in order to exist. On this view one may countenance the existence of memories and other mental states generally, which are not current objects of introspective awareness, so long as they may be brought to consciousness. It is clear enough that some memories may only be brought to consciousness with great difficulty. The mere inability to introspect some mental item on a particular occasion, even after great effort, is thus insufficient to show that it does not exist. Mental phenomena might easily escape one's introspective notice on such a view; they need only be accessible to introspection in principle.

Even this view, however, is almost certainly false, although the reasons for thinking so were not available to Descartes. Work in experimental psychol-

ogy has for some time now required the postulation of mental states which are not accessible to introspection. Two brief examples should suffice to make the point. First, in order to explain our responsiveness to features of the environment of which we are not consciously aware, it is necessary to postulate mental mechanisms which register information about the environment and integrate this information with other facts to which we are sensitive. No amount of introspective attention can acquaint us with the operation of these mental processes or the contents of the mental states which register the information on which they draw. Second, as Noam Chomsky's work has shown, the process of language acquisition involves the generation and testing of detailed hypotheses about the structure of the language spoken around one; language use requires that the rules of one's language be mentally represented (see CHOMSKY, N). These hypotheses and rules, however, while explicitly represented in the mind, are not accessible to introspection. No amount of introspective scrutiny can acquaint us with any of these features of the mind.

The picture of the mind which is thus emerging from work in experimental psychology and psycholinguistics is quite different from that portrayed by Descartes. On Descartes' view, theorizing about the mind is unnecessary because the data provided by introspection already encompass all that there is to the mind. In this respect, psychology contrasts with the other sciences where theories need to be constructed to explain the data collected, and entities and processes need to be postulated to account for the regularities in observed phenomena. Current work in psychology, however, presents the mind as an object of study as fit for theorizing as those in any other science and, indeed, as requiring theoretical investigation if it is to be properly understood. Indeed, once we recognize the existence of memories which are not current objects of awareness, we have taken the first step in theorizing about the mind. On current accounts, introspection gives us access to only a very small corner of the mental world – comparable to the access unaided vision provides us to chemical phenomena. By far the greatest part of our mental life is simply inaccessible to introspection.

One might think that although current work in psychology undermines Descartes' view that introspection gives us access to a complete account of the mind, it leaves his claim that introspection provides an infallible guide to the mind, at least as far is it goes, untouched. This is not, however, the case. Once it is acknowledged that the mind is a fit object of scientific theorizing, it becomes impossible to insulate the judgments of introspection from the encroachment of theory. Introspection provides people with a certain perspective on their mental states. It is but one perspective, however. Our best available theories of the mind draw on other sources of information as well, and may in principle provide us with reasons for thinking that the perspective provided by introspection is not always an accurate one, just as our best available theories of vision may allow us to recognize situations in which visual appearances are likely to mislead. In the case of introspection, as with vision, one need not appeal to subtle work in experimental psychology to see its fallibility at work. The fallibility of introspection is not merely a theoretical possibility, but a fact of everyday life.

Works of literature have long portrayed characters whose introspective understanding of their own mental states fall far short of perfection, not merely by being incomplete, but by being inaccurate as well. Failure to recognize accurately one's own emotions, desires, beliefs, motivations and traits of character are all familiar. Indeed, it is simply a part of the common-sense conception of the mental that introspection is subject to error in making these kinds of judgments. The current experimental literature in psychology both supports and deepens this common-sense view. Introspective judgments of current mental states simply are not infallible. This is not to say, of course, that introspection cannot provide us with knowledge of our own mental states, for, at least on most views, knowledge does not require infallibility.

The limitations of introspection were recognized by Kant in the *Critique of Pure Reason* (1781/1787): introspection, according to Kant, 'represents to consciousness even our own selves only as we appear to ourselves, not as we are in ourselves' (B153).

3 Cartesian projects in contemporary perspective

Even if we acknowledge that introspection provides neither a complete nor a completely accurate account of the mind, it is not obvious what implications this has for the Cartesian doctrine of the epistemic priority of self-knowledge – that is, the view that knowledge of one's own mental states is in an important sense prior to knowledge of the physical world. Many have suggested that this last Cartesian doctrine survives the downfall of the others, and that the projects to which it gives rise must still be carried out, although perhaps with some minor modifications. Others have argued that the doctrine of the epistemic priority of self-knowledge must fall with the other Cartesian doctrines, and that the projects to which it gives rise are thereby completely undermined.

One project which is clearly undermined is the constructive project of radical foundationalism. The radical foundationalists, following Descartes, sought to provide empirical knowledge with an infallible foundation. On this view, a belief is shown to be justified either by showing it to be infallible or by appropriately basing it on a foundation of infallible beliefs. Because the foundation consists of beliefs about which mistakes are impossible, it can need neither revision nor correction in light of new information. Introspection was thought to provide such a foundation of judgments about the current contents of one's mind. The fallibility of introspection, however, clearly vitiates this project by robbing it of the required foundation. This need not, of course, be taken to show that radical foundationalism provides a mistaken account of the requirements for justified belief. Rather, it shows that the requirements which radical foundationalists set out cannot be met. Thus, either radical foundationalism does not correctly lay out the requirements for justified belief, or scepticism about the external world is inevitable.

The constructive projects associated with weaker versions of foundationalism, however, are not so obviously undermined. Introspection might be thought to provide one with a fallible foundation for one's beliefs about the physical world. Such a foundation would be subject to revision, but one would still need to show, as with radical foundationalism, how to ground judgments about the physical world in the deliverances of introspection. Many of the justificatory projects faced by radical foundationalism will have analogues within this more modest foundationalist enterprise; the problems of the external world, of other minds, and of the past and the future, for example, will present the modest foundationalist with justificatory projects (see FOUNDATIONALISM).

Coherence theorists – who hold, roughly, that a belief is justified if it fits in with one's other beliefs – may also accept the doctrine of the priority of self-knowledge. Indeed, on one natural way of presenting a coherence theory, agents who wish to justify their beliefs must begin by introspecting in order to discover what beliefs they have; only then can the project of justifying one's beliefs begin. In holding such an account of justification, one need not hold that introspection gives one complete or infallible access to one's beliefs. Introspection is used here, as in modest foundationalism, simply to provide a starting point for the task of justification. Having provided such a starting point, the deliverances of introspection may subsequently be revised in light of considerations of overall coherence (see KNOWLEDGE AND JUSTIFICATION, COHERENCE THEORY OF).

These versions of foundationalism and the coherence theory share a commitment to the doctrine of the epistemic priority of self-knowledge. On these versions of both views, knowledge of the physical world is possible only when appropriately founded in knowledge of (certain of) one's own mental states. Some have argued, however, that both foundationalism and the coherence theory thus understood are misguided for precisely this reason, for it may be thought that the doctrine of the epistemic priority of self-knowledge is also undermined once introspection is seen as a source of only an incomplete and partially accurate view of the mind. On such a view, the special epistemic status of self-knowledge depends upon the infallibility of introspection. If introspection is a source of knowledge which is both incomplete and fallible, then it fails to distinguish itself from perception of the external world as a privileged source of belief. Introspection may be, on the whole, a source of accurate information about the mind, but on this view it can occupy no special place in a theory of justification once the claim of infallibility is rejected. There is no more reason to begin the project of justifying one's beliefs with the deliverances of introspection than with the deliverances of sense perception. The reflective believer, on this view, does not begin reflection by focusing exclusively on the contents of their own mind, and then determining what can be justified in light of such contents; instead, perceptual judgments are taken at face value from the beginning, just as introspective judgments are, and the project of justification proceeds against the background of one's total body of belief. Such a view makes a complete break with Cartesian doctrine by assigning no special status whatsoever to introspection.

4 Introspection and the metaphysics of mind

Thus far, we have examined the significance of introspection for epistemology, but introspection has also been pressed into service to support important metaphysical doctrines. Descartes argues in the Sixth Meditation that we recognize our existence as thinking beings by way of introspection, and this provides the key premise in an argument for dualism (see DUALISM). Once again, there is substantial scholarly debate on the precise nature of the argument, but this much is clear: Descartes points out that he can conceive that the world could be such that he should have no body and yet, at the same time, his introspective understanding should guarantee that he exists as a thinking thing. Thinking alone, he argues, is essential to him. From these premises, he concludes that the mind may exist without the body; it is an immaterial substance.

This argument was attacked from its first presentation. Descartes' critics contend that the mere fact that one can conceive of the mind existing without the body does not show that, in fact, it can exist without the body. I can imagine, for example, that my computer should continue to work even if its plug should be removed from the outlet, but this of course does not show that it is a genuine possibility that it should continue to work in such circumstances. My ability to conceive of my mind existing without my body may similarly reflect no genuine possibility. Although the argument is clearly defective when presented in just this way, it continues to remain a source of interest in discussion of the mind and its nature, and many still argue that some version of this argument, or considerations in some way similar to those Descartes brought forth, may be used to defend dualism. Thus, a number of authors have recently argued that a complete physical description of the universe inevitably leaves something out which introspection reveals, namely the qualitative nature of mental states. There is something it is like to be a bat, for example, but any physical description of the bat's brain, central nervous system, sensory equipment and so on, inevitably leaves this out. This shows, it is argued, that a physical account of the bat is thus incomplete. Some have taken this to show that a proper account of the mind must inevitably appeal to something nonphysical. Once again, introspective evidence is called upon to support dualism. More than this, the argument assumes, with Descartes, that introspection provides us with some deep insight into the essential properties of our mental states, properties which are fundamentally incompatible with those of the physical realm.

5 Introspection and self-improvement

Just as introspection has long been thought to provide a special route and a special insight into the self, it has also been thought to provide an indispensable tool in projects of self-improvement, both epistemological and moral. On the epistemological side, the special connection thought by Cartesians to hold between introspective access to one's mental states and the justification of one's beliefs dictates that those who wish to improve their epistemic situation must allow introspection to play a central role in that project. By the same token, many have thought that the first step on the road to moral self-improvement involves introspective self-scrutiny, examining one's motivations and character traits. Indeed, it has frequently been held that introspective self-monitoring is a crucial constituent of a moral life. One might reasonably wonder, however, given the possibility of self-deception, whether introspection is really the best tool for carrying out such a project of moral self-evaluation. It has even been argued, on empirical grounds, that introspection is not well suited to the task of epistemic self-evaluation because introspection may be especially insensitive in locating and identifying beliefs held on inadequate grounds. Even the most radical anti-Cartesians, however, grant that introspection must play some role in these projects. While it can no longer be claimed that introspection presents the final word on the character of one's mind, there can be no doubt that it plays an important role in the project of self-understanding.

See also: CONSCIOUSNESS; INTROSPECTION, PSYCHOLOGY OF; NATURALIZED EPISTEMOLOGY; UNCONSCIOUS MENTAL STATES

References and further reading

Alston, W.P. (1971) 'Varieties of privileged access', *American Philosophical Quarterly* 8 (3): 223–41. (Important discussion of the wide spectrum of views available on the kind of special access which introspection might provide.)

Armstrong, D.M. (1968) *A Materialist Theory of the Mind*, London: Routledge & Kegan Paul. (Defends a perceptual model of introspection, arguing that introspective judgment is fallible.)

Chomsky, N. (1980) *Rules and Representations*, New York: Columbia University Press. (Gives an account of the reasons stemming from linguistic theory, discussed in §2 above, for thinking that a large portion of the mind is inaccessible to introspection.)

Churchland, P.M. (1985) 'Reduction, qualia and the direct introspection of brain states', *Journal of Philosophy* 82 (1): 8–28. (Responds to the kind of argument for dualism, discussed above in §4, which is based on introspection.)

* Descartes, R. (1641) *Meditations on First Philosophy*, in *The Philosophical Writings of Descartes*, trans. J. Cottingham, R. Stoothoff and D. Murdoch, Cambridge: Cambridge University Press, 3 vols, 1985. (The tranparency view may be found in Meditation Two, the argument for dualism is in Meditation Six.)

Gopnik, A. (1993) 'How we know our minds: The illusion of first-person knowledge of intentionality', *Behavioral and Brain Sciences* 16 (1): 1–14. (A vigorous defence of a radically anti-Cartesian view of introspection. Contains an excellent bibliography of the experimental literature and is followed by comments from a large number of philosophers and psychologists of varying perspectives.)

Hume, D. (1739) *A Treatise of Human Nature*, Oxford: Clarendon Press, 1978. (Hume's discussion of personal identity can be found at bk I, pt 4, §6.)

* Kant, I. (1781/1787) *Critique of Pure Reason*, trans. N.K. Smith, New York: St Martin's Press, 1965. (Kant's discussion of introspection appears in B131–6; B152–8; A341–66; B406–32.)

Kornblith, H. (1989) 'Introspection and misdirection', *Australasian Journal of Philosophy* 67 (4): 410–22. (Argues on empirical grounds that introspection is either useless or counterproductive in providing a check on the manner in which we arrive at our beliefs.)

Lehrer, K. (1991) *Metamind*, Oxford: Oxford University Press. (Presents a Cartesian perspective on the importance of introspective understanding for a wide range of rational activities.)

Lyons, W. (1986) *The Disappearance of Introspection*, Cambridge, MA: MIT Press. (Critically examines accounts of introspection in psychology and philosophy of mind.)

Nagel, T. (1974) 'What is it like to be a bat?', *Philosophical Review* 83 (4): 435–50. (Presents the classic statement of the difficulties, discussed in §4 above, which introspective understanding presents for a physical account of the world. Nagel stops short of endorsing dualism.)

Nisbett, R. and Wilson, T. (1977) 'Telling more than we can know: Verbal reports on mental processes', *Psychological Review* 84 (3): 231–59. (Important contribution to the experimental literature on the kinds of errors to which introspection is susceptible.)

Ryle, G. (1949) *The Concept of Mind*, New York: Barnes & Noble. (Offers a behavioural account of the mind and mental concepts generally, including introspection.)

Shoemaker, S. (1988) 'On knowing one's own mind', *Philosophical Perspectives* 2: 183–209. (Defends the Cartesian view that the essence of certain mental states lies in our special introspective access to them.)

HILARY KORNBLITH

INTROSPECTION, PSYCHOLOGY OF

Introspection is the process of directly examining one's own conscious mental states and processes. Since the seventeenth century, there has been considerable disagreement on the scope, nature and epistemic status of introspection. Descartes held that all our mental states are subject to introspection; that it is sufficient to have a mental state to be aware of it; and that when we introspect, we cannot be mistaken about what we 'see'. Each of these views has been disputed. Nineteenth-century psychology relied heavily on introspection, but with the exception of important work in psychophysics and perception, it is now primarily of historical interest. Recently, Nisbett and Wilson have argued that when people attempt to report on the processes mediating the effects of a stimulus on a response, they do not do so on the basis of introspection but, rather, on the basis of an implicit common-sense 'theory'. Ericsson and Simon have developed a model of the mechanisms by which 'introspective' reports are generated and have used that model to identify the conditions under which such reports are reliable.

1   The classical conception
2   The scope of introspection
3   The nature of introspection
4   Epistemic status and scientific role

1   The classical conception

The term 'introspection' comes from the Latin 'spicere' (to look) and 'intra' (within). In ordinary English, it means 'the observation of one's own mental states or processes'. As we shall see in §3, whether introspection truly constitutes a form of observation is a matter of dispute. However, it is generally agreed that introspection involves awareness of certain aspects of one's mind, specifically, an awareness that involves a 'higher-order' belief or representation that one is in some 'lower-order' mental state. (A thought about cats is a 'first-order' mental state, whereas a belief *that one has a thought about cats* is 'second-order'.)

The first important treatment of introspection is that of DESCARTES (1641), who held that there is nothing to the mind but what is in consciousness and available to introspection (see CONSCIOUSNESS §7; INTROSPECTION, EPISTEMOLOGY OF). Introspective awareness of our mental states and processes might be thought to be the result of a separate higher-order process trained on lower-order states and processes. However, for Descartes, the connection is much closer than that: mental states and processes are, on his view, 'self-intimating'. It is sufficient simply for a mental state or process to be 'within us' for us to be aware of it. Indeed, Descartes held that the beliefs that result from introspection are infallible. As long as we consider our mental states only as they are 'in themselves', they cannot be false.

2   The scope of introspection

Does the set of states and processes that can be introspected exhaust the mental? Philosophical responses to this question fall into two traditions. Until well into the nineteenth century, most Anglo-American philosophers, including, in particular, the British Empiricists (LOCKE, J., HUME, D., MILL, J.) and the American, William JAMES, followed Descartes in answering in the affirmative (see EMPIRICISM; SENSE-DATA). In contrast, many German philosophers, beginning with Leibniz and including Kant and Schopenhauer, have argued that there are aspects of mind that are hidden from introspective awareness.

The current view is largely anti-Cartesian. Both Freudian psychoanalytic theories and contemporary cognitive science posit the existence of unconscious mental states and processes, that is, mental states and processes to which introspection has no access (see UNCONSCIOUS MENTAL STATES). A popular view among psychologists, in fact, is that introspective accessibility is not simply a black and white affair but, rather, that there are multiple levels of consciousness, each with its own conditions of accessibility.

3   The nature of introspection

There is substantial disagreement about the role of introspection and the kind of process introspection might be. Many disagree, for example, about whether one can be in a conscious mental state without being introspectively aware that one is in that state. The received view (see, for example, Armstrong 1968; Rosenthal 1986; Dretske 1993) is that one can; Shoemaker (1994) has argued to the contrary.

Second, there is disagreement over what 'order' of belief or representation is required for introspective awareness. Most philosophers who adopt the 'higher-order thought' view opt for a second-order thought as sufficient. Rosenthal, however, suggests that second-order thoughts are simply what makes a state conscious; introspective awareness requires that we be conscious of those second-order thoughts and, hence, that there be a *third*-order thought that one is having the second-order ones.

Finally, there is considerable discussion over whether introspection is correctly considered to be a form of perception or observation, a view associated with Locke (1689). For example, in perception, there is both object-awareness and fact-awareness. I perceive the tree and perceive that there is a tree. Are there also two forms of awareness in introspection? Do I both perceive my pain and perceive that I am in pain? Shoemaker and Dretske argue that introspection does not involve awareness of any (mental) object

843

such as a 'pain'. Furthermore, in perception, the relation between the objects perceived and the state of perceiving is causal. Is the same thing true for introspection, or is the relation also conceptual, as Shoemaker has argued? In other words, are there mental states whose introspectibility is essential to their very nature? This would be the case if one adopts Descartes' view that mental states are self-intimating or Shoemaker's view that mental states are defined by their functional role, and this role includes producing introspective awareness of the states in question (see CONSCIOUSNESS §10).

4 Epistemic status and scientific role

Many philosophers have taken issue with the Cartesian view that introspection is infallible. For example, James held that because introspection involves conceptualization, it suffers from fallibility just as any mode of observation does. Armstrong agrees that introspective awareness is fallible, but for a different reason, namely, that the state being introspected and the introspecting state are 'distinct existences', and, hence, connected only contingently.

Psychologists have focused not so much on the epistemic status of introspective awareness *per se* but on whether introspection can constitute a reliable method for the scientific study of the human mind. There were considerable efforts in the nineteenth century to found psychology on careful introspective reports, and the work of WEBER, FECHNER and HELMHOLTZ gave rise to important work on the 'psychophysics' of sensation (or the relation of introspected to physical magnitudes of, for example, light and sound) that continues to the present day (see Stevens 1951; Sekuler and Blake 1994). In contrast, the 'structuralist' programme of WUNDT and Titchener, which sought to discover the basic elements of thought and the laws by which they combine into more complex mental experiences, was far less successful.

In the early nineteenth century, Comte (1830) issued two challenges to a general introspective psychology. First, he asserted that introspection of intellectual (as opposed to emotive) activity is impossible. The conscious self is, in some sense, essentially unified. Hence, it cannot 'split' itself into two, one portion engaged in first-order intellectual activity with a second portion looking on. Second, even supposing that introspection is possible, it is worthless, presumably, because it is unreliable (see CONSCIOUSNESS §6).

Psychologists and philosophers interested in scientific psychology have responded to these challenges in a variety of ways. For example, James (1890) agreed

with Comte that introspective awareness of 'on-line' intellectual activity is impossible. However, since we clearly are often aware of what passes in our minds, we must ask how this can be. His view, following Mill (1865), was that introspection is actually retrospection. We are not aware of our occurrent states as we have them but, rather, of our *immediate memories* of those states. Since these memories are not part of the stream of consciousness, the impossible split in the conscious self is avoided (see CONSCIOUSNESS §10).

Comte's second challenge is, perhaps, the more serious of the two. For it might well be the case that although introspection is possible, the process of introspecting distorts the first-order mental activity being introspected. The threat of such distortion was a serious problem for the introspectionist psychologists of the late nineteenth and early twentieth century. In fact, some have argued that Titchener's failure to take the problem of unreliability sufficiently to heart contributed not only to the downfall of introspectionist psychology in particular, but also to the radical behaviourist 'revolution' and the eclipse of any mentalistic psychology for much of the twentieth century (see BEHAVIOURISM, METHODOLOGICAL AND SCIENTIFIC).

Behaviourism has itself now been overthrown in favour of an approach that, once again, takes the mental seriously. As a consequence, psychologists are struggling with the question of whether and to what extent introspective awareness can give us information about our mental states and processes. A contemporary challenge to the reliability of introspection comes from the work of Nisbett and Wilson (1977) who considered the psychological causes of our judgments and behaviour. They argued that people have little or no privileged introspective access to such causal information. Instead, their reports are based on implicit, cultural 'theories' that they apply to themselves as they do to others.

In one classic study cited by Nisbett and Wilson, subjects were asked to tie together the ends of two cords hung from the ceiling that were placed far enough apart so that one cord could not be reached while holding on to the other. To solve the problem, subjects were permitted to use any of the various objects strewn about the room. There were several solutions, one of which involved attaching a weight to the end of one cord, and then swinging it so that it could be caught while holding on to the second cord. Most subjects could not discover this solution on their own. However, when cued by the experimenter casually putting one of the cords in motion in the periphery of the subjects' vision, they typically solved the problem within 45 seconds. Subsequently, though, when subjects were asked how they arrived at this solution, the experimenter's hint was mentioned by less than a third of the subjects.

The most powerful defence of introspection in recent years comes from two cognitive scientists, Ericsson and Simon (1980). They argued that verbal reports of mental activities constitute important data, but that we can only assess the epistemic value of this data if we understand the mechanisms by which the reports are generated. They then proposed a model according to which cognitive information can be stored in various memories, including short-term memory (STM), which has a limited capacity and a short duration, and long-term memory (LTM), which has a very large capacity and is relatively permanent. Information that is attended to is kept in STM and is directly accessible for verbal report. Information stored in LTM must be retrieved before it can be reported (see MEMORY).

There are many different kinds of verbal report. First, we can distinguish reports that are concurrent with the execution of the primary task (such as solving a problem in mathematics) from reports that are retrospective. Second, some verbal reports ('level I') require no additional processing. This is so when information used in the primary task is already in verbal form (in STM) and simply requires articulation. In contrast, there are verbal reports that do require additional processing, either recoding, say, from visual to verbal form ('level II'), or filtering and providing information (such as the reasons for certain behaviour or choices) to which attention would not ordinarily be paid ('level III').

The Ericsson and Simon model predicts what a host of experimental studies have borne out; that each of these different types of verbal report will differ in accuracy. In particular, concurrent level I reports neither change nor slow the course or structure of the primary-task cognitive process. Concurrent level II reports may slow the primary-task cognitive processes, but also do not change them. However, for level III reports, there may well be substantial effects on task performance. Finally, the accuracy of retrospective reports depends not only on the level involved but also on the duration of the task and the lag between completion and the report. As both the duration and lag time increases, accuracy will decrease.

Ericsson and Simon claim that their model is quite consistent with Nisbett and Wilson's findings. In particular, in the studies reviewed by Nisbett and Wilson, the retrospective procedures used to elicit the actors' reports were not those the model identifies as eliciting valid reports. For example, in the cord-tying task, subjects do not report the causal role of the hint

because by the time they are queried, this information is no longer in short-term memory.

See also: CONSCIOUSNESS; INTROSPECTION, EPISTEMOLOGY OF; QUALIA; UNCONSCIOUS MENTAL STATES

References and further reading

* Armstrong, D.M. (1968) *A Materialist Theory of the Mind*, London: Routledge. (Discussion of the nature and epistemic status of introspection in the context of a defence of central state materialism. Presents arguments mentioned in §§3, 4.)

Churchland, P.M. (1985) *Matter and Consciousness*, Cambridge, MA: MIT Press. (Chapter 4 includes several arguments against the infallibility of introspective awareness.)

* Comte, A. (1830) *Introduction to Positive Philosophy*, trans. and ed. F. Ferre, Indianapolis, IN: Hackett Publishing Company, 1988. (The classic statement of objections to the possibility and reliability of introspection.)

Danziger, K. (1980) 'The History of Introspection Reconsidered', *Journal of the History of the Behavioral Sciences* 16: 241–62. (A useful discussion of the history of introspective psychology with emphasis on the period from 1880 to 1914.)

Dennett, D.C. (1978) 'Toward a Cognitive Theory of Consciousness', in *Brainstorms*, Cambridge, MA: MIT Press. (Sketch of an information-processing model of consciousness, including an account of introspection.)

* Descartes, R. (1641) 'Meditationes de prima philosophia', in *Oeuvres de Descartes*, vol. 7, ed. C. Adam and P. Tannery, Paris: CNRS/Vrin, 1964; trans. 'Meditations on First Philosophy, including Objections and Replies', in *The Philosophical Writings of Descartes*, vol. 2, ed. J. Cottingham, R. Stoothoff and D. Murdoch, Cambridge: Cambridge University Press, 1984. (The classical philosophical treatment of consciousness and introspection.)

* Dretske, F. (1993) 'Conscious Experience', *Mind* 102: 263–83. (Presents argument mentioned in §3.)

* Ericsson, K.A. and Simon, H.A. (1980) *Protocol Analysis: Verbal Reports as Data*, Cambridge, MA: MIT Press; revised edn, 1993. (A classical cognitive science treatment of the reliability of introspective verbal reports.)

Farthing, G.W. (1992) *The Psychology of Consciousness*, Englewood Cliffs, NJ: Prentice Hall. (A useful psychology text on consciousness, with two chapters on introspection.)

Hill, C. (1991) *Sensations: A Defense of Type Materialism*, Cambridge: Cambridge University

Press. (An interesting treatment of introspection which emphasizes its active nature.)

Howe, R.B.K. (1991) 'Introspection: A Reassessment', *New Ideas in Psychology* 9: 25–44. (A defence of introspection as a method in psychology.)

* Locke, J. (1689) *An Essay concerning Human Understanding*, with notes by A.C. Fraser, New York: Dover, 1959. (The classical statement of the view that introspection is a form of perception.)

Lycan, W. (1995) 'Consciousness as Internal Monitoring', in *Consciousness and Experience*, Cambridge, MA: MIT Press, ch. 2. (Defends the Lockean view that introspection is inner sense, mentioned in §3, against numerous objections.)

Lyons, W. (1986) *The Disappearance of Introspection*, Cambridge, MA: MIT Press. (A useful overview of the various historical and contemporary views on introspection.)

* James, W. (1890) *The Principles of Psychology*, New York: Holt. (Chapter 7, volume 2 includes James' response to Comte, discussed in §4.)

* Mill, J.S. (1865) *Auguste Comte and Positivism*, Ann Arbor, MI: University of Michigan Press, 1968. (Includes Mill's response to Comte's arguments mentioned in §4.)

* Nisbett, R. and Wilson, T. (1977) 'Telling More Than We Can Know: Verbal Reports on Mental Processes', *Psychological Review* 84 (3): 231–59. (An extensive review of the psychological literature that argues that people are often unaware of what causes their actions.)

* Rosenthal, D.M. (1986) 'Two Concepts of Consciousness', *Philosophical Studies* 49: 329–59. (Contrasts the Cartesian and a non-Cartesian conception of consciousness.)

—— (1993) 'Thinking that One Thinks', in M. Davies (ed.) *Consciousness: Psychological and Philosophical Essays*, Oxford: Blackwell. (Develops an argument for the higher-order thought view of consciousness.)

* Sekuler, R. and Blake, R. (1994) *Perception*, New York: McGraw-Hill. (A good recent textbook on psychophysics.)

* Shoemaker, S. (1994) 'Self-Knowledge and "Inner Sense"', *Philosophy and Phenomenological Research* 54 (2): 249–315. (An extended argument against the view that introspection is a form of perception. Presents arguments mentioned in §3.)

Stevens, S.S. (1951) *A Handbook of Experimental Psychology*, New York: Wiley & Sons. (A classic contemporary anthology including works in psychophysics.)

White, P.A. (1988) 'Knowing More About What We Can Tell: "Introspective Access" and Causal Report Accuracy 10 Years Later', *British Journal of Psychology* 79: 13–45. (A review of the literature published in response to Nisbett and Wilson (1977) that calls some of their conclusions into question.)

BARBARA VON ECKARDT

INTUITIONISM

Ultimately, mathematical intuitionism gets its name and its epistemological parentage from a conviction of Kant: that intuition reveals basic mathematical principles as true a priori. Intuitionism's mathematical lineage is that of radical constructivism: constructive in requiring proofs of existential claims to yield provable instances of those claims; radical in seeking a wholesale reconstruction of mathematics. Although partly inspired by Kronecker and Poincaré, twentieth-century intuitionism is dominated by the 'neo-intuitionism' of the Dutch mathematician L.E.J. Brouwer. Brouwer's reworking of analysis, paradigmatic for intuitionism, broke the bounds on traditional constructivism by embracing real numbers given by free choice sequences. Brouwer's theorem – that every real-valued function on a closed, bounded interval is uniformly continuous – brings intuitionism into seeming conflict with results of conventional mathematics.

Despite Brouwer's distaste for logic, formal systems for intuitionism were devised and developments in intuitionistic mathematics began to parallel those in metamathematics. A. Heyting was the first to formalize both intuitionistic logic and arithmetic and to interpret the logic over types of abstract proofs. Tarski, Beth and Kripke each constructed a distinctive class of models for intuitionistic logic. Gödel, in his Dialectica *interpretation, showed how to view formal intuitionistic arithmetic as a calculus of higher-order functions. S.C. Kleene gave a 'realizability' interpretation to the same theory using codes of recursive functions. In the last decades of the twentieth century, applications of intuitionistic higher-order logic and type theory to category theory and computer science have made these systems objects of intense study. At the same time, philosophers and logicians, under the influence of M. Dummett, have sought to enlist intuitionism under the banner of general antirealist semantics for natural languages.*

1 **Kantian epistemology, constructivism and 'semi-intuitionism'**
2 **Brouwer and Dutch intuitionism**
3 **Elements of Brouwerian intuitionism**
4 **Heyting's logic and the proof interpretation**
5 **Metamathematics: intuitionistic systems and**

1 Kantian epistemology, constructivism and 'semi-intuitionism'

The thesis from which mathematical intuitionism draws its name is Kant's: that we exercise a pure intuition to apprehend the correctness of basic mathematical claims directly and a priori. Kant defended the thesis – for arithmetic and geometry – in the 'Transcendental Aesthetic' of his first *Critique*. Twentieth-century intuitionists, under the leadership of L.E.J. Brouwer, founder of Dutch or neo-intuitionism, adopted a modification of Kant's view. Intuition in elementary arithmetic and analysis was to be identified with a pure intuition of the subdivision of time intervals. Kant's account of geometry was refused and only elementary arithmetic retained intuitive primacy (see MATHEMATICS, FOUNDATIONS OF §2). By Brouwer's lights, the role of intuition cannot be understudied by empirical inquiry, linguistic understanding or logical reasoning. Brouwer's intuitionism, then, opposes both empiricism and logicism. Moreover, since intuitionists think to know intuitively principles which are infinitary and contentful, intuitionism is also at odds with finitism and formalism.

Deprecation of logic's influence on mathematics has been characteristic of intuitionism and is reminiscent of the attitudes Schopenhauer expressed in *Die Welt als Wille und Vorstellung* (*The World as Will and Representation*). According to Schopenhauer, mathematics is not best developed *more geometrico*, since deductions from axioms obscure the true grounds for mathematical results. He argued that each mathematical truth S has its own intuitable ground of being G and that the premier means to intuit the truth of S would be to uncover G and construct it in time without the aid of explicit deduction. Schopenhauer recommended that mathematics be reformulated accordingly.

Since before the time of Brouwer, intuitionistic mathematics has been constructive. In general, the demand for constructivism is the demand that E be respected:

(E) The correctness of existential claim $\exists x A(x)$ is to be guaranteed by warrants from which both an object a and a further warrant for $A(a)$ are constructible.

Constructivism is commonly deemed revisionary of conventional mathematics, requiring alteration in standard notions of mathematical objects, canons of adequate proof and fundamental principles of reasoning (see CONSTRUCTIVISM IN MATHEMATICS). Intuitionists trace their constructive lineage at least as far back as Leopold KRONECKER (1823–91), who initiated a programme for arithmetizing higher algebra; in this, he demanded for arithmetic a primacy irreducible to natural science or logic and refused to countenance non-constructive existence proofs.

Writings of the so-called 'semi-intuitionists', particularly Poincaré and Borel, exerted a strong influence on Brouwer and his followers. Poincaré, considered the leading European mathematician of his day, also rejected the idea that geometric truths express synthetic judgments known a priori but embraced the intuitive aprioricity of elementary arithmetic, with mathematical induction holding pride of place (see POINCARÉ, J.H. §§3, 5). In common with the Dutch intuitionists, Poincaré construed infinite totalities as potential, rather than completed. Accordingly, he rejected, along with Russell's type theory, Zermelo's axioms for set theory as guarantors of transfinite arithmetic. Borel was a prominent member of the 'Paris school' of mathematicians, which included Baire and Lebesgue. He advocated constructivism to the extent that existence was to be tied to explicit definability: specific functions and real numbers were only to be accepted once they were fully defined. Borel distinguished, as did the young Brouwer, a 'geometric' from a 'practical' continuum. The former was deemed the object of a general intuition, not analysable into individual reals. The latter was the totality of definable real numbers. It was probably in writings by Borel (or an earlier book by Du Bois Reymond) that Brouwer came upon the idea that real numbers be given by choice sequences of rationals generated randomly, as if by successive throws of a die.

2 Brouwer and Dutch intuitionism

The intuitionism of the twentieth century is that of Brouwer: a radical extension of constructive mathematics incorporating anti-classical principles of logic and analysis. Brouwer held the chair in set theory and axiomatics at the University of Amsterdam from 1912 until 1955. He first achieved fame for discoveries in algebraic topology, particularly proofs of the invariance of dimension and of the fixed-point theorem that bears his name. In articles published between 1907 and 1930, Brouwer combined a battery of influences with an austere personal philosophy of life to create a programme for intuitionistic mathematics. The programme called for trenchant criticism of presuppositions of conventional mathematics as well as thorough reconstruction of arithmetic, analysis and set theory so as to free them of those presuppositions.

In accordance with his subjectivistic, even solipsistic, personal philosophy, Brouwer insisted that intuitionistic mathematics be a private study of mental mathematical constructions. Language and interpersonal communication, indeed all intellectual activity, played diminished roles in Brouwer's scheme of things. He thought language an instrument so defective as to make mathematicians incapable of conveying the precise sense of their constructions to others. Hence, if mathematics is to retain certainty and exactness, it was not to consist in linguistic representations but in languageless construction. Brouwerian mathematics would not be able to derive its authority from the application to mathematics of a universal logic, valid for all domains of thought.

After Brouwer, the principal exponent of Dutch intuitionism was his student and colleague, Heyting. In addition to major contributions to the formalization of intuitionistic logic, arithmetic and set theory and to the interpretation of that formalism, Heyting pursued studies in intuitionistic algebra, geometry and the theory of Hilbert space. Among early intuitionists were M.J. Belinfante, G.F.C. Griss, H. Freudenthal, B. van Rootselaar and, for a time, H. Weyl. The most distinguished proponents of Dutch intuitionism during the last quarter of the twentieth century are students of Heyting: A.S. Troelstra and D. van Dalen. Notable as well has been a group of intuitionists from Nijmegen including H. de Swart and W. Veldman.

3 Elements of Brouwerian intuitionism

Already in his 1907 dissertation, 'On the Foundations of Mathematics', Brouwer was advancing the intuitionistic idea that mathematics is a 'free creation' of the mind unfettered by empirical data or linguistic constraints. Beginning with 'The Unreliability of the Logical Principles' (1908 [1975]), Brouwer took critical aim at the ground rules of conventional mathematics, challenging the validity of the law of the excluded middle (LEM). (The 1908 article may also reflect views held by Brouwer's teacher and colleague G. Mannoury.)

The validity of LEM does conflict with a natural view of constructivity. At present, it is unknown whether there exist an infinite number of twin primes, that is, pairs of prime numbers that differ by 2. Let the predicate $P(x)$ hold of p just in case $\langle p, p+2 \rangle$ is the greatest twin prime pair, if such a pair exists, or of 1, if there are an infinite number of twin primes. If LEM is

valid, there exists a determinate m such that $P(m)$. However, short of solving the problem of twin primes, no one can provide, in accordance with E, a recipe for computing m in decimal notation. It is noteworthy, first, that Brouwer did not think that this style of reasoning proved the negation of LEM. Rather, he maintained that it affords LEM a 'weak counterexample', a proof that the intuitionist will, most likely, never be able to endorse that law. (Quantified versions of LEM are refuted by intuitionistic continuity principles, described below.) Second, a direct mathematical connection is here forged between the truth of disjunctions and the availability of recipes for deciding an issue.

Brouwer also constructed weak counterexamples to such conventional theorems as that every real is either rational or irrational and that the continuum is totally ordered. In the case of the former, generate in parallel the decimal expansions of π and of ρ, where ρ's expansion begins 0.33333... but is to be halted when a string of seven 7s appears in the expansion of π. Clearly, ρ cannot be irrational, for then the desired string neither appears nor fails to appear. But, to assert that ρ is rational, E requires that one locate integers m and n such that ρ is their quotient. This is not possible, for we would then know where a string of seven 7s appears in the expansion of π, something now unknown.

Prior to 1920, Brouwer adopted the notion of 'choice sequences', also called 'infinitely proceeding' sequences. These need be neither law-like – governed by computable recipes for generating terms – nor even fully determinate in advance. Brouwer permitted restrictions imposed by a spread law (see below) but, beyond that, nothing about the future course of the sequence may be known, other than the fact that its terms are freely and independently chosen.

Brouwer employed two intuitionistic analogues for the conventional notion of a class of numbers. These are the concepts now called 'species' and 'spread'. Species are properties determined by extensional mathematical predicates and are themselves individuated extensionally: pairs of species are identical when they apply to the same items. Spreads are either species of choice sequences constrained to obey a spread law or species of sequences obtained from these via continuous mappings. A 'spread law' is a decidable property of finite sequences which holds of the empty sequence and culls out from the tree of all sequences a subtree containing branches unbounded in length. A choice sequence is an 'element' of a spread S when it determines a branch in S's tree. A spread with a tree which always branches finitely often was called by Brouwer a 'fan'.

These notions in hand, Brouwer proved the most

celebrated result of intuitionistic mathematics, now known as 'Brouwer's theorem': every real-valued function of a real variable defined on a closed, bounded interval is uniformly continuous. This theorem is known to follow from two distinctively intuitionistic principles. The first, originally isolated by Heyting, is weak continuity (WC-N). Let 'α' and 'β' range over choice sequences and 'n' over natural numbers. Neighbourhoods of α are determined by its initial segments s: β lies in the s-neighbourhood of α ($\beta \in s$) whenever it shares s with α.

(WC-N) If $\forall\alpha\exists nA(\alpha,n)$, then, $\forall\alpha\exists n\exists$ neighbourhood s of α $\forall\beta \in sA(\beta,n)$.

E and the indeterminacy of choice sequences are thought to secure plausibility for WC-N. When we have $\forall\alpha\exists nA(\alpha,n)$, there is to hand a uniform method M for constructing, from each choice sequence α, an n such that $A(\alpha,n)$. Since M is uniform, it can take cognizance, in calculating a specific n from α, of no more than an initial segment of α. After all, we may know nothing more of the course of α than the terms already calculated. Hence, M must yield a proof, for that n, of $\forall\beta \in sA(\beta,n)$. WC-N is alone sufficient to yield strong counterexamples to quantified forms of LEM. Contemporary proofs of Brouwer's theorem also rely on the 'fan theorem', an intuitionistic correlate of König's lemma, which asserts that, with respect to the neighbourhoods just described, every fan is constructively a compact topological space.

In such articles as 'Über Definitionsbereiche von Funktionen' (On Domains of Definitions for Functions, 1927 [1975]), Brouwer attempted a detailed proof of Brouwer's theorem and explained how to deduce the fan theorem from another assertion about spreads, the 'bar theorem'. The latter is, in effect, a principle of 'reverse induction' up from the bottom nodes in a countable, well-founded tree. Let S be a spread. A set of finite sequences B in S is a 'bar' when all α in S have initial segments in B. A set of finite sequences A in S is 'hereditary' if A holds of sequence s in S whenever it holds of all s's descendants in S. The bar theorem asserts that, whenever A is hereditary and contains a decidable bar B, the empty sequence belongs to A. Unfortunately, Brouwer's attempt to prove it suffered from a non sequitur and is widely considered inconclusive.

Most controversial of Brouwer's innovations, even for fellow intuitionists, was his theory of the 'creative subject'. In articles published after 1947, Brouwer put to work, in defining choice sequences, a representation in temporal series of the discoveries of an idealized mathematician. From this representation, Brouwer looked to derive strong counterexamples – direct refutations – for findings of conventional

analysis, among them that every linear equation with non-zero coefficients has a real solution. Some see the creative subject as a child of Brouwer's subjectivistic philosophy because of Brouwer's assumption that any claim which is permanently unknown to the ideal mathematician is false. Due to difficulties attending its formal analysis, the creative subject remains a subject of debate.

4   Heyting's logic and the proof interpretation

To win a prize offered by the Dutch Mathematical Association, Heyting made the first efforts at a comprehensive formalization for Brouwerian logic, arithmetic and set theory. His system, published in 1930 and 1931, was anticipated in part by the incomplete systems of A.N. Kolmogorov and V.I. Glivenko. Notational details aside, Heyting's predicate logic, now treated as definitive of intuitionistic logic, is equivalent to Gentzen's later natural deduction system NJ. Standard formalizations of intuitionistic predicate logic and elementary arithmetic are still called 'Heyting predicate logic' – or HPL, for short – and 'Heyting arithmetic' – HA – in honour of his achievement.

In a monograph of 1934, Heyting advanced an interpretation of the logic which, he believed, expressed its Brouwerian meaning. He gave, by recursion on claims A, conditions on abstract intuitionistic proofs of A. The 'proof interpretations' for '$\vee$', '$\to$' and '$\forall$' statements are, roughly, as follows.

($\vee$)   A proof of $A \vee B$ consists in both a number and a further proof such that, if the number has value 0, the further proof is one of A and, if the number has value 1, the proof is of B.

($\to$)   A proof of $A \to B$ affords a construction converting any proof of A into one of B.

($\forall$)   A proof of $\forall nA(n)$ affords a construction f such that, for any number m, $f(m)$ proves $A(m)$.

If constructions are computable operations, logics sound for this interpretation may not validate LEM. Let $A(n)$ define an undecidable set of natural numbers. Then, $\forall n(A(n) \vee \neg A(n))$ plausibly lacks proof. Were there such a proof – one satisfying ($\to$) and ($\forall$) – it would yield, computably in n, an $f(n)$ correctly marking the truth or falsity of $A(n)$, thus contradicting $A(n)$'s undecidability.

The idea of testing logical principles with abstract constructions and proofs is visible in Brouwer's writings. In 1932, Kolmogorov had offered, independently of Heyting, a structurally similar interpretation of intuitionistic reasoning as a 'calculus of problems'. Consequently, the proof interpretation is also known as the 'BHK interpretation', after Brouwer, Heyting and Kolmogorov. The adequacy of certain aspects of the BHK has been a matter of academic dispute. For example, if condition ($\rightarrow$) defines the concept 'abstract proof of $A \rightarrow B$', then the definition is impredicative: it contains a quantification – 'any proof of A' – over all proofs (see CONSTRUCTIVISM IN MATHEMATICS).

5 Metamathematics: intuitionistic systems and translation theorems

In the first decades after 1945, S.C. Kleene and G. Kreisel, together with their students and colleagues, led a host of metamathematical explorers into traditional intuitionistic territory. Kleene's system for Brouwer's analysis, 'FIM' after Kleene's book with R.E. Vesley, *The Foundations of Intuitionistic Mathematics* (1965), brought to it standard formalization. Among Kreisel's innumerable contributions are formal systems for choice sequences, higher-order arithmetic and the theory of constructions. Of special interest to post-war proof theorists was the system T invented by Gödel to express, for his *Dialectica* interpretation, the behaviours of primitive recursive functionals of finite type (see §6 below).

The 1970s brought out a bumper crop of intuitionistic formal theories for sets, types and higher-order functions. Troelstra (1973a) subjected HAS, a second-order version of Heyting arithmetic containing variables for species and an impredicative comprehension axiom, to logical examination. For computer scientists (see §7), Martin-Löf's unconventional ML type theories acquired a certain celebrity. The ML systems were not invented, as was FIM, to formalize Brouwer's analysis but to represent a mixture of traditional ideas with Martin-Löf's own approach to constructivism. Among the ideas ML assimilates are the BHK interpretation and Frege's distinction between thought and assertion as well as such proof-theoretic mainstays as normalization and W. Howard's 'formulas-as-types'.

As for set theories, IZF – 'intuitionistic Zermelo–Fraenkel' – was a formalism of choice for studying universes of Heyting-valued sets (see §6). H. Friedman's system B was intended to formalize E. Bishop's constructive analysis but is no stronger, proof-theoretically, than HA. P. Aczel's 'constructive Zermelo–Fraenkel' CZF is translatable into an ML system with a type for well-founded trees. CZF is close kin to J. Myhill's constructive set theory CST.

In 1933, Gödel – and, independently, Gentzen and Bernays – showed how to embed the theorems of conventional Peano arithmetic (PA) faithfully into the negative ($\lor$, $\exists$-free) fragment of HA. So, PA is seen to be conservative over HA for negative formulas and, as far as consistency goes, HA is commensurate with its classical cousin. Unknown to Gödel and Gentzen, Kolmogorov had already proposed, in 1925, a similar negative translation for a fragment of HPL. More recently, negative translations have been discovered for higher-order arithmetic, type theory and set theory. Gödel also constructed (in 1933) a translation from Heyting's propositional logic into the modal calculus S4. H. Rasiowa and R. Sikorski later applied Gödel's idea to quantified systems. During the 1980s, modal interpretations for intuitionistic arithmetic motivated N. Goodman and S. Shapiro to recommend systems for 'intensional mathematics'.

6 Metamathematics: algebraic, functional and realizability interpretations

Just as conventional logical signs represent Boolean operations, the logical signs in HPL can also be read algebraically. The relevant algebraic operations act on the open sets of a topological space or, more generally, on elements of Heyting algebras – kinds of distributive lattices with greatest element T. So construed, every formula of HPL gets assigned a topological or lattice-theoretic 'truth-value' such that HPL-theorems always evaluate to T. In 1936, S. Jaśkowski seems to have been the first to interpret Heyting's propositional logic over finite distributive lattices. In the next two years, M. Stone and A. Tarski independently interpreted the logic over topological spaces. Tarski's article (1938) includes a proof, in conventional metalogic, that every propositional formula which is not an intuitionistic theorem has a countermodel over the open subsets of $\mathbb{R}^n$. A. Mostowski gave topological semantics to HPL. D.S. Scott (1968) showed how to extend topological interpretations to intuitionistic analysis, thereby constructing models for Brouwer's theorem. In the 1970s, Scott was among the prime movers in the study of Heyting-valued algebraic semantics for intuitionistic higher-order logic and set theory.

Close relatives of topological models (and of Cohen forcing) are Beth and Kripke models. In 1947, E.W. Beth introduced the idea of interpreting HPL over domains attached to nodes in finitely branching trees. He later argued that Heyting's logic is sound and complete with respect to his notion of model and that this fact is provable intuitionistically. (In the latter, Beth was shown to have erred.) S. Kripke (1965) proposed, in effect, that formulas be assigned upward closed subsets of partially ordered sets as 'truth-values'. He gave conventional proofs that HPL is sound and complete with respect to these assignments and that validity in Kripke structures and in Beth structures are equivalent. Both types of models have been extended to other intuitionistic systems, including set theory. Later researchers saw that sets of Kripke or of Beth models can be 'glued' together to prove that HA, not to mention other systems, possesses the disjunction property (DP) and explicit definability for numbers (EDN). A system S has DP just in case, whenever A and B are sentences and S derives $A \vee B$, then S derives A or S derives B. S has EDN if, whenever $\exists n A(n)$ is a sentence that S derives, there is a number term t such that S derives $A(t)$.

The premier functional interpretation for HA was Gödel's 1959 *Dialectica*, named for the journal in which it first appeared. The point of the interpretation, conceived by Gödel as early as 1941, was to obtain a consistency proof for arithmetic via an extension of Hilbertian finitistic reasoning to higher types. Here, each arithmetic formula is replaced by a quantifier-free translation in the formal system T. The logic of HA is thereby subsumed within combinatorics for higher-type objects. Gödel maintained that the correctness of T is sufficiently evident that the interpretation gives a convincing proof for HA's consistency. Extensions and applications of Gödel's ideas were soon forthcoming: in the late 1950s and early 1960s, Kreisel and C. Spector constructed *Dialectica*-style interpretations for analysis; J.-Y. Girard found functional interpretations for HAS in 1971.

Generally, a 'realizability interpretation' is an association between formulas A and items i such that i serves, intuitively, to encode information available from a constructive proof of A. When i is so associated with A, it is said to 'realize' A or to be a realizability witness for A. On Kleene's original realizability interpretation from 1945, witnesses are natural numbers that encode the computational information given by A. Witnesses of conditionals, for example, are Turing machine indices such that, if $[[A]]$ and $[[B]]$ are the sets of witnesses for A and B, respectively, then $[[A \rightarrow B]]$ is the set of all indices of machines which, given inputs from $[[A]]$, output in $[[B]]$. Kleene proved each HA-theorem to have a non-empty set of witnesses. Realizability also shows HA to be consistent with Church's thesis, the assertion that every arithmetical function is Turing computable. Kleene later devised a realizability interpretation for FIM in which witnesses are functions rather than numbers. He also enlarged the idea of realizability to incorporate his q-realizability and 'slash' interpretations; these permit straightforward proofs of DP and EDN for HA. Many forms of realizability have been invented, extending the concept to most intuitionistic systems.

7 Category theory and computer science

In the 1970s and 1980s, applications of formal systems to category theory and to computer science stimulated new interest in intuitionism. During 1969, F.W. Lawvere isolated axioms for categories which are elementary topoi – generalizations of Grothendieck topoi. Together with M. Tierney, he verified that topoi represent categorial versions of set-theoretic universes which are intuitionistic, rather than conventional, in their logic. The set of truth-values within a topos is always a Heyting, rather than a Boolean, algebra. Research has shown that the theory of interpretations over categories encompasses not only algebraic and topological models but also Kripke models, Beth models and realizability. (See CATEGORY THEORY, APPLICATIONS TO THE FOUNDATIONS OF MATHEMATICS.)

Computer scientists have put formal constructive proofs to work extracting programs. As E would have it, a proof p of A is constructive to the extent that there are methods M for extracting from p computational information relevant to A. For instance, if p is a constructive proof of $\forall n \exists m A(n,m)$, M should extract from p a recipe guaranteed to compute a function f such that, for all n, $A(n, f(n))$. The power of high-level programming languages makes it possible to ask for software to play the role of methods M: to extract automatically, from formal proofs p, programs guaranteed to compute functions with the behaviours p specifies. Such software would convert a formal constructive proof that a specification is satisfiable into a program certain to satisfy it. During the 1980s, a number of researchers looked to implement constructive program extraction, among them R.L. Constable and his associates at Cornell (1986), creators of the PRL ('proof refinement logic') systems inspired by Martin-Löf's ML.

8 Intuitionism and antirealism

Since the 1970s, Michael Dummett has been principal sponsor for the view that foundational issues for intuitionism and its logic are properly addressed in philosophical discussions over programmatic 'antirealist' semantics for natural language. Dummett proposed that debates between proponents of conventional and of intuitionistic logics gain a solid footing only when viewed as one skirmish within a wider battle between proponents of realist and of antirealist semantics. Dummett's semantic realist insists that the meaning of statements be explicated by theories associating each statement with bivalent truth-conditions which obtain or fail independently of human knowledge. Dummett's conjectured antirealist would have it that the meanings of statements can only be given in terms of operations people have been taught to employ in verifying or falsifying claims, and not in terms of truth-conditions which may prove ineffable. Intuitionism, then, is supposed to represent an expression of antirealism for which the relevant semantic operations would be those entering into the fashioning of intuitionistic proofs. (See ANTIREALISM IN THE PHILOSOPHY OF MATHEMATICS §2.)

Obstacles to the antirealist programme include the difficulties inherent in designing, even in outline, a coherent antirealist semantics that covers all the territory Dummett has suggested it might cover, including antirealism about psychology and the past. Also, it is in no way clear that features of intuitionistic logic and mathematics can be well understood from the vantage of a semantic theory. It remains to be shown that intuitionistic mathematics, rather than finitism or Markovian constructivism, is the true ally of antirealist semantics. Lastly, it is a concern that Dummett's ideas flout one of the main planks of Brouwer's intuitionism: that mathematics must be independent of metaphysics. For traditional intuitionists, there can be no final explanation for intuitionistic mathematics other than the mathematics itself.

See also: LOGICAL AND MATHEMATICAL TERMS, GLOSSARY OF

References and further reading

Beeson, M.J. (1985) *Foundations of Constructive Mathematics*, Berlin: Springer. (An overview of the metamathematics of constructive formal systems; requires considerable formal experience.)

* Brouwer, L.E.J. (1975) *Collected Works*, vol. 1, ed. A. Heyting, Amsterdam: North Holland. (An invaluable compendium of Brouwer's writings, some in English and others in German; the articles 'The Unreliability of the Logical Principles' and 'Über Definitionsbereiche von Funktionen' (On Domains of Definitions for Functions) and sections of his dissertation appear. The level of technical difficulty is high.)

—— (1981) *Brouwer's Cambridge Lectures on Intuitionism*, ed. D. van Dalen, Cambridge: Cambridge University Press. (A compact sample of Brouwer's thinking; well edited but quite technical.)

* Constable, R.L. *et al.* (1986) *Implementing Mathematics With the NuPrl Proof Development System*, Englewood Cliffs, NJ: Prentice-Hall. (An admirable introduction to the computer system but no substitute for 'hands-on' experience.)

Dummett, M.A.E. (1977) *Elements of Intuitionism*, Oxford: Clarendon Press, 1990. (An influential text in which great emphasis is placed upon the metalogic of intuitionism.)

—— (1978) *Truth and Other Enigmas*, London: Duckworth, and Cambridge, MA: Harvard University Press. (Essential reading on intuitionism and antirealism; the preface is especially recommended.)

Fourman, M.P. and Scott, D.S. (1979) 'Sheaves and Logic', in M.P. Fourman *et al.* (eds) *Applications of Sheaves*, Springer Lecture Notes in Mathematics, vol. 753, Berlin: Springer, 302–401. (A mathematically sophisticated but lucid introduction to Heyting-valued interpretations of intuitionistic systems.)

Gödel, K. (1986–95) *Collected Works*, ed. S. Feferman *et al.*, New York and Oxford: Oxford University Press, 3 vols. (Authoritative compendium of Gödel's published works and very fine source books. The clear and painstaking introductions are especially recommended.)

Heijenoort, J. van (ed.) (1967) *From Frege to Gödel: A Source Book in Mathematical Logic, 1879–1931*, Cambridge, MA: Harvard University Press. (An invaluable collection of significant articles by Gödel, Hilbert, Brouwer, Skolem and others; technical knowledge often required.)

Heyting, A. (1956) *Intuitionism: An Introduction*, Amsterdam: North Holland; 3rd revised edn, 1971. (The first – and still the most charming – popular technical account of Brouwer's intuitionism.)

* Kant, I. (1781/1787) *Critique of Pure Reason*, trans. N. Kemp Smith, New York: St Martin's Press, 1965. (The 'Transcendental Aesthetic' section includes Kant's highly influential views on a priori intuition.)

Kleene, S.C. (1945) 'On the Interpretation of Intuitionistic Number Theory', *Journal of Symbolic Logic* 10: 109–24. (Technical but wonderfully clear and amazingly prescient.)

* Kleene, S.C. and Vesley, R.E. (1965) *The Foundations of Intuitionistic Mathematics*, Amsterdam: North Holland. (Mathematically exacting, historically important but dauntingly formal.)

Kreisel, G. (1965) 'Mathematical Logic', in T.L. Saaty (ed.) *Lectures in Modern Mathematics*, vol. 3, New York: Wiley, 95–195. (A challenging sampler of Kreisel's – and others' – thoughts and theorems on the foundations of mathematics.)

* Kripke, S.A. (1965) 'Semantical Analyses of Intuitionistic Logic', in J. Crossley and M.A.E. Dummett (eds) *Formal Systems and Recursive Functions*, Amsterdam: North Holland, 92–130. (Includes formal results on the completeness of intuitionistic

logic but also nontechnical explications of the model theory.)

Lambek, J. and Scott, P. (1986) *Introduction to Higher-Order Categorical Logic*, Cambridge: Cambridge University Press. (A fine introduction to a highly technical subject.)

Martin-Löf, P. (1984) *Intuitionistic Type Theory*, Naples: Bibliopolis. (Based on lectures delivered by the author. Offers a helpful introduction to a detailed subject.)

Rasiowa, H. and Sikorski, R. (1963) *The Mathematics of Metamathematics*, Warsaw: PWN. (A standard reference on algebraic semantics; requires technical proficiency.)

* Schopenhauer, A. (1818, 1844) *Die Welt als Wille und Vorstellung*, trans. E.F.J. Payne, *The World as Will and Representation*, New York: Dover, 1969, vol. 1, §15. (Schopenhauer's reflections on mathematics.)

* Scott, D.S. (1968) 'Extending the Topological Interpretation to Intuitionistic Analysis I', *Compositio Mathematica* 20: 194–210. (A topological treatment of Brouwerian analysis that calls for metamathematical experience.)

Smorynski, C. (1973) 'Applications of Kripke Models', in A.S. Troelstra (ed.) *Metamathematical Investigation of Intuitionistic Arithmetic and Analysis*, Lecture Notes in Mathematics, vol. 344, Berlin: Springer, 324–91. (A lucid technical introductory overview to the model theory of intuitionistic arithmetic.)

* Tarski, A. (1938) 'Der Aussagenkalkül und die Topologie' (The Propositional Calculus and Topology), *Fundamenta Mathematica* 31: 103–34; repr. and trans. in *Logic, Semantics, Metamathematics*, ed. J. Corcoran, Indianapolis, IN: Hackett Publishing Company, 1983, 421–54. (Characteristically careful and clear exposition of early results on topological interpretations.)

* Troelstra, A.S. (1973a) 'Notes on Intuitionistic Second-Order Arithmetic', in A. Mathias and H. Rogers (eds) *Cambridge Summer School in Mathematical Logic*, Berlin: Springer, 171–205. (Remains a fine example of the metamathematics of higher-order intuitionistic systems. A companion piece to Troelstra (1973b).)

—— (ed.) (1973b) *Metamathematical Investigation of Intuitionistic Arithmetic and Analysis*, Lecture Notes in Mathematics, vol. 344, Berlin: Springer. (Terse and highly technical. For metamathematicians of the 1970s and 1980s, the bible of intuitionistic systems.)

Troelstra, A.S. and Dalen, D. van (1988) *Constructivism in Mathematics: An Introduction*, Amsterdam: North Holland, 2 vols. (A comprehensive technical overview of the current state of constructive mathematics, with emphasis on intuitionism and mathematical logic.)

DAVID CHARLES McCARTY

INTUITIONISM IN ETHICS

To intuit something is to apprehend it directly, without recourse to reasoning processes such as deduction or induction. Intuitionism in ethics proposes that we have a capacity for intuition and that some of the facts or properties that we intuit are irreducibly ethical. Traditionally, intuitionism also advances the important thesis that beliefs arising from intuition have direct justification, and therefore do not need to be justified by appeal to other beliefs or facts. So, while intuitionism in ethics is about the apprehension of ethical facts or properties, traditional intuitionism is principally a view about how beliefs, including ethical beliefs are justified. Varieties of intuitionism differ over what is intuited (for example, rightness or goodness?); whether what is intuited is general and abstract or concrete and particular; the degree of justification offered by intuition; and the nature of the intuitive capacity. The rejection of intuitionism is usually a result of rejecting one of the views that lie behind it.

Note that 'intuition' can refer to the thing intuited as well as the process of intuiting. Also, somewhat confusingly, intuitionism is sometimes identified with pluralism, the view that there is a plurality of fundamental ethical properties or principles. This identification probably occurs because pluralists often accept the epistemological version of intuitionism.

1   The motivation for intuitionism
2   Varieties of intuitionism
3   Why not intuitionism?

1   The motivation for intuitionism

Traditional intuitionism in ethics is not so much an attempt to establish that we have justification for ethical beliefs as an attempt to explain how ethical beliefs get their justification. That some ethical beliefs have justification is taken as a datum to be explained.

The form this explanation takes is determined by an explicit or implicit commitment to three views: moral realism, the autonomy of ethics and foundationalism in the theory of knowledge. Moral realism is the view that there are ethical facts or properties that are in some way objective or mind-independent, although the exact nature of the objectivity or mind-independence is controversial (see MORAL REALISM). That ethics is autonomous means that ethical facts cannot be 'reduced' to, or fully explained in terms of, nonethical ones (see AUTONOMY, ETHICAL §5). For example, this would preclude something's goodness being analysable in terms of someone's desire for it. Foundationalism is a general theory about the justification of beliefs, asserting that all justification has as a foundation beliefs that have direct justification (see FOUNDATIONALISM). Nonfoundational beliefs must rely for their ultimate justification on beliefs that have direct justification.

If it is accepted that we sometimes have justification for ethical beliefs and the explanation of their justification has to be consistent with these three views, then traditional intuitionism is almost inevitably the result. It should be noted, however, that some modern philosophers, such as Jonathan Dancy (1983), hold that some ethical facts or properties must be apprehended (intuited) directly, but reject foundationalism and the view that beliefs arising from intuition have direct justification. In what follows I shall focus on traditional intuitionism.

Moral realism, the autonomy of ethics, and foundationalism lead to traditional intuitionism as follows. The combination of moral realism and the autonomy of ethics ensures that ethical beliefs are about irreducibly ethical facts or properties and, thus, that ethical beliefs are irreducibly ethical. According to foundationalism, justification of beliefs about these irreducibly ethical facts or properties has as a foundation beliefs that have direct justification (that is, they are self-evident or need no evidence). Irreducibly ethical beliefs cannot have nonethical beliefs as their foundation. For if they could, the contents of the ethical beliefs would have to be so intimately related to the contents of the foundational nonethical beliefs as to be inconsistent with the autonomy of ethics. For example, if beliefs about desires provide the foundation for beliefs about goodness, then desiring and goodness would have to be intimately related. So, for any ethical beliefs to have justification, there must be some ethical beliefs that have direct justification and arise from direct apprehension (intuition). (If the foundational beliefs could arise from indirect apprehension, they could also be justified indirectly.)

Adding the 'datum' that we do sometimes have justification for ethical beliefs, we can conclude that some of our ethical beliefs arise from intuition and have direct justification. This is traditional intuitionism in ethics.

2 Varieties of intuitionism

Although elements of intuitionism have always had a place in ethical debate, it was only in the seventeenth century that it became a distinctive view (see CAMBRIDGE PLATONISM). More accurately, it became the distinctive core of a group of views, which has been developed in different ways.

For a start, in developing this core, we can ask what intuitions are about. For example, are they about rightness and wrongness, as according to H.A. Prichard (1949) and Joseph BUTLER (§3), goodness and badness, as held by G.E. Moore (1903), or defeasible moral reasons for performing and not performing actions, as W.D. Ross argued (1930; 1939) (see PRICHARD, H.A. §2; MOORE, G.E.; ROSS, W.D.)? Is what we intuit general and abstract, as Richard PRICE (§2) and Henry SIDGWICK (§2) maintained, or concrete and particular (Prichard and Butler)? For example, if intuitions are about the rightness of actions, would we intuit that it is morally right to perform any action of a certain general type or would we intuit that a particular act we are contemplating is morally right?

Since justification comes in degrees, there can be divergent views about the degree of justification conferred on beliefs arising from intuition (see MORAL KNOWLEDGE §3). Although intuition has usually been taken to confer justification at least sufficient for knowledge, it could be held to confer any degree of justification from certainty (which guarantees truth) to a mere presumption in favour of the fact intuited. If complete justification is not conferred on a belief by intuition, then, of course, it may acquire additional justification on other grounds, such as the degree to which it coheres with other beliefs. Also, intuitionists can take different sides on the externalism/internalism question about justification (see INTERNALISM AND EXTERNALISM IN EPISTEMOLOGY). Typically, internalists say that there has to be an awareness of the features that give a belief justification, while externalists deny this. Intuitionists who are internalists might say, for example, that a belief arising from intuition has justification only if the believer holds it to be indubitable (impossible not to believe) or, alternatively, merely difficult not to believe. On the other hand, externalists deny that such psychological features are required for the justification of beliefs arising from intuition.

There are also differing views about the nature of the intuitive capacity. It can be taken to be an intellectual capacity, as it was by Price and Moore, or a capacity for something more like perception, as it was by Prichard and Thomas REID. Those who take the intuitive capacity to be intellectual usually hold that the contents of the intuitions are general or abstract principles. Those who take it to be more like perception usually believe that intuitions have particular, concrete contents.

It could be held that we have the capacity for both kinds of intuition, intellectual and perceptual, and each kind gives us foundational beliefs. It is more usual, however, to hold that we have the capacity for only one kind of intuition, that its contents (general or particular) are foundational and beliefs of the other kind are indirectly justified, if at all.

If we have the capacity only for intellectual intuition and we intuit general principles, then particular ethical beliefs might be justified by recognizing that some situation involves an instance of the general principle. For instance, if we intuit a general principle like 'There is some ethical reason not to do any act that results in harm to anyone', we might recognize that a particular act falls under the principle and conclude that we have an ethical reason not to do it. Alternatively, if the capacity is taken to be perceptual and the intuitions to be about particular situations, then the general principles may be justified by some kind of induction on the particular cases. For example, we might intuit something like 'The harm this action would cause gives me an ethical reason not to do it' and use some form of induction to arrive at the general principle.

In any case, it is important to distinguish between the order of justification and the order of discovery. It could be that general principles are discovered through consideration of particular cases, but are justified directly, while the particular beliefs are justified only indirectly, as instances of the general principle or content. For example, we may have to experience a number of instances of lying before we can intuit the general principle that lying is, *ceteris paribus*, wrong, while we are justified in believing that a particular instance of lying is, *ceteris paribus*, wrong, only by applying the general principle.

Finally, the capacity for ethical intuition needs grounding in some mechanism. Those who believe that the intuitive capacity is intellectual and the contents of intuition general usually hold that these contents are necessary, synthetic truths, that there are other such truths, such as those of mathematics, and that the same capacity and mechanism is used in apprehending all such truths (Price and Ross). Some who hold that that intuition is particular and similar to perception postulate a 'moral sense' (Reid and Prichard) (see MORAL SENSE THEORIES). In neither case is the mechanism well understood.

3 Why not intuitionism?

The rejection of intuitionism is usually a consequence of rejecting one or more of the views that motivate it: moral realism, the autonomy of ethics and, in the case of traditional intuitionism, foundationalism. Although each of these views is controversial, the combination of moral realism and the autonomy of ethics is the source of objections to any form of intuitionism in ethics.

Intuitionism, and its commitment to irreducibly ethical facts or properties that we can apprehend directly, is incompatible with a broadly scientific, or naturalistic, picture of the world and how we learn about it. According to this picture, irreducibly ethical facts or properties would have to be occult. They would not be the sort of things that we can have scientific theories about. Matters are only made worse by claiming that we have some faculty that allows us to apprehend directly these irreducibly ethical properties or facts, to say nothing of the claim that beliefs arising from this direct apprehension are justified directly. Since the properties or facts are occult, so too must be the faculty that allows our awareness of them. Since persons would have an occult faculty, we could not have a complete scientific theory about persons. Indeed, the fact that moral realism and the autonomy of ethics lead to the claim that we have a capacity for intuition does not provide support for intuitionism; rather, it gives us ample reason to believe that at least one of the views leading to it must be wrong. Or so goes the objection.

Those who reject intuitionism by rejecting the autonomy of ethics usually argue that ethical properties or facts are actually nonethical ones, whose apprehension is compatible with the scientific picture of the world (see NATURALISM IN ETHICS). For example, it might be argued that to say that something is morally required is to say that it brings about more pleasure than its alternatives. Note that such views involve moral realism and may involve foundationalism.

Rejecting intuitionism by rejecting moral realism is consistent with accepting the autonomy of ethics. For example, it could be held that what seem to be ethical judgments are actually irreducibly ethical prescriptions, the expression of irreducibly ethical attitudes or the projection of such attitudes (see ANALYTIC ETHICS; EMOTIVISM; PROJECTIVISM).

Another possibility is to accept that our moral practices and beliefs are committed to intuitionism and that intuitionism's incompatibility with the scientific picture of the world shows that our ethical practices and beliefs involve fundamental error (see MORAL SCEPTICISM §3; MORAL REALISM §7).

There are several possible responses to the claim that intuitionism is incompatible with a scientific picture of the world. The compatibility of these outlooks rests, it can be argued, on a proper understanding of the scientific picture of the world. In the same vein, this compatibility can be said to depend on a proper understanding of intuition. A further possible response is to say 'so much for the scientific picture'.

See also: COMMON SENSE ETHICS; EPISTEMOLOGY AND ETHICS; MORAL JUDGMENT

References and further reading

Audi, R. (1996) 'Intuitionism, pluralism, and the foundations of ethics', in W. Sinnott-Armstrong and M. Timmons (eds) *Moral Knowledge?: New Readings in Moral Epistemology*, Oxford: Oxford University Press, 101–36. (A modern defence of a view which is quasi-intuitionistic.)

* Dancy, J. (1983) 'Ethical particularism and morally relevant properties', *Mind* 92: 530–47. (An example of nontraditional intuitionism, arguing that what we intuit is particular and concrete.)

* Moore, G.E. (1903) *Principia Ethica*, Cambridge: Cambridge University Press, esp. chaps 5, 6. (Holds that intuitions are general, that the truth of utilitarianism is self-evident and that we can intuit the goodness of some properties.)

* Prichard, H.A. (1949) *Moral Obligation*, Oxford: Oxford University Press. (Argues that we intuit the rightness of particular actions.)

Ross, W.D. (1930) *The Right and the Good*, Oxford: Clarendon Press, esp. ch. 2. (Classic exposition of pluralist intuitionism.)

—— (1939) *The Foundations of Ethics*, Oxford: Clarendon Press, esp. 79–86 and ch. 8. (Holds that we intuit general principles about the moral relevance of types of actions.)

Schneewind, J.B. (1990) *Moral Philosophy from Montaigne to Kant*, Cambridge: Cambridge University Press, 2 vols. (Contains descriptions of, and extracts from, many of the early intuitionists, including Richard Cumberland, Samuel Clarke, Shaftesbury, Francis Hutcheson, Joseph Butler, Richard Price and Thomas Reid.)

ROBERT L. FRAZIER

INTUITIONISTIC LOGIC AND ANTIREALISM

The law of excluded middle (LEM) says that every sentence of the form $A \lor \neg A$ ('A or not A') is logically true. This law is accepted in classical logic, but not in intuitionistic logic. The reason for this difference over logical validity is a deeper difference about truth and meaning. In classical logic, the meanings of the logical connectives are explained by means of the truth tables, and these explanations justify LEM. However, the truth table explanations involve acceptance of the principle of bivalence, that is, the principle that every sentence is either true or false. The intuitionist does not accept bivalence, at least not in mathematics. The reason is the view that mathematical sentences are made true and false by proofs which mathematicians construct. On this view, bivalence can be assumed only if we have a guarantee that for each mathematical sentence, either there is a proof of the truth of the sentence, or a proof of its falsity. But we have no such guarantee. Therefore bivalence is not intuitionistically acceptable, and then neither is LEM.

A realist about mathematics thinks that if a mathematical sentence is true, then it is rendered true by the obtaining of some particular state of affairs, whether or not we can know about it, and if that state of affairs does not obtain, then the sentence is false. The realist further thinks that mathematical reality is fully determinate, in that every mathematical state of affairs determinately either obtains or does not obtain. As a result, the principle of bivalence is taken to hold for mathematical sentences. The intuitionist is usually an antirealist about mathematics, rejecting the idea of a fully determinate, mind-independent mathematical reality.

The intuitionist's view about the truth-conditions of mathematical sentences is not obviously incompatible with realism about mathematical states of affairs. According to Michael Dummett, however, the view about truth-conditions implies antirealism. In Dummett's view, a conflict over realism is fundamentally a conflict about what makes sentences true, and therefore about semantics, for there is no further question about, for example, the existence of a mathematical reality than as a truth ground for mathematical sentences. In this vein Dummett has proposed to take acceptance of bivalence as actually defining a realist position.

If this is right, then both the choice between classical and intuitionistic logic and questions of realism are fundamentally questions of semantics, for whether or not bivalence holds depends on the proper semantics. The question of the proper semantics, in turn, belongs to the theory of meaning. Within the theory of meaning

Dummett has laid down general principles, from which he argues that meaning cannot in general consist in bivalent truth-conditions. The principles concern the need for, and the possibility of, manifesting one's knowledge of meaning to other speakers, and the nature of such manifestations. If Dummett's argument is sound, then bivalence cannot be justified directly from semantics, and may not be justifiable at all.

1   **Standard intuitionistic logic**
2   **Logic from the intuitionistic viewpoint**
3   **Bivalence and the meaning of the logical constants**
4   **Dummett on antirealism and semantics**
5   **The relation between realism and bivalence**
6   **Dummett's antirealist argument**

1   Standard intuitionistic logic

The term 'intuitionistic logic' is used in two related senses. In the first sense, intuitionistic logic is the set of logical principles which are valid according to general intuitionism, as originally proposed by the Dutch mathematician L.E.J. Brouwer (1908). In the second, more standard, sense, intuitionistic logic is the logic determined by any one of several equivalent sets of logical rules and axioms. Such an axiom system, motivated by Brouwer's ideas, was first proposed by the Dutch logician Arend Heyting (1930) (see INTUITIONISM).

Usually, the phrase 'intuitionistic logic' is taken to mean the logic you get by accepting classical logic and withdrawing your acceptance of the law of excluded middle (LEM). LEM is the law according to which every sentence of the form $A \vee \neg A$ is logically true. Intuitionistically, this law is rejected. This means that the intuitionist is not allowed to assert a sentence $A \vee \neg A$ purely on logical grounds. It does not mean that the negation of that sentence may be asserted. Intuitionistically, as much as classically, the sentence $\neg(A \vee \neg A)$ is a contradiction.

Because of the inconsistency of $\neg(A \vee \neg A)$ we are allowed to infer its negation, $\neg\neg(A \vee \neg A)$. Classically, we could now infer $A \vee \neg A$, because the rule of double negation elimination (DNE), that is, the rule that from $\neg\neg A$ you may infer A, is valid in classical logic. Therefore, DNE is also not intuitionistically valid. By equally simple, intuitionistically acceptable reasoning, you can infer DNE from LEM. In fact, in natural deduction, systems for intuitionistic logic differ from their classical counterparts precisely by not containing DNE.

Classically, LEM is valid in virtue of the truth table explanations of the propositional constants. By the explanation of '$\neg$', either A is true or $\neg A$ is true, and by the explanation of '$\vee$', nothing more is needed for the truth of $A \vee \neg A$. So those who reject LEM must understand these logical constants in a different way.

2   Logic from the intuitionistic viewpoint

L.E.J. Brouwer is commonly regarded as the father of intuitionism, but he himself traces the intuitionist tradition back at least to Kant, who thought of intuitions of space and time as basic to mathematics (see KANT, I. §5). In Heyting 1934 the following two theses characterize intuitionism:

(1)   Mathematics has not only formal significance, but also content.

(2)   Mathematical objects are immediately grasped by the thinking subject; therefore mathematical knowledge is independent of experience.

Heyting then subdivides intuitionism into 'half-intuitionism' and intuitionism proper. The half-intuitionist holds that mathematical objects exist independently of our thinking, but can be known by means of our mathematical constructions. The full-blown intuitionist denies this, or at least rejects the idea that the thesis of mind-independent existence of mathematical objects can be used as a means of mathematical proof.

How can the realistic view of mathematical objects be used as a means of proof? Precisely because that view licenses the use of the law of excluded middle. If mathematical objects exist independently, and have all their properties independently, then, for instance, either, as a matter of fact, the sequence of digits 0123456789 does occur somewhere in the decimal expansion of π, or, as a matter of fact, it does not. For each mathematical statement, either mathematical reality renders that statement true, or else it does not, in which case the statement is false. In this way mathematical realism justifies LEM. LEM, in turn, is used as a means of proof.

Brouwer rejected mathematical realism. He thought that mathematics is an activity where propositions are proved by means of mental constructions, and above all that such mental constructions are precisely what make mathematical propositions true. The statement that 0123456789 does occur somewhere in the decimal expansion of π is rendered true by a construction, for example, by the construction of the decimal expansion up to the point where the sequence occurs, and is rendered false by a construction which proves that it cannot ever occur. And (roughly) a disjunction is rendered true by having one of its disjuncts rendered true. On this view, we are not in advance justified in asserting that the sequence either does or does not occur, for we have no guarantee, before a proof is actually found, that either we can carry out the verifying construction or else we can carry out the falsifying construction.

On these grounds Brouwer rejected LEM. He went further, in that, in sharpest contrast to the formalist school in the philosophy of mathematics (see HILBERT'S PROGRAMME AND FORMALISM), he refused to accept logic at all as a separate source of knowledge in mathematics. In particular, that a set of mathematical axioms is consistent is not in itself a good reason, according to Brouwer, for accepting them. The relation between logic and mathematics is the opposite. Logical validity depends on insight in the nature of mathematical truth. And this leads to an understanding of the logical operators themselves.

3 Bivalence and the meaning of the logical constants

The truth table explanations give the meaning of the classical propositional constants. For instance, the meaning of '$\rightarrow$' is given by the fact, or stipulation, that $A \rightarrow B$ is false if A is true and B false, and true in the other three cases. This gives the classical meaning of '$\rightarrow$' for the reason that these four truth-value combinations exhaust all possibilities, which, in turn, involves the principle of *bivalence*, the principle that each statement is either true or false.

Under default assumptions, bivalence holds if and only if LEM is valid. The default assumptions are two: first, that $(A \vee B)$ is true if A is true or B is true. Second, that $\neg A$ is true if A is false.

The intuitionist does not accept the principle of bivalence. Again, this means that the intuitionist is not allowed, without further justification, to assert of a sentence A that it is either true or false. It does not mean that the intuitionist may assert that there are sentences which are neither true nor false. In fact, the question whether there are such sentences is a quite separate issue (see VAGUENESS §3; PRESUPPOSITION §2; MANY-VALUED LOGICS, PHILOSOPHICAL ISSUES IN). However, the intuitionist as well as the classical logician may adopt the view that some sentences are neither true nor false, for example, because of non-referring singular terms. The modified classical logician will then claim that each sentence is either true, or false, or neither true nor false, and the modified intuitionist will not accept this principle.

The intuitionist also accepts the truth tables, but for the intuitionist they do not explain the meaning of the constants. Since the principle of bivalence is not accepted, it cannot be assumed that the entries in the truth tables exhaust all possibilities. The intuitionist may be allowed to assert $A \rightarrow B$, on the basis of a deduction of B from A, without being allowed to assert that either A is false or B is true.

On the intuitionistic conception, a mathematical proposition is true only if there is a proof of it. Moreover, the *meaning* of a mathematical sentence is closely tied to what counts as a proof of it. This is the leading idea in the Brouwer–Heyting or Brouwer–Heyting–Kolmogorov interpretation of the logical constants. Heyting once suggested that a mathematical sentence expresses an expectation of finding a proof of it. The meaning of '$\vee$' is then recursively explained by saying that a sentence $A \vee B$ expresses an expectation which is fulfilled just in case at least one of the expectations expressed by A and by B is fulfilled.

The modern version of this kind of explanation is due primarily to Michael DUMMETT (1973). Dummett suggests that we can correlate forms of sentence to forms of proof. There is no one form that is common to all proofs of a sentence $A \vee B$, but we can make a distinction between 'canonical' and 'non-canonical' proofs, proposed by both Dummett and the Swedish logician Dag Prawitz (1974), such that a canonical proof of $A \vee B$ is a proof consisting of either a proof of A or a proof of B. Non-canonical proofs are constructions which give us *effective* methods of finding canonical proofs. An effective method is a method which is guaranteed to yield the result after a finite number of elementary steps.

Then a proof of $A \vee B$ either consists of a proof of A or a proof of B, or of an effective method of finding the one or the other. A canonical proof of $A \& B$ is a pair of proofs, of A and of B respectively. A canonical proof of $A \rightarrow B$ is an effective method of transforming any proof of A into a proof of B. A canonical proof of $\neg A$ is an effective method of transforming any proof of A into a proof of '$\perp$' (absurdity, a sentence constant that is false by definition), and therefore a proof of the impossibility of a proof of A. A canonical proof of $\forall x A$ is an effective method for finding, for any term t, a proof of At. A canonical proof of $\exists x A$ is a proof of At, for some term t.

These are the intended intuitionistic interpretations of the logical constants. It follows from these meaning explanations that a non-canonical proof of $A \vee \neg A$ is an effective method for finding either a proof of A or a proof of $\neg A$. If there is such a non-canonical proof of $A \vee \neg A$, then A is called 'effectively decidable' (in Dummett's terminology, which we follow in §6; more technically, the term applies to predicates, or infinite classes of sentences). However, the notion of an absolutely undecidable sentence, that is, of a sentence A such that neither A nor $\neg A$ can be proved at all, does not make sense intuitionistically. A cannot be proved only if it can be proved that A cannot be proved (since truth amounts to provability), but such a proof constitutes a proof of ¬*A*, contradicting the second assumption that ¬*A* cannot be proved.

A semantic idea that is closely related to the Brouwer–Heyting–Kolmogorov interpretation is the idea that the meaning of the logical constants is given by the rules for them in natural deduction, as first devised by Gerhard GENTZEN (1934) and later developed by Prawitz (1965) (see LOGICAL CONSTANTS §4). In particular there is a close analogy between the introduction rules in natural deduction and the forms of canonical proofs. For instance, the introduction rule for '&' is that *A* & *B* may be inferred from the joint premises of *A* and *B*. From this alternative perspective, introduction rules are valid by definition, and all other rules are to be justified with respect to these.

From both these kinds of meaning-explanation, standard intuitionistic logic is justifiable and LEM is not. But the question is whether further rules than the standard ones are valid. This could be answered in the negative by a proof of semantic completeness, that is, of the statement that all intuitionistically valid principles are derivable from standard intuitionistic logic. Such a proof would have to invoke the intended interpretations rather than some other semantics, and it would have to employ only intuitionistically valid modes of reasoning. At the time of writing, it is not clear that such a proof can be found.

4 Dummett on antirealism and semantics

Brouwer rejected mathematical realism, rejected the law of excluded middle and adopted the idea that mathematical statements are true in virtue of mental constructions. These views naturally go together, but their interrelations are non-trivial.

Antirealism, that is, rejection of realism, comes in many forms. The most direct form is a denial of the existence of entities, for example, the existence of universals. Brouwer denied the existence of extramental mathematical objects. If this is denied, then there is a question of evaluating mathematical sentences. Since we want to preserve standard arithmetical judgments, we must understand a sentence such as '2 + 2 = 4' so that neither its meaningfulness, nor its truth, depends on the existence of entities of the rejected kind. One possibility is to interpret the sentence in terms of mental constructions, as Brouwer did, but it is not the only one. You can also reinterpret arithmetical sentences, for example, so as to make them true or false by virtue of facts about numerals and their operators. You can even do it in such a way that, if you are a realist about numerals, the principle of bivalence remains valid. So not every form of antirealism will necessitate a change

of logic. It will always depend on the way the sentences are reinterpreted.

The form of view suggested, combining a denial of the existence of entities (numbers) with an affirmation of bivalence for (arithmetical) sentences, has been categorized by Dummett as a form of sophisticated realism, rather than a form of antirealism. On Dummett's view, belief in the determinacy of facts is more central to realism than belief in the existence of entities. A mathematical antirealist can accept the existence of numbers and reject the statement that every mathematical state of affairs either obtains or does not obtain. On this view we just cannot take for granted that every mathematical question has an answer in mathematical reality.

These reflections suggest a central place for the principle of bivalence in questions of realism, and that is just what Dummett has proposed. However, there are two more specific features of Dummett's views on bivalence and realism. First, Dummett places bivalence, as a criterion of realism, in an epistemic perspective. In this perspective, realism is in the first place opposed to the knowability principle, that is, the view that if a sentence is true, then it can be known to be true (see MEANING AND VERIFICATION §5). If you accept bivalence, then, from the epistemic perspective, what is important is that you hold every sentence to be either true or false whether or not it is possible to find out which. And if you reject bivalence, the default reason, from the epistemic perspective, is that on the one hand you accept the knowability principle and, on the other, you do not think there is any guarantee that each sentence can be either known to be true or known to be false.

Second, Dummett regards acceptance of bivalence not just as characteristic of the realist, but as actually defining what it is to be a realist. Similarly, rejection of bivalence by definition makes you an antirealist. Although Dummett recognizes further aspects of realism and antirealism, bivalence is taken as the main dividing line. In this way realism becomes a semantic issue (hence the terms 'semantic realism' and 'semantic antirealism' in discussion of Dummett's views).

There are three interconnected reasons for this change of perspective. First, Dummett holds that traditional metaphysical disputes are framed in pictorial language, with pictures like that of an ethereal realm of abstract entities. These pictures should be replaced by more precisely stated claims. Secondly, the conflict about, for example, the reality of the past, is a conflict about what makes our sentences about the past true, and therefore the question of the reality of the past will involve the question of the proper semantics for sentences about the past. The realist thinks that a sentence can be made true by past facts even if it is impossible for us to know what they are, and the antirealist rejects this as incoherent. Similarly for other disputes over realism. Third, if the conflict is taken as a conflict about semantics, then it can actually be resolved. It will be resolved once it has been shown what a correct meaning theory for the language in question must look like.

5   The relation between realism and bivalence

However, it may seem that Dummett has overstated the role of bivalence in metaphysics. Semantics is what connects bivalence, for some range of sentences, and the determinacy of facts in the corresponding area. What connection there is depends on the kind of semantics, that is, on how the sentences are interpreted. But it also depends on how well the meanings of the sentences are determined.

Suppose that you interpret sentences about the past according to a correspondence model, so that they are made true or false by past facts or events. The sentence 'George Washington crossed the Potomac' is then true, if it is true, in virtue of the event of Washington's crossing the Potomac. Suppose further that all sentences concerned have a well-determined meaning. If a sentence has a well-determined meaning, then it depends only on reality whether or not the sentence is true.

Under these assumptions realism and bivalence are equivalent. If past reality is fully determinate, so that all past states of affairs either obtained or did not obtain, and the meanings of the sentences are such that this and nothing else is needed for making them true or false, then each sentence is true or false. And similarly, if bivalence holds, so does realism.

You may doubt that reality is fully determinate, suspecting that there might be gaps, as it were, and take this as a reason for accepting the knowability principle, thinking that our only guarantee that some state of affairs does or does not obtain is that we can get to know either that it obtains or that it does not. In that case, under the same initial assumptions, bivalence will fail. Conversely, if you accept the knowability principle for another reason, then you have a reason to reject bivalence, since there is no guarantee that each sentence can be known either to be true or to be false. Again under the same assumptions, you must reject realism.

However, if one of these two assumptions is dropped, then the equivalence is lost. Suppose that you give up the second assumption, about the determinacy of meaning. You may think, for example, that the application of a predicate such as

'...crossed...' to a pair of objects, such as Washington and the Potomac, is determinately either correct or incorrect only if it is within our present capacity to decide whether it is the one or the other. If we do not have that capacity, then, on this view, the meaning of the predicate is underspecified for these arguments. This view leads to the rejection of bivalence. We cannot assert that each sentence is either true or false, since if we cannot either verify or falsify a particular sentence, then, on this view, its truth-value is left indeterminate. In this case, however, there are no consequences for reality. Reality may be fully determinate. The failure of bivalence depends on meaning only, not on the world.

We get the same result if the first assumption is dropped. Suppose that we adopt a kind of verificationism for sentences about the past. We interpret them so that they are made true or false not by past facts or events, but by present evidence, that is, by such present facts as we take as grounds for asserting those sentences, such as facts about written documents or memories. Then again we have a reason to reject bivalence, for there is no guarantee that we will, for each sentence about the past, be in possession either of truth-making evidence or of falsity-making evidence. And again nothing seems to follow about realism. If sentences about the past are not made true or false by past facts, then failure of bivalence implies nothing about the determinacy of past reality.

The natural reply to the objection is that we have no conception whatsoever about the reality of the past save as that which is represented by our sentences about the past. If these sentences cannot reasonably be given a semantics according to which they are true or false in virtue of past facts, then the notion of an independent past reality must be rejected, for it is only as the truth-maker of our sentences that we have a reason to be realists about it. Moreover, we cannot then use the sentence 'Past facts are fully determinate' for stating an independent metaphysical truth, for this sentence must itself be evaluated according to the proposed alternative semantics.

If this reply is correct, then questions of metaphysics are *eo ipso* questions of semantics. And then, as Dummett thinks, metaphysical conflicts are to be settled within the theory of meaning. Indeed, according to Dummett 1991, expressions of metaphysical pictures of reality have no content at all in addition to the semantic views that go with them.

6   Dummett's antirealist argument

We have seen that the principle of bivalence is of central importance both for realism and for classical logic. Bivalence itself, for any kind of sentence, or for some particular kind, is to be justified by the proper semantics for the kind of sentence in question. And what the proper semantics is, is a question in the general theory of meaning.

Within the theory of meaning Dummett has, notably in 'What is a Theory of Meaning? (II)' (1976), proposed general principles, from which an argument is drawn to the conclusion that a semantics of bivalent truth-conditions cannot be correct.

The first step in Dummett's reasoning is the observation that an account of linguistic meaning must be an account of linguistic understanding, that is, of knowledge of meaning. The thesis that meaning consists of truth-conditions is acceptable if and only if it is acceptable that understanding a sentence consists of knowing its truth-conditions, and similarly for other accounts of meaning.

Second, understanding must be publicly manifestable. That is, if I understand a particular sentence, then I must be able to reveal to my interlocutors that I do. This is because language is a means of communication. If there were ingredients in meaning such that knowledge of them could not be made manifest to others, then speakers could not know whether they attached the same meanings to the same expressions, and then communication, as far as those ingredients in meaning are concerned, would be impossible (see PRIVATE STATES AND LANGUAGE).

Thus, if meaning consists of truth-conditions, knowledge of truth-conditions must be manifestable. But how do you manifest your knowledge of the truth-conditions of a sentence? Sometimes you can manifest your understanding by means of a verbal explanation of the meaning of the sentence, but in this way the problem is transferred to the question of your knowledge of the meaning of the sentences you use in your explanation. When you cannot, without circularity, explain further, then you must manifest your understanding in a more primitive way. Dummett says that such a manifestation is a manifestation of a particular capacity, namely, the capacity to get to know that the sentence is true, if it is true, and to get to know that it is false, if it is false. According to Dummett, this is what counts as manifesting knowledge of truth-conditions.

The next step concerns the possibility of such manifestations. If the sentence in question is effectively decidable (see §3 above), then manifesting knowledge of its truth-conditions is possible in principle, but perhaps not in practice. If a sentence is practically decidable, that is, deciding it is within the scope of ordinary human abilities, then I can manifest my knowledge of its truth-conditions by applying a decision method, like making an observation or a small number of calculations, and arrive at a knowl-

edge of its truth-value. If the sentence is effectively decidable, but not in practice, for example, because the number of calculations needed is too large, then I can at least manifest my knowledge of a decision method for it.

The problem appears, according to Dummett, when we come to sentences which are not effectively decidable. A sentence such as 'Two million days before the birth of Benjamin Franklin, an even number of birds landed on Mount St Helen' is not effectively decidable, for we have no method today which is guaranteed to give the right answer. In this case I do not have a capacity to get to know the truth-value, and therefore I cannot manifest my knowledge of its truth-conditions.

The sentence is clearly meaningful, and I clearly understand it. Since knowledge of meaning must be manifestable, and I cannot manifest my knowledge of bivalent truth-conditions in this case, knowledge of its meaning cannot be knowledge of bivalent truth-conditions. Hence, Dummett concludes, meaning does not in general consist of bivalent truth-conditions.

If this argument is sound, then the principle of bivalence cannot be justified in the most natural way, that is, directly from the proper semantics of the sentences it concerns, for that is not a semantics of bivalent truth-conditions. As Dummett points out, this does not in itself invalidate the bivalence principle, since the argument allows that bivalence may be justified in some other way. It seems plausible, however, that bivalence cannot be justified in any way allowed for by Dummett's meaning-theoretical principles.

If bivalence cannot be justified for some particular class of sentences, then neither can semantic realism for that class of sentences. And, since logical principles are perfectly general and topic neutral, if there is some class for which bivalence fails, then, under the default assumptions about the relation between bivalence and LEM (§3), LEM is not a logical law.

This is the destructive aspect of Dummett's enterprise. It has been criticized by a number of philosophers. One objection, due to McDowell 1987, is that the requirement of (full) manifestability is too strong, and another is that Dummett has a rigid and unjustified view of how knowledge of truth-conditions may be manifested.

The constructive aspect is a project of outlining a kind of semantics that satisfies Dummett's own requirements. The model for such a semantics, according to Dummett, is precisely the intuitionistic interpretation of the logical constants. The question is whether this idea can be generalized, in particular from logic and mathematics to empirical sentences. Such a generalization would amount to some form of verificationism, that is, a view according to which the meaning of a sentence is somehow given by the method, or methods, of verifying the sentence. There are, however, many ways of verifying a verifiable sentence, and only some are directly connected with its meaning. In accordance with the intuitionistic interpretation of the logical constants we should therefore distinguish between canonical and non-canonical, or direct and indirect, verifications of a sentence. Then we can say that the meaning of a declarative sentence is given by what counts as a direct verification of it. On this model, understanding of a sentence would be manifested by exercising an ability to decide, for every proposed piece of evidence, whether or not it constitutes a verification of the sentence. The point is that we can be credited with such an ability even in cases where we in fact do not know how to find a verification. It is enough that we can recognize it if we find it. Therefore the requirement of manifestability is taken to be fulfilled.

However, it has been claimed by Wright 1987 that if full manifestability is required, then problems begin already with sentences not decidable in practice, for example, sentences whose shortest proofs are too long to be surveyable by humans. But, as Wright points out, a finite upper bound on the length of proofs cannot be acknowledged within intuitionism.

Dummett rejects such finite upper bounds, but in fact leaves it open whether intuitionistic logic meets all the meaning-theoretic requirements. He does not, however, see any *principled* reason for doubting it, as he does in the case of classical logic, with its accompanying realism.

See also: ANTIREALISM IN THE PHILOSOPHY OF MATHEMATICS; LOGICAL AND MATHEMATICAL TERMS, GLOSSARY OF; MEANING AND TRUTH; REALISM AND ANTIREALISM; REALISM IN THE PHILOSOPHY OF MATHEMATICS

References and further reading

* Brouwer, L.E.J. (1908) 'De onbetrouwbaarheid der logische principes', *Tijdschrift voor wijsbegeerte* 2: 152–8; trans. A. Heyting, 'The Unreliability of the Logical Principles', in *Collected Works*, vol. 1, *Philosophy and Foundations of Mathematics*, ed. A. Heyting, Amsterdam and Oxford: North Holland, 1975. (Brouwer's original proposal that intuitionistic logic is the set of logical principles which are valid according to general intuitionism.)

—— (1913) 'Intuitionisme en formalisme', *Wiskundig Tijdschrift* 9: 180–211; trans. A. Dresden, 'Intuitionism and Formalism', in P. Benacerraf and H. Putnam (eds) *Philosophy of Mathematics: Selected Readings*, Cambridge, MA: Cambridge University Press, 1964. (One of several papers on the nature of intuitionism and logic, originally read in 1912.)

* Dummett, M. (1973) 'The Philosophical Basis of Intuitionistic Logic', in *Truth and Other Enigmas*, London: Duckworth, 1978. (This paper includes the canonical proof kind of interpretation of the logical constants and presents the antirealist argument.)

* —— (1976) 'What is a Theory of Meaning? (II)', in G. Evans and J. McDowell (eds) *Truth and Meaning: Essays in Semantics*, Oxford: Clarendon Press. (Dummett's classic paper on the theory of meaning, including a presentation of the antirealist argument.)

—— (1977) *Elements of Intuitionism*, Oxford: Clarendon Press. (A thorough introduction to intuitionistic mathematics and logic. Densely written.)

* —— (1991) *The Logical Basis of Metaphysics*, London: Duckworth. (A comprehensive treatment of logic, meaning and metaphysics; partly technical, partly difficult.)

* Gentzen, G. (1934) 'Untersuchungen über das logische Schliessen', *Mathematische Annalen* 39: 176–210; trans. 'Investigations into Logical Deduction', in *Collected Papers*, ed. M.E. Szabó, Amsterdam: North Holland, 1969. (Gentzen's presentation of natural deduction.)

* Heyting, A. (1930) *'Die formalen Regeln der intuitionistischen Logik'* (The Formal Rules of Intuitionistic Logic) , in *Sitzungsberichte der Preußische Akademie der Wissenschaften*, Berlin. (Heyting's formalization of intuitionistic propositional logic.)

* —— (1934) *Mathematische Grundlagenforschung. Intuitionismus. Beweistheorie* (Foundations of Mathematics. Intuitionism. Proof Theory), Berlin: Springer; repr. 1974. (Includes an excellent 25-page introduction to intuitionism, as known at the time.)

* McDowell, J. (1987) 'In Defence of Modesty', in B. Taylor (ed.) *Michael Dummett: Contributions to Philosophy*, Dordrecht: Nijhoff. (A criticism of Dummett's requirements on meaning theories, including the requirements on manifestability. The book contains other good papers on Dummett, with extensive replies.)

McGuinness, B. and Oliveri, G. (eds) (1994) *The Philosophy of Michael Dummett*, Dordrecht: Kluwer. (A good collection of critical comments on Dummett, with extensive replies.)

* Prawitz, D. (1965) *Natural Deduction: A Proof Theoretic Study*, Stockholm: Almqvist & Wiksell. (A classic study of properties of natural deduction systems for both classical and intuitionistic logic.)

* —— (1974) 'On the Idea of a General Proof Theory', *Synthese* 27: 63–77. (Introduces the notion of a

canonical argument in the context of defining the concept of a valid argument.)

Tennant, N. (1987) *Antirealism and Logic: Truth as Eternal*, Oxford: Clarendon Press. (A well-written and useful introduction to, and overview of, the issues, both philosophical and formal, and a defence of antirealism.)

* Wright, C. (1987) 'Strict Finitism', in *Realism, Meaning and Truth*, Oxford: Blackwell. (This paper concerns among other things whether the strict finitist has not got equally good arguments against the intuitionist as the intuitionist has against classical logic. The book as a whole is to a great extent concerned with Dummett's projects, both the negative and the positive.)

PETER PAGIN

IQBAL, MUHAMMAD (1877–1938)

Muhammad Iqbal was an outstanding poet-philosopher, perhaps the most influential Muslim thinker of the twentieth century. His philosophy, though eclectic and showing the influence of Muslims thinkers such as al-Ghazali and Rumi as well as Western thinkers such as Nietzsche and Bergson, was rooted fundamentally in the Qur'an, which Iqbal read with the sensitivity of a poet and the insight of a mystic. Iqbal's philosophy is known as the philosophy of khudi *or Selfhood. Rejecting the idea of a 'Fall' from Eden or original sin, Iqbal regards the advent of human beings on earth as a glorious event, since Adam was designated by God to be God's viceregent on earth. Human beings are not mere accidents in the process of evolution. The cosmos exists in order to make possible the emergence and perfection of the Self. The purpose of life is the development of the Self, which occurs as human beings gain greater knowledge of what lies within them as well as of the external world. Iqbal's philosophy is essentially a philosophy of action, and it is concerned primarily with motivating human beings to strive to actualize their God-given potential to the fullest degree.*

1 **Life**
2 **Works**
3 **Philosophy of the self**
4 **Epistemology**
5 **Political philosophy**
6 **Critical evaluation**

1 Life

Muhammad Iqbal was born at Sialkot in India in 1877. His ancestors were Kashmiri Brahmans; his forefathers had a predilection for mysticism, and both his father, Nur Muhammad, and his mother, Imam Bibi, had a reputation for piety. An outstanding student, Iqbal won many distinctions throughout his academic career. He passed the intermediate examination from the Scotch Mission School in Sialkot in 1893 and then moved to the Government College in Lahore, where he graduated in 1897. In 1899 he obtained a master's degree in Arabic. Having been deeply influenced by Sir Thomas Arnold, the well-known scholar of Islam, while he was at the Government College, Iqbal followed his advice and proceeded to Trinity College, Cambridge in October 1905, graduating in 1907 having studied philosophy under J.M.E. McTaggart. His doctorate was taken at Munich University, with a thesis entitled *The Development of Metaphysics in Persia*.

On his return from Europe in July 1908, Iqbal took up the post of Professor of Philosophy and English Literature at the Government College in Lahore, and also began his law practice. In 1911 he gave up his teaching career because he felt that he had a message to deliver and could do it better if he adopted an independent profession such as law. However, he always remained interested in education and was associated with the Oriental College, the Government College and the Islamia College in Lahore, and with the Jami'a Millia in Delhi. During the sessions of the Round Table Conferences in London he worked on the various committees connected with educational reforms. In 1933 Iqbal, along with some others, was invited by the Afghan government to visit the country and advise the government and Kabul University on educational matters.

Iqbal also took an interest in the workings of the Muslim League, but did not participate actively in politics. During the period 1910–23 he tried instead to create political consciousness and bring about an awakening of Indian Muslims. In 1924 Iqbal became a member of the National Liberal League of Lahore; in 1926 he was elected a member of the Punjab Legislative Assembly, and in 1930 was elected president of the All-India Muslim League, where he delivered a historic address. He took part in the Second and Third Round Table Conferences held in London, and was most disappointed with the outcome. Iqbal was knighted on 1 January 1923. His last years were clouded with ill health. After his death in 1938 he was buried near the gate of the Badshahi Mosque in Lahore, with many attending and millions in mourning.

2 Works

A precocious youth, Iqbal began to write poetry at a very early age, and soon after he came to Lahore he became known through his participation in poetic symposia. As a young poet, he came under the influence of Mirza Dagh Dehalvi, one of the renowned exponents of Urdu poetry. An organization to which Iqbal was devoted all his life was the Anjuman-e-Himayat-e-Islam (Society for the Support of Islam). The annual sessions of the Anjuman fulfilled an acute emotional need of Indian Muslims and became national festivals. Iqbal read his poems regularly at these sessions, and in fact his poems were the main attraction for the thousands who flocked to Lahore, almost on an errand of pilgrimage, to see and hear him. It was at an Anjuman meeting in April 1911 that Iqbal read his famous 'Shikwa' (The Complaint), a poem which commands such a unique place in Urdu literature that Iqbal's fame could rest securely on it alone.

The publication of *Asrar-e-khudi* (The Secrets of the Self) in 1915 was a significant event. It was followed by *Rumuz-e-bekhudi* (The Mysteries of Selflessness), which dealt with the development of the communal ego, in 1918; *Payam-e-mashriq* (The Message of the East), Iqbal's answer to Goethe's *West–Östlicher Divan*, in 1923 (see GOETHE, J.W. VON); *Zabur-e-'ajam* (The Persian Psalms) in 1927; *Javid nama* (The Pilgrimage of Eternity), Iqbal's magnum opus modelled on Dante's *Divine Comedy*, in 1932; *Musafir* (The Traveller) in 1934; *Bal-e-Jibril* (Gabriel's Wing) in 1935; *Zarb-e-Kalim* (The Stroke of Moses) and *Pas che bayad kard ai aqwam-i-sharq?* (So What Should be Done, O Nations of the East?) in 1936. *Armaghan-e-hijaz* (The Gift of Hijaz), containing both Persian and Urdu verse, appeared posthumously in 1938. As well as his poetical works, Iqbal wrote three works in prose. *'Ilm-ul-iqtisad* (The Study of Economics), which was the first book on political economy to be published in Urdu, appeared in 1903; Iqbal's doctoral thesis, *The Development of Metaphysics in Persia* was published in 1908; and his lectures, *The Reconstruction of Religious Thought in Islam*, were first published in 1930. Iqbal also wrote numerous articles in Urdu and English in various journals and newspapers.

3 Philosophy of the self

Iqbal's philosophy is often described as the philosophy of *khudi*, or the Self. For him, the fundamental fact of human life is the absolute and irrefutable consciousness of one's own being. For Iqbal, the advent of humanity on earth is a great and glorious event, not an event signifying human sinfulness and degradation. He points out that according to the Qur'an, the earth is humanity's 'dwelling-place' and 'a source of profit' to it. Iqbal does not think that having been created by God, human beings were placed in a supersensual paradise from which they were expelled on account of an act of disobedience to God. Pointing out that the term 'Adam' functions as the symbol of self-conscious humanity rather than as the name of an individual in the Qur'an, Iqbal describes the 'Fall' as a transition from 'a primitive state of instinctive appetite to the conscious possession of a free self, capable of doubt and disobedience' (Iqbal 1930: 85). For Iqbal, Adam's story is not the story of the 'First Man' but the ethical experience, in symbolic form, of every human being. Following the Qur'anic teaching that though human beings come from the earth, God's spirit has been breathed into them, Iqbal holds on the one hand that human beings are divinely created, and on the other hand that they have evolved from matter. Unlike dualists, Iqbal sees no impassable gulf between matter and spirit, nor does he see human beings as a mere episode or accident in the huge evolutionary process. On the contrary, the whole cosmos is there to serve as the basis and ground for the emergence and perfection of the Ego. Humanity's evolution has not come to an end, for the destiny of human beings lies 'beyond the stars'.

The purpose of life is the development of the Self. In order that they may achieve the fullest possible development, it is essential for human beings to possess knowledge. Following the Qur'an, Iqbal maintains that there are two sources of knowledge: the inner consciousness of human beings and the outer world of nature. Starting with the intuition of the Self, human beings become aware of the Not-Self, the confronting 'other' which provides a constant challenge for them. Nature, however, does not confront God in the same way as it confronts humanity, since it is a phase of God's consciousness. God is immanent since God comprehends the whole universe, but also transcendent since God is not identical with the created world. All life is individual. There is a gradually rising scale of selfness running from the almost inert to God who is the Ultimate Ego. God is not immobile nor is the universe a fixed product; God is constantly creative and dynamic and the process of Creation still goes on. The Qur'anic saying, 'Toward God is your limit' (Surah 53: 42), gives Iqbal an infinite worldview, and he applies it to every aspect of the life of humanity and the universe.

Iqbal distinguishes between two aspects of the Self, the efficient and the appreciative. The efficient self is that which is concerned with, and is itself partially formed by, the physical world. It apprehends the succession of impressions and discloses itself as a series of specific, and consequently numerable, states. The appreciative self is the deeper self, of which one becomes aware only in moments of profound meditation when the efficient self is in abeyance. The unity of the appreciative self is that in it, each experience permeates the whole. The multiplicity of its elements is unlike that of the efficient self. There is change and movement, but this change and movement are indivisible; their elements interpenetrate and are wholly non-serial in character.

Corresponding to the two aspects of the Self are the two levels of time, serial time and pure duration. Serial time is spatialized or clock time, whereas pure duration is a ceaseless continuous flow in which all things live and move and have their being. As human beings perfect their egohood, they cast off the girdle of serial time and gain a measure of eternity.

Iqbal believes ardently that human beings are the makers of their own destiny and that the key to destiny lies in one's character. He constantly refers to the Qur'anic verse, 'Verily God will not change the condition of a people till they change what is in themselves' (Surah 13: 12). Humanity's mission on earth is not only to win greater freedom but also to gain immortality, which according to Iqbal 'is not ours by right; it is to be achieved by personal effort. Man is only a candidate for it' (Iqbal 1930: 119).

Though humanity is the pivot around which Iqbal's philosophy revolves, yet as pointed out by Schimmel, Iqbal's 'revaluation of Man is not that of Man qua Man, but of Man in relation to God' (Schimmel 1963: 382). Iqbal's Ideal Person is the Servant of God. The relation between humanity and God is a personal one; hence the great importance of prayer in the thought of Iqbal. The belief in the one living God gives humanity freedom from all false deities and fortifies it against forces of disintegration. Iqbal sees his concept of the Ideal Person realized in the Prophet of Islam, whose life exemplifies all the principles dearest to Iqbal's heart. In his view art, religion and ethics must be judged from the standpoint of the Self. That which strengthens the Self is good and that which weakens it is bad. Iqbal does not admit the absolute existence of evil but regards it as being necessary for the actualization of moral purpose as vital activity in the world. His Iblis (or *al-Shaytan*, Satan) is the counterpart to his Ideal Person (see FREE WILL; SELF, INDIAN THEORIES OF).

4 Epistemology

Iqbal cannot be easily or exclusively classified as an empiricist, rationalist or intuitionist since he combines sense-perception, reason and intuition in his theory of knowledge (see EPISTEMOLOGY IN ISLAMIC PHILOSOPHY). He defines knowledge as 'sense-perception elaborated by understanding' ('understanding' here does not stand exclusively for 'reason' but for all non-perceptual modes of knowledge). There are two ways of establishing connections with the Reality that confronts us. The direct way is by means of observation and sense-perception; the other way is through direct association with that Reality as it reveals itself within.

Iqbal compares the classical spirit with its contempt for sense-perception with the empirical attitude of the Qur'an 'which sees in the humble bee a recipient of Divine inspiration and constantly calls upon the reader to observe the perpetual change of the winds, the alterations of day and night, the clouds, the starry heavens and the planets swimming through infinite space' (Iqbal 1930: 91) The cultures of the ancient world failed, says Iqbal, because their approach to reality was entirely introspective as they moved from within outwards. This gave them theory without power, and no durable civilization can be based on mere theory.

Iqbal distinguishes between 'logical understanding', which has a sectional nature and 'the deeper movement of thought', which is identical with intuition. He frequently points out (particularly in his poetry) the limitations of the former, but this does not mean that he was an anti-rationalist or anti-intellectual. Iqbal cites enthusiastically the Qur'anic verses (2: 28, 31) which state that Adam's superiority over angels lay in his power to 'name' things, that is, to form concepts. Concepts are not abstract logical entities: they are based on, and indissolubly linked with, facts of sensation. It is the knowledge of things and their inherent nature that exalted Adam over celestial creatures, and it is only through an unceasing struggle to attain the knowledge of things that humanity can maintain its superiority with justice in the world. Without discursive 'intellect' science would be impossible, and without science very little progress would be made in the material sphere. Iqbal believed strongly in the power and utility of science, but he did not regard science as the measure of all things. Science seeks to establish uniformities of experience, that is, the laws of mechanistic repetition, but does not take account of feelings, purposes and values. In Iqbal's opinion, the predicament of present-day humanity is that its life is wholly overshadowed by the results of its intellectual activity and it has ceased to live soulfully, or from within, having been cut off from the springs of life.

Like the existentialists, Iqbal sounds a warning that an idolatrous attitude towards reason and science leads in the direction of dehumanization. Since he puts great emphasis on intuition as a mode of knowledge, there has been much debate on the apparent conflict between reason and intuition in his works. However, Iqbal regarded reason and intuition as organically related and considered both to be necessary for the fulfilment of human destiny. Equating scientific knowledge with *'aql* (reason) and mystic knowledge with *'ishq* (love), Iqbal struggles constantly against separating the former from the latter since he believes that without love, reason becomes demonic.

5 Political philosophy

Of all the parts of his thought, Iqbal's political philosophy is perhaps the most commonly misunderstood. This misunderstanding is largely the result of dividing his political philosophy into phases, such as the nationalistic phase, the pan-Islamic phase and the last phase in which he pioneered the Muslim independence movement. By regarding each phase as being quite different from and independent of the other phases, one almost always reaches the conclusion that either Iqbal's political views changed with astonishing rapidity or that he could not make up his mind and was inconsistent. One can indeed see Iqbal first as a young poet with rather narrow parochial sympathies which gradually widened into love of homeland, and then gave way to love of Islam which later became transformed into love of humanity. However, he can also be seen as a visionary, whose ideal from first to last was the realization of God's Kingdom on Earth, who believed in the interrelatedness, equality and freedom of human beings, and who strove at all times to achieve these goals; and by viewing Iqbal in this one light, one attains a much better understanding of his political philosophy.

Iqbal's interest in politics was secondary not primary. In his historic address at Lahore, in 1932, he made this clear:

> Politics have their roots in the spiritual life of Man. It is my belief that Islam is not a matter of private opinion. It is a society, or if you like, a civic Church. It is because present-day political ideals, as they appear to be shaping themselves in India, may affect its original structure and character that I find myself interested in politics.
>
> (Iqbal 1964: 288)

Iqbal's impact on the political situation of the Muslims in India was so great that he is hailed as the 'spiritual' founder of Pakistan. Undoubtedly, there was much focus on the Islamic community in his major works written between 1908 and 1938. Nevertheless, when accused by Lowes Dickinson of

being exclusive in his thinking, Iqbal denied the allegation and said:

> The humanitarian ideal is always universal in poetry and philosophy, but if you make it an effective ideal... you must start, not with poets and philosophers, but with a society exclusive in the sense of having a creed and well-defined outline.... Such a society according to my belief is Islam. This society has so far proved itself a more successful opponent of the race-idea which is probably the hardest barrier in the way of the humanitarian ideal.... All men and not Muslims alone are meant for the Kingdom of God on earth, provided they say goodbye to their idols of race and nationality and treat one another as personalities. The object of my Persian poems is not to make out a case for Islam: my aim is simply to discover a universal social reconstruction, and in this endeavour, I find it philosophically impossible to ignore a social system which exists with the express object of doing away with all the distinctions of caste, rank and race.
>
> (Iqbal 1964: 98–9)

6 Critical evaluation

Iqbal undertook the task of uniting faith and knowledge, love and reason, heart and mind. In the case of a writer at once so prolific and so provocative, there is bound to be considerable controversy in the evaluation of the measure of his success. Some regard Iqbal's thought as mainly eclectic, while others regard it as exciting and original. But surely it is true that if any thinker has succeeded – to whatever degree – in the task of building a bridge between East and West, it is Iqbal.

One of the most important questions to be asked regarding Iqbal's work as a philosopher is, from what point of view is it to be judged? Inevitably the work of every philosopher must be subjected to the test of coherence and consistency. On the whole, Iqbal's philosophy sustains this test. Like any other philosopher he has first principles which seem to him self-evident, and which he therefore does not seek to defend. Like most other philosophers, there are times and places where he is not very clear or is evasive and unwilling to commit himself. Many writers have also seen a number of contradictions (which appear in some specific part of his thought, usually in his socio-political philosophy) disappear when viewed in the larger context of his total philosophy.

See also: ISLAMIC PHILOSOPHY, MODERN; SOUL IN ISLAMIC PHILOSOPHY

List of works

Iqbal, M. (1903) *'Ilm-ul-iqtisad* (The Science of Economics), Lahore: Iqbal Academy, 1961. (Iqbal's first published book in Urdu was also the first book on economics to be published in Urdu, and contains a number of important socioeconomic ideas which were to become important elements of his philosophy of the individual and communal ego.)

—— (1908) *The Development of Metaphysics in Persia*, Cambridge: Cambridge University Press; Lahore: Bazm-Iqbal, 1964. (Iqbal's doctoral dissertation in which he traces the logical continuity of Persian thought.)

—— (1915) *Asrar-e-khudi* (The Secrets of the Self), Lahore: Shaikh Ghulam Ali and Sons; trans. R.A. Nicholson, Lahore: Shaikh Muhammad Ashraf, 1950. (Iqbal's first volume of poetry in Farsi, in which he laid the foundations of his philosophy of life based on the mysticism of the struggle, the continuing endeavour of the self to fully actualize its potential.)

—— (1918) *Rumuz-e-bekhudi* (The Mysteries of Selflessness), Lahore: Shaikh Ghulam Ali and Sons; trans. A. Arberry, London: John Murray, 1953. (This volume of Farsi poetry is concerned with the role of the individual in a community and forms the basis of Iqbal's social and political philosophy.)

—— (1923) *Payam-e-mashriq* (The Message of the East), Lahore: Shaikh Muhammad Ashraf. (This volume of Farsi poetry was inspired by Goethe's *West–Östlicher Divan*, and highlights those social and religious ideas which have a bearing on the spiritual development of individuals and communities.)

—— (1924) *Bang-e-dara* (The Sound of the Caravan Bell), Lahore: Shaikh Ghulam Ali and Sons. (Iqbal's first collection of poetry in Urdu, which contains some of his best known and most inspiring poems such as 'Shikwa' (The Complaint) and 'Jawab-e-shikwa' (The Response to the Complaint).)

—— (1927) *Zabur-e-'ajam* (The Persian Psalms), Lahore: Shaikh Ghulam Ali and Sons. (In this volume of Farsi poetry, Iqbal's philosophy of love finds exquisite expression.)

—— (1930) *The Reconstruction of Religious Thought in Islam*, Lahore: Shaikh Muhammd Ashraf. (This is one of the most important works of philosophy in modern Islam, in which Iqbal formulates a new Muslim metaphysics in the light of the philosophical tradition of Islam and recent developments in various domains of human knowledge.)

—— (1932) *Javid nama* (The Pilgrimage of Eternity), Lahore: Shaikh Ghulam Ali and Sons. (This volume of Farsi poetry is Iqbal's magnum opus, modelled on the Prophet's *me'raj* or ascension to the presence of God, which is a symbol of self-realization.)

—— (1933) *Musafir* (The Traveller), Lahore: Shaikh Mubarak Ali. (This volume of Farsi poetry records Iqbal's visit to Afghanistan at the invitation of King Nadir Shah.)

—— (1935) *Bal-e-Jibril* (Gabriel's Wing), Lahore: Shaikh Mubarak Ali. (Iqbal's second volume of poetry in Urdu is an acknowledged masterpiece in terms of its literary quality and its prophetic call to action.)

—— (1936) *Zarb-e-alim* (The Stroke of Moses), Lahore: Shaikh Ghulam Ali and Sons. (This volume of Urdu poetry contains Iqbal's critique of the modern age in the light of the symbol of Moses, a seeker of God who insisted on seeing God.)

—— (1938) *Armaghan-i-hijaz* (The Gift of Hijaz), Lahore: Shaikh Ghulam Ali and Sons. (This volume, containing both Farsi and Urdu poetry, was published posthumously and sums up what Iqbal believed to be the teaching of the Prophet from the Hijaz, the symbol of the desert which represents a life of struggle and austerity.)

—— (1948) *Speeches and Statements*, ed. Shamloo, Lahore: Al-Manar Academy. (Collection of shorter works on a variety of subjects.)

—— (1961) *Stray Reflections*, ed. J. Iqbal, Lahore: Shaikh Ghulam Ali and Sons. (Collection of Iqbal's reflections on a number of topics, ranging from the philosophical to the practical.)

—— (1964) *Thoughts and Reflections of Iqbal*, ed. S.A. Vahid, Lahore: Shaikh Muhammad Ashraf. (Contains Iqbal's historic addresses and significant writings on a number of subjects.)

References and further reading

Arnold, T.W. (1928) *The Islamic Faith*, London: Benn. (An important work on Islam by Iqbal's teacher, mentor and friend.)

Hassan, R. (ed.) (1977) *The Sword and the Sceptre*, Lahore: Iqbal Academy. (A collection of historic writings on the life and work of Iqbal.)

—— (1979) *An Iqbal Primer*, Lahore: Aziz. (An introduction to Iqbal's philosophy, analysing the salient ideas in each of his works.)

* Schimmel, A.M. (1963) *Gabriel's Wing*, Leiden: Brill. (By far the best treatment of Iqbal's poetic metaphysics.)

Sinha, S. (1947) *Iqbal, the Poet and his Message,*

Allahabad: R.N. Lal. (Interesting discussion of Iqbal's poetic style and its philosophical relevance.)

Vahid, S.A. (1959) *Iqbal: His Art and Thought*, London: John Murray. (A comprehensive overview of Iqbal's literary and philosophical ideas by a noted Iqbal scholar.)

RIFFAT HASSAN